The Professional Reference NetWare

Karanjit Siyan

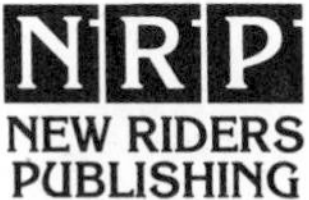

New Riders Publishing, Indianapolis, Indiana

NetWare: The Professional Reference, Third Edition

By Karanjit Siyan

Published by:
New Riders Publishing
201 West 103rd Street
Indianapolis, IN 46290 USA

Printed in the United States of America 4 5 6 7 8 9 0

Library of Congress Cataloging-in-Publication Data

Siyan, Karanjit, 1954-
NetWare: The professional reference / Karanjit Siyan. —3rd ed.
p. cm.
Includes index.
ISBN 1-56205-318-3 : $45.00
1. Operation systems (Computers) 2. NetWare (Computer file)
I. Title.
QA76.76.063S58 1994
005.7' 1369—dc20 94-21980
CIP

Warning and Disclaimer

This book is designed to provide information about the NetWare computer program. Every effort has been made to make this book as complete and as accurate as possible, but no warranty or fitness is implied.

The information is provided on an "as is" basis. The author and New Riders Publishing shall have neither liability nor responsibility to any person or entity with respect to any loss or damages arising from the information contained in this book or from the use of the disks or programs that may accompany it

Publisher *Lloyd J. Short*
Associate Publisher *Tim Huddleston*
Product Development Manager *Rob Tidrow*
Marketing Manager *Ray Robinson*
Director of Special Projects *Cheri Robinson*
Managing Editor *Matthew Morrill*

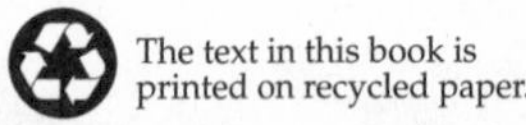

About the Author

Karanjit Siyan is president of Kinetics Corporation. He has authored international seminars on Novell networks, TCP/IP networks, Windows NT, and Solaris SunOS and PC network integration. He also teaches advanced technology courses in the United States, Canada, and Europe. He has published articles in *Dr. Dobbs Journal*, *The C Users Journal*, and *Databased Advisor*. Mr. Siyan has authored *NetWare Training Guide: NetWare 4 Update*, *NetWare Training Guide: NetWare 4 Administration*, and coauthored *Downsizing to NetWare*, *LAN Connectivity*, *Banyan VINES: The Professional Reference*, and *NetWare 4 for Professionals*. Mr. Siyan has been involved with installing, configuring, and designing Novell-based networks since 1985 and is an Enterprise CNE. He is also a Microsoft Certified Professional for Windows NT. Before he became an independent consultant, Mr. Siyan worked as a senior member of the technical staff at ROLM Corporation. He originally trained as an electronics engineer at the Indian Institute of Technology, Kharagpur, India, where he graduated with a Bachelor of Technology degree in Electronics and Electrical Communication Engineering. He later completed his Master of Technology degree in Computer Science from Indian Institute of Technology, Madras, India, and received an MS in Engineering from the EECS department, University of California, Berkeley. Mr. Siyan is based in Montana where he lives with his wife. He is currently working on his Ph.D. in the area of fuzzy logic and neural networks for computer network management.

Trademark Acknowledgments

Acknowledgments

One of the most pleasurable tasks of being an author is to thank the people responsible for the success of a book. My heartfelt thanks to my wife Dei for her love and support. I wish to thank my father, Ahal Singh, and my mother, Tejinder; my brothers, Harjit and Jagjit; and my sisters, Kookie and Dolly. Special thanks to Mother. Without her spiritual support, this book would not have been possible.

I wish to thank Learning Tree International for permission to use the material from my seminars. The contents of this book were inspired from that work. Readers interested in additional information about these seminars (Courses 255 and 261) may call (800) 421-8166 (US), (800) 267-1696 (Canada), or 0800282353 (U.K.). Also, thanks to John Moriarty and Rick Adamson of Learning Tree International for "getting on my case" and teasing me about errors in the first edition of *NetWare: The Professional Reference.* What are friends for, right? Special thanks to Bob Sanregret and Anders Amundoson who initially asked me to author Learning Trees Novell courses on which some of the topics in this book are based. Thanks also to Dr. Jerry Cole who read many parts of the second edition and suggested many improvements.

I would like to thank the Institute of Electrical and Electronics Engineers, Inc. for permission to use some of their illustrations. These illustrations are reprinted from IEEE Std 802-1990, IEEE Standard for Local and Metropolitan Area Networks: Overview and Architecture, copyright © 1990 by the Institute of Electrical and Electronics Engineers, Inc.

Many thanks to the staff of Macmillan Computer Publishing. In particular, I want to thank Ray Robinson for his patience and willingness to listen to my suggestions; Drew Heywood for his insightful comments; Rob Lawson for his attention to this book's details; Stacey Beheler for her help in lining up technical editors; Suzanne Snyder, John Sleeva, Lillian Yates, Sarah Kearns, Laura Frey, Geneil Breeze, and Amy Bezek for their excellent job of editing; and the rest of the staff of New Riders Publishing.

Product Director
Drew Heywood
Team Leader/Production Editor
Rob Lawson
Editors
Suzanne Snyder
Sarah Kearns
Laura Frey
Geneil Breeze
Amy Bezek
John Sleeva
Lillian Yates
Acquisitions Editor
Alicia Krakovitz
Technical Editors
Eric Bowden
Dennis Williams
Acquisitions Coordinator
Stacey Beheler
Editorial Assistant
Karen Opal
Publisher's Assistant
Melissa Lynch
Cover Designer
Sandra Stevenson
Book Designer
Roger S. Morgan
Production Imprint Manager
Juli Cook
Production Imprint Team Leader
Katy Bodenmiller
Graphics Image Specialists
Clint Lahnen
Tim Montgomery
Dennis Sheehan
Susan VandeWalle
Production Analysts
Dennis Clay Hager
Mary Beth Wakefield
Production Team
Nick Anderson
Troy Barnes
Don Brown
Elaine Brush
Cheryl Cameron
Stephanie Davis
Kimberly K. Hannel
Angela P. Judy
Ayanna Lacey
Stephanie McComb
Jamie Milazzo
Michelle M. Mitchell
Wendy Ott
Shelly Palma
Chad Poore
Casey Price
Ryan Rader
Clair Schweinler
Kim Scott
Marc Shecter
Susan Shepard
Tonya R. Simpson
SA Springer
Marcella Thompson
Scott Tullis
Indexers
Jeanne Clark
Michael Hughes

Contents at a Glance

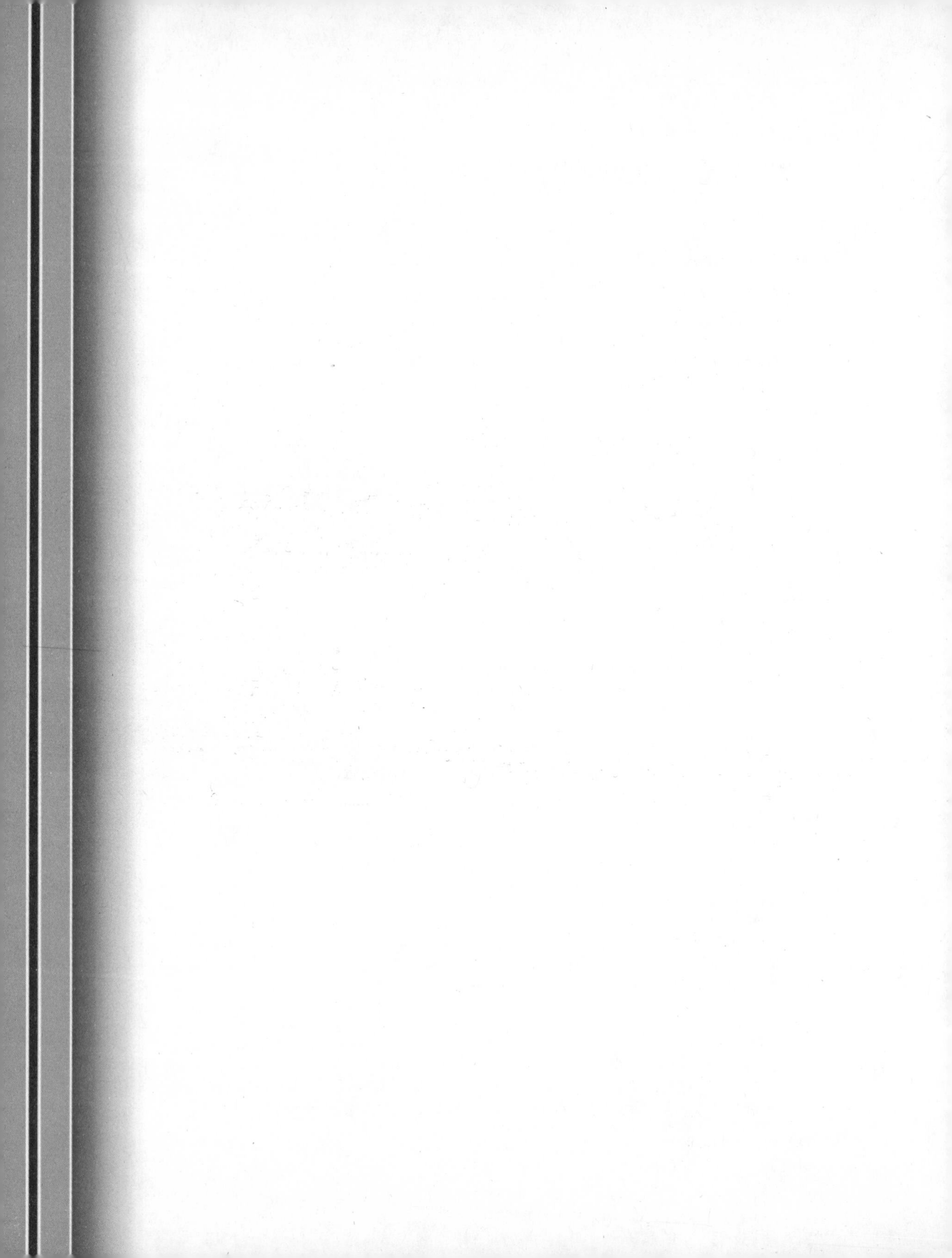

Table of Contents

Introduction

This is the third edition of *NetWare: The Professional Reference*. In the two years since the first edition was published, this book has established itself as the foremost single-volume reference on NetWare and related products. This third edition significantly expands coverage. Here are some of the areas you will want to examine:

- NetWare 3.1x coverage has been expanded to include version 3.12.
- Extensive coverage of NetWare 4.01 has been added, including coverage of the related technologies such as SPX II.
- New material covers high-speed LAN technologies such as 100 megabit Ethernet and switching hubs.
- Coverage of ATM has expanded to reflect the growing importance of this technology.
- A new chapter has been added on Category 5 unshielded twisted-pair cable.
- Other new technologies that are discussed include: *NetWare Link State Protocol* (NLSP), virtual LANs, AppWare Foundation, and Visual AppBuilder.

Your interest in *NetWare: The Professional Reference, 3rd Edition*, indicates that you have more than a casual acquaintance with local area networks. You may be the manager of a network or a consultant whose business revolves around LANs. It seems safe to assume that the LANs you support have grown to a size that makes more basic books insufficient to meet your needs. The School of Hard Knocks has probably convinced you that LANs are far more complex than advertisers would have us believe. They can be so demanding of your knowledge and skills, in fact, that you probably have examined many books for information that expands on the basic and intermediate NetWare products that are commonly available.

The author and publisher of this book are confident that you will find this to be such a book. *NetWare: The Professional Reference, 3rd Edition* is more than a guide to managing Novell NetWare; it is a book about the whys as well as the hows of managing a LAN.

This additional depth should be apparent in the second chapter, which presents complete rules for configuring Ethernets, Token Rings, and ARCnets. Similar depth is found in the discussions about the architecture of NetWare, wide area networking, NetWare bridges, server maintenance, and so forth. As your networks grow in scale and complexity, you will appreciate this added information.

Although you are probably not a newcomer to local area networks, you should review the landscape by briefly scanning some terms and concepts.

Some Thoughts About LANs

Although, depending on the definition, local area networks have been around for at least two decades, they have become a popular technology only fairly recently. The following are reasons for the newfound popularity of LANs:

- The availability of low-cost, high-performance microcomputers
- The development of inexpensive network components
- The introduction of cost-effective, powerful networking software

The use of microcomputers in a LAN environment led to the concept of client/server computing, as opposed to the traditional terminal/host computing architecture used in mini- and mainframe computers. The NOS became the centerpiece of the LAN and enabled applications stored on the server to run on LAN workstations. This book is devoted to the most popular LAN NOS: NetWare, developed by Novell, Inc.

LANs provide efficient, optimized communications over a moderately sized geographic area (such as an office building, warehouse, campus, or factory). A *LAN* can be defined as a communications vehicle for interconnecting computing elements by means of well-defined interface mechanisms. The *computing elements* can be microcomputers, minicomputers, or mainframe computers. The *interface mechanisms* can be cables, network cards, software, and so on. Of the several interesting characteristics of LANs, the most important are short distances and high data rate.

The first characteristic, short distances, reflects the letter L in LAN, which stands for Local. Studies have shown that 80 percent of an organization's communications needs are within a small geographical area. (Most LANs do not exceed distances of 10 km.) There are important exceptions to this, such as the *Fiber Distributed Data Interface* (FDDI), which is a ring-based LAN that can span distances of 200 km.

The second characteristic of a LAN is its high-speed data rate over channels that are relatively error free. Although most LANs operate over speeds between 1 Mbs to 100 Mbs, a few LANs operate at lower or faster speeds. The words *high speed* are relative: LANs utilize high speeds compared to modems and typical wide area networks. Because applications and data are stored centrally (on servers), but are used on workstations (clients), this extra speed is essential for supporting high-volume data transfers.

Nodes on a LAN

A LAN consists of a number of nodes that are connected through a shared transmission medium. The term *node*, in a network context, refers to any intelligent device that can be addressed by another intelligent device on the network. These intelligent devices are the computers on the network.

The computers on a LAN can be classified as servers or clients (workstations). *Servers* may be general- or special-purpose microcomputers that provide a service to other nodes. A few examples of server types are the following:

- File server
- Database server
- Communication server
- Gateway server
- Management server

Servers provide services to *client workstations* on the LAN. These workstations are general-purpose computers (such as IBM PCs, Macintoshes, and UNIX workstations) that have been equipped with network-interface hardware and software. The network interface enables the workstation to perform local computer functions or to take advantage of network services, as required.

Novell NetWare comprises a family of products that provides LAN services and that enables workstations to become clients on the network. The NetWare *network operating system* (NOS) is sufficient for configuring a network server to provide file and printing services to clients. Additional products from the NetWare product family and from third-party vendors greatly expand the capability of the LAN to provide database services, electronic mail, communication services, and much more.

The basic NetWare NOS is the focus of this book. NetWare is available in three versions: 2.2, 3.12, and 4.01. Version 3.11 is the more flexible and advanced product. In the course of reading this book, you will gain an understanding of the features of these two products and how they are installed and managed.

Beyond an understanding of the NetWare software, however, you will be exposed to detailed information about the environment in which NetWare operates. The NetWare NOS runs on more than 180 different variations of network hardware technologies. Network administrators find that a knowledge of these technologies is essential whenever their LANs grow to more than a trivial size. Knowing how to expand networks and how to fix them when they break requires a great deal of technical expertise.

Besides supporting communications, LANs enable users to share resources, which is a sophisticated capability of the operating system. The network administrator needs to understand the complexities so that users can share applications and data effortlessly and safely. To enable you to properly configure multiuser applications, this book demonstrates the ways that NetWare enables applications to implement special concurrency-control mechanisms, such as record and file locking.

In addition to demonstrating techniques for sharing application and data files, *NetWare: The Professional Reference, 3rd Edition* examines techniques for sharing peripheral devices, such as printers, modems, and large-capacity disks. LANs are economical, in part because they promote the sharing of expensive resources.

The Trend toward Downsizing

The cost efficiency of local area networks has inspired an industry trend to move appropriate applications to smaller, more affordable platforms. Increasing numbers of corporations are considering downsizing alternatives, and LANs appear prominently in the strategies that are being considered.

This downsizing trend means that LANs are increasingly being used to support mission-critical computing services. More than ever, it is necessary for managers of LANs to ensure that their networks are efficient and reliable. This book is intended to provide the kind of detailed information you require as the manager of a NetWare LAN to ensure that your network meets the highest expectations of your users.

How This Book Is Organized

This book starts with background information and extends through the details of installing and managing NetWare LAN components. The chapters are organized as follows:

Part 1: Network Technologies

Chapters 1 through 5 introduce the various pieces of local and wide area networks. Taken together, the chapters in this section give you a solid technical foundation for understanding how NetWare and LANs work.

Chapter 1, "NetWare Protocols," describes the most common protocols that are associated with NetWare. Protocols such as IPX/SPX, TCP/IP, NCP, and AppleTalk are discussed within the context of the *Open Systems Interconnnect* (OSI) seven-layered networking model.

Chapter 2, "LAN Standards for the Physical and Data Link Layers," discusses Ethernet, Token Ring, and ARCnet in the perspective of the OSI networking model. You learn the components of these network standards and the rules for extending networks as they must grow in size.

Chapter 3, "Bridging and Routing," explores devices that are used to enable networks to grow beyond a limited number of devices and beyond a limited geographic area. Coverage of NLSP has been added for this edition.

Chapter 4, "WANs and MANs," considers the issues raised when networks grow to several servers and span metropolitan or larger geographic areas. ATM coverage has been expanded for this edition.

Chapter 5, "Hardware for NetWare Servers," gives you the information you need to configure high-performance servers for use with NetWare.

Part 2: NetWare 2.2, 3.11, and 3.12

This part focuses on the NetWare product on the server. You will examine the fine points of installing and configuring the NetWare operating system. Most readers of this book will have performed at least one NetWare installation. Chapters 7–10 give you a little more perspective on how the NetWare products are designed and configured.

Chapter 6, "Features of NetWare 2.2, 3.11, and 3.12," introduces general concepts of network operating systems and examines how NetWare is designed for performance, reliability, and richness of features. Issues of interoperability and management are also addressed.

Chapter 7, "Installing NetWare 3.12 Servers," is a new chapter covering installation of NetWare 3.12.

Chapter 8, "Managing NetWare 2.2, 3.11, 3.12 Users," addresses the task of configuring and maintaining user network accounts.

Chapter 9, "Managing NetWare 2.2, 3.11, 3.12 Security," analyzes the need for security on a network and presents techniques for ensuring that your network will not be threatened by security problems.

Part 3: NetWare 4

This is a new part that provides detailed coverage of NetWare 4.01.

Chapter 10, "Features of NetWare 4," explores the new features of NetWare 4.

Chapter 11, "Understanding NetWare 4 Directory Services," covers the most important features of NetWare Directory Services. Later chapters will cover some features in greater depth.

Chapter 12, "Installing NetWare 4.*x*," covers installation procedures.

Chapter 13, "NetWare Directory Services Security," shows how to manage NDS to provide high levels of network security.

Chapter 14, "NetWare Directory Services Schema and X.500," shows how NDS is related to the X.500 directory standard.

Chapter 15, "NetWare Directory Services Name Resolution," explores the intricate details of NDS naming conventions.

Chapter 16, "NetWare Directory Services Partitions," describes the procedures for setting up and replicating NDS database partitions in order to build a fault-tolerant directory system.

Chapter 17, "NetWare Directory Services Time Synchronization," explains how to manage time synchronization of various NetWare 4 time servers.

Chapter 18, "Managing NetWare 4 Users," describes the procedures required to manage user accounts.

Chapter 19, "NetWare Directory Services Auditing," shows how to set up and use the NetWare 4 auditing capabilities.

Part 4: The NetWare Network Environment

As mentioned earlier in the introduction, NetWare employs a client/server architecture. Because the server is only half of the total architecture, this part turns its attention to the client side. You will examine various workstation operating systems and how they are used with NetWare. You also will examine the tools available for configuring a user's NetWare environment, such as login scripts, menus, and print job management. You also will look at the big picture of internetworking, viruses, and network management. These are all features that must be dealt with as your NetWare LANs grow in scope.

Chapter 20, "Supporting DOS Workstations," describes the process of configuring DOS workstations for NetWare. DOS remains the most popular PC operating system; however, system administrators will find that a lot needs to be done to optimize the setup of a DOS workstation. New in this edition is coverage of the DOS VLM Requestor.

Chapter 21, "Supporting Non-DOS Workstations," examines the growing nontraditional workstation. Although DOS remains the operating system of most PC users, more powerful operating systems are currently attracting more attention. Common examples are Apple System 7, OS/2 2, and UnixWare, all of which integrate nicely into NetWare LANs. Each of these operating systems is discussed in this chapter. This chapter now includes coverage of Windows NT.

Chapter 22, "Performance Tuning in NetWare 2.2, 3.*x*, and 4.*x* Servers," demonstrates detailed procedures for enhancing performance of NetWare servers.

Chapter 23, "Managing User Sessions," examines login scripts, menus, and other tools that determine the user's environment when using resources on a NetWare LAN. The new NMENU system for NetWare 3.12 and 4.*x* is covered in this edition.

Chapter 24, "The NetWare File System," is concerned with the server-disk subsystems and with the volumes, directories, and file systems that are used to store applications and data on the server. This edition adds discussion of the NetWare 4 NDS syntax for volume and file names.

Chapter 25, "NetWare Printing" presents options for configuring printers as server-attached or workstation-attached network devices. Techniques for managing print servers, remote printers, print queues, and print jobs are examined.

Chapter 26, "Internetworking," describes how NetWare connects to other types of networks, such as TCP/IP, X.25, Appletalk, and SNA. LANs no longer exist in isolation, and NetWare has products to solve many internetworking problems.

Chapter 27, "NetWare/IP," explains how this new product can be used to build a NetWare network that uses TCP/IP as the native protocol.

Chapter 28, "Network Management," looks at the tools with which you can monitor your network and ensure that it offers top performance. This chapter now includes coverage of *NetWare Management Services* (NMS).

Chapter 29, "Network Applications," discusses some of the issues that are encountered when installing network and non-network applications on a LAN server. New coverage includes discussion of *Mail Handling System* (MHS) and Novell's new AppWare product line.

Part 5: Network Troubleshooting

Chapter 30, "Network Cable Troubleshooting," discusses the techniques used for cable troubleshooting. The electrical parameters for category 3,4,5 cabling are covered in detail.

Chapter 31, "Network Troubleshooting," describes the principles of network troubleshooting. In particular, this chapter discusses in detail the use of LANalyzer for troubleshooting Ethernet and Token Ring networks.

Other NetWare Titles from New Riders

New Riders Publishing offers an expanding line of books about Novell NetWare. These books are addressed at various levels of user requirements and experience.

7 Keys to Managing NetWare is both an introduction to NetWare and a task-oriented guide to managing a NetWare network. New administrators will find that this book enables them to set up a NetWare server properly, with a minimum of fuss. Experienced administrators will find that the task-oriented approach makes this an effective reference guide to NetWare management procedures.

Inside NetWare 3.12, 3rd Edition is New Riders' general-purpose tutorial and reference for Novell NetWare. This is an excellent first book for new systems administrators; it also covers the subject in sufficient depth that it is sure to find a permanent place among your NetWare documents.

Downsizing to NetWare is a manual of tools and techniques for downsizing large applications for local area networks. Many corporations are reducing computing costs through downsizing, and this book will tell you what you need to know to plan and implement a downsizing strategy.

The *NetWare Training Guide* series consists of four volumes that assist in preparing NetWare administrators for Certified NetWare Engineer testing:

- *Managing NetWare Systems* covers the System Administration and Advanced System Administration tests for NetWare 3.1x and 2.2.

- *Networking Technologies* covers DOS and Microcomputer Concepts, NetWare Service and Support, and Networking Technologies.

- *NetWare 4 Administration*, by Karanjit Siyan, covers the NetWare 4.*x* Administration and Advanced Administration tests.
- *NetWare 4 Update*, by Karanjit Siyan, covers the NetWare 4.*x* Update test. This book is the fast way for CNEs and ECNEs to upgrade their certifications to cover NetWare 4.*x*.

Publisher's Note

The staff of New Riders Publishing is committed to bringing you the very best in computer reference material. Each New Riders book is the result of months of work by authors and staff who research and refine the information contained within its covers.

As part of this commitment to you, the NRP reader, New Riders invites your input. Please let us know if you enjoy this book, if you have trouble with the information and examples presented, or if you have a suggestion for the next edition.

There are several ways to contact NRP. You may write us at:

New Riders Publishing
Attn: Associate Publisher
201 W. 103rd Street
Indianapolis, IN 46290

If you prefer, you can fax New Riders Publishing at (317) 581-4670.

NRP is an imprint of Macmillan Computer Publishing. To obtain a catalog or information, or to purchase any Macmillan Computer Publishing book, call (800) 428-5331.

You can send electronic mail to New Riders from a variety of sources. NRP maintains several mailboxes organized by topic area. Mail in these mailboxes will be forwarded to the staff member who is best able to address your concerns. Substitute the appropriate mailbox name from the list below when addressing your e-mail. The mailboxes are:

ADMIN	Comments and complaints for NRP's Publisher
APPS	Word, Excel, WordPerfect, other office applications
ACQ	Book proposal inquiries by potential authors
CAD	AutoCAD, 3D Studio, AutoSketch, and CAD products
DATABASE	Access, dBASE, Paradox, and other database products
GRAPHICS	CorelDRAW!, Photoshop, and other graphics products
INTERNET	Internet
NETWORK	NetWare, LANtastic, and other network-related topics
OS	MS-DOS, OS/2, all OS except UNIX and Windows
UNIX	UNIX
WINDOWS	Microsoft Windows (all versions)
OTHER	Anything that doesn't fit the above categories

If you use an MHS e-mail system that routes through CompuServe, send your messages to:

mailbox @ NEWRIDER

To send NRP mail from CompuServe, use the following To address:

MHS: *mailbox* @ NEWRIDER

To send mail from the Internet, use the following address format:

mailbox@newrider.mhs.compuserve.com

We will respond to as many readers as we can. Please note that New Riders cannot serve as a technical resource for hardware- or software-related problems. Refer to the documentation that accompanies your product for help with specific problems.

Networking Technologies

NetWare Protocols

Knowledge of *protocols*, which represent the mechanisms that enable the systems on a network to talk to each other, is important for configuring, troubleshooting, and understanding networks. Protocol knowledge also is very useful in understanding the reasons that networking software from different vendors (and sometimes the same vendor!) do not interoperate.

Before you can understand networking protocols, you must understand the terminology used to define and understand them. The preeminent model for comparing protocols is the *Open Systems Interconnection* (OSI) reference model. Today, all vendors compare their proprietary, industry-standard, or international-standard protocol implementations against the OSI reference model.

Understanding the OSI Model

The OSI reference model was developed in 1978 by the *International Organization of Standards* (ISO) to specify a standard to be used for the development of open systems and as a yardstick to compare different communication systems. Network systems designed according to OSI framework and specifications speak the same language; that is, they use similar or compatible methods of communication. This type of network system allows systems from different vendors to interoperate.

In the early days of computer networks (prior to the OSI model), the proprietary computer network architecture reigned supreme. In those days, an organization interested in installing a computer network examined the choices available, including IBM, DEC, HP, Honeywell, and Sperry and Burroughs (now Unisys). Each of those choices had its own proprietary architecture; the capability to interconnect networks from different vendors was almost nonexistent.

After they committed to buying equipment from a specific vendor, the organization was virtually "locked in." Updates or modifications to the system were provided by the vendor, and because the vendor had a closed proprietary architecture, no one could compete with that vendor in supplying equivalent services. Prices were determined based on what the customer could bear without complaining too much!

Today's users probably realize that in many areas of the computer industry, this picture has not changed much. Proprietary architecture history is still around, but the good news is that OSI can change the way it works. In fact, the big debate in computer circles today centers on the amount of time it will take to have the ISO-recommended protocols for the OSI layers to become the dominant standard in the networking industry.

For now, the OSI model can, at the very least, provide you with a clearer picture of how the different components of a network relate to each other.

Layers of the OSI Model

The OSI model has seven layers, as shown in figure 1.1. The layers, working from the bottom up, are as follows:

- Physical
- Data Link
- Network
- Transport
- Session
- Presentation
- Application

Figure 1.1
The OSI reference model.

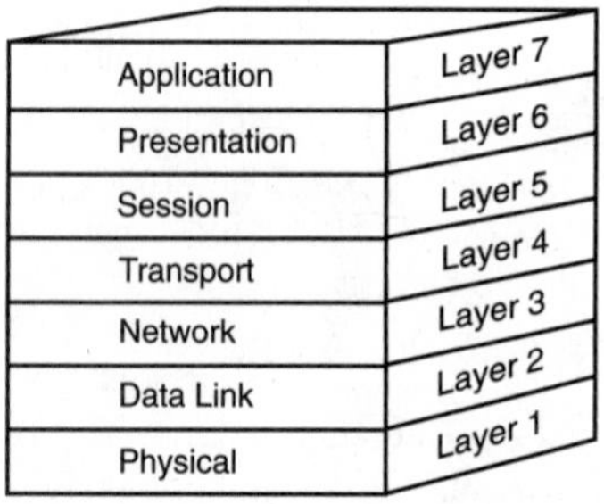

The ISO applied the following five principles when creating the OSI reference model:

1. A layer should be created only when a different level of abstraction is needed.

2. Each layer should provide a well-defined function.

3. The function of each layer should define internationally standardized protocols.

4. The layer boundaries should minimize the information flow across layer interfaces.

5. Distinct functions should be defined in separate layers, but the number of layers should be small enough that the architecture does not become unwieldy.

The following sections summarize the functions of the seven layers.

Physical Layer

The *physical layer* transmits bits over a communication channel. The bits can represent database records or file transfers; the physical layer is oblivious to what those bits represent. The bits can be encoded as digital 1s and 0s or in analog form. The physical layer deals with the mechanical, electrical, and procedural interfaces over the physical medium.

Data Link Layer

The *data link layer* builds on the transmission capability of the physical layer. The bits transmitted or received are grouped in a logical unit called a *frame*. In the context of LANs, a frame can be Token Ring or Ethernet.

The bits in a frame have special meanings. The beginning and ending of a frame is marked by special bit patterns. Additionally, the bits in a frame are divided into an address field, control field, data field, and error control field. Figure 1.2 shows a typical data link frame. You see more specific examples of the data link frame in the discussion of Ethernet and Token Ring LANs.

Address Field(s)	Control Field	Data Field	Error Control Field

Figure 1.2
A typical data link layer frame.

The *address* field(s) contains the sending and receiving node address. The *control* field is used to indicate the different types of data link frames, which include data frames and frames used for managing the data link channel. The *data* field contains the actual data being transmitted by the frame. The *error control* field usually detects errors in the data link frame. The *data link* layer also is the first layer in which you see error control concerns. The error control field is usually a hardware-generated *checksum* used to detect errors in the data link frame.

Network Layer

The *network layer* builds on the node-to-node connection provided by the data link layer. The node-to-node data link services are extended across a network by this layer. An additional service provided by the network layer is how to route *packets* (units of information at the network layer) between nodes connected through a network.

Besides routing, the network layer helps eliminate congestion as well as regulate flow of data. The network layer also makes it possible for two networks to be interconnected by implementing a uniform addressing mechanism. Token Ring or Ethernet LANs, for example, have different types of data link addresses. To interconnect these two networks, you need a uniform addressing mechanism that can be understood by both Token Ring and Ethernet. For NetWare-based networks, this capability is provided by the *Internet Packet Exchange* (IPX), a network layer protocol.

Transport Layer

The *transport layer* provides enhancements to the services of the network layer. This layer helps ensure reliable data delivery and end-to-end data integrity. To ensure reliable delivery, the transport layer builds on the error control mechanisms provided by the lower layers. If the lower layers do not do a good enough job, the transport layer has to work harder. This layer is the last chance for error recovery. In fact, when it comes to providing error free delivery, you could say "The buck stops here" at the transport layer.

The transport layer also may be responsible for creating several logical connections over the same network connection, a process called *multiplexing*. Multiplexing (or time sharing) occurs when a number of transport connections share the same network connection.

The transport layer is the middle layer of the OSI model. The three lower layers constitute the *subnet* (portion of the network model), and the three upper layers are usually implemented by networking software on the node. The transport layer is usually implemented on the node also; its job is to convert an unreliable subnet into a more reliable network.

Because of multiplexing, several software elements (OSI terminology uses the term *protocol entity*) share the same network layer address. To uniquely identify the software elements within the transport layer, a more general form of addressing is necessary. These addresses, called *transport addresses*, usually are a combination of the network layer address and a transport *Service Access Point* (SAP) number. Sometimes the names *sockets* or *port numbers* are used to identify transport addresses.

Examples of transport protocols used by NetWare are *Sequenced Exchange Protocol* (SXP) and *Packet Exchange Protocol* (PXP).

Session Layer

The *session layer* uses the transport layer to provide enhanced session services. Examples of a session include a user being logged in to a host across a network or a session being established for the purpose of transferring files.

The session layer can provide some of the following enhancements:

- Dialog control
- Token management
- Activity management

A session, in general, allows two-way communications (*full duplex*) across a connection. Some applications may require alternate one-way communications (*half duplex*). The session layer has the option of providing two-way or one-way communications, an option called *dialog control*.

For some protocols, it is essential that only one side attempt a critical operation at a time. To prevent both sides from attempting the same operation, a control mechanism, such as the use of *tokens*, must be implemented. When using the token method, only the side holding a token is permitted to perform the operation. Determining which side has the token and how it is transferred between the two sides is known as *token management*.

The use of the word *token* here should not be confused with Token Ring operation. Token management is a much higher level concept at layer five of the OSI model. IBM's Token Ring operation belongs to layers two and one of the OSI model.

If you are performing a one-hour file transfer between two machines and network crashes occur approximately every 30 minutes, you may never be able to complete the file transfer. After each transfer aborts, you have to start all over again. To avoid this problem, you can treat the entire file transfer as a single activity with checkpoints inserted into the datastream. That way if a crash occurs, the session layer can synchronize to a previous checkpoint. This operation of managing an entire activity is called *activity management*.

Presentation Layer

The *presentation layer* manages the way data is represented. Many ways of representing data exist, such as ASCII and EBCDIC for text files, and 1s or 2s for numbers. If the two sides involved in communication use different data representations, they cannot understand each other. The presentation layer represents data with a common syntax and semantics. If all the nodes use and understand this common language, misunderstanding in data representation is eliminated. An example of this common language is *Abstract Syntax Representation, Rev 1* (ASN.1), an OSI recommendation.

Application Layer

The *application layer* contains the protocols and functions needed by user applications to perform communication tasks. Examples of common functions include the following:

- Protocols for providing remote file services, such as open, close, read, write, and shared access to files
- File transfer services and remote database access
- Message handling services for e-mail applications
- Global directory services to locate resources on a network
- A uniform way of handling a variety of system monitors and devices
- Remote job execution

Many of these services are called *Application Programming Interfaces* (APIs). APIs are programming libraries that an application writer can use to write network applications.

In NetWare, *NetWare Control Protocol* (NCP) is an example of an application layer protocol. NCPs allow NetWare resources to be accessed by NetWare clients.

ODI Protocol Layering and the OSI Model

NetWare protocol stacks are implemented using the *Open Data Link Interface* (ODI) mechanism. The ODI protocol layering provides a mechanism for systematically using the protocol components to build the protocol stack.

Strictly speaking, the ODI mechanism, the NetWare protocols, and protocols from most vendors are not in complete compliance with the OSI reference model. The only protocols that comply closely with the OSI reference model are the ISO recommendations for each of the OSI layers.

ODI Architecture

The ODI specification allows a large number of network adapters to support different protocol stacks, such as TCP/IP, OSI, SPX/IPX, and AppleTalk. Prior to ODI and similar mechanisms (NDIS Packet Driver now called Crynwr drivers), a separate driver had to be written for each protocol stack. It also was difficult to get these separate drivers to coexist on a workstation, making it difficult to support more than one protocol stack.

The key components of ODI layers are the *Link Support Layer* (LSL) and the *Multiple Link Interface Driver* (MLID), as shown in figure 1.3.

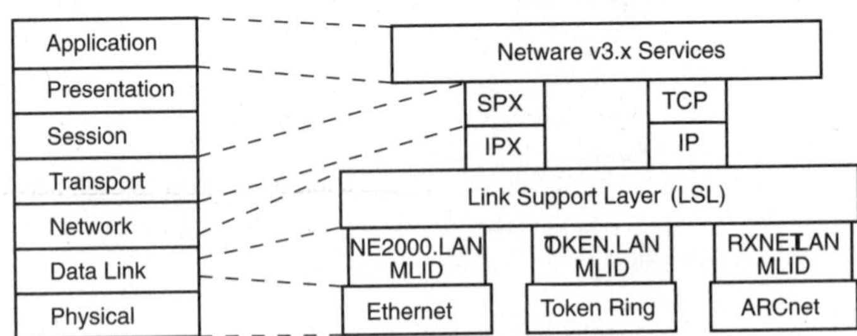

Figure 1.3
ODI components versus the OSI model.

In figure 1.3, the Ethernet, Token Ring, and ARCnet networking technologies correspond to the first and second layers of the OSI model. The NE2000.LAN, TOKEN.LAN, and RXNET.LAN are the names of the MLID drivers. Other types of network boards can have different names. These drivers correspond to a portion of the data link layer. The drivers are written to interface with the link support layer (LSL). The LSL, which does not map well onto the OSI model, represents the boundary between the data link and the network layers. Because the LSL provides the interface between MLID drivers and the upper-layer protocols, you can think of the LSL as covering a portion of the data link layer and the lower portion of the network layer of the OSI model.

The link support layer is a key element in the ODI specification. It *virtualizes* the network adapter by providing a logical view of the network adapter. The network layer software does not have to be rewritten to understand the low-level mechanics and operational details of a new network adapter. The network layer software "sees" a well-defined virtual interface to any network adapter. The well-defined virtual interface means that protocol stacks can be written to interface with the network adapter in a standard way.

The practical significance of this is that the network layer protocol needs to be written just once to this virtual interface. When a new type of network adapter is built, the manufacturer writes an MLID driver for it that can hook into the LSL layer. The LSL provides the same virtual interface to this board, and the protocol software does not need to be rewritten for the new network adapter.

The same MLID driver can support new types of protocol software, as long as the protocols are written to the virtual interface provided by LSL. The MLID driver can handle packets from different protocol stacks delivered to it by the LSL.

On receiving the different protocol packets from the network, MLID forwards the packet to the LSL without interpreting the packet contents. The LSL is responsible for sending the packets to the correct protocol stack.

The LSL acts as a software switch through which multiple protocol packet types travel and are delivered to the correct MLID or the correct protocol stack. To provide this routing, the LSL contains information about the MLIDs and the protocol stacks it supports. When MLID drivers or protocol stacks are loaded, they register information about themselves with the LSL. The LSL keeps track of this information in a *data segment* (OSdata). This segment includes items such as network adapter information, protocol stack information, and binding information.

When the MLID loads, the LSL assigns a logical number to each network adapter. When a protocol stack loads and registers with the LSL, it also is assigned a logical protocol stack number. Up to 16 such protocol stacks can be supported.

The LSL also keeps information on the send-and-receive *event control blocks* (ECBs). Event control blocks are data structures used for transmitting and receiving packets, and contain packet ID information. LSL uses the packet ID information in ECBs, and information on network adapters and protocol stacks registered with it, to route packets.

The LSL has a set of routines for the LAN adapters below it and the protocol stacks above it. The LSL calls these routines to move data packets (see fig. 1.4). Each network adapter registers a send routine and a control routine, for example. Also associated with each network adapter is a *packet buffer area.* The packet buffer area makes it possible for multiple adapters of the same type to have only one MLID loaded reentrantly. In this case, even though the adapters have the same send and control routines, those adapters have a different data area. The protocol stacks above the LSL also register a similar set of support routines with the LSL. Poor network performance can often be attributed to poorly optimized LAN drivers—especially when dealing with multiple protocol stacks. It is always important to ask for, and use, the latest drivers for your LAN adapter.

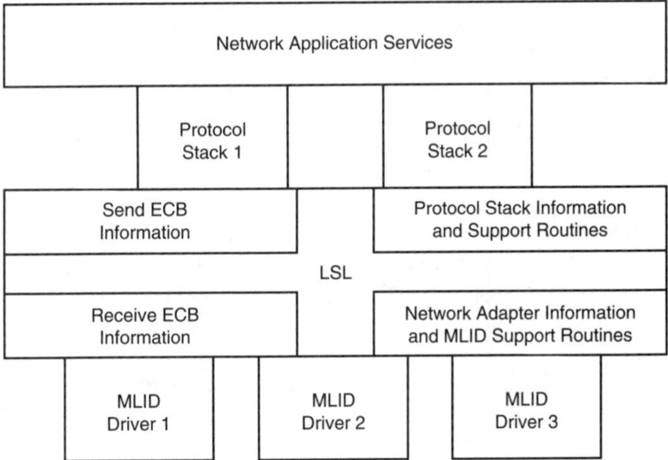

Figure 1.4
Information stored in the LSL.

The LSL module is specific to an operating system platform. That means that the actual LSL module cannot be interchanged between operating systems even though LSL is available for DOS, OS/2, NetWare 3.*x*, and NetWare external routers. In DOS, for example, LSL is loaded as a TSR, which is implemented in the file LSL.COM, and in OS/2 it is loaded as a device driver called LSL.SYS.

Every packet on a network has a *Media Access Control* (MAC) frame that encapsulates the communications protocol packet (IPX, AppleTalk, TCP/IP). The MAC is the lower sublayer of the data link layer. For LANs, it represents the mechanisms by which a node on the LAN acquires access to the physical LAN. Within the ODI-based node, a *protocol ID* (PID) consisting of one to six bytes is prepended to the frame. This PID identifies the MAC frame and the communications protocol contained in the MAC frame. A code of 8137 (hexadecimal), for example, is used to indicate an Ethernet II MAC frame that has IPX data inside it. The LSL uses the PID value to route the packet to the appropriate protocol stack. More information about MAC frames is available in Chapter 2, "LAN Standards for Physical and Data Link Layers."

Streams Interface and ODI

In the NetWare 3.*x* server, the *Streams* interface can be used to encapsulate the communications protocols and to provide a uniform transport interface. Streams, an interface developed by AT&T in UNIX System V and originally proposed by Dennis Ritchie, creator of the popular C language, defines a stream head that can be used as a common interface by applications, and a stream tail that interfaces with the drivers. Because the preferred driver in NetWare is ODI-based, the stream tail interfaces with the LSL. Between the stream head and the stream tail, a number of protocol modules can be *pushed* (see fig. 1.5).

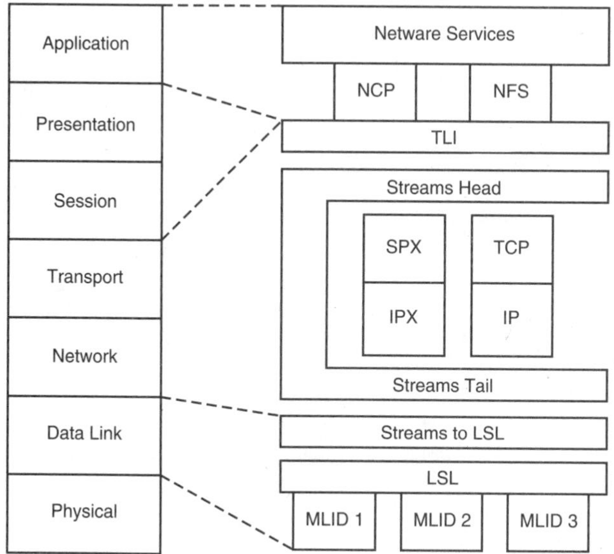

Figure 1.5
Streams and ODI.

Think of the Streams interface as providing a common *software wrapper* around the transport modules. Because Streams is a very low-level interface, an alternate *Transport Layer Interface* (TLI) that makes use of Streams and simplifies the writing of applications is often used.

NetWare Native Protocols

The NetWare native protocols are NCP, SPX, and IPX. Of these, SPX and IPX are based on Xerox's XNS protocol suite. The *Sequenced Packet Exchange* (SPX) protocol is based on the *Sequenced Packet Protocol* (XNS SPP). *Internet Exchange Protocol* (IPX) is based on the *Internet Datagram Protocol* (XNS IDP). IPX corresponds to layer three of the OSI model and is a connectionless datagram protocol. SPX, a connections-oriented protocol, corresponds to the fourth layer of the OSI model.

NetWare Core Protocol (NCP) was developed by Novell to support NetWare services. The Service Advertising Protocol (SAP) is used by NetWare to advertise NetWare services on a NetWare-based network.

In addition, Novell uses a modified form of XNS RIP as its routing protocol.

1

Internet Packet Exchange (IPX)

The IPX protocol is a network layer protocol that provides connectionless datagram services on top of the data link protocols such as Ethernet, Token Ring, ARCnet, and PPP (Point-to-Point) protocols. The IPX protocol can be made to work on virtually all existing data link protocols. The use of the term *connectionless* implies that prior to data transmission, no control packets are sent to establish a connection. Therefore, after the data is transmitted, no teardown or breakdown of the connection is required.

Messages are sent by breaking them into packets and sending complete source address and destination information per packet. No guarantees are made about the successful arrival of the packet (called a *datagram* when a packet for a connectionless protocol). If guarantees are to be made, an upper-layer protocol such as SPX or NCP must provide this capability. The datagram-oriented nature of IPX makes it easier to implement the underlying network technology. Datagrams work well with network services that require a broadcast capability.

A unique network address also is available from the IPX layer, per NetWare node. The IPX network address consists of a 32-bit network number and a 48-bit node address pair, making a total of 10 bytes of network address. When configuring NetWare servers, the 32-bit network number must be supplied by the installer and kept unique per physical network. If you are interested in obtaining a unique network number, contact Novell for registering your number. Later chapters suggest internal procedures on ways to manage this network number within your network environment without creating duplicate network number conflicts.

Because of IPX's origin in the XNS IDP protocol, a 48-bit node address is used (IDP originally ran on Ethernet, which has a 48-bit address). A NetWare node can have several software processes running, such as NCP, SAP, and RIP services. To uniquely identify packets to each of these processes, a *socket number* is used. The socket number is a 16-bit number assigned to each process that wants to communicate using IPX services. Internally, the socket number is used to access data structures used to communicate with the IPX protocol. A few of the well-known socket numbers are 451 hex for NCP; 452 hex for SAP; 453 hex for RIP; 455 hex for NetBIOS; and 456 hex for diagnostics. A complete address description of a process on a NetWare node consists of the following 3-tuple:

<network number, node address, socket number>

Figure 1.6 shows the IPX packet structure. The *Checksum field* is usually set to FFFF hex to indicate that checksums are disabled. IPX expects the data link layer to inform it about packet errors because the data link protocols, such as Ethernet and Token Ring, have a hardware *Cyclic Redundancy Checksum* (CRC).

The *Length field* is the length of the IPX packet in bytes. This includes the IPX header length of 30 bytes plus the data field. IPX originally inherited a 576-byte limit from the XNS IDP packet structure. New IPX drivers can handle larger size packets, even though most of Novell's documentation still refers to the 576-byte limit.

The *Transport Control field* is used as a hop count field to count the number of routers traveled by the IPX packet. This field is used by IPX routers and incremented each time the IPX packet goes through a router. When the hop count reaches 16, the IPX packet is dropped. The 16 hop count limit is inherited from XNS RIP, which was used as the basis for Novell's RIP.

2 bytes	2 bytes	1 byte	1 byte	4 bytes	6 bytes	2 bytes	4 bytes	6 bytes	2 bytes	
Checksum	Length	Transport Control (heps)	Packet Type	Destination Network	Destination Node	Destination Socket	Source Network	Source Node	Source Socket	Data

Figure 1.6
IPX packet structure.

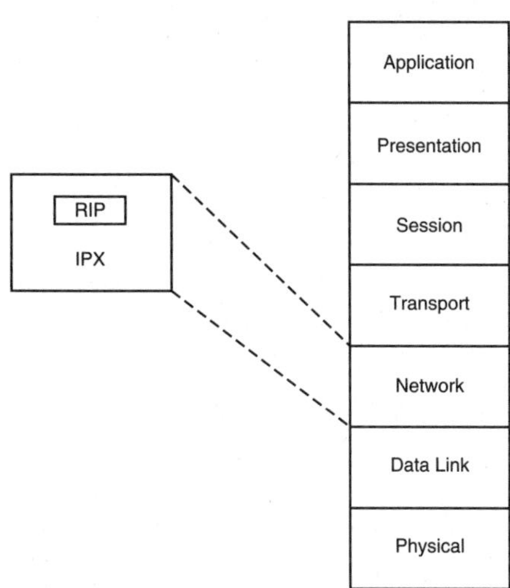

The *Packet Type field* is used for protocol multiplexing and de-multiplexing between the IPX layer and upper-layer protocols. The Packet Type identifies which upper-layer protocol must receive the data portion of the IPX packet. Some of the packet type codes are 4 for *Packet Exchange Protocol* (PXP); 5 for SPX; and 17 for NCP. A packet type code of 0 is reserved for an unknown packet type.

The *Destination Network, Destination Node,* and *Destination Socket fields* uniquely identify a process in the destination node; and the *Source Network, Source Node,* and *Source Socket fields* identify a process in the source node.

The destination network number of an IPX packet is used to decide if an IPX packet should be sent locally on an IPX network or to a local router. All nodes on the same physical network must have the same network number. A node discovers its IPX network number from an IPX router on that network. Typically, the IPX router also is the NetWare file server, because all NetWare file servers contain an IPX router software module.

If the destination network number is the same as the local network number, the IPX packet is sent directly to the node on the local network. If the destination network number is different from the local network number, and this is the first time an IPX packet is being sent to the destination network, a *route request packet* is sent via the *Routing Information Protocol* (RIP) to determine the fastest route.

The reply contains the address of a local router capable of forwarding the packet. The IPX packet is then forwarded to this router. IPX routers hold *routing tables* that contain routing information on all networks reachable by that router. These routing tables are updated by sending routing information using the RIP protocol every 60 seconds.

Sequenced Packet Exchange (SPX)

The SPX protocol is a transport layer protocol that provides connection-oriented services on top of the connectionless IPX protocol. SPX is used when a reliable virtual-circuit connection is needed between two stations. The SPX protocol takes care of flow control and sequencing issues to ensure that packets arrive in the right order. SPX also ensures that destination node buffers are not overrun with data that arrives too rapidly.

Prior to data transmission, SPX control packets are sent to establish a connection, and a connection ID is associated for that virtual circuit. This connection ID is used in all data transmissions. At the end of data transmission, an explicit control packet is sent to break down the connection. SPX uses an acknowledgment scheme to make sure that messages arrive at the destination. Lost packets are re-sent, and sequencing is used to keep track of packets so that they arrive in the proper order and are not duplicated.

SPX uses a timeout algorithm to decide when a packet needs to be retransmitted. The timeout is dynamically adjusted based on the delay experienced in packet transmission. If a packet times out too early, its value is increased by 50 percent. This process can continue until a maximum timeout value is reached or the timeout value stabilizes. To verify that a session is still active when there is no data activity, SPX sends probe packets to verify the connection. The frequency of these probe packets can be controlled by settings in the NET.CFG file discussed in later chapters.

An interesting aspect of SPX is that many SPX connections can use the same IPX socket (see fig. 1.7). This allows multiple connection IDs to be multiplexed and de-multiplexed across the same IPX socket.

Figure 1.7
SPX Connection IDs and Sockets.

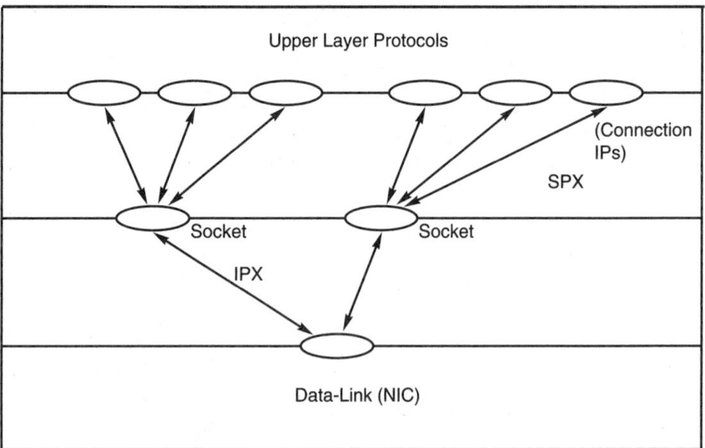

Figure 1.8 shows the SPX packet structure. The *Connection Control* field is used for regulating flow of data across the connection. The bit sequence 0001000, for example, is used as an end-of-message signal, and the bit sequence 01000000 indicates that an acknowledgment is requested.

The *Data Stream Type* indicates the nature of the data contained in the SPX data field. It is used to identify the upper-layer protocol to which the SPX data must be delivered. It serves a similar role to the Packet Type field in the IPX packet.

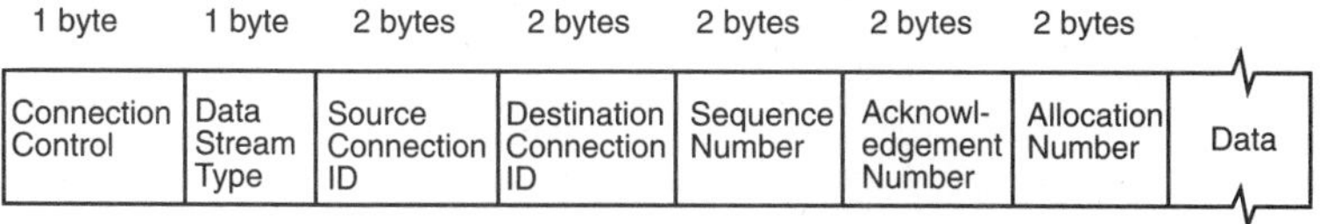

Figure 1.8
SPX packet structure.

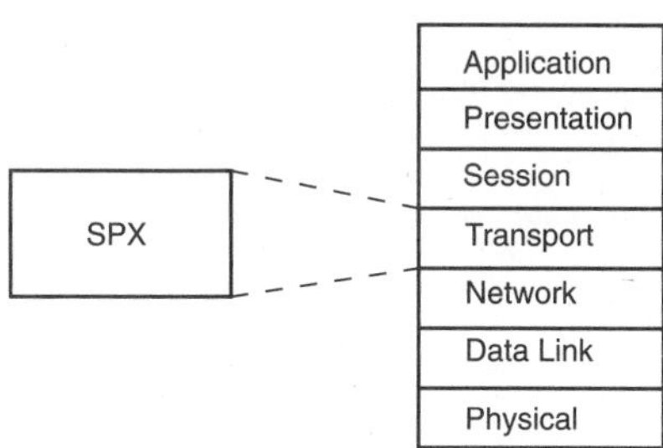

The *Source Connection ID* and the *Destination Connection ID* are the virtual circuit numbers used to identify a session. These IDs are used to de-multiplex separate virtual circuits on a single socket.

The *Sequence Number* field numbers every packet sent. This is used by SPX to detect lost and out-of-sequence packets.

The *Acknowledgment Number* field is used to indicate the next packet the receiver expects. It means that all packets prior to the Acknowledgment value have been received correctly.

The *Allocation Number* indicates how many free buffers the receiver has available on a connection. This value is used by the sender to pace the sending of data. The use of the Allocation Number helps avoid overwhelming the receiver with packets that do not have a corresponding buffer available to hold them.

The NetWare workstation does not usually use the SPX protocol; it uses the IPX protocol directly. Reliability of transmission is maintained by the NCP protocol. SPX is used to establish remote connections between the Print Server and remote printers. SPX also is used in NetWare SQL and remote connections to the NetWare file server through RCONSOLE.

Sequenced Packet Exchange II (SPX II)

SPX II was introduced by Novell in 1993 to provide improvements over the older SPX protocol in the following areas:

- Window flow control
- Larger packet sizes

- Improved negotiation of network options
- Safer method of closing connections

Novell cited the following reasons for providing a newer SPX protocol (SPX II):

- The poor performance of SPX when compared with IPX
- The small packet size (maximum 576 bytes) used by SPX because of an absence of a facility to negotiate a larger packet size between two end-points
- Lack of proper *flow control* (the sending of additional data packets before the acknowledgment of a previous packet is sent)
- Lack of an orderly release (*graceful close*) mechanism, which ensures that data is not lost when a connection is closed

Like SPX, SPX II is a connections-oriented transport layer (OSI Layer 4) protocol (see fig. 1.9). SPX II is designed to be backwards compatible with SPX. This means that SPX II is designed to recognize SPX packets as well as the enhanced SPX II packet. To achieve this goal, the SPX II packet format is designed to be a superset of the SPX packet structure. Figure 1.10 compares the packet structure of SPX II. You can see that the SPX II has an additional field called the *Negotiation Size* that is 2 bytes long. The additional Negotiation Size field makes the SPX II header (including the IPX header) 14 bytes. Whereas the data portion of the SPX packet is limited to 534 bytes (576 bytes minus12 bytes of SPX header and 30 bytes of IPX header), the data portion of the SPX II packet is as follows:

> Maximum Media Packet size – SPX II Header Size – IPX Header Size = Maximum Media Packet size – 44

Figure 1.9
SPX and SPX II and the OSI model.

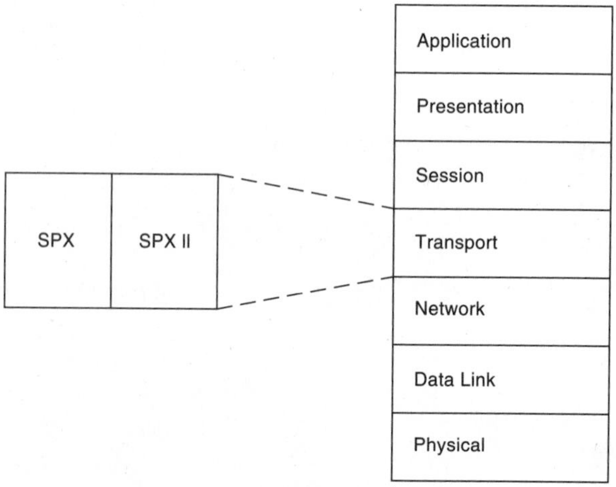

	1 byte	1 byte	2 bytes	2 bytes	2 bytes	2 bytes	2 bytes	2 bytes
SPX II	Connection Control	Data Stream Type	Source Connection ID	Destination Connection ID	Sequence Number	Acknowledgement Number	Allocation Number	Negotiation Size

	1 byte	1 byte	2 bytes	2 bytes	2 bytes	2 bytes	2 bytes
SPX	Connection Control	Data Stream Type	Source Connection ID	Destination Connection ID	Sequence Number	Acknowledgement Number	Allocation Number

Figure 1.10
SPX and SPX II packet structure.

Apart from the additional Negotiation Size, additional bits are defined for the first field of the SPX II packet called the *Connection Control* field. Figure 1.11 shows these additional bits, and table 1.1 describes them. SPX II uses the bit fields defined in figure 1.11 to operate in an SPX-compatible mode or the SPX II-enhanced mode. If the SPX II (Bit 5) in the Connection Control field is set, it indicates an SPX II packet. If such a packet is received from a remote end, it indicates that the remote end supports SPX II. If the SPX II bit is not set in the Connection Control field, it indicates the older SPX packet.

Table 1.1
SPX II Connection Control Field Definitions

Field Abbreviation	Bit Position	Description
XHD	8	Reserved for extended header
RES	7	Reserved. Must be 0.
NEG	6	Negotiate Size Request/Response
SPX II	5	Indicates an SPX II packet structure
EOM	4	End of Message; indicates end of message
ATN	3	Gains attention of the remote end
ACK	2	Requests that the remote end acknowledge the reception of the data packet
SYS	1	Indicates a system packet. System packets are used for controlling the SPX connection and are not sent to the application process. System packets are not numbered by the Sequence Number field.

1

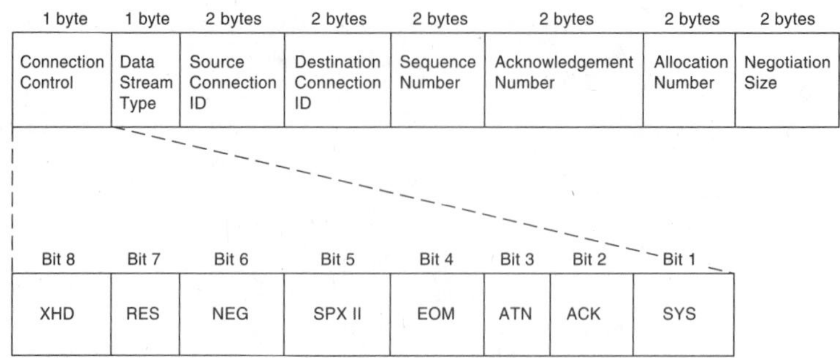

Figure 1.11
SPX Connection Control field.

You can switch from SPX to SPX II enhanced mode during connection establishment by the SPX protocol software. During connection establishment, the SPX protocol software can negotiate the maximum packet size to be used for the connection. To do this, set the NEG bit (bit 6) to 1 in the connection request. Figure 1.12 shows the connection establishment and packet size negotiation sequence for SPX II. In this example, Side A initiates the open connection request and is the active side. Side B receives the request and responds to it and is the passive side. Side A makes an open connection request and sets the NEG field in the *Connection Control* field. When the receiving Side B sees an open connection request and the NEG field set to 1, it sends an acknowledgment to this packet and sets the maximum packet size it is willing to use in the *Negotiation Size* field. In this example, Side B negotiates a maximum packet size of 1,500 bytes. Side A on receiving an acknowledgment of its open connection request sent earlier, reads the maximum size from its local interface. On NetWare nodes, this information is contained in the LSL layer for ODI drivers. In the example, Side A's maximum packet size is 4,096 bytes. Side A sets the negotiated size to the minimum of the maximum packet sizes of the local and the remote interface as illustrated in the following formula:

> Negotiated size = min (Max. packet size of local interface, Maximum packet size of remote interface)

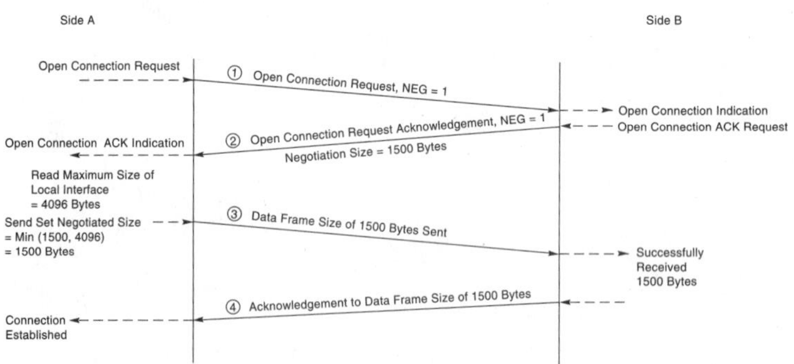

Figure 1.12
SPX II Open Connection Negotiation.

Side A transmits a packet size of 1,500 bytes, the negotiated packet size, to Side B. If Side B successfully receives this packet, it acknowledges the negotiated packet size, and the connection is established.

After connection is established, the data transfer phase begins. SPX II uses a *windowing* algorithm for flow control. With NetWare 4.*x*, a default window size of eight packets is used. This means that up to eight packets can be sent before an acknowledgment is received for the packets sent. SPX II uses the Sequence Number field, the Acknowledgment Number field, and the Allocation Number field to ensure proper reception of packets. Each packet is numbered by the value in the Sequence Number field. The Sequence Number field is incremented for each data packet in the send direction.

Figure 1.13 shows data transfer that uses a window size of eight. The ACK packet from the receiver contains a Sequence Number (seq) value of zero; an Acknowledgment Number (ack) value of 101; and an Allocation Number (alloc) value of 108. The Acknowledgment Number represents the number of the next expected packet. The Allocation Number is the Sequence Number of the last packet the receiver expects to see in the current window. In other words, the number of packets to be received have a sequence number from ack to alloc. The window size can be computed as shown in the following formula:

Window Size = alloc – ack + 1

In the example in figure 1.13, ack = 101 and alloc = 108. The current window size can be computed as follows:

Window Size = 108 – 101 + 1 = 8

After eight packets are sent (see fig. 1.13), the receiver sends an ACK packet containing an *ack* value of 119, the next expected data packet. If the *alloc* value is set to its old value of 118, the ACK packet closes the window. Another ACK packet with an *alloc* value greater than or equal to *ack* must be sent to open a window of size *alloc - ack* + 1. In the example in figure 1.13, the last ACK packet has an *ack* of 109 and an *alloc* of 118, which opens a window size of 10.

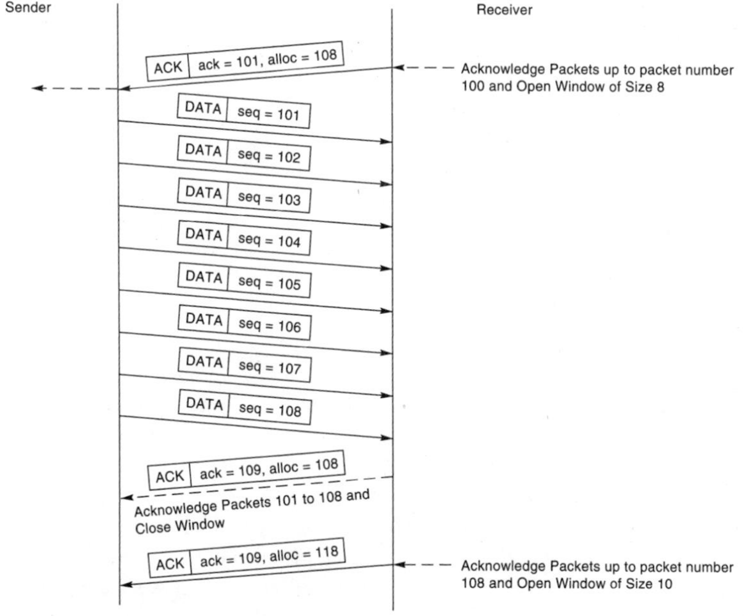

Figure 1.13
Data Transfer using SPX II windows.

A number of data packets can be acknowledged by a single acknowledgment packet. The acknowledgment (ACK) packet has the ACK and SYS bits in the Control Field set. The Sequence Number field of the ACK packet is zero. If the Sequence Number field of an ACK packet is non-zero, it represents a Negative Acknowledgment (NAK) packet. The Sequence Number field of a NAK packet is the number of data packets that need to be re-sent. Figure 1.14 shows the use of a NAK packet. The ACK packet from the receiver has an *ack* of 1 and an *alloc* value of 5. This opens a window of size 5. The sender sends packets with Sequence Numbers of 1 to 5. Packets with Sequence Numbers of 2 to 4 are not received correctly. A NAK packet is sent by the receiver containing a *seq* value of 3 (the number of packets lost), and an *ack* value of 2 (the first of the bad packets). The *alloc* value is unchanged in the NAK packet. The receiver upon receiving these NAK packets retransmits 3 packets starting with sequence number 2. These are packets 2, 3, and 4 that were not received correctly. After receiving all the packets in the window, the receiver acknowledges all the packets with a single ACK packet whose *ack* is set to 6.

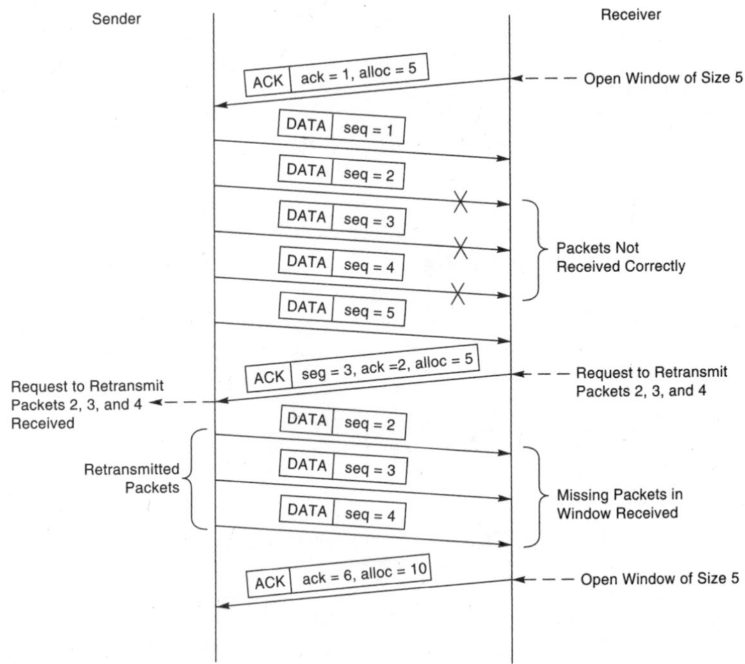

Figure 1.14
Use of the NAK packet to retransmit lost packets in SPX II.

At the end of the data transfer phase, the connection is closed. Connection close in SPX II is done using the orderly release mechanism in which the connection close is negotiated by both sides. This allows each communication end point to delay the acknowledgment of a connection close request until all its data is transmitted and acknowledged. Figure 1.15 shows the orderly release mechanism. Side A makes a request to terminate the connection by issuing an orderly release request. Side B responds by sending an ACK packet for the orderly release request. This ACK packet means that Side B received the orderly release request. Connection is not terminated, however, unless Side B also issues an orderly release request. Side B may prefer to send additional data to side A. When Side B completes sending its data, it sends an orderly release request. If the side that sent the original orderly release request (Side A) receives an orderly release request from the remote end point (Side B), it terminates the connection.

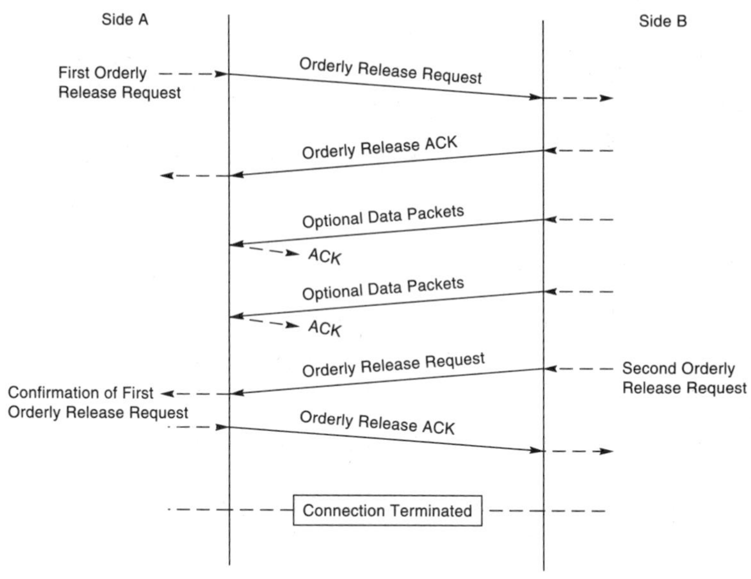

Figure 1.15
Orderly release mechanism of SPX II.

SPX II provides enhanced option management functions that allow applications to query, verify, or negotiate network-specific options. SPX II provides for the following two types of option negotiations:

- Negotiation between an application and its local end point
- Negotiation between an end point and its remote end point

The type of options negotiated between an application and its local end point include the following:

- The size of the local interface's window
- Whether an application can negotiate options with a remote end point
- Maximum size of incoming and outgoing packets
- Number of times to retransmit a packet if a transmission failure occurs
- Minimum time-out value before retransmitting a packet. A value of zero instructs SPX II to use its own internal default.
- Maximum time-out increment added to the minimum time-out value for retransmitting a packet
- Maximum amount of time that a connection can remain idle before SPX II must send a *watchdog query packet* (also called *keep alive packet*) to determine if the connection is still valid
- Maximum amount of time for a session setup packet to arrive after the connection request is made

The type of options negotiated between an end point and its remote end point include the following:

- Maximum size of incoming and outgoing packets from remote end
- Retrieving the value of the remote window size
- SPX II packet characteristics: checksum, data encryption, data signing

An application can negotiate an option with the local end point; but if the local end point negotiates a different value for this option from the remote end point, the application does not have the correct value for this option. The option must query SPX II for the current value.

To see the advantages of SPX II over SPX, consider an example of a the transfer of a 20 KB file over an Ethernet LAN. Using SPX, the number of packets needed can be estimated as follows:

1. Maximum packet size for SPX is 534 bytes. A 20 KB packet requires the following:

   KB/534B = 20*1024/534 = 38.4 packets

   The 38.4 packets refers to 38 packets of 534 bytes and one packet of 188 bytes.

2. The receiver sends back 39 ACK packets for each of the 39 data packets. A total of 39 data packets *plus* 39 ACK packets are sent during the data transfer phase for a total of 78 packets.

If SPX II is used for transmitting the same 20 KB file, the maximum packet size for Ethernet is used. This allows each SPX II packet to hold the following:

Maximum Media Packet size - SPX II Header Size - IPX Header Size

= Maximum Media Packet size - 44

= 1,500 - 44

= 1,456 bytes

Assume that SPX II uses a window size of 8 (default for NetWare 4.*x*).

The number of packets needed for SPX II can be estimated as follows:

1. Maximum packet size for SPX is 1,456 bytes. A 20 KB packet requires the following:

   KB/534 B = 20*1024/1456 = 14.1 packets

   The 14.1 packets refers to 14 packets of 1,456 bytes and one packet of 96 bytes—a total of 15 data packets.

2. Because the window size is eight packets, the 14 packets can be sent in two windows. The receiver sends back two ACK packets for each of the two windows. The last window has only seven packets, and the last 96-byte packet has an EOM flag set in the Connection Control field. This is a signal to the receiver to reassemble the packets into a single message for delivery to the application on the receiver.

A total of 15 data packets plus two ACK packets are sent during the data transfer phase, for a total of 17 packets.

The packet ratio during the data transfer phase between SPX and SPX II is 78/17 = 4.5.

Extensive studies by Novell indicate that SPX II out-performs SPX by a factor of as much five, despite the fact that SPX II was used with the TLI (Transport Layer Interface), which introduces an extra overhead. SPX II is used with TLI because TLI provides a general transport layer API that can be used for a large number of transport layer protocols (such as TCP, SPX, and SPX II).

The Packet Exchange Protocol

The *PXP* (Packet eXchange Protocol) is derived from the XNS *PEP* (Packet Exchange Protocol) and is a transport layer protocol. PXP provides a lower reliability of service than SPX, but is more reliable than IPX. It is used to transmit a request and to receive a response. The request/response sequence is called a *transaction.* PXP does not keep track of duplicate requests and therefore is suitable for idempotent transactions, or upper-layer protocols that can handle duplicate requests. An *idempotent* transaction is one that causes no undue side effects even if the transaction is duplicated by mistake. An example of this is the reading of a data block from a file. If this request is mistakenly duplicated, no harm is done.

An example of an application that makes use of PXP is the NetBIOS emulation software that can run on NetWare workstations.

Figure 1.16 illustrates the structure of the PXP packet. The ID field is a 32-bit field that identifies the requesting packet. This field serves as a transaction ID used to match the PXP packet request and its reply.

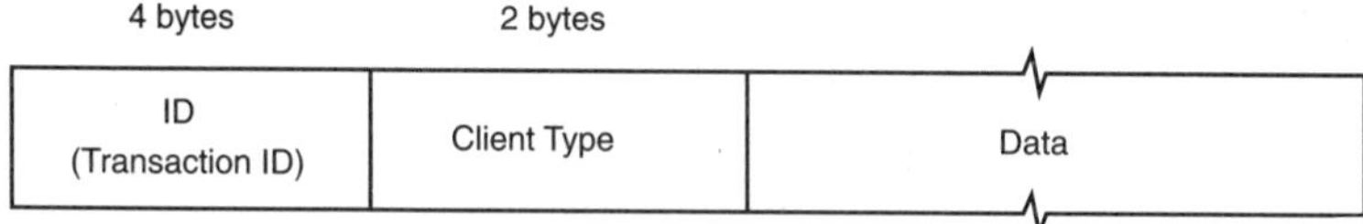

Figure 1.16
PXP packet structure.

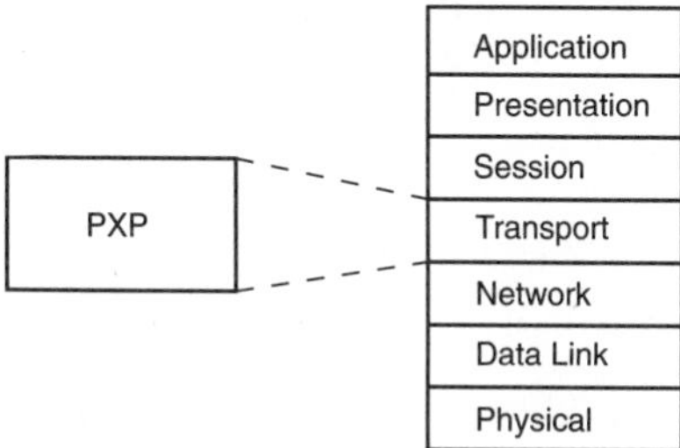

The *Client Type* identifies the user of the PXP protocol. The user of the PXP protocol is called the *Client Protocol.*

NetWare Core Protocol

The *NetWare Core Protocol* (NCP) is used to implement NetWare's file services, print services, name management services, file locking, synchronization, and bindery operations. A *bindery* refers to the internal database of network objects kept on the NetWare server.

NCP is implemented at the workstation and the NetWare server. On the workstation side, NCP is implemented in the NetWare shell and is limited to making requests for services to an NCP server. The NetWare server (NCP server) contains a full implementation of NCP that can execute or process requests for NCP services. NCP provides transparent remote file and print services to a NetWare client. These remote services have the appearance of being local to the client.

NCP directly uses the IPX protocol, avoiding the use of SPX or PXP. This enables NCP to be more efficient because it avoids the protocol overhead of the SPX and PXP protocols. NCP provides its own mechanism for session control, error detection, and retransmission. Figure 1.17 shows an NCP packet structure.

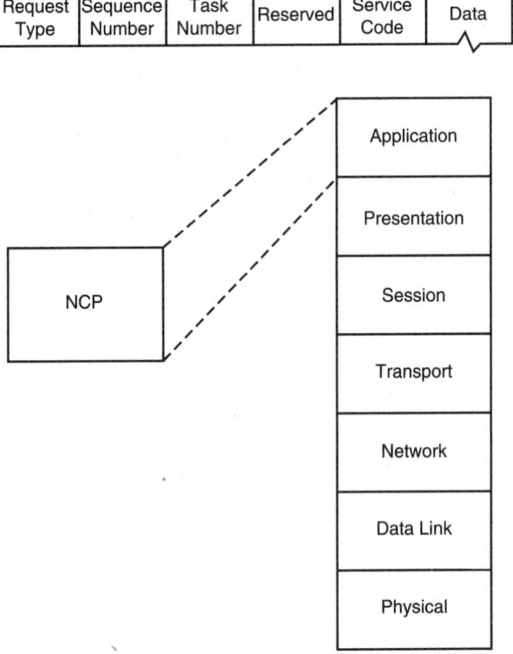

Figure 1.17
NCP packet structure.

In figure 1.17, the *Request Type* field indicates the type of NCP request. Examples of NCP request types are Create Service Connection, Negotiate Buffer Size, Logout, Get Server Date and Time, Get Station Number, and End of Job. The *sequence number* is used as a transaction ID field and identifies an NCP request and its corresponding response. The *service code* further identifies the service requested by the workstation.

Packet Burst Mode

The NCP Protocol numbers each request and reply packet with a sequence number. This *sequence number* is used as a transaction ID field to identify an NCP request and its corresponding response for a particular session. The session is identified by the connection number and is placed in every NCP transaction.

The NCP transaction models the client/server interaction between a workstation and a NetWare server quite well. This transaction, however, introduces a new set of problems when NetWare servers are used in wide area networks. Typically, WAN link capacities today are in the range of tens of kilobits per second. This is quite small in relationship to the megabits-per-second speed used in LANs, causing WANs to run at slower speeds than LANs. In addition, WANs have longer delays because they span longer distances. Using a single request and single response model as shown in figure 1.18 means that the effective throughput of the transaction is as follows:

$$E = (Q + N^*Pn)/(N^*Td) \qquad (1)$$

E = effective throughput of the NCP transaction

Q = size of the request packet

N = number of reply packets

Pn = size of the *N*th single reply packet

Td = round-trip delay

As can be seen in figure 1.18, if the reply is larger than a single packet, it has to be sent in a series of successive transactions, each of which takes additional time equal to the round-trip delay. Many earlier NetWare routers have a limit of 512 bytes per packet, which means that if a 64 KB file had to be transferred, 128 of the 512 bytes would have to be sent.

To get an idea of what the throughputs are like, substitute numerical values in the preceding equation. Assume the size of the request packet is 128 bytes, and the reply is a 1,000-byte packet. Also, assume that the round-trip delay on the link is one second, and the reply consists of four packets. Plugging these values into the equation, you get the following:

$$E = (128 + 4^*1000)/(4^*1) = 1032 \text{ bytes/sec} = 8{,}256 \text{ bits/sec}$$

In Packet Burst mode, a single read reply can be sent as a series of successive packets that do not have to wait for an NCP acknowledgment of every message sent. Also, an NCP request can consist of a series of requests that do not have to wait to be acknowledged by a reply. Figure 1.19 shows a request and a three-packet reply using packet burst. The effective throughput is now computed by the equation:

Ep = (Q + N*Pn)/Td (2)

Ep = effective throughput of the NCP transaction using packet burst

Q = size of the request packet

Pn = size of the *N*th single reply packet

Td = round-trip delay

N = number of reply packets

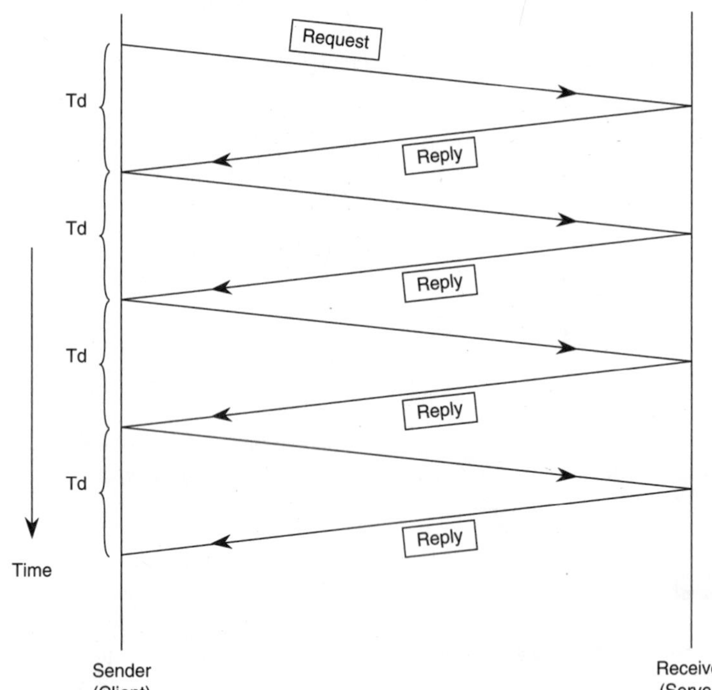

Figure 1.18
Single request/reply transactions.

Using the preceding numerical example, you can calculate the effective throughput using packet burst as follows:

Ep = (128 + 4*1000)/1 = 4,128 bytes/sec = 33,024 bits/sec

You can see that the effective throughput for packet burst, in this example, is four times that of the normal throughput. This is not surprising because dividing equation (2) by equation (1) reveals the following:

$$Ep/E = N \qquad (3)$$

or that:

$$Ep = N*E \qquad (4)$$

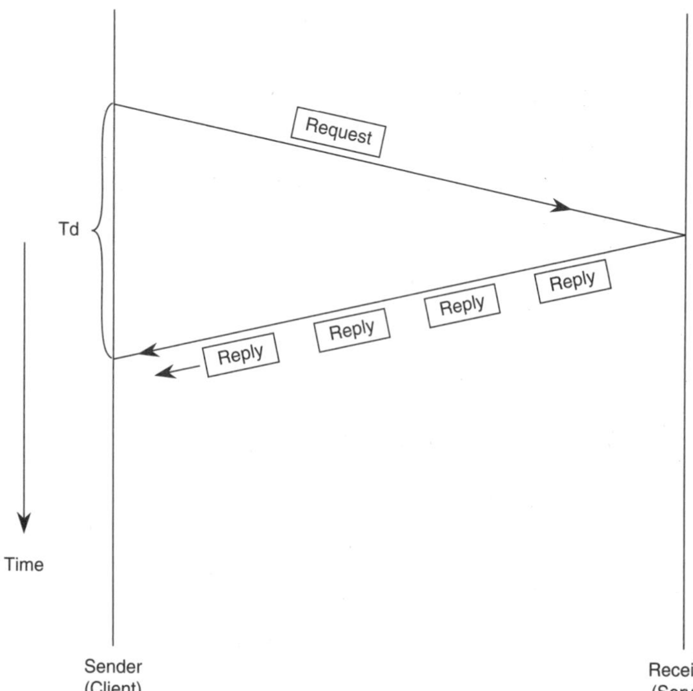

Figure 1.19
Single request/multiple reply.

Effective throughput of packet burst, therefore, is *N* times that of a normal NCP. Tests done by Novell reveal that performance improvements of up to 300 percent can be achieved on a WAN. Packet burst also can improve performance in a LAN by up to 50 percent. Burst mode also can be used in situations in which a transaction consists of a multiple request/single reply sequence (see fig. 1.20).

Burst mode implements a dynamic window size algorithm and dynamic timeout mechanism. The dynamic window size allows burst mode to adjust the number of frames that can be sent in burst mode. The *dynamic timeout* (also called *transmission metering*) adjusts itself to line quality, line bandwidth, and line delay.

To set up packet burst, you need the PBURST NLM to run on the NetWare server, and the special burst shell called BNETX.COM to run at the DOS workstation. You can get the latest copies of these through the NetWire forum on CompuServe. To configure packet burst, perform the following steps:

1. Load the PBURST NLM on the NetWare server.

2. As an optional step, to observe the statistics screen on PBURST, issue the following command on the NetWare server console:

```
SET ENABLE PACKET BURST STATISTICS SCREEN=ON
```

This is a new command that is added when the PBURST NLM loads.

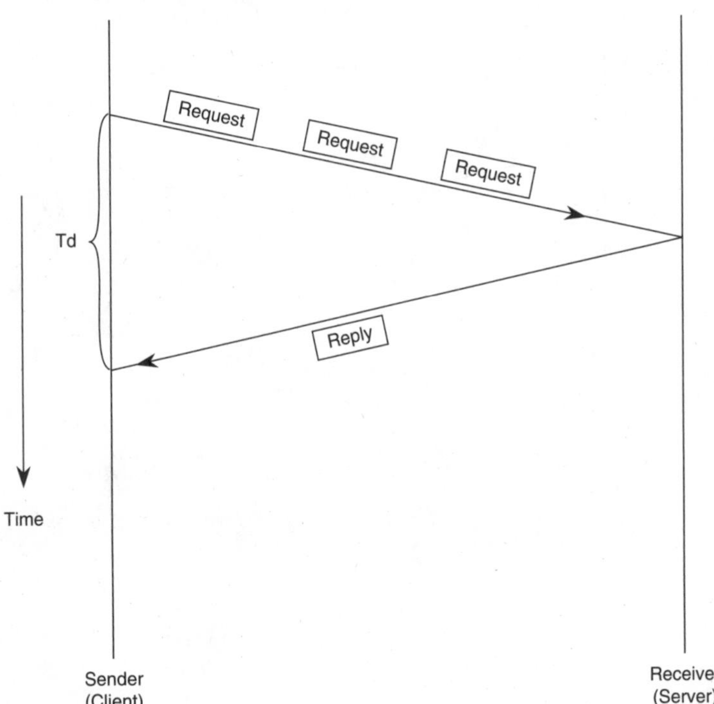

Figure 1.20
Multiple request/single reply.

3. At the workstation, configure the following in NET.CFG:

```
PB BUFFERS = N
```

in which *N* is from 2 to 10.

If the NIC driver can handle larger size packets, configure it using the following command:

```
IPX PACKET SIZE LENGTH=N
```

in which *N* is the packet size.

4. Load BNETX.COM at the workstation.

5. The statistics screen should show the packet burst activity.

BNETX uses about 7 to 8 KB more RAM compared to the conventi performance should offset the additional memory requirement. The BNETX also depends on the PB BUFFERS parameter set in NET to additional PB BUFFERS parameters, use the following formul

Buffer Memory Requirement = PB BUFFERS * (102 +

The 102 bytes is the combined protocol overhead of IPX, NCP *event control block* and is a data structure in memory used to manage packe

Other NetWare Protocols

This section on native NetWare protocols has focused on the major NetWare protocols and their packet structure. Other protocols such as RIP, SAP, Watchdog, Echo, Serial, and Error are discussed in other sections of this book in which their discussion is more appropriate. To fully understand IPX and its relationship to RIP and SAP, for example, you need to understand the intricacies of routing techniques and routing protocols. These protocols are discussed in detail in Chapter 3, "Bridging and Routing." In this chapter, some fundamental protocols, such as IPX, also are revisited, but in greater detail.

TCP/IP

Today, most people agree that the Transmission Control Protocol and the Internet Protocol (TCP/IP) is the de facto mechanism by which interoperability can be achieved. When people talk about TCP/IP, they usually refer to a variety of communication protocols such as TCP, IP, ICMP, ARP, FTP, TELNET, and NFS. The list is quite long and impressive, as new protocols and services are continually added.

The TCP/IP protocols evolved from the former ARPANET and from Internet. *Internet* is the largest network in the world, connecting thousands of nodes. TCP/IP is used as the primary transport and network protocol on the Internet.

The initial Internet protocols were developed at Stanford University and *Bolt, Beranek, and Newman* (BBN) in the 1970s. The impetus for this development came from *DOD* (Department of Defense) *Advanced Research Project Agency* (DARPA). DARPA funded the development of the *Advanced Research Project Agency NETwork* (ARPANET). ARPANET was one of the earliest packet-switched networks.

The TCP/IP protocol was integrated in the kernel of a very popular and seminal version of UNIX called the *Berkeley Software Distribution* (BSD) UNIX. BSD UNIX was a very popular version of UNIX used in many university computer science departments. Many of the commercial versions of UNIX based their TCP/IP implementation on BSD UNIX. In the mid 1980s, vendor interest in TCP/IP became very high, and it became the de facto standard for interoperability.

TCP/IP is important for the NetWare system manager because NetWare 3.*x* comes with a TCP/IP stack that allows the NetWare server to function as an IP router. If you want TCP/IP application services,

...h as *File Transfer Protocol* (FTP) and *Network File System* (NFS), you can use a product like NetWare NFS to run on the NetWare server. Figure 1.21 shows the relationship of TCP/IP to the OSI model.

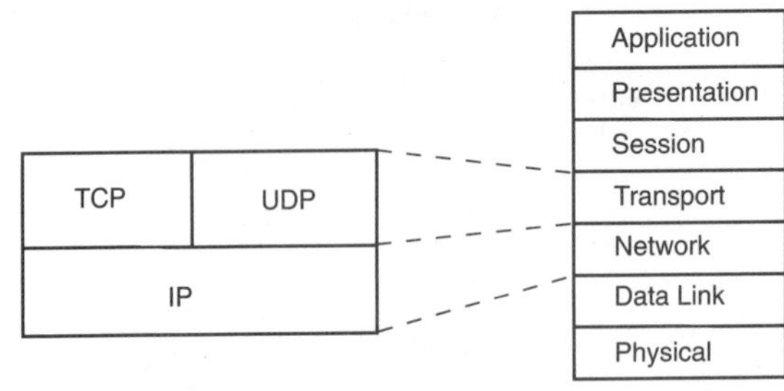

Figure 1.21
TCP/IP and the OSI model.

Transmission Control Protocol (TCP) is a transport layer protocol, and *Internet Protocol* (IP) is a network layer protocol. Figure 1.22 shows a partial list of the TCP/IP protocols. As you can see from this list, TCP/IP protocols are numerous, and a detailed discussion of these is beyond the scope of this book. Only a few of these protocols, such as IP and TCP, are discussed.

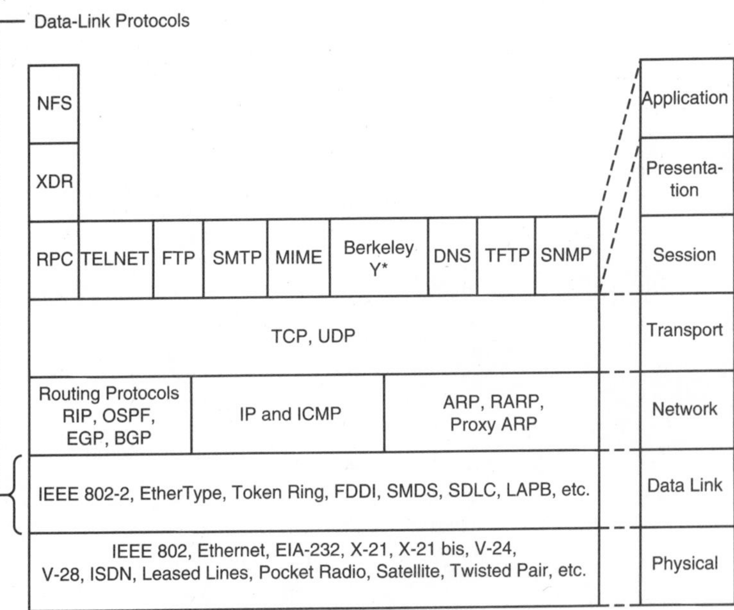

Figure 1.22
A few TCP/IP protocols.

The IP Protocol

The IP protocol is a network layer protocol that provides connectionless datagram services on top of many data link protocols (see fig. 1.22).

IP does not guarantee delivery of datagrams; it makes the best effort it can to deliver data. Upper-layer protocols, such as TCP, can be used to build guaranteed delivery services on top of IP. IP provides a number of interesting services that have become the basis of design of other protocols.

IP provides the notion of a *logical network address* independent of the underlying network. It makes use of an *Address Resolution Protocol* (ARP) to provide the binding between this logical address (called the *IP address*) and the physical node address of a node.

IP datagrams can be fragmented into smaller units to accommodate the *Maximum Transmission Unit* (MTU) of the underlying network. If fragmentation takes place, the fragments are created with sufficient information so that they can be reassembled. Reassembly of fragments to make up the original datagram is done at the destination node. Problems with IP, such as unreachable destinations and reassembly timeouts, are reported to the sender by the *Internet Control Message Protocol* (ICMP).

IP addresses are represented by a 32-bit number. Each network interface in a node that supports an IP stack must have an IP address assigned to it. The IP address is a two-part address consisting of a network ID and a host ID, as shown in figure 1.23. The most significant bits are used to determine how many bits are used for the netid and the hostid. Five address classes are currently defined: A, B, C, D, and E. Of these, class A, B, and C addresses are assignable. Class D is reserved for multicasting and is used by special protocols to transmit messages to a select group of nodes. Class E is reserved for future use.

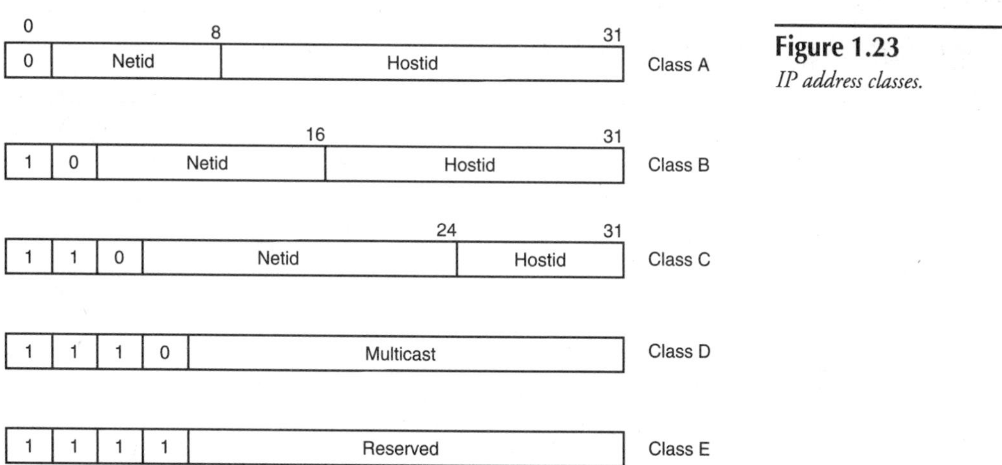

Figure 1.23
IP address classes.

The netid portion of the IP address is similar to the network number used in IPX protocols. It identifies the network uniquely. Interconnected networks must have unique netids. If your network is going to be connected to other networks, such as the Internet, you must apply to a central authority to obtain a unique netid (network number) not in use by anyone else. The central *Internet Address Network Authority* (IANA) is as follows:

DDN Network Information Center
14200 Park Meadow Drive, Suite 200
Chantilly, VA 22021, USA
e-mail address: HOSTMASTER@NIC.DDN.MIL

Older reference works on TCP/IP may list the *Stanford Research Institute* (SRI) as the *Network Information Center* (NIC). This no longer is true; but you can still obtain *Request For Comments* (RFCs) from SRI. Request For Comments are documents that define the Internet protocol standards and other information pertaining to the Internet. The standards that define IP and TCP protocols are RFC 791 and RFC 793, for example. RFC documents are in the public domain, and their distribution is unlimited.

The different types of IP address classes are defined to address the needs of networks of different sizes. Table 1.2 shows the number of networks and nodes possible with each address class.

Table 1.2
Reasons for Using Specific Address Class

Address Class	Number of Networks	Number of Nodes
A	127	16,777,214
B	16,383	65,534
C	2,097,151	254

A class A network is suited for very large networks, but because its netid field (see fig. 1.23) is only seven bits, there can be only 127 such networks. The original ARPANET is an example of a class A network. Class B networks are medium-size networks and are suited for medium to large organizations. Class C networks are suited for small organizations, in which each network can have no more than 254 nodes.

The 32-bit number is represented for convenience as four decimal numbers corresponding to the decimal value of the four bytes that make up the 32-bit IP address. Each decimal number is called an *octet.* The decimal numbers are separated by periods (.). This shorthand notation for IP addresses is called *dotted decimal notation.* Figure 1.24 shows the format of an IP packet. The following shows an IP address in its binary form and also as a dotted decimal notation:

IP Address = 10010000 0001011 01001010 1001010

IP Address = 144.19.74.202

In figure 1.24, the version number field is four bits long and indicates the format of the IP header. This allows future IP packet structures to be defined. The current version number is four. Table 1.3 shows the other possible values of the version number field. IP version seven may be the next possible IP format that allows for longer IP addresses; however, this is still the subject of considerable debate.

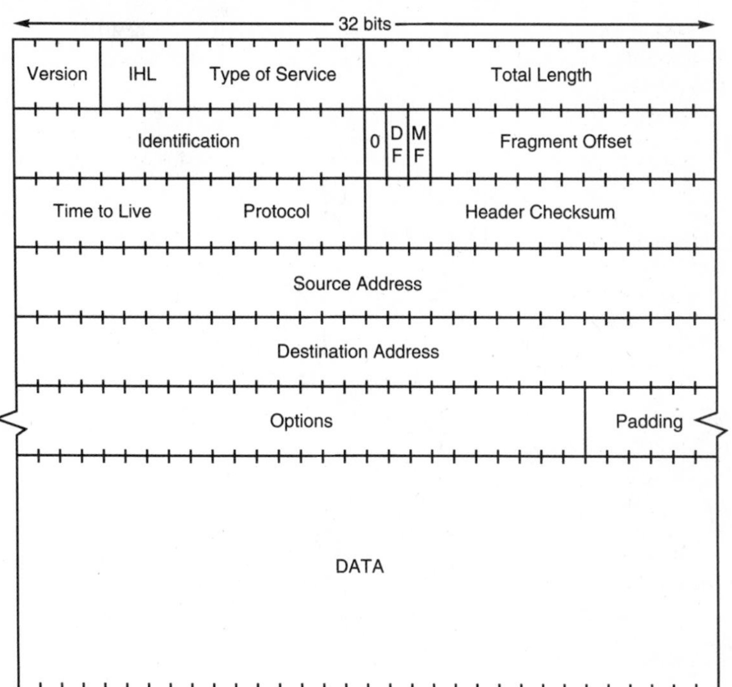

Figure 1.24
IP packet structure.

Table 1.3
IP Version Number Values

IP Version	Meaning
0	Reserved
1_3	Unassigned
4	IP
5	Stream IP (Experimental IP)
6_14	Unassigned
15	Reserved

The *Internet Header Length* (IHL) is the length of the header in 32-bit words. This field is required because the IP header contains a variable-length option field.

The *Type Of Service* (TOS) field informs the networks of the *Quality Of Service* (QOS) desired, such as precedence, delay, throughput, and reliability. Figure 1.25 shows the meaning of this eight-bit field.

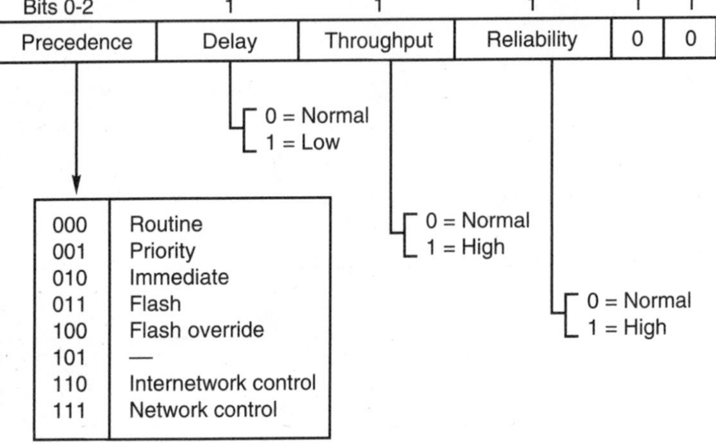

Figure 1.25
Type Of Service field for IP packets.

The *Precedence* field reflects the military origin of IP networks. The following are the meanings of some of the precedence values:

- Flash: ASAP (As Soon As Possible); maximum priority on all circuits
- Immediate: Within four hours
- Priority: Same day
- Routine: Within one day

Most IP implementations and routing protocols (RIP, HELLO, and so on) ignore the Type of Service field.

The Precedence field is intended for Department of Defense applications of the Internet protocols. The use of nonzero values in this field is outside the scope of the IP standard specification. Vendors should consult the *Defense Information Systems Agency* (DISA) for guidance on the IP Precedence field and its implications for other protocol layers.

Vendors should note that the use of precedence most likely requires that its value be passed between protocol layers in much the same way as the TOS field is passed. The IP layer must provide a means for the transport layer to set the TOS field of every datagram sent; the default is all zero bits. The IP layer should pass received TOS values up to the transport layer.

Although little used in the past, the TOS field is expected to play an increasing role in the near future with routing protocols such as OSPF that could use the TOS field. The TOS field is expected to be used to control two aspects of router operations: routing and queuing algorithms. The TOS field also can be mapped into the data link layer for effective sharing of serial lines by different classes of TCP traffic.

The *Total Length* field contains the length of the IP header and data in bytes. The maximum size of the datagram is 65,535 bytes. All IP nodes must be prepared to receive a minimum size of 576 bytes (512 bytes of data plus 64 bytes of protocol overhead).

The *Identification* field is set uniquely for each datagram, and is the datagram number. It is used in conjunction with the fragment flags *DF* (Don't Fragment), *MF* (More Fragments), and Fragment Offset fields to reassemble the datagram. If the DF flag is set to one, the datagram should not be fragmented. The MF flag set to one indicates to the receiver that more fragments are to come. An MF set to zero indicates the last fragment.

The *Fragment Offset* field indicates the position of the fragment's data relative to the start of the original datagram. This is a 13-bit field and is measured in eight-byte groups. This means that the Fragment Offset value must be multiplied by eight to get the byte offset.

The *Time To Live* (TTL) is measured in seconds and represents the maximum time an IP datagram can live on the network. It should be decremented at each router by the amount of time taken to process the packet. The intent is that TTL expiration causes a datagram to be discarded by a router, but not by the destination host. Hosts that act as routers by forwarding datagrams (such as NetWare 3.*x*) must follow the router rules for TTL. The TTL field has two functions: limit the lifetime of TCP segments and terminate Internet routing loops. Although TTL is time in seconds, it also has some attributes of a hop count because each gateway is required to reduce the TTL field by at least one. This is why some implementers mistakenly set it to 16, because 16 is infinity for RIP. But TTL is independent of RIP metrics.

Other considerations for TTL fields are the following:

- A host must not send a datagram with a TTL value of zero, and a host must not discard a datagram just because it is received with TTL less than two.
- An upper-layer protocol may want to set the TTL to implement an expanding scope search for some Internet resource. This is used by some diagnostic tools and is expected to be useful for locating the "nearest" server of a given class using IP multicasting, for example. A particular transport protocol also may want to specify its own TTL boundary on maximum datagram lifetime.
- A fixed value must be at least big enough for the Internet *diameter*, the longest possible path. A reasonable value is about twice the diameter, which allows for continued Internet growth.
- The IP layer must provide a means for the transport layer to set the TTL field of every datagram sent. When a fixed TTL value is used, that value must be configurable. Unfortunately, most implementations do not allow the initial TTL value to be set. A default value of 32 or 64 is very common.

The *Protocol* field indicates the upper-layer protocol that is to receive the IP data. It is similar in function to the Packet Type field for IPX packets. The "Assigned Numbers" RFC 1060 contains the defined values for this field; for example, TCP has a protocol field value of six; UDP has a value of 17; and ICMP has a value of one.

The *header checksum* is used for the IP header only. The 1's complement of each 16-bit value making up the header is added (excluding the Header Checksum field). Then the 1's complement of the sum is taken. This field is recomputed at each router because the TTL field is decremented, and the header modified.

The *source address* and *destination address* are the 32-bit IP addresses of the source and destination nodes.

The IP options are security, loose source routing, strict source routing, record route, and Internet timestamp.

The TCP Protocol

TCP is the primary transport protocol used to provide reliable, full-duplex, virtual-circuit connections. The connections are made between port numbers of the sender and the receiver nodes. TCP has an octet-stream orientation. An *octet* is a group of eight bits. Therefore, an *octet stream* is an eight-bit stream. There is no inherent notion of a block of data. TCP can be used to provide multiple virtual-circuit connections between two TCP hosts.

Figure 1.26 shows the TCP packet structure. The *source port* and *destination port* numbers identify the end-point processes in the TCP virtual circuit. Some port numbers are well-known, whereas others are dynamically assigned. RFC 1066 contains a description of some of the well-known port numbers. A few of these are shown in table 1.4.

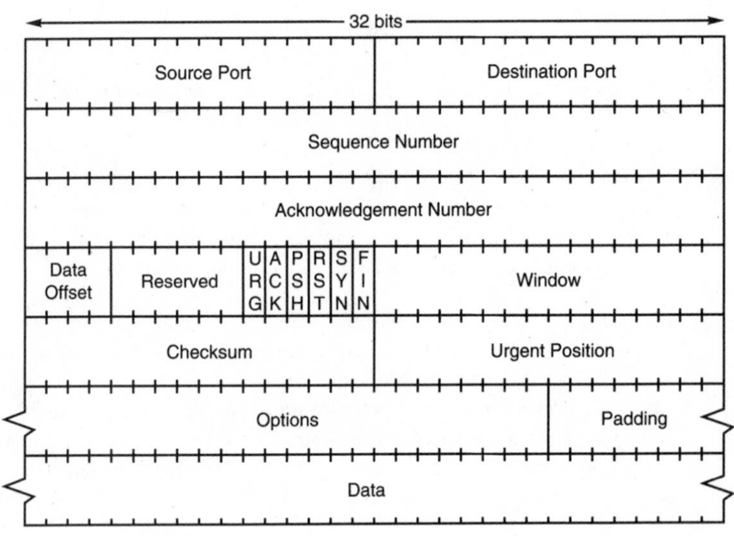

Figure 1.26
TCP packet structure.

Table 1.4
Some Well-Known TCP Port Numbers

Port Number	Description
0	Reserved
5	Remote Job Entry
7	Echo
9	Discard
11	Systat
13	Daytime
15	Netstat
17	Quotd (Quote of the day)
20	ftp_data
21	ftp (Control)
23	telnet
25	smtp
37	time
53	name server
102	ISO-TSAP
103	X.400
104	X.400 sending service
111	Sun RPC
139	NetBIOS session source
160-223	Reserved

The 32-bit *sequence number* is the number of the first byte of data in the current message. If the SYN flag is set to one, this field defines the initial sequence number to be used for that session. A 32-bit value is used to avoid using old sequence numbers that already may be assigned to data in transit on the network.

The *acknowledgment number* indicates the sequence number of the next byte expected by the receiver. TCP acknowledgments are cumulative—that is, a single acknowledgment can be used to acknowledge a number of prior TCP message segments.

The *Data Offset* field is the number of 32-bit words in the TCP header. This field is needed because the TCP options field can be variable in length.

The flags that follow have the following meanings:

- **URG.** This flag is used to send out-of-band data without waiting for the receiver to process octets already in the stream. When the URG flag is set, the Urgent Pointer field is valid. RFC 1122 states that the urgent pointer points to the sequence number of the LAST octet (not LAST+1) in a sequence of urgent data, and that RFC 793 describes it incorrectly as LAST + 1. A TCP implementation must support a sequence of urgent data of any length. A TCP layer must inform the application layer asynchronously whenever the TCP layer receives an Urgent pointer with no previous pending urgent data, or whenever the Urgent pointer advances in the data stream.

  There must be a way for the application to learn how much urgent data remains to be read from the connection, or at least to determine whether more urgent data remains to be read. Although the Urgent mechanism can be used for any application, it is normally used to send interrupt-type commands to a Telnet program. The asynchronous, or *out-of-band*, notification allows the application to go into urgent mode, reading data from the TCP connection. This allows control commands to be sent to an application whose normal input buffers are full of unprocessed data.

- **ACK.** The ACK flag indicates that the Acknowledgment Number field is valid.

- **PSH.** This flag tells TCP to immediately deliver data for this message to the upper-layer process. When an application issues a series of send calls without setting the PSH flag, the TCP may aggregate the data internally without sending it. Similarly, when a series of segments is received without the PSH bit, a TCP may queue the data internally without passing it to the receiving application.

  The PSH bit is not a record marker and is independent of segment boundaries. Some implementations incorrectly think of the PSH as a record marker, however. The transmitter should collapse successive PSH bits when it packetizes data to send the largest possible segment.

  A TCP can implement PSH flags on send calls. If PSH flags are not implemented, then the sending TCP must not buffer data indefinitely and must set the PSH bit in the last buffered segment (for example, when no more queued data is to be sent).

  RFC-793 erroneously implies that a received PSH flag must be passed to the application layer. Passing a received PSH flag to the application layer is now optional.

An application program is logically required to set the PSH flag in a send call whenever it needs to force delivery of the data to avoid a communication deadlock. A TCP should send a maximum-size segment whenever possible to improve performance, however. This means that on the sender side, a PSH may not result in the segment being immediately transmitted.

When the PSH flag is not implemented on send TCP calls (or when the application/TCP interface uses a pure streaming model), responsibility for aggregating any tiny data fragments to form reasonable-size segments is partially borne by the application layer. Generally, an interactive application protocol must set the PSH flag at least in the last send call in each command or response sequence. A bulk transfer protocol like FTP should set the PSH flag on the last segment of a file, or when necessary to prevent buffer deadlock.

At the receiver, the PSH bit forces buffered data to be delivered to the application (even if less than a full buffer is received). Conversely, the lack of a PSH can be used to avoid unnecessary wake-up calls to the application process; this can be an important performance optimization for large time-sharing hosts.

- **RST.** The RST bit resets the virtual circuit due to unrecoverable errors. The reason could be a host crash or delayed duplicate SYN packets.
- **SYN.** This flag indicates the opening of a virtual-circuit connection. TCP connections are opened using the *three-way-handshake* procedure. The SYN and the ACK flags are used to indicate the following packets:

  SYN = 1 and ACK = 0 Open Connection Packet

  SYN = 1 and ACK = 1 Open Connection Acknowledgment

  SYN = 0 and ACK = 1 Data packet or ACK packet
- **FIN.** The FIN flag terminates the connection. Connection termination in TCP is accomplished by using a graceful close mechanism. Both sides must agree to terminate by sending a FIN = 1 flag before connection termination can occur; doing this ensures that data is not unexpectedly lost by either side by an abrupt connection termination.

The *Window* field is used to implement flow control and is used by the receiver to advertise the number of additional bytes of data it is willing to accept.

The *Checksum* field is 1's complement of the sum of all the 16-bit words in the TCP packet. A 96-bit pseudoheader (see fig. 1.27) is pre-pended to the TCP header for checksum computation. The pseudoheader is used to identify if the packet has arrived at the right destination. The pseudoheader has the protocol ID (6 for TCP), source, and destination IP address. Because the TCP header contains the source and destination port number, this describes the connection between the endpoints.

The *Options* field currently defines only the *Maximum Segment Size* (MSS) option, which is negotiated during connection establishment.

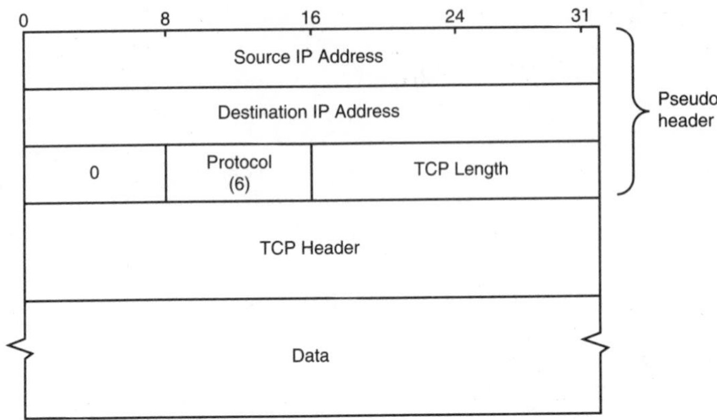

Figure 1.27
Pseudoheader in TCP checksum.

AppleTalk

AppleTalk is a set of proprietary protocols used by Apple Computers to network its Macintosh desktop computers. AppleTalk protocols are important to NetWare users and Administrators because the Macintosh computer can be found in many organizations, and Macintosh users and other NetWare users often need to share information. You learn in later chapters of this book that Novell supports Macintosh users in NetWare-based networks by running the AppleTalk protocols directly on the NetWare server, enabling the NetWare user to emulate an AppleShare server to Macintosh clients.

Macintosh users can use their familiar graphical user interface to access the NetWare/AppleShare server. The AppleShare emulation solution also is used to connect Macintosh users to other network architectures, such as DEC VAX computers, UNIX computers, and Windows NT Advanced servers. This section helps you understand the background and protocol architecture of AppleTalk.

Development of AppleTalk protocols began in 1983 and became available in 1984. What is unusual about Apple's approach is that the AppleTalk protocols were implemented in the Macintosh OS; it was not a separate piece of client networking software that had to be loaded onto the Macintosh OS.

Also, no additional networking hardware had to be added to provide the equivalent of a Network Adapter interface. The networking hardware was built into the Macintosh system board in the form of the LocalTalk interface. LocalTalk is RS-422 based at the physical layer and can operate at up to 230.4 Kbps. Whereas this speed is much less than that of Ethernet and Token Ring, it is adequate for small networks and applications that do not have high network bandwidth requirements.

The first set of AppleTalk protocols had a limitation of 254 nodes per physical network and ran on LocalTalk hardware. This was called AppleTalk Phase I. In 1989, Apple released an updated set of protocols called AppleTalk Phase II. AppleTalk Phase II overcomes the 254 node/network limit by allowing a range of network numbers to be associated with a physical network. A node is identified by a pair of numbers: the network number and the node number. When a specific network number is used up to form the network number/node number pair, another network number from the network range can be used.

AppleTalk Phase II, besides providing support for LocalTalk, also supports other data link access protocols such as Ethernet, IEEE 802.3, and the IEEE 802.5 Token Ring. These hardware technologies are discussed in greater detail in the next chapter. The Ethernet and Token Ring network boards used in Macintosh networks are called *EtherTalk* and *TokenTalk* respectively. The FDDI boards for Macintosh workstation are called FDDITalk. Figure 1.28 shows the link access technologies used in AppleTalk in relationship with the OSI model.

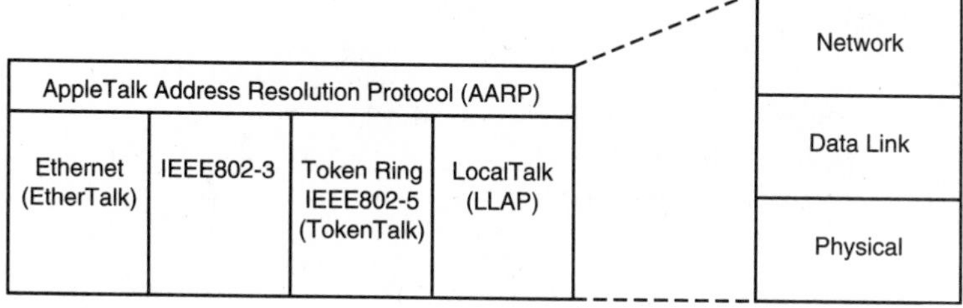

LLAP = LocalTalk Link Access Procedure

Figure 1.28
AppleTalk link access technologies.

AppleTalk Data Link Layer

The *AppleTalk Address Resolution Protocol* (AARP) is modeled after TCP/IP's ARP protocol and provides a binding between upper-layer network addresses and data link layer addresses. AARP makes it possible to run AppleTalk protocols on different data link layer technologies with the data link layer address of a destination node being determined dynamically.

Figure 1.29 shows examples of how AARP can be used. AARP can be used in a situation in which a sender station knows the destination's upper-layer protocol address, but does not know the data link layer address. The data link layer address is needed by the AppleTalk drivers to send the AppleTalk frame over the physical link. In this case, an AARP broadcast request is sent that contains the destination's upper-layer protocol address.

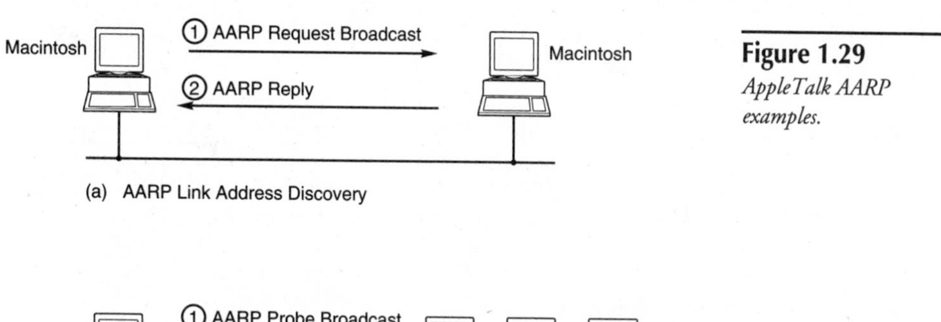

Figure 1.29
AppleTalk AARP examples.

All nodes receive the broadcast, but only the node that has the same upper-protocol address as in the AARP request packet responds with its data link address. The protocol address and data link address mappings are kept in a local cache in memory and are called the *Address Mapping Table* (AMT). Before sending a data transmission, the AMT is consulted to discover the data link address of the destination. If no entry is in the AMT, AARP is used to discover the mapping. Old AMT entries are automatically timed-out and purged from the AMT table.

Another situation in which AARP can be used is in *dynamic address selection.* When a Macintosh computer is booted on a network, it picks a node address randomly and sends an AARP request broadcast with the same node address. If a reply is received, it implies that the node address is in use. In this case, the station must pick another address and repeat the process until a unique node address is determined. Figure 1.30 shows the AARP packet structure.

The meanings of the fields in figure 1.30 are described as follows:

- **Hardware Type and Protocol Type.** These fields together define the data link and protocol address type used by AARP. The hardware type could be EtherTalk, TokenTalk, or LocalTalk; and the protocol type is AppleTalk.
- **Hardware Address Length and Protocol Address Lengths.** These fields are needed because AARP was designed to provide mappings between a number of different hardware and protocol technologies. Because the length of the hardware address (data link address) and protocol address could be different, their length values are placed in the AARP packet.
- **Function Code.** This field determines the type of AARP packet. Currently, three codes are defined for the three AARP packets. Function Code 1 indicates an AARP request; Function Code 2 indicates an AARP reply; and Function Code 3 indicates an AARP probe used for dynamic address selection.
- **Source Hardware Address, Source Protocol Address, Destination Hardware Address, and Destination Protocol Address.** These fields have lengths specified by the Hardware Address Length and Protocol Address Length fields. These fields contain the hardware address and protocol address of the nodes involved in the AARP exchange.

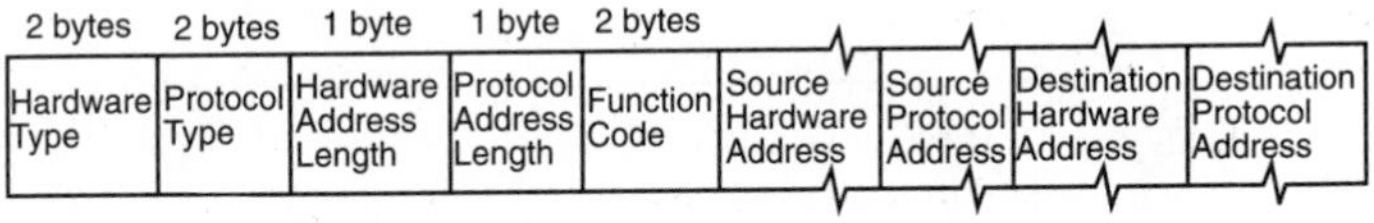

2 bytes	2 bytes	1 byte	1 byte	2 bytes				
Hardware Type	Protocol Type	Hardware Address Length	Protocol Address Length	Function Code	Source Hardware Address	Source Protocol Address	Destination Hardware Address	Destination Protocol Address

Figure 1.30
AARP packet structure.

AppleTalk Network Layer

Figure 1.31 shows the network layer used in AppleTalk that is related to the OSI model. The *Datagram Delivery Protocol* (DDP) is the major protocol used by the network layer. Other protocols such as *Routing Table Maintenance Protocol* (RTMP), *Zone Information Protocol* (ZIP), and *Name Binding Protocol* (NBP) also help support the operation of the network layer.

The DDP is a connectionless protocol between two processes running on separate nodes on the network. Because it is connectionless, DDP by itself cannot be used to guarantee delivery of the datagram. Upper-layer protocols at the transport layer must be used to guarantee delivery.

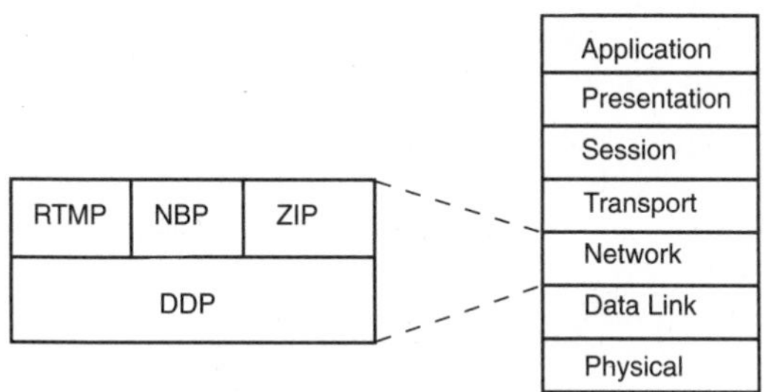

Figure 1.31
AppleTalk network layer.

Sockets define the boundary points between DDP and the upper layers through which data exchange takes place. DDP sockets are similar in concept to IPX sockets and TCP/IP port numbers discussed earlier. The sockets are described by numbers ranging from 1 to 255. Numbers 1 to 127 have well-defined meanings and are *Statically Assigned Sockets* (SASs). Socket numbers from 128 to 254 are assigned dynamically on demand and are called *Dynamically Assigned Sockets* (DASs).

DDP contains a provision for assigning unique network addresses for each node by using a combination of a 16-bit network number and an eight-bit node number. To further distinguish *Upper Layer Processes* (ULPs) running on a node, the socket number can be used. Thus a complete process address consists of the following 3-tuple:

<network number, node number, socket number>

Older networks such as LocalTalk are limited to a single network number and an eight-bit node number associated with that network number. Each node number of these *nonextended networks* is unique. In AppleTalk Phase II, data link layer technologies can support more nodes than the eight-bit value of Phase I. To support these networks the concept of extended networks was introduced. Extended networks can have a range of network numbers assigned to them. This allows for more nodes than can be accommodated by an eight-bit value.

Figure 1.32 shows an example of a short header DDP packet structure. The short header DDP packet is designed for nonextended networks. The extended header packets have additional fields for the network number, node numbers, hop count, and checksum. The network numbers are used by routers to distinguish between the different networks. The hop count is also used by routers to determine the distance a packet has to traverse.

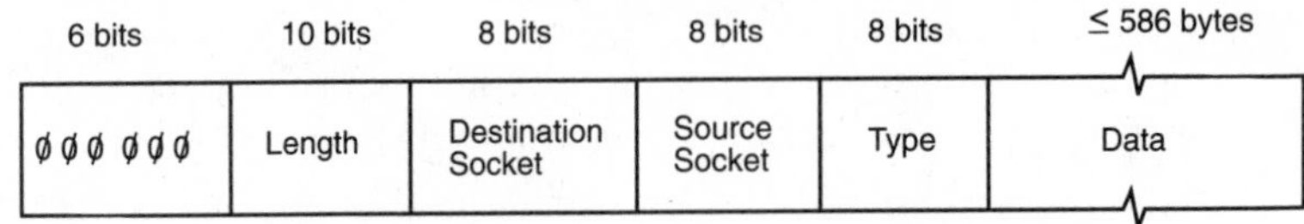

Figure 1.32
Short header DDP packet structure.

The first six bits are unused and set to zero. The next ten bits represent the length of the datagram, which cannot exceed 586 bytes. The destination and source socket numbers follow next and identify the processes on the nodes. The Type field is used to indicate to which Upper Layer Process the DDP packet data should be sent.

In an AppleTalk Internet, several physical AppleTalk networks are connected by routers. The routers are responsible for directing the packet to the correct destination network. The source node must determine if the packet is to be sent to a router or the local network. It does this by examining the destination network number. If this number is in the range assigned to the local network, the destination node is in the local network.

If the number is not in the range assigned for the local network, it is sent to one of the AppleTalk routers. The routers exchange information using the RTMP protocol. The RTMP protocol was derived from the XNS RIP protocol and is an example of a Distance-Vector routing protocol. These classes of protocols are discussed in Chapter 3, "Bridging and Routing."

The Name Binding Protocol provides a logical association between AppleTalk names and network addresses. It is similar in concept to the *Domain Name System* (DNS) protocol used in TCP/IP networks. AppleTalk names are symbolic names used to designate services on the network and are therefore easier for users to deal with than network addresses, which are numeric quantities. These services include such things as printers or shared modems. AppleTalk services are called *Network Visible Entities* (NVEs). Examples of NVEs are sockets and mailboxes. NVEs have names called entity names and attributes that specify the characteristics of the NVE. NBP is used to build an association (called *name binding*) between the NVE name and its network address. The name and address associations are kept in name tables.

All the name tables on the AppleTalk Internet make up the *name directory*. When an application wants to use a name, it consults its local name table. If it cannot find the name, it issues an NBP lookup packet to find the name's address. The address is returned by NBP. Because DDP does not perform Internet broadcasts, NBP lookups across the entire Internet are not possible. To make it possible to look up names on an Internet, the concept of a zone was created. NBP lookups can be done on a zone basis.

A *zone* represents a group of logically related AppleTalk nodes. They are a means of categorizing how nodes are typically used on the internetwork. They can span multiple networks. A zone can include a few nodes from one network, some nodes from another network, and so on. Or, a zone can include all the nodes in one physical network or only a few of the nodes on that network. When a node is powered up, the zone it belongs to is selected from a list of zones for that network. All nodes in a nonextended network must belong to the same zone.

A zone-wide NBP lookup is sent to the local router responsible for broadcasting the NBP lookup request to all networks in the specified zone. Only nodes in the selected zone can reply to the NBP lookup packet.

When the concept of zone was created to solve the NBP broadcast problem, a mechanism was needed to maintain the mapping between network numbers and zones. The Zone Information Protocol was created to maintain this mapping. This mapping is maintained in tables called *Zone Information Tables* (ZITs). ZITs are maintained in AppleTalk routers. When a node starts up, it uses a ZIP request packet to discover the zone it belongs to. When a router discovers new networks via the RTMP protocol, that router sends a ZIP request for obtaining the zone list for the new network.

AppleTalk Transport Layer

Figure 1.33 shows the transport layer used in AppleTalk that is related to the OSI model. AppleTalk uses two transport protocols: *AppleTalk Transaction Protocol* (ATP) and *AppleTalk Data Stream Protocol* (ADSP).

The ATP protocol is based on the concept of completing a transaction reliably. A *transaction* is defined as a request/response sequence between a client and a server. Each transaction is numbered by a transaction ID, which enables the client to associate a transaction response with the correct transaction request. Because either a transaction request or response can get lost in transmission, it is important for the client to know which transactions must be *executed once* (XO) only, and which must be done *at-least-once* (ALO).

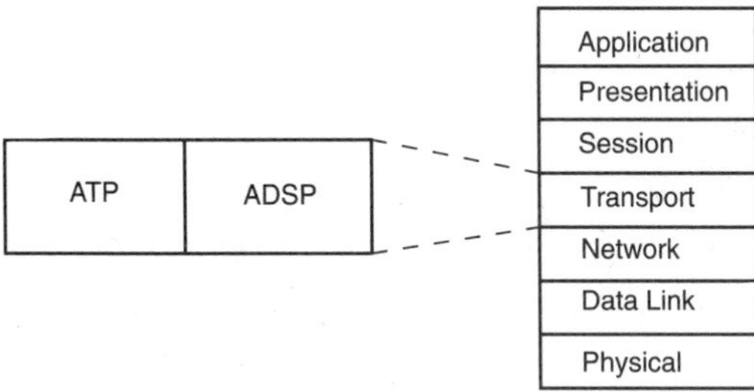

Figure 1.33
AppleTalk transport layer.

The ALO transactions can be repeated without any harm; an example of this is a read request for a block of data in a file. ALO transactions also are called *idempotent transactions.* The XO transactions must not be repeated because they could have undesirable consequences. An example of an XO transaction is a request by a client to append a data block to the end of a file. If this command is repeated, an additional data block is added to the end of the file. XO transactions also are called *non-idempotent transactions.*

If the data to be transmitted is larger than can be transmitted by the underlying network, ATP can fragment and reassemble data with the limitation that the original message must be limited to eight fragments. Because of varying delays and errors in transmission, a packet could get out of sequence or become lost. A bitmap/sequence number field is used in the ATP header to keep track of packets. For a transaction request, this field represents a bitmap; for a transaction reply, it represents a sequence number. The *bitmap* refers to the number of responses expected by the client. The client allocates a buffer to hold each response.

Figure 1.34 shows an initial transaction request with a bitmap of 00000111. Each bit position that is a 1 corresponds to an expected response. The responses contain sequence numbers. In the example in the figure, responses 0 and 2 are received correctly, but response 1 is lost. The client makes a request with a bitmap of 00000010, which indicates to the server that packet 1 is outstanding and needs to be sent again. If the number of responses is less than the expected number, an end-of-message packet is sent.

Figure 1.34
An ATP transaction example.

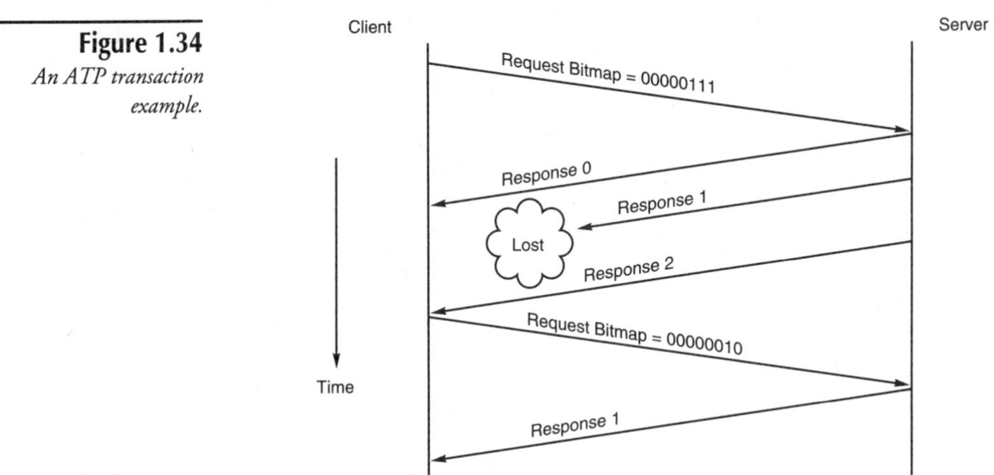

The *Control Information* field in an ATP packet (see fig. 1.35) indicates the type of ATP packet such as request, response, XO, or ALO. The *Bitmap/Sequence number* field indicates the expected response and the sequence number of the response packet. The *Transaction ID* field matches a response with a request.

Another AppleTalk transport layer protocol is the ADSP. The ADSP protocol provides full duplex virtual circuit capability between two sockets. The data flow is stream-oriented in a manner similar to TCP. Each byte in the stream has a sequence number. Flow control is achieved by a sliding-window mechanism. The window size is adjusted based on the amount of data the other side is willing to accept and has a maximum size of 64 KB.

Two types of ADSP packets are defined: *control* and *data packets.* ADSP control packets are defined so that they can be used for virtual circuit operation, such as creation and teardown. The ADSP protocol, unlike ATP, does not have any inherent client/server orientation. Any side can initiate the virtual circuit connection.

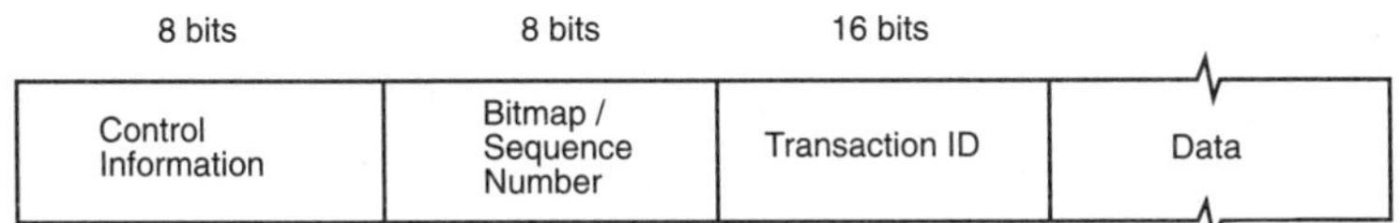

Figure 1.35
AppleTalk transaction protocol.

AppleTalk Session Layer Protocol

Figure 1.36 shows the session layer used in AppleTalk in relationship with the OSI model. AppleTalk uses two session protocols: *AppleTalk Session Protocol* (ASP) and *Printer Access Protocol* (PAP).

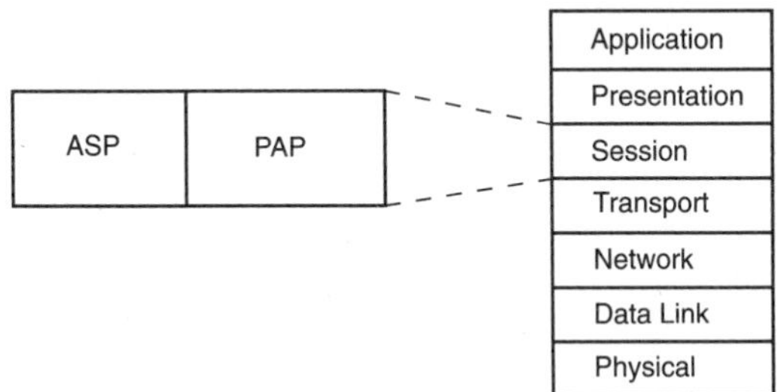

Figure 1.36
AppleTalk session layer.

ASP is used to create, maintain, and destroy sessions that use the underlying transport mechanism provided by the ATP layer. ASP builds on the concept of the transaction to provide a *session* consisting of a series of transactions. The ASP user, such as a workstation, does not have to deal in terms of transactions; the workstation can open an ASP session with the server, over which it can send commands and not have to worry about commands being sent out of order, lost, or duplicated.

ASP can be used by a client to obtain status information on the server. The server also can send an ASP attention command to workstations informing them of a change in server status.

The PAP session protocol is used to create, maintain, and destroy connections to remote printer services. Although designed to be used with printers, PAP is quite general and can be used to provide connections to other services as well. PAP uses the NBP protocol to obtain the address of the server and establishes a connection by building on the services provided by ATP. All transactions are sent using the XO mode of ATP. PAP can be used to read data from the server or write data to it.

AppleTalk Application Layer

AppleTalk does not have an explicit presentation layer. Its most common application layer protocols are the *Apple Filing Protocol* (AFP) and *AppleTalk Print Services* (APS) (see fig. 1.37). The APS is used to provide remote printer services to a client; it uses the PAP protocol to provide printer services.

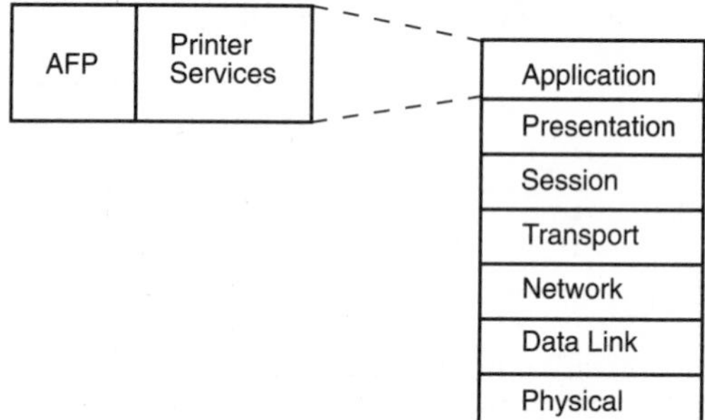

Figure 1.37
AppleTalk application layer.

The AFP protocol uses ASP to provide remote file services. It is similar in concept to NetWare's NCP and the NFS protocols used in TCP/IP networks.

File access requests from application programs are processed by AFP to determine if they are for local or remote file access (see fig. 1.38). AFP sends local file requests to the local file system. If the file request is remote, AFP uses the *AppleTalk Filing Interface* (AFI) to transmit the file request across the network. The AFI uses the AppleTalk protocols (ASP, ATP, DDP) to send the request to the server. The request is processed by the AppleTalk protocols on the server and communicated to the file server control program.

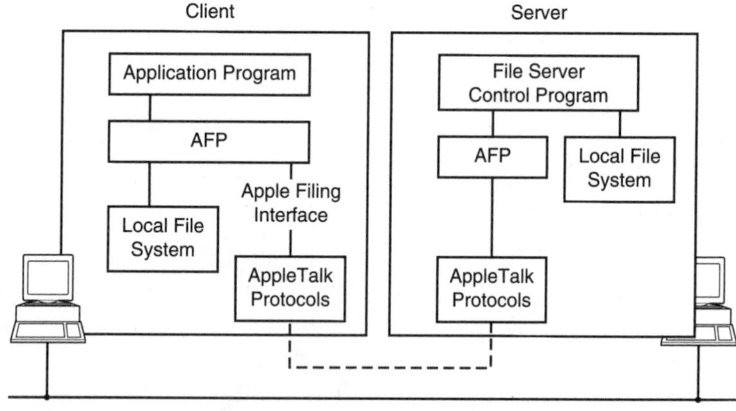

Figure 1.38
AppleTalk filing protocol.

AFP includes security mechanisms through a user/password authentication mechanism, volume passwords, and directory access control. Directory access control consists of Search, Read, and Write privileges.

Summary

This chapter laid the foundation for a better understanding of network protocols. The OSI reference model was discussed as a means to compare different protocol architectures. The ODI protocol architecture was compared with respect to the OSI reference model.

The protocol structure of some of the major protocols such as NCP/SPX/IPX, TCP/IP, and AppleTalk was discussed. These protocols are commonly found in a NetWare environment.

LAN Standards for the Physical and Data Link Layers

You must understand LAN wiring schemes to install the LAN media and identify the locations of the servers, workstations, hosts, routers, gateways, and bridges in a LAN. You can use a variety of wiring schemes used by LANs such as coaxial cable, twisted-pair wiring, and fiber optics. Even for the same media such as twisted-pair wiring, the rules are different for Ethernet, Token Ring, and ARCnet. This chapter explores wiring schemes for common LANs.

A working knowledge of LAN wiring schemes is important for the LAN manager who needs to know when distance limitations for a LAN are exceeded. Many LAN problems can be attributed to poorly designed and installed LAN wiring schemes or to wiring schemes that do not follow the wiring design rules.

Wiring schemes are just one LAN component. Other components include the following:

- Network Interface Cards (NICs)
- Network drivers
- Protocols
- Network operating systems (NOSs)
- Network shells and redirectors

The relationships among components are not always clear. The OSI model helps you keep a global vision of the components and how they interrelate.

The IEEE Local Area Network Standards

As you work with NetWare, you encounter references to the *Institute of Electrical and Electronic Engineers* (IEEE) 802 standards. The first two OSI layers are most closely related to the network components of Ethernet, Token Ring, or ARCnet. The IEEE defines Ethernet as an 802.3 standard and Token Ring as an 802.5 standard. These standards constitute the majority of networks that run Novell NetWare.

The IEEE undertook Project 802 in February of 1980 to identify and formalize LAN standards for data rates not exceeding 20 megabits per second (Mbps). Standardization efforts resulted in the IEEE 802 LAN standards. The number 802 was chosen to mark the calendar date when IEEE undertook the LAN standardization efforts (80 for 1980, 2 for February).

Figure 2.1 shows the IEEE LAN standards in relationship to the OSI model. You can see that the primary emphasis of the IEEE committee was to standardize the hardware technologies used at the physical and data link layers. This is not surprising considering that networking hardware, such as network interface cards and LAN wiring, can be modeled completely by the two lower OSI layers.

Figure 2.1
Relationship of the IEEE 802 standard to the OSI model. (Courtesy IEEE Standard 802-1990)

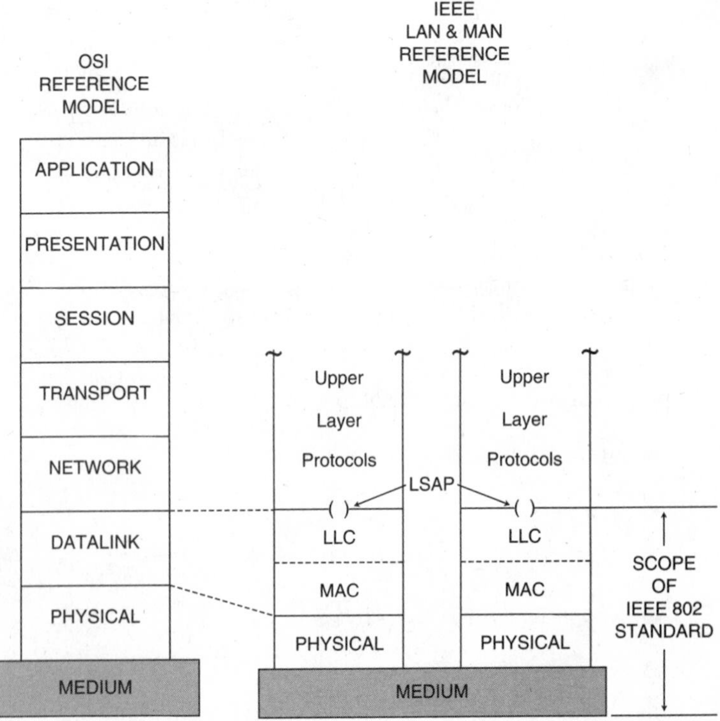

The IEEE standards divide the OSI data link layer into two sublayers: the *Media Access Control* (MAC) and the *Logical Link Control* (LLC). The MAC layer deals with media access techniques utilized to control access to a shared physical medium. Token Ring and Ethernet have different implementations of the MAC layer because they use different methods to share the physical media.

All IEEE LANs have the same LLC layer as defined by standard 802.2. The advantage of a common sublayer such as the LLC is that upper-layer mechanisms can be the same regardless of what kind of networking hardware you use.

Figure 2.1 shows the interface between upper-layer protocols and the LLC layer defined by *Link Service Access Points* (LSAPs). LSAPs are logical data link addresses. A single MAC address, such as an Ethernet address, can have multiple LSAP addresses. These multiple addresses allow multiple end-point connections between two nodes on a LAN.

The LLC layer also provides the options of virtual circuit (connections-oriented) or datagram (connectionless) services or a combination of these two.

Unacknowledged, datagram services are modeled after postal services. In the datagram approach, every packet contains complete addressing information such as destination and source addresses. No special effort is made to ensure that packets arrive intact or in the correct order. Unacknowledged, datagram services are called Type 1 services.

In a *virtual-circuit,* a special effort is made to ensure that packets arrive error-free in the order they were sent. Virtual circuits are modeled after the telephone system and require that a connection be established between two nodes before they exchange data. When data transfer is complete, this virtual circuit needs to be closed or terminated. Virtual-circuit services are called Type 2 services.

Acknowledged, datagram services, a combination of datagram and virtual circuits, are called Type 3 services. Type 3 correct data errors by retransmitting packets.

In summary, the types of services provided by LLC are as follows:

- **Type 1.** Unacknowledged, datagram service. Supports point-to-point, multipoint, and broadcast transmission.

- **Type 2.** Virtual-circuit service. Provides sequenced, flow-controlled, error-free services between LSAPs.

- **Type 3.** Acknowledged, datagram service. Provides datagram point-to-point service with acknowledgments.

Figure 2.2 shows how the IEEE committee identifies the choices at the different layers. Each of the choices represents a standard protocol or specification. Their IEEE numbers and meaning are described in table 2.1.

Table 2.1
IEEE Standards

IEEE Standard	Meaning
IEEE 802.1	LAN bridging
IEEE 802.2	Logical Link Control (LLC)
IEEE 802.3	Standardization of Ethernet Technology. Includes 100BASE-TX, 100BASE-TF, and 100BASE-T4 (Fast Ethernet)
IEEE 802.4	Token Bus standard
IEEE 802.5	Token Ring standard
IEEE 802.6	Metropolitan Area Network (MAN)
IEEE 802.7	Broadband technical advisory
IEEE 802.8	Fiber-optic technical advisory
IEEE 802.9	Integrated Voice/Data (IVD)
IEEE 802.10	LAN security
IEEE 802.11	Wireless LANs
IEEE 802.12	100BASE-VG (100VG-AnyLAN)

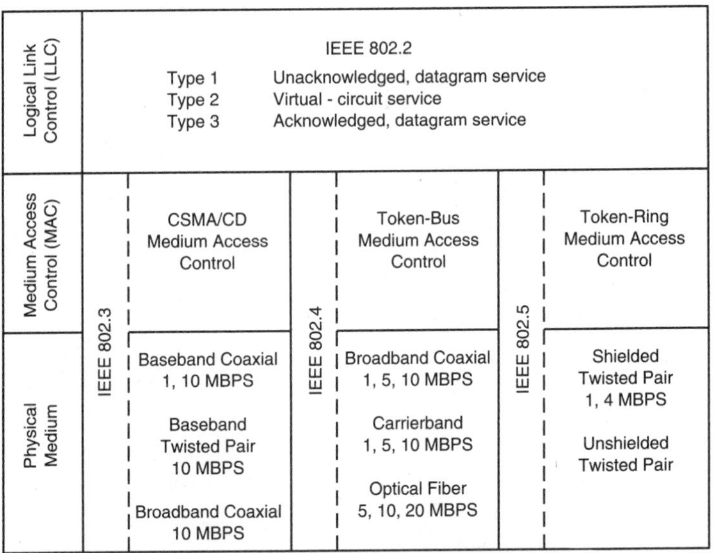

Figure 2.2
Services defined by various IEEE 802 standards.

LAN Wiring Topologies

Each LAN standard has its own rules for LAN wiring. These rules define the connecting media, the hardware requirements, and the various component arrangements. Two primary concerns exist in regard to media: the media type (usually some type of cable) and the way the various cables in the network are laid out.

The geometrical arrangement of the wiring scheme is called the *topology*. The topologies common in LANs are the star, bus, and ring. These are shown in figure 2.3.

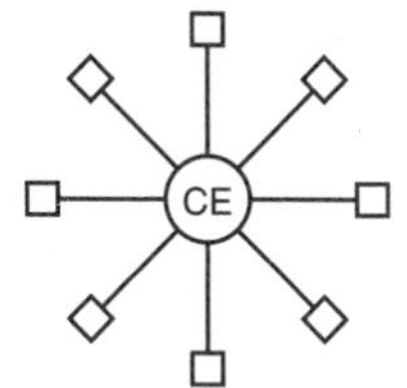

Star Topology

CE = Central Element

- Media not shared
- CE performs centralized switching/connection function

Bus Topology

- Shared media
- Access to shared media done by distributed control
- Bidirectional broadcast

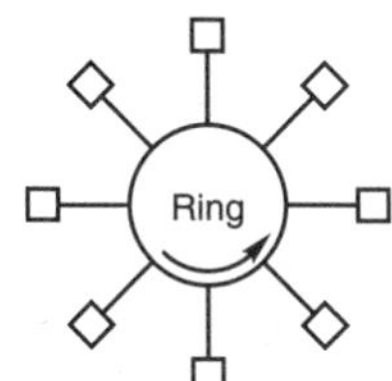

Ring Topology

- Shared media
- Access to shared media done by distributed control
- Unidirectional broadcast

Figure 2.3
LAN topologies.

In the *star* topology, communication between any two nodes must go through a central device or switching element. The devices that connect to the central switch tend to be simple, with all the complexity residing in the central switch. The central switching element should be reliable and provide signal isolation between ports so that failures at any one port are not propagated to other ports.

Classic examples of star topology are mainframe and minicomputer architectures in which the host is the central switch. If the host breaks down, it is time to take a coffee break! This points out the vulnerability of the star wiring topology: it is vulnerable to a single point of failure.

If, on the other hand, the central switching element is both reliable and provides signal isolation between the ports, the star topology is one of the best topologies. This is why it is used in ARCnet, Token Ring, *Fiber Distributed Data Interface* (FDDI), and 10BASE-T LANs. Another advantage is that it is easy to connect or remove stations from a central location. In many LANs, these central elements (hubs) come with advanced network management features like *Simple Network Management Protocol* (SNMP).

The *bus* topology consists of a linear cable to which stations are attached. Signals sent by a station on the bus propagate in both directions. Every transmission is available to every station on the network more or less simultaneously. A classic example of a bus topology is Ethernet.

The *ring* topology consists of a cable in the form of a loop with stations attached to it. Signals are sent in only one direction, and the ring can be implemented by point-to-point simplex (one direction flow) links. Stations see only the transmissions that pass them in the ring. An example of a network that uses the ring topology is a Token Ring LAN.

An important distinction should be noted between physical and logical network topologies. The *physical* topology of a network describes the way in which the actual cables are routed. The *logical* topology describes the way that the network behaves.

Token Ring is described as a ring topology because data is passed from station to station until it returns to the starting point. Data behaves as though it travels around a ring. Token Ring networks always are wired with an individual cable that extends from a central wiring hub to each workstation. Because the wiring system looks like a star, Token Ring has a star logical topology. Similarly, Ethernet always has a logical bus topology even when it is wired in a star using the new and popular 10BASE-T system.

You can see and touch the physical topology of the network. You cannot see the logical topology; it is the network from the perspective of how data is sent through the network.

Media Choices

This section briefly reviews common LAN media choices, such as coaxial, twisted pair, and fiber optic, as seen in figure 2.4.

Coaxial Cable

Coaxial cable consists of an inner conductor (usually made of a copper alloy) used for sending a signal. The return signal flows through the shield separated from the central conductor by a *dielectric* (electrically insulating material). There can be several concentric shields surrounding the common axis where the inner conductor is placed, hence the name common axis or coaxial cable. The shield provides good bandwidth capabilities and electrical noise immunity. This cable type is the "granddaddy" of LAN media because some of the earliest LANs were built using it. Coaxial cables typically are found in bus LAN topologies.

Twisted-Pair Wiring

Twisted-pair (TP) wiring consists of a pair of wires wrapped around each other. These wires are twisted to minimize radiation and electrical interference. Twisted-pair wiring can have a shield around it to improve its data transmission quality. Both *shielded twisted-pair* (STP) and *unshielded twisted-pair* (UTP) wiring are available for LANs. One wire is used for sending the signal, and the other wire acts as a signal return. Twisted-pair wiring is cheap and easy to install. Many buildings are prewired with data-grade twisted-pair wiring.

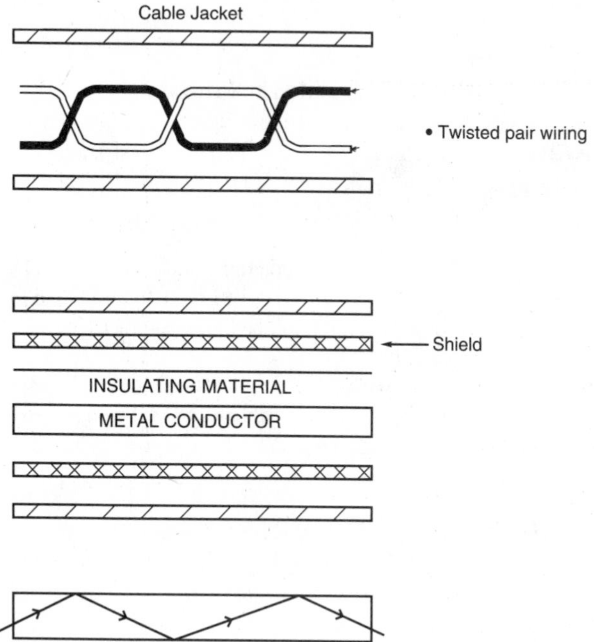

Figure 2.4
Twisted-pair, coaxial, and fiber-optic cables.

Shielded Cables

Shielded cables surround the center conductors with a jacket of fine, braided wires. The shield helps prevent outside electrical interference from affecting the conductors and also reduces the risk of broadcasting signals that can interfere with nearby electronic devices. Although shielded cables once were required for nearly all local area network installations, recent developments permit more use of unshielded twisted-pair wire, which is similar to that used for telephone communications. Networks often can use already-installed telephone wire.

Fiber-Optic Cable

Fiber-optic cables consist of a strand of fiber material, usually glass, inside a protective jacket. Signals are transmitted in the form of reflected light pulses. Signals can propagate over long distances before they need amplification (provided by repeaters). Fiber-optic has the best noise immunity characteristics compared to other wiring, is secure because it cannot be tapped easily, and has the best bandwidth characteristics. Today's high-speed LANs use fiber-optic media. The end-component costs for fiber-optic cables and the required connecting equipment, however, are higher than those of twisted-pair and coaxial cables. Fiber-optic cables, therefore, are most commonly used for high-speed connections or in situations requiring long cables or better immunity to electrical interference.

Ethernet LANs

Robert Metcalfe, along with David Boggs and others who worked for Xerox Corporation, developed a LAN based on carrier-sensing mechanisms. This LAN spanned a distance of one kilometer, supported 100 personal stations, and achieved data rates of 2.94 Mbps. This system was called Ethernet in honor of that elusive substance called ether through which electromagnetic radiation was once thought to propagate.

Ethernet was proposed as a standard by Digital Equipment Corporation, Intel, and Xerox. The first Ethernet standard was published in September 1981 and was called the DIX 1.0. DIX stood for **D**igital (DEC), **I**ntel, and **X**erox. DIX 1.0 was followed by DIX 2.0 published in November 1982.

Meanwhile, Project 802 from the IEEE had undertaken LAN standardization efforts. Not surprisingly, Digital, Intel, and Xerox proposed the adoption of Ethernet as a standard. IBM, based on prototypes built at its Zurich Lab, proposed the Token Ring as a standard. The Ethernet proposal became known as the IEEE 802.3, and the Token Ring proposal became the IEEE 802.5.

True to the nature of committee design, the IEEE 802.3 standard is not quite the same as the Ethernet standard; there are important differences. Although 802.3 and Ethernet are incompatible standards, the term *Ethernet* is used in NetWare LANs to designate 802.3-compliant networks. This book bows to common usage and uses the term Ethernet for both standards, making distinctions as required when a specific standard is discussed.

Ethernet Operation

Before an Ethernet station transmits, it listens for activity on the transmission channel (see fig. 2.5). Ethernet frequently is described as a "listen before talking" protocol. *Activity* is any transmission caused by other Ethernet stations. The presence of a transmission is called a *carrier*. The station electronics can sense the presence of a carrier.

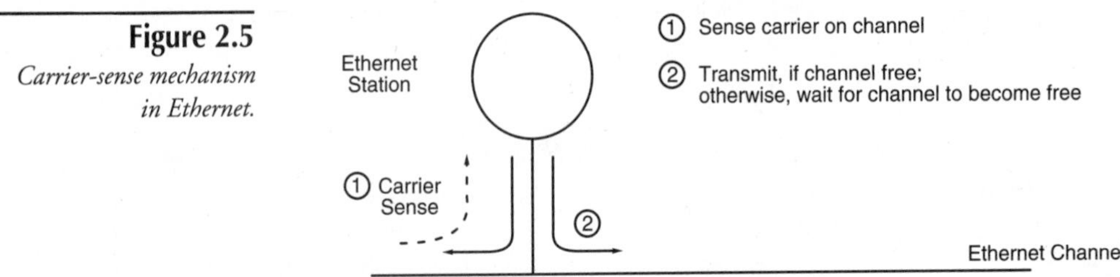

Figure 2.5
Carrier-sense mechanism in Ethernet.

If a station detects a busy channel, the station refrains from transmission. After the last bit of the passing frame, the Ethernet data link layer continues to wait for a minimum of 9.6 microseconds to provide proper interframe spacing. At the end of this time, if a data frame is waiting for transmission, and the channel is free, transmission is initiated. If the station has no data to transmit, it resumes the carrier sense (listening for a carrier) operation. The interframe gap provides recovery time for other Ethernet stations.

If a station tries to transmit when the channel is busy, a garbled transmission results. Garbled transmissions are called *collisions.*

If the channel is free (no carrier is detected), the station is free to transmit. Because multiple stations attached to the Ethernet channel use the carrier-sense mechanism, it is called a *Carrier Sense with Multiple Access* (CSMA).

If two stations decide to transmit at the same time, and no activity is on the channel, a collision occurs. Collisions occur during the normal operation of Ethernet LANs because stations transmit based on only one condition: the presence of a carrier on the channel. They do not know if packets are queued for transmission on other stations. Furthermore, the CSMA operation is complicated by propagation delay in LANs. In Ethernet, for example, signals propagate at 0.77 times the speed of light on standard (thick) cables and 0.65 times the speed of light on thin Ethernet cables. A delay occurs before a transmission is heard by all stations, and a station may transmit because it has yet to hear another station's transmission.

Collisions are a fact of life in Ethernet LANs. Ethernet stations minimize the effects of collisions by detecting the collisions as they occur. Hence the name CSMA/CD to describe the Ethernet media access mechanism (CD stands for *Collision Detect*). The stations involved in the collision abort their transmissions. The first station to detect the collision sends out a special jamming pulse to alert all stations that a collision has taken place. After a collision occurs, all stations set up a random interval timer. Transmission takes place only after this interval timer expires. Introducing a delay before transmission can reduce the probability of collisions.

When successive collisions occur, the average random time-out value is doubled. This doubling takes place for the first ten consecutive collisions. Beyond that, doubling the average random time-out value does not improve the performance of the network significantly. This mechanism is called the *truncated binary exponential back-off algorithm.*

How long does a station have to wait under heavy load conditions to transmit a frame? A station may experience a string of bad luck during which every time it transmits some other station has the bus. When collisions occur, stations introduce a delay using the random timer. But what if a station has the misfortune of timing out after the other stations already have timed out? Under the worst-case scenario, a station may have to wait indefinitely. This is not acceptable for real-time applications. Hence Ethernet is not suited for real-time applications.

The next section examines different Ethernet options.

Ethernet Cable Options

Coaxial cable serves as the medium for two variations of Ethernet: the Standard Ethernet and the Thin Ethernet. A newer Ethernet version (called the 10BASE-T standard) also can run on UTP wiring. These options are shown in figure 2.6.

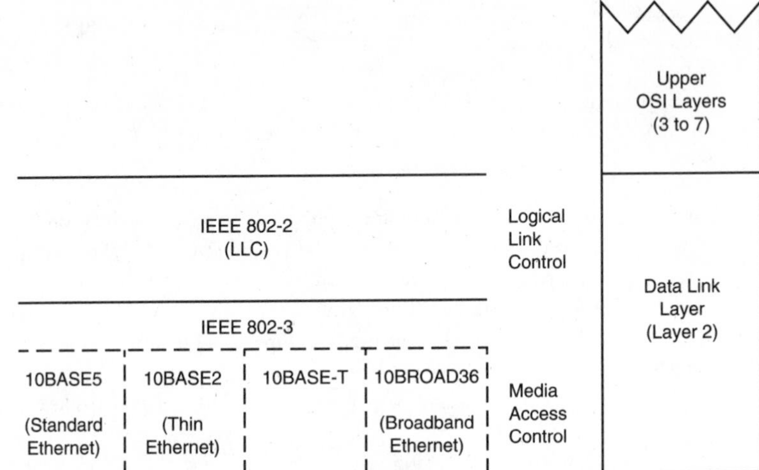

Figure 2.6
IEEE options for 802.3 Ethernet.

Although the packet structures for Ethernet and IEEE 802.3 differ, many vendors now manufacture cards that can operate in both modes by changing the network driver setting. In NetWare, for example, you can configure the workstation and server software to operate an NE2000 or SMC (previously Western Digital) network card with the Ethernet packet structure or IEEE 802.3 packet structure.

Under most circumstances, standard Ethernet devices can coexist on a network with devices using the 802.3 standard. The two devices, however, cannot exchange data.

Standard Ethernet Wiring Rules

Another name for Standard Ethernet is Thick Wire Ethernet because the coaxial cable it uses is much thicker than that used for Thin Wire Ethernet. The IEEE version of standard Ethernet is called 10BASE5. The 10 stands for 10 Mbps operation; the BASE stands for baseband operation; and the 5 stands for 500 meters per segment.

Figure 2.7 shows some standard Ethernet components. The network board or NIC shown in this figure has a DIX connector socket and a coaxial connection. The coaxial connection is used to connect to Thin Wire Ethernet. This particular card can be used with both Thick/Thin Wire Ethernet.

Stations on Thick Ethernet communicate with the external network through external transceivers attached to the shared media. The shared media is called the trunk segment cable, or just segment. Because of signal attenuation, a segment cannot be longer than 500 meters.

The external transceiver and the NIC are connected by a transceiver cable. The DIX connector plug mates with the DIX connector socket on the NIC. A slide lock is used to secure this connection. The other end of the transceiver fits into a connector on the external transceiver.

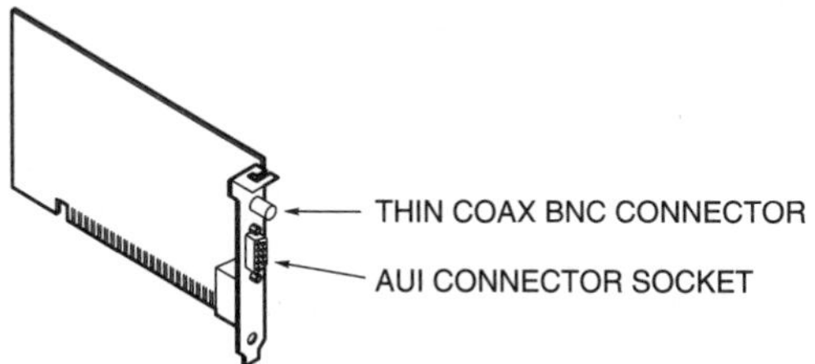

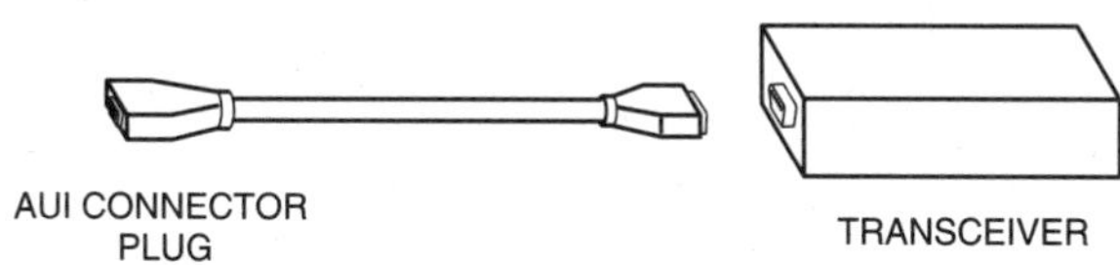

Figure 2.7
Thick Ethernet network cable and hardware.

Figure 2.8 shows the Thick Ethernet cable used to make up the trunk segments. Thick Ethernet cable has a 0.4-inch diameter and 50-ohm cable, and is available in various precut lengths with an N-series connector plug attached to each end. You also can purchase Thick Ethernet cable in spools or bulk quantities. These come without the N-series connectors attached at the ends.

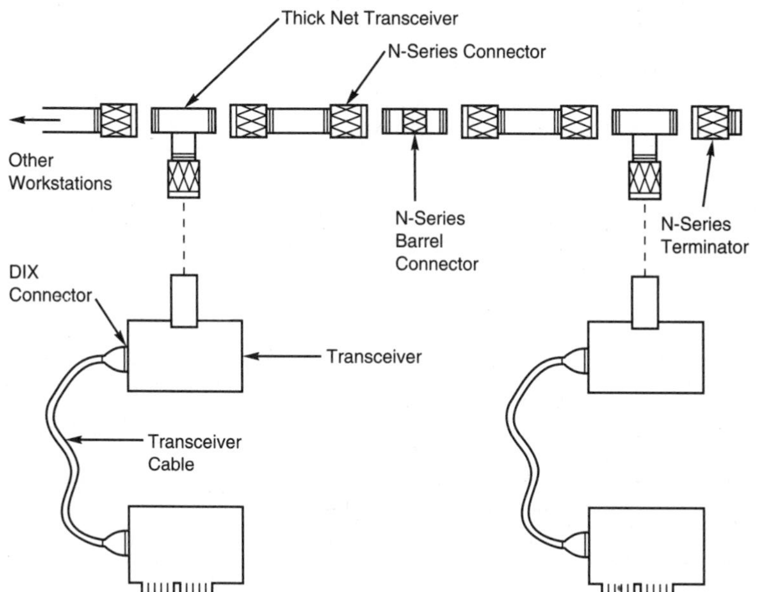

Figure 2.8
Thick Ethernet Coaxial Cable Connectors.

Figure 2.8 also shows the N-series *barrel connector* that can be used to join two lengths of Ethernet cable. A trunk segment must be terminated with an N-series *terminator*. The N-series terminator is a 50-ohm resistor that blocks electrical interference on the segment. Additionally, it cancels out any signal

reflections caused by signals reaching the end of the cable. The N-series terminator is attached to the male N-series terminator on the end of the segment. N-series terminators come with a grounding wire. One end of the cable must be grounded; the other end must remain ungrounded to avoid *ground-loop* currents.

Figure 2.9 shows an example of a Thick Ethernet network. Two trunk segments are joined by a device called a repeater in Thick Ethernet networks. A *repeater* is an active device that allows an Ethernet LAN to expand beyond a single segment by linking two segments. The repeater amplifies and regenerates the signal so that the signal can be transmitted over longer distances. A multiport repeater such as a DEMPR (Digital Equipment's multiport repeater) can link a number of Ethernet segments.

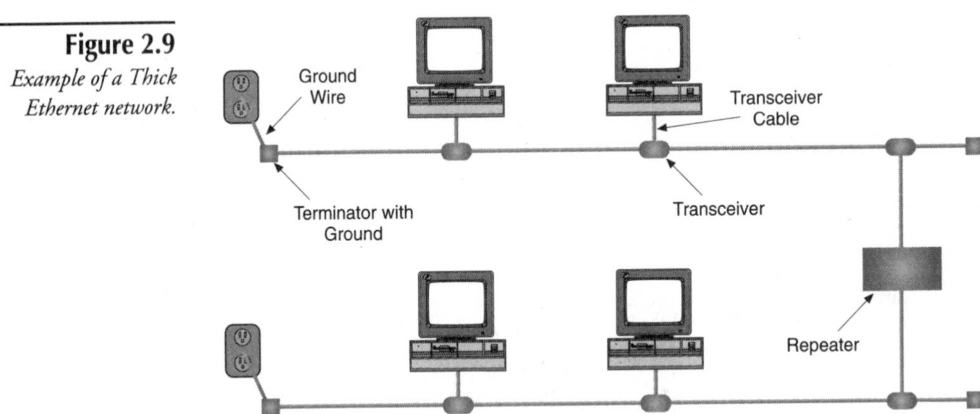

Figure 2.9
Example of a Thick Ethernet network.

Table 2.2 describes the rules you must follow with Thick Ethernet wiring.

Table 2.2
Thick Ethernet Parameters and Wiring Rules

Thick Ethernet Parameters	Value
Max data rate	10 Mbps
Max repeaters without IRLs	2
Max repeaters with IRLs	4
Max coaxial segment length	500 meters
Max transceiver cable length	50 meters
Max number of link segments	2

Thick Ethernet Parameters	Value
Max combined link segment length	1,000 meters
Max stations per segment	100
Max number of stations	1,024
Distance between stations	Multiples of 2.5 meters

To travel from one station to another station on an Ethernet LAN that consists of coaxial trunk segments only (see fig. 2.10), a signal cannot travel through more than two full repeaters. A *full repeater* joins two coaxial segments together directly. A coaxial segment is distinct from a link segment. A link segment made of fiber-optic or twisted-pair cable can be used to join two coaxial segments over a longer distance. The purpose of a link segment is to extend the range of an Ethernet LAN. You can have a maximum of two link segments on an Ethernet LAN. Link segments do not have stations attached to them and are connected to coaxial segments by repeaters. Another name for them is *Inter-Repeater Link-segment* (IRL).

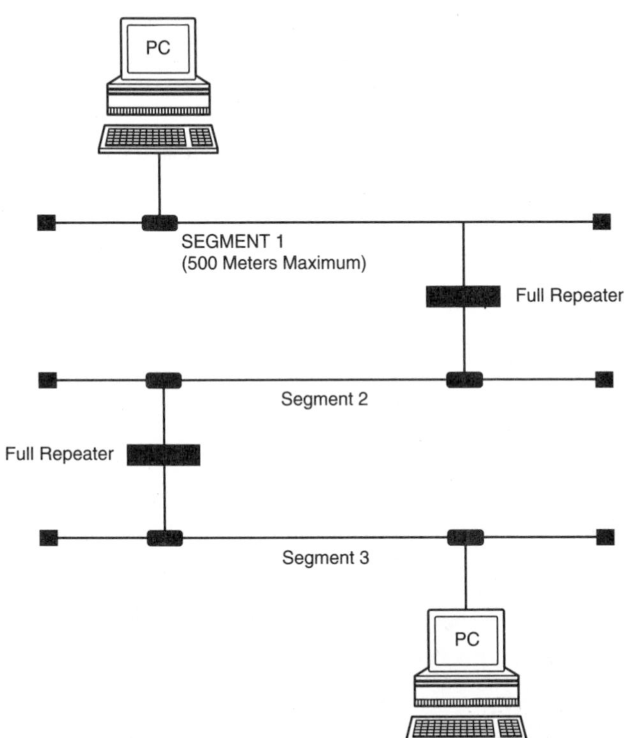

Figure 2.10
The longest possible Thick Ethernet.

A *half-repeater* joins a coaxial segment to a link segment. Another name for a half-repeater is a remote repeater. The trunk coaxial segment length cannot exceed 500 meters. The combined lengths of the two link segments cannot exceed 1,000 meters. Using these wiring parameters, you can deduce the maximum length of an Ethernet LAN.

Figure 2.11 illustrates the longest possible Ethernet. T1 through T6 represent transceivers. Using this diagram, you can calculate the length of this network as follows:

Coax segment 1 length	500 meters
Coax segment 2 length	500 meters
Coax segment 3 length	500 meters
Combined link segment 1 and 2 length	1,000 meters
Total Ethernet length	2,500 meters

Some people cheat and add the transceiver cable lengths to transceivers T1, T2, T3, T4, T5, and T6 in figure 2.11. Because the maximum transceiver cable length is 50 meters, this gives a combined transceiver length of 300 meters. The following calculations show how to arrive at this number:

Transceiver cable length of transceiver T1	50 meters
Transceiver cable length of transceiver T2	50 meters
Transceiver cable length of transceiver T3	50 meters
Transceiver cable length of transceiver T4	50 meters
Transceiver cable length of transceiver T5	50 meters
Transceiver cable length of transceiver T6	50 meters
Combined transceiver cable length	300 meters

The maximum Ethernet length is 2,800 meters (2,500 meters plus 300 meters for the transceiver drops).

The repeater attachment to a segment counts as one station. The maximum number of stations you can attach to a Thick Ethernet segment is 100, including repeater attachments, and the total number of stations cannot exceed 1,024. The repeater attachments do not count toward the limit of 1,024 for maximum number of stations. The minimum distance between any two stations is 2.5 meters. It is recommended that you separate stations at distances of multiples of 2.5 meters to minimize interference caused by standing waves on an Ethernet segment. *Standing waves* are formed by the presence of electrical signals on the segment.

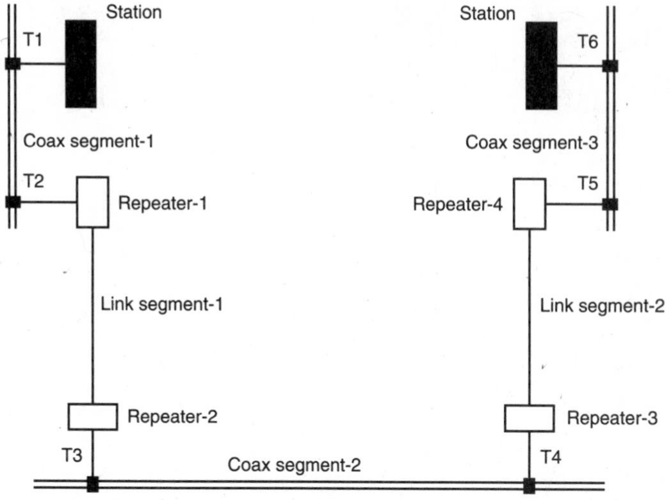

Figure 2.11
Longest Ethernet possible.

Thin Wire Ethernet Wiring Design Rules

Other names for Thin Wire Ethernet are *Thinnet* and also *Cheapernet* (because it is cheaper than Standard Ethernet). The coaxial cable it uses is much thinner than that used for Thick Wire Ethernet. The IEEE version of Thin Wire Ethernet is called *10BASE2.* The 10 stands for 10 Mbps operation; the BASE stands for baseband operation; and the 2 stands for approximately 200 meters (actually, 185 meters) per segment.

Figure 2.12 shows some of the Thin Wire Ethernet components. The network board or NIC in this figure has a coaxial connection.

The transceiver functions for a Thin Wire Ethernet are performed by the on-board NIC electronics. No external transceiver connections are made to the NIC. BNC T-connectors are used to connect the NIC with the cable. The two opposing jacks of the T-connector are used to join two lengths of Thin Wire Ethernet cable. The remaining plug is attached to the BNC connector jack on the NIC.

The shared media is called the *trunk segment cable* or just *segment.* Due to signal attenuation, a thin wire segment cannot be longer than 185 meters. Thin Ethernet cable has a 0.2-inch diameter and RG-58 A/U 50-ohm cable, and is available in various precut lengths with a standard BNC plug attached to each end. Thin Ethernet cable can be purchased also in spools or bulk quantities that come without the BNC connectors attached at the ends.

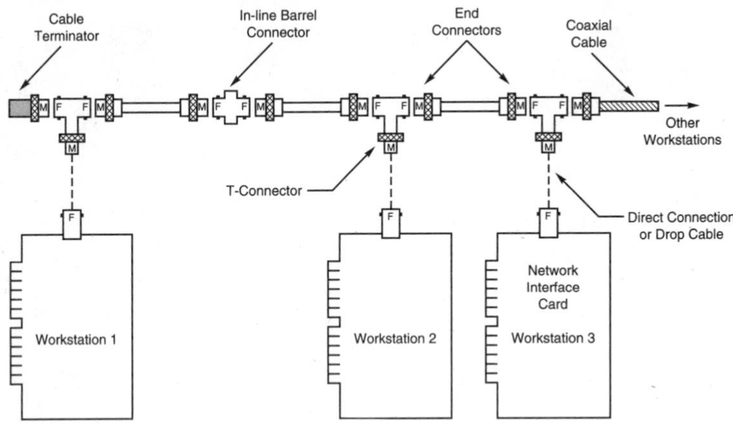

Figure 2.12
Thin Ethernet components.

You also can use the BNC barrel connector to join two lengths of Ethernet cable. A trunk segment must be terminated with a BNC terminator. The BNC terminator is a 50-ohm resistor that blocks electrical interference on the segment. Additionally, it cancels any signal reflections caused by signals bouncing off the end of the cable. The BNC terminator is attached to one of the two jacks on a T-connector to which no cable is attached. A grounded BNC terminator has a grounding wire. One end of the cable must be grounded; the other end must remain ungrounded to avoid ground loop current.

Figure 2.13 shows an example of a Thin Ethernet network. In this network, two trunk segments are joined by a repeater. The repeater in figure 2.13 has two ports to attach a maximum of two segments.

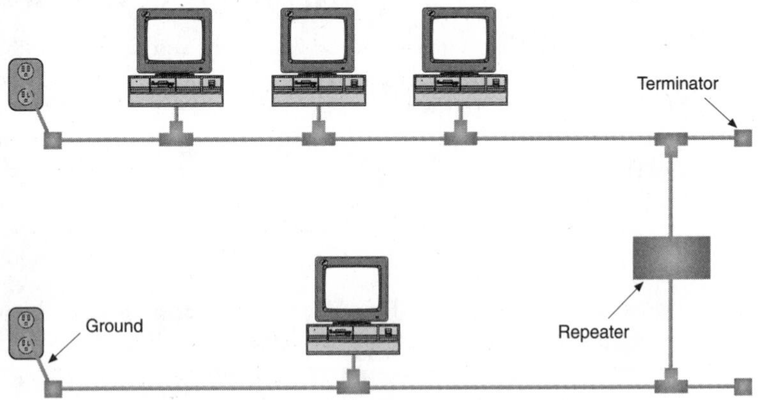

Figure 2.13
Example of a Thin Ethernet network.

A number of rules are related to Thin Ethernet wiring; table 2.3 summarizes these rules.

Table 2.3
Thin Ethernet Parameters and Wiring Rules

Thin Ethernet Parameters	Value
Max data rate	10 Mbps
Max repeaters without IRLs	2
Max repeaters with IRLs	4
Max coaxial segment length	185 meters
Max number of link segments	2
Max stations per segment	30
Max number of stations	1,024
Min distance between stations	0.5 meters

The repeater rules for Thin Ethernet are the same as for Thick Ethernet.

The trunk coaxial segment length for Thin Ethernet cannot exceed 185 meters. The maximum number of stations that can be attached to a Thin Ethernet segment is 30, and the total number of stations cannot exceed 1,024. The repeater attachment to a segment counts as one station. The minimum distance between any two stations is 0.5 meters.

10BASE-T Wiring Design Rules

An increase in interest for 10BASE-T began in 1990 due to the lower cost components and ease of configuring networks based in UTP wiring. The 10 stands for 10 Mbps operation; the BASE stands for baseband operation; and the T stands for twisted-pair wiring.

In figure 2.14, the NIC has a telephone-type RJ-45 port, which is officially called a *Media Dependent Interface* (MDI) port. The NIC shown in the figure also has a DIX connector. The DIX connector is used to connect to Thick Wire Ethernet by means of a transceiver. This particular card can be used with both 10BASE-T and Thick Ethernet. Many NICs require a switch setting to enable either the 10BASE-T or DIX port, whereas others like the SMC Elite16T card have an auto-sense mechanism.

The transceiver functions for a 10BASE-T are performed by the onboard NIC electronics.

The 10BASE-T uses a physical star topology with the 10BASE-T concentrator serving as the central switching element. Figure 2.15 shows the 10BASE-T plug and connector. Each concentrator accepts cables to several workstations, usually twelve. UTP wiring is used to connect a 10BASE-T concentrator to the workstation. This wiring normally consists of 0.4 to 0.6 mm diameter (26 to 22 AWG) unshielded wire in a multipair cable. The performance specifications are generally met by 100 meters of 0.5 mm telephone twisted pair.

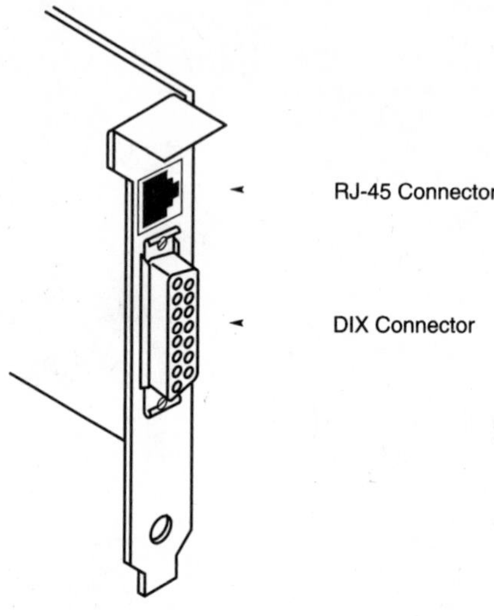

Figure 2.14
Connectors on a 10BASE-T network adapter card.

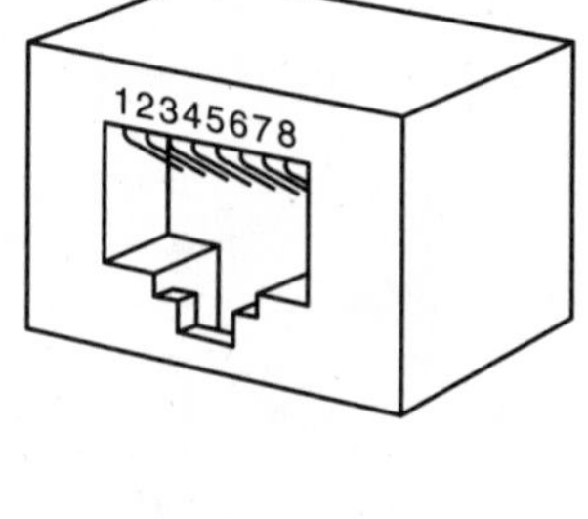

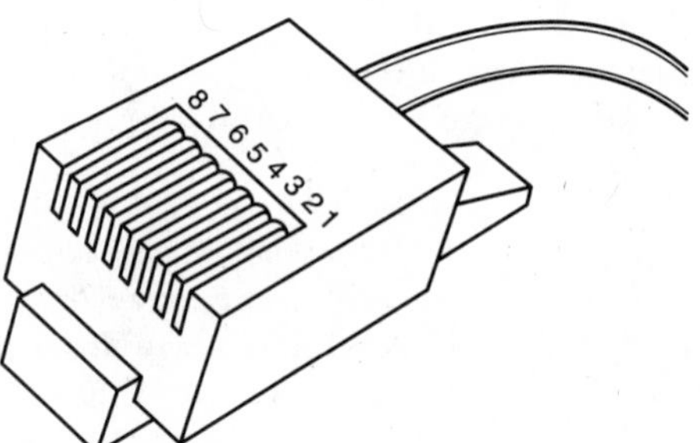

Figure 2.15
10BASE-T plug and connector. (Source: IEEE Standard 802.3i-1990)

Two twisted pairs (four wires) are between each NIC and the concentrator, as shown in figure 2.16. Each two-wire path forms a simplex link segment. One simplex segment is used for transmitting, and the other for receiving. Table 2.4 shows the pin assignments for a four-pair twisted-pair wiring. Only two pairs, one for transmission (TD) and another for receiving (RD), are used.

Table 2.4
Pin Assignments for the MDI Connector

Contact	MDI signal	Wire Color Code in AT&T T568B	Wire Color Code in TIA 2840 for T568B-UTP
1	TD+	white with orange band	white-green
2	TD_	orange with white band	green
3	RD+	white with green band	white-orange
4	Not used by 10BASE-T	blue with white band	blue
5	Not used by 10BASE-T	white with blue band	white-blue
6	RD_	green with white band	orange
7	Not used by 10BASE-T	white with brown band (or solid orange)	white-brown
8	Not used by 10BASE-T	brown with white band (or solid gray)	brown

A crossover function is implemented in every twisted-pair link so that the transmitter at one end will be connected to the receiver at the other. Figure 2.17 shows the two ways of implementing crossover functions. One way to do this is to use an external crossover UTP cable that reverses the transmit and receive pairs at the RJ-45 connector at one end of the UTP cable. A second way is an internal crossover function in which the crossover is designed as part of the internal circuitry in the 10BASE-T device. An MDI port with this function is marked with the symbol "X".

Figure 2.18 shows a single concentrator 10BASE-T network. The concentrator has 12 RJ-45 ports. If the station's NIC has a 10BASE-T (RJ-45) connector, the connections can be made directly through UTP cable. For stations with 10BASE5 network boards, a 10BASE-T MAU (10BASE-T transceiver) is needed to connect the AUI cable to the station.

2

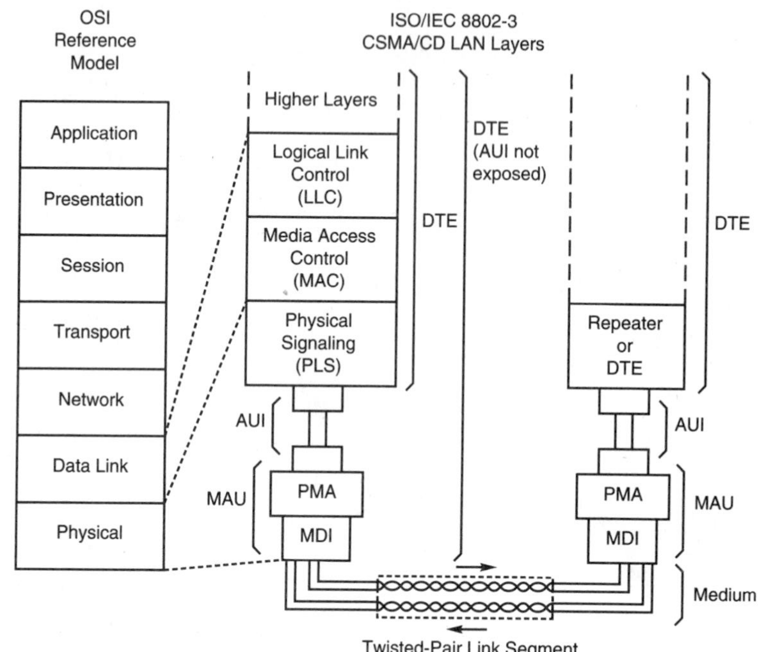

Figure 2.16 *Simplex segments used in 10BASE-T. (Source: IEEE Standard 802.3i-1990)*

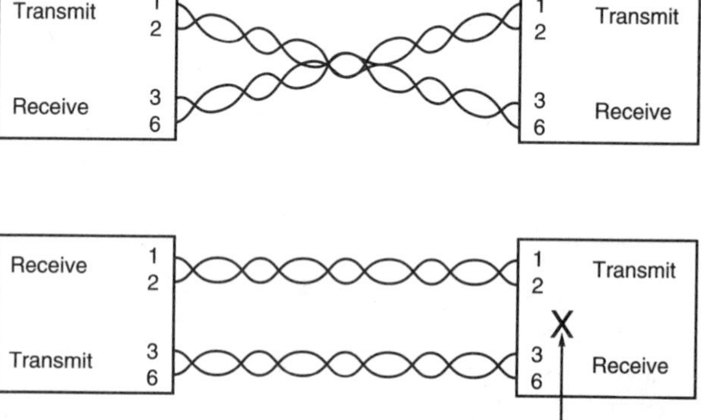

Figure 2.17 *10BASE-T crossover wiring.*

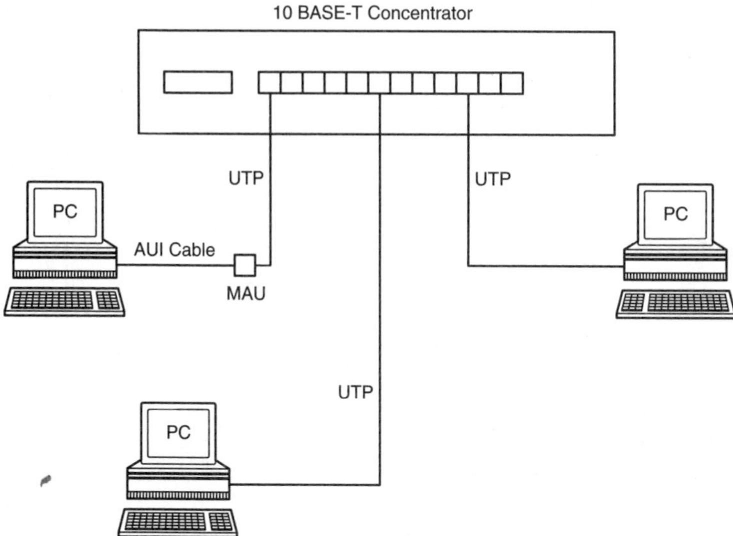

Figure 2.18
A single concentrator 10BASE-T network.

The 10BASE-T concentrator serves the role of a repeater. It performs the following functions:

- Data packet retiming (IEEE 802.3 standard)
- Per-port Link Integrity Test ("Good Link Test")
- Per-port autopartitioning, which disconnects the port in the event of 30 consecutive collisions, an excessively long single collision, or jabber input

The proper operation of the CSMA/CD 10BASE-T network requires network size to be limited to control round-trip propagation delays (the time it takes a signal to reach the extremity of a network and return). The configuration rules for more than one concentrator are as follows:

- A maximum of four concentrators in the data path between any two stations
- UTP segments no longer than 100 meters

UTP Wiring Considerations

UTP wiring for data communications has come a long way from its initial use of transmitting analog voice signals to its use in 10BASE-T and *CDDI* (Copper Distributed Data Interface), which is a variation of the FDDI LAN that runs at 100 Mbps. More recently there has been a rise of interest in the use of UTP for a 100 Mbps version of Ethernet called 100BASE-T. Other names for this technology are 100BASE-TX (formerly called 100BASE-X) and 100BASE-VG (or 100VG-AnyLAN).

Although using UTP for LAN wiring needs can simplify installation and reduce wiring costs, it can, if not done properly, do just the opposite: complicate installations and increase maintenance costs. The factors to consider for an effective UTP installation are discussed next.

The lack of a shield in UTP makes it cheaper than other types of wiring and also easier to install because it is more flexible than the shielded twisted-pair wiring. However, because it is unshielded, UTP can become a good antenna and susceptible to *Electro-Magnetic Interference* (EMI) and *Radio-Frequency Interference* (RFI). At such frequencies as 10 to 100 Mbps, UTP wiring results in loss of signal due to attenuation. Inductance and capacitance effects also become dominant at these high frequencies. The inductance is caused by the electromagnetic field that surrounds the UTP wire when the high-frequency signals pass through it. It can be likened to the transformer effect that induces a voltage on the secondary of the transformer due to electromagnetic coupling. The capacitance effect occurs because the conductors that make up the twisted-pair wire are separated by an insulating material. These effects reduce the quality of the signal and limit the distance that can be used between devices connected by UTP. The twists used in twisted-pair wiring help reduce inductance by creating a magnetic field that essentially cancels out inductance. For this reason, an important parameter in measuring the quality of a cable is the twists per inch of the wire. This can reduce the amount of *crosstalk,* which is the inductive coupling to other pairs of wires or noise sources. Crosstalk can lead to signal distortion (often called *jitter*), and in the case of Ethernet networks can be mistaken for collisions, which can degrade network performance. In token ring networks, crosstalk can generate hard errors that can cause the token ring networks to reconfigure. Reconfigurations are time-consuming and result in slow networks.

Flat silver satin wire, which works fine in low-speed data networks such as 19.2 Kbps, has zero twists per inch. This type of cabling is common in telephone networks; however, if voice telephone cable is used in data networks that operate in the Mbps range, it can result in disaster. Besides causing the network to fail, it can create a great deal of EMI noise that can cause other devices to fail also.

The signal used in both Ethernet and Token Ring networks is a baseband signal. *Baseband signals* are digital signals that have sharp edges. The capacitance effect in a wire causes the signal to lose some of its sharpness so that it becomes rounded. The resistance effect causes the signal to lose its strength (attenuation). The inductance and capacitance effect can make the signal vulnerable to external noise sources to the point that the signal can be completely distorted. Figure 2.19 illustrates these effects.

Another factor to consider is that signals with sharp edges or rapidly changing signals result in high-frequency harmonics. Mathematically speaking, the *ds/dt*—the rate at which the signal changes—is high for the edges of the baseband signal. If the signal is periodic, it can be expressed as the sum of sine wave harmonics of the fundamental frequency of the signal, in which the sine wave may have different phase (starting point) differences. This means that a 20 Mbps signal is not just a 20 Mbps signal, but a sine wave with 20 MHz fundamental frequency and harmonic components of 40 MHz, 60 MHz, 80 MHz, 100 MHz, 120 MHz, and so on. The higher harmonics are smaller in magnitude. In practical terms, this means that the cable must be able to carry the higher harmonic components of the data signal. If it does not do this well, the signal can become distorted.

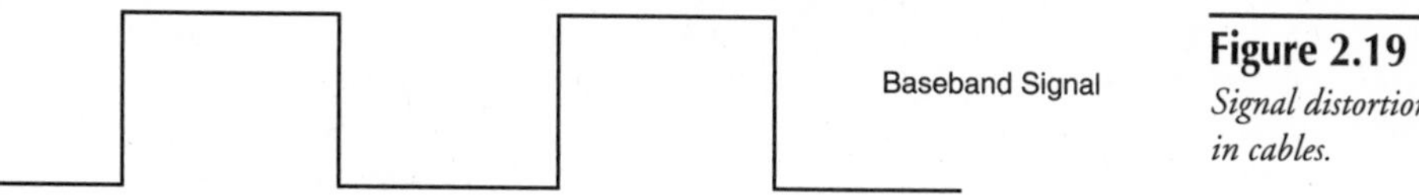

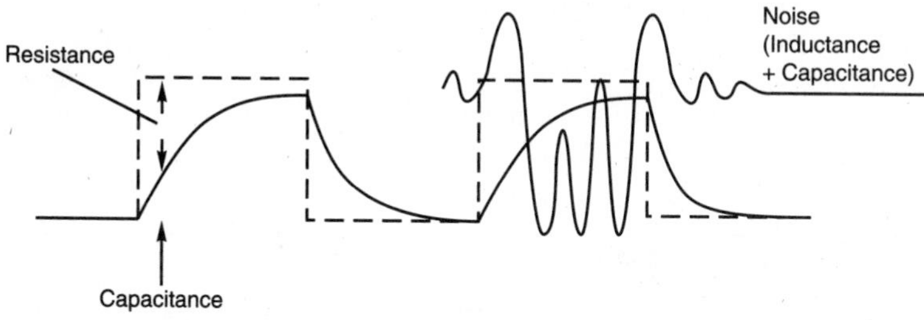

Figure 2.19
Signal distortion and noise in cables.

Some of these factors can be mitigated by using high-quality twisted-pair wiring. The characteristics of cables can be defined in terms of attenuation, which is measured in decibels per 100 feet. *Decibels* is a logarithmic scale (to the base 10) for comparing power levels. It is defined as follows:

log (P2/P1)

P2 = Power at output

P1 = Power applied at input

LAN designers specify maximum distance lengths for cable segments based on attenuation characteristics of the cable medium for the frequency of data transmission. For this reason, 10BASE-T networks have a limit of 100 meters between station and wiring concentrator.

The following examples of twisted-pair wiring meet the requirements for Token Ring and Ethernet installations:

- AT&T DIW 24/4
- AT&T PDS Systimax 2061
- EIA/TIA 568 Type 3, Level 3, Category 3
- Bell System 48007
- NT BDN 24 AWG

The type of sheath used to enclose the twisted-pair wire affects its plenum rating. *Plenum rating* determines whether the cable must be encased in a conduit for fire resistance as required by some building codes. PVC (polyvinyl chloride) is the most common coating used and is not fire resistant.

Another type of cable coating called *TFEP* (teflon fluorinated ethylene propylene) is rated as fire resistant. It also has a lower dielectric constant. The lower the dielectric constant, the lower the capacitance, and, therefore, the lower the signal distortion. Because of these characteristics, TFEP-coated wire can transmit the signal over longer distances with less signal distortion compared to PVC-coated wires.

In telephone networks, it is common to use a punch-down block called the 66 Block. Although this type of punch-down block works fine for telephone networks, it is not designed to carry data. For data networks that need to carry data in the Mbps range, you must use punch-down blocks specifically designed for data. These include punch-down blocks known as the 110s, 3m 7000D, and Krone. Data grade punch-down blocks include gold-plated or silver-plated contact points, labeling, and so forth. Data-grade patch panels also are available. Some of their features are cross-connect circuits etched on the wafer board itself. These patch panels can carry high-frequency signals in a manner similar to printed circuit boards.

Mixed Media Ethernet Networks

You can combine the different media (coaxial, twisted pair, and fiber) into one Ethernet LAN. If you combine mixed media networks, use a fiber-optic, twisted-pair, or coaxial cable to implement the link segment. Figures 2.20 and 2.21 show examples of mixed media networks.

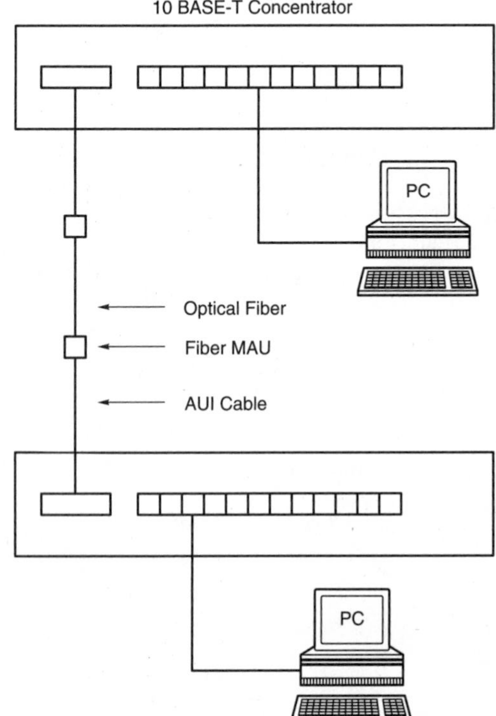

Figure 2.20
An 802.3 network using fiber-optic cable.

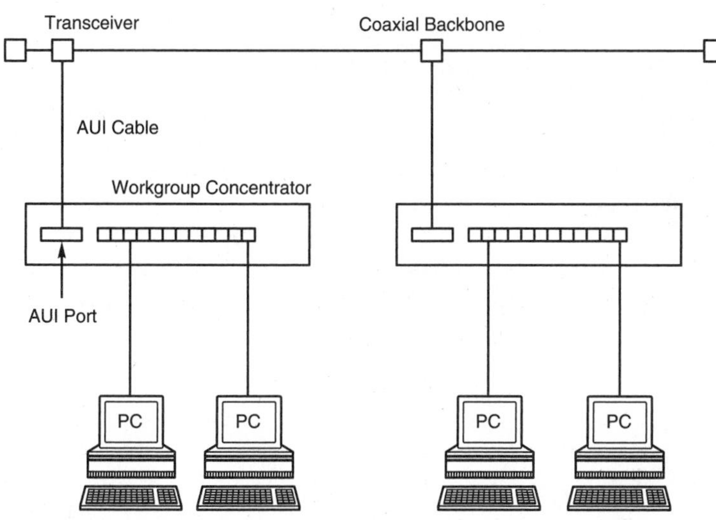

Figure 2.21
An 802.3 network incorporating a coaxial backbone.

Table 2.5 summarizes the maximum delays of the various media segments. This table is important for the LAN manager because Ethernet segments can be built by combining cables from different vendors, each of which may differ from the specifications by small amounts. Test equipment like *Time Domain Reflectometers* (TDRs) can be used to verify that the delays are within the specifications.

Table 2.5
Maximum Delays for Ethernet Media

Media Segment Type	Max MAUs per Segment	Max Segment Length (meters)	Min Propagation Velocity (ns)	Max Delay per Segment
Coaxial Segment				
10BASE5	100	500	0.77c	2165
10BASE2	30	185	0.65c	950
Link Segment				
FOIRL	2	1000	0.66c	5000
10BASE-T	2	100	0.59c	1000

continues

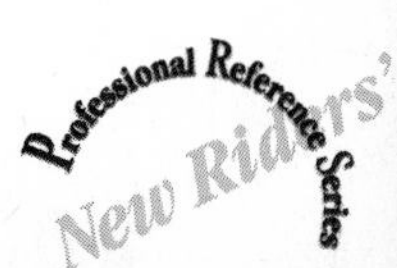

Table 2.5, Continued
Maximum Delays for Ethernet Media

Media Segment Type	Max MAUs per Segment	Max Segment Length (meters)	Min Propagation Velocity (ns)	Max Delay per Segment
AUI (Transceiver Cable)				
AUI	DTE/1 MAU	50	0.65c	257

c = 300,000,000 meters/sec (Velocity of light in vacuum)
FOIRL = Fiber-Optic Inter-Repeater Link

The following network topology rules apply for mixed media networks:

1. Repeater sets are required for all segment interconnections.
2. The maximum transmission path between any two stations can consist of up to five segments, four repeater sets (including optional AUIs), and two MAUs.
3. If a network path consists of five segments and four repeater sets, up to three segments can be coaxial trunks, and the remainder must be link segments. If five segments are present and *Fiber-Optic Inter-Repeater Link* (FOIRL) is used as the link segment, the link segment should not exceed 500 meters.
4. If a network path consists of four segments and three repeater sets, the maximum allowable length of the FOIRL segments is 1,000 meters each.

Rule two is illustrated in figure 2.22. Notice that this rule does not establish how many segments are coaxial trunks with multiple station attachments, and how many are link segments with no station attachments. Rule 3 clarifies this problem.

Rule three is illustrated in figure 2.23. This figure shows a multimedia Ethernet network. The media used in this network is a combination of coaxial, fiber, and twisted pair. Notice in figure 2.23 that there are five repeater sets. At first glance, this may seem to contradict the rule of a maximum of four repeater sets. Between any two stations, however, are no more than four repeaters in the transmission path. There is a total of ten segments: seven twisted pair, two fiber optic, and one coaxial. However, no more than five segments exist between any two stations. Also, there is a maximum of one coaxial segment, which is within the maximum of three coaxial segments. When the coaxial segment is included in the transmission path, the remaining four segments are link segments: three twisted-pair and one fiber-optic link segment. Because there are a maximum of five segments and four repeaters in the transmission path, the maximum FOIRL length is 500 meters, in compliance with rule three. The maximum span of this network is 1,300 meters, not including AUI drops.

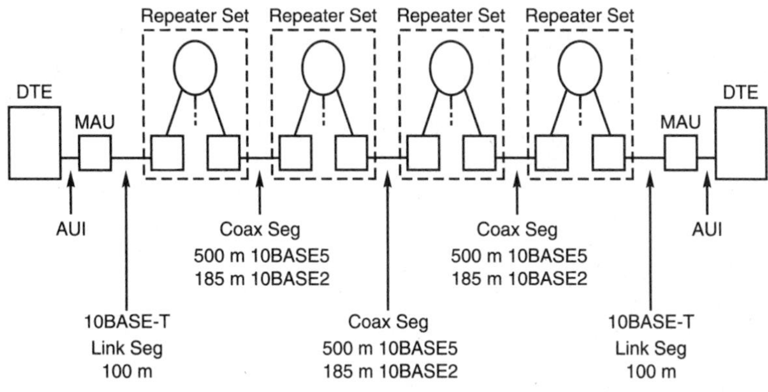

Figure 2.22
Maximum Ethernet transmission path with three coaxial segments. (Source: IEEE Standard 802.3i-1990)

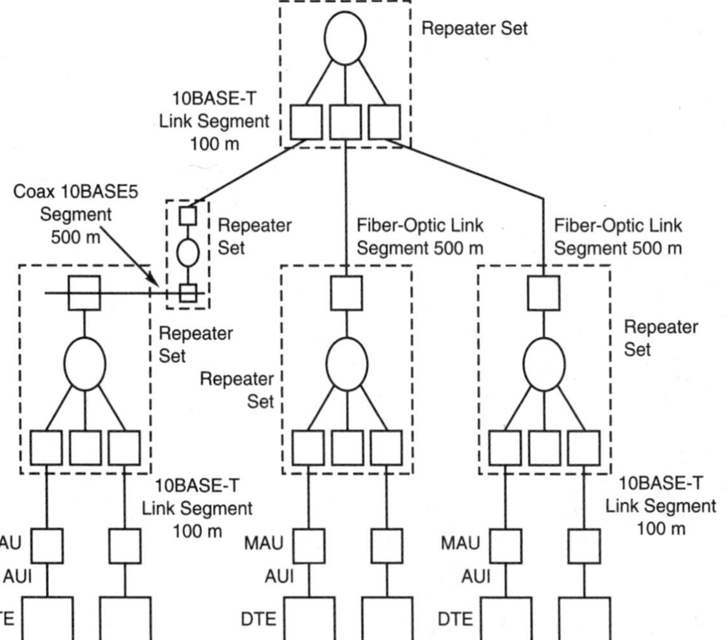

Figure 2.23
Maximum transmission path using 802.3 coaxial segments, 10BASE-T link segments, and fiber-optic link segments. (Source: IEEE Standard 802.3i-1990)

Rule four is illustrated in figure 2.24. There are three repeater sets and four segments: four twisted pair and two fiber optic. There are no coaxial segments in this figure. Between any two stations is a maximum of four segments and three repeaters. The four segments consist of two fiber-optic and two twisted-pair cables. Each of the FOIRL links has a maximum length of 1,000 meters. The maximum span of this network is 2,200 meters, not including AUI drops.

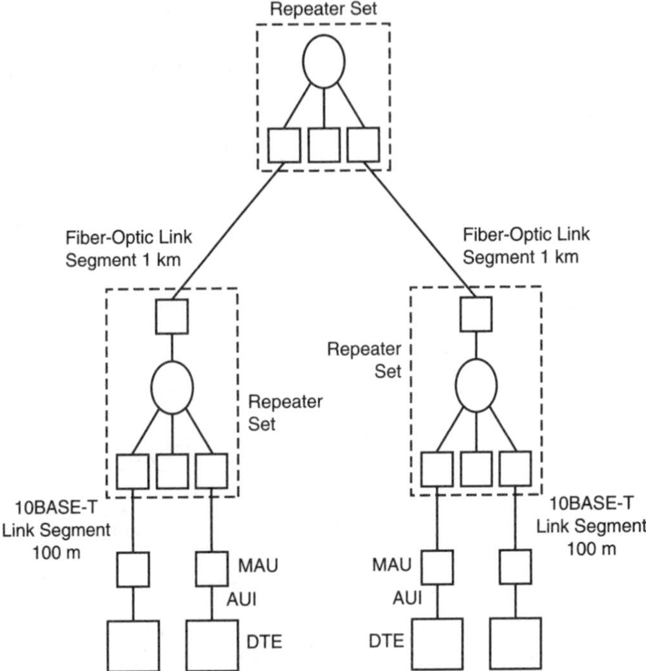

Figure 2.24
Maximum transmission path with three repeater sets and four link segments. (Source: IEEE Standard 802.3i-1990)

Combining Thin/Thick Cable in a Segment

You can combine thin and thick Ethernet cable in a single segment by using as much thin cable as possible. Thin cable is cheaper and easier to install than thick cable. Figure 2.25 illustrates a network layout using segments made up of a combination of thin and thick cable.

Combined thin/thick cables are between 185 meters and 500 meters long. The minimum length is 185 meters because coaxial segments shorter than 185 meters can be built with thin cable exclusively. The maximum of 500 meters is the limit for a segment made of thick coaxial exclusively.

To compute the maximum amount of thin cable you can use in one combination trunk segment, use the following equation:

thinLen = (500-trunkLen)/3.28 meters

(trunkLen equals the length of the trunk segment you want to build, and thinLen equals the maximum length of the thin length cable you can use.)

If you want to build a trunk segment of 400 meters, for example, the maximum length of thin coaxial cable you can use is as follows:

thinLen = (500_400)/3.28 = 30.48 meters

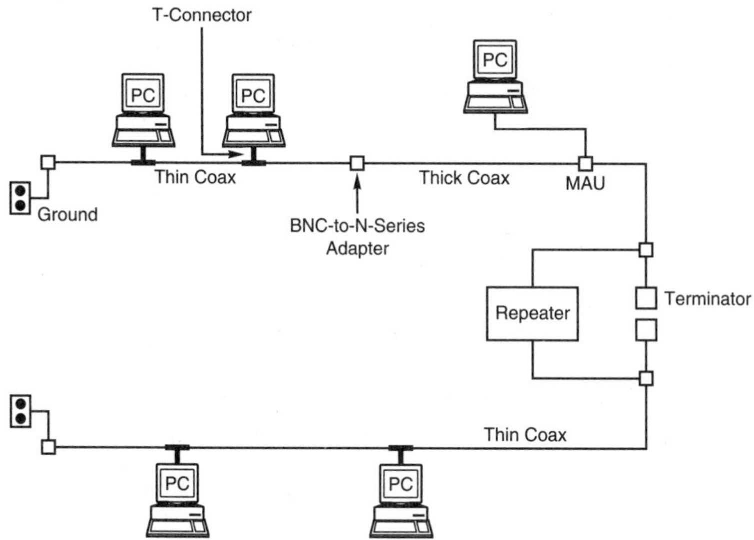

Figure 2.25
Combining Thick and Thin coaxial Ethernet.

You can use 30.48 meters of thin coaxial with 400_30.48 = 369.52 meters of thick cable. Thin and thick coaxial cable must be connected by means of an N-series to a BNC jack.

IEEE 802.3 versus Ethernet-II (DIX 2.0)

Both Ethernet-II and IEEE 802.3 have a minimum frame size of 64 bytes and a maximum frame size of 1,518 bytes. The next section examines their respective frame structures.

Ethernet-II

The Ethernet frame (see fig. 2.26) begins with a preamble of eight octets (one octet = eight bits) consisting of an alternating pattern 1010 that ends in 101011. At 10 Mbps, this preamble is of 6.4 microseconds' duration and is sufficient time for the receiving station to synchronize and get ready to receive the frame.

The *Destination Address* (DA) and the *Source Address* (SA) field follow this preamble. Each address field is six octets long. The first three octets represent a manufacturer's code, and the remaining three octets are assigned by the manufacturer. This assignation is made so that an Ethernet card has a unique six-octet address. This address usually is burned into a ROM chip on the Ethernet card. The *least significant bit* (LSB) of the first octet is the Physical/Multicast bit. It is zero for an Ethernet address. A value of one for this LSB indicates a multicast address. For instance, a hex value of FFFFFFFFFFFF, all 1s, for the DA field represents a broadcast. The manufacturer's code formerly was assigned by Xerox; it now is assigned by IEEE.

The Type field, also referred to as Ethertype, is a two-octet field used to indicate the type of data in the data field. Thus, if the Ethernet frame is used to carry NetWare data, the Ethertype value is 8137 hex. If it is used to carry DoD *Internet Packet* (IP) data, it has the value 0800 hex. XNS packets used in 3COM

networks have the value 0600hex. This field is used by network drivers or the network layer to demultiplex data packets to the appropriate protocol stack. It allows multiple protocol stacks to run on a single Ethernet card.

Ethernet - II	IEEE 802.3
Preamble 8 OCTETS	Preamble 7 OCTETS
	Start Frame Delimiter 1 OCTET
Destination Address 6 OCTETS	Destination Address 2 or 6 OCTETS
Source Address 6 OCTETS	Source Address 2 or 6 OCTETS
Type 2 OCTETS	Length 2 OCTETS
Data Unit 46-1500 OCTETS	LLC Data 46-1500 OCTETS
Frame Check Sequence 4 OCTETS	Frame Check Sequence 4 OCTETS

Figure 2.26
Comparison of Ethernet II and 802.3 frame structures.

The Data Unit field is a variable length field that can range from 46 to 1,500 octets. The remaining fixed length fields add up to 18 bytes.

The FCS field is generated by the Ethernet hardware at the end of the data field and is a 32-bit *Cyclic Redundancy Checksum* (CRC) over the address, type, and data fields. It is used to detect errors in transmission. Bad frames are retransmitted.

IEEE 802.3

The IEEE frame shown in figure 2.26 begins with a preamble of seven octets (one octet = eight bits) consisting of an alternating pattern 1010. At 10 Mbps, this preamble is of 5.6 microseconds' duration, sufficient time for the receiving station to synchronize and get ready to receive the frame.

The *Start Frame Delimiter* (SFD) follows after the preamble and is defined by the pattern 10101011. Note the following:

IEEE 802.3 preamble + SFD = Ethernet preamble

The IEEE 802.3 preamble and the SFD field combined are identical to the eight-octet Ethernet preamble.

The DA and the SA fields follow the SFD. Each address field can be six octets or two octets long. The six-octet addressing is the most common. The first three octets represent a manufacturer's code, and the remaining octets are assigned by the manufacturer. This assignation is made so that any two Ethernet and IEEE cards will have a unique six-octet address. This address is usually burned into a ROM chip on the IEEE 802.3 card. The LSB of the first octet represents the Individual/Group field and is similar to the Physical/Multicast field in Ethernet. The next bit is the *Universe/Local* (U/L) field and indicates if the addressing is global or local.

The Length field follows the address fields and is two octets long. It indicates the data size of the 802.3 frame. A minimum of 46 octets of LLC is required to make up the minimum size of 64 octets. The maximum value of this field is 1,500 to make a maximum frame size of 1,518 octets.

The Data Unit field is a variable length field containing 46 to 1,500 octets of LLC data.

The FCS field is generated by the IEEE 802.3 hardware at the end of the Data field and is a 32-bit CRC over the Address, Type, and Data fields. It is used to detect errors in transmission. Bad frames are retransmitted.

Differences between Ethernet-II and IEEE 802.3

There are differences between Ethernet-II and IEEE 802.3. You can see that Ethernet-II uses a two-byte Type field to indicate the type of data. The Type field values were at one time assigned by Xerox; they are now assigned by IEEE. Rather than the Type field, IEEE 802.3 has a two-byte Length field. The length information for Ethernet packets is supplied by a higher layer. In some cases, the NIC can determine the length of the frame based on hardware mechanisms, find out the bits received, and pass this information to upper layers. For IEEE 802.3 frames, the "type" information is supplied by the IEEE 802.2 (Logical Control Layer) frame that is part of the Data Unit field. Figure 2.27 illustrates the LLC frame format.

For example, a hex code of E0 indicates a NetWare packet. A hex code of AA is reserved to transmit upper-layer packets generated by non-IEEE LANs. This is referred to as the *Sub Net Access Protocol* (SNAP) mechanism. A complete description of SNAP can be found in RFC-1042 obtainable from Stanford Research Institute, Network Information Systems Center, 333 Ravenswood Ave., Menlo Park, CA 94025, (415) 859-6387. This discussion is beyond the scope of this book.

Ethernet has no provision to pad the data to make a minimum Ethernet frame of 64 bytes. IEEE 802.3 frames have a Length field to encode the pad information. In Ethernet, the padding has to be performed by upper layers.

Incompatibility between LattisNet UTP and 10BASE-T

Before 10BASE-T became an official standard, a number of vendors jumped the gun and announced the 10BASE-T–compliant network cards and concentrators. These older cards are not compliant with the 10BASE-T cards. These cards include the popular Western Digital 8003 EtherCard PLUS series. The reasons for incompatibility follow:

- Voltage levels for old cards are 2 V peak-to-peak. The new cards have 5 V peak-to-peak.
- Low DC current was used in old cards to indicate link integrity. The new cards use a "good link beat" message.
- Jabber detection was done at the concentrator for old cards. The new cards perform this at the concentrator and the transceiver.
- Equalization of signal timing was done after packet reception in old cards. The new cards do this after packet transmission.
- The noise squelch is done differently in the two cards.

Figure 2.27
"Type" information in IEEE 802.3.

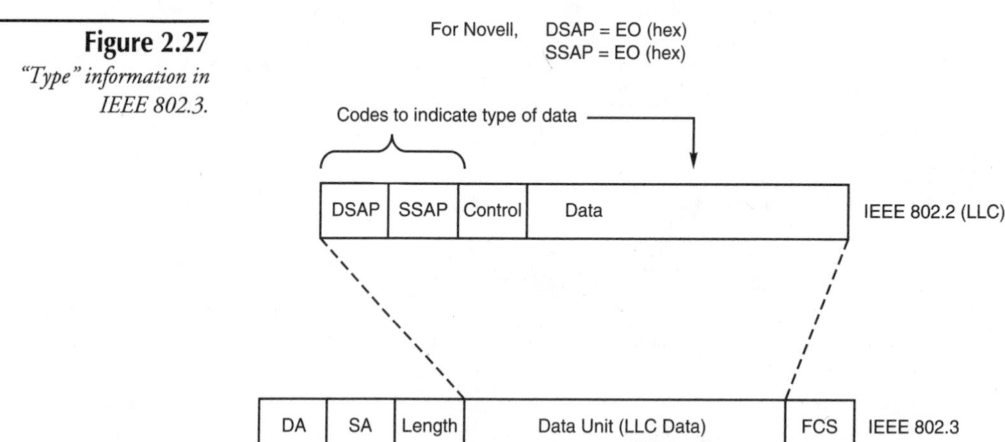

One way of integrating the older cards with 10BASE-T is to use the Intellicom Model 312M concentrator. The Intellicom Model 312M has an RS-232 management port that can be used to connect to a terminal or a PC running terminal emulation software (such as PROCOMM+). Using the terminal, you can program each of the 12 individual ports in the Intellicom 312M to be compatible with the older UTP cards or 10BASE-T cards.

Fast Ethernet

As network-based applications become more common and complex, they place greater demands on network bandwidth. Examples of applications that need greater network bandwidth are computer-aided design, computer-aided training, document management, image processing, real-time video, and multimedia. Although Ethernet with its maximum data rate of 10 Mbps has been used for these applications, a faster network is needed. Examples of faster networks are Fast Ethernet and the 100 BASE-VG specification, both of which operate at 100 Mbps.

Before discussing the high-speed Ethernet standards, a brief background of the position of these standards in relationship to the installed base of existing Ethernet networks is helpful.

The original 1982 Ethernet specification defined a bus-based network that used CSMA/CD and operated at 10 Mbps. The original Ethernet specification was for a coaxial cable about one-half inch in diameter and was referred to as "thick" coax. Because of the large diameter cable, this Ethernet technology is called *Thick Ethernet.* Thick Ethernet, although adequate for connecting large machines such as minicomputers and mainframes, was prohibitively expensive for the emerging PC-based LAN market. To meet the demands of the PC-based LAN market, a cheaper solution was devised that consisted of a thin coax cable (RG-58) and that eliminated the need of the external transceiver and transceiver cable assembly. This less expensive Ethernet based on a thinner coax cable was called *Cheapernet* or *Thin Wire Ethernet* or *Thin Ethernet.* The transceiver functions of Thin Ethernet were integrated on the network interface board, making it simpler to install, and the reduced cost made it more suitable for the PC LAN market. When IEEE formally adopted the Ethernet standard it was called IEEE 802.3.

The IEEE 802.3 specification defines a communication protocol that consists of LLC/MAC layer and PMD layer (see fig. 2.28). The LLC and MAC layers correspond to layer 2, the data link layer of the OSI model. The *Physical Media Dependent* (PMD) layer corresponds to layer 1, the physical layer of the OSI model. The distinguishing characteristic of IEEE 802.3 is the MAC layer. The MAC layer is responsible for the format of the Ethernet frame and the arbitration mechanism used to gain access to a shared media. The arbitration mechanism used by the Ethernet MAC layer is the CSMA/CD mechanism described in detail earlier in this chapter. Keeping the MAC layer independent of the physical layer allows the IEEE 802.3 specification to specify a number of different media types (see fig. 2.29). It also allows the MAC layer to be defined in a speed-independent fashion. With the exception of the *interpacket gap* time, which is the minimum time that must elapse between packets that are sent, all MAC time parameters are expressed in bit-time intervals. This means that it is possible to use Ethernet at faster data rates than the original 10 Mbps operation speed for Ethernet.

The Fast Ethernet Alliance, a group of vendors interested in promoting Fast Ethernet technology, consists of DAVID Systems, Digital Equipment Corporation, Grand Junction Networks, Inc., Intel Corporation, National Semiconductor, SUN Microsystems, SynOptics Communications, and 3COM Corporation.

Fast Ethernet as it is currently defined operates at 100 Mbps, and represents a ten-fold scaling of the Ethernet 10 Mbps MAC layer operation. The scaling is possible because of the independence of the physical layer from the MAC layer. The physical layer for IEEE 802.3 is responsible for sending and receiving the data bit stream to and from the attached medium, encoding and decoding the bit stream, carrier sense, collision detection, and from electrical and mechanical interface to the attached medium.

Fast Ethernet's maximum network diameter is 250 meters. This is in contrast with the 10 Mbps Ethernet whose diameter is 2,500 meters. The maximum diameter of Fast Ethernet is one-tenth that of the 10 Mbps Ethernet, although its speed is ten times more. There is a trade-off of speed versus distance for CSMA/CD networks. For CSMA/CD to work, a station must transmit long enough to detect a collision with a station transmitting from the farthest end of the network. At 10 Mbps and a maximum diameter of 2,500 meters, the packet must be transmitted for at least 57.6 microseconds to meet these requirements. The minimum number of bits to be transmitted therefore is computed as shown in the following:

Minimum transmitted bits = 10 Mps * 57.6 microseconds = 576 bits

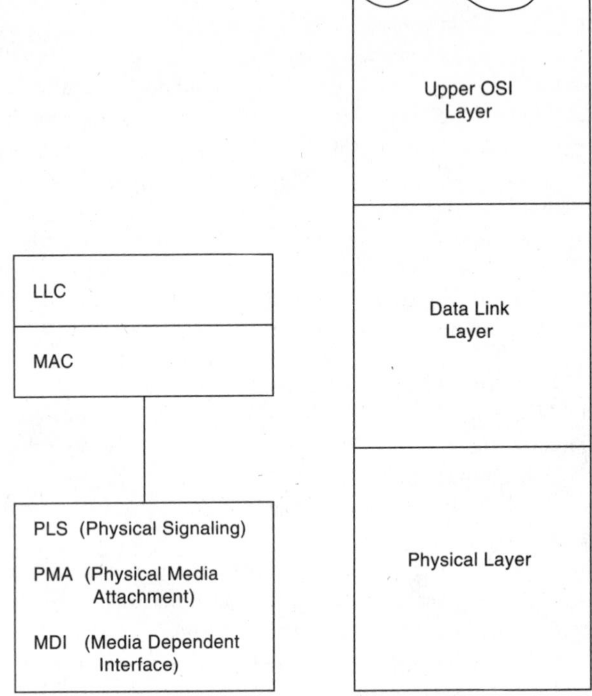

Figure 2.28
IEEE 802.3 specification components.

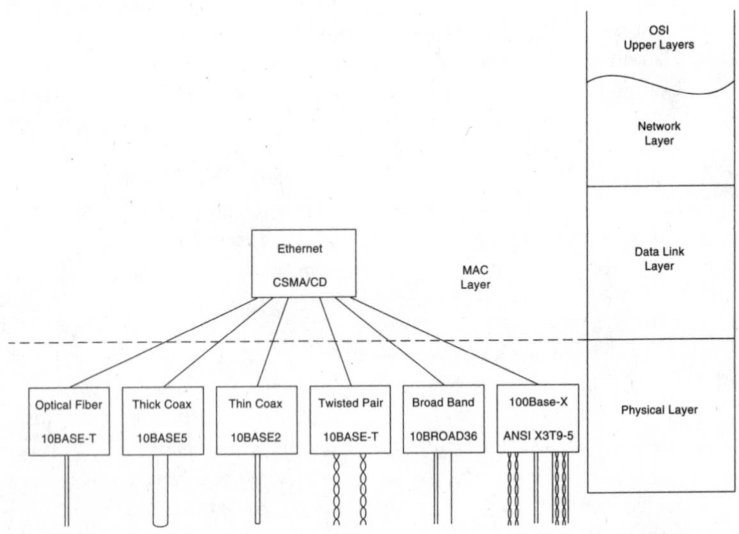

Figure 2.29
IEEE 802.3 physical media support.

The 576 bits includes the Ethernet/IEEE 802.3 preamble, which is 64 bits long. So the minimum Ethernet/IEEE 802.3 frame size is 576 - 64 = 512 bits (64 bytes). In Fast Ethernet, the MAC layer is the same as for Ethernet. This means that the Ethernet frame format and size is the same for these versions of Ethernet. The minimum Ethernet frame size for Fast Ethernet is also 64 bytes. A collision must be detected while transmitting the preamble and the minimum frame size (576 bits). Because Fast Ethernet transmits data ten times faster than Ethernet, 576 bits are transmitted in 5.76 microseconds, instead of the 57.6 microseconds for Ethernet. The network diameter therefore must be ten times smaller to detect a collision with a station transmitting from the farthest end of the network. That is, Fast Ethernet's diameter is 2,500/10 = 250 meters.

In general, if the data transfer rate is R Mbps for a CSMA/CD network, the network diameter (D) for maintaining compatibility with the Ethernet frame format and size is as follows:

$D = 25000/R$ meters

For a 10 Mbps CSMA/CD Ethernet, the diameter is 25,000/10 = 2,500 meters.

For a 100 Mbps CSMA/CD Fast Ethernet, the diameter is 25,000/100 = 250 meters.

For a 500 Mbps CSMA/CD (hypothetical) Ethernet, the diameter is 25,000/500 = 50 meters.

An AT&T study done in the late 1980s showed that the majority of the networks (greater than 90 percent) have desktops within 100 meters of the local wiring closet. This is within the 250 meter maximum diameter of Fast Ethernet.

Fast Ethernet supports a variety of different types of physical media. One such physical layer specification is the 100BASE-X proposal from Grand Junction Networks, Inc., an early player in the Fast Ethernet specification. The 100BASE-X proposal defines three cable options: two pairs for category 5 UTP, IBM Type 1 (two pairs of shielded twisted-pair data grade), and optical fiber. 100BASE-X uses the ANSI twisted-pair X3T9.5 PMD layer. ANSI TP-X3T9.5 PMD was endorsed in 1992 as technology for reliably and economically transmitting a 100 Mbps signal over twisted-pair wiring for CDDI. CDDI is the twisted-pair version of FDDI. Figure 2.30 shows the relationship between Fast Ethernet MAC and the ANSI X3T9.5 PMD layer. 100BASE-X combines the Ethernet MAC layer with the ANSI X3T9.5 PMD standard. The ANSI X3T9.5 standard supports Category 5 UTP, IBM Type 1, and optical fiber cabling.

The TP-PMD uses stream cipher scrambling for security and MLT-3 bit encoding. 100 BASE-TX (formerly called 100BASE-X) also can use the FDDI Fiber PMD that uses the 62.5/25 micron fiber multimode cable. The Fiber PMD is unscrambled and uses 4B/5B encoding and *Non Return to Zero Inverted* (NRZI) signaling. The 4B/5B uses 4 out of 5 bits for data symbols. This results in 16 data symbols and 16 control symbol bit patterns. The bit patterns for the data symbols are such that long strings of 0s and 1s are avoided. This allows NRZI signaling to be used, which cannot encode clocking information if a long string of 0s and 1s is used. To use FDDI's Fiber PMD, the 100BASE-X specifies the use of a special *convergence sublayer* (see fig. 2.31). The convergence sublayer translates continuous signaling of the Fiber PMD to the start-stop, half-duplex signaling expected by the Ethernet MAC.

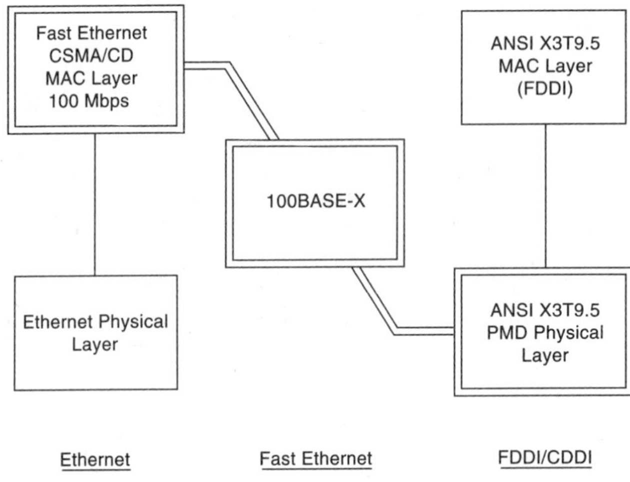

Figure 2.30 *Relationship between Fast Ethernet, 100BASE-X, and ANSI X3T9.5 PMD.*

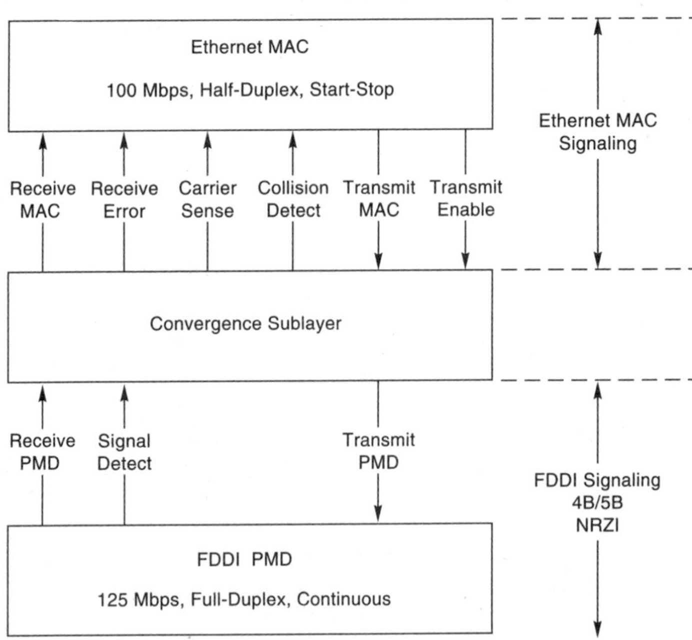

Figure 2.31 *Convergence sublayer for Fiber PMD in 100BASE-TX.*

100 BASE-TX supports unshielded twisted-pair wiring consisting of two pairs of Category 5 UTP. The 10BASE-T specification is designed to use two pairs of Category 3 UTP (voice grade UTP). For those sites that want to use Fast Ethernet but only have category 3 UTP and do not want to upgrade their cabling to Category 5 UTP, an alternate proposal called the *4T+* was specified by the Fast Ethernet Alliance. The 4T+ uses four pairs of Category 3 UTP. The workstation-to-repeater hub distance is 100 meters for 4T+ signaling, but hub-to-hub distance is ten meters. This type of network is called *100BASE-T4*.

The 4T+ is a new encoding method that uses an eight binary/six ternary (8B/6T) code set. It is similar to the MLT-3 signaling used with Category 5 UTP, but has a limited bandwidth of 30 MHz. Figure 2.32 shows how the four pairs of Category 3 UTP are used. Pair 1 is used for collision indication; pairs 2, 3, and 4 are used for carrying data.

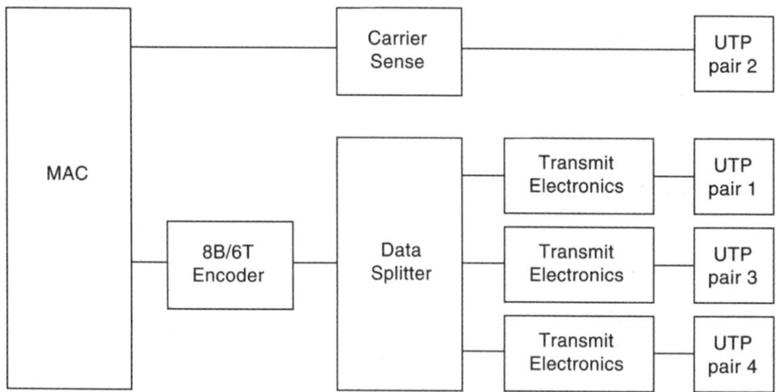

Figure 2.32
4T+ twisted-pair usage.

Another variation of the Fast Ethernet is the use of fiber-optic cable for transmission. This type of standard is called *100BASE-TF.*

Table 2.6 shows the parameter values used by Fast Ethernet.

Table 2.6
Parameter Values for Fast Ethernet versus Ethernet

Parameter	Ethernet	Fast Ethernet
slotTime	512 bit-times	512 bit-times
interFrameGap	9.60 microseconds	960 nanoseconds
attemptLimit	16	16
backoffLimit	10	10
jamSize	32 bits	32 bits
maxFrameSize	1,518 octets	1,518 octets
minFrameSize	64 octets (512 bits)	64 octets (512 bits)
addressSize	48 bits	48 bits

An alternative to Fast Ethernet has been proposed by Hewlett-Packard and AT&T. This scheme uses a Demand Priority Access Method in which a network hub device controls access to the network based on a priority scheme. Because this scheme uses a different access method from CSMA/CD, it cannot be classified as an "Ethernet" scheme even though it retains the frame format structure of Ethernet. This scheme is the subject of study by the IEEE 802.12 committee.

The HP and AT&T proposal (IEEE 802.12) uses four pairs of Category 3 UTP. This Demand Based Priority Access method is called 100BASE-VG because it uses a voice grade Category 3 UTP. It also can be configured to use shielded twisted pair, Category 5 UTP, and fiber-optic cables.

Figure 2.33 summarizes the wiring approaches used by the Fast Ethernet and the IEEE 802.12.

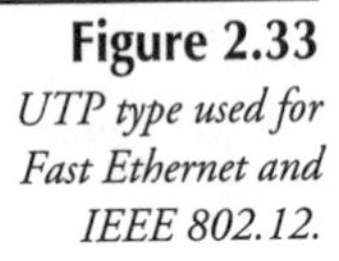

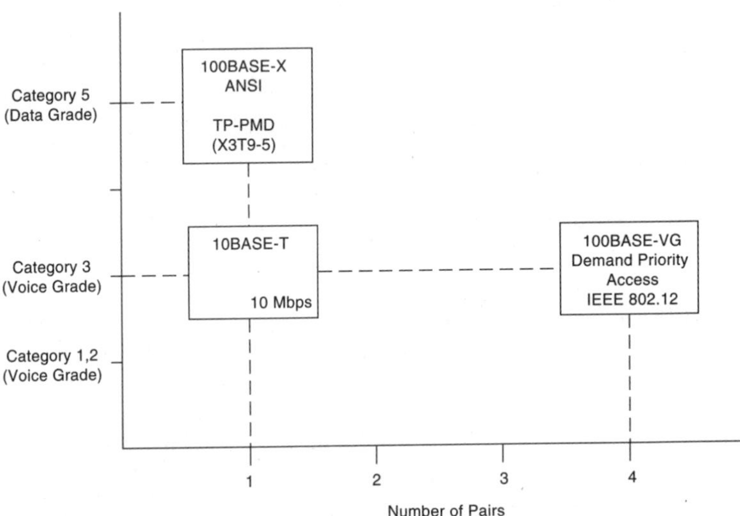

Figure 2.33
UTP type used for Fast Ethernet and IEEE 802.12.

The Politics of Numbering: IEEE 802.13, IEEE 802.14, IEEE 802.30, or IEEE 802.3?

This may be a strange section in a book of this nature, but you should understand why the Fast Ethernet proposal has been, at different times, called the IEEE 802.14 and the IEEE 802.30.

The Fast Ethernet was initially considered as part of the IEEE 802.3 specification. The chairman of the committee felt that the use of TP-PMD (Twisted Pair-Physical Media Dependency) warranted sufficient changes to the MAC layer that a new working group was needed. The next number after IEEE 802.12 would have been IEEE 802.13. It was felt that the number 13 in the IEEE 802.13 designation would place the Fast Ethernet proposal at a disadvantage, because 13 is considered to be "unlucky" in western culture. Consequently, the number designation of IEEE 802.14 was used for Fast Ethernet. This number designation was later changed to IEEE 802.30. The chair of the IEEE 802 committee said that allowing the Fast Ethernet to remain in the IEEE 802.3 committee would give the Fast Ethernet proponents an unfair advantage over the IEEE 802.12 proposal. At the next meeting of the IEEE 802 working group in 1993, the chair resigned to head the IEEE 802.12 group. The new chairman brought the IEEE 802.30 group back under the aegis of the IEEE 802.3 group where it originally began.

Understanding the IEEE 802.12

The primary sponsor of the IEEE 802.12 Demand Priority access method is Hewlett-Packard (HP). Other vendors who have expressed support for IEEE 802.12 include AT&T Microelectronics, IBM, Proteon, and Ungermann-Bass. This standard is also referred as the 100BASE-VG or the 100VG-AnyLAN.

In the IEEE 802.12 proposal, networks are designed around a central repeater called the *root repeater.* The root repeater polls its ports in the *port order* to determine if a station or another repeater hub attached at the port is waiting to transmit. Figure 2.34 shows an example of an IEEE 802.12 network. The root repeater polls its port number 1, then port number 2, and then port number 3. At port number 3, another repeater is attached. This is called a Level 2 repeater, to distinguish it from the Level 1 repeater, which is the root repeater. Polling port number 3 of the root repeater results in the Level 2 repeater polling its ports in the port order. If the Level 2 repeater has eight ports, the polling action continues as 3-1, 3-2, 3-3, 3-4, 3-5, 3-6, 3-7, 3-8. After the Level 2 repeater connected to port 3 finishes its polling, the polling action is transferred back to the root repeater that continues polling its port 4, 5, and so on. In figure 2.34, another Level 2 repeater is attached to port 8 of the root repeater. After polling port 7 of the root repeater, the polling action continues to the Level 2 repeater attached to port 8 of the root repeater. This results in the following ports being polled in the order specified: 8-1, 8-2, 8-3, 8-4, 8-5, 8-6, 8-7, 8-8. After this, the polling action reverts to the root repeater, which repeats the polling starting from its port 1.

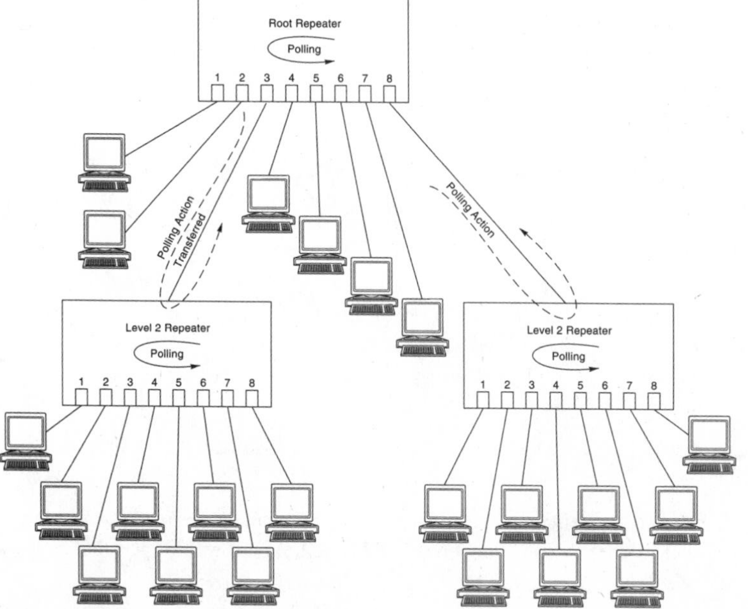

Figure 2.34
IEEE 802.12 polling scheme.

In the diagram in figure 2.34 only two levels of repeaters are shown. IEEE 802.12 permits the cascading of up to three levels of repeater hubs. The distance between a workstation and a repeater hub can be a maximum of 100 meters. An IEEE 802.12-based network can span a maximum distance of 4,000 feet.

Because of the polling action of IEEE 802.12, the time an application has to wait for gaining access to the network can be predicted with precision. This is of great importance in real-time applications. To further support applications that may need immediate access to the network, a priority scheme is introduced. In this priority scheme, requests for transmission can be classified as high priority requests or normal priority requests. High-priority requests are serviced before normal priority requests. Multiple levels of priority are proposed to support real-time traffic.

With any priority-based scheme, it is possible for low-priority stations to be denied access for long periods of time. To ensure fairness, normal priority requests waiting for more than 250 milliseconds are given a boost in priority so that they can be satisfied. Additionally, no station can transmit twice in a row if another station has a request pending at the same level. At the root repeater, a high-priority request cannot preempt a lower priority request in progress. At lower level repeaters, such as Level 2 and Level 3 repeaters, a high-priority request can preempt a lower priority request even if the lower priority request is in progress.

The 802.12 standard can use either an Ethernet frame or a Token Ring frame format. In its current form, the 802.12 proposal requires all hubs in a priority domain to support either the Ethernet or Token Ring format, but not both. An extension to the 802.12 standard is being considered so that a hub can support both Ethernet and Token Ring frame types.

The encoding method used by 802.12 is a *quartet* signaling encoding scheme. This method uses four sequential code streams sent on four twisted pairs of a Category 3 UTP. The encoding used is the *Non Return to Zero* (NRZ) with 5B/6B encoding scheme. The NRZ encoding minimizes the signal changes needed to send information. The 5B/6B encoding scheme uses 5 out of 6 bits for data symbols. This results in 32 data symbols and 32 control symbol bit patterns. The bit patterns in the data symbols are such that continuous strings of 1s or 0s are avoided. This is important because with NRZ encoding a continuous string of 1s or 0s results in a loss of clocking information needed by the receiving station to recover the encoded data.

The 802.12 proposal contains an option for using two pairs of Category 5 or two pairs of STP, or one strand of fiber-optic cable. With these wiring options, the four sequential code streams normally sent over four pairs of Category 3 UTP are multiplexed on two pairs of Category 5 or STP, or a single strand of fiber.

Additionally, MIB variable definitions for using SNMP to manage 802.12 hubs are available. This makes it possible for the 802.12 hubs to be managed using SNMP managers.

Ethernet Switches

An interesting variation of Ethernet implementation are the Ethernet switching hubs made by vendors such as Kalpana (Kalpana EtherSwitch), Grand Junction (Grand Junction FastSwitch), 3COM (LinkBuilder), and Microaccess, Inc. (OptiLAN).

Ordinarily, Ethernet uses a media shared by all the attached devices that participate in the CSMA/CD arbitration mechanism. The maximum bandwidth on Ethernet is 10 Mbps. This bandwidth must be shared by the devices that attach to the Ethernet LAN (see fig. 2.35). If this data bandwidth was divided equally among N attached devices, each device must be allocated a bandwidth of the following:

$10/N$ Mbps

For $N = 1{,}024$, which is the maximum number of devices on a single Ethernet LAN, the average bandwidth per attached device is 10 Kbps. In actual practice, not all the N devices are actively transmitting on the network. Even assuming that 10 devices ($N = 10$) are actively participating on the Ethernet LAN, the average bandwidth is 1 Mbps.

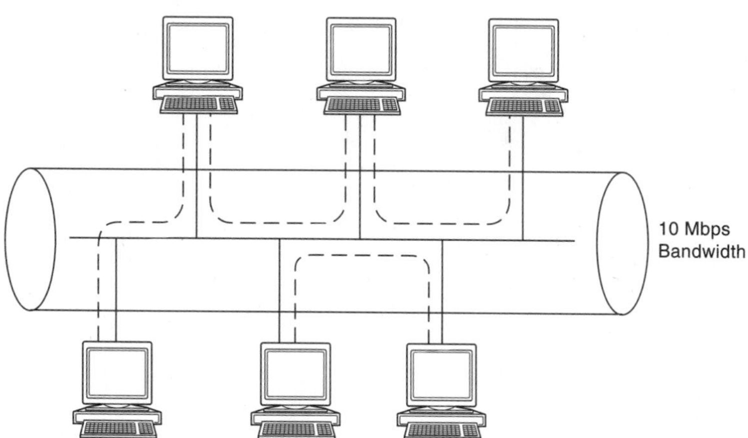

Figure 2.35
Ethernet bandwidth for shared media.

To increase the bandwidth available for applications, some vendors make a special hub called the Ethernet switch (see fig. 2.36) in which each port of the Ethernet switch is attached to a LAN that operates at 10 Mbps. Each port of the Ethernet switch stores the addresses of the devices attached to that port. It must, therefore, have sufficient memory associated with each port to store the addresses of all the nodes that can be attached to that node. The Ethernet switch uses the addresses stored at each port to send a packet received on one port to the appropriate destination port. This action is called *switching.* The criterion used to perform the switching function is the destination address of the Ethernet frame. Each Ethernet segment attached to a port of the Ethernet switch forms a separate CSMA/CD collision domain. Collisions generated on one Ethernet segment are not transmitted to other Ethernet segments. In this regard, the Ethernet switch can be seen as a bridge. The aggregate capacity of a network that uses an Ethernet switch is multiplied by the number of ports on the Ethernet switch. If M ports are in the Ethernet switch, the formula for aggregate capacity is as follows:

$10 \times M$ Mbps

Thus for a 12 port Ethernet switch, the Ethernet switch must be able to switch data rates up to 120 Mbps.

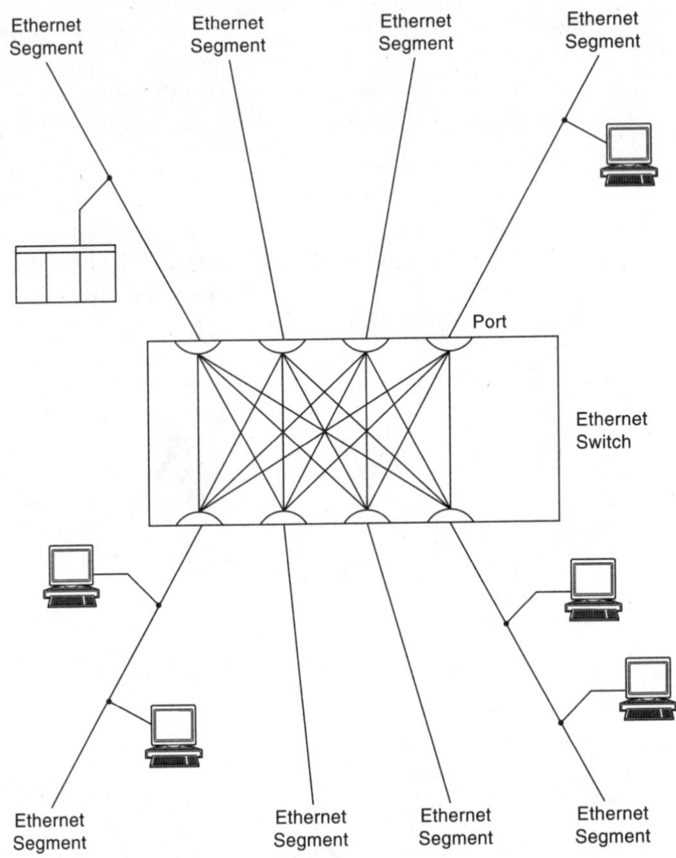

Figure 2.36
Ethernet switch.

Some vendors offer a variety of switching options with their Ethernet switch. A few of the common ones are *store and forward switching, fast forward switching,* and *fragment free switching.*

In store and forward switching, the entire packet is received at the port before a decision is made to switch the packet to its appropriate port. Receiving the entire packet allows the Ethernet switch to check the Ethernet packet for CRC errors. Packets with an invalid CRC are rejected. This mode, although the most reliable, is the slowest of the switching modes because the entire packet has to be stored before being switched.

In fast forward switching, a decision is made to switch the packet after receiving the address header only. This reduces the latency or the wait time for a packet, but can result in packets with a bad CRC being sent to another port because the CRC is not checked. This mode is the fastest and the least reliable of the switching modes. Errors in the packet can still be detected by upper-layer protocol software running on Ethernet stations.

Fragment free switching represents a compromise between the store and forward switching and fast forward switching. In fragment free switching, the Ethernet switch examines the packet long enough to determine that it is at least 64 bytes long, which is the minimum packet size for Ethernet and the size of the Ethernet collision window. Packets smaller than 64 bytes are called *fragments* and can result from collisions on an Ethernet segment or a malfunctioning card at an Ethernet station.

Another distinguishing characteristic of Ethernet switches is whether they allow only a single station to attach to the Ethernet switch port or an entire segment. An example of a product that allows a single station to attach to the Ethernet switch is FastSwitch 10 and FastSwitch 10/100 from Grand Junction. These products provide a private 10 Mbps channel for each attached workstation. Kalpana's EtherSwitch can attach Ethernet segments to a port on the Ethernet switch, and can be used to relieve congestion at high traffic locations on the network by providing a higher aggregate bandwidth at these locations than is possible with non-switched Ethernet hubs.

Because network traffic can be concentrated at the server's port, faster ports such as the 100 Mbps port in Grand Junction's FastSwitch 10/100 can be used. An alternate solution is to install 20 Mbps full duplex Ethernet cards at the server. Ethernet operates in a half-duplex mode at 10 Mbps. By attaching two ports to a single Ethernet card that have a separate link to the Ethernet switch, you can double the bandwidth of traffic between the server and the switch. Kalpana offers a special NLM called the SwitchBalance NetWare Loadable Module that runs on NetWare servers and evenly balances the traffic between Kalpana's EtherSwitch and the 20 Mbps full duplex Ethernet connections.

Some Ethernet switch products offer a *secure address* mode in which the station addresses associated with each port can be entered into a table. This prevents nonauthorized users from using the Ethernet switch. In Ethernet switches in which only a single station can attach to a port, the port can be disabled if an unauthorized station is detected.

Other options that exist for Ethernet switches are SNMP support that allows the switch to be managed by SNMP managers, such as HP's OpenView, SUN's SunConnect Manager, and Novell's NMS.

In many networks, a major network bottleneck is the network traffic handled by the server. Consider an Ethernet Switch that provides a 10 Mbps private channel for each station attached to its port, and in which the server is attached to one of the Ethernet switch's ports. If *M* stations were to access the server simultaneously, the server would have to handle 10**M* Mbps of data (see fig. 2.37). If ten stations needed to access the server at 10 Mbps, the server would have to handle 10*10 = 100 Mbps of data. An ordinary Ethernet switch can not provide a solution to this problem. What is needed here is an Ethernet switch that has dedicated ports that can handle 100 Mbps of data. An example of such a switch is Grand Junction's FastSwitch 10/100 that has 24 ports that provide 10 Mbps private Ethernet channels to stations and two ports that provide 100 Mbps Fast Ethernet channels to which servers can be attached. The servers must be installed with the FastNIC 100 EISA network boards. Twelve simultaneous conversations can exist between the 10 Mbps private Ethernet channels and a 100 Mbps port. This yields an aggregate bandwidth of the following:

$$12 \times 10 + 1 \times 100 = 120 + 100 = 220 \text{ Mbps}$$

Whereas Grand Junction's FastSwitch 10/100 provides aggregation of Ethernet traffic to Fast Ethernet, other products provide Ethernet switching to either FDDI, ATM (asynchronous transfer mode), or proprietary backbones. 3COM's LinkBuilder 3 GH switches 88 Ethernet segments to an FDDI

backbone, and Ungermann-Bass's Dragon Switch switches private Ethernet channels to Access One's proprietary 320 Mbps PlusBus backplane. Chipcom's 10BASE-FB star coupler is an all-fiber Ethernet switch with eight ports; each port provides a private 10 Mbps Ethernet channel.

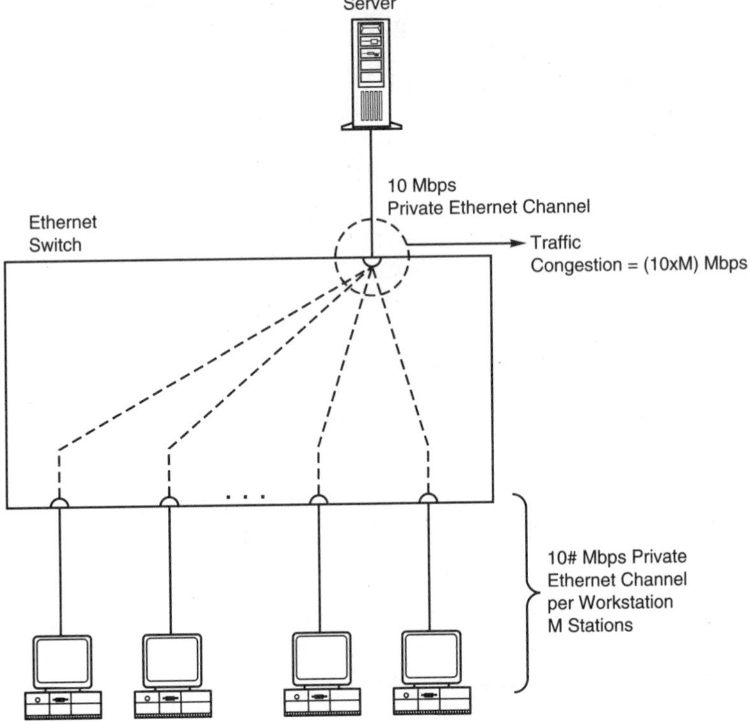

Figure 2.37
Traffic problem at server port for Ethernet switch.

Understanding Virtual LANs

A new method of organizing LAN workstations into logical domains or *virtual domains* has developed out of the work done with integrating existing LANs into ATM networks. This new organizational scheme creates a *Virtual LAN* (VLAN). The members of the VLAN are workstations/servers that can be dynamically assigned by the network administrator.

Figure 2.38 shows a conventional LAN consisting of several LAN segments connected using bridge/router combinations. The bridges/routers provide traffic isolation between the LAN segments and allow LAN segments to be treated as separate management domains. To physically reorganize such networks can be daunting, because you have to physically relocate the machines and change their software configuration. Virtual LANs simplify the reorganization/configuration of the tasks without physically relocating the workstations and servers.

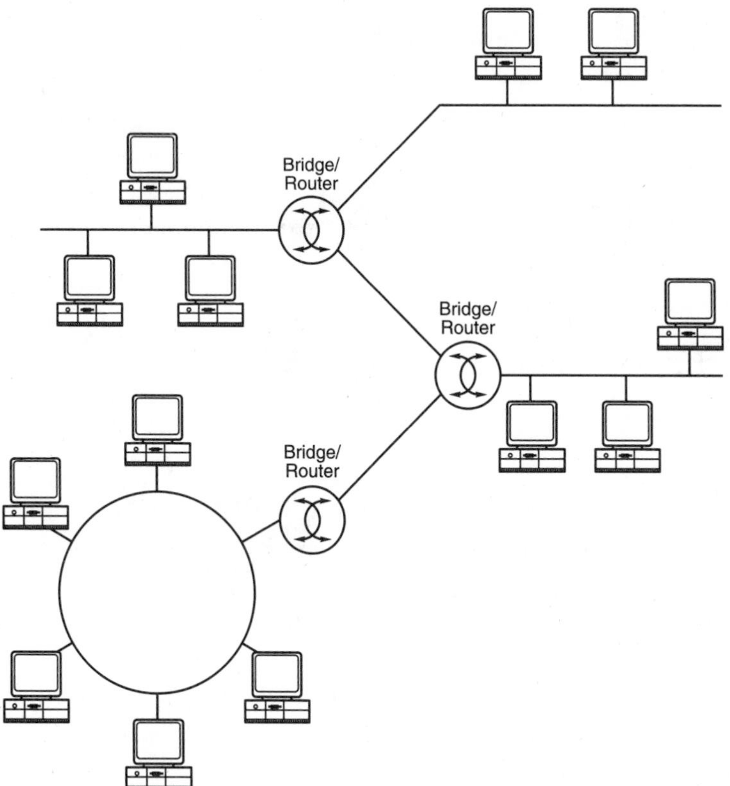

Figure 2.38
Bridge/router based LAN.

Virtual LANs are built around switching hubs using conventional technologies such as Ethernet and Token Ring, although nothing prevents these hubs from being based on ATM technology. The switching hubs are tied together to form a physically distributed star topology. Using software that runs at the switching hubs, the administrator can dynamically assign ports on hubs to a particular LAN domain. Figure 2.39 shows a number of virtual LANs formed out of several switching hubs. Workstations that form a VLAN are part of the same broadcast domain. A broadcast sent by a workstation in a VLAN is received only by workstations in that Virtual LAN domain. This allows VLANs to behave like their physical counterparts (Ethernet, Token Ring, and so on).

If virtual LANs can be formed by grouping ports from different switching hubs (see fig. 2.39), the hubs are called *segment-switching hubs.* Another type of hub, the *port-switching* hub, also can be used to form VLANs. Port-switching hubs are limited to forming a VLAN out of ports on a single hub only (see fig. 2.40). Segment-switching hubs, on the other hand, are more flexible because they allow a VLAN to be formed by aggregating ports from different hubs, at potentially different locations, into one logical LAN. Linking VLANs that use port-switching hubs, requires using external bridges and routers. In segment-switching hubs, VLANs within the same hub can be bridged. VLANs that span several segment-switching hubs can be bridged or routed. Many of the segment-switching hubs do not require any external bridging and routing, as these functions are included in the hub.

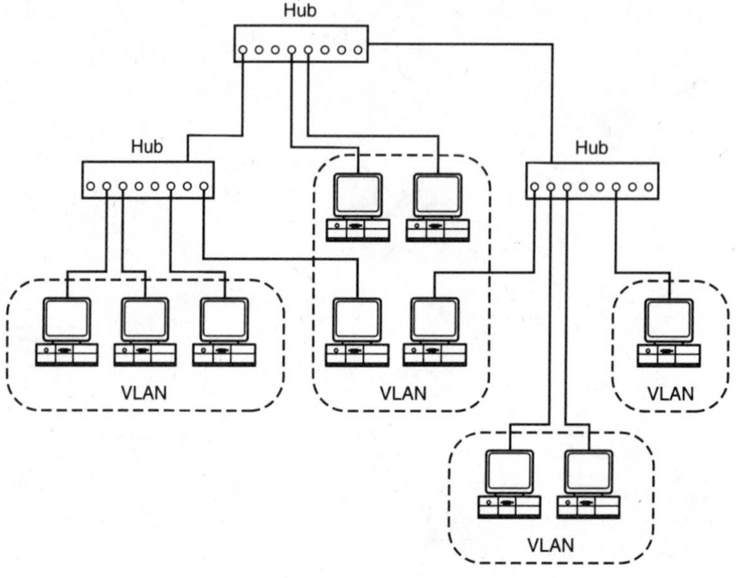

Figure 2.39
Virtual LANs formed using segment-switching hubs.

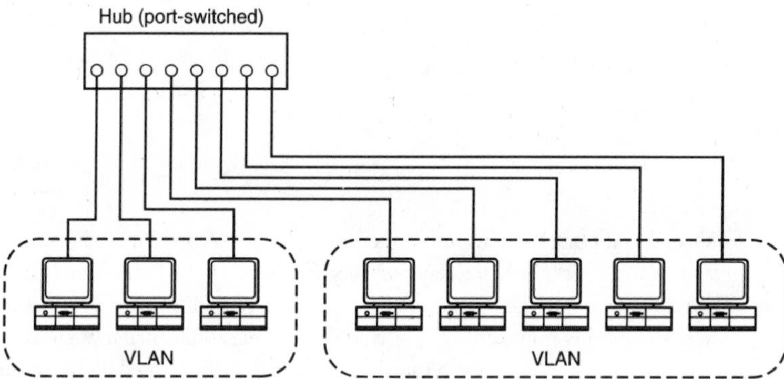

Figure 2.40
Virtual LANs formed using port-switching hubs.

Virtual LANs offer the following advantages:

- Partitioning of networks to better utilize network bandwidth by restricting high volume traffic to within a VLAN
- Flexible and dynamic traffic isolation
- Easy node manipulation
- Separation of logical network management from physical infrastructure by allowing network administrators to change VLAN configurations and manage network bandwidth

VLAN technology is particularly useful in collision-based networks, such as Ethernet, because it helps to restrict the number of workstations that see a collision on the network.

Segment-switching and port-switching hub products are available for Ethernet, Token Ring, FDDI, and ATM. Examples of port-switching hubs are SynOptics Communication System's Lattis System 5000 and 3COM's LinkBuilder MHS/II. Examples of segment-switching hubs are Alantec, Inc.'s PowerHub; Cabletron System, Inc.'s Multi Media Access Center; and Ungermann-Bass, Inc.'s DragonSwitch.

Examining the 10BASE-FB and 10BASE-FL Standards

In the preceding section, Chipcom's 10BASE-FB star coupler is mentioned as an example of an all-fiber Ethernet switch. The 10BASE-FB and 10BASE-FL standards are used to extend the range of existing Ethernet networks. 10BASE-FL is used for synchronous Ethernet connections, and 10BASE-FB is used for asynchronous connections between a station and the Ethernet segment. The 10BASE-FB was ratified by the IEEE 802 committees in September 1993. Prior to the 10BASE-FL and 10BASE-FB standards, the *Fiber-Optic Inter-Repeater Link* (FOIRL) was used to link Ethernet segments at distances up to one kilometer. The 10BASE-FB and 10BASE-FL extend the range between Ethernet segments to two kilometers (an IEEE specification limit). Commercial products such as Chipcom's products can go beyond the two kilometer limit, to distances of up to four kilometers.

Exploring Other Names for Ethernet

Ethernet was originally introduced as Ethernet Version 1.0 in 1980 by Digital, Intel, and Xerox. This was followed in 1982 by Version 2.0 of Ethernet, also by DIX. The IEEE adopted Ethernet with slight but important variations and called it the IEEE 802.3 standard ("Standard 802.3 Carrier Sense Multiple Access with Collision Detect (CSMA/CD) Access Method and Physical Layer Specifications").

In 1982, the *European Computer Manufacturers Association* (ECMA) adopted it as the ECMA 80/82/82 standard. The United States federal government adopted "Ethernet" in the FIPS PUBS 107 publication in 1984. In 1989, the International Organization of Standards and International Electrotechnical Commission adopted it as the ISO/IEC 8802-3 standard.

Exploring Token Ring LANs

Ring-based networks have been around for many years. Ring LANs are a concatenation of point-to-point links, and as such are not broadcast LANs like Ethernet. They are considered to be sequential broadcast LANs with the point-to-point links forming a circle. The technology of ring LANs is digital, unlike that of Ethernet LANs in which the carrier sense mechanism can be analog. Another attractive feature of ring-based LANs is their deterministic response time even under heavy load conditions.

The Token Ring LAN you encounter most often is the IEEE 802.5. This LAN is often referred to as the IBM Token Ring because IBM was the prime mover behind the IEEE 802.5 standard.

Token Ring Operation

Figure 2.41 illustrates Token Ring operation. The Token Ring LAN is a concatenation of point-to-point links. Each station acts like a repeater providing the necessary amplification and correcting for signal jitter. The links can be made up of any medium such as coaxial, twisted pair, and fiber optic. For the IBM Token Ring, twisted pair is the medium of choice. Fiber-optic links can be used to extend Token Ring operation over longer distances.

Figure 2.41
Token Ring operation.

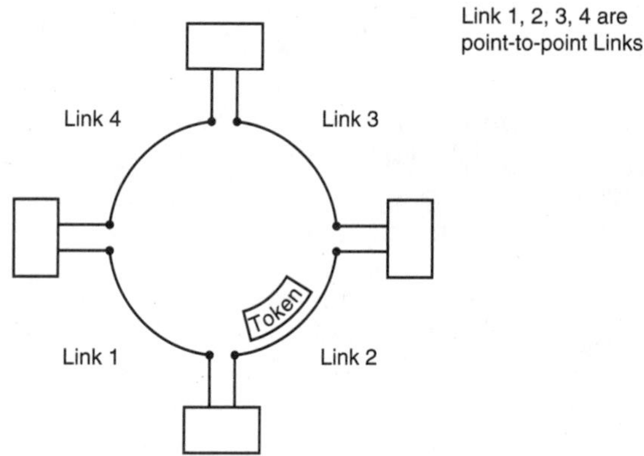

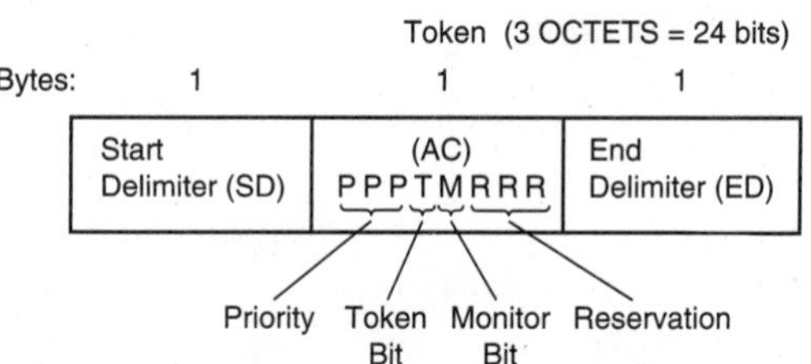

For proper operation of the ring, the token must circulate continuously even if no activity is on the ring. Twenty-four bits (three octets) are in the token, and the ring must have enough latency or delay to hold 24 bits. If the bit rate on the ring is 4 Mbps, the ring must have a latency of 24/4 Mbps = 6 microseconds. Six microseconds may seem like a very short delay, but consider a twisted-pair medium in which the propagation velocity is 0.59 times the speed of light. To compute the size of the ring that has a latency of 6 microseconds, use the following formula:

Size of Ring	= Latency × Propagation
Speed of media	= 0.0000006 × 0.59 × 3 × 100,000,000 meters
	= 1062 meters
	= 1.062 km

Thus the minimum size of the ring would be 1 km! This size is enormous, considering that you may want to install a few stations in a single room. For this reason, a special station designated as the *Active Monitor* adds a 24-bit delay buffer to the ring. This buffer also compensates for any accumulated phase jitter on the ring. The Active Monitor is important for maintaining normal operation of the ring.

Under normal operation of the ring, stations can be powered down. What happens to the bits that need to go across an inactive station? Token Ring networks are wired as star networks with a hub or wiring center. Each station's connection is controlled by a relay in the hub. In figure 2.42, the relays are held open by power from the station. When a station is powered down, the relay closes, bypassing the inactive station.

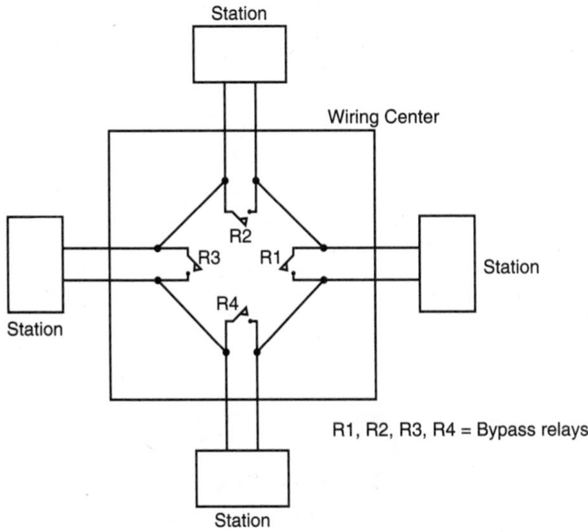

Figure 2.42
Token Ring relay bypass mechanism.

As illustrated by figure 2.43, a Token Ring station operates in one of the four following modes:

- Transmit mode
- Listen mode
- Bypass mode
- Receive mode

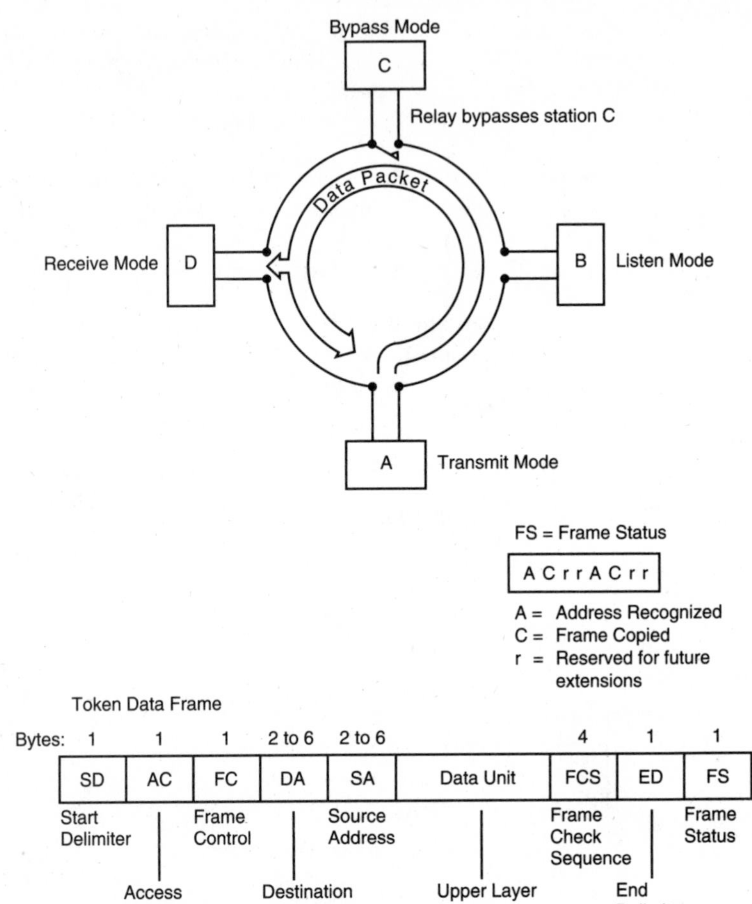

Figure 2.43
Token Ring station modes.

Figure 2.43 shows four stations operating in these modes. Station A is in transmit mode. To enter this mode, station A seizes a free token. The token has a token bit called the *T bit,* which has a value of 0 for a token and 1 for a data frame. The transmitting station changes this T bit to a 1 (data frame), indicating a busy token with accompanying data, and transmits the data frame. Because station A is sending this data frame to station D, the destination address field holds station D's address, and the source address field holds A's address.

Station B is operating in listen mode, and checks the destination address field of the frame to see if the frame holds its (B's) address. Because the frame is addressed to station D, it enters listen mode. In listen mode, a station copies the incoming bits to the output link.

Station C is powered down and is therefore in bypass mode. The bits flow through the bypass relay.

Station D examines the destination address field. Station D discovers that it is indeed the addressed station and, therefore, enters receive mode. In receive mode, the data frame is copied into the station's memory and also sent along the ring. A number of flags called *Frame Status flags* are modified to indicate proper reception of the data frame. Station A receives the data frame that it sent and examines the Frame Status flags. The Frame Status flags serve the purpose of a hardware-based acknowledgment. The sending station can determine these flags and determine if the frame was received correctly. The Frame Status flags are the Address-recognized (A) flag, Frame-copied (C) flag, and the Error (E) flag. The E flag is computed and set by every station. The A and C flags are set by the destination station only. Table 2.7 defines these flags.

Table 2.7
Frame Status Flags

Frame Flags	Value	Meaning
A	1	Address recognized
A	0	Address not recognized
C	1	Frame copied successfully
C	0	Frame not copied
E	1	Bad frame (CRC error)
E	0	Good frame

The legal combinations of these flags are as follows:

- **AC = 00.** This implies that the address was not recognized, and, therefore, the copy operation did not take place.
- **AC = 10.** This implies that the station exists, but the frame was not copied. If E = 1, a bad frame was received. If the E flag is 0, then the frame was not copied for unknown reasons.
- **AC = 11.** This implies that the station exists and the frame was copied to the station. If E = 1 and AC = 11, this indicates that the error was produced after the frame was copied.
- **AC = 01.** This implies that the station was not recognized, but a station still copied the frame! This condition should not occur in a Token Ring network that does not have bridges. If bridges are used, the bridge sets the AC to 01, indicating that the frame was not addressed to the bridge, but the bridge has copied the frame for forwarding to another network.

As the bits sent by station A come back to station A, they are removed from the ring.

If station A is powered down before the frame it sent comes back, the frame circulates endlessly because the sending station must remove the frame it sends. Many similar scenarios could disrupt normal ring operation. What if the token was destroyed by noise on the ring? Would stations wait for the token indefinitely? The token ring operation contains self-healing mechanisms to correct for these and many

other possibilities. These situations are detected and handled by special control frames called MAC frames, which is one of the reasons why the IEEE 802.5 operation is more complex than IEEE 802.3. The following discussion describes just a few of these self-healing mechanisms.

Although all stations seem equal, some stations are more equal than others. One such station is the Active Monitor. A *monitor bit* (M-bit) in the token is set to 0 by the transmitting station. The Active Monitor examines this M-bit and changes it to a 1, if it is a 0. If the Active Monitor bit sees an M-bit value of 1, it concludes that this data frame has been circulating once too often! This might be because the transmitting station crashed and failed to remove the data frame from the ring.

If the token is lost because it got mangled by noise on the ring, the Active Monitor times out and generates a new token. The Active Monitor keeps track of this *Token Rotation Time* (TRT) and times out if it exceeds a threshold value. For small Token Ring networks, the typical value of TRT is eight microseconds. Under heavy load conditions this value can rise.

The Active Monitor is not a station with special networking hardware. Any station on the Token Ring can become an Active Monitor. All other stations act as Standby Monitors. The choice of which station becomes an Active Monitor is realized through a ring-initialization procedure. If the Active Monitor fails, one of the Standby Monitors becomes the Active Monitor.

When no data frames are circulating around the ring, the Active Monitor issues an *Active Monitor Present* (AMP) MAC frame. This frame is sent at regular intervals of usually seven seconds. Other stations in the role of Standby Monitor send *Standby Monitor Present* (SMP) MAC frames. Standby Monitors detect the AMP frame and conclude that the Active Monitor is doing its job. If the Active Monitor skips a beat—if it does not send out the AMP frame when it should—one of the Standby Monitors takes over the role of the Active Monitor. The Standby Monitor that detects the failure of the Active Monitor sends its claim on the Token Ring in the form of Claim Token (CL_TK) MAC frames. The Standby Monitor stops sending these frames if one of the following conditions occurs:

- Another CL_TK frame is received, and the sender's address is greater than this station's address. If two or more stations send out CL_TK, the station with the higher address becomes the Active Monitor.

- A *Beacon* (BCN) MAC frame is received. This frame is sent as a result of a major ring failure such as a ring break. The BCN frame is used to locate and isolate the fault. In this case, the ring needs to be healed before deciding the winner of this contest.

- A *Purge* (PRG) MAC frame is received. This frame is sent out at the end of the Claim Token procedure by the station that has become the new Active Monitor. This means that the race already has been won by another station, and so there is no point in continuing.

In any of the preceding cases, the Standby Monitor backs off. If a station receives the CL_TK frame it generated, it becomes the Active Monitor (new king of the hill!) and issues an RG MAC frame to inform other stations of the new Active Monitor. At this point, the new Active Monitor adds the 24-bit latency buffer to the ring and commences monitoring the network.

Before joining a ring, a new station sends out the *Duplicate Address Test* (DAT) MAC frame as part of the ring initialization procedure. The DAT frame is sent with its own address in the DA (Destination Address) field. If another station responds with the AC bits set to 11, then another station has the same address. The new station returns an appropriate status code. Network monitoring software can detect this code and process it with an appropriate error message.

Another feature of the IEEE 802.5 is the priority access mechanism. The token has two fields, called the Priority field and the Reservation field, that each consist of three bits. A total of eight priority values can be defined (0 to 7). The Reservation field is set to 0 by the transmitting station. If a station wants priority access, it can place its priority value in the Reservation field. After the transmitting station receives the frame it sent, it copies the Reservation field value in the Priority field of the new token that it generates. The token now has the requested Priority value. Only stations with higher or equal priority can access this token.

Token Ring Options

The IEEE 802.5 specifies Token Ring options (see fig. 2.44) at data rates of 1 Mbps, 4 Mbps, and 16 Mbps. The 1 Mbps uses UTP wiring. Initially, the 16 Mbps used STP wiring. A demand within the industry was to have 16 Mbps data rate on UTP wiring. Several products are available to support UTP wiring for 4 and 16 Mbps token rings. For a long time, a 16 Mbps UTP version was not available from IBM. IBM has teamed with Synoptics Communications to propose a 16 Mbps UTP standard to the IEEE 802.5 committee.

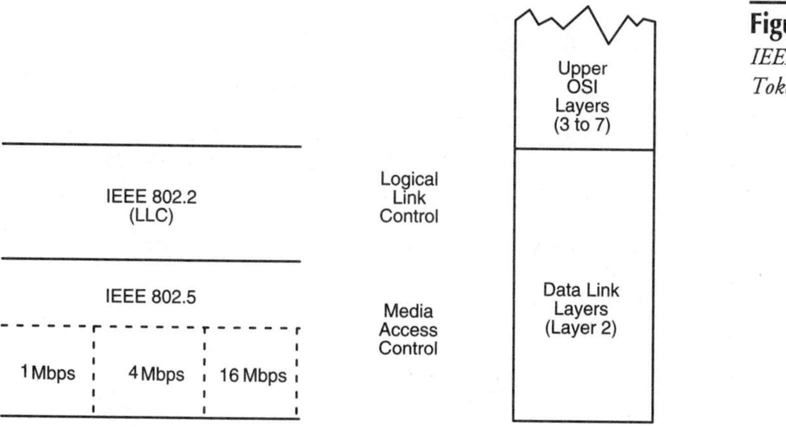

Figure 2.44
IEEE 802.5 options for Token Ring.

The 16 Mbps stations have an option called the *early token release mechanism.* In this option, the 16 Mbps stations do not wait for the return of the data frame to place the token on the network. This mechanism allows up to two data frames to be transmitted on a Token Ring LAN at a time.

Token Ring LAN Components

For standard-bus (ISA) stations, the following adapter cards are available from IBM:

IBM Token Ring PC Adapter
IBM Token Ring 16/4 Adapter
IBM Token Ring PC Adapter II

For Micro Channel Architecture stations, the following cards are available from IBM:

IBM Token Ring PC Adapter/A
IBM Token Ring 16/4 Adapter/A
IBM Token Ring 16/4 Busmaster Server Adapter

The Token Ring network board (NIC) has a 9-pin socket used to connect the network adapter cables. Various manufacturers provide network adapter cards. Some manufacturers' cards are equipped with RJ-45 connectors, which makes them ready to connect directly to UTP (Type 3) wiring.

The IBM 8228 *Multistation Access Unit*, also called MAU but not to be confused with the *Media Attached Unit* (MAU) in IEEE 802.3, is a wiring center that allows up to eight stations to be connected to it. The two end ports, called *Ring In* (RT) and *Ring Out* (RO), are not used to connect Token Ring stations. These are used to connect multiple MAUs together. Four port wiring centers (also called *hubs*) also are available. MAUs also are available that contain a number of network management features. These are called *smart* or *intelligent* MAUs.

The IBM 8228 Setup Aid is used to test each port in the IBM 8228 before it is installed. It is used to check the operation of the bypass relay mechanism for each port.

The IBM Token Ring network adapter cable is made of eight feet of IBM Type 1 cable. Type 6 cable also can be used, although these are recommended as patch cables between wiring centers. One end of this cable connects to the Token Ring adapter, and the other end is a dual-gender connector that plugs into one of the station ports in the IBM 8228 MAU.

The method of interconnecting 8228 MAUs and workstations is illustrated in figure 2.45.

IEEE 802.5 Design Rules

Table 2.8 summarizes the rules for Token Ring wiring:

Table 2.8
Token Ring Wiring Rules

Token Ring Parameters	Type 1, 2	Type 3
Max devices per ring	260	96
Tested data Rates	16 Mbps	4 Mbps

Token Ring Parameters	Type 1, 2	Type 3
Station to single MAU LAN	300 M	100 M
Station to multiple MAU LAN	100 M	45 M
Max MAUs per LAN	12	2
MAU-to-MAU distance	200 M	120 M

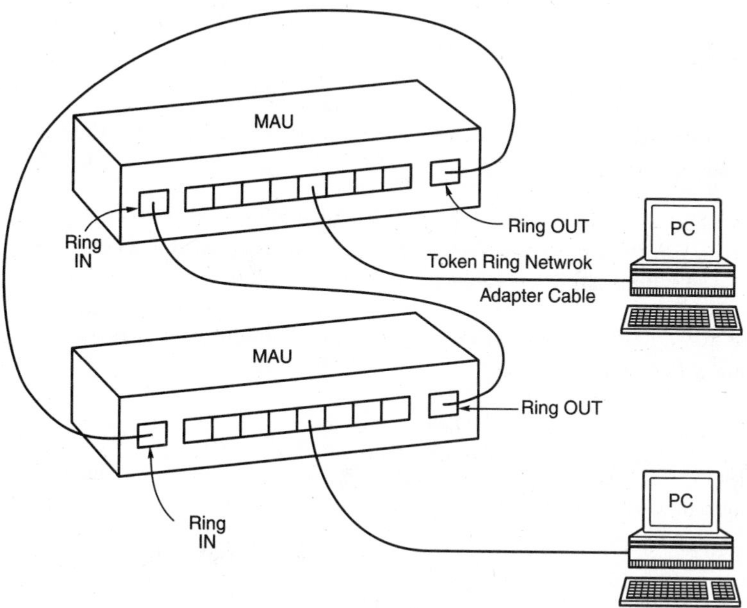

Figure 2.45
Token Ring network cabling components.

Types 1 and 2 Cabling

Although a maximum of 260 stations can be used with Type 1 and 2 cables, a more reasonable number is 100. The limit on the maximum stations is due to accumulated clock jitter. Interestingly enough, if you use the IBM 8228 MAU, which has a maximum of eight ports, you only use 12 MAUs (refer to table 2.8). (There is a maximum of 8 × 12 = 96 stations on the Token Ring.)

For Type 1 and 2 cables, the maximum distance between workstation to MAU is 300 meters for a single MAU LAN, but this distance drops to 100 meters for multiple MAU LANs. As a practical measure, it is better to work with the tighter constraint of 100 meters, even for a single MAU LAN, because LANs have a tendency to grow and, as you add more stations, you eventually need a multiple MAU LAN.

The maximum MAU-to-MAU distance for a Token Ring LAN is 200 meters for Type 1 and 2 cables.

Type 3 Cabling

For Type 3 cabling, the maximum distance between workstation to MAU is 100 meters for a single MAU LAN, but this distance drops to 45 meters for multiple MAU LANs. As a practical measure, it is better to work with the tighter constraint of 45 meters even for a single MAU LAN. The reason for this is that LANs have a tendency to grow, and as you add more stations, you eventually need a multiple MAU LAN.

Guidelines for Token Ring Cabling

General guidelines for token ring cabling are as follows:

1. Stations located within eight feet of the MAU can be connected by using eight-foot adapter cable.
2. Stations farther than eight feet from the MAU can be connected by using extension cords (or you can build longer adapter cables).
3. To form a ring by using multiple MAUs, connect a patch cable from the RO of the first MAU to the RI of the second MAU. Continue doing this for all the MAUs until you reach the last MAU. Connect the RO of the last MAU to the RI of the first MAU.
4. You cannot connect stations to the RI and the RO ports. The RI and RO ports are only used for interconnecting multiple MAUs.
5. Patch cables (IBM Type 6) should not be spliced.
6. Patch cables (IBM Type 6) should not be used in any duct, plenum, or other space used for air handling. IBM Type 9, which is a plenum-rated cable, can be used instead.
7. You cannot place Token Ring workstations operating at 4 Mbps and 16 Mbps in the same physical Token Ring cable. The stations must all be 4 Mbps or 16 Mbps for the Token Ring to work.

Token Ring Troubleshooting Considerations

For the Token Ring to work correctly, the physical token loop must be maintained. Any problems that disrupt the flow of data on the physical wire can cause the Token Ring to malfunction. Also, because the data flows through each workstation (each station acts as a repeater), a malfunctioning workstation can cause the entire ring to fail. For these reasons, troubleshooting Token Ring networks is challenging.

The Size of the Ring

Token Ring networks using STP cabling such as the IBM Type 1 and Type 2 cables have a limit as to the maximum number of stations that can be placed in a single physical ring. This limit is 260 stations for the IBM Token Ring using STP cables. Adding workstations above this limit causes clock jitter problems that make the ring fail. To have a useful ring, the minimum number of physical stations is 2. The actual number of stations on a ring is a number between these two limits: 2 and 260.

An important consideration when determining the number of stations is to keep a physical ring large enough to provide useful work, but small enough to make troubleshooting easier. In a smaller ring, it is much easier to physically isolate the offending station or isolate the problem in the ring.

One way to keep a ring to a reasonable size to facilitate troubleshooting is to use token ring bridges as illustrated in figure 2.46. *Bridges* are devices that allow physical rings to be separate in terms of MAC layer operation. For example, in figure 2.46, two rings are joined by a bridge. Each ring has its own token, which is used to implement the MAC mechanism. The token is restricted to the physical ring on which it operates. Using this approach, you can construct complex ring networks, in which each ring operates independently of the others but can still communicate to other stations in other rings through the bridges. The bridges participate in the MAC mechanism of the rings to which they are connected.

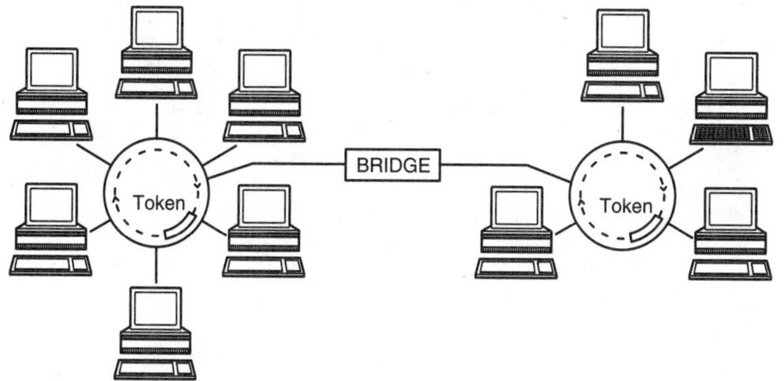

Figure 2.46
Separate token mechanism of rings connected with a bridge.

Built-In Diagnostics

The IEEE 802.5 specification for the Token Ring specifies built-in diagnostics used by workstations to isolate problems. Many of these diagnostics refer to the concept of a fault domain or failure domain.

The *fault domain* is a section of the ring (see fig. 2.47) that consists of the following three components:

- The station transmitting the BCN (beacon) Frame
- The beaconing station's *Nearest Active Upstream Neighbor* (NAUN)
- The cable between the beaconing station and its NAUN

Because the data flow in a ring is unidirectional, every station has a neighbor that is upstream with respect to its position in the ring. This *upstream neighbor* is the station from which the data frame is received and is called the NAUN. The use of the word *Active* implies that the NAUN may not be the nearest physical upstream neighbor because the physically closest neighbor may not be participating in the ring. The NAUN for each station is set in the Neighbor Notification process activated by the Active Monitor.

Figure 2.47
Fault domain.

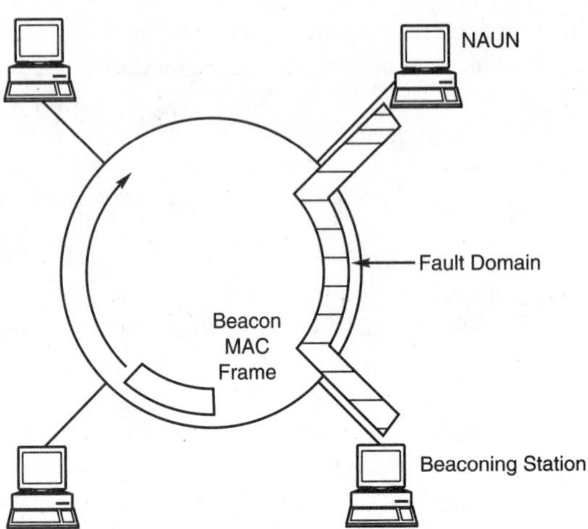

When a station discovers a hard error, it sends a beacon MAC frame that contains its NIC address, the NAUN, and the beacon type. The contents of the beacon frame essentially define the fault domain. The beacon type is helpful in diagnosing the cause of the error. An example of a beacon type is a cable fault. The beacon frame is broadcast to all stations. All other stations enter the Beacon Repeat mode in which they copy and repeat the frame around the ring. The beacon frame is generated repeatedly by the station that detects the hard error. After the NAUN copies the beacon frame eight times, it removes itself from the ring and conducts a series of self-tests such as the DAT and the Lobe Media Test. In the Lobe Media test, the NIC transmits a Lobe Test MAC frame to the MAU port to test if it receives the frame correctly. If it receives the frame incorrectly, the lobe (cable between the NIC and the MAU port) is suspect.

If the NAUN station fails, it removes itself from the ring. Because the NAUN, which was the cause of the problem, is off the ring, the beaconing station receives the BCN frames it sends. At this point, the station stops beaconing and retransmits the token frame onto the ring. The ring now has auto-recovered.

If the NAUN station passes its self-test, it reinserts itself in the ring. After a certain time, the beaconing station assumes that the NAUN passed the self-test. The problem could then be with the beaconing station. Therefore, the beaconing station goes through the same series of self-tests. If the beaconing station fails its tests, it removes itself from the ring. The Active Monitor then initiates a Ring Recovery by issuing a Ring PRG (Purge) followed by a Claim Token MAC frame. If the beaconing station passes its test, it reinserts itself in the ring. If the beaconing condition persists, the problem requires manual troubleshooting. The problem is most likely caused by the cabling media (including the MAU) between the beaconing station and its NAUN.

Token Ring Cable Problems

One of the areas of great vulnerability in Token Ring operation is the failure of the physical cable. When the physical cable fails, the token cannot flow, and, therefore, the ring cannot function. Consult *Token Ring Troubleshooting* (New Riders Publishing) for an excellent guide to troubleshooting many of the common cable and operational problems in Token Ring networks. The discussion that follows is based on this material.

Cabling problems can be repeatable or intermittent. Repeatable problems are the easiest because they indicate a recurring condition on the network, and you can use standard divide-and-conquer troubleshooting techniques to isolate the problem. These problems are often called *hard faults* or *solid problems.* Intermittent problems, by their very definition, exist only under certain conditions. Because these conditions are often unknown or hard to reproduce, isolating these problems can be particularly difficult. If it is possible to convert an intermittent problem to a repeatable problem by simulating the conditions under which the problem occurs, troubleshooting is much easier.

The following are some of the more common problems with Token Ring cables:

- Open cables
- Shorted cables
- Crossed conductors
- Bad connectors
- Bad cable terminations
- Improper cable placement

Open cables are caused by a physical break in the cable conductor, which prevents the signal from flowing. These cables can be the result of faulty manufacture, damage to the cable during installation such as excessive crimping pressure, or physical tension. Open cables also can result from careless construction work near the proximity of the cable.

Shorted cables result from the internal conductors touching each other. Like open cables, this problem can be the result of bad manufacture, excessive force during installation, and so on.

Open and shorted cables caused by improper installation usually occur at the ends of the cables because this is where the end connectors are installed. Carelessness in installing connectors at the end can damage the cable. Besides causing physical breaks in the cable, open and shorted faults can cause signal reflection. Open and shorted cables can be detected using *Time Domain Reflectometer* (TDR) instruments. It also is possible for a damaged cable, even though no short nor opening is present, to generate enough signal reflection to bring down the network.

Crossed conductors are caused by cable conductors improperly connected to their end connectors. The Token Ring cable uses a color code standard—red (Pin 1 Receive Plus), green (Pin 6 Receive Minus), orange (Pin 9 Transmit Plus), and black (Pin 5 Transmit Minus). If this standard is not adhered to while attaching the connectors, improper signaling on the Token Ring can occur. The problem may appear as failure at the station or MAU.

Bad connectors are problems in the physical connector itself, such as shorted connectors.

Bad cable terminations result from improper connections between the internal conductors and the physical connector. This can be caused by loose or disconnected conductors or crossed conductors.

Improper cable placement also can cause problems. Placing the cable near high voltage or current sources, such as High Voltage lines, can induce sufficient noise into the internal conductor to override the data signals. Improperly shielded cables can cause similar problems. This problem is even more pronounced when UTP cables are used.

To solve complex problems when troubleshooting Token Rings, a common approach is to divide and conquer. Because the Token Ring is wired in a physical star topology, the best way to solve Token Ring cable-related problems is to isolate the lobe cables from the main ring path cable and test the ring with and without the lobe cable. A *lobe cable* is the workstation-to-MAU cable. The main ring path cable consists of the MAU and the patch cables used to interconnect the MAUs. Removing the patch cables can isolate the MAUs, which can then be tested individually.

Sometimes a problem may be due to a port on the MAU or the failure of the NIC to generate a sufficiently strong phantom DC current to insert itself into the ring.

Token Ring NIC Failures

If an NIC encounters a solid internal fault, it generates a hard error, such as a BCN MAC frame, onto the ring. A protocol analyzer such as LANalyzer or Sniffer can be used to discover the station that causes the hard error. Hard errors result in the Token Ring stations entering the beaconing fault/domain process for ring recovery. At the conclusion of this process, the offending node is removed from the ring.

Sometimes the cause of an NIC failure may not be an internal hardware problem at all, but an improperly configured NIC. There may be an improper hardware setting such as the I/O Base Address, *Interrupt Request* (IRQ) line, *Direct Memory Access* (DMA) line, slot setting, or NIC microcode level. Other things to check are speed settings and possible incompatibility between the NIC, lobe cable, MAU, or cabling terminator.

Another type of NIC error is a soft error. *Soft errors* can result from improper configuration of ring speed settings or NIC firmware microcode versions. When an NIC detects a soft error, it may be detecting a marginal internal failure. Soft errors are reported in a special Report Soft Error MAC frame that is addressed to the *Ring Error Monitor* (REM) that has the functional address of C00000000008. This functional address can be seen through a protocol analyzer and represents the REM that has the special task of gathering ring errors and forwarding them to the Token Ring LAN Manager station at the functional address of C00000002000.

The NIC actually waits for a period of time defined by the parameter T (Soft_Error_Report)—about two seconds—to acquire software-error information. When a software error is encountered, the NIC increments the count of software errors, which is then transmitted to the REM functional address. Along with the number of software errors, the Report Soft Error MAC frame also includes the transmitting station address, its NAUN, and the type of software error. The software error counter is reset after transmission of the Report Soft Error MAC frame.

A high occurrence of soft errors can cause ring performance degradation and initiate a Ring Recovery process. This includes the Claim Token process to determine the Active Monitor and the Neighbor Notification process so that each station can determine its NAUN. This Ring Recovery process can consume a great deal of time and degrade the Token Ring's performance. The *soft error counter* is a

12-byte field, with each byte reserved for a special type of error. Currently, ten error types are defined with the remaining two bytes being reserved for future use.

Exploring ARCnet LANs

In 1976, four engineers from Datapoint Corporation built a LAN that evolved into a widely used, but relatively unknown, LAN in the industry—*Attached Resource Computer Network* (ARCnet). The goal of the design team was to develop network links between Datapoint's computer systems to allow customers to share resources while still retaining the benefits of stand-alone processing.

A data rate of 2.5 Mbps was selected, primarily because that was the transfer rate of the disks Datapoint was using at the time. A small frame size of a maximum of 508 bytes was chosen because a study done by ARCnet's designers revealed that more than 90 percent of all messages transmitted on a network were small. The designers wanted to make the network reliable so that failures in stations and cables had a minimal impact on the rest of the network. Another requirement was to make ARCnet work with a variety of media such as coaxial, twisted pair, and fiber optic. Today, products exist that support these media.

By 1977, the project was complete. It did not make a big splash in the industry, however, primarily because ARCnet was not a separate product; it was embedded in Datapoint's computing machines.

ARCnet technology predates Ethernet technology even though many people think that Ethernet technology is older. The reasons for ARCnet being relatively unknown are many. As mentioned, Datapoint kept the technology proprietary. It was not until 1982 that Datapoint enabled *Standard Microsystems Corporation* (SMC) to market an ARCnet chip set to other OEMs. Ethernet had already become popular by this time.

Datapoint—unlike Digital, Intel, and Xerox—did not propose ARCnet to the IEEE committee, and it had less market influence compared to other companies behind Ethernet and the Token Ring standard. The SMC chip set, developed in 1982, started a grass-roots movement. More than a dozen vendors have used this chip set to manufacture ARCnet network cards.

ARCnet uses the RG/62 93-ohm coaxial cable used with IBM 3270 terminals. There are many stories about whether this was done as part of the design or was an accident. This coaxial cable is cheaper than the 50-ohm coaxial cable used in Ethernet. Additionally, many older office buildings and airport complexes are wired with this type of cabling, making the transition to ARCnet easy.

ARCnet uses the token passing bus mechanism, which makes ARCnet deterministic. There is a fixed upper bound on the amount of time a station has to wait before it can transmit.

Despite its many advantages, ARCnet has the disadvantage of a low data rate (2.5 Mbps). A number of ARCnet vendors have banded together to form the *ARCnet Trader's Association* (ATA), which disseminates information to users about ARCnet technology. Membership in ATA is open to vendors, system integrators, and users. ATA is located at 3365 N. Arlington Heights Rd., Arlington Heights, IL 60004, (708) 255-3003. Under its auspices, a new ARCnet standard (ARCnet Plus) has been developed, which operates at a data rate of 20 Mbps.

Figure 2.48 shows an ARCnet LAN. Station transmission is broadcast in the same manner as for a bus LAN, but access to the bus is determined by a token, hence the name *Token Passing Bus.*

Figure 2.48
ARCnet LAN operation.

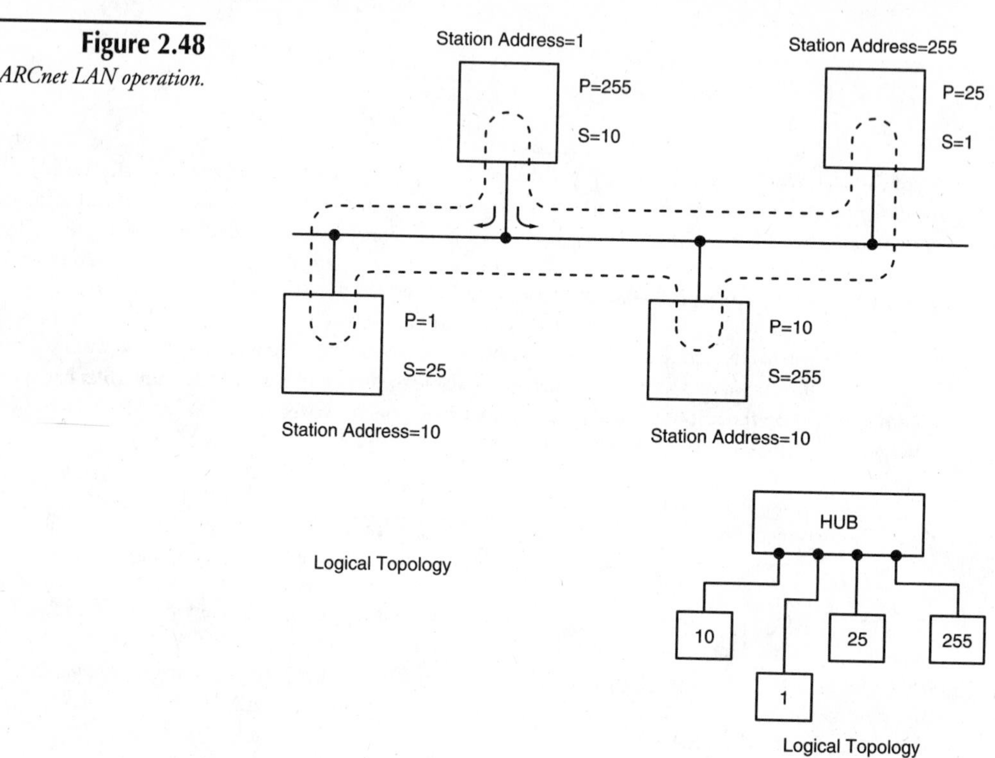

Figure 2.48 shows stations with node addresses of 1, 10, 25, and 255 on a bus. At startup time, a logical ordering is made so that these stations form a logical ring. Each station keeps track of two pieces of information: its successor and its predecessor. This information is shown by the letters S (successor) and P (predecessor) for each station. A *successor* for a station is the station on the ring with the next highest address. A *predecessor* for a station is the station with the next lowest address.

A maximum of 255 stations is allowed in ARCnet, with the lowest station address being 1. Station address 0 is used for broadcast. The successor for station 255 is 1, and the predecessor for station 1 is 255. The predecessor and successor information for the stations in figure 2.48 is as follows:

Station	Predecessor (P)	Successor (S)
1	255	10
10	1	25
25	10	255
255	25	1

A special frame, called the *token frame*, is passed from a station to its successor. The passing of this frame from station to station forms a logical ring. The token frame is called the *Invitation To Transmit* (ITT) frame. Its structure is as follows:

ITT =	ALERT	EOT	DID	DID

All ARCnet frames are preceded by an ALERT burst, similar to the preamble for Ethernet. An *ALERT burst* consists of six-bit intervals of mark (1). A *mark (1)* is represented by a dipulse pulse, which consists of a positive pulse followed by a negative pulse. A *space (0)* is represented by the absence of a pulse. The EOT is the ASCII EOT (04 hex) and is followed by two bytes. Each of the bytes contains the successor information called the *Destination ID* (DID) number. The DID field is repeated for reliability.

A station that has the ITT frame can transmit at most one frame before passing the frame to its successor (next DID). Before a data frame is sent to a destination node, it must be queried to see if it has enough buffer space to accept the frame. A special frame called the *Free Buffer Enquiry* (FBE) performs this function.

FBE =	ALERT	ENQ	DID	DID

The *ENQ (ENQUERY)* is the ASCII ENQ (05 hex) and is followed by two bytes. Each of the bytes contains the DID of the station whose free buffer status is desired. The DID field is repeated for reliability. If the destination node sends a positive response, known as an *Acknowledgement* (ACK) frame, the sending node can send the data frame.

A positive ACK frame consists of two bytes, as follows:

ACK =	ALERT	ACK

The ACK is the ASCII ACK (06 hex). When sent in response to an FBE frame, it indicates availability of buffer space at the receiver. There is no DID field in the ACK frame because it is sent as a broadcast frame.

A *Negative Acknowledgment* (NAK) is the ASCII ACK (15 hex). It indicates nonavailability of buffer space at the receiver. The NAK is not sent to indicate improper data frame reception. No DID field exists because NAK is sent as a broadcast frame.

A NAK frame consists of two bytes, as follows:

NAK =	ALERT	NAK

When an ACK frame is received in response to an FBE frame, a data frame can be sent. Data frames are transmitted by the PAC (packet) frame, as follows:

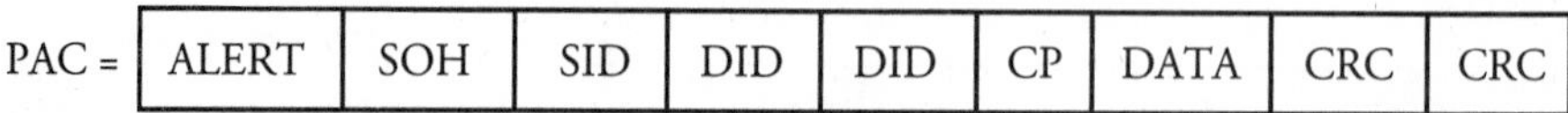

The *Start of Header* (SOH) is the ASCII SOH (01 hex). The source and destination address are indicated by the *Source ID* (SID) and DID fields. Again, the DID field is repeated for reliability. The *Continuation Pointer* (CP) field indicates where in its memory the station finds the beginning of the transmitted data. The data field DATA is of variable length between 1 to 508 bytes. A two-byte CRC, determined by the DATA field, is appended by the sender for error-checking purposes.

If a fault occurs to disrupt the proper passing of the token, the network must be reconfigured. Reconfiguration or resequencing also takes place when a station is added or removed from the token passing ring.

If an active node fails to receive an ITT token frame after 840 milliseconds (or if it is powered up), a RECON pattern, consisting of eight mark intervals followed by one space, is sent 765 times. This pattern is illustrated by figure 2.49.

Figure 2.49
A RECON pattern.

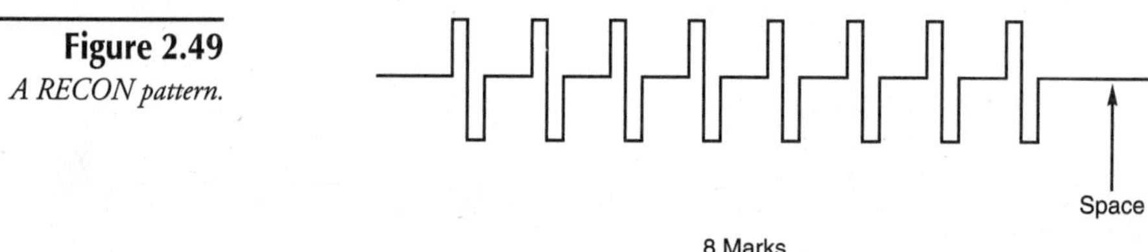

This RECON burst lasts for 2,754 microseconds, which is long enough to disrupt any token frame transmission under way. The result is that the token frame is lost. The stations wait for another 78 microseconds, and if no activity occurs, it is safe to assume that a reconfiguration is in progress. Each station then sets its successor (NID) to its own address (ID) plus one, and it sets a time out value according to the following equation:

Time out = $146 \times (255\text{-ID})$ microseconds

The node with the highest address has the first time out and issues an ITT to its successor (NID). A station with address 255 has a time out value of 0. If no activity occurs after 74 microseconds (less than 78 microseconds), the highest address station assumes that the node with the successor address of NID does not exist. The highest address station, then, increments the NID value and sends another ITT with the DID field set to the new NID value. This procedure is repeated until the highest address station discovers its successor. At this time, the token is transferred to the successor, and the successor repeats this process.

When all active nodes are found, the normal token-passing operation is resumed. Reconfiguration can take between 24 to 61 milliseconds, depending on the number of active nodes and the value of their node addresses. To minimize the initial time out value to zero and to reduce the reconfiguration time, set at least one ARCnet node to address 255. This should be a node such as a server, which is likely to be up all the time.

Deleting a node is a simpler process under ARCnet and does not invoke the full reconfiguration mechanism. If, in the preceding example, station 10 drops from the ring and does not respond to the ITT sent from station 1 for a period of 74 microseconds, station 1 assumes that station 10 is no longer active. Node 1 then increments its NID value (new value 11) and sends an ITT to station 11. If there is no response, the process repeats in another 74 microseconds. Because the next station address is 25, within (25_10) × 74 microseconds = 1.1 milliseconds, station 1 figures out that its successor is station 25.

If station 10 wants to reenter the network, it waits for a period of 840 milliseconds for the token. If it has not been invited to transmit through an ITT frame sent to it, it invokes the full reconfiguration mechanism.

ARCnet Components

Figure 2.50 shows some typical ARCnet components. An RG-62/U 93-ohm cable is used to connect the components of an ARCnet LAN. BNC twist-lock connector plugs are attached to both ends of the cable. BNC connector jacks mate with the BNC connector plugs and are located on several pieces of ARCnet hardware such as active and passive hubs, network cards, and active links.

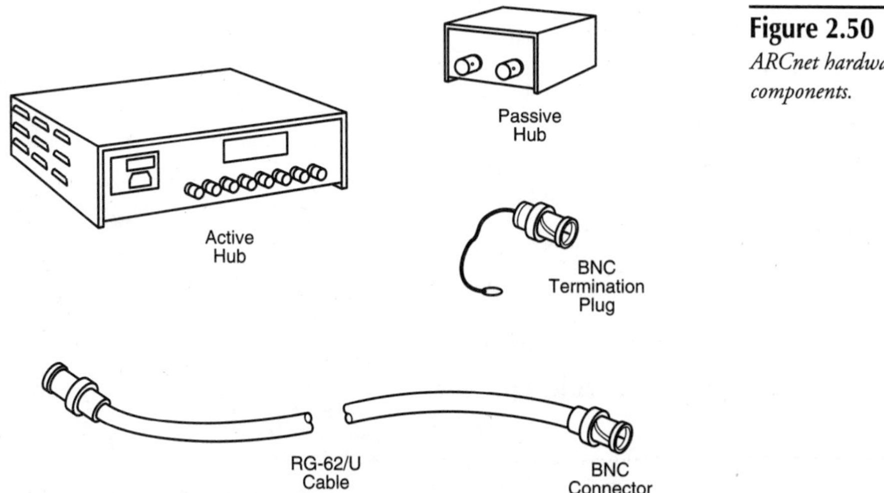

Figure 2.50
ARCnet hardware components.

Active hubs serve as repeaters in other LANs. An active hub amplifies and reconditions the signal. They usually have eight ports, although active hubs with more ports are available. Terminating unused ports on an active hub is recommended, but not necessary because of the isolation circuitry used in most ARCnet active hubs.

Passive hubs usually come with four ports to which network cables such as the RG-62/U can be attached. Unused ports in passive hubs must be terminated. Unlike the active hubs, they do not have special isolation circuits.

ARCnet Star Wiring Design Rules

Figure 2.51 illustrates the design rules for an ARCnet LAN using distributed star topology. Table 2.9 summarizes these rules. All distances in the figure are maximum distances.

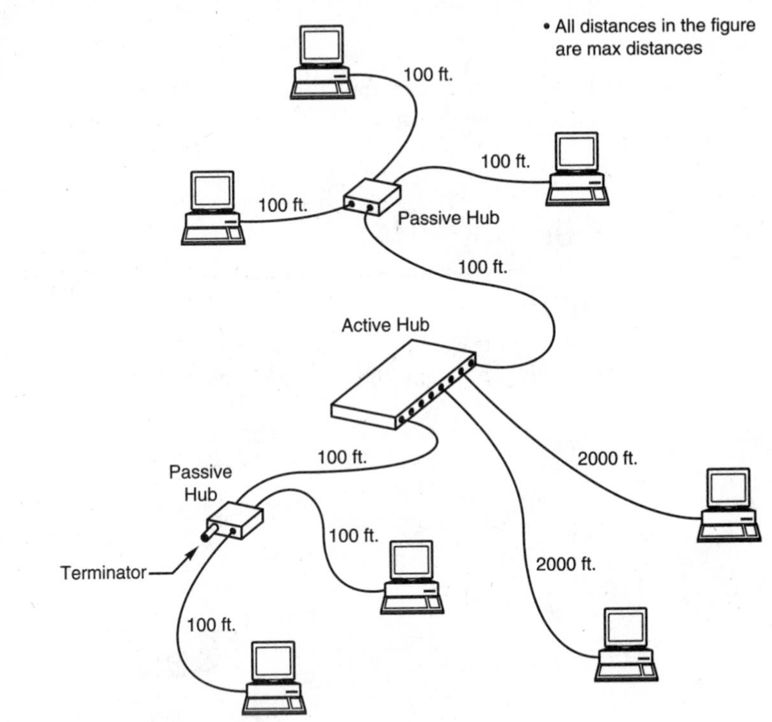

Figure 2.51
ARCnet using star-wiring rules.

Table 2.9
Cable Distance Limitations

From	To	Max Distance (feet)
One network end	The other end	20,000
Network station	Active hub	2,000
Network station	Passive hub	100

From	To	Max Distance (feet)
Active hub	Active hub	2,000
Active hub	Passive hub	100
Passive hub	Passive hub	Does not work

Thus, the maximum span of an ARCnet network is 20,000 feet (3.8 miles). ARCnet LANs are quite resilient to out-of-spec installations for distances between active components. They can span distances of 4.5 miles, even though this is outside the ARCnet specification. When passive hubs are employed, the distances cannot exceed 100 feet. Also, a passive hub cannot be connected in a series with another passive hub—the signal attenuation is too great for this to work.

The following are general rules for ARCnet networks:

1. Active hubs can connect to other hubs (active and passive) and ARCnet stations.
2. Passive hubs can connect to active hubs and ARCnet stations. They cannot connect to other passive hubs directly.
3. Do not create loops in an ARCnet LAN. A *loop* is created when a cable coming from a hub goes through other hubs and then connects back into the original hub.
4. Always terminate unused ports in a passive hub.
5. Keep a log of station addresses. Two stations cannot have duplicate addresses. No automatic mechanism exists to prevent this from occurring, as is the case in IEEE 802.5.
6. To minimize reconfiguration time, set the most reliable station that is active most of the time to station address 255, which can be your file server.
7. Many ARCnet NICs enable you to set the token rotation time threshold before reconfiguration ensues. For Pure Data cards, token rotation times can be set to 74.7, 283.4, 561.8, and 1,118.6 microseconds. All cards that participate in the token mechanism—that is, belonging to the same ARCnet LAN—need to have the same setting. Usually, the 74.7 microsecond setting is large enough for a 20,000-foot ARCnet LAN. For an unusually large number of active and passive hubs, this value may need to be increased. In general, such large configurations should be avoided. It is better to use routers or bridges, discussed in Chapter 3, "Bridging and Routing," for connecting many small LANs.

ARCnet Coaxial Bus Design Rules

ARCnet can be used in a bus topology in which up to eight stations can be daisy-chained with RG-62/U cables over a maximum distance of 1,000 feet (see fig. 2.52). In the bus topology, a T-connector is used to connect the workstations; a single bus segment must be terminated with a 93-ohm impedance at both ends.

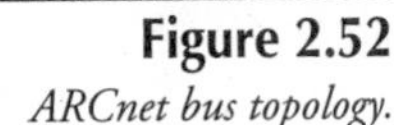

Figure 2.52
ARCnet bus topology.

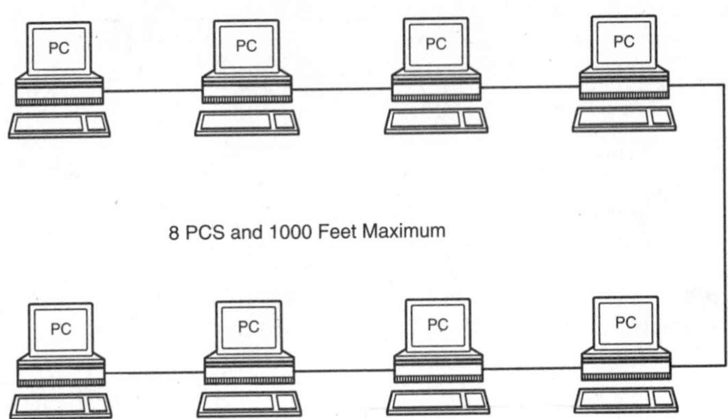

ARCnet coaxial bus topology can be mixed with the distributed star topology provided by an active hub. One end of the bus can be connected to an active hub. The total number of workstations that can be connected to a single eight-port active hub in this manner is 8 × 8 = 64. If two active hubs are to be connected, one port in each active hub is used up for connecting the active hubs. Therefore, each active hub supports 56 stations; the two active hubs support a total of 112 stations. Table 2.10 summarizes the configuration rules for the coaxial bus.

Table 2.10
Configuration Rules for ARCnet Coaxial Bus

Parameters	Value
Max stations per bus	8
Max length of bus	1,000 feet
Max stations on single 8-port active hub	64

ARCnet Twisted-Pair Wiring Design Rules

Twisted-pair wiring can be used for ARCnet LANs (see fig. 2.53). With ARCnet, twisted-pair bus topology is functionally and logically equivalent to the coaxial bus topology. Only one pair of twisted-pair wiring is needed. The twisted pair ARCnet board has two six-pin modular jacks that can be used to daisy-chain the ARCnet board, unless the board is at the beginning or end of the daisy-chain segment. Terminators must be placed on unused plugs. A maximum of ten stations can be used in the twisted-pair daisy chain, whose length cannot exceed 400 feet. The minimum spacing between stations in the daisy chain is six feet.

Twisted-pair bus topologies can be mixed with the distributed star topology provided by an active hub. One end of the bus can be connected to an active hub. Table 2.11 summarizes the configuration rules for the twisted-pair bus.

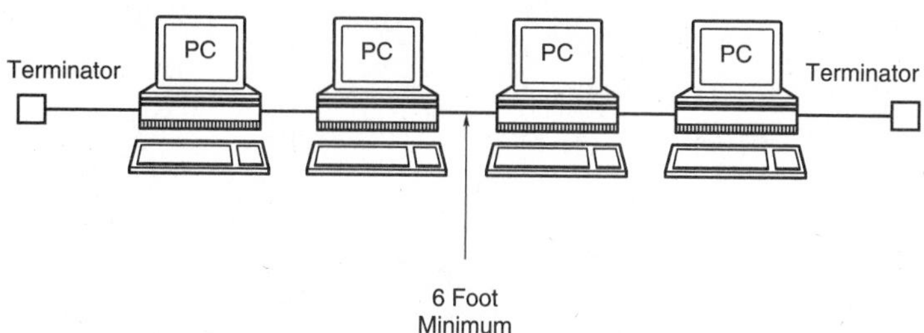

Figure 2.53
ARCnet with twisted-pair wiring.

Table 2.11
Configuration Rules for ARCnet Twisted-Pair Bus

Parameters	Value
Max stations per TP bus	10
Max length of TP bus	400 feet
Min distance between nodes	6 feet
Max stations on single 8-port active hub	80

Large ARCnet Networks

The total number of stations in a single ARCnet LAN cannot exceed 255, and its maximum span is 20,000 feet. Within these limitations any combination of distributed star, coaxial bus, or twisted-pair bus can be used. Figure 2.54 shows an ARCnet LAN using XINET components and a mix of cabling technologies.

20 Mbps ARCnet Plus

One of the most amazing features of the 20 Mbps ARCnet Plus is that it improves the performance of ARCnet by a factor of 8; yet it retains downward compatibility with the 2.5 Mbps ARCnet. Figure 2.55 shows the differences between ARCnet Plus and ARCnet.

Nodes on the standard ARCnet signal a logical 1 by a single cycle of a 5 MHz sine wave, followed by a silence of equal length. A logical 0 consists of two intervals of silence. (The interval is 1/5MHz = 200 nanoseconds' duration.) Two such intervals are necessary to send one bit (0 or 1) of information, which works out to a duration of 400 nanoseconds (a maximum data rate for ARCnet of 1/400 nanoseconds = 2.5 Mbps).

ARCnet sends data in integral multiples of bytes. Each byte is preceded by a three-bit calibration pattern (110) to keep the receiver in pace with the transmitter. An overhead of three bits exists for every eight bits of data. Therefore, the effective data rate for ARCnet is 8/11 × 2.5 Mbps = 1.82 Mbps, which is a great deal of wasted bandwidth. The periods of silence are wasteful, and the calibration overhead takes up 27 percent of the bandwidth.

Figure 2.54
A large, mixed media ARCnet. (Source: XINET)

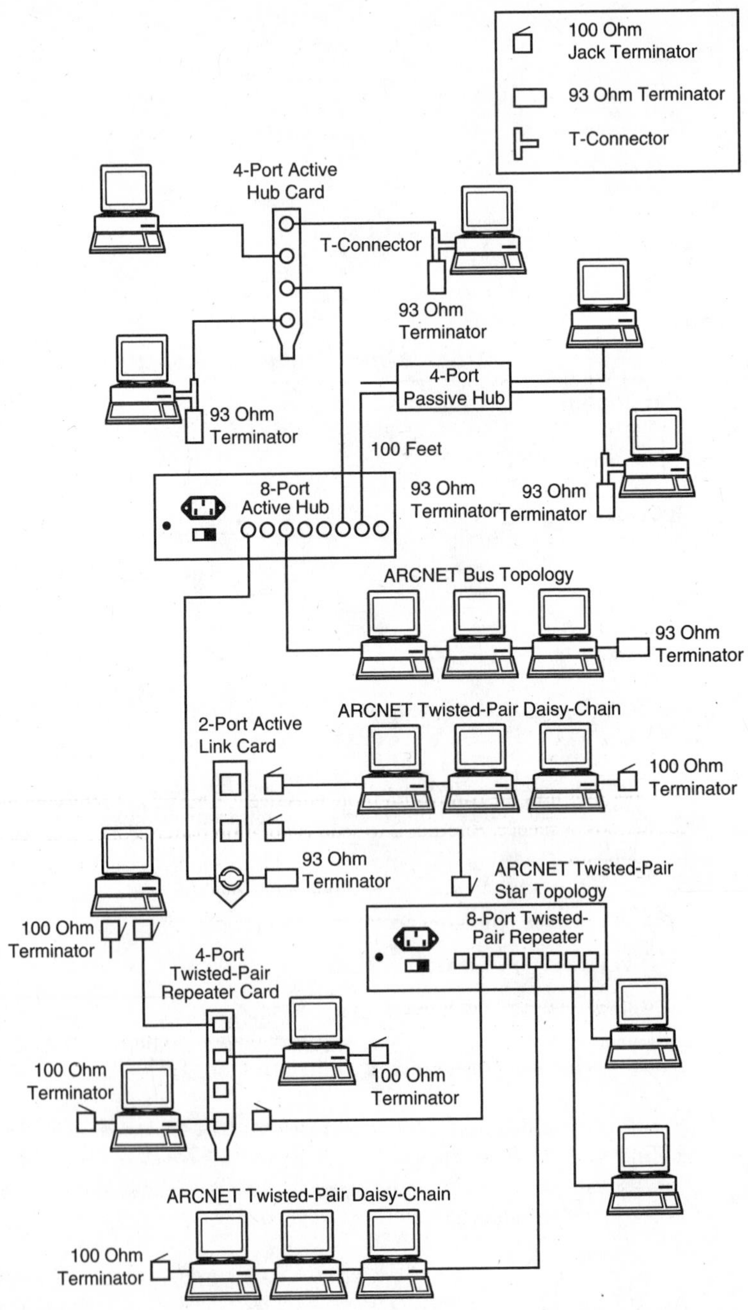

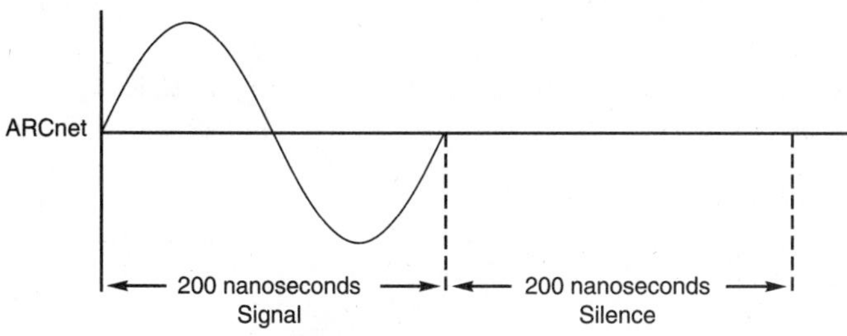

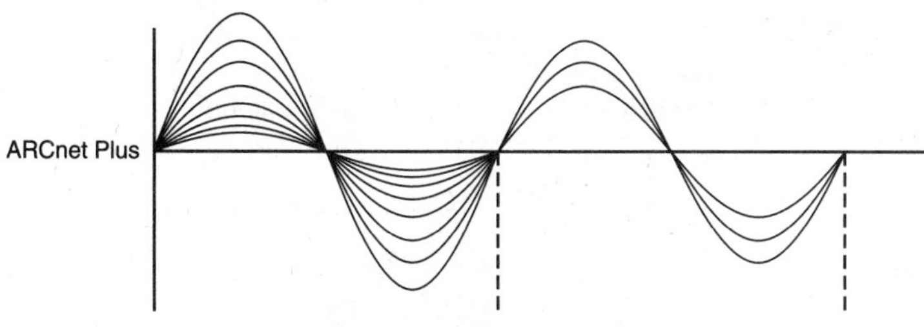

Figure 2.55
ARCnet and ARCnet Plus signals.

ARCnet Plus uses the bandwidth more effectively. One way of achieving higher data rates is to cut out the periods of silence. Another is to send calibration patterns once every eight bytes. The most ingenious technique it uses is Amplitude Modulation, which squeezes four bits of information into every 200-nanosecond interval. A pulse can be either a positive or negative sine wave with eight possible amplitudes from 0 to 12 volts. This gives a total of 2 × 8 = 16 combinations of pulses, enough to represent four bits of data.

Hence, the total ARCnet Plus data rate = 4 bits × 5 million pulses per second = 20 Mbps, excluding overhead. When you take into account the calibration overhead, this yields an effective data rate of 16.84 Mbps, which is faster than Ethernet and the 16 Mbps Token Ring.

During initialization, the ARCnet Plus node sends a special signal that informs others that it can operate at higher speeds. This signal also is sent when an ARCnet Plus node passes the token. An ARCnet Plus node communicates to another ARCnet Plus node at 20 Mbps, but steps down gracefully to 2.5 Mbps to communicate with a 2.5 Mbps ARCnet node.

The new standard enables packet lengths of up to 4,096 bytes and a maximum of 2,047 nodes. IEEE 802.2 or DoD IP addressing mechanisms can be used for easier integration with Ethernet, Token Ring, and TCP/IP networks.

If you want to upgrade to ARCnet Plus, consider the following:

- To mix the two types of cards together, the cabling can remain the same but the active hubs have to be replaced with ARCnet Plus active hubs. If older active hubs are used, the high-speed ARCnet Plus signals are filtered out.
- Another way to solve this problem is to use older ARCnet active hubs, but to make sure that you do not put two ARCnet Plus nodes on opposite sides of the older active hub.

Exploring LocalTalk

LocalTalk is Apple Computer's proprietary physical LAN used to connect Macintosh computers. LocalTalk corresponds to layers 2 and 1 of the OSI model (see fig. 2.56). As the layer 2 (data link) protocol, it is known as the *LocalTalk Link Access Protocol* (LLAP). LocalTalk initially was conceived in 1983, but formally announced in 1984. It is unusual, in the sense that the LocalTalk protocols are built into the motherboard of every Macintosh computer. All that is required are the physical connector cables and the AppleTalk protocols.

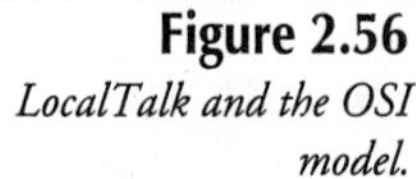

Figure 2.56
LocalTalk and the OSI model.

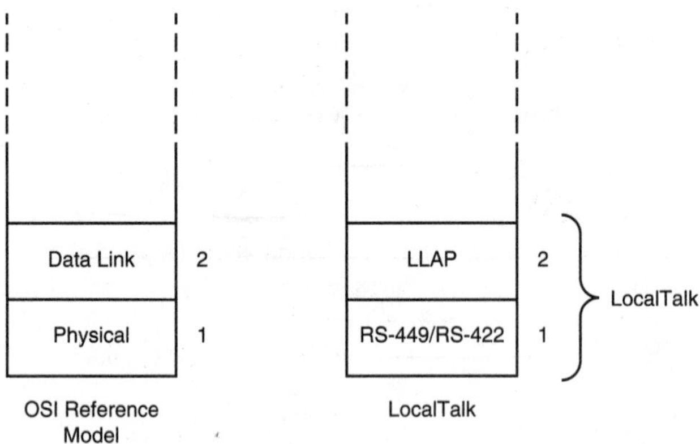

LocalTalk uses STP wiring. The physical interface is RS-449 with the RS-422 balanced option. The balanced option allows LocalTalk to reject common mode noise. This principle is illustrated in figure 2.57. Signals are split into positive- and negative-going signals. The receiver electronics takes the difference of these two signals. Legitimate signals are doubled in strength; noise signals, which appear as a common signal (common mode noise), are canceled. The encoding method used in LocalTalk is a bi-phase encoding scheme referred to as *FM-0,* also called *bi-phase space.* Bi-phase encoding requires at least one transition per bit time and is self-clocking. That is, clocking information is encoded in the same signal used to represent data. The Manchester encoding scheme used in Ethernet and the Differential Manchester encoding scheme used in Token Ring (IEEE 802.5) are examples of bi-phase encoding.

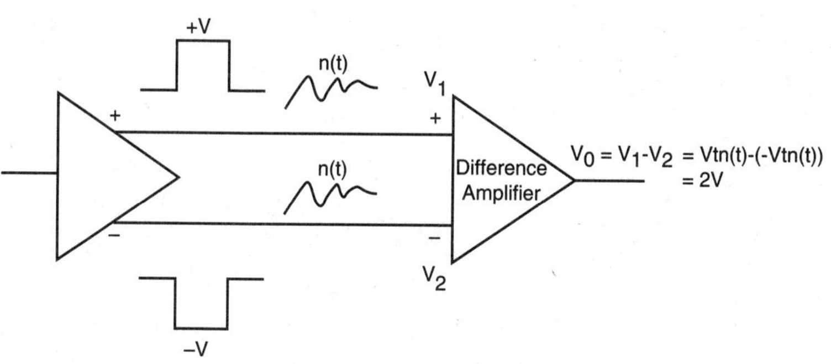

LocalTalk networks are limited to speeds of 230.4 Kbps and distances of 300 meters. Each LocalTalk segment can support a maximum of 32 devices.

LocalTalk uses an unusual scheme for determining physical addresses of LocalTalk stations. Physical addresses are not preassigned—they are determined dynamically using a dynamic address assignment process. When a LocalTalk station (Macintosh computer) boots, it picks an address at random and broadcasts it in an *AppleTalk Address Resolution Protocol* (AARP) request (see fig. 2.58). The AARP request essentially asks the question "Is there anyone out there with the address listed in this packet?". If a reply is heard, it means that the address is in use, or a duplicate address exists; the LocalTalk station picks another address and repeats the process until a unique address is discovered.

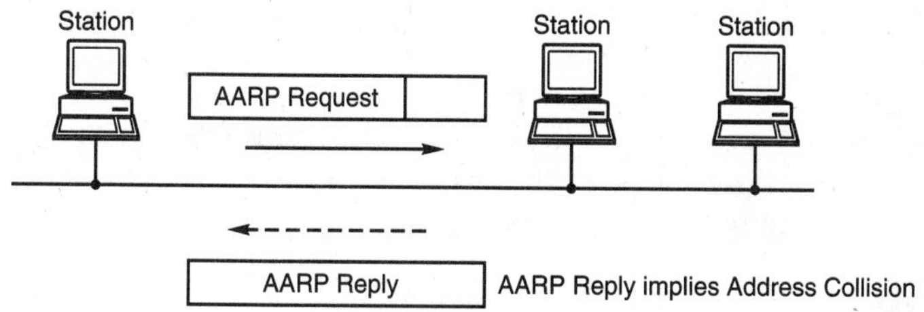

Figure 2.58
Dynamic address assignment in LocalTalk.

LocalTalk addresses can range from 1 to 255 and are divided into two groups: user and server addresses. Addresses ranging from 1 to 127 are assigned to the user, and addresses from 128 to 254 are assigned to servers. The address 255 is a special address used for broadcasts. This address division allows LocalTalk to quickly determine clients from servers. This is useful in situations in which clients and servers must be treated differently. Servers, for example, are usually more overworked than clients and therefore can be given more time to respond to Duplicate Address AARP queries.

LocalTalk Access Mechanism

LocalTalk defines its own vocabulary to distinguish between ordinary and broadcast transmissions. Ordinary transmissions consist of a sequence of frames called a *transmission dialog*. The frames in a transmission dialog must be separated by a minimum time called the *Inter Frame Gap* (IGP), which is 200 microseconds. The minimum gap between transmission dialogs is called the *Inter-Dialog Gap* (IDG) and is 400 microseconds. Figure 2.59 illustrates these concepts.

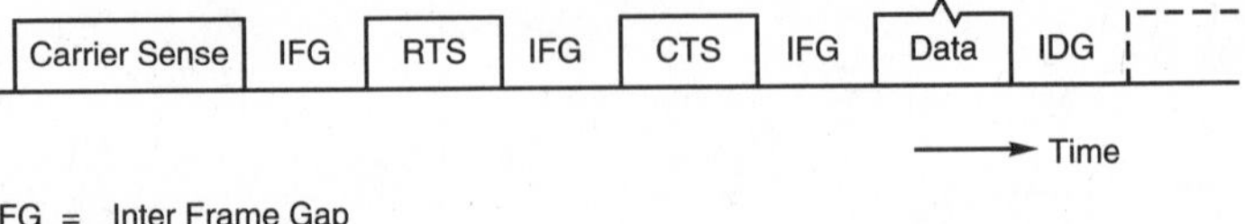

Figure 2.59
LocalTalk transmission.

The mechanism used to arbitrate access to the common LocalTalk bus is *Carrier-Sense with Multiple Access/Collision Avoidance* (CSMA/CA). Unlike Ethernet, which uses collision detection, LocalTalk does not detect collisions. It attempts to avoid collisions by prefacing each transmission dialog with a *Request To Send* (RTS) and *Clear To Send* (CTS) signal sequence. The RTS/CTS sequence warns all other nodes of an impending transmission. Also, because this exchange is relatively small compared to an actual data transmission, it is better to have collisions in the smaller time period used in this exchange. If a collision does take place, LocalTalk does nothing to handle it. LocalTalk leaves it to the upper-layer protocols to timeout if the data transmission is delayed. All data transmissions in LocalTalk have a 2-byte *Frame Check Sequence* (FCS). The receiving node accepts the data transmission only if the FCS it calculates matches that in the transmitted frame. If the FCS does not match, the data transmission is assumed to be in error, and the data frame is discarded without informing upper-layer software of the incident.

LocalTalk uses the carrier sense mechanism to determine if the LocalTalk bus is busy. The carrier- sense period lasts for at least the minimum IDG, which is 400 microseconds. Because dialog transmissions are separated by the IDG, this gives a fairly reasonable assurance that the collision interval is within the carrier-sense interval. Before transmitting, LocalTalk nodes sense the channel for the carrier.

If the channel is busy, the LocalTalk node waits and defers from transmitting. The waiting period is a function of the deferral history and a random time out element. Under heavy network loads, many deferrals can take place. The waiting period is adjusted to become longer. This effectively causes the stations to perform a back-off, similar to an Ethernet operation.

If the channel is free, the transmitting node sends an RTS frame. It then waits for the IFG of 200 microseconds for the receiving node to respond with a CTS frame. If a proper CTS frame is not received, the transmitting node assumes that a collision has taken place, and the transmitting node goes into the deferral mode. If the CTS frame is received correctly, the transmitting node must send a data frame within the IDG time period.

Broadcast transmission dialogs in LocalTalk occur in a manner similar to directed transmissions. The difference is that the RTS is broadcast with a destination address of 255. This RTS broadcast informs the nodes on the network of an impending transmission. The transmitting node does not expect a CTS in response. If the channel remains free, the broadcast message is sent.

LocalTalk Frame Format

LocalTalk uses control frames and data frames. The control frame is used by the MAC layer operation of LocalTalk, and the data frame is used for actual data transmission.

The packets are preceded by a two-byte preamble, followed by a one-byte destination and a one-byte source address. Figure 2.60 shows the structure of the LocalTalk frame.

2-byte	1-byte	1-byte	1-byte		2-byte		1-byte	1-byte	
Preamble	Destination ID	Source ID	Type	Reserved 6 bits	Length 10 bits	Data Field	FCS	Trailer Flag	Abort Sequence 12-18 bits

Figure 2.60
LocalTalk frame structure.

The *preamble* consists of the bit pattern 01111110 repeated twice. Its purpose is to inform the receiver of an impending frame, so that the receiver can synchronize itself to receive the frame.

The *destination and source IDs* are each one-byte and describe an address from 0 to 255.

The *type* field is one-byte and specifies if this is a control or data frame. Values of 1-127 are used for control frames, and 128-255 are used for data frames. If the type field indicates a control frame, the data field is absent. For data frames, the value classifies the content of the data field, so that it can be delivered to the correct upper-layer protocol software. This value is used by upper-layer protocol software for multiplexing and de-multiplexing purposes.

If the type field indicates a data frame, a data length field is present and indicates the length of the data field. This is a two-byte field, with the lower ten bits used to indicate the length in bytes of the data field. The upper six bits are reserved for use by upper-layer protocol software.

The *Data* field contains the actual data delivered to upper-layer protocols. It can consist of from 0 to 600 bytes.

The FCS is a 16-bit CRC value. It is calculated on the destination address, source address, type, data length, and data fields.

A *Trailer Flag,* consisting of the bit sequence 01111110, is used to mark the end of the frame.

The *Abort Sequence* consists of a run of 12 to 18 "1" bits. This run forces nodes to lose synchronization with respect to the bi-phase encoding scheme. It is used to confirm that the transmitting node has finished using the LocalTalk bus.

Understanding Network Adapters

This section focuses on the network adapters inside LAN nodes. These devices go by the following names:

- Network adapter unit/board/cards
- Network controllers
- Network interface cards (NICs)

- Network cards
- Network adapters
- Intelligent network interface cards (INICs)

These terms all refer to the network electronics that fit inside a node on a LAN and implement layers 2 and 1 of the OSI model. You can use any of the names for a network adapter.

Functional Description of a Network Adapter

A number of modules on the network adapter perform specialized processing. These modules include the following:

- Transmit/receive module
- Encode/decode module
- Frame buffers area
- MAC layer processing module
- Host-bus interface module

These modules and their functions are described in the next sections. A functional description of a network adapter is shown in figure 2.61.

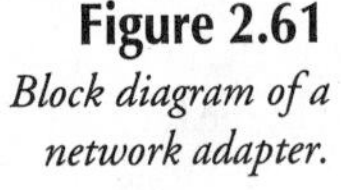

Figure 2.61
Block diagram of a network adapter.

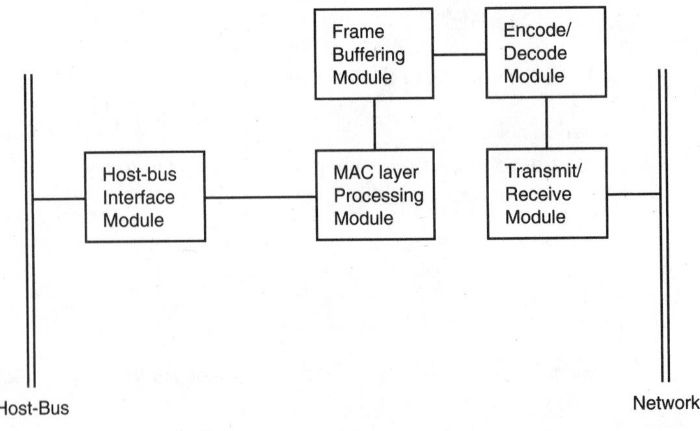

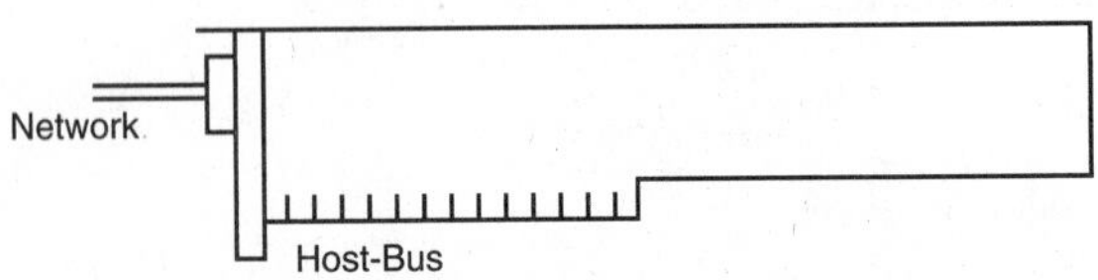

Transmit/Receive Module

The *transmit/receive module* contains the interface electronics to drive the signal on to the network media and receive the signal from the network. As signals propagate through the network media, they are reduced in strength. The transmitting station must send the signal with sufficient power to be understood by the farthest node that needs to hear the signal.

For example, in the case of 10BASE5, the signal must be sent with sufficient power to span a distance of 500 meters. The transmit/receive module contains the amplifier electronics to perform this function. This module corresponds roughly to the *Physical Layer Signaling* (PLS) and the *Media Attachment Unit* (MAU) in the IEEE standards.

Encode/Decode Module

Before a signal is transmitted, it can be encoded to put clock information as part of the data stream. The clocking information is necessary for the receiving station to keep its clock synchronized to the transmitter clock. When a signal is received by a station, it needs to decode the signal; that is, to recover the data bits. The *encode/decode module* performs these functions.

A variety of encoding techniques is used by different LANs. Ethernet and IEEE 802.3 use Manchester Encoding; IEEE 802.5 uses Differential Manchester Encoding; and FDDI uses a combination of *Non Return to Zero Inverted* (NRZI) and 4B/5B encoding.

Frame Buffer Area

When a frame is to be transmitted to the network or has just been received from the network, it is kept in a special area of memory on the adapter card for processing. In many network adapters, this *frame buffer area* is implemented by RAM chips on the network adapter. The amount of memory reserved for frame buffering can vary from a few kilobytes to a megabyte.

Many network adapters implement intelligent buffer management algorithms in firmware. Some use scatter algorithms that can keep the header separate from the data portion of the frame, which eliminates the need to move header and data into a contiguous block of memory prior to transmission.

MAC Layer Processing Module

The MAC layer processing module is perhaps the most important module in the network adapter. It performs the following important functions:

- Encapsulation/decapsulation. The *encapsulation* function is performed by the transmitting station and includes generation of the correct address, control, and frame check sequence fields. The *decapsulation* function is performed by the receiving station and includes processing of the address, control, and frame check sequence fields. Error detection also is performed by the decapsulation function.

- Implementation of the MAC algorithms (the CSMA/CD access mechanism for Ethernet and the token access mechanism for Token Ring).

These functions require processing power. Earlier network cards borrowed this processing power from the station's CPU. Needless to say, these network cards were very slow. Today, all network adapters have their own processing functions. These processing functions are implemented on special microprocessors that have their own ROM or microcode containing the MAC algorithms. These network controller chips have their own RAM for processing the MAC algorithms.

Host-Bus Interface Module

The exchange of control and data information between the network adapter and the station is performed through the host-bus interface. The host-bus interface module must have a built-in understanding of the protocol used for data transfer on the host bus. Many bus standards exist; network cards are classified by whether they work for an ISA bus, EISA bus, or a Micro Channel bus. Apple's Macintosh machines use Nu-Bus, and must have their own network cards.

Many NIC vendors have shown their support for the bus mastering *Peripheral Component Interconnect* (PCI) bus standard. This 32-bit bus is processor independent and offers self-configuration. When the computer is powered up, it automatically assigns itself a unique address and interrupts.

The width of a bus is defined by the number of data bits it can transmit in parallel. The wider the data bus, the more efficient the network adapter. For IBM PCs, 8-bit network cards are very common. 16-bit cards provide better performance, and 32-bit network cards for EISA and Micro Channel give the best performance.

Hardware Elements of a Network Adapter

When installing a network adapter and setting up networking software, such as NetWare, you may have to set several hardware parameters such as IRQ, DMA, Base Address, I/O address, and so on. This section discusses these hardware elements.

Interrupt Lines

When a packet arrives at a station, the station is busy performing other tasks for the user and needs to be informed that a packet has arrived so it can process it. The network adapter informs the station's CPU of this event through a mechanism called an *interrupt.*

When an interrupt occurs, the CPU stops (after making a careful record of the last thing it is doing) and examines on which line the interrupt occurred. The CPU uses the interrupt line number to consult a table that it keeps in the lower memory. This table, called the *interrupt vector table,* is organized like an address book and contains the address of the program (interrupt service routine) that knows how to handle this packet. The CPU transfers control to this program. When it finishes processing the packet, the program transfers control back to the CPU, which resumes the task it was performing prior to the interrupt.

Interrupts also are used by peripheral devices, such as the keyboard, disk, or printer, to communicate with a CPU. The Intel processors used in IBM PCs have a number of IRQ lines. Some of these lines are dedicated for special functions. Table 2.12 shows some common IRQ assignments. (This table shows only the common devices used in an XT and AT.)

Table 2.12
IRQ Assignments

IRQ	XT	AT
2	EGA/VGA	EGA/VGA
3	COM2	COM2
4	COM1	COM1
5	Hard disk	LPT2
6	Floppy controller	Floppy controller
7	LPT1	LPT1
10	N/A	Unused
11	N/A	Unused
15	N/A	Unused

To install a network adapter, you must set its IRQ to an unused interrupt. For example, the hard disk inside an XT is likely to use IRQ 5, and the LPT2 port in an AT is likely to use IRQ 5. Avoid using IRQ 5 for these components.

Sometimes conflicts are acceptable if you are not using a specific device. Many network cards use a default configuration of IRQ 3, which means that serial port COM2 cannot be used. Many common station configurations do not use COM2, so this conflict is acceptable.

Some IRQ levels may be usable, even though there may be a conflict. For example, IRQ 2 is a default setting for many ARCnet cards. Although this may conflict with EGA/VGA cards, many stations work fine with such a configuration. The reason for this is that not many applications use the interrupt mechanism in EGA/VGA cards. Likewise, you may not have any conflict using IRQ 7, even though a printer is installed at LPT1, because many applications do not use LPT1 with interrupts.

DMA Lines

How is a packet transferred from the network adapter's buffers to the station's memory? One mechanism for doing this is through *Direct Memory Access* (DMA). Using DMA, the network card can transfer the packet to the station's memory without involving the station's CPU. This is desirable because the CPU can continue processing without interruption. When the CPU is not accessing its memory, the DMA mechanism steals memory cycles and transfers data to the station's memory.

DMA channel 0 is used to refresh Dynamic RAM chips. No two devices should share a DMA channel.

Shared or Base Memory

Many network adapters do not use DMA to transfer data. Instead, they use a technique called *Direct Memory Mapping* or *Shared Memory.*

The network adapter's buffers are mapped to an area of memory above 640 KB. The area of memory between 640 KB to 1 MB is used by devices such as video adapters, network adapters, and the PC's BIOS (Basic Input/Output System).

By sharing a common address space for applications and the network adapter's buffers, programs can be written to access the network adapter's buffers as easily as accessing any other area of memory. There is no need to move packets in RAM because the packets can be processed while they reside on the network adapters.

When installing network adapters that use shared memory, you need to specify the base address. The base address is the start of the area above 640 KB, in which the network adapter's buffer memory is to be mapped. Switch settings can specify the size of buffer memory to be used. Typical values of buffer memory size range from 4 KB to 64 KB. Care must be exercised to ensure that RAM addresses for various devices do not overlap. Figure 2.62 shows RAM above 640 KB (A0000 hex) used by some common devices.

I/O Port Addresses

Network adapters contain status and control registers. Networking software such as network drivers use these registers to control the operation of the adapter and find its status.

The control and status registers are accessed through *Input/Output* (I/O) ports. I/O ports form an address space that can be accessed by the PC's IN and OUT instructions. I/O ports are defined for some common devices as shown in table 2.13. I/O port addresses must be selected to avoid conflicts with other devices.

Table 2.13
Input/Output Ports for Common Devices

Possible I/O Base Address (hex)	Devices and Their Typical I/O Addresses
200	Game controller/Joystick (200_20F) Expansion Unit (210_217)
220	Novell NetWare Key Card (older NetWare)
260	LPT2: (278_27F)
280	LCD display on Wyse 2108 PC Western Digital EtherCard factory setting

Possible I/O Base Address (hex)	Devices and Their Typical I/O Addresses
2E0	COM4: (2E8_2EF) GPIB-Adapter 0 (2E1) COM2: (2F8_2FF) Data Acquisition (2E2_2E3)
300	Prototype Card (300_31F) 3COM EtherLink factory setting (300_31F)
320	XT Hard Disk Interface (320_32F)
360	LPT1: (378_37F)
380	SDLC/Secondary Bi-Sync Interface (380_38C)
3A0	Primary Bi-Sync Interface (3A0_3A9) Monochrome Display (3B0_3BB)
3C0	EGA Display (3C0_3CF) CGA Display (3D0_3DF)
3E0	COM3: (3E8_3EF) Floppy Disk Controller (3F0_3F7) COM1: (3F8_3FF)

Performance Considerations for Network Adapters

Many LAN Administrators ask which network adapter is faster—Token Ring, Ethernet, or ARCnet. The answers are not always obvious because studies can be biased or skewed in favor of one adapter. The studies all conclude that 10-Mbps Ethernet and 16-Mbps Token Ring are faster than ARCnet at 2.5 Mbps. These results are not surprising considering their data rates. The ARCnet Plus at 20 Mbps can be expected to be faster than both Ethernet and ARCnet. FDDI at 100-Mbps is the fastest among these. The 100BASE-X and 100BASE-NG Network Adapters also operate at 100 MBs and are low-cost alternatives to FDDI. The use of ATM in LANs will lead to even faster network adapters.

In designing a network interface card, a vendor makes several design choices that affect the price/performance trade-off. The four major characteristics that contribute to NIC performance are the following:

- Media access scheme
- Raw bit rate
- Onboard processor
- NIC-to-host transfer
- Efficiency of software NIC driver

Figure 2.62
RAM usage between 640 KB and 1 MB.

Device	Memory Range
MONO	B0000 – B1000
CGA	B8000 – C0000
EGA	A0000 – C0000
VGA	A0000 – C4000
EXP. MEM	D0000 – E0000
XT BIOS	F4000 – 10000
IBM AT BIOS	E0000 – 10000
CLONE AT BIOS	F0000 – 10000

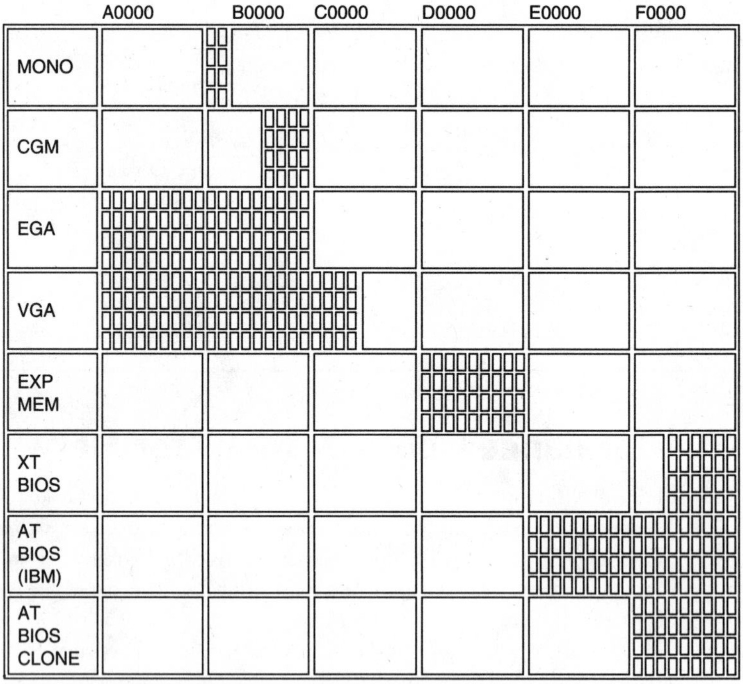

A0000 B0000 C0000 D0000 E0000 F0000

MONO
CGM
EGA
VGA
EXP MEM
XT BIOS
AT BIOS (IBM)
AT BIOS CLONE

Media Access Scheme

The *media access scheme,* such as CSMA/CD or Token Access, is an important parameter in NIC performance. Token Access gives a deterministic performance; CSMA/CD does not. On the other hand, CSMA/CD is simpler and faster under light loads compared to Token Access.

Raw Bit Rate

The *raw bit rate* is the maximum bit rate possible on a given media. The actual effective bit rate is much less, taking into account protocol overhead and timing delays. Nevertheless, the raw bit rate represents an upper limit for the given media.

Fiber-optic media can be used for data rates in the hundreds of Mbps range. FDDI at 100 Mbps is only the beginning—you can expect higher-speed LANs based on fiber-optic cables.

Coaxial cable can generally accommodate data rates up to 50 Mbps and STP wiring around 20 Mbps.

ARCnet Plus uses a 5-MHz sine wave, but by using special encoding techniques can pack four bits of information in every cycle, yielding a maximum of 20 Mbps.

Onboard Processor

Effective use of an onboard processor can speed up an NIC. If the firmware for the NIC is poorly written, however, it can have just the opposite effect. Some vendors implement upper-layer protocol processing on the NIC card itself for better overall throughput. An example of such an NIC is the Federal Technologies EXOS series board that has onboard TCP/IP processing.

When NetBIOS was created by IBM for the IBM PC Broadband LAN, it was implemented in firmware on the NIC itself. However, because of an inefficient implementation, it ran slower than NetBIOS implemented in software.

NIC-to-Host Transfer

The NIC-to-host channel can be implemented in several ways: shared memory, DMA, or I/O ports. NICs can use any of these methods or a combination of them. Observations have shown that shared memory is the fastest; I/O ports are next; and DMA is the slowest.

The data width of the bus interface has a dramatic effect on NIC-to-Host transfer speeds. This width can be 8, 16, or 32 bits. The wider the data width, the faster the data transfer.

The type of host bus also affects the transfer rate. EISA and Micro Channel NICs are faster than ISA NICs.

Efficiency of the Software NIC Driver

The efficiency of the software NIC driver is often evaluated as a factor that can reduce the performance of an NIC. The software driver for the NIC provides an interface between the NIC and the communications software represented by OSI layers 3 and higher. If the software driver is poorly written, the overall throughput of the NIC can be dramatically reduced.

Summary

The physical network is a complex combination of tangibles and intangibles. The tangibles include cables, connectors, hubs, and a wide variety of other devices. The intangibles include electrical signals and protocols that organize the electrical signals into meaningful communications. NetWare professionals need a thorough understanding of these network characteristics.

NetWare has a long history of supporting a wide variety of network cabling systems, and a book might be required to describe them all. The tendency in the LAN industry, however, is toward support of a relatively small number of standards that offer reliability, low or moderate cost, high performance, and broad industry support. This chapter examined the most prominent physical layer standards used to implement NetWare LANs.

IEEE 802.3 Ethernet and IEEE 802.5 Token Ring are used to implement the majority of local area networks. Therefore, these standards received extensive treatment. ARCnet and LocalTalk are well established in certain niches, and most NetWare technicians encounter them from time to time. A thorough understanding of the control mechanisms and cabling systems employed with these standards enables you to plan reliable networks and troubleshoot them effectively when problems arise.

Discussion in this chapter focused on fairly simple LANs. At a certain point, however, it may become necessary to subdivide your network. You may, for example, have too much traffic on your Ethernet or too many stations for a single Token Ring. In the next chapter, you see how bridges and routers are used to expand networks to support large numbers of devices and large physical areas, and to control data traffic.

Bridging and Routing

If the network manager must go beyond the capabilities of a single LAN and access network or computing resources on other networks, he must determine which devices to use to extend the range of a LAN. Bridges, repeaters, and routers are often the choices to extend the range of a single LAN or to combine a number of LANs in a single internetwork.

In this chapter, you learn to connect NetWare LANs. This chapter first lays the foundation for understanding bridges, repeaters, and routers, and then discusses the way to configure and install NetWare routers. The latter part of this chapter examines NetWare 2.*x* routing problems and the way NetWare 3.*x* overcomes these problems. You also learn about performance issues for internal/external and dedicated/nondedicated routers.

Understanding Repeaters, Bridges, and Routers

Repeaters, bridges, and routers are devices that extend the range of a LAN. Most LANs such as Ethernet, ARCnet, and Token Ring have distance limitations. The maximum span of an Ethernet LAN, for example, is 2,500 meters using multiple segments and repeaters. Although you can use repeaters to go beyond a single coaxial segment, you cannot use more than four repeaters. If you use bridges and routers, you can go beyond the 2,500-meter Ethernet limitation. Each Ethernet LAN still has the 2,500-meter and four repeater rule, but after a packet crosses a bridge it is on another logical LAN and subject to the restrictions of that LAN only.

Bridges and routers do more than extend the range of a LAN. You can use them to connect dissimilar LANs and to alleviate traffic bottleneck problems. The IBM 8209 bridge, for example, can be used to connect an Ethernet and a Token Ring LAN. Conceptually, these devices *bridge* the gap between dissimilar LANs. They also can connect to LANs of the same type, such as two Ethernet LANs.

Although bridges and routers are described as devices, you may wonder exactly what that means. They consist of a computer that runs algorithms to perform bridging or routing functions. If high performance is desired, these devices are special dedicated computers that can perform bridging and routing functions efficiently. For bridges, the algorithms are usually encoded in EPROM (firmware) for rapid execution. Routers, as you learn shortly, are more complicated than bridges and may require frequent fixes by the vendor to correct problems. It is easier to implement the routing algorithms in software so that they can be changed more easily.

Many vendors allow incremental expanding of their bridges and routers. Hardware modules that consist of one or more network boards can be used to connect to different types of networks. These hardware modules fit into a slot in the bridge or router and connect to a high-speed backplane bus used for data transfer between the modules.

Vendors who make routers and bridges include Cisco, DEC, Vitalink, Wellfleet, New Bridge, 3COM, Timeplex, BBN, Novell, and many others. Novell does not make a specialized router product like the other vendors. Routers from Novell are workstations or servers that run routing software. Up to four NICs (16 in NetWare 3.*x*) can be added to a server or a workstation so that it can perform routing among the network boards.

In earlier Novell literature, the routing function provided by NetWare was called a *bridge.* To be compatible with the rest of the industry, Novell now calls it a *router.*

Repeaters

A *repeater* operates at the physical layer of the OSI model. It takes a signal from one LAN, reconditions and re-times it, and sends it to another LAN. The reconditioning usually amplifies and boosts the power level of the signal. The repeater has no knowledge of the meaning of the individual bits in the packet. A repeater cannot be addressed individually; no address field exists in the packet for a repeater.

The repeater's job is simple. Detect the signal, amplify and retime it, and send it through all the ports except the one on which the signal was seen. In the case of Ethernet, the signals transmitted include data packets and even collisions. The segments of the LAN that are connected participate in the media access mechanism such as CSMA/CD or Token Access (see Chapter 2, "LAN Standards for Physical and Data Link Layers"). For Token Ring LANs, each station performs the repeater function so that usually no separate repeater device is needed. Some fiber-optic media extensions to the Token Ring may use special repeater devices to boost the signal over long distances.

Bridges

Bridges connect two separate networks to form a logical network. Figure 3.1 shows an example of a bridge between an IEEE 802.3 and IEEE 802.5 LAN. This bridge has two network cards: a Token Ring card and an Ethernet card. The Token Ring card is used to connect the bridge to the Token Ring LAN, and the Ethernet card connects to the Ethernet LAN.

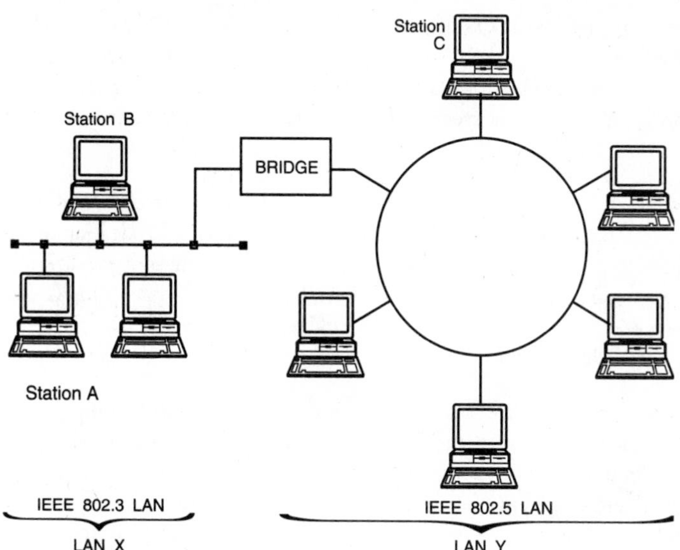

Figure 3.1
Bridge between IEEE 802.3 and IEEE 802.5 LAN.

One way of looking at this concept is that a bridge has a split personality. It behaves as a Token Ring station and also as an Ethernet station, and herein lies the key to understanding its function. In figure 3.1, a packet sent from station A to station B does not cross the bridge in its normal mode of operation. The bridge detects that stations A and B are on the same LAN, and a bridging function is not required.

If, however, station A sends a packet to station C, the bridge realizes that station C is on another LAN (Token Ring) and places the packet on the Token Ring LAN. It cannot place the Ethernet packet directly on the Token Ring LAN because the Ethernet frame cannot be understood by the Token Ring LAN. The bridge must remove the Ethernet header and replace it with a Token Ring header containing C's address. The bridge also must wait for a free token before placing the packet on the Token Ring LAN. As it waits, other packets can be sent to it for transmission to the Token Ring LAN. These packets must be queued for processing. A bridge, therefore, must have storage capacity to store frames and acts as a store-and-forward device.

In figure 3.1, most of the stations on LAN X communicate among themselves. Occasionally, stations in LAN X may need to communicate with stations in LAN Y. Another way of saying this is that most of the traffic is intra-LAN (within a LAN), and a small fraction is inter-LAN (between two LANs). A good rule of thumb is the 80/20 rule. About 80 percent or more of traffic should be intra-LAN traffic, and 20 percent or less should be inter-LAN traffic.

If the 80/20 rule is violated frequently, the stations generating excessive inter-LAN traffic should be detected and relocated to another LAN so that they do not cause excessive inter-LAN traffic. Stations generating excessive traffic can be detected by using protocol analyzers, such as LANalyzer, or SNMP (Simple Network Management Protocol) managers, such as LANtern Services Manager. Novell makes both of these products.

A bridge operates at the data link layer of the OSI model. A bridge performs most of its work at layer 2. Bridges examine the *Media Access Control* (MAC) header of a data packet. The MAC address corresponds to the layer 2 address and represents the physical station address or the hardware address of the network board. MAC addresses are unique for every station. Bridges rely on MAC addresses for their operation.

Unlike a repeater, a bridge actually sees the data packet. Bridge ports have unique MAC addresses. A bridge has an understanding of the data packet up to the data link layer and can decode it up to this level. Bridges isolate the media access mechanisms of the LANs to which they are connected. Thus, collisions in a CSMA/CD LAN do not propagate across a bridge. In the case of Token Ring LANs joined by a bridge, the token does not cross a bridge. Because bridges are selective about which data packets can be transferred, they help solve traffic bottleneck problems.

Bridges are effective for a small number of LANs, but as the number of LANs grow, the number of possible paths between the sender and receiving station become very large. Not all the possible paths are optimal—some paths involve roundabout ways of getting to the destination, and this can create unnecessary traffic. If a bridge is to be effective for large LANs, it must have knowledge about the optimal path. A bridge only operates at the data link layer, however, and the routing information is part of layer 3 (network layer) operation. Most bridges cannot make decisions about routes through the network because information on routes is encoded in the network address. An exception to this is source routing bridges that use routing information. However, the routing is based on MAC layer (data link layer) addresses and not network layer addresses.

Although a bridge can seem limited, it is a simple and inexpensive way to interconnect two LANs. To perform intelligent routing decisions, you need a router.

Routers

A *router* operates at the network layer of the OSI model. A router performs most of its work at layer 3. Bridges are limited to examining the MAC address of a data packet, but routers can examine the network address. Because the network address usually has routing information encoded in it, routers can use this capability to make intelligent decisions. Thus, a *route* in a network consists of network addresses and paths. Routers are aware of many possible paths to get to a destination and also are aware of which path is the most optimal. The optimum path can be determined by various cost metrics. A *cost metric* is a formula that can be based on the following parameters:

- Is the destination reachable?
- How many hops does it take to reach the destination? The link between two store-and-forward devices is one hop.
- What is the time delay to reach the destination?
- What is the cost of transmission for the paths along the route?
- What is the data transfer capacity (bandwidth) of various paths?
- What is the status of links along the path?

The cost metric for determining the best route can become complex. Routers can be distinguished on the basis of the criteria they use to determine the optimal path.

Because routers have much more information to work with, they can do more things with a packet than a bridge, and they also are more complex. Because they are more difficult and costly to develop, routers cost more. They do more processing of the packets than a bridge; therefore, they tend to be slower than bridges.

Routers are the devices of choice to use to interconnect large LANs. You also can use routers to connect LANs over long distances. In figure 3.2, a gateway device is shown operating at layer 7. In general, a *gateway* is a device that can operate at any layer of the OSI model and provides translation between two incompatible protocols. A gateway operating at layer 7 is an application layer gateway. Examples of this concept are X.400 gateways. Devices that connect to IBM's SNA networks are usually called gateways because SNA (Systems Network Architecture) protocols are proprietary and wholesale translation must be done to connect to IBM's SNA networks.

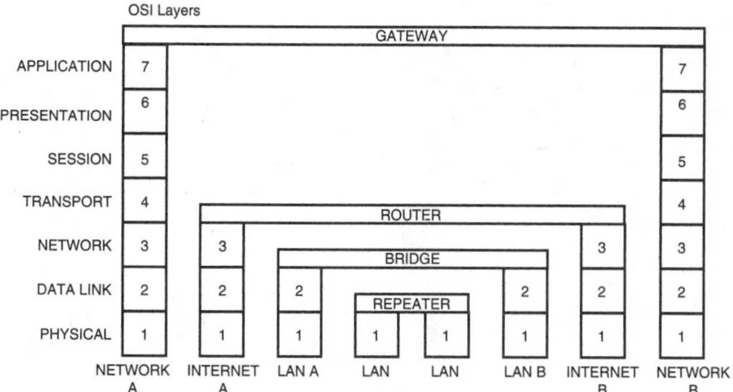

Figure 3.2
OSI model for repeaters, bridges, and routers.

Repeaters, Bridges, Routers, and the OSI Model

The best way to understand the difference between repeaters, bridges, and routers is in reference to the OSI model. If you are not familiar with the OSI model, you may want to review the discussion in Chapter 1, "NetWare Protocols."

Figure 3.2 shows a model for several interconnection devices in relationship to the OSI model. The model shown in this figure is for a repeater, bridge, and router.

Local versus Remote Connections

Bridges and routers also can be classified on the basis of whether they are local or remote (wide area network). The difference depends on their network interfaces or ports.

Local bridges and routers have ports that connect them to local transmission media over relatively short distances. An example of this setup is the transceiver cable used in Ethernet LANs. You can choose from a variety of choices such as coaxial, twisted-pair, and fiber-optic media to connect local devices to a network. The actual media choice often is dictated by the LAN being connected.

Remote bridges and routers require ports that can connect them to long-haul transmission media. You have fewer interface choices for long transmission media. Some popular choices include RS-232 ports and V.35 ports. Many remote devices have two or more remote connections and at least one local connection. LANs separated by large distances, therefore, can be connected by two remote devices as shown in figure 3.3. Router A has two local ports and one remote port. Router B has one remote port and one local port. The remote ports are connected by a point-to-point link. You can run a number of protocols on these point-to-point links. Some of the choices include X.25, Frame Relay, T1, SONET, and SMDS (see Chapter 4, "WANs and MANs").

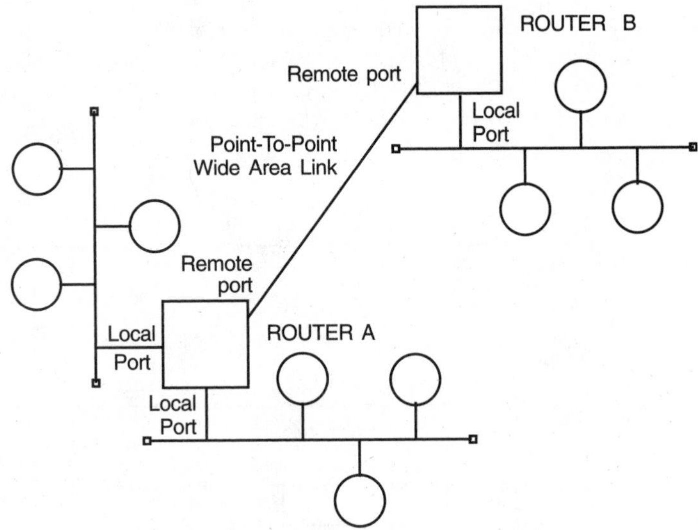

Figure 3.3
Remote routers.

Besides point-to-point links, you also can use *cloud* technologies to connect LANs. *Point-to-point* links are telephone circuits, or T1 circuits, that you can lease from telephone companies or other vendors. Because these lines are dedicated for the communications from the sender point to a destination point, they are named point-to-point. *Cloud* technologies, such as the type shown in figure 3.4, are based on switching systems. The router, acting as the *Customer Premise Equipment* (CPE) is used to connect to the cloud. The details of the cloud are not known to the LAN. It may use an X.25/X.75 protocol, Frame Relay, SMDS switches, or a proprietary technology. The cloud or *wide area network* (WAN) is managed by the organization that provides the long-haul service.

A difference between local and remote bridges and routers is the cost of the connection. Because local connections are managed entirely by the organization that owns the LAN, no additional cost is incurred. For remote connections, you must pay for the services provided by the long-haul vendor. Typical costs of such services are $2,000 per month or higher. This amount is beyond the budget of small organizations. With advances in technology, it is hoped that these costs will come down.

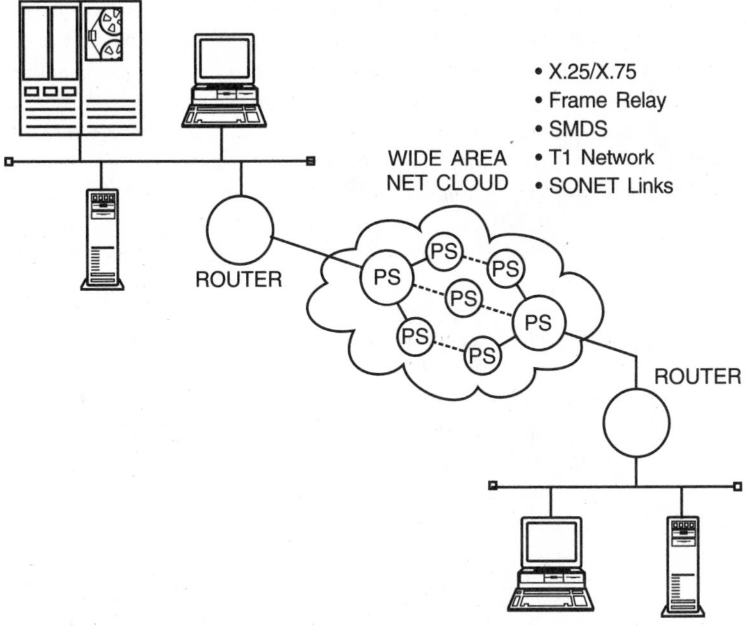

Figure 3.4
Routers connected by means of WAN cloud technologies.

Transparent Bridges versus Source-Routing Bridges

The two predominant methods of bridging are the *Transparent Bridge* (TB) and the *Source-Routing* (SR) bridge. In transparent bridging (also called *spanning tree bridges*), the decision to relay packets is performed by the bridge and is transparent to workstations.

Figure 3.5 shows a transparent bridge network. Each bridge maintains a table that keeps track of station addresses. Transparent bridges examine the source address of every packet they see and record this source address in the bridge table along with the number of the port on which the packet was seen. Transparent bridges also maintain a timeout field for each table entry so that old entries can be periodically purged.

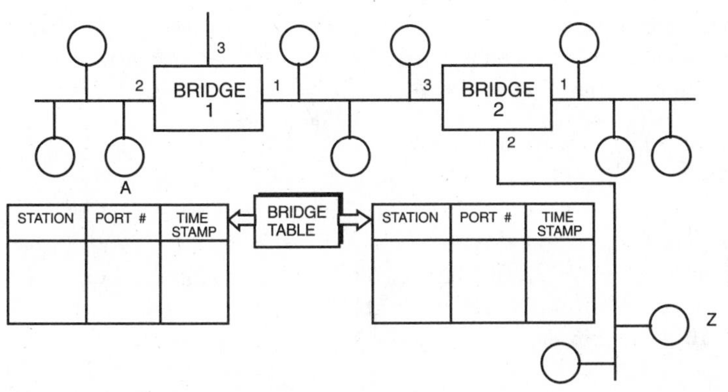

Figure 3.5
Transparent bridge network.

Consider what happens if station A transmits a packet to station Z. Bridge 1 sees the packet and consults its table to see whether it has an entry for station Z. If it does not, it forwards the packet through all its out ports, excluding the port on which the packet was observed. Bridge 1 also checks the source address field of the packet and records in its table that station A can be reached at its port 2. When Bridge 2 sees the packet, it repeats the algorithm just described. If no entry exists for station Z, it forwards the packet through all its outgoing ports (flooding). It also records the fact that station A can be reached through its port 3. When station Z acknowledges the message from A, it sends a packet with source address Z and destination address A. After Bridge 2 consults its table, it notes that A can be reached through port 3 and forwards the packet only through port 3. It also records that station Z can be reached through its port 2.

To prevent endless circulation of packets, transparent bridge networks cannot have loops. The transmission path forms a spanning tree that covers all the stations on the network. If there are bridges that can form a loop, as shown in figure 3.6, these bridges must remain inactive. The inactive bridges act like redundant bridges. Redundant bridges are activated after the spanning tree topology changes. Topology changes are transmitted by *Bridge Protocol Data Units* (BPDUs). This special protocol is used to maintain the overall spanning tree topology. The process of arriving at the spanning tree is called the *spanning tree algorithm.* One bridge in the spanning tree becomes the *root,* and all other bridges transmit frames in the direction of the root by using a least-cost metric.

Figure 3.6
Avoiding loops on transparent bridge networks.

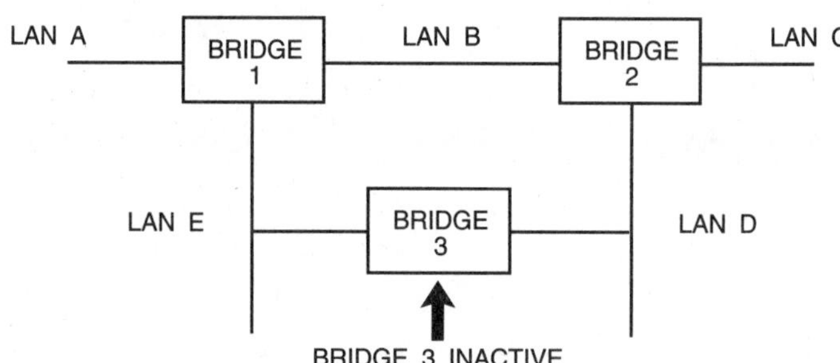

The spanning tree bridge is the preferred method for Ethernet and IEEE 802.3 networks and is supported by vendors that manufacture bridges for these LANs.

Source routing, a different method sponsored by IBM, connects bridges to its Token Ring networks. In Source Routing, the source (sender) must determine the best path to get to a destination. After this path is discovered, the source station maintains this path in its routing table and includes this path in the *Routing Information* (RI) field for every packet sent. Figure 3.7 shows the RI field along with its relationship to the Token Ring packet. The RI field is present whenever the I/G bit of the source address is set to 1. This I/G bit also is referred to as the *Routing Information Indicator* (RII) bit. The Token Ring frame structure is discussed in Chapter 2, "LAN Standards for Physical and Data Link Layers." The *Routing Designator* (RD) fields contain the path the packet must follow to arrive at the destination. RD fields consist of a ring number and a bridge number pair. SR bridges simply follow the directions in the routing information field. A total of 14 RD fields are possible, which limits the largest transmission path to 13 bridges or hops. IBM's implementation currently limits total RD fields to eight, which corresponds to seven bridges or hops.

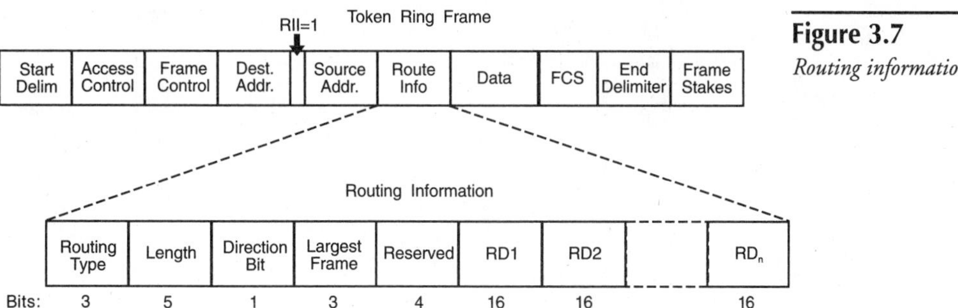

Figure 3.7
Routing information field.

Figure 3.8 shows the path from station A to Z using source routing. The details of the routing field also are shown.

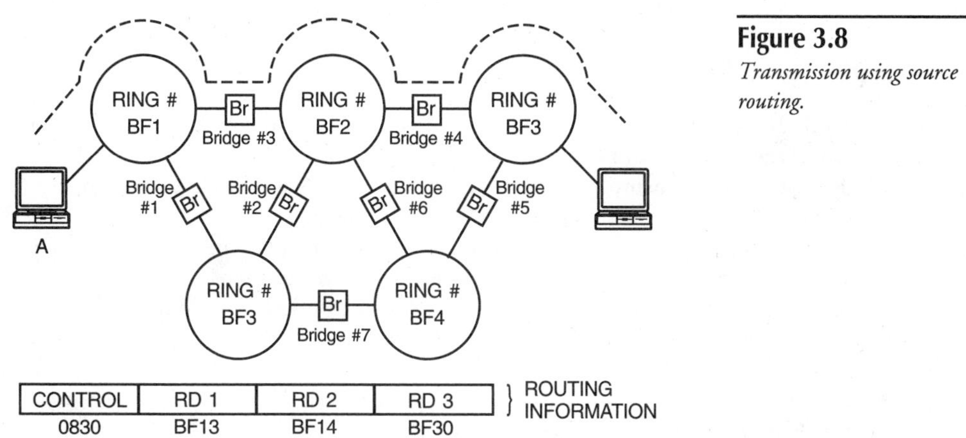

Figure 3.8
Transmission using source routing.

The key to the operation of source routing is discovering the initial route. This is done by sending a *discovery frame* sent by the source node when it wants to discover the best path to a destination. The discovery frame circulates on the network and arrives at the destination with a record of the path taken. The discovery frames are returned to the sender, who then selects the best possible path.

IEEE 802.5 networks prefer the source routing method. To connect IEEE 802.3 networks that use transparent bridges with IEEE 802.5 networks that use source routing, you can use several methods. One method is to have a bridge, such as the IBM 8209 bridge, that provides translation of routing information between the two separate bridge mechanisms. Another method is to use a bridge that is a combination of source routing and transparent bridges. These bridges are called *Source Routing Transparent* (SRT) bridges. In SRT, transparent bridging is used when no RI field exists; otherwise, source routing is used. Figure 3.9 shows the model for SRT bridges. The MAC layer entity consists of SR and TB algorithms. These algorithms are invoked depending on the setting of the RII bit.

Figure 3.9
Source Routing Transparent (SRT) bridges.

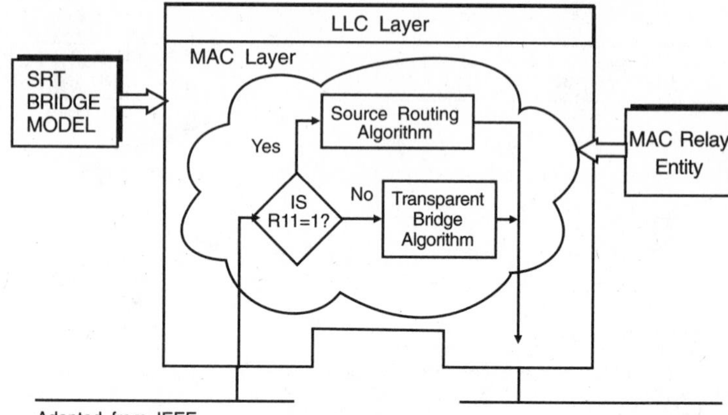

How Does Routing Work

An internetwork based on routers consists of many distinct logical networks (see fig. 3.10). A logical network is characterized by having its own unique network address. This network address is common to all the nodes in the logical network. The individual nodes in a logical network are distinguished by their own unique addresses. For LANs, this is the MAC layer or physical address, such as an Ethernet address or Token Ring address. Therefore, to address a node on a different logical network, the sending station must know the network address and the node address of the destination node. This information is then encoded in the packet sent. Routers that connect these two networks rely on the network address information in the packet to forward the packet to its correct destination.

Figure 3.10
Internetworking addressing.

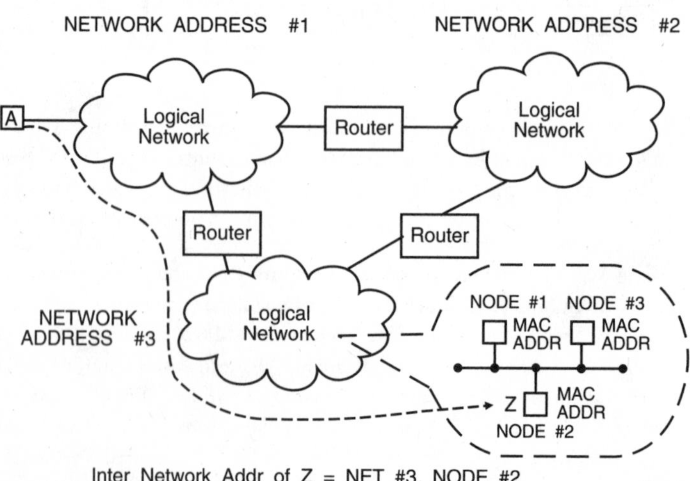

The logical networks in the internetwork can be managed by potentially independent organizations and can be viewed as separate administrative domains. These separate administrative domains make their own decisions about which kind of networking software to run. Because different networking software uses different protocols, the internetwork runs a variety of protocols. Any router used to connect the logical networks must understand all these different protocols. Most routers made today, therefore, are multiprotocol routers. Some of the common protocols supported by multiprotocol routers are as follows:

- IPX/SPX
- XNS Protocols
- TCP/IP
- SLIP (Serial Line Internet Protocol)
- PPP (Point-to-Point Protocol)
- SNAP (Sub-Net Access Protocol)
- DECnet
- SNA (Systems Network Architecture)
- X.25
- CLNP (Connectionless Network Protocol)
- IS-IS (Intermediate System to Intermediate System)
- ES-IS (End System to Intermediate System)
- NLSP (NetWare Link Service Protocol)

NetWare routers are designed to connect NetWare-based networks. NetWare 3.*x*-based routers can be extended to provide IP routing and AppleTalk routing. The *NetWare Multiprotocol Router* (MPR) provides general-purpose routing of most of the industry standard protocols.

Not all protocols are routable. Examples of nonroutable protocols are *Local Area Transport* (LAT) from DEC, LU 6.2, and NetBIOS protocols from IBM. These protocols do not have an explicit network layer. Routers depend on the network layer for their operation. Protocols that do not have a network layer are unroutable. Unroutable protocols must be bridged.

Routers examine the network layer source and destination address in the packet to determine where a packet came from and where it needs to be delivered. Routers are expected to figure out the best possible path. A number of criteria, such as cost and distance, help determine the best possible path. The information related to determining the best possible path is kept in an internal database called the *routing table*. A fundamental requirement of a router is to initialize and maintain its routing table. Based on the routing table information, a router should determine the next hop in the journey of the packet.

Routing tables can be global or local. Global routing tables have a table entry for every network and can therefore use global optimization techniques to determine the best possible path. For large networks, the cost of maintaining a very large routing table with the most recent information can become prohibitive. Modern routing protocols use local routing information, by which routers know information about the "local" portion of the internetwork they connect to. The routing tables for such routing protocols tend to be smaller and more manageable.

Another distinction between routers is the manner in which the information in routing tables is updated. Two approaches are static and dynamic. In static routing, the Administrators manually must set each entry in the routing table. Although this approach may be advantageous for total security and control, it also is inflexible and does not automatically adapt to network changes. In dynamic routing, the routing tables are set automatically by each router. Special packets that contain routing information are exchanged by routers. These packets contain updates on path information and are used by routers to update their routing tables. The manner in which these special packets exchange information constitutes a routing protocol. Many types of routing protocols exist. The *Routing Information Protocol* (RIP) used in NetWare routers is based on Xerox's XNS protocols. Another protocol used in Novell routers, called *NetWare Link Service Protocol* (NLSP) is based on ISO's IS-IS link state routing protocol.

Dynamic routing always involves the use of some routing protocol and is more flexible than static routing. Dynamic routing is the preferred approach in most modern routers.

To make the most current information available to the network, a router broadcasts information whenever it detects a change in the network. If a certain link goes down or a new link is available to form an additional path, the information concerning it is broadcast by using a routing protocol. The amount of information sent can vary from an incremental update to an entire routing table. The number of routers to which this information is sent and the actual amount of information sent depends on the routing protocol used.

After a router sees a packet, it examines its routing table for the destination address to send the packet along the best possible path. The determination of the best possible path depends on the following factors:

- The routing metric
- The routing algorithm
- Available information in the routing table
- The topology of the network and the locations of the routers in the network

If the routing metric is based on distance, the best possible path is the shortest path. Most routers use a simplifying metric, which is called the *hop metric*, to measure distances. A *hop* is a path between two store-and-forward devices, such as a router or a station. The number of hops, therefore, is a measure of the number of times a packet has to be processed by a router.

The shortest path can turn out to be the most expensive path. A metric is needed that can factor other variables, such as economic cost, line speed, and transmission delay. The routing algorithms that use these metrics can be classified into two broad categories: *Distance Vector Algorithms* (DVAs) and *Link State Algorithms* (LSAs).

A knowledge of these classifications is important. LSA-based networks, for example, adapt more quickly to network changes and are more robust than their DVA counterparts. Because of their quick response time, LSA-based networks make better use of communications facilities and have better performance figures.

The major distinction between DVA and LSA is the manner in which they compute the cost for each path. In DVA, the model of the network is computed by each router telling its neighboring routers information about the rest of the network. This process is much like the party game in which a message is whispered to one individual who whispers it to another and so on, until everyone has heard the information. The last person to hear the information often hears an entirely different message. Although routers tend to transmit information more reliably than people, this example points out the weakness of the DVA algorithm. As information is propagated from router to router, not all routers have the same view of the network. Also, it takes a while for the information to propagate. During this period of time, the routing tables will be inconsistent with the network topology, and this may lead to transient anomalies such as packets being lost or delivered by inefficient routes. NetWare routers handle this problem by providing a RESET ROUTER command that can cause routing tables to be updated immediately.

LSAs compute the model of the network based on each router telling the rest of the network about its connections. Because each router knows exactly who its neighbors are and the type of connections it has, other nodes on the network have a more complete picture. LSA-based routers contribute to network traffic only when the link state information changes (links going up or down). If the network is stable, link state protocols do not generate much network traffic. This is one reason why a link state protocol such as NLSP is preferable to a distance vector protocol such as RIP in a large NetWare-based network. An advantage of LSA is that the topological map of the network can be more easily constructed from LSA information. Topological maps are a great help in routing hierarchical networks.

Hierarchical networks are useful in the construction of large networks (see fig. 3.11). To make routing more manageable, the network is divided into regions or areas. Each area has its own routers. The routers within an area only perform routing for nodes in that area. These intra-area routers are called level 1 routers. Areas are joined together by inter-area routers called level 2 routers. The level 2 routers form a logical router backbone, which is used for transmitting inter-area traffic. An example of a hierarchical network is DECnet or the DoD internet.

The other type of network is a *flat network*, which consists of only one level. This network contains no hierarchy of areas and routers. All routers are on the same logical level with no distinction between parts of the network. Flat area networks are suited for small networks. An example of a flat network is NetWare LANs connected by NetWare routers.

Both DVA- and LSA-routing algorithms can be used for either flat or hierarchical networks. LSA works better, however, with hierarchical networks because the network topology can be derived more easily from it.

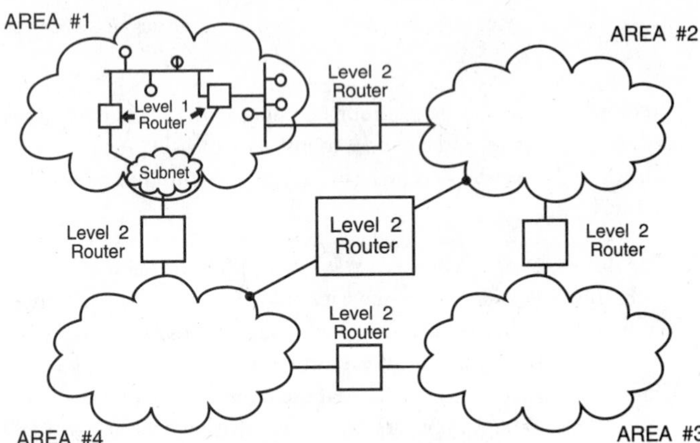

Figure 3.11
Hierarchical networks.

Until recently, most routing protocols have been DVA-based and implemented on flat networks. The XNS routing protocol on which Novell's routing protocol is based is DVA-based. The XNS routing protocol is called the *Routing Information Protocol* (RIP). Do not confuse it with the protocol of the same name, RIP, that is used for TCP/IP-based networks. The TCP/IP RIP and XNS RIP are different. TCP/IP RIP also is DVA-based.

Newer protocols, such as *Open Shortest Path First* (OSPF) for TCP/IP networks, *Intermediate System to Intermediate System* (IS-IS) for OSI-based networks, and NetWare Link Service Protocol (NLSP) for Novell network use LSA techniques.

DVA- and LSA-based routing techniques have been used for flat and hierarchical networks. The LSA algorithm, because it deals with topological maps of the network, can be used more easily to partition networks into areas. This is exactly what is required for hierarchical networks divided into special areas. Therefore, LSA techniques adapt better to hierarchical networks.

As networks grow in size, DVA-based routers do not perform very efficiently. They transmit their entire routing tables, which can get very large as networks grow in size. Networks that use LSA-based routers scale much better as networks grow.

Initially, most of the networks started using DVA-based routers. The problems with DVA did not surface until the networks began growing in size. A classic example of this is the TCP/IP-based internet, in which networks that connect to the backbone still use DVA-based RIP. Many of the DVA-based protocols were derived from XNS routing protocol, also called RIP, which also stands for Routing Information Protocol. This includes the TCP/IP RIP and Novell's RIP. All three RIPs (XNS, TCP/IP, and Novell) are different, and unfortunately, they all use the same acronym. If you are dealing with a multivendor network, you are likely to see all three on the internet, and this can cause some confusion.

The two LVA-based routing protocols that you should be aware of are OSPF for TCP/IP networks and IS-IS for OSI-based networks. Both protocols use LSA techniques. As networks evolve to more open standards, vendors may be forced to adopt these routing protocols.

A discussion of these protocols is beyond the scope of this book. This book focuses on Novell's RIP.

Bridges versus Routers

Bridges and routers can both be used to consolidate networks. They provide a wide range of functionality and features that can be helpful in simplifying the task of network administration. Bridges and routers have their own unique advantages and disadvantages. Table 3.1 summarizes the pros and cons of bridges, and table 3.2 examines the advantages and disadvantages of routers.

Table 3.1
Bridging: Pros and Cons

Pros	Cons
Simple to install, load, and configure	Cannot perform effective balancing
Perform automatic reconfiguration	Can cause traffic overload problems
Can be used with protocols that cannot be routed	Ineffective in preventing broadcast storms
Can be moved easily with bridge networks	Certain applications may not run on bridge networks
Have good cost/performance ratio	

Table 3.2
Routing: Pros and Cons

Pros	Cons
More flexible than bridges	More difficult to set up
Can perform load balancing/sharing	Moving stations can be difficult
Are effective in controlling broadcast storms	Routers based on static routing can cause problems
More effective for large networks with arbitrary topologies	Some protocols cannot be routed
Can accommodate growth more easily	

Bridges do not require complex configurations. You can power them on and connect them to networks without any problem. This makes them easy to install. Some of the more advanced bridges may require some configuration if you want to manually enter routing information in the bridges' tables, but the interface is easy to use.

Because bridges do not have a network address (they operate below the network layer), the networking software on the nodes does not need to be configured to recognize newly installed bridges. In other words, under typical circumstances, bridges are transparent to the network software. The only time you may have to do any configuring at the nodes is if you are dealing with IBM bridges that use source routing.

Because bridges operate below the network layer of the OSI model, they need to know about protocol details of upper layers. Numerous upper-layer protocols exist, and the complexity of dealing with them is hidden from bridges. A consequence of this is that bridges do not have to be configured for upper-layer protocols as long as they can understand the data link protocols, such as Ethernet, Token Ring, and so on. Certain upper-layer protocols, such as NetBIOS (PC networks), LU6.2 (IBM SNA networks), and LAT (DECnet), cannot be routed effectively, but they can be used with bridges because bridges do not need to know the details of upper-layer protocols.

Bridges form a single logical network that has the same network address. The stations and bridge ports in a bridge internetwork have their own unique node address, but because they share the same network address, they can be moved around in the same logical network without having to configure them for new network addresses.

Bridges provide very rapid packet transfer at relatively low cost. In many situations, a negligible penalty is paid (1 to 5 percent drop in data rate) when transferring data between two networks.

Because bridges are not aware of redundant paths on the network, they cannot perform load sharing across these paths. A single path can get heavily congested by internet traffic even though alternative paths can be used to reduce the congestion.

Bridges can flood the network unexpectedly. This results in very slow networks.

Large networks connected by bridges may experience *broadcast storms.* As the name suggests, a sudden rise in the number of broadcast packets occurs. Broadcast packets are used by the upper-layer protocols (layers 3 and above) to communicate general information about themselves to the rest of the network. An example of this is the SAP and RIP protocols used by NetWare (discussed later in this chapter). Bridges use BPDUs that are broadcast to all other bridges. All this extra traffic can cause significant network load. Most of these broadcast protocols use a 60-second (or a multiple) interval, and if they get synchronized, very high-peak loads can occur at 60-second intervals.

Bridges can prevent certain types of applications from running on the networks. Some applications need unique network names based on the network address. Because one network address exists for a bridged network, multiple copies of the application cannot run on the same network.

Routers have more options for partitioning networks in different ways. For example, they can perform load sharing if alternate paths of equal cost are available. They can associate a cost metric called the *Route*

Path Cost (RPC) for each route and select the optimum route. The route-path cost can be determined as a function of economic cost, data rate, path delays, security cost, and priorities.

Routers can be configured to prevent broadcast storms. They can be used to selectively filter out certain types of traffic for networks. For example, it does not make sense to broadcast a NetWare SAP packet to an interconnected AppleTalk network if no NetWare servers are on that network. Routers can be used to contain broadcast traffic within a single network because they have knowledge of the broadcast protocols.

Routers are more effective than bridges for maintaining and configuring large networks. They can support arbitrary topologies and can more easily accommodate network growth.

Setting up routers may require specialized training. Many router vendors offer week-long training classes. Each individual protocol that will be routed needs to be set up independently. The information on protocols in this book helps you to understand a router's configuration parameters.

Moving end systems (ES-OSI terminology for user stations) between network segments is more difficult because their network addresses have to be changed to the network address of the relocated end system.

Some routers use static routing. This means that routing information has to be entered manually into the router's table by the network manager. This can be a very laborious and tedious process. Also, manual entry is always prone to errors and can easily become outdated when network changes are made. Many networking problems on large networks can be traced to incorrect entries in static routing tables.

Some protocols, such as NetBIOS, LU6.2, and LAT, cannot be routed. Many of these protocols do not follow the OSI model in terms of having an explicit network layer. The router needs an explicit network header from which a network address can be extracted. If the protocol cannot provide a router with this information, it cannot perform routing. For this reason, some vendors provide a product that is a combination of a bridge and a router (*Brouter*=Bridge + Router). A brouter tries to route a protocol. If it cannot do so, it tries to bridge it.

Examining NetWare Routers

This section discusses NetWare-based routers. The actual routing mechanism used is discussed followed by a discussion about the IPX, RIP, and SAP mechanisms essential to routing. This section also discusses limitations of NetWare-based routers and how to manage the network number assignment for routers.

Understanding NetWare Routing

All NetWare servers can act as internetwork routers. Additionally, you can configure ordinary PC workstations to act as routers. Because servers perform the dual role of router and server, such configurations are called *internal routers.* If a PC workstation is set up to perform DOS and routing functions, it also is a *nondedicated router*; if it is set up to perform routing functions only, it is called a *dedicated router.* Because the routing is done on a separate external device, such routers are called *external routers.*

Figure 3.12 shows the routing processes running on a router. This routing process is an integral part of a NetWare server. The routing software also can be generated and configured for external routers by using Novell's ROUTEGEN utility. The use of this utility is discussed later in this chapter.

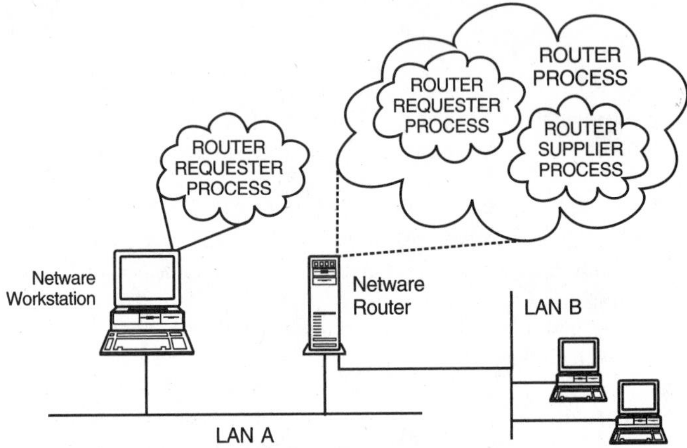

Figure 3.12
NetWare router processes.

All stations on a NetWare LAN are somewhat aware of routing. They all have a *router requester process* used for requesting routing information from other routers. NetWare routers additionally have a *router supplier process* used to supply routing information to the router requester process. In short, all stations, including routers, have a router requester process. Only NetWare routers have the router supplier process (see fig. 3.12). The request for routing information and the reply to it are transmitted by using the routing information protocol.

When a packet is sent to a router (see fig. 3.13), the NIC card in the router observes the packet and reports it to the network driver by using the hardware interrupt mechanism. The network driver performs data link layer processing (layer 2 of OSI model) on the packet. This process strips the data link layer header and passes the data to the next higher layer, which is the network layer. The network layer in NetWare routers implements the IPX protocol. If the destination network address of the IPX packet differs from the network address of the network on which the IPX packet was seen, the IPX packet is sent to the routing process. The routing process determines which of its NIC ports should be used to forward the packet.

Figure 3.14 shows two LANs connected by a NetWare router. Each network to which the router connects has a unique logical network address. In a pure NetWare-based network that only uses NetWare routers, stations on the same cabling plant or logical network have the same unique network address (also called the network number). If stations have the same network address, no routing is necessary to transfer packets between them. Destinations on the same logical network are reached using the broadcast mechanism inherent in LANs. If the destination has a different network address, a router is needed to route the packet to the appropriate destination LAN. If a packet is sent from station A to station B, no routing is necessary because both stations are on the same LAN and have the same network number. If a packet is sent from station A to station C, routing is necessary because station C has a different network number from station A.

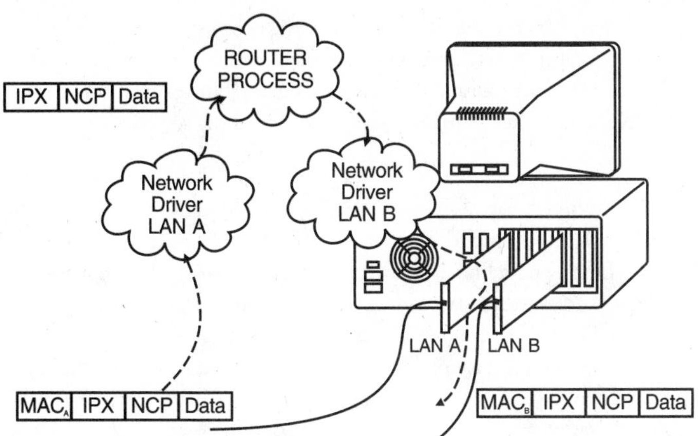

Figure 3.13
NetWare router packet processing.

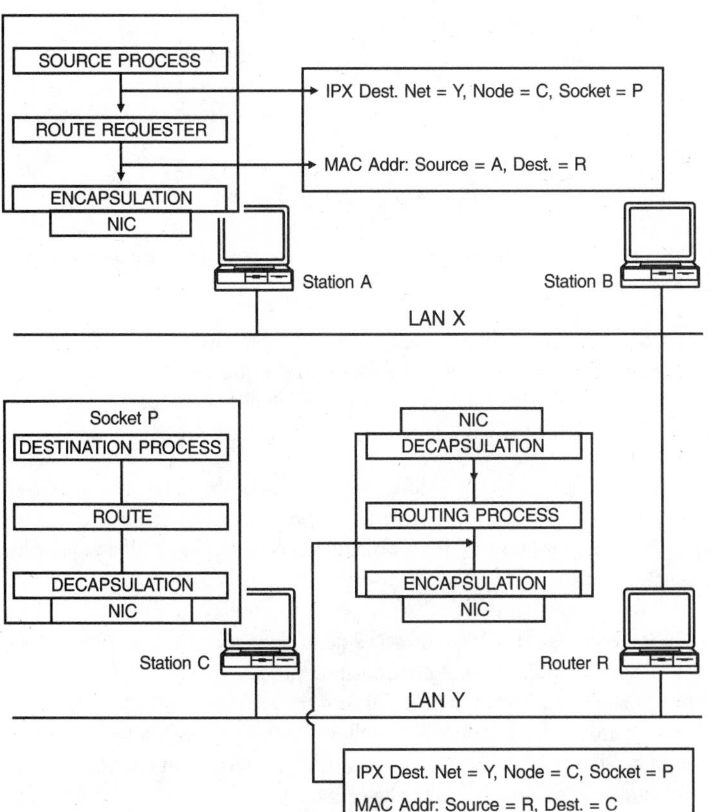

Figure 3.14
NetWare routing model.

The full destination address of a packet is encoded in the IPX header and consists of the network number, the node address, and the socket number. The node address is the data link layer address of a station and is the address of the NIC card in a station. This address is fixed (burned in ROM on NIC) or set by switch settings on the NIC. The socket number uniquely identifies the software process running on the station.

Figure 3.14 shows the internet IPX address of a packet sent from station A to station C. The routing requester process at station A realizes that the network destination is different from LAN X. Station A knows of router R on the network. During data link encapsulation, the destination data link address is set to that of the router. The router receives the packet addressed to it and decapsulates the data link header. This process recovers the original IPX packet sent from station A. The IPX packet's destination address is examined by the routing process in the router. The routing process consults its routing table and determines that the destination network is connected to one of its ports. It then sends the packet to the appropriate NIC port for encapsulation and transmission. Finally, destination C receives the packet and decapsulates it. On further examination of the IPX destination address, station C determines that it is indeed the correct recipient of the packet.

If the router had determined after examining its routing table that the destination LAN was not directly attached to one of its ports, then the router would forward the packet on one of its ports. The decision on which port to send the packet would be based on the hops and delays it would take to reach the destination.

In general, the three possibilities for forwarding a packet are as follows:

- If the router is an internal router and the destination is the internal router, the packet is passed directly to the *File Service Process* (FSP).
- If the destination number of the IPX packet is the same as that of the network number to which the router is directly connected, the router forwards the packet to the directly-connected network. Before sending this packet, it properly encapsulates it by using the MAC header (data link layer header). This situation is essentially the same as that discussed in figure 3.14.
- If the destination number of the IPX packet is different from that of the directly connected networks, the router must determine the next router responsible for transmission of the packet. This determination is based on the entry for the destination network in its routing table, which contains the fastest path to get to the destination network.

As the packet passes through the routers, the IPX source and destination addresses do not change. Only the MAC header changes by the encapsulation and decapsulation process. The MAC header contains the immediate source and immediate destination address to forward the packet on its next hop. The IPX header essentially remains the same so that all routers can follow the same algorithm to reach the destination. The only modification is that the transport control field (discussed in the next section) is incremented to count the number of routers the packet has passed through.

Internet Packet Exchange (IPX)

To understand NetWare routing, you should understand the manner in which stations are addressed in a NetWare LAN. This address is encoded in the IPX packet and is used by routers. RIP and the algorithms associated with it are based on the semantics of the IPX packet structure. This section introduces the fundamentals of IPX semantics. Some of the information in this section may seem a little too detailed, but if as a LAN manager, you are involved in managing your LAN with a protocol analyzer, this information is invaluable.

Figure 3.15 shows an IPX packet encapsulated by an Ethernet packet. The IPX packet encapsulates upper-layer protocols, such as SPX or NCP. Table 3.3 summarizes the meaning of the fields in the IPX packet. The diagram is shown for descriptive purposes. In actual practice, Novell avoids the use of the SPX protocol to minimize protocol overhead, and a typical NetWare packet consists of the IPX datagram encapsulating an NCP packet with no intervening SPX packet.

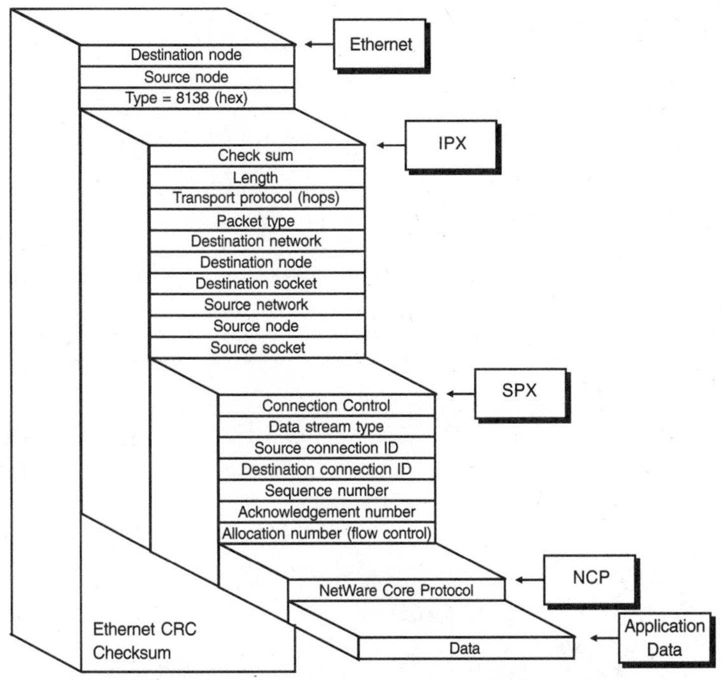

Figure 3.15
IPX packet. (Drawing courtesy of Learning Group International)

The *checksum* field is a 1s complement add-and-left-cycle (rotate) of all the 16-bit words in the IPX packet. The checksum does not include the checksum word itself and is designed to be easily computable. Another characteristic of the checksum is that it can be incrementally computed if only a few words change, such as a change in the network address fields. The checksum is inherited from the XNS *Internet Datagram Packet* (IDP) from which IPX is derived. It is in addition to any hardware-generated checksums used at the data link layer of the OSI model.

Table 3.3
IPX Packet Structure

Field	Meaning
Checksum	Optional 1s complement checksum
Length	Byte length of IPX packet
Transport Control	Used by routers as a "hop count" field
Packet Type	Identifies type of data encoded in the data portion of IPX packet
Destination Network	Uniquely identifies destination network from a number of interconnected networks
Destination Number Node Address	Uniquely identifies the node address of the destination station
Destination Socket	Software address in destination node
Source Network Number	Uniquely identifies source network from a number of interconnected networks
Source Node Address	Uniquely identifies the source node of the sending station
Source Socket	Software address in sending node

At the time XNS was designed, hardware and memory systems were not very reliable. One of the functions of this checksum is to verify the data path between the NIC and memory in the station. IPX is typically configured to ignore the checksum field and places all 1s (FFFF hex) in this field to indicate that the field is not used. NetWare-based networks rely on the data link control and other upper-layer mechanisms for error control. This avoids the processing overhead of computing the checksum.

The *length* field contains the complete maximum length of the IPX packet measured in bytes. This figure includes the IPX header length of 30 bytes plus the data. If the packet contains an odd number of bytes in the data portion of the packet, an extra "garbage" byte is added to make the packet an integral number of 16-bit words. The garbage byte is not included in the length field. Originally, IPX packets had a nominal maximum length of 576 bytes. Allowing for 30 bytes of IPX header, this allowed a maximum of 576 – 30 = 546 bytes of data. This maximum length was inherited from the specification of the XNS IDP packets. Many LANs can accommodate larger packet sizes (1,518 bytes for Ethernet), and the 576 byte maximum length restriction has been removed by Novell. IPX packets that use a longer packet length than 576 bytes do not interoperate with pure XNS routers that use smaller packet sizes. Because there are few installed examples of the original XNS routers, this is not a serious problem.

The *transport control* field is used for transporting internet packets across routers. This field is used only by routers. Workstations set this field to zero when sending a packet. The transport control field is an eight-bit field, but only four bits are used:

	Transport Control							
Bit:	7	6	5	4	3	2	1	0
	X	X	X	X	H	H	H	H

Bits marked X X X X are unused and set to zero. Bits marked H H H H represent the hop count field. The hop count field is increased by one each time it is processed by a router. A router can determine the number of routers encountered by the packet. The four-bit hop count field limits the maximum number of routers in any path. A maximum of 15 routers is permissible on any transmission path. After the hop count field reaches a value of 16 (that is, when it reaches the sixteenth router), it is discarded. The XNS Error protocol is used to transmit this fact to the source. But because a datagram protocol (IPX) is used for this, there is no guarantee that the message will be seen by the source. Applications that need greater reliability must use the SPX protocol or some other internal mechanism.

The maximum hop count field ensures that IPX packets are not routed indefinitely in a loop. With a maximum value of 15 for the hop count field, you can have a maximum of 16 networks in any transmission path.

The *packet type* field is used to identify the data contents of the data portion of the IPX packet. This field is used for protocol multiplexing. It allows a number of client protocols to reside on top of IPX and allows the IPX module to determine which of the client protocols, SPX, PXP, NCP, Echo, Error, Serial (copy protection), Watch Dog, RIP, or SAP to send the packet to (see fig. 3.16). Table 3.4 shows some of the more common packet types. Developers interested in a new packet type assignment must contact Xerox.

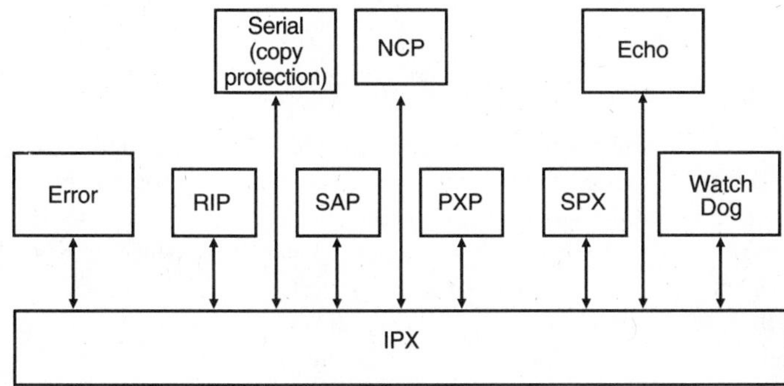

Figure 3.16
IPX clients.

Table 3.4
Common Packet Type Assignments for IPX

Packet Type	Protocol
1	Routing Information Protocol (RIP)
2	Echo
3	Error
4	Packet Exchange Protocol (PXP)
5	Sequenced Packet Exchange (SPX)
17	NetWare Core Protocol (NCP)
20–37	Experimental

Network numbers uniquely identify the logical network to which a station is attached. Network numbers are primarily used for routing. The router routes the packet to the LAN that has the same destination number as the destination number in the IPX packet. This network number field in the IPX packet is four bytes. This field can, therefore, accommodate a network number size of eight hexadecimal digits. If the routing is to work correctly, all logical networks in an internetwork must have a unique network number. The network number must be different from the internal network number for NetWare 3.*x* servers. The network number is assigned at the time of installation for each logical network connected to the router. A value of zero for the destination network number means that the packet is not to be processed by an internetwork router.

From an administrative point of view, you must exercise control in keeping these network numbers unique within an organization. This administrative control is essential if LAN operations within an organization are decentralized. The node address uniquely identifies the station NIC within a logical network. After a packet is routed to the correct destination LAN, it must be sent to the correct station. The node address uniquely identifies the station to receive the packet. The IPX packet has a six-byte field for the node address and can accommodate a 12-digit hexadecimal number. XNS networks were originally designed for Ethernet, which has a six-byte address field. Fortunately, the six-byte address field is the same size used for IEEE LANs and FDDI. For LANs that use a smaller address size for stations, such as ARCnet or Proteon-10, the address field can be padded with zeros in the most significant digits. A node address of all 1s (hexadecimal FF FF FF FF FF FF) indicates a broadcast packet.

The *socket number* identifies the software or client process running at a station. A station can have a number of client processes running (see fig. 3.17). Because they run on the same station, they each have the same network number and node address. If a packet is to be sent to a specific client process, a means should exist to identify it uniquely. The socket number is used to identify the client process uniquely. Socket numbers are analogous to mailboxes. A client process is notified when a packet is delivered to its mailbox. Sockets are implemented as data structures that can be used to send and receive packets at a unique software address within a station. They are inherently bidirectional in their nature.

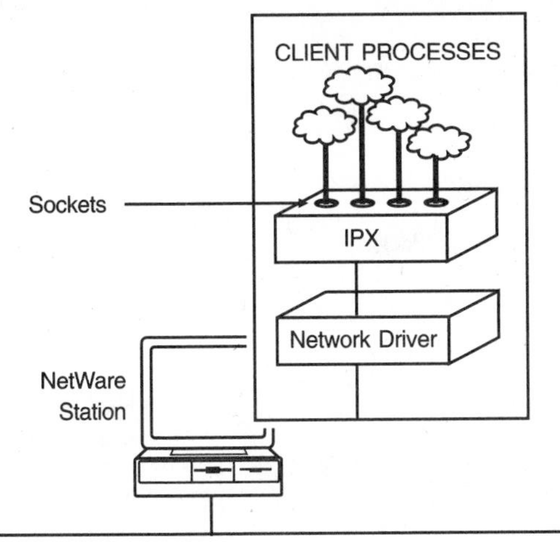

Figure 3.17
IPX socket numbers.

Certain protocols use a standard socket number. These standard socket numbers are called *well-known socket numbers.* Table 3.5 lists some well-known socket numbers. You can obtain well-known socket numbers by contacting Xerox or Novell. Socket numbers above 8000 (hex) are assigned by Novell.

Table 3.5
Well-Known Socket Numbers for IPX

Socket Number (hex)	Meaning
1	XNS Routing Information Protocol (RIP)
2	Echo Protocol Packet
3	Error Handler Packet
20 _ 03F	Experimental
1 _ BB8	Registered with Xerox
BB9 _	Dynamically Assignable
451	NetWare File Service Packet
452	NetWare Service Advertising Packet (SAP)
453	NetWare Routing Information Protocol (RIP)
455	NetBIOS Packet

continues

Table 3.5, Continued
Well-Known Socket Numbers for IPX

Socket Number (hex)	Meaning
456	NetWare Diagnostic Packet
4001	NetWare Watchdog Packet
4003	NetWare Shell Socket
8000 _	Well-Known Socket Numbers Assigned by Novell

Using RIP and SAP

Routers use the RIP protocol to maintain a cache containing routing information (routing table). The routing algorithms used by routers serve the following purposes:

- Quickly initialize the routing table after the router starts
- Ensure that the routing table adapts quickly to changes in network topologies
- Ensure that if routers come up or go down, other routers learn about this change as quickly as possible

Every routing table contains at least the following information for every network that can be reached by the router:

- Timing delay to reach the network
- Number of hops to network
- A list of networks directly connected to the router
- Node address of a router on the directly connected network by which packets will reach the specified network for the amount of time delay and hops in the table entry
- A timer used for routing table maintenance to age out old entries

Figure 3.18 illustrates the routing table in a router.

During initialization, the router initializes the routing table to contain network numbers for directly connected networks. In figure 3.18, the directly connected networks LAN A, LAN B, LAN C, and LAN D have network numbers 1001, 1002, 1003, and 1004. This information is built into the router during installation time, and the routing process simply reads this information and initializes its routing table.

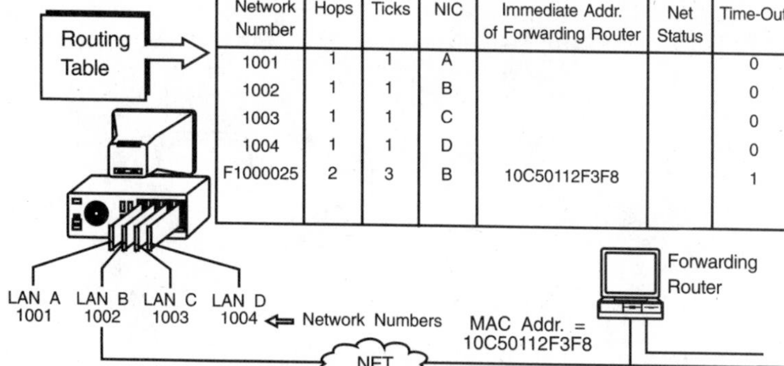

Figure 3.18
Routing table in a NetWare router.

Requests for routing information and their corresponding replies are encoded in a RIP packet. Because transmission on the LAN is through a broadcast mechanism, routers see all RIP responses. Some responses answer RIP requests originated by the router and others are gratuitous information in reply to RIP requests from other routers. The router updates its tables if any of the following conditions is true:

- The RIP reply originated from an internetwork router connected to the directly connected network
- The existing entry in the routing table has not been updated for 90 seconds
- A better route was discovered to the specified network

Every time the router entry is updated, its timeout value is reset to 90 seconds. If a table entry has not been updated for three minutes (twice 90 seconds), it is assumed to be suspect. The number of hop fields is set to infinity (actually set to 16) to indicate that the network is no longer reachable. These entries are kept for another 60 seconds before being purged so that other routers know that the network cannot be reached.

Routers also broadcast a copy of their routing table in the RIP packet to other routers on all the networks to which it is connected. This response packet is sent at intervals of 60 seconds. In addition, whenever a router modifies its routing table entry, the change is broadcast to all routers on its directly connected networks. As the recipients of this information modify their routing table entries, they too send RIP response packets to routers on their directly connected networks. This ripple effect quickly transmits the changes throughout the network.

When routers broadcast information, they follow the "best information algorithm." The first rule is that the router does not broadcast routing information about networks to a directly connected network that was obtained from the same directly connected network. In figure 3.19, when router ROUTER_BC sends information on segment B, it should not include any information that it received from ROUTER_AB about segment A. If it did, a user might think that segment A could be reached directly through ROUTER_AB and ROUTER_BC. The second rule is similar to the first rule. It states that a router should not include information about a directly connected network to which it is sending routing information broadcasts. In the example in figure 3.19, ROUTER_BC cannot broadcast information about segment B on segment B. It can broadcast only on segment B information on segments C and D.

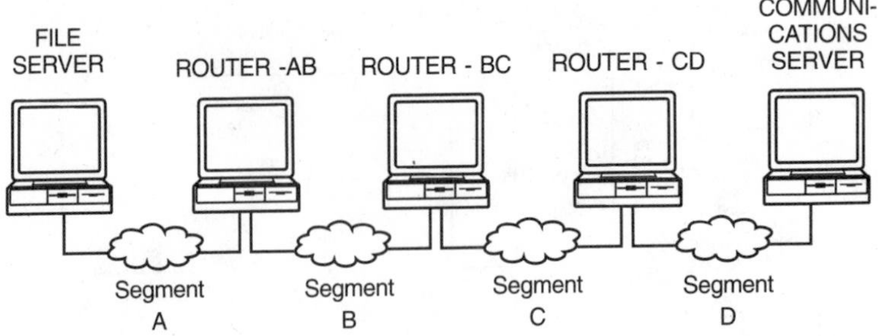

Figure 3.19
Multiple LAN segments joined by NetWare routers.

Figures 3.20 to 3.23 illustrate the router operations. When the router ROUTER_BC is first brought up, it initializes its routing tables with information on its directly connected networks. Next, the router sends an initial RIP response (see fig. 3.20) to inform routers on its directly connected segments (ROUTER_AB and ROUTER_CD) of the segments it now makes available (segments B and C).

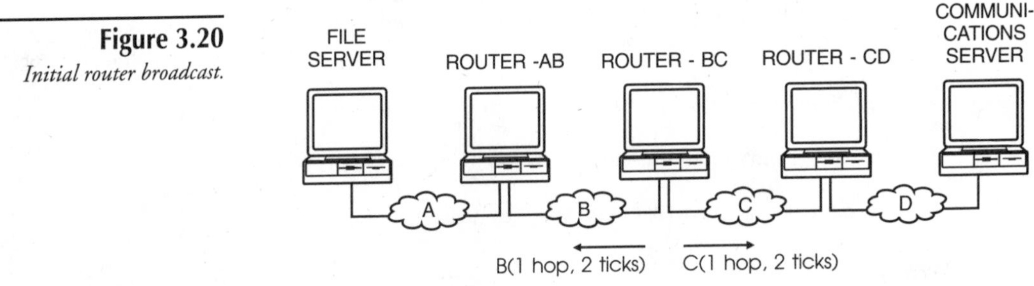

Figure 3.20
Initial router broadcast.

Next, the router broadcasts a general RIP request on its directly connected networks for information on all network segments that exist on the internetwork (see fig. 3.21). All routers on its directly connected segment (ROUTER_AB and ROUTER_CD) send a RIP response to this request by using the best information algorithm. The router then initializes its routing table with this information. At periodic intervals, the router is the recipient of routing information from other routers (see fig. 3.22).

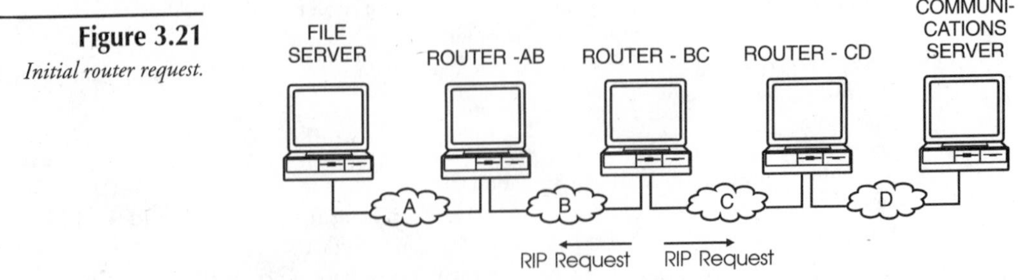

Figure 3.21
Initial router request.

After the router is up, it broadcasts its routing information in a RIP response packet at 60-second intervals (see fig 3.23).

When routers are shut down gracefully by using the DOWN command (the power plug is not pulled suddenly), they broadcast a RIP response packet, which sets the delay for all networks it can reach to infinity. This response packet informs other routers that the router has been shut down and cannot be used.

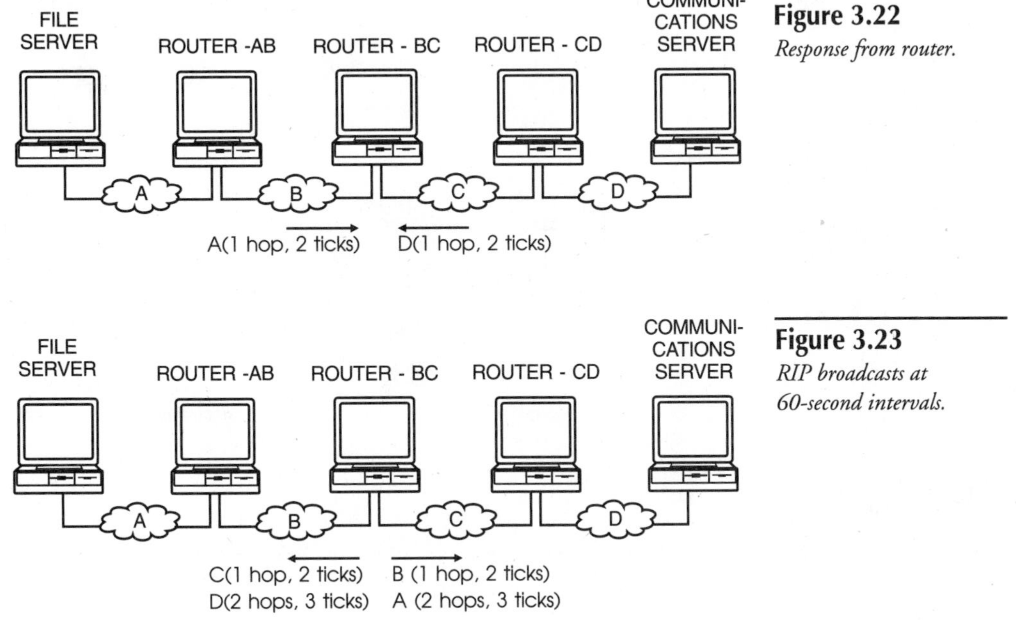

Figure 3.22
Response from router.

Figure 3.23
RIP broadcasts at 60-second intervals.

This mechanism is illustrated in figure 3.24. When ROUTER_BC is shut down, it sends a RIP response to other routers, such as ROUTER_AB and ROUTER_CD, that it is no longer available. These routers then update their tables.

If you do not use the DOWN command to shut down a router or you have an unexpected power failure or hardware glitch, the neighboring routers are not immediately aware that a change has occurred. Unexpected shutdown can cause transient routing problems until the timeout mechanism for routing table entries goes into effect. It takes a delay of three minutes before other routers remove the entries in their routing table for the failed router.

When a router receives a request for information, it supplies the information in a RIP response packet. If it does not have the information, it returns a delay of infinity for the requested network to indicate that the network cannot be reached.

The RIP protocol is crucial so that routers can keep their routing tables up-to-date. Figure 3.25 shows the structure of the RIP packet, and figure 3.26 shows a RIP packet captured and decoded through Novell's LANalyzer. Figure 3.27 shows the RIP packet structure defined by Xerox. The only difference between the Novell RIP and the Xerox RIP is the addition of the Time Delay measured in ticks, with each tick being approximately 1/18 second. (18.21 ticks occur per second.) This change improves a NetWare router's capability to select the fastest route to a destination. It also prohibits a straight integration between Novell's RIP and pure XNS implementations.

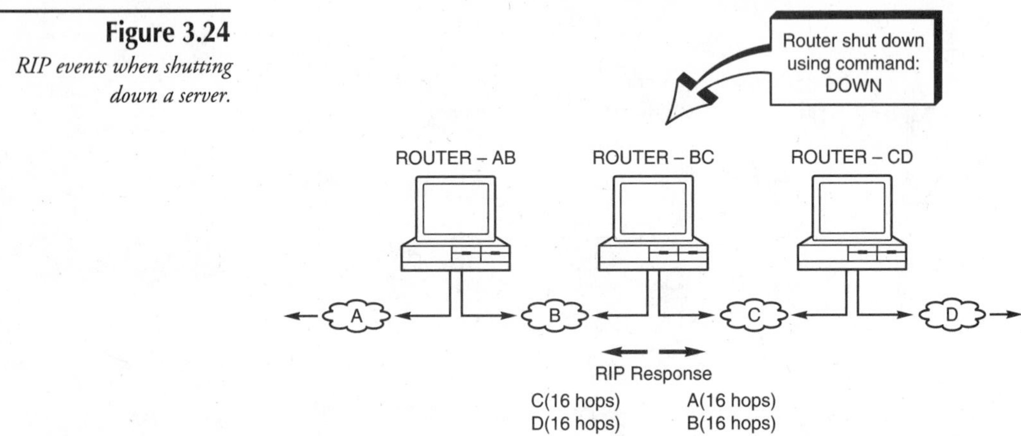

Figure 3.24
RIP events when shutting down a server.

The *operation* field of the RIP packet indicates whether the packet is a request or response. The following codes are used for the operation field:

Operation	Description
1	Request
2	Response

After the operations field comes the contents field, which describes one or more sets, or *tuples,* of routing information. Each tuple describes an object network's network number and the number of hops and time ticks it takes to get to that network number.

A hop is counted every time a packet goes through a router. The maximum number of permissible hops is 15. A value of 16 is synonymous to infinity and means that the destination is unreachable.

The time delay field measures (in clock ticks) how much time it takes to get to the network number. Novell added the time field to better determine the fastest path. The time delay also permits better integration with IBM SNA or T1 networks that are more time-sensitive.

If the operation specified in the RIP packet is a request (1), then each tuple represents the object network for which the requester wants routing information. If the requester wants information on all object networks, only one tuple is included whose network number field is set to all 1s. If the operation specified in the RIP packet is a response (2), then each tuple represents routing information for the object network in the form of number of hops and clock ticks to reach the network number. If the number of hops field is set to infinity (16), it indicates that the destination is unreachable.

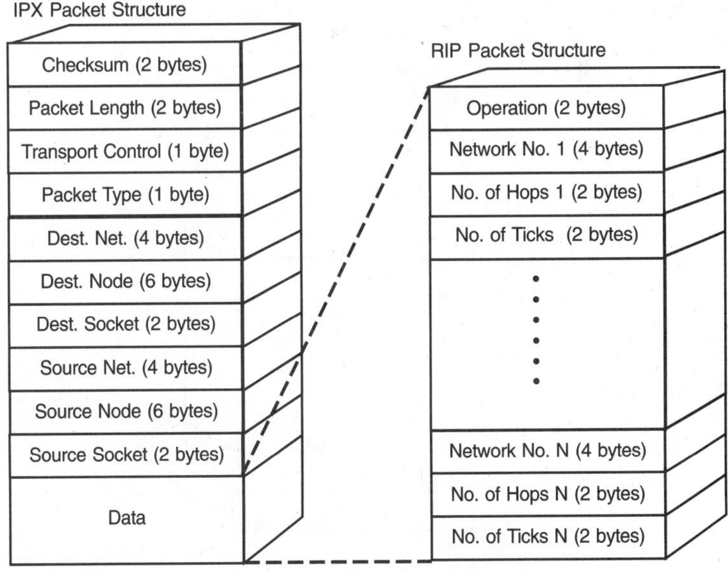

Figure 3.25
Novell RIP packet structure.

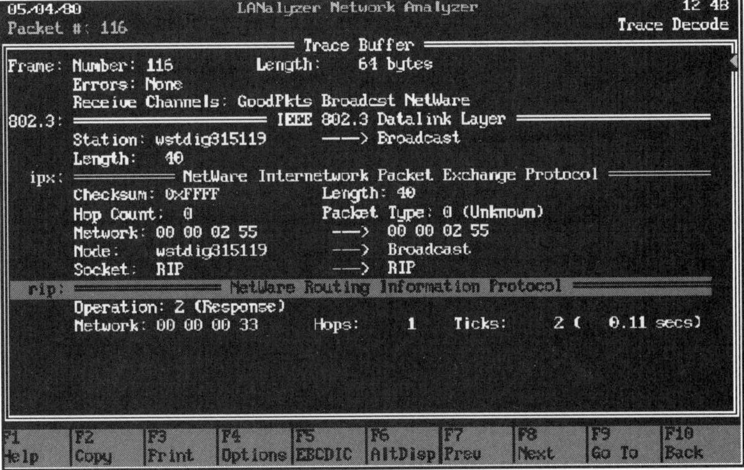

Figure 3.26
RIP packet captured and decoded by LANalyzer.

NetWare routers also act as repositories of other information. They contain a database of services provided by servers on the network. They obtain this information through *Service Advertising Protocol* (SAP). The SAP follows the spirit of the Xerox Clearinghouse Protocol, but differs from it in detail and implementation.

The Service Advertising Protocol permits servers such as file servers, print servers, and gateway servers to advertise their services and addresses. These services are dutifully recorded by Novell routers in a table

called the *Server Information Table* (SIT). The Server Address field includes the full internetwork address, the network number, node address, and socket number of the server. The Server Type holds the type of service being performed. Examples of some server type designations are shown in table 3.6.

Figure 3.27
XNS RIP.

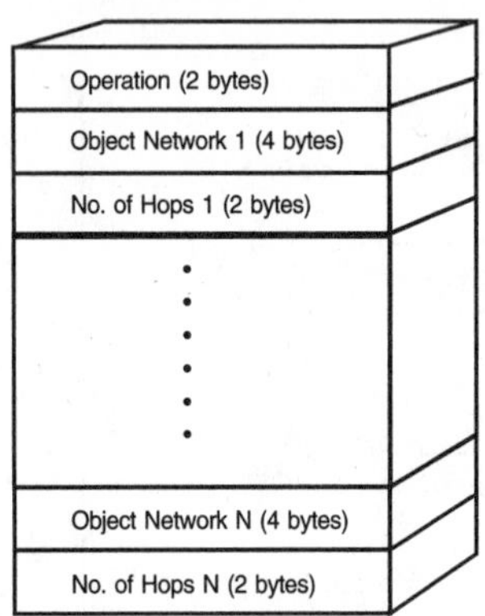

Table 3.6
Server Type Designations

Type of Service (Server Type)	Object Type Code (Hex)
File Server	4
Job Server	5
Gateway	6
Print Server	7
Archive Server	9
Administration	B
NAS SNA Gateway	21
Remote Bridge Server	24
Bridge Server	26
TCP/IP Gateway	27
Time Synchronization Server	2D
Advertising Print Server	47

Type of Service (Server Type)	Object Type Code (Hex)
TES - NetWare for VMS	7A
NetWare Access Server	98
Portable NetWare	9E
NNS Domain	133

The Time Since Changed or Time-Out field is used to age and retire entries for servers that unexpectedly go down. Currently, the SIT information is not organized for quick database-type queries. To rapidly access SIT information, this information is copied to the file server's bindery, which is an internal database used to keep track of certain resources on the server. SAP agents in the file server periodically update the file server's bindery so that any client attached to a server can obtain information on other services on the internetwork. If a client needs to determine which services are available on the network, it can query a nearby router or server.

The SAP packet uses the IPX packet for its transport. Figure 3.28 details the SAP packet.

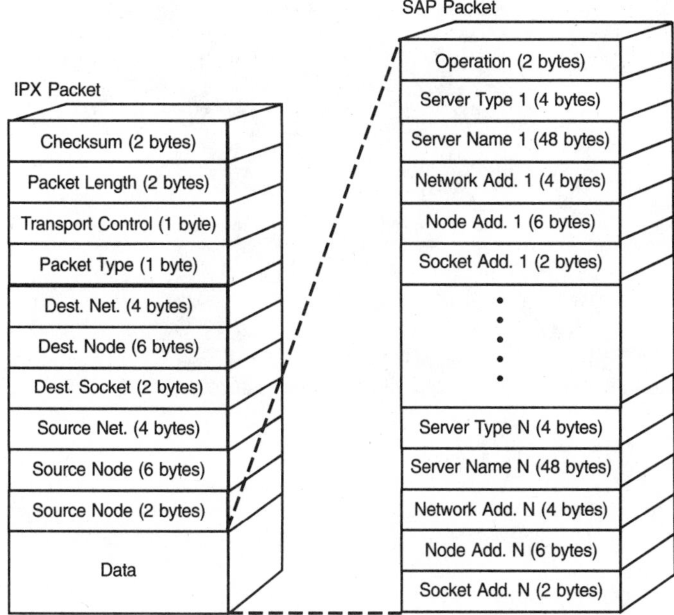

Figure 3.28
Service Advertising Protocol (SAP).

The *operation* field in the SAP packet defines the type of operation being performed. The four possible values for this operation code are as follows:

- A request by a client for the name and address of a server of a certain type (such as file server, print server, and communications server). If the client loads the NetWare shell, it issues this SAP request.
- A response to the nearest server query
- A general request for information on all servers of a certain type
- A response to the general request

Figures 3.29 to 3.31 illustrate these SAP packets obtained by using Novell's LANalyzer.

The Server Information Table in a router is updated in a manner similar to the RIP table, except that the request/response packets are SAP packets. SAP request/responses also follow the best information algorithm for RIP packets. After a server is brought up for the first time, it broadcasts information about itself to all routers. At every 60-second interval, the router process broadcasts SAP packets that contain information about all servers of which they are aware. After a server is shut down, it broadcasts a SAP packet to indicate that its services are no longer available.

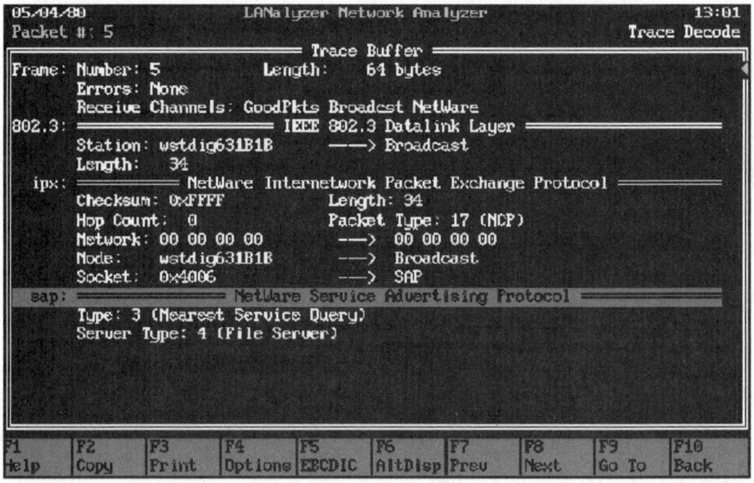

```
05/04/80              LANalyzer Network Analyzer                    13:01
Packet #: 5                                                   Trace Decode
========================== Trace Buffer ==================================
Frame: Number: 5              Length:    64 bytes
       Errors: None
       Receive Channels: GoodPkts Broadcst NetWare
802.3: ==================== IEEE 802.3 Datalink Layer ====================
       Station: wstdig631B1B       ---> Broadcast
       Length:   34
  ipx: =========== NetWare Internetwork Packet Exchange Protocol ==========
       Checksum: 0xFFFF             Length: 34
       Hop Count:   0               Packet Type: 17 (NCP)
       Network: 00 00 00 00          ---> 00 00 00 00
       Node:    wstdig631B1B         ---> Broadcast
       Socket:  0x4006               ---> SAP
  sap: =============== NetWare Service Advertising Protocol ===============
       Type: 3 (Nearest Service Query)
       Server Type: 4 (File Server)

F1   F2   F3    F4      F5     F6      F7   F8   F9    F10
Help Copy Print Options EBCDIC AltDisp Prev Next Go To Back
```

Figure 3.29
SAP request packet.

Tracking Network Numbers

You must keep network numbers unique within an organization. If you do not keep network numbers unique, you encounter problems. The NetWare router detects duplicate routing number assignments.

When network numbers are not kept unique, the NetWare router detects a conflict in the routing number assignment. You see the following displayed:

```
1/11/93 7:18am: 1.1.112 Router configuration error detected
Router at node C0DC3F19 claims network 00000333 should be 00000255
1/11/93 7:18am: 1.1.112 Router configuration error detected
Router at node C0DC3F19 claims network 00000333 should be 00000255
1/11/93 7:18am: 1.1.112 Router configuration error detected
```

```
Router at node C0DC3F19 claims network 00000333 should be 00000255
1/11/93 7:18am: 1.1.112 Router configuration error detected
Router at node C0DC3F19 claims network 00000333 should be 00000255
```

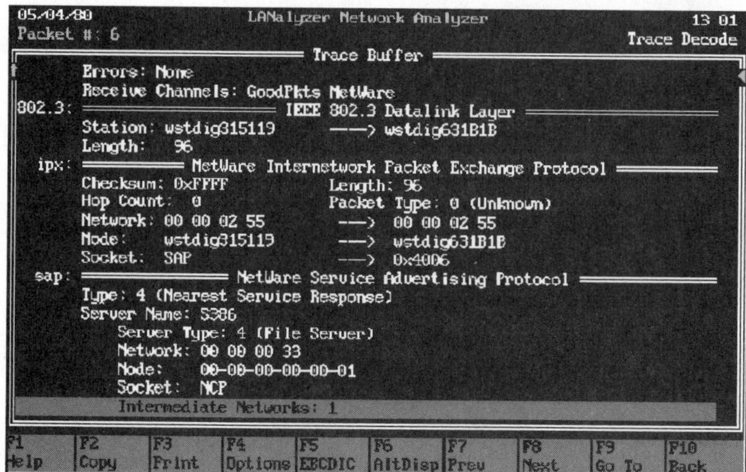

Figure 3.30
SAP response packet.

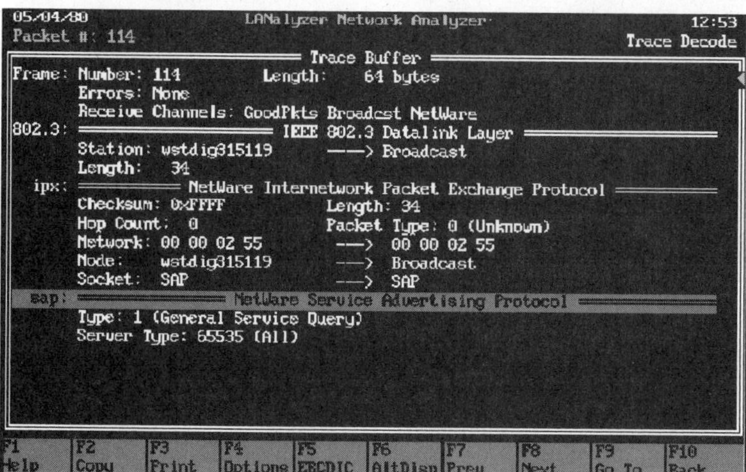

Figure 3.31
SAP general request packet.

The router error message is saying that another node claims the network number is incorrect. In this case, network number 00000333 should be 00000255 because the other node (router) has this number in its configuration. Set the same network number in the configuration for both routers to solve this problem.

In many large organizations, LAN operations are decentralized. As a result, different installers may select the same network numbers, with the default network number of 1 being the most common. When it is time to internetwork the separate departmental LANs, the network number conflicts become painfully apparent. You can avoid these conflicts by using a universal network number assignment scheme. This scheme is not something mandated by Novell; it is a recommendation to simplify network administration.

The network number field in IPX packets is four bytes long, which means that the network number can be eight hexadecimal digits. These eight hexadecimal digits can be assigned the meanings as shown in table 3.7.

Table 3.7
Meanings Assigned to Hexadecimal Digits

Byte 3 **I D**	**Byte 2** **D N**	**Byte 1** **N N**	**Byte 0** **N N**
I =	1-digit hexadecimal code for network number or internal network number (NetWare 3.*x*, 4.*x*). A value of D (hex) indicates a network number. A value of F (hex) indicates an internal network number.		
D D =	2-digit hexadecimal number for department code.		
N N N N N =	5-digit hexadecimal number for each logical network or internal network number.		

An example of departmental codes for a fictitious organization follows in table 3.8. This list can be updated, if necessary, to add additional departments that have networks installed for them.

Table 3.8
Example of Assigned Departmental Codes

Department	**Code (D D)**	**Hex**
Unassigned		00–0F
Corporate	10	
Accounting	11	
Manufacturing	12	
Food Services	13	
Telecommunication Services	14	
Research	15	
Unassigned		16–FF

The five hexadecimal digits *N N N N N* that follow the department code can be assigned by the individual departments. This section provides some suggestions for assigning these hexadecimal digits.

For network numbers, the *N N N N N* can be used for the network cable segments. This cable number can be assigned as outlined in the following paragraphs.

The first *N* hexadecimal digit can be a code for the frame type used on that network. If you are using Ethernet with NetWare 3.12 and NetWare 4.*x*, you may want to have ETHERNET_802.3 and ETHERNET_802.2 frame types loaded at the server/router. NetWare 3.12 and 4.x default to using ETHERNET_802.2. Each of these different frame types requires a different network number. Assigning a code for the frame type for the first *N* hexadecimal digit can accomplish this task. The codes listed in table 3.9 can be used.

Table 3.9
Code Assignments for Frame Types

Frame Type	First *N* Value
RX_NET	0
TOKEN-RING	1
ETHERNET_802.2	2
ETHERNET_802.3	3
TOKEN-RING_SNAP	4
ETHERNET_SNAP	A
ETHERNET_II	E

For internal network numbers, the frame types do not matter, so the first *N* hexadecimal digit can be 0.

The remaining *N N N N* hexadecimal digits are assigned a sequential number 1, 2, 3 and so on, for cable numbers or server numbers. For example, the first cable installed in a department has the last *N N N N* hexadecimal digits numbered 0001, the second cable installed is numbered 0002, and so on. Similarly, the first file server installed has the last *N N N N* for the internal network number assigned as 0001, the second server installed is 0002, and so on.

In situations in which departments are connected by an IPX router, the question arises as to what should be the network numbers for the router's port. The network numbers should be consistent with the numbers assigned to file servers on the cable segment connected to the router's ports. For a cable segment that does not have file servers connected to the router's port, the network number should have the department code assigned for the department that has the majority of workstations connected to the router's port.

If the shared IPX router is NetWare 3.*x*- or NetWare 4.*x*-based, it also must be assigned an internal network number. The internal network number should have a department code for the department that has the primary duty for maintaining the IPX router.

An example may clarify the preceding discussion. Assume that the Accounting department network, the Business Office network, and the Food Processing network are to be connected by a shared IPX router. The Accounting department has an ARCnet card and an Ethernet card on a server called FSA. The Ethernet cable connected to FSA needs to support the following frame types:

- ETHERNET_802.3
- ETHERNET_802.2
- ETHERNET_II

The Corporate server FSB has one server with a single ARCnet card. The Manufacturing department does not have a server. They use workstations on an ARCnet cable connected to the router to access servers on the Accounting and Corporate networks. Assume that proper access permissions are set to prevent unauthorized access.

The following are the internal network numbers of file servers and network numbers that can be used:

- Server FSA (Accounting):

Internal network number	= F1100001
ARCnet network number	= D1100001
Ethernet network number for ETHERNET_802.3	= D1130001
Ethernet network number for ETHERNET_802.2	= D1120001
Ethernet network number for ETHERNET_II	= D11E0001

- Server FSB (Corporate):

Internal network number	= F1000001
ARCnet network number	= D1000001

- IPX Router:

ARCnet network number for port connected to Accounting	= D1100001
ARCnet network number for port connected to Corporate	= D1000001
ARCnet network number for port connected to Manufacturing	= D1200001

You can tell at a glance whether the network number assignment is for a cable segment or NetWare 3.*x* internal number by examining the first hexadecimal digit. The next two digits indicate the department responsible for administering the network number. Within the department, they can keep track of their network number assignments (such as that based on frame types). Using this scheme greatly simplifies the problem of network number assignments.

Limitations of NetWare Routers

NetWare routers understand only IPX. Multiple protocol routers tend to be protocol-independent. Pure NetWare routers cannot be used to connect networks that use multiple protocols because they do not have an understanding of other protocols such as DECnet and SNA.

NetWare routers are limited by the performance of the PCs and the type of NICs installed in them. Despite these limitations, NetWare routers are extremely useful for pure NetWare environments. One big advantage of NetWare routers is low cost. The routing software is bundled with NetWare, which enables you to install a NetWare router for the cost of the PC and NICs.

Configuring an Internal Router

Figure 3.32 shows two drivers selected for NetWare 2.2 during the installation process. If the NetWare 2.2 is generated with the configuration shown, it acts as an internal router that performs routing between two LANs.

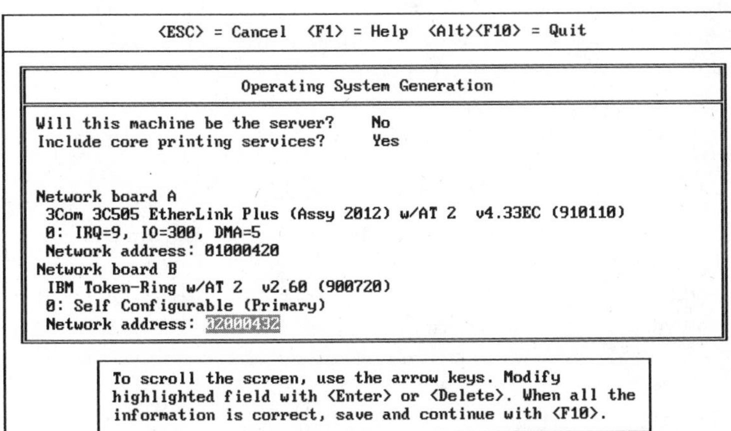

Figure 3.32
NetWare 2.2 internal router configuration.

Figure 3.33 shows the AUTOEXEC.NCF file for NetWare 3.*x*. Notice that two drivers (WDPLUSSV and NE2000) are loaded. To bind the two loaded drivers to the IPX protocol stack, two BIND commands were used. Each BIND command specifies a different network number. With this configuration, NetWare 3.*x* acts as an internal router that performs routing between two LANs.

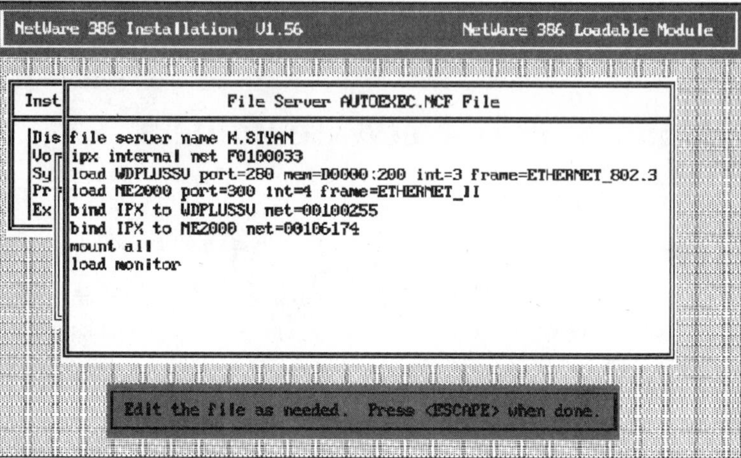

Figure 3.33
NetWare 3.x internal router configuration.

Installing and Managing External NetWare Routers

This section discusses installation procedures for NetWare routers. You learn to configure NetWare routers through a guided tour. You can configure NetWare routers in several ways: dedicated/nondedicated and protected/real mode. You learn about the differences between these configurations in the following sections.

Dedicated and Nondedicated Mode Routers

A *dedicated router* is a computer that performs only routing functions. It cannot be used as a DOS workstation. Because all the computer resources are set aside for routing functions, dedicated routers have better performance. Another advantage of the dedicated router approach is greater reliability and security. No applications are running on the computer that could cause it to hang, and because users cannot use it as a workstation, it also is more secure from inadvertent reboot of the router computer.

A *nondedicated router* is a computer that performs both routing and workstation functions. It can be used as a DOS workstation to run applications while the routing function is performed in the background. Because computer resources are shared between routing functions and applications running on the router, nondedicated routers have poorer performance. The advantage of the nondedicated router approach is that it saves the cost of an extra workstation. Because nondedicated routers are exposed to applications and users, they are less reliable and secure compared to dedicated routers.

Dedicated router configuration should be selected if possible because of potential problems with the nondedicated approach. Choose the nondedicated router approach only if severe budgetary constraints do not permit the purchase of an additional computer.

The dedicated mode router can be set up in the protected mode or real mode depending on the microprocessor inside the workstation. If an Intel 8086 microprocessor is being used, the router can operate only in real mode. Real-mode routers can use memory up to 1 MB (see fig. 3.34). If the workstation has an Intel 80286, 80386, or higher microprocessor, and if it has sufficient extended memory, it can run in protected mode (see fig. 3.35).

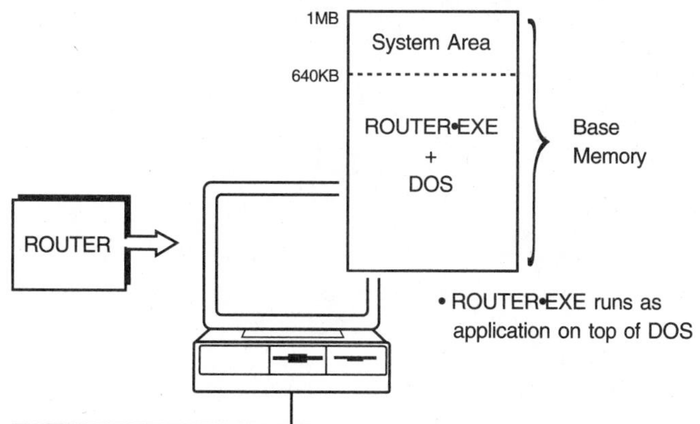

Figure 3.34
Real-mode router.

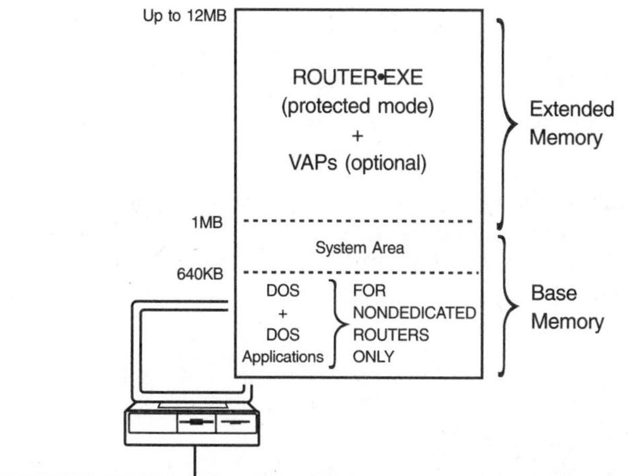

Figure 3.35
Protected-mode router.

In protected mode, only 12 MB of RAM is used for external routers. This 12 MB is currently a NetWare router limitation. Nondedicated routers can operate only in protected mode.

Router Hardware and Software Requirements

Each PC that must act as a router must be installed with two or more NICs. The limit is four NICs for external routers. The NICs should have no hardware conflicts with each other or with other hardware

inside the PC. Hardware parameters such as interrupt request line, DMA channels, I/O ports, and base memory addresses must be set uniquely. If a protected-mode router is to be configured, you must allow at least 500 KB of extended memory for the router process. You can have up to 12 MB of RAM in the protected-mode router. Extra memory can be used for router buffers to improve the performance.

The software requirements are as follows:

- ROUTEGEN disk
- Network driver disks such as LAN_DRV_XXX
- DOSUTIL-1 disk containing CONSOLE.COM if nondedicated router is to be set up

Installing a NetWare Router

Figure 3.36 shows the process of generating the routing software. The utility to generate the routing software is ROUTEGEN, which can be found in the ROUTEGEN disk that comes with NetWare (2.*x* and 3.*x*). The ROUTEGEN utility is the same for NetWare 2.*x* and NetWare 3.*x*.

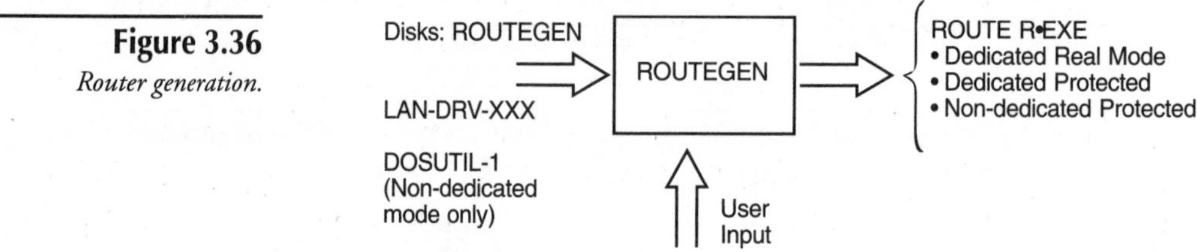

Figure 3.36
Router generation.

The end result of the ROUTEGEN.EXE is a ROUTER.EXE program that implements the router. This ROUTER.EXE program file must be copied to the router boot disk. The router must then be configured to boot correctly. The boot process is slightly different between dedicated and nondedicated routers and is discussed after a guided tour of the router installation.

Router Generation

To install a router, follow these steps:

1. Install the NICs into the workstation to be used as a router. You can install up to four NICs. Base address must not conflict with any other hardware in the router. Only two IBM Token Ring network boards can be used in a router.

2. Boot the workstation to be used as a router with DOS 3.*x* or higher.

3. Insert the ROUTEGEN disk in drive A and enter **ROUTEGEN**. After a `Please Wait` message, a screen appears.

4. Press Enter to continue. The Router Generation screen appears with the following fields:

   - **Operating system mode.** You have a choice between two modes of configuration: dedicated and nondedicated. If you select nondedicated mode, you must assign a process address.

   - **Nondedicated process address.** This address is a unique hexadecimal number. It identifies the workstation DOS environment to the router process.

   - **Number of communication buffers.** Communication buffers are temporary areas in the router's RAM to hold incoming/outgoing packets. The default number is 150, which is adequate for most router configurations. If you anticipate heavy router traffic, the number of communication buffers should be increased. The maximum number of communication buffers is 1,000.

   - **Network board.** This field shows information on the router's NICs. The first NIC is called Network board A, the second Network board B, and so on.

   - **Driver.** For a given network board, the driver to be used is shown. To deselect a driver, press Del. To see a list of available drivers, press Enter. If the driver you want is not listed, press Ins and follow the instructions to select another driver.

   - **Configuration option.** A driver can have a number of combinations of its parameter settings. You must select the setting that corresponds to the NIC's settings. Some NICs and drivers are software-configurable.

   - **Network address.** Every cabling segment attached to the Network boards A, B, C, and D must have a unique address. This address is expressed as an eight-digit hexadecimal number and is used by the IPX packets to uniquely identify the different networks. It is part of the internetwork address, which consists of network address, node address, and socket number.

5. Select either the dedicated or nondedicated router operating mode.

6. Increase the number of communication buffers to 200.

7. Highlight the Driver field under Network board A and press Enter.

   A list of drivers for network board A is displayed. If the driver you want is not listed, you must press Ins and follow the instructions to add it to the list.

   ROUTEGEN contains a bug; therefore, if you are adding a driver to the list and it does not work, copy the drivers to the ROUTEGEN disk and repeat the preceding steps.

8. After you select the driver, highlight Configuration option and press Enter. A list of configuration options appears.

9. Highlight the configuration option that matches the NIC's setting and press Enter.

10. Assign a unique network address for the LAN connected to the NIC. This address is an eight-digit hexadecimal number. You do not need to enter leading zeros.

11. Repeat steps 7 to 10 for as many NICs as are in the router. These steps must be done for network boards B, C, and D.

12. Review the information. Make any corrections. If satisfied, press F10 to continue. A series of messages appears to inform you that the router is being linked.

Creating the Router Boot Disk

The ROUTER.EXE file created in the preceding section must be copied to the router boot disk. The router can be booted from either the hard disk or a floppy disk.

Both of these disks must be DOS-bootable and run DOS 3.*x* or higher. To make the DOS disk bootable, use the FORMAT command with the /S parameter.

Installing a Dedicated Router

After you create the DOS boot disk, perform the following steps:

1. Copy the ROUTER.EXE file from the ROUTEGEN disk to a DOS bootable disk.

2. Create an AUTOEXEC.BAT file with the ROUTER command.

3. Boot the router machine. ROUTER.EXE loads and activates the router.

Installing a Nondedicated Router

To install a nondedicated router, follow these steps:

1. Copy the ROUTER.EXE file from the ROUTEGEN disk to a DOS bootable disk.

2. Create an AUTOEXEC.BAT file with the following commands:

   ```
   ROUTER
   NETx
   F:
   LOGIN
   ```

   After the ROUTER program loads, it activates the router. NET*x* (*x* can be 3, 4, 5, or X for generic shell) loads the shell, which permits the router to be used as a workstation. IPX.COM is not needed because the IPX protocols are implemented by ROUTER.EXE.

3. Create a CONFIG.SYS file on the boot device with the FILES= and BUFFERS= parameters set to 20 each.

4. Boot the router machine. ROUTER.EXE loads and activates the router and NETx.COM activates the workstation.

Note that if you forget that you are on the router and reboot the workstation, you reboot the router!

5. To switch to the router console from DOS mode, type **CONSOLE**. To switch to DOS mode from console mode, type **DOS**.

Running VAPs at the Router

If the router is running in protected mode (dedicated or nondedicated), *Value Added Process* (VAP) applications also can run at the router. The VAP files can be copied to the boot disk used for the router. If the router detects a VAP file during the boot process, it asks you the following:

```
Value added processes have been defined. Do you wish to load them?
```

Press Y to load or press N to ignore VAPs.

You may want to have VAPs load automatically. You can create the ROUTER.CFG file in the same directory as the ROUTER.EXE file. In the ROUTER.CFG file, you include the following command:

```
VAP WAIT number
```

In the preceding syntax, *number* is the number of seconds the router should wait before loading the VAPs automatically. A waiting period of 10 to 360 seconds can be specified. If the *number* is omitted, the default is ten seconds.

If the VAPs cannot fit in the same directory as the ROUTER.EXE file, you can specify the path to locate the files in the ROUTER.CFG file. The general syntax of this command is the following:

```
VAP DISK path
```

If *path* is omitted, a default of drive A is assumed.

If the VAP files are kept on drive C under the directory VAP_APPS, the ROUTER.CFG file may look like the following:

```
VAP DISK C:\VAP_APPS
VAP WAIT 15
```

Using the Router Commands

You must type all router commands at the router console. The RESET ROUTER command initializes the router table if you suspect that this table is inaccurate or corrupted.

If you use the DOWN command to shut down routers, they broadcast a RIP response to indicate that the networks connected to it can no longer be reached. All other routers that see this broadcast update their tables. But if a router goes down unexpectedly, the RIP response is not sent, and it may take up to three minutes before other routers discover that the router is down. During this time, the router tables are inaccurate. Routing decisions made using inaccurate information can result in undeliverable packets or inefficient routing paths.

If you issue the RESET ROUTER command at a router, it sends a RIP request to nearby routers and rebuilds an accurate routing table.

The TRACK ON command provides three types of information as follows:

- Routing information (RIP packets)
- Server information (SAP broadcast packets)
- Workstation connection requests (SAP request/response)

Figure 3.37 shows the Router Tracking screen for a NetWare 3.*x* internal router. Use the Alt+Esc and Ctrl+Esc key combinations to switch between the track screen and the console screen for NetWare 3.*x*.

Figure 3.37
NetWare 3.x internal router track screen.

```
Router Tracking Screen
OUT [00000033:FFFFFFFFFFFF] 6:59:44am   S386         1   S386         2
OUT [00000255:FFFFFFFFFFFF] 6:59:44am   S386         1   S386         2
IN  [00000033:000000000001] 6:59:51am   S386         1
OUT [00000033:FFFFFFFFFFFF] 7:00:14am   00000255  1/2
OUT [00000255:FFFFFFFFFFFF] 7:00:14am   00000033  1/2
IN  [00000033:000000000001] 7:00:19am   S386         1
OUT [00000033:FFFFFFFFFFFF] 7:00:43am   S386         1   S386         2
OUT [00000255:FFFFFFFFFFFF] 7:00:43am   S386         1   S386         2
IN  [00000033:000000000001] 7:00:46am   S386         1
OUT [00000033:FFFFFFFFFFFF] 7:01:13am   00000255  1/2
OUT [00000255:FFFFFFFFFFFF] 7:01:13am   00000033  1/2
IN  [00000033:000000000001] 7:01:14am   S386         1
IN  [00000033:000000000001] 7:01:41am   S386         1
OUT [00000033:FFFFFFFFFFFF] 7:01:42am   S386         1   S386         2
OUT [00000255:FFFFFFFFFFFF] 7:01:42am   S386         1   S386         2
IN  [00000033:000000000001] 7:02:08am   S386         1
OUT [00000033:FFFFFFFFFFFF] 7:02:12am   00000255  1/2
OUT [00000255:FFFFFFFFFFFF] 7:02:12am   00000033  1/2
IN  [00000033:000000000001] 7:02:36am   S386         1
OUT [00000033:FFFFFFFFFFFF] 7:02:42am   S386         1   S386         2
OUT [00000255:FFFFFFFFFFFF] 7:02:42am   S386         1   S386         2
IN  [00000033:000000000001] 7:03:03am   S386         1
<Use ALT-ESC or CTRL-ESC to switch screens, or any other key to pause>
```

The Route information for NetWare 3.*x* has the following syntax:

```
InOut [LAN:NodeAddr] Time NetNum Hops/Ticks NetNum Hops/Ticks ...
```

The NetWare 2.*x* route information differs slightly by not having the Time field and has the following general syntax:

```
InOut [LAN:NodeAddr] NetNum Hops/Ticks NetNum Hops/Ticks ...
```

InOut specifies whether the information is being received from the network (IN) or the router is transmitting the information (OUT).

LAN specifies which LAN card (NIC) received/transmitted the routing information. The LAN cards are labeled A, B, C, and D.

NodeAddr specifies a six-byte (12 hex digits) node address of the NIC. In figure 3.37, node address FFFFFFFFFFFF indicates a broadcast to all nodes on the local network.

Time is displayed in hours, minutes, and seconds and is the time that the information was transmitted/ received.

NetNum is the network number of the logical network or the internal number of a NetWare 3.*x* server.

Hops is the number of routers that a packet must traverse to reach the indicated network number.

Ticks is the time delay to reach the specified network number and is measured in 1/18-second increments. For low-speed asynchronous lines, this number can be as high as 999. For asynchronous and X.25 routers, *Ticks* is computed as the following:

Ticks = 4 × One-way transport time in 1/18th second increments + 10

For LANs such as ARCnet, Ethernet, and Token Ring one hop represents one tick, even if the actual transmission takes less time.

The server information is broadcast by using SAP packets, and these also are reported by means of the TRACK screen. The server information for NetWare 3.*x* has the following syntax:

```
InOut [LAN:NodeAddr] Time NetNum ServName Hops  ServName Hops ...
```

The NetWare 2.*x* server information differs slightly by not having the Time field and has the following general syntax:

```
InOut [LAN:NodeAddr] NetNum ServName Hops  ServName Hops ...
```

ServName is the name of the server on the network for which information is being propagated, and *Hops* indicates the number of routers a packet must traverse to get to the server. VAPs and NLMs that advertise services also are reported on the TRACK screen.

To turn off the TRACK screen enter **TRACK OFF** at the server console.

You can use the TRACK command to help solve `Unknown File Server` errors. If network numbers are set incorrectly, a server may not be seen through the SLIST command. Workstations attempting to log in see `Unknown file server` errors. Turning the TRACK screen on may cause the `WARNING!! MULTIPLE ROUTER WITH SAME INTERNET ADDRESS!` or `ROUTER CONFIGURATION ERROR!!! ROUTER xxxxxxxxxxxx claims LAN A is yyyyy!` errors to occur. To fix these problems, follow the guidelines in this chapter's earlier section "Tracking Network Numbers."

Using NetWare 3.*x* as an IP Router

Novell is striving to integrate their proprietary architecture with non-Novell networks. One such trend is with UNIX-based networks. Novell is a major shareholder of USL (Unix Systems Lab), which manages the UNIX product line for AT&T. NetWare integration with UNIX-based networks is currently available only through NetWare 3.*x*.

NetWare 3.*x* allows the integration of NetWare with TCP/IP- and IPX-based networks.

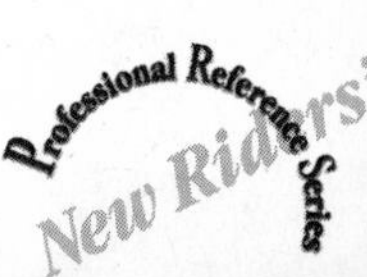

Understanding TCP/IP-Based Networks

Before you can understand how TCP/IP and NetWare integration works, you must understand TCP/IP and how it differs from Novell's native SPX/IPX protocols.

TCP/IP

TCP/IP is two protocols: TCP and IP. *TCP* is a transport protocol that fits into layer four of the OSI model. *IP* is a network protocol that fits into layer three of the OSI model. Figure 3.38 illustrates the relationship between TCP/IP and the OSI model. The *User Datagram Protocol* (UDP) is a cousin of TCP, but is simpler and not as reliable as TCP.

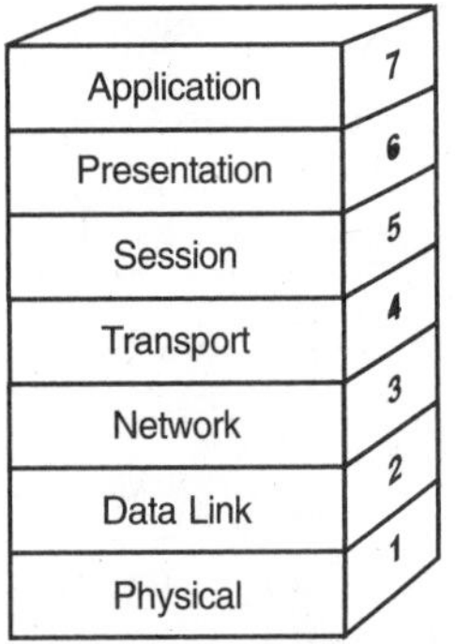

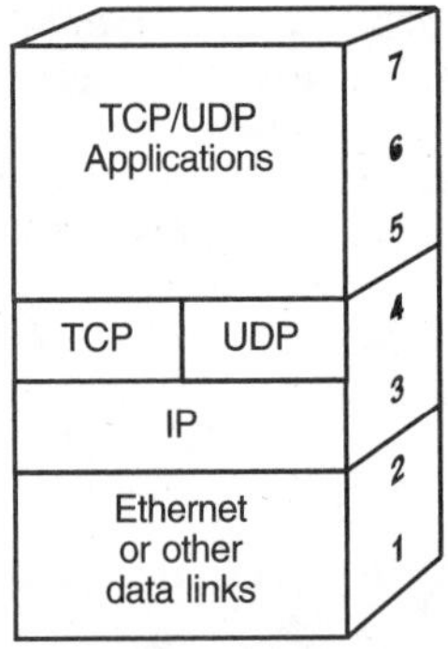

Figure 3.38
TCP/IP comparison with the OSI model.

Note that the OSI model is commonly used as a means of describing the functionality of a protocol such as TCP/IP; it is not meant to imply that TCP/IP is an International Organization of Standards recommendation. The transport layer's job is to ensure end-system to end-system data integrity.

Over the years, TCP has acquired a reputation for robustness and reliability. TCP has had its trial by fire and has had to undergo changes to fix problems dealing with data transmission integrity. In addition to reliability, TCP allows software processes within a node to be referred to by unique addresses. This address is called the *TCP port number.* This port number is similar in concept to the IPX/SPX sockets discussed earlier.

Whereas the TCP protocol runs on an end-system, such as a user system or a host/server, the IP protocol can run on intermediate systems used to connect the end-system together (see fig. 3.39). Examples of these intermediate systems are IP routers. The job of the IP layer is to prepare the messages from the TCP layer. The IP layer must know the address of the destination IP layer. This address is a 32-bit address called the *IP address* (or the *internet address*). In general, the destination node can be on a different network, so a portion of this IP address is used to refer to the network number of the destination network. The remaining portion is used to refer to the host number within that network.

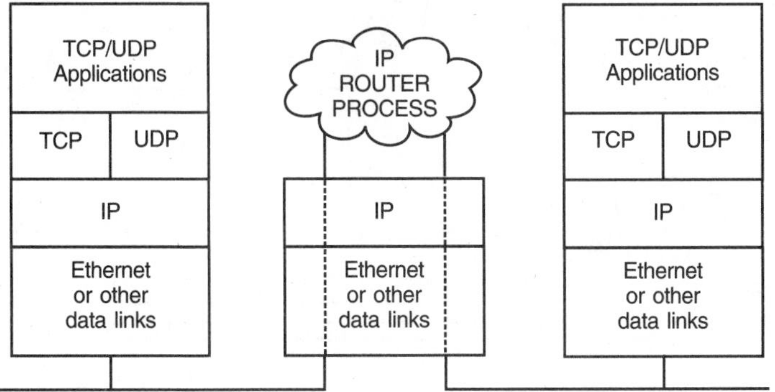

Figure 3.39
IP router connecting end-systems.

The IP layer must send the message by the best route it can. If the message is too large, it can be broken down into smaller pieces (fragmented or segmented) by the sender or at any point along the path to the destination. At the destination, the fragments must be put back together in the correct order. The IP layer adds enough information to each piece of message to accomplish this task.

The IP layer provides a means of connecting a large number of networks. An IP packet can go across 255 routers. NetWare LANs are limited to 15 routers along a transmission path. One benefit of integration with IP networks is that a NetWare packet can be routed across larger networks using the more flexible IP mechanism.

NetWare TCP/IP Architecture

The BSD 4.3 socket interface and the AT&T *Transport Layer Interface* (TLI) are *application programming interfaces* (APIs) that come with the Network C Language Compiler (see fig. 3.40). The *Network File System* (NFS) server comes with NetWare for NFS, an implementation of SUN's NFS. The *Open Datalink Interface* (ODI) is a flexible mechanism to write network card drivers so that multiple protocol stacks can be associated with an NIC.

Simple Network Management Protocol (SNMP) is a popular network management protocol for TCP/IP-based networks. SNMP agents can run on NetWare servers and report information on configuration and status of nodes. The information available is a set of managed objects referred to as a *Management Information Base* (MIB). SNMP clients such as TCPCON.NLM can access TCP/IP protocol stack managed objects.

The SNMPLOG.NLM processes SNMP trap messages and logs them in to a file in SYS:ETC/SNMP$LOG.BIN.

The TCPLOG.NLM presents a menu-driven interface that enables you to use SNMP to access TCP/IP MIB locally or from a remote node. It also allows access to the SNMP log file.

3

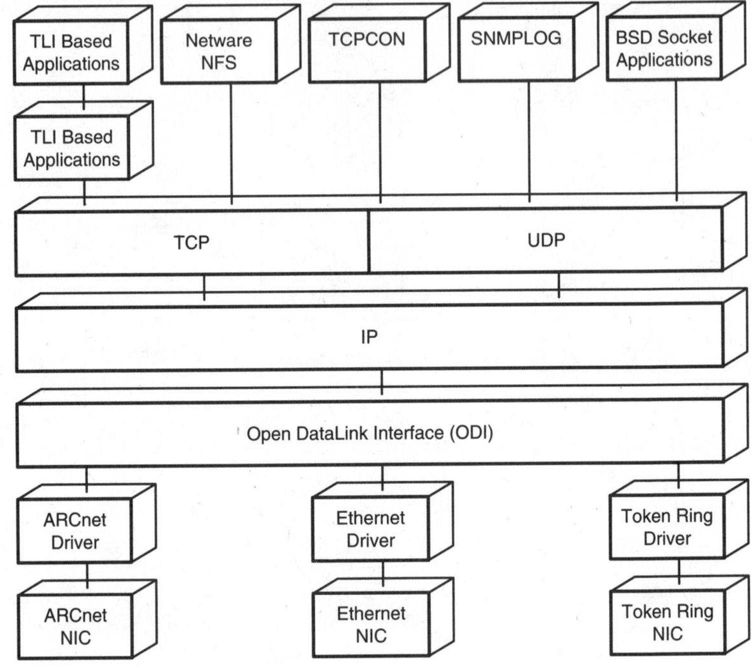

Figure 3.40
The NetWare TCP/IP architecture.

Configuring NetWare 3.*x* as an IP Router

Novell has added a mechanism for adding new protocol support in the NetWare 3.*x* network operating system. This mechanism is the *NetWare Loadable Module* (NLM) architecture. NLMs are software engines or tasks that can be dynamically loaded and unloaded from the server console. The TCP/IP protocols are implemented as an NLM (TCPIP.NLM) in NetWare 3.11 and beyond.

To load TCP/IP on the NetWare 3.11 server, enter the following command at the server console:

```
LOAD TCPIP
```

Protocol dependencies are built into TCPIP.NLM so that any NLM that it requires that is not loaded in server memory is automatically loaded. The TCPIP.NLM requires that STREAMS, CLIB, and SNMP.NLMs be loaded first. If these NLMs are not loaded, loading TCPIP.NLM results in an automatic load of these NLMs.

The LOAD TCPIP command has a number of interesting options. The general syntax is the following:

```
LOAD TCPIP [FORWARD = {YES¦NO}] [RIP={YES¦NO}] [TRAP=IP_ADDR]
```

The FORWARD parameter is used to turn the NetWare 3.11 server into an IP router. Use this parameter to connect two or more IP networks. The default value is NO.

The RIP parameter is used to enable or disable the IP routing information protocol. This RIP protocol is different from that used by Novell.

When the RIP protocol is enabled, the RIP traffic is monitored and updates are made to an internal routing table. If FORWARD is set to YES, the router broadcasts RIP updates to other IP routers. If disabled, the router does not monitor RIP traffic. The default RIP value is YES.

The TRAP parameter is used to specify the IP address to which the server sends SNMP trap messages.

After the TCP/IP protocol is loaded, it must be bound or associated with a network card driver that will be used to access the TCP/IP network.

The BIND command is used to build the logical association between the TCP/IP stack and the driver. The following is an example list of commands necessary to complete this binding:

```
LOAD NE2000 INT=3 PORT=2E0 NAME=ENG_NIC FRAME=ETHERNET_II
LOAD TCPIP
BIND TCPIP TO ENG_NIC ADDR=10.1.1.5
```

The `ADDR=` parameter represents an IP address. IP addresses are 32 bits or four bytes long. The conventional way of representing IP addresses is to use the dotted decimal notation in which each number represents one of the four bytes that make up the IP address. These numbers are separated by the period (.) symbol.

The BIND command for IP has the following general syntax:

```
BIND IP TO boardName
[ADDR=ipAddress] [MASK=maskAddress]
[BCAST=bcastAddress] [GATE=gateAddress]
[DEFROUTE={YES¦NO}] [ARP={YES¦NO}]
[COST=numberOfHops] [POISON={YES¦NO}]
```

Table 3.10 describes the parameter values.

Table 3.10
BIND Parameters for IP Routing

Parameter	Description
ADDR	IP address assigned to NIC connected to this interface.
MASK	Subnet mask assigned to IP network.
BCAST	Default IP address to be used for broadcasting. If not specified, it is FF FF FF FF.
GATE	Default gateway on IP network. When not specified, routing is performed by using RIP.

continues

Table 3.10, Continued
BIND Parameters for IP Routing

Parameter	Description
DEFROUTE	If TCPIP was loaded with FORWARD=Yes, the node is to be used as a default gateway through RIP. Default value is No.
ARP	Used to determine whether the Address Resolution Protocol to map IP addresses to hardware addresses is used. Default value is Yes.
COST	Number of hops of cost assigned to this interface. Default cost is 1. Maximum is 15.
POISON	Used to control poisoned reverse for routing updates sent to this interface. The default value of No reduces IP traffic at a small cost to stability.

Integrating IPX and IP Networks

In this section, you examine different scenarios that show how IPX and IP networks can be integrated.

Scenario 1

Suppose that you have a single Ethernet network that contains the following setup:

- Several NetWare and UNIX clients
- NetWare 3.*x* server
- UNIX server

Figure 3.41 shows how these network elements can be integrated. Notice that because this network is an IP network and an IPX network, it must have unique IP and IPX network numbers. The IPX network number is 01700022, and the IP network number is 130.1.0.0. Each IP node must have a unique IP address. The NetWare server has a single Ethernet NIC interface shared by IPX and IP stacks. The NetWare 3.*x* AUTOEXEC.NCF file would contain commands similar to the following:

```
LOAD NE2000 PORT=300 INT=3 NAME=IPX_NETWORK
LOAD NE2000 PORT=300 INT=3 NAME=IP_NETWORK FRAME=ETHERNET_II
LOAD TCPIP
BIND IPX TO IPX_NETWORK NET=01700022
BIND TCPIP TO IP_NETWORK ADDR=130.1.0.0
```

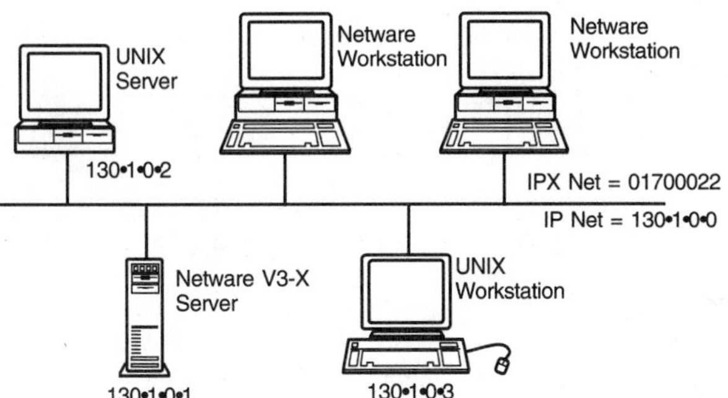

Figure 3.41
Single network with IPX and IP nodes.

Scenario 2

Suppose, for example, that you have an IPX Token Ring network connected to an IP Ethernet with a NetWare 3.*x* server with the following elements:

- Several NetWare and UNIX clients
- NetWare 3.*x* server used to connect the two networks
- UNIX server

Figure 3.42 shows how these network elements can be integrated. Notice that the separate IP and IPX networks have unique IP network and an IPX network numbers. The IPX network number is 01700022, and the IP network number is 130.1.0.0. Each IP node must have a unique IP address. The NetWare server has an Ethernet NIC interface and a Token Ring NIC. The NetWare 3.*x* AUTOEXEC.NCF file would contain commands similar to the following:

```
LOAD TOKEN NAME=IPX_NETWORK
BIND IPX TO IPX_NETWORK NET=01700022
LOAD NE2000 PORT=300 INT=3 NAME=IP_NETWORK FRAME=ETHERNET_II
LOAD TCPIP
BIND TCPIP TO IP_NETWORK ADDR=130.1.0.0
```

Note that NetWare 3.*x* acts as an IPX node and an IP node. It can be used to provide file services to both IPX and IP networks.

Scenario 3

For this scenario, suppose that you have an IPX Token Ring network connected to an IP Ethernet with a NetWare IP router. The network also has the following elements:

- Several NetWare and UNIX clients
- NetWare 3.*x* server used as a router
- UNIX servers

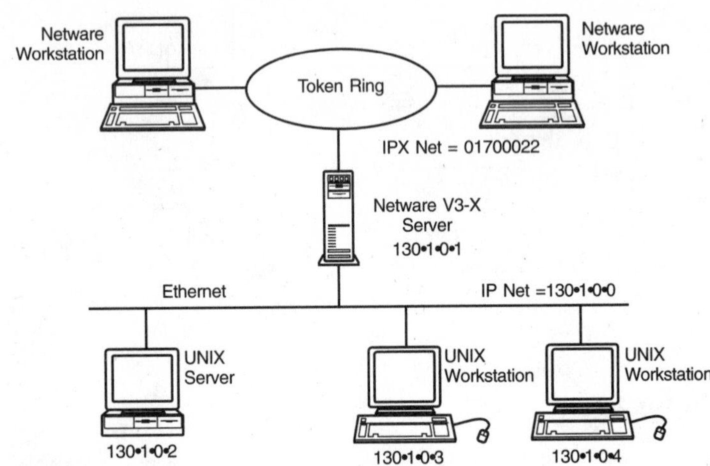

Figure 3.42
Separate IPX and IP networks.

Figure 3.43 shows how these network elements can be integrated.

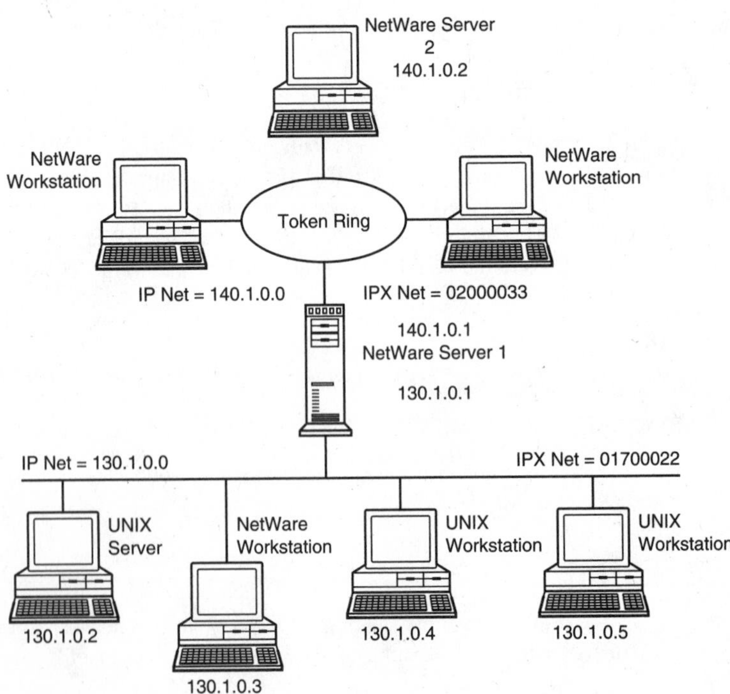

Figure 3.43
IPX Token Ring network connected to IP Ethernet with NetWare IP router.

Notice the two separate IP and IPX networks. Each of these networks must have unique IP network and IPX network numbers. The IPX network numbers are 01700022 and 02000033, and the IP network numbers are 130.1.0.0 and 140.1.0.0. The NetWare server has an Ethernet NIC interface and a Token

Ring NIC. Each NIC is shared by IPX and IP protocol stacks. The two NetWare 3.*x* servers' AUTOEXEC.NCF files contain commands similar to the following:

```
NetWare 3.x server 1

LOAD TOKEN NAME=IPX_TOKEN
LOAD TOKEN NAME=IP_TOKEN FRAME=TOKEN-RING_SNAP
LOAD NE2000 PORT=300 INT=3 NAME=IPX_ETHER
LOAD NE2000 PORT=300 INT=3 NAME=IP_ETHER FRAME=ETHERNET_II
BIND IPX TO IPX_TOKEN NET=02000033
BIND IPX TO IPX_ETHER NET=01700022
LOAD TCPIP FORWARD=YES
BIND IP TO IP_TOKEN ADDR=140.1.0.1
BIND IP TO IP_ETHER ADDR=130.1.0.1

NetWare 3.x server 2

LOAD TOKEN NAME=IPX_TOKEN
LOAD TOKEN NAME=IP_TOKEN FRAME=TOKEN-RING_SNAP
BIND IPX TO IPX_TOKEN NET=02000033
LOAD TCPIP
BIND IP TO IP_TOKEN ADDR=140.1.0.2
```

IP Tunneling

The IP tunnel LAN driver (IPTUNNEL NLM) can be run on a NetWare 3.*x* server that allows IPX packets to be encapsulated by UDP/IP packets for transmission across a potentially large IP network. IP tunneling allows IPX nodes to communicate with other IPX nodes by using an IP cloud (see fig. 3.44). The IP tunnel driver converts the IP cloud into a logical network interface so that IPX protocols can communicate with it as if it were another NIC driver.

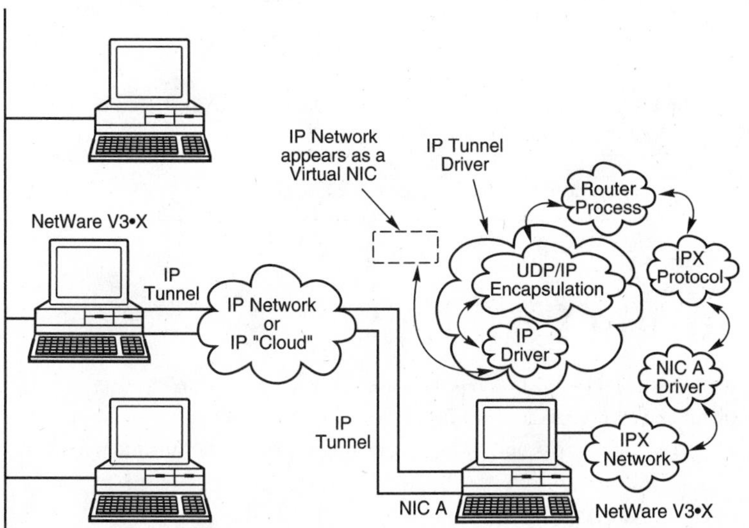

Figure 3.44
IP tunneling.

The IPX packet is encapsulated by a user datagram protocol packet and transported across the IP network. At the destination, the UDP header is stripped to recover the IPX packet. The UDP checksum is used to ensure data integrity of the IPX packet.

The NetWare 3.*x* IP tunnel driver can be used with SK-IPX/IP gateway from Schneider & Koch to connect NetWare 3.*x* nodes to NetWare 2.*x* nodes. It also works with IP tunnel client driver from LAN WorkPlace for DOS or the Schneider & Koch DOS end-node product.

To configure the NetWare 3.*x* server to use the IP tunnel, you must load it as a LAN driver. The TCPIP.NLM must be loaded prior to loading IPTUNNEL.NLM.

The LOAD IPTUNNEL command line has the following syntax:

```
LOAD IPTUNNEL [PEER=remoteIpAddr]
[CHKSUM={Yes¦NO}] [LOCAL=localIpAddr]
[PORT=udpPortNumber] [SHOW={YES¦NO}]
```

Table 3.11 summarizes the parameters.

Table 3.11
IPTUNNEL Parameters

Parameter	Description
PEER	Adds IP address to peer list. Peers are IPX routers to which NetWare RIP broadcast messages should be sent. IP networks have limited broadcast capabilities and, to avoid excessive traffic over a large IP network, the peer list is used.
CHKSUM	Enables UDP checksums. The default is to enable checksums.
LOCAL	Specifies a local IP address for the tunnel.
PORT	Specifies the UDP port number for the tunnel. Default value is 213, the officially assigned UDP port number for IPX packets.
SHOW	Requests a configuration report on the tunnel driver.

Avoiding Routing Problems

Novell reports that NetWare 2.*x*-based internal routers have some unique routing problems. You learn about some of these problems and how to avoid them in the following sections. You also learn about how NetWare 3.*x*-based routers avoid these problems by introducing the concept of the internal network number.

NetWare 2.*x* Routing Problems

Redundant paths often are used to improve the reliability of the network. In NetWare 2.*x*-based networks, these redundant paths can lead to inefficient routing.

Figure 3.45 shows a NetWare 2.*x*-based network on which the file servers FS_1 and FS_2 act as internal routers. The network contains a redundant path between the two servers. Consider what happens when workstation WS_B4 tries to attach to server FS_1. The shortest path to FS_1 is through segment B. But there is a good chance that the packets may go through router FS_2 onto segment A and reach FS_1 through NIC A on FS_1.

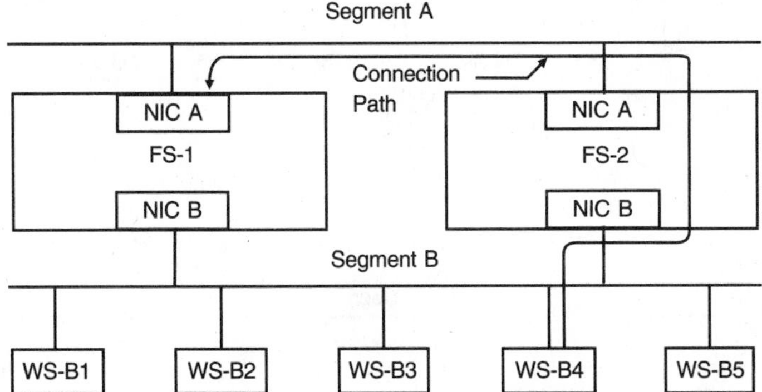

Figure 3.45
NetWare 2.x routing problem.

When the server advertises itself through service advertising protocol, the SAP packet must be encapsulated in an IPX packet for transmission. The network number and node address used in this IPX packet constitutes the internetwork address of the file service process. NetWare 2.*x* uses the internetwork address of NIC A in the file server for the file service process. Figure 3.46 shows the logical representation of this file service addressing. When the workstation on segment B seeks to connect to a file server FS_1, it wants to connect to the file service process whose internet work address is the same as NIC A. The file service process is logically on segment A. Figure 3.47 shows this logical positioning of the file service processes for FS_1 and FS_2.

When WS_B4 tries to make a connection to FS_1, it sends a RIP request for the fastest route to file service process FS_1. Two routers respond to this request: router FS_1 and router FS_2. Because they both report the same distance, as far as the workstation is concerned, they are both equally good paths. If FS_2 responds to the RIP request before FS_1, the workstation sends a create connection NCP request through FS_2. After a connection path is established by a workstation, it remains for the duration of the connection.

Solving NetWare 2.*x* Routing Problems

One way to solve the problem described in the preceding section is shown in figure 3.48. The workstations are connected to the same segment as the file server's NIC A if there are redundant paths.

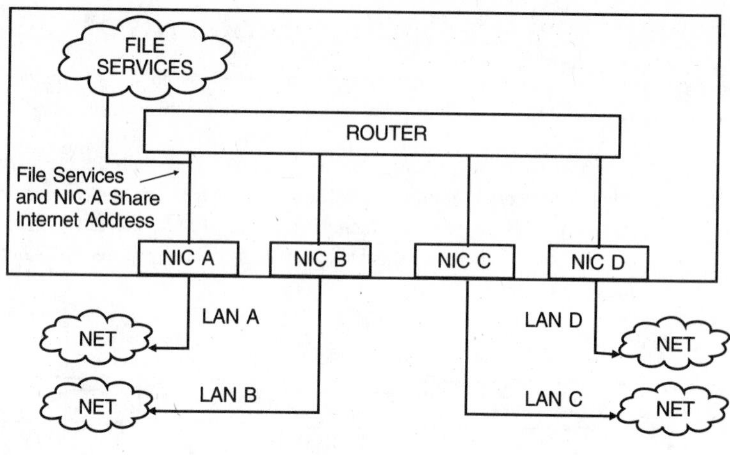

Figure 3.46
NetWare 2.x file services addressing.

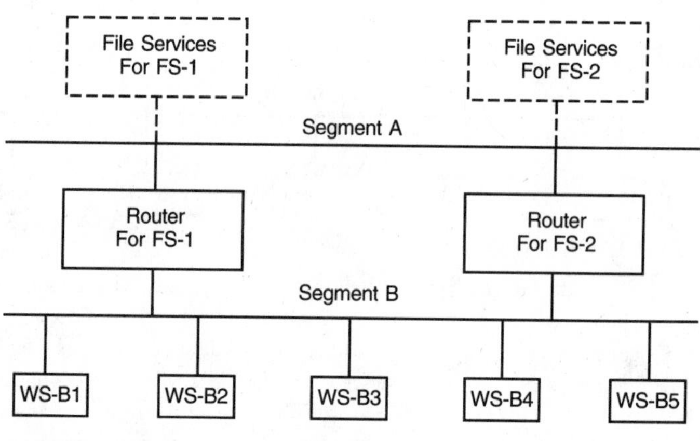

Figure 3.47
Logical positioning of file services.

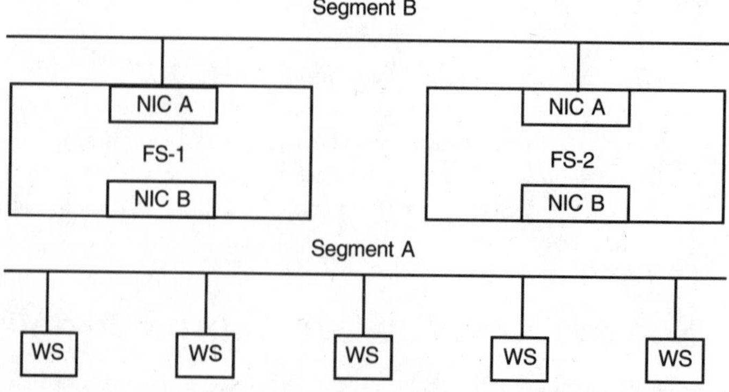

Figure 3.48
NetWare 2.x routing solution with stations connected to one segment.

The logical positioning of the file service processes for FS_1 and FS_2 is on the same segment as the workstations, and there is no need to go through a router to get to the file service process.

If workstations are connected to both segments, the solution in figure 3.49 can be used. Workstations that connect most often to FS_1 are on the same segment as FS_1's NIC A. Workstations that connect most often to FS_2 are on the same segment as FS_2's NIC A.

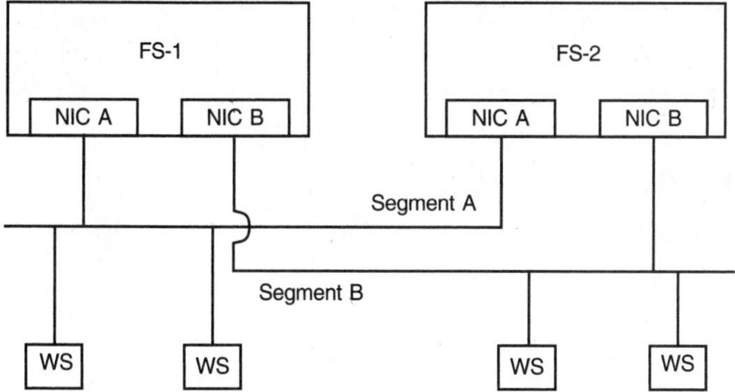

Figure 3.49
NetWare 2.x routing solution with stations connected to both segments.

Solving NetWare 3.*x* Routing Problems

NetWare 3.*x* avoids the NetWare 2.*x* routing problem by having a separate internetwork address for the file service process that is not tied to the internet address of LAN A or any other NIC in the server. Figure 3.50 shows the addressing for NetWare 3.*x*.

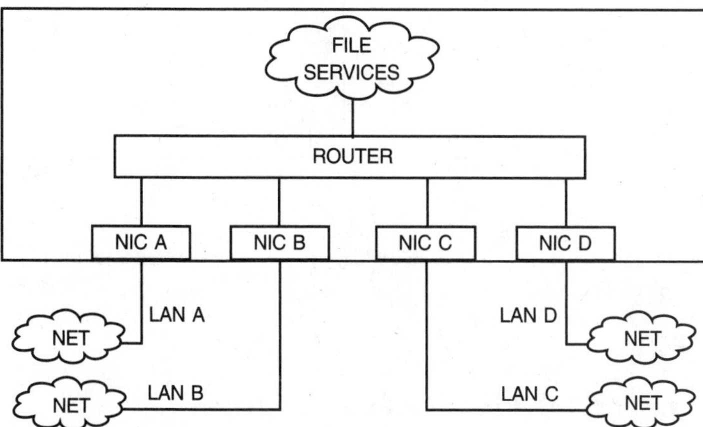

Figure 3.50
NetWare 3.x file services addressing.

The internetwork address of the file service process is referred to as the *internal network number* and is assigned during NetWare 3.*x* installation. This internal network number must be distinct from all other internal network numbers and network numbers on the internet.

Understanding Router Efficiency

Novell has performed a number of studies measuring performance of internal and external routers. These studies are a great help in designing optimal router configurations. The tests were done with NE2000 and NE1000 NICs on AT 286 and Compaq 386 25 MHz machines. Although the tests were done for SFT NetWare 2.15 and NetWare 386 3.0 and are, therefore, somewhat dated, the trend they represent can be extrapolated for NetWare 2.*x* and NetWare 3.*x*.

Throughput of Internal Routers

Figure 3.51 shows throughput for internal routers set up in the following configurations:

- No router
- Busy and non-busy SFT NetWare 2.15
- Busy and non-busy NetWare 3.0

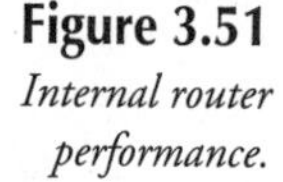

Figure 3.51
Internal router performance.

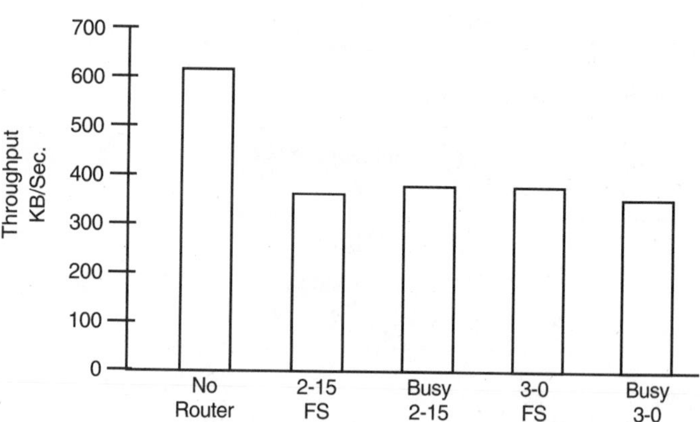

The tests show that a substantial performance drop occurs when a packet goes through a router. This drop can be as much as 41 percent compared to the no router test. Another interesting point is that SFT NetWare 2.15 and NetWare 3.0 routers have comparable performance.

Throughput of External Dedicated Routers

The test performed consisted of adding from one to six routers in series and testing the throughput of the system as each router was added. Figure 3.52 shows the performance degradation curve that was measured.

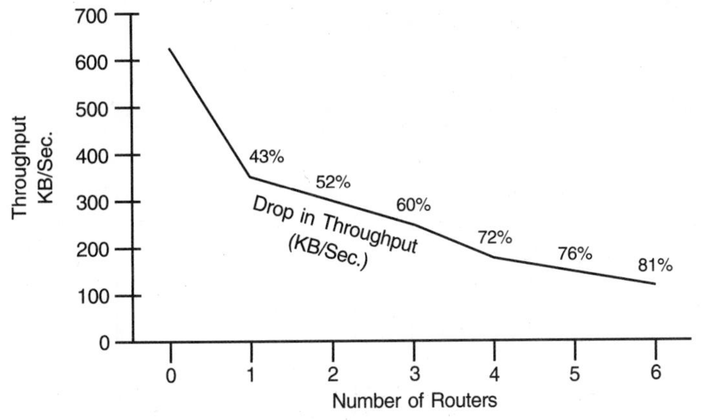

Figure 3.52
Multiple router performance.

The performance drop after going through one router was 43 percent. After that, a four- to eight-percent drop occurred for every router added. With six routers in the series, the performance drop was 81 percent. The effective bandwidth of the network was only 19 percent of the bandwidth available on a network without routers.

Throughput of External Nondedicated Routers

The test for external dedicated routers was repeated for nondedicated routers. The nondedicated routers performed some background processing to simulate their typical use. After going through only one router, the performance dropped by 60 percent. And after two routers, it dropped to 67 percent (see fig. 3.53).

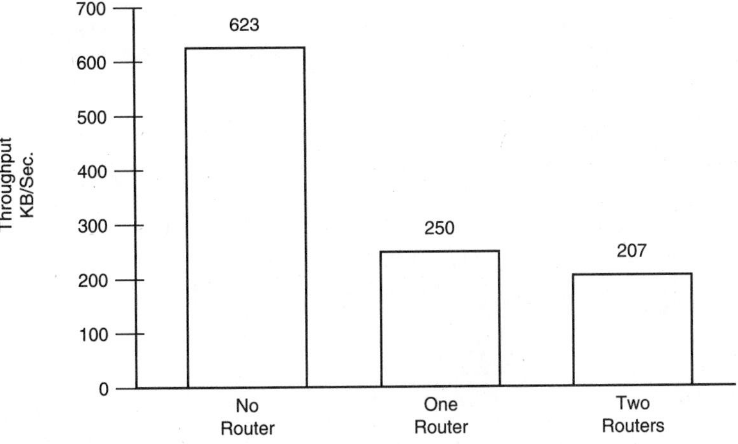

Figure 3.53
Throughput drop of external nondedicated routers.

These results point out that the nondedicated router configuration is the slowest of the router configurations. Figure 3.54 compares the performance of dedicated and nondedicated external routers. These results underscore the author's opinion that nondedicated router configurations should be avoided.

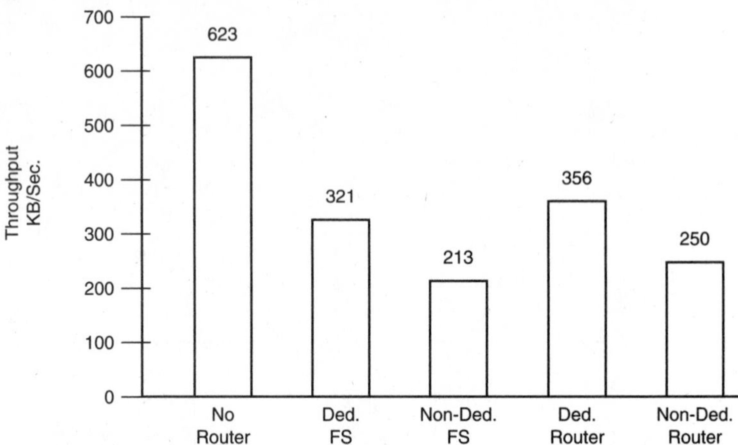

Figure 3.54
Performance of dedicated and nondedicated external routers.

NetWare Multiprotocol Router

For those who want support for routing of protocols other than IPX, there is the multiprotocol router. This NLM runs on a NetWare server and performs routing for OSI, AppleTalk, NetBIOS, IPX, and TCP/IP. When used in conjunction with WAN Links, it can provide routing over wide-area links. Routers from vendors such as Cisco perform similar functionality but at a higher performance and cost. The NetWare Multiprotocol router, on the other hand, can provide routing for small networks at a much lower cost.

In addition to routing, the Multiprotocol router provides Telnet, X-Windows, SNMP, and *Point-to-Point Protocol* (PPP) support. The Telnet service is particularly valuable because it allows stations running a Telnet client session to log in remotely to the router and perform basic administration functions. X-Windows support allows the router to be managed by UNIX workstations running X-Windows and TCP/IP protocols. The PPP capability permits point-to-point connection with other routers, such as Cisco routers, that support this protocol.

The network management station can be Novell's Network Services Manager for Windows and for third-party network management stations such as SUN's SunNet Manager, Hewlett-Packard's OpenView, and IBM's NetView 6000.

The router runs a SAP filter that can be used to limit the number of times SAP broadcasts are made on a wide-area link. Without this filter, the frequent SAP broadcasts done to advertise networks consume the already limited bandwidth of many wide-area links.

WAN Links can be run with multiport serial boards, and a WANIS interface is defined that can enable third-party manufacturers to support WAN Links. WANIS extends Novell's ODI to the WAN environment.

The multiprotocol router includes NetWare Hub Services. This is a monitoring and management system for hubs that can run on a NetWare platform. These hubs, installed in PC workstations, allow the PC to be controlled by the NetWare hub services.

Hardware-Based Routers

Although internal routers based on NetWare and the NetWare multiprotocol router can be used for most networks, they are not designed to handle heavy traffic loads. For handling heavy traffic loads, special computers designed for routing functions are used. Besides handling heavy loads, these computers can be used for routing almost any industry-standard protocol. These hardware-based routers are made by a number of companies such as Cisco, Wellfleet, Proteon, Digital, Timeplex, and Advanced Computer Communications.

The hardware-based routers use a multiprocess architecture and proprietary high-speed buses to facilitate high-speed routing. The diagram in figure 3.55 models the general architecture for most hardware-based routers.

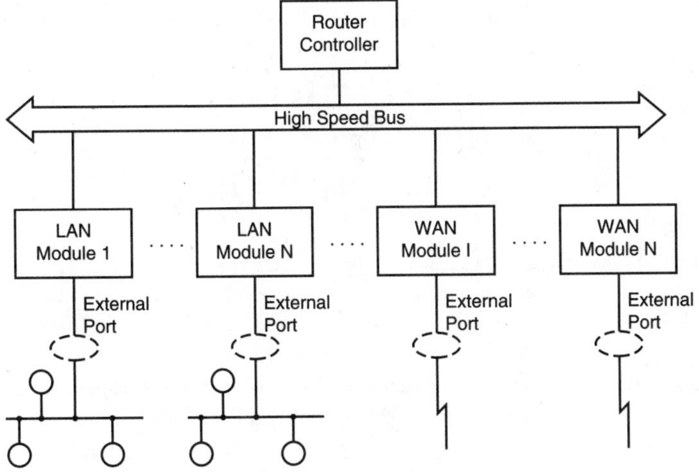

Figure 3.55 *Model for high-speed routers.*

The router architecture is modular and allows for network hardware modules to be installed in bus slots. Addition of each of these modules gives the router the capability to connect to a specific type of network. These network modules can be designed for LANs and WANs. Each network module is designed for a specific type of network. To connect to an Ethernet network, for example, an Ethernet network module needs to be installed. To connect the Ethernet network to an FDDI network, an Ethernet and an FDDI module need to be installed. The router controller in figure 3.55 is usually implemented on the router's motherboard.

Routers can be purchased with standard network module configurations. Popular choices are Ethernet and Token Ring for LAN modules, and T1, leased-line, or dial-up lines for WAN modules. These routers permit multiple links to a network. The secondary links can be used as a backup and, in some routers, also can be used for *load balancing*—when traffic is diverted equally among the links to achieve a higher sustained throughput. This feature is particularly valuable for point-to-point wide-area links, as shown in figure 3.56.

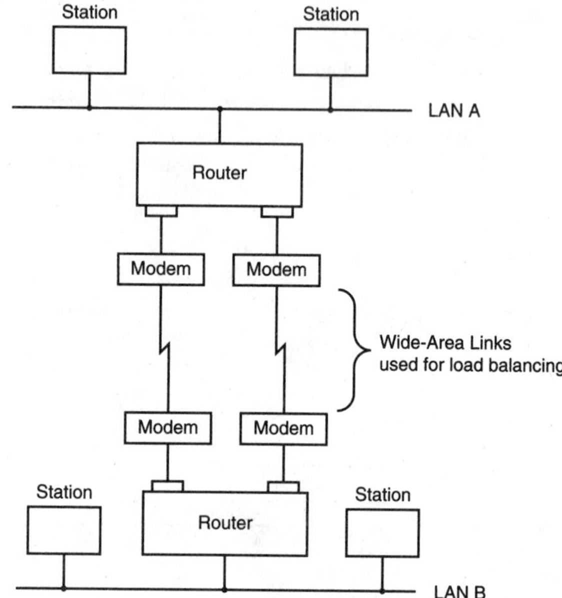

Figure 3.56
Load balancing on wide-area links.

Some hardware-based routers can be booted from a special floppy disk that contains the routing software. The advantage of this is that the routing logic can be easily updated when bug fixes and new features need to be released. An example of this kind of router is ACS 4200 from Advanced Computer Communications. Many of the routers available today also can be configured to act as bridges. As mentioned earlier in this chapter, these routers are called *brouters*. The bridge operation is particularly useful for protocols such as *NetBIOS Extended User Interface* (NetBEUI) and LAT that are not routable because they do not have a network layer.

Routers can be configured through a local terminal attached to an RS-232 port on the router box. If a dumb terminal is not available, a computer running terminal emulation software such as PROCOMM or SmartCom can be used. Some of the high-end routers also provide TELNET server services. This means that any computer running TELNET client services can log in remotely to the router and configure the router. Figure 3.57 shows the variety of configuration options.

The router configuration is typically done through a command-line or menu-driven interface. The TimeLan 100 router, for instance, has a menu-driven interface. Many of the Wellfleet and ACC routers have a command-line interface.

The router must be configured for each protocol it needs to route. An example of the configuration commands needed for the IP network routing in figure 3.58 is shown next. The example commands are shown for the ACS 4200 router connecting two LANs over a wide-area link. Other routers have similar commands. The syntax details are different, but the semantics are very similar.

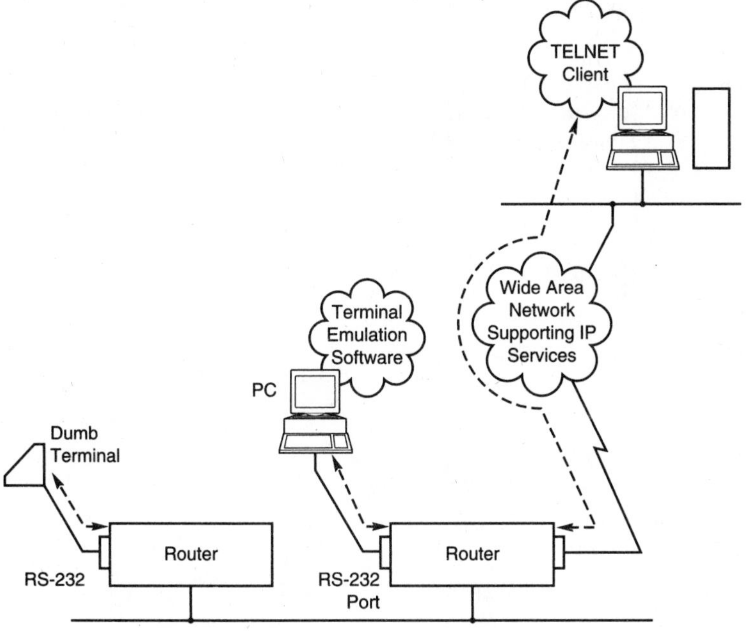

Figure 3.57
Router configuration options.

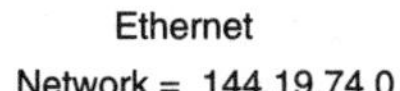

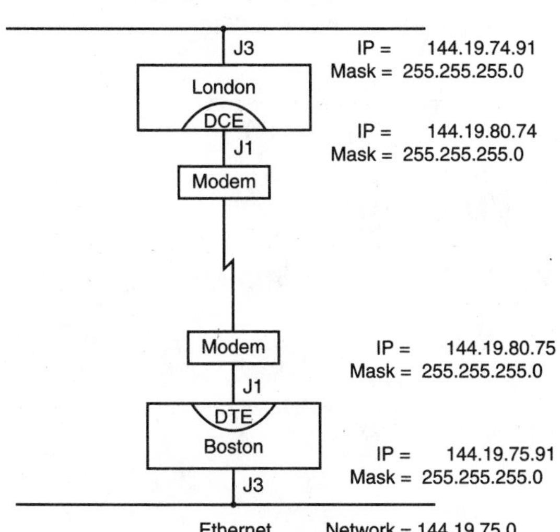

Figure 3.58
Simple IP routing example.

Configuration for the London router is as follows:

```
login netman            # Login to the router
set prompt to london    # For descriptive purpose only
add ip network entry 144.19.74.91 255.255.255.0 j3
add ip network entry 144.19.80.74 255.255.255.0 j1
# The above commands assign IP address and subnet masks
# to the router's J3 and J1 ports.

set rip protocol on
# This activates the IP RIP protocol. Other choices

add ip network entry 144.19.75.91 255.255.255.0 j3
add ip network entry 144.19.80.75 255.255.255.0 j1
# The above commands assign IP address and subnet masks
# to the router's J3 and J1 ports.

set rip protocol on
# This activates the IP RIP protocol. Other choices
# are OSPF and so on

delete ip route entry 144.19.74.0
# This command deletes any routing table entry for the
# network 144.19.74.0

add ip route entry 144.19.74.0 255.255.255.0 144.19.80.74 1
# This command adds an entry to the routing table that
# says that network 144.19.74.0 can be reached by sending
# IP traffic to port 144.19.80.74. The network is 1 hop
# away.

reset                   # This makes the change permanent
```

Understanding NetWare Link Service Protocol

NetWare Link Service Protocol (NLSP) is a link state protocol designed to overcome the limitations of *distance-vector* based protocols such as RIP and SAP. Before discussing the NLSP protocol, it is useful to examine some of the limitations of RIP and SAP, and why Novell has a new protocol to accomplish routing and service advertising.

RIP Problems

The RIP (Routing Information Protocol) is used by NetWare servers and clients to find the best route to a given destination. One problem of RIP is that it takes a longer time to stabilize compared to link state protocols. The technical description of this problem is that RIP has a slower convergence.

IPX routers exchange routing information using RIP at periodic intervals (60 seconds). The RIP message contains a list of all routes known to that router. In other words, each RIP message contains the entire routing table of the router. For large networks, the routing table tends to be large, and the RIP messages are proportionately large. A router, upon receiving a RIP message from its neighbor, recomputes the routes in its table based on the new information and sends the recomputed routing table on its next broadcast interval. It may take several broadcast intervals before the routers have a consistent view of the network. This problem is known as *slow convergence.* In addition to slow convergence, RIP has no authentication mechanism to prevent an intruder from broadcasting an incorrect RIP message. Other known problems that plague distance-vector based methods are *count-to-infinity* problems and lack of capability to set up *routing domains* so that routing in a designated area or domain can be done without impacting other areas of the network.

The count-to-infinity problem is a classic problem associated with distance-vector schemes. This problem arises when a router (router A) sends recomputed information about a route to a router (router B) from which it originally received the information (see fig. 3.59). If a link connected to router A is broken, router A waits for its next broadcast interval to send information about unreachable destinations to its neighbor. Meanwhile, router B, not knowing about unreachable destinations, sends its routing table to router A before router A can send its broadcast. This routing table contains old information about the status of the links including the link that is down. Router A thinks that the unreachable destinations are reachable through router B and updates its table with incorrect information. Because router B is a neighbor, router A adds its distance from router B to the route path information received from router A. When router A broadcasts its incorrect routing table to B, router B adds its distance from router A to reach destinations through A. At each broadcast interval the distance-metric to reach the unreachable destinations grows until it reaches a value assumed to be infinity. In RIP, this value is 16 hops.

One solution to the count-to-infinity problem of RIP *is split-horizon,* and another is *triggered update.* In split-horizon, you do not report information about destinations from routers from which you originally received the information. In triggered updates, changed information is sent immediately without waiting for the next broadcast interval.

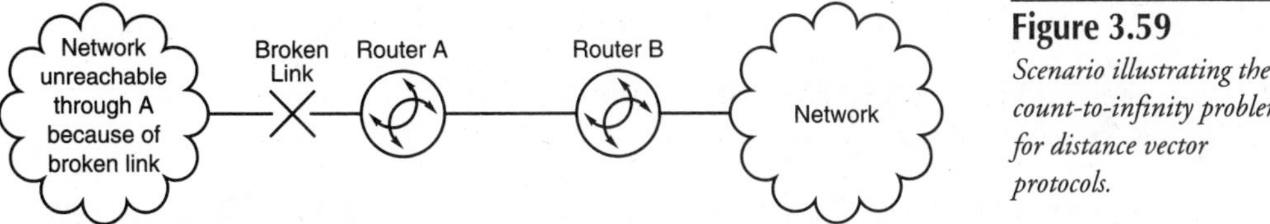

Figure 3.59
Scenario illustrating the count-to-infinity problem for distance vector protocols.

Both RIP and SAP messages can consume a substantial fraction of the network bandwidth. In SAP, the server advertises the name of a service at periodic intervals of 60 seconds, and this too has the characteristics of a distance vector protocol. The destinations in the SAP protocol are the text strings that represent the name of advertised services. Both SAP and RIP are expensive in terms of the bandwidth they consume. In a LAN, the bandwidth used by SAP and RIP broadcasts is not significant, but it is significant on the slower WAN links. In NetWare 4.*x,* the periodicity of broadcasts can be customized to reduce the bandwidth requirements, but in general a better protocol is needed. For all the previously mentioned reasons, Novell created NLSP.

NLSP Messages

NLSP is designed to provide exchange of routing information between routers, and the building of a routing table at each router that has a global view of the network. It also can be used as a replacement for SAP. To provide backwards compatibility, it can co-exist and interoperate with existing RIP/SAP based networks. NLSP also can be expanded to provide hierarchical or *area* routing (discussed earlier in this chapter). Areas are defined using a *<network number, network mask>* pair. The network number and network mask are each four bytes long. The network mask is used to define the area to which a router belongs. It also can be used for specifying multicast broadcasts for WAN networks.

Novell's NLSP implementation is based on ISO's IS-IS standard. Novell chose to create their own protocol rather than adopt ISO's IS-IS to have greater flexibility for enhancing the protocol for NetWare-based networks. The IS-IS standard has been completed, and it is difficult to affect and influence changes on an international standard. The NLSP protocol has the following three types of messages:

- Hello
- LSP
- SNP

The NLSP Hello messages are used by NLSP routers to verify the up/down status of a router's link to its neighbor.

The *Link State Protocol* (LSP) message is used to broadcast the identity of the router and the status of the links connected from it to the router's neighbors. The LSP lists link state information used to reach the router's neighbors. On a LAN that has several routers directly connected to it, the link state information reported by any router about the neighbor routers connected to the LAN are very similar. It, therefore, makes sense to have only one router, called the *Designated Router* (DR), send link state information rather than have all routers connected to the LAN send link state messages. In general, if *N* routers are on a LAN and each router sends link state messages, there would be *N***N* messages on the LAN. Using a designated router, the LAN can be treated as a logical or pseudo-node on a network consisting of many LANs and WAN links. The designated router can be selected based on a priority assigned to each router. This priority can be adjusted to influence the selection of a designated router. Assigning priorities to the DR is one improvement of NLSP over IS-IS.

The LSP messages are used to compute the best route to a destination using Edsgar Djikstra's *Shortest Path First* (SPF) algorithm. The SPF algorithm is noteworthy because of the optimal route paths it yields for any router. It is run whenever the link state information for a router changes, and is described next.

Computation of the Forwarding Database in NLSP

NLSP uses Djikstra's Shortest Path First algorithm to compute the forwarding database for a router. To compute the shortest path from router R, perform the following steps:

1. Place router R at the root of a tree and label it R(0). The number in parentheses represents the route path cost, which is 0 for router R to reach itself.

2. For any new router, N, placed in the tree, examine the LSP messages. If for any neighbor X of N, the path from R to X through N is the best path so far to the neighbor X, put the router X on the tree with the label X (cost to N + cost from N to X).

3. If alternative paths exist to a node X from router R, use the path with the least cost.

An example can clarify the previously stated rules for computing the routing table (also called forwarding database) based on the SPF algorithm. In figure 3.60 it is required to compute the best routes from router B. The nodes in this figure represent routers, and the numbers on the arcs represent route path cost of the links. Therefore the cost of reaching nodes C, G, and A from B are 2, 3, and 5, respectively.

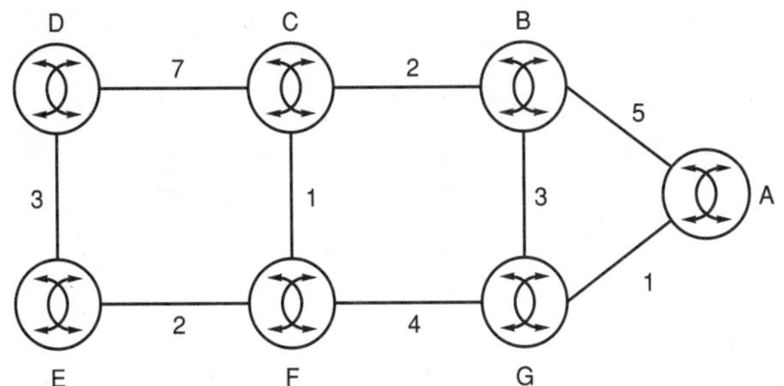

Figure 3.60
Example network used to show the SPF algorithm.

In figure 3.61, node C is placed at the root of the tree, and the neighbor nodes reachable through C are placed next to it (see fig. 3.62). Each node is shown with the route path cost to reach it in parenthesis.

In figure 3.62, nodes D and F as neighbors of node C are placed on the tree with costs to reach them from the root node B. The costs to D and F are computed as follows:

Cost to D = Cost to C + Cost from C to D = 2 + 7 = 9

Cost to F = Cost to C + Cost from C to F = 2 + 1 = 3

In figure 3.63, nodes F and A are shown reachable from node G. The costs to F and A are computed as follows:

Cost to F = Cost to G + Cost from G to F = 3 + 4 = 7

Cost to A = Cost to G + Cost from G to A = 3 + 1 = 4

The cost to F is 7 and is *greater* than the previously computed cost of 3 through node C, and therefore node F(7) is deleted from the tree. The cost to node A is 4, and this is *less* than the previously computed cost of 5 through node B. The previous node A(5) is therefore deleted from the tree.

In figure 3.64, nodes E and G are shown reachable from node F. The costs to E and G are computed as follows:

Cost to E = Cost to F + Cost from F to E = 3 + 2 = 5

Cost to G = Cost to F + Cost from F to G = 3 + 4 = 7

The cost to G is 7 and is *greater* than the previously computed cost of 3 from node B, and therefore node G(7) is deleted from the tree.

In figure 3.65, node D is shown reachable from node E. The cost to D is computed as follows:

Cost to D = Cost to E + Cost from E to D = 5 + 3 = 8

The cost to D is 8 and is *less* than the previously computed cost of 9 from node B, and therefore node D(9) is deleted from the tree and is replaced with node D(8) under E(5).

The SPF algorithm yields the tree shown in figure 3.66, from which the forwarding database from C is computed as shown in table 3.12.

Table 3.12
Forwarding Database of Router B

Destination	Forwarding Router	Cost
A	G	4
B	Not Applicable (Self)	0
C	C	2
D	C	8
E	C	5
F	C	3

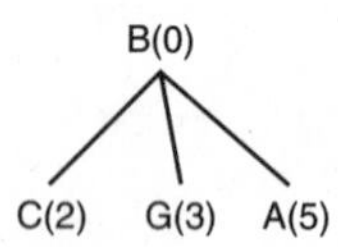

Figure 3.61
SPF Algorithm: Cost to reach immediate neighbors of B.

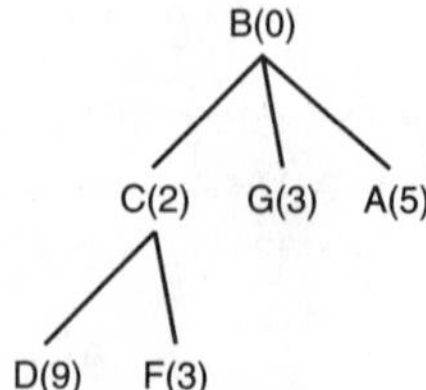

Figure 3.62
SPF Algorithm: Cost to reach immediate neighbors of C.

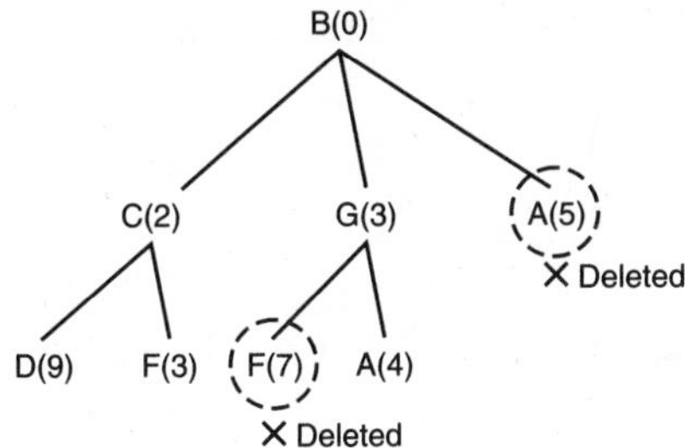

Figure 3.63
SPF Algorithm: Cost to reach immediate neighbors of G.

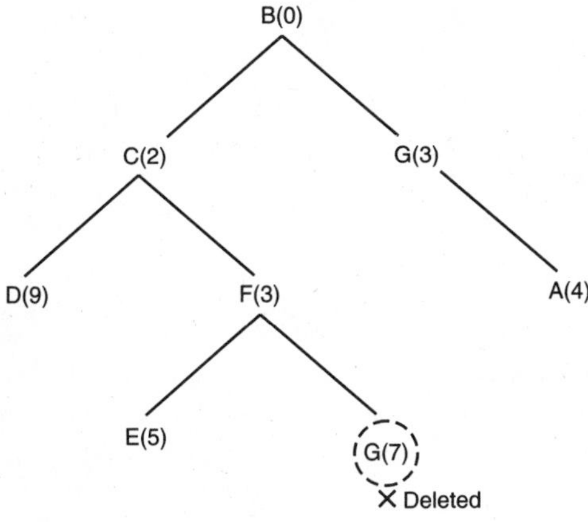

Figure 3.64
SPF Algorithm: Cost to reach immediate neighbors of F.

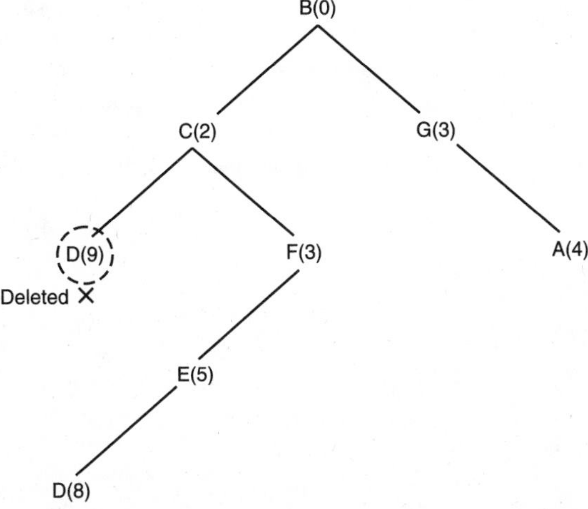

Figure 3.65
SPF Algorithm: Cost to reach immediate neighbors of E.

3

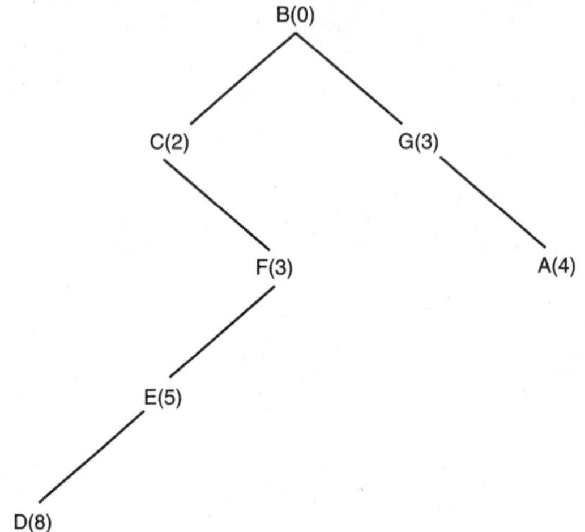

Figure 3.66
SPF Algorithm: Optimal path to reach nodes from B.

Use of SNP in NLSP

The *Sequence Number Packet* (SNP) summarizes the information in the LSP database. Instead of sending the complete LSP database information, a summary of information about the LSP database is sent. The two types of SNP messages are partial and complete. *Partial SNP* (PSNP) messages are used to acknowledge specific LSP messages and *Complete SNMP* (CSNP) messages summarize LSPs in a specified range. An example of PSNP usage is in a point-to-point link to acknowledge one or more LSP messages. For a LAN, the designated router can use CSNP to summarize the LSP database. If the CSNP indicates a discrepancy, you can request the missing information using PSNP.

LSP messages can contain SAP information. The router closest to the service can place SAP information in the LSP message. The SAP information need not be transmitted periodically, and only one router transmits it. The link state protocol ensures that only changes in link state and service information are sent, and there is no need for periodic broadcasts. As a precaution, NLSP forces a broadcast of service and link state information every two hours just in case of unforeseen problems caused by previous link state information being lost.

Migrating to NLSP

To support existing RIP/SAP based networks, the NLSP can run on a router (or NetWare server acting as router) at the boundary between an NLSP routing domain and an RIP/SAP domain (see fig. 3.67). The routing information and service information acquired by the NLSP router can be translated into RIP/SAP information for networks based on these protocols.

NLSP software is available for NetWare 3.11 and higher. If you are using a router built using ROUTEGEN, you may consider upgrading to the NetWare Multiprotocol Router that has NLSP support.

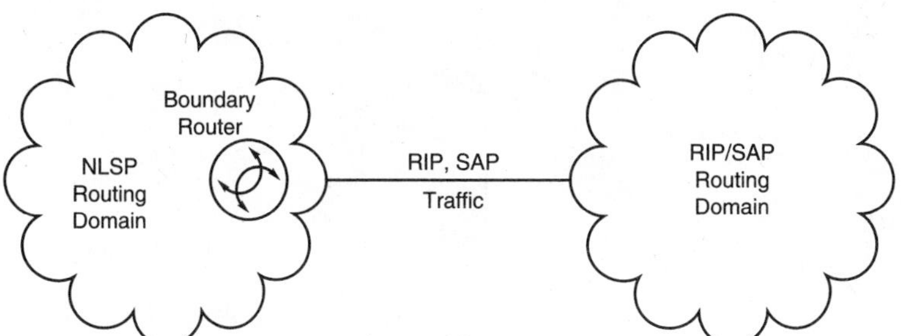

Figure 3.67
Coexistence of NLSP and RIP/SAP.

When converting from RIP to NLSP, you can convert gradually. If you convert WAN links to use NLSP, you see an immediate reduction in network bandwidth used by routing messages.

It is difficult to define an exact procedure for migrating to NLSP. The optimum strategy depends on the network topology, the speed at which you want to make the conversion, and the resources you have for troubleshooting problems that may arise because of the conversion. A general strategy for performing the conversion is outlined next.

The general strategy for converting to NLSP should be to convert the core of the WAN links to use NLSP for routing messages. *Campuses* (areas) that have LANs joining the core WAN infrastructure can continue using RIP when the WAN links are converted to using NLSP. You can then, gradually, convert routers in each campus area to use NLSP.

Assign addresses so that the campuses can be treated as a single area or multiple areas. Initially, you may not use hierarchical routing, but if you select your network addresses wisely, you can create areas and domains by changing only the network masks for a network address.

If your network topology contains loops, convert all the routers within the loop to use NLSP at the same time to avoid convergence problems associated with RIP and to reduce the network bandwidth used by RIP routing messages.

Mesh Networks and NLSP

Mesh networks allow for the most flexible network topology (see fig. 3.68) because they are characterized by redundant paths to reach a destination. Because of the redundant links, mesh networks lead to a more reliable design. However, if SAP and RIP are used in mesh networks, the broadcast traffic generated by these protocols can quickly overwhelm the network. For this reason, a collapsed backbone or tree configuration (see figs. 3.69 and 3.70) is often preferred to RIP/SAP-based NetWare networks.

NLSP makes use of mesh networks in NetWare-based networks more practical because NLSP does not rely on excessive use of broadcasts for its operation. NLSP reacts quickly to changes in the status of links in a mesh network.

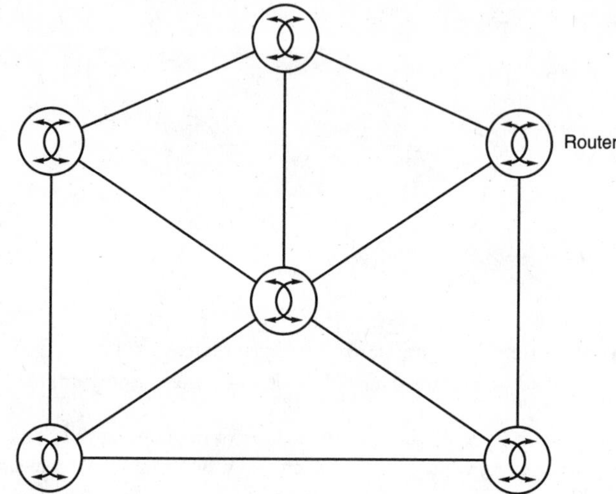

Figure 3.68
Mesh networks.

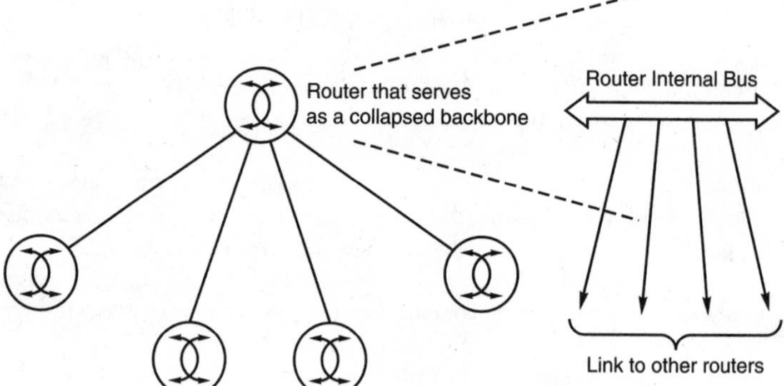

Figure 3.69
Collapsed backbone networks.

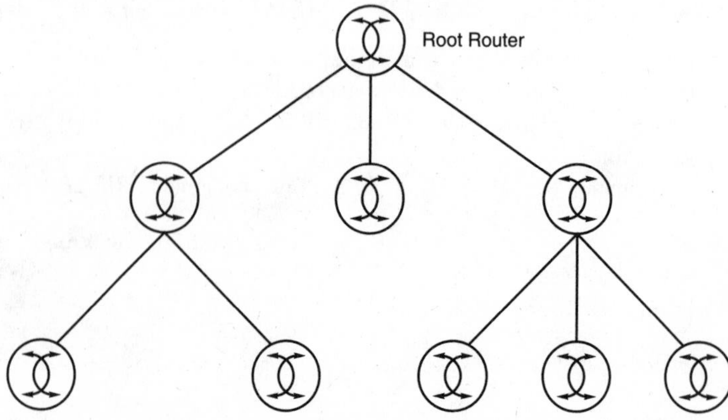

Figure 3.70
Tree configuration.

Hierarchical Routing in NLSP

NLSP can be used to organize networks into hierarchical routing domains. Several networks can be connected by routers to form a *routing area.* Routers connecting networks within a routing area are called Level 1 routers. Routing areas can be connected together to form a *routing domain* (see fig. 3.71). The routers connecting routing areas within a routing domain are called Level 2 routers. A routing domain is generally administered by a single network administration authority, such as the MIS department or *Network Operations Center* (NOC) for an organization, or a public carrier. Routing domains administered by different organizations can be connected using Level 3 routers. Figure 3.71 shows the different levels of routers.

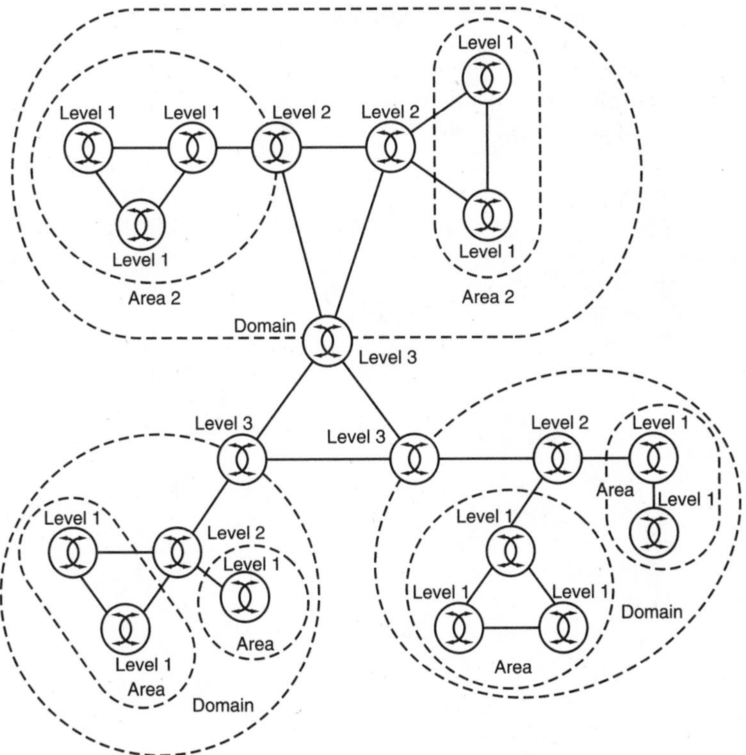

Figure 3.71
Hierarchical routing in NLSP.

Level 2 routers also act as a Level 1 area routers within their own areas. Also, a Level 3 router acts as Level 2 router within its domain. Use of Level 2 routers reduces the amount of information that routers at each level need to know and process, and leads to improvements in the efficiency of the routing mechanism. For instance, Level 1 routers need to store link state information in their areas only. They do not need to be aware of link state information for routers in other areas. To send traffic to other areas, a Level 1 router needs to know its nearest Level 2 router. Level 2 routers need to advertise the area addresses of the areas within their domains only. Similarly, Level 3 routers need to advertise addresses of their domains only.

3

Managing Addresses for Hierarchical Routing Using NLSP

IPX uses a 32-bit address for each LAN segment. Additionally, NetWare 3.*x* and NetWare 4.*x* servers have unique internal network numbers. Routing areas and domains can be defined by network addresses and 32-bit network masks.

Consider a routing area that has a network address of D1127000 and a network mask of FFFFF000. Each F (hex) in the network mask represents a bit pattern of four 1s (1111). The network mask has the following meaning:

- A grouping of 1s in the network mask represents corresponding bits in the network address that refer to the network address of that area or domain.
- A grouping of 0s in the network mask represents corresponding bits in the network address that must be assigned to network segments within areas (or domains).

Thus a network mask of FFFFF000 applied to an area with a network address of D1127000 means that the address prefix D1127 is common to all network segments within the area. Each network segment within the area must have a network address unique in the last three hexadecimal digits (because of three zero hexadecimal digits in the network mask). Figure 3.72 shows examples of such network segments. With three hexadecimal digits assigned to a network segment in an area, 12-bit combinations can be assigned to network segments. This works out to be 4,096 network segments.

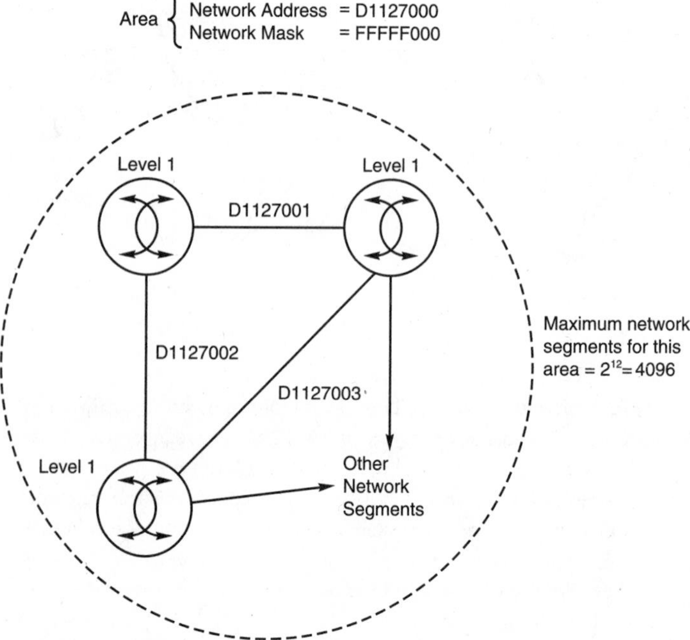

Figure 3.72
Example of network masks and network addresses for areas.

The network mask should be selected to allow for growth in the network segments or segment areas.

Consider an example of hierarchical routing that uses Level 3 routers (routing between domains). A domain with a network address of E3324600 and an associated network mask of FFFFFF00 means that all areas within the domain must have E33246 as their address prefix. Because a group of 24 1-bits is in the network mask, the first 24 bits of the address (E33246) must be common. The last two hexadecimal digits (8-bits) must be assigned to areas and network segments within an area. This enables you to have 256 network segments in each domain. Level 2 routers that connect areas in the domain must have an appropriate network mask set to indicate which of the remaining bits in the network address are used to indicate areas and network segments. If Level 2 routers use a mask of FFFFFFF0, a four-bit number can be assigned to areas—that is, there can be 16 areas, and each area can have 16 network segments (see fig. 3.73).

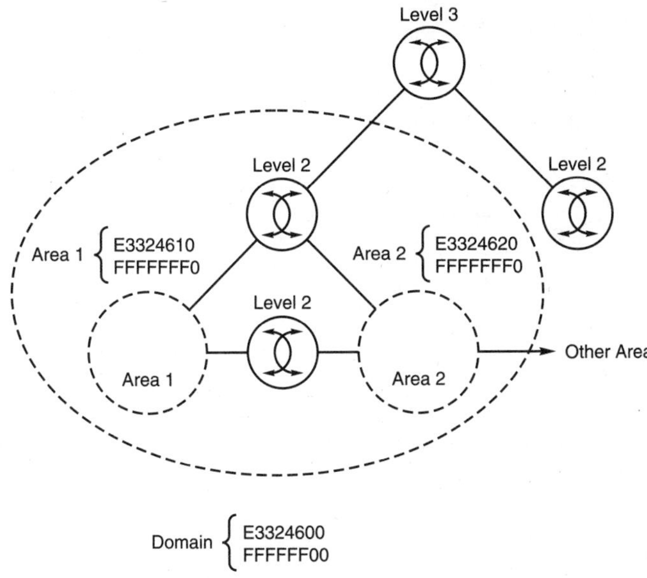

Figure 3.73
Example of network masks and network addresses for domains.

The number of bits you assign for domains, areas, and network segments depends on network growth considerations and the number of domains, areas, or network segments that you plan on having in your network. In the preceding example, if you plan to have up to 20 network segments within an area, you can assign five bits (32 network segments) for the network segments, and the remaining three bits for the area. This enables you to have eight areas within the domain, and 32 network segments within the area, making a maximum of 256 network segments within a domain.

Assigning addresses in a hierarchical manner, as described in the earlier examples, makes *inter-domain routing* (also called *cross-domain routing*) more efficient because of the following reasons:

- Level 3 routers can process routing information to domains by examining the common prefix for that domain. Level 3 routers do not have to know about network addresses and area addresses within the domain. This saves compute cycles and storage space for storing addressing information about networks within the domain.

- There is no need to send a full area address of a domain to other domains. This results in savings in network bandwidth. Domains can hide their internal topology from outsiders, improving an organization's security.
- Data stored at each domain router is compact because it includes the common prefixes of other domains.

Figure 3.74 uses common prefixes for domains. Domain A has a common prefix of D3441; domain B has a common prefix of D3442; and domain C has a common prefix of D3443. Domain A is further divided into four areas A1, A2, A3, and A4. Domain B is divided into three areas of B1, B2, and B3. Domain C is divided into two areas of C1 and C2. Areas within a domain are distinguishable from areas within other domains by the fifth hexadecimal digit. Areas in domain A have "1" as the fifth hexadecimal digit; areas in domain B have a "2"; and areas in domain C have a "3" as the fifth hexadecimal digit. A Level 3 router for domain B needs to know that all addresses in domain A begin with D3441 and addresses in domain C begin with D3443. If this router receives a packet with address prefix D3441, it forwards it to the Level 3 router for domain A; if it receives a packet with address prefix D3443, it forwards it to the Level 3 router for domain C; and if it receives a packet with address prefix D3442, it forwards it to the Level 3 router for domain B. Level 3 routers for other domains A and C work in a similar manner.

Figure 3.74
Common-prefix routing.

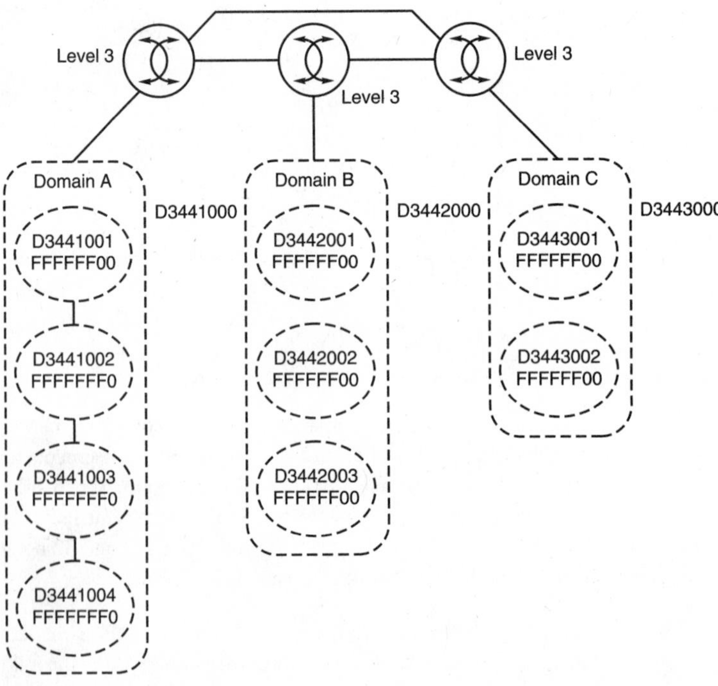

Assigning Multiple Addresses for an NLSP Area

An NLSP area can have up to three different area addresses, each with a different network mask. NLSP treats the multiple addresses as synonyms for the routing area. Typically, the new addresses are added to represent alternate views of the network. NLSP allows routing areas to be organized without disrupting the network. For example, you could split a routing area into areas by introducing new addresses to some of the routers and gradually phasing out the old addresses. When all routers in the area have separate area addresses, the area is split into two.

IPX Registry Service

Novell provides an IPX network address registry service. If you plan to connect networks to other organizations, you can apply to Novell to obtain a range of unique IPX addresses. Contact Novell at 408-321-1506 or send Internet mail to registry@novell.com or the MHS NHUB e-mail to registry@novell.

Summary

In this chapter, you learned the differences between bridges and routers and the advantages and disadvantages of using them. The operation of two types of bridges—the spanning tree and source routing—were examined.

The operation of routers was discussed in some detail, both from a general point of view and a Novell-specific point of view. Guidelines for installing NetWare routers were discussed. Integration techniques for NetWare 3.*x* and UNIX networks also were discussed.

You also learned about performance issues for internal/external and dedicated/nondedicated routers and routing problems with NetWare 2.*x* networks.

WANs and MANs

As networks expand, you must connect islands of LANs to provide an integrated network computing platform. This chapter discusses the technologies you use to create large LANs.

You may want to interconnect LANs for the following reasons:

- Integrating existing LANs
- Extending the capabilities of existing LANs
- Increasing performance by providing access to faster networks or networks with more powerful servers and hosts
- Improving network availability by providing redundant network links, hosts, and servers

Exploring Wide Area Networks

Local area network (LAN) technologies offer high performance, but they are suited for use only in limited geographic areas, usually within a building or campus setting. If you need to connect LANs for longer distances, you must use other technologies. Networks that span long distances frequently are referred to as *wide area networks* (WANs). This section introduces the methods you can use to interconnect LANs over large geographic areas. Each method has advantages and disadvantages based on cost, availability, and performance.

FDDI

Fiber Distributed Data Interface (FDDI) is regarded by many as a high speed LAN (100 Mbps). Because it can span a distance of 100 kilometers, however, it can be used as a WAN to interconnect LANs or serve as a backbone to LANs. FDDI spans layers one and two of the OSI model and can be used to provide IEEE 802.2 or LLC services to upper layers (see fig. 4.1). FDDI can be used to run client/server applications that rely on IEEE 802.2 services, including NetWare, which provides IEEE 802.2 encapsulation. The FDDI physical station address follows the IEEE 48-bit (six octet) addressing convention.

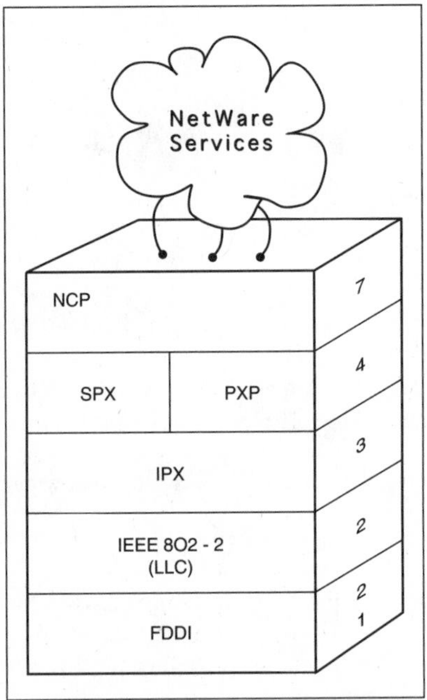

Figure 4.1
FDDI spans layers 1 and 2 of the OSI model.

A full FDDI configuration consists of two fiber rings. The primary ring is used for data transfer, and the secondary ring serves as a backup ring in case the primary ring fails. If the primary ring fails, an auto-sense mechanism causes a ring wrap so that traffic is diverted to the secondary ring (see fig. 4.2). Only stations that have a *dual-attachment* (connected to primary and secondary rings) tolerate this failure.

FDDI is based on the Token Ring access method that runs at 100 Mbps. A token is used to control access to the ring, but the details of token management are different from IEEE 802.5 LANs (see Chapter 2, "LAN Standards for Physical and Data Link Layers"). The maximum length of FDDI is 200 kilometers (100 kilometers for dual rings), and the distance between two nodes on a FDDI LAN cannot exceed two kilometers. Distance parameters are based on a maximum latency (delay) of 1.617 milliseconds. Maximum FDDI frame size is 4,500 bytes. This size makes it suited for high-speed file transfers, such as graphic, image, and other data files. Because the frame size is larger, more data can be packed into the frame, and fewer packets are needed to send the file. The total number of connections to an FDDI ring cannot exceed 2,000 (1,000 for dual-attached stations).

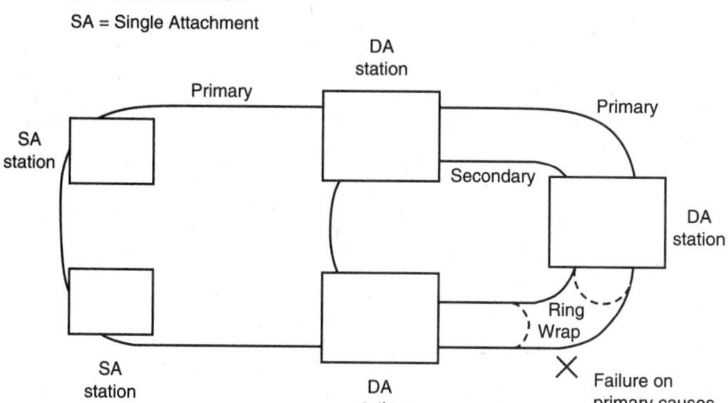

Figure 4.2
FDDI ring with dual and single attachments.

The FDDI networks expect that PC workstations will not be attached directly to them, but attached by means of an FDDI concentrator or router (see fig. 4.3). PC workstations are turned on and off often in normal usage. If workstations are connected directly to the FDDI ring, their powering on and off causes frequent ring reconfigurations that may become costly in a large FDDI network. PC workstations connected directly to FDDI networks also may not keep up with the high data rates in FDDI. The newer AT computers, based on Intel 80386, 80486, or 80586 chips, may keep pace with the FDDI data rates, but they are hampered by slow I/O buses.

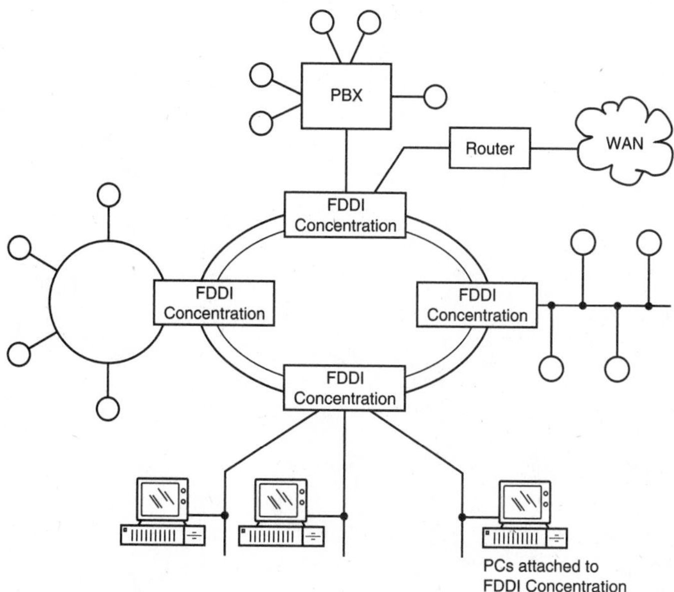

Figure 4.3
FDDI network with router.

The FDDI concentrators, or *Multi Access Station Units* (MAUs), also serve as a fan-out box so that multiple stations can be connected. Several FDDI concentrators can be cascaded to increase the fan-out.

Although the FDDI concentrator has a dual attachment, the stations attached to the concentrator have a single attachment to save on FDDI NIC costs. FDDI concentrators should be powered on all the time to reduce ring reconfigurations.

FDDI token management enables several FDDI frames to be resident on the ring at a time, which better utilizes the data bandwidth on the ring.

The FDDI ring operates in two modes: synchronous and asynchronous. In *synchronous mode*, stations are guaranteed a percentage of total bandwidth available on the ring. This bandwidth allocation is calculated in terms of percentage of *Target Token Rotation Time* (TTRT). The TTRT is the expected token rotation time for the expected traffic on the network and is negotiated during ring initialization. A station with synchronous bandwidth allocation can transmit data for a period of time not to exceed the percentage of TTRT allocated to it. Any remaining time left after all stations finish synchronous transmission is allocated to the remaining nodes. Thus, if the actual *Token Rotation Time* (TRT) is less than TTRT, the leftover time (TTRT_TRT) is used for asynchronous transfer.

In *asynchronous mode*, transfer can take place in two modes: restricted and nonrestricted. A station can perform an extended transfer in restricted asynchronous mode. The *Station Management* negotiates a maximum restricted time. Stations running in restricted asynchronous mode should not take up the entire ring for a period of time greater than TTRT.

In *nonrestricted mode*, leftover time is divided between any node that wants to send data. This mode of operation is the default. The division of time can be based on priority schemes in which stations have a threshold TRT. Stations with lower threshold TRT are cut off earlier.

FDDI uses multimode fiber. Extensions to FDDI that use single-mode fiber currently are in development. Although multimode can use a mix of light frequencies, a single-mode fiber uses laser and a smaller-core diameter fiber. Single-mode fiber has less signal attenuation and can be used over longer distances. With these FDDI extensions, two stations can be up to 60 kilometers apart. FDDI-II permits circuit switching in the synchronous mode with up to 16 synchronous channels of 6.144 Mbps each.

Many vendors are interested in running the FDDI protocols over a copper medium. Some vendors propose *Unshielded Twisted-Pair* (UTP) wire, whereas other vendors favor *Shielded Twisted-Pair* (STP) wire. ANSI's goal is to have one unifying protocol, rather than separate protocols for STP and UTP wiring. Using copper-based FDDI wiring is cheaper than using the fiber-based products. One problem of using twisted-pair wiring is compliance with FCC regulations and signal attenuation that limits the distance between a workstation and the FDDI concentrator. It is the goal of copper-based FDDI to have at least distances of 100 meters between workstations and FDDI concentrators.

Some vendors, such as Crescendo Communications, Inc. of Sunnyvale, California, have copper-based FDDI products. Crescendo Communications' *Copper Distributed Data Interface* (CDDI) runs on UTP wiring. Crescendo currently offers an eight-station MAU (1,000 Workgroup Concentrator) that connects workstations at distances of 50 meters. An SBus CDDI adapter can be used as the FDDI interface for the Sun Microsystems, Inc. SPARC station. IBM offers a version of FDDI on STP wiring.

Defining HIPPI

The *High Performance Parallel Interface* (HIPPI) is a LAN standard that the ANSI X3T9.3 committees currently are investigating to provide data rates between 800 Mbps to 1,600 Mbps.

HIPPI transfers 32 bits of data in parallel across distances of about 25 meters. The parallel transmission runs over a 50-pair twisted-pair wire cable—32 pairs are used for data lines, and the remaining lines are used for control.

HIPPI evolved from the proprietary HSX I/O bus that CRAY supercomputers use. Graphic workstations require high I/O data rates to perform real-time modeling and display.

Figure 4.4 shows how you can adapt HIPPI for LAN usage. The HIPPI standard proposes a HIPPI Framing Protocol Layer that allows IEEE 802.2 protocol to run on top of it. Any protocol stack that uses IEEE 802.2, such as NetWare, can use HIPPI.

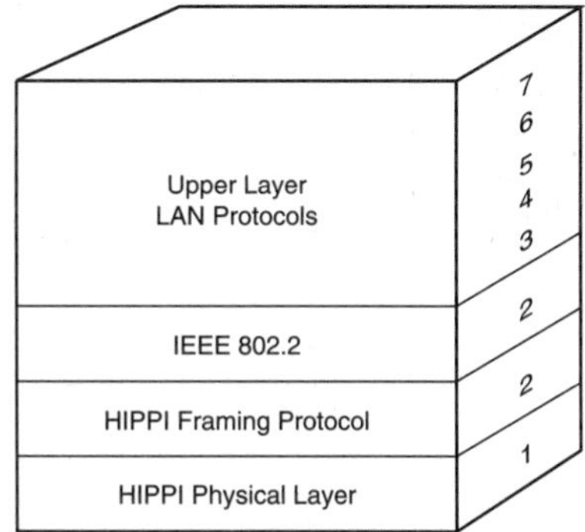

Figure 4.4
Adapting HIPPI for LAN usage.

Because of distance limitations and cabling costs, the current HIPPI probably will not be used for the backbone or WAN connectivity. Nevertheless, it represents an interesting development for those applications that require very high speed LANs.

Metropolitan Area Network

Metropolitan Area Networks (MANs) are an interesting development in computer network standards. The MAN standard originally was intended for local area networking, but its size and scope mandate that it be managed by a central body, such as the telephone company or other commercial organizations. In this regard, it is similar to WANs.

You can implement city-wide MANs that can carry data rates as high as 155 Mbps. The IEEE 802.6 committee is trying to standardize MANs. The MAN standard has a checkered past. MAN structure originally was based on coaxial technology with a slotted ring approach, but that standard was superseded by growth in fiber-optic technology.

The following list summarizes the differences between LANs and MANs:

- City and suburban areas employ MANs, whereas areas that cover smaller geographical distances employ LANs.
- Public operation of MANs through a telephone company raises issues of security, reliability, cost, and central billing that do not arise in LAN setups.
- MANs can serve as high-speed backbones faster than FDDI.
- MANs can carry a mix of voice, video, and data traffic more effectively than LANs.
- MANs cross public rights-of-way. Service utilities such as telephone companies have these permissions; LAN owners typically do not.

MANs can transmit a mix of voice and data traffic. Another possible use of MAN technology is to provide LAN connectivity. The media access technology used by MAN, *Dual Queue Dual Bus* (DQDB), unlike FDDI, scales very well across longer distances and higher data rates than the current MAN specification. For this reason, perhaps, that Bell Communications Research (Bellcore) is interested in using DQDB as one of the techniques for its *Switched Multi-Megabit Data System* (SMDS) services.

MAN services can be supplied city-wide by phone companies or by commercial organizations. You can use routers with a MAN connection to interconnect LANs at data speeds up to 100 Mbps; or the MAN can be used as a backbone for LANs.

MAN networks are of two types: private and public. These types are similar to private and public X.25 networks. For organizations that have stringent security or large data transfer requirements, a private MAN, such as that depicted in figure 4.5, can be used. Private MANs use dedicated cables; because only the organization's data is on the MAN, this simplifies security and billing issues. This type of MAN is like a very large LAN. Not all organizations, however, can justify the expense of a private MAN. Most organizations use shared cables that have traffic from a variety of sources, including city and state governments and private organizations.

DQDB is the media access protocol used in MAN and is based on a proposal by Telecom Australia and its subsidiary QPSX. Originally, this protocol was known as the *Queued Packet and Synchronous Exchange* (QPSX) protocol, but was later changed to DQDB to avoid confusion with the QPSX company. It consists of two loops of fiber in the form of a bus (see fig. 4.6). DQDB is arranged in the form of a ring so that a central station can provide clocking and synchronization information for transmission of frames. Data frames are sent on both buses but in opposite directions. Fault isolation mechanisms can bypass malfunctioning nodes or breaks in the cable. The dual bus architecture permits the use of a clever MAC protocol that enables requests for transmission from stations to be placed in a distributed queue. This distributed queue mechanism provides access characteristics independent of network size and speeds.

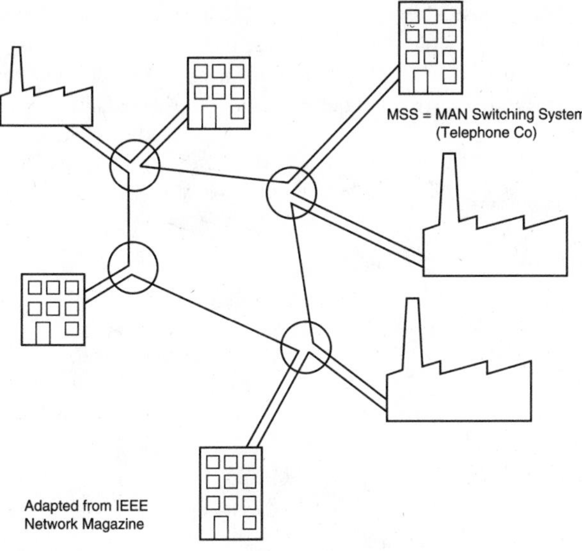

Figure 4.5
A MAN configuration.

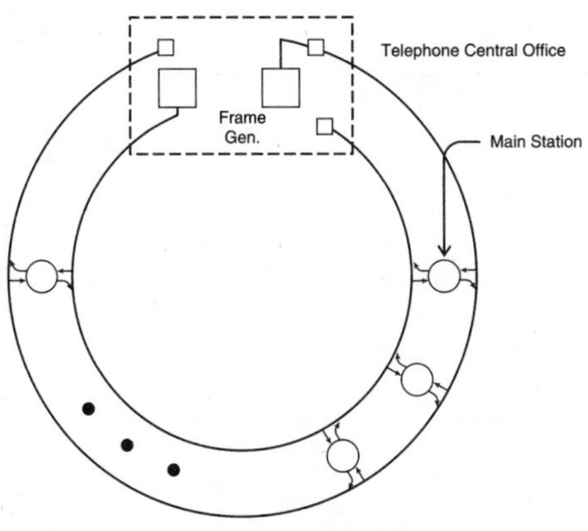

Figure 4.6
DQDB architecture and frame format for MANs.

The MAN data frame is shown in figures 4.6 and 4.7. Each slot contains two control bits, BUSY and REQ. A BUSY bit indicates that a slot is busy, and REQ is used by a station to request an empty slot. A station that wants to send data on a bus makes its request on the reverse bus by setting the REQ bit flag. The REQ bit informs the upstream neighbors that a station downstream wants access to a slot. Each node keeps track of requests downstream from it by counting the REQ bits as they pass on the reverse bus (see fig. 4.7). The REQ counter is incremented for requests on the reverse bus. The REQ counter contents are transferred to the *Count Down* (CD) counter (see fig. 4.8). The CD counter is decremented

for each free slot on the forward bus because a free slot will be used by a station downstream that previously made its request through the REQ bit. A station can use the first free slot after its CD counter reaches zero. Using these counters, a first-in-first-out queue is formed. The queue position is indicated by the value of CD in each station. It is truly a distributed queue that is 100 percent fair.

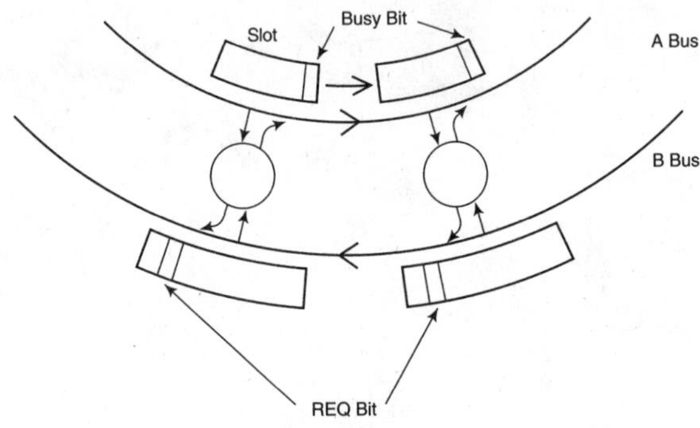

Figure 4.7
Distributed Queue formation on a bus for MAN.

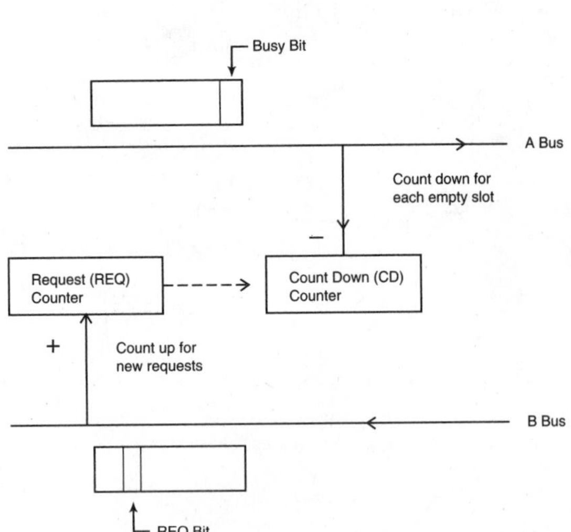

Figure 4.8
DQDB operation used in MAN.

X.25

Figure 4.9 shows the elements of an X.25 network, and figure 4.10 shows how these elements can be used to connect LANs. An X.25 network contains a number of packet switches that switch and route packets transmitted between two nodes, such as a terminal and host machine. Although data transfer takes place using packets, the appearance to higher layers of software is that a single continuous logical channel (or virtual circuit) exists between two nodes. Typical packet sizes of X.25 networks are 128 bytes, although other sizes are possible and can be negotiated at connection time.

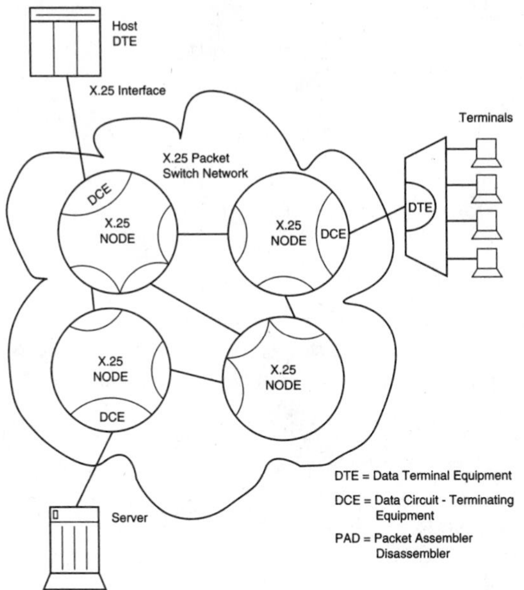

Figure 4.9
Elements of an X.25 network.

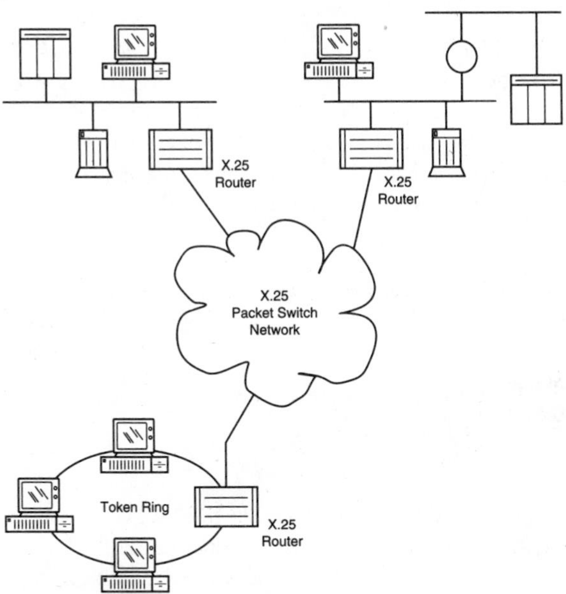

Figure 4.10
Connecting LANs through the X.25 network.

Although terminals are attached to the X.25 network through a *Packet Assembler Disassembler* (PAD), host machines can be attached directly or through synchronous modems. The X.25 network uses the X.25 protocols, which actually are three protocols. These protocols include the X.21 or X.21bis at the physical level, *Link Access Procedure Balanced* (LAPB) at the data link level, and X.25 *Packet Level Protocol* (PLP) at the network level. Figure 4.11 shows this relationship.

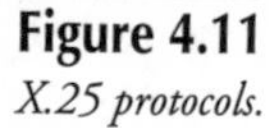

Figure 4.11
X.25 protocols.

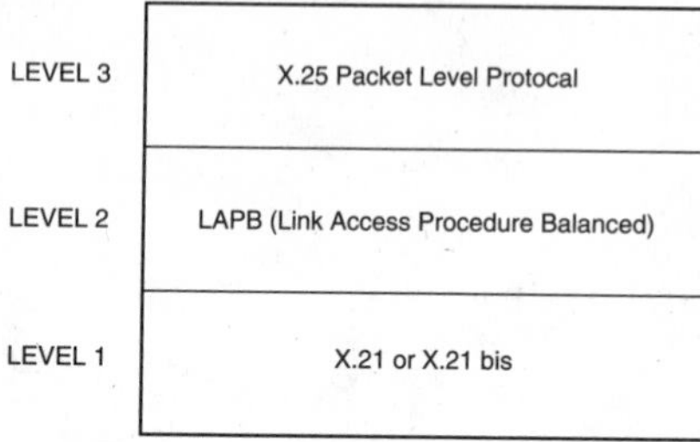

The X.25 protocol enables a maximum of 4,095 virtual circuits to be time-multiplexed across a physical link between the node and an X.25 network. In actual practice, fewer virtual circuits are used because most physical links cannot support the aggregate data rate for 4,095 virtual circuits.

Typical transmission speeds of X.25 networks are 64 Kbps, but higher speeds are available. If two LANs are connected through an X.25 network, data transfer between the LANs is limited to this speed. This setup limits the kind of applications that you can run across X.25 networks. Many LAN applications require data-transfer rates of at least 1 Mbps to run efficiently. File transfers and terminal emulation applications run efficiently across an X.25 network, but workstation applications run slowly.

Frame Relay

Frame Relay technology was developed for *Broadband Integrated Services Digital Network* (B-ISDN). It can provide higher transfer-data rates by eliminating much of the overhead inherent in an X.25 network. Multiplexing and switching are provided at the lower data link layer rather than the network layer. The flow control and error control that exists between packet switch nodes for X.25 does not exist in Frame Relay. Frame Relay relies on higher-level software mechanisms to provide this service if necessary. Frame Relay assumes that the media used for data transmission is inherently reliable. It does error checking, but does not perform error recovery, leaving this to higher layers.

Interest in Frame Relay is rising. Frame Relay overcomes the limitations of X.25 networks by enabling you to connect LANs at speeds up to 2 Mbps. These speeds, which rival LAN speeds, allow workstation applications to run well. As the need for LAN interconnectivity over wide area networks increases, so will the interest in Frame Relay technology.

T1

The *T1 circuit* is a point-to-point full-duplex digital circuit originally intended for carrying digitized voice. You can connect several point-to-point circuits to form a T1 network. The T1 circuit can use a variety of media besides copper, such as coaxial cables, fiber optics, infra red, 18- and 23-GHz microwave radio, or satellite links.

T1 networks provide a physical level connection with a data rate of 1.544 Mbps. This rate is in the range that can run workstation applications efficiently across T1 networks. The basis for T1 networks is the T1 circuit. Figure 4.12 shows two LANs connected by a T1 circuit.

Broadband ISDN

X.25, Frame Relay, and T1 networks can be used to interconnect LANs at 2 Mbps or less. One technology under development to interconnect LANs at higher data rates is based on B-ISDN. B-ISDN was developed to respond to the need to improve the basic and primary rates provided by ISDN (Narrowband ISDN). Voice, video, data, image, and multimedia are examples of applications that require high bandwidth.

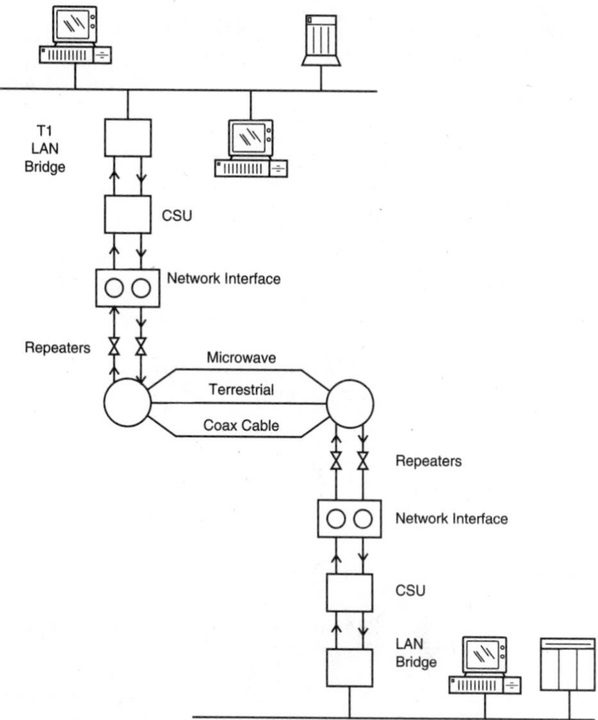

Figure 4.12
LANs connected by means of T1 circuit.

Initial B-ISDN interfaces provide data-rate transmission of 51 Mbps, 155 Mbps, or 622 Mbps over fiber-optic media. Figure 4.13 shows that the physical-layer support for B-ISDN is provided by ATM and SONET, which are described in the following sections. With appropriate adaptation layers, SONET and ATM can be used for LAN interconnectivity. A client layer in figure 4.13 can be frame relay, SMDS, or IEEE 802.2, for example.

SONET

The *Synchronous Optical Network* (SONET) was first proposed as a standard by Bellcore for a family of interfaces to be used in optical networks. The lack of standards for high-speed digital transport to be used for single-mode fiber led to a number of proprietary standards. SONET is now an international standard accepted by ANSI.

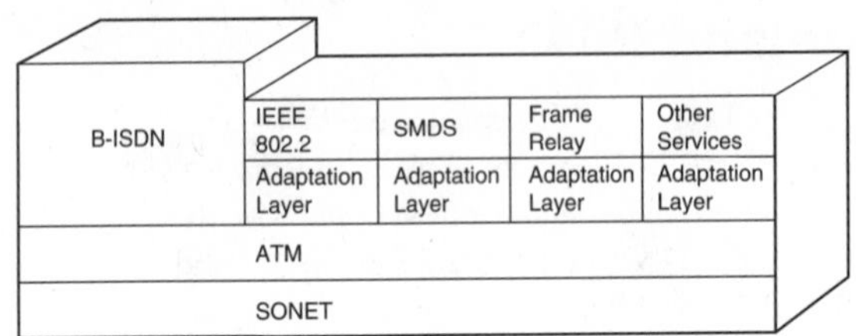

Figure 4.13
B-ISDN support infrastructure.

The SONET standard provides a point-to-point link over fiber-optic media. It provides the physical layer connection for B-ISDN and is defined in terms of a hierarchy of data rates. This hierarchy is defined in terms of the *Optical Carrier* (OC) speeds and the corresponding electrical signals (*Synchronous Transport Signals*) used to interface with electrical components. Table 4.1 shows this hierarchy.

Table 4.1
SONET Data Rates

OC Hierarchy	STS Hierarchy	Data Rate
OC-1	STS-1	51.84
OC-3	STS-3	155.52
OC-9	STS-9	466.56
OC-12	STS-12	622.08
OC-18	STS-18	933.12
OC-24	STS-24	1244.16
OC-36	STS-36	1866.24
OC-48	STS-48	2488.32

The OC and STS rates are multiples of 51.84 Mbps. The basic building block is the 51.84 Mbps line rate. Thus OC-48 is 48 × 51.84 Mbps = 2488.32 Mbps. The standard defines up to OC-240; that is, 240 × 51.48 = 12.4416 Gbps rate. STS-1 rates are roughly equivalent to the T3 (45 Mbps) data rates available today.

Design goals of SONET included providing a way to accommodate T3 data rates and resolving the incompatibility between the North American and European digital hierarchies, as expressed in the T1, T2, and T3 signals. The North American standard is based on a T1 rate of 1.544 Mbps, whereas the European standard is based on 2.048 Mbps. As a result of this incompatibility, T1-based routers for NetWare LANs operate differently in North America than they do in Europe.

STS data streams can be combined to yield higher STS rates. Three STS-1 rates multiplexed together, therefore, can yield a data rate of STS-3.

The STS-1 frame is 810 bytes and is made up of a 90 column-by-9-row matrix with each cell of this matrix being one byte long. This data matrix is transmitted in one STS-1 frame, as seen in figure 4.14. The first three bytes of each row contain overhead information. The first three rows contain nine bytes of section overhead, and the remaining six rows contain 18 bytes of line overhead. The combined section and line overhead of each frame is 27 bytes. The remaining 87 columns contain the payload or data. This frame payload is called the *synchronous payload envelope* (SPE) and works out to be 783 bytes (9 × 87). Not all the SPE contains data; the first nine bytes contain path information.

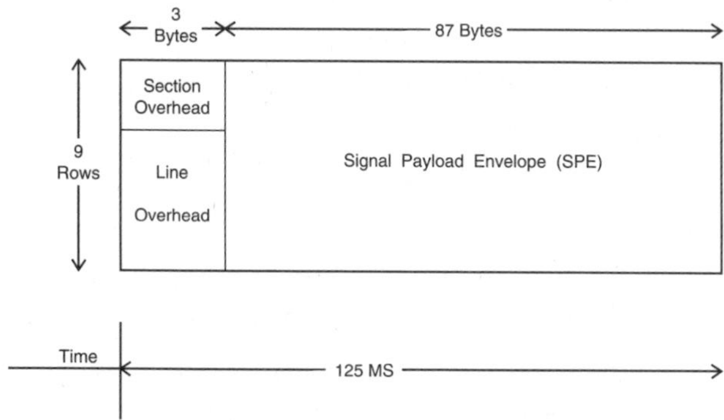

Figure 4.14
STS-1 frame in SONET.

The STS-1 frame is sent once every 125 microseconds or at the rate of 8,000 frames every second. Because each byte in the frame is eight bits, the data for each byte of data in a frame corresponds to an 8,000 × 8 = 64,000 bps channel. You can use this data rate to transport digitized speech or data.

Of the 783 bytes that make up the SPE, nine bytes are used for transport overhead for every row. This transport overhead contains a pointer to the location in the SPE that the actual data begins, thus allowing data to float.

Detailed consideration of section, line, and path overhead is beyond the scope of this book. A table of their definitions is included, however, to show the reader the rich functionality and robustness of SONET, as well as the reasoning for an interest in it for WAN/LAN communications.

Understanding Asynchronous Transfer Mode (ATM)

Asynchronous Transfer Mode (ATM) has its origins in the evolving Broadband ISDN (B-ISDN) networks and provides high-bandwidth, low-delay switching technology that multiplexes data over cells of a fixed size. While its origins are in the B-ISDN public Wide Area Networks, vendors are very interested in ATM as a technology for LANs that need high bandwidths. Examples of LAN applications that can

benefit from the high bandwidth of ATM are desk-to-desk video conferencing, desk-to-desk multimedia conferencing for local and remote users, medical imaging, CAD/CAM, distance learning, scientific visualization, data fusion, animation, video libraries, multimedia e-mail, supercomputer access, and communications.

Consider a desk-to-desk video conferencing that requires 1.544 Mbps. If 30 users on a LAN perform desk-to-desk video conferencing, the aggregate bandwidth requirement would be the following:

$$1.544 \times 30 = 46.32 \text{ Mbps}$$

Moreover, video conferencing applications need a sustained bandwidth and low delays. Current LAN access methods such as CSMA/CD and Token Access require modification to be capable of sustaining such high data rates and low delays. ATM, on the other hand, because it uses B-ISDN technology, can easily meet these requirements.

In figure 4.13, ATM is used above SONET to provide services for ISDN signaling or Frame Relay applications.

ATM is one of a general class of packet switching services that relays and routes information based on the address contained in the packet. Unlike other packet switching technologies such as X.25 or Frame Relay, however, ATM uses fixed-length packets called *cells.*

The fixed length ATM cells are made available on demand to applications and provide a flexible and fast packet switching service. The packets are 53 bytes in size. The 53-byte cell size includes five bytes of header information. Therefore, the actual cell size in terms of data transmitted is 48 bytes. The cells are the fundamental unit for data transport. Data traffic from multiple channels are multiplexed at the cell level. The fixed-packet size of ATM is in contrast to the variable length information field in other packet switching technologies. For example, frame relay, which relays frames of data, can have packet sizes from 64 bytes to 1,500 bytes.

Synchronous Transfer Mode versus Asynchronous Transfer Mode

Packet-switching technologies such as ATM exploit communication channels more efficiently than *Synchronous Transfer Mode* (STM) technologies. A classic example of an STM technology is the T1 carrier. In T1, a period of time called the *frame* is divided into 24 time slots. Each time slot is assigned to a separate voice channel, making it possible to *time multiplex* 24 voice channels in a single frame. The time slots are combined with a frame bit from the T1 signal. Each time slot is synchronized with respect to the frame bit, hence the name Synchronous Transfer Mode. In STM, the data for a particular voice channel is identified by its position in the frame. This type of technique uses *position multiplexing.* In ATM, the data is identified by a label (address information) in the five-byte header of the ATM cell. For this reason, ATM is sometimes referred to as a *label multiplexing* technique. Both STM and ATM use time multiplexing techniques. One of the fundamental differences between the two is the method used to identify a data slot: STM uses position multiplexing, and ATM uses label multiplexing.

In STM, because a time slot is assigned per voice channel, each voice channel is guaranteed a certain bandwidth. If a voice channel is not used, the bandwidth goes unutilized. Even if the voice signals obtain additional unutilized time slots, the voice communications do not improve significantly. If, however, unutilized time slots become available for data traffic, data transfer rates improve dramatically. In ATM, access can be given to data traffic or voice traffic on demand. In general, data traffic tends to occur at random intervals and for random lengths of time. ATM is well-suited for transporting this type of traffic because additional data cells can be generated on demand. Voice, video, and other real-time traffic that is time sensitive and needs immediate access to data cells, never has to wait for more than one 53-byte cell. For one 53-byte cell, this works out to be the following:

53 Bytes/155 Mbps = 53 Bytes × 8 bits/Byte/155000000 = 2.7 micro seconds

By keeping the cells short, real-time traffic is guaranteed ready access. For data traffic, however, the longer the packet size, the greater the efficiency of transfer. Because of this, the size of the ATM cell is the subject of much controversy. Originally, the voice people wanted small cell sizes of 32 bytes. This increases the likelihood of cells being available when they are needed on short notice. The data people felt that small cells introduce greater overhead in packet splitting and recombination because data packet sizes in LAN applications tend to be large. They were willing to settle for a cell size of 64 bytes. A compromise of 48 data bytes per cell was adopted. Together with an additional header of five bytes, the ATM cell size became 53 bytes. Breaking a large data packet into small cells introduces a certain inefficiency for data traffic, but enables the cells to be used for voice services and multimedia applications. Cells from different traffic types are multiplexed into a common path called the *virtual path.* The cell multiplexing in ATM provides a better bandwidth utilization. Cells are allocated on demand. This is well-suited for LAN applications, which typically have *bursty* traffic. When no traffic exists, no new data cells are generated. The term *asynchronous* in ATM refers to the fact that the recurrence of cells containing information from individual users does not occur periodically. That is, the cells for individual users occur asynchronously.

Each user on an ATM network is ensured that, although the ATM network contains cells from other users and other communication sessions, the user's data can be transmitted in a manner consistent with the subscribed *Quality of Service* (QOS). To provide the desired QOS, the user's data is sent on a *virtual channel* (VC). The virtual channel is unidirectional and is identified by the *Virtual Channel Identifier* (VCI). To provide bi-directional communications, two virtual channels are needed. The bandwidth for the return virtual channel can be assigned symmetrically (same as the sending channel), asymmetrically (different from the sending channel), or can be zero (unidirectional session).

ATM Interfaces

Figure 4.15 shows an ATM interface between two desktop computers. In this example, the desktop computers obtain a physical link of a certain capacity, such as 155 Mbps. Other data rates also are possible. The initial path created is called a virtual path and is identified by the *Virtual Path Identifier* (VPI). The VPI can represent a high-speed trunk line between the desktop computers or a LAN connection using ATM devices. Within the virtual path, a number of separate virtual circuits are possible. Virtual circuits within the VPI are identified by a VCI. These virtual circuits can be used by data, voice, or multimedia applications being shared by the two desktop computers. The VPI and VCI values have a local significance only, and a new VPI/VCI value can be assigned at the receiving end.

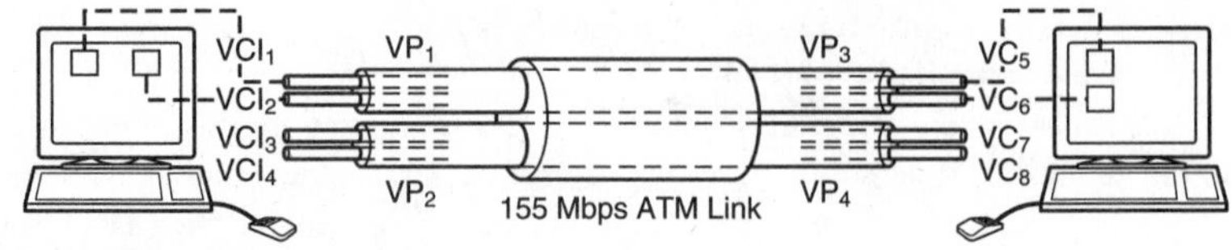

Figure 4.15
ATM interface between two computers.

The VPI/VCI addressing mechanism can be viewed as a hierarchical addressing scheme. Figure 4.16 shows the frame structure of an ATM cell. The VPI is a one-byte field, followed by a two-byte VCI field. ATM switching equipment can route the ATM cell on the basis of the first byte. When the cell reaches the destination, the VCI can be used to further determine the exact location to send the cell. The VPI/VCI together make a three-byte field, which allows a maximum of 16 million circuits to be used over a single interface. From a practical point of view, fewer virtual circuits are used. Many vendors of ATM equipment provide a maximum of 4,096 virtual circuits per user interface. The virtual circuit capacity in the ATM switches used in an ATM network have to be much higher. The ATM switches use the VPI/VCI label information in the header of the ATM cell to uniquely identify the virtual circuit to which the cell belongs.

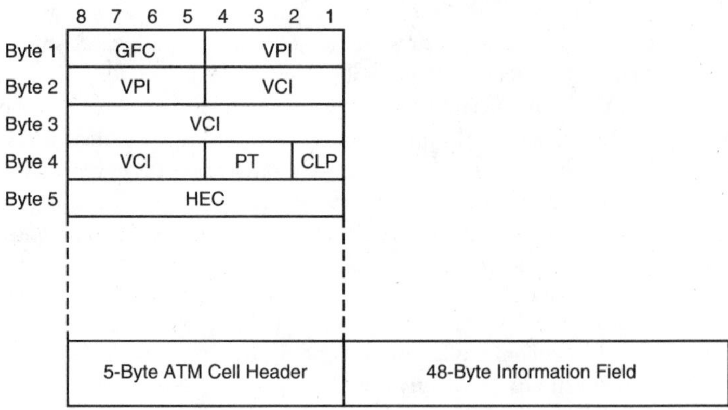

Figure 4.16
ATM cell structure.

The VPI/VCI have a local significance only and undergo a mapping based on the routing tables kept at each ATM switch. When a virtual path is created, each ATM switch in the virtual path is assigned a set of lookup tables. The lookup tables identify an incoming cell by its header address and the port to which the ATM cell should be routed. They also contain information to overwrite the incoming VPI/VCI address with a new address recognizable by the next ATM switch as an entry in its local routing table. The cell is passed from ATM switch to ATM switch over the prescribed route set during the call establishment phase. The path used is *virtual* in the sense that the physical communications facility is dedicated to the cell only when the cell *traverses* it. At other times, the physical communications facility may be used by other cells belonging to other virtual circuits. By sharing the physical communications facility among several virtual circuits, the communications efficiency for ATM can be much higher than for STM. It is possible to push the communications efficiency and the network utilization as high as the user is willing to push. Public ATM networks tariff parameters can be used to assign different grades of service. Users have the option of paying higher rates for guaranteed service or lower rates for "best-efforts" service.

The transfer capacity on the virtual circuit is determined on a per-call basis and is influenced by the Quality of Service parameters requested during the call establishment phase, network capacity, and other factors. The other fields in figure 4.16 deal with flow control (*Generic Flow* Control—GFC), type of data being sent (*Payload* Type—PT), and header integrity (*Header Error* Control—HEC). The *Cell Loss Priority* (CLP) field, if set to one, indicates that the cell is subject to discarding on the network. When set to zero, the CLP indicates that the cell has a high priority and should not be discarded.

ATM Protocol Stack

Figure 4.17 shows a typical protocol stack used with ATM communications. The physical layer for ATM consists of two sub-layers: the *Physical Media Dependent* (PMD) layer and the *Transmission Convergence layer* (TC). The PMD layer deals with physical functions such as bit transmission, bit alignment, encoding, and electrical conversion. ATM can support diverse media types such as twisted-pair wiring, fiber optic, and coaxial. If fiber-optic cables are used, the PMD layer performs the electrical conversion between light and electrical signals. The TC layer provides a conversion between the ATM cells used by upper layers and bits used by the PMD layer. It also performs transmission frame generation and recovery, transmission frame adaptation, cell delineation, header error control sequence generation and verification, and cell rate decoupling.

The *transmission frame adaptation* is used for formatting the data in the cells to the transmission frame structure to be used for transmission. In the United States, SONET is used as one of the transmission frame options for ATM. This means that data in the cells must be extracted and placed in the DS3 envelope format used by SONET. When data is received in a DS3 payload format, it must be extracted and placed in the ATM cell format.

The *transmission frame generation and recovery* is responsible for the physical generation and reception of the transmission frame (such as SONET).

The *cell delineation* prepares the flow of cells so that the cell boundaries can be recovered by the receiver. The ATM cells are scrambled and placed in the cell stream to protect against malicious users. Either a polynomial-based, self-synchronizing scrambler or a modulo addition of a pseudo-random sequence can be used. At the receiver, the cell boundaries must be identified by reversing the scrambling process and the cells recovered.

The *header error control sequence generation and verification* is used to compute the header checksum at the transmitter. The header checksum also is computed at the receiver to detect errors in the ATM cell header. The checksum can be used to perform single-bit error correction or multiple-bit error detection.

Figure 4.17
ATM communications protocol stack.

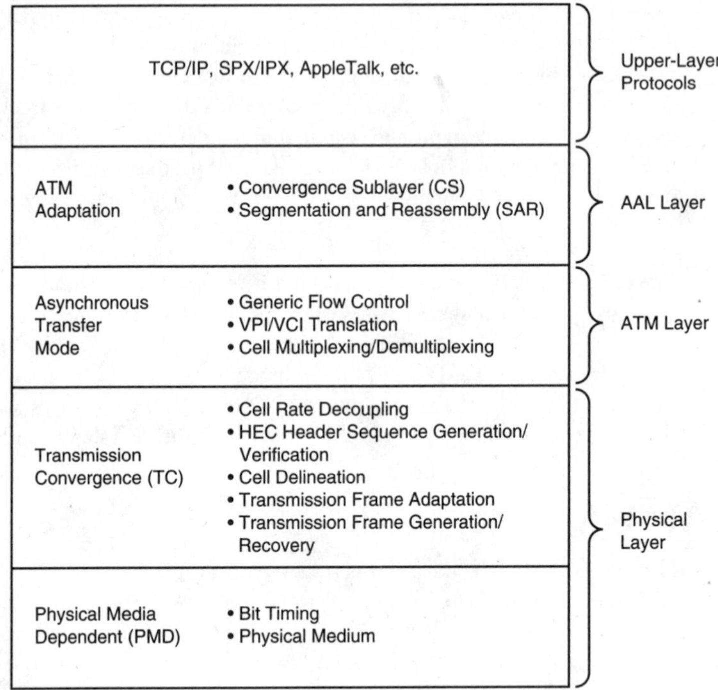

The *cell rate decoupling* is used to insert or suppress idle cells so that the rate of valid cells matches the payload capacity of the physical transmission system used.

The ATM layer (see fig. 4.17) provides cell multiplexing and demultiplexing, VPI and VCI translation, and cell header generation and extraction.

The *cell multiplexing and demultiplexing* function of the ATM layer performs cell multiplexing functions in the transmit direction and cell demultiplexing function in the receive direction. In the transmit direction, cells from individual virtual paths and virtual channels are placed in a cell flow. In the receive direction, the cells are sent to the appropriate VP or VC.

The *VPI and VCI translation* occur within ATM switches. The values of the VPI and VCI fields in the incoming ATM cells are mapped to a new VPI and VCI value based upon the lookup tables within the ATM switch.

The *cell header generation and extraction* are performed at the end-points of the ATM connection, such as desktops and servers that need to send the ATM cells for processing to a higher layer. At the transmitting ATM station, the cell header generation function receives the data from an upper layer and generates an ATM cell header except for the *Header Error Control* (HEC) field, which is computed by the ATM physical layer. At the receiving station, the ATM cell header information is stripped, and the resulting 48-byte cell sent to the upper layer.

The *ATM Adaptation Layer* (AAL) maps the upper-layer *Protocol Data Units* (PDUs) from protocols such as TCP/IP, SPX/IPX, and so on, to the ATM cells required by the ATM layer. The AAL functions can be divided into two sublayers. These sublayers are the *Convergence Sublayer* (CS) and the *Segmentation And Reassembly* (SAR) sublayer. The *Convergence Layer* (CL) is specific to each type of upper-layer protocol that is supported by and interfaces with the characteristics of the upper-layer protocol it must support. On the transmitting station, the SAR layer segments upper-layer PDUs into 48-byte cells. On the receiving side, it assembles the 48-byte cells received from the ATM layer to upper-layer PDUs.

ATM Services

The services used over the AAL are classified into five classes based on the following service parameters:

- **Time relation between source and destination.** This service can be required or not required. Certain applications such as sending 64 Kbps *Pulse Code Modulated* (PCM) voice signals require a timing relation between source and destination for the voice sample values to be decoded at the receiver. Most traffic from computer applications does not require a timing relationship between source and destination.

- **Bit Rate.** Some services require a *Constant Bit Rate* (CBR) whereas other services do not. Services that do not require a constant bit rate are called *Variable Bit Rate* (VBR) services.

- **Connection Mode.** Applications may need connection-oriented service or connectionless service.

Based on the preceding service parameter descriptions, the five classes of AAL services are defined as follows:

- **Class A.** Timing Required, Constant Bit Rate, Connection-oriented

- **Class B.** Timing Required, Variable Bit Rate, Connection-oriented

- **Class C.** Timing Not Required, Variable Bit Rate, Connection-oriented

- **Class D.** Timing Not Required, Variable Bit Rate, Connectionless

- **Class X.** Unrestricted, Variable Bit Rate, Connectionless or Connection-oriented

In addition to the preceding classifications, another recommendation by CCITT has resulted in four types of AAL protocols. These are Type AAL 1, Type AAL 2, Type AAL 3/4, and Type AAL 5. The ATM Forum that consists of computer communication vendors has specified that they will use AAL Type 5 (AAL 5) for computer communications.

One of the most active areas of ATM applications is the use of ATM for LANs. This approach uses ATM to provide the media access control mechanism traditionally used by LANs. LANs traditionally use datagram services at the MAC layer in which reliable delivery is not guaranteed. Reliable services are provided by upper-layer mechanisms, such as the transport layer. In some applications such as real-time modeling, it is sensible to provide a guaranteed service between a supercomputer and a graphic workstation to perform image transfers at high rates, at the lower OSI layers.

ATM supports a broad spectrum of traffic types including LAN traffic. In the case of LAN traffic, the longer packet sizes are broken down to small cells by LAN Terminal Adapters that implement the adaptation layer. As seen in figure 4.13, the packet switch services provided by ATM also can be used by other transport services such as Frame Relay.

Traditional LAN applications such as Ethernet, Token Ring, and FDDI depend on sharing of the media to provide low cost media access. Media sharing was important in the early days of LANs when Thick Ethernet networks were prevalent. In Thick Ethernet networks, the cost of the coaxial cable was higher, and therefore it was important to share the expensive media between the LAN stations. Because the media is shared in traditional LANs, arbitration techniques, such as CSMA/CD for Ethernet, Token Access for Token Ring, and FDDI, have been devised that select a single station for accessing the media for a certain duration of time. These techniques avoid conflicts when multiple stations need access to the media at the same time. The disadvantage of shared media access LANs is that stations can access the media only one at a time, and because packet sizes on LANs can be large, other stations have to wait for longer times for the media to become "free." This is a drawback for real-time applications that need more immediate access to the transmissions facility. The other disadvantage of traditional LANs is that all stations run at the same data rate regardless of their data throughput requirements. The only exception to this is ARCnet PLUS LANs that can run a mix of stations at 2.5 Mbps and 20 Mps. It is interesting to note that to overcome some of the limitations of the shared media access technique of Ethernet, vendors have developed Ethernet switches that dedicate the 10 Mbps communications facility to a single workstation. Chapter 3, "Bridging and Routing," covers Ethernet switches.

Local ATM

ATM-based LANs, often called *Local ATM* (LATM), replace the shared media of traditional LANs with a dedicated communications facility between the station and an ATM switch. The control of the network resides in the ATM switch, which routes messages and controls access in case of congestion. This is in contrast to traditional LANs in which control is distributed in each LAN interface. Figure 4.18 shows an example of an ATM LAN that uses ATM switches and ATM interfaces at the workstation. Each workstation communicates through a dedicated link to the ATM switch. A message sent from a workstation is routed by the ATM switch to the appropriate destination. Because each link is dedicated, its full bandwidth can be assigned to the workstation and there is no contention or wait delay for the media. Unlike conventional LANs, users do not have to communicate at the same data rate. For instance, a few of the ports in the ATM switch can be 155 Mbps fiber-optic ports, and others can be lower cost 1.544 Mbps, 10 Mbps, or 45 Mbps over twisted pair. This flexibility makes it possible to customize the network for different needs without paying for excess capacity upfront.

Conventional LANs use a set of physical layer protocols different from WANs. Consequently, conventional LANs need a separate device, such as a bridge or router, to convert LAN protocols, data rates, and signals to the protocols used for WANs (see fig. 4.19). The ATM protocol on the other hand can be used for both WANs and LANs. This makes it possible to build a LAN/WAN network comprising of ATM switches only. To connect a LATM to a Wide Area Network, you can use a single port in the LATM switch to connect to a network of ATM switches. Figure 4.20 shows an ATM LAN/WAN network. If you compare figure 4.20 with the router-based solution in figure 4.19, you can see that a router for a LAN can require multiple port connections to connect to different sites. As the number of WAN ports on a router increases so does the Wide Area Communication cost. The connections for these ports are typically leased lines, T1 carrier, and so on, and are typically paid on a monthly basis regardless of the actual usage. Using ATM it is possible to perform billing on a per-cell (or giga-cell basis because many cells are used by users) basis, and this results in more accurate billing of actual usage.

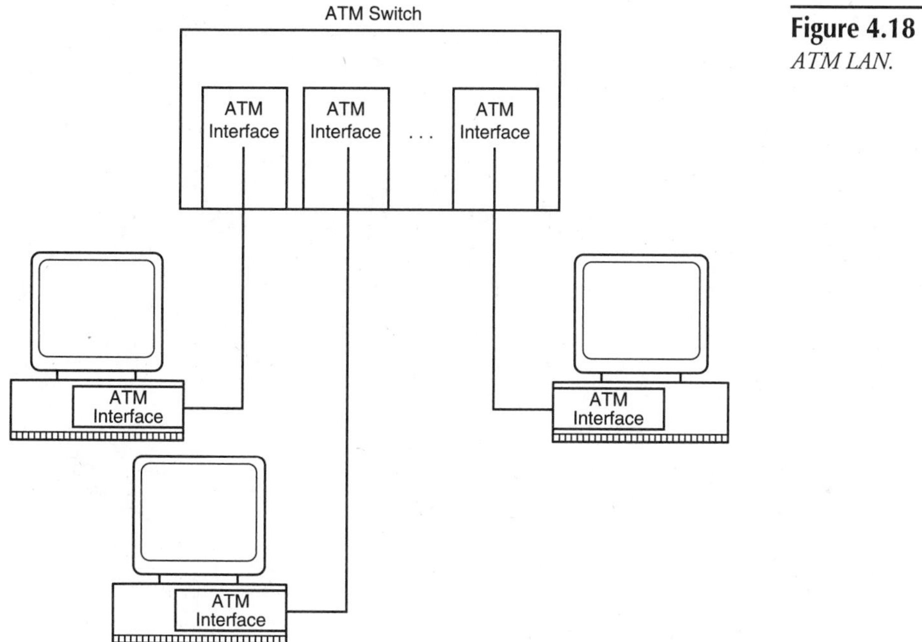

Figure 4.18
ATM LAN.

The switches that make up the ATM WAN can be part of a public network or private to an enterprise. In the former case, the switches are owned by the public carrier, and network management of these switches is performed by the public carrier. In the latter case, the ATM switches are owned by a private enterprise that also is responsible for maintaining the switches.

Other possible uses of ATM in LANs include the following:

- Simple point-to-point links
- ATM ports on routers
- Private ATM switch connecting conventional LANs
- Public ATM switch network connecting conventional LANs

Figure 4.21 shows a point-to-point ATM link connecting two ATM-configured devices. Such a configuration is used in special dedicated applications or for initial testing of ATM technology.

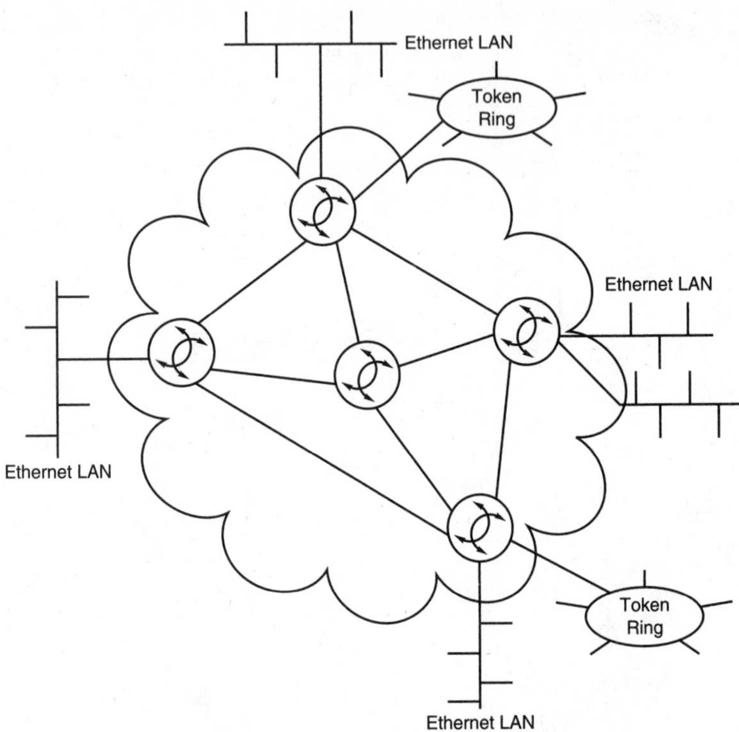

Figure 4.19
Router based LAN/WAN.

Figure 4.22 shows two conventional LANs using routers to communicate between themselves. The routers have an ATM port, and can therefore use ATM communications for transferring messages. This allows networks to use existing LAN technology and still use ATM communications for evaluation purposes and lower costs. (A cost analysis should be done to see if the ATM link provides the desired service at a reduced cost.)

Figure 4.23 shows a private ATM switch connecting several conventional LANs. Each LAN has a router with an ATM port. A link from the router's ATM port connects to the ATM switch. LAN traffic from the router is forwarded to the private ATM switch, which routes the LAN traffic to the appropriate router on another LAN. The advantage of this solution is that if *N* sites need to be connected, *N* links are needed to the private ATM switch. If *N* sites are connected to each other using router-based technology, $N(N-1)/2$ links are needed. As the number of sites grows, the number of such links and their cost grows exponentially.

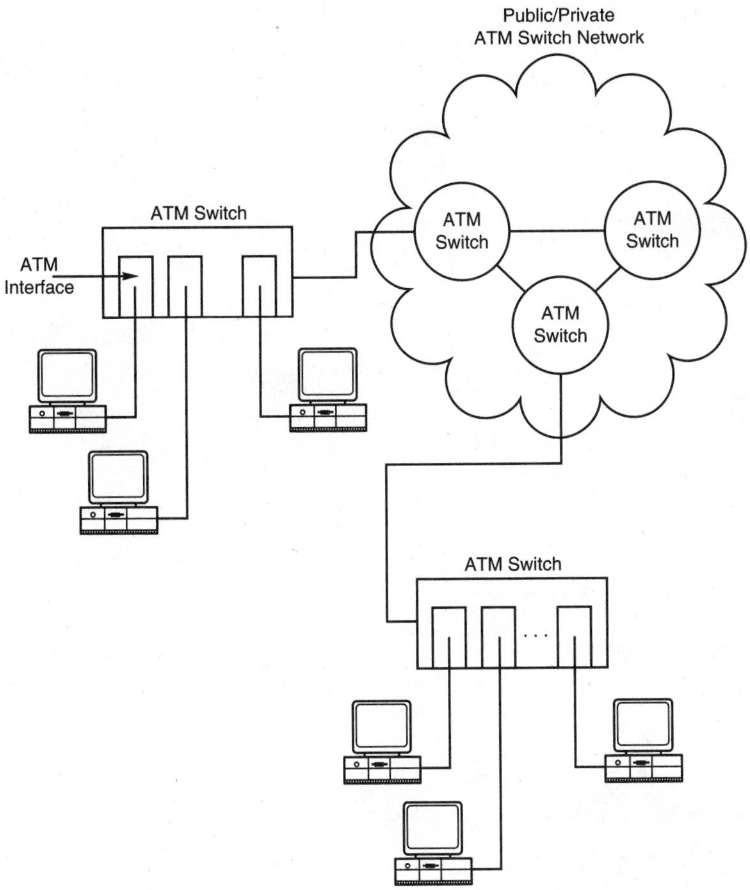

Figure 4.20
ATM LAN/WAN.

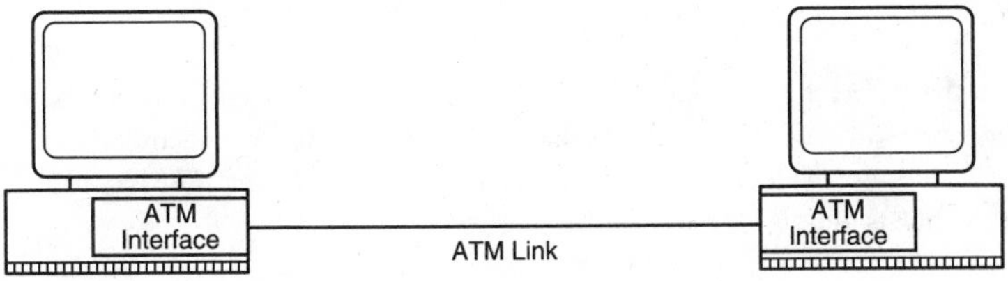

Figure 4.21
Simple point-to-point Links.

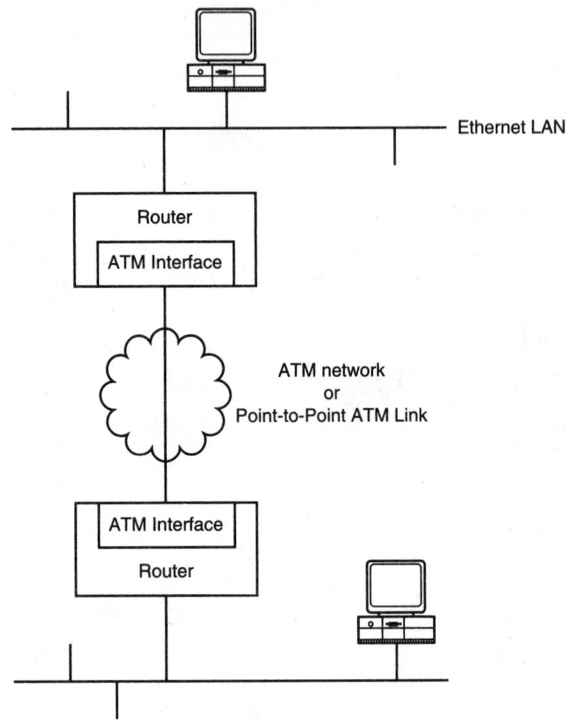

Figure 4.22
ATM ports on Routers.

Figure 4.24 shows an ATM switch network connecting several conventional LANs. The ATM switches are provided by a public network, which relieves the network manager from having to acquire, maintain, and manage this network.

Figures 4.22 to 4.24 show ATM-based solutions that can be used with conventional LAN-based technology. The ATM switch is used to provide the WAN communications for the network. Figure 4.20 shows an LATM solution that uses ATM for both LANs and WANs.

Another interesting aspect is that ATM is a scaleable technology. The ATM technology is not tied to any specific media or particular bandwidth. Figure 4.25 shows that the physical media dependent layer can use coaxial, twisted pair, or fiber optic. Data rates can vary from 64 Kbps, 1.544 Mbps, 45 Mps, 155 Mbps, and higher. Users send bursts of cells for as much data they need to send.

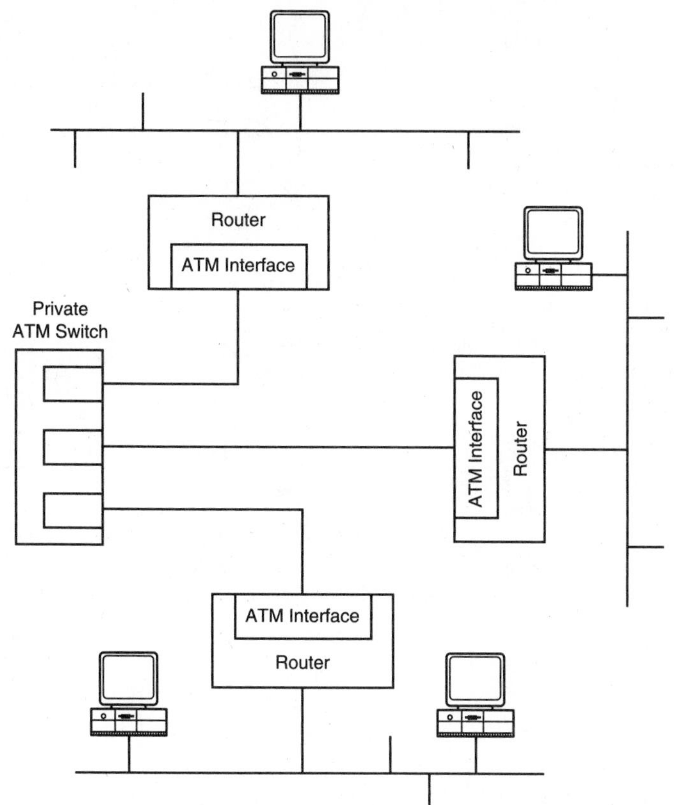

Figure 4.23
Private ATM switch connecting conventional LANs.

Comparing ATM and NetWare-Based Networks

Novell's plan to integrate NetWare services with ATM is a two-step process. The first step is to provide interconnection services to legacy LANs. *Legacy LANs* are any non-ATM–based LANs such as Ethernet, Token Ring, FDDI, and so on. Services to interface legacy LANs include the following:

- ATM LAN interconnection services
- ATM LAN emulation

ATM LAN interconnection services are provided through extending NetWare *Multi-Protocol Router* (MPR) to interface with an ATM LAN. ATM LAN emulation consists of providing a virtual LAN interface of existing LAN topology and interfaces over ATM.

4

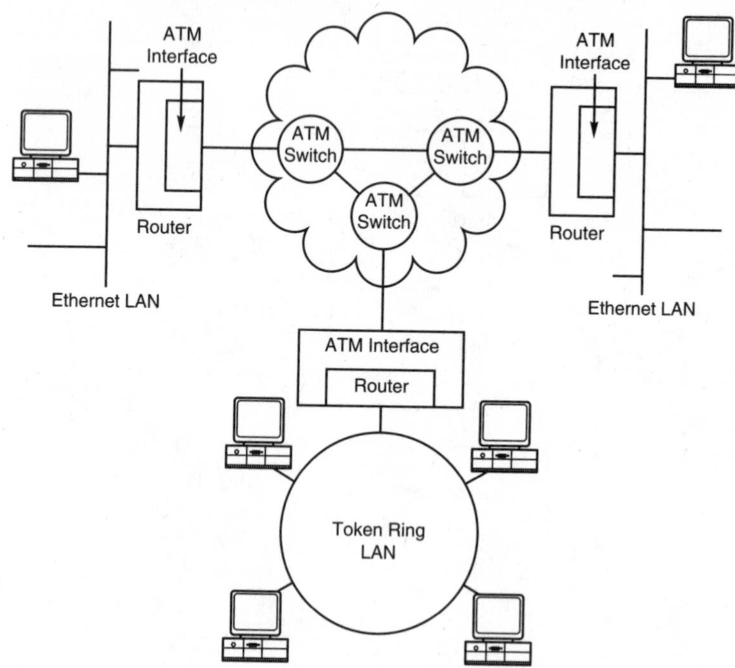

Figure 4.24
Public ATM switch network connecting conventional LANs.

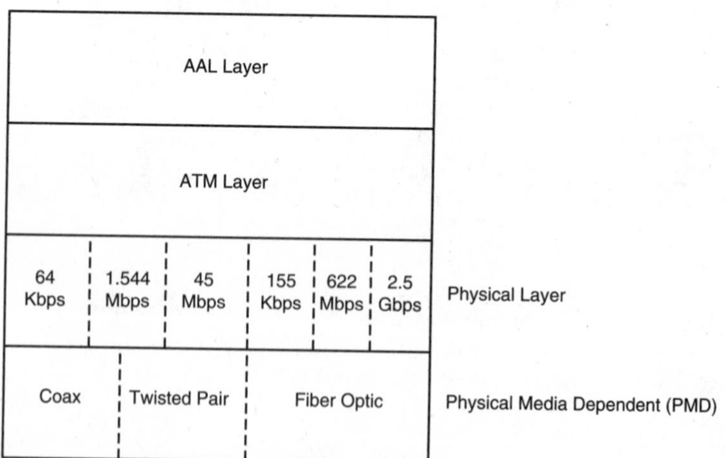

Figure 4.25
ATM scaleable technology.

In the long term, Novell will provide native ATM services. Native ATM services include the following:

- Connection-oriented IPX (CON-IPX)
- IPX media services

- ATM management services
- NetWare Directory Services (NDS)

ATM LAN Interconnect Services

ATM LAN interconnect services consist of NetWare servers or MPRs configured to interface with an ATM network using ATM's *User Network Interface* (UNI) specification (see fig. 4.26). These devices essentially act as routers between LAN topologies and ATM networks. Either *Permanent Virtual Circuits* (PVCs) or *Switched Virtual Circuits* (SVCs) are statically configured between the routers. The routers treat the ATM network as a point-to-point circuit. These circuits are statically configured at each router and are created when the router powers up. The data traffic across ATM LANs use *Sub-Net Access Protocol* (SNAP) encapsulation.

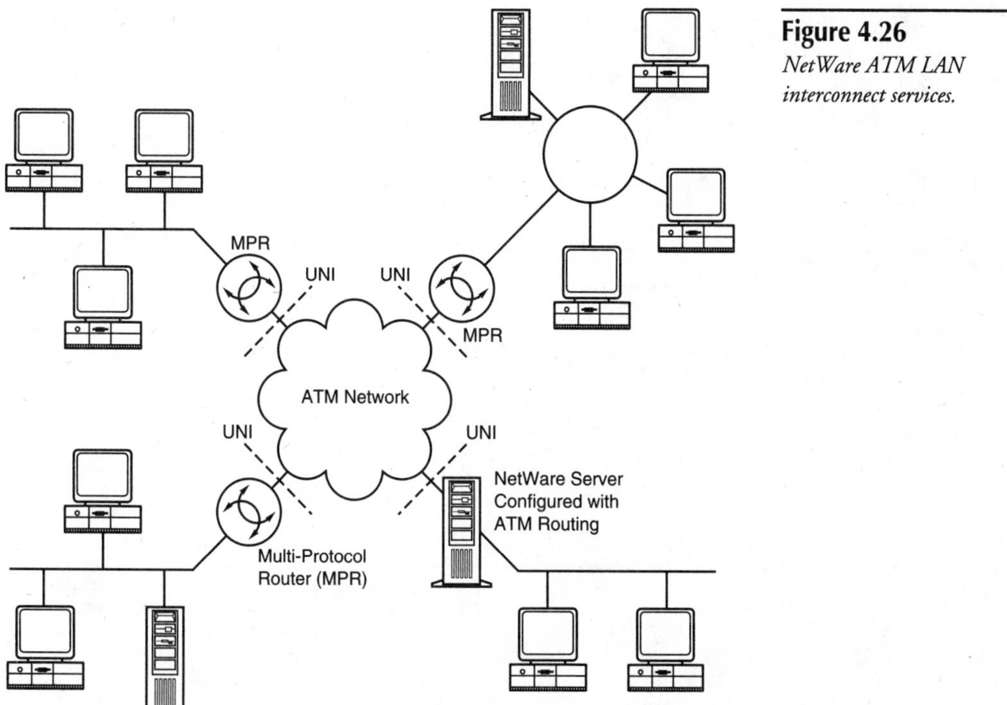

Figure 4.26
NetWare ATM LAN interconnect services.

Initially, the lines used to build the ATM network can be either T1, T3, or SONET operating at speeds up to 155 Mbps. The line efficiency of the ATM circuit is based on the following:

- SONET STS-1 line efficiency of 96.7%
- ATM cell efficiency of 90.5% (48 bytes/53 bytes)

- AAL5 frame efficiency of about 99.8% (variable)
- IPX packet efficiency of about 99% (variable)

The AAL5 and IPX packet efficiencies are variable. To obtain the overall line efficiency, multiply these percentage efficiencies:

$$\text{Total line efficiency} = 0.967 \times 0.905 \times 0.998 \times 0.99 = 0.865\ (87\ \%)$$

Therefore, a 45 Mps T3 circuit can carry 39 Mbps of data, and a 155 Mbps SONET circuit can carry 134 Mbps of data.

The ODI driver stack at the Multi-Protocol Router with ATM interconnection services (see fig. 4.27) has drivers for the ATM UNI and the LAN or WAN interface.

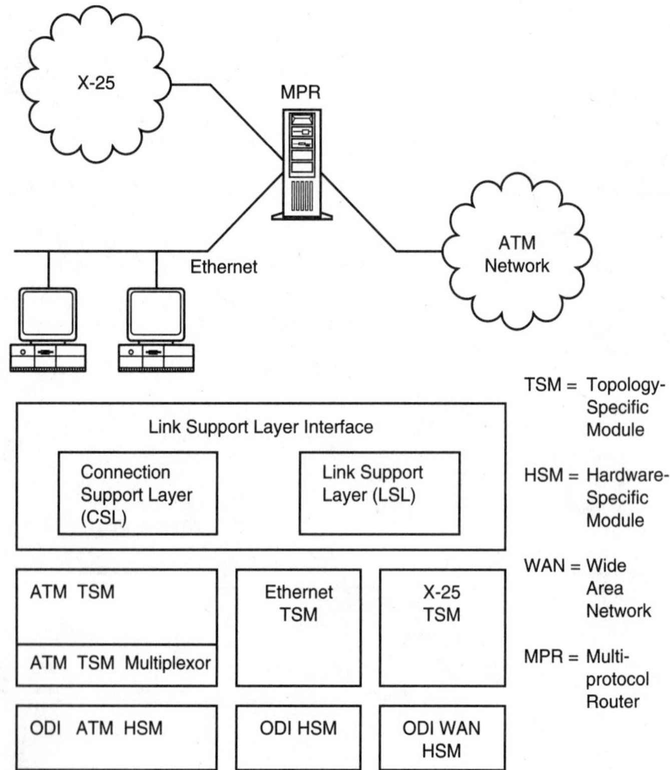

Figure 4.27
ODI Driver Stack for the ATM LAN Interconnect.

ATM LAN Emulation

ATM LAN emulation is meant to leverage existing software interfaces for legacy LANs, such as Ethernet and Token Ring. This allows the operation of existing NetWare protocol stacks for IPX, IP, and

AppleTalk. It is possible for a NetWare server to have multiple emulated LAN interfaces through a single ATM interface (see fig. 4.28). The emulated LANs can operate at higher speeds than the corresponding physical LAN because the underlying speed of an ATM network usually exceeds that of legacy LANs.

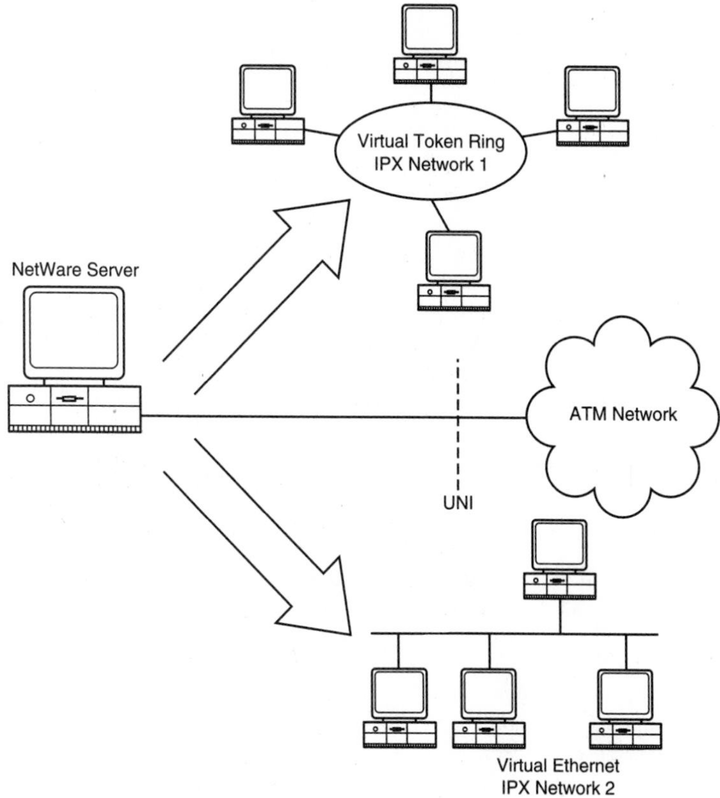

Figure 4.28
ATM LAN emulation.

To provide LAN emulation services the following components are needed:

- LAN emulation server (LE Server)
- Multicast server (MC Server)
- LAN emulation client (LE Client)

These components can be implemented as NLMs on NetWare servers. Figure 4.29 shows the model for LAN Emulation.

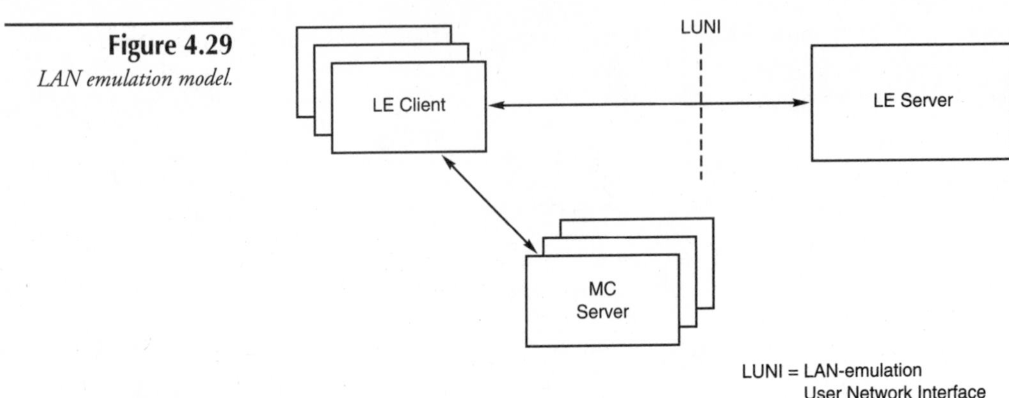

Figure 4.29
LAN emulation model.

The LE server responds to LAN emulation registration packets and manages the LAN emulation registration information. It also is responsible for LAN emulation control packet forwarding.

The MC Server is needed to support the broadcasting of various service and control packets on a LAN-emulated ATM network. The ATM network is a connection-oriented network at the data link layer, and is not inherently suited for broadcast traffic. The MC server is responsible for maintaining multicast domains. It is responsible for distributing multicast requests to multicast receivers within the multicast domain.

The LE Client is responsible for forwarding and receiving MAC frames; establishing connection with the LE server; joining a multicast domain; and issuing LAN emulation registration packets to the LE server.

Figures 4.30 and 4.31 show the ODI Driver stack for LAN emulation. Figure 4.30 shows the ODI driver stack for 32-bit clients and figure 4.31 shows the ODI driver stack for 16-bit clients. The model in figure 4.30 includes a general-purpose ODI ATM Topology Specific Module that virtualizes any legacy LAN and requires a 32-bit client because of larger memory requirements.

Native ATM Services

Native ATM services can be equipped to provide APIs compliant with existing IPX services and new APIs for CON-IPX (connection-oriented IPX) called *ATM IPX Media Services.*

The older API is provided to maintain backwards compatibility with applications that use existing IPX API datagram services. The older API runs on top of the newer APIs provided through ATM IPX Media services.

Newer applications can use the ATM IPX Media service that uses CON-IPX and provides new capabilities, such as control of Quality-of-Service parameters. QOS parameters include error rate, latency, and circuit bandwidth.

Summary

In this chapter, you learned some of the reasons why you need to expand the range of a LAN to include WANs. Technologies discussed included X.25, Frame Relay, MANs, SONET, SMDS, and FDDI. You learned the principles behind MANs, SONET, SMDS, and FDDI.

Hardware for NetWare Servers

System Managers generally want to optimize the throughput they can obtain from a given hardware configuration. Many factors determine the ideal hardware for a NetWare server. This chapter explores some of the components that affect server performance and examines some of the choices that are available in designing the optimal hardware platform. Many different server-platform possibilities are currently available. To fully exploit your options, you should be familiar with the following hardware features that can influence the performance and reliability of servers:

- CPU power
- BUS configuration
- Network I/O
- Disk I/O

CPU Power

CPU Power or bandwidth refers to the processing speed of the server. In general, a faster CPU gives better performance, all other factors being equal. Sometimes running NetWare on a faster CPU may not give expected performances if the bottleneck in system throughput is due to other factors such as bus speed, network I/O or disk I/O.

Because of historical reasons and the success of the Intel processors in providing low-cost computing solutions, the dominant server platform for NetWare is Intel-based. NetWare 3.*x* and 4.*x* can run on Intel 80386 or higher microprocessors, such as the 80486, the P5 (Pentium), and chips that are upward-compatible to the 80386 architecture.

Compaq and other computer vendors have developed multiprocessor-based machines that can run NetWare. Multiprocessor servers fall into two general categories: *symmetrical multiprocessing* (SMP) and *asymmetrical multiprocessing* (AMP). Figure 5.1 demonstrates some of the differences between these two approaches.

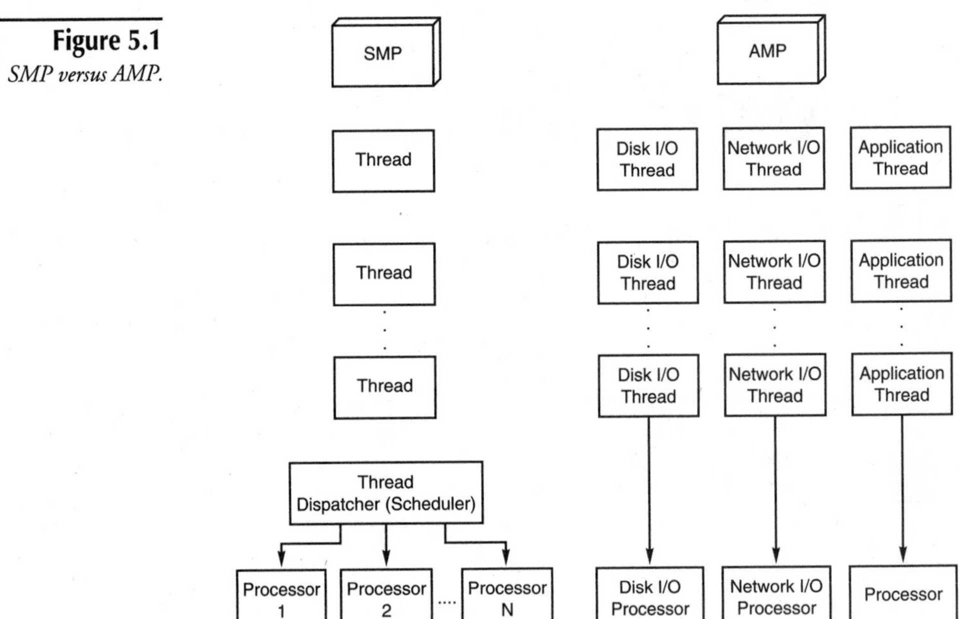

Figure 5.1
SMP versus AMP.

In symmetrical multiprocessing, the threads of a server process can run on whichever CPU is available. That is, execution can take place on any of the available processors. (A *thread* is a sequence of instructions that is executed. A NetWare *process* or *task* can have many threads, which allows parallelism in computation.)

In asymmetrical multiprocessing, certain threads are dedicated to run on special processors. A processor, for example, could be dedicated for disk I/O, another could be dedicated for network I/O, and another for application computation.

It is generally agreed that SMP is a more flexible architecture than AMP because SMP keeps all the processors busy. In AMP, it is quite possible for some processors to be very busy while others are idle, waiting for a specific type of job. To use SMP servers effectively, software in the operating system must be aware of the multiple-processor architecture so that it can schedule threads on the processors.

The NetWare architecture is currently being modified to take advantage of multiprocessor computers, though this feature is not available at the time of this writing.

An exciting area of development is a *processor-independent* version of NetWare that allows NetWare to be ported on other processor architectures, such as RISC-based platforms. NetWare for HP's RISC Precision Architecture is one example of this new technology. More recently, a joint venture has been formed between SUN Microsystems and Novell to port NetWare to the SPARC Architecture. The SPARC architecture is one of the earlier RISC architectures and still commands a market lead over other RISC platforms. NetWare may well become the first non-SunOS operating system to run on SPARC stations. SPARC stations come in scalable platforms ranging from the low-end SPARC Classic to the mainframe-performance SPARC-Center 2000 that is multiprocessor-based. The SPARC Classic has a better price/performance ratio than the 80486-based systems and is in the same price range. Computers with DEC's 64-bit Alpha RISC processor are another platform that NetWare can run on natively.

Figure 5.2 shows the architecture of a processor-independent version of NetWare. The basic NetWare services comprising the NetWare OS, NLMs, and CLIB are separated out and interact with the hardware-specific platform through a well-defined *NetWare system interface* (NSI). Existing application NLMs that use CLIB for system services and do not use undocumented hooks to the operating system can be recompiled to work under the new platform.

The hardware-specific platform details are below the NSI layer (see fig. 5.2) and consist of the peripheral devices and software specific tools, such as compilers, linkers, and libraries, for the new platform.

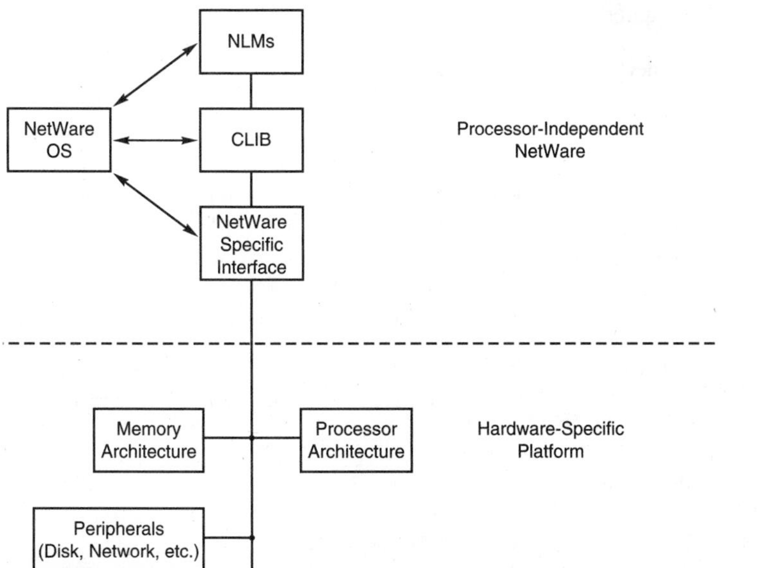

Figure 5.2
Architecture of processor-independent NetWare.

NetWare services have been hosted on other operating system platforms, such as UNIX, VMS, and Stratus VOS. These were at one time referred to as *portable NetWare.* More recent names are NetWare for UNIX, NetWare for VMS, and so on. NetWare SunLink is a product from SUN Connect that provides NetWare services on SunOS 4.1.*x* and Solaris. Whereas other operating systems and the underlying hardware they support can be used as a server platform for NetWare, there is a performance

penalty for interfacing through another operating system. If the underlying hardware is fast, as in the case of Stratus XA 2000 and XA/R Continuous Processing minicomputers and mainframes, then there are gains in performance over the Intel platforms.

Also available are super-server hardware platforms that are Intel-based (from Compaq Computer Corp. and NetFrame Systems, Inc.). Both of these support NetWare 3.*x*.

The Compaq SystemPro LAN Server is built around the high-end Intel processor family and consists of a number of system processor modules that have a microprocessor, a numeric coprocessor, separate cache memory, and a cache memory controller. The system processor modules communicate through a 32-bit processor/memory bus. A shared system memory module also is connected to the processor/memory bus. The shared system memory module cannot only hold programs that are executing on the system processor modules but also synchronize processing between the system processor modules. I/O peripherals are supported by an EISA bus. The EISA bus controller connects to both the processor/memory bus and the EISA bus.

The NetFrame Systems super-servers, although based on Intel processors, represent a radical departure in terms of I/O bus design. When compared to minicomputers and mainframes, PC-based servers have a slow I/O bus. EISA and MCA buses do not measure up to the I/O bandwidths of mini-computers and mainframes. To overcome the PC bus limitations, NetFrame has designed a proprietary I/O bus that borrows from the architecture used in mainframes.

NetFrame uses a hierarchical bus design. These buses are arranged in a hierarchical tree, with the lower speed buses represented by the leaf nodes of the tree. The lower-speed buses actually are 32-bit 25 megabytes/sec buses, and they funnel data to higher-speed buses as they travel up toward the root of the tree. The root of the tree represents multiple Intel-based processor modules that receive data through a 64-bit 64 megabyte/sec bus. A shared memory module with a 64 MB or higher capacity also is attached to this bus. A dedicated diagnostic processor module called the Server Activated Maintenance (SAM) module is used for detecting and correcting errors. The SAM module can interrogate other system modules and record status information for recovery and repair.

SAM also has some other interesting capabilities such as remote diagnostics. It can be configured to dial predefined telephone numbers, to leave voice-synthesized messages, or to dial pagers (beepers). The system manager then can dial into SAM and perform a certain amount of remote diagnostics over any touch-tone telephone.

Devices such as I/O servers and application servers connect to the 32-bit 25 megabyte/sec bus. The I/O server boards contain support for a variety of disk and network technologies. A single I/O server can contain Ethernet or Token Ring network connections, and ports for RS-232, LocalTalk, and SCSI-II. An Intel processor runs on each I/O server and executes the drivers for the various peripheral devices.

Another example of a scalabale processor architecture is the Pyramid SMP (from Pyramid Technologies, 408-428-8449) that runs NetWare services on a UNIX SVR4-based operating system. This is an example of NetWare for UNIX technology hosted on an SMP architecture. NetWare for Pyramid SMP performs load balancing by symmetrically distributing communication (IPX, SPX, NCP) and file service tasks over multiple processors. As far as users are concerned, the Pyramid SMP machine appears as a very fast NetWare server.

Host-Bus Interface and Bus Mastering

The exchange of control and data information between the network adapter and the server's CPU is performed by means of the host-bus interface. The host-bus interface module must have a built-in understanding of the nature of the host bus. A network card is designed to interface with a very specific I/O bus such as the *Industry Standard Architecture* (ISA) bus, *Extended Industry Standard Architecture* (EISA) bus, or a *Micro Channel Architecture* (MCA) bus. Apple's Macintosh machines use Nu-Bus, and SUN's Sparcstations use S-Bus; these must have their own network cards.

The *width of a bus* is defined by the number of data bits it can transmit in parallel. The wider the data bus, the more efficient the network adapter will be. For the IBM PCs, 8-bit network cards are very common. 16-bit cards provide better performance but also cost a little more. 32-bit network cards for EISA and Micro Channel are available. Another important consideration is the speed of the bus measured in MHz (megahertz) and the data transferred per cycle of the bus.

The EISA and Micro Channel buses have a *bus-mastering capability*. This means that network adapters designed for these buses can transfer data to the computer at high data rates with minimal interaction from the CPU. ISA bus network adapters can be placed on an EISA bus, but these will not benefit from the bus-mastering capability of the EISA bus. In other words, EISA buses are downward-compatible with ISA buses. ISA network adapters, on the other hand, cannot interoperate with Micro Channel buses. Micro Channel buses require specially designed network adapters.

The data transfer rate of a bus can be characterized by the following formula:

$$B = S * (D/C)$$

In this formula, B = bus transfer rate (bus throughput), S = speed of bus (MHz), D = width of data transferred, and C = cycles to transfer D bits.

For ISA buses, the bus speed is 8.33 MHz, and 16-bits are transferred in 2 cycles. Therefore, the ISA bus throughput is as follows:

B (ISA) = 8.33 MHz * (2 bytes/2 cycles) = 8.33 Megabytes/sec

For EISA buses, the bus speed is 8.33 MHz, and 32-bits are transferred per cycle. Therefore, the EISA bus throughput is as follows:

B (EISA) = 8.33 MHz * (4 bytes/1 cycle) = 33.32 Megabytes/sec

For MCA bus, the bus speed is 10 MHz, and 32-bits are transferred in per cycle. Therefore, the MCA bus throughput is:

B (MCA) = 10 MHz * (4 bytes/1 cycle) = 40 Megabytes/sec

A new type of bus called the *Local Bus* has become popular to bypass the ISA, EISA, or MCA bus for video traffic between the CPU and the video adapter. This bypass is useful for avoiding the bus bottleneck. The local bus on many systems operates at 33 MHz and transfers 32-bits per cycle. Using the preceding formula, the throughput of the local bus works out to be:

B (Local Bus) = 33 * (4 bytes/1 cycle) = 132 Megabytes/sec

For the S-bus used in SUN Microsystem's SPARC station, the bus speed is 50 MHz, and 32-bits are transferred in per cycle. Therefore, the S-bus throughput is:

B (S-Bus) = 50 MHz * (4 bytes/1 cycle) = 200 Megabytes/sec

This is one of the reasons running native NetWare on SPARC stations yields higher performance than Intel platforms.

Network I/O

Network Input/Output determines the overall performance of a file server. *Network I/O* is a measure of how rapidly data can be transferred between a server and a workstation. Because the server acts as a repository of data files on a remote file system, it is important to understand what the factors are that affect it.

A few of the more important factors that make up a server configuration and that have a direct impact on network I/O are:

- Network interface cards (NIC)
- Network drivers
- Protocols
- Network operating system
- Bus speeds at the server

These elements can conspire with each other to either improve or worsen network performance. The discussion that follows addresses some of these issues.

Understanding Network Adapters

Network adapters provide the physical connection between a node (workstation or server) on a LAN and the LAN cable.

These devices go by several names:

Network Adapter Unit/Board/Cards

Network Controllers

Network Interface Card (NIC)

Network Cards

Network Adapters

Network Interface Module (NIM)

Intelligent Network Interface Cards (INIC)

They all refer to the network electronics that fit inside a node on a LAN and implement layers 2 and 1 of the OSI model.

A functional description of a network adapter is shown in figure 5.3.

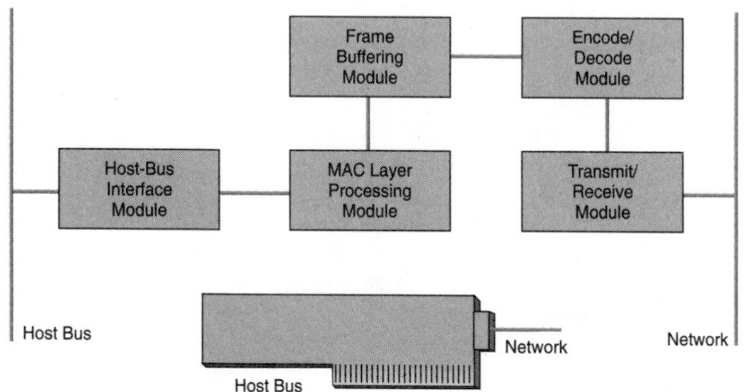

Figure 5.3
Block diagram of a network adapter.

A number of modules on the network adapter perform specialized processing. These are:

Transmit/Receive module

Encode/Decode module

MAC layer processing

Frame buffers

Host-Bus interface

The discussion that follows explains how these modules interact with each other. It is important to understand this interaction because it can help pinpoint potential adapter-related network I/O bottlenecks.

The transmit/receive module contains the interface electronics to drive the signal to the network media and to receive the signal from the network. As signals propagate through the network media, they are reduced in strength. The transmitting station must send the signal with sufficient power to be understood by the furthest node that needs to hear the signal.

Before a signal is transmitted, it may be encoded to add clock information to the data stream. The clocking information is necessary for the receiving station to keep its clock synchronized to the transmitter's clock. When a signal is received by a station, it needs to decode the signal; that is, recover

the data bits. The Encode/Decode module performs these functions. A variety of encoding techniques are used by different LANs. Ethernet and IEEE 802.3 use Manchester Encoding, IEEE 802.5 uses Differential Manchester Encoding, and FDDI uses a combination of *non return to zero inverted* (NRZI) and 4B/5B encoding.

When a frame is to be transmitted to the network or has just been received from the network, it is kept in a special area of memory on the adapter card for processing. In many network adapters, this frame buffer area is implemented by RAM chips on the network adapter. The amount of memory reserved for frame buffering can vary from a few kilobytes to a megabyte. Many network adapters implement, in firmware, intelligent buffer management algorithms to efficiently process packets received from the network. Some use scatter algorithms that can keep the header separate from the data portion of the frame. This eliminates the need for moving header and data into a contiguous block of memory prior to transmission.

The MAC layer processing module is perhaps the most important module in the Network Adapter. It performs several important functions:

1. **Encapsulation/decapsulation functions.** The encapsulation function is performed by the transmitting station and includes the generation of correct address, control, and frame check sequence (CRC) fields. The decapsulation function is performed by the receiving station and includes processing of the address, control, and frame check sequence fields. Error detection is also performed by the decapsulation function.

2. **Implementation of the MAC algorithms.** This would be the CSMA/CD access mechanism for Ethernet and the token access mechanism for Token Ring.

These preceding functions require processing power. Earlier network cards borrowed this processing power from the station's CPU. Needless to say, these network cards were very slow. Today, all network adapters have their own processing functions. These are special microprocessors that have their own ROM or microcode containing the MAC algorithms. These network controller chips also have their own RAM to process the MAC algorithms.

Performance Considerations for Server Network Adapters

Many LAN administrators would like to know which network adapter is faster—Token Ring, Ethernet, or ARCnet? This is an important question because the network adapter can become a bottleneck, and it is useful to know which one of the networking alternatives can eliminate the problem. Studies all conclude that 10 Mbps Ethernet and 16 Mbps Token Ring are faster than ARCnet at 2.5 Mbps. These results are not so surprising considering the data rates. The ARCnet Plus at 20 Mbps can be expected to be faster than both Ethernet and standard ARCnet. FDDI at 100 Mbps is the fastest of these. Thomas-Conrad has a 100 Mbps fiber optic proprietary LAN that is a combination of ARCnet and FDDI.

In designing a network interface card, a vendor makes several design choices that affect the price/performance tradeoff. The following four major characteristics contribute to NIC performance:

1. Media Access Scheme
2. Raw Bit Rate
3. Onboard Processor
4. NIC to Host Transfer

These characteristics are considered next.

Media Access Scheme

The media access schemes such as CSMA/CD and Token Access are important factors to consider in determining NIC performance. Token Access gives a deterministic performance whereas CSMA/CD does not. On the other hand, CSMA/CD is simpler and faster under light loads compared to Token Access.

Raw Bit Rate

This is the maximum bit rate that is possible on a given media. The actual effective bit rate, taking into account protocol overhead and timing delays, is much less. Nevertheless, the raw bit rate represents an upper limit for the given media.

Fiber-optic media can be used for data rates in the 100s of Mbps range. FDDI at 100 Mbps is only the beginning. We can expect higher speed LANs based on fiber-optic cables.

Coax cable can generally accommodate data rates up to 50 Mbps and shielded twisted pair wiring around 20 Mbps.

ARCnet Plus uses a 5 MHz sine wave but by using special encoding techniques it can pack 4 bits of information in every cycle, yielding a maximum of 20 Mbps.

Onboard Processor

Effective use of an onboard processor can speed up an NIC. If the firmware for the NIC is poorly written, however, it can have just the opposite effect. When NetBIOS was created by IBM for the IBM PC Broadband LAN, it was implemented in firmware on the NIC itself. However, because of an inefficient implementation, it ran slower than NetBIOS implemented in software. Some vendors implement upper-layer protocol processing on the NIC card for better overall throughput. An example of such an NIC is Federal Technologies' EXOS series board that has onboard TCP/IP processing. (The EXOS product line was sold by Excelan to Federal Technologies, after the merger of Excelan with Novell.)

NIC to Host Transfer

The NIC to host channel can be implemented in several ways: shared memory, DMA, or I/O ports. NICs may use any of these methods or a combination of them. Observations have shown that shared memory is the fastest, I/O ports are next, and DMA is the slowest.

The data width of the bus interface has a dramatic effect on NIC-to-Host transfer speeds. This width can be 8, 16, or 32 bits. The wider the data width, the faster the data transfer.

The type of host bus also affects the transfer rate. EISA and Micro Channel NICs are faster than ISA NICs.

Disk I/O

Disk mirroring/duplexing is an option that can be used with NetWare to improve the fault tolerance of the server disk subsystem should the server disk fail. This fault tolerance is obtained at the expense of purchasing twice as much storage as would normally be required, since each disk holding programs and data has a secondary backup disk. The performance of a mirrored disk subsystem is approximately the same for disks that are not mirrored. Actually, reads are slightly faster, and writes to the disk are slightly slower, but these are not significant changes.

Another solution to the mirrored disk approach was proposed in a paper by David A. Patterson, Garth Gibson, and Randy Katz of the University of California, Berkeley (Report no. UCB/CSD 87/39, December 1987). The report titled "A Case for Redundant Array of Inexpensive Disks or RAID" discusses the concept of using an array of disks to distribute data that can provide reliability and improve disk performance. Because disk performance continues to be a bottleneck on PC server-based solutions, there has been a great deal of interest in RAID technology.

The key concept behind RAID is a technique called striping. *Striping* allows data blocks to be interleaved across several drives that have the same performance and storage characteristics, instead of storing them on the same drive. Each drive operates independently of the others, and this allows data to be transferred in parallel from each drive. This means that if an array of *n* disks is operating in parallel, the data will be transferred in $1/n$ the time compared to data transferred using a single disk, resulting in an *n*-fold improvement in disk transfer rate. Figure 5.4 shows data being read in a RAID subsystem using 3 drives. The numbers in the figure represent data blocks and show that they are interleaved across the 3 disks.

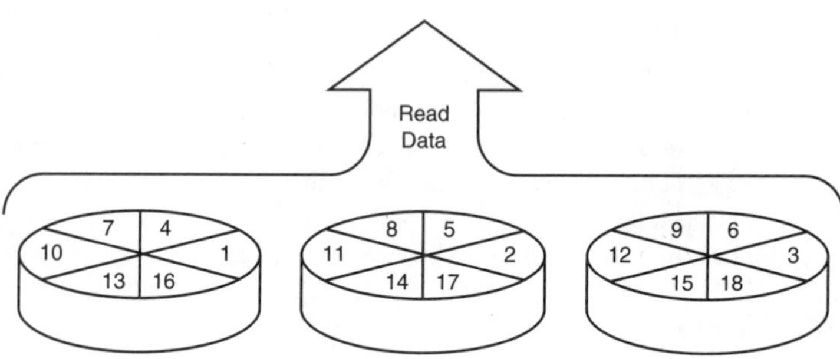

Figure 5.4
Disk striping.

Reliability in RAID is achieved by using one of the disks for storing a *check byte*. The check byte is constructed in such a way that should one of the drives fail, the data in that drive can be reconstructed from the remaining data drives (including the check byte drive). A popular algorithm to construct the check byte is the exclusive OR (XOR) operation. Figure 5.5 shows how the XOR checksum byte can be used to reconstruct the data in a 3-disk RAID drive. Two of the drives are used to hold the data, and the third drive is the "check" drive. The first data drive in this example has a bit pattern of 11100011, and the second drive has the data pattern 11101101. The check byte using the XOR operation is 11010111 (see table 5.1). If drive 2 fails, its data can be recovered by an exclusive OR (XOR) operation of the bytes in the remaining drives (see fig. 5.5).

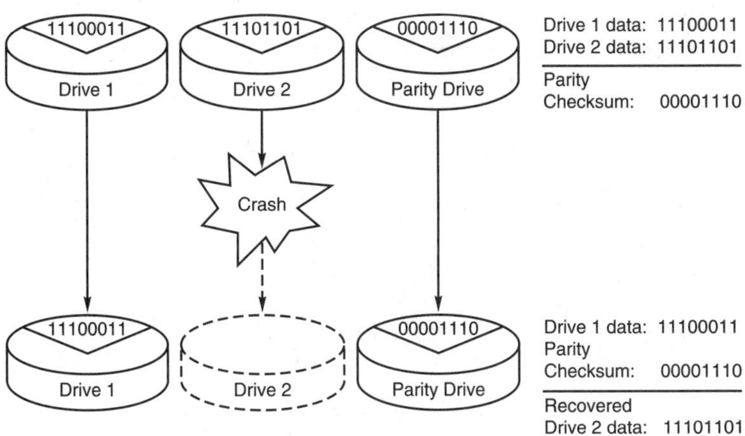

Figure 5.5
Reconstructing data for a failed drive.

Table 5.1
Exclusive OR Operation for Computing Check Byte

Drive	Drive Status	Bit Pattern
Data drive 1	Running	11100011
Data drive 2	Running	11101101 XOR

Check Byte drive	Running	00001110

If data drive 2 fails, table 5.2 shows how data can be reconstructed.

Table 5.2
Recovering Data from a Failed Drive

Drive	Drive Status	Bit Pattern
Data drive 1	Running	11100011
Check Byte drive	Running	00001110 XOR
--		
Data drive 2	Failed	11101101

The check byte is recomputed if a byte location is changed and if the changed check byte has to be written to the check disk. If the check byte is maintained on a single drive, it could result in a bottleneck that would negate the speed improvements of the interleaved drives. For this reason, the check byte is distributed across the disks for improving performance.

The check byte disk represents a storage overhead, but for an *n*-array RAID system, it is 1/*n* of the total storage. For a value of *n* larger than 2, it represents a smaller overhead than a mirrored/duplexed system.

Disk arrays that use RAID technology are classified in terms of RAID levels 0 to 5.

RAID level 0 only makes use of the striping feature of RAID but has no provision for redundancy. Striping improves the performance of the disk array, but because no check bytes are used, there is no improvement in fault tolerance compared to a single-disk system.

RAID level 1 provides disk mirroring along with striping. Every disk has a mirror that has an exact data copy of the primary disk. For best performance, the disks should be designed so that the reads and writes can be performed independently. This will result in speed improvements because the read request will be completed by the first drive that returns the result.

RAID level 2 has a provision for data recovery with one disk reserved for data recovery. The striping function is performed at the bit level. This means that the bits are scattered consecutively across the disks. The first bit, for example, is written on the first disk in the array, and the second bit on the second disk, and so on. RAID 2 is not commonly implemented for microcomputers.

RAID level 3 provides striping at the byte level, with one disk reserved for the check byte. The check-byte disk is called the parity drive and, as already explained, can be used to recover information on the failed drive. It is common to design the spindle rotation of disks so that parallel reads can be done efficiently.

RAID level 4 provides striping at the block level. A block is the amount of data transferred in a single read/write operation. Like RAID level 3, a disk is reserved for a parity drive.

RAID level 5, like RAID level 4, provides striping at the block level. Unlike RAID level 4, however, it spreads the error-correcting block data evenly across the disks. This avoids the bottleneck of writing error-correcting data to a single disk.

RAID disk drivers are available from the manufacturers of the drives for NetWare and other operating system platforms such as OS/2, UNIX, and Windows NT.

Regardless of whether one chooses the disk mirroring/duplexing approach or the RAID approach, the disk subsystem should be fast and reliable. You can build server disk subsystems using IDE, ESDI, or SCSI. The best choice is SCSI because of its flexibility for both disk mirroring/duplexing approaches and RAID.

Summary

This chapter discussed some of the factors that determine the ideal hardware for a NetWare server. System managers should consider such hardware features as CPU speed, server bus type, network I/O, characteristics of NICs, and the speed and reliability of disk subsytems.

These factors have to be balanced against the amount of money one is willing to spend on the server platform. An exciting area of development for NetWare servers is native NetWare running on powerful RISC-based workstations. RISC platforms offer greater speeds and freedom from the PC-based bus approaches such as EISA and MCA which do not rival the performance of mainframe and minicomputer-based bus architectures. An important development in disk subsystem performance is the availability of cost-effective RAID solutions to improve disk speed and reliability.

NetWare 2.2, 3.11, and 3.12

Features of NetWare 2.2, 3.11, and 3.12

This chapter examines some of the capabilities of a *network operating system* (NOS) based on NetWare 2.2, 3.11, and 3.12. NetWare 4.*x* is covered in Part III of this book. This chapter looks at some of the functions of a NOS and examines its relationship to the OSI model. Other issues that are examined include security, management, and interoperability features.

Understanding Network Operating Systems

Before understanding what a network operating system is, you must understand what an operating system is. An *operating system* (see fig. 6.1) is a program that manages resources of a single computer. Operating systems typically manage the following resources:

- Local file system
- Memory in a computer
- Loading and execution of application programs that run in the computer memory
- Input/output to peripheral devices attached to a computer
- CPU scheduling among application programs

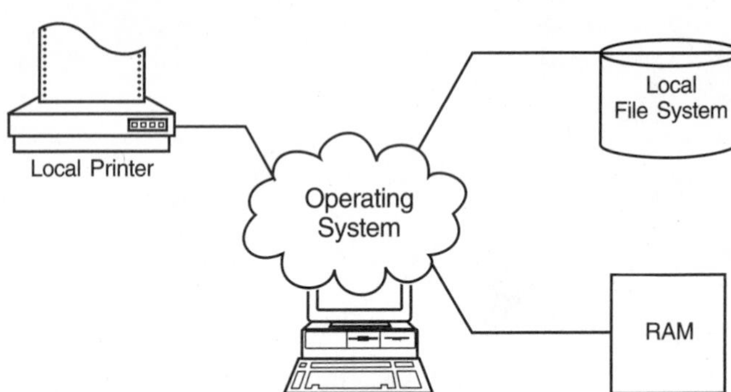

Figure 6.1
Resources managed by an operating system.

A network consists of resources, such as stations and printers, and communication devices, such as bridges, routers, and gateways. The job of a network operating system is similar to that of an operating system except that it has to manage resources on a much larger scale. A *network operating system* (see fig. 6.2) is a program that manages resources across an entire network. The following is a list of some of the resources a network operating system manages:

- Remote file systems that are accessible by other workstations
- Memory on the computer that a NOS runs on
- Loading and execution of shared application programs
- Input/output to shared network devices
- CPU scheduling among NOS processes

Examining the Features of a Network Operating System

NOS software can be distributed equally among all nodes, or a major portion of the NOS can reside in a central node. A NOS that is distributed equally among all nodes is called a *peer-to-peer NOS.* An example of this is NetWare Lite. A NOS whose major portion runs on a central node is a *centralized NOS.* The central node is called the *server.* Applications that make use of resources managed by the central node NOS are called *clients.* This architecture generally is referred to as the *client/server architecture.*

Because the client software runs on workstations, the workstations are sometimes referred to as *clients.* Only applications that make use of services, however, should be called *clients.* Applications or system software that provide services to other applications are called *servers.*

When a client communicates with the server, it must have a small portion of the NOS running on it. In NetWare terminology, the NOS running on the client is called the *shell* (NetWare 2.2, 3.11) or the *requester* (NetWare 3.12 and higher). Examples of the centralized NOS are NetWare 2.*x* and NetWare 3.*x*.

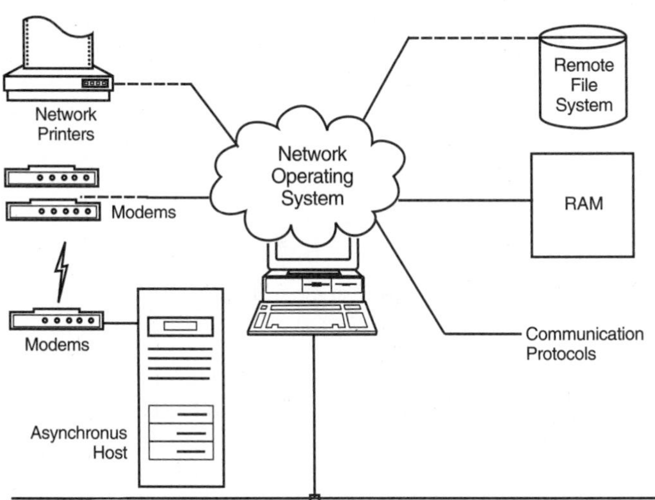

Figure 6.2
Resources managed by a network operating system.

When a NOS runs on a user node (workstation), it must communicate and interact with the native operating system on the user node. The native operating system that runs on the workstation is called a *workstation operating system* (WOS). Examples of WOSs are DOS, OS/2, UNIX, and Macintosh's System 7.

NOS and the OSI Model

Figure 6.3 shows the NOS in relationship with the OSI model. You can see in this figure that the NOS spans layers 3 to 7 of the OSI model. The NOS has three major aspects:

- Network driver
- Subnet protocols
- Application layer protocols

The NOS communicates with the LAN hardware by means of a network driver. The network driver acts as a liaison between the Network Interface Card (NIC) and the subnet protocols. The subnet protocols are communication protocols needed to send application and system messages across the network. The application layer protocols implement the NOS services and communicate with the subnet protocols. Each of these major aspects of a NOS are discussed in the next few sections.

Figure 6.3
The relationship between the NOS and OSI.

OSI Model		NOS
APPLICATION	Layer 7	NOS
PRESENTATION	Layer 6	a) APIs b) Subnet protocols c) Network Driver
SESSION	Layer 5	
TRANSPORT	Layer 4	
NETWORK	Layer 3	
DATA LINK	Layer 2	Ethernet/ Token Ring or other LANs
PHYSICAL	Layer 1	

Network Drivers

A *network driver* is a program that spans portions of layers 2 and 3 of the OSI model. It provides an interface between the NIC and the upper-layer protocols.

The network driver masks the complexities of the way a NIC must be controlled for transmitting and receiving packets from upper layers. The network driver has an intimate understanding of the hardware operation of the NIC, such as the various control/status registers, DMA, and I/O ports. Vendors producing NICs according to LAN standards, such as the IEEE 802.5, implement the details of the NIC differently. This means that two IEEE 802.5 nodes may be able to communicate across a LAN despite differences in implementation, such as IRQ lines, DMA, and I/O port mechanisms. Because the implementations are different, each NIC must have a different network driver even though NICs can communicate with each other by using the same IEEE 802.5 protocol.

Network installers select the correct network driver for the card and integrate this network driver with the NOS. As you will see later in this chapter, in NetWare 2.*x* this process is done by generating NetWare. NetWare 3.*x* uses a more flexible dynamic binding mechanism to accomplish this task.

NetWare comes with drivers for some popular cards. Drivers not included with the NetWare disks must be obtained from the manufacturer of the card. Usually, a NIC comes with a floppy disk containing drivers for operating systems such as NetWare, LANMAN, VINES, and UNIX. Many NIC vendors maintain their own bulletin boards, and you can download network drivers for them. Some vendors supply drivers through the NetWire forum on CompuServe.

Subnet Protocols

Subnet protocols span layers 3 to 5 of the OSI model. These layers provide the network services that are essential for sending data across a LAN. The functions of layers 3 to 5 are discussed in Chapter 1, "NetWare Protocols." Review the discussion in that chapter for a better understanding of the subnet protocols.

Subnet protocols play an important role in the performance and functionality of a NOS. Fast subnet protocols result in a fast NOS. On the other hand, slow subnet protocols make for a sluggish NOS. Also, a subnet protocol that is fast on a LAN may be slow on a *wide area network* (WAN).

The native subnet protocols used by NetWare are IPX for layer 3 and either SPX or PXP for layer 4.

In most situations, a layer 5 protocol is not necessary for NetWare. If an application is written to make use of the NetBIOS protocol, an optional layer 5 can be provided that implements the NetBIOS protocol. The NetBIOS software emulator implements its services by making use of the SPX protocols.

The subnet protocols and their relationship to the OSI model are shown in figure 6.4.

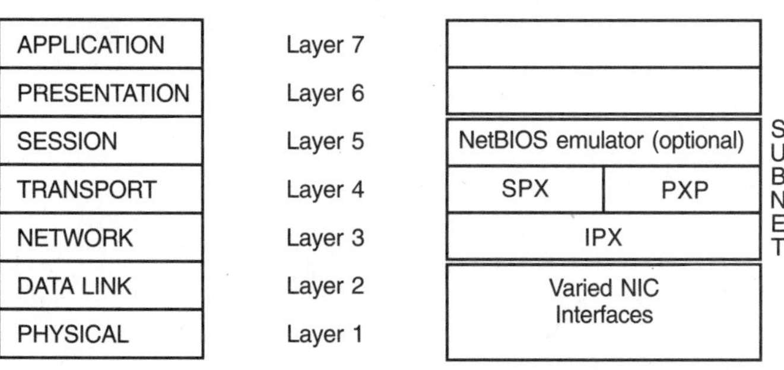

Figure 6.4
The relationship between OSI and the NetWare subnet protocols.

The native NetWare protocols were derived from Xerox's *XNS* (Xerox Network Standard) protocols. The relationship between XNS and NetWare protocols is shown in table 6.1.

Table 6.1
XNS and NetWare Protocols

XNS Protocol	NetWare Protocol
IDP (Internet Datagram Protocol)	IPX (Internet Packet Exchange)
PEP (Packet Exchange Protocol)	PXP (Packet Exchange Protocol)
SPP (Sequence Packet Protocol)	SPX (Sequence Packet Exchange)

Novell based its subnet protocols on XNS because these protocols had the reputation of working efficiently in a LAN environment. XNS protocols were not designed to be used for wide area networks, which have larger time delays. Because of this, Novell's IPX, PXP, and SPX protocols suffer from the same limitations as XNS protocols for WAN applications. Novell offers a streamlined version of its protocols for WANs to overcome some of these limitations. This streamlined version—the *packet burst* NLM—is available for only NetWare 3.x and higher.

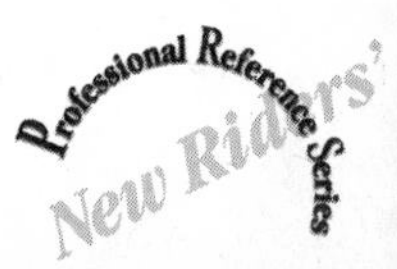

In retrospect, Novell could have avoided some of these problems and gained an early lead in WANs had they chosen the Internet UDP/TCP/IP protocols. User Datagram Protocol works efficiently across LANs, and Transmission Control Protocol works efficiently across WANs. The Internet protocols and others are available for NetWare 3.*x*.

The IPX protocol provides the capability to send data across different interconnected LANs. IPX is a datagram (connectionless) service. SPX provides a virtual circuit (connections-oriented) service for those applications that need it. SPX has a larger overhead in terms of processing time and additional packets, so NetWare avoids this for its internal operation. PXP is a transport protocol that is connectionless. It is patterned after Xerox's PEP protocol.

Application Layer Protocols

The single most important application layer protocol that NetWare provides is *NetWare Core Protocol* (NCP). Without NCP, none of the file services offered by NetWare would be possible. A number of reference materials mistakenly show the NCP protocol as belonging to layer 5 or layer 6. NCP provides remote file services to client nodes and rightfully belongs in layer 7 of the OSI model.

Some of the misunderstanding about NCP protocol functions probably arises because the definition of the NCP protocols is not publicly available. Novell is extremely reluctant to reveal details about the NCP protocol. Developers can, for a lot of money, obtain details of NCP protocols after they sign appropriate nondisclosure agreements.

The following are some of the functions that NCP provides:

- Opens files under different modes
- Closes open files
- Reads data blocks from open files
- Writes data blocks to open files
- Gets a list of directory entries
- Manipulates the server database (bindery)
- Provides high-level connection services
- Provides synchronization operations

Multitasking versus Single-Tasking NOS

Operating systems like DOS are single-tasking. This means that DOS can perform only one thing at a time. For the environment and applications for which DOS was originally conceived, this was not a problem. The operating system needed to manage only one user and one application at a time.

Some of the earlier NOSs, such as MS-NET from Microsoft and its derivatives, provided NOS services on top of DOS. A big performance penalty was paid by these earlier NOSs. Consider, for example, what would happen if several packet requests came to a server that was running MS-NET on top of DOS. MS-NET would have to make use of DOS to provide access to the hard disks on the server. If a second packet request was allowed to be processed while the first one was in progress, the MS-NET server would crash. Why? Because DOS is nonre-entrant.

Nonre-entrant means that a piece of program code can be entered or executed only once at any given time. *Re-entrant* code can be entered or executed by a number of processes at any time. 3+SHARE from 3COM, an earlier NOS based on MS-NET, also was based on DOS. It avoided the DOS bottleneck by providing a re-entrant piece of code that could access the server's resources. 3COM called this piece of re-entrant code *CIOSYS* (concurrent I/O system). Earlier MS-NET versions queued packet requests and allowed only one packet to be processed at a time.

Microsoft solved the MS-NET problem in LAN Manager because LANMAN runs on top of OS/2. OS/2 is a multitasking operating system and is re-entrant; it can process several packet requests at a time.

Another popular NOS, *virtual network system* (VINES) from Banyan, runs on top of a modified UNIX System V. UNIX is multitasking and re-entrant and can process multiple packet requests.

A NOS must be multitasking and re-entrant. If a NOS runs on top of another operating system, that operating system must, in turn, be multitasking and re-entrant.

NetWare is multitasking and re-entrant, but it is not based on a general purpose operating system like OS/2 or UNIX. (Novell does have a version of NetWare that runs on UNIX called NetWare for UNIX, but it is another product line.) NetWare is built from the ground up as a multitasking operating system.

In a general purpose operating system, issues of fairness are more important than throughput and efficiency. Consider a general purpose multitasking operating system (such as UNIX) that is running several user applications. Although some applications (foreground tasks) may be more important than others (background tasks), it is important that no applications are starved for CPU time. To achieve this goal, a process is given a certain amount of time, and then the CPU turns its attention to another process, regardless of what it may be doing at the time. Although this procedure may be more democratic and fair, it has an adverse effect on the system throughput, especially when critical processes are interrupted.

NetWare adopts the philosophy that a process can monopolize the CPU for as long as it needs to complete critical tasks. Processes need to yield the CPU to others when done performing critical tasks. This *nonpremptive scheduling* mechanism is used in the design of many real-time operating systems.

The NetWare Network Operating System

NetWare was first developed in 1983 as a NOS that ran on a proprietary Motorola 68000 microcomputer that acted as the central element in a star topology. This network was called the S-Net. Novell abandoned the proprietary hardware approach and developed NetWare for the IBM XT platform, calling it NetWare 86. NetWare 86 was followed by the Advanced NetWare 286 and SFT NetWare 286 products. Macintosh support was added to SFT NetWare 286 2.15. Novell then announced ELS NetWare, which was developed to compete with entry-level LANs. ELS NetWare was not very successful and has given way to NetWare Lite.

When the Intel 80386-based AT personal computer was designed, Novell released a completely revamped version of NetWare to run on 386-based ATs. This NetWare version was rewritten by using Watcoms 32-bit C compiler and became NetWare 386. The NetWare 386 product line now is called NetWare 3.*x*, and the NetWare 286 product line merged into a unified NetWare 2.2. The rewrite of NetWare in C led to the development of Portable NetWare, which consists of NetWare services ported to different operating system platforms. Portable NetWare has since been retitled NetWare for UNIX. Novell continues to form strategic alliances with major networking vendors, such as IBM, DEC, HP, and AT&T, to make NetWare available on as wide a range of platforms as possible.

NetWare has pioneered features such as *System Fault Tolerant* (SFT) servers, security services, and performance improvement mechanisms. Many of the other network operating systems now support these features. Novell did not invent these features because similar features existed and exist on minicomputer and mainframe-based systems. Novell, however, was the first to use these features on PC-based networks.

Other NOS Choices

Several excellent NOS choices are available in the NOS market place, including LAN Manager from Microsoft, VINES from Banyan, and IBM LAN Server from IBM. The history of these products is shown in figure 6.5.

Today, NetWare's main competitor is LANMAN. LANMAN was first marketed through 3COM and other OEMs. For many years, the most advanced version of LANMAN was available from 3COM and was called 3+OPEN. Microsoft made the decision to market LANMAN through 3COM because 3COM was then the well-known archrival of Novell. 3COM added many improved features to LANMAN, such as sophisticated network administration, *demand protocol architecture* (DPA), and Macintosh support. 3COM, however, quit the NOS business by early 1991.

LANMAN now is supported and marketed by Microsoft. Many of the 3+OPEN features are being integrated into LANMAN. LANMAN runs on the OS/2 platform. Microsoft has announced that future versions of LANMAN will run on its *New Technology* (NT) operating system platform. LANMAN also is available on UNIX platforms through a port made by AT&T. Initially, HP and AT&T worked on this port, but HP eventually dropped out. Micro-Tempus has a LANMAN version for the IBM MVS mainframe platform. Many other licenses of LANMAN exist.

IBM's first NOS offering was the IBM *PC LAN Program* (PCLP). PCLP was based on MS-NET and suffered from all the performance problems of running on DOS. PCLP still is available from IBM and is an example of a peer-to-peer NOS. When Microsoft released LANMAN as part of OS/2, IBM, through a license agreement with Microsoft, developed a NOS based on LANMAN. This NOS from IBM is the IBM LAN Server. It is based on OS/2 *EE* (Extended Edition). OS/2 EE has the additional components of a Communications Manager to interface with IBM SNA networks and a Database Manager that supports the IBM mainframe database (DB2). Although IBM has its own NOS offering, it became a reseller of Novell's NetWare in early 1991.

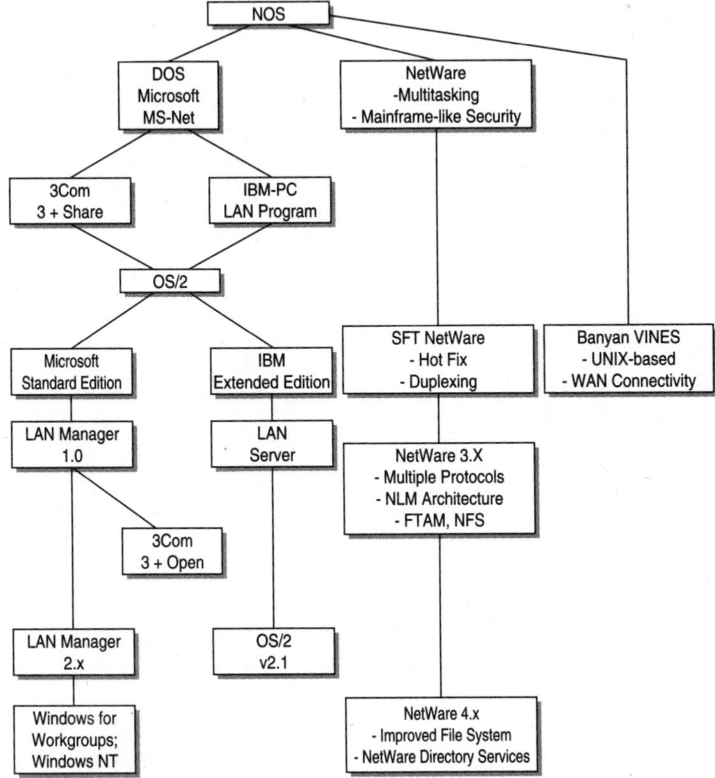

Figure 6.5
The history of network operating systems. (Graphic courtesy of Learning Group International)

VINES from Banyan is based on a modified UNIX System V. It is a robust NOS with features comparable to NetWare and LANMAN. Because UNIX comes with protocols like TCP/IP that work well with WANs, it is not surprising that VINES has very good support for wide area networking. Banyan went one step further and designed a powerful distributed naming service that enables network resources to be accessed by a symbolic name, regardless of their location anywhere on the network. This naming service is called StreetTalk and is one of the reasons VINES enjoys an edge in LAN/WAN integration. Novell uses NetWare Directory Services based on the CCITT X.500 in NetWare 4.*x*.

Understanding NetWare's NOS Security

When NetWare came out in 1984, it quickly acquired a reputation of being a secure NOS. Other NOSs that were based on MS-NET, such as MS-NET, IBM PCLP, and 10NET, had very poor security. In contrast to these NOSs, NetWare provided security features that rivaled those of minicomputer and mainframe operating systems.

The next few sections briefly examine some of the security features of NetWare.

User Account Security

All versions of NetWare have a user name/password security feature. To use NetWare, a user must have an account and a valid password on the system. In earlier versions of NetWare, passwords were sent over the LAN in unencrypted form. When protocol analyzers became quite common, unencrypted passwords became an obvious security deficiency. Protocol analyzers examine packets on a LAN and easily see the password that is sent by a user workstation during the log-in sequence. Now, all versions of NetWare encrypt the password at the station before sending it across the LAN.

Time Restrictions

By using the system administration utility SYSCON, a NetWare administrator can impose time restrictions on when a user can log in. The time restrictions can be imposed in terms of half-hour intervals and can be set for any of the weekdays.

The time restriction feature is designed for network sites that have strict security measures in which access to the network needs to be denied to users.

Station Restrictions

NetWare administrators can use the system administration utility SYSCON to impose station restrictions on where a user can log in. The station restriction enables a user to log in from only stations that have a specified station address.

The station restriction feature is designed for network sites that have strict security measures in which access to the network is possible through certain physical areas only. Station restrictions prevent users from wandering to other areas of the building and using workstations that do not belong to them.

Space Restrictions

One of the questions a network administrator has to ask is: How much server disk space should a user be allowed? If a user does not have any restrictions, the user can, by design or accident, use up all the space on the server disk.

Suppose, for example, that a user runs an application that creates a temporary file on the server disk. If a bug is in the application, the application can keep on entering data in the temporary file until it expands and fills all available disk space on the server. This situation is not too uncommon and when it occurs, all the users on that server are affected.

You can safeguard available disk space by limiting disk space on an individual user basis, based on the applications a user runs. Typical values allocated per user on the server range from 1 MB to 20 MB.

Diskless Workstations

When LANs began to become popular and became a legitimate platform for running business applications in corporations, some MIS managers had misgivings about the LAN client/server technology. One reason for this misgiving was that user workstations had removable media, such as disks. It would be possible for an unscrupulous user to download sensitive information to a floppy disk or hard disk and walk away with the disk. With the traditional terminal/host architecture, the user can view this information on-screen but cannot walk away with a disk containing sensitive information.

One way to keep users from copying sensitive information onto floppy disks is to install diskless workstations. Diskless workstations do not have any storage media, such as floppy disk drives or hard disks. They boot their native operating system, such as DOS, from a copy of the operating system boot image that is stored on the server. The NIC cards on diskless work-stations have a special boot *programmable read only memory* (PROM) that enables the NIC to fetch the boot image from a public directory on the server. In the case of NetWare, this is the SYS:LOGIN directory under volume SYS: on the server.

Media Security

In many applications, LAN media security is a big concern. The LAN cabling should be installed so that it is not possible for an unauthorized user to access the LAN cables. Coaxial cables and twisted pair cables are easy to tap and read data. They also emit electromagnetic radiation. A determined person with sufficient resources can read LAN traffic through these emanations. Some military applications install LAN cabling in a metal conduit to prevent noise emanations and bury the cable in concrete to prevent physical access to the LAN cables.

The best LAN media for security purposes is fiber optic because it is more difficult to tap. If a probe is inserted into the fiber optic conductor, it can cause additional reflections and interference to the light signals and cause the fiber optic link to crash.

Encryption

How do you secure data on the file server? One way is to make use of the security permissions provided by the NOS. The network administrator with supervisor or equivalent privileges, however, can read all files and directories on the server. This becomes a problem with sensitive information that you do not want other users, including the supervisor, to see. One way of handling this is to encrypt databases and files that contain sensitive information. Some database systems, such as Novell's Btrieve record manager, have the capability to encrypt data files. The file is decrypted when it is opened and encrypted when it is closed. As you can imagine, however, performance suffers because of the encryption and decryption operations.

A number of encryption programs are available. Some encryption programs are bundled with software tools, such as Borland's SideKick and Central Point's PC-TOOLS. Many use the *Data Encryption Standard* (DES) algorithms for encryption.

Encryption also can be done in hardware at the NIC level before transmitting packets across the LAN media. When encrypting LAN packets, only the data portion of the packet is encrypted. The network address and control fields in the packets usually are not encrypted so that devices such as bridges and routers can interpret the network address and control fields.

Motorola's wireless LAN uses encryption to prevent users from tapping into the microwave frequency used for transmission. Wireless LANs have sophisticated encryption algorithms in which the seed used for encryption is changed randomly every 2 milliseconds. The *seed* is a number or code that is used as the key for the encryption algorithm.

Audits

LAN audits are very helpful for performing an analysis of the threats to which a NOS has been subjected.

A hostile user, for example, might try to guess passwords by repeatedly trying password combinations. In NetWare, one way to prevent this is to lock out the user after a certain number of failed password attempts. Another way is to have an audit of all password attempts. Some audit messages are reported directly to the server console, whereas others are kept in an audit trail file.

Computer Viruses

Computer viruses are a form of networking terrorism of which network managers must be aware. A few misguided programmers spend countless hours devising techniques to terrorize innocent users by wiping out their data, or infecting the data in such a manner that the software virus can propagate itself.

It is much more difficult for virus writers to break the security of a NOS such as NetWare. A network manager can use a number of preventive measures to reduce the threat of viruses. Virus detection and correction software also are available that can be used in a network environment.

Managing Interoperability Issues in a NOS

As networks grow in size, one of the major problems a network administrator faces is *interoperability*. When all the hardware and software components are from the same vendor, the system usually functions flawlessly. This is the reason why many users and corporations prefer a single vendor solution.

Many MIS departments are pure IBM, or pure DEC, or pure Novell. Network applications and requirements have become so broad and diverse that it is difficult for a single vendor to supply all possible needs. The larger vendors, such as IBM, DEC, and HP, come very close to supplying these needs, but many of their solutions require the purchase of a proprietary platform. The vendor then can lock the user into a particular computing architecture, which makes it difficult to purchase equipment that is not from the same vendor.

Some end users are perfectly happy to be locked into a vendor's solution because they do not have to deal with interoperability issues—the vendor does instead. Solutions from a single vendor, however, usually are not the most cost-effective. Competition and the free market system tend to drive down equipment prices and increase performance. Also, vendors have strengths in different areas. Many network managers exploit the strengths of various vendors, leading to multivendor networks.

One solution to the interoperability dilemma is the adoption of open systems in which vendors make products compliant to universally accepted standards. The development of the OSI model and standardization efforts of organizations, such as ISO, ANSI, IEEE, and ECMA, are steps in the right direction. Only time will tell the success of these efforts.

The following section discusses some of the more important aspects of interoperability as it relates to multivendor networks.

Defining Interoperability

Interoperability means that all the hardware and software components in a system cooperate at all levels. This is a broad, yet accurate, definition of interoperability and encompasses a wide range of issues. Although the term interoperability may be difficult to define, you begin to appreciate the *lack* of interoperability when your network stops working because of conflicting components.

As the following examples point out, interoperability usually is not discussed unless the hardware and software do not interoperate.

You can, for example, buy a telephone from a variety of sources and plug it in any telephone socket. You do not have to be a technician or electrical engineer to perform this task. As long as that telephone jack is enabled by the telephone company, you can dial any telephone in the world. This is an example of interoperability at the highest level.

Another example is Centronics parallel printer cable for IBM personal computers. You can buy it from any source, and it works just fine with any IBM PC clone. Likewise, all FAX machines can "talk" to each other because they use the same Group 3 FAX as the language used in sending facsimile data.

All of these examples have one thing in common. They all conform to the same standard. In the case of telephones, the phone jacks and the signals used for communications comply to a standard. For the Centronics parallel printer cable, the cable connectors and the wiring conform to a standard. In the FAX machine example, all FAX machines use the same Group 3 FAX code. When components operate as they should operate, interoperability usually is not a topic of discussion.

On the other hand, if you install a NetWare server on the same LAN as a VINES server and try to get the two servers to share data and applications, you begin to realize the importance of interoperability. Because NetWare and VINES use different architectures, they cannot communicate. This is an example of network software interoperability. Hardware interoperability issues also exist.

You cannot, for example, connect a Token Ring station directly to an Ethernet bus because each system uses different connectors and cables. Even if you manage to connect the Token Ring NIC to the

Ethernet bus by a liberal use of a soldering iron and a wire cutter, the two stations will not be able to talk to each other. Ethernet uses a carrier-sense mechanism and Token Ring uses token access. In other words, the two stations are incompatible at the physical and data link layers of the OSI model.

On the other hand, you can connect a 10BASE5 Ethernet LAN and a 10BASE-T Ethernet LAN and expect them to interoperate. Both use different cable types; 10BASE5 uses coaxial cable and 10BASE-T uses unshielded twisted pair wiring. You can, however, join these two LANs by a 10BASE-T transceiver, enabling the stations on the two LANs to communicate as if they were part of the same network. This is possible because both 10BASE5 and 10BASE-T use the same carrier-sense access mechanism. In this example, the two LANs are compatible at the data link layer of the OSI model.

The OSI model is indispensable in analyzing problems concerning inter-operability issues within networks. As you learned earlier in the chapter, interoperability problems stem from lack of standardization. If all networks followed the same standards, the term *interoperability* probably would not have been created by the networking industry. (The term does not yet exist in the English dictionary.) Read Chapter 1, "NetWare Protocols," for a description of the OSI model.

Interconnectivity versus Interoperability

Sometimes the term *interconnectivity* is confused with *interoperability*. You can, for example, put a Token Ring NIC in a NetWare server, an IBM LAN Server, and a VINES server, and then connect them to the same Token Ring LAN. The token in this Token Ring circulates through each of these servers. Data and control packets generated by each of these servers circulate to other servers. Compatibility exists at the data link layer of the OSI model because each of these servers uses the same token access mechanism. These servers, however, cannot share and exchange applications and data. In this example, you have *interconnectivity* among these servers but not *interoperability*. Figure 6.6 shows compatibility at the physical (layer 1) and data link (layer 2) layers of the OSI model, but no compatibility at the upper layers.

Figure 6.6
Server compatibility at the physical and data link layer only.

NetWare	Layer	IBM LAN Server	Layer	VINES
NCP	7	SMB	7	File Services
	6		6	
NetBIOS (opt)	5	NETBEUI	5	NetBIOS, RPC
SPX, PXP	4	NETBEUI	4	VSPP
IPX	3	NETBEUI	3	VIP
IEEE 802.5	2	IEEE 802.5	2	IEEE 802.5
IEEE 802.5	1	IEEE 802.5	1	IEEE 802.5

In the preceding figure, NETBEUI is IBM's NetBIOS extended user interface, SMB is IBM's file services protocol (Server Message Block), VIP is VINES Internet Protocol, VSPP is VINES Sequenced Packet Protocol, and RPC is VINES remote procedure call.

You can compare interconnectivity and interoperability to a room full of English-speaking and French-speaking people talking at the same time. Interconnectivity exists because each person can hear the utterances of each speaker. The English and French speakers, however, cannot understand each other (unless they understand both languages). In other words, *interoperability among the people speaking in the room does not exist.*

Different Levels of Interoperability

Interoperability should be considered in terms of the applications used by users. Can these applications run on different platforms? Can data files and information be exchanged between them? If a user can perform these general tasks, you will not hear much about interoperability problems.

In terms of the OSI model, interoperability exists when you have compatibility at the application layer (layer 7). How does layer 7 interoperability affect the other layers 1 to 7 of the OSI model? In the OSI model, a layer depends on the services provided by the layer below it. Layer 7 of the OSI model, therefore, uses the services provided by layer 6, which in turn uses the services provided by layer 5 and so on all the way down to layer 1. In order to have interoperability at layer 7, or the application layer, you must have interoperability at layers 1 to 6. The sole purpose of layers 1 to 6 is to provide interconnection between the application layers of two stations that are sharing information.

File transfer protocols, such as Kermit, XMODEM, and *File Transfer Protocol* (FTP), are examples of interoperability. Kermit and XMODEM can be found on many different systems, and yet you can exchange files by using asynchronous dial-up lines (telephone lines) between these systems. FTP implementations exist on DOS machines, NetWare 3.*x* servers, and UNIX machines. You can use FTP to transfer files between these systems.

In the preceding discussion, *interconnectivity* is compatibility at layers 1 to 6 of the OSI model. *True interoperability* is compatibility at layer 7 (the application layer) of the OSI model and the application software that makes use of it. True interoperability cannot exist without the interconnectivity support of layers 1 through 6 of the OSI model.

Examining Levels of Interoperability

The preceding section discussed interpretability issues at the different layers of the OSI model. The OSI model is used as a yard stick only because not many commercial implementations make use of ISO recommendations for the protocols at the OSI layers. Even among the OSI recommendations, several options are available from which to choose. Some of the layers have incompatible options. Two implementations, therefore, can both claim to be OSI compatible, but because they use incompatible options at some of the layers, no interoperability exists between them.

Interoperability at the Physical Layer

If stations are attached to the same physical media, such as coaxial cable, twisted pair cable, or fiber optic, then they have interoperability at the physical media, or layer 1, of the OSI model. Examples of this are Ethernet stations that are connected by coaxial cable, or Token Ring stations connected by IBM Type 1 twisted pair wiring. Figure 6.7 shows the OSI model for two stations connected by the same media.

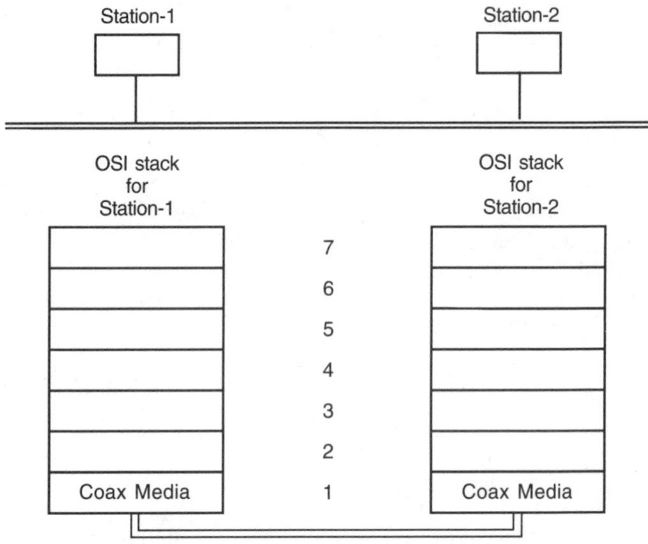

Figure 6.7
Interoperability at the physical layer with same cable.

You also can have physical layer interoperability even when stations are connected by different media types. You can, for example, interconnect stations on a coax Ethernet LAN and on a 10BASE-T LAN. Interoperability is established between the two LANs by a *10BASE-T transceiver* that joins a 10BASE-T link to the transceiver cable and provides the signal conversion. Figure 6.8 shows the interoperability between these stations as it relates to the OSI model.

Interoperability at the Data Link Layer

Figure 6.8 also shows interoperability at the data link layer. Both stations use the same IEEE 802.3 mechanism for accessing the LAN, which assures inter-operability at the data link layer.

You also can have interoperability for Ethernet and Token Ring LANs indirectly through a translating device, even though they use different data link layer mechanisms. The translating device that provides interoperability between dissimilar data link layers is called a *bridge.* The IBM 8209 bridge, for example, can be used to connect Ethernet and IBM Token Ring LANs. Figure 6.9 shows an example of a bridge.

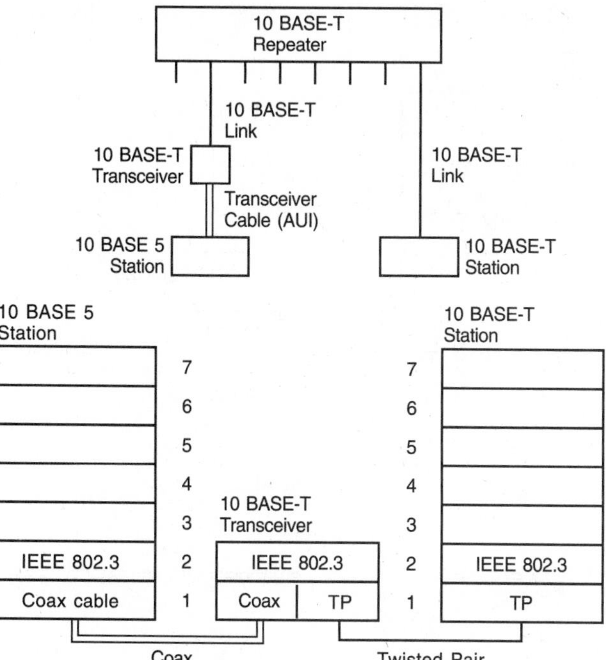

Figure 6.8
Interoperability at the physical layer with coaxial and twisted pair cables.

Interoperability at the Subnet Layers

Two NetWare stations can communicate with each other because they use the same protocols at the subnet layers. Subnet layers are defined as layers 3 to 5 of the OSI model. Figure 6.10 shows two NetWare stations that are interoperable at the subnet layer. In examining their OSI representations, you can see that the NetWare stations use the same protocols at layers 3, 4, and 5. In this example, the stations are using Novell's NetBIOS implementation to communicate. Two NetWare stations can use just layer 3 (IPX) to communicate. Many applications that run on NetWare use just the IPX layer for interoperation. An important point illustrated in figure 6.10 is that to have interoperability at the subnet layers, you must have interoperability at the physical and data link layers (layers 1 to 2).

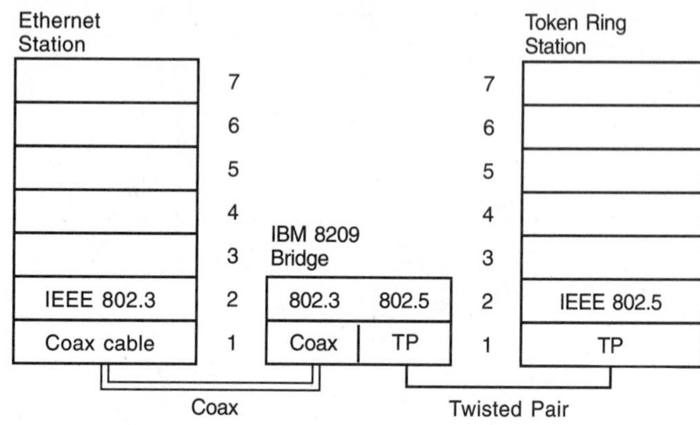

Figure 6.9
Interoperability at the data link layer through a bridge.

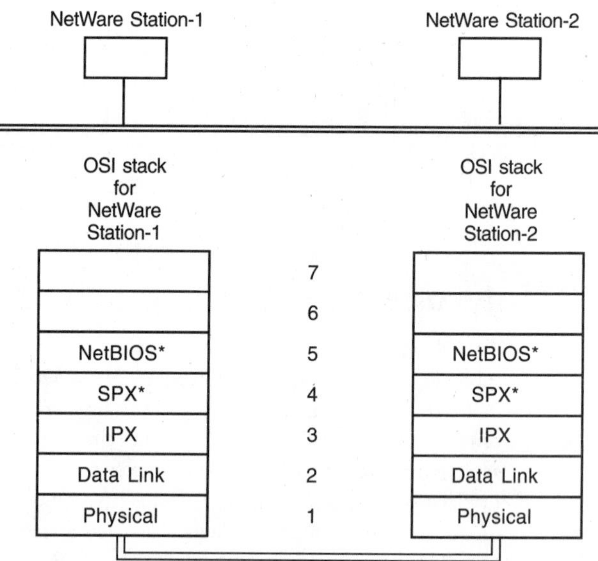

Figure 6.10
Interoperability at subnet layers for NetWare stations.

Interoperability at the Application Layer

Earlier in this chapter, you saw that transferring files is an example of interoperability at the application layer. One area of great interest to many corporations is interoperability of different electronic mail systems. For PC-based networks, a defacto standard is Novell's *message handling system* (MHS). MHS was developed by Action Technologies of Emeryville, California, and now is controlled by Novell. Many electronic-mail packages, like DaVinci Mail and cc:Mail (a subsidiary of Lotus Corp.), use and support MHS. You even can use MHS on CompuServe. If you do not have a need to go outside PC-based LANs, MHS provides sufficient capabilities for interoperation between electronic-mail systems. If you need to send electronic mail to an IBM mainframe or to stations on DECnet, however, MHS does not work. The bigger vendors, such as IBM and DEC, have their own electronic-mail standards.

Electronic mail is represented by an international standard called X.400. X.400 is a general standard that enables text, binary, voice, and facsimile data to be sent in an electronic-mail message. All the major vendors in the United States, such as IBM and DEC, and the network industries in Europe and Japan support X.400. Many vendors use their own proprietary systems, but to interoperate with each other, vendors use X.400 gateways. X.400 gateways translate the proprietary message format into the X.400 format and vice-versa. A related standard exists that is called the X.500 and handles network name services on a worldwide scale that is used in conjunction with X.400.

Other interoperability issues at the application layer deal with application-level interoperability. The following section discusses how to run applications on both IBM PC and Macintosh computers. You also learn how to exchange application data files between the IBM and Macintosh.

Data Interoperability for DOS

Lotus 1-2-3 and Microsoft Excel spreadsheets can run on both the IBM PC and Macintosh platforms. These applications contain conversion routines to import and export spreadsheets between these two platforms. These conversion routines are necessary because the IBM PC and Mac operating systems use different file systems and methods to represent data. Data transparency does not exist between these systems. Excel and 1-2-3, for example, have built-in support for this conversion. Not all applications provide conversion routines, but third-party support tools that provide data conversion are available. Conversion between text files from IBM PC to Macintosh is easy. More complex file structures require special utilities. The following are some utilities (and their manufacturers) that you can use to convert more complex files between IBM PCs and the Macintosh:

- AutoImport (White Crane Software)
- Catapult (Tangent Group)
- DataLens Driver (Digital Networks)
- PC/SQL-Link Database Gateway (Micro Decisionware)
- Ally (Unisys)

Data Interoperability Provided by NetWare

A network operating system such as NetWare 3.*x* enables Macintosh, DOS, OS/2, and UNIX workstations to store files on the server. (NetWare 2.*x* supports DOS, OS/2, and Macintosh file systems.) Figure 6.11 shows that each of these workstations sees its own file system on the same NetWare server. Macintosh users see folders and iconic representations of files, and DOS users see file names (eight-character file name and three-character extension) on the server. NetWare supports this file transparency by using a general representation for files on the server called the *Universal File System.*

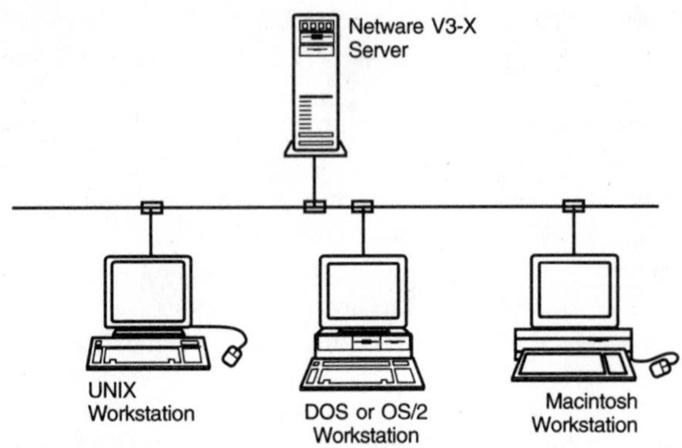

Figure 6.11
Multi-workstation support on NetWare 3.x.

Data Interoperability under Microsoft Windows and OS/2

Applications running in the Microsoft Windows or OS/2 environments can export and import data between applications. The most primitive mechanism for doing this is the cut-and-paste operations that can copy application data into a temporary buffer. This data then can be imported into other applications that are running under Windows or OS/2. A much more powerful mechanism for providing data exchange is *Dynamic Data Exchange* (DDE). DDE enables you to set up an interprocess communications link between two applications operating in a Windows or OS/2 environment. When data changes are made in one application, the changes are automatically sent to the linked application.

The problem with DDE is that it works with only true Windows or OS/2 Presentation Manager applications. Also, DDE does not provide data transparency. The applications linked by DDE need to understand each other's message format. DDE is concerned only with getting the message across. In this sense, DDE is similar to the transport and session layer protocols in the OSI model.

Data Interoperability Using Object Linking and Embedding

To better support data transparency, vendors, such as Microsoft, have developed *object linking and embedding* (OLE). OLE provides a way to share data between different applications. OLE introduces the notion of *data ownership*. The application that first creates the data, owns the data. This association between application and data exists even when the data is exported to other applications.

If, for example, you have OLE-aware versions of AutoCAD and PageMaker, you can create an illustration under AutoCAD, and then export it to PageMaker. Because the illustration was created in AutoCAD, an ownership association exists between AutoCAD and the illustration and is retained even though the drawing now is in a PageMaker document. You can modify the illustration by using PageMaker, but each time you do this, AutoCAD is invoked to change the illustration. Pointers associated with the illustration notify the OLE-aware application as to what you are trying to accomplish and transparently take care of the operation by invoking the owner of the imported data. Although the illustration appears in the PageMaker document, it physically belongs to AutoCAD.

OLE manages data by treating it as an object. An *object* (see fig. 6.12) is a specific instance of a user-defined data class and consists of the data representation and the programs required to manipulate it. To manipulate and link (import) an object to other applications, the object is placed in a *container*. The container has simple controls for the object. In most situations, these controls are all that you need to manipulate the object. If greater control is desired, OLE can be used to call the owner of the application directly.

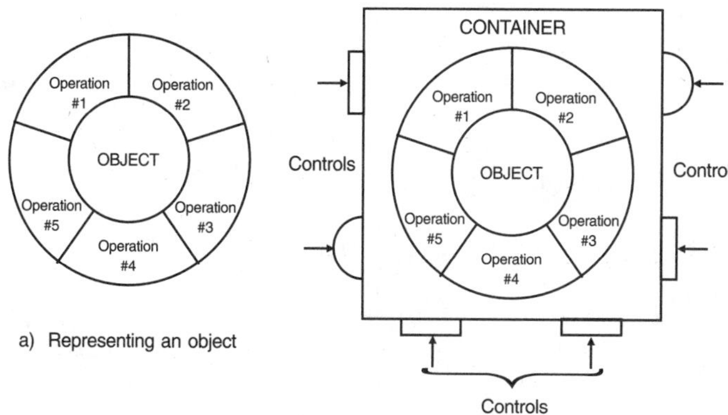

Figure 6.12
Data object definitions.

The problem with the OLE approach is that currently it is not easy to transport or convert documents to non-OLE systems. In the preceding example, if the AutoCAD illustration is moved to a system that does not have AutoCAD, the illustration vanishes.

Data Interoperability Using OMF

Hewlett-Packard's NewWave is an object-oriented system that runs under Microsoft Windows. In NewWave, data export and import is controlled by a centralized *Object Management Facility* (OMF). NewWave's inter-process data communications capability enables it to interoperate with non-Windows systems. OMF also runs under UNIX with a distributed network version that can run on a server.

HP and SUN Microsystems have collaborated to develop a plan for a *distributed object management facility* (DOMF) and have submitted it to the *Object Management Group* (OMG). *OMG* is a consortium of vendors whose goal is to establish a network object management architecture. DOMF is ambitious; its goal is to provide data transparency on different computing platforms across mixed types of networks.

Examining NetWare's Management Tools

NetWare comes with several management tools. Most of these tools are software-based; that is, they do not require any hardware other than the server and workstations on the network. Hardware-based tools,

such as the SNMP LANtern Monitor and SNMP LANtern Management Station, also are available from Novell, but they must be purchased as separate products. SNMP-based products are discussed in Chapter 4, "WANs and MANs."

Some of the NetWare built-in management tools run directly on the server, whereas others run at the workstation and access management information from the server. The purpose of these management tools is to report the status of the server, such as server memory utilization, server cache statistics, and status of disk drives. By monitoring the server and network-wide parameters, the LAN manager can determine whether the network is behaving normally. If a failure occurs in any part of the network, one or more of the monitored parameters indicate an abnormal value.

The NetWare management tools are distinct from other tools, such as SYSCON. SYSCON performs server administration, such as managing user accounts, groups, and server accounting.

Monitoring the File Server Console

The TRACK console command can be used to monitor some types of server traffic. The TRACK ON command initiates a tracking display on the console monitor. You can cancel tracking by using the TRACK OFF command.

Both versions of NetWare support a console MONITOR facility, but they are similar only in name. The MONITOR NLM is the primary server monitoring utility for NetWare 3.*x*. The MONITOR command in NetWare 2.*x* displays only the file activity for active workstations. Under NetWare 2.*x*, FOCONSOLE is the closest equivalent to the MONITOR NLM in NetWare 3.*x*.

When you use the MONITOR command at a NetWare 2.*x* console, NetWare displays a screen that shows the server utilization and six window panels that contain information on activities of stations 1 to 6. The MONITOR command accepts the station number as a parameter. To see stations 6 to 11, however, type the following command:

```
MONITOR 6
```

The server utilization is the server CPU utilization and must not be confused with the network utilization, which measures the amount of traffic on the network. Typical values for server CPU utilization are in the range of 0 to 60 percent. Execution of some server applications can bring this utilization to as high as 90 to 99 percent. Some users even reported a server utilization of over 100 percent. This usually happens when older versions of NetWare 2.*x* are running on a very fast AT 386 or 486 (33 MHz or more). These older versions of NetWare 2.*x* have a bug in the formula for computing server utilization on machines with a very fast clock rate.

Using Workstation Monitoring Tools

The workstation monitoring tools that come with NetWare run on the workstation and monitor server performance and volume utilization.

The two workstation monitoring tools are FCONSOLE. These tools run on both NetWare 2.*x* and NetWare 3.*x*. VOLINFO is a simple tool that shows the server disk volume utilization.

FCONSOLE is a much more sophisticated tool and displays information on server statistics at the workstation and works well for NetWare 2.*x* servers. FCONSOLE's functions have been largely replaced by the MONITOR NLM in NetWare 3.*x*. It is invoked by typing the command **FCONSOLE** at the workstation.

Using the Remote Management Facility

A useful tool that is available only on NetWare 3.*x* is the *remote management facility* (RMF). RMF enables a supervisor or remote console operator to perform console operations from a remote location, such as from another workstation. This means that you can set up a virtual server console at any workstation, and then control any server that has the appropriate RMF software loaded on it. Because server console operations can be performed at the workstation, you can keep the server in a restricted area with the keyboard locked or removed. This makes for a more secure networking environment.

Table 6.2 lists the components that make up the RMF software, and figure 6.13 shows how these components can be used to control a server through a workstation. The server can be controlled by a direct link across the network, through an asynchronous link, or by any combination of these two methods.

Table 6.2
Remote Management Facility Components (RMF)

Utility	Description
REMOTE.NLM	Acts as the console and keyboard manager. REMOTE.NLM interfaces with communications drivers in RSPX.NLM and RS232.NLM.
RSPX.NLM	Provides SPX support for REMOTE.NLM. RSPX.NLM is an NLM communications driver.
RS232.NLM	Provides asynchronous communications support to REMOTE.NLM. RS232.NLM is an NLM communications driver.
RCONSOLE.EXE	Runs at the workstation to provide a virtual console direct link across the network.
ACONSOLE.EXE	Runs at the workstation to provide a virtual console asynchronous link through modems and dial-up lines.

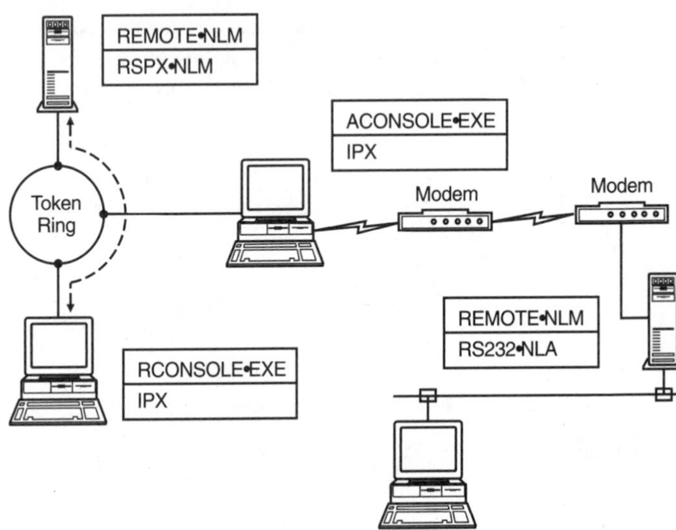

Figure 6.13
Remote management.

Configuring the NetWare NOS

As you configure NetWare, you need to make a number of choices. Some of these features are selected at the time NetWare is configured and generated. NetWare generation is required in NetWare 2.*x* because the NetWare object modules need to be statically linked. These procedures are discussed in the following sections.

Setting Up Nondedicated and Dedicated Servers

In NetWare 2.*x*, the server can be set up in one of two modes: dedicated or nondedicated. This decision is made at the time of NetWare generation and has a big impact on server performance and the way the server is used.

Nondedicated NOS

A nondedicated NOS is a station that can be used as a server and as a workstation simultaneously. In the case of NetWare, this is possible by having two partitions on the server disk: one for NetWare and one for DOS. The NetWare partition must be the one that is active and bootable. You can set up a nondedicated server only with NetWare 2.*x*—not with NetWare 3.*x*.

The server's RAM is divided into an area for DOS and NetWare. DOS programs run in real mode, and NetWare runs in protected mode. The real mode is used in AT 286 and higher machines to maintain compatibility with DOS that was designed to run on Intel 8086 microprocessors. The 8086 has a maximum addressable memory (physical RAM) of 1 MB. NetWare on an AT 286 requires more RAM and makes use of the protected mode of Intel 80286 chips. This allows for a maximum addressable memory of 16 MB.

To run DOS and NetWare, simultaneously, the microprocessor must switch between real and protected modes rapidly. When the Intel 80286 is first powered on, it comes up in real mode. Programs can issue an instruction to switch the microprocessor to protected mode. After the microprocessor has switched to protected mode, however, it cannot switch back to real mode without resetting (rebooting) the microprocessor.

For ATs made after 1986, the BIOS was modified to distinguish between a fake and a real reboot. To switch between protected and real mode, a fake reboot is initiated by the keyboard processor. This causes the 80286 to reset, switch to real mode, and execute the BIOS reset code, but the modified BIOS recognizes this as a fake reboot and does not execute the reset code. This explains why nondedicated mode does not run on old ATs that do not have a modified BIOS. Also, some ATs display sluggish performance because they use a different design for the keyboard whose processor is used to initiate a reboot. To correct this problem, use an IBM keyboard or a true IBM-compatible keyboard.

Dedicated NOS

A dedicated NOS is one that only the NOS can run on. DOS and the NOS do not coexist on the server. The server RAM is used exclusively for their NOS.

Choosing between Dedicated and Nondedicated NOS

In the nondedicated mode, DOS is run as an application on top of NetWare. The server's CPU is shared between DOS and the NOS, thus slowing them both down. Also, if the DOS application crashes, it would crash the NOS. In the nondedicated mode, exposing the server machine to users is a security risk.

Not all DOS applications can run on the server in the nondedicated mode, such as the following types of applications:

- Applications that require extended and expanded memory drivers. NetWare takes over all memory above 640 KB for its own purpose. Extended and expanded memory drivers conflict with NetWare memory usage.
- Applications that try to directly manipulate interrupt vectors, I/O ports, and other hardware in the PC. NetWare controls the hardware. DOS and application software run as applications on top of NetWare. Direct control of hardware conflicts with NetWare usage of the server machine.

For all these reasons, nondedicated mode is no longer as attractive as it was once thought to be. The real reason behind a nondedicated NOS is to save the cost of an extra machine. With the AT prices under a thousand dollars, the problems of nondedicated NOS are not worth it.

6

Understanding SFT Levels

Novell has defined three *System Fault Tolerant* (SFT) levels for its NetWare NOS to improve its reliability:

- SFT Level I Hot fix
- SFT Level II Disk mirroring Disk duplexing
- SFT Level III Server duplexing

SFT Level I, or the hot fix level, is defined as read-after-write verify (see fig. 6.14). In all versions of NetWare, whenever a block is written, it is immediately read to verify that what was read is the same as what was written. If the two blocks are different, the area on the disk is bad, and the block is rewritten into a special area called the *redirection area.* About 2 percent of the disk is reserved as the redirection area. The bad spot on the disk is recorded in a bad-block table. That area of the disk is never written into until the disk is formatted and prepared again for server installation by using a utility called *comprehensive surface analysis* (COMPSURF).

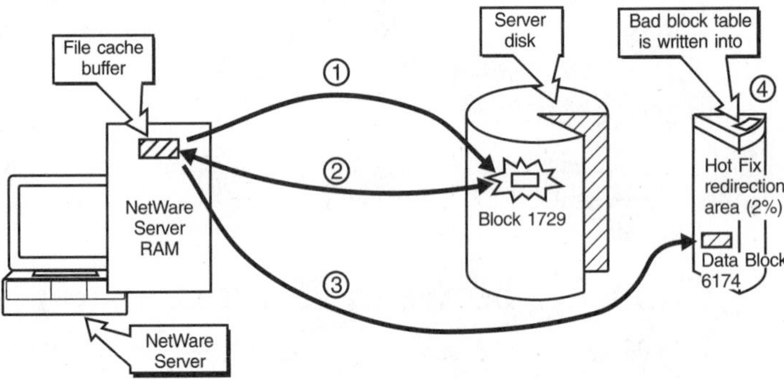

Figure 6.14
SFT Level I (hot fix). (Graphic courtesy of Learning Group International)

SFT Level II has two options. The first option is disk mirroring. Most ISA disk controllers support two disk channels. Two disks of the same size are attached to the disk controller. One of the disks is designated as the primary controller, and the other disk is designated as the secondary disk (see fig. 6.15). The secondary disk acts as a mirror image of the primary. When a block is written, it is written to both disks. When a block is read, the read command is issued to both disks. The fastest disk read response is the one that is used.

If the primary disk fails, the secondary disk takes over. When the primary disk is repaired, the secondary disk information is transferred to the primary disk. If the disk controller fails, a secondary disk attached to the same controller is not useful. Disk duplexing (see fig. 6.16) enables the primary and secondary disks to be attached to separate disk controllers. This makes the server fault-tolerant toward disk controller failures. SFT Level II includes SFT Level I.

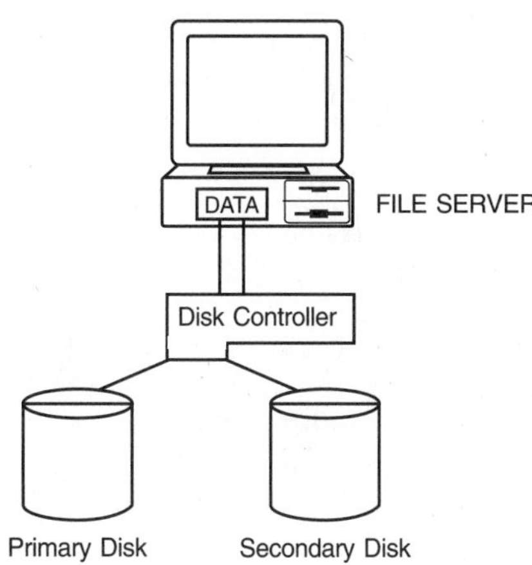

Figure 6.15
SFT level II (disk mirroring).

SFT Level III enables a second server to act as a backup for a primary server. The two servers are connected by a high speed bus. If the primary server fails, the secondary server takes over. SFT Level III includes SFT Level II.

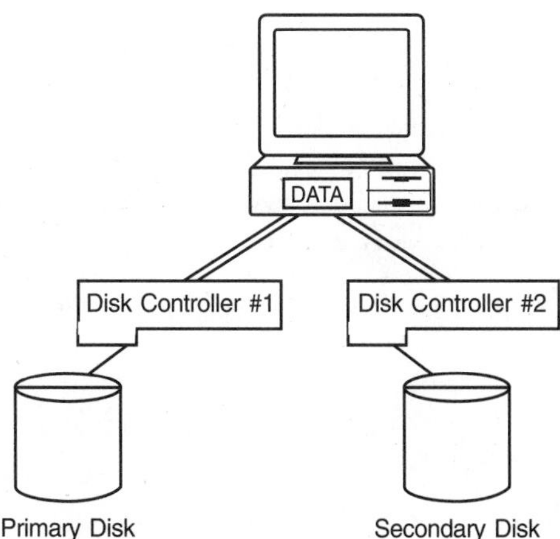

Figure 6.16
SFT level II (disk duplexing).

Examining Peer-to-Peer Network Operating Systems

Peer-to-peer NOS offers an attractive low-cost alternative to the more expensive centralized servers. For small networks, a peer-to-peer NOS can be adequate for most networking needs. This section briefly examines peer-to-peer network operating systems.

A peer-to-peer NOS, such as NetWare Lite, enables any DOS machine to become a server. A DOS station can be a server, a workstation, or both.

Many small businesses are intimidated by the complexity involved in setting up a NOS like NetWare, IBM LAN Server, LANMAN, or VINES. All they would like to do is be able to share files, printers, and a few applications. Many such organizations already have stand-alone PCs. All they really need is networking hardware and a simple and cheap NOS. The easiest small-business solution is a peer-to-peer NOS, also called an entry-level NOS.

Advantages of a Peer-to-Peer NOS

The following are the advantages of the peer-to-peer NOS over the central-server approach:

- Peer-to-peer NOSs are cheaper and easier to install and administer for a small number of users compared to most central-server NOSs like NetWare, LANMAN, IBM LAN Server, and VINES.
- Any DOS machine (usually with a hard disk) can be converted into a server for a peer-to-peer NOS. This is useful for quick sharing of files between users. Most central-server NOSs require special preparation of hard disks. Also, in the dedicated mode, servers on central-server NOSs cannot be used as a DOS station. Even in the nondedicated mode, central-server NOSs may have limitations as to the amount of memory available for applications, and you may not be able to use special memory management drivers, such as expanded and extended memory management drivers.
- You do not need to dedicate a special machine as a server on peer-to-peer NOSs. This results in reduced costs for LANs.

Limitations of a Peer-to-Peer NOS

Compared to the central server approach to LANs, the peer-to-peer NOS does have disadvantages. For a larger number of nodes (over 25 or 50), the peer-to-peer NOS may quickly become unmanageable. Because users can set their workstation as a server, they can spend an inordinate amount of work time playing with and administering their server. Network administration can become an absorbing and interesting task. Consider an organization of 50 users of a peer-to-peer LAN who spend several hours a day putting special files, such as games, on their server and administering and fine-tuning their server. You can imagine what would happen to the productivity of the organization. For a large number of servers and nodes, central control still is one of the most effective ways of administering the network.

In stark contrast to this model of centralized control is the network administration on Internet, which can be best described as near anarchy! Luckily, there is no shortage of Internet experts and hackers (in the good sense of the word) who fix problems as they arise.

Because DOS is used as a server, the performance of peer-to-peer NOSs are limited by the DOS file system and DOS memory limitations. A DOS-based server can support fewer nodes effectively compared to the central-server. This may not be a big disadvantage because peer-to-peer NOS-based LANs generally have fewer nodes to support.

Another disadvantage of peer-to-peer NOSs is that organizations tend to grow in size, and when companies grow, networks must grow. When the number of nodes becomes very large, the networks may become difficult to manage. Also, for a larger number of nodes, the peer-to-peer LANs may become more expensive. If this happens, consider switching to NetWare 2.*x*, which costs approximately $30 per user node. NetWare Lite, a peer-to-peer NOS, costs $50 per node. For a 60-node LAN, the cost of NetWare Lite is $3000. For a larger number of nodes, the cost actually gets more expensive than NetWare 2.*x*. Although these costs are not fixed and will probably change by the time you read this, you can apply the same reasoning to decide when NetWare Lite becomes too expensive.

Examining Multipurpose NOSs

The earliest NOSs that were introduced in the networking industry were disk servers. *Disk server technology* provided remote disks to users on a LAN, but the users could not share files easily. Disk server technology was replaced by *file server technology*, in which files could be shared among users. File server technology gave LAN users a remote file system that could be accessed by the WOS commands and software interfaces. Generally speaking, file server technology gave birth to the client/server model for PC networks.

Depending on the application that is run on a server, the file server can be treated as a special application server. A file server that has gateway software to networks, such as IBM's SNA network, can be called a *gateway server*. A file server that supports a pool of modems that can be used to dial out or dial in is called an *asynchronous communications server*. A file server can be treated as a general purpose computing platform and not just a provider of file services. Today, these computing platforms are called *servers*.

Servers are multifaceted and can provide a number of dedicated services. The following describes some of these services.

Internal Routers

A number of NIC cards can be placed in a server, and a LAN can be connected to each NIC. The server software performs routing functions between the different LANs. In NetWare 2.*x*, up to four NIC cards can be placed in a server. In NetWare 3.*x*, this number is 16.

To perform this routing function, each LAN needs to have a unique network address. A *network address* is used in the IPX packet to send data packets across an Internet LAN. This network address, or network number, can be considered to be associated with the cabling system used to interconnect the LAN.

The first NIC in the server is called LAN A, the second LAN B, the third LAN C, and the fourth LAN C.

Because NetWare supports over 180 different NIC cards, the server can perform routing functions between over 180 different LANs for IPX packet traffic.

External Routers

A routing function can be performed by a dedicated workstation, rather than by a server. The same number of NICs can be placed in a workstation, and routing software generated by the ROUTEGEN utility can be run at the dedicated workstation. A router built in this manner is called an *external router.* The rules for a unique network address for the different LANs are the same for internal routers.

Internal Routers versus External Routers

The advantage of internal routers is that the server machine does double duty as a server and as a router. An extra machine is not needed to perform routing functions. The disadvantage of this approach is the performance penalty for sharing a single machine. When router traffic is heavy, the file server performance suffers, and when the file server is busy, the router performance suffers.

External routers, because they are dedicated machines, have a better performance than internal routers. They are recommended over internal routers for networks with heavy Internet traffic. The disadvantage is the price of an extra machine for the external router.

Major Differences between NetWare 3.11 and NetWare 3.12

NetWare 3.12 is for the most part the same as NetWare 3.11. The major differences are the following:

- Change from a default frame type of ETHERNET_802.3 to ETHERNET_802.2.
- Simplified Installation of server.
- Use of NetWare Requester implemented as *virtual loadable modules* (VLMs) instead of the NetWare shell. Older NetWare shells can still be used.
- Bundling of Basic MHS and Macintosh client utilities.

Detailed discussion of the above issues are covered in later chapters.

Summary

In this chapter, you learned about some of the capabilities of network operating systems and the types of services they provide. You learned how to analyze a NOS in relationship to the OSI model and how the NOS functions map to the OSI model.

You also learned about the different types of interoperability and interconnectivity issues in a network environment.

Installing NetWare 3.12

In the preceding chapters, you saw the process of installing NetWare 2.2 and NetWare 3.11. NetWare 3.11 is a very successful Network Operating System. With its widespread deployment in many application areas, it has been subjected to rigorous testing. Over the years, many patches have been added to fix problems encountered in many situations. Not all sites need to implement these patches; many sites function just fine without them.

With the release of NetWare 3.12, the known problems with NetWare 3.11 were fixed, and these fixes were integrated into the operating system. This means that if your site has been loading the NLMs that fix the known problems, you will not have to load these NLMs when you upgrade to NetWare 3.12.

Installing NetWare 3.12—An Overview

The NetWare 3.12 installation is simple compared to NetWare 3.11. This chapter first describes a new installation for NetWare 3.12, and later describes the upgrade process from earlier versions of NetWare.

Perhaps the biggest improvement in NetWare 3.12 is the capability to install from a CD-ROM. The CD-ROM includes Novell's on-line help for 3.12, called the *Electro Text*. It follows the pattern of NetWare 4.*x*, which also comes on CD-ROM and includes the on-line Electro Text. Electro Text is installed as an Microsoft Windows application and includes the full set of NetWare 3.12 manuals in electronic form.

Another difference between NetWare 3.11 and NetWare 3.12 installation is a program called INSTALL, used to start the installation. This is different from the INSTALL NLM used in NetWare 3.11 and later in the NetWare 3.12 installation. The INSTALL program used to start the installation is currently a batch file on the INSTALL disk or the in startup directory \NETWARE.312\ENGLISH on the CD-ROM media. The purpose of the INSTALL program is to do some of the initial work of preparing the server disk. When this program runs, it guides you through the process of creating a small DOS partition on the server disk to hold the server boot files. It also copies the essential server boot files from the SYSTEM-1 disk onto this DOS partition. The INSTALL program also can create a NetWare partition and a volume name (SYS:). It can optionally modify the AUTOEXEC.BAT file on the server DOS partition to automatically start the SERVER.EXE program to initiate the NetWare 3.12 boot sequence. No printed manuals are included, but can be purchased as an option.

A number of steps and decisions need to be made during installation. These steps are as follows, listed in the order in which they should be performed:

1. Run the INSTALL.BAT program from the distribution media.
2. Decide between creating a new DOS partition or retaining the existing partition on the server disk.
3. Create the NetWare partition.
4. Select a name for the file server.
5. Assign an internal number to the server.
6. Copy server boot files to the DOS partition.
7. Enter locale information.
8. Select file-name format.
9. The INSTALL program runs the SERVER.EXE from the DOS partition at the server, loading NetWare. This is the end of the INSTALL.BAT program.
10. Load and configure disk drivers.
11. Load INSTALL.NLM.
12. Optionally, create additional NetWare partitions, mirror the partitions, create volumes, and assign volume names.
13. Mount volumes.
14. Load and configure network drivers.
15. Bind IPX to LAN drivers. If other protocol stacks are loaded, they also should be bound to a LAN driver.
16. Assign a network address for the cabling segment connected to the NICs.

17. Optionally, load any other NLMs.

18. Create STARTUP.NCF and AUTOEXEC.NCF files.

19. Copy NetWare system and utility files to NetWare SYS volume.

Understanding Installation Decisions and Parameters

The best way to understand the individual installation steps is to actually perform them. The guided hands-on approach in this chapter helps you to perform the installation. However, before you perform the installation, you should have an understanding of the major parameters and decisions that need to be made.

The next few sections discuss the following issues and parameters:

- Using the SERVER.EXE program
- Selecting file server name
- Assigning internal network number and network address
- Selecting file name format
- Loading disk drivers
- Loading NIC drivers
- Binding protocol stacks to NIC drivers by using the BIND command
- Running the INSTALL NLM

The SERVER.EXE Program

The SERVER.EXE program is run by the INSTALL program after the startup files are copied to the server boot directory.

If you want to start the server after installation, you must run the SERVER.EXE program from a DOS partition at the server. The SERVER.EXE can run only on an Intel 80386-based machine or higher. The SERVER.EXE loads in extended memory and switches the Intel 80386 microprocessor to the protected mode where it can address RAM up to 4 GB.

The SERVER.EXE program must be run when the server first is installed and also after rebooting the server after installation. On loading, SERVER.EXE looks for and executes STARTUP.NCF and AUTOEXEC.NCF. The STARTUP.NCF file is similar to the CONFIG.SYS file used in DOS and must exist on the DOS partition from which the server is booted. It loads disk driver and optional certain other configuration parameters. If STARTUP.NCF does not exist, as is true for a first time installation, SERVER.EXE assumes that an installation is being performed, and prompts the user for the information that the STARTUP.NCF file provides. If the SYS: volume was created in a prior installation step, and the STARTUP.NCF file exists, the SERVER.EXE program mounts (activates) the volume. It then looks for AUTOEXEC.NCF on the SYS:SYSTEM directory on the server. Again, if this is a first time installation, SYS: will not exist and hence cannot be mounted; and SERVER.EXE will not search for AUTOEXEC.NCF.The SERVER.EXE program can be invoked from the DOS prompt with a number of interesting parameters. If you are doing your first NetWare 3.*x* installation, the discussion on the SERVER.EXE parameters may not be of much interest to you. Nevertheless, it is included here for future reference.

If the STARTUP.NCF file exists on the DOS boot partition, it is executed by SERVER.EXE. After this, the AUTOEXEC.NCF file is executed from the SYS:SYSTEM directory. At times, you might want to experiment with a different boot sequence. The SERVER.EXE has a number of options to make this job easy.

Suppose that you want to use a different startup file than STARTUP.NCF. You can start the server by typing the following command:

```
SERVER -S ALTSTART.NCF
```

ALTSTART.NCF contains an alternate set of startup commands.

Suppose that you want to ignore the processing of STARTUP.NCF and AUTOEXEC.NCF and experiment with a different boot sequence. You can do this by using the following command:

```
SERVER -NS
```

If you want to stop the processing of AUTOEXEC.NCF, but not STARTUP.NCF, use this command:

```
SERVER -NA
```

Table 7.1 summarizes these different parameters.

Table 7.1
SERVER.EXE Parameters

Parameter	Meaning
-NS	Do not process STARTUP.NCF
-NA	Do not process AUTOEXEC.NCF
-S *alternateFile*	Use *alternateFile* rather than the STARTUP.NCF file
-D	Enter internal debugger mode; not used during installation
-C *cacheSize*	An alternate way to specify the cache buffer size

File Server Name

All servers on a NetWare internetwork must have a unique name used to identify the server from all other servers. This must be a name from 2 to 47 characters with no spaces. The first character cannot be a period (.), and alphanumeric characters, hyphens, and underscores can be used.

On practical note, keep the server name descriptive of the function it performs and keep it to a reasonable length as the server name is used in many NetWare commands. Future network managers who are not fast and accurate touch typists will bless you for a reasonably short server name.

Internal Network Number and Network Address

A unique internal number must be assigned to identify the server process. This number must be different from all other internal network numbers for other servers and the network addresses used to identify different cabling segments.

The internal network number is used to identify a logical network distinct from the physical network. Its real use is to solve some routing problems inherent with NetWare 2.*x* servers, in which the server process is identified by the network address assigned to the first NIC (LAN A) in the server.

A unique network address must be assigned to every cabling segment. NetWare 3.12 allows up to 16 LAN cards to be connected to a server. Each of these must have a unique number. This network address must be different from all other network addresses on all servers on the internal network and is referred to as the network number during the installation. The network address used in this context must not be confused with the "network address" of the LAN card. The network address of a LAN card is referred to as the *node address.*

Figure 7.1 shows a LAN with three servers, with one server being used as a router. The internal network numbers F0000033, F000003A, and F000003F are distinct from each other and the network address of A73B and BC47 used for the two cabling segments. The NICs attached to the same cabling segment have the same network address. Their node addresses of 02, 03, 04, and 05 are distinct.

Internal network number and network address are up to eight-digit hexadecimal numbers. Leading zeros are omitted when entering their values in the installation process.

File Name Format

NetWare 3.12 enables you to set locale-specific format settings such as country code, code page, keyboard mapping, and so on. In addition, NetWare 3.12 enables you to select the type of file-name characters that can be used for storing files on the server. The file-name format setting can be done during the installation process. During installation, you are asked to choose between DOS format file names and NetWare format file names.

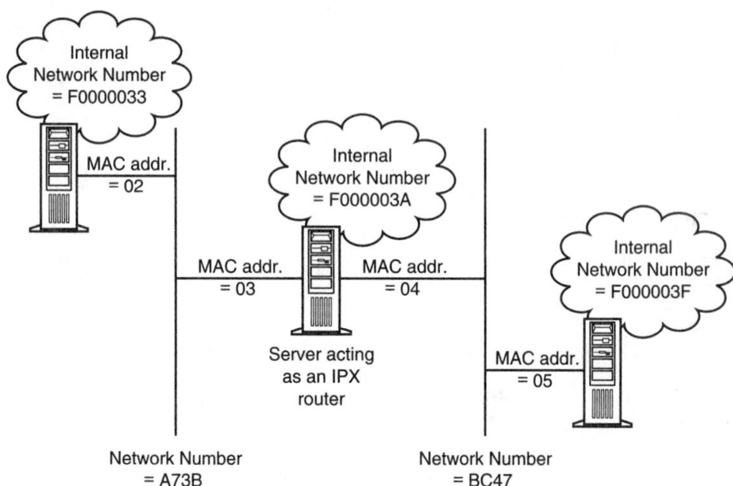

Figure 7.1
Internal network numbers versus network numbers.

A little bit of background can help you understand the ramifications of using this option. NetWare has always allowed extended ASCII codes from 128 to 255 to be included as part of file names. These characters include many of the line drawing characters and characters in non-English languages, such as accent characters. This allows NetWare to support file names with special characters.

In NetWare 3.12 (and 4.*x*), the installer is given the choice of conforming to DOS legal file-name characters, or of retaining the original NetWare legal file-name characters allowed, which include characters with codes from 128 to 255. The choice you make determines the legal character names NetWare 3.12 uses, and not legal character names used by an application program running under the NETX shell or the DOS Requester.

The NetWare DOS Requester used by NetWare 3.12 is fundamentally different from the NETX shell. NETX intercepts DOS function calls (by trapping the software interrupts such as INT 21 hex). NETX examines the commands to determine if DOS or the network should handle it. Commands passed to DOS undergo the DOS validation process for legal file-name characters. Commands sent to the network, however, bypass the DOS validation process for legal character names. DOS never sees these "invalid" file names. So if an application issues a command to create a file name on a network drive, the server creates the file according to its own rules of what is legal and illegal. Because NetWare 3.*x* allows characters between 128 to 255 as legal, an application could create on a network drive file names with special codes.

The DOS Requester does not trap the commands first. It lets DOS decide if the function being invoked should be sent locally or transmitted across the network. This feature is possible with DOS versions 3.*x* and higher and is called the DOS *redirector* function. (Unfortunately, it often is confused with the DOS Requester.) The DOS redirector decides if the function requested should be handled by DOS or by the network. Because DOS sees all commands first, it decides whether the command is valid. It does file-name verification before passing it onto the DOS requester (implemented by VLMs).

If DOS file-name format is selected at the NetWare server, lowercase and accented characters are converted to uppercase characters; therefore, file-name character translation is done at the server. If the file-name request originates from a station running VLMs, the character translation is done at the workstation. If the file-name request originates from a station running the NETX shell, character translation is not done at the workstation, but is handled by the server because the DOS file-name format was selected at the server.

If NetWare file-name format is selected at the NetWare server, lowercase and accented characters are *not* converted to uppercase characters at the server. The workstation must do the character translation. If the file-name request originates from a workstation running VLMs, the character translation is done at the workstation. But if the file-name request originates from a workstation running the NETX shell, character translation is not done at the workstation and, because the server does not handle character translation (because the NetWare file-name format was selected at the server), the accented characters are not converted, but are left lowercase.

The preceding discussion implies that a potential problem exists with networks running a mix of NETX and VLM software at the workstations. If the behavior of NetWare 4.*x* was the same as NetWare 3.*x*, then only the NetWare file-name format would exist at the server. Workstations running NETX then could create file names not recognizable by workstations running VLMs.

For this reason the DOS file-name format was created in NetWare 4.*x*. DOS file-name format gives greater assurance that the behavior at the server for file names is the same for NETX or VLM workstations.

It is best to install NetWare 3.12 with DOS file format to avoid incompatibility between workstations running NETX and VLM software.

You might be tempted to think that the problem could be avoided if all workstations were running NETX and the NetWare server was configured for NetWare file format. Not all versions of DOS perform file-name validation the same way, however. DOS from different vendors can use different rules for valid file-name characters. It is possible for workstations running DOS from different vendors to create files on a NetWare server (configured with NetWare file format) that are not accessible by another workstation.

Interestingly enough, this problem always existed with NetWare 3.11 and earlier versions (set to NetWare file format), but most sites never saw it because they ran the same version of DOS. Sites that support DOS from different vendors can encounter the problem described in the preceding paragraph.

DOS 3.3 and higher can do file-name character validation based on the language-specific configuration information given to it. What if two workstations on the same network are configured for different languages? They would then use different *code page tables.*

This means that workstations potentially could create files on the server that could not be understood by another workstation configured with a different code page. If the DOS file-name format is selected at the server, the server may remap certain file-name characters. For this reason, if workstations are set to

different language configurations, it may be preferable to select NetWare file-name format, so that the server does not try to remap any characters in the 128 to 255 range.

The preceding issues become important when trying to upgrade a NetWare 3.11 or 2.*x* server that could have file names containing characters in the 128 to 255 range. If the NetWare 3.12 server is selected with DOS file-name format, some of the file-name characters are now illegal. The server, in this case, remaps the illegal file-name character the first time the volume mounts. VREPAIR can be run when the illegal characters are detected during the volume mount. VREPAIR translates any lowercase accented characters to uppercase accented characters, according to the rules for the country code and code page installed on the server. Name collisions after character translation are handled by substituting a number for the last character in the file name. Be aware that if you have applications that reference these renamed files, you need to reconfigure the applications.

If NetWare file-name format is selected during the upgrade process, no files are renamed, but you do have the potential problems listed earlier—that is, a NetWare format file name at the server and different workstation configurations could produce file names other workstations may not understand.

Loading Disk Drivers

Disk drivers are written as DSK files and must be loaded so that the server can communicate with the disks. They are loaded with the LOAD command.

To load the ISADISK driver, issue the following command:

```
LOAD ISADISK
```

Type the following command to load the PS/2 ESDI driver:

```
LOAD PS2ESDI
```

Hardware parameters, such as port numbers and interrupt numbers, can be specified as parameters to the LOAD DiskDriverNLM command; but if they are not specified, the disk driver prompts you for a value.

The parameter settings for the ISADISK driver are shown in table 7.2.

Table 7.2
ISADISK Parameters

Parameter	Supported Values (hex)	Default (hex)
INT	B, C, D, E	E
PORT	170, 1F0	1F0

If more than one ISADISK controller exists on the server, the LOAD ISADISK command can be issued a second time. When the driver is loaded a second time, it loads itself reentrantly and only accepts an alternate set of parameters.

Thus to specify the ISADISK parameters at the command line, use the following command:

```
LOAD ISADISK  INT=E  PORT=1F0
```

The PS/2 SCSI driver can be loaded four times, and it loads itself reentrantly. For the Micro Channel and EISA architectures, you must specify the SLOT parameter, as in the following example:

```
LOAD PS2SCI   SLOT=2
```

Loading NIC Drivers

The network adapters (NICs) are activated by loading their NLM drivers.

Thus to load the TOKEN ring driver one must use the following command:

```
LOAD TOKEN
```

To load the Novell Ethernet driver for NE2000 and define a logical name ETHER for it, issue the following command:

```
LOAD NE2000 NAME=ETHER
```

Because multiple NICs in a server can form an internal router, you must issue a the LOAD command for every NIC.

Hardware parameters such as port numbers and interrupt numbers can be specified as parameters to the LOAD *NetDriver* command; but if they are not specified, the NIC driver prompts you for a value.

The remaining discussion in this section is not necessary for a first-time simple installation. The information is included here for your future reference in dealing with more complex installations.

Most NIC drivers use one or more of the following parameters:

DMA=*number*

INT=*number*

MEM=*address*

PORT=*address*

NODE=*number*

RETRIES=*number*

SLOT=*number*

NAME=*board name*

FRAME=*name*

For the actual parameter values, you must consult the vendor's documentation.

Table 7.3 gives a brief explanation of these parameters. Table 7.4 lists the parameters specifically used for Token Ring networks.

Table 7.3
Network Card Parameters in LOAD *LAN_DRIVER* Command

Parameter	Meaning
DMA	DMA channel number of NIC.
INT	IRQ level NIC is set.
MEM	Base memory address of RAM on driver.
PORT	I/O Port address setting of NIC.
NODE as NICs	Overrides node address on NICs that permit it, such as those using IEEE MAC addressing schemes.
RETRIES	Number of times NIC driver retries failed packet transmissions; default for most adapters is 5; can be set to as high as 255.
SLOT	Used for microchannel and EISA bus computers; tells NOS which NIC to link driver to. Hardware parameters like I/O port and IRQ are set with the reference disk.
NAME	Up to a 17-character unique name for an NIC; useful for many NICs of the same type. Name can be used in the BIND command.
FRAME	Type of MAC layer encapsulation to be used; provides support for Ethernet and Token Ring.

Table 7.4
Token Ring-Specific Parameters for LOAD TOKEN Command

Parameter	Meaning
LS	Number of IEEE 802.5 link stations.
SAPS	Number of Service Access Points for Token Ring driver.
TBC	Transmit Buffer Count for Token Ring driver; default is set to 2.
TBZ	Transmit Buffer Size for Token Ring driver; values range from 96 to 65,535, though not all values are supported. The default value is 0 and implies maximum that works for the NOS or the NIC.

Most of these parameters are fairly straightforward; the FRAME parameter, however, requires a little explanation.

The FRAME parameter can be used for Ethernet and Token Ring NICs and tells the NIC driver the type of header to be used for packets. In other words, this parameter controls the MAC layer encapsulation.

In Chapter 2, "LAN Standards for Physical and Data Link Layers," you saw that many modern Ethernet NICs can generate either IEEE 802.3 encapsulation or Ethernet II (version 2.0) encapsulation. NetWare 3.12's default Ethernet encapsulation is IEEE 802.2 (see fig. 7.2). This corresponds to a FRAME value of ETHERNET_802.2. In practical terms, it means that the NetWare 3.12 server by default can speak only to stations or other computers that can understand the IEEE 802.2 headers in the packets. Many non-Novell networks, such as UNIX-based networks or DECnet, use Ethernet II encapsulation. To communicate with these networks, NetWare provides the flexibility of changing the MAC layer encapsulation to Ethernet II. This is done by setting the FRAME parameter in the LOAD NIC_DRIVER command to ETHERNET_II. Another value for the FRAME parameter for Ethernet is ETHERNET_SNAP.

If ETHERNET_802.2 is used for the FRAME parameter, it implies an IEEE 802.3 MAC layer encapsulation, but in addition, the data portion of the IEEE 802.3 frame contains an IEEE 802.2 frame. IEEE 802.2 or *Logical Link Control* (LLC) is discussed in Chapter 2, "LAN Standards for Physical and Data Link Layers." Using LLC, multiple sessions are possible between *Link Service Access Points* (LSAPs). In the case of ETHERNET_802.2, a protocol identifier value of E0 (hexadecimal) is used for the DSAP (Destination Service Access Point) and the SSAP (Source Service Access Point) fields. The DSAP and SSAP fields are used for protocol multiplexing/demultiplexing in a manner similar to the way the Ether Type field is used in Ethernet II.

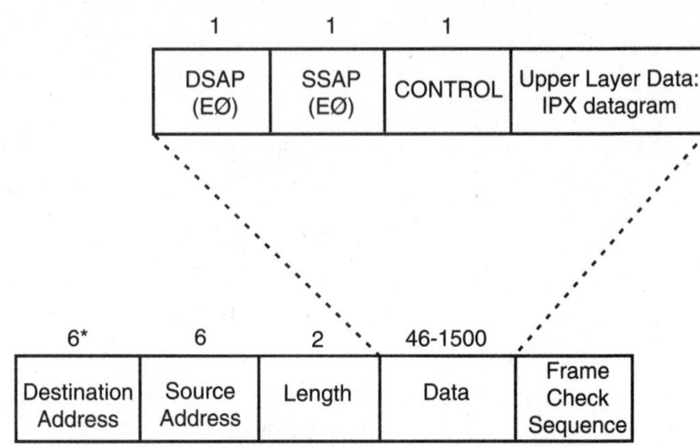

Figure 7.2
NetWare 3.12 (and higher) default frame encapsulation for Ethernet (ETHERNET_802.2).

For further discussion of other frame types, refer to the discussion in Chapter 6, "Features of NetWare 2.2, 3.11, and 3.12," about SNAP and Token Ring frames. Because NetWare 3.12 evolved from NetWare 3.11, the frame type definitions remain the same. The only difference is the use of ETHERNET_802.2 as the default frame type for NetWare 3.12 rather than ETHERNET_802.3 used in NetWare 3.11. Novell's definition of ETHERNET_802.3 is incomplete according to the IEEE specifications and is therefore often called the "raw" frame type, as it omits the LLC header.

Table 7.5 summarizes the different frame types.

Table 7.5
Server Frame Types Supported

Frame	FRAME Parameter Name	Description
IEEE 802.3	ETHERNET_802.3	Novell's raw Ethernet frame type. Does not include an LLC (IEEE 802.2) frame.
IEEE 802.2	ETHERNET_802.2	Default frame type for NetWare 4.*x*. Essentially IEEE 802.3 frame with an LLC (IEEE 802.2) sublayer.

Frame	FRAME Parameter Name	Description
IEEE 802.3 with SNAP extension	ETHERNET_SNAP	Used for AppleTalk networks. Essentially an IEEE 802.2 frame with an additional 3-octet *Organization Unit Identifier* (OUI) and a 2-byte Ether Type field. Also can be used with some TCP/IP software.
Ethernet II	ETHERNET_II	Ethernet II frame that differs from IEEE 802.3. Main distinction is the presence of a 2-octet Ether Type field rather than a 2-octet length field (IEEE 802.3).
IEEE 802.5	TOKEN-RING	Standard IEEE 802.5 frame.
IEEE 802.5 with SNAP extension	TOKEN-RING_SNAP	Used for AppleTalk and TCP/IP networks. Essentially an IEEE 802.5 frame with an additional 3-octet Organization Unit Identifier (OUI) and a 2-byte Ether Type field.
ARCnet	RX-NET	Only one frame type is used with ARCnet.

BINDing Protocol Stacks to NIC Drivers

Before an NIC driver can receive a packet and send it to the appropriate protocol stack, you must specify which protocol stack the NIC must work with. This is done by process called *binding*, whereby an NIC driver is logically associated with a protocol stack.

Thus, when the token ring driver TOKEN is loaded, it must be bound to the IPX protocol stack. Other protocol stacks if loaded also can be used. To use SPX/IPX, Novell's native protocol stack, it must be bound using the following BIND command:

```
BIND IPX TO TOKEN
```

If the network address is entered incorrectly, the servers on that cable segment will receive a "Router Configuration Error." To correct this problem, unbind the driver and issue the BIND command again—this time specifying the correct network address. The BIND command accepts a number of parameters, the most important being the NET parameter that must be set to the value of the network address (cabling number) of the cabling segment to which the NIC is connected. If this is not specified, the BIND command prompts you for a unique network address. To specify the NET parameter with value AA3F (hex) in the BIND command, use this command:

```
BIND IPX TO TOKEN NET=AA3F
```

The BIND command must be issued for every NIC in the server. If you have more than one NIC of the same type on the server, the BIND command needs to distinguish between the different driver instances. This can be done by including that driver's parameters along with the BIND command. You do not need driver parameters if you bind a protocol to a board name. To register a board name for the driver, it must be loaded using the NAME parameter.

Running the INSTALL NLM

After the drivers are loaded and protocol stacks bound to their appropriate drivers, you must run the INSTALL NLM to complete the installation. Do this by entering the following command:

```
LOAD INSTALL
```

The INSTALL.NLM is a menu-driven utility and can be used for a number of tasks, including the following:

- Format server disk drives and perform surface analysis
- Create NetWare partitions
- Mirror/duplex server disks
- Create and configure server volumes
- Create/edit STARTUP.NCF and AUTOEXEC.NCF files
- Copy system and public files

Understanding Installation Requirements of NetWare 3.12

NetWare 3.12 can support up to 4 GB of RAM and 32 TB of disk storage requirements. Because most sites have considerably less resources on a server, you should also know what the minimum requirements are.

Server RAM Requirements

The minimum server RAM requirement for NetWare 3.12 is 4 MB. Most sites want to have more if they are using application and management NLMs on the server.

You need at least 4 MB to load the operating system, disk drivers, LAN drivers, and INSTALL.NLM. Other considerations for estimating server memory are listed next:

1. Amount of server RAM must be 0.008 times the disk space in megabytes.
2. The amount of server RAM needed is determined by multiplying 5/1048576 by the number of files that have an additional name space entry and the number of additional name spaces. For example, if a Macintosh, NFS, OS/2, or FTAM name space is added to a volume, an additional directory entry is added to the directory entry table that contains the file name and attributes for that name space. DOS name space is not used in the preceding calculations.
3. A cache size of 1 to 4 MB should be added. Allocating server RAM for caching can have a dramatic affect on server performance.
4. Add 2 MB for installing one or both of the CLIB or BTRIEVE.NLMs if you are running an application that uses one of these NLMs, such as PSERVER.NLM, which implements printer server on the NetWare server.
5. Add an estimated memory requirement for any additional NLMs that you want to run on the server.

Using the preceding requirements, you can come up with an equation for estimating server RAM. The equation below takes into account the six factors listed earlier.

E = D*0.008 + F*N*5/1048576 + C + S + 2*A + O

E = Estimated Server RAM in Megabytes

D = Disk space in Megabytes

F = Number of files that have a name space

N = Number of name spaces per file

C = Cache size (1 to 4 MB)

S = Memory needed for server (4 MB)

A = 1 if application uses CLIB or BTRIEVE.NLM, NetWare NFS or NetWare for Macintosh; 0 otherwise

O = Memory for other NLMs loaded on the server

The following example helps to clarify the use of the preceding equation:

SCS has decided to install a NetWare 3.12 server on an Intel 80486 33 MHz computer with a 200 MB hard disk. They plan to run NetWare for Macintosh on the server, and therefore the server has to support an additional Macintosh name space. An estimated 15,000 files will be on the server volume. The NetWare server also will be used as a print server, but will not run any other application servers. For improved server performance, it was decided to have at least 2 MB for caching. Other application NLMs loaded at the server need about 2 MB of RAM.

The parameters for this example are as follows:

D = Disk space in megabytes = 200

F = Number of files that have a name space = 15,000

N = Number of name spaces per file = 1

C = Cache size (1 to 4 MB) = 2

S = Memory needed for server = 4

A = 1 if an application uses CLIB or BTRIEVE.NLM = 1

O = Memory for other NLMs loaded on the server = 0

NetWare 3.12 server memory requirements can be estimated by using the preceding parameters in the following formula:

$$E = D*0.008 + F*N*5/1048576 + C + S + 2*A + O$$

$$= 200*0.008 + 15000*1*5/1048576 + 2 + 4 + 2*1 + 2$$

$$= 1.6 + 0.07 + 2 + 4 + 2 + 2$$

$$= 11.67 \text{ MB}$$

Therefore, a server RAM of 12 MB should meet the needs of the preceding example. If no optional NLMs (O parameter) are needed, the server RAM would be 10 MB.

Installing a New NetWare 3.12 Server

You can install a NetWare 3.12 server from floppy disks, hard drive/network drive, or CD-ROM.

To install from a hard disk or network drive, you can load the floppy disks onto the drive. You probably want to use this method to bypass the floppy load, which can be time-consuming, and if you want to install several NetWare 3.12 servers.

Uploading Files to a Network Drive

To upload the files to a network drive or hard disk, follow these steps:

1. Log in to a server with the Supervisor account.
2. Create a directory called NETWARE.312 on the network volume.
3. Copy disks manually to a hard disk or network volume if you have diskettes and don't want to install from them. This is done by creating a directory such as NETWARE.312, and creating a subdirectory structure under this directory, where each subdirectory represents a disk and whose name is the same as the disk's volume label. The main disks to include are the Install, Unicode, and System_x disks.
4. Enter the letter of the source drive (A:) and press Enter.
5. Enter the letter of the network drive and press Enter.
6. Insert disks as requested.

Selecting the Boot Method

As with NetWare 3.11, you need a DOS partition on the server disk to boot the server or boot the server machine with a bootable DOS floppy. Most sites prefer the hard disk partition method because server startup times using the bootable floppy are considerably slower. You may decide to use the bootable floppy for security purposes or as a backup in case of a problem with the DOS partition on the server disk. Some sites lock the bootable floppy for security reasons after the server is started so that an unauthorized user cannot start the server.

If you decide to use a bootable floppy, you need to have a DOS bootable high-capacity (1.2 MB or 1.44 MB) disk. You can format a disk using the /S option, or use the DOS SYS command to transfer system files to the floppy.

Next, copy the following files from the SYSTEM-1 disk to the server boot floppy:

- SERVER.EXE (contains the license serial number)
- NWSNUT.NLM
- NUT.NLM

In addition to the preceding files, copy the NetWare disk drivers for your server disk from the SYSTEM-2 disk to the server boot floppy. You may optionally want to copy the following on the server boot disk:

- Name space support NLMs (NFS.NAM, MAC.NAM, OS2.NAM, FTAM.NAM)
- VREPAIR.NLM and support modules for additional name spaces such as V_NFS.NLM for NFS and so on
- LAN drivers (These normally load from the SYS:SYSTEM directory; but in case of a corrupted copy in SYS:SYSTEM, it is good to have a copy on the server boot disk.)

You may want to create an AUTOEXEC.BAT file that loads the SERVER.EXE program.

If you are using a COMPAQ computer, you can force the server to switch to high speed mode by adding the following to the AUTOEXEC.BAT file:

```
MODE SPEED=HIGH
```

The Install Process

Whether you are loading from floppy disk, network drive, or CD-ROM, the install process is initiated by going to the directory that contains the INSTALL.BAT program and typing **INSTALL:**

```
A: (Goto the directory containing INSTALL)
INSTALL
```


One of the fundamental changes in NetWare 3.12 from version 3.11 is the use of the ETHERNET_802.2 frame—rather than the ETHERNET 802.3 frame—as the default frame type. As a result, you see a warning message for Ethernet users (see fig. 7.3). For more information about differences between Ethernet_802.2 and Ethernet_802.3 frames, refer to Chapter 2, "LAN Standards for Physical and Data Link Layers." The main point to note is that if the workstation and server use different frame types, they cannot communicate.

The INSTALL disk also is bootable, so you can start your installation by booting from it. It automatically runs the INSTALL program upon booting.

If you are installing from a network drive or CD-ROM, make sure that the SYSTEM-1 disk is copied to the appropriate directory on the server DOS partition, usually C:\SERVER.312.

If you plan to use a disk driver not supported in the distribution media, copy the necessary driver files to the server boot directory (default name C:\SERVER.312) to make it easier for you in the installation process.

Figure 7.3
Warning message for Ethernet users.

```
*************************************************************
*                 ETHERNET USERS PLEASE NOTE:               *
*   Netware v3.12 sets the default Ethernet frame type      *
*   to 802.2. The default Ethernet frame type for older     *
*   versions of NetWare is 802.3.                           *
*   If you are installing NetWare v3.12 in an existing      *
*   NetWare environment that is currently using Ethernet    *
*   802.3 frame types, you may wish to load both frame      *
*   types or change the default Ethernet frame type to      *
*   802.3.                                                  *
*   Machines running Ethernet frame type 802.2 will not     *
*   see machines running Ethernet frame type 802.3.         *
*   Please refer to the NetWare v3.12 manuals for more      *
*   information.                                            *
*************************************************************
Press any key to continue . . .
```

The rest of the installation steps are as follows:

1. When the INSTALL program loads and after you press Enter for the warning message, you should see a screen with the following options (see fig. 7.4):

    Install new NetWare v3.12

    Upgrade NetWare v3.1x

    Display Information (README) File

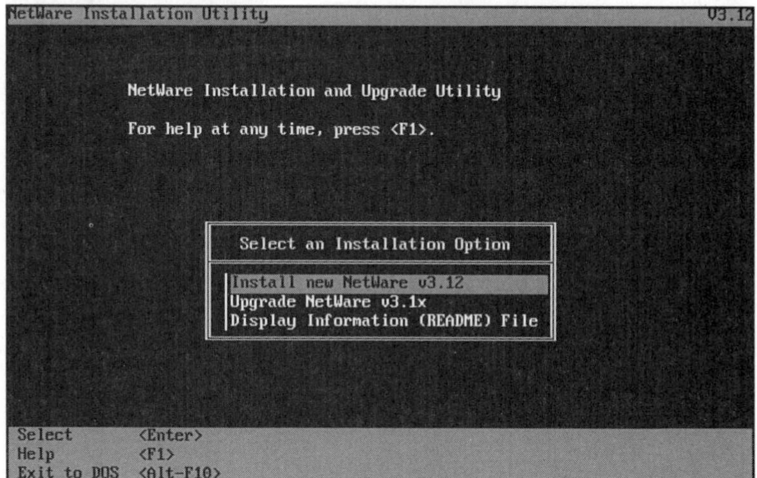

Figure 7.4
NetWare 3.12 installation options.

7

    Browse through the README files by selecting Display Information (README) File for tips on resolving installation problems.

2. Select Install new NetWare v3.12, to install a new NetWare 3.12 server. A screen similar to figure 7.5 appears, showing the disk partition options.

3. You can retain the existing DOS partitions or create a new one.

    If the hard disk is not configured, choose Create a New DOS Partition. If you already configured your hard disk by manually creating a partition and installing DOS, choose Retain Current Disk Partitions.

4. If you select Create a New DOS Partition, you should see a screen similar to figure 7.6.

    If you select Retain Existing Partitions, skip to step 10.

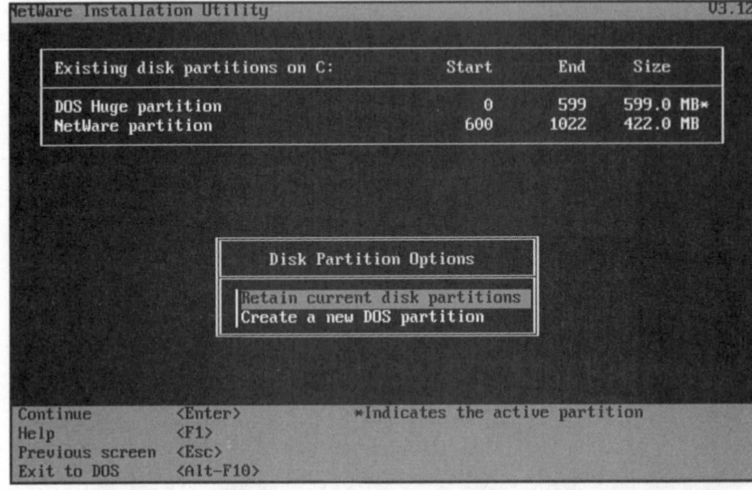

Figure 7.5
NetWare 3.12 Installation—disk partition options.

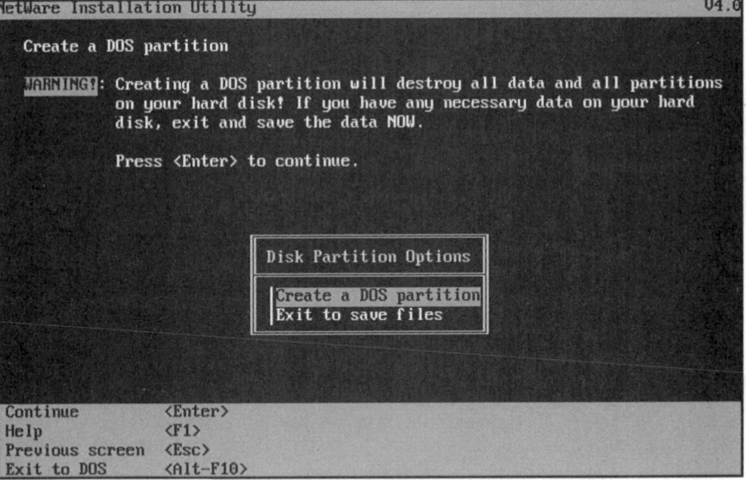

Figure 7.6
Create a DOS partition.

5. Select Create a DOS Partition from the Disk Partition Options screen. If you have data on your hard disk that you want to save, you can select Exit to Save Files, back up your data, and restart the installation.

6. You are prompted to enter the size of the DOS partition. The default is 5 MB, but you can create any size partition.

7. After entering the DOS partition size, you are then asked to verify `Add this partition and destroy the data on your hard disk?` Answer Yes.

8. A message screen appears informing you that a new DOS partition has been created, and the computer reboots to allow DOS to recognize the new partition. Press Enter.

   If installing from NetWare distribution disks, the system is restarted.

   If you are using any other method (CD-ROM, network, and so one) you should manually restart INSTALL the way you did at the beginning of this installation. Make sure that the DOS programs, such as FORMAT.COM, are in the search path.

9. After INSTALL is restarted, you are then informed that the DOS partition will now be formatted. Press Enter to accept this choice.

   Occasionally, the FORMAT of the DOS partition fails. If it does, format the DOS partition manually (FORMAT C: /S), and restart INSTALL.

10. You are then prompted for the server name (see fig. 7.7).


```
NetWare Installation Utility                                          V3.12
  Name the new server

          Enter a unique name for this NetWare server. For guidelines, press
          <F1>.

          (Example: MY_SERVER)

          Press <Enter> to continue.


                         Enter Server Name:
       Server name:

Continue         <Enter>
Help             <F1>
Previous screen  <Esc>
Exit to DOS      <Alt-F10>
```

Figure 7.7
Prompted for server name.

   Enter server name, which can be from 2 to 47 characters and include alphanumeric characters (A-Z, 0-9), hyphens, and underscores. You cannot use a period as the first character.

   After installation, the server name is saved in the AUTOEXEC.NCF file. When the SERVER.EXE program loads during normal startup of the NetWare server, the server name is read from this file.

11. You are then prompted for an internal network number (see fig. 7.8). The installation program generates a number at random. You can select this internal network number, because it is not likely to conflict with an existing internal network number, or use the system for network number assignments described in Chapter 3, “Bridging and Routing.”

It is best to select your own internal network number according to your own scheme or use Novell's IPX Registry. Novell has created an IPX number registry in which you can reserve a range of network numbers to allow the creation of a global IPX network, similar to the existing Internet (global network primarily based on TCP/IP).

Internal network numbers can be eight hexadecimal digits long and must be different from other internal network numbers and the network numbers used to identify the cable segments.

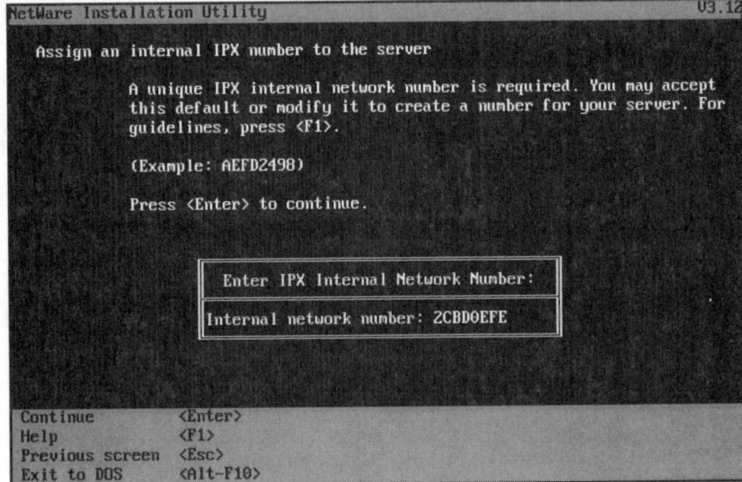

Figure 7.8
NetWare 3.12 installation—internal network number assignment.

The internal network number describes a logical network that uniquely identifies the *NetWare Core Protocol* (NCP) processing engine at the heart of the NetWare server. Internal network numbers were introduced in NetWare 3.0 to solve routing anomalies common in NetWare 2.*x* networks, where the NCP processing engine had a network number the same as that of the network installed on LAN A (the first network adapter on the server). Refer to Chapter 3, "Bridging and Routing," for a more detailed discussion of this topic.

12. You are asked to verify the source and destination paths for copying the server boot files (see fig. 7.9). To change the source path, use the function key F2; to change the destination path, use the function key F4.

    The default source path is the drive from which you booted. Normally, you do not have to change the source path if you are installing using the floppy disk or local CD-ROM method. If you are installing from across the network, you can press F2 and specify the network drive and path from which to read the software distribution.

    The default destination is C:\SERVER.312. Accept this default, unless you have your own standard as to where the server files are copied.

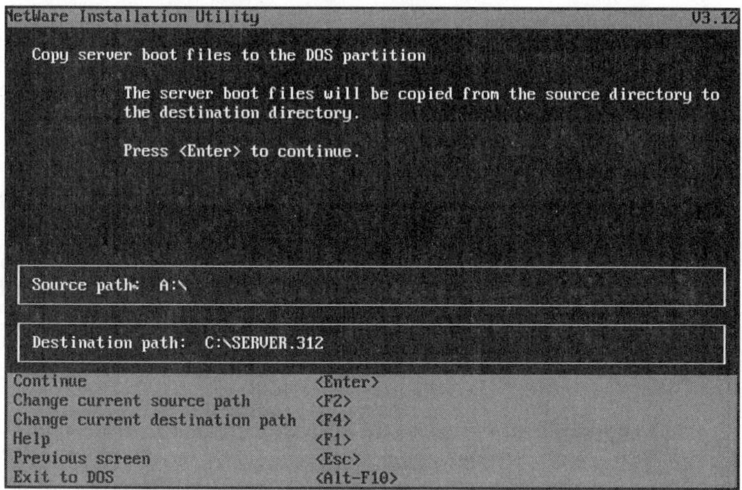

Figure 7.9
NetWare 3.12 installation—copying server boot files.

13. Press Enter to verify the source and destination paths.

    You should see a status display of the files copied to the DOS partition. If you are installing from floppy disks, you are prompted to enter the distribution disks (see fig. 7.10). The files copied are from essential files needed to start the server from the DOS partition.

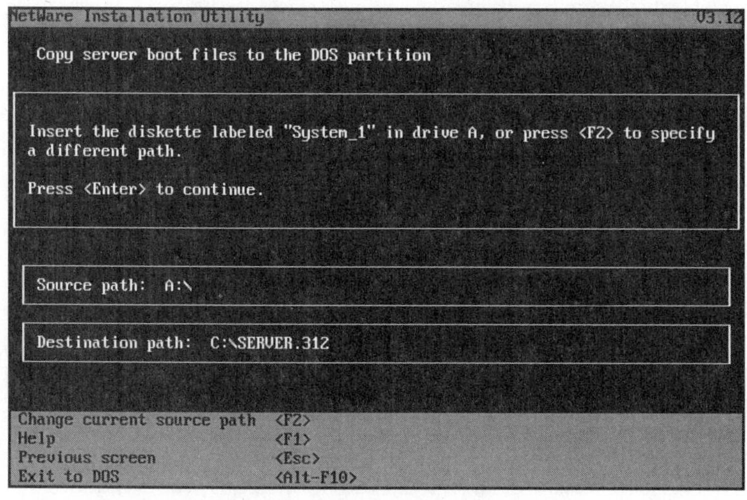

Figure 7.10
Server boot files being copied.

If installing from floppy disks, follow the directions on-screen to insert the disks.

14. You are asked to select a locale configuration for the server (see fig. 7.11). The configuration displayed is that for the server, but its default values displayed are taken from the DOS configuration you are using to run the INSTALL program.

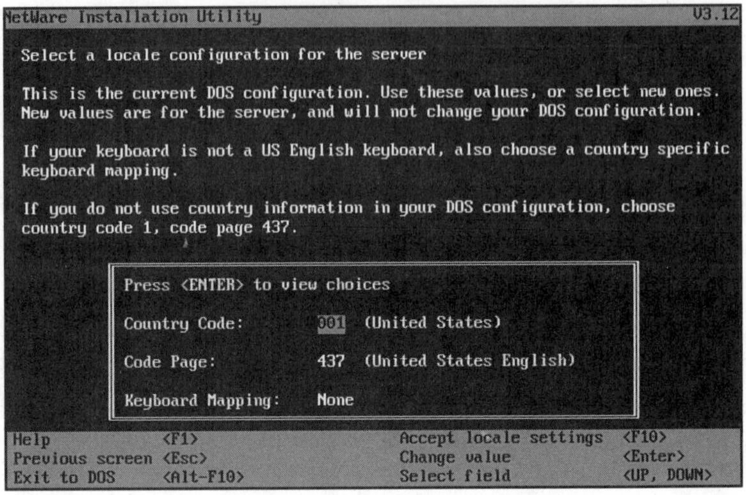

Figure 7.11
The Locale Information screen.

```
NetWare Installation Utility                                              V3.12

 Select a locale configuration for the server

 This is the current DOS configuration. Use these values, or select new ones.
 New values are for the server, and will not change your DOS configuration.

 If your keyboard is not a US English keyboard, also choose a country specific
 keyboard mapping.

 If you do not use country information in your DOS configuration, choose
 country code 1, code page 437.

          Press <ENTER> to view choices

          Country Code:        001  (United States)

          Code Page:           437  (United States English)

          Keyboard Mapping:    None

Help            <F1>                       Accept locale settings  <F10>
Previous screen <Esc>                      Change value            <Enter>
Exit to DOS     <Alt-F10>                  Select field            <UP, DOWN>
```


The *country code* is a three-digit number. Consult the COUNTRY.SYS entry in your DOS manual for the applicable country code. For the United States, the country code is 001.

The *code page* is a country-dependent three-digit number. For United States English, the code page value is 437. This defines the character sets used for screen display.

The *Keyboard Mapping* choice supports keyboard layout differences specific to a language. The Keyboard Mapping values supported are France, Germany, Italy, Spain, and the United States.

When finished making changes, press F10 to accept local changes. If you press Enter at any time, you will be editing the highlighted field.

15. Next you must select the file-name format (see fig. 7.12). The file-name format choices are as follows:

    DOS Filename Format (recommended)

    NetWare Filename Format

    NetWare Filename format allows extended lowercase file names; whereas DOS maps lowercase letters to uppercase for file names.

    Select DOS Filename format, unless you are using NETX shell to create extended lowercase file names. The NETX shell allows the creation of extended lowercase file names, but these file names are not readable by the DOS requester (VLM).

    Press F9 to view uppercase mapping information (see fig. 7.13).

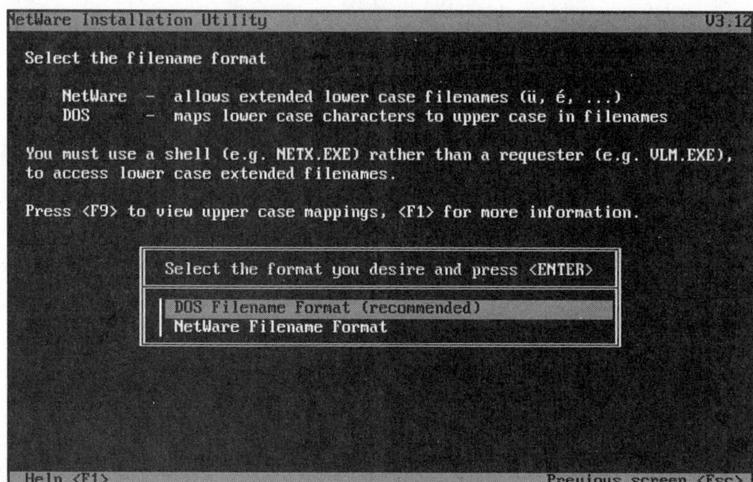

Figure 7.12
Selecting file name format.

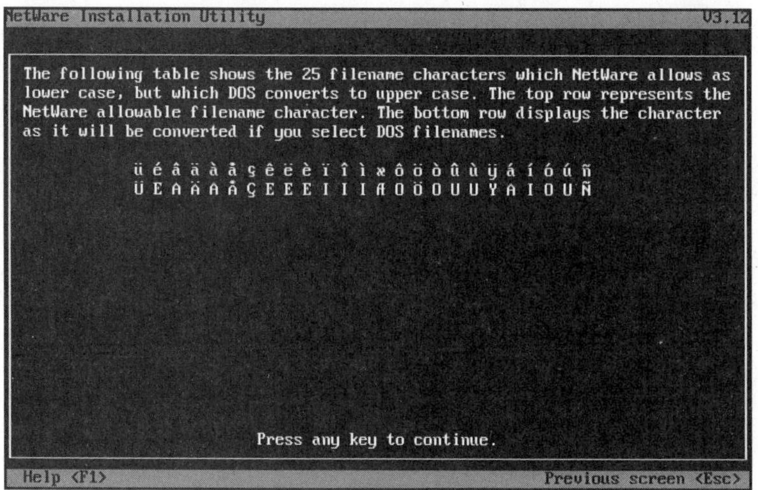

Figure 7.13
Uppercase mapping information.

A detailed discussion on file-name format issues occurs later in this chapter.

16. You are asked if you want to specify any special startup SET commands (see fig. 7.14).

    Several SET commands can be placed in the STARTUP.NCF file only. The STARTUP.NCF file resides on the DOS partition and in the directory where SERVER.EXE program was copied. It contains commands to load disk drivers and name spaces, and special commands such as `SET AUTO REGISTER MEMORY ABOVE 16 MEGABYTES=OFF` (set to ON to automatically add memory above 16 MB for EISA bus server machines).

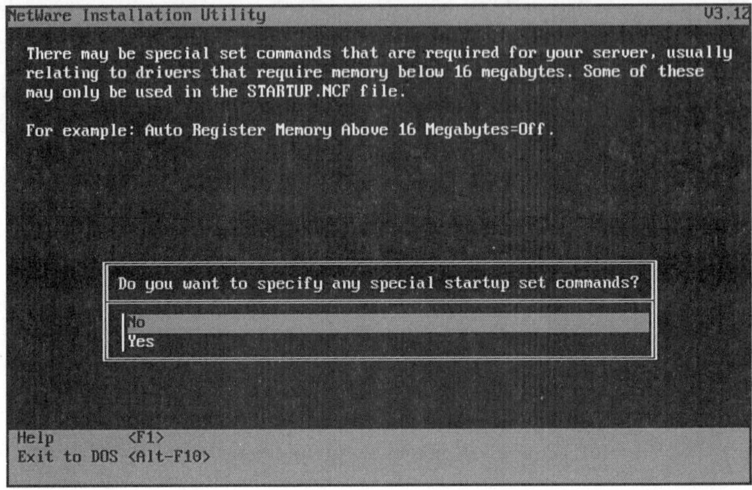

Figure 7.14
Special startup SET commands.

Select Yes only if your server configuration demands that you need to set special parameters in STARTUP.NCF file. Otherwise, select No. You can always edit the STARTUP.NCF file at a later stage.

17. You are asked if you want AUTOEXEC.BAT to load SERVER.EXE. If you answer Yes, your AUTOEXEC.BAT is modified to contain the following commands to start the server automatically, every time the machine is booted:

```
REM The following lines were created by the server installation program.
REM They will cause the server to come up whenever this computer is booted.
:BEGIN_SERVER
C:
cd C:\SERVER.312
SERVER
:END_SERVER
```

    If you select No, you must manually start the SERVER.EXE program.

    Select Yes, unless you have special circumstances. You can always edit the AUTOEXEC.BAT file at a later stage to add other commands, such as the DOS PAUSE command, to give you a chance to break out of AUTOEXEC.BAT.

18. If you select Yes, to have the install program add SERVER.EXE to the AUTOEXEC.BAT file, you are asked to verify the location of the AUTOEXEC.BAT file.

19. The SERVER.EXE program loads, at this point.

    From this point, the installation choices are similar to NetWare 3.11. The INSTALL.BAT file returns you to the command prompt (c:), and you must continue manually with the installation.

20. Enter the command **LOAD ISADISK.**

    Replace ISADISK with the name of the driver for the server disk. Other examples are IDE.DSK, AHA1540.DSK for ISA Adpatec SCSI, and so on. NetWare server disk drivers have a DSK extension. You can find them on the SYSTEM-1 disk or the C:\SERVER.312 directory to which they are copied. If the disk driver type you need is not in the distribution disks, you may want to contact the disk vendor.

    As the ISADISK loads, messages similar to the following appear on-screen:

    ```
    Loading module ISADISK.DSK
    NetWare 386 ISA Device Driver
    Version Number    Date of manufacture
    Copyright 1993 Novell, Inc. All rights reserved.
    Supported I/O port values are 1F0, 170
    I/O port: 1F0
    ```

    The ISA disk controller board can be set at either port address of 1F0 (hex) or 170 (hex). Your NetWare 386 server has one primary disk controller set at port address 1F0 (hex).

    If you are loading an ESDI disk driver, you get better performance using the following command:

    ```
    LOAD ISADISK /B
    ```

21. Select the appropriate port address.

    You should see a list of supported interrupt values, as follows:

    ```
    Supported interrupt number values are E, F, B, C
    Interrupt number: E
    ```

    The default is E. Unless your configuration is very different, your disk controller is probably set to use interrupt E (hex).

22. Select the interrupt number to match your disk controller board.

    If your server disks are attached through the *Disk Coprocessor Board* (DCB) you must run LOAD DISKSET after running `LOAD DiskDriver`. If this is not the case for your server disks, you can bypass this step.

23. Load the network board driver.

    Enter the following command to load the network driver:

    ```
    LOAD NetworkDriver
    ```

    Replace *NetworkDriver* with the name of the driver you will be using. Enter the parameters for the NIC installed on the server machine, when prompted to do so.

You can enter the FRAME type value to be used with the board. The frame type values supported are shown in table 7.5.

The Ethernet default frame type for NetWare 3.12 is ETHERNET_802.2, and the default frame type of NetWare 3.11 is ETHERNET_802.3. If you need to support a mix of NetWare 3.11 and NetWare 3.12 servers, load both Ethernet frame types at the server. Loading both frame types can adversely affect network speed and performance, so you may not want to load both drivers unless absolutely necessary.

The default frame type for NetWare 4.*x* is Ethernet_802.2. NetWare 3.12 was changed to support this preferred frame type after NetWare 4.0 was released.

For Token Ring networks, the default frame type is TOKEN-RING.

To load a driver for an alternative frame type, use the following command:

```
LOAD NetworkDriver   FRAME=FrameValue
```

in which *FrameValue* is one of the names specified in table 7.1. Therefore, to load the driver a second time with ETHERNET_802.2, use this command:

```
LOAD EthernetNetworkDriver   FRAME=802.3
```

EthernetNetworkDriver is the LAN driver for the Ethernet NIC.

If you load the NIC driver twice, the driver is loaded reentrantly. This means that the program code copy of the NIC driver is shared, but the parameter details are kept in different data segments.

24. NetWare 3.12 allows transport protocols other than IPX/SPX to function on the network. At this point, you can choose the protocols to be supported on the server. The native protocol used by NetWare 3.12 is the IPX/SPX NetWare protocol.

    The next step is to bind the IPX/SPX protocol to the network card driver by issuing the following command:

    ```
    BIND IPX TO NetworkDriver
    ```

    When asked for a network number, select the network number assigned (or to be assigned, if this is the first server on the cable) to the cable. If you are binding to another protocol, you are asked for the appropriate address. For example, if you are binding to the IP protocol, you are asked for the IP Address of the interface.

    Each network card must be assigned the network number that identifies the cabling system to which it is attached. The number is entered as a hexadecimal number and is eight hexadecimal digits long. It is not necessary to enter leading zeroes.

Values of 0 and FFFFFFFF are reserved and should not be used. A value of FFFFFFFF indicates an IPX broadcast packet. An example of its use is in SAP and RIP protocols. A value of 0 indicates an unknown network number. These conventions were first defined in the Xerox Network Standard (XNS) protocol suite from which IPX/SPX was derived.

25. Enter the network number for the physical network segment you are connecting to. A message similar to the following should appear on-screen:

    ```
    IPX LAN protocol bound to NetworkDriver Driver.
    ```

    Next, prepare the server disk and load the NetWare system files.

26. Enter the command to load the INSTALL NLM:

    ```
    LOAD INSTALL
    ```

    The INSTALL program is an NLM and can be used to format server disks, create NetWare partitions, perform surface analysis, mirror disks, create volumes, create file server initialization files, and load the operating system on the server disk.

27. The NetWare partition and first system volume SYS: should already have been created for you in a preceding step when you ran the INSTALL program from the floppy disk, CD-ROM, or network drive. Consequently, you should not have to use INSTALL to create a NetWare partition and volume; skip to the next step. The following instructions are to help those who are having unusual problems with creating a NetWare partition during the INSTALL program.

    Occasionally, things do not work as they are supposed to, and you might have to restart the installation because of a server crash. To do this, type the name of the SERVER.EXE from the server boot directory, load the disk driver and LAN driver, bind the protocols to the LAN driver, and load INSTALL. You may now need to destroy a previous partition and create a new one.

    To re-create a new partition and volume, do the following:

    a. Highlight Disk Options and press Enter. The Available Disk Options menu is displayed. The Format option is only necessary if the drive has never been formatted on DOS or NetWare.

    b. Highlight Partition Tables and press Enter. If you loaded disk drivers for multiple installed disks, you are presented with an Available Disk Drives menu. If only one disk is installed, then a Partition Options menu showing the two partitions created by you (one DOS, one NetWare) appears. If the partition to be used for NetWare 3.*x* shows a partition type other than NetWare Partition (partitions created with NetWare 3.11 appear as NetWare 386 Partition), delete it using the Delete Partition option. However, be warned that deleting a NetWare partition deletes all data contained in that partition. Make sure that you have a reliable backup of any important data.

c. Next, create a NetWare partition using the Create NetWare Partition option. During partition creation, you should see a screen that shows the Partition Size in cylinders and Megabytes, and also Hot Fix Information that contains the size of the data area and the redirection area. The redirection area used for hot fix is nominally two percent of the partition space. This can be increased or decreased.

d. Press Esc from the Partition Information screen. You are asked if you want to create the partition. Reply with a Yes. You should see the NetWare partition type created.

e. Press Esc to go back to the Available Disk Options screen. The Surface Test option can be executed next. It is optional because hot fix is operational during the server installation.

f. Press Esc one more time to go to the Installation Options screen.

g. Highlight the Volume Options choice and press Enter. A list of volumes is displayed. Press Ins to add a new volume. You should see a screen on the new volume to be created. The NetWare installation enables you to combine separate NetWare partitions, called volume segments, into a single, logical volume that spans multiple disks.

h. Press Esc and answer Yes to the question `Create Volume?`.

i. Press Alt+Esc to go back to the console prompt.

j. From the console prompt type the command **`MOUNT ALL.`** This command mounts all the volumes just created. Alternatively, you can give separate commands such as MOUNT SYS to mount individual volumes. Messages similar to the following should appear after executing the MOUNT ALL command:

```
Mounting Volume SYS:
Initializing Transaction Tracking System
10/16/93 10:09pm:  1.1.60 Bindery open requested by the SERVER
```

k. Press Alt+Esc to get back to the INSTALL NLM.

Next, create the AUTOEXEC.NCF and STARTUP.NCF files.

28. From the Installation Options menu, select the System Options.

29. Highlight Create AUTOEXEC.NCF File and press Enter.

    The commands in AUTOEXEC.NCF are executed to complete the boot process after SERVER.EXE executes commands in STARTUP.NCF. Because AUTOEXEC.NCF is saved in and runs from SYS:SYSTEM, place most of the boot commands in SYS:SYSTEM for added protection.

30. Use the cursor-movement keys to go the end of the file and add the following command:

    `MOUNT ALL`

You can optionally add the `SET ALLOW UNENCRYPTED PASSWORDS=ON` if you have a different copy of NetWare utilities on NetWare 2.*x* and NetWare 3.*x* servers on your network. Press Esc and save the changes.

31. From the Available System Options menu, select the Create STARTUP.NCF File option. The Path For STARTUP.NCF File should display. The path should be the server boot directory.

32. Press Enter to see the contents of the newly created file. If you need to add any special commands to STARTUP.NCF, you can do so at this point.

    The commands in the STARTUP.NCF file are executed by the SERVER.EXE program. The STARTUP.NCF is usually stored on the same drive and subdirectory you boot from, either a DOS partition or disk. It contains the commands to load disk drivers and non-DOS name support for the server.

33. Press Esc and answer Yes to save the STARTUP.NCF file.

34. Copy the system and public files. Press Esc to get back to the Available System Options screen. Select the Copy System and Public Files option. If you are copying from floppy disks, a window appears prompting you to insert NetWare 386 SYSTEM_1 Disk in drive A. Follow the instructions to insert the floppy disk. You can alternatively specify another source besides A: by pressing F6. If you are installing from CD-ROM, use the following path:

    ```
    DriveOrVolumeName:\NETWARE.312\ENGLISH
    ```

    You can press F5 to skip a disk.

    If you are installing from a network drive, specify the directory to which the installation disks were copied:

    ```
    DriveOrVolumeName:\NETWARE.312\ENGLISH
    ```

35. After the system and public files are copied, the server is installed. At the end of the copy operation the message `File Upload Complete` appears.

36. Press Esc a few times and when asked `Exit Install?`, answer Yes.

37. Bring the server down by typing the following commands from the server console:

    ```
    DOWN
    EXIT
    ```

38. Bring up the server and verify that all modules load as expected.

Upgrading from NetWare 2.*x* and 3.11 to NetWare 3.*x*

Whereas NetWare 2.*x* is adequate for small to medium sized networks, NetWare 3.12 is more suitable for large networks. Advances in NetWare technology are likely to be seen first in NetWare 3.12 (and NetWare 4.*x*).

To upgrade from NetWare 2.*x* or 3.11 to 3.12, you must take into account the following actions and considerations:

1. Run BINDFIX to clean up and repair any bindery errors. Next, perform a full back up of server data as a precautionary measure.
2. Restore, using SALVAGE, any deleted files that you want to retain as part of the upgrade process.
3. Perform any maintenance tasks, such as making file names consistent with the file format selected for the NetWare 3.12 server. NetWare 2.*x* actually allows directory names to be 14 characters long. Rename these directories to be consistent with DOS file-naming conventions.
4. If you are upgrading an *NetWare Name Service* (NNS)-based network, upgrade all servers in a domain at the same time.

The Migration Utility

NetWare 3.12 comes with a migration utility called MIGRATE.EXE that allows the upgrading of NetWare servers. The MIGRATE utility must be run from a workstation. It can be used to upgrade a NetWare 2.*x* or 3.*x*, or IBM LAN server, or the IBM PCLP (PC LAN Program) 1.3 Extended Services to a NetWare 3.12 server.

You can use the following two methods to upgrade servers using the MIGRATE utility:

- Across-the-wire migration
- Same-server migration

Across-the-Wire Migration

Figure 7.15 shows how across-the-wire migration works. The hardware requirements for this technique are as follows:

- A source server that needs to be converted—a NetWare 2.*x* or 3.*x*, or IBM LAN server, or IBM PCLP 1.3 Extended Services
- A destination server that is an existing NetWare 3.12 server already installed (using the methods described earlier)

- A workstation with sufficient disk storage to hold the migrated bindery information and for running the MIGRATE.EXE utility

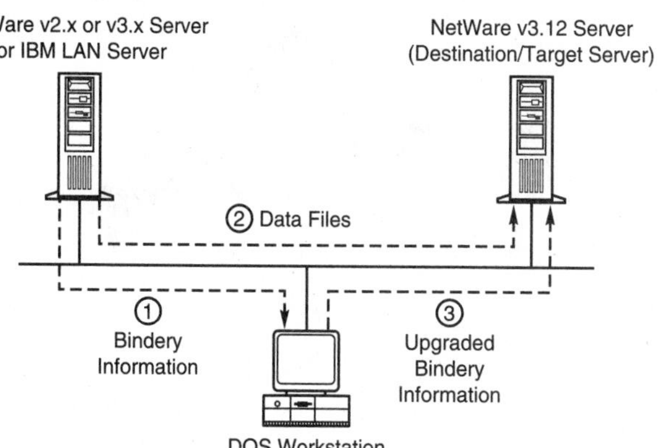

Figure 7.15
Across-the-wire migration.

As you can see from figure 7.15, across-the-wire migration assumes that you already have a NetWare 3.12 server installed and you want to migrate data files, user accounts, and other setup information from a source server (NetWare 2.*x* or 3.*x*, or IBM LAN server) to the NetWare 3.12 server.

Across-the-wire migration involves the following three-step process:

1. The bindery and setup information is copied from the source server to a working directory on the workstation running MIGRATE.

2. The data files are copied directly *across-the-wire* from the source server to the destination server.

3. The bindery information is migrated to the NetWare 3.12 server from the working directory on the workstation where it was copied to in step 1.

Across-the-wire migration enables you to preserve your data files and user environment. User accounts are translated to user objects. Default account restrictions, accounting methods, print queues, and print servers are preserved. The installer has the choice of allowing users to log in to the new system without a password or assigning passwords generated randomly (stored in SYS:SYSTEM\NEW.PWD).

Because across-the-wire migration does not modify the source server, it is a very safe method for upgrading.

The following steps explain the procedure for migration:

1. Install a NetWare 3.12 server using the steps outlined in this chapter.

2. Copy the contents of MIGRATE to a workstation that will be used for migration. You can run the MIGRATE.EXE program from the MIGRATE disk, but it is faster and more convenient to run it from a hard disk.

3. Log in to the source and destination servers. You can log in to the source and destination server at a later step from within MIGRATE. To do this, you must at least have the NetWare shell (or requester) loaded.

4. Run MIGRATE. You should see the MIGRATE main menu (see fig. 7.16). The Custom Migration Option enables you to select the information that you want to migrate. Use this option for greater control over the information that you want to migrate from the source server. For example, you can decide to migrate or not migrate any of the following information:

   - All information
   - Data files
   - Trustee assignments
   - Users
   - User restrictions
   - Groups
   - Group restrictions
   - Default account restrictions
   - Accounting information
   - Print queues and print servers

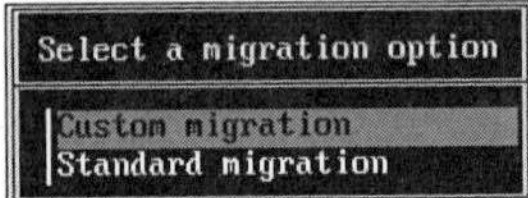

Figure 7.16
The MIGRATE main menu.

Source server refers to the v2.*x*, v3.*x*, or IBM LAN server, or IBM PCLP being migrated. *Destination server* refers to the NetWare 3.12 server to which bindery and data information is to be copied.

The Standard Migration option migrates all information from the source server. That is, all data files and bindery objects are migrated to the NetWare 3.12 server. Use this option if you do not want to be selective about what information to migrate.

5. If you choose the Custom Migration option from the Migration menu, you can select the type of migration (see fig. 7.17). The choices are across-the-wire or same-server migration. Whether you select across-the-wire or same-server, you must select the source LAN type (see fig. 7.18) and destination LAN (see fig. 7.19) type.

Figure 7.17
Select the type of migration.

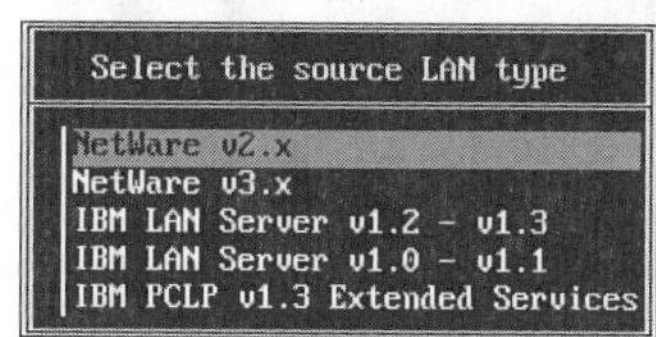

Figure 7.18
Select the source LAN type for migration.

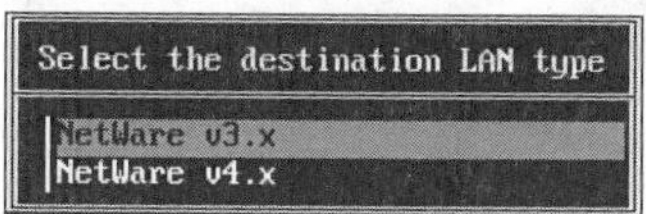

Figure 7.19
Select the destination LAN type for migration.

6. After selecting the source and destination LAN types, you have to configure the migration process, including defining the working directory for migration. You must have at least 5 MB of space available for the working directory. Figure 7.20 shows the configuration options. The screen shown is for the Custom Migration option, which gives you the greatest flexibility and control. You are presented with similar choices for the Standard Migration option. For the source server, you must define the source server name, the type of information to migrate (see fig. 7.21), and the volumes on the source server to migrate (see fig. 7.22). For the destination server, you also must define the destination server name, the type of information to migrate, and the volumes on the source server to migrate.

   If you are not already logged on to the servers, you must do so from within MIGRATE (see fig. 7.23).

   You must select the volume destinations for the destination server. Figure 7.24 shows that the NWCS\SYS: volume is to be migrated to the NW3CS:SYS: volume. You can select this choice or edit the destination path.

   For migrating user accounts and print servers, you can specify a choice of assigning no passwords or random passwords to the destination user accounts (see fig. 7.25). Random passwords are kept in SYS:SYSTEM\MEW.PWD.

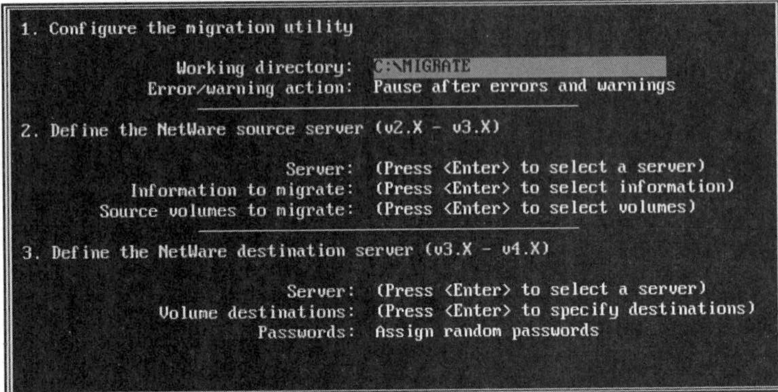

Figure 7.20
Configuring migration.

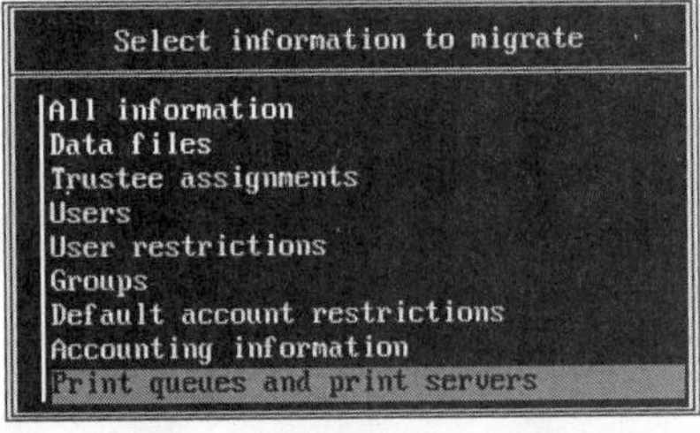

Figure 7.21
Types of information to migrate.

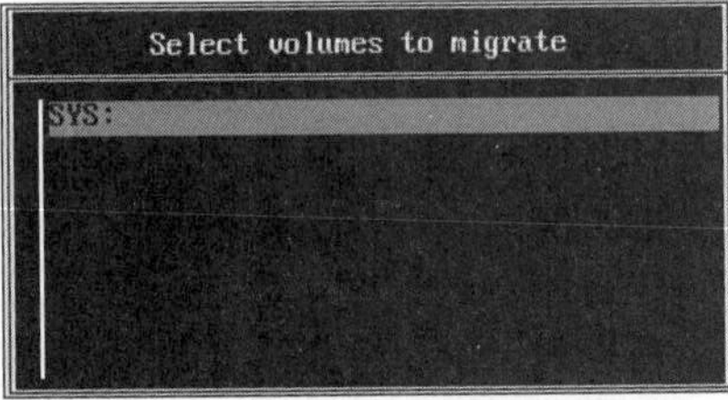

Figure 7.22
Volumes on source server to migrate.

User Name:

Figure 7.23
Logging on to a server from within MIGRATE.

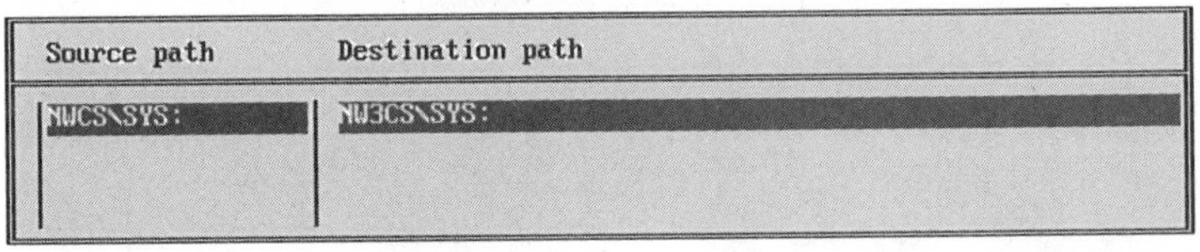

Source path	Destination path
NWCS\SYS:	NW3CS\SYS:

Figure 7.24
Selecting volume destination to migrate to.

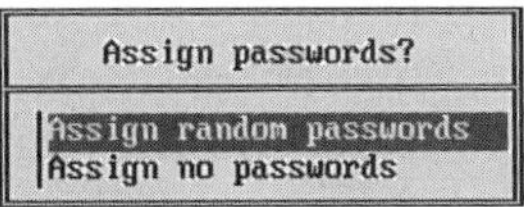

Figure 7.25
Password migration strategy.

7. When the migration configuration is made, press F10 to continue with migration. You are presented with a list of migration actions that can be performed. Select Start Migration to begin the migration process. A list of actions taken during the migration process is displayed on-screen (see fig. 7.26). You can press the space bar to pause the actions, or Esc to stop the migration. The migration report is created in a file called MIG*nnn*.RPT, where *nnn* is a number identifying the report. Errors in migration are displayed if you selected the option to pause on error when configuring the migration process (see fig. 7.27). You can choose to continue, stop, or ignore migration errors.

   At the end, a message displays informing you of the completion of the migration process (see fig. 7.28).

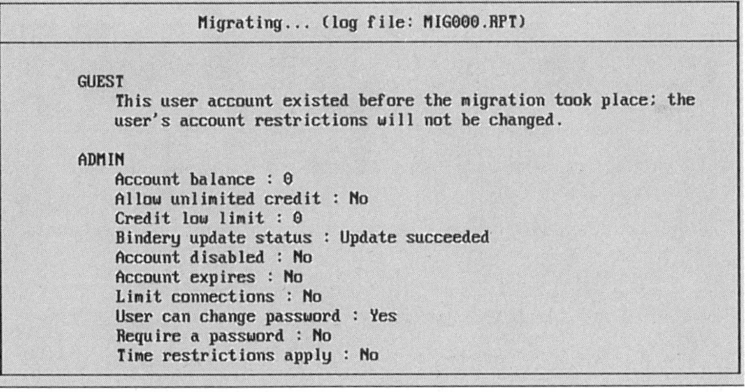

Figure 7.26
Migrated information being displayed.

8. When finished, exit the MIGRATE utility.

Same-Server Migration

Figure 7.29 shows how the same-server migration technique works. The hardware requirements for this technique are as follows:

- A source server that needs to be converted. This can be a NetWare 2.*x* (running on a 386 class machine) or 3.*x*; IBM LAN server 1.0, 1.1, 1.2, or 1.3; or IBM PCLP 1.3 Extended Services. There is no separate destination server.

- A workstation with sufficient disk storage and backup device, to hold the migrated bindery information and the data files. The MIGRATE utility runs at the workstation.

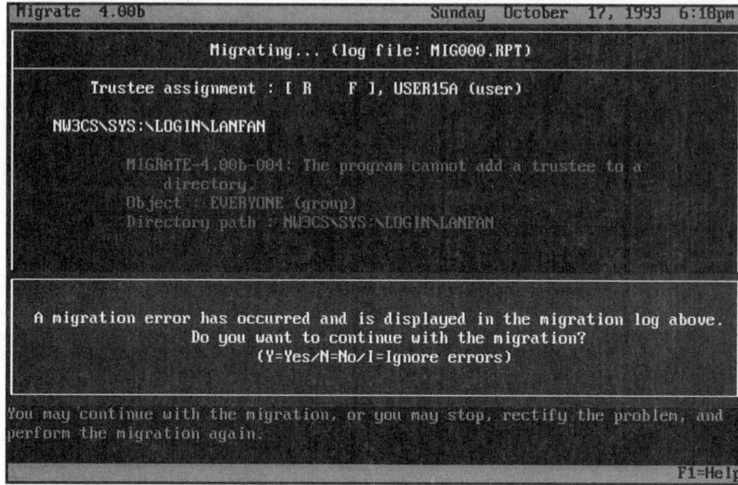

Figure 7.27
Migration error.


```
Migration from the source server to the destination server is complete.
Press <Enter> to continue.
```

Figure 7.28
Migration complete.

As you can see from figure 7.29, unlike across-the-wire migration, same-server migration does not assume that you already have a NetWare 3.12 server installed. You can use only a single server that is to be converted and a workstation for running MIGRATE. This workstation also is used for backup and restore of data and bindery.

Same-server migration involves a five-step process as follows:

1. The data files are backed up to the backup device attached to the workstation.
2. The bindery and/or setup information is copied from the source server to a working directory on the workstation.
3. The NetWare 3.12 server needs to be installed on the server. Note that to do this, any prior information on the server disk will be lost. This is why doing steps 1 and 2 reliably is very important.
4. Restore backed up data files from backup device to the newly installed NetWare 3.12 server.
5. Run the MIGRATE utility to migrate bindery information to the NetWare 3.12 server. The bindery information was stored in the working directory in step 2.

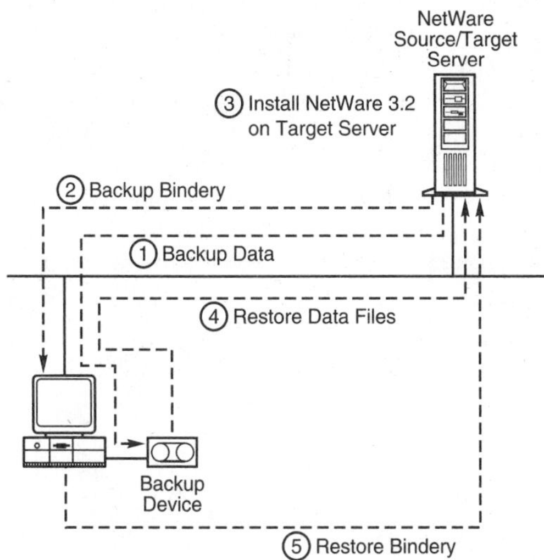

Figure 7.29
Same-server migration.

Same-server migration enables you to preserve your data files and user environment. If the name of the destination server is changed in same-server migration, then during migration of intermediate file data to the destination server, a precautionary step is taken to break the connection to the source server. This is to avoid inadvertently copying the files to the source server again, but with a different server name. The MIGRATE utility informs you that the connection is broken and gives you a choice of re-initializing the connection. You should answer No to this query for MIGRATE to work correctly.

Because same-server migration modifies the source server, there is a small risk that data could be lost. The risk is minimized by making sure that a good backup of the data and bindery is done, in steps 1 and 2.

Other Migration Issues

If you are migrating a data file that has the same name as a file that already exists on the destination server, the file is not copied. Instead, an error message is displayed and written to a migration report.

If you are migrating a directory with the same name as a directory that already exists on the destination server, the files from both directories are merged under the destination directory.

Summary

In this chapter, you learned about the installation choices to be made during a NetWare 3.12 installation. It is quite possible to install a NetWare 3.12 operating system without understanding the reasons behind design choices. One of the goals of this chapter was to give you an understanding of why a design choice has to be made a certain way. This helps you to identify and solve installation and configuration problems more effectively. A guided tour of a NetWare 3.12 installation was presented to give you a better understanding of the installation process.

Understanding NetWare 3.12 installation is a key to understanding the changes made to this network operating system. Many decisions about parameters must be made throughout the installation process. Incorrect choices for these parameters can cause an installation to fail or have an adverse impact on server performance.

Managing NetWare 2.2, 3.11, 3.12 Users

This chapter helps you understand the different ways that user and group accounts can be created and managed. Managing user accounts is the most common task that the network supervisor has to perform. To simplify this task, the Supervisor can delegate responsibilities and tasks to assistant Supervisors called *workgroup managers*. In this chapter, you learn how to set up workgroup managers.

NetWare delegates the responsibility for Supervisor tasks one step further by defining file-server console operators who can perform administrative tasks at the file-server console.

Also, you can manage the server console remotely by means of the Remote Management Facility (RMF). The MONITOR NLM utility enables you to monitor users. You learn about remote management later in the chapter.

Understanding User Administration

User account administration can be divided into two phases: creating and establishing the user account and maintaining the user accounts.

User accounts can be created in several ways. The most popular way is by using the SYSCON utility because it is an interactive menu-driven utility that is easy to work with. Most NetWare administrators are familiar with its use.

In many environments, user accounts must be created for a large number of users with similar needs. Creating users one at a time with SYSCON can become a daunting task. In these situations, the MAKEUSER utility can be used for a batch creation of users. MAKEUSER defines its own script language, which can be used for creating or deleting users and setting up individual parameters for them.

Colleges and universities are good examples in which user accounts are created in batch. As new students enroll every semester or quarter, old accounts must be deleted and new accounts must be created. The deletion and creation of these accounts can easily be done by using the MAKEUSER utility.

In large networks, multiple servers can be organized as *domains*. Instead of creating user accounts for each server in the domain, a domain user account can be created by using the NETCON utility.

The second phase, maintaining user accounts, involves maintenance of the network. User accounts are never static because the needs of the organization (and thus the needs of the users in the organization) change and evolve with time. The SYSCON and NETCON utilities can be used for the maintenance of most of the user parameters that need to be modified.

Managing User Accounts

This section focuses on managing user accounts. You learn how to perform user-account management for accounts that use SYSCON. In a later section, you learn how to use MAKEUSER to manage a batch of user accounts.

Creating User Names

Before a user account can be created, you must decide which user name will be used to identify the account. A uniform and consistent method should be used for assigning the user names for the user accounts. The following lists some of the conventions for creating user names:

- **User's first name.** The user's first name works well in small LANs, in which everyone is on a first-name basis. Examples of user names for accounts are MARY, JOHN, DAVID, and so on. If there is more than one user with the same first name, there is a name-collision problem—use another naming scheme.

- **User's last name.** The user's last name is common in more formal organizations. If there is more than one user with the same last name, again there is a name-collision problem—again, another naming scheme can be used.

- **User's first name and last name initial.** Although the first name and last name initial usually works to avoid most name collisions, it is not foolproof. If more than one user has the same first name and last name initial, use another naming scheme.

- **User's first name initial and last name.** The user's first name initial and last name also works well to avoid most name collisions.

- **User's initials.** Although the user's initials for the user name is not very common, it can be used in organizations in which people are usually identified by their initials. To avoid name collisions, the initials of first, middle, and last names can be used. Examples of user names are KSS, DGS, JFK, and so on. Unless these names are easily recognizable, they should be avoided. (Some users may not like to be referred to by their initials.)

User names can be up to 47 characters long, but it is preferable to limit them to no more than 8 characters. It is convenient, when assigning home directories, to make the home directory name the same as the user name (see fig. 8.1). Because directory names under DOS cannot contain more than 8 characters, the user name also should contain 8 characters or fewer.

Creating Groups and Group Names

Sometimes users need the same type of access from the server, particularly if they are on the same project team, or if their jobs are similar. NetWare provides a convenient scheme to manage these users. Users with common needs are considered to be part of the same *group*, which has a group name (up to 47 characters long) associated with it. The group is assigned a set of access privileges. All users who are members of the group can then inherit the access rights assigned to the group.

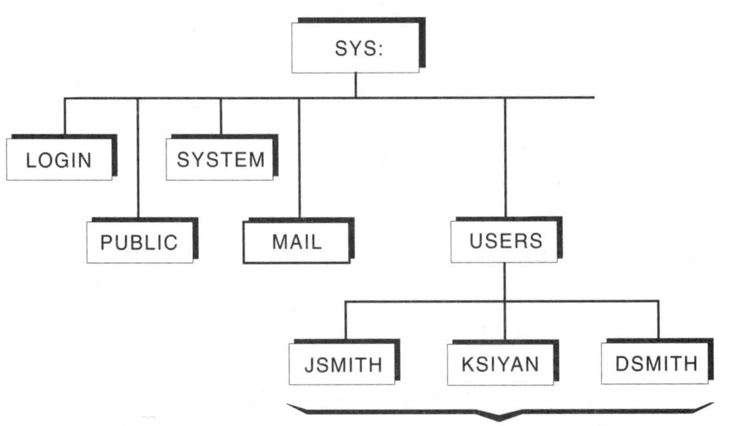

Figure 8.1
User names assigned to home directories.

Groups simplify user account administration. Instead of assigning access privileges individually, for example, the privileges can be assigned to a group—the users then automatically inherit the privileges of the group. Other benefits of groups are the following:

- Access privileges can be revoked from all users in a group.
- Access privileges can be granted to all users in a group.
- If a user no longer is a part of the workgroup, he or she can be removed from the membership list for that NetWare group.
- When a new user joins the workgroup, he or she can be made a member of the NetWare group.

Thus, groups make user account administration easier. They do not have home directories or mail directories, as do user accounts. The concept of groups is used extensively for simplifying user-account management with SYSCON.

System configuration (SYSCON), a menu-driven utility that creates and modifies user accounts, is commonly used to manage user accounts. You also can use the USERDEF and MAKEUSER utilities to manage these accounts.

The following sections give you the steps to follow for the various tasks that SYSCON performs, and show you the SYSCON screens for NetWare 3.*x*. (SYSCON from NetWare 3.*x* also can be used for administering user accounts for NetWare 2.*x*.)

SYSCON's many options reflect the fact that almost all system administration tasks can be performed with this utility. Because choosing these tasks can be bewildering, the user administration tasks discussed in this chapter are grouped by logical functions. These tasks also are presented in a logical order, so if you are setting up users for the first time, you can follow the discussion to simplify creation and maintenance of users. (If a batch creation of users is desired, MAKEUSER/USERDEF can be used. For setting up workgroup administrators, SYSCON can be used.)

The following sections discuss in detail three important system-administration tasks:

- Setting up user accounting
- Creating and assigning group accounts
- Creating a user account

Setting Up User Accounting

Before setting up user accounts, you must plan your account setup. The NetWare manuals include planning sheets you can use for this purpose. You also can use the planning sheet designed by the author. The difference between this and other planning sheets is that user information is presented in a one-user-per-worksheet form (see table 8.1), rather than on one large sheet containing information about many users.

Table 8.1
User Information Worksheet

1. User name: ____________________
2. Full name: ____________________
3. Home directory: ____________________
4. Security equivalences: ____________________

5. Trustee Directory Assignments:

Directory	*Trustee Assignment*
______	______________
______	______________

6. Trustee File Assignments:

File	*Trustee Assignment*
______	______________
______	______________

7. Member of groups: ____________________________

8. Managed by workgroup managers: ______________

9. Workgroup Manager for:

Users	*Groups*
______	______

10. Password restrictions: ____________________________

11. Account restrictions:____________________________

12. Station restrictions:____________________________

13. Time restrictions:______________________________

14. User ID (hexadecimal number): ______________________

For a large network, keeping this information up-to-date can be critical. Store your planning worksheets in a secure place in case of a server disk crash or the loss of the server bindery (internal database) that is used to keep track of user information. These worksheets can help to rebuild the system.

It also is important to keep these worksheets current because user needs evolve with time. Network administrators often are too overworked (or do not set aside the time) to maintain good user-account documentation. If the server disk crashes, it is usually the network administrator who must "rebuild" the system.

The table 8.1 worksheet can be used throughout this book to compile information about the user. Another way to manage worksheets is to utilize an application database in which the worksheet corresponds to a record in a database (or table). Some excellent database-management packages include Paradox, Btrieve, dBASE, or any SQL-based package.

Database worksheets have a disadvantage, however. If you want to share the database, you probably want to keep it on the server, and if the server disk crashes, you lose this database. For this reason, it is best to maintain a hard copy (or paper record) of all information as a backup.

Creating and Assigning Group Accounts

A worksheet similar to table 8.1 can be used to keep track of group information (see table 8.2). Again, the information is presented in the form of one worksheet per group for easy reference.

Table 8.2
Group Information Worksheet

1. Group name: ______________________________

2. Full group name:______________________________

3. Member list:______________________________

   ____

   ____

4. Trustee Directory Assignments:

   Directory *Trustee Assignment*

   ________ ________________

   ________ ________________

5. Trustee File Assignments:

   File *Trustee Assignment*

   ________ ________________

   ________ ________________

After you have filled out the worksheet for groups you want to define, follow these steps to create the groups by using SYSCON:

1. Log in to the server as the Supervisor. The following instructions assume that you are logging in to a NetWare 3.*x* server. The procedure for NetWare 2.*x* servers is very similar.

2. Invoke the SYSCON program. A menu appears, showing the SYSCON options.

3. Select the Group Information option from the Available Topics box. The Group Names box displays the groups defined on the server, as shown in figure 8.2.

Figure 8.2
Group Name box, showing groups defined on the server.

4. To add a new group, press Ins. The New Group Name dialog box appears, prompting you for the new group name (see fig. 8.3).

Figure 8.3
New Group Name dialog box.

5. Enter the new group name and press Enter. The group name that you just added—in this case, DBASE—should display in the Group Names box, as shown in figure 8.4.

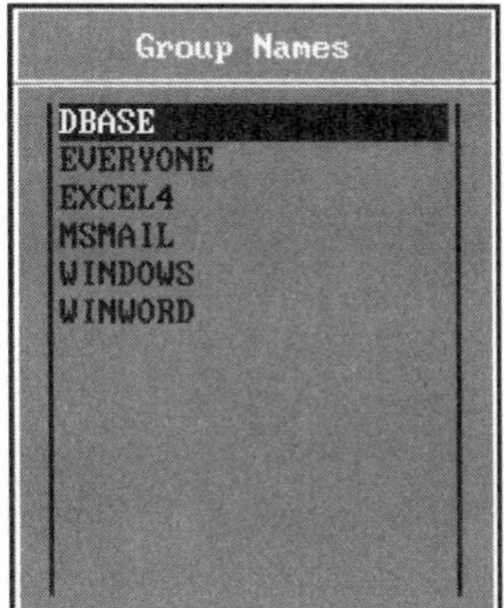

Figure 8.4
New group name displays.

6. Repeat the preceding steps to add new group names.
7. From the list of groups in the Group Names box, select a newly created group and press Enter. The Group Information box for the selected group appears, as shown in figure 8.5.
8. Select the Full Name option and enter a descriptive name for the group.
9. Both the Managed Users And Groups option and the Managers option can be used to set up other groups and users managed by this group, and to set up managers for members of this group.

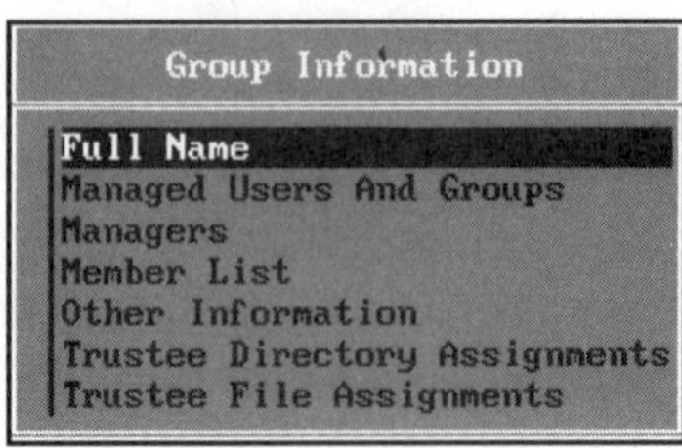

Figure 8.5
Group Information box.

10. To add new members to the group, select the Member List option from the Group Information box. The Group Members box appears, as shown in figure 8.6.

Figure 8.6
Group Members box.

11. To add members, press Ins. To delete members, press Del. The Not Group Members box appears, as shown in figure 8.7.

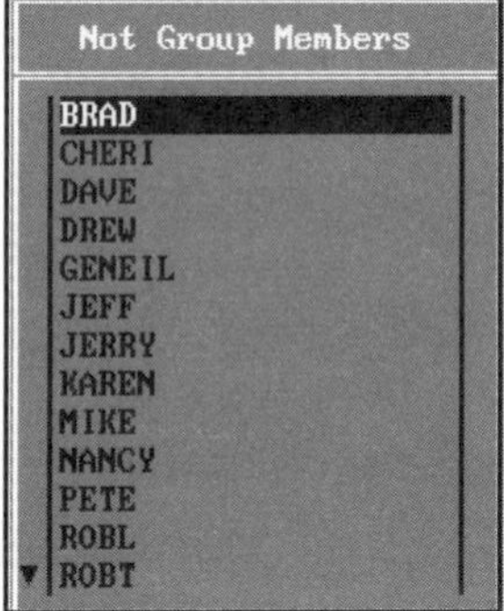

Figure 8.7
Not Group Members box.

12. From the list of user names that are not members of the group, mark the new members by pressing F5, and then Enter. (You also can highlight a new member, press Enter, and then repeat the process.) The new member names appear in the Group Members box (see fig. 8.8).

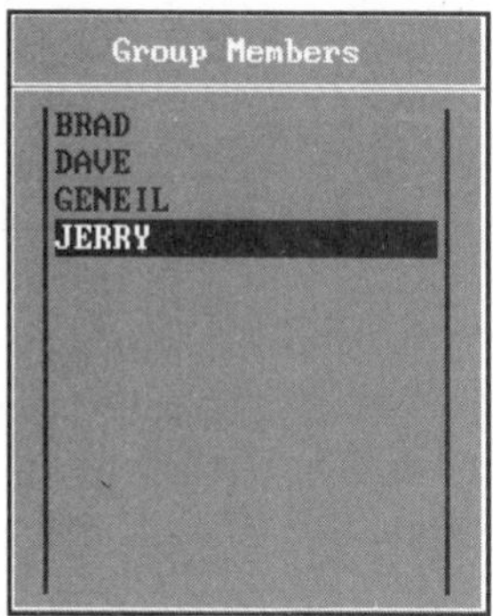

Figure 8.8
New members listed in the Group Members box.

13. Select the Other Information option from the Group Information box. A box displays, as in figure 8.9, showing the group ID and whether the group members are file server console operators.

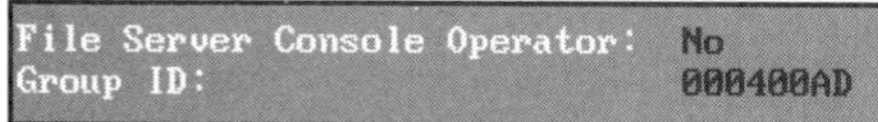

Figure 8.9
File Server Console Operator and Group ID box.

14. Press Esc to return to the Group Information box, and select the Trustee Directory Assignments option. A box displays, showing a list of Trustee Directory Assignments for the group. If this is a new group, the list will initially be empty. Figure 8.10 shows this box.

15. To make other trustee directory assignments, press Ins. A dialog box appears, prompting you to enter the directory in which the trustee should be added (see fig. 8.11).

    In the current release of NetWare, the default rights assigned for a directory assigned to a group are Read and File Scan. To change the trustee directory assignment, highlight the trustee directory assignment that is displayed, and then press Enter. The Trustee Rights Granted box appears.

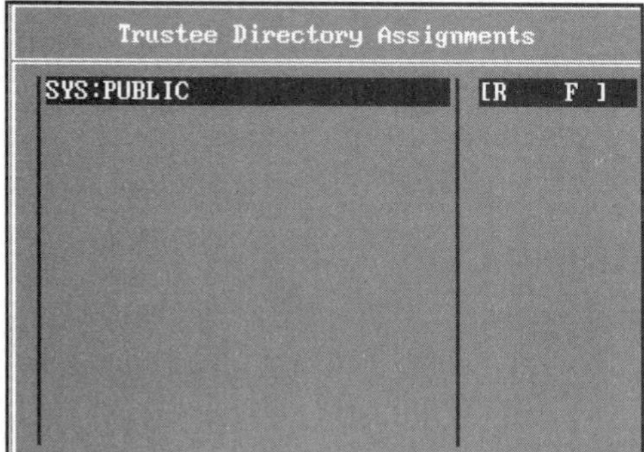

Figure 8.10
Trustee Directory Assignments dialog box.

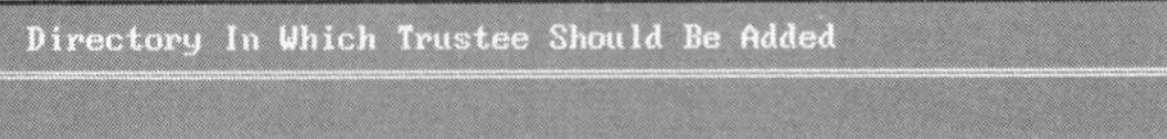

Figure 8.11
Directory In Which Trustee Should Be Added dialog box.

To add to this list, press Ins; to delete from this list, highlight the entry to be deleted and press Del. If the Ins key is pressed, the Trustee Rights Not Granted box appears. Mark the trustee assignment to be made by pressing F5, and then press Enter. Press Esc a few times to return to the Trustee Directory Assignment box.

16. To make trustee file assignments, select the Trustee File Assignments option from the User Information box. The Trustee File Assignments box appears (see fig. 8.12).

17. To make other trustee file assignments, press Ins. A dialog box appears that asks you to enter the path name of the file for which the trustee assignment is being set, as shown in figure 8.13. To modify the trustee file assignment, follow the same steps used for modifying trustee directory assignments.

18. Press Esc several times or press Alt+F10 and answer YES to exit SYSCON.

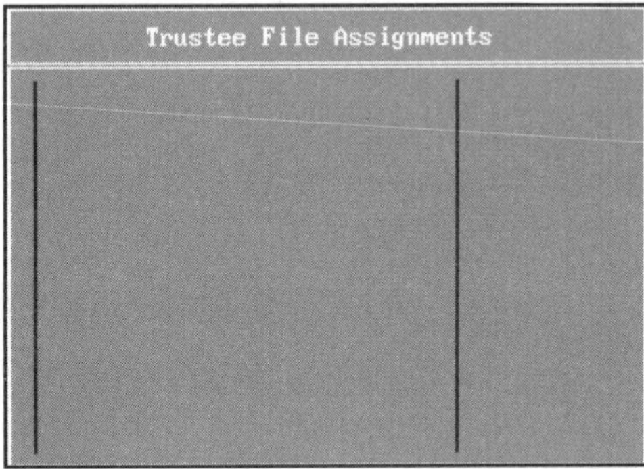

Figure 8.12
Trustee File Assignments dialog box.

Select the Directory To Select A File From

Figure 8.13
Select the Directory To Select A File From dialog box.

Creating a User Account

In this section, you learn how to use SYSCON to create a user account. The assumption is that you have used SYSCON to create groups. (If you are not sure how to do this, consult the previous sections.)

Suppose, for example, that you are setting up an account for a single user. (Multiple-user accounts can be set up by repeating the steps for a single-user account.) Before you start, you must know the user's trustee assignments and the groups that the user belongs to (fill out the worksheets shown in tables 8.1 and 8.2). Then follow these steps:

1. Log in to the server as Supervisor. The assumption is that you are logging in to a NetWare 3.*x* server. The procedure for NetWare 2.*x* servers is very similar.

2. Invoke the SYSCON program. The SYSCON Available Topics box displays, as shown in figure 8.14.

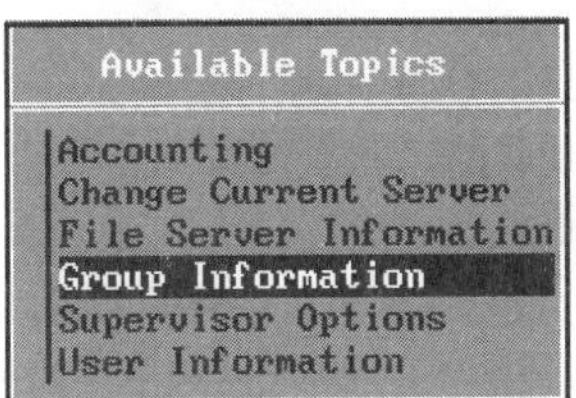

Figure 8.14
Available Topics box.

8

3. Select the User Information option from the Available Topics box. The User Names box appears, showing the names of the users defined on the server (see fig. 8.15).

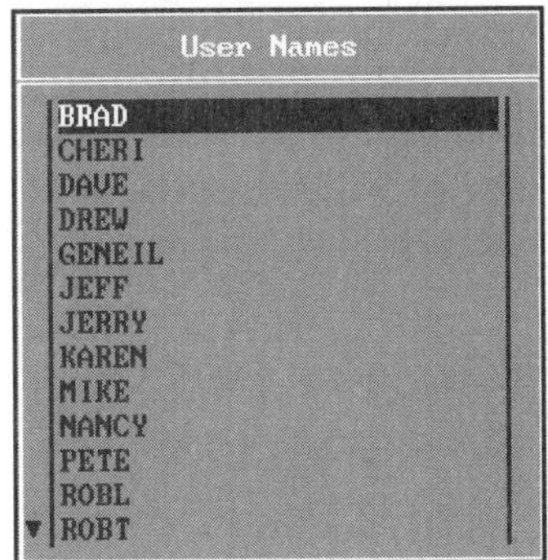

Figure 8.15
User Names box.

4. Press Ins to add a new user. A dialog box appears, asking for the new user name, as shown in figure 8.16.

Figure 8.16
User Name dialog box.

5. Enter the user name for the user to be created, and then press Enter. A screen with a default path name for the user's home directory displays.

6. Change the home directory for the user to SYS:USERS/*UserName*, and then press Enter. If asked to verify creation of the home directory, select YES. The new user that has been created—in this case, ADMIN—is highlighted in the User Names box (see fig. 8.17).

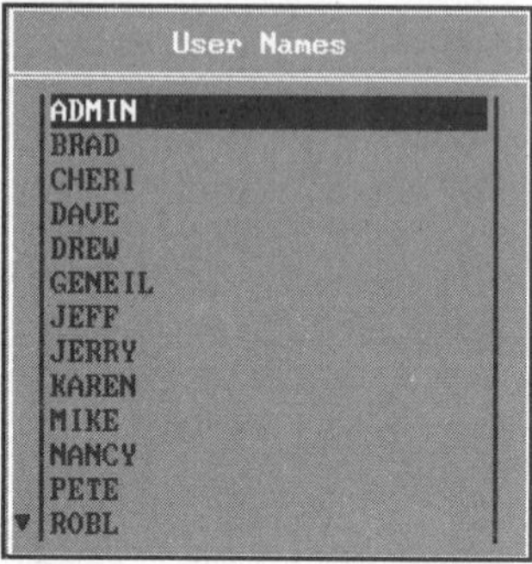

Figure 8.17
New user highlighted in User Names box.

7. Highlight the user name from the dialog box, and then press Enter. The User Information box appears, displaying a list of user attributes, as in figure 8.18.

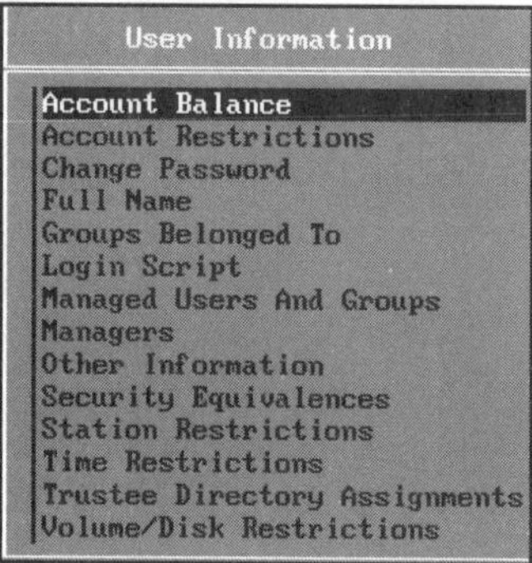

Figure 8.18
User Information box, showing user attributes.

8. Select the Full Name option, and enter the full name when asked to do so.

9. Select the Groups Belonged To option. A box appears, with a list of groups to which the user belongs, as shown in figure 8.19. By default, the user belongs to the group EVERYONE.

10. Press Ins to display a list of groups the user does not belong to. A box appears, with a list of groups the user does not belong to (see fig. 8.20).

11. Press F5 to mark the groups you want to make the user a member of, and then press Enter. Alternatively, you can highlight a group name and press Enter. After adding the user to new groups, the Groups Belonged To box reappears, showing the new list of groups that the user is a member of (see fig. 8.21).

Figure 8.19
The default group EVERYONE highlighted in the Groups Belonged To box.

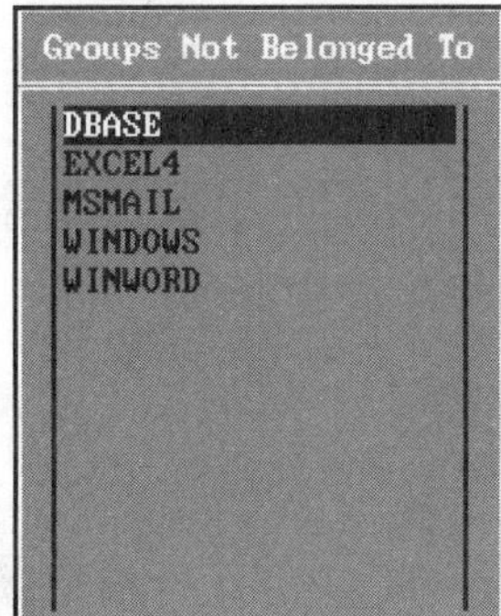

Figure 8.20
Groups Not Belonged To dialog box.

8

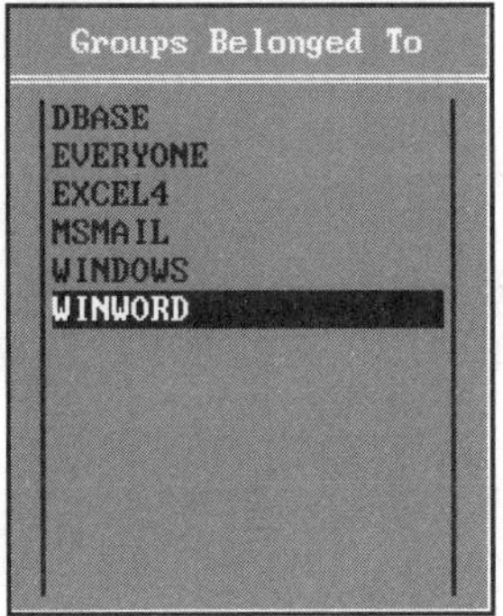

Figure 8.21
New groups listed in the Groups Belonged To box.

12. Press Esc to return to the User Information box. (For information on creating log-in scripts, see Chapter 25, "Printing in NetWare 2.2, 3.*x*, and 4.*x*.")

13. Select the Other Information option from the User Information box and press Enter. A dialog box appears (see fig. 8.22).

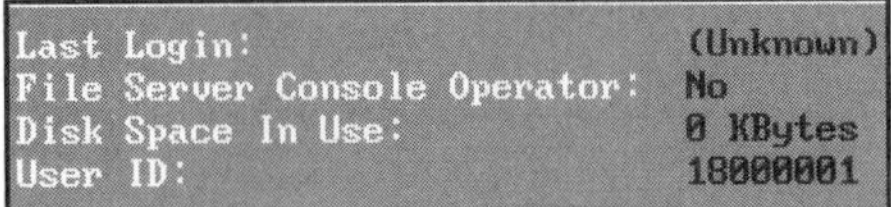
Last Login: (Unknown)
File Server Console Operator: No
Disk Space In Use: 0 KBytes
User ID: 18000001

Figure 8.22
Dialog box for Other Information.

14. Record the User ID in the worksheet in table 8.2. (The *user ID* is the internal name under which the user's information is kept in the bindery. It also is the name of the directory under SYS:MAIL, in which the user's log-in script is kept.)

15. To create a Trustee Directory Assignment for a user, press Esc to return to the User Information box, and then select the Trustee Directory Assignments option. A Trustee Directory Assignments box appears, as shown in figure 8.23.

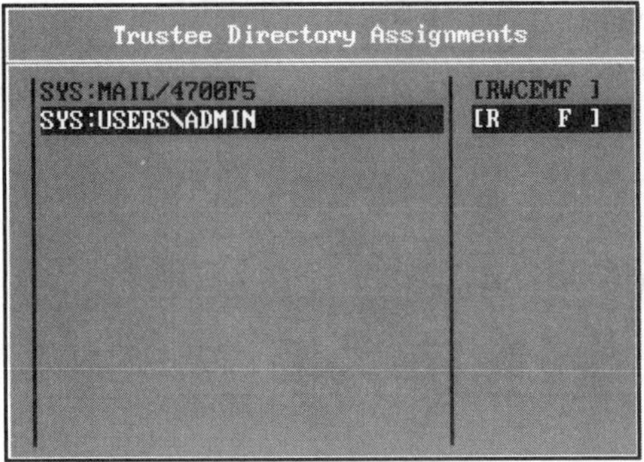

Figure 8.23
Trustee Directory Assignments box.

16. To make other trustee directory assignments, press Ins. A dialog box displays, in which you add the trustee directory (see fig.8.24).

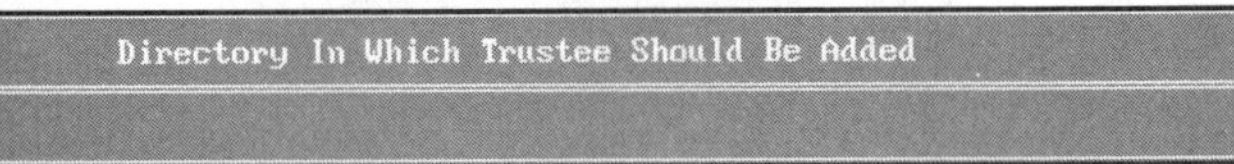

Figure 8.24
Directory In Which Trustee Should Be Added dialog box.

In the current release of NetWare, the default rights assigned for a directory other than the home directory are Read and File Scan. To change the trustee directory assignment, highlight the trustee directory assignment that is displayed and press Enter. The Trustee Rights Granted box appears. To add to this list, press Ins; to delete from this list, press Del. When Ins is pressed, the Trustee Rights Not Granted box appears. Press F5 to mark the trustee assignment to be made, and then press Enter. Press Esc a few times to return to the Trustee Directory Assignments box.

17. To make trustee file assignments, select the Trustee File Assignment option from the User Information box. A dialog box showing a list of Trustee File Assignments appears, as in figure 8.25.

Figure 8.25
Trustee File Assignments dialog box.

18. To make other trustee file assignments, press Ins. A dialog box appears (see fig. 8.26) and expects you to enter the path name of the file for which the trustee assignment is being set.

Select the Directory To Select A File From

Figure 8.26
Select the Directory To Select A File From dialog box.

To modify the trustee file assignment, follow the same steps used for modifying trustee directory assignments.

19. Press Esc several times, or press Alt+F10 and answer YES to exit SYSCON.

Creating Users with the MAKEUSER and USERDEF Utilities

NetWare comes with a powerful user batch-creation utility, MAKEUSER, that can be used to automate user creation. A script language, consisting of statements (or directives), can be used to specify the information to be entered into the system bindery.

The following is a sample list of a script file, SAMPLE.USR, that can be used to create a user in batch mode. The MAKEUSER script files have a default extension of USR. The MAKEUSER command language consists of a number of reserved words, described in table 8.3. These reserved words are preceded by the pound symbol (#). The only exception to this rule is the reserved word REM (# is optional). To continue on to the next line, the continuation symbol (+) can be used at the end of a line. The sample of the script file is as follows:

```
rem
rem * Create a batch of users. This template file is meant
rem * as a sample MAKEUSER file only.
rem
rem Establish the home directory
```

```
#home    sys:users
rem * Users will be members of group students and engineers
#groups   students; engineers
rem * Users will use a common login script specified by
rem * the contents of the file specified below.
#login_script sys:public/scripts/eng.scr
rem * Max disk space per user=10MB=10MB/4KB=2500 blocks
rem * Note: block #'s = disk space/ block size
#max_disk_space SYS,2500
rem #create User; FullName;Password;groups;rights
#create User1; Full Name;reimman$gauss;wpusers;sys:apps rwcemf^
#create User2; Full Name;laplace#cauchy;sysop;sys:apps rwcemf^
```

The #HOME statement specifies that the home directory for users created by #CREATE will be the user name under the directory SYS:USERS. Statements like #HOME, #GROUPS, #LOGIN_SCRIPT, and #MAX_DISK_SPACE establish a context for user creation. This *context* means that the values defined by these statements are valid for all users created by the #CREATE statements, until explicitly cleared by the #CLEAR directive.

The #GROUPS statement specifies that users are members of the groups students and engineers.

The #LOGIN_SCRIPT statement specifies that the login script for the users is described by the contents of the file SYS:PUBLIC/SCRIPTS/ENG.SCR.

The maximum disk space allowed for users is specified by the #MAX_DISK_SPACE statement—it is 2500 blocks or 10 MB, assuming a disk block size of 4 KB.

The two #CREATE commands create two users. Their passwords are specified as REIMANN$GAUSS and LAPLACE$CAUCHY. For security reasons, the users must be forced to change these passwords because anyone with access to the MAKEUSER file can see them.

User1 and User2 have membership to groups other than what is specified in the #GROUPS statement. User1 is a member of group WPUSERS and User2 is a member of group SYSOP. Both users have an explicit trustee assignment of RWCEMF to the directory SYS:APPS.

The MAKEUSER script file can be created with a text editor or through the menu-driven front end to MAKEUSER, USERDEF. An additional benefit of MAKEUSER is that it contains the documentation about user information that can be used to re-create user accounts if the bindery becomes corrupted or if the server disk file crashes.

There are a number of commands that can be used to create or delete assign rights to users. In the sample, you saw the use of some of these commands. The first word of the command following the pound symbol (#) is the *keyword.* All commands must be preceded with this character. Comments can be placed by preceding them with the semicolon (;) or the keyword REM.

Table 8.3 lists the different statements that can make use of these keywords; it also contains a description of their meanings. At a minimum, the #CREATE or #DELETE keyword must be in every USR script file.

The NetWare manuals state that #CREATE must have a caret symbol (^) to terminate the statement (or if all the options are not used). Although the caret (^) can be omitted for the current releases of NetWare, it may become mandatory in the future. It is thus a good idea to specify it to terminate the #CREATE statement.

Table 8.3
MAKEUSER Statements

Statement	Description
#ACCOUNT_EXPIRATION *M,D,Y*	Specifies the date on which the accounts expire: *M* is the month number, *D* is the day number, and *Y* is the year number.
#ACCOUNTING *B,L*	Specifies the balance *B* to be used for users, and the lower limit value *L* for this balance.
#CLEAR or #RESET	Resets the values of keywords and the contexts they define.
#CONNECTIONS *N*	Specifies the maximum concurrent connections *N* for users.
#CREATE *U[;F][;P] [;G][;D [R]]*	Creates user *U*, whose full name is *F* and has password *P*. *G* is a list of groups the user is a member of. The directory trustee assignment and rights of the user group are specified by *D* and *R*.
#DELETE *U [;U]*	Deletes user *U*.
#GROUPS *G [;G]*	Specifies the group context so that all users created with #CREATE are members of the group *G*.
#HOME_DIRECTORY *P*	Specifies the home directory context so that all users created with #CREATE have their home directory under the directory specified by *P*.
#LOGIN_SCRIPT *P*	Specifies the path name *P* of the file that will be used for the log-in script file for the users that are created by #CREATE.
#MAX_DISK_SPACE *V,N*	Specifies maximum disk space allowed by created users in terms of number *N* of disk blocks for volume *V*. (The actual disk space depends on the disk block size. For NetWare 3.*x*, the disk block size has a default value of 4 KB and is set during volume creation. For NetWare 2.*x*, the disk block size is fixed at 4 KB.)

continues

Table 8.3, Continued
MAKEUSER Statements

Statement	Description
#PASSWORD_LENGTH	Specifies the minimum password length for the user.
#PASSWORD_REQUIRED	Specifies that passwords are mandatory.
#PASSWORD_PERIOD *D*	Specifies the number of days *D* between password expirations.
#PURGE_USER_	Works in conjunction with #DELETE.
DIRECTORY	Deletes the home directory when #DELETE is processed.
#REM or REM	Specifies comments in the script file.
#RESTRICTED_TIME *D,S,E [;D,S,E]*	Specifies the day *D* during the week, the start *S*, and the end *E* times that a user is allowed to log in to the server. The *D* value can be mon, tue, wed, thu, fri, sat, sun. To specify all days, use *everyday*. The *S* and *E* values are the time of the day in *hh:mm am_pm* format. Examples of *S* and *E* values are 12:00 a.m. and 2:30 p.m.
#STATIONS *N,S [,S] [N,S [,S]]*	Restricts a user to log in from the specified station only. *N* is the network address, and *S* is the station address of the station a user is allowed to log in from. *N* can be up to 8 hexadecimal digits long, and *S* can be up to 12 hexadecimal digits long. If all stations are to be included with any network address, the keyword "all" can be used.
#UNIQUE_PASSWORD	Specifies that the user cannot use a password that was used previously.

The following script file is an example of a more elaborate use of these statements. This script file shows that it is possible to set complex account restrictions, such as password length, and time and station restrictions through the MAKEUSER script file. The #CLEAR statement can be used for defining new user contexts in the same script file.

```
rem
rem * Create a batch of users.
rem
rem
rem * Establish the user context
rem
#home    sys:users
#groups  advgroup
#login_script sys:public/scripts/adv.scr
#max_disk_space SYS,1000
```

```
#password_length 9
#password_period 35
#password_required
#unique_password
#restricted_time mon,8:00am,6:00pm;+
  tue,7:00am,7:00pm;+
  wed,7:00am,7:00pm;+
  thu,7:00am,7:00pm;+
  fri,7:00am,7:00pm;+
  sat,7:00am,1:00pm
#stations  01200344,all;01300451,22,34,42
#create KARANJIT;KARANJIT SIYAN;$ama;;sys:apps rwcemfa^
#create DEI;DEI SIYAN;$ita;sysop;sys:apps rwcemfa^
#clear
#home    sys:users
#groups  sales;support
#login_script sys:public/scripts/sales.scr
#max_disk_space SYS,500
#password_length 12
#password_period 45
#password_required
#unique_password
#restricted_time everyday,8:00am,6:00pm
#stations    01300451,563
#create BALI;;moti;sysop^
```

To delete user accounts, the following script file can be used. The #HOME and the #PURGE_USER_DIRECTORY ensure that, when the user account is deleted, the user's home directory also is deleted (purged).

```
rem
rem * Delete a batch of users.
rem
rem
rem * Establish the user context
rem
#home    sys:users
#purge_user_directory
#delete user1;user2;user3
#delete user4
```

Using the USERDEF Utility

The USERDEF utility can be used for the following tasks:

- Creating users by using the default or previously defined template
- Setting up a customized template
- Creating users based on the template

These tasks are described in the following sections.

Creating Users by Using the Default Template

To create users by using the default or previously defined template, follow these steps:

1. Log in as a Supervisor and enter the command **USERDEF**. The Available Options box displays, as shown in figure 8.27.

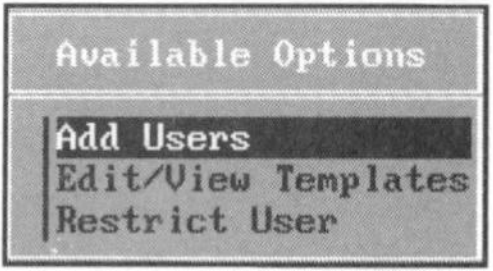

Figure 8.27
Available Options box.

2. Select the Add Users option from the Available Options box. A box appears showing a list of templates that can be used for creating users (see fig. 8.28). One of these templates is the DEFAULT template. The others, if displayed, are templates created by the Edit/View Templates option.

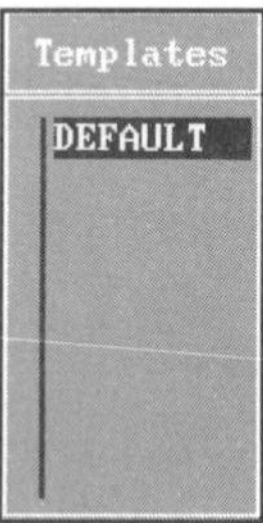

Figure 8.28
Templates box.

3. Select a template for creating a user. The Users box displays (see fig. 8.29), showing a list of those users that have been created.

4. To create a new user, press Ins.

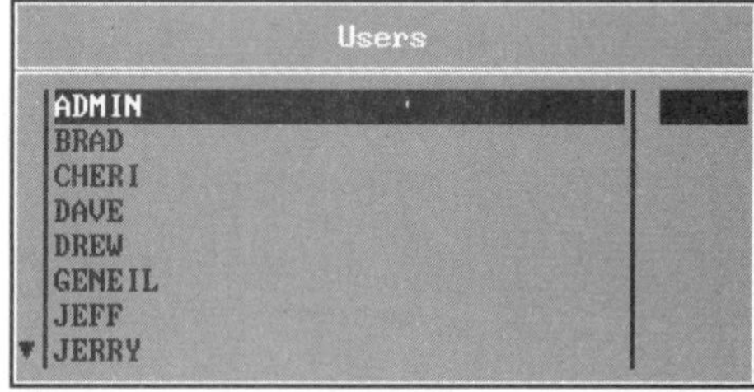

Figure 8.29
Users box.

5. Enter the appropriate responses when prompted for the following information:

   Full name

   Login name

The new user that is created should be displayed in the Users box and should have a `(new)` tag next to it, as shown in figure 8.30.

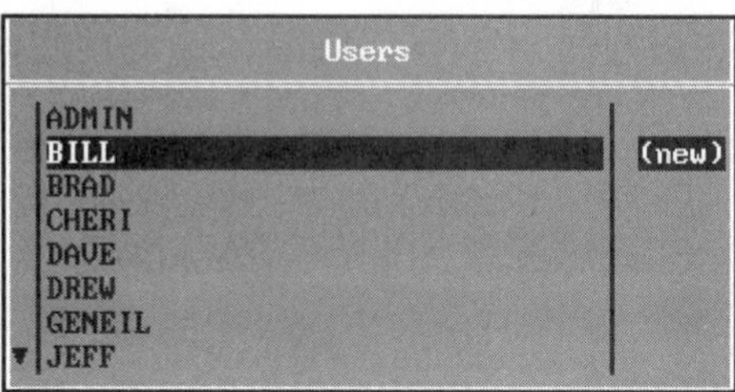

Figure 8.30
Users box showing new user with tag.

6. Press Esc, and when prompted to Create New Users by using Template, select Yes. The MAKEUSER utility should be run to create the user. If error messages are generated, make sure that you are in a directory in which the default MAKEUSER script is accessible.

7. Press Esc several times, or press Alt+F10 and answer Yes to exit USERDEF.

Creating a Customized Template

To create a customized template, follow these steps:

1. Log in as a Supervisor and enter the command **USERDEF**. The Available Options box for USERDEF displays.

2. Select the Edit/View Templates option from the Available Options box. The Templates box that can be used for creating users displays (see fig. 8.31). One of the templates should be the DEFAULT template. The others, if displayed, are templates created by the Edit/View Templates option.

3. Press Ins to add a new template to be used for creating a user. You are prompted for the name of the new template, as shown in figure 8.32.

Figure 8.31
Templates box showing DEFAULT template and other templates.

Figure 8.32
Template prompt.

4. Type the new template name and press Enter. A box displays with the list of the new template options (see fig. 8.33).

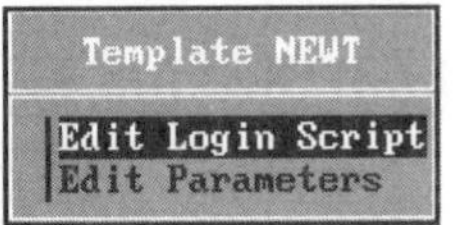

Figure 8.33
Template NEWT box showing new options.

5. Select the Edit Login Script option for the new template. A default login script for the new template displays, as shown in figure 8.34.

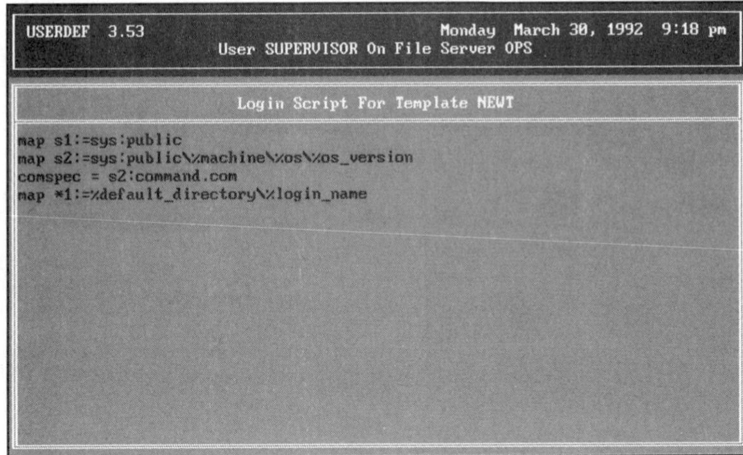

Figure 8.34
Login Script For Template NEWT box.

To modify the login script, see Chapter 23, "Managing User Sessions," for different options. Press Esc to exit. If the login script is modified, save the changes.

6. Select the Edit Parameters option from the Template NEWT box for the new template. The Parameters for Template NEWT box displays (see fig. 8.35).

   To modify the parameters, see Chapter 25, "Printing in NetWare 2.2, 3.*x*, and 4.*x*," for print job definitions for a user, and see this chapter for account restrictions. At the minimum, change the default directory to the home directory of SYS:USERS. Press Esc to exit, and then save any changes. Press Esc to return to the Templates box. The newly created template should be highlighted.

7. Press Esc several times, or press Alt+F10 and answer Yes to exit USERDEF.

```
Parameters for Template NEWT

Default Directory:  SYS:
Copy PrintCon From: (see list)
Groups Belonged To: (see list)
Account Balance:                      1000
Limit Account Balance:                No
      Low Limit:
Limit Concurrent Connections:         No
      Maximum Connections:

Require Password:                     Yes
      Minimum Password Length:        5
Force Periodic Password Changes:      Yes
      Days Between Forced Changes:    90
Require Unique Passwords:             Yes
Limit Disk Space:                     No
      Maximum Disk Space (in KB):
```

Figure 8.35
Parameters for Template NEWT box.

Restricting a User by Using USERDEF

1. Log in as a Supervisor and enter the command **USERDEF**. The Available Options box displays.

2. Select the Restrict User option. The Users On Server box displays, showing the users that can be restricted (see fig. 8.36).

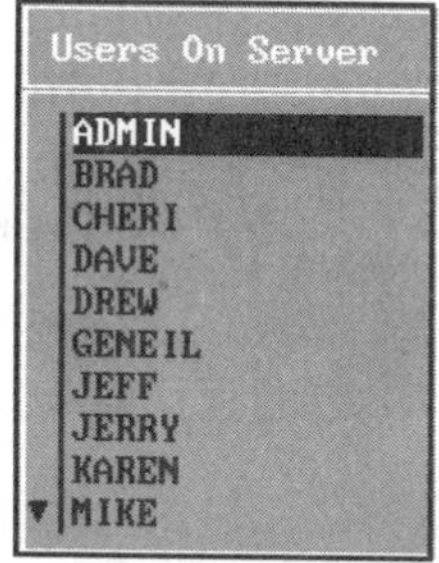

Figure 8.36
Users On Server box.

3. Select a user to be restricted. Select the volume to restrict for the user. The User Disk Space Limitation Information dialog box appears (see fig. 8.37), containing user disk-space restrictions.

4. To restrict disk space, change the Limit Space: field to YES, and enter the amount of disk space for the user in the Available*:* field.

5. Press Esc several times, or press Alt+F10 and answer YES to exit USERDEF.

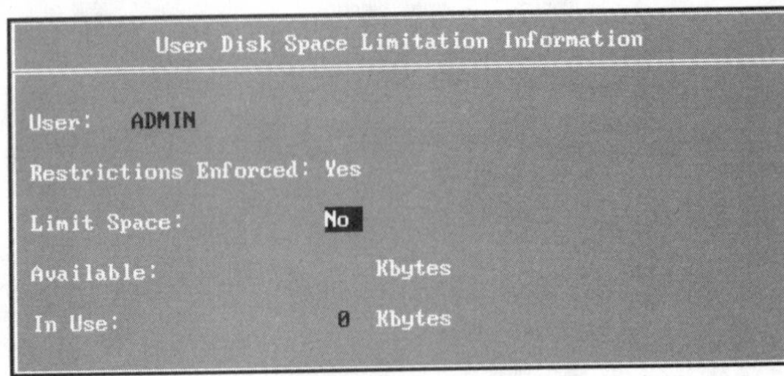

Figure 8.37 *User Disk Space Limitation Information box.*

Using Workgroup Managers

The Supervisor can delegate responsibilities for user administration to other special users, called *workgroup managers.* Workgroup managers can administer a group of users or groups assigned to them. This section shows you how to set up a workgroup manager.

Suppose, for example, that you have at least two user accounts, called USER1 and USER2, and that you want to set up USER1 as a workgroup manager over USER2.

Setting Up the Workgroup Manager

1. Log in as a Supervisor on the S386 server. Once logged in, invoke the SYSCON utility.
2. Select the User Information option from the Available Topics box, and then press Enter.
3. Highlight a user name in the window titled User Names, and then press Enter. A User Information box displays, as shown in figure 8.38.

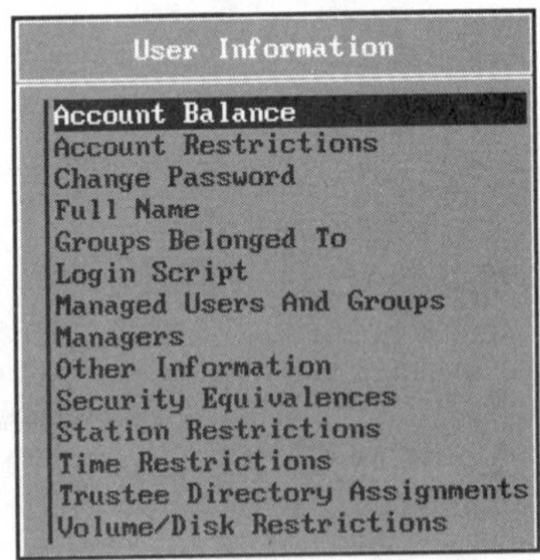

Figure 8.38 *User Information box.*

4. Select the Managed Users And Groups option, and then press Enter. The Managed Users And Groups box displays (see fig. 8.39) and contains all users and groups managed by the user.

Figure 8.39
Managed Users And Groups box.

5. Press Ins to add a user or group to be managed. The Other Users And Groups box displays, as shown in figure 8.40.

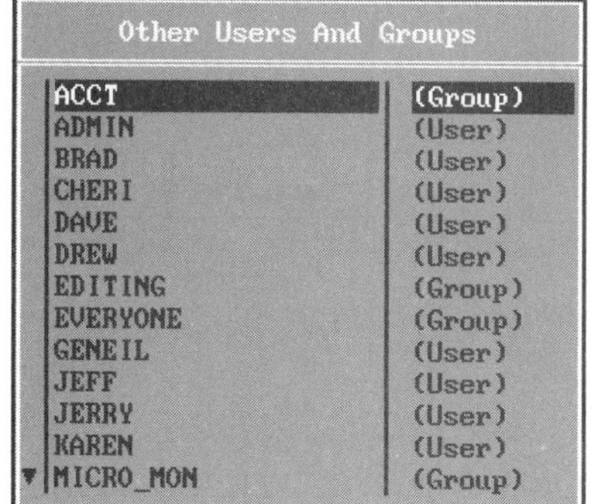

Figure 8.40
Other Users And Groups box.

6. Highlight the user that is to be managed. Press Enter to redisplay the Managed Users And Groups box (see fig. 8.41).

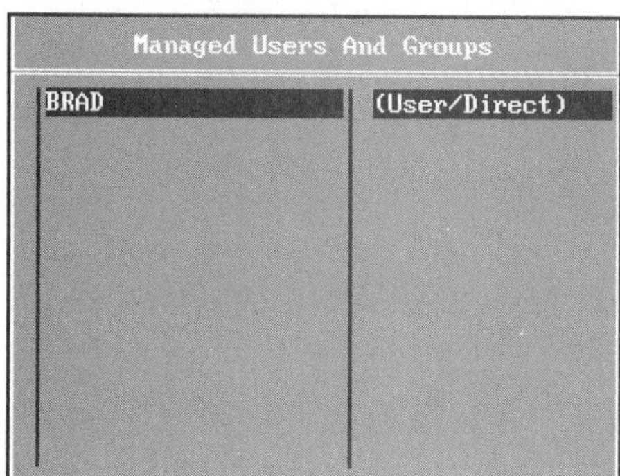

Figure 8.41
A group highlighted in the Managed Users And Groups box.

Steps 7 to 9 are optional. By following these steps, you verify that the manager/managed relationship between the two users is created.

7. Press Esc a few times to return to the User Names dialog box.
8. Highlight the user selected in step 6, and then press Enter.
9. Select the Managers option from the User Information box and press Enter. The Managers box displays the designated Manager for this user, as shown in figure 8.42.

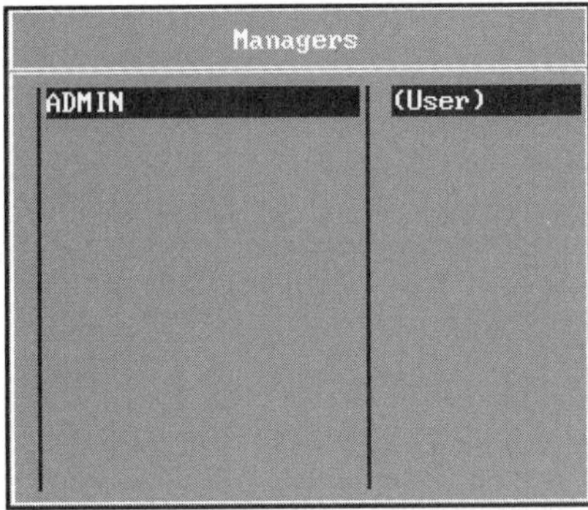

Figure 8.42
Managers box showing designated Manager.

The list in the Managers box shows all users and groups that are managers of the user designated as USER2.

10. Select Supervisor Options from the Available Topics box in SYSCON. The Supervisor Options box appears, showing the available options (see fig. 8.43).

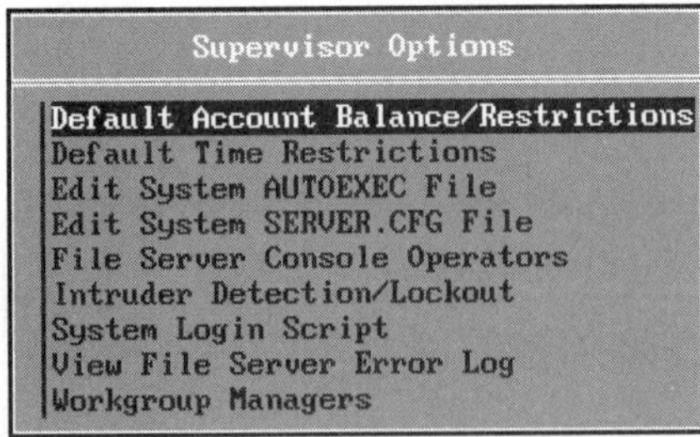

Figure 8.43
Supervisor Options box.

11. Highlight the Workgroup Managers option and press Enter. The Workgroup Managers box appears (see fig. 8.44).
12. Press Ins to create a workgroup manager. The Other Users And Groups box appears (see fig. 8.45), showing a list of users and groups who are not workgroup managers.

Figure 8.44
Workgroup Managers box.

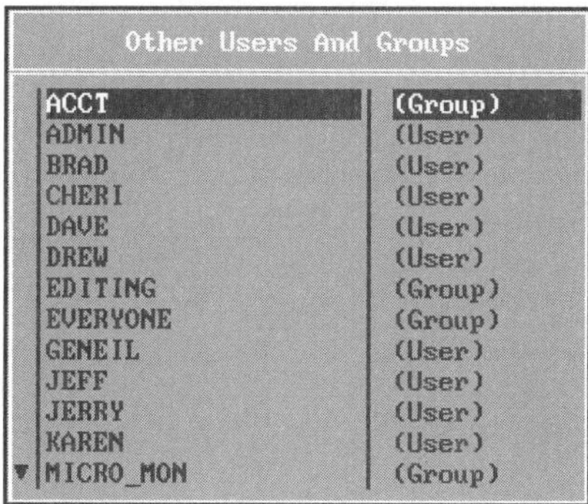

Figure 8.45
Other Users And Groups box.

13. Highlight a user name, and press Enter. The user is added to the box of workgroup managers (see fig. 8.46).

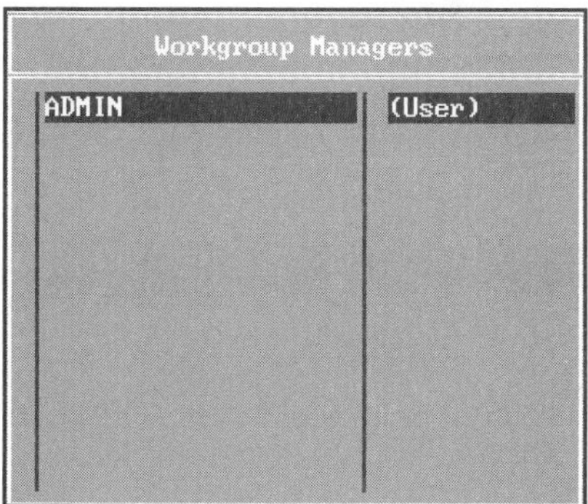

Figure 8.46
User added to Workgroup Managers box.

14. Press Esc several times, or press Alt+F10 and answer Yes to exit SYSCON.

Managing User Accounting

With the release of NetWare 2.*x*, Novell provided resource accounting tracking. *Resource accounting* provides the functionality of a billing system in which users can be charged for services used at the file server. The resources that can be tracked include connection time, disk blocks read/written, service charges, and disk space utilized. For logging in to a *bulletin board service* (BBS), for example, there is a connect-time cost (the telephone call cost) and sometimes a surcharge for using features of the BBS. NetWare resource accounting mimics these functions.

In reality, very few installations make use of NetWare resource accounting directly to bill users for services. There are two reasons for this. First, NetWare servers are administered and used by departments that own the network, so they do not charge for services provided internally.

Second, NetWare resource accounting, by itself, is not a complete system for charging and billing users. To provide a complete system, third-party products must be used that are written with NetWare Accounting *application programming interfaces* (APIs).

NetWare resource accounting, while not sophisticated enough to provide direct billing of users, is still valuable because it provides statistics on server usage. The accounting usage data is logged in to an internal audit file (NET$ACCT.DAT) at the server. Two utilities, ATOTAL and PAUDIT, can be used to interpret the internal audit files.

Other reasons to use resource accounting are to justify the purchase of a LAN or to compare costs of downsizing from a minicomputer or mainframe environment.

A university computer lab, for example, can use resource accounting to fix the amount of network usage for a semester. A certain quota of resource usage, for example, can be assigned to the user on the basis of the duration of the semester, the typical amount of disk space used, and so on. As the students use network resources, their resource usage is subtracted from their initial quota by the resource-accounting software. When their quota expires, they may request an additional resource quota from the network administrator. Such a system can prevent indiscriminate use of server resources.

Resource accounting also keeps track of dates and times of log-in and log-out attempts. This information is invaluable if you suspect that someone is trying to break in to the system.

Overview of NetWare Resource Accounting

NetWare resource accounting can be used to track the following resources:

- Disk blocks read (number of blocks)
- Disk blocks written (number of blocks)
- Disk storage (number of block-days)
- File service requests (number of services)

To install NetWare resource accounting, you, as the Supervisor, must select the Accounting option from the SYSCON main menu. When asked if you want to install resource accounting, answer YES. Resource accounting needs to be enabled just once when the server is installed.

Tracking Connect Time

Connect time is recorded in minutes; it measures the amount of time a user is logged in to the server. Connect-time costs are similar to those used in BBSs and time-share systems. Connect time can be used as the basis for billing users; it also can discourage users from leaving unattended workstations that are logged in to the server. Unattended stations can be a big security risk—imagine what could happen if an unscrupulous user has access to a station logged in with a Supervisor account.

Figure 8.47 shows the resource accounting screen for connect charges.

```
SYSCON  3.62                             Tuesday  March 31, 1992  8:30 am
                     User SUPERVISOR On File Server OPS

                                                 Sun  Mon  Tue  Wed  Thu  Fri  Sat
    Connect Time Charge Rates          8:00am     1    1    1    1    1    1    1
                                       8:30am     1    1    1    1    1    1    1
                                       9:00am     1    1    1    1    1    1    1
Sunday                                 9:30am     1    1    1    1    1    1    1
8:00 am To 8:29 am                    10:00am     1    1    1    1    1    1    1
                                      10:30am     1    1    1    1    1    1    1
Rate  Charge       Rate  Charge       11:00am     1    1    1    1    1    1    1
 1  No Charge       11                11:30am     1    1    1    1    1    1    1
 2                  12                12:00pm     1    1    1    1    1    1    1
 3                  13                12:30pm     1    1    1    1    1    1    1
 4                  14                 1:00pm     1    1    1    1    1    1    1
 5                  15                 1:30pm     1    1    1    1    1    1    1
 6                  16                 2:00pm     1    1    1    1    1    1    1
 7                  17                 2:30pm     1    1    1    1    1    1    1
 8                  18                 3:00pm     1    1    1    1    1    1    1
 9                  19                 3:30pm     1    1    1    1    1    1    1
10                  20                 4:00pm     1    1    1    1    1    1    1
     (Charge is per minute)            4:30pm     1    1    1    1    1    1    1
```

Figure 8.47
Connect Time Charge Rates screen.

To get to the menu shown in the figure, log in to the server as the Supervisor and invoke SYSCON. Make the following menu selections:

Accounting

Connect Time Charge Rates

The connect-time charge is based on half-hour intervals. A charge of 1 signifies No Charge. To change a charge, highlight a half-hour interval and press Enter. When the Select Charge Rate menu appears, highlight Other Charge Rate, and then press Enter. The New Charge Rate box appears. Figure 8.48 shows this process.

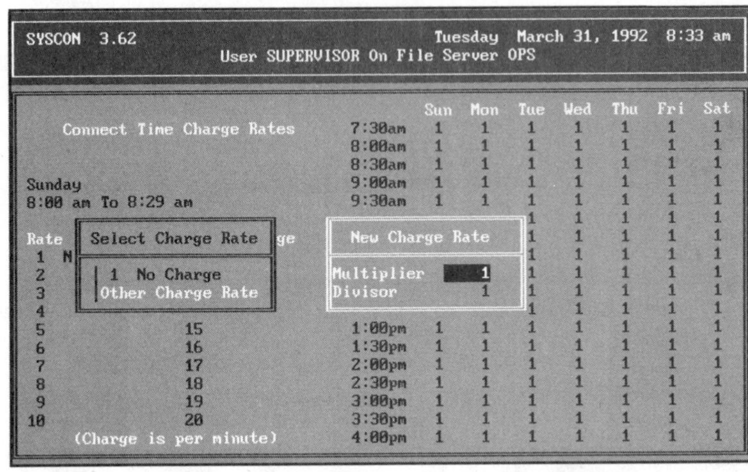

Figure 8.48
Setting connection-time charges.

The actual charge amount is computed by the following formula:

ChargeAmount = AmountUsed 5 Multiplier/Divisor

AmountUsed represents the units of resources that are consumed; Multiplier and Divisor represent scale factors to convert this figure into a monetary value. Because the AmountUsed resource is a large number, the Divisor should be larger than the Multiplier to scale down resource usage to reasonable cost values. To set the charge to 0, enter **0** for the multiplier value.

Tracking the Number of Disk Blocks Read

A *block* is a unit of storage information. In NetWare 2.*x*, the disk-block size is fixed at 4 KB. NetWare 3.*x* gives you the option of changing the disk-block size during the time of volume definition. The default disk-block size for NetWare 3.*x* is 4 KB, which is adequate for most systems (most installations use the default disk-block size).

The actual usage depends on the type of application that is running. Database applications that do a large number of disk I/Os, for example, can have a large impact on this statistic.

NetWare accounting can be used to keep track of charges for the number of disk blocks read. It is not realistic to charge users for disk blocks read because even the execution of a program or NetWare utility at the server increases this number. (This is because the entire program is read from the server disk into the workstation memory, which contributes a large number to the number of disk blocks read.)

Figure 8.49 shows the resource accounting screen for disk blocks read charges. To get to the menu shown in the figure, do the following:

1. Log in to the server with a Supervisor account and invoke SYSCON.

2. Make the following menu selections:

Accounting

Blocks Read Charge Rates

The blocks read charge is based on half-hour intervals. A charge of 1 signifies No Charge. To change a charge, highlight a half-hour interval and press Enter. When the Select Charge Rate menu appears, highlight the Other Charge Rate option, and press Enter. The screen shown in figure 8.50 appears, showing the New Charge Rate box.

The actual charge amount is computed by the following formula:

ChargeAmount = AmountUsed 5 Multiplier/Divisor

```
SYSCON  3.62                               Tuesday  March 31, 1992  8:35 am
                    User SUPERVISOR On File Server OPS

                                          Sun  Mon  Tue  Wed  Thu  Fri  Sat
    Blocks Read Charge Rates      8:00am   1    1    1    1    1    1    1
                                  8:30am   1    1    1    1    1    1    1
                                  9:00am   1    1    1    1    1    1    1
Sunday                            9:30am   1    1    1    1    1    1    1
8:00 am To 8:29 am               10:00am   1    1    1    1    1    1    1
                                 10:30am   1    1    1    1    1    1    1
Rate  Charge      Rate  Charge   11:00am   1    1    1    1    1    1    1
 1  No Charge      11            11:30am   1    1    1    1    1    1    1
 2                 12            12:00pm   1    1    1    1    1    1    1
 3                 13            12:30pm   1    1    1    1    1    1    1
 4                 14             1:00pm   1    1    1    1    1    1    1
 5                 15             1:30pm   1    1    1    1    1    1    1
 6                 16             2:00pm   1    1    1    1    1    1    1
 7                 17             2:30pm   1    1    1    1    1    1    1
 8                 18             3:00pm   1    1    1    1    1    1    1
 9                 19             3:30pm   1    1    1    1    1    1    1
10                 20             4:00pm   1    1    1    1    1    1    1
      (Charge is per block)       4:30pm   1    1    1    1    1    1    1
```

Figure 8.49
Blocks Read Charge Rates.

AmountUsed represents the units of resources that are consumed; Multiplier and Divisor represent scale factors to convert the number into a monetary value. Because the AmountUsed resource is a large number, the Divisor amount should be larger than the Multiplier amount to scale down resource usage to reasonable cost values. To set the charge to 0, enter **0** for the multiplier value.

Tracking the Number of Disk Blocks Written

You also can keep track of the number of disk blocks written by the user to the server disk. The actual usage depends on the type of application that is running. Database applications that do a large number of disk I/Os have a large impact on this statistic; word processing applications have relatively few disk-block writes. Word processing applications perform most of the editing functions on file buffers kept at the workstation—disk blocks are written only when the file is saved to the server disk.

Figure 8.51 shows the resource accounting screen for disk block written charges.

To get to the menu in the figure, perform the following:

1. Log in to the server with a Supervisor account and invoke SYSCON.
2. Make the following menu selections:

   Accounting

   Blocks Written Charge Rates

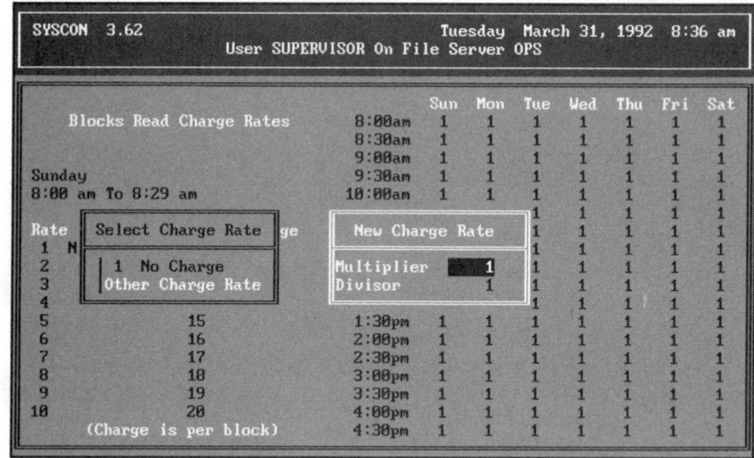

Figure 8.50 *Setting blocks read charges.*

```
SYSCON 3.62                              Tuesday  March 31, 1992  8:36 am
                       User SUPERVISOR On File Server OPS

                                              Sun  Mon  Tue  Wed  Thu  Fri  Sat
   Blocks Written Charge Rates       8:00am    1    1    1    1    1    1    1
                                     8:30am    1    1    1    1    1    1    1
                                     9:00am    1    1    1    1    1    1    1
Sunday                               9:30am    1    1    1    1    1    1    1
8:00 am To 8:29 am                  10:00am    1    1    1    1    1    1    1
                                    10:30am    1    1    1    1    1    1    1
Rate  Charge       Rate  Charge     11:00am    1    1    1    1    1    1    1
 1  No Charge       11              11:30am    1    1    1    1    1    1    1
 2                  12              12:00pm    1    1    1    1    1    1    1
 3                  13              12:30pm    1    1    1    1    1    1    1
 4                  14               1:00pm    1    1    1    1    1    1    1
 5                  15               1:30pm    1    1    1    1    1    1    1
 6                  16               2:00pm    1    1    1    1    1    1    1
 7                  17               2:30pm    1    1    1    1    1    1    1
 8                  18               3:00pm    1    1    1    1    1    1    1
 9                  19               3:30pm    1    1    1    1    1    1    1
10                  20               4:00pm    1    1    1    1    1    1    1
      (Charge is per block)          4:30pm    1    1    1    1    1    1    1
```

Figure 8.51 *Blocks Written Charge Rates screen.*

The blocks written charge is based on half-hour intervals. A charge of 1 signifies No Charge. To change a charge, highlight a half-hour interval and press Enter. When the Select Charge Rate menu appears, highlight the Other Charge Rate option, and press Enter. The screen shown in figure 8.52 appears. The actual charge amount is computed by the following formula:

ChargeAmount = AmountUsed **5** Multiplier/Divisor

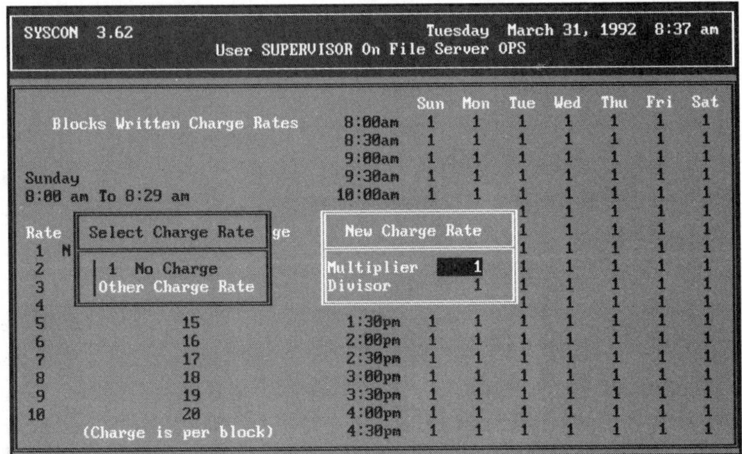

Figure 8.52
Setting blocks written charges.

AmountUsed represents the units of resources that are consumed; the Multiplier and Divisor represent scale factors to convert the figure into a monetary value. Because the AmountUsed resource is a large number, the Divisor should be larger than the Multiplier amount to scale down resource usage to reasonable cost values. To set the charge to 0, enter **0** for the multiplier value.

Tracking Server Disk Space Charge Rates

The amount of server disk space utilized for a user can be measured in terms of *block-days.* One block-day can be interpreted as one disk block of storage kept by the user for one day; or two disk blocks, each kept for one-half day. The block-day is the product of the amount of disk space and the time over which the disk space is used.

If users are charged for disk space, they are encouraged to clean their files on the server by deleting useless files, or by removing files that are seldom used and can be backed up. The Limit Disk Space option in SYSCON also can be used to prevent users from using large amounts of disk space.

Figure 8.53 shows the resource accounting screen for disk block storage charges.

To get to the menu shown in the figure, perform the following:

1. Log in to the server with a Supervisor account and invoke SYSCON.
2. Make the following menu selections:

   Accounting

   Disk Storage Charge Rates

```
SYSCON  3.62                                    Tuesday  March 31, 1992  8:37 am
                        User SUPERVISOR On File Server OPS

                                              Sun  Mon  Tue  Wed  Thu  Fri  Sat
      Disk Storage Charge Rates      8:00am
                                     8:30am
                                     9:00am
Sunday                               9:30am
8:00 am To 8:29 am                  10:00am
                                    10:30am
Rate  Charge        Rate  Charge    11:00am
 1                   11             11:30am
 2                   12             12:00pm
 3                   13             12:30pm
 4                   14              1:00pm
 5                   15              1:30pm
 6                   16              2:00pm
 7                   17              2:30pm
 8                   18              3:00pm
 9                   19              3:30pm
10                   20              4:00pm
      (Charge is per block-day)      4:30pm
```

Figure 8.53
Disk Storage Charge Rates screen.

The disk storage charge is based on half-hour intervals. A charge of 1 signifies No Charge. To change a charge, highlight a half-hour interval, and then press Enter. The New Charge Rate box, shown in figure 8.54, appears.

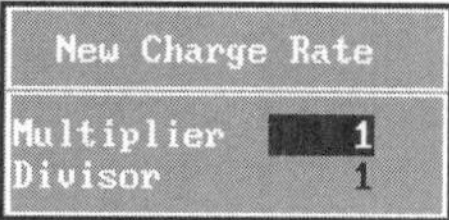

Figure 8.54
Setting disk storage charges.

The actual charge amount is computed by the following formula:

ChargeAmount = AmountUsed 5 Multiplier/Divisor

AmountUsed represents the units of resources that are consumed; the Multiplier and Divisor represent scale factors to convert the figure into a monetary value. Because the AmountUsed resource is usually a large number, the Divisor should be larger than the Multiplier amount to scale down resource usage to reasonable cost values. To set the charge to 0, enter **0** for the multiplier value.

Tracking Services Used

Figure 8.55 shows the resource accounting screen for service requests charges.

To get to the menu in figure 8.55, perform the following:

1. Log in to the server with a Supervisor account and invoke SYSCON.

2. Make the following menu selections:

   Accounting

   Service Requests Charge Rates

```
SYSCON  3.62                              Tuesday  March 31, 1992  8:38 am
                        User SUPERVISOR On File Server OPS

                                              Sun  Mon  Tue  Wed  Thu  Fri  Sat
  Service Requests Charge Rates      8:00am    1    1    1    1    1    1    1
                                     8:30am    1    1    1    1    1    1    1
                                     9:00am    1    1    1    1    1    1    1
Sunday                               9:30am    1    1    1    1    1    1    1
8:00 am To 8:29 am                  10:00am    1    1    1    1    1    1    1
                                    10:30am    1    1    1    1    1    1    1
Rate  Charge       Rate  Charge     11:00am    1    1    1    1    1    1    1
 1  No Charge       11              11:30am    1    1    1    1    1    1    1
 2                  12              12:00pm    1    1    1    1    1    1    1
 3                  13              12:30pm    1    1    1    1    1    1    1
 4                  14               1:00pm    1    1    1    1    1    1    1
 5                  15               1:30pm    1    1    1    1    1    1    1
 6                  16               2:00pm    1    1    1    1    1    1    1
 7                  17               2:30pm    1    1    1    1    1    1    1
 8                  18               3:00pm    1    1    1    1    1    1    1
 9                  19               3:30pm    1    1    1    1    1    1    1
10                  20               4:00pm    1    1    1    1    1    1    1
(Charge is per request received)     4:30pm    1    1    1    1    1    1    1
```

Figure 8.55
Service Requests Charge Rates screens.

The service requests charge is based on half-hour intervals. A charge of 1 signifies No Charge. To change a charge, highlight a half-hour interval, and press Enter. When the Select Charge Rate box appears, highlight the Other Charge Rate option, and press Enter. The screen shown in figure 8.56 appears.

```
SYSCON  3.62                              Tuesday  March 31, 1992  8:39 am
                        User SUPERVISOR On File Server OPS

                                              Sun  Mon  Tue  Wed  Thu  Fri  Sat
  Service Requests Charge Rates      8:00am    1    1    1    1    1    1    1
                                     8:30am    1    1    1    1    1    1    1
                                     9:00am    1    1    1    1    1    1    1
Sunday                               9:30am    1    1    1    1    1    1    1
8:00 am To 8:29 am                  10:00am    1    1    1    1    1    1    1
                                                         1    1    1    1    1
Rate  | Select Charge Rate | ge   | New Charge Rate |    1    1    1    1    1
 1  N                                                    1    1    1    1    1
 2    |  1  No Charge      |      |Multiplier     1 |    1    1    1    1    1
 3    | Other Charge Rate  |      |Divisor        1 |    1    1    1    1    1
 4                                                       1    1    1    1    1
 5                  15               1:30pm    1    1    1    1    1    1    1
 6                  16               2:00pm    1    1    1    1    1    1    1
 7                  17               2:30pm    1    1    1    1    1    1    1
 8                  18               3:00pm    1    1    1    1    1    1    1
 9                  19               3:30pm    1    1    1    1    1    1    1
10                  20               4:00pm    1    1    1    1    1    1    1
(Charge is per request received)     4:30pm    1    1    1    1    1    1    1
```

Figure 8.56
Setting service requests charges.

The actual charge amount is computed by the following formula:

ChargeAmount = AmountUsed × Multiplier/Divisor

AmountUsed represents the units of resources that are consumed; Multiplier and Divisor represent scale factors to convert this figure into a monetary value. Because the AmountUsed resource is normally a large number, the Divisor should be larger than the Multiplier amount to scale down resource usage to reasonable cost values. To set the charge to 0, enter **0** for the multiplier value.

Using the ATOTAL and PAUDIT Utilities

If accounting services have been enabled, the resource usage-per-user data is stored in records in an internal database file called NET$ACCT.DAT. The chargeOrNote field of an accounting record can hold connect-time charges, disk-storage charges, log-in/log-out times, account-lock events, or server time-modified events.

The information in the NET$ACCT.DAT file can be accessed by the ATOTAL utility, which produces a report on resource usage. This report, consisting of daily and weekly totals of accounting usage, includes connect time, blocks read and written, block-days, and server requests. If there is no charge for a resource, the corresponding entry for that charge is zero. The ATOTAL utility can be invoked from the DOS prompt after logging in to a server. Running ATOTAL produces a list similar to the following:

```
2/13/92:
   Connect time:     32    Server request: 457
   Blocks read:       0    Blocks written: 0
   Block days:       21
2/14/92:
   Connect time:     17    Server request: 2333
   Blocks read:       0    Blocks written: 0
   Block days:       46
Totals for week:
   Connect time:     49    Server request: 2790
   Blocks read:       0    Blocks written: 0
   Block days:       67
```

The PAUDIT utility also makes use of the NET$ACCT.DAT file by displaying an audit report of user activities, such as the log-in and log-out times of a server. The following is a sample list produced by running PAUDIT:

```
9/24/91 14:02:18  File Server KSS
   NOTE: about User KARANJIT during File Server services.
   Login from address 00000352:42608C3C6A93.
9/24/91 14:30:58  File Server KSS
   NOTE: about User KARANJIT during File Server services.
   Logout from address 00000352:42608C3C6A93.
9/24/91 14:31:28  File Server KSS
   NOTE: about User KARANJIT during File Server services.
   Login from address 00000352:42608C3C6A93.
9/24/91 14:33:46  File Server KSS
   NOTE: about User KARANJIT during File Server services.
   Logout from address 00000352:42608C3C6A93.
9/24/91 15:31:55  File Server KSS
   NOTE: about User KARANJIT during File Server services.
   Login from address 00000355:42608C3C6A93.
10/24/91 9:49:38  File Server KSS
   NOTE: about User SUPERVISOR during File Server services.
   Login from address 00000255:0080C8706571.
10/24/91 10:03:14  File Server KSS
   NOTE: about User SUPERVISOR during File Server services.
   Logout from address 00000255:0080C8706571.
```

Each entry in the report consists of three lines. The first line indicates the date and time of the audit event and the name of the server on which the event took place. In the second line, the NOTE item in the report indicates which user account and file services are involved. The third line indicates the event, such as login, logout, and so on. Intruder alerts caused by unauthorized access attempts also are reported in the PAUDIT report. Whenever the file server's time is changed, the event also is recorded in the file.

After a certain period of time (usually a month), the NET$ACCT.DAT file becomes very large, and it is necessary to reduce its size. If the file NET$ACCT.DAT is deleted, it is automatically created the next time a resource entry is made to this file. To reduce the size of the NET$ACCT file, follow these guidelines:

1. Generate hard copies of reports by using the ATOTAL and PAUDIT utilities. The following commands can be used to generate a text file containing the reports, which can then be printed and/or archived:

   ATOTAL 28MAY92.ATO (generated May 28, 1992)

   PAUDIT 28MAY92.PAU (generated May 28, 1992)

2. Archive (back up) the NET$ACCT.DAT file, and then delete it. It will be automatically created by the resource accounting administrator to have console capability at any workstation.

To set up the RMF capability, use the following programs to perform these steps:

RCONSOLE.EXE or ACONSOLE.EXE (workstation)

RSPX.NLM or RS232.NLM (server)

1. Create a customized boot disk for the remote server
2. Bring up the new file server with a remote boot disk
3. Install NetWare from a remote workstation
4. Copy the NetWare file remotely to the server

Managing User Support Remotely

A number of tools are available to enable you to take over a user's workstation remotely. These tools are designed for you to support users remotely and walk them through a problem. Although the process is similar to that described for the Remote Management Facility for the server console, a user's monitor and keyboard are now available remotely to the user. Table 8.4 lists some of the tools that are available for this purpose.

Table 8.4
User Remote Management Support Tools

Software Tool	Publisher
Close-Up/LAN	Norton Lambert
NetRemote+	Brightwork Software
Commute	Central Point Software

In NetRemote+, for example, stations that can be taken over by the network administrator must run a program called NRLISTEN. This program loads as a TSR and can be configured so that a password must be entered before the user workstation can be taken over. Typically, NRLISTEN is loaded automatically during the log-in process and takes up about 8 KB of RAM. The network administrator who wants to support a user remotely runs the program NRCALL.

Figure 8.57 shows the NRCALL screen. A list of users that are logged in to the network are displayed. The users that have NRLISTEN running at their workstations are highlighted. To take over the user's workstation, the user name must be highlighted and the Enter key used to select the user. At this time, the user workstation is under the control of the network administrator. To relinquish control and invoke the NetRemote menu, press F1. A useful feature of NetRemote+ is its memory map of the user workstation that can be displayed (see fig. 8.58). The memory map enables the administrator to view remotely the programs that are running at the user workstation. You also can view the version of the IPX/SPX and NetWare shell being run at another workstation.

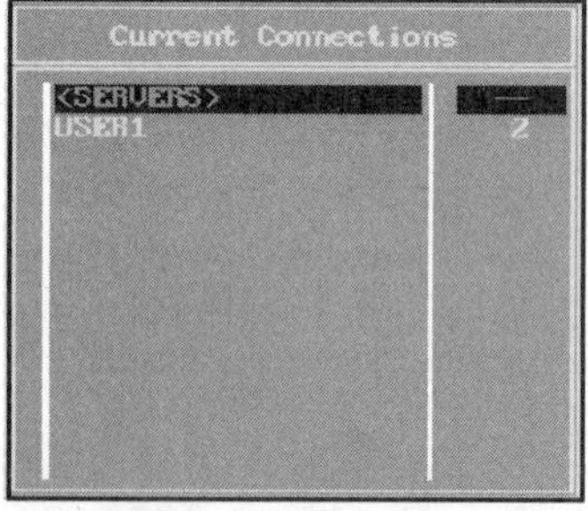

Figure 8.57
NetRemote+ NRCALL screen.

Programs In Memory

PSP	BYTES	PROGRAM	HOOKED VECTORS
11D3	3456	DOSEDIT.COM	
12B4	4000	UNKNOWN	
13AF	4032	UNKNOWN	0B
14AC	14624	UNKNOWN	64 7A FE
1B3F	41488	NRLISTEN.EXE	17 1B 20 21 24 27 F1

Figure 8.58
NetRemote+ user workstation memory map.

Summary

This chapter showed you the two ways that user and group accounts can be created and managed using the SYSCON and MAKEUSER utilities.

The SYSCON utility can be used for setting up user accounts and for creating groups and user accounts. It also can be used for controlling user accounting, restricting passwords, and restricting stations and times.

Use the MAKEUSER utility when you need to create several users with similar accounts. MAKEUSER is a command-line utility that uses a text file, containing special statements, to create and delete user accounts. Several examples of using MAKEUSER—from the simple to the more complex—were presented. You also learned specifically how to do common tasks using the SYSCON utility.

This chapter discussed a special class of users, the workgroup manager, that can delegate supervisor responsibilities. The supervisor makes this assignment through SYSCON. You learned how the server can be managed remotely by using the RMF facility in NetWare 3.*x*. To manage users remotely, several third-party products are available.

Managing NetWare 2.2, 3.11, 3.12 Security

Sharing resources in a network environment has its advantages. Along with these advantages, however, come a variety of security problems. These concerns usually take the form of making sure that only the *right* amount of information is shared by users. On a network, there is a need for a mechanism that prohibits unauthorized access to the system or to certain files. For example, a user's personal files on the server should be kept private—other users should not be able to access these files. Also, system files should be accessible only by a network administrator—an ordinary user should not be able to modify or remove applications installed on the server.

NetWare provides security features rivaling those of many mainframe/minicomputer environments. Unless these security features are understood and implemented correctly, however, they do not protect the network. This chapter gives you an overview of NetWare security features and how to implement them.

Exploring NetWare Security Features

To address the rising concern of network security, Novell has published a research report, titled "NetWare Security: Configuring and Auditing a Trusted Environment." The report is lengthy and fairly involved, but it presents a global view of network security that is very relevant for today's network environment. It also discusses specific methods that NetWare uses to meet many of the security requirements published in the *Orange Book* and the *Red Book*.

The *Orange Book* and *Red Book* are U.S. Department of Defense (DoD) publications and, collectively, have become the standard for security of computer systems and networks. (The nicknames come from the color of their covers.)

The *Orange Book* is formally titled *Trusted Computer System Evaluation Criteria* (or the DoD85 standard) and was published in 1985. These standards were later applied to networks, and were then published in 1987: *Trusted Network Interpretation of the Trusted Computer System Evaluation Criteria* (known as the *Red Book*). A companion document, *Trusted Network Interpretation Environments Guideline*, was published in 1990.

For information on these publications contact:

National Computer Security Center
9800 Savage Road
Fort George G. Meade, MD 20755-6000

(410) 859-4371

A discussion of these documents' coverage of security requirements would make a complete book in itself. Some definitions from these documents are necessary, however, as you examine NetWare security features.

Seven security classifications can be applied to computers or networks. These classifications define progressively more secure systems and are presented in table 9.1. For example, DOS is classified as a class D system because it has minimal protection.

Table 9.1
Security Classifications from DoD Orange Book

Security Class	Description
D	Minimal Protection
C1	Discretionary Security Protection
C2	Controlled Access Protection
B1	Labeled Security Protection
B2	Structured Protection
B3	Security Domains
A1	Verified Design

Source: Trusted Computer System Evaluation Criteria, U.S. Department of Defense

Each of the classes defines a security policy that is defined in table 9.2. This table is used by the Department of Defense to determine the security classification of computer systems. Table 9.3 presents simplified versions of these classifications that can be applied to commercial systems such as NetWare.

Table 9.2
Requirements for DoD Security Ratings

Criteria	Classes						
Security Policy:	**D**	**C1**	**C2**	**B1**	**B2**	**B3**	**A1**
Discretionary Access Control	x	R	R	-	-	R	-
Object Reuse	x	x	R	-	-	-	-
Labels	x	x	x	R	R	-	-
Label Integrity	x	x	x	R	-	-	-
Exportation of Labeled Info	x	x	x	R	-	-	-
Label Human-Readable Output	x	x	x	R	-	-	-
Mandatory Access Control	x	x	x	R	R	-	-
Subject Sensitivity Labels	x	x	x	x	R	-	-
Device Labels	x	x	x	x	R	-	-
Accountability:	**D**	**C1**	**C2**	**B1**	**B2**	**B3**	**A1**
Identification/ Authentication	x	R	R	R	-	-	-
Audit	x	x	R	R	R	R	-
Trusted Path	x	x	x	x	R	R	-

continues

Table 9.2, Continued
Requirements for DoD Security Ratings

Criteria	Classes						
Assurance:	**D**	**C1**	**C2**	**B1**	**B2**	**B3**	**A1**
System Architecture	x	R	R	R	R	R	-
System Integrity	x	R	-	-	-	-	-
Security Testing	x	R	R	R	R	R	R
Design Spec/ Verification	x	x	x	R	R	R	R
Covert Channel Analysis	x	x	x	x	R	R	R
Trust Facility Management	x	x	x	x	R	R	-
Trust Recovery	x	x	x	x	x	R	-
Trusted Distribution	x	x	x	x	x	x	R
Documentation:	**D**	**C1**	**C2**	**B1**	**B2**	**B3**	**A1**
Security Features User Guide	x	R	-	-	-	-	-
Trusted Facility Manual	x	R	R	R	R	R	-
Test Documentation	x	R	-	-	R	-	R
Design Documentation	x	R	-	R	R	R	R

x = no requirement

- = same requirements as the next lower class

R = additional requirements over the lower classes

Source: Trusted Computer System Evaluation Criteria, U.S. Department of Defense

Table 9.3
Commercial Interpretation of Security Classifications

Criteria	Classes			
Security:	**D**	**C**	**B**	**A**
Discretionary Access Control	x	R	R	-
Object Reuse	x	R	-	-
Labels	x	x	R	-
Label Integrity	x	x	R	-
Exportation of Labeled Information	x	x	R	-
Labeling Human-Readable Output	x	x	R	-
Mandatory Access Control	x	x	R	-
Subject Sensitivity Labels	x	x	R	-
Device Labels	x	x	R	-
Accountability:	**D**	**C**	**B**	**A**
Identification and Authentication	x	R	R	-
Audit	x	R	R	-
Trusted Path	x	x	R	-
Assurance:	**D**	**C**	**B**	**A**
System Architecture	x	R	R	-
System Integrity	x	R	-	-
Security Testing	x	R	R	R
Design Specification/Verification	x	x	R	R
Covert Channel Analysis	x	x	R	R

continues

Table 9.3, Continued
Commercial Interpretation of Security Classifications

Criteria	Classes			
Assurance:	**D**	**C**	**B**	**A**
Trust Facility Management	x	x	R	-
Trust Recovery	x	x	R	-
Trusted Distribution	x	x	x	R
Documentation:	**D**	**C**	**B**	**A**
Security Features User Guide	x	R	-	-
Trusted Facility Manual	x	R	R	-
Test Documentation	x	R	R	R
Design Documentation	x	R	R	R

x = no requirement

- = same requirements as the next lower class

R = additional requirements over the lower classes

Source: Trusted Computer System Evaluation Criteria, U.S. Department of Defense

Many systems claim to satisfy a certain security classification when, in fact, they do not. The certification process for any security system is lengthy and expensive, and it must be conducted by a U.S. government agency. A class A system is not necessarily the most desirable solution for commercial environments—such a system is very expensive to purchase, and the overhead costs for implementing all of the security features are tremendous.

A newly installed NetWare operating system has a security classification of D (minimal protection) because the security features have not yet been activated. For example, there is not yet a password on the Supervisor account. A properly configured NetWare system has a class C security rating. In this chapter, you learn to implement the various security features of NetWare.

Using Log-in Security

At the very minimum, the log-in security of NetWare should be enabled. When a user invokes the LOGIN.EXE program from the SYS:LOGIN directory on the server, a copy of this program is transferred to the workstation memory. The LOGIN.EXE program acts as the guardian of the NetWare NOS.

In current NetWare releases, the user password is encrypted before transmission to prevent devices, such as protocol analyzers, from "seeing" the password in the clear. This encryption does not, however, prevent a clever user from capturing the encrypted password and replaying the log-in sequence from another workstation to gain unauthorized access to a user account. To foil such attempts, NetWare employs a special *log key* that is unique from session to session and is difficult to duplicate.

The complete log-in process is described in the following steps:

1. The LOGIN program asks for the user name.

2. The user inputs his user name, or enters the server/user name combination. If the user specifies a new server, LOGIN locates and attaches to the specified server. The details of the workstation attachment mechanism are discussed in Chapter 20, "Supporting DOS Workstations."

3. The workstation then issues an NCP LOGOUT request to clear any connection information left from a previous session. This request is made because of a feature of the LOGIN program that automatically logs you out of the current session if you run LOGIN while logged in to the server.

4. The workstation requests the object ID of the user name account.

5. The workstation requests a log key from the server. This log key is unique for a given session. The server responds to this request by sending out an 8-byte variable log key.

6. LOGIN requests the user password, and then performs a non-reversible encryption using the user's object ID and password to calculate a 16-byte encrypted password value.

7. The workstation encrypts the 16-byte encrypted value and the variable 8-byte log key by using a non-reversible encryption algorithm to get a new 8-byte password value that is transmitted to the server for authentication. This process is essentially double-encryption.

8. The server repeats the double-encryption performed by the workstation to get an 8-byte password value.

9. If the values from the workstation and the server match, user access is granted; otherwise, the log-in attempt is rejected and the intruder lockout counter for that user is incremented. This counter limits the number of unsuccessful log-in attempts that can be made.

Using Password Security

In this section, you learn some general methods for selecting passwords and ways to safeguard password security. You also learn how to implement NetWare's password security restrictions.

Protecting Passwords

NetWare security is password-based. Passwords are the first line of defense. If a user knows or guesses your password, however, he can access your account. After the password is verified by the LOGIN

utility, the intruder has access to all privileges for your account. (The user is limited only by the limitations imposed on the account.) If he manages to invade a Supervisor account, the entire network is in jeopardy. Therefore, Supervisor passwords must be guarded with extreme care and changed often. Unfortunately, many Supervisors consider themselves exempt from the security restrictions imposed on normal users. Intruders who want to break into the system thus focus their attention on obtaining the Supervisor passwords.

Another important aspect of NetWare security is the physical security of the servers. The NetWare server machines must be kept in a physically secure location, with limited access. It is possible, however, to boot the server machine under DOS—perhaps when no one is logged in to the server—and use programs to obtain a *binary dump* of critical locations on the disk. These dumps can be used to decrypt the Supervisor password. (Novell will probably make this process more difficult in the future because of some adverse publicity.)

The following guidelines can be followed to protect passwords:

- Make passwords mandatory for all users. This control is accessed through SYSCON under NetWare.

- Change the defaults that come with the system. For example, the initial defaults for SUPERVISOR and GUEST are no password.

- Do not write down your password anywhere, especially on or near the PC. Take the extra trouble to remember your password.

- Do not type your password while others are watching, especially if you are not a touch typist. If you suspect that you are being observed as you type in your password, change your password at the first secure opportunity.

- Never let another user use or share your password. If your password is revealed—whether deliberately or inadvertently—change it as soon as you can.

Selecting Passwords

If the network administrator allows you to chose your own passwords, pick passwords that are not easy to guess. NetWare passwords can be up to 127 characters long. The following lists some general guidelines for creating good passwords:

1. Create passwords that are not found in any dictionary. Words that are found in a dictionary are subject to a "dictionary attack" program that can systematically try dictionary entries to obtain your password.

2. Avoid passwords that are names of people or pets (especially family members or family pets). Good hackers usually do their homework.

3. Passwords that are a mix of alphabetic and numeric characters are better than passwords that are made up of one or the other. Especially avoid all numeric passwords, such as phone numbers, birth dates, and social security numbers.

4. Create passwords that are relatively long—they should contain no fewer than eight characters. Short passwords are vulnerable to an automated attack in which all possible combinations can be tried. If you are a network administrator, you can implement a minimum password length through SYSCON (or when the user account is created with MAKEUSER). A longer password may take an extra second or two to enter, but the extra security is well worth the effort.

5. Do not use the names of machines and servers you access as passwords.

6. When making a password, use a combination of short words, special characters, and numbers. An example of such a password is $lock;not9he.

7. Avoid meaningless passwords that you are tempted to write in a book or some place for future reference.

8. To remember passwords, use contractions of phrases such as: "Better not forget this password" can be Bet!fogt:pwd or the phrase "Remember to water plants today" can be abbreviated as Remb^wtr%plnts[tdy].

9. Pick passwords that are pronounceable such as: Hick*Enuf, O2.beRich, and O2be.Sprt.

Some security-conscious organizations insist that employees agree in writing to comply with documented guidelines for creating passwords and other security matters. Others use machine-generated passwords consisting of random letters and numbers. Again, the problem with this method is that users are tempted to write down these hard-to-remember passwords, providing the opportunity for discovery.

Implementing NetWare Password Security

Figure 9.1 shows the account balance/restrictions box for a user (in this case ANNE), which can be used to control password permissions.

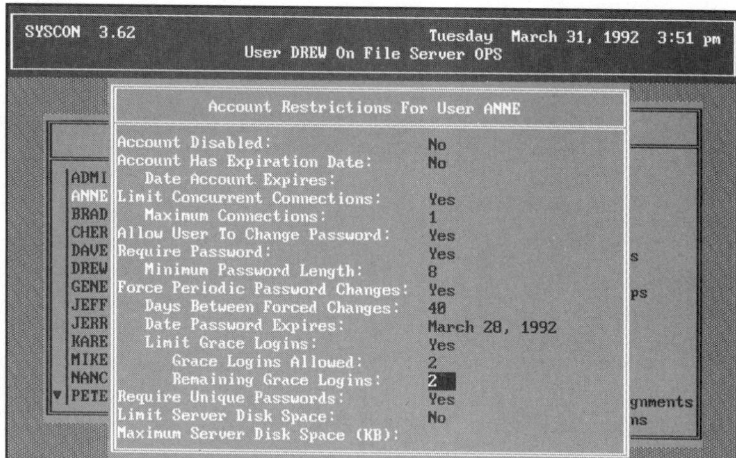

Figure 9.1
Account Restrictions For User box.

To display this box, perform the following steps:

1. Log in to the server with a Supervisor account and invoke SYSCON.
2. Make the following menu selections:

   User Information

   Select a user

   Account Restrictions

From the box shown in the figure, the following password restrictions can be noted about the user named ANNE:

- The number of *concurrent connections*, or the workstations that USER1 can log in to simultaneously, is limited to one.
- ANNE can change her password, but the minimum password length is eight characters.
- ANNE is required to change her password every 40 days, and her current password expires on March 28, 1992.
- The number of *grace logins* are limited to two. That is, ANNE receives two warnings that her password is expiring and must be changed. If she fails to assign a new password after the second warning, it expires and a Supervisor must assign a new one.
- ANNE cannot reuse old passwords when the current password expires. Passwords that differ from each other by two digits, such as the number of the month that the password is changed, should be avoided. These passwords are easy to guess.

Any of these restrictions can be changed for a user account. To change the default password restrictions for all users that will be created in the future, use the dialog box shown in figure 9.2. To display this dialog box, perform the following steps:

1. Log in to the server with a Supervisor account and invoke SYSCON.
2. Make the following menu selections:

   Supervisor Options

   Default Account Balance/Restrictions

```
Default Account Balance/Restrictions

Account Has Expiration Date:              No
   Date Account Expires:
Limit Concurrent Connections:             No
   Maximum Connections:
Create Home Directory for User:           Yes
Require Password:                         Yes
   Minimum Password Length:               5
Force Periodic Password Changes:          Yes
   Days Between Forced Changes:           40
   Limit Grace Logins:                    Yes
      Grace Logins Allowed:               6
Require Unique Passwords:                 Yes
Account Balance:                          0
Allow Unlimited Credit:                   No
   Low Balance Limit:                     0
Limit Server Disk Space:                  No
Maximum Server Disk Space (KB):
```

Figure 9.2
Default Account Balance/ Restrictions dialog box.

Understanding the Intruder/ Detection Lockout Feature

The Intruder Detection/Lockout feature of NetWare limits the number of unsuccessful log-in attempts a user can make. After a predefined number of attempts, NetWare assumes that the user is an intruder and locks the user out for a period of time set by the administrator. The Intruder Detection/Lockout dialog box, shown in figure 9.3, controls the intruder lockout mechanism. To display this dialog box, perform the following steps:

1. Log in to the server with a Supervisor account and invoke SYSCON.

2. Make the following menu selections:

   Supervisor Options

   Intruder Detection/Lockout

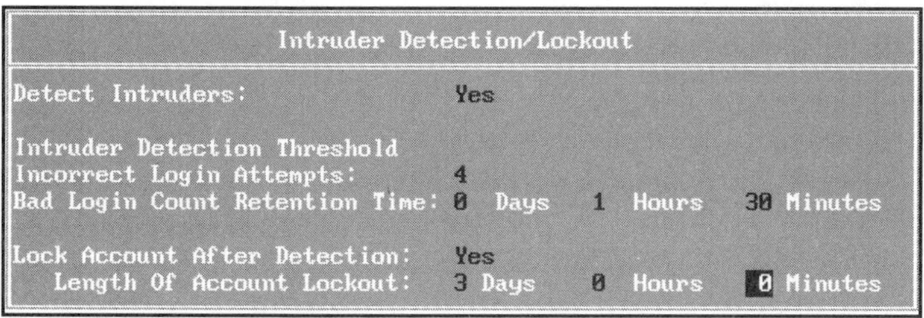

Figure 9.3
Intruder Detection/ Lockout box.

When an intrusion attempt is discovered, it is displayed on the server console and also logged in the NET$ACCT.DAT file, where it can be seen by using the PAUDIT utility. The record indicates the user name, the date and time of the attempted log-in, and the physical node address from which the attempt was made. Intruder attempts are logged only for valid user names. If an invalid user name is used, NetWare password security rejects the log-in attempt, but no intrusion attempt is registered.

In the Intruder Detection/Lockout box, the Bad Login Count Retention Time field controls the sensitivity of the intruder detection/lockout mechanism; it can be defined as the time period over which unsuccessful log-in attempts are evaluated as intrusions. This sensitivity can be set between one minute and 40 days. The Length Of Account Lockout field defines the time for which the intruder is locked out and, just as the preceding setting, can be set to a value between one minute and 40 days. During this time, the user cannot log in unless reinstated by the Supervisor.

The intruder detection/lockout feature also can be used to foil the automated attacks discussed earlier in this chapter. This mechanism can be enabled for the Supervisor account; using it can be dangerous, however, if there is only one Supervisor account (SUPERVISOR). Anyone can then lock out the Supervisor account by deliberately trying out a few incorrect passwords. The Supervisor account is then locked out for the time delay specified by SYSCON—in the worst case, for up to 40 days!

Restricting Access Based on User Profile

The most effective way to secure system and user data is to correctly use the following features:

- Directory trustee assignment
- File trustee assignment (NetWare 3.*x* only)
- Directory attribute security
- File attribute security
- File server security

The Directory trustee assignment feature controls access to files in a directory and can be set explicitly for users, or these assignments can be inherited by virtue of membership to a group. The File trustee assignment feature is defined in NetWare version 3.*x* and provides a finer level of control over individual files in a directory. Trustee assignments have the following meanings:

- Supervisory (NetWare 3.*x* only)
- Read
- Write
- Create
- Modify

- File Scan
- Access Control

The Directory attribute and File attribute security features are flags that can be set on a directory and file to modify ways that files can be accessed. For example, all program files must be flagged with at least Copy Inhibit, Delete Inhibit, and Rename Inhibit. For extreme security, the Execute Only flag also can be added, preventing the file from being copied and backed up (even by the Supervisor). When assigned, the Execute Only flag cannot be removed from the file, but the file can be deleted, and then reinstalled. Unfortunately, some programs do not operate correctly with the Execute Only flag, so care must be exercised in its use.

The Read audit (Ra) and Write audit (Wa) flags mentioned in the NetWare manuals are not implemented for NetWare 3.11 and 2.2.

Enabling Default Security Options

As previously discussed, most of NetWare's security features are not enabled when initially installed, which eases the job of initial system administration.

Figure 9.4 shows the Default Account Balance/Restrictions dialog box as seen by using the SYSCON utility. You can see that there are no account expiration date, no limit on concurrent connections, and no password requirements.

```
            Default Account Balance/Restrictions

Account Has Expiration Date:                    No
   Date Account Expires:
Limit Concurrent Connections:                   No
   Maximum Connections:
Create Home Directory for User:                 Yes
Require Password:                               No
   Minimum Password Length:
Force Periodic Password Changes:
   Days Between Forced Changes:
   Limit Grace Logins:
      Grace Logins Allowed:
Require Unique Passwords:
Account Balance:                                0
Allow Unlimited Credit:                         Yes
   Low Balance Limit:
Limit Server Disk Space:                        No
Maximum Server Disk Space (KB):
```

Figure 9.4
Default Account Balance/ Restrictions box, with the Allow Unlimited Credit field set to Yes.

If the Limit Concurrent Connections and Require Password fields are set to Yes, the Default Account Balance/Restrictions are changed to that shown in figure 9.5. The minimum password length is changed to five, but there is no requirement on unique passwords; that is, a user can reuse old passwords.

Figure 9.5
Default Account Balance/Restrictions with the Limit Concurrent Connections and Require Password fields set to Yes.

```
                Default Account Balance/Restrictions
Account Has Expiration Date:                              No
   Date Account Expires:
Limit Concurrent Connections:                             Yes
   Maximum Connections:                                   1
Create Home Directory for User:                           Yes
Require Password:                                         Yes
   Minimum Password Length:                               5
Force Periodic Password Changes:                          No
   Days Between Forced Changes:
   Limit Grace Logins:
      Grace Logins Allowed:
Require Unique Passwords:                                 No
Account Balance:                                          0
Allow Unlimited Credit:                                   Yes
   Low Balance Limit:
Limit Server Disk Space:                                  No
Maximum Server Disk Space (KB):
```

If the Force Periodic Password Changes field is set to Yes, the defaults shown in figure 9.6 are displayed. You see that the days between forced changes of passwords is set to 40, and six grace log-ins are allowed after the password expires.

9

Figure 9.6
Default Account Balance/Restrictions with the Force Periodic Password Changes field set to Yes.

```
                Default Account Balance/Restrictions
Account Has Expiration Date:                              No
   Date Account Expires:
Limit Concurrent Connections:                             Yes
   Maximum Connections:                                   1
Create Home Directory for User:                           Yes
Require Password:                                         Yes
   Minimum Password Length:                               5
Force Periodic Password Changes:                          Yes
   Days Between Forced Changes:                           40
   Limit Grace Logins:                                    Yes
      Grace Logins Allowed:                               6
Require Unique Passwords:                                 No
Account Balance:                                          0
Allow Unlimited Credit:                                   Yes
   Low Balance Limit:
Limit Server Disk Space:                                  No
Maximum Server Disk Space (KB):
```

The intruder detection/lockout mechanism is not automatically enabled. It can be enabled by selecting Supervisor Options from SYSCON, and then selecting the Intruder Detection/Lockout option. When enabled, the default values, shown in figure 9.7 are selected. The intruder threshold is set to 7 attempts, the retention time is set to 30 minutes, and the length of lockout is 15 minutes. With these default settings, a clever intruder can try a maximum of 6 attempts every hour without completely locking up the account.

```
                 Intruder Detection/Lockout
Detect Intruders:                  Yes

Intruder Detection Threshold
Incorrect Login Attempts:          7
Bad Login Count Retention Time:  0  Days    0  Hours    30 Minutes

Lock Account After Detection:      Yes
   Length Of Account Lockout:    0 Days     0  Hours    15 Minutes
```

Figure 9.7
Default values in Intruder Detection/Lockout box.

Although you should not be too liberal with threshold setting, keep in mind that everyone makes occasional typing errors. If the user is legitimate and simply makes a mistake, he should be able to enter the correct information on the second or third try. An intruder, however, may need several attempts to successfully open the account.

Establishing a Class C Installation

The Default Account Balance/Restrictions settings are not adequate for secure installations. Instead, use the default settings shown in figures 9.8 and 9.9, which are adequate for most installations. By using these settings, the NetWare installation can be classified as a class C system.


```
          Default Account Balance/Restrictions
Account Has Expiration Date:                  No
   Date Account Expires:
Limit Concurrent Connections:                 Yes
   Maximum Connections:                       1
Create Home Directory for User:               Yes
Require Password:                             Yes
   Minimum Password Length:                   8
Force Periodic Password Changes:              Yes
   Days Between Forced Changes:               40
   Limit Grace Logins:                        Yes
      Grace Logins Allowed:                   1
Require Unique Passwords:                     Yes
Account Balance:                              0
Allow Unlimited Credit:                       Yes
   Low Balance Limit:
Limit Server Disk Space:                      No
Maximum Server Disk Space (KB):
```

Figure 9.8
Recommended Default Account Balance/Restrictions settings for a class C security rating.

```
                 Intruder Detection/Lockout
Detect Intruders:                  Yes

Intruder Detection Threshold
Incorrect Login Attempts:          3
Bad Login Count Retention Time:  1  Days    0  Hours    0  Minutes

Lock Account After Detection:      Yes
   Length Of Account Lockout:    7 Days     0  Hours    0  Minutes
```

Figure 9.9
Recommended Intruder Detection/Lockout default settings.

Using Bindery Audit Tools

Two excellent bindery audit tools are the SECURITY.EXE utility (which comes with NetWare) and BINDVIEW+ (available from the LAN Support Group, (713) 789-0882).

The SECURITY.EXE utility can be run by Supervisors to assist network administrators in determining how secure their NetWare configuration is. The utility must be run by a user with Supervisor privileges. It provides a list of potentially weak areas of the network's security, checks the bindery (system internal database) for user and group objects, and notifies you of potential problems due to excessive security imposed on a user or group (or due to unrestricted access because of no passwords).

The following report was produced by running the SECURITY utility. Notice that a number of security holes, or weaknesses, are reported; the main ones involve excessive rights to directories and the lack of passwords on many critical user accounts.

```
User AMAR (Full Name: AMAR RAMA)
  Has [ R  FA] rights in SYS:PUBLIC (maximum should be [ R  F ])
  Does not require a password
User DEI
  Account has not been used for more than 3 weeks
    Last Login: Thursday  October 24, 1992  9:45 am
  Does not require a password
  No Full Name specified
User ADMIN
  Is security equivalent to user SUPERVISOR
  Account has not been used for more than 3 weeks
    Last Login: Thursday  October 24, 1992  1:19 pm
  Does not require a password
  No Full Name specified
User USER15 (Full Name: USER NAME)
  Does not require a password
User KARANJIT (Full Name: Karanjit S. Siyan)
  Is security equivalent to user SUPERVISOR
  Account has not been used for more than 3 weeks
    Last Login: Friday  September 27, 1992  10:12 am
  Does not require a password
User GUEST
  Has no LOGIN_CONTROL property
  No Full Name specified
User SUPERVISOR
  Does not require a password
  No Full Name specified
```

In general, SECURITY reports the following problems (note that the word "object," when referring to security permissions in the NetWare bindery, means a user or a group):

- Objects without assigned passwords.
- Objects with insecure passwords (passwords that are easily guessed).
- Objects that have the security equivalence of Supervisor.

- Objects with privileges in the root directory of a volume.
- Objects without login scripts.
- Objects with excessive rights in standard directories. An object's rights in the standard directories must be limited, as follows:

Standard Directory	Trustee Assignment
SYS:PUBLIC	[R F]
SYS:SYSTEM	[ ]
SYS:LOGIN	[R F]
SYS:MAIL	[WC]

Another tool for generating bindery reports or for viewing the bindery is BINDVIEW+, which can automate security audits and locate major security holes on NetWare file servers. An auditor or network administrator can define a list of security-violation criteria called the *base line*; BINDVIEW+ searches for users, groups, files, directories, print queues, or print servers that violate this base line.

BINDVIEW+ comes with a *Query By Example* (QBE) report generator, which can be used to generate customized reports. It provides sample reports and templates that can be modified to your needs.

Traveling BINDVIEW+ is a customized version of the BINDVIEW+ report generator. It can select a large variety of security options for evaluating a LAN, such as the following:

- User password analysis (checks for insecure passwords)
- Data security analysis of user and directory of file data
- User rights analysis
- Virus security holes or security weaknesses that a virus can exploit

Restricting Log-ins Time, Station, and Space

NetWare can restrict log-ins on certain days and times of the week, prohibiting users from working at certain times of the day or from logging in to the network from a remote location. In a secure environment, for example, you may not want users on the network after a certain time in the evening or on weekends.

Another useful capability restricts a user to a specific station only. A security problem in many organizations stems from users' unrestricted access to any workstation on the network. If a user is on a terminal that is not his regular workstation, he also may have access to sensitive papers and files lying on somebody's desk.

User accounts also can be assigned a disk quota to prevent them from "hogging" too much disk space.

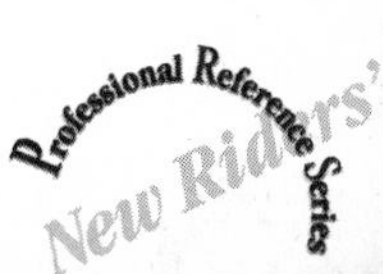

The security restrictions discussed in this chapter must be balanced with ease of use. Excessive security can prevent intruders from accessing the network, but it also can be a great hindrance and annoyance to legitimate users.

Restricting Log-ins by Time

Figure 9.10 shows the Default Time Restrictions dialog box for users to log in to a server.

To display this dialog box, perform the following tasks:

1. Log in to the server with a Supervisor account and invoke SYSCON.
2. Make the following menu selections:

   Supervisor Options

   Default Time Restrictions

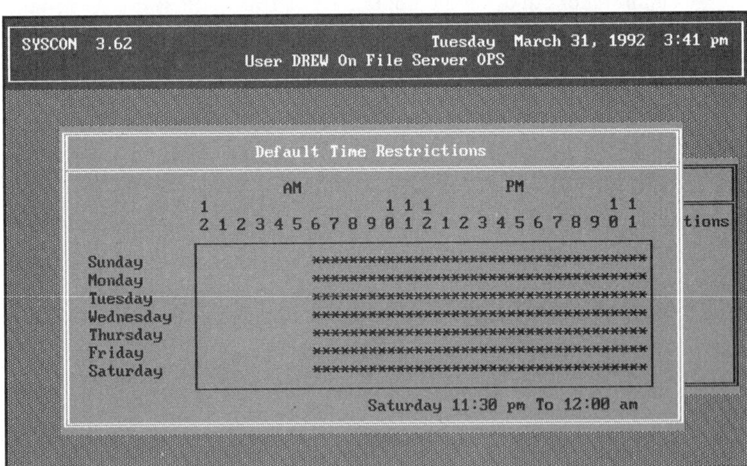

Figure 9.10
Sample default time restrictions.

Each asterisk (*) represents a 30-minute interval. If a user is allowed to log in during a period, it is marked with an asterisk. A blank space indicates that the user is not allowed to log in. To disallow access during a half-hour time interval, press Del at the desired interval. To allow access, use Ins or type an asterisk. To toggle the state of the interval, press Enter. To delete a block of * values, mark the block by pressing F5, and then press Del.

In this example, you see that, by default, users are not allowed access to the file server on Saturday, or daily between 12:00 a.m. and 6:00 a.m.

Figure 9.11 shows the default time restrictions for all new users that are created. (These restrictions can be overridden for individual accounts.) This figure shows the time restrictions for a specific user (ANNE).

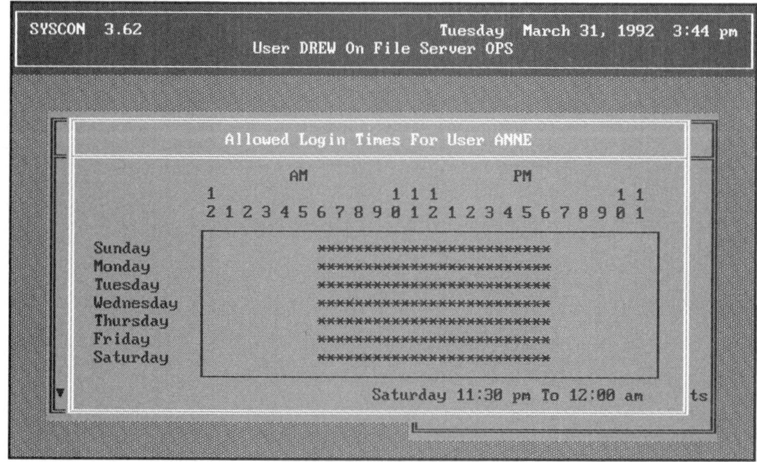

Figure 9.11
Allowed Login Times For User screen, showing specific user.

To display the box, perform the following tasks:

1. Log in to the server with a Supervisor account and invoke SYSCON.
2. Make the following menu selection:

   User Information

3. Select a user name for time restriction and highlight:

   Time Restrictions

Restricting Log-ins by Station

Figure 9.12 shows the Allowed Login Addresses box, which restricts stations.

Figure 9.12
Allowed Login Addresses box.

To display this dialog box, perform the following tasks:

1. Log in to the server with a Supervisor account and invoke SYSCON.
2. Make the following menu selections:

   User Information

   Select a user for station restriction

   Station Restrictions

Figure 9.12 shows an empty list of allowed log-in addresses for the user. This list is initially empty because there are no station restrictions for a user by default. To add station restrictions, press Ins at this screen. When prompted for the network address, enter up to an eight-digit hexadecimal network address for the workstation the user is allowed to access, and then press Enter. The screen in figure 9.13 is displayed.

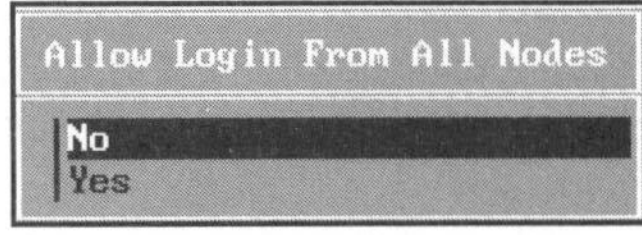

Figure 9.13
Station restriction choice.

To disallow access to all stations, select No; when prompted for the node address, as shown in figure 9.14, enter up to a 12-digit hexadecimal node address.

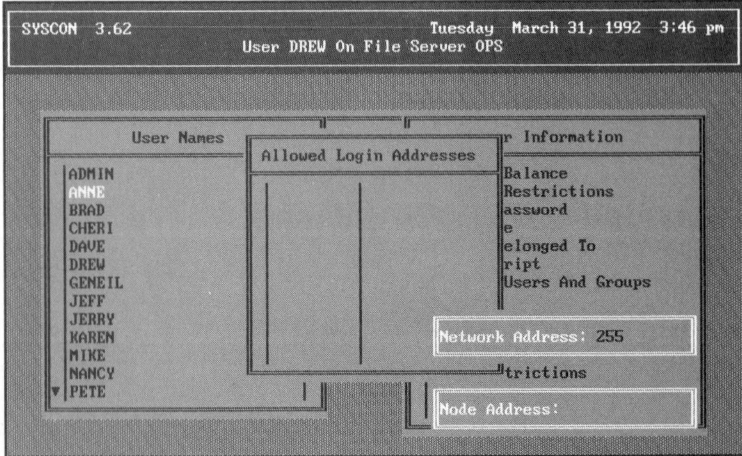

Figure 9.14
Node Address prompt.

Figure 9.15 shows a station restriction on network address 00000255 and node address 000C00123456. The user can only log in from the listed station address.

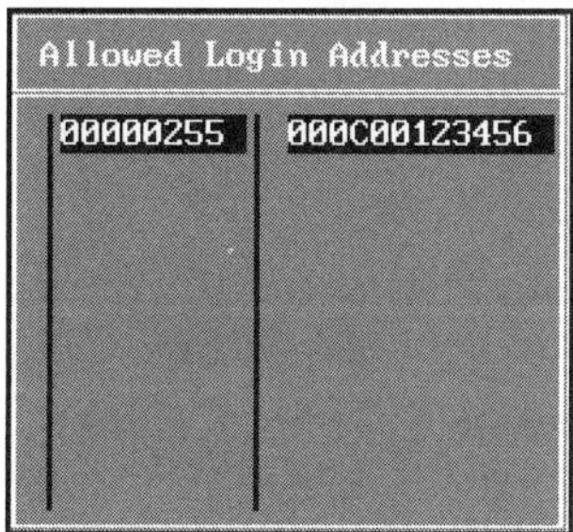

Figure 9.15
Allowed Login Addresses box, showing restrictions.

Restricting by Space

Figure 9.16 shows the User Volume/Disk Restrictions box, which restricts disk space.

Figure 9.16
User Volume/Disk Restrictions dialog box.

To display this dialog box, perform the following tasks:

1. Log in to the server with a Supervisor account and invoke SYSCON.
2. Make the following menu selections:

   User Information

   Select a user for station restriction

   Volume/Disk Restrictions

   Select a volume to place the restriction

By default, the user's space is not limited. Change the Limit Volume Space? field to Yes. Specify the Volume Space Limit field in kilobytes. Press Esc a few times to exit SYSCON.

Ensuring Server Console Security

NetWare 3.*x* has a server console security feature, ensuring that only users with proper security can access the server. This protects the server console from misuse.

The following features can be used:

- The SECURE CONSOLE command can be issued at the server console. This command does the following:

  Prevents loadable modules from being loaded from any directory other than SYS:SYSTEM.

  Prevents keyboard entry into the NetWare debugger.

  Prevents anyone but the console operator from changing the system date and time.

  Removes DOS from the file server. The intruder then cannot down the server, exit to DOS, and then run programs. With DOS removed, the system reboots if it is downed. You also can use a server machine with a power-on password feature.

- Select Lock File Server Console from MONITOR.NLM and supply a password to protect the server (see fig. 9.17).

- Protect RCONSOLE.NLM with a password so that a user cannot access the console remotely.

Finally, the best way to secure the server console is to place the server machine in a location that is not easy to access without detection, such as a locked room or office.

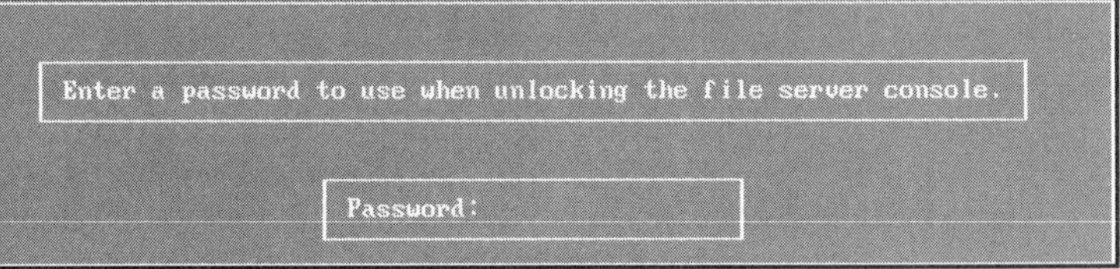

Figure 9.17
Lock File Server Console in MONITOR.NLM.

Summary

In this chapter, you learned about different security classes and how NetWare can be used to implement a class C security system. Among the many NetWare security features are the following:

- Log-in security
- Password security
- Intruder detection/lockout security
- Time/Station/Space security
- Server console security

NetWare 4

Features of NetWare 4

In Part 2 of this book, you learned about NetWare 2.2, 3.11, and 3.12. NetWare 4.*x* is an evolutionary step from earlier versions of NetWare with an emphasis on enterprise networking. NetWare 4.*x*, with its many server disk optimization features, also is an attractive choice for workgroup computing. While NetWare 4.*x* installation is more automated, it requires more attention to design of the NetWare Directory Services, a new feature of the operating system.

In this chapter, you learn some of the motivation behind the NetWare 4.*x* features beneficial in building secure, large-scale enterprise-wide networks. NetWare 4.*x* is in many ways very similar to the architecture of the earlier NetWare 3.*x* operating system, and in other ways represents a radical departure in terms of how the network can be viewed and managed.

Exploring the Motivation for New NetWare 4 Features

A network can consist of several LANs tied together with wide area links as shown in figure 10.1. For a user to use printer or network volume storage resources, the user needs to know the location of the resources. In figure 10.1, a user of earlier versions of NetWare must know the names of the file servers to which the printer and volume resources are attached. Before accessing a resource on a server, the user must log in to that server. If the user needs to access a volume resource on another server, the user has to attach to that server and then create a separate drive mapping. Attaching to a server implies that the user needs accounts on each server to which the user needs access. This approach works well in small networks that have a workgroup orientation (called *workgroup networks*); but on large networks with many servers, users cannot easily remember what resources are available on each server. A logical view of the network that hides the network's non-essential, physical details is much easier for the user. Figure 10.2 shows a logical view of the network depicted in figure 10.1.

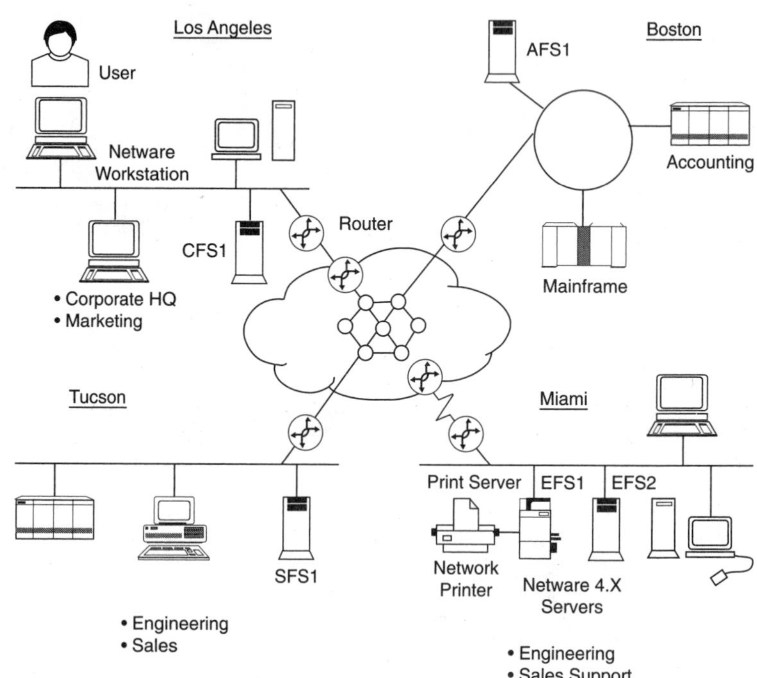

Figure 10.1
Example of a NetWare-based network.

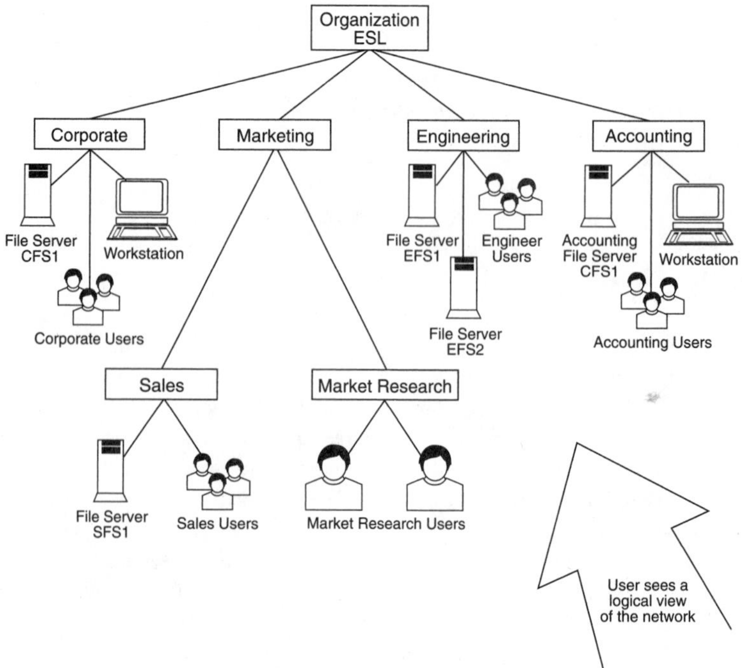

Figure 10.2
Logical view of a network.

In the logical view of the network, resources are organized into groups that are in turn organized into a hierarchy that reflects their usage, function, or geographical location. If a user wants to use the resources on this network, the user logs in to this logical view of the network. Access to resources on the network can be controlled by security mechanisms that are global in scope and apply to the entire network. In NetWare 3.*x* and NetWare 2.2, access to resources is controlled by security mechanisms local to each server (called the *bindery*). The bindery does not have network-wide significance. Bindery-based services are, therefore, *server-centric.* To provide a single access to the network, the designers of NetWare 4.*x* created a global data base called the *NetWare Directory Service* (NDS). The NetWare Directory Service is the mechanism used in NetWare 4.*x* to provide a logical view of the network.

The NetWare Directory Service provides a *global database* service not confined to a single server and represents network-wide resources. This is the single most important difference between NetWare 4.*x* and NetWare 3.*x*/2.2. The NDS is also the feature that affects many network administration tasks and network utilities. Many pre-NetWare 4.0 network administration tasks and network utilities modified the network information in the bindery. NetWare 3.*x* and 2.2 utilities cannot be used for NetWare 4.*x* because the information in a global database needs to be modified, and the older utilities understand the bindery but have no concept of a global database. Because of this, several older utilities were consolidated into new utilities that need to understand how to correctly modify the global database.

Examining NetWare 4.*x* Features

Some of the more significant NetWare features are as follows:

- NetWare Directory Services (NDS)
- Improvements in NetWare File System support
- Improved file system security and management
- Support for network auditing
- Simplified and more efficient memory management architecture
- Improvements in client networking services
- Integrated Storage Management Services (SMS)
- Improvements in network print services architecture
- Multiple language support (Internationalization)
- Simplified installation and upgrade procedures
- On-line NetWare manuals through Electro Text

Understanding NetWare Directory Services

NetWare Directory Services is perhaps the most distinct feature of NetWare 4.*x*. It provides the network administrator and the user with a logical view of the network that hides the sometimes bewildering complexity of the actual physical topology and configuration. The logical view of the network can be organized into what makes sense and what is easily recognizable to the users of the network. For example, in figure 10.3 the view of the network is hierarchical and reflects the organization chart of the company, which can be recognized by the users in that organization. The physical details of the network such as the type of cabling, and interconnecting devices such as routers and bridges, are absent in figure 10.3. In other words, the network Administrator and the user do not need to be aware of the physical nature of the network to use the network.

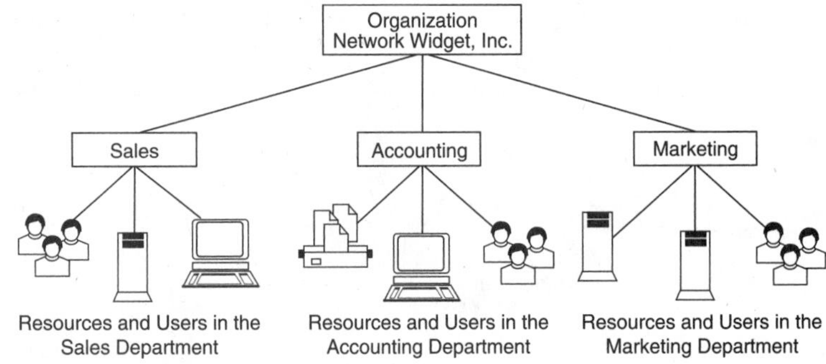

Figure 10.3
Logical network reflecting hierarchy of organization.

10

The logical view is possible because of the Network Directory Services. NDS provides a *distributed* database that can act as a repository of information on all the shared resources on the network. The database is distributed because it does not physically reside on any single server on the network. The database is *hierarchical* because it provides a convenient grouping of resources by function, location, or organization structure.

NDS is essentially a replacement for the *bindery* services that were part of the pre-NetWare 4.0 product line. The bindery in earlier NetWare releases was also a way of organizing resources, but the resources were specific to the server on which the bindery resided. The bindery could not easily support information on other nodes on the network, and because it was organized as a *flat* database rather than a hierarchical database, it did not have any natural way of representing usage or organizational relationships between resources.

Some benefits of using NDS are as follows:

- Provides logical organization of the network
- Requires single login to the network

- Offers global network management view
- Provides independence from physical location of resources

Logical Organization of the Network

The logical organization of the network is a benefit derived directly from the way resources can be grouped in a hierarchical fashion in the NDS representation for an organization (see fig. 10.3). This grouping reflects the way users want to use the network and makes it easy for users and network Administrators to find network resources without knowing the physical details of network connectivity. A user who needs to use a network resource has a *logical pointer* to the NDS database. These pointers are called *objects*, and they contain information on the resource. In NetWare 4.*x*, all network resources that can be accessed by a NetWare user are represented by objects.

A file server is an example of a network resource that can be modeled as a file server object. Inside this file server object (see fig. 10.4) is information such as the file server's name, network address, location, and so on. Information about the file server is called *properties* of the file server object.

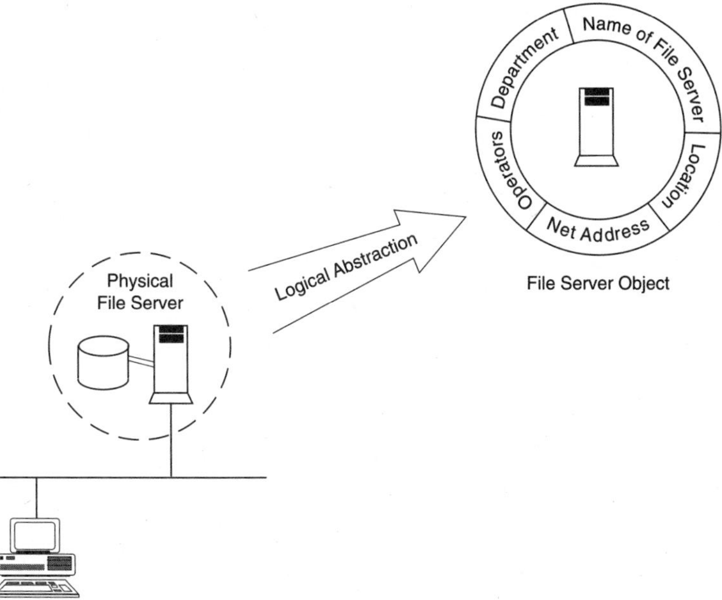

Figure 10.4
File server represented as an object.

Single Login to the Network

A single login to a network (see fig. 10.5) authenticates a user just once to access all the resources on the network. When a user logs in, the network Administrator can limit access to resources on the network. For example, all users by default can see the structure of an organization's directory even though they

cannot access all the objects in this directory unless explicitly given this access by a network Administrator. A single login to a network also simplifies the use of the network because a user does not need to perform separate logins to multiple servers on the network.

Figure 10.5
A single login to the network.

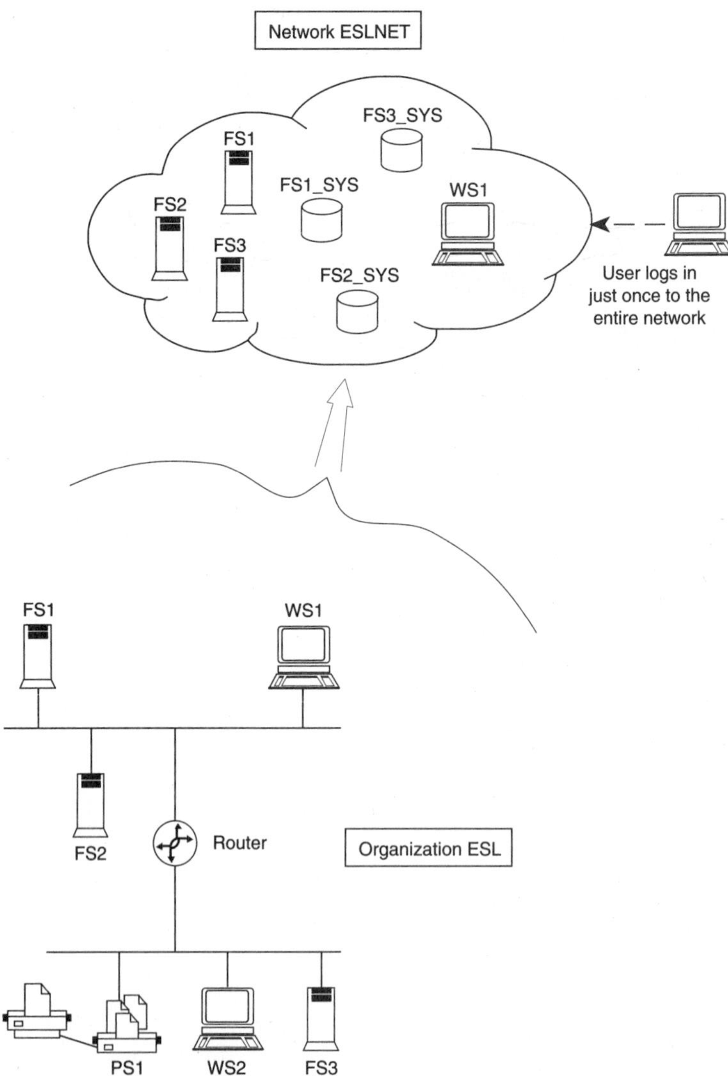

Before NetWare 4.0, the user had to log in (or attach) explicitly by supplying a user name and password for every server that the user wanted access to. The number of such concurrent connections was limited to eight. In addition, the network Administrator had to create separate accounts on each server that the user needed access to. This easily became burdensome on a large network.

The single login to a network is possible because the user authentication takes place against a global network directory, which is not specific to any server. In figure 10.6, you can see that the first step to logging in to a network is authentication of the user against information in the global directory. After the user authentication is successful, the user is granted access to any resource on the network. The maximum number of concurrent connections to different NetWare servers is now increased to 50 (although the default maximum is still 8).

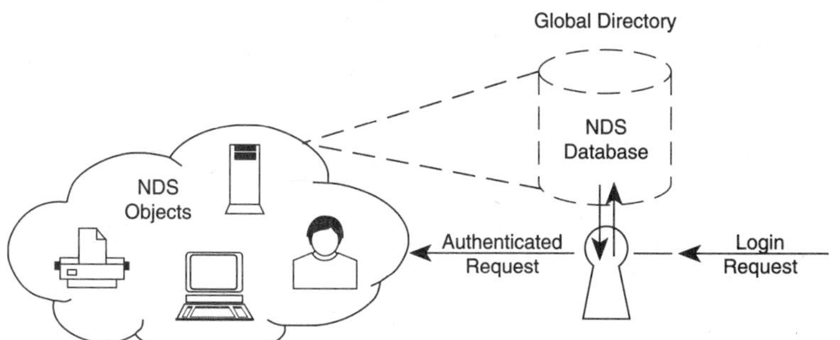

Figure 10.6
User authentication to the network.

Global Network Management

Before NetWare 4.0, network management tasks had to be performed separately on each NetWare server because network management usually resulted in a modification of the bindery, and the bindery was specific to each server.

Because the NDS is a global database, *global network management* in which network resources can be changed by the network Administrator from any place on the network is possible (see fig. 10.7). As you learn later, the network Administrator can delegate responsibility to other users who serve as network Administrators. Prior to NetWare 4.0, the responsibility could be delegated to a fixed number of user account managers, workgroup managers, and other operators; whereas, NetWare 4.*x* can have many levels of network Administrators with varying degrees of responsibilities.

Independence from Physical Location of Resources

In pre-NetWare 4.0 networks, the resources were described in a server bindery and dependent on that server. A classic example of this is the NetWare printer definitions tied to a specific server. If the printer had to be relocated to another server, the bindery representation of the printer had to be moved to another server (see fig. 10.8). If a large network is in a state of constant change, this can become a major task.

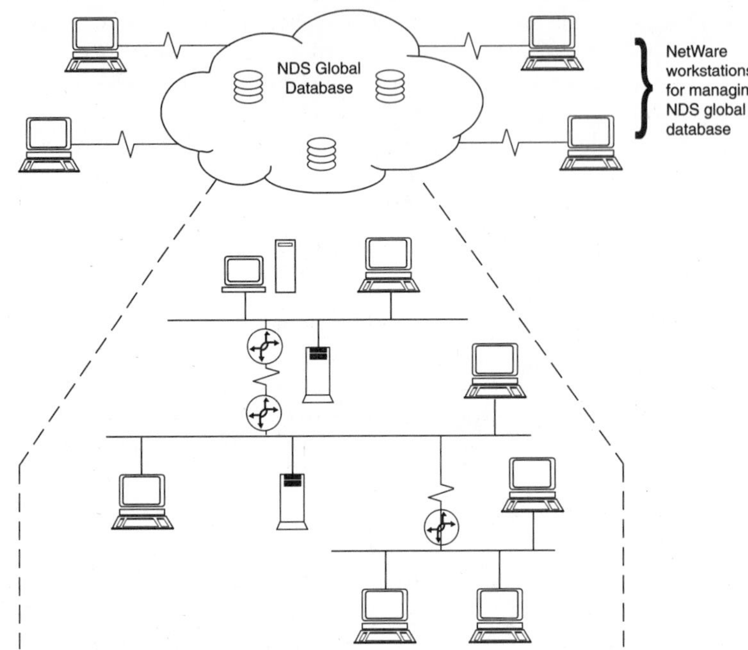

Figure 10.7
Global network management.

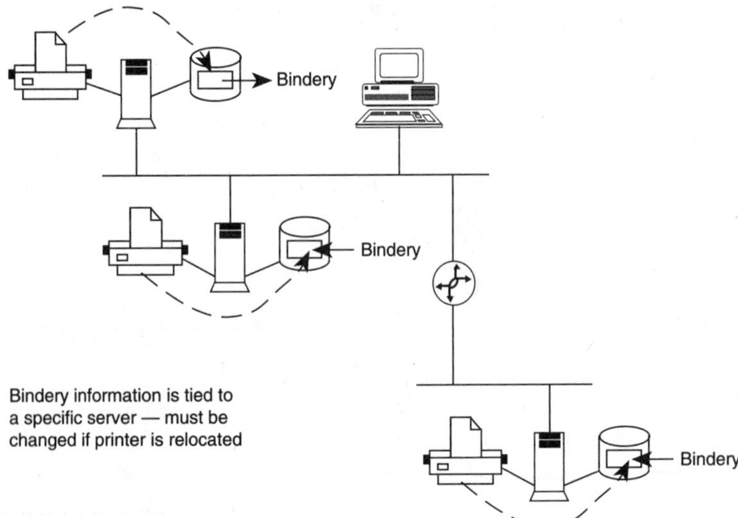

Figure 10.8
Bindery representations of printer definitions.

In NetWare 4.*x*, the resource definitions are not tied to any specific server or physical location on the network. This means that a user can access a resource without worrying about the physical location of the resource and how it can be reached. Changes to network resources are made to the NDS object that is part of a global database. The NDS object can be accessed from any station on the network, provided the user is granted security permission for the resource.

Exploring Improvements in the NetWare File System

One of NetWare's strengths is a fast and efficient file system. This has always been central to NetWare's popularity and capability to act as a file server. In NetWare 4.*x*, the file system is improved. Some improvements are because of the following new features: *block suballocation, compression,* and *migration.*

Block Suballocation

NetWare 4.*x* allows the disk block size selected at installation time to be 4 KB, 8 KB, 12 KB, 16 KB, or 64 KB (1 KB is 1,024 bytes). This capability also exists in NetWare 3.*x*; but in NetWare 3.*x*, if a 200-byte file is created on a volume that has a disk block size of 4 KB, a 4 KB block of storage is allocated and the remaining 3,896 bytes (4,096 - 200) are not available for use. This represents a wasted space of 95 percent; if the disk block size is 64 KB, the wasted space is even greater. Figure 10.9 shows how block suballocation in NetWare 4.*x* works. In NetWare 4.*x*, the unused disk block space is used in 512-byte suballocation units. If a 200-byte file is created, for example, a 512-byte suballocation within the 4 KB disk block is used. The remaining seven 512-byte suballocation blocks are available for sharing by leftover fragments of other files. If all these suballocation blocks are used, then in the preceding example only 312 (512 - 200) bytes are wasted out of a total of 4,096 bytes—only eight percent. If the disk block size is 64 KB, an even smaller percentage of wasted space occurs (about 0.5 percent). If the file sizes and leftover fragments are multiples of 512-bytes, no space is wasted.

Block suballocation can be defined as a mechanism in NetWare 4.*x* to allow small files and files that are not multiples of the disk block size to share space in a disk block that otherwise would be wasted. The improved disk space utilization is accompanied by the extra overhead in the operating system to maintain status of disk blocks that have been suballocated, but because disk writes are done in the background, the impact of this overhead is minimal.

Disk suballocation is enabled by default during a NetWare volumes installation. It can be explicitly disabled during installation. Always allocate a disk block size of 64 KB for maximum gain in server disk performance because the software and disk subsystems perform at an optimum at this block size.

NetWare File System Compression

Studies show that the processor utilization of many NetWare servers in real-life networks does not often exceed 50 percent. In heavily loaded servers, it is not uncommon to see processor utilization higher than

90 percent, but such situations are relatively rare. The designers of NetWare 4.*x* decided to use this unutilized processor "bandwidth" for useful background tasks, such as file system compression. Today, many disk compression utilities are available for DOS. These utilities decompress disk blocks as they are read and compress them back when they are written. This process causes the disk to appear slow because of the compression operation that accompanies each read or write operation. In NetWare 4.*x*, file compression is done in the background. Certain parameters can be set at the file server to control the frequency at which compression can be done in the background. When a file is retrieved, it is decompressed. The file blocks immediately decompressed are available for use, even as the rest of the file is being decompressed by special *decompression threads* (see fig. 10.10). Usually, the file remains in the decompressed state until a certain period of time that can be controlled at the server. The compression of files is always done in the background.

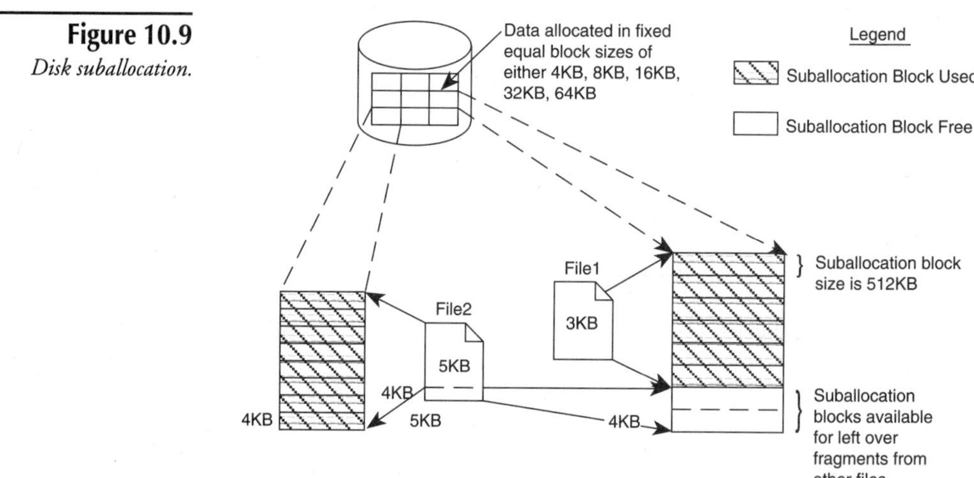

Figure 10.9
Disk suballocation.

Using the file compression feature, the effective disk space can be increased without adding new server drives. The amount of savings in disk space depends on the nature of repeated characters or binary patterns in the file and is very high for text files. It is not uncommon to see savings of up to 63 percent or more because of file compression. This means that 500 MB of files can take up as little as 185 MB (at 63 percent compression) of disk space. With disk space being at a perennial premium on file servers, this is a great advantage.

A file will not be compressed unless NetWare sees a certain gain in disk space. The network Administrator can exercise explicit control by flagging files and directories for immediate compression, or never to be compressed.

The compression option can be disabled or enabled during installation of a volume on the NetWare server. The default is that compression is enabled, which means that NetWare tries to compress a file if it has not been used for some time, provided a minimum savings in disk space can be achieved.

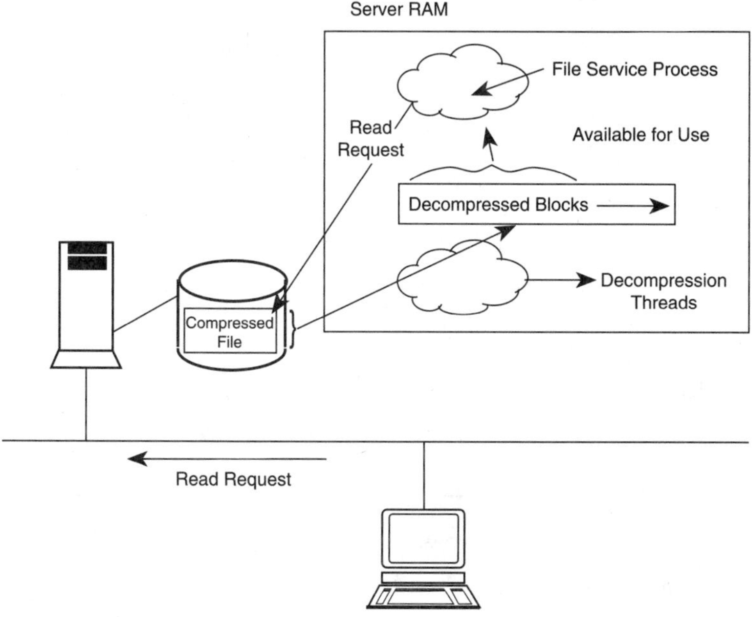

Figure 10.10
A read of a compressed file.

10

Data Migration

Data Migration allows infrequently used files to be moved to a *near-line* or *off-line* storage medium. Examples of near-line storage are *optical disk libraries* (also known as *juke-boxes*), and examples of off-line storage are *tape backup devices.* When data migration occurs, NetWare 4.*x* still sees the data on the NetWare volumes because the directory entries for the migrated files are still on the NetWare volume. If a migrated file is accessed, the file is brought back in (*demigrated*) to the NetWare volume (see fig. 10.11). The net effect of data migration is that valuable disk space is freed. When combined with compression, data migration is a very effective way of saving disk space.

Some of the earlier Control Data Corporation's super computers used data migration, but NetWare 4.0 is the first to popularize its use among PC-based *Network Operating Systems* (NOS).

Data migration can be enabled or disabled at the time of installing the NetWare volume. The files also can be marked for migration by using the NetWare utilities.

Data migration can be implemented using the *High Capacity Storage System* (HCSS). The HCSS is a storage and retrieval system that can extend the capacity of a NetWare server by integrating optical libraries into the NetWare file system. HCSS can work in conjunction with data migration so that migrated files can be moved from the faster but lower-capacity NetWare volumes to the slower but higher-capacity media that comprise the HCSS.

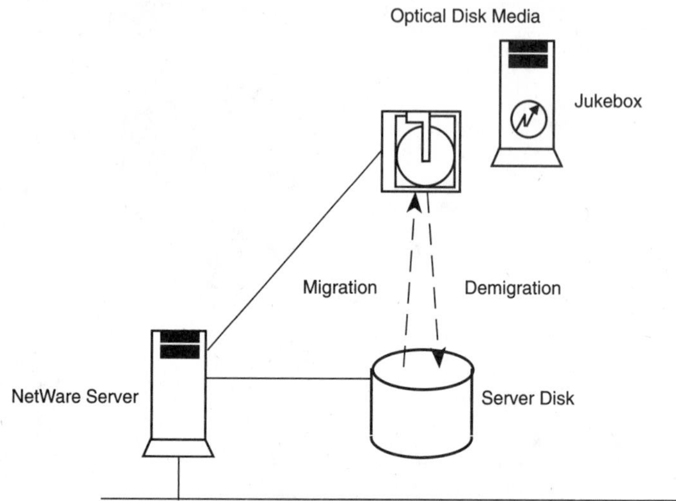

Figure 10.11
Data migration.

As far as the user is concerned, the operation of data migration and HCSS is transparent. Files migrated to the HCSS are accessed with the same commands as files that reside on the NetWare volume. If a migrated file is accessed, it is automatically demigrated.

Migration is performed on an individual file basis depending on the last time the file was accessed, called the *least recently used* criteria, and the current volume usage. Least recently used criteria for files refers to the least-active files, or files not accessed the longest. If the current volume usage exceeds a *capacity threshold*, data migration occurs. Capacity threshold is the percentage of the server's disk used before data migration begins.

Improved File System Security and Management

Access to the NetWare 4.*x* network is performed when the user logs in to the NetWare Directory for a network. Each organization can have its own network directory tree that reflects the usage and security needs of network users. As part of implementing network security, access to parts of the network directory tree are controlled by explicit trustee assignments. Figure 10.12 shows the different steps that must occur before a user is granted access to a file on a volume. These include login authentication, NDS security, and NetWare file system security.

When a user logs in to the network, the user specifies the name of the NDS object that represents the user account. The user's login name and password are used to build a personalized key used to *authenticate* a user's right to access the network. The actual algorithm used to build the personalized key is RSA, which stands for *Rivest, Shamir and Adelman*, the original creators of a public encryption key algorithm. Novell licensed this technology from RSA, Inc. for use with NetWare 4.*x*.

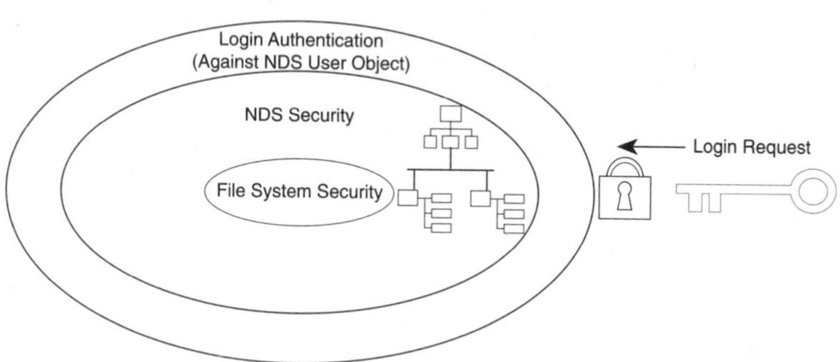

Figure 10.12
NetWare 4.x security.

After the user is authenticated on the network, the user must have rights to directory objects that represent resources on the network. This is seen in figure 10.12, in which a user has to pass through the NetWare Directory Services security. To access files on a volume, for example, the user must have certain rights to the volume object in the directory tree.

After the user passes through the NetWare Directory Services, the user's access to a file is controlled by the File and Directory Trustee rights. These rights are the same as those for the NetWare 3.*x* servers.

Network management is done by the network Administrator. An initial user account called ADMIN is created when a directory tree is first established. This is equivalent to the SUPERVISOR user in versions of NetWare before 4.0 except that the ADMIN user has network-wide responsibility. The ADMIN user account can be deleted or renamed, and in that sense does not have any special significance as does the SUPERVISOR account in NetWare 3.*x* and 2.*x* servers, which cannot be renamed or deleted. Because the ADMIN account can be deleted, make sure that other users have the equivalent of supervisory rights to the directory tree before the ADMIN account is deleted. For secure environments, you may want to rename the ADMIN account so that an unauthorized user cannot know and use the Supervisor's user name to try to break system security.

The ADMIN user can create other user objects anywhere in the directory tree. This is usually done in such a manner that the users can access resources in the directory tree easily and for ease in implementing security on the network.

The network Administrator can delegate to users different levels of network responsibility. For example, a user can be delegated the authority to create other user objects, but not delete them; or a user can be assigned the responsibility of managing part of a directory tree, but not accessing the information represented by the objects. This makes it possible to have multiple levels of network Administrators in a more flexible manner than the NetWare 3.*x* approach of workgroup and user account managers.

Security in NetWare 4.*x* can be more finely controlled by creating assistant "supervisors" who can administer network resources, but do not have access to data that needs to be protected from view, such as payroll data or other financial data.

Exploring Support for Network Auditing

In NetWare 4.*x*, you can set up a class of users called *auditors* that can act independently of the network Administrator to audit critical activities on the network. The auditors also can audit past and present transactions on the network for any security breaches (see fig. 10.13). It is important to understand why network auditors need to be independent of the network Administrator. The network Administrator of the directory tree, unless specifically restricted, has unrestricted access to data and resources on the network. As a result, an organization places great trust in the network Administrator. If this trust is betrayed, the network Administrator can cause a great deal of damage to an organization's data and privacy of data.

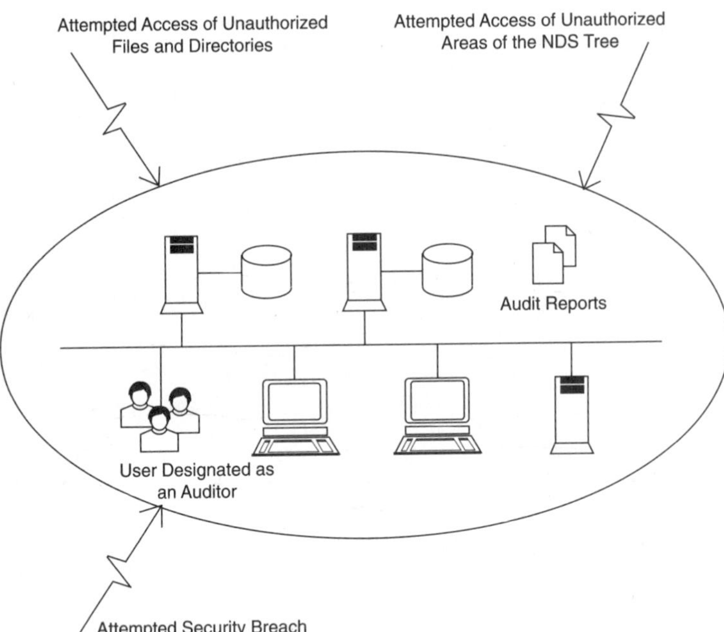

Figure 10.13
*Auditing in NetWare 4.*x.

Auditing allows auditor users to monitor actions on the network including those of the network Administrator. For this reason, an auditor should not have Supervisor rights or equivalence. The auditors' main function is to track events on the network, but they are unable to modify data on the network, other than the Audit Data and the Audit History files.

Auditing should not be confused with accounting features of earlier NetWare versions. Accounting allows the tracking of resource usage on the networks, such as disk blocks read and written, storage charges, and service requests. This accounting capability is still available in NetWare 4.*x*.

Auditing allows the monitoring of critical events on the network, such as logins and logouts, file operations, directory services object operations (creations, deletions, reads and writes), directory object events, user events, and trustee modifications. To audit files, auditing is enabled at the volume level. For directory objects, auditing must be enabled at the container object level. Container objects are used in the NDS tree for organizational purposes and are discussed in the next chapter. When enabled, log files are created to track audited operations. The primary utility for implementing auditing is AUDITCON.

Understanding Improvements in Memory Management

NetWare 3.*x* memory management is a great improvement over the way NetWare 2.2 managed memory on the server. However, NetWare 3.*x* still has a few problems with memory management, as seen in figure 10.14. In NetWare 3.*x*, memory is managed in five pools, each serving a different purpose. The pools are for purposes such as permanent memory, cache movable, cache non-movable, temporary allocated memory, and semi-permanent memory. To meet temporary high demands, memory pools could borrow memory from the file cache buffer memory; but once borrowed, this memory is not returned. Under certain conditions, memory leakage can occur to the point that the file cache buffer memory is severely depleted resulting in a severe degradation of server performance. To reset the memory pools, the server must be restarted.

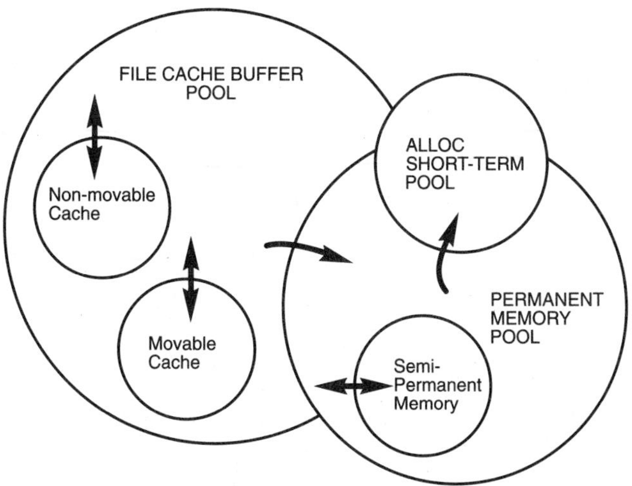

Figure 10.14
NetWare 3.x memory management.

10

Similar to how NetWare 3.*x* improves on NetWare 2.*x*, NetWare 4.*x* memory management is a considerable improvement over NetWare 3.*x*. First, no separate memory pools are used (see fig. 10.15); only one main pool exists and that is the file cache memory. All memory used by processes running on the server are borrowed against this pool and completely returned to it when the process terminates. The memory returned to the file cache can be reused by other processes. Consequently, memory management is simpler because there is only one pool rather than five; memory management also takes fewer processor cycles to accomplish, making memory allocation faster. The effects of fragmentation are

minimized in NetWare 4.*x* because NLMs treat memory as being logically continuous. The logically continuous address space is translated by the processor memory management hardware to physical memory pages that are 4 KB in size.

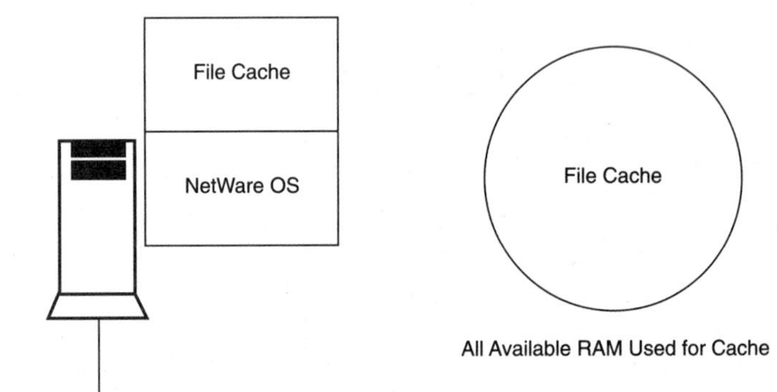

Figure 10.15
NetWare 4.x memory management.

Some features of NetWare 4.*x* memory management are as follows:

- Improved server performance because memory management is an important resource for server processes
- Integration with the paged memory architecture of the Intel processors
- Ring protection to control damage caused by misbehaved NLMs
- Ease of writing applications for the NLM developer because memory management is simpler

A controversial aspect of NetWare 3.*x* memory usage is that all programs—the kernel and applications—run in Ring 0 of the Intel 80386 architecture. The Intel 80386 architecture defines four rings—rings 0 to 3 (see fig. 10.16). The idea is to have the operating system kernel run at ring 0, and other programs at one of the outer rings. Programs running at, say, ring 3 can access the RAM used by programs running in ring 3, but cannot *directly* access RAM for programs running at rings 2, 1, and 0. Therefore, if the operating system kernel is running in ring 0, a program at ring 3 must make an *inter-ring gate call* to make service requests from the operating system kernel. If the program crashes, it cannot affect the operating system kernel. This architecture makes the system more reliable at the cost of reduced speed because of the inter-ring call overhead. OS/2 is an example of an operating system that uses the ring architecture.

NetWare 3.*x* does not use the ring architecture. The NetWare 3.*x* operating system, NLMs, and all server processes run in ring 0. What NetWare 3.*x* loses in reliability, it gains in simplicity and speed.

In NetWare 4.*x*, all NLMs by default run in ring 0. The network Administrator, however, can configure the server to run NLMs loaded in an outer ring so that offending programs cannot cause the operating system kernel that runs in ring 0 to crash. As new NLMs are added to the server, they can be loaded in an outer ring for a trial period. They run a little slower here because they have to make an inter-ring call. If the NLMs prove to be reliable, they can be added to ring 0, in which they can run faster.

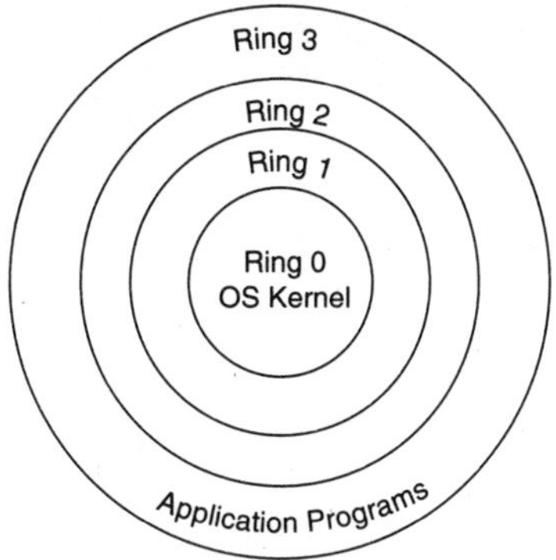

Figure 10.16
Intel 80386 processor ring architecture.

When purchasing NLMs from third parties, check to see if they are designed to run in an outer ring of the Intel processor (80386 and higher). Not all NLMs can run in an outer ring.

Understanding Improvements in Client Networking Services

The NetWare 4.*x* networking software for workstation operating system clients includes better support for DOS, MS Windows, and OS/2 (see fig. 10.17). DOS and MS Windows now use a DOS requester, ODI support, and Packet Burst Protocol support.

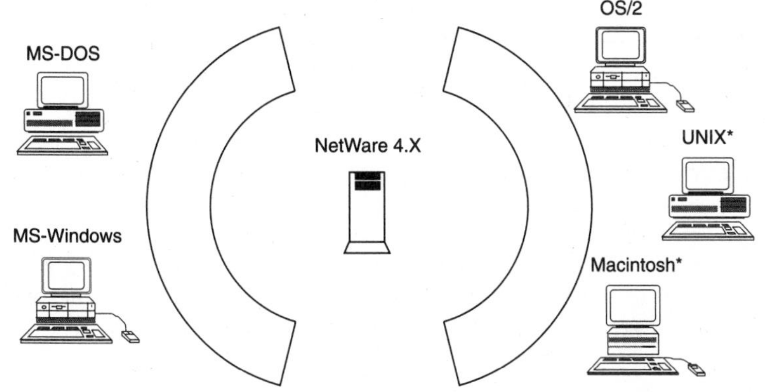

Figure 10.17
*Multiple client support in NetWare 4.*x.

The DOS requester allows the redirector capability of later releases of DOS through the interrupt mechanism INT 2F (hex) to be used. The earlier NetWare shell used the DOS INT 21 (hex) mechanism and a software multiplexor mechanism to direct the request to appropriate system services. Because of the additional overhead of the software multiplexor mechanism, it was slightly less efficient. In

NetWare 4.*x*, the DOS requester actually consists of a number of smaller components that must be loaded only if the service is necessary. These smaller components are called *Virtual Loadable Modules* (VLMs) and are loaded and managed by the VLM Manager (VLM.EXE). VLMs give you the flexibility of selectively loading only the services needed. VLMs are designed to understand NetWare Directory Services, and even a VLM component (NETX.VLM) can be used to communicate with bindery based servers.

The ODI support is the *Open Datalink Interface* that provides an interface for protocol stacks to talk to network boards that represent layer 2 (data-link layer) of the OSI model. The ODI interface was also available in earlier NetWare client software.

The Packet Burst protocol allows transmission of multiple packet requests and packet replies. It is similar to the window flow control mechanism used in other protocol suites and is an improvement over the single packet request/response behavior of the earlier NCP packet transmissions. The Packet Burst protocol was added to later releases of NetWare 3.*x* and also is available for NetWare 4.*x*. The Packet Burst protocol is particularly useful for multiple NCP packet requests and packet replies in which a number of requests or replies can be acknowledged by a single acknowledgment packet. This eliminates some of the overhead of the round-trip delay when a sender has to wait for the last packet sent to be acknowledged before transmitting the next packet. It also results in fewer packets being sent, which results in reduction of network traffic and reduced time for processing packets. Although Packet Burst comes bundled with NetWare 4.*x*, it is an option with NetWare 3.11 involving the PBURST.NLM on the server and the new client shell called BNETX.

Another enhancement in NetWare 4.*x* is support for *Large Internet Packet* (LIP). Earlier NetWare routers were limited in the size of the internet packet supported. With LIP, this limit is removed and larger packet sizes, common in token ring (4 KB to 16 KB) and Ethernet networks (13.5 KB), are possible.

Understanding Integrated Storage Management Services (SMS)

Storage Management Services (SMS) in NetWare 4.*x* provide data on the network to be backed or restored in a common data format and in a manner that is hardware and software independent. A *Target Service Agent* (TSA) program is run on each device that needs to be backed up and is the target for the SBACKUP program. These targets include workstations and NetWare 3.*x* and NetWare 4.*x* servers (see fig. 10.18).

In SMS, the SBACKUP program is responsible for backup and restore operations. SBACKUP is an NLM that runs on a NetWare server. The NBACKUP functionality of earlier NetWare releases is now consolidated in SBACKUP.

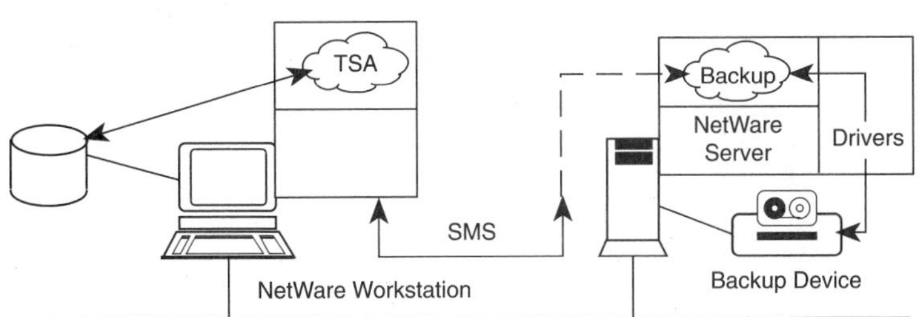

Figure 10.18
SMS and TSAs.

SMS consists of a number of other modules, such as the *Storage Management Data Requester* (SMDR) used to pass commands between the SBACKUP and the TSAs and device drivers that use the *Storage Device Interface* (SDI) to communicate between the SBACKUP program and the storage devices (see fig. 10.19).

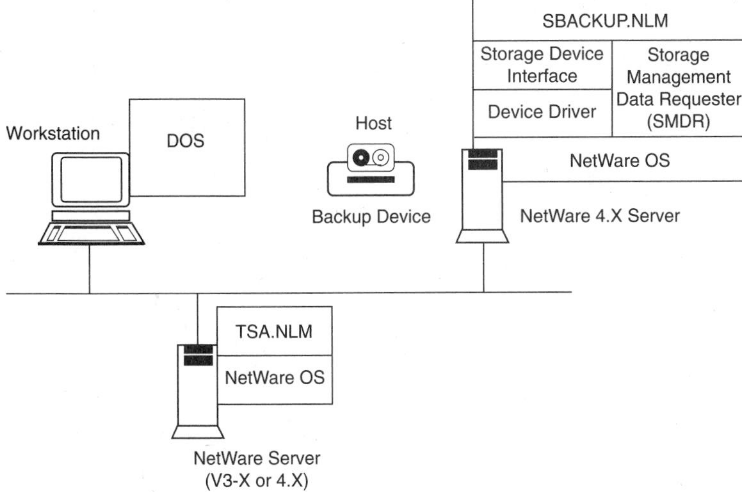

Figure 10.19
SMS architecture.

Besides SBACKUP you may want to consider a number of third-party backup schemes that use SMS. These provide a simpler and streamlined user interface and many advanced backup options.

Improvements in Network Print Services Architecture

In NetWare 3.*x*, print services are defined as part of the print server definition, and the only way to do a network print job is to submit the print job to a print queue. In NetWare 4.*x*, the network print jobs can be still sent to the network print queue, but in addition print jobs can be sent to the printer object in the NDS tree.

Other improvements in NetWare 4.*x* printing include the following:

- Simpler installation in comparison to NetWare 3.*x*
- Support for a larger number of printers (up to 256) on a single print server
- Remote printers can be set up on NetWare servers

Multiple Language Support (Internationalization)

Because the character of NetWare has become international in scope, NetWare 4.*x* introduces support for international languages to NetWare Loadable Modules and network utilities. This means that messages and options associated with utilities can be set in the language of the user. The default language is English, but other languages can be supported during installation when running the SERVER.EXE program. After installation, the INSTALL.NLM can be used to configure date, time, and number formats.

It is even possible to have different language NLMs running on the server at the same time; or to have one user using the system utility NETADMIN in French and another user using the same utility in Italian. It is important to understand that the language support does not mean that NetWare is capable of translating messages between users using different languages. For example, if the SEND utility is used by a French language user to send a message in French to another user who is set up to use Italian, NetWare cannot translate the message from French to Italian.

Even though the language may be the same, differences in the way that date, time, and numbers are formatted can exist. A classic example of this is English, which is spoken in both the United States and the United Kingdom. The default format for representing dates in the United States is *mm/dd/yy* (example: 10/16/93). In the United Kingdom, the default date format is *dd/mm/yy* (example: 16/10/93). The formatting is not just dependent on the language, but can change across different locales for the same language.

Table 10.1 shows examples of the date, time, and number formats for the United States, United Kingdom, France, and Germany.

Table 10.1
Format Differences for Countries

Country	Number Format	Time Format	Date Format
U.S.A.	355,113.22	11:55:00 p.m.	10/16/93
U.K.	355,113.22	23:55:00	16/10/93

Country	Number Format	Time Format	Date Format
Germany	355.113,22	23:55:00	16.10.93
France	355 113,22	23:55:00	16.10.93

The capability to support differences in language and format representations is called *internationalization.* Internationalization in NetWare is supported through *unicode* representation, which is a standard for representing data in 16-bits rather than the familiar 8-bit ASCII.

Understanding Simplified Installation and Upgrade Procedures

NetWare 4.*x* distribution comes in CD-ROM. Distribution on high-density floppy disks is an additional cost and can be obtained by sending in a request form that accompanies the NetWare 4.*x* distribution.

Installing NetWare 4.*x* on CD-ROM saves time during installation because copying the files from the distribution media is much faster, resulting in a simpler and faster implementation.

The CD-ROM drive can be attached to the server being installed, or it can be attached to a remote workstation. Figure 10.20 shows the different possibilities; the CD-ROM drive is shown as an external unit to the workstation or server. Internal CD-ROM's are also possible.

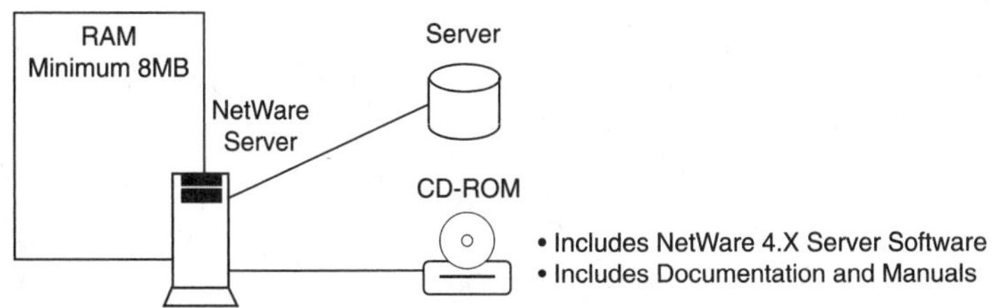

Figure 10.20
NetWare 4 installation using CD-ROM distribution.

On-line NetWare Manuals through Electro Text

NetWare Electro Text is a graphical utility that works with Windows 3.1 (or higher), to give on-line manuals that can be accessed through a *graphical user interface* (GUI). Figure 10.21 shows a sample Electro Text screen.

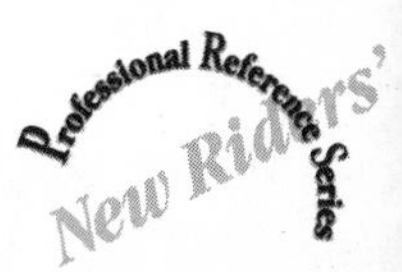

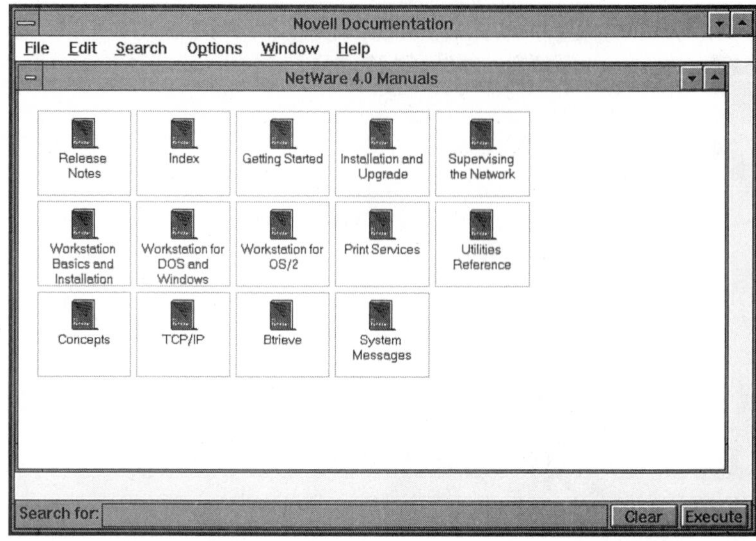

Figure 10.21
Sample Electro Text screen.

All the NetWare manuals are available in Electro Text format. Following is a list of these manuals and a brief description of their contents:

- **Index.** The index links to all places in the manuals. Click on a link marker to go to a place in the manual in which a term or topic can be found. The link markers can be made visible within the manual by selecting the INDEXED style from the Text option in the View menu. This is a useful feature because clicking on a link marker in a manual takes you back to the Index manual, which also lists link markers to other related concepts.

- **Release Notes.** Release notes consist of general issues in the area of utilities, High-Capacity Storage System (HCSS), Workstation for DOS/Windows and OS/2, Backing up and restoring data, and Print Services. Usually, last-minute changes that did not get into the manual are kept here.

- **Getting Started.** This contains many NetWare 4.0's new features and a brief tutorial on understanding and planning NDS. This is meant to be quick-start into the important concepts behind NetWare 4.*x*.

- **Installation and Upgrade.** This contains information on how to install a new NetWare 4.*x* server or upgrade to NetWare 4.*x* from other NetWare servers, such as NetWare 2.*x* or 3.*x* and IBM LAN Server.

- **Supervising the Network.** This helps you to set up and administer the network after you complete the NetWare 4.*x* installation. It covers issues such as managing NDS, NetWare files and directories, creating login scripts, NetWare server maintenance, network auditing, and backing up and restoring data.

- **Workstation Basics and Installation.** This helps you install and configure your workstation software. It also guides you on issues such as logging on to a NetWare server and covers the workstation tools that you can use to manage a workstation connected to a NetWare 4.*x* server.
- **Workstation for DOS and Windows.** This contains information on the NetWare DOS requester and configuring it for your workstation. It provides help with improving the security of the NetWare workstation and setting up multiple protocol support.
- **Workstation for OS/2.** This provides information for DOS users who need to migrate to OS/2. It contains information on accessing network services form Virtual DOS machines, and setting up Named Pipes and NetBIOS protocol support.
- **Print Services.** This helps you with NetWare 4.*x* printing concepts and how you can set up, load, and use network printing utilities. It contains some troubleshooting tips and guidelines for network print services.
- **Utilities Reference.** This contains information on how to use NetWare utilities, such as Text workstation utilities, server utilities, and GUI-based utilities. It also contains information on NDS bindery objects and their properties.
- **Concepts.** This is a glossary of NetWare-related terms with a tutorial description of what each term means. Topics are listed alphabetically in categories ranging from AAA to ZZZ.
- **TCP/IP (Transmission Control Protocol /Internet Protocol).** TCP/IP is a de facto protocol for connecting heterogeneous systems together. This talks about how TCP/IP can be configured and managed on the NetWare 4.*x* server. It explains the concepts in relationship to NetWare's implementation of TCP/IP.
- **Btrieve.** Btrieve is a popular and efficient record manager bundled as an NLM in NetWare servers. This talks about the installation and configuration issues of Btrieve.
- **System Messages.** This is a list of all possible system and warning messages that you may encounter in configuring NetWare 4.*x*. It lists the messages according to the modules that generate them, and there are over 150 modules. It explains the possible cause of the error message and the action you can perform to fix it.

The command line utilities now have a */?* switch that gives additional help information on how to use these utilities. This switch is very convenient, providing help from the command line without invoking any other on-line documentation. In reality, typing illegal command line parameters also results in help screens being displayed.

Help also is available in the menu utilities through function key F1. This help is context sensitive. The menu utilities such as FILER and PCONSOLE use the familiar C-Worthy Menu interface. Unlike previous versions of NetWare, pressing F1 twice (F1,F1) does not display extended help information.

Examining NetWare 4.*x* Utilities

When upgrading from NetWare 3.*x* to NetWare 4.*x*, many people discover that some very familiar utilities such as SYSCON are no longer present in NetWare 4.*x*. SYSCON was a bindery-based network administration tool and has been replaced by the more powerful NETADMIN tool based on NDS.

Some utilities have disappeared or were consolidated into a more functional utility. For example, the utilities VOLINFO, SALVAGE, and PURGE were consolidated into FILER. Table 10.2 lists some of these changes.

Table 10.2
NetWare 4.x Utility Changes

NetWare 4.0 Utility	Description
NETADMIN.EXE	Menu driven text utility used to create NDS objects. Also can be used to assign property values and rights. Consolidates some of the features of pre-NetWare 4.0 utilities, such as SYSCON, SECURITY, USERDEF, and DSPACE.
NWADMIN.EXE	MS Windows and OS/2 graphical utility to manage NDS tree and perform operations on it. Is a consolidated graphical tool for network management.
UIMPORT.NLM	Text utility for batch creation of users. Replaces the function of the pre-NetWare 4.0 MAKEUSER utility.
DOMAIN.NLM	Enables the creation of protected domains that allow NLMs to run in rings 1, 2, or 3 of the Intel processors. Runs as a server NLM.
MONITOR.NLM	General purpose server monitor utility for monitoring the server. Runs as a server NLM and consolidates the functions of the pre-NetWare 4.0 MONITOR and FCONSOLE.
SERVMAN.NLM	Facilitates the easy viewing and changing of the many server SET parameters. Allows these changes to be stored in AUTOEXEC.NCF and STARTUP.NCF files. Runs as a server NLM.
RCONSOLE.EXE REMOTE.NLM	RCONSOLE also performs the function of ACONSOLE (asynchronous console). Used for remote management of server.
NWSNUT.NLM	Library interface for C-Worthy style graphical functions used by server-based graphical tools, such as MONITOR and SERVMAN.

NetWare 4.0 Utility	Description
PARTMGR.EXE	Text utility for managing partitions and their replicas.
Partition Manager	GUI equivalent of the PARTMGR utility.
DSREPAIR.NLM	Repairs inconsistencies and problems in the NDS database. Provides the functionality of the BINDFIX and BINDREST utilities used to repair the bindery.
DSMERGE.NLM	Used for combining separate NDS trees.
TIMESYNC.NLM	Performs time synchronization. Is set up to load through AUTOEXEC.NCF during NetWare 4.0 server installation.
CDROM.NLM	CD-ROM support for CD drives attached to the NetWare 4.0 server.
RTDM.NLM	Real Time Data Migration utility that runs at the server.
LIST DEVICES	Server console command. Lists device information.
SCAN FOR NEW DEVICES	Server console command. Scans for any new devices added to the server.
MEDIA	Server console command. Used to confirm if requests to insert/remove media on the server were performed.
MAGAZINE	Server console command. Used to confirm if requests to insert/remove magazine on the server were performed.
MIRROR STATUS	Server console command. Used to display status of mirrored partitions.
ABORT REMIRROR	Server console command. Used to stop mirroring of partitions.
REMIRROR PARTITION	Server console command. Used to remirror partitions.
AUDITCON.EXE	Allows independent users to act as auditors. Is a superset of the pre-NetWare 4.0 ATOTAL and PAUDIT.
RIGHTS.EXE	Consolidates functions of pre-NetWare 4.0 RIGHTS, GRANT, REVOKE, REMOVE, and ALLOW utilities.
FLAG.EXE	Consolidates functions of pre-NetWare 4.0 FLAG, FLAGDI,R and SMODE utilities.

continues

Table 10.2, Continued
NetWare 4.*x* Utility Changes

NetWare 4.0 Utility	Description
FILER	Consolidates functions of pre-NetWare 4.0 FILER, SALVAGE, PURGE, DSPACE, and VOLINFO utilities.
NPRINTER.EXE	Allows a printer attached to a workstation (DOS or OS/2) or a server to be used as a network printer.
SBACKUP.NLM	Used to perform backup across the network. Consolidates the pre-NetWare 4.0 SBACKUP and NBACKUP.
RPL.NLM	Allows remote booting for diskless workstations (PCs).
KEYB	Server console command. Allows the selection of a nationality or language for the keyboard device.
LANGUAGE	Server console command. Sets up the use of the specified language at the server.
CX.EXE	Allows users to navigate the NDS tree by changing the context. Does for NDS directory what the CD command does for file directories.
LOGIN.EXE	Used to log in or attach to a server. Uses NDS objects and consolidates pre-NetWare 4.0 LOGIN and ATTACH utilities.
NMENU.BAT MENUMAKE.EXE MENUCNVT.EXE	NMENU is the batch utility; MENUMAKE is the menu compiler utility; and MENUCNVT is the menu conversion utility. Menus are based on Saber menus.
NDIR.EXE	Consolidates the pre-NetWare 4.0 NDIR, LISTDIR, CHKDIR, and CHKVOL utilities.
NETUSER.EXE	Replaces pre-NetWare 4.0 SESSION. Text graphical tool for performing drive mappings, printing, and network attachments.
SEND.EXE	Consolidates the pre-NetWare 4.0 SEND, CASTON, and CASTOFF utilities.
NLIST.EXE	Consolidates the pre-NetWare 4.0 USERLIST and SLIST utilities.
Tools Group for Windows and OS/2	Tools installed as a group in the MS Windows Program Manager and OS/2's desktop.

Summary

In this chapter, you examined the features of NetWare 4.*x*. NetWare 4.*x* represents an exciting change in the way large enterprise-wide area networks can be supported. The principal change is the introduction of NetWare Directory Services, which enables you to superimpose a logical structure or view on a physical network, making the network easier to use and administer.

Because NDS is central to accessing resources on the network, security is integrated into NDS. When a user logs in, that user is authenticated at the NDS level. Auditing can be used to further monitor activity on the network.

Other improvements are in the area of Storage Management Services, Enhanced client support, Enhanced and integrated utilities, and better on-line documentation.

Understanding NetWare 4 Directory Services

NetWare Directory Services (NDS) is perhaps the single most important feature of NetWare 4.*x*. It allows a network consisting of many servers to be treated as a single network that can be very simply administered. NDS allows network resources to be treated as logical resources. The logical resources are grouped together to represent their logical relationship. Network administration consists of primarily managing the resources in the NDS database. This chapter will teach you basic NDS concepts and how NDS can be used to access and manage network resources. Understanding of NDS services is fundamental to managing NetWare 4.*x*, because access of network resources revolves around how the NDS is represented, accessed and managed.

Understanding NDS

NDS is a distributed global database of services and resources that is available on the network. The term *global* implies that there is a single database that is shared by all servers on the network and is available to users from any point on the network. Most resources of importance to network management on the network have an entry in this global database.

Conceptually, this database exists when directory services is installed, and it is not tied to any physical resource such as a server. In practice, because NDS is implemented as a database, it must be stored on storage devices on the network such as physical volumes that are associated with physical servers. Since the size of the NDS database can become very large, and also for reliability reasons, the NDS database is not stored at any central site (except for very small networks). Portions of the NDS database are distributed on volume storage devices at strategic locations on the network. These subdivided elements of the NDS are called *partitions*.

NDS Logical Resources

NDS logical resources are represented by *objects.* Since these logical resources are associated with NDS, they are often called *NDS objects.* NDS objects can be conceptually seen as records in a global database (see fig. 11.1). The network resources that can be represented as NDS objects include network printers, network volumes, NetWare file servers, Apple Filing Protocol servers, user accounts, and so on.

Figure 11.1
NDS global database.

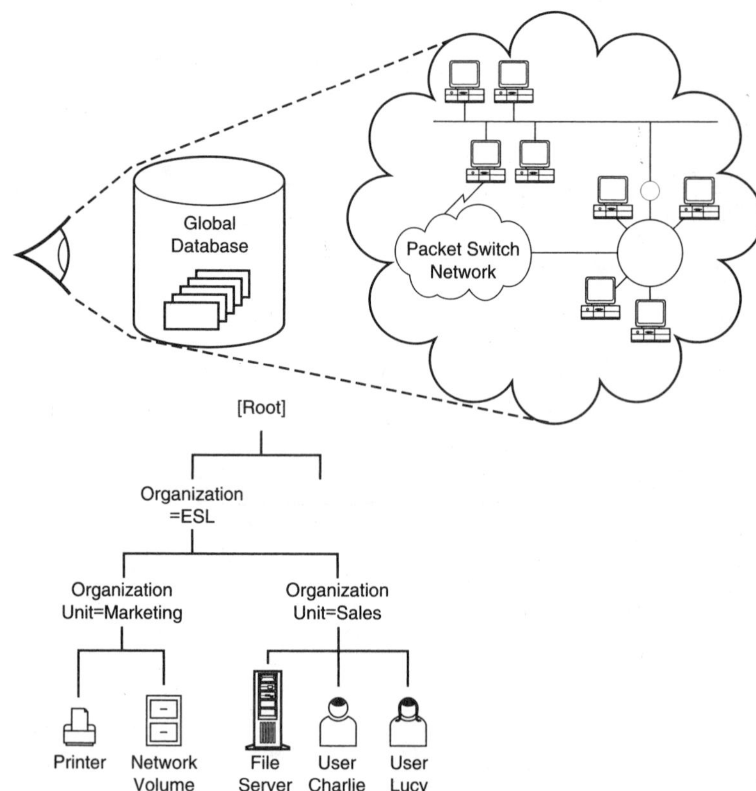

Each NDS object holds information about the logical resource it represents. Information on an object is stored as *properties* of the object. Since an NDS object can be viewed as a record, the properties are similar to the fields of a record (see fig. 11.2). For example, the properties of a user object are the user's login name, last name, groups the user belongs to, user's telephone number, and so on. Figure 11.3 shows examples of NDS resource objects and their properties. The figure shows some of the properties of a user object and a NetWare server object. The properties are listed in the property column and represent the *categories* or *type* of information that can be stored in the object. The actual information stored in a property is listed in the Value column and is called a *property value.* Some properties are crucial and must have a value associated with them. These are *mandatory* or *required* properties. An example of a mandatory property for all NDS objects is the name property, called the *common name.* If the name property is not defined, an object cannot be referenced. The *last name* property for user objects is mandatory. Some of the NetWare server object's properties are also shown in figure 11.4. These properties can be viewed using the NetWare Administrator GUI tool. This figure shows that one can specify the *Department* and *Organization* properties for the server object. The properties *Net Address, Status,* and *Version* cannot be changed by the administrator and represent the current status of the physical file server.

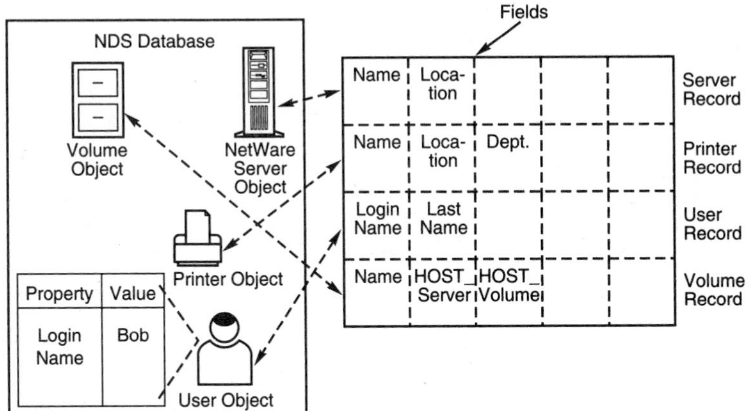

Figure 11.2
Properties of objects.

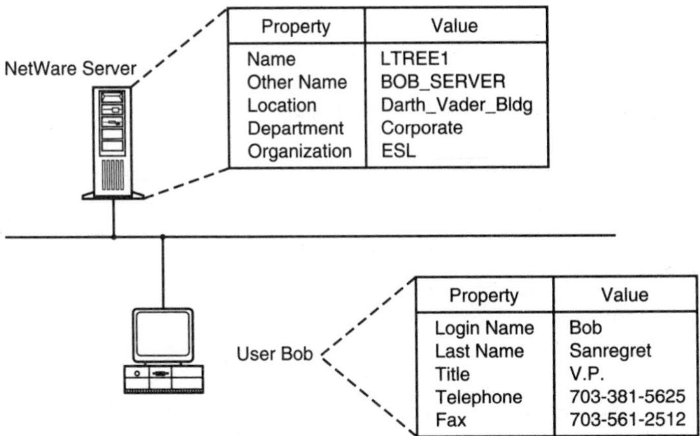

Property	Value
Name	LTREE1
Other Name	BOB_SERVER
Location	Darth_Vader_Bldg
Department	Corporate
Organization	ESL

Property	Value
Login Name	Bob
Last Name	Sanregret
Title	V.P.
Telephone	703-381-5625
Fax	703-561-2512

Figure 11.3
Example NDS objects and property values.

Figure 11.4
NetWare server properties.

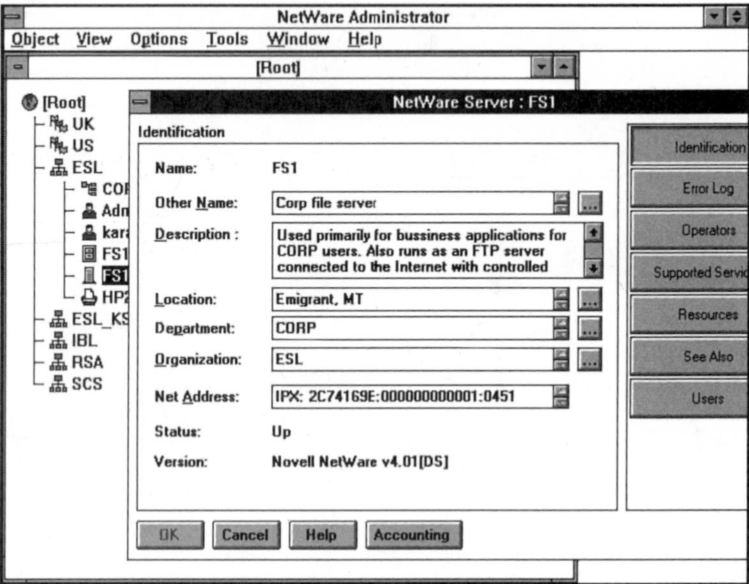

In NetWare 3.*x*, there was a *Full Name* property for user accounts that was optional. But in NetWare 4.*x* the *last name* property is mandatory. This may at first seem strange, because the *last name* property does not seem to serve any crucial technical function in the NDS database. The answer to this mystery lies with X.500 on which the NDS is based. In X.500, certain properties are explicitly defined as being mandatory while others are optional. Many of the properties defined in NDS user objects are taken directly from the X.500 definition. In X.500, the last name property for user objects is called *surName* property and this is mandatory. NDS defines the *last name* property to be mandatory to be compliant with X.500.

Certain properties in NDS are defined for informational purposes and are *optional* properties. Examples of these are a user's telephone number, fax number, user's title, and electronic mail address. Many objects have a "See Also" property which is optional.

Property values can be single valued or multi-valued. If a property is single valued, no more than one value can be defined for that property. An example of this is the network address property of a NetWare File Server object. Multi-valued properties can have more than one value defined for it. An example of this is the telephone number property for user objects. Multiple telephone numbers can be defined for a user object.

Property values can be a numeric value, a string, or some special format as in the case of a network address on an IPX network (4-byte network address, 6-byte node address, 2-byte socket number).

For your organization, define which of the optional properties will have values defined for them. It is generally a good idea to define the optional properties for information purposes, so that the NDS database can be queried for information on these property values. However, certain oragnizations may not wish to give out the telephone number or other information on the users. In this case certain properties may not be defined, or NDS security may be used to allow only certain users to view information on the NDS objects.

Comparing NDS to the NetWare Bindery

NDS treats all resources on the network as objects belonging to a global database. This global database (directory) represents the network, and has a structure that corresponds to a logical view of the network. The directory is not kept in a centralized location, but portions of it (partitions) are distributed across servers on the network, and it is therefore a *distributed database.* This is different from the approach used in pre-NetWare 4.0 based networks, where the resources on a server were centrally located in a flat database called the bindery. Because the bindery served as a centralized database, it could become a single point of failure.

The directory database in NDS is organized in a hierarchical fashion. This hierarchical structure maps well into the organizational structure of most organizations. And it can be used to represent logical relationships between network resources, such as grouping of resources under a node representing a department of an organization. It is interesting to contrast the differences between the NDS and the NetWare 3.*x* bindery, because this gives an insight into the improved manner in which network resources are managed in NetWare 4.*x*. Table 11.1 summarizes the differences between the NDS and the NetWare bindery.

Table 11.1
NDS vs. Bindery

Attribute/Feature	NDS	Bindery
Structure	Hierarchical	Flat
Users	Network-wide	Server-centric
Login	Network-wide	Server-centric
Passwords	Single password	Password per server
Groups	Network-wide	Server-centric
Location	Distributed	Server-centric

The bindery was used in earlier versions of NetWare to keep information on network resources in a flat database. This flat database did not represent the logical relationship between network resources. The bindery was server-centric, and was used to store information on resources available at a NetWare server, and not the entire network. As a result of this, tasks such as user account creation had to be performed on each server separately. User and group accounts had to be stored in the bindery of the server on which they were defined. There was no concept of a network wide user account. (There was an attempt to provide this capability using NNS, NetWare Name Service, but this was not a very successful attempt and was never popular because of a number of problems dealing with the implementation of NNS).

The NDS structure is hierarchical. This allows NDS to represent relationships between network resources in a manner that is more comprehensible for the user and the network administrator. The logical representation of resources in the NDS are called NDS objects. The NDS can also be used to store information about objects so that this information can be queried in much the same way the *white* and *yellow* pages of a telephone directory can be used. For instance, the user object information can be used to keep information such as phone numbers, fax numbers, electronic mail address, address, location, and so on. User and group accounts in the NDS are network wide in scope and this eliminates the need of the network administrator for creating user and group accounts on each server the user needs access to.

Many of the tasks such as user/group account creation, which in earlier releases of NetWare had to be done separately on each server, are eliminated, because the user/group account creation needs to be created just once in the directory. Once created this user account can be assigned rights to any network resource that is represented in the NDS, such as NetWare volumes and network printers. Other benefits of the NDS is that the user needs to remember just one password to the network. Once validated, the user's trustee assignments will give the user the necessary access privileges to network resources.

It is important to understand that NDS provides control of directory resources such as servers and volumes; but not control over the contents of volumes such as files and directories. Access to files and directories are provided by the trustee right mechanisms used in NetWare 3.*x*.

Understanding the NetWare Directory Database

NDS is a global, distributed database that keeps information on network resources in a hierarchical manner. The distributed nature of NDS allows it to store information on many types of objects such as users, printers, servers, and volumes that are of interest to the network user community (see fig. 11.5). The distributed information is actually stored on NetWare servers throughout the network in a manner that is transparent to the user. A directory synchronization mechanism is used, so that directory changes on any part of the NDS database are propagated throughout the network. In other words, NDS synchronizes itself to present a consistent view of itself to the rest of the network. The directory synchronization takes place automatically without user intervention. The network administrator can set certain parameters to minimize the affect of directory synchronization on network traffic.

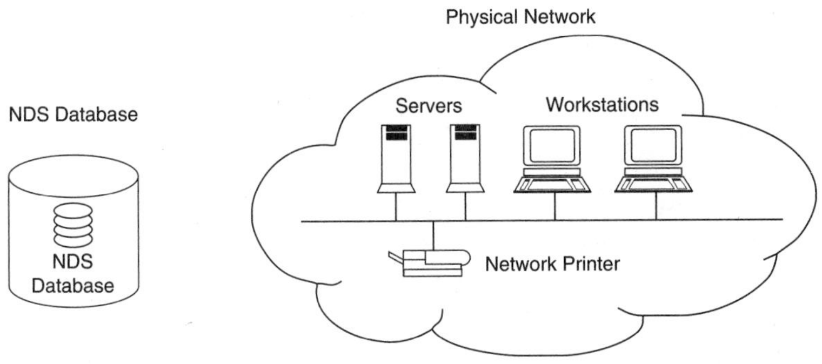

Figure 11.5
NDS database.

For security reasons, NDS is kept as a hidden data area on a storage volume. The NDS presents a hierarchical view of itself to the rest of the world. Access to any portion of the NDS is controlled by a new set of *object trustee assignments* made on NDS objects.

The hierarchical relationship in NDS is often described in terms of a directory tree, such as the one shown in figure 11.6

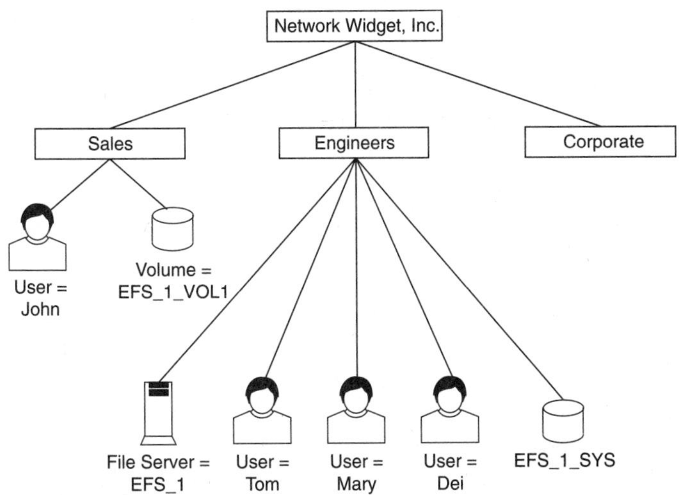

Figure 11.6
Hierarchical NDS tree for Network Widgets, Inc.

The hierarchical relationship allows network resources to be organized in a manner that reflects how the network is used, instead of the physical topology and connectivity of the network. The directory organization can be made to more closely match the user's view of the network. For example, in figure 11.6, the engineers Tom, Mary and Dei of the organization Network Widget, Inc. have user accounts defined under the departmental unit (called organizational unit, in NDS terminology) Engineers. Figure 11.7 shows that the users are not in the same physical location. In figure 11.7, engineers Tom and Mary are in the city of Dallas whereas user Dei is in the city of Los Angeles; but, since they all belong to the group Engineers, they will have similar needs to access network resources. Under these circumstances it makes sense to group them in an organizational unit called Engineers, regardless of their physical location.

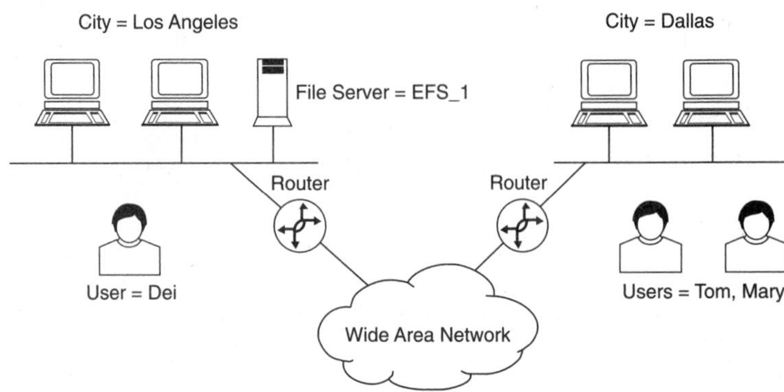

Figure 11.7
Physical network for Network Widgets, Inc.

The file server for the engineers of Network Widget, Inc. is currently defined in Los Angles. Should there be a need in the future to physically move the server to Dallas, the file server can be moved without changing the NDS view of the network. The file server EFS_1 still is under the organizational unit of Engineers in the NDS tree. In figure 11.6, you can see that volume EFS_1_SYS that is physically attached to the server EFS_1 is in the organizational unit Engineers, because it is primarily used by the engineers of the company. Another volume, called EFS_1_VOL1 is also physically attached to the server EFS_1, but its NDS representation is kept in the organizational unit SALES because it is primarily used by members of the sales team. One reason for the volume EFS_1_VOL1 to be kept in the SALES organizational unit, could be that the group SALES does not as yet have their own file server. From this discussion you can see that network resources can be placed in the NDS tree according to their use and the user's view of the network, rather than by physical location of the resource.

The NDS is based on the CCITT X.500 standard. CCITT is the Consultative Committee for International Telephone and Telegraphy. It is an international body that developes standards in the area of data communications. Many of its members are the standards making bodies of countries. CCITT publishes standards, and updates to existing standards at periodic intervals of 4 years.

NDS is not in complete compliance with X.500, because NDS is largely based on the 1988 X.500 recommendations. The X.500 standard has further evolved into the 1992 X.500 specification, but this was not available to the designers of NDS who started working on NDS before 1992.

For strategic reasons you can expect Novell's implementation of NDS to comply with the international consensus on X.500. Another area of expected change is the protocol mechanisms for keeping the NDS database updated, when changes are made to it (*directory synchronization*). These have not been completely specified in the X.500 standards. As a result of this Novell, like many other X.500 vendors (DEC, Retix, and so on), had to design their own directory services synchronization protocol to deal with directory synchronization. Many X.500 vendors, including Novell, are seeking common ways to implement X.500 complaint synchronization methods and services. Novell does provide an API to exchange data between other name services. This makes it possible to build name service gateways to other name services.

NDS complies closely with the X.500 recommendations. The details of the kind of objects that make up the directory are specific to NetWare-based networks. Other general classes of objects which are not

Novell-specific can be added to the NDS directory by making use of the NDS programming APIs. This makes it possible to integrate it with other vendors' X.500 directory implementations.

NDS Components

NDS has a hierarchical structure, and it uses a specific terminology to describe its components. Some of the terms have been derived from CCITT's X.500 recommendations, while others are specific to Novell. Before you can get a working understanding of NDS, you must understand the vocabulary and terms used to describe NDS.

Tree Structure of NDS

The NDS database is organized as a hierarchical tree. A *tree* is a computer science term used to describe a way of representing data starting from a single point called the *root*. The root of this tree has *branches*, which can in turn branch-off to other branches or *leaves*. Figure 11.8 illustrates this concept of tree, along with a picture of the NDS tree.

The tree has a single root (see fig 11.8). This is important to realize, because the NDS data base also has a single root. If you have several NDS databases constructed separately from each other, they will have separate roots. At the moment there is no way of dynamically exchanging NDS information between NDS trees with their own separate roots. Tools exist for combining several separate NDS trees (each with its own root) into a single larger NDS tree. An example of such a tool is DSMERGE which allows two NDS trees to be merged.

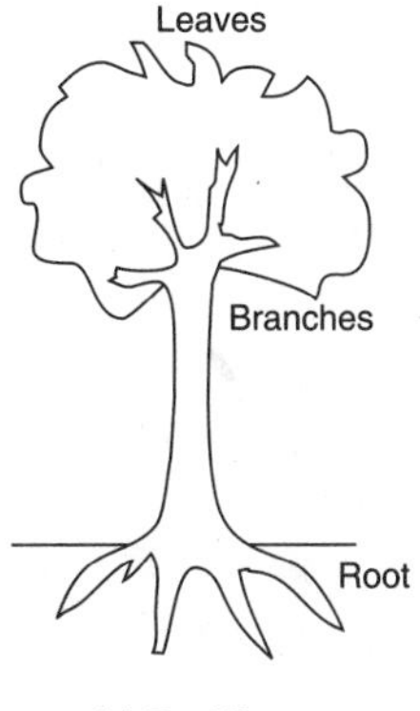

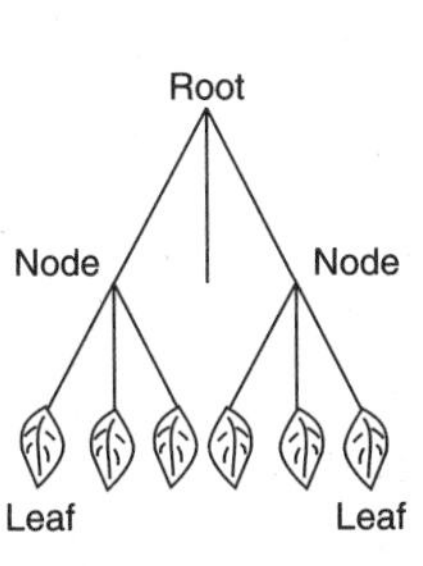

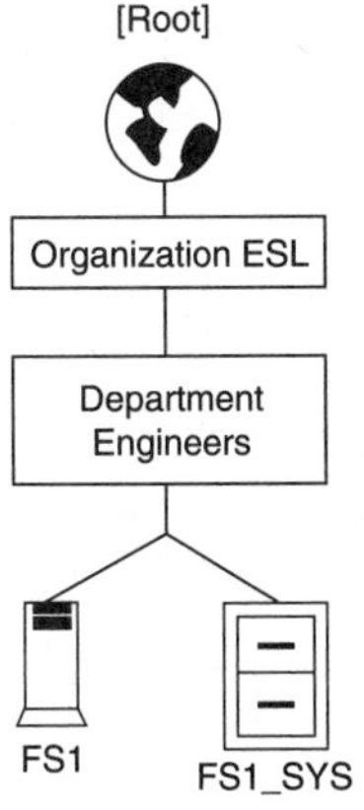

Figure 11.8
NDS Tree Components.

The root of a tree describes the first level of the tree, and is used to describe the entire tree. The [Root] object cannot be created using any of the NetWare adminstration tools; it is created during the installation of a NetWare 4.*x* server object, where you have the opportunity to install the server object in an existing NDS tree or define a separate NDS tree with its own [Root]. Once defined the [Root] object cannot be renamed, moved or deleted.

A *branch* from the root of a tree leads to another *node* on the tree, and describes a complete subtree (see fig. 11.8). A *node* on the tree that contains other nodes is called a *container object*. (All nodes of a tree represent a logical concept of an organization or a resource and are called *objects*.) A branch of a tree can therefore be seen as a container object and all the objects underneath it.

Container Objects

A *container* in NDS is an object that contains other objects such as other containers and resource and service objects. Containers provide a practical way of organizing objects by departments, geographic location, work groups, projects, common usage of network resources, or any other criteria that make it easier to use the network.

The container objects provide a convenient way for organizing other nodes into *groups* (see fig. 11.9). This is a very key advantage of NDS; that is, besides facilitating a logical organization of the NDS tree, container objects can be used as groups that can be assigned certain security rights, which then affect the security rights of all nodes in that container.

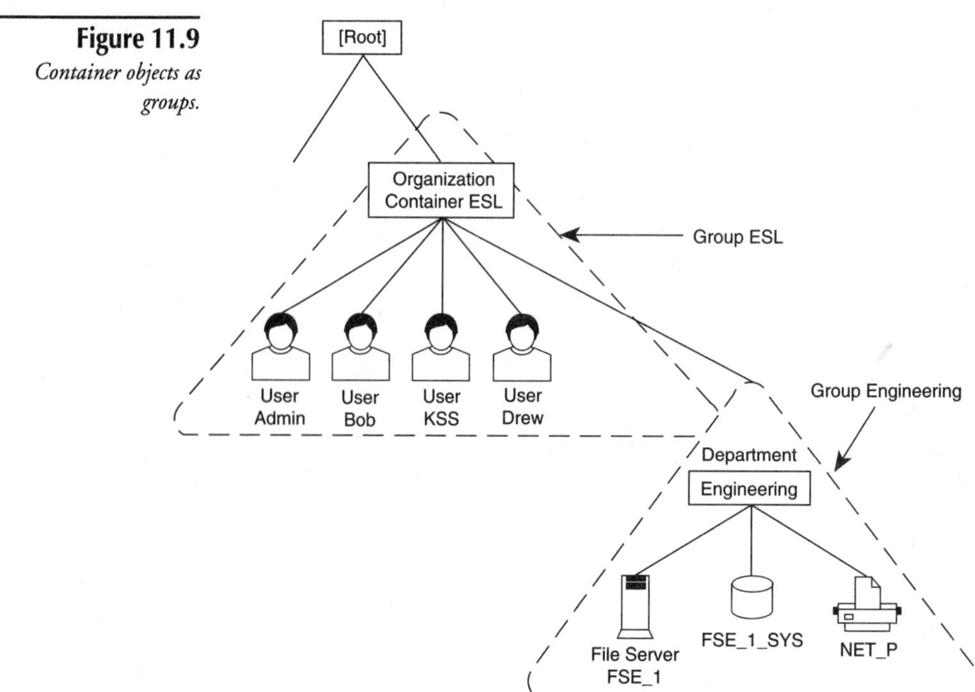

Figure 11.9
Container objects as groups.

The NDS defines the following container objects besides the [Root] object:

- Country
- Organization
- Organizational Unit

The *type* of a container is referred to as its object class. Each of the container types listed above have a separate object class definition. An object class definition defines the rules that govern the object's existence in the NDS tree. An example of such a rule is that the Country container can exist directly underneath the [Root] object. It cannot be contained in the Organization or Organizational Unit containers. This rule is described by the *Containment Classes* structure rules for NDS objects.

Leaf Objects

A node in the tree that does not (and cannot) contain any other nodes is called a *leaf object*. A leaf object is similar to the leaves of a real tree that do not have any branches and other leaves coming from it. A leaf object acts as a terminal point in the tree and represents a network resource or service (see fig. 11.10). A leaf object can only exist inside a container object.

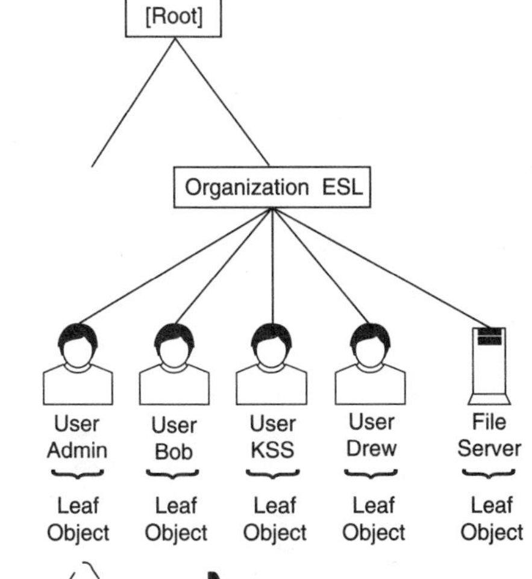

Figure 11.10
Leaf objects.

Object Class and Schema

A NetWare 4.*x* based network can have many different types of network resources and services, and each of them is described by a special type of leaf object. In our earlier discussion, you learned about file server and print server objects. These are all examples of leaf objects. The object definition (also called object type) for an object in the NDS database is called its *object class.* In database technology terms, the collection of the different object definitions possible in the database, and their scope and rules of existence and operation within the database, is called the *schema.* Since the NDS tree is a global distributed database, database terms are sometimes used to describe the NDS tree, and you should be familiar with them. The NDS schema is therefore a collection of object class definitions, for objects such as file servers, computers, printers, print servers, and so on (see fig 11.11). When an object of a type that can exist in the NDS schema is created, the object class is said to be *instantiated.* The object class implies a potential for an object of that class to exist in the database; it does not imply an existence of an object of that type. The object class must be instantiated (created) before an object belonging to that category can exist.

Figure 11.11
NDS schema.

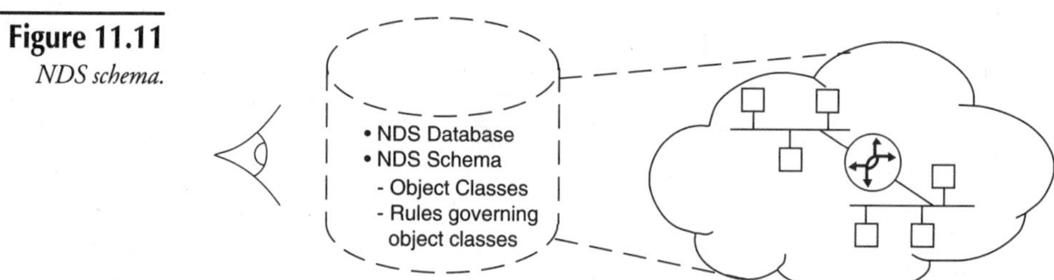

In the example in figure 11.8, the nodes ESL and Engineers are examples of container objects. They are container objects, because they can in turn *contain* other objects. The leaves FS1 and FS1_SYS are examples of leaf objects. These leaves are the terminal points in the tree, and cannot contain other objects.

A container that has objects defined in it is a *parent container* to the objects that it contains. Some object classes can contain other objects while other objects cannot. For instance leaf object classes cannot contain any other object classes. Container object classes can contain other object classes, but there are rules that govern what container class objects can exist in other container class objects. These structural rules are called *Containment Classes rules* and define where one type of object class may occur in relationship with other object classes. An object can exist in or *be subordinate to* only the objects listed among the object's containment classes. Table 11.2 shows the containment class rules for container objects.

Table 11.2
Containment Class Rules for Container Objects

Container Object	Containment Classes (can exist in)	Can Contain
[Root]	*Cannot* exist under any object. Parent to all objects.	Country *Alias* (Alias can be to another country object only)
Country	[Root]	Organization Organizational Unit *Alias* (Alias can be to an Organization or Organizational Unit object only)
Organizational	[Root]	Country Organizational Unit Leaf objects
Organizational Unit	Organization Organizational Unit	Organizational Unit Leaf objects

Containers and Directories in File Systems

Containers are similar to directories in a file system. A directory in a file system can contain other subdirectories and files. In a similar manner a container in NDS contains other sub-containers and leaf objects (network resources and services) (see fig 11.12). A directory in a file system can be used for organizing files. Containers in NDS are used to organize network resources. One difference between an NDS tree and a file system directory tree is that there are limitations in the NDS tree where container and leaf objects can occur.

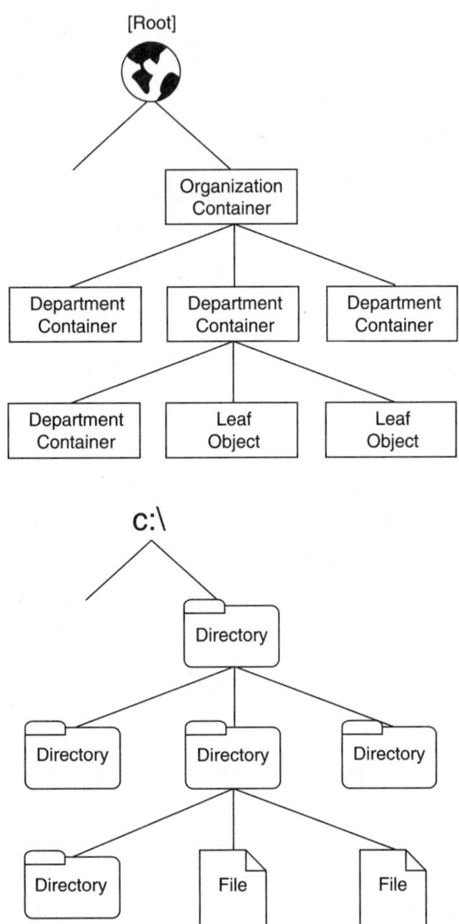

Figure 11.12
Containers vs. Directories for File System.

There is no limit to the NDS tree depth. For practical reasons of NDS tree management, you may want to limit the depth of the NDS tree.

The container typically represents an organization, department within an organization, work group center, responsibility center, geographical location, shared information, or network usage. The container and its relationship with other objects in the tree must be planned carefully. Once the NDS tree is constructed, it is difficult, at the moment, to make changes. Tools for major restructuring of NDS are expected to become available.

Object Names

All nodes of the NDS tree must have a name, called the *object name*. The root of the tree has the fixed object name of [Root]. Object names are case insensitive. This means that two objects with the name NW4CS_SYS and nw4Cs_sYs have the same object name. Therefore, [root] and [Root] refer to the same object—the root of the directory tree.

Objects that are directly in the same container cannot have the same name. Therefore, in figure 11.13, the container ENGINEERS cannot have two volume objects with the names NW4CS_SYS and nw4Cs_sYs. It is not possible to have the same name even for two objects that have a different object class. Therefore container ENGINEERS cannot have a file server object named ZAPHOD and a user object named ZAPHOD These two objects can, however, exist in different containers as seen in figure 11.14.

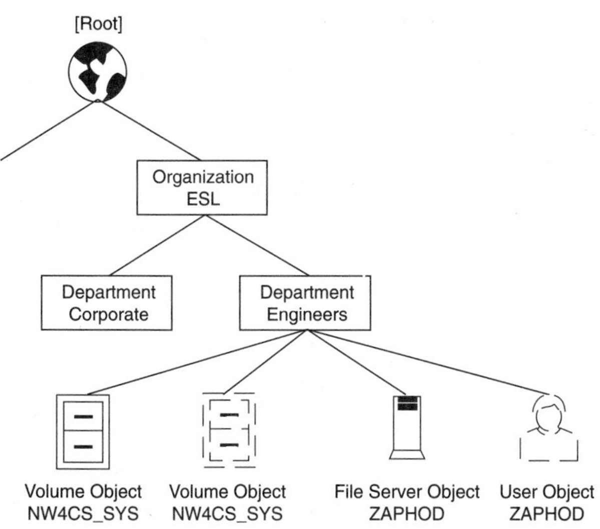

Figure 11.13
Object names in a container.

Even though object names are case insensitive, the case of the name at the time of creating the object, is preserved for display purposes. This means that if you create an object named mY_worKstation, it will appear in the case used for the object name at the time the object was created. Leaf objects can be renamed, but not container objects.

To make object names consistent, and more readily understandable, it is important for an organization to have guidelines about object naming conventions.

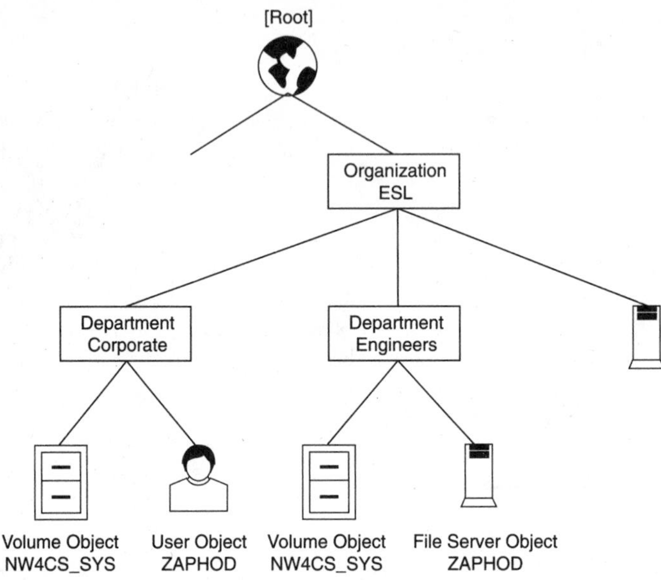

Figure 11.14
The same object names in different containers.

An object name can be up to 64 characters long, and can consist of alphanumeric characters, dashes, underscores, parenthesis, and even spaces. If spaces are used, you will have to enclose the object name in quotation marks (") for it to be recognized in command line utilities and login scripts. For simplicity, you may wish to avoid this. It is even possible to construct a name with a single blank. Figure 11.15 shows an interesting example of an NDS tree that has two objects with a blank name. The first container object under ESL and the user object underneath it have a blank object name. Even though blank names may be permitted, it is a good idea to avoid them, as the utilities that query NDS do not handle them in a consistent manner.

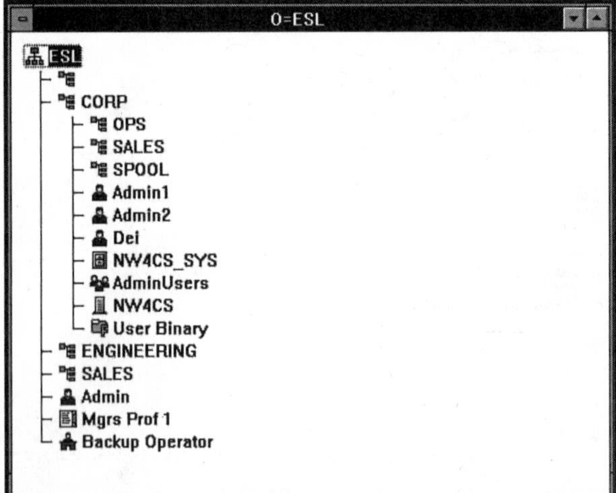

Figure 11.15
Blank name objects.

Brackets, periods, and percent signs are not permitted in object names. A few special characters such as plus(+), period(.), and equals (=) must be preceded by a backslash (\). In general, it is a good idea to avoid using special characters in object names, as the names then become confusing and difficult to use and remember.

NDS may even allow you to use characters that are designated illegal in the documentation for creating names of objects. However, they are not guaranteed to work in a consistent manner in the NDS-based commands and utilities. For this reason, it is best to avoid them.

Types of Container Objects

NDS supports four types of container objects:

- The [Root] object
- The Country object
- The Organization Object
- The Organizational Unit object

Figure 11.16 shows the icons used to represent these different container objects. These icons are displayed when using the Windows based network administration tools. The US container, in this figure, represents the Country object. The containers AT&T, DEC, ESL, ESL_KSS, LG, LTREE, MITEL, RSA, SCS, WELFLEET, WIDGET all represent Organization container objects. The containers ACCOUNTING, CORP, R&D, SALES represent Organizational Unit container objects.

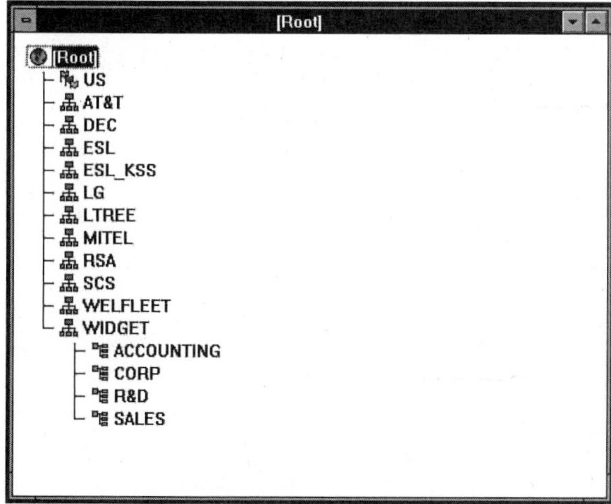

Figure 11.16
Symbolic representations of container objects.

The [Root] Container Object

Of these the most frequently used container objects are the Organization object and the Organizational Unit object. There can be only one [Root] object per NDS tree. The [Root] object cannot be renamed or deleted. It can have rights to other objects, or other objects can have rights to it.

It is possible to install NetWare 4.*x* on separate LANs, each with their own [Root] object. This could easily happen if the network was built in different segments, and final connectivity of the separate network segments was done at a later time. Under these circumstances, several [Root] objects could exist, each describing a different tree. Now, if you connect the network segments together, the networks represented by the different [Root] objects will not be able to communicate (see fig. 11.17) through normal NDS mechanisms.

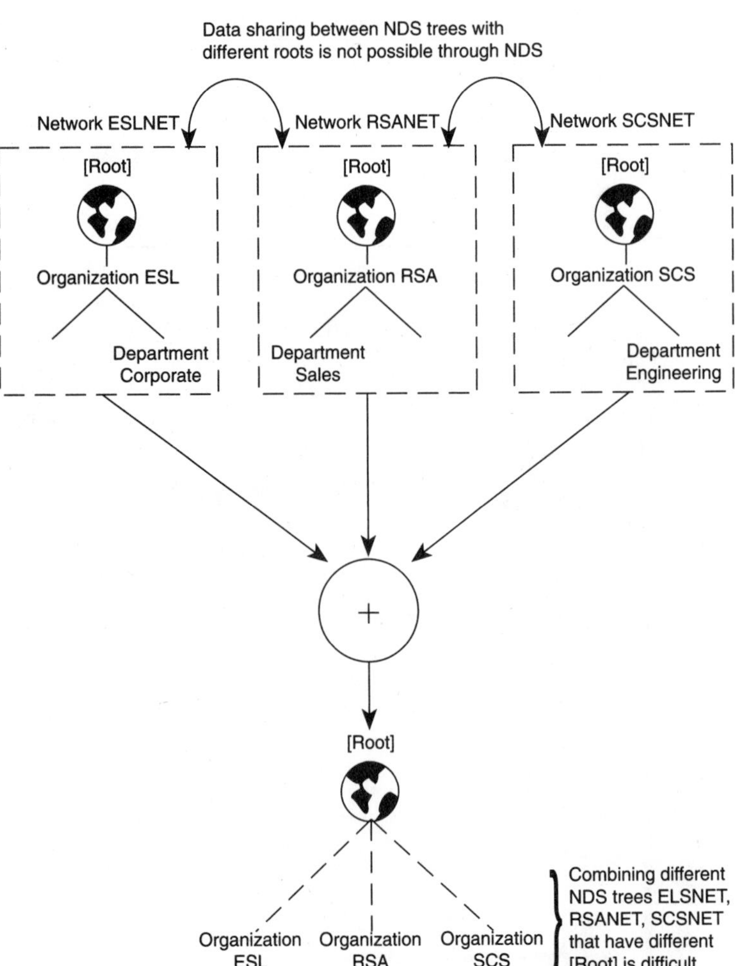

Figure 11.17
Multiple [Root] objects and sharing of data.

It is possible, however, to have two servers, FS1 and FS2, each defined in its own unique tree, TREE1 and TREE2. You could login to FS1 under TREE1 as a valid NDS user. If you were to map a drive to a volume on FS2 using the NetWare 3.*x* syntax, NetWare will automatically switch to bindery emulation mode and attempt to connect you. You could then have access to the FS2 object, even though it is in a separate NDS tree.

1. Login to TREE1 as a valid NDS user
2. MAP N FS2/SYS:

This is the NetWare 3.*x* syntax, which will cause NetWare to switch to bindery emulation mode.

When installing a NetWare 4.*x* server that is *not the first server* that was installed, you should have physical connectivity from this NetWare 4.*x* server to the rest of the network, so that the server can be installed as part of the NDS tree.

For extremely secure environments, it may be desirable to have separate [Root] objects. This will ensure that users in a directory tree under one [Root] cannot access or communicate with users under another [Root].

The [Root] object can contain only Country, Organization, and Alias objects. Of these, Country and Organization are container objects, and Alias is a leaf object.

The Country Container Object

The Country object is part of the X.500 recommendations, but it is seldom used in commercial networks based on NetWare 4.*x*, because many organizations are multi-national in character and are not organized along country boundaries. Also, if a country object is used, then that branch of the NDS tree cannot use simplified object names (you will learn more about this later). Country object names are limited to two characters. They can be any two characters, but it is recommended that the CCITT's two-letter designations for countries be used. Figure 11.18 shows an NDS tree with the two-letter designations for several countries. From this figure you can see that the Country object must be placed directly below the [Root] object. The Country object is optional. If used, it must occur directly under the [Root] object.

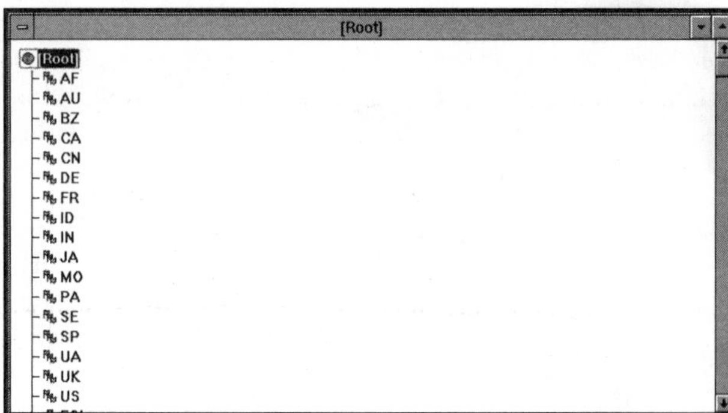

Figure 11.18
Country objects in an NDS tree.

The Country object can contain only Organization and Alias objects.

The Organization Object

The Organization object represents the name of the organization. Figure 11.19 shows an NDS tree that has the Organization objects. Notice the special icon used to represent the Organization object. At least one Organization object must be used in an NDS tree. It can occur directly under the [Root] object or a Country object. In figure 11.19, the organization objects CISCO, HP, IBL, IBM, MS, NOVELL are placed directly underneath the Country object US. Also, organizations AT&T, DEC, ESL, ESL_KSS, LG, LTREE, MITEL, RSA, SCS, WELLFLEET, WIDGET are placed directly underneath the [Root] object. These are the only places that the NDS schema allows an organization object to be placed.

Figure 11.19
Organization objects.

The Organization object can contain any leaf object and Organizational Unit object, but it cannot contain another Organization object.

The Organizational Unit Object

Since an organization is usually subdivided into specialized functions, such as by department, network usage, common jobs, location, work groups, responsibility centers, and so on, the Organizational Unit object can be used to represent the organization's subdivision. The Organizational Unit must occur under an Organization object or another Organizational Unit object. An Organizational Unit cannot occur directly under the [Root] object or Country Object.

Figure 11.20 shows examples of an Organizational Unit object and the different locations in the NDS tree that it can occur. The organizations HP, MS, NOVELL that are in the Country container object have organizational units such as CORP, ENGINEERING, MARKETING and DISTRIBUTION directly underneath them. The organization ESL_KSS that is directly underneath the [Root] has organizational units CORP, ENG, SALES underneath it. Notice that CORP is used as an organizational unit name in more than one organization. The object naming rules require an object name to be unique only within the same *level* of the container, and this allows the same object names to be used in different containers.

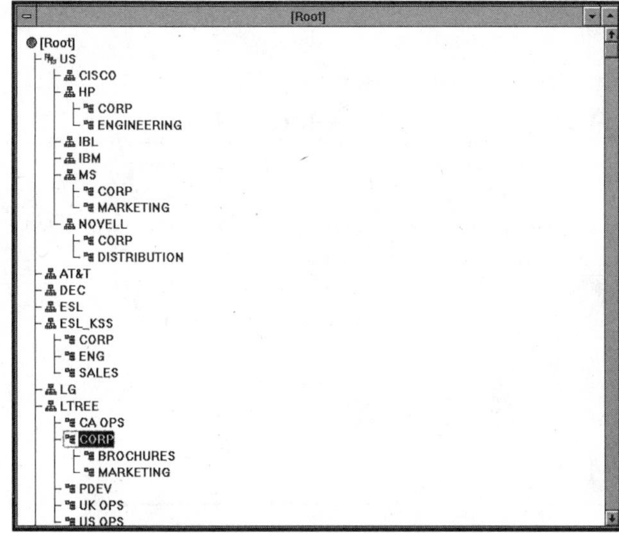

Figure 11.20
Organizational Unit objects.

In figure 11.20, organization LTREE has an organizational unit CORP underneath it. And CORP has two other organizational units, BROCHURES and MARKETING, directly underneath it. This is typical of many organizations that can be expected to have subdivisions within a department of an organization.

The Organizational Unit object can contain any leaf object and Organizational Unit object.

Attribute Types

As part of the X.500 system of naming objects, each object type is represented by an attribute designator. For example, Country objects have the attribute type C. This means that the Country object US is represented as:

```
C=US
```

The other container objects, Organization and Organizational Unit, have the attribute types of O and OU, respectively. Therefore the organization IBM will be represented by:

```
O=IBM
```

and an organizational unit SALES would be represented by:

```
OU=SALES
```

A leaf object that represents a resource or a service has the attribute type designator CN (Common Name). Therefore, the file server named NW4CS, would be represented as

```
CN=NW4CS
```

The different attribute types are summarized in table 11.3. All attribute types except the one for [Root] are part of the X.500 recommendations.

Table 11.3
Attribute Type Designators

Object	Container/Leaf	Attribute Type
[Root]	Container	No special attribute type. Designated by [Root] itself.
Country	Container	C
Organization	Container	O
Organizational Unit	Container	OU
Leaf Object	Leaf	CN

Leaf Object Types

Leaf objects are the actual representations of network resources. The other objects such as [Root], Country, Organization, and Organizational Unit are logical in nature and are used for organizational purposes.

The NDS schema, by default permits only the following leaf objects:

- AFP Server
- Alias
- Computer

- Directory Map
- Group
- NetWare Server
- Organizational Role
- Print Server
- Printer
- Print Queue
- Profile
- User
- Volume
- Bindery Object
- Bindery Queue
- Unknown

These are the only standard leaf objects that are currently available.Each of these leaf objects are discussed next.

AFP Server Object

The AFP Server leaf object is currently used for informational purpose only. It represents an *AppleTalk Filing Protocol* (AFP) server that is on your network. This could be a Macintosh computer running the AFP protocols, or even a VAX server emulating AFP protocols. The AFP server can be used to store information such as the network address, users, and operators. One of the benefits of NDS is that it can be queried for information in a manner similar to databases. So if for each AppleTalk server on your network, you have an AFP Server object (see fig. 11.21) , then you can make general queries such as: "Show me all AppleTalk servers in container O=ESL."

Figure 11.21
AFP Server object.

AFP Server : AFP1

Identification

Name:	AFP1
Other Name:	AFP_SRV_1
Description:	VAX Server Emulating AppleTalk Protocols.
Location:	SALES Building 2, Computer Room
Department:	PCB sales
Organization:	SCS Inc.
Version:	Test Version
Serial Number:	1728121729
Connections:	

Identification | Resources | See Also | Users | Network Addresses

OK | Cancel | Help

Alias Object

The NDS system is hierarchical in nature, and the object naming syntax (as you will learn later in this chapter) consists of enumerating the NDS objects starting from the leaf, all the way up to the top of the tree. If you try to reference an object that is not in your container, then the naming syntax becomes a little complicated, especially for end users who do not have the training to understand the NDS naming convention (see fig 11.22).

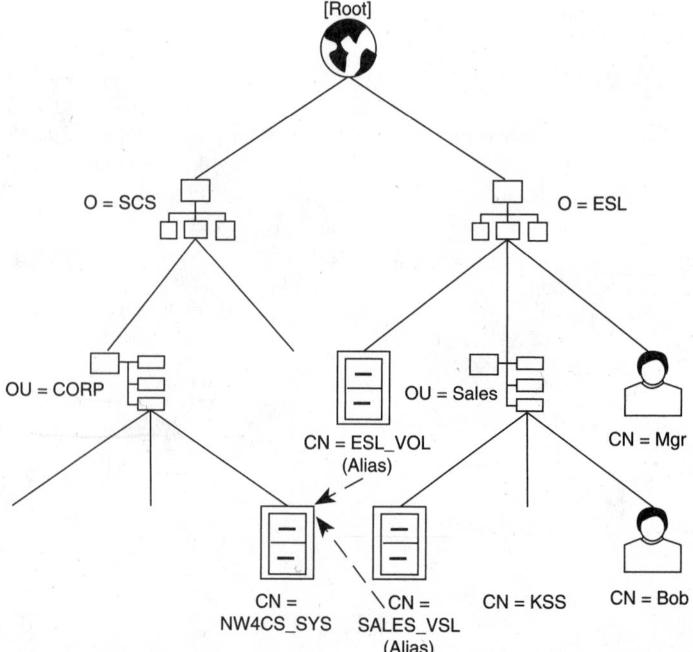

Figure 11.22
Accessing another object via alias.

NDS permits the definition of an object called the alias object. An alias object can point to a leaf or a container object. This is similar to the concept of symbolic links used in operating systems such as UNIX, except that UNIX symbolic links apply to file systems, whereas alias objects are links to leaf objects in the NDS tree. Figure 11.23 shows the information that you need to supply at the time of creating an alias object. In this dialog box, the name MyAliasName is going to be the new name of the alias object which is going to be created under [Root] (shown highlighted in the figure). The value for the aliased object can be entered directly or by selecting the browse icon next to this field, which shows the select object dialog box. Since the alias object is being created under [Root], the only possible objects that can be aliased are the organization and country objects. An attempt to alias another object produces an error message.

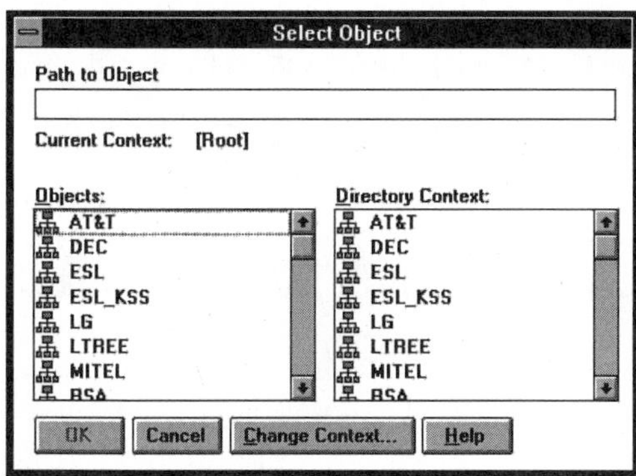

Figure 11.23
Alias Object Creation.

Computer Object

A computer object is used to represent a non-server computer such as a workstation, minicomputer, or mainframe. It can even be used to represent a router, which can be seen as a specialized computer with multiple network boards and routing logic implemented in firmware or software. A computer object can contain information such as network address, computer serial number, computer operator, etc., (see fig. 11.24).

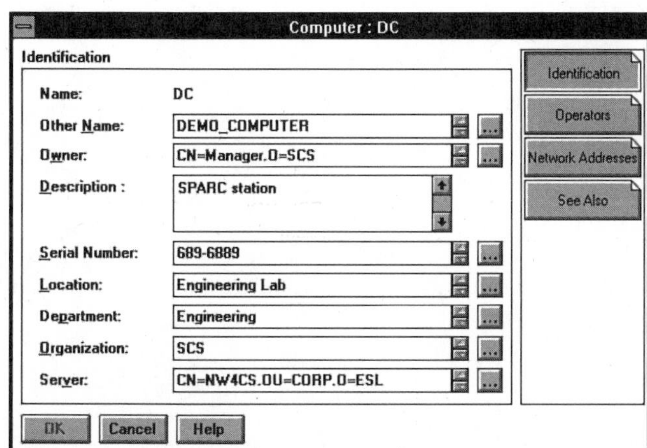

Figure 11.24
A computer object.

Directory Map

A directory map object contains a reference or pointer to a directory on a volume object anywhere in the NDS tree. Currently, MAP objects are only used in the MAP command which allows a workstation drive letter to refer to network directory on a server. Use of the directory map objects can simplify the MAP command that is used to point to volume objects in other containers.

A very important use of the MAP command is in login scripts. Login scripts are a sequence of instructions that get executed when a user logs in. They are primarily used to set up a user's network environment. Consider the situation in which a login script that contains the MAP command to map the drive letter G is mapped to a directory in the volume object named FS1_VOL in container O=ESL. If at a later point the volume object is moved to another container, or if the directory path is changed, the mapping would be invalid and all references to the former location of the volume object and directory would have to change. If the Directory Map object was used to perform the mapping in the login script, only the Directory Map reference to the new volume/directory location would have to change, and the login scripts would not change. Figure 11.25 shows a Directory Map object in an NDS tree with some of its properties.

Figure 11.25
A directory map object.

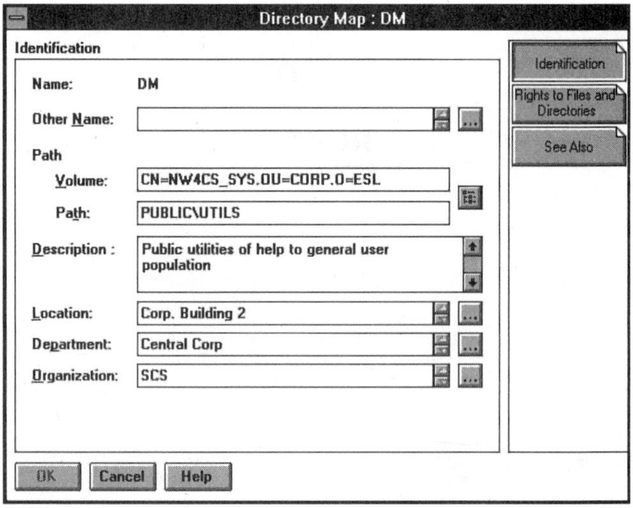

Group Object

A *group object* is used to refer to a collection of users in the NDS tree. The group object can only refer to a collection of user objects. The group object is used as a convenience for assigning a number of users the same security rights. Figure 11.26 illustrates the concept of groups. In figure 11.27, the users belong to the same container. This is the most common use of groups. The group object permits users from other containers to belong to the same group.

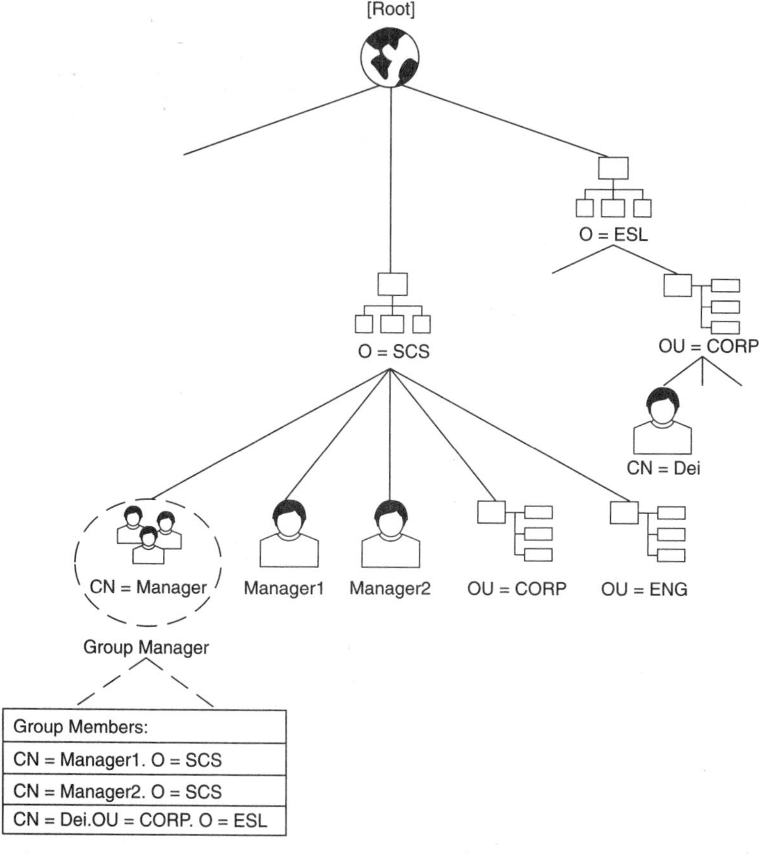

Figure 11.26
The concept of groups.

The group object is similar to the concept of groups in NetWare 3.*x*, except that Group is an NDS object, instead of a bindery object. Also, there are no default groups such as group EVERYONE that, by default, contains all users that were created on the NetWare 3.*x* server. To achieve the effect of a group such as EVERYONE, container objects can be used. All objects created in a container can be treated as a group by using the container name. A group object has a group membership property that is a list of user objects defined anywhere in the NDS tree. Members of a group object can only be user objects. Container objects, on the other hand, can be used as groups, but members of a container object can be any leaf object or other container objects. Container groups can be used to provide a hierarchical relationship between groups which is not possible with group objects and the groups used in NetWare 3.x. For instance, in NetWare 3.*x*, a group cannot contain other groups. This means the subset relationship between groups does not exist. Subset relationships between groups is possible when using containers that have a natural hierarchical relationship between them.

Figure 11.27 shows the group object membership property.

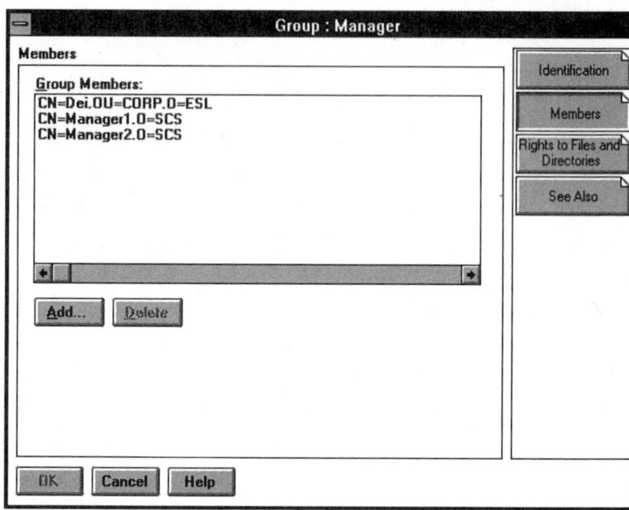

Figure 11.27
Group object membership property.

NetWare Server Object

The NetWare server object represents the physical NetWare server on a network. This is the object that provides *NetWare Core Protocol* (NCP) services. Some of the services provided by this object are represented as special objects in the NDS tree that reference the NetWare server. An example of this is the volume object, which may be part of the physical NetWare server, but is represented as a separate volume object.

The NetWare server object is created during installation. One of the parameters that you specify as part of the installation is the container in which the NetWare server should be placed. The NetWare server object contains information such as the physical location of the server object, its network address, the service it provides, and so on.

The NetWare server object is referenced by other objects in the NDS tree. An example of this is the Volume Object that references the NetWare server that acts as its host server. Without the NetWare server object you could not reference the volume object, and hence the files on the volume.

Figure 11.28 shows a NetWare server object in an NDS tree and some of its properties. Notice that the status of the server is shown as being Up, and its IPX address is IPX:F0000055:000000000001:0451. The F0000055 refers to the 8-hexadecimal digit internal number of the NetWare server; 000000000001 refers to the 12-hexadecimal digit node number; and 0451 refers to the 4-hexadecimal digit socket number for receiving NCP requests. The 000000000001 is a 12-hexadecimal digit node number and is different from the hardware address of the board, sometimes also called the node address or the MAC (Media Access Control) address. The version number of the server is reported as Novell NetWare 4.0[DS]. The DS stands for Directory Services.

NetWare Server : NW4CS

Identification

Name: NW4CS

Other Name: CS

Description : Main server for CORP

Location: Corp Building 4, Room 517

Department: CORP MAINT.

Organization: SCS

Net Address: IPX: F0000055:000000000001:0451

Status: Up

Version: Novell NetWare v4.0[DS]

Identification | Error Log | Operators | Supported Services | Resources | See Also | Users | Blocks Read | Blocks Written

OK | Cancel | Help | Accounting

Figure 11.28
The NetWare Server object.

Organizational Role Object

The Organizational role refers to a position or role within a department or organization. Usually a set of responsibilities and tasks are associated with that position. An example of such a role is the backup operator who needs access to certain volumes to perform the backup operation. Another example could be the print server operator. A user object can be assigned to be an occupant of the organizational role object. In this case, the user object inherits all the rights that have been assigned to the organizational role object (see fig. 11.29). If the responsibility for performing the task is passed on to another user, the user occupant of the organizational role object can be changed to reflect this.

11

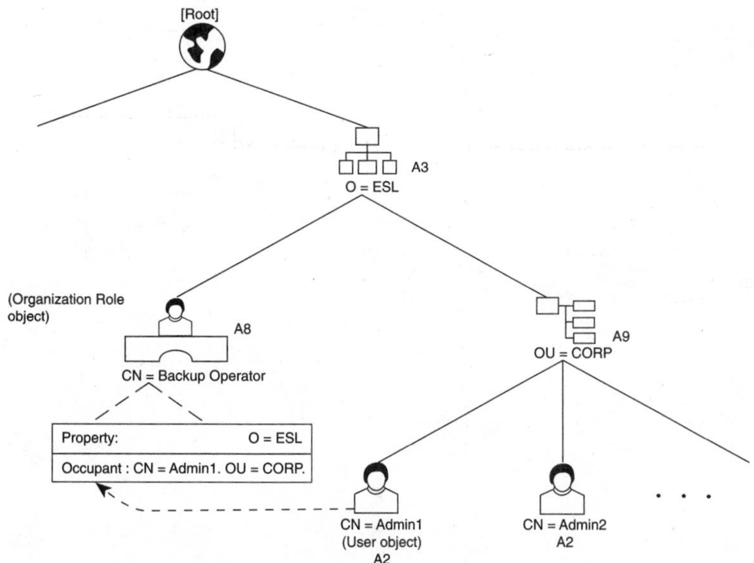

Figure 11.29
The relationship between a user object and an organizational role object.

The organizational role object is useful in situations where the task performed by the organization role does not change, but the persons fulfilling that role changes. For example, the person assigned to perform backup tasks could change depending on the workload of individuals in an organization. Instead of changing the rights of the user for performing a certain task, these rights could be assigned just once to the organizational role object. The occupant of the organizational role object could be changed, and this would give the assigned occupant sufficient rights to perform the organizational role's task. Figure 11.30 shows the organizational role object and the individual occupying that role at the moment. Only user objects can be assigned to the property Occupant. Figure 11.30 indicates that the occupant of the organization role is the user object CN=Admin1.OU=CORP.O=ESL

Figure 11.30
An organizational role object.

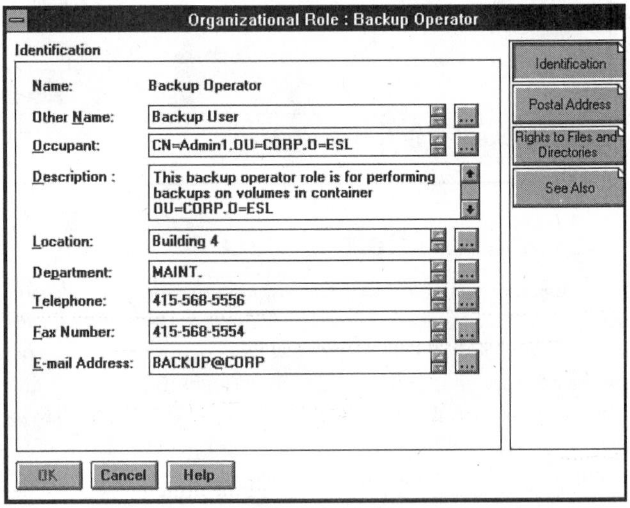

Print Server Object

A print server object describes the services provided by the NetWare Print Server. The print server object is created by utilities PCONSOLE and *NetWare Administrator Tool* (NWADMIN). It contains a reference to all the Printer objects it services.

Figure 11.31 shows the print server object and some of its properties in the NDS tree. Notice that the print server has a property called the Advertising Name. This is the name used by the print server to advertise its services using *Service Advertising Protocol* (SAP). The status of the print server indicates that it is down.

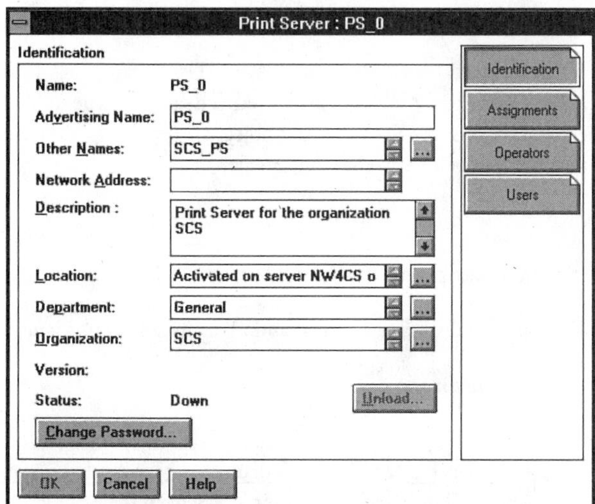

Figure 11.31
A print server object.

Print Queue Object

The print queue object is used to describe the network print queues. The print queue has a reference to the volume object on which the actual print jobs are stored. The print queue is assigned to a printer object. Print jobs sent to the printer object are sent to the associated print queue. As in NetWare 3.*x*, print jobs can also be sent to the print queue.

Figure 11.32 shows the print queue object in the NDS tree. Notice that the Volume property indicates the volume object that is used to support the print queue. Print queues are stored in the QUEUES directory on the specified volume.

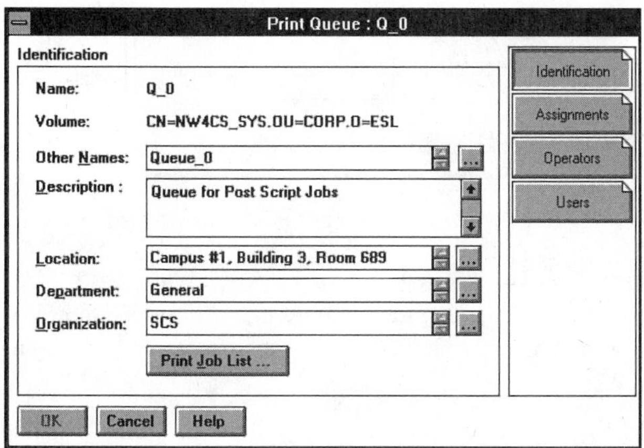

Figure 11.32
A print queue object.

11

Printer Object

The printer object is used to describe the physical network printer device. The print queue object has a reference to the volume object on which the actual print jobs are stored. The print queue in turn is assigned to one of the printer objects. Print jobs sent to the printer object are sent to the associated print queue. As in NetWare 3.*x*, print jobs can also be sent to the print queue.

There are currently more restrictions when sending jobs to printer objects. For instance,

1. You must be a user of *all* the queues assigned to the printer object.

2. You must have Browse NDS rights to the printer object and all assigned print queue objects.

3. You need to designate a default queue for the printer object.

Figure 11.33 shows a printer object in the NDS tree and the properties of the print object that contain references to other printer related objects. In this figure the Print Queue's property list has just one queue object assigned to it at a priority of 1 (highest). This means that print jobs sent to the printer object will be sent to the queue represented by the object: CN=QUEUE_0.OU=CORP.O=SCS. The print server this printer services is CN=PS_0.OU=CORP.O=SCS.

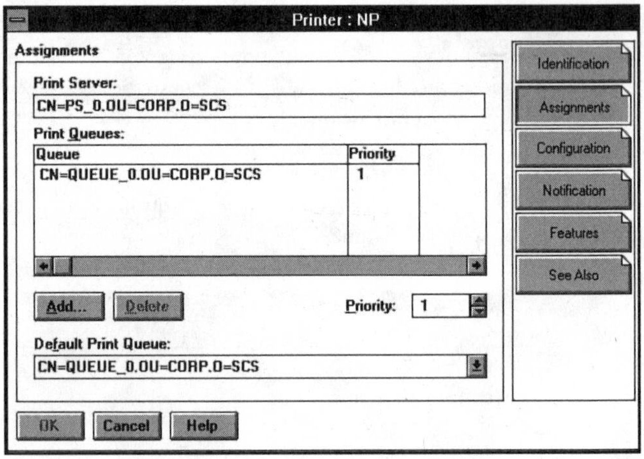

Figure 11.33
A printer object and the assignment properties.

Profile Object

This is an object that represents common actions that are performed during the login processing. It represents a login script that is shared by a number of users. The user objects that share the login script can be in different containers.

The profile object is listed as a property of a user object. It is executed when an individual uses the user object to log in to the network. Other types of login scripts such as the system login script and user login scripts exist. However, these are properties of the container object and the user object, and do not exist as separate NDS objects. The Profile object is the only login script type that can exist as an independent NDS object.

Figure 11.34 shows a profile object in an NDS tree, and the login script contained in the profile object.

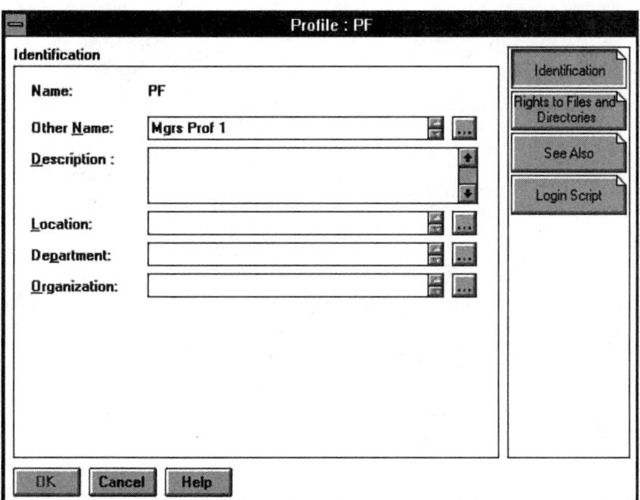

Figure 11.34
A profile object.

User Object

A user object represents the user account of the individual that logs in to the network. This is the most important object as far as the user is concerned. Changes made to this object affect the user directly. The user object must exist for every user that needs to login to the network. The user object is defined in the NDS tree, which makes it different from NetWare 3.*x*, where user objects were defined on a server. Using this single user object, an individual can access all the servers and other network resources to which the user has been assigned rights.

Some of the attributes (called *properties* in NDS terms) of the user object are a home directory on a volume object that the user has rights to, login restrictions, enabling/disabling intruder lock out mechanism, and so on.

Figure 11.35 shows a user object defined in the NDS tree and some of its properties.

A user object with the special name USER_TEMPLATE can be used as a template for creating default property values for user objects within that container. There can be only one USER_TEMPLATE object within a container (Organization, Organizational Unit containers) that allows the creation of such objects.

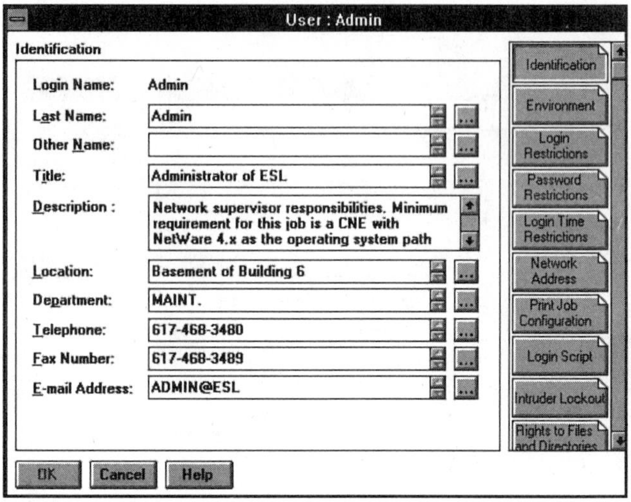

Figure 11.35
A user object.

Volume Object

The volume object represents the physical volume that is attached to the server. It represents data storage on the network and is used to represent the file system on the network and for storing print jobs associated with a network queue.

Though the volume object appears to be an object that is independent of the NetWare server, the volume object has a logical connection to the NetWare server object, to which it is attached. For this reason, volume objects have a property called the *host server* that associates the volume with its host NetWare server (see fig. 11.36).

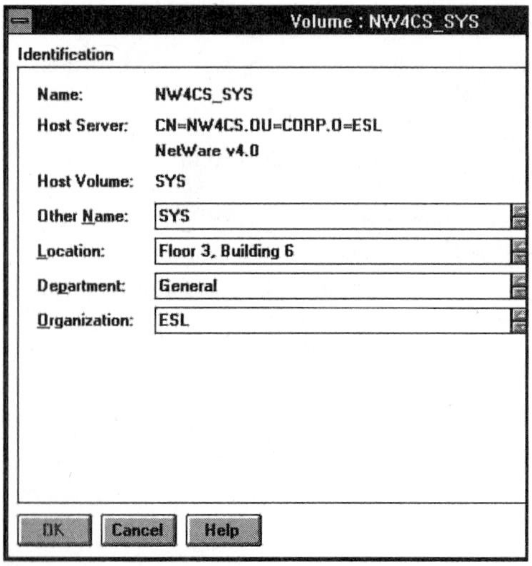

Figure 11.36
A volume object.

The volume object is created when the NetWare 4.*x* server is first installed in a container. The volume is given a default NDS name that consists of the name of the NetWare 4.*x* server, followed by an under score, followed by the name of the physical volume such as SYS, VOL, and so on. The physical name of a volume is the name given when the volume was first initialized as part of the installation process using the INSTALL NLM.

```
NDS volume object name = Object Name of Server _ Physical     Volume Name
```

Therefore, if the NetWare server object name is NW4CS, the first physical volume on it, which has the name SYS, will have an NDS name of NW4CS_SYS. If the server has a second volume named VOL1, its NDS name will be NW4CS_VOL1.

If you were to bring a server down, and bring it up with a different name, the new volume object names based on the new name of the server will appear. The old volume names will become Unknown objects.

Bindery Object

The bindery object is created when placing a NetWare 3.*x* server/service in the NDS tree as part of the upgrade or migration utility. The internals of this object cannot be managed by NDS. The bindery object is used to provide bindery emulation services, which allow a NetWare 4.*x* server to be accessed by NetWare 3.*x* client software that expects to see a bindery based server.

For NetWare 4.*x* servers to be accessed by NetWare 3.*x* client software, the SET BINDERY CONTEXT parameter needs to be set at the NetWare server. This parameter is set by default during the NetWare server installation. Certain utilities such as SBACKUP.NLM and AUDITCON.EXE use bindery emulation. These will not work correctly if BINDERY CONTEXT is not set.

Bindery Queue Object

The bindery queue object represents a queue placed in the NDS tree as part of the upgrade or migration process. It represents a NetWare 3.*x* print queue and is used to provide compatibility with bindery-based utilities and applications.

Unknown Object

The unknown object represents an NDS object whose object class cannot be determined because its NDS information has been corrupted. Figure 11.37 shows an object of unknown type under the container O=ESL. The unknown object is the first one listed under O=ESL, and has the question mark (?) icon next to it.

An unknown object can appear if you bring the server down and then up again specifying a different server name. The new volume names will appear, and the old volume names will become unknown objects. Also, if the object that an alias volume object points to is removed, the alias object appears as an unknown object.

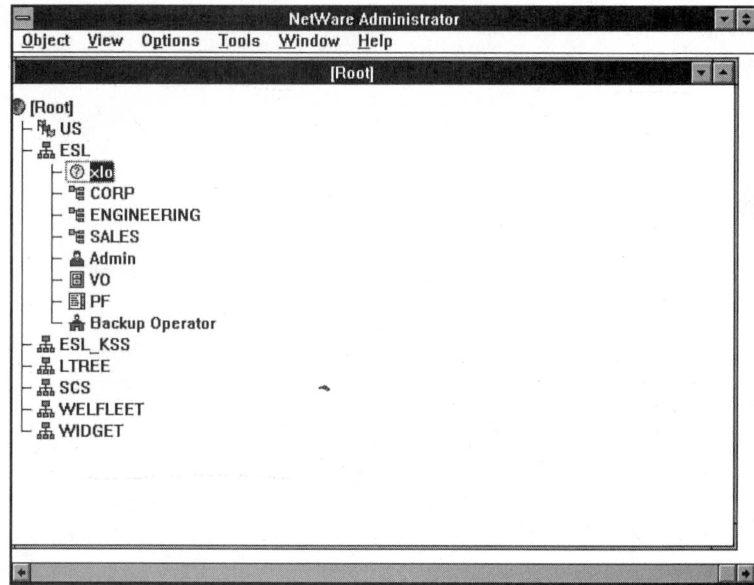

Figure 11.37
An unknown object.

Too many unknown objects in an NDS tree can signal an NDS directory corruption problem. Running DSREPAIR utility can fix this problem.

Table 11.4 summarizes the preceding discussion and gives a brief description of each type of leaf object.

Table 11.4
Leaf Object Descriptions

Leaf Object Class	Meaning
AFP Server	An AppleTalk File Protocol Server. Used for informational purpose.
Alias	A link to another object. This is a substitute name for an object that points to another object in the NDS tree.
Computer	An object that represents a computer: workstation, minicomputer, mainframe, and so on. It is used for informational purposes.
Directory Map	An object that makes it possible to perform a simple drive mapping to another container. Makes it easier to maintain login scripts.

Leaf Object Class	Meaning
Group	An object that has members that can be other objects. Similar to the concept of groups in NetWare 3.*x*, except that Group is an NDS object, instead of a bindery object.
NetWare Server	Represents a NetWare server on a network. This is the object that provides *NetWare Core Protocol* (NCP) services. Some of the services provided by this object are represented as special objects in the NDS tree that reference the NetWare server.
Organizational Role	Represents a position that has a certain set of defined tasks and responsibilities, and can be performed by a user assigned that role.
Print Server	Represents the Print Server service.
Print Queue	Represents the network print queue that holds the print jobs before they are printed.
Printer	Represents a network printer that can accept print jobs sent to it.
Profile	Represents an object that can be used for sharing of common actions that are performed during the login processing, regardless of whether they are in the same container.
User	The object that represents the user account. Used to contain information on the users who use the network.
Volume	The object that represents data storage on the network. Used to represent the file system on the network used for storing files and print jobs associated with a network queue.
Bindery Object	The object created when placing a NetWare 3.*x* server/service in the NDS tree as part of the upgrade process. Internals of this object cannot be managed by NDS. It is used to provide bindery emulation services.

continues

Table 11.4, Continued
Leaf Object Descriptions

Leaf Object Class	Meaning
Bindery Queue	Created as part of the upgrade process. It represents a NetWare 3.*x* print queue.
Unknown	Represents an NDS object whose object class cannot be determined because its NDS information has been corrupted. Running DSREPAIR can fix this problem.

Object Properties

An object has attributes called properties that represent the types of information that can be stored in the object. In this sense, an NDS object is similar to a record in a database; and the properties of the object are similar to the different field types that can be in a record.

Figure 11.38 shows the File Server object. The file server object in this figure shows the properties such as Name, Network Address, and Location. The actual values assigned for each of these properties is called the *property value.* A property value is an instance of the property type. Some of the properties of an object are mandatory and critical for the object to be used properly. Other properties are descriptive and used for informational and documentation purposes which allows the NDS to be used as a database of management information. The critical values are filled out by the network administrator at the time of creating the object. The values that are used for information and documentation can be filled out at a later time by the network supervisor who has *write* access to these properties. An example of properties for the user object that are for informational purposes is the list of telephone and fax numbers for that user, the postal address, and the job title of the user. The name property for a user object is mandatory.

Fill out as many property values for an object as you have information for, because the NDS tree can be used as a database of information that can be queried by using tools such as NLIST

Properties can be single-valued or multi-valued. A property such as the login name of the user is single-valued, whereas the telephone number for a user is multi-valued and represented as a list of values.

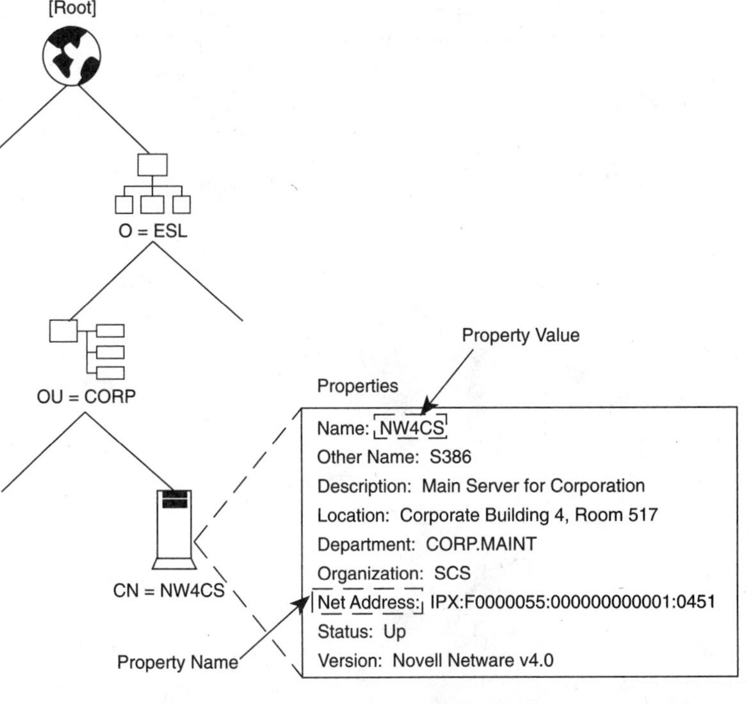

Figure 11.38
An NDS object and properties.

NDS Tree Case Study

Consider the organization MICROCON that makes advanced semiconductor devices. It has its manufacturing plants and research labs in San Jose, but its marketing and sales department is in New York. The San Jose facility has a VAX computer, a NetWare 4.*x* file server used for manufacturing and testing, and another NetWare 4.*x* server for R & D. The R & D engineers are Rick and James; the manufacturing engineers are Tom and Bill. Ed is the network administrator of the entire network.

The New York facility has two file servers NY_FS1 and NY_FS2 that are shared by all users at that facility. Kirk is the overall network administrator. The SALES department is a department within the MARKETING group. Currently, the sales persons are Janice, Jane and John. Ron works in the Marketing department, which at the moment is under-staffed.

A diagram of the physical network for MICROCON is shown in figure 11.39. Figure 11.40 shows the NDS tree structure for this organization. Notice that since users Ed and Kirk have a network administrator responsibility, their user objects are defined directly under the container OU=ENGINEERING and OU=MARKETING. Shared resources that are used by all users of the San Jose and New York networks

are also assigned directly within these containers. Examples of these shared resources are the printer FS1_PRT and the file servers NY_FS1 and NY_FS2. File servers FS1 and FS2 are placed in the containers OU=MANUFACTURING and OU=R&D. The SALES division is defined as a sub-container of OU=MARKETING. The salespersons user objects are defined in the OU=SALES container.

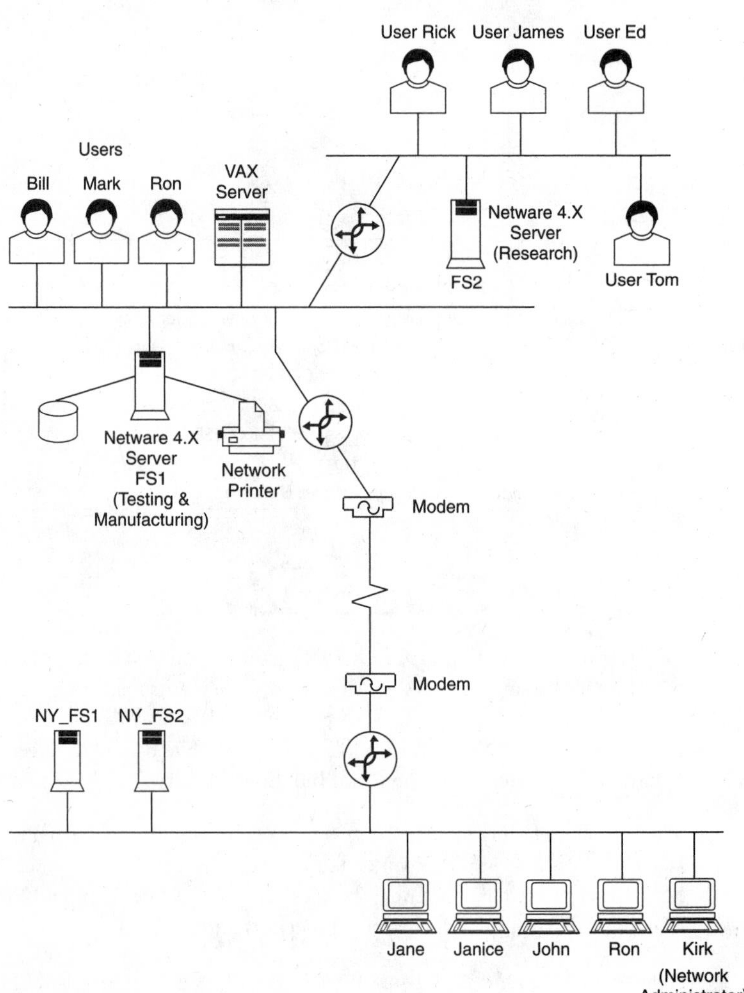

Figure 11.39 *The MICROCON physical network.*

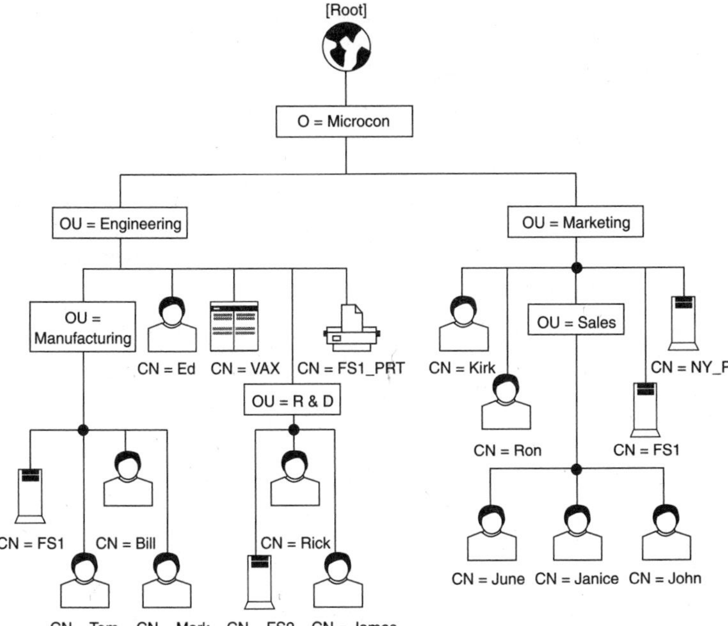

Figure 11.40
The MICROCON NDS Tree.

Using the preceding example, draw a physical network and an NDS tree for the organization, *Electronic Systems Lab* (ESL), based in London, with facilities in Toronto, New York and Paris. Research labs are located in Paris and Toronto, with marketing in New York and administration and sales in London. There is a support staff of network administrators in London that manages the entire network. Network services and hardware support at other sites are performed by local contractors. Each location has its own servers and printers. London and New York both have two file servers each and three network printers, while other locations have a single file server and two network printers attached to the file server. As the company grows, it is expected that additional servers will be added. All locations have their own print servers. The locations are tied together with communications links that run at 1.544 Mbps. The local networks used at each site are based on Ethernet.

Make reasonable assumptions for data that is not provided in this case study. For instance, you may have to invent names for users at each of the locations, and decide which of the users are going to be network administrators.

When you design the NDS tree for ESL, consider the following:

1. Decide on the depth of the tree. How many container levels do you need?
2. List all container objects that you need. Justify why you need each container.
3. Give appropriate names for container objects. Should they correspond to departments or geographical location?
4. Do you need one organizational unit, or more than one?

NDS Tools

The two primary tools for creating, deleting, and moving NDS objects are

- Network Administrator Tool (NWADMIN.EXE)
- NETADMIN

Another tool for batch creation of users is UIMPORT. UIMPORT is similar to the NetWare 3.*x* MAKEUSER tool. Since UIMPORT is not part of the scope of this book, it is not discussed.

The Network Administrator Tool is Windows and OS/2 *Graphical User Interface* (GUI) tool that can be used for managing NDS objects, whereas the NETADMIN tool is a text utility for creating NDS objects using C-Worthy menus.

Setting Up the Network Administrator Tool (NWADMIN.EXE)

To set up the NWADMIN.EXE tool, you must have installed the NetWare 4.*x* server and the DOS/ Windows client software. The following steps outline how to set up the NWADMIN tool for MS Windows.

From within Windows, perform the following:

1. If the NetWare group does not exist, do step 2. Otherwise skip to step 3.
2. Make sure that you are logged in to the NetWare 4.*x* network.

   Create a new program group called NetWare (or any other name you prefer) by doing the following:

   - From the Program Manager, select the File Menu.
   - Select the New option from the File menu.
   - Select the Program Group from the New Program Object dialog box and select the OK box.
   - In the Program Group Properties box, enter the following information for the Description and Program Group File.

Description:	**NetWare**
Group File:	**C:\WINDOWS\NWUTILS.GRP** (or whichever is the Windows directory)

3. If the program item for the NetWare Administrator Tool is set, you can skip this step. Otherwise, perform the following to create a program item for NetWare Administrator Tool.

   - Highlight the NetWare program group.
   - From the Program Manager, select the File Menu.
   - Select the New option from the File menu.
   - Select the Program Item from the New Program Object dialog box and select the OK box.
   - In the Program Item Properties box, enter the following information and select OK.

     Description: **`NetWare Administrator Tool`**

     Command Line: **`Z:\PUBLIC\NWADMIN`**

     Working Directory: **`Z:\PUBLIC`**

   Answer Yes to the question `The specified path points to a file that may not be available during later Windows sessions. Do you want to continue?` This message appears because the path is a network drive, and unless you are logged in to the network, the network drive will not be available.

   Also, you can specify a network drive other than Z. Z is used because you are likely to have at least one search drive, and this will be mapped to search drive Z. You will have to make sure that this search drive is not "root mapped", though.

   - The program item for NWADMIN should appear in the program group.

11

Using the NetWare Administrator Tool

This section will give you a guided tour in creating the NDS tree structure of figure 11.41 by using the NetWare Administrator Tool. This section assumes that you are familiar with using MS Windows. The term *click* on an icon means to position the mouse pointer on the icon and to click the left key once. The term *double-clicking* on an icon means to position the mouse pointer on the icon and to click the left key twice in rapid succession.

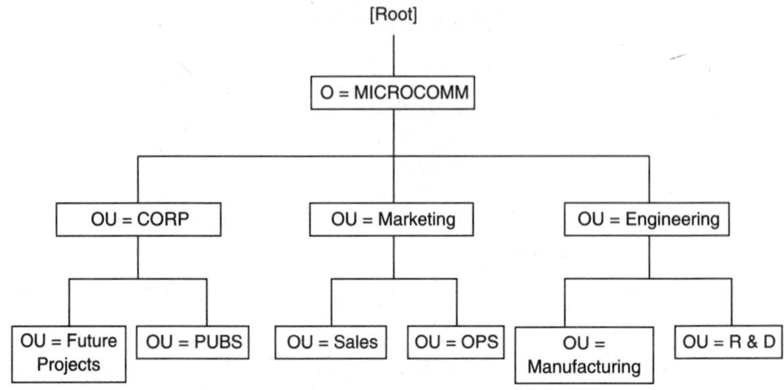

Figure 11.41
A sample NDS tree.

1. Log in to the network as an Administrator account.

   When the NDS services are first installed (at the time the first NetWare 4.*x* server is installed), a default network administrator user object Admin is created that has supervisor privileges to the entire NDS tree. You can use the Admin user object to log in to the network.

2. Activate the NetWare Group and start the NetWare Administrator Tool program item (you can do this *double-clicking* on the NetWare Administrator icon).

   You should see a screen similar to that shown in figure 11.42.

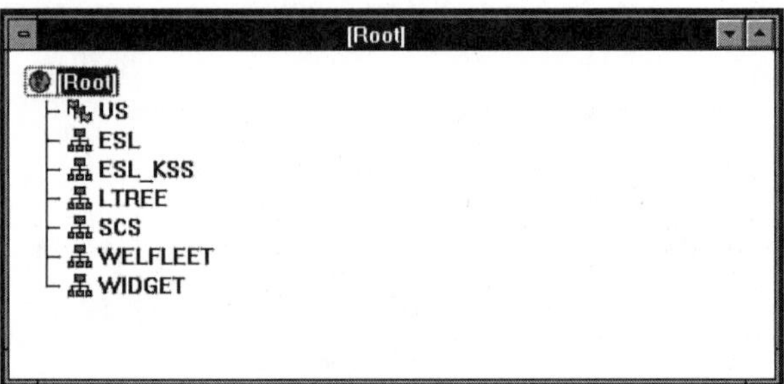

Figure 11.42
The NetWare Administrator menu.

The NDS tree in figure 11.42 shows the NDS tree starting from the current container. To see the NDS tree starting from the [Root], perform the following steps:

- Select the View menu
- Select the Set COntext option

Set the current context to [Root]. You can set this entering [Root] or by using the browse icon to browse through the NDS tree and select the context that you want to set as the current context.

3. Highlight the [Root] object. You can do this by clicking on it once.

   Right click on the [Root] object to see a list of operations that can be performed under the [Root].

   - Select Create

   You should see a list of objects that can be created under the [Root] object, as seen in figure 11.43.

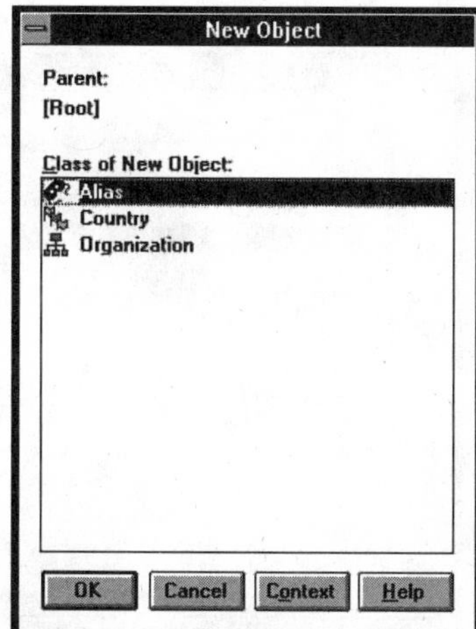

Figure 11.43
New objects under [Root] container.

4. Select the organization object and click OK.

   You should see a dialog box for creating the organization object (see fig. 11.44).

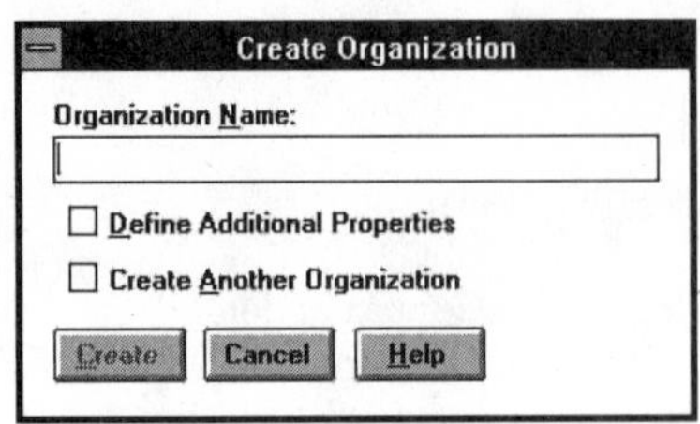

Figure 11.44
The dialog box for creating an organization container.

Enter the name of the organization shown in figure 11.44, and select the Create button.

You should see the name of the newly created organization, MICROCOMM, appear in the NDS tree.

5. Highlight MICROCOMM and right click.

   - Select Create.

You should see a list of objects that can be created under the organization object (see fig. 11.45). Compare figure 11.45 with figure 11.43. Notice that the list of objects that can be created under an organization object is much larger.

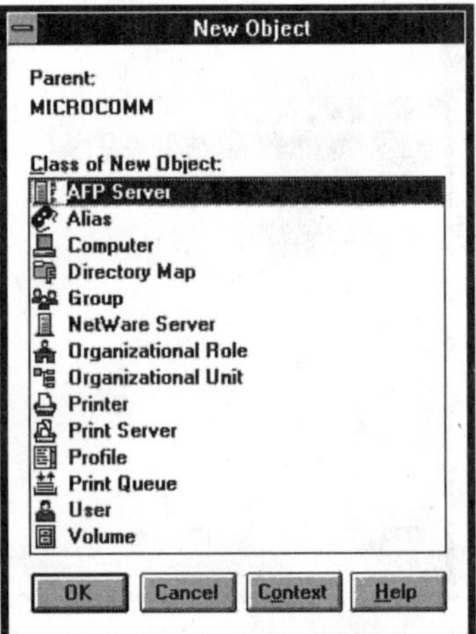

Figure 11.45
New objects under an organization container.

11

6. Select the organizational unit object and click OK.

   You should see a dialog box for creating the organization object (see fig. 11.46).

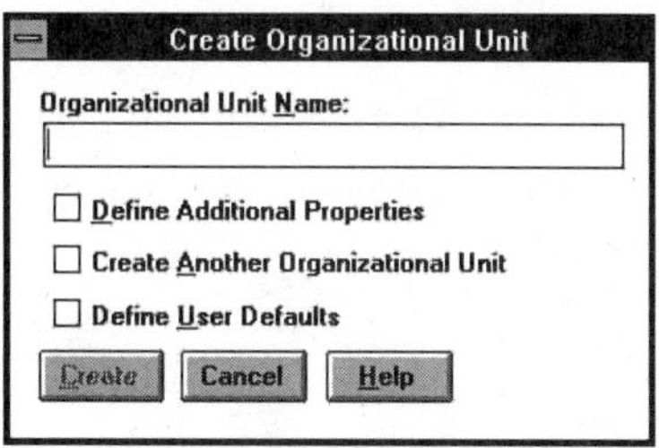

Figure 11.46
The dialog box for creating an organizational unit container.

Enter the name of the organizational unit CORP, shown in figure 11.41, and select the Create button.

You should see the name of the newly created organizational unit CORP appear in the NDS tree, if you double click on MICROCOMM.

7. Repeat steps 5 and 6 to create organizational unit container objects for MARKETING and ENGINEERING, as shown in figure 11.41.
8. Repeat preceding steps to create the rest of the organization, as shown in figure 11.41.
9. Delete the NDS tree you have just created. You cannot delete a container object that has objects defined in it. You must, therefore, start with the bottom most objects, and delete them first.

To delete an object, right click on the object and select the Delete operation. Alternatively, highlight the object and select the Object menu, and select the Delete operation from the menu.

To delete a group of objects, you can perform the following:

1. Open the container by double-clicking on it.
2. Highlight the first object to be deleted. Click on the last object to be deleted while holding SHIFT. You should see the objects between the first and the last object highlighted.
3. Press Del.

Using the NETADMIN Utility

This section will give you a guided tour in creating the NDS tree structure of figure 11.35 using the NETADMIN Tool. The NETADMIN is a text based utility that provides a similar functionality to the NetWare Administrator Tool. As a system administrator, it is very useful to be able to perform NDS operations using NETADMIN, because you may run into situations where MS Windows is not installed at a NetWare workstation. NETADMIN can work directly on top of DOS, and does not require MS Windows.

For this section, the guided tour will be to accomplish the same objectives as in the previous section so that you can compare the differences between using NetWare Administrator and the NETADMIN tools.

1. Log in to the network as an Administrator account.

   When the NDS services is first installed (at the time the first NetWare 4.*x* server is installed), a default network administrator user object Admin is created that has supervisor privileges to the entire NDS tree. You can use the Admin user object to login to the network.

2. Invoke the program NETADMIN, by typing its name:

   ```
   NETADMIN
   ```

   You should see the NETADMIN screen shown in figure 11.47.

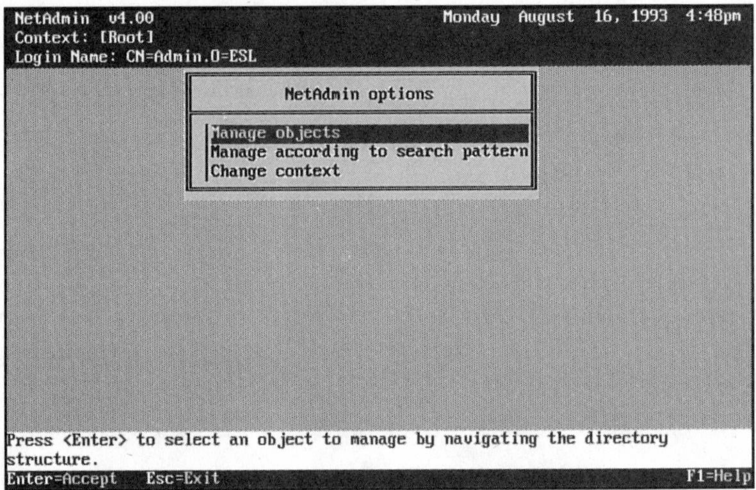

Figure 11.47
The NETADMIN screen.

The NETADMIN utility is located in SYS:PUBLIC directory, and you must have a search path to that directory for the NETADMIN command to work correctly.

The current context is seen on top of the screen under the label Context. If this is not set to [Root], perform the following steps to set it to [Root].

- Select "Change context."
- Enter [Root] when asked to "Enter context:."
- Press Enter to go back to the NETADMIN main menu with the changed context.

3. Select "Manage objects."

   You should see a list of objects and their class under the [Root] container (see fig. 11.48).

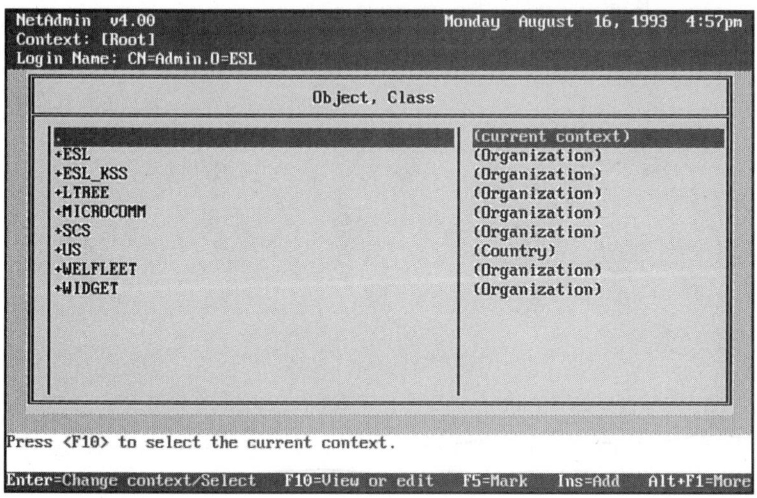

Figure 11.48
Object, Class under the [Root] container.

4. Press Ins.

   You should see a list of objects that can be created under [Root] (see fig. 11.49).

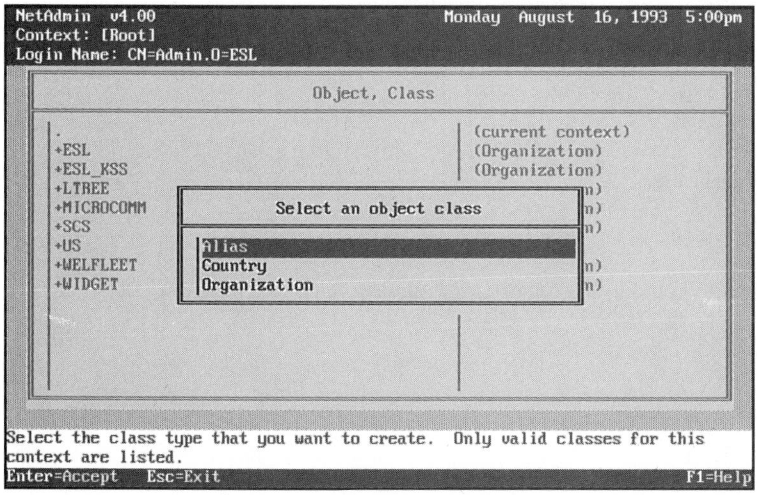

Figure 11.49
Selecting an object Class under the [Root] container.

5. Select the "Organization" choice to create an organization object.

   You should see a dialog box for creating the organization object (see fig. 11.50).

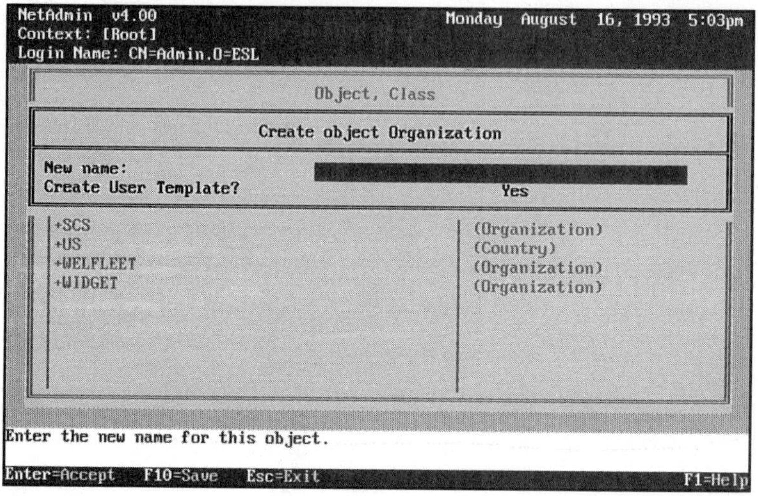

Figure 11.50
The NETADMIN dialog box for creating an organization container.

Enter the name of the organization shown in figure 11.41. You can elect to create a User Template for the organization object at this point or defer this action till later.

6. Press F10 to save changes and perform the create operation.

   When prompted to create another organization object, answer No.

   You should see the name of the newly-created organization appear in the Object, Class list.

7. Highlight the newly-created organization and press Enter. Notice that your context has changed to the organization.

8. Press Ins to create an object.

   You should see a list of objects that can be created under the Organization object (see fig. 11.51).

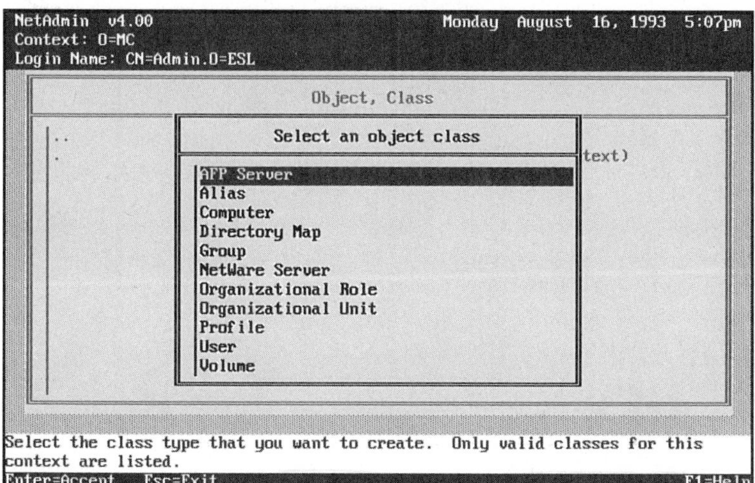

Figure 11.51
Select an Object Class under Organization container.

9. Select the "Organizational Unit" choice to create an organization object.

   You should see a dialog box for creating the Organizational Unit object (see fig. 11.52).

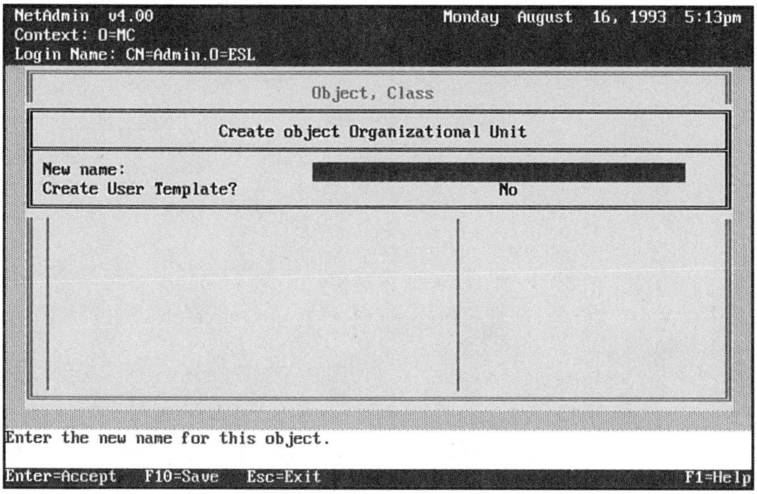

```
NetAdmin  v4.00                              Monday  August  16, 1993  5:13pm
Context: O=MC
Login Name: CN=Admin.O=ESL

                         Object, Class

                 Create object Organizational Unit

  New name:
  Create User Template?                          No

Enter the new name for this object.

Enter=Accept   F10=Save   Esc=Exit                                     F1=Help
```

Figure 11.52
The NETADMIN dialog box for creating an organizational unit container.

   Enter the name of the Organizational Unit shown in figure 11.41. You can elect to create a User Template for the organization object at this point or defer this action until later.

10. Press F10 to save changes and perform the create operation.

11. When asked to create another organizational unit object, answer Yes and repeat the preceding steps to create all the other organizational unit objects.

12. Review figure 11.41 and repeat preceding steps to create the rest of the organization as shown in figure 11.41.

13. Delete the NDS tree you have just created. You cannot delete a container object that has objects defined in it. You must, therefore, start with the bottom most objects, and delete them first.

    To delete an object, highlight it from the Object, Class list and press Del. You will be asked to confirm your delete operation.

NDS Context

The NDS context is a term used to describe the position of an object in the NDS tree. The position is described in terms of the container that contains the object. For example, in figure 11.53 the context of object Admin is container ESL, and the context of the file server object FS1 is in container CORP.

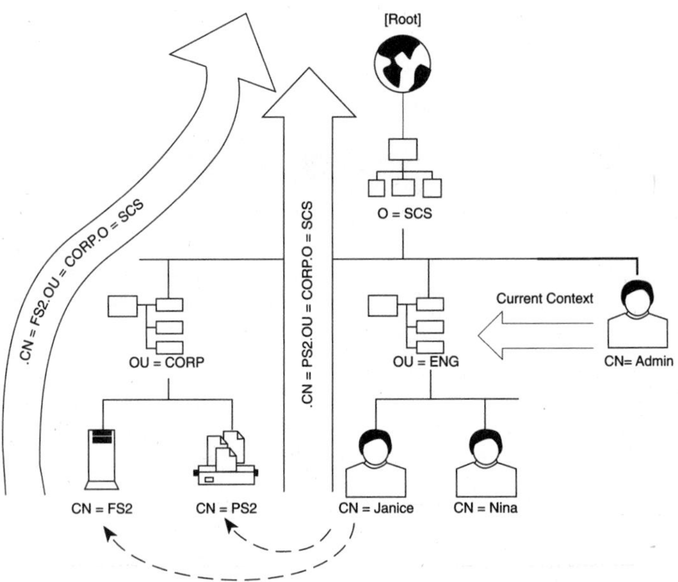

Figure 11.53 *Referencing objects in another context.*

The context of an object is important because some NDS utilities require you to know the position (or location) of the object in the NDS tree. In general, you must know the object's position (context) so that you can find it. (There are commands such as the NLIST command that will help you find the object's position in the NDS tree, if you know its name. These will be discussed at a later point in this chapter.) The context of an object affects how the object is referenced.

The context can also be seen as a *pointer* that locates the object's position in the NDS tree. The context is described in terms of listing, from left to right, the NDS names of the container objects, separated by periods (.). The order of listing the container objects is to start with the immediate container and working your way up to the root. Therefore, the context of object Admin in figure 11.53 is

```
ESL
```

or

```
O=ESL
```

since there is only one container. The [Root] container object is not listed, since it is always implied that the top-most container is [Root]. In the second form of representing the NDS context, the object type designator such as O (Organization) is used. Both forms are valid, with the second form using attribute type designators.

Another example is the context of object FS2 in figure 11.53.

```
CORP.ESL
```

or

```
OU=CORP.O=ESL
```

The [Root] container object is not listed, since it is always implied that the top-most container is [Root]. In the second form of representing the NDS context, the object type designator OU (Organizational Unit) and O (Organization) is used.

A special type of context called the *current context* is the current position of the *attached* workstation in the NDS tree. An attached workstation is one that is connected (logically speaking) via the network to the NDS tree.

When the network client software loads, it makes a connection to the NDS tree. If DOS is used as the workstation software, it can maintain only one current context for each DOS session. The workstation's current context can only be set to container objects, and *not* leaf objects, because a context is defined to be the position of the immediate *container* that contains the object in the NDS tree.

The current context is the default reference point used by the workstation to find other objects in the NDS tree. It is used in the same manner as the concept of the *current directory* in a file system. Just as the current directory cannot be set to a file name, the current context cannot be set to a leaf object.

Objects that are in the current context of a workstation can be referred to by their leaf object names. For instance, in figure 11.53, if the workstation's current context is CORP.ESL, and the user of that workstation can reference the objects FS2 and PS2 by their common names:

```
FS2
```

or

```
CN=FS2
PS2
```

or

```
CN=PS2
```

It is not essential to use the full NDS name of the object, in this case. This is a great convenience to the user of the workstation, because the user does not have to type the full NDS name of the object. Resources that are not in the current context cannot be referred to by their leaf names only; you must specify the NDS path name of the object. Objects FS2 and PS2, in figure 11.53, must be referenced by their NDS path name.

NDS Naming

In the previous section, you observed that objects that are not in the current context of a workstation must be defined by their NDS path name. There are three ways of specifying the NDS path names:

- Complete name
- Typeless name
- Partial name

Complete Name

A complete name is the name of an NDS object that includes the leaf name and the names of the containers that contain the leaf object, starting from the leaf object and going up the tree to the [Root] object. The object names are specified with their attribute name abbreviation (attribute type). The complete name must always begin with a period (.). Periods between object names that make up the NDS name are used as separators for the object names. This is an important point to note: The leading period has a different meaning than other periods used in the NDS object name; it signifies that the name is a complete name, and the object can be referenced by *enumerating* its path all the way to the root. The path is enumerated by listing the object name and its containers all the way to the root object.

The general syntax of the complete name of an object is:

```
.CN=leaf_object.[OU=org_unit_.{OU=org_unit}].O=organization.[C=country]
Bottom of tree ————————————————————————————————> Top of tree
```

In the preceding syntax, the [] brackets and the {} braces are *meta characters* that have special meaning. The [] indicates that the contents between the [] are optional. The {} indicates that there can be zero or more occurrences. The leading period is required for complete names. Without the leading period, the complete name becomes a partial name.

To summarize some of the rules of a complete name: the syntax for a complete name always begins with a period, followed by the NDS path of the object all the way up to the root. Since there can be only one [root] per NDS tree, the [root] object is not listed as part of the NDS tree. If an attribute type is used to qualify the object name in the NDS path, it will have the following form:

```
attribute_type_abbreviation=object_name
```

The *attribute_type_abbreviation* will be **CN** for leaf object, **OU** for Organizational Units, **O** for Organization, and **C** for Country. After the name of the object, the list of containers starting with the most *immediate* container, and continuing all the way to the [Root] container are enumerated. Since there can be only one [Root], the root object is not listed. The square brackets around the Organizational Unit list indicate that the OU's are optional. Examples of types of complete names aıe listed as follows:

```
.CN=leaf_object.O=organization.C=country
```

or

```
.CN=leaf_object.O=organization
```

or

```
leaf_object.org_unit      (typeless complete name that does not have the
attribute types)
```


The C=*country* has been left out in the last syntax example of the complete name, because the Country object is optional.

The most general case of the complete name would list the Organizational Units, a single organization, and a country name as shown in the following:

```
.CN=leaf_object.OU=org_unit.OU=org_unit.O=organization.C=country
```

In the preceding syntax example, only two Organizational Unit objects are shown, but there could be any number of these objects.

In figure 11.54, the complete names of the objects FS1, PS1, PRINT_1, PRINT_2, and PS2 are shown as follows:

```
.CN=FS1.OU=REGION_A.O=HAL
.CN=PS1.OU=REGION_A.O=HAL
.CN=PRINT_1.OU=OPS.OU=SALES.O=HAL
.CN=PRINT_2.OU=SALES.O=HAL
.CN=PS2.O=HAL
```

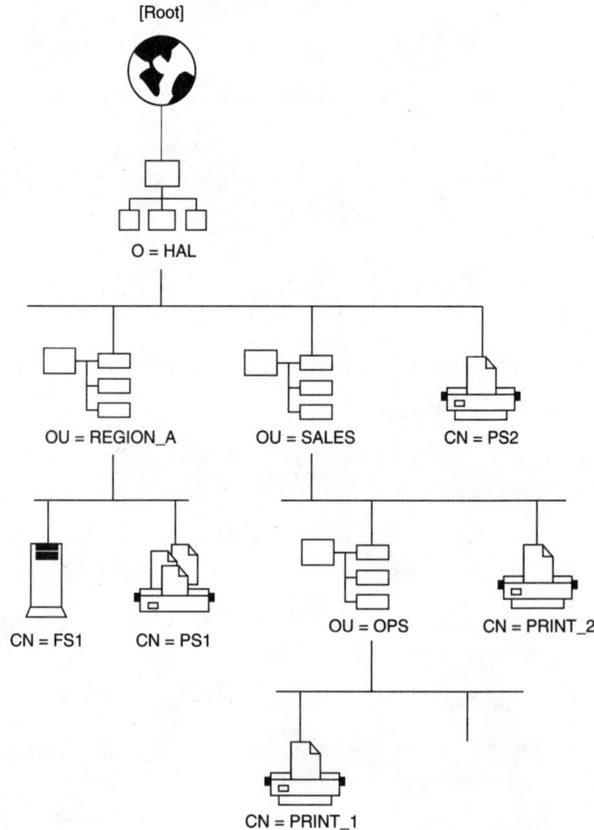

Figure 11.54
The NDS tree for complete name examples.

Partial Name

A partial name for an NDS object is its NDS path relative to the current context. This is in contrast to the complete name that lists the NDS path objects, relative to the root of the tree. A partial name is similar to specifying the name of a file relative to the current directory, and a complete name is similar to specifying the name of a file, using its complete path name that lists all the directories starting from the root.

Resolving a Partial Name

The NDS must resolve the partial name to a complete name. This is done by appending the current context to the partial name and adding a period at the beginning to indicate a complete name, as in the following:

```
Complete Name = .Partial Name.Current Context
```

An example will help clarify the preceding rule:

If the current context is OU=CORP.O=ESL, the partial name for object HP_PR1 that is in the same context is CN=HP_PR1. NDS forms the complete name by appending the current context OU=CORP.O=ESL to the partial name CN=HP_PR1, and adding a period at the beginning.

```
Current Context is      OU=CORP.O=ESL
Partial Name is   CN=HP_PR1
Complete Name is: . concatenated with CN=HP_PR1 concatenated with
OU=CORP.O=ESL
```

The main purpose of a partial name is to simplify the names for NDS objects that are in the current context or in the vicinity of the current context.

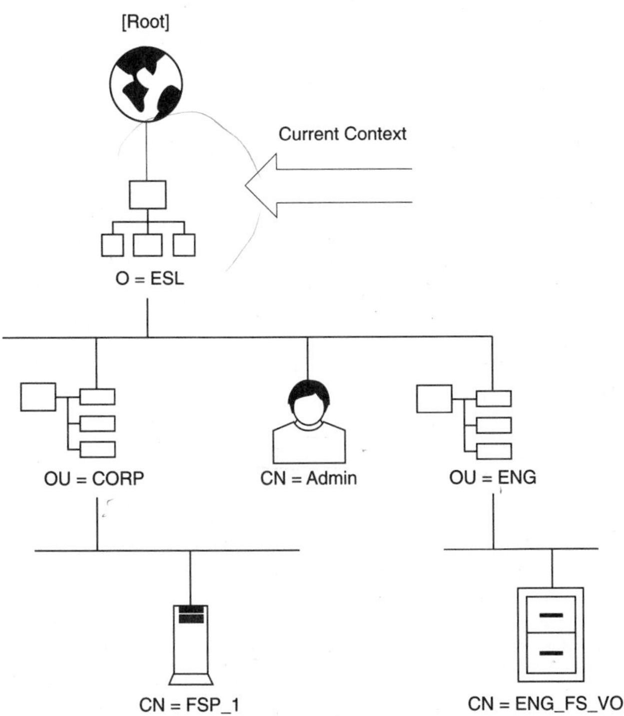

Figure 11.55
The partial name for objects not in the current context, but in the same tree branch.

The examples so far have been of objects in the current context. In figure 11.55 the object FSP_1 is not in the same context as the current context that is set to O=ESL. In this case, the partial name of FSP_1 is the object name plus the list of all the containers leading up to the current context O=ESL. That is, the partial name for FSP_1 is

```
CN=FSP_1.OU=CORP
```

Similarly the partial name of ENG_FS_VOL, if current context is O=ESL is

```
CN=ENG_FS_VOL.OU=ENG
```

and partial name of Admin, if current context is O=ESL is

```
CN=Admin
```

What if the current context is *not* set to a container that is part of the complete name leading up to the root. In this case, appending a period (.) at the end of the NDS name refers to the container above. In figure 11.56 the current context is OU=ENG.O=SCS. If the object DEI_FS in OU=CORP is to be referenced, you can use the partial name:

```
CN=DEI_FS.OU=CORP.
```

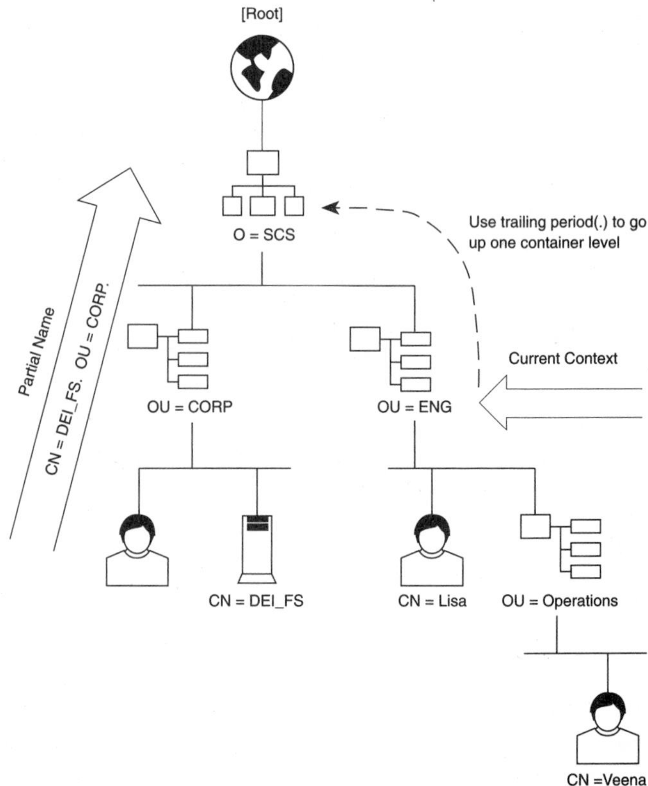

Figure 11.56
The partial name for an object when its current context is in a different branch of the NDS tree.

The trailing period (.) at the end refers to the parent container of the current context, which in this case is O=SCS. The partial name of the object DEI_FS with respect to the container O=SCS is CN=DEI_FS.OU=CORP. But because the current context is in a different tree branch (current context is OU=ENG.O=SCS and not O=SCS), a trailing period must be added at the end.

If the current context in figure 11.56 was OU=OPERATIONS.OU=ENG.O=SCS, then the same object CN=DEI_FS could be referred to by the partial name of

```
CN=DEI_FS.OU=CORP..
```

Two trailing periods, means two parent containers above the current context. Since the current context is OU=OPERATIONS.OU=ENG.O=SCS, the two trailing periods refer to the container O=SCS.

The trailing period can occur *only* in partial names.

The trailing period rules can be summarized as follows:

1. A single trailing period rule at the end of the NDS partial name removes a *single* object name from the current context.
2. The resulting name formed by removing a left most object from the current context is appended to the partial name.
3. A leading period is added to form a complete name.

Figure 11.57 shows a partial name with a trailing period.

```
CN=LUCY.
```

and a current context value of

```
OU=OPS.OU=SALES.O=SCS
```

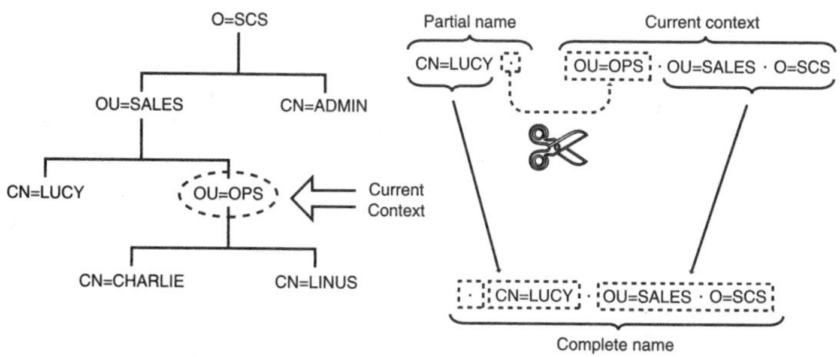

Figure 11.57
Trailing period rules.

When the trailing period rule 1 is applied, the trailing period (.) results in the removal of the left most OU=OPS from the current context, and the resulting name is

```
OU=SALES.O=SCS
```

From rule 2, this name is appended to the partial name, forming

```
CN=LUCY.OU=SALES.O=SCS
```

From rule 3, a leading period is added to form the resolved complete name:

```
.CN=LUCY.OU=SALES.O=SCS
```

Partial Name Example Exercise

The partial names for objects HP_PR1, FS1, VOL1, FS2, and BOB in figure 11.58 are listed in table 11.5 for different current context settings.

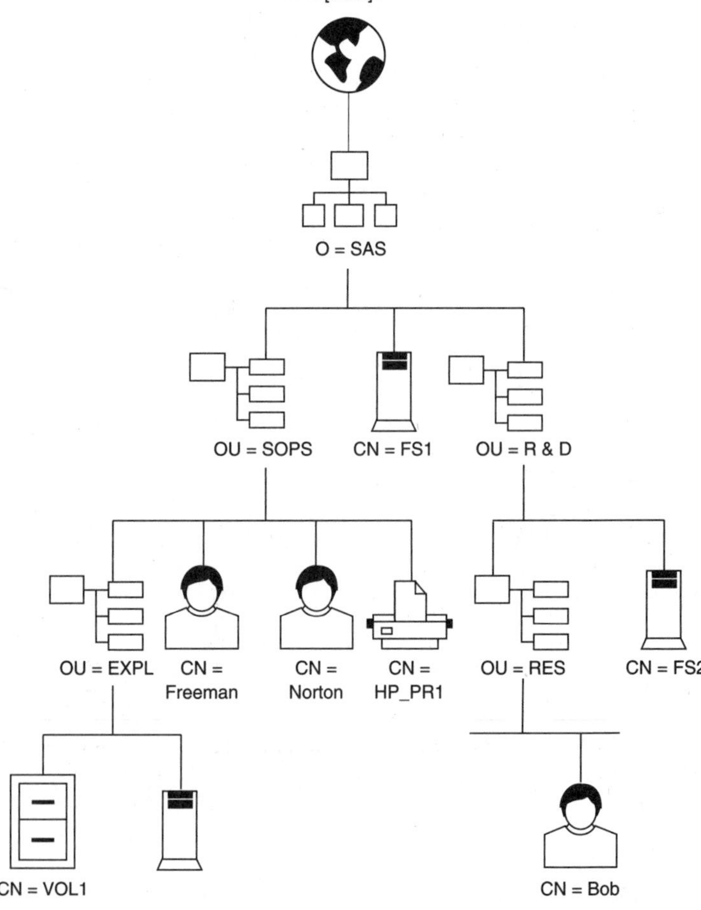

Figure 11.58
The NDS tree for partial name examples.

Table 11.5
Partial Name Examples

NDS Object Name		Current Context Partial
HP_PR1	O=SAS	CN=HP_PR1.OU=SOPS
HP_PR1	[Root]	CN=HP_PR1.OU=SOPS.O=SAS
HP_PR1	OU=SOPS.O=SAS	CN=HP_PR1
HP_PR1	OU=R&D.O=SAS	CN=HP_PR1.OU=SOPS.
HP_PR1	OU=RES.OU=R&D.O=SAS	CN=HP_PR1.OU=SOPS..
HP_PR1	OU=EXPL.OU=SOPS.O=SAS	CN=HP_PR1.
FS1	[Root]	CN=FS1.O=SAS
FS1	O=SAS	CN=FS1
FS1	OU=SOPS.O=SAS	CN=FS1.
FS1	OU=EXPL.OU=SOPS.O=SAS	CN=FS1..
FS1	OU=R&D.O=SAS	CN=FS1.
FS1	OU=RES.OU=R&D.O=SAS	CN=FS1..
FS1_VOL1	[Root]	CN=FS1_VOL1.OU =EXPL.OU=SOPS.O=SAS
FS1_VOL1	O=SAS	CN=FS1_VOL1.OU=EXPL.OU=SOPS
FS1_VOL1	OU=SOPS.O=SAS	CN=FS1_VOL1.OU=EXPL
FS1_VOL1	OU=EXPL.OU=SOPS.O=SAS	CN=FS1_VOL1
FS1_VOL1	OU=R&D.O=SAS	CN=FS1_VOL1.OU =EXPL.OU=SOPS.
FS1_VOL1	OU=RES.OU=R&D.O=SAS	CN=FS1_VOL1.OU =EXPL.OU=SOPS..
FS2	[Root]	CN=FS2.OU=R&D.O=SAS
FS2	O=SAS	CN=FS2.OU=R&D

continues

Table 11.5, Continued
Partial Name Examples

NDS Object Name		Current Context Partial
FS2	OU=SOPS.O=SAS	CN=FS2.OU=R&D.
FS2	OU=EXPL.OU=SOPS.O=SAS	CN=FS2.OU=R&D..
FS2	OU=R&D.O=SAS	CN=FS2
FS2	OU=RES.OU=R&D.O=SAS	CN=FS2..
BOB	[Root]	CN=BOB.OU=RES.OU=R&D.O=SAS
BOB	O=SAS	CN=BOB.OU=RES.OU=R&D
BOB	OU=SOPS.O=SAS	CN=BOB.OU=RES.OU=R&D.
BOB	OU=EXPL.OU=SOPS.O=SAS	CN=BOB.OU=RES.OU=R&D..
BOB	OU=R&D.O=SAS	CN=BOB.OU=RES
BOB	OU=RES.OU=R&D.O=SAS	CN=BOB

NDS Naming Rules

This section will summarize the naming rules that have been discussed in many of the examples in this chapter. There are three important concepts dealing with NDS Path, Typeless Naming and Period Rules, which will be discussed next.

NDS Path

The NDS Path name is consists of a list of object names, that are written left to right, beginning with the referenced object, and leading up to either the [Root] object or the current context. If the object name is preceded with a period (.), the object names refer to the complete name and must lead up to the [Root]. If the NDS path name does not have a leading period, then it refers to a partial name.

Typeless Name

The complete name of the object, in addition to beginning with a period, uses the attribute type names CN, OU, O, C to designate the type of the object as being a Common Name, Organizational Unit, Organization and Country object respectively.

If certain assumptions are made about the type of names, then specifying the attribute names is not necessary. For instance if the assumption is made that the left-most name is a Common Name and the right most is an Organization name, then the intervening objects must be of type Organizational Unit. This is a safe assumption to make, since all leaf objects must have a common name, and the Organization container is mandatory for an NDS tree. This means that object names have the following syntax.

```
CN.OU.OU .... .O
```

The OU objects are optional, though in actual practice most NDS trees will have at least one OU object.

With the preceding assumptions, the object name can be specified without the CN=, OU=, O= attribute names preceding the object name. This results in a simplification of the name, and such names are called *typeless* names. Typeless names do not have attribute names.

Therefore, the complete name

```
.CN=DEI.OU=CORP.O=ESL
```

can be expressed as a typeless complete name using

```
.DEI.CORP.ESL
```

When NDS encounters a typeless complete name that has more object names then the current context, it must resolve it into a complete name with attribute specifiers using the following Default Typing Rule:

1. The leftmost object is of type CN.
2. The rightmost object is of type O.
3. All intervening objects are of type OU.

Under special conditions, it is possible to use typeless names when the Country object is part of the NDS path. You will learn more about this in the following paragraphs.

It is possible to come up with a general typeless naming scheme that works for country objects also. The problem is knowing if the rightmost object is of type Country or type Organization. Country names can only be two letters, so if the right most object name is longer than 2 letters, it must be an Organization object.

The problem is that Organization objects can also be 2 letters. One solution would be to restrict organization objects to be more than 2 letters. This would allow the distinction between Country and Organization objects to be made based on the length of their names. Another solution would be to use the CCITT abbreviations for country codes. These are recommended two-letter codes to be used for all known countries and is updated regularly by CCITT. These two-letter country codes could be in a standard *country file* that comes with the NetWare distribution, and if this is an ASCII text file, additions and deletions could be made easily to it as geo-political boundaries of countries change. The rule then would be that if the right-most name in a typeless name is listed in this country file, it must indicate a country object. If country object is in the typeless name, the second right-most name must be an Organization object.

You can have mixed typeless and typed name to specify NDS objects under the Country container. For instance, the complete name .CN=FS1.O=ESL.C=US could be expressed as

```
.FS1.ESL.C=US
```

NetWare has a number of utilities that recognize the type of object they are working on. For example, utilities such as CX and NETADMIN work on container objects while changing NDS context because you cannot change your context to that of a leaf object. These utilities do not assume that the left-most object is a leaf object (attribute type CN), when they see a typeless name. They assume that the left most object is of type OU or O and attempt complete name resolution based on this. In general, NetWare utilities are aware of the type of objects they should work on and may override any default typing rules.

The Default Typing rule stated earlier applies to NDS names that have more objects than the current context. Suppose that the current context is


```
OU=CORP.O=SCS
```

This context has 2 NDS objects: OU=CORP and O=SCS.

If a typeless name such as .FS1.MKTG.SCS is submitted, it has 3 NDS object: OPS, MKTG and SCS. In this case the default typing rule will apply, and the left-most object will be treated as of type CN and the right-most will be of type O. The intervening objects will be of type OU. Therefore, the typeless name .FS1.MKTG.SCS will resolve to

```
.CN=FS1.OU=MKTG.O=SCS
```

Consider the same example where the typeless name .FS1.MKTG.SCS was used with the CX command:

```
CX .FS1.MKTG.SCS
```

The CX command would assume that the leftmost object is of type OU or O (in this case OU is the only possibility):

```
.OU=FS1.OU=MKTG.O=SCS
```

If there is no container with the complete name .OU=FS1.OU=MKTG.O=SCS, the CX command will fail.

When NDS encounters a typeless complete name that has the *same* number of object names as the current context, it must resolve it into a complete name using the attribute specifiers of the current context:

Consider the same previous example where the current context is

```
OU=CORP.O=SCS
```

If a typeless name such as .MKTG.SCS is submitted, it has two NDS objects which is the same as the number of NDS objects in the current context. In this case NDS will resolve the left most name to be of type OU because the left-most name in the current context is of type OU, and it will resolve the right-most name of type O because the right-most name in the current context is of type O. Therefore, the typeless name .MKTG.SCS will resolve to

```
OU=MKTG.O=SCS
```

What if the current context is as follows:

```
O=ESL.C=MX
```

If a typeless name such as .NTE.SC is submitted, it has two NDS objects which is the same as the number of NDS objects in the current context. In this case NDS will resolve the left most name to be of type O because the left-most name in the current context is of type O, and it will resolve the right-most name of type C because the right-most name in the current context is of type C. Therefore, the typeless name .NTE.SC will resolve to

```
.O=NTE.C=MX
```

If this object does not exist, NDS will report it as an incorrect NDS object.

If your current context is in a country container and you submit a name that has the same number of NDS objects as the current context but is in an Organization container, the previously stated rule will resolve it as an object in the country container. Similarly, if your current context is in an Organization container and you submit a name that has the same number of NDS objects as the current context but is in a Country container, the previously stated rule will resolve it as an object in the organization container. In both these cases the resolution to complete names will be incorrect. You can resolve this by specifying the type of the right-most object, such as that shown in the following examples:

```
.ESL.C=US
.CORP.O=SCS
```

Also, if the NDS utilities expect the typeless NDS names to be leaf objects, then they will override the previously stated rule and assume that the left-most object is of type CN. Examples of utilities that expect to work on leaf objects are LOGIN, MAP and CAPTURE.

Name Context at Workstation

NetWare 4.*x* client software provides the ability to set the current context before a user logs into the workstation. This is provided by the **Name Context** configuration setting in the NET.CFG file. The NET.CFG file is processed at the time the NetWare client software drivers and the network requester software are started.

The format of the name context is the following:

```
NAME CONTEXT = "NDS Path of Context"
```

The NET.CFG statements are case insensitive and can be entered in upper- or lowercase.

Suppose it is desired to set the current context at the time of login for user Bob to

```
OU=CORP.O=SCS
```

then this can be done by including the statement

```
Name Context = "OU=CORP.O=SCS"
```

in the NET.CFG file.

You cannot enter a leading period (.) in the name context parameter. For example, the following is illegal:

```
NAME CONTEXT = ".OU=CORP.O=SCS"
```

A sample NET.CFG file that has the name context set to OU=CORP.O=ESL follows. The Name Context specification must occur in the *NetWare DOS Requester* section.

```
LINK DRIVER SMC8000
   FRAME ETHERNET_802.2
   INT   3
   PORT 280
   MEM  D0000

NetWare DOS Requester
   FIRST NETWORK DRIVE = F
   NAME CONTEXT = "OU=CORP.O=SCS"
```


The name context can be explicitly changed by using the *Change Context* (CX) command before logging in to the network. Placing the name context statement in the NET.CFG is a convenience to the user, as it can simplify access to the network resources the user most frequently uses. For this reason, it is best to place the name context to the container that contains the resources a user is most likely to use. If the name context of a user is set to the container that contains the user object, log in to the network is possible by using the command

```
LOGIN UserLoginName
```

For user BOB, this would be as simple as

```
LOGIN BOB
```

If the name context is set to a different context than the location of the user object, the user would have to use the NDS path to the user object.

```
LOGIN NDSPathToUserObject
```

For user BOB whose user object is defined in OU=CORP.O=SCS, this would be

```
LOGIN .CN=BOB.OU=CORP.O=SCS
```

or

```
LOGIN .BOB.CORP.SCS
```

The second form demonstrates the use of the typeless complete name, whereas the first form shows the user object being referenced by its complete name with attribute type designators.

NDS Queries From the Command Line

The two primary command line utilities for browsing the NDS tree are:

- *Change Context* (CX)
- *Network List* (NLIST)

Used together, the CX and NLIST utilities provides a flexible and powerful mechanism for browsing and searching NDS object names and properties.

The CX utility

The CX utility is used to change the current context. When used by itself, without any parameters and options it can be used to find out the current context. Thus the command CX from the DOS prompt, as shown below, displays that the current context is set to O=ESL.

```
F> CX
O=ESL
F> CD
F:\SYSTEM
```

The command in bold is the command a user types in, and the other text is the system's response. In the above commands F> is the system (DOS) prompt and the O=ESL and the F:\SYSTEM are the results that are displayed on executing the CX and the CD commands, respectively.

The CX command is very similar to the CD command that allows the user to display current directory or change the current directory for a file system. It is important to keep in mind that the CX operates on the NDS directory and not the file system directory. Changing NDS directory context does not change the current file system directory. Therefore, in the above example, the CX command reveals that the

current context is O=ESL and the CD command reveals that the current directory is F:\SYSTEM. Changing the current context will have no effect on the current directory setting, and changing the current directory will not have any effect on the current context setting..

The commands that follow will refer to the NDS tree in figure 11.59 to make them more meaningful.

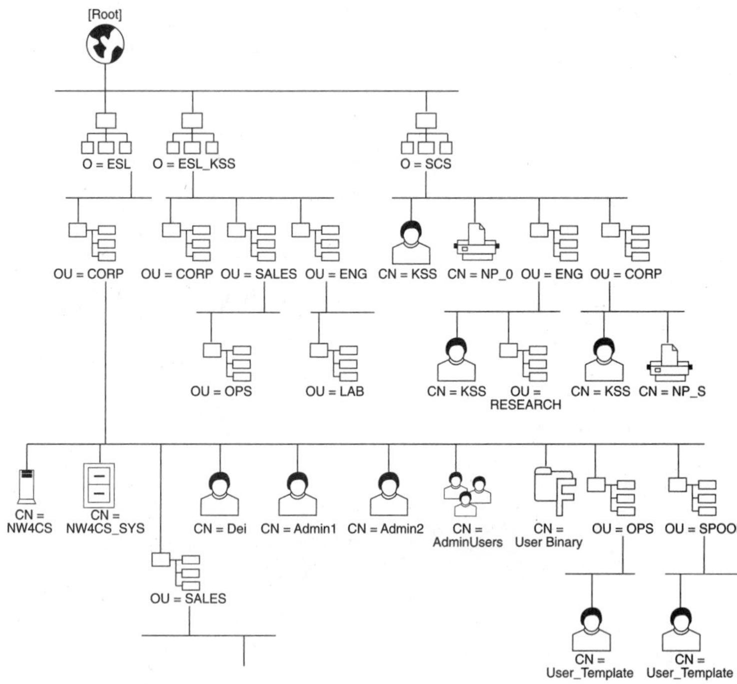

Figure 11.59
An NDS tree example for CX commands.

To change the current context to OU=CORP.O=ESL, the following command can be issued:

```
F> CX .OU=CORP.O=ESL
OU=CORP.O=ESL
```

Notice that the CX command always returns the current context, and this is a quick check to see if the CX command worked correctly.

In the preceding command the complete name .OU=CORP.O=ESL was used. Typeless names can also be used, since there is no Country object in the NDS tree. For instance, the following command has the same effect as the preceding command.

```
F> CX .CORP.ESL
OU=CORP.O=ESL
```

To go back one container level above, you can issue the command

```
F> CX  .
O=ESL
```

The period (.) following the CX command means that you wish to change your context to the parent container. Periods can be combined to go up several container levels. The example that follows illustrates this:

```
F> CX
OU=CORP.O=ESL
F> CX ..
[Root]
```

In the preceding example, the current container is OU=CORP.O=ESL. Using the command CX .. goes two container levels up, which in this case is the [Root] container.

What would happen if you tried to go three container levels above if your current context is OU=CORP.O=ESL?

```
F> CX
OU=CORP.O=ESL
F> CX ...
CX-4.00-260: An internal system error occurred during CX's attempt to
canonicalize the context: (...)
```

If an attempt is made to change the context to a location that does not exist in the NDS tree an error message is displayed. In the above error message the term *attempt to canonicalize the context* refers to the attempt the NDS made to transform the user's input into a standard X.500 naming syntax form. The term *canonical form* in Computer Science refers to a uniform or standard form.

To change the context to the [Root] you can use the /R option

```
F> CX /R
[Root]
```

To view all container objects (tree structure) below your current context or specified context you can use the /T option

```
F> CX
[Root]
F> CX /T
```

Figure 11.60 shows the output of the CX /T command issued from the [Root].

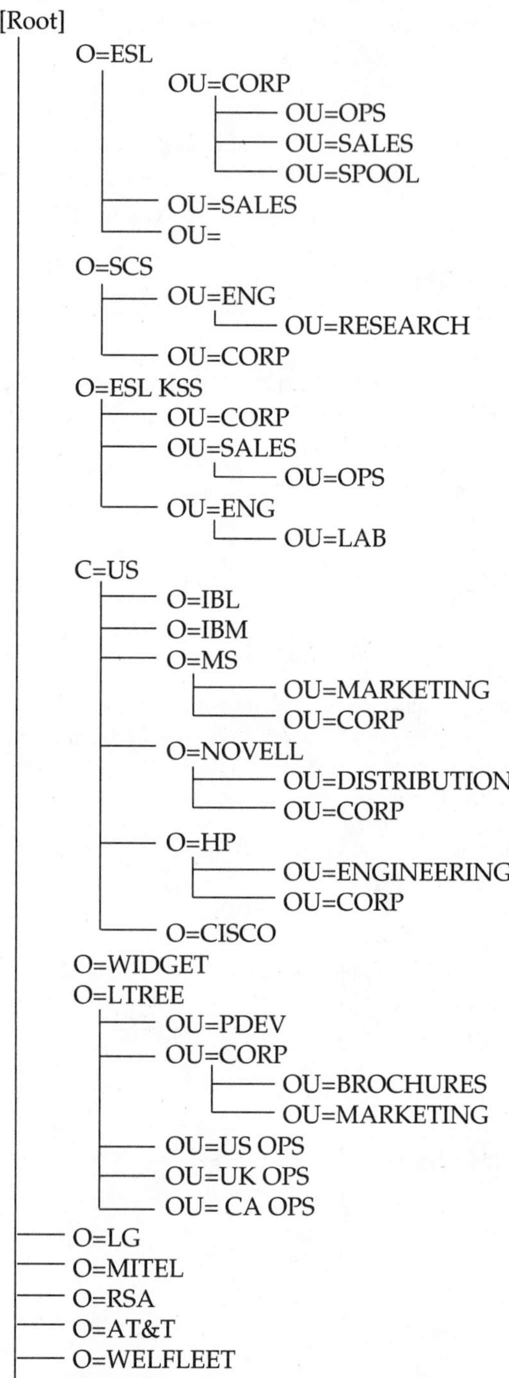

Figure 11.60
The CX /T command issued from the [Root] context.

11

You can combine the /R with other options such as /T. If /R is combined with /T, the CX /T command is issued from the root of the tree, but the context is not changed. Type the following:

```
F> CX
OU=CORP.O=ESL
F> CX /T /R

F> CX
OU=CORP.O=ESL
```

The command CX /T /R produces the same output as in figure 11.61; the context before and after executing the command remains the same (OU=CORP.O=ESL).

The /A (or /ALL) option enables you to view all objects at or below the current context. It is meant to be used in conjunction with options like the /T option.

```
F> CX
OU=CORP.O=ESL
F> CX /T /A
```

The command CX /T /A produces an output that is shown in figure 11.61.

```
OU=CORP.O=ESL
   ├─ CN=NW4CS
   ├─ CN=NW4CS_SYS
   ├─ CN=Dei
   ├─ CN=Admin1
   ├─ CN=Admin2
   ├─ CN=AdminUsers
   ├─ CN=User Binary
   ├─ OU=OPS
   │     └─ CN=USER_TEMPLATE
   ├─ OU=SALES
   │     └─ CN=USER_TEMPLATE
   └─ OU=SPOOL
         └─ CN=USER_TEMPLATE
```

Figure 11.61
The CX /T /A command issued from the OU=CORP.O=ESL context.

The CX /T /A command can be combined with the /R option. For instance:

```
F> CX
OU=CORP.O=ESL
F> CX /T /A /R
F> CX
OU=CORP.O=ESL
```

The CX /T /A /R will show all objects starting from the [Root], but the context will remain the same (OU=CORP.O=ESL) before and after executing the commands.

To view only container objects at a specified level, you can use the /CONT option

```
F> CX
OU=CORP.O=ESL
F> CX /CONT
```

The /CONT command can be combined with /A to see all objects within the container only

```
F> CX
OU=CORP.O=ESL
F> CX /CONT /A
```

Figure 11.62 shows the output of using the CX /CONT /A command in the current context OU=CORP.O=ESL.

Figure 11.62
The CX /CONT /A command issued from the OU=CORP.O=ESL context.

```
OU=CORP.O=ESL
 |— CN=NW4CS
 |— CN=NW4CS_SYS
 |— CN=Dei
 |— CN=Admin1
 |— CN=Admin2
 |— CN=AdminUsers
 |— CN=User Binary
 |— OU=OPS
 |— OU=SALES
 └— OU=SPOOL
```

What is the difference between the CX /CONT /A and the CX /T /A command? Compare figure 11.63 with figure 11.62. The CX /CONT /A will display all objects in the current context only, whereas the CX /T /A displays all objects in the current context and in the containers below the current context.

If the CX /CONT /A is combined with the /R option, what output will be displayed?

```
F> CX
OU=CORP.O=ESL
F> CX /CONT /A /R
F> CX
OU=CORP.O=ESL
```

Figure 11.63 shows the output of using the CX /CONT /A /R command in the current context OU=CORP.O=ESL. Notice that the current context before and after executing this command does not change, even though the /R option starts displaying the tree starting from the [Root] object.

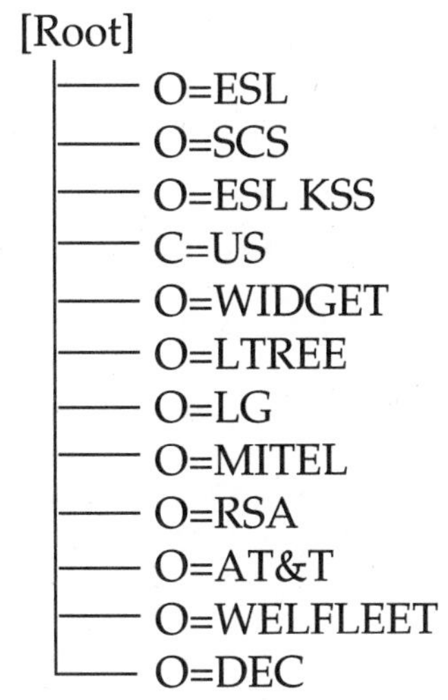

Figure 11.63
The CX /CONT /A /R command issued from the OU=CORP.O=ESL context.

The CX command can be used with typeless and partial names. For instance if the current context in figure 11.60 is O=ESL, the partial typeless name to change the context to OU=CORP.O=ESL would be:

```
F> CX
O=ESL
F> CX CORP
OU=CORP.O=ESL
```

If current context is O=ESL, the partial typeless name to change the context to OU=SALES.OU=CORP.O=ESL would be:

```
F> CX
O=ESL
F> CX SALES.CORP
OU=SALES.OU=CORP.O=ESL
```

If the current context is [Root], the partial typeless name to change context to O=SCS would be:

```
F> CX
[Root]
F> CX SCS
O=SCS
```

If the current context is O=SCS, the partial typeless name to change context to O=ESL would be:

```
F> CX
O=SCS
F> CX ESL.
O=ESL
```

The preceding example uses the trailing period rule, to go one container above the current context.

If the current context is OU=CORP.O=SCS the partial typeless name to change context to OU=SALES.OU=CORP.O=ESL is:

```
F> CX
OU=CORP.O=SCS
F> CX SALES.CORP.ESL..
O=ESL
```

The preceding example uses the trailing period rule, to go two containers above the current context.

To view additional help on using the CX command, type the command:

```
CX /?
```

The screens in figure 11.64 show the two help screens that are displayed when typing the CX /? command. Table 11.6 also summarizes many of the common CX options.

Table 11.6
Common CX Options

Command	Description
CX .	Change context to one container above current context
CX	Display current context
CX /R	Change context to root of NDS tree
CX /T	View all container objects below current or specified context
CX /T /A	View all objects in current context and below
CX /CONT	View container objects at current or specified context only
CX /CONT /A	View all objects at current context or specified context only
CX *new_context*	Changes context to specified context
CX /?	Obtain CX help screens

CX	Options Help	v4.00
Syntax: CX [new context] [R] [/T I CONT] [/ALL]] [/C] [/?]		
To:	Use:	
view all container objects below the current or specified context.	/T	
view container objects at the current or specified level.	/CONT	
modify /T or /CONT to view ALL objects at or below the context	/ALL	
change context or view objects relative to root	/R	
For example, to:	Type:	
view directory tree below the current context	CX /T	
view containers within a specific context	CX .O=Novell /CONT	

CX	General Usage Help	v4.00
Purpose: View and set current context. Syntax: CX [new context] [/Root] [/[Tree I CONT] [/All]] [/C] [/?]		
New context: A context can be entered either relative to your current context or as a distinguished name relative to the directory root. Use trailing periods (.) to change to a context relative to a higher level of your current context. To change to a context relative to the root of the directory put a period at the beginning of the new context or use the /Root flag.		
To view your current context type CX Current context is OU=Engineering.O=Novell		
For example, to change context:	Type:	
O=Novell	CX	
OU=Testing.OU=Engineering.O=Novell	CX OU=Testing	
OU=Marketing.O=Novell	CX OU=Marketing.	

Figure 11.64
The CX /? Help Screen.

The NLIST Command

The NLIST command views information on different object classes. The information is displayed in a convenient tabular form. NLIST is the fundamental command line utility for extracting information on NDS objects. It can be used to set up general purpose queries that will search NDS objects based upon a number of search criteria such as:

- Search on property values
- Search on existence of properties
- Search on a specific branch of the NDS tree

If you wish to search for all active users that are connected to the network, use the /A option, such as the command:

```
F> NLIST USER /A
Object Class: USER
Current context: O=ESL
Conn          = The server connection number
*        = The asterisk means this is your connection
User Name = The login name of the user
Address      = The network address
Node          = The network node
Login time   = The time when the user logged in
User Name                                         Address          Node
 *Admin                                           [    E8022][       C024282D]
One user object was found in this context.
One user object was found.
```

The output of all NLIST commands produces a legend that describes the columns for the tabular information that is displayed.

The asterisk next to a connection means that this is your connection to the server. The output of this command is equivalent to the USERLIST /A command in NetWare 3.*x.*

To see all user objects defined in the current context and sub-containers, use the /S option

```
F> CX
OU=CORP.O=ESL
F> NLIST USER /S
Object Class: USER
Current context: OU=CORP.O=ESL
User name= The name of the user
Dis           = Login disabled
Log exp   = The login expiration date, 0 if no expiration date
Pwd        = Yes if passwords are required
Pwd exp  = The password expiration date, 0 if no expiration date
Uni          = Yes if unique passwords are required
Min         = The minimum password length, 0 if no minimum
User Name                                 Dis  Log Exp Pwd  Pwd Exp Uni Min
-----------------------------------------------------------------------------
CN=Dei                                    No   0-00-00 No   0-00-00 No   0
CN=Admin1                                 Yes  0-00-00 Yes  0-00-00 No   8
CN=Admin2                                 No   9-01-99 No   0-00-00 No   5
A total of 3 USER objects was found in this context.
Object Class: USER
Current context: OU=SPOOL.OU=CORP.O=ESL
User Name                                 Dis  Log Exp Pwd  Pwd Exp Uni Min
-----------------------------------------------------------------------------
```

```
CN=USER_TEMPLATE              No   0-00-00 No   0-00-00 No   0
One USER object was found in this context.
Object Class: USER
Current context: OU=SALES.OU=CORP.O=ESL
User Name                     Dis  Log Exp Pwd  Pwd Exp Uni Min
--------------------------------------------------------------------------------
CN=USER_TEMPLATE              No   0-00-00 No   0-00-00 No   0
One USER object was found in this context.
Object Class: USER
Current context: OU=OPS.OU=CORP.O=ESL
User Name                     Dis  Log Exp Pwd  Pwd Exp Uni Min
--------------------------------------------------------------------------------

CN=USER_TEMPLATE              No   0-00-00 No   0-00-00 No   0
One USER object was found in this context.
A total of 6 USER objects was found.
```

As you can see from the last two NLIST commands, the output always begins with the Object Class that was specified in the NLIST command. The Current Context is listed next, and then the information returned by NLIST for the current context.

The NLIST USER /S command was issued from the context OU=CORP.O=ESL. It lists all the users found in the context OU=CORP.O=ESL and all users defined in sub containers below this context. There were a total of 3 user objects defined in the context OU=CORP.O=ESL. User Dei was not disabled and had no login expiration dates. Also, user Dei did not have any restrictions of unique passwords or minimum password length. User Admin1, on the other hand, was disabled, and had the restrictions of password being required, and passwords being unique and of a minimum of 8 characters. User Admin2 was not disabled, but the login account would expire on 9-1-99, and although no password uniqueness is enforced for this user, the minimum password length is 5 characters. The sub containers OU=SPOOL.OU=CORP.O=ESL,

OU=SALES.OU=CORP.O=ESL and OU=OPS.OU=CORP.O=ESL were searched next. Each revealed a user object with the name USER_TEMPLATE, that like user Dei in the container above, had no restrictions. You will learn later that the user USER_TEMPLATE in a container can be used as a model for other users created within that container.

To see property details for a specific user, such as user DEI, use the command:

```
F> NLIST USER=DEI  /D
Object Class: USER
Current context: OU=CORP.O=ESL
User: CN=Dei
    Name: Dei
    Access Control List (ACL):
        Subject: Dei
        Property:  [All Properties Rights]
        Property Rights: [ R   ]
```

```
    Access Control List (ACL):
        Subject: Dei
        Property: Login Script
        Property Rights: [ RW  ]
    Access Control List (ACL):
        Subject: [Public]
        Property: Default Server
        Property Rights: [ R   ]
    Access Control List (ACL):
        Subject: [Root]
        Property: Group Membership
        Property Rights: [ R   ]
    Access Control List (ACL):
        Subject: Dei
        Property: Print Job Configuration
        Property Rights: [ RW  ]
    Access Control List (ACL):
        Subject: [Root]
        Property: Network Address
        Property Rights: [ R   ]
    Home Directory:
        Volume Name: NW4CS_SYS
        Path: \users\Dei
        Name Space Type: DOS
    Language:
        English
    Default Server: NW4CS
    Object Class: User
    Object Class: Organizational Person
    Object Class: Person
    Object Class: Top
    Password Allow Change: True
    Password Required: False
    Password Unique Required: False
    Last Name: Siyan
One USER object was found in this context.
One USER object was found.
```


The output of the NLIST USER=Dei /D command gives detailed information on the properties for that object. Some of the properties that are listed for the user are [All Properties Rights], Login Script, Default Server, Group Membership, Printer Job Configuration, Network Address, Home Directory, Language, Password Allow Change, Password Required, Password Unique Required, and Last Name. Many of the properties are listed under the heading of *Access Control List* (ACL).

Notice that in the NLIST USER=Dei /D command, the following lines are displayed at the end:

Object Class: User

Object Class: Organization Person

Object Class: Person

Object Class: Top

The preceding lines indicate the derivation hierarchy for user object Dei. The base class for user object Dei is User class. This is derived from the Organizational Person super class, which is in turn derived from the super class Person, which is in turn derived from super class Top.

To search for user KSS in current container and all sub-containers:

```
F> CX
O=SCS
F> NLIST USER=KSS /S
Object Class: USER
Current context: O=SCS
User name= The name of the user
Dis          = Login disabled
Log exp   = The login expiration date, 0 if no expiration date
Pwd         = Yes if passwords are required
Pwd exp  = The password expiration date, 0 if no expiration date
Uni          = Yes if unique passwords are required
Min         = The minimum password length, 0 if no minimum
User Name                                      Dis  Log Exp Pwd  Pwd Exp Uni Min
CN=KSS                                         No   0-00-00 No   0-00-00 No   0
One USER object was found in this context.
Object Class: USER
Current context: OU=CORP.O=SCS
User Name                                      Dis  Log Exp Pwd  Pwd Exp Uni Min
---------------------------------------------------------------------------------
CN=KSS                                         No   0-00-00 No   0-00-00 No   0
One USER object was found in this context.
Object Class: USER
Current context: OU=ENG.O=SCS
User Name                                      Dis  Log Exp Pwd  Pwd Exp Uni Min
CN=KSS                                         No   0-00-00 No   0-00-00 No   0
One USER object was found in this context.
```

The NLIST USER=KSS /S command finds all occurrences of user object KSS in current context and all sub containers.

To see all printer objects within current context and all sub containers

```
F> CX
O=SCS
F> NLIST PRINTER /S
Current context: O=SCS
Partial Name                                                Object Class
---------------------------------------------------------------------------------
CN=NP_0                                                     Printer
One PRINTER object was found in this context.
```

```
Current context: OU=CORP.O=SCS
Partial Name                                                Object Class
CN=NP_0                                                     Printer
One PRINTER object was found in this context.
A total of 2 PRINTER objects was found.
```

To search for a specific property value for an object class such as the user object class, in the current context and all sub-containers:

```
F> CX
O=SCS
F> NLIST USER SHOW "Telephone Number"  /S
Object Class: USER
Current context: O=SCS
User name= The name of the user
Dis           = Login disabled
Log exp   = The login expiration date, 0 if no expiration date
Pwd         = Yes if passwords are required
Pwd exp  = The password expiration date, 0 if no expiration date
Uni          = Yes if unique passwords are required
Min         = The minimum password length, 0 if no minimum
User Name                                    Dis  Log Exp Pwd  Pwd Exp Uni Min
CN=KSS                                       No   0-00-00 No   0-00-00 No   0
One USER object was found in this context.
Object Class: USER
Current context: OU=CORP.O=SCS
User Name                                    Dis  Log Exp Pwd  Pwd Exp Uni Min
CN=KSS                                       No   0-00-00 No   0-00-00 No   0
One USER object was found in this context.
Object Class: USER
Current context: OU=ENG.O=SCS
User Name                                    Dis  Log Exp Pwd  Pwd Exp Uni Min
CN=KSS                                       No   0-00-00 No   0-00-00 No   0
One USER object was found in this context.
A total of 3 USER objects was found.
```

If the /S option was left out in the preceding command (NLIST USER SHOW "Telephone Number"), only the phone numbers for users in the current context of OU=CORP.O=SCS would be displayed.

To see a specific value for a specific object, use

```
F> CX
OU=CORP.O=ESL
F> NLIST SERVER=NW4CS SHOW "Network Address"
Object Class: SERVER
Current context: OU=CORP.O=ESL
Server: CN=NW4CS
    IPX/SPX Network Address
        Network: F0000055
        Node: 1
        Socket: 451
```

```
One SERVER object was found in this context.
One SERVER object was found.
F> CX .O=SCS
O=SCS
F> NLIST PRINTER="NP_0" SHOW "Location" /S
Current context: O=SCS
Printer: CN=NP_0
    Location: Building 6, Room 404
------------------------------------------------------------------------------
One PRINTER object was found in this context.
Current context: OU=CORP.O=SCS
Printer: CN=NP_0
    Location: Engineering Lab Bldg, Printer Room 5
------------------------------------------------------------------------------
One PRINTER object was found in this context.
A total of 2 PRINTER objects was found.
```

In the NLIST SERVER command, the network address of server NW4CS is queried. The network address that is reported is the internal software address of the server that consists of a the *internal network number*, the *socket number* and the node number which is always set to 1. The internal network number is selected during installation, and the socket number identifies the file service process that handles incoming requests. The NLIST PRINTER command shows the location of the printer object NP_0. The /S option helps find this printer object in the current context of O=SCS and all sub-containers. Without the /S option, only the printer object located at Building 6, Room 404 would be found, and the printer object at location Engineering Lab Bldg, Printer Room 5 would not show up.

To search for all objects with a specific property value, use the WHERE option with the NLIST command.

```
F> CX
O=SCS
F> NLIST USER WHERE "Title" EQ ENGINEER
Object Class: USER
Current context: O=SCS
User name= The name of the user
Dis         = Login disabled
Log exp   = The login expiration date, 0 if no expiration date
Pwd         = Yes if passwords are required
Pwd exp  = The password expiration date, 0 if no expiration date
Uni         = Yes if unique passwords are required
Min         = The minimum password length, 0 if no minimum
User Name                                    Dis  Log Exp Pwd  Pwd Exp Uni Min
------------------------------------------------------------------------------
KSS                                          No   0-00-00 No   0-00-00  No  0
One USER object was found in this context.
One USER object was found.
F> NLIST USER=KSS SHOW TITLE
```

```
Object Class: USER
Current context: O=SCS
User: CN=KSS
    Title: Engineer
One USER object was found in this context.
One USER object was found.
```

In the preceding commands, the quotes (") are placed around property names and values that have spaces around them; otherwise, they are optional. Also the EQ operator for comparison can be replaced by the equal symbol (=). This means that each of the following commands are equivalent and produce the same results.

```
NLIST USER WHERE "Title" EQ ENGINEER
NLIST USER WHERE "Title" = ENGINEER
NLIST USER WHERE "Title" = "ENGINEER"
NLIST USER WHERE Title = "ENGINEER"
NLIST USER WHERE Title = ENGINEER
```

The common NLIST options are summarized in table 11.7.

Table 11.7
Common NLIST Options

Command	Description
NLIST USER /A	Display active users logged on to the network
NLIST VOLUME /S	Display all volumes in the current context and sub containers
NLIST USER=Dei /D	Show detail property values for a user
NLIST USER=KSS /S	Search for a specific object in current context and all sub containers
NLIST SERVER=FS1 SHOW "Network Address"	Show a specific property for a specific server object
NLIST PRINTER WHERE "LOCATION"=LAB	Search for objects that have a specific property value
NLIST /?	Displays top level help screen for NLIST

The help screens obtained from using the NLIST /? command are displayed in figures 11.65 through 11.69. Figure 11.65 is the top level help, and the other figures are the specific help screens described in the top-level help. These help screens are shown here for your reference.

```
NLIST                       General Help Screen                      v4.00
---------------------------------------------------------------------------
Purpose: View information about users, groups and other objects.
Syntax: NLIST class type [proerty search option]
                  [display option] [basic option]
---------------------------------------------------------------------------
For details on:                          Type:
   Property search options                 NLIST /? R
   Properties                              NLIST /? P
   Display options                         NLIST /? D
   Basic options                           NLIST /? B
   All Help Screens                        NLIST /? ALL
---------------------------------------------------------------------------
Class types:                  User                    Queue
   * (all class types)        Group                   Printer
   Server                     Volume                  Print Server
   Computer                   Profile                 Organization
   Directory Map              Alias                   AFP Server
   Organization Unit
---------------------------------------------------------------------------
Enclose in double quotes all class types or properties conating spaces>
```

Figure 11.65
The top-level help screen for NLIST.

```
NLIST                     Basic Options Help Screen                  v4.00
---------------------------------------------------------------------------
Purpose: Specify basic options for viewing objects.
Syntax: NLIST class type [= object name] [basic option]
---------------------------------------------------------------------------
To display:                                   basic options:
   Active users or servers                      /A
   Objects throughtout all subordinate contexts /S
   Objects in a specified context               /CO <context>
   Continuously without pausing                 /C
   Bindary information                          /B
   Available Directory Services trees           /TREE
---------------------------------------------------------------------------
For example to:                               Type:
   See all servers in current context
    and all subordinate contexts              NLIST Server /S
   See all logged in users (active)           NLIST User /A
   See all volumes in the context O=My Org    NLIST Volume /CO "O=My Org"
   See all servers in bindery mode            NLIST Server /B
   See all Directory trees in bindery mode    NLIST /Tree = *
```

Figure 11.66
NLIST /? B: Basic options help screen.

```
NLIST                   Property Search Help Screen                  v4.00
---------------------------------------------------------------------------
Purpose: Spearch for objects by property value
Syntax: NLIST object class [= object name]
           WHERE property <operator> value
---------------------------------------------------------------------------
Operators:                                LE = Less than or equal
   EQ = Equal                             GT = Greater than
   NE = Not Equal
   LT = Less than
   EXISTS = property exists
---------------------------------------------------------------------------
For example to:                           Type:
   See all users whose
    Login Grace Limit is greater          NLIST User WHERE
    than 0                                     "Login Grace Limit" GT 0
   See all users whose
    telephone number begins               NLIST User WHERE
    with 801                                   "Telephone Number" EQ 801
   See all queues which have
    an operator                           NLIST Queue WHERE Operator EXISTS
```

Figure 11.67
NLIST /? R: Property search options help screen.

Figure 11.68
NLIST /? P: Properties help screen.

```
NLIST                    Properties Help Screen                    v4.00
------------------------------------------------------------------------
Purpose: Show examples of some properties
------------------------------------------------------------------------
Properties for class type User include:
   EMail Address
   Group Membership
   Login Script
   Default Server
------------------------------------------------------------------------
Properties for class type Server include:
   Network Address
   Oranization Name
   Department
   Version
------------------------------------------------------------------------
Refer to "Utils Doc" for complete list of properties
   and class types.
```

Figure 11.69
NLIST /? D: Display options help screen.

```
NLIST                 Display Options Help Screen                  v4.00
------------------------------------------------------------------------
Purpose: Select how data is to be displayed
Syntax: NLIST class type [= object name] [display option]
------------------------------------------------------------------------
To display:                              display options
   Detailed information                     /D
   Only the ojbect name                     /N
   Specific properties                      SHOW property [, property . . .]
------------------------------------------------------------------------
For example, to:                         Type:
   See detailed information for
    group ADMIN                          NLIST Group = Admin /D
   See the telephone numbers and street
    addresses of all users               NLIST User SHOW "Telephone Number",
                                         "Street Address"
   See only the names of the queues in
    current and all subordinate contexts NLIST Queue /N /S
```


NDS Queries Using the NetWare Administrator Tool

NDS queries can also be generated using a Graphical User Interface tool such as the NetWare Administrator Tool.

The Search option is started by performing the following steps:

1. Start NetWare Administrator Tool.

2. Highlight the container object from which the search is to be carried out. If you wish to search the entire NDS tree, highlight the [Root] object.

3. Select the **O**bject menu.

4. Select the Searc**h** option from the Object menu.

After the preceding steps, you should see a screen similar to that shown in figure 11.70. The Start From is the starting point of the search, and can be set to any container object in the NDS tree. The Browse icon, next to this value can be used to browse for an appropriate container, as can be seen in figure 11.71. The default is to search the entire subtree as indicated by default check mark on the "Search Entire Subtree" box.

Several other object classes are listed in the Search For files. In addition to the standard object classes, additional classifications can be used to aid in finding the objects. These additional classifications are listed in table 11.8

The Properties list box allows you to select from the different properties that you want to search for. The comparison operators include Equal, Not Equal To, Not Present, Present. There is a field for entering the actual property value that you want to search for.

Table 11.8
Additional Object Classifications for Search Option

Object Classification	Description
Device	Includes all computer and printer objects
Locality	This classification is not used by NDS, currently; but may be used by third-party products and tools
Organizational Person	Lists all users
Partition	Used by the Partition Manager tool to indicate containers that are on the top of a separate partition
Person	Includes all users
Resource	Includes Printer Queue and Volume Objects
Server	Includes NetWare Server, Print Server, and AFP server
Top	Includes every object in the container that is being searched

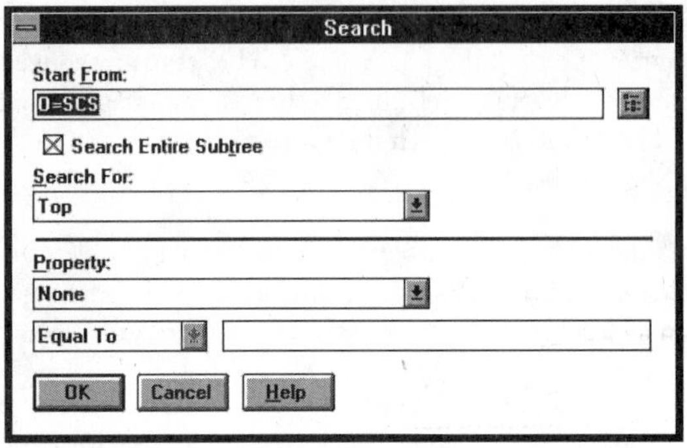

Figure 11.70
The Search option in the NetWare Administrator Tool.

Search
Start From:
O=SCS
☒ Search Entire Subtree
Search For:
Top
Property:
None
Equal To
OK Cancel Help

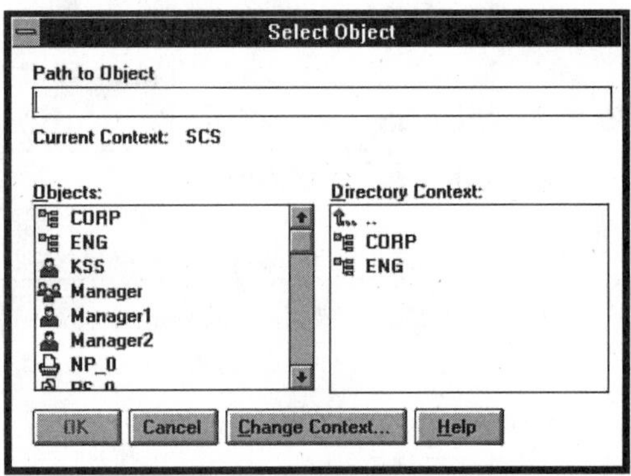

Figure 11.71
The Select Object panel used for browsing to set the value of Start From in the Search option.

The figure 11.72 shows the results of searching all organizational unit objects in the container O=SCS, and its sub containers. This figure shows that there are three organizational unit objects that were found:

```
OU=CORP.O=SCS
OU=ENG.O=SCS
OU=RESEARCH.OU=ENG.O=SCS
```

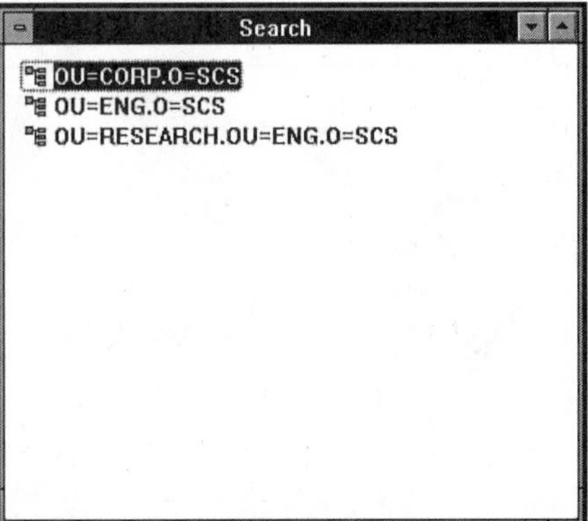

Figure 11.72
The Search results for all organizationalal unit objects in O=SCS NDS database.

The Volume Object

There is one object that is both an NDS object and a file system object. This is the volume object. It has characteristics of both a file system object and an NDS object. As an NDS object, the volume is managed by NDS, but its components consist of directories and files.

Summary

In this chapter, you have learned the basics of NetWare Directory Services. The NDS represents an exciting way of managing the network as a logical entity. Because NDS is a key service in NetWare 4.*x*, many details of its operations were provided in this chapter. One of the concepts covered was NDS as global database for network management. This global database is accessible from any point on the network. The nature of the NDS objects was examined, and each of the different type of leaf and container objects were described in detail. The NDS naming rules were described with respect to several examples. Among the key concepts that were covered were Current Context, Complete Names, Typeless Names, Partial Names, Period rules.

The NDS utilities CX, NLIST and their most important options were discussed, and numerous examples of how they could be used were provided. The chapter concluded with a discussion on partitioning, replication and time synchronization.

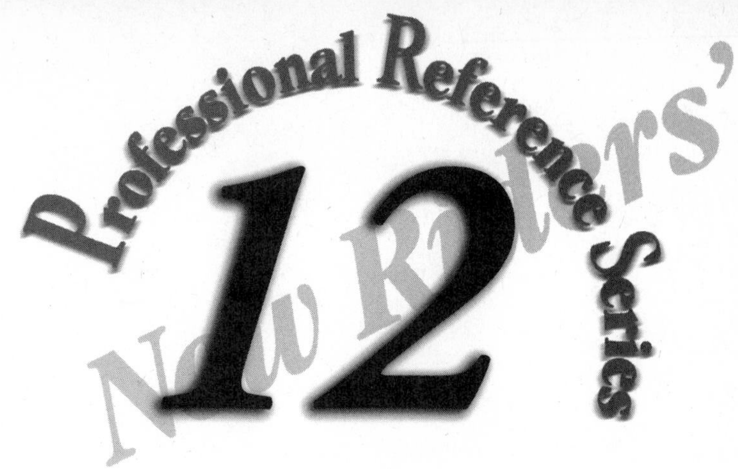

Installing NetWare 4.*x*

In this chapter, you learn about the NetWare 4.*x* installation and upgrade process. Normally, software installation can be performed as a first step without considering serious design issues. NetWare 4.*x* is a complex operating system, and its installation should be attempted only after careful planning. A very important aspect in the design of a NetWare 4.*x*-based network is the NDS tree structure. During NetWare 4.*x* installation, you are asked to make decisions about the NDS tree structure for your network. It is, therefore, essential that you have a good understanding of the NDS directory tree for your organization. Remember that once you have chosen the basic NDS tree structure, it is difficult to make changes. You can save yourself a great deal of time and effort by doing things right the first time.

Besides learning how to install NetWare 4.*x*, you learn in this chapter how existing NetWare 3.*x* servers can be upgraded to NetWare 4.*x*. Several options are available for migrating to NetWare 4.*x*. Preplanning and proper design are key in accomplishing these tasks efficiently.

Installation Changes

Earlier versions of NetWare, such as NetWare 3.*x* and 2.*x*, were distributed on disks. Because NetWare is a complex piece of software, it takes an inconveniently large number of disks and a long time to install. A fundamental change in NetWare 4.*x* is that it is distributed on a single CD-ROM disk. In this regard, NetWare 4.*x* has followed the path set by some popular versions of UNIX that are also distributed on CD-ROM. The NetWare 4.*x* distribution comes with the CD-ROM distribution media and a license disk that has a serial number and a code for the maximum number of users supported by the NetWare OS.

In NetWare 3.*x*, the server disk had to be partitioned and formatted for DOS. The DOS system had to be installed to load the NetWare server program (SERVER.EXE). To continue with the installation, the INSTALL.NLM had to be run, and this was used to create a NetWare partition and a NetWare volume.

NetWare 4.*x* also requires a DOS partition, either on the hard disk or a floppy disk, to start the server (SERVER.EXE) program. However, if you do not have the server disk prepared, NetWare 4.*x* installation performs these tasks for you. The NetWare 4.*x* installation program can be used for creating a DOS partition and installing DOS. The version of DOS that is installed is DR-DOS (now called Novell DOS). DR-DOS was purchased by Novell when it acquired Digital Research, the makers of CP/M and DR-DOS.

NetWare 4.*x* installation creates a directory called SERVER.40 in the DOS partition and copies the minimum set of programs it needs to start the SERVER.EXE program and continue with the installation. The NetWare 4.*x* installation program starts the SERVER.EXE program, load the INSTALL.NLM, and guide you through the appropriate options to complete the installation.

Though the installation steps are automated, and there is no need to copy numerous floppy disks on to the server, you must still make key decisions to complete the installation successfully.

The experience and knowledge an installer has with NetWare 3.*x* is still applicable. As you go through this chapter, you recognize that many of the tasks and concepts are similar to those in NetWare 3.*x*. For example, the concept of NLMs as extensions to the NetWare OS is the same. The same file extension conventions are used to indicate the different type of NLMs. The disk drivers still have a .DSK extension, and the LAN drivers have a .LAN extension. All NLMs are, by default, loaded from the SYSTEM directory. The PUBLIC directory has the same meaning as in NetWare 3.*x*.

Installation Requirements

The installation requirements for NetWare 4.*x* can be divided into hardware and software categories.

Hardware Requirements

In terms of hardware, the server must be an Intel 80386 or higher processor with at least 8 MB of RAM (this is double the requirement for NetWare 3.11), and an internal or external hard disk of at least 60 MB. The server must also have at least one NIC (Network Interface Card) with the correct NLM driver. One of the other areas of improvement in NetWare 4.*x* is that the distribution comes with a list of a larger number of network drivers. Table 12.1 shows the initial list of drivers supported for NetWare 4.*x*. This list is expected to grow as newer network boards become available. Also, if support for the NIC of your choice is not listed here, consult with the NIC vendor. Drivers downloaded from bulletin board systems (BBSs) contain instructions on how to use them in the NetWare 4.*x* installation process. Other optional pieces of hardware are a tape backup and an optical jukebox for data migration.

Minimum hardware requirements for NetWare 4.*x* are as follows:

- Intel 80386 processor (or better)
- 8 MB of RAM
- Server disk size of at least 60 MB

- Supported Network Interface Card (NIC)
- CD-ROM drive, if NetWare 4.*x* is on CD-ROM media

An important but often overlooked attribute is that the server should have an accurate time clock, especially if it is going to act as a Single Reference Time Server, Primary Time Server, or Reference Time Server. Reference Time Servers should, by definition, have an accurate time clock. But the Single Reference Time Server and the Reference Time Server are usually ordinary computers, and should have a reasonably accurate clock.

Table 12.1
Partial List of NetWare 4.x Supported LAN Drivers for the Server

LAN Driver File Name	Description
3C503.LAN	3COM 3C503 EtherLink II Driver 3COM 3C503 EtherLink II TP Driver 3COM 3C503 EtherLink II/16 Driver 3COM 3C503 EtherLink II/16 TP Driver
3C509.LAN	3COM EtherLink III Family Driver
3C523.LAN	3COM 3C523 EtherLink II Driver/MC Driver 3COM 3C523 EtherLink II Driver/MC TP Driver
3NW391R.LAN	Proteon p1391 RapiDriver
3NW392R.LAN	Proteon p1392 RapiDriver
3NW89XR.LAN	Proteon p189x RapiDriver
E21N4X.LAN	Cabletron Ethernet E21xx (ISA/EISA) ODI Server Driver
EXP16.LAN	Intel EtherExpress ISA Family Intel EtherExpress MCA Family
HP386A16.LAN	Hewlett-Packard PC LAN/AT 16
HP386A32.LAN	Hewlett-Packard PC LAN Adapter/16 Plus
IBMETHR.LAN	IBM Personal System/2 Adapter for Ethernet Networks

continues

Table 12.1, Continued
Partial List of NetWare 4.x Supported LAN Drivers for the Server

LAN Driver File Name	Description
INTEL593.COM	Intel LAN593 Driver
IPTUNNEL.LAN	IP Tunnel Driver
MADGEODI.LAN	MADGE Hardware Support Module
NCRWL06.LAN	NCR WaveLAN AT/MC
NE1000.LAN	Novell Ethernet NE1000
NE1500T.LAN	Ansel M1500 All-In-One-Networking Novell Ethernet NE1500T
NE2.LAN	Novell Ethernet NE/2
NE2000.LAN	Novell Ethernet NE2000
NE2100.LAN	Ansel M2100 All-In-One-Networking EXOS 105 Novell Ethernet NE2100 Wearness 2110T or Wearness 2107C
NE2_32.LAN	Novell Ethernet NE/2-32
NE3200.LAN	INTEL EtherExpress32 Microdyne EXOS235T Novell Ethernet NE3200
NE32HUB.LAN	Novell Ethernet NE32HUB
NI9210.LAN	Racal-Datacom NI9210
NTR2000.LAN	Novell Token Ring
PCN2L.LAN	Novell PCN II and PCN Baseband Driver
SMC8000.LAN	SMC EtherCard PLUS Family Server Driver

LAN Driver File Name	Description
SMCARC.LAN	Standard Microsystems Corp. ISA or MCA ARCNET Driver
T20N4X.LAN	Cabletron Token Ring T20XX (ISA/EISA) ODI Server Driver
TCARCH.LAN	Thomas-Conrad ARCNet/TCNS Server Lan Driver
TCE16ATH.LAN	Thomas-Conrad TC5045 Server Lan Driver
TCE16MCH.LAN	Thomas-Conrad TC5045 16-bit Server Lan Driver
TCE32MCH.LAN	Thomas-Conrad TC5045 32-bit Server Lan Driver
TCNSH.LAN	Thomas-Conrad TCNS Server Lan Driver
TCTOKH.LAN	Thomas-Conrad Token-Ring Server Lan Driver
TOKEN.LAN	Token Ring
TOKENDMA.LAN	IBM Token-Ring Busmaster
TRXNET.LAN	Novell Turbo RX-Net
UBPCETP.LAN	Ungermann-Bass MIUpc/EOTP MicroChannel adapter
UBPSETP.LAN	Ungermann-Bass MicroChannel adapter

Hardware Requirements for the Root Server

The first NetWare 4.*x* server that you install defines the initial NDS partition, which also contains the [Root] object of the NDS tree. For this reason, the first NetWare 4.*x* server that is installed is called the *root server*. The root server should be a 25 MHz Intel 80486 computer or better.

A faster machine is preferred as a root server, because the root server contains the master replica of the NDS root partition. A user logged on to a sub-partition (see fig. 12.1) and who needs to access an object on another sub-partition, needs to access (albeit transparently) the root server, which contains the linkage information to other partitions. Even though the object in another sub-partition can be contacted transparently, a fast root server minimizes access time to other sub-partitions.

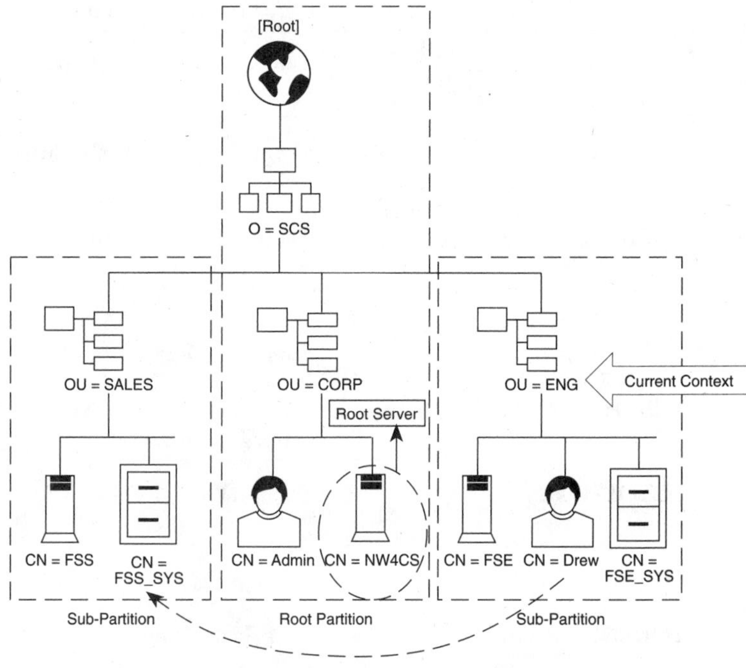

Figure 12.1 *Accessing objects in other sub-partitions.*

Software Requirements for NetWare 4.*x*

The software requirements for NetWare 4.*x* include DOS for the initial loading of the server software. The versions of DOS that are supported are DOS 3.1 and higher for a standard Intel platform with an ISA (Industry Standard Architecture) or EISA (Enhanced Industry Standard Architecture) bus. Micro Channel Adapter (MCA) computers must use a DOS 3.3 or higher. The other requirement is the NetWare 4.*x* software and license disk. A registration disk (different from the license disk) is also included. This is used to copy registration information on the installed NetWare 4.*x* software. Registration is done by sending the completed registration disk to Novell. Though recommended, registration is not a requirement for completing NetWare 4.*x* installation.

NetWare 4.*x* requires DOS for the initial load of the server:

- ISA/EISA bus servers need DOS version 3.1 or higher
- MCA bus servers need DOS version 3.3 or higher

The NetWare 4.*x* software normally comes on CD-ROM, but can be obtained on disks. For NetWare 4.0, there were 36 high density disks, 25 being for the operating system and client, 9 for documentation, 1 for the server license, and 1 for registration.

The hardware and software requirements are shown in figures 12.2 and 12.3.

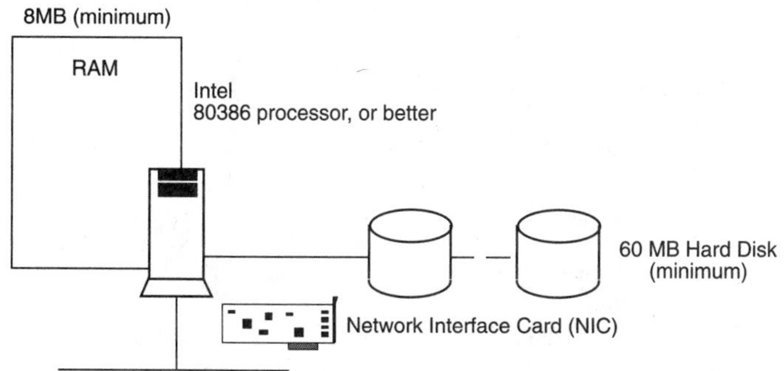

Figure 12.2
The hardware requirements for NetWare 4.x.

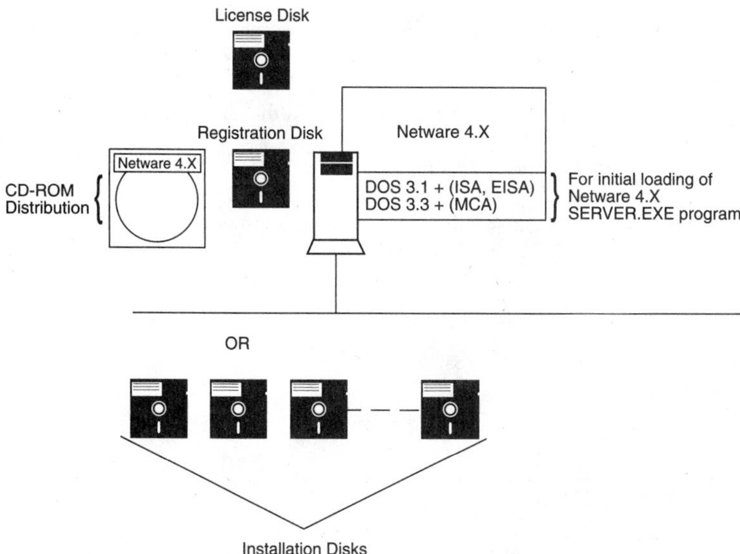

Figure 12.3
The software requirements for NetWare 4.x.

Computing Server Memory Requirements

NetWare documentation contains two ways of computing memory requirements. The first method is documented in the *NetWare Application Notes*, April 1993, and in the Installation and Upgrade

NetWare 4.0 manual. The second method is also documented in the Installation and Upgrade NetWare 4.0 manual. The first method is a simplified formula, and the second method is more detailed. This section presents both methods.

Simplified Method for Estimating Server Memory Requirements

NetWare 4.*x* server memory requirements can be estimated based on the following factors:

1. Disk space supported on the NetWare server.

   Amount of server RAM needed is 0.008 times the disk space in megabytes.

2. Number of files that have a name space entry other than DOS name space.

   For instance, if a Macintosh, NFS, OS/2, or FTAM name space is added to a volume, an additional directory entry is added to the directory entry table that contains the file name and attributes for that name space.

   Amount of server RAM needed is 5/1048576 multiplied by the number of files that have an additional name space entry, and the number of additional name spaces.

   DOS name space, which is the default name space, is not used in the above calculations.

3. Cache memory needed for increased server performance.

   Allocating server RAM for caching can have a dramatic effect in improving server performance.

   In general, a cache size of 1 MB to 4 MB should be added.

4. Memory used by the operating system software.

   Allocate 5 MB to 6 MB for loading the NetWare operating system, directory services, LAN and disk drivers, and the INSTALL.NLM.

5. Memory for CLIB or BTRIEVE.NLM.

   If you are running an application that uses CLIB or BTRIEVE.NLM, you need to add 2 MB to the server RAM. An example of an application that needs these NLMs is PSERVER.NLM (implements printer server on the NetWare server).

6. Any additional NLMs that you wish to run on the server.

   Add an estimated memory requirement for these NLMs.

Using the preceding factors, you can come up with an equation for estimating server RAM. The following equation takes into account the six factors listed previously:

$E = D \times 0.008 + F \times N \times 5/1048576 + C + S + 2 \times A + O$

E = Estimated server RAM in megabytes

D = Disk space in megabytes

F = Number of files that have a name space

N = Number of name spaces per file

C = Cache size (1 MB to 4 MB)

S = Memory needed for server. Novell Installation manuals use a value of 6 MB; NetWare Application Notes use a value of 5.5 MB.

A = 1 if an application uses CLIB or BTRIEVE.NLM; 0 otherwise

O = Memory for other NLMs loaded on the server

An example helps clarify the use of the preceding equation.

SCS has decided to install a NetWare 4.*x* server on an Intel 80486 33 MHz computer with a 200 MB hard disk. They plan to be running NetWare for Macintosh on the server, and therefore the server must support an additional Macintosh name space. There are an estimated 1,500 files on the server volume. The NetWare server also is used as a print server, but does not run any other application servers. For improved server performance, it is has been decided to have at least 2 MB for caching.

The preceding example's parameters are as follows:

D = Disk space in megabytes = 200

F = Number of files that have a name space = 1500

N = Number of name spaces per file = 1

C = Cache size (1 MB to 4 MB) = 2

S = Memory needed for server = 6

A = 1 if an application uses CLIB or BTRIEVE.NLM = 1

O = Memory for other NLMs loaded on the server = 0

NetWare 4.*x* server memory requirements can be estimated by using the following formula.

Using the preceding parameters in the equation for estimated server RAM:

$$\begin{aligned} E &= D \times 0.008 + F \times N \times 5/1048576 + C + S + 2 \times A + O \\ &= 200 \times 0.008 + 1500 \times 1 \times 5/1048576 + 2 + 6 + 2 \times 1 + 0 \\ &= 1.6 + 0.007 + 2 + 6 + 2 + 0 \\ &= 11.607 \text{ MB} \end{aligned}$$

Therefore, a server RAM of 12 MB should meet the preceding needs.

Detailed Method for Estimating Server Memory Requirements

NetWare 4.*x* server memory requirements can be estimated based on the following detailed factors:

1. Core operating system requirement is 5 MB.
2. Cache memory needed for increased server performance:

   1 MB + (D × 5) KB

   in which D = online disk space in MB.

   Allocating server RAM for caching can have a dramatic effect in improving server performance.

   This formula is based on the assumption that the number of users accessing the server increase with disk space. It is designed to give reasonable performance per user.

3. Memory used by the media manager:

   150 KB + (0.2 × D) KB

   in which D = online disk space in MB.

4. Memory for connection in use:

   (2 × U) KB

   in which U = number of user connections.

   If the server is already installed, you can use the MONITOR.NLM to get a more accurate value.

   The 2 KB per user is used for holding connection state information for the user.

5. Memory for packet receive buffers:

   $(2.3 \times R)$ KB

   in which R = number of packet receive buffers.

   If the server is already installed, you can use the MONITOR.NLM to get a more accurate value.

6. Memory for directory cache buffers:

   $(4.3 \times Db)$ KB

   in which Db = number of directory cache buffers.

   If the server is already installed, you can use the MONITOR.NLM to get a more accurate value.

7. Memory for service processes:

   $(9 \times P)$ KB

   in which P = number of service processes.

   If the server is already installed, you can use the MONITOR.NLM to get a more accurate value.

8. Memory needed to support file compression, if it is enabled on any volume:

   250 KB

9. Volume requirements:

   a. File Allocation Table:

      $(8.2 \times Vb)$ Bytes

      in which Vb = Volume Blocks.

   Volume Blocks can be computed by dividing the size of a volume by the block size in use for that volume. Thus:

      Vb = V / B

      in which V = Volume size and B = Block size.

   b. Block suballocation (if enabled):

      $((B \times 2 - 1) \times 4096 + 5 \times Nf)$ Bytes

in which

B = Block size

Nf = Number of files and Nf can be estimated by dividing the volume size by average file size.

c. Directory Entry Tables:

$10 \times Nf$ Bytes

in which Nf = Number of files.

10. NLM Requirements.

Add up all the NLMs that are needed at the server. The following table can be used to estimate memory requirements for some common NLMs.

If the server is already installed, you can use the MONITOR.NLM to get a more accurate estimate for memory used by NLMs.

NLM	Function	RAM Usage
BTRIEVE.NLM	Needed by database managers and NetWare NFS, NetWare for Macintosh	700 KB
CLIB.NLM	Needed by PSERVER.NLM and other NLMs	500 KB
INSTALL.NLM	For installation and maintenance	600 KB
PSERVER.NLM	Implements the print server	200 KB

12

Using the preceding factors, you can come up with an equation for estimating server RAM. The following equation takes into account the six factors listed previously:

$$E = S + (1\text{ MB} + (D \times 5)\text{ KB}) + (150\text{ KB} + (0.2 \times D)\text{ KB}) + (2 \times U)\text{ KB}$$

$$+ (2.3 \times R)\text{ KB} + (4.3 \times Db)\text{ KB} + (9 \times P)\text{ KB} + 250 \times Fc\text{ KB}$$

$$+ (8.2 \times Vb) + ((B \times 2 - 1) \times 4096 + 5 \times Nf) + 10 \times Nf$$

$$+ O$$

E = Estimated Server RAM in megabytes

S = Core operating system requirements = 5 MB

D = Online disk space in MB

U = Number of user connections

R = Number of packet receive buffers

Db = Number of directory cache buffers

P = Number of service processes

Fc = 1 if file compression enabled on a volume; 0, otherwise

Vb = Volume Blocks

B = Block size

Nf = Number of files

O = Memory for other NLMs loaded on the server

The same example is used for the simplified memory estimation.

SCS has decided to install a NetWare 4.*x* server on an Intel 80486 33 MHz computer with a 200 MB hard disk. There are an estimated 1,500 files on the server volume and file compression is enabled on the volume. The NetWare server also is used as a print server, but does not run any other application servers. It is estimated that 50 users are on the server. Assume that the media manager is active, and the number of packet receive buffers is 50, directory cache buffers is 50, and number of service processes is 10.

This example's parameters are as follows:

S = Core operating system requirements = 5 MB

D = Online disk space in MB = 200

U = Number of user connections = 50

R = Number of packet receive buffers = 50 (assumption)

Db = Number of directory cache buffers = 50 (assumption)

P = Number of service processes = 10 (assumption)

Fc = 1

Vb = Volume Blocks = 200 MB / 4 KB = 50,000

B = Block size = 4 KB

Nf = Number of files = 1,500

O = Memory for other NLMs loaded on the server = 200 KB
(from table of NLM memory usage)

NetWare 4.*x* server memory requirements can be estimated by using the following formula.

Using the preceding parameters in the equation for estimated server RAM:

$E = S + (1\ MB + (D \times 5)\ KB) + (150\ KB + (0.2 \times D)\ KB) + (2 \times U)\ KB$

$+ (2.3 \times R)\ KB + (4.3 \times Db)\ KB + (9 \times P)\ KB + 250 \times Fc\ KB$

$+ (8.2 \times Vb) + ((B \times 2 - 1) \times 4096 + 5 \times Nf) + 10 \times Nf$

$+ O$

$= 5\ MB + (1\ MB + 200 \times 5\ KB) + (150\ KB + 0.2 \times 200\ KB) + 2 \times 50\ KB$

$+ 2.3 \times 50\ KB + 4.3 \times 50\ KB + 9 \times 10\ KB + 250 \times 1\ KB$

$+ 8.2 \times 50000 + (4 \times 2 - 1) \times 4096 + 5 \times 1500$

$+ 200\ KB$

$= 5\ MB + 2\ MB + 190\ KB + 100\ KB$

12 $+ 115\ KB + 215\ KB + 90\ KB + 250\ KB$

$+ 410000 + 28672 + 7500$

$+ 200\ KB$

$= 7.29\ MB$

$+ 0.67\ MB$

$+ 0.43\ MB$
(assuming 1024 KB=1 MB and 1024 Bytes =1 KB)

$+ 0.2\ MB$

$= 8.59\ MB$

Therefore, a server RAM of 12 MB should meet the preceding needs and leave plenty of space for normal file caching needs.

Computing Server Disk Requirements

A NetWare 4.*x* server needs DOS for initial loading of its SERVER.EXE program. DOS can be loaded from a floppy disk or from a DOS partition on the server disk. It is much more convenient and faster to start NetWare 4.*x* from a DOS partition on the server disk, so you should plan on having at least a 5 MB partition to store SERVER.EXE, STARTUP.NCF, Disk drivers, Name Space NLMs, DOS system files and COMMAND.COM, and other useful utilities (VREPAIR.NLM, and so on).

The minimum disk space requirements for NetWare 4.*x* are represented in figure 12.4 and described in the following table:

NetWare utilities (SYS:PUBLIC)=	24 MB	(38.1%)
System files and programs (SYS:SYSTEM)=	7 MB	(11.1%)
Login utilities (SYS:LOGIN)=	2 MB	(3.2%)
Online help (Electro Text)=	25 MB	(39.7%)
DOS/Windows Client software=	5 MB	(7.9%)
Total	6 MB	(100%)

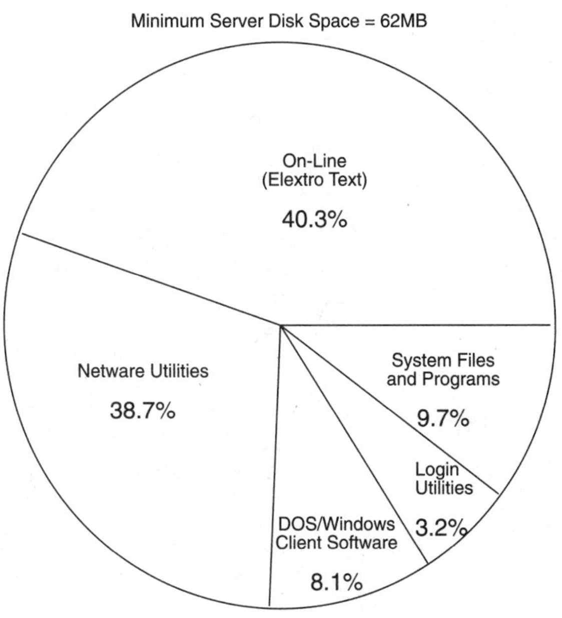

Figure 12.4
NetWare 4.x. disk space requirements.

If OS/2 workstations are being used, you should add another 5 MB for the OS/2 client installation and software programs.

As can be seen from the estimate of disk space requirements, the Online help takes up the largest amount of disk space (39.7 percent).

These figures are for NetWare 4.*x* configured for English language support. As additional language modules are installed, the disk space requirements can be expected to increase.

To save disk space in a multiple server network, install NetWare documentation on a single server. However, if all users on the network access this single server for online documentation, you may have to go to a larger user license version of NetWare 4.*x*. You may decide to split the documentation between two servers in order to keep the server license cost down and to increase availability of the documentation in case one of the documentation servers is down.

Determining the Installation Method

NetWare 4.*x* provides the installer with a number of choices for performing server installation. You can install from:

1. CD-ROM attached to the server being installed
2. CD-ROM on an existing NetWare server
3. Floppy disks
4. Network disks

The INSTALL program is the same for each of the preceding methods. The difference is in terms of time and cost.

A rough estimate of the installation time is presented in table 12.2. The figures are approximate because of variability in network speeds, CD-ROM data transfer rate, and the fact that floppy disk installation requires close attention from the installer. Most of the time is spent copying the online documentation and the public utilities and files.

Table 12.2
Estimated Installation Time

Network Installation Method	Installation Time (Minutes)
Network drive	30
CD-ROM	40
Floppy disk	90

As can be seen from table 12.2, the fastest method is to use a network drive (assuming Ethernet speeds). However, this implies the availability of an already installed server. Also, to use the network drive method, the NetWare server distribution must be copied on to an existing server, and this itself could be a time-consuming process.

Though the time estimate for the floppy-disk method seems to be only twice as much as the CD-ROM method, you may want to take into account the annoyance factor of having to insert the many installation disks.

To install over the network, you must have a logical connection from the server machine to the network source that has a copy of the distribution software (see fig. 12.5). This can be done by installing the network client software on the server machine being installed and making a network connection to the NetWare distribution source (another NetWare server). Figure 12.5 shows that the network drive F is used to access the distribution source. Any other network driver besides F can be used for this purpose. The server distribution software can be either on a server disk or a CD-ROM.

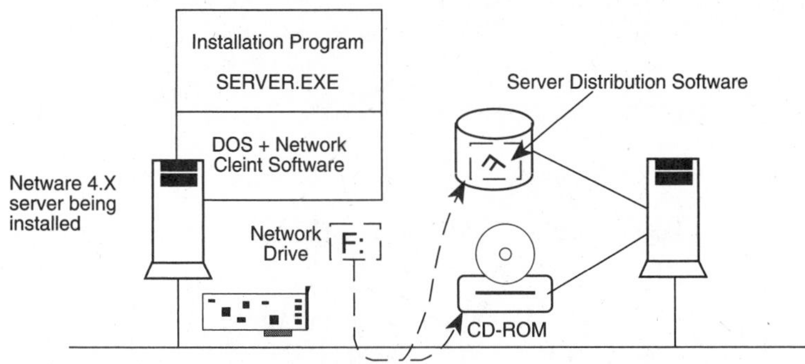

Figure 12.5
Installing over a network.

Do not use a memory manager such as HIMEM, 386MAX, QEMM on the server being installed, as these memory managers conflict with NetWare's use of the server's extended memory.

While installing using the network method, do not load the server LAN driver to use the same NIC as the NetWare client software. This can be done by using two NICs at the server, or by using a single NIC, but performing the LOAD and BIND statements that load and bind the LAN driver to the protocol stack, after copying the distribution software. When you load the LAN driver, it imitates the LAN board, but for some LAN boards this can disrupt the network drive connection. If all that is left to copy are the ElectroText and CBT files, you can repeat this step later or use RCONSOLE to copy these files.

NetWare 4.*x* Installation

This section reviews the installation procedure and then presents you with the details of performing the installation. Figure 12.6 shows you an overview of the NetWare 4.*x* installation.

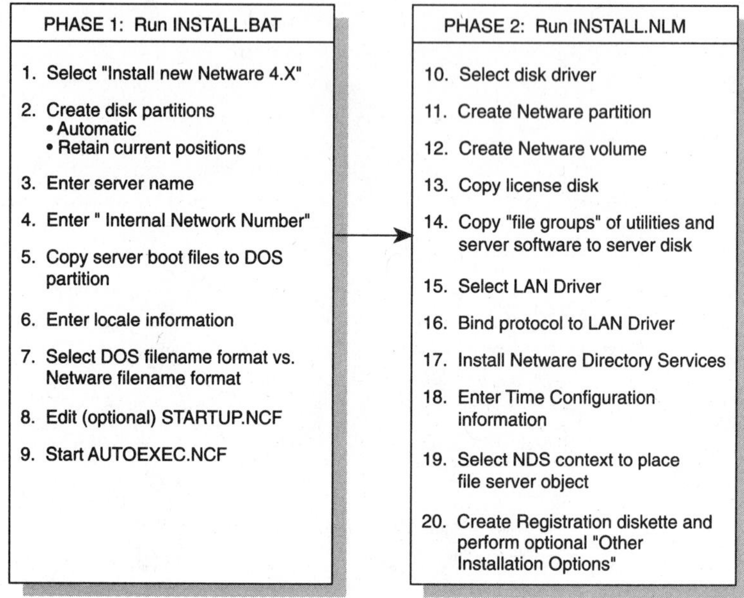

Figure 12.6
An overview of a NetWare 4.x installation.

Here is a guided tour of the NetWare 4.*x* installation:

1. You begin the installation by booting with the INSTALL disk if you are using the floppy disk method.

   If you are using the CD-ROM method, you can go to the \NETWARE.40*language* directory on your CD-ROM device and run INSTALL.

   12

   The CD-ROM must be recognizable by DOS. This means that you must load all the essential drivers to recognize the CD-ROM device. Since each CD-ROM manufacturer has a different set of installation procedures and CD-ROM drivers, you should follow their instructions.

   CD-ROM installation users should follow these steps:

   a. Change your directory to the CD-ROM drive.

   b. The directory structure on the CD-ROM looks similar to that shown in figure 12.7.

   c. Change your current directory to \NETWARE.40\ENGLISH. If you wish to install and configure NetWare 4.*x* for another language, replace ENGLISH in the above directory name with the name of one of the supported languages (DEUTSCH, ESPANOL, FRANCAIS, ITALIANO, etc.). If you select another language, it becomes the default server language from now on. The default server language can be changed by copying the SERVER.MSG file from one of the language directories.

   d. Run the INSTALL.BAT file.

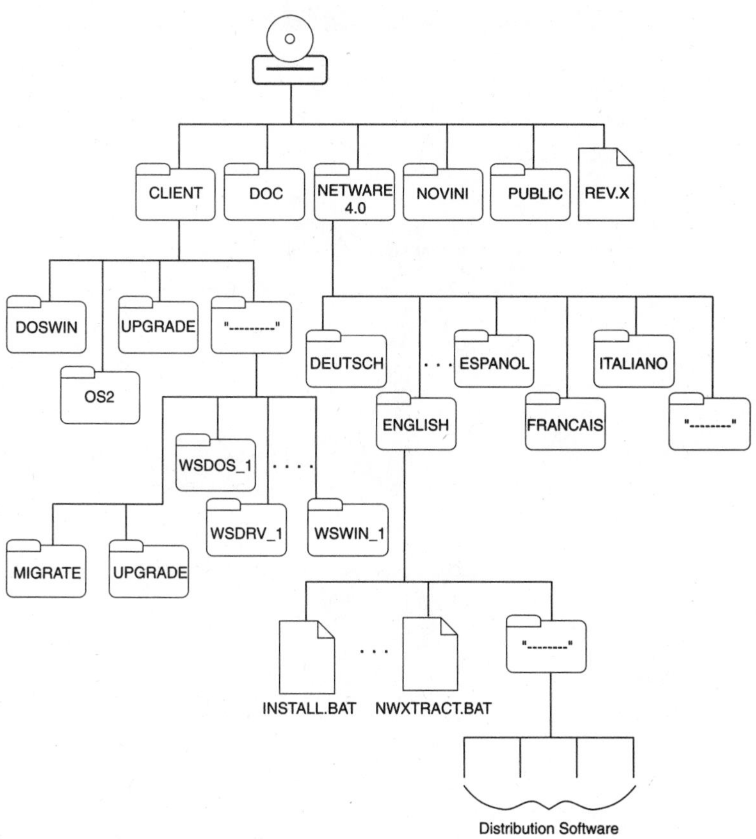

Figure 12.7
The CD-ROM Distribution Directory Structure.

2. You should see a screen that looks similar to figure 12.8. The screen has the following options:

   - Install new NetWare 4.*x*
   - Upgrade NetWare 3.1*x* or 4.*x*
   - Display Information (README) File

   Browse through the README files (by selecting the Display Information (README) File option) for tips on resolving installation problems. Figure 12.9 shows some of the files that are available. You may also see the Release Notes for the Netware 4 version that you are installing.

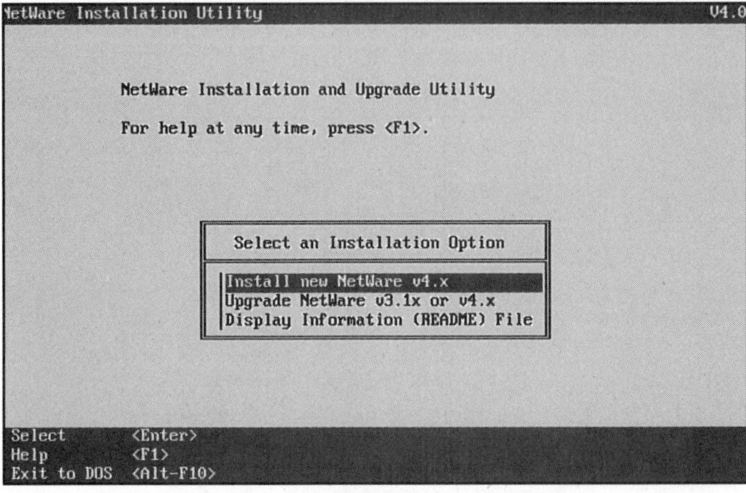

Figure 12.8
NetWare 4.x installation options.

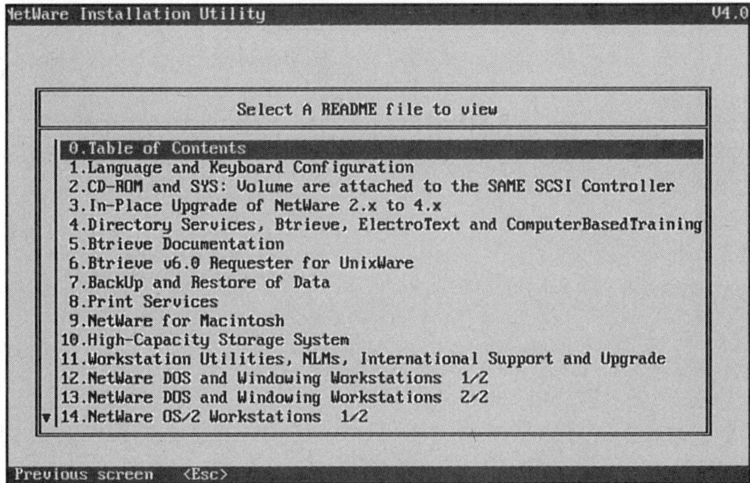

Figure 12.9
NetWare 4.x installation options.

3. Select the Install new NetWare 4.*x* option to install a new NetWare 4.*x* server. You should see a screen similar to figure 12.10.

   If you are selecting the Upgrade NetWare 3.1*x* or 4.*x* option, back up your data before performing the upgrade, even though no existing data files are deleted.

4. You can retain existing DOS partitions or create a new one.

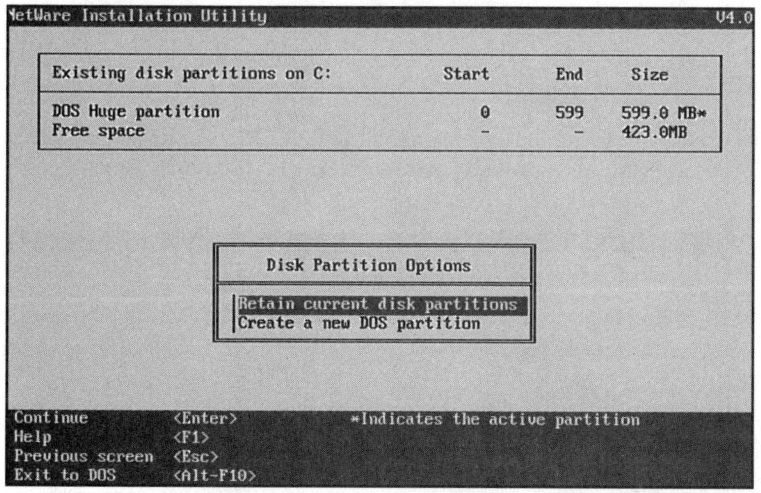

Figure 12.10
NetWare 4.x Installation: Disk Partition Options.

If the hard disk has not been configured, you should select the Create a new DOS partition option. If you have already configured your hard disk by manually creating a partition and installing DOS, you should select the Retain current disk partitions option.

The instructions that follow describe the steps necessary to create a new DOS partition; this is the case if you have selected a new NetWare 4.*x* installation.

5. If you select the Create a new DOS partition option, you should see a screen similar to figure 12.11.

   If you select the Retain current disk partitions option, skip to step 11.

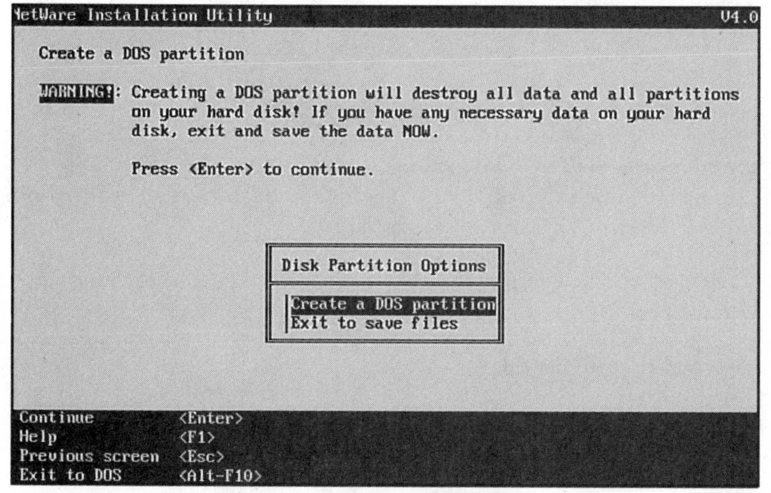

Figure 12.11
Create a DOS partition.

6. Select Create a DOS partition from Disk Partition Options. If you have data on your hard disk that you wish to save, you can select the Exit to save files option and back up your data and restart the installation.

7. You are prompted to enter the size of the DOS partition (see fig 12.12). The default is 5 MB, but you can create any size partition, provided you leave at least 60 MB for NetWare 4.*x*.

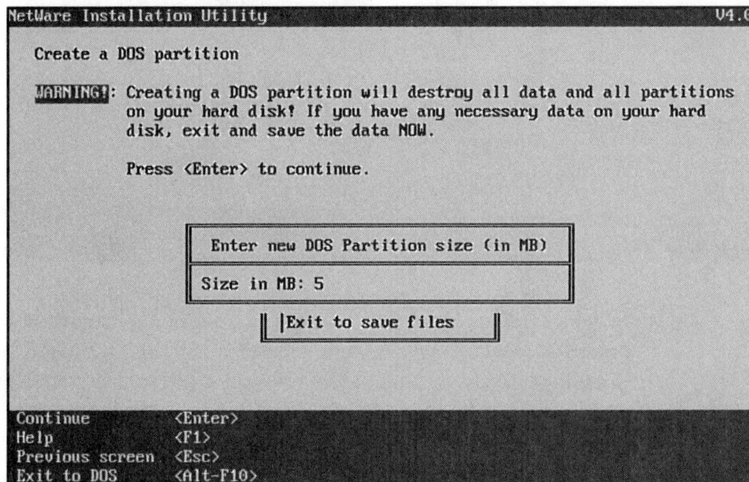

Figure 12.12
DOS partition size.

8. After entering the DOS partition size, you are asked to verify `Add this partition and destroy the data on your hard disk.` Answer Yes.

9. A message screen should appear informing you that a new DOS partition has been created, and the computer reboots to allow DOS to recognize the new partition.

   Press Enter.

   If installing from NetWare distribution disks, the system is restarted.

   If you are using any other method (CD-ROM, network, and so on), you should manually restart INSTALL the way you did at the beginning of this installation. Make sure that the DOS programs such as FORMAT.COM are in the search path.

10. After INSTALL is restarted, you are informed that the DOS partition can now be formatted. Press Enter to accept this choice.

    The DOS partition is now being formatted.

11. You are prompted for the server name (see fig 12.13).

Enter a server name, which can be from 2 to 47 characters and include alphanumeric characters (A-Z, 0-9), hyphens and underscores. You cannot use a period as the first character.

After installation, the server name is saved in AUTOEXEC.NCF file. When the SERVER.EXE program loads during normal startup of the NetWare server, the server name is read from this file.

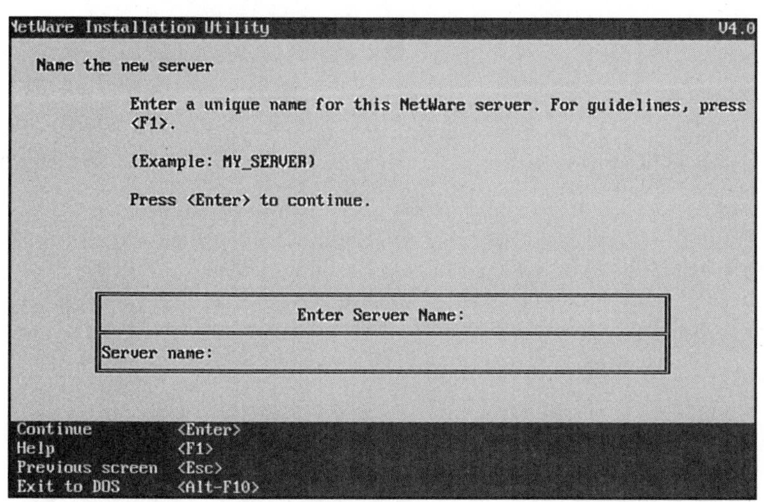

Figure 12.13
Prompting for server name.

12. You are prompted for an Internal network number (see fig 12.14). The installation program generates a number at random. You can select this internal network number, since it is not likely to conflict with an existing internal network number.

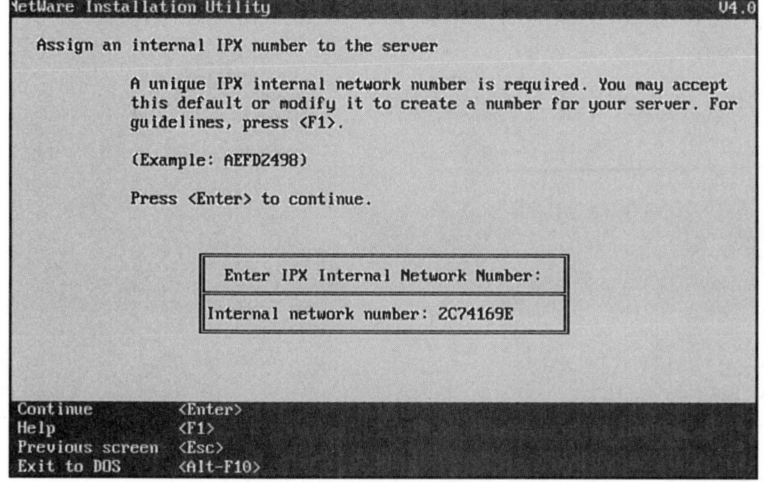

Figure 12.14
NetWare 4.x Installation: Internal Network Number.

After formatting the DOS partition, NetWare 4.*x* installation asks you to enter:

- Server name
- Accept a random Internal IPX network number

It is best to select your own internal network number according to your own scheme, or to use Novell's IPX Registry. Novell is creating an IPX number registry where you can reserve a range of network numbers to allow the creation of a global IPX network, similar to the existing Internet (global network based primarily on TCP/IP).

Internal network numbers can be eight-hexadecimal digits long and must be different from other internal network numbers and the network numbers used to identify the cable segments.

The *internal network number* describes a logical network that uniquely identifies the NCP (NetWare Core Protocol) processing engine that is at the heart of the NetWare server. Internal network numbers were introduced in NetWare 3.0 to solve routing anomalies that were common in NetWare 2.*x* networks, where the NCP processing engine had a network number that was the same as that of the network installed on LAN. A (the first network adapter on the server).

13. If you are not running INSTALL from \NETWARE.40*language*, you are asked to verify the source and destination paths for copying the server (see fig 12.15) boot files. To change the source path use F2; to change the destination path use F4.

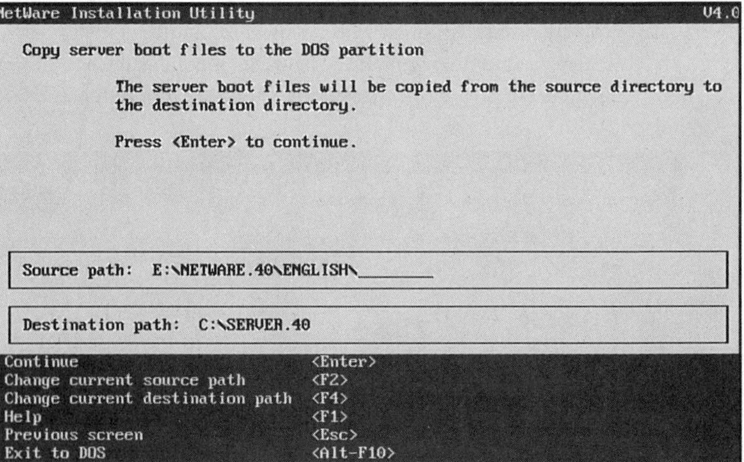

Figure 12.15
NetWare 4.x Installation: Copying server boot files.

The default source path is the drive you booted from. Normally, you should not have to change the source path if you were installing using the floppy disk or local CD-ROM method. If you were installing from across the network, you can press F2 and specify the network drive and path to read the software distribution from.

The default destination is C:\SERVER.40. You should accept this default, unless you have your own standard as to where the server files are copied.

14. Press Enter to verify the source and destination paths.

    You should see a status display of the files that are copied to the DOS partition (see fig. 12.16).

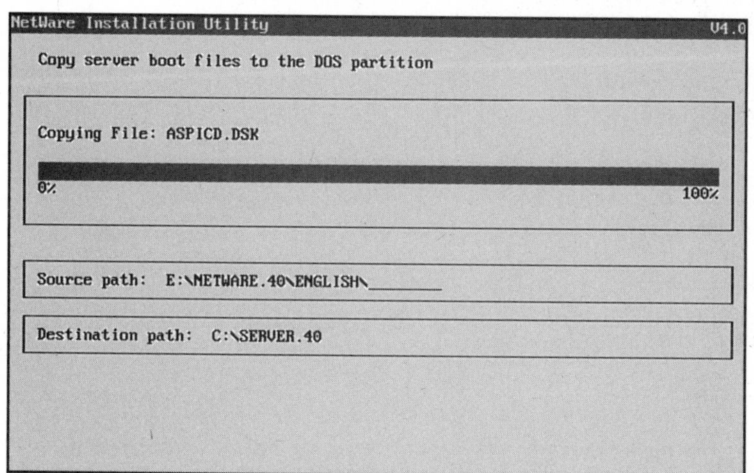

Figure 12.16
NetWare 4.x: server boot files being copied.

15. You are asked to select a locale configuration for the server (see fig. 12.17). The configuration that is displayed is that for the server, but its default values that are displayed are taken from the DOS configuration you are using to run the INSTALL program.

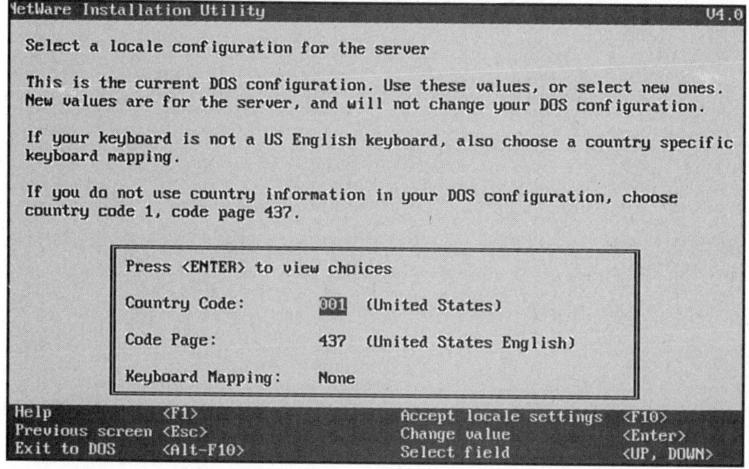

Figure 12.17
NetWare 4.x: locale information.

Prior versions of NetWare did not support country-specific conventions such as differences in keyboard layout. NetWare 4.*x* supports internationalization and allows other keyboard layouts.

The *Country Code* is a three-digit country code. Consult the COUNTRY.SYS entry in your DOS manual for the applicable country code. The U.S. country code is 001.

The *Code Page* is a country-dependent three-digit page code. For U.S. English, the code page value is 437. This defines the character sets that are used for screen display.

The *Keyboard Mapping* supports keyboard layout differences that are specific to a language. The Keyboard Mapping values that are supported are France, Germany, Italy, Spain, and United States.

When you are done making changes, press F10 to accept local changes. If you press Enter at any time, you are editing the field that has been highlighted.

16. You must next select the file name format (see fig. 12.18). The file name format choices are:

    a. DOS Filename Format (recommended)

    b. NetWare Filename Format

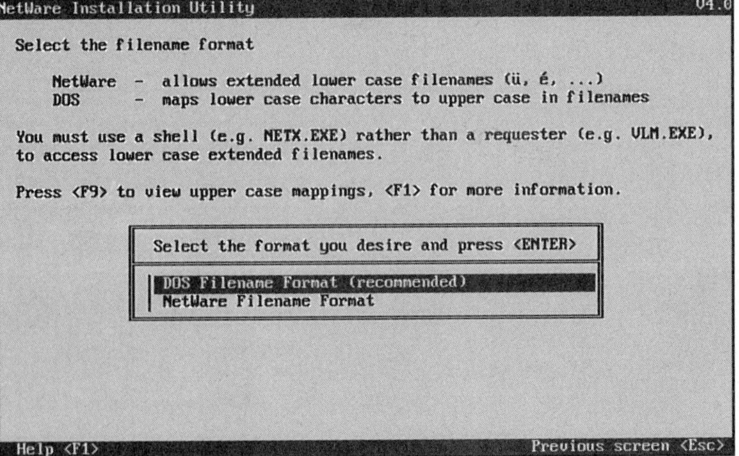

Figure 12.18
NetWare 4.x: Filename Format.

NetWare file format allows extended lowercase file names, whereas DOS maps lowercase letters' characters to uppercase for file names.

Select the DOS Filename Format option, unless you are using the NETX shell to create extended lowercase file names. The NETX shell allows the creation of extended lowercase file names, but these file names are not readable by the DOS requester (VLM).

For a detailed discussion on file name format issues, see the section on "Setting File Name Format," later in this chapter.

17. You are asked if you want to specify any special startup SET commands.

    There are several SET commands that can be placed in the STARTUP.NCF file only. The STARTUP.NCF file resides on the DOS partition and in the directory where SERVER.EXE program was copied. It contains commands to load disk drivers and name spaces, and special commands such as SET AUTO REGISTER MEMORY ABOVE 16 MEGABYTES=OFF. (Set to ON to automatically add memory above 16 MB for EISA bus server machines.) With NetWare 4.02 and higher, set Reserved Buffers below 16 MB to 200 if the server has devices that use the ASPI interface.

    Select Yes only if your server configuration demands that you need to set special parameters in STARTUP.NCF file. Otherwise, select No. You can always edit the STARTUP.NCF file at a later stage.

18. You are asked if you want AUTOEXEC.BAT to load SERVER.EXE. If you answer Yes, your AUTOEXEC.BAT is modified to contain the following commands to start the server automatically, every time the machine is booted:

    ```
    REM The following lines were created by the server
    installation program.
    REM They will cause the server to come up whenever this computer is
    booted.
    :BEGIN_SERVER
    C:
    cd C:\SERVER.40
    SERVER
    :END_SERVER
    ```

    If you select No, you have to manually start the SERVER.EXE program.

    Select Yes, unless you have special circumstances. You can always edit the AUTOEXEC.BAT file, at a later stage, to add other commands such as the DOS command PAUSE to give you a chance to break out of the AUTOEXEC.BAT file.

19. If you selected Yes to have the install program add SERVER.EXE to the AUTOEXEC.BAT file, you are asked to verify the location of the AUTOEXEC.BAT file.

20. The SERVER.EXE program loads at this point.

21. You are informed of the path from which NetWare loads (see fig 12.19). If you wish to change this (such as specify a network drive), you must use F3 to select a different path.

    Press Enter to select the default path.

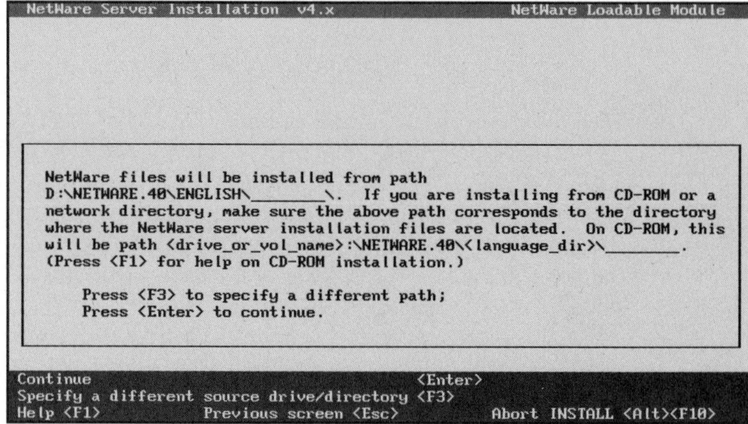

Figure 12.19
NetWare 4.x Installation Path.

22. You are presented with information that NetWare is scanning for available drivers, after which you see a list of disk drivers.

23. Select the disk driver that matches the server disk controller. If the driver you want is not listed, press Ins to load the disk driver from a distribution medium.

24. You are presented with a screen for selecting the parameter settings for your disk controller. These include Port value, Interrupt number, DMA value, ABOVE16 (Y for Yes, N for No), and so on.

    Make any corrections and verify that the parameter settings match disk controller settings.

    Press F10 to save changes and continue with installation. Follow instructions to load the driver and continue with installation.

25. You are given a choice of creating disk partitions "Manually" or "Automatically." "Manually" allows you to specify partition sizes, Hot Fix, and mirroring. "Automatically" allows you to create an unmirrored NetWare partition in the disk space available.

26. After you create the NetWare partition, you are presented with the Manage NetWare Volumes screen. This screen shows a summary of all the proposed volume changes. The volume SYS: is always the first volume that is created. It is created automatically on device 0, and must have a minimum size of 50 MB.

If you have multiple volumes, Novell documentation says that they are given the default names of VOL1 (device 1), VOL2 (device2), and so on. You can choose a different name by using F3 or Ins. You can also modify the volume parameters (see fig. 12.20), and you can change all volume names, except the volume name SYS:.

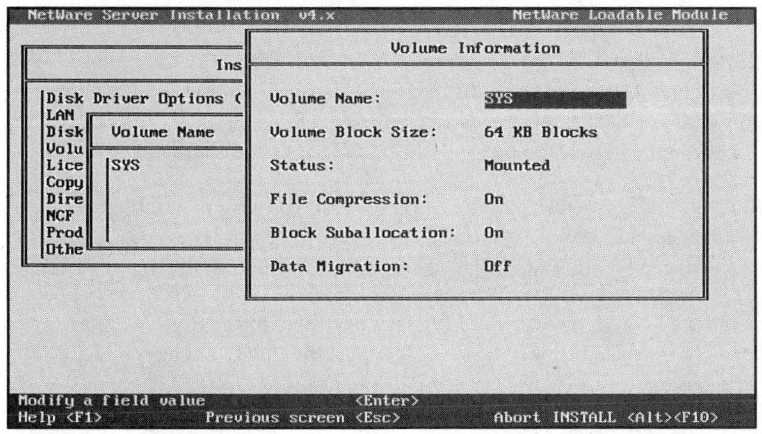

Figure 12.20
Volume Information.

Other parameters you can change on a volume are as follows:

a. **Volume Block Size.** The volume block size can be set to multiples of 4 KB, up to 64 KB (4 KB, 8 KB, 16 KB, 32 KB, 64 KB).

   The volume block size has a default value that is set according to the size of the volume. Table 12.3 shows the default volume size that is selected.

Table 12.3
Default Block Size versus Volume Size

Default Block Size (KB)	Volume Size (Range is in MB)
4	0 to 31
8	32 to 149
16	150 to 499
32	500 to 1,999
64	2,000 and above

Because of disk suballocation, a larger block size is not wasted for small files. Once selected, the disk block size cannot be changed.

Select a block size of 64 KB because most disk controllers perform best at this block size. Also, disk block suballocation ensures that space is used efficiently, even for larger block sizes.

b. **File Compression.** This ensures that files that have not been accessed for a specified period of time are compressed to save on disk space. Once file compression for a volume is enabled, it cannot be disabled. After installation, individual files and directories can be marked with or without compression by using the FLAG command (or the FILER utility).

c. **Block Suballocation.** This feature optimizes disk space by ensuring that unused fragments of disk blocks are not wasted. Actual disk space is used in 512-byte sizes. Left over space in a block is shared by other files. The default value for Blocks Suballocation is On.

d. **Data Migration.** This allows movement of files to a near-line storage device such as an optical jukebox. The default value for Data Migration is Off. Unless you have a High-Capacity Storage System (HCSS) installed, leave this value set to Off.

27. Press F10 to save volume changes.

28. You are asked to insert the license disk. Follow instructions to insert the license disk.

29. You are asked to verify the NetWare 4.*x* source path. Modify the path, if necessary, by using F3, and press Enter.

30. You are given a choice of file groups that you may want to load. These file groups should include:

    - NetWare 4.*x* DOS Utilities
    - NetWare 4.0 OS/2 Utilities
    - NetWare 4.0 Windowing Utilities
    - Setup a Network Directory for Client Install and Upgrade

    Check the boxes for the file groups you wish to install. You should install at the very minimum NetWare 4.*x* DOS Utilities and NetWare 4.0 Windowing Utilities.

    Press F10 to accept and save your selections, and confirm your selections. After this, you should see a status list of files that are copied to your server disk.

31. When file copying is completed, you see a message on the screen informing you to press Enter to continue. Press Enter.

32. A message `Scanning for available drivers` should appear, and you are presented with a list of LAN drivers.

    Please note that at this point the NetWare 4.*x* server cannot transmit or receive messages on the network. Only after you load and bind the driver to the protocol stack does the NetWare 4.*x* server become an active participant on the network.

33. Scroll through the list (see fig. 12.21) and select the correct LAN driver for your NIC. If your driver is not listed, press Ins to load a driver from a floppy disk. If the driver is different from floppy drive A, use F3 to specify an alternate source.

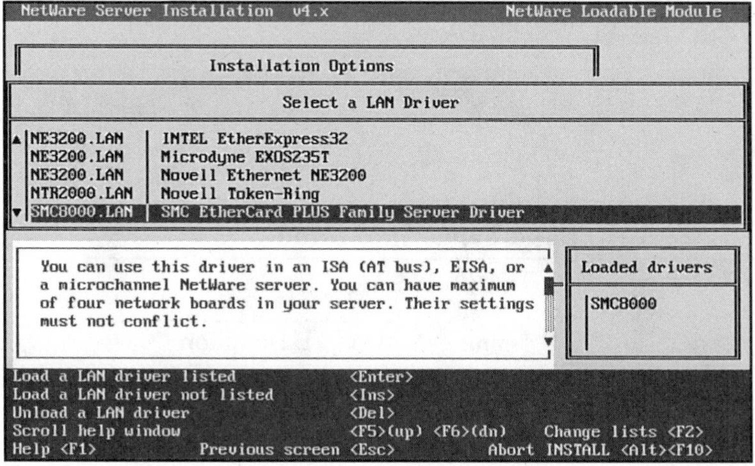

Figure 12.21
The Select a LAN Driver option.

34. You are presented with a default set of parameter values for your driver such as the following (see fig. 12.22):

    - Port value
    - Memory address
    - Interrupt number
    - DMA value (if your NIC uses Direct Memory Access)
    - Frame types

The port value, memory address, interrupt number, and DMA values should match the hardware settings on the NIC.

The frame type values that are supported are shown in table 12.4.

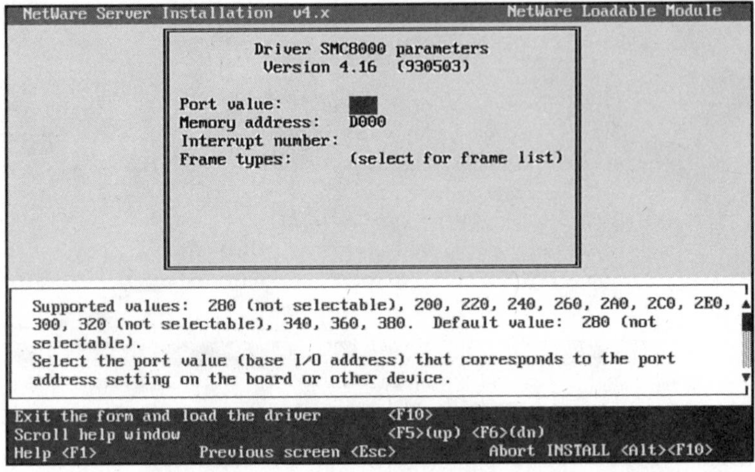

Figure 12.22
LAN Driver Parameters.

Table 12.4
Server Frame Types Supported

Frame	FRAME Parameter Name	Default Logical Name	Description
IEEE 802.3	ETHERNET _802.3	*boardname* _1E_802.3	Novell's raw Ethernet frame type. Does not include an LLC (IEEE 802.2).
IEEE 802.2	ETHERNET _802.2	*boardname* _1E_802.2	Default frame type for NetWare 4.*x*. Essentially IEEE 802.3 frame with an LLC (IEEE 802.2) sublayer.
IEEE 802.3 with SNAP extension	ETHERNET _SNAP	*boardname* _1E_SNAP	Used for Appletalk networks. Essentially an IEEE 802.2 frame with an additional 3-octet Organization Unit Identifier (OUI) and a 2-byte Ether Type field.
Ethernet II	ETHERNET _II	*boardname* _1E_II	Ethernet II frame, which differs from IEEE 802.3. Main distinction is the presence of a 2-octet Ether Type field instead of a 2-octet length field (IEEE 802.3).

Frame	FRAME Parameter Name	Default Logical Name	Description
IEEE 802.5	TOKEN-RING	*boardname* _1T_RING	Standard IEEE 802.5 frame.
IEEE 802.5 with SNAP extension	TOKEN-RING_SNAP	*boardname* _1T_SNAP	Used for Appletalk networks. Essentially an IEEE 802.5 frame with an additional 3-octet Organizational Unit Identifier (OUI) and a 2-byte Ether Type field.
ARCnet	RX-NET	*boardname* _RX-NET	There is only one frame type that is used with ARCnet.

For Token Ring frames, you can specify a local address that overrides the *Media Access Control* (MAC) address of the Token Ring that is on the board (each IEEE specification LAN board has a unique 6-octet address). You should normally not have to override this address, unless interacting with other networks (such as SNA networks).

The default order of Token Ring frame transmission is that the *Most Significant Bit* (MSB) is transmitted first. Normally, you should not have to change this, unless the board vendor recommends it. To change this value to an LSB (Least Significant Bit) order, use the toggle key F4 on the highlighted frame in the Frame Type List. You can get to the Frame Type List by selecting the field Frame Types.

If you decide to change the bit order of address transmission, you must also specify that the order of node (MAC) address transmission is MSB or LSB. The default is MSB. The node address transmission order is changed by selecting the value in the Node Address field.

You can change a frame's default logical name by highlighting it in the Frame Type List and using F3. Alternatively, you can edit the LOAD *BoardDriver* statement in the AUTOEXEC.NCF file, after the installation.

For Ethernet, the default frame types that are loaded are EHERNET_802.3 and ETHERNET_802.2. Though ETHERNET_802.2 is the default frame type for NetWare 4.*x*, the ETHERNET_802.3 frame type is also loaded for compatibility with existing NetWare 3.*x* clients.

For Token Ring, the default frame type is TOKEN-RING.

35. After you select the LAN drivers, they are loaded. If the LAN driver cannot recognize the board, the loading of the LAN driver fails. You must have a LAN board installed on your server that matches the LAN driver settings.

The LAN driver is loaded *reentrantly* if you specified more than one frame type for the driver (loading reentrantly means that the program code for the driver is shared and differences in the frame type information are kept in a separate data area for each frame type).

The Installation program then asks you to specify a network address (same as network number for IPX) for each of the frame types you have selected. A random address is generated if this is the first server on a new network, but you should select a network number according to your own standards (see discussion in step 12).

If you are installing on an existing IPX network, NetWare 4.*x* installation searchs the network for the network number on the LAN segment.

Complete the binding of the LAN driver by following the instructions displayed on the server screen.

When done loading the LAN driver, you can select another LAN driver or select the Continue with installation option.

36. The NetWare server then searches the network for the existence of a directory tree. If it finds one, it displays the name of the directory tree. You can select this tree, or create a new tree by pressing Ins.

    If this is the first server on the network, you must select a name for the directory tree.

    If you are installing on an existing network, make sure that your server is connected to the network. If a new [Root] and directory tree is created, you are not able to integrate this with an existing network.

    If you attempt to create a new tree when one already exists, a warning message is displayed informing you of some of the consequences of your actions. Starting with NetWare 4.02, you can select a simple NDS installation or custom NDS installation. The simple NDS installation creates a single-level NDS tree with a single organization container. If you select the simple NDS installation, follow the screen instructions. The remaining numbered instructions describe the custom NDS installation.

37. You are prompted to select a time zone. Selecting the correct time zone is important, if you are going to connect to networks in other time zones. When prompted, make any changes to STARTUP.NCF and AUTOEXEC.NCF. Perform any Installation Options such as creating the Registration Disk.

38. You are presented with a form for entering time configuration information for the installed server:

    For *Time Server Type*, enter either a Single Reference Time Server, Reference Time Server, Primary Time Server, or Secondary Time Server. If you select the Single Reference Time Server, you cannot have a Primary Time Server or another Reference Time server. With Single Reference Time Server, only the Secondary Time Servers can exist.

    For *Standard time zone abbreviation*, enter the abbreviation code for your time zone. This string is for display purposes only. You can enter any value, but it is best to enter a value that is standard for your time zone. The important parameter to set for time zone offset is *Standard time offset from UTC*. The standard time zone abbreviation can also be changed in the AUTOEXEC.NCF file.

For *Standard time offset from UTC*, verify that the time-offset for your zone is correct. You can set the time offset in the format *hh:mm:ss* (hours:minutes:seconds) behind or after UTC.

Many areas of the world have daylight savings time, and several others do not. NetWare 4.*x* gives you the flexibility of changing the daylight savings time criteria, or disabling it altogether.

To enable daylight savings time, answer Yes to `Does your area have daylight savings time (DST)?` To disable daylight savings time, answer No to this parameter.

The DST time zone abbreviation specifies a string for daylight savings time that is used for display purposes only. The daylight savings rules are set by the DST offset from standard time, DST Start, and DST End parameters. The DST time zone abbreviation can also be changed in the AUTOEXEC.NCF file.

The DST offset from standard time is a parameter that represents the time difference between daylight savings time and standard time. This can have the value *hh:mm:ss* and can be set to be *ahead* or *behind* the standard time.

The DST Start and the DST End times indicate the start and end of daylight savings time. The values for these parameters can be programmed to be on a weekday of a specified month at a specific time, or on a specific day of the month at a specific time. For example, in the U.S.A., in areas that use daylight savings time, the daylight savings time commences at 2:00 a.m. on the first Sunday of the month of April and ends at 2:00 a.m. on the last Sunday of the month of October. Should the laws change to a different daylight savings start and end, NetWare 4.x provides the flexibility to provide for these changes from the server console.

The time settings are recorded in the AUTOEXEC.NCF file. The listing that follows shows a sample AUTOEXEC.NCF file that has the time settings. The commands dealing with time settings have been highlighted.

12

```
set Time Zone = MST7MDT
set Daylight Savings Time Offset = 1:00:00
set Start Of Daylight Savings Time = (APRIL SUNDAY
FIRST  2:00:00 AM)
set End Of Daylight Savings Time = (OCTOBER SUNDAY LAST
2:00:00 AM)
set Default Time Server Type = SINGLE
set Bindery Context = O=ESL
file server name FS1
ipx internal net 2C74169E
load SMC8000 mem=D0000 int=3 PORT=280 FRAME=Ethernet_802.3
NAME=SMC8000_1E_802.3
bind IPX to SMC8000_1E_802.3 net=255
load SMC8000 mem=D0000 int=3 PORT=280 FRAME=Ethernet_802.2
NAME=SMC8000_1E_802.2
bind IPX to SMC8000_1E_802.2 net=E8022
```

39. Press F10 to save changes in the time configuration information for the server. Verify that you want to save the time configuration.

40. You should see a screen that asks you to specify a context in which this server should be placed.

    In the Company or Organization field, enter the name for your primary organization. This should be a name that is readily recognizable by the users of the network. For instance, the company International Business Machines can simply use the abbreviation IBM for the organization name.

    You are given the option to specify three sub-organization units:

    Level 1 Sub-Organizational Unit (optional)

    Level 2 Sub-Organizational Unit (optional)

    Level 3 Sub-Organizational Unit (optional)

    The organizational unit levels are optional, because a minimal NDS tree can consist of only the organization container. To create the context in which the newly installed server should be placed, you should consult your NDS tree design.

    You are building only a partial tree here. The full directory tree can be built using the NETADMIN or the NetWare Administrator tool. If you have created a new directory tree, the root partition is installed on the NetWare server that you have just installed.

    Once the server is installed it cannot be moved using the INSTALL.NLM. If you desire to change its location, you must use the NETADMIN or NetWare Administrator.

    The server object is created at installation only. The INSTALL.NLM can create the server object but cannot be used to perform general NDS management. The NETADMIN and the NetWare Administrator can be used for managing the NDS tree.

    The first server installed in a container gets a Master replica of that partition if the container does not exist. Other servers installed in the same context receive a Read/Write replica of that partition. If the container that holds the server already exists, all servers installed in that container get a Read/Write replica of the partition holding the container. These partitions can be further modified by using the PARTMGR utility or the Partition Manager tool.

    As you enter the values for the organization unit levels, you see the Server Context value change to reflect the names of the organization unit levels that you have entered.

    If you want to place the server in a tree branch containing the country object, you can modify the server context fields by adding **.c=xx** at the end of the server context, where xx is the two-letter country code.

    The Administrator Name field describes the Common Name (NC) for the administrator of the network. It is set to Admin by default, and is placed in the organization container. The Admin user object can be renamed, moved, and even deleted. Before deleting the Admin user object, you must make sure that there are other user objects that have Supervisor rights so that the NDS tree can be maintained.

You must know the context of the Admin user, and decide on the initial Admin password, when designing the directory tree.

The Password field is for the Admin user object password. Setting a password is not a requirement for completing the installation, even though it is highly recommended that a password be set as early as possible. The password for the Admin object can be set using the NETADMIN or NetWare Administrator Tool.

41. After making the changes, press F10 to save them. You see a message informing you that NDS services are being installed.

    INSTALL reports the number of volume objects installed in the directory. The volume objects are installed with a Common Name that consists of the file server name and the following physical volume name:

    ```
    servername_volumename
    ```

    If the server name is FS1, its first volume name (SYS) has the Common Name:

    ```
    CN=FS1_SYS
    ```

42. Press Enter to continue. You are asked to note the following information:

    ```
    Directory tree name
    Directory context
    Administrator name
    ```

    The Directory Context is the NDS context in which the server was placed.

    Press Enter to continue.

43. If the STARTUP.NCF file is displayed (see fig. 12.23). Edit this file as necessary and press F10 to save changes and continue.

44. If the AUTOEXEC.NCF file is displayed (see fig. 12.24). Edit this file as necessary and press F10 to save changes and continue.

45. You are presented with the Other Installation Options screen (see fig. 12.25). The following options are available:

    - Create a registration disk
    - Upgrade v3.1*x* Print Services
    - Configure Communication Protocols
    - Copy On-line Documentation From CD-ROM to the Server

- Copy Computer Based Training Files From CD-ROM to the Server
- Create Optional Diskettes
- Install an Additional Server Language
- Install NetWare for Macintosh (5-User)
- Install NetWare for NFS
- Install NetWare for SAA

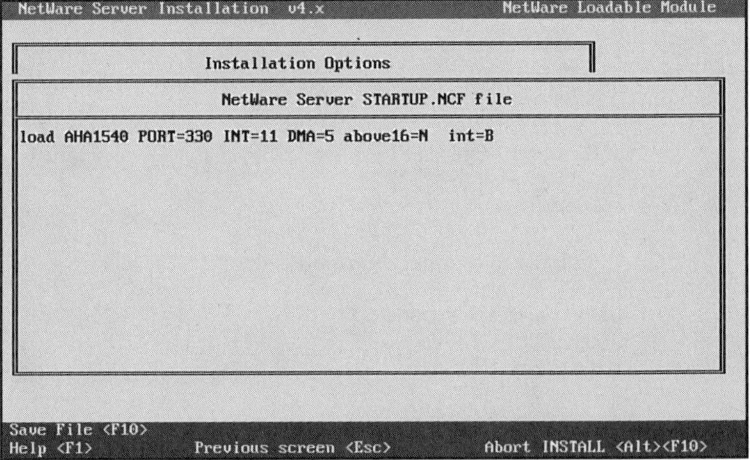

Figure 12.23
The STARTUP.NCF file displayed during INSTALL.

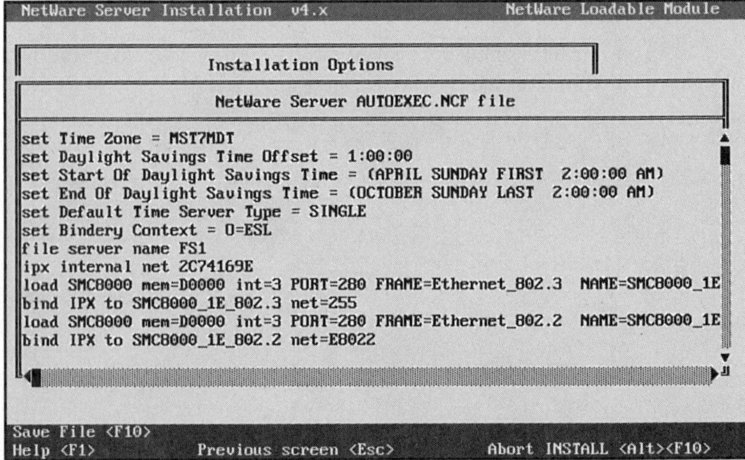

Figure 12.24
The AUTOEXEC.NCF file displayed during INSTALL.

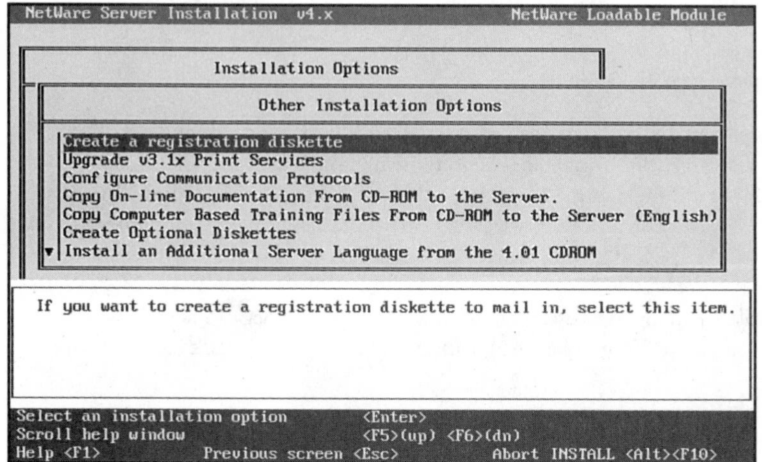

Figure 12.25
The Other Installation Options Menu.

Of the installation products, NetWare for Macintosh (5-User) version is bundled with NetWare 4.*x*. The other products, such as NetWare for NFS and NetWare for SAA must be purchased separately.

Select Create a registration diskette and follow instructions to create a registration disk and mail it to Novell.

46. Press F10 to go to the final installation screen that contains advice on the manuals to refer to for managing the network.

    Press Enter to exit to system console screen.

    Bring the server down and then up to verify your installation.

Setting File Name Format

Among the NetWare 4.*x* locale-specific format settings such as date and time, currency, sorting tables, uppercase tables, and so on, are the legal file name characters that can be used for storing files on the server. The file name format setting can be done during installation process. During installation, you are asked to choose between DOS format file names and NetWare format file names.

A little bit of background helps you understand the ramifications of using this option. NetWare has always allowed extended ASCII codes from 128 to 255 to be included as part of file names. These characters include many of the line drawing characters and characters in non-English languages (such as accent marks). This allowed NetWare to support file names with special characters.

In NetWare 4.*x*, the installer is given the choice of conforming to DOS legal file name characters, or of retaining the original NetWare legal file name characters that are allowed, which include characters with

codes from 128 to 255. The choice you make determines only the legal character names NetWare 4.*x* uses, and not legal character names used by an application program running under the NETX shell or the DOS Requester implemented by VLMs.

The NetWare DOS Requester used by NetWare 4.*x* is fundamentally different from the NETX shell. NETX intercepts DOS function calls (by trapping the software interrupts such as INT 21 hex). NETX examines the commands to see if DOS or the network should handle them. Commands that are passed to DOS undergo the DOS validation process for legal file name characters. However, commands that are sent to the network bypass the DOS validation process for legal character names. DOS never sees these "invalid" file names. So if an application issues a command to create a file name on a network drive, the server would create the file according to its own rules of what was legal and illegal. Since NetWare 3.*x* allowed characters between 128 to 255 as legal, an application could create a network file name with special codes.

The DOS Requester does not trap the commands first. It lets DOS decide if the function being invoked should be sent locally or transmitted across the network. This feature is possible with DOS versions 3.*x* and higher, and is called the DOS *redirector* function. (Unfortunately, it is often confused with the DOS Requester.) The DOS redirector decides if the function that is requested should be handled by DOS or by the network. Since DOS sees all commands first, it decides whether the command is valid or not. It verifies the file name before passing the file on the DOS Requester (implemented by VLMs).

If DOS Filename Format was selected at the NetWare server, lowercase and accented characters are converted to uppercase characters. File name character translation would be done at the server. If the file name request originated from a station running VLMs, the character translation would have been done at the workstation. If the file name request originated from a station running the NETX shell, character translation would not be done at the workstation, but would be handled by the server, because the DOS file name format was selected at the server.

If NetWare Filename Format was selected at the NetWare server, lowercase and accented characters are *not* converted to uppercase characters at the server. It would be up to the workstation to do the character translation. If the file name request originated from a station running VLMs, the character translation would have been done at the workstation. But, if the file name request originated from a station running the NETX shell, character translation would not be done at the workstation, and because the server does not handle character translation (because the NetWare Filename Format was selected at the server), the accented characters are not converted, but are left as lowercase.

The preceding discussion implies that there is a potential problem with networks running a mix of NETX and VLM software at the workstations. If the behavior of NetWare 4.*x* was the same as NetWare 3.*x*, then only the NetWare Filename Format would exist at the server. Workstations running NETX could then create file names that would not be recognizable by workstations running VLMs.

This is the reason why the DOS Filename Format was created in NetWare 4.*x*. DOS Filename Format gives greater assurance that the behavior at the server for file names would be the same for NETX or VLM workstations.

You might be tempted to think that the problem just discussed could be avoided if all workstations were running NETX (and using bindery emulation to access NetWare 4.*x* server) and the NetWare server was configured for NetWare Filename Format. However, not all versions of DOS perform file name validation the same way. DOS versions obtained from different OEM vendors use different rules for valid file name characters. In this situation, it is possible for a workstation running DOS from a different vendor to create files on a NetWare server (configured with NetWare Filename Format) that is not accessible by another workstation.

Interestingly enough, this problem always existed with NetWare 3.*x* (set to NetWare Filename Format), but most sites never saw it because they ran the same version of DOS. Sites that supported DOS from different vendors can run into the problem described here.

DOS 3.3 and above can do file name character validation based on the language-specific configuration information given to it. What if two workstations on the same network were configured for different languages? They would then use different *code page tables.*

This means that workstations potentially could create files on the server that would not be understandable by another workstation configured with a different code page. If the DOS Filename Format has been selected at the server, the server may remap certain file name characters. For this reason, if workstations are set to different language configurations, it may be preferable to select the NetWare Filename Format so that the server does not try to remap any characters in the 128 to 255 range.

The above issues become important when trying to upgrade a NetWare 3.*x* or 2.*x* server that could have file names containing characters in the 128 to 255 range. If the NetWare 4.*x* server was selected with DOS Filename Format, some of the file name characters are now illegal. The server, in this case, remaps the illegal file name character the first time the volume mounts. In NetWare 4.*x*, VREPAIR automatically is invoked when the illegal characters are detected during the volume mount. VREPAIR translates any lowercase accented characters to uppercase accented characters, according to the rules for the country code and code page that the server has installed. Name collisions after character translation are handled by substituting a number for the last character in the file name. Be aware that if you have program files that reference these renamed files, you need to reconfigure them.

If NetWare Filename Format was selected during the upgrade process, no files are renamed, but you would have the potential problems listed earlier: a NetWare format file name at the server and different workstation configurations could produce file names other workstations may not understand.

Resolving Conflicts with CD-ROM Sharing SCSI Controller with Server Disk

One of the nicer features of NetWare 4.*x* is that it can be installed from a CD-ROM. Many of the CD-ROMs use the SCSI (Small Computer Systems Interface) interface. The advantages of using a SCSI interface are not only faster speeds, but the capability of the SCSI bus to allow several devices to be daisy-chained.

Consider the situation in figure 12.26, where a CD-ROM and the server hard disk are daisy-chained and share the same SCSI controller. One would expect the scheme to work, but it actually produces a problem during the installation. While copying the files from the CD-ROM to the server disk, the installation process freezes. The reason for this is a conflict among the NetWare SCSI driver, DOS SCSI hard disk driver, DOS CD-ROM driver, and DOS BIOS routines when they try to access the same SCSI controller. This conflict is detected when an attempt is made to copy PUBLIC and SYSTEM, or any other files, from the CD-ROM.

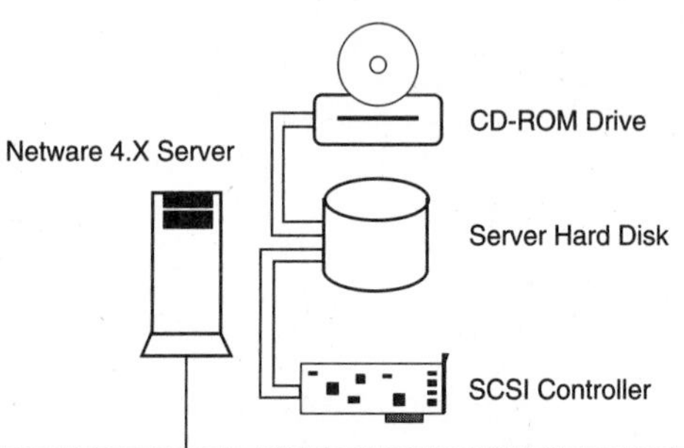

Figure 12.26
Shared SCSI controller problem during installation.

The real problem here is that NetWare relies on DOS for its initial load and access to the CD-ROM during installation. And DOS SCSI drivers conflict with NetWare's use of the SCSI controller.

One way to avoid the problem is *not* to share the SCSI controller between the server disk and the CD-ROM (see fig. 12.27). This can be done by attaching the CD-ROM through a parallel port using a device such as Trantor's Mini-SCSI parallel port cable. Another way is to use a separate controller for the CD-ROM during the installation. The CD-ROM could be connected to another SCSI controller, or if you are using a non-SCSI CD-ROM, you would attach it to the non-SCSI controller card. In either case, conflict is avoided. Yet another way is to follow the procedure described as follows that allows installation even if the CD-ROM and server disk share the same SCSI controller.

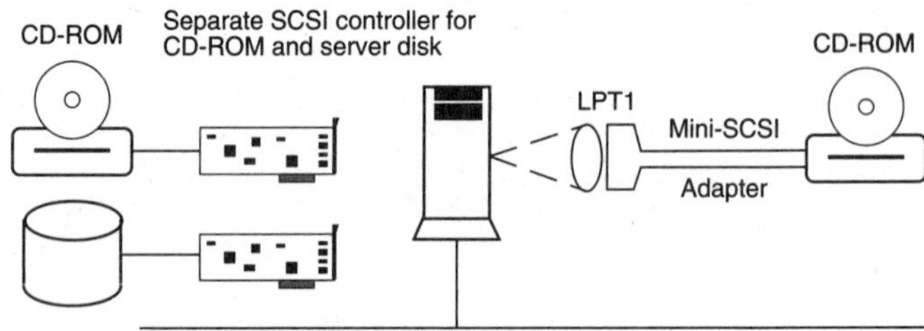

Figure 12.27
Avoiding shared SCSI controller problem during installation.

1. Go through the following normal NetWare 4.*x* installation procedure:

   a. Create a small DOS partition on the server disk and format it.

   b. Install the DOS drivers to support the CD-ROM device, so that it is installed as a DOS device. This may involve adding CD-ROM device driver configuration in the CONFIG.SYS and the AUTOEXEC.BAT file in the DOS partition on the server.

   An example of such statements is shown as follows (the actual statements depend on the vendor-specific drivers):

File CONFIG.SYS:

```
DEVICE=ASPI4DOS.SYS
DEVICE=ASWCDSNY.SYS /D:ASPICD0
```

File AUTOEXEC.BAT:

```
MSCDEX /D:ASPICD0 /l:D /m:20
```

In the last example, drive letter D is assigned to the CD-ROM drive:

c. Ensure that you have a NetWare 4.*x* disk driver that supports CD-ROM media as a mounted NetWare volume.

2. Go to the D:\NETWARE.40*language* directory; in which *language* is the server language to be installed such as DEUTSCH, ENGLISH, ESPANOL, FRANCAIS, or ITALIANO.
3. Start INSTALL by typing its name.
4. Make the following selections:
   - Install New NetWare 4.0
   - Retain Current Disk Partition

   Use the details in the previous section on NetWare 4.*x* installation as a guide.
5. Enter the server name and IPX number.
6. Verify the source and destination paths in the Copy server boot files to the DOS partition screen.
7. Enter the correct Country Code, Code Page, and Keyboard Setting.
8. Make a choice between DOS and NetWare Filename Formats.
9. Optionally add SET commands to the STARTUP.NCF file.
10. Make a choice to have the server installation program modify the AUTOEXEC.BAT file on the DOS partition.
11. Select the correct disk driver.
12. Select the choice to create NetWare partitions "Automatically."
13. You are warned about having the CD-ROM and server disk on the same controller. Ignore these warning messages because this is the problem you are attempting to solve.
14. Create the server volumes.
15. Insert the license disk when prompted to do so.

16. When the Copy NetWare Files screen appears, DO NOT PRESS F10 to save changes and continue. Use Alt+F10 to break out of the install. Down the server and exit to DOS.

17. Copy NetWare CD-ROM drivers to the server boot directory. If D: is the CD-ROM drive, use the commands:

```
copy D:\NETWARE.40\________\BC\CDROM.NLM C:\SERVER.40
copy D:\NETWARE.40\________\DISKDRV\ASPICD.DSK C:\SERVER.40
```

    If you prefer using the CDNASPI.DSK rather than Adaptee's ASPICD.DSK, you can copy CDNASPI.DSK using the following:

```
copy D:\NETWARE.40\________\DISKDRV\CDNASPI.DSK C:\SERVER.40
```

18. Remove DOS CD-ROM drivers that conflict with NetWare CD-ROM drivers:

    a. Remove ASPI driver from CONFIG.SYS.

    b. Remove MSLDEX program from AUTOEXEC.BAT.

19. Reboot the server, and start SERVER.EXE:

    a. CD \SERVER.40

    b. SERVER -NA

    c. SEARCH ADD C:\SERVER.40 (to search C:\SERVER.40)

    d. LOAD AHA1540 (use your SCSI disk driver)

    e. MOUNT SYS

20. Load the ASPI CD-ROM driver if CD-ROM is attached via an ASPI controller. Otherwise, go to the next step.

```
LOAD driver
```

    in which *driver* is ASPICD or CDNASPI.DOS.

21. Load the CDROM NLM:

```
LOAD CDROM
```

22. Run the command:

```
CD DEVICE LIST
```

    You should see the CD device displayed.

23. Mount the CD-ROM device:

```
CD MOUNT volumename
```

or

```
CD MOUNT volumenumber
```

The *volumename* and *volumenumber* can be obtained from:

```
CD DEVICE LIST
```

or

```
CD VOLUME LIST
```

Ignore error messages during the mounting of the CD volume.

You should see messages similar to the following:

```
**   Reading in FAT
**   Verifying Directory FAT chain
**   Scanning the Directory
**   Checking Subdirectories
**   Scanning Files with Trustee Nodes
**   Scanning Deleted Files
**   Linking the Name Spaces
```

Some of the messages display because the CD-ROM is a read-only volume. The mounting process appears to be slow, so please be patient. If your server hangs, try the preceding steps again!

24. Unload INSTALL and then reload it:

```
UNLOAD INSTALL
LOAD INSTALL
```


25. Start the installation again by selecting Install a New 4.0 Server.

26. Press F3 to specify a different path.

    Enter the name of the directory that contains the distribution software. This is the directory that contains the file NETMAIN.ILS. Currently this file is in the directory \NETWARE.40*language*________. The last directory is eight underscore (_) characters strung together; it is not a continuous line!

```
volumename:NETWARE.40\language\________
```

    in which *language* is DEUTSCH, ENGLISH, ESPANOL, FRANCAIS, or ITALIANO.

27. For *volumename* use NETWARE_40.

    Wait for the file to be copied.

28. Press F10 and proceed with the installation as outlined earlier.

Upgrading to NetWare 4.*x*

Upgrading to NetWare 4.*x* can be done from the following:

- NetWare 3.*x*
- NetWare 2.*x*
- Another network operating system

Of the above choices, only the NetWare 3.*x* option is within the scope of this training guide, and so most of this section is devoted to this option.

To upgrade from NetWare 3.*x* to 4.*x*, you must take into account the following actions and considerations:

1. Run BINDFIX to clean up and repair any bindery errors. Next, perform a full backup of server data as a precautionary measure.

2. Restore, using SALVAGE, any deleted files that you wish to retain as part of the upgrade process.

3. Perform any maintenance tasks such as the following:

   a. Rename user accounts to be consistent. If you are upgrading user accounts to a single container, you must make sure that user login names are unique, as NDS rules require objects in the same context to have unique Common Names.

      If name collisions do occur (user accounts with the same name on two different servers), the first user account that is created takes precedence. For this reason it is best to start upgrading a NetWare 3.*x* server that has the largest number of user accounts and other settings.

   b. If a new NetWare 4.*x* server is to be added to a new branch, create the NDS branch. You can use NETADMIN or NetWare Administrator to perform this task.

4. If you are upgrading an NNS (NetWare Name Service) based network, upgrade all servers in a domain at the same time. Servers in the same domain should be placed in the same container. The domain in NNS roughly corresponds to the grouping of objects in a single container. When the first NNS server is upgraded, the installation adds a directory property called *NNS_Domain* to the upgraded bindery object's container.

Translation of Bindery in Upgrade Process

When a NetWare 3.*x* server is upgraded, bindery objects are placed in a container as part of the upgrade process. Certain rules are applied to ensure the greatest compatibility between the NetWare 3.*x* setup and the new way of managing resources with NetWare 4.*x*.

User accounts in NetWare 3.*x* are translated to NDS user objects. User account information such as login scripts, login restrictions, and passwords become properties of the user objects.

The File and Directory Trustee assignments (for the NetWare file system, and *not* NDS trustee assignments) are retained. There is no difference between the file system rights of NetWare 3.*x* and NetWare 4.*x*, except for certain name changes. Inherited Rights Mask (IRM) is called Inherited Rights Filter (IRF) and the Supervisory rights of NetWare 3.*x* are called Supervisor rights.

NetWare 3.11 groups are converted to NDS group objects. The members of the group become a property of the NDS group object. The security equivalence and file system trustee assignments for groups are retained.

The default account restrictions and print queue objects are carried over from NetWare 3.*x*. The NetWare 3.*x* print queue becomes the Bindery Queue object under NetWare 4.*x*.

The NetWare 3.*x* console operator becomes an operator property of the server object, and Security Equivalence becomes the Security Equivalence property of the user object.

A utility called PUPGRADE.NLM is available that allows NetWare 3.*x* print servers, print definitions, and print job configurations as objects and properties of objects. For instance, the printer definition can be converted to an NDS print object, but the print job configuration is assigned as a property of a container object.

Table 12.5 summarizes the translation of bindery information to NetWare 4.*x*.

Table 12.5
Bindery Translation Summary

Bindery Information	**Translated To**
User accounts	NDS user objects. NetWare 3.*x* login scripts, login restrictions, and passwords become properties of user objects.
Group accounts	NDS group objects. Group membership, file and directory trustee assignments, and security equivalencies become properties of user objects.
File System Trustee Assignments	Remain the same for NetWare 4.*x*. There are minor changes in terminology; for example, IRM becomes IRF, and Supervisory right becomes Supervisor right.
Security Equivalence	Becomes a property of the user object. Property is also called Security Equivalence.
Console Operator	Becomes a property of the server object. Property is called the Operator property.

continues

Table 12.5, Continued
Bindery Translation Summary

Bindery Information	Translated To
Print Queues	Become Bindery Queue object that allows their function to be retained.
Default Account Restrictions	Are carried over from NetWare 3.*x*.

The Upgrade Process

The NetWare 4.*x* INSTALL NLM has an option called Upgrade NetWare v3.1*x* or v4.*x* Server (see fig. 12.8). This allows a NetWare 3.*x* server to be upgraded to a NetWare 4.*x* server using the NetWare 3.*x* server hardware only (see fig. 12.28).

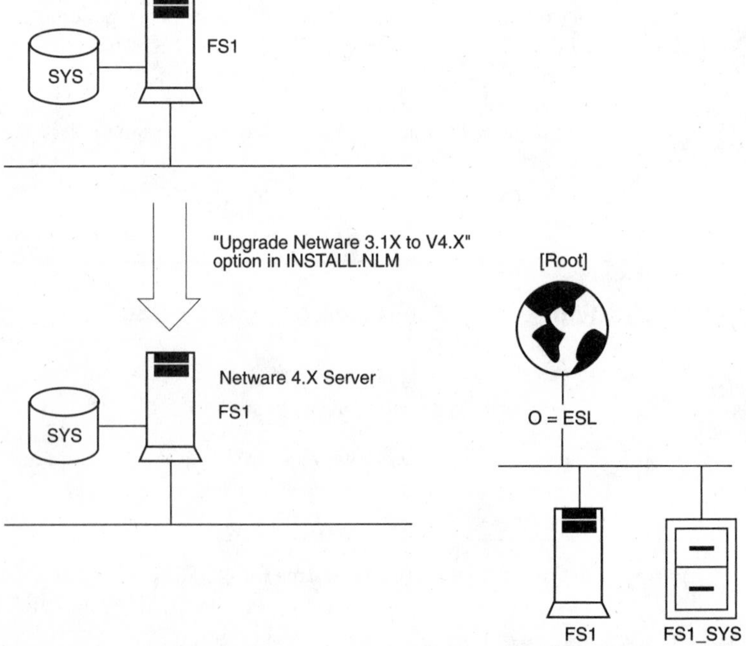

Figure 12.28
Upgrade 3.1x to NetWare 4.0 option in INSTALL.NLM.

The following is a guided tour of the installation process. Many similarities exist between the upgrade process and installing a new NetWare 4.*x* server. The procedure is presented here for your reference and review. Detailed commentary on some of the steps was presented on the NetWare 4.*x* Installation section earlier in the chapter.

1. You can begin the upgrade by booting with the INSTALL disk if you are using the floppy disk method.

   If you are using the CD-ROM method, the CD-ROM must be recognizable by DOS. This means that you must load all the essential drivers to recognize the CD-ROM device. Since each CD-ROM manufacturer has a different set of installation procedures and CD-ROM drivers, you should follow their instructions.

   CD-ROM installation users should follow the following steps:

   a. Change your directory to the CD-ROM drive.

   b. Change your current directory to \NETWARE.40\ENGLISH. If you wish to install and configure NetWare 4.*x* for another language, replace ENGLISH in the above directory name with the name of one of the supported languages (DEUTSCH, ESPANOL, FRANCAIS, ITALIANO, and so on).

   c. Run the INSTALL.BAT file.

2. You should see the INSTALL main screen (see fig. 12.8). The upgrade option is Upgrade a v3.*x* or 4.*x* Server.

   Select the Upgrade a v3.*x* or 4.*x* Server.

   You should see a screen (see fig. 12.29) for copying server boot files to a directory on the server's DOS partition. Use F4 to enter a destination directory, such as C:\SERVER.40. If you need to change the source directory, use F3. NetWare creates the boot directory, if it does not exist.

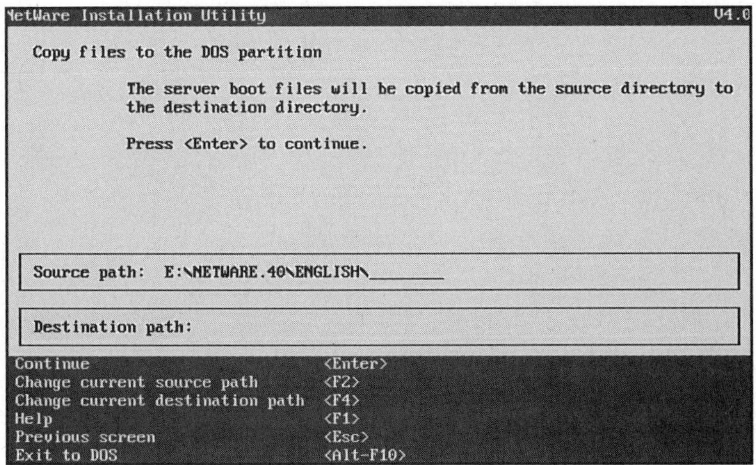

Figure 12.29
Upgrading to NetWare 4.x: Copying server boot files.

Press Enter to start the copying of files.

If you specified a boot directory that does not contain your existing SERVER.EXE, you are prompted to enter its name.

You should see a status message of files that are being copied. The files that are copied include the following:

SERVER.EXE

INSTALL.NLM

NWSNUT.NLM (Graphical interface utility for running certain NLMs)

LAN and disk drivers (*.LAN, *.DSK)

Message and help files

Older drivers found on the DOS partition cannot be upgraded. The Upgrade process reports this to you.

3. You should see a locale configuration screen (see fig. 12.30). Select the values for the appropriate locale.

   After making changes, press F10 to save choices and continue.

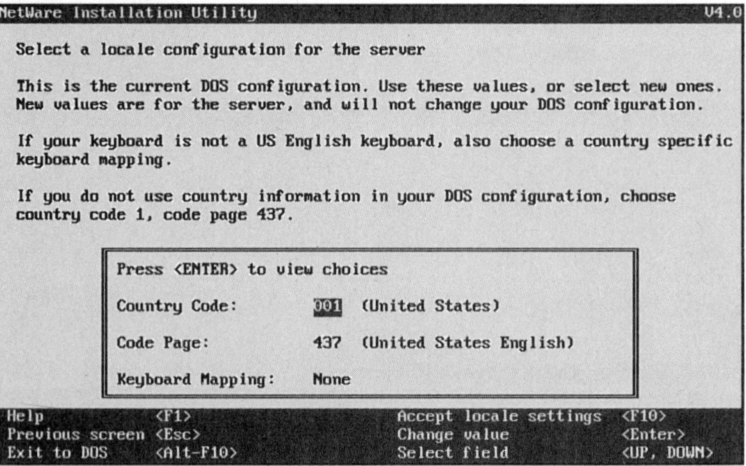

Figure 12.30
NetWare 4.x Upgrade: Locale Information.

4. You must next select the file name format. The file name format choices are the following:

   a. DOS Filename Format (recommended)

   b. NetWare Filename Format

NetWare format allows extended lowercase file names, whereas DOS maps lowercase characters to uppercase for file names.

Select DOS Filename Format, unless you are using the NETX shell to create extended lowercase file names. The NETX shell allows the creation of extended lowercase file names, but these file names are not readable by the DOS requester (VLM).

5. You are asked if it is OK to invoke the existing STARTUP.NCF file. Select Yes, unless your disk configuration has changed and you need to load new drivers.

6. You see a message that some drivers may not load, and should be updated to their more recent versions. Press Enter to see a list of drivers that failed to load.

7. You are informed of the path from which NetWare loads. If you wish to change this (by specifying a network drive, for example), you must use F3 to select a different path.

   Press Enter to select the default path.

8. You are presented with information that NetWare is scanning for available drivers, after which you see a list of disk drivers.

9. If the correct disk driver is not loaded, select the disk driver that matches the server disk controller. If the driver you want is not listed, press Ins to load disk driver from a distribution medium.

   Press F10 to continue.

10. You are asked to insert the license disk. Follow instructions to insert the license disk.

11. You are asked to verify the NetWare 4.*x* source path. Modify the path, if necessary, by using F3, and press Enter.

12. You are given a choice of file groups that you may want to load. These file groups should include the following:

    - NetWare 4.*x* DOS Utilities
    - NetWare 4.0 OS/2 Utilities
    - NetWare 4.0 Windowing Utilities
    - Setup a Network Directory for Client Install and Upgrade

    Check the boxes for the file groups you wish to install. You should at the very minimum install NetWare 4.*x* DOS Utilities and NetWare 4.0 Windowing Utilities.

    Press F10 to accept and save your selections, then confirm your selections. After this, you should see a status list of files that are copied to your server disk.

13. When file copying is completed, you see a message on the screen informing you of the drivers that were not updated. If these drivers are important to you, you should get their latest versions that work with NetWare 4.*x*.

    Press Enter to continue.

14. A message appears that the AUTOEXEC.NCF file is being scanned for LAN drivers that have no frame specified.

    LOAD statements for loading the LAN driver that do not have an explicit FRAME parameter default to use the IEEE 802.2 frame (FRAME=ETHERNET_802.2) under NetWare 4.*x*. In NetWare 3.*x*, the default, if no FRAME parameter was specified, was Novell's raw ETHERNET_802.3. If ETHERNET_802.3 is used with NetWare 4.*x*, workstations would be unable to log in to the network. To avoid this problem, make sure that you explicitly specify the correct FRAME parameter while loading the LAN driver from the AUTOEXEC.NCF file.

15. You see a screen informing you that the original AUTOEXEC.NCF file now can be executed. You should monitor it closely to see which drivers fail to load. Alternatively, you can edit the AUTOEXEC.NCF file by pressing F3 before AUTOEXEC.NCF runs.

    To continue without executing the AUTOEXEC.NCF file, press F4.

    To execute the AUTOEXEC.NCF file, press Enter.

16. A message `Scanning for available drivers` should appear, and you are presented with a list of LAN drivers.

12

17. Scroll through the list and select the correct LAN driver for your NIC. If your driver is not listed, press Ins to load a driver from a floppy disk. If the driver is different from floppy drive A, use F3 to specify an alternate source.

18. The Upgrade process searches the network for the existence of a directory tree. If it finds one, it displays the name of the directory tree. You can select this tree or create a new tree by pressing Ins.

    If this is the first server on the network, you must select a name for the directory tree. If you attempt to create a new tree when one already exists, a warning message is displayed informing you of some of the consequences of your actions.

19. You are presented with a form for entering time configuration information for the installed server:

    For Time Server Type, enter either a Single Reference Time Server, Reference Time Server, Primary Time Server, or Secondary Time Server. If you select the Single Reference Time Server, you cannot have a Primary Time Server or another Reference Time server. With Single Reference Time Server, only the Secondary Time Servers can exist.

For Standard time zone abbreviation, enter the abbreviation code for your time zone. This string is for display purposes only. You can enter any value, but it is best to enter a value that is standard for your time zone. The important parameter to set for time zone offset is Standard time offset from UTC. The standard time zone abbreviation also can be changed in the AUTOEXEC.NCF file.

For Standard time offset from UTC, verify that the time-offset for your zone is correct. You can set the time offset in the format *hh:mm:ss* (hours:minutes:seconds) behind or after UTC.

Many areas of the world have daylight savings time, and several others do not. NetWare 4.*x* gives you the flexibility of changing the daylight savings time criteria, or disabling it altogether.

To enable daylight savings time, answer Yes to `Does your area have daylight savings time (DST)?` To disable daylight savings time, answer No to this parameter.

The DST time zone abbreviation specifies a string for daylight savings time that is used for display purposes only. The daylight savings rules are set by the DST offset from standard time, DST Start, and DST End parameters. The DST time zone abbreviation can also be changed in the AUTOEXEC.NCF file.

The DST offset from standard time is a parameter that represents the time difference between daylight savings time and standard time. This can have the value *hh:mm:ss* and can be set to be *ahead* or *behind* the standard time.

The DST Start and the DST End time indicate the start and end of daylight savings time. The values for these parameters can be programmed to be on a weekday of a specified month at a specific time, or on a specific day of the month at a specific time. For example, in areas in the U.S. that use daylight savings time, the daylight savings time commences at 2:00 a.m. on the first Sunday of the month of April and ends at 2:00 a.m. on the last Sunday of the month of October. Should the laws change to a different daylight savings start and end, NetWare 4.*x* provides the flexibility to provide for these changes from the server console.

The time settings are recorded in the AUTOEXEC.NCF file.

20. Press F10 to save any changes in the time configuration information for the server. Verify that you want to save time configuration.

21. You should see a screen that asks you to specify a context in which this server should be placed.

    In the Company or Organization field, enter the name for your primary organization. This should be a name that is readily recognizable by the users of the network. For instance, the company International Business Machines can simply use the abbreviation IBM for the organization name.

    You are given the option to specify three sub-organization units:

        Level 1 Sub-Organizational Unit (optional)

Level 2 Sub-Organizational Unit (optional)

Level 3 Sub-Organizational Unit (optional)

The organizational unit levels are optional because a minimal NDS tree can consist of only the organization container. To create the context in which the newly installed server should be placed, you should consult your NDS tree design.

You are building a partial tree here only. The full directory tree can be built using the NETADMIN or the NetWare Administrator tool. If you have created a new directory tree, the root partition is installed on the NetWare server that you have just installed.

The Administrator Name field describes the *Common Name* (CN) for the administrator of the network. It is by default set to Admin, and is placed in the organization container. The Admin user object can be renamed, moved, and even deleted. Before deleting the Admin user object, you must make sure that there are other user objects that have Supervisor rights so that the NDS tree can be maintained.

You must know the context of the Admin user, and decide on the initial Admin password, when designing the directory tree.

The Password field is for the Admin user object password. Setting a password is not a requirement for completing the installation, even though it is highly recommended that a password be set as early as possible. The password for the Admin object can be set using the NETADMIN or NetWare Administrator Tool.

22. After making the changes, press F10 to save changes. You see a message informing you that NDS services are being installed.

    You should see a status screen informing you of the bindery objects that are converted to equivalent NDS objects.

    The Upgrade process reports the number of volume objects installed in the directory. The volume objects are installed with a Common Name that consists of the file server name and the physical volume name:

    ```
    servername_volumename
    ```

    If the server name is NW4CS, its first volume name (SYS) has the Common Name of

    ```
    CN=NW4CS_SYS
    ```

23. Press Enter to continue. You are asked to note the following information:

    ```
    Directory tree name
    Directory context
    Administrator name
    ```

The Directory Context is the NDS context in which the server was placed.

Press Enter to continue.

24. The AUTOEXEC.NCF file is scanned to verify that the Ethernet 802.2 frame type is loaded for Ethernet drivers. AUTOEXEC.NCF also is scanned for time and directory context information. It makes changes to the AUTOEXEC.NCF file. You can make further edits to these changes.

25. Press Enter to continue. You are shown the old AUTOEXEC.NCF and the new AUTOEXEC.NCF, side-by-side. Make any edits you want, and press F10 to save changes and continue.

26. You are presented with the Other Installation Options screen. The options that are available here are:

    - Create a registration disk
    - Upgrade v3.1*x* Print Services
    - Configure Communication Protocols
    - Copy On-line Documentation from CD-ROM to the Server
    - Copy Computer Based Training files from CD-ROM to the Server
    - Create optional disks
    - Install an Additional Server Language
    - Install NetWare for Macintosh (5-User)
    - Install NetWare for NFS
    - Install NetWare for SAA

    Of the installation products, NetWare for Macintosh (5-User) version is bundled with NetWare 4.*x*. The other products, such as NetWare for NFS and NetWare for SAA, must be purchased separately.

    You may want to create a Registration disk and mail it to Novell.

27. Press F10 to go to the final installation screen, which contains advice on the manuals to refer to for managing the network.

    Press Enter to exit to system console screen.

    Bring the server down and up, in order to verify your installation.

The Migration Utility

NetWare 4.*x* comes with a migration utility called MIGRATE.EXE that allows the upgrading of NetWare servers. This is different from the Upgrade process discussed in the previous section; that is done by selecting the Upgrade NetWare 3.1*x* or 4.*x* option from the INSTALL NLM. The Migrate utility requires that it be run from a workstation. It can be used to upgrade for a NetWare 2.*x*, 3.*x*, or IBM LAN Server to a NetWare 4.*x* server.

The following two methods can be used to upgrade servers using the MIGRATE utility:

1. Across-the-Wire migration
2. Same-server migration

Across-the-Wire Migration

Figure 12.31 shows how the Across-the-Wire migration technique works. The hardware requirements for this technique are the following:

1. A source server that needs to be converted. This could be a NetWare 2.*x*, 3.*x*, or an IBM LAN server.
2. A destination server is an existing NetWare 4.*x* server that has already been installed (using the methods described earlier).
3. A workstation with sufficient disk storage to hold the migrated bindery information, and for running the MIGRATE.EXE utility.

Across-the-Wire migration assumes that you already have a NetWare 4.*x* server installed, and that you wish to migrate data files, user account, and other setup information from a source server (NetWare 2.*x*, 3.*x*, or IBM LAN server) to the NetWare 4.*x* server.

Across-the-Wire migration involves a three-step process:

1. The bindery and/or setup information is copied from the source server to a working directory on the workstation running MIGRATE.
2. The data files are copied directly across-the-wire from the source server to the destination server.
3. The bindery information is migrated to the NetWare 4.*x* server from the working directory on the workstation to which it was copied in step one.

Across-the-Wire migration allows you to preserve your data files and your user environment. User accounts are translated to user objects. Default account restrictions, accounting methods, print queues, and print servers are preserved, but passwords are not preserved. The installer has the choice of allowing users to log in to the new system without a password, or assigning passwords that are generated randomly (stored in SYS:SYSTEM\NEW.PWD).

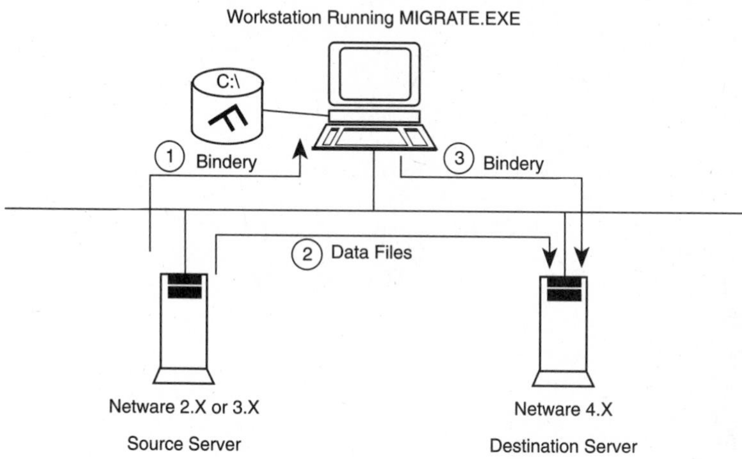

Figure 12.31
Across-the-Wire migration.

User login scripts are migrated but not modified to match the new environment. These are placed in the SYS:SYSTEM\UIMPORT.DAT file. A corresponding SYS:SYSTEM\UIMPORT.CTL file also is created. You can place the login scripts in the NDS by using the following command from SYS:SYSTEM:

```
UIMPORT UIMPORT.CTL UIMPORT.DAT.
```

The bindery emulation feature of NetWare 4.*x* allows NDS to emulate a "flat" bindery structure for objects within an Organization or Organization Unit container. This allows compatibility with existing workstations.

Because the Across-the-Wire migration does not modify the source server, it is a very safe method for doing an upgrade.

Same-Server Migration

Figure 12.32 shows how the Same-Server migration technique works. The hardware requirements for this technique are:

1. A source server that needs to be converted. This could be a NetWare 2.*x*, 3.*x*, or an IBM LAN Server. There is no separate destination server.

2. A workstation with sufficient disk storage and a backup device to hold the migrated bindery information and the data files. The MIGRATE utility runs at the workstation.

As you can see from the preceding, unlike the Across-the-Wire migration, Same-Server does not assume that you already have a NetWare 4.*x* server installed. You can use only a single server that is to be converted and a workstation for running MIGRATE. This workstation is also used for backing up and restoring data and the Bindery.

Same-Server migration involves a five-step process:

1. The data files are backed up to the backup device attached to the workstation.
2. The bindery and/or setup information is copied from the source server to a working directory on the workstation.

Figure 12.32
Same-Server migration.

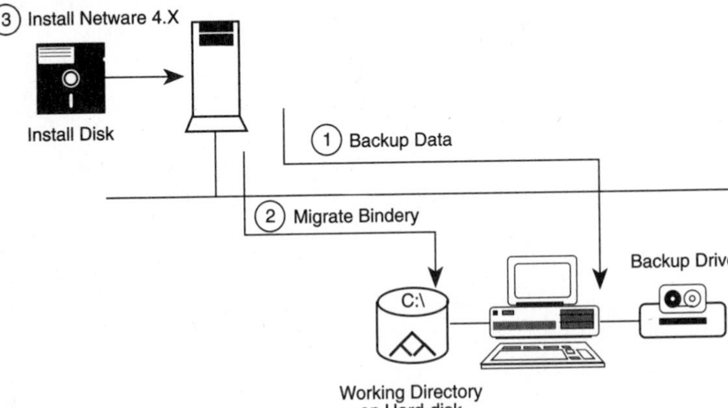

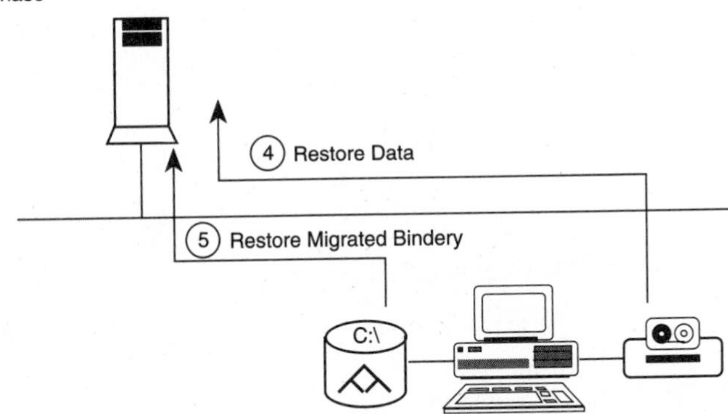

3. The NetWare 4.*x* server needs to be installed on the server. Note that to do this, for a NetWare v2.*x* server upgrade, any prior information on the server disk is lost. This is why doing steps 1 and 2 reliably is very important. NetWare 3.*x* uses the same partition/volume structure as NetWare 4.*x*.

4. Restore backed-up data files from the backup device to the newly installed NetWare 4.*x* server.
5. Run the MIGRATE utility to migrate bindery information to the NetWare 4.*x* server. The bindery information was stored in the working directory in step 2.

The Same-Server migration allows you to preserve your data files and your user environment. User accounts are translated to user objects. Default account restrictions, accounting methods, print queues, and print servers are preserved, but passwords are not. The installer has the choice of allowing users to log in to the new system without a password, or assigning passwords that are generated randomly (stored in SYS:SYSTEM\NEW.PWD).

The bindery emulation feature of NetWare 4.*x*, allows NDS to emulate a "flat" bindery structure for objects within an Organization or Organization Unit container. This allows compatibility with existing workstations.

Because the Same-Server migration modifies the source server, this method has a small risk that data could be lost. The risk is minimized by making sure a good backup of the data and bindery is done in steps 1 and 2.

Other Migration Issues

If you are migrating a data file that has the same name as a file that already exists on the destination server, the file is not copied. Instead, an error message is displayed, and written to a migration report. If you are migrating a directory that has the same name as a directory that already exists on the destination server, the files from both directories are merged under the destination directory.

The system login script is not migrated, but user login scripts are migrated.

You may want to use the UIMPORT utility to migrate user accounts. This is similar to the MAKEUSER utility in NetWare 3.*x*. If you have a CD-ROM disc, you can create the MIGRATE disk by performing the following:

1. Go to the directory \CLIENT\UPGRADE in the NetWare 4.*x* distribution.
2. Run the MAKEDISK command:

   ```
   MAKEDISK A: language
   ```

   in which *language* is one of the following:

   ENGLISH

   FRENCH or FRANCAIS

   ITALIAN or ITALIANO

GERMAN or DEUTSCH

SPANISH or ESPANOL

You must have two formatted disks. One of them should be DOS bootable and should have the FDISK.COM and FORMAT.COM programs on it. You should also have the DOS utilities on the search path. The MAKEDISK batch file uses the DOS LABEL command to label the disks that you produce. The DOS bootable disk that you produce is the "NetWare In-Place Upgrade" disk and the other disk is the "NetWare Migration Utility."

Summary

In this chapter, you have learned the basics of NetWare 4.*x* installation and how to upgrade from NetWare 3.*x* to 4.*x*. Before commencing an installation or an upgrade, you should have a design of the NDS tree. If the server is to be installed in an existing NDS tree, you must make the decision if the server should be installed in a new container or an existing container.

You were shown how to estimate server memory and disk requirements. A guided tour was presented to install a NetWare 4.*x* server, and many of the installation choices were discussed in detail. Toward the end of the chapter you were presented with a brief look at migration techniques and issues.

NetWare Directory Services Security

NetWare Directory Services provides a logical view of the network resources and provides access to these resources in a uniform manner. The user needs to log in to the network just once. Once logged in, access to network resources is controlled by NDS security.

In this chapter you learn how NetWare 4.*x* NDS security is implemented and how it can be used to provide access to only those parts of the NDS tree to which the user should have access. You learn about the default security assignments for many NDS objects. It is important to understand the default security assignments to NDS objects before one can further enhance and customize NetWare security.

The rules for computing effective rights are presented, along with the different ways rights can be acquired. You also learn how to implement a network administration strategy by delegating network responsibility.

Overview of Network Security

NetWare 4.*x* security includes the traditional NetWare 3.*x* security dealing with login security and file system security. NetWare 4.*x* adds an additional component called the NDS security. The three elements of NetWare 4.*x* security are:

- Login Security
- NDS Security
- File System Security

Figures 13.1 and 13.2 show the NetWare 3.*x* and NetWare 4.*x* security. At each of the levels (or elements) of security, a number of tools and options exist. To implement security effectively on a network, you need to understand how to implement the different options at each level, and what tools NetWare 4.*x* provides to implement network security.

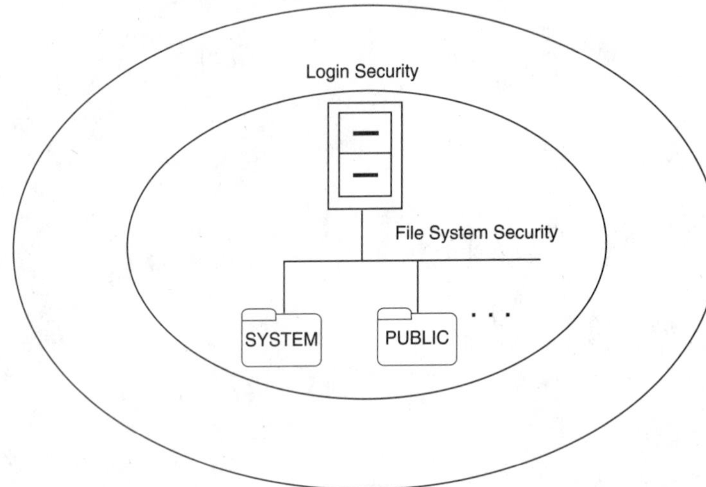

Figure 13.1
NetWare 3.x network security.

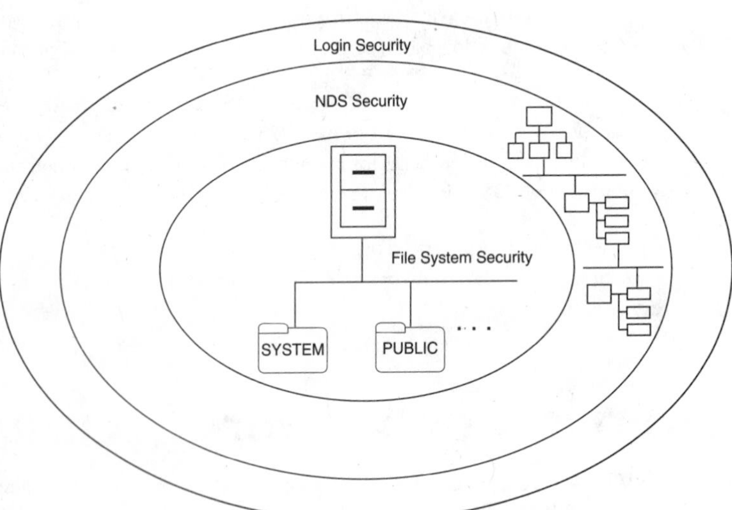

Figure 13.2
NetWare 4.x network security.

Login Security

The Login security in figures 13.1 and 13.2 has a number of components. Login security controls who can gain initial entry into the network. The login authentication of a user must be done against the user object stored in the global NDS database. For instance, a user logging in as an object CN=KARANJIT in container O=ESL, must after initial attachment to the network, type in the following command:

```
LOGIN .CN=KARANJIT.O=ESL
```

or

```
LOGIN .KARANJIT.ESL
```

The first login command specifies the complete name of the user object. The second form uses the typeless complete name. This assures that the user can log in from any context in the NDS tree. The context is the location (pointer) in the NDS tree. Partial names can also be used by the user to log in to the network. For example, if the current context is [Root], the following commands could be used:

```
LOGIN CN=KARANJIT.O=ESL
```

or

```
LOGIN KARANJIT.ESL
```

If the current context is O=ESL, the container that holds the user object being logged into, the following command could be used:

```
LOGIN CN=KARANJIT
```

or

```
LOGIN KARANJIT
```


Before a user can successfully log in, the user has to pass through several login restriction checks (see fig. 13.3). These login restrictions are as follows:

1. Account Restrictions
2. Password Restrictions
3. Station Restrictions
4. Time Restrictions
5. Intruder Limits

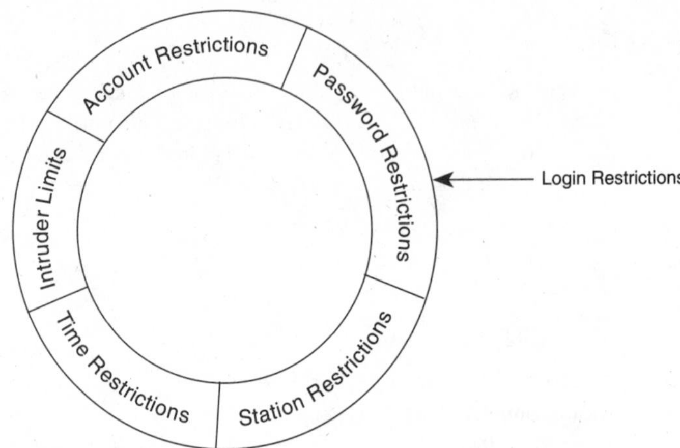

Figure 13.3
Login Restrictions.

The login restrictions in figure 13.3 are done on NDS objects, and they are done through the NetWare Administrator and the NETADMIN tool.

The procedure for setting these restrictions is briefly described in the following sections. There are five types of login restrictions in NetWare 4.*x*:

- Account Restrictions
- Password Restrictions
- Station Restrictions
- Time Restrictions
- Intruder Limits

Account Restrictions

Account Restrictions can be controlled by changing the account restriction properties for a user object. Account restrictions includes the ability to restrict a user object in the following ways:

- Disabling the user account
- Setting an expiration date on the user account
- Limiting Concurrent Connections

Figure 13.4 shows the Account Restriction properties for a user object. In this figure the account is enabled. This is indicated by the absence of the check box on Account Disabled. The Account Has Expiration Date shows that the expiration date on the account is 8/22/99 at 2:00:00 AM. Also, the concurrent connections are limited to 3. This means that the user CN=KARANJIT.O=ESL can log in on no more than 3 stations at the same time.

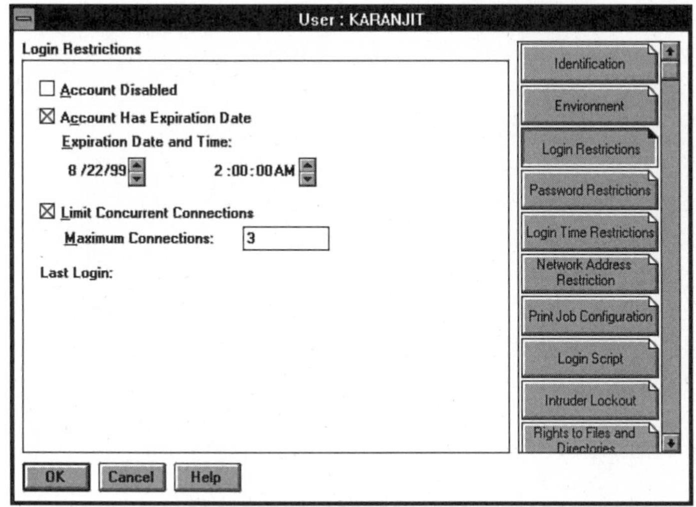

Figure 13.4
Account Restrictions Dialog Box.

To get to figure 13.4, you need to perform the following actions:

1. Log in to the network with Administrator privileges to at least a portion of the NDS tree that has user objects defined.

2. Start the NetWare Administrator Tool. You should see a screen similar to figure 13.5.

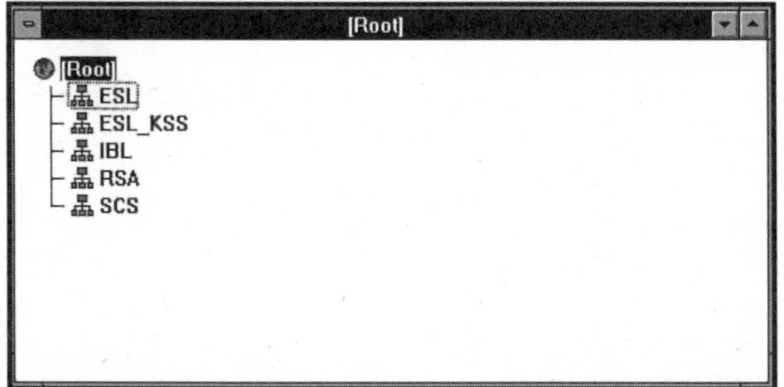

Figure 13.5
NetWare Administrator showing NDS tree.

Set the context of the NDS tree so you can see the entire NDS tree. You can set the context by performing the following:

Select View menu

Select Set Context from the View menu

3. Examine a container that has user objects defined. Figure 13.6 shows a portion of the NDS tree that has several users defined.

[Root]
[Root]
ESL
CORP
Cathy
Craig
Dei
Harjit
Heidi
USER_TEMPLATE
Admin
karanjit
FS1_SYS
FS1
ESL_KSS
IBL
RSA

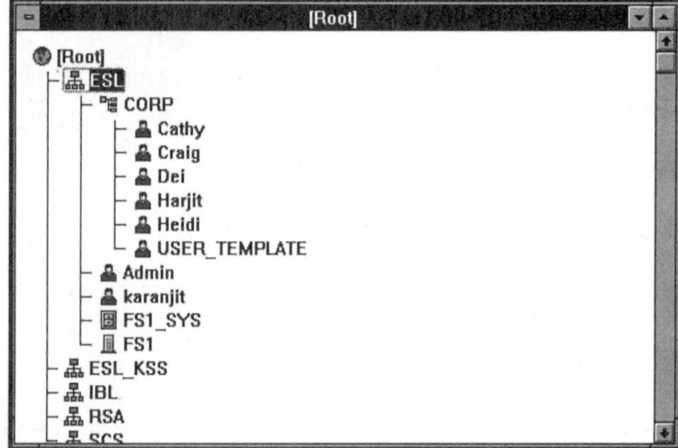

Figure 13.6
NDS Tree with several user objects defined.

Highlight a user object and examine its properties. You can do this by double-clicking on the user object, or right click on user object and select the Details option.

Figure 13.7 shows the properties of the user object.

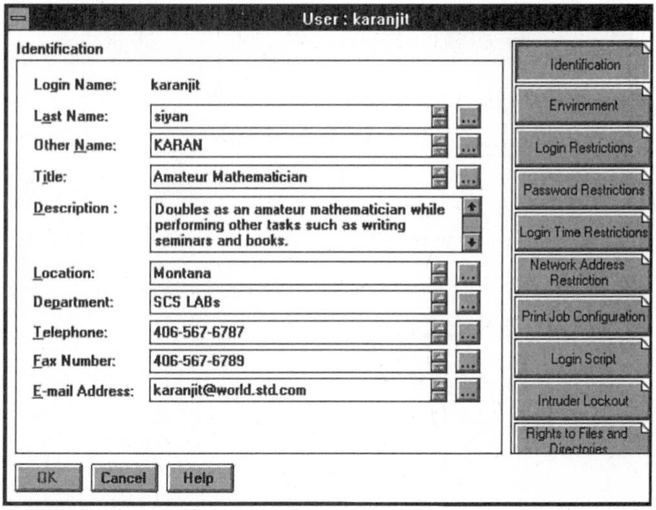

User : karanjit
Identification
Login Name: karanjit
Last Name: siyan
Other Name: KARAN
Title: Amateur Mathematician
Description : Doubles as an amateur mathematician while performing other tasks such as writing seminars and books.
Location: Montana
Department: SCS LABs
Telephone: 406-567-6787
Fax Number: 406-567-6789
E-mail Address: karanjit@world.std.com
Identification
Environment
Login Restrictions
Password Restrictions
Login Time Restrictions
Network Address Restriction
Print Job Configuration
Login Script
Intruder Lockout
Rights to Files and Directories
OK
Cancel
Help

Figure 13.7
Properties of user object CN=KARANJIT.O=ESL.

4. Select Login Restrictions page button, and you see the dialog now for setting Account Restrictions.

Password Restrictions

Password Restrictions is a property of a user object. Password restrictions includes the ability to restrict a user's password in the following ways:

- Allow user to change (or not change) the user password.
- Require that a password be always set, or disable this requirement.
- Enforce a minimum password length, or have no control on the minimum password length.
- Force (or do not force) users to change passwords periodically. The periodicity of change can be set from 1 to 999 days, and can be set to start at any date and time.
- Force (or do not force) users to set unique passwords.
- Limit grace logins to a specific number 0 to 999.

Figure 13.8 shows the Password Restriction properties for a user object. In this figure the user is allowed to change his password. A password is required, and its minimum length is 5 characters. The user is forced to change passwords periodically starting from 10/1/94 at 2:00:00 AM, and intervals of 40 days after that. The password that a user enters must be unique from previous passwords the user may have used. The user is allowed a limit of 6 grace logins after the password expires, and currently there are 5 grace logins left. If the user does not change the password in the specified number of logins, the account is disabled. It can be enabled by an Administrator.

To get to figure 13.8, you need to perform the following actions:

1. Log in to the network with Administrator privileges to at least a portion of the NDS tree that has user objects defined.
2. Start the NetWare Administrator Tool.
3. Examine a container that has user objects defined.
4. Highlight a user object and examine its properties. You can do this by double-clicking on the user object, or right click on user object and select the Details option.
5. Select the Password Restrictions page button, and you see the dialog box for setting Password Restrictions (see fig. 13.8).

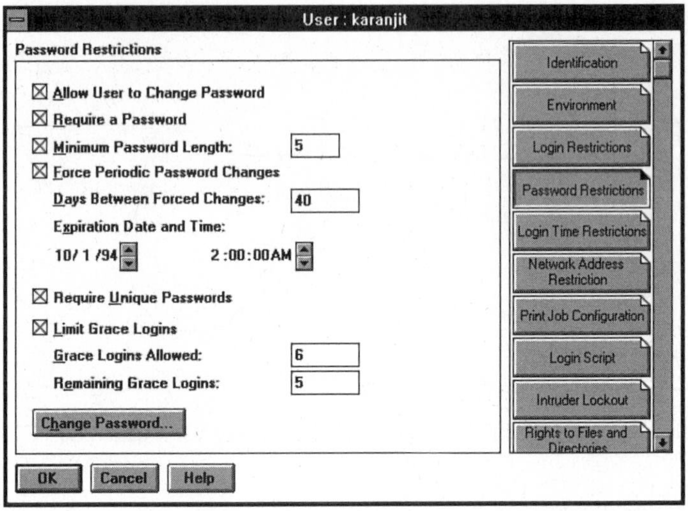

Figure 13.8
Password Restrictions Dialog Box.

Time Restrictions

Time Restrictions is a property of a user object. Time Restrictions includes the capability to restrict a user's ability to log in in the following ways:

- The user can log in during specific days of the week only.
- The user can be restricted to log in at specific times only.
- The granularity of time interval that can be set for logging in is 30 minutes.

Figure 13.9 shows the Login Time Restriction properties for a user object. In this figure the user is allowed to log in on weekdays only. Access on Sunday and Saturday is denied by the times during those days shaded in gray. On weekdays, the user is not allowed to log in from 10 p.m. to 12 a.m., and from 12 a.m. to 4 a.m. This means that the user can only log in from Monday to Friday between 4 a.m. and 10 p.m.

To get to figure 13.9, you need to perform the following actions:

1. Log in to the network with Administrator privileges to at least a portion of the NDS tree that has user objects defined.
2. Start the NetWare Administrator Tool.
3. Examine a container that has user objects defined.
4. Highlight a user object and examine its properties. You can do this by double-clicking on the user object, or right click on user object and select the Details option.
5. Select the Login Time Restrictions page button, and you see the dialog box for setting Time Restrictions (see fig. 13.9).

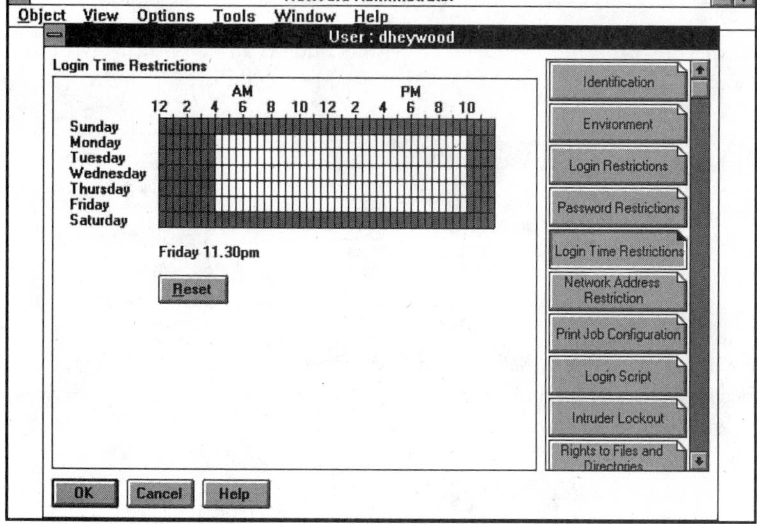

Figure 13.9
Time Restrictions Dialog Box.

Station Restrictions

Station restrictions (also called Network Address restrictions) includes the capability to restrict a user's ability to log in from specific workstations. In NetWare 4.*x* Station restrictions is more powerful and general than NetWare 3.*x*. Station restrictions in NetWare 3.*x* could only be done on the hardware address (MAC address) of the workstation's network board. In NetWare 4.*x*, Station restrictions includes the capability to restrict based on a protocol address. For this reason, the station restriction is also called Network Address Restriction in NetWare 4.*x*. Network Address Restrictions is a property of a user object and allows you to restrict logins based on Network Addresses such as:

- IPX/SPX
- SDLC
- AppleTalk
- OSI
- TCP/IP
- Ethernet/Token-Ring

The Network Address formats for some of the address formats are shown in figure 13.10 to 13.12.

IPX/SPX Address format (see fig. 13.10) consists of a 4-byte network number and a 6-byte hardware address. The hardware address is the MAC (Media Access Control) address of the network board.

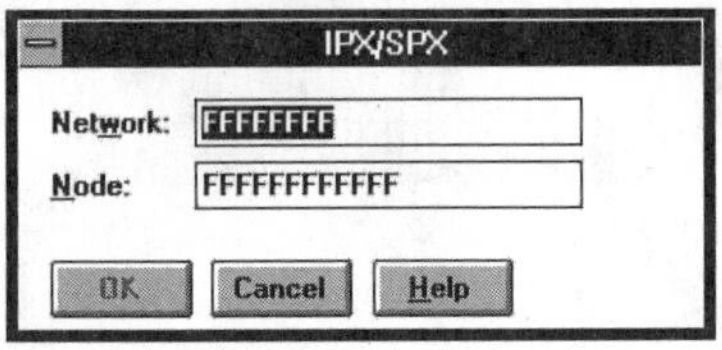

IPX/SPX
Network: FFFFFFFF
Node: FFFFFFFFFFFF
OK
Cancel
Help

Figure 13.10
IPX/SPX Address Restriction.

The TCP/IP Address format (see fig. 13.11) is the IP address and consists of a 4-byte logical address that is expressed in a dotted-decimal notation. Each of the 4 bytes that make up the IP address are expressed in their equivalent decimal number (range 0 to 255) and separated by the dot (.).

TCP/IP
IP Address: 255 . 255 . 255 . 255
OK
Cancel
Help

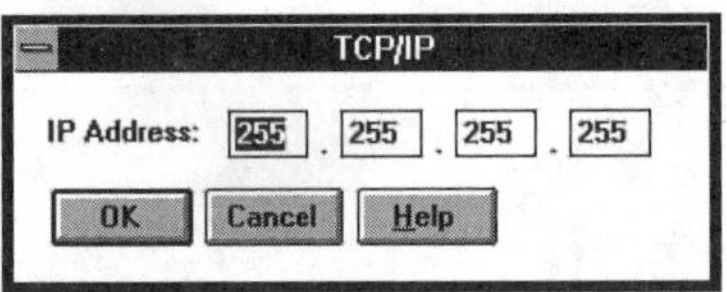

Figure 13.11
TCP/IP Address Restriction.

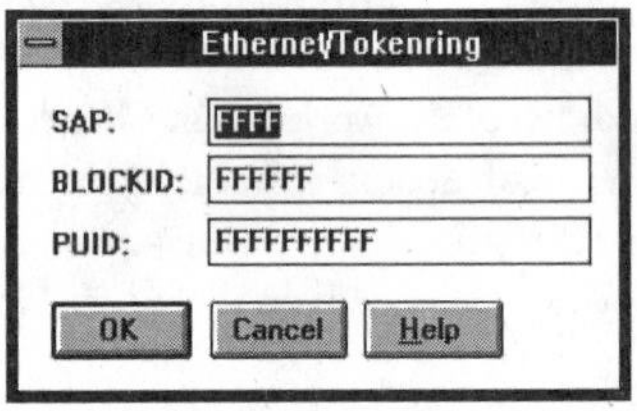

Ethernet/Tokenring
SAP: FFFF
BLOCKID: FFFFFF
PUID: FFFFFFFFFF
OK
Cancel
Help

Figure 13.12
Ethernet/Token-Ring Address Restriction.

13

The Ethernet/Token-Ring address format shows the SAP (Service Access Point) address and a 6-byte MAC address. The SAP is a 2 byte field that is part of the *Logical Link Control* (LLC, also called IEEE 802.2), that could be used with frame types such as ETHERNET_802.2, ETHERNET_SNAP, TOKEN-RING, and TOKEN-RING_SNAP. The 6-byte MAC address is broken down into a 3-byte BLOCKID and a 5-byte *Physical Unit ID* (PUID). The terms BLOCKID and PUID are used with IBM's SNA or SAA networks. For LAN usage, these fields can be considered to be one long field that can be used to code the station's MAC address.

To see the Network Address restriction screens shown in figures 13.10 to 13.12, you need to perform the following actions:

1. Log in to the network with Administrator privileges to at least a portion of the NDS tree that has user objects defined.

2. Start the NetWare Administrator Tool.

3. Examine a container that has user objects defined.

4. Highlight a user object and examine its properties. You can do this by double-clicking on the user object, or right click on user object and select the Details option.

5. Select Network Address Restrictions page button, and you see the dialog box for setting Address Restrictions.

Intruder Limits

Intruder Limits is set in a container object and applies to all user objects within the container. It limits the user's access to the network if an incorrect password was typed in too many times. The account is then locked, and you can use the screen in figure 13.13 to see the number of incorrect login attempts and the station address that was used by the intruder. To enable login for a locked user, select the Account Locked check box.

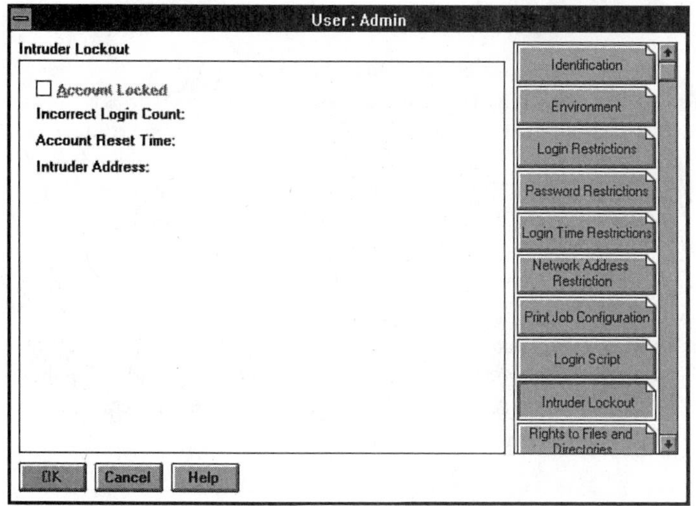

Figure 13.13
Intruder Lockout Screen.

To get to figure 13.13, you need to perform the following actions:

1. Log in to the network with Administrator privileges to at least a portion of the NDS tree that has user objects defined.

2. Start the NetWare Administrator Tool.

3. Examine a container that has user objects defined.

4. Highlight a user object and examine its properties. You can do this by double-clicking on the user object, or right click on user object and select the Details option.

5. Select Intruder Lockout page button, and you see the dialog box for accessing the Intruder Lockout screen (see fig. 13.13).

Login Authentication

When a user first logs in to the network, the network authenticates the user against the information stored in the user's object, such as the user's login name and password. Once authenticated, further requests are validated to ensure that the requests originate from the user's workstation, and that they have not been illegally altered in transit across the network. NetWare 4.*x*'s authentication mechanism takes place in the background, with no more direct user involvement once the user types in the object and password correctly. In other words, further authentication takes place in the background and is transparent to the user. The authentication of a user is done on each session basis. If the user were to log out of the network, background authentication ceases until the user attempts to log in to the network again.

Authentication is used to ensure that only a valid user could have sent the message, and that the message came from the workstation where the initial authentication data was created. It validates that only the sender could have built the message, and that the message has not been illegally modified during transit across the network. It also guarantees that the message is for the current session only, thus eliminating the threat from play-back attacks, where an attempt is made to capture a valid session and play it back on the network.

NetWare 4.*x* authentication is based on the RSA (Rivest, Shamir, Adleman) algorithm. This is a public key encryption algorithm that is extremely difficult to break. The public and private key are strings of numbers that are independent of each other. The independence means that one cannot derive one key from the other. Prime numbers (numbers divisible only by 1 and themselves) have this property, so they are typically used for public and private keys. One of the keys is kept private, which means only a designated user knows about it, and the other key is public which means that all users on the network can have access to it. If a message is encrypted with a private key, it can be decrypted with a public key. And, if a message is encrypted with a public key, it can be decrypted with a private key. This means that a workstation can encrypt its name M, with a private key Kp to form an encrypted message. Any entity on the network, such as a NetWare server, can decode this message with the public key (Kg), using the decryption algorithm (such as RSA), and discover that only the user M could have sent it (because the message contains a coding for the user name).

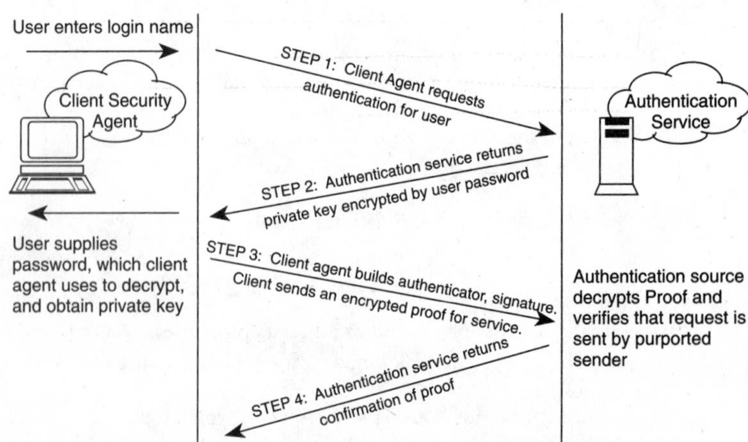

Figure 13.14
NetWare 4.x Login Authentication.

This relationship can be expressed mathematically as:

> Message M, encrypted with private key Kp, using encryption algorithm E = E(M,Kp)
>
> Decrypting message N using public key Kg, using decryption algorithm D = D(N, Kg)
>
> If message N is an encrypted message; that is, N = E(M,Kp), it follows that
>
> D(E(M,Kp), Kg) = M

In step 1 of figure 13.14, the client agent (on behalf of the user) requests authentication. The authentication services on the network return the private key for the user encrypted with the user's password (Pu). This is shown as step 2 in figure 13.14.

That is, authentication services return

```
E(Kp, Pu)
```

The user types in the password and the client agent uses the password supplied by the user (Pu) to decrypt the message. That is, the private key is known to the user, by using:

```
D(E(Kp,Pu), Pu)  = Kp
```

The password is then erased from memory to prevent a hacker (correctly speaking cracker) from illegally obtaining it. With the private key, the client agent creates a credential (also called an authenticator). The authenticator contains the user's complete name, the workstation's address, and a validity period which is the duration of time the authenticator can expect to be valid. There are other undocumented values that make up the authenticator also. In other words, the authenticator (A) is a mathematical function of the above named values:

> A = f(Complete Name of user, Workstation's Address, Validity Period, ...)
>
> The client then creates a signature (S), by encrypting the Authenticator (A) with its private key Kp.
>
> S = E(A, Kp)
>
> A proof (P) is then constructed that contains values derived from the Signature (S), the request for authentication (Rq), and a random number generated value (Rn), and is further encrypted by the user's public key (Kg).
>
> P = E (f(S, Rq, Rn), Kg)

The (S, Rq, Rn) in the equation above is a mathematical combination of the Signature (S), request for authentication (Rq), and a random number generated value (Rn).

The proof is then sent across the network, instead of the signature (S). This prevents anyone from illegally obtaining the signature. The proof (P) accompanies each authentication request, and is unique for a request, or a session. The random number generator makes it different for each message.

The final request for service (see step 3 in fig. 13.14) contains the request for authentication, the authenticator, and the proof.

```
Final Request = Rq+A+P
```

The authentication services check that the proof contains the signature and the message request. They can do this by decoding the proof with the private key (Kp).

```
D (P, Kp)  = D (E(f(S, Rq, Rn),Kg), Kp) = f(S,Rq,Rn).
```

Once S has been obtained, it can decode S with a public key (Kg). Remember that,

```
S = E(A, Kp)
```

So decoding S would give back the Authenticator

```
D(S, Kg) = D(E(A,Kp), Kg) = A
```

The Authenticator (A) was as follows:

```
A = f(Complete Name of user, Workstation's Address, Validity Period, ...)
```

From the above, the authentication services can discover the complete name of the user, its workstation address, and the validity period, and any other parameters that were encoded. It would be extremely difficult for any other workstation to spoof another workstation's identity.

The proof assures the authentication service that the message has not been modified.

As you can see, the scheme is clever and sufficiently complicated and makes breaking the authentication security a daunting task.

NetWare 4.*x* provides a scheme for continual background authentication, once the initial authentication is complete. This makes it difficult to assume the identity of a legitimate user connection.

NDS Security Concepts

Once the user is validated for network services, the NDS security is used to determine what network resources (NDS objects) the user is allowed access to. The kind of operations a user is permitted to perform on an NDS object (and files and directories in volumes on the network) are called rights. The operations permissible on NDS objects are called NDS object rights, and the operations permissible on a NetWare file system are the file system rights.

There are several examples of how an NDS object right could be useful. Suppose a user wants to view the structure of a tree. Should the user be allowed to view the directory structure? Viewing the structure (also called browsing) of a tree would be very valuable for a user, if the user is to find out what network resources are available on the network. One of the object rights is called Browse, which allows the user to view the directory structure. Other types of rights are useful to Create, Delete, or Rename objects. You would not want an ordinary user to have these rights. An administrator user should have a special right called the Supervisor right that would grant the administrator all privileges to a directory object.

Figure 13.15 shows that if object rights could not be inherited, explicit rights would have to be assigned at each directory and container level. This would involve greater security administration than is needed in most cases. Using inheritance can simplify the assignment of rights, as seen in figures 13.16 and 13.17.

When a right is assigned to a container directory object, should all objects in that container get those rights? Objects in a container that receive rights from a parent (superior object) container are said to inherit rights. Inheritance is a very important property and is used in object rights to simplify the assignment of rights. Consider the situation of an organization unit container that has 1,000 objects underneath it (see fig. 13.16). For the most part, a user/group needs the same right to all the objects in that container. If objects could not inherit rights from their parent container, each one of the 1,000 objects would have to be granted a right individually! Most administrators would not appreciate performing such a task. If, on the other hand, objects could inherit rights, the desired object right could be granted just once for the organization unit container (see fig. 13.16). What if some objects in the container needed a different set of rights (see fig. 13.17)? In this case, there needs to be a mechanism to block the flow of rights below a certain container. This mechanism is called the *Inheritance Rights Filter* (IRF) and is discussed in greater detail in another section.

Another important question is: Do you want any network administrator to have complete control over the NDS tree for the entire organization? Such control would give this user access to all network resources. Many large organizations are reluctant to do this. NDS object rights give the ability to restrict access to portions of the NDS tree, even to administrator users. Care should be used to prevent a situation where no one has administrative rights to a portion of the NDS tree.

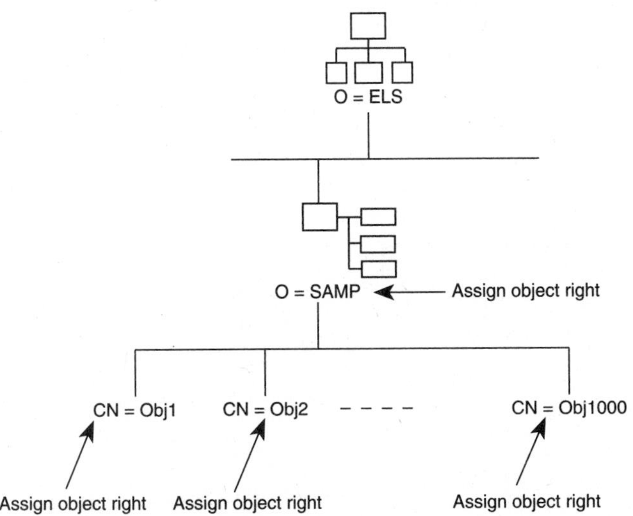

Figure 13.15
If object rights could not be inherited.

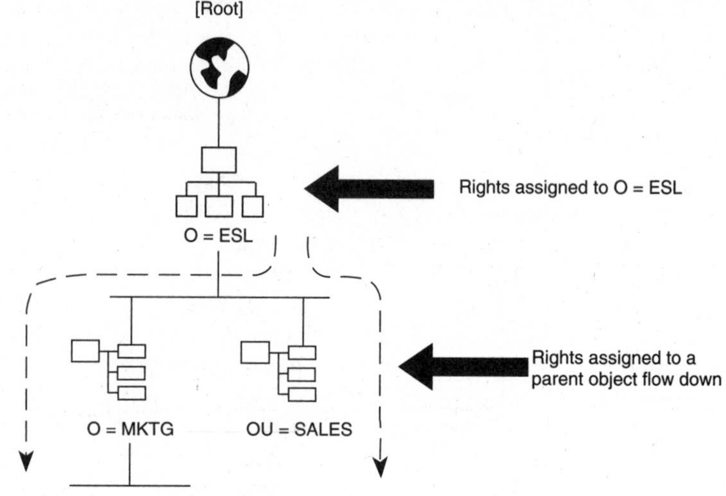

Figure 13.16
Inheritance in object rights for NetWare 4.x.

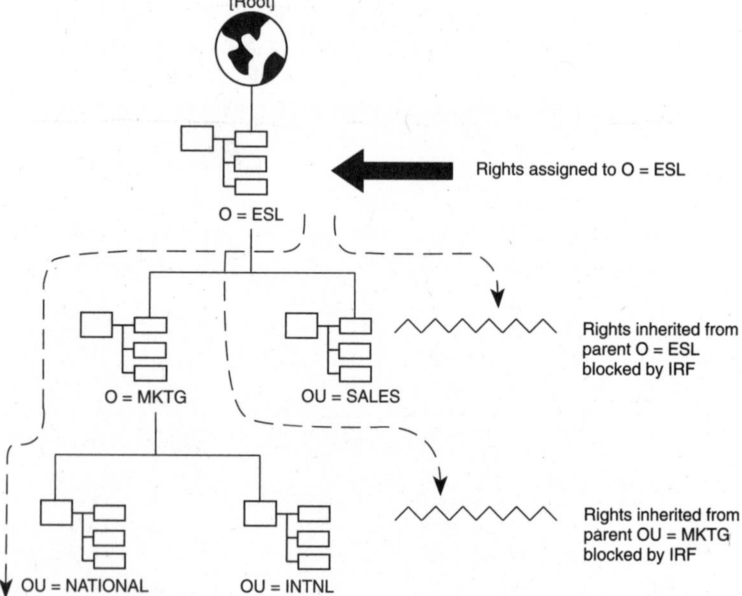

Figure 13.17
Blocking inheritance of object rights in NetWare 4.x.

NDS Rights

NDS provides for two types of rights—the rights to perform operations on the NDS tree structure, and the rights to perform operations on properties of an object (see fig. 13.18). These two rights are quite different.

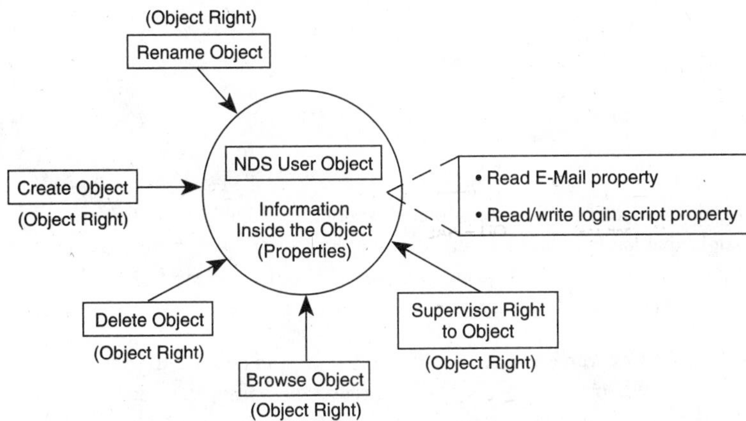

Figure 13.18
Object versus Property rights.

For instance, when working with the NDS structure, you may wish to browse the tree, or rename an object. When you are examining the properties of an object, the browse right is not meaningful. You would typically want to be able to read the value of a property or write to it. An example of this would be that you may want a user to have Read access to their E-mail address property, but you may not want users to change their E-mail address. You may, on the other hand, allow a user to modify their login scripts. In this case they need to have Write access to the login script property for the user object.

NDS rights that deal with the structure of objects in the NDS tree are called Object rights. These are used to view and manage objects in the NDS tree.

NDS rights that deal with being able to access the values stored in the properties of an object are called Property rights. Property rights deal with what a user can do with the values of a property.

An NDS object that is granted a specific right is called the trustee of the object (see fig. 13.19). The trustee can be any object in the NDS tree. It is easy to understand that user objects and group objects can be trustees, because they all deal with users. But it may seem strange, at first, to think of a container object as a trustee to another object. Container objects can be considered as groups where the members of the container are the NDS objects in the container. Making a container a trustee to another object gives all objects in that container rights to the designated object. Moreover, these rights flow down to other containers and objects, unless explicitly blocked at a tree level.

In summary, there are two types of NDS rights:

1. Object rights

2. Property rights

The next few sections discuss object rights, followed by a discussion of property rights.

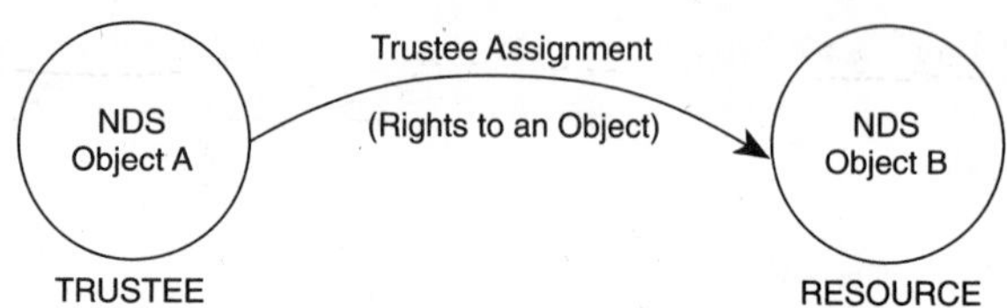

Figure 13.19
Trustee of an Object and Rights to an Object.

Clarifying Terminology

When a right is assigned to an object A for another object B, the object A is called a trustee of object B. The process of granting this right is called a trustee assignment. Oftentimes the object that has been granted the right, and the right that has been granted, are called a trustee assignment. A trustee can be any other object. In NetWare 3.*x*, a trustee could be a user account or a group account. In NetWare 4.*x*, other leaf objects and container objects can also be made trustees.

When a user object is a trustee, the user who is logged in as the user object can perform the operations allowed by the trustee assignment. When a container is made a trustee of an object, all objects in that container can perform the operations allowed by the trustee assignment. Similarly, when a group object is made a trustee for an object, all user objects that are listed in the group object's Group Membership property, can perform the operations allowed by the trustee assignment.

Object Rights

13

Object rights are assigned to an object in the NDS tree and control the operations that can be performed on the object as a whole. They do not control access to information within the object, but for one important exception. This is a situation when a Supervisor object right has been granted to an NDS object. Granting the Supervisor object right gives full control over the information inside the object, but the Supervisor right, like any other right, can be blocked by an *Inherited Rights Filter* (IRF).

Control of information kept inside the object (property) is accomplished by property rights.

Table 13.1 shows the different object rights that are possible.

Table 13.1
Object Rights

Object Right	Abbreviation	Meaning
Supervisor	S	Grants all rights. Assigning this right automatically gives Supervisor rights to the objects All Properties (discussed in a later section).
Browse	B	Grants the right to see an object in the NDS tree. When a request is made to search for an object, its name is returned.
Create	C	Applies to container objects only. Gives the right to create a new directory object within the container. Cannot be given to leaf objects, because they cannot contain subordinate objects.
Delete	D	Grants right to delete an NDS object. Only leaf objects and empty container objects can be deleted.
Rename	R	Grants right to rename object. Applies to leaf objects only.

Supervisor Object Right

The Supervisor right grants all possible rights to the user object. An object with Supervisor rights has full access to the information inside the object. This is an exception. Normally the object rights do not affect access to the contents of the object.

A special right called the All Properties property is used to describe all the properties. When a Supervisor right is assigned, a Supervisor property right is also assigned to All Properties. For this reason, all access to the information inside the object is given if an object has the Supervisor right. Needless to say, this right must be given with care. If you find it necessary, you can block the Supervisor right to branches of an NDS tree by removing this right from the Inheritance Rights Filter for the top-level container for a tree branch.

Browse Object Right

The Browse object right is perhaps the most common right which is given. For readers familiar with NetWare file system security, the browse object right is similar to the File Scan right for file systems. A browse right for an object gives the trustee the ability to see the object's name in the NDS tree. Without this right (if a Supervisor right is not given), the object is hidden from the user's view.

If a browse right is not granted to a trustee for a container, the trustee is denied access to all containers and objects within that tree branch. The default is to give everyone the Browse right to the [Root] object. Since all objects in a directory tree are under the [Root] object, the Browse right is inherited (it also can be said that it *flows down)* by all objects in the NDS tree.

If you wish to deny access to users in a specific part of the NDS tree for security reasons, you can do this by blocking the Browse right (using the IRF) for the container that represents the tree branch.

Create Object Right

The Create object right gives the trustee the ability to create subordinate objects underneath the container. Since leaf objects cannot have subordinate objects beneath them, the create right is not assignable to leaf objects. Figure 13.20 shows an attempt to assign an object right to a leaf object, such as the User1.CORP.ESL_XXX. Notice that the object right Create is not shown as an option for this user.

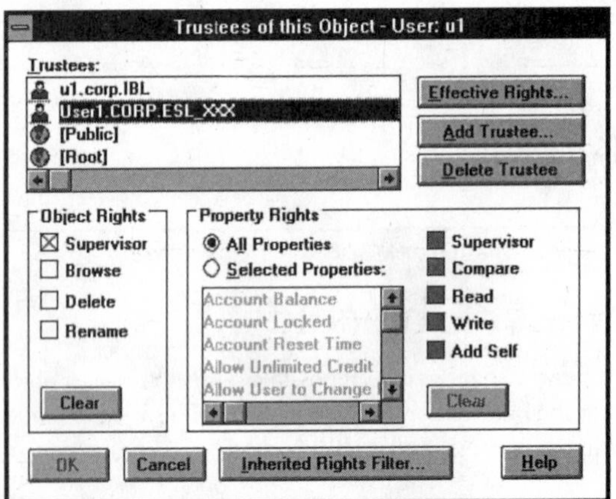

Figure 13.20
Create right not possible for leaf objects.

You must also have Browse rights in addition to Create rights to a container before you can create an object underneath the container using a tool such as the NetWare Administrator. The Browse right is usually inherited, because [public] is assigned the Browse right to [Root]. You do not need the Browse right to change to a context using the CX command.

Delete Object Right

This grants the trustee the right to delete an object. A container object can be deleted only if it has no other objects beneath it. You must delete the leaf and sub container objects before you can delete a container. This rule is primarily there to prevent inadvertent damage to the NDS tree.

If a file server is active, its object cannot be deleted. Again, this is for reasons of security, so that access to the file server is not lost while users are connected to it.

You can, however, delete a file server's volume object, even while users are logged in to it! This can have disastrous consequences, because users cannot access the volume using NDS. Don't try this on a production system! If someone does manage to delete the volume object, try this fix:

1. Create a volume object using NetWare Administrator or NETADMIN.
2. If an error message is generated,
   a) reboot the server
   b) connect to the server using VLM /PS=servername. Replace the servername with the name of the server that has the physical volume whose volume object representation was deleted.
3. Log in to the server and create a volume object.
4. Specify the Host Server property to be the NDS name of server, and Host Volume to be SYS.

Alternatively, you can try the following:

1. LOAD INSTALL.NLM at the server.
2. Select Maintenance/Selective Install option.
3. Select Directory Options.
4. Select Install/Reinstall mounted volumes into the directory. You are asked to log in to the NDS as Admin. INSTALL then prompts you to add deleted volumes back into the NDS structure. The volume is placed in the current server context.

Rename Object Right

The Rename object right allows the trustee to change the Name property for the object. Only leaf objects can be changed. Once a name is assigned to a container object, it cannot be changed. The only way to change the name of a container object is to delete it first, and then re-create it with a different name. This may not be possible on a production system.

There is good justification for not being able to change the container name with impunity. What would happen to all the references to NDS names in scripts if a container name were to change? The scripts and commands that reference the old name have to change. On a large network, which is geographically dispersed, this can create difficult problems.

Decide on the names of the container objects, using great care. You may want to take into account how easily the container name is recognized by users of the network. It should not be too long, and its appearance as seen in the NDS tree (lowercase, uppercase, or combination of both) should be considered. Once created, a container name cannot be changed.

The [Public] Trustee

Earlier, it was mentioned that everyone is given the [Browse] right. Readers familiar with NetWare 3.*x* may recall that almost everyone was given the Read File scan (RF) rights to SYS:PUBLIC. This was done using the group called EVERYONE. There are no default groups called EVERYONE (or a similar name) in NetWare 4.*x*. So the problem is, how do you assign the Browse right to everyone?

The problem is further compounded by the fact that the Browse right would be nice to have for users who are not logged in to the network, but merely attached.

The difference is that users who are logged in to the network have been authenticated by NDS. Users who are attached have a connection to the SYS:LOGIN directory of a NetWare file server. This gives them access to the LOGIN.EXE, CX.EXE, NLIST.EXE, and other programs, that they can use to log in to the network, or search the NDS tree for the name of a resource. The network security, in most cases, is not threatened if a user can see the names of network resources. In extremely secure environments, the Browse right can be revoked from any part of the NDS tree. Another advantage of a Browse right available for attached users/workstations, is that it permits the NDS to interface with third-party tools or other X.500 implementations that may wish to search Novell's implementation of NDS (DIB—Directory Information Base, in X.500 terms) for names of resources and its tree structure.

13

In order to solve this problem, the designers of NDS created an implicit group called [Public]. An implicit group is different from other groups, called explicit groups (such as group objects), in the sense that it does not have an explicit membership. Membership to an implicit group is implied by other means. In the case of the group [Public], all workstations that are attached (connected to but not logged in as yet) to a NetWare 4.*x* network, are automatically members of the group [Public]. This makes it possible to assign rights to workstations that are not authenticated by NetWare 4.*x*. You must take care to assign to [Public] a minimal set of rights. Otherwise, non-authenticated connections to the network can have excessive rights to the network. Other operating systems, such as Windows NT, also have the concept of an implicit group, where membership to certain groups is implied when users access a Windows NT station across a network.

When the system is first installed, the group [public] is made a trustee of [root] and given the Browse object right to the root object [Root]. Figure 13.21 illustrates this trustee assignment, and figure 13.22 shows the NetWare Administrator screen that shows the assignment of these rights. The Browse object right is inherited by all containers and their sub-containers, down to the individual leaf objects. This allows a user to browse the directory tree.

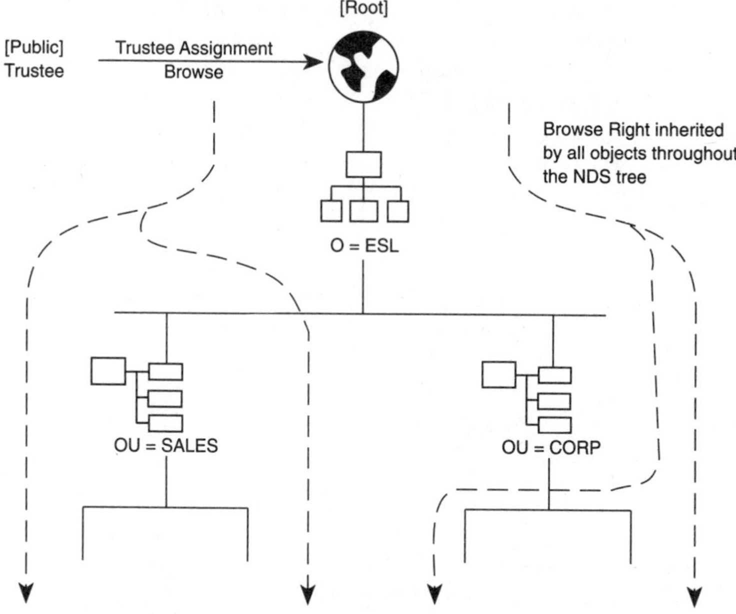

Figure 13.21
Browse right to trustee [public] on [Root] object.

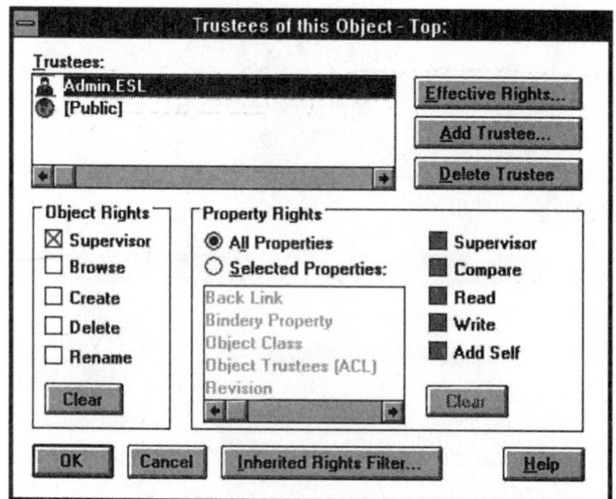

Figure 13.22
NetWare Administrator showing default trustee assignments to [Root] object.

There may be situations in which you want users to browse only portions of the NDS tree, rather than allow the entire NDS tree to be browsed. In this case the default trustee assignment of Browse for [public] to [Root] object can be removed, and this right assigned to the root container (top of tree branch) for which the user needs to see directory resources. Figures 13.23 and 13.24 illustrate this concept. These figures show that the Browse right can be granted to all connected users to a specific tree branch. In figures 13.23 and 13.24, the root of this tree branch is at the organization object level O=ESL; it could also be at a lower level in the tree, such as at an Organization Unit level.

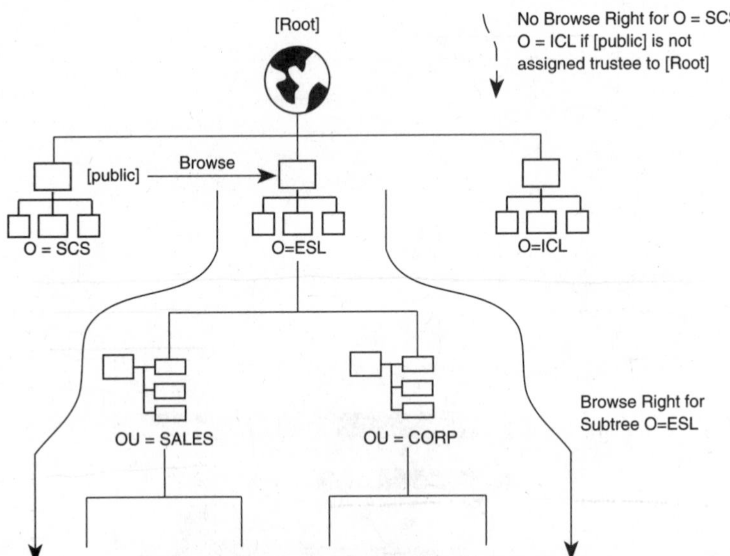

Figure 13.23
Browse right to trustee [public] for container O=ESL.

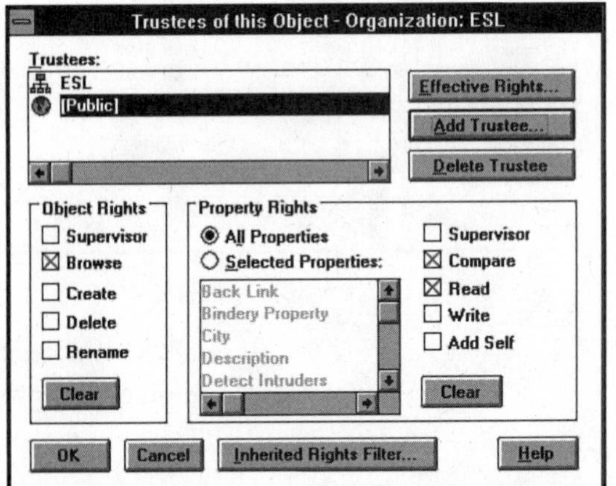

Figure 13.24
NetWare Administrator showing Browse right to [public] for container O=ESL.

Default Object Rights

NetWare 4.*x* sets certain default system rights to simplify the number of administration tasks that would otherwise have to be performed. One of these default rights was the Browse right that the [public] trustee was given to the [Root] object. Some of the other default rights are discussed below.

The container object that contains the SYS volume object is given the Read and File scan (RF) rights to the SYS:PUBLIC directory of the volume object. This is shown in figure 13.25. This figure shows that the CORP.ESL container, that is the parent container of the server volume object, is given the Access Rights of Read and File scan. This allows all objects, such as user and group objects, defined in that container to inherit these rights. In essence, this is equivalent to assigning Read and File scan rights to group EVERYONE in NetWare 3.*x*. If you have upgraded your server from NetWare 3.*x* to NetWare 4.*x*, and if the group EVERYONE had Read and File scan rights to SYS:PUBLIC, you see the group object Everyone in the container where the upgraded NetWare 4.*x* server and volume objects are installed. You should also see the group object Everyone as a trustee to SYS:PUBLIC with Read and File scan rights.

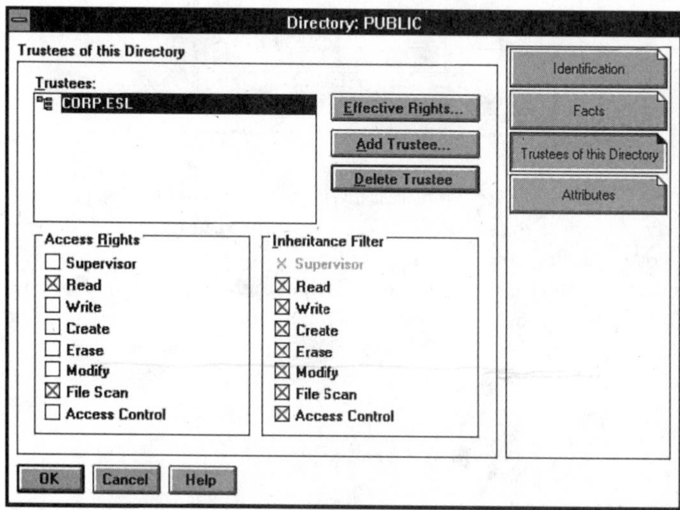

Figure 13.25
Rights to SYS:PUBLIC.

The initial user Admin is by default given the Supervisor object right to [Root]. This means that the Admin user inherits Supervisor object rights to all objects and their contents in the NDS tree. For this reason the password to the initial Admin user must be guarded with care. The Admin user by default is placed in the Organization object container and is named Admin. For security reasons, it may be advisable to rename this user object and move it to another context.

The user object, by default, has the following object trustees assigned to it:

1. The [Root] object is made a trustee to the user object and given the Browse object right (see fig. 13.26). This means that any NDS object can browse the user object.
2. If the creator of the user object is not the Admin user, who has Supervisor rights, the creator is made a trustee with Supervisor rights to the newly created object.

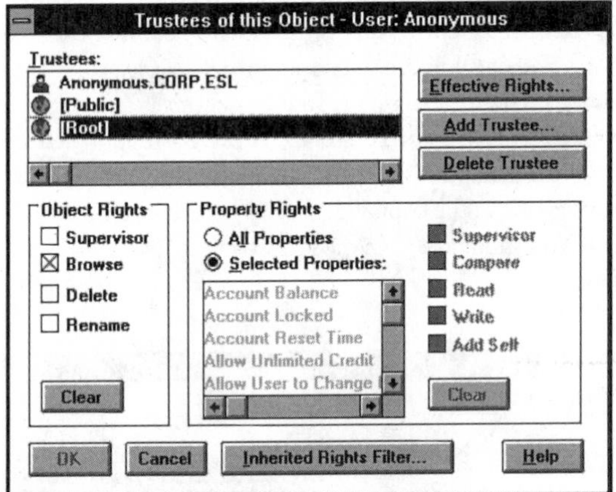

Figure 13.26
Default [Root] trustee assignment for user object.

Another default right is that the creator of the server object is given the Supervisor object right to the server object. Assigning Supervisor right to the server object also gives Supervisor rights to All Properties of the supervisor object. Supervisor All Properties right also implies Write property right to the ACL property of the server object. Anyone who has the Write property right to the ACL property of the server object is given the Supervisor right to the root of the server's volumes. This implies that assigning the Supervisor right to a server object gives *all* file system rights to volumes attached to that server.

Inheritance of Object Rights

When an object trustee assignment is made, the right granted to the trustee is inherited by all objects that are subordinate to it. In the case of container objects, this means that all leaf objects in the container, and all subcontainers, inherit this right. This inheritance of rights is sometimes called *flowing down of rights.* If an object is given an explicit trustee assignment at a lower level in the tree, any object rights that were inherited from above are overwritten.

Figure 13.27 shows an example of an NDS tree, where user object KSS is made a trustee of the organization container O=ESL. The trustee assignment that has been given is the [B C D] rights. This is the right to Browse Create and Delete objects. The container O=ESL has two sub-containers: the organization units OU=CORP and OU=ENG. The rights assigned to user KSS for O=ESL flow to these sub-containers. The sub-container objects inherit the [B C D] right. The [B C D] right for trustee KSS, in turn, flows down to the sub-containers below OU=CORP and OU=ENG. It is important to realize that the [B C D] right is only for a specific trustee; in this case, the trustee is the user object. The rights assigned to Organization Unit container OU=ENG flow to its two sub-containers OU=OPS and OU=LAB. The rights inherited by the OU=LAB container flow further down the tree, but the OU=R&D sub-container has an explicit trustee assignment of [B] for user object KSS. This explicit trustee assignment overrides the trustee assignment user KSS inherits for OU=R&D from the parent container OU=LAB. The trustee assignment for user object KSS then becomes the new right of [B]. This new right flows down to subordinate containers below OU=R&D. In figure 13.27 these subordinate containers are OU=LASER and OU=NNET. User object KSS inherits the rights of [B] to these containers.

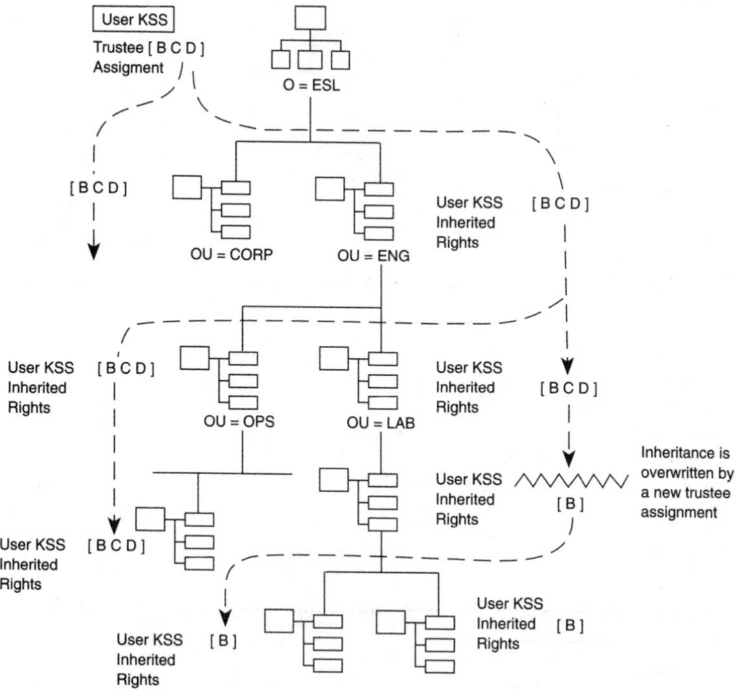

Figure 13.27
Example of Inheritance of Object Rights.

It is also interesting to see that in OU=OPS underneath the OU=ENG container, no explicit trustee assignment was given to user KSS. In this case, the trustee assignment [B C D] flows down and is inherited by the OU=MAINT container that is subordinate to OU=OPS.

Besides an explicit trustee assignment that overrides any inherited rights, inheritance can also be controlled by the use of the Inheritance Rights Filter. This topic is discussed next.

13

Inherited Rights Filter

The Inherited Rights Filter is a part of a property of the object, called the ACL property (also called the Object Trustees property). It can be used to control what inherited rights are allowed to be received from above.

Every NDS object has an Inherited Rights Filter (IRF). The default value of the IRF is all object rights [S B C D R]. This means that an NDS object has the potential to inherit all rights. The IRF is often confused with the actual object right. The sole purpose of IRF is to block a right from flowing further down. The IRF cannot be used to block an explicit trustee assignment. The explicit trustee assignment overrides any Inherited rights received from above, and causes the IRF to be ignored.

The IRF functions in a manner similar to the Inherited Rights Filter for NetWare 4.*x* file system (same as NetWare 3.*x*, Inherited Rights Mask, except for the name change). The important difference is that the Supervisor right can be removed for IRF for NDS. In the NetWare file system, the Supervisor right could not be removed, from the IRF for a file or directory.

When the Supervisor right is removed from the IRF for an NDS object, the Supervisor right is essentially blocked from that tree branch. Before removing a Supervisor right from the IRF of an NDS object, you must make another object a trustee with Supervisor rights for that object.

In the first NetWare 4.0 release, you were given a warning message when you attempted to remove the Supervisor object right from an IRF. You could, however, override this warning and remove the Supervisor right from the IRF anyway. This essentially produced a black hole in the tree that no one could have access to. Starting with NetWare 4.01, the warning was changed to an error message. If you attempt to remove the Supervisor right from an IRF, an error message is produced instead. This error message informs you that:


```
You cannot filter the Supervisor object right because no object has explicit
Supervisor object right to this object.
```

Figure 13.28 shows an attempt to remove the Supervisor right for an NDS object. The trustee CORP.ESL is highlighted in the Trustees box, which means that the operations that are performed are in relationship to this trustee object. An attempt was made to remove the Supervisor right from the IRF. Figure 13.28 shows the Supervisor box still checked, but the error message that you see in the figure was produced when an unsuccessful attempt was made to clear this box.

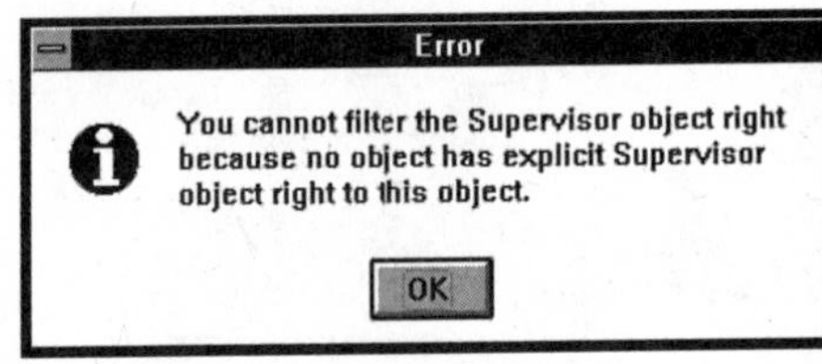

Figure 13.28
An attempt to remove Supervisor right from an IRF for a container object.

The reader who is interested in experimenting with this should try the following:

1. Log in as an Admin user and start the NetWare Administrator.
2. Right-click on a container and select Trustees of this Object. You should see a screen similar to figure 13.29.
3. Highlight the container in the Trustee List box and select the Inherited Rights Filter button.
4. You should see the Inherited Rights Filter screen.
5. Click on any of the object rights in the Filter panel. The rights should be exposed for your view.
6. Try to remove the Supervisor object right by clicking on the box next to it. You should see the error message in figure 13.28.

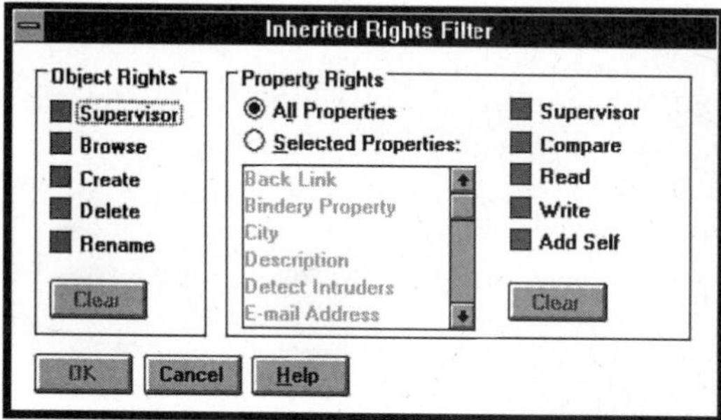

Figure 13.29
The Inherited Rights Filter Screen.

If at least one Supervisor trustee assignment to an object exists, the Supervisory object right can be removed from the IRF. In this case, though the Supervisor right is blocked, there is at least one object that can manage the object and its subordinate objects.

Though the Supervisor right can allow a trustee to perform all operations on an object, it is a good practice to assign other rights, in case the Supervisor right is accidentally removed. From the above discussion, you can see that NetWare 4.01 (and higher) checks to see if there exists at least one trustee that has a Supervisor right before allowing the Supervisor right to be removed; but you may still want to assign other rights as a precautionary measure, in case of failures or bugs in an NDS release.

Security Equivalence

A user object can be granted all the security rights of another NDS object. This is called security equivalence, and is a property of the user object. Figure 13.30 shows that user Dei is made security equivalent to the user CN=Admin1.OU=CORP.O=ESL and the Organization Unit OU=CORP.O=ESL_XXX. This means that Dei inherits by the definition of security equivalence, whatever rights the user object CN=Admin1.OU=CORP.O=ESL has, plus the rights the container object OU=CORP.O=ESL_XXX has. These rights are in addition to the rights that user Dei already has.

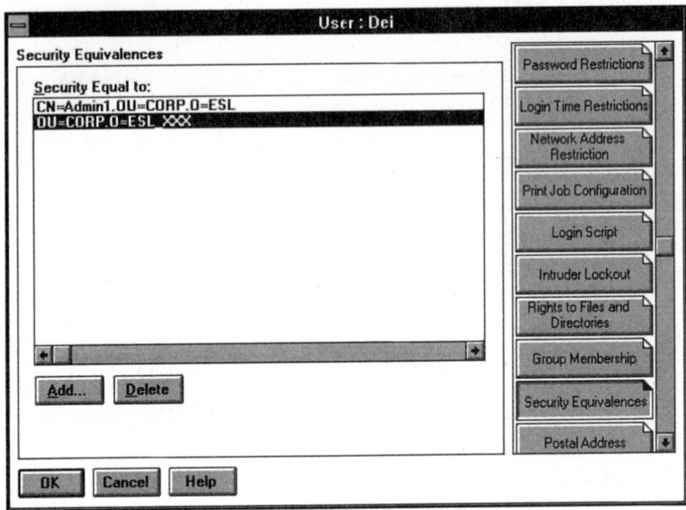

Figure 13.30 *Security Equivalence Property of a user object.*

Because Security Equivalence is a property of the user object, care should be taken that the user does not have the right to make changes to this property. If a user does have the Write property right to the security equivalance property and the Write property right to the ACL property of an Admin user object, the user could assign an Admin user object as one of the values for the security equivalence property. This would give the user all the rights the Admin user has. The default for a newly created user is that a user can read their security equivalence property, and you should not normally have to change this value.

One situation where security equivalence may be particularly useful is when a user in an organization needs access to files and directories of another user. This user could be made security equivalent to the user whose files and directories need to be accessed. To perform this task, you need to have the Write property right for the user object (property rights are discussed later in this chapter).

Object Effective Rights

An object's Effective rights are the rights that a user actually has to the object. The Effective right is not the same as the rights inherited from a parent container because these could be blocked by the IRF. Also, a user may have a right blocked for it, but may inherit a right because a group that the user belongs to, has an explicit or inherited trustee assignment for the object. By the same token, an Effective right is not the same as an explicit trustee assignment, because a user can inherit other rights because a group that the user belongs to, has an explicit or inherited trustee assignment for the object.

The Effective rights need to be calculated for each situation. Because of the hierarchical structure of the NDS tree, a right may be inherited from a number of sources. This makes the determination of NDS rights an interesting and challenging task.

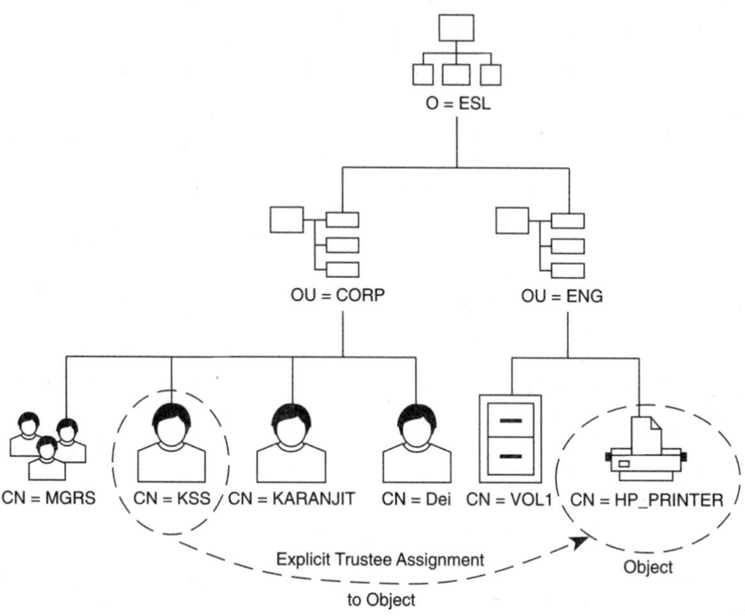

Figure 13.31
Sources for computing Effective Rights.

Consider the example in figure 13.31. To compute the effective rights of user KSS to the printer object HP_PRINTER, you must consider effective rights that come from any of the following sources:

1. Explicit trustee assignment: This includes the trustee assignment on HP_PRINTER that lists user KSS as a trustee (see fig. 13.32).

2. Inherited from trustee's parent container: Trustee assignment on HP_PRINTER that lists OU=CORP as a trustee. This also includes trustee assignment on HP_PRINTER that lists other parent containers such as O=ESL and [Root] as trustees, since the user KSS is in the tree branch with these objects as roots of the tree branch (see fig.13.33).

3. Inherited from direct assignment to object's container: Trustee assignment on the container OU=ENG that lists user KSS as a trustee (see fig. 13.34). The rights so assigned must pass through the object HP_PRINTER's IRF.

4. Inherited from assignment of trustee's container to object's container: Trustee assignment on the container OU=ENG that lists user object KSS's parent containers such as OU=CORP, O=ESL and [Root] as a trustee (see fig. 13.35). The rights so assigned must pass through the object HP_PRINTER's IRF.

5. Trustee assignment to a group object: Any trustee assignment made to the group object MGRS which the user KSS is a member of (see fig. 13.36).

6. Trustee assignment to a security equivalent object: If user KSS is made a security equivalent to object KARANJIT, any right that the user KARANJIT has to HP_PRINTER is automatically inherited by user KSS (see fig. 13.37).

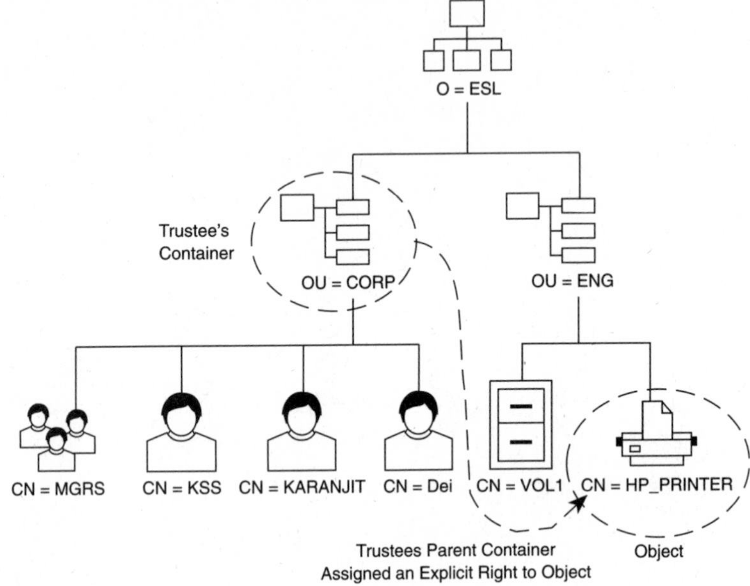

Figure 13.32
Effective Object Rights: Explicit trustee assignment.

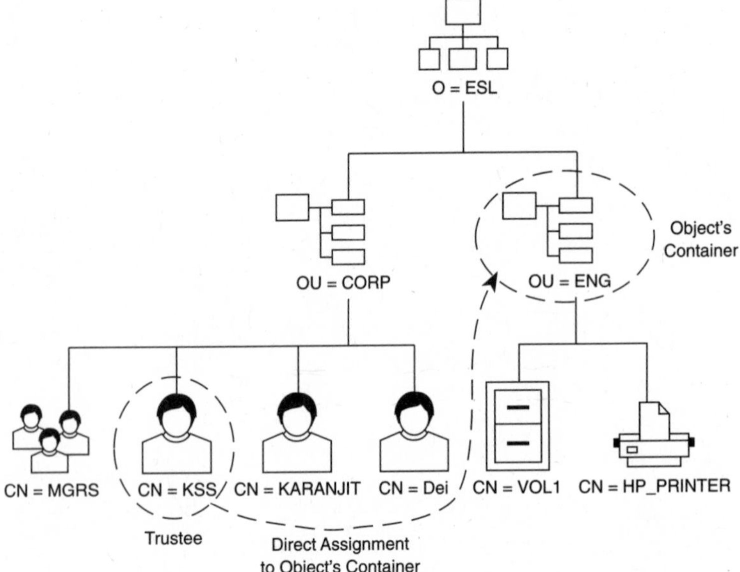

Figure 13.33
Effective Object Rights: Inherited from trustee's parent container.

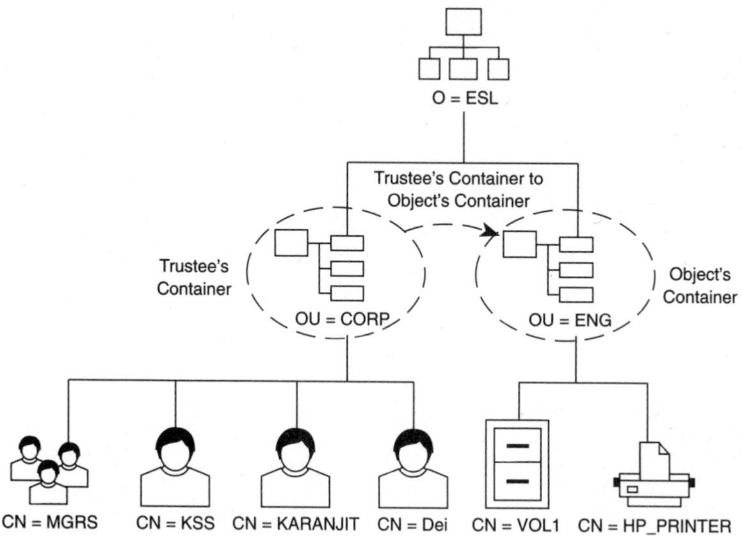

Figure 13.34
Effective Object Rights: Inherited from direct assignment to object's container.

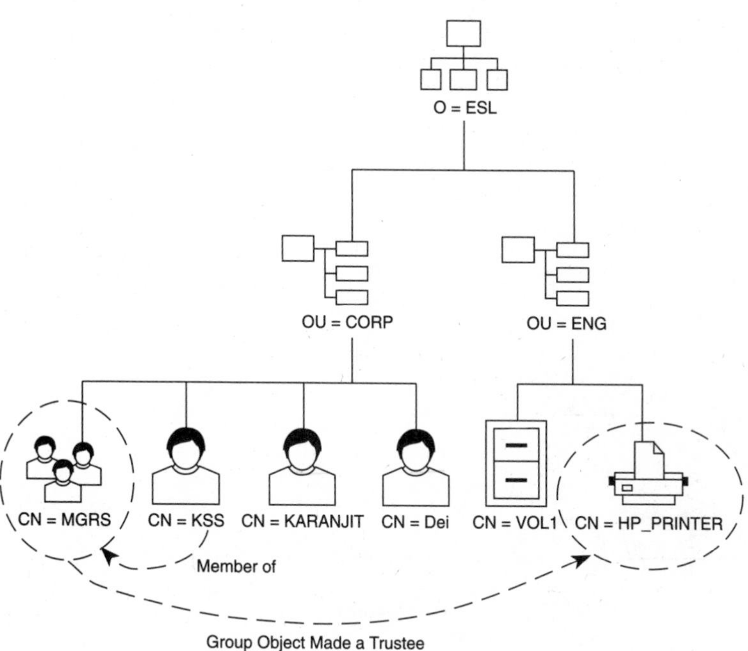

Figure 13.35
Effective Object Rights: Inherited from assignment of trustee's container to object's container.

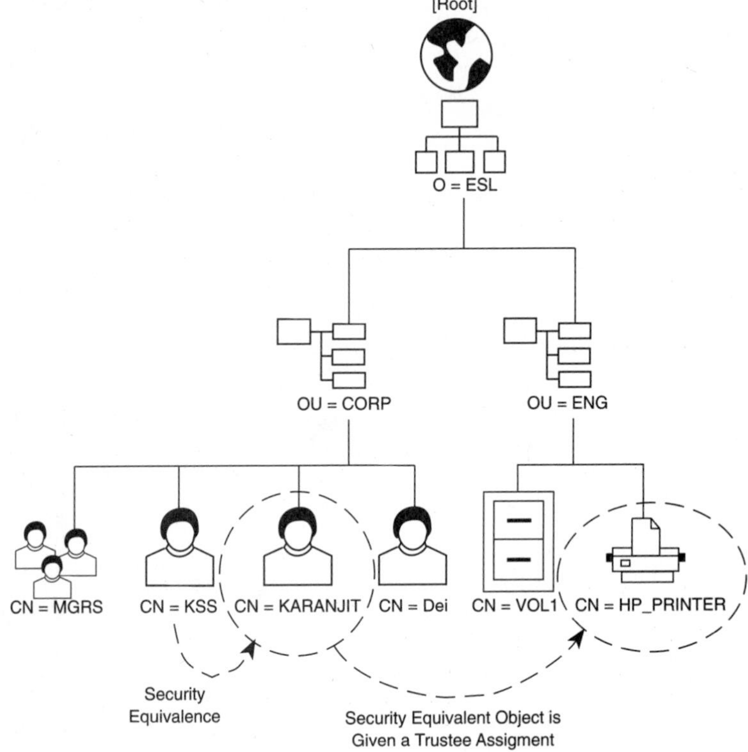

Figure 13.36
Effective Object Rights: Trustee assignment to a group object.

Figure 13.37
Effective Object Rights: Trustee assignment to a security equivalent object.

O = ESL		
	IRF	
	Inherited Rights	
	Trustee Assignment	
	Effective Rights	
O = CORP		
	IRF	
	Inherited Rights	
	Trustee Assignment	
	Effective Rights	
O = ACCTG		
	IRF	
	Inherited Rights	
	Trustee Assignment	
	Effective Rights	

Simple Organization Directory Tree
O = ESL
OU = CORP
OU = ACCTG

As you can see from the above discussion, to compute effective rights one must consider the following:

- The rights explicitly granted to a user object.
- The rights inherited from above minus the rights revoked by the IRF. If an explicit trustee assignment exists, it overrides any inherited rights for that particular trustee.
- The rights granted to container objects between the object and the [Root]. This applies to container objects that are between the object and the [Root] and the trustee and the [Root].
- The rights granted through security equivalence.

The next section presents case studies that give you practice in computing effective rights.

Calculating Object Effective Rights

Understanding how effective rights are computed for an object in the NDS tree is extremely important for NetWare 4.*x* administration. For this reason, a number of case studies are presented that help you understand how effective rights work in NetWare 4.*x*.

Figure 13.38 shows a worksheet that can be used for computing effective rights. This figure also shows a partial directory tree with the containers O=ESL, OU=CORP and OU=ACCTG. The worksheet for computing effective rights shows the entries for each of these containers. For each container, there are entries for

- Inherited Rights Filter (IRF)
- Inherited Rights
- Trustee Assignment
- Effective Rights

While practicing how to compute effective rights, the worksheet is an invaluable aid, as it systematically shows the rights at each level. With more experience and practice in computing effective rights, you may be able to dispense with the use of a worksheet, and be able to compute effective rights more directly.

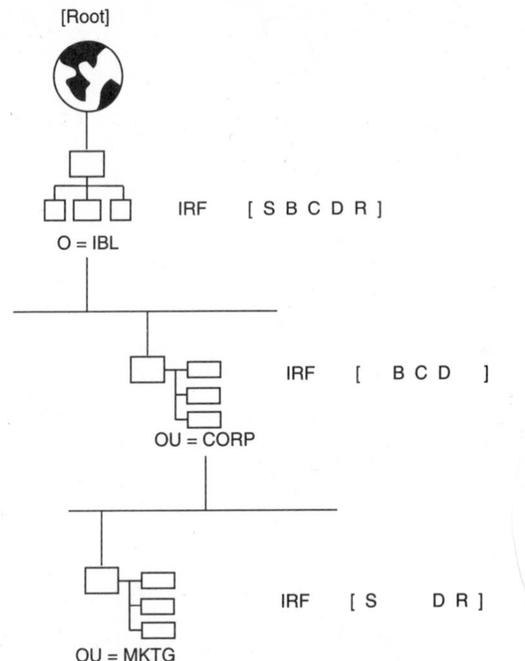

Figure 13.38
Worksheet for computing Effective Rights.

Computing NDS Effective Rights

To compute effective rights for an NDS object, you must consider the following:

- The rights explicitly granted to a user object.
- The rights inherited from above minus the rights revoked by the IRF. If an explicit trustee assignment exists, it overrides any inherited rights for that particular trustee.
- The rights granted to container objects between the object and the [Root]. This applies to container objects that are between the object and the [Root] and the trustee and the [Root].
- The rights granted through security equivalence.

The next few sections present case studies that further explain the rules for computing effective rights.

Effect of Making an Explicit Trustee Assignment

Figure 13.39 shows an NDS tree where user Sean has [B C D R] rights to O=ESL. The IRF for O=ESL, OU=CORP and OU=OPS is [S B C D R]. User Sean is given an explicit assignment of [B R] to OU=OPS.

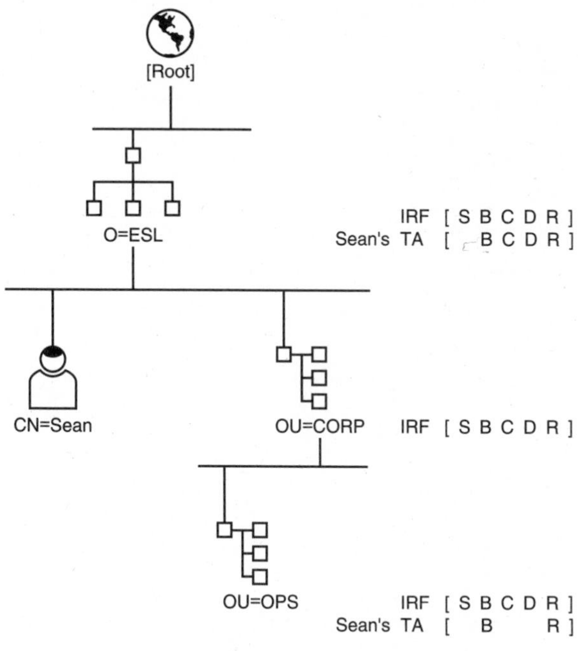

Figure 13.39
Example NDS tree—Explicit trustee assignment.

Figure 13.40 shows the completed worksheet containing the answers and the effect of the explicit trustee assignment to OU=OPS. The explanations for entries in the worksheet are presented next.

Entries for O=ESL

13

According to the case study, the IRF is [S B C D R]. There are no rights inherited from above, and therefore the entry for Inherited rights is None. An explicit trustee assignment of [B C D R] has been given to the user. The explicit trustee assignment overrides any other Inherited rights, so the Effective rights for the user in container O=ESL are the same as the explicit trustee assignment. That is, Effective rights of the user for O=ESL are [B C D R].

Entries for OU=CORP

According to the case study, the IRF is [S B C D R]. The rights inherited from above are the Effective rights of the parent container masked with the IRF for this container:

```
IRF                             [S B C D R ]
Effective rights of parent      [  B C D R ]
--------------------------------------------
Inherited rights                [  B C D R ]
```

The Inherited rights for OU=CORP are [B C D R]. Since no trustee assignment is made in OU=CORP, the Effective rights are the same as the Inherited rights. That is, Effective rights for OU=CORP are [B C].

Entries for OU=OPS

According to the case study, the IRF is [S B C D R]. The rights inherited from above are the Effective rights of the parent container masked with the IRF for this container:

```
IRF                          [S  B C D R ]
Effective rights of parent   [   B C D R ]
--------------------------------------------
Inherited rights             [   B C D R ]
```

The Inherited rights for OU=SOPS are [B C D R] for the user Sean. An explicit trustee assignment of [B R] has been made to OU=OPS for user Sean. This explicit trustee assignment overrides any Inherited rights for user Sean. That is, Effective rights for OU=OPS is [B R], the same as the explicit trustee assignment.

Figure 13.40
Worksheet for case study—Explicit trustee assignment.

Container	Entry	S	B	C	D	R	
O=ESL							
	IRF	S	B	C	D	R	
	Inherited Rights	None					
	Trustee Assignment		B	C	D	R	User Sean
	Effective Rights		B	C	D	R	User Sean
OU=CORP							
	IRF	S	B	C	D	R	
	Inherited Rights		B	C	D	R	User Sean
	Trustee Assignment						
	Effective Rights		B	C	D	R	User Sean
OU=OPS							
	IRF	S	B	C	D	R	
	Inherited Rights		B	C	D	R	User Sean
	Trustee Assignment		B			R	User Sean
	Effective Rights		B			R	User Sean

13

Explicit Trustee Assignment and Security Equivalent Assignments

Figure 13.41 shows an NDS tree where user Sean has [C D R] rights to O=ESL. The IRF for O=ESL, OU=CORP and OU=OPS is [S B C D R]. User Sean is given an explicit assignment of [R] to OU=OPS. User Sean is made security equivalent to user James who is a member of group Agents. Group Agents has been given an explicit trustee assignment of [C D] to OU=OPS. The [public] group has been given [B] rights to [Root].

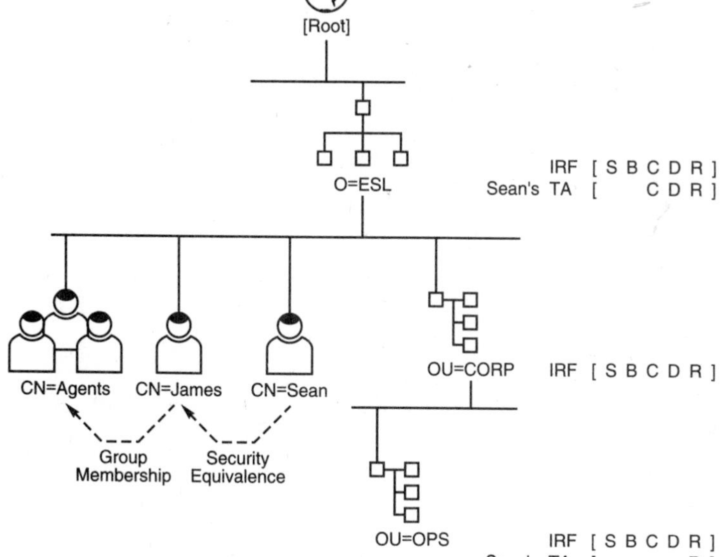

Figure 13.41
Example NDS tree—Explicit trustee assignment and security equivalents.

Figure 13.42 shows the completed worksheet containing the answers and the effect of the explicit trustee assignments and security equivalents for OU=OPS. The explanations for entries in the worksheet are presented next.

Entries for O=ESL

The IRF, according to the case study, is [S B C D R]. [public] has Browse object right to [Root], and therefore the rights inherited from [Root] are computed as shown below:

```
IRF                             [S  B C D R ]
Inherited rights from [Root] [    B       ]
---------------------------------------------
Inherited rights                [    B       ]
```

Inherited rights from security equivalence to [public] are [B].

An explicit trustee assignment of [C D R] has been given to the user Sean. The explicit trustee assignment overrides any other Inherited rights for user Sean. Notice that the Inherited rights are through [Public] and there are no Inherited rights for user Sean. So the Effective rights for the user Sean in container O=ESL are the explicit trustee assignment plus any Inherited rights through other sources, such as through [public].

Effective rights of the user for O=ESL are [B C D R]. The [B] rights are from [public] and the [C D R] rights are through an explicit assignment.

Entries for OU=CORP

The IRF, according to the case study, is [S B C D R]. The rights inherited from above are the Effective rights of the parent container masked with the IRF for this container:

```
IRF                            [S B C D R ]
Effective rights of parent     [  B C D R ]
--------------------------------------------
Inherited rights               [  B C D R ]
```

The Inherited rights for OU=CORP are [B C D R]. The [B] rights are inherited from [public] and the [C D R] rights are Inherited rights for user Sean.

Since no trustee assignment is made in OU=CORP, the Effective rights are the same as the Inherited rights. That is, Effective rights for OU=CORP are [B C D R].

Entries for OU=OPS

According to the case study, the IRF is [S B C D R]. The rights inherited from above are the Effective rights of the parent container masked with the IRF for this container:

```
IRF                            [S B C D R ]
Effective rights of parent     [  B C D R ]
--------------------------------------------
Inherited rights               [  B C D R ]
```

The Inherited rights for OU=OPS are [B C D R] for the user Sean. The [B] rights are inherited from [public] and the [C D R] rights are Inherited rights for user Sean.

An explicit trustee assignment of [R] has been made to OU=OPS for user Sean. This explicit trustee assignment overrides any inherited rights for user Sean. This means that the Inherited rights of [C D R] are overridden by the explicit assignment of [R] for user Sean. The [B] right is not overridden, because it is inherited from [public].

13

User Sean acquires the rights given to group Agents because user Sean is security equivalent to user James, and James is a member of group Agents. The rights acquired through security equivalence are the [C D] rights.

The effective rights for OU=OPS are as follows:

1. The explicit trustee assignment of [R] for user Sean *plus*
2. The Inherited rights of [B] from security equivalence to [public] *plus*
3. The explicit rights assignment of [C D] assigned through security equivalence to user James

Therefore, the Effective rights for OU=OPS are [B C D R].

Object		S	B	C	D	R	
O=ESL							
	IRF	S	B	C	D	R	
	Inherited Rights		B				[Public]
	Trustee Assignment			C	D	R	Sean
	Effective Rights		B	C	D	R	Sean, [Public]
OU=CORP							
	IRF	S	B	C	D	R	
	Inherited Rights		B	C	D	R	Sean, [Public]
	Trustee Assignment						
	Effective Rights		B	C	D	R	Sean, [Public]
OU=OPS							
	IRF	S	B	C	D	R	
	Inherited Rights		B				[Public]
				C	D	R	Sean
	Trustee Assignment			C	D		Group Agents
						R	Sean
	Effective Rights		B	C	D	R	Sean, [Public], Group Agents

Figure 13.42
Worksheet for case study—Explicit trustee assignment and security equivalencies.

Using IRF To Restrict Rights

Figure 13.43 shows an NDS tree where user Sean has [S B C D] explicit rights to O=ESL. The IRF for O=ESL is [S B C D R], for OU=CORP it is [S B], and for OU=OPS it is [B C D R].

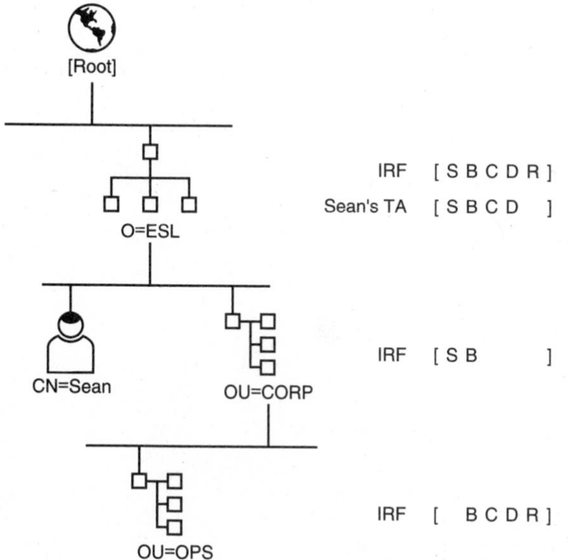

Figure 13.43
Example NDS tree—Using IRF to restrict trustee assignment.

Figure 13.44 shows the completed worksheet containing the answers and the effect of the blocking of rights using IRF. The explanations for entries in the worksheet are presented next.

Entries for O=ESL

According to the case study, the IRF is [S B C D R]. No rights are inherited from above, and therefore the entry for Inherited rights is None. An explicit trustee assignment of [S B C D] has been given to the user. The explicit trustee assignment overrides any other Inherited rights, so the Effective rights for the user in container O=ESL are the same as the explicit trustee assignment. That is, Effective rights of the user for O=ESL are [S B C D (R)]. The R right is shown in parenthesis to remind you that this right was not explicitly granted, but is implied from the Supervisor right.

Entries for OU=CORP

According to the case study, the IRF is [S B]. The rights inherited from above are the Effective rights of the parent container masked with the IRF for this container:

```
IRF                             [S B             ]
Effective rights of parent      [S B C D (R) ]
-----------------------------------------------------
Inherited rights                [S B (C D R) ]
```

The Inherited rights for OU=CORP are [S B (C D R)]. The actual Inherited rights are [S B], but the (C D R) rights are implied from the Supervisor right. Since no trustee assignment is made in OU=CORP, the Effective rights are the same as the Inherited rights. That is, Effective rights for OU=CORP are [S B (C D R)].

Entries for OU=OPS

According to the case study, the IRF is [B C D R]. The rights inherited from above are the Effective rights of the parent container masked with the IRF for this container:

```
IRF                             [  B  C D R  ]
Effective rights of parent      [S B (C D R) ]
-----------------------------------------------------
Inherited rights                [  B         ]
```

The Inherited rights for OU=OPS are [B] for the user Sean. Notice that because the [S] right was blocked, the (C D R) rights that were implied because of the presence of the [S] right are removed from the Inherited rights. Since no trustee assignment is made in OU=OPS, the Effective rights are the same as the Inherited rights. That is, Effective rights for OU=OPS are [B].

O=ESL			
	IRF	S B C D R	
	Inherited Rights	None	
	Trustee Assignment	S B C D	User Sean
	Effective Rights	S B C D (R)	User Sean
OU=CORP			
	IRF	S B	
	Inherited Rights	S B (C D R)	User Sean
	Trustee Assignment		
	Effective Rights	S B (C D R)	User Sean
OU=OPS			
	IRF	B C D R	
	Inherited Rights	B	User Sean
	Trustee Assignment		
	Effective Rights	B	User Sean

Figure 13.44
Worksheet for case study—Blocking rights through IRF.

Using Containers To Assign Rights

Figure 13.45 shows an NDS tree where OU=CORP.O=ESL has [B C D] Explicit rights to OU=SALES.O=ESL. The IRF for O=ESL is [S B C D R]; for OU=CORP it is [S B C D R]; for OU=SALES it is [ ]; and for OU=OPS it is [B]. User objects Nina and Janice are defined in the context OU=CORP.O=ESL. User Nina has an explicit trustee assignment of [S B] to O=ESL and an explicit trustee assignment of [D R] for OU=OPS. What are the rights for user object Nina in container OU=OPS.OU=SALES.O=ESL?

Figure 13.46 shows the completed worksheet containing the answers and the effect of the blocking of rights using IRF. The explanations for entries in the worksheet are presented next.

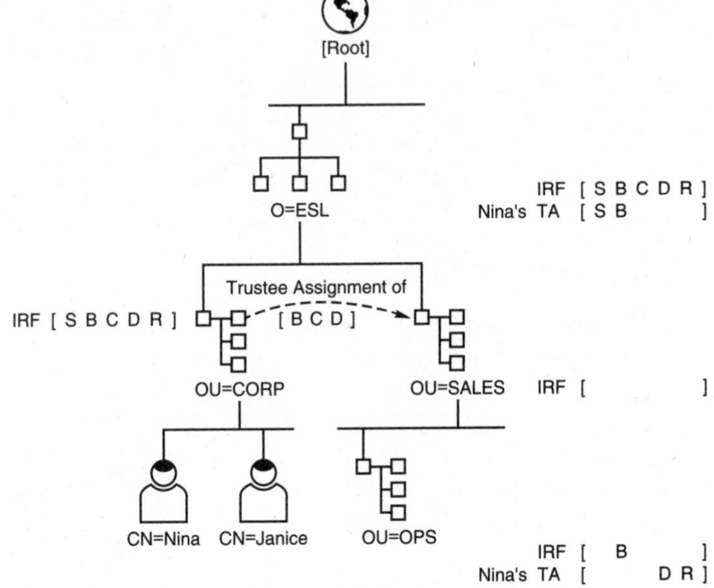

Figure 13.45
Example NDS tree—Assigning rights through containers.

Figure 13.46
Worksheet for case study—assigning rights through containers.

Container		Rights	
O=ESL			
	IRF	S B C D R	
	Inherited Rights	None	
	Trustee Assignment	S B	User Nina
	Effective Rights	S B (C D R)	User Nina
OU=SALES			
	IRF		
	Inherited Rights	No Rights	
	Trustee Assignment	B C D	Container OU=CORP
	Effective Rights	B C D	Container OU=CORP
OU=OPS			
	IRF	B	
	Inherited Rights	B	Container OU=CORP
	Trustee Assignment	D R	User Nina
	Effective Rights	B D R	User Nina

Entries for O=ESL

According to the case study, the IRF is [S B C D R]. There are no rights inherited from above, and therefore the entry for Inherited rights is None. An explicit trustee assignment of [S B] has been given to the user Nina. The explicit trustee assignment overrides any other inherited rights, so the Effective rights for the user in container O=ESL are the same as the explicit trustee assignment. That is, Effective rights of the user for O=ESL are [S B (C D R)]. The (C D R) right is shown in parentheses to remind you that these rights are not explicitly granted, but are implied from the Supervisor right.

Entries for OU=SALES

The IRF, according to the case study is [ ]. The rights inherited from above are the Effective rights of the parent container masked with the IRF for this container:

```
IRF                             [                 ]
Effective rights of parent      [S  B C  D (R) ]
----------------------------------------------------
Inherited rights                [                 ]
```

The Inherited rights for Nina in OU=SALES are [ ]; that is, no rights.

The container OU=CORP is given an explicit trustee assignment of [B C D] to OU=SALES. The Effective rights of OU=CORP in OU=SALES are the same as the explicit trustee assignment, that is [B C D].

Entries for OU=OPS

According to the case study, the IRF is [B]. The rights inherited from above are the Effective rights of the parent container masked with the IRF for this container:

```
IRF                             [   B         ]
Effective rights of parent      [   B C D     ]
----------------------------------------------------
Inherited rights                [   B         ]
```

The Inherited rights for OU=OPS are [B] for the container OU=CORP. User Nina has an explicit trustee assignment of [D R] for OU=OPS. Therefore, the Effective rights of Nina are the Inherited rights via OU=CORP *plus* the Explicit rights to OU=OPS.

```
Inherited Rights from CORP      [   B            ]
Explicit TA                     [          D R ]
----------------------------------------------------
Effective rights                [    B     D R ]
```

Nina's Effective rights are [B D R] in OU=OPS.OU=SALES.O=ESL.

13

Property Rights

Property rights are used to control access to information inside an NDS object. All objects have properties, since all objects are used to store information. An object can have many properties, and different objects can be expected to have different properties. For example, a volume object has a host server property, whose value is the name of the NetWare server the volume is associated with. But this property does not exist for a user object. Similarly, a user has a group membership property that does not exist for a volume object. The group membership is an example of a property that is multi-valued. Another example is the telephone number property. A user can have several phone numbers, so the telephone property for the user has the characteristic of accommodating multiple values. The location property of an object is single valued, since an object can have only one location.

The X.500 term for a property is an attribute. An attribute can consist of a type and one or more values. In NDS these are termed property values. The attribute type determines the characteristic of the attribute, such as its syntax, number of values allowed, how the values can be tested for comparison, and so on. If an attribute value can contribute to the name of an object, it is called a distinguished attribute value. An example of this would be the name attribute of an object.

Table 13.2 lists the Property rights that are defined for an NDS object.

Table 13.2
Property Rights Summary

Property Right	Abbreviation	Meaning
Supervisor	S	Grants all rights to All properties.
Compare	C	Grants the right to compare the value to a property. Does not allow you to see the value.
Read	R	Grants right to read the value of a property. Read includes the Compare right, even if the Compare is not explicitly given.
Write	W	Grants the right to add, remove, or change any values of the property.

Property Right	Abbreviation	Meaning
Add or Delete Self	A	Applies to list property values such as group membership. Grants the trustee the right to add or remove itself from the property value. The trustee cannot add or delete other values of the property. Useful for mailing lists, group lists.

The Supervisor property right grants all rights to a property. If desired, this property can be blocked by the Inherited Rights Filter.

The Compare property right grants the right to compare the value of a property. A trustee with the Compare property right allows a trustee to compare the property value to any value. The result of this comparison is a logical True if there is a match, and a logical False if there is no match. This property right would be useful for NDS tools that need to check for the existence of a specific value. The Compare right does not give you the right to read a property value. This right is granted by a special property value.

The Read property right grants the right to read a value for a property. This property right would be useful for NDS tools that need to display selected property values of an NDS object. If a trustee can read the value, it follows that the trustee should be able to compare the property value against another value. For this reason, a Read property right includes the Compare property right.

The Write property right allows the property value to be changed. Some property values are multi-valued. In this case, the Write property allows the trustee to remove from or add values to the property.

The Add or Delete Self property right allows the addition of a new property value or the removal of an existing property value. This right applies to multi-valued properties such as group memberships, mailing lists, or the Access Control List (ACL). The Add or Delete Self property right cannot be used to change the value of a property other than itself.

The Write property right includes the Add or Delete Self property.

All Properties Right vs. Selective Property Right

The property rights can be assigned selectively to specific properties, or they can be applied to all the properties of an object. When a property right is assigned to all the properties of an object, it is called the All Properties right. When a property right refers to an individual or selected property, it is called Selected Property right. An example of property right assignment is when a user object is created in a container. The user object is given the Read property right to all of its properties (All Properties). It is

also given a Read/Write property right to its login script property and the Print Job Configuration Property. This allows the user to modify their user login script and print job configuration. Should you wish to prevent a user from performing these activities, you have to restrict these property rights.

The All Properties Right is a convenient way of assigning default property rights to all properties. If there are some exceptions to this default, the Selected Property right can be used to individually set the property right of any property. The Selected Property right overrides the property right set by the All Properties right.

The Access Control List property

Every object has an *Access Control List* (ACL) property, also called the Object Trustees property. This property contains a list of all trustees that have a trustee assignment to the object or its property. It does not list other objects this object may have a right to. Because of this, to grant a right you must go to the object, and then assign a trustee. You cannot go to the trustee and add objects that this trustee may have rights to.

The ACL property value can be used to specify any of the following:

1. An object right, such as the [S B C D R] rights
2. A right to all properties of the object, called the "All Properties Right"
3. A right to a specific property

Since an ACL is a property of the object that describes the trustee assignments to the object, it can include a trustee assignment to itself. This trustee assignment to the ACL property would describe which of the operations described by the property rights [S C R W A] a trustee could perform.

Consider what would happen if a trustee had a Write property right to the ACL. Such a trustee could then modify the ACL, and grant and revoke privileges by changing the ACL value. To do this a trustee would in addition need the Read property right and the Browse object right to the object. The trustee could grant itself Supervisor rights to the object. And this would give the trustee complete control over the object and its subordinates (unless blocked by an IRF or explicit assignment).

In actual practice, it is unlikely that you would want to give an Admin user just the Write right to the ACL property. You would probably want to give the Admin user Supervisor object right. This would give complete control over the object and its subordinates, unless as noted earlier, you block the Supervisor right.

Normally, you would probably not single out the ACL property (appears as Object Trustee property in the NetWare Administrator Tool) to give property rights to. But you could inadvertently grant the Write right to All Properties. This in turn would grant the Write right to the ACL property, and then the problem described earlier would exist.

NDS Rights and the File System

A trustee who has the Write property right to the NetWare server's ACL property is granted the Supervisor file system right to the root of each server's volume. It is therefore important that you do not inadvertently give the Write right to the server's ACL property, or the Write right to the server object (All Properties of the server object).

Normally, the NDS rights are independent from the file system rights. The only exception is the one mentioned above. Actually, the exception is necessary to provide an easy way for a trustee with Supervisor rights to access files and directories in volume objects.

Consider the Admin user, who is normally given the Supervisor object right to the root container of the tree branch that user is expected to manage. This user would then have Supervisor rights to all objects in the tree branch, unless the Supervisor right is explicitly blocked. The Supervisor object right would grant to the user the Supervisor property right to All Properties for all objects, including the server object. If the user has the Write property right to the server object, the user then inherits the Supervisor NetWare File System right to the root of all volumes for which the server is a host.

The Admin user could be explicitly granted the Supervisor NetWare File System right to a volume object also. In general, any NDS object can be granted an explicit NetWare File System right to a file or directory in any volume object, even though an NDS object is usually granted NDS security rights. Figure 13.47 shows a situation in which the user Admin1.CORP.ESL has been granted Supervisor, Read and File Scan rights to the SYSTEM directory of a volume. Figure 13.48 shows that the NDS group object NETMGRS.CORP.ESL_XXX has been granted Read and File Scan rights.

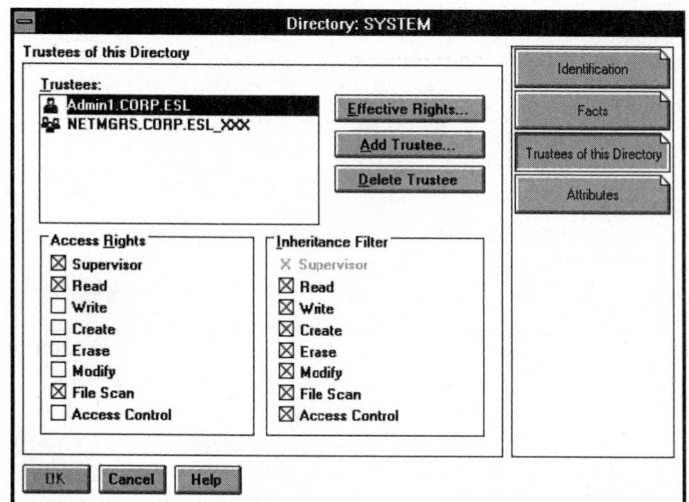

Figure 13.47
NetWare File System right assigned to a user NDS object.

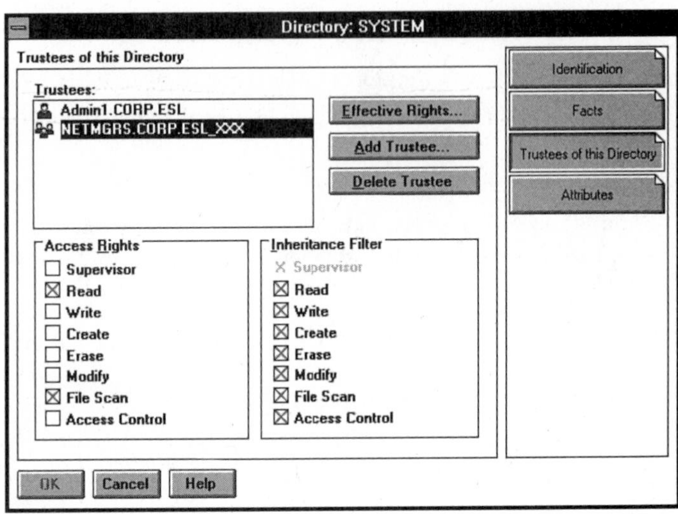

Figure 13.48
NetWare File System right assigned to a group NDS object.

Care must be exercised when assigning a container object a right to another NDS object or a NetWare File System. A right assigned to a container object is inherited by all objects within that container, because a container acts as a logical group of NDS objects.

For instance, if a Supervisor NetWare File System right is assigned to the [Root] object, all objects in the [Root] directory are assigned the Supervisor NetWare File System right. And since [Root] is the top-most container of an NDS tree, this includes all objects in the NDS tree.

Calculating Property Effective Rights

Calculating Property Effective rights is similar to calculating Object Effective rights. The same rules of inheritance apply.

Object property rights can be dealt with in terms of their All Property rights or Selective Property rights. Only All Property rights can be inherited. Selective Property rights cannot be inherited. Consider what would happen if a Selective Property were allowed to be inherited. A selected property may have no meaning for objects further down in the tree. For instance, intruder detection is a property of a container object, and if this property was inherited to an object (such as a user object that does not have an intruder detection property), it would not make sense. On the other hand, it may be convenient to assign rights to information inside objects, regardless of the different types of properties NDS objects can have. This can be done by allowing the All Properties right to be inherited.

The All Properties right and Selected Properties right each have a separate Inherited Rights Filter, so a right can be blocked at any level. Also, a right assigned to a Selected Property overrides the rights that may be inherited through the All Properties rights.

Case Study 1—Computing Property Effective Rights

Figure 13.49 shows a directory tree for organization IBL. Drew is made a trustee of Organization O=IBL and given the All Properties right of Create, Read, Add/Delete Self. The All Properties IRF for the containers are shown below:

IRF for O=IBL	[S C R W A]
IRF for OU=CORP	[C R W]
IRF for OU=MKTG	[S W A]

Calculate Drew's Property Effective rights in containers O=IBL, OU=CORP and OU=MKTG. Assume that Drew does not inherit rights from any other source than the ones listed in the case study.

Figure 13.50 shows the completed worksheet containing the answers. The explanation for entries in the worksheet is presented next.

Entries for O=IBL

According to the case study, the IRF is [S C R W A]. There are no rights inherited from above, and therefore the entry for Inherited rights is None. An explicit trustee assignment of [C R A] has been given to the user. The explicit trustee assignment overrides any other inherited rights, so the Effective rights for the user in container O=IBL are the same as the explicit trustee assignment. That is, the Property Effective rights of the user for O=IBL are [C R A].

Entries for OU=CORP

According to the case study, the IRF is [C R W]. The rights inherited from above are the Effective rights of the parent container masked with the IRF for this container:

```
IRF                           [     C R W    ]
Effective rights of parent    [     C R     A]
-------------------------------------------------
Inherited rights              [     C R      ]
```

The masking operation is a logical AND operation, which means that an entry needs to be in both of the rights for it to be in the final result.

The Inherited rights for OU=CORP are [C R]. Since no trustee assignment is made in OU=CORP, the Effective rights are the same as the Inherited rights. That is, Property Effective rights for OU=CORP are [C R].

Entries for OU=MKTG

According to the case study, the IRF is [S W A]. The rights inherited from above are the Effective rights of the parent container masked with the IRF for this container:

```
IRF                             [S     W A ]
Effective rights of parent      [  C R     ]
--------------------------------------------
Inherited rights                [          ]
```

The Inherited rights for OU=MKTG are [ ], or No rights. Since no trustee assignment is made in OU=MKTG, the Effective rights are the same as the Inherited rights. That is, Property Effective rights for OU=MKTG are No rights.

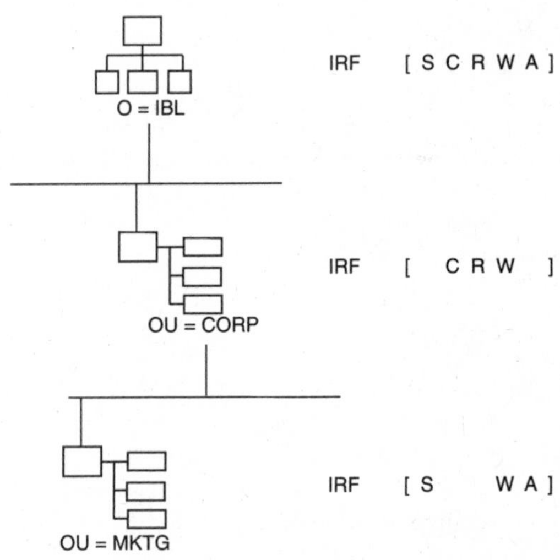

Figure 13.49
Property Effective Rights: NDS tree for case study 1.

Figure 13.50
Property Effective Rights: Worksheet for case study 1.

O = IBL		
	IRF	S C R W A
	Inherited Rights	None
	Trustee Assignment	C R A
	Effective Rights	C R A
OU = CORP		
	IRF	C R W
	Inherited Rights	C R
	Trustee Assignment	None
	Effective Rights	C R
OU = MKTG		
	IRF	S W A
	Inherited Rights	No Rights
	Trustee Assignment	None
	Effective Rights	No Rights

Case Study 2—Computing Property Effective Rights

Figure 13.51 shows a directory tree for organization IBL. James is made a trustee of Organization O=IBL and given the All Properties right of Create, Read and Write. James is also made a trustee of organization unit OU=MKTG, and given the All Properties right of Write. The All Properties IRF for the containers are shown below:

IRF for O=IBL	[S C R W A]
IRF for OU=CORP	[S C R W A]
IRF for OU=MKTG	[S R]

Calculate James's Property Effective rights in containers O=IBL, OU=CORP and OU=MKTG. Assume that James does not inherit rights from any other source than the ones listed in the case study.

Figure 13.52 shows the completed worksheet containing the answers. The explanations for entries in the worksheet are presented next.

Entries for O=IBL

According to the case study, the IRF is [S C R W A]. There are no rights inherited from above, and therefore the entry for Inherited rights is None. An explicit trustee assignment of [C R W] has been given to the user. The explicit trustee assignment overrides any other Inherited rights, so the Effective rights for the user in container O=IBL are the same as the explicit trustee assignment. That is, the Property Effective rights of the user for O=IBL are [C R W (A)]. The [(A)] right is implied from the Write right.

Entries for OU=CORP

According to the case study, the IRF is [S C R W A]. The rights inherited from above are the Effective rights of the parent container masked with the IRF for this container:

```
IRF                           [S C R W  A  ]
Effective rights of parent    [  C R W (A) ]
-------------------------------------------
Inherited rights              [  C R W (A) ]
```

The masking operation is a logical AND operation, which means that an entry needs to be in both the rights for it to be in the final result.

The Inherited rights for OU=CORP are [C R W (A)]. Since no trustee assignment is made in OU=CORP, the Effective rights are the same as the Inherited rights. That is, Property Effective rights for OU=CORP are [C R W (A)].

Entries for OU=MKTG

According to the case study, the IRF is [S R]. The rights inherited from above are the Effective rights of the parent container masked with the IRF for this container:

```
IRF                           [S    R       ]
Effective rights of parent    [  C  R W (A)]
---------------------------------------------
Inherited rights              [ (C) R       ]
```

The Inherited rights for OU=MKTG are [(C) R]. The [(C)] Inherited right is implied because of the presence of the Read right in the Inherited rights. Because no trustee assignment is made in OU=MKTG, the Effective rights are the same as the Inherited rights. That is, Property Effective rights for OU=MKTG are [(C) R].

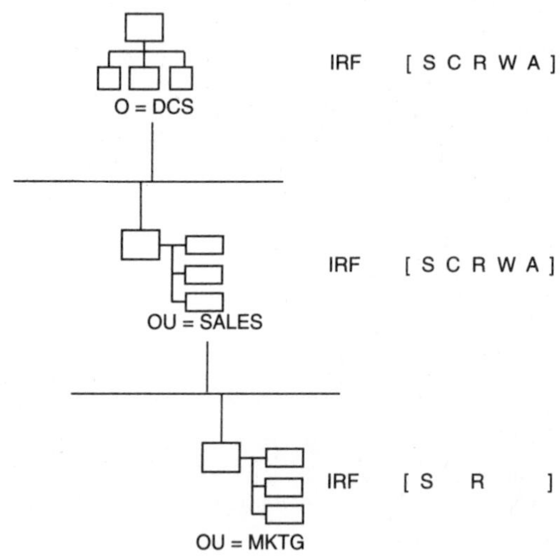

Figure 13.51
Property Effective Rights: NDS tree for case study 2.

Figure 13.52
Property Effective Rights: Worksheet for case study 2.

O = IBL			
	IRF	S C R W A	
	Inherited Rights	None	
	Trustee Assignment	C R W	James
	Effective Rights	C R W (A)	James
OU = CORP			
	IRF	S C R W A	
	Inherited Rights	C R W (A)	
	Trustee Assignment	None	
	Effective Rights	C R W (A)	James
OU = MKTG			
	IRF	S R	
	Inherited Rights	(C) R	
	Trustee Assignment		
	Effective Rights	(C) R	James

13

Case Study 3—Computing Property Effective Rights

Figure 13.53 shows a directory tree for organization DCS. James is made a trustee of Organization O=DCS and given the All Properties right of Create, Read and Write. James is a member of the group ATEAM. ATEAM is given the All Properties right Write and Add/Delete Self to OU=SALES. The All Properties IRF for the containers are shown below:

IRF for O=DCS	[S C R W A]
IRF for OU=SALES	[S C R W A]
IRF for OU=MKTG	[S R]

Calculate James's Property Effective rights in containers O=DCS, OU=SALES and OU=MKTG. Assume that James does not inherit rights from any other source than the ones listed in the case study.

Figure 13.54 shows the completed worksheet containing the answers. The explanations for entries in the worksheet are presented next.

Entries for O=DCS

According to the case study, the IRF is [S C R W A]. There are no rights inherited from above, and therefore the entry for Inherited rights is None. An explicit trustee assignment of [C R W] has been given to the user. The explicit trustee assignment overrides any other Inherited rights, so the Effective rights for the user in container O=DCS are the same as the explicit trustee assignment. That is, the Property Effective rights of the user for O=DCS are [C R W (A)]. The [(A)] right is implied from the Write right.

Entries for OU=SALES

According to the case study, the IRF is [S C R W A]. The rights inherited from above are the Effective rights of the parent container masked with the IRF for this container:

```
IRF                           [S  C R W  A  ]
Effective rights of parent    [   C R W (A) ]
---------------------------------------------
Inherited rights              [   C R W (A) ]
```

The masking operation is a logical AND operation, which means that an entry needs to be in both of the rights for it to be in the final result.

The Inherited rights for OU=SALES are [C R W (A)]. A trustee assignment is made to group object SALES of Write and Add/Delete Self. This would override any inherited trustee assignments for group object ATEAM. But since no trustee assignments are inherited for group object ATEAM, there are no rights to override. You cannot override the Inherited rights of [C R W (A)], because these rights are for user object James and not group object ATEAM.

Since James is a member of group ATEAM, his rights to OU=SALES are the sum of the Inherited and Effective rights.

```
Inherited rights for user James      [    C R W (A)]
Trustee assignment for ATEAM         [        W  A ]
---------------------------------------------------------------------
Effective rights for James           [    C R W  A ]
```

Property Effective rights of user object James for OU=SALES are [C R W A]. Notice that the Add/Delete to Self right is no longer an implied right [(A)], since it was explicitly assigned to group ATEAM. Also, the Write right is derived from both the Inherited rights and trustee assignment to group object ATEAM. If this right were removed from the Trustee Assignment, the Write right would still exist in the Effective rights because it would then be derived from the Inherited rights.

Entries for OU=MKTG

According to the case study, the IRF is [S R]. The rights inherited from above are the Effective rights of the parent container masked with the IRF for this container:

```
IRF                            [S      R       ]
Effective rights of parent     [    C  R W A   ]
-----------------------------------------------
Inherited rights               [   (C) R       ]
```

The Inherited rights for OU=MKTG are [(C) R]. The actual right inherited is [R], but the [(C)] Inherited right is implied because of the presence of the Read right in the Inherited rights. Both of these rights are due to rights assigned to user James. Since an explicit trustee assignment is made in OU=MKTG to user James, the explicit trustee assignmnet of [W] overrides the Inherited rights. Property Effective rights for OU=MKTG are [W (A)].

```
Inherited rights for James     [  (C)  R          ]
Trustee assignment for James   [            W (A) ]
----------------------------------------------------
Effective rights for James     [            W (A) ]
```


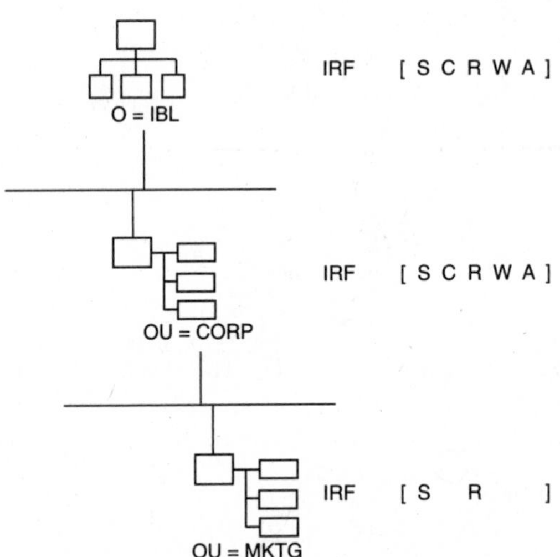

Figure 13.53
Property Effective Rights: NDS tree for case study 3.

O = DCS			
	IRF	S C R W A	
	Inherited Rights	None	
	Trustee Assignment	C R W	James
	Effective Rights	C R W	James
OU = SALES			
	IRF	S C R W A	
	Inherited Rights	C R W (A)	
	Trustee Assignment	W A	ATEAM
	Effective Rights	C R W A	James, Group ATEAM
OU = MKTG			
	IRF	S R	
	Inherited Rights	(C) R	James
	Trustee Assignment	W (A)	James
	Effective Rights	W (A)	James

Figure 13.54
Property Effective Rights: Worksheet for case study 3.

Comparing NetWare File System Security with NDS Security

The similarities are that both NDS and NetWare file system security make use of the concepts of trustees, trustee rights, inheritance, and Inherited Rights Filter. For a user to gain access to an object (NDS of file/directory), the user must be made a trustee to an object and given appropriate rights. The rights flow down the tree and can be blocked by the IRF. The actual rights a user has at any level of the tree are called Effective rights.

The differences between NDS and NetWare file system security include the following:

- NDS rights are further sub-divided into Object rights and Property rights.
- In NDS rights, the Supervisor object right and Property right can be blocked by the IRF. In NetWare file system right the Supervisor right cannot be blocked.
- NDS rights do not flow to a NetWare file system right, except in the following case: Any user that has the Write property right to the ACL of the server object has the Supervisor right to the root of each of the server's volumes.

When a user object is created, no automatic file system rights are created (except to the user's home directory, if one was specified at the time of creation). Figure 13.55 shows the rights to newly created user CN=KSS.O=IMF to the home directory USERS\KSS in volume CN=FS1_SYS.OU=SALES.O=ESL. Notice that the user has [S R W C E M F A] rights to his home directory; that is, the user has All Rights to his home directory.

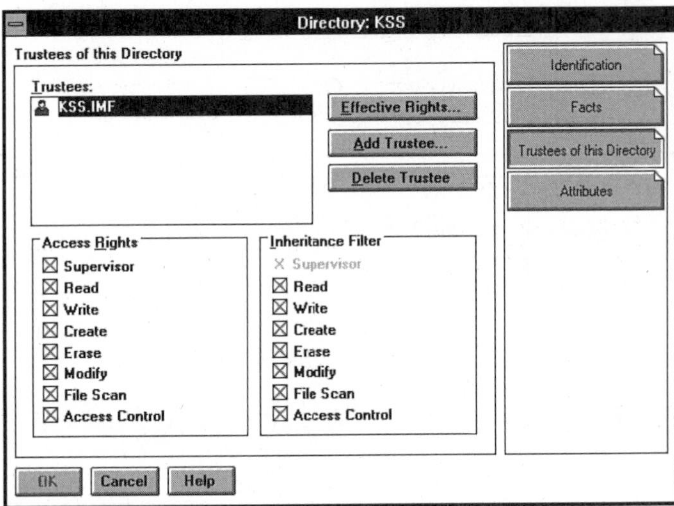

Figure 13.55
Right of user KSS in home directory.

In NetWare 3.*x*, the term Inherited Rights Mask (IRM) was used to describe the mechanism to block the flow of NetWare file system rights. In NetWare 4.*x*, the term *Inherited Rights Filter* (IRF) is used for both file system rights and NDS object rights.

13

Another minor distinction, though not documented in the Novell manuals, is that in NetWare 3.*x* the Supervisor file system rights were called Supervisory. They are now called Supervisor in NetWare 4.*x*.

As in NetWare 3.*x*, the file system supervisor right granted to a directory also grants Supervisor rights to files and directories below the directory.

One major conceptual difference between NetWare 3.*x* and NetWare 4.*x* file systems is the scope of the trustee. In NetWare 3.*x*, the trustee could only be a user account or a group account defined in the server's bindery. In NetWare 4.*x*, user objects and group objects in containers other than where the volume is installed, can be assigned trustees. The trustee is not limited to the user and group objects—it can be any NDS object, such as another container object. If a container object is made a trustee of file/directory, all objects within it (including, of course, user and group objects) inherit the trustee rights to the file or directory. When dealing with assigning file/directory rights it is easier to assign the rights using a container object, if the NDS containers and the leaf objects are properly designed to reflect usage of resources.

Any NDS object that has a Write right to the ACL property (Object Trustee property) of the NetWare server object, is also granted the Supervisor right to the root of each of the volumes hosted by the NetWare server. Since a Supervisor file/directory right cannot be blocked by an IRF, this should be a consideration in setting up Security rights.

The Write property right can be granted through:

1. Write right to All Properties of the NetWare server object.
2. Write right to the Selected Property ACL (Object Trustee) for the NetWare server object.
3. Supervisor right to the All Properties right or ACL property (Selected Property) for the NetWare server object.
4. Supervisor object right to the NetWare server object. This causes the object to have Supervisor right to the All Properties of the NetWare server object.
5. Security equivalence to an object that has any of the rights listed above.

Directory and File Attribute rights in NetWare 4.*x* are a superset of the rights for NetWare 3.*x*. That is, NetWare 4.*x* directory and file attributes include all those for NetWare 3.*x*, and additionally, the rights listed in table 13.3.

Table 13.3
Additional NetWare 4.*x* Attributes

Attribute	File/ Directory	Abbreviation	Description
Migrate	File	M	Indicates that the file has migrated to near-line storage
Don't Migrate	File/ Directory	Dm	Prevents a file or the files in a directory from migrating
Compress	File	Co	Indicates if a file has been compressed
Don't Compress	File/ Directory	Dc	Prevents a file or the files in a directory from being compressed
Immediate Compress	File/ Directory	Ic	Specified file or files in a directory are marked for compression as soon as the OD can perform compression

continues

Table 13.3, Continued
Additional NetWare 4.x Attributes

Attribute	File/ Directory	Abbreviation	Description
Can't compress	File	Cc	Indicates that a file cannot be compressed because of limited space saving benefit

The attributes *Migrate* (M), *Compress* (Co), and *Can't Compress* (Cc) are status attributes and indicate the status of individual files only. The other attributes—*Don't Migrate* (Dm), *Don't Compress* (Dc), and *Immediate Compress* (Ic)—apply to both files and directories and specify actions that are to be performed or prevented from occurring.

The Data Migration feature is installed using INSTALL.NLM and requires a near-linestorage medium that acts as a secondary to the primary hard disk storage area.

The compression feature is enabled or disabled on a volume-by-volume basis during installation. It can be further controlled by a variety of SET parameters.

Default NDS Security

13

When the NDS tree is first installed, the *implicit* group [public] is made a trustee of [Root] and given the Browse object right. The Browse object right is then inherited by all subcontainers under the NDS tree unless explicitly blocked by revoking rights from the Inherited Rights Filter. By definition, [public] includes all user objects that are connected to an NDS tree, including those that are simply attached to a NetWare 4.*x* server and not logged (not authenticated) into the network (see fig. 13.56). You should avoid assigning excessive rights through [public]. For example, if rights are assigned through [public] to a NetWare file system, all users that attach to the network can access the file system *without logging in* to the network. You can run the DSREPAIR.NLM at the server to remove any [public] trustee assignments to the NetWare file system.

To run DSREPAIR for removing file system trustee assignments to [public], follow these steps:

1. Type the following at server console:

   ```
   LOAD DSREPAIR
   ```

2. Select "1. Select Options"

3. Make sure that "5. Check file system for valid trustee IDs" is selected.

   Selected DSREPAIR options have an asterisk (*) next to them.

4. Select "8. Return to selection menu"

5. Select "2. Begin Repair"

6. Select "3. Exit"

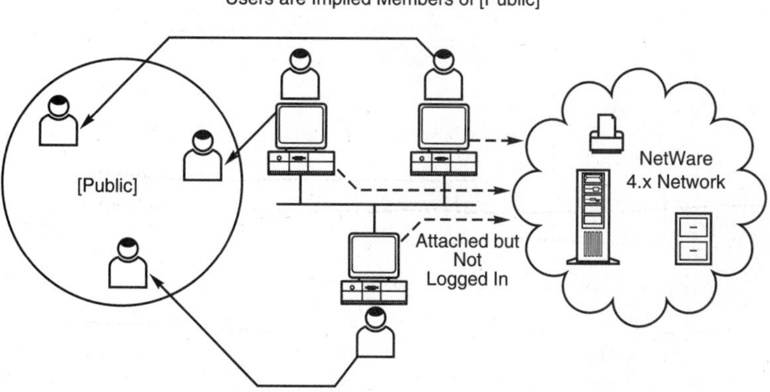

Figure 13.56
[public] implicit group membership.

Rights can be assigned explicitly, in which case they are called *explicit trustee assignment.* Another way of obtaining rights is by *inheritance.* Rights assigned to a container of an NDS tree *flow down* to all objects in the container unless they are explicitly blocked. The rights inherited by an NDS object are called *inherited rights.* Blocking of rights is done by using the Inherited Rights Filter (IRF). The actual rights inherited by an NDS object are the *logical AND* of the rights inherited from the parent of the NDS object and the IRF assigned to the NDS object. The IRF can be assigned to any NDS object in the NDS tree except the [Root] object. An explicit trustee assignment for an NDS object *overrides any inherited rights for that NDS object.* This new explicit trustee assignment flows down, until restricted by an IRF for an object, or until another explicit trustee assignment is made. You cannot set an IRF on an object for a particular trustee. The IRF that is set for an NDS object applies to all trustees of the NDS object.

Property rights can be granted on a selected property basis, in which case these rights are called *Selected Property Rights.* For example, a user object may have an explicit Read and Write right to the Login Script property. This means that the user can read and modify the contents of his user login script. It is sometimes desirable to grant the same property rights to all properties of an NDS object. An example of this could be assigning the right Read and Compare to all properties of an NDS object. The rights assigned in this manner are called *All Property Rights.* All Property Rights is a collective way to grant rights to all properties of an NDS object. The rights assigned through All Properties can be inherited, but the rights granted through Selected Properties cannot be inherited. The NDS security maintains separate Inherited Rights Filters for

- Object rights
- All Properties rights
- Selected Property rights

Because object rights and All Properties rights can be inherited (or flow down), it makes sense that there are Inherited Rights Filters for them. But at first glance, it does not make sense that Selected Property rights has an IRF since it has been stated that Selected Property rights cannot be inherited. The reason why Selected Property rights have a separate filter is that the All Property rights apply to all the properties of an NDS object, and you may wish to block out rights to a specific property. One way of doing this is to block out the rights by removing them from the Inherited Rights Filter for that specific property. Another way of modifying the property right for a specific property is to grant an explicit property right for that property. Explicit rights granted to a specific property override the All Property rights.

An example of the use of the mechanisms described so far are the default property rights assigned to user objects. A user is granted the Read and Compare All Properties to their user object. This allows the user to examine the property values set for the user object. The user is also granted the Read and Write selected property rights to the Login Script and Print Job Configuration properties. These selected property rights override the All Property rights of Read and Compare.

The NDS object rights are independent of the NDS property rights, except in one important case. A Supervisor object right to an NDS object gives to the trustee the Supervisor property right of All Properties for that NDS object. The Supervisor property right of All Properties gives to the trustee complete control over the objects properties, including any critical properties used to determine security rights for that object.

The ACL Property

A critical property that exists for all NDS objects is the Access Control List (ACL) property. The ACL property contains a list of all trustee assignments to that object. The ACL property is also called Object Trustees property in the NetWare Administrator (see fig. 13.57). For example, if a user object has a Supervisor object right granted for it to user CN=Admin.O=ESL, and a Read/Write property right for property E-Mail granted to CN=MailKeeper.O=ESL, then the ACL for the user object contains two entries in the ACL list:

1. Trustee CN=Admin.O=ESL granted [S] object right
2. Trustee CN=MailKeeper.O=ESL granted [R W] property right

These two additional entries are a record of the trustee assignments given to the user object, and are in addition to any other entries that may have been granted to the user object, such as the trustee assignments to implement default rights for the user object.

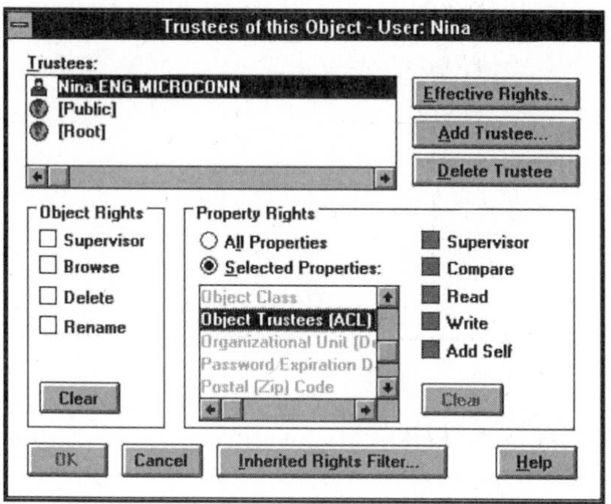

Figure 13.57
Object Trustee (ACL) Selected Property.

The ACL property right lists only explicit trustee assignments. It does not, for instance, contain Inherited rights and Effective rights, which are computed based on considerations that are discussed later in this chapter. A conceptual view of the ACL property list is shown in figure 13.58. This figure shows that the volume object NW4KS_SYS has two trustee assignments (ACEs—Access Control Elements) in its ACL property. User object CN=Peter.OU=CORP.O=ESL has the object rights of Browse and Read, and container object OU=MKTG.O=ESL has the object right of Supervisor. The latter ACE implies that all objects under the container grouping OU=MKTG inherit the Supervisor rights to volume object NW4KS_SYS.

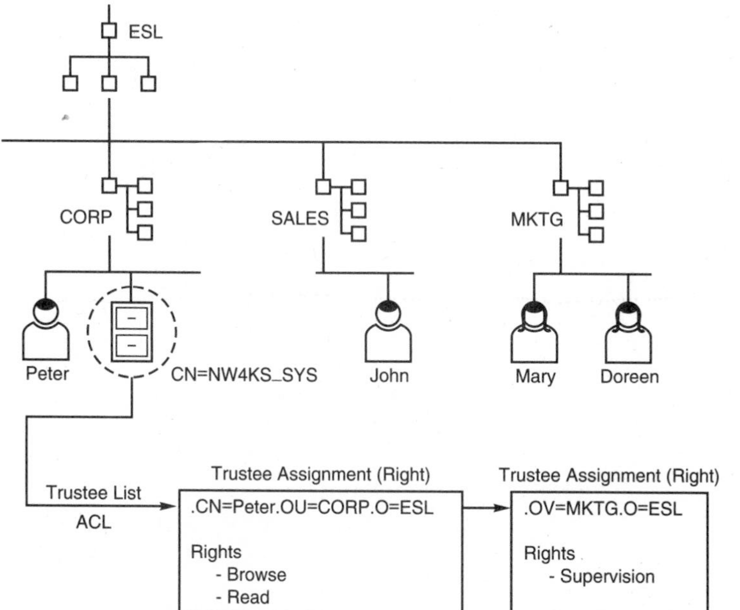

Figure 13.58
ACL and ACE.

If a user object has the Write property right to the ACL property right, the user can modify the ACL property. For instance, the user can modify the ACL property right and grant to himself the Supervisor object right.

Also, if a user has Supervisor object rights, the user automatically has Supervisor All Property rights to that object. The Supervisor All Properties right implies that the user has the Write property right to the ACL property right.

If a user has the Write property right to the ACL of a file server object, the user automatically has the Supervisor NetWare File System right to the root of all volumes attached to the server (see fig. 13.59). This is the only case where NDS security rights affect the NetWare file system security rights. Figure 13.59 shows that user CN=Dei.OU=CORP.O=ESL has the Write property right to server object CN=NW4KS.OU=CORP.O=ESL. The server NW4KS has two volumes attached to it whose volume object names are NW4KS_SYS and NW4KS_VOL1. User Dei is given Supervisor NetWare file system right to the root of these volumes. The Supervisor file system rights once assigned cannot be blocked.

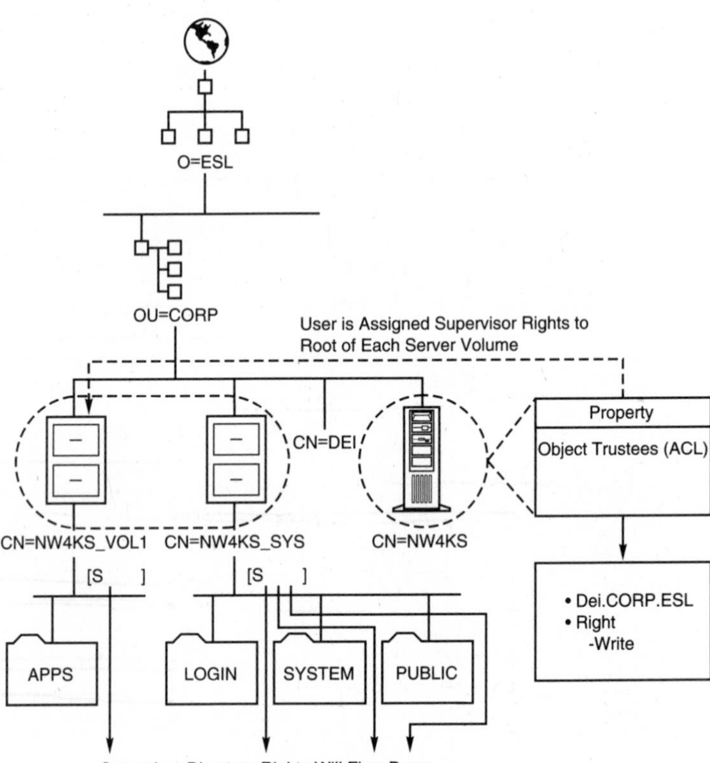

Figure 13.59
Write property right and ACL of NetWare server object.

Figure 13.60 shows that the ACL for NetWare server NW4KS has been given the Write property right. Figure 13.61 shows the Effective rights for Dei.CORP.ESL for the volume object NW4KS_SYS that is attached to the NetWare server NW4KS. Notice that figure 13.61 shows the Effective rights for user Dei to be *all rights*, because user Dei has Supervisor rights. When a Supervisor file system right is explicitly assigned, it cannot be blocked using an IRF or an explicit assignment further down the file system directory tree. Even though the Supervisor file system right assigned to a user through Write property right is not explicitly assigned, it cannot be overridden by an explicit assignment. Figure 13.62 shows that user Dei.CORP.ESL has been granted an explicit assignment of *No Rights* to the root directory of volume NW4KS_SYS. You can use the Effective Rights button on the screen in figure 13.62 to see the effect of these new trustee assignments. Figure 13.63 shows that the Effective rights of Dei.CORP.ESL to root of volume are still All rights.

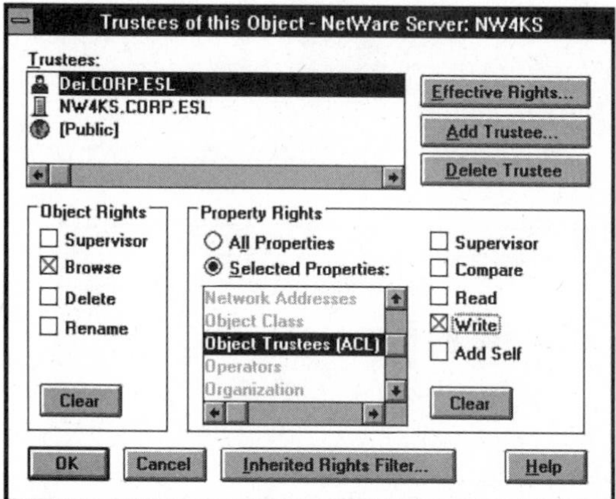

Figure 13.60
Write property right assigned to ACL of NetWare server object.

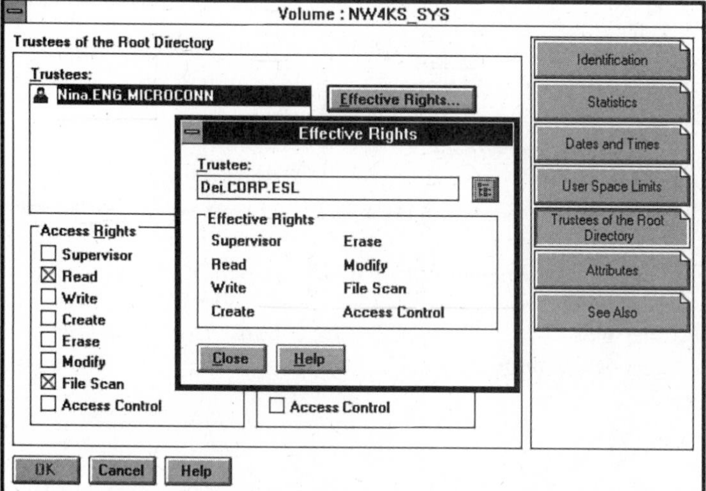

Figure 13.61
Effective rights of user to root of volume.

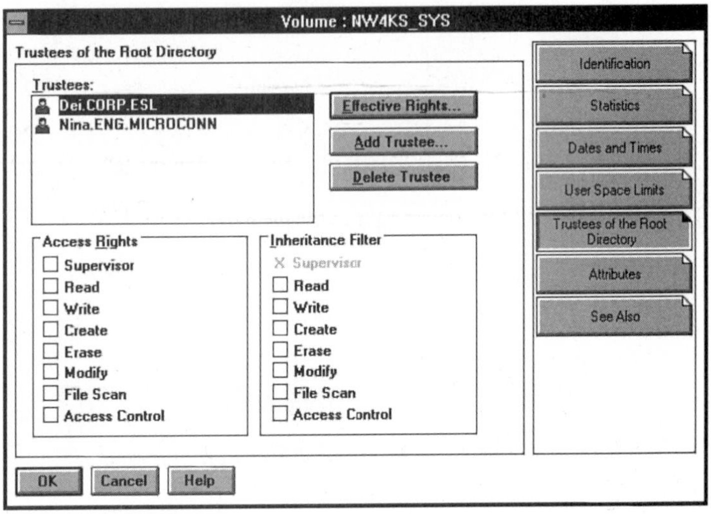

Figure 13.62
Explicit assignment of No Rights to root of volume.

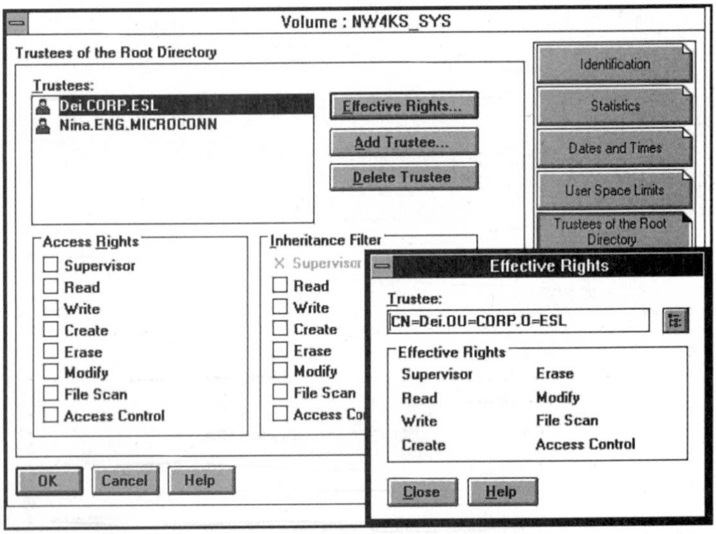

Figure 13.63
Effective Rights to root of volume not affected by explicit assignment.

If you want users to manage the server object and you do not want a user to inherit the Supervisor right to the NetWare file system through the Supervisor object right or the Supervisor All Properties right to the file server object, you can assign the user an alternate set of rights to the file server object. You can assign the user the [B D R] object right to the file server object and the [C R W A] All Properties right to the server object, except the ACL property. You can assign the selected property right of [R C] to the ACL property of the server object, to prevent a user from inheriting the Write property through All Properties, or use the IRF for the ACL property to block the Write property right.

If you wish a user to manage a NetWare server object and prevent the user from inheriting the Supervisor right to the NetWare file system, you can assign the following rights to the user:

- The [B D R] object right to the file server object
- The [C R W A] All Properties right to the server object
- The explicit [R C] (or [R] because [R] implies [C]) Selected Property right to the ACL property of the server object

Figure 13.64 shows that user Dei.CORP.ESL has been granted [B D R] object rights to NetWare server NW4KS. Notice that the Create right is not listed as it applies to container objects only. Figure 13.64 also shows that user Dei.CORP.ESL has been granted [C R W A] All Properties rights to NetWare server NW4KS. Figure 13.65 shows that an explicit Selected Properties trustee assignment of Read and Compare ([R C]) has been made to the Object Trustees (ACL) to override the All Properties assignment of [C R W A] that includes the Write property right.

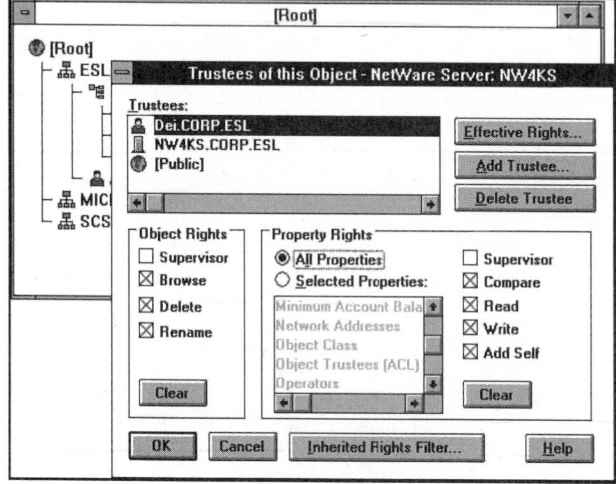

Figure 13.64
Restricted rights to manage server object.

13

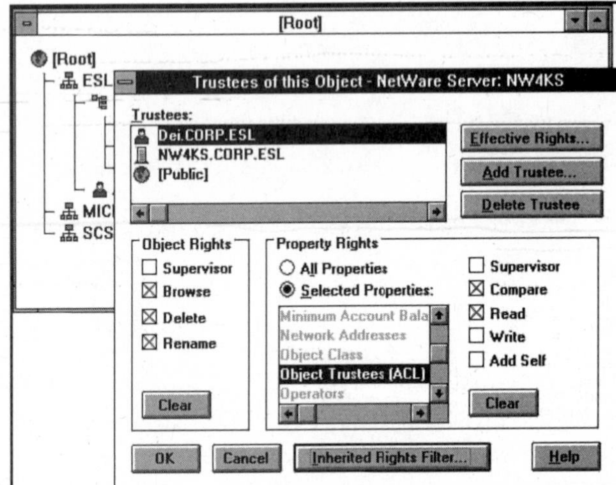

Figure 13.65
Restricting rights to ACL property of server object.

Security Equivalence

Another feature of NetWare 4.*x* security is security equivalence. Security equivalence is a property of a user object and is used to temporarily assign a user the same rights as another user. If a user is security equivalent to another user, called the *target* user in the discussion that follows, the user acquires the following:

- Explicit trustee assignments of the target user
- Membership to groups that the target user is a member of
- Organizational Roles that the target user occupies
- Inherited rights from parent containers of the target user up to the [Root]
- All rights granted through [public]. All attached users are implicit members of group [public]

Security equivalencies to users, groups, and organizational role objects are called *explicit* security equivalencies. Security equivalencies through containers and [public] are called *implicit* security equivalencies.

In order to make a user object security equivalent, you need Write property right to the Security Equivalent property of the user object and the Write property right to the ACL of the target user object. Figure 13.66 shows the Security Equivalence property for a user. In figure 13.66, user Dei is security equivalent to the users:

```
CN=Jan.OU=CORP.O=SCS
CN=Lisa.O=ESL
CN=Nina.OU=ENG.O=MICROCONN
```

User Dei is also security equivalent to the group object CN=Mgrs.O=ESL, the organization unit OU=SALES.O=ESL, the organization O=SCS and the organization role object CN=BackupOp.OU=CORP.O=ESL. The security equivalence can be made to user objects, group objects, organizational role objects, and container objects such as organization unit, organization, and country objects. A user cannot be made security equivalent to [Root].

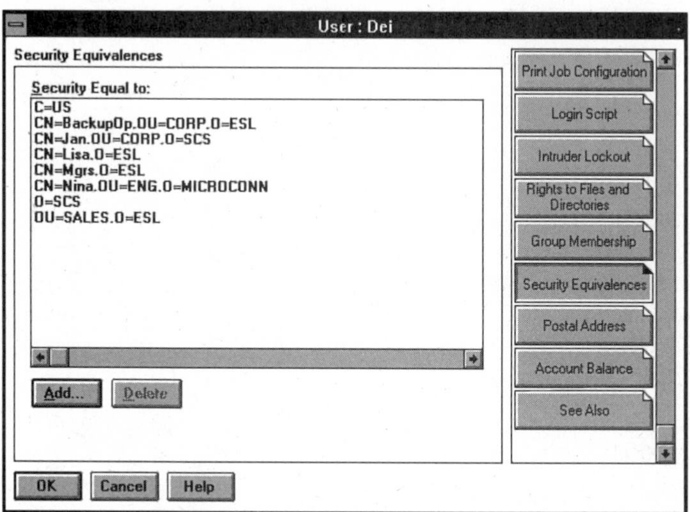

Figure 13.66
Security Equivalence property.

In general, Security Equivalence should be used on a temporary basis to quickly assign security rights. It is preferred that explicit trustee assignments be made for acquiring rights. Excessive use of security equivalencies can make tracing the source of rights difficult on networks with large NDS trees. Please note that in NetWare 3.*x*, to make a user a supervisor equivalent, you use the SYSCON utility to give them supervisor equivalency to the user Supervisor. In NetWare 4.*x*, you make a user a supervisor of an NDS tree branch by giving them Supervisor rights to the root container for that tree branch.

Default Rights Assignment

Proper assignment of rights is essential for implementing network security. Creating a secure network environment is one of the most potentially complex areas of NetWare 4.*x* network management. To aid in the implementation of NDS security, a default set of rights is assigned to key NDS objects. The default rights are designed in such a manner that they can be used to meet the most likely security configuration requirements for most organizations. The default rights make it possible to get a NetWare 4.*x* network running with the required security configuration with minimal effort.

This default security configuration can be further modified to meet any custom security requirements. The default rights are assigned during NDS installation, file server installation, and NDS object creation. These default assignments are considered next.

Default Rights Assigned to [Root]

The NDS database is created during installation. If you are installing the first NetWare 4.*x* server on the network, the NDS is installed as part of the server installation. NDS services can also be installed or removed by running the INSTALL.NLM at the server, and selecting:

Maintenance/Selective Install from the INSTALL main menu

Directory Options from the Installation Options menu

From Directory Services Option menu, you can select either

- Install Directory Services onto this server
- Remove Directory Services from the server

When NetWare Directory Services are first installed, the [Root] is given certain trustee assignments to simplify NDS administration. During NDS creation, the Admin user object is created. The Admin user object is given the Supervisor object right to the [Root]. Additionally, the group [public] is given Browse object rights to [Root].

Making trustee assignments to the [Root] causes the trustee rights to flow down the entire NDS tree. In other words, assignments made to [Root] have a global effect. The user object Admin gets the Supervisor object rights to all objects in the NDS tree. This allows the Admin user to administer all resources in the NDS tree. The NDS Supervisor right can be blocked from a tree branch (or any NDS leaf object) by removing the Supervisor right from the IRF for a tree branch or an NDS leaf object. This allows the creation of multiple levels of Administrators, where administrators have rights to manage parts of the NDS tree, but not the entire NDS tree.

Giving the group [public] the Browse object right assignment, gives to all users Browse rights to the entire NDS tree. The group [public] includes all users that are attached to the network. This includes even users that have not yet logged in. As soon as a user loads the VLM.EXE and makes a connection to a server, the user is automatically a member of group [public]. Giving users the Browse right to the NDS tree allows users to navigate the NDS tree using the CX and NLIST commands that are found in the LOGIN directory of the server that the user initially attaches to. The CX command is particularly useful for changing current context and displaying a graphical NDS tree that shows the resources that are available. It should be emphasized that the Browse right gives a user the ability to list NDS objects in a container, and does not imply any other rights such as accessing information in the NDS object or the ability to create, delete or rename objects. The Browse right to [Root] for group [public] can be removed after installation. If you do not have Browse rights to the NDS tree, you can still use the CX command to change your context, but the only objects you can see (using the CX/T/A command) are Bindery emulation objects.

The Browse rights are assigned to all users so that they can navigate the NDS tree and look for resources. In some secure environments, there may be concerns about users being able to "see" resource objects in the entire NDS tree. In this case the Browse trustee assignment can be removed from [Root]. As explained earlier, it is possible for a user to log in as a user object without having Browse rights to the user object. You can use the NAME CONTEXT configuration parameter in the NET.CFG file to place the user in the appropriate context, and lessen the need for a user to navigate the NDS tree.

If [public] is removed as a trustee of [Root], and [Root] is made a trustee of [Root] and given the Browse object rights, only logged in users can browse the NDS tree. Other users can still log in to the NDS tree if they know their complete NDS name, or they know their login name and are initially placed in the same context as their default NetWare server.

Figure 13.67 shows the default rights for a newly installed NDS tree. This figure shows that Admin and [public] are trustees of [Root]. This figure also shows that Admin has Supervisor object rights to [Root]. Figure 13.68 shows that [public] has Browse object rights to [Root].

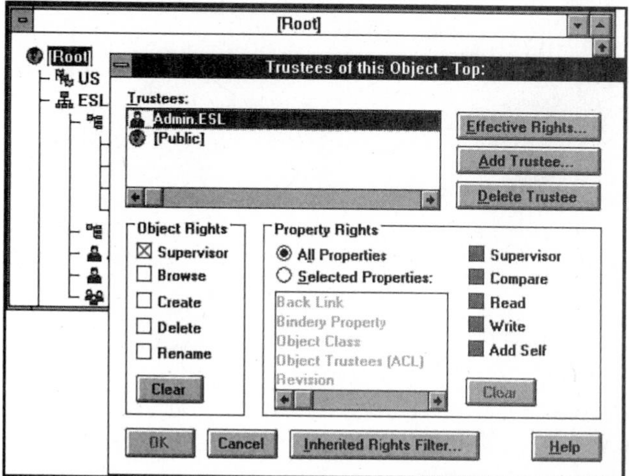

Figure 13.67
Default rights for Admin.

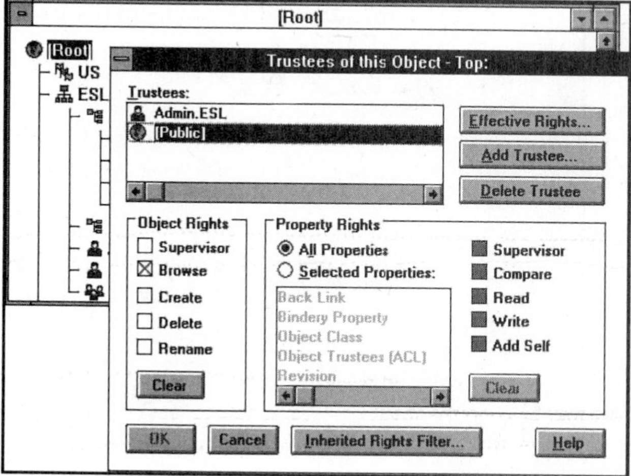

Figure 13.68
Default rights for [public].

Default Rights Assigned for NetWare Server Object

When a NetWare 4.*x* server is installed it can be installed in a newly created NDS tree, or in a container in an existing NDS tree. The creator of the server object is automatically assigned the Supervisor object right. The creator of the server is the server object itself (see fig. 13.69). Figure 13.70 also lists [public] as a trustee to the NetWare server object. This may seem puzzling at first, as excessive rights assigned to [public] can potentially bypass NetWare security. The group [public] is given the Read property right to the Network Address property of the server object (see fig. 13.70). The Network Address property contains the IPX address of the NetWare server (see fig. 13.71). The Network Address includes the Internal Network Number for the file server which is F0000066 in figure 13.71, the node address which is always 1 for a NetWare server on the internal logical network, and the socket number 451 (hexadecimal) at which NCP (NetWare Core Protocol) services are registered.

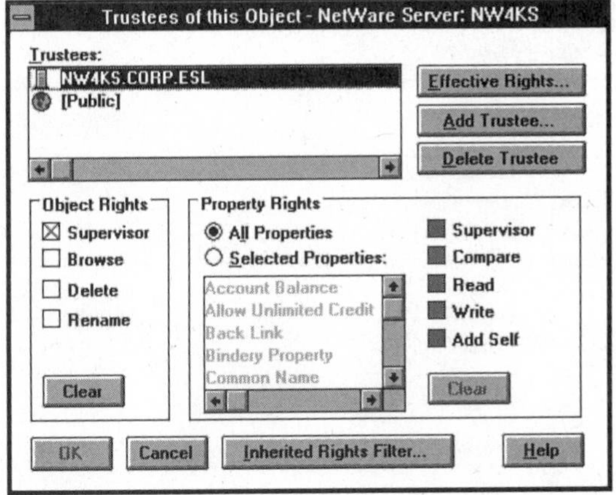

Figure 13.69
Default trustees for server object.

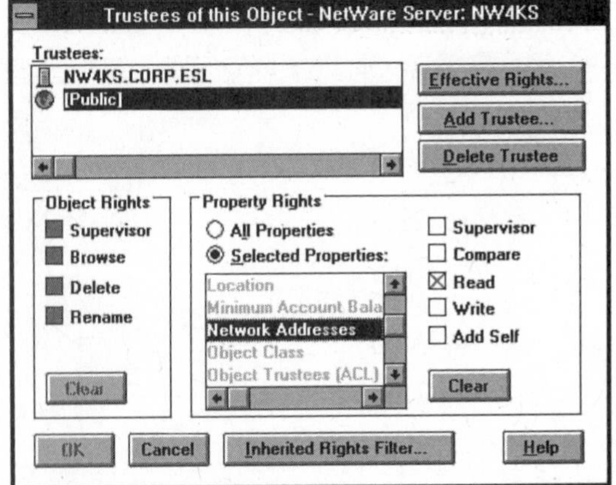

Figure 13.70
Default rights assigned to [public] for server object.

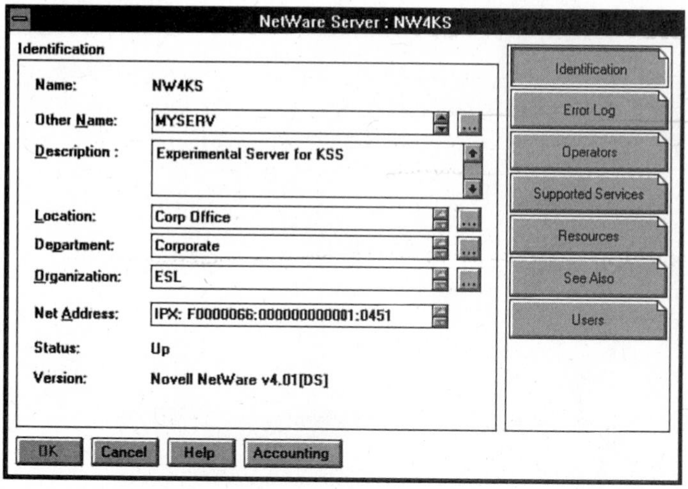

Figure 13.71
Network Address property for server object.

Any user, such as Admin, who has Supervisor Object right to the server object also has Supervisor File System rights to the volumes attached to the server. Such a user can perform file system administration for the server. If the Supervisor File System right is deemed to be excessive rights, then the user can be granted [B C D R] object rights to the server, and [C R W A] All Properties rights to the server object, except for the ACL property. The ACL property can be assigned [C R] Selected Property rights. It is important to safeguard users from having the Write property right to the NetWare server object's ACL property, because this would imply that the user has Supervisor File System right to all volumes attached to the server.

The container in which the NetWare server object and its volumes are installed is automatically given certain default file system rights. This container is given Read and File Scan ([R F]) rights to directory SYS:PUBLIC and the Create ([C]) right to directory SYS:MAIL.

Figure 13.72 shows the trustees for directory PUBLIC. The trustee CORP.ESL is the organization unit under which the server was installed. Notice that the trustee CORP.ESL has a trustee assignment of [R F]. Figure 13.73 shows the trustees for directory MAIL. The container CORP.ESL is the organization unit under which the server was installed, and is listed as a trustee. The container CORP.ESL has a trustee assignment of [C].

Figure 13.72
Default trustees for the PUBLIC directory.

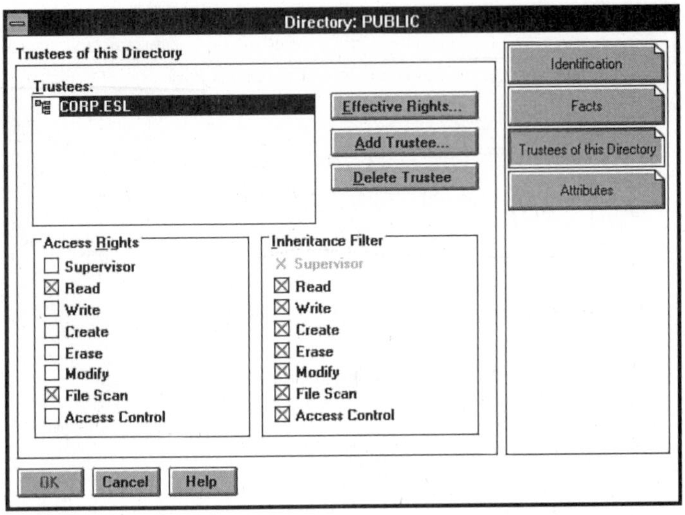

Figure 13.73
Default trustees for the MAIL directory.

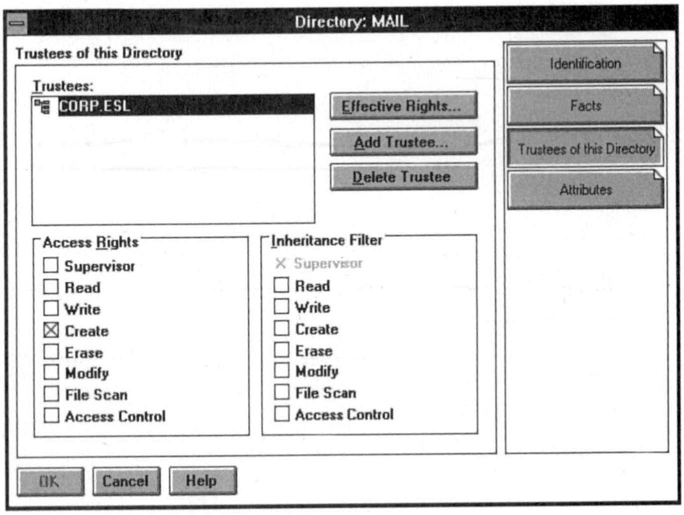

The advantage of giving the file server's container object certain default rights is that all users in that container inherit those rights because container objects act as groups for assignment of rights. Since users that need access to the shared file system of a volume object are likely to be created in the same container as the volume object, assigning the container default rights simplifies file system administration. The container is given a default right of [R F] to PUBLIC, because users in the container need to map a search drive to PUBLIC, where the network utilities are kept. The MAIL directory is used in NetWare 3.*x* systems, and for this reason the default right of Create is given to MAIL, for bindery emulated users that are migrated from a bindery-based server.

If the volume object is moved to another container, the new container is not automatically granted rights to the PUBLIC and MAIL directories in the volume object. You must explicitly assign to the new container appropriate rights to the volume's PUBLIC and MAIL directories.

Another default trustee assignment that is made is that the [Root] has the Read property right to the Host Server property of the installed server's volume object. Figure 13.74 shows the trustees of the volume object NW4KS_SYS. [Root] is listed as a trustee and has the Read selected property right to the volume's Host Server property. This right allows all logged in users to determine the name of the host server to which this volume is attached.

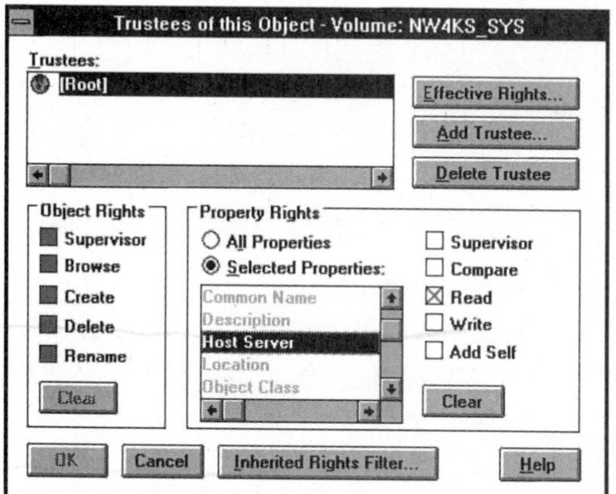

Figure 13.74
Default trustees for the volume object.

Default Rights Assigned to Containers

In a previous section, you learned that the [Root] container is given certain default rights for simplifying network administration. The organization and organization unit containers are given certain default rights when they are created. Both the organization and organization unit containers are given the Read property right to their Login Script property. Figures 13.75 and 13.76 show that the organization and organization containers are trustees of themselves and have a Read selected property to their Login Script property.

The Country container object does not have any default trustee assignments.

The following are default rights for container objects:

- Organization and Organization Unit objects are given the [R] selected property right to their Login Script property
- Country objects are given no default rights

A container's login script property acts as the system login script for user objects directly in that container. Assigning a container the Read property right to the Login Script property ensures that users in that container can Read (and process) the system login script.

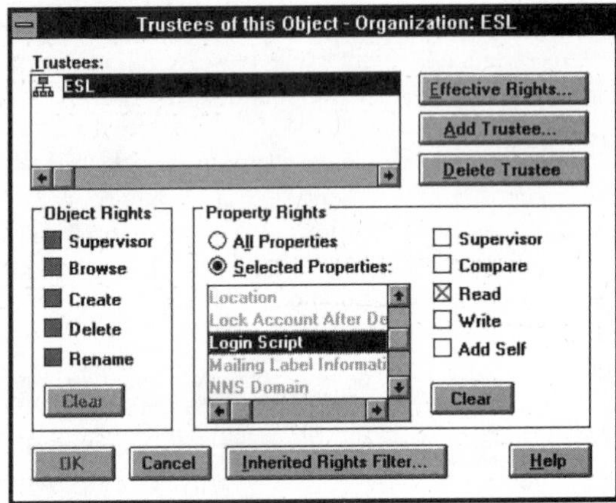

Figure 13.75
Default trustees for organization object.

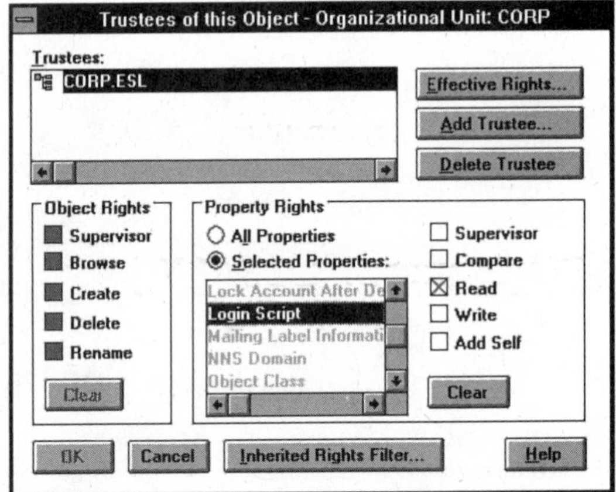

Figure 13.76
Default trustees for organization unit object.

Using the Organization and Organization Unit objects as trustees is a very convenient way of assigning rights to other NDS objects and the NetWare File System. The rights assigned to these containers are inherited by all objects in that container and its subcontainers. Containers have a natural grouping which reflects the organizational structure or usage within an organization.

If all users in an organization need a specific right, it is easier to assign the Organization (O) as a trustee rather than assigning each of the Organization Units (OU) as trustees. In any case, you must ensure that you only assign the necessary rights to those users that need it.

If assigning rights to an Organization or Organization Unit leads to assigning rights to users who should not have these rights, you can assign rights using Group objects or Organizational Role objects. You should assign only users who need rights as members of these objects. Another advantage of using Group or Organizational Role objects is that the members of these group objects can be from different containers. You can only assign user objects as members of the Group or Organizational Role objects. For Group objects, membership is assigned by adding user objects to the Group Members property list. For Organizational Role objects, membership is assigned by adding user objects to the Occupant property list.

Both Group objects and Organizational Role objects can be used for assigning trustee rights. A reasonable question to ask is, what (if any) are the differences between them? Group objects are defined in the NetWare environment. Organizational Role objects have a formal definition in the X.500 specification from which NDS is derived. This makes it possible for third-party X.500 implementations to more easily access the information in the Organizational Role objects.

Organizational Role objects are more formal definitions of network responsibilities. For instance, you could have a job description (organizational role) for a Backup Operator. The occupants of this Organizational Role object could change, but the rights assigned the Organizational Role object are such that they are sufficient for performing the job description, and change only when the NDS tree is reorganized or the job description is changed.

Another distinction between these two types of group objects is that the Organizational Role has the additional properties of Telephone Number, Fax Number, and E-mail address, as per X.500 schema requirements for Organizational Role objects. The Group object does not have these additional properties.

Default Rights for User Objects

When a user object is created, the user is given a set of default rights to simplify the administration for the user object. Figure 13.47 shows the default trustees of a newly created user. The trustees for user object Lisa are Lisa.ESL, [Public] and [Root]. The user object has three trustees:

- The user object
- [Public]
- [Root]

The user object is given the Read and Write ([R W]) property right to its Login Script property and its Print Job Configuration property. Figure 13.47 also shows that user Lisa has the selected property right of Read and Write to her Login Script property. Figure 13.48 shows the Print Job Configuration property right for the same user. If the user's home directory is created using NetWare utilities, such as NETADMIN and NetWare Administrator, the user is given [S R W C E M F A] File System rights to its home directory.

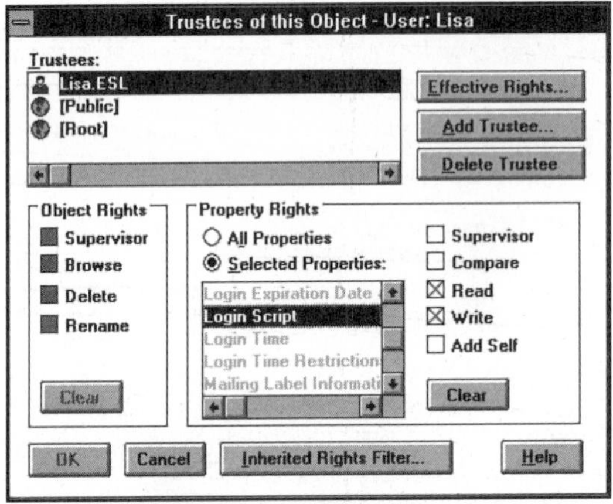

Figure 13.77 *Default Login Script property right for user object.*

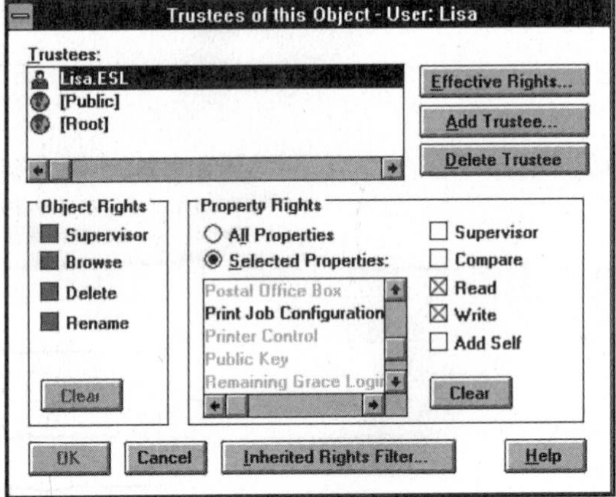

Figure 13.78 *Default Print Job Configuration property right for user object.*

13

The [R W] property right for a user object allows the user object to modify their login scripts. If you wish to prevent the user from modifying their login script, you must assign the [R] right for the user login script. A user must, at a minimum, have the Read property right to their login script so that it can be processed.

If you do not wish a user to modify their print job configurations, you must revoke the Write property right form their Print Job Configuration property.

The [Public] group is given a default property right of Read to the user's default server. Figure 13.79 shows that user Lisa has been given the Read property right to the Default Server. This allows all users that are connected to the network to find out the default server name for that user. Figure 13.80 shows that the default server property for user Lisa is set to CN=NW4KS.OU=CORP.O=ESL. This property can be changed to another file server object. The Default Server is the NetWare server that the user object connects to when logging in to the network. It can be specified in the NET.CFG file using the DEFAULT SERVER parameter, or the *Preferred Server* (PS) option when loading the VLM Manager.

The Default Server for a user is also used to store SEND messages for that user. The Default Server is the server used to synchronize your workstation's time when the SYSTIME utility is run without any parameters, and when you first connect to the network (unless explicitly disabled in NET.CFG).

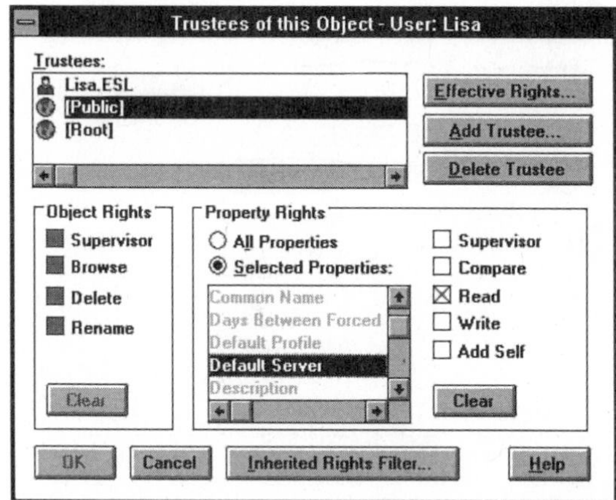

Figure 13.79
Default Server property right for user object to trustee.

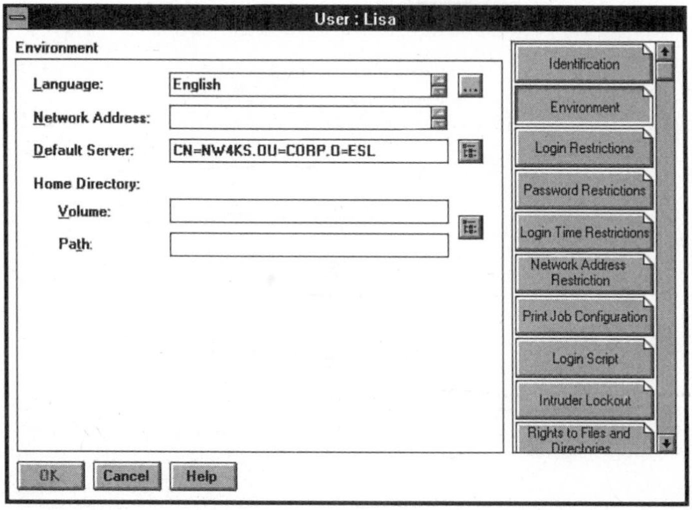

Figure 13.80
Default Server property for user object.

The [Root] is given the Read property right for the Group Membership property of a user object (see fig. 13.81). This Read property implies that all logged in users can find out which groups the user is a member of. The [Root] is also given the Read property right for the Network Address property of a user object (see fig. 13.82). This Read property implies that all logged in users can find out the workstation address a user is logged in from. The Network Address property shows a value for logged in users only. If a user is not currently logged in, the Network Address property is not defined. The user's Network Address property is the workstation's network address from which they are logged in. If IPX is used as the protocol transport, the Network Address consists of the network number (cable segment number), the node address (also called the MAC or hardware address), and the IPX socket number 400F (hexadecimal) that is used by the workstation networking software.

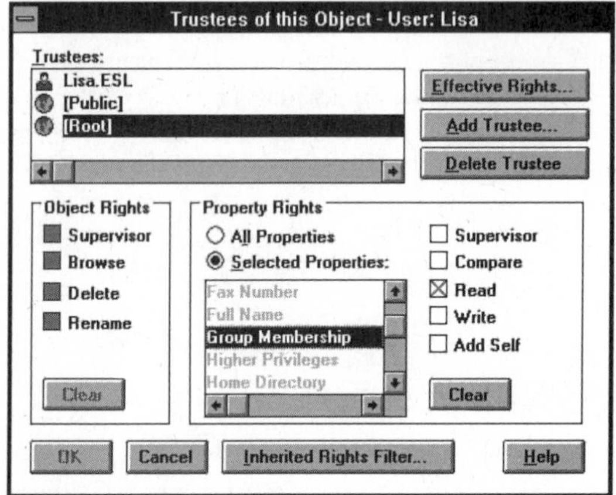

Figure 13.81 *Default Group Membership property right to trustee [Root].*

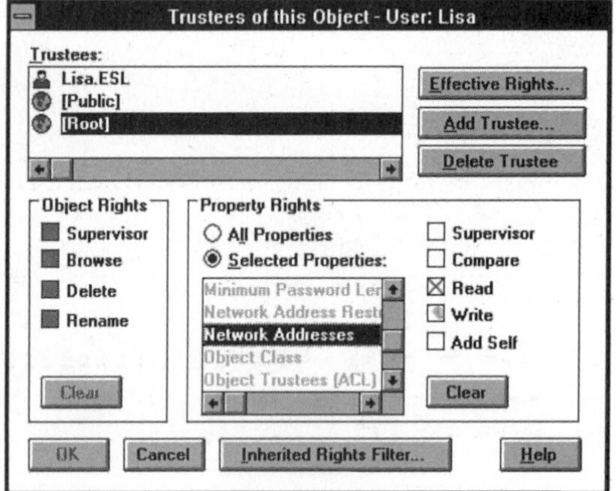

Figure 13.82 *Default Network Address property right to trustee [Root].*

The user object has the following default trustee assignments to it:

- The user object is given the Read and Write ([R W]) property right to their Login Script property and their Print Job Configuration property, and the [S R W C E M F A] file system rights to their home directory.
- [Public] is given the Read Selected Property right to the user's default server.
- [Root] is given the Read property right for the Group Membership property and the Network Address property of the user object.

Guidelines for Determining Excessive Rights

Occasionally you may discover that a user or group of users have excessive rights. Excessive rights are any rights that are above and beyond those required by users to complete their tasks. Excessive rights can also give users the ability to acquire additional rights or restrict rights of other users. To correct the problem of excessive rights you must be able to trace the origin of these rights. In a NetWare 4.*x* environment, this can be particularly challenging because of the many levels of NetWare security and the large number of sources rights can be acquired from. The following is a guideline for determining excessive rights:

1. Determine the explicit rights granted to the following objects:

   a) User objects

   b) Group and Organizational Role objects

   c) Containers between the user and the [Root]

   d) Security Equivalencies

2. Determine rights inherited through explicit trustee assignments to any of the objects listed in the previous item. Also, determine if a user inherits rights through group membership, container membership, or security equivalence.

3. Use the NetWare tools to determine Trustee Assignments and Effective Rights. For NDS rights you can use NETADMIN or NWADMIN. For File System Rights, you can use NWADMIN, NETADMIN, FILER, or the RIGHTS command.

Guidelines for Determining the Cause of Insufficient Rights

This is the opposite of the problem discussed in the previous section. Occasionally you may run into a situation where a user does not have sufficient rights to perform a task or has just lost these rights because of changes made to the NDS. In this case, you must consider the following:

1. Check to see if any explicit rights the user is supposed to have, have been granted. You may wish to check if IRFs are blocking the user's rights. If they are, you can set the IRF to pass the desired rights or make an explicit trustee assignment.

2. Check to see if the user is a member of the group or organizational role objects that have been assigned the rights needed by the user.

3. If the user was given rights through security equivalence, check the user's security equivalence property to see if the security equivalencies exist.

4. Check the rights of the container through which the user inherits the rights. If a reorganization of the NDS tree has taken place, certain rights may not have been properly assigned to container objects.

Network Administration Strategies

The NDS tree can be potentially very big because it is used to represent network resources in an organization. For a small organization, the NDS tree can be managed by a single Administrator user. For larger organizations, it is more practical for the functions of network administration to be carried out by a number of users. In this case, the network administration tasks need to be divided among several network administrators. One way of doing this is to assign an Administrator per tree branch.

Figure 13.83 shows the NDS tree for organization O=ESL, with several Administrators for the department tree branches. Each of the tree branches with the organization units OU=CORP, OU=SALES, and OU=MKTG have administrators CN=Admin.OU=CORP.O=ESL, CN=Admin.OU=ENG.O=ESL, and CN=Admin.OU=MKTG.O=ESL, respectively. Typically, these administrators have complete responsibility for managing their NDS tree branch, but no rights to manage another tree branch. The department administrators do not have rights to manage objects in the context O=ESL. Resources in context O=ESL are managed by user CN=Admin.O=ESL that is defined in the O=ESL context. The CN=Admin.O=ESL administrator can create new organization containers and manage rights to the [Root] object, but typically does not have rights to manage the tree branches for the individual departments.

Figure 13.83
Administrators per NDS tree branch.

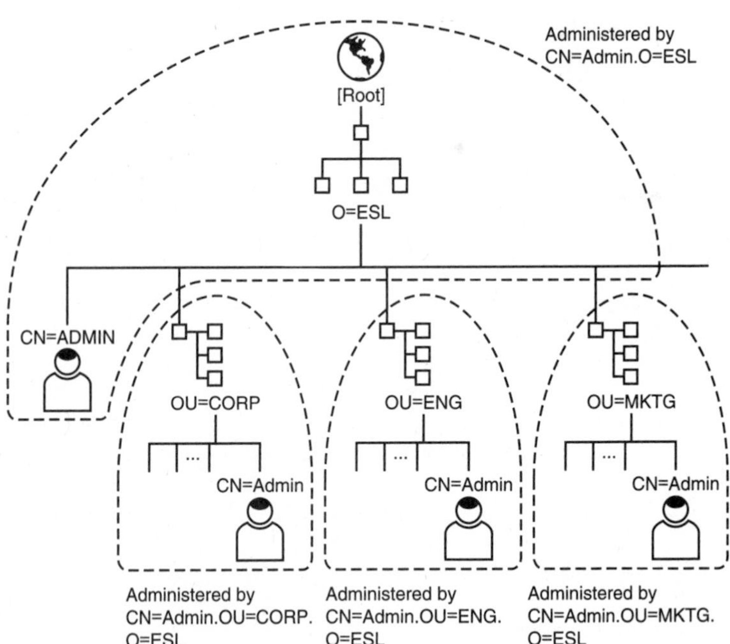

Assigning Administrators for each tree branch can be used to provide decentralized network management. It is possible for an organization to use this scheme effectively. You might even argue that because of decentralization, each department has jurisdiction over their network resources (their *turf*), and *turf wars* can be avoided. However, complete decentralization introduces another problem. Can the central MIS department (if one exists) trust the individual departments to manage their NDS tree properly? How much technical expertise and how many well-trained network administrators are there that can be trusted to manage their NDS tree branch? If there is a need to enforce global networking changes, how easy will it be to get the individual departments to comply, if you do not have any rights to the individual tree branches?

Because of the issues raised by some of these questions, many organizations consider it prudent to not lose control over individual tree branches. They have a special administrator account that has access rights for managing all of the tree branches. This user object may not be used for day-to-day administration tasks, but it exists as a *back-door* administrator user account, should the need arise to enforce a central network management policy. You should also enable auditing so that you can monitor attempts by individual departments to weaken the access rights of the special administrator account.

A second way to manage the NDS tree is to have one administrator account that manages the entire NDS tree and assistant network administrators who help the main network administrator. This is similar to the work group manager concept used in NetWare 3.*x*.

The procedures for implementing each of these network management approaches are discussed next.

Distributed Management: Single Administrator per NDS Tree Branch

As figure 13.83 indicates, in this approach you must block the rights of the original Administrator account CN=Admin.O=ESL. The general procedure for creating a separate Admin account for a department is shown below. The description is given in terms of creating a separate Administrator for OU=CORP.O=ESL (see fig. 13.83). The administrator account for the OU=CORP.O=ESL tree branch is referred to by the name CN=Admin.OU=CORP.O=ESL. If you need to perform this procedure on your NDS tree, you probably have different names for the root of the tree branch and the Admin user accounts, and you have to make appropriate substitutions for these names.

1. Create an Admin account in the department container. In the case of figure 13.83, this is the user CN=Admin.OU=CORP.O=ESL.

2. Assign to the newly created Admin account the following rights:

   Object rights of [S B C D R] to OU=CORP.O=ESL

   All Property rights of [S C R W A] to OU=CORP.O=ESL

3. Revoke rights from the IRF for OU=CORP.O=ESL to block access rights for other network administrators outside the tree branch.

   The reason for doing this is to prevent CN=Admin.O=ESL from inheriting access rights to OU=CORP.

   As an example, you may wish to set the IRF for object rights to [B] and IRF for All Properties for OU=CORP to [R]. Keeping the Browse right in the IRF for object rights allows users to see the objects in the CORP tree branch. The All Properties Read right allows other network administrators to read the properties of NDS objects in the tree branch, unless an object has a selected property right to override this.

4. Remove any trustee assignments to OU=CORP and any of its subcontainers for user CN=Admin.O=ESL.

5. Make sure that CN=Admin.OU=CORP.O=ESL has rights to itself. Also ensure that no other user such as CN=Admin.O=ESL has rights to CN=Admin.OU=CORP.O=ESL. If another user has access rights to CN=Admin.OU=CORP.O=ESL, they can restrict the right to this user.

6. Make sure that no other user is a security equivalent to the newly created Administrator and that there are no aliases to this user object.

Before revoking the Supervisor object right from the IRF for a container, you must have a user who has Supervisor object right to that container. Otherwise, the system prevents you from revoking the Supervisor IRF right, and you get an error message that "you cannot filter the Supervisor object right because no object has explicit Supervisor object right to this object."

The NetWare utilities do not prevent you from deleting the only user object that has Supervisor object rights to the tree branch. You can, therefore, lose control of an NDS tree branch, if you inadvertently (or by design) delete the user object that has Supervisor object rights to the NDS tree branch. If you delete the only user object that has Supervisor object rights to the NDS tree branch, you have created a black hole in the NDS tree. A later section discusses the NDS Black Hole problem in more detail.

Central Management: Assistant Administrators

Because of the risk of losing control over a tree branch by either delegating responsibility to a department administrator or through inadvertent creation of a "black hole" in the NDS tree, you may wish to use central network administration with work group managers that act as assistant administrators. You must implement security in such a manner that you can prevent loss of control over a tree branch. You can use the procedure that follows as a guideline. The description is given in terms of creating an assistant Administrator for OU=CORP.O=ESL (see fig. 13.84). The administrator account for the OU=CORP.O=ESL tree branch is referred to by the name CN=WMgr.OU=CORP.O=ESL. If you need to perform this procedure on your NDS tree, you probably have different names for the root of the tree branch and the Admin user accounts, and you have to make appropriate substitutions for these names.

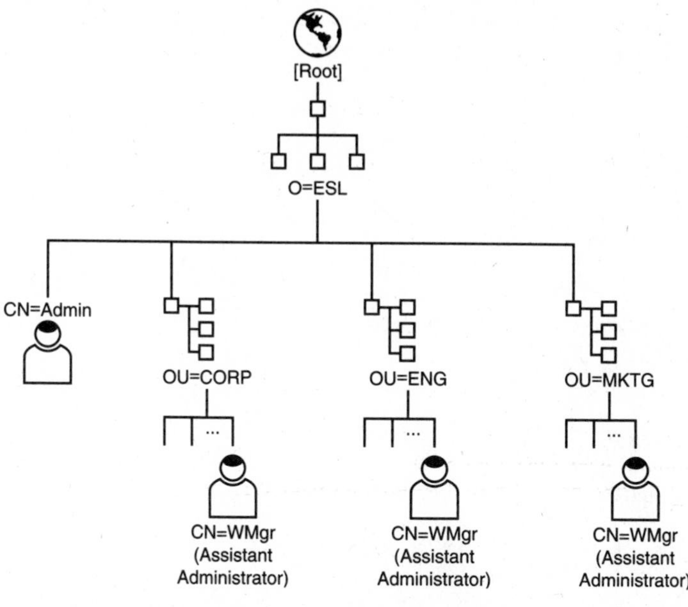

Figure 13.84
Creating a Workgroup Manager Account.

1. Create a Workgroup Manager account, CN=WMgr, in the department container. In the case of figure 13.84, this is the user CN=WMgr.OU=CORP.O=ESL.

2. Assign to the newly created Workgroup Manager account the following rights:

   Object rights of [B C D R] to OU=CORP.O=ESL

   All Property rights of [C R W A] to OU=CORP.O=ESL

   Selected Property rights of [C R] to Object Trustees (ACL)

   Assigning the Selected Property rights of [C R] to the ACL property is important, otherwise the Workgroup Manager can inherit the Write property right for the ACL property through the All Properties rights, and this gives the Workgroup Manager the ability to modify the trustees for the CORP container, and even give himself the Supervisor object right to the CORP container.

3. Make sure that CN=Admin.O=ESL has an explicit Supervisor trustee assignment to manage OU=CORP. You can do this by assigning the following rights to CN=Admin.O=ESL:

   Object rights of [S B C D R] to OU=CORP.O=ESL

   All Property rights of [S C R W A] to OU=CORP.O=ESL

4. Make sure that CN=Admin.O=ESL has an explicit Supervisor trustee assignment to CN=WMgr.OU=CORP.O=ESL. This can be done by assigning the following rights to CN=Admin.O=ESL:

   Object rights of [S B C D R] to CN=WMgr.OU=CORP.O=ESL

   All Property rights of [S C R W A] to CN=WMgr.OU=CORP.O=ESL

5. Remove rights except from IRF for CN=WMgr.OU=CORP.O=ESL. This is to prevent the Workgroup Manager from inheriting excessive management rights. Set the IRF as follows:

   IRF for Object rights for CN=WMgr.OU=CORP.O=ESL set to [B]

   IRF for All Properties rights for CN=WMgr.OU=CORP.O=ESL set to [C R]

6. Restrict Workgroup Manager, CN=WMgr.OU=CORP.O=ESL, rights as follows:

   Object rights for CN=WMgr.OU=CORP.O=ESL set to [B]

   Selected Property right for CN=WMgr.OU=CORP.O=ESL set to [C R] for ACL property

   Selected Property right for CN=WMgr.OU=CORP.O=ESL set to [R W] for Login Script property

   Selected Property right for CN=WMgr.OU=CORP.O=ESL set to [R W] for Print Job Configuration property

The NDS "Black Hole" Problem

To study the black hole problem in NDS, you should be working on an experimental NDS tree. You can create an NDS tree branch as shown in figure 13.85. The name of the organization container is O=BLACK-HOLE. It is so named because you are about to create a black hole in the NDS tree and study the kinds of problems you can get into when you lose control over an NDS tree branch.

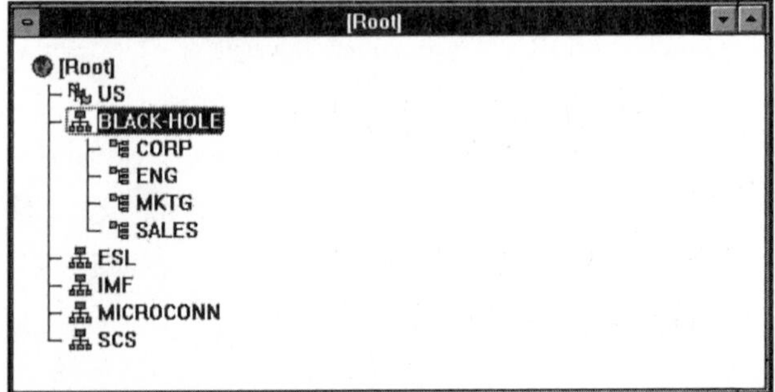

Figure 13.85
Experimental NDS Tree for studying the Black Hole problem.

To create a black hole in the NDS tree, use the steps that follow as a guideline:

1. Log in as the Administrator for the NDS tree.
2. Create an Admin account for O=BLACK-HOLE. Create this Admin account in another container called O=TEST.
3. Give to CN=Admin.O=TEST [S B] object rights to the O=BLACK-HOLE container.
4. Set the Object rights Inherited rights Filter for O=BLACK-HOLE to [B].

   This blocks all object rights except the Browse object right.
5. If you try to access the Trustees of this Object option from the NetWare Administrator, you are unable to access this option, as it is grayed out. This is because the IRF setting of [B] for O=BLACK-HOLE blocks out all but the Browse rights.

   You may wish to log in as the newly created user Admin.TEST to see that you have Supervisor object rights to the O=BLACK-HOLE container. If you do this, make sure that the Admin.TEST has at least [R F] file system rights to the PUBLIC directory, so the user can access the NetWare tools.
6. Make sure that you are logged in as the original Admin user and delete the user account that has Supervisor rights to O=BLACK-HOLE. That is, delete the Admin.TEST user.
7. Now try to access the container object O=BLACK-HOLE, and try to create or delete NDS objects in it. Also, try to change the Trustee Assignments to the O=BLACK-HOLE container.

   You have created a black hole in the NDS tree, as that tree cannot be managed.

Solution to the NDS Black Hole Problem

The easiest solution is to prevent the black hole problem from occurring. One way is to make sure that a central network administrator has explicit Supervisor object rights to all the critical NDS tree branches.

Another solution based on using the SBACKUP program is outlined in the following steps:

1. On another NetWare 4.*x* server, create an NDS tree with the same tree name as the one that has the black hole.
2. Create the NDS objects with the same structure as the existing tree, but with the correct object rights set so you can access the tree branches. You can create the NDS tree structure for only the NDS tree branch that has the black hole problem, and the Admin user object that was deleted.

   Back up this NDS tree using SBACKUP.

3. Restore the backed up NDS tree, using SBACKUP, on the server that has the black hole problem.

   In the Restore Options for SBACKUP, set the following options:

   Overwrite existing parent: Yes

   Overwrite existing child: Yes

The SBACKUP writes over the existing NDS tree that has the black hole problem. The new set of NDS rights assigned to the tree branch with the black hole problem allows you to manage that tree branch.

Danger of Giving a Workgroup Manager Write Property Right to ACL of Container

A common problem in setting up a workgroup manager who acts as an assistant Administrator is the failure to revoke Write property rights from the ACL property of the container.

Consider a workgroup manager CN=WMgr.OU=CORP.O=ESL who has been given the following rights to manage the OU=CORP.O=ESL tree branch:

Object rights of [B C D R] to OU=CORP.O=ESL

All Property rights of [C R W A] to OU=CORP.O=ESL

Figure 13.86 shows the [B C D R] object rights and [C R W A] All Properties rights assigned for WMgr.CORP.ESL. Because the [C R W A] All Properties implies that the user WMgr.CORP.ESL has Write property right to the OU=CORP.O=ESL container's ACL property, the user WMgr.CORP.ESL can modify this ACL property.

Figure 13.87 shows that WMgr.CORP.ESL has acquired Supervisor object rights by selecting the Trustees of this Object for the CORP container, using the NetWare Administrator.

To prevent the previous scenario from occurring, you should explicitly assign to the Workgroup Manager the Selected Property right of [C R] to the ACL property for the container.

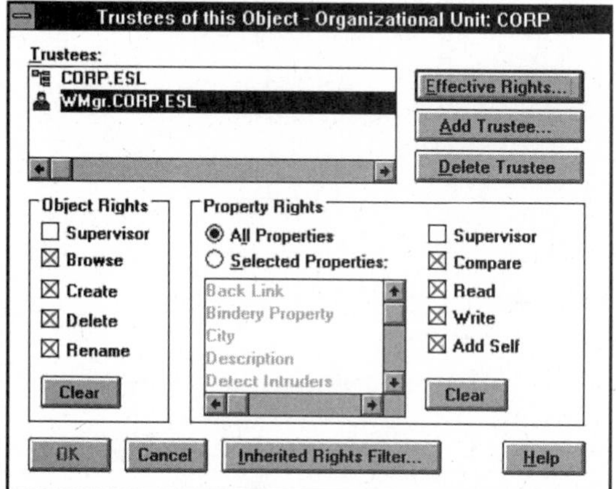

Figure 13.86
Workgroup Manager rights to container object.

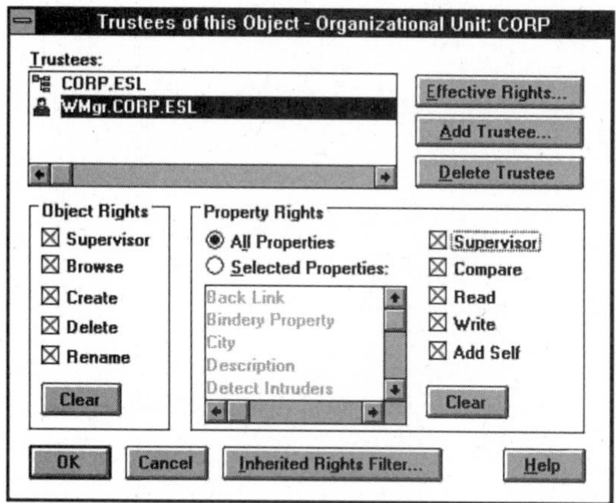

Figure 13.87
Workgroup Manager acquires Supervisor object rights because of Write property right to container.

Case Study: Implementing a NetWare Administrator Strategy

Consider the NDS tree in figure 13.88. It is proposed that the Admin.ESL user account manages the entire NDS tree for organization ESL. The department CORP has an Admin account Admin.CORP.ESL that has management jurisdiction over the CORP tree branch. The department SALES has a network Administrator whose name is James. James is relatively new to NetWare 4.*x* Administrator, and it has been decided that the Admin.ESL retains control over OU=SALES, and James performs limited network administration and serves in the capacity of a Workgroup Manager for the SALES department.

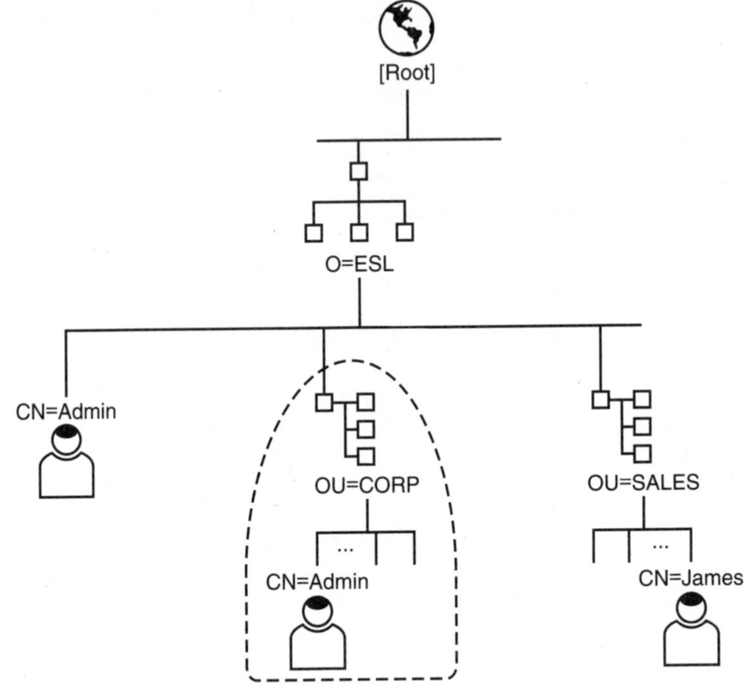

Figure 13.88
NDS Tree for Implementing a NetWare Administrator strategy.

1. What should be Admin.CORP.ESL object rights and property rights to the OU=CORP container?

   Answer: The Admin.CORP.ESL should have the following object and property rights:

   Object rights of [S B C D R] to OU=CORP.O=ESL

   All Property rights of [S C R W A] to OU=CORP.O=ESL

   These rights allow Admin.CORP.ESL to manage the tree branch OU=CORP.

2. What should be the IRF settings on OU=CORP to revoke rights from Admn.ESL?

   Answer: The OU=CORP should have the following IRF settings:

   Object rights IRF set to [B]

   All Properties IRF set to [R]

   These IRF settings block Supervisor rights of Admin.ESL from flowing down to the CORP container.

3. Should any trustee assignments to the OU=CORP be removed for user Admin.ESL?

   Answer: Yes. If explicit trustee assignments for Admin.ESL are not removed, the user is able to manage the NDS tree. Explicit trustee assignments override any inherited rights restricted by IRF settings.

4. What trustee rights should Admin.CORP.ESL have to himself? What additional precautions should be taken for user Admin.CORP.ESL?

   Answer: The Admin.CORP.ESL should have [S] object rights to Admin.CORP.ESL.

   Additionally, you should ensure that user Admin.ESL does not have any trustee assignments to Admin.CORP.ESL.

5. User James.SALES.ESL needs to perform the following management tasks:

   - Create, Delete, Rename user accounts
   - Change property values for user accounts
   - Browse the SALES tree branch

   Additionally, James should not be able to change the trustee assignments to SALES.

   What minimal rights should be assigned to James?

   Answer: User James should have the following minimal rights:

   Object rights of [B C D R] to OU=SALES.O=ESL

   All Property rights of [C R W A] to OU=SALES.O=ESL

   Selected Property rights of [C R] for property Object Trustees (ACL) of container OU=SALES.O=ESL.

   Assigning the Selected Property rights of [C R] to the ACL property of the container is important, otherwise the Workgroup Manager can inherit the Write property right for the ACL property through the All Properties rights. This gives the Workgroup Manager the ability to modify the trustees for the SALES container, and even give himself the Supervisor object right to the SALES container.

6. What explicit trustee assignments should Admin.ESL have over OU=SALES?

   Answer: Admin.ESL should have the following explicit trustee assignments:

   Object rights of [S B C D R] to OU=SALES.O=ESL

   All Property rights of [S C R W A] to OU=SALES.O=ESL

7. What explicit trustee assignments should Admin.ESL have over James?

   Answer: Admin.ESL should have the following explicit trustee assignments over James:

   Object rights of [S B C D R] to James.SALES.ESL

   All Property rights of [S C R W A] to James.SALES.ESL

8. What rights should James have to himself to prevent him from assigning additional rights to himself?

   Answer: James should have the following explicit trustee assignments over himself:

   Object rights of [B] to James.SALES.ESL

   Selected Property right of [C R] for ACL property for James.SALES.ESL

   Selected Property right of [R W] for Login Script property for James.SALES.ESL

   Selected Property right of [R W] for Print Job Configuration property for James.SALES.ESL

9. What should be the IRF filter for James so that he does not inherit any rights to manage himself?

   Answer: James should have the following IRF settings on his user object to prevent himself from inheriting rights to manage himself:

   IRF for Object rights for James.SALES.ESL set to [B]

   IRF for All Properties rights for James.SALES.ESL set to [C R]

Rights Needed for Management Tasks

This section considers the rights that are needed to perform some common management tasks. The rights for the following management tasks are discussed:

- Printing on a network
- Mailing List Administration
- Using Directory Map objects
- Assigning Profile Login scripts
- Using alias user objects

Printing on a Network

Printing on a network does not require any special NDS rights. Access to printing functions is controlled by the users and operator properties of print-related objects. Access to a print queue object is provided through the print queue's Operators and Users property. Figure 13.89 shows that the creator of the queue is automatically assigned to the Operators property list when a new queue object is created. Figure 13.90 shows the Users property of a print queue object. This figure shows that the container in which the print queue is defined, by default, becomes the print queue user. This means that all users defined in that container can print jobs to the queue. Also, the creator of the queue is assigned as a user of the print queue object. If the print queue object is moved to another container, its Users property is not automatically changed. In other words, the new container does not automatically get added to the Users property of the print queue object.

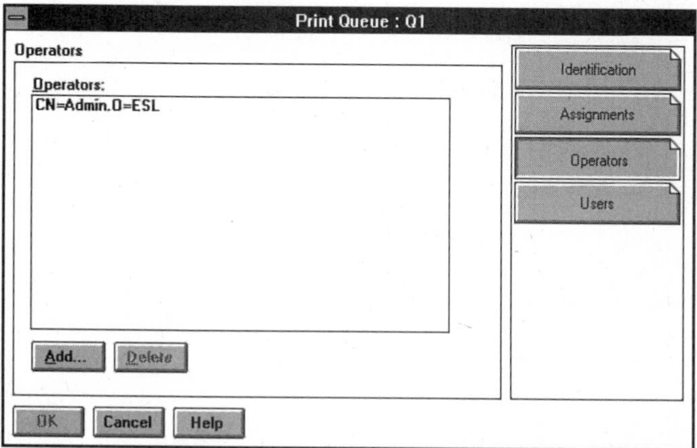

Figure 13.89
Default Operators property for print queue objects.

Figure 13.90
Default Users property for print queue object.

Figure 13.91 shows that the creator of the print server object is automatically assigned to the Operators property list of the print server object. Figure 13.92 shows the Users property of a print server object. This figure shows that the container in which the print queue is defined, by default, becomes the print server user. This means that all users defined in that container can print jobs to the queue. If the print server object is moved to another container, its Users property is not automatically changed. In other words, the new container does not automatically get added to the Users property of the print server object. The print server object has a password property, which if set, controls access to loading the print server at a server console. To load a print server at a server console no special NDS rights are needed. That is, the print server does not need to have any special rights to the file server object; and the file server object does not need to have any special file system rights to the print server object.

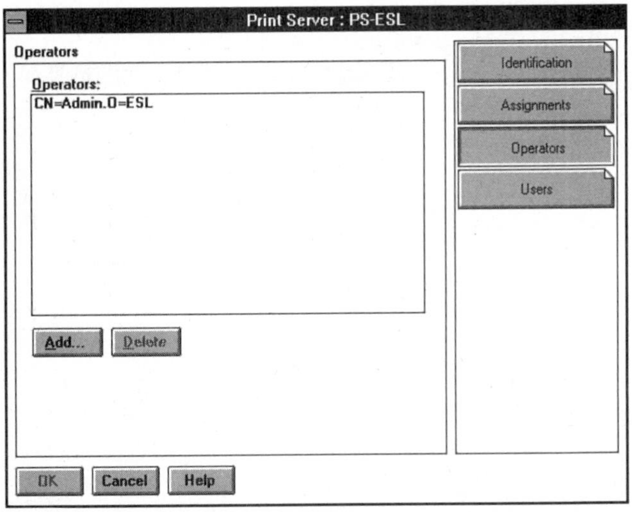

Figure 13.91
Default Operators property for print server object.

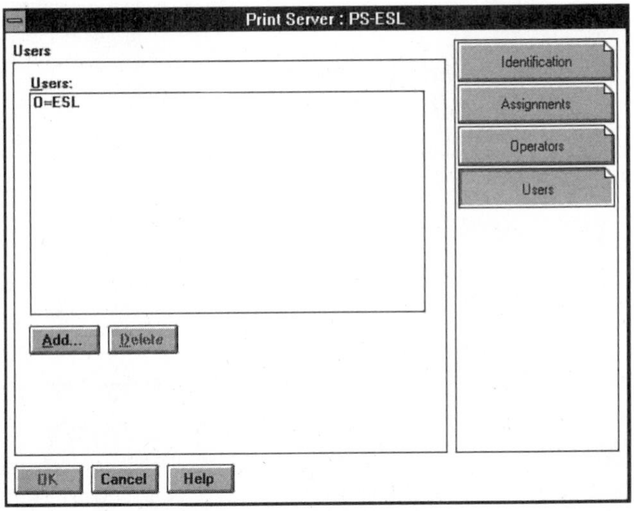

Figure 13.92
Default Users property for print server object.

When the print queue, printer, and print server objects are created, they are given a default set of NDS rights. These NDS rights are not required for printing. They are needed for managing the printing objects.

Figure 13.93 shows the default trustees for a newly created print server object. The trustees of the print server object are:

- the creator of the print server object (Admin.ESL)
- the print server object (PS-ESL.ESL)
- [Public]
- [Root]

Figure 13.93 also shows that the creator of the print server object has the object rights of [S B C D R] to the print server object, and the All Properties rights of [S C R W A] to the print server object.

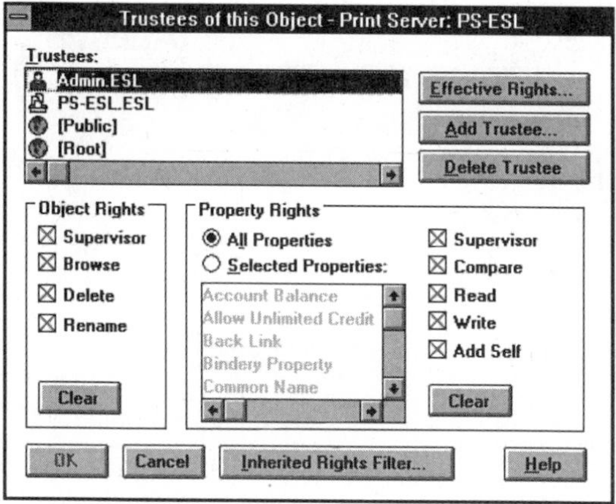

Figure 13.93
Default rights for creator of print server object.

Figure 13.94 shows that the print server object has the default object rights of Supervisor to the print server object.

Figure 13.95 shows that [Public] has the default Selected Property rights of Read for the Network Address property of the print server object. This allows any user connected to the network (but not necessarily logged in) the ability to read the network address at which the print server object is installed. The Network Address property contains the IPX address of the NetWare server. The Network Address includes the Internal Network Number for the NetWare server on which the print server is running, and the node address (which is always 1 for the NetWare server on the internal network). The Network Address property value appears only if the print server is running.

Figure 13.94
Default rights for print server object.

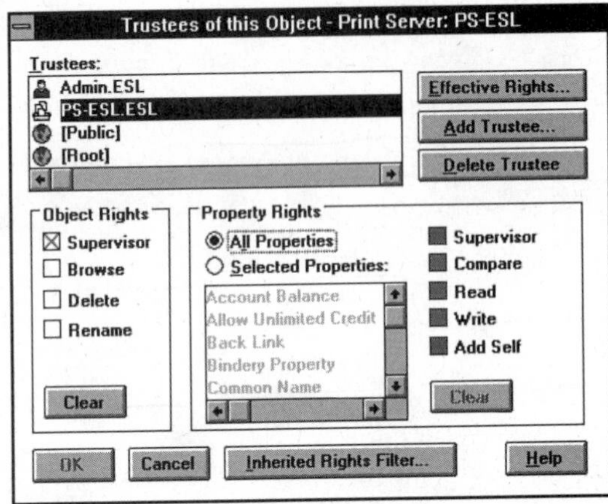

Figure 13.95
Default rights for [Public] to print server object.

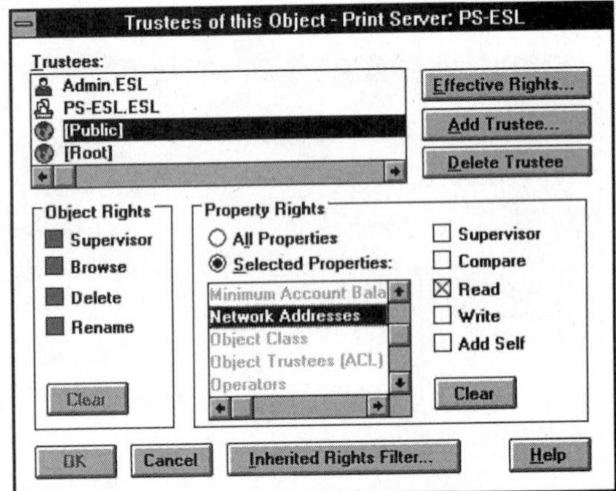

Figure 13.96 shows that [Root] has the default object rights of Browse to the print server object. This gives any user logged in to the network the ability to see the name of the print server object.

The Print Server object has the following default trustee assignments:

- The creator of the print server object has [S B C D R] object rights and [S C R W A] All Properties rights to the print server object
- The print server object has [S] object rights to the print server object
- [Public] has the [R] Selected Property right for the Network Address property of the print server object
- [Root] has the [B] object rights to the print server object

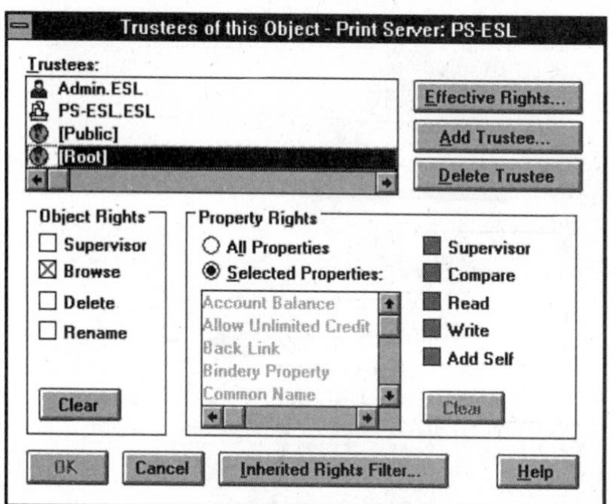

Figure 13.96
Default rights for [Root] to print server object.

Figure 13.97 shows the default trustees for a newly created print queue object. The trustees of the print queue object are:

- The creator of the print queue object (Admin.ESL)
- [Root]

Figure 13.97 also shows that the creator of the print queue object has the object rights of [S B C D R] to the print queue object, and the All Properties rights of [S C R W A] to the print queue object.

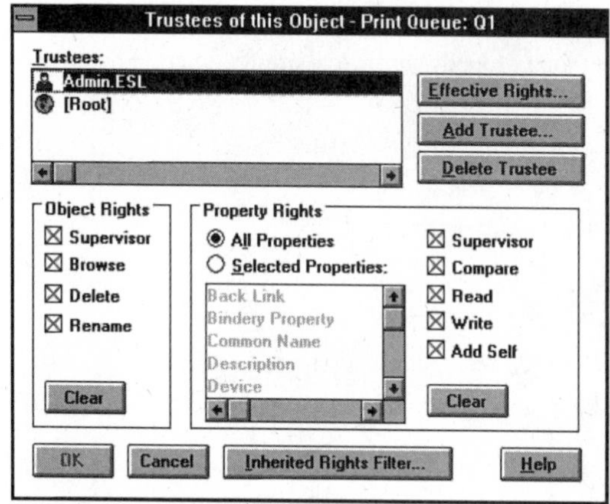

Figure 13.97
Default rights for creator of print queue object.

Figure 13.98 shows that [Root] has the default object rights of Browse to the print queue object and the default All Properties right of Read to the print queue object . This gives any user logged in to the network the ability to see the name of the print queue object and read its property values.

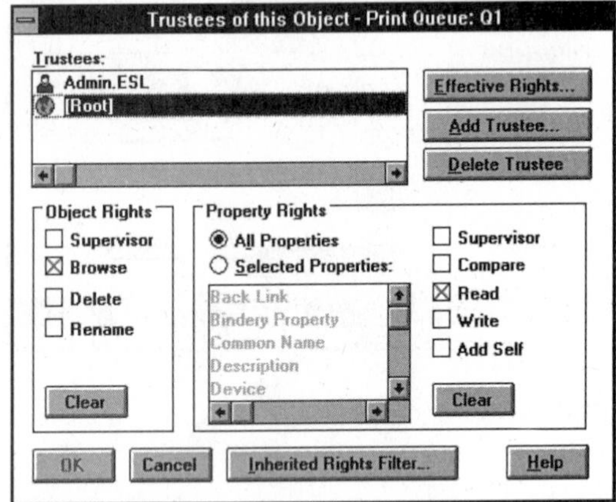

Figure 13.98
Default rights for [Root] to print queue object.

The Print queue object has the following default trustee assignments:

- The creator of the print queue object has [S B C D R] object rights and [S C R W A] All Properties rights to the print queue object.
- [Root] has the [B] object rights and the [R] All Properties rights to the print queue object.

Figure 13.99 shows the default trustees for a properly configured printer object. The trustees of the printer object are:

- The creator of the print queue object (Admin.ESL)
- The print server object to which the printer object is assigned
- [Root]

Please note that, if the printer object is created by itself and is not yet assigned to a print server object, the print server object is not a trustee of the printer object.

Figure 13.99 also shows that the creator of the printer object has the object rights of [S B C D R] to the printer object, and the All Properties rights of [S C R W A] to the printer object. The printer object shown in figure 13.99 was created using the Quick Setup option of PCONSOLE, which correctly configures the print objects.

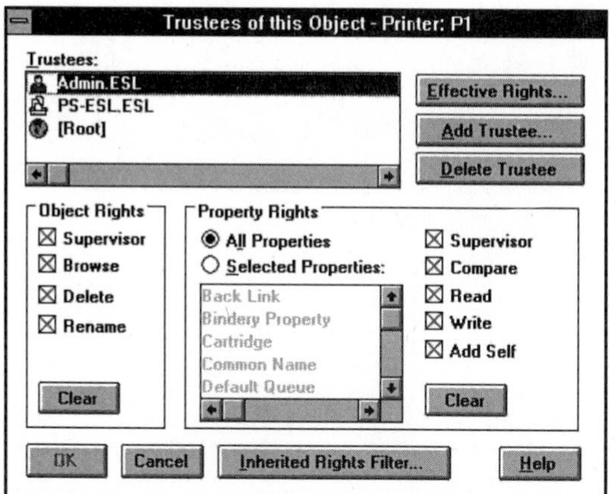

Figure 13.99
Default rights for creator of printer object.

Figure 13.100 shows that the print server object to which the printer is assigned has the default object rights of Browse to the printer object and the default All Properties right of Read to the printer object. This gives any user logged in to the network the ability to see the name of the printer object and read its property values.

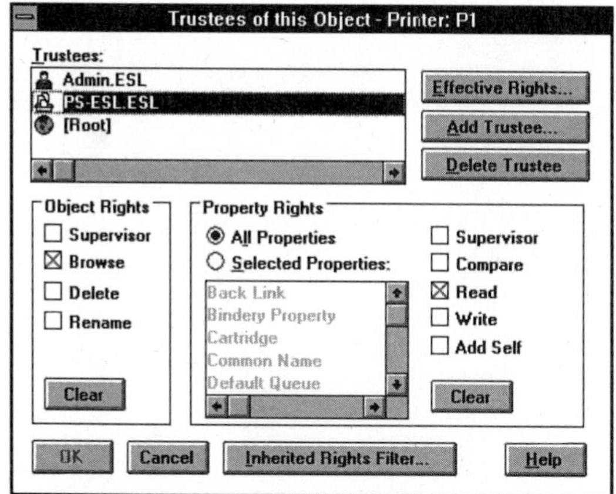

Figure 13.100
Default rights for print server object to which the printer object is assigned.

Figure 13.101 shows that [Root] has the default object rights of Browse to the printer object and the default All Properties right of Read to the printer object . This gives any user logged in to the network the ability to see the name of the printer object and read its property values.

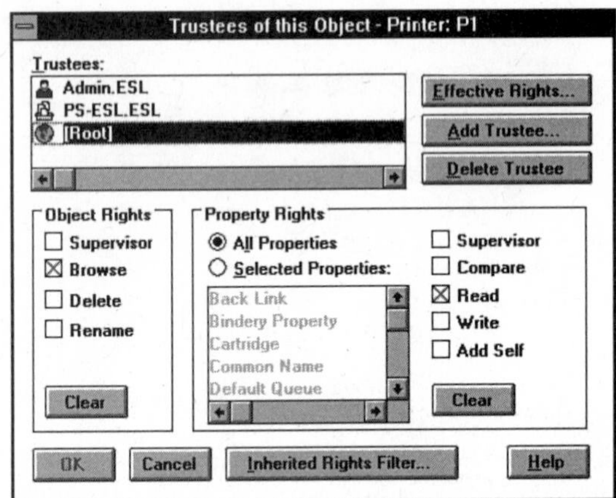

Figure 13.101
Default rights for [Root] to printer object.

When a printer object is created using NetWare Administrator (or PCONSOLE—but not using the Quick Setup option), the trustees assigned to it are:

- The creator of the printer object
- [Root]

The print server object is not a trustee of the printer object, because the printer has not been assigned to a print server. When the printer object is assigned to the print server, the print server is made a trustee of the printer object.

A properly configured printer object has the following default trustee assignments:

13

- The creator of the printer object has [S B C D R] object rights and [S C R W A] All Properties rights to the printer object.
- The Print Server object to which the printer is assigned has the [B] object rights and the [R] All Properties rights to the printer object.
- [Root] has the [B] object rights and the [R] All Properties rights to the printer object.

Mailing List Administration

One of the properties of user objects, organization role objects, organization unit objects, and organization objects is the E-mail Address property. This property can be used to enter the electronic mail address for the object. The actual value of the E-mail Address depends on the type of e-mail system that is being used. Some organizations prefer to delegate the responsibility of maintaining properties such as E-mail Address, Telephone Number, FAX Number, and Postal Address to a special user called the Mailing List Administrator. The Mailing List Administrator should be able to modify these properties and should therefore have Read and Write property rights to the properties they manage. The Mailing

List Administrator account can be implemented as a user object. If a more formal designation is needed for the Mailing List Administrator, it can also be implemented as an Organizational Role object.

The Mailing List Administrator should have the [R W] property rights for the following properties that the Mailing List Administrator manages:

- E-mail address
- Telephone Number
- FAX Number
- Postal Address

The trustee rights assigned to the Mailing List Administrator must be assigned for each NDS object the Mailing Administrator manages. For a large organization, this can become a very laborious process. You might be tempted to give to the Mailing List Administrator rights for the users they manage through a group object or a container object, but you end up giving the Mailing Administrator more rights than it should have. Also, assigning the All Properties rights to the Mailing List Administrator would give the Write property right for the ACL property. If the Mailing List Administrator has the Write property to the ACL of an object, the Mailing List Administrator can modify the trustee assignments to the object.

Using Directory Map objects

The Directory Map Object is used for simplifying the use of the MAP command, and for making the MAP command independent of changes to the location of the directory being mapped to. In order to use the Directory Map object, you must have the Read All Properties right to the Directory Map Object. When a Directory Map object is first created it does not have any default trustee assignment. You must explicitly assign the [R] All Properties right to the Directory Map object.

The following shows an attempt to map a Directory Map Object CN=DirMap.O=ESL by a user who does not have the Read All Properties right to the Directory Map Object:

```
F:\>MAP G: = .CN=DirMap.O=ESL
MAP-4.01-195: Directory [CN=DIRMAP.O=ESL] cannot be located.
```

If the user is assigned the [R] All Properties right to the CN=DirMap.O=ESL, the above command works correctly as shown:

```
F:\>MAP G: = .CN=DirMap.O=ESL
Drive G: = NW4KS_SYS.CORP: \DOC
```

In the previous example, the Directory Map Object, CN=DirMap.O=ESL, was set to point to the NW4KS_SYS:DOC directory. The user should have at least [R F] file system right to the directory being pointed to for the MAP command to work.

When a Directory Map object is first created it does not have any default trustee assignment. Before you

can use the Directory Map object, you must have the [R] All Properties right to the Directory Map Object.

You may wish to make the container in which the Directory Map object is defined a trustee to the Directory Map object and give to the container the [R] All Properties right. This gives all users in the container the [R] All Properties right to the Directory Map object, and allows them to use it. It is quite possible that future releases of NetWare 4.*x* may provide this as a default trustee assignment when a Directory Map object is created.

The Directory Map object has a property called Rights to Files and Directories. Assigning rights to a file system via this property does not cause these rights to be inherited by the users mapping to the Directory Map object.

Assigning Profile Login Scripts

The Profile object contains the profile login script. User objects have a property called the Profile, which can be set to point to a profile object. The profile login script is a way of implementing a common login script that is shared by any user that has their Profile property pointing to the same profile object. The profile login script is executed after the system login script (if one exists), but before the user's login script (if one exists). The system login script is the login script for the user's container. If the user's login script does not exist, and the NO_DEFAULT directive has not been specified in the system or profile login script, the default login script is run.

The following simple exercise demonstrates the rights needed to run a profile login script:

1. Create a container O=IBL, and a user object James in that container.
2. Create the profile object CProf in O=IBL and examine its default trustees.
   Notice that the profile object CN=CProf.O=IBL does not have any default trustees.

13

3. In the Profile Login script for the profile object CN=CProf.O=IBL, place the following login script statement:

   write "Profile login script for CProf is executed"

4. Set the Profile property for user James to point to the CN=CProf.O=IBL object.
5. Log in as the user CN=James.O=IBL.

   Notice that the profile login script for the user James is not executed. The reason for this is that user James does not have [R] property rights to the profile object's Login Script property.

6. Log in as Admin.

   Make user CN=James.O=IBL a trustee of CN=CProf.O=IBL with the [R] Selected Property rights to the Login Script property.

7. Log in as the user CN=James.O=IBL, again.

   Notice that the profile login script for the user James is executed. The reason for this is that user James now has [R] property rights to the profile object's Login Script property.

When a profile object is created, it does not have any default trustees. A user who has their Profile property set to a profile object must be able to read the profile login script in order to execute it. This means that the user must have the Read property right to the profile object's Login Script property.

The Novell documentation says that if the user and the Profile object are in the same container, no additional rights to the Profile object are needed. If the container in which the profile login script was created was made a trustee of the profile object and given the Read property write to its Login Script, this would be true. As the exercise above indicates, this is not true for NetWare 4.*x*, and a user must have the Read property right to the profile login script, even if the user and the profile object are in the same container.

The following are the steps needed to set up a profile login script for a user:

1. Create the profile object and set its profile login script.

2. Set the Profile property of a user to point to the profile object.

3. Assign the user the [R] property rights to the profile object's Login Script property.

   If all users are in the same container, you can assign the container a trustee of the profile object and give it the [R] property rights to the profile object's Login Script property.

   Typically, users who share a profile login script are in different containers. If they are in the same container, using the system login script for that container is usually sufficient. If the users are members of a group object or an organizational role object, you can make the group object or organizational role object a trustee of the profile object. Alternatively, you may wish to individually assign users trustees of the profile object.

Using Alias User Objects

To understand the rights needed by alias users to execute their login scripts, consider the situation in Figure 13.102, which shows an NDS tree for organizations IBL and UNE.

Figure 13.102
Alias user object and login scripts.

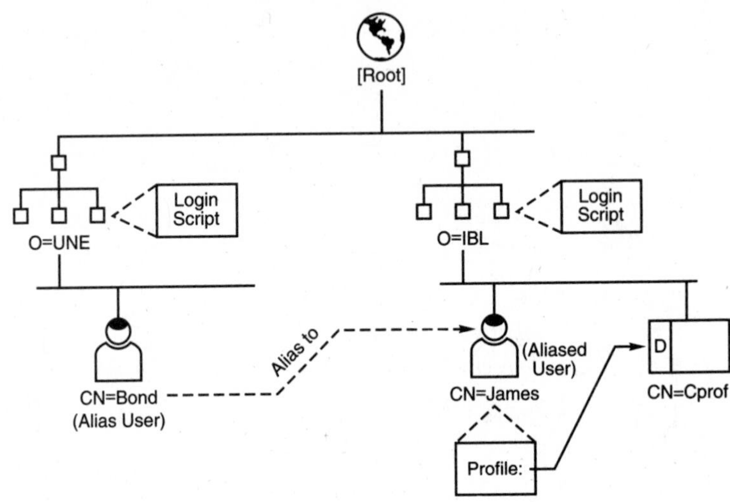

Organization IBL has a user James defined in the container O=IBL, and organization UNE has an alias object Bond that is an alias to CN=James.O=IBL. The user CN=Bond.O=UNE is the *alias* user, and the user CN=James.O=IBL is called the *aliased user*. The O=IBL has a system login script set that has the following login script statements:

```
WRITE "Executing login script for container IBL"
```

User CN=James.O=IBL has his Profile property set to the profile object CN=CProf.O=IBL. The profile login script has the following login statement:

```
WRITE "Executing profile login script CProf"
```


User CN=James.O=IBL has the following statements in his user login script:

```
WRITE "Executing login script for user James"
```

Additionally, user CN=James.O=IBL is a trustee of the profile object CN=CProf.O=IBL and has the [R] property right to the profile object's Login Script property. Since Bond is an alias to user James, Bond is automatically a trustee of CN=CProf.O=IBL with the same rights. The NetWare Administrator does not allow you to add the alias and the aliased user as trustees of the same object. (Try it, to verify this for your NetWare 4.*x* server.)

If you log in as user CN=James.O=IBL, you see messages similar to the following:

```
Executing login script for container IBL
Executing profile login script CProf
Executing login script for user James
```

If you log in as the alias user CN=Bond.O=UNE, you see messages similar to the following:

```
Executing profile login script CProf
Executing login script for user James
```

Notice that the login script for O=IBL container is not executed for the user CN=Bond.O=UNE. When an alias user logs in, it runs the container login script for the container the alias user is in, and not the container login script for the aliased user.

If you were to create a system login script for container O=UNE and place in it the statement:

```
WRITE "Executing login script for container UNE"
```

Then log in as the alias user CN=Bond.O=UNE, and you see messages similar to the following:

```
Executing profile login script CProf
Executing login script for user James
```

Notice that the login script for O= UNE container is not executed for the user CN=Bond.O=UNE, even though it has been set. In order for an alias user to execute the login script of the container it is defined in, the alias user must be granted the [R] property right to the Login Script property of its container. If this is done, logging in as alias user CN=Bond.O=UNE produces messages similar to the following, showing that the alias user's container login script is executed.

```
Executing login script for container UNE
Executing profile login script CProf
Executing login script for user James
```

It may seem a little strange that the alias user needs to be granted an explicit trustee assignment to the Login Script property of the container, especially because the container is made a trustee of itself and given the [R] Selected Property right to its Login Script property.

The reason for assigning the alias user an explicit trustee assignment to the Login Script property of the container is because the alias user is really a "phantom" user whose true existence is in the container that holds the aliased user, even though the aliased user does not execute the system login script of the aliased user. The aliased user needs to have [R] property rights to the alias' container's Login Script property.

If you assign the alias user the [R] property rights to its container, and then go back to re-examine the trustee assignments of the alias' container, you see that the aliased user is listed as a trustee, even though you initially made the alias user a trustee of the container.

Summary

In this chapter, you have learned the basics of NetWare 4.*x* security. NetWare security is layered. The first layer you must pass through is Login Authentication and Login Restriction. The second layer is NDS security. The last (third) layer is the NetWare File System security.

You were presented with a detailed explanation of how Login Authentication is done. Certain mathematical equations were presented, to show you how authentication works. You can use this as a reference, and to further your understanding.

You also learned about the default security assignments for many NDS objects such as [Root], container, user, and NetWare server objects. It is important to understand the default security assignments to NDS objects before attempting to change it to fine-tune NetWare security. The default rights are assigned to simplify network administration. If you change the default rights, you should make sure that the users can perform network tasks.

You were shown how to implement a network administration strategy by delegating network responsibility. This can be done using a distributed approach of assigning an Administrator per NDS tree branch or a centralized approach of having a central Admin account, and assigning assistant administrators that act as workgroup managers.

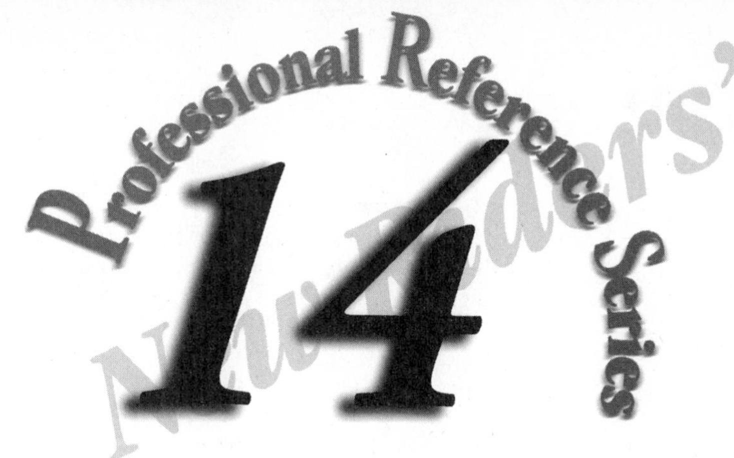

NetWare Directory Services Schema and X.500

The term *schema* describes the structure of a database and the rules of operation on the database. When applied to *NetWare Directory Services* (NDS), it refers to the structure of the NDS database, the structure of the NDS objects, the properties of NDS objects and so on. It describes the different types of *object classes* allowed and how these objects interrelate to each other. Because NDS is based on X.500 and, over time, is expected to evolve to become even more like X.500, this chapter also discusses X.500, the terminology used in X.500, and its equivalent concept used in NDS.

The purpose of this chapter is to give you greater insight and knowledge about the structure of NDS. Detailed knowledge of X.500 is not essential to performing day-to-day NetWare 4.*x* administration tasks.

Understanding the X.500 Standard

The X.500 is a set of *Open Systems Interconnection* (OSI) standards that describes the interconnection of information systems from different manufacturers, at different levels of complexity, under different management, and of different ages. The last criteria of *different ages* implies that systems which comply with X.500 will be compatible with future evolution of the X.500 standards. This is an important criteria because it ensures that current X.500 systems should interoperate with future systems based on the evolving X.500 standard.

The information systems and their directory information is called the *Directory.* The information inside the Directory is called the *Directory Information Base* (DIB). In NetWare terms, the DIB is called the *NetWare Directory Services* (NDS).

The Directory provides information on services such as OSI applications, OSI management processes, OSI layer entities, and telecommunication services. As in the case of NDS, however, the Directory can be used as a model to define directory services for other non-OSI systems.

The Directory provides a single, unified, name space directory for applications and users on the network. Figure 14.1 shows a simple usage model for the Directory. The *Directory user* refers to computer programs that act on behalf of end users or applications and request services to read or modify information in the DIB. The *Directory User Agent* (DUA) is the program that actually makes the request. In NetWare 4.*x*, the Directory Services for DOS workstations is implemented by the NDS.VLM.

Figure 14.1
Model of directory use.

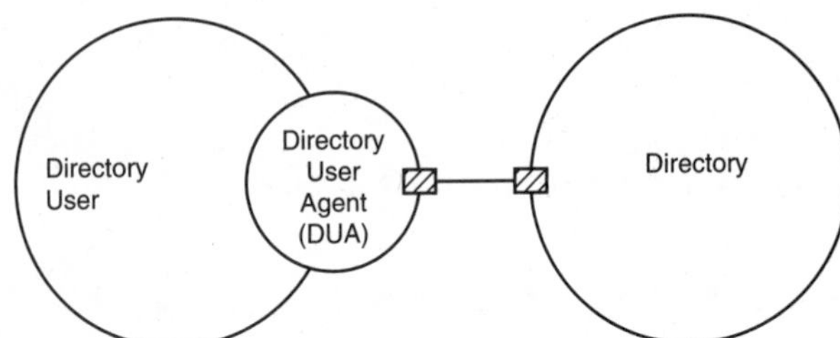

In the marketing literature of different organizations, the Directory is often cited as an example of a general purpose database. This is not true, even though the Directory may be built using general purpose database technology. The assumptions in X.500 Directory services, and also NDS, are the following:

- Queries are more frequent than updates. This is true for a variety of directories such as the telephone directory published once every few months. The Directory is used for looking up information far more often than it gets updated.
- The updates are determined by the dynamics of people and organizations rather than the dynamics of networks.
- Updates to directories need not take place instantaneously. There may be transient conditions in which both new and old versions of the information may exist in the directory.
- Except for situations in which users have different access rights to the directory, the results of a directory query should be the same regardless of the location from which they are issued. This means that directory services such as NDS cannot be used for holding information, such as routing tables of a network, when the information queried depends on the location of the query.

X.500 is not just one standard, but a series of standards. Table 14.1 shows the names of the X.500 standard documents and their equivalent *ISO/IEC* (International Organization of Standards/International Electrotechnnical Commission). This chapter covers the fundamental concepts behind CCITT X.500. For a more detailed discussion, you can refer to the standards listed in the table.

Table 14.1
X.500 Recommendations

CCITT Recommendation	Equivalent ISO/IEC Standard
X.500	ISO 9594-1, Information processing system—Open Systems Interconnection. The Directory—Part 1: Overview of concepts, model and service.
X.501	ISO 9594-2, Information processing system—Open Systems Interconnection. The Directory—Part 2: Models.
X.509	ISO 9594-8, Information processing system—Open Systems Interconnection. The Directory—Part 8: Authentication framework.
X.511	ISO 9594-3, Information processing system—Open Systems Interconnection. The Directory—Part 3: Abstract service definition.
X.518	ISO 9594-4, Information processing system—Open Systems Interconnection. The Directory—Part 4: Procedures for distributed operation.
X.519	ISO 9594-5, Information processing system—Open Systems Interconnection. The Directory—Part 5: Protocol specifications.
X.520	ISO 9594-6, Information processing system—Open Systems Interconnection. The Directory—Part 6: Selectedattribute types.
X.521	ISO 9594-7, Information processing system—Open Systems Interconnection. The Directory—Part 7: Selected object classes.

The Directory Information Base (DIB)

The DIB is the X.500 term for the NDS database. The DIB is composed of information on objects in the form of *directory entries*. A directory entry consists of *attributes*. The attributes have a *type* and one or more values. The directory entries in a DIB are arranged in the form of a tree (see fig. 14.2) called the *Directory Information Tree* (DIT). The DIT is the X.500 term for the NDS tree.

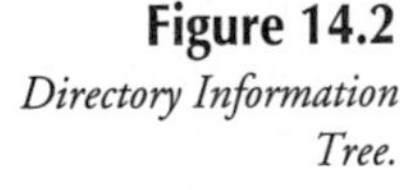

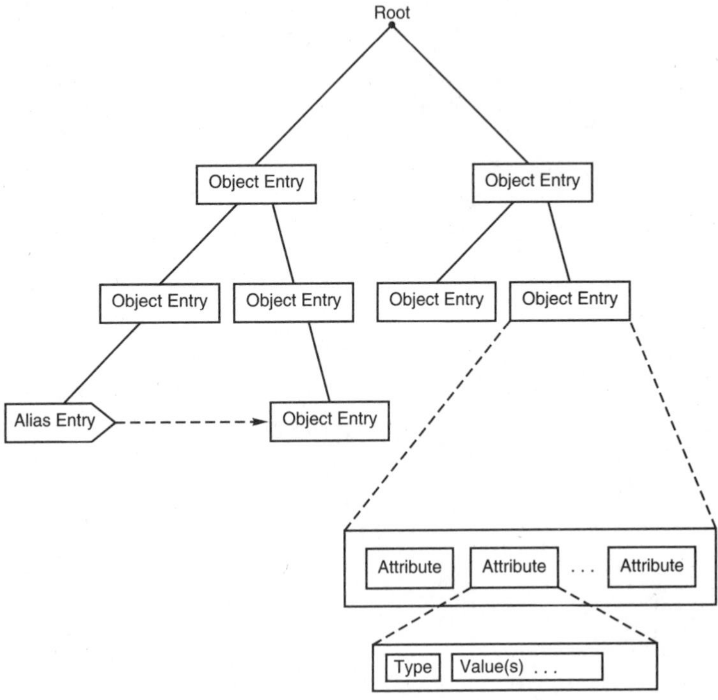

Figure 14.2
Directory Information Tree.

Directory Names

Every directory entry has a *Distinguished Name* (DN) that uniquely and clearly identifies the entry and its location in the DIT. The Distinguished Name can consist of a combination of certain designated directory entry attributes. The Distinguished Name for a directory entry is made up of the Distinguished Name of its *superior* (immediate parent) and the *Relative Distinguished Name* (RDN) for the directory entry. Each directory entry has one or more "name" attribute values called *distinguished values* that serve to uniquely identify that directory entry from its siblings. The unordered collection of these values is called the Relative Distinguished Name. The RDN must distinguish a directory entry from its siblings. Most objects defined in NDS have only one attribute—the *Common Name* (CN)—that distinguishes the object from its siblings. The directory entries can be for object entries or alias entries (see fig. 14.2). The object entries refer to the actual objects, and the alias entries provide an alternate name for the objects they point to.

Figure 14.3 shows a DIT. Notice how DNs for objects such as Bill are represented.

The X.500 standard does not define how the textual strings for Distinguished Names are to be represented, but the X.500 standard does define how Distinguished Names are exchanged between OSI systems. Typically, this is done using the ASN.1 (Abstract Syntax Notation 1) that unambiguously transmits the Distinguished Names across the network. When dealing with implementations of NDS, you must have a textual representation of these distinguished names, which can differ between implementations.

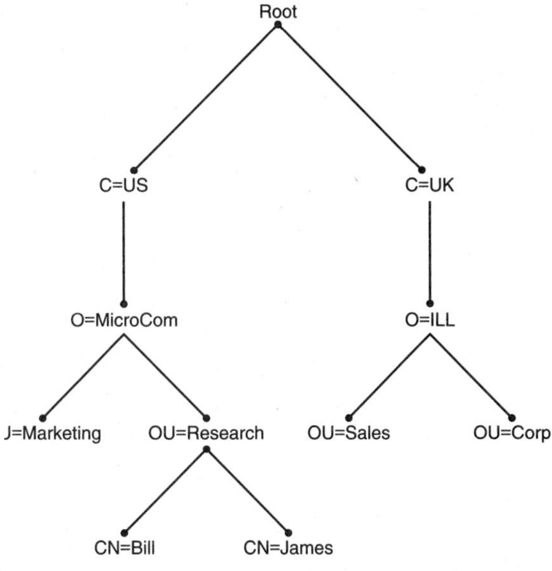

Figure 14.3
Distinguished Names in a DIT.

Contrary to popular belief, Novell's syntax for complete names for the NDS is not the only way to represent Distinguished Names. This does not mean that Novell is not compliant with X.500, because the standard does not define the textual representation of the DN. In the X.500 standard document, the Distinguished Name for object Bill in figure 14.3 would be represented as the following:

```
{C= US, O=MicroCom, OU=Research, CN=Bill}
```

Compare this to the following NDS representation of the Distinguished Name for Bill:

```
.CN=Bill.OU=Research.O=MicroCom.C=US
```

From the preceding example, you can see that the term *Distinguished Name* is the X.500 term for the term *Complete Name* used in NDS.

Another interesting X.500 implementation that uses a different Distinguished Name syntax is *QUIPU,* developed at University College, London, and available as part of the *ISO Development Environment* (ISODE) release. ISODE can be obtained by contacting the following address:

University of Pennsylvania
Department of Computer and Information Science
Moore School
Attn: ISODE Distribution
200 South 33rd Street
Philadelphia, PA 19104-6319
U.S.A.
(215) 898-8560

QUIPU (pronounced *kwi-poo*) is named after the manner in which information was stored by the Inca of Peru. These people did not use writing, instead they used colored strings knotted to encode information. The strings were attached to a larger rope to form a device known as the *Quipu.* The Quipu could only be read by trained people and contained information about property locations and rights throughout the Inca empire.

The user Bill of figure 14.3 is named as follows in QUIPU:

```
@C=US@O=MicroCom@OU=Research@CN=Bill
```

Notice that in QUIPU, objects are written left to right, but starting from the root of the DIT and moving down the tree to the object. This is in contrast to NDS in which objects, although written from left to right, are listed starting from the object and moving up the tree.

To move up one level from the current context the syntax in NDS is as follows:

```
CN=KSS.OU=SCS.
```

To move up one level in QUIPU, the syntax is as follows:

```
..@OU=SCS.CN=KSS
```

The X.500 standard describes the existence of a *Locality* object that describes a location. Figure 14.4 shows a DIT that uses a Locality object. Currently, the NDS schema does not implement the Locality object. The X.500 notation for the Distinguished Name for Janice is as follows:

```
{CN=US,  L=Berkeley, CN=Janice}
```

The Locality object acts as a container object and is meant to describe information for a person residing at a location such as a town, city, etc. It could be used for organizing an electronic directory for locations that are similar to the paper telephone directories that exist in many parts of the world.

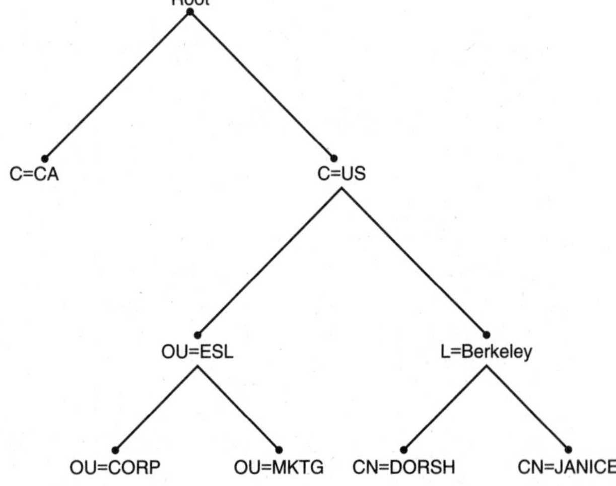

Figure 14.4
DIT using Locality object.

Understanding the Directory Schema for the NDS

The Directory enforces a set of rules on how the different types of directory entries are organized in the DIT and the types of operations that can be performed on them. These rules are called the *Directory schema* and help maintain consistency in the DIB.

The structure rules for how the different objects in the DIT are organized are described in an annex to the X.521 Recommendation and is shown in figure 14.5. This figure is interesting for a number of reasons. It shows the major classes of objects that can exist in the DIT, and where they can occur in relationship to each other. Except for the Locality object, Application process, and Application entity, you can see that the rules for the DIT are the same as for the NDS tree. The Application process class is intended for OSI applications integrated with X.500. These are not currently implemented in NDS. The Locality object is not supported by NetWare utilities, although the NDS can support it.

In figure 14.5, an arrow is drawn from a superior (parent) object class to its immediate subordinate (child). For example, an arrow is drawn from the root object class to the Country, Locality, and Organization object classes, respectively. This means that the Country, Locality, and Organization object classes can exist directly underneath the root of the DIT. In the NDS tree, only the Country and Organization classes can exist under the root. The Locality and Organizational Unit object classes have an arrow coming from themselves and going into themselves. This means that there can be several levels of the Locality and Organizational Unit object class in a DIT.

The NDS schema consists of the following three major components:

- Object classes
- Attribute types
- Attribute syntaxes

Object classes describe the different types of objects that can exist in the NDS. To describe the different object classes, you need to specify the structural rules for the object class, super class of the object class, mandatory attributes, and optional attributes.

The structural rules define the relationship of the object to other objects in the NDS tree. For example, you should know whether a certain object can appear in a specified container. In the example in figure 14.5, the Organizational Unit object can exist in an Organization or Locality container, but not directly underneath a Country or root object.

The *attribute type* is a particular piece of information in the object class. Examples of attribute types are Account Balance (occurs in a user object class), ACL (occurs in the Top object class), and Detect Intruder (occurs in the Organization and Organizational Unit object class).

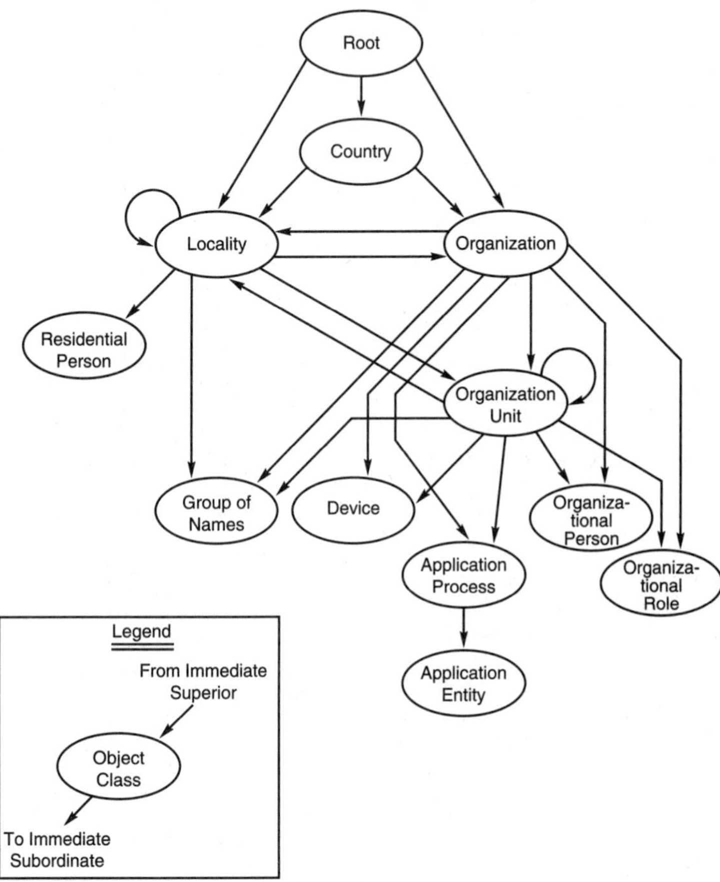

Figure 14.5
Objects in a DIT.

An *attribute syntax* defines the type of data stored in an attribute type. An attribute type is made up of an attribute syntax (also called *property syntax*), and can have a constraint placed on it. Examples of attribute syntaxes are Counter, Integer, and Boolean. The attribute type Account Balance has the attribute syntax Counter; the attribute type Detect Intruder is made up of the attribute syntax Boolean; and the Common Name attribute type is made up of the attribute type Case Ignore String and can have 1 to 64 elements.

In general, an attribute syntax can consist of one or more data types with rules that express an ordering relationship between them. These rules are called *matching rules* and can be substring, equality, or ordering (less than, equal to, greater than). The set of attribute syntaxes is the only element of the NDS schema that is nonextensible. The other elements: object class and attribute types can be extended by Directory Services APIs.

Table 14.2 shows constraints that can be placed on the attribute type.

Table 14.2
Constraints on Attribute Types

Constraint	Description
Hidden	The user cannot see or modify the attribute. The NDS name server is responsible for maintaining this attribute. Defined by DS_HIDDEN_ATTR in the NWDSDEFS.H file.
Non-removable	This attribute type cannot be deleted from the schema. For example, all attribute types that make up the base schema are flagged with this attribute to prevent an application from deleting attribute types from the base schema. Defined by DS_NONREMOVABLE_ATTR in the NWDSDEFS.H file.
Public Read	Anyone can read the attribute type. No object property rights are needed to read the attribute type. Also, the IRF cannot be used to prevent the reading of this attribute type. Defined by DS_PUBLIC_READ in the NWDSDEFS.H file.
Read Only	The user cannot modify the attribute. The NDS name server is responsible for maintaining this attribute. Defined by DS_READ_ONLY_ATTR in the NWDSDEFS.H file.
Single-valued	The attribute has a single value only. If an attribute does not have this constraint, it is a multi-valued attribute. For example the attribute ACL does not have this attribute because it consists of multiple values. Defined by DS_SINGLE_VALUED_ATTR in the NWDSDEFS.H file.
Sized	The attribute has an upper and lower bound such as length of strings or values of integers. Defined by DS_SIZED_ATTR in the NWDSDEFS.H file.
String	The attribute is a string of characters. Primarily used for naming objects and text descriptions of objects. Defined by DS_STRING_ATTR in the NWDSDEFS.H file.

continues

Table 14.2, Continued
Constraints on Attribute Types

Constraint	Description
Server Read	Server class objects are given special read access to this attribute even though read right is not explicitly or implicitly given to the attribute. IRF cannot be used to block read right for server class objects. An example of an attribute type that uses this constraint is the Default Queue in the printer object. The NCP server can access the name of the default queue in the printer object regardless of any permission setting on the Default Queue property. Defined by DS_SERVER_READ in the NWDSDEFS.H file.
Sync Immediate	Modifications made to this attribute type are synchronized immediately rather than at the next synchronization interval. An example of an attribute type that uses this constraint is the CA (Certification Authority) Private Key and CA Public Key that describe the Certification Authority private and public keys for the object class partition. Defined by DS_SYNC_IMMEDIATE in the NWDSDEFS.H file.
Write Managed	You must have managed rights on the object that contains this attribute before you can change the attributes value. Defined by DS_WRITE_MANAGED in the NWDSDEFS.H file.
Suppress Synchronization	The information in this attribute is not synchronized to other replicas. Currently the only attribute type that uses this constraint in the NDS base class schema is the *Reference* attribute defined in the Top object class. The Reference class object is used for internal book keeping purposes. For example, if objects A, B, and C have privileges granted to object X (through the ACL attribute type), the Reference attribute of object X contains the object names A, B, and C. This makes it easy to find the objects that reference a given object. The Reference attribute is not synchronized to other replicas. Defined by DS_SF_PER_REPLICA in the NWDSDEFS.H file.

Class Inheritance in NDS

A very important attribute for directory entry (object) is the *object class.* The value of the object class determines the type of the NDS object and the type of other attributes it can contain. NDS has a formal definition of all the different object classes that it can contain. The definition for NDS objects is based on *class inheritance.* Class inheritance uses a definition hierarchy similar to that used in object-oriented programming languages.

The structural rules for objects define the concept of an *immediate super class.* An *object class* can be defined as a sub-class of another object, with some additional refinements in terms of new attributes. Another way of saying this is that an object's definition is "derived" from its immediate superior class.

At the "top-most" level is an object called *top.* Top is the super class of all objects. All NDS objects are directly or indirectly derived from top. Figure 14.6 shows the derivation hierarchy of the different NDS object classes. Top is the only class that has no super class. When an object has a super class, the object's definition is said to be *derived* from this super class. This means that the object's attributes (properties) are those defined by the super class object *plus* any additional properties peculiar to that object. In other words, an object *inherits* some of its properties from its super class.

The definition of the top object class can be expressed using the format of ASN.1 as follows:

```
Top OBJECT-CLASS
    MUST CONTAIN {Object Class}
    MAY CONTAIN  { ACL,
            Back Link,
            Bindery Property,
            Obituary,
            Reference }
```

ASN.1 is a standard that deals with rules of encoding and describing structural properties of application-level data. ASN.1 is part of the *International Organization of Standards* (ISO) recommendations for the presentation layer (layer 6) of the *Open Systems Interconnection* (OSI) reference model. It is the language used by protocol designers to describe upper-layer application protocols.

In the preceding definition of the top object class, the *clause* MUST CONTAIN means that the properties listed in { } must have a value. The clause MAY CONTAIN means the properties listed in { } need not have values. In other words, the values of the properties listed in MAY CONTAIN are optional.

Other clauses that may be used in the definition are SUBCLASS OF, CONTAINMENT, and NAMED BY.

The SUBCLASS OF is used to indicate that the object is *derived from* another object. In the definition of the top object class, no SUBCLASS OF clause exists because the top class is not derived from any other object. The CONTAINMENT clause is used to describe the containers in which the defined object can be placed. For example, the CONTAINMENT clause for user objects is Organization and Organizational Unit objects. The user object cannot occur in any other container. The NAMED BY

clause is used to indicate the object attributes used to name the object. Usually, the NAMED BY attribute contains attributes such as Common Name (CN) that are used for leaf objects. For container objects, attributes such as the Organization name and Organizational Unit can be used.

The derivation of NDS objects from its super classes are defined in the following sections.

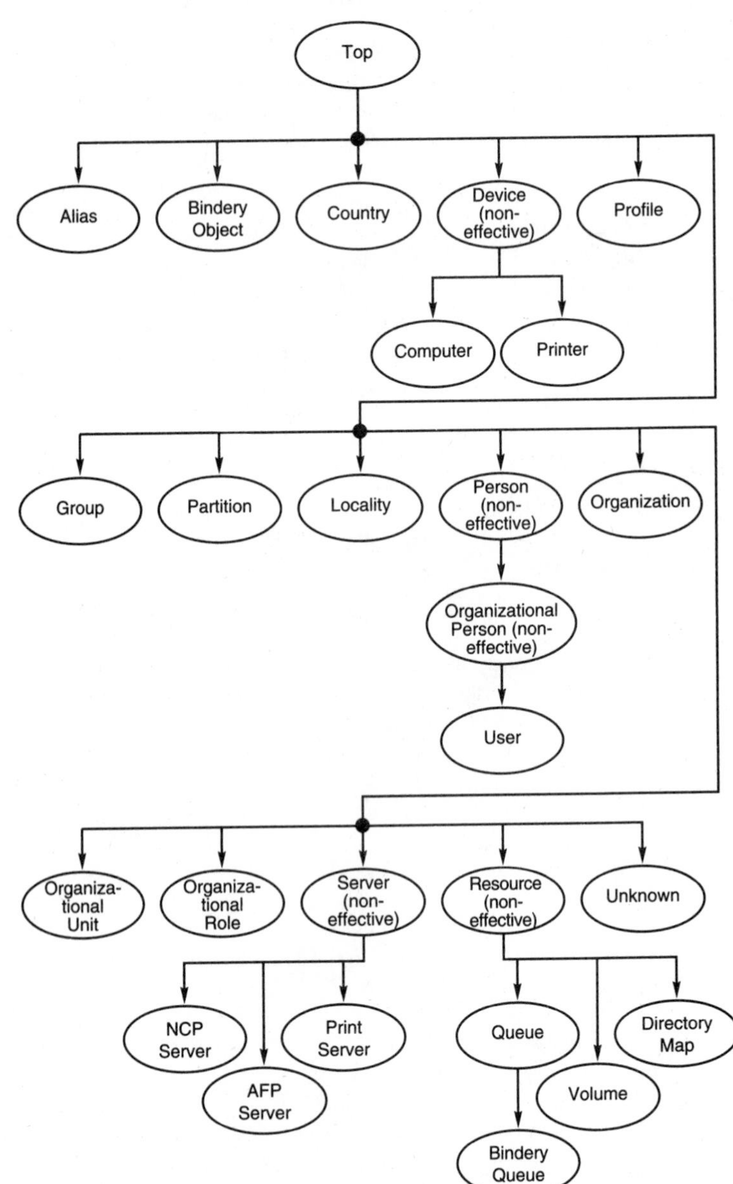

Figure 14.6
Overview of schema for NDS object classes.

Defining Alias Objects

The derivation of the alias class is shown in figure 14.7. The formal definition of the alias object class follows the figure.

```
Alias OBJECT-CLASS
    SUBCLASS OF Top
    MUST CONTAIN { commonName, // Called Name in NWADMIN
             surName // Called Last Name in NWADMIN
                }
    MAY CONTAIN  { Description, Telephone Number,
             Full Name, See Also }
```

Figure 14.7 shows an example of derivation in which the alias object class is derived from the top super class. The only new attribute/property defined in the alias object class is the *aliasObjectName*; all other properties of the alias object class are inherited from the top super class.

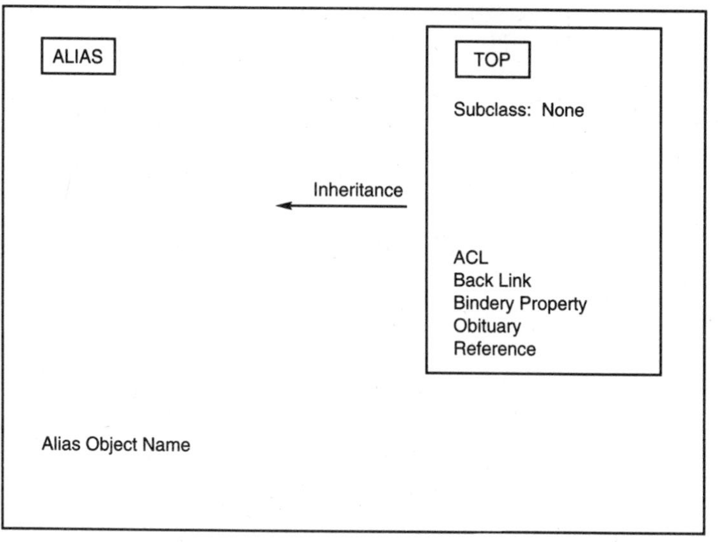

Figure 14.7
Alias object derived from the top class object.

The following is a definition of the alias object:

```
alias OBJECT-CLASS
    SUBCLASS OF Top
    MUST CONTAIN {aliasObjectName}
```

Definition of a User Object

The user object class is actually derived from the super class *organizational person.* This means that the user class has all information types defined in the Organizational Person super class as well as any additional attributes defined for the user class. The organizational person class is itself derived from the *person* class which is in turn derived from the top super class. This inheritance is shown in figure 14.8.

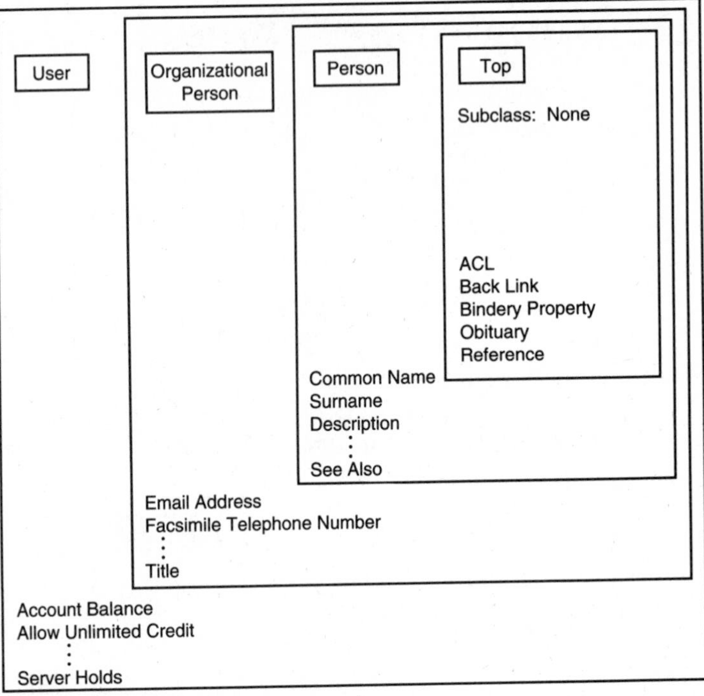

Figure 14.8
User object class derivation.

In formal terms the derivation of the user class is defined as follows:

```
Person OBJECT-CLASS
    SUBCLASS OF Top
    MUST CONTAIN { Common Name, // Called Name in NWADMIN
                   SurName // Called Last Name in NWADMIN
                   }
    MAY CONTAIN  { Description, Telephone Number,
                   Full Name, See Also }

Organizational Person OBJECT-CLASS
    SUBCLASS OF Person
    MAY CONTAIN {    EMail Address,
                 Facsimilie Telephone Number,
                 Locality Name, // Not implemented in NDS
                 Organizational Unit Name,
                 Physical Delivery Office Name,
                 Postal Address,
                 Postal Code,
                 Postal Office Box,
                 State or Province name,
                 Street Address,
                 Title }
    CONTAINMENT {    Organization,
                 Organizational Unit }
```

```
    NAMED BY       {    Common Name,
            Organizational Unit }

User OBJECT-CLASS
    SUBCLASS OF Organizational Person
    MAY CONTAIN {    Account Balance,
            Allow Unlimited Credit,
            Group Membership,
            Higher Privileges, // Not implemented
            Home Directory,
            Language,
            Last Login Time,
            Locked By Intruder,
            Login Allowed Time Map,
            Login Disabled,
            Login Expiration Time,
            Login Grace Limit,
            Login Grace Remaining,
            Login Intruder Address,
            Login Intruder Attempts,
            Login Intruder Reset Time,
            Login Maximum Simultaneous,
            Login Script,
            Login Time,
            Message Server,
            Minimum Account Balance,
            Network Address,
            Network Address Restriction,
            Password Allow Change,
            Password Expiration Interval,
            Password Minimum Length,
            Password Required,
            Password Unique Required,
            Passwords Used,
            Print Job Configuration,
            Printer Control,
            Private Key,
            Profile,
            Public Key,
            Security Equals,
            Server Holds }
```

The X.500 standard defines two *sub classes* (derived classes) from the person class. These are the *residential person* and *organizational person.* The residential person object class is not defined in NDS. This is used in X.500 to define directory services similar to those found in telephone books. From figure 14.5 you can see that the residential person occurs under the Locality object.

Objects belonging to object classes, such as person and organizational person, do not exist as objects in an NDS database. They are used for object derivation and construction only and are therefore called *non-effective classes.* Classes such as user, group and so on can have their objects exist in an NDS tree. Such classes are called *effective classes.* Only an effective class can be used to create NDS objects. An object class used to create NDS objects is called the created object's *base class.* It therefore follows that only an effective class can be used as a base class for an object. Sometimes in object-oriented programming languages, the term *parent class* is the same as the base class. In NDS vocabulary, the term *parent class* is used for container objects that contain other objects, and is not used to describe the object derivation hierarchy.

The NDS base schema defines the following non-effective classes:

- Device
- Organizational Person
- Person
- Resource
- Server
- Top

The NDS base schema defines the following effective object classes:

- Alias
- AFP Server
- Bindery Object
- Bindery Queue
- Computer
- Country
- Directory Map
- Group
- Locality
- Partition
- NCP Server
- Organization
- Organization Role
- Organizational Unit
- Printer

- Print Server
- Profile
- Queue
- Unknown
- User
- Volume

The CONTAINMENT clause (see definition of Organizational Person) defines the container in which the object can have an existence. The NAMED BY clause defines the Relative Distinguished Name used to identify the object.

The Higher Privileges attribute in the user class definition is not currently implemented. It is meant to activate certain privileges on a temporary basis and then deactivate them. Users of UNIX systems will readily recognize that the su (supervisor command) on a UNIX system allows an already logged in user to assume *root* (supervisor) privileges after proper password authentication. The Higher Privileges attribute, if implemented, can provide a similar capability.

The Message Server attribute for the user object class is set to the server object that stores and forwards broadcast type messages.

The Bindery Object

The *Bindery object* is an effective-class object and is derived from Top (see fig. 14.6). Its formal definition is as follows:

```
Bindery Object OBJECT-CLASS
    SUBCLASS OF Top
    MUST CONTAIN { Bindery Object Restriction,
                 Bindery Type,
                    Common Name }
    MAY CONTAIN  { Any }

    CONTAINMENT {Organization,
                  Organizational Unit}
    NAMED BY { Bindery Type,
                  Common Name }
```

Defining a Country

The *Country object* is an effective-class object and is derived from Top (see fig. 14.6). Its formal definition is as follows:

```
Country OBJECT-CLASS
    SUBCLASS OF Top
    MUST CONTAIN { Country Name // C=
               }
    MAY CONTAIN  { Description }

    CONTAINMENT { Root}
    NAMED BY {Country Name }
```

Defining Device Objects Computer and Printer

The *Computer* and *Printer objects* are effective-class objects derived from the non-effective class object *Device*, which is in turn derived from the object class Top (see fig. 14.6). Their formal definitions are as follows:

```
Device OBJECT-CLASS
    SUBCLASS OF Top
    MUST CONTAIN { Common Name // CN=
               }
    MAY CONTAIN  { Description,
                 Locality name,  // L=
                 Network Address,
                 Organization,
                 Organizational Unit,
                 Owner,
                 Serial Number,
                 See Also }

    CONTAINMENT {     Organization,
                 Organizational Unit}
    NAMED BY {Common Name }

Computer OBJECT-CLASS
    SUBCLASS OF Device
    MAY CONTAIN  { Operator,
                 Server,
                 Status }

Printer OBJECT-CLASS
    SUBCLASS OF Device
    MAY CONTAIN  { Cartridge,
                 Default Queue,
                 Host Device,
                 Memory,
                 Network Address Restriction,
                 Notify,
                 Operator,
                 Page Description Language,
                 Printer Configuration,
                 Print Server,
                 Queue,
                 Status,
                 Supported Typefaces }
```

Defining a Group

The *Group object* is an effective-class object and is derived from Top (see fig. 14.6). Its formal definition is as follows:

```
Group OBJECT-CLASS
    SUBCLASS OF Top
    MUST CONTAIN { Common Name // CN=
               }
    MAY CONTAIN  { Description,
                Full Name,
                Group ID (GID),
                Locality Name,
                Member,
                Organization,
                Organizational Unit,
                Owner,
                See Also }

    CONTAINMENT { Organization,
                Organizational Unit}
    NAMED BY {Common Name }
```

Defining a Locality

The *Locality object* is an effective-class object and is derived from Top (see fig. 14.6). Its formal definition is as follows:

```
Locality OBJECT-CLASS
    SUBCLASS OF Top
    MAY CONTAIN  { Description,
                Locality Name,
                State or Province Name,
                Street Address,
                See Also }

    CONTAINMENT { Root,
                Country,
                Organization,
                Organizational Unit}
    NAMED BY {Locality Name,
                State or Province Name }
```

Defining an Organization

The *Organization object* is an effective-class object and is derived from Top (see fig. 14.6). Its formal definition is as follows:

```
Organization OBJECT-CLASS
    SUBCLASS OF Top
    MUST CONTAIN { Organization } // O=
```

```
MAY CONTAIN  { Description,
              Detect Intruder,
              Email Address,
              Telephone Number,
              Facsimilie Telephone Number,
              Intruder Attempt Reset Interval,
              Intruder Lockout Reset Interval,
              Locality Name,
              Lockout After Detection,
              Login Script,
              Login Intruder Limit,
              NSS Domain,
              Physical Delivery Office Name,
              Postal Address,
              Postal Code,
              Postal Office Box,
              Print Job Configuration,
              Printer Control,
              State or Province Name,
              Street Address,
              See Also }

CONTAINMENT { Root,
              Country,
              Locality }
NAMED BY { Organization } // O=
```

Defining an Organizational Role

The *Organizational Role object* is an effective-class object and is derived from Top (see fig. 14.6). Its formal definition is as follows:

```
Organizational role OBJECT-CLASS
    SUBCLASS OF Top
    MUST CONTAIN { Common Name } // CN=
    MAY CONTAIN  { Description,
                  Email Address,
                  Telephone Number,
                  Facsimilie Telephone Number,
                  Locality Name,
                  Organizational Unit,
                  Physical Delivery Office Name,
                  Postal Address,
                  Postal Code,
                  Postal Office Box,
                  Role Occupant,
                  State or Province Name,
                  Street Address,
                  See Also }

    CONTAINMENT { Organization
                  Organizational Unit }
    NAMED BY { Common Name } // CN=
```

Defining an Organizational Unit

The *Organizational Unit object* is an effective-class object and is derived from Top (see fig. 14.6). Its formal definition is as follows:

```
Organizational unit OBJECT-CLASS
    SUBCLASS OF Top
    MUST CONTAIN { Organizational Unit } // OU=
    MAY CONTAIN  { Description,
                Detect Intruder,
                Email Address,
                Telephone Number,
                Facsimilie Telephone Number,
                Intruder Attempt Reset Interval,
                Intruder Lockout Reset Interval,
                Locality Name,
                Lockout After Detection,
                Login Script,
                Login Intruder Limit,
                NSS Domain,
                Physical Delivery Office Name,
                Postal Address,
                Postal Code,
                Postal Office Box,
                Print Job Configuration,
                Printer Control,
                State or Province Name,
                Street Address,
                See Also }
    CONTAINMENT { Organization,
                Organizational Unit,
                Locality }
    NAMED BY { Organizational Unit } // OU=
```


Defining a Partition

The *Partition object* is an effective-class object and is derived from Top (see fig. 14.6). This object can only be created using the Partition Manager and PARTMGR tools. Its formal definition is as follows:

```
Country OBJECT-CLASS
    SUBCLASS OF Top
    MAY CONTAIN  { Authority Revocation,
                CA Private Key,
                CA Public Key,
                Certificate Revocation,
                Convergence,
                Cross Certification Pair,
                High Convergence Sync Interval,
                Inherited ACL,
                Low Convergence Reset Time,
```

```
                 Low Convergence Sync Time,
                 Partition Creation Time,
                 Received Up To,
                 Replica,
                 Synchronized Up To }
```

Because the Partition object does not occur in the NDS tree as a normal NDS object, it cannot be referenced by NDS naming syntax. The Partition object does not have a NAMED BY or CONTAINMENT definition.

Defining a Profile Object

The *Profile object* is an effective-class object and is derived from Top (see fig. 14.6). Its formal definition is as follows:

```
Profile OBJECT-CLASS
    SUBCLASS OF Top
    MUST CONTAIN { Common Name,      // CN=
                Login Script }
    MAY CONTAIN  { Description,
                Locality Name,
                Organization,
             Organizational Unit,
                See Also }

    CONTAINMENT { Organization,
            Organizational Unit }
    NAMED BY { Common Name } // CN=
```

Defining a Resource Object

The *Resource object* is a non-effective class object and is derived from Top (see fig. 14.6). This object is used in the derivation of the effective class objects Print Queue/Bindery Queue, Directory Map, and Volume objects. Its formal definition is as follows:


```
Resource OBJECT-CLASS
    SUBCLASS OF Top
    MUST CONTAIN { Common Name }      // CN=
    MAY CONTAIN  { Description,
                Host Resource Name,
                Locality Name,
                Organization,
                 Organizational Unit,
                See Also }

    CONTAINMENT { Organization,
                Organizational Unit }
    NAMED BY { Common Name } // CN=
```

Defining a Print Queue Object

The *Print Queue object* is an effective class object and is derived from the Resource non-effective class object. Its formal definition is as follows:

```
Print Queue OBJECT-CLASS
    SUBCLASS OF Resource
    MUST CONTAIN { Queue Directory }
    MAY CONTAIN  { Device,
                Host Server,
                Network Address,
                Operator,
                Server,
                User,
                Volume }
```

Defining a Bindery Queue Object

The *Bindery Queue object* is an effective class object and is derived from the Resource non-effective class object. Its formal definition is as follows:

```
Print Queue OBJECT-CLASS
    SUBCLASS OF Print Queue
    MUST CONTAIN { Bindery Type }
    NAMED BY { Common Name, Bindery Type }
```

Defining a Directory Map Object

The *Directory Map object* is an effective class object and is derived from the Resource non-effective class object. Its formal definition is as follows:

```
Directory Map OBJECT-CLASS
    SUBCLASS OF Resource
    MUST CONTAIN { Volume,
                Path }
```


Defining a Volume Object

The *Volume object* is an effective class object and is derived from the Resource non-effective class object. Its formal definition is as follows:

```
Directory Map OBJECT-CLASS
    SUBCLASS OF Resource
    MUST CONTAIN { Host Server }
                Host Volume }
    MAY CONTAIN { Status }
```

Defining a Server Object

The *Server object* is a non-effective class object and is derived from Top (see fig. 14.6). Its formal definition is as follows:

```
Server OBJECT-CLASS
    SUBCLASS OF Top
    MUST CONTAIN { Common Name } // CN=
    MAY CONTAIN  { Description,
                Allow Balance,
                Allow Unlimited Credit,
                Full Name,
                Host Device,
                Locality Name,
                Minimum Account Balance,
                Network Address,
                Organization,
                Organizational Unit,
                Private Key,
                Public Key,
                Resource,
                Status,
                User,
                Version,
                See Also }

    CONTAINMENT { Organization,
                Organizational Unit}
    NAMED BY { Common Name } // CN=
```

Defining an NCP Server Object

The *NCP Server* (or *NetWare Server*) *object* is an effective class object and is derived from the non-effective class Server. Its formal definition is as follows:


```
Server OBJECT-CLASS
    SUBCLASS OF Server
    MAY CONTAIN  {Operator,
                Supported Services }
```

Defining a Print Server

The *Print Server object* is an effective class object and is derived from the non-effective class Server. Its formal definition is as follows:

```
Print Server OBJECT-CLASS
    SUBCLASS OF Server
    MAY CONTAIN  {Operators,
                Printers,
                SAP Name }
```

Defining an AFP Server

The *AFP Server object* is an effective class object and is derived from the non-effective class Server. Its formal definition is as follows:

```
AFP Server OBJECT-CLASS
    SUBCLASS OF Server
    MAY CONTAIN  {Operator,
                Supported Connections }
```

Defining an Unknown Object

The *Unknown object* is an effective-class object and is derived from Top (see fig. 14.6). Its formal definition is as follows:

```
Unknown OBJECT-CLASS
    SUBCLASS OF Top
    MAY CONTAIN { Any }
```

Understanding Exotic Properties

When searching for properties (or attribute types) for NDS objects, you may see a number of *exotic* properties that have *intriguing names* but are not documented in the on-line reference. With some of the property names, you can take an educated guess, but with others this is not always easy. Some of these properties are discussed next for your reference.

The *Authority Revocation* property is used in Partition non-effective object class. The Partition object class encapsulates information required for directory synchronization and connectivity for partitions of the directory. The Authority Revocation property is a time-stamped list of public keys that have been revoked. This attribute is used internally by NDS.

Back Link is defined in the top super class. Because all NDS objects are inherited from the top super class, they all inherit the Back Link property. This property is used to define a list of servers that need to be notified of changes in the status of the object. The user cannot modify this property. It is used by name servers. Server class objects can read this property without being given an explicit trustee assignment to read this property. Inheritance masks also cannot be used to restrict the reading of this property by server class objects.

Bindery Object Restriction is used in bindery objects and stores an error code that indicates the reason why the bindery object cannot be represented as a directory object.

The *Bindery Property* is defined in super class top and is used to emulate bindery properties that cannot be represented as NDS properties.

Bindery Type is used in a Bindery Object or Bindery Queue to describe the type of the bindery object.

CA Private Key is used in the Partition object class and contains the certification authority private key. User applications cannot access this key because it is hidden. This is used to validate public keys. The private key is encrypted using the certification authority's password.

CA Public Key is used in the Partition object class and contains the certification authority public key and other certification information.

Cartridge is used in printer objects and contains a list of font cartridges present in the printer.

Certificate Revocation is used in the Partition object class and contains a time-stamped list of public keys revoked by the certification authority.

Convergence is defined for the Partition object class. It indicates the degree of effort a partition should make in attempting to keep replicas synchronized. A value of zero indicates *low convergence.* This means that updates should not be propagated immediately, but should wait for the next synchronization interval. A value of zero indicates that synchronization is done at low frequency to save on network resources. Partitions with low convergence should be synchronized at least once every 24 hours.

A value of one indicates *high convergence.* This means that an immediate attempt should be made to propagate updates. If this attempt fails, synchronization should be done at the next synchronization interval. The default setting for this attribute is one, which means that high convergence is in effect.

High Convergence Sync Interval is defined for the Partition object class. It is the interval at which partition synchronization takes place if no directory events have caused synchronization to occur. When high synchronization is in effect, changes in partition information cause immediate synchronization to other replicas. If no changes take place in the high convergence sync interval (default value 60 minutes), synchronization is started.

Low Convergence Sync Interval is defined for the Partition object class. It is the interval in seconds that must elapse from one partition synchronization to the next. This has an effect only if *Convergence* is set to low (value of zero).

Low Convergence Reset Time is defined for the Partition object class. This property is used to store the time of day at which low convergence synchronization takes place. After this, the interval counter is reset. The next synchronization takes place only after the *Low Synchronization Sync Interval* time has passed. The *Low Convergence Reset Time* has an effect only if *Convergence* is set to low (value of zero).

Cross Certificate Pair is defined for the Partition object class. It provides a pair of public keys that can be used to provide a simpler and shorter certification.

GID is defined for the object class group. It is the group ID used by UNIX clients.

UID is defined for the object class user. It is the user ID used by UNIX clients.

Higher Privileges is defined for the user object class, but is not currently implemented. Its purpose is to enable a logged-in user to temporarily acquire a higher set of privileges. After a function is performed with the higher set of privileges, the higher privileges can be surrendered.

Message Server is defined for the user object class. It contains the name of the server used to store and forward broadcast messages for the user.

Obituary is defined in the top super class, and is therefore a property of all NDS objects. This attribute is used internally by NDS for name resolution during directory operations, for example, renaming an object. When an object is renamed an *obituary timestamp* is recorded for the renamed object allowing it to be identified by its old name. Meanwhile, if changes are made to the renamed object in another partition, those changes refer to the older name of the object. Moreover, these changes are not immediately seen in the partition in which the renamed object resides. When changes to the object finally reach the partition in which the renamed object resides, it cannot find the original name of the object. The obituary attribute is then used to identify the object and implement the changes.

Object Class is defined in the top super class, and is therefore a property of all NDS objects. It is a list of all the super classes from which the object is derived.

Partition Creation Time is defined for the partition object class and contains a timestamp identifying the "incarnation" of the replicas of a partition.

Received Up To is defined for the partition object class and contains a timestamp identifying the last time the replica received an update.

Reference is defined in the top super class and is therefore a property of all NDS objects. It is used internally by NDS and contains a list of objects that reference an object. For example if objects X, Y, Z have trustee assignments to U, then the Reference attribute of U lists objects X, Y, Z. This makes it easier for NDS to find all objects that reference object U. The Reference attribute type is not replicated.

Replica is defined for the partition object class and contains the name servers that store replicas of the partition.

Synchronized Up To is defined for the partition object class and contains the timestamp with which servers that have a copy of the partition's replica were synchronized.

Server Holds is defined for a user class object. This attribute is used when NetWare Accounting is active and describes the number of accounting charges pending while the server performs an operation. Before performing an operation, the server does the following:

14

1. Ensures that the user has sufficient balance

2. Places the correct charges and user identification in Server Holds attribute

3. After operation is complete, deducts the charges from the user balance

Type Creator Map is used by user object class and identifies the user as a Macintosh file system client. It is used by NetWare for Macintosh to identify users who should be given type and creator descriptions when information on files is requested.

Unknown Base Class is used to identify the class of an object before it was changed to an unknown class.

Summary

This chapter discussed the NDS schema and how it was derived from the X.500 schema. Because NDS is based on X.500 and, over time, has been expanded to become even more like X.500, this chapter also discussed X.500, the terminology used in X.500, and its equivalent concept used in NDS.

The components of the NDS schema are object classes, attribute types, and attribute syntaxes. The object class is defined in terms of attribute types and rules for building the object class. The attribute types are the properties that make up an object class and are defined in terms of attribute syntaxes. The attribute syntaxes are the different data types. The attribute syntax is the only nonextensible part of the NDS schema. New attribute types and object classes can be defined using the NDS APIs.

NetWare Directory Services Name Resolution

When an NDS object name is submitted to the NDS name service, it must be able to locate the network resource represented by the NDS object name. The NDS stores information on network resources in a distributed database. This means that portions of the NDS information may be kept on servers in different locations on the network. The NDS name service has to figure out which servers to contact to find information on the NDS object. Because a server may hold only a portion of the NDS tree, the request for the NDS object may have to be "bounced" around before the answer is found. One of the considerations in the NDS design is to have an optimal mechanism to resolve an NDS name. This chapter will give you a deeper understanding on the name resolution process.

Overview of Distributed Operations in NDS

Objects in the directory are organized in a hierarchical fashion, in the same manner that a file system organizes subdirectories and files. This object hierarchy is also called a *tree* or a *directory tree.* The tree can be divided into smaller pieces or subtrees called *partitions.* Each partition is named by the object at the root of the subtree. Thus, the partition describing the entire tree is called the [Root] partition. A copy of a partition is called a *replica.* Replicas are useful for providing an online backup of partition data and for minimizing the distance an NDS query has to travel to be satisfied. Replicas are kept synchronized with the original copy of the partition (master partition), and the NDS query can be satisfied by a replica that is close to the source of the query.

NetWare 4 supports multiple replicas of a partition that can be read-only or read-write.

Partitioning and replication enable distribution of the directory information among servers. This enables distribution of the work of the name service, as well as more convenient access to the data. NetWare 4 Directory Services, therefore, is a hierarchical, distributed, replicated name service. The job of a name service is to maintain information about objects and to locate the objects and the associated object information for clients.

Partitions are described in the NDS schema as a type of NDS object. A partition that represents a portion of the NDS tree can have a subordinate partition that represents a subtree linked to its parent tree. The parent partition (superior partition) is called a partition root. Objects that are partition roots have additional properties that are used by NDS for synchronization. One of these properties is the *replica pointer*, which contains the name and internal net address of the server where the replica is located for every replica of a partition. The replica pointers of a partition form a list of the locations of the replicas.

The commonly recognized replica types are Master, Read Write (sometimes called a *Secondary replica*), and Read Only. Another less well-known replica type is that of Subordinate Reference. The Subordinate Reference connects the tree. A Subordinate Reference (Sub Ref for short) is a complete copy of a partition root object. It exists on servers where the superior partition exists and the subordinate partition does not. Because a Sub Ref is a partition object and has a replica pointer property, it has a list of all the replica locations. From that list, the directory can locate a replica of objects in that partition. You can think of the Subordinate Reference as a pointer to the locations of subordinate replicas.

It is not a requirement that one server hold a copy of the entire object hierarchy. The directory tree can be both distributed and replicated. There has to be, therefore, a method of finding the physical location of objects. That method is called tree walking, or resolving a name.

What Is Tree Walking?

When an NDS client agent submits a request to resolve an NDS name, the request may not be received by the name server (NetWare 4 server that has directory services installed) that has the information to fulfill the request. If the name server is not able to fulfill the request by consulting its NDS database, it must contact another name server that can fulfill the request. It is possible to have a situation in which several name servers may have to be contacted before finding the name server that can fulfill the request. To find the information, the name server searches through the hierarchy of partitions until the requested information is found. This process is called *tree walking* or *name resolution.*

Understanding Name Resolution

Tree walking or name resolution consists of resolving a name to an address of the object. The address of the object is the physical location of the object. This process performed by Directory Services is an essential part of the distributed, replicated name service of NetWare 4. It eliminates the necessity that clients be aware of the physical location of resources they use. Clients need only know the name of the resource or (using a NDS search utility like NLIST.EXE) the type of resource. The term *client* is used to describe anything that uses the services provided by the network or a server on the network. Users are the most common type of client in the networking environment.

The X.500 specification discusses three models for name resolution:

- Chaining
- Multicasting
- Referral

The Chaining Model of Name Resolution

The X.500 specification describes *chaining* as a mode of interaction that may be used by one *Directory System Agent* (DSA) to pass on a request to another DSA, when the former DSA has knowledge about naming contexts held by the latter.

Figure 15.1 shows the chaining method of name resolution. In this figure, the *Directory User Agent* (DUA) refers to the network entity submitting a request, such as resolving a name. In NetWare 4.*x* networks, the DUA corresponds to an NDS client, such as a NetWare 4.*x* workstation submitting a request for resolving an NDS name. The DSA is the network entity within which the *Directory Information Base* (DIB) is stored and managed. In NetWare 4.*x* networks, the DSA corresponds to NetWare 4.*x* servers that store and manage the NDS database. In figure 15.1, the numbers associated with the interaction lines show the order of interactions.

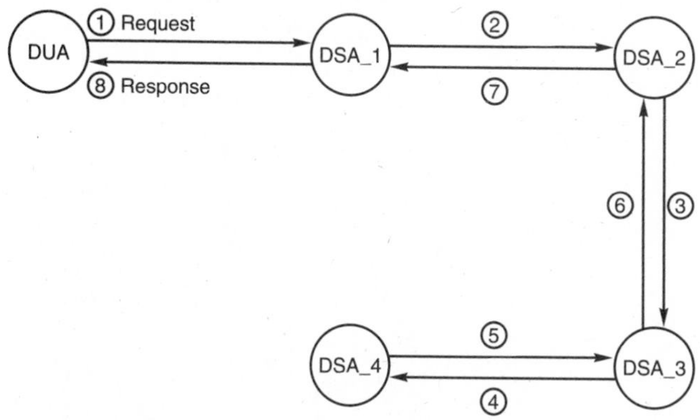

Figure 15.1
Chaining mode.

The DUA submits an object name and desires the address for the object. The original request goes to DSA_1, which cannot fulfill the request. DSA_1 contacts another DSA_2 that it thinks has the information. DSA_2 also cannot fulfill the request, and thus contacts DSA_3. This process continues until the object is finally located on DSA_4. In a NetWare 4.*x* network, the DSA_1, DSA_2, DSA_3, and DSA_4 directory system agents will be implemented in NetWare 4.*x* servers. DSA_4 returns the information on the physical location of the object back along the request chain until it is returned to the DUA client.

Multicasting Model for Name Resolution

The X.500 specification describes *multicasting* as a mode of interaction that may be used by a DSA to chain an identical request in parallel or sequential manner to one or more DSAs when the former DSA does not have complete knowledge about naming contexts held by the latter.

Figure 15.2 shows the multicasting method of name resolution done in parallel. In this figure, the numbers associated with the interaction lines show the order of interactions. In figure 15.2, the DUA submits an object name and desires the address for the object. The original request goes to DSA_1, which cannot fulfill the request. DSA_1 submits an identical request simultaneously (in parallel) to DSA_2, DSA_3, and DSA_4. Each of these DSAs sends back a response. DSA_1 uses the response returned by the DSAs to fulfill the original request.

Figure 15.2
Multicasting mode done in parallel.

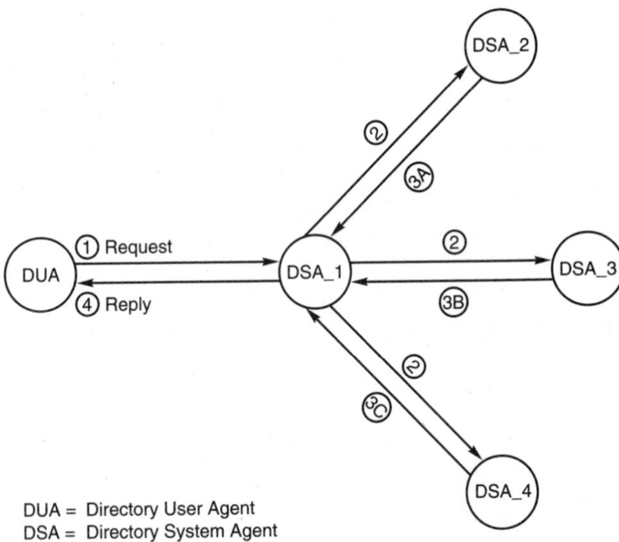

Figure 15.3 shows the multicasting method of name resolution done sequentially. In this figure, the numbers associated with the interaction lines show the order of interactions. In figure 15.3, the DUA submits an object name, and then wants the address for the object. The original request goes to DSA_1, which cannot fulfill the request. DSA_1 submits the request to DSA_2 and waits for a response. If the response is negative, the request is submitted to DSA_3. If DSA_3's response indicates a success in finding an answer to the request, the result is returned by DSA_1, and there is no need to send the request to DSA_4.

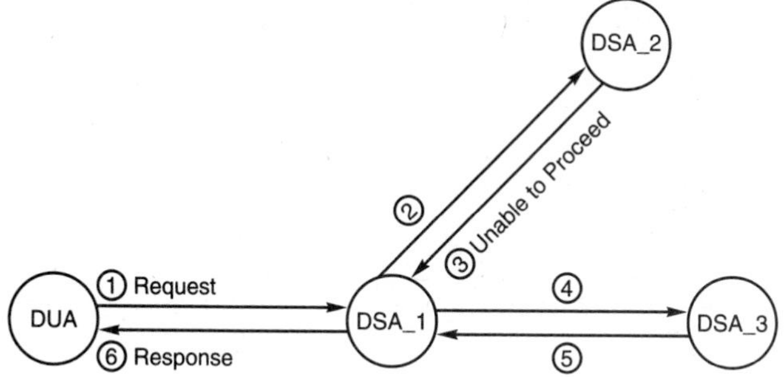

Figure 15.3
Multicasting mode done sequentially.

Referral Model for Name Resolution

The X.500 specification describes *referral* as a mode of interaction in which a referral to another DSA is returned instead of the desired response. The referral contains a knowledge reference to another DSA. A knowledge reference associates the object name (DIT entry, DIT = Directory Information Tree) with the DSA (NetWare 4.*x* server) in which it is located. The referral is then used by the requesting agent, either a DSA or a DUA (NetWare 4.*x* client workstation), to query another DSA.

If the requesting agent is a DSA agent, it must use the knowledge reference in the referral to chain or multicast the original request to other DSA. Figure 15.4 shows a DSA handling a referral response, and figure 15.5 shows a DUA handling a referral response. In these figures, the numbers associated with the interaction lines show the order of interactions.

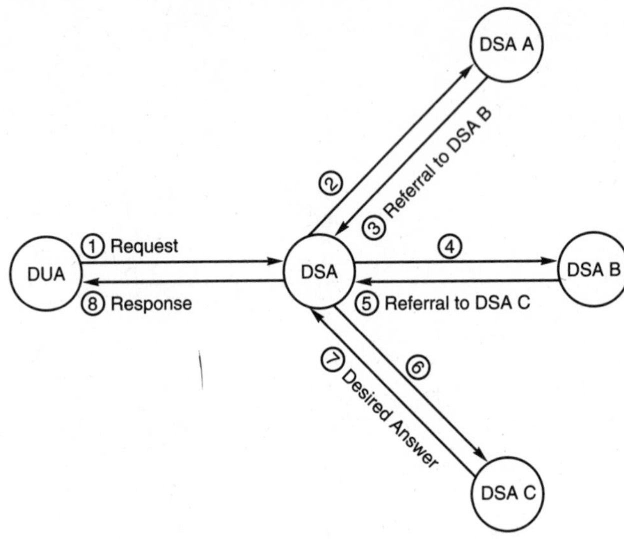

Figure 15.4
Referral mode—DSA makes requests.

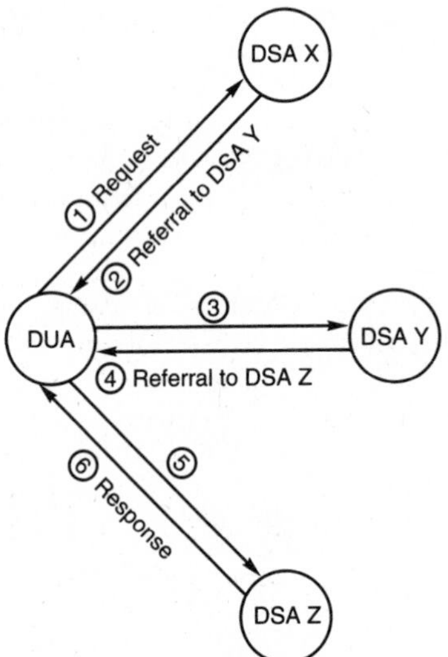

Figure 15.5
Referral mode—DUA makes requests.

Tree Walking in NetWare 4

NetWare 4 does not use chaining as a method of name resolution, but uses instead a sequential form of multicasting that may be combined with the referral mode. Figure 15.6 shows how NetWare 4 might perform name resolution.

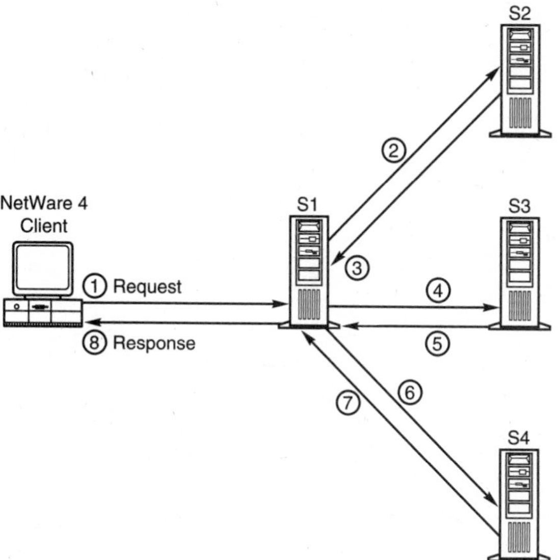

Figure 15.6
NetWare 4 Name Resolution.

The client makes the original request for the object from the DSA, server S1. Unable to fulfill the request, S1 contacts the server S2. Server S2 returns its lack of success to S1, which then contacts server S3. This continues until the object is located on S4. The information as to the location of the object is then returned to the client. Once requested to walk the tree on behalf of the client, the server S1 DSA does not chain the request through the next server, but waits for each server in turn to reply to its request. Rather than appearing as part of a chain of requests, S1 looks like the hub in a wheel; it is in charge of locating the object. S1 returns to the client the physical location of the object requested.

Specific Examples of Tree Walking

Figure 15.7 shows the object hierarchy of a directory tree, which will be used to illustrate tree walking. Three partitions are in the EXAMPLE_TREE—[Root], DEPT_C.ESL, and DEPT_E.DEPT_C.ESL. The partition boundaries are indicated in figure 15.7 by a dashed line. Figure 15.8 shows the physical view of the same tree—EXAMPLE_TREE. This figure shows what the actual object hierarchy looks like on each of the three servers. Server S1 has the Master replica of the partition [Root]. The partition object DEPT_C.ESL is a subordinate reference on S1. The Master replica of DEPT_C.ESL is located on server S2 with a subordinate reference of DEPT_E.DEPT_C.ESL. Server S3 has the Master replica of DEPT_E.DEPT_C.ESL. The external references on servers S2 and S3 are indicated by a dashed line.

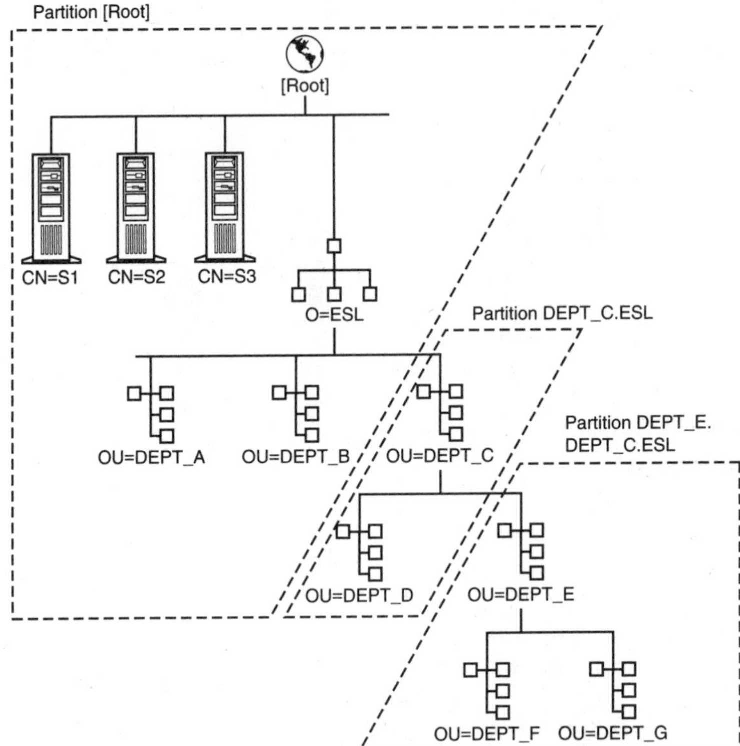

Figure 15.7
Object hierarchy of a directory tree.

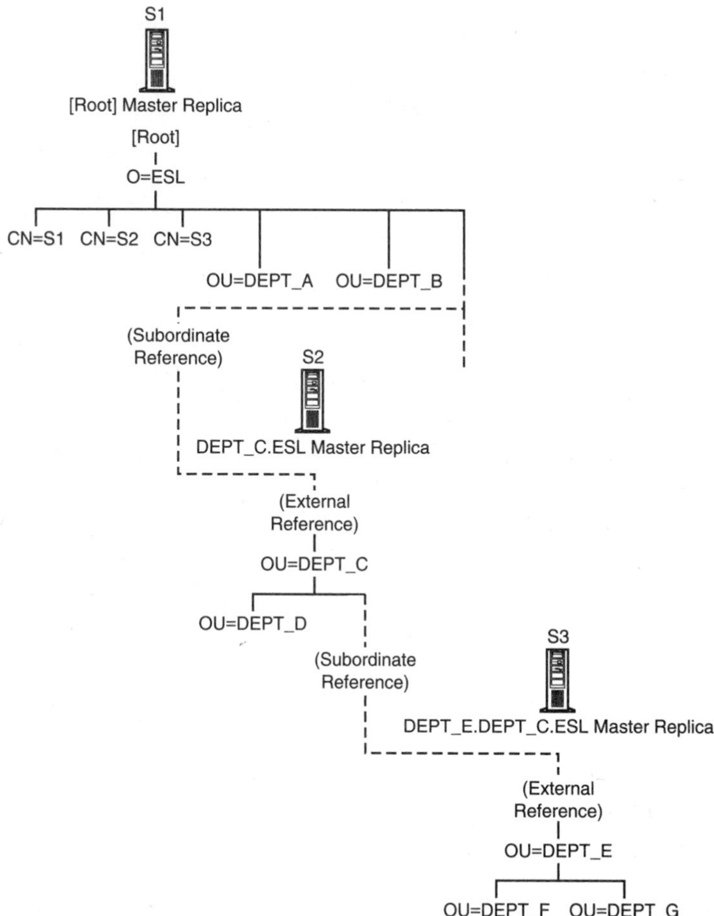

Figure 15.8
Replicas, Subordinate, and External References.

This tree is set up for illustration purposes only. This is not a useful tree design for fault tolerance purposes because only one copy (replica) exists for each partition.

Object Found on Initial Server

In the first example, the client is attached to server S2 (shown in figure 15.9) and is asking for the location of object DEPT_D.DEPT_C.ESL. Figure 15.9 shows that server S2 has a copy of the object DEPT_D.DEPT_C.ESL (S2 holds a replica of partition DEPT_C.ESL, in which DEPT_D.DEPT_C.ESL is located). S2 returns the physical location of DEPT_D.DEPT_C.ESL to the client. The physical location is the network address of the DSA S2.ESL that holds the desired object.

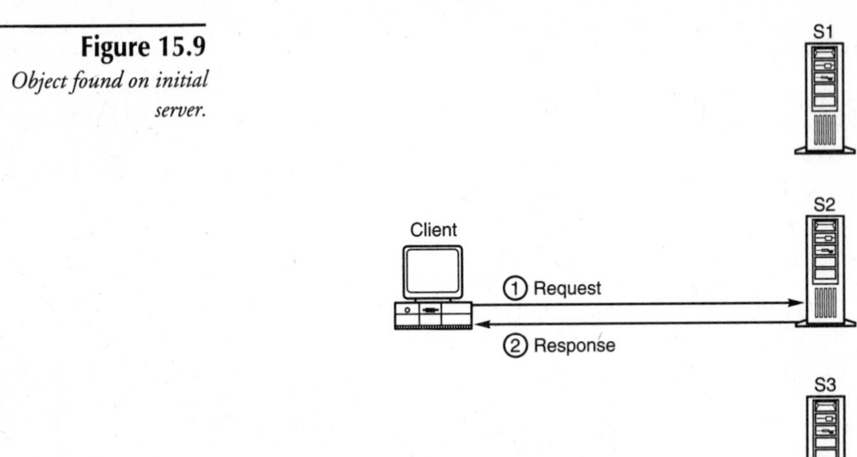

Figure 15.9
Object found on initial server.

Object Not Found on Initial Server

In the second example, the client is attached to server S2 (see fig. 15.10) and is asking for the location of object DEPT_F.DEPT_E.DEPT_C.ESL. S2 will check first to see if it has a copy of the object. Because that is not the case in this example, S2 must look on another server. These steps are followed:

1. From the replica pointer property of DEPT_E.DEPT_C.ESL (a Subordinate Reference) contained in partition object DEPT_C.ESL (see fig. 15.8), S2 finds the address of server S3.

2. S2 contacts server S3.

3. S3 verifies to S2 it has a copy of the desired object DEPT_F.DEPT_E.DEPT_C.ESL.

4. S2 returns to the client the physical location of DEPT_F.DEPT_E.DEPT_C.ESL. This is the network address of S3, the DSA that has a copy of the desired object.

5. The client connects to server S3 for access to the information associated with DEPT_F.DEPT_E.DEPT_C.ESL.

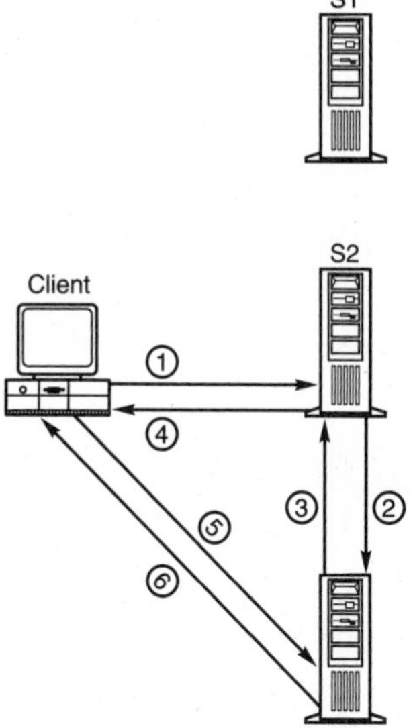

Figure 15.10
Object not found on initial server.

This example shows that NDS performs a referral mode operation to resolve the name.

Walking Up the Tree

The previous example illustrates how the subordinate reference might be used to locate an object lower in the tree. The subordinate reference also is used in walking up the tree. Consider the example of the client request again going to server S2, and the object requested is [Root]. S2 does not have a copy of [Root], so it must walk the tree on behalf of the client. Remember that subordinate reference replicas reflect servers that hold the partition root object (parent or superior partition), but not the child (subordinate) partition. In this case, [Root] is the superior partition and DEPT_C.ESL. is the child partition. Looking at the replica pointers of the partition DEPT_C.ESL, the subordinate reference replica type indicates there is a subordinate reference of DEPT_C.ESL—and therefore a replica of its parent partition—on server S1. Server S2 knows the location of a server (S1) that contains partitions higher in the tree. Server S2 is able to contact server S1 looking for the object [Root]. The physical location of the object [Root] then is returned to the client.

This is a simplistic example because there is only one replica of each partition. If a server does not have a replica of the object being requested by another server, it also returns additional addresses at which the object might be found.

As a user logs in to a NetWare 4 directory tree, the name service locates a writable copy of the user's object. Because the name service is concerned with the physical location of the object, the user need not be.

Name Resolution While Logging In to the Network

Clients log in to a network to use the services provided by the network. The login process makes use of name resolution. The process and end result of logging in are described in this section.

Logging In—Bindery-Based Servers

As the user of a bindery-based server logs in, the following happens:

1. User JOHN enters "login NW4CS/JOHN" as he logs in to the bindery-based server NW4CS from his DOS workstation using the utility LOGIN.EXE.

2. The NetWare shell locates the server NW4CS using the bindery of the server to which it attached during the bootup of the client workstation.

3. The utility first tries to log in to NW4CS without a password. If that fails, JOHN is prompted to enter his password.

4. If the password is correct, JOHN is considered logged in to the server NW4CS. His security equivalencies (any object on the server that has the same rights as JOHN) are calculated and stored in the connection table, along with his user name and his workstation's address.

5. LOGIN.EXE then executes John's login script.

If JOHN wishes to use the file system on the bindery-based server ATHENA, he uses the utility MAP.EXE and enters "map h:=ATHENA/sys:" on the command line. Steps 2, 3, and 4 also are executed by MAP.EXE. Notice that the only differences are the name of the utility used, and that the login script is not executed in the case of MAP.EXE. The end result is the same: the bindery-based server NW4CS and the bindery-based ATHENA know the identity and the rights (security equivalencies) of the user object JOHN. He now is able to use the services (file and print) provided by these two servers.

Conceptually, the process of logging in can be viewed as that of establishing an identity with the server. At the end of the login process, the server knows the name and the address of the client requesting services. The client's security equivalencies also have been established.

John's user name and password on the server NW4CS might be different than his user name and password on the server ATHENA. All the information about JOHN (login script, last login time, passwords used, security equivalencies, and so on) is stored independently on each of these servers.

Logging In—NetWare 4 Servers

For the purposes of the following discussion, the NetWare 4 servers being referred to form a single object hierarchy or tree. The name of the organization is ESL, and the name of the tree is ENET. The object hierarchy is shown in figure 15.11. This is a small tree with one user, Admin.ESL. Figure 15.12 shows the physical location of the data associated with the object hierarchy.

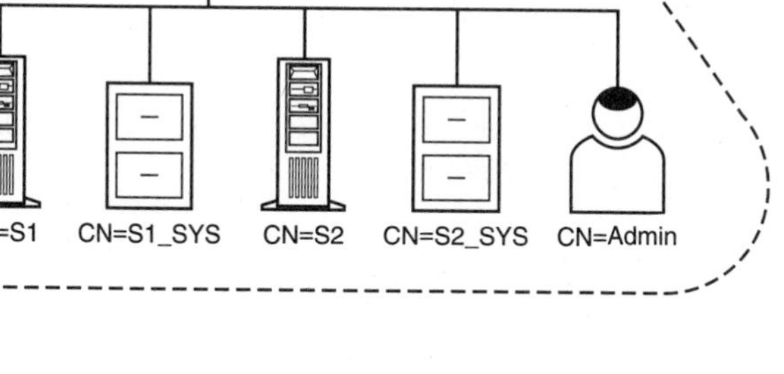

Figure 15.11
The logical view of the ENET tree.

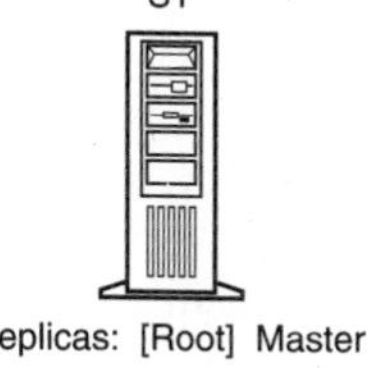

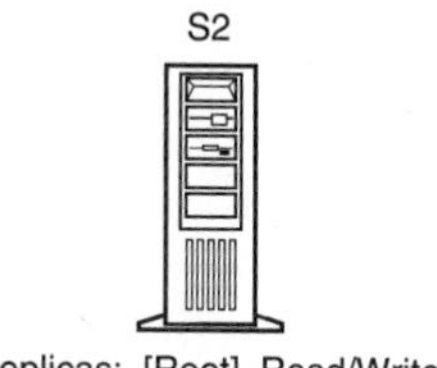

Figure 15.12
Replicas in the ENET tree.

When Admin.ESL logs in to the network, the following happens:

1. User Admin enters "login admin" on the command line as he logs in to the tree ENET from his DOS workstation using the utility LOGIN.EXE.

2. The NetWare DOS Requester locates the server S1 which first answers the broadcast for any server in the tree ENET during the bootup of the client workstation.

3. Using the name context (O=ESL) in the NET.CFG located at Admin's workstation, LOGIN.EXE uses Directory Services—the name service in NetWare 4—to locate the object Admin.ESL. Figure 15.12 shows that S1 has a copy of the object Admin.ESL.

4. Using the connection to S1, LOGIN.EXE tries to log in as "Admin.ESL" with no password. If that fails, Admin is prompted to enter his password.

5. If the password is correct, Admin is considered logged in to the tree, ESL. His network address is added as a property to the object Admin.ESL. His last login time and login time properties are updated to reflect the current login. Because an object's properties are modified during the login process, a writable replica of the object logging in must be available. These property modifications are synchronized to the replica on server S1.

Having proved knowledge of the password, the authentication materials necessary for proving his identity to other servers in the tree are sent to the workstation.

6. The workstation now has all the pieces necessary to authenticate connections to any server in the ESL tree. LOGIN.EXE now authenticates the connection to S1. Admin's user name and workstation addresses are stored in the connection table on the server S1. In addition, Admin's security equivalencies are calculated for use in the connection table.

7. The commands in the login script now can be executed.

If Admin.ESL wishes to use the file system on S2, he enters "map h:=S2_SYS" at the command line. The utility MAP.EXE uses the directory to locate S2_SYS.ESL, connect to the server S2, and authenticate the connection to S2. Admin is not prompted for a password. The authentication process uses the material received during the login to generate the proof of identity to the server. Once again, the end result is the same. The identity of Admin.ESL has been proven to the server S2. The name, network address, and security equivalencies are stored in the connection table of S2.

On bindery-based servers, the process of establishing an identity with the server is called logging in to the server. In NetWare 4, the same process is called *authenticating* to a server. The end result of the process of authentication is the same as that of login in bindery-based servers: the client is identified to the server. The client's name and workstation address are stored in the server's connection table along with the client's security equivalencies, which were calculated by the name service (Directory Services, in the case of NetWare 4).

Differences in the process of logging between NetWare 4 servers and bindery-based servers include the following:

- Users of NetWare 4 do not need to be concerned with the physical location of resources. Directory Services provides this service through walking the tree, as described earlier.
- NetWare 4 login is network-wide, not server-centric.
- After the initial login, users are not prompted for user names and passwords (as long as they are using services in the same tree). The materials necessary to generate proof of identity to servers are stored on the client's workstation.

Using an Upgrade Tip

During the process of upgrading from 3.*x* and 2.*x*, it is possible to encounter the following:

- A user has bindery accounts on two servers.
- The two servers get upgraded into a NetWare 4 Directory tree.
- The user now has two unique names in the tree.

For example, after the upgrade, John.Marketing.Apex and John.Engineerig.Apex represent the same user. (John had user accounts on two servers upgraded into different contexts in the tree.) NetWare 4 permits each user in the network of servers to be represented by the same object. During the upgrade process, however, some duplication of objects might exist. An administrator could remove duplicate entries when time permits.

A potential problem, however, during the period of time in which multiple objects exist for the same user is to make changes in reference to one object and have the results show up on the other object.

In this example, John logs in and does his work as the object John.Engineering.Apex. John needs rights to SYS:SYSTEM on the server Mktg1. Container Admin.Marketing.Apex maps a drive to SYS:SYSTEM on the server Mktg1 and enters on the command line: "RIGHTS . R F /NAME=John". The context of Container Admin is set to Marketing.Apex. John then tries to map a drive to SYS:SYSTEM on Mktg1 and receives the message that volume SYS: does not exist on Mktg1.

The problem here is that the object that was granted the file system rights is John.Marketing.Apex, because Container Admin typed "John" and the name was completed using the context, Marketing.Apex.

Container Admin.Marketing.Apex should enter "RIGHTS . R F /NAME=John.Engineering." on the command line. Also, the object John.Marketing.Apex should be deleted because it is not being used and is causing some confusion. The "." following Engineering is important here. It causes the name context to be shortened from "Marketing.Apex" to "Apex".

Using the Same Tree as a Different User

At any one time, a workstation supports a single login to a directory tree; this is because only one set of authentication information can be stored in the workstation. This authentication information is used for the background authentication.

It is sometimes desirable, however, to be able to log in to the same tree as more than one user. You can do that by using bindery emulation for the second login. As an example, Joe.Eng.ABC is logged in to the ABC_TREE. He needs to temporarily access an application on the server IS1, also in the ABC_TREE. Joe.Eng.ABC does not have any rights on IS1, but there is a well-known user object, IS_User, on the server IS1. IS_User has no password and limited file rights on the server.

Joe can use the NetWare 4 LOGIN.EXE to gain IS_User's rights on the server IS1 by entering "login is1/is_user /ns /b" on the command line. This is equivalent to ATTACH.EXE in 3.*x* and 2.*x* versions of NetWare. The "/ns" option tells LOGIN not to execute the login script. The "/b" option tells LOGIN to use bindery emulation.

Understanding Server Objects

NCP Server is an object class defined in the base schema of NetWare 4. Objects whose base class is NCP Server represent the servers in the Directory Services hierarchy or tree. As each server is installed into a tree, an object is created in that object hierarchy that represents the server. Each server in the tree also is given a version property that describes the version of NetWare 4 running on that server. "[DS]" is added to the end of the version string at the time of installation.

It is possible to add through the administrative utilities 3.*x*, 2.*x*, and even other NetWare 4 servers as objects in the tree. Please note that while these servers appear in the tree as NCP server objects, they were not added through the installation process but rather through an administrative utility. These objects also have a version property. However, "[DS]" does not appear at the end of the version string on these servers.

It follows, therefore, that all NetWare 4 servers installed into an object hierarchy or tree have "[DS]" appended to the version property. These servers can be thought of as all belonging to the same tree. Server objects that do not belong to the same tree ("non tree" servers) are not important in the operation of the directory.

Server objects in the tree are very important to the operation of Directory Services. The names and addresses of the server objects are used to keep track of the physical location of the replicas. A property of partitions objects (replica pointer) contains the name and address of the server on which the replica is located.

A server object can be moved to another location in the tree by using an administrative utility, such as NETADMIN.EXE or NWADMIN.EXE. The server's *relative distinguished name*, or leaf portion of the name (RDN) can be changed only in the AUTOEXEC.NCF file located in SYS:SYSTEM on the server itself. The server's internal address can be modified in the same manner. In order for these changes to take place, the server must be downed and brought back up again. The server itself then takes care of notifying the directory hierarchy of the name and/or address change.

Servers in a NetWare 4 tree should be thought of as part of a system of servers rather than as an isolated server. Although servers and links might go down, synchronization cannot complete until all the servers involved have been updated. In addition, partition and replication operations require that all the servers be contacted in order to successfully conclude. Hardware failure may necessitate removing a server from the system.

One very useful option of NetWare 4 Directory Services is the capability to have a server that contains no replicas. External references make this possible. Because a Read Write replica is required for bindery emulation, servers with no replicas will not be available for bindery emulation. It is also important to observe the following:

- The server does not need to hold a replica of its own object.
- Bindery emulation does not require that the server's bindery emulation context contain the server's own object.

Servers as Clients

Clients of the network are usually considered users accessing services from a workstation. NetWare 4 adds another dimension to this model, as the servers themselves become clients of other servers in the tree. Servers use the same authentication protocol as the more traditional clients in identifying themselves to other servers. Because the object hierarchy is distributed as well as replicated, one server might need directory information held by another server in order to fulfill a request.

Rebuilding Replicas

Both the partition management utilities NWADMIN.EXE and PARTMGR.EXE have an option labeled "Rebuild Replicas." This option is necessary to correct a specific condition in NetWare 4 Directory Services. That condition occurs when the SET command is used on a server's console to set time back. This condition manifests itself with a certain error return from the server—`0XFD6D` or `-659`.

As modifications to the NDS objects are made by a client, a timestamp is issued by the server where the modification took place. This timestamp is part of the information maintained by each server for each replica located on the server. If a server "issues a timestamp" for a replica of a partition at a certain time (10/12/94 05:15:05, for example) and then the time on that server is set back to 10/10/94 10:14:12, no further modifications to that replica may be made until the server's time reaches and exceeds the previously issued timestamp (10/12/94 05:15:05). The reason is that issuing timestamps for a previous point in time might duplicate a timestamp that already had been issued.

The "Rebuild Replicas" option will correct this condition. This is a significant network operation. The Master replica re-timestamps every object in the replica being rebuilt. This means that a new timestamp is issued for every object and every property of every object in the entire partition. The Master replica then resends all the objects (with their new timestamps) to every replica.

During the time the Master replica is resynchronizing the objects in the replica, there is a period of time on the other replicas that the objects appear as having base class Unknown. These objects act as placeholders for the "real" object—the name and creation time of the object is known, but the property information has been deleted to be replaced with the data received from the Master. When the "real" object is received from the Master replica, the "real" object will take the place of the placeholder object.

This option also causes the partition creation time to increase. The *partition creation time* is a property of every partition object. It has two parts: the instance of the partition and the replica number where the instance was created. Remember that each replica is given a number when the replica is created. When a partition is initially created, the instance of the partition is 1 and the replica number is 1. If the Rebuild Replicas option were to be executed, the instance would be incremented to 2.

It is possible to change the replica type of a replica on a server through the partition management utilities. Replica 4 could be made the Master replica. If the "Rebuild Replicas" option was executed after this change in replica types, the instance of the partition would be 3 and the replica number 4.

Note that the replica number is used internally by NetWare 4 Directory Services. It is not visible to clients through the utilities, and is only useful for those interested in understanding the underlying technology of the product. Clients see the logical presentation of the tree—as an object hierarchy—and need not be concerned with the internals, such as timestamps, partition creation time, replica number, and so on.

Summary

In this chapter, you learned how name resolution is performed according to X.500 specifications, and how NetWare 4 implements name resolution. NetWare Directory Services is a name service. One of the functions of this name service is to find the physical location of objects so that clients can be concerned with the names of objects rather than their physical location. Resolving an object returns to the client the physical location of that object. This process relies on a property of partition objects called the replica pointer—a list of replica locations by server name and server address. Because the directory uses the name and address of servers to locate objects, the object representing the server is very important.

Clients use the process of name resolution during the login as they identify themselves (authenticate) to servers in a directory tree.

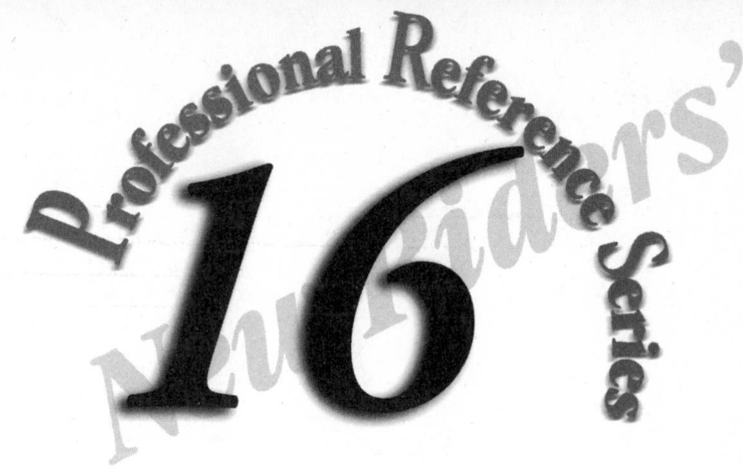

NetWare Directory Services Partitions

This chapter presents the mechanisms used to store and manage the NDS database on the server. You are introduced to the concept of partitions and replicas and how they can be used to improve fault tolerance of the NDS database. You will learn about the different replica types that can exist, replica synchronization, and the rules for creating replicas on NetWare servers. You also will learn about the NetWare tools that can be used to manage replicas and partitions.

Understanding NDS Partitions and Replicas

The NDS database that represents an NDS tree must physically reside on a storage volume. There are two options to consider regarding where this NDS database should be kept:

- Should the entire NDS database be centralized?
- Should you take subsets of the NDS database and distribute the database? If the database is distributed, what factors should determine how it is to be distributed?

If the NDS database is kept at a central location, a failure in the network at the central location would make the NDS database unavailable to the entire network. For small LANs, the issue of centralization is not of much concern. For large networks that are separated by Wide Area Network links, having a single NDS database becomes a single point-of-failure problem.

You should distribute the database in such a manner that a single failure does not disable the entire NDS service. The logical division (subset) of an NDS database is called a *partition.* The partition contains the resources and the organizational structure of a portion of the NDS tree. The partition does not contain any information on the file system structure of a network volume.

NDS partitions can be used to divide the NDS database logically. Because the NDS database has the logical structure of a tree, partitioning divides the NDS database into subtrees, with each partition storing NDS objects of that subtree. The partition is often described in terms of its *Parent container* or its *Root container.* The Parent container of a partition is the top container (root) of the subtree that it represents. A partition's Parent container defines the boundary of that partition.

Figure 16.1 shows an NDS tree that is logically divided into three partitions. The Parent containers of the three partitions are [Root], OU=SALES, and OU=ENG. These Parent containers are the root of the subtree for their partition.

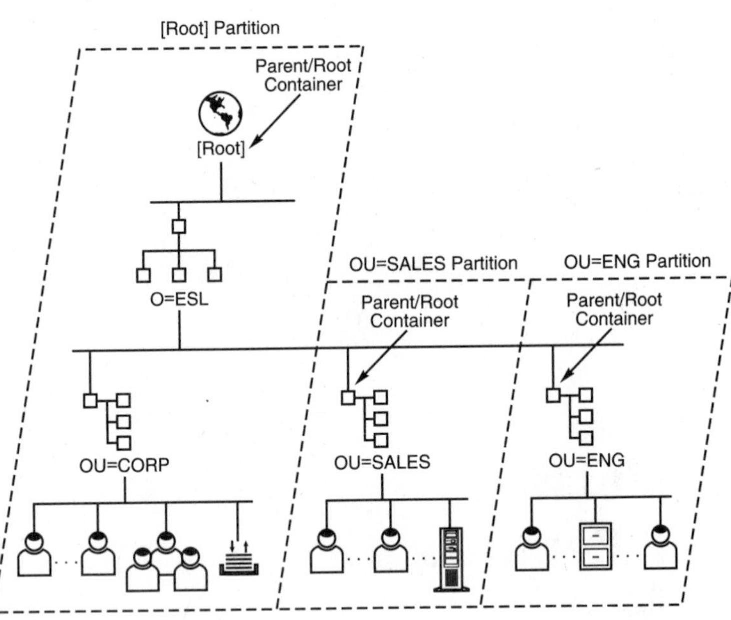

Figure 16.1
Logical division of a tree into partitions.

A partition is stored at a NetWare server's volume. In figure 16.1, the partition for [Root] is stored on the server FSC.ESL, the partition for OU=SALES is stored on the server FSS.SALES.ESL, and the partition for OU=ENG is stored on server FSE.ENG.ESL.

When talking about the location where a partition is stored, it is quite common to refer to the partition as being stored on a server, although a more accurate description would be that the partition is stored on a server's volume. Partitioning allows the distribution of the NDS database across the network. An advantage of distributing the NDS database is that if a server goes down, only the NDS information stored in the partition being stored on the downed server is unavailable. As you will learn later, you can minimize the risk of losing this NDS information by keeping duplicate copies of the partition at other locations.

At the introduction of NetWare 4.0, Novell recommended that a partition should not contain more than 500 objects. Later releases have increased this limit to 100,000 objects per partition.

Partitions can help the NDS performance by:

- Dividing NDS databases so that each NDS database serves local users
- Reducing the need for NDS searches and lookups to be performed over the slower Wide Area Links

Figure 16.2 shows an NDS database that is split into two partitions, with each partition residing on a server volume on LAN segments separated by a slow Wide Area Link. In this case, most of the NDS lookups and searches are done against the local NDS partition, without having to go over the slow Wide Area Link.

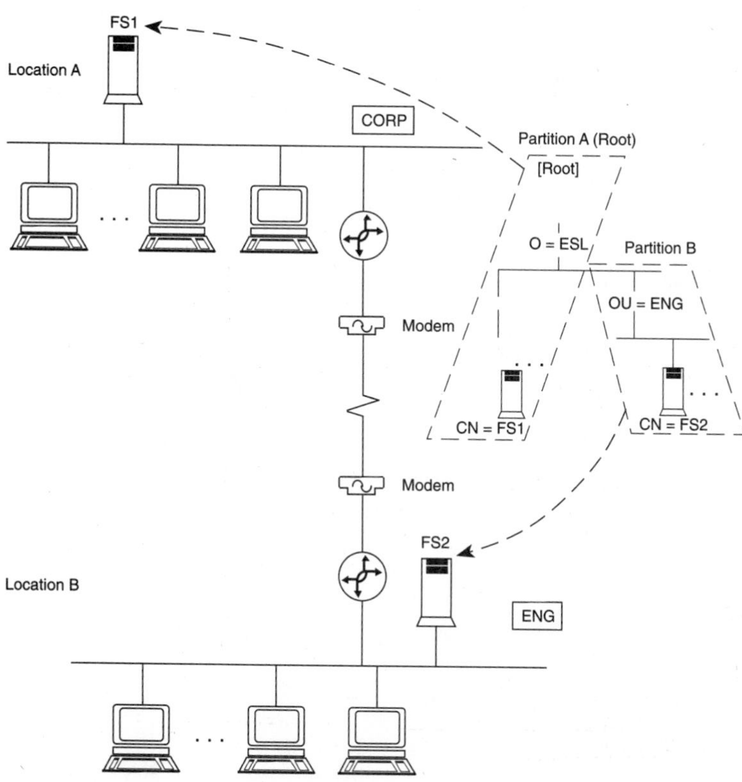

Figure 16.2
NDS partitions across a Wide Area Link.

A problem can arise with the example in figure 16.2. What if the storage volume or file server on which the NDS partition resides crashes? Then, the portion of the NDS that is implemented by the NDS partition is unavailable, and users are not able to access the resources represented by the failed NDS partition. To solve this problem, a technique called *replication* can be used.

Replication consists of keeping a copy of an NDS partition at another location. The copy of the partition is called a *replica* of the partition. The replica is kept at a strategic location on another NetWare 4.*x* server. In figure 16.3, Location A keeps a copy of the NDS partition for Location B on its NetWare 4.*x* server, and Location B keeps a copy of the NDS partition for Location A on its NetWare 4.*x* server. If a user at Location A tries to access resources described by the NDS database in Location B, and if the remote server at Location B is temporarily unavailable or the Wide Area Link is down, the NDS queries for objects at the remote location serviced by the replica stored on the server at Location A.

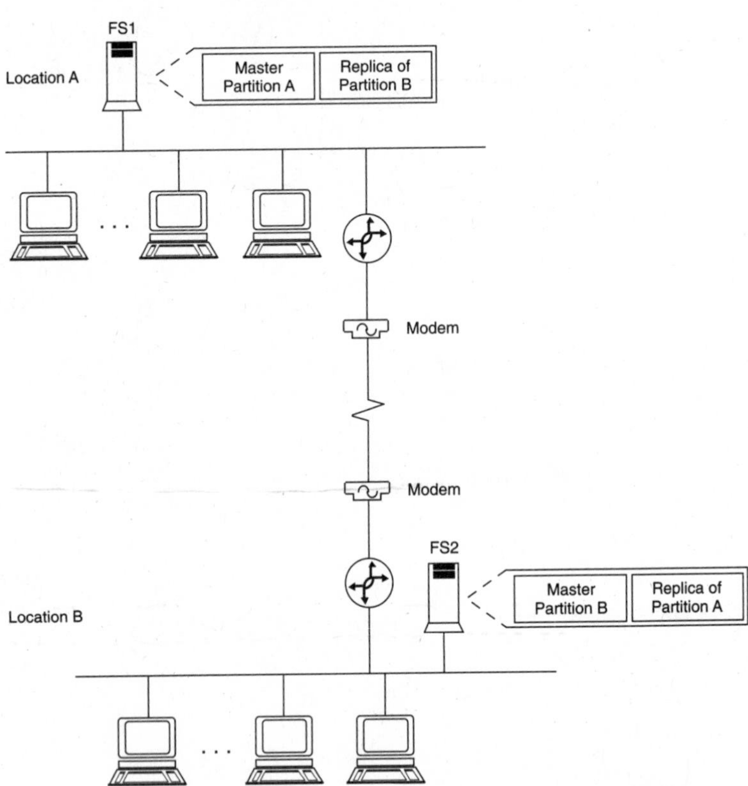

Figure 16.3
NDS replicas across a Wide Area Link.

The previous example illustrates that replicas provide fault tolerance for the NDS database by providing online backup copies of a partition. This eliminates any single point of failure for the NDS database and provides fault tolerance in the NDS database. Without replication, if a server containing the NDS partition goes down, the NDS objects in that partition are no longer available. Because access to most network resources is provided through NDS objects, these network resources are not available.

There is no limit to the number of replicas that may be established for each partition. Having a large number of replicas for a partition, however, means that the synchronization overhead can be excessive when a replica is modified. As a matter of practicality, you should limit the number of replicas to no more than 8 to 10 per partition. You also should limit the number of replicas on a particular server to 8.

The first server on the network contains the [Root] partition and typically receives a replica of all new partitions that are installed. Making the [Root] server your fastest computer improves the performance of NDS operations carried out on the [Root] server. The context in which a server is placed in a partition has no bearing on the performance of NDS operations or the type of replicas it can contain. Servers anywhere in the NDS tree can contain any type of replica.

Another advantage of using replicas is that NDS queries for objects at remote locations can be satisfied by the local replica. This makes it possible for a user logging in to a network to be authenticated by information in the local replica. If the NDS partition at the remote location changes as a result of new objects added or old objects deleted, the NDS partitions can synchronize themselves by sending only the *new* information that has changed. This is a much more efficient way of doing NDS lookups and maintaining consistency of the NDS database.

Partitions represent logical portions of the NDS database *that can be copied,* and replicas are the physical parts of the NDS database *that are copied.*

Replicas thus provide the following advantages:

- Increased NDS fault tolerance and reduced risk of any single point of failure
- Fast access to NDS services across slow Wide Area Links
- Login access to the network, even when some NetWare servers are unavailable

Essentially, replication provides fault tolerance for the NDS, but does not provide fault tolerance for the file system.

Recognizing Types of NDS Partitions

Because a replica is a copy of the NDS partition, NDS makes the following distinctions for replicas:

- Master replica
- Read Only replica
- Read Write replica

Master Replica

The *Master replica* is the original partition that is created for representing a subset of the NDS database. The Master replica contains the *authority* for the objects defined on it. All other replicas must defer to information contained in the Master replica; that is, the Master replica, by definition, contains the most recent information, and there can be only one Master replica per partition. This replica is used by the NDS synchronization mechanism to update all other replicas. All other replicas are created from the Master replica.

A Master replica is created when an NDS partition is first created, and resides on the NetWare server on which the partition is created. The Master replica is the source used to create all other replicas for that partition, and for making updates to other replicas. If the partition has to be redefined, you can do so only by redefining the Master replica. A restructuring of the Master replica causes other replicas of the partition to be deleted automatically and new replicas of the Master partition to be created.

Figure 16.4 shows the Master replica for the [Root] partition. It shows that the replica stored on server CN=NW4KS.OU=CORP.O=ESL is of type Master. In this example, the [Root] partition contains only one Server object (CN=NW4KS.OU=CORP.O=ESL). When a partition contains only one Server object, there are no additional replicas for that partition unless you create one. If a new Server object is placed in the same partition as the server that contains the Master replica, the new Server object will have the option of copying a Read Write partition of the Master replica.

Figure 16.4
Master replica.

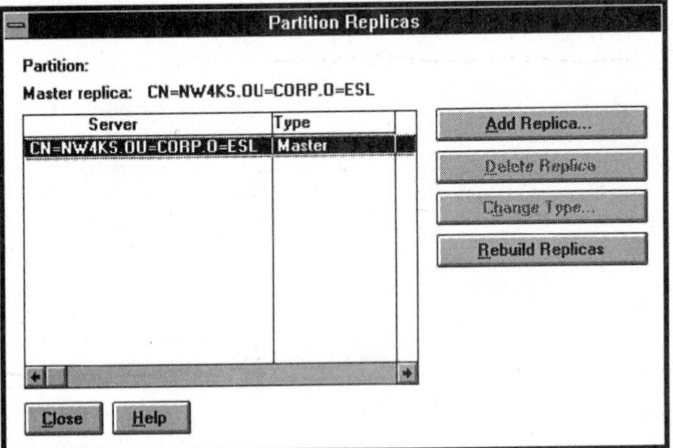

Read Only Replica

A *Read Only replica* contains a copy of the Master replica that cannot be modified by ordinary users. The Read Only replica can be the recipient of update information from the Master replica or the Read Write replica. The Read Only replica cannot initiate changes on its own, however.

Read Only replicas are similar to the concept of yellow pages on other directory systems and can be used for searching for information. The Read Only replica is used as a database that can be queried against, but it cannot be used for logging into the network because that modifies the NDS tree. For instance, the Network Address property of the User object is altered to contain the station address of the workstation that the user is using. Also, the Last Login property of the User object is modified to contain the date and timestamp of the last login.

16

Read Write Replica

A *Read Write* replica is a copy of the Master replica and can be used to update the NDS database and provide information to NDS queries. NDS objects in the Read Write replica can be modified, deleted, or created. When these changes are made to a Read Write replica, it generates update traffic to modify other Read Write replicas and the Master replica. Changes made to the Read Write replica result in directory synchronization network traffic that is sent to all replicas of the corresponding partition.

If the Master replica becomes corrupt, the Read Write replica can be used to re-create it. For this reason, it is advisable to have several Read Write replicas of a partition. You cannot split or merge a partition using Read Write replicas. Only the Master replica, because it has authority for the partition, can be used for restructuring a partition. Examples of restructuring a partition are splitting a partition and merging partitions into a single partition.

Because the Read Write replica is modifiable, it can, unlike the Read Only replica, be used for logging in to the network.

Figure 16.5 shows the three replica types. The Master replica is on the CN=NW4CS.OU=CORP.O=ESL server, the Read Write replica is on the CN=NW4KS.OU=CORP.O=ESL server, and the Read Only replica is on the CN=NW4KS.OU=ENG.O=ESL server.

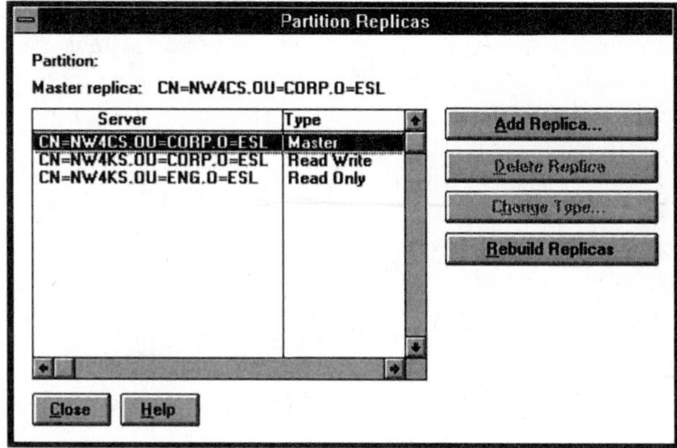

Figure 16.5
Master replica, Read Write replica, and Read Only replica.

Replica Ring

The servers that hold the replica of a given partition are called the *replica ring* for that partition. Figure 16.6 shows a replica ring for a partition OU=CORP. This replica ring consists of servers FSC.ESL, FSS.SALES.ESL, and FSE.ENG.ESL. Server FSC.ESL holds the Master partition for [Root], and servers FSS.SALES.ESL and FSE.ENG.ESL hold the Read Write replica for the [Root] partition.

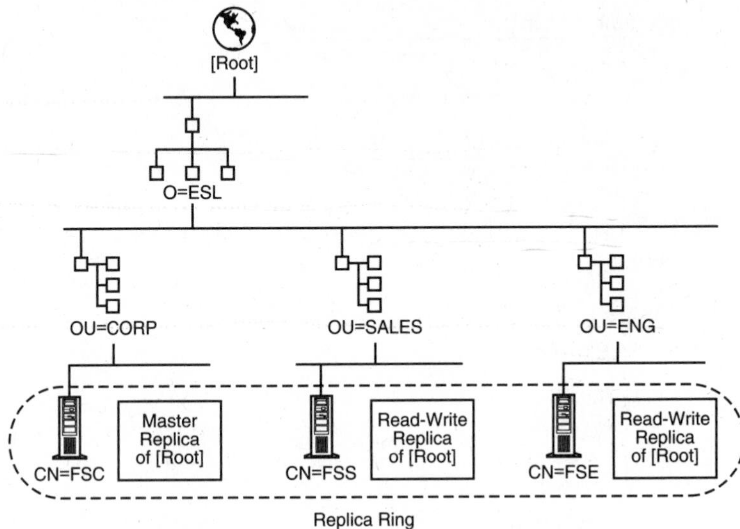

Figure 16.6
Replica ring.

Changes made to any replica, such as the Read Write replica on server FSE.ENG.ESL, must be sent to the other servers, FSC.ESL and FSS.SALES.ESL, that make up the replica ring for the [Root] partition. If a server is down when the changes are initiated, it is unable to receive the changes. The members of a replica ring still will initiate changes, regardless of the status of other members of the replica ring. If a server that is down is brought up again, its replica is synchronized to the Master replica.

If the servers of the replica ring are down during ordinary NDS changes, such as NDS object deletion, creation, or modification, they can be resynchronized when they are brought up again. However, if major changes such as partition splitting and merging are being attempted, all servers in a replica ring should be online and reachable through the network for the changes to be successful.

If a server in a replica ring must be taken down during a split/merge of the partition, you must perform the following precautionary tasks:

- If the server holds a Read Write or Read Only replica, you should delete this replica.
- If the server holds a Master replica, you should make this a Read Write replica. Because the split/merge can be done only through a Master replica, you have to make another Read Write replica the Master replica.

Designing Partitions

When designing partitions, you should be aware of the following rules for partitions and replicas:

- Partitions can be created only at the container level of the NDS tree.
- You do not have to have a replica of the entire NDS database at any location, because the NDS database is designed to be usable in partitions. The Master replica of a partition can be split into smaller partitions.
- A NetWare server can hold only one replica type of a partition. An attempt to store another replica of a partition on a server that already holds a replica of that partition will be denied (see fig. 16.7). Also, it is not essential for a NetWare server to have a replica.
- There can be only one Master replica for a partition and any number of other replica types for the partition.

```
135: The master replica is already located on this
server and another replica of this partition can not
be created on server NW4KS.CORP. Error code: FD70.
            Press <Enter> to continue.
```

Figure 16.7
Denial of an attempt to store more than one replica of a partition on a server.

Partitions should be created to organize the NDS database in logical manageable units that provide easy and efficient access. You should use replicas for partitions to increase the fault tolerance of an NDS database. Fault tolerance is important for preserving the integrity of a database, in case the server where a partition is maintained is not available.

You should take into account the following factors when designing partitions and replicas for improving fault tolerance and efficient access:

- Location of replicas
- Number of replicas
- Size of replicas
- Expensive/low-speed WAN links

Replicas should be located at strategic locations to improve fault tolerance and provide efficient access. To protect yourself from natural disasters that can plague a site (lightning or fire, for example), you should consider placing replicas on servers at different geographic locations (see fig.16.8). This provides a high level of fault tolerance. Storing replicas at a single geographic location provides a relatively low degree of fault tolerance (see fig. 16.9). As a practical consideration, you also should backup the NDS database frequently. This can be done using SBACKUP.

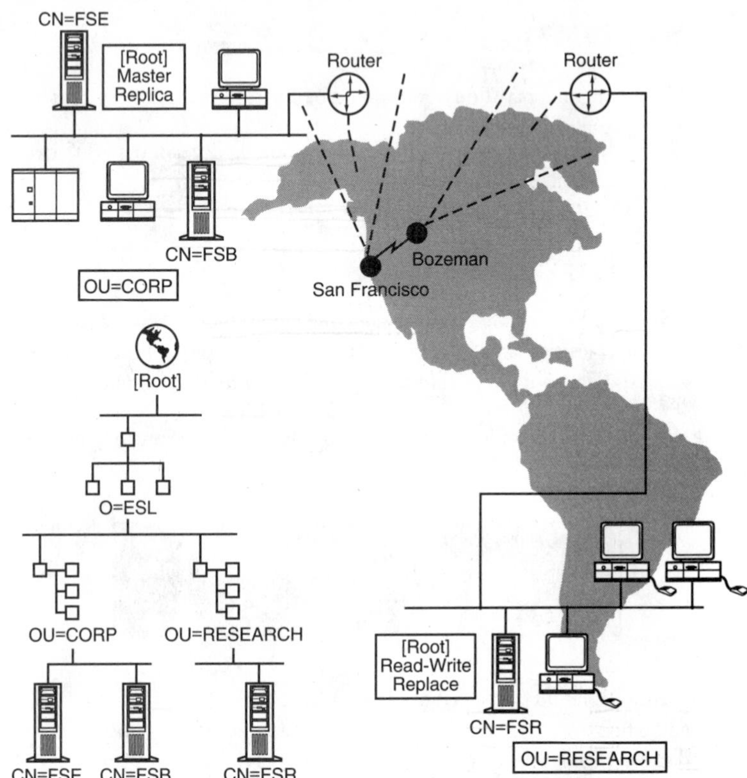

Figure 16.8
High degree of fault tolerance.

If network resources are used for the most part by a certain group of users, those user objects and their resources should be kept in the same partition. Figure 16.10 shows a partition where users and the network resources they use are in the same partition. Figure 16.11 shows an example of a poor design, where users and their network resources are in different partitions. If the users and their network resources are in different partitions, additional traffic is generated to access these resources. If the replicas are separated by a slow and/or expensive wide area link, it further compounds the problem. If users need frequent access to a partition at a remote location, they should consider storing a replica of the partition on the user's local server to avoid traffic over the wide area link. Figure 16.12 shows a solution to the problem in figure 16.11, by keeping a Read Write replica of the partition containing network resources local to the users who need to access them.

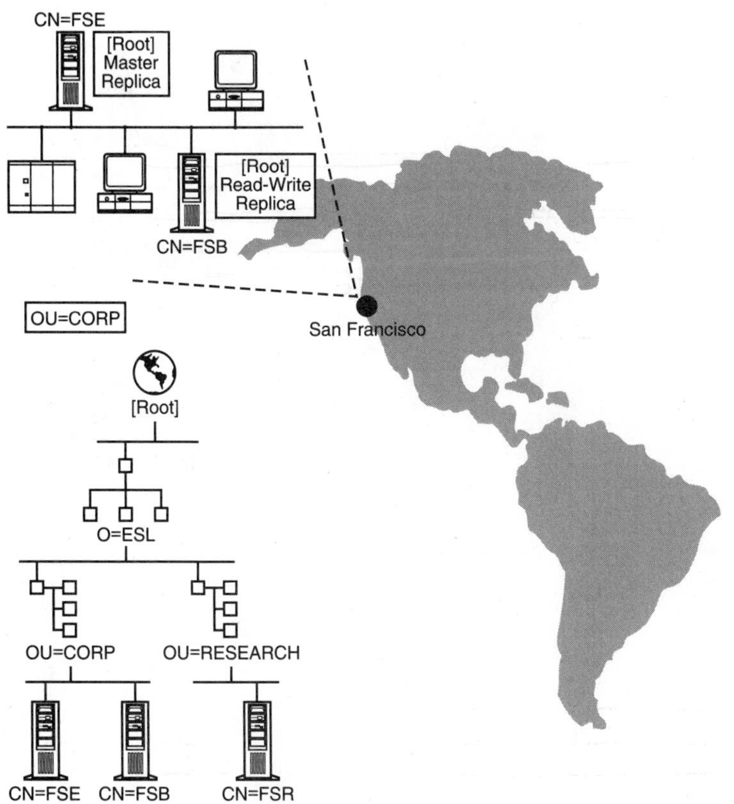

Figure 16.9
Low degree of fault tolerance.

As the number of replicas of a partition increase, so does the fault tolerance of that partition. This should be balanced against the fact that as the number of replicas increases, so does the amount of network traffic to keep the servers in the replica ring properly synchronized. Each replica also takes up storage space on the server on which it resides. The average number of replicas on a server can be 4 to 5, but should not exceed 8.

You should consider carefully the locations where critical replicas should be kept. If Master replicas are on servers in disaster-prone cities, you should try to select another city that is relatively safe to keep a replica of this partition.

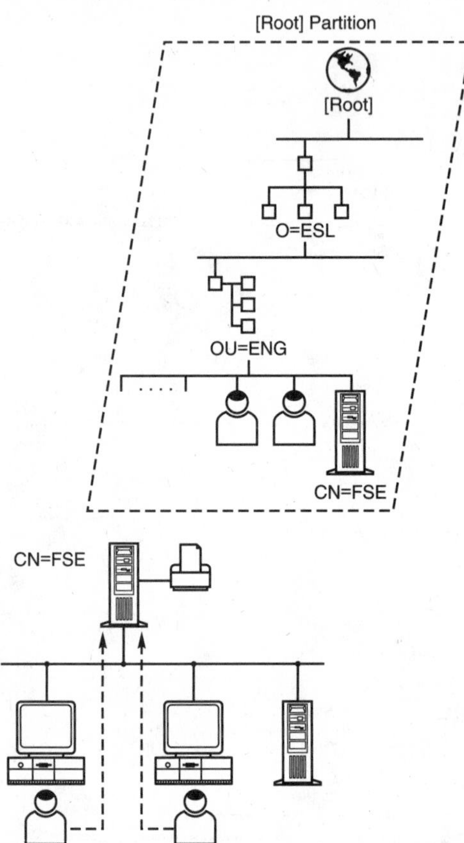

Figure 16.10
Example of a good design that has users and the network resources they use in the same partition.

You should take into account the size of a replica before you decide to place it on a server. An NDS object in a replica takes up approximately 1 KB of disk space. A good rule of thumb is to try to keep a partition size to no more than 500 NDS objects. The NDS database is stored in the SYS volume. You should make sure that you have enough free disk space in the volume so that TTS is not shut down. If TTS shuts down, it could seriously impair the integrity of the NDS database.

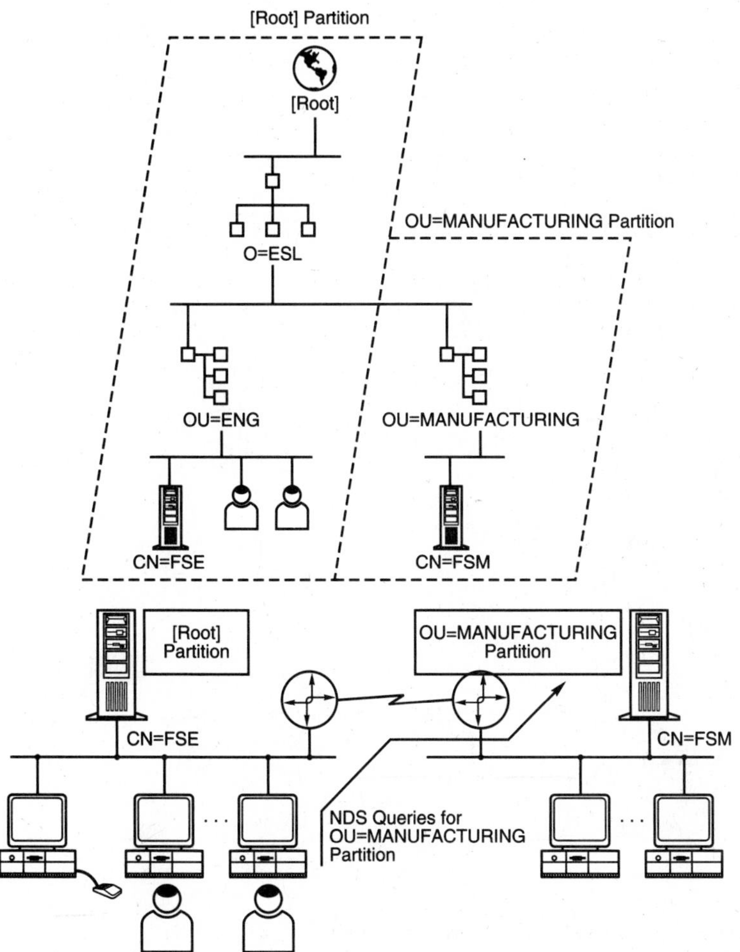

Figure 16.11
Example of a poor design that has users and the network resources they use in different partitions.

Before you decide to store replicas at remote sites, you should take into account the speed and expense of the wide area link, and the anticipated NDS traffic across these links. You should know the type of wide area link you are using. Is it a 9.6 Kbps dial-up link, an X.25 or Frame Relay link, a T1 (1.544 Mbps) or better link? If the link is too slow, you may be better off not keeping a replica at a remote location.

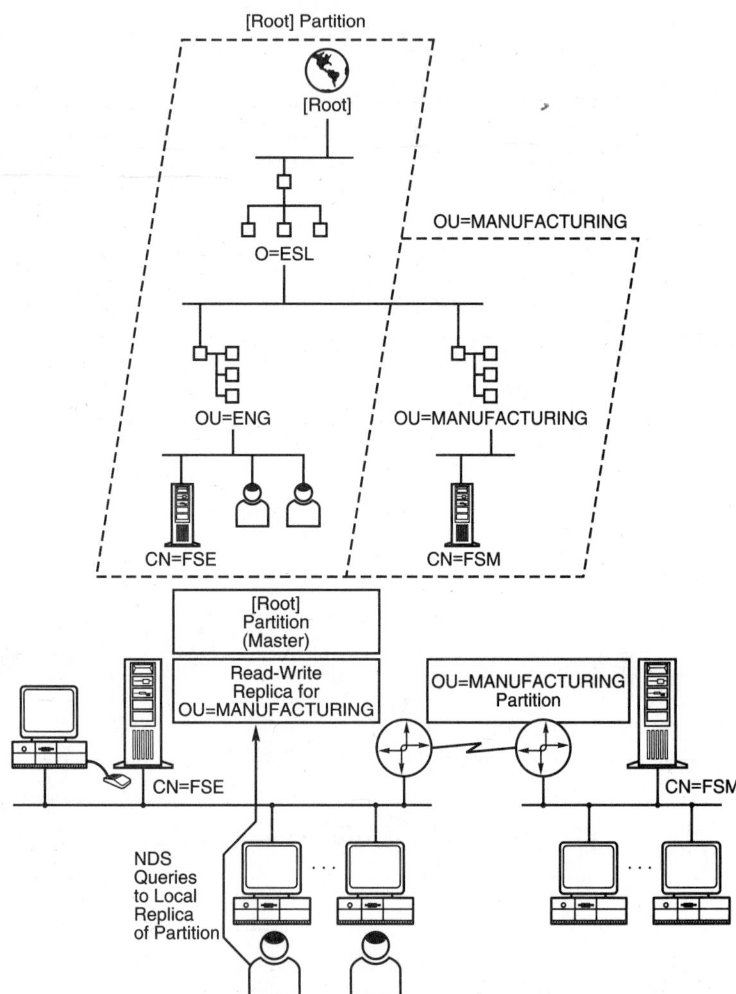

Figure 16.12
Example of a poor design that has users and the network resources they use in different partitions.

Understanding Replication

When you install or upgrade a new NetWare 4.*x* server using the INSTALL.NLM program, you have the option of creating the server in an existing container or a new container. If you select a new container, this container is added to the NDS tree. The type of replicas that are placed on the installed server depends on whether the server is being installed in an existing or new container.

If you are installing the server in an existing container, no new partitions are created. The new server has the option of receiving a Read Write replica of the container's partition. Figure 16.13 shows the operation of installing a new server in an existing container. The new server FS_S has the option of receiving a Read Write replica of the [Root] partition.

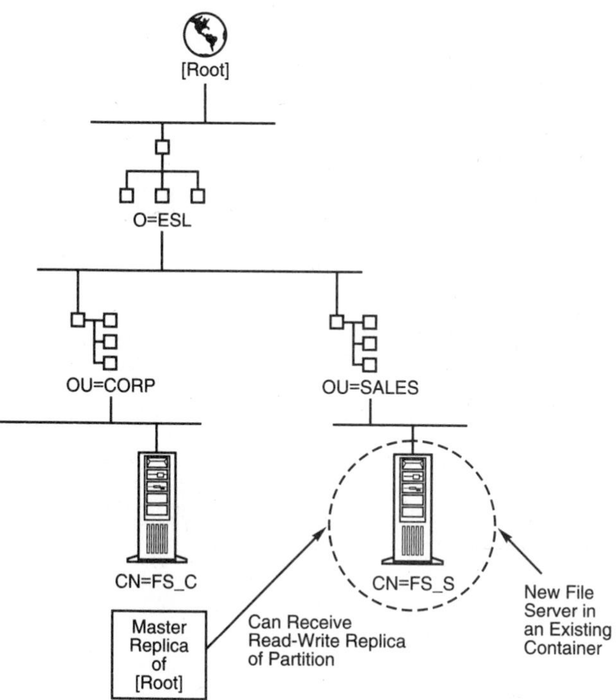

Figure 16.13
Installing a server in an existing container.

If the Server object is created in a new container, you are creating a new partition with the container as the root of that partition. The server will have a Master replica of this new partition placed on it. Additionally, a Read Write replica of the new partition is placed in the servers that contain the Master replica of the parent partition. Figure 16.14 illustrates this operation. The FS_E server installed in the new container OU=ENG receives the Master replica for the new partition with OU=ENG at its root. The server FS_C in the parent partition [Root] receives a Read Write replica of the new partition OU=ENG.

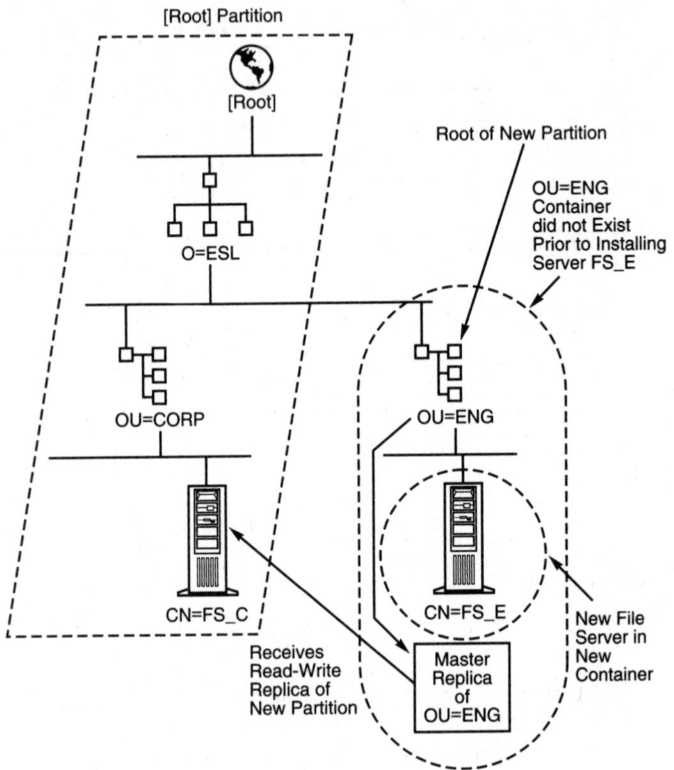

Figure 16.14
Installing a server in a new container.

When the NDS tree is created, NetWare 4.*x* uses certain default configurations for creating the replicas. The rules for newly installed servers have been discussed previously. The other rules are discussed in the context of an example. Consider the NDS tree in figure 16.15 that shows there are three partitions that cover the entire NDS tree.

Partition 1 contains the [Root] partition, organization O=ESL, and organization unit OU=CORP. The Master replica is stored on the file server FS_C.CORP.ESL.

Partition 2 contains the OU=SALES organization unit. The Master replica for partition OU=SALES is stored on the file server FS_S.SALES.ESL.

Partition 3 contains the OU=ENG organization unit. The Master replica for partition OU=ENG is stored on the file server FS_E.ENG.ESL.

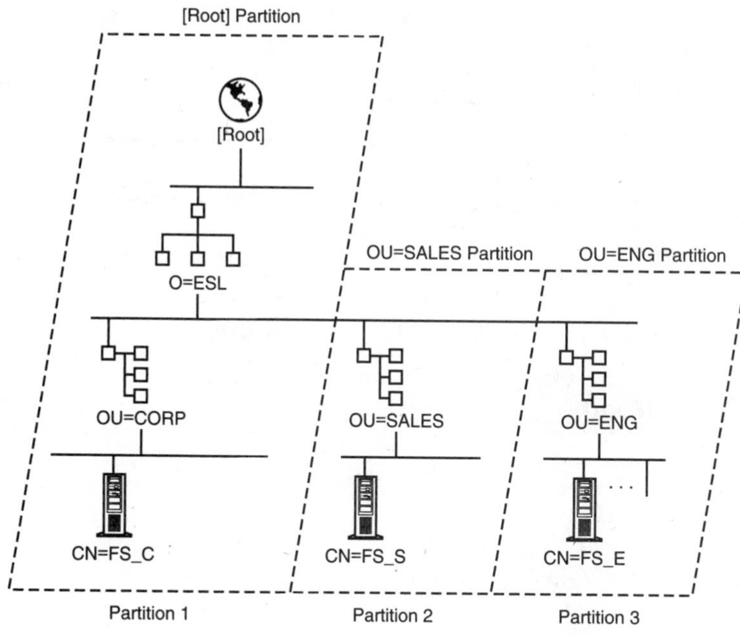

Figure 16.15
Example NDS partitions before splitting.

Additionally, assume the following:

- Server FS_C has a Read Write replica of Partitions 2 and 3.
- Server FS_S has a Read Write replica of Partition 1 and a Read Only replica of Partition 3.
- Server FS_E has a Read Write replica of Partitions 1 and 2.

Table 16.1 summarizes the replicas in each of the different partitions.

Table 16.1
Initial State of Replicas on Three Partitions

	Server for [Root]	Server for OU=SALES	Server for OU=ENG
Partition [Root]	Master	Read Write	Read Write
Partition OU=SALES	Read Write	Master	Read Write
Partition OU=ENG	Read Write	Read Only	Master

Now assume that the PARTMGR (or Partition Manager) is used to split Partition 1 into two partitions with roots at [Root] and OU=CORP. Table 16.2 shows the new distribution of replicas. This table shows that after splitting the original [Root] partition in two, any servers that had a replica of the old partition received a replica of the new partitions that is of the same type as the old replica. Server for [Root] originally contained the Master replica for [Root]. It now has Master replicas for [Root] and OU=CORP. Servers OU=SALES and OU=ENG contained a Read Write replica of the original [Root] partition. They both now contain Read Write replicas of [Root] and the new OU=CORP partition.

Table 16.2
Final State of Replicas on Four Partitions

	Server for [Root]	Server for OU=SALES	Server for OU=ENG
Partition [Root]	Master	Read Write	Read Write
Partition OU=CORP	Master	Read Write	Read Write
Partition OU=SALES	Read Write	Master	Read Write
Partition OU=ENG	Read Write	Read Only	Master

Understanding Replica Synchronization

To keep the replicas properly updated, directory synchronization is used. This is done by a process called the *skulk* process that synchronizes the replicas with the updated information.

Any kind of global synchronization mechanism needs an accurate time reference that should be the same throughout the network. This ensures that the NDS operations would be timestamped accurately, regardless of where they were performed on the network. Timestamps are unique codes that identify when the event took place and the replica that originated the event.

All NDS events such as adding, deleting, and updating NDS objects must be performed consistently on all replicas of a partition. This is called *replica synchronization*, and takes place in the background between servers of a replica ring. Replica synchronization is a background process which is user-transparent. It is an automatic process and is not configurable by users.

Accurate timestamps on NDS operations are essential to ensure that the NDS database is updated and synchronized correctly. The timestamps are used for ordering the directory events that occur. It is important that all servers have the same time. Ideally, this time should match the *Universal Time Coordinated* (UTC) time, but this is not essential for NDS operations to be done reliably. To maintain the UTC time, an external time source is needed. NetWare 4.*x* time synchronization mechanism allows for the use of external time sources.

The changes to NDS objects are done in the order in which the NDS modification requests are timestamped. If the timestamps on the modification requests do not have a common time reference, no guarantee can be made that the changes are made in the correct order. This could lead to inconsistencies in the NDS database.

NDS timestamps are based on a common network time that is maintained by time servers on the network. A common network time is important for replica synchronization. It ensures that NDS changes can be applied in the correct order. Timestamps also are used by NDS to set expiration times on temporary NDS entries.

Consider the case in which two servers, FSA and FSB, have a replica of a partition and are not properly synchronized. Assume that the time clock on FSA is 2 minutes ahead of the time clock on FSB. If an update is sent by FSA and the same update is sent by FSB 1 minute later, the update sent by FSB should be the one that is considered by other replicas as being the most recent. Because the clock in FSA is 2 minutes ahead of the clock in FSB, however, the FSA update will be registered by other servers as being the most recent.

In small networks, the server times will be apart by just a few seconds, and in very large complex networks they can be expected to be within 10 to 15 seconds from each other. This time differential between the server times is called the *get caught interval.* Any changes occurring in the get caught interval will be resolved in an unpredictable order. In real-life networks, most events occur outside the get caught interval, and it is very unlikely that users will experience the situation just described.

When a user logs in, the Network Address and Last Login property of an object in a replica are modified. These login changes are sent out every 5 minutes (300 seconds).

Collecting updates and sending them at periodic intervals minimizes the network traffic. This is particularly true for network logins, which tend to occur at about the same time when the office day starts.

The server sending the update information keeps track of the time the information was sent. Other servers in the replica ring keep track of the times the update was received. If the sender does not get back an acknowledgment, it waits for a certain period of time before retrying the update. If a server in a replica ring has not received an update for a certain time interval, it sends out a query asking for updates.

Managing Partitions and Replicas

As the needs of an organization change, networks must adapt to these changes and meet new requirements. The following are some of the changes you might have to make to adjust to new requirements:

1. Move replicas to other NetWare servers if the server needs to be replaced.

2. Split partitions that become too large.

3. Split/merge partitions to avoid excessive network traffic for directory operations.

4. Merge partitions to consolidate information and reduce synchronization overhead.

In addition, monitor storage on the SYS volume and keep sufficient disk space to prevent shutting down of TTS—replicas on the server can become too big.

NDS partitions can be managed by one of the following:

- PARTMGR.EXE, a DOS-based text utility
- The partition Manager option in the NetWare Administrator Tool

The partition manager tools can be used to perform the following tasks on NDS partitions:

- Viewing existing NDS partitions
- Splitting partitions
- Merging partitions

Splitting a partition involves creating a new partition out of an existing partition. Merging a partition results in deleting old partitions.

Figure 16.16 shows an NDS partition displayed using the Partition Manager GUI tool, and figure 16.17 shows the same partition using the PARTMGR tool.

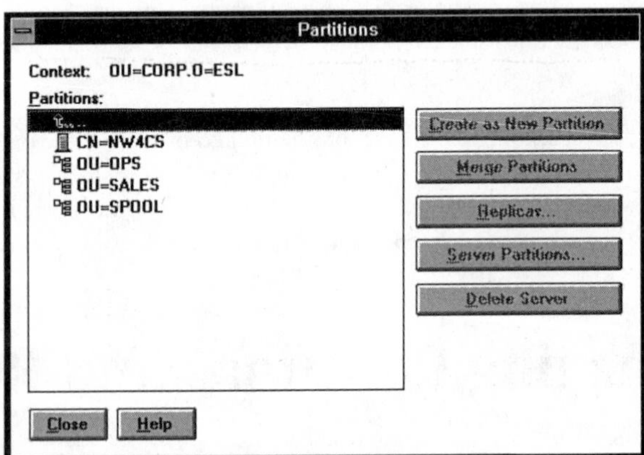

Figure 16.16
Partition Manager used for viewing partitions.

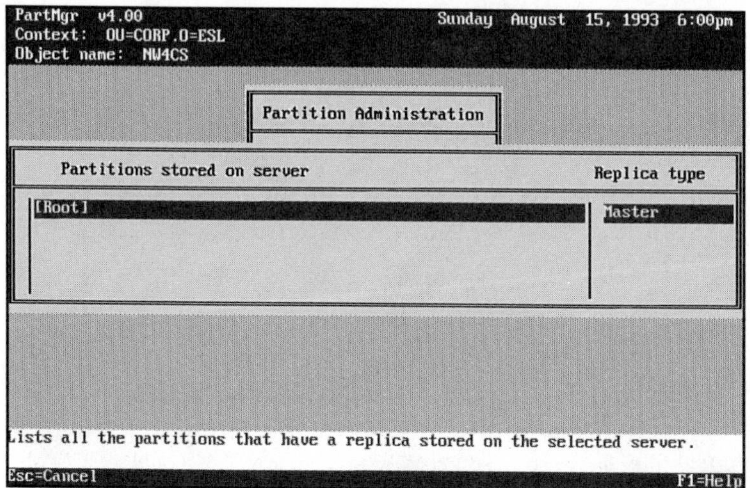

Figure 16.17
PARTMGR used for viewing partitions.

RAM requirements at the workstation are 6 MB for the Partition Manager and 512 KB for the PARTMGR.

Viewing Replicas

You can display replica information in two ways:

- View replicas for a given partition.
- View replicas stored on a particular NetWare server.

The Partition Manager and PARTMGR can be used to view replicas of a partition.

To view replicas, you need the Write property right to the ACL property of the Server object on which the replicas reside.

Viewing Replicas for a Given Partition

The following is the general procedure for viewing replicas for both tools:

1. Select the container that is the root of the partition.
2. If you are using Partition Manager, select the **R**eplicas button. You should see the list of replicas for that partition (see fig. 16.18).

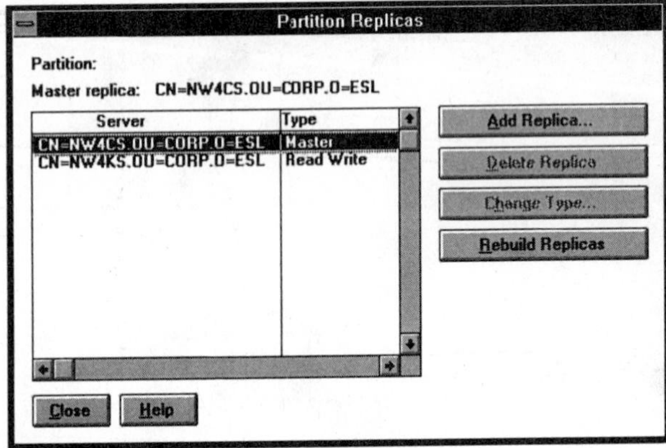

Figure 16.18 *Viewing replicas for a partition using Partition Manager.*

3. If you are using PARTMGR, press F10 and select View/Edit replicas. You should see a list of replicas for that partition (see fig.16.19).

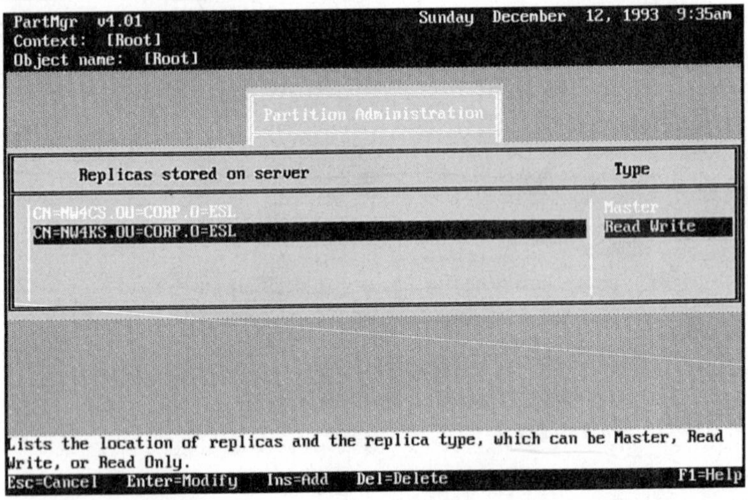

```
PartMgr v4.01                                  Sunday December 12, 1993 9:35am
Context: [Root]
Object name: [Root]

                    Partition Administration

      Replicas stored on server                                  Type
 CN=NW4CS.OU=CORP.O=ESL                                          Master
 CN=NW4KS.OU=CORP.O=ESL                                          Read Write

Lists the location of replicas and the replica type, which can be Master, Read
Write, or Read Only.
Esc=Cancel   Enter=Modify   Ins=Add   Del=Delete                       F1=Help
```

Figure 16.19 *Viewing replicas for a partition using PARTMGR.*

4. The list contains the servers on which a replica is stored and the replica type.

Viewing Replicas Stored on a Particular NetWare Server

To view replicas stored on a NetWare server:

1. Manager or PARTMGR.

2. If you are using Partition Manager, select the **S**erver Partitions button and you should see the list of replicas on that server (see fig. 16.20).

Figure 16.20
Viewing replicas on a server using Partition Manager.

If you are using PARTMGR, press F10. You should see a list of replicas on that server (see fig. 16.21).

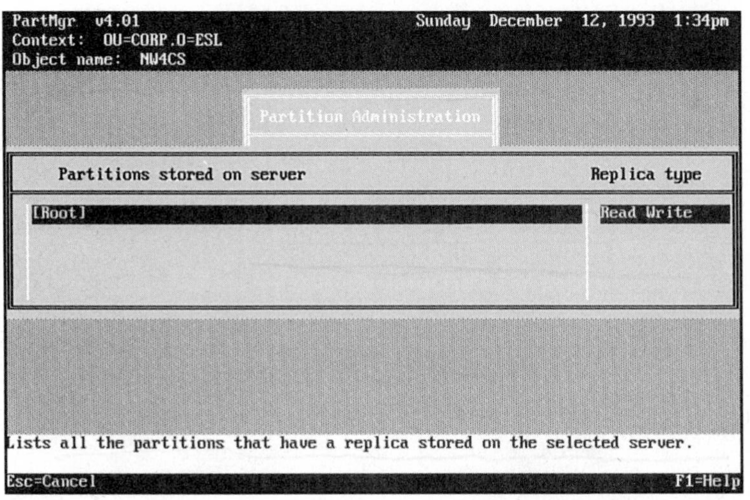

Figure 16.21
Viewing replicas on a server using PARTMGR.

The list contains the name of the replica and its replica type.

Splitting Partitions or Creating New Partitions

When a partitioned tree becomes very large, it may be necessary to split the partition. You also should split a partition if a portion of the partition needs to reside at a different location. A classic example of this situation is when NDS objects in a subtree are used primarily at a remote location (that is, separated from the location where the partition now resides) by a slow wide-area link. To minimize NDS traffic queries across a network, split the partition in two.

Any container in the NDS tree can be used as the starting point for creating a new partition. This container becomes the first object in the NDS partition and is called the root or Parent container of the partition.

To create a new partition, you need the Supervisor object right to the container that is being partitioned.

The new partition can be created using Partition Manager or the PARTMGR utility. These tools can be used to make a selected container in the NDS tree the root of a new partition. Because you are creating the partition for the first time, a Master replica of the partition is placed on the current server.

When you split a partition, all servers that have a replica of the partition receive a copy of the replicas of the new partitions resulting from the split.

The procedure for splitting the partition is described in the context of the examples in figure 16.22, which shows an NDS tree for a LAN that has a single [Root] partition stored on the NW4CS server at site A. It has been decided that the SALES department has been relocated to a remote site B that is connected to site A with a slow wide-area link. Because users in the sales department are now at site B, it is preferable to split the partition, create a new partition whose root is OU=SALES, and keep this partition on a server at site B.

Creating (Splitting) a New Partition Using Partition Manager

When the Partition Manager is started, each container that is the root of a partition will have a partition icon next to it (see fig. 16.23). Certain color codes are used to assist you in determining the meaning of the different objects. Containers that are at the root of a partition are red, the NetWare servers that hold replicas are blue, and the objects that are part of the [Root] partition are black.

To create a new partition using the Partition Manager:

1. Log in as Admin and start the Partition Manager from the NetWare Administrator.

2. Browse the NDS tree and highlight the container that should be the root of a new partition. Figure 16.24 shows that container OU=SALES is the root of a new partition.

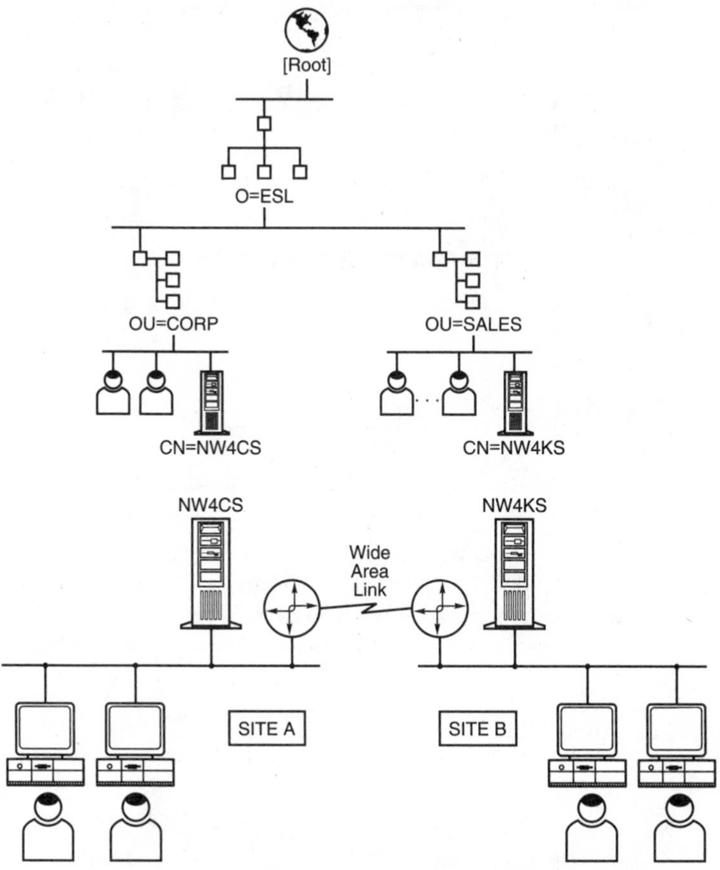

Figure 16.22
Case Study: Need for splitting a partition.

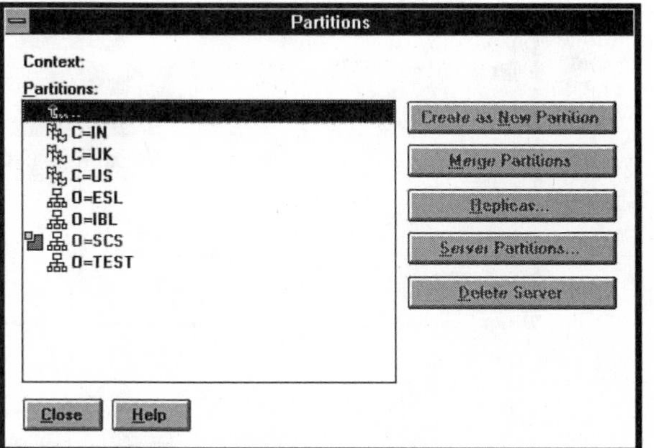

Figure 16.23
Containers that are roots of partitions.

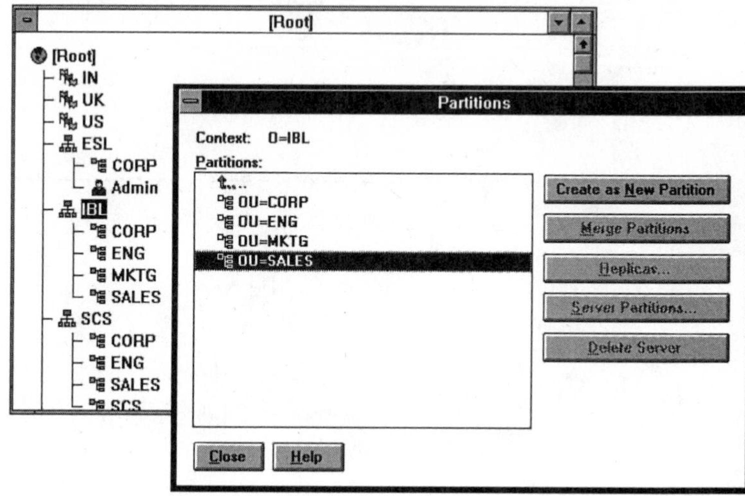

Figure 16.24
Container to become the root of a new partition.

Select the button Create as New Partition. When asked to verify whether you want to make this container the start of a new partition, select Yes. This can take from 1 to 10 minutes depending on the number of replicas, their size, and their location. When the operation is successful, you should see the partition icon next to the container that is the root of the newly created partition (see fig. 16.25).

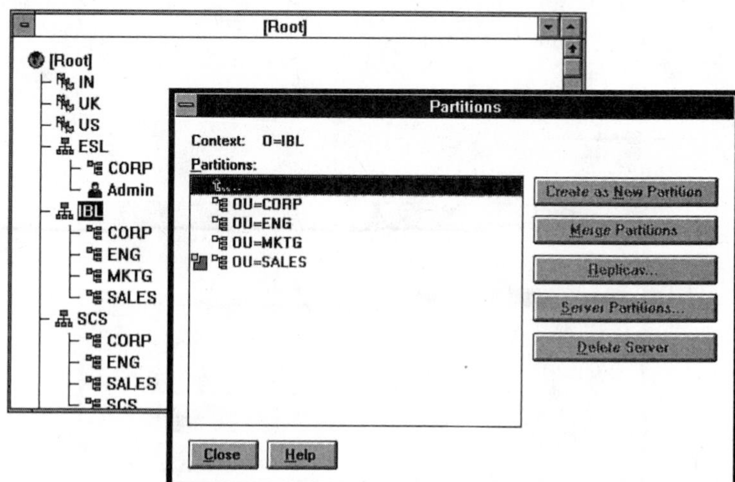

Figure 16.25
Container that is the root of a new partition.

To view the partition that you have created, select the container that you just partitioned and select Replicas. The complete name of the server on which you created the partition appears in the server column, and the type of replica appears in the Type column. Because you have just created the partition, the replica type should be Master. You can make additional replicas of this partition on other servers.

Creating (Splitting) a New Partition Using PARTMGR

To create a new partition using the PARTMGR:

1. Log in as Admin, and start the PARTMGR.
2. Select Manage Partitions.

   Those containers that are the root of a partition will have an object class of partition (see fig. 16.26).

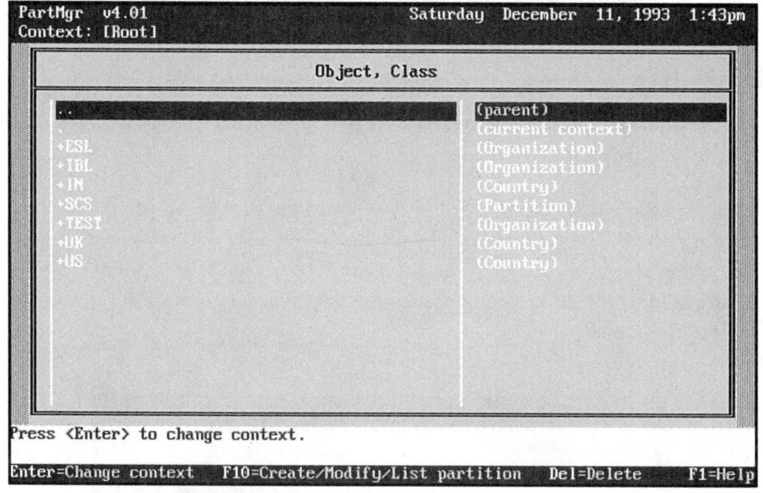

Figure 16.26
Object, Class container screen.

3. Browse the NDS tree and highlight the container that should be the root of a new partition.
4. Press F10.

When asked to verify whether you want to make this container the start of a new partition, select Yes. This can take 1 to 10 minutes depending on the number of replicas, their size, and their location.

When the operation is successful, you will see that the name of the new partition is the same as the container name, but the object class is changed to Partition (see fig. 16.27).

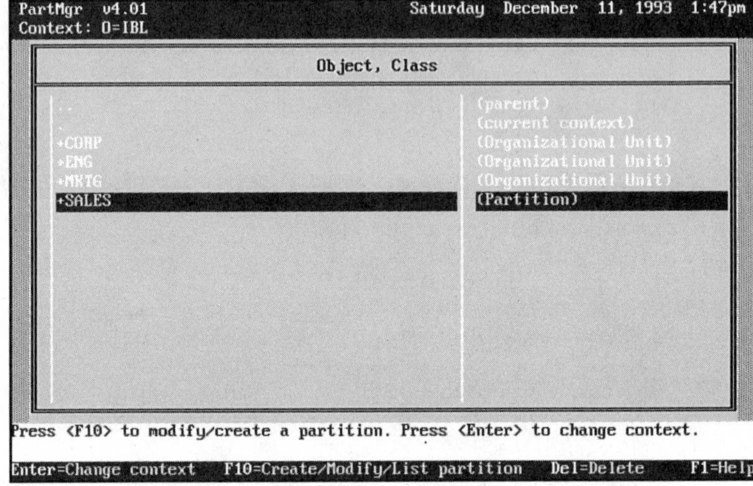

Figure 16.27
OU=SALES as the root of a new partition.

Merging Partitions

You may decide to merge partitions to consolidate resources. When merging partitions, a subordinate partition is merged with the parent partition.

In the example in figure 16.28, if the SALES department is moved from site B to site A, you may want to merge the SALES partition into the [Root] partition. The partition OU=SALES is *subordinate* to the *parent* partition [Root]. To merge partitions, you need the Supervisor object right to the root of the parent partition. In the example in figure 16.28, you need the supervisor object right to [Root] to merge the OU=SALES partition into the [Root] partition.

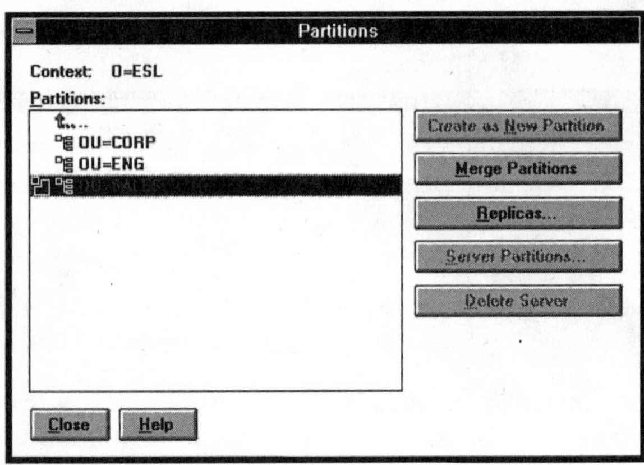

Figure 16.28
Container to be merged with the partition.

If you are merging and splitting several partitions one after another, you may get a message that the partition is busy. You may have to wait a minute or longer for the replicas to synchronize.

For 20 servers in a single location, the synchronization can take 20 to 30 minutes. For 20 servers in multiple locations, the synchronization can take up to 60 minutes or longer.

The procedures shown in the next sections outline how a merge operation can be performed.

Merging Using Partition Manager

To merge using Partition Manager:

1. Log in as Admin and start the Partition Manager from the NetWare Administrator.

2. Browse the NDS tree and highlight the container that you want to merge with the parent partition (see fig. 16.29).

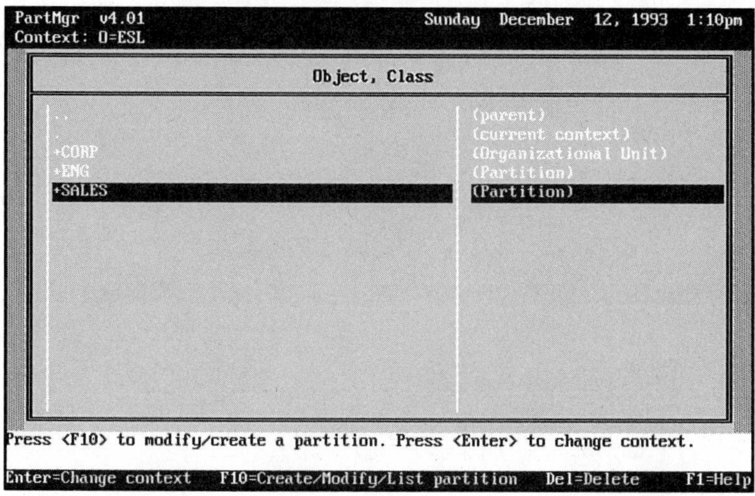

Figure 16.29
Container to be merged with PARTMGR.

3. Select the button Merge Partitions. When asked to verify that you want to merge the partition, select Yes. This usually takes from 1 to 60 minutes (or longer) depending on the number of replicas, their size, and their location.

   If you do not see the partition icon next to the partition that was merged disappear, you should go one level up the tree and browse that tree branch again. This will refresh the display.

Merging Using PARTMGR

To merge using PARTMGR:

1. Log in as Admin.
2. Run PARTMGR.
3. Browse the NDS tree and highlight the container that you want to merge with the parent partition (see fig.16.30).

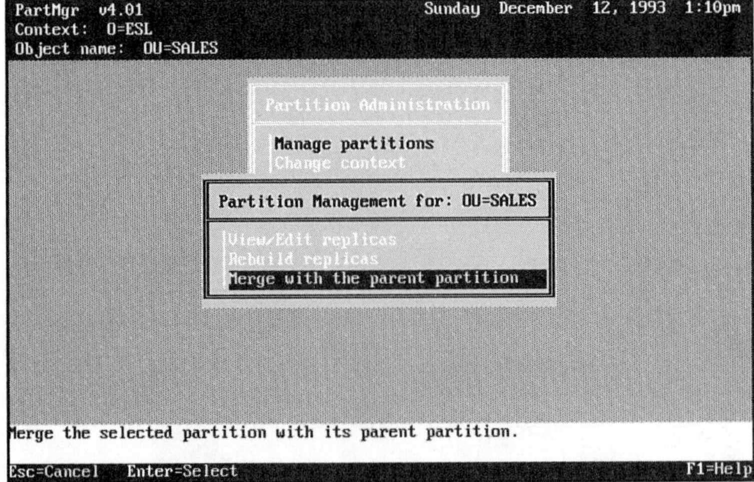

Figure 16.30
Operations that can be performed on the partition.

4. Press F10.

   You should see a list of operations that can be performed on the partition (see fig. 16.31).

5. Select Merge with the parent partition.

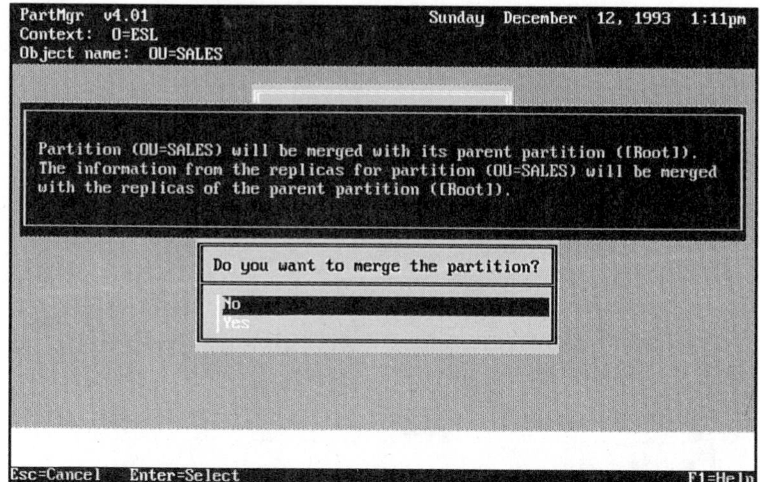

Figure 16.31
Message showing the name of the partition to be merged with the parent partition using PARTMGR.

Searching for Partitions

When the NDS tree is very large, it is helpful to find all the partitions that are defined on the NDS tree. You can do this using the NetWare Administrator.

To search for all partitions in the NDS tree, use the following as a guideline:

1. Start the NetWare Administrator.

2. Select Search... from the Object menu. You should see the search panel displayed. Set the fields in the Search dialog box as follows (see fig. 16.32):

   Start From: [Root] (or any container from which you want to start the search)

   Check the box Search Entire Subtree

   Search For: Partition

3. Select OK.

Figure 16.33 shows that three partitions were found: [Root], OU=SALES, and OU=ENG.

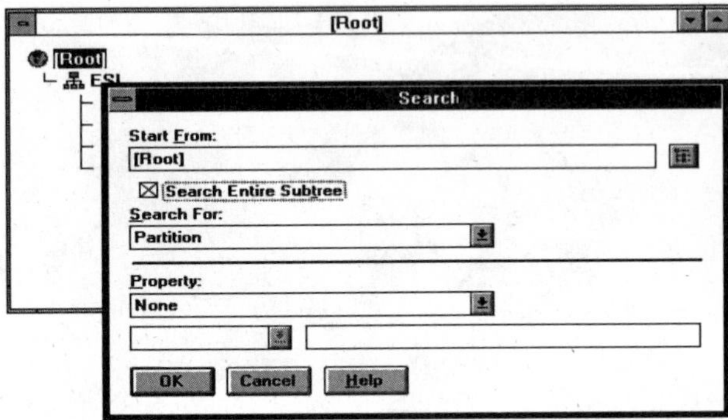

Figure 16.32
Search options for partitions.

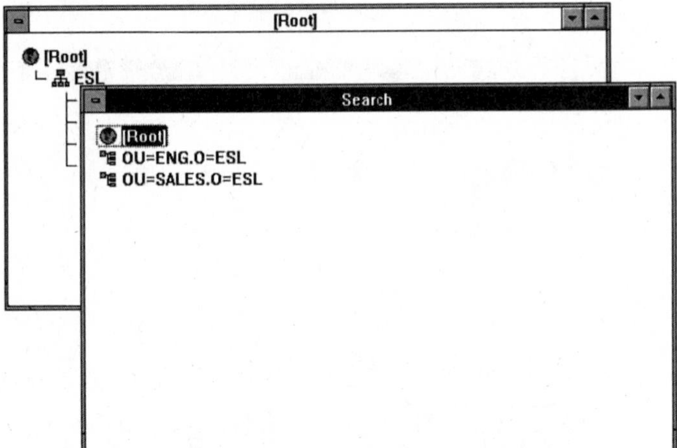

Figure 16.33
Partitions searched for in the NDS tree.

Repairing NDS Partitions

If the Master replica becomes corrupt, it can propagate inaccurate information about the NDS partition. A corrupt Master replica also prevents you from performing partition restructuring, such as splitting and merging.

The causes of a corrupt Master replica can range from problems with the server's disk storage, the server being powered off unexpectedly, or the server crashing in the middle of an NDS operation, to simply having a bug in the NDS software.

You can use any of the following techniques to correct problems with replicas:

- Changing replica types
- Rebuilding a replica
- Using DSREPAIR.NLM

Changing Replica Types

If the Master replica is corrupted, you can replace it with a Read Write replica. This is done by changing the replica type of a Read Write replica to a Master replica. When this is done, the original Master replica (also, the corrupt Master replica, in this case) is downgraded to a Read Write replica and is synchronized with the information in the new Master replica.

To change a replica type, you need the Supervisor object right to the root of the partition whose replica type is being changed. You can perform this task using the Partition Manager of PARTMGR.

Making a Read Write Replica a Master Replica Using Partition Manager

The following can be used as a guideline for changing a replica type using Partition Manager:

1. Log in as Admin, and start the Partition Manager from the NetWare Administrator.
2. Browse the NDS tree and highlight the container whose replica type you want to change.

   You should see a list of servers and the replica types they have (see fig. 16.34).

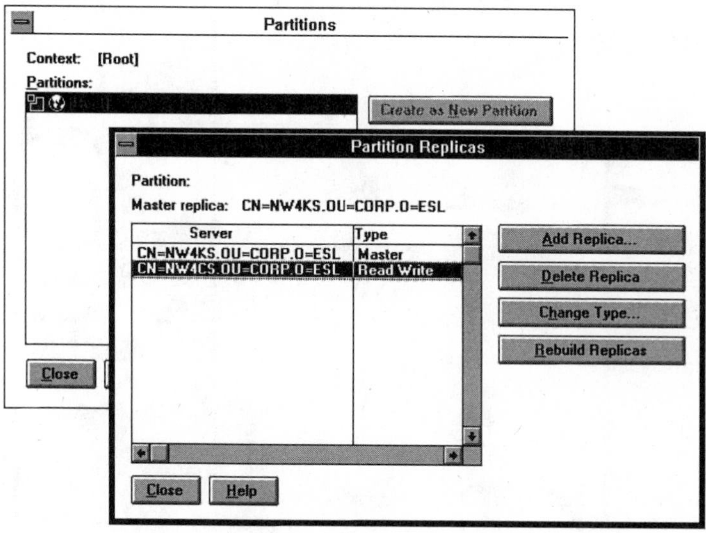

Figure 16.34
Replicas on the server using Partition Manager.

3. Select the server that contains the replica type you want to change.

   Select the button Change Type.

   You should see a panel to change the replica type (see fig. 16.35).

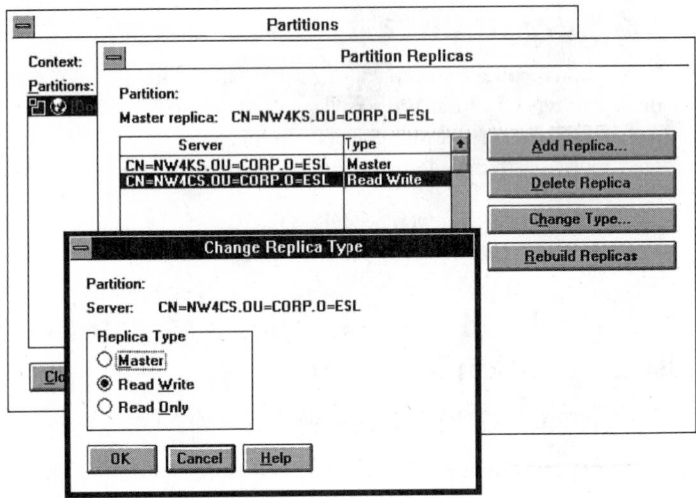

Figure 16.35
Change Replica Type options.

Select the **M**aster replica type and select OK.

You should see a list of servers and the changes in the replica types (see fig. 16.36).

4. Select the **C**lose buttons to exit the Partition Manager.

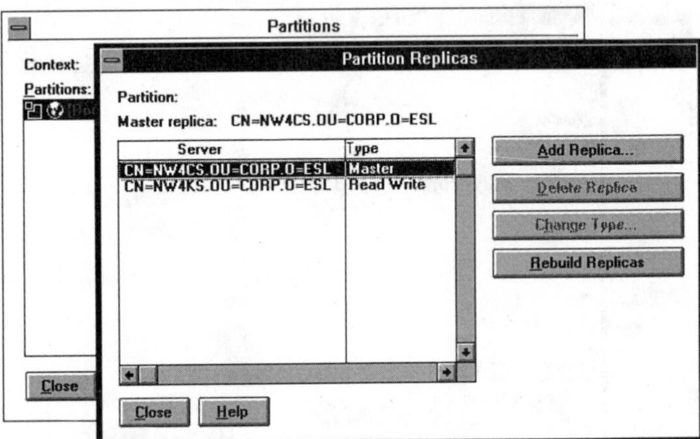

Figure 16.36
Replicas on the server.

Making a Read Write Replica a Master Replica Using PARTMGR

The following can be used as a guideline for changing a replica type using PARTMGR:

1. Log in as Admin.

2. Run PARTMGR.

3. Browse the NDS tree, and highlight the container whose replica type you want to change.

   Press F10.

   Select View/Edit replicas.

   You should see a list of servers and their replica types (see fig. 16.37).

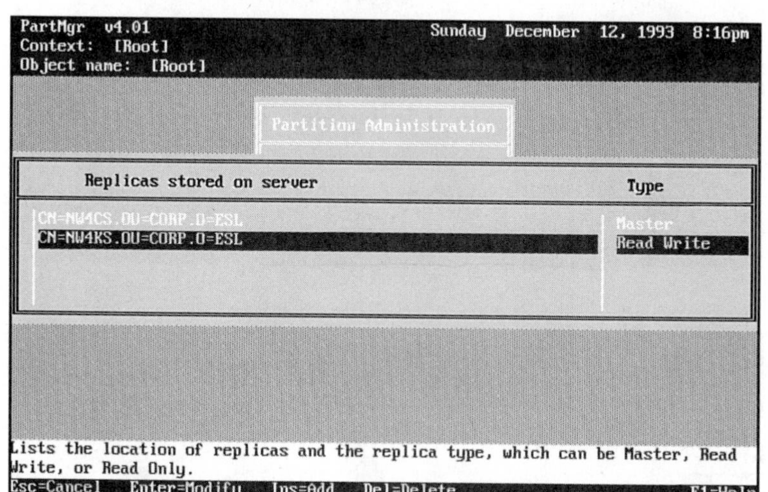

Figure 16.37
Replicas on the server using PARTMGR.

4. Highlight the server that contains the replica type you want to change, and press Enter.

   You should see an editable field for the current replica type. Press Enter to change.

   You should see the list of replica types to which you can change (see fig. 16.38).

   Highlight the Master option and press Enter.

   Press F10 to save your changes.

   You should see a list of servers and the changes in the replica types (see fig.16.39).

5. Press Alt+F10 and exit PARTMGR.

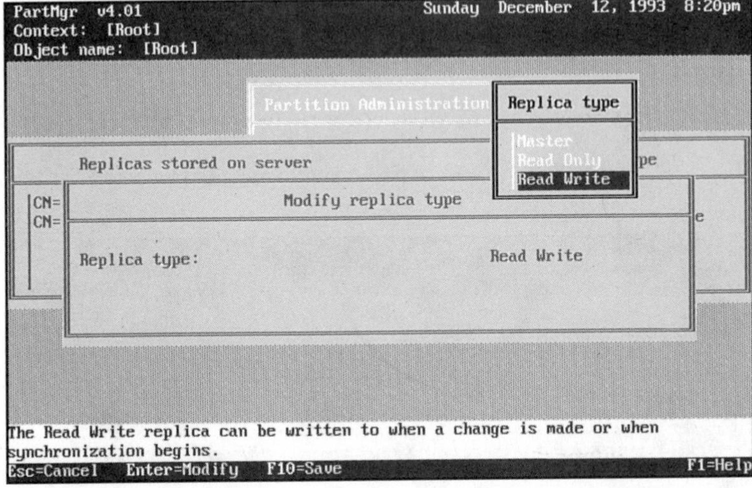

Figure 16.38
List of replica type options.

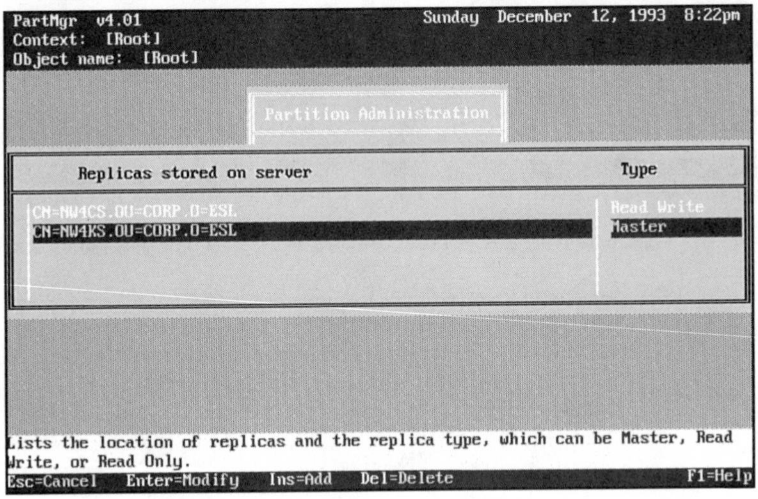

PartMgr v4.01
Sunday December 12, 1993 8:22pm
Context: [Root]
Object name: [Root]
Partition Administration
Replicas stored on server
Type
CN=NW4CS.OU=CORP.O=ESL
Read Write
CN=NW4KS.OU=CORP.O=ESL
Master
Lists the location of replicas and the replica type, which can be Master, Read Write, or Read Only.
Esc=Cancel Enter=Modify Ins=Add Del=Delete
F1=Help

Figure 16.39
Changed replicas on the server.

Rebuilding a Replica

If the replicas on a partition are not synchronized with the Master replica, or become corrupted, you can use the Partition Manager or PARTMGR to rebuild the replicas. To do this, you need Supervisor object rights to the root of the partition whose replicas you are rebuilding.

Using the Rebuild Replicas Option in Partition Manager

Use the following steps as a guideline for rebuilding a replica using Partition Manager:

1. Log in as Admin and start the Partition Manager from the NetWare Administrator.

2. Browse the NDS tree, and highlight the container whose replicas you want to rebuild.

3. Select the **R**eplicas button.

4. Highlight the Master replica; select the button **R**ebuild Replicas.

When asked whether you want to replace another replica's data with data from this replica, answer Yes.

Rebuilding Replicas Using PARTMGR

Use the following steps as a guideline for rebuilding a replica using PARTMGR:

1. Log in as Admin.

2. Run PARTMGR.

3. Browse the NDS tree, and highlight the container whose replicas you want to rebuild.

   Press F10.

   Select Rebuild replicas.

   You should see a list of servers and their replica types.

4. Highlight the Master replica and press F10.

   Press Enter and select Yes to confirm your choice.

5. Press ALT+F10 and exit PARTMGR.

Using DSREPAIR.NLM

If the Master replica is corrupt or the server on which it resides is no longer available, you can run DSREPAIR at the server to re-create the Master replica from the information in the Read Write replicas in the replica ring. You must use caution in using DSREPAIR and ensure that you have only one Master replica in the ring.

DSREPAIR will select a Read Write replica to become a new Master, and the old Master replica will be downgraded to a Read Write replica.

To use DSREPAIR to repair a ring with no Master replica, perform the following:

1. Run DSREPAIR at the server:

   LOAD DSREPAIR

2. Select option 1. Select Options.

3. Select option 4. Do not check consistency of local replicas.

This option should change to 4. Repair replica ring with no Master.

4. Select option 8. Return to selection menu.
5. Select option 2. Begin repair.
6. Exit DSREPAIR by selecting 3. Exit.

Removing a Server Object from an NDS Tree

Occasionally, you may need to remove a NetWare server from the NDS tree. If you attempt to perform this on a server that is active, you will see the error message shown in figure 16.40. Because a Server object may contain replicas of partitions, it should be deleted using the Partition Manager or PARTMGR utility. If you do succeed in deleting an inactive server using NETADMIN or the NetWare Administrator, it could damage the replica ring and cause serious problems.

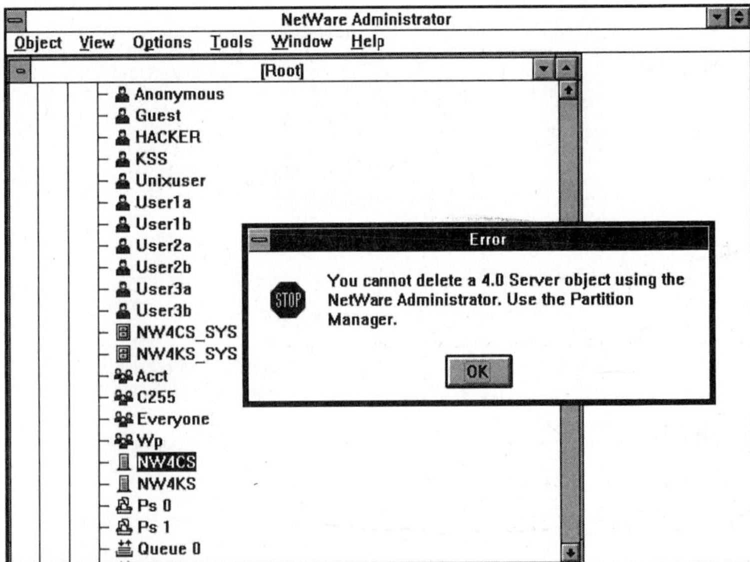

Figure 16.40
An attempt to remove the Server object from an NDS tree.

The procedures for deleting a Server object using the Partition Manager and PARTMGR are outlined next.

Deleting the NetWare Server Using the Partition Manager

To delete the NetWare server using the Partition Manager:

1. Log in as Admin.
2. Start the Partition Manager from the Tools menu of the NetWare Administrator.
3. Browse the NDS tree using the Partition Manager browse function and locate the Server object(s) that need to be deleted. Figure 16.41 shows the NetWare servers that hold partition replicas.

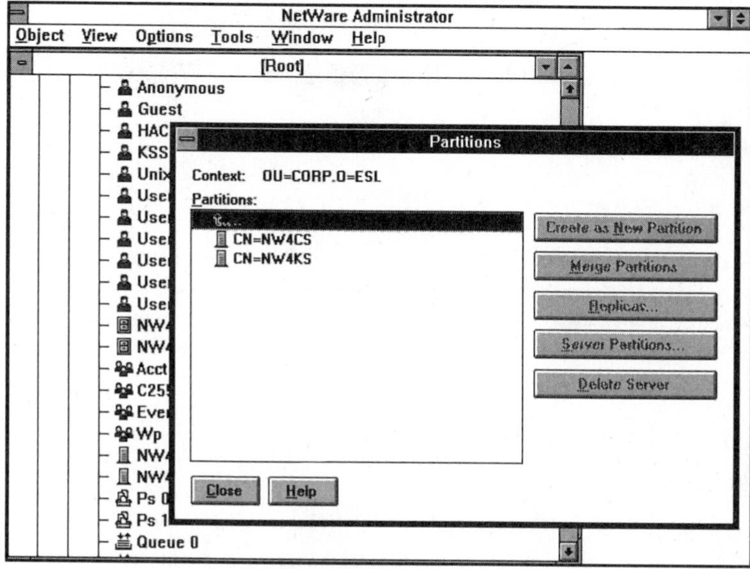

Figure 16.41
NetWare Server objects that hold replicas.

4. Highlight the Server object and select the Delete Server button.

Deleting the NetWare Server Using the PARTMGR

To delete the NetWare server using the PARTMGR:

1. Log in as Admin.
2. Run the PARTMGR utility.
3. Browse the NDS tree and locate the Server object(s) that need to be deleted. Figure 16.42 shows the NetWare servers that hold partition replicas.

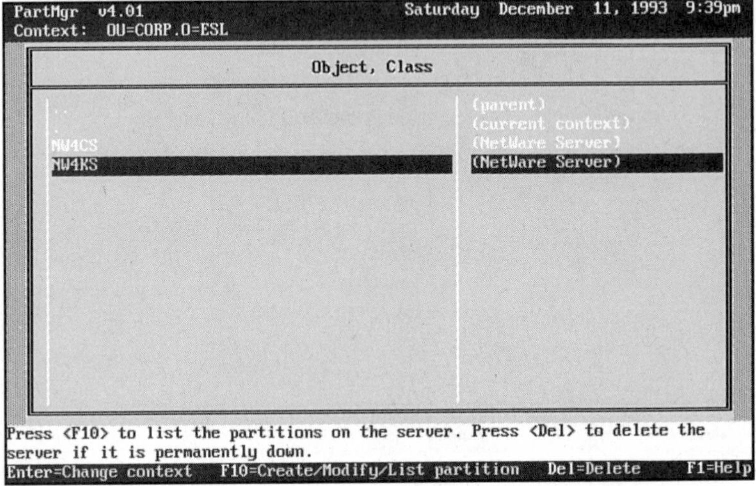

Figure 16.42
NetWare Server objects that hold replicas.

4. Highlight the Server object and press Del.

5. When asked whether you want to delete the Server object, select Yes.

When you select the delete option for deleting the Server object using PARTMGR or Partition Manager, the replicas on the server are deleted first, and then the Server object is deleted. You should not bring the server down immediately after it has been deleted from the NDS tree. You should wait until all servers in the replica ring are notified of the deleted server; you will then stop receiving replica updates.

Status of Server Volume Objects with Server Object ID Deleted

When the server is deleted from the NDS tree, the Volume objects for which the Server object is host are changed to object class Unknown. This prevents the volume from being accessed. You then can use the NetWare Administrator or NETADMIN to delete the Unknown objects.

Reinstalling the NDS Tree

If you run into a situation where the NDS database is corrupted beyond repair, you may be left with no other alternative than to create a new NDS database. Fortunately, this can be done without losing the files and directories on the server volume. You will, however, lose trustee assignments to files and directories that you have added since the server was last installed. Trustee assignments are granted to NDS objects such as User objects, Group objects, and Container objects. As part of the process of reinstalling the NDS, you have to remove the existing NDS database first. When this takes place, the trustee assignments made to the objects in the NDS database are lost.

Before reinstalling the NDS tree, take the usual precautionary measure of backing up the files and directories on the server. The reinstalling of the NDS tree is a reliable process and you should not encounter any problems. The nature of computers and software being what they are, however, it is prudent to take precautions that enable you to recover from the unexpected.

When you remove the directory services from a server, you also remove the Server object from the NDS tree, and *downgrade* the server's volumes to bindery volumes. The downgraded volumes and the servers are still available for access through bindery-based utilities. For example, RCONSOLE is a bindery-based utility, and you can use this to access the server's console, even though directory services are removed from the server.

If you remove the directory services from a server that has a Master replica or has the only replica that has links to subordinate partitions, the subordinate partitions on other servers become invalid. For this reason, you should change the replica type of the Master replica to a Read Write replica, using the procedure outlined in this chapter. Then make replicas of any critical partitions on other servers.

To reinstall the directory service on a server, you need to have the Supervisor object right to the Server object and its associated Volume objects.

The following describes the procedure for reinstalling directory services on a server:

1. Ensure that all the servers' volumes are mounted.

   If all the servers' volumes are not mounted, you have to repeat the procedure for removing NDS from a server with the other volumes.

2. Run the INSTALL NLM at the server console:

   LOAD INSTALL

3. Make the following menu selections:

   Select Maintenance/Selective Install.

   Select Directory Options.

   Select Remove Directory Services from this Server.

4. When asked to confirm whether you want to remove directory services, select Yes.

5. Log in to the directory services, when prompted to do so, with the Admin password.

   The servers' volumes are downgraded, and a message appears informing you of the number of volumes that have been downgraded.

   At this point, you are ready to reinstall NDS services on the server.

6. From the Directory Options of the INSTALL.NLM, select Install Directory Services onto this server.

7. You will be asked the name of the NDS tree. If you are connected to the rest of the network, INSTALL will remember the tree name that was used.

   You will be presented with a number of screens dealing with the context in which you want to install this server and the time services that will be installed on the server. Make the appropriate choices based on your NDS tree design. You may want to examine the AUTOEXEC.NCF file on the server to see the current configuration at the server. You can examine the AUTOEXEC.NCF options through the NCF Files Options in the Installation Options menu.

8. Run DSREPAIR on the server to update and fix the NDS database.

Instructions on running DSREPAIR are presented earlier in this chapter.

Summary

In this chapter, you learn about the mechanisms used to store and manage the NDS database on the server. You are introduced to the concept of partitions and replicas. Partitions enable you to manage a large NDS database using smaller manageable units. Replicas are copies of partitions and can be used to improve the fault tolerance of an NDS database. Placing replicas in strategic locations minimizes network traffic due to directory lookups. There are three types of replicas: Master, Read Write, and Read Only. This chapter explains the differences between them and the reason for using each replica type.

This chapter also explores partition design and management issues and how replica synchronization works. Partitions can be managed by using the Partition Manager or PARTMGR.

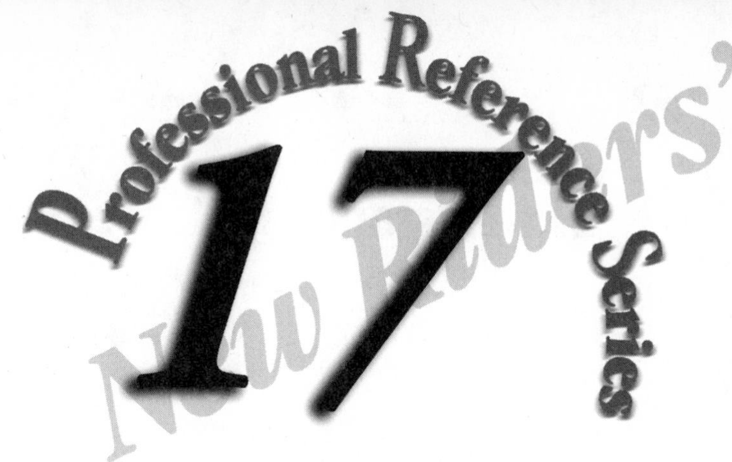

NetWare Directory Services Time Synchronization

Time synchronization is important in NetWare 4.*x*-based networks because NDS operations and changes must occur in the proper sequence on the network.

The NDS database is distributed on the network. Time synchronization is implemented in NetWare 4.*x* to solve the problem of keeping a consistent view of the NDS database because portions of the NDS tree are kept on different servers that use separate hardware time clicks. When objects are added to the Directory, they are first added in a local copy of the database (*replica*). The changes in the NDS database are propagated throughout the network to other replicas. If the same object is modified in two different local copies of the database, or modified twice in the same local copy, the order in which the modifications were made must be preserved because these changes must be performed on other replicas. For example, deleting a user object, adding a new user object with the same name, and changing it has a different effect than changing it first, deleting it, and then adding the user object.

On a distributed network consisting of many servers, there is a tendency for server clocks and times to drift even if they are initially set to the same time. The amount of drift depends on each machine and the accuracy of its time clock. A mechanism is needed to ensure that the server clocks are synchronized to within a predefined tolerance. This is called *time synchronization,* and it ensures that a common network-wide time exists throughout the network.

Although time synchronization is not part of the NDS schema, without it NDS would not work reliably. Time synchronization is implemented by the NetWare Loadable Module, TIMESYNC.NLM. This module must be run at each server and is loaded automatically when the NetWare 4.*x* server is started.

Understanding Time Server Types

All NetWare 4.*x* servers are required to synchronize their time to a common network time for NDS operations to be performed in a consistent manner; therefore, each NetWare 4.*x* server acts as a time server. Time servers fall into two categories: *time providers* and *time consumers.* Time providers act as sources of time (also called *time sources*).

When a NetWare 4.*x* server is installed, you see the following choices of time server types during installation:

- Single Reference Time Servers (SRTS)
- Reference Time Servers (RTS)
- Primary Time Servers (PTS)
- Secondary Time Servers (STS)

Single Reference Time Servers

The SRTS is the default choice during a first time installation. The first installed NetWare 4.*x* server can be designated as the SRTS. The SRTS is the authoritative time source on the network. All other servers synchronize their time to match the SRTS. Although the SRTS can be made to work for all kinds of networks, it is primarily recommended for small networks (see fig. 17.1). For larger networks, the SRTS acts as a single point of failure, and other mechanisms should be used. When SRTS is used, other types of time servers such as PTS or RTS cannot be used.

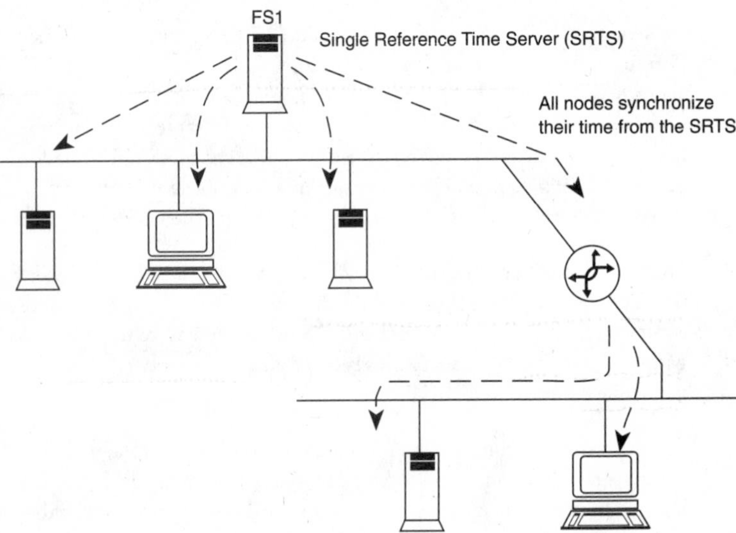

Figure 17.1
The Single Reference Time Server.

All servers on the network must be able to contact the SRTS because it is the only source of time.

Time synchronization can exist on a physical network even if a physical network is divided into separate logical directory trees. A physical network can contain several directory trees that do not normally share resources. Although each directory tree is treated as a separate logical network, they share a common network time because the time servers in the separate directory trees are reached through a physical connection. The default behavior is that you cannot have an SRTS for each directory tree if the servers in the directory trees can be reached through physical network connections. To override this default behavior of a common time synchronization across multiple directory trees, the SET TIMESYNC DIRECTORY TREE MODE parameter can be used. This parameter is discussed in table 17.2 later in this chapter.

For a small network that uses an SRTS, time synchronization is trivial or non-existent because all other servers synchronize their time to the SRTS. In larger networks, use of the SRTS poses a *single-point-of-failure* problem, and other types of time servers, such as Primary Time Servers and Reference Time Servers, can be used as sources of time. When more than one time source exists, a common network time is computed based on a voting process that occurs between the time providers.

Single Reference Time Servers, by definition, do not use another time provider to remain synchronized. A Single Reference Time Server is the sole authority for time on the network, and its time is used as the common network time.

Reference Time Servers

Reference Time Servers are used to provide an external time source. They are designed to be accurate and usually synchronize their time from a radio clock slaved to the Naval Observatory or some other equally accurate time source. Another way to design the RTS is by using a time synchronization NLM that contacts an accurate time source through a modem at regular intervals. An RTS can synchronize itself by an external time source, but it never adjusts its time from any other source on the network. For reliability, additional RTSs can be used, which should be strategically located at other points on the network (see fig. 17.2). Because there can be differences in the time provided by RTSs, a voting method is used to decide the reference time to be used on the network. All Reference Time Servers participate in this vote. If any Primary Time Servers exist, they too participate in the vote. The Primary Time Servers adjust their time to match the consensus reached as a result of the vote.

Use an RTS when you need to have a central point to control accuracy of network time with respect to an external source. For large networks in which synchronization with an accurate external clock is needed, a backup RTS is recommended.

A Reference Time Server, by definition, does not initialize its clock with the common network time. It is used for the sole purpose of determining an accurate common network time.

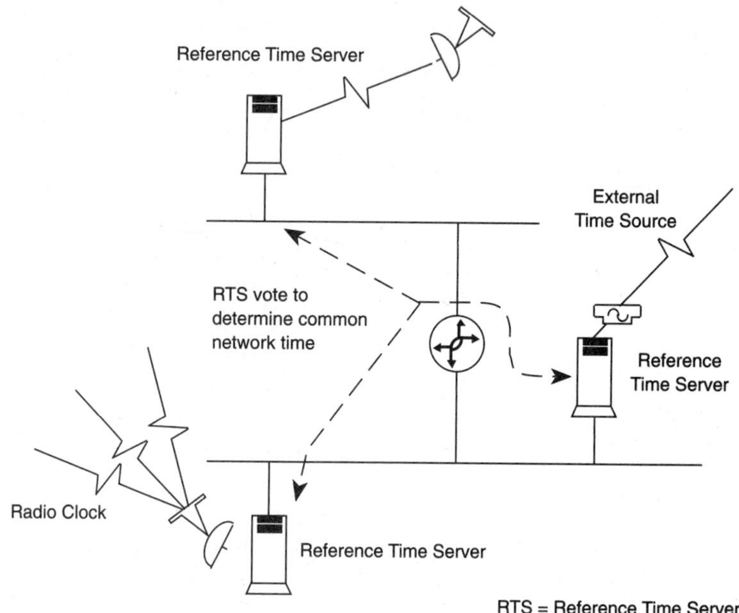

Figure 17.2
Reference Time Servers.

Primary Time Servers

A Primary Time Server synchronizes its time by voting with at least one other PTS or RTS (see fig. 17.3). In other words, a PTS must have another PTS or another RTS to synchronize its time. The network might have several PTSs and RTSs, in which case, all the PTS and RTS time servers participate in the vote.

Unlike an RTS, a PTS adjusts its time to match the common network time (result of the vote). The RTS and PTS servers poll each other to determine each other's time before casting their votes. During the time PTSs are adjusting their clocks, the network time may drift slightly during the synchronization process. The other clients and servers take their time from the PTS. Having several PTSs on the network provides a measure of fault tolerance because as one PTS goes down, another PTS can be used to provide an alternate time source. It is recommended that you use one PTS for about every 125 to 150 secondary time servers. If greater fault tolerance is required, you can increase the number of PTSs.

The PTS provides time to other secondary time servers. You should, therefore, locate the PTS so that requests by secondary servers to synchronize their time from a PTS do not have to travel over expensive long-distance links. If the network consists of several locations, each location should have its own PTS.

Please note that Reference Time Servers and Primary Time Servers require another time provider with which they must be able to exchange timing information to remain synchronized. A Reference Time Server or Primary Time Server cannot claim to be synchronized unless it can contact other time provider(s), which are used to compute a common time used by the Primary Time Servers and Secondary Time Servers to initialize their time clocks.

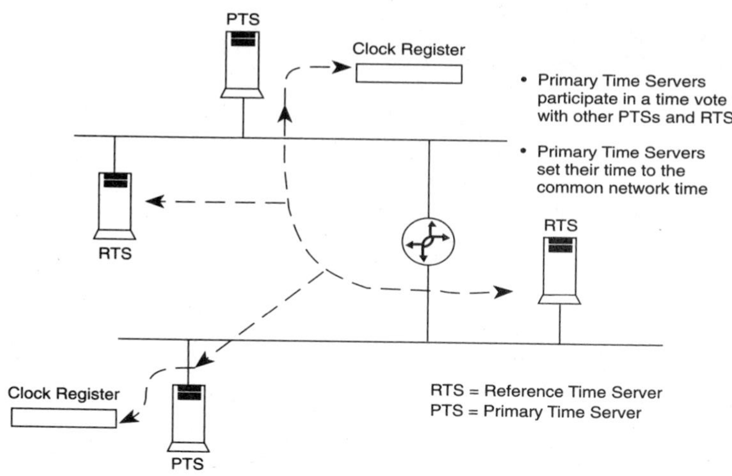

Figure 17.3
Primary Time Servers.

Secondary Time Servers

Secondary Time Servers synchronize their time from a PTS, RTS, or SRTS (see fig. 17.4). Secondary Time Servers do not participate in the vote to obtain a common network time. If an SRTS is used, then all other servers must be Secondary Time Servers and must have a path to the SRTS. If an SRTS is not used, the STS can obtain its time through a PTS. To minimize network traffic and time synchronization delays, the STS should contact the nearest PTS, with a minimum of router hops and network segments between an STS and its time source.

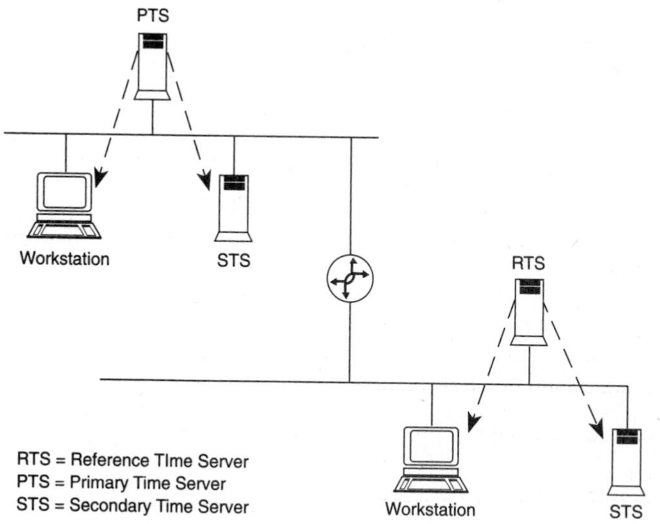

Figure 17.4
Secondary Time Servers.

Implementing Time Synchronization

The timestamps used for synchronization consist of the following two parts:

- The date and time measured in seconds since January 1, 1970
- An event counter that uniquely identifies all events occurring in the same second

To determine the network time, each NetWare 4.*x* server keeps track of time zone information and daylight savings time information.

The time zone setting provides the following information:

- An abbreviation for the local time zone name
- Offset of the local time zone from Universal Time Coordinated (UTC)
- An abbreviation for the local time zone name to be used during daylight savings time

The city of Bozeman is in Montana in the United States; therefore, its time zone setting is set by the following command:

```
SET TIME ZONE= MST7MDT
```

The time zone without any daylight savings is represented by the characters preceding the start of the time zone offset, which can be any of the following characters: plus (+), minus (-), colon (:), or a digit (0–9). In the preceding example, the string *MST* represents the normal time for the city of Bozeman.

The characters following the time zone offset represent the daylight savings time abbreviation. The time zone offset in this example is seven hours from UTC. In general the time zone offset can be expressed as the following:

```
[+¦-]HH:MM:SS
```

It is customary to simplify the time zone offset and omit the plus sign or the MM:SS, if these fields are zero. For example, a time zone offset of +07:00:00 can be simplified to the single digit 7.

Locations West of zero degrees longitude have a positive time offset, and locations East of zero degrees longitude have a negative time offset. The following formula expresses the relationship between UTC, local time, time zone offset, and daylight savings time offset:

17

```
UTC = local time + time zone offset - daylight savings time offset
```

In earlier versions of NetWare, the time zone setting was used by routines in the CLIB.NLM and did not directly affect server time. Starting with NetWare 4.*x* the time zone string is used in determining the local time.

Table 17.1 shows the SET parameters that control the daylight savings time in NetWare 4.*x*.

Table 17.1
Daylight Savings Time SET Parameters in NetWare 4.*x*

SET Parameter	Description
SET Daylight Savings Time Offset	Is converted to seconds and added to the local time when daylight savings time begins for a location. The default value is +1:0:0.
SET Start of Daylight Savings Time	Specifies the rules for computing when daylight savings time commences.
SET End of Daylight Savings Time	Specifies the rules for computing when daylight savings time ends.
SET Daylight Savings Time Status	Can have a value of OFF (default) or ON. Changing the value of this parameter does not change local time, but causes UTC to be computed based on the adjusted time offset.
SET New Time with Daylight Savings	Can have a value of OFF (default) or ON. Changing the value of this parameter changes local time based on daylight savings time, but does not change the UTC time.

The preferred method of setting daylight savings time status is to use the SET Start of Daylight Savings Time and SET End of Daylight Savings Time console commands.

These commands are stored in the AUTOEXEC.NCF file during initial server installation.

Be careful when changing daylight savings time information using SET commands on a server. In particular, be careful not to inadvertently change the UTC time. This can be done if the SET Daylight Savings Time Status is used (see table 17.1). The SET New Time with Daylight Savings Time Status can be used to avoid the recalculation of UTC time and force local time to be recalculated instead.

The goal of time synchronization is to maintain the same UTC time on all NetWare 4.*x* servers. Time synchronization deals only with UTC time, but changing UTC time does indirectly change local time to maintain the following time relationships discussed earlier:

```
UTC = local time + time zone offset - daylight savings time offset
```

Changing the local time, time offset, or daylight savings time offset can cause the UTC time to be recalculated. When time synchronization is active, be cautious about changing local time information.

Time Synchronization Algorithm

Every server on which time synchronization is active shares a fundamental synchronization algorithm, described in the following pseudocode:

```
loop forever
// a polling loop or polling interval
begin
Find a time source (using SAP or direct data communication)
Exchange time information with the time source.
Adjust the time information to account for transmission delays.
Calculate the difference between the local UTC clock and that of
the time source.
Modify the tick rate to correct for difference during the next
sleep.
Go to sleep for the duration of the polling interval.
end loop
```

Each time-synchronized server performs the following three fundamental functions:

- Provides UTC time to any NLM or client workstation that requests it
- Provides status information indicating whether the UTC time is synchronized
- Adjusts its internal clock rate to correct for drift and maintain UTC synchronization

Each server determines if its internal UTC clock is within a maximum error interval, called the *synchronization radius*, of the common network time (the time sources agree to be the network time). If the server time is within the synchronization radius, it sets a synchronization flag in its status information to TRUE. This indicates to TIMESYNC.NLM that the server's internal UTC time can be exchanged as a time stamp with other servers on the network that also have their synchronization flags set. This condition provides a degree of assurance that the UTC time on the server does not differ from the time on other synchronized servers by more than a predictable error. Because time synchronization packets encounter delays and servers poll each other at intervals of time, there is no way to guarantee that the synchronization status on a server is correct at any given instant. Also, the maximum network delay experienced by time synchronization packets must be less than the time synchronization radius. If this is not so, the delays in sending time synchronization packets are excessive. Assuming a default time synchronization radius of two seconds and a signal speed through copper of *0.7 x velocity of light in vacuum*, the maximum span of the network is as follows:

17

```
=2 * ( 0.7 x velocity of light in vacuum)
=2 secs *(0.7 x 300000000 meter/sec)
=420000000 meters = 420000 km
```

Such a network is large enough to span the Earth. It is just about large enough to span the distance between the Earth and the moon!

This frequency with which time servers perform synchronization is controlled by the following SET parameter:

```
SET TIMESYNC POLLING INTERVAL = n
```

In the preceding parameter, *n* is in seconds and has a minimum value of 10 and a maximum value of 2678400 (31 days). Its default value is 600 seconds (ten minutes).

The type of time synchronization used on the network is identified during the NetWare 4.*x* server installation. The actual time is stored as *Universal Time Coordinated* (UTC), which is the modern name for *Greenwich Mean Time* (GMT).

Because servers can reside in different time zones, the time zone must be selected accurately, and the local daylight savings time convention set correctly. For example, within the continental United States, certain areas do not use daylight savings time. The NetWare 4.*x* server is flexible enough to use whatever method is used locally. If necessary, even the Daylight Savings Time rules can be changed by programming them through SET commands on the NetWare 4.*x* server. All the time synchronization parameters can be set by the server SET command.

Exchange of Time Information between Time Servers

Time servers poll each other to exchange their timestamps. Figure 17.5 shows how the time exchange may proceed between two servers. This figure shows two time servers attempting to synchronize. The first time server sends a packet containing its local clock reading, *t1*, to the second time server. The second time server notes the timestamp, *t2*, at which this initial packet arrives. The second time server takes a reading of its local time stamp, *t3*, and sends a packet containing *t2* and *t3* to the first time server. The first time server notes the timestamp, *t4*, when the second packet arrives.

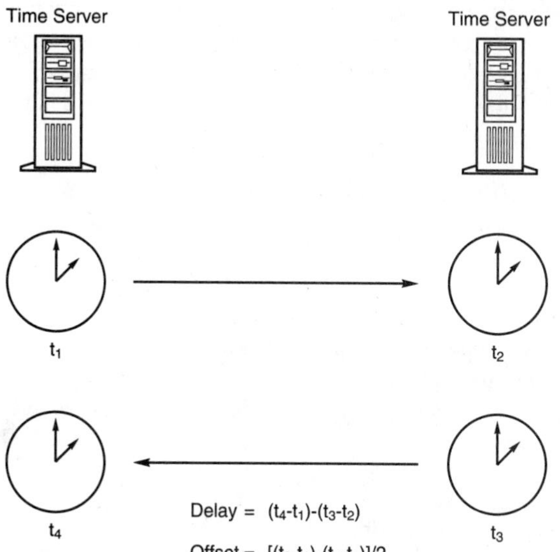

Figure 17.5
Time exchange between servers.

From the readings *t1, t2, t3,* and *t4,* the first time server can compute the transmission delay to the second server and the *time offset* between the two clocks. These values are calculated as follows:

```
Delay  = Time elapse between sending initial packet and receiving response  -
 Time spent in processing packet at second server
Time elapse between sending initial packet and receiving response = t4 - t1
Time sent in processing packet at second server = t3 - t2
Delay = (t4 - t1) - (t3 - t2)
```

The time offset is computed as the difference between the time servers' initial readings (*t1* and *t2*) and their second readings (*t3* and *t4*). The resulting time offset value is split between the two time servers; that is, it is divided by two. The offset is computed as follows:

```
Offset = [ (t2 - t1) - (t4 - t3) ] / 2
```

The time server collects a number of offsets through the synchronization check mechanism just described before applying a time correction to its clock. The set of offsets may be obtained through a series of synchronization checks with several other time servers. For example, if the server performed synchronization checks with four other time servers and obtained a time offset value of *O1, O2, O3,* and *O4* using the offset equation discussed earlier, then the set of time offsets is as follows:

```
{ 01, 02, 03, 04 }
```

The time server processes this set of offsets so obtained to compute the *probable clock error.* This process is called *offset filtering.* The probable clock error is computed as the average of the offsets. In the preceding example, probable clock error is computed as follows:

```
Probable Clock Error = ( 01 + 02 + 03 + 04 ) / 4
```

For primary time servers, the clock is corrected at half the probable clock error value. The sign of the correction value is reversed before it is applied because a clock that is ahead must be retarded, and a clock that is behind must be advanced. The following formula shows the corrected time as a function of old network time and the probable clock error.

```
Corrected time = Old Time - (Probable Clock Error) / 2
```

Role of the Clock

Intel microprocessor-based NetWare 4.*x* servers have two types of clocks: *hardware clocks* and *software clocks.* Hardware clocks are battery powered and maintained even when the computer is powered off. Software clocks are maintained by the operating system software and are initialized by the hardware clock during the computer boot process. The software maintains the time using the hardware-based timer interrupts, which occur every *tick* (1/18.26th of a second). After the boot process, the hardware clock is essentially ignored unless explicitly set by a server console command.

The hardware clocks on most computers are susceptible to errors. The term *clock jitter* describes a short-term variation; the term *wander to* describes long-term variation; and the term *clock drift* describes variations due to aging and ambient (temperature, humidity, and so on) conditions. The purpose of time synchronization is to correct these deviations among multiple clocks in remote locations to within the synchronization radius.

The software clock is maintained by the server in a data structure consisting of several registers and counters modified by the operating system *Time Synchronization Services* (TSS). The Time Synchronization Services control the clock by modifying three 64-bit registers and one 32-bit counter. The 64-bit register contains unsigned values. The most significant 32 bits contain the number of whole seconds, and the lower 32 bits contain the fractional seconds. A value of 1.5 seconds, for example, is represented by the following 64-bit value:

```
00000000000000000000000000000001 10000000000000000000000000000000
<-------- msb 32 bit (seconds) ----------> <----lsb 32 bit (fractional
seconds) ---->
```

The TIMESYNC NLM

Time synchronization is implemented by the TIMESYNC.NLM, which can be configured using a number of console SET parameters or by placing configuration parameters in the TIMESYNC.CFG file kept in the SYS:SYSTEM directory. The TIMESYNC.CFG file is a text file and can be edited using any text editor. Alternatively, SERVMAN can be used to make changes in the SET parameters; save these changes in the TIMESYNC.CFG file.

It is generally better to make time synchronization changes in the TIMESYNC.CFG file rather than in the AUTOEXEC.NCF file or by using the SET commands at the server console. The TIMESYNC.CFG file is specially designed for time synchronization, whereas the AUTOEXEC.NCF file is used for general purpose server configuration. Also, TIMESYNC.CFG is processed earlier than AUTOEXEC.NCF. TIMESYNC.CFG is processed when the server boots up and TIMESYNC.NLM loads. TIMESYNC.NLM loads before the SYS: volume is mounted, after which AUTOEXEC.NCF is processed.

Using Time Synchronization Parameters

The following steps serve as a guide for using SERVMAN to configure time synchronization parameters:

1. Load SERVMAN from the server console.

2. Select Console Set Commands from Available Options. You should see the Set Categories menu.

3. Select Time. You should see the Time parameters form (see fig. 17.6) showing the parameters that affect time synchronization. These time parameters are described in detail in table 17.2.

4. After making changes in the SET parameters, press Esc until you see the Update options menu (see fig. 17.7).

5. Select Update TIMESYNC.CFG now to save parameters in the TIMESYNC.CFG file. Figure 17.8 shows the contents of the TIMESYNC.CFG file created using the Update TIMESYNC.CFG now option. Unless explicitly mentioned, the SET parameters in table 17.1 can be placed in the TIMESYNC.CFG file without the TIMESYNC keyword prefix.

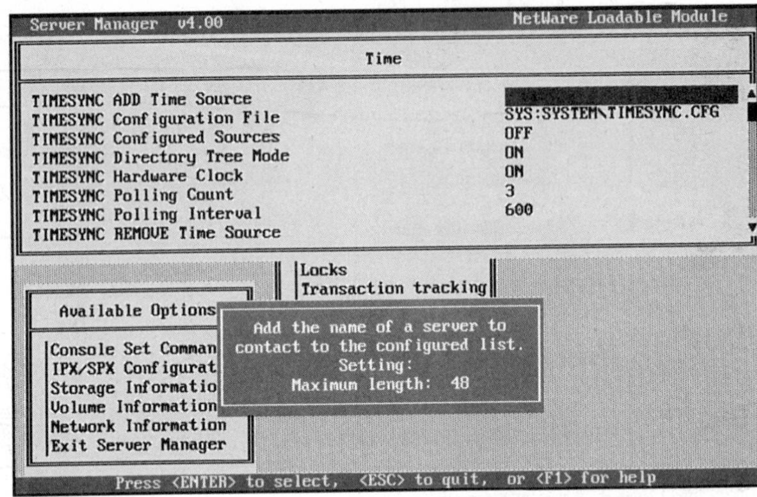

Figure 17.6
Setting Time parameters in SERVMAN.

6. To save parameter settings to a selected file (called *flushing to a file*), select Copy all set parameters to file. Figure 17.9 shows the contents of the file SETCMDS.CP created by selecting this option. As can be seen from this figure, not only the SET TIMESYNC parameters are changed, but all SET commands are changed.

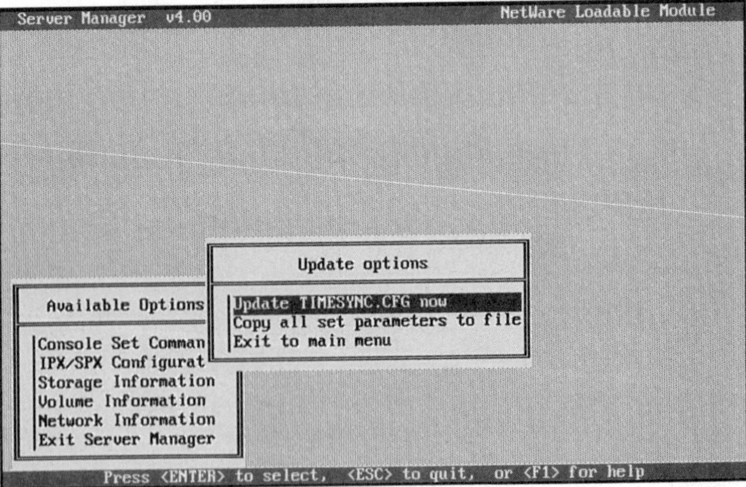

Figure 17.7
Update options for time synchronization parameters in SERVMAN.

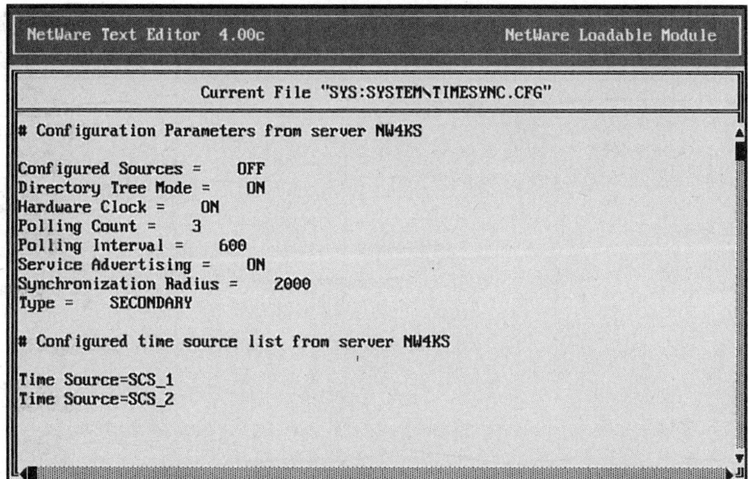

Figure 17.8
Sample TIMESYNC.CFG file in SERVMAN.

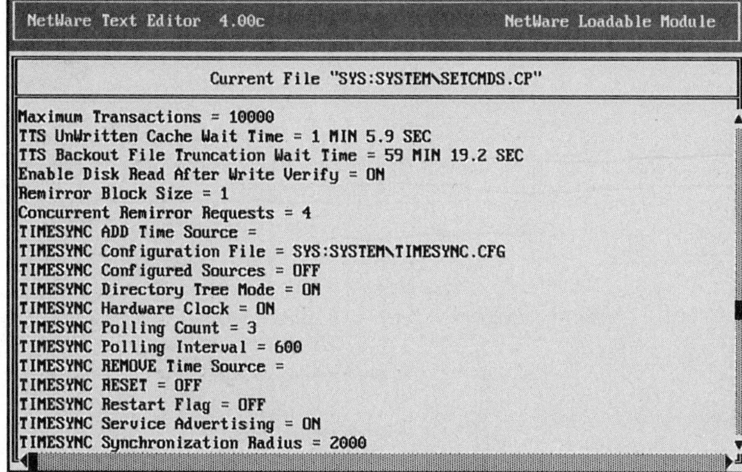

Figure 17.9
SET commands flushed to a file in SERVMAN.

Table 17.2
SET TIMESYNC Parameters

TIMESYNC Parameter	Description
TIMESYNC ADD Time Source=*ts*	This is used to specify the time source, *ts*, to be contacted for obtaining the time. The time source name, *ts,* can be up to 48 characters long. You can use this to build a list of time servers that your server can

continues

Table 17.2, Continued
SET TIMESYNC Parameters

TIMESYNC Parameter	Description
	contact to obtain its time. Normally, SAP is used to obtain the common network time. If this parameter is set, your server contacts the time servers in the order specified until it obtains the time. Only if none of the specified time servers are available will the SAP method be used (unless disabled by TIMESYNC Configured Sources Default parameter). By default this parameter is not set.
TIMESYNC Configuration File Default=*pathname*	This parameter is used to specify the default path for the configuration file. The default value is SYS:SYSTEM\TIMESYNC.CFG. You can use an alternate path name. You cannot specify this parameter in the TIMESYNC.CFG or AUTOEXEC.NCF file. You can only specify this parameter in the STARTUP.NCF file.
TIMESYNC Configured Sources Default=[ON|OFF]	This parameter is used to control whether your server uses SAP to obtain the time source or a preconfigured list of time servers (set by TIMESYNC ADD Time Source parameter). The default value is OFF, which means SAP will be used. To use a preconfigured list of time servers, set the value to ON. If you set the value to ON, you must use the TIMESYNC ADD Time Source parameter to specify a list of time servers.
TIMESYNC Directory Tree Mode =[ON|OFF]	This parameter is used to specify the NDS tree scope of SAP broadcasts. If you set this parameter to ON, only SAP broadcasts from servers in your NDS tree are used for time synchronization. SAP broadcasts from servers that are not part of your NDS tree are ignored. The default value is ON, which enables you to maintain a tighter control for time synchronization in the NDS tree. If you set this parameter to OFF, SAP broadcasts from any server, regardless of the NDS tree it belongs to, are used for time synchronization.
TIMESYNC Hardware Clock Default=[ON|OFF]	This parameter is used to determine if the NetWare server uses an external time source or reads its internal time clock. If this parameter set to OFF, your server contacts an external time source (such as an atomic clock or radio clock) to obtain its time. The default is

TIMESYNC Parameter	Description
	ON, which means that your server reads its internal clock. If this parameter is set to ON for Single or Reference time servers, these servers read their clocks. If this parameter is set to ON for Primary or Secondary time servers, these servers set their clocks based on the common network time.
TIMESYNC Polling Count Default=*n*	This parameter sets the number of time synchronization packets that will be exchanged during a polling cycle. The polling cycle is used for time synchronization. The default value is 3 and can range from 1 to 1,000. If you increase the value, the amount of synchronization traffic increases. Novell recommends that you do not increase this setting (unless you have a very good reason).
TIMESYNC Polling Interval Default=*t*	This parameter sets the amount of time, in seconds, that elapses between polling cycles. The default is 600 seconds (10 minutes), and the value can range from 10 to 2,678,400 seconds (31 days). If you decrease this time parameter, your servers will be more closely synchronized, but the network time increases. If you want to decrease the network traffic due to polling cycles, you should increase this value. For slower WAN links, you may want to increase the polling interval.
TIMESYNC Remove Time Source=*ts*	This parameter is used to remove the specified time source from a list of configured time sources. It is primarily meant to be issued from the server console to make deletions in the list. This command is usually not added in the TIMESYNC.CFG or AUTOEXEC.NCF file.
TIMESYNC Reset = [ON | OFF]	This parameter resets the values changed by the TIMESYNC.CFG or SET TIMESYNC commands to their default values and removes the list of time sources. It does not alter the contents of the TIMESYNC.CFG or AUTOEXEC.NCF file. It only resets the current values of the parameters for the server. After the value is changed to ON, it executes the actions described and resets to OFF. The default value is OFF.

continues

Table 17.2, Continued
SET TIMESYNC Parameters

TIMESYNC Parameter	Description
TIMESYNC Restart Flag=[ON I OFF]	This parameter is used to restart TIMESYNC.NLM with a new set of values from the TIMESYNC.CFG file without rebooting the server. After the value is changed to ON, it executes the actions described and resets to OFF. The default value is OFF.
TIMESYNC Service Advertising =[ON|OFF]	This is used by time providers *only,* not time consumers (secondary time servers), to determine the method by which the time source should advertise. This parameter has no effect on secondary time servers. The default value is ON, which means that time providers use SAP broadcasts for advertising time. If you set the TIMESYNC Configured Sources to ON, you should set the value of this parameter to OFF.
TIMESYNC Synchronization Radius Default=*t*	This parameter determines the "error" bounds for time synchronization. It determines how far apart the times on the servers can be before adjustment is necessary. If you set this parameter to a high value, you allow for larger differences between times on servers. If the error margin is too large, it can reduce the integrity of NDS transactions being done in the correct sequence. If the radius is small, the servers are more closely synchronized but generate greater synchronization traffic. If the radius is made too small, time synchronization becomes difficult, if not impossible, to achieve. The value is measured in milliseconds and has a default of 2,000 milliseconds. It can range from 0 to 2,147,483,647 milliseconds.
TIMESYNC Time Adjustment =[+|-]*hh:mm:*ss[[*ATmm/dd/yy* Single *hh:mm:ss* [AM|PM]] [CANCEL]]	This parameter can be used to manually adjust time on a Reference or Primary time server. Use this command sparingly to correct network-wide time errors. Frequent use of this command can corrupt time synchronization on the network, and this causes inconsistencies in the order of events performed on the network. The AT option can be used to schedule a time adjustment on the specified day *mm/dd/yy* and time *hh:mm:ss.* To cancel a previously scheduled time adjustment, use CANCEL instead of AT. The maximum length of the value is 99 characters. The default date and time is six polling intervals or one hour from now, whichever is larger.

TIMESYNC Parameter	Description
TIMESYNC Time Source = *ts*	This adds the name of the time source, *ts*, to the configured list of servers. When used without specifying a value, it displays a list of current time servers.
TIMESYNC Type = *type*	This is used to set the *type* of time server active on the file server. The *type* can have any of the following values: SINGLE, REFERENCE, PRIMARY, SECONDARY. SINGLE refers to Single Reference Time Servers; REFERENCE refers to Reference Time Servers; PRIMARY refers to Primary Time Servers; SECONDARY refers to Secondary Time Servers. The default value is SECONDARY.
TIMESYNC Write Parameters =[ON|OFF]	When set to ON, this causes certain parameters (controlled by TIMESYNC Write Value parameter) to be written to the TIMESYNC.CFG file. The default is OFF.
TIMESYNC Write Value = *n*	The value of *n* controls the type of parameters written to the TIMESYNC.CFG file, if TIMESYNC Write Parameters is ON. If *n* is set to 1, only internal parameters from this file server are written to TIMESYNC.CFG. If *n* is set to 2, only external parameters from servers on the TIMESYNC TIME SOURCE list are written to TIMESYNC.CFG. If *n* is set to 3, both internal and external parameters from servers on the TIMESYNC TIME SOURCE list are written to TIMESYNC.CFG. The default value is 3.
Time Zone = *sssNddd*	This parameter determines the offset from UTC. *sss* refers to the standard time zone. Examples are PST, MST, CST, and EST. These are three letter abbreviations for U.S. Pacific Standard Time, U.S. Mountain Standard Time, U.S. Central Standard Time, and U.S. Eastern Standard Time, respectively. *N* refers to the number of hours offset from UTC. U.S. Pacific Coast is eight hours from UTC, and U.S. East Coast is five hours from UTC. The *ddd* indicates if daylight savings time is in effect. PDT = U.S. Pacific Daylight savings Time. MDT = U.S. Mountain Daylight savings Time. CDT = U.S. Central Daylight savings Time. EDT = U.S. Eastern Daylight savings Time.

Service Advertising Protocol (SAP) versus Custom Time Synchronization

Time servers discover the existence of other time servers by using either of the following methods:

- Service Advertising Protocol
- Direct communication (custom configuration)

The SAP is used by services, including time servers, to broadcast their existence across the network. For small networks, this is a very effective and simple way to discover services on the network, because it does not require extra configuration. On large networks, however, the SAP can use up large amounts of bandwidths. Use of the NLSP (see chapter 3, "Bridging and Routing") protocol to advertise services can eliminate some of the proliferative nature of SAP. Another solution is to use direct communication between time servers. The time servers are initialized with a list of other time sources using the following SET parameter:

```
SET TIMESYNC TIME SOURCE = time server
```

In addition, you must use the following SET commands to disable the use of SAP in conjunction with time servers.

```
SET TIMESYNC CONFIGURED SOURCES DEFAULT= ON
SET TIMESYNC SERVICE ADVERTISING = OFF (on time sources)
```

Custom configuration involves determining which servers on the network are time sources and which servers follow what time source. Each server is then given a configuration file (TIMESYNC.CFG) that lists the authorized time sources for that server and its parameters.

Secondary servers attempt to contact the time sources in the order listed and stop as soon as any time source is reached. It is even possible, at the risk of a greater time synchronization error, to have a secondary time server contact another time server. In most situations, the secondary servers can contact the other source time servers.

Some of the advantages of custom configuration are as follows:

- You have complete control of the time synchronization hierarchy.
- You can distribute time sources around the network based on the strategy of minimizing network traffic and improving reliability of time synchronization.
- You can increase the reliability of time synchronization by adding alternate time sources to be used in case of network failures.
- You can eliminate the excessive traffic caused by the use of SAP for finding out other time servers.

Custom configuration has the following disadvantages:

- Customization is more complex and requires careful planning, especially for large networks.
- If a new time source is added, the configuration files on other time servers have to be updated. The only way other time servers will discover the new time source is if they are explicitly told about it in their configuration files. Otherwise, the new time server will never be contacted.

In larger networks, a number of decisions need to be made concerning time synchronization. Some of the more important issues are included in the following list:

1. Which servers will be time sources (PTS, RTS) and which will be Secondary servers?
2. Will time synchronization use SAP exclusively to discover time servers, a configured sources list, or a combination of the two?

   To keep network design simple, you may decide to use either SAP or custom configuration. You can eliminate use of SAP for time synchronization by using the SET TIMESYNC SERVICE ADVERTISING = OFF and SET TIMESYNC CONFIGURED SOURCES DEFAULT= ON parameters in the TIMESYNC.CFG file.
3. If servers are to use a configured sources list, which servers will contact which time sources?
4. If more than one NDS tree is on the same network, will the trees be time synchronized independently or together?
5. Figure out how you will set the value of the polling interval, the polling count, and the synchronization radius. In most cases, the default values are adequate. You can consult the description of these parameters in table 17.2 and the discussion on determining network traffic due to synchronization, in the next section, to optimize these parameters.
6. Will there be more than one RTS? What external time sources will be used to synchronize the RTS?

Determining the Effects of Time Synchronization Traffic

The network traffic generated by time synchronization is determined by the size of the time synchronization packets and the number of time exchanges during each polling loop. The number of exchanges during each polling loop is determined by the following polling count parameter:

```
SET  TIMESYNC POLLING COUNT DEFAULT = n
```

The default value of this parameter is three—that is, it takes three time exchanges, which each involve an NCP send/receive pair. Each NCP send/receive pair totals 332 bytes of data. Thus, the default three exchanges involve six packets—a total 996 bytes of data.

The frequency of polls is determined by the following SET parameter:

```
SET TIMESYNC POLLING INTERVAL DEFAULT=t
```

The default value of this parameter is 600 seconds (ten minutes), although when time synchronization is first begun, polling occurs every ten seconds.

At the beginning of time synchronization, the time synchronization traffic is represented by the following equation:

```
= 996 Bytes/10 seconds = 996 Bytes * 8 Bits/Byte /10

= 797 bits/sec
```

When time synchronization stabilizes, the default time synchronization traffic is as follows:

```
= 996 Bytes/600 seconds = 996 Bytes * 8 Bits/Byte /600

= 13 bits/sec
```

As the number of PTS and RTS servers increases, the number of time synchronizations increases. If there are *N* time servers, the number of separate server exchanges is as given by the following:

$N(N-1)/2$

For a network with five time servers, the number of exchanges is computed as follows:

$5(5-1)/2 = 10$

For a network with ten time servers, the number of exchanges is computed as follows:

$10(10-1)/2 = 45$

Table 17.3 shows the traffic rates for different numbers of time servers. As the network grows and requires additional time servers, the amount of synchronization traffic grows. You can increase the polling interval to reduce the amount of time synchronization traffic as long as the server clocks do not drift beyond the synchronization radius during the polling interval. Increasing the polling interval may become necessary if the synchronization traffic is occurring over a slow WAN link. As you can see from table 17.3, on most networks the amount of synchronization traffic is small compared with traffic associated with network use.

Table 17.3
Estimates for Time Synchronization Traffic Assuming a Default Poll Count of Three

Polling Interval (secs)	Number of Time Servers	Time Synchronization Traffic
10	2	797 bps
10	5	8.0 Kbps

Polling Interval (secs)	Number of Time Servers	Time Synchronization Traffic
10	10	35.9 bps
10	50	976.3 Kbps
10	100	3.94 Mbps
600	2	13 bps
600	5	130 bps
600	10	585 bps
600	50	15.9 Kbps
600	100	64.4 Kbps

Building a Time Synchronization Hierarchy

On large networks, it is useful to build a hierarchy of time servers. The time servers at the top level of this hierarchy are closely synchronized, and servers at lower levels are synchronized to servers on the next higher level. The hierarchical structure of the time servers is based on physical location of servers and synchronization traffic considerations and is independent of the hierarchical structure of the NDS tree.

As the number of levels in the time server hierarchy grows, the synchronization error between the top level and lower level time servers increases. In general, the time synchronization error between the top level and any lower level is directly proportional to the number of intervening levels.

The following are some suggestions to help you organize your time synchronization hierarchy:

1. Have Secondary servers synchronize to time sources such as the Primary, Reference, or Single Reference servers.

2. If Secondary servers must follow other Secondary servers, keep the depth of the tree as small as possible.

3. Minimize the number of time sources to keep network traffic low. The number of packet exchanges between *N* time servers is proportional to *N*N*.

4. On large networks, use multiple time sources to reduce time synchronization network traffic. Use local time sources in separate geographic locations.

Repairing Time Synchronization

The best laid plans of network designers can sometimes go astray, and it is possible to lose time synchronization on the network. This can occur when links go down and the time servers are unable to contact each other to maintain proper time synchronization. The clock drift on most computers is such that they are accurate for a few hours without correction. If time synchronization is lost for a long period of time, it is possible for replicas on different servers to contain inconsistent views of the Directory tree. Timestamp problems can be repaired using the partition manager client utilities. These utilities assume that the master replica of the partition contains the most up-to-date information. The master replica of a partition is copied over to other replica types of the partition and overwrites these replicas. If the master replica does not contain the most recent information, more recent changes made to other replicas are lost.

If you can determine that some replica other than the master partition contains the most recent information, you must use the partition manager to change the most current replica to a master replica.

Several hidden parameters in TIMESYNC can be used for fine-tuning the synchronization algorithm. These parameters may be eliminated in future releases of TIMESYNC. Although they are still available, they may prove to be useful in debugging time synchronization activities.

You can enable time synchronization using the following command:

```
SET TIMESYNC DEBUG = 7
```

The preceding command displays time synchronization activity on the server console. To disable it, use the following command:

```
SET TIMESYNC DEBUG = 0
```

The TIMESYNC DEBUG parameter can be set to other values, in which each bit value in the number controls a group of messages or disables output altogether.

Information on decoding these message types is provided next. Consider a message of the following type:

```
TIMESYNC: Polled server NW4CS
Weight = 1, OFFSET.H = FFFFFFFF OFFSET.L = FFF03453
```

In the preceding message, the name of the polled server is NW4CS. The Weight value of 1 indicates that time synchronization exchange was successful. A value of 0 indicates that time synchronization did not take place because out-of-range data was detected. This might be because the time server is unreachable (not up or network link is down). The values for OFFSET.H and OFFSET.L are the calculated difference of the server's time from the polled server's time. The two values form a 64-bit signed number with an implied hexadecimal point separating the whole and fractional parts. In the preceding message, the OFFSET values form the number FFFFFFFF.FFF03453, which means that the server is a fraction ahead of NW4CS.

A reported Weight of 0 with non-zero offset values indicates that the synchronization data is out of range. For example, this might occur if one server is 10 years ahead of the other.

If a message of the preceding type does not appear at all, it implies that this time server does not know about any other time servers. This might be because the configured time source list is empty, or no SAP time source can be found, or both. If you disabled the use of SAP, the only possible cause is that the configured time source list is empty.

To examine the current setting of the time source list, use the following command on the server console:

```
SET TIMESYNC TIME SOURCE =
```

Consider another message type that appears as follows:

```
Uniform Adjustment Requested = -0.0E0F98DD
Server type = 2
```

This message shows the actual adjustment (Uniform Adjustment Requested) to be applied to the clock during the next polling period. The server type values reported have the following meanings:

```
2=Secondary Time Server
3=Primary Time Server
4=Reference Time Server
5=Single Reference Time Server
```

The time adjustment value is displayed as signed hexadecimal. In this case, the sign is a minus, so the time will be subtracted because the server is ahead of the polled server. The value 0.0E0F98DD corresponds to one tick. Generally, one-tick or half-tick errors are caused by random time behaviors and network delays between the two time servers. If an adjustment of +0.00000000 is seen, the time servers are in exact synchronization. You also may see this value stabilize at a small negative value, such as -0.00000094, due to a small round-off error in the synchronization algorithm. An error of 0.00000094 corresponds to 34 nanoseconds, which is much smaller than the resolution of the time server clock.

Consider another message type that commonly appears as follows:

```
Adjustment smaller than Correction Floor was ignored.
```

This message means that the clock adjustment is so small that it is being ignored. The parameter that determines the "cut-off" value is set by the following command:

```
SET TIMESYNC CORRECTION FLOOR = t
```

The default value of this parameter is 1 millisecond and can be set to a value of *t* milliseconds. This value must always be less than the synchronization radius or synchronization does not occur. You can use this parameter to eliminate the correction for the one-tick jitter that sometimes occurs.

Another interesting undocumented time synchronization parameter is the following:


```
SET TIMESYNC IMMEDIATE SYNCHRONIZATION = ON
```

The preceding SET command awakens the synchronization process immediately and causes it to start a polling loop. After synchronization it automatically resets to OFF. You can use this to observe the effects of parameter setting changes immediately by forcing a time synchronization rather than waiting for time synchronization at the end of the polling interval.

If time servers fail to synchronize, check for obvious errors. The most common reason is that there are no reachable time sources. In this case, check the time source list or network connections. You can turn on the debug option by using the following command:

```
SET TIMESYNC DEBUG = 7
```

From the messages displayed, you can determine if the server is attempting to contact a time source. If the server's time is set far ahead, time synchronization may take a long time. The server's time does not move backwards. It could takes two hours to lose two hours. Check the server's time and manually adjust the clock, if necessary.

When booting a new server, it may take several seconds before the new server learns about the other time servers. If using SAP, the SAP messages are received at the next SAP broadcast interval. Also, before exchanging time synchronization messages, a route request can be used to discover the address of the forwarding router. All this adds a few seconds of delays initially.

As long as one time source remains active, other time sources can be shut down and rebooted. A time server, upon joining the network, polls for and uses the network time. If only two time sources are on a network and these are booted for the first time, the time on the first server that polls is used as the initial value of the network time.

Occasionally, NDS may report the following error even though the SET TIME command reveals that the server times are synchronized:

```
Time_Not_Synchronized - Error 659 (FD6D)
```

This error actually occurs when NDS receives a timestamp older than information already in the Directory. This could happen if the server's time was set backwards, such as in the situation of losing the Complementary Metal Oxide Semiconductor (CMOS) battery or the server time being set incorrectly when the server was booted.

If the local time is misconfigured while time synchronization is active, the UTC time is also incorrect. The Time Synchronization mechanism attempts to adjust UTC time to correspond to the network time, which in turn changes local time. Time synchronization may therefore fight efforts to correct misconfigured local parameters. If the local time is badly misconfigured while time synchronization is active, you can rest time synchronization by using the following command:

```
SET TIMESYNC RESTART = ON
```

You also can bring the server down and up again. TIMESYNC.NLM is automatically loaded when the server is started. NetWare 4.01 does not ship with a separate TIMESYNC.NLM, so if you unload it using the UNLOAD command, you cannot load it without bringing the server down and up. You can contact Novell Technical Support to obtain a copy of TIMESYNC.NLM.

Summary

In this chapter, you learned about the importance of time synchronization on a distributed network consisting of many servers. Time synchronization is accomplished by running the TIMESYNC.NLM on each NetWare 4.*x* server. You learned about the different time server types that can be used in NetWare 4.*x* networks and when to use a particular time server type.

You also learned about the different SET parameters that can be used to affect time synchronization, and how the SAP and direct communication methods are used by time servers to find each other.

Managing NetWare 4 Users

This chapter helps you understand how NetWare 4.*x* user accounts can be created and managed. NetWare 4 user accounts are defined as *NetWare Directory Services* (NDS) user objects in the NDS tree. Managing such user accounts consists largely of creating and managing NDS user objects using tools such as NWADMIN and NETADMIN.

This chapter examines the different ways that user and container accounts can be created and managed. Managing user accounts is the most common task the network Administrator has to perform. To simplify this task, the Administrator can delegate responsibilities and tasks to other users. In this chapter, you learn how to set up users with these additional capabilities.

This chapter points out the importance of setting up a good NDS structure for your company. You learn that proper delegation of capabilities and placement of container objects makes network management easier.

Also, you can manage the server console remotely by means of the *Remote Management Facility* (RMF). The MONITOR NLM utility enables you to monitor users. You learn about remote management later in this chapter.

Understanding User Administration

User account administration can be divided into two phases: creating and establishing a user account, and maintaining user accounts.

User accounts can be created in several ways. The most popular way is by using the NETADMIN utility, an interactive menu-driven utility that is easy to use. Another method is to set up users by using NWADMIN, a Windows equivalent to NETADMIN (and several other DOS-based utilities).

In many environments, user accounts must be created for a large number of users with similar needs. Creating users one at a time with NETADMIN can become a daunting task. In these situations, the UIMPORT utility can be used for a batch creation of users. UIMPORT is designed primarily to import comma-delimited ASCII-text databases, such as a telephone list, into the NDS database. You design a control file that determines which fields in your ASCII database will be imported.

Colleges and universities are good examples of areas in which user accounts are created in batches. As new students enroll every semester or quarter, old accounts must be deleted and new accounts must be created. These accounts easily can be deleted and created by using the UIMPORT utility.

The second phase, maintaining user accounts, involves maintenance of the network. User accounts are never static because the needs of the organization (and thus the needs of users in the organization) change and evolve with time. The NETADMIN and NWADMIN utilities can be used to maintain most of the user parameters that need to be modified.

Managing User Accounts

This section focuses on managing user accounts. You learn how to perform user-account management for accounts that use NETADMIN. In a later section, you learn how to use NWADMIN and then UIMPORT to manage a batch of user accounts.

Creating User Names

Before a user account can be created, you must decide which user name to use to identify the account. A uniform and consistent method should be used for assigning user names for the user accounts. The following are some conventions for creating user names:

- **User's first name.** The user's first name works well in small LANs, in which everyone is on a first-name basis. Examples of user names for accounts are MARY, JOHN, DAVID, and so on. If more than one user has the same first name, a name-collision problem occurs, so use another naming scheme.

- **User's last name.** The user's last name is common in more formal organizations. If more than one user has the same last name, a name-collision problem occurs—again, another naming scheme can be used.

- **User's first name and last initial.** Although the first name and last name initial usually works (preventing most name collisions) it is not foolproof. If more than one user has the same first name and last initial, use another naming scheme.

- **User's first name initial and last name.** The user's first name initial and last name also works well to avoid most name collisions.

- **User's initials.** Although making the user's initials the user name seldom is done, this scheme can be used in organizations in which people usually are identified by their initials. To avoid name collisions, the initials of first, middle, and last names can be used. Examples of such user names are KSS, DGS, JFK, and so on. Unless these names are easily recognizable, they should be avoided. (Some users may not like to be referred to by their initials.)

User names can be up to 64 characters long, but limiting them to no more than eight characters is preferable. When assigning home directories, making the home directory name the same as the user name is convenient. Because directory names under DOS cannot contain more than eleven characters including the extension, the user name also should contain eight or fewer characters.

In NDS, the user is classified as a *leaf object.* NDS enables you to define not only a user's login name, but also the user's full name and other names (such as nicknames). The user's login name then is combined with the NDS context to form the complete name.

Creating Containers and Container Names

Sometimes users need the same type of access from the server, particularly if they are on the same project team or if their jobs are similar. NetWare provides a convenient scheme to manage these users. Users with common needs are considered to be part of the same container, which has a container name (up to 64 characters long) associated with it. The container is assigned a set of access privileges. All users who are members of the container then can inherit the access rights assigned to the container.

Containers simplify the administration of user accounts. Instead of assigning access privileges individually, for example, the privileges can be assigned to a container; the users then automatically inherit the privileges of the container. Other benefits of containers include the following:

- Access privileges can be revoked from all users in a container
- Access privileges can be granted to all users in a container
- If a user is no longer a part of the workgroup, the user can be moved from the NetWare container
- If a user no longer is a part of the workgroup, the user can be moved from the original container to a new or existing container

Thus, containers make user-account administration easier. Unlike user accounts, containers do not have home directories. The concept of containers is used extensively to simplify user-account management with NETADMIN.

NETADMIN (NETwork ADMINistration), a menu-driven utility that creates and modifies user accounts, commonly is used to manage user accounts. You also can use the NWADMIN and UIMPORT utilities to manage these accounts.

The following sections give you the steps to follow for the tasks NETADMIN performs and show you the NETADMIN screens for NetWare 4.*x.* To a limited extent, SYSCON, from NetWare 3.*x,* can be used on a NetWare 4.*x* server to manage user accounts. This can be done under bindery emulation. The 3.*x* SYSCON can manage objects in the same container as the file server object only.

NETADMIN's many options reflect the fact that almost all system administration tasks can be performed with this utility. Because choosing these tasks can be bewildering, the user administration tasks discussed in this chapter are grouped by logical functions. These tasks also are presented in a logical order, so that if you are setting up users for the first time, you can follow the discussion to simplify the process of creating and maintaining users. (If you want a batch creation of users, MAKEUSER/ USERDEF can be used. To set up workgroup administrators, NETADMIN can be used.)

The following sections discuss in detail three important system-administration tasks:

- Setting up user accounting
- Creating and assigning container objects
- Creating a user object

Understanding NDS Objects and Properties

An important aspect of managing users and containers in NetWare 4.*x* is understanding the difference between objects and properties.

An object is an item in the NDS structure. An NDS object is similar to a bindery object in earlier versions of NetWare. Objects are divided into two general categories: *container* and *leaf*. The objects this chapter focuses on are Users and Organizational Units. Along the way, several other related objects also are discussed. A *user object* represents a network user in the NDS database. An *organizational unit* (OU) represents a grouping of related NDS objects, such as users, printers, and NetWare file servers. A user object is categorized as a leaf object. An OU is a container object.

A *property* is a characteristic that belongs to an object. Each type of object has a different set of properties. The properties of a user object include its login script, password, time restrictions, and so on. Properties of an organizational unit object include its login script and its intruder-detection capability.

When you create a user or an OU, you create an object. When you manage a user or an OU, you are changing its properties.

Setting Up User Accounting

Before you start setting up user accounts, you must plan your account setup. The NetWare manuals include planning sheets you can use for this purpose. You also can use the planning sheet designed by the author. The difference between this and other planning sheets is that user information is presented in a one-user-per-worksheet form (see table 18.1), instead of on one large sheet containing information about many users.

Table 18.1
User Information Worksheet

1. NDS Context ______________________________

2. Login Name ______________________________

3. Full Name ______________________________

4. Address/Phone No.______________________________

5. Object Rights

Context	*Rights*
__________	______
__________	______
__________	______

6. Property Rights

Context	*Rights*
__________	______
__________	______
__________	______

7. Directory Rights

Context	*Rights*
__________	______
__________	______
__________	______

8. File Rights

Context	*Rights*
__________	______
__________	______
__________	______

9. Group Memberships ______________________________

10. Security Equivalences ______________________________

11. Profile Login Script ______________________________

12. Password Restrictions ______________________________

13. Account Restrictions ______________________________

14. Station Restrictions ______________________________

15. Time Restrictions ______________________________

16. Other Info ______________________________

For a large network, keeping this information up-to-date can be critical. Store your planning worksheets in a secure place in case of a server disk crash or the loss of the NDS database used to keep track of user information. These worksheets can help you rebuild the system.

Keeping these worksheets current is important also because user needs evolve with time. Network Administrators often are too overworked (or do not set aside the time) to maintain good user-account documentation. If the server disk crashes, the network Administrator is usually the person who must "rebuild" the system.

The table 18.1 worksheet can be used throughout this book to compile information about the user. Another way to manage worksheets is to use an application database in which the worksheet corresponds to a record in a database (or table). Some excellent database-management packages include Paradox, Btrieve, dBASE, and any SQL-based package.

Database worksheets have a disadvantage, however. If you want to share the database, you probably want to keep it on the server, and if the server disk crashes, you lose this database. For this reason, it is best to maintain a hard copy of all information as a backup.

Creating and Managing Container Objects

The four types of container objects are the following:

- Root
- Country
- Organization
- Organizational Unit

You need to do some careful planning to chart out the structure of your network. Eventually, you will arrive at a plan in which the NDS structure meets the structure of your company. You must plan for the eventuality that all the networks in the company will be linked together. When this happens, all trees on the network should be merged. This means that even an isolated network today might be linked with other networks one year from today. All NDS trees in a company must be planned as though they were going to be a single tree.

The preceding hierarchy—Root, Country (C), Organization (O), and Organizational Unit (OU)—must be observed. That is, Root is higher than Country, and OU is lower than O. You can skip the Country level if you want.

On a simple network, you can skip the OU level in favor of just one Organization under the Root. In a more complicated network, you probably will use OUs.

Table 18.2 helps you plan your container objects. This worksheet can be used to plan for Organizations and Organizational Units.

Table 18.2
Container Information Worksheet

1. NDS Context______________________________________

2. Container Name______________________________________

3. Other Names______________________________________

4. Users and Other______________________________________

Leaf Objects______________________________________

5. Object Rights

Context *Rights*

6. Property Rights

Context *Rights*

7. Directory Rights

Context *Rights*

8. File Rights

Context *Rights*

continues

Table 18.2, Continued
Container Information Worksheet

9.	Other Info
	_______________
	_______________
	_______________
	_______________
	_______________

The word *context* identifies the position of the object in the NDS hierarchy. NDS names are specified from left to right and from lowest object to highest object. *Typeful* names include O and OU designations, and so on. *Typeless* names leave out these identifiers.

The following is an example of a typeful name:

```
.CN=JSMITH.OU=MARKETING.OU=US.O=INTCO
```

The following is an example of a typeless name:

```
.JSMITH.MARKETING.US.INTCO
```

Note that proper management of container objects can make managing a 4.*x* network extremely easy. All values assigned to the container's properties are inherited by users placed under the container. The container login script, for example, becomes a user's System Login Script. All rights assigned to the container apply automatically to users in the container. Figure 18.1 illustrates the NDS hierarchy for a small company.

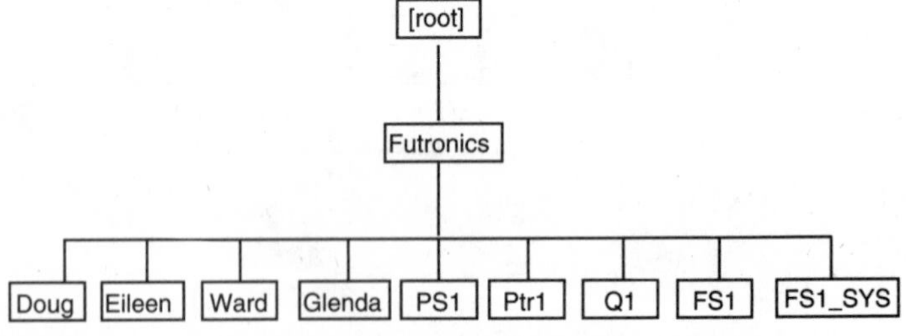

Figure 18.1
The NDS structure for a small company.

The following steps show you how to set up a structure for a large company. You are shown how to set up the .OU=ACCOUNTING.OU=US.O=INTCO side of the tree, using NETADMIN.

1. Log in to the server as an Admin User by entering the following:

   LOGIN .ADMIN.INTCO

2. Get into NETADMIN by entering the following:

   NETADMIN

3. Change context to the root by selecting Change Context and entering **[root]**. To move down to a container object, select that object and press Enter. To move up one level, press Enter after highlighting the double dots (..). The single dot indicates that you accept the current context. Press F10 after highlighting any object to take you to the management details screen for that object.

4. Select Manage objects from the main menu. Select the IntCo Organization object and press Enter. Note that the Organization object and Organizational Units (if any) are created at the time you install the server. The server and its volumes appear as objects in the server context selected when you install the server. In this example, the server context is as follows: `.OU=Marketing.OU=US.O=IntCo`. Highlight the `.OU=US` object and press Enter.

5. You now can create the new Organizational Unit by pressing Ins. A screen appears, giving you a list of possible objects you can create at this point (see fig. 18.2).

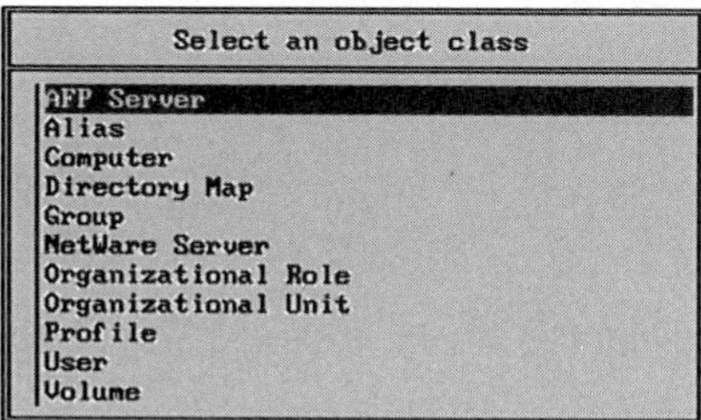

Figure 18.2
Creating an object in NETADMIN.

6. Select Organizational Unit, press Enter, and then type **Accounting.** Select NO after the question, `Create User Template?.` Press F10 to save the selection. Answer NO when asked whether to create another Organizational Unit.

7. Select the new OU just created—Accounting—and press Enter. This takes you to a blank screen. Your current context is displayed at the top left of the screen:

   ```
   .OU=Accounting.OU=US.O=IntCo
   ```

8. Create two more Organizational Units, AR, and AP, as in step 6. For the OU=AP, answer YES to the prompt about creating a user template.

A *user template* is a set of defaults you can use when you are creating any user under an Organization or Organizational Unit. These defaults replace the Default Account Balance/Restrictions NetWare 3.*x* and 2.*x* provide for using SYSCON. Values assigned to the user template are assigned automatically to any new user created under this container. You learn more about the user template later in this section.

In the following section, you learn about the properties of an OU and the way to assign a trustee right. Properties of an object vary depending on the object. Table 18.3 summarizes the properties of an O or OU. This table assumes that O and OU objects represent departments in your company. According to your circumstances, however, you might prefer to use "workgroup" instead of "department." Note that only the object's name is required: all other fields are optional.

Table 18.3
Organization or Organizational Unit Properties

Menu Selection	Property	Description
Identification	Name	The department's common NDS name.
	Other Name	Any other names you use to refer to this department. (For your information only.)
	Description	A description of this department.
	Telephone	The department's telephone number.
	Fax Number	The department's fax number.
	E-Mail Address	The e-mail address for the department or organization; could be an Internet address.
	Location	Location of this department.
Login Script	Login Script	The login script for a container object becomes the system login script for any users in the container.
Postal Address	Street	The department's street.
	Post Office Box	The department's P.O. box.
	City	City in which the department is located.
	State or Province	State or province in which the department is located.

Menu Selection	Property	Description
	Postal (ZIP) Code	The department's postal (ZIP) code.
	Copy the address	If you answer Yes, the preceding information is transferred to the Mailing Label section.
	Mailing Label	The next five fields are part Line 1 of a mailing label. Currently, this feature is not used. You could use NLIST to extract this information and redirect it to an ASCII file, which could then be edited and printed.
	Mailing Label Line 2	
	Mailing Label Line 3	
	Mailing Label Line 4	
	Mailing Label Line 5	
	Mailing Label Line 6	
Intruder	Detect Intruders	YES or NO. If set to YES, the Detection system detects people trying to log in to your network as users in this container, using invalid passwords. The default is NO.
	Incorrect Login	The number of times you allow a user to enter an invalid password; values range from 1 to 10,000.

continues

Table 18.3, Continued
Organization or Organizational Unit Properties

Menu Selection	Property	Description
	Intruder Attempt	The number of days, hours, Reset Interval, and minutes you allow incorrect login attempts. If you set the number of incorrect attempts to 3, for example, and the number of days to 1, you allow someone 3 incorrect passwords in 1 day. Ranges of values are as follows: Days—0 to 40; Hours—0 to 23; Minutes—0 to 62.
	Lock Account	YES or NO. If you set this After Detection property to YES, the account the user is trying to get into will be locked for the specified Intruder Lockout Reset Interval. This security feature is meant to prevent hackers from getting into your system. The disadvantage is that an intruder might lock any account in this container. The default is NO.
	Intruder Lockout	This value is the amount of Reset Interval time the account in this container is locked after an intruder is detected. Ranges of values are as follows: Days—0 to 40; Hours—0 to 23; Minutes—0 to 62.

Menu Selection	Property	Description
See Also	See Also	This property is for your reference only. It enables you to specify other objects that have some sort of association with this object.
Edit the User		This object, which looks like a Template user object, is covered in the next section. Properties of the User Template can be assigned a set of values. When you create a new user under this container, the properties of that user take on the values you assign here. This makes managing users much easier.

Understanding Organizational Unit Properties

Now you learn how to manage an Organizational Unit. Follow these steps:

1. Select the .OU=AR object and press F10. Note that if you press <Enter> you will change context instead of moving to the management screen. A screen with some management options appears. Options include the following:

   - View or edit properties of this object
   - Delete
   - View or edit rights to files and directories
   - View or edit the trustees of this object

2. Select the View or Edit Properties menu choice and, using table 18.3 as reference, enter various values. When you finish the properties, press Esc to move back to the Actions for Organizational Unit: AR menu.

3. To assign a Trustee right to the container, select the View or Edit Rights to Files and Directories menu option. The screen you see is similar to the one shown in figure 18.3.

Figure 18.3
Managing an Organizational Unit in NETADMIN.

Rights to files and/or directories

Volume object name: FS1_SYS.CA.
Beginning Path:
Directories/Files: Directory
Trustee Search Depth: All subdirectories

Volume object name is the NDS name for the volume that contains the directory to which you want to assign a Trustee right.

Beginning Path usually is the root of the volume. If you have a complicated directory structure, you might want to start one or two directories down off the root.

Directories/Files indicates the types of rights you want to assign. Select Directory if you want to assign directory Trustee rights only. Select File if you want to assign file Trustee rights only. Select Directory and File for both.

Trustee Search Depth indicates how deep you want the newly assigned rights to go. If you select All subdirectories, the Trustee rights "trickle down" to subdirectories beneath the currently assigned directory. If you select Current directory only, the rights are assigned to the current directory only.

4. After you complete this screen, press F10 to assign Trustee rights. When a blank screen appears, press Ins to add trustee assignments. Now you can fill in the directory and/or file name you want, or press Ins again to browse through the directory structure. When you are finished, you see a directory and file listed. The default rights are RF (Read and File Scan). Figure 18.4 shows an assignment for APPS\EXCEL.

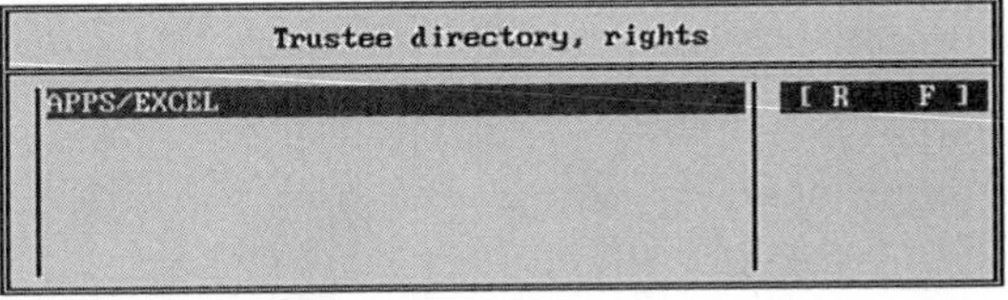

Figure 18.4
NETADMIN—adding trustee assignments.

To modify the rights, press Enter. You see a list of currently assigned rights. Press Ins to add rights or Del to remove rights. Press F5 to mark several rights at a time. Press Esc when you finish.

5. You can view the trustees of this container by selecting the View or Edit the Trustees of this Object option from the Actions for Organizational Unit: AR menu (see fig. 18.5).

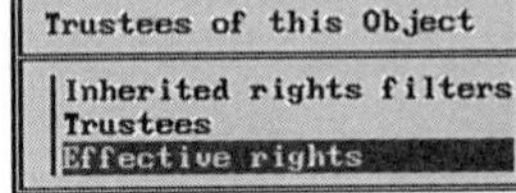

Figure 18.5
NETADMIN—The Trustees of this Object menu.

Inherited Rights Filters (IRFs) enables you to add, edit, or delete filters to properties and objects. An IRF controls access rights inherited from higher levels of the NDS tree.

Effective Rights enables you to see which objects have rights to this object. This option is like a rights calculator: it takes into account rights inherited from containers; rights that flow down from higher levels; and explicit assignments.

Trustees enables you to assign another object as a trustee of this object. To make BOB the Administrator of the AR container, proceed as follows:

a. Select the Trustees option. You see a list showing all current trustees and of which property they are the trustee. Press Ins to make BOB a trustee over the AR container object; a list of properties appears, as shown in figure 18.6.

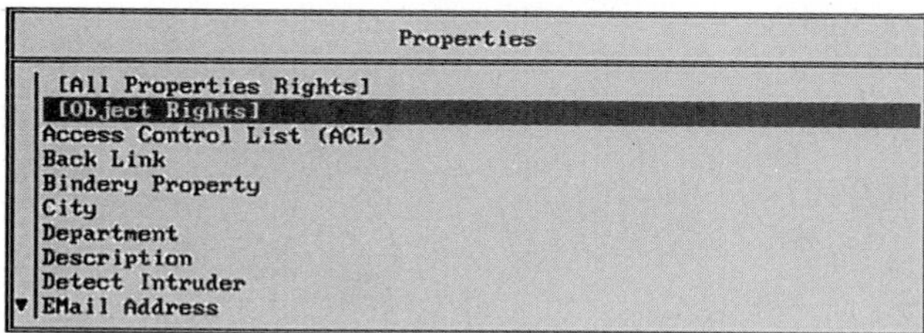

Figure 18.6
NETADMIN—object and property rights selection screen.

Select [Object Rights] and press Enter.

b. Enter BOB's NDS name by typing **.CN=Bob.OU=AR.OU=Accounting.OU =US.O=IntCo**, or press Ins and browse through the NDS tree until you find BOB's name.

Bob's name will appear on the list with Browse rights. Press Enter to alter his rights and then press Ins to add all other rights (see fig. 18.7). After you finish tagging all other object rights, press Enter to finalize them and Esc to return to the Property, Rights, Trustee list.

Now exit NETADMIN by pressing Esc several times or by pressing Alt+F10.

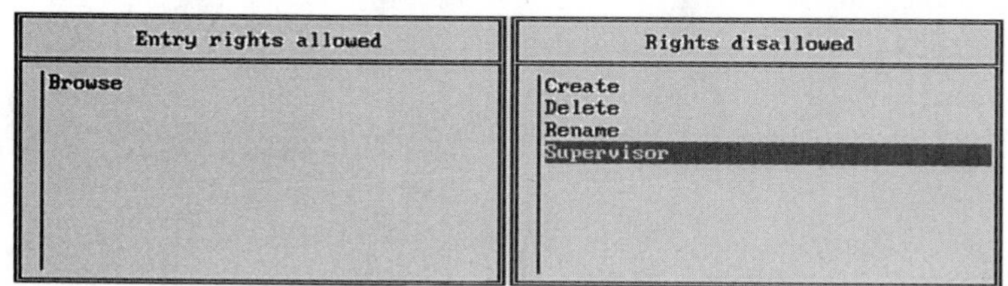

Figure 18.7
NETADMIN—adding object rights.

Creating and Managing a User Account

In this section, you learn how to use NETADMIN to create a user account. The assumption is that you have used NETADMIN to create containers. (If you are not sure how to do this, consult the preceding sections.)

Suppose that, for example, you are setting up an account for a single user. (Multiple-user accounts can be set up by repeating the steps for a single-user account.) Before you start, you must determine the user's NDS context, NDS object and property Trustee rights, directory and file trustee rights, and other information. Review the worksheets in tables 18.1 and 18.2 to assist you in gathering this information.

Creating a User Account

The following steps show you how to create a new user account. You will create a user BOB in the AR container object created in the preceding section.

1. Log in to the server as the Administrator:

   LOGIN .cn=Admin.o=IntCo

2. Invoke the NETADMIN utility.

3. Select Manage Objects. Locate the AR organizational unit under Accounting by selecting the appropriate container objects. One object, USER TEMPLATE, should already be under the container.

   The following current context should be displayed at the top of the screen for AR:

   OU=AR.OU=Accounting.OU=US.O=IntCo

4. Press Ins to add another user; a list of object classes appears. Select User and press Enter; a screen appears, similar to the one in figure 18.8. Fill in the values shown on-screen. Table 18.4 summarizes each of these fields.

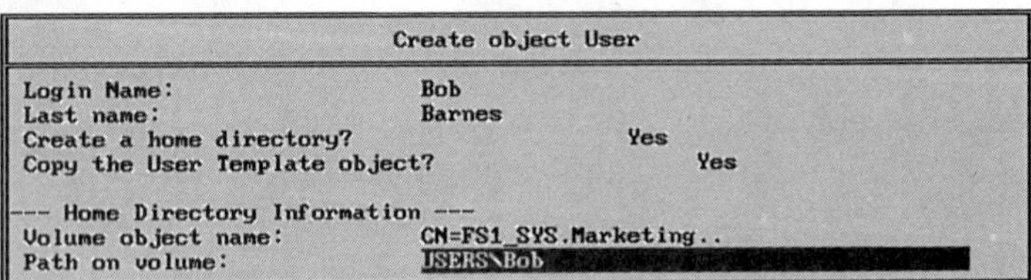

Figure 18.8
Adding a user object in NETADMIN.

Table 18.4
Creating a User Object in NETADMIN

Property	Description
Login Name	The new user's login name (a required field).
Last name	The new user's last name (a required field).
Create a home directory?	YES or NO. The default is NO. If you select YES, NETADMIN creates a directory for this user on the specified volume and path you enter. NETADMIN assumes that you want the directory name to be the same as the Login Name and takes the first eight characters. NETADMIN then assigns this user RWCEMFA directory trustee rights to his home directory. You must have at least Create and Access Control directory Trustee rights for this volume and path to be able to create a home directory for a user.
Copy the User Template object?	YES or NO. The default is YES. If you leave this option at the default, the User Template discussed earlier is copied to the user. You can make additional changes at any time.
Volume object name	This option enables you to specify the volume in which the user's home directory is located. (Valid only if you answered YES to Create a home directory?) Volumes are specified by their NDS name. If you are not sure about the name, press Ins; you can browse through the NDS tree to locate the volume you want.
Path on volume	Completely identify the user's new home directory from the root of the volume. If, for example, you want to create a user BOB with a home directory SYS:USERS\BOB, enter **USERS/BOB** in this field. If you are not sure which path to use, press Ins; you can browse through the directory tree to locate the desired path.

5. When you finish using this screen, press F10 to save the information you provided. You are asked whether you want to create another user object. For the purposes of this exercise, answer NO.

Managing a User Account

The next series of steps familiarizes you with the procedures for managing a user account, using NETADMIN. You make changes to the settings for .BOB.AR.Accounting.US.IntCo—the user you just created.

1. Log in to the network as the Administrator.

2. Invoke the NETADMIN utility. Select the Change Context option and change to the OU=AR.OU=Accounting.O=IntCo context. Remember to press F10 when you see the AR organizational unit; otherwise, Change Context does not change your context to the right place.

3. Select Manage Objects. You should see the user BOB and the USER TEMPLATE objects listed. Select BOB and press Enter or F10.

   From this menu you can work with properties for this user; rename, move, or delete the user; and work with Trustee rights.

4. From the Actions for User menu for BOB, select View or Edit Properties of this Object. The next menu you see is similar to the one shown in figure 18.9.

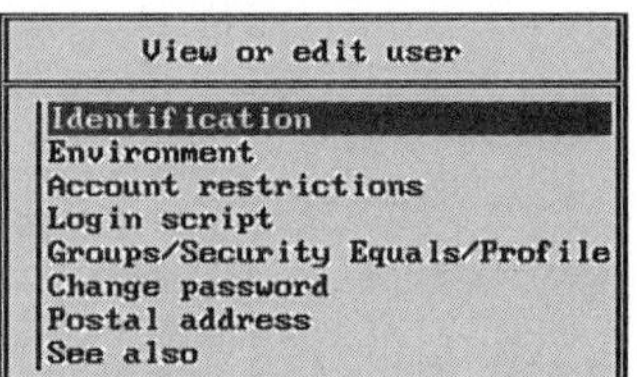

Figure 18.9
Managing user object properties in NETADMIN.

Table 18.5 summarizes the possible values for each property accessible through this menu. (The steps continue after the table.) Many of these properties are multivalued, which means that you can enter more than one value for them. To add a value, press Ins. TELEPHONE, for example, enables you to add as many telephone numbers (voice mail, pager, desk telephone, home telephone, cellular telephone, and so on) as are appropriate for a user. Defaults for the values shown in table 18.5 are set in the USER TEMPLATE object.

Table 18.5
User Object Properties

Menu Selection	Property	Description
Identification	Login Name	User's common NDS name (required).
	Last Name	User's last name (required).
	Other Name	Any other names by which you refer to this user; (For your information only).
	Title	User's title (if any).
	Description	A description of this user.

Menu Selection	Property	Description
	Telephone	User's telephone number.
	Fax Number	User's fax number.
	E-Mail Address	The e-mail address for the user or organization; could be an Internet address.
	Location	This user's location.
	Department	User's department in the company.
Environment	Language	User's default language; can be changed by setting the NWLANGUAGE DOS variable to one of the languages supported on your server.
	Default Server	The NDS name of the server on which the user receives messages from a SEND command or a server broadcast.
	Network Address	Read automatically when the user next logs in. You cannot change this field. The network address is the address of the cabling segment from which the user logs in.
	Volume Object Name	Volume on which user's home directory is located.
	Path on Volume	The exact subdirectory on the volume on which user's home directory is located.
	Create a Home Directory	Use this option to create a home directory for the user if one does not already exist.

continues

Table 18.5, Continued
User Object Properties

Menu Selection	Property	Description
Login Script	Login Script	The user's personal login script.
Login	Account Disabled Restrictions	Yes or No. If you set this to YES, this user cannot log in. This generally is done when the user is on vacation or extended leave of absence.
Account Restrictions—the Account Restrictions menu includes the following items, up to Login Script:		
	Account Has Expiration Date	Yes or No. If YES, you can set a date when this account will no longer be valid. This is useful when you set up accounts for temporary employees who will leave at a specified date.
	Date Account Expires	If this option is set to YES, you can enter an expiration date here.
	Limit Concurrent Connections	Yes or No. If set to NO, the user can log in to the network simultaneously, from different workstations, as many times as he wants. If set to YES, you can set a limit on the number of concurrent logins.
	Maximum Connections	If this option is set to YES, you can enter the number of logins here. Values range from 1 to 32,000. Note that you are limited by the number of user licenses your version of NetWare supports.
	Time Zone	This field, which reports the workstation's time zone,

Menu Selection	Property	Description
		cannot be modified. (The time zone comes from its default server or from the DOS TZ variable, if set.)
Password Restrictions	Allow User to Change Password	Yes or No. If set to NO, user cannot change his own password. If set to YES, password can be changed.
	Require a Password	Yes or No. If set to NO, the user can choose whether to have a password. If set to YES, the user must have a password. Users who do not have a password are asked to enter a new password the next time they log in.
	Minimum Password Length	Sets the minimum number of characters needed for the password; values range from 1 to 20.
	Force Periodic Password Changes	Yes or No. If set to YES, user is prompted to change his password after a specified number of days.
	Days Between Forced Changes	The interval between forced password changes; values range from 1 to 365 days.
	Date Password Expires	You can "pre-expire" a password by setting a date in the past. Otherwise, you can set a limit on the user's current password. This option is useful when you set up new users. Generally, you assign a password when users first start. For a more secure network, users should be

continues

Table 18.5, Continued
User Object Properties

Menu Selection	Property	Description
		encouraged to change their passwords as soon as possible.
	Limit Grace Logins	Yes or No. A *grace login* is the number of times a user is allowed to log in after his password expires. If set to YES, user must change the password when asked.
	Grace Logins Allowed	The number of times the user can log in until he is forced to change the password; values range from 1 to 200 days.
	Remaining Grace Logins	This value reports the number of grace logins remaining for this user.
	Require Unique Passwords	Yes or No. If you set this options to YES, the system "remembers" the last eight passwords the user entered. Users cannot reuse a password until after the eighth password.
	Date and Time of Last Login	This field, which displays the last date and time the user logged in, cannot be modified.
	Time Zone	This field, which reports the workstation's time zone, cannot be modified. The time zone comes from the default server or from the DOS TZ variable, if set. (This field is identical to the

Menu Selection	Property	Description
		one on the Login Restrictions menu.)
Time Restrictions		You will see a 7-days x 24-hour grid that enables you to set when this user can log in to the network. Time intervals are in half-hour segments. An asterisk (*) indicates that a user can log in; a space indicates a time at which the user cannot log in.
Network Address		A list of network cable segments Restrictions from which the user can log in. This option prevents users from logging in to the network from certain cable segments on the LAN. Suppose, for example, that you have a restricted area in your building. You can make this area off-limits by restricting users to all segments except this one. Limitations are by protocol (such as IPX/SPX or TCP/IP), Network Address, and Node Address. If you limit a user to a particular node address, you effectively limit that user to one station.
Intruder Lockout	Account Locked Status	Yes or No. This field tells you whether the Intruder Detection System (set up at the container level) has disabled this account.

continues

Table 18.5, Continued
User Object Properties

Menu Selection	Property	Description
	Incorrect Login Count	The number of times the intruder attempted to get in with an invalid password.
	Account Reset Time	The total amount of time the account is locked.
	Time Until Reset	The amount of time remaining before the account is unlocked.
	Last Intruder Address	The network and node address of the workstation at which the intrusion occurred.
	Time Zone	The time zone of the workstation at which the intrusion occurred.
Account Balance	Account Balance	Represents the amount of credit in units remaining for this user; ties into the Accounting System (described later in this chapter). Values range from 99,999,999 to -99,999,999.
	Allow Unlimited Credit	Yes or No. If set to YES, this user is not affected if his credit goes below the Low Balance Limit. Otherwise, the user is locked out of the system when the credit balance is depleted.
	Low Balance Limit	The lower limit allowed before the user is locked out of the system. If a user is logged in and his or her Account Balance goes below

Menu Selection	Property	Description
		this limit, the OS sends the user an `Out of Funds` message, giving the user five minutes to save work and log out.
Volume Space	Volume Object Restrictions	Name of the volume in which the user has a space restriction added.
	Limit Volume Space	Yes or No. If set to YES, you can limit the amount of disk storage this user can have available per volume. The user is not allowed to see more disk space than this limit. When a user exceeds the limit, he starts receiving `Out of Disk Space` messages.
	Volume Space Limit	The amount of storage space (in kilobytes) allowed; values can range from 0 to the size of the volume. Setting this value to 0 prevents the user from creating any files on this volume. If users' print queues are located in the volume, they cannot print. Any program that creates temporary files is impacted also.
	Volume Space in Use	The amount of disk space this user is using.
Login Script		This screen is a limited text editor that enables you to enter the user's login script.

continues

Table 18.5, Continued
User Object Properties

Menu Selection	Property	Description
Groups/Security	Group Equals/Profile	This list shows to which groups the user belongs. *Groups* are objects that can be created when you want to assign Trustee rights to users in different containers.
	Security Equal To	User gains all the rights of any object you place on this list. This is a quick way to assign rights. A user automatically has the same level of security as his container.
	Profile	A profile object is used to store a login script common to several users in one or more containers. When you enter the NDS name of the profile object here, the user automatically starts using the login script of the profile object. You also must be sure to assign Browse object rights for this user to the Profile object, as well as Read property rights to the Profile's Login Script property.
Change Password		Use this option to change the user's password.
Postal Address	Street	Street on which the user is located.
	Post Office Box	User's P.O. box.

Menu Selection	Property	Description
	City	City in which the user is located.
	State or Province	
	Postal (ZIP) Code	
	Copy the address to the mailing label?	If you answer YES to this question, the preceding information is transferred to the Mailing Label section.
	Mailing Label Line 1	The next five fields are part of a mailing label. Currently, this feature is not used. You can use NLIST to extract this information and redirect it to an ASCII file, which then can be massaged and printed.
	Mailing Label Line 2	
	Mailing Label Line 3	
	Mailing Label Line 4	
	Mailing Label Line 5	
	Mailing Label Line 6	
See Also		Contains references to other objects to which this user might be related. (For your information only.)

5. After you have made any changes you want to the properties, return to the Actions for User: Bob menu. To assign a file trustee right, select the View or edit rights to files and directories option. The screen you see is similar to the one described earlier (refer to fig. 18.7). Fill in the screen as follows:

   - Next to Volume object name, enter the NDS name for volume SYS.
   - Do not make any entries next to Beginning Path because the root of the volume is assumed.
   - Select File to assign a file trustee right.
   - Trustee Search Depth is not important because you are assigning a file trustee right here only.

6. After you fill out this screen, press F10 to assign trustee rights. When you see a blank screen, press Ins to add the file trustee assignment. Enter **SYSTEM** when you are prompted to enter a directory. Then when you are prompted to enter the name of a file, type **RCONSOLE.EXE** or press Ins and locate the file through the list.

7. NetWare 4.*x* provides support for all utilities in a number of languages. Most utilities have two files (in addition to the EXE file) that provide this support. In the case of RCONSOLE, you need to add these two files to the file trustee list, as follows:

```
SYS:SYSTEM\NLS\ENGLISH\RCONSOLE.MSG
SYS:SYSTEM\NLS\ENGLISH\RCONSOLE.HEP
```

   After you finish, you see a screen similar to the one shown in figure 18.10.

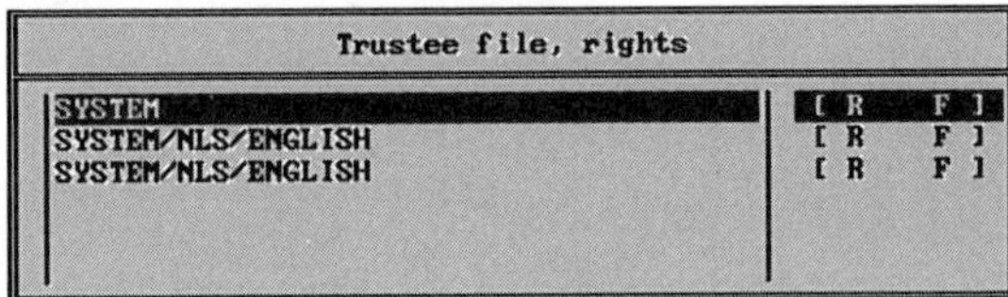

Figure 18.10
File trustee rights in NETADMIN.

   Note that the names of the files are not displayed. When you exit NETADMIN and then get back in, file trustee assignments do not appear. They can be verified from FILER or from the DOS prompt. To verify the assignments in this example, type the following line:

```
RIGHTS SYS:SYSTEM\RCONSOLE.*  /T  /SUB
```

   Figure 18.11 shows you the results of this command.

8. Exit NETADMIN by pressing Esc several times or by pressing Alt+F10.

18

```
F:\>RIGHTS SYS:SYSTEM\RCONSOLE.* /T /SUB
FS2\SYS:SYSTEM\RCONSOLE.EXE
User trustees:
     CN=Bob.OU=ar.OU=accounting.OU=us.o=intco          [ R     F ]
------------
No group trustees have been assigned.

FS2\SYS:SYSTEM\NLS\ENGLISH\RCONSOLE.HEP
User trustees:
     CN=Bob.OU=ar.OU=accounting.OU=us.o=intco          [ R     F ]
------------
No group trustees have been assigned.

FS2\SYS:SYSTEM\NLS\ENGLISH\RCONSOLE.MSG
User trustees:
     CN=Bob.OU=ar.OU=accounting.OU=us.o=intco          [ R     F ]
------------
No group trustees have been assigned.

F:\>
```

Figure 18.11
Verifying file trustee assignments by using RIGHTS. Double-clicking on container objects expands or collapses the NDS tree at that point.

Creating Objects with the NWADMIN Utility

NetWare 4.*x* includes a Windows-based management utility, NWADMIN. This utility can do everything NETADMIN can do and more. It also includes, among other features, the Windows equivalent of PCONSOLE, PARTMGR, and RCONSOLE.

NWADMIN presents you with a graphical overview of your network. Double-clicking on leaf objects takes you to a management detail screen.

Using NWADMIN To Create a Profile Object

You already learned the way to create an organizational unit object and a user object through NETADMIN. The process is similar when done through NWADMIN. The next series of steps shows you the way to use NWADMIN to create a profile object, give it a login script, and assign the profile to a user.

1. Make sure that you are logged in as an Admin user.

2. Go into Windows and invoke the NWADMIN utility.

3. Select the .AR.Accounting.US.IntCo container object. Positioning your context in NWADMIN is very important. When you are going to create an object, what you create and where it is placed depends on your current context. Because you are creating a profile object under AR, it is important that you position yourself accordingly. Figure 18.12 illustrates the NWADMIN screen at this point.

4. From the Object menu, select Create. Then from the list of possible objects to create under AR, select Profile; the New Object dialog box appears, as shown in figure 18.12. From the New Object dialog box, select Profile and click on OK. A new dialog box appears with a place for you to enter the name of the profile.

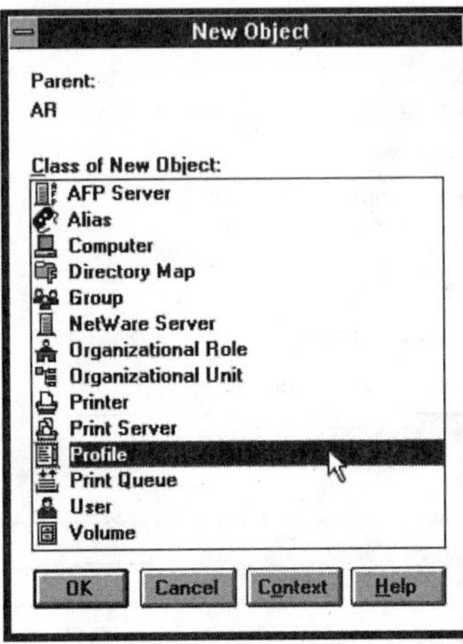

Figure 18.12
The New Object dialog box.

5. Enter the name of the profile. For this example, type **AR_Profile**. Place a check mark in the Define Additional Properties box. This causes NWADMIN to take you immediately to the Properties management screen instead of returning to the main screen. Select Create to create the new profile object.

6. Enter whatever details you want about the profile (see fig. 18.13). The buttons with three dots next to the Other Name, Location, Department, and Organization fields indicate that these are multivalued fields. Press one of these buttons to access the list for a multivalued property. The large rectangular buttons to the right of the screen take you to different sets of properties for this object.

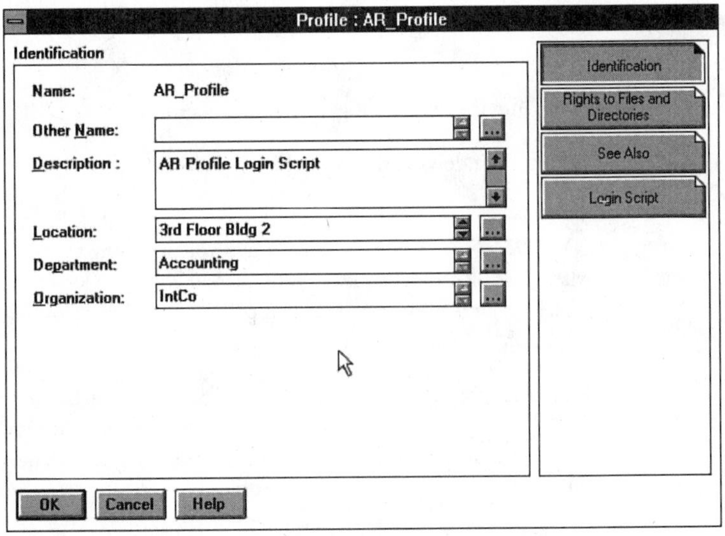

Figure 18.13
The profile object properties screen in NWADMIN.

7. Click on the Login Script button at the right and then enter the following simple login script:

```
WRITE "This is the Profile Script..."
```

   Click on OK to exit and save this information. Notice that a new profile object, AR_Profile, is added to the AR container. Next, you need to assign the profile to user BOB.

8. Double-click on user BOB. On the new screen, which looks like the one shown in figure 18.14, click on the Login Script button.

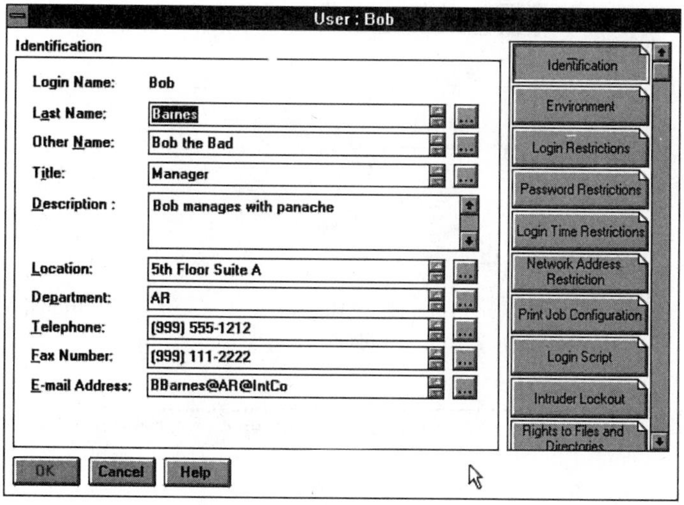

Figure 18.14
The user object properties screen in NWADMIN.

9. Under the login script itself, locate the field labeled Profile. This is where you identify the AR_Profile. You can type the complete NDS name or click on the Browse button to the right of the field.

To browse through the NDS structure, use the box labeled Directory Context. When you are ready to select an object, highlight it in the box labeled Objects.

User BOB now is assigned to the AR_Profile. When he logs in, he gets the following login scripts:

- The AR container login script
- The AR_Profile login script
- His personal login script

Login scripts are covered in greater detail in Chapter 23, "Managing User Sessions."

Using NWADMIN To Create a Group Object

Groups play a less-significant role in NetWare 4.*x* than they do in earlier versions of NetWare. In NetWare 4.*x*, the primary purpose of a Group is to assign trustee rights to a group of users other than all users in a container, such as the following:

- A group of users in more than one container
- A subset of the users in one container

In this process, you first create the group, next assign members, and then assign trustee rights. Perform the following steps, using NWADMIN:

1. Log in as the Admin user.
2. Go into the NWADMIN utility from Windows.
3. Select the organizational unit .OU=US.O=IntCo.
4. From the Object menu, select Create and then choose Group from the menu that appears.
5. Type **Managers** as the name of the group and then check the box next to Define Additional Properties. Finally, select Create. When the Group details box appears, enter any appropriate identifying details.
6. To assign members to the group, select the Members property button on the right of the screen. The list currently is empty. Browse through the NDS structure by selecting objects in the Directory Context box after choosing the Add button. To add members, select them from the Objects box and click on OK. Figure 18.15 shows the completed screen.

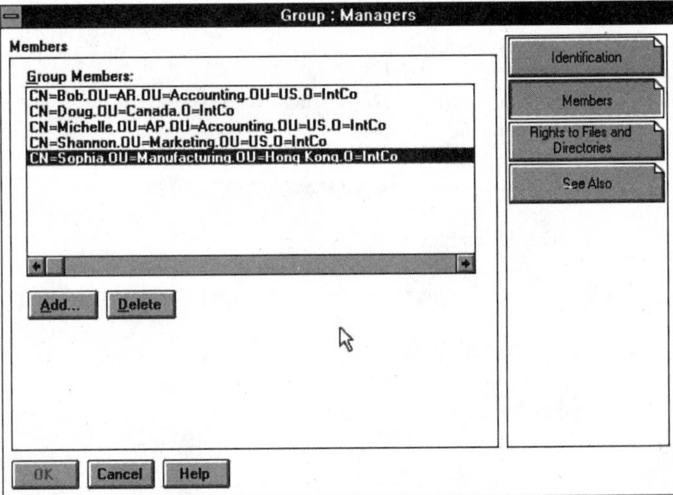

Figure 18.15
Using NWADMIN to add members to a group.

7. To assign rights to the group, click on the Rights to Files and Directories button. To display current rights, click on the Show button. Add new rights now by clicking on the Add button.

8. Browse through the NDS structure to locate the volume in which to add rights. Be sure to select a subdirectory, not the entire volume. If you select the volume, NWADMIN assumes that you want to assign trustee rights at the root. In figure 18.16, you can see subdirectories in the browse screen's Files and Directories box.

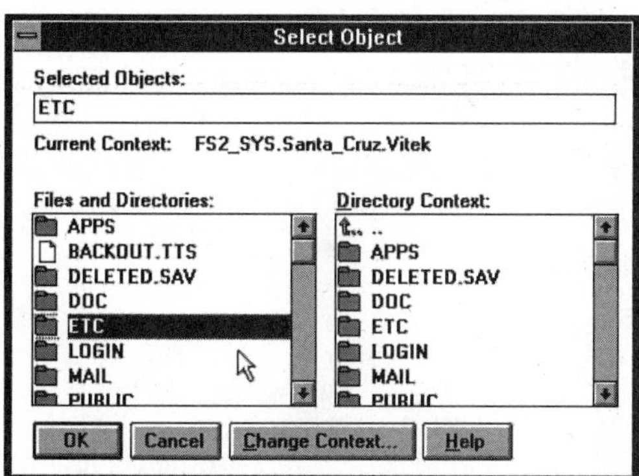

Figure 18.16
Browsing through files and directories in NWADMIN.

9. After you select the directory, place a check mark next to the box that corresponds to the rights you want to assign. Figure 18.17 shows the completed rights screen.

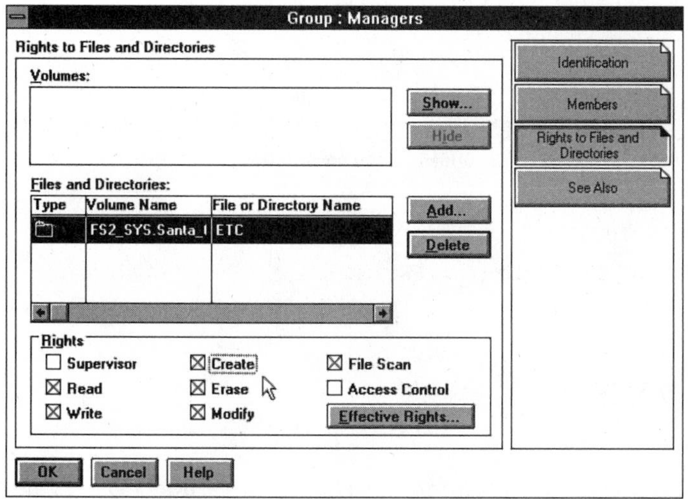

Figure 18.17
Assigning trustee rights to a group, using NWADMIN.

10. Finally, click on OK and exit NWADMIN.

Importing Users with the UIMPORT Utility

The UIMPORT (User IMPORT) utility is designed to enable you to import users from an ASCII file. The idea behind this utility is that many companies already maintain a list of employees. Most systems enable you to write out this information in ASCII format. In dBASE, for example, if you open a database with the USE command, you can perform a COPY TO XYZ DELIMITED command. This command writes the data to a file XYZ, in ASCII format with commas separating the data elements.

The UIMPORT utility can be used only for adding users. It does not build other objects in the NDS structure. You must prepare the structure by adding organization and organizational unit objects prior to adding users using UIMPORT. UIMPORT will not create Os and OUs.

UIMPORT uses two files, a control file and a data file, both of which must be ASCII text files. In the data file, commas separate the data elements. If one of the data elements (such as a Notes or Comments field) contains commas, that field must be enclosed in quotation marks. The following is an example of a data file:

```
Palmer, Laura, Single, AP, 666-2323, "Entrepreneur, dealer, clerk"
Haywood, Donna, Single, AP, 777-3434, "Pure, but wants to be like Laura"
Cooper, Dale, Married, Marketing, 555-1212, "Sharp-eyed and tireless"
Gordon, Gordon, Married, Marketing, 334-5671, "Hard of hearing; shouts a lot"
Lady, Log, Single, AR, 444-5151, "Talks to logs and foresees future"
Frere, Jacques, Married, Canada, 314-555-6262, "Canadian Ops Manager"
```

The control file tells NetWare which fields in the data file to place into which properties in the NDS structure. In addition, the control file tells UIMPORT how to treat the data. An example of a control file follows:

```
Import Control
    User Template=Y
    Create Home Directory=Y
    Home Directory Path="USERS"
    Home Directory Volume=".CN=FS2_SYS.OU=Marketing.OU=US.O=IntCo"
Fields
    Last Name
    Name
    Skip
    Department
    Telephone Number
    Description
```

The syntax for UIMPORT is the following:

```
UIMPORT   ControlFilename   DataFilename
```


Figure 18.18 illustrates the UIMPORT process. The control file dictates the way UIMPORT takes the data file. The results of the UIMPORT process end up in the NDS database.

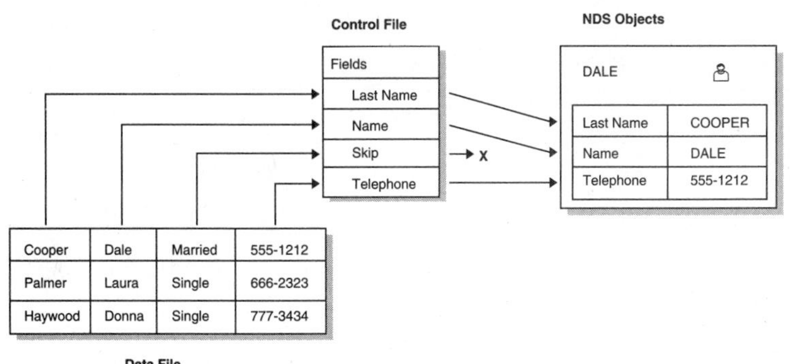

Figure 18.18
The UIMPORT process.

Figure 18.19 shows a sample UIMPORT process using the control and data files listed in the two examples just shown. Table 18.6 summarizes the parameters available in the control file. Parameters available under FIELDS in the control file are the same as the user-object properties listed in table 18.5. The only difference is an additional field, SKIP, which causes UIMPORT to skip that particular parameter in the data file. In the sample data file, for example, marital status (Single or Married) has no place in the NDS database. To prevent the marital status data from appearing in the NDS, you place a SKIP in the control file in which the marital status data comes in.

```
F:\USERS>UIMPORT CTRL.TXT DATA.TXT
Import context: OU=marketing.OU=us.o=intco
Creating user Laura, Copying Template User, Adding to group everyone,+ Done.
Creating user Donna, Copying Template User, Adding to group everyone,+ Done.
Creating user Dale, Copying Template User, Adding to group everyone,+ Done.
Creating user Gordon, Copying Template User, Adding to group everyone,+ Done.
Creating user Log, Copying Template User, Adding to group everyone,+ Done.
Creating user Jacques, Copying Template User, Adding to group everyone,+ Done.

F:\USERS>
F:\USERS>
F:\USERS>
F:\USERS>
F:\USERS>
F:\USERS>
F:\USERS>
F:\USERS>
F:\USERS>
F:\USERS>
F:\USERS>
F:\USERS>
F:\USERS>
F:\USERS>
F:\USERS>
```

Figure 18.19
A sample UIMPORT process.

Table 18.6
UIMPORT Control File's Import-Control Parameters

Parameter	Description
Separator	Identifies the punctuation that separates data elements in the data file. The default is a comma (,). If you want to change the separator—to use an ampersand, for example—type **SEPARATOR=&** in the Import Control section.
Quote	Identifies the character used to enclose string data. The default character is a quotation mark ("). If you want to use a slash instead, enter the follow ing: **QUOTE=/**
Name Context	Identifies the NDS container in which to import users. The default is your current context. If you are not sure of your current context, type **CX** at the DOS prompt. Otherwise, identify the alternate context using complete NDS syntax. To import into the Canada OU, for example, enter the following:**NAME CONTEXT=".ou=Canada.O=IntCo"**
Replace Value	Tells UIMPORT what to do with duplicate values. If you enter Y, UIMPORT overwrites existing values. The default is N. When this parameter is set to N, data in the file is added to existing values. This is how you get more than one data element into a multivalued field.
User Template	Set this to Y when you want new users you have created to take on the properties you assigned to the User Template. The default is N.
Import Mode	Controls how user objects are imported. The following are possible values: C = Create new objects only. Where data matches an existing object, ignore the data. B = Create a new object if there is no conflict; otherwise, update the object. This is the default. R = Remove objects.
Delete Property	Used to remove specified properties from the NDS user database. The character you use to represent a property to be deleted is discretionary. Suppose, for example,

<table>
<tr><th>Parameter</th><th>Description</th></tr>
<tr><td></td><td>that a new company mandate is issued instructing you, for reasons of privacy, to remove all telephone numbers and street address information from the NDS database. To implement this policy you would have to create a control file, as follows:

<code>Control File:
Import Control
    Delete Property=&&
    Fields
    Name
    Last Name
    Telephone Number
    Postal Address</code>

Inside the data file, place the delete character next to the names of the users affected. The following is a sample data file that corresponds to the preceding control file:
<code>Data File:
Dale, Cooper, &&, &&
Laura, Palmer, &&, &&</code>
These changes would cause deletion of the Telephone Number and Postal Address properties for these users.</td></tr>
<tr><td>Create Home Directory</td><td>If you set this to Y, UIMPORT creates a directory for this user in the Path and Volume specified by the next parameter. The user also is assigned RWCEMFA directory trustee rights. The name of the home directory will be the same as the user's name.</td></tr>
<tr><td>Home Directory Path</td><td>The directory under which the home directory is created. Do not specify a file server or volume for this parameter.</td></tr>
<tr><td>Home Directory Volume</td><td>The NDS name of the volume to contain the home directory.</td></tr>
</table>

The following control and data files show how you can use UIMPORT to update telephone numbers:

```
Control File = CTRL2.TXT
Import Control
    Replace Value=Y
Fields
    Last Name
    Name
    Telephone Number
Data File = DATA2.TXT
Cooper, Dale, 222-3456
Haywood, Donna, 777-4429
Palmer, Laura, 891-5544
```

The following control and data files are an example of how you can use UIMPORT to remove NDS users:

```
Control File = CTRL3.TXT
Import Control
    Import Mode=R
Fields
     Last Name
     Name
Data File = DATA3.TXT
Cooper, Dale
Haywood, Donna
Palmer, Laura
```

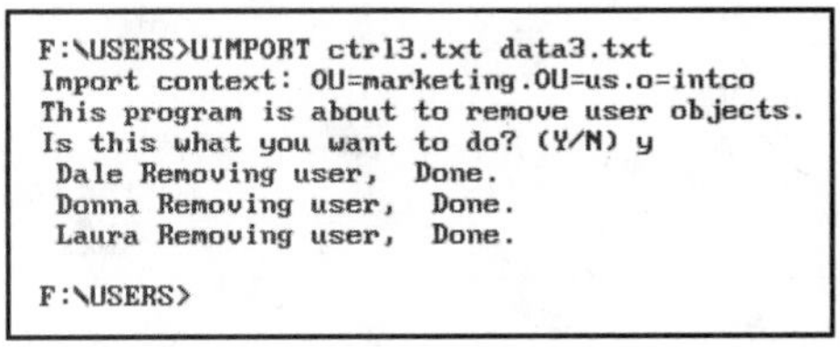

```
F:\USERS>UIMPORT ctrl3.txt data3.txt
Import context: OU=marketing.OU=us.o=intco
This program is about to remove user objects.
Is this what you want to do? (Y/N) y
 Dale Removing user,  Done.
 Donna Removing user,  Done.
 Laura Removing user,  Done.

F:\USERS>
```

Figure 18.20
Using UIMPORT to remove user objects.

Figure 18.20 shows the results of this operation. The following command was typed:

```
UIMPORT  ctrl3.txt  data3.txt
```

The following control and data files are examples of using UIMPORT to remove telephone numbers:

```
Control File = CTRL4.TXT
Import Control
    Delete Property=*DELETE*
Fields
    Last Name
    Name
    Telephone Number
Data File = DATA4TXT
```

```
Cooper, Dale, *DELETE*
Haywood, Donna, *DELETE*
Palmer, Laura, *DELETE*
```

Figure 18.21 shows the results of this operation. The NLIST command in the lower half of the figure confirms the removal of the telephone numbers. Note that the names Dale, Donna, and Laura are not on the list of users with telephone numbers.

```
        Telephone Number: 314-555-6262
A total of 6 user objects was found in this context.

A total of 6 user objects was found.

F:\USERS>uimport ctrl4.txt data4.txt
Import context: OU=marketing.OU=us.o=intco
 Updated, Dale,+ Done.
 Updated, Donna,+ Done.
 Updated, Laura,+ Done.

F:\USERS>nlist user show "telephone number"
Object Class: user
Current context: OU=marketing.OU=us.o=intco
User: CN=Gordon
        Telephone Number: 334-5671
User: CN=Log
        Telephone Number: 444-5151
User: CN=Jacques
        Telephone Number: 314-555-6262
A total of 3 user objects was found in this context.

A total of 3 user objects was found.

F:\USERS>
```

Figure 18.21
Using UIMPORT to remove telephone number properties.

Managing User Accounting

With the release of NetWare 2.*x*, Novell provided resource-accounting tracking. *Resource accounting* provides the functionality of a billing system in which users can be charged for services used at the file server. Resources that can be tracked include connection time, disk blocks read/written, service charges, and disk space used. For logging in to a *bulletin board service* (BBS), for example, there is a connect-time cost (the telephone call cost) and sometimes a surcharge for using features of the BBS. NetWare resource accounting mimics these functions.

In reality, very few installations use NetWare resource accounting directly to bill users for services, for two reasons. First, because NetWare servers are administered and used by departments that own the network, they do not charge for services provided internally.

Second, NetWare resource accounting, by itself, is not a complete system for charging and billing users. To provide a complete system, third-party products written with NetWare Accounting APIs (Application Programming Interfaces) must be used.

Although NetWare resource accounting is not sophisticated enough to provide direct billing of users, it is valuable because it provides statistics on server usage. The accounting usage data is logged in to an internal audit file (NET$ACCT.DAT) at the server. The ATOTAL utility is provided to interpret the internal audit files.

Other reasons to use resource accounting are to justify the purchase of a LAN or to compare costs of downsizing from a minicomputer or mainframe environment.

A university computer lab, for example, can use resource accounting to fix the amount of network usage for a semester. A certain quota of resource usage, for example, can be assigned to the user on the basis of the duration of the semester, the typical amount of disk space used, and so on. As the students use network resources, the resource-accounting software subtracts their resource usage from their initial quota. When their quota expires, they can request an additional resource quota from the network Administrator. Such a system can prevent indiscriminate use of server resources.

Resource accounting also keeps track of dates and times of login and logout attempts. This information is invaluable if you suspect that someone is trying to break into the system

Overview of NetWare Resource Accounting

NetWare resource accounting can be used to track the following resources:

- Disk blocks read (number of blocks)
- Disk blocks written (number of blocks)
- Disk storage (number of block-days)
- File service requests (number of services)

To install NetWare resource accounting, you, as the Administrator, must select the Accounting option from the NETADMIN or NWADMIN utilities. Select the File Server object and locate the accounting option. When asked whether you want to install resource accounting, answer YES. Resource accounting needs to be enabled just once when the server is installed.

Tracking Connect Time

Connect time is recorded in minutes; it measures the amount of time a user is logged in to the server. Connect-time costs are similar to those in BBSs and time-share systems. Connect time can be used as the basis for billing users; it also can discourage users from leaving unattended workstations logged in to the server. Unattended stations can be a big security risk—imagine what could happen if an unscrupulous user has access to a station logged in with an Administrator account.

Figure 18.22 shows the resource accounting screen for connect charges.

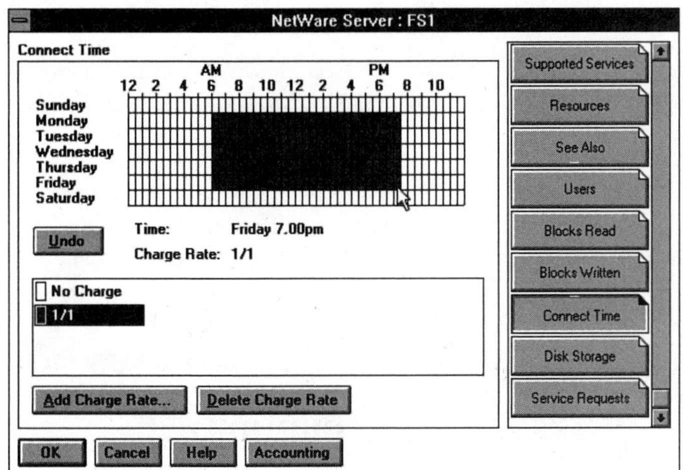

Figure 18.22
Connect time charge rates screen.

To get to the menu shown in the figure, log in to the server as the Administrator and then invoke the NWADMIN utility from Windows. Proceed as follows:

1. Double-click on the file server object.
2. Click on the Connect Time button.
3. Click on the Add Charge Rate button.
4. Enter the Multiplier and Divisor charges and click on OK.
5. Using the mouse, highlight on the time grid an area corresponding to the times you want this new charge to be effective.

The connect-time charge is based on half-hour intervals. A charge of 1 signifies No Charge. To change a rate to another rate, highlight the charge rate you want (in the list over the Add Charge Rate button) and highlight a block of time. The Undo button undoes the last change you made. The Delete Charge Rate button removes the currently selected charge rate.

The actual charge amount is computed by the following formula:

```
ChargeAmount = AmountUsed × Multiplier/Divisor
```

AmountUsed represents the units of resources consumed; *Multiplier* and *Divisor* represent scale factors to convert this figure into a monetary value. Because the *AmountUsed* resource is a large number, the *Divisor* should be larger than the *Multiplier* to scale down resource use to reasonable cost values. To set the charge to 0, enter **0** for the *Multiplier* value.

Tracking the Number of Disk Blocks Read

A *block* is a unit of storage information. In NetWare 2.*x*, the disk-block size is fixed at 4 KB. NetWare 4.*x* gives you the option of changing the disk-block size during the time of volume definition.

The actual usage depends on the type of application running. Database applications that do many disk I/Os, for example, can impact this statistic dramatically.

NetWare accounting can be used to keep track of charges for the number of disk blocks read. Charging users for disk blocks read is not realistic because even the execution of a program or NetWare utility at the server increases this number. (The reason is that the entire program is read from the server disk into the workstation's memory, which contributes a large number to the number of disk blocks read.)

Figure 18.23 shows the resource accounting screen for disk blocks read charges, using the NETADMIN utility. To get to the menu shown in the figure, do the following:

1. Log in to the server with an Administrator account and invoke NETADMIN.
2. Select the Manage Objects menu. Locate the file server object and press Enter.
3. Make the following menu selections:
   - View or Edit Properties of this Object
   - Accounting
   - Blocks Read Charge Rate

Figure 18.23
The blocks read charge rates.

```
        Blocks read charge rates                         Sun Mon Tue Wed Thu Fri Sat
                                             8:00         1   1   1   1   1   1   1
                                             8:30         1   1   1   1   1   1   1
                                             9:00         1   1   1   1   1   1   1
Rate                  Rate                   9:30         1   1   1   1   1   1   1
    Charge                Charge            10:00         1   1   1   1   1   1   1
 1 No charge          11                    10:30         1   1   1   1   1   1   1
 2                    12                    11:00         1   1   1   1   1   1   1
 3                    13                    11:30         1   1   1   1   1   1   1
 4                    14                    12:00         1   1   1   1   1   1   1
 5                    15                    12:30         1   1   1   1   1   1   1
 6                    16                    13:00         1   1   1   1   1   1   1
 7                    17                    13:30         1   1   1   1   1   1   1
 8                    18                    14:00         1   1   1   1   1   1   1
 9                    19                    14:30         1   1   1   1   1   1   1
10                    20                    15:00         1   1   1   1   1   1   1
                                            15:30         1   1   1   1   1   1   1
          (Charge per block)                16:00         1   1   1   1   1   1   1
```

The blocks read charge is based on half-hour intervals. A charge of 1 signifies No Charge. To change a charge, highlight a half-hour interval and press Enter. You also can use the F5 and arrow keys to highlight a block of time. When the Select Charge Rate menu appears, highlight the Other Charge Rate option, and press Enter. The screen shown in figure 18.24 appears, showing the New charge rate box.

Figure 18.24
Setting a new charge rate.

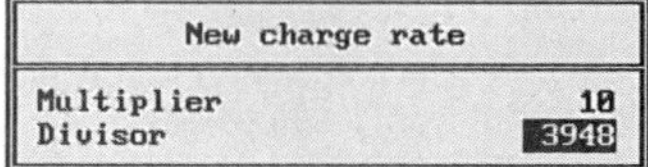

The actual charge amount is computed by the following formula:

```
ChargeAmount = AmountUsed × Multiplier/Divisor
```

AmountUsed represents the units of resources consumed; *Multiplier* and *Divisor* represent scale factors to convert the number into a monetary value. Because the *AmountUsed* resource is a large number, the *Divisor* amount should be larger than the *Multiplier* amount to scale down resource usage to reasonable cost values. To set the charge to 0, enter **0** for the *Multiplier* value.

Tracking the Number of Disk Blocks Written

You also can keep track of the number of disk blocks written by the user to the server disk. The actual usage depends on what type of application is running. Database applications that do a large number of disk I/Os have a large impact on this statistic; word processing applications have relatively few disk-block writes. Word processing applications perform most of the editing functions on file buffers kept at the workstation—disk blocks are written only when the file is saved to the server disk.

To get to the menu in the figure, follow these steps:

1. Log in to the server with an Administrator account and invoke NETADMIN.

2. Select the Manage Objects menu, locate the file server object, and press Enter.

3. Make the following menu selections:

   - View or Edit Properties of this Object

   - Accounting

   - Blocks Written Charge Rate

The blocks-written charge is based on half-hour intervals. A charge of 1 signifies No Charge. To change a charge, highlight a half-hour interval and press Enter. When the Select Charge Rate menu appears, highlight the Other Charge Rate option and press Enter. The screen shown in figure 18.25 appears. The actual charge amount is computed by the following formula:

```
ChargeAmount = AmountUsed × Multiplier/Divisor
```

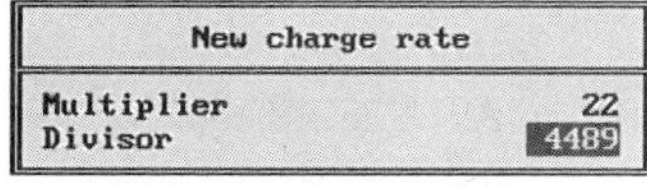

Figure 18.25
Setting blocks-written charges.

18

AmountUsed represents the units of resources consumed; the *Multiplier* and *Divisor* represent scale factors to convert the figure into a monetary value. Because the *AmountUsed* resource is a large number, the *Divisor* should be larger than the *Multiplier* amount to scale down resource usage to reasonable cost values. To set the charge to 0, enter **0** for the *Multiplier* value.

Tracking Server Disk Space Charge Rates

The amount of server disk space utilized for a user can be measured in terms of *block-days.* One block-day can be interpreted as one disk block of storage kept by the user for one day; or two disk blocks, each kept for one-half day. The block-day is the product of the amount of disk space and the time over which the disk space is used.

If users are charged for disk space, they are motivated to clean their files on the server by deleting useless files or by removing files that are seldom used and can be backed up. The Limit Disk Space option in NETADMIN also can be used to prevent users from using large amounts of disk space.

Figure 18.26 shows the resource accounting screen for disk block storage charges.

Figure 18.26
The Disk storage charge rates screen.

```
      Disk storage charge rates                       Sun Mon Tue Wed Thu Fri Sat
                                              8:00
                                              8:30
                                              9:00
Rate                 Rate                     9:30
   Charge               Charge               10:00
 1                   11                      10:30
 2                   12                      11:00
 3                   13                      11:30
 4                   14                      12:00
 5                   15                      12:30
 6                   16                      13:00
 7                   17                      13:30
 8                   18                      14:00
 9                   19                      14:30
10                   20                      15:00
                                             15:30
      (Charge per block day)                 16:00
```

To get to the menu shown in figure 18.26, follow these steps:

1. Log in to the server with an Administrator account and invoke NETADMIN.
2. Select the Manage Objects menu. Locate the file server object and press Enter.
3. Make the following menu selections:
   - View or Edit Properties of this Object
   - Accounting
   - Disk Storage Charge Rate

The disk storage charge is based on half-hour intervals. A charge of 1 signifies No Charge. To change a charge, highlight a half-hour interval and then press Enter. The New Charge Rate box, shown in figure 18.27, appears.

Figure 18.27
Setting disk storage charges.

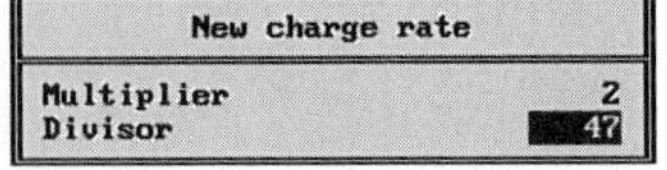

The actual charge amount is computed by the following formula:

```
ChargeAmount = AmountUsed × Multiplier/Divisor
```

AmountUsed represents the units of resources consumed; the Multiplier and Divisor represent scale factors to convert the figure into a monetary value. Because the AmountUsed resource usually is a large number, the Divisor should be larger than the Multiplier amount to scale down resource usage to reasonable cost values. To set the charge to 0, enter **0** for the multiplier value.

Tracking Services Used

Figure 18.28 shows the resource accounting screen for service requests charges.

```
   Service requests charge rates                    Sun Mon Tue Wed Thu Fri Sat
                                          8:00       1   1   1   1   1   1   1
                                          8:30       1   1   1   1   1   1   1
                                          9:00       1   1   1   1   1   1   1
Rate                 Rate                 9:30       1   1   1   1   1   1   1
   Charge               Charge           10:00       1   1   1   1   1   1   1
 1 No charge         11                  10:30       1   1   1   1   1   1   1
 2                   12                  11:00       1   1   1   1   1   1   1
 3                   13                  11:30       1   1   1   1   1   1   1
 4                   14                  12:00       1   1   1   1   1   1   1
 5                   15                  12:30       1   1   1   1   1   1   1
 6                   16                  13:00       1   1   1   1   1   1   1
 7                   17                  13:30       1   1   1   1   1   1   1
 8                   18                  14:00       1   1   1   1   1   1   1
 9                   19                  14:30       1   1   1   1   1   1   1
10                   20                  15:00       1   1   1   1   1   1   1
                                         15:30       1   1   1   1   1   1   1
         (Charge per request)            16:00       1   1   1   1   1   1   1
```

Figure 18.28
The Service requests charge rates screen.

To get to the menu in figure 18.28, follow these steps:

1. Log in to the server with an Administrator account and invoke NETADMIN.
2. Select the Manage Objects menu. Locate the file server object and press Enter.
3. Make the following menu selections:
   - View or Edit Properties of this Object
   - Accounting
   - Service Requests Charge Rate

The service requests charge is based on half-hour intervals. A charge of 1 signifies No Charge. To change a charge, highlight a half-hour interval and press Enter. When the Select Charge Rate box appears, highlight the Other Charge Rate option and press Enter. The screen shown in figure 18.29 appears.


```
       New charge rate
Multiplier              49
Divisor               5527
```

Figure 18.29
Setting service requests charges.

The actual charge amount is computed by the following formula:

```
ChargeAmount = AmountUsed × Multiplier/Divisor
```

AmountUsed represents the units of resources consumed; *Multiplier* and *Divisor* represent scale factors to convert this figure into a monetary value. Because the *AmountUsed* resource normally is a large number, the *Divisor* should be larger than the *Multiplier* amount to scale down resource usage to reasonable cost values. To set the charge to 0, enter **0** for the *Multiplier* value.

Using the ATOTAL and NLIST Utilities for Accounting Purposes

If accounting services are enabled, the resource usage-per-user data is stored in records in an internal database file called NET$ACCT.DAT. The chargeOrNote field of an accounting record can hold connect-time charges, disk-storage charges, login/logout times, account-lock events, or server time-modified events.

The information in the NET$ACCT.DAT file can be accessed by the ATOTAL utility, which produces a report on resource usage. This report, consisting of daily and weekly totals of accounting usage, includes connect time, blocks read and written, block-days, and server requests. If there is no charge for a resource, the corresponding entry for that charge is zero. The ATOTAL utility can be invoked from the DOS prompt after logging in to a server. Running ATOTAL produces a list similar to the following:

```
 F:\SYSTEM>atotal
ACCOUNTING SERVICES TOTAL UTILITY, version 2.02
    Connect time:    2084    Server request: 4080
    Blocks read:      932    Blocks written: 94
    Blocks day:      2927
 Totals for week:
    Connect time:    14922    Server request: 17992
    Blocks read:      1814    Blocks written: 307
    Blocks day:         67
```

The NLIST utility can be used to view user account balances. The syntax is as follows:

```
NLIST user=[login name] SHOW "Account Balance" /S
```

The login name can be the name of any user in the NDS database. If you want to see all users, type **user=*** or just **user**. The SHOW command instructs NLIST to display the value of a property. The Account Balance parameter is the property to be displayed. The /S option tells NLIST to display users below the current NDS context. To view or change your current NDS context, use the CX command.

Figure 18.30 shows you the result of the NLIST command.

```
F:\SYSTEM>NLIST USER SHOW "ACCOUNT BALANCE" /S
Object Class: USER
Current context: OU=Santa_Cruz.O=VITEK
User: CN=Doug
        Account Balance: 99992
User: CN=Ward
        Account Balance: 100000
A total of 2 USER objects was found in this context.

A total of 2 USER objects was found.

F:\SYSTEM>
```

Figure 18.30
Using NLIS to show account balances.

After a certain period of time (usually a month), the NET$ACCT.DAT file becomes very large and its size must be reduced. If the file NET$ACCT.DAT is deleted, it is automatically created the next time a resource entry is made to this file. To reduce the size of the NET$ACCT file, follow these guidelines:

1. Using the ATOTAL utility, generate hard copies of reports. The following command can be used to generate a text file containing the reports, which then can be printed and archived:

   ```
   ATOTAL  28MAY94.ATO (generated May 28, 1994)
   ```

2. Archive (back up) the NET$ACCT.DAT file and then delete it. It will be created automatically by the resource accounting system the next time the OS records an accounting charge.

Managing User Support Remotely

A number of tools are available to enable you to take over a user's workstation remotely. These tools are designed for you to support users remotely and walk them through a problem. Although the process is similar to that described for the Remote Management Facility for the server console, a user's monitor and keyboard now are available remotely to the user. Table 18.7 lists some of the tools available for this purpose.

Table 18.7
User Remote Management Support Tools

Software Tool	Publisher
Close-Up/LAN	Norton Lambert
NetRemote+	Brightwork Software
Commute	Central Point Software

In NetRemote+, for example, stations that can be taken over by the network Administrator must run a program called NRLISTEN. This program loads as a TSR and can be configured so that a password must be entered before the user workstation can be taken over. Typically, NRLISTEN is loaded automatically during the login process and takes up about 8 KB of RAM. The network administrator who wants to support a user remotely runs the program NRCALL.

Figure 18.31 shows the NRCALL screen, which displays a list of users logged in to the network. Users with NRLISTEN running at their workstations are highlighted. To take over the user's workstation, you must select the user by highlighting the user name and pressing Enter. After this is done, the user workstation is under the control of the network Administrator. To relinquish control and invoke the NetRemote menu, press F1. A useful feature of NetRemote+ is its memory map of the user workstation, which can be displayed (see fig. 18.32). The memory map enables the Administrator to view remotely the programs running at the user workstation. You also can view the version of the IPX/SPX and NetWare shell being run at another workstation.

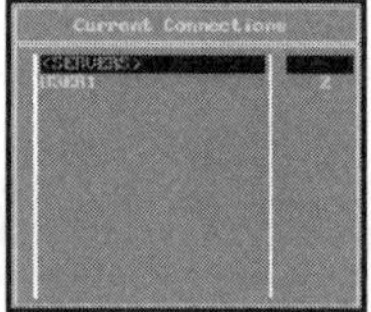

Figure 18.31
NetRemote+ NRCALL screen.

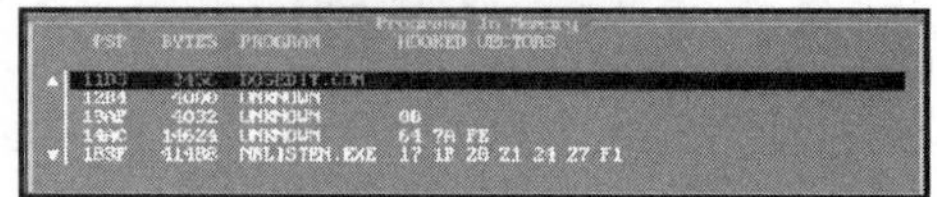

Figure 18.32
NetRemote+ user workstation memory map.

Summary

This chapter showed you the two ways that users and accounts can be created and managed by using the NETADMIN, NWADMIN, and UIMPORT utilities.

The NETADMIN utility can be used for setting up user accounts and for creating groups and user accounts. It also can be used for controlling user accounting, restricting passwords, and restricting stations and times. The NWADMIN utility can do all that NETADMIN can do and more. NWADMIN is a graphical, Windows-based utility. Both the NETADMIN and NWADMIN utilities can be used to assign trustee rights. The rights examined in this chapter include NDS object and property rights, and file/directory rights.

18

Use the UIMPORT utility when you need to create several users with similar accounts. UIMPORT is a command-line utility that uses a control file, containing special statements, to create and delete user accounts in conjunction with a data file. Several examples of how to use UIMPORT—from the simple to the more complex—were presented. You also learned specifically how to use the NETADMIN and NWADMIN utilities to do common tasks.

This chapter briefly examined remote user management tools. These tools can be used to manage and monitor user activities from a distance.

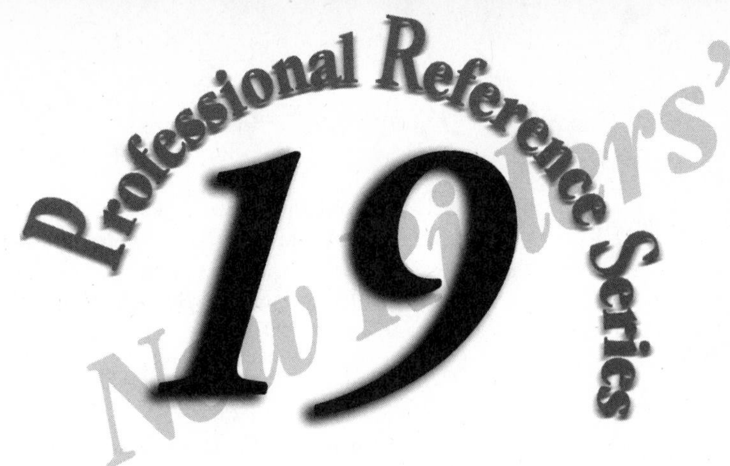

Network Directory Services Auditing

With NetWare 4.*x*, the NetWare operating system includes a powerful feature called *auditing* that can be used to augment NetWare security. In large systems, such as the operating systems that run on mainframes and minicomputers, it is common to have an auditing capability that allows selected events, such as access of a specified file or directory, to be monitored. Moreover, the person performing the auditing is independent of the system administrator. This avoids concentrating power with a single individual.

In this chapter you will learn about the auditing features and capabilities of NetWare 4.*x*. In particular, you will learn about the role differences between the network administrator and the auditor, the AUDITCON tool for auditing, how events in the file system and the NDS can be audited, how to customize the auditing environment, and how reports can be prepared from the audit log.

Examining the Need for Auditing

NetWare 3.*x* (and earlier versions) contained a feature called *accounting* that could be activated on a newly installed server using the SYSCON utility. Once the accounting feature was activated, the system administrator could keep track of the number of blocks read from and written to, the services requested from the NetWare server, and the number of blocks of storage utilized by a user over a period of time. Although these statistics were interesting, their value was somewhat limited; most NetWare 3.*x* system managers did not make use of these accounting functions in any serious way. What was often needed was a way to track the usage of individual files and directories.

For example, the accounting feature could not determine the number of times an application was accessed over a particular period of time, which would enable the network administrator to determine if the number of licenses purchased for a particular application was appropriate. If an organization has purchased a 50-user license for an application when there are, at most, 20 users who use the application, it is better to implement a 20- or 25-user version.

In addition, accounting does not report who is accessing system administrator tools such as NETADMIN.EXE or RCONSOLE.EXE. This could help in discovering a breach in security. NetWare 4.*x* auditing is designed to alleviate these and other limitations of NetWare 3.*x* network management.

The NetWare 3.*x* accounting feature remains available in NetWare 4.*x*, but NetWare *accounting* is quite different from the NetWare 4.*x* *auditing*. While accounting provides interesting information on such things as the number of blocks read and written to, or the amount of time a user is logged in, it cannot tell you how or when a specific file or directory was accessed. Auditing, on the other hand, can be used to obtain information on individual files and directories and how they are accessed over a period of time. It can also be used to audit server event changes in the NDS tree, or creation/deletion of queues.

Auditing on the network is used for recording network transactions and determining if the network activity represented by these transactions is in accordance with the network policy for the organization. These auditing transactions are called *events*, and they can be used to track user actions on the network, how a resource is being used and by whom, access to the file system, and access to the NDS.

Auditing can be used to track:

- File/directory events
- Server events
- Directory service events

As networks grow and become more complex, control over the network can become decentralized. As this happens, it is very difficult for management to determine if proper procedures are being followed to prevent security breaches or misuse of the network. Auditing, if properly implemented, can be used to determine who is performing security-sensitive tasks. Auditing can also be used to troubleshoot network-related problems and to determine if proper procedures are being followed and if procedures are in accordance with the organization's network policy.

A few of the motivations for implementing auditing are as follows:

1. Keeping track of application software usage for determining if the application licenses are adequate.
2. Determining if users have more privileges than they need. This could occur if users are made security equivalents to other NDS objects (to give them temporary privileges), but the security equivalencies are not removed; or, if a user's job responsibilities have changed.
3. Determining if users have less privileges than they need. Usually you find out about this quickly, when users complain that they cannot perform a certain task. A reason for this is that

job responsibilities may have changed, but the trustee assignments to perform different job responsibilities have not changed.

4. Discovering newly created files that are left unsecured. This can happen if new files and directories are created, but appropriate access restrictions are not placed.

5. There are too many users on the network, and it is difficult to monitor what everyone is doing. It may not even be desirable to monitor all activities of users, as this may not be within the domain of network management and could compromise the job functions of some users. What *is* important to monitor is any deviation from the network policies of an organization.

Understanding the Function and Role of a Network Auditor

On most networks administrators are all-powerful, in the sense that they can access all resources on the network without any restrictions. Such unrestricted power is necessary if the network supervisor is to be able to effectively support the users. However, this unlimited power also means that the network supervisor can access sensitive and classified data on the network without any checks (other than management's confidence that the network supervisor will not abuse this trust). From a practical and political viewpoint, it may be desirable to have a deterrence against a potentially dishonest network supervisor. This deterrence can be implemented using auditing.

Sensitive files can be audited for events that perform an operation on the files such as a read and write. Any time a user, including the network supervisor, accesses the audited file, that action is recorded in an *audit log*. This audit log can be used to discover the users who access the audited file. The network supervisor is very unlikely to surreptitiously access classified files if he or she knows that the file is audited. Auditing cannot prevent a network supervisor from accessing a file, but should such an access be performed, the event will be stored in the audit log and will be discovered by the auditor.

For this reason, it is not advisable to have the network supervisor and the auditor be the same person. The auditor can be any user on the network. What makes the network auditor user special is that the auditor user has knowledge about the audit password, which is needed to access the auditing functions of the audit tool called AUDITCON. Because the only distinction between an ordinary user and an auditor user is knowledge of the password, the audit password must be guarded from non-auditor users, including the network supervisor. Typically, the network supervisor enables auditing and creates a password for the auditor user. Once this password is given to the auditor, the auditor should immediately change the password without telling the network supervisor what the new password is.

In many organizations, a degree of mistrust exists between the network supervisor and the management structure. This mistrust is often fueled by the following facts:

- The management of the company is forced to rely on the network supervisor for providing access to critical and confidential data within the company.

- The network supervisor often has access to data that even top-level managers in an organization do not have.
- The management is forced to place a high level of trust with the network supervisor.

In the majority of cases, network supervisors are trustworthy and do not abuse the trust placed in their hands. However, an occasional supervisor may be tempted to step over the line. There is sometimes an opinion shared by network supervisors that they are not paid well enough for the high degree of responsibility they are charged with.

With NetWare 4.*x* auditing, a check can be placed on the network supervisor so that this trust is not abused. This helps the management of an organization and also the honest network supervisor. If there is a security breach, the audit log can be examined to discover the guilty party. Without proper auditing, the network supervisor is often automatically under suspicion if confidential data is lost or leaked to a competitor.

If auditing is enabled, the network supervisor can be exonerated of any potential suspicion. Therefore, the auditing feature, if enabled, can be used for the administrator's protection as much as it is for management's. The following precautions should be taken when auditing:

- The auditor should be independent of the network supervisor.
- The auditor should change the initial audit password assigned by the supervisor as soon as possible.
- The network supervisor should not have knowledge of the changed audit password.

Reviewing Auditing Features in NetWare 4.*x*

NetWare 4.*x* auditing allows the auditor to act independently of the network supervisor to perform the following functions:

1. Keep track of file system events such as changes and access to files and directories.
2. Track events such as changes and access to NDS objects.
3. Track server events such as bringing down a server, deleting bindery objects, and mounting/dismounting volumes.

The auditor does not have to be a specially created user. Any existing user can be set up to perform the role of an auditor. Some organizations may prefer that the auditor be an outside contractor who is not part of the organization and can verify network security and procedures independently.

The network supervisor (or administrator) must act in accord with management to implement auditing. The management of the company designates a particular user to be an auditor, and discusses with the auditor what the goals of the auditing process are. The network usage policy, if an organization has one, should be clarified at this point.

Management then informs the network administrator who the auditor is. The network administrator should set up the auditor's environment. This includes the following:

- Creating a User object for the auditor and assigning appropriate file system and NDS rights. The auditor should have [R F] rights to SYS:PUBLIC where the AUDITCON tool is kept.
- Creating a home directory for the auditor to prepare and store audit reports.
- Setting the login environment and login script. A search drive should be mapped to the directory containing the AUDITCON files. This is normally the SYS:PUBLIC directory.

The network administrator should enable auditing. Auditing can be enabled at a volume or a container. To audit file system events, auditing should be enabled at the volume level. For NDS events, auditing is enabled at the container level. The tool for enabling auditing and implementing auditing is AUDITCON. AUDITCON operates in the bindery-emulation mode when used to track file system events, and operates in the NDS mode when tracking NDS events.

Novell recommends having one auditor per volume or container. When you enable auditing for a volume or container, you enable it for that container only. In the case of containers, auditing is not automatically enabled for the subcontainers of a container. If you want to enable auditing for subcontainers, you must do so as a separate task.

The network administrator then creates an auditor password and notifies a designated user (the auditor) of the password. The network administrator empowers a user to be an auditor by giving the user the auditor password.

The network administrator may have to train the auditor on the use of the AUDITCON utility and how it can be used to change the password.

The auditor must then set up the auditing environment. This is done by:

- Running AUDITCON
- Changing the auditor password assigned by the supervisor
- Customizing the auditing environment

The AUDITCON utility must be run to access the auditing functionality. Before auditors can use AUDITCON to customize the auditing environment, they must log in *to* the volume or container using the supervisor-assigned password. AUDITCON is password-protected because it is kept in the SYS:PUBLIC directory where it can be accessed by any user. Only the user with knowledge of the AUDITCON password can *log in to* the AUDITCON utility.

The next step is for the auditors to change their passwords and establish their independence from the network administrator, who knows of the old auditor password but not the new one that has been assigned. This is a very crucial step, because the auditor, by design, is kept independent of the network administrator. If the network administrator knows the audit password, he or she can perform auditing functions.

If the auditor is in charge of several volumes or containers, the password for each of these must be changed. The auditor should take precautions not to lose the password, or leave the AUDITCON running unattended at a workstation after logging into AUDITCON. An unscrupulous user could then change the password of an unattended AUDITCON. If the password is lost for a container, you will have to reinstall the container. This usually means deleting the container and then re-creating it. If the password is lost for a volume, it means that the volume must be reinstalled.

After the password has been changed, the auditor can customize the auditing environment. The auditor can customize a number of parameters for setting the auditing environment. The auditor has complete control over this auditing environment and the log files in which auditing records are kept.

The auditor can then select events to be audited that are logged in audit log files. The auditor can create audit reports and maintain the audit files.

The auditor performs auditing functions using the AUDITCON utility that can be found in SYS:PUBLIC. Because most users have Read and File Scan trustee rights to this directory, no special trustee rights assignment has to be made for the auditor to access these files. The auditor should not have access to the SYS:SYSTEM directory; the network supervisor and auditor tasks need to be kept separate.

Even though the auditor does not have full access to a directory or a file, the auditor can audit file/directory events.

It is important for the auditor to select the right kind of events to be tracked. A common mistake is to flag too many events that are not of consequence to network security. This causes voluminous audit reports to be generated, which often go unread and therefore are ignored. The auditor should be trained in the use of the AUDITCON features and functions.

While the auditor can be any network user (other than the network supervisor), the auditor should have the capacity to be trained in the features and functions of AUDITCON. The AUDITCON options, in the author's opinion, are not easily understood by the average end user. Some of the vocabulary used in deciding if the event is global, or user and directory, or user and file, could have been better defined. You will learn more about this in later sections of this chapter.

Once the audit events have been identified, the auditor can generate audit reports and view the audit report on screen, or print the audit report. These steps will be described in details in the sections that follow. The steps needed for auditing are shown in figure 19.1.

The auditor can:

- Keep track of file system events
- Track events such as changes and access to NDS objects and trustee rights

The Admin user (or user with Supervisor object rights) can enable auditing on a volume or a container basis.

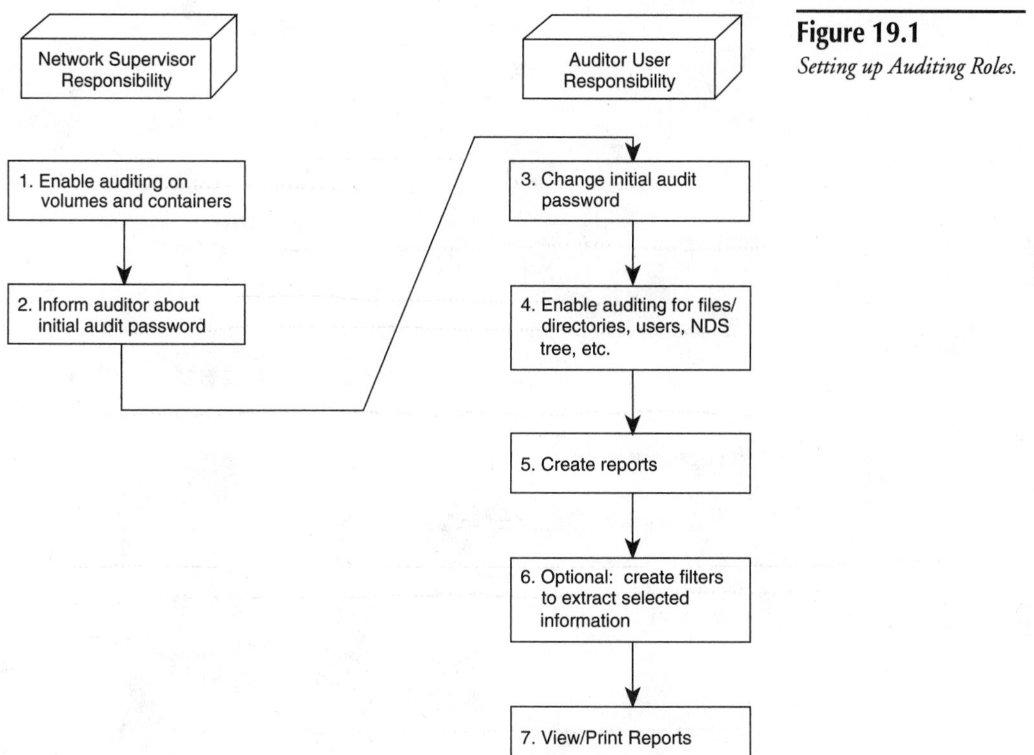

Figure 19.1
Setting up Auditing Roles.

Using the AUDITCON Tool

The AUDITCON.EXE file is the primary tool for performing network auditing. Figure 19.2 shows the main menu for the AUDITCON tool; it shows that one of the options is "Enable Volume Auditing." Presence of this option in the main AUDITCON screen indicates that auditing has not been enabled for this volume. This option should be selected to enable auditing for that volume.

When the Audit Directory Services option is selected (see fig. 19.3), you have a choice of selecting the NDS sub-tree starting from a particular container that should be audited (option "Audit Directory Tree"). There is also an option to change the context for the session (option "Change Session Context"). The session context is displayed at the top of the screen. In the example in figure 19.3, the session context is [Root].

The option "Change Current Server" allows you to log in to other servers for the purpose of auditing volumes on other servers.

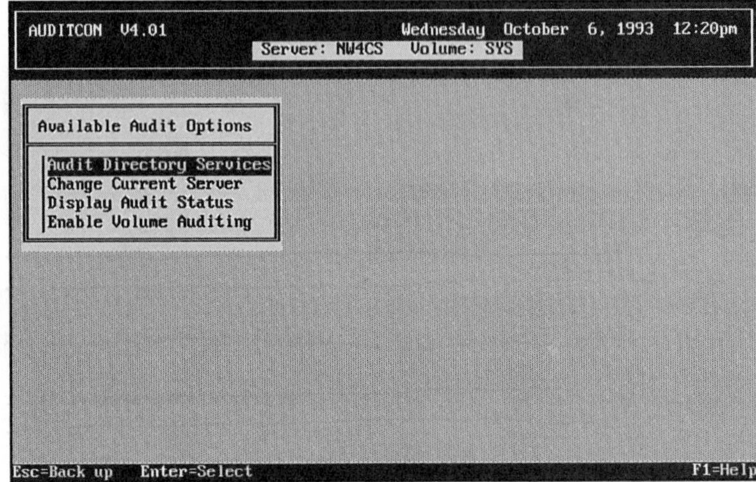

Figure 19.2 *The AUDITCON main screen when auditing has not been enabled.*

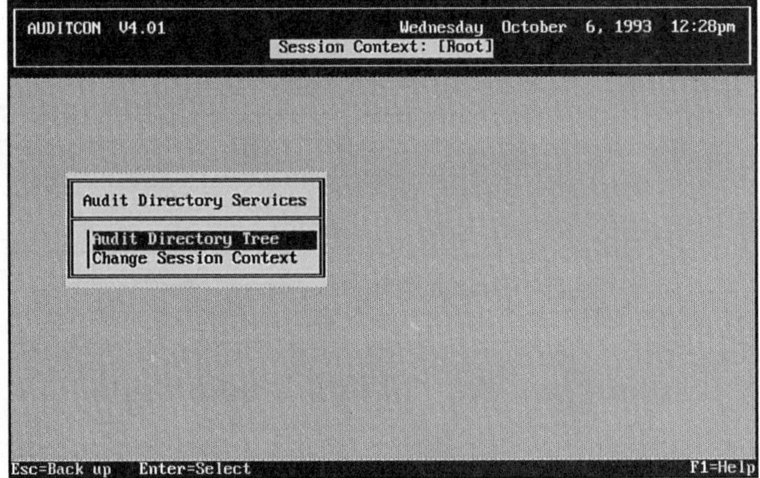

Figure 19.3 *The Audit Directory Services screen.*

The option "Display Audit Status" shows the status of audit files on the current volume. For the example under discussion where auditing has not been enabled, selection of this option should indicate an auditing status of OFF (see fig. 19.4).

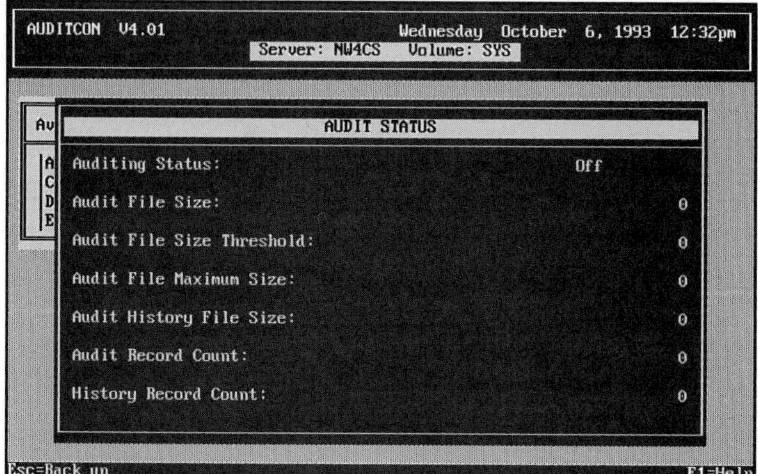

Figure 19.4
Display Audit Status when auditing is disabled.

Using the Audit Files

When an audit event occurs, it is logged in a file named NET$AUDT.DAT. This file is kept at the root of each volume and is flagged "open." Flagging this file open ensures that non-auditors on the network cannot access this file. The NET$AUDT.DAT file only contains auditing information for volume auditing for this volume. NDS auditing data is stored in the NDS database.

It may be desirable on some networks to keep track of the auditor's activities. The purpose of this is to have a deterrence against the power that an auditor has. For example, it would be useful to know which auditor accessed the audit log file NET$AUDT.DAT. NetWare 4.*x* solves this problem by keeping an Audit History file called AUD$HIST.DAT that is also kept in the root of a volume and is flagged "open."

This audit history file keeps track of the auditor's access to the audit log file NET$AUDT.DAT and records the date, the time, and the auditor who accessed this file. Any enabling or disabling of monitor functions on the volume is also kept in the audit history file. If the auditor clears the history file to "hide" a questionable event, the first entry in the new history file will record the fact that the history file was cleared.

If there are multiple auditors on the network, they should be given separate user accounts. This is so that their auditing activities are recorded under their respective user names.

The information in the NET$AUDT.DAT file is kept in binary form. The auditor uses the binary audit files to generate an audit report. The audit report is a text file and is stored on the network. Because a text report file can be read by anyone, it must be guarded to ensure that an ordinary user does not have access to it. Otherwise, any user who has read access rights to this file will become privy to its contents. The audit report can also be viewed on-screen. This process creates a temporary file that is deleted upon exiting the view.

Enabling Auditing

One of the steps shown in figure 19.1 was for the network supervisor to enable auditing for a volume or container and select an audit password. These steps are described in this section. Screen captures are presented to help you review.

1. You must determine the volume to be audited. This decision is based on which volume is used for keeping sensitive data to be tracked, or the volume that contains program files whose usage needs to be monitored.

2. Log in to the network as an Admin user and run AUDITCON.

3. From the main menu option, select "Enable volume auditing."

4. Enter the volume password (see fig. 19.5). You will be asked to retype the password for verification purposes. If there is an audit data file on the volume, it will be moved to an old audit data file. If there is an old data file that already exists, it will be deleted.

   After enabling volume auditing, the main screen of AUDITCON will change (see fig. 19.6). The "Enable Audit Status" option will be missing from the "Available Audit Options."

   If you select the "Display Audit Status" option, you will see that the volume auditing has been enabled (see fig. 19.7).

5. Exit AUDITCON.

6. Give the audit password to the auditor and instruct the auditor to change the password immediately.

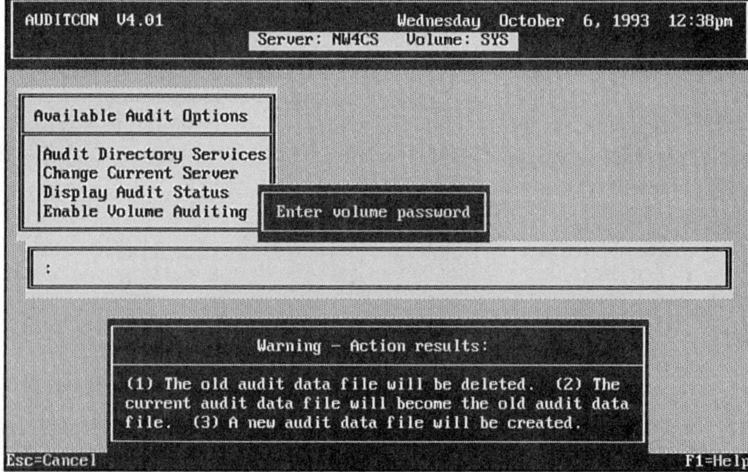

Figure 19.5
The Enable Volume Auditing screen.

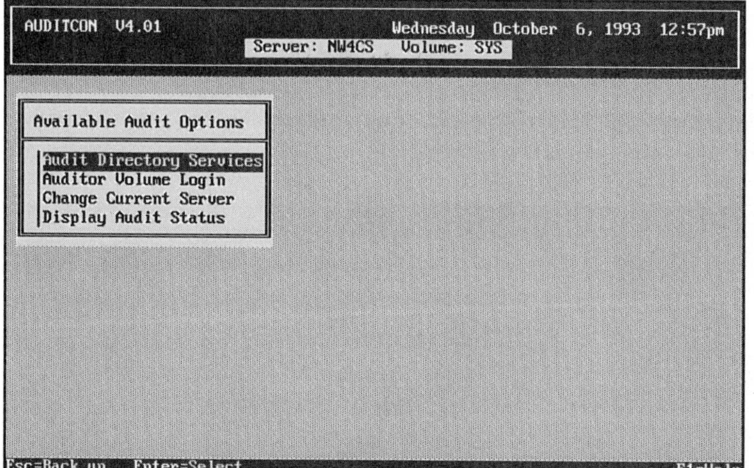

Figure 19.6
The AUDITCON main screen with volume auditing enabled.

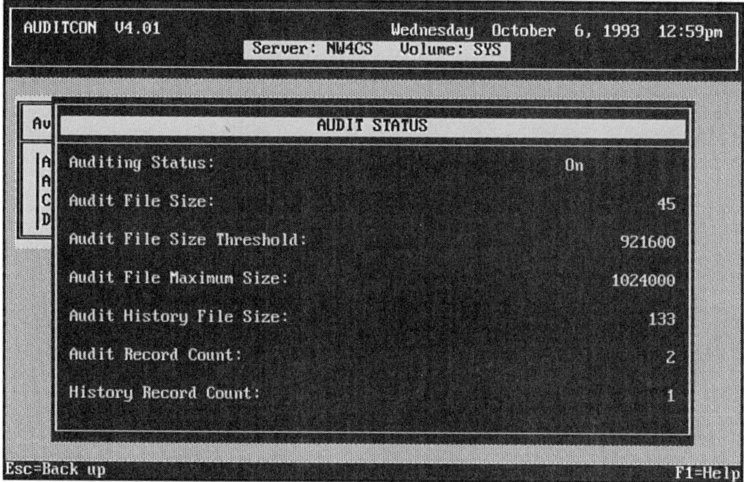

Figure 19.7
Display Audit Status when auditing is enabled.

Changing the Audit Password

The network supervisor empowers a user to be an auditor by informing the user about the volume password. The auditor must change the password at the earliest opportunity to maintain independence from the network supervisor.

The auditor password must be guarded with care to maintain the independence of the auditor. If the auditor password is forgotten, it cannot be recovered. Disabling of auditing requires knowledge of the auditor password and can only be done using AUDITCON. If this password is forgotten, the only way to disable auditing would be to delete the volume and re-create it.

The following steps guide you through the process of changing the auditor password:

1. Log in to the network as an auditor user and run AUDITCON.
2. From the main menu of the AUDITCON utility, select "Auditor Volume Login." You should be prompted for a password (see fig. 19.8).

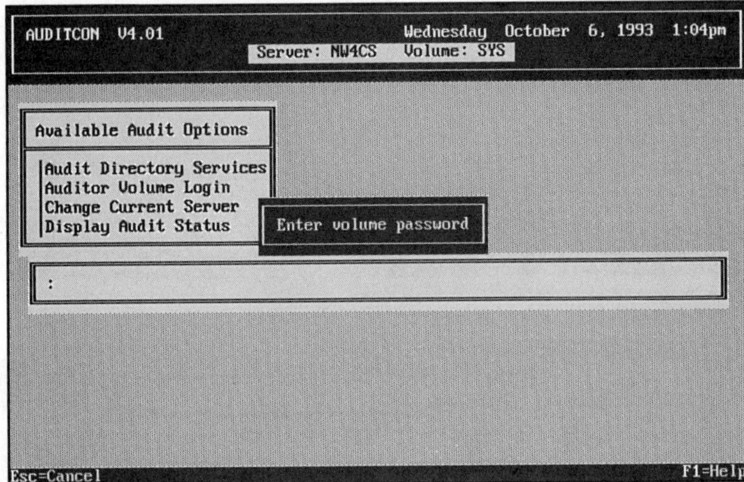

Figure 19.8
The AUDITCON Auditor Volume Login.

3. Enter the password that was initially defined by the network supervisor. This password is needed to gain access to the AUDITCON functions. You should see that the main AUDITCON screen changes (see fig. 19.9) with the following new options:
   - Audit Files Maintenance
   - Auditing Configuration
   - Auditing Reports
4. Select "Audit Configuration" from Available Audit Options. You should see a list of Auditing Configuration Options (see fig. 19.10).
5. Select "Change Audit Password" from "Audit Configuration Options."
6. You will be presented with a screen to enter the current volume password (see fig. 19.11). This is to validate the auditor.
7. You will then be asked to enter a new audit password. You should enter a *new* password—AUDITCON does not check to see if the password you entered is different from the initial password given to you by the network supervisor.

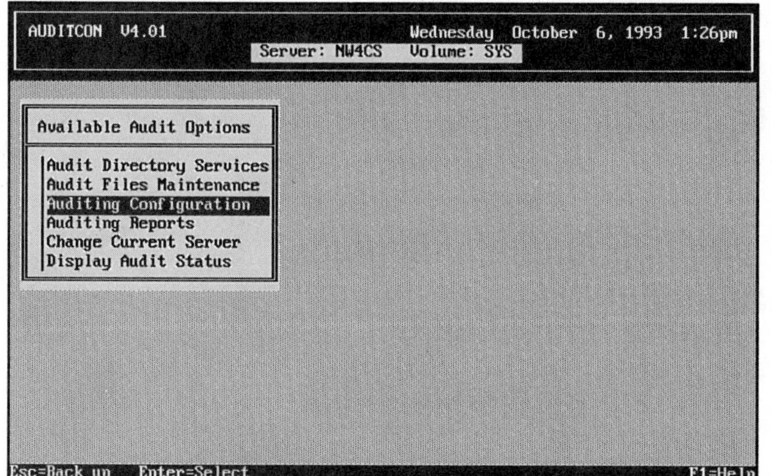

Figure 19.9
The AUDITCON Main Screen after volume login.

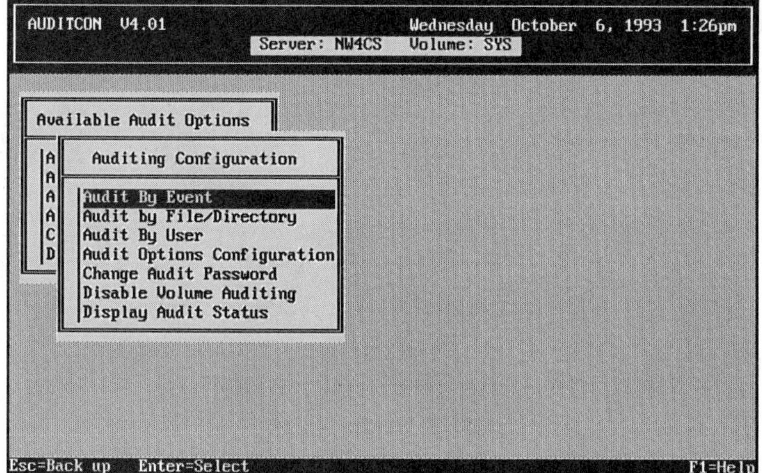

Figure 19.10
The AUDITCON Auditing Configuration options.

8. Exit AUDITCON.

Use the new password with AUDITCON.

Once the auditor password has been changed for the purpose of being independent of the network supervisor, the auditing function can be performed. Some of the common auditing functions are outlined in the following sections.

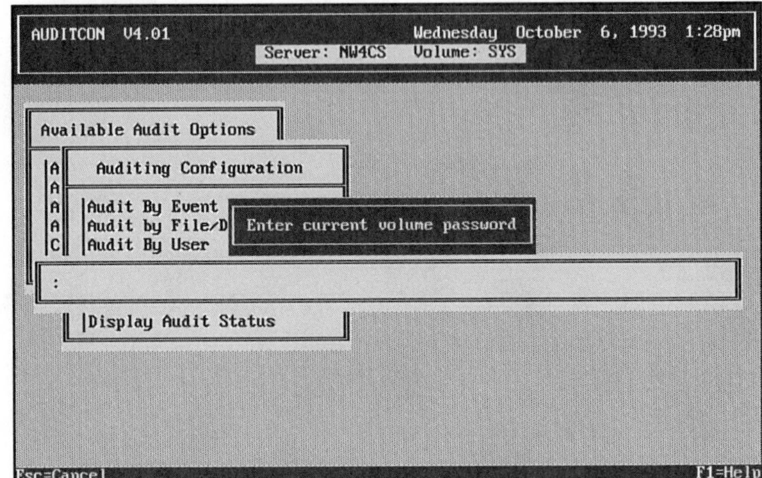

Figure 19.11
The AUDITCON Change Audit Password option.

Auditing Configuration Options

The screen for Auditing Configuration Options is presented to an auditor (see fig. 19.10) when the auditor is authenticated by supplying the correct Audit Volume Login password. This menu option presents a number of interesting choices that are listed here:

- Audit By Event
- Audit By File/Directory
- Audit By User
- Audit Options Configuration
- Change Audit Password
- Disable Volume Auditing
- Display Audit Status

The more important of these configuration options are explained in the following sections.

Audit By Event

The *Audit By Event* option allows you to select among four different types of events (see fig. 19.12) to be audited. These events are:

1. File events

2. QMS events

3. Server events

4. User events

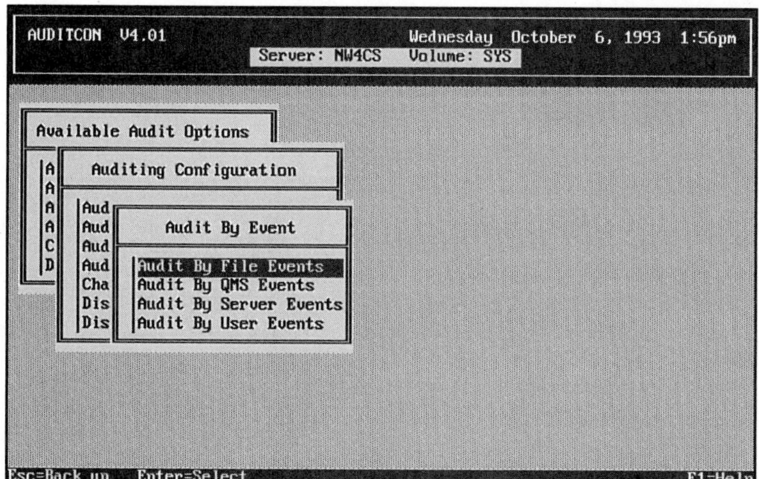

Figure 19.12
The Audit By Event option.

Audit By File Events

The *File Events* option audits file and directory operations such as open/read/write file, create file/directory, and delete file/directory. These events can be monitored on a global basis, by *user or file*, and by *user and file*. *Global* auditing means that the operations will cause the event to be logged, regardless of the user, file, or directory name on the audited volume. Auditing on a *user or file* basis means that the event will be recorded if it applies to an audited user or an audited file. Auditing on a *user and file* basis means that the event will be recorded if it applies to an audited user and an audited file or directory.

The "or" and "and" in these options act as the Boolean logical "or" and "and" operators. These options act as filters and control the amount of audit data that goes into the audit files.

Audit By QMS Events

The *QMS Events* option allows auditing of operations that affect the printer queues, such as creating and deleting of print queues.

Audit By Server Events

Server Events enables you to monitor events such as bringing down the server, restarting the server, or mounting a volume attached to the server. All server events are recorded globally.

Audit By User Events

User Events refer to creation/deletion of user objects, and user logins and logouts. Trustee assignment changes affecting users are also audited by this event type.

Table 19.1 summarizes the Audit By Event types.

Table 19.1
Audit By Event Types

Event Type	Description
File events	Audits file and directory operations such as open/read/write file, create file/directory, and delete file/directory.
QMS events	Audits operations such as creating and deleting of print queues.
Server events	Audits events such as bringing down the server, restarting the server, or mounting a volume.
User events	Audits creation/deletion of User objects, user logins and logouts, and trustee assignment changes.

Audit By File/Directory

When this option is selected, you are presented with a list of files and directories (see fig. 19.13) in the current directory that can be audited. You can select any of the files and directories in the list to be audited. A column next to the file or directory contains the audit status (OFF or AUDITED). If a file or directory is selected for auditing, an audit record is entered in the NET$AUDT.DAT file whenever an operation is performed on the selected file or directory.

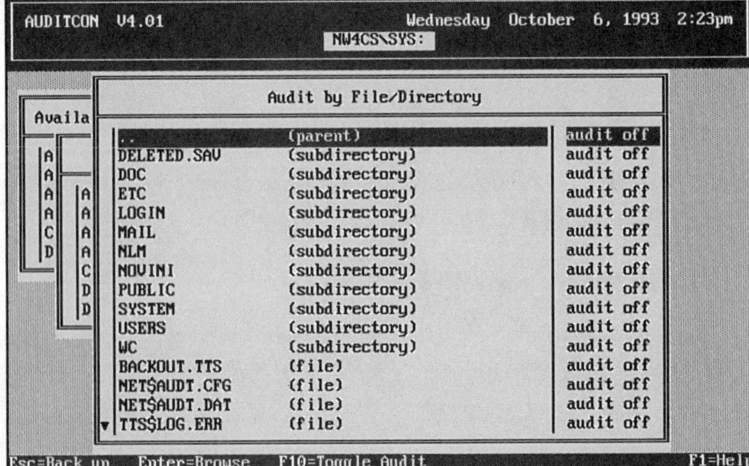

Figure 19.13
The Audit by File/Directory option.

F10 can be used to toggle the audit status. A dot-dot (..) symbol indicates the parent directory, and can be used to "move up" one directory level. In general, pressing Enter when any directory is highlighted allows you to examine the contents of that directory.

Audit By User

Audit by User gives you a list of users who can be audited (see fig. 19.14). You can select any of the users whom you want to audit. A column next to the user name contains the audit status (OFF or AUDITED) for that user. If a user is selected for auditing, an audit record is entered in the NET$AUDT.DAT file whenever that user performs an audited operation.

The list of users in figure 19.14 are bindery emulation users. To audit other users outside the file server's bindery context you will have to use NDS Auditing. When you do volume auditing by user, it offsets only bindery-emulated users, and the events are stored in the NET$AUDT.DAT file. When you select NDS Auditing, any user can be audited regardless of the context in which the user is defined.

F10 can be used to toggle the audit status for the user.

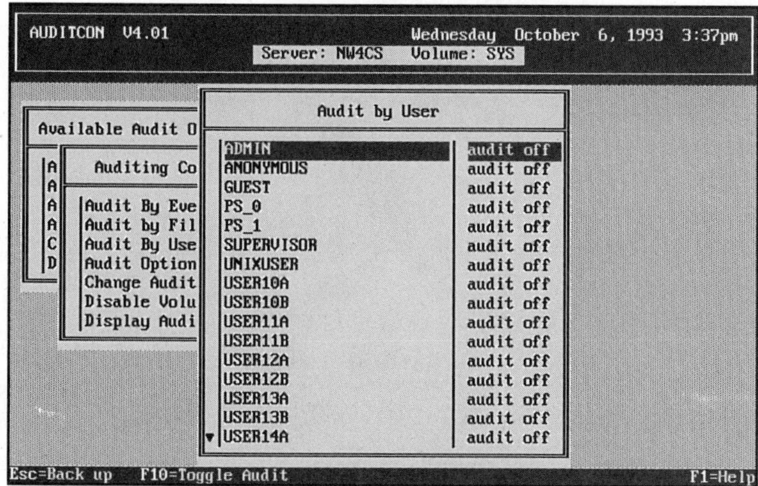

Figure 19.14
The Audit by User option.

Auditing Options for NDS

In the previous discussion you learned about the auditing options for a volume. At the volume level, the auditor can audit by user, events, or by files/directories.

At the NDS container, the auditor can audit by user or by NDS events. The general procedures for selecting the events to audit in a container are:

1. Run AUDITCON and log in to the container to be audited.

2. Select Auditing Configuration.

3. Select Audit By DS Events or Audit By User.

4. Once you have completed your selections, press Esc to save your changes.

If you select Audit By DS Events, you will see a list of NDS events that can be selected. When auditing is enabled for an NDS event, all occurrences of that event in the container will be logged. Figures 19.32 and 19.33, discussed in a later section of this chapter, show the different types of DS Events that can be audited.

If you select Audit By User, a list of NDS objects is shown. You can select the User objects from this list or browse the NDS tree and select any other User object. You can use F10 to toggle the status of the user from "audit off" to "AUDITED."

Audit Configuration

The Audit Configuration option can be selected from the Available Audit Options (see fig. 19.15), and allows the auditor to configure auditing parameters. The auditing parameters are kept in the NET$AUDT.CFG file on the root of the audited volume.

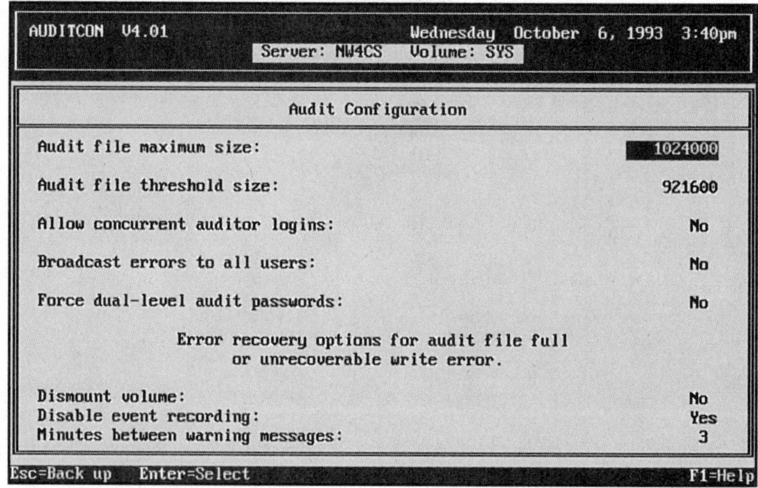

Figure 19.15
The Audit Configuration option.

The following parameters can be changed:

- Audit file maximum size
- Audit file threshold size
- Allow concurrent auditor logins
- Broadcast errors to all users

- Force dual-level audit passwords
- Recovery options when audit file is full or unrecoverable write error occurs:

```
Dismount volume
Disable event recording
Minutes between warning messages
```

Audit File Maximum Size

The *Audit file maximum size* parameter allows you to enter the NET$AUDT.DAT audit log file size in bytes. The default file size is 1,024,000 bytes. When the file size is full, it must be reset or deleted. Certain recovery options such as dismounting a volume or disabling event recording can also be triggered when the audit log file fills up. If you want to increase the audit log file size, you should consult with the network administrator; this will affect available disk space on a volume.

Audit File Threshold Size

The *Audit file threshold size* parameter is used to specify a size of the audit log file, upon reaching which the system should start sending warning messages. The warning messages are sent at a default interval of three minutes, but can be changed by the *Minutes between warning messages* field. The default value is set to about 90 percent of the *Audit file maximum size.*

Allow Concurrent Auditor Logins

The *Allow concurrent auditor logins* parameter, when set to Yes, can be used to allow more than one auditor access to a volume or container. Because audit access is allowed by password, auditors must share the same password. If this value is set to its default value of No, an attempt by a second auditor to log in to a volume or container that is already in use will produce the error in figure 19.16.

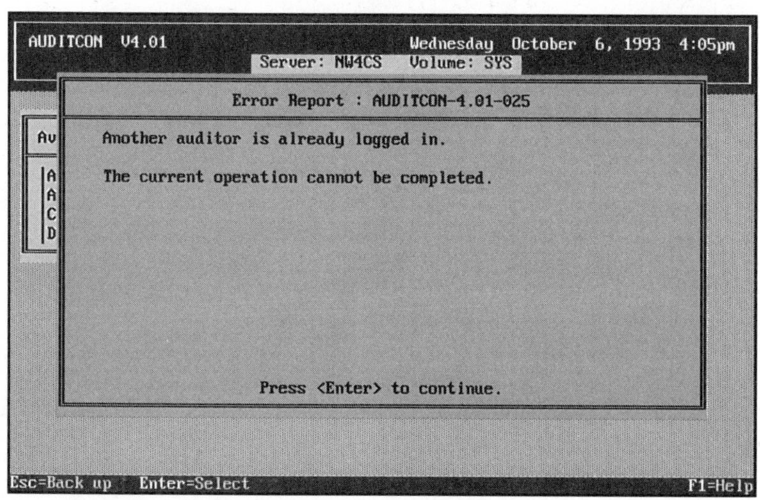

Figure 19.16
Audit error disallowing concurrent usage when Allow Concurrent Auditor Logins is set to No.

Broadcast Errors to All Users

The *Broadcast errors to all users* parameter sends a message to all attached workstations when the NET$AUDT.DAT file reaches its threshold value defined in *Audit file threshold size.*

Force Dual-Level Audit Passwords

The *Force dual-level audit passwords* parameter implements a second password that must be entered to save configuration or change settings. This second password is in addition to entering the first password for volume or container login for auditing purposes. By default, the *Force dual-level audit passwords* field is set to No.

When the audit log is full, certain recovery options such as dismounting a volume or disabling event recording can be triggered. If the *Dismount volume* field is set to Yes, the volume is automatically dismounted when the audit file is full. The network supervisor will have to remount the volume, at which point you can take actions such as deleting/saving the audit log file and resetting it. Before setting this option to Yes, the auditor should consult the network supervisor because it can cause a serious disruption to users on the network. Unless applications running at the client workstations are written in a robust manner, they can get locked if the volume is dismounted. This option must only be selected if the security requirements of maintaining a complete audit log are more important than the disruption of network applications. By default the value of the *Dismount volume* field is set to No.

Alternatively, if the audit log file is full, you can set the *Disable event recording* to Yes in order to stop the recording of any additional audit events. By default the value of this parameter is set to Yes.

The *Minutes before warning messages* is the time in minutes a warning message is sent to the server console (and also to attached workstations if *Broadcast errors to all users* is set to Yes) when the audit file size reaches the *Audit file threshold size.*

Auditing a Network User for a Specific Directory

It is sometimes useful to audit the actions a user can perform. Examples of these operations can be file creation/deletion/read or directory creation and deletion. The following steps outline how a network user can be audited for file read operations in a specific directory called SYS:PAYROLL.

1. Log in to the network as an auditor user and run AUDITCON.
2. From the main menu of the AUDITCON utility, select Auditor Volume Login.
3. From the main menu, select Auditing Configuration.
4. From the Auditing Configuration (see fig. 19.10) select Audit By Event.

5. From the Audit By Event menu, select Audit By File Events. You should see a screen similar to that in figure 19.17.

The screen does not show all the operations that can be audited for files and directories. You can use the cursor keys or PgDn and PgUp to examine other entries. Using PgDn, you can see the other entries for operations that can be audited (see fig. 19.18). The second screen shows an entry for File Read—User and File. This is the entry you must select for auditing a specified user for reading a file in a specified directory. It means that the system will track events that apply to an audited user and an audited file/directory.

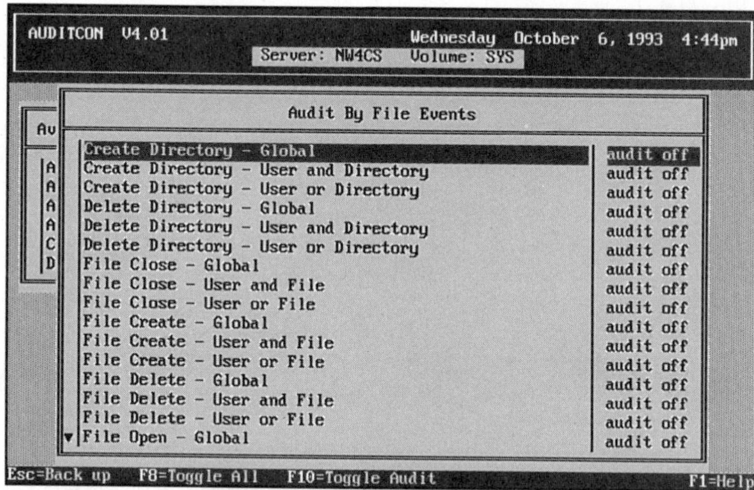

Figure 19.17
The Audit By File Events screen.

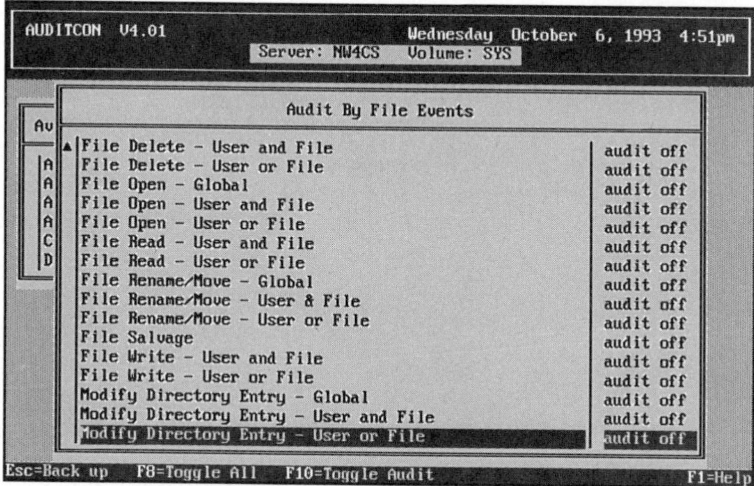

Figure 19.18
The Audit By File Events Screen—second screen.

6. Selecting File Read—User and File can be done by using F10 (see fig. 19.19). Answer Yes to save changes.

   Up to this point, you have only turned on auditing for a file event of the type File Read—User and File. You must next specify the directory and the user to be audited.

7. Press Esc a few times to go back to the Auditing Configuration menu.

8. From the Auditing Configuration menu select Audit by File/Directory. You should see a screen similar to that in figure 19.20.

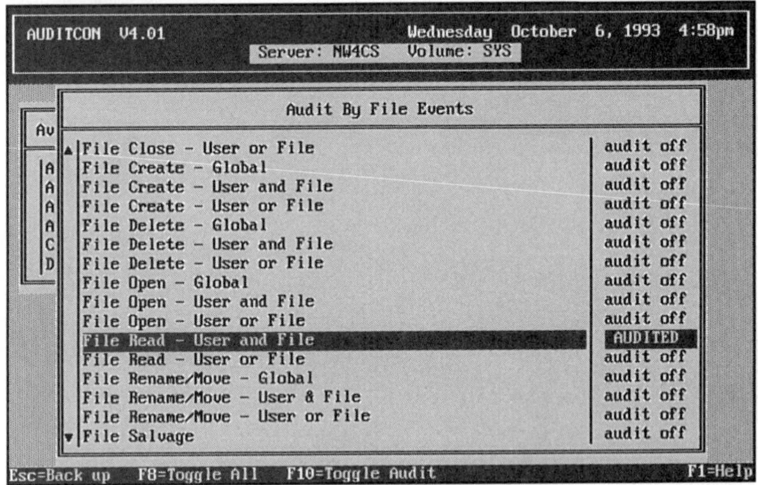

Figure 19.19
Auditing File Read—User and File.

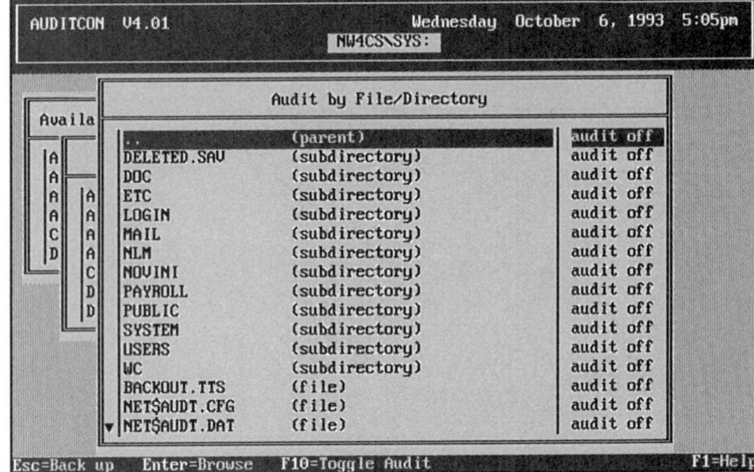

Figure 19.20
The Audit by File/Directory for directory selection.

9. Use the cursor keys and Enter to select the directory to be audited. Use F10 to toggle audit. Figure 19.21 shows the screen after selecting SYS:PAYROLL directory to be audited.

   Press Esc and answer Yes to save changes.

10. Press Esc to go back to the Auditing Configuration menu.

11. From the Auditing Configuration menu, select Audit by User. You should see a screen similar to that in figure 19.22.

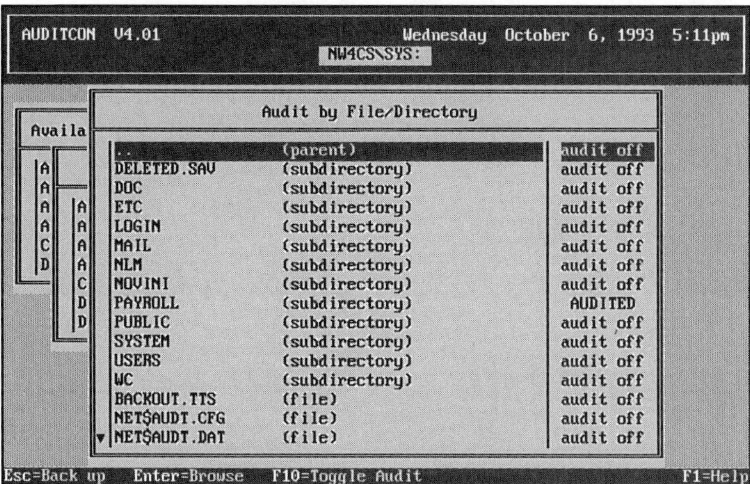

Figure 19.21
An audited directory.

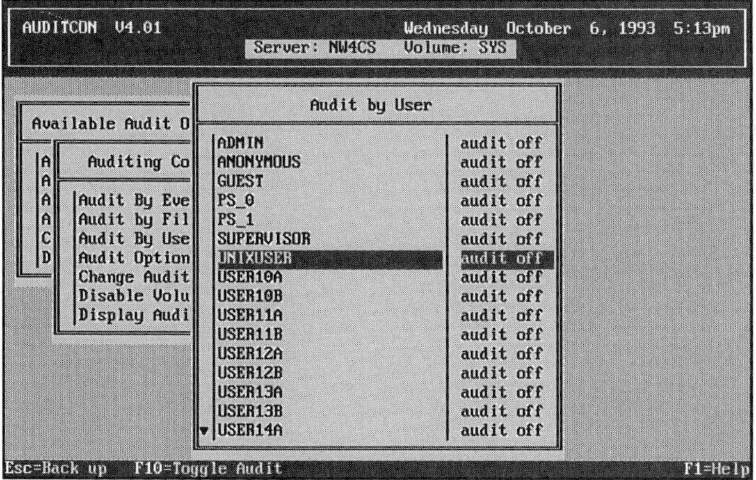

Figure 19.22
A user selection in the Audit by User screen.

12. Use F10 to mark a user for auditing, and answer Yes to save changes. Figure 19.23 shows the screen after selecting user HACKER to be audited.

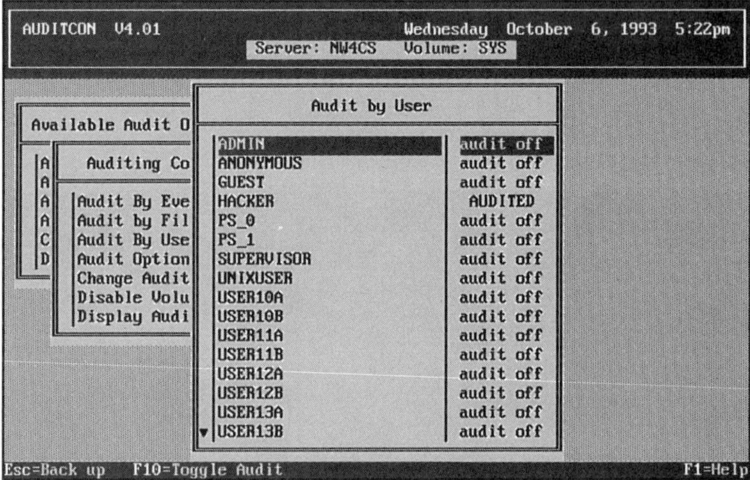

Figure 19.23
An audited user.

Auditing a Specific File

The auditor can flag files and directories to be audited. This is done by performing the steps that follow. The steps show how a particular file can be audited. An example of auditing a file could be to audit all attempts to access an application program-executable file such as NETADMIN.EXE to find out the frequency of access to this file. This knowledge could be used to determine all users who attempted to access this program file.

1. Log in to the network as an auditor user and run AUDITCON.

2. From the main menu of the AUDITCON utility, select Auditor Volume Login.

3. You must specify the password for the volume. Select Audit Configuration from the main menu.

4. From the Audit Configuration menu (see fig 19.10), select Audit by Event.

5. You can audit a specific file by selecting the option File Open—User or File from the Audit by File Events menu.

   Specifying File Open—User or File means that you will track all occurrences of an event when it applies to an audited user or an audited file. In this case, you are interested in an audited file.

   Press Esc and answer Yes to save changes.

6. Press Esc a few times to go back to the Auditing Configuration menu.

7. From the Auditing Configuration menu, select Audit by File/Directory. You should see a screen similar to that in figure 19.20.

8. Use the cursor keys and Enter to select the directory to be audited. Use F10 to toggle audit. Figure 19.24 shows the screen after selecting SYS:PUBLIC\NETADMIN.EXE file to be audited.

   Press Esc and answer Yes to save changes.

9. Exit AUDITCON.

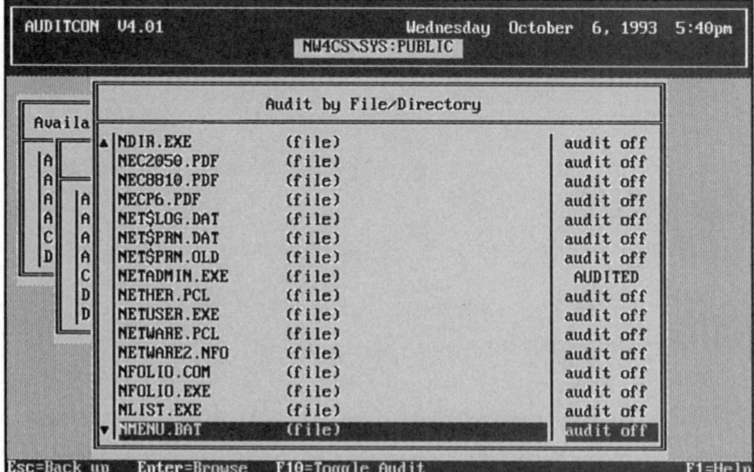

Figure 19.24
The audited file NETADMIN.EXE.

Auditing a Volume for Directory Creations and Deletions

There are situations when it is useful to audit operations such as creation and deletion of directories and subdirectories. It may also be useful to audit these events throughout the volume, regardless of the user performing the event. The following steps outline how this can be done.

1. Log in to the network as an auditor user and run AUDITCON.

2. From the main menu of the AUDITCON utility, select Auditor Volume Login.

3. You must specify the password for the volume. Select Audit Configuration from the main menu.

4. From the Audit Configuration menu (see fig 19.10), select Audit by Event. You should see the screen shown in figure 19.19.

5. You can audit creation or deletion of any directory by selecting from the Audit By File Events menu the option Create Directory—Global and Delete Directory—Global.

   Specifying "Global" mode means that you will track all occurrences of an event throughout the volume regardless of the user.

   Use F10 to toggle the audit status. Press Esc and answer Yes and save changes.

   Figure 19.25 shows the screen after making the previous selections.

6. Exit AUDITCON.

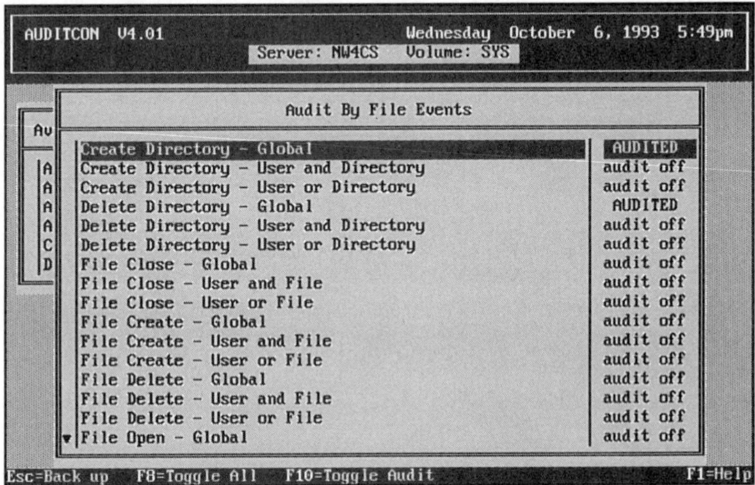

Figure 19.25
Audited create/delete directories.

Auditing the NDS

AUDITCON can be used to keep track of NDS object creation/deletion. The auditor must have Browse object rights to the container that is audited. The following steps outline how the audit password can be changed for a container, and also how a User object can be audited. When auditing NDS events, you can audit any User object in the NDS tree for operations on that container. This is different from auditing files and directories where the audit operations are done in bindery-emulation mode. This means that only bindery-emulated users in the context of the Server object can be audited.

1. Log in to the network as an auditor user and run AUDITCON.

2. From the main menu of the AUDITCON utility, select Audit Directory Services.

3. From the Audit Directory Service menu, select Audit Directory Tree. You should see a screen similar to figure 19.26.

4. Highlight the container that should be audited. In our example, the O=ESL container is selected. Use F10 to toggle the audit status. You should see a screen similar to figure 19.27 showing the Available Audit Options.

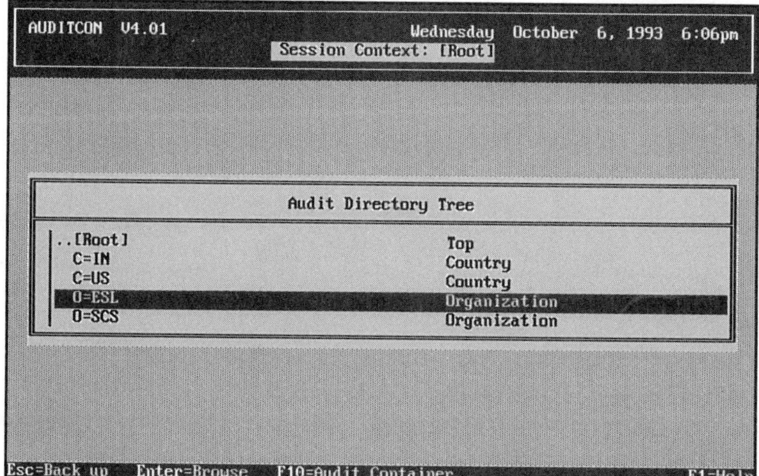

Figure 19.26
The Audit Directory Tree.

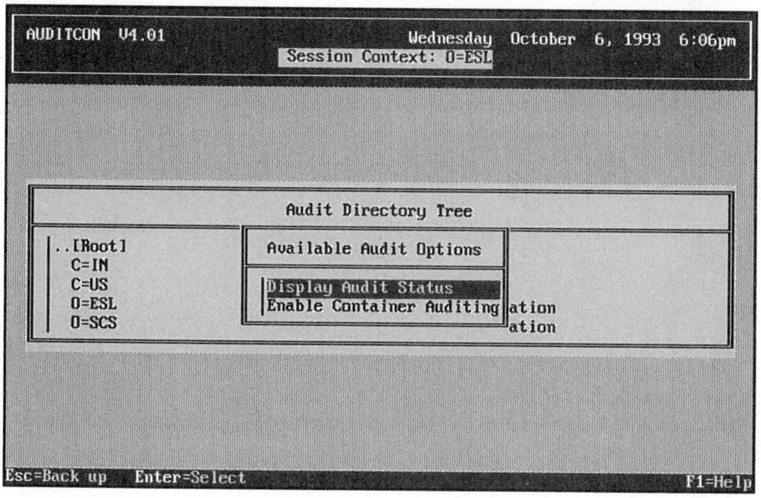

AUDITCON V4.01
Wednesday October 6, 1993 6:06pm
Session Context: O=ESL
Audit Directory Tree
..[Root]
C=IN
C=US
O=ESL
O=SCS
Available Audit Options
Display Audit Status
Enable Container Auditing
Esc=Back up Enter=Select F1=Help

Figure 19.27
Available Audit Options for a container when auditing is disabled.

The Display Audit Status option shows the audit status of the Container object. If auditing has not been enabled for this container, you should see the screen in figure 19.28. If the auditing is enabled, you should see a screen similar to figure 19.29.

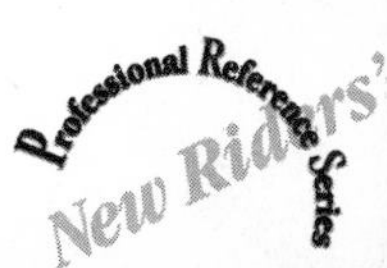

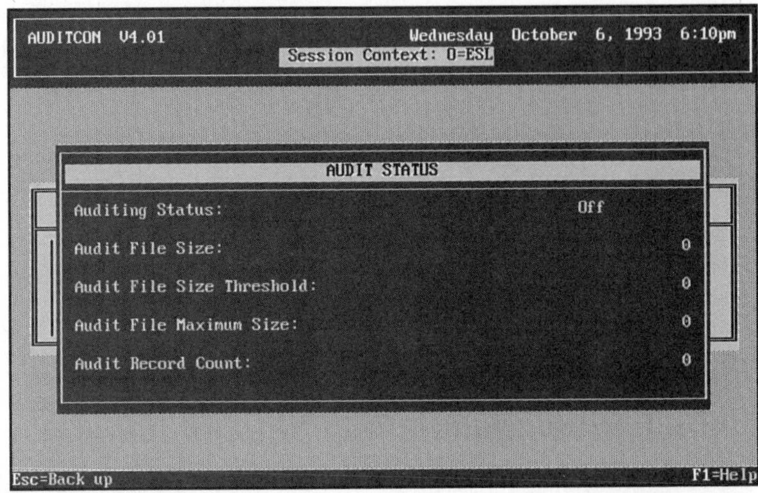

Figure 19.28 *Display Audit Status for container when auditing is disabled.*

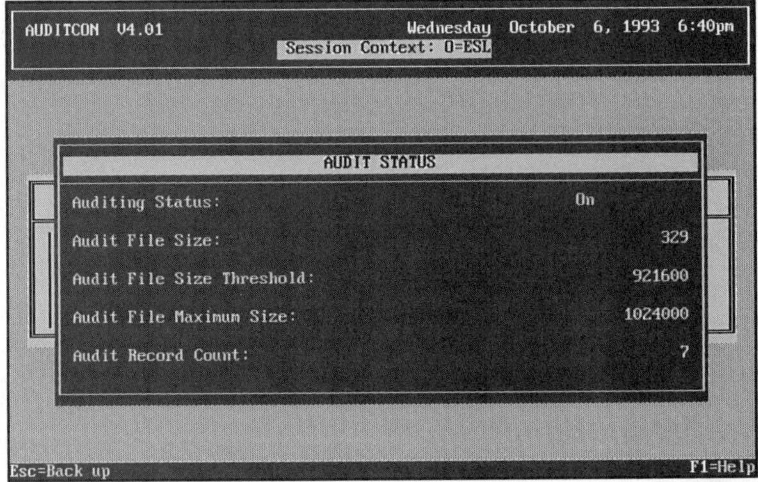

Figure 19.29 *Display Audit Status for container when auditing is enabled.*

The Admin user, or a user with Supervisor file system rights, must select the Enable Container Auditing option to enable auditing.

5. You will be prompted to enter the container password.

6. The Available Audit Options will change for the audited container (see fig. 19.30).

7. From Available Audit Options, select Auditor Container Login.

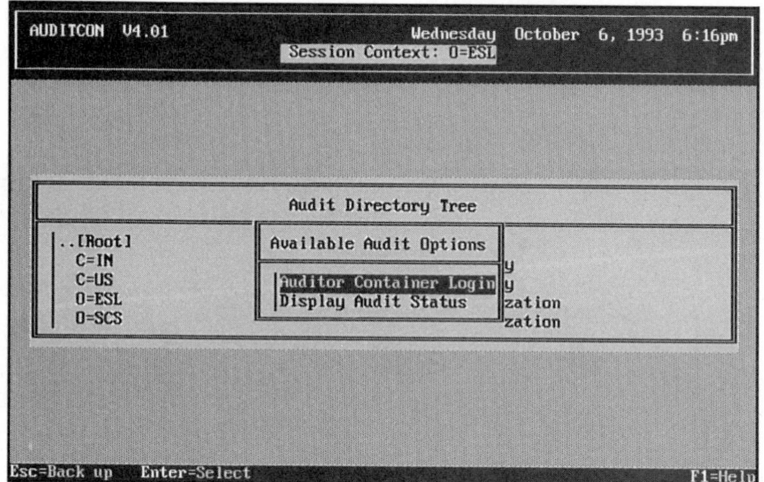

Figure 19.30
Available Audit Options for a container when auditing is enabled.

8. Select Auditing Configuration. You should see the Auditing Configuration options menu (see fig. 19.31).

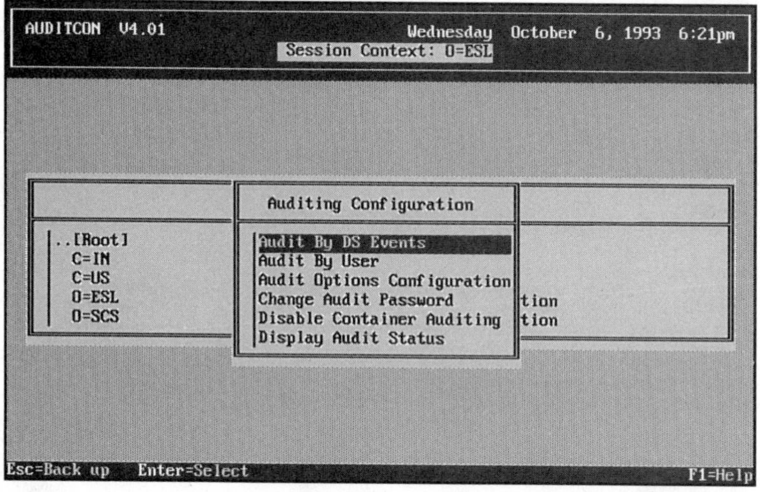

Figure 19.31
Auditing Configuration for containers.

9. To change the password, select Change Audit Password. You will be asked to enter the current password. After this, you will be asked to enter a new password, and asked again to retype it. The retyping of the password is for verification purposes.

10. From Auditing Configuration menu, select Auditing By DS Events. You should see the different types of events that can be audited (see fig. 19.32). You may have to use the cursor keys or PgDn and PgUp to see all of the directory service events that can be audited. Figure 19.33 shows the other DS events.

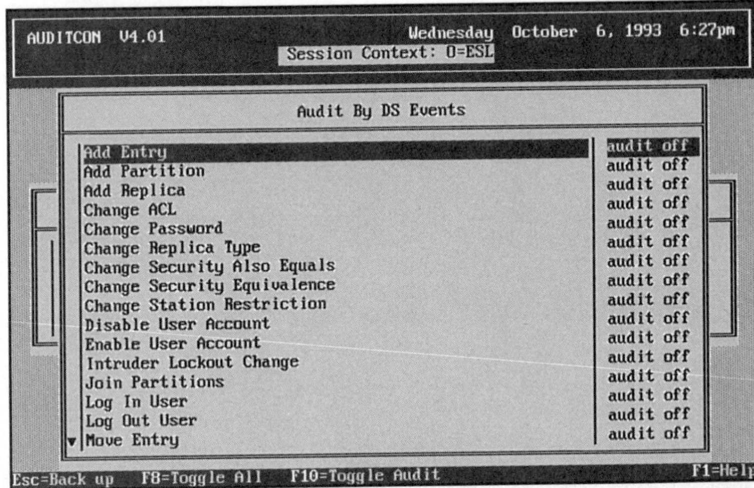

Figure 19.32
Audit By DS Events.

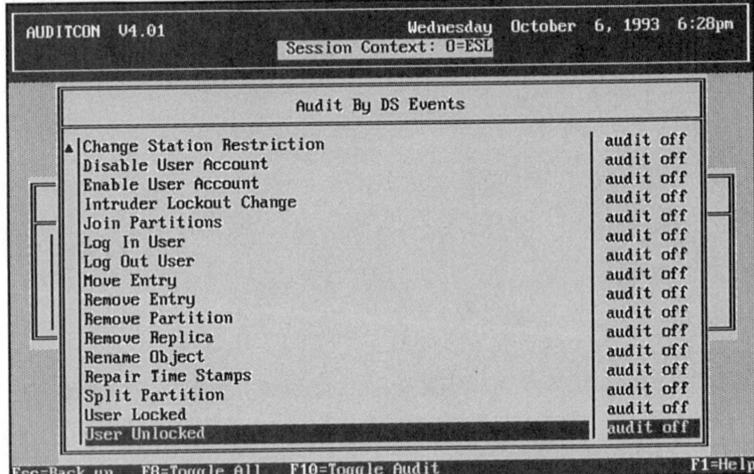

Figure 19.33
Audit By DS Events—second screen.

11. To audit the following events,

    - Change Password
    - Log In User
    - Log Out User
    - Change ACL

    highlight each event and use F10 to toggle them to the AUDITED status. Figure 19.34 shows that these events have been enabled.

    Press Esc and answer Yes to save changes.

12. Exit AUDITCON.

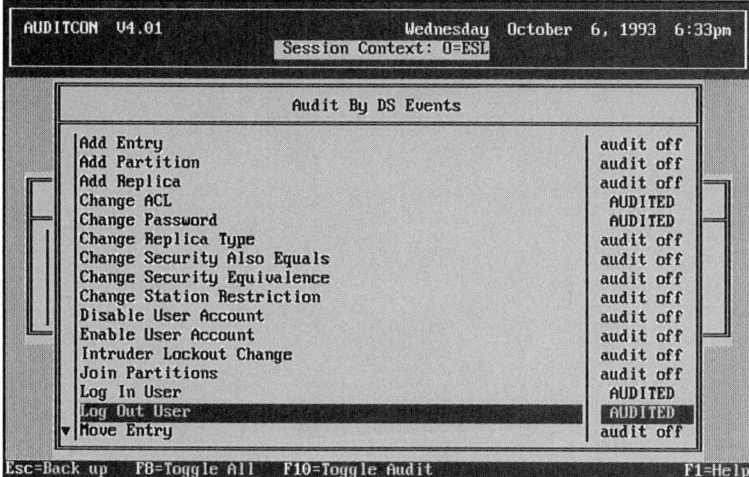

Figure 19.34
Audit By DS Events showing events that are audited.

Generating Audit Reports

The AUDITCON tool has the ability to view the contents of the NET$AUDT.DAT and the AUD$HIST.DAT file through a simple report-generation option. The reports are written to a text file, and can be printed or stored for safekeeping. Because the report is a text file, you should exercise caution to make sure that ordinary users do not have access to this text file. For example, it is not a good idea to keep the report in the SYS:PUBLIC directory where users typically have Read and File Scan access rights. It is best to print the file and delete and purge it from the network.

The report option also allows the setting of filters to view selected data. This is useful in situations where large amounts of audit data are generated.

Typical steps the auditor needs to perform to generate reports are as follows:

1. Create and apply a filter. An existing filter can be edited and modified also.
2. Generate the report in a DOS text file.
3. Print the report or view the audit report online.

The following steps will guide you in generating an audit report.

1. Log in to the network as an auditor user and run AUDITCON. Next, log in to Volume Auditing or Directory Services Auditing.
2. From the main menu of the AUDITCON utility, select Auditing Reports. You should see a screen similar to that in figure 19.35.

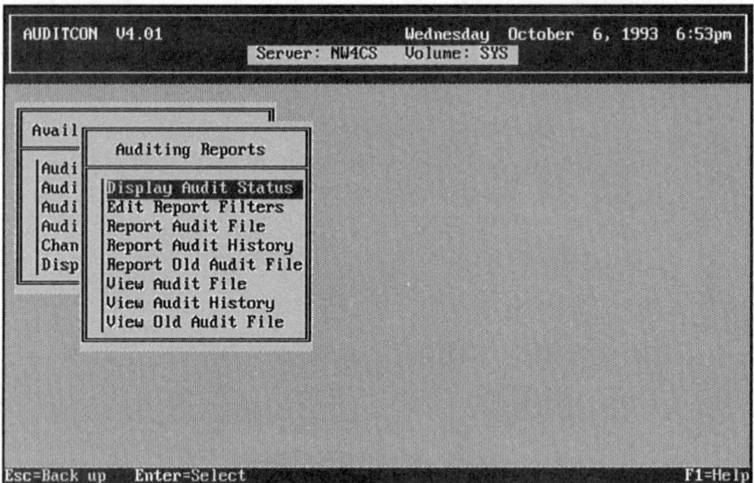

Figure 19.35
Auditing Reports menu.

3. You can create new filters by selecting Edit Report Filters or view the audit log and audit history files. You can also view a filter that you have created previously.

   A later section in this chapter will guide you in creating a filter.

4. To view the Audit file, select Report Audit File from the Auditing Reports menu.
5. You will be asked to enter the file name for the report. You can accept the default name of AUDITDAT.TXT or choose another (see fig. 19.36). The auditor must have [RWCEM] rights to the current directory. These rights are needed because the auditor creates temporary files.

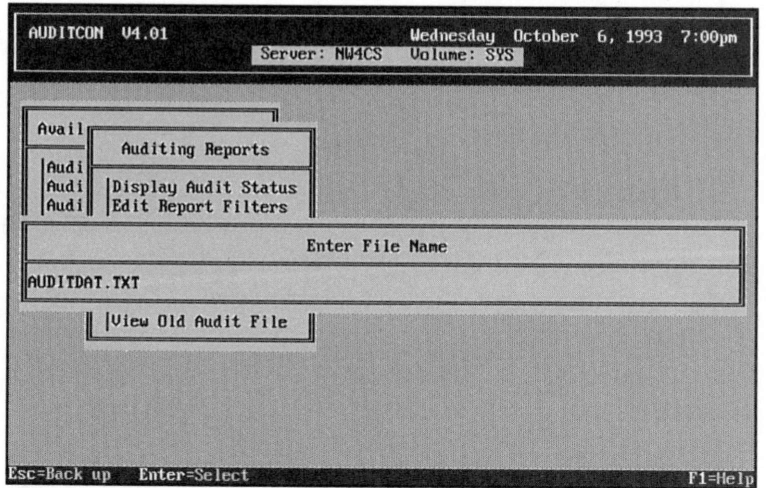

Figure 19.36
Auditing Reports—Enter File Name.

6. You will be asked to select a filter. If a filter has not been defined, only the default filter _no_filter_ will be displayed (see fig. 19.37).

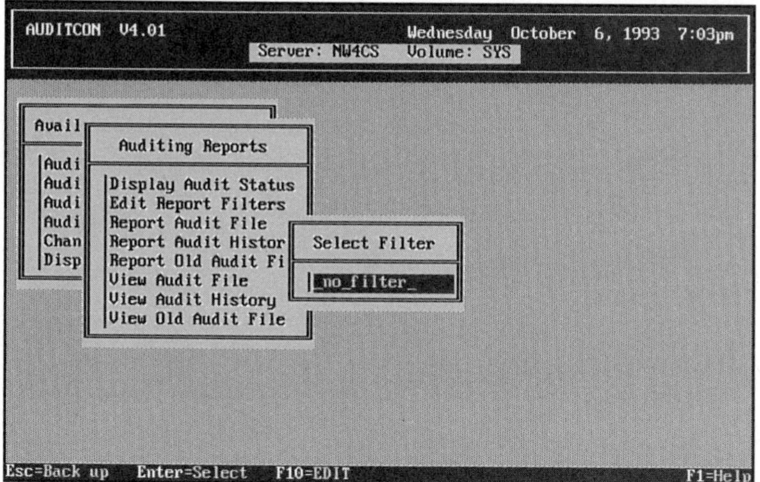

Figure 19.37
Auditing Reports—Default Filter _no_filter_.

7. To view a report, you can select View Audit File from Auditing Reports. Figure 19.38 shows an example report.

8. To view the history file, you can select View Audit History from Auditing Reports. Figure 19.39 shows a sample history report.

9. Exit AUDITCON.

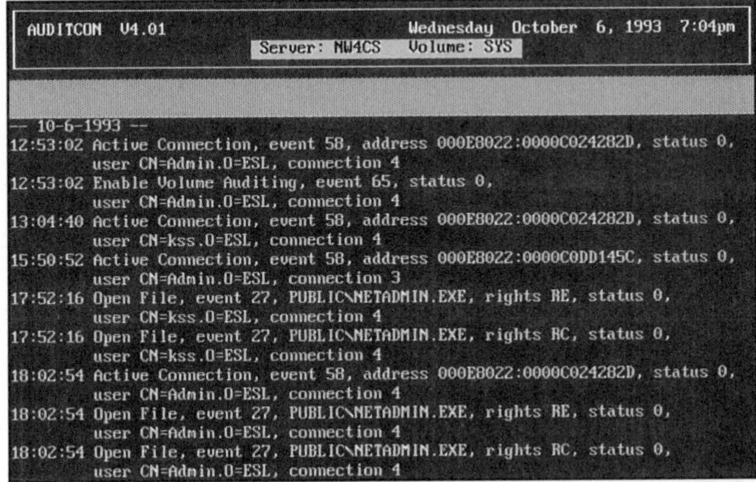

Figure 19.38
Audit Reports—Viewing Audit Report.

```
AUDITCON V4.01                                Wednesday October 6, 1993 7:06pm
 Server: NW4CS   Volume: SYS                                      -- MORE --
-- 10-6-1993 --
18:02:54 Enable Volume Auditing, event 65, status 0,
         user  , connection 4
13:04:40 Auditor Login, event 59, address 000E8022:0000C024282D, status 0,
         user CN=kss.O=ESL, connection 4
13:29:34 Auditor Logout, event 66, status 0,
         user CN=kss.O=ESL, connection 4
13:29:34 Auditor Login, event 59, address 000E8022:0000C024282D, status 0,
         user CN=kss.O=ESL, connection 4
13:37:04 Change Audit Password, event 61, status 0,
         user CN=kss.O=ESL, connection 4
13:39:44 Auditor Logout, event 66, status 0,
         user CN=kss.O=ESL, connection 4
13:40:22 Auditor Login, event 59, address 000E8022:0000C024282D, status 0,
         user CN=kss.O=ESL, connection 4
13:41:28 Auditor Logout, event 66, status 0,
         user CN=kss.O=ESL, connection 4
13:42:04 Auditor Login, event 59, address 000E8022:0000C024282D, status 0,
         user CN=kss.O=ESL, connection 4
15:50:52 Auditor Login, event 59, address 000E8022:0000C0DD145C, status 166,
         user CN=Admin.O=ESL, connection 3
```

Figure 19.39
Audit History Reports—Viewing Audit History Report.

Creating a Report Filter

Because of the large amounts of audit data that can be generated, it is useful to know how filters can be created to select only the audit data of interest. Once you create a filter, you can store it and reuse it later. When you create reports, you can select from a list of previously defined filters, and if necessary modify an existing filter and use it.

The following steps will guide you through creating a simple filter.

1. Log in to the network as an auditor user and run AUDITCON.

2. From the main menu, select Auditor Volume Login and supply the audit password.

3. From the main menu of the AUDITCON utility, select Auditing Reports. You should see a screen similar to that in figure 19.35.

4. You can create new filters by selecting Edit Report Filters. When a list of filters appears, press Ins. You should see the Edit Report Filter menu (see fig. 19.40).

   You can set a filter using any of the following criteria:

   - Date/Time
   - Event
   - Exclude/Include Paths and Files
   - Exclude/Include Users

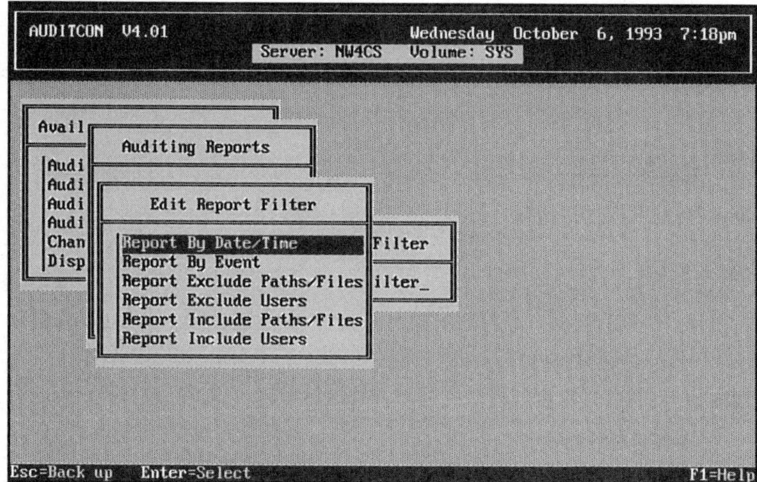

Figure 19.40
Edit Report Filter.

5. To select a report by its date and time, select Report By Date/Time and press Ins (see fig. 19.41). This enables you to select the start date/time and the end date/time for the audit events that are of interest. Once you make your changes, press Esc.

   Figure 19.42 shows a date/time filter set up from October 1, 1993, 12:00:00 p.m. to October 31, 1993, 11:59:59 p.m.

   Press Esc to go back to the Edit Report Filter menu.

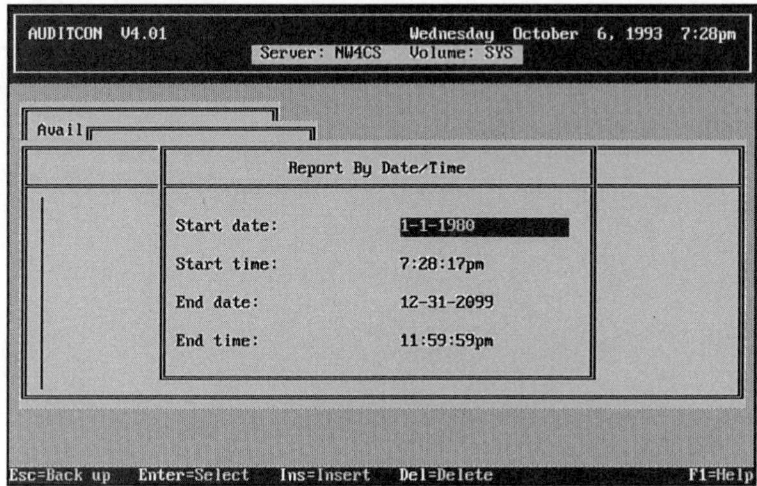

Figure 19.41
Edit Report Filter—Date/Time Form.

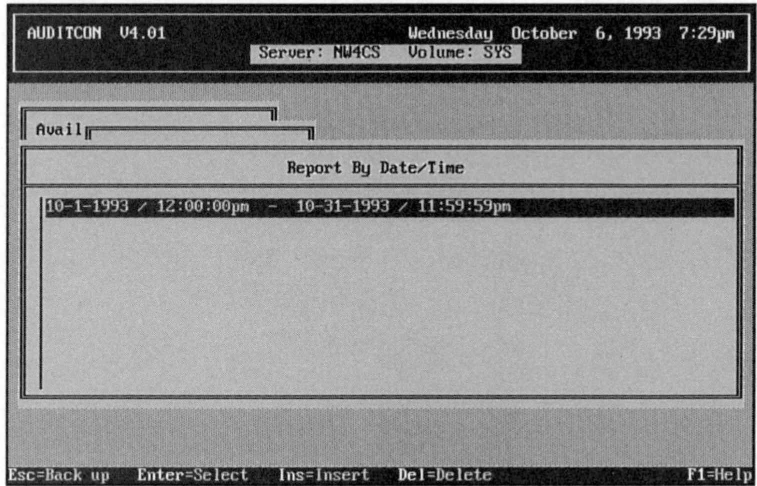

Figure 19.42
Edit Report Filter—Date/Time Filter.

6. To select a report by file events select Report By Event (see fig. 19.43). You should be able to set up a filter by file events, QMS events, server events, and user events.

   Figure 19.44 shows the Report By File Events. There are two columns against file events. These show the audit status and the report status. By default, an audited event is also reported. In figure 19.44, the File Open—User or File and File Read—User or File events are audited, and also reported. To toggle the report status, F10 can be used.

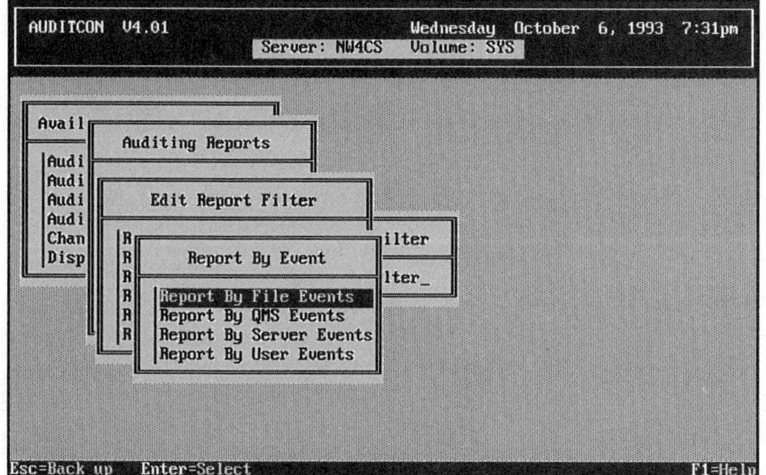

Figure 19.43
Edit Report Filter—Report By Event.

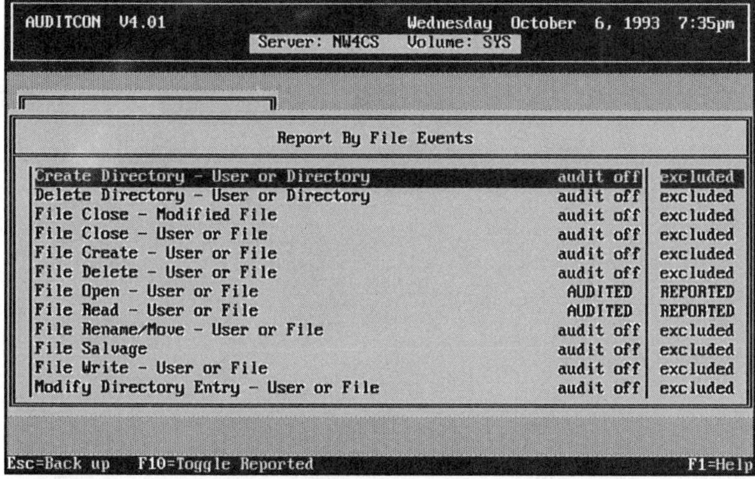

Figure 19.44
Edit Report Filter—Report By File Events.

7. The Report Exclude Paths/Files option and the Report Include Paths/Files option can be selected to exclude or include information on specific files or directories.

8. The Report Exclude Users option and the Report Include Users option can be selected to exclude or include information on specific users. The Report Exclude Users list is by default empty, and the Report Include Users option contains the asterisk (*) entry indicating all users are included. You can use Ins and Del to insert and delete user names from this list.

   Figure 19.45 shows that auditing information for only the user HACKER will be presented.

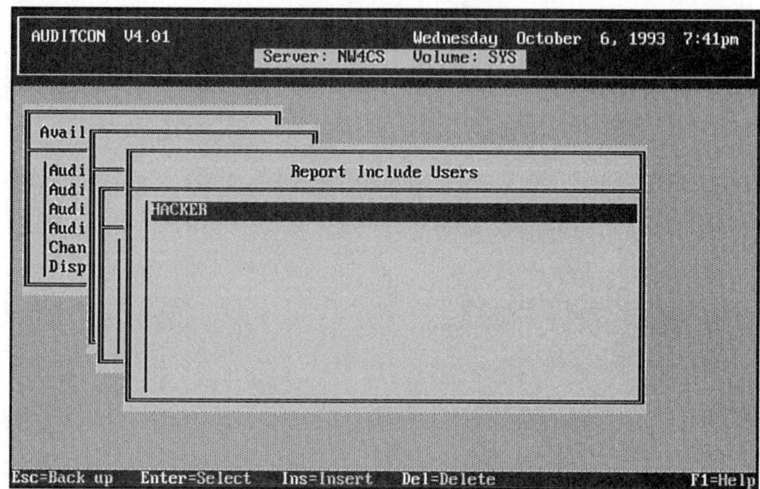

Figure 19.45
Edit Report Filter—Report Include Users.

9. After making the filter edits, press Esc a few times. You will be presented with an option of saving the filter under a name (see fig. 19.46). Enter a suitable filter name and press Enter.

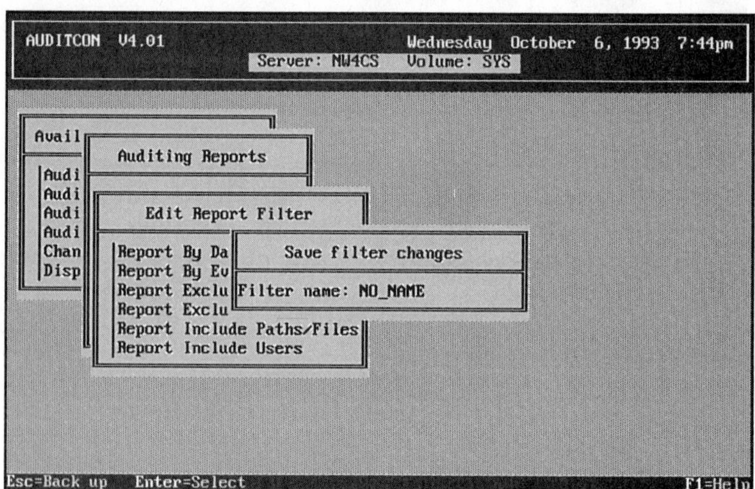

Figure 19.46
Edit Report Filter—Save filter changes.

10. You can test your filter by selecting View Audit File from Auditing Reports, and selecting the newly defined filter.

Figure 19.47 shows an example of a report that uses a filter for looking at information for the user HACKER. Notice that the information is on user HACKER only. Also, in this filter the File Open—User or File event has been filtered out, but the File Read—User or File file event has been retained in the filter.

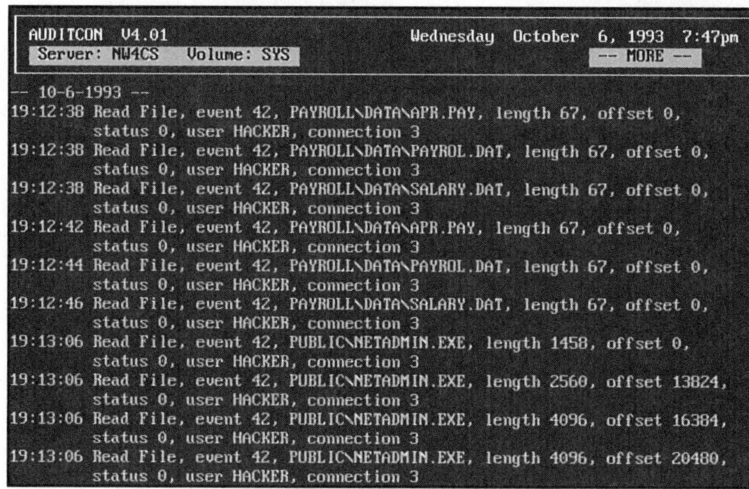

Figure 19.47
Edit Report Filter—Using a filter on a report.

Managing Audit Reports

The audit reports are generated as text files. While the original audit files NET$AUDT.DAT and AUD$HIST.DAT are flagged open and not accessible to non-auditors, the text files can be read by any user who has Read rights to them. For this reason, it is best to print the audit report and delete and purge the original. If an electronic text file of the report is desired, it can be downloaded onto a floppy disk.

The following steps outline the procedure to print an audit report:

1. Log in to the network as an auditor user and run AUDITCON. Next, log in to Volume or Directory Services auditing.

2. From the main menu of the AUDITCON utility, select "Auditing Reports."

3. Select Report Audit File or Report Audit History from the Auditing Reports menu.

4. You will be asked to enter the file name for the report. Enter the full pathname for the report.

5. Exit AUDITCON.

6. Print the Audit Report text file. You can use the NPRINT, NETUSER, PCONSOLE, or CAPTURE commands for printing. Alternatively, you can import the text file into a word processor and use the print function within the word processor.

7. Optionally, you can copy the report file onto a floppy disk and delete and purge the report file from the network.

Maintaining Audit Files

AUDITCON has options to manage existing audit log files. These options are typically used when the audit log files get full. Using these options, the auditor can move existing audit log files to old audit log files, and reset audit log files.

The following steps outline how this can be accomplished:

1. Log in to the network as an auditor user and run AUDITCON.

2. From the main menu of the AUDITCON utility, select Auditor Volume Login.

3. You must specify the password for the volume.

4. From the Available Audit Options menu, select Audit Files Maintenance. You should see the Audit Files Maintenance menu (see figure 19.48).

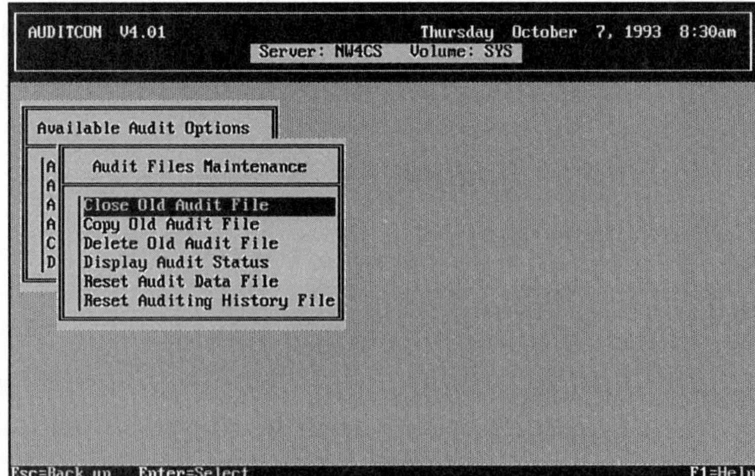

Figure 19.48
The Audit Files Maintenance menu.

The Close Old Audit File option is used for closing an old audit file so that it can be accessed outside AUDITCON. This option closes the file so that it can be accessed. A user must have appropriate trustee rights to access the closed file.

The Copy Old Audit File option allows you to copy an old audit file. This file is copied as a compressed, non-readable file. You can specify the name and the destination of the file. The default name is AUDITOLD.DAT. If you want to copy this file in a readable report format, you can do this by activating the Auditing Reports menu and selecting Report Audit file.

The Delete Old Audit File option allows you to delete an old audit file. The current audit file is not affected.

The Display Audit Status option allows you to view the audit status on files such as audit file size, audit file threshold, the maximum audit file size, the history file size, the audit record count, and the history record count.

The Reset Audit Data File option moves current data in the audit file to the Old Audit Data file. Any data that exists in the Old Audit Data file is overwritten. For this reason, you may wish to use the Copy Old Audit File to save the data in the Old Audit File before using the Reset Audit Data File option. The Audit Data File is reset to zero records, and will continue gathering audit events based on the current configuration settings.

The Reset Auditing History File deletes the entries that have been recorded in this file, and leaves space for new entries. This option applies to audited volumes and not to audited containers.

Auditing Guidelines

If you want to determine if there is a security breach, you can audit:

- Changes to the ACL for an object (NDS event)
- File opens and reads of critical files

If you suspect security breaches by a particular user, you can audit:

- File opens/reads/writes by the user
- File opens/reads/writes to those files that you suspect the user is tampering with

If you suspect that there is a security breach at the file server, you can audit:

- NetWare server events
- Server volume mounts/dismounts
- Logins to the network
- Read/opens to RCONSOLE program for remote access

If you want to troubleshoot performance problems with an application, you can audit:

- File operations by the application that you suspect is slow
- File opens to the application program, to determine simultaneous use of the program

If you want to justify purchase of a higher license version of an application, you can audit the following events to determine if such a purchase is justified:

- Audit writes to the application's data and program files
- If the application prints to a queue, audit use of print queues

If you want to monitor usage of sensitive files, you can audit file opens/reads to that file.

Summary

In this chapter you learned about the auditing capabilities of NetWare 4.*x*. The principal tool for auditing is AUDITCON. AUDITCON can be used for monitoring file system events, QMS events, server events, user events, and NDS events. The differences between these different types of events were described in this chapter. You also learned about the different parameters for audit configuration, such as setting audit file maximum size and specifying what recovery options to select in case the audit file is full.

This chapter also presented an outline of steps to be performed for setting up different auditing scenarios. Toward the end of the chapter you learned about report generation and filter creation for generating reports on selected events.

The NetWare Network Environment

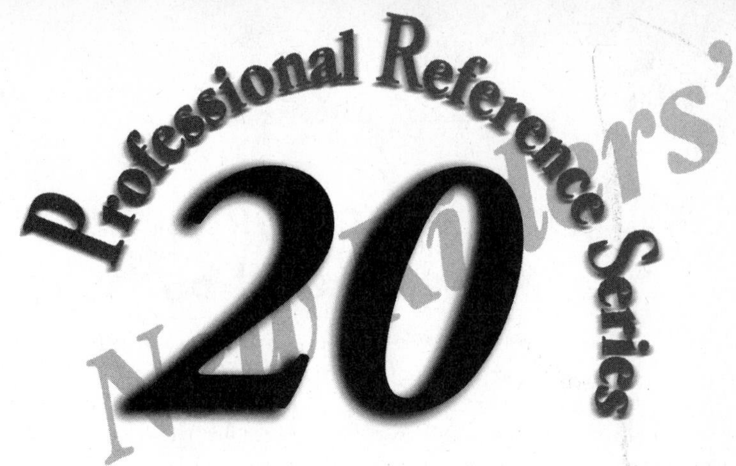

Supporting DOS Workstations

As far as the end user is concerned, the workstation is the most important component of the network. If the workstation is slow or does not have an adequate amount of RAM or disk space, users may not be able to do their work efficiently or even at all. Even if the network has the fastest server and a great deal of RAM, these do not help the user if the workstation is inadequate.

In this chapter, you learn how to manage the workstation. You also learn how to perform the following tasks:

- Generate IPX for NetWare workstations
- Install ODI components
- Use source routing drivers for IBM Token-Ring networks
- Configure NetWare workstations for Ethernet II LANs
- Install OS/2 NetWare workstations

This chapter concludes with an in-depth discussion of the NetWare workstation connection mechanism. An understanding of this connection mechanism can help you solve problems, such as those that result in the `File server not found` message.

NetWare workstations comprise both hardware and software components. The following sections examine these components.

Understanding NetWare Workstation Hardware and Software

On a NetWare LAN, the workstations can be IBM personal computers or compatibles, Macintosh computers, or UNIX workstations. The PC is by far the most popular hardware platform for NetWare workstations; in fact, the PC is one of the earliest workstation platforms supported by Novell. (Historically, CP/M machines were the first.) This is not surprising when you consider that most computers in use today are IBM PCs and compatibles.

Other platforms, such as Macintosh and UNIX workstations, are increasing in popularity but are fewer in number than PCs. This chapter, therefore, focuses on the PC running DOS.

Eventually, Novell plans to develop NetWare so that it can run at the workstation—or server—level on every popular microcomputer or workstation architecture. Novell's strategic alliances with IBM, Apple, Sun, DEC, and Hewlett Packard are steps in that direction.

From a network manager's point of view, the capability of running NetWare on many hardware and operating-system platforms is a welcome step toward multiple-vendor integration. An enterprise-wide network usually has a mix of different hardware and operating system platforms such as PCs, Macintoshes, engineering workstations that run UNIX, minicomputers, and mainframes. Users usually interact with PC, Macintosh, or engineering workstations, although terminals still are used in some instances.

Each workstation platform can use a variety of operating systems. Many operating systems have a preferred *Graphical User Interface* (GUI). Table 20.1 lists the dominant workstation/OS platforms of today. Note, however, that this list is not complete; many other OS and GUI choices are available, such as PC-MOS, PICK, DESQview, and NewWave, but a discussion of all these operating systems and GUIs is beyond the scope of this book.

Table 20.1
Popular Workstation/OS Combinations

Workstation	Operating System	GUI
IBM PC XT	DOS	No standard GUI
IBM PC AT 286	DOS OS/2 1.*x*	Microsoft Windows Presentation Manager
IBM PC AT 386	DOS OS/2 2.*x* UNIX	Microsoft Windows Presentation Manager and Microsoft Windows X Windows

Workstation	Operating System	GUI
Eng. workstations (SUN, HP, DEC, and so on)	UNIX	X Windows
Macintosh	System 7	System

The IBM PC Family and PC Compatibles

The IBM PC family currently includes the IBM PC XT, IBM PC AT 286, IBM PC AT 386, Pentium-based, and IBM PS/2 microcomputers, as well as numerous compatible microcomputers produced by other manufacturers. The 486 and higher compatibles fall into the 386 category because the architecture of the Intel 80486 and Pentium machines is essentially the same as the Intel 80386 machine. The common denominator for all IBM PC platforms is DOS. DOS-based applications usually run in the Intel processors' real mode. By using tools such as the Phar Lap memory extender and special compilers, however, developers can write DOS applications that run in protected mode with the Intel 80286 and higher microprocessors.

The distinction between real and protected modes is important because the mode determines what size application can run on the workstation. Real mode exists in the Intel microprocessor architecture to maintain compatibility with Intel 8086-based machines (IBM PC and IBM PC XT).

In real mode (fig. 20.1), DOS and applications can run in 640 KB of RAM. An additional 384 KB—a total of 1024 KB—also is available, but typically is used by adapters in the workstation to carry out direct memory mapping of their internal buffers. This additional 384 KB is sometimes called *high memory.* More recent versions of MS-DOS and *Digital Research DOS* (DR DOS) use clever techniques to utilize unused RAM in this additional 384 KB high-memory range. This allows more space for applications that must run within the 640 KB. As applications have grown more complex, developers have taken many stop-gap measures to make as much RAM as possible available for applications. These techniques include the use of extended memory, the conversion of extended memory to expanded memory, and the use of high memory to load DOS, device drivers, and *Terminate-and-Stay-Resident* (TSR) programs.

Protected mode is available only on Intel 80286 and higher microprocessors. In protected mode, the Intel 80286 can use up to 16 MB of RAM corresponding to the 24-bit address lines of the microprocessor. The Intel 80386 provides up to 4 GB of RAM in protected mode; therefore, protected mode is the logical choice if you want to run large applications. But things are not as simple as they appear. Applications are dependent on DOS, and DOS runs in real mode. DOS applications, therefore, also must run in real mode. Even those DOS applications that use special techniques to run in protected mode—the Intel 80286 and higher—must switch to real mode to use DOS. A few other minor problems exist. For example, the BIOS in most PCs operates in real mode and is nonre-entrant. Protected-mode operating systems, such as NetWare, OS/2, and UNIX, bypass most real-mode services offered by the BIOS. (This explains why certain BIOS-based functions, such as Shift-PrtScrn, do not work under these operating systems.)

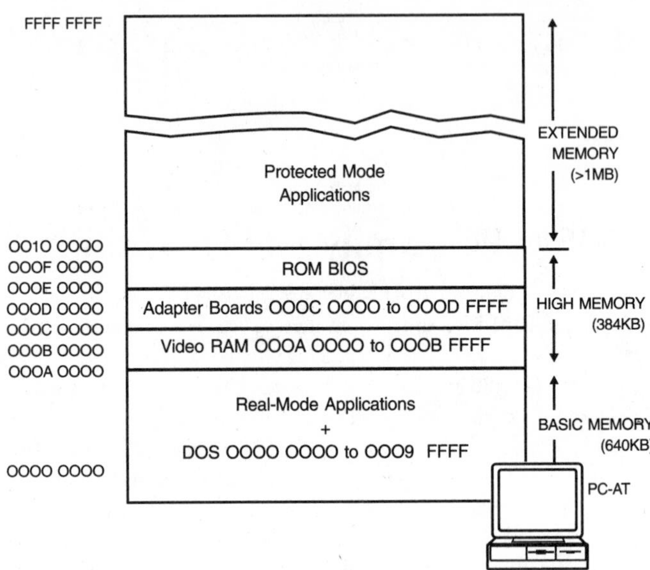

Figure 20.1
Real-mode versus protected-mode applications.

DOS continues to be a real-mode OS so that it can run the large installed base of DOS real-mode applications. If DOS ever becomes a protected-mode, multitasking OS, many applications may have to be recompiled or rewritten to run in protected mode.

The minimum requirements you need for an IBM PC NetWare workstation that runs DOS are as follows:

- At least 640 KB of RAM
- Workstation NIC with no conflicts with other hardware devices in the workstation
- Monochrome, EGA/VGA or higher display adapters (CGA adapters also can be supported but, because of their poor quality, are usually avoided)
- Floppy disk drive to boot DOS and run NetWare workstation software
- NICs with remote boot PROMs to boot with workstation operating system image kept on the server in the absence of floppy drives

DOS-based PCs must run DOS 3.*x* or higher. Support for DOS 2.*x* and below has been dropped.

To use a DOS machine as a NetWare workstation, you must run networking software at the workstation. This networking software ordinarily takes up 66 KB of space. Because DOS consumes about 64 KB of space, this leaves about 520 KB of space to run an application. In later chapters, you learn how MS-DOS 5 and DR DOS use even less memory.

The workstation's networking software (often called the *shell*) uses a certain number of software interrupts. Only applications that do not conflict with these software interrupts can run on the NetWare workstation. Conflicts of this type have become less frequent because of Novell's market dominance. Most application vendors maintain compatibility with Novell to avoid these conflicts, but if a conflict arises, the application vendor usually can be convinced to use some other software interrupt. Table 20.2 lists the software interrupts used by a NetWare workstation.

Table 20.2
Software Interrupts Used by NetWare Workstation

Network Component	Interrupts	Memory Size (Bytes)
IPX.COM	08 0B 2F 64 7A C8 F0 F3 F5 FD FF	19,840
NETX.COM	10 17 1B 20 21 27	41,472

OS/2 1.*x* runs on Intel 80286 or higher machines, but the future of OS/2 is with 2.*x* and higher versions. OS/2 2.*x* runs on Intel 80386-based and higher machines. The minimum requirement for OS/2 2.*x* is 4 MB.

To use OS/2 at a NetWare workstation, networking software must run in the form of device drivers. The most important piece of the networking software for OS/2 is the OS/2 NetWare Requester. The NetWare Requester allows OS/2 workstations to access the NetWare server.

Configuring DOS Workstations for NetWare

The workstation needs to be set up with the networking software before it can access the NetWare server. Two forms of network software exist for DOS workstations. The older combination of IPX and NET*x* remains the most common method used to configure DOS workstations. The newer *Open Data Link Interface* (ODI) approach represents Novell's future strategy and offers some advantages when multiple protocols must be supported. In DOS workstations, the networking software is loaded as TSR programs. For OS/2 workstations, the networking software is set up as device drivers.

You can use the NETX shells to login into NetWare 2.*x*, 3.*x*, and 4.*x* servers (bindery emulation mode). You can also use the NetWare Requester implemented using VLMs (Virtual Lodable Modules) to log into the NetWare 2.*x*, 3.*x* and 4.*x* servers. The VLMs have a bindery compatible module called NETX.VLM that emulates the shell to log in to bindery-based servers. Bindery-based servers are NetWare 2.*x*, 3.*x*, and 4.*x* servers in bindery-emulation mode.

This chapter first discusses the requirements for the installed base of NetWare workstations that use NETX.COM or NETX.EXE. A later section covers the requirements for workstations that use the NetWare Requester.

IPX/NETx Workstation Software

Two major components make up the networking software for a DOS workstation. These are as follows:

- IPX.COM
- NET*x*.COM (or NETX.COM or NETX.EXE)

Both IPX.COM and NET*x*.COM are TSR programs that must be loaded after you boot the workstation in DOS. IPX must be loaded at the workstation first, followed by NET*x*.COM. (The *x* refers to the major DOS rev number—3 for DOS 3.*x* and 5 for DOS 6.*x*.) There is also a generic version of NETX called NETX.COM or NETX.EXE. The shell with the EXE extension is a later release. These programs typically are run in the AUTOEXEC.BAT file or some other DOS batch file. Together, IPX.COM and NET*x*.COM set up the DOS NetWare workstation environment.

IPX.COM contains an implementation of the SPX/IPX protocols that are linked with the NIC drivers. That is, IPX.COM implements layers 3 (network) and 4 (transport) of the OSI model (see fig. 20.2). The IPX protocol interfaces with the rest of the network by using the NIC drivers linked with it. Figure 20.2 illustrates the IPX.COM in relationship to the NIC driver. Because workstations can have a variety of NICs, a different driver must be linked with IPX.COM for each NIC type. NetWare does not come with a separate IPX.COM for each driver type. NetWare gives you the pieces to create the IPX.COM, such as the object module IPX.OBJ and the network drivers for a number of NICs. Other network drivers not included with NetWare can be obtained from the NIC vendor or CompuServe. The NetWare installer must link these individual pieces together to create an IPX.COM file. Such a file implements the transport protocols necessary for packet transmission across the network.

The process of creating a new copy of IPX.COM by linking with a NIC driver is called *generating the shell.* This can be confusing because *shell* refers to NET*x*.COM rather than IPX.COM, but IPX.COM is the file being generated. The NET*x*.COM file does not have any NIC driver components and does not need to be generated. NET*x*.COM is a generic program for a specific DOS version *x* and is used with IPX.COM. NET*x*.COM is the workstation shell because it surrounds DOS and processes each command before the command is passed on to DOS or the network. The NET*x*.COM is a program that extends the workstation environment. Like IPX.COM, NET*x*.COM is loaded as a TSR at the workstation. NET*x*.COM must be loaded after IPX.COM is loaded. NET*x*.COM runs on top of DOS and creates a network environment for the user.

The user can still use DOS commands while the shell is loaded because a NetWare workstation views the network as a series of DOS drives. Drives A to E usually are reserved for local hard disks and RAM drives at the workstation, and drives F to Z generally are assigned to the network.

The server's file system is accessible to the user by drive letters F to Z. The NetWare MAP command enables the user to map a drive letter to a directory on the server disk. This network drive letter can be used when a drive letter is needed for network and most DOS commands. In other words, the work environment of the client includes the server's file system. Access to the file server's system is not automatic; you need a valid user account and password on the server.

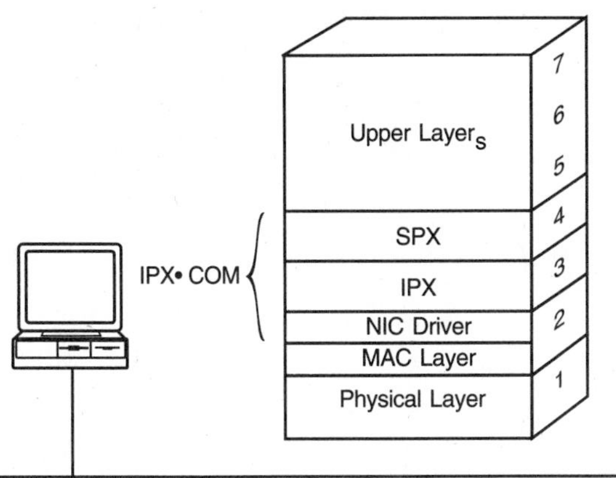

Figure 20.2
IPX components.

The *x* in NET*x*.COM stands for the DOS version being used at the workstation. NET3.COM is used for DOS 3.*x*, and NET5.COM is used for DOS 5.*x*. To simplify management of NetWare workstations, Novell now has a generic NETX.COM shell that can be used for all DOS 3.*x* and later versions. Support for earlier DOS versions has been discontinued.

NET*x*.COM is not bound to any drivers and runs on top of the IPX/SPX protocols implemented by IPX.COM; therefore, it is not generated by the shell or workstation-generation process.

The shell can be viewed as a network traffic director. It distinguishes local commands from network commands. Local commands are sent to DOS, where they are processed by the workstation operating system. Network commands are sent across the network. Consider the following command:

```
COPY C:\DATA.22 A:
```

The shell recognizes this as a local command that deals with local resources only. No network resources are referred to in the source (local hard disk file C:\DATA.22) or destination (floppy drive A). This command is processed locally by DOS.

Now consider the following command:

```
COPY F:\USERS\DEI\DATA.22 A:
```

If you assume that the drive letter F refers to a network drive, this command means to copy the file DATA.22 from the network drive F:\USERS\DEI to the local floppy. The shell recognizes this as a network command and performs the file transfer from the network drive to the local floppy. The transfer involves software and hardware network components, including the shell (NCP requests and replies), IPX.COM (transport protocols IPX/SPX), network drivers, the workstation NIC, and the LAN. The user does not see all the behind-the-scenes work that satisfies a simple DOS COPY request. And herein lies the power of the system: the network is as easy to use as DOS commands.

Connecting to the Server

When the shell NET*x*.COM loads, it initializes the workstation environment. An important part of this initialization is finding a server to connect to. The shell broadcasts a SAP packet asking for the nearest server. The servers on the network that receive this SAP request respond with a Give Nearest Server SAP response.

The server's response tells the client how far away the server is (number of hops) and the name of the server. This information enables the client to attach to the server. This attachment is a logical connection for which control commands are sent to manage the client-to-server connection. This connection is not the same as being logged in to the server. Logging in to the server is done through the LOGIN.EXE command stored in the server's SYS:LOGIN directory.

After the initial handshake has formed an attachment to the server, the shell maps the first available network drive to the server's SYS:LOGIN directory. Drive F is usually the first available drive because it follows drive E—the default value of the LASTDRIVE parameter in CONFIG.SYS. Most workstations do not have the LASTDRIVE parameter set in their CONFIG.SYS file; therefore, the DOS system defaults to E for the LASTDRIVE parameter.

The SYS:LOGIN directory to which F is mapped contains the program files LOGIN.EXE and SLIST.EXE. LOGIN.EXE implements the LOGIN command, and SLIST.EXE implements the server list command that displays a list of all servers that can be reached by the workstation.

To invoke the LOGIN.EXE file, the user must change to the F drive and issue the LOGIN command. LOGIN.EXE then is downloaded to the workstation's RAM and runs on the workstation's CPU. The LOGIN command prompts the user for a login name and password. If this is entered correctly, the user is then logged in to the server.

Thus, the login commands take the following sequence:

```
IPX
NETX
F:
LOGIN
```

A more general form of the LOGIN command that specifies the user name is as follows:

```
LOGIN [[ServerName/]UserName]
```

For example, if you want to log in to a server named KSS, type the following command:

```
LOGIN KSS/UserName
```

The server name distinguishes between several servers on the network. When several servers are available, each one responds to the shell's initial request for the nearest server. The server that has the fastest response is the one selected for the attachment. This may not be the server on which you want to log in.

The IPX.COM Workstation Software

The workstation-generation program, or WSGEN, is common to both NetWare 2.2 and NetWare 3.11 and later versions. Prior to these versions, a program called SHGEN was used. Older versions of NetWare, such as Advanced NetWare 2.0a, used a program called GENSH.

You can find WSGEN on the NetWare disk labeled WSGEN. The workstation-generation process can be performed on any PC with a floppy drive and sufficient memory to run WSGEN. WSGEN runs from the DOS prompt.

WSGEN links the NIC drivers to the program file IPX.OBJ to produce an IPX.COM file that implements the SPX/IPX protocols. The IPX.COM file also contains the linked NIC driver that can communicate with the NIC. NETX.COM is a generic program that can be used with all linked IPX.COM versions; NETX.COM is not customized by WSGEN.

This section gives you a detailed look at the WSGEN process. You must have the following software/hardware components to perform these exercises:

- An IBM PC with 640 KB RAM and one floppy drive
- The WSGEN disk containing the generation program
- LAN driver disks such as LAN_DRV_001 or LAN_DRV_XXX
- DOS 3.*x* or higher to boot the PC

To prepare the NetWare workstation for generation, take the following steps:

1. Boot the workstation with the DOS boot disk.
2. Place the disk labeled NetWare WSGEN in drive A. Enter the following command to start the generation process:

   ```
   WSGEN
   ```

   The WSGEN opening screen appears, as shown in figure 20.3.
3. Press Enter to continue workstation generation. After a few seconds of the `Please Wait` message, WSGEN displays a screen showing a list of the network drivers (see fig. 20.4).

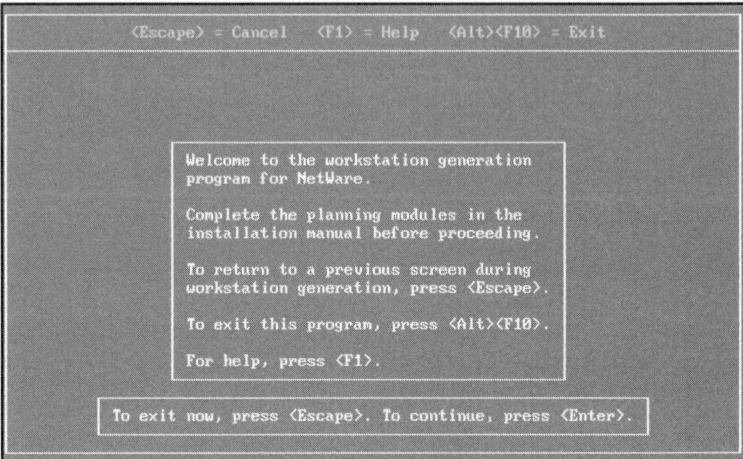

Figure 20.3
The Workstation Generation program opening screen.

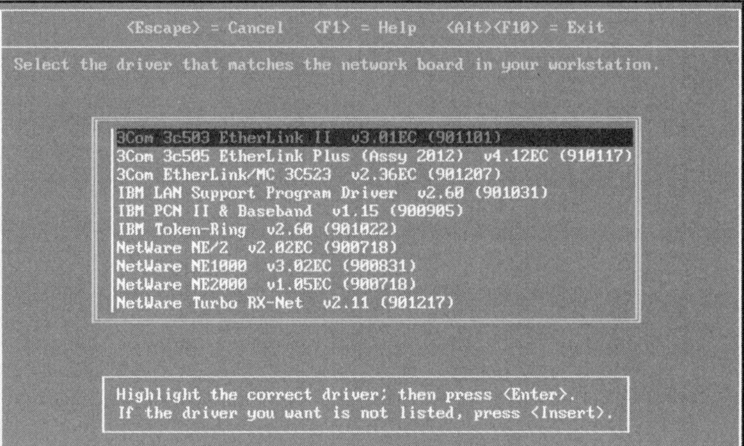

Figure 20.4
The Workstation Generation select network driver screen.

4. If you find the driver for the NIC card installed at your workstation, select it by highlighting the LAN Driver. (If the driver you need is not listed, press Ins and proceed with step 5, or skip to step 9.)

5. A message appears asking you to insert a disk labeled LAN_DRV_???. Drivers not listed in the default list of drivers must be obtained from the driver manufacturer. These drivers come in disks labeled LAN_DRV_???. The symbol "???" is a code assigned to the manufacturer.

6. Insert the disk labeled LAN_DRV_XXX in a drive and press Enter to continue. A message appears that states the driver for the NIC was read successfully.

7. Press Enter to continue. A screen that displays the list of network card drivers on the LAN_DRV_XXX disk appears.

8. Use the cursor keys to scroll down the list of drivers and locate the NIC driver.

9. Highlight the NIC driver and press Enter.

10. A list of configuration options should appear. Figure 20.5 shows a sample screen of typical configuration options.

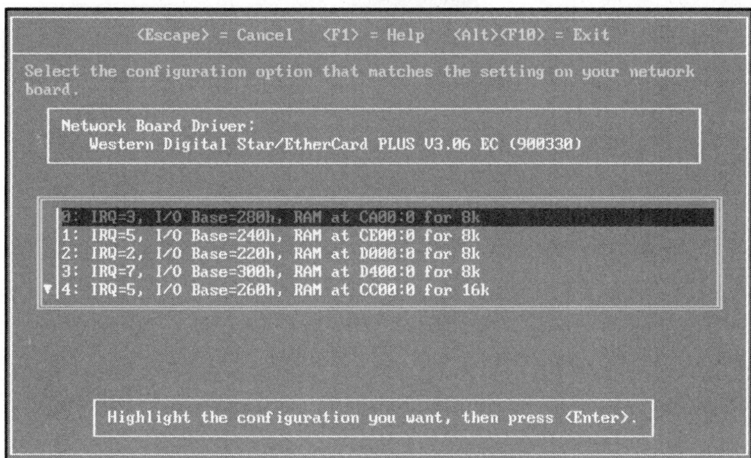

Figure 20.5
The Workstation Generation configuration options screen.

11. Highlight the configuration option that matches the NIC setting and press Enter.

12. Highlight the *Yes, generate workstation software* option and press Enter.

13. If the disk WSGEN is not in a drive, insert it when prompted to do so.

    The following messages appear:

    ```
    Creating DOS Workstation.
    Novell Linker, Version 2.1
    Linking WSGEN:IPX.COM.
    Insert disk LAN_DRV_200 in any drive
    Strike a key when ready . . .
    ```

14. Insert the following disks, in this order:

    LAN_DRV_001 or LAN_DRV_XXX

    WSGEN

    The following messages appear, as does the screen shown in figure 20.6:

    ```
    Novell configuration utility:
    Configuring WSGEN:IPX.COM
    ```

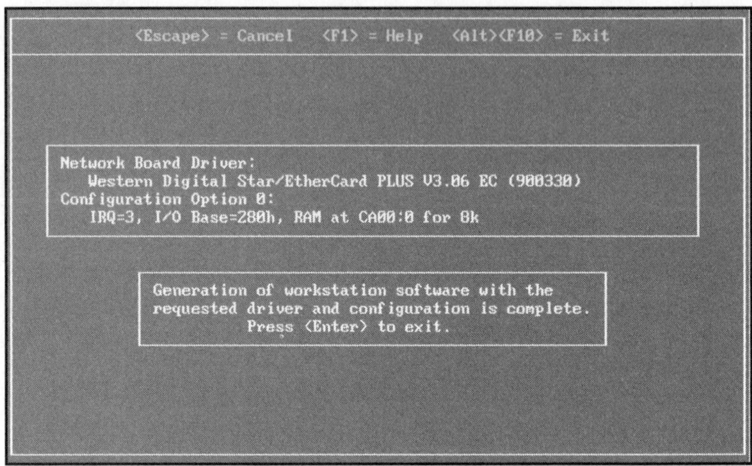

Figure 20.6
The Workstation Generation complete screen.

15. Workstation generation is now complete. Press Enter to exit.

16. Copy the files IPX.COM and NET3.COM from the WSGEN disk onto a NetWare workstation boot disk. You can prepare this disk by using the DOS format command, as follows:

    ```
    FORMAT A: /S
    ```

    If you have a single floppy system, copy these files to your hard disk first, and then copy from the hard disk to the floppy.

17. Create a batch file NETLOG.BAT that has the following commands (or put the commands in the AUTOEXEC.BAT file):

    ```
    IPX

    NET3

    F:

    LOGIN
    ```

18. Use the batch file to log in to the NetWare server, as follows:

    ```
    NETLOG
    ```

    If you have an account on the server, you can log in to the server. If the workstation cannot find a server, a `File server not found` message appears.

NET and IPX Options

Both NET*x* and the IPX programs have options that can be used to alter their behavior. One useful option, the I option, reveals the following important information:

```
IPX I

Novell IPX/SPX v3.04 (910703)

Copyright 1985, 1991 Novell Inc. All Rights Reserved.

LAN Option: D-Link Pocket Ethernet DE-600 V2.01 (910321) Hardware
Configuration: Printer port & IRQ channel auto-detected

NET5 I

NetWare V3.10 - Workstation Shell for PC DOS V5.x (910307)

(c) Copyright 1990 Novell, Inc. All Rights Reserved.

NETX I

NetWare V3.22 - Workstation Shell (910731) (c) Copyright

1991 Novell, Inc. All Rights Reserved.
```

The IPX I command in the preceding examples states the version number of the IPX module—version 3.04. The date stamp reveals that the driver was released on March 21, 1991 (910321). The NIC driver linked is the D-Link (David Systems) Pocket Ethernet DE-600 driver. The version number of the driver is V2.01, and the hardware configuration tells you that the printer port and the IRQ level are automatically detected by the driver.

The NET5 I and NETX I commands reveal similar information. You can tell that NETX is a more recent version—version 3.22 versus V3.10—than NET5. This fact is confirmed if you examine the date of release and the copyright year.

Whereas the I option was available for older versions of IPX and NET*x*, newer versions of these programs have more useful options. To find these options type the NET*x* /? and IPX /? commands, as follows:

```
IPX /?

Usage: IPX [options]
valid options:
   I or /I      Displays version information
   D or /D      Displays hardware options
   O or /O<num>   Load using hardware option <num>
   C or /C=[path]<filename>  Specifies an alternate
                             configuration file
   ? or /?                   Displays this help screen
```

The option letters can be preceded by either the hyphen (-) or forward slash (/) character. The -I option is the information option. The /D option displays the hardware configuration. An example of the use of the /D option is as follows:

IPX /D

```
Novell IPX/SPX v3.04 (910703)(c)
Copyright 1985, 1991 Novell Inc. All Rights Reserved.

LAN Option: D-Link Pocket Ethernet DE-600  V2.01 (910321) Hardware options
available:

 *  0. Printer port & IRQ channel autodetected
```

Each driver has a number of selectable configuration options. The asterisk (*) is placed next to the option currently selected in the driver. You can load IPX with an alternate hardware option by using the /O parameter to specify the hardware option. IPX also can be loaded with a number of configurable options to be placed in the specified text file. If the text file is not specified, the configuration file has the default name NET.CFG.

NETX /?

```
NetWare V3.22  Workstation Shell (910731)
(c) Copyright 1991 Novell, Inc. All Rights Reserved.

Usage : NETX  [<option>]
Valid <options>:

/?                          Displays shell usage
/I                          Displays shell version and type
/U                          Unloads the NetWare shell from memory
/F                          Forcibly unloads the NetWare shell, in spite of
                            TSRs loaded after the shell (CAUTION: The
                            /F option can hang your workstation.)
/PS=<server>                Specifies a preferred server
/C=[path\]<filename.ext>    Names your NetWare shell configuration file (For
                            use with DOS 3.0 through 5.0.)
```

The -I option is the information option.

The /U unloads the shell and releases the RAM space occupied by the shell. This enables you to experiment with memory configurations without having to reboot the workstation. Prior to the /U option, the only way to unload the shell—if third-party software or shareware utilities were not used—was to reboot the workstation.

Before the shell unloads, other TSRs that were loaded after the shell must be removed. Some TSRs cannot be unloaded. In this situation, you can force an unload of the shell by using the /F option. The /F option can create gaps of unused space in the workstation RAM and can cause your workstation to "hang."

The /PS=*server* option forces a connection to the specified server. This is useful when multiple servers are on the network. To reconnect to the desired server, use the LOGIN command that specifies the server name, or invoke NET*x* with the preferred server name. Therefore, to ensure a connection to the server named KSS, type the following:

```
NETX /PS=KSS
```

The /C option specifies the shell configuration file. If you do not specify the shell configuration file, the NET.CFG file in the current directory—if it exists—is used as the configuration file.

Shell Configuration Files SHELL.CFG and NET.CFG

The shell configuration can be customized by placing commands in the NET.CFG file. These commands must be placed at the beginning of the NET.CFG file and also can be placed in the older SHELL.CFG file. Novell, however, is replacing the SHELL.CFG file with the more versatile NET.CFG file.

The configuration commands can be grouped into configuration options for:

- IPX
- NET*x*
- NETBIOS

Tables 20.3 to 20.5 summarize these parameters for your reference. For more detailed information, refer to the NetWare 2.2 *Using the Network* manual.

The following is a sample NET.CFG file for DOS workstations:

```
                              ; IPX.COM configuration options
CONFIG OPTION=1               ; Uses configuration option 1
IPX RETRY COUNT=30            ; Increases retry count
IPX SOCKETS=60                ; Increases IPX sockets
SPX CONNECTIONS=50            ; Increases SPX connections

                              ; NETx.COM parameters
FILE HANDLES=60               ; Increases file handles
LOCAL PRINTER=0               ; Disables Shift PrtScrn
LONG MACHINE TYPE=KSS_PC      ; Changes %MACHINE
PREFERRED SERVER=KSS_SRV      ; Specifies server to connect to
SEARCH MODE=2                 ; Never searches for data files in search
                                drives
SET STATION TIME=OFF          ; Special timing clock at workstation
TASK MODE=0                   ; Plain Old DOS - no multitasking

                              ; NETBIOS parameters
NETBIOS COMMANDS=22           ; Increases command queue
NETBIOS RECEIVE BUFFERS=10    ; Increases IPX receive buffers
NETBIOS SEND BUFFERS=10       ; Increases IPX send buffers
NETBIOS SESSIONS=20           ; Reduces sessions
```

Table 20.3
NET.CFG IPX.COM Parameters

Parameter	Value
CONFIG OPTION=*n*	Overrides the network driver configuration option selected by WSGEN or DCONFIG.
INT64=[ON|OFF]	Configures IPX to use software interrupt 64 hex. Primary purpose is for compatibility with earlier versions of NetWare. Default is ON.
INT7A=[ON|OFF]	Configures IPX to use software interrupt 7A hex. To be used for compatibility with NetWare 2.0a. Default is ON.
IPATCH=*a*	Fixes "bugs" in IPX.COM. Any location in IPX.COM can be replaced ("patched") with a specified value.
IPX PACKET SIZE LIMIT=*n*	Changes the maximum packet size set by a LAN driver—if the driver supports this.
IPX RETRY COUNT=*n*	Specifies number of times a workstation tries to resend a packet. Default is 20 retries.
IPX SOCKETS=*n*	Specifies maximum number of sockets that can be opened by the workstation. Default is 20 sockets.
SPX ABORT TIMEOUT=*n*	Specifies number of clock ticks SPX waits without receiving response from the remote side before it terminates the connection. Default is 540 ticks (about 30 seconds).
SPX CONNECTIONS=*n*	Specifies number of simultaneous SPX connections allowed at a workstation. Default is 15 connections.
SPX LISTEN TIMEOUT=*n*	Specifies number of clock ticks SPX waits for a response from the remote side. If there is no response, it times out and sends "probe" packets to see if remote is still alive. Default is 108 ticks (about 6 seconds).
SPX VERIFY TIMEOUT=*n*	Specifies number of clock ticks SPX waits before sending a packet to the remote side to verify if a connection is still alive. Default is 54 ticks (about 3 seconds).

Table 20.4
NET.CFG NETx.COM Parameters

Parameter	Value
ALL SERVER=[ON|OFF]	Sends End of Task signal to all connected servers, if set to ON. If set to OFF, sends End of Task signal only to the servers interacting with the task. Default is OFF.
CACHE BUFFERS=*n*	Specifies number of cache buffers. Cache buffers are 512-byte buffers that the shell uses for local caching of nonshared, nontransactional files. Default is 5 buffers.
EOJ=[ON|OFF]	Specifies if files, locks, and semaphores are closed automatically at the end of the job. Default is ON.
FILE HANDLES=*n*	Specifies an upper limit on number of files the workstation can have opened at the network simultaneously. Default is 40 files. Local files are controlled FILES= in CONFIG.SYS.
HOLD=[ON|OFF]	Specifies if workstation files should be held open if they were opened and closed. Default is OFF.
LOCAL PRINTERS=*n*	Changes the BIOS setting for the number of local printers at a workstation. Setting *n* to 0 prevents the workstation from hanging if the Shift-PrtScrn key is pressed when no local printer exists.
LOCK DELAY=*n*	Specifies the number of ticks the shell waits before obtaining a lock. Default is 1.
LOCK RETRIES=*n*	Specifies the number of times the shell attempts to get a lock on a network resource.
LONG MACHINE TYPE=*typeName*	Changes the value of the %MACHINE login script variable. The default value is IBM_PC. The variable *typeName* is 6 characters or less.
MAX CUR DIR LENGTH=*n*	Defines the current directory length as a value that can be from 64 to 255. Default is 64.
MAX PATH LENGTH=*n*	Defines the network path length as a value that can be from 64 to 255. Default is 255.

continues

Table 20.4, Continued
NET.CFG NETx.COM Parameters

Parameter	Value
MAX TASKS=*n*	Defines the maximum number of tasks that can be active simultaneously at the workstation. Used in DESQview and MS Windows environment. The value ranges from 20 to 128 with a default of 31.
PATCH=*n*	Patches any address in the shell.
PREFERRED SERVER= *serverName*	Forces the shell to attach to the specified server.
PRINT HEADER=*n*	Sets the size of the initialization string for the printer that is sent before each print job. The value ranges from 0 to 255 with a default of 64 bytes.
PRINT TAIL=*n*	Sets the size of the reset string for the printer that is sent after each print job. The value ranges from 0 to 255 with a default of 16 bytes.
READ ONLY COMPATIBILITY= [ON|OFF]	Specifies if a file marked Read Only attribute can be opened for read/write. Default value is OFF.
SEARCH MODE=*mode*	Specifies the search mode for the shell. Can be used to extend the normal DOS search for a data file on the search drives. The value can be from 1 to 7 with a default of 1. Search mode has the following meanings: 1. Search if path not specified for data file 2. Never search 3. Search if path not specified, and request is to read a file but not to modify it 4. Reserved 5. Always search 6. Reserved 7. Always search if request is only to read the file
SET STATION TIME= [ON|OFF]	Synchronizes the shell's workstation time to servers time when set to ON. Default is ON.
SHARE=[ON|OFF]	Enables a process to inherit all the resources of a parent process, such as file handles, when set to ON. Default is ON.

Parameter	Value
SHORT MACHINE TYPE=*typename*	Sets %SMACHINE login variable to this specified value. The default value is IBM. The variable *typeName* is 4 characters or less.
SHOW DOTS=	Enables shell to emulate the DOS [ON|OFF] FindFirstMatching and FindNextMatching calls for dot (.) and dot-dot(..) entries when set to ON. The default is ON. Must be ON for MS Windows.
SPECIAL UPPER CASE=[ON|OFF]	Causes the shell to call DOS to provide translation for ASCII characters above 128 when set to ON. Used for foreign language and special characters support. Default is OFF.
TASK MODE=*n*	Affects the manner in which the shell handles virtual machine task management. The default value of 2 works well with MS Windows 3.0. Earlier Windows versions used a task mode of 1. If you are not using multitasking, you can speed up the shell by using a task mode of 0.

Table 20.5
NET.CFG NETBIOS.EXE Parameters

Parameter	Value
NETBIOS ABORT TIMEOUT=*n*	Specifies the number of ticks to wait for an acknowledgment After this time, NetBIOS times out and terminates the connection. Default value is 540 ticks (about 30 seconds).
NETBIOS BROADCAST COUNT=*n*	Specifies the number of times NetBIOS broadcasts a query/claim for a name. The value ranges from 2 to 65535. Default value is 4 if internet is ON, or 2 if internet is OFF.
NETBIOS BROADCAST DELAY=*n*	Specifies the number of ticks NetBIOS waits between query/claim broadcasts. Value can be from 18 to 65535. Default value is 36 if internet is ON, or 18 if internet is OFF. NOTE: When multiplied by NETBIOS BROADCAST COUNT, this determines the total time taken to broadcast a name-resolution packet across the network.
NETBIOS COMMANDS=*n*	Specifies the number of outstanding NetBIOS commands that can be waiting for completion at the workstation. The values range from 4 to 250 with a default of 12.

continues

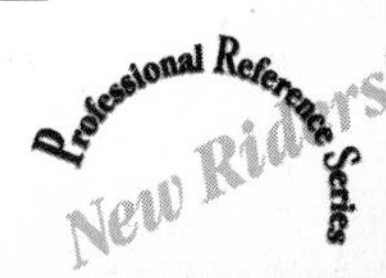

Table 20.5, Continued
NET.CFG NETBIOS.EXE Parameters

Parameter	Value
NETBIOS INTERNET= [ON|OFF]	Sends claim-name packets to all stations on the internet if set to ON. If internet is OFF, NetBIOS sends claim-name packets to stations on the local network and ignores them from outside the local network. Claim-name packets are sent to establish the uniqueness of the NetBIOS name of a station. The default value is ON. If more than one LAN segment is used or if a nondedicated server is used, this value must be ON.
NETBIOS LISTEN TIMEOUT=*n*	Specifies the number of ticks NetBIOS waits for a packet from a remote station before requesting the remote station to verify its connection. Value can be from 1 to 65535. Default value is 108 (about 6 seconds).
NETBIOS RECEIVE BUFFERS=*n*	Specifies the number of receive IPX buffers used by NetBIOS. Value can be from 4 to 20. Default value is 6 buffers.
NETBIOS RETRY COUNT=*n*	Specifies the number of times NetBIOS transmits a request to establish a connection or to retransmit a failed communication before it gives up. The value ranges from 10 to 65535 with a default value of 20.
NETBIOS RETRY DELAY=*n*	Specifies the number of ticks NetBIOS waits between packet transmissions while establishing a connection or resending a data packet. The value ranges from 10 to 65535 with a default value of 10 ticks (about 0.5 second).
NETBIOS SEND BUFFERS=*n*	Specifies the number of send IPX buffers used by NetBIOS. Value can be from 4 to 20. Default value is 6 buffers.
NETBIOS SESSIONS=*n*	Specifies the number of NetBIOS sessions the workstation can have. The values can range from 4 to 250 with a default of 32.
NETBIOS VERIFY TIMEOUT=*n*	Specifies the number of ticks NetBIOS waits before attempting to send a packet to the remote station to confirm the connection. Value can be from 4 to 65535. Default value is 54 ticks (abut 3 seconds).
NPATCH=*n*	Patches a location in the NETBIOS.EXE file.

ODI Shells and Drivers

Novell and Apple developed a specification called the ODI to support multiple protocols in a workstation and a server. Network drivers for NIC cards can be written to this ODI specification, and this enables multiple protocol stacks to share the same network driver. NIC drivers for NetWare 3.*x* servers are written to the ODI specification.

NetWare workstations can use either the generated-workstation software or the ODI drivers. But if you need to run multiple protocol stacks, you must use the ODI drivers. An example of an application that uses ODI drivers is LAN Workplace for DOS. This product, available from Novell, enables a workstation to use SPX/IPX protocols to log in to a NetWare server or use TCP/IP protocols to log in to a TCP/IP host.

ODI offers a number of advantages, including the following:

- Multiple protocol support, such as TCP/IP, SPX/IPX, and AppleTalk, can be added to the same NIC driver without adding extra NICs.
- Sessions with a variety of servers and hosts using different protocol stacks at the workstation can be established. In general, you use a protocol stack at the workstation that the server or host understands.
- All protocol stacks written to the ODI specification can communicate with any NIC driver written to the ODI specification.
- Multiple protocols support is simplified because only one LAN driver exists. Improvements in the ODI LAN driver (or bug fixes) benefit all protocols that work with the improved LAN driver.
- More configuration choices are available through the NET.CFG configuration file. This makes it possible to change the workstation software configuration more easily.

The ODI Specification

The three important components that make ODI work at the workstation level are as follows:

- LSL.COM
- ODI LAN driver
- Protocol stacks

LSL.COM implements the *Link Support Layer* (LSL), and the ODI LAN driver constitutes layer 2 of the OSI model (data link layer). The protocol stacks implement layer 3 and above.

Understanding the ODI Driver Load Sequence

ODI drivers eliminate the need to generate the workstation software, but they still require the individual components to be loaded in a specific order.

In terms of workstation RAM and logical connections between the components, you must load the Link Support Layer first because when the ODI LAN driver is loaded, it expects to logically connect to the LSL layer. The LSL layer and the ODI LAN driver have interface points that dovetail with each other. Next, you load the ODI LAN driver. With the LSL.COM and the ODI LAN driver loaded, the data layer (OSI model) is complete.

You then load the communications protocols on top of the link support layer. When the communications protocol loads, it automatically binds itself to the link support layer. This completes the communications protocol stack down to the NIC interface. You also can load additional protocol stacks at this time.

To make use of the communications protocol, you must run an application or network program, such as the NetWare shell.

For DOS NetWare stations, the communications protocol SPX/IPX is implemented in the file IPXODI.COM.

To summarize the preceding steps, the commands that must be issued to set a NetWare station with an NE2000 NIC to log in to a NetWare server are as follows:

```
LSL
NE2000
IPXODI
NETX
F:
LOGIN
```

The NE2000.COM is the program name for the NE2000 ODI LAN driver.

ODI Component Options

All ODI components have optional parameters that can be used to modify their behavior. At the very least, they all have the ? parameter to obtain help, and the U parameter to unload the components. You must unload the ODI components in the reverse order of the loading sequence. The unload order is NET*x*.COM, IPXODI.COM, ODI LAN Driver, and LSL.COM.

The ODI components are on the NetWare Lite DRIVERS disk, or the disk labeled DOS ODI WORKSTATION SERVICES. LSL.COM, IPXODI.COM, and the LAN drivers accept a ? parameter that instructs them to display the file version and help list.

```
LSL ?

NetWare Link Support Layer  v1.10 (910625)
(c)Copyright 1991 Novell, Inc. All Rights Reserved.
```

```
Available command line options:

   LSL         Installs the LSL
   LSL U       Removes resident LSL from memory
   LSL ?       Displays this help screen
```

WDPLUS ?

```
Western Digital LAN Adapter MLID v1.02 (910621)
(c) Copyright Western Digital Corporation 1991, All Rights Reserved.

Available command line options:

   WDPLUS      Installs the MLID
   WDPLUS U    Removes resident MLID from memory
   WDPLUS ?    Displays this help screen
```

IPXODI ?

```
NetWare IPX/SPX Protocol  v1.10 (910625)
(c)Copyright 1991 Novell, Inc. All Rights Reserved.
```

Available command line options:

PX or the Remote Diagnostic Responder. The Remote Diagnostic Responder is useful for some third-party applications that gather diagnostic information. By not loading these components, you can save workstation memory. The SPX and the Remote Diagnostic Responder each take up roughly 4 KB of RAM. If you need more memory to run applications, IPXODI can be invoked using the A or D option.

Table 20.6 shows the amount of memory consumed when IPXODI is running with various options:

Table 20.6
IPXODI Options Memory Usage

Command	Meaning	Memory Used (Bytes)	Memory Saved (Bytes)
IPXODI	Load full IP	15904	N/A
IPXODI D	Load IPX and SPX only	12272	3632
IPXODI A	Load IPX only	7088	5184

The Workstation ODI Boot Disk

To prepare the workstation boot disk containing the ODI drivers, perform the following steps:

1. To prepare a DOS bootable disk, type the following command:

   ```
   FORMAT A: /S
   ```

2. Copy the following files from the DOS ODI WORKSTATION SERVICES BOOT disk to the DOS bootable disk:

   LSL.COM

   IPXODI.COM

   ODI Network Driver (such as NE2000.COM)

   NET*x*.COM

3. Create a batch file and enter the following commands in the batch file:

   ```
   LSL
   ODI Network Driver
   NETx
   F:
   LOGIN
   ```

   (In your actual batch file, replace *ODI Network Driver* with the name of the appropriate driver file.)

4. Create AUTOEXEC.BAT and CONFIG.SYS files to suit your workstation environment. For instance, you can put FILES= and BUFFERS= parameters along with any device drivers particular to your workstation. You also may want to increase the size of memory set aside for the DOS environment variables by placing the following in CONFIG.SYS:

   ```
   SHELL=COMMAND.COM /P /E:800
   ```

   The preceding statement in the CONFIG.SYS file increases the size of environment variable memory to 800 bytes for DOS 3.2 and higher versions.

   In the AUTOEXEC.BAT file, you may want to add the PROMPT PG command to change the prompt to include the current working directory.

5. If your NIC card is set to a nondefault setting or if you need to support protocols other than SPX/IPX, you must create a NET.CFG file.

NET.CFG Configuration File Options for ODI Workstations

NET.CFG is a text file that contains commands to alter the behavior of ODI workstation components. SHELL.CFG also contains shell configuration information. Information in the SHELL.CFG file is now included in the more versatile NET.CFG file. The contents of the SHELL.CFG file can be placed at the beginning of the NET.CFG file. If both the SHELL.CFG and NET.CFG file exist on the workstation disk, both are processed, but any SHELL.CFG commands in NET.CFG are ignored.

The main section headings for NET.CFG are left-justified. The entries under each heading are indented by a space or a tab. The three section headings are as follows:

- LINK SUPPORT
- PROTOCOL
- LINK DRIVER

(Comments are preceded by a semicolon, and statements in NET.CFG are case-insensitive.)

The LINK SUPPORT section establishes the number of communication buffers and the memory size set aside for those buffers.

The PROTOCOL section maintains the binding between a specific protocol and the ODI Network Driver. Some protocols maintain several simultaneous sessions. The PROTOCOL section also can be used to control the number of sessions.

The LINK DRIVER section changes the hardware-configuration settings in the ODI Network Driver. Examples of hardware settings are DMA, Interrupt Line, Base Memory address, and I/O Port address. Use the LINK DRIVER section when the workstation NIC uses nondefault settings.

Not all main section headings need to be in the NET.CFG file. For example, if the Western Digital EtherCard PLUS must be set to the nondefault settings of IRQ=5, I/O Port address=300 (hex), and memory base address of D8000, then NET.CFG looks something like the following:

```
LINK DRIVER WDPLUS
   ; Interrupt Request Line is set to 5
   int   5
   ; I/O Port address is 300 hex
   port 300
   ; Base memory address is D8000
   mem D8000
```

The PROTOCOL and LINK SUPPORT sections are not listed because the default protocol and link support settings need not be changed.

Link Support

You can change the BUFFERS and MEMPOOL parameters in the LINK SUPPORT section.

The BUFFERS parameter takes the following general form of the BUFFERS parameter:

```
BUFFERS bufferNumber [bufferSize]
```

The BUFFERS parameter changes the number (*bufferNumber*) and size (*bufferSize*) of communication buffers for non-SPX/IPX protocols. SPX/IPX protocols implemented by the IPXODI protocol stack do not use the LSL buffers; they use a separate set of communication buffers. An example of a protocol that needs LSL buffers is TCP/IP, which needs at least two buffers. The size of a buffer must be large enough to hold the MAC header and the maximum data size encapsulated by the MAC header.

The *bufferSize* is optional and has a minimum value of 618 bytes and a default value of 1130 bytes. The total amount of buffer space for LSL buffers must not exceed approximately 59 KB:

bufferNumber × bufferSize <= 59 KB

The MEMPOOL parameter takes the following general form:

```
MEMPOOL memSize [k]
```

The MEMPOOL parameter specifies the size of the memory-pool buffer (*memSize*) that is set aside. This number can be expressed in kilobytes by including the k after *memSize*. SPX/IPX protocols do not use memory-pool buffers. Protocols such as TCP/IP need at least 2048 bytes of memory pool.

For the exact setting of BUFFERS and MEMPOOL, you must consult the third-party protocol settings.

Protocol

You can specify the BIND and SESSIONS parameters in the PROTOCOL section.

The PROTOCOL section main heading must specify the protocol name to which the parameters BIND and SESSIONS apply. An example of the protocol section is as follows:

```
PROTOCOL IPX
   BIND NE2000
```

The BIND parameter refers to IPX because this protocol was specified in the main section heading: PROTOCOL IPX.

The BIND parameter takes the following general form:

```
BIND networkDriver
```

BIND makes a logical association between the protocol specified in the PROTOCOL section heading and the ODI network driver (*networkDriver*). This logical association establishes a data path between the NIC and the protocol stack. The BIND parameter also is useful if a number of NICs are in a workstation. When the protocol stack IPXODI loads, it binds to the first NIC driver loaded. This may not be the NIC that you want to use with the SPX/IPX protocol stacks. To change the default binding, use the BIND parameter. For example, if a workstation has the EXOS215 board and the Token Ring board, and you want IPX to bind to the TOKEN ring driver, you can use the following statements in NET.CFG:

```
PROTOCOL IPX

     ; Force IPX binding to TOKEN ODI driver.
     bind TOKEN
```

Even if the TOKEN driver is loaded last, the IPX protocol binds to the TOKEN driver.

In the DOS environment, IPX can be bound to only one NIC driver.

Some protocols can be used to establish multiple sessions. The SESSIONS parameter can be used to specify the number of sessions (*numberSessions*):

```
SESSIONS numberSessions
```

Link Driver

The *driverName* in the LINK DRIVER section heading must specify the ODI network driver name. All parameters included in the LINK DRIVER section heading apply to *driverName*. These parameters are described in table 20.7.

Table 20.7
Link Driver Parameters

Parameter	Meaning
DMA	DMA channel number
INT	Interrupt line number
MEM	Memory address range
PORT	I/O Port address
NODE ADDRESS	Assigns a new MAC address
SLOT	Associates NIC driver with a slot
FRAME	Specifies MAC layer frame encapsulation
PROTOCOL	Registers a new protocol
SAPS	Service Access Points for LANSUP driver
LINK STATIONS	Link Stations for LANSUP driver
ALTERNATE	Use alternate adapter for LANSUP, TOKEN, PCN2
MAX FRAME SIZE	Specifies maximum frame size for Token Ring
* DMA [#1 | #2]	*channelNumber*

The DMA parameter can be used to configure up to two DMA channels. Some NICs have two configurable DMA channels. The first configurable channel is number 1, and the second configurable channel is number 2. When the number is omitted, the first configurable channel is configured.

The *channelNumber* refers to the DMA channel value used by the NIC.

LAN DRIVER 3C505

```
; Set the DMA channel to 3.
; Since there is only one DMA configurable channel
; the #1 parameter can be omitted.
DMA 3
```

LAN DRIVER DriverWithTwoDmaChannels

```
; The driver has two configurable DMA channels
; Set the second DMA channel to 4 and the first
; DMA channel to 3.
DMA #2 4
DMA 3
; Notice that since #1 or #2 was omitted, it
; refers to the first configurable DMA channel
```

* INT [#1 | #2] interruptRequestNumber

The INT parameter can be used to configure up to two interrupt lines. Some NICs have two configurable interrupt lines. #1 refers to the first configurable line, and #2 refers to the second configurable line. When the number is omitted, it is assumed that the first configurable line is being configured.

The *interruptRequestNumber* refers to the interrupt line value used by the NIC.

Examples:

LAN DRIVER EXOS05

```
; Set the interrupt line to 2.
; Since there is only one configurable
; interrupt line the #1 parameter can be omitted.
int 2
```

LAN DRIVER DriverWithTwoInterruptLines

```
; The driver has two configurable interrupt lines
; Set the second interrupt line to 4 and the first
; interrupt line to 3
int #2 4
int 3
; Notice that since #1 or #2 was omitted, it
; refers to the first configurable interrupt line.
```

* MEM [#1 | #2] hexStartAddr [hexLengthInParagraphs]

The MEM parameter can be used to configure up to two memory-address ranges. Some NICs may have two configurable address ranges. Number 1 refers to the first configurable range, and number 2 refers to the second configurable range. When the number is omitted, the first configurable memory-address range is configured.

The *hexStartAddr* variable refers to the start address of NIC memory, and *hexLengthInParagraphs* refers to the size of the NIC memory in paragraphs. Paragraphs are memory blocks of 16 bytes. The *hexLengthInParagraphs* variable usually can be omitted because the ODI drivers can determine this length from the NIC.

Examples:

LAN DRIVER WDPLUS

```
; Set the base address to D8000 and
; the memory size to 4000 hex bytes         ; (400 paragraphs).
; Because there is only one configurable
; address range the #1 parameter can be omitted.
mem D8000 400
```

LAN DRIVER DriverWithTwoMemoryRanges

```
; The driver has two configurable memory ranges
; Set the second range to DC000 and the first
; range to D0000
mem #2 DC000
mem D0000
; Notice that since #1 or #2 was
; omitted, it refers to
; the first configurable range.
```

* PORT [#1 | #2] hexStartAddr [hexNumberPorts]

The PORT parameter can be used to configure up to two I/O port address ranges. Some NICs may have two configurable I/O ports. Number 1 refers to the first configurable port, and number 2 refers to the second configurable port. When the number is omitted, the first configurable port address range is configured.

The *hexStartAddr* variable refers to the start address of the I/O port, and the *hexNumberPorts* variable refers to the number of I/O ports. The *hexNumberPorts* usually can be omitted because the ODI drivers can determine this number from the NIC, or it can be hard-coded in the NIC driver.

Examples:

LAN DRIVER NE1000

```
; Set the I/O port address to 300.
; Since there is only one configurable
; I/O port, #1 can be omitted.
port 300
```

LAN DRIVER DriverWithTwoPorts

```
; The driver has two configurable I/O ports
; Set the first port to 280 and the second
; port to 300
port #1 280
port #2 300
```

* NODE ADDRESS hexNodeAddress

The NODE ADDRESS parameter overrides the MAC address that may be set for the NIC. Many NICs use the IEEE MAC layer addressing scheme. Examples of such NICs are IEEE 802.3, IEEE 802.4, IEEE 802.5, and FDDI NICs. These NICs allow a local addressing mode whereby the MAC address stamped on the NIC board can be replaced by a local address.

The *hexNodeAddress* variable refers to the new MAC address of the NIC. You must be careful when you set the *hexNodeAddr* because it may conflict with other NICs. In normal circumstances, the NIC address need not be changed. You may need to change the NIC address, however, if either of the following unusual circumstances exists:

1. A bug in the NIC causes two NICs to report the same MAC address. Normally, the NIC vendor sets MAC addresses. Occasionally, the NIC vendor can make an error and give two NICs the same MAC address.

2. Certain protocols—transparent bridge, Token Ring—may use contention schemes based on MAC addresses for their operation. If you change the MAC address, you can favorably alter the behavior of these protocols.

   Examples:

   ```
   LAN DRIVER 3C501

        ; Set the node address to C1002.
        node address C1002
   ```

* SLOT slotNumber

The SLOT parameter can be used to disable the default slot scan in Micro Channel or EISA machines. The LAN driver refers to the NIC in the specified slot.

The *slotNumber* variable refers to the slot number that is usually found on the back of these machines.

In the following example, two NE/2 NICs are being used in a workstation. They are inserted in slots 1 and 2. The NET.CFG file can contain the following lines:

```
LAN DRIVER NE2

     ; Set the slot number to 1.
     ; Actually, if the slot parameter was left out,
     ; the default scan would start with slot 1 and
     ; this would be OK
     slot 1
     ; Other parameters can be set for NE/2 in slot 1.
     ;
```

```
LAN DRIVER NE2

        ; Set the slot number to 2.
        ; The slot parameter is required to make a
        ; distinction
        ; between the NICs in slots 1 and 2.
        slot 2
        ; Other parameters can be set for NE/2 in slot 2.
        ;
```

If the NET.CFG is set up as indicated, the batch file to load the ODI components can then contain commands to load the two NE2 drivers:

```
LSL
NE2
NE2
```

FRAME frameType

The FRAME parameter specifies alternate MAC-layer encapsulations for the NIC boards. Most Ethernet NICs can be set up to have IEEE 802.3 encapsulation or ETHERNET_II encapsulation. When the frame parameter is not specified, the default is IEEE 802.3 for Ethernet NICs. Certain upper-layer protocols such as IP (from TCP/IP) or AppleTalk may require a different MAC-layer encapsulation than the default value. The FRAME parameter changes the MAC framing used for the upper-layer protocols.

The *frameType* refers to frame type values, such as:

- ETHERNET_802.3
- ETHERNET_802.2
- ETHERNET_II
- ETHERNET_SNAP
- TOKEN_RING
- TOKEN_RING_SNAP
- IBM_PCN2_802.2
- IBM_PCN2_SNAP
- NOVELL_RX-NET

* PROTOCOL uprotocolName hexProtocolId frameType

The PROTOCOL parameter registers new protocols to be used with existing ODI drivers.

You can replace *protocolName* with the new protocol being registered. For example, replace *hexProtocolId* with the protocol ID assigned to the new protocol and replace *frameType* with a valid frame type to be used for MAC-layer encapsulation.

If, for example, you want to add a new protocol NEWP to a EXOS215 NIC, the protocol ID assigned to NEWP is 99AF and the MAC encapsulation is ETHERNET_SNAP. The NET.CFG file contains lines similar to the following to register the NEWP protocol:

```
LINK DRIVER EXOS215
        frame ETHERNET_SNAP
        protocol NEWP 99AF ethernet_snap
```

If you use IPX and the new protocol, NEWP, you must specify the PROTOCOL parameter. Also, you must specify the protocol ID for IPX. The default frame of ETHERNET_802.3 has a protocol ID of 0. The NET.CFG file looks similar to the following:

```
LINK DRIVER EXOS215
        frame ETHERNET_SNAP
        protocol NEWP 99AF ethernet_snap
        frame ETHERNET_802.3
        protocol IPX 0 ethernet_802.3
```

Table 20.8 lists frame types and protocol IDs for IPX.

The SAPS and LINK STATIONS parameters are used for the LANSUP drivers to specify the number of service access points and link stations needed. They are specific for IBM LANSUP driver. If you do not use this driver, you do not need these parameters. These parameters must be set to values recommended by the IBM LAN Support Program documentation which comes with the NICs that use these drivers.

The LANSUP, TOKEN, and PCN2 drivers can be the primary or alternate adapter. If you use an alternate adapter, you must use the ALTERNATE parameter as shown in the following example:

```
LINK DRIVER LANSUP
        alternate
```

Table 20.8
Protocol IDs for IPX

Frame Type	Protocol ID (hex)
ETHERNET_802.3	0
ETHERNET_802.2	E0
ETHERNET_II	8137
ETHERNET_SNAP	8137
TOKEN-RING	E0

Frame Type	Protocol ID (hex)
TOKEN-RING_SNAP	8137
IBM-PCN2_802.2	E0
IBM-PCN2_SNAP	8137
NOVELL_RX-NET	FA
IP	800
ARP	806
RARP	8035

* MAX FRAME SIZE *frameSize*

This parameter specifies the maximum frame size (*frameSize*) used on the Token Ring LAN. For Token Ring NICs with 8 KB of shared RAM, this parameter has a default value of 2,168 bytes. For larger shared-RAM sizes, the default value is 4,216 bytes.

The value of *frameSize* must be a multiple of 8 and must be large enough to include the largest frame size plus 6 bytes of adapter overhead. The largest frame size must be the largest data packet plus the largest header. The largest header can be determined as follows:

MAC header	=	35 bytes
SNAP header	=	5 bytes
Upper layer protocol header	=	74 bytes
Largest header	=	114 bytes

If 2 KB data packets were to be sent, maximum frame size would be the following:

Data packet size	=	2,048 bytes
Largest header	=	114 bytes
Adapter overhead	=	6 bytes
Largest frame size	=	2,168 bytes

To obtain maximum frame size, the largest frame size must be rounded to a multiple of 8. This number is 2168. The NET.CFG entry looks similar to the following:

```
LINK DRIVER TOKEN
        max frame size 2168
```

ODI Workstation and Token Ring Source Routing

NetWare workstations that need to communicate across an IBM source routing bridge must run the IBM Token-Ring Source Routing Driver contained in the file ROUTE.COM on the DOS ODI WORKSTATION SERVICES disk.

To install ROUTE.COM, copy it from the DOS ODI WORKSTATION SERVICES disk to the workstation boot disk. Include ROUTE.COM after you load the ODI NIC driver but before you load the protocol stack.

For workstations that use the LANSUP driver, the ODI load sequence is as follows:

```
LSL
LANSUP
ROUTE
IPXODI
```

The ODI load sequence for workstations that use the TOKEN driver is shown below:

```
LSL
TOKEN
ROUTE
IPXODI
```

ROUTE.COM can be loaded with a number of parameters specified on the command line. To obtain a brief list of these parameters, use the ROUTE ? command, as follows:

ROUTE ?

```
NetWare Source Routing Driver  v1.11 (910123)
 (c)Copyright 1991 Novell Inc. All Rights Reserved.

ROUTE   U,BOARD=dd,CLEAR,DEF,GBR,MBR,NODES=dd,REMOVE=xxxxxxxxxxxx

U                 Unloads a previously installed Source Router from memory.
BOARD=dd          A DECIMAL board number as Assigned by ODI. Do NOT use this
                  parameter if you are using an OLD IPX Driver.
CLEAR             CLEAR ALL Nodes from a previously loaded Source Router.
DEF               Send DEFault (Unknown) Node Addresses ALL ROUTES Broadcast.
                  If NOT entered, SINGLE ROUTE Broadcast is ASSUMED.
GBR               Send Broadcast (FFFF FFFF FFFF) Addresses ALL ROUTES
                  Broadcast. If NOT entered, SINGLE ROUTE Broadcast is AS-
                  SUMED.
```

```
MBR              Send MultiCast (C000 xxxx xxxx) Addresses ALL ROUTES
                 Broadcast. If NOT entered, SINGLE ROUTE Broadcast is AS-
                 SUMED.
NODES=dd         The number of NODE Addresses to support. dd is a DECIMAL
                 number between 0 and 255. If dd is LESS THAN 08, then 08 is
                 ASSUMED. If NOT entered, dd DEFAULTS to 16.
REMOVE=xxxxxx    A HEXADECIMAL NODE Address to REMOVE from a previously
                 loaded Source Router. If LESS THAN 09 HEXADECIMAL DIGITS are
                 entered, 4000 xxxx xxxx is ASSUMED.
```

All parameters are optional, are not case-sensitive, and can be entered in any order. They can be used to set the Source Router being loaded to or change the configuration of a previously loaded Source Router.

Most of these parameters have default values that work with simple networks. For larger networks, some of the parameters can be changed to reduce network traffic on some paths. Table 20.9 describes these parameters. With the exception of the NODES parameter, these parameters can be entered on a second ROUTE command to alter the behavior of the ROUTE program already loaded.

For example, the following command means that source routing is done through board 2. Frames for stations that have addresses not in the source routing table are sent as *All Routes Broadcast* (DEF) frames. *General Broadcast* (GBR) and *Multicast Broadcast* (MBR) frames also are sent as All Routes Broadcast frames. The source routing table has 20 entries:

```
ROUTE BOARD=2,DEF,GBR,MBR,NODES=20
```

If a major crash on the network affects many SR bridges, type the following command to force a rebuild of the source routing table:

```
ROUTE CLEAR
```

Table 20.9
ROUTE.COM Command Line Parameters

Parameter	Meaning
BOARD=number	Specifies a board number for the Token Ring board. The board number is determined in the order in which the LAN driver is loaded.
CLEAR	Forces a rebuild of the source routing table. Can be used if the SR (Source Routing) bridges are down or an alternate path is available.
DEF	Sends frames that do not have addresses in the Source Routing table as All Routes roadcast frames, which prevents them from being forwarded across Single Route IBM ridges. When DEF is not specified, these frames are forwarded as Single Route Broadcast frames.

continues

Table 20.9, Continued
ROUTE.COM Command Line Parameters

Parameter	Meaning
GBR	Sends General Broadcast frames as All Routes Broadcast frames. When GBR is not specified, GBR frames are forwarded as Single Route Broadcast frames.
MBR	Sends Multicast Broadcast frames as All Routes Broadcast frames. When MBR is not specified, GBR frames are forwarded as Single Route Broadcast frames.
NODES=*entries*	Specifies the number of entries in the source routing table. The value ranges from 8 to 255 with a default of 16.
REMOVE=*address*	Removes a specified node address from the source routing table. This forces the workstation to find an alternate route. Can be used when an SR bridge is down. The address is a 12-digit hex number. If fewer than 9 digits are entered, the IBM prefix of 4000 hex is added.

DOS NetWare Workstations and Ethernet II LANs

When a NetWare workstation is used to connect to a VAX host running NetWare for VMS, the workstation must be set up for Ethernet II encapsulation. This is because DEC uses Ethernet II encapsulation at the MAC layer. Many UNIX-based LANs also use Ethernet II.

The default MAC-layer encapsulation for NetWare Ethernet stations is IEEE 802.3. To work with LANs where hosts and servers are set up for Ethernet II encapsulation, the MAC-layer encapsulation must be changed to ETHERNET II. In this section, you learn how to change the MAC encapsulation.

IPX.COM for Ethernet II

The utility ECONFIG can be used to change the frame encapsulation for IPX. This utility can be found on the WSGEN disk. When you type **ECONFIG** at the DOS prompt, you get the following information about its usage:

```
Usage: econfig [volume:]file [parameter list]
[parameter list] is one of the following:

SHELL:[configuration type]
AD:[configuration type]
[configuration type] = N, E [type constant]
[type constant] = 0 FFFF (8137 is Novell's assigned type constant)

Example: econfig os.exe a:n; b:e 8137; c:e 15af
         econfig shell.com shell:e 8137
```

You can use ECONFIG to configure IPX.COM and NetWare 2.*x* NOS. You cannot use it with ODI workstation software or NetWare 3.*x*. For ODI workstations, the configuration must be done through the FRAME parameter in the NET.CFG file. For NetWare 3.*x* NOS, configuration must be done by the FRAME parameter on the LOAD command in file AUTOEXEC.NCF.

The steps outlined next show how to use ECONFIG to configure IPX.COM:

1. Copy the ECONFIG utility to the directory that contains IPX.COM, or make ECONFIG available through the DOS search path.

2. Type the following command to configure IPX.COM:

   ```
   ECONFIG IPX.COM SHELL:E 8137
   ```

   The constant 8137 is the Ethernet Type field value assigned to Novell.

3. To verify the configuration change, type the following:

   ```
   ECONFIG IPX.COM
   ```

   You see the following message:

   ```
   SHELL: Ethernet Typefield: 8137 (Assigned Novell type constant)
   ```

   Type the following command to change the shell back to the Novell IEEE 802.3 encapsulation:

   ```
   ECONFIG IPX.COM SHELL:N
   ```

ODI Workstations for Ethernet II

To configure ODI workstations for Ethernet II, include the FRAME parameter in the NET.CFG file under the LINK DRIVER section. The NET.CFG file for NE2000 driver may look similar to the following:

```
LINK DRIVER NE2000
        frame ETHERNET_II
```

The frame ETHERNET_II parameter changes the MAC-layer encapsulation to Ethernet II.

Windows 3.1

Installing Windows 3.1 on a NetWare-based network can be done by installing Windows individually at each workstation or by loading a copy of Windows onto a server, and then running setup to download and install Windows at each workstation. The latter approach is much easier and consists of running Windows setup with the /a option to install Windows on the server, and then running Windows setup with the /n option from each station logged in to the server. To do this legally, you should have a license for each Windows workstation you are installing.

Depending on the location of the shared files, user files, and swap files, Windows can be installed at the workstation in four possible configurations.

Shared files are Windows utilities (TERMINAL.EXE, CLOCK.EXE, and so on), font files, device drivers, and help files. All of the shared files can take up to 16 *MB* of disk space. A Windows installation normally installs only those files needed by the workstation hardware configuration, and these can be anywhere between 8 to 11 *MB*. User files include INI, PIF, and GRP files that contain a user's system configuration, and these occupy about 300 KB of disk space. The swap file is used by the Virtual Memory Manager and can be on a local or network drive. Because keeping it on a network can generate a great deal of network traffic when this swap area is used, it is strongly recommended that you keep the swap file local. It also is best to allocate this file permanently in one contiguous chunk of disk space in order to speed up swap-file access.

Installation Configurations

The four configurations mentioned earlier are as follows:

- Local installation only
- Network installation only
- Shared and user files on network
- Shared files on network, user files local

One can derive other permutations of these four basic configurations by keeping the swap file on the network; but as mentioned earlier, this is not a recommended option.

Local Installation Only

This configuration—shown in figure 20.7—has the largest amount of local disk space requirement and does not have any sharing of files on the server. This could be a valid option if sufficient disk storage space is available locally. The advantage of this approach is that all files needed to operate Windows in case of server downtime are available locally.

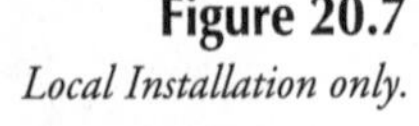

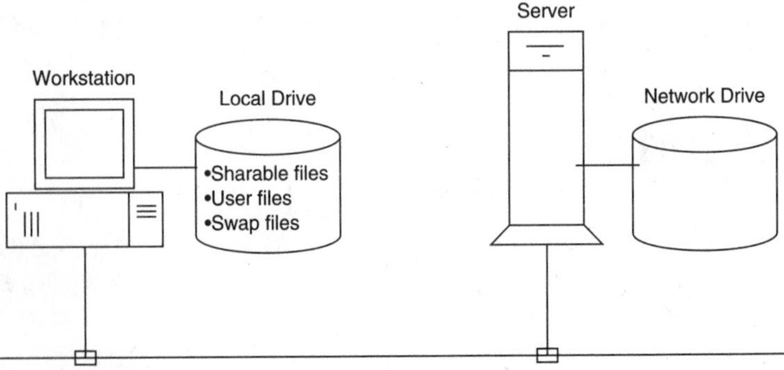

Figure 20.7
Local Installation only.

Network Installation Only

This configuration—shown in figure 20.8—is the complete opposite of the previous configuration in that all files are stored on the server. Shared files need to be on a shared directory on the server and marked with the shareable flag using FLAG. User files and swap space can be in the user's home directory. This configuration also implies that the swap file is kept on the server, which can slow down the network; Windows' performance is a little slower when swapping is involved. This may be the only option for diskless workstations. The advantage of this approach is that it requires a minimal (zero, actually) local storage requirement.

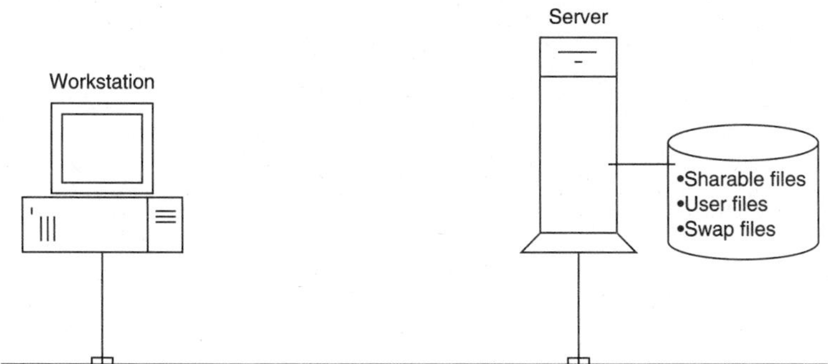

Figure 20.8
Network Installation only.

Shared and User Files on Network

This configuration—shown in figure 20.9—is a variation of the "Network Installation Only" approach in the sense that the swap file is kept locally, and the shared and user files are stored on the server. Shared files need to be on a shared directory on the server and marked with the shareable flag using FLAG. User files and swap space can be in the user's home directory. Swap file is kept on a local disk so that swapping does not generate any additional network traffic that can slow down the network and reduce Windows' performance. This is the best option if there is local storage space, but you wish to conserve it for other uses.

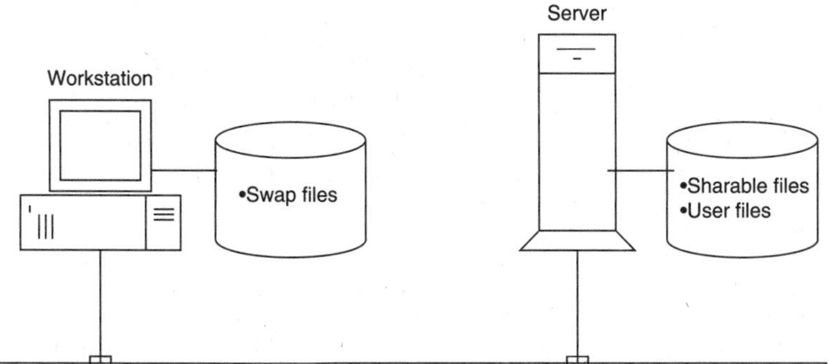

Figure 20.9
Shared and user files on network.

Shared Files on Network, User Files Local

Figure 20.10 demonstrates this configuration choice. Shared files need to be on a shared directory on the server and marked with the shareable flag using FLAG. User files and swap space are on the local disk. This option is attractive if you wish to conserve server disk space. Unless the user workstation is secured by other means, this is a less secure configuration than the preceding one in which user files are kept on the server. Keeping the user files on the server implies that they are protected using the server network operating system permission. Keeping it local on a DOS workstation implies that any user can gain access to the user files.

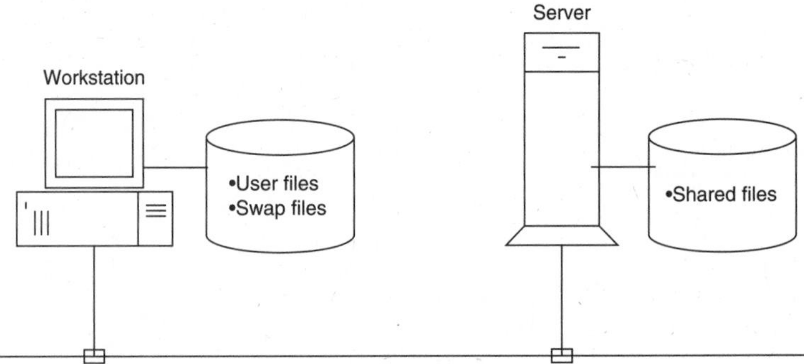

Figure 20.10
Shared files on network, user files local.

Network Drivers

It is best to use ODI drivers that come with Windows because this gives you the flexibility of changing the IRQ, Base Address, Shared Memory, and other network settings easily. These drivers also can be obtained through the NetWire forum on CompuServe or through the Windows Resource Kit.

The Windows Resource Kit comes with a NEWIPX utility that can generate traditional (non-ODI) IPX.COM files conveniently during network login. NEWIPX determines if the workstation's IPX needs to be updated, and if it does, it generates a new IPX. To set up NEWIPX, do the following:

1. Create a directory on the server and give users [R F] privileges to this directory.

   If you create the directory under SYS:PUBLIC, the [R F] rights are inherited.

2. Copy the files IPX.OBJ and NEWIPX.EXE from the Windows Resource kit to the new subdirectory you have created.

3. Copy the NIC drivers to be linked with IPX.OBJ to the same directory.

Next, set up the following in the login script file for the user:

```
rem Invoke NEWIPX and pass it the directory containing the user's IPX.COM
F:\PUBLIC\NEWIPX  C:\NETLOG

rem Check Error_Level codes:
rem
```

```
rem   Error_Level 0               No upgrade necessary
rem   Error_Level 1               Upgrade successful
rem   Error_Level > 1             Upgrade failed

if  "%ERROR_LEVEL" > "1" then begin
      rem  Problem running NEWIPX
      write "IPX upgrade failed. Please inform your Supervisor"
      pause
end

if  "%ERROR_LEVEL" = "1" then begin
      rem  Ran NEWIPX with no problems
      write "New IPX installed"
      pause
end
```

NET.CFG Settings

The following parameter settings in the NET.CFG can alter Windows behavior:

SHOW DOTS

FILE HANDLES

ENVIRONMENT PAD

SEARCH DIR FIRST

Set SHOW DOTS=ON in NET.CFG. The default is OFF. This causes DOS System Calls FindFirstMatching and FindNextMatching to work correctly for current (.) and parent (..) directories.

The default setting for FILE HANDLES is 40. The recommended value is 60 for Windows. Using smaller values may cause error messages about files not being available.

When a *Virtual DOS Machine* (VDM) is created, it inherits the parent's environment space but does not allow for any growth in this environment space. The ENVIRONMENT PAD allows additional memory to be allocated for the environment space when a VDM session is created.

The SEARCH DIR FIRST parameter has a default value of OFF. This means that if handle-oriented directory searches are being done, the files are searched first, and then the directories. Setting SEARCH DIR FIRST=ON, causes the directories to be searched before files.

INI File Settings

Windows distribution contains additional NetWare related files:

NETWARE.DRV

NETWARE.HLP

NETWARE.INI

NWPOPUP.EXE

VNETWARE.386

VIPX.COM

TBMI2.COM

The NETWARE.DRV file contains program code to implement many of the NetWare-related command functions. For instance, setting NetWareHotKey=1 in the Options section of NETWARE.INI file causes the NETWARE.DRV command functions to be invoked by using the F6 hot key. NETWARE.HLP contains help information for NETWARE.DRV functions. The NETWARE.INI file controls the configuration for NETWARE.DRV.

The NWPOPUP.EXE program handles broadcast messages that appear in a Windows pop-up screen. During Windows Setup of NetWare workstations, a LOAD= line is placed in WIN.INI file to cause this to be loaded when Windows runs.

The VNETWARE.386 file virtualizes multiple sessions to the NetWare server. VIPX.386 virtualizes IPX communications between sessions. The 386 extension indicates that this file can be used in 386 enhanced mode only.

The TBMI2.COM program is the task-switched buffer manager for IPX/SPX used to support non-Windows programs that need to talk directly to the SPX/IPX protocol stack.

NETWARE.INI

The NETWARE.INI file and its sections are discussed in tables 20.10 and 20.11.

Table 20.10
NETWARE.INI Options Section

Parameter	Description
NetWareHotKey=	Setting this enables the hot key to invoke the functions in the NETWARE.DRV. The following codes can be used: To use F6, set the value to 1. For other function keys, use the formula: 111 + Function Key Number. Therefore, to use the function key F10 as a pop-up, set the value to 111 + 10 = 121.
Messages=	A value of 0 blocks broadcast messages, and a value of 1 enables broadcast messages. Default value is 1.

Parameter	Description
RestoreDisplay/Timeout=	Specifies the number of seconds the "Restore Connections" message is to be displayed when reconnecting permanent drive and printer mappings. A value of 0 disables the message. The maximum value is 30 seconds.

Table 20.11
NETWARE.INI MSW30-PrtQ Section

Parameter	Description
MaxJobs=	This is the number of print jobs displayed by the Print Manager. The default value is 50 with a minimum of 1 and a maximum of 250.
MaxBufSize=	This is the buffer size in bytes for sending jobs to be queued. The default is 3,500. The value can range from 3,500 to 30,000 bytes.
UpdateSeconds=	This specifies the frequency in seconds that Print Manager should update the print queue display. The value can range from 1 to 65 seconds and has a default of 30 seconds.

SYSTEM.INI

The SYSTEM.INI file has a NetWare section that contains the parameters described in table 20.12.

Table 20.12
SYSTEM.INI NetWare Section

Parameter	Description
NWShareHandles=	If set to TRUE, drive mappings have a global effect on all DOS sessions. The default value is FALSE, which means drive mappings in a DOS session are local to that DOS session only.
RestoreDrives=	If set to TRUE, drive mappings are restored to their previous state when exiting Windows. The default value is TRUE.

WIN.INI

The WIN.INI can affect a NetWare station's behavior by setting parameters defined in the Windows and Network sections. Tables 20.13 and 20.14 document this behavior.

Table 20.13
WIN.INI Windows Section

Parameter	Description
NetWarn=	Specifies if a warning message should be displayed when the shell is not loaded. A value of 1 enables the warning and a value of 0 disables the warning. The default value is 1.

Table 20.14
WIN.INI Network Section

Parameter	Description
DriveMapping	This contains the drive mappings from the DOS session. These have the following entries: F:=[FS1/SYS:] APPS\DB F:= [FS1/SYS:APPS\DB] for root maps
LPT1:=	This contains the printer attachments from the DOS session.
LPT1-OPTIONS=	For each permanent printer attachment, there is an options entry that looks like the following: LPT1-OPTIONS=Flag,C,T,TO,F,BT,BN Flag = 8 (No Form feed sent at end of job) Flag = 16 (Notify On) Flag = 64 (Tabs Enabled) Flag =128 (Banner On) C = Number of Copies T = Tab Size TO = Timeout in Seconds F = Form Number BT = Banner Text BN = Banner Name

Using TBM12

TBMI2 is used for non-Windows applications that need to multitask and that make direct calls to the SPX/IPX stack. To determine if your application needs to use TBMI2, perform the following test:

1. Load TBMI2. Just type the name, and it becomes memory resident.
2. Run Windows.
3. Run the non-Windows applications.
4. Exit Windows.
5. Type the command to obtain diagnostic information on TBMI2:

   ```
   TBMI2   /D
   ```

6. If the parameter TBMI2 Old int usage count or TBMI2 Far call usage count is non-zero, the application has made direct calls to the SPX/IPX stack.

The TBMI2's command-line parameters are the following:

/? or **/H**	Help on program usage.
/Cfilename	Configuration file. If not specified, NET.CFG is used.
/D	Diagnostic information.
/I	Version information.
/U	Unload TBMI2 from memory.

The TBMI2 configuration parameters are as follows:

```
INT 64=[ON ¦ OFF]
INT 7A=[ON ¦ OFF]
```

The INT 64 parameter, if set to ON, allows applications to access SPX/IPX by the software interrupt INT 64 (hex). It is used to provide compatibility with earlier versions of IPX. The default value is ON. If an application needs to access interrupt 64 (hex), it can be set to OFF.

The INT 7A parameter, if set to ON, allows applications to access SPX/IPX by the software interrupt INT 7A (hex). It is used to provide compatibility with applications written for NetWare 2.0a. The default value is ON. If an application needs to access interrupt 7A (hex), it can be set to OFF.

Exploring the Workstation Connection Mechanism

This section explains the behind-the-scenes mechanism that makes a workstation connection possible. The actual connection mechanism is discussed first, and then the tables kept at the workstation and the server to manage the connection are discussed.

Making the Connection

When the NetWare shell or OS/2 NetWare requester loads, it has no knowledge of any servers on the network. Because all servers keep track of services available on the network through the SAP protocol, the shell can connect to any one server. Once this connection is made, the shell can query the server about other services on the network.

You must perform the following steps to make the connection:

1. Obtain a server's address
2. Obtain a route to the server
3. Request and negotiate a connection

Server's Address

To obtain a server's address, the shell issues a SAP broadcast request for the nearest server. All routers—including servers that act as internal routers— on the workstation's segment that have knowledge of the nearest server respond with a SAP response.

This sequence of events is illustrated by the first two packet transmissions in figure 20.11. Figure 20.11 also shows other packet transmissions necessary to complete a connection. The SAP request and SAP response packets are decoded by a LANalyzer in figures 20.12 and 20.13. Figure 20.13 shows that the SAP response contains the server name, its full internet address, and the number of hops required to reach the server.

```
05/11/80                 LANalyzer Network Analyzer                    11:06
Press ALT-T to toggle between summary modes                    Trace Summary
                             Trace Buffer
Created On 05/11/80 11:05:02  Elapsed Time 00:00:16   Total Packets      790

 Pkt# Source        Destination   Layer  Highest Layer
    1 wstdig631B1B  Broadcast     sap:  Query Nearest Service File Server
    2 wstdig315119  wstdig631B1B  sap:  Resp Nearest Service server=S386
    3 wstdig631B1B  Broadcast     rip:  Req  network=F0 10 00 33
    4 wstdig315119  wstdig631B1B  rip:  Resp network=F0 10 00 33; 1 hops
    5 wstdig631B1B  wstdig315119  ncp:  Req  Create Service Connection
    6 wstdig315119  wstdig631B1B  ncp:  Rply Create Service Connectio; Success
    7 wstdig631B1B  wstdig315119  ncp:  Req  Negotiate Buffer Size
    8 wstdig315119  wstdig631B1B  ncp:  Rply Negotiate Buffer Size; Success
    9 wstdig631B1B  wstdig315119  ncp:  Req  Logout
   10 wstdig315119  wstdig631B1B  ncp:  Rply Logout; Success
   11 wstdig631B1B  wstdig315119  ncp:  Req  Get File Server Date and Time
   12 wstdig315119  wstdig631B1B  ncp:  Rply Get File Server Date and; Success
   13 wstdig631B1B  wstdig315119  ncp:  Req  Get Station Number
   14 wstdig315119  wstdig631B1B  ncp:  Rply Get Station Number; Success
   15 wstdig631B1B  wstdig315119  ncp:  Req  End Of Job
   16 wstdig315119  wstdig631B1B  ncp:  Rply End Of Job; Success

F1   F2   F3    F4      F5   F6     F7      F8   F9    F10
Help Load Print Options Save Decode Compare Find Go To Back
```

Figure 20.11

Packet transmissions in making a connection.

```
05/18/80                 LANalyzer Network Analyzer                    02:15
Packet #: 1                                                     Trace Decode
                                nwslog
Frame: Number: 1          Length:   64 bytes
       Errors: None
       Receive Channels: GoodPkts Broadcst NetWare
802.3: ================ IEEE 802.3 Datalink Layer ================
       Station: wstdig631B1B        ---> Broadcast
       Length:  34
  ipx: ========== NetWare Internetwork Packet Exchange Protocol ==========
       Checksum: 0xFFFF              Length: 34
       Hop Count:  0                 Packet Type: 17 (NCP)
       Network: 00 00 00 00          ---> 00 00 00 00
       Node:    wstdig631B1B         ---> Broadcast
       Socket:  0x4006               ---> SAP
  sap: ============= NetWare Service Advertising Protocol =============
       Type: 3 (Nearest Service Query)
       Server Type: 4 (File Server)

F1   F2   F3    F4      F5     F6      F7   F8   F9    F10
Help Copy Print Options EBCDIC AltDisp Prev Next Go To Back
```

Figure 20.12

A Get Nearest Server SAP request.

The Get Nearest Server/Give Nearest Server request/response also can be observed through the router tracking screen by typing **TRACK ON** at the server console.

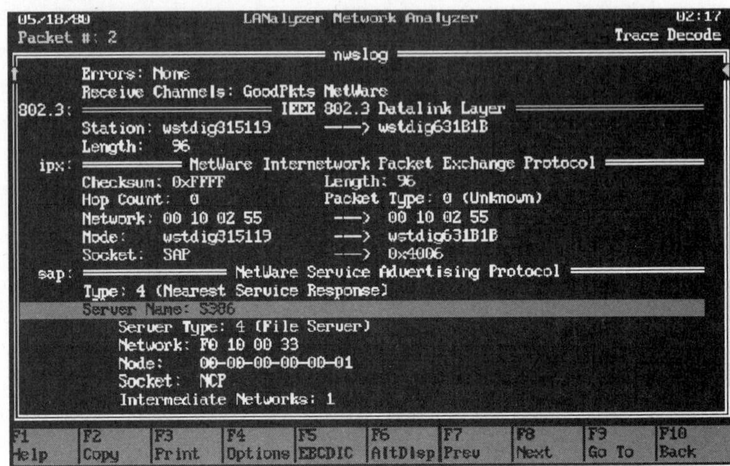

Figure 20.13
A Give Nearest Server SAP response.

The Get Nearest Server/Give Nearest Server information for NetWare 3.*x* has the following syntax:

```
InOut [LAN:NodeAddr] Time        Give Nearest Server

InOut [LAN:NodeAddr] Time        Give Nearest Server serverName
```

The NetWare 2.*x* Get Nearest Server/Give Nearest Server information, which does not have the Time field, has the following syntax:

```
InOut [LAN:NodeAddr]      Give Nearest Server

InOut [LAN:NodeAddr]      Give Nearest Server serverName
```

The NetWare 3.*x* TRACK screen displays Get Nearest Server/Give Nearest Server information as follows:

```
IN    [A:400000000010]    01:00:12pm    Get Nearest Server

OUT   [A:400000000010]    01:00:13pm    Give Nearest Server KSS
```

NetWare 2.*x* TRACK screen shows Get Nearest Server/Give Nearest Server information in this manner:

```
IN    [A:400000000010]    Get Nearest Server

OUT   [A:400000000010]    Give Nearest Server KSS
```

A Route to the Server

After the workstation has the name and internet address of the server, it determines the best route to the server. It sends a RIP request (Get Local Target) and waits for a RIP response (Give Local Target). The RIP request and response are shown as packets 3 and 4 in figure 20.11. The details of these packets are shown in figures 20.14 and 20.15.

If the server's network number is the same as the workstation's number, the server and the workstation are on the same network. If the server's network number is different from the workstation's network number, the shell broadcasts a RIP request for the fastest route to the server. If several routers respond with a route equal to the shortest route, the first response is selected.

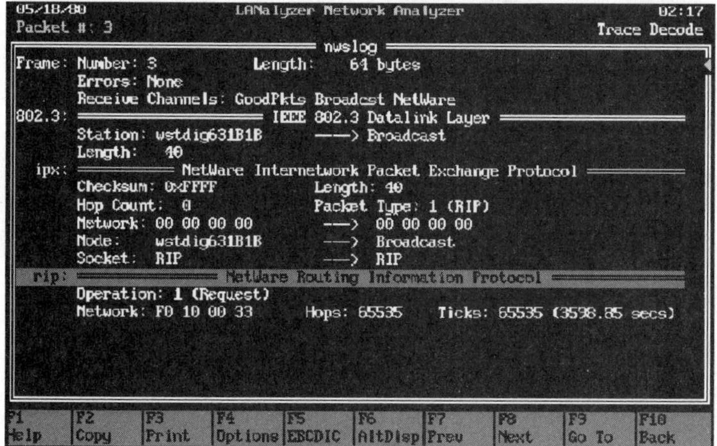

Figure 20.14
A RIP request packet for best route to server.

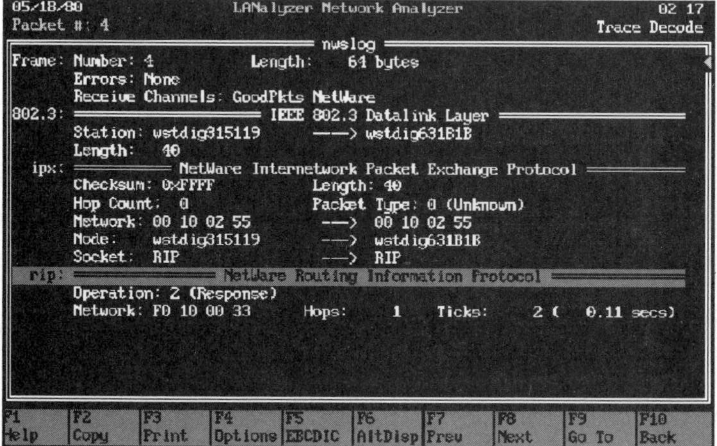

Figure 20.15
A RIP response packet for best route to server.

The MAC address of the router or the server is used to forward the NCP connection request.

Connection Request and Negotiation

After the workstation knows the internet address of the server—and the router to get to it, if necessary—it issues an NCP connection request to create a connection to the server. The NCP connection request and response are shown as packets 5 and 6 in figure 20.11. These packets are shown decoded in figures 20.16 and 20.17.

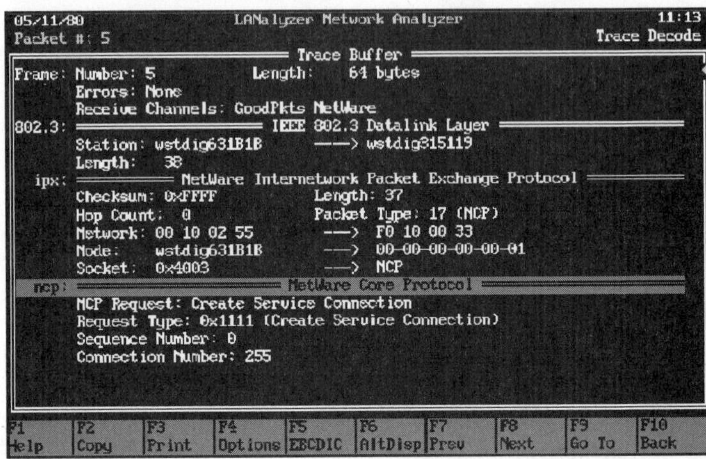

Figure 20.16
An NCP service connection request packet.

After the connection to the server is established, the shell negotiates the maximum packet size it can use. Packets 7 and 8 show this negotiation. The shell issues an NCP Negotiate Buffer Size request (fig. 20.18), and the server responds with an NCP Negotiate Buffer Reply (fig. 20.19).

The Preferred Server Shell

The preferred server shell (v3.01 and higher) adds features not offered by older shells. The server to which an attachment is made can be specified by parameters on the command line (NET*x* PS=*serverName*) or by a parameter in the NET.CFG file.

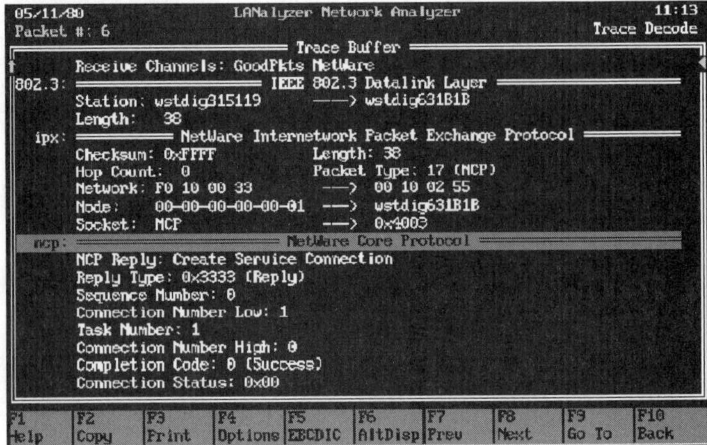

Figure 20.17
An NCP service connection reply packet.

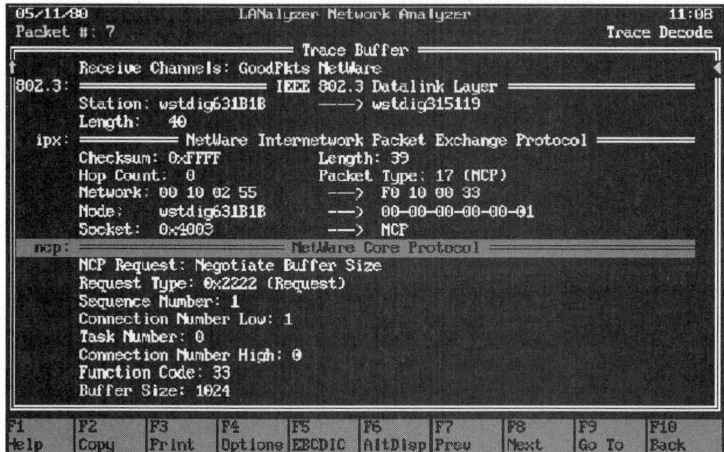

Figure 20.18
NCP Negotiate Buffer Size request packet.

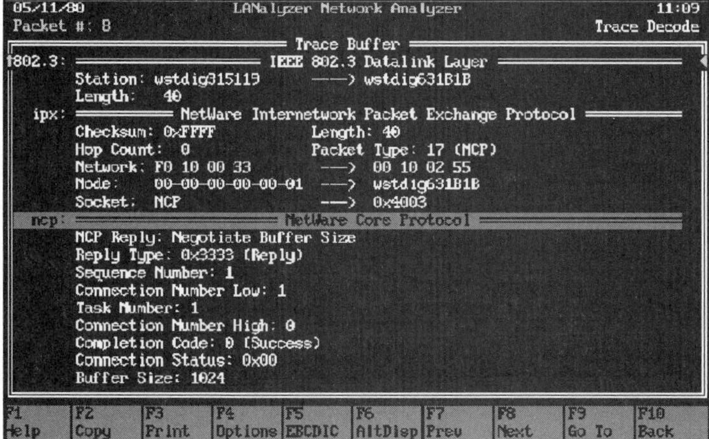

Figure 20.19
NCP Negotiate Buffer reply packet.

The first eight steps in table 20.15 to make a connection are the same for the older shells and the preferred server. If the server that the preferred shell initially connects to is not the one specified by the user, you must perform several additional steps as shown in table 20.16. The preferred shell obtains the IPX internet address of the preferred server from the bindery of the attached server (steps 9 and 10). It then obtains a route to the preferred server (steps 11 and 12), creates the connection (steps 13 and 14), negotiates maximum packet size (steps 15 and 16), and destroys the service connection made in steps 5 and 6. Steps 11 to 16 repeat steps 3 to 8, except that the interaction takes place with the preferred server rather than the first attached server.

The preferred shell saves the Give Nearest Response up to four additional servers, in case the server that responds first does not have any free connection slots.

Table 20.15
Initial Connection Packet Sequence

Packet Type	Protocol	Source	Destination
1. Get Nearest Server	SAP	client	broadcast
2. Give Nearest Server	SAP	router	client
3. Route Request (GetLocalTarget)	RIP	client	broadcast
4. Route Response (GiveLocalTarget)	RIP	router	client
5. Create Connection	NCP	client	server
6. Connection Assigned	NCP	server	client
7. Negotiate Packet Size	NCP	client	server
8. Maximum Packet Size	NCP	server	client

Table 20.16
Connection Sequence for Preferred Server Shell

Packet Type	Protocol	Source	Destination
1. Get Nearest Server	SAP	client	broadcast
2. Give Nearest Server	SAP	router	client
3. Route Request (GetLocalTarget)	RIP	client	broadcast
4. Route Response (GiveLocalTarget)	RIP	router	client
5. Create Connection	NCP	client	server
6. Connection Assigned	NCP	server	client
7. Negotiate Packet Size	NCP	client	server
8. Maximum Packet Size	NCP	server	client
9. Query Server Bindery for Preferred Server	NCP	client	server

Packet Type	Protocol	Source	Destination
10. Address of Preferred Server	NCP	server	client
11. Route Request (GetLocalTarget)	RIP	client	broadcast
12. Route Response (GiveLocalTarget)	RIP	router	client
13. Create Connection	NCP	client	preferred server
14. Connection Assigned	NCP	preferred	client server
15. Negotiate Packet Size	NCP	client	preferred server
16. Maximum Packet Size	NCP	preferred	client server
17. Destroy Service Connection	NCP	client	preferred server

NetWare Core Protocol (NCP)

The NCP (layer 7) is used for all requests for services by the client and for the responses to these requests. The NCP provides its own session control and sequence control instead of relying on SPX—a transport layer protocol—to provide this function. This streamlines the NCP protocol that runs on IPX by avoiding the overhead of layers 4, 5, and 6.

The Request Type field determines the type of NCP packet, such as Connection Request or Negotiate Buffer Size. The client assigns the Sequence Number field starting with a value of 1 after the connection is established. Every request by the client is assigned a sequence number, one greater than the previous request. The server's NCP response contains the same sequence as the corresponding NCP request. This ensures that the client is receiving the correct response for its request. It also enables the shell and the server to determine when a packet is lost.

When a client establishes a connection to the server, a connection number is assigned for the duration of the session. This connection number is placed in the Connection Number field of every NCP request/response packet. The Connection Number field identifies NCP requests and responses as belonging to a specific session.

Connection Management

The connection between a client and the server is identified by a connection number that remains the same for the duration of the session. The client and the server keep track of this and other information in special tables. These tables enable the client and server to manage the session.

The Shell's Connection Table

The shell's connection table is used to keep track of the client's connections. A DOS client can support up to eight server connections. Each entry of the shell connection table contains the server name and the internet address of the server to which it connects. If the packets need to be forwarded to a router to reach the server, the router's MAC address is stored in the table entry (Router Node Address). The current value of the NCP sequence number and the connection number for the session also are stored in the table.

Two timeout values are maintained for every connection: maximum timeout and receive timeout. The maximum timeout is the maximum time the shell waits for a response from the server before it resends the request. This timeout is based on the initial estimate of the time delay between the client and the server, obtained during the RIP response to the nearest server route request, and is measured in clock ticks.

```
Maximum Timeout = 16 × Td + 10
```

Td=Time delay between client and server. If the server and client are on the same LAN, Td equals one tick, and maximum timeout equals 16 × 1 + 10 = 26 ticks.

The receive timeout is dynamically adjusted based on current delays on the network. The initial value is set by the following formula:

```
Initial Receive Timeout = 4 × Td + 10
```

The receive timeout increases by 50 percent if the server does not respond within the current setting of the timeout value.

```
New Increased Receive Timeout = 1.5 × Current Receive Timeout
```

The increase continues by 50 percent every time the server does not respond in the specified time, until the maximum timeout value is reached.

The shell reduces the receive timeout value every time the shell does not have to issue a retry request. To decrease the receive timeout, the shell takes the time necessary to receive a response to the last request that did not require a retry, multiplies that value by 2, and adds 10. The new receive timeout is set to the mean of this calculated value and the current receive timeout.

```
New Decreased Receive Timeout= [ (2 × Time to receive response)+ 10)   +
Current receive timeout ] / 2
```

The IPX Retry Count parameter determines the number of times the shell sends the request. This parameter can be set in the NET.CFG—previously SHELL.CFG—file. If this count is exceeded, the error message `Network error on server XXXX. Error XXXX from network. Abort, Retry?` appears. Some network drivers may ignore the IPX Retry Count parameter setting in the NET.CFG file and use a hard-coded default.

The Server Connection Table

A portion of the connection table keeps track of the clients it services. This table contains an entry for every connection to a client. The Network Address, Node Address, and Socket Number refer to the internet address of the client. Each time a connection request from a client arrives, the server compares the IPX internet source address with these fields. If these addresses do not match, a security breach has occurred.

The Sequence Number field keeps track of request/response packets between a client and the server. The NIC Number field holds the number of the NIC (A, B, C, D), or network number of the NIC, used to send the packet to the client. If the server was reached by routers, the MAC address of the router on the server's segment is placed in the Intermediate Router Address field. Because of this, the server does not need to determine a route to the client. To send a reply to the client, the server simply copies the Intermediate Router Address field in the packet's MAC destination address field. The packet's IPX destination address field contains the destination internet address of the client. The routers then route the server reply packet to the client.

The Watchdog Timer field is discussed a little later. A 100-byte Reply Buffer is maintained for every client connection. If the response to a client is less than 100 bytes, a copy of the response is kept in the Reply Buffer field. If the client does not receive a response and resends the request, the server uses the Reply Buffer field to reply to the client. The server then does not have to reprocess the client request because most server responses are less than 100 bytes.

Watchdog Process

The server maintains a watchdog process to monitor shell connections that may have crashed because of network problems or a workstation crash. At the end of the watchdog timer, files that were opened by the workstation before the crash are closed, and the connection information for the workstation in the server connection table is removed.

The server uses the watchdog process to poll clients not heard from in the last 5 minutes. Figure 20.20 shows the watchdog packets captured using the LANalyzer. An active shell responds to the watchdog packet request. Figures 20.21 and 20.22 show the details of the watchdog packet request and response. If the shell fails to respond, the server sends a watchdog request packet every minute until it has sent a total of 11 watchdog request packets. If the shell fails to respond to the last watchdog packet, the station is cleared.

NetWare 3.*x* servers enable you to set a parameter that monitors workstations cleared by the watchdog process. This parameter can be set by typing the following on the NetWare 3.*x* console:

```
SET CONSOLE DISPLAY WATCHDOG LOGOUTS=ON
```

NetWare 3.*x* watchdog parameters can be changed by typing the following SET command:

```
SET NUMBER OF WATCHDOG PACKETS=numbWatchdogPackets
```

The preceding command, which can be placed in an NCF file, sets the number of times the server polls an inactive station before it terminates the connection. This value ranges from 5 to 100 and has a default value of 10.

```
SET DELAY BEFORE FIRST WATCHDOG PACKET=delayFirstWatchdogPacket
```

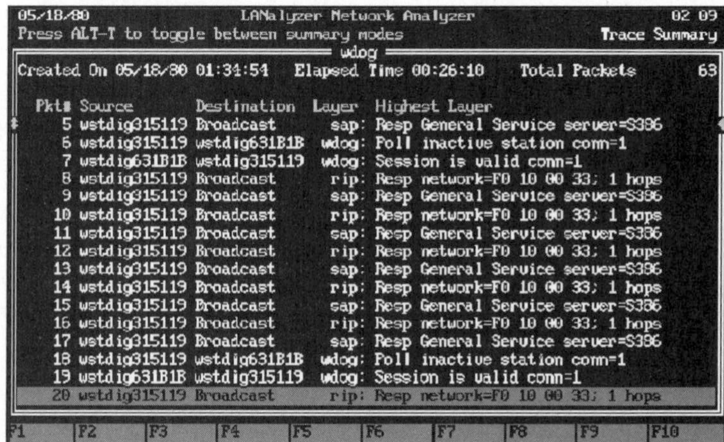

Figure 20.20
Watchdog packets captured using the LANalyzer.

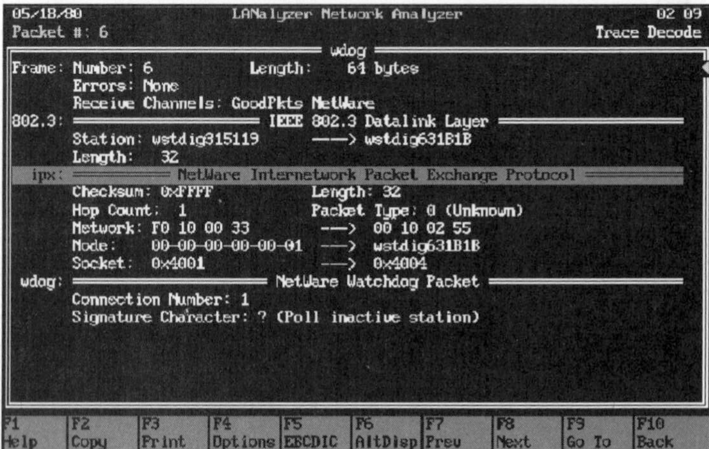

Figure 20.21
Watchdog packet request.

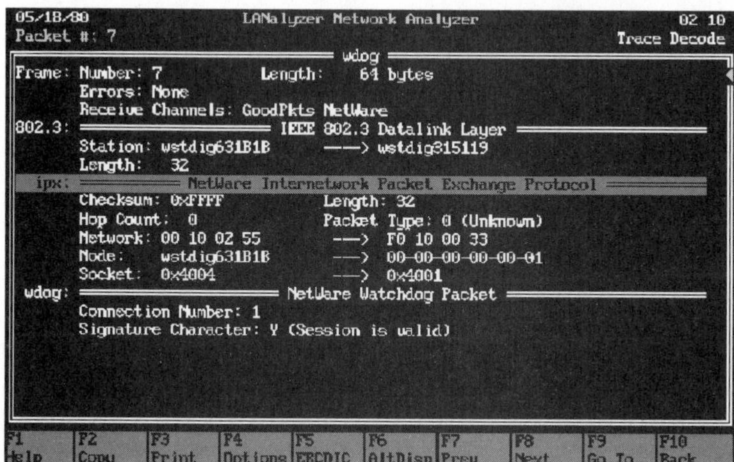

Figure 20.22
Watchdog packet response.

In the preceding command, *delayFirstWatchdogPacket* is the normal delay between the time a watchdog poll packet is sent to an active station and a valid response is received from that station. This value ranges from 15.7 seconds to 20 minutes 52.3 seconds and has a default value of 4 minutes 56.6 seconds.

```
SET DELAY BETWEEN WATCHDOG PACKETS=delayWatchdogPackets
```

The *delayWatchdogPackets* command controls the time between repeated sendings of watchdog poll packets if no response is received. This value ranges from 9.9 seconds to 10 minutes 26.2 seconds and has a default value of 59.3 seconds.

In NetWare 2.2, the WATCHDOG command can be issued from the server console to change the watchdog-process timing parameters. The general syntax of this command is as follows:

```
WATCHDOG [START=n] [INTERVAL=n] [COUNT=n]
```

The START value designates the number of seconds the server waits to send a watchdog request packet to verify the connection. The value ranges from 15 to 1200 with a default of 300 seconds.

The INTERVAL represents the number of seconds the server waits to send repeated watchdog request packets after the client fails to respond. The value ranges from 1 to 600 with a default of 60.

The COUNT refers to the number of intervals the server waits after START before clearing the connection. The value ranges from 5 to 100 with a default of 10.

Preparing the PC as a Workstation

When DOS is used to boot a PC, the PC has no idea that it is used as a workstation on a NetWare LAN. The CONFIG.SYS file does not contain network drivers. The network software that is needed to turn the PC into a workstation on a NetWare LAN is loaded as TSR programs. These TSRs are

IPX.COM and NETX.COM. If ODI drivers are being used, then you need the ODI Driver.COM file, the Link Support Program LSL.COM, and the IPXODI.COM that implements the SPX/IPX protocols. The ODI drivers also are loaded as TSRs.

Although CONFIG.SYS does not contain commands that suggest that the PC is being used as a NetWare workstation, certain configuration commands in the CONFIG.SYS file can have an important effect on using the PC as a NetWare workstation.

The following discussion is for DOS-based workstations. For OS/2, the CONFIG.SYS file contains direct network driver support.

Loading DOS

You might find that it is helpful to have a knowledge of what takes place behind the scenes when DOS first loads. Certain problems during the processing of network login scripts become clear when you understand the DOS load process.

When a system is first powered up, it automatically jumps to location 0FFFF0 hex, and begins executing the program starting at that location. This is a feature of all Intel 8086 family of microprocessors (the 80286, 80386, and 80486), and is independent of any operating system (such as DOS, OS/2, and UNIX) that may be running on the PC. The special location 0FFFF0 hex lies in a location in the ROM of the PC, and performs a power on self-test (POST) that checks memory (RAM) integrity, the keyboard, system clock, and other devices. After a successful POST, control is transferred to the bootstrap program, which is part of the BIOS (see figs. 20.23, 20.24, and 20.25).

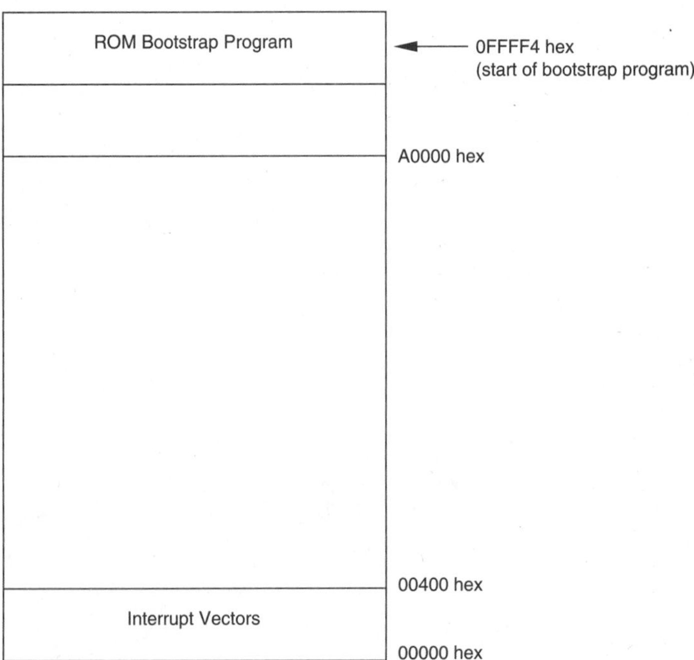

Figure 20.23 *Memory map when control is transferred to bootstrap program.*

The bootstrap program reads the first sector on the boot media (either the floppy disk in drive A or hard disk in drive C), which contains the remainder of the bootstrap program and information on the disk. After reading the rest of the bootstrap program into an arbitrary location in memory, the system transfers control to it. The bootstrap program then checks for the existence of a copy of the operating system. For MS-DOS, this is done by checking for the two files IO.SYS and MSDOS.SYS in that order. For IBM PC-DOS, these two files are IBMBIO.SYS and IBMDOS.SYS. If these files are missing, the system responds with the following error message:

```
Non-System disk or disk error
Replace and strike a key when ready
```

You receive this message also when the NetWare workstation software is copied to a floppy disk that has not been properly prepared by using the FORMAT /S or SYS commands in DOS.

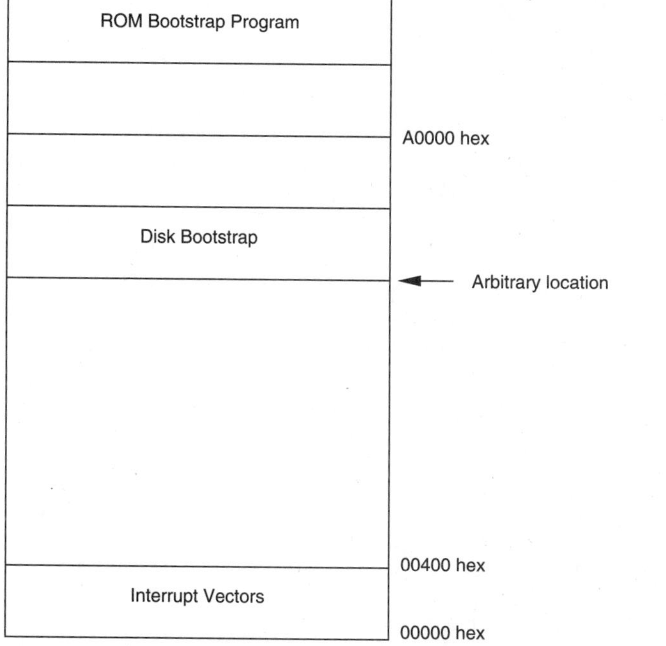

Figure 20.24
Memory map on loading disk bootstrap.

If the two system files are found, they are read into memory and control is transferred to the program in IO.SYS. In some systems, the IO.SYS loads first, and this in turn reads MSDOS.SYS in memory. The IO.SYS file actually consists of the following two parts:

- **BIOS.** Contains a linked set of resident device drivers for standard PC devices, such as CON, AUX, PRN, COM1, COM2, COM3, and NUL. Also, some hardware-specific initialization code is run to initialize certain devices.

- **SYSINIT.** Contains code from Microsoft and the BIOS supplied by the manufacturer of the PC. SYSINIT is called by the manufacturer's BIOS initialization code. It determines the amount of contiguous RAM, and then relocates itself so it can "get out of the way" of the DOS kernel that is loaded next.

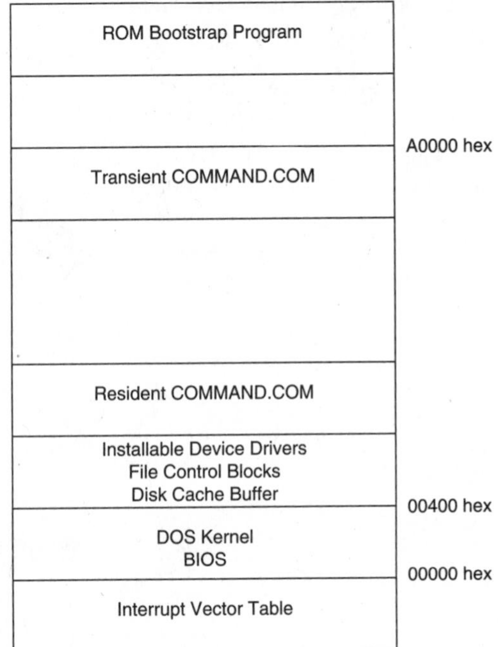

Figure 20.25
Final DOS map showing COMMAND.COM components.

Next, SYSINIT executes the initialization code in MSDOS.SYS, to accomplish the following:

- Setting up internal system tables
- Setting up interrupt vectors in locations 20 hex to 2F hex
- Calling the initialization function for each resident device driver

After the system initialization code displays, the MS-DOS copyright message displays, and the basic MS-DOS system loads. SYSINIT uses the MS-DOS file services to open the CONFIG.SYS file. (CONFIG.SYS processing is discussed in more detail in the following section.) If it is found, the entire CONFIG.SYS file is loaded in memory and each line in the file is processed. Any device drivers loaded by DEVICE= or DEVICEHIGH= commands are processed in the order in which they are found and loaded in memory. For DR DOS, statements with a ? before them cause the system to prompt the user if that statement should be processed.

After all the installable device drivers are loaded, SYSINIT closes all the files it has opened. SYSINIT then opens the console (CON), printer (PRN), and auxiliary (AUX) devices as standard input, standard output, and standard error devices.

Finally, SYSINIT calls the MS-DOS EXEC function to load the command-line interpreter COMMAND.COM, which is located on the boot media or specified by the SHELL= statement in CONFIG.SYS. To conserve memory, COMMAND.COM actually loads two parts. The *resident part* loads in lower memory, and the *transient part* loads just below the 640 KB limit.

The resident part of COMMAND.COM always is resident in RAM. The transient portion of COMMAND.COM can be written over by applications that are big enough to fill the entire 640 KB. After the application exits, DOS reloads the transient portion from a copy of COMMAND.COM. The location of COMMAND.COM is indicated by the COMSPEC environment variable, whose default value is set by the COMMAND.COM path in the SHELL= statement in the CONFIG.SYS file. The value of COMSPEC is important because an invalid COMSPEC can be the cause of the `Invalid COMMAND.COM—System Halted` error message that sometimes is encountered with NetWare LANs. This issue is discussed later on in this chapter. After SYSINIT performs its job, it is no longer needed and is discarded (see fig. 20.25).

If an AUTOEXEC.BAT file is in the root directory of the boot media, it is read into memory and processed by using the command line interpreter COMMAND.COM. If the AUTOEXEC.BAT file is not found, DOS prompts you for the date and time, which is a good reason to create an AUTOEXEC.BAT file and have at least a statement such as PROMPT PG in the file.

Understanding the CONFIG.SYS File

The following statements may appear in the CONFIG.SYS file and are important for a PC that you want to set up as a NetWare workstation:

```
SHELL=<pathname>/COMMAND.COM /P /E:<space>
FILES=<number of file handles>
BUFFERS=<number of buffers>
LASTDRIVE=<lastdrive>
DEVICEHIGH=<device path>
BREAK=[ON ¦ OFF]
```

The SHELL= statement uses the /P switch to run AUTOEXEC.BAT and make the command-line interpreter permanent. The /E switch tells DOS the amount of space it should reserve for the environment variables. In a NetWare environment in which many applications are being run, you might want to increase this value if you get the message Out of environment space. A good value to use is 800 bytes. The SHELL= statement, then, might look like the following:

```
SHELL=C:\DOS\COMMAND.COM /P /E:800
```

The C:\DOS\ statement specifies the *pathname* in which the DOS COMMAND.COM file can be found. If you are using an earlier version of DOS, such as DOS 3.1, the environment space is measured in number of paragraphs. Each paragraph is 16 bytes.

The FILES= statement controls the number of files the workstation can have open locally. It does not have any effect on the number of files opened on the network. FILES= still is important for applications that need to open a combination of local and network files. You can control the number of files that can be opened on NetWare servers by using the FILE HANDLES= statement in the NET.CFG (or older SHELL.CFG) file. The default is 40 open files on the network per workstation.

You can, for example, set the number of files a workstation can open locally to 30 by including **FILES=30** in the CONFIG.SYS file. You also can set the number of files that can be opened on the network to 50 by including **FILE HANDLES=50** in the NET.CFG file.

The BUFFERS= statement specifies the number of 512-byte blocks set aside for read and write operations. DOS reads and writes data in 512-byte sectors. If a sufficient number of buffers are in RAM, this can speed up file operations. In DR DOS, the HIBUFFERS= statement can be used to allocate buffers in high memory rather than conventional memory. A general rule of thumb is to have one buffer for every file you might want to open simultaneously.

The LASTDRIVE= statement specifies the last drive letters recognized by DOS. Its default value is E. This is the reason that the first network drive usually defaults to drive F. Under certain conditions, such as running NetWare Lite and NetWare on the same workstation, you might want to use the LASTDRIVE= statement to set a different last drive. If you set the LASTDRIVE= parameter to M, for examples, drives A to M can be used for local devices and network drives for NetWare Lite. Drives N to Z then can be used by NetWare.

When some applications are installed, they may add the LASTDRIVE=Z statement in the CONFIG.SYS file. Under these conditions, you do not have any assignable network drives for NetWare. You have to change the LASTDRIVE= statement to a value with which NetWare can work.

Another application for LASTDRIVE= is to use drive letters C, D, and E, which normally are used for local disks as network drives. You might want to do this for diskless workstations or workstations with floppy drives and no hard drives. In the latter case, if you have two floppy drives and no virtual RAM disks, you can use the statement **LASTDRIVE=B** so that the first available network drive is C. This setup is useful if you are running out of drive letters to assign to network directories.

The DEVICEHIGH= and DEVICE= statements load device drivers in memory. The DEVICE= statement loads device drivers in conventional memory. DEVICEHIGH= loads the drivers in upper memory, leaving more space for applications to run in conventional memory. If you want to conserve conventional memory for applications, you should load as many device drivers as possible in upper memory by using DEVICEHIGH=. In DR DOS, the equivalent command for loading drivers in upper memory is HIDEVICE=.

By setting the BREAK= statement to BREAK=OFF, you cannot break out of programs by using the Ctrl+C or Ctrl+Break keys until the program performs an I/O operation on the screen or printer. Setting the BREAK=OFF statement can prevent users from breaking out of batch files.

This section has covered only the CONFIG.SYS parameters that have a more direct bearing on the network environment. For a more complete and comprehensive description of CONFIG.SYS parameters, consult your DOS manual. In general, most other CONFIG.SYS parameters can be specified in the CONFIG.SYS file without adversely affecting the network workstation environment.

The following is an example of a CONFIG.SYS file used in a network workstation. This example should give you a sense of what you can place in the CONFIG.SYS file without having any problems.

```
DEVICE=C:\DOS5.0\HIMEM.SYS
DOS=HIGH,UMB
DEVICEHIGH=C:\DOS5.0\SETVER.EXE
DEVICEHIGH=C:\DOS5.0\EMM386.EXE RAM
FILES=40
BUFFERS=40
SHELL=C:\COMMAND.COM /P /E:800
LASTDRIVE=M
```

In the preceding example, the LASTDRIVE= statement is set to M because the workstation also is used for NetWare Lite. The first available network drive then becomes N for NetWare LANs.

Understanding the AUTOEXEC.BAT File

After the CONFIG.SYS file processes, DOS uses the command-line interpreter to execute the commands in the AUTOEXEC.BAT file. DOS looks for the AUTOEXEC.BAT file in the root directory of the boot media. The statements that you can place in CONFIG.SYS files are fundamentally different than the ones you can place in AUTOEXEC.BAT files. The statements in CONFIG.SYS files are special statements dealing with system configuration. On the other hand, the statements in AUTOEXEC.BAT files can be any DOS internal or external commands and any applications that you normally load from the DOS command line.

You can, for example, place the following commands in your AUTOEXEC.BAT file to set up an automatic startup script for logging in to a NetWare network:

```
@ECHO OFF
PROMPT $P$G
PATH C:\LOCAL\APPS;C:\LOCAL\BIN
IPX
NETx
REM * Remove NETBIOS if applications do not need it
NETBIOS
REM * Next line is only needed, if NETBIOS applications are
REM * poorly written and check for IBM PC LAN product before
REM * running. Most of these applications have been
REM * fixed and you would not normally need the INT2F program
INT2F
F:
LOGIN serverName/userName
```

In DOS 3.3 or higher, the @ character instructs the batch file not to display that line. The ECHO OFF command stops the commands in the AUTOEXEC.BAT file from being displayed as they are executed. The PATH command sets up a local path environment. When the login processing continues, a special login script is processed that sets up the network environment. This login script contains commands to set up the network search path. In earlier versions of the shell (NETX.COM), the network search path would override the local path. This problem has been fixed in more recent releases so that, as new network search paths are added, the PATH in the AUTOEXEC.BAT file is preserved and added at the end of the search path.

In the preceding example, the NETBIOS and IN2F commands are optional and are needed only if you are running applications that need the NETBIOS protocol stack. Because of NetWare's popularity, most applications are written to make direct use of the IPX protocols. You should seldom have a need to use Novell's NETBIOS emulation.

If you are using the ODI drivers, then you probably want to use an AUTOEXEC.BAT file similar to the following:

```
@ECHO OFF
PROMPT $P$G
PATH C:\LOCAL\APPS;C:\LOCAL\BIN
LSL
REM * Replace SMCPLUS with the ODI driver for the
REM * network adapter.
SMCPLUS
IPXODI
NETx
F:
LOGIN serverName/userName
```

In the preceding example, the LSL is loaded first, which is followed by the ODI driver for the network adapter in the workstation. In the preceding example, the ODI driver for an SMC Elite 16T network adapter (*SMCPLUS*) is used. The IPXODI program that implements the SPX/IPX protocols is loaded next, and finally the NETx shell program. ODI drivers require that a NET.CFG file be set up appropriately as discussed in an earlier chapter.

You can load the IPX.COM and the NETX.COM in upper memory by using the LOADHIGH command from DOS 5.0, or the HILOAD command in DR DOS.

Examining the Login Process

When the NetWare shell (NETX.COM) loads, it sets up the first network drive to map to the SYS:LOGIN directory on the specified server. The first network drive usually is F. By changing to this drive and invoking the LOGIN program, you can initiate the user authentication process. The user has to supply the correct login name and password before access to a NetWare server is granted.

After you log in, the commands that you type are checked by the shell to see if they are network commands. Network commands are sent to the server, where they are processed and the results sent back. Local commands are processed by the local workstation operating system. The advantage of this approach is that, as far as DOS is concerned, it has little awareness that the workstation is being used on a network. The networking software makes it appear as if the network is an extension of the workstation operating environment. This makes it possible for single-user applications to run on the network if they are set up correctly.

Figures 20.26 and 20.27 show the kind of processing that takes place at the workstation and the server to keep the network transparent to DOS.

When a DOS application wants to make use of DOS system services, such as request for file open, it issues a software interrupt by using the instruction INT 21H. When NETx loads, it takes over several software interrupts and steals the DOS interrupt by placing an address to its own code in the interrupt vector for 21 (hex). In this manner the shell can monitor all DOS system calls. If the DOS system call is for NetWare services, such as access to a file on a network drive, the shell directs this request across the network to the server. In this sense, the shell plays the role of a traffic policeman or a redirector.

The request is sent as an NCP packet encapsulated in an IPX datagram and passed on to the LAN drivers for the workstation. The LAN drivers encapsulate the IPX packet with data link headers and send this packet across the network to the server. The server's LAN drivers strip the data link headers and pass the IPX packet to the IPX process on the server. The IPX process passes the IPX packet to the router process on the server. Remember, every NetWare server is capable of acting as an IPX router. The router process examines the destination address on the IPX packet and checks if the IPX packet is destined to a different network than the one on which the IPX packet was received. If the IPX packet belongs to a different network, the router process consults its routing table to determine to which router the IPX packet should be sent. The IPX header then is replaced by the address of the next router. This process continues until the IPX packet gets to its final destination.

If the router process discovers that no routing is necessary, it strips the IPX header and sends the original NCP request to the file server process on the server. The file server processes the request and sends an NCP reply packet to the router and IPX process. The router process determines whether or not the packet needs to be routed. The NCP packet is encapsulated in an IPX packet and sent to the LAN drivers, which send it back to the workstation that made the request. At the workstation, the LAN drivers strip off the data link header and pass it on to the IPX software running at the workstation (IPX.COM or IPXODI.COM). The IPX process at the workstation strips off the IPX header and sends the NCP reply packet to the NetWare shell, which translates the original DOS request to a DOS system reply. The application that was waiting for the DOS system service then resumes its work.

Figure 20.26
NetWare workstation makes a system request.

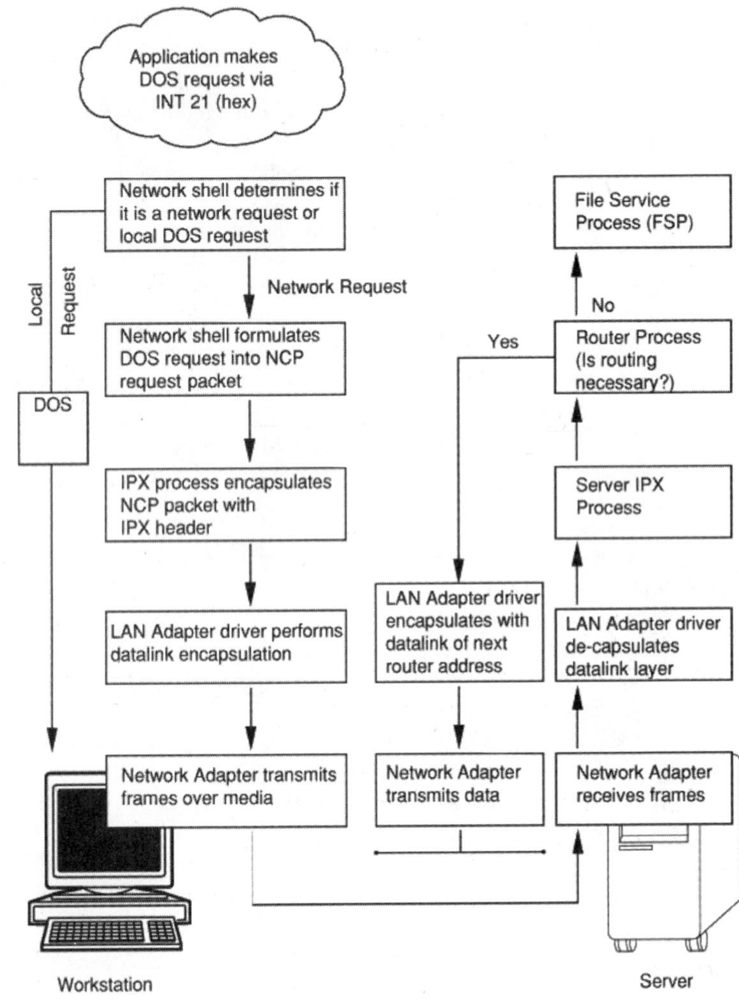

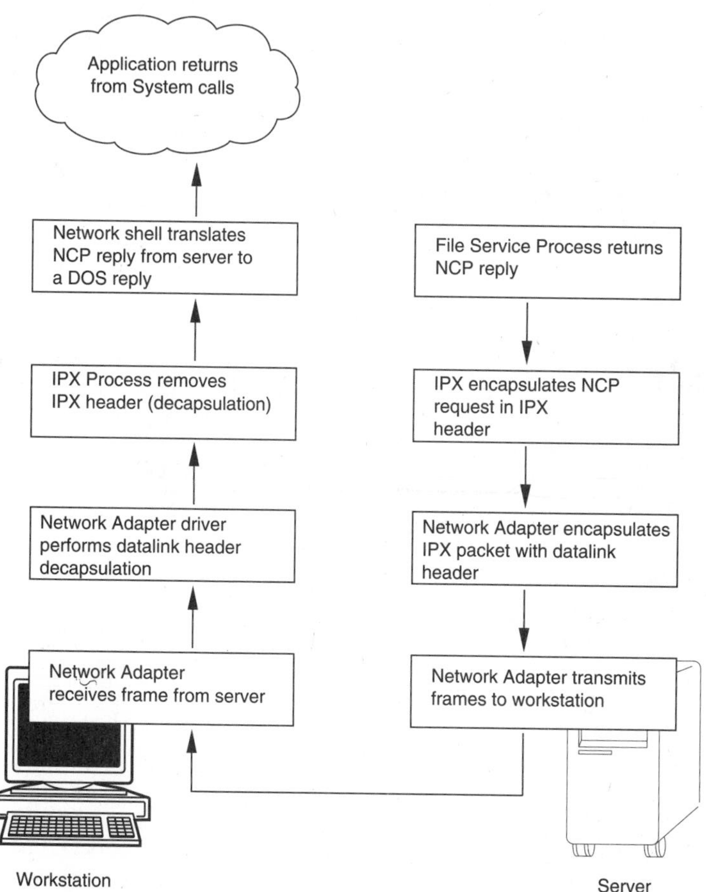

Figure 20.27
NetWare server replies to workstation request.

Examining NetWare Requester Architecture and Components

The NetWare Requester software is modular, and its components are diagrammed in figure 20.28. From an architectural point of view, the workstation consists of the following:

1. DOS Requester
2. Communication Protocol
3. Link Support Layer
4. LAN Driver

20

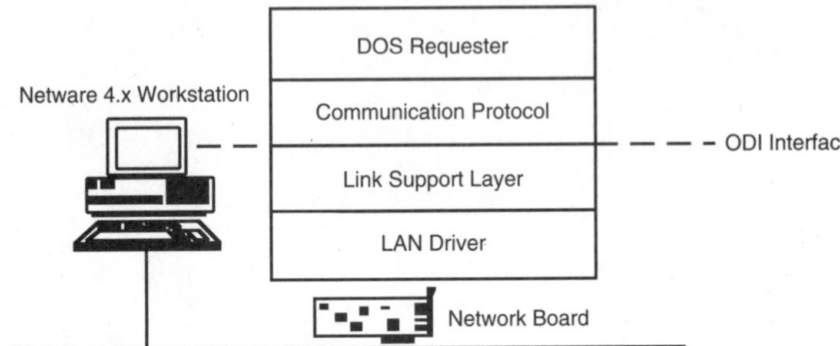

Figure 20.28
NetWare 4.x client components.

The DOS Requester

When an application makes a request for services, DOS examines this request. If the request is for local resources, the request is handled by DOS. If the request is for network resources, the request is sent to the DOS Requester. Starting with DOS 3.1, DOS has had the capability of providing redirection services. The DOS Requester for NetWare (also called the NetWare DOS Requester) shares system tables, such as the drive table, with DOS (see fig. 20.29). DOS keeps track of which drive letter entries in the table are for DOS and the DOS Requester. When an application makes a request for a file on a particular drive letter, DOS is able, after consulting the shared drive table, to direct the request to the DOS Requester or local DOS system services.

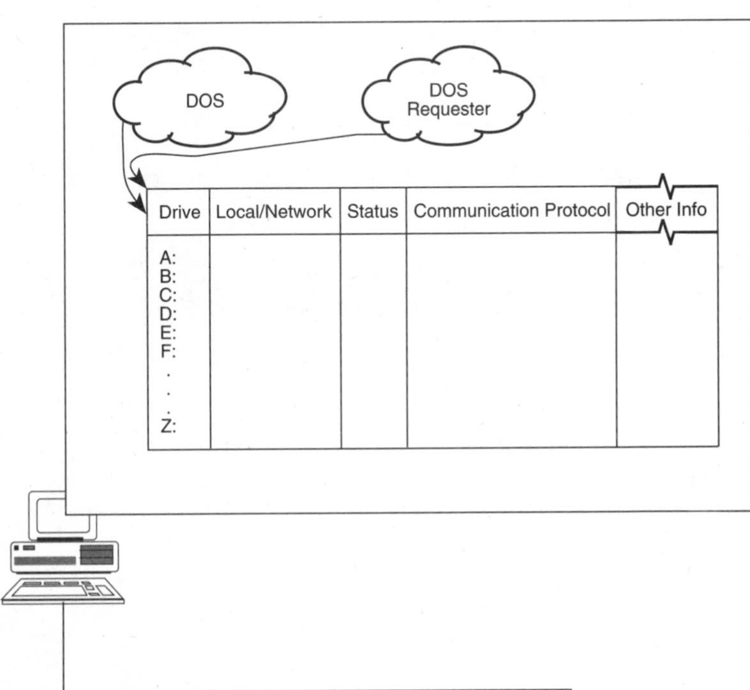

Figure 20.29
The DOS requester and DOS drive tables.

The DOS Requester takes the application request and translates it into an equivalent NCP request. NCP stands for *NetWare Core Protocol*, which is the protocol used to carry requests for services to a NetWare file server. The NetWare file servers have an NCP server process that can handle multiple requests for network services and then send the result of processing the NCP requests back to the sender. The NCP requests are carried across the network by a transport communication protocol. The default communication protocol for a NetWare client is IPX (Inter-network Packet eXchange protocol).

The DOS Requester is able to support from 2 to 50 connections. Without any explicit configuration, it supports 8 connections by default.

The DOS Requester includes support for multiple languages. The message files for different languages are stored in the \NWCLIENT\NLS*language* directory at the workstation, where *language* is replaced by one of the supported languages. For English this directory is \NWCLIENT\NLS\ENGLISH.

The DOS Requester provides for background authentication after an initial connection is made to the user. The background authentication occurs transparent to the user. A special area in the workstation's memory called *tagged data storage* is allocated for this purpose.

The DOS Requester is actually implemented as a number of smaller modules called *Virtual Loadable Modules* (VLMs). This modular structure allows you the option to place these individual components in expanded, extended, conventional memory or in memory used by protected-mode DOS extenders. Another advantage of the modular structure is that Novell or a third-party vendor can easily extend the functionality of the DOS Requester by supporting additional VLMs. If the workstation has insufficient memory to load all the VLMs, unneeded VLMs are swapped out.

The DOS Requester provides backward compatibility with the previous NETX.EXE and NETX.COM DOS shells through a special VLM called NETX.VLM.

The Communication Protocol

The communication protocol uses the network board to send the packets across the network. Between the communication protocol and the network board is the *Open Datalink Interface* (ODI). The ODI interface is a modular method of implementing communication components that correspond to the ODI interface.

There are many choices of communication protocols, such as SPX/IPX, TCP/IP, AppleTalk, OSI, and so on.

The Link Support Layer and MLID Drivers

The *link support layer* (LSL) provides an ODI interface to the communication protocol. This interface enables multiple protocol stacks to coexist in harmony and even share the same network board driver. The LSL acts as a software switchboard that provides a communication path between the communication protocol and the LAN driver to which the protocol is bound.

The ODI driver is also called the *Multiple Link Interface Driver* (MLID) because it can support multiple interfaces to communication protocols via the link support layer. The communication protocols are written to the DDI interface, and so is the MLID driver.

Implementing the NetWare Client Architecture Components

The software components that correspond to the architectural components (DOS Requester, communication protocol, link support layer, and network driver) are shown in Figure 20.30.

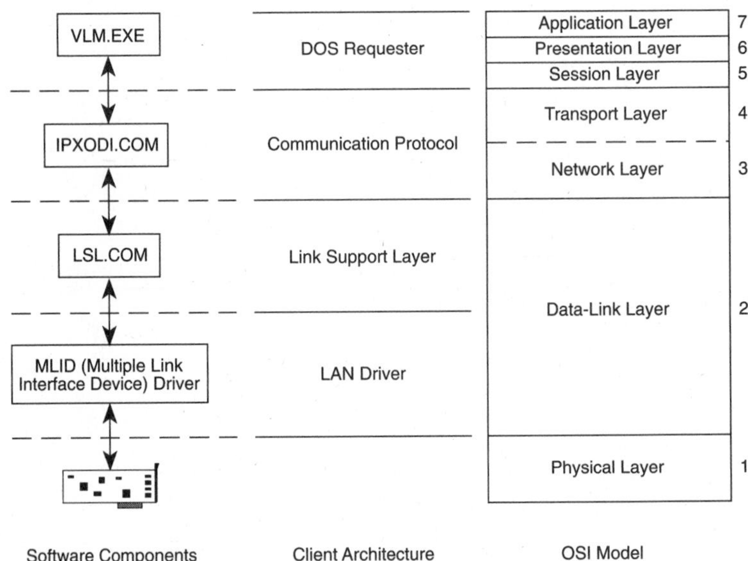

Figure 20.30
NetWare client software components.

The DOS Requester is implemented by VLMs. Virtual Loadable Modules are a way of breaking up the monolithic NetWare shell (NETX.COM or NETX.EXE) in earlier versions of NetWare and dividing it into smaller components, each of which you can load selectively.

The communication protocol is implemented by Terminate-and-Stay-Resident (TSR) programs. The default IPX protocol is implemented by the IPXODI.COM program. Other protocol stacks that can be used are TCP/IP (TCPIP.EXE).

Although the name of the IPXODI.COM file makes no mention of *Sequenced Packet Exchange* (SPX) protocol, IPXODI.COM includes the SPX protocol. The SPX protocol is not normally used by NetWare 4.*x* but is used in applications such as RCONSOLE (Remote Console) and for establishing connections between print servers and remote printers. These applications require a reliable virtual-circuit connection, which is implemented with the SPX protocol. The IPXODI technology has not changed from NetWare 3.*x*. The same IPXODI switches and options that were used in NetWare 3.*x* are also used in NetWare 4.*x*.

The link support layer is implemented by LSL.COM for DOS. Like IPXODI.COM, the LSL.COM program is also a TSR. You must load LSL.COM before loading the ODI driver.

Comparing the NetWare DOS Requester with the NetWare Shell

The NetWare shell was used in pre–NetWare 4.*x* versions such as NetWare 3.*x*. Figure 20.31 shows the architectural overview of the NetWare 3.*x* shell components and the NetWare 4.*x* client architecture.

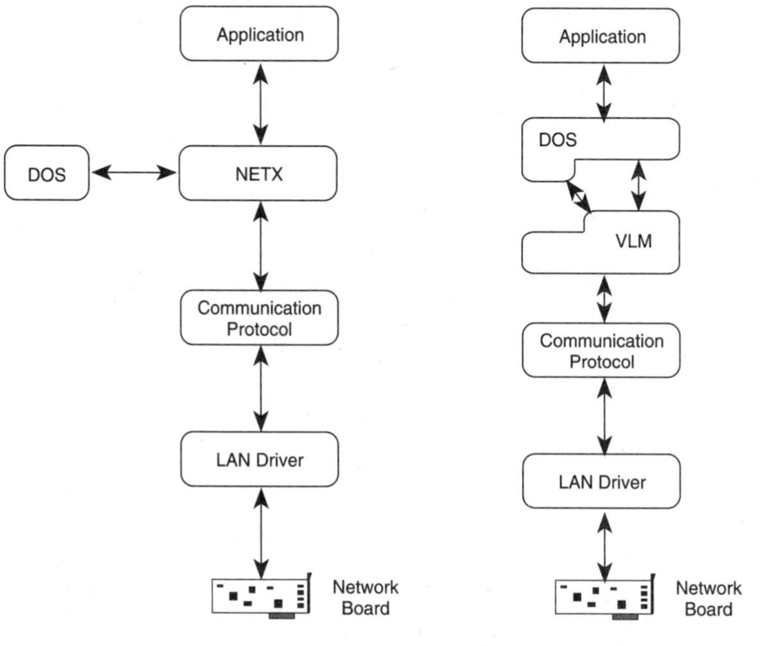

Figure 20.31
NetWare shell and NetWare 4.x client architecture.

The NetWare 3.*x* shell is the front end to DOS and can be seen as a component that provides the interface between an application and DOS. Application requests for system services are intercepted by the shell. Most system services use the INT 21 (hexadecimal) software interrupt. The NetWare shell takes over this interrupt (see fig. 20.32), and when a system request arrives, the shell determines whether the request should be passed to DOS or sent as an NCP request to the communication protocol. Besides intercepting system calls via INT 21 (hexadecimal)—called hooking to an interrupt vector by programmers, the shell intercepts other system calls via software interrupts 24 (hexadecimal) and 17 (hexadecimal). The shell keeps a different drive table than DOS and does not share data structures with DOS. The shell also keeps track of a Drive Connection ID table, Drive Handle table, Drive Flag table, and File

Server name table. When used to log in to the server, the shell initializes its tables with information on that connection. The drive mappings for a particular session, for example, are stored in the Drive Connection ID table.

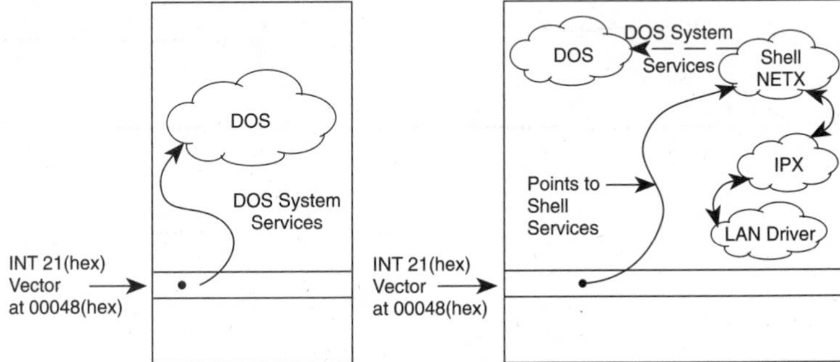

Figure 20.32
The NetWare shell and INT 21 (hex).

A limitation of the NetWare 3.*x* shell is that it has a maximum of eight connection slots in the table and a 64 KB size. The eight-connection table size means that the shell can be used to make connections to no more than eight servers at a time. For large networks consisting of many servers, this restriction can turn out to be a true limitation. The 64 KB size comes from the fact that the shell is implemented as a COM file (NETX.COM). A COM file cannot be larger than 64 KB. Later versions of the shell have been implemented as EXE files that can have more than 64 KB. You want the shell to be as small as possible, but increased functionality and capability require larger-sized shells.

The NetWare 3.*x* shell supports DOS 2.*x* and above, and the NetWare 4.*x* DOS Requester requires DOS 3.1 and higher. The reason that the DOS Requester requires DOS 3.1 and above is because DOS 3.1 was the first version of DOS that included a redirector capability.

The DOS Requester shares tables with DOS, which reduces memory used for system tables. Network file and print services are sent by DOS to the NetWare DOS Requester. The NetWare DOS Requester is a collection of software modules, each implementing a specialized function of the NetWare requester. Some of these functions are equivalent to those that were implemented in NetWare 3.*x*, and others are new to NetWare 4.*x*. An example of one function that is new to NetWare 4.*x* is NetWare Directory Services; another is the authentication module that implements the RSA encryption used as part of the login authentication.

The DOS Requester approach provides support for 2 to 50 connections and uses the DOS software interrupt INT 2F (hexadecimal) to provide the DOS redirection capability. The requester requires more memory than the NetWare 3.*x* shell for background authentication and added functionality. But the requester is broken into smaller software modules (called VLMs), which can be managed more easily by memory managers that can place them in expanded memory or high memory. The NetWare DOS Requester includes support for multiple languages such as English, French, Spanish, German, and Italian.

Table 20.17 summarizes the differences between the DOS Requester and the NetWare shell.

Table 20.17
Comparing the DOS Requester with the NetWare Shell

NetWare DOS Requester	NetWare 3.*x* Shell
Uses DOS redirector via INT 2F hex.	Intercepts system services via INT 21 hex.
Requires DOS 3.1 or higher.	Supports DOS 3.*x* and higher.
Can have 2 to 50 simultaneous connections.	Can have up to 8 simultaneous connections.
Memory requirements are larger because of background authentication and added functionality.	Memory requirements are limited to 64 KB.
Shares drive and status tables with DOS, reducing system table memory requirements.	Keeps its own set of drive tables that are independent of DOS. Intercepted call for network services makes use of the separate system tables.
Multiple language support.	Lack of multiple language support.

Examining NetWare DOS Requester Components

The NetWare DOS Requester consists of a Manager program called VLM.EXE. When you load VLM.EXE, it in turn loads the Virtual Loadable Modules (VLMs). Virtual Loadable Modules, program files that provide specific functions, are readily identified by a VLM extension.

Comparing VLMs with NLMs

With the introduction of VLMs at the workstation, Novell hopes to add the same flexibility that exists when you use *NetWare Loadable Modules* (NLMs) at the server. Figure 20.33 shows a comparison of these approaches. Novell has specified how NLMs can be written, and many third-party vendors provide management capabilities and applications that you can connect directly to internal NetWare resources, with the NLM acting as an extension of the operating system itself. As the use of VLMs becomes more popular, third-party products that extend the workstation's network capability increases. As new VLMs become available, they can connect to the VLM bus shown in figure 20.33 and provide a clean way of extending the capability of the network client software.

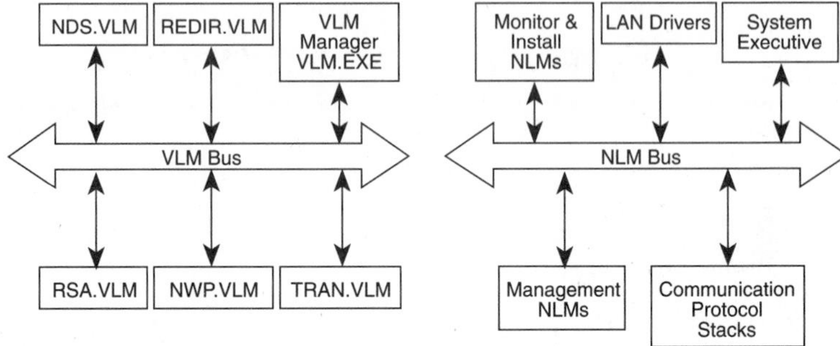

Figure 20.33
The VLM bus and the NLM bus.

Examining the VLM Manager

The VLM Manager, implemented by VLM.EXE, is a TSR, and it can manage any VLM program file written to the VLM specification.

The data flow and communications between VLMs are managed by the VLM Manager. The VLM Manager is also responsible for handling application requests and forwarding them to the appropriate VLM that can process the request. It also manages memory services, such as the need for memory allocation and deallocation, on behalf of the VLMs.

The VLM Manager loads the VLM program files in a default order if you have specified the USE DEFAULT=ON option in the NetWare DOS Requester section of the NET.CFG file. If the USE DEFAULT=ON option is not specified, the VLMs must be loaded in another order, which you must specify in the NET.CFG file. If you are not using all of the default VLMs, you may wish to explicity specify which VLMs you are loading. You can do this by specifying

```
VLM = nameOfVLM
```

in the NetWare DOS Requester section of the NET.CFG file. The VLMs are loaded in the order in which the VLM= *nameOfVLM* is placed in the NET.CFG file. An example of using the previous statement is shown below:

```
NetWare DOS Requester
    VLM = CONN.VLM
    VLM = IPXNCP.VLM
    VLM = TRAN.VLM
    VLM = SECURITY.VLM
    VLM = NDS.VLM
    VLM = BIND.VLM
    VLM = RSA.VLM          ; Not loaded by DEFAULT
    VLM = NWP.VLM
    VLM = FIO.VLM
    VLM = GENERAL.VLM
    VLM = REDIR.VLM
    VLM = PRINT.VLM
    VLM = NETX.VLM
    VLM = AUTO.VLM          ; Not loaded by DEFAULT - Requires RSA.VLM
```

Loading VLMS in the Default Order

If you specify the USE DEFAULT=ON option in the NetWare DOS Requester section of the NET.CFG file, the VLM Manager loads 12 VLMs. The order in which they are loaded reflects the order in which they are used for a NetWare 4.*x* client that has been enabled for directory services.

The default load order is as follows:

1. CONN.VLM
2. IPXNCP.VLM
3. TRAN.VLM
4. SECURITY.VLM
5. NDS.VLM
6. BIND.VLM
7. NWP.VLM
8. FIO.VLM
9. GENERAL.VLM
10. REDIR.VLM
11. PRINT.VLM
12. NETX.VLM

Understanding the Types of VLMs

VLMs can be classified into two types: those that are responsible for controlling the interactions between VLMs, and those that perform specific functions.

The VLMs that perform specific functions are called child VLMs. A *child VLM* is able to perform a designated task but does not have complete knowledge of how to obtain requests for processing from other VLMs. This job is the responsibility of the multiplexor VLMs. *A multiplexor VLM* is able to direct specific tasks, such as an application request, to the appropriate child VLM (see fig. 20.34).

Figures 20.35 and 20.36 show examples of the relationship between multiplexor VLMs and child VLMs. The multiplexor VLMs include NWP.VLM and TRAN.VLM.

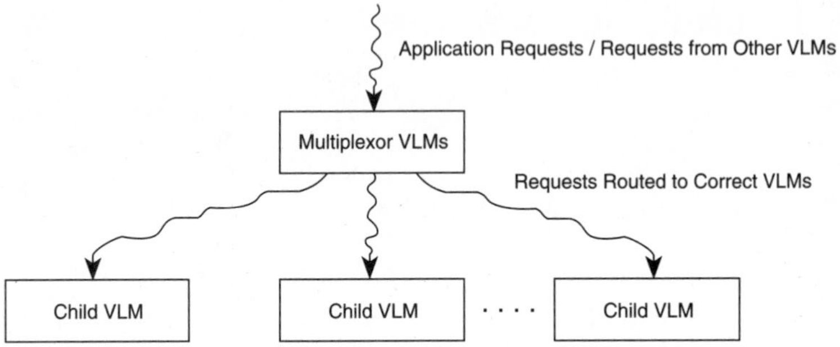

Figure 20.34
Multiplexor and child VLMs.

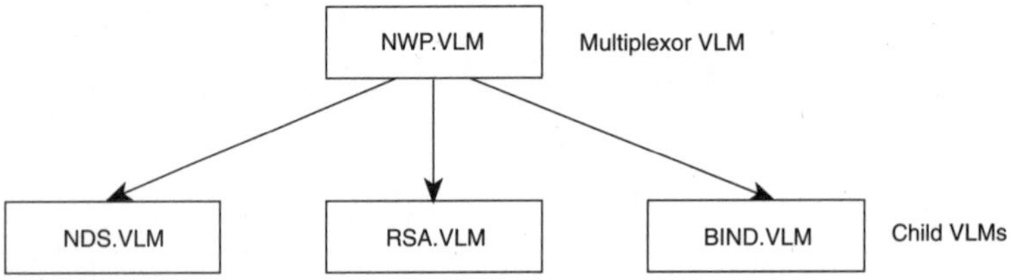

Figure 20.35
The NWP.VLM multiplexor VLM.

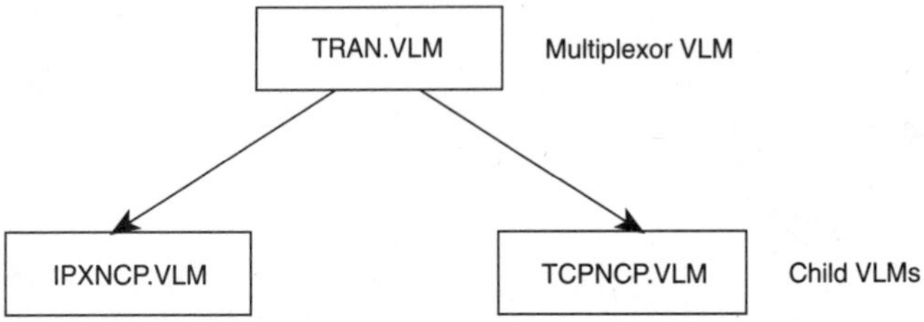

Figure 20.36
The TRAN.VLM multiplexor VLM.

NWP.VLM is the NetWare protocol multiplexor VLM whose child VLMs are those that deal with NetWare Directory Services: NDS.VLM, RSA.VLM, BIND.VLM, and PNW.VLM. NDS.VLM implements the client portion of the NetWare Directory service that is capable of making requests for NDS services against the NDS database. RSA.VLM implements the Rivest, Shamir, Adleman public key encryption that is used in the login and background authentication of NetWare client services. BIND.VLM enables a NetWare 4.*x* server's resources to be viewed as part of a fictitious bindery. In other words, BIND.VLM provides a virtual bindery view of a NetWare 4.*x* server. This feature is called bindery emulation. For bindery emulation to work, you must load another VLM called NETX.VLM to provide the equivalent of the NetWare 3.*x* NETX.EXE (or NETX.COM) functionality. The PNW.VLM (called LITE.VLM in earlier Novell documentation) contains the support for the Personal NetWare product.

TRAN.VLM is the transport multiplexor VLM whose children are IPXNCP.VLM and TCPNCP.VLM. This multiplexor VLM is responsible for sending the data from an application process to the correct network service protocol for processing. An example of the network service protocol is the NetWare Core Protocol (NCP).

The names of the children IPXNCP.VLM and TCPNCP.VLM are misleading. You might think of IPXNCP.VLM, for instance, as a replacement for IPXODI.COM, which implements the SPX/IPX protocol for ODI drivers. On the contrary, IPXNCP.VLM implements the proper formatting of a network service request into an NCP request packet. This request is sent via the appropriate ODI communication protocol stack. In the case of IPXNCP.VLM, this protocol is the IPX protocol implemented by IPXODI.COM. Novell or third-party solution providers can add additional protocol stacks.

TCPNCP.VLM is used by the NetWare/IP product. This product enables NCP calls to be transported across an IP internet. You have to load NLMs on a NetWare server to turn it into a "NetWare/IP Server." To support the use of TCP/IP for NCP services on the workstation, you would load the following files:

1. LSL.COM
2. NE2000.COM (or a suitable MLID)
3. TCPIP.EXE (same as is used in the LAN Workplace for DOS product)
4. NWIP.EXE (NetWare/IP client module)
5. VLM.EXE

You must load child VLMs before you load their multiplexor VLM. Thus you must load NDS.VLM, BIND.VLM, or RSA.VLM before loading the multiplexor VLM NWP.VLM. The first child VLM to be loaded becomes the default VLM for that multiplexor. This means that this VLM is checked first to see if it needs to handle the data. If NDS.VLM is loaded before BIND.VLM, for example, the default VLM for NWP.VLM is NDS.VLM. If there is only one child VLM that is used, you do not need multiplexing. If you do not need a multiplexor, it need not be loaded in memory. An easy way to prevent a module from loading is to rename it.

Working with Virtual Loadable Modules

VLMs implement specific functions of the DOS Requester. The redirector function is provided by REDIR.VLM, for example, and the printing function is provided by PRINT.VLM. Isolating the functionality of the requester into separate modules called VLMs gives you the flexibility of loading only the service that you need. Also, because the VLMs are smaller program files, they can be better managed by the different extended and expanded memory managers.

Figure 20.37 shows the VLMs and the interrelationships between them.

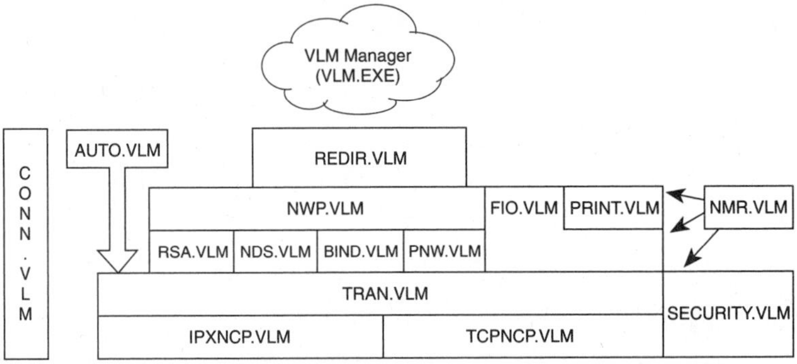

Figure 20.37
VLMs and their interrelationships.

The VLMs shown in figure 20.37 can be grouped into three service categories:

- DOS Redirection
- Service Protocol
- Transport Protocol

These three categories are also sometimes called the DOS Redirection Layer, the Service Protocol Layer, and the Transport Protocol Layer, with the DOS Redirection Layer being at the top and the Transport Protocol Layer being at the bottom (see fig. 20.38).

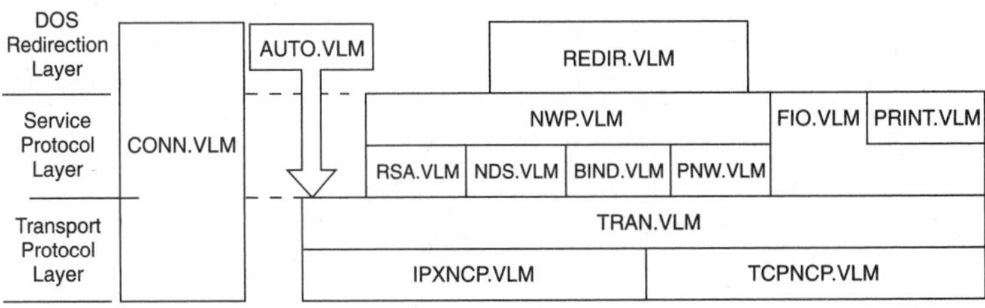

Figure 20.38
The VLM service categories.

The DOS Redirection Layer is implemented by REDIR.VLM, which provides a client application with access to remote network file and print services.

The Service Protocol Layer handles specific functions such as connection management, network file input/output, network printing, and other miscellaneous services such as message broadcast. Most of these services are used by REDIR.VLM to implement its function. Examples of modules that are in this layer are NWP.VLM (NetWare protocol multiplexor) and its child VLMs (NDS.VLM, RSA.VLM, BIND.VLM, and PNW.VLM), FIO.VLM (file input/output VLM), and PRINT.VLM (network print redirector). NWP.VLM is the Personal NetWare VLM used to support the peer-to-peer capabilities of the Personal NetWare product.

The NWP.VLM, which is part of the Service Provider Layer, is used for connection management (establish and maintain conneections, logins, logouts) broadcast messages. It also handles particular server implementations such as NDS, Bindery(BIND), and Personal NetWare (PNW — older name is NetWare Lite).

The FIO.VLM, which is part of the Service Provider Layer, is the file input/output module. It is used for basic file operations, and provides for cached/non-cached reads and writes, burst mode reads and writes, and Large Internet Packet read/write operations. Novell refers to the packet burst protocol implementation used by the FIO.VLM as PBODI (Packet Burst ODI).

The remaining major Service Provider Layer component is the PRINT.VLM, which implements print redirector function.

The Transport Protocol Layer is responsible for maintaining server connections and for converting the service requests generated by the Service Protocol Layer VLMs into appropriate network requests for services. The network requests are formatted into the proper NCP (NetWare Core Protocol) packets by VLMs such as IPXNCP.VLM and TCPNCP.VLM. The transport VLMs (IPXNCP.VLM and TCPNCP.VLM) provided at this layer are managed by the TRAN.VLM multiplexor VLM.

Table 20.18 contains a summary of the different VLMs, whether they are optional or required, and their load default order number. The load default order number is for those VLMs that are loaded by default. For VLMs that are not loaded by default, the column contains information on where to insert these VLMs. The details of these VLMs is presented in the next few sections.

Table 20.18
VLM Summary

VLM Name	Load Default Order Number	Optional/ Required	Description
CONN	1	Required	Connection Table Manager
IPXNCP	2	Required unless using NetWare/IP	Transport protocol using NCP/IPX. Child of TRAN.VLM
TRAN	3	Required	Transport Protocol Multiplexor
SECURITY	4	Optional	Used to implement packet signatures and general security functions

continues

Table 20.18, Continued
VLM Summary

VLM Name	Load Default Order Number	Optional/ Required	Description
NDS	5	Required	NetWare Directory Services; child of NWP.VLM
BIND	6	Required for NW3.*x* support. Optional for NW 4.*x*	Bindery emulation; child of NWP.VLM
NWP	7	Required	NetWare protocol multiplexor
FIO	8	Required	File input/output for network requests
GENERAL	9	Required	Miscellaneous functions for other VLMs such as NETX.VLM and REDIR.VLM
REDIR	10	Required	DOS Redirector
PRINT	11	Optional	Print Redirector
NETX	12	Optional	Older NetWare Shell compatibility
AUTO	After NETX	Optional	Auto-reconnect and auto-retry. Must have RSA.VLM loaded.
RSA	After BIND Before NWP	Optional	Background authentication service using RSA. NDS re-authentication used by AUTO.VLM.
NMR	Any order	Optional	NetWare Mangement Responder
PNW	Before NWP	Optional	Personal NetWare

AUTO.VLM

AUTO.VLM is used to reestablish a connection with a server after the loss of an NCP connection. A loss of connection could occur, for instance, if the NetWare server crashes or is downed unexpectedly. As the server is activated again, AUTO.VLM reconnects to the server and reestablishes the necessary user environment, such as drive mappings, connection status, printer connections, and so on. Figure 20.39 shows how AUTO.VLM establishes this environment in the case of server crash.

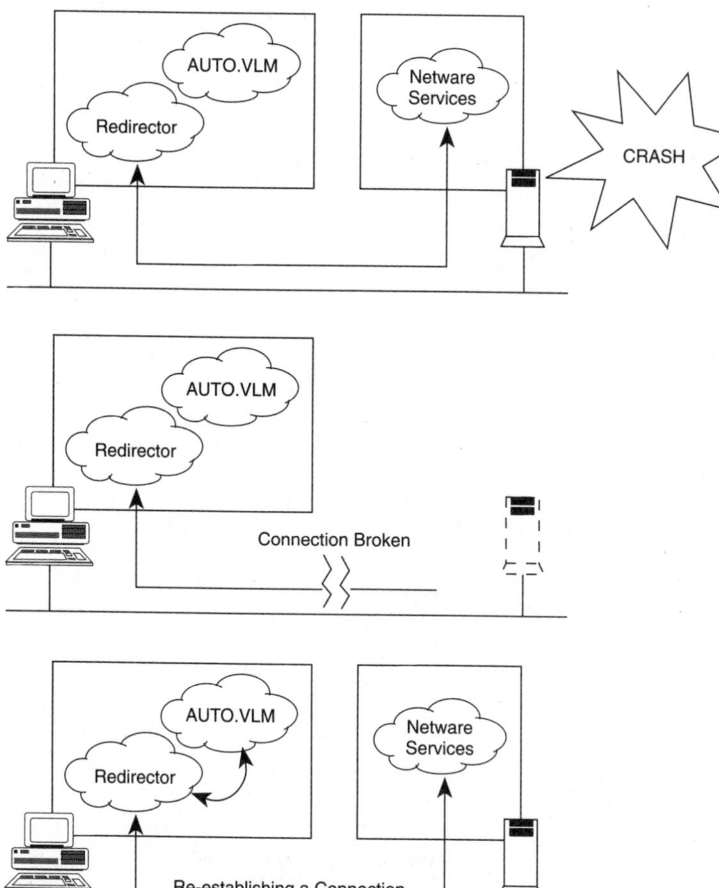

Figure 20.39
Establishing reconnections by using AUTO.VLM.

If files were open at the time the server was downed, AUTO.VLM opens the files, but any further recovery depends on how the application running at the workstation is able to deal with the connection loss.

AUTO.VLM is able to restore the connection status because the status of the workstation is maintained in the workstation's RAM. If the workstation crashes, however, this status information is lost. When detecting the loss of the connection, the server clears it. Bringing the workstation up again does not restore the connection status.

AUTO.VLM does not load automatically and is not part of the default loading order. To load AUTO.VLM, you must explicitly specify it in the NetWare DOS Requester section of the NET.CFG file, using this line:

```
VLM = AUTO.VLM
```

BIND.VLM

BIND.VLM, a child VLM of the NWP.VLM multiplexor VLM, implements bindery emulation services for a NetWare workstation client. Bindery emulation enables access to NetWare 3.*x* bindery objects placed in the NDS tree as a result of the Migrate process. BIND.VLM and NETX.VLM provide access to bindery-based NetWare 3.*x* servers (see fig. 20.40). BIND.VLM maintains compatibility with NetWare 3.*x* servers and enables you to view their bindery information. It also enables NetWare 3.*x* servers to be more easily integrated with NetWare 4.*x*–based networks.

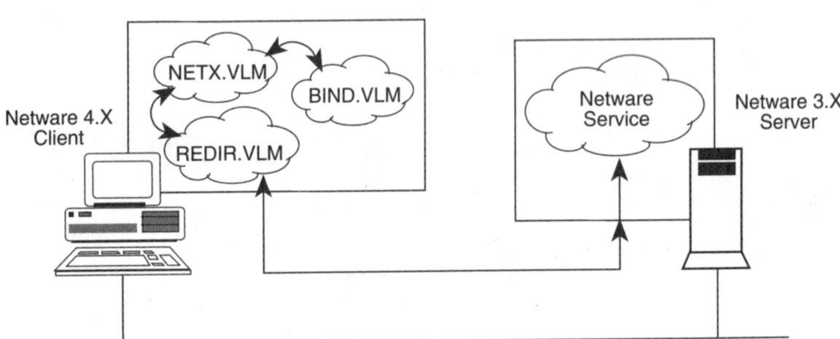

Figure 20.40
Bindery emulation by BIND.VLM.

CONN.VLM

CONN.VLM implements the connection table manager. The connection table manager spans the DOS Redirection Layer, the Service Protocol Layer, and the Transport Layer and is a vital component of the NetWare requester, providing support for all three service layers. CONN.VLM also keeps track of the connections between a DOS Requester and a NetWare server. Examples of information maintained in the table are the connection number, the services and transport protocols used by a connection, and the status of connection.

The number of supported connections can be configured in the range from 2 to 50. Information on the connections is kept in a special connection table (see fig. 20.41) that can be accessed by other VLMs. A number of APIs are provided by CONN.VLM; these APIs give to the caller statistics on connections.

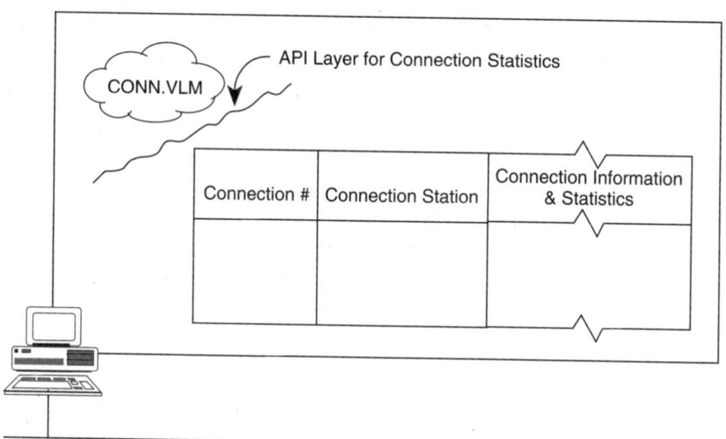

Figure 20.41
The connection table managed by CONN.VLM.

FIO.VLM

FIO.VLM is used to provide the file input/output services. Access to network files that are needed by an application are sent to FIO.VLM via REDIR.VLM (see fig. 20.42). This module implements a local workstation file cache, packet burst support, and Large Internet Packet (LIP) capability.

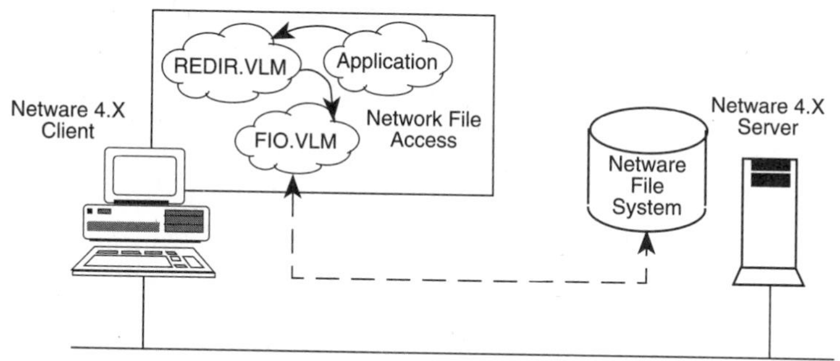

Figure 20.42
The file input/output VLM.

GENERAL.VLM

This VLM implements general services that can be used by other VLMs such as NETX.VLM and REDIR.VLM. Examples of these services are obtaining connection information, managing drive mappings, implementing the different search modes, and supporting long and short machine names.

IPXNCP.VLM

IPXNCP.VLM, a child VLM of the TRAN.VLM multiplexor VLM, is responsible for taking network file requests from the FIO.VLM module and formatting them into the correct NCP requests for delivery to the appropriate ODI communication stack, such as IPXODI.COM (see fig. 20.43). The name IPXNCP for this VLM is perhaps a little misleading, as it seems to suggest that the VLM might

implement both the NCP and the IPX protocol stack. This is not true. The IPX protocol stack is implemented by the appropriate communication stack that is loaded before the VLM Manager, VLM.EXE, is loaded.

Figure 20.43
IPXNCP.VLM processing functions.

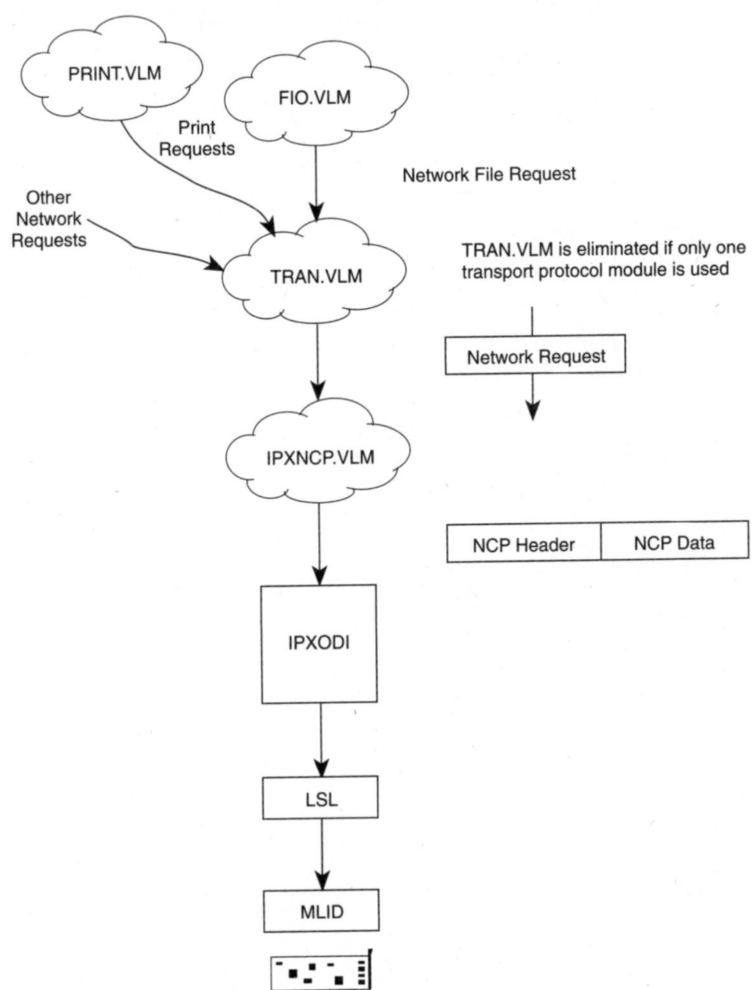

NDS.VLM

NDS.VLM, a child of the multiplexor NWP.VLM, implements the client NetWare Directory Services. In the X.500 model on which NDS is based, a component called the Directory User Agent (DUA) makes requests on behalf of an application for directory services. NDS.VLM is an implementation of the X.500 DUA. NDS.VLM provides access to the NetWare NDS-based server, such as NetWare 4.*x*.

NETX.VLM

NETX.VLM implements the functionality of the NETX.EXE and NETX.COM files that were used with NetWare 3.*x*. That is, NETX.VLM implements the NetWare shell for bindery-based servers. You cannot use the NETX.EXE and NETX.COM programs with VLMs. If used, they conflict with REDIR.VLM and cause the workstation to crash or malfunction.

NETX.VLM has been provided for backward compatibility in supporting applications that might rely on a shell. As mentioned before, the shell intercepts DOS system calls and routes network requests for NCP processing and local requests to DOS system services.

NMR.VLM

NMR.VLM implements the NetWare Management Responder Module. This VLM collects diagnostic information on the workstation environment, which the module can communicate to any requesting application running locally or on the network. Software from Novell or a third party can use this information to provide diagnostic information about the workstation.

The NetWare Management Responder Module is loaded with the DOS Requester but is not part of the DOS Requester. The module makes use of the memory-management functions provided by the *Virtual Memory Manager* (VLM.EXE) to load into memory but operates independently of the NetWare requester functions. NMR.VLM serves as a network management agent that reports on diagnostic information for the workstation (see fig. 20.44). Examples of the information NMR.VLM can gather are workstation network statistics, memory allocation, and other configuration information. It also can report on ODI-related statistics and information.

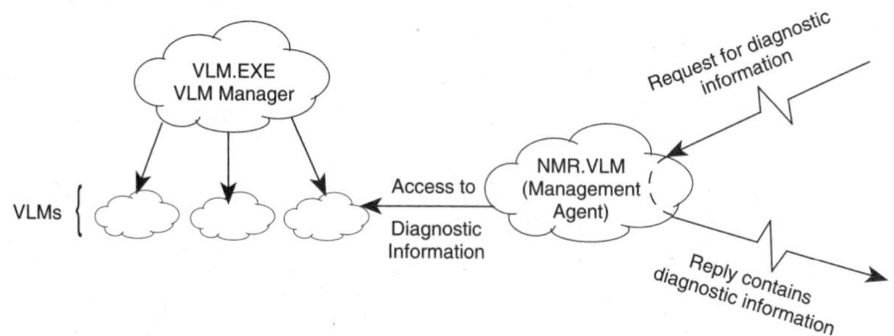

Figure 20.44
The NetWare Management Responder Module.

NWP.VLM

NWP.VLM is the NetWare protocol multiplexor VLM. It directs requests to the appropriate child VLM, such as NDS.VLM, RSA.VLM, BIND.VLM, or PNW.VLM. (PNW.VLM is the Personal NetWare VLM, which provides services to NetWare desktop-based servers.)

NWP.VLM provides access to the appropriate network service via its child VLMs. It is used to provide connections to (log in or out of) NDS-based servers (NetWare 4.*x*), bindery-based servers (NetWare 3.*x*), and NetWare desktop servers.

PRINT.VLM

PRINT.VLM implements the network printing functions. Applications making direct use of network printing, or printing to local printers redirected to network printers (using the CAPTURE command), use PRINT.VLM to submit print jobs.

Printing services are needed for both directory and bindery services. It is the job of PRINT.VLM to provide services for both.

RSA.VLM

This module implements the RSA public-key encryption algorithm. RSA.VLM is used by *NetWare Directory Services* (NDS.VLM) and for background authentication and for the auto-reconnect features provided by AUTO.VLM. RSA.VLM is also available for use by third-party applications.

SECURITY.VLM

SECURITY.VLM implements enhanced security services and is independent of RSA.VLM, which is used to authenticate a network login and validate the resulting connection on an ongoing basis. SECURITY.VLM protects every NCP request by maintaining at the workstation and the server a session state that is a function of the current activity and the past activity on that session. A special signature precedes an NCP packet request. This signature is based on past and prior activity on the session. The receiving station computes the expected signature based on its session state information and compares the signature with the signature found in the received NCP packet. If the signatures do not match, the packet is rejected. The signature is generated using session activity and a 64-bit session key that never crosses the network.

The algorithm used to provide the signature is *Message Digest 4* (MD4). MD4 is used by the Internet protocol suite and is documented in RFC 1320. RFC, which stands for Request for Comment, is the vehicle that is used to publish standards and proposals for new standards for the Internet suite of protocols.

Using SECURITY.VLM might result in a performance degradation. You must balance that risk against the additional security gains that accrue from using the module.

TRAN.VLM

TRAN.VLM is the transport protocol multiplexor, which directs network requests to the appropriate upper-layer protocol-processing module such as IPXNCP.VLM or TCPNCP.VLM. This architecture ensures that adding support for other protocol modules is possible. Network requests are sent from the TRAN.VLM to the appropriate transport protocol used to send the request. The default protocol that is used is IPX. Like the availability of the NetWare IP product, the TCP/IP transport protocol can be used. The IPXNCP.VLM is used to provide a communication path to the PIX protocol, and the TCPNCP.VLM is used to provide a communication link to the TCP/IP transport protocols.

Understanding DOS Client Installation

In earlier NetWare versions, you had to use a program such as WSGEN or SHGEN to provide a communication protocol module IPX.COM that implemented the SPX/IPX stack and was linked to the appropriate network driver. The ODI drivers eliminated the need for static linking by providing a flexible way of binding the protocol stack (such as IPXODI.COM) to the driver.

NetWare 4.*x* provides an install program file (INSTALL.BAT) that you can run to set up the client software in the language of your choice. The language support includes English, French, German, Spanish, and Italian. As you learned in the preceding sections, the NETX shell has been replaced by the Virtual Memory Manager (VLM.EXE), which loads a number of VLMs. The installation program installs the VLMs in the appropriate workstation directories and creates the necessary batch files to load the ODI drivers and protocol stacks and run the VLM.EXE program.

You can install the NetWare DOS Requester from either the CD-ROM or floppy disk distribution. If you are installing from the CD-ROM distribution, you need to go to the \CLIENT\DOSWIN directory on the CD-ROM distribution and type **INSTALL**. If installing from a floppy disk, you need the disks labeled WSDOS-1, WSWIN-1, and WSDRV-2.

If you have only the CD-ROM distribution and want to create the installation floppy disks for network client software, you must run the MAKEDISK command that you can find in the \CLIENT\DOSWIN directory. You must have three blank, preformatted, high-density disks. You also should have the DOS utilities on the search path. The MAKEDISK batch file uses the DOS LABEL command to label the disks that you produce. Use this command:

```
MAKEDISK A: language
```

where *language* is one of the following:

ENGLISH

FRENCH or FRANCAIS

ITALIAN or ITALIANO

GERMAN or DEUTSCH

SPANISH or ESPANOL

The following steps describe the procedure for installing NetWare from floppy disks. Unless a CD-ROM drive is attached to a workstation, this method is perhaps the most common one used for a first-time installation. You also can copy the NetWare workstation client software to a network drive and run the installation program from that drive. The directory structure on the network drive is the same as that on the CD-ROM. You must make the directory in which the client INSTALL program is located your current drive, and then run the INSTALL command.

Follow these steps to install NetWare from floppy disks:

1. Insert the disk labeled NetWare Client DOS/Windows (WSDOS-1) in a floppy drive. Change your current directory to this drive.

2. Run the batch file INSTALL.BAT to start the NetWare client software installation. You then should see a screen on NetWare client installation (see fig. 20.45).

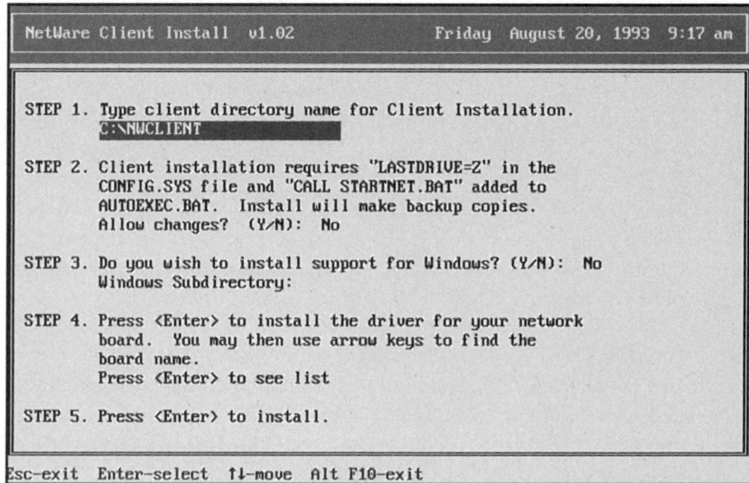

Figure 20.45
The NetWare Client Install screen.

In Step 1, you can change the destination where the client software is installed or select the default destination directory of C:\NWCLIENT. Unless you have a strong preference or reason, using the default name is best, especially if you are installing a number of VLM client installations and want to use a standard convention.

In Step 2, you can allow the installation program to make changes to your CONFIG.SYS and AUTOEXEC.BAT files. If you allow the installation program to make the changes, it adds a LASTDRIVE=Z statement to the CONFIG.SYS file. Ordinarily, you should allow the installation program to make these changes; otherwise, you have to make these changes manually. You cannot then use this file for the NetWare shell (NETX.EXE or NETX.COM) for normal operation. With LASTDRIVE=Z, the NetWare shells assign the next available "drive", which is "[:" as a network drive. In the AUTOEXEC.BAT file, the program adds the following statement:

```
@CALL C:\NWCLIENT\STARTNET
```

(If you use a directory other than NWCLIENT for the client installation, the NWCLIENT in the CALL statement is replaced with the appropriate directory name.)

When you use LASTDRIVE=Z:, the NETX shells take the next available drive, which is "[:". This causes problems and causes the login script to have fits. When you do not use Z: as the LASTDRIVE, the VLM shells still load, but full NETX.VLM capability is not realized. With LASTDRIVE=X in the CONFIG.SYS file, the following message comes up:

```
VLM.EXE   -NetWare virtual loadable module manager v1.02 (930510)
(C) Copyright 1993 Novell, Inc.  All Rights Reserved.
Patent pending.

The VLM.EXE file is pre-initializing the VLMs............
The VLM.EXE file is using extended memory (XMS).
DOS is only configured for 24 drives, NETX.VLM requires 26 drives
for full functionality.  The NETX.VLM file will load with partial
support.
Add LASTDRIVE=Z to the CONFIG.SYS file, reboot the workstation; then
load the NETX.VLM file.
You are attached to server FS1
```

In Step 3, you can choose to install MS Windows support for your workstation. The default directory for MS Windows support is C:\WINDOWS. If your Windows installation is another directory, you have to edit this field and enter the Windows directory.

3. When you are done making changes in Steps 1, 2, and 3, press Enter in Step 4 to install the LAN driver for your workstation network board. You should see a message that prompts you to `Insert the Driver Disk.`

4. Insert the driver disk labeled *NetWare Client DOS/Windows*, and press Enter. You then should see a list of drivers supported on the network (see fig. 20.46).

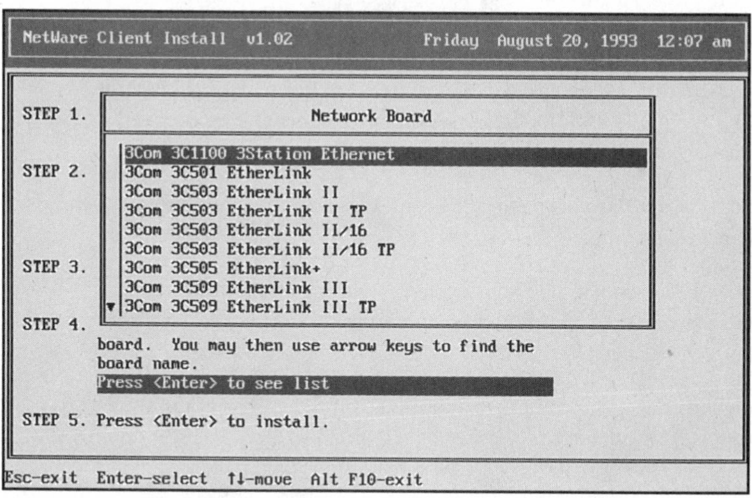

Figure 20.46
NetWare 4.x Client Install: Network boards supported.

If you already have the driver loaded (from a previous installation), the installation program recognizes it and gives you the choice of loading this LAN driver.

5. Select from the list of drivers the driver that matches the NIC in your workstation. You then should see a list of NIC parameters for the board that you have selected. Figure 20.47 shows the default settings for the SMC EtherCard PLUS Family Adapter.

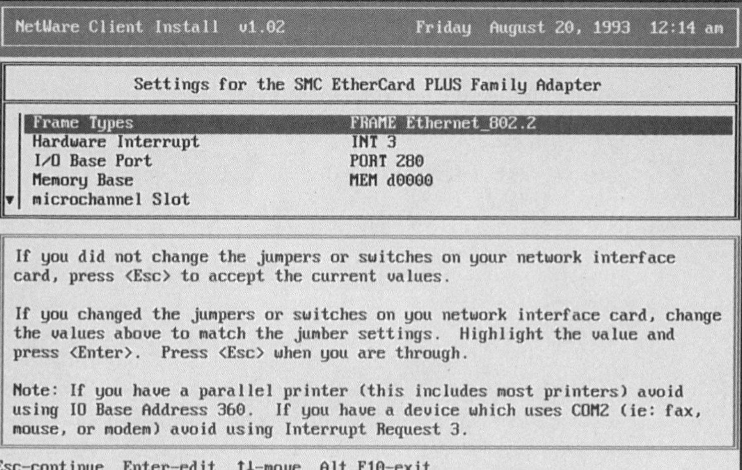

Figure 20.47
NetWare 4.x Client Install: Network board parameters.

6. To change a value of a parameter, highlight it and press Enter. If you do not know the parameter settings for your board, you might have to abort the installation and restart it after you determine the network board settings. You can determine the network board settings by examining the jumper and switch settings (sometimes in consultation with the network board manual) or if your network board ships with a software setup utility, you can use this. Or if you have an IPX.COM and IPXODI.COM installed for your board, you can use IPX I or IPXODI. (Alternatively, examine the NET.CFG file.)

   You should select the correct frame type for the board. Figure 20.48 shows the values that are available for Ethernet frame type.

   The default order of Token Ring frame transmission is that the *Most Significant Bit* (MSB) is transmitted first. Normally, you should not have to change this setting, unless the board vendor recommends this change.

7. After making parameter changes, press Esc to continue. You should be back to the NetWare Client Install screen with the driver selected (see fig. 20.49).

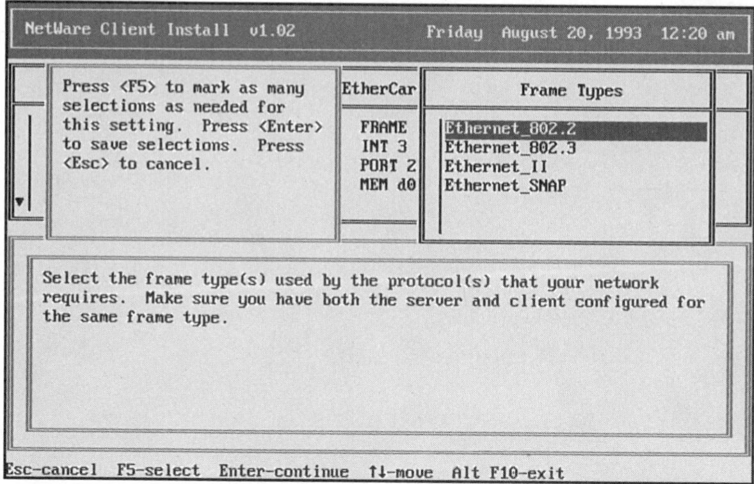

Figure 20.48
NetWare 4.x Client Install: Ethernet frame types.

```
NetWare Client Install  v1.02              Friday  August 20, 1993  12:25 am

STEP 1. Type client directory name for Client Installation.
        C:\NWCLIENT

STEP 2. Client installation requires "LASTDRIVE=Z" in the
        CONFIG.SYS file and "CALL STARTNET.BAT" added to
        AUTOEXEC.BAT.  Install will make backup copies.
        Allow changes?  (Y/N):  No

STEP 3. Do you wish to install support for Windows? (Y/N):  No
        Windows Subdirectory:

STEP 4. Press <Enter> to install the driver for your network
        board.  You may then use arrow keys to find the
        board name.
        SMC EtherCard PLUS Family Adapter

STEP 5. Press <Enter> to install.

Esc-exit  Enter-select  ↑↓-move  Alt F10-exit
```

Figure 20.49
NetWare 4.x Client Install: Shows selected driver.

In Step 5, press Enter to continue with installation.

You next see a status message that the selected driver is being installed, and you are asked to insert the WSDOS-1 disk.

8. Insert the WSDOS-1 disk in the floppy drive and press Enter. You should see a status display of files being copied to the workstation and then a completion message (see fig. 20.50) informing you of the changes that have been made.

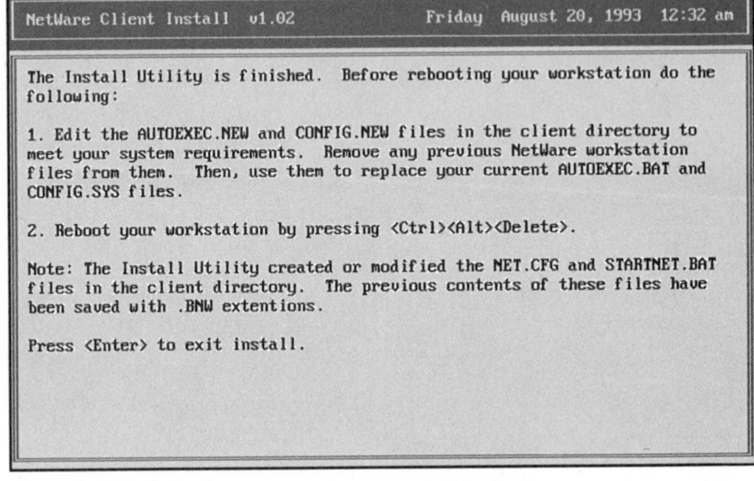

Figure 20.50
NetWare 4.x Client Install: Installation summary.

The changes made to the AUTOEXEC.BAT and CONFIG.SYS files are stored in the AUTOEXEC.NEW and CONFIG.NEW files in the client directory.

9. Edit the files AUTOEXEC.NEW and CONFIG.NEW in the client directory, and reboot the workstation. Samples of AUTOEXEC.NEW and CONFIG.NEW are shown here. Notice that CONFIG.NEW has LASTDRIVE set to Z. The client software is started by the following statement in the AUTOEXEC.NEW file:

```
@CALL C:\NWCLIENT\STARTNET
```

AUTOEXEC.NEW:

```
@CALL C:\NWCLIENT\STARNET
@ECHO OFF
PROMPT $P$G
C:\WIN\SMARTDRV.EXE
PATH C:\HJWIN;c:\hj2;c:\bin;c:\windows;c:\scsi
doskey
set FTP_ETC=c:\pctcp\etc
set NSE_DOWNLOAD=D:\DOWNLOAD
SET TEMP=C:\WINDOWS\TEMP
```

CONFIG.NEW:

```
DEVICE=C:\DOS\SETVER.exe
DEVICE=C:\scsi\ASPI4DOS.SYS
DEVICE=C:\scsi\ASWCDSNY.SYS /D:ASPICDO
files=50
buffers=50
DEVICE=C:\WINDOWS\HIMEM.SYS
shell=command.com /p /e:800
DEVICE=C:\WINDOWS\SMARTDRV.EXE /DOUBLE_BUFFER
STACKS=9,256
LASTDRIVE=Z
```

Optimizing Workstation Memory

You might want to use the LOADHIGH commands to load some of the TSRs high. For instance, you might try the following sequence in the STARTNET.BAT file:

```
@ECHO OFF
C:
CD \NWCLIENT
SET NWLANGUAGE=ENGLISH    (Replace ENGLISH with the language of choice)
LOADHIGH LSL
LOADHIGH SMC8000           (Replace with name of your ODI driver)
LOADHIGH IPXODI
VLM
CD \
```

You might also try running MEMAKER for MS-DOS 6.*x* and above to see how memory optimization can be done.

Using VLM Options

You can load the VLM Manager with a number of interesting options. These options are reminiscent of the options that are used in the NETX shell program, but new options have been added also.

You can conveniently display the list of available options by typing this command:

```
VLM /?
```

The following listing shows the help messages displayed when you execute the VLM /? command:

```
VLM.EXE      - NetWare virtual loadable module manager  v1.02 (930510)
(C) Copyright 1993 Novell, Inc.  All Rights Reserved.
Patent pending.
Available command line options:
/?     Display this help screen.
/U     Unload the VLM.EXE file from memory
/C=[path\]filename.ext
       Specify a configuration file to use (Default is NET.CFG).
/Mx    The memory type the VLM.EXE file uses where x is one of the following:
       C = Conventional memory.
       X = Extended memory (XMS).
       E = Expanded memory (EMS).
/D     Display the VLM.EXE file diagnostics.
/PS=<server name>
       Preferred server name to attach to during load.
/PT=<tree name>
       Preferred tree name to attach to during load.
/Vx    The detail level of message display where x is one of the following:
       0 = Display copyright and critical errors only.
       1 = Also display warning messages.
```

```
2 = Also display VLM module names.
3 = Also display configuration file parameters.
4 = Also display diagnostics messages.
```

Unloading VLM.EXE

If you do not have TSRs loaded after loading VLM.EXE, you can unload VLM.EXE by typing this command:

```
VLM /U
```

If the VLM Manager thinks that it is unsafe to unload itself, it does not unload and displays a warning message instead.

Specifying the Configuration File

When VLM.EXE loads, it looks for configuration information in the NET.CFG file. Specifically, it looks for the NetWare DOS Requester section of the NET.CFG file and processes configuration statements in that section. Earlier, you saw examples of the statements USE DEFAULTS=ON and USE DEFAULTS=OFF, which you can use to enable or disable the default load order.

You can use the /C option to specify another configuration file besides the default NET.CFG. If you want to specify the configuration file C:\CONFIG\STAND.CFG, for example, use the command

```
VLM  /C=C:\CONFIG\STAND.CFG
```

Specifying the Memory Type

You can load the VLMs in conventional, extended, or expanded memory. To load in extended and expanded memory, you should have the appropriate extended and expanded memory drivers loaded.

To load in extended memory, use the command

```
VLM /MX
```

To load in expanded memory, use the command

```
VLM /ME
```

To load in conventional memory (default), use the command

```
VLM /MC
```

The DOS Requester uses the LIM XMS 2.0 specification. When VLM.EXE loads, it selects XMS memory by default, unless the /M*x* switch is used to specify a different memory. If it is unable to use XMS, it tries to use EMS. The EMS driver must be loaded for the EMS option to work. If VLM.EXE is not able to use EMS, it uses conventional memory. You can use the DOS LOADHIGH statement to load VLM.EXE in high memory, but there is no special built-in parameter to provide this.

Indicating the First Network Drive

When the VLM loads, it attaches to the nearest server. It does this by issuing a GetNearestServer SAP (Service Advertising Protocol) request, and waiting for all NetWare servers to respond. The VLM then connects to the server that was returned in the first GiveNearestServer SAP response. Next, the VLM attaches the next available drive in the workstation's drive table to the SYS:LOGIN volume of this server (see fig. 20.51).

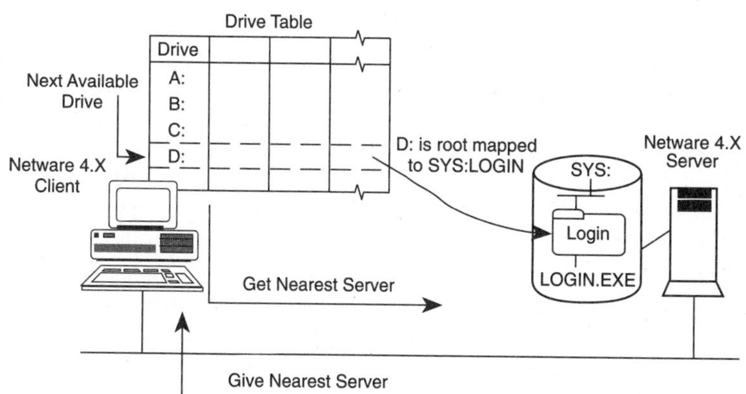

Figure 20.51
Attaching the network drive to SYS:LOGIN.

The SYS:LOGIN directory contains a number of programs that can be used to access the network. Some of the main programs are LOGIN.EXE, CX.EXE, and NLIST.EXE. Also, OS/2 workstations can use a subdirectory called OS2 in SYS:LOGIN to connect to the network. To maintain compatibility with the NETX behavior, you can specify the first network drive to be used in the NetWare DOS Requester section by adding this statement under the NetWare DOS Requester section:

```
FIRST NETWORK DRIVE=F
```

Without this statement, the next available drive D is mapped to SYS:LOGIN. For instance, if the FIRST NETWORK DRIVE parameter is not specified, the next available drive depends on what devices are in use. If you have a hard drive set up as C: and a CD-ROM unit set up as D:, you would get E: as the first network drive.

After the network drive attaches to SYS:LOGIN, you must change the current drive to the attached network drive and type the LOGIN command. Thus, the typical login sequence is

```
F:
LOGIN  SpecifyLoginName
```

You can place all these commands in a batch file for automation.

Specifying the Initial Server

If you want to specify the server to which you want to log in initially, you must use the preferred server (/PS) option. If you want to log in to the server FS1, for instance, you must use the following command:

```
VLM /PS=FS1
```

The /PS option works in a similar manner to the preferred option for the NETX shell. You also can use the PREFERRED SERVER parameter in the NET.CFG file. This parameter is primarily meant for clients who use BIND.VLM rather than NDS.VLM. For a NetWare 4.*x* client, an initial connection is made to the preferred server. If this server happens to be a NetWare 4.*x* server, an attachment to the preferred tree is made.

Specifying a Preferred Tree

In a NetWare 4.*x* network, multiple NetWare Directory Service trees are possible. Most organizations prefer having a single tree because of the difficulty in restructuring and merging trees; and also because a single tree meets the needs of complex organizational structures. In some situations, however, multiple NDS trees might be useful, perhaps for security reasons so that you can prohibit information exchange between two NDS trees. Another reason could be the establishment of an experimental NDS tree on a production network that already has an NDS tree in use. Many system administrators might want to work with an experimental network to learn about structuring an NDS tree before making these changes on a production network.

Using the preferred tree (/PT) option gives you a choice of connecting to a particular tree. If you want to connect to an experimental NDS tree called EXPNET, for instance, use the following command:

```
VLM /PT=EXPNET
```

To connect to a production network called CNET, you might want to unload the VLM and reconnect. You thus would use these commands, the first to unload, and the second to connect to the CNET tree:

```
VLM  /U
VLM  /PT=CNET
```

You also can use the PREFERRED TREE=*treeName* option in the NET.CFG file to specify a preferred tree option.

Requesting Messages

During the loading of the VLM, you can obtain important messages relating to warning, error, and diagnostic information. These messages can provide a valuable diagnostic aid when you are trying to figure out the load order of the VLMs.

The general command for loading VLMs with different verbosity levels for messages is

```
VLM /Vx
```

in which *x* is a number from 0 to 4.

If you want to display copyright and critical error messages only, use the following command to load the VLMs:

```
VLM /V0
```

If in addition to copyright and critical error messages you want to display warning messages, use the following command to load the VLMs:

```
VLM /V1
```

If in addition to copyright, critical error messages, and warning messages, you want to display the names of the VLM modules as they load, use the following command to load the VLMs:

```
VLM /V2
```

If in addition to copyright, critical error messages, warning messages, and names of the VLMs as they load, you want to display configuration file parameters, use the following command to load the VLMs:

```
VLM /V3
```

If in addition to copyright, critical error messages, warning messages, names of the VLMs as they load, and configuration file parameters, you want to display diagnostic information, use the following command to load the VLMs:

```
VLM /V4
```

The following sample listing shows the messages produced when you load the VLM with a /V3 option:

```
C:\NWCLIENT> VLM /V3
VLM.EXE       - NetWare virtual loadable module manager  v1.02 (930510)
(C) Copyright 1993 Novell, Inc.  All Rights Reserved.
Patent pending.
The VLM.EXE file is pre-initializing the VLMs............
The VLM.EXE file is using conventional memory.
CONN.VLM      - NetWare connection table manager  v1.02 (930510)
IPXNCP.VLM    - NetWare IPX transport module  v1.02 (930510)
TRAN.VLM      - NetWare transport multiplexor module  v1.02 (930510)
SECURITY.VLM  - NetWare security enhancement module  v1.02 (930510)
NDS.VLM       - NetWare directory services protocol module  v1.02 (930510)
BIND.VLM      - NetWare bindery protocol module  v1.02 (930510)
NWP.VLM       - NetWare protocol multiplexor module  v1.02 (930510)
FIO.VLM       - NetWare file input-output module  v1.02 (930510)
GENERAL.VLM   - NetWare general purpose function module v1.02 (930510)
FIRST NETWORK DRIVE F
REDIR.VLM     - NetWare DOS redirector module  v1.02 (930510)
PRINT.VLM     - NetWare printer redirection module  v1.02 (930510)
NETX.VLM      - NetWare workstation shell module  v4.00 (930510)
FIRST NETWORK DRIVE F
```

Obtaining VLM Diagnostic Information

After you have loaded the VLM Manager, you can obtain diagnostic information on it by running VLM with the diagnose option (/D). Many of the numbers displayed (especially those in columns) are expressed as hexadecimal numbers, as you can see in the following example:

```
F:\> VLM  /D
VLM.EXE      - NetWare virtual loadable module manager  v1.01 (930402)
(C) Copyright 1993 Novell, Inc.  All Rights Reserved.
Patent pending.

The VLM.EXE file v1.1  is currently loaded
VLM transient switch count : 2766
VLM call count             : 24596
VLM current ID             : 0040h
VLM memory type            : XMS
VLM modules loaded count   : 14
VLM block ID (0 if CON)    : A908h
VLM transient block        : 2D10h
VLM global seg (0 if CON)  : 2411h
VLM async queue (h, t, s)  : 0000:0000, 2320:0030, 0
VLM busy queue (h, t, s)   : 0000:0000, 2320:003C, 0
VLM re-entrance level      : 1
VLM full map count         : 2764

VLM Control Block information      Address   TMemSize  GMemSize  SMemSize
ID   Flag Func Maps Call TSeg GSeg Low  High Para K    Para K    Para K
---- ---- ---- ---- ---- ---- ---- ---- ---- ---- ---- ---- ---- ---- ----
0001 A000 0005 0000 2078 2320 08FE FFFF FFFF 0100 0004 0000 0000 0000 0000
0010 B000 0011 0000 1461 2411 24B4 FFFF FFFF 00A3 0002 000F 0000 01AE 0006
0021 B000 000B 0000 01B9 24C3 25A7 FFFF FFFF 00E4 0003 00A2 0002 0066 0001
0020 E000 000B 0001 0362 24C3 25A7 FFFF FFFF 00E4 0003 00A2 0002 0066 0001
0061 A000 0005 0036 0035 2D10 2649 0000 0000 0101 0004 0000 0000 00D2 0003
0032 A000 0010 010A 0139 2D10 2649 1010 0000 0170 0005 00B9 0002 003E 0000
0031 A000 0010 0037 0036 2D10 2702 2710 0000 00B6 0002 001C 0000 002D 0000
0034 A000 0005 0035 0034 2D10 271E 3270 0000 03C3 0015 00C1 0003 0022 0000
0030 A000 0011 007E 0066 2D10 27DF 6EA0 0000 00B0 0002 0071 0001 0048 0001
0041 A000 000B 0057 0099 2D10 2850 79A0 0000 0197 0006 0282 0010 002B 0000
0043 A000 000A 00D3 00E4 2D10 2AD2 9310 0000 006B 0001 001E 0000 0050 0001
0040 A000 0009 045B 1656 2D10 2AF0 99C0 0000 0233 0008 0063 0001 004A 0001
0042 A000 000E 004B 005B 2D10 2B53 BCF0 0000 00D9 0003 00AC 0002 0059 0001
0050 A000 0007 029B 0B7C 2D10 2BFF CA80 0000 0213 0008 00EE 0003 007D 0001
0060 A000 0006 0038 0035 2D10 2CED EBB0 0000 0084 0002 0022 0000 0041 0001
Total                                        11C6      0777
Maximum                                      03C3      0282      01AE
```

Explanations of the diagnostic information follow in the next several sections.

VLM Transient Switch Count

When the VLMs have been loaded in expanded and extended memory, the VLM Manager might swap the VLMs into a temporary area of memory called the *transient switch block*. As it does so, the VLM

Manager keeps track of the number of times this switch takes place for the different modules. The switch count for the individual VLM modules is reported in the Maps column under VLM control block information. The total for all the VLMs is reported in the VLM transient switch-count parameter at the top of the screen.

The transient switch block takes up about 8.4 KB of conventional memory.

VLM Call Count

The VLM Manager facilitates the interaction between the different VLMs and keeps track of the number of times it has to call the different VLMs. The number of times an individual VLM is called is shown in the Call column under VLM control block information. The total VLM count for all the VLMs is reported in the VLM call count parameter at the top of the screen.

You can use the entries in the Call column to estimate the most frequently used VLMs. Under heavy usage, however, this number can roll over. For this reason, you need to exercise care in monitoring these numbers frequently before making an estimate on the most frequently used VLMs.

VLMs are reported by a VLM ID, which is in the leftmost column of the diagnostic information screen. Refer to table 20.19 in the next section to find out the correspondence between VLM ID and the VLM name.

You can use the VLM call count to estimate how the VLMs at a particular workstation are used. This information could be useful if you are trying to reduce workstation memory usage by determining which VLMs are not used.

VLM Current ID

The VLM current ID indicates the VLM that is currently loaded in the VLM transient swap block area. Each of the VLMs has an internal ID representation, which is listed in table 20.19.

Table 20.19
VLM ID Table

VLM ID	VLM Name
01	VLM.EXE (the VLM Manager)
10	CONN.VLM
20	TRAN.VLM
21	IPXNCP.VLM
22	TCPNCP.VLM

continues

Table 20.19, Continued
VLM ID Table

VLM ID	VLM Name
30	NWP.VLM
31	BIND.VLM
32	NDS.VLM
33	PNW.VLM
34	RSA.VLM
40	REDIR.VLM
41	FIO.VLM
42	PRINT.VLM
43	GENERAL.VLM
50	NETX.VLM
60	AUTO.VLM
61	SECURITY.VLM
100	NMR.VLM

You can use the VLM ID column to determine the VLMs that are loaded in memory. AUTO.VLM, for example, is an optional VLM that reestablishes a connection with a NetWare server if the server was downed unexpectedly and is brought up again. To determine whether the AUTO.VLM feature has been loaded, you would examine the VLM ID column for the VLM ID code of 60. Similarly, to find out whether the SECURITY.VLM module that implements the NCP packet signatures (using MD4 algorithm) has been loaded, you would scan for the VLM ID code of 61.

VLM Memory Type

As you know, the VLM Manager can use conventional, extended, and expanded memory. If you want to know the memory type that is in use at a workstation, look at the VLM memory-type parameter. This examination is important to determine whether the workstation is using the memory type that you intended. A value of CON indicates that conventional memory is being used, XMS indicates that extended memory is used, and EMS indicates that expanded memory is being used.

Normally, you specify the memory type by using this command:

```
VLM  /Mx
```

where *x* is C (Conventional), E (Expanded), or X (Extended). If the workstation has not been configured correctly, you might not be able to load the VLMs in the intended memory type. With DOS 5.*x* and above, for instance, the following statements in CONFIG.SYS load the expanded memory manager EMM386.SYS and tell DOS to manage the *Upper Memory Block* (UMB):

```
DEVICE=C:\DOS\HIMEM.SYS
DEVICE=C:\DOS\EMM386.SYS
DOS=UMB
```

Many system administrators prefer to load DOS in high memory, so they also specify the last statement to be:

```
DOS=HIGH,UMB
```

If you are using DR DOS 6.*x* (or Novell DOS), you do not need to include the HIMEM.SYS driver because the DR DOS memory manager EMM386.SYS provides the management functions of HIMEM.SYS. To load DOS in high memory, however, you must use this command to place DOS in high memory and use the upper memory blocks:

```
HIDOS=ON
```

VLM Modules Loaded Count

This number indicates the number of VLMs that have been loaded. To determine the individual VLMs that have been loaded, you must use the VLM ID codes and table 20.19. Options in the NET.CFG file enable you to control the VLMs that are loaded. If you have changed the default order or number of VLMs that have been loaded, you can use the diagnostic screen to check whether any of the VLMs failed to load.

VLM Block ID

This ID is the enhanced memory handle used for the expanded and extended memory managers. Its primary use is for debugging by software development engineers when writing VLM program code.

The VLM block ID is always 0 for conventional memory because no handle is associated with conventional memory.

VLM Transient Block

The VLM transient block shows the start of the transient block memory area, which is used to swap VLMs. You can use this number for debugging purposes to obtain offsets for code and data in VLMs that are being debugged.

The transient block start is shown in paragraphs, with a paragraph being 16 bytes. Thus you must append a hexadecimal 0 digit to the value to get the start of the transient block as a byte address.

The VLM Manager tries to allocate the transient block area in upper memory. If unable to do so, the VLM Manager allocates the transient memory block in conventional memory. The transient block must be allocated as a contiguous block of memory; it cannot be split for purposes of memory allocation.

The transient block is about 8.4 KB in size.

VLM Global Seg

The VLM global seg parameter shows the start of the global memory area. Programmers use this number for debugging.

The global memory start area is shown in paragraphs, with a paragraph being 16 bytes. Thus you must append a hexadecimal 0 digit to the value to get the start of the global block as a byte address.

The VLM Manager tries to allocate the global block area in upper memory. If unable to do so, the VLM Manager allocates the global memory in conventional memory. The global area must be allocated as a contiguous block of memory; it cannot be split for purposes of memory allocation.

The global memory is used by the VLMs for allocating data and as a means of sharing global variables.

The global block is about 22 KB in size.

VLM Async Queue (h, t, s) and VLM Busy Queue (h, t, s)

These queues are used by VLMs to represent lists of data structures and are primarily needed by programmers. In computer science, a *queue* is a method of organizing data for easy access. Figure 20.52 shows an example of a queue. The queue is described by a pair of values called the head (h) and the tail (t). The size (s) field is not essential for describing the queue, but having this value along with the head and tail values is convenient because it quickly describes the number of data elements that make up the queue (see fig. 20.53).

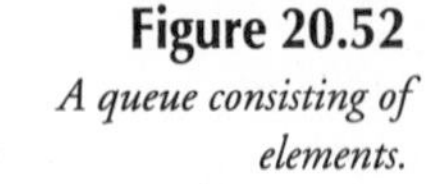

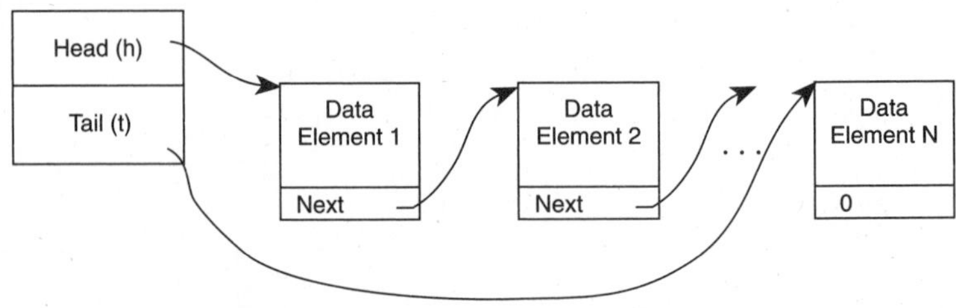

Figure 20.52
A queue consisting of elements.

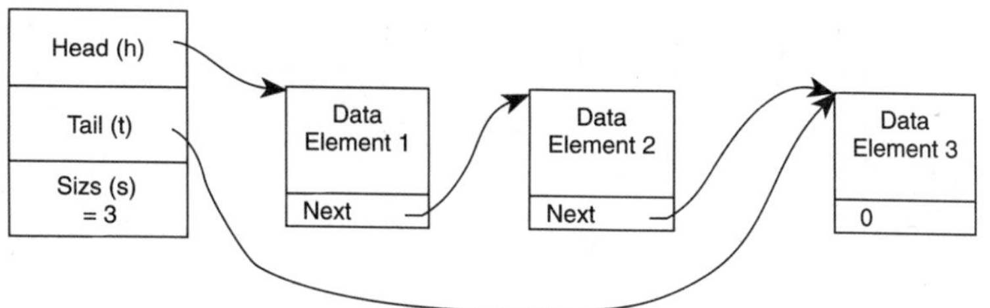

Figure 20.53
A queue with the size parameter information included.

The normal status of the VLM async and VLM busy queues is that they should be empty. Data elements entered in the queues are processed quickly, so by the time you type the command VLM /D to obtain diagnostic information, these queues should be empty. If the queue appears to be non-empty, it indicates a problem with some date elements being orphaned or unprocessed.

A legitimate question to ask, then, is "What constitutes an empty queue?" In figure 20.54, you can see that an empty queue must have a zero value for the size (s) parameter. Because no elements are in an empty queue, the head (h) pointer should also have a zero value. The tail pointer for an empty queue is initially set to point to the structure containing the head pointer. Thus the normal values of the VLM async queue (h, t, s) and VLM busy queue (h, t, s) are for the head (h) to have the value of a null pointer, represented as 0000:0000; the size (s) of the queue to be 0; and the tail to have a non-zero pointer value, expressed as *ssss:xxxx*, where at least one of the *ssss* or *xxxx* values is non-zero.

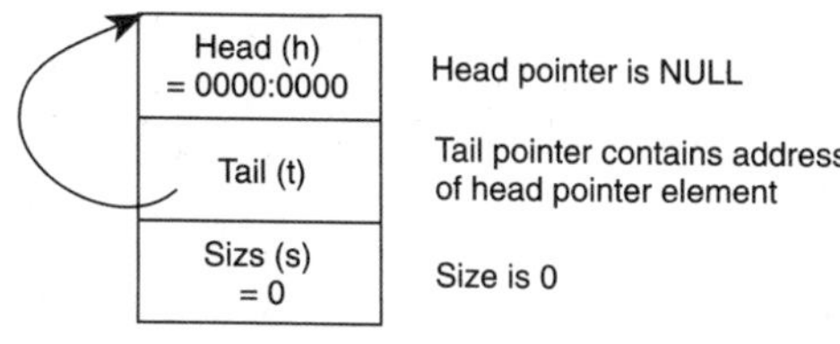

Figure 20.54
An empty queue.

VLM Re-entrance Level

When a multiple-level request is performed, the VLM Manager keeps track of its nesting level, using the VLM re-entrance parameter. If the value of this parameter is different from 1, it indicates that one or more VLMs is misbehaving. This problem could happen if a VLM receives a request to perform a specific function but never returns from processing the request. In any case, the re-entrance parameter serves as an indication of a problem with the VLMs. You also might want to check the VLM async and VLM busy queues for a non-empty status as a further indication of a related problem.

VLM Full Map Count

The VLM full map count indicates the number of VLM "map out" requests. A "map out" occurs if a memory block that is needed is in expanded or extended memory and must be brought back into the transient block area. Because the VLM transient switch count parameter keeps track of the number of times the VLM Manager swapped modules into the transient switch block area, the VLM full map count should be close to this number.

If all the VLMs are loaded in conventional memory, no interaction should occur with extended or expanded memory, and the full map count number should be 0.

VLM Control Block Information

The VLM control block information section of the diagnostics display screen contains additional information about the VLMs. As you might remember, you learned earlier in this section that the first column indicates the IDs for the VLMs that are loaded. (Table 20.19 lists the VLM ID codes.) The rest of the columns in the diagnostics display are discussed in the following paragraphs.

Flag

The Flag column contains codes for the status of VLMs. A code of A000 indicates that the corresponding VLM is valid and is loaded. A status code of B000 indicates that the VLM is valid and loaded in low memory. A status code of E000 indicates that the VLM is valid and loaded, but its function is subsumed by another VLM. An example of this situation is the multiplexor VLM TRAN.VLM, which is not needed if only one child VLM, IPXNCP.VLM, exists. In this case, the input to TRAN.VLM is diverted to IPXNCP.VLM, and the TRAN.VLM is not needed because this service is provided directly by IPXNCP.VLM.

Func

The Func column indicates the number of functions that are available for calling that particular VLM. VLM functions are numbered and can be called by a call-by-number interface.

Maps

The Maps column indicates how often the specified VLM needs to be mapped into memory. A VLM needs to be loaded in conventional or upper memory to be executed.

Call

The Call column indicates how often a VLM was called. You can use this information to make decisions about unloading VLMs that are not needed. You should heed two caveats concerning the Call column:

- Heavily used VLMs have their counter reset to zero (they roll over) quite often.
- Multiplexor VLMs might not show a count that is incremented, but they are needed for routing a VLM request.

Examples of VLMs that you could unload are AUTO.VLM, PRINT.VLM, NETX.VLM, NMR.VLM, SECURITY.VLM, NDS.VLM, and BIND.VLM. (Keep in mind that one of the two VLMs, NDS.VLM or BIND.VLM, must be loaded for the VLMs to work.)

TSeg and GSeg

The TSeg column shows the transient segment for the VLM, and the GSeg column shows the global segment. These segments refer to temporary areas of memory and global memory areas, respectively.

Address Low/High

Address Low/High takes up two columns in the middle of the screen. These values indicate the memory location of the transient memory for VLM.EXE and the VLMs.

A value of FFFF indicates that the VLM is loaded in conventional memory. Any other value indicates that the VLM is loaded in extended or expanded memory. If the VLM is loaded in EMS memory, the Low column indicates the EMS handle, and the High column indicates the EMS logical page. If the VLM is loaded in XMS memory, the Low and High columns together indicate the relative 32-bit (D-Word) address in extended memory.

TMemSize Para/K

The numbers in this column represent the transient memory size for each of the VLMs that have been loaded. Different VLMs, because of differences in size, can be expected to have different needs for transient memory. The transient block that gets allocated depends on the size of the largest TMemSize value for a VLM.

The memory size is shown in two columns titled Para and K. The Para column shows the memory size in paragraphs, where a paragraph is 16 bytes. The K column shows the memory size in kilobytes, but the value is truncated and not rounded (as you might expect). Thus a memory size of 4.8 KB is reported as 4 and not 5. If you want to get the memory size in exact kilobytes (where 1 KB = 1,024 bytes), you must multiply the value in the Para column by 16 and divide the result by 1,024.

In the listing of VLM /D presented previously, the largest-sized transient block is for the VLM with the code of 34, and the next highest is code 40. Using table 20.19, you can see that this code 34 refers to RSA.VLM and code 40 refers to REDIR.VLM. RSA.VLM is optional. If this is not loaded, the largest-sized transient block is used by REDIR.VLM.

The RSA.VLM transient block size is 3C3 paragraphs, or 3C30 bytes (multiplying a hexadecimal number by 16 is equivalent to adding a 0 at the end). This value works out to a size of 15,408 bytes, computed as follows:

3C30 = 3*4,096 + C*256 + 3*16 + 0*1

= 3*4,096 + 12*256 + 3*16 + 0*1

= 15,408 bytes

GMemSize Para/K

The GMemSize value is the global memory size for each of the VLMs that have been loaded. Different VLMs can be expected to have different needs for global memory. The global block that gets allocated depends on the sum of the global data area requirements of all the VLMs.

The memory size is shown in two columns titled Para and K. The Para column shows the memory size in paragraphs, where a paragraph is 16 bytes. The K column shows the memory size in kilobytes, but the value is truncated and not rounded (as you might expect). Thus a memory size of 4.8 KB is reported as 4 and not 5. If you want to get the memory size in exact kilobytes (where 1 KB = 1,024 bytes), you must multiply the value in the Para column by 16 and divide the result by 1,024.

The bottom of the screen should show the sum of the entries in each column and the maximum valued entry. Typically, the largest-sized global block is for the VLM with the code of 41. Using table 5.3, you can see that this code refers to FIO.VLM. The FIO.VLM global block size is 282 paragraphs or 2,820 bytes (multiplying a hexadecimal number by 16 is equivalent to adding a 0 at the end). This value works out to a size of 10,272 bytes, computed as follows:

$$2830 = 2 \times 4{,}096 + 8 \times 256 + 2 \times 16 + 0 \times 1 = 10{,}272 \text{ bytes}$$

The sum of the global data areas is 777 paragraphs or 7,770 bytes, which computes to 30,576 bytes as follows:

$$7{,}770 = 7 \times 4{,}096 + 7 \times 256 + 7 \times 16 + 0 \times 1 = 30{,}576 \text{ bytes}$$

SMemSize Para/K

The SMemSize is the start memory size for each of the VLMs that have been loaded. The start memory size is the initial size for the loaded VLMs.

The memory size is shown in two columns titled Para and K. The Para column shows the memory size in paragraphs, where a paragraph is 16 bytes. The K column shows the memory size in kilobytes, but the value is truncated and not rounded (as you might expect). Thus a memory size of 4.8 KB is reported as 4 and not 5. If you want to get the memory size in exact kilobytes (where 1 KB = 1,024 bytes), you must multiply the value in the Para column by 16 and divide the result by 1,024.

Exploring New NET.CFG Options

NET.CFG is a text file that contains configuration statements dealing with configuring the ODI driver, providing the binding between the communication protocol and the ODI driver and the NetWare requester. A new section called the NetWare DOS Requester has been defined for the NetWare 4.*x* clients. You need to indent the configuration statements under the NetWare DOS Requester heading at least two spaces.

Table 20.20 shows the configuration statements in the NetWare
NET.CFG file. The parameters in table 20.20 are indented ur
NET.CFG file. A sample NET.CFG file, used by the author i

```
Link Driver CEODI
    FRAME Ethernet_802.2        ; Used by NW4.
    FRAME Ethernet_802.3        ; Compatibilit
    FRAME Ethernet_II            ; For TCP/IP
    INT              5        ; Interrupt
    PORT            300        ; I/O Port base add
    MEM            d0000        ; Base memory address
    SOCKET        1        ;  Specific to PCMCIA catd
    IOWORDSIZE     16              ;  Specific to PCMCIA catd
    SOCKETSERVICES     Y        ;  Specific to PCMCIA catd
    CARDSERVICES     Y        ;  Specific to PCMCIA catd

Protocol IPX
    bind 1          ; Bind to ETHERNET_802.3
                ; Also default binding, if not specified

NetWare DOS Requester
;    LARGE INTERNET PACKETS=ON ; Default is ON
;    SIGNATURE LEVEL=1          ; Default signature level is 1
    PB BUFFERS=4          ; Default is 3. 4 provides best thoughput for me
    FIRST NETWORK DRIVE = F
    PREFERRED TREE = CNET
    PREFERRED SERVER = NW4KS
    NAME CONTEXT = "OU=CORP.O=ESL"
    MESSAGE LEVEL = 4         ; Highest level verbosity on loading
    AVERAGE NAME LENGTH = 15 ; Limit server name (2-48) to 15 characters
    CONNECTIONS = 5    ; Save space by limiting connections (2-50)
    LOCAL PRINTERS=9
    USE DEFAULTS=OFF
    VLM = CONN.VLM
    VLM = IPXNCP.VLM
    VLM = TRAN.VLM
    VLM = SECURITY.VLM
    VLM = NDS.VLM
    VLM = BIND.VLM
    VLM = RSA.VLM    ; Not loaded by DEFAULT
    VLM = NWP.VLM
    VLM = FIO.VLM
    VLM = GENERAL.VLM
    VLM = REDIR.VLM
    VLM = PRINT.VLM
    VLM = NETX.VLM
    VLM = AUTO.VLM    ; Not loaded by DEFAULT - Requires RSA.VLM
```

Also, the more common and useful statements in the NET.CFG file are discussed in more detail, next.

Table 20.20
NetWare DOS Requester NET.CFG Parameters

arameter	Used By	Description
Auto Reconnect = [ON|OFF]	auto.vlm nds.vlm nwp.vlm	AUTO.VLM must be loaded for this parameter to be effective. When set to ON (default value), AUTO will attempt to reconnect to the server if there is a break in the network connection. After AUTO reconnects to the server, it will reauthenticate the client, and if necessary, rebuild the client environment. AUTO makes use of RSA.VLM to reauthenticate the client. AUTO.VLM requires that RSA.VLM be loaded. When set to OFF, AUTO will not attempt to reconnect to the server. You may wish to set the value to OFF to eliminate network traffic due to AUTO.VLM's attempt to reconnect to the server.
Average Name Length=*n*	conn.vlm	This specifies the average name length of the server name. The DOS Requester uses this parameter and the CONNECTIONS parameter to determine the memory it needs to set aside for a connection table. The value can range from 2 to 48 characters and has a default of 48 characters. If you use short server names, you can save some memory by setting this parameter to the average name length for your servers.
Cache Buffers=*n*	fio.vlm	This sets the number of cache buffers the DOS Requester uses for caching non-shared, non-transactional files at the workstation. Only non-shared, non-transactional files can be cached at the workstation, because if a file is shared or transactional, it's data must be cached at the server for other clients to share the file data. Also, transactional tracking is implemented at the server and not at the workstation. The value can range from 0 to 64 cache blocks and has a default value of 5. Increasing the number of cache buffers increases the processing speed for files accessed sequentially, but also increases memory usage. You can reduce this parameter to decrease memory usage. The size of the cache buffers is set by the Cache Buffer Size parameter.

Table 20.20 shows the configuration statements in the NetWare DOS Requester section of the NET.CFG file. The parameters in table 20.20 are indented under the NetWare Requester Section in the NET.CFG file. A sample NET.CFG file, used by the author for his workstation, is shown below:

```
Link Driver CEODI
    FRAME Ethernet_802.2        ; Used by NW4.x
    FRAME Ethernet_802.3        ; Compatibility with NW 3.11 and earlier
    FRAME Ethernet_II            ; For TCP/IP support for PC/TCP package
    INT              5        ; Interrupt
    PORT            300        ; I/O Port base address
    MEM            d0000        ; Base memory address
    SOCKET        1        ;  Specific to PCMCIA catd
    IOWORDSIZE     16            ;  Specific to PCMCIA catd
    SOCKETSERVICES    Y        ;  Specific to PCMCIA catd
    CARDSERVICES    Y        ;  Specific to PCMCIA catd

Protocol IPX
    bind 1        ; Bind to ETHERNET_802.3
                ; Also default binding, if not specified

NetWare DOS Requester
;    LARGE INTERNET PACKETS=ON ; Default is ON
;    SIGNATURE LEVEL=1          ; Default signature level is 1
    PB BUFFERS=4          ; Default is 3. 4 provides best thoughput for me
    FIRST NETWORK DRIVE = F
    PREFERRED TREE = CNET
    PREFERRED SERVER = NW4KS
    NAME CONTEXT = "OU=CORP.O=ESL"
    MESSAGE LEVEL = 4          ; Highest level verbosity on loading
    AVERAGE NAME LENGTH = 15 ; Limit server name (2-48) to 15 characters
    CONNECTIONS = 5    ; Save space by limiting connections (2-50)
    LOCAL PRINTERS=9
    USE DEFAULTS=OFF
    VLM = CONN.VLM
    VLM = IPXNCP.VLM
    VLM = TRAN.VLM
    VLM = SECURITY.VLM
    VLM = NDS.VLM
    VLM = BIND.VLM
    VLM = RSA.VLM    ; Not loaded by DEFAULT
    VLM = NWP.VLM
    VLM = FIO.VLM
    VLM = GENERAL.VLM
    VLM = REDIR.VLM
    VLM = PRINT.VLM
    VLM = NETX.VLM
    VLM = AUTO.VLM    ; Not loaded by DEFAULT - Requires RSA.VLM
```

Also, the more common and useful statements in the NET.CFG file are discussed in more detail, next.

Table 20.20
NetWare DOS Requester NET.CFG Parameters

Parameter	Used By	Description
Auto Reconnect = [ON|OFF]	auto.vlm nds.vlm nwp.vlm	AUTO.VLM must be loaded for this parameter to be effective. When set to ON (default value), AUTO will attempt to reconnect to the server if there is a break in the network connection. After AUTO reconnects to the server, it will reauthenticate the client, and if necessary, rebuild the client environment. AUTO makes use of RSA.VLM to reauthenticate the client. AUTO.VLM requires that RSA.VLM be loaded. When set to OFF, AUTO will not attempt to reconnect to the server. You may wish to set the value to OFF to eliminate network traffic due to AUTO.VLM's attempt to reconnect to the server.
Average Name Length=*n*	conn.vlm	This specifies the average name length of the server name. The DOS Requester uses this parameter and the CONNECTIONS parameter to determine the memory it needs to set aside for a connection table. The value can range from 2 to 48 characters and has a default of 48 characters. If you use short server names, you can save some memory by setting this parameter to the average name length for your servers.
Cache Buffers=*n*	fio.vlm	This sets the number of cache buffers the DOS Requester uses for caching non-shared, non-transactional files at the workstation. Only non-shared, non-transactional files can be cached at the workstation, because if a file is shared or transactional, it's data must be cached at the server for other clients to share the file data. Also, transactional tracking is implemented at the server and not at the workstation. The value can range from 0 to 64 cache blocks and has a default value of 5. Increasing the number of cache buffers increases the processing speed for files accessed sequentially, but also increases memory usage. You can reduce this parameter to decrease memory usage. The size of the cache buffers is set by the Cache Buffer Size parameter.

Parameter	Used By	Description
Cache Buffer Size=*n*	fio.vlm	This sets the size of the local cache buffers used by the DOS Requester. The value can range from 64 to 4096 bytes, and has a default of 512 bytes. Increasing the value can improve performance because larger amounts of data are cached at the workstation, but this also increases memory used at the workstation. The parameter value should not exceed the maximum packet size of the network board. If the parameter is less than the maximum packet size, the maximum packet size should be a multiple of the cache buffer size.
Cache Writes = [ON|OFF]	fio.vlm	This parameter can be used to enable (ON) or disable (OFF) the writing of data to the cache. The default value is ON, which means that cache writing is enabled. Setting the parameter to OFF can improve data integrity but decrease the performance of write operations.
Checksum= *n*	ipxncp.vlm nwp.vlm tcpncp.vlm	This can be used for enabling or disabling checksums for NCP packets. The data-link layer ordinarily performs hardware checksums. You can further increase reliability by performing checksums within the NCP packets. But this is done at the expense of decreasing network performance because of the extra time needed to compute and validate NCP checksums. The value can be an integer from 0 to 3 and has a default value of 0. The meanings of these values are as follows: 0 = NCP checksums disabled (default) 1 = Enabled but not preferred 2 = Enabled and preferred 3 = NCP checksums required The values of 1 to 3 indicate the priority of performing NCP checksums at the server. If the value is set to 1, and the server is busy, it may not perform the NCP checksum. If the value is set to 2, the server will attempt to perform the checksum. However, under extremely busy conditions, it may elect not to perform the checksum. A value of 3 indicates that the server will always perform the checksum regardless of how busy the server is.

continues

Table 20.20, Continued
NetWare DOS Requester NET.CFG Parameters

Parameter	Used By	Description
Connections=*n*	conn.vlm fio.vlm	This is the maximum number of simultaneous connections the DOS Requester supports. The value can range from 2 to 50 and has a default value of 8. The default value maintains compatibility with the older NETX shell (NETX.COM or NETX.EXE). You can reduce this number to save memory, if you expect to use few connections. Values higher than 8 (default) may not be supported by software that is explicitly written for the older shell. Changing the value from the default value of 8 may decrease NETX compatibility.
DOS Name = *name*	netx.vlm general.vlm	Defines the name of the operating system that is used in the login script variable %OS. The default value is MSDOS, but can be set to any 5-character name.
First Network Drive = *X*	general.vlm	This sets the drive letter that will be used to access the server when the workstation attaches to a server. The network drive specified is, by default, mapped to the SYS:LOGIN directory of the server. The available drive letters are A to Z, and must be specified without the colon after the letter. If this parameter is not specified, the default is the first available drive. If you have a floppy drive and only one hard disk partition C: on your workstation, the first network drive will be D: (if the parameter is not specified).
Handle Net Errors = [ON|OFF]	ipxncp.vlm tcpncp.vlm	This sets the default method used to handle network errors. If the value is set to ON (default), network errors generate the software interrupt INT 24 (hex). An interrupt service routine that is hooked to interrupt vector 24 (hex) handles the error. If the value is set to OFF, an actual error code is returned, but no further actions taken. It is sometimes useful to see the actual error code, but if the error is not handled, the application can become unstable or crash.

Parameter	Used By	Description
Large Internet Packets = [ON|OFF]	ipxncp.vlm tcpncp.vlm	When set to ON (default) an attempt is made to use the largest packet size negotiated between server and workstation regardless of intervening routers. Intervening routers must be configured to handle the largest size. Older IPX routers (external routers created using ROUTEGEN) were restricted to handling 576 bytes of data. If the IPX router cannot be configured to handling the negotiated packet size, then packet size is restricted to the smaller router packet size. When the value is set to OFF, and an intervening IPX router is detected, the largest packet size is restricted to 576 bytes.
Load Low Conn = [ON|OFF]	conn.vlm	When set to ON (default), the connection manager (CONN.VLM) is loaded in conventional memory. When set to OFF, the CONN.VLM is loaded in upper memory. This frees space in conventional memory, but degrades performance.
Load Low IPXNCP = [ON|OFF]	ipxncp.vlm	When set to ON (default), the IPXNCP.VLM transport module is loaded in conventional memory. When set to OFF, the IPXNCP.VLM is loaded in upper memory. This frees space in conventional memory, but degrades performance.
Local Printers = *n*	print.vlm	This is used to override the number of printers attached locally to the workstation. The default value is determined by the BIOS when the workstation boots up. The value can range from 0 to 9 and is set to 3 for most workstations. Setting a value of 0 prevents the workstation from hanging if the user presses the <Shift><PrtScr> keys and there is no local printer attached or the printer port is not redirected ("captured") to a network printer. If the value is set to 0, PRINT.VLM will not load.
Long Machine Type = *name*	netx.vlm general.vlm	Defines the name of the machine that is used in the login script variable %MACHINE. The default value is IBM_PC, but can be set to any 6-character name.

continues

Table 20.20, Continued
NetWare DOS Requester NET.CFG Parameters

Parameter	Used By	Description
Max Tasks = *n*	conn.vlm	Sets the maximum number of tasks that can be active simultaneously. The value can range from 20 to 128 tasks and has a default value of 31. This is used in multitasking environments, such as MS Windows and DESQview, that can have several applications running concurrently. Increase this number if you have problems running an additional program in these environments.
Message Level = *n*	nwp.vlm	This is used to control the amount of information that is displayed when VLM.EXE loads. The message-level numbers have the same meaning as the numbers used in the /V option. Each message-level number includes information displayed by message numbers below that number. The values range from 0 to 4 and have a default value of 1. These meanings are as follows: 0 = Only copyright message and critical errors are displayed 1 = Warning messages (default) 2 = Program load information for VLMs 3 = Configuration information 4 = Diagnostic information
Message Time Out = *n*	nwp.vlm	This sets the number of ticks (1/18.26 sec) after which broadcast messages will be cleared from the screen, without user intervention. The value can range from 0 to 10,000 ticks and has a default value of 0. A value of 0 indicates that user intervention is required to clear the broadcast message.
Name Context = "*context*"	nds.vlm	This is used to specify the workstation's default NDS context when the DOS Requester loads. The context is the workstation's position in the NDS tree. If not specified the workstation's context is set to [Root].
Network Printers = *n*	print.vlm	This is used to set the number of ports (LPT1: to LPT9:) that the DOS Requester can capture. The value can range from 0 to 9 and has a default value of 3. To disable sending jobs to the network printer, set the value to 0. If set to 0, PRINT.VLM will not

Parameter	Used By	Description
		load, and this effectively disables network printing from the workstation.
PB Buffers = *n*	fio.vlm	This sets the number of packet buffers used by packet burst. The value can range from 0 to 10 and has a default value of 3. Setting a value of 0 disables packet burst. Generally speaking, a larger value results in better performance, as long as the workstation can handle the data in the packet burst. However, a larger value can also increase the amount of memory used at the workstation.
Preferred Server = *name*	bind.vlm	Forces the DOS Requester to attach to the specified NetWare server. There is no default value. Without this option, the workstation attaches to the server that returns the fastest Give Nearest Server SAP response to the workstation's Get Nearest Server SAP request. This has the same meaning as the /PS option used in VLM.EXE. However, the /PS option will override this parameter setting. If both PREFERRED SERVER and PREFERRED TREE are specified, connection is established with the first server that meets the criteria in either parameter.
Preferred Tree = *name*	nds.vlm	Forces the DOS Requester to attach to the specified NDS tree. There is no default value. This has the same meaning as the /PT option used in VLM.EXE. However, the /PT option will override this parameter setting. If both PREFERRED SERVER and PREFERRED TREE are specified, connection is established with the first server that meets the criteria in either parameter.
Print Buffer Size = *n*	print.vlm	This sets the size of the print buffer used for 1-byte print requests. In some applications, 1-byte print requests may occur in the middle of a print job. The value can range from 0 to 256 and has a default value of 64. Increasing the parameter value can increase performance in certain cases at the expense of increased memory requirements.

continues

Table 20.20, Continued
NetWare DOS Requester NET.CFG Parameters

Parameter	Used By	Description
Print Header = *n*	print.vlm	Sets the maximum size of the initialization string that is sent to the printer at the beginning of a job. This initialization string is sent to set the printer into the desired mode for the print job that follows. The value can range from 0 to 1024 and has a default value of 64. If your printer is not being initialized correctly, try increasing this parameter.
Print Tail = *n*	print.vlm	Sets the maximum size of the initialization string that is sent to the printer at the completion of a print job. This initialization string is sent to reset the printer into the desired mode for the next print job. The value can range from 0 to 1024 and has a default value of 64. If your printer is not being reset correctly, try increasing this parameter.
Read Only Compatibility = [ON|OFF]	redir.vlm	When set to ON, a file flagged as read-only can be opened with a read/write access call. The system will still prevent the program from writing to the file. Prior to NetWare 2.1, you could open a read-only file with read/write access but could not write to it. When set to OFF (default), a file flagged as read-only cannot be opened with a read/write access call. This is also the behavior for DOS. To maintain compatibility with DOS, NetWare 2.1 and above were changed so that a read-only file cannot be opened with a read/write access call. Set the value to ON only if you are running applications that need to open a read-only file with a read/write access call.
Search Mode = *n*	general.vlm	This is used to change the method for searching data files on NetWare search drives, if files are not found in the current directory. The value can range from 0 to 7 and has a default value of 1. The search mode values have the following meaning: 0 = No special search instructions 1 = Search if path not specified for data file 2 = Do not search drives for data files

Parameter	Used By	Description
		3 = Search if path not specified for data file, and file is opened for read access and *not* modify access 4 = Reserved 5 = Always search regardless if path is specified for a file or not 6 = Reserved 7 = Always search if request is to read a file, regardless if path is specified for a file or not
Set Station Time = [ON|OFF]	vlm.exe	If set to ON (default), this sets the workstation date and time the same as that of the server's date and time. If set to OFF, it disables time synchronization of workstation time with server.
Show Dots = [ON|OFF]	redir.vlm	When set to ON (default), it allows the DOS Requester to emulate the DOS system calls FindFirstMatching and FindNextMatching on the directory entries dot (.) and dot-dot (..). This emulation is needed because NetWare does not support the dot (.) and dot-dot (..) entries in its file system.
Short Machine Type = *name*	netx.vlm general.vlm	Defines the name of the machine as it is used in the login script variable %SMACHINE. The default value is IBM, but can be set to any 4-character (or less) name.
Signature Level = *n*	nwp.vlm	Specifies the level of packet signature support that is used at the workstation. 0 = Packet signatures disabled 1 = Enabled but not preferred (default) 2 = Preferred 3 = Required
True Commit = [ON|OFF]	fio.vlm	If set to ON, it causes an NCP commit message to be sent for every DOS commit message. This can improve data integrity, but decrease performance. The default is OFF, which means that performance is preferred over data integrity. Set this to ON to guarantee data integrity for critical data events such as those in database applications.

continues

Table 20.20, Continued
NetWare DOS Requester NET.CFG Parameters

Parameter	Used By	Description
Use Defaults = [ON|OFF]	vlm.exe	If set to ON (default), a default set of VLMs is loaded in the order described in this chapter. If set to OFF, you must use the VLM = *name* parameters to specify the VLMs that must be loaded.
VLM = *name*	vlm.exe	The VLM that is specified is loaded. You can specify the full path name of the VLM, if it is to be loaded from a different directory. This option allows VLMs not listed in the default to be loaded.

Other NET.CFG Sections

The parameters in table 20.20 are placed in the NetWare DOS Requester section of the NET.CFG file. There are two other major sections in the NET.CFG file. These are the Link Driver and Protocol and Link Support Section. The statements in each major section are indented by a tab or at least one space under that section. The following shows the general structure of the NET.CFG section:

```
# This is a comment
; This is also a comment
Link Driver DriverName
    DMA [#1¦#2] dmachannel
    INT [#1¦#2] interruptnumber
    MEM [#1¦#2] hexstartaddress [hexlength]
    PORT [#1¦#2] hexstartaddress
    FRAME  frametype

Protocol protocolname
;  This section is optional
    BIND [#1 ¦ #2]

Link Support
; This is required by protocols such as TCP/IP
    BUFFERS number [size]
    MEMPOOL number
    MAX BOARDS number
    MAX STACKS number

NetWare DOS Requester
;  The parameters in table 20.20 go here, and are
;  indented by a tab or at least one space
```

Using NAME CONTEXT

You use the NAME CONTEXT statement to establish the context of the workstation on attachment to the NDS tree. The statement's syntax is

```
NAME CONTEXT = "complete name path"
```

Replace *complete name path* with the complete name of the context to be set initially. You should set the initial name context for users to the container that contains most of the resources they are likely to use. You must include the complete name in the quotation marks.

An example of the use of NAME CONTEXT is

```
NetWare DOS Requester
    NAME CONTEXT = "OU=CORP.O=ESL"
```

Using PREFERRED TREE

Use the PREFERRED TREE option to specify the NDS tree to which the VLMs are to attach initially when they are loaded. The PREFERRED TREE option has meaning when the NDS.VLM is loaded because the option refers to an NDS tree. The syntax for using the PREFERRED TREE option is

```
PREFERRED TREE = tree name
```

Replace *tree name* with the name of the NDS tree.

An example of the use of PREFERRED TREE is

```
NetWare DOS Requester
    PREFERRED TREE = CNET
```

Using FIRST NETWORK DRIVE

In the NetWare 4.*x* client, the DOS drive table is shared between DOS and the DOS Requester. When the VLMs load, the redirector assigns the first available DOS drive letter to the network drive. If the workstation has a single hard disk partition (drive C), drive D becomes the first network drive. To maintain compatibility with applications and batch/script files that might require the first network drive to be F (the default with the NETX shell programs), a new statement called FIRST NETWORK DRIVE has been provided.

The syntax for using the FIRST NETWORK DRIVE option is

```
FIRST NETWORK DRIVE = drive letter
```

Replace *drive letter* with a drive letter that is not in local use.

An example of the use of FIRST NETWORK DRIVE is

```
NetWare DOS Requester
    FIRST NETWORK DRIVE = F
```

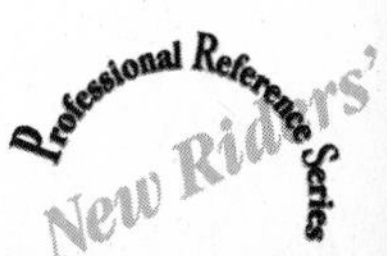

Using PB BUFFERS

The packet burst capability can be configured with the PB BUFFERS statement in the NetWare DOS Requester section. The default value is PB BUFFERS = 3, if PB BUFFERS is not specified in the NET.CFG file. This capability also exists with NetWare 3.*x*.

The syntax for using the PB BUFFERS option is as follows:

```
PB BUFFERS = n
```

Replace *n* with a number from 0 to 10. A value of 0 disables the packet burst option. Any other value from 1 to 10 enables the packet burst and also specifies the number of buffers for the packet burst.

This sample command enables the PB BUFFERS option and specifies four buffers for the burst mode:

```
NetWare DOS Requester
    PB BUFFERS = 4
```

Using USE DEFAULTS and the VLM Statement

The VLMs are loaded by default in the load sequence described previously in this chapter (see "Loading VLMs in the Default Order"). To disable the default load sequence, you must use this command:

```
USE DEFAULTS=OFF
```

If the default load sequence is disabled, you must specify the VLMs to load, using the VLM statement:

```
VLM=nameOfVLM
```

Replace *nameOfVLM* with the name of the VLM to load.

An example of the use of these statements is

```
NetWare DOS Requester
    USE DEFAULTS=OFF
    VLM=CONN.VLM
    VLM=IPXNCP.VLM
        :
        :
    (and other VLMs)
```

You also can use the VLM statement with the default load order to specify optional VLMs to be loaded. To load the RSA.VLM and AUTO.VLMs after the default load sequence, for example, use these commands:

```
NetWare DOS Requester
    USE DEFAULTS=ON
    VLM=RSA.VLM
    VLM=AUTO.VLM
```

Specifying Frame Types

The default frame type for NetWare 4.*x* has been changed to ETHERNET_802.2. You need to specify this frame type in the Link Driver section. If you have on the network NetWare 3.*x* servers that use their default frame type of ETHERNET_802.3, you must additionally specify the ETHERNET_802.3 frame type. If you are using TCP/IP protocol stack software such as LAN WorkPlace or FTP Software's PC/TCP (running on top of ODI drivers), you must additionally specify the ETHERNET_II frame type.

The following lines show an example of the frame type for SMC8000 boards for NetWare 3.*x* server compatibility:

```
Link Driver SMC8000
    int         3
    port         280
    mem         D0000
    frame         ETHERNET_802.2
    frame         ETHERNET_802.3
```

The following lines show an example of the frame type for SMC8000 boards for NetWare 3.*x* server and TCP/IP compatibility:

```
Link Driver SMC8000
    int         3
    port         280
    mem         D0000
    frame         ETHERNET_802.2
    frame         ETHERNET_802.3
    frame         ETHERNET_II
```

Understanding Requirements for Windows Workstations

When the NetWare 4.*x* client software is installed, you can specify that MS Windows support files can be copied to the directory containing MS Windows. When this is done, the following files are copied:

1. **NETWARE.DRV.** This is the network driver that is used to access the NetWare 4.*x* network from within MS Windows. It implements many of the NetWare-related command functions. NETWARE.DRV makes use of two additional support files: NETWARE.INI and NETWARE.HLP. The NETWARE.INI file contains configuration information for customizing NETWARE.DRV. For instance, if the HotKeyEnabled=1 is placed is placed in the Options section of NETWARE.INI, the hot key F6 (default value), can be used to invoke NetWare functions.

2. **VIPX.386.** This is used for running DOS applications in the enhanced mode under MS Windows. VIPX.386 virtualizes IPX communications between DOS sessions and synchronizes network calls and responses from DOS applications.

3. **VNETWARE.386.** This is used to process broadcast messages and virtualize multiple sessions to the NetWare server (see fig.20.55). It works with NETWARE.DRV and NWPOPUP.EXE.

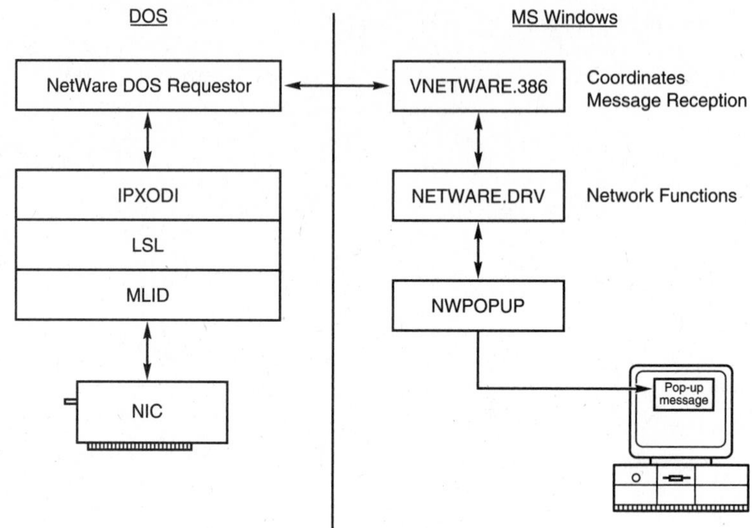

Figure 20.55
Processing of broadcast messages.

The NetWare-specific MS Windows files are:

- NETWARE.INI
- NWADMIN.INI
- ET.INI

The contents of a sample NETWARE.INI file are shown next. You can use the NWUSER tool to customize NETWARE.INI for information on device setup, print redirections, drive mappings, network connections, message handling, and hot keys.

```
[Options]
HotKeyEnabled=1

[NeWt.Settings]
SaveSettings=1
ViewResources=1
ViewBind=0
ViewNDS=1
ViewPNW=1
ViewConnections=0
ViewVolumes=1
ViewQueues=1
ViewUsers=1
ViewGroups=1
ControlBar=1
StatusBar=1
48,Personal NetWare=1, 22,0,1,-1,-1,0,0,636,408, 1001,1000,0,Personal NetWare
```

```
[NeWt.Windows]
124,NetWare=1, 22,0,1,15663125,-1,0,0,540,223, 1001,1000,267,NetWare
202,Drives=1, 22,0,2,15663125,-1,22,22,562,245, 1001,1000,271,Drives
204,Printers=1, 22,0,2,15663200,-1,44,44,584,267, 1001,1000,271,Printers
```

Notice that the [Options] section has the HotKeyEnabled=1, which means that hot key is enabled, and is set to a default value of F6. To use a different function key, set the value to 111 + *n* where n is the function key number, F*n* (F3, F4, etc.). Therefore, to use the function key F11, you would set the value of HotKeyEnabled to 111 + 11 = 122. The [NetWt.Settings] section contains the setting for viewing network resources.The [NetWt.Windows] contains settings for establishing network drive and printer redirections.

The NWADMIN.INI is used for setting options for the MS Windows based NetWare tools. The contents of a sample NETWARE.INI file is shown next.

```
[Snapin Object DLLs]

[Browser Preferences]
Filters=none
Confirmations=Move, Delete
Scope=Any
```

The [Snapin Object DLLs] is used for supporting new extensions to NDS objects. The [Browser Preferences] section, as the name suggests, contains browser settings for the NetWare Administrator Tool. There are no filters set for viewing objects, and no specific Scope is set. The NetWare Administrator Tool confirms the Move and Delete operations.

The ET.INI is uses for setting Electro Text help options. The contents of a sample ET.INI file is shown next. This file is well commented, and explains itself.

```
; This file, ET.INI, tells Novell ElectroText where documents and
; other essential files are located on your system or network.  A
; copy of this ET.INI file must reside in your local Windows
; directory (usually C:\WINDOWS).  You should update the drive
; letters and/or directory paths listed in this file after copying
; it into your Windows directory so that they point to the correct
; locations of the specified files.

[DYNATEXT]

; This section specifies files and directories used by the viewer
; program itself.

; The following line points to a directory containing viewer icons
; and other program data.
DATA=Z:/DOC/DATA

; The following line authorizes your viewer to work with certain
; categories of electronic books.  You can change the drive letter
; and path to point wherever the authorization file is located.
AUTH=Z:/DOC/DATA/SECURITY/AUTH
```

```
; The following line specifies a directory for notes that are made
; available to everyone on your system.
PUBLIC_NOTES=Z:/DOC/PUBNOTES

; The following line specifies a directory for your private bookmarks or
; other annotations.  The directory must be one for which you have
; write permission.  It will automatically be created if it does
; not already exist.
PRIVATE_NOTES=C:/PRVNOTES

[DOCSETS]

; This section specifies the physical location of docsets (document
; collections) on your system or network and associates each docset
; with an abstract name used in making libraries and bookshelves.
; All books in a particular docset must occupy a single directory
; structure, but that directory structure can be put anywhere on
; your network as long as its path specification below is changed
; accordingly.  The environment variable NWLANGUAGE, set in your
; AUTOEXEC.BAT file, is used to switch among different language
; versions of Novell manuals.
NW40=Z:/DOC/$NWLANGUAGE/NW40
ETHELP=Z:/DOC/$NWLANGUAGE/ETHELP

[LIBRARIES]

; This section makes libraries available to the ElectroText viewer.
; The contents of each library are specified by a file with an .ETL
; extension.

; The following line gives the path down which the viewer will look
; for .ETL files.  The ETLPATH may consist of any number of
; directory specifications separated by semicolons.
ETLPATH=Z:/DOC/$NWLANGUAGE

; The following line specifies which library to open when the
; viewer is started.  If you have more than one library, you can
; change this line to open a different one when you start the viewer.
OPEN=LIB1

; The following list associates each library with an abstract name.
; Each name must correspond to a file with an .ETL extension
; located somewhere in the ETLPATH given above.  For example, the
; first entry implies the existence of a file named NOVELL.ETL that
; specifies the Novell Technical Documentation Library.
LIB1=NOVELL

[HELP]

; These entries set up ElectroText help files.  They should
; ordinarily not be changed.
```

```
LIBWIN=ETHELP;HLP_LIBR
BOOKWIN=ETHELP;HLP_BOOK

[TABLES]

; This section regulates the appearance of tables and should
; ordinarily not be changed.
WVGA=1/1;12;12
WSVGA=1/1;12;12
WXGA=1/1;12;12
WLCDVGA=1/1;12;12

[PREFERENCES]

; This section records user choices set in the Preferences section
; of the viewer's library and book windows.
DEFAULT=QUERYLANG:SIMPLE
WVGA=OUTLINE:LEFT;SEARCH:VISIBLE
WSVGA=OUTLINE:LEFT;SEARCH:VISIBLE
WXGA=OUTLINE:LEFT;SEARCH:VISIBLE
WLCDVGA=OUTLINE:LEFT;SEARCH:VISIBLE

; If you have a greyscale or monochrome display, add the
; following line:
; DISPLAY=WLCDVGA
```

Other files that are modified during the MS Windows client software installation are the PROGRAM.INI and SYSTEM.INI files. The original versions of these files are saved as PROGRAM.BNW and SYSTEM.BNW.

In the PROGRAM.INI file, a new group file NWUTILS.GRP is added under the section [Groups]. The SYSTEM.INI file is modified to contain the line `NETWORK.DRV=Novell NetWare (4.0)` in the [Boot.Description] section. The [386enh] section is also modified, to load the virtual drivers VNETBIOS, VNETWARE.386, VIPX.386, and VCLIENT.386, and statements for enhanced support are added.

The following shows partial sections of the SYSTEM.INI and PROGRAM.INI files that are modified by NetWare 4.*x* client installation.

Partial contents of SYSTEM.INI

```
[boot]
network.drv=netware.drv


[boot.description]
network.drv=novell netware (v4.0)

[386enh]
network=*vnetbios, vipx.386, vnetware.386
 [standard]
```

```
[nonwindowsapp]
localtsrs=dosedit,ced

[mci]
waveaudio=mciwave.drv
sequencer=mciseq.drv
cdaudio=mcicda.drv

[drivers]
timer=timer.drv
midimapper=midimap.drv
```

Partial contents of PROGRAM.INI

```
[Groups]
; New group for NetWare tools added.
Group10=C:\WINDOWS\NWUTILS.GRP
```

Upgrading Client Files

NetWare 4.*x* comes with two utilities that can be used for updating files and upgrading IPX LAN drivers to equivalent ODI drivers. These utilities are:

- WSUPDATE
- WSUPGRD

Using WSUPDATE

WSUPDATE is designed to update files in workstation directories with the latest version of files from the network. This is very useful for simplifying changes that need to be made on a large number of workstations on the network. The WSUPDATE can be executed as a command-line utility, or it can be placed in a login script file (system, profile or user login script file). If placed in a login script file, it must be preceded by the # character. Placing it in a login script file ensures that the change is made when the user logs in. A simple example makes the use of WSUPDATE clear.

Suppose that you have obtained the latest version of the VLM.EXE file (from CompuServe or your Novell dealer) that fixes a known bug and you wish to install this latest version of VLM.EXE on user workstations. If the VLM.EXE is placed in a network drive H:, running the following command at each workstation ensures that the latest VLM.EXE is copied on all workstations:

```
WSUPDATE  H:VLM.EXE
```

If the previous command is placed in a login script file, the update takes place whenever the user executes the login script file. When this command is run, WSUPDATE searches all local drives at the workstation and replaces VLM.EXE on the workstation with the latest version from drive H:. WSUPDATE makes use of date and timestamps on the file to determine which file is more recent.

Using WSUPDATE /? gives an overview of the help screens for WSUPDATE. To see all the help screens, use WSUPDATE /? ALL. Figures 20.56 to 20.59 show all the help screens for WSUPDATE for your study, as these contain examples of the use of WSUPDATE. The general syntax of WSUPDATE is shown below, and the options are explained in table 20.21.

```
WSUPDATE sourcepath  [destination:[destpath\filename]] [/options]
```

sourcepath	This is the location of the source file.
destination:	This can be either a drive letter to search for outdated files, or a volume name to search for outdated file.
destpath\filename	If this is not specified, the destination drive is searched from the root.
options	These are explained in table 20.21.

Table 20.21
WSUPDATE Options

/Option	Description
/ALL	Searches all mapped drives
/C	Copies a new file over the old one, and does not keep a backup
/E	Erases the existing log file
/F=*commandfile*	Specifies the path name for the command file for WSUPDATE that contains the commands for updating files
/LOCAL	Searches all local drives at the workstation
/L=*logfile*	Specifies the path for the log file used to store WSUPDATE log information
/P	Prompts the user to proceed before performing the update
/O	Specifies all files, even those that are Read-Only, should be updated
/R	Renames the updated files with a .OLD extension, instead of deleting them
/S	Searches all subdirectories in the destination for files to update
/?	Displays on-line help screens. Can be further qualified by options such as /? BA Basic /? AD Advanced /? SYN Syntax /? ALL All help screens

Figure 20.56
WSUPDATE /? ALL—Help Screen 1.

```
WSUPDATE                      General Help Screen                        v4.01

Purpose: Update workstation files from the network.
Syntax:  WSUPDATE <source file name> [destination drive:] [path] [option]

For help on:              Type:
  Basic options             WSUPDATE /? BA
  Advanced options          WSUPDATE /? AD
  Syntax                    WSUPDATE /? SYN
  All                       WSUPDATE /? ALL

For example:                              Type:
  To update NET5.COM on drive C:
  from drive Z:                             WSUPDATE Z:NET5.COM C:

>>>  Enter = More   Esc = Cancel   C = Continuous
```

Figure 20.57
WSUPDATE /? ALL—Help Screen 2.

```
WSUPDATE                      Basic Options Help                         v4.01

Syntax:  WSUPDATE <source file name> [destination drive:] [path] [option]

To:                                                               Use:
  Copy the new file over the old one                               /C /n

  Rename the old file with an .OLD extension before copying        /R

  Search all mapped drives for the outdated file                   /ALL

  Search all local drives for the outdated file                    /LOCAL

  Search all subdirectories for the outdated file.             /S

For example, to:                  Type:
  Update NETX.COM in all
  subdirectories of all             WSUPDATE Z:NETX.COM /LOCAL /S
  local drives

>>>  Enter = More   Esc = Cancel   C = Continuous
```

```
WSUPDATE                    Advanced Options Help                      v4.01
Syntax: WSUPDATE <source file name> [destination drive:] [path] [option]
To:                                               Use:
  Specify command file name                        /F=<path\filename>

  Specify log file name                            /L=<path\filename>

  Erase the existing log file                      /E

  Update regular and read-only files               /O

  Allow program halt before file search            /P
For example,to:                            Type:
  Update regular and read-only
  copies of NE2000.COM in all
  subdirectories of                          WSUPDATE NE2000.COM C: /O /S
  drive C: and record changes in                 /L=LOG.FIL
  the log file LOG.FIL
>>>  Enter = More    Esc = Cancel    C = Continuous
```

Figure 20.58 *WSUPDATE /? ALL—Help Screen 3.*

```
WSUPDATE                          Syntax Help                          v4.01
Syntax:  WSUPDATE <source file name> [destination drive:]
                  [destination path\file name] [option]
To:                                                Use:
  Copy over old file                                /C
  Rename old file, then copy                        /R
  Search all drives                                 /ALL
  Search local drives                               /LOCAL
  Search subdirectories                             /S
  Command file                                      /F = <path\file name>
  Log file                                          /L = <path\file name>
  Erase log file                                    /E
  Read-only files                                   /O
  Abort                                             /P

F:\>
```

Figure 20.59 *WSUPDATE /? ALL—Help Screen 4.*

To update all copies of the IPXODI.COM from SYS:PUBLIC\IPXODI.COM on local drive C: and all subdirectories in that local drive, and create a log file C:\WSUPDATE.LOG, use:

```
WSUPDATE  SYS:PUBLIC\IPXODI.COM C: /S /L=C:\WSUPDATE.LOG
```

Figure 20.60 shows the results of running the previous command. The contents of the log file are shown here:

```
CN=Admin.O=ESL  01/09/94 15:47:55
Network number: [   E8022]  Node number: [  80C7D66F0F]
Copy a file
     From path NW4CS/SYS:PUBLIC\
     To path C:\\BIN\
       IPXODI.COM
Copy a file
     From path NW4CS/SYS:PUBLIC\
     To path C:\\NOVELL\
       IPXODI.COM

Source file: NW4CS/SYS:PUBLIC\IPXODI.COM
Destination path: C:
Search subdirectories: YES
Destination file: IPXODI.COM
Copies found:      5
Copies outdated:   2
Copies updated:    2
```

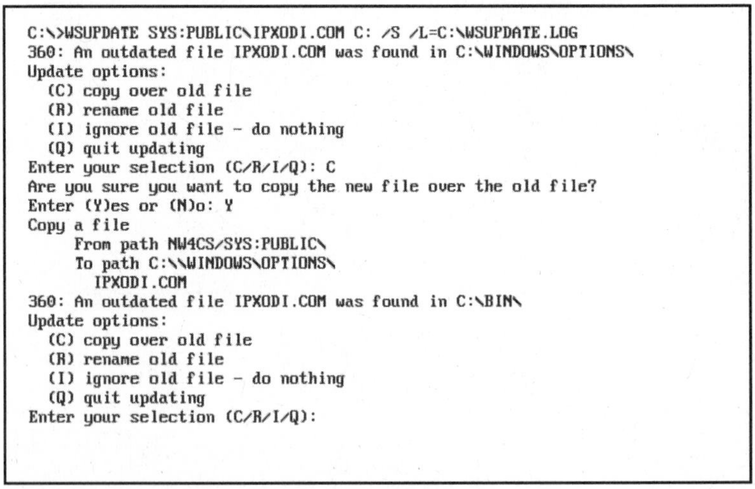

```
C:\>WSUPDATE SYS:PUBLIC\IPXODI.COM C: /S /L=C:\WSUPDATE.LOG
360: An outdated file IPXODI.COM was found in C:\WINDOWS\OPTIONS\
Update options:
  (C) copy over old file
  (R) rename old file
  (I) ignore old file - do nothing
  (Q) quit updating
Enter your selection (C/R/I/Q): C
Are you sure you want to copy the new file over the old file?
Enter (Y)es or (N)o: Y
Copy a file
     From path NW4CS/SYS:PUBLIC\
     To path C:\\WINDOWS\OPTIONS\
       IPXODI.COM
360: An outdated file IPXODI.COM was found in C:\BIN\
Update options:
  (C) copy over old file
  (R) rename old file
  (I) ignore old file - do nothing
  (Q) quit updating
Enter your selection (C/R/I/Q):
```

Figure 20.60
Sample run of the WSUPDATE command.

To run WSUPDATE and use the commands stored in file C:\WSUPDATE.CM, use:

```
WSUPDATE /F=C:\WSUPDATE.CM
```

The contents of a sample command file to update IPXODI.COM and VLM.EXE are shown below:

```
SYS:PUBLIC\IPXODI.COM      C:\NWCLIENT\IPXODI.COM
H:VLM.EXE                  C:\NWCLIENT\VLM.EXE
```

The IPXODI.COM in SYS:PUBLIC and VLM.EXE in H: are used as source files to update corresponding files in C:\NWCLIENT.

To search all mapped drives and rename the old files with a .OLD extension, use:

```
WSUPDATE F:\SOURCE\HOSTS  /ALL /R
```

To search all local drives and copy over the old files, use:

```
WSUPDATE VOL1:SOURCE\INET.CFG  /LOCAL /C
```

Using WSUPGRD

This is used to convert workstations using IPX.COM to using ODI-based software. WSUPGRD analyzes the driver file, and extracts from it the parameters needed for the NET.CFG file. This utility is helpful if all your workstations have the same network board configuration and driver types. If you have a mix of many different types of network boards and drivers, you should peform the upgrade manually. WSUPGRD cannot be used to upgrade software for diskless workstations, such as those that use the Remote Program Load (RPL) capability.

Using WSUPGRD /? gives a help screen for using WSUPGRD. This help screen is shown in figure 20.61. (In v1.02 of the help screen the name of the utility is incorrectly spelled as WSUPGRDE.)

```
WSUPGRD              Workstation LAN Driver Upgrade                v1.02

Purpose: Upgrade a DOSIPX LAN driver to the corresponding DOSODI driver.
Run after the workstation is logged into a Netware server.

Syntax:          WSUPGRDE [path] [/C] [/N] [/E0|1|2] [/S]

to:
exit with errorlevel 1 if no upgrade is performed              /C
not delete the DOSIPX driver                                   /N
not edit AUTOEXEC.BAT                                          /E0
edit AUTOEXEC.BAT                                              /E1
create NWSTART.BAT and edit AUTOEXEC.BAT                       /E2
suppress generation of NET.CFG lines from the DOSIPX driver    /S

path is the path to and name of the existing DOSIPX driver.

For example, to:
upgrade an NE2000 driver named NE2000.COM, and load the
driver and IPX in AUTOEXEC.BAT (rather than NWSTART.BAT.)  WSUPGRD NE2000 /E1

C:\>
```

Figure 20.61
WSUPGRD help screen.

The general syntax of WSUPGRD is shown below, and the options are explained in table 20.22.

```
WSUPGRD [driverfile]  [/options]
```

driverfile	This is the path name of the driver file. The default value is \IPX.COM, if this is not specified.
options	These are explained in table 20.22

Table 20.22
WSUPGRD Options

/Option	Description
/C	This is the Cancel Code or exit code. When this option is set, a DOS error-level code of 1 is returned if the upgrade was performed. Without this option no exit code is set if the upgrade is performed. Using this option allows you to write batch files to test the succesful operation of WSUPGRD and take further actions. If there is an error in the execution of WSUPGRD, an error level of 3 is returned regardless of whether the /C option was specified.
/N	This is the No Delete option. By default, the old driver is deleted before the ODI driver file is installed. Using the /N option informs WSUPGRD not to delete the old driver file. If the old driver and the ODI driver have the same name, the old driver file is deleted even though the /N option is set.
/E*n*	Controls the type of changes made to the workstation's AUTOEXEC.BAT file. If *n* is set to 0, no changes are made to AUTOEXEC.BAT. If *n* is set to 1, the line which loads the IPX driver (if present) is to be deleted and replaced with commands to load LSL, MLID (ODI drivers) and IPXODI. If *n* is set to 2, the line which loads the IPX driver (if present) is to be deleted and replaced with a command to a batch file called NWSTART.BAT which loads LSL, MLID (ODI drivers) and IPXODI. The default value of *n* is 2.
/S	This is the Suppress option. This option causes the suppression of the generation of the NET.CFG file based on the IPX driver configuration.
/I	This is the information option. This causes WSUPGRD to display the hardware ID in the master configuration table of the ODI driver. If this switch is used, all other options are ignored.

The following examples use SMC8000 as the LAN driver.

To save the IPX driver and modify AUTOEXEC.BAT to include a call to NWSTART.BAT, use:

```
WSUPGRD SMC8000  /N /E2
```

To save the IPX driver and modify AUTOEXEC.BAT to include lines for loading LSL, MLID and IPXODI, use:

```
WSUPGRD SMC8000  /N /E1
```

To replace the old IPX driver (and delete it) and modify AUTOEXEC.BAT to include lines for loading LSL, MLID and IPXODI, use:

```
WSUPGRD SMC8000  /E1
```

Summary

In this chapter, you learned how to manage the workstation setup, including the following activities:

- Generating IPX for NetWare workstations
- Installing ODI components
- Using source routing drivers for IBM Token-Ring networks
- Configuring NetWare workstation for Ethernet II LANs
- Configuring NetWare Requester and the VLM components
- Using WSUPGRD and WSUPDATE

You also learned details of the NetWare workstation-connection mechanism. Knowledge of this connection mechanism can help troubleshoot many configuration problems.

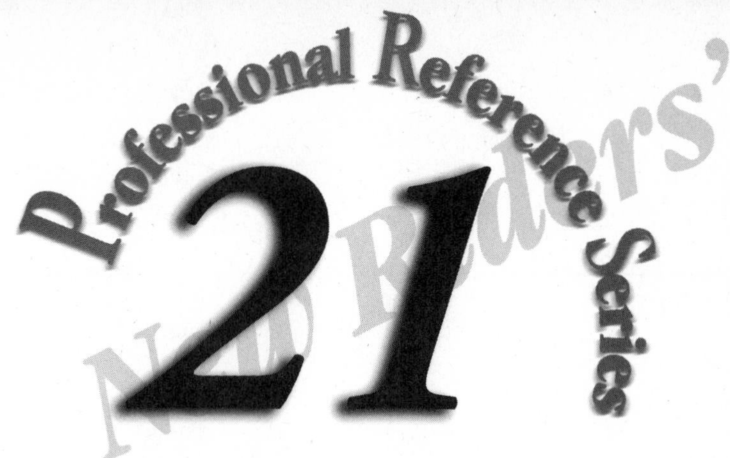

Supporting Non-DOS Workstations

NetWare has long provided services for DOS/Windows clients. Other clients such as OS/2, UNIX and Windows NT are becoming more important. Therefore, Novell has aggressively pursued the goal of enabling NetWare to provide services to a variety of computer environments.

Currently NetWare provides connectivity for Macintosh, OS/2, UNIX and Windows NT computers. This connectivity is provided through a variety of protocol and file-support options. By adding AppleTalk protocol support for connectivity, Apple Filing Protocol support for file access, and AppleTalk Print Service Protocol support for printing, you enable your Macintosh users to access files on a NetWare server and print to NetWare printers as though the resources were installed on a standard Mac network.

This chapter discusses the support NetWare provides for Macintosh and OS/2 workstations. It also introduces you to Novell's UnixWare product, a UNIX environment that can utilize standard IPX/SPX protocols to access NetWare servers.

Macintosh

Every Macintosh station comes with a built-in LocalTalk adapter that communicates at speeds up to 254 KB per second. If you want higher communication speeds, Token Ring or Ethernet NICs can be used on Macintosh stations equipped with expansion slots. The protocol used by Macintosh workstations is AppleTalk. For a NetWare server to coexist with Macintosh workstations, the NetWare server must support AppleTalk protocols.

Figure 21.1 shows that the NetWare server runs a dual protocol stack that consists of the native NCP/SPX/IPX stack and the AppleTalk protocol stack. The *Service Protocol Gateway* (SPG) translates Apple File Protocol requests issued by Macintosh workstations to NCP requests at the server. The SPG then translates the NCP responses of the NetWare server to AFP responses before they are relayed to the requesting workstation. This procedure creates the illusion that the NetWare server is a Macintosh server.

Figure 21.1
Macintosh workstation. (Graphic courtesy of Learning Group International.)

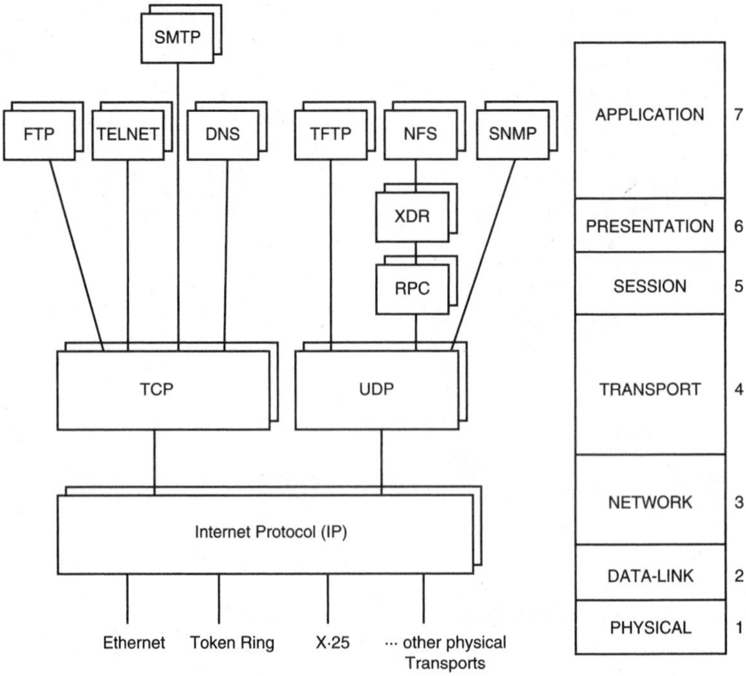

The AppleTalk protocol stack is implemented as an NLM on NetWare 3.*x* and as a VAP on NetWare 2.*x*. The client software that runs on Macintosh workstations is AppleShare. Macintosh workstations see the NetWare servers as AppleShare servers. This enables Macintosh users to use the familiar AppleShare interface; for instance, they can use the Chooser program to select the NetWare server.

From the Macintosh workstation's perspective, the NetWare server looks just like an AppleShare server, and the Macintosh user can use the familiar Chooser program to log in to the NetWare server and access the NetWare volumes.

Most of the complexity of setting up Macintosh stations on a NetWare network is at the server. The discussion that follows is for configuring the NetWare 3.*x* server to act as an AppleShare server.

The sequence of steps necessary to configure a NetWare 3.*x* server to act as an AppleTalk server is outlined as follows:

1. At the file server, type the following to load the Macintosh name space and add it to the server volume:

   ```
   load mac
   add name space macintosh to volume SYS
   ```

   Replace SYS with the name of the server volume that will support Macintosh files.

2. Load INSTALL NLM and install NetWare for Macintosh. This involves copying the Macintosh support files to the server and can be done by selecting Product Options from the Installation Options screen.

3. Edit STARTUP.NCF file and add the following:

   ```
   load mac
   set minimum packet receive buffers=100
   ```

4. Edit AUTOEXEC.NCF and add the following:

   ```
   load appletlk net=50001 zone={"Admin"}

   load  ne2000 int=2  port=300  frame=ethenet_snap name=EtherNet1
   load  dl2000  int=3  port=200  name=LocalTalk1

   bind  appletlk EtherNet1 net=1-4 zone={"Admin", "Dept1"}
   bind  appletlk  LocalTalk1  net=6  zone={"Dept2"}

   load afp
   load atps
   ```

The APPLETLK.NLM contains the AppleTalk protocols and the AppleTalk router. The AFP.NLM and ATPS.NLM implement the Apple Filing Protocol and the Apple Print Services (see fig. 21.2). The AppleTalk routing in figure 21.2 is performed at the level of the *Datagram Delivery Protocol* (DDP) by the *Routing Table Maintenance Protocol* (RTMP).

When the LOAD APPLETLK command is issued, the AppleTalk routing and communication protocols (ASP, ATP, DDP) are loaded.

The LOAD NE2000 and LOAD DL2000 commands load the drivers for Ethernet and LocalTalk respectively. This configuration is for a network of the type shown in figure 21.3 that has an Ethernet and LocalTalk board installed in the server. The Ethernet network must use the SNAP protocol for encapsulating upper-layer AppleTalk protocols, and, therefore, the FRAME=ETHERNET_SNAP parameter must be specified when the driver is loaded. Because the DL2000 driver uses the standard *LocalTalk Link Access Protocol* (LLAP), no frame parameter is required.

The BIND statements specify the binding of the AppleTalk protocols to the NIC drivers. The NET=1-4 may look peculiar but is used to refer to the fact that Extended network addressing is being used to support Extended Networks. Extended Networks were defined at the time AppleTalk Phase 2 protocols were defined to overcome the shortcomings of AppleTalk Phase 1 protocols. AppleTalk Phase 1

protocols could not have more than 254 node addresses per physical network segment. This was due to the fact that the network address field in LLAP is 8 bits long. Modern networks, such as Ethernet and Token Ring, can easily have more than 254 node addresses on a physical network segment. To support these networks, a network range was defined. The actual node address consisted of network number and a node number pair. Each network number could have associated with it 254 node addresses. Thus, a network range of NET=1-4 can have 4 × 254 = 1,016 node addresses. LocalTalk networks are unchanged in AppleTalk Phase 2. Thus, you see the NET=6, which is a single network number. This is semantically equivalent to using a NET=6-6 network range. The network range is a pair of numbers that must be between 1 and 65,279. Physical segments cannot have overlapping numbers, otherwise the AppleTalk router would get confused. All AppleTalk routers connected to the same physical network must have the same network-number range. This is similar to the rule for connecting IPX routers to the same physical network.

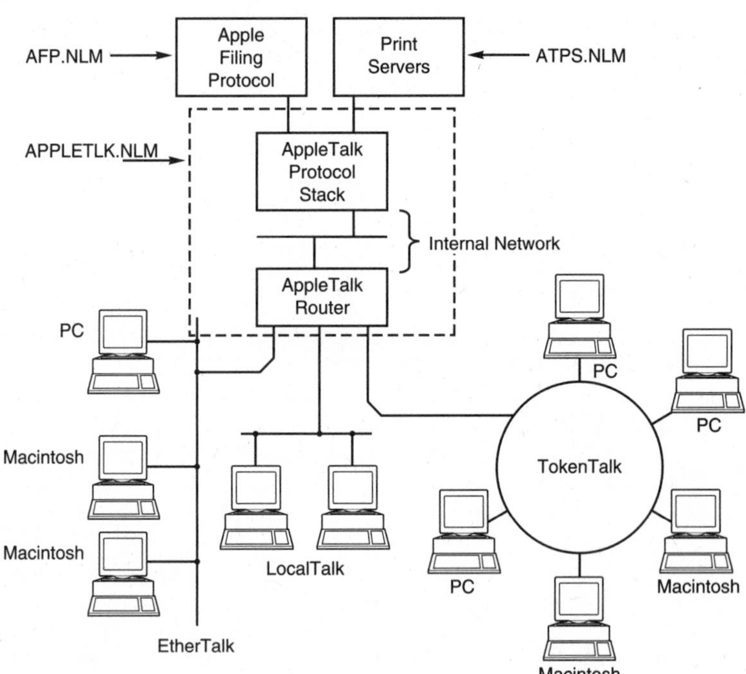

Figure 21.2
AppleTalk modules and Internal Routing.

The BIND parameters specify a zone parameter. Zones are a logical grouping of devices on an AppleTalk network that make it easier to locate devices through the Chooser panel. Searches for resources on a network are always done in the context of the currently selected zone. The user is free to pick other zones through the Chooser panel. Normally, the current zone is the same as the default zone. The default zone can be changed by the user through the Macintosh Control Panel.

The LOAD AFP and LOAD ATPS commands load the AppleTalk Filing Protocol and Print Service protocols.

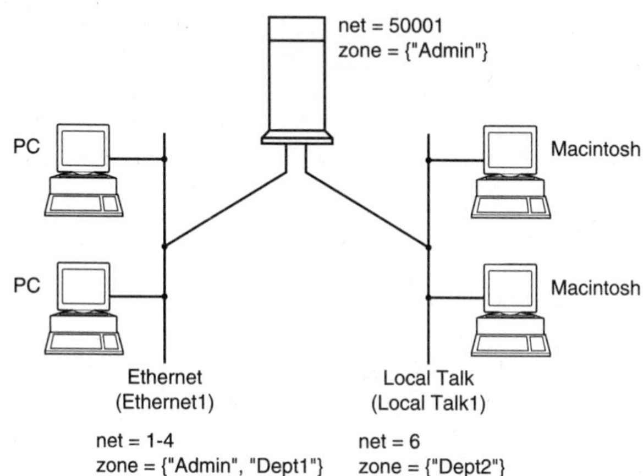

Figure 21.3
Example AppleTalk network.

One of the areas of potential confusion experienced by network administrators for Macintosh networks is the assignment of zone names. The following discussion will clarify some of these issues.

Zones are used to narrow the search for resources on the network. A user belonging to the "Engineering" department, for example, normally needs to see only those resources belonging to his department and should not be presented with resources for other departments. Occasionally, a user may need to access network resources belonging to another department, in which case, a facility exists to make the selection. In this discussion, departments of an organization are used to logically divide the network. Other logical groupings are possible such as grouping by physical location for "Building1," "Building2," and so on. These logical divisions have a name assigned to them called the *zone name.*

In the example of the AUTOEXEC.NCF file, several zone names are used. The first is the zone name used with the LOAD APPLETLK command. This zone name refers to the internal AppleTalk network within the server. This internal network number must have a network number and a zone name assigned to it. It is treated as a non-extended Phase 2 network and, therefore, has a single network number assigned to it. It is a good idea to choose network numbers with a high value for internal network numbering to distinguish between other network numbers. The internal network is contained within the AppleTalk module (fig. 21.2) and does not have any physical components. When the internal AppleTalk receives a file request for the AppleTalk server, it routes it as it would any other packet. Because the AppleTalk server is in the same module as the AppleTalk router, the packet is sent directly through the internal network to the server. The AppleTalk server with the given zone name and its print services will show up in the list for the zone name to which they belong. Zone names are represented as quoted (") strings. They can be 32 characters long and can even include spaces.

Zone names also must be specified in the BIND command. For extended networks, multiple zone names (up to 255) are possible. This is seen in the BIND NE2000 example. For non-extended networks (Phase 1 networks), a single zone name must be used as seen in the BIND DL2000 example. In extended networks, the first zone name listed becomes the default zone. If there are several routers connected to the same physical network segment, they must agree about the zone name or zone list assigned to it. Because the default zone is the first zone name, the zone list for each router must begin with the same zone name.

For complex networks, the number of possible zones—the zone list, in other words—can become large. Because there is a limit of 82 characters for the BIND command, it is not always possible to list all the zone names on the command line. To solve this problem, the -z option can be used when the AppleTalk protocol stack is loaded:

```
LOAD APPLETLK  NET=5001 -Z
```

The -z option causes the LOAD APPLETLK command to look for the file ATZONES.CFG in the SYS:SYSTEM directory. This file can be created by a text editor and is a list of the network range and zone list pairs. An example of an ATZONES.CFG file is shown as follows:

```
net=50002 zone={"Control"}
net=50003 zone={"Control"}
net=50004 zone={"Control"}

net=10-15 zone={"Control", "Building1", "Building2"}
net=16-20 zone={
"Building3",
"Building4",
"Building5"
}

net=21-25 zone={"Manufacturing", "Marketing }
```

Essentially, the ATZONES.CFG file contains a mapping between net numbers and associated zone names.

Typically, a user selects the zone name as top-level organizer for accessing the network resources in the Chooser Panel. After a zone name is selected, the user clicks on the service icon. This causes the Macintosh station to send *Name Binding Protocol* (NBP) broadcasts for the service in the selected zone. Any intervening routers will re-broadcast the NBP request to the appropriate networks. The routers directly connected to the selected zone broadcast the NBP request to all nodes in that zone. The nodes that provide the service send an NBP reply packet containing their names. These names are then displayed in the Chooser panel.

Zone names are maintained by the AppleTalk network routers. After a router discovers a new router through the RTMP protocol, it sends a *Zone Information Protocol* (ZIP) request to that router querying it for its zone information. The zone information is cached by all the routers, and as long as the router has a good entry in the RTMP table, another zone query is not issued. Routers are not automatically informed about changes in zone configuration. This becomes a problem if the zone name is deleted; it will show up as a valid zone name in the Chooser for Macintosh computers, even though it does not exist. The only way to update zone information in the list is to force the RTMP tables to change. This can be done by isolating a network segment and waiting for the RTMP protocol to detect the change. This procedure can take between 10 to 20 minutes, or longer, in a large AppleTalk internet. The other approach is to reset all routers by bringing them down and up again.

OS/2 LAN Requester and Drivers

The components of an OS/2 NetWare workstation resemble the ODI architecture discussed for DOS workstations because OS/2 NIC drivers are based on the ODI specification. The Link Support Layer provides a logical network interface for the protocol stacks to bind to. Protocol support includes IPX, SPX, and Named Pipes. The NetWare LAN requester assumes the role of the NetWare shell in DOS workstations.

To install an OS/2 NetWare station follow these steps:

1. Install OS/2 at the workstation. (Follow the instructions that come with OS/2.)

2. Install OS/2 NetWare requester and workstation drivers on the OS/2 workstation.

3. Install NetWare utilities for OS/2 on the file server.

4. Optionally, install *Remote Initial Program Load* (RIPL) capability for diskless workstations.

The NetWare OS/2 Requester

Before you install the NetWare OS/2 requester, you must install OS/2 on the workstation. OS/2 requires a hard disk for installation. Consult the OS/2 documentation to learn how to install OS/2.

To install the NetWare requester, the associated drivers for link support, and the SPX/IPX protocols, run the INSTALL program located on the REQUESTER disk. Install the NetWare OS/2 components in the C:\NETWARE directory on the OS/2 workstation hard disk.

To install the OS/2 NetWare requester follow these steps:

1. Boot the workstation with OS/2 and select either OS/2 window or OS/2 full screen from the Group-Main window.

2. Insert the REQUESTER disk in drive A and type the following at the OS/2 prompt:

   A:INSTALL

3. Follow the instructions to select the installation directory. The default is C:\NETWARE. The installation program guides you through the process.

4. Edit the CONFIG.SYS file to enable the network driver for the NIC in the OS/2 workstation. You usually must remove the REM (remark) comment that precedes the *DEVICE=* statement for the NIC driver.

The following list shows the CONFIG.SYS file for an OS/2 NetWare workstation. The CONFIG.SYS statements are grouped for easy identification. Most of the CONFIG.SYS commands deal with OS/2

configuration. Toward the end of the CONFIG.SYS are the NetWare requester components. Before the NetWare requester component (NWREQ.SYS) is activated, a number of support components, such as link support, NIC driver, and protocol stack, must be activated. A number of statements dealing with other protocols such as SPX, Named Pipes, and NetBIOS are commented out. If these components are needed for the OS/2 NetWare workstation, the REM that precedes them must be removed.

The NetWare requester components and protocol stacks are all implemented as device drivers. For example, IPX is implemented by the IPX.SYS device driver, SPX by the SPX.SYS device driver, Named Pipes by the NMPIPE.SYS device driver, and NetBIOS by the NETBIOS.SYS device driver. This contrasts with DOS workstations that implement these components by terminate-and-stay resident (TSR) programs.

```
IFS=C:\OS2\HPFS.IFS  /CACHE:512 /CRECL:4 /AUTOCHECK:C
PROTSHELL=C:\OS2\PMSHELL.EXE
SET USER_INI=C:\OS2\OS2.INI
SET SYSTEM_INI=C:\OS2\OS2SYS.INI
SET OS2_SHELL=C:\OS2\CMD.EXE
SET AUTOSTART=PROGRAMS,TASKLIST,FOLDERS,CONNECTIONS
SET RUNWORKPLACE=C:\OS2\PMSHELL.EXE
SET COMSPEC=C:\OS2\CMD.EXE
LIBPATH=.;C:\OS2\DLL;C:\OS2\MDOS;C:\;C:\OS2\APPS\DLL;C:\NETWARE;
SET PATH=C:\OS2;C:\OS2\SYSTEM;C:\OS2\MDOS\WINOS2;C:\OS2\INSTALL;C:\
;C:\OS2\MDOS;C:\OS2\APPS;L:\OS2;P:\OS2;C:\NETWARE;
SET DPATH=C:\OS2;C:\OS2\SYSTEM;C:\OS2\MDOS\WINOS2;C:\OS2\INSTALL;C:\
;C:\OS2\BITMAP;C:\OS2\MDOS;C:\OS2\APPS;C:\NETWARE;P:\OS2;
SET PROMPT=$i[$p]
SET HELP=C:\OS2\HELP;C:\OS2\HELP\TUTORIAL;
SET GLOSSARY=C:\OS2\HELP\GLOSS;
SET IPF_KEYS=SBCS
PRIORITY_DISK_IO=YES
FILES=20
DEVICE=C:\OS2\TESTCFG.SYS
DEVICE=C:\OS2\DOS.SYS
DEVICE=C:\OS2\PMDD.SYS
BUFFERS=30
IOPL=YES
DISKCACHE=64,LW
MAXWAIT=3
MEMMAN=SWAP,PROTECT
SWAPPATH=C:\OS2\SYSTEM 2048 2048
BREAK=OFF
THREADS=256
PRINTMONBUFSIZE=134,134,134
COUNTRY=001,C:\OS2\SYSTEM\COUNTRY.SYS
SET KEYS=ON
REM SET DELDIR=C:\DELETE,512;D:\DELETE,512;
BASEDEV=PRINT01.SYS
BASEDEV=IBM1FLPY.ADD
BASEDEV=OS2DASD.DMD
```

```
SET EPMPATH=C:\OS2\APPS
SET FAXPM=C:\OS2\APPS
DEVICE=C:\OS2\APPS\SASYNCDA.SYS
PROTECTONLY=NO
SHELL=C:\OS2\MDOS\COMMAND.COM C:\OS2\MDOS /P
FCBS=16,8
RMSIZE=640
DEVICE=C:\OS2\MDOS\VEMM.SYS
DOS=LOW,NOUMB
DEVICE=C:\OS2\MDOS\VDPX.SYS
DEVICE=C:\OS2\MDOS\VXMS.SYS /UMB
DEVICE=C:\OS2\MDOS\VDPMI.SYS
DEVICE=C:\OS2\MDOS\VWIN.SYS
DEVICE=C:\OS2\MDOS\VCDROM.SYS
REM DEVICE=C:\OS2\PCMCIA.SYS
REM DEVICE=C:\OS2\MDOS\VPCMCIA.SYS
BASEDEV=OS2CDROM.DMD /Q
IFS=C:\OS2\CDFS.IFS /Q
BASEDEV=OS2SCSI.DMD
BASEDEV=NECCDS1.FLT
BASEDEV=AHA154X.ADD
DEVICE=C:\OS2\MDOS\VMOUSE.SYS
DEVICE=C:\OS2\POINTDD.SYS
DEVICE=C:\OS2\MOUSE.SYS SERIAL=COM2
DEVICE=C:\OS2\COM.SYS
DEVICE=C:\OS2\MDOS\VCOM.SYS
CODEPAGE=437,850
DEVINFO=KBD,US,C:\OS2\KEYBOARD.DCP
DEVINFO=SCR,VGA,C:\OS2\VIOTBL.DCP
SET VIDEO_DEVICES=VIO_VGA
SET VIO_VGA=DEVICE(BVHVGA)
DEVICE=C:\OS2\MDOS\VSVGA.SYS

REM - NetWare Requester statements BEGIN -
DEVICE=C:\NETWARE\LSL.SYS
RUN=C:\NETWARE\DDAEMON.EXE
DEVICE=C:\NETWARE\NE2000.SYS
DEVICE=C:\NETWARE\IPX.SYS
DEVICE=C:\NETWARE\SPX.SYS
RUN=C:\NETWARE\SPDAEMON.EXE
rem DEVICE=C:\NETWARE\NMPIPE.SYS
rem DEVICE=C:\NETWARE\NPSERVER.SYS
rem RUN=C:\NETWARE\NPDAEMON.EXE NP_COMPUTERNAME
DEVICE=C:\NETWARE\NWREQ.SYS
IFS=C:\NETWARE\NWIFS.IFS
RUN=C:\NETWARE\NWDAEMON.EXE
rem DEVICE=C:\NETWARE\NETBIOS.SYS
rem RUN=C:\NETWARE\NBDAEMON.EXE
DEVICE=C:\NETWARE\VIPX.SYS
DEVICE=C:\NETWARE\VSHELL.SYS
REM - NetWare Requester statements END -
```

OS/2 NetWare Utilities

21

OS/2 NetWare workstations cannot use the DOS NetWare utilities installed during the server installation. Novell has written OS/2 versions of utilities, such as SYSCON, FCONSOLE, FILER, and SESSION. These utilities are on disks labeled OS2UTIL-1, OS2UTIL-2, and so on. The utilities must be installed on the server for OS/2 NetWare workstations to use them. This must be accomplished as a separate step.

To install the OS/2 NetWare utilities complete the following steps:

1. Boot up the workstation with OS/2 and select either OS/2 window or OS/2 full screen from the Group-Main window.

2. Insert the OS2UTIL-1 disk in drive A and use the LOGIN program to log in as SUPERVISOR to the NetWare server (*serverName*):

   ```
   A:\LOGIN\LOGIN serverName/SUPERVISOR
   ```

   (Replace *serverName* with the name of the server.)

3. Change to the drive that contains the OS2UTIL-1 disk and type the following command:

   ```
   SERVINST serverName
   ```

4. Follow the instructions until the OS/2 NetWare utilities are installed.

After the OS/2 NetWare utilities are installed, the OS/2 utilities are located in the directories indicated in the preceding list. The separate directories SYS:LOGIN/OS2, SYS:PUBLIC/OS2, and SYS:SYSTEM/OS2 are created to avoid name conflicts with DOS utilities.

When the OS/2 NetWare workstation logs in to a NetWare server that has the NetWare utilities installed, drive L is mapped to the SYS:LOGIN/OS2 directory. This enables you to invoke the OS/2 LOGIN program in that directory. SYSCON must be used to modify the user's login script to include drive mappings to SYS:PUBLIC/OS2.

To invoke the OS/2 LOGIN program, when attached to a NetWare server without the OS/2 NetWare utilities installed, you must copy the OS/2 LOGIN program onto the OS/2 workstation's hard disk.

NET.CFG for OS/2 NetWare Workstations

To configure the NetWare requester for non-default settings, you must use the NET.CFG configuration file. The NET.CFG file for OS/2 is similar to that used for DOS workstations, but some differences exist. The main section headings for the OS/2 NET.CFG file are left-justified, and the entries under each heading are indented by a space or a tab.

The BUFFERS parameter can be changed in the LINK SUPPORT section.

The general form of the BUFFERS parameter is as follows:

```
BUFFERS bufferNumber [bufferSize]
```

The BUFFERS parameter changes the number (*bufferNumber*) and size (*bufferSize*) of communication buffers.

The *bufferSize*, which is optional, has a default value of 1130 bytes. The total amount of buffer space for LSL buffers must not exceed 64 KB:

```
bufferNumber × bufferSize <= 64 KB
```

The *protocolName* in PROTOCOL STACK can be IPX or SPX. Each of the protocol stacks—IPX and SPX—has a different set of parameters. Tables 21.1 and 21.2 describe the parameters for IPX and SPX.

Examples:

```
PROTOCOL STACK IPX

        socket 128    ; Increase socket count to max of 128
        bind trxnet    ; Bind IPX to Novell RX-Net driver

PROTOCOL STACK SPX

        sessions 19    ; SPX session to 19
        abort timeout 450000    ; Abort time out to 45 secs.
        verify timeout 20000    ; Verify time out to 40 secs.
        listen timeout 15000    ; Listen timeout to 15 secs.
        retry count 10    ; Reduce retries to 10
```

Table 21.1
OS/2 IPX Parameters for Protocol Stack

Parameter	Meaning
socket count	Specifies the maximum number of sockets (count) that IPX can have open at a workstation. The number of sockets can be from 9 to 128. The default value is 32.
router mem size	Specifies the memory size in bytes in the router memory pool allocated for routing. Default value is 450.
bind name	Specifies the NIC driver name that is bound to the IPX protocol stack. Primarily used for workstations with several NICs.

Table 21.2
OS/2 SPX Parameters for Protocol Stack

Parameter	Meaning
sessions count	Specifies number of SPX connections (count) to be supported. Acceptable values are between 8 and 256 with a default of 16.
abort timeout val	Specifies the number of milliseconds (val) SPX must wait for an acknowledgment before terminating a connection. Minimum value is 10 milliseconds, and the default is 30000 milliseconds (30 seconds).
verify timeout val	Specifies the number of milliseconds (val) SPX must wait between packet transmissions before asking for an acknowledgment that the connection is still intact. Minimum value is 10 milliseconds, and the default is 3000 milliseconds (3 seconds).
listen timeout val	Specifies the number of milliseconds (val) SPX waits for a packet from the connection. Minimum value is 10 milliseconds and the default is 6000 milliseconds (6 seconds). If no packet arrives in the specified time, SPX includes a request for immediate acknowledgment in every packet sent. If no acknowledgment is received, SPX uses the abort timeout value.
retry count val	Specifies the number of times (val) the workstation attempts to resend a packet. Acceptable values are from 1 to 255 with a default of 20.

The NETWARE REQUESTER Section

The OS/2 NetWare requester can be configured in the NETWARE REQUESTER section. The parameters that can be controlled are described in table 21.3.

Example:

```
NETWARE REQUESTER

        sessions 15            ; Set to 15 sessions
        cache buffers 20       ; 20 read/write buffers
        request retries 5      ; Reduce retries to 5
        preferred server KSS   ; Attach to server with name KSS
```

Table 21.3
OS/2 NetWare Requester Parameters

Parameter	Meaning
cache buffers cnt	Specifies number of buffers (cnt) at workstation to be used to cache data from open files. Acceptable values range from 0 to 128 with a default of 8.
sessions cnt	Specifies number of file server connections (cnt) that the requester supports. Acceptable values range from 8 to 20 with a default of 8. (Each connection uses at least 3 IPX sockets.)
request retries cnt	Specifies number of times (cnt) the requester tries to resend a request following a communication error. Minimum value is 5 and the default value is 20.
preferred server sn	Specifies the server name (sn) to attach to when the NetWare requester loads.

The NETWARE NETBIOS Section

The NETWARE NETBIOS section is used only if the NetBIOS protocol stack is loaded (DEVICE=NETBIOS.SYS in CONFIG.SYS). Configuration of NetBIOS protocol includes name management, session creation, and session management. Table 21.4 describes the NetBIOS parameters.

Example:

```
PROTOCOL NETBIOS

        names 28        ; Name table size 28
        sessions 20     ; NetBIOS sessions
        internet off    ; Turn claim-name packets off across
                          internet
```

Table 21.4
OS/2 NetWare NetBIOS Parameters

Parameter	Meaning
names *cnt*	Specifies the number of names *cnt* the workstation can have in its name table. The values can range from 4 to 128 with a default of 26.

continues

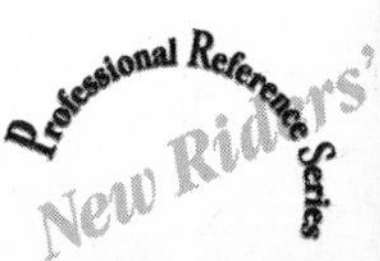

Table 21.4, Continued
OS/2 NetWare NetBIOS Parameters

Parameter	Meaning
sessions *cnt*	Specifies the number of NetBIOS sessions *cnt* the workstation can have. The values can range from 4 to 128 with a default of 32.
commands *numb*	Specifies the number of outstanding NetBIOS commands *numb* that can be waiting for completion at the workstation. The values range from 4 to 128 with a default of 12.
sessions *cnt*	Specifies the number of NetBIOS sessions *cnt* the workstation can have. The values range from 4 to 128 with a default of 32.
retry delay *numb*	Specifies delay in milliseconds *numb*. If no response is received to a NetBIOS connection request or a packet transmission, it waits for the specified amount of time before trying again. The default value is 500.
retry count *numb*	Specifies the number of times *numb* NetBIOS tries to establish a connection or send data, if there is no response the first time. The default value is 20.
internet [on|off]	The internet parameter determines the behavior of the claim-name packet. NetBIOS requires all stations to have a unique logical name. Claim-name packets establish a unique NetBIOS name. When set to ON, NetBIOS broadcasts claim-name packets to all stations on the internet to establish the uniqueness of the claim-name packet. When internet is OFF, NetBIOS sends name-claim packets to stations on the local network only. It ignores responses from outside the local network.
broadcast count *N*	Specifies the number of times *N* NetBIOS broadcasts a claim for a name. Minimum value is 1. Default value is 4 if internet is ON, or 2 if internet is OFF.
broadcast delay *N*	Specifies delay in milliseconds *N*. NetBIOS waits for the specified time between a query and claim broadcasts. Value can be from 100 to 65,535. Default values are 2000 if internet is ON or 1000 if internet is OFF.
abort timeout *N*	Specifies timeout value in milliseconds *N*. If no acknowledgment is received in the timeout interval, NetBIOS terminates the connection. Minimum value is 500. Default value is 30,000.

Parameter	Meaning
verify timeout *N*	Specifies the timeout in milliseconds *N*. NetBIOS waits for at least the specified value before sending a "probe" packet to the remote station to confirm the connection. Value can be from 100 to 65,535. Default value is 3000.
listen timeout *N*	Specifies timeout in milliseconds *N*. NetBIOS waits for the specified time for a packet from a remote station. It then sends a "probe" packet to verify its connection. Value can be from 200 to 65,535. Default value is 6000.

The LINK DRIVER *driverName* Section

The *driverName* in the LINK DRIVER section heading must be replaced with the OS/2 network driver name. All parameters included in the LINK DRIVER section heading apply to *driverName*. These parameters are as follows:

- DMA
- INT
- MEM
- PORT
- NODE ADDRESS
- SLOT
- FRAME
- PROTOCOL

These parameters have the same meaning and syntax as described for ODI LINK DRIVER parameters. Refer to the section on ODI drivers to see how to use these parameters. The only difference is the SLOT parameter. SLOT has an additional option—the "?" parameter. The SLOT ? parameter tells the OS/2 NetWare requester to find the first board corresponding to the board designated in the LINK DRIVER *driverName*.

If OS/2 NetWare stations are used with IBM Source Routing bridges, the source routing driver must be enabled by placing the following statement in the OS/2 CONFIG.SYS file:

```
DEVICE=C:\NETWARE\ROUTE.SYS
```

The router parameters can be configured through the PROTOCOL ROUTER main-section in the OS/2 NET.CFG file. The general syntax of the parameters for this section is as follows:


```
PROTOCOL ROUTE
        source route def gbr mbr nodes n board n
```

The parameters for the source route are DEF, GBE, MBR, NODES N, and BOARD N. These parameters have the same meaning as the corresponding DOS ODI source routing parameters. For details about these parameters, consult Chapter 20, "Supporting DOS Workstations."

For example, to enable DEF, GEBR, and MBR at the OS/2 NetWare station, place the following in the NET.CFG file:

```
protocol route
        source route def gbr mbr
```

The NetWare SPOOLER Section

The NetWare spooler controls print jobs initiated at the workstation.

The NetWare SPOOLER section takes the following general syntax:

```
netware spooler
    form n
    copies n
    [keep ¦ no keep]
    size n
    [tabs ¦ no tabs]
    file s
    name s
    [banner ¦ no banner]
    [form feed ¦ no form feed]
    maxsetup n
    maxreset n
```

Table 21.5 explains each of the parameters of the NetWare SPOOLER syntax.

Table 21.5
OS/2 NetWare SPOOLER Parameters

Parameter	Value
form *n*	Specifies the form number *n* to be used for printing. Default is form 0.
copies *n*	Specifies the number *n* of copies to be printed. Default is 1 copy.
[keep|no keep]	Specifies that printing should continue keep even if capture is interrupted. Default is keep.

Parameter	Value
space *n*	Specifies the number *n* of spaces in a tab. Default is 8.
[tabs|no tabs]	Spooler expands tab to the number of spaces specified in the space n parameter. Default is tab.
file *s*	Specifies the filename *s* to be printed in the banner.
name *s*	Specifies the user name *s* to be printed in the banner.
[banner|no banner]	Enables/disables printing of banner.
[form feed|no form feed]	Enables/disables form feed at end of job.
maxsetup *n*	Specifies the maximum number of characters (*n*) setup string that is sent to the printer.
maxrest *n*	Specifies the maximum number of characters (*n*) in the reset string that is sent to the printer.

UNIX Workstations

UNIX is an operating system that runs on a broad range of hardware platforms. UNIX was originally used on minicomputers, mainframes, and supercomputers before becoming available on engineering workstations and the IBM PC.

Most engineering workstations that run UNIX use the Motorola 68000 family of microprocessors. Many UNIX vendors also have ported their version of UNIX to the Intel 80XXX microprocessor. At one time, a version of UNIX ran on an IBM PC/XT—an Intel 8086 microprocessor. Today, most of the interest in the Intel family is focused on the Intel 80386 or higher. These microprocessors have the power to run UNIX efficiently.

Because UNIX runs on a variety of hardware platforms and because so many varieties of UNIX exist, UNIX hardware requirements cannot be generalized. The UNIX vendor can help to determine the hardware requirements you need. Minimum RAM for most UNIX versions that run on the PC family is 4 MB. Experts recommend that you use at least 12 MB of RAM for serious work. Hard disk size depends on the UNIX components installed, but generally a 200 MB or larger disk is best.

Because UNIX workstations commonly use TCP/IP as the transport protocol for networking, integration with NetWare requires that NetWare also run TCP/IP. Currently, TCP/IP support is available only in NetWare 3.11 or higher. NetWare 3.*x* enables the server to act as a NFS server and an IP router (see Chapter 3, "Bridging and Routing").

UnixWare

21

UnixWare is UNIX System V Release 4 that supports a built-in NetWare SPX/IPX protocol stack. This product has been developed by UNIVEL, a joint venture of USL and Novell. Because USL has been purchased by Novell from AT&T, it is now a wholly owned subsidiary of Novell. The UnixWare product comes in two main versions: a personal edition and an Application Server. The personal edition is meant for the end-user who needs to run 32-bit UNIX applications on a desktop and has no need for the complexity of a full UNIX version with its development tools. The Application Server is meant for developers who want to write client/server applications with the server applications running on the UnixWare Application server back-end. The Application Server provides the developer with the full range of UNIX development tools.

One of UnixWare's attractive features is its ease of installation. It can be installed from CD-ROM and is much simpler to install compared to other UNIX versions. An X-Windows-based graphical interface is provided. The user has a choice of using either MOTIF or OpenLook interface. UnixWare uses the term MOOLIT to describe its MOTIF and OpenLook option.

Figure 21.4 shows UnixWare used on a NetWare network. The UnixWare Application Server also is positioned as a down-sizing platform for Mainframe-based applications. It comes with a complete set of development tools, such as COBOL compilers, linkers, and libraries, to port mainframe applications. The down-sized applications or new server applications can serve as back-ends to either DOS-based applications running an SPX/IPX stack or to other UnixWare Personal Edition desktops. The UnixWare desktop has built-in SPX/IPX protocol stack and a NetWare requester. It can be used as a NetWare client to a NetWare server by making a connection through the SPX/IPX protocol stack. Because UnixWare supports TCP/IP, this can be used to access other UNIX servers and NetWare running NetWare for NFS. NetWare for NFS provides NFS, FTP, and remote XCONSOLE services.

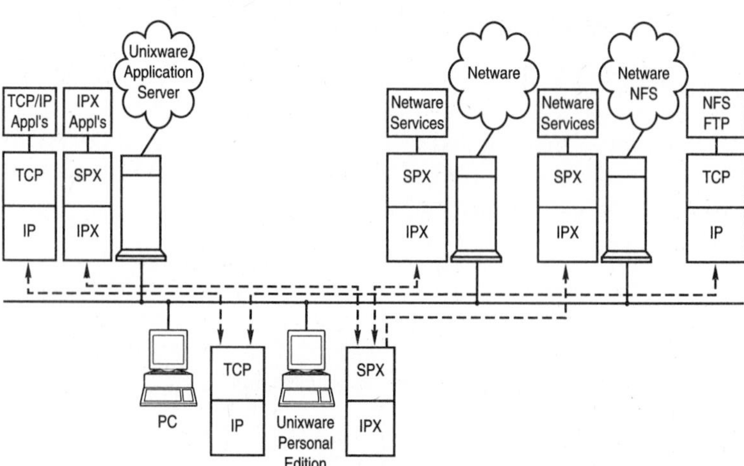

Figure 21.4
Example of a UnixWare network.

From a user's perspective, UnixWare provides the following features:

- **Graphical desktop.** Choice of MOTIF or OpenLook.
- **NetWare networking.** You can access a NetWare server using SPX/IPX.
- **Application compatibility.** Thousands of UNIX applications, including those that run on the popular SCO UNIX.
- **Multitasking.** This enables the user to run several applications simultaneously.
- **Multiuser capability.** The Personal Edition supports 2 users and the Application server has an unlimited number of users.

Windows NT

Windows NT is a 32-bit multitasking operating system which has a GUI interface based on the latest releases of Microsoft's Windows family products.

Support for Windows NT is available from both Microsoft and Novell. Before installing any of the client software, you should check with Microsoft and Novell to see if any patches to the Windows NT clients are required. You can obtain the requesters from Microsoft and Novell. They are also available on CompuServe and the Internet (host ftp.microsoft.com or ftp.novell.com). The client software kits contain detailed instructions on installing the software and you should consult these as there could be last minute changes that are usually documented in these sources.

Microsoft's NetWare Workstation Compatible Service (NWCS)

Microsoft's NetWare Requester, called the *NetWare Workstation Compatible Service* (NWCS) uses an IPX-compatible protocol implemented by Microsoft called NWLink. The NWLink protocol module in Windows NT contains Microsoft's implementation of IPX, SPX. With NWCS, you can configure the Windows NT clients to use packet burst provided the NetWare server supports it.

You can use NWCS to connect to NetWare 2.*x*, 3.*x* servers. You can only connect to NetWare 4.*x* servers in the bindery emulation mode. At the moment, NWCS does not include support for NetWare Directory services that require extended NCP services. You can use tools such as FILER, SYSCON, MAP to access and configure network services.

NWCS provides a gateway that can be implemented on a Windows NT station and allows users connecting to the Windows NT machine to access resources on the NetWare server. The Windows NT machine that acts as a gateway logs in to the NetWare server on behalf of the Windows NT users (see fig. 21.5). The Windows NT gateway machine logs in to the NetWare server as a user that is defined on

the NetWare server. This NetWare user must be a member of the NetWare group NTGATEWAY. If such a group does not exist, you must create one on the NetWare server and make the NetWare user account a member of this group. You must also assign to this user any rights/permissions that you would like the Windows NT users to have. If several Windows NT machines need access to the same NetWare server, you should define separate NetWare user accounts and make them members of group NTGATEWAY.

Figure 21.5
NWCS Gateway.

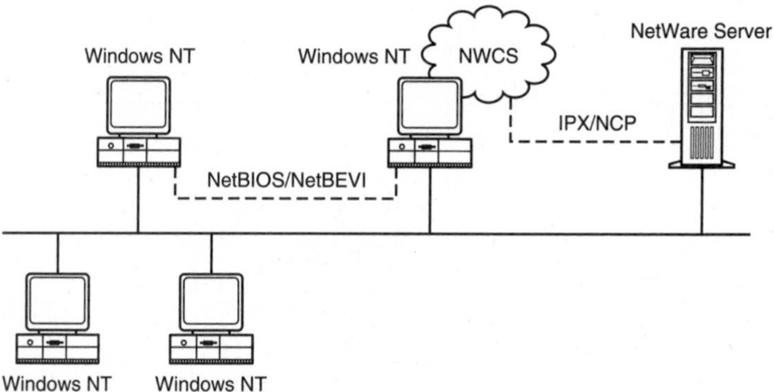

To enable the NWCS to NetWare Gateway you must have NWCS installed first. Next, you can use the steps below as a guideline to enable the NetWare gateway:

1. Open Control panel and activate (click using mouse button) the NWCS icon.
2. Click on the Gateway button.
3. Fill in the name and password of the NetWare user account on the screen.
4. Fill in the share names using Microsoft's *Universal Naming Convention* (UNC). For example if you are sharing volume SYS on server KSS, the UNC share name will be as follows:

   ```
   \\KSS\SYS
   ```

5. Windows NT or Windows clients can map to this share name using their native NetBEUI/NetBIOS protocols and access services on the NetWare server.

Novell's NetWare Client for Windows NT

Novell allows the use of either the NWLink protocol module and the NDIS drivers or you can use the ODI drivers that come with the NetWare Client for Windows NT software. At the moment of writing this packet burst support can be configured only if you use the ODI drivers.

The NetWare client can be used to connect to NetWare 2.*x*, 3.*x* or 4.*x* servers. Support for accessing NetWare Directory Services comes with Novell's version of the client software.

Novell's client software supports a Novell DOS box icon. Clicking on this opens a DOS session that enables you to log in and access network services. You can use this box to access utilities such as SYSCON, FILER, MAP. At the moment of writing this, you cannot access these utilities from the NT command prompt.

Beame & Whiteside's MultiConnect for Windows NT

Beame & Whiteside offer MultiConnect for Windows NT that allows NetWare clients to access Windows NT servers. This product runs on Windows NT and causes it to appear as a bindery-based NetWare server to NetWare clients. In other words, it emulates NetWare services on a Windows NT machine (see fig. 21.6). The MultiConnect implements IPX/SPX/NCP protocols on the Windows NT machine.

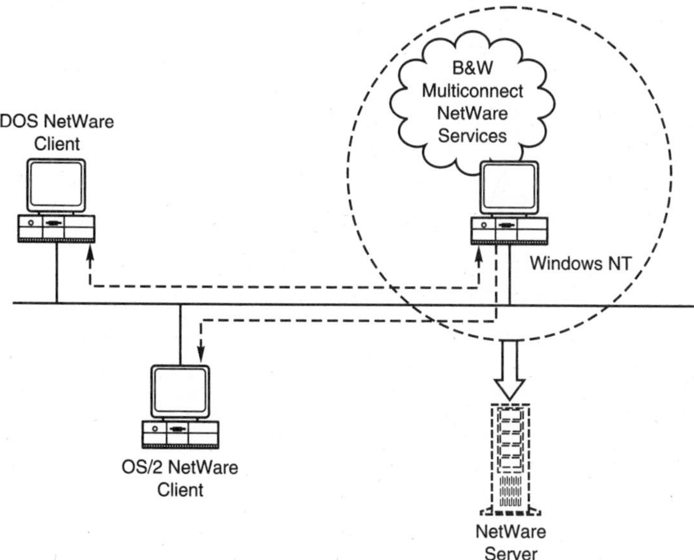

Figure 21.6
MultiConnect for Windows NT.

Summary

This chapter discussed NetWare's support for Macintosh and OS/2 workstations and introduced you to Novell's UnixWare product, a UNIX environment that can access NetWare servers by means of standard IPX/SPX protocols.

Performance Tuning in NetWare 2.2, 3.*x*, and 4.*x* Servers

In the previous chapters, you learned how to install and configure NetWare 2.2, 3.11, 3.12, and 4.*x*-based servers. Several factors affect network performance. In this chapter you learn what these factors are and how you can improve the performance of your network. Some of the decisions that affect network performance can be made before installing a network, whereas others can be made only after installation. Decisions made prior to network installation include the choice of server machine platforms, network adapters, disk subsystems, and so on. To fine-tune the network after installation, you must monitor how well the network is performing. Some of these tools, such as MONITOR NLM for NetWare 3.*x* and 4.*x*, are provided by Novell. Third-party tools such as the Frye Utilities perform similar functions and work on both NetWare 2.*x* and 3.*x*.

Future versions of NetWare are expected to improve on network management and performance monitoring functions. Protocol analyzers such as LANalyzer are powerful tools for improving network performance. The purpose of such monitoring tools is to analyze current performance, checking for bottlenecks. When you discover the bottlenecks, you can take steps toward eliminating them.

Understanding the Factors Affecting Network Performance

Because the network is made up of hardware and software components, the factors that affect network performance are hardware- and software-related.

This section enables you to have better understanding of the hardware and software performance factors. There is a strong relationship between hardware and software factors, and both must be considered together to evaluate the performance of a network. This chapter first examines the hardware performance factors, and then the software factors.

Hardware Components Affecting Server Performance

The following major hardware-related factors affect network performance:

- Disk subsystem: speed and storage capacity
- Network adapters: speed, bus width, and network access technology
- Server bus characteristics
- Speed of server and workstation computers

The hardware-related factors are not confined to any single piece of equipment, such as the server machine, but also include the type of network adapters at the server and the workstation, and the network access speed and method (CSMA/CD, Token Access, and so on). One of the most important hardware elements is the server computer, its disk subsystem, and the type of network adapter inside the server. In NetWare LANs, the server computer plays a central role; any improvements on the server hardware directly affect network performance.

Sometimes, installing a faster computer as the server does not necessarily improve performance. Understanding this point is important because the performance of the entire network is limited by its slowest component. If the physical layer is the slowest component of the network, for example, replacing the server machine or disk subsystem with a faster component does not improve performance in general.

Some of the tools described here can help you determine which component is the cause of the bottleneck. Generally, however, no cut-and-dry formulas for determining performance bottlenecks currently exist. Most experienced network managers use a combination of knowledge of their network, knowledge of underlying technology, and good common sense and intuition to detect and isolate performance-related problems. Some promising technology exists in the area of expert systems to better solve these problems. But expert systems are only as good as the people programming them; they can help guide you to a solution to the problem but cannot necessarily solve the problem for you.

Disk Subsystem

The most important function a NetWare server performs is to provide file services. Because the server files are stored on the server disk, a fast disk subsystem results in faster file services and, from a user's perspective, a faster network. The disk subsystem is responsible for filling and emptying the contents of the operating system cache to satisfy network requests for data retrieval and storage. The operating system cache should be large enough to satisfy most network read retrieval requests from cache. The disk subsystem should be fast enough to keep the operating system cache full of needed data.

The data-transfer rate between the CPU and the disk is determined by the disk, the disk controller, and the bus interfaces. The older PC AT disks that used MFM encoding are among the slowest hard disks. Today, most disks use a higher level of RLL encoding, allowing them to pack more data per sector, which means that the disk has to rotate smaller distances (requiring less time) to deliver the same amount of data. This translates to faster data-transfer rates.

The types of disks that give the best performance in the marketplace today are disks based on *Integrated Device Electronics* (IDE), *Enhanced Small Devices Interface* (ESDI), and *Small Computers Systems Interface* (SCSI).

The IDE disks replace the older AT-style disks and provide a higher performance interface between the computer and the disk, enabling them to be faster than the AT-style disks. IDE implements most of its logic on the electronics on the drive itself. However, IDE uses the computer's CPU to perform many of its tasks. It is limited to drives per controller, has a data transfer rate of 2 to 3 MB/sec, and has a maximum file size limit of 528 MB owing to PC BIOS limits. Some of the more recent IDE drives perform close to SCSI speeds, if only one drive is used. If two drives are used, IDE usually performs at less than SCSI speed owing to the fact that the device electronic controls have to be shared by two drives.

The ESDI interface developed out of the I/O interface used in minicomputer environments and is faster than the IDE disks. The SCSI interface is the most versatile because it enables multiple devices to be connected to an external I/O bus. SCSI disk drives usually are external; they have their own power supply and therefore tend to be more reliable.

The disk manufacturers seem to have voted on the SCSI interface as the best technique for providing high-capacity, high-speed disks. The most recent version of SCSI interface, called the *SCSI-II interface*, has some performance improvements over the older SCSI-I interface.

SCSI devices can transfer data at rates up to 40 MB/sec (320 Mbps), which is well over the speed of Ethernet (10 Mbps), Token Ring (16 Mbps), ARCnet PLUS (20 Mbps) and FDDI (100 Mbps). In actual practice, these devices achieve smaller data-transfer rates if used with the ISA-style bus because the ISA bus currently is limited to transfer rates of 4 Mbps to 8 Mbps. Therefore, for best performance, use SCSI devices with either the microchannel or EISA bus that can support higher data rates.

SCSI-I uses an 8-bit bus and has a data rate of 5 MB/sec. There can be 7 devices per master device (the SCSI controller) that are daisy-chained on the SCSI bus. Also, only one command can be pending for a SCSI device.

SCSI-II supports the SCSI-I command set and uses parity checking on the bus to detect errors. It also supports a *bus disconnect* feature where a SCSI device releases the bus while performing a command. This makes the SCSI bus available for other devices. SCSI-II overcomes the SCSI-I limitation of one command per SCSI device. With SCSI-II, multiple commands can be issued to a SCSI-II compatible device which are kept in the *Tag Command Queue* (TCQ). Because the device holds commands in a queue, it can execute them in sequence as each command finishes, and does not have to wait for the next command from the SCSI controller as in the case of SCSI-I. This leads to a dramatic improvement in performance. Other performance improvement features of SCSI-II are double the bus clock speed of SCSI-I, and double bus width (16 bits). The current classifications that are used in the industry for classifying SCSI features are shown in table 22.1

Table 22.1
SCSI Classifications

Classification	Bus Width (bits)	Data Transfer Rate (MB/sec)	Command Queuing
SCSI-I	8	5	Single command only
SCSI-II	8,16,32	5, 10, 20	Supports Tag Command Queuing
Fast SCSI-II	8	10	Supports Tag Command Queuing
Fast and Wide SCSI-II	16	20	Supports Tag Command Queuing
Fast and 32-bit Wide SCSI-II	32 (most devices do not support 32 bits)	40	Supports Tag Command Queuing

A new type of disk subsystem, called RAID, is also popular. It has the potential of providing a high degree of reliability through a fault-tolerant architecture. *Redundant Array of Inexpensive Disks* (RAID) enables data to be distributed across multiple inexpensive disks, so that if any disk were to fail, data can be recovered based on information on the other active disks.

Network Adapters

In a networking environment, the network adapters determine the data-transfer rate through the network media. Not all adapters for a network technology are created equal. There are many manufacturers of Ethernet adapters, for example; although they all comply with the Ethernet standard of 10 Mbps, they have different effective data rates. Network adapters from 3COM are quite popular, but there are at least two types of adapters for IBM PCs: 3COM EtherLink and 3COM EtherLink Plus. The 3COM EtherLink Plus is a higher-performance card, and is therefore more expensive. It has more packet buffers and faster circuitry. Ideally, all stations on a network should have high-performance cards to obtain the maximum possible data-transfer rate. If cost is a major factor, at least the server computer and external routers should have a high-performance card. Using a high-performance network adapter for the server can dramatically improve the network performance.

The following factors affect the performance of a network adapter:

- Media access scheme
- Raw bit rate
- Onboard processor
- NIC-to-host transfer

The *media access scheme* refers to the arbitration mechanism, inherent in baseband LANs, that limits how the messages are placed on the media. Examples of this are CSMA/CD, used in Ethernet and IEEE 802.3, and Token Access, used in IBM Token Ring (IEEE 802.5). Token Access gives a deterministic performance even under heavy network loads, whereas CSMA/CD is susceptible to reduced throughput because of collisions under heavy loads. Under light loads, on the other hand, the CSMA/CD access method is simpler and faster than Token Access.

The *raw bit rate* is the maximum bit rate possible on a given medium. The effective bit rate (taking into account protocol, overhead, and queue and processing delays) is much less. The raw bit rate represents an upper limit for the medium.

Effective use of an onboard processor can speed up a network adapter. If the firmware for the NIC is poorly written, however, it can have just the opposite effect as that seen in the earlier IBM PC Broadband LAN adapters. Some vendors implement upper-layer protocol processing on the NIC card itself for better overall throughput. An example of such an NIC is Federal Technologies' EXOS series board that has onboard TCP/IP processing.

Data arriving on the network adapter needs to be transferred into the host computer's memory. The NIC connection to the host channel can be implemented using shared memory, DMA, or I/O ports. NICs may use any of these methods or a combination of them. Observations have shown that shared memory is the fastest, followed by I/O ports, with DMA the slowest. Avoid NICs that use DMA exclusively for transferring data, as these probably are slow NICs. Some cards use a combination of shared memory and DMA, which gives them a certain level of parallelism that can improve their performance.

The data width of the bus interface has a dramatic effect on NIC-to-host transfer speeds. Current data widths are 8, 16, or 32 bits. The wider the data width, the faster the data transfer. EISA and Micro Channel NICs are faster than ISA NICs. It is a good strategy to use an EISA or Micro Channel machine with an EISA or Micro Channel adapter at the server because network traffic is concentrated at this point.

Try to avoid mixing network adapters from different vendors on one LAN. Although all vendors claim to follow a standard, important implementation differences that can affect the performance of a network may exist between them. Some Ethernet vendors implement the random-time backoff algorithm differently, for example, so that in case of Ethernet bus contention and collision, they will timeout before network adapters from other vendors. In practical terms, this means that these network adapters access the LAN bus before network adapters from other vendors. Another way to look at this is to see these network adapters as "poor citizens" on the network. One way to handle these network adapters is to isolate them in their separate LAN segment, where they have minimum impact on other stations on the network.

Another property of most PC LANs, and LANs based on the IEEE standards, is that the bigger (in geographical size) they are, the smaller their network utilization is. This factor is often overlooked during the design of backbone LANs to span large distances. Network administrators are surprised by the drop in network utilization, and hence data throughput, as LAN size increases. The reason for this is a bit technical but very interesting, and is explained next.

Network utilization is defined as the percentage of time spent in transferring data, not including the time spent in packet processing and transmission delays. One can estimate the maximum utilization achievable by assuming that under the best possible conditions, there will be zero processing delay and queue delay, but you cannot avoid the transmission delay due to the finite propagation speed of the signal.

The data *transmit time* (Tx) is the time it takes to deliver data to the LAN media for a given transmission rate. The *transmission delay* (Td) is caused by the finite propagation speed of signals in the LAN media. Under the highest possible data-transfer rate, the messages are sent one after another with minimal delays. The message consists of a channel-use time of Tx and a propagation delay (nonuse) time of Td. The actual utilization (U) is the fraction of useful time spent transmitting data. You can make this determination by using the following formula:

$$U = Tx / (Tx + Td)$$

$$= 1 / (1 + Td/Tx)$$

$$U = 1 / (1 + a) \quad (1)$$

in which $a = Td/Tx$.

If the LAN data rate for transmitting a packet of size P bits is D bps, then

$$Tx = P/D \text{ seconds} \qquad (2)$$

If the propagation velocity of signal in media is V meters/sec and the size of the LAN is L meters, then

$$Td = L/V \text{ seconds} \qquad (3)$$

Studies show that the average packet size for most LAN applications is small (about 128 bytes). Using this, you can compute the network utilization of the 10BASE-T LAN.

In the 10BASE-T LAN of figure 22.1, the maximum length of the LAN will be 200 meters, not including the backplane. The backplane CSMA/CD bus in the 10BASE-T concentrator has a length of about 0.5 meters. Using the formulas for 10BASE-T LAN, and assuming a signal propagation speed of 0.7 times speed of light in vacuum, you can make the following calculation:

P (Packet size) = 128×8 bits = 1024 bits

D (Data Transfer Rate) = 10 Mbps (fixed for Ethernet)

L (Length of LAN) = 200.5 meters

V (Signal Propagation speed) = $0.7 \times$ speed of light sin vacuum

$= 0.7 \times 3 \times 100{,}000{,}000$

$= 2.1 \times 100{,}000{,}000$

Tx = P/D = 1024/10 Mbps = 102.4 microseconds

Td = L/V = 200.5 / (2.1 × 100,000,000) = 0.95 microseconds

a = Td/Tx = 0.95/102.4 = 0.0093

U (10BASE-T) = 1 / (1 + a) = 1 / (1 + 0.0093) = 99 percent

Figure 22.1 also shows a larger LAN, such as an IEEE 802.3 10BASE-5 LAN that has a maximum size of 2800 meters. Repeating the calculations with the 10BASE-5 parameters gives the following result:

P (Packet size) = 128 × 8 bits = 1024 bits

D (Data Transfer Rate) = 10 Mbps (fixed for Ethernet)

L (Length of LAN) = 2800 meters

V (Signal Propagation speed) = 2.1 × 100,000,000 meters/sec

Tx = P/D = 1024/10 Mbps = 102.4 microseconds

Td = L/V = 2800/(2.1 × 100,000,000) = 13.3 microseconds

a = Td/Tx = 13.3/102.4 = 0.13

U (10BASE-5) = 1/(1 + a) = 1/(1 + 0.13) = 88.4 percent

A drop in performance of about 10 percent is noted between 10BASE-T (99%) and 10BASE-5 (88.4%). These calculations do not include processing and queuing delays at the network adapters. Actual network utilization is much less if these additional delays are taken into account; nevertheless, it explains why connecting a 10BASE-T LAN to a 10BASE-5 by means of a repeater results in a drop in performance for the 10BASE-T stations. One solution to this problem is to connect the 10BASE-T LANs to the 10BASE-5 through bridges, so that the CSMA/CD mechanism is partitioned into separate domains (see fig. 22.2).

For faster network performance, you may wish to consider EtherSwitches, Fast Ethernet, ATM, and Virtual LANs.

Server Bus Characteristics

The server bus reliability and performance has a an effect on server performance. For instance, if you are using a high performance Fast and Wide SCSI-II interface with a slow ISA bus, the ISA bus speed could be a bottleneck in I/O operations. Some of the parameters to consider in evaluating the server bus requirements are:

- Data integrity
- Reliability
- Performance
- Compatibility with existing hardware and software

- Industry acceptance
- Flexible architecture that allows for growth and increased functionality

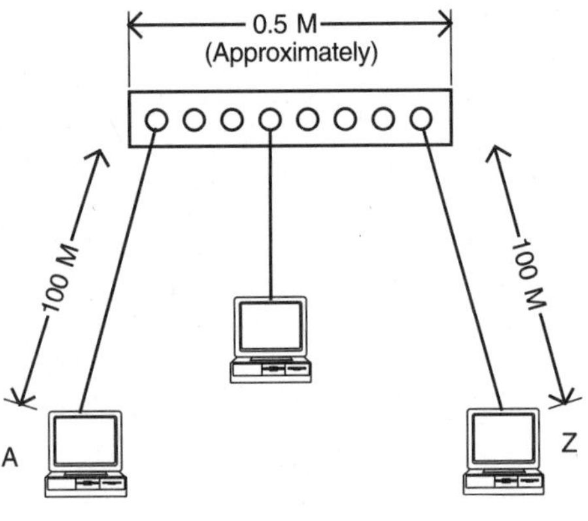

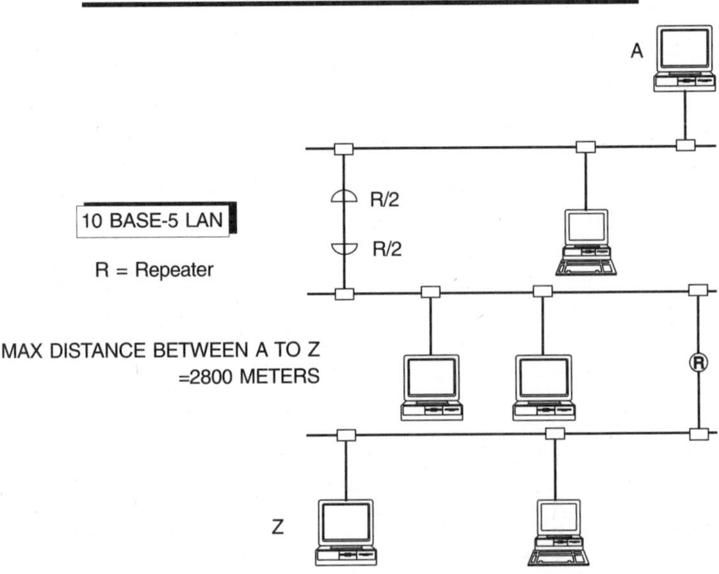

Figure 22.1
A larger 10BASE-T LAN.

Data integrity and reliability implies that the data should be transferred reliably over the server bus without errors. A bus should implement at least a parity scheme to detect single bit errors. Errors can be caused by faulty electronics, electrical interference, particle bombardments, and radiation from other devices. If such errors are detected, the receiving device on the server bus can request that the corrupt data be re-sent.

Performance can be increased by using a bus with a wide data path and by using bus mastering. Bus mastering is a technique that allows a device to gain control of the bus and transfer data. This allows I/O to be performed without processor intervention and overhead.

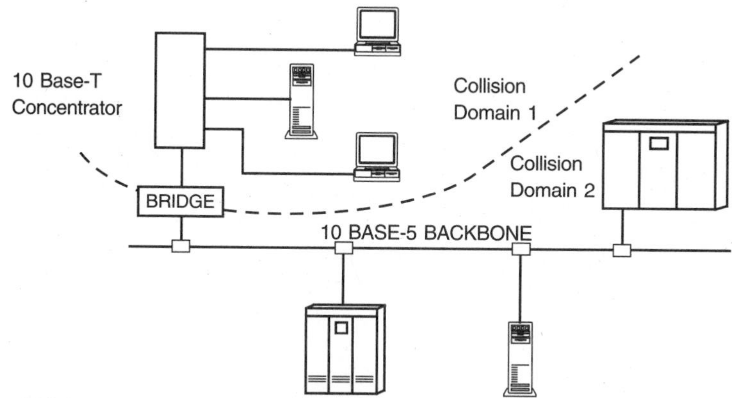

Figure 22.2
Partitioned CSMA/CD mechanism.

Common server buses on Intel based servers are:

- ISA
- EISA
- Micro Channel
- PCI

The *Industry Standard Architecture (ISA)* bus is used in old AT designs and has a data path width of 16 bits. It transfers data at 10 MB/sec and does not use bus mastering or bus parity.

The *Extended Industry Standard Architecture (EISA)* uses software configuration to automatically configure EISA boards, and uses a 32-bit wide bus. It can be used to support the older ISA bus cards. It uses full bus mastering but does not have bus parity. It can transfer data up to 66 MB/sec.

The Micro Channel bus developed by IBM is a complete redesign of the bus and is not compatible with ISA or EISA cards. It is a 32-bit wide bus and has auto configuration capability and full mastering and bus parity. It can transfer data between 10 MB/sec to 160 MB/sec. Besides IBM PCs, it is used in the RS/6,000 workstations, Communications Controllers (IBM 3172) and mainframes (IBM 9370).

The *Peripheral Component Interconnect (PCI)* is a redesign of the system bus by Intel. It is a 64-bit wide bus and has auto configuration capability and full mastering and bus parity. It can transfer data between 132 MB/sec to 264 MB/sec. It can accommodate fast video transfers needed with client operating systems that have a graphical interface.

CPU Speed of Server

A fast server computer executes the NetWare operating system code faster and gives better performance. Server CPU performance is often rated in *millions of instructions per second* (MIPS).

The overall performance of the server system speed can be measured for NetWare 3.*x* and 4.*x* servers, and this number can be used as a speed index to fine-tune the server's performance.

When NetWare 3.*x* or 4.*x* loads, using the SERVER.EXE program, it performs a system speed test. The purpose of this speed test is to inform the network administrator of the server's operating speed. Some Intel 80386-based machines come with selectable speeds; during system startup time they may be operating at speeds as low as 6 MHz or 8 MHz. A low speed is an indication that the server is not operating at its maximum clock speed and that server performance will be affected accordingly. Actually, the speed rating is a function of more than the CPU clock speed. It is a measure of the following factors:

- CPU type
- CPU clock speed
- Memory speed
- Memory wait states
- Speed and size of CPU cache
- Overall system design

Because of the preceding factors, the speed rating is a good indication of the server's overall performance. A higher rating indicates a faster system. Table 22.2 shows the speed ratings of different server machines. From this table, you can see that the Compaq 386S, which has a 80386SX CPU at 16 MHz, has a speed rating of 98, whereas a 80386 CPU running at the same 16 MHz clock has a speed rating of 121 because of its wider data bus. Properly designed 80486 machines can have speed ratings of over 600. The speed rating also indicates that computers requiring memory wait states should be avoided as server machines.

Table 22.2
Speed Index Rating

Computer	Chip	Clock speed	Wait state	Rating
Compaq	386S	80386SX	1	98
Novell	386AE	80386	1	121
Compaq	386/25	80386	0	242
AT Clone	486/25	804860	0	686

The server speed test is a simple loop that runs for approximately 0.16 seconds and counts the number of times a given piece of code can be executed in less than 2/100ths of a second. A larger number of iterations indicates a faster machine. The flowchart in figure 22.3 shows the speed test. Before the speed test begins, the floppy drive is shut off. (Some computers automatically switch to a slower speed when the system floppy is accessed, which affects the speed rating.) The piece of code executed checks the timer to see whether three clock ticks (0.16 seconds) have elapsed. This operation involves a number of instructions that move data from CPU registers and memory. A faster CPU and faster memory increment the counter to a larger value in the same amount of time. The counter is divided by 1,000; the result is displayed as the speed index. A speed rating of 242 means that the counter was incremented 242,000 times in three clock ticks.

When running database NLMs or other application NLMs on the NetWare server that use numerical computations, it is important to have a floating point coprocessor on the server. For Intel 80486 and higher, the *Floating Point Processor* (FPU) is built into the microprocessor chip. For file services, the IO bus speed is more critical than CPU speed. But for application NLMs, the CPU and the FPU speed can also be critical. For memory intensive NLMs the memory transfer burst rates can also be significant. Intel 80486 processors can do 160 MB/sec burst transfers to memory. Pentium processors can do 528 MB/sec burst transfers to memory.

For faster server CPU performance, you may wish to consider other alternatives to Intel processors, such as *Symmetrical Multi-Processing* (SMP) machines, *Processor Independent NetWare* (PIN) that uses RISC processors, or NetWare for UNIX running on SMP and RISC platforms.

Software Aspects Affecting Server Performance

The software factors that determine network performance focus primarily on the Network Operating System. Because the bulk of the NOS runs on the server computer, software performance usually is concerned with fine-tuning the NOS operation on the server.

Aspects that affect server performance are as follows:

- Server memory management
- Server file caching, directory caching, and hashing
- Elevator seeking
- Tuning server parameters

Server Memory NetWare 2.*x*, 3.*x*, and 4.*x*

Server memory is allocated in NetWare 3.*x* and 4.*x* on a dynamic basis, depending on the situation at hand. These versions of NetWare do the best job they can to allocate memory so that overall system performance is improved. It occasionally needs some help from the network administrators through use of SET parameter commands, which are examined in greater detail later.

The NetWare 2.*x* scheme of memory allocation is not so flexible. Most of these problems occur because of the 64 KB-segmented architecture of the Intel 80286 microprocessor on which NetWare 2.*x* is based. NetWare 2.*x* is written in assembly language. To keep the code efficient, it tries to avoid using segment arithmetic for data access. This means that internal data segments end up confined to memory segments of no more than 64 KB. This has some direct consequences in NetWare 2.*x* performance, such as a limit to the number of File Service Processes at the server, which limits the number of file requests that can be handled simultaneously.

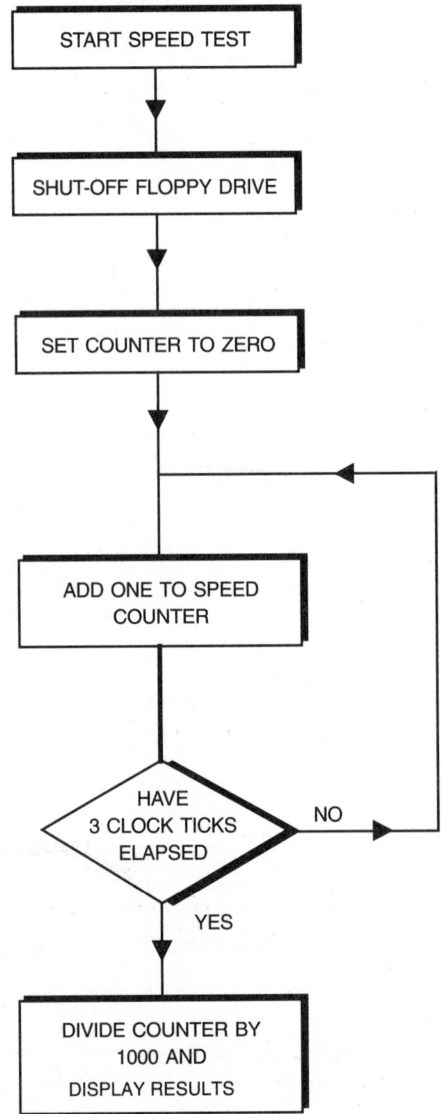

Figure 22.3
The speed test.

Segmentation remains with NetWare 3.*x* and 4.*x* and the Intel 80386 microprocessor, but the segment size is 4 GB (gigabytes). NetWare uses 4 GB segments for program code and data (called the *flat memory* model). Because the segment size is larger than the RAM available on most machines, this is not a problem.

NetWare 3.*x* memory, while an improvement over NetWare 2.*x*, is allocated in pools whose sizes can change dynamically (see Chapter 8). In NetWare 4.*x*, there is just one global pool that is used by the OS and the application NLMs. When memory is released by a process, it is returned to this global pool. NetWare 4.*x*'s memory allocation is consequently simpler and faster.

Another fact to keep in mind is that servers configured with larger amounts of memory are more likely to experience failures in memory. The probability of failure in memory increases linearly with the amount of memory. Consider that the probability of failure in a 1 MB over a period of 1 month is *p*. Then the number of failures in *M* megabytes over *T* months is as follows:

$$F = M \times T \times p$$

The value of *p* is typically 0.00033 for most memory chips on the market, and therefore the expected number of failures of 16 MB of RAM over a period of 60 months (5 years) is as follows:

$$16 \times 60 \times 0.00033 = 0.32$$

Many NetWare servers are typically configured with 16 MB of RAM and seldom experience any memory problem, because the expected failure is only 0.32. Consider a server configured with 64 MB or 128 MB of RAM. Using the previous formula, the failure rates work out as follows:

Failures over 60 months for 64 MB of RAM = $64 \times 60 \times 0.00033$

$=1.3$

Failures over 60 months for 128 MB of RAM = $128 \times 60 \times 0.00$

$=2.6$

You can see from the previous calculations that one can expect at least one failure in server memory for memory sizes greater than 64 MB over a period of 5 years. When a single bit memory failure occurs, the parity check on memory on most Intel based machines will detect the error and generate a *Non-Maskable Interrupt* (NMI). The NMI causes most operating systems, including NetWare, to crash. This is unacceptable in mission critical applications. A solution to this is to use special servers that use *Error Correcting Checks* (ECC) that can detect and correct memory problems dynamically without user intervention, or use SFT III or some specialized fault tolerant server architecture (NetFRAME, Pyramid, and so on).

Caching and Hashing

Memory that remains after allocating space for the NetWare operating system kernel, data tables, and NLM processes and applications is used for file caching. *File caching* is an attempt to substitute fast RAM for the slower disk memory. The difference in speed between RAM and most disks is in the order of 100 to 1. Substituting the use of RAM wherever possible can result in a file access 10 to 100 times faster than disk access. If disk speeds were the same as RAM speeds, there would be no need for file caching. As long as disks are slower than RAM, file caching can be used to improve file access.

In file caching, server RAM is used to keep the most frequently used disk blocks. Disk blocks ahead of the one currently being read may be perfected in server RAM, in anticipation of subsequent disk-block needs. These techniques can improve server performance on server reads. For server file writes, the disk block is written out first to cache and then to the server disk by a background process controlled by the SET parameter value of `DIRTY DISK CACHE DELAY TIME`.

Normally, a copy of the server directory is kept on the server disk. Many file operations require the reading of the disk's directory entries. These operations can be accelerated if the directory is maintained in RAM. (This is called *directory caching*.) To further accelerate access to the desired directory entry, a directory hashing function can be used to localize the search for a directory entry. Both NetWare 3.*x* and NetWare 2.*x* implement file caching and directory caching and hashing, provided that enough RAM space is available to implement these features.

Elevator Seeking

NetWare uses elevator seeking to minimize excessive arm movements of the disk when satisfying multiple read/write requests from several workstations. If the I/O operations were performed in the order in which they arrive, disk requests arriving in random order could lead to excessive disk arm movements, called *disk thrashing*. One way to avoid this problem is to sort the disk operations by the track number of the disk blocks being accessed, rather than by their order of arrival. The disk arm needs to make fewer sweeps to handle the disk requests. This is called *elevator seeking*.

Elevator seeking not only results in faster I/O operations but also reduces wear and tear on the disk.

File Server Performance Characteristics

An interesting study on file server performance was done by IBM using *Comprehensive LAN Application-performance Report Engine* (CLARE) at the IBM LAN Systems Performance Laboratory in Boca Raton, Florida. The CLARE application benchmark is an alternative to other popular approaches in performance bench marking and system measurement. The benchmarks are designed to be more realistic, using the unique I/O patterns of applications such as WordPerfect, Lotus 1-2-3, cc:Mail, FoxBASE+, and File Copy (DOS COPY).

Systematic measurements of server performance yielded a graph similar to that in figure 22.4. This graph shows the Transactions per second versus Number of active server users. The transactions per second are measured at the server and are not the individual transaction rates at each workstation.

Transactions per second indicate how many *units of work* were done per second. A transaction is any arbitrary unit of work. The problem in many benchmarks is defining the unit of work that is being measured. For example, it could be a user loading a spreadsheet, processing it, and saving it to the server's file system. Given a definition of a transaction that involves network file I/O, it follows the performance characteristics shown in figure 22.4.

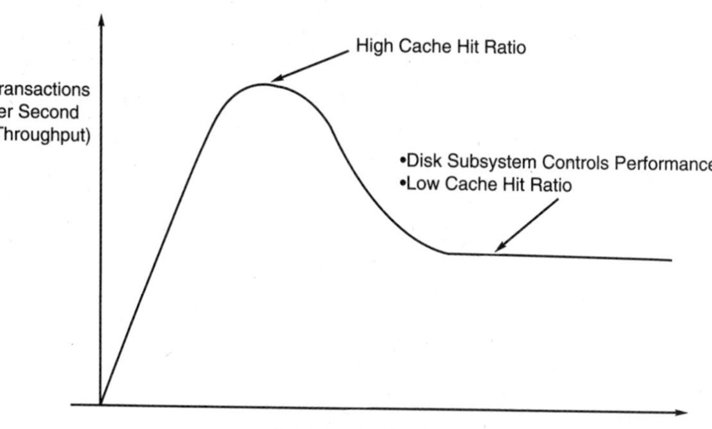

Figure 22.4
General file server performance characteristics.

The graph shows that initially as the number of active users increase, the transactions increase at a constant rate. This is because the server has enough capacity to be able to satisfy immediate demands placed on it. It also represents the fact that the server is able to satisfy I/O requests directly from cache. As the number of users increase, they will issue requests to perform transactions on their behalf, and the server is able to do so because it has the capacity to perform them without any bottlenecks. The initial slope of the curve, which is a constant, is dependent on how quickly the transactions are processed at the server, which in turn depends on how quickly the network and LAN adapter is able to transfer data between the workstation and the server. The peak of the curve represents the maximum transfer rate that the server configuration can sustain for a specific transaction type and network adapter. Figure 22.5 shows the file server performance with different network adapters. Using a faster network adapter increases the initial slope and the peak. With a faster network adapter user requests are delivered quicker to the server, and therefore more transactions can be processed per second.

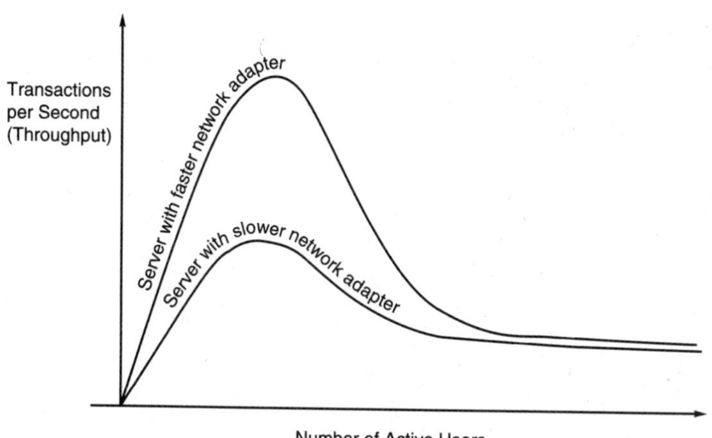

Figure 22.5
File server performance with different network adapters.

Beyond a certain number of active users, the curve begins to flatten out and the curve begins to slope downward as the transactions per second drop. This is caused by an increased amount of I/O activity that starts breaking down the "caching engine" at the server. As the number of active users increases, the users need an additional data space in the cache to satisfy their requirements. If the user's request cannot be satisfied from the cache, it must be satisfied directly from the disk. This increases the time for a transaction, which in turn reduces the rate at which transactions can be performed. Users will experience long delays in their network requests.

As additional users are added beyond the peak, the ratio of requested data to the servers cache size increases. This ratio (U) can be defined as follows:

$$U = T/C$$

in which

T = Total requested data by active users

C = Server data cache size

As the value of U becomes greater than 1, the disk cache loses its effectiveness. Furthermore, as active users increase, the portion of the cache used to store write-data increases. Write-data must be written to disk ("flushed") to free up space in the available cache. Thus the cache size is reduced by the amount of write-cache data in the disk at any time. Correctly speaking, the previous equation should be written as

$$U = T / (C - W)$$

in which

T = Total requested data by active users

C = Server data cache size

W = Total write-data in the server cache

You can use the previous formula to work out an interesting case study.

Assume a cache size of 6 MB on a server, and that an active user submits a transaction that needs 200 KB of read-cache data and 2 KB of write-data in the server's cache constantly. How many active users (N) will cause the server cache size to saturate?

Cache will saturate when $U = 1$

From the case study,

$$T = N \times 200 \text{ KB}$$

in which N is the number of active users.

$$C = 6\ MB = 6000\ KB$$

$$W = N \times 2$$

Plugging the previous values in

$$U = T / (C - W)$$

you get

$$1 = N \times 200 / (6000 - N \times 2)$$

Solving this equation

$$6000 - N \times 2 = N \times 200$$

$$N \times (200 + 2) = 6000$$

$$N = 6000 / (202) = 29.7$$

Rounding up this result, you get a value of 30 users as the number that will cause the server cache to saturate. In this simplified case study, it is assumed that the server cache requirements are the same for each user. In real life, you will have to estimate a user's cache requirements based on that individual's activity. Another assumption made in this case study is that the user constantly ties up the cache with a certain amount of data. In real-life, many users need the cache only occasionally, and there are periods of time when they do not have any data in the server cache.

Performance can be improved by adding a faster disk subsystem that does not allow the write-cache data (*W*) in the server cache to build up. A faster disk I/O subsystem will flush the write-cache data quickly, and this will give a flattened peak in the server performance curve (see fig. 22.6), which means that the peak performance will be sustained over a longer period of time.

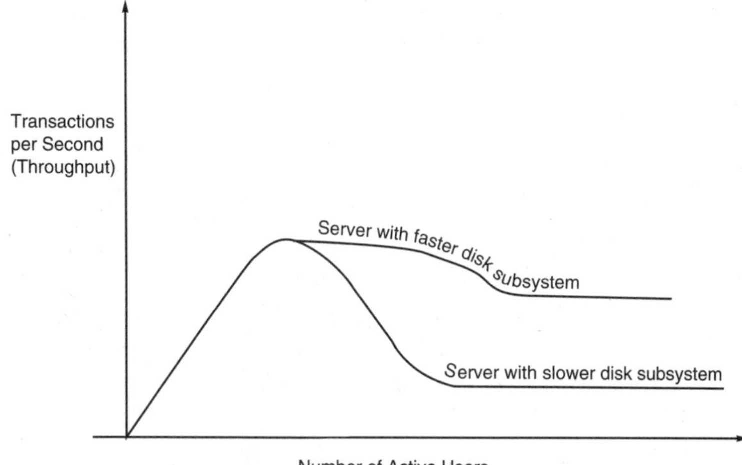

Figure 22.6
File server performance with different disk subsystems.

Tuning NetWare 3.*x*, 4.*x* Performance

NetWare 3.*x* and 4.*x* do a good job of monitoring the server's resources, and change parameters automatically to try to improve server performance. For most system resources, the parameters specify minimum and maximum limits as well as a wait-time limit that specifies how rapidly a resource is allocated. The wait-time limit parameters smooth out peak load demands for system resources so that the operating system does not overreact to a transient demand situation.

These parameters also can be controlled or viewed through the SET command. When you type **SET** at the DOS prompt, NetWare 3.*x* lists the following configuration categories and asks which category you want to view:

1. Communications
2. Memory
3. File caching
4. Directory caching
5. File system
6. Locks
7. Transaction tracking
8. Disk
9. Miscellaneous

From a performance point of view, many of these parameters are closely associated. The SET commands for memory, file caching, and directory caching affect the server's memory performance. The SET commands for the file system, locks, and transaction tracking categories, for example, affect file system performance. Because of this interrelationship, the SET commands are grouped and discussed here as follows:

- Memory performance tuning
- File system performance tuning
- Communications performance tuning
- Operating system processes tuning
- Threshold and warning parameters

To change a SET parameter value, the general command is as follows:

```
SET parameter description=New parameter value
```

To view a parameter's current setting, use:

```
SET parameter description
```

Certain parameters cannot be set at the console prompt or in the AUTOEXEC.NCF file. They can be set only in the STARTUP.NCF file. A list of these parameters follows:


```
AUTO REGISTER MEMORY ABOVE 16 MEGABYTES
AUTO TTS BACKOUT FLAG
CACHE BUFFER SIZE
MAXIMUM PHYSICAL RECEIVE PACKET SIZE
MAXIMUM SUBDIRECTORY TREE DEPTH
MINIMUM PACKET RECEIVE BUFFERS
```

In the discussion that follows, unless explicitly stated, the parameters are for NetWare 3.*x* and NetWare 4.*x*. In some situations, a SET parameter applies to NetWare 3.12 and higher only. This will also be explicitly stated.

Memory Performance Tuning for NetWare 3.*x* and 4.*x*

NetWare 3.*x* manages memory in dynamic pools, which is a more flexible manner than NetWare 2.*x*. Generally, this memory management is transparent to the user, but you need to understand some principles that can help you take corrective action if memory becomes a bottleneck.

The NetWare 3.*x* server memory is divided into three NetWare NOS application areas:

1. File-cache buffer pool
2. Permanent memory pool
3. Alloc memory pool

The permanent and alloc memory pools grow or shrink according to actual demand. Memory not allocated to these pools and the NOS kernel is used for file caching.

The file-cache buffer pool is used to store file blocks from the most frequently used files. Two pools (called *movable* and *nonmovable*) interact with the file-cache buffer pool. They obtain their memory from the file-cache buffer pool and, when done, return memory to it. The movable pool is used for system tables that change size, such as FATs and hash tables. Tables and objects in the movable pool can be moved in memory to prevent excessive memory fragmentation. The nonmovable pool is used for *NetWare Loadable Modules* (NLMs).

The permanent pool is used for long-term memory needs such as directory cache buffers and packet receive buffers. Although it is called permanent memory, it is quite dynamic. A portion of it is static but the rest is semi-dynamic. Communications buffers are an example of permanent pool memory usage. When NetWare loads and initializes itself, it sets up a certain number of communication buffers. With rising network activity, NetWare allocates additional communication buffers to store the extra data packets. These buffers are allocated from permanent memory. Once allocated, they will not be released even if network activity subsides. The reasoning behind this approach is to allocate enough resources to handle peak loads on the network.

The alloc memory pool is used to store information about the following:

- Drive mappings
- Service request buffers
- SAP tables
- Open/Lock files and semaphores
- User connection information
- NLMs
- Queue manager tables
- Messages queued for broadcasting

The alloc memory is used temporarily for fulfilling short-term processing needs. During NetWare execution, data objects may need to be created dynamically and destroyed after the NOS finishes using them. Memory used for the alloc pool is managed by a linked list of free memory blocks. Using this linked list approach, the NOS can quickly find the memory it needs. When memory is needed, it is allocated from this free list. When released, it returns to the free memory list where it can be reused.

NetWare tries to allocate memory for NLMs from the alloc pool. As memory requirements for NLMs increase, the alloc pool is depleted. To satisfy the NLM memory requirement, NetWare borrows memory from the file-cache buffer pool. Once borrowed, this memory is not returned to the file-cache pool, even if the NLMs are unloaded. The worst-case situation would be that many NLMs are frequently loaded and unloaded. Under these circumstances, permanently borrowing memory from the file-cache area could deplete it severely, which would degrade the server performance. NetWare has control mechanisms to prevent this *memory leakage* from occurring. SET commands can be used to limit the size of the alloc pool. The alloc pool has a default of 2 MB but can be set as high as 16 MB and as low as 50 KB.

The following SET command restricts the size of the alloc pool and can be used to solve the file-cache buffer pool leakage problem:

SET MAXIMIMUM ALLOC SHORT TERM MEMORY= *n* (for NetWare 3.*x* Only)

in which *n* is the maximum size (in bytes) of alloc pool memory. The valid range is from 50,000 bytes to 16,777,216 (16 MB). The default value is 209,712 bytes (2 MB).

File caching also affects server memory performance. File caching allows data blocks from files that are being read or written to be kept in RAM, thus speeding access to these files. File caching is independent of other caching techniques such as those used by disk-caching controllers. The file-caching tunable parameters deal with the number of file-cache buffers, concurrent disk writes, and disk synchronization (cache-write delays).

Other SET parameters that affect server memory performance are described next. To use the parameters with the SET command, the SET command must precede the parameter, as shown in the preceding example (for changing the maximum alloc short-term memory).

MAXIMUM ALLOC SHORT TERM MEMORY= *n* (for NetWare 3.*x* Only)

This determines the amount of memory (*n*) the server allocates (when it is booted) for alloc pool. Its value can range from 50,000 to 16,777,216 bytes, with a default value of 2,097,152. Normally, you should not have to change this value, but you can decrease it if you need some additional memory, such as loading other NLMs. Increasing this value is easier to determine; if there is insufficient memory in the alloc pool, the server starts issuing warning messages that operations cannot be completed. Increment the value in units of 1 KB until the messages disappear.

AUTO REGISTER MEMORY ABOVE 16 MEGABYTES= [ON¦OFF]

EISA machines can support more than 16 MB of RAM. Under certain circumstances, you may have to use this parameter to allow NetWare to handle extra memory correctly. Setting this parameter in the STARTUP.NCF file allows NetWare to register this memory when it first comes up. This parameter cannot be set at the console prompt or in the AUTOEXEC.NCF file. NetWare needs to know all the memory available when it first boots up. The default value is ON. If you are using a board that can address only 24 bits of RAM, you may have to set this value to OFF, or you may have corrupted lower memory because 24 bits can address only 16 M. Any higher address value maps to lower memory.

CACHE BUFFER SIZE= *n* (for NetWare 3.*x* Only)

Because NetWare 3.*x* can support variable disk block sizes, NetWare enables you to set the size of the cache buffer that can hold disk blocks. The default value of 4,096 bytes also is the default size of the disk block and should be adequate in most situations. If a larger disk block size is being used, you may want to increase this value because it can improve performance. Be aware that NetWare does not mount any volume disk block size smaller than the cache size. This parameter must be set in the STARTUP.NCF file; it cannot be set in the AUTOEXEC.NCF file or at the console prompt. Legal parameter values are 4,096; 8,192; and 16,384. A convenient way to experiment with different parameter values is the cache size -c parameter that can be used with SERVER.EXE (SERVER -c cacheSize).

MINIMUM FILE CACHE BUFFERS= *n*

File caching can be used to improve the performance of file I/O operations. NetWare uses memory remaining after allocation of the operating system and NLMs for file caching. In NetWare 3.*x*, you can set aside a certain amount of memory for file caching. The file-cache memory also acts as a memory reserve. The server draws on this memory reserve for its needs. The problem with this is that the file-cache memory can be severely depleted, which can seriously affect server performance. A certain amount of memory should always be reserved for file caching (this parameter can be used to set the minimum amount reserved for file caching). If file I/O seems slow, or long delays and timeouts occur for network operations, the file cache may have fallen below the minimum value necessary for acceptable server performance. If such is the case, the value of this parameter should be increased. The default value for this parameter is 20, which also is the minimum value. The number should be increased gradually to a maximum of 1,000 (the file-cache buffer's usage using MONITOR NLM). Using an extremely high value for this parameter could result in wasted memory that could impact other critical data structures that need memory. The NetWare server should give warning if the file-cache buffer reserve falls below the minimum level.

GARBAGE COLLECTION INTERVAL= *n* (for NetWare 4.*x* Only)

Garbage collection is the process of cleaning up the fragmented memory on the server. Memory returned to file cache (such as unloading an NLM) can become fragmented. The garbage collection process makes this memory available to new processes. Garbage collection interval refers to the maximum time between the activation of consecutive garbage collections. This can range from 1 minute to 1 hour, and has a default value of 15 minutes.

MINIMUM FREE MEMORY FOR GARBAGE COLLECTION= *n* (for NetWare 4.*x* Only)

This parameter specifies the minimum number of allocated bytes that need to be free before garbage collection can occur. The system will not perform garbage collection until at least the specified number of bytes can be made free. Set this value low, if you want garbage collection to occur and do not care if only a small amount of memory is made free at each garbage collection. You may wish to do this if you are short on memory at the server. Set this value high if you have plenty of RAM and do not need garbage collection to occur frequently. The parameter can be set from 1,000 to 1,000,000 bytes. The default is 8,000.

NUMBER OF FREES FOR GARBAGE COLLECTION= *n* (for NetWare 4.*x* Only)

When an NLM wants to allocate memory, it makes a call to the *malloc()* function. When an NLM releases memory, it makes a call to the *free()* function. NetWare 4.*x* keeps track of the total number of times NLMS make a "free" request. This parameter sets a limit to the minimum number of frees needed before garbage collection can take place. The parameter value can range from 100 to 100,100 frees, and has a default value of 5,000.

Tuning Server File System Performance (for NetWare 3.*x* and 4.*x*)

File caching allows faster access of frequently used files by keeping the disk blocks in fast RAM for read and write operations. Write operations are performed in a delayed fashion, with the writes being done first to RAM. A background process writes these disk buffers (dirty buffers) to the disk during less critical moments but within the time specified by the Dirty Disk Cache Delay Time parameter.

File caching affects both memory and file system performance. The minimum file-cache buffers parameter, discussed in the section on memory performance tuning, affects both memory performance and file system performance.

Directory caching also plays an important role in file system performance, because it allows fast access to frequently used directories. Directory tables are kept in directory buffers in RAM, and the server uses a "least recently" algorithm to keep the directory entries in memory. When the server starts, NetWare starts with a *minimum directory cache buffers* (default is 20). When the minimum directory cache buffers is used up, the server must wait for a *directory cache allocation wait time* (default 2.2 seconds) before allocating another buffer. Under periods of sustained directory access, the number of directory entries could increase to the *maximum directory cache buffers* (default 400). As directory-cache buffers increase, the number of buffers available for file caching decreases. Hence, there is a trade-off between directory caching and file caching; they must be carefully balanced for optimum performance.

The following are SET parameters for file system performance.

READ AHEAD ENABLED= [ON¦OFF] (for NetWare 3.12 and 4.*x* Only)

NetWare 3.12 and NetWare 4.*x* contain heuristics to determine if the network I/O pattern issued by a workstation is sequential or random. If the READ AHEAD ENABLED parameter is set to ON and the server determines that a file is being accessed sequentially, it will read the next disk block when the workstation crosses the mid-point of the current block being processed. This feature has tremendous benefits for applications that access network file data sequentially. An example of this is database sort where records are accessed sequentially. The default for this parameter is ON. There is no need to normally turn this parameter OFF. One possible reason would be to measure the difference in performance with read ahead and without read ahead. Another possible reason would be if you suspect that the NetWare heuristics is incorrectly classifying the network I/O pattern as sequential when it is in fact random. Turning this parameter OFF will avoid waste of file cache buffer space used for reading ahead file blocks that are never used.

READ AHEAD LRU SITTING TIME THRESHOLD= *n* (for NetWare 3.12 and 4.*x* Only)

Read ahead occurs in the background and is a low priority process. If the LRU sitting time for a cache block is below this parameter, it indicates that the server is busy performing file I/O. In this case, read-ahead will not be performed. The default for this parameter is 10 seconds and it can range from 0 to 1 hour. To disable the behavior described below you can set the parameter to 0.

MAXIMUM CONCURRENT DISK CACHE WRITES= *n*

Unlike DOS, NetWare can perform several disk writes concurrently. One reason for this is that NetWare does not rely on the single-threaded BIOS on the machine to perform I/O. The disk drivers for NetWare allow multi-threaded or concurrent I/O. To speed up disk I/O operations, a number of requests can be placed on the elevator mechanism. The *elevator mechanism* allows the disk head to move in continuous sweeps across the disk, which are more efficient than the random back-and-forth

movements. This mechanism can be used to set the number of write requests (*n*) that can be queued on the disk elevator for a single sweep across the disk surface. A high value for this parameter makes write requests more efficient; a lower number makes read requests more efficient. One way to decide how to set this parameter is to monitor the number of dirty cache buffers using MONITOR. If this number says that a majority of the buffers (70 percent or more) are dirty buffers, the writes are more predominant than reads. In this case, you can improve performance by increasing this parameter. The value ranges from 10 to 100, with a default of 50.

DIRTY DISK CACHE DELAY TIME= *n*

To improve disk I/O, the server performs delayed writes by writing first to RAM and then from RAM to disk during idle times. NetWare enables you to control how long this wait period should be. If there are many small requests, buffering the writes in RAM before writing them out to the disk is more efficient. This is especially true if the write requests are contiguous sectors on the disk because these can be combined as a smaller number of disk writes. A disk-cache delay time that is too small is the same as disabling the delayed write mechanism. Without delayed writes, server performance could suffer. The default value of 3.3 seconds is long enough for a typical mix of disk I/O operations that take place on the server. The value can be as small as 0.1 seconds, but not more than 10 seconds. An extremely high value can make the server file system more vulnerable in the event of a server crash because many disk I/O operations would be in RAM and not committed to the disk.

MINIMUM FILE CACHE BUFFER REPORT THRESHOLD= *n*

NetWare issues a warning if the number of file-cache buffers falls below a certain threshold. The first warning that the number of cache buffers is getting too low is issued when the following condition is met: Current number of cache buffers + minimum file-cache buffers <= minimum file-cache buffer report threshold. Suppose that the minimum file-cache buffers parameter is set to 20, and the minimum file-cache buffer report threshold is set to 30; when the current number of cache buffers is 50, the previously described condition is met and a warning message is issued. If the number of cache buffers continues to fall to the minimum file-cache buffers, the warning `Cache memory allocator exceeded minimum cache buffer left limit` is issued on the server console. The default value of the threshold is 20, which means that if the minimum file-cache buffer is set to its default of 20, the first warning is issued when the cache number falls to 40. The minimum value of this parameter is 0; it cannot exceed 1,000.

MINIMUM FILE DELETE WAIT TIME= *n*

When a file is deleted, it is not purged immediately from the volume. This parameter controls the minimum amount of time a file should remain on the volume before being purged. Files that have been deleted will not be purged for at least this time, even if the volume is full and the user is unable to create new files. The parameter value ranges from zero to seven days, with a default of 1 minute 5.9 seconds.

FILE DELETE WAIT TIME= *n*

When a file is deleted, it is not purged immediately from the volume. This parameter controls the amount of time a file should remain on the volume before being purged. Files that have been deleted will not be purged for this time. After this time, the server is free to purge these files. The server keeps at least 1/32nd of its disk space free, and starts purging files (starting with the oldest file) to meet this criteria. The parameter value ranges from zero seconds to seven days, with a default of 5 minutes 29.6 seconds. A small value for this parameter could slow down the server if many deletions are being made. A large value could adversely impact availability of disk space if the server disks were almost full.

MINIMUM DIRECTORY CACHE BUFFERS= *n*

In NetWare, directories are cached in RAM for fast directory searches and directory updates. The directories are kept in directory cache buffers, whose minimum number is controlled by this parameter. This number must be high enough to perform most directory searches quickly. If the number is set too high, the unused portion is not available for file caching and other server operations. If the server responds slowly to directory searches, especially when it is first booted, monitor this number through the MONITOR NLM. The delay could be caused because the minimum directory cache-buffers parameter is set too low and the server spends time allocating new directory buffers. The value ranges from 10 to 2,000, with a default of 20.

MAXIMUM DIRECTORY CACHE BUFFERS= *n*

As the number of directory entries and files increases, the server allocates more directory-cache buffers to hold the directories. To prevent the situation from getting out of hand with all available space being used for directory caching, the server enables you to set a limit on the maximum number of directory-cache buffers. If the file server continues to respond slowly, this parameter can be increased after consulting the MONITOR NLM on the directory-cache usage. If the MONITOR NLM reports a shortage of available RAM, and if this parameter is too high, the parameter value should be reduced. Because the server does not release memory automatically if this parameter value is reduced, it must be restarted to free up the unused memory. The parameter value ranges from 20 to 4,000, with a default of 500.

DIRECTORY-CACHE BUFFER NONREFERENCED DELAY= *n*

Only a finite amount of space is in the directory-cache buffers. As new directory entries are loaded into RAM, the older ones can be overwritten. Overwriting older directories too quickly can be a waste, especially if the older directory entries are needed again. This parameter controls the amount of time a directory entry should remain in RAM in the nonreferenced state before it can be overwritten by another directory entry. A higher value indicates that the directory entry is more likely to be cached in memory when needed. This not only speeds up directory access, but also increases the number of directory-cache buffers because directory entries are held longer in the cache. A lower value can slow down directory access because they can be overwritten by new directory entries and will not be in RAM when needed. The parameter value ranges from 1 second to 5 minutes, with a default of 5.5 seconds.

DIRTY DIRECTORY CACHE DELAY TIME= *n*

Directory entries that are modified in RAM need to be written out to disk to keep the directory on the server disk synchronized with changes in the file system. This parameter controls how long a directory entry can remain in RAM before it must be written to disk. Keeping this parameter high results in faster directory writes but also increases the chance of directory tables getting out of synch with those on disk

in the event of a crash. A low value for this parameter reduces the possibility of directory tables becoming corrupt, but the more frequent writes can reduce the performance. The parameter value ranges from zero seconds to 10 seconds, with a default of 0.5 seconds. A zero setting disables the cache delay. Directory entries must be written immediately to disk, which causes slower directory writes.

MAXIMUM CONCURRENT DIRECTORY CACHE WRITES= *n*

To speed up directory operations, several requests can be placed on the elevator mechanism. The elevator mechanism allows the disk head to move in continuous sweeps across the disk, which are more efficient than the random back-and-forth movements for disk I/O. This parameter controls the number of directory writes that can be queued on the elevator. A high value makes write requests more efficient; a lower number makes read requests more efficient. The parameter value ranges from 5 to 50, with a default of 10.

DIRECTORY CACHE ALLOCATION WAIT TIME= *n*

NetWare does not respond immediately to a demand for new cache buffers. It waits for a period of time before satisfying this demand. This period of time, which is set by this parameter, is used to smooth out peak transient requests that may cause allocation of more directory-cache buffers than are needed. If the wait time is too low, the server will seem too eager to satisfy transient loads and may allocate more directory-cache buffers than are needed. If the server delays too long to satisfy the request, it will seem sluggish and seem to adapt slowly to user needs. The parameter value ranges from 0.5 second to 5 minutes, with a default of 2.2 seconds.

NCP FILE COMMIT= [ON¦OFF]

This parameter controls the behavior of an NCP FILE COMMIT request by a client. If this parameter is set to ON, an NCP FILE COMMIT request causes all pending writes to be written immediately to disk. If the parameter is set to OFF, the cache manager flushes the pending writes to disk later. The default value for this parameter is ON. Changing this parameter to OFF can lead to small speed improvements, at the risk of a small chance of data corruption should the server crash before the disk writes are done.

TURBO FAT RE-USE WAIT TIME= *n*

Turbo FATs (indexed tables) are used for indexed files (files with more than 64 entries) and take time to build. If a number of indexed file operations are being performed, releasing the turbo FATs when they may be used again does not make sense. On the other hand, not releasing turbo FATs after their use consumes RAM space that could be used by NetWare. This parameter can be used to set the period of time turbo FAT buffers should remain in memory after an indexed file is closed. After the wait time value, the turbo FAT buffer can be reused for another indexed file. If applications perform random accesses and close many large files, this parameter value should be increased to avoid the overhead of rebuilding the turbo FAT index. If you want memory to be released for other operating system resources, this parameter can be increased. The parameter value ranges from 0.3 seconds to 1 hour 5 minutes 54.6 seconds, with a default of 5 minutes 29.6 seconds.

ENABLE DISK READ AFTER WRITE VERIFY= [ON¦OFF]

This enables and disables the hot-fix mechanism, which performs a read after a write, and compares the block read with that in memory. You should leave this parameter set to its default value of ON. If disk mirroring or duplexing is used and you are ensured of disk reliability, turning this parameter OFF can lead to faster disk writes.

ALLOW DELETION OF ACTIVE DIRECTORIES= [ON¦OFF] (for NetWare 4.*x* Only)

If this parameter is ON, a user with sufficient file system rights can delete a directory that another user has in use. A directory is considered to be in use if the user has a drive mapping to it and is performing operations in the directory, such as copying in to or out of the directory. The default for this parameter is ON.

Transaction Tracking System (TTS) Parameters

The following group of parameters places limits on the TTS system. TTS is the ability to ensure that either all operations defined in a transaction are done or none are.

AUTO TTS BACKOUT FLAG= [ON¦OFF] (for NetWare 3.*x* Only)

In NetWare 3.*x*, the TTS feature is built into the operating system. In the event of a server crash, files that have been flagged transactional can be restored to a previous consistent state. Setting this parameter to ON causes the server to back out any incomplete transactions automatically at start-up time. The default value is OFF, which means that the user is prompted with the message `Incomplete transaction(s) found. Do you wish to back them out?` This parameter can be set only in the STARTUP.NCF file, not at the console prompt or AUTOEXEC.BAT file.

TTS ABORT DUMP FLAG= [ON¦OFF] (for NetWare 3.*x* Only)

The TTS feature allows incomplete writes to a transactional file to be backed out in the event of a server crash. With this parameter set to ON, NetWare creates a file called TTS$LOG.ERR on the SYS volume, to back out incomplete writes for transactional files. The default value is OFF, which means that the information to perform the backout is not saved. The result is faster writes and less reliability.

MAXIMUM TRANSACTIONS= *n* (for NetWare 3.*x* Only)

Because NetWare is multitasking, the transaction operations can occur simultaneously. NetWare enables you to set the number of transactions that can be performed simultaneously on the server. Decrease this value if few transactions are used on the server. The parameter value ranges from 100 to 10,000, with a default of 10,000.

TTS UNWRITTEN CACHE WAIT TIME= *n* (for NetWare 3.*x* Only)

Transactional data is held in RAM to be written out later. NetWare enables you to control the amount of time transactional data can be held in memory. If a transactional block is held in memory after this time, other write requests are held up until the transactional data is written. The default value of 1 minute 5.9 seconds is adequate for most purposes. Increasing this value can result in small speed improvements if the TTS feature is used extensively by applications. The parameter value ranges from 11 seconds to 10 minutes 59.1 seconds.

TTS BACKOUT FILE TRUNCATION WAIT TIME= *n* (for NetWare 3.*x* Only)

The TTS backout file holds backout information for files, so that the files can be backed out if the server crashes. NetWare clears the backout file when the file is not in use. NetWare enables you to determine how long an allocated block remains available for the TTS backout file when these files are not being used. The parameter value ranges from 1 minute 5.1 seconds to 1 day 2 hours 21 minutes 51.3 seconds, with a default of 59 minutes 19.2 seconds. The default value works well in most situations.

File and Record Locking Parameters

The following group of parameters control how the operating system responds to file and record locks.

MAXIMUM RECORD LOCKS PER CONNECTION= *n*

NetWare allows any station to issue record locks. Every record lock consumes server resources. NetWare enables you to limit the number of record locks any workstation can issue, to prevent any one station from consuming too many resources. The number of locks can be monitored also through the MONITOR NLM. The parameter should be increased if an application fails while locking records. The parameter should be decreased if the workstation is consuming too many server resources. The parameter value ranges from 10 to 10,000, with a default value of 500.

MAXIMUM FILE LOCKS PER CONNECTION= *n*

NetWare enables any workstation to issue file locks. NetWare enables you to limit the number of file locks any workstation can issue, to prevent any one station from consuming too many resources. The number of locks can be monitored also through the MONITOR NLM. The parameter should be increased if an application fails while locking records. The parameter can be decreased if the workstation is consuming too many server resources. The parameter value ranges from 10 to 10,000, with a default value of 250.

MAXIMUM RECORD LOCKS= *n*

NetWare enables you to set a system-wide global parameter that sets a limit on the total number (*n*) of record locks NetWare can process simultaneously. The purpose of this parameter is to prevent too many record locks from consuming too many server resources. Increase this number if applications are failing and receiving messages about insufficient record locks. The parameter value ranges from 100 to 200,000, with a default value of 20,000.

MAXIMUM FILE LOCKS= *n*

NetWare enables you to set a system-wide global parameter that sets a limit on the total number (*n*) of file locks NetWare can process simultaneously. The purpose of this parameter is to prevent too many file locks from consuming too many server resources. Increase this number if applications are failing and receiving messages about insufficient file locks. The parameter value ranges from 100 to 100,000, with a default value of 10,000.

Tuning File-Compression Performance

This group of parameters is used to control file compression in NetWare 4.*x*. File compression occurs after a user has accessed a file and certain conditions, set by SET parameters have taken place.

COMPRESSION DAILY CHECK STARTING HOUR= *n* (for NetWare 4.*x* Only)

This parameter controls when the file compression process starts. The value can range from 0 (midnight) to 23, and has a default value of 0. A value of 23 represents 11:00 PM. You can flag a file for immediate compression by setting the *Immediate Compression* (Ic) flag. The *Ic* flag is reset automatically after compression has taken place. Otherwise, a file is compressed after a certain minimum time interval (DAYS UNTOUCHED BEFORE COMPRESSION) has elapsed.

COMPRESSION DAILY CHECK STOP HOUR= *n* (for NetWare 4.*x* Only)

This parameter controls when the automatic file compression process stops. The value can range from 0 (midnight) to 23 (11:00 pm), and has a default value of 6. You may wish to control this parameter if you have an automatic backup that runs during the hours that the automatic file compression process is active.

MINIMUM COMPRESSION PERCENTAGE GAIN= *n* (for NetWare 4.*x* Only)

This parameter controls the minimum percentage savings that must occur on a file before compression can proceed. If the file compression process determines that the savings are less than that specified by this parameter, the file will not be compressed. An example of this is if you already have files compressed using a utility such as PKZIP. The percentage you can gain by compressing such files is typically low (about 1%). Trying to compress these files is wasteful of CPU time as the savings are small. The parameter can be set to a value from 0 to 50 percent. The default is 5 percent.

ENABLE FILE COMPRESSION= [ON¦OFF] (for NetWare 4.*x* Only)

When set to OFF, this parameter prevents the server from performing file compression. The default value is set when you first install the file server.

MAXIMUM CONCURRENT COMPRESSIONS= *n* (for NetWare 4.*x* Only)

This parameter controls the number of compressions the server can perform simultaneously. A high setting speeds up compression but takes CPU time away from other processes, and may result in a degradation of server performance for network file I/O. The parameter can range from 1 to 8 and has a default value of 4.

CONVERT COMPRESSED TO UNCOMPRESSED OPTION= *n* (for NetWare 4.*x* Only)

This parameter controls the disposition of a file that has been uncompressed. The parameter can range from 0 to 2 and has a default value of 1. The meaning of the parameter values are described next.

Parameter Value	Description
0	Always leave the file uncompressed.
1	If the compressed file is read only once within the time period described by the DAYS UNTOUCHED BEFORE COMPRESSION parameter, leave the file compressed. On any future access of this file within this time period, leave the file uncompressed.
2	Always leave the file uncompressed.

If you wish to conserve disk space, set the value to 0. If you wish to leave the file uncompressed after it has been accessed just once, set the parameter to 2.

DECOMPRESS PERCENT DISK SPACE FREE TO ALLOW COMMIT= *n* (for NetWare 4.*x* Only)

This represents the percentage of disk space that must be free before NetWare will attempt to uncompress the file permanently. Set this value high if you are concerned that you have many compressed files which, if uncompressed, could fill up the hard drive. The parameter can range from 0 to 70 percent and has a default value of 10 percent.

DECOMPRESS FREE SPACE WARNING INTERVAL= *n* (for NetWare 4.*x* Only)

This parameter sets the number of seconds between warning messages that tell you when there is not enough disk space to uncompress a file. The parameter can range from 0 seconds to 29 days, 15 hours, 50 minutes, 3.8 seconds. The default value is 31 minutes and 18.5 seconds.

DELETED FILES COMPRESSION OPTION= *n* (for NetWare 4.*x* Only)

This parameter controls the disposition of files that have been deleted. The parameter can range from 0 to 2 and has a default value of 1. The meaning of the parameter values are described next.

Parameter Value	Description
0	Do not compress deleted files
1	Compress the next day
2	Compress immediately

Choose a value of 2 if you do not want to recover a deleted file immediately, or if you want to conserve disk space. Choose a value of 0 if the network users tend to salvage deleted files soon after they have been deleted.

DAYS UNTOUCHED BEFORE COMPRESSION= *n* (for NetWare 4.*x* Only)

This parameter sets the time period before automatic compression occurs for files that have not been accessed. The parameter value can range from 0 (compress the same day) to 100,000 days and has a default value of 7 days. The setting may be overridden by the *Ic* (Immediate Compress) attribute on a file or directory. Set this parameter to the average number of days files remain active.

Tuning Communications Performance

The communications parameters control characteristics of communication buffers. *Communication buffers* are areas in the server RAM dedicated for holding packets. The packets remain in memory before they are processed by the *File Service Processes* (FSPs).

The following sections describe how these SET parameters can affect the communications performance of a server.

MAXIMUM PHYSICAL RECEIVE PACKET SIZE= *n*

The size of a packet that can be transmitted is determined by the networks physical access mechanism and driver limitations. On the server side, NetWare enables you to define the maximum size (*n*) of a packet that can be processed by the file server. When a workstation makes a connection to the server, the packet size is negotiated, based on the settings of the network driver being used at the workstation. This parameter value needs to be large enough to accommodate the maximum packet size used by a workstation. The parameter value ranges from 618 to 4,202 bytes, with a default of 1,130 bytes. Generally, a large packet size can speed communications but consumes more RAM. The parameter can be set only in the STARTUP.NCF file.

MAXIMUM PACKET RECEIVE BUFFERS= *n*

The server needs to keep a certain number of packet buffers in RAM to avoid being overrun by data. Normally, the server allocates receive buffers dynamically, based on its needs. NetWare enables you to set an upper limit on the number of packet receive buffers (*n*) the operating system can allocate. The MONITOR NLM can be used to monitor current usage of this parameter. If this parameter is close to the maximum value, increase the value until you have at least one packet receive buffer per workstation. For OS/2 and MS Windows, increase this value, based on the number of simultaneously running network applications at the workstations. Allow for at least one buffer per application. The MONITOR NLM can be used also to monitor the No ECB available count errors. If these errors are being reported, increase this parameter in increments of 10. For EISA and Micro Channel server machines, increase this parameter to allow for five to 10 packet receive buffers per EISA/Micro Channel network board. If the number of file service processes reported by MONITOR NLM is close to its maximum, you can increase the parameter maximum number of service processes to reduce the need for more packet receive buffers. The parameter value ranges from 50 to 2,000, with a default of 100.

MINIMUM PACKET RECEIVE BUFFERS= *n*

NetWare enables you to set a minimum number of packet receive buffers (*n*) at the server. The MONITOR NLM can be used to monitor current packet receive buffers. The default value is 10. Too few receive buffers will cause the server to respond sluggishly when it first comes up. If No ECB available count errors are reported through the MONITOR NLM after the server boots, increase this parameter. For EISA and Micro Channel server machines, increase this parameter to allow for at least five packet receive buffers per EISA/Micro Channel network board. The parameter value ranges from 10 to 1,000.

REPLY TO GET NEAREST SERVER= [ON¦OFF]

This parameter determines if the file server will respond to Get Nearest Server SAP requests. These requests are generated by workstations when they first log in to the network. If you are using diskless workstations you may wish to limit the diskless workstation requests to one physical server. You can do this by turning this parameter OFF on other servers on the segment. Another reason for using this parameter is to hide certain servers on the network for security reasons. You can still log in to servers that have this parameter set OFF by explicitly specifying the name of the server.

NEW PACKET RECEIVE BUFFER WAIT TIME= *n*

NetWare enables you to set a waiting period before a request for a new packet receive buffer is satisfied. The reason for this wait is to smooth out peak demands for receive buffers and to allocate receive buffers for sustained loads only. Otherwise, you could end up with more receive buffers than are needed for optimal performance. However, if the parameter is set to too high a value, the server will be slow to respond to sustained needs for additional packet receive buffers. If the parameter is set too low, the server may be too quick to respond to transient demands for additional receive buffers and may end up allocating more receive buffers than are necessary. Novell recommends that this parameter not be changed for EISA bus master boards on the server. The parameter can range from 0.1 to 20 seconds, and has a default value of 0.1 second.

NEW PACKET RECEIVE BUFFERS= *n* (for NetWare 3.*x* Only)

NetWare enables you to set up a waiting period before a request for a new packet receive buffer is satisfied. The reason for this wait is to smooth out peak demands for receive buffers and allocate receive buffers for sustained network loads only. Otherwise, you would end up with more receive buffers than are needed for optimal performance. If the parameter is set to a high value, the server will be slow to respond to sustained peak loads. If it is set too low, the server may respond too quickly to peak loads, and may end up allocating more receive buffers than are necessary. Novell recommends that this parameter not be changed for EISA bus master boards in the server. The parameter value ranges from 0.1 to 20 seconds, with a default of 0.1 second.

DELAY BETWEEN WATCHDOG PACKETS= *n*

This is the time interval (*n*) between watchdog packets sent from the server to the workstation after there is no response to the first watchdog packet. The watchdog packet is sent to see whether the workstation is still "alive" on the network. If this parameter is set too low, this could generate excessive network traffic because the watchdog packet is sent to every station attached to the server. The parameter value ranges from 1 second to 10 minutes 26.2 seconds, with a default of 4 minutes 56.6 seconds. Normally, the default value is adequate for most networks. For workstations and servers connected by wide area networks, the parameter value can be increased to avoid extra overhead and to account for extra delays. On a wide area network, the setting of this parameter can be critical. Setting the delay too low causes a second watchdog packet to be sent without waiting to receive a response from the first. The delay between watchdog packets must be set greater than the round-trip delay to the workstation.

DELAY BEFORE FIRST WATCHDOG PACKET= *n*

The server sends watchdog packets to a station that has been quiet for some time. NetWare enables you to set how long a server should wait before polling a station that has been inactive; then a watchdog packet is sent as a probe to see whether the station is still alive. The parameter value ranges from 15.7 seconds to 20 minutes 52.3 seconds.

NUMBER OF WATCHDOG PACKETS= *n*

The NetWare server sends repeated watchdog packets if the workstation does not respond to a poll from the first watchdog packet. In a heavily congested network, the workstation response to a watchdog packet or the server watchdog packet can get lost. The NetWare server gives the workstation a few more chances (*n*) before declaring it dead and clearing the connection. The parameter ranges from 5 to 100, with a default value of 10. Setting a low delay between watchdog packets when the number of watchdog packets is high can cause excessive network traffic and affect the network performance.

Tuning Operating System Processes in NetWare 3.*x* and 4.*x*

A number of parameters deal with tuning the process scheduling time in the NetWare 3.*x* and 4.*x* operating system. These SET parameters for operating system processes are described in the following sections.

PSEUDO PREEMPTION TIME= *n* (for NetWare 3.*x*)

NetWare uses nonpreemptive scheduling. Processes must relinquish control voluntarily. This parameter forces certain NLMs to relinquish control if they use too much CPU time. The parameter value should be set along the guidelines that come with the NLMs you run. The values range from 1,000 to 10,000, with a default of 2,000. Each value represents a raw CPU time of approximately 0.84 microseconds.

PSEUDO PREEMPTION COUNT= *n* (for NetWare 4.*x* Only)

NetWare uses nonpreemptive scheduling. Processes must relinquish control voluntarily. This parameter forces certain NLMs to relinquish control if they have made this number of reads and writes. The parameter value should be set along the guidelines that come with the NLMs you run. The values range from 1 to 4,294,967,295 with a default of 10. Setting this parameter to a value higher than the default allows each thread to perform more I/O before it is forced to relinquish control.

GLOBAL PSEUDO PREEMPTION TIME= [ON¦OFF] (for NetWare 4.*x* Only)

If set to ON, this parameter causes all threads to use pseudo preemption. The default value is OFF.

WORKER THREAD EXECUTE IN A ROW COUNT= *n* (for NetWare 4.*x* Only)

This parameter places restrictions on the operating system scheduler. The parameter value represents the number of times the scheduler can consecutively schedule new work before allowing other threads to do their work. The parameter value ranges from 1 to 20 and has a default value of 10. By setting this value high, you enable the OS to handle more requests at the cost of slowing down existing requests. Set this value to low if you want to force the server to finish existing work in a thread before dispatching new work.

UPGRADE LOW PRIORITY THREADS= [ON¦OFF] (for NetWare 4.*x* Only)

If you set this parameter to ON, low priority threads, such as file compression threads, will be upgraded to regular priority. The file server will display a warning message on the server console telling you to adjust this parameter if an ill-behaved NLM freezes a low-priority thread. The default for this parameter is OFF.

MAXIMUM SERVICE PROCESSES= *n*

In NetWare 3.*x* and 4.*x*, file service processes are created on demand. NetWare enables you to set an upper limit on the number of file service processes (*n*) it can create. This number also can be monitored by the MONITOR NLM. Increase this parameter if the server is always near its maximum. The parameter ranges from 5 to 40, with a default value of 20.

NEW SERVICE PROCESS WAIT TIME= *n*

NetWare creates file service processes on demand. Under transient peak loads, too many file service processes can be created. NetWare enables you to smooth out transient demands for file service processes by setting up a waiting period. The parameter ranges from 0.3 seconds to 20 seconds, with a default value of 2.2 seconds. This parameter prevents NetWare from reacting too quickly to peak loads and from allocating too many file service processes.

MAXIMUM OUTSTANDING NCP SEARCHES= *n*

Directory searches for existing files are common on a NetWare server because of the flexibility of NetWare's search-mode feature. Normally, only one NCP search operation is permitted per workstation connection. If your applications support it, multiple NCP searches can speed up the application. This parameter enables you to set a limit on the maximum number of *NetWare Core Protocol* (NCP) searches that can be outstanding at any time. The parameter ranges from 10 to 100, with a default value of 51.

Threshold and Warning Parameters

NetWare 3.*x* and 4.*x* have many parameters that generate warning messages when their threshold values are crossed. These parameters do not affect the performance of the system directly, but are important for status alert messages and system operation. These SET threshold and warning parameters and their descriptions follow.

CONSOLE DISPLAY WATCHDOG LOGOUTS= [ON¦OFF]

The watchdog process clears inactive connections with workstations. Normally it does this silently. If you want a report of when the connection is cleared on the server console, set this parameter ON. The default value is OFF.

IMMEDIATE PURGE OF DELETED FILES= [ON¦OFF]

NetWare allows deleted files to be salvaged by the SALVAGE utility. When this parameter is set to ON, all files are immediately purged on deletion; that is, the salvage file feature is disabled. The default value (OFF) permits deleted files to be salvaged.

VOLUME LOW WARN ALL USERS= [ON¦OFF]

NetWare enables users to be informed when a volume is almost full. The default value is ON; users are alerted when the volume is almost full.

VOLUME LOW WARNING THRESHOLD= *n*

NetWare enables you to set how many free disk blocks (*n*) remain on a volume before it issues a warning. To estimate this number, you must divide the desired free-space threshold by the disk-block size. The value for this parameter can range from 0 to 100,000 blocks, with a default value of 256.

VOLUME LOW WARNING RESET THRESHOLD= *n*

The VOLUME LOW WARNING THRESHOLD issues the first warning that disk space is low. NetWare enables you to set the number of disk blocks that must be freed (*n*) before a second warning is issued. This parameter is used to prevent repeated warning messages being sent if free space hovers around the threshold set by VOLUME LOW WARNING THRESHOLD. When the first warning `VOLUME LOW WARN ALL USERS` is issued, and users reduce disk space just below the threshold, having a warning message may not be desirable if disk-space utilization rises above the threshold. Actually, this process could repeat several times—dipping below the threshold and then rising again—and the repeated warning messages could be a source of great annoyance to the user. The value for this parameter can range from zero to 100,000 blocks, with a default value of 256.

MAXIMUM PERCENT OF VOLUME USED BY DIRECTORY= *n*

NetWare enables you to set an upper limit on the percentage (*n*) of a volume that may be used as directory space. This percentage value ranges from 5 to 50, with a default value of 13.

MAXIMUM PERCENT OF VOLUME SPACE ALLOWED FOR EXTENDED ATTRIBUTES= *n*

NetWare 3.*x* and 4.*x* support multiple file-name spaces such as Macintosh, NFS, OS/2, and FTAM. These names spaces require extended attribute support. NetWare enables you to set and limit the percentage (*n*) of a volume that may be used for extended attribute storage. When the volume is being mounted, the setting becomes effective. This percentage value ranges from 5 to 50, with a default value of 10.

MAXIMUM EXTENDED ATTRIBUTES PER FILE OR PATH= *n*

NetWare enables you to set an upper limit on the number of extended attributes (*n*) that can be assigned to a file or path. This parameter setting affects all server volumes. The parameter value ranges from 4 to 512, with a default value of 32.

MAXIMUM SUBDIRECTORY TREE DEPTH= *n*

NetWare enables you to set the number of directory levels supported by the NetWare file system. The default value of this parameter is 25, even though some DOS applications cannot support more than 10 levels. The parameter value ranges from 10 to 100. This parameter can be set from the STARTUP.NCF file only. It cannot be set from the console prompt.

ALLOW UNENCRYPTED PASSWORDS= [ON¦OFF]

When set to OFF, this parameter enables users to use encrypted passwords only. The OFF setting is used if all file servers are NetWare 3.*x* and 4.*x*. If servers on the network are below NetWare 3.*x*, this parameter can be set to OFF to avoid login problems. If the servers are 2.12 and above, the NetWare 3.*x* or 4.*x* utilities can be copied to these servers and password encryption can be enabled by keeping this parameter value OFF. For NetWare servers below 2.12 (such as NetWare 2.0a), this parameter should be set to ON.

DISPLAY SPURIOUS INTERRUPT ALERTS= [ON¦OFF]

NetWare enables you to be alerted about spurious interrupts. *Spurious interrupts*, caused by IRQ conflicts between devices on the server, generate the message `Spurious hardware interrupt <number> detected`. The default setting is ON because spurious interrupts need to be resolved for the proper functioning of the server. A value of OFF is provided as a convenience (to turn off the messages while waiting for a resolution of the problem).

DISPLAY LOST INTERRUPT ALERTS= [ON¦OFF]

NetWare enables you to be alerted about lost interrupts. This message is generated when a driver or adapter generates an interrupt request and then drops the request before the CPU can respond to it. This generates the message `Interrupt controller detected a lost hardware interrupt`. The default setting is ON because lost interrupts can degrade server performance. A value of OFF is provided as a convenience (to turn off the messages while waiting for a resolution of the problem). This usually indicates a driver or board problem.

DISPLAY DISK DEVICE ALERTS= [ON¦OFF]

NetWare enables you to be alerted to disk events such as a hard disk added, activated, deactivated, mounted, or dismounted. The default setting is OFF. Setting the parameter to ON during disk testing and debugging can yield information that may be helpful.

DISPLAY RELINQUISH CONTROL ALERTS= [ON¦OFF]

NetWare enables you to be alerted when an NLM uses the server CPU continuously for more than 0.4 seconds, without relinquishing control to other processes. This parameter is meant for software developers during the testing phase of their NLM product. Its default value is OFF.

DISPLAY OLD API NAMES= [ON¦OFF]

Some of the API names were changed in NetWare 3.1*x*, and resource tracking was added for better monitoring and control of NLMs and their use of system resources. Also, resource tracking forces NLMs to release all their resources when they are unloaded. The default value of this parameter is OFF. Set this parameter to ON to monitor whether old APIs are being used. If older APIs are being used, contact the vendor of the software to get a more compatible version of the API.

HALT SYSTEM ON INVALID PARAMETERS= [ON¦OFF] (for NetWare 4.*x* Only)

Setting this parameter to ON causes the server to stop when an invalid parameter or condition is detected in executing the operating system or NLM code. This parameter can be set in the STARTUP.NCF or AUTOEXEC.NCF file. You may wish to set this parameter to ON when debugging new NCF files or new NLMs. Normally, you should set this value to OFF to allow the server to boot despite anomalous conditions. The default for this parameter is OFF.

SERVER LOG FILE OVERFLOW SIZE= *n* (for NetWare 4.*x* Only)

This value controls the maximum size that the server log file (SYS$ERR.LOG)can achieve. The size can be set between 65,536 and 4,294,967,295 bytes. The default value is 4,194,304 bytes.

SERVER LOG FILE STATE= *n* (for NetWare 4.*x* Only)

This setting controls the action to be taken if the server log file exceeds the overflow size set by the preceding parameter. The parameter values have the following meaning:

Parameter Value	Meaning
0	Take no action
1	Delete the log file (default)
2	Rename the log file

`VOLUME LOG FILE OVERFLOW SIZE=` *n* (for NetWare 4.x Only)

This value controls the maximum size that the volume log file (VOL$ERR.LOG) can achieve. The size can be set between 65,536 and 4,294,967,295 bytes. The default value is 4,194,304 bytes.

`VOLUME LOG FILE STATE=` *n* (for NetWare 4.*x* Only)

This setting controls the action to be taken if the volume log file exceeds the overflow size set by the preceding parameter. The parameter values have the following meaning:

Parameter Value	Meaning
0	Take no action
1	Delete the log file (default)
2	Rename the log file

`VOLUME TTS LOG FILE OVERFLOW SIZE=` *n* (for NetWare 4.*x* Only)

This value controls the maximum size that the TTS log file (TTS$ERR.LOG)can achieve. The size can be set between 65,536 and 4,294,967,295 bytes. The default value is 4,194,304 bytes.

`VOLUME TTS LOG FILE STATE=` *n* (for NetWare 4.*x* Only)

This setting controls the action to be taken if the TTS log file exceeds the overflow size set by the preceding parameter. The parameter values have the following meaning:

Parameter Value	Meaning
0	Take no action
1	Delete the log file (default)
2	Rename the log file

Setting Time Synchronization Parameters

NetWare 4.*x* has a number of parameters dealing with Time Synchronization.

Monitoring Tools

Several monitoring tools are available. Some are among the NetWare products; others, such as the Frye Utilities, must be purchased through the product vendor.

The following sections examine the console NLM, Frye Utilities, and Protocol Analyzers for network monitoring.

Console MONITOR NLM for NetWare 3.*x*

MONITOR is one of the most useful utilities for monitoring server performance. The MONITOR utility, an NLM that can be run from the server console, can be used to view information about any of the following:

- Server CPU utilization and overall activity
- Cache memory status
- Disk drives
- Mounted volumes
- LAN drivers
- Loaded NLMs
- File lock status
- Memory usage

The most important screens are displayed and discussed in this section. Menu selections to reach a particular screen from the MONITOR NLM are described by the following convention:

MONITOR -> Selection 1 -> Selection 2

which shows that from the MONITOR main menu, you select the `Select 1` option and then the `Select 2` option.

MONITOR Main Screen

When invoked from the console, the main screen shown in figure 22.7 is displayed. The main screen displays a wealth of information, most of which is related to server utilization and caching. The top part of the screen displays the operating system version, server name, and how long the server has been up. The *Utilization* shows the percentage of time the server is busy. This value can give an indication of server activity.

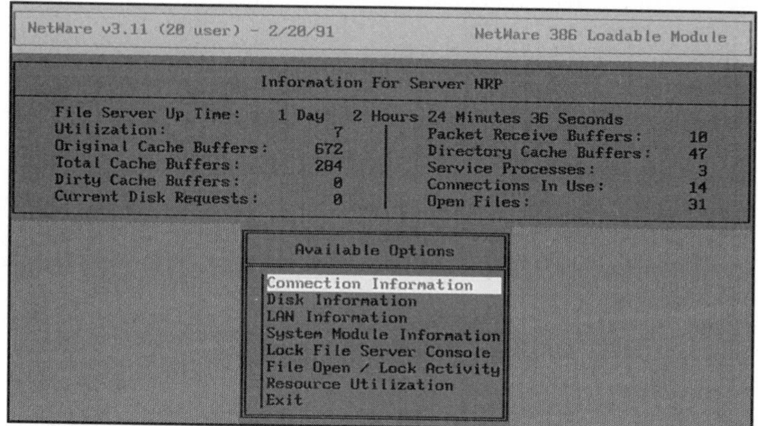

Figure 22.7
The MONITOR main screen.

When the server starts, several file-cache buffers are available to it. (The number is indicated by Original Cache Buffers.) The server satisfies memory requests for new NLMs from this cache pool, and over a period of time the number of cache buffers available may decrease. The current number of file-cache buffers is indicated by Total Cache Buffers. The server writes to a disk block by first writing to a copy of the disk block in a file-cache buffer in RAM. These buffers eventually need to be written to disk by a delayed background process controlled by the SET parameter DIRTY DISK CACHE DELAY TIME. While it is waiting to be written out, these buffers are called *dirty cache buffers.*

As the I/O activity on the server disk rises, not all disk requests can be processed simultaneously, and some have to wait in queue to be serviced. The number of disk requests waiting in queue is indicated by Current Disk Requests.

A certain number of buffers (indicated by Packet Receive Buffers) must be available to handle workstation requests.

The total number of buffers allocated to speed directory access are indicated in Directory Cache Buffers. The number of processes dedicated for handling file service requests is indicated by Service Processes. This number can increase on demand, and never decreases unless the server is restarted. The total number of connections in use at the server is indicated by the Connections In Use, and the total number of files opened at the server is indicated by Open Files.

MONITOR Connection Information

The MONITOR connection information screen is shown in figure 22.8. This screen can be reached through:

MONITOR -> Connection Information

Users who are logged out are indicated by NOT-LOGGED-IN. They show up in the connection information list because the shell at the workstation is still attached to the server.

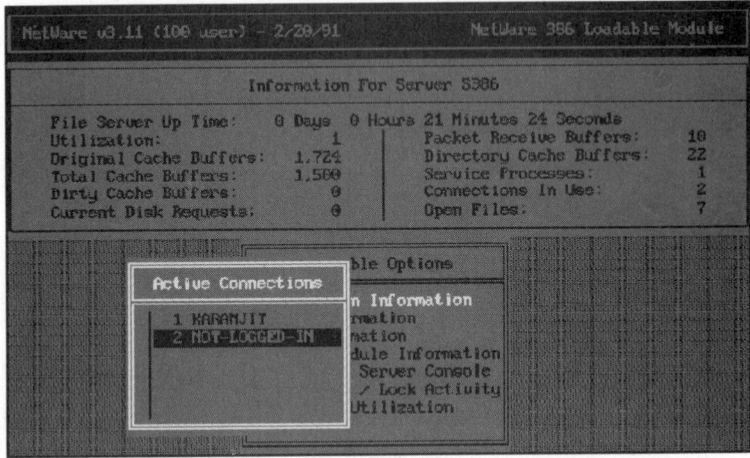

Figure 22.8 *The MONITOR connection information screen.*

If a displayed user is selected, information on that user is displayed as shown in figure 22.9. The top half of the screen in figure 22.9 displays statistics on the user; the bottom half indicates the files opened by the user. The statistics for the user indicate the following:

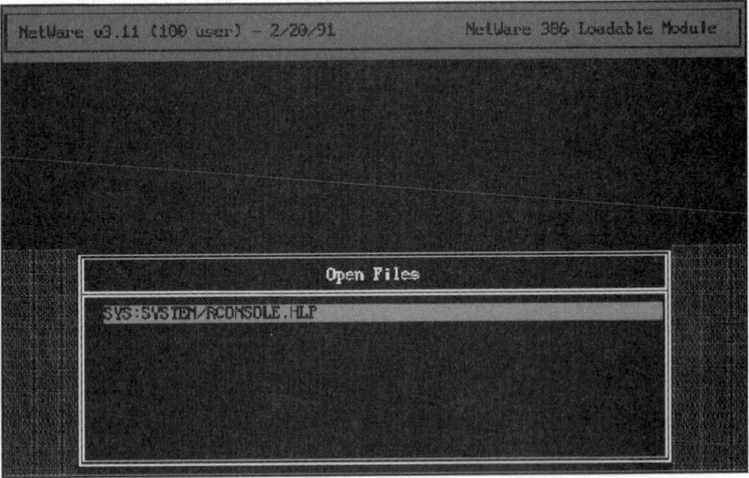

Figure 22.9 *MONITOR user information.*

- **Connection time.** Measured in days, hours, and minutes.
- **Network Address.** This address consists of three parts: network number (cable segment number), node address, and socket address. The socket address for the workstation shell is 4003 (hex); this is the software address of the workstation shell process.
- **Requests.** The total number of NCP requests generated by the workstation connection are displayed.
- **Kilobytes Read.** Measure of amount of information read. If enabled through accounting services, a user can be charged for this service.

- **Kilobytes Written.** Measure of amount of information written. If enabled through accounting services, a user can be charged for this service.
- **Status.** A user status can be *Normal*, which means the user is logged in; *Waiting*, which means the station is waiting for a file to be unlocked; or *Not-logged-in*, which means the shell attached to the server by the user is not logged in.
- **Semaphores.** Displays the number of semaphores used by the station. Semaphores can be used to arbitrate access to resources (NICs, areas of RAM, bus), and also to limit the number of workstations that can use a shared application.
- **Logical Record Locks.** Displays the number of logical locks used by a connection. A *logical lock* is implemented by assigning a logical name to a resource and locking that name. Other applications check for a lock on the name before accessing the resource. A logical record is enforced by applications. (This is different from physical locks that are enforced by the network operating system and can lock a range of bytes on a file. If another user attempts to access a range of bytes that is physically locked, the user receives an `Access Denied` error message.)

The physical locks for an open file can be displayed by selecting an open file and pressing Enter. Figure 22.10 shows the headings for the physical locks. The Start and End columns indicate the byte offset at which the lock begins and ends. The Record Lock column indicates one of the four types of record locks defined in table 22.3.

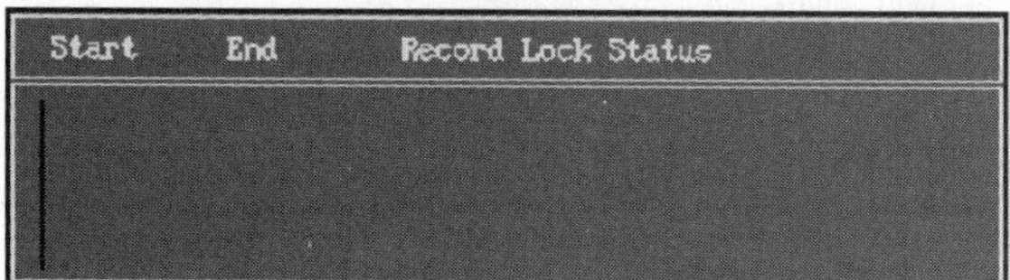

Figure 22.10
MONITOR physical locks for user connection.

Table 22.3
Types of Physical Locks

Physical Lock	Description
Locked Exclusive	Locked so that no one else can read or write to the specified range of bytes
Locked Shareable	Locked so that reads are allowed but only one station can write
Locked	Logged for future locking
TTS Holding Lock	Unlocked by application but still locked by TTS because transactions are not complete

The Status column indicates a Not Logged status, which signifies that no lock requests are pending. A Logged status indicates that several records are being prepared for locking. The server logs each lock before performing the lock, to avoid deadly embrace or deadlock conditions.

MONITOR Disk Information

The MONITOR disk information screen is shown in figure 22.11. This screen can be reached through:

MONITOR -> Disk Information -> Select a hard disk

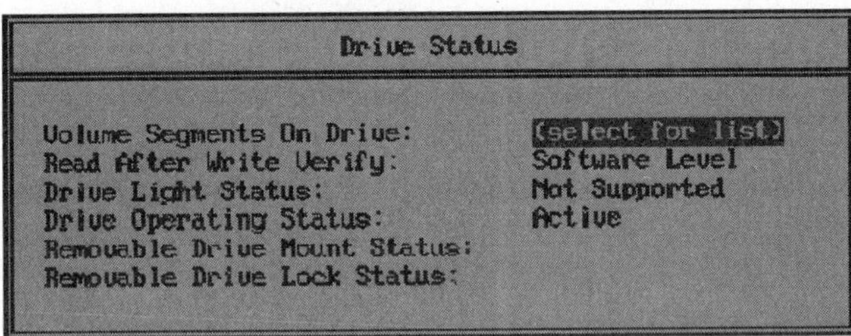

Figure 22.11 *MONITOR disk information.*

Figure 22.11 displays driver information for the selected hard disk. The top part of the screen indicates information on the disk driver; the bottom half of the screen, the Drive Status. The driver information includes the following:

- **Driver.** This is the driver name.
- **Disk Size.** Size in megabytes of all partitions on the disk.
- **Partitions.** Number of partitions defined on the hard disk.
- **Mirror Status.** The values are *Mirrored*, which indicates that disk mirroring is in place; *Not Mirrored*, which indicates that disks are being used independently; and *Remirroring*, which indicates that data is being transferred between disks so that they can be mirrored.
- **Hot Fix Status.** *Normal* indicates that hot fix is enabled. *Not-hot-fix* indicates that hot fix has been disabled or has failed.
- **Partition Blocks.** Total space in disk blocks on the server disk.
- **Disk Blocks.** Number of blocks from the total partition blocks that can be used for data.
- **Redirection Blocks.** Number of blocks reserved for the Hot Fix Area.
- **Redirected Blocks.** Number of bad blocks found and redirected by hot fix.
- **Reserved Block.** Used for hot-fix tables.

The Drive Status fields are explained in the following list:

- **Volume Segments On Drive.** A volume can be made up of many disk partitions or disks; they are listed if this field is selected.
- **Read After Write Verify.** Normally set to Software Level Verify, because Hot Fix performs read-after-write verify. Some disk controllers can perform this test, in which case Hardware Level Verify may be selected. The Disable Verify disables the read-after-write verify. This option should be selected only for benchmark tests. Under normal operation, always have some form of read-after-write verify check.
- **Drive Light Status.** Can be used to physically flash the drive-light status indicator at regular intervals, so that you can identify the physical disk. This option may not be supported for some disk drivers/drive types.
- **Drive Operating Status.** Used to manually deactivate/activate disk; used primarily for testing disk drives.
- **Removable Drive Mount Status.** Used to manually mount/dismount removable media. The values can be Mounted/Dismounted.
- **Removable Drive Lock Status.** Used to lock a removable medium to prevent its physical removal. The values can be Locked/Unlocked. If the status value is Unlocked, the removable medium can be dismounted and removed.

MONITOR LAN Information

The MONITOR LAN information screen is shown in figure 22.12. This screen can be reached through:

MONITOR -> LAN Information -> Select a LAN driver

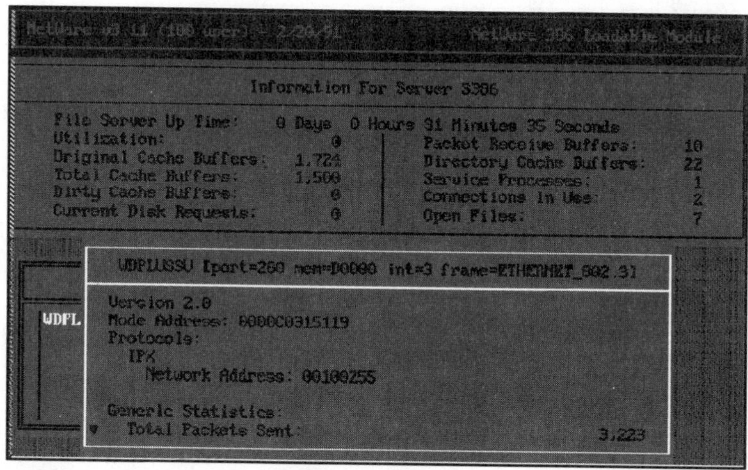

Figure 22.12
MONITOR LAN driver information.

Figure 22.12 displays the LAN driver information for the selected LAN driver. The bottom half of the screen shows a window titled with the name of the LAN driver selected. The LAN driver information indicates the version number, node address of the NIC in the server, protocols bound to the LAN driver, and the network address of the cabling segment on which the LAN driver is working.

Figure 22.13 shows more of the Generic Statistics information. The statistical information for a LAN driver cannot fit on-screen, but you can use the cursor or PgDn keys to see the rest of the information.

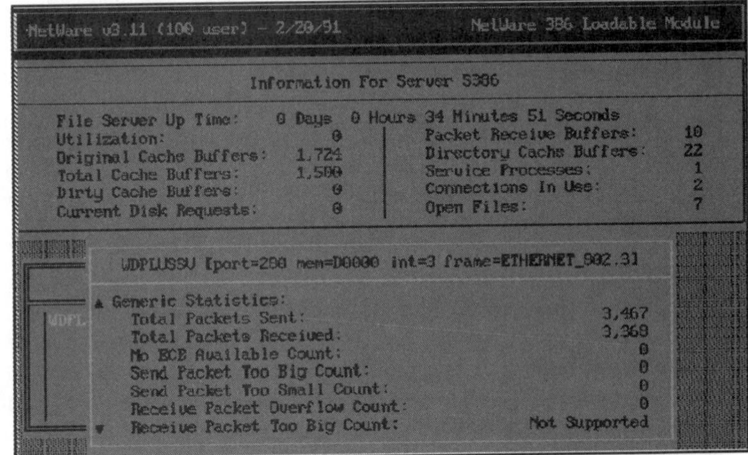

Figure 22.13
MONITOR LAN Generic Statistics.

Generic Statistics information, available for all LAN drivers, is described in table 22.4.

Table 22.4
MONITOR Generic Statistics for LAN Drivers

Parameter	Description
Total Packets Sent	Total packets sent through this LAN driver; indicates which driver is handling most of the traffic, and how much traffic.
Total Packets Received	Total packets received by this LAN driver; indicates which driver is handling most of the traffic, and how much traffic.
No ECB Available Count	A counter that increments when a packet receive buffer is not available for an incoming packet. Server allocates packet receive buffers on demand until the MAXIMUM PACKET RECEIVE BUFFERS is reached (see the earlier section in this chapter on SET parameters).

Parameter	Description
Send Packet Too Big Count	A counter that increments when server transmits a packet too big for the NIC to handle; indicates an incorrect setting of MAXIMUM PHYSICAL RECEIVE PACKET SIZE or a problem with the server software or NIC driver.
Send Packet Too Small Count	A counter that increments when server transmits a packet too small for the NIC to handle; indicates a problem with the server software or NIC driver.
Receive Packet Overflow Count	A counter that increments when server receives a packet too big to store in a cache buffer; indicates a problem with workstation software in negotiating a proper packet size; could also be a problem with NIC driver or card at sender.
Receive Packet Too Big Count	A counter that increments when server receives a packet too big for the NIC to handle; indicates an incorrect setting of MAXIMUM PHYSICAL RECEIVE PACKET SIZE or a problem with sender software or NIC driver.
Receive Packet Too Small Count	A counter that increments when server too small count receives a packet too small for the NIC to handle; indicates problem with sender software or NIC driver.
Send Packet Miscellaneous Errors	A catch-all error counter that increments when an error occurs during transmission of a packet that does not fit any other category. A large value could indicate problems with network hardware.
Receive Packet Miscellaneous Errors	A catch-all error counter that increments when an error occurs during reception of a packet that does not fit any other category. A large value could indicate problems with network hardware.

continues

Table 22.4, Continued
MONITOR Generic Statistics for LAN Drivers

Parameter	Description
Send Packet Retry Count hardware	A counter that increments when server retries sending a packet because of a error; indicates a problem with cabling or NIC hardware, or a problem with long delays across a Wide Area Network. Try increasing the retry count using the LOAD driver command.
Checksum Errors	A counter that increments when a data error is detected by the CRC checksum at the end of the MAC frame (packet); indicates a problem with NIC hardware, noise, or cabling.
Hardware Receive Mismatch Count	A counter that increments when the packet length indicated by the length field in a packet does not match the size of the packet received by the NIC; indicates a problem with NIC or NIC driver.

In addition to Generic Statistics, Custom Statistics specific to the NIC hardware are being used. These are reported by the driver for that NIC and are different for different network hardware. Figure 22.14 shows the custom statistics for an Ethernet NIC. Among other statistics, a variety of custom statistics deal with collision count. This is in keeping with the operation of Ethernet.

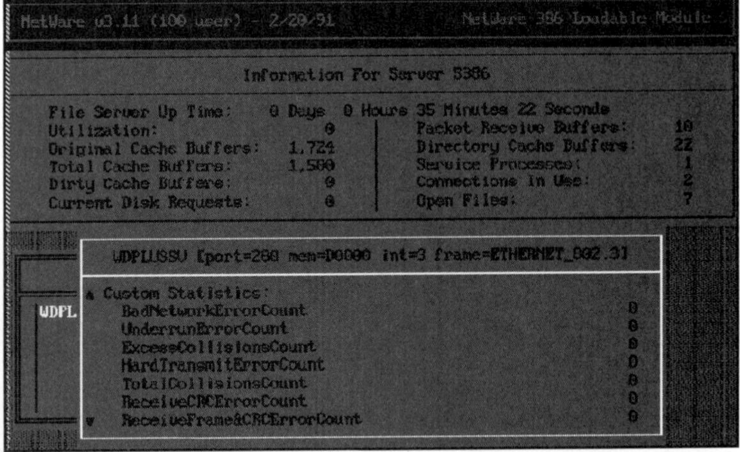

Figure 22.14
MONITOR LAN Custom Statistics.

MONITOR System Module Information

The MONITOR System Module List screen is shown in figure 22.15. This screen can be reached through:

MONITOR -> System Module Information

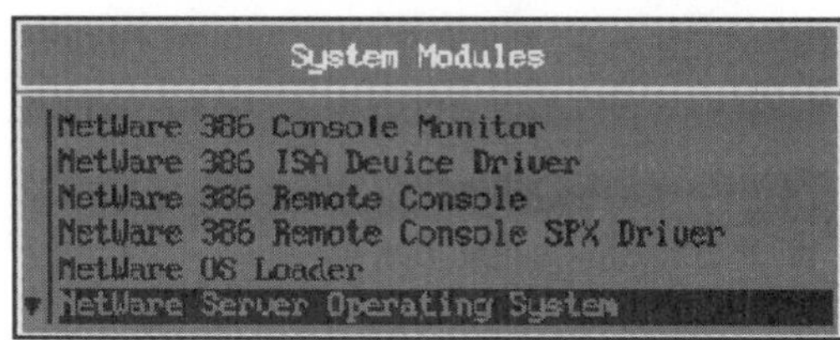

Figure 22.15
MONITOR system module list.

Figure 22.16 displays the information for the selected system module. The top part of the screen indicates the module size in RAM and the file name under which the system module was loaded. The bottom half of the screen shows the resource tags for that system module. A *resource tag* is a mechanism introduced in NetWare 3.10 to keep track of system resources. It also allows NetWare to ensure that all tagged resources are released when the system module is unloaded. Because the system modules can be written by third-party vendors over whom Novell has little control, this is a useful addition to the NetWare operating system, allowing it to release resources when a module unloads.

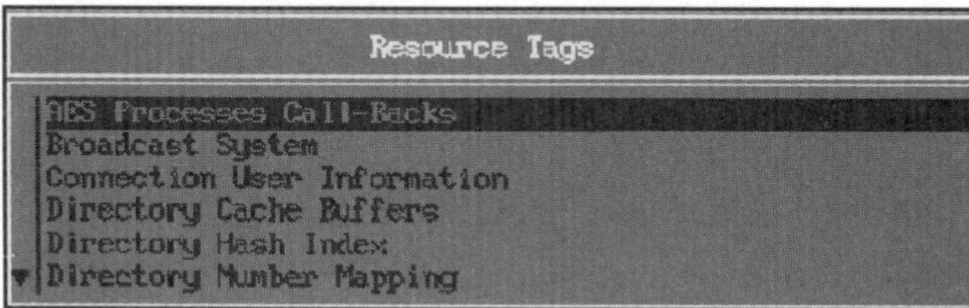

Figure 22.16
MONITOR system module information.

Selecting a resource (see fig. 22.17) displays the tag name (Tag), the name of the parent module this resource belongs to (Module), the type of resource (Resource), and the amount of memory used by the resource (In Use).

Figure 22.17
MONITOR resource tag information.

MONITOR File Open/Lock Activity

The MONITOR File Open/Lock Activity screen is shown in figure 22.18. This screen can be reached through:

MONITOR -> File Open/Lock Activity -> Select path name of a file

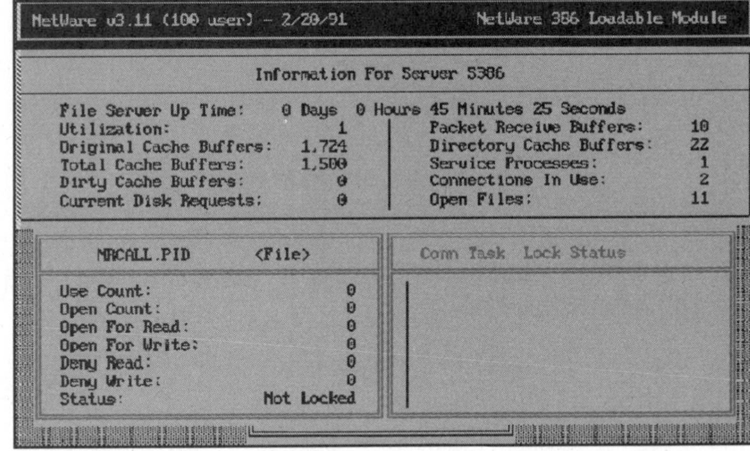

Figure 22.18
MONITOR File Open/Lock activity.

Use Count is the number of connections that have the file opened or locked. Open Count defines the number of connections that currently open the file; Open Read indicates the number of connections reading from the file; and Open Write, the number of connections writing to the file. The following relationship holds true at all times:

Open Count = Open Read + Open Write

The Deny Read and Deny Write fields indicate whether the file lock for the open operation is exclusive or shared. Deny Read indicates the number of connections that have opened the file, but denies even the read operation (exclusive file lock). Deny Write indicates the number of connections that have opened the file, but denies writes to other stations (shared read).

The Status field indicates whether the file is Locked or Unlocked. The Conn column indicates a list of connections using that field. The Task is an internal number used by the NetWare shell for the application using the file. The lock status can have the values of Exclusive, Shareable, TTS Holding Lock, Logged, or Not Logged. The Exclusive lock means that no one else can read or write to the record; Shareable means that others may read but not write to the record. TTS Holding Lock means that the file was unlocked by an application, but because the transactions are not complete, the TTS has the file locked. Logged means that a set of records is being prepared for locking, to avoid a deadly-embrace situation. Not-Logged, the normal condition, indicates that no locks are pending.

MONITOR Resource Utilization

The MONITOR Resource Utilization screen is shown in figure 22.19. This screen can be reached through:

MONITOR -> Resource Utilization -> Select a resource

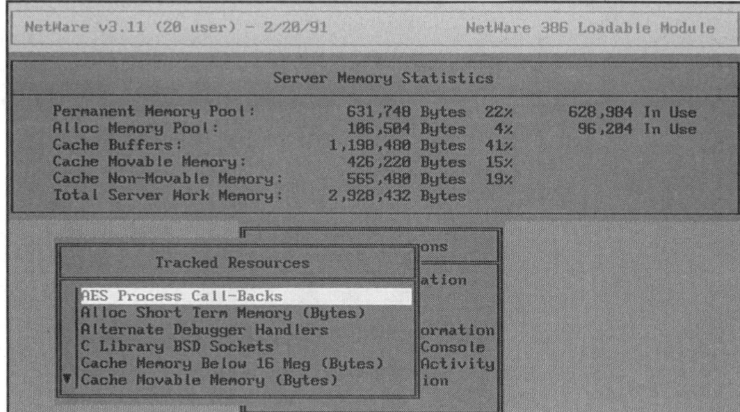

Figure 22.19
MONITOR tracked resources.

In figure 22.19, the bottom part of the screen shows a list of resources tracked by NetWare. The server tracks resources such as the Alloc Memory Pool by forcing procedures to use a resource tag when doing an allocation. The top part of the screen contains server memory statistics. The individual fields are as follows:

- **Permanent Memory Pool.** Memory used by processes when they do not intend to return it for awhile (if ever). When more memory is needed, cache buffers are transferred to this pool; these cache buffers will never be returned to the cache buffer pool. The directory-cache buffers, as well as the packet-receive buffers, are contained in this pool.

- **Alloc Memory Pool.** Memory used by processes when they do not intend to use it for long periods of time. When more memory for this pool is needed, it is transferred from the Permanent Memory Pool; this memory will never be returned to the Permanent Memory Pool. This is the preferred memory pool for loadable modules to use when allocating small pieces of memory.

- **Cache Buffers.** The amount of memory in the cache buffer pool. This memory currently is being used for file caching. The amount of memory in this area should be greater than that in any other area.

- **Cache Movable Memory.** Memory allocated directly from the cache buffer pool. When freed, this memory will be returned to the cache buffer pool. It differs from Cache Non-Movable Memory in that the memory manager may move the location of these memory blocks to optimize memory usage. Volume tables and hash tables typically use this memory.

- **Cache Non-Movable Memory.** Memory allocated directly from the cache buffer pool. When freed, this memory will be returned to the cache buffer pool. Used when large pieces of memory are needed.
- **Total Server Work Memory.** This is the sum of all the memory pools.

To view the list of resource tags with a specific resource type, highlight the resource type and press Enter. You may then select a specific resource tag and view additional information associated with it.

Figure 22.20 shows resource tags for the tracked resource process. The resource tags are listed on the screen's right. Notice that the resources under the tracked resource processes are NLMs. This is to be expected because the NLMs act as processes. Selecting a specific resource tag gives more information on that resource. Figure 22.21, for instance, shows the resource information for the process RSPX.NLM.

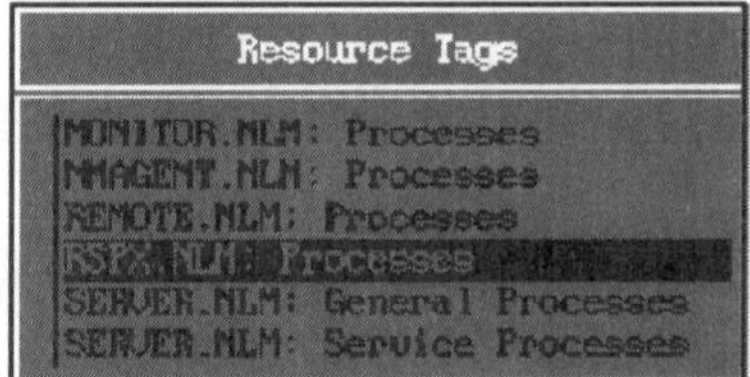

Figure 22.20 *MONITOR Resource Tags.*

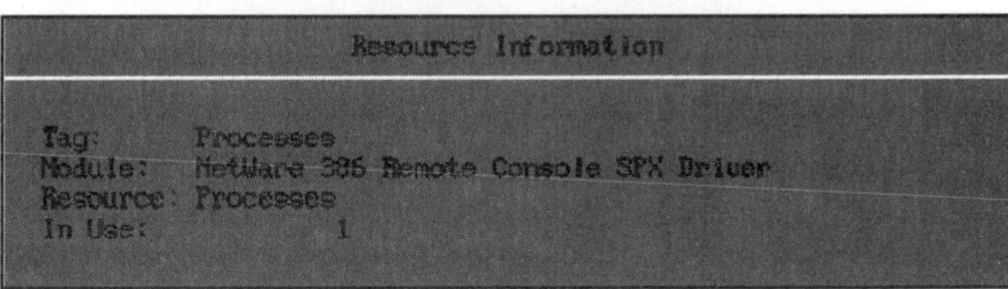

Figure 22.21 *MONITOR Resource Information.*

Undocumented MONITOR OPTION LOAD MONITOR -P

If the MONITOR utility is loaded using an undocumented option, a new option, Processor Utilization, is displayed.

```
LOAD MONITOR -P
or
LOAD MONITOR P
```

Selecting Processor Utilization gives a screen similar to that shown in figure 22.22, which lists the Available Processes and Interrupts. The list includes active processes (or threads) as well as all available hardware interrupts. To select multiple processes for observation, mark them with the F5 key and press Enter.

The screen in figure 22.23, for example, shows the process activity for seven processes marked with the F5 key. The Time column indicates the amount of time the CPU spent executing the code in the context of that process. For interrupts, this is the amount of time spent in the *Interrupt Service Routine*

(ISR) associated with that interrupt. The Count column represents the number of times the process ran during a sample period. For interrupts, this number indicates the number of interrupts serviced during a sample period. The Load column gives the percentage of time the CPU spent in this process or interrupt.

Name	Time	Count	Load
Cache Update Process	251	4	0.02 %
Directory Cache Process	155	4	0.01 %
FAT Update Process	309	9	0.02 %
Monitor Main Process	0	0	0.00 %
Polling Process	1,126,794	25	96.89 %
RSPX Process	0	0	0.00 %
Interrupt 3	354	2	0.03 %
Total Sample Time:	1,179,609		
Histogram Overhead Time:	16,709	(1.41 %)	
Adjusted Sample Time:	1,162,900		

Figure 22.22

Available processes and interrupts.

NetWare v3.11 (100 user) - 2/20/91 NetWare 386 Loadable Module

Name	Time	Count	Load
Cache Update Process	251	4	0.02 %
Directory Cache Process	155	4	0.01 %
FAT Update Process	309	9	0.02 %
Monitor Main Process	0	0	0.00 %
Polling Process	1,126,794	25	96.89 %
RSPX Process	0	0	0.00 %
Interrupt 3	354	2	0.03 %
Total Sample Time:	1,179,609		
Histogram Overhead Time:	16,709	(1.41 %)	
Adjusted Sample Time:	1,162,900		

Figure 22.23

Process activity.

At the bottom of the screen, an overhead summary displays the total sample time, the amount of time spent generating the utilization information (along with the percentage), and the adjusted sample time—the amount of time available for all the processes and interrupts to use. All the process and interrupt statistics are relative to the adjusted sample time.

Note that the utilization information is generated only when MONITOR is in this screen. When you enter this screen, MONITOR turns on the statistics-generation engine in NetWare. When you leave this screen, MONITOR turns off the statistics-generation engine, and the operating system returns to its normal mode of operation.

When the server is idle, the CPU will spend most of the time in the Polling Process and the STREAMS Q Runner Process if STREAMS is loaded. This can be used as an indication of low CPU utilization. Server Processes are used to service workstation requests. If other processes or interrupts have an unusually high percentage of the CPU's time, it may indicate bad hardware, drivers, or NLMs, or simply a busy server.

As you can see from figure 22.24, most CPU time is allocated to the Polling Process. Because there was no other activity on the system on which this measurement was taken, most of the time was spent in the polling process. The NIC setting on the server was set to Interrupt 3; as packets are processed by the NIC, Interrupt 3 shows activity. Whenever packets were transferred between workstation and server, the Interrupt 3 activity jumped up, as figure 22.24 shows.

Figure 22.24
Polling Process time and increase in Interrupt 3 activity.

Name	Time	Count	Load
Cache Update Process	314	5	0.02 %
Directory Cache Process	193	5	0.01 %
FAT Update Process	306	9	0.02 %
Monitor Main Process	0	0	0.00 %
Polling Process	1,126,728	26	96.88 %
RSPX Process	0	0	0.00 %
Interrupt 3	355	2	0.03 %
Total Sample Time:	1,179,654		
Histogram Overhead Time:	16,754	(1.42 %)	
Adjusted Sample Time:	1,162,900		

Console MONITOR NLM and SERVMAN NLM for NetWare 4.*x*

Many of the parameters in the MONITOR for NetWare 4.*x* are similar to NetWare 3.*x*. There are some important differences, also. This section will briefly describe the MONITOR NLM for NetWare 4.*x*.

The MONITOR and SERVMAN NLMs can be activated using the LOAD command. The MONITOR command has a few optional parameters, as shown in table 22.5.

Table 22.5
Monitor Options

Monitor Option	Description
/L or L	Locks the server console.
/NS or N	Disables the "snake" screensaver, which is otherwise activated after 10 minutes of inactivity.
/NH	Disables the Help screens for MONITOR Note: Although this switch is included in the Novell documentation, it does not work with MONITOR version 4.01.

The MONITOR NLM can be used for monitoring:

- Server utilization
- Status of cache memory
- Network connections (licensed and attached connections) and their status
- Disk drive information
- File lock status
- LAN driver information
- NLMs loaded at server
- Memory usage
- Mounted volumes
- Scheduling information
- Resource utilization

Additionally, the MONITOR NLM can be used to lock the server console.

The SERVMAN NLM can be used for

- Viewing and configuring NetWare OS parameters
- Viewing and Updating SET parameters in STARTUP.NCF and AUTOEXEC.NCF
- Viewing network adapter, device, and partition information
- Viewing volume information

- Configuring IPX/SPX parameters
- Viewing network information

Understanding General Server Statistics

The main MONITOR screen (see fig. 22.25) and main SERVMAN (see fig. 22.26) screen show a number of general statistics for the server and the network. The parameters that are displayed on the screen give an overview of the network and server status.

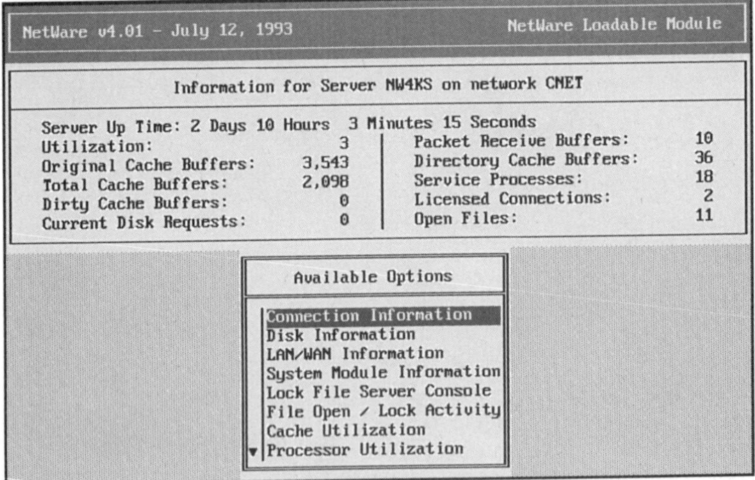

Figure 22.25
General MONITOR statistics.

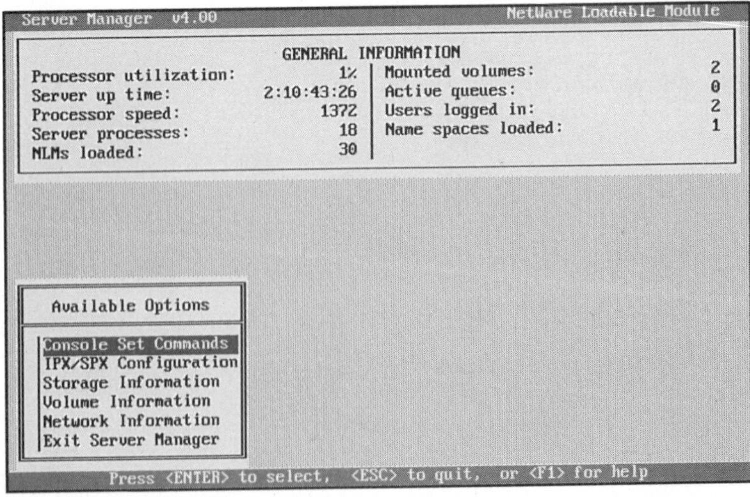

Figure 22.26
General SERVMAN statistics.

The top part of the screen in figure 22.25 displays the NetWare 4.*x* version and release date. The Information for Server field shows the name of the server being monitored and the name of the NDS tree on which the server is located. Figure 22.25 shows that the name of the server is NW4KS and the NDS tree name is CNET.

The Server Up Time field on the MONITOR (see fig. 22.25) and the SERVMAN screen (see fig. 22.26) shows how long the server has been up since the last time it was started. The *Utilization* field in MONITOR and *Processor Utilization* field in SERVMAN show the CPU utilization of the server. This is expressed as the percentage of time the server is busy.

The Original Cache Buffers field in the MONITOR screen shows the total number of cache buffers that were available when the server was first started.

Original Cache Buffers = (M – N – D) / B

in which

M = Total server memory

N = Memory used by NetWare 4.*x* kernel

D = Memory used by DOS on server

B = Block size

The Original Cache Buffers value as reported by the screen in figure 22.25 is 3,543. Assuming a block size of 4 KB (4,096 bytes), the initial memory allocated for cache buffers is 3,543*4,096 = 14,512,128 bytes. The server in figure 22.25 had a total memory of 16 MB (16,777,216 bytes). This means that the memory used by the NetWare OS kernel and DOS is 16 MB – 14,512,128 bytes = 2,265,088 bytes, or 2.2 MB.

The Total Cache Buffers field in the MONITOR screen is the number of buffers currently available. As NLMs are loaded, this number decreases. The number in figure 22.25 is 2,063 buffers. This means that *Original Cache Buffers – Total Cache Buffers* = 3,543 – 2,063 = 1,480 cache buffers are used by additional NLMs. On the server in figure 22.25, the additional NLMs were MONITOR, SERVMAN and TCPIP NLMs. The total number of NLMs that are loaded can be seen in the *NLMs loaded* field in the SERVMAN screen (see fig. 22.26).

The Dirty Cache Buffers field in the MONITOR screen is the number of buffers that contain file data that is yet to be written to the disk. These buffers are called *dirty* because the information in them is not synchronized to the disk. The SET Dirty Disk Cache Delay Time parameter can be used to control the minimum amount of time the server waits before synchronizing a dirty disk cache buffer to disk. It has a default value of 3.3 seconds and can range from 0 to 10 seconds. For applications where data integrity is very important, you can set this parameter to 0, to avoid dirty disk blocks being not synchronized to disk. If *Dirty Cache Buffers* is consistently high, it indicates a high level of write I/O activity where the background process that writes file cache buffers to disk is unable to keep up with the I/O activity.

The Current Disk Requests field in the MONITOR screen indicates the number of disk I/O requests that are in queue waiting to be serviced. If *Current Disk Requests* is consistently high, it indicates a high level of I/O activity. Using a faster disk controller/disk combination, or splitting the I/O activity across several volumes or servers, will generally improve I/O response times.

The Packet Receive Buffers field in the MONITOR screen is the number of communication buffers at the server that can process workstation requests. This parameter is in the range controlled by the SET Minimum Packet Receive Buffers and the SET Maximum Packet Receive Buffers parameters.

The Directory Cache Buffers field in the MONITOR screen is the number of buffers reserved for directory caching. In NetWare 4.*x*, portions of the directory entry tables are cached to improve directory search response times.

The Service Processes field in the MONITOR and SERVMAN screen is the number of processes dedicated by the NetWare 4.*x* OS to handle station requests. During peak server activity, when workstation requests exceed the number of service processes that have been assigned, additional service processes are assigned. Once assigned, the memory allocated to the service processes is not reduced, unless the server is restarted. You can control the rate at which new service processes are allocated by the SET New Process Service Wait Time that delays the request for a new service process. This parameter can range from 0.3 to 20 seconds and has a default value of 2.2 seconds. The SET Maximum Service Processes parameter limits the growth of the number of processes that handle packets, and can be set to a value between 5 and 100. It has a default value of 40.

The Licensed Connections field on the MONITOR screen, and the Users logged in field on the SERVMAN screen, is the number of licensed connections to the server. This number reflects the number of users that are using resources on this server. This value is different from the "Active Connections" that can be displayed by selecting the "Connection Information" option on the MONITOR screen. The Active Connections includes the licensed connections and any other network devices (usually workstations) that are attached to the server but are not making use of server resources.

The Open Files field in the MONITOR screen is the number of files that are currently open at the server. NetWare 4.*x* can support 100,000 open files. To view file names that are opened by a particular user, you must select the Connection Information option, highlight the user name, and press Enter.

The SERVMAN General Information reports other information (see fig. 22.26) such as Processor Speed, which is an index that indicates how fast the processor is. The Mounted volumes field indicates the number of server volumes that are mounted, including any CD-ROM volumes that may be mounted. The Active queues field refers to the number of print queues that are active on the server. The Name spaces loaded field shows the number of name spaces that are supported. This value should be at least 1, because the DOS name space is always supported.

Monitoring Storage and Volume Information

You can see the Storage and Volume information on the server by using either MONITOR or SERVMAN. The information shown by these tools complement each other, and in some cases the same information is shown in the MONITOR and SERVMAN NLMs.

You can optimize server disk utilization by enabling sub-allocation, compression, and data migration (if you have the hardware support). To improve response times for the server disk, you can use high performance disk and disk controllers. Many high performance servers use SCSI controllers that come with custom disk drivers that are optimized to take advantage of the special hardware features of the disk controllers. Use of a 32-bit bus and bus mastering technique, such as that used in EISA and MCA adapters, can further improve data transfer rates for the server disk.

Viewing Disk Information in MONITOR

To view disk information using MONITOR, select "Disk Information" from "Available Options." Highlight a system disk driver and press Enter. You should see a screen similar to figure 22.27. The top half of the screen shows the Driver, Disk Size, and Partitions on the disk. The DOS partition on a server disk is counted as a partition. This screen shows the Mirror Status and the Hot Fix Status of the disk. The Partition Blocks field shows the total number of 4 KB-disk blocks that are available. A certain number of redirection blocks—shown in the Redirection Blocks field—are reserved for hot fix, and the actual number of 4 KB data blocks—shown in the Data Blocks field—that are available is the difference between the values in the Partition Blocks and Redirection Blocks fields.

Partition Blocks = Data Blocks + Redirection Blocks

The Redirection Blocks field indicates the number of blocks that were relocated because of hot-fix errors. If this number increases rapidly, it usually indicates a rapidly deteriorating disk. You should reformat the disk and perform surface analysis, or replace the disk.

The Reserved Blocks field represents the number of redirection blocks reserved for system use. When the following condition holds, hot-fix on the volume has failed.

Redirected Blocks + Reserved Blocks = Redirection Blocks

The lower half of the screen indicates the following information: The Volume Segments On Drive field shows the volume segments that make up the logical volume. A NetWare volume can consist of 32 volume segments. The Read After Write Verify field indicates if the read-after-write feature is supported by the volume. Figure 22.27 shows that the read-after-write feature is hardware supported for the volume. The Drive Light Status field indicates the current drive light flash status. If a parameter is not supported by the hardware, a value of `Not Supported` is displayed. The Drive Operating Status field indicates if the drive is `Active` or `Deactivated`. For removable disks, two other parameters—Removable Drive Mount Status and Removable Drive Lock Status—are displayed. These indicate if the removable drive is currently mounted or if the drive is locked.

Viewing Storage Information in SERVMAN

To view storage information using SERVMAN, select `Storage Information` from Available Options. You will see information on the top half of the screen for the object that is highlighted in the Storage objects menu in the lower part of the screen. Figure 22.28 shows information on the adapter that is highlighted on the bottom half of the screen. Adapter objects in the Storage objects menu are not indented. Device, Magazines, and Changer objects are indented once, and Partition objects are indented twice.

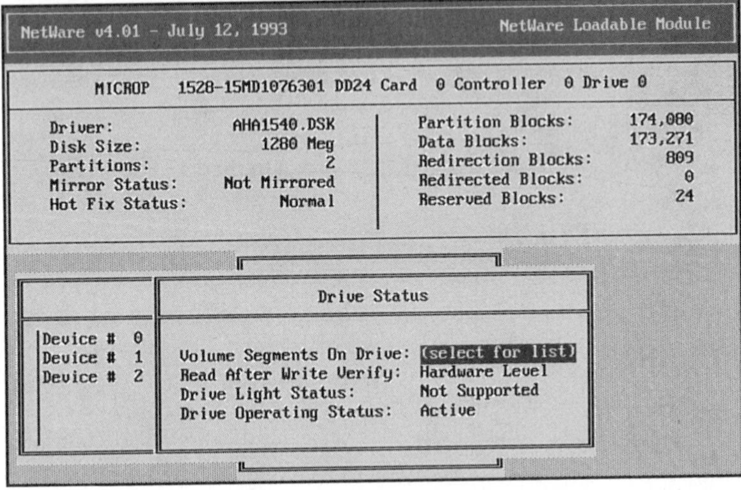

Figure 22.27
Disk Information using MONITOR.

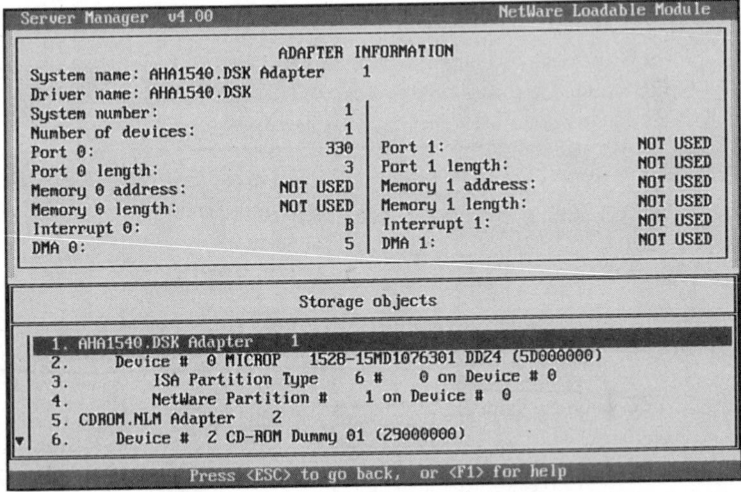

Figure 22.28
Disk controller adapter information using SERVMAN.

The disk controller adapter information in figure 22.28 shows the system name of the adapter, its system number (internal number used by system to identify the adapter), driver name, and number of devices on the adapter. The hardware settings for the adapter are also displayed. For instance, figure 22.28 shows that the adapter uses a port of 330 (hex), port length of 3 bytes, interrupt value of B (hex), and DMA channel 5.

Highlighting option 2 (`Device # 0 MICROP`) shows information about the device attached to the adapter (see fig. 22.29). The device information shows the heads, cylinders, sectors per track, block size and disk capacity of the device attached to the adapter. It also shows the device type of the attached device and the adapter number to which the device is attached.

```
Server Manager  v4.00                          NetWare Loadable Module

                          DEVICE INFORMATION
Adapter number:                    0 |
Heads:                            64 | Block size (bytes):          64 KB
Cylinders:                      1280 | Device type:             Hard Disk
Sectors per track:                32 | Capacity (bytes):    1,342,177,280

                         Storage objects

  1. AHA1540.DSK Adapter    1
  2.      Device #  0 MICROP   1528-15MD1076301 DD24 (5D000000)
  3.           ISA Partition Type     6 #    0 on Device # 0
  4.          NetWare Partition #     1 on Device #  0
  5. CDROM.NLM Adapter    2
  6.      Device #  2 CD-ROM Dummy 01 (29000000)

              Press <ESC> to go back,  or <F1> for help
```

Figure 22.29
Device information using SERVMAN.

Highlighting option 4 (`NetWare Partition # 1 on Device # 0`) shows information about a NetWare partition on the device. Figure 22.30 shows the NetWare partition type (101) as recorded in the partition manager table, the partition size in blocks, total number of hot fix blocks available, used hot fix blocks, mirror status and condition, number of mirrors, and partition offset in blocks.

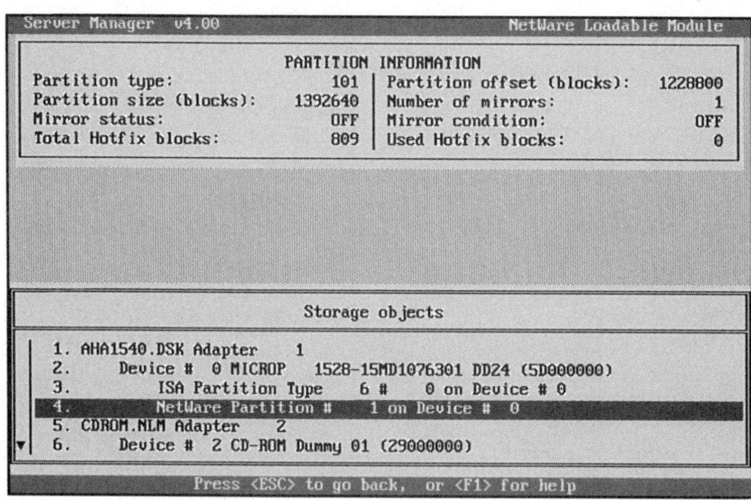

Figure 22.30
Partition information using SERVMAN.

Viewing Volume Information in SERVMAN

To view volume information using SERVMAN, select Volume Information from Available Options. You will see volume information on the top half of the screen for the volume object that is highlighted in the Volume Objects menu in the lower part of the screen. Figure 22.31 shows information about volume SYS: that is highlighted on the bottom half of the screen.

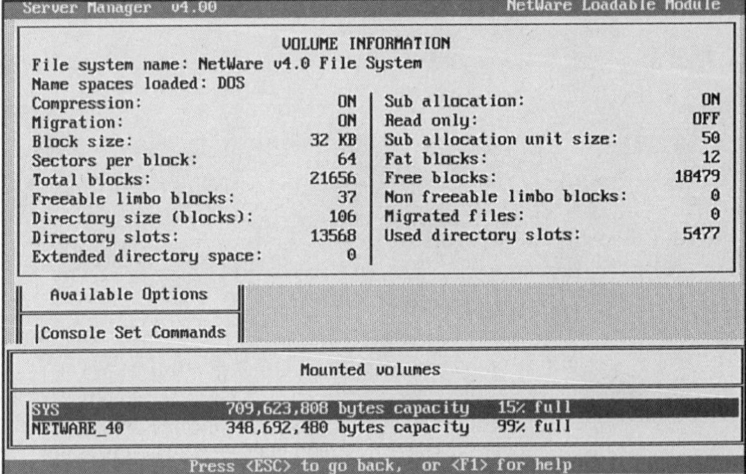

Figure 22.31
Volume information using SERVMAN.

The Volume information in SERVMAN includes information such as file system name, name spaces that are loaded, status of compression, sub-allocation, migration, number of migrated files, volume block size, sectors per block, total blocks, free blocks, directory size in blocks, directory slots, used directory slots and read-only status (ON for CD-ROM volumes), freeable limbo blocks and non-freeable limbo blocks. For most of these parameters, their meaning is self-evident and contained in the name of the parameter. However, a few of the parameter names do not easily reveal their meaning and are discussed next.

Directory slots means directory entries. *Limbo blocks* refers to disk blocks that are in a state of "limbo" in which they are not usable. *Freeable limbo blocks* refers to the number of blocks that would be usable if they could be freed. Examples of these freeable limbo blocks are blocks holding deleted files. To regain these blocks, you can use the PURGE command. *Non freeable limbo blocks* refers to the number of blocks that are not in use by the system and are not freeable by ordinary means. These blocks indicate potential problems with the server volume. You may be able to free some of these blocks by running VREPAIR. Use of VREPAIR is described at the end of this chapter.

Controlling Turbo FAT Reuse Time

NetWare 4.*x* uses the Turbo FAT feature to improve access to large randomly accessed files. Normally files are accessed by the *File Allocation Table* (FAT). The FAT is shared by all files on a NetWare volume, and is cached in server RAM to provide faster access to its contents. The FAT contains a chain of pointers to data blocks for files. When a file needs to be accessed, the server finds the start of the chain in the *Directory Entry Table* (DET), and follows the chain in the FAT table.

For files that have more than 64 FAT entries and that are randomly accessed, NetWare 4.*x* builds a special FAT table for that file in the server RAM. This special table is called the *Turbo FAT table* (also called *Index table*), and contains an index of blocks for that specific file only. This makes it possible to very quickly find data blocks for the indexed file.

The system has built-in heuristics to determine if a file is accessed randomly, and only uses Turbo FATs for files that are randomly accessed files. Files that are accessed sequentially do not have Turbo FATs built for them.

When an indexed file is closed, its Turbo FAT is not immediately released, in case that file is to be reused again. This delay is controlled by the SET Turbo FAT Re-Use Wait Time parameter that has a default value of 5 minutes 29.6 seconds. Indexed files that are reused within this SET parameter value will find their Turbo FATs in RAM and be able to reuse it. If the indexed file is used after this time, the Turbo FAT will have to be rebuilt again. You can increase the value of this parameter, if you expect that there will be longer delays in the reuse of a file.

Examining Memory Utilization

NetWare 4.*x* manages memory in 4 KB page sizes. The memory for NLMs is allocated from a common file cache pool and released to this common pool when the NLM is unloaded. An NLM can also issue the system *free()* call to release memory that it has dynamically allocated.

The memory needed by an NLM is the memory for itself, plus any other NLMs it depends on. Because common NLMs, such as CLIB, STREAMS, and TLI can be shared by a number of NLMs, the overall system memory requirements is reduced. The memory used by an NLM is approximately the same as the size of the NLM file. Certain NLMs allocate additional memory when they are running, and this must be factored into the estimated memory usage for that NLM.

Viewing System Module Information

Figure 22.32 shows the System Module Information for the NetWare Directory Services. To see this figure, select "System Module Information" from "Available Options" in MONITOR. Highlight the desired system module, and press Enter. From figure 22.32, you can see that the name of the NetWare Directory Services is DS.NLM and it uses 376,345 bytes. You can also see a list of *resource tags* used by the NLM. When an NLM makes use of resources, it can register the name of the resource and other information on the resource as a set of *resource tags*. This enables the server to monitor and track how these resources are used. Figure 22.33 shows that the Alloc memory tag uses 39,888 bytes of memory. To view the memory used by a resource tag, highlight the resource and press Enter.

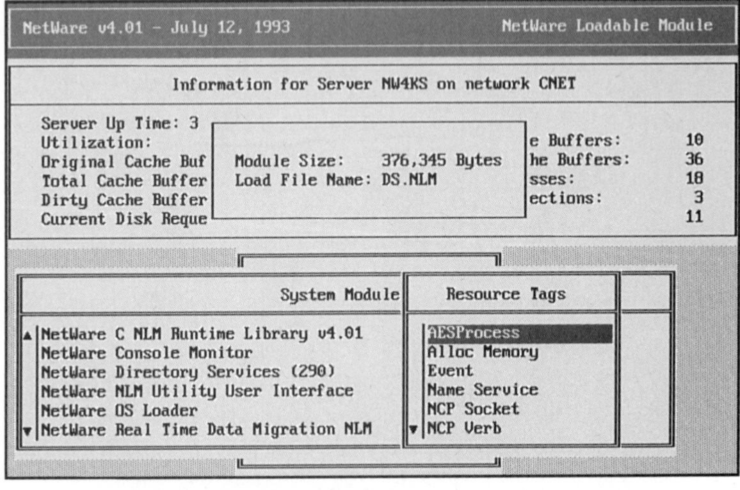

Figure 22.32 *System Module information for DS.NLM.*

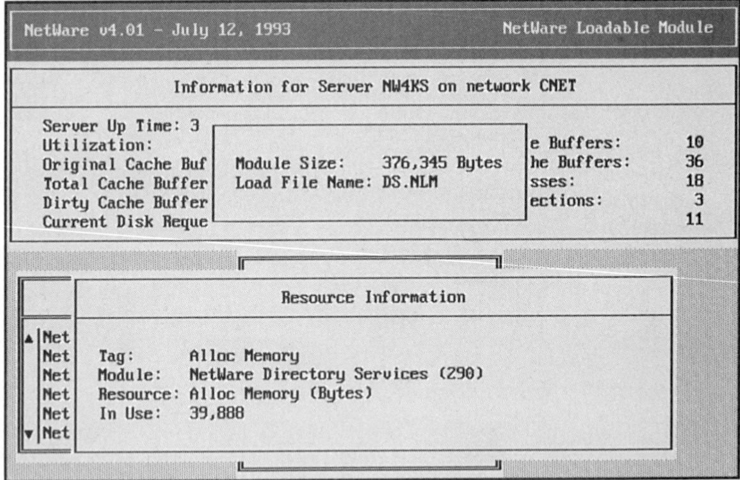

Figure 22.33 *Memory used by resource tag in MONITOR.*

Viewing Memory Utilization

When you select Memory Utilization from Available Options in MONITOR, the top part of the screen changes to show allocated memory information for all modules (see fig. 22.34).

The 4 K Cache Pages field shows the number of cache pages in the memory allocation pool. This pool is the set of pages from which memory is allocated.

The Cache Page Blocks field represents the memory that has already been allocated and is in the allocated memory pool.

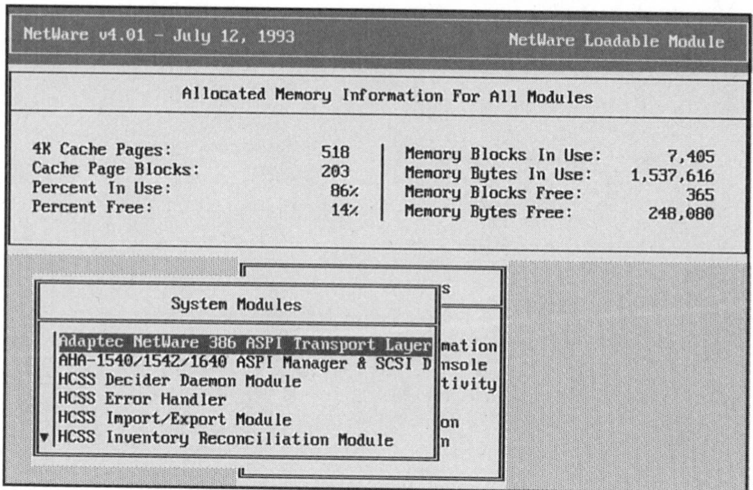

Figure 22.34
Allocated Memory Information for all Modules using MONITOR.

The Percent In Use field is the percentage of memory in the allocated memory pool (Cache Page Blocks) that is in use, and the Percent Free field is 100 minus the Percent In Use value.

The Memory Blocks In Use field is the number of pieces of memory that have been allocated and are currently in use.

The Memory Bytes In Use field is the number of bytes of memory that have been allocated and are currently in use.

The Memory Blocks Free field is the number of pieces of memory that have been freed and are available for reuse.

The Memory Bytes Free field is the number of bytes of memory that have been freed and are available for reuse.

To see memory allocation for an individual system module, highlight the module and press Enter. The lower part of the screen displays the memory allocated for that module. Figure 22.35 shows the memory utilization for the NetWare Directory Services. The description of these parameters is the same as that discussed for all the system modules, except that the values refer to the individual system module rather than all the system modules.

You can perform garbage collection from the screen in figure 22.35. *Garbage collection* looks for whole pages in the free area of the allocated memory pool and returns them to the system. To perform garbage collection for the selected module, press F3, and to perform garbage collection for the entire system, press F5.

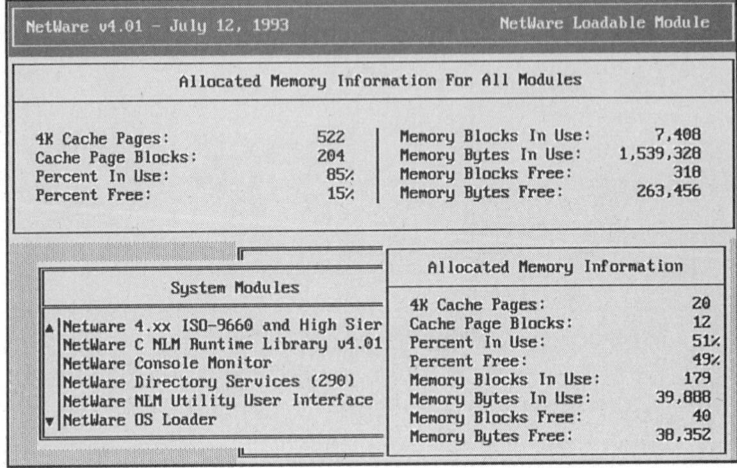

Figure 22.35
Allocated Memory Information for NetWare Directory Services using MONITOR.

Examining Cache Utilization

NetWare improves the performance of disk reads and writes by allocating an area of server RAM called the *file cache*, and by reading disk blocks into the file cache area. Subsequent reads of the same disk block can be satisfied from the file cache. Reads from the file cache are much faster than reading directly from the disk. Similarly, writes are done to the cache and returned as being completed. A background process called the *lazy cache write process*, flushes the written blocks to server disk. When a read request is satisfied from the file cache, it is called a *cache hit*. Cache utilization can be defined as the percentage of cache hits.

Managing Cache Utilization

To observe cache utilization, select Cache Utilization from Available Options in MONITOR (see fig. 22.36). The parameters for cache utilization are described in table 22.6.

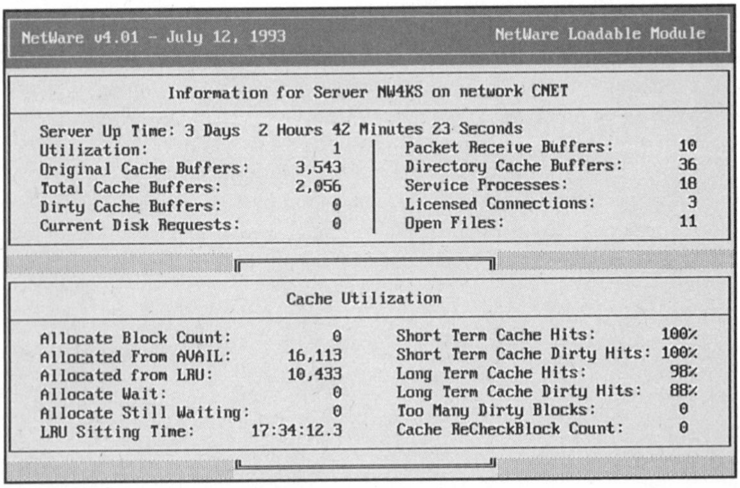

Figure 22.36
Cache Utilization using MONITOR.

```
NetWare v4.01 - July 12, 1993                     NetWare Loadable Module

            Information for Server NW4KS on network CNET

Server Up Time: 3 Days  2 Hours 42 Minutes 23 Seconds
Utilization:                    1 | Packet Receive Buffers:        10
Original Cache Buffers:     3,543 | Directory Cache Buffers:       36
Total Cache Buffers:        2,056 | Service Processes:             18
Dirty Cache Buffers:            0 | Licensed Connections:           3
Current Disk Requests:          0 | Open Files:                    11

                          Cache Utilization

Allocate Block Count:          0   Short Term Cache Hits:        100%
Allocated From AVAIL:     16,113   Short Term Cache Dirty Hits:  100%
Allocated from LRU:       10,433   Long Term Cache Hits:          98%
Allocate Wait:                 0   Long Term Cache Dirty Hits:    88%
Allocate Still Waiting:        0   Too Many Dirty Blocks:          0
LRU Sitting Time:     17:34:12.3   Cache ReCheckBlock Count:       0
```

Table 22.6
Cache Utilization Parameters

Cache Parameter	Description
Allocate Block Count	This indicates the number of disk cache block requests that have been made since the server was started.
Allocated From AVAIL	This indicates the number of disk cache block requests that were satisfied from the AVAIL list which consists of blocks that are not currently used.
Allocated from LRU	This indicates the number of disk cache block requests that were satisfied from the LRU list, which consists of blocks that are Least Recently Used (oldest blocks not referenced).
Allocate Wait	This indicates the number of times a cache block request had to wait because there were no available cache blocks.
Allocate Still Waiting	This indicates the number of times a cache block request had to wait behind another cache block request in the queue that was still waiting because there were no available cache blocks. This indicates the number of times the queue size for memory allocation requests was more than 1.
LRU Sitting Time	This indicates the time since the oldest block in the LRU list was last referenced.
Short Term Cache Hits	This indicates the percentage of disk cache requests that were satisfied with cache blocks that were already in the file cache *over the last one second.*
Short Term Cache Dirty Hits	This indicates the percentage of disk cache requests that were satisfied with cache blocks already in the file cache, but the disk block was *dirty* (not yet flushed to disk), *over the last one second.*
Long Term Cache Hits	This indicates the percentage of disk cache requests that were satisfied with cache blocks that were already in the file cache. *Long Term* means longer than a second.
Long Term Cache Dirty Hits	This indicates the percentage of disk cache requests that were satisfied with cache blocks that were already in the file cache, but the disk block was *dirty* (not yet flushed to disk). This parameter indicates how often a request was made for a block that was just recently written to the cache. Blocks written to the cache are

continues

Table 22.6, Continued
Cache Utilization Parameters

Cache Parameter	Description
	written to the disk in a time interval controlled by the SET the Dirty Disk Cache Delay Time, whose default value is 3.3 seconds. *Long Term* means longer than a second.
Too Many Dirty Blocks	This indicates the number of times a write request was delayed because there were too many dirty blocks.
Cache ReCheckBlock Count	This indicates the number of times disk cache requests had to be retried, because the target block was being used.

If the *Long Term Cache Hits* falls below 90 percent, you can improve performance by adding more server RAM. Meanwhile, you can make more RAM available to the system by unloading NLMs that are not needed. You can also remove DOS (used to boot the server machine) by using the REMOVE DOS command. However, this typically frees up only 104 KB of server RAM.

You can also improve cache utilization by making the cache buffer size and the volume block size the same. NetWare requires that the cache block size be equal to the smallest volume block size. If you are using volumes with different volume block sizes, you cannot make the cache buffer and volume block size the same.

Novell makes the following recommendations for the SET parameters for improving speeds of disk reads and writes. These changes can be made by the SET command or by the SERVMAN.NLM.

Increase Concurrent Writes to improve speed of disk writes. This can be done by changing the Maximum Concurrent Disk Cache Writes to 100. The default value is 50 and can be set to a value from 10 to 4,000.

```
SET MAXIMUM CONCURRENT DISK CACHE WRITES= 100
```

To change disk and directory caching for faster writes, set the Dirty Disk Cache Delay Time to 7 seconds, Maximum Concurrent Directory Cache Writes to 25, and Dirty Directory Cache Delay Time to 2 seconds.

```
SET DIRTY DISK CACHE DELAY TIME= 7 SECONDS
SET MAXIMUM CONCURRENT DIRECTORY CACHE WRITES= 5
SET DIRTY DIRECTORY CACHE DELAY TIME= 2 SECONDS
```

To change disk and directory caching for faster reads, set the Maximum Concurrent Disk Cache Writes to 10, Maximum Concurrent Directory Cache Writes to 5, and Dirty Directory Cache Buffer NonReferenced Delay to 60 seconds.

```
SET MAXIMUM CONCURRENT DISK CACHE WRITES= 10
SET MAXIMUM CONCURRENT DIRECTORY CACHE WRITES= 5
SET DIRTY CACHE BUFFER NONREFERENCED DELAY= 60 SECONDS
```

The Dirty Disk Cache Delay Time has a default value of 3.3 seconds and can range from 0.1 to 10 seconds. This is the minimum amount of time the system waits before writing a dirty file cache buffer to server disk.

The Maximum Concurrent Directory Cache Writes has a default value of 10 and can range from 5 to 50. This is the maximum number of simultaneous writes of the directory cache buffers.

The Dirty Directory Cache Delay Time has a default value of 0.5 seconds and can range from 0 to 10 seconds. This is the minimum time the system waits before flushing a dirty cache buffer to disk.

The Dirty Cache Buffer NonReferenced Delay Directory Cache Delay has a default value of 5.5 seconds and can range from 1 second to 5 minutes. This is the time to wait after a directory cache buffer was referenced before reusing it.

Understanding the Disk Read Ahead Mechanism

NetWare 3.12 and NetWare 4.*x* implement a disk Read Ahead mechanism. For files that are sequentially accessed, it is an advantage to read the next few blocks after the current block is being read, and cache them in memory, because subsequent sequential reads will find these blocks in cache. NetWare 4.*x* has built-in heuristics to determine if a file is being accessed sequentially or randomly. If NetWare 4.*x* determines that the file is being read sequentially it begins to *stage* data beyond the current block that is being read in cache.

Using a large volume block size is an advantage, as larger amounts of read-ahead data can be cached, and a disk read can often be processed in a single rotation of the disk. For example, if the volume block size is 64 KB, a 64 KB data can be read in a single read. If the volume block size is 4 KB, the server has to perform 16 read operations to read the same 64 KB of data.

Whenever a file on the server is open, NetWare begins tracking the patterns in which data blocks in the file are read. If NetWare determines that the file is being accessed sequentially, it activates an internal read-ahead process. When the workstation requester accesses data beyond the midpoint of the current block, the next block of data is read into cache. For a 64 KB data block, the requester has to reach the 32 KB midpoint mark, and the next sequential data block is read.

NetWare keeps a watchful eye on the pattern of data access even after it has determined that a file is being accessed sequentially. If the access to a file changes from sequential access to random access, NetWare detects this, and deactivates the Read Ahead process. NetWare does not use read-ahead for randomly accessed files because read-ahead can introduce an extra overhead, where data that is read ahead of its time is not likely to be used.

Read-ahead requests are placed in a queue and processed in the background at a lower priority than normal read and write requests. Because read-ahead requests are processed in the background, they do not significantly impact the normal I/O operations. The "scheduling mechanism" in NetWare ensures that under peak-load conditions, fewer read-ahead requests are performed in comparison with normal reads and writes.

22

Understanding Disk Request Prioritization in NetWare 4.x

In earlier versions of NetWare, it was possible to run into certain rare situations where read requests would be ignored. This situation would occur in situations involving a large number of Write requests. Write requests are written to cache buffers and a background process flushes the dirty cache buffers to disk. If the number of dirty write cache buffers increased beyond a certain threshold, the server would switch the task of flushing the dirty disk buffers from the background to the foreground mode, so that it could quickly recover the use of the dirty cache buffers. When the server switched to foreground writes, it did so to the exclusion of processing other tasks. If a high priority read request occurred when the server was performing foreground writes of dirty cache buffers, it would get ignored.

To prevent the previous problem from occurring in NetWare 4.*x*, disk requests are prioritized into four queues:

- Critical events
- Read requests
- Write requests
- Read-ahead requests

The priority of these queues is in the order in which they are listed, with Critical events being at the highest priority and Read Ahead requests at the lowest priority. The four queues are often called *disk elevators* by Novell.

Critical events are those that must be guaranteed to be completed. Examples of critical events are file commits and TTS log writes.

Read requests are the next priority, because they are generated by foreground client tasks that depend on the results of the read (read of directory or a file). Read requests also constitute the bulk of the work done at a server.

Write requests are at the next priority, because most write requests can be performed in the background (write requests are typically written to the cache and await the *lazy-cache write process* that flushes them to disk). When a client makes a write request, it expects the request to be performed, but very often the subsequent actions the client performs does not depend on the results of the write request. Even if the client needs to access the data that was immediately written, the dirty cache buffer can be read, as it holds the most current data. When this occurs, the number of writes to the server disk can be occurred. You can monitor the occurrence of this event through MONITOR's cache utilization statistics Long Term Cache Dirty Hits and Short Term Cache Dirty Hits fields.

Read-ahead requests are performed at the lowest priority, as they can generally improve the performance of sequential reads, but are not critical to the operation of the server.

NetWare 4.*x* does not require that the higher priority queue requests always be fulfilled before a lower priority queue can be fulfilled. Instead, NetWare takes a percentage of requests from each request queue and services them in the order of their priorities. The higher the priority of the queue, the greater the percentage of requests serviced from that queue. This mechanism guarantees that requests from each queue are processed, regardless of the fact that there may be a large number of requests in a high priority queue.

Examining Processor Utilization and Scheduling Information in NetWare 4.*x*

The general MONITOR and SERVMAN statistics show the overall processor utilization (see fig. 22.25 and 22.26). NetWare 4.*x* can be used to see processor utilization on a per process basis. This enables you to determine where most of the processor time is being spent. Under continuous heavy processor loads, it is usually just a few processes that contribute to most of the processor load. You can use MONITOR to quickly identify which processes use most of the processor cycles. You may then decide to load these applications on separate servers dedicated to running them.

To view Processor Utilization using MONITOR, select Processor Information: from Available Options. You can highlight any process and press Enter to see its processor utilization statistics. To see several processes together, you can mark them with F5 and press Enter. Alternatively, you can select all the processes by pressing F3. Figure 22.37 shows the processor utilization for processes selected using F3. You can also see process utilization when you select Scheduling Information from Available Options (see fig. 22.38).

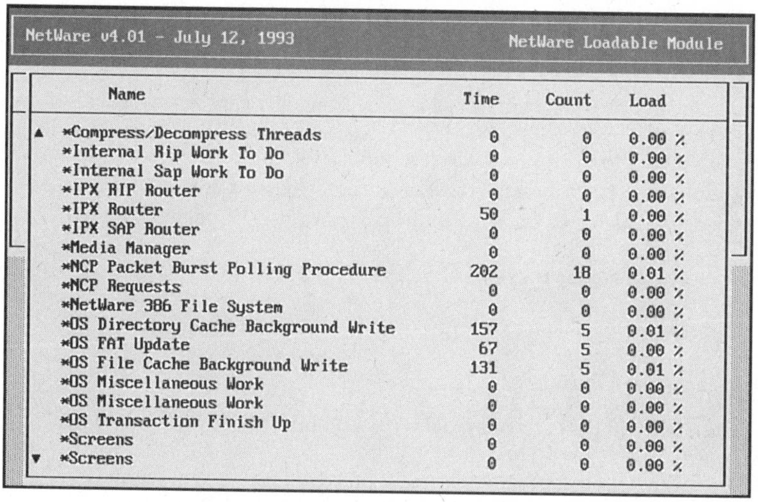

NetWare v4.01 - July 12, 1993 NetWare Loadable Module

Name	Time	Count	Load
*Compress/Decompress Threads	0	0	0.00 %
*Internal Rip Work To Do	0	0	0.00 %
*Internal Sap Work To Do	0	0	0.00 %
*IPX RIP Router	0	0	0.00 %
*IPX Router	50	1	0.00 %
*IPX SAP Router	0	0	0.00 %
*Media Manager	0	0	0.00 %
*NCP Packet Burst Polling Procedure	202	18	0.01 %
*NCP Requests	0	0	0.00 %
*NetWare 386 File System	0	0	0.00 %
*OS Directory Cache Background Write	157	5	0.01 %
*OS FAT Update	67	5	0.00 %
*OS File Cache Background Write	131	5	0.01 %
*OS Miscellaneous Work	0	0	0.00 %
*OS Miscellaneous Work	0	0	0.00 %
*OS Transaction Finish Up	0	0	0.00 %
*Screens	0	0	0.00 %
*Screens	0	0	0.00 %

Figure 22.37
Processor Utilization for all processes.

In figure 22.25, process utilization information is sampled, processed and displayed in 1 second, and for figure 22.26, information is sampled, processed, and displayed every 2 seconds.

The Name column displays the name of the process being displayed. The Time column indicates the time the CPU spent executing code in that process or interrupt service routine. The Count column shows the number of times the process or interrupt service routine ran during the sample period. The Load column indicates the percentage of time the CPU spent in this process or interrupt service routine.

If you scroll through the screen, you will see an overhead summary at the bottom. The summary includes Total Sample Time, Histogram Overhead Time, and Adjusted Sample Time. All statistics are displayed relative to the Adjusted Sample Time which is the difference between the Total Adjusted Time and Histogram Overhead Time values. The statistics collection is turned ON only when the screens in figures 22.25 and 22.26 are displayed, and turned OFF when you exit these screens.

Figure 22.38
Scheduling Information for processes.

```
NetWare v4.01 - July 12, 1993                         NetWare Loadable Module

        Name                          Sch Delay       Time      Count     Load

▲ ServMan Backgroun Process              0              0          0    0.00 %
  ServMan Main Process                   0              0          0    0.00 %
  SNMP Agent        0 Process            0              0          0    0.00 %
  Sync Clock Event Process               0              0          0    0.00 %
  TCP Test Server Process                0              0          0    0.00 %
  TCP Timing Loop Process                0            710         36    0.02 %
  TCP/IP            0 Process            0          1,263          2    0.05 %
  TCP/IP Packet Process                  0              0          0    0.00 %
  TCP/IP Utility Process                 0             54          2    0.00 %
  TimeSyncMain Process                   0            104          2    0.00 %

  Interrupts                                        2,829         41    0.11 %
  Idle Loop                                     2,316,729         37   96.16 %
  Work                                              3,239        136    0.13 %

  Total Sample Time:                            2,425,187
  Histogram Overhead Time:                         16,087   ( 0.66 %)
  Adjusted Sample Time:                         2,409,100
```

If the server is idle, it spends most of its time in the idle loop process. This indicates a low server utilization.

The Scheduling Information displays only processes whose scheduling delay can be adjusted. You can use the + or – key to increase or decrease the scheduling delay of the highlighted process. If the server CPU utilization for a process is too high, you can reduce it by increasing the scheduling delay.

Another way to change the scheduling delay is to use SCHDELAY.

The general syntax for this NLM is

`LOAD SCHDELAY [`*`processName`*` = `*`number`*`]`

in which *processName* is the name of the process and *number* is the amount of delay.

Loading SCHDELAY without any parameters shows the list of processes that are running and their current delay. For example, to increase the delay of the Media Manager process to 5, the command would be as follows:

```
LOAD SCHDELAY MEDIA MANAGER=5
```

To change the delay for a particular process to 0 (no delay), use the command:

`LOAD SCHDELAY `*`processName`*` = 0`

To change the delay for all processes to 0 (no delay), use the command:

```
LOAD SCHDELAY ALL PROCESSES = 0
```

Resource Utilization

When an NLM allocates resources, the server forces the NLM to register a resource tag for identifying the resource. NetWare 4.*x* keeps track of resources by using this resource tag.

When you select Resource Utilization from Available Options, the lower left side of the screen shows the resource types that are tracked by the server (see fig. 22.39). If you highlight a tracked resource and press Enter, you can see the resource tags for that resource type. Figure 22.40 shows the resource tags for the SNMP Abstract Object resource type. If you highlight a resource tag and press Enter, you can see the Tag name, Module name (NLM name), Resource type the resource tag belongs to, and the amount of the resource type that has been allocated (In Use) by the resource tag (see fig. 22.41).

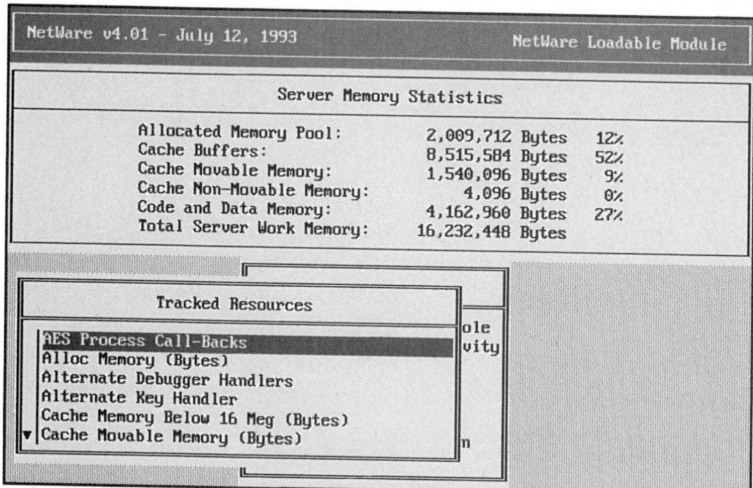

Figure 22.39
Resources tracked by the server.

```
NetWare v4.01 - July 12, 1993                 NetWare Loadable Module

                    Server Memory Statistics
        Allocated Memory Pool:        2,071,152 Bytes   13%
        Cache Buffers:                8,458,240 Bytes   52%
        Cache Movable Memory:         1,540,096 Bytes    9%
        Cache Non-Movable Memory:         4,096 Bytes    0%
        Code and Data Memory:         4,158,864 Bytes   26%
        Total Server Work Memory:    16,232,448 Bytes

        Tracked Resources                Resource Tags
 SMILE Manager                   SNMP.NLM SNMP Internal Objects
 SMILE Manager Requests          TCPIP.NLM TCP/IP MIB Registration
 SNMP Abstract Objects
 SNMP Trap Handlers
 Stack Memory (Bytes)
 STREAMS Active Handles
```

Figure 22.40
Resource tags for a tracked resource type.

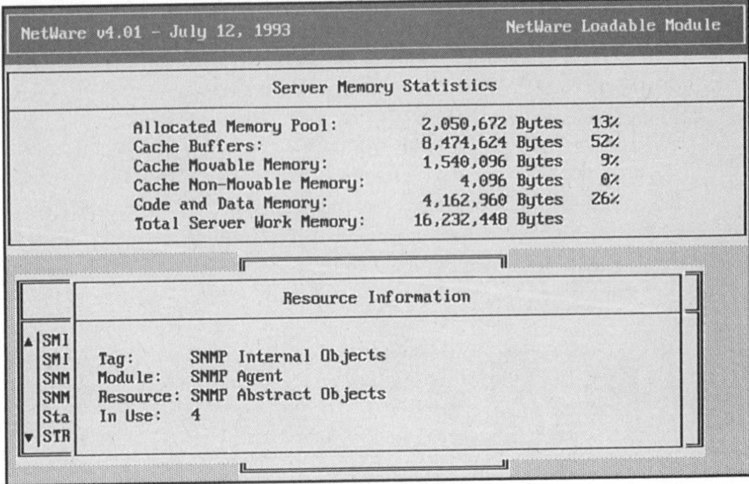

Figure 22.41
Resource tags details.

Frye Tools

Other third-party tools provide performance-related information for NetWare. One such tool—the Frye Utilities for Network Management, from Frye Computer Systems, Inc. (617-451-5400)—can monitor performance of both NetWare 3.*x* and NetWare 2.*x* servers. In addition to performance tuning, the utilities also provide diagnostic reports, server documentation, and weekly maintenance reports. The Frye Utilities for NetWare includes an Early Warning System that indicates automatic notification of errors when certain threshold conditions are met. Figure 22.42 shows some of the parameters that can be monitored. Notification alert messages can be sent to designated users on the network through electronic mail, fax, or a pager system.

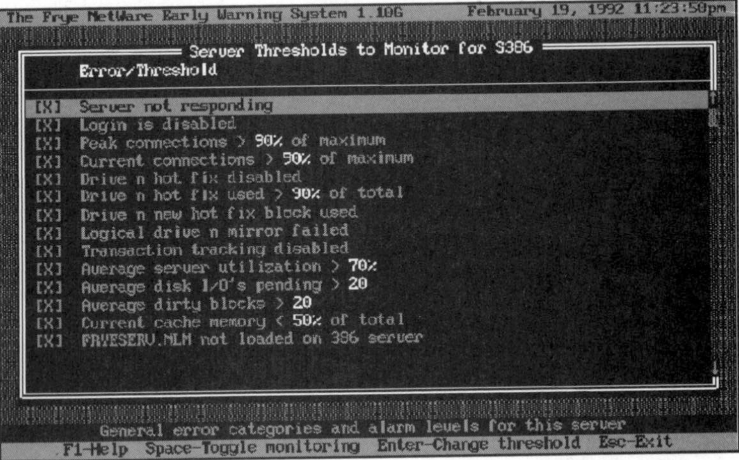

Figure 22.42
Frye Tools: Parameter thresholds.

The performance-monitoring capability of Frye Utilities goes beyond what the MONITOR utility currently offers.

Nu-Mega Technology Tools

When a new application or system NLM is installed, it must share the CPU resources with the NetWare operating system. Depending on how NLMs are written, they can have a serious impact on server—and hence network—performance. This is particularly true if an NLM contains bugs, is poorly written, and starts monopolizing the server CPU time or starts writing to areas of memory to which it is not supposed to write.

Nu-Mega Technologies, Inc. (603-889-2386) provides Net-Check and the NLM-Profile tools, which are invaluable for detecting and monitoring ill-behaved NLMs in NetWare 3.*x*. NetWare 4.*x* includes the ability to load NLMs in different ring domains, and the tool is not needed for this version of NetWare.

The NET-Check tool can be used to monitor NLMs and prevent them from writing into another NLM's code or data area. Normally the developer should catch such behavior, so users should not see the problem. But if a software bug escapes the software developer (as it often does), you have to deal with it. NET-Check is able to detect NLMs that make an out-of-bounds memory overwrite. It can be configured to prevent these overwrites from taking place, or to allow them to take place and inform you of these overwrites.

NET-Check provides this protection by running most of the NLMs in ring 3 of the Intel 80386 microprocessor. Normally, NetWare and NLMs run in ring 0, where they have access to all the hardware resources and there is no protection. By running at ring 3 and making use of pages, NET-Check is able to use the hardware protection mechanisms of the Intel 80386 microprocessor to catch ill-behaved NLMs.

Run NET-Check whenever you install a new NLM application on your NetWare 3.*x* server, and when you want to monitor for any illegal actions, until you are satisfied that the installed NLMs are behaving properly. Because NET-Check monitors for illegal activities, it also can help in detecting viruses attached to NLMs. Nu-Mega claims that NET-Check can be run all the time without affecting server performance.

The NET-Profile tool gives a profile of CPU usage for the processes and NLMs running on the server. The NetWare scheduling mechanism is nonpreemptive. (It is up to a process to relinquish control of the CPU.) Although this makes for a very efficient scheduler, a poorly written NLM can hog CPU time to the detriment of overall server performance. NET-Profile can detect these errant NLMs. The NET-Profile tool adds a small amount of overhead to the server operation. If performance is a critical issue, NET-Profile should be run to monitor behavior of newly installed NLM applications. When you are sure that all the NLMs are behaving, NET-Profile can be unloaded from the server memory.

PERFORM3 Benchmarking

One of the most difficult aspects of improving the performance of a network is not knowing to what extent a particular network component contributes to the overall network performance. The PERFORM3 utility can help you measure the performance of various configurations. To evaluate the impact of a network component, replace the component and use PERFORM3 to observe how much impact the replacement has on network performance.

PERFORM3 is a performance-measurement utility that measures data-transfer throughput, which is dependent on several factors, such as the following:

- Server speed (type of server, bus type, and so on)
- Network hardware/topology
- LAN driver
- Server disk subsystem
- Network operating system

PERFORM3, an improved successor to the earlier PERFORM and PERFORM2 utilities, is available through NetWire on CompuServe. The operation of PERFORM3 is independent of the type of Network Operating System used, as long as DOS workstations running on Intel microprocessors are supported. PERFORM3 can be used, for example, to measure performance of networks based on NFS, LANMAN, VINES, PATHWORKS, and NetWare.

PERFORM3 measures average and peak data throughput for single or multiple stations performing a benchmark test. The results can be displayed in graph form or printed.

Some of the many applications of PERFORM3 are mentioned here:

- Measuring performance improvements caused by a higher priced or higher throughput network card at the server. You can use this to verify vendor's claims about their network cards.
- Measuring the effect on network throughput of a faster server machine.
- Measuring the effect on system throughput of faster workstations with high-performance network cards.
- Measuring the effect on system throughput of faster server disks.

A study published by Novell in *LAN Evaluation Report 1986* is an example of the usefulness of the performance studies. The study was done using PERFORM to measure throughput of 286A, 286B, PC AT, and PC XT file servers running on different network hardware. The partial report reproduced in table 22.7, for available maximum bandwidth, was performed using six IBM PC AT workstations running at 6 MHz. Performance of the specialized 286A server made by Novell is much higher. Although Novell has discontinued this server, the report points out an important fact—specialized server machines (Compaq SystemPro and so on) result in higher data throughput.

Table 22.7
Available Maximum Bandwidth Using PERFORM (Numbers represent kilobytes/second)

Network Type	286A	PC AT	PC XT
SMC ARCnet	115.31	104.54	76.34
3COM EtherLink	235.15	167.40	81.61
3COM EtherLink+	410.11	278.30	125.65
IBM PC Network	34.83	33.62	26.88
IBM Token Ring/4 Mbps	241.33	226.17	130.30

To find out how to use PERFORM3, simply type **PERFORM3** at the DOS prompt. The following is displayed:

```
PERFORM3 version 1.61
Syntax is:

.PERFORM3 <graph name> <...configurable options...>
where options are:
 <test time seconds to test (12 to 65535)>     default = 12
 <start size  (1 to 65535)>                    default = 1
 <stop size   (start size to 65535)>   default = (stop-start+1)/128
C:\PERFORM>
```

Figure 22.43 shows the results of using PLOTOUT on a test run using the command:

```
PERFORM3 WDPLUS1 12 1 2048 64
```

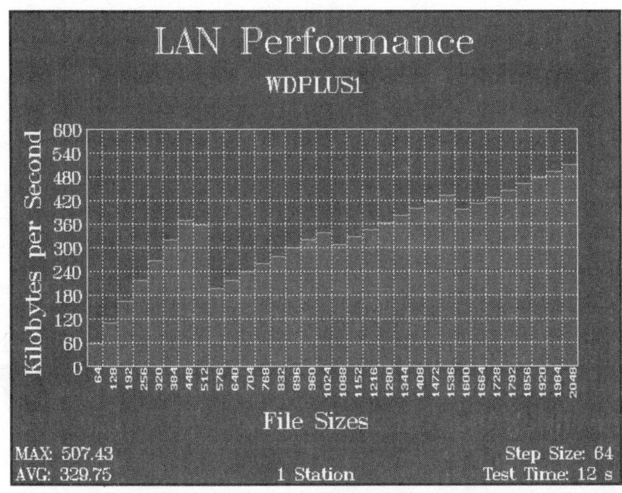

Figure 22.43
PERFORM3 plot results for file sizes up to 2,048 bytes.

The command line tells you that the plot file was WDPLUS1, test time was 12 seconds, and from 1 to 2,048 bytes were transferred at increments of 64 bytes. The peak transfer rate was 507.43 Kbps and the average transfer rate was 329.75 Kbps.

Figure 22.44 shows the results of PERFORM3 done on the same network using the command **PERFORM3 WDPLUS3 12 1 8192 256**. If you compare figure 22.44 to figure 22.43, you can see that the data throughput is higher (Peak: 810.69 Kbps, Average = 613.55 Kbps) for large file transfers.

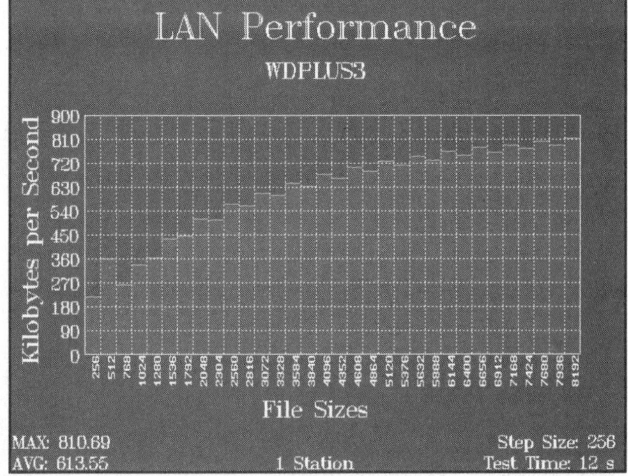

Figure 22.44
PERFORM3 plot results for file sizes up to 8192 bytes.

Protocol Analyzers

Protocol analyzers are another tool that can be used to monitor performance of networks. A protocol analyzer tool called LANalyzer allows the monitoring of a variety of statistics on the network. LANalyzer is a hardware/software package that can be installed in an IBM-compatible PC with a hard drive. The hardware consists of a special Ethernet or Token Ring board that can operate in *promiscuous mode*—it can capture and store all packets, even those not directly addressed to the LANalyzer. Special digital processing techniques are used on the network boards to obtain timing and collision information that would not be possible with ordinary network boards.

Figure 22.45 shows LANalyzer in the process of collecting traffic on a NetWare Ethernet LAN. As it captures packets and stores them in a trace buffer, LANalyzer also reports conditions on the network such as local collisions, remote collisions, CRC/Alignment errors, and illegal packet lengths. LANalyzer uses the concept of traffic channels to classify traffic. A *channel* is a user-definable category of network traffic. If a packet satisfies the user-defined criteria, it is counted by that channel and saved into the trace buffer. A packet may satisfy more than one channel and therefore be counted more than once. Only one copy of the packet will be saved, however. The bar graph window in figure 22.45 corresponds to the *Rate* column. The musical symbol represents an alarm that sounds if the rate exceeds a certain threshold indicated by the position of the musical symbol.

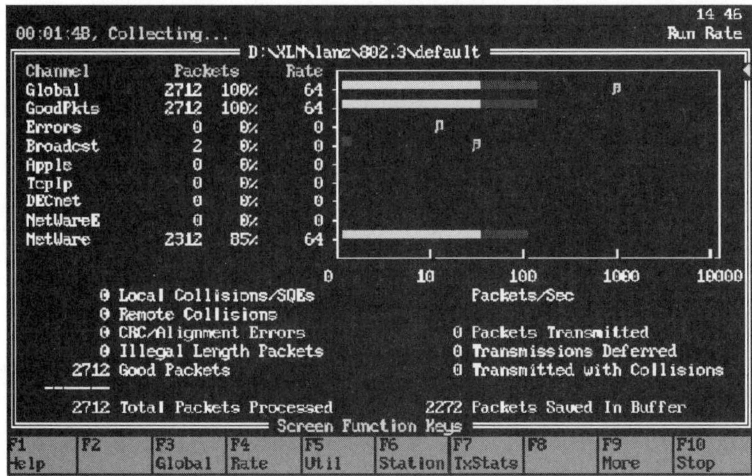

Figure 22.45
Novell LANalyzer capturing traffic.

In addition to capturing and decoding packets, LANalyzer comes with several preconfigured applications designed for NetWare LANs. The applications listed in figure 22.46 are for a NetWare Ethernet LAN.

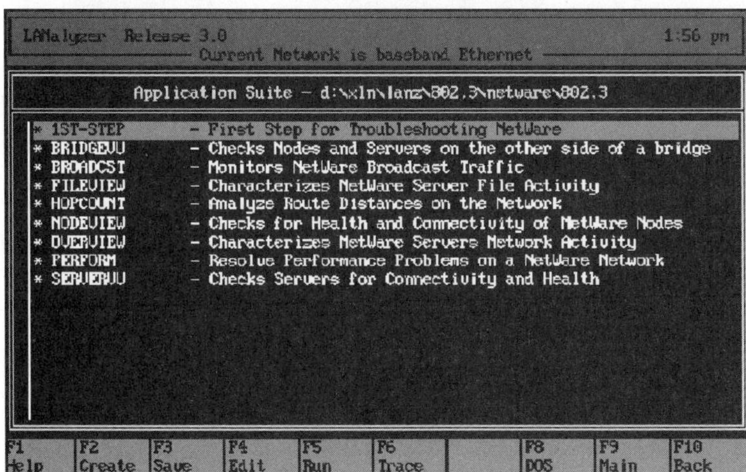

Figure 22.46
Novell LANalyzer NetWare-specific applications.

Besides providing trace decodes of NetWare protocols, LANalyzer also can be used for decoding the following classes of protocols:

AppleTalk I & II	SMB
DECnet	SNA
NetWare	TCP/IP
NetWare Lite	Vines

NFS XNS

OSI

Protocol analysis tools such as LANalyzer from Novell or The Sniffer from Network General can be quite expensive. Fortunately, relatively inexpensive software-based protocol analysis tools also are available. These tools, which use the network board inside a workstation, consist of software that can capture and decode network traffic. One such tool is LANWATCH, from FTP Software (508-685-4000); another is LANdecoder, from Triticom (612-937-0772).

Figures 22.47 and 22.48 show NetWare traffic captured using LANWATCH and LANdecoder.

Figure 22.47 *FTP Software's LANWATCH decode.*

```
Time   Length: Type:                                        FTP Software LANWatch 2.0
003.37 (0110): 802: Novell WDgtl dc3f19 ->           *       SAP: general response
003.37 (0060): 802: Novell WDgtl dc3f19 -> WDgtl 664e19      11:
011.23 (0060): 802: Novell WDgtl 664e19 ->           *       SAP:
011.24 (0110): 802: Novell WDgtl dc3f19 -> WDgtl 664e19      SAP: nearest response
011.24 (0060): 802: Novell WDgtl 664e19 ->           *       RIP: request
011.24 (0060): 802: Novell WDgtl dc3f19 -> WDgtl 664e19      RIP: response
011.24 (0060): 802: Novell WDgtl 664e19 -> WDgtl dc3f19      FILE:
011.25 (0060): 802: Novell WDgtl dc3f19 -> WDgtl 664e19      FILE:
011.25 (0060): 802: Novell WDgtl 664e19 -> WDgtl dc3f19      FILE:
011.25 (0060): 802: Novell WDgtl dc3f19 -> WDgtl 664e19      FILE:
011.25 (0060): 802: Novell WDgtl 664e19 -> WDgtl dc3f19      FILE:
011.29 (0060): 802: Novell WDgtl dc3f19 -> WDgtl 664e19      FILE:
011.29 (0060): 802: Novell WDgtl 664e19 -> WDgtl dc3f19      FILE:
011.29 (0060): 802: Novell WDgtl dc3f19 -> WDgtl 664e19      FILE:
011.56 (0060): 802: Novell WDgtl 664e19 -> WDgtl dc3f19      FILE:
011.57 (0062): 802: Novell WDgtl dc3f19 -> WDgtl 664e19      FILE:
011.58 (0110): 802: Novell WDgtl dc3f19 ->           *       SAP: general response
011.58 (0060): 802: Novell WDgtl 664e19 -> WDgtl dc3f19      FILE:
011.59 (0062): 802: Novell WDgtl dc3f19 -> WDgtl 664e19      FILE:
011.59 (0060): 802: Novell WDgtl 664e19 -> WDgtl dc3f19      FILE:
011.62 (0060): 802: Novell WDgtl dc3f19 -> WDgtl 664e19      FILE:
011.62 (0070): 802: Novell WDgtl 664e19 -> WDgtl dc3f19      FILE:
011.62 (0084): 802: Novell WDgtl dc3f19 -> WDgtl 664e19      FILE:
'?' for help                                                 Mode: EXAMINE 15:09:14
```

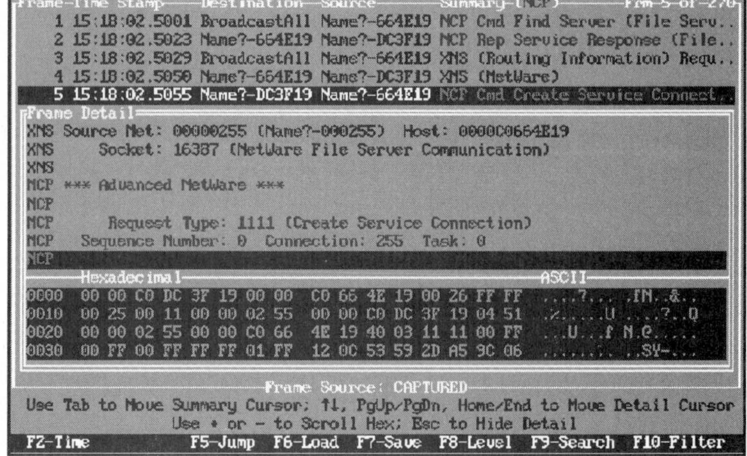

Figure 22.48 *Triticom's LANdecoder.*

Understanding How FSPs Affect Server Performance

The number of *File Service Processes* (FSPs) is vital for good server performance. An FSP is a process that handles file service requests (NCP requests) from workstations. For optimum performance, there need to be as many FSPs as there are simultaneous file service requests.

In NetWare 3.*x* and 4.*x*, the number of FSPs is increased on demand, in keeping with the flexible nature of NetWare 3.*x* and 4.*x*'s memory and resource-allocation architecture. In NetWare 2.2, resource allocation is not so flexible. The number of FSPs in NetWare 2.2 is fixed. This number, which is determined by the installation parameters, cannot be changed easily without reconfiguring NetWare 2.2. NetWare versions earlier than 2.2 suffer from the same problem and have fewer FSPs than NetWare 2.2. A symptom of this problem is that the server seems to slow down under heavy loads.

This section examines the NetWare 2.2 File Service Limitation problem. The information is based on application notes (*NetWare Application Notes, June, 1990*) describing the FSP problem, published by Novell.

Role of FSP in NetWare 2.*x* Server Performance

To understand exactly why a lower number of FSPs can cause problems, one needs to understand the role the FSP plays on the server.

When a workstation sends an NCP request to read a block of data, the FSP servicing the NCP request schedules the appropriate process to retrieve the information from the disk. The FSP then instructs this disk process to wake it up after it has completed the read operation; then it goes to sleep. If all FSPs are sleeping or otherwise occupied, no other NCP requests can be processed until an FSP becomes available. The server delays or ignores any new NCP requests that come in during this time, and as the packet receive buffers get full, additional packets that are received are dropped. When the workstations do not receive a reply from the server, they timeout and retransmit the request, further aggravating the situation and causing excessive network traffic.

Using FCONSOLE To Monitor FSP Shortage in NetWare 2.*x*

You can use FCONSOLE statistics to determine whether your server has FSP problems. This statistic can be seen from the LAN I/O Statistics screen that can be reached through:

FCONSOLE -> Statistics -> LAN I/O Statistics

The field File Service Used Route number indicates how many File Service Packets had to wait for an FSP. You should monitor the value of this field periodically. The difference between two readings gives you the number of NCP requests delayed because of lack of FSPs.

You can use the total File Service Packets to determine the total number of packets processed and compute the percentage of packets that experienced FSP shortage (this percentage should not exceed 10 percent). One word of caution: the field values roll over at 65,536. You may have to take this into account if a latter reading is less than the first.

Also, because of the way some drivers (such as the Racal-Interlan NP600 NIC) are written to prefetch receive buffers, the File Service Used Route counter increments for every File Service Packet delivered

to the server, and this field will be incorrect. You cannot rely on the FCONSOLE technique to make a determination on FSP shortage.

Reason for FSP Limitation in NetWare 2.*x*

The real reason for FSP limitation is that buffers used by FSPs for incoming File Service Packets are allocated out of a 64 KB data segment called the *DGroup segment.* The 64 KB segment is a limit on the data-segment size for pre-Intel 80386 processors. Because the DGroup segment is used also for many other purposes, it limits the number of File Service Packet buffers that can be allocated. The number of buffers available for File Service Packet requests also determines the number of FSPs that can be running on the server. By improving on the scheme for allocating this space, used in NetWare 2.1*x* servers, NetWare 2.2 can have more FSPs.

For comparison purposes, figure 22.49 shows the memory allocation used for NetWare 2.15 and NetWare 2.2. This figure also explains how data in the DGroup segment is allocated. The *Global Static Data* (GSD) area is used for global variables defined in NetWare 2.2, as well as for variables defined by NIC drivers and disk controller drivers. The Process Stacks area provides stack space for all the different NetWare processes. The Volume and Monitor Tables contain information about all disk volumes mounted on the server, as well as information for the server's MONITOR screen. Dynamic Memory Pool 1 is used by virtually all NetWare processes and routines as either a temporary or semipermanent workspace.

Figure 22.49
DGroup data-segment map for NetWare 2.15 versus NetWare 2.2.

Netware V2.15	Netware V2.2
Global Static Data (28kb Minimum)	Global Static Data (23kb Minimum)
Process Stacks (7kb Minimum)	Process Stacks (12kb Minimum)
Volume and Monitor Tables (0-2kb Minimum)	Volume and Monitor Tables (0-2kb Minimum)
Dynamic Memory Pool 1 (16kb + FSP buffer division)	Dynamic Memory Pool 1 (10kb + FSP buffer division)
File Service Process Buffers (Up to 10 FSP buffers)	File Service Process Buffers (Up to 10 FSP buffers)

The major improvements in memory allocation in NetWare 2.2 are that the Global Static Data area and Dynamic Memory Pool 1 have decreased. The Global Static Data area has decreased by 5 KB, which is offset by a 5 KB increase in the Process Stacks area.

The Global Static Data area was decreased by moving some information out of the DGroup data segment and into other memory areas. Also, installers can now choose to configure the server with or without core printing services. When core printing services are not linked, an additional reduction occurs in the Global Static Data area.

Reductions in Dynamic Memory Pool 1 are achieved by removing drive mappings for workstations to a new Dynamic Memory Pool 4 area.

One of the design goals for NetWare 2.2 was to correct the problem of FSP shortages. The removal of drive mappings to a separate dynamic memory pool, and a decrease in the GSD area, provide additional RAM for FSP Buffers. After upgrading to 2.2, users can expect to have two to four additional FSPs.

FSP Buffer Size in NetWare 2.*x*

Table 22.8 shows the memory requirements for each FSP buffer.

Table 22.8
FSP Buffer Components

Buffer Component	Size (bytes)
Reply buffer	94
Workspace	106
Stack space	768
Receive buffer	512–4,096

As you can see from this table, the total size of the FSP buffer depends on the receive buffer size. The receive buffer size is the largest packet size of any NIC driver configured into the operating system. If you have configured an Ethernet driver with a packet size of 1,024 bytes and an ARCnet driver using 4,096 byte packets, for example, the size of the FSP buffers for this server is as follows:

94 + 106 + 768 + 4,096 = 5,064 bytes

Also, the Ethernet packets use only 1,992 bytes (94 + 106 + 768 + 1,024 = 1,992); the remaining 3,072 bytes in the Ethernet packet are wasted.

This shows that configuring a server with NIC drivers that use different packet sizes can be very inefficient. Try to keep all of the NIC driver packet sizes the same to avoid wasted space. Table 22.9 shows three types of NIC drivers, their respective possible packet sizes under NetWare, and their DGroup buffer sizes.

Table 22.9
FSP Buffer Sizes

NIC Driver	Packet Size (bytes)	FSP Buffer Size (bytes)
Ethernet	1,024	1,192
Token Ring	1,024–4,096	1,192–5,064
ARCnet	512–4,096	1,480–5,064

Increasing FSPs in NetWare 2.*x*

To increase FSPs, you must increase FSP buffers. Before you do this, you should estimate how close you are to gaining another FSP for your NetWare 2.2 configuration. To do so, follow these steps:

1. Figure out the FSP buffer size, using the tables described earlier in this chapter.

2. Take the maximum RAM in Dynamic Memory Pool 1 and subtract it from the fixed size of Dynamic Memory Pool 1 (16 KB for 2.1*x*, or 10 KB for 2.2).

3. Subtract the number in Step 2 from the FSP buffer size. The result is the number of bytes that must be made available before you gain an additional FSP.

For example, if a NetWare 2.2 server has a 1,992-byte FSP buffer size and the maximum Dynamic Pool Memory 1 of 10,660 bytes, to get an additional FSP you would have to free an additional 1,572 bytes of DGroup. Here is the computation:

1,992 – (10,660 – 10,240) = 1,572

To free this much space, you must know which items have the biggest impact on DGroup RAM allocation. In order of importance they are as follows:

1. NIC driver packet size. The NIC driver packet size has the biggest impact on FSP allocation because it determines the divisor used to allocate FSP buffers. The larger the packet size, the larger the FSP buffer size (and hence the smaller the number of FSPs).

2. Amount of disk space mounted and directory entries allocated. Disk configurations have the second largest impact on DGroup RAM allocation. Mounting a single volume of 2G with 10,000 directory entries would require 13,584 bytes of DGroup RAM.

3. NIC and disk-driver global variables. The size of NIC and disk variables can be significant. The Async WNIM driver alone requires 9,942 bytes of DGroup RAM.

4. Possible RAM lost to DMA workaround. In some PCs, the DMA hardware cannot handle receive buffers that straddle a 64 KB boundary; NetWare will skip memory which, depending on the size of the receive buffer, could be from 0 to 4,095 bytes. By changing to a non-DMA NIC driver, this problem can be avoided.

Here is the reasoning used to define this list:

1. The NIC driver packet size has the biggest impact on FSP allocation because it determines the divisor used to allocate FSP buffers. The larger the packet size, the larger the FSP buffer size (and hence the smaller the number of FSPs).

2. Disk configurations have the second largest impact on DGroup RAM allocation. Mounting a single volume of 2 GB with 10,000 directory entries would require 13,584 bytes of DGroup RAM.

3. NIC and disk variables can be significant in size. The Async WNIM driver alone requires 9,942 bytes of DGroup RAM.

4. The maximum DGroup RAM that can be lost to this DMA workaround is 4,095 bytes.

5. The maximum DGroup RAM that can be allocated to print spooler stacks is 3,340 bytes. (Because NetWare 2.2 allocates these stacks from Dynamic Memory Pool 1, this applies only to 2.1*x*.)

6. For NetWare 2.1*x*, the TTS process stack uses 250 bytes of DGroup RAM. Also, GSD variables for TTS in 2.1*x* can run from 142 to 152 additional bytes.

Based on the preceding list, you can devise an action plan for gaining additional FSP buffer space. These steps are listed in order of increasing impact on the server.

1. For NetWare 2.1*x*, remove spooled printers.

2. Decrease the number of directory entries, if you have directory entries to spare. The current directory entry usage can be monitored using VOLINFO.

3. Exchange DMA NIC drivers with non-DMA ones.

4. Decrease the NIC driver packet size.

5. Remove TTS (2.1*x* only).

6. Decrease disk space.

7. Use Dynamic Memory Pool 1 patch for qualified servers (2.1*x* only). This can be obtained from NetWire Forum on CompuServe.

Limiting FSP Buffers in NetWare 2.*x*

The title of this section may seem to run counter to the previous discussions because the goal all along has been to increase the number of FSP buffers, and hence the number of FSPs.

Limiting FSP buffers is useful when additional Dynamic Memory Pool 1 memory is needed. Whatever memory is not made into an FSP buffer is used for Dynamic Memory Pool 1.

To limit the FSP buffers, place the following statement in the SERVER.CFG file and restart the server. The value of *n* can range from 3 to 10.

```
FILE SERVICE PROCESSES=n
```

Managing Complex NetWare Networks

One of the main problems of managing complex NetWare-based networks is server management. NetWare servers are available in licenses of 20, 50, 100, or 1,000 users. Long before a server reaches the license limit, it may become necessary to add additional servers.

You may want to add additional servers for the following reasons:

- To increase server processing power available to users
- To prevent network traffic from becoming a bottleneck at a single server
- To increase remote file system storage capacity on the network
- To split application usage across servers for better performance

The server must process file requests from workstations. In NetWare 2.*x*, a fixed number of task engines called *File Server Processes* (FSPs) are available (see fig. 22.50). Because each FSP processes only one request at a time, the number of simultaneous requests that can be processed are limited. NetWare 3.*x* has a more flexible technique for managing the number of FSPs, and uses dynamic memory management to create more FSPs if needed. As the number of users increases, the probability of file service requests waiting in a queue to be processed increases. You can increase the number of FSPs and CPU power by adding servers.

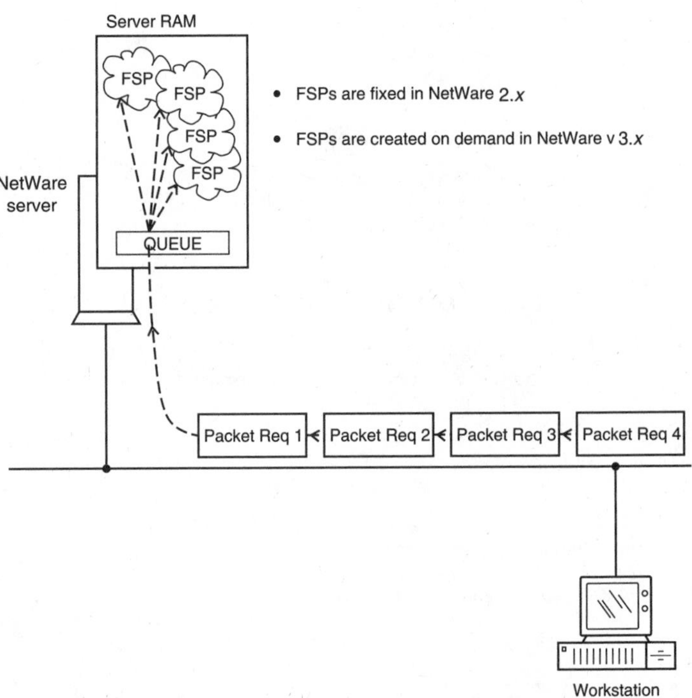

Figure 22.50
File server processes in NetWare.

The nature of server-based computing is such that the majority of file service requests are directed to the server. If you have a single server, this server and the NIC in the server can become overloaded. Introducing a second server can reduce the amount of network traffic directed to a single server (see fig. 22.51). Cost-conscious organizations often add a second NIC card on a single server and divide the LAN into two LANs interconnected by a server (see fig. 22.52). This scheme also increases effective NIC bandwidth at the server. The second approach does not, however, add more processing power for the server.

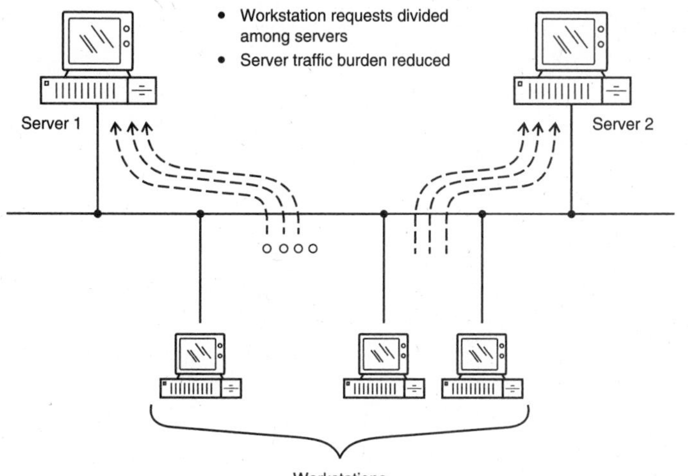

Figure 22.51
Reducing network traffic with multiple servers.

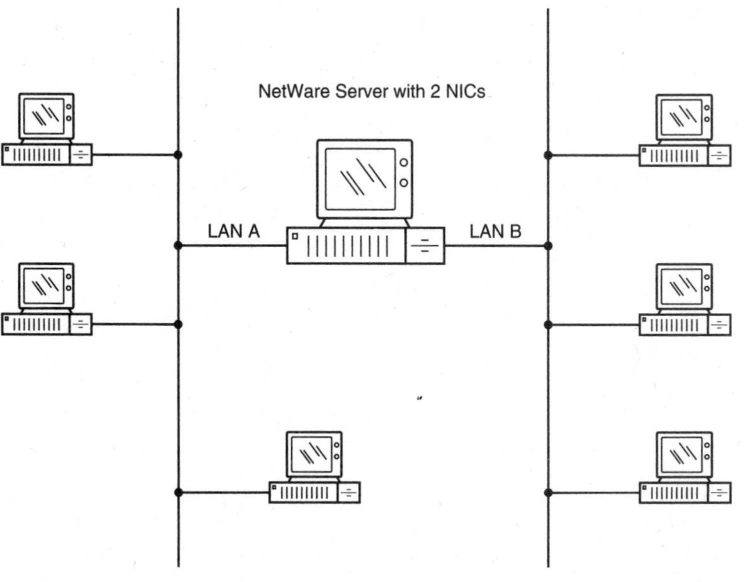

Figure 22.52
Reducing network traffic with multiple NICs.

If the disk storage on the server is not sufficient to support the users, you can add a second disk or a second server with additional storage capacity.

You can use a server to run a variety of network applications. Some applications, primarily those that are database-intensive, place great demands on processing power and server disk storage. These applications are best placed on their own server platform so that they have the dedicated resources of their own server without impacting other applications.

Figure 22.53 shows a LAN with a number of servers. This LAN contains five file servers, six database servers, and a communications server. A user can log in to a number of these file servers to access the resources. NetWare limits the number of servers to which a user can attach to no more than eight.

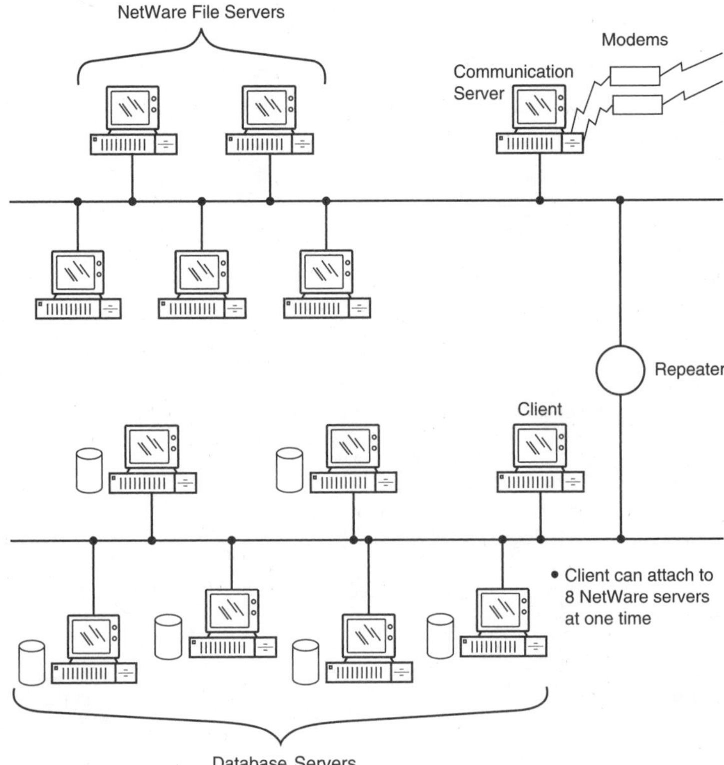

Figure 22.53
Multiserver configuration.

Managing a Multiserver Configuration

Figure 22.53 depicts a setup in which the user must have an account on each of the servers. To log in to the first server, the user must execute the LOGIN command. To log in to additional servers, you must use the NetWare ATTACH command, and you must make a drive mapping to a directory on the server.

Figure 22.53 demonstrates that when you add an account for a new user, you must create the account on each server. If each server does not contain the accounts, the user cannot access resources on the server.

If the user profile, or login script, must be changed for a user, the login script may need to be changed on all servers. You cannot have one account for all the servers. As the internetwork grows in size, more users need access to resources on several sources. Keeping track of these resources can become difficult.

The Domain Concept

The *domain concept* solves some of the problems of managing a multiserver configuration. The domain consists of a number of servers. To workstations on the network, however, the domain appears as a single logical server. The users are presented with a logical view of the server resources on the network. Note that the domain concept and NetWare name service work only on NetWare 3.*x* and that this package must be purchased separately.

Rather than logging in to multiple servers one by one, users can log in to the domain and access the resources on the network. One server is designated as the *domain controller*, which manages access to the domain. The domain and domain controller concepts are illustrated in figure 22.54. You need to add a user account just once to the domain, rather than adding the account to each individual server. The user accounts are distributed to the servers on the domain.

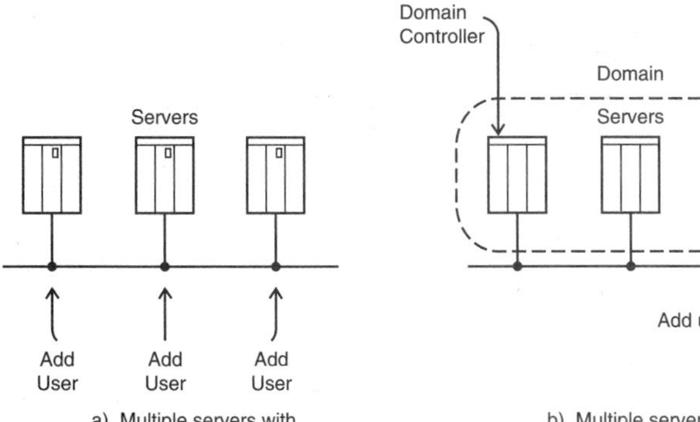

Figure 22.54
Domain concept.

Each server has the same users, groups, and print queues as all the other servers in the domain. Each user has the same password on each server in the domain. A user can access multiple servers in the domain with a single login command and can print to any print queue in the domain. The domain is set up and maintained by the *domain administrator*.

NetWare Name Service (NNS)

To support the domain concept, Novell designed a distributed name service called the *NetWare Name Service*. NNS is an optional product, which is supported by NetWare 3.11 only. The following rules apply to NNS domains:

- Domains cannot overlap. A server can be in one, and only one, domain. Not all servers on the internetwork must be in a domain.

- A domain can contain a maximum of 400 servers. A more practical limit is 10 to 30 servers per domain.
- No limit applies to the total number of domains in the internetwork.
- Membership of a server in a domain is independent of geographical location, networking topology, or cabling. All servers must, however, be reachable through the internetwork.

Figure 22.55 shows servers for the engineering, corporate, and manufacturing departments of an organization. Using NetWare Name Service, these servers are divided into three domains. The engineers do not log in to each server separately; they log in to the engineering domain and access all three servers. The manufacturing and corporate personnel also log in once to their respective domains.

Figure 22.55
Departmental LAN with domains.

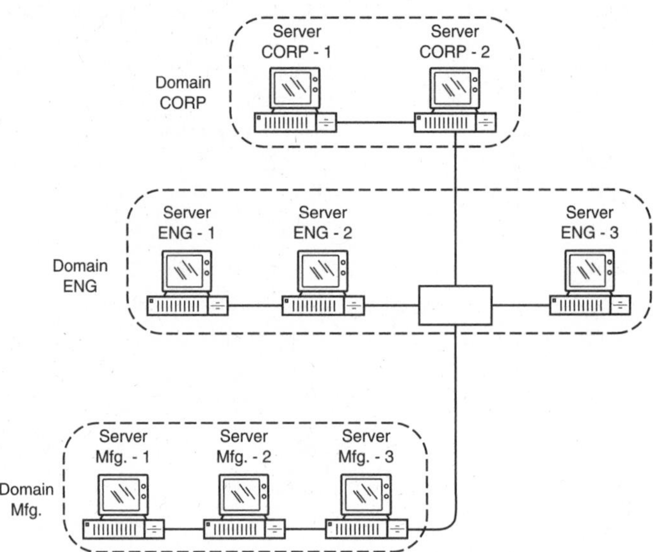

Server access is determined by a user profile. The user profile is a group-level login script that sets up the user's network environment.

The profile has a name that distinguishes it from other profiles and a list of users or groups who are members of this profile. Users have a default profile. Unless otherwise specified, a user logs in by using the default profile. The profile can contain up to eight servers, to which the user automatically attaches after log-in. The profile also contains a profile login script that is executed after the domain login script. Then the user's login script is executed. (Login scripts are covered later in the book.) Under the NetWare work group manager feature, managers can be assigned to profiles. Profile managers can modify the profile they manage.

In the example in figure 22.56, PROFILE_A and PROFILE_B can be defined for the engineering domain. Half of the engineers are assigned to PROFILE_A and can access servers ENG_1 and ENG_2. The remaining engineers are assigned to PROFILE_B and can access all the engineering servers.

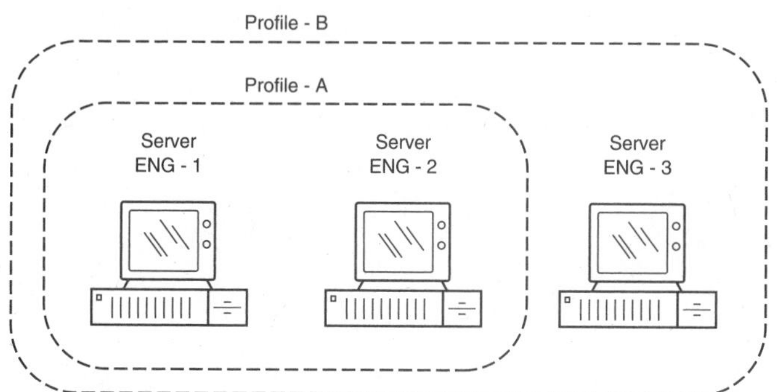

Figure 22.56
Profiles in a single domain.

If a user or group is added, deleted, or modified on one server in the domain, the change is replicated to every server in the domain. The servers in the domain are synchronized; they have the same copy of the Name Service Database.

You use the NSINSTAL program to install NNS. You must install NNS on every server in the domain. Most NetWare utilities behave the same under NNS. Some utilities may have enhanced options to support the domain concept.

System Configuration (SYSCON), which is examined later in this book, is replaced by NETCON on the NNS database. You must use NETCON instead of SYSCON on servers that are part of a domain. An NNS-aware SYSCON ships with the NNS disks. You must install this version on servers that are not part of a domain. It is designed to protect the NNS database from accidental corruption by nondomain users.

NNS is not exactly transparent to the user. Trustee rights, users object ID, disk space restrictions, intruder lockout, grace logins, and accounting are specific to each server. More importantly, if a server in the domain is down when the Name Service database is changed, synchronization is not automatic when the server is brought up again. You must use the NETCON utility to resynchronize the domain.

NetWare 4.*x* corrects many of these shortcomings by providing a true distributed database (based on X.500) for name services called NetWare Directory Services. Instead of keeping several server binderies synchronized, NDS provides a distributed database for keeping track of all network resources. Also, NDS is hierarchical whereas the bindery is flat and cannot be used to represent hierarchical relationship between network resources. Many of the former bindery objects are converted to NDS objects when upgrading to NetWare 4.*x*.

Starting with NetWare 4.1, a utility called NETSYNCH is provided that allows bindery based servers to synchronize their binderies to NDS. Also, in this version of NetWare 4, the bindery objects in the NDS tree can be managed by NetWare 4.*x* tools.

Summary

In this chapter, you learned about the factors that affect network performance. These factors can be hardware-based and software-based. The most important factors in each category were discussed.

Some of the monitoring and performance tools discussed in this chapter are the MONITOR NLM, SERVMAN NLM (for NetWare 4.*x*) Frye Utilities, Nu-Mega Utilities, PERFORM3, LANalyzers, LANWATCH, and LANDecoder. These tools can be used to fine-tune the network after installation, and to monitor how well the network is performing.

You also learned about the importance of the File Service Process and learned about key aspects of managing complex networks.

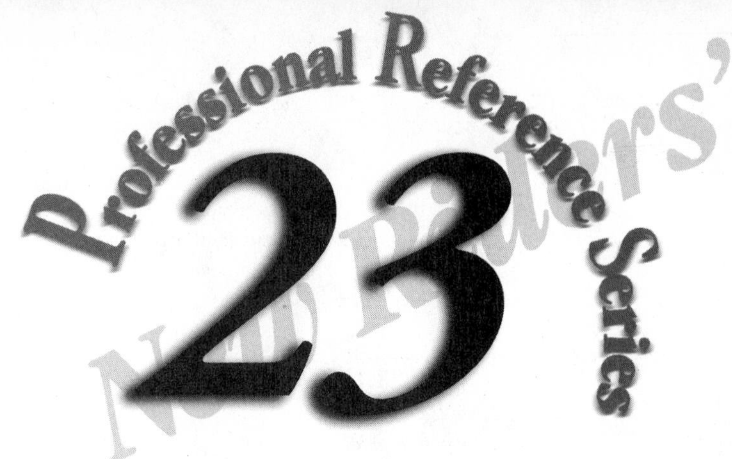

Managing User Sessions

The network environment is where the user lives and breathes on the network, and therefore must be configured with a great amount of planning and attention to detail. This chapter discusses the different types of start-up files for the individual DOS workstation and the network environment. Network start-up files are called *login scripts.*

The following sections discuss the login script commands and script variables that make up the network start-up files. Recommendations are presented on how to organize the login scripts to keep them simple and understandable. You also learn about the NetWare MENU system.

Understanding Login Scripts

After the user logs in successfully, a network login script is processed, which sets up the network environment. The login script file is kept on the server and plays a role similar to that of the AUTOEXEC.BAT file for a single-user PC.

When a user logs in to a server, login scripts associated for that user are executed. First, the system login script is executed. The system login script sets up a global environment for the user. Besides system login scripts, there are other login scripts. The order of execution of the remaining scripts depends on the NetWare version.

Login Scripts in NetWare 2.*x*, 3.11, and 3.12

After the LOGIN utility authenticates a user's login request, it looks for a file called NET$LOG.DAT in the SYS:PUBLIC directory (see fig. 23.1). This file contains the location of the system login script. A *system login script* is used for commands that affect all the users. Examples of the commands that can be placed within the system login script are commands for displaying messages, mapping network drives, searching drives, and setting environment variables. Because the system login script file can be viewed by other users, do not keep sensitive information in this file. The system login script can be created or edited by using SYSCON. The system login SCRIPT is stored as a text file in NET$LOG.DAT for the current releases of NetWare.

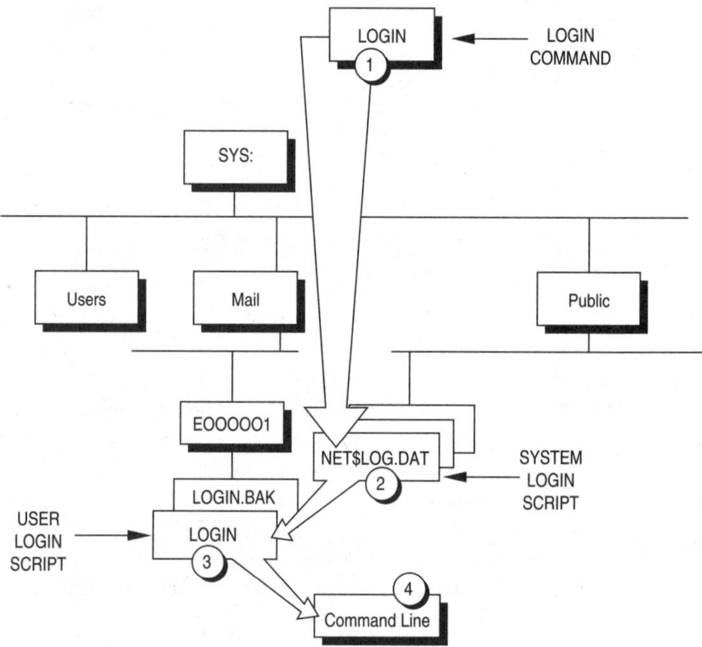

Figure 23.1
The order of login script processing. (Graphic courtesy of Learning Group International.)

After the system login script is executed, the user login script is processed. The *user login script* is kept in a text file called LOGIN in the MAIL directory for that user. Earlier in this book, you learned that the MAIL directory was originally created for a Novell e-mail program that has been discontinued. The MAIL directory is a subdirectory in the SYS:MAIL directory and has the user's internal hexadecimal ID.

The individual login script serves to customize the user environment even further. The same type of commands that can be executed in the system login script file also can be placed in the individual login script file. The LOGIN.BAK file holds a backup version of the LOGIN script file, which is created when the LOGIN script file is changed by using the SYSCON utility.

After the user's individual login script utility is executed, control is returned to the DOS prompt, and the user's environment is considered to be set.

If a user's login script is not set, the default login script executes.

Default Login Script for NetWare 2.*x* and 3.*x*

The first time the Supervisor logs in to the server, no login script files are set. The server uses a default login script file so that the Supervisor can perform basic functions. If a user is created, and the Supervisor forgets to set up a login script file for the user, the default login script file is executed. The default login script is executed only if no individual login script exists and is ignored if the system finds an individual login script.

The default login script for NetWare 2.*x* and 3.*x* looks similar to the following one. Comments have been added to illustrate certain points.

```
REM This sets up a greeting for the user.
WRITE "Good %GREETING_TIME, %LOGIN_NAME."

REM This is similar to the DOS ECHO OFF command.
REM It stops the display of commands as they are executed.
MAP DISPLAY OFF

REM Error processing is not shown
MAP ERRORS OFF

REM Map the first network drive (*1:) to the
REM user's home directory, which by default is the
REM user's name under the root directory on volume SYS:
MAP *1:=SYS:%LOGIN_NAME

REM Map the first search drive to the SYS:PUBLIC directory
REM which contains some basic system utilities that can
REM be executed by the user.
MAP S1:=SYS:PUBLIC

REM Turn on display of commands as they are processed
REM so that when the MAP command is executed, a list
REM of the current drive mappings is displayed.
MAP DISPLAY ON
MAP
```

You can see that the MAP command in the preceding file can be executed from the command line as well as directly in the login script. Some login script commands, such as WRITE, MAP DISPLAY ON, and MAP DISPLAY OFF, cannot be executed from the DOS prompt.

The commands in the login script files are interpreted by the LOGIN utility, including the MAP command. The MAP command is in the SYS:PUBLIC directory. The first time you execute the MAP command in the login script, you do not have a search drive mapping to the SYS:PUBLIC directory. The MAP commands, however, still work, regardless of the absence of a search path to the SYS:PUBLIC directory. The reason for this is that the MAP command is interpreted and not invoked as an external program.

If you want to invoke external utilities, you must precede them with the # character. To invoke the utility CHKVOL, for example, use the following command in the login script file:

```
#CHKVOL
```

Another item to notice in the preceding login script file example is the use of the %GREETING_TIME and %LOGIN_NAME variables. These are called *login script identifier variables* and are examined later in this chapter. These variables evaluate to character strings, which then can be used in commands, such as WRITE Good %GREETING_TIME, %LOGIN_NAME. This statement, for example, may produce the following message:

```
Good Morning, KARANJIT.
```

The %GREETING_TIME evaluates to Morning, and %LOGIN_NAME evaluates to the user's login name, in this case, KARANJIT. When you use these variables in a string, such as Good %GREETING_TIME, %LOGIN_NAME., the script variables must be in uppercase letters to evaluate correctly. Outside string variables, the script variables can be in upper- or lowercase.

Complex Login Script Files

One of the more powerful commands that can be used in a login script is the IF ... THEN conditional statement. This type of statement has the following general form:

```
IF expression THEN BEGIN
    statements
ELSE
    statements
END
```

or

```
IF expression THEN statement
```

The IF statement in the login script file gives you the power to conditionally execute statements; that is, the IF statement executes statements only if a certain condition is true. It can be used to customize a login script. The login script, however, might become too complicated when you use the IF ... THEN statement. The following is an example of a complicated login script:

```
MAP DISPLAY OFF
BREAK OFF
FIRE PHASERS 3 TIMES
WRITE ""
WRITE "Good %GREETING_TIME, %LOGIN_NAME"
WRITE ""
WRITE "You have logged in to file server %FILE_SERVER"
WRITE "from station %NETWORK_ADDRESS:%P_STATION."
WRITE ""
WRITE "Your connection number is %STATION and you are"
WRITE "using shell %SHELL_TYPE on machine %SMACHINE."
WRITE "Your internal userid is %USER_ID"
WRITE ""
WRITE "Today is %DAY_OF_WEEK %MONTH_NAME, %DAY %YEAR"
IF MEMBER OF "NONCIVILIAN" THEN
    WRITE "System time is %HOUR24:%MINUTE:%SECOND"
ELSE
    WRITE "System time is %HOUR:%MINUTE:%SECOND %AM_PM"
END
```

```
IF MONTH = "1" AND DAY = "1" THEN BEGIN
    WRITE "Happy new year %YEAR, %FULL_NAME"
END

IF SHORT_YEAR = "00" THEN WRITE "Have a nice new century!"

IF NDAY_OF_WEEK = "6" THEN
    WRITE "Have a good weekend!"

IF NDAY_OF_WEEK > "1" AND NDAY_OF_WEEK < "7" THEN
    FDISPLAY SYS:MESSAGES/DAILY.MSG

ELSE
    DISPLAY SYS:MESSAGES/WEEKEND.MSG
END

IF MEMBER OF "ENGINEERING" THEN BEGIN
    IF DAY_OF_WEEK="TUESDAY" THEN
        WRITE "STAFF MEETING AT 3:00 PM"
    IF DAY_OF_WEEK="FRIDAY" THEN BEGIN
        WRITE "STATUS MEETING AT 3:30 PM."
        WRITE "BE THERE OR BE SQUARED!"
    END
END

MAP INS S1:=SYS:PUBLIC
MAP INS S2:=SYS:PUBLIC/%MACHINE/%OS/%OS_VERSION

IF MEMBER OF "PAYROLL" THEN BEGIN
    IF DAY_OF_WEEK="MONDAY" THEN
        WRITE "STAFF MEETING AT 1:00 PM IN CONF.RM. 303"
    IF DAY_OF_WEEK="FRIDAY" THEN
        WRITE "REVIEW MEETING AT 11:00 AM."
    END

    ATTACH LAKSHMI/%LOGIN_NAME
    MAP L:=LAKSHMI/SYS:USERS/%LOGIN_NAME
END

COMSPEC=S2:COMMAND.COM

IF MEMBER OF "ACCOUNTING" THEN
    MAP INS S16:=SYS:APPS/AMRIT
END

IF MEMBER OF "WPUSERS" THEN
    MAP INS S16:=SYS:APPS/WP
END

IF MEMBER OF "PAYROLL" OR MEMBER OF "ACCOUNTING" THEN BEGIN
    MAP INS S16:=SYS:APPS/ADP
    MAP *2:=SYS:PAYROLL
END
```

```
IF LOGIN_NAME = "SUPERVISOR" THEN BEGIN
    MAP *1:=SYS:USERS/SUPER
    MAP *2:=SYS:SYSTEM
    MAP INS S2:=*2:
    MAP INS S3:=SYS:SYSTEM/NMUTILS
END

IF MEMBER OF "ACCOUNTING"
    #CAPTURE Q=ACCT_LASERQ NB TI=25

IF MEMBER OF "ENGINEERING" THEN BEGIN
    #CAPTURE Q=ENG_LASERQ NB NT TI=15
    IF ERROR_LEVEL <> "0" THEN BEGIN
        SEND "ERROR IN CAPTURE" TO TOM
        #EMAIL TOM "ERROR IN CAPTURE FOR %LOGIN_NAME"
    END
END

IF <EDITOR>="BRIEF" THEN
    MAP INS S16:=SYS:APPS/BRIEF
END

DOS SET X = "1"
ALOOP:
    SET X = X 1 "1"
    WRITE "VICTORY PARADE!"
IF <X> IS LESS THAN 7 THEN GOTO ALOOP

DRIVE *2:
DOS VERIFY ON
SET PROMPT = "$P$G"
MAP DISPLAY ON
MAP
EXIT "MENU *1:TOPAPPS"
```

The preceding system login script resembles a BASIC program more than a simple login script. Its only redeeming feature, besides the fact that it may work for a specific environment, is that it uses almost every type of script variable and login statement. The system login script's complexity makes it difficult to maintain. When making changes for a specific group, an inadvertent mistake is easy to make, which can affect all the users on the system.

Recommendations for Organizing Script Files in NetWare 2.*x* and 3.*x*

Over a period of time, the system login script file can get complex (such as the one in the preceding section) as you try to adapt a common system login script file to a changing network environment. You can, however, organize script files in a way that avoids most of the preceding complexity and yet provides a flexible mechanism that can be adapted as new needs arise. Figure 23.2 shows a recommended organization.

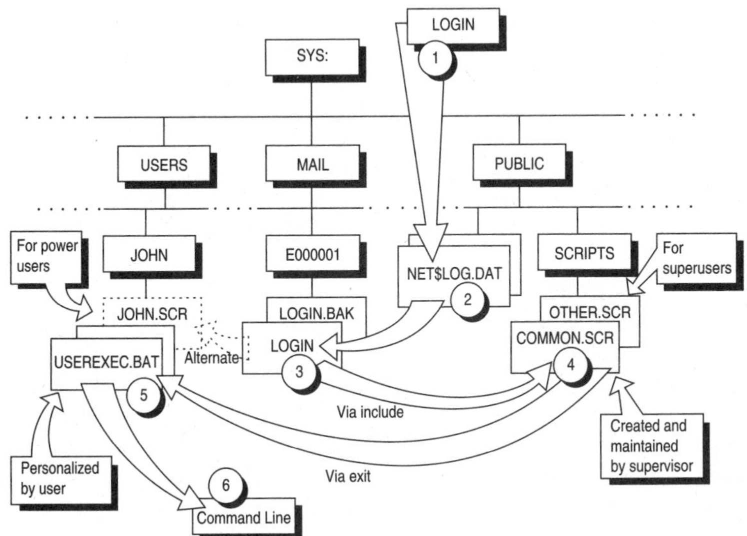

Figure 23.2
Recommended structure for user login scripts for NetWare 2.x and 3.x. (Graphic courtesy of Learning Group International.)

The system login script file is kept as simple as possible. IF ... THEN statements should not be used in the system login script. The system login script file can contain statements to display messages that are system wide, such as the following:

```
REM ****************************************************
REM *                                                  *
REM * The system login script can only have           *
REM * simple statements of the type FDISPLAY           *
REM *                                                  *
REM ****************************************************

REM * Send a global display message
FDISPLAY SYS:MESSAGES/GLOBAL.MSG
```

When the preceding system login script file is processed, it displays any global system messages that the supervisor may have kept in the message file SYS:MESSAGES/GLOBAL.MSG. Control then is transferred to the individual login script file.

The individual login script can contain a statement such as the following:

```
INCLUDE SYS:PUBLIC/SCRIPTS/COMMON.SCR
```

The INCLUDE statement means that the contents of the specified file, in this case SYS:PUBLIC/SCRIPTS/COMMON.SCR, are processed as login script commands. If all the users have a common script file, the COMMON.SCR statement can be used for them. The advantage of using the INCLUDE statement is that if the login script for the users is to be changed, only the COMMON.SCR file needs to be changed once. Suppose, for example, that you are not using the INCLUDE statement. Then, to change the login script for users, you have to use SYSCON to change every login script for all the users. This can become a tedious process and can be avoided entirely by using the INCLUDE statement and a common script file.

The first few statements can be greeting statements. These are followed by drive mappings, including search drives. The COMSPEC variable then must be set to point to the correct copy of COMMAND.COM.

Next, individual messages can be printed. Avoid using too many IF .. THEN statements, otherwise the statements can become too complex. If you want to use conditional statements, such as IF MEMBER OF GROUP THEN ...., you can create a separate *group*.SCR file and specify it in the INCLUDE statement in the login script file for members of the group, as follows:


```
INCLUDE SYS:PUBLIC/SCRIPTS/group.SCR
```

In the preceding example, you can replace *group* with a name of the group for which special processing needs to be done. The users must have Read and File Scan rights ([R F]) in the SYS:PUBLIC/SCRIPTS directory.

Within members of the group, most of the login script commands are the same, but a small amount of customization may need to be done for individual users. This customization can be placed in a batch file called USEREXEC.BAT that is the home directory for every user as in the following example:

```
EXIT "F:USEREXEC.BAT"
```

The EXIT statement terminates processing of the login script. If an argument such as F:USEREXEC.BAT is specified, the argument is treated as a command executed immediately when the login script terminates. The F: drive is usually the first network drive, and it points to the home directory for the user. It is typically created using the following MAP command:

```
MAP *1:=SYS:USERS/%LOGIN_NAME
```

The *1 refers to the first network drive. The home directory for the user contains the USEREXEC.BAT file. This USEREXEC.BAT file can contain any customization commands for the user.

As an Administrator, you may have to deal with users who like to play with and customize their own login script files. These users often are called *power users*, and they probably will balk at being placed in the same category as common users through the COMMON.SCR file. For these users, you can create a login script file containing the following command:

```
INCLUDE SYS:USERS/%LOGIN_NAME/%LOGIN_NAME.SCR
```

The preceding command looks in the user's home directory for processing a file that has the same name as the user's login name with a SCR extension. The SCR extension is the author's convention for SCRipt files. You can use your own, if you prefer.

Because the power users have rights to their home directory, they can freely edit their script files. If they make a mistake that hurts them, they only have themselves to blame and not you.

Login Scripts in NetWare 4.*x*

NetWare 4.*x* supports the following four types of login scripts:

- System

- Profile
- User
- Default

The system login script is a property of the organization and organization unit container objects. The profile login script is a property of the profile leaf object. The user login script is a property of the user object. The default login script does not exist as an object or a property; it is contained in the LOGIN.EXE utility used for logging in to the network. Because login scripts are properties of objects, NDS tools such as the NETADMIN or the NetWare Administrator can be used for creating and modifying login scripts.

Each of these different login script types is discussed in the following sections.

System Login Script

The system login script is a property of the organization and organization unit container objects, and its scope is the user objects defined in that container. This means that system login scripts are a convenient way to specify the commands that should be executed for all users belonging to an organization or department (organization unit) within the organization.

The system login script is executed for only the immediate users in that container. In figure 23.3, the system login script for organization O=SCS applies only to users Admin, KSS, and Dei defined in that container. It does not apply to users Lisa, Janice, and Bill in container OU=ENG.O=SCS. The container OU=ENG has its own system login script, and this applies to users Lisa, Janice, and Bill. The container OU=SALES.O=SCS in figure 23.3, does not have a system login script. This means that for users Nina, John, and Dorsch no system login script exists. If a container does not have a system login script, it *does not inherit* the system login script from a parent container.

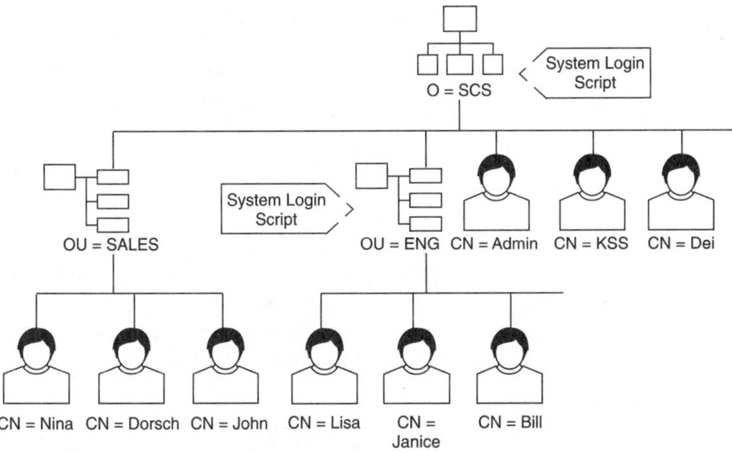

Figure 23.3
The scope of system login script.

The system login script is the first type of login script executed and can be used to set up the general environment for all users in that container.

To create a system login script, you must highlight the container object using NETADMIN or the NetWare Administration tool, and select its login script property for modification.

Profile Login Script

A profile login script is a property of the profile object. The profile object is a leaf object whose sole purpose is to contain the profile login script (see fig. 23.4). If a group of users has common needs, they fit a certain *profile*. In this case, a profile object can be assigned to each of the users.

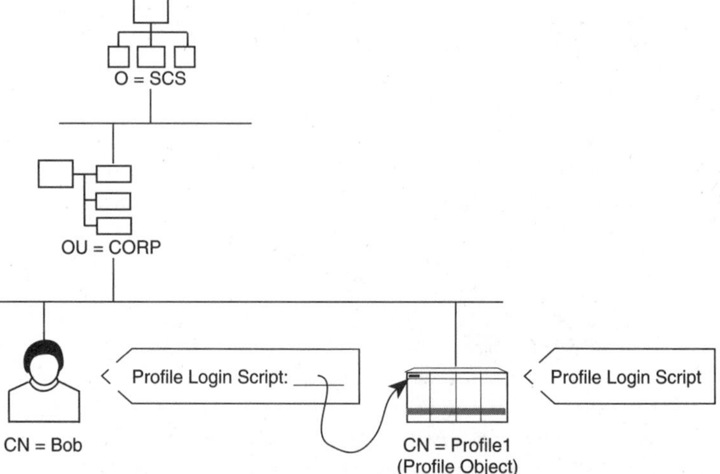

Figure 23.4
Profile login script.

Every user object has a profile login script property (as well as a user login script property). The profile login script property for a user can contain the name of a profile object. If the profile login property for a user object is set to a profile object, the profile login script (property of the profile object) is executed every time that user logs in. If the profile login property for a user object is *not* set, no profile login script is executed when that user object is logged in.

The profile login script is executed after the system login script, and a user object can have only one profile login script.

The profile login script is similar to the system login script, but its purpose is different. The system login script applies only to user objects in the immediate container. In certain situations, users belonging to different containers have a need for setting up a common user environment. The profile login script property for users can be set to the same profile object, even if the user objects are defined in different containers. This makes it possible for users in different containers to have a common login script.

User Login Script

Every user object has a login script property (see fig. 23.5). The value for the login script property can be a sequence of login script commands. The same type of login script commands used for the system and profile login scripts can be used for user login scripts.

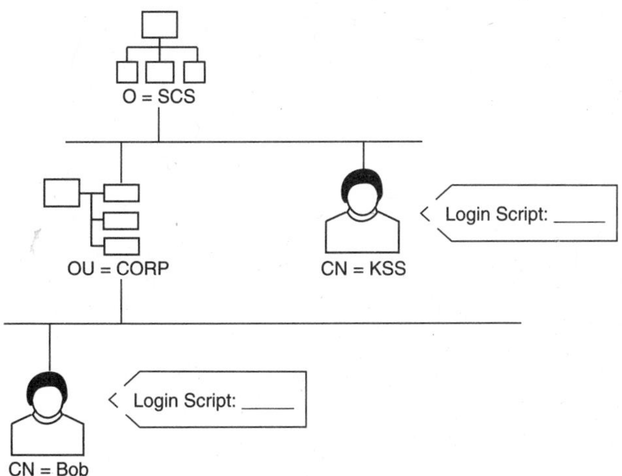

Figure 23.5
User login script.

The user login script is executed after the profile login script (if any).

The user login script can be used to customize a user's login environment. The other login scripts (system and profile) are used to share common login script commands with other users. A user may have special needs not addressed by these "group" login scripts. In that case, the user login script can further customize the user's environment.

Default Login Script for NetWare 4.*x*

The default login script for NetWare 4.*x*, unlike the other login script types, cannot be modified. The default login script is fixed, and can be considered to be "contained" in the login program, LOGIN.EXE. The default login script provides a minimum user environment in case a user logs in and does not have a user login script. This is certainly true the first time the user Admin logs in to a newly installed network. A newly installed network does not have any system, profile, or user login scripts set up. The Admin user can at least perform some basic administration without having to create drive mappings.

After a user login script is created for a user, the default login script does not execute for that user. In some situations, all the login script needs of a user can be met by the system login script or the profile login script. In this case, a user login script is not necessary. Because the user login script has not been set, however, the default login script executes *in addition to* any system and profile login scripts. One of the default actions the default login script performs is to set up a search drive mapping to SYS:PUBLIC. If

the system or profile login script already maps a search drive to SYS:PUBLIC, a second search drive mapping to SYS:PUBLIC is created unless the user login script property is set, or a NO_DEFAULT login directive exists in the system or profile login script.

The default login script for NetWare 4.*x* looks similar to the following. Comments were added to illustrate certain points.

```
REM This sets up a greeting for the user.
WRITE "Good %GREETING_TIME, %LOGIN_NAME."

REM This is similar to the DOS ECHO OFF command.
REM It stops the display of commands as they are executed.
MAP DISPLAY OFF

REM Error processing is not shown.
MAP ERRORS OFF

REM Map the first network drive (*1:) to the
REM root directory on volume SYS:
MAP *1:=SYS:

REM Map the first search drive to the SYS:PUBLIC directory
REM which contains some basic system utilities that can
REM be executed by the user.
MAP S1:=SYS:PUBLIC

REM Turn on display of commands as they are processed
REM so that when the MAP command is executed, a listing
REM of the current drive mappings is displayed.
MAP DISPLAY ON
MAP
```

As you study this default login script, you can see that the MAP command, which can be executed from the command line, also can be executed directly in the login script. Certain login script commands such as WRITE, MAP DISPLAY ON, and MAP DISPLAY OFF cannot be executed from the DOS prompt.

The commands in the login script files are *interpreted* by the LOGIN utility, and this includes the MAP command. The MAP command is in the SYS:PUBLIC directory, and the first time you execute the MAP command in the login script, you do not have a search drive mapping to the SYS:PUBLIC directory. Yet somehow the MAP commands still work, regardless of the absence of a search path to the SYS:PUBLIC directory. This is because the MAP command is interpreted and not invoked as an external program.

The NO_DEFAULT Directive

The NO_DEFAULT directive in the system or profile login script can explicitly disable the execution of the default login script (see fig. 23.6). This is useful if you want to override the default mappings created when the user login script property is not set, but do not want to set the user login property because the login scripts of the system and/or profile login script are sufficient to set up the required user environment.

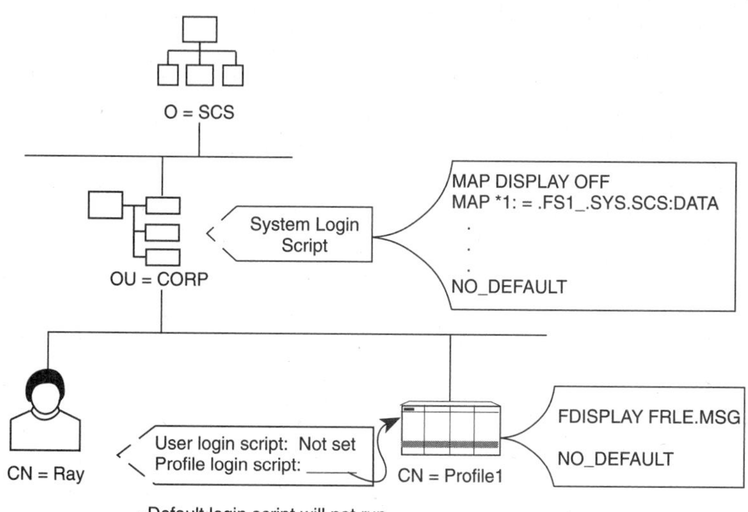

Figure 23.6
The NO_DEFAULT login script command.

Login Script Execution Order for NetWare 4.*x*

The order of execution for the login script types is illustrated in figure 23.7 and in the following list. These steps are executed when the user logs in to a NetWare 4.*x* network.

1. If a user's container has the system login script property set, the system login script is executed for that user.

2. If a user's profile login script property is set to a profile object, the profile login script for that profile object is executed for that user.

3. If a user's user login script property is set, the user login script for that user object is executed.

4. If a user's user login script property is *not* set, the default is executed *unless* the NO_DEFAULT login script command is included in the system or profile login script.

Some examples may help illustrate the preceding rules. Figure 23.8 shows an example of the NDS tree for organization O=TEC that has a system login script. Under O=TEC are two organization unit objects. One of the organization unit objects OU=ENG has a system login script, whereas the other OU=EXP does not have a system login script. The users Admin, KSS, and Bill have user login scripts, but user Charles does not have a login script. The user KSS also has a profile login script property set to the profile object CN=Profile1.OU=ENG.O=TEC. The order of execution of login scripts for the different users are as follows:

- **User KSS.** User KSS's container has a system login script, so the system login script for OU=ENG is executed first. User KSS also has a profile login script. This is executed next. Finally a check is made to see if user KSS has a user login script. Because user KSS has a user login script, this is executed next. The order of login script executions for user KSS is as follows:

- System login script for OU=ENG
- Profile login script for profile object PROFILE1.ENG.TEC
- User login script for KSS

Figure 23.7
Login script order.

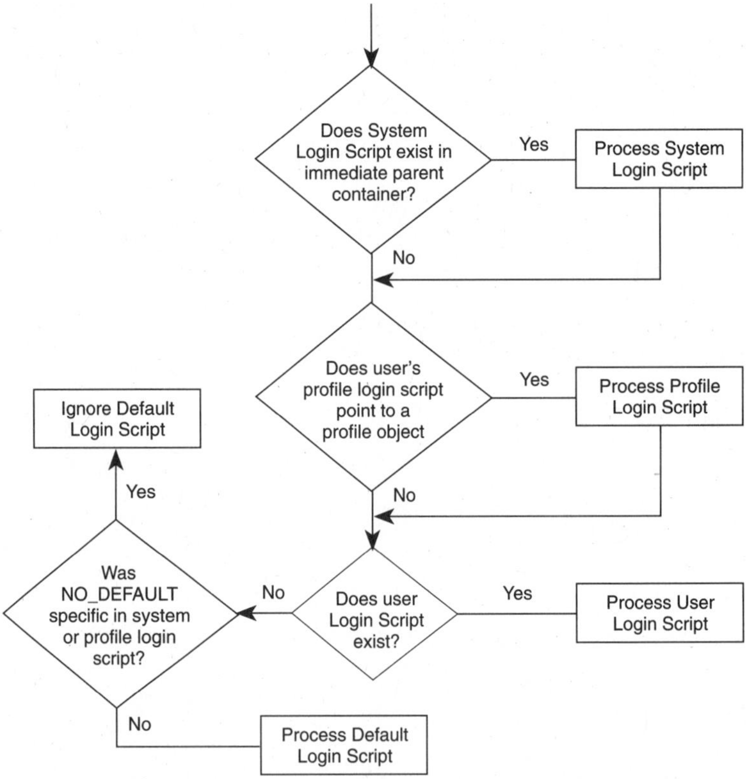

- **User Bill.** User Bill's container has a system login script, so the system login script for OU=ENG is executed first. User Bill does not have a profile login script. A check is made to see if user Bill has a user login script. Because user Bill has a user login script, this is executed next. The order of login script executions for user KSS is as follows:
  - System login script for OU=ENG
  - User login script for Bill
- **User Admin.** User Admin's container has a system login script, so the system login script for O=TEC is executed first. User Admin does not have a profile login script. A check is made to see if user Admin has a user login script. Because user Admin has a user login script, this is executed next. The order of login script executions for user Admin is as follows:

- System login script for O=TEC
- User login script for Admin

- **User Charles.** User Charles's container OU=EXP does not have a system login script, so no system login script is executed. User Charles does not have a profile login script. A check is made to see if user Charles has a user login script. Because user Charles does not have a user login script, the default login script is executed next.

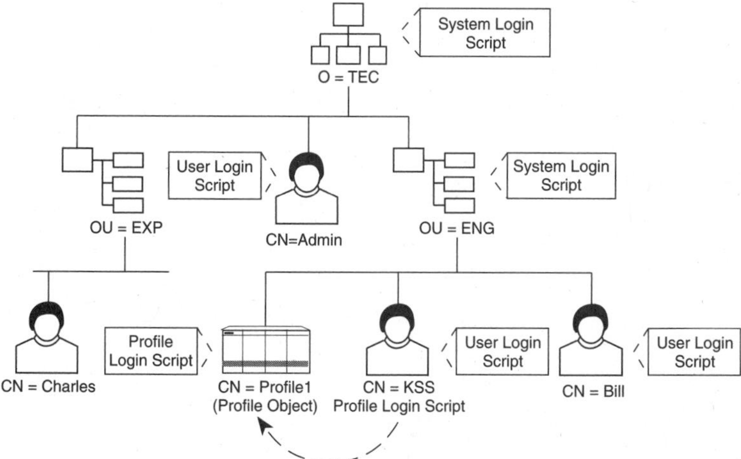

Figure 23.8
Example of login script execution.

When To Use the EXIT Command

Avoid using the EXIT command in all but the last line in the individual login script because the EXIT command terminates the processing of the login script, and this may not be what you want to do.

If used in the system login script file, the EXIT command stops the processing of the system login script and returns control to the DOS prompt. The other login scripts are bypassed.

The EXIT command sometimes can be placed in the individual login script file to serve as a convenient means of escaping to the DOS prompt. For properly designed script files, however, this should not be necessary.

Understanding Login Script Commands

The following commands can be used in login scripts:

# (Execution of external commands)	FIRE PHASERS
ATTACH	GOTO
BREAK	IF ... THEN ... ELSE

DOS BREAK

COMSPEC

DISPLAY

FDISPLAY

DOS SET or SET

DOS VERIFY

DRIVE

EXIT

INCLUDE

MAP

PAUSE

PCCOMPATIBLE

REMARK or REM

SHIFT

WRITE

In addition, the following commands are specific to NetWare 4.*x*:

- CLS
- ATTACHB
- CONTEXT
- DOS SET or SET
- DOS VERIFY
- NOSWAP and SWAP
- LASTLOGINTIME

The following sections discuss these commands.

The # Character

When placed before an external command, the # character provides external program execution. The following is the general syntax of the command:

```
# [path]filename parameters
```

The *[path]filename* statement specifies the full path name of the external command. The # character must be the first character in the command line. Under DOS, you can execute any EXE and COM file. To execute a DOS batch file or a DOS internal command, you must invoke the command-line processor by using the following command:

```
#COMMAND /C batch or internal
```

In the preceding command, *batch or internal* is replaced by the name of a batch file or an internal command. To clear the screen from the login script, you can use the DOS CLS internal command, as shown in the following command:

```
#COMMAND /C CLS
```

In NetWare 4.*x*, you can use the explicit login command CLS to clear the screen, as follows:

```
CLS
```

When executing an external command, you must make sure that the proper drive mappings and search drives have been set. This is because the external command executes in the context of the NetWare environment set up at the time of execution. You must have sufficient network rights in the directory in which the program is located—minimum rights should be [R F].

When the external command is executed, the login program is still resident in RAM and is not released until termination of the login script processing. Therefore, do not load TSRs during login processing because it leaves a hole in memory (where the login program was) when login script processing terminates.

The ATTACH Command (NetWare 2.2 and 3.*x*)

The ATTACH command, which can be executed as a NetWare command from the DOS prompt, enables you to attach to other servers. You can attach to a maximum of eight file servers. This command enables you to attach to other file servers without interrupting the current execution of the login script. The general syntax of the command is as follows:

```
ATTACH [fileserver[/username[;password]]]
```

If the *fileserver*, *username*, and *password* are not specified, you are prompted for them.

You need to be careful about including password information in the login script file. Anyone with Read access to the login script file can read the password, which compromises the security of your network.

Login Script Command: ATTACHB (NetWare 4.*x*)

The ATTACHB command can be used to attach to bindery based servers. You can attach to a maximum of *eight* file servers. This command allows the attachment to other file servers without interrupting the current execution of the login script. The general syntax of the command is as follows:

```
ATTACHB [fileserver[/username[;password]]]
```

If the *fileserver*, *username*, and *password* are not specified, you are prompted for the variables you have not entered.

The BREAK Command

The BREAK ON command enables you to terminate the execution of your login script. The general syntax of the command is as follows:

```
BREAK [ON ¦ OFF]
```

If the command is set to BREAK ON, the command enables you to terminate the processing of your login script by pressing Ctrl+C or Ctrl+Break. The default value is OFF.

The BREAK command is different from the DOS BREAK command, explained next.

The DOS BREAK Command

If DOS BREAK is set to ON, it enables Ctrl+Break checking for DOS. With Ctrl+Break checking enabled, whenever a program sends a request to DOS, it can be terminated by pressing Ctrl+Break. This command is equivalent to the BREAK command available under MS-DOS.

The COMSPEC Command

COMSPEC specifies the directory that DOS should use to load the command-line processor COMMAND.COM. The general syntax is the following:

```
COMSPEC=[path]COMMAND.COM
```

You can use a command-line processor other than COMMAND.COM, but such implementations are rare. The COMSPEC command directly sets the COMSPEC DOS environment variable.

When a large program loads, it can overwrite the transient portion of DOS. When this program exits, the transient portion of COMMAND.COM needs to be restored. DOS uses the COMSPEC environment variable to obtain a copy of COMMAND.COM. If the COMMAND.COM in memory and the one indicated by COMSPEC are for different versions of DOS, the workstation crashes with an `Invalid COMMAND.COM` message. On a network, chances are that users may be using different versions of DOS, and therefore COMSPEC may be pointing to an incorrect version of DOS. The COMSPEC variable should be set to the correct directory. This can be done by using the following commands:

```
MAP S2:=SYS:PUBLIC/%MACHINE/%OS/%OS_VERSION
COMSPEC=S2:COMMAND.COM
```

In the first command, for example, you can use the following command for MS-DOS 5:

```
SYS:PUBLIC/IBM_PC/MSDOS/V5.00
```

You can place in this directory the MS-DOS utilities to be used by the users on the network, and also a copy of MS-DOS 5.0 COMMAND.COM. This enables you to share DOS 5 utilities on the network and have a single place in which you can locate COMMAND.COM.

Another technique that can be used for users who boot from the hard disk is to set COMSPEC as follows:

```
COMSPEC=C:\COMMAND.COM
```

The preceding command takes care of different versions of DOS on the workstation's hard disk.

OS/2 users should not set their COMSPEC variable as indicated earlier. In case a login script needs to be shared by OS/2 users and users using the *Virtual DOS Machine* (VDM), the OS/2 users should reset their value of the COMSPEC variable.

The DISPLAY Command

This command shows the contents of the specified file on the workstation screen. The exact characters are displayed, including any control codes for printer and word processing formats. The following is the general syntax:

```
DISPLAY [pathname]file
```

The [*pathname*]*file* statement is the name of the file whose contents are displayed.

The FDISPLAY Command

The FDISPLAY command shows the contents of the specified text file on the workstation screen. The text is formatted and filtered so that only the text is displayed. The general syntax is the following:

```
FDISPLAY [pathname]file
```

The [*pathname*]*file* statement is the name of the file whose contents are displayed.

The DOS SET or SET Command

This command can be used to set a DOS environment variable from within a login script. The general syntax is as follows:

```
[option] [DOS] SET name = "value"
```

The [*option*] parameter can be replaced by an optional keyword, such as TEMP, TEMPORARY, or LOCAL, to signify that the variable is set only during the login script processing and does not affect the DOS environment. Replace *name* with the name of the environment variable and *value* with its actual value. The *value* must always be enclosed in quotation marks (").

The following are examples of the use of the SET command:

```
SET PROMPT = "$P$G"  (For setting DOS prompt)
SET FNAME =          (For removing the definition of the environment variable)
SET Y = "1"
SET Y = <Y> 1 1
SET UDIR = "*1:\\USERS\\%LOGIN_NAME"
```

If you want to use the backslash character (\) in a string value, you must specify two backslashes, as shown in the following example:

```
SET FILENAME = "F:\\PUBLIC\\TEMP\\KSSFILE"
```

The reason for providing two backslashes is that the single backslash character indicates special character codes, as shown in the following list:

- **\r.** Indicates a carriage return
- **\n.** Specifies a new line

- **\".** Embeds quotation marks in string
- **\7.** Generates a beep sound (bell)

The DOS VERIFY Command

When set to ON, the DOS VERIFY command verifies that the data copied to a local drive can be written without errors. The default is OFF, and the general syntax is the following:

```
DOS VERIFY [ON¦OFF]
```

The NCOPY command automatically does a read-after-write verify check and can be used to copy files to floppy disks. If you want to use the MS-DOS COPY command, you should have the following command in your login script for added reliability in making copies to floppy disks:

```
DOS VERIFY ON
```

The /V option also can be used with the MS-DOS COPY command to produce the same effect.

The DRIVE Command

The DRIVE command can be used to specify which network drive is the default drive. The general syntax is as follows:

```
DRIVE [driveletter: ¦ *n:]
```

Replace the *driveletter* statement with a drive letter, and **n* with the network drive number, such as ***1**, ***2**, and so on. The first network drive *1 is the default drive, but you can change this by specifying the new default drive in the DRIVE command.

The EXIT Command

Normally, execution of the login scripts terminates at the end of processing the individual user login script. The EXIT command can be used to prematurely terminate the login script processing or to specify the command to be executed upon termination. The general syntax is the following:

```
EXIT [filename]
```

Replace the *filename* statement with the program name and arguments of any command to be executed after the login script terminates. If an error message about limitations in the size of the command string that can be executed is displayed, you can try to minimize the characters in the command string by leaving out file extensions.

The following are examples of the use of the EXIT command:

`EXIT`	(Terminates login processing.)
`EXIT MENU`	(Executes the MENU utility upon termination.)
`EXIT "F:USEREXEC.BAT"`	(Executes USEREXEC.BAT in the default drive upon termination.)

The FIRE PHASERS Command

The FIRE PHASERS command produces sound effects of firing phasers. It does not work from the DOS command line. The general syntax is as follows:

```
FIRE PHASERS n TIMES
```

Replace *n* with a number from 1 to 9. Some examples of this command follow:

```
FIRE PHASERS 4 TIMES

FIRE PHASERS %NDAY_OF_WEEK TIMES
```

The GOTO Command

Use the GOTO command to repeat processing of portions of the login script. The following is the general syntax:

```
GOTO label
```

You can replace the *label* with an identifier, but it must be specified in the current login script. The following example shows how to use the command:

```
SET X = "1"
REM The line below shows how labels can be defined.
LOOP:
    REM The indentation shown below is for purposes
    REM of clarity and readability of the login script.
    REM It is not a requirement.

    REM Placing <> around X tells the login processor
    REM that this is an environment variable whose value
    REM needs to be evaluated.
    SET X = <X> 1 "1"

    REM Do whatever login script processing
    REM that needs to be repeated, here.

REM Place a condition for terminating the loop, otherwise
REM you will repeat this loop indefinitely!
IF <X> <= "10" THEN GOTO LOOP
```

Set BREAK ON in the login script before experimenting with loops just in case you want to break out of a loop you create unintentionally.

The IF … THEN … ELSE Command

This statement enables you to execute certain commands conditionally. The general syntax is as follows:

```
IF conditional(s) [AND¦OR¦NOR] conditional(s) THEN
    command
```

```
ELSE
    command
END
```

If the command is a series of statements, you must include the BEGIN command on the previous line.

In the preceding syntax, the *conditional(s)* statements can be generated by using the following operators:

The following operators are equivalent to Equal:

=

==

EQUAL

EQUALS

The following operators are equivalent to Not Equal:

!=

<>

Not equal

Does not equal

Not equal to

The following are used as greater-than and less-than relational operators:

>	Is greater than
<	Is less than
>=	Is greater than or equal to
<=	Is less than or equal to

The INCLUDE Command

The INCLUDE command indicates a level of indirection for processing login scripts. The content of the file specified in the INCLUDE statement is to be processed next, after which processing returns to the statement following the INCLUDE command. The general syntax is as follows:

```
INCLUDE [pathname]filename
```

The *[pathname]filename* statement is the location of the file to be processed.

You can nest INCLUDE commands up to any level limited only by the memory available for processing. As a practical matter, do not use more than two levels of nesting, or your login script will be difficult to figure out by others. You must have a minimum of [R F] rights to the INCLUDE file.

In NetWare 4.*x*, you can specify an NDS object that has a login script property. This type of INCLUDE statement has the following form:

```
INCLUDE objectname
```


The [*pathname*]*filename* statement is the location of the file to be processed, and *objectname* is the name of the object whose login script you want to use. Container objects, profile objects, and user objects have login scripts associated with them. For example to execute the login script for the container OU=CORP.O=SCS, use the following command:

```
INCLUDE OU=CORP.O=SCS
```

The MAP Command

The MAP command has the same syntax and meaning as the NetWare MAP command found in the SYS:PUBLIC directory, with only a few extensions. Use the following extensions to the MAP command for login script processing:

```
MAP DISPLAY [ON¦OFF]
```

```
MAP ERRORS [ON¦OFF]
```

The MAP DISPLAY ON command shows the drive mappings when you log in. This is the default setting. To disable the MAP processing, messages use MAP DISPLAY OFF.

MAP ERRORS ON displays error messages that occur, for example, if the path to which you are mapping does not exist (not relocatable). The default setting is ON. To disable the display of MAP errors, you can use MAP ERRORS OFF. Leave the MAP ERRORS command to its default setting of ON.

The PAUSE or WAIT Command

This command pauses the execution of the login script. Its general syntax is the following:

```
PAUSE
```

or

```
WAIT
```

This command can be used to pause the execution of the login script so that the messages do not scroll by before you have time to read them.

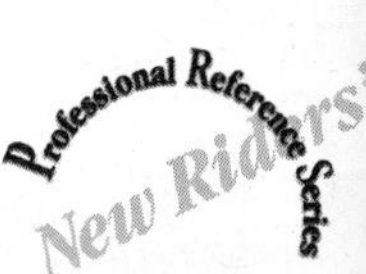

The PCCOMPATIBLE or COMPATIBLE Command

This command indicates that the workstation PC is IBM PC-compatible. Its general syntax is as follows:

```
PCCOMPATIBLE
```

or

```
COMPATIBLE
```

If your machine is IBM PC-compatible, but you changed the long machine or short machine name by using the LONG MACHINE TYPE= or SHORT MACHINE TYPE= statements in the NET.CFG (older SHELL.CFG) file, you must use the PCCOMPATIBLE command to indicate to the shell that your machine is IBM PC-compatible. If you do not do this, graphic NetWare utilities, such as SYSCON and FILER, which use the C-Worthy library routines, do not work correctly.

The REMARK or REM Command

This command places comments in the login script file for enhancing the readability of the login script. You can use REMARK or REM. The general syntax is the following:

```
REM [text]
```

or

```
* text
```

or

```
; text
```

The SHIFT Command

The SHIFT command can be used to pass variables after the LOGIN *servername*/*username* command. These variables are referred to as %0, %1, %2, and so on.

In the LOGIN command, you might have typed something like the following:

```
LOGIN WE_SERVE/LYDIA PUBS GRAPHIC
```

The following shows how the variables of the general syntax are replaced with statements in the preceding command:

%0= WE_SERVE

%1= LYDIA

%2= PUBS

%3= GRAPHIC

The %0 variable always is assigned to the file server being logged in to, even if the file server name is not explicitly specified in the LOGIN command. The %1 variable always is mapped to the user's login name. The %2 variable and other variables are mapped to the additional arguments on the LOGIN command line.

The SHIFT command shifts the variable assignments. Its general syntax is as follows:

```
SHIFT [n]
```


The *n* variable can be a positive number for the number of variables you want to shift to the right, or it can be a negative number for shifting to the left. If *n* is left out, the default value of 1 is assumed.

The primary use of the SHIFT command is to sequence through the parameters specified in the command line. The following loop, for example, can be used to assign %2 to each of the parameters specified in the LOGIN command line after the user name:

```
LOOP:
    IF "%2" = "VAL1" THEN Command
    IF "%2" = "VAL2" THEN Command
    IF "%2" = "VAL3" THEN Command

    SHIFT 1
IF "%2" <> "" THEN GOTO LOOP
```

The preceding loop checks each parameter against a specific value and, if a match is found, performs the action specified. The SHIFT 1 command causes the %2 variable to be assigned to the next parameter to the right until no more parameters are left to process. When no more parameters are left, the conditional expression in the IF statement evaluates to false, and execution proceeds to the statement following the IF statement.

The WRITE Command

The WRITE command displays a text message on-screen. Its general syntax is the following:

```
WRITE text
```

You can use the semicolon (;) to concatenate text strings. The following two WRITE commands, for example, result in the same output:

```
WRITE Good ; GREETING_TIME; , %LOGIN_NAME

WRITE Good %GREETING_TIME, %LOGIN_NAME
```

Login Script Command: CONTEXT (NetWare 4.*x*)

The CONTEXT statement can be used to change a user's context from the login script. The general syntax is as follows:

```
CONTEXT  context
```

To set your context to OU=LAB.OU=INVE.O=ETC, you can use the following login command:

```
CONTEXT OU=LAB.OU=INVE.O=ETC
```

or

```
CONTEXT LAB.INVE.ETC
```

To move one container above current context, you can use this command:

```
CONTEXT .
```

To move two containers above current context, issue the following command:

```
CONTEXT ..
```

Login Script Command: MACHINE (NetWare 4.*x*)

This can be used to set the value of the MACHINE login script variable. The MACHINE value also can be changed from the NET.CFG file. The general syntax of the command is as follows:

```
MACHINE = machinename
```

The *machinename* statement is replaced by a name that can be up to 15 characters long. If a machine name is longer than 15 characters, it is truncated to conform to this limit. For example, to specify that a machine name is NECULTRA, use the following command:

```
MACHINE=NECULTRA
```

NO_DEFAULT (NetWare 4.*x*)

If you do not want to create a user login script and do not want the default login script to run, you can use the NO_DEFAULT command. Using NO_DEFAULT disables the execution of the default login script, which normally runs if the user login script is not set.

NOSWAP and SWAP (NetWare 4.*x*)

The LOGIN.EXE is normally in conventional memory when an external command is executed through the #. If insufficient memory is available, LOGIN.EXE is swapped out to high memory, if available, or to the local hard disk. If you want to disable this swapping action, use the NOSWAP login command. In this case, if LOGIN.EXE cannot be held in conventional memory and run the external command, execution of the external command fails.

You can revert to the default behavior by using the SWAP command.

Login Script Command: LASTLOGINTIME (NetWare 4.*x*)

This command displays the last time the user logged in; it is used for informational purposes only.

SET TIME [ON | OFF] (NetWare 4.*x*)

The command SET TIME ON in the login script synchronizes workstation time to the server to which it is first attached. This is the default behavior.

The command SET TIME OFF disables synchronization of workstation time to the server to which it was first attached.

Login Script Variables

This chapter makes many references to login variables, and many examples are used throughout the chapter. Table 23.1 gives a formal definition of each of these script variables. The script variables also are sometimes referred to as login macros because they evaluate to a specific value. When used as part of a string or a path name, the percent character must be used before the script variable name.

Table 23.1
Identifier Variables

Conditional Items	**Screen Display**
ACCESS_SERVER	Displays TRUE if access server is functional. Displays FALSE if not functional.
ERROR_LEVEL	Displays the number of errors. If 0, no errors are found.
MEMBER OF *group*	Displays TRUE if the user is a member of a specified group. Displays FALSE if the user is not a member of a specified group.
Date	**Screen Display**
DAY	Displays the day from 01 to 31.
DAY_OF_WEEK	Displays the day of the week.
MONTH	Displays the month from 01 to 12.
MONTH_NAME	Displays the name of the month.
NDAY_OF_WEEK	Displays the number of the weekday.
SHORT_YEAR	Displays the year in short format, such as 92, 93, and so on.
YEAR	Displays the year in full format, such as 1992, 1993, and so on.

continues

Table 23.1, Continued
Identifier Variables

DOS Environment	Screen Display
<>	Enables you to use any DOS environment variable as a string.
NETWORK_ADDRESS	Displays the network number of the cabling system in eight hex digits.
FILE_SERVER	Displays the name of the file server.
Time	**Screen Display**
AM_PM	Displays the time as day or night, using a.m. or p.m.
GREETING_TIME	Displays the time of day as morning, afternoon, or evening.
HOUR	Displays the time of day in hours, from 1 to 12.
HOUR24	Displays the hour in 24-hour time, from 00 to 23.
MINUTE	Displays the minutes from 00 to 59.
SECOND	Displays the seconds from 00 to 59.
User	**Screen Display**
FULL_NAME	Displays the full name of the user by using SYSCON information.
LOGIN_NAME	Displays the user's login name.
USER_ID	Displays the ID number of each user workstation.
MACHINE	Displays the machine for which the shell was written, such as IBMPC.
OS	Displays the workstations operating system, such as MS-DOS.
OS_VERSION	Displays the DOS version of the workstation.
P_STATION	Displays the station address or node address in 12 hex digits.
SMACHINE	Displays the name of the machine in short format, such as IBM.
STATION	Displays the connection number.

Examining Novell Menus in NetWare 2.*x* and 3.11

All NetWare versions ship with the MENU utility. This utility takes as its input a text file containing a description of how the menus should appear. This text file has an MNU extension and can be created with any text editor. The basic syntax of this text file is as follows:

```
%Title V,H,C
Option1
    Executable commands
Option2
    Executable commands
Option3
    Executable commands
Option4
    %Sub Menu
%Sub Menu,V,H,C
OptionSub1
    Executable commands
OptionSub2
    Executable commands
```

The following sample menu script is an example of a menu text file:

```
%Dei's Menu,0,0,1
File Manager
    FILER
System Configuration
    SYSCON
File Console
    FCONSOLE
Applications
    %Applications

%Applications,14,60,1
WordProcessing
    MAP G:=SYS:APPS\WP
    G:
    WP
    F:
Database
    MAP G:=SYS:APPS\DBX
    G:
    DB
    F:
Spread Sheet
    MAP G:SYS:APPS\SS
    G:
    SS
    F:
```

As can be seen in the preceding examples, main and submenu titles always are preceded by the percent (%) character placed on the left margin. The percent character serves as an indication to the MENU parsing function that what follows is the title of the menu.

The menu title is followed by three numbers separated by commas. The first number is the distance (measured in lines) of the center of the menu from the top of the screen. The second number represents the distance (measured in columns) of the center of the menu from the left edge of the screen. These two numbers represent the vertical (V) and horizontal (H) coordinates of the center of the menu. A value of zero indicates that the menu is to be centered with respect to that coordinate. Thus, in the preceding example, you can see that Dei's main menu has the coordinates of 0,0, which means the menu is to be placed perfectly in the center. The third number is the color palette. The color palette is the color scheme for the foreground and background.

The color palette can be changed or a new one defined by using the utility COLORPAL. For most situations, the default color palette should suffice. There are five predefined color palettes, and these are numbered zero to four. If the color palette number is left out, a default color palette of zero is used.

The option lines are placed on the left margin also, but without the % character. One or more commands is placed below each option line. The commands are placed on separate lines and must be indented. The MENU utility can be invoked by using the following command:

```
MENU MenuFile
```

If you leave out the menu file, the default menu file MAIN.MNU, which is defined in the SYS:PUBLIC directory is used. It is customary to define a menu file for each user name and to give the menu file the same name as the user's login name. Therefore, for the user DEI, the menu file can be DEI.MNU. This menu for the user can be invoked by using the following command:

```
MENU DEI
```

This command can be placed in the user's login script by using the following command:

```
#MENU DEI
```

or

```
EXIT "MENU DEI"
```

or

```
EXIT  "MENU %LOGIN_NAME"
```

The last EXIT command automatically expands to the file name that has the same name as the user's login name.

If the EXIT command exits to a batch file called USEREXEC.BAT, defined in the user's home directory, then the USEREXEC.BAT file can contain the MENU FileName command as follows:

```
EXIT "F:USEREXEC.BAT"
```

When designing menus, an important consideration is the placement of the menus. This can be done in an ad hoc fashion by trial and error until you get the placement desired. Or better still, a more systematic method can be used, which uses the following formulas in which V and H are the coordinates specified in the menu title definition:

V = number of lines above menu 1 (number of lines in height of menu)/2

H = number of columns to left of menu 1 (number of columns in width of menu)/2

Suppose, for example, that the height of the menu is eight lines, and its width is 20 columns. Suppose also you have decided to place the top of the menu ten lines from the top of the screen, and the left edge of the menu 50 columns from the left of the screen. Using the preceding formulas, you get the following values:

V = 10 1 8/2 = 10 1 4 = 14

H = 50 1 20/2 = 50 1 10 = 60

The title would then be placed as the following:

```
%Title,14,60,0
```

If the `File Missing` message appears when the MENU command is invoked, it indicates that the file cannot be found in the current directory or on the search path. In this case, you need to make sure that the file exists in the current directory or in the search path.

Sometimes it is useful to give the user the option to enter information on the commands. An example of this is an option to copy files or send messages. A portion of the menu script file can then be the following:

```
%Interactive Commands,10,20,1
File Copy
    NCOPY @1"Source file name" @2"Destination"
Send Message
    SEND @1"Type a message" @2"Send to?"
```

The variables @1 and @2 in the preceding example become placeholders for whatever value the user types. The user is prompted to type these values. The text that follows the @ variables is displayed so that the user knows what kind of information is expected by the MENU system.

When the MENU utility displays the options, it sorts the options in alphabetical order. This can sometimes lead to undesirable consequences when the options appear in a different order from the one intended. Some system Administrators, therefore, resort to prefixing the option title with a number such as the following:

```
%Title,0,0

1. Option A
    Executable
```

```
2. Option B
    Executable

3. Option C
    Executable
```

23

Using this approach sorts the menu titles in the order of the numbers. This scheme works well for options that do not exceed nine. An option number of ten, for example, appears between options 1 and 2. You can of course resort to using two or more digit numbers, such as 01, 02, 03, and so on, to solve this problem.

Examining Novell Menus in NetWare 3.12 and 4.*x*

The NetWare 3.11 Novell Menus are adequate in simple situations, but many network Administrators prefer to use more robust third-party tools, such as the Saber menus. In NetWare 3.12 and 4.*x*, Novell has licensed the Saber menu technology. Currently, the NetWare 3.12 and 4.*x* menus do not have the full functionality of the commercial Saber menu system package, but they are a vast improvement over the NetWare 3.*x* Novell Menus. Starting with NetWare 3.12, the NetWare 3.*x* product line uses the NMENU utility. The NMENU implements the Novell Menus. It is currently a batch file (NMENU.BAT) that invokes other utilities such as MENUEXE.EXE and MENUREST.EXE.

One of the improvements in the NMENU utility is the requirement of less memory, which allows programs that need more memory to be run.

A scripting language is used to create the source file for the NMENU utility. The source (.SRC extension) file is then compiled to produce a data file (DAT extension). The data file is then used with a NMENU.BAT utility that interprets and executes the DAT file. Figure 23.9 depicts the steps to perform these operations.

Older menu script files (.MNU extension) used with the scripting language of the NetWare 3.11 Novell Menu utility, can be converted to the NetWare 4.*x* menu script language by using a conversion tool called MENUCNVT.EXE. Figure 23.10 shows the conversion process.

If the older Novell Menu script file is named MAIN.MNU, then to convert, compile, and run the menu using the NetWare 4.*x* menu system, you can perform the following steps:

1. MENUCNVT MAIN.MNU (Produces a MAIN.SRC file).

2. Examine MAIN.SRC file and edit as necessary.

3. MENUMAKE MAIN.SRC (Produces a MAIN.DAT file).

4. NMENU MAIN.DAT

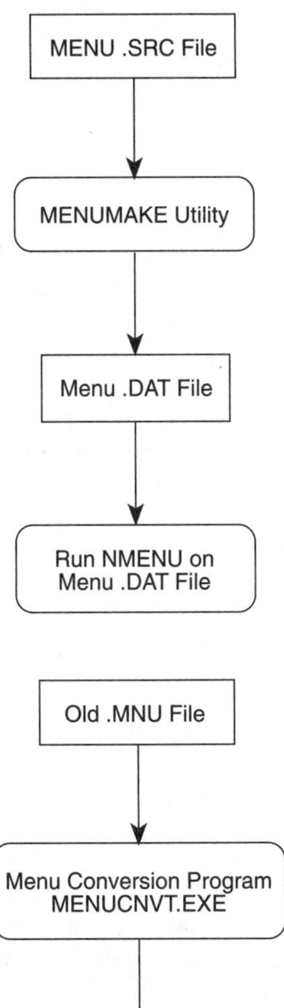

Figure 23.9
Novell Menu compilation steps.

Figure 23.10
The Novell Menu conversion process.

Menu Temporary Files

When the Novell Menus are executed using the following command:

```
NMENU   compiledfile
```

in which *compiledfile* contains the compiled menu description, a number of temporary files are created. These default files are created in the current directory unless special environment variables are set. To create these temporary files, the user needs the following permissions:

- Read (R)
- Write (W)
- Create (C)
- Erase (E)
- Modify (M)
- File Scan (F)

The user has these rights in their home directory and their local hard disk, so these commands can be run from the home directory or local hard disk. If the machine is turned off or stops while running the NMENU program, temporary files are left behind. Some Administrators may prefer to define a common directory in which these temporary files are kept because it makes it easy for the Administrator to clean up old temporary files. To set NMENU to use a specific directory for holding NMENU temporary files, you can set the S_FILEDIR environment variable. For instance, to set the NMENU to use Z:\MENUDAT as a temporary directory, you can use the following command in the workstation's AUTOEXEC.BAT file.

```
SET S_FILEDIR=Z:\MENUDAT
```

Alternatively, you can set the following command in a login script file, such as the system, profile, or user login script file:

```
SET S_FILEDIR="Z:\MENUDAT"
```

A problem with using a common directory for holding temporary files is that the temporary file names are based on the user name. As long as the user names are unique, the temporary files are unique per user, and the Novell Menus work just fine. But, what if a user logs in more than one time using the same user name and uses the Novell Menus? This is possible unless the number of concurrent connections restriction is kept to one. In this case, the Novell Menus try to create a separate set of temporary files with names that already exist. The resulting name collisions cause Novell Menus not to work as expected. The solution to this is to have Novell Menus create temporary files based on station connection number, which is unique per user session. Therefore, if a user logs in using the same user account, each user session has a different connection number, and a different set of temporary files for Novell Menus.

The S_FILE environment variable can be used to determine how temporary files are to be named. This can be used to change temporary files to use the station connection number using the following command in a login script:

```
SET S_FILE="%STATION"
```

To set the Novell Menus to use the user's home directory for temporary files, use the following command in a login script:

```
SET S_FILEDIR="SYS:USERS/%LOGIN_NAME"
```

Example Menu Script

The following is a sample menu script file, and figure 23.11 shows the Novell Menus resulting from it:

```
menu 01,Network Utilities
    item NetAdmin
        exec NETADMIN
    item NetUser
        exec NETUSER
    item DOS Prompt
        exec DOS
    item Logout
        exec LOGOUT
```


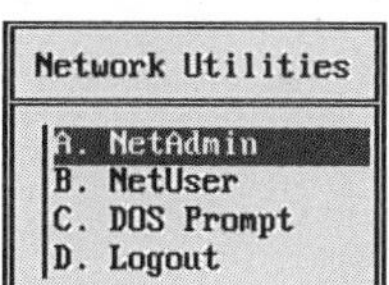

Figure 23.11
NMENU display.

The name of the menu is called the *menu title* and is defined by the MENU command. Each option in the menu item is defined by the ITEM statement. The names of the programs to be executed when an option is selected are defined by the EXEC statement.

You examine the details of the menu script next.

Menu Parts

A NetWare Menu can consist of four components (see fig. 23.12). The components are specified in the Menu source file and are given in the following list:

- A main menu that has a title and at least one option
- Commands to be executed when an option is selected
- Submenus displayed when an option is selected
- Prompts for user input

The first two items in the preceding list are necessary. The remaining parts, the submenus and prompted user input, are optional.

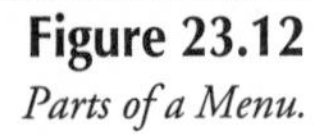

Figure 23.12
Parts of a Menu.

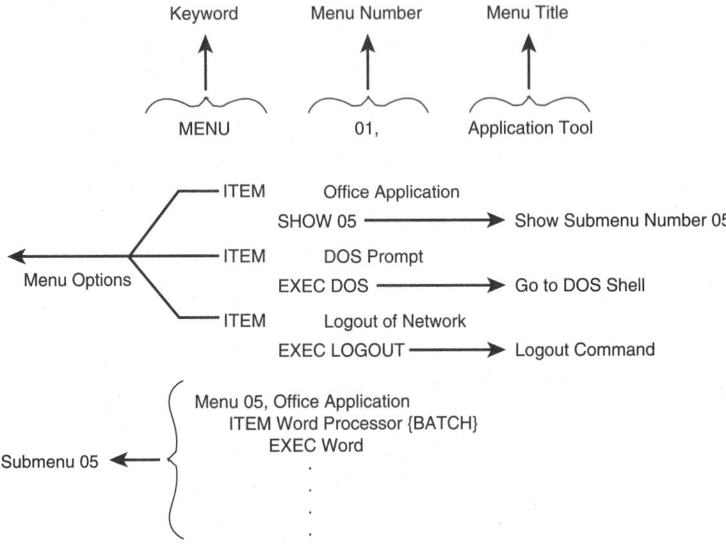

Menu Commands

As you saw earlier, the principle menu commands are MENU, ITEM, and EXEC. The MENU and ITEM commands are used for organizing the structure and appearance of the menu. The EXEC command is used to control the execution of commands when a particular item is selected. In general, menu commands can be divided into the following two categories:

- Organizational commands
- Control commands

These two categories of commands are discussed in greater detail in the following sections.

Organizational Commands

Organizational commands are responsible for the overall organization and contents of the menu; they also determine the appearance of the menu on-screen. Currently, only two commands are defined for this category, which are the following:

- MENU
- ITEM

Every menu and submenu is defined by a MENU command. The parameters for the MENU command are a menu number and the title of the menu. Its general syntax is the following:

```
MENU menuNumber,menuTitle
```

The *menuNumber* is unique per menu, and it can be any number between 1 and 255. No special ordering relationship exists between the menu numbers and the menus displayed. The only requirement is that they be unique. No spaces should be between the *menuNumber*, the comma, and the *menuTitle*. The *menuTitle* is a string of characters that should not exceed 40 characters and is displayed at the top of the menu. It is used to identify the title of the menu.

For example, if a menu is given a number of five and a title of Available Options, its menu command appears as follows:

```
MENU 5,Available Options
```

The preceding command defines the start of the menu Available Options identified by the menu number five.

The ITEM organizational command defines the option displayed for a menu. The items are listed in the order in which you want them to appear in the menu. An option consists of a text string parameter to the ITEM command. The general syntax of the ITEM command is as follows:

```
ITEM  itemText { itemOption itemOption ... }
```

or

```
ITEM  ^tagchar itemText { itemOption itemOption ... }
```

In the first format for the ITEM command, every *itemText* is preceded by a letter automatically assigned by the MENU utility. The letters are from A to Z, with the first ITEM command assigned A, the next B, and so on. These letters or *item tags* serve as a short-cut to selecting the option. Pressing the letter key corresponding to an option causes that menu item to be selected. The item tags do not determine the order in which the menu is displayed. The display order is determined by the order in which the items are listed. The *itemText* is the text string that you want displayed for the menu option. The *itemOptions* are placed within { } braces, and can consist of zero or more item options that further qualify the menu option. The *itemOption* statement is discussed in greater detail in the following section. An example of the syntax for the first format is the following:

```
ITEM    NetAdmin Tool { }
```

The *itemText* is NetAdmin Tool; no *itemOptions* are specified, and therefore the {} the braces are empty. If the braces { } are empty, they can be omitted, as in the following example:

```
ITEM Display Context
        EXEC CX
```

If this were the first ITEM listed under a MENU command, it would have a tag character of A; if this were the second item its tag character would be B, and so on.

The second format for the command is similar to the first format. The difference is that ^*tagchar* can precede the *itemText*. The caret (^) character followed by a single character, the *tagchar*, allows this character to override the default letter assignment for that item. For example, if you want to use digits 1 to 6 to designate the menu options, use the following command:

```
ITEM  ^1First Option { }
ITEM  ^2Second Option { }
ITEM  ^3Third Option { }
ITEM  ^4Fourth Option { }
ITEM  ^5Fifth Option { }
ITEM  ^6Sixth Option { }
```

The item options are displayed in the order in which they are listed. The MENU utility makes no attempt to sort them based on any tag characters specified. It is possible to mix ITEM statements with tag characters and the ITEM statements without tag characters as in the following example:


```
MENU 01, NLIST and NDIR Menu
ITEM     Show all objects  {PAUSE}
    EXEC NLIST * /D /S /CO "[Root]"
ITEM     NLIST Help
    EXEC NLIST /? ALL
ITEM     Change Context    {PAUSE}
    EXEC CX %
ITEM     ^XEXIT
    EXEC EXIT
ITEM     ^LExit and Logout
    EXEC LOGOUT
```

ITEM Options

The *itemOptions*, placed in the { } braces in the ITEM command, further qualify how the commands associated with the ITEM are executed. The following example shows the ITEM command and the commands executed when an item is selected:

```
ITEM Menu Option Text { }
    command 1
    command 2
           :
    command N
```

The commands executed when the ITEM is selected are listed immediately following the ITEM. These commands are preceded by one of the following key words: EXEC, LOAD, SHOW, GETO, GETR, and GETP, and are discussed in greater detail in the next section.

The *itemOption* that can be placed in {} can be any of the following:

- BATCH
- CHDIR
- SHOW
- PAUSE

The BATCH item option is used to free up additional memory when running an application. The Novell NetWare 4.*x* MENU Utility by itself takes up 32 KB of RAM. For applications that take up a large amount of memory, it is desirable to use as much RAM as possible for the application. By using the BATCH option, the commands associated with the Menu are written in a temporary batch file. The MENU utility is removed from memory, and the batch file runs. The last command in the batch file re-invokes the MENU utility. To run the NETADMIN utility using a batch file, use the following:

```
ITEM NetAdmin Utility {BATCH}
    EXEC NETADMIN
```

The CHDIR item option is used to restore the default directory to the one that existed prior to executing the command. Some programs give you the option of changing the default directory or changing the default directory when they are run. After exiting these programs, you may be placed in a default directory different from the one in use prior to executing the program. It is often desirable to have the same default directory when a program is excepted from the MENU utility. For example, to keep the same default directory for a program called TELNET, throughout the execution of the MENU utility, you can use the following:

```
ITEM Remote login via TELNET {CHDIR}
    EXEC TELNET
```

The different item options can be combined. For example, to execute FILER as a batch file and to retain the same default directory, you can use the following:

```
ITEM Filer Utility {BATCH CHDIR}
    EXEC FILER
```

The order in which the item options are placed inside { } is not significant. Therefore, the preceding statements are equivalent to the following:

```
ITEM Filer Utility {CHDIR BATCH}
    EXEC FILER
```

The SHOW item option displays the name of the DOS command executed from the MENU utility on the upper-left hand corner of the screen as it executes. This is particularly useful if the DOS command that is executing is passed a parameter, which also is displayed as the command executes. An example of this usage is shown in the following command:

```
ITEM Directory Contents Listing {SHOW}
    EXEC DIR %
```

The PAUSE option causes the message `Press any key to continue` at the end of executing the command(s). This gives the user an opportunity to read the screen before proceeding to the next step. The MENU utility does not proceed to the next step unless the user presses a key. The following is an example of using the PAUSE option:

```
ITEM Search for files that have "SCS (C)opyright"  {PAUSE}
    EXEC GREP  "SCS (C)opyright"  *.*
```

Table 23.2 summarizes the ITEM different options discussed earlier.

Table 23.2
ITEM Options

Item Option	Description	Example
BATCH	Frees up RAM occupied by MENU utility (32 KB) when a program runs.	ITEM Application X {BATCH}
CHDIR	Restores default directory to that which existed prior to running the commands associated with the menu item.	ITEM Application X {CHDIR}
SHOW	Shows DOS commands on upper-left corner of screen as they execute.	ITEM Application X {SHOW}
PAUSE	Pauses display and waits for user to press a key, at end of executing a command.	ITEM Application X {PAUSE}

Menu Control Commands

The MENU and ITEM commands discussed in the preceding section are used to determine the contents of a menu or submenu and the manner in which options should be displayed or run. The actual commands processed occur after the ITEM command. These commands are called *control commands*, and are used to execute applications from within the MENU utility (NMENU), to load menu definitions kept in separate files, to show submenus, and to obtain user input. Six control commands that begin with key words are the following:

- EXEC
- LOAD
- SHOW
- GETO
- GETR
- GETP

The first three of the preceding control commands (EXEC, LOAD, and SHOW) deal with executing programs and loading and displaying submenus. The last three of these commands (GETO, GETR, and GETP) solicit input from the user, which can then be used as parameters for commands and programs executed.

The EXEC Control Command

The EXEC (or EXECUTE) command is used to run an application. The command that is run can be an EXE, COM, BAT, an internal DOS command, or any of the following:

- DOS
- EXIT
- LOGOUT

An example of using the EXEC command for a DOS internal command is as follows:

```
ITEM    ^DShow Directory listing {SHOW}
    EXEC DIR
```

The following is an example of using the EXEC command for a NetWare .EXE program file:

```
ITEM    ^UNetwork User {BATCH}
    EXEC NETUSER
```

The EXEC DOS command runs a second copy of the command shell. For DOS, this is the COMMAND.COM command processor. When a second copy of the command shell runs, the user is presented with a command prompt and can type in any DOS or application command. The NMENU utility and the previous copy of the command shell are still loaded, so you are limited by the remaining memory available for your DOS application. The following is an example of the use of the EXEC DOS command:

```
ITEM  Exit to DOS { }
    EXEC DOS
```

To return to the Novell Menu Utility, you must type the **EXIT** command at the command prompt. This terminates the second shell and returns you to the MENU utility.

For secure environments, you may want to control the applications a user can run on the network. In this case, you may want to restrict the user's access to the command prompt and not use the EXEC DOS command.

If you want to give users the option of exiting the menu program completely and going to the DOS prompt, you can use the EXEC EXIT command. This command terminates the MENU utility program, which causes the system to remove the program from memory. Control is returned to the command shell and the command prompt. If, for security reasons, you want to control a user's access to the command, do not use the EXEC EXIT command. An example of the use of the EXEC EXIT command is as follows:

```
ITEM  Exit NMENU { }
    EXEC EXIT
```

In many environments, it is desirable to control a user's access to the command prompt. So none of the options, EXEC DOS or EXEC EXIT, are suitable for this purpose, because these give a user access to the command prompt. Yet, it is necessary for a user to terminate the use of the network and the Novell Menus. To accomplish this, a special EXEC LOGOUT command has been defined. When the EXEC LOGOUT option is used, it logs the user out of the network and simultaneously terminates the Novell Menu utility.

An example of the use of the EXEC LOGOUT command is as follows:

```
ITEM  Exit Novell Menus and logout { }
    EXEC LOGOUT
```

Table 23.3 summarizes the different EXEC commands that can be used.

Table 23.3
EXEC Command Summary

EXEC type	Description
EXEC *command*	Replace *command* with a DOS internal/external command, an .EXE or .COM program file, or a DOS batch file.
EXEC DOS	Starts a secondary shell and gives user access to the command prompt through the secondary shell.
EXEC EXIT	Terminates the Novell Menu (NMENU) utility and returns control to the command shell and the command prompt.
EXEC LOGOUT	Terminates the Novell Menu (NMENU) utility and logs user out of the network. Provides a secure option to exit the Novell Menus.

The SHOW Control Command

A menu is defined using the MENU command in which you must define the menu number and title. There can be many such menu commands in a single file. The first menu command in a complied file (produced by running MENUMAKE), that is passed as a parameter to the NMENU command, becomes the first menu displayed. This is the main menu. All other menus in the file are displayed by using the SHOW command. The syntax of the SHOW command is as follows:

```
SHOW menuNumber
```

The *menuNumber* should be replaced with a number that represents the menu number defined in the MENU statement for the submenu that should be displayed. A single menu file can have up to 255 submenus or menu commands (menu definitions).

The submenu displayed is *cascaded* in relationship to the previous menu. Its position on-screen is determined automatically by the Novell Menu utility.

Figure 23.13 shows the SHOW commands in a menu script file. The two SHOW commands: SHOW 3 and SHOW 8 refer to the indicated submenus in the script file.

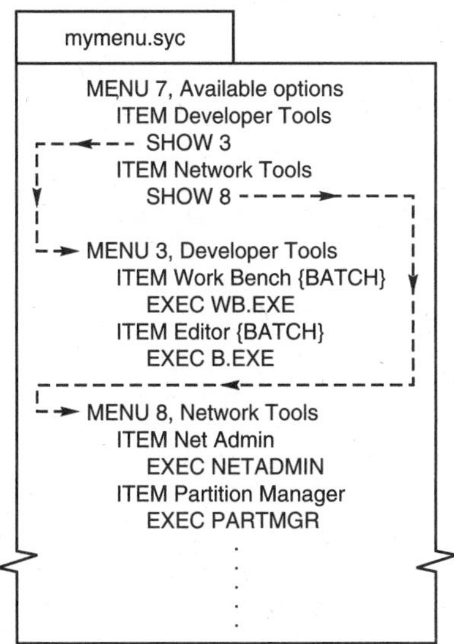

Figure 23.13
SHOW commands in a menu script file.

The LOAD Control Command

A menu is defined using the MENU command in which you must define the menu number and title. Up to 255 submenus or menu commands (menu definitions) can exist in a single menu file. For large menu systems, it is necessary to place the menu definitions in separate files. You also may decide to use separate files for smaller menu systems because doing so can help you organize and manage the menu definitions. To load a menu in a separate file, you must use the load command. The syntax of the LOAD command is as follows:

```
LOAD menuName
```

The *menuName* should be replaced by the file name of the compiled menu file. When the LOAD command is executed, the original menu system is left running, but a second menu is added to the screen.

Figure 23.14 shows the use of the LOAD command. It shows how a large menu can be broken into smaller menus. In this figure, three menus MENU1, MENU2, and MENU3 are shown defined in separate files MENU1.DAT, MENU2.DAT, and MENU3.DAT.

Figure 23.14
Use of menu LOAD command.

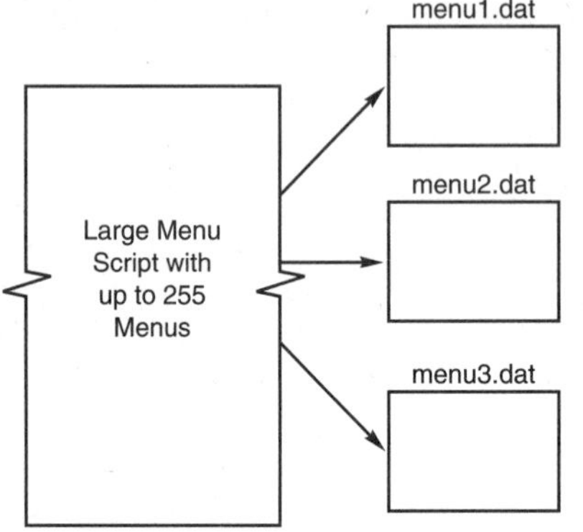

MENU 01, Operations Menu
ITEM Word Processing Application
LOAD MENU1

ITEM Database Application
LOAD MENU2

ITEM Spread Sheet Applications
LOAD MENU3

The GET*x* Commands

The three forms of the GETx commands are GETO, GETR, and GETP. Like the other control commands, GET*x* commands are listed after an ITEM command and are executed when the menu item is selected. The following is an example of some of the GETx commands:

```
ITEM   ^LDirectory Listing
    GETO  Enter directory name: {} 45,, {}
    EXEC DIR
```

The GETO Command

The GETO command is used for obtaining an optional input from the user. The "O" in GETO stands for "optional." When the GETO command is executed, as shown in the preceding example, a dialog box is displayed. The message text in the dialog box, the width of the user input, the initial value of the user input, and so on are passed as parameters to the GETO command.

With the GETO, GETR, and GETP commands the Enter key signals that you have completed the information. If you press F10 without completing the user input, it signals that you want to continue with the menu execution.

The user has the choice of making an entry or not making an entry (optional GET). In either case, when the user presses the F10 key, execution continues. If the user makes an entry, the entered value is passed as a parameter to the command that follows. In the preceding example, the command that follows is the EXEC DIR command. In this example, if a user makes the entry **F:\SYSTEM**, the following EXEC command executes:

```
EXEC DIR F:\SYSTEM
```

The preceding command displays the contents of the directory F:\SYSTEM. If the user does not make any entry, but just presses F10, the EXEC command that executes is as follows:

```
EXEC DIR
```

The preceding command displays the contents of the current directory.

The % character can be used as a placeholder for a single user input. The preceding example of the use of the GETO command can be alternatively expressed using the % placeholder.

```
ITEM   ^LDirectory Listing

    GETO  Enter directory name: {} 45,, {}

    EXEC DIR %
```


The GETR Command

The GETR command works similarly to the GETO command just described. The big difference is that the GETR command *requires* users to enter information. Just pressing F10 (or Enter if GETR is in its own dialog box), does not cause the GETR command to continue execution. The menu display pauses and does not continue until a valid input is entered.

The following is an example of the use of GETR:

```
ITEM  User Command
    GETR Enter a user command: {}80,,{}
    EXEC %
```

The preceding example passes the user typed string as a command to be executed by the EXEC command.

The GETP Command

The GETP command works similarly to the other GETx commands described earlier. The special feature of GETP is that it assigns a variable to the user input. This variable can then be used in other commands. The following is an example of the use of GETP:

```
ITEM     Network Copy {PAUSE SHOW}
    GETP    Source: {} 60,, {}
    GETP    Destination: {} 60,,{}
    EXEC    NCOPY  %1 %2
```

The first GETP parameter assigns the user input to the variable %1, and the second GETP command assigns its user input to %2. These parameters are used in the EXEC NCOPY command as the source and destination, respectively. Table 23.4 summarizes the different GETx commands.

Table 23.4
GET*x* Commands

GET*x* Command	Description
GETO	Used to obtain optional user input.
GETR	Used to obtain required user input.
GETP	Used to obtain user input assigned to variables %1, %2, and so on.

Comparing GETP, GETR, and GETO Command User Input Processing

Whereas the GETR and GETO commands append the input they receive to the next EXEC command, the GETP command parses the input and breaks it down into words assigned to parameter variables %1, %2, %3, and so on.

Thus if the user input is as follows:

```
MONTHS  12 YEARS 25
```

the parameter variables have the following values:

```
%1 = MONTHS
%2 = 12
%3 = YEARS
%4 = 25
```

These parameter variables can be used in the next EXEC command, as in the following example:

```
EXEC CalcInt  %3=%4  TYPE %1=%2
```

Given the previously discussed parameter values, the above EXEC command evaluates to the following:

```
EXEC CalcInt YEARS=25 TYPE MONTHS=12
```

As you can see, the GETP enables you greater control over how you can use the user typed-in values.

GET*x* Parameter Options

In the examples of the GET*x* commands in the preceding section, you saw the use of the {} braces and the commas (,) as part of the syntax of the GET*x* command. This syntax is part of a general syntax that gives you options to control the width of the user input and the initial value displayed for the user. You also can modify the user input by prepending or appending special text string values to the user input. The syntax of these parameters is as follows:

```
GETx  promptString, {prependString} length,prefillString,{appendString}
```

or

```
GETx  promptString,{prependString} length,prefillString,SECURE {appendString}
```

The *x* in GET*x* is O, R, or P for the different types of GET commands. The *promptString* is the text displayed for the GET command and is meant as an aid to the user to enter the appropriate value. The *prependString* placed inside the {} is a string attached to the beginning of the data the user enters. If there is no value that you want to prepend to the entered data, you must enter the *empty string* inside {}. The following is an example of the use of the prepend string:

```
ITEM    ZIP code for Montana Residents
    GETR    {MT }5,,{}
    EXEC RecZip %
```

In the preceding example, the prepend string "MT" is prepended to the supplied user input. The RecZip represents a custom application that processes user-supplied data.

Please note that the difference between the {} braces with no space between them and the { } braces with a space between them. The former represents a *null* or *empty* string and means that no value will be prepended to the user data. The latter represents a blank character prepended to the user data. These comments also apply to the {*appendString*} in the GET*x* command syntax.

The *length* specifies the size of the user input field. It is the number of characters the user can enter for the GET command. The *length* field is mandatory and can have a maximum value of 80 characters. The following example shows a maximum length field of 80 being used:

```
ITEM    Address Information
    GETR  Enter your street address {}80,,{}
    EXEC RecData %
```

The RecData in the EXEC command in the preceding example is meant as an example of a custom application (RecData) that can process the user supplied information.

The *prefillString* is the initial value placed in the user's response field. It is used as the default value that the user can accept, if the user chooses not to enter a different value. The *prefillString* is optional. The *prefillString* is separated from the *length* field by a comma (,) and no spaces. If no prefill string is used, it can be omitted as shown in the following example:

```
ITEM    Get user information
    GETO Enter your company name:{}50,,{}
    EXEC RecData  %
```

The following example shows a prefill string being used:

```
ITEM    Get user information
    GETO Enter your company name:{}50,IBM,{}
    EXEC RecData  %
```

In the preceding example, the Enter your company name: field in the dialog box for the GETO command has an initial value of IBM. The user can accept this value or override it with a different value. The user-supplied value is used as a parameter to a custom application called RecData.

The SECURE keyword is optional. If present, it must occur between the *prefillString* parameter and the {*appendString*} parameter. If the SECURE keyword exists as part of the GET command syntax, it means that the typed-in user data is not displayed (hidden). This is useful if the user wants to enter a password, security code, or some other confidential data. The following is an example of the use of the SECURE keyword:

```
ITEM    Security Information
    GETR    Enter Personal Identification Number(PIN): {}4,,SECURE{}
    EXEC  ValidPIN %
```

The ValidPIN in the EXEC command signifies a custom application—one that, perhaps, validates the user-supplied PIN data.

The *appendString* placed inside the {} is a string attached to the end (appended) of the data the user enters. If there is no value that you want to append to the entered data, you must enter the *empty string* inside {}. The following is an example of the use of the append string:


```
ITEM    Security Information
    GETR    Enter Personal Identification Number(PIN): {}4,,SECURE{KXVZ}
    EXEC ProcPIN
```

In the preceding example, the append string "KXVZ" is appended to the supplied user input. The ProcPIN represents a custom application that processes the user supplied data. In this example, the append string is used as a special security code sent in conjunction with the user-supplied data to the processing program ProcPIN.

If several GET commands are listed under an ITEM command, the GET fields are grouped in the order of occurrence with ten GETs per dialog box. In other words, there can be a maximum of ten GET command prompts per dialog box. If you want to override this default behavior and have a GET command appear in its own dialog box, you must use the caret (^) at the beginning of the prompt text for the GET command. The following example shows how each of the GET commands can appear in its own dialog box:

```
ITEM  Enter User Information
    GETP    ^User Name:{}50,,{}
    GETP  ^Address:{}80,,{}
    GETP  ^Password:{}30,,SECURE{}
    EXEC ProcUser %1 %2 %3
```

The ProcUser represents a custom application that processes the user supplied input.

The following example shows another use of the GET commands that prompts users for options. The user is prompted for the source and destination directories. These are used as parameters %1 and %2 in the NCOPY command.

```
ITEM    Network Copy {PAUSE SHOW}
    GETP    Source: {} 60,, {}
    GETP    Destination: {} 60,,{}
    EXEC    NCOPY  %1 %2
```

The following examples illustrate other uses of the GET commands.

Example 1:

```
ITEM    Authenticate User
    GETR    User ID:  {} 10,guest,{}
    GETR    Password: {} 25,,SECURE{}
    EXEC    CHKUSER.EXE
```

In Example 1, the user is asked for a password. The user's response is not displayed because of the SECURE option. The user's response is used as an argument to CHKUSER.EXE.

Example 2:

```
ITEM    Directory Listing
    GETO    Directory Path: {  } 40,,{}
    EXEC    dir
```

In Example 2, the user is asked for the directory path for which a listing should be displayed. If one is not specified, the DIR command is executed without an argument, in which case, a listing for the current directory is displayed.

Example 3:

```
ITEM    Compute Mortgage {SHOW}
    GETP    Enter loan amount:      {}10,0,{}
    GETP    Interest Rate:          {}5,6.5,{}
    GETP    Enter period (/m=months or+
    /y=years) : {} 8, /y=30,{}
    EXEC    echo  Loan amount   = %1
    EXEC    echo  Interest rate   = %2
    EXEC    echo  Period                = %3
    EXEC    MortCalc    /l=%1  /r=%2  %3
```

In Example 3, the loan amount and interest are passed as parameters to the program MORTCALC (Mortgage Calculation). The loan amount is passed as a parameter of the form /l=*amount*. The interest rate is passed as a parameter of the form /r=*rate*. The period is displayed with a default field value of "/y=30" (30 years). The user can enter the value using the /m=*months* or /y=*years* format. This is passed as the %3 argument to the program MORTCALC.

No more than 100 GET commands are allowed per ITEM command. Also, the GETO and GETR commands must be entered between the ITEM and the EXEC line associated with them.

The general syntax of the GET*x* command is as follows:

```
GETx promptString,{prependString}length,prefillString,[SECURE]{appendString}
```

The [ ] brackets around SECURE imply that SECURE is optional; it is not part of the syntax for GET*x*.

Table 23.5 summarizes the different GET parameters discussed in this chapter.

Table 23.5
GET Parameters

GET*x* Parameter	Description
promptString	Message that must be displayed to the user.
prependString	User-entered data is prepended with the *prependString* placed in the first set of {}.

continues

Table 23.5, Continued
GET Parameters

GET*x* Parameter	Description
length	Maximum number of characters for the user field. Its maximum value is 80 characters.
prefillString	Used as the default response, in case the user does not enter a value.
SECURE	User typed-in information is not displayed. Used for secure data such as passwords and codes.
appendString	User-entered data is appended with the *appendString* placed in the first set of {}.

NMENU Limitations

The following list outlines the menu limitations:

- Up to 255 submenus or menu commands (menu definitions) can be in a single menu file.
- Maximum number of characters for the user field is 80.
- Maximum number of characters on a line in the menu script is 80. Longer lines can continue to the next line by ending the preceding line with the line continuation character +.
- No more than 100 GET commands are allowed per ITEM command.
- If several GET commands are listed under an ITEM command, the GET fields are grouped in the order of occurrence with ten GETs per dialog box.
- The Novell Menus can have no more than one main menu and ten submenus (using the SHOW command) on the screen at any time. This means that the maximum level of sub-menu nesting cannot exceed ten.
- You cannot mix EXEC and SHOW submenu commands under an ITEM option. Therefore, the following example is illegal:

```
ITEM Telmail option
   EXEC MAP T:=FS1/SYS:INET/BIN
   SHOW 06
```

Customizing NMenu Colors

The MENU utility COLORPAL can be used to customized color palettes for the menu utilities. The color schemes and the default color scheme are defined in the following file:

```
shortmachine_RUN.OVL
```

in which *shortmachine* is replaced by the SHORT MACHINE TYPE parameter defined in the NET.CFG file. The default value of SHORT MACHINE TYPE is IBM, and therefore the default name of the color schemes file (C-Worthy overlay file) is as follows:


```
IBM_RUN.OVL
```

If you set the SHORT_MACHINE type to a different value, such as NEC, using the following command:

```
SHORT MACHINE TYPE=NEC
```

in the NET.CFG file, you must define the overlay file NEC_RUN.OVL. This allows custom color palettes to be defined for user workstations with unusual displays that need to use a set of color combinations different from the default.

Summary

In this chapter, you learned the different types of startup scripts necessary to set up a NetWare workstation. These include the familiar DOS startup files CONFIG.SYS and AUTOEXEC.BAT. Certain statements in these files can be specifically configured for the network environment.

In NetWare 2.*x* and 3.*x*, you can have system, user, and default login scripts. NetWare 4.*x* uses these types of login scripts and adds another called profile login script. The order of execution of these login scripts was discussed in this chapter, along with details of the login script commands and variables that can be used to set up a customized network environment.

Finally, you saw how the Novell menu systems—MENU(NetWare 3.11) and NMENU (NetWare 3.12 and NetWare 4.*x*)—can make it easier for users to access network services.

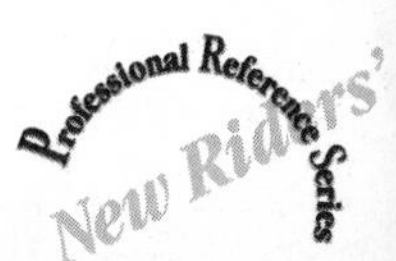

The NetWare File System

The NetWare server provides a remote file system that can be accessed by NetWare clients. Because many users share this remote access file system, the following points are important:

- The server's remote file system must be well-organized and easy to maintain.
- Users must share the server's file system without violating system security or another user's privacy.
- Access to the file system must be intuitive and consistent with the workstation operating system used by the client.
- Access to the file system must be nearly as fast as access to a workstation's local hard disk.

NetWare combines all of these features. The NetWare system and utilities are organized into standard directories, such as LOGIN, SYSTEM, and PUBLIC. Users can be assigned a home directory to store their personal files. If a directory contains system programs used for network administration, access to these programs can be restricted. Access to the network files is simple and intuitive; you can access the server files by using the workstation's operating system commands. And because most LANs operate at speeds of megabits per second, access to the server's file system is fast. You can read and write to a network file about as fast as you can read and write to a local disk.

Looking at Directory Organization

The server's disk is an important component of the server. A high-performance disk subsystem has a dramatic effect on the server's overall performance. Many types of disk subsystems exist. A knowledge of disk subsystem features helps you to choose the correct disk to improve a server's performance.

The user sees a logical view of the server disk. This logical view must be consistent with the workstation operating system used by the client. For example, a user of a Macintosh station sees the remote file system by using the FINDER interface, and a user of a DOS workstation sees the file system as a number of remote drives designated by letters, such as F, G, H, and so on.

Disk Subsystems

Disk systems are internal or external. The computer's chassis houses the internal disk; you can access internal disks only by removing the chassis, which usually involves powering down the computer. External disk systems exist outside the computer. A host bus adapter in the computer acts as a bus interface for the external disk. External disks are more convenient for the network administrator because you do not have to turn off the computer to access an external disk.

A good disk subsystem for a server has the following characteristics:

- Large capacity
- High-data, throughput-fast disks and system bus
- Low cost
- Capability to withstand long periods of use
- Reliability

Choose a disk subsystem based on how well it satisfies the preceding criteria.

Because the server is a repository for programs and data shared by many network users, it should have as large a disk system as is practical based on drive cost and drive support. A fast disk system improves server performance as long as other factors, such as LAN speed and server system bus, are not bottlenecks. The type of system bus must be considered carefully if fast disk performance is required because the data has to travel through the system bus. AT-style buses currently handle 4 Mbps to 8 Mbps data rates. These data rates can become bottlenecks for disk subsystems that transfer at higher data rates—ESDI and SCSI drives. Faster disks are better suited for the EISA—Enhanced Industry Standards Architecture-Micro Channel buses.

Because the disk acts as a repository for applications and data, reliability is one of the most important criterion of the servers disk subsystem. If the disk subsystem fails, the network may be unusable. Loss of critical data on the server can result in loss of revenue for an organization. To avoid this, proper backups must be made.

Table 24.1 shows the results of a study done by the Yankee Group concerning the cost of system down time for over 250 U.S. corporations. From this you can see that disk subsystems must be very reliable to keep network down-time costs low. For this very reason, Novell has defined its *System Fault Tolerant* (SFT) architecture. SFT Level II—discussed in Chapter 6, "Features of NetWare 2.2, 3.11, and 3.12"—enables a secondary disk to act as a backup to the primary disk for all operations. If the primary disk fails, the secondary disk can be used without any loss in network downtime.

Table 24.1
Cost of System Downtime

Cost per Hour	Percentage of U.S. Corporations
$1,000	42 %
$10,000	26 %
$50,000	5 %
$50,000	4 %
Unknown	23 %

The common disk subsystems for microcomputers are ISA, IDE, SCSI, and ESDI.

Be sure that you purchase the disk controller and adapter from the same source or vendor. If you try to mix and match disk controllers and drives, you may not get optimum performance.

Data Encoding Techniques

Some disk controllers use special encoding techniques to place more data per disk track. These disk controllers work with specially designed disks that have the capability to retain high-density data. If you use these controllers with a disk that is not designed for high-density encoding, you can lose data. An understanding of data encoding techniques helps you recognize these problems.

A disk is composed of platters that have magnetic surfaces divided into tracks. The tracks are divided into sectors, which are further subdivided into bytes of information. Sectors are preceded by sector IDs set during the low-level format of a disk. High-level formats deal with the logical organization of the disk sectors.

Disk drives encode the data on magnetic media inside the tracks on each disk platter. The type of magnetic media can be oxide, plated, or sputtered. The bit information is stored in terms of magnetic charges on the disk. The disks rotate at speeds of 3600 to 7200 revolutions per minute (RPM). As the disk rotates, the disk controller electronically positions the heads—one per surface—to the correct track so that sectors can be read or written. As the track spins under the disk head, the magnetic media is read as a series of digital pulses. These pulses are decoded as a binary digit of 1 or 0. An encoding scheme represents data on the disk.

Table 24.2 shows an encoding scheme used for *Modified Frequency Modulation* (MFM) drives. In this scheme, every bit of information is represented as two half-bits on the disk. A half-bit is defined as a *silence* (no magnetic charge) or a *pulse* (magnetic charge). To represent a data bit of 1, the half-bits are defined as a silence followed by a pulse. To represent a 0, two half-bit combinations are used: if the previous half-bit was a pulse, two half-bits of silence are used; if the previous half-bit was a silence, the half-bits are a pulse followed by a silence.

Table 24.2
MFM or RLL 1,3 Encoding

Data	Half-Bit Encoding
0	1 0 (if previous half-bit is 0)
	0 0 (if previous half-bit is 1)
1	0 1

Table 24.3 shows the half bit encodings for any two consecutive data bits. With two data bits, only four combinations exist: 00, 01, 10, and 11. From this table you see that the minimum number of silence bits is 1, and the maximum number of silence bits is 3. This type of encoding is called *Run Length Limited* (RLL) *1,3.* MFM uses RLL 1,3 encoding. Drives in IBM-XTs and earlier IBM-ATs are MFM drives. ESDI drives use RLL 2,7 or RLL 3,9 and can pack more bits of information. Because the sector size is usually 512 bytes, more sectors can be used per track.

Table 24.3
RLL 1,3 Half-Bit Patterns

Data Pattern	Half-Bit Encoding
0 0	0: 1 0 1 0 (previous bit 0)
	1: 0 0 1 0 (previous bit 1)
0 1	0: 1 0 0 1 (previous bit 0)
	1: 0 0 0 1 (previous bit 1)
1 0	0: 0 1 0 0 (previous bit 0)
	1: 0 1 0 0 (previous bit 1)
1 1	0: 0 1 0 1 (previous bit 0)
	1: 0 1 0 1 (previous bit 1)

Table 24.4 shows the encoding for a RLL 2,7 drive. With this type of encoding, drives can pack 26 sectors per track. Twenty-five sectors are used for data, and the remaining sector can be used to remap a bad sector on the track. This technique—called *sector sparing*—accepts up to 25 × 512 = 12,800 bytes per sector, which is nearly double that of MFM drives that have 17 sectors per track. Another technique—*track sparing*—marks the entire track as bad, but this results in an inefficient utilization of disk space.

Table 24.4
RLL 2,7 Encoding

Data Pattern	Half-Bit Encoding
0 0	1 0 0 0
0 1	0 1 0 0
1 0 0	0 0 1 0 0 0
1 0 1	1 0 0 1 0 0
1 1 1	0 0 0 1 0 0
1 1 0 0	0 0 0 0 1 0 0 0
1 1 0 1	0 0 1 0 0 1 0 0

ST-506/412 Disk Subsystems

ST-506/412 disk subsystems are the most common disks found in microcomputers. Shugart Technologies, which later changed its name to Seagate Technologies, originally developed this interface standard.

The disk controller for ST-506 supports two disks. A 34-pin ribbon cable carries control signals that connect to the hard disks, and a 20-pin ribbon cable carries data. Up to two disks can be daisy-chained—that is, connected in a series—on the same control cable.

Some controllers employ a 34-pin cable with a twist in the middle that causes wires 24 and 29 to be "twisted." This twist enables both hard drives to be jumpered to identical settings. The twist makes one drive appear to be drive 0 (the first drive), and the other drive appear to be drive 1 (the second drive) despite the identical jumper settings.

5T-506 disk controllers typically use MFM encoding to store data.

IDE Disk Subsystems

In the 5T-506 disk interface, the controller electronics are on a separate adapter installed in an expansion bus slot. Disk manufacturers have come up with a scheme to integrate the disk controller electronics in the system board. Cables from the system board connect to disks. IDE stands for Intelligent Device Electronics or Integrated Device Electronics.

IDE drives are faster than 5T-506 drives, but appear to NetWare to be ST506 drives. Both usually use the same NetWare drivers as the ISADISK.DSK driver program.

ESDI Disk Subsystems

Maxtor developed the *Enhanced Small Devices Interface* (ESDI) in 1983, and a number of disk drive manufacturers have adopted it since then. The I/O interface used for many minicomputer environments is the foundation of the ESDI.

ESDI drives use 2,7 or 3,9 RLL encoding that enables them to compress more sectors per track. The number of sectors per track can be 26, 53, or a higher number. Because ESDI drives can use different RLL encodings, make sure that you buy a matched disk controller and disk—that is, buy them from the same source.

Many ESDI controllers implement track buffering. When a request for a single sector is made, the entire track is read and cached in fast RAM on the disk controller. This is done in anticipation of subsequent sector requests from the same track. ESDI track buffering works only for read operations, not write operations.

Track buffering does not replace NetWare's file caching mechanism, but complements it. NetWare's file caching mechanism provides cache buffering for both read and write operations, which improves the file system's overall performance.

SCSI Disk Subsystems

The *Small Computer Systems Interface* (SCSI), pronounced "Scuzzy," is a *bus interface* for peripheral devices. SCSI enables devices such as disk drives and tape drives to be connected to an external I/O bus. Developed by Adaptec, SCSI became an *American National Standards Institute* (ANSI) standard in 1982. Apple's Macintosh PLUS and later models made the SCSI popular. These machines are equipped with a SCSI port that enables you to plug in disk drives and tape units externally.

Because the SCSI is a bus interface, I/O devices are connected serially—or daisy-chained—to the bus. Up to eight such devices can be connected to the bus. Some SCSI products integrate the device controller with the SCSI adapter; others integrate the device controller and the SCSI adapter on the drive itself. The latter solution is called an embedded SCSI disk drive. Although these solutions reduce the cost of the product, they impose a limit on the number of devices that can be connected to the SCSI adapter.

The SCSI architecture is based on the block-multiplexor I/O channel interface of IBM mainframes and can transfer data at rates up to 32 Mbps.

Logical View of Disk Subsystem

The NetWare NOS presents a logical view of the server's disk. A NetWare client sees the server's disk as being organized into volumes, directories, and files. Internally, NetWare manages the disk as a sequence of disk blocks of fixed size. This block size is 4 KB for NetWare 2.*x* and is available for NetWare 3.*x* and 4.*x* at installation time with values of 4 KB, 8 KB, 16 KB, 32 KB and 64 KB. Because NetWare manages the disk as a sequence of blocks, NetWare remains independent of the physical disk structure, such as number of sectors per track, number of cylinders, and number of disk platters (surface area).

To use the server's disk, unused drive letters (usually F to Z) are assigned to directories on the server. After this logical association is made, you can treat the server directories as extensions to the local disk subsystem. Access to the server's remote file system can be made with the workstation operating system commands by using a network drive letter.

Volumes

A server's disk is organized into *volumes*. Volumes are a logical division of the space available on a server's disk.

In NetWare 2.*x*, a volume has a maximum size of 254 MB. If a disk is smaller than or equal to 254 MB, a volume can span the entire disk. This is the preferred way to make volume assignments for the NetWare 2.*x*—that is, whenever possible a volume spans an entire disk.

If the disk is larger than 254 MB, it must be divided into volumes no larger than 254 MB. Figure 24.1 shows a NetWare 2.*x* disk with a capacity of 680 MB. It is divided into three volumes: two volumes of 254 MB, and one volume of 172 MB. The 254 MB volume size limitation also limits the maximum file size to 254 MB because a file cannot exceed volume size. For applications that use very large files, this can be a serious limitation.

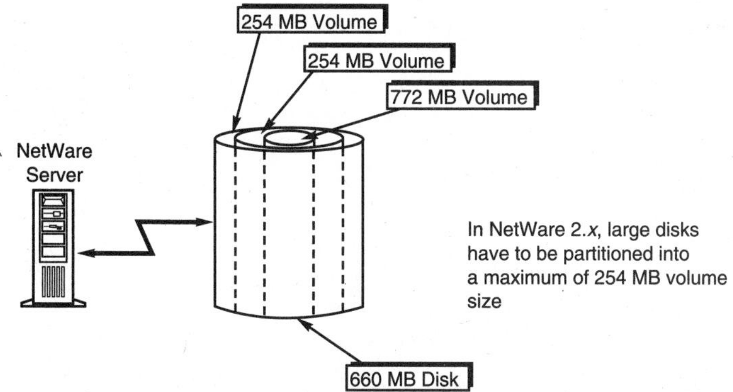

Figure 24.1
NetWare 2.x partitioning of large disk.

In NetWare 3.*x* and 4.*x*, a server supports 64 volumes that have a maximum size of 32 TB. Because this is greater than the size of disks available today, you do not need to partition a large disk into logical volumes in NetWare 3.*x*. In the example in figure 24.1, the entire 680 MB disk can be assigned to a single volume.

In NetWare 3.*x*, a logical volume can span several server disks, which is called *volume spanning*. A volume consists of up to 32 volume segments. Each volume segment can be a disk partition or an entire disk. The volume segments are defined by using the Disk Options in the INSTALL NLM.

To perform volume spanning, you must follow these steps:

1. After you load INSTALL.NLM, select the following choices:

   Installation Options

   Volume Options

2. After a list of volumes appears, press Ins to add a new volume. If you have more than one hard disk that potentially can be used for volume spanning, a list of these partitions appears.

3. From the Free Space Available for Volume Segments list, select the disk to be used as a volume segment.

4. In the New Volume Information menu, enter the Volume Name, Volume Block Size, and Initial Segment Size fields.

   The Initial Segment Size field holds the total number of blocks available for that volume segment. If you want to use a smaller value, you can compute the new block size by using the formula:

   Disk blocks = (Amount of space to be allocated in MB × 1024) / Block size in KB

   If you want to use only 25 MB for a volume configured with 4 KB blocks, the number of disk blocks for Initial Segment Size is:

   Disk blocks = 25 × 1024 / 4 = 6400 blocks

   The block size must be the same for all volume segments.

5. Press Esc, and save the volume definition.

The *Volume Definition Table* stores the details of volume name, size, and segments. Every volume contains a Volume Definition Table in its partition.

Volume spanning enables applications to have large files that cannot fit on a single disk. Another advantage is that multiple simultaneous I/O operations can be done on the volume in *parallel* because the volume now has a number of separate disks and disk controllers that provide concurrent access to it. This also means that requests to access a volume do not have to be queued up as long as they refer to an area of the volume on a separate disk, because the requests can be processed by the separate disk controllers and drives.

The disadvantage to volume spanning is that if any of the disks comprising a volume fails, the entire volume fails. Novell recommends that you use SFT Level II to avoid this problem, but this approach can be expensive when very large disks are involved.

The first volume in a NetWare server always is named SYS:. This volume holds the NetWare NOS and its program and data files. Other volumes can have names consisting of from two to 15 characters. Try to keep volume names simple and easy to remember. For instance, the first volume after SYS: can be labeled VOL1:, the next one VOL2:, and so on.

Volumes hold data in blocks that have a size of 4 KB. In NetWare 2.*x* the block size is fixed to 4 KB, but in NetWare 3.*x* and 4.*x* you can select larger block sizes, such as 8 KB, 16 KB, 32 KB, or 64 KB.

Larger block sizes provide more efficient file access for large files because fewer blocks must be accessed for a given file. Larger disk blocks also require fewer entries in the *File Allocation Tables* (FATs) and, therefore, less RAM to keep track of them. Smaller size disk blocks use more RAM for their FAT tables.

If you have a volume intended for large database files, you can configure it for larger block sizes to provide more efficient file access. If you have a large number of small files on a volume, larger block sizes waste space because the last block is on the average only half full. After you select a block size, you cannot change it without destroying the data on the disk. You must be careful, therefore, if you select a nondefault block size when you install NetWare 3.*x*. NetWare 4.*x* minimizes wastage of block space by using a feature called data suballocation (see Chapter 12, "Installing NetWare 4.*x*").

Directories and Files

A volume can be further divided into directories and files. NetWare supports a hierarchical file structure. Figure 24.2 illustrates the hierarchy of dividing a volume into directories and files. For DOS workstations, the files and directories follow the 8.3 naming rule—that is, 8 characters, a period, and a 3-character extension.

To specify a file on a particular server, the full path name of the file is used. Use the following syntax:

```
[serverName/]volName:dir1{/dir2}/fileName
```

The directory separator delimiter character is / or \. The following are examples of NetWare path names:

```
KSS/SYS:PUBLIC/SCRIPTS/STUDENTS.SCR
SYS:APPS\README.DOC
VOL1:BRIGHT/DOC\MANUAL.DOC
```

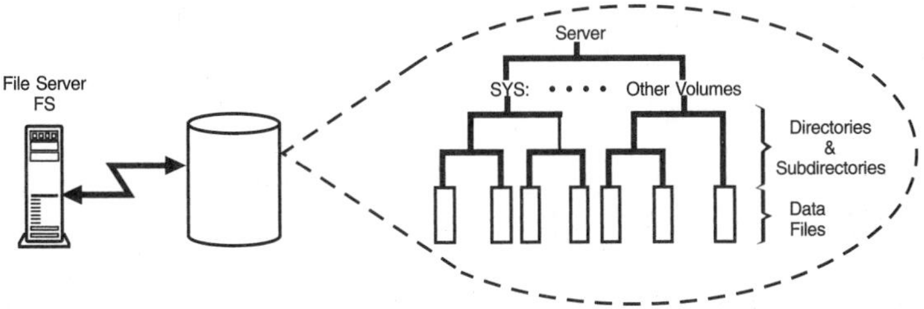

Figure 24.2
Logical organization of NetWare server file system.

In the first example, the path name includes the name of the server KSS. The server name is separated from the rest of the path name by either the / or \ character. This example uses /. The volume name is SYS:. The first directory is PUBLIC, and the subdirectory name is SCRIPTS. The file name is STUDENTS.SCR.

In example two, the optional server name is left out. This implies that the name of the default server is used. The directory APPS that contains the file README.DOC is under the volume name SYS:.

In example three, the optional server name is left out. The volume name is VOL1:. The directory name is BRIGHT. BRIGHT has a subdirectory named DOC, which contains the file MANUAL.DOC. In example 3, both / and \ are used as directory separators. As a matter of style, one or the other character should be used consistently.

Using Volume Object Names (NetWare 4.*x* Only)

In NetWare 4.*x* a Volume Object Name is created at the time of creating the physical volume name during server installation (see fig 24.3). Every physical volume name has an NDS object name counterpart. The Volume Object Name for a physical volume is its NDS object name. The Volume Object is placed in the same context as the file server object, and its name is derived from the file server using the following rule: *The default volume object name is a concatenation of the file server object name, the underscore character (_), and the physical object name.*

Therefore for a volume that has the physical name *PhysicalVolumeName,* that is attached to the server whose name is *ServerName,* the volume object name is ServerName_PhysicalVolumeName.

Examples of the application of this rule are shown next:

Physical Volume Name	Server Name	Volume Object Name
SYS:	FS1	FS1_SYS
VOL1:	LTREE1	LTREE1_SYS
CORP_VOL:	FS_CORP	FS_CORP_CORP_VOL
APP$ENG!VOL	KSS_FS	KSS_FS_APP$ENG!VOL

The volume object contains properties such as the *Host Server Name* and the *Physical Volume Name* that refer to the server object and its physical name. Though the volume objects are created in the context in which the file server object is placed, they can be moved to a different context. However, it is advisable to keep the volume objects in their default context (same as server context), since it is most likely to be used by user objects defined in this context, and to avoid confusion about the location of volume objects.

Since volume object names refer to the volume object in the NDS tree, you can use the NDS syntax to refer to its name. To refer to the volume object name FS1_SYS in the context OU=CORP.O=SCS, you can use any of the following:

```
.CN=FS1_SYS.OU=CORP.O=SCS
.FS1_SYS.CORP.SCS
FS1_SYS                  (if current context is OU=CORP.O=SCS)
```

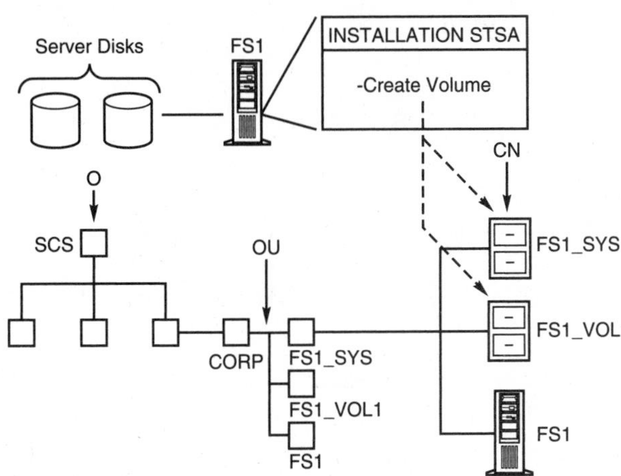

Figure 24.3
Volume Object Naming.

Using NDS Syntax to Access NetWare 4.*x* Files

You can refer to a file on a NetWare 4.*x* server using the NetWare 3.*x* file naming syntax. In this case, bindery emulation is used to resolve the file name. In the NetWare 3.*x* syntax, the full path name of the file consists of:

```
[serverName/]volName:dir1{/dir2}/fileName
```

Because a NetWare 4.*x* volume is a leaf object in the NDS tree, the directories' and files' path names can use the NDS syntax to refer to the volume name (see fig. 24.4). This figure shows the path name for subdirectories ENG and CORP that are in the COMMON subdirectory in the volume object FSDEV_SYS. The volume object is in the context OU=CORP.O=LGROUP. If the current context is O=LGROUP, the partial NDS name of

```
FSDEV_SYS.CORP.LGROUP
```

or

```
CN=FSDEV_SYS.OU=CORP.O=LGROUP
```

can be used to refer to the volume object. To refer to the subdirectory CORP or ENG, the volume object name must be prefixed with the file directory path COMMON/CORP or COMMON/ENG. The volume object name and the directory path are separated by the colon (:) delimiter. Therefore, the CORP and ENG directories can be referred to by the following syntax, if current context is O=LGROUP

```
FSDEV_SYS.CORP.LGROUP:COMMON/CORP
CN=FSDEV_SYS.OU=CORP.O=LGROUP:COMMON/ENG
```

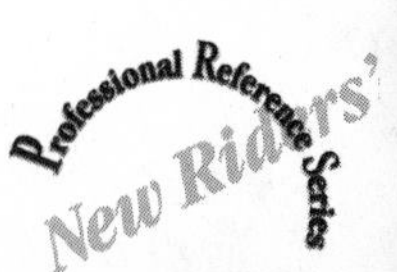

If the current context is OU=CORP.O=LGROUP, the partial NDS name of

```
FSDEV_SYS
```

or

```
CN=FSDEV_SYS
```

can be used to refer to the volume object. To refer to the subdirectory CORP or ENG, the volume object name must be prefixed with the file directory path COMMON/CORP or COMMON/ENG. Therefore, the CORP and ENG directories can be referred to by the following syntax, if current context is OU=CORP.O=LGROUP

```
FSDEV_SYS:COMMON\CORP
CN=FSDEV_SYS:COMMON/ENG
```

Notice that either the backslash (\) or forward slash (/) characters can be used to separate file directory names.

Instead of using partial names for the volume object, as in the previous examples, you can also use complete names. Examples of complete name syntax for referring to the file directory are shown here. Notice, that complete names must have a leading period (.)

```
.FSDEV_SYS.CORP.LGROUP:COMMON/CORP
.CN=FSDEV_SYS.OU=CORP.O=LGROUP:COMMON/ENG
```

The first example uses typeless complete names for the volume object, and the second example uses complete names with attribute type designators (CN, OU, O).

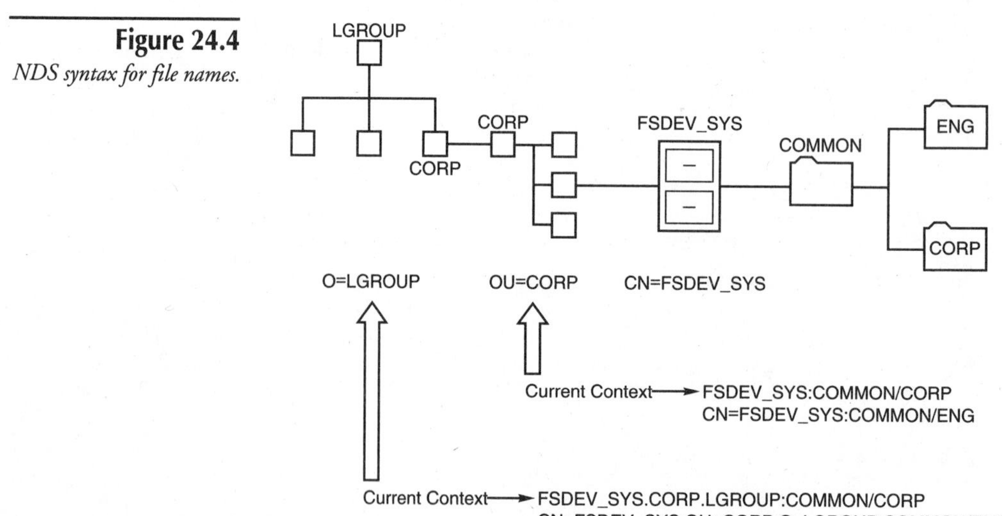

Figure 24.4
NDS syntax for file names.

What is often confusing to beginners about the syntax examples in figure 24.4, is that the normal convention of naming files is to start from the top of the file directory tree, and enumerate the directories separated by the delimiters backslash (\) or forward slash (/), all the way down to the file or directory. The NDS naming convention, on the other hand is the complete opposite. In NDS naming, you start with the *bottom* of the tree, and list the object names separated by the delimiter period (.) all the way up to the [Root] object. The [Root] object is not listed, because a NDS tree can have only one root.

When you name file directories using the NDS syntax, you are combining the NDS and File naming conventions. Figure 24.5 shows graphically that these two conventions can be thought of as going up the *hill* to list the NDS path name. At the peak, you list the colon (:) separator. The colon character is listed at the *peak* of the hill, and marks the switch-over to the file naming convention. The file naming convention lists the file directories starting with the root directory and goes *down* the hill to the file or directory.

In summary, when combining NDS syntax for volume names with NetWare file system directory syntax remember that

Path names in NDS syntax are listed from bottom to top

Path names in NetWare file system are listed from top to bottom

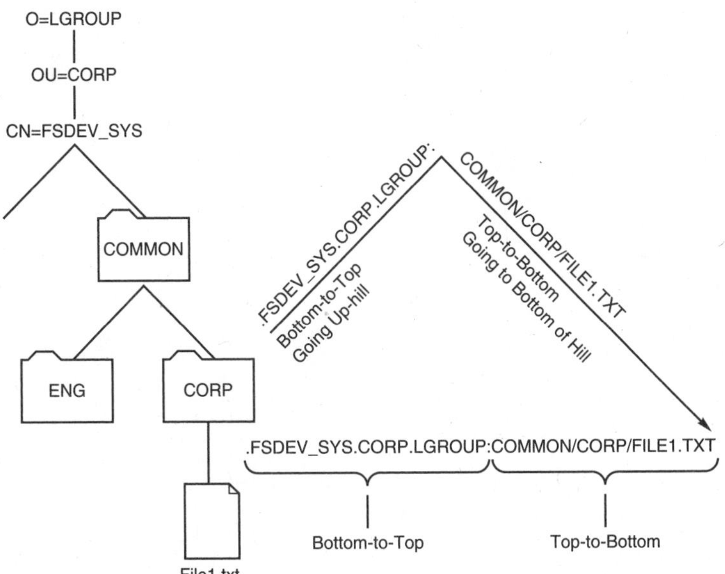

Figure 24.5
Combining NDS syntax and file naming syntax.

Drive Mappings

To use the NetWare server's file system, the user assigns an network drive to a directory on the server. The process of assigning a workstation drive letter to a server directory is called *mapping a network drive.* Figure 24.6 shows the available drive letters. Driver letters from A to E usually are reserved for local drives because the default LASTDRIVE parameter for CONFIG.SYS is drive E. Drives F to Z are used for network drives.

Figure 24.7 shows drive mappings to the file system on the server. Use the MAP command to set up the drive mappings. The syntax of the MAP command is as follows:

```
MAP [INS ¦ DEL ¦ ROOT] driveName: [ = networkDirectory]
```

24

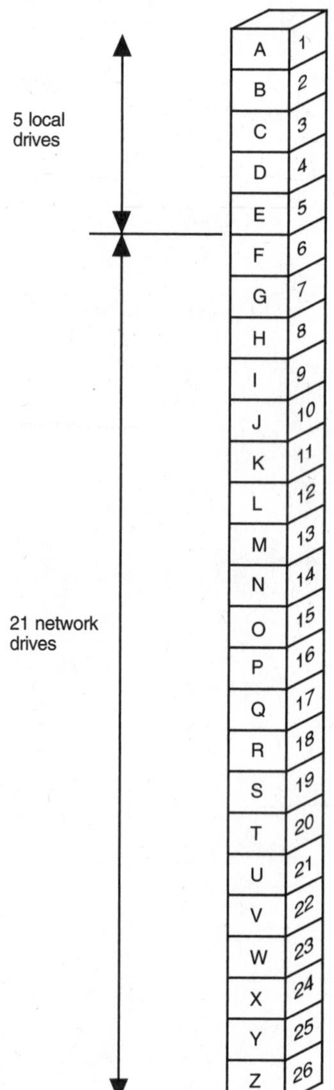

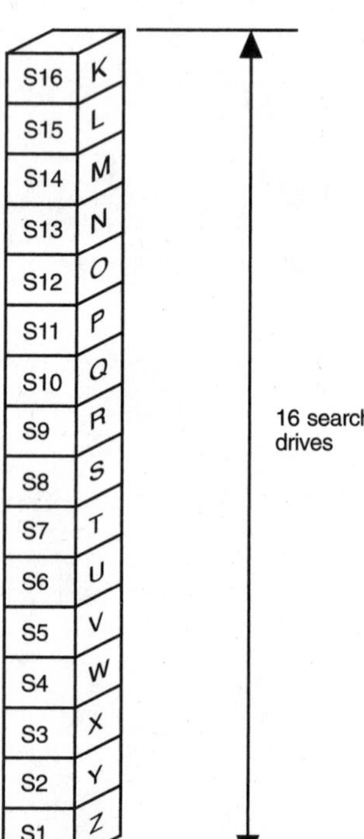

Figure 24.6
Search drives. (Graphic courtesy of Learning Group International)

DriveName is a drive letter or a search drive (see next section). The [= *networkDirectory*] means that the assigned network directory is optional if the DEL option is used.

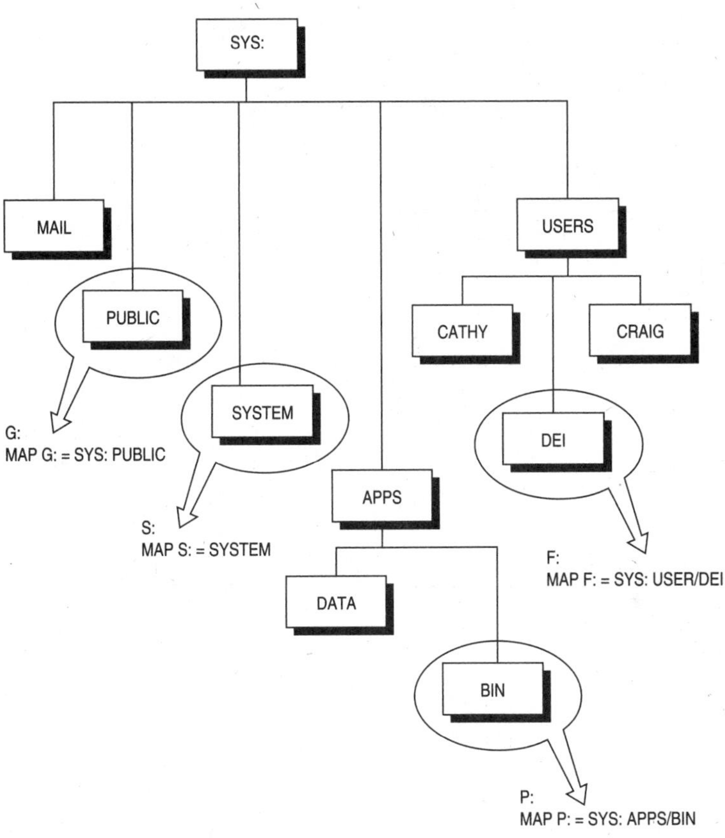

Figure 24.7
Drive mappings to server's file system.

Examples of how to use the MAP command are as follows:

```
MAP F: = SYS:PUBLIC
MAP ROOT G: = KSS/VOL1:DEVELOP/BIN
MAP DEL F:
```

Example one maps drive F to SYS:PUBLIC on the default server.

Example two maps drive G to VOL1:DEVELOP/BIN on server KSS. In addition, G is *rooted* (ROOT) to the network directory KSS/VOL1:DEVELOP/BIN. When a drive is rooted to a network directory, the network directory acts as the root of the file system. Because the root directory is the top-level directory, you cannot go up the directory by using the following DOS command:

```
CD ..
```

This fake root protects the security of the network directory. You also can use the fake root to install single-user applications on the NetWare server. Some single-user applications are installed in the root directory. If these applications are installed on the server, they can clutter up the root directory on the server volume. A fake root enables you to install a single-user application in a subdirectory on the server.

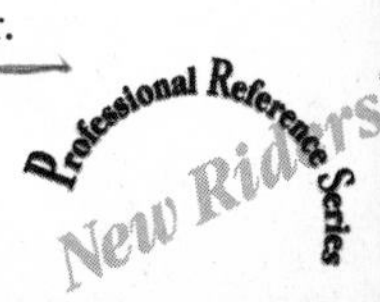

To legally install a single-user application on the server, you must have a license for every user of the application on the network.

Example three deletes (DEL) the drive mapping for F. If you delete a drive mapping, the [= *networkDirectory*] is omitted.

You cannot map to a network directory unless you have access rights to that directory. If you attempt to map to a network directory for which you do not have access rights, the error message `DIRECTORY XXX NOT LOCATABLE` appears.

In NetWare the CD command alters the drive mapping, so you should use it with care. Consider what would happen if you used the following command from the local C: drive prompt:

```
C:\> CD SYS:COMMON\DATA
```

This would map your C: drive to SYS:COMMON\DATA. You would then lose access to your C: drive. You can regain access to the local drive C: by typing:

```
MAP DEL C:
```

The MAP NEXT or MAP N command assigns the next available drive as a network drive. Consider the following example, in which only on network drive F: has been assigned:

```
MAP  F: = SYS:USERS\JOHN
```

Then, using the following MAP NEXT commands

```
MAP NEXT SYS:USERS\JOHN\DATA
MAP N       SYS:DATA
MAP NEXT FS1/VOL1:DATA
```

assigns network drive G to SYS:USERS\JOHN\DATA, network drive H: to SYS:DATA and network drive I: to FS1/VOL1:DATA. The second form of the MAP command shows that the letter "N" is an abbreviation for option "NEXT."

When the MAP NEXT command executes, it reports the network drive that has been assigned. Therefore, MAP NEXT is a convenient way to provide network drive mappings, using a simpler syntax, when it does not matter which network drive is assigned, as long as it is not a network drive that is already in use.

NetWare 4.*x* provides for a NP option in the MAP command. The MAP NP option allows a local or search drive mapping to be overridden without prompting the user. Its general syntax is

```
MAP NP  [Option] Drive: = DirectoryPath
```

Thus, to override the local drive mapping D:, you can use

```
MAP NP C: = SYS:USERS/KSS/BIN
```

To override a search drive mapping for search drive S3:, that may already exist, use:

```
MAP NP S3: = SYS:USERS/DORSH/BIN
```

The MAP CHANGE option can be used in NetWare 4.*x* to toggle between a search drive and a network drive.

Consider a network administrator who has just installed an application in a network drive J: that is mapped to NW4CS_SYS:APPS\WP. The network administrator now wants to test the application by placing it in the search drive. In that case, the administrator can issue the command.

```
MAP CHANGE J:
```

or the abbreviated form

```
MAP C J:
```


If the next available search drive is S10:, you should see the following displayed as a result of executing any of the previous MAP CHANGE commands:

```
c1
S10: = J:.  [NW4CS_SYS: \]
```

If you wish to remove the search drive and make it a regular drive, you can use the MAP CHANGE to toggle back to the network drive:

```
MAP C S5:
```

Throughout the preceding operations, the drive J: is still mapped to SYS:APPS\WP. Even when J: is mapped as a search drive, the association between J: and SYS:APPA\WP is maintained.

Search Drives

In DOS, the PATH command specifies the order that directories are searched if a program file is not found in the current directory. The directories specified in the PATH command are stored in a DOS environment variable of the same name (PATH).

You cannot include NetWare directories as part of the DOS PATH command by using the NetWare syntax for a directory. For example, a DOS station has the following setting for the PATH environment variable before logging into a NetWare server:

```
PATH=C:\WP51;C:\BIN;C:\BC\BIN;C:\WC386\BIN
```

To add the NetWare directory SYS:PUBLIC\UTIL to the beginning of the search path, you might be tempted to try the following DOS PATH command:

```
PATH=SYS:PUBLIC\UTIL;C:\WP51;C:\BIN;C:\BC\BIN;C:\WC386\BIN
```

This DOS PATH command does not work. DOS cannot process the NetWare syntax SYS:PUBLIC\UTIL in the PATH environment variable because DOS only recognizes a one-letter drive in this location. To solve this problem, NetWare uses *search drives* to specify network directories as part of the search path.

Figure 24.3 shows search drives. Sixteen search drives exist, and they are labeled SEARCH1 to SEARCH16. You can abbreviate SEARCH by using S. The first search drive, therefore, is abbreviated as

S1, and the sixteenth search drive is abbreviated as S16. Use the MAP command to make search drive assignments. Search drives specify the order that directories, including network directories, are searched. This is similar to the way the DOS PATH command operates, except that search drives enable you to work with network directories.

In the preceding example, therefore, if you want to include the network directory SYS:PUBLIC\UTIL as part of the search path, you can use the following MAP commands:

```
MAP S1:=SYS:PUBLIC\UTIL
```

or

```
MAP INS S1:=SYS:PUBLIC\UTIL
```


The first MAP command maps search drive 1 (S1) to the network directory SYS:PUBLIC\UTIL, and this directory is searched first. The second MAP command inserts (INS) SYS:PUBLIC/UTIL as the first search drive. If the first search drive was assigned previously, the INS option pushes it down the list to become the second search drive. Figure 24.8 illustrates this "push-down" effect. This figure shows the search drives before and after the user issues the MAP INS command.

Figure 24.8
The push-down effect of the MAP INS command.

Search Drive	Single Drive Letter Assignment	Search Directory
S1	Z:	SYS:PUBLIC
S2	Y:	SYS:SYSTEM

→

Search Drive	Single Drive Letter Assignment	Search Directory
S1	Z:	SYS:PUBLIC/UTIL
S2	Y:	SYS:PUBLIC
S3	X:	SYS:SYSTEM

MAP INS S1: = SYS : PUBLIC/UTIL

When the user issues the **MAP S1:=SYS:PUBLIC\UTIL** command to map search drive 1, the DOS PATH environment variable changes also. It assigns an unused drive letter starting with Z to the network directory, and inserts Z in the DOS PATH environment variable. Therefore, the DOS PATH environment variable before the MAP S1:=SYS:PUBLIC/UTIL command looks like this:

```
PATH=C:\WP51;C:\BIN;C:\BC\BIN;C:\WC386\BIN
```

After using the MAP command, the DOS PATH environment variable looks like this:

```
PATH=Z:.;C:\WP51;C:\BIN;C:\BC\BIN;C:\WC386\BIN
```

DOS recognizes the single letter Z as another directory letter, and it searches drive Z as it does any local drive. The period (.) stands for the current directory, and when used in the PATH environment variable, it indicates that the current directory Z, mapped to SYS:PUBLIC\UTIL, is to be searched.

NetWare assigns search drive letters beginning with Z and moving backward through the alphabet to K. Figure 24.6 illustrates this—search drive 1 uses Z, and search drive 16 uses K. Letter assignments for applications usually begin with F: and move through J. The reverse order of letter assignment for search drives minimizes conflicts between the applications and search drives. Applications drive letters are assigned safely up to drive J. If applications use drives beyond J, you will have a conflict when you reach the maximum of 16 search drives because search drive 16 also uses K. This situation is not uncommon in complex NetWare user environments, and the network manager may wish that the English alphabet had more than 26 letters or that DOS used a different scheme.

Search drive mappings affect the user's current session only. When a user issues a MAP command to map to a network directory, the mapping is only for the user who issues the command. Other users on the network are not affected by this drive mapping. The shell holds the drive mappings only for a session. When the user logs out of a server by using the LOGOUT command, the drive mappings disappear from the drive map table. To make the drive mappings permanent, the user must automate the execution of the MAP commands. One way to do this is with a login script. MAP commands used to build a network search path can be placed in a login script file. A *login script* defines a user's network environment and is the equivalent of the DOS AUTOEXEC.BAT file. Login scripts are discussed in detail in Chapter 23, "Managing User Sessions."

If an attempt is made to map a search drive that does not exist, the next logical search drive is assigned as a search drive. Consider the following example in which a NetWare session has three search drive mappings as shown:

```
MAP INS S1:=SYS:PUBLIC
MAP INS S2:=SYS:PUBLIC\BIN
MAP INS S3:=SYS:APPS\BIN
```

If an attempt is made to perform the following mapping:

```
MAP INS S16:=SYS:APPS\DB
```

the next search drive mapping that is assigned is S4: and *not* S16:. This is because search drive S16: does not exist, and the next available search drive is S4:. Search drive S16: is typically used for this purpose, since it is the last search drive. Any other search drive that is not used will exhibit the same behavior, when used in the MAP command. Thus, if the only search drives that exist are described by the MAP commands that follow:

```
MAP INS S1:=SYS:PUBLIC
MAP INS S2:=SYS:PUBLIC\BIN
MAP INS S3:=SYS:APPS\BIN
```

Then, using search drive S6: that does not exist, in the following MAP command:

```
MAP INS S16:=SYS:APPS\WP
```

will map search drive S4: to SYS:APPS\WP.

Since the last possible search drive in NetWare is search drive 16 (S16:), the MAP INS S16 is most commonly used to assign the next search drive letter.

The order of the search drive mappings should include the most frequently used search drives listed first, to minimize unnecessary searches. This is particularly true for network search drives, as searching network search drives generate network traffic. For example, a user needs applications and programs stored in the local drives more often than access to programs on network drives. If the network drives are listed before local drives in the search path, unnecessary traffic will be generated searching for programs in network drives, when the program actually resides in the local drives. In this case, the user should have local search drives listed before network search drives.

Network Drive Assignments

The best way to learn about network drive assignments is to experiment with them. This section gives you hands-on experience with drive mappings.

To follow the exercises listed in this section, you must have access to the user SUPERVISOR account and a non-supervisor user account.

1. Log in as SUPERVISOR or use a valid user account. (See Chapter 10, "Features of NetWare 4," if you are not sure how to log in to a server.)

2. Type:

   MAP

   The MAP command examines the current drive mappings. The response to this command looks like the following output. The details depend on the way your login script is set up.

   ```
   Drive  A:   maps to a local disk.
   Drive  B:   maps to a local disk.
   Drive  C:   maps to a local disk.
   Drive  D:   maps to a local disk.
   Drive  E:   maps to a local disk.
   Drive  F: = S386\SYS:  \
   SEARCH1:  = Z:. [S386\SYS:  \PUBLIC]
   SEARCH2:  = Y:. [S386\SYS:  \PUBLIC\IBM_PC\MSDOS\V3.31]
   ```

3. Issue a MAP command to map drive I to SYS:PUBLIC:

   MAP I:=SYS:PUBLIC

   To verify that your mapping has been successful, type:

   MAP

4. Try to map to a directory that does not exist.

   MAP J:=SYS:DEVELOP

   The `Directory SYS:DEVELOP is not locatable` message appears.

5. Map to a directory for which you do not have access rights. To perform this step you must create a directory called SYS:DEVELOP/BIN using a supervisor account, and then log in as a user that does not have SUPERVISOR rights. Type:

   MAP J:=SYS:DEVELOP/BIN

If you do not have access to this directory, you will get an error message that states that the directory is not locatable.

You also can log in as a supervisor, assign Read and File scan rights of SYS:DEVELOP to the user you are working with, and then map drive H to the directory SYS:DEVELOP while logged in as a non-supervisor user:

```
MAP J:=SYS:DEVELOP/BIN
```

This time the mapping is successful.

6. To delete the drive J mapping, type:

```
MAP DEL J:
```

7. To map drive J to the same directory as I, type:

```
MAP J:=I:
```

Use the MAP command to verify this mapping.

8. You do not need to use the NetWare network directory syntax to specify the volume name to map to a network directory. Try the following:

```
MAP H:=F:\PUBLIC
```

The preceding command maps H to the same volume as F, starting from the root, and going down to the PUBLIC directory.

9. You can experiment with search drives in the next few sections.

To note the current search drives, type:

```
MAP
```

Current drive mappings and search drive mappings similar to the following appear (for a NetWare 3.*x*) server. In NetWare 4.*x*, the output is similar but has a few formatting differences:

```
Drive  A:   maps to a local disk.
Drive  B:   maps to a local disk.
Drive  C:   maps to a local disk.
Drive  D:   maps to a local disk.
Drive  E:   maps to a local disk.
Drive  F: = S386\SYS:  \
Drive  H: = S386\SYS:  \PUBLIC
Drive  I: = S386\SYS:  \PUBLIC
Drive  J: = S386\SYS:  \PUBLIC
--
SEARCH1:  = Z:. [S386\SYS:  \PUBLIC]
SEARCH2:  = Y:. [S386\SYS:  \PUBLIC\IBM_PC\MSDOS\V3.31]
```

In the preceding example, search drive 1 is mapped to S386\SYS:\PUBLIC.

To display the current DOS search path, type:

PATH

The following response appears:

```
PATH=Z:.;Y:.;
```

Notice that the PATH command is consistent with the current search drive mappings.

10. Insert SYS:DEVELOP/BIN as the first search drive. Type:

    MAP INS S1:=SYS:DEVELOP/BIN

    To examine the changed drive mappings, type:

    MAP

    The following response appears:

```
Drive  A:   maps to a local disk.
Drive  B:   maps to a local disk.
Drive  C:   maps to a local disk.
Drive  D:   maps to a local disk.
Drive  E:   maps to a local disk.
Drive  F: = S386\SYS:  \
Drive  H: = S386\SYS:  \PUBLIC
Drive  I: = S386\SYS:  \PUBLIC
Drive  J: = S386\SYS:  \PUBLIC
--
SEARCH1:  = X:. [S386\SYS:  \DEVELOP\BIN]
SEARCH2:  = Z:. [S386\SYS:  \PUBLIC]
SEARCH3:  = Y:. [S386\SYS:  \PUBLIC\IBM_PC\MSDOS\V3.31]
```

    Compare the search drive mappings with those in step 9.

    To examine the DOS PATH environment variable type:

    PATH

    The following results appear:

```
PATH=X:.;Z:.;Y:.;
```

    Compare the DOS PATH environment variable with that in step 9. Notice that the DOS PATH environment variable reflects the changed search drive mappings.

11. Delete the first search drive mapping, by typing:

    MAP DEL S1:

To examine the new search drive mappings and the DOS PATH environment variable, use the commands outlined in step 10. These should have the same values, as in step 9.

12. Try to delete a drive that does not exist by typing:

    MAP DEL S16:

    If the search drive S16 does not exist, an error message appears.

13. Add a search drive at the end.

    You probably have fewer than 16 search drive mappings for your current log-in session. If you do, type the following command:

    MAP INS S16:=SYS:DEVELOP

    To examine the search drive mappings, type:

    MAP

    Notice that you did not create search drive 16, but you did create a search drive with a number one greater than the last search drive. When you want to create a search drive, but do not know the number of the last search drive, use the MAP INS S16: command. This command automatically assigns the next available number to the new search drive.

14. The MAP command also can be applied to a local directory:

    MAP INS S16:=C:\

    To examine the new search drive mappings and the DOS PATH environment variable, use the MAP and PATH commands. Notice that directory C:\ is now in the search drive list and the DOS PATH environment variable.

    If you do not have a hard drive, you can use floppy drive A. If you have a diskless workstation, you cannot perform this part of the exercise.

15. To map drive H to SYS:PUBLIC, type:

    MAP H:=SYS:PUBLIC

    Make H the current drive, and use the DOS change directory command to go one level up to the root SYS:.

    ```
    H:
    CD ..
    ```

    Type the MAP command to find out the current search drive mappings.

    The change directory command changes the drive mapping of Drive H.

16. Repeat step 15 with a fake root MAP command. For instance, to map Drive H to SYS:PUBLIC with a fake root, type:

```
MAP ROOT H:=SYS:PUBLIC
```

Make sure that H is the current drive, and use the DOS change directory command to move up one level to the root SYS:.

```
H:
CD ..
```


Now use the MAP command to find out the current search drive mappings. Unlike step 15, the change directory command does not go above the fake root.

17. If you inadvertently wipe out the DOS PATH environment variable, the search drives also are deleted.

To delete the DOS PATH, type:

```
F:
CD \
SET PATH=
```

Unless your current directory is SYS:PUBLIC, which stores the MAP command, type **MAP**. The following message appears:

```
Bad command or file name
```

To change to the SYS:PUBLIC directory that holds the MAP.EXE (command program file) type:

```
CD \PUBLIC
```

Next, type **MAP**. Note that the search drive mappings also have been wiped out.

Using Directory Map Objects in NetWare 4.*x*

In NetWare 4.*x*, if a volume object is moved to another location in the NDS tree or renamed (see fig. 24.32), all batch files and login scripts that refer to old position of volume would have to be changed. In figure 24.32, the volume object ENG_VOL is moved from the context OU=ENGINEERING.O=ESL to OU=CORP.O=ESL. Prior to moving the object, the drive K: was mapped to the PUBLIC directory of the ENG_VOL, using the NDS path name for the volume object:

```
MAP K: = .ENG_VOL.ENGINEERING.ESL:
```

After the relocation of the volume object name, the previous drive mapping K: will no longer be valid. To map drive K: using the NDS path name, the new drive mapping would be:

```
MAP K: = .ENG_VOL.CORP.ESL:
```

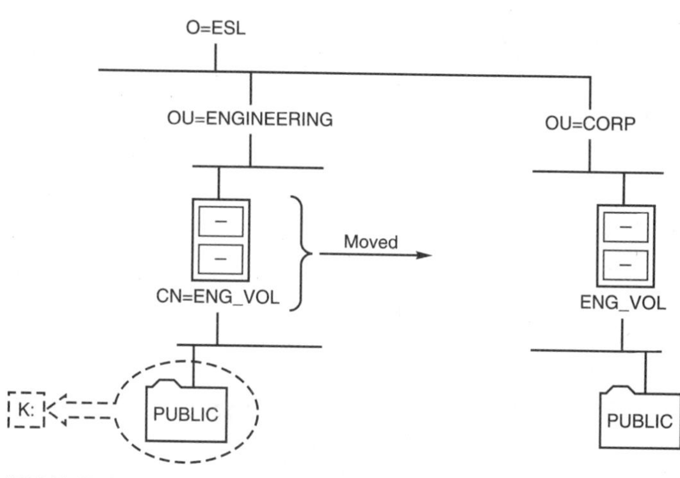

Figure 24.9
Moving a volume object to a different context.

To avoid problems of the kind mentioned previously, there needs to be a way of creating a drive mapping that is independent of the position of the volume object. This can be done using a directory map object.

The *Directory Map Object* can be used to provide *location independent* mapping. This object contains as one of its property, a volume/directory path (see fig. 24.10). Figure 24.11 shows a directory map object in the context OU=ENGINEERING.O=ESL. The directory map object refers to the PUBLIC directory in the ENG_VOL. To map a drive to the PUBLIC directory using the directory map object, use:

```
MAP K: = ENG_PUBLIC
```

If the ENG_VOL volume object is moved to the context, OU=CORP.O=ESL, the volume/directory path property of the directory map object ENG_PUBLIC needs to change, but the mapping to PUBLIC directory does not change.

Figures 24.12 and 24.13 show another example of the use of directory map objects.

Figure 24.12 shows directory mappings to different volume objects. Assume that the current context in the NDS tree is OU=CORP.O=ESL. A drive mapping of I: to the APPS\SS\DATA directory for the volume object FS1_SYS can be written in any of the following forms:

```
MAP I: = .CN=FS1_SYS.OU=CORP.O=ESL:APPS\SS\DATA
```

or

```
MAP I: = .CN=FS1_SYS.OU=CORP.O=ESL:APPS\SS\DATA
```

or

```
MAP I: = SYS:APPS\SS\DATA
```

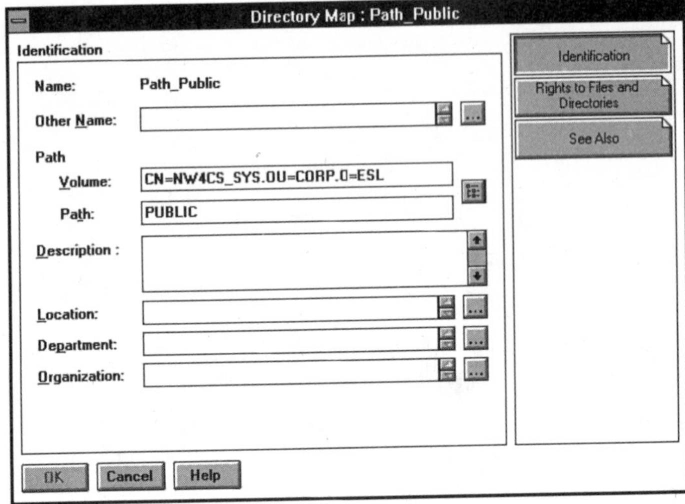

Figure 24.10
Directory Map Object properties.

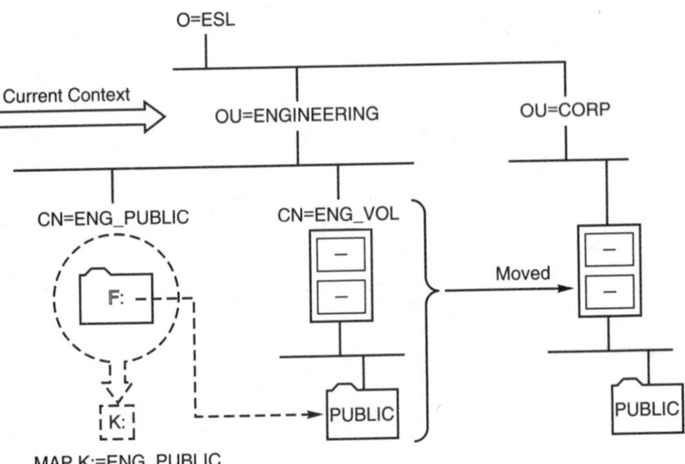

Figure 24.11
Location independent mapping using Directory Map Object.

The first form of the MAP command uses a complete name for the volume object with attribute type designators (CN, OU, O). The second form refers to the partial name of the volume object, and because the volume object is in the current context, the common name of the volume object can be used. The third form uses the physical name of the volume object and can be used if the user initially connects to the file server FS1.

In the tree branch under the container OU=SALES, a drive mapping of J: to the SHARED\DOCS directory for the volume object FS2_VOL can be written in any of the following forms:

```
MAP J: = .FS2_VOL.SALES.ESL:SHARED/DOCS
```

or

```
MAP J: = .CN=FS2_VOL.OU=SALES.O=ESL:SHARED/DOCS
```

or

```
MAP J: = FS2_VOL.SALES.:SHARED/DOCS
```

The first form refers to the typeless complete name of the volume object. The second form of the MAP command uses a complete name for the volume object with attribute type designators (CN, OU, O). The third form uses the partial name of the volume object (relative to the current context OU=CORP.O=ESL).

The mappings shown in figure 24.12 can be simplified using directory map objects as shown in figure 24.13. In figure 24.13, two directory map objects CN=Path_Docs and CN=Path_Data are created. The directory map object CN=Path_Docs contains a mapping to the SHARED\DOC directory for volume object CN=FS2_VOL.OU=SALES.O=ESL, and the directory map object Path_Data contains a mapping to the APPS\SS\DATA directory for volume object CN=FS1_SYS.OU=CORP.O=ESL. The drive mappings of I: and J: in the example in figure 24.35, can now be expressed in terms of the directory map objects.


```
MAP I: = .CN=Path_Data.OU=CORP.O=ESL
```

or

```
MAP I: = .Path_Data.CORP.ESL
```

or

```
MAP I: = Path_Data
```

The first form of the MAP command uses complete name with attribute types (CN, OU, O) for the directory map object. The second form uses a typeless complete name, and the second form uses a partial name for the directory map object. Since the directory map object is in the current context, the common name of the directory map object can be used for the partial name.

The drive mappings for J:, using directory name object are the following:

```
MAP J: = .Path_Docs.CORP.ESL
```

or

```
MAP J: = .CN=Path_Docs.OU=CORP.O=ESL
```

or

```
MAP J: = Path_Docs
```

The first form of the MAP command uses the typeless complete name of the directory map object. The second form of the MAP command uses complete name with attribute types (CN, OU, O) for the directory map object. The third form uses a partial name for the directory map object. Since the directory map object is in the current context, the common name of the directory map object can be used for the partial name.

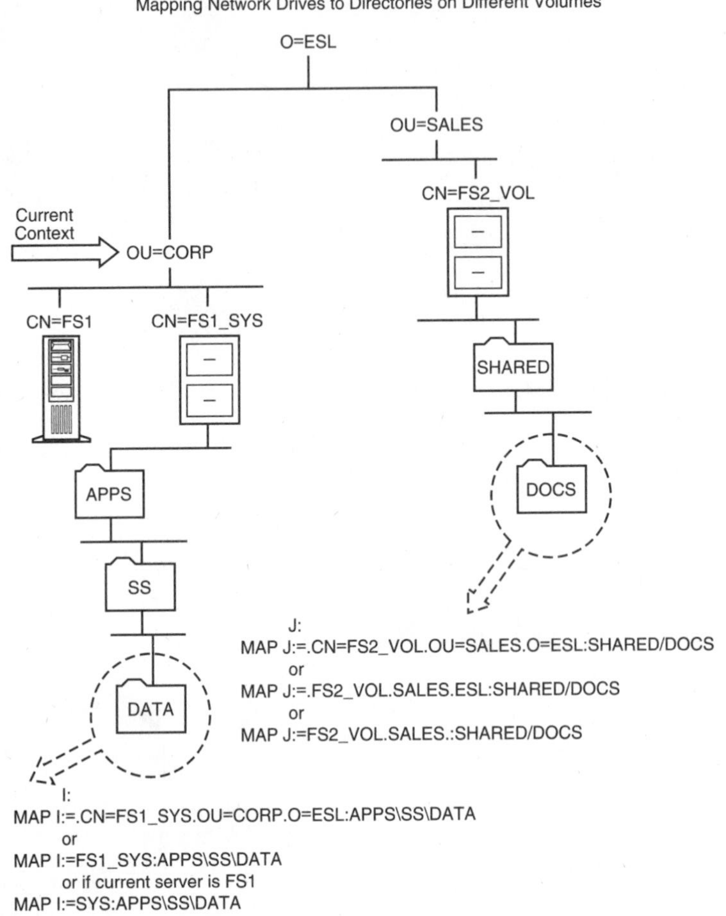

Figure 24.12
Network drive mappings to directories on different volumes.

Alternate Name Space Support

NetWare 3.*x* and 4.*x* support alternate file systems, such as the Macintosh file system. These alternate file systems also are called *alternate name spaces.* Macintosh workstations see the NetWare file systems in terms of folders. A Macintosh file has two components—a *data fork* and a *resource fork.* A data fork holds the data portion of the file and the resource fork contains file attributes, such as the icon used to display the file and access rights to a file. To support the Macintosh file system, NetWare 2.*x* must run the Macintosh VAP, and NetWare 3.*x* must run the Macintosh Name Space NLM (MAC.NAM). When you select a backup utility for a NetWare server that implements the Macintosh name space, make sure that it can back up both data forks and resource forks.

In addition to the Macintosh name space, NetWare 3.*x* and 4.*x* support OS/2 name space, NFS name space and FTAM name space. These name spaces have longer file and directory names (typically 254 characters). If OS/2 uses the FAT file system (a DOS-compatible file system), the OS/2 name space is *not* needed. The OS/2 name space *must* be installed if the *High Performance File System* (HPFS) is used.

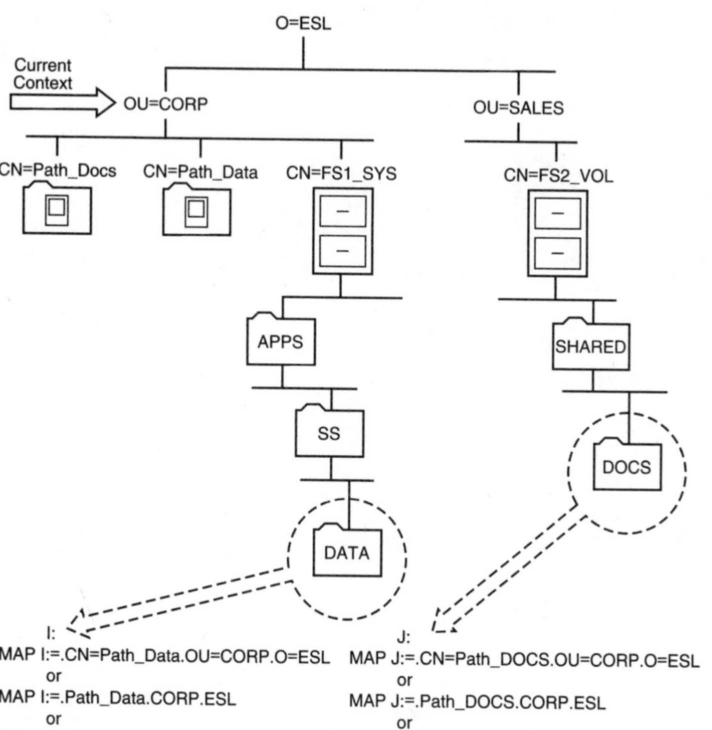

Figure 24.13
Network drive mappings using directory map objects.

To add name space support, load the name space module in the STARTUP.NCF file and use the ADD NAME SPACE command in the AUTOEXEC.NCF file.

For example, to add name space support for a Macintosh file system, perform the following steps:

1. Load the disk driver and add the following line in STARTUP.NCF:

   ```
   LOAD MAC
   ```

2. After you mount the volume to which you want to add the name space, type the following line in AUTOEXEC.NCF:

   ```
   ADD NAME SPACE MACINTOSH TO VOLUME SYS
   ```

   To add name space support for a volume other than SYS, replace SYS with the volume name. To examine current name-space modules use the command:

   ```
   ADD NAME SPACE
   ```

   After you add the Macintosh name space, you must run the MACINST program to complete the Macintosh installation on the file server.

To add name space support for OS/2, NFS, or FTAM, replace MACINTOSH with OS2, NFS, or FTAM.

Organizing a Directory

Upon its installation on the server, NetWare creates a standard directory structure to store its program and system files. To install applications and user's data on the server, you can augment this directory structure. This section examines how the standard directory structure can be augmented.

Default Directory Organization

During installation, NetWare creates a standard directory structure shown in figure 24.14. The SYSTEM, PUBLIC, LOGIN, and MAIL directories are created on volume SYS: for both NetWare 2.*x*, 3.*x* and 4.*x*.

In addition to these directories, NetWare 3.*x* and 4.*x* create a directory called ETC under SYS:SYSTEM. The ETC directory holds tables and configuration information for TCP/IP support. This directory is modeled after the UNIX /ETC directory.

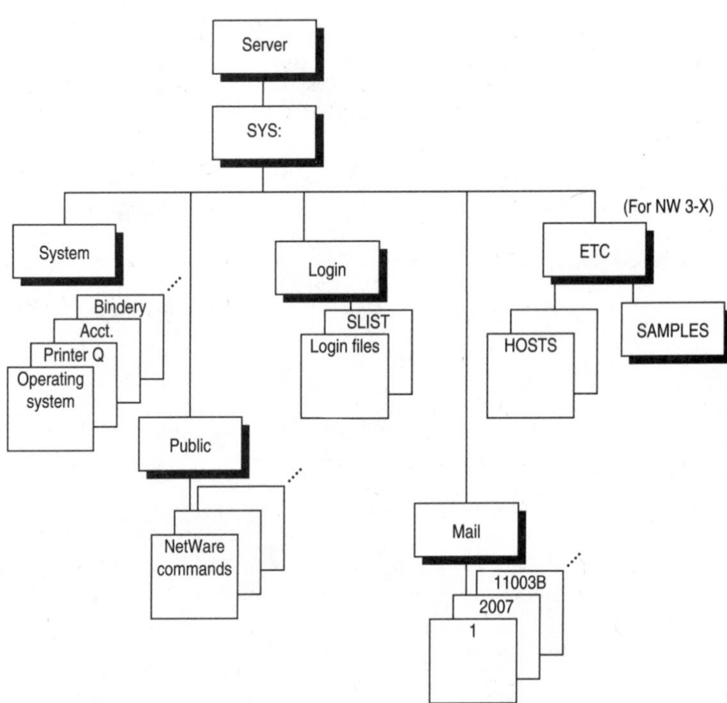

Figure 24.14
Server SYS: structure as installed. (Graphic courtesy of Learning Group International)

The root directory also has a file called DELETED.SAV that holds the names of the files that have been deleted but can be recovered by the SALVAGE command.

In the sections that follow, you learn about the kinds of files in each of these directories.

LOGIN Directory

The LOGIN directory contains the NetWare utilities LOGIN.EXE, SLIST.EXE(NetWare 2.*x*, 3.*x*), NLIST.EXE, and CX.EXE (NetWare 4.*x* only). The LOGIN directory also holds the operating system boot images created by the DOSGEN program for diskless workstations. Some LAN managers use this directory to store other programs that they want to be widely available to users without restrictions. An example of such a program is a virus scan program.

The default access rights to the SYS:LOGIN directory prevent modification of programs in this directory. You must make sure that these default access rights are not changed. Otherwise, the LOGIN directory can become a place through which a virus can spread.

The LOGIN directory for NetWare 4.*x* contains a subdirectory called NLS that includes national language support for login utilities.

PUBLIC Directory

The PUBLIC directory contains the NetWare utilities that are most commonly used. It also holds a copy of LOGIN.EXE and SLIST.EXE as a backup in case they are corrupted in the LOGIN directory. Again, care must be exercised to limit access to SYS:PUBLIC so that NetWare utilities may be run but not modified.

For a description of the utilities in the PUBLIC directory, refer to the NetWare *User's Manual*. A description of these utilities is beyond the scope of this book, but the more important files in SYS:PUBLIC are listed in table 24.5 for your ready reference. This list is for NetWare 3.*x*. The program files for NetWare 2.*x* and 4.*x* are similar to those for NetWare 3.*x*. NetWare 4.*x*'s PUBLIC directory contains programs specific to NetWare 4.*x* such as NETUSER.EXE, NETADMIN.EXE, NLIST.EXE, and so forth.

The PUBLIC directory for NetWare 4.*x* contains a subdirectory called NLS that includes national language support for public utilities.

Table 24.5

Important Files in SYS:PUBLIC (for NetWare 3.*x*)

File Name	Description
ALLOW.EXE	Enables user to view, edit, set, or modify IRM for a directory or a file.

continues

24

Table 24.5, Continued
Important Files in SYS:PUBLIC (for NetWare 3.*x*)

File Name	Description
ATTACH.EXE	Attaches to a server other than the one that you are logged in on—up to a maximum of eight servers.
CAPTURE.EXE	Redirects local printer output to a network printer. Used for single-user applications that print to the local printer only.
CASTOFF.EXE	Blocks the receipt of messages, except those sent by a supervisor through FCONSOLE.
CASTON.EXE	Enables the receipt of messages through the SEND command.
CHKVOL.EXE	Displays statistics on volume usage.
COLORPAL.EXE	Selects the color palettes to be used with NetWare graphic utilities.
DSPACE.EXE	Sets disk space restrictions for directories and network paths.
ENDCAP.EXE	Ends redirection of local printer output to network printer.
FCONSOLE.EXE	Monitors server utilization and performance statistics. (Limited in NetWare 3.*x* because these functions are performed by the MONITOR NLM.)
FILER.EXE	Manages files and directory rights, rights mask, and attributes.
FLAG.EXE	Sets file attributes.
FLAGDIR.EXE	Sets directory attributes.
GRANT.EXE	Grants rights to directories and files for users and groups.
LISTDIR.EXE	Lists all subdirectories below the current directory.
LOGIN.EXE	Authenticates users' request to log in to the server and executes the login.
LOGOUT.EXE	Logs out from the server.
MAKEUSER.EXE	Adds or deletes users from directives in a script file.
MAP.EXE	Assigns drive letters to network directories.
MENU.EXE	Runs menu script files.
NBACKUP.EXE.	Backs up server files to various backup devices.

File Name	Description
NCOPY.EXE	Copies network files. More efficient than DOS COPY commands.
NDIR.EXE	Lists network information about directories and files. Similar to DOS DIR commands, but gives network-specific information on files.
NPRINT.EXE	Prints on network printers.
NVER.EXE	Lists NetWare version on server.
PCONSOLE.EXE	Configures and manages shared printers and queues.
PRINTCON.EXE	Creates and modifies print job configurations.
PRINTDEF.EXE	Configures form and printer device driver information.
PSTAT.EXE	Displays printer status.
PSC.EXE	Controls/displays status of network printers.
PSERVER.EXE	Sets up a dedicated print server at a workstation.
PURGE.EXE	Removes files erased in the current login session.
REMOVE.EXE	Removes a user or group from the list of trustees for a path.
RENDIR.EXE	Renames a directory.
REVOKE.EXE	Revokes directory or file rights for a user or group.
RIGHTS.EXE	Displays effective rights of a user for directories and files.
RPRINTER.EXE	Sets up a remote nondedicated printer.
SALVAGE.EXE	Recovers deleted files.
SEND.EXE	Sends a message to other stations.
SESSION.EXE	Manages session parameters, such as drive mappings, and sends messages.
SETPASS.EXE	Sets or changes user passwords.
SETTTS.EXE	Sets transaction tracking level.
SLIST.EXE	Displays a list of file servers on the network.

continues

Table 24.5, Continued
Important Files in SYS:PUBLIC (for NetWare 3.*x*)

File Name	Description
SMODE.EXE	Sets the search mode of an executable file.
SYS$ERR.DAT	System error data file.
SYS$HELP.MSG	System help data files.
SYS$MSG.DAT	System message data files.
SYSCON.EXE	Manages user accounts and groups.
SYSTIME.EXE	Displays server time and synchronizes workstation time to server time.
TLIST.EXE	Displays a directory's trustee list.
USERDEF.EXE	Provides a menu-driven front end to MAKEUSER.
USERLIST.EXE	Lists users logged in.
VERSION.EXE	Displays version of utility.
VOLINFO.EXE	Displays real-time volume utilization.
WHOAMI.EXE	Displays information about your connection.

SYSTEM Directory

The SYSTEM directory contains the NetWare operating system files and system programs. Access to SYS:SYSTEM must be limited to system administrators and special management utilities that may need to access SYS:SYSTEM. The print spooler queues are implemented as subdirectories in the SYS:SYSTEM directory. Certain types of print servers may therefore need access to these directories.

For a description of the utilities in the SYSTEM directory, refer to the NetWare manuals of the command reference included on the disk with this book. Table 24.6 lists the more important SYS:SYSTEM files for your reference. The list is for NetWare 3.*x*. The program files for NetWare 2.*x* are similar to the NetWare 3.*x* files. The fundamental difference is that NetWare 3.*x* and 4.*x* SYSTEM directories contain NLMs, and NetWare 2.*x* SYSTEM directories contain VAPs.

The SYSTEM directory for NetWare 4.*x* contains a subdirectory called NLS that includes national language support for system utilities.

Table 24.6
Important Files in SYS:SYSTEM for NetWare 3.*x*

File Name	Description
ACONSOLE.EXE	Provides remote console connection over an asynchronous link.
ATOTAL.EXE	Generates an accounting summary of server resource usage.
AUTOEXEC.NCF	Contains system configuration information.
BCONSOLE.EXE	(Btrieve console.) Executes Btrieve operations and observes Btrieve status.
BINDFIX.EXE	Attempts to repair damaged bindery (system database).
BINDREST.EXE	Restores bindery to previous state. Used when BINDFIX does not work.
BROUTER.EXE	Routes Btrieve record manager requests.
BSTART.NCF	Loads Btrieve NLM from the server console—a NetWare Command File.
BSTOP.NCF	Unloads Btrieve NLM—a NetWare Command File.
BTRIEVE.NLM	Provides Btrieve Record Management service.
CLIB.NLM	Supports utilities requiring C library routines and functions.
DCB.DSK	Disk Coprocessor Board driver NLM.
DOSGEN.EXE	Creates boot image files for diskless stations.
EDIT.NLM	Text editor NLM that can be run from server console.
INSTALL.NLM	Installs and configures 3.*x* NOS.
IPCONFIG.NLM	NLM for configuring IP addressing.
IPXS.NLM	STREAMS interface to IPX protocols.
ISADISK.DSK	ISA disk driver NLM.
MAC.NAM	Macintosh file system Name Space support NLM.
MATHLIB.NLM	Math library routine interface for the Intel 80387 coprocessor.

continues

Table 24.6, Continued
Important Files in SYS:SYSTEM for NetWare 3.*x*

File Name	Description
MATHLIBC.NLM	Math library routine emulation of the Intel 80387 coprocessor. Used if coprocessor does not exist.
MONITOR.NLM	Monitors server resources.
NET$REC.DAT	Contains bindery data.
NMAGENT.NLM	Manages multiple LAN drivers on server.
PAUDIT.EXE	Displays server accounting log.
PROTO.NLM	Views protocol identification numbers.
PSERVER.NLM.	Loads printer server on file server.
REMOTE.NLM	Monitors server console remotely in Remote Management Facility.
ROUTE.NLM	Supports source routing for IBM Token Ring bridges.
RS232.NLM	Support for remote console connection over an asynchronous link.
RSETUP.EXE	Creates custom server boot disk to support remote server control.
RSPX.NLM	Supports remote management of server console.
SECURITY.EXE	Reports security holes on the server.
SNMP.NLM	SNMP Agent on server.
SPXCONFG.NLM	Provides configuration of SPX parameters.
SPXS.NLM	SPX protocol for STREAMS.
STREAMS.NLM	Implements STREAMS protocol. Used as a common transport interface for multiple transport protocols.
SYS$ERR.DAT	System error message file.
SYS$ERR.LOG	System error log file.
SYS$MSG.LOG	System messages file.
TCPIP.NLM	Implements TCP/IP protocols on NetWare 3.*x* server.

File Name	Description
TLI.NLM	Transport Layer Interface NLM. Common transport interface.
TCPCONFG.NLM	Configures TCP/IP.
TOKENRPL.NLM	Enables remote boot for IBM Token Ring network boards.
UPGRADE.EXE	Upgrades from NetWare 2.*x* to NetWare 3.*x*.
UPS.NLM	Implements the software link between server and UPS (Uninterrupted Power Supply) device.
VREPAIR.NLM	Repairs minor volume problems.
WSUPDATE.EXE	Updates shell files from the file server.

MAIL Directory

The MAIL directory contains the login scripts for the users who are defined on the NetWare server. Every object on the system, including users, has a unique internal hexadecimal ID, called the *user ID*. This user ID is an internal reference variable used to keep track of user information in the system bindery. When a user account is created on the server, a subdirectory with the same name as the user ID also is created in the SYS:MAIL directory. Access rights to the user ID directory in SYS:MAIL are set up automatically. The user ID subdirectory contains the user's login script in a file called LOGIN. If a login script file is changed, NetWare keeps a copy of the old login script, in a file called LOGIN.BAK.

Earlier versions of NetWare distributed an electronic mail program called MAIL. The electronic mail messages were stored in the user ID subdirectory in SYS:MAIL along with the user's login script. Distribution of the electronic mail program was discontinued, but the name of the directory MAIL remains.

In NetWare 4.*x*, the MAIL directory is kept for bindery emulation purposes.

DOC Directory

This is an optional directory at the root of a volume for NetWare 3.12 and 4.*x* servers. It contains the Electro Text help files. Electro Text is a graphical user interface help system that contains all of the Novell manuals on-line.

ETC Directory

Contains files for configuring TCP/IP on NetWare 3.*x* and 4.*x* servers. SYS:ETC/SAMPLES contain sample files that can be customized.

QUEUES Directory

This is an optional directory that can exist at the root of a NetWare 4.*x* server volume, and contains the print queue associated with a NDS print queue object.

Command Reference On-Line Help

Because all NetWare commands and utilities are found in the SYS:PUBLIC or SYS:SYSTEM directory, tables 24.5 and 24.6 are a summary of the command reference. By using this table and the NetWare 3.11's HELP utility or NetWare 3.12 and 4.*x*'s Electro Text utility, you can learn about any command.

For instance, if you want to learn about the NetWare command PSC on a NetWare 3.11 server, perform the following steps. (The screens shown are for a NetWare 3.11 server, but the help utility is similar for NetWare 2.2. The help utility was written using NFOLIO from Folio Corporation of Provo, Utah.)

1. Log in to the server and type:

   HELP

   A screen similar to figure 24.15 appears.

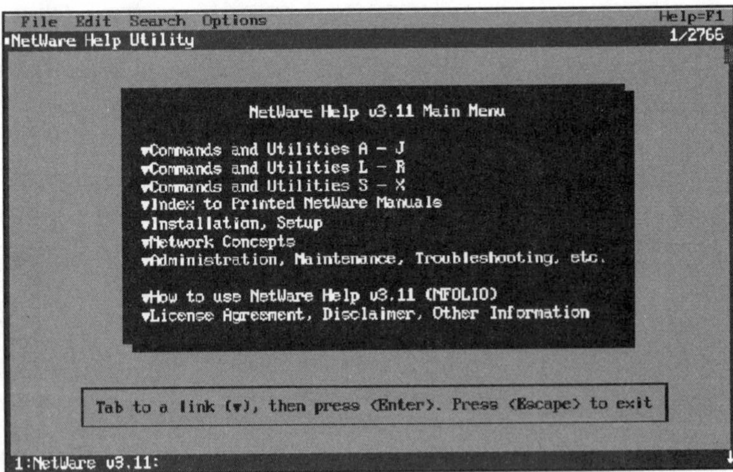

Figure 24.15
NetWare 3.11 Help Main Menu.

2. Press Tab to get to the first link help option. Then use the arrow keys to move the cursor to the desired help section and press Enter. For getting information about the command PSC, for instance, move to the Commands and Utilities L - R option and press Enter (see fig. 24.16).

3. Now use Tab and the arrow keys to position the cursor on the command you want to learn about, and press Enter.

   To find out more about the PSC command, for example, select it by moving the cursor to the PSC option, and then press Enter. The main PSC help screen appears, as shown in figure 24.17.

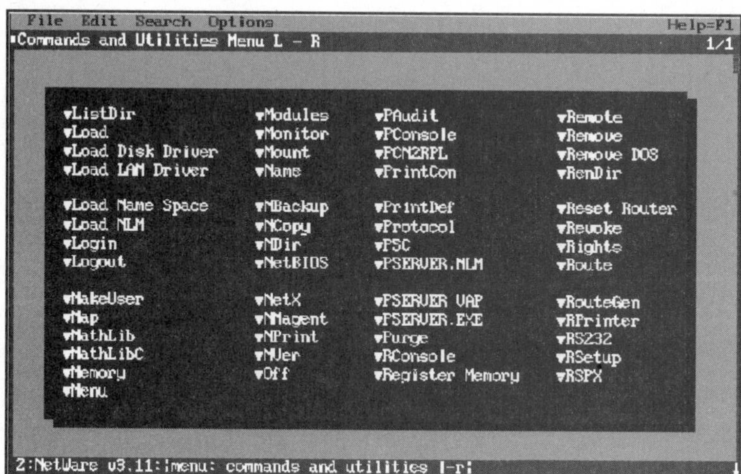

Figure 24.16
NetWare 3.11 Commands and Utilities Menu L - R.

4. You can explore a number of items in detail on this screen. If you select the Parameters field, for example, a screen displays that shows you how to format parameters to the PSC command (see fig. 24.18).

5. If you select the Notes option from the PSC main help screen, the screen illustrated in figure 24.19 is displayed.

6. If you select the Examples option from the PSC main help screen, the information illustrated in figure 24.20 is displayed.

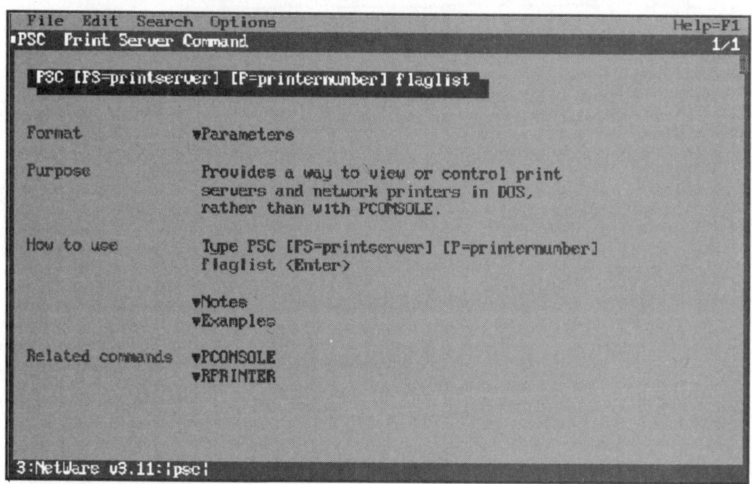

Figure 24.17
The NetWare 3.11 PSC (Print Server Command) screen.

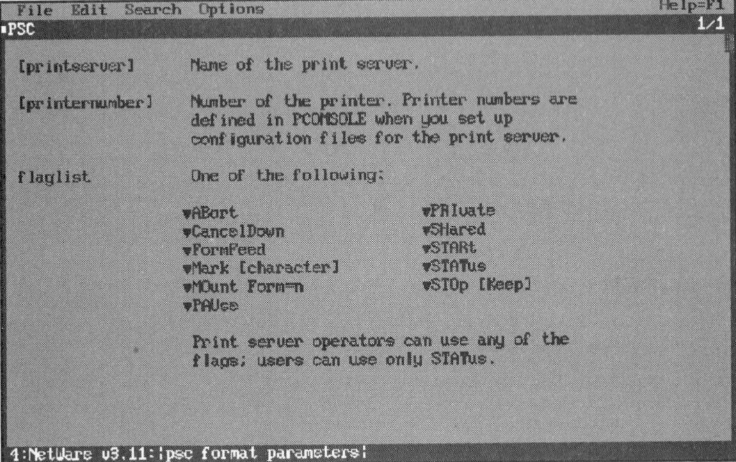

Figure 24.18
The NetWare 3.11 PSC format parameters screen.

The preceding screen shows you many examples. If you want to see how to use PSC to view the status of all printers, select the View status of all printers option. Figure 24.13 shows the information that appears.

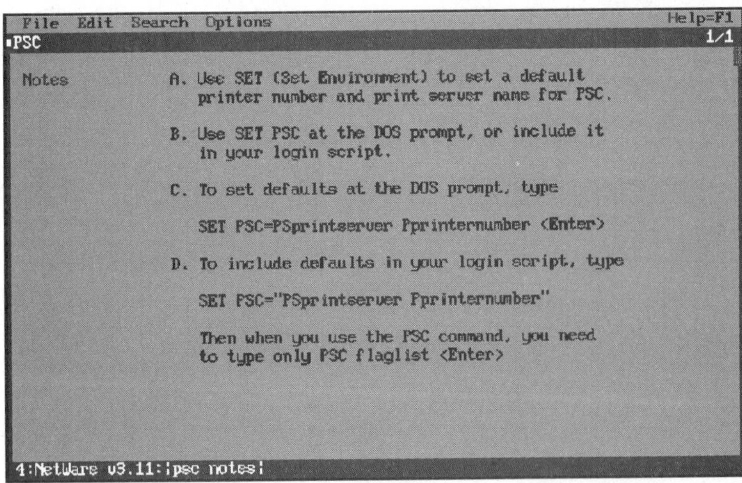

Figure 24.19
The NetWare 3.11 PSC Notes screen.

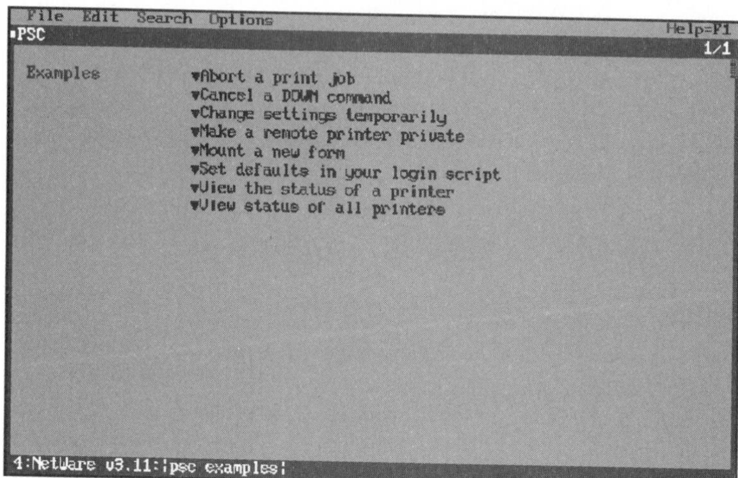

Figure 24.20
The NetWare 3.11 PSC Examples screen.

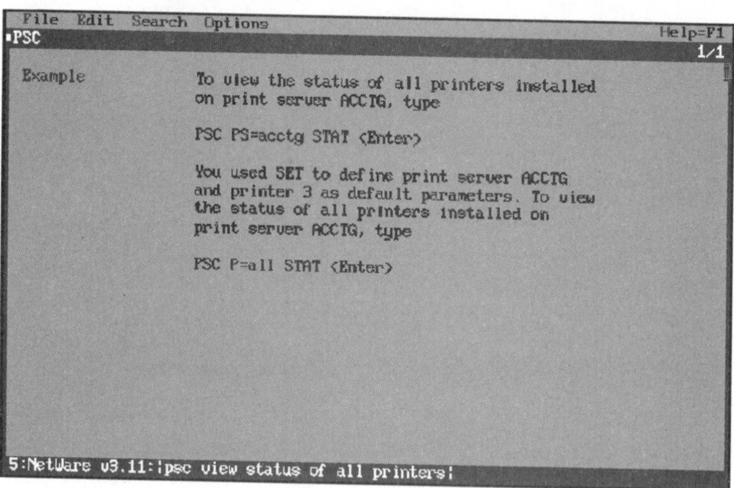

Figure 24.21
The NetWare 3.11 PSC view status of all printers screen.

7. Press Esc to return to the main PSC help menu. Notice the links to Related Commands near the bottom of the screen display (in this case, RCONSOLE and RPRINTER). You can examine these commands by using HELP.

8. To exit HELP, press Esc several times.

As you can see, with only a few keystrokes, you can obtain a wealth of information about PSC or any command.

Applications Directories

In the previous section, you learned about the standard directory structure created by NetWare during installation. When you want to install applications or user's directories, you must define directories to keep these applications separate from the NetWare NOS files. This separation results in easier maintenance and upgrades of NetWare and application programs.

Directory Organization for Few Applications on Server

Figure 24.22 shows application directories installed directly under the root directory of a volume. For instance, the network version of WordPerfect 5.1 can be installed in a directory called SYS:WP51; dBASE can be installed in a directory called SYS:DBASE. This approach works only when relatively few applications are installed on the server. If many applications are installed on the server, the root directory becomes cluttered with a large number of directories. If you keep the number of directories in the root small, the directory structure is easy to comprehend and manage.

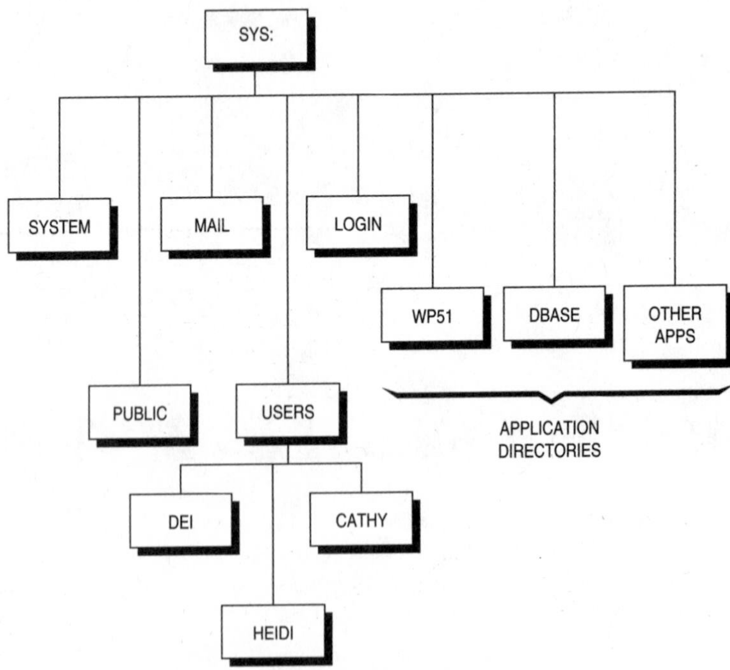

Figure 24.22
Directory organization for few applications on server.

An application directory can have many subdirectories for data and programs, or a single application directory can store all programs and data. Applications may require a specific structure for the application directory.

Directory Organization for Many Applications on Server

When many applications are installed on the server, a two-level structure for defining application directories is best. Similar applications are grouped together in a directory named to reflect the specific kind of application. Figure 24.23 illustrates this concept.

Consider a server that needs more than one word processor, for instance. A class directory called SYS:WP can be created, within which individual application directories for the separate word processors can be created. Word Perfect 6.0 can be installed in the directory SYS:WP/WP60, Microsoft Word can be installed in the directory SYS:WP/WORD, and a text editor such as Brief can be installed in SYS:WP/BRIEF.

Another example is a software developer who uses C compilers from different vendors. The class directory can be SYS:C. Microsoft C compiler can be installed in the directory SYS:C/MSC, and the Borland C++ compiler can be installed in SYS:C/BC.

In these examples, the volume SYS: is used for the application directories. If other volumes are available, they also can be used to install applications. In general, applications used simultaneously can be distributed across multiple volumes. This improves performance because disk controller and device electronics are not shared by all the applications. Some applications enable you to store data files in more than one data directory. If frequently used data files are stored on separate server physical disks, the application's speed increases.

Other OS Applications OS/2, Mac, and Windows

If the server supports more than one kind of workstation operating system, you must keep the applications for the different operating systems separate. This improves organization and makes installation and removal of applications on the server easier. Figure 24.24 shows a sample directory organization that has OS/2, DOS, Mac, and Windows applications installed on the server. In many instances, a spreadsheet, such as Excel, also is installed for different operating system platform types.

Home Directory Organization

A *home directory* on the server disk stores a user's personal files. Users usually have unrestricted access to their home directories because the home directory is an extension of the local disk space at the user's workstation.

NetWare uses a default home directory structure of SYS:HOME (HOME is directly under SYS:). Users have subdirectories under the SYS:HOME directory named after their log-in names. With this approach, user TOM has a home directory of SYS:HOME/TOM. The home directory also can have a directory structure of SYS:USERS. This is a common name for home directories used by many operating systems. In this case, the user TOM has a home directory of SYS:USERS/TOM.

Figure 24.25 shows the home directories for a number of users. Within the home directories, users create subdirectories to organize their files.

Figure 24.23
Directory organization for many applications on server.

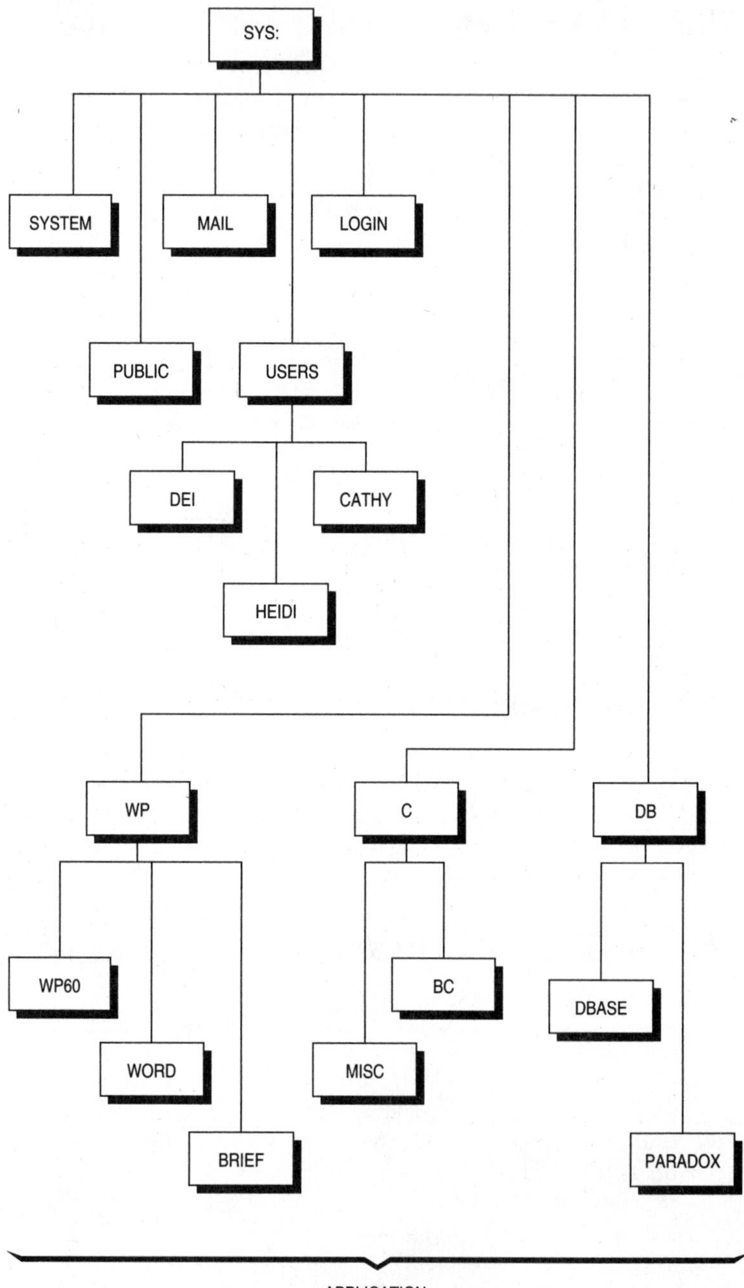

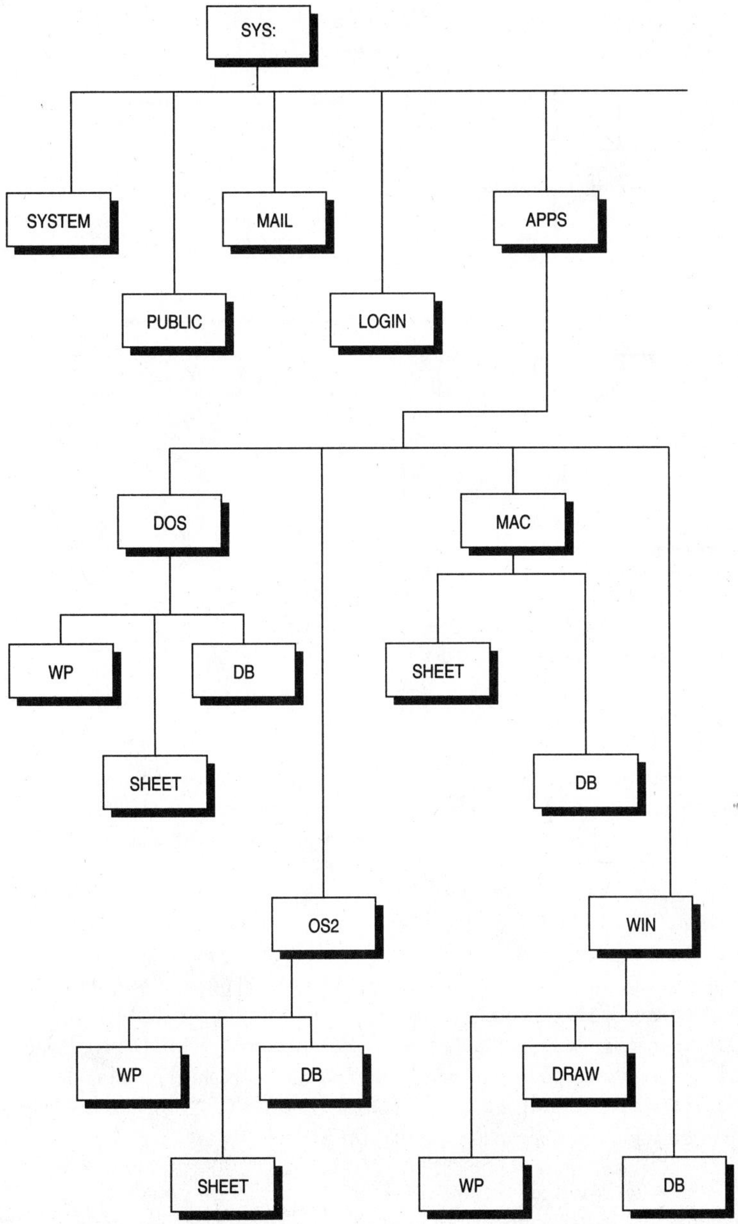

Figure 24.24
Multiple OS application support on server.

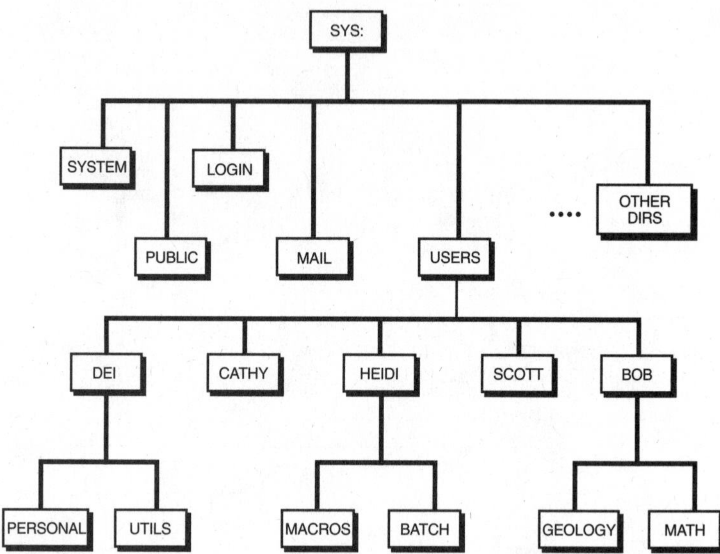

Figure 24.25 *Home directory organization on server.*

The NetWare utility SYSCON creates home directories as part of a user account. See Chapter 9, "Managing NetWare 2.2, 3.11, and 3.12 Security," for details on how to use SYSCON.

DOS Directories

A copy of the DOS program files should be kept on the server. This simplifies access to DOS programs when the user logs in to the server. You also should include the network directory that contains the DOS programs as one of the search drives so that DOS programs can be invoked from any directory.

Because many versions of DOS can be used by users on the network, Novell recommends that you use the directory structure shown in figure 24.26 to store DOS programs. To support this directory structure, NetWare defines a number of script variables shown in figure 24.26 by the % sign. These script variables are used to specify directories in the login script and are mapped into values as shown in figure 24.26. Thus the script variable %MACHINE can map into values IBM_PC or COMPAQ; the script variable %VERSION can map into version numbers such as V3.20, V3.31, V5.0. Depending on the DOS version and machine type, the appropriate network directory can be specified by using the generic script variables. The LONG MACHINE TYPE parameter in the NET.CFG workstations configuration file determines the value of script variables like %MACHINE.

Ordinarily, the network administrator strives to have one version of DOS for all users on the network. Conflicts between DOS versions and applications, and DOS versions tailored to the workstation hardware and specific DOS applications, make it difficult to have only one version of DOS. Under these circumstances, you can use the directory structure in figure 24.26.

If you use the scheme shown in figure 24.26, you must make sure to avoid license infringements. That is, you must have a license for each user who could use DOS workstations at any time.

File System Performance

Several factors can improve a disk subsystem's performance. These factors include optimum selection of disk block size, file caching, directory hashing and caching, and the use of Turbo FATs.

Disk Block Size

In NetWare 3.*x* and 4.*x*, you have the option to select a disk block size different from the default. You select this block size at the time you define a volume by using INSTALL NLM. The disk block size values that are legal in NetWare 3.*x* are 4 KB (default), 8 KB, 16 KB, 32 KB, and 64 KB.

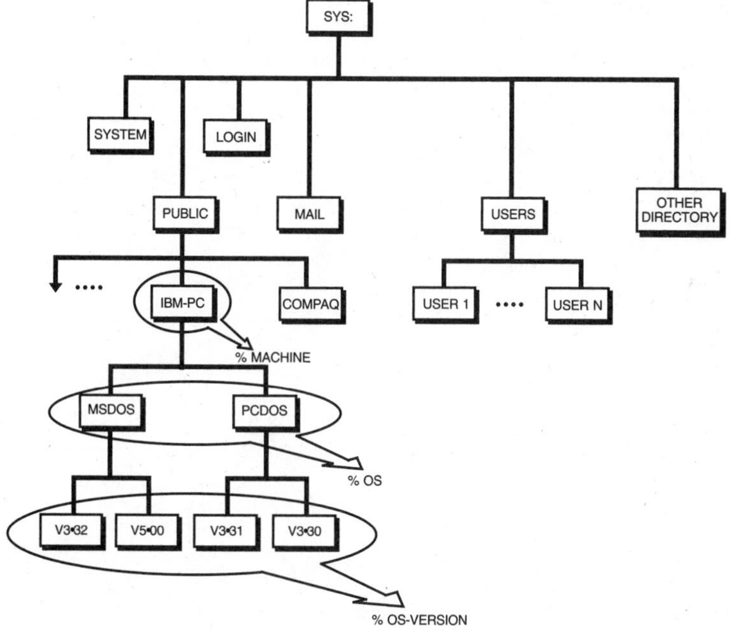

Figure 24.26
DOS directory structure on server.

In a database consisting of a small number of very large data files, a large disk block size is best. Database operations typically are executed in a local region of a data file. If the disk block size is large, fewer blocks must be fetched compared to a volume that has a smaller disk block size. In addition, the fewer the disk blocks you have in a volume, the smaller the size of the FAT to keep track of them in RAM.

In a system that contains many files, large disk block size results in a higher proportion of unused disk space. In this situation, a smaller disk block size gives better space utilization.

Memory for File Caching and Directory Caching and Hashing

Server RAM left over after allocation has been made to the NOS is used for file caching. The larger the amount of RAM that is used in the server, the greater the amount of space that is left for file caching. Additional file cache results in better server performance. Directory hashing and caching are enabled by default, and they speed up directory access.

In NetWare 3.*x* and 4.*x*, the SET command controls some of the parameters that affect file and directory caching. Chapter 7, "Installing NetWare 3.12 Servers," discusses these parameters in greater detail.

Turbo FATs

If a file is more than 2 MB in size, and you flag it with an indexed attribute, a separate index table is built for every indexed file. These special index tables are called *Turbo FATs*. The FLAG command flags a file with an indexed attribute. NetWare 3.*x* and 4.*x* automatically indexes files having over 64 regular FAT entries.

Disk Space Management

Because users share disk space on the server, you can limit disk space per user. In NetWare 2.*x*, you must enable the option to limit disk space during installation. Disk-space limiting enables individual disk quotas to be assigned by using SYSCON or DSPACE utilities.

One reason to restrict disk space is to prevent a user from using an inordinate amount of disk space. Suppose that a user runs an application that has a software bug. This bug causes it to go in a loop while it writes to a data file. The data file can become large enough to consume all available disk space on the server and to prevent others from using the server's disk. In the NetWare 3.*x* and 4.*x* , the SET command can be used to monitor volume usage.

NetWare 3.*x* and 4.*x* SET Command for Volume Utilization

You can use the SET VOLUME command to set thresholds and warnings for volume utilization. These commands are as follows:

SET VOLUME LOW WARN ALL USERS

SET VOLUME LOW WARNING THRESHOLD

SET VOLUME LOW WARNING RESET THRESHOLD

The SET VOLUME LOW WARN ALL USERS command warns all users that the volume is almost full. The values can be set to either ON or OFF, but ON is the default. Some LAN managers turn this value to OFF so that the beginning network user is not confused by unfamiliar system messages. In this case, you must run the utility CHKVOL or VOLINFO for the server volumes on a daily basis.

Example:

```
SET VOLUME LOW WARN ALL USERS=OFF
```

The SET VOLUME LOW WARNING THRESHOLD command controls how many free disk blocks remain on a volume before NetWare issues a warning. To estimate this number, you must divide the desired free space threshold by the disk block size. The value for this parameter ranges from 0 to 100,000 blocks, with a default value of 256.

If you want to set the threshold to 1 MB, for a nondefault disk block size of 8 KB, for example, the number of free blocks is estimated by:

Free blocks = Free disk space/Disk block size = 1 MB/ 8 KB = 128

The SET command would be as follows:

```
SET VOLUME LOW WARNING THRESHOLD=128
```

For a disk block size of 4 KB (default), the free block count will be 1 MB/ 4 KB = 256—the default value.

The SET VOLUME LOW WARNING RESET THRESHOLD command determines how many disk blocks must be freed up before a second warning is issued. This parameter prevents repeated warning messages from being sent if the free space hovers around the limit established by SET VOLUME LOW WARNING THRESHOLD. When the first warning is issued (SET VOLUME LOW WARN ALL USERS), and the users reduce disk space to just below the threshold, you may not want another warning message to appear if the disk space utilization soon rises above the threshold again. This process of dipping below the threshold and then rising again can occur repeatedly, and a repeated warning message is very annoying to the user. The value for this parameter ranges from 0 to 100,000 blocks, with a default value of 256.

To set this threshold value to 256 blocks (1 MB for 4 KB size blocks), the command is as follows:

```
SET VOLUME LOW WARNING RESET THRESHOLD=256
```

These SET values can be recorded in the STARTUP.NCF file.

CHKVOL and VOLINFO

CHKVOL and VOLINFO commands monitor disk space. CHKVOL is a command-line utility similar to the DOS's CHKDISK utility, and it displays the results just once. As illustrated in figure 24.27, you can use CHKVOL to quickly find out how much disk space is available. VOLINFO is an interactive utility that displays disk utilization in real-time. VOLINFO monitors disk space and directory entries available on server volumes. You can change the time intervals at which the information is updated in the Available Options box (see fig. 24.28).

DSPACE (NetWare 3.*x* Only)

DSPACE is a disk space management utility that limits the maximum size of a directory and its subdirectories on a per user basis.

In NetWare 4.*x* disk space management is performed using the FILER utility.

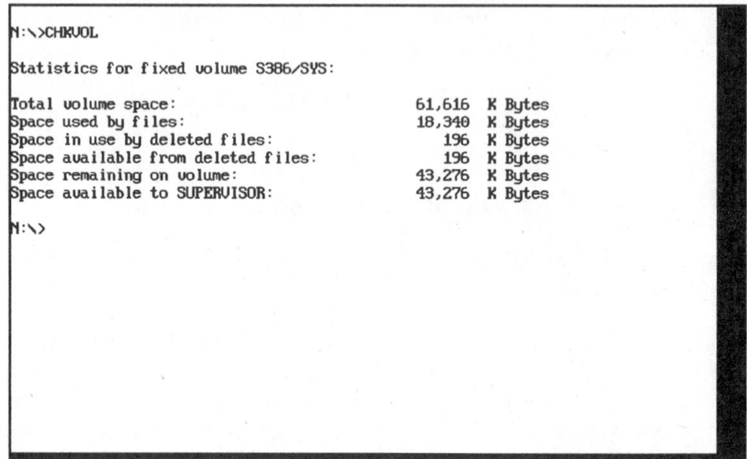

Figure 24.27
The CHKVOL utility.

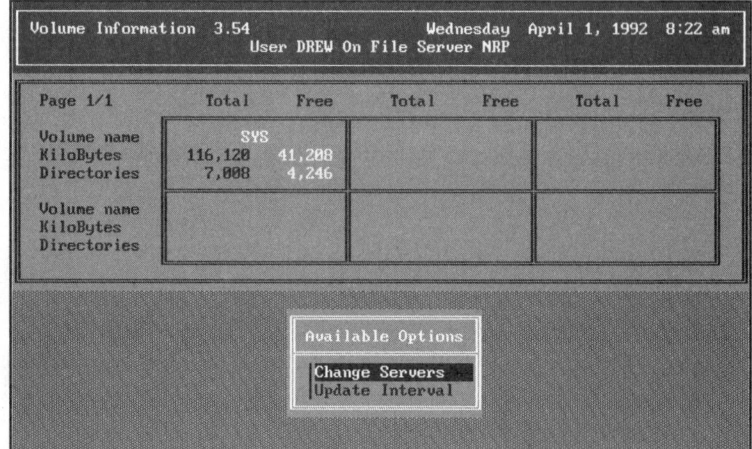

Figure 24.28
Figure CaptionThe VOLINFO utility.

To invoke this utility perform the following steps:

1. Log in to a server as a SUPERVISOR, and type **DSPACE**.
2. Select User Restrictions. When a list of users appears, select the user that you want to work with. Then, when a list of volumes appears, select the volume that you want to work with.
3. A screen similar to the one shown in figure 24.29 appears:

```
User Disk Space Limitation Information

User:   GUEST
Volume: SYS
Limit Space:      Yes
Available:       1024 Kilobytes
In Use:             0 Kilobytes
```

Figure 24.29
User Disk Space Limitation Information screen.

The Limit Space field tells you if the disk space limitation is enabled for that user. The Available field tells you the current disk space restriction for the user, and the In Use field shows the amount of space used by the user.

4. From the Available Options menu, select Directory restrictions. (You may need to press Esc a few times to get this menu to appear.)

5. A window appears that contains the current directory. Enter the directory you want to perform the restriction for, and press Enter. Or, use Ins to build the directory path one level at a time.

6. A screen similar to that shown in figure 24.30 appears with the following fields:

7. The Path Space Limit specifies the minimum size limit for all the directories along the selected path. If a directory above the selected directory has a smaller space limit, that limit applies to the current directory.

8. The Limit Space field specifies if any restrictions exist on the current directory. Enter Yes for restriction or No for no restriction.

9. The Directory Space Limit specifies the space restriction on the selected directory.

10. The Currently Available field specifies the space currently available for the selected directory.

```
Directory Disk Space Limitation Information

Path Space Limit:       1024 Kilobytes
Limit Space: Yes
Directory Space Limit:        1024 Kilobytes
Currently Available:       1004 Kilobytes
```

Figure 24.30
Directory disk space limitation information.

Restricting Space Using Other Utilities

The utility SYSCON, in NetWare 3.*x*, restricts space on a per-user basis. The steps to perform this task are as follows:

1. Log in to a server as a SUPERVISOR, and type **SYSCON**.

2. Select User Information and, when a list of users appears, select the user you want to work with. From the User Information window, select Volume/Disk Restrictions, and then select the volume that you want to restrict. A screen similar to figure 24.31 displays.

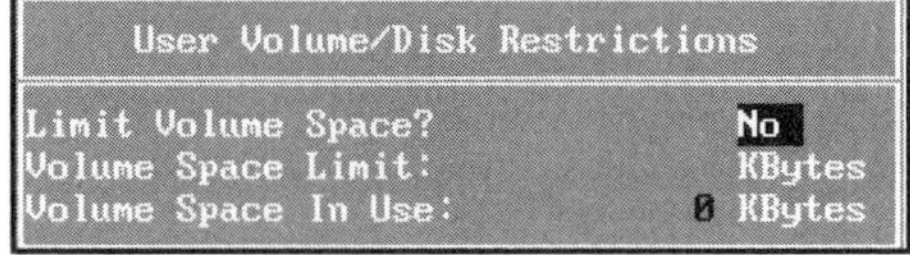

Figure 24.31
User/Volume Disk Restrictions screen.

Change the Limit Volume Space? field from No to Yes, and specify the amount of disk space in kilobytes in the Volume Space Limit field. The Volume Space In Use field reports the space currently used by the user.

Rights Access

After a user successfully logs in to the server, NetWare controls access to directories and files on the server. In this section, NetWare 3.*x* and 4.*x* rights security are discussed first. Because NetWare 3.*x* rights security is a superset of NetWare 2.2 security, you easily can understand both NetWare 3.*x* security and NetWare 2.2 security. Toward the end of this section, you learn the differences between NetWare 3.*x*/4.*x* and NetWare 2.2 security.

Trustee Rights

In NetWare, users are assigned rights to perform operations such as Read, Write, Create, and Erase in files in a directory. The user entrusted with these rights is called a *Trustee*, and the actual rights assigned are called *Trustee Assignment*—or TA.

A user can be given a trustee assignment explicitly. In other words, the trustee assignment can be given on an individual-user basis. To set individual rights for a large number of users, however, is very tedious and difficult to maintain. In addition, many users have similar needs; they access the same directories and files on the server. For instance, all engineers in the engineering department need access to the same directories. To help with the management and administration of users with similar needs, NetWare uses groups.

A *group* is a collection of network users who has the same access privileges to directories and files on the server. For instance, all engineers are members of a group called ENGINEERS. The group ENGINEERS can be given a trustee assignment in a manner similar to that for individual users. The difference is that all members of the group automatically inherit the trustee assignments for that group (see fig. 24.32). If new members are added to the engineering department, they are made members of the group ENGINEERS. If engineers leave the department, they are removed from the group ENGINEERS. This automatically removes the privileges for the user as a member of the group ENGINEERS.

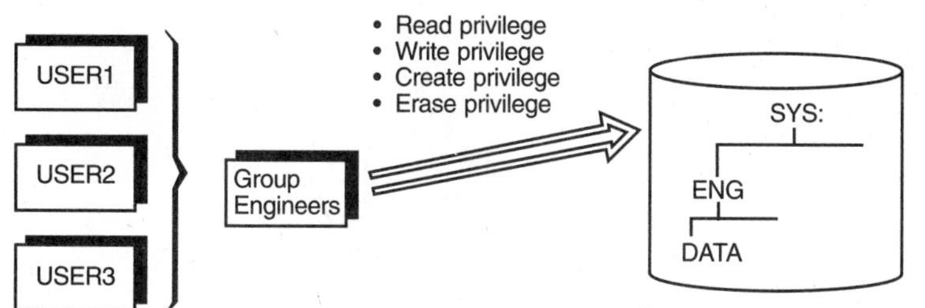

Figure 24.32
Trustee assignment on a group basis. (Graphic courtesy of Learning Group International)

Most users are members of more than one group. They are at least members of a predefined group called EVERYONE. The total rights for a group is the sum of all the rights inherited by virtue of membership to all groups. Therefore, if a user has Read and Write TA (trustee assignment) to directory SYS:COMMON/DATA because of membership in group EVERYONE and Read, Create, and Erase TA to the same directory because of membership in group ENGINEERS, then the user has a TA of Read, Write, Create, Erase to SYS:COMMON/DATA—that is, the sum of the user's rights by virtue of membership to groups EVERYONE and ENGINEERS. Groups and their membership are defined through the NetWare utility SYSCON.

Directory Rights and File Rights

Table 24.7 shows the NetWare 3.*x* directory rights, and table 24.8 shows the differences between NetWare 3.*x* and pre-NetWare 2.2 rights. NetWare 2.2 rights are similar to NetWare 3.*x* rights except that NetWare 2.2 does not have supervisory rights.

Table 24.7
NetWare Directory Trustee Rights

Name	Description
S*	Gives rights to all directory/subdirectories/files. Called *Supervisory* rights in NetWare 3.*x* and *Supervisor* rights in NetWare 4.*x*.
R	*Read* rights to open files in a directory, read contents, and execute.
W	*Write* rights to open and write (modify) contents of files.

continues

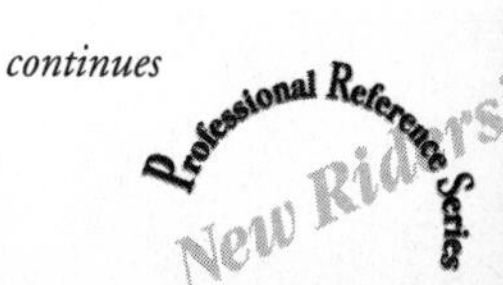

24

Table 24.7, Continued
NetWare Directory Trustee Rights

Name	Description
C	*Create* rights to create files and subdirectories in a directory.
E	*Erase* rights to delete a directory, its files, and its subdirectories.
M	*Modify* rights to change directory and file attributes and rename.
F	*File scan* rights to view names of subdirectories and files.
A	*Access Control* rights to other users, modify trustee rights, and IRM (for NetWare 3.*x*) or IRF (for NetWare 4.*x*).

Table 24.8
Comparison Between NetWare 3.x/4.x and Pre-NetWare 2.2 Rights

3.*x*	Pre 2.2	Comments
S		No equivalent concept of supervisory rights in pre-NetWare 2.2.
R	R O	Read includes opening and writing to a file in NetWare 3.2.
W	W O	Write includes opening and writing to a file in NetWare 3.*x*.
C	CP	Parental rights eliminated in NetWare 3.*x* and 2.2.
E	DP	Parental rights eliminated in NetWare 3.*x*; name different.
M	M	Modify is same in pre-NetWare 2.2 and NetWare 3.*x*.
F	S	Names different; concept is same.
A		Closest concept in pre-NetWare 2.2 is parental rights.

The Read and Write rights in table 24.7 enable the user to read and write files in a directory. The user needs both of these rights to perform updates on files in a directory. Reading and writing also imply that the user has a right to open files in a directory. Earlier versions of NetWare (pre-NetWare 2.2) had an explicit Open right that always had to be set to do anything useful with a file. Newer versions of NetWare do not have an explicit Open right—it is implied by the Read and Write rights.

The User needs the Create and Erase rights to create and remove files and subdirectories. Modify rights can be used to change file attributes. Without Modify rights, you cannot use NetWare commands, such as FLAG, to change file attributes.

The File Scan right enables a user to view names of files and subdirectories. If you do not want a user to see file names in a directory, you can remove the File Scan right. With this right removed, the user can issue DIR or NDIR (NetWare DIR command) but cannot see the name of files in the directory.

The Access Control right enables other users to modify trustee rights and the *Inherited Rights Mask* (IRM). In NetWare 4.*x*, the IRM is called *Inherited Rights Filter* (IRF). They serve the same purpose. IRM and IRF are discussed a little later in the chapter. This means that a user who has Access Control rights to a directory can use a NetWare utility, such as FILER, to assign rights to other users for this directory. Access Control rights must be assigned only to trusted users.

Table 24.9 shows file level rights for NetWare 3.*x*. In NetWare 3.*x* Trustee Assignment can be made at the file level. This is unlike NetWare 2.*x* in which a TA can be made only at the directory level. NetWare 3.*x* gives you more control over files in a directory. In most situations, such a high level of control is not needed, but this control is nice to have if you do encounter a situation that needs it. Trustee rights for files are similar to those for directories, except that the scope of these rights is limited to an individual file. File trustee rights use the same symbols as directory trustee rights. The Create right for a file gives the user the right to salvage a file after it has been deleted. This is different from the Create right for a directory, which enables you to create files and subdirectories in a directory.

Table 24.9
NetWare 3.x File Trustee Rights

Name	Description
S	*Supervisory* rights to all rights to the file.
R	*Read* rights to open a file, read contents, and execute the program.
W	*Write* rights to open and write (modify) contents of a file.
C	*Create* rights to salvage a file after the file has been deleted.
E	*Erase* rights to delete a file.
M	*Modify* rights to change a file's attributes and rename the file.
F	*File Scan* rights to view name of a file and its full path name.
A	*Access Control* rights to modify file's trustee assignments and IRM.

In NetWare 3.*x*, you can determine Trustee Assignments by using the utilities SYSCON and FILER or the command-line utilities GRANT and REVOKE. In NetWare 4.*x*, you can use FILER, the *NetWare Administrator* (NWADMIN), and the RIGHTS command.

Examples of Controlling Rights in NetWare 3.*x*

The following examples illustrate the control of the command-line utilities GRANT and REVOKE in NetWare 3.*x*.

To give user BALI a Trustee Assignment of Read, Write, Create, Erase, and File Scan to directory SYS:WP/DATA, type the following command:

```
GRANT R W C E F FOR SYS:WP/DATA TO BALI
```


To remove from user MOTI the Trustee Assignment of Write, Create, and Erase for directory SYS:WP/DATA type:

```
REVOKE  W C E  FOR SYS:WP/DATA FROM MOTI
```

Examples of Controlling Rights in NetWare 4.*x*

The following examples illustrate the control of file system rights using the command-line utility RIGHTS in NetWare 4.*x*.

The RIGHTS command allows you to:

- View/set the rights of a directory or file
- View trustee assignments to a specified directory
- See inherited rights
- View and set the inherited rights filter

The examples that follow show the control of file system rights.

To view the rights for user KSS in SYS:USERS/KSS directory, the command is as follows:

```
RIGHTS SYS:USERS/KSS
```

To list trustees use the /T option. For example, to view the trustee assignments for a specified directory such as SYS:USERS/KSS, use the command:

```
RIGHTS SYS:PUBLIC  /T
```

The following is a sample display output:

```
NW4CS\SYS:\PUBLIC
User trustees:
     CN=KSS.OU=CORP.O=SCS                                    [ R     F ]
----------
Group trustees:
     CN=Everyone.OU=CORP.O=ESL                               [ R     F ]
----------
Other trustees:
     OU=CORP.O=ESL                                           [ R     F ]
```

Please note that group Everyone is not a predefined group under NetWare. It appears example because the server was upgraded from NetWare 3.*x* to NetWare 4.*x*.

The output of the previous RIGHTS command shows that a user, a group object and a co... have rights to NW4CS\SYS:\PUBLIC. The user object CN=KSS.OU=CORP.O=SCS, the group obje... CN=Everyone.OU=CORP.O=ESL, and the container object OU=CORP.O=ESL all have Read and File Scan rights to NW4CS\SYS:\PUBLIC.

Since the container object OU=CORP.O=ESL all have Read and File Scan rights to NW4CS\SYS:\PUBLIC, all user objects in the container OU=CORP.O=ESL have the same Read and File scan rights to NW4CS\SYS:\PUBLIC.

Notice that the /T option lists all trustees that have been given an explicit trustee assignment to SYS:PUBLIC. Whereas NWADMIN and NETADMIN can also display this information, using the previous RIGHTS command is simpler (and usually faster).

You can grant and revoke rights using the /NAME= option. The general syntax of RIGHTS using the /NAME= option is as follows:

```
RIGHTS  directory_file_name  [+¦-]rights  /NAME=objectname
```

To set the rights for user KSS in SYS:USERS/KSS directory so that the user has all rights except Supervisor rights, type:

```
RIGHTS SYS:USERS/KSS  CRWEMFA /NAME=.KSS.CORP.SCS
```

To remove the Erase and Create rights for user KSS in SYS:USERS/KSS directory, type:

```
RIGHTS SYS:USERS/KSS  -C-E  /NAME=.KSS.CORP.SCS
```

You can use RIGHTS to assign rights to more than one user using a single RIGHTS command. Consider two user objects KSS in contexts CORP.ESL and CORP.SCS. To assign both users all rights, except Supervisor right, to the current directory, the following command could be used:

```
RIGHTS . ALL /NAME=.CN=KSS.OU=CORP.O=ESL,.CN=KSS.OU=CORP.SCS

NW4CS\SYS:USERS
Directories                                             Rights
------------------------------------------------------  ---------------
KSS                                                     [ RWCEMFA]
```

Rights for one directory were changed for .CN=KSS.OU=CORP.O=SCS

```
W4CS\SYS:USERS
Directories                                             Rights
------------------------------------------------------  ---------------
KSS                                                     [ RWCEMFA]
```

Rights for one directory were changed for .CN=KSS.OU=CORP.O=ESL

Notice that the period (.) can be used for the current directory name. Also, that ALL means all rights except Supervisor right. The /NAME= option enables you to list a number of NDS names.

To remove all rights (except Supervisor, if given) for the two user objects KSS in contexts CORP.ESL and CORP.SCS, you can use the following command:

```
RIGHTS . -ALL /NAME=.CN=KSS.OU=CORP.O=ESL,.CN=KSS.OU=CORP.SCS
NW4CS\SYS:USERS
Directories                                                  Rights
----------------------------------------------------------  ------------
KSS                                                          [          ]
```

Rights for one directory were changed for .CN=KSS.OU=CORP.O=SCS

```
NW4CS\SYS:USERS
Directories                                                  Rights
----------------------------------------------------------  ------------
KSS                                                          [          ]
```

Rights for one directory were changed for .CN=KSS.OU=CORP.O=ESL

Notice, that all rights have been removed for the two user objects.

Table 24.10 shows the rights letter codes that can be used with the RIGHTS command.

Table 24.10
Rights Letter Codes in the RIGHTS Command

Rights Letter Codes	Description
ALL	Grant all rights except supervisor
N	Revoke all rights
S	Supervisor right
C	Create right
R	Read right
W	Write right
E	Erase right
M	Modify right
F	File scan right
A	Access Control right
+	Adds the right to existing rights
-	Removes a right from existing rights

When you precede the /NAME= with the keyword REM, the names listed in the /NAME parameter are removed as trustees to the file or directory. This is different from removing trustee rights. Removing trustee rights can remove rights, including all rights but the user is still listed as a trustee.

To remove user .KSS.CORP.ESL as a trustee of SYS:USERS/KSS, you can use the following command:

```
NW4CS\SYS:USERS\KSS
User .KSS.CORP.ESL is no longer a trustee of the specified directory.
Trustee .KSS.CORP.ESL was removed from one directory.
```


Inherited Rights Mask and Inherited Rights Filter

In NetWare 3.*x*, the *Inherited Rights Mask* (IRM) is the filter that blocks the inheritance of rights from parent directories. NetWare 3.*x* assigns an IRM to each subdirectory and file. In NetWare 4.*x* the IRM is called the Inherited Rights Filter. Their meanings are the same, and they behave in the same manner.

When a user creates a new directory (or file), the maximum potential rights that it can inherit from the parent directory are all rights. That is, the Inherited Rights Mask (or Inherited Rights Filter in NetWare 4.*x*) is [SRWCEMFA]. (The individual letters in the square brackets represent the first letter of the individual right.) The IRM or IRF can be restricted to limit the effective rights a user has to a directory (or file).

You can use the NetWare utility FILER or the command-line utility ALLOW to modify the IRM (or IRF).

Controlling IRM in NetWare 3.*x*

The following example illustrates the use of the ALLOW command on a NetWare 3.*x* server. To see the IRM for a directory for the user KIPLING, type the following:

```
ALLOW SYS:USERS/KIPLING
```

To assign an IRM of Read, Write, Create, File, Scan, and Access Control for user KIPLING, type:

```
ALLOW SYS:USERS/KIPLING TO INHERIT R W C F A
```

Controlling IRF in NetWare 4.*x*

You can use the /F option to examine or change the Inherited Rights Filter. To see the current IRF for SYS:USERS/KSS, use the following command:

```
RIGHTS SYS:USERS/KSS  /F

NW4CS\SYS:USERS
Directories                                                Rights
---------------------------------------------------------- ---------------
KSS                                                        [SRWCEMFA]
```

You can precede a right with a + or – to add or remove that right from the IRF. You can remove all rights from the IRF, except the Supervisor right.

To remove the Write right from the IRF for SYS:USERS/KSS, use the command:

```
RIGHTS SYS:USERS/KSS  -W   /F

NW4CS\SYS:USERS
Directories                                                  Rights
------------------------------------------------------------ ------------
KSS                                                          [SR CEMFA]
```

To set the IRF for SYS:USERS/KSS to [SR F], use the command:

```
RIGHTS SYS:USERS/KSS  SRF   /F

NW4CS\SYS:USERS
Directories                                                  Rights
------------------------------------------------------------ ------------
KSS                                                          [SR    F ]
```

In NetWare 4.*x*, the /I option of the RIGHTS command allows you to see how the inherited rights contribute to effective rights.

To see your rights that have been inherited for SYS:PUBLIC for the user KSS defined in container OU=CORP.O=SCS, use the command:

```
RIGHTS SYS:PUBLIC  /NAME=.KSS.CORP.SCS  /I
Name= .KSS.CORP.SCS
Path Rights
---------------------------------------------------------------------------
NW4CS\SYS:

Inherited Rights Filter: [                          ]

Inherits from above:[                          ]
--------------
Effective Rights = [                          ]
---------------------------------------------------------------------------
NW4CS\SYS:\PUBLIC

Inherited Rights Filter:  [SRWCEMFA]

Inherits from above:[                          ]
KSS.CORP.SCS [ R            F   ]
--------------
Effective Rights = [ R            F   ]
---------------------------------------------------------------------------
```

The /I option enables you to see inherited rights. It shows you the sequence of steps as to how rights are computed.

Effective Rights

Figure 24.33 illustrates how effective rights can be determined from Trustee Assignments and the Inherited Rights Mask by applying some *rules of combination.* These rules of combination are illustrated in figures 24.34 and 24.35 for directories and files. In the computation examples of rights, the term IRM is used. If you are using NetWare 4.*x*, you can replace IRM with IRF in these examples, and they behave the same as in NetWare 3.*x*.

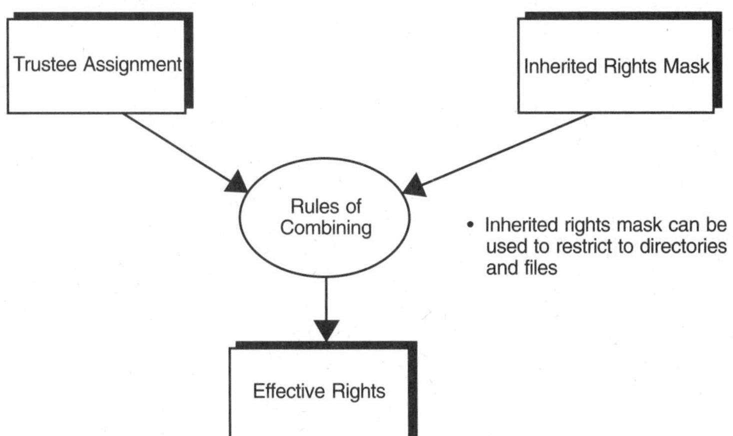

Figure 24.33
Effective Rights and Inherited Rights Mask. (Graphic courtesy of Learning Group International)

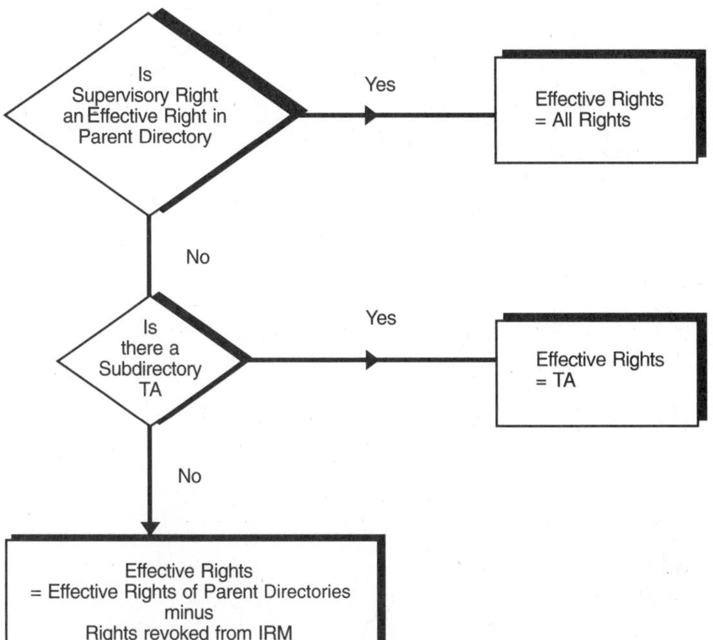

Figure 24.34
Effective Rights for directories.

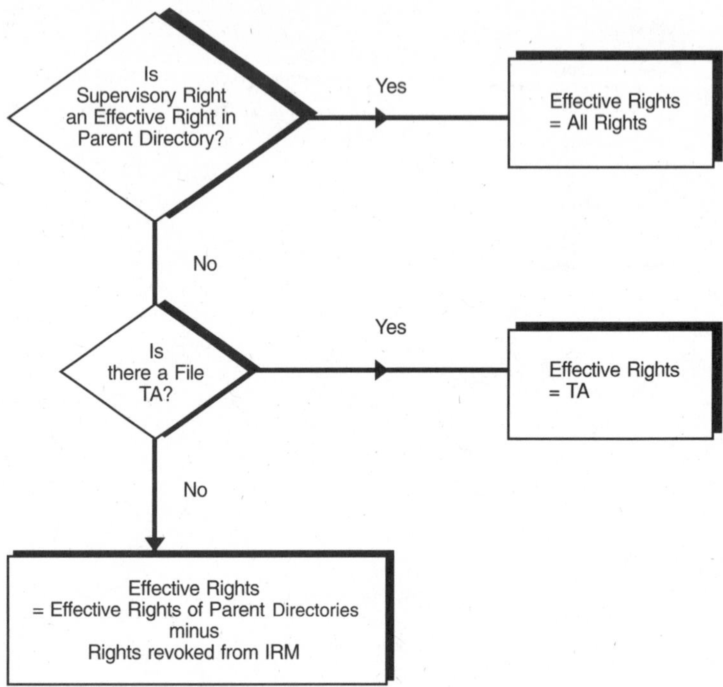

Figure 24.35 *Effective Rights for files.*

At first glance, the rules of combination look complex, but after you study a few examples, you can appreciate the logic behind them. The examples that follow determine effective rights for directories.

Example 1: If no explicit Trustee Assignment has been granted to a subdirectory, the effective rights for the subdirectory are determined by the *logical* AND of the subdirectory's Inherited Rights Mask and the parent directory's effective rights. The effective rights of SUBDIR01 and the logical AND operation are shown in figure 24.36.

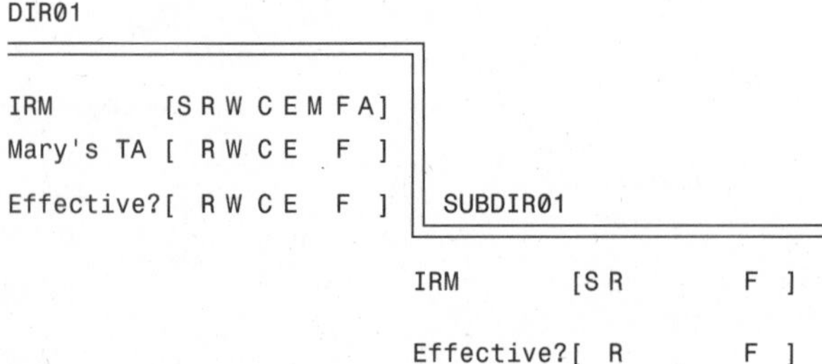

Figure 24.36 *No explicit trustee assignment in subdirectory. (Graphic courtesy of Learning Group International)*

Example 2: If explicit Trustee Assignment has been granted to a subdirectory, the effective rights for the subdirectory are the same as the explicit Trustee Assignment regardless of the subdirectory's Inherited Rights Mask. In other words, an explicit TA overrides any IRM setting. The effective rights to subdirectory SUBDIR02 are shown in figure 24.37.

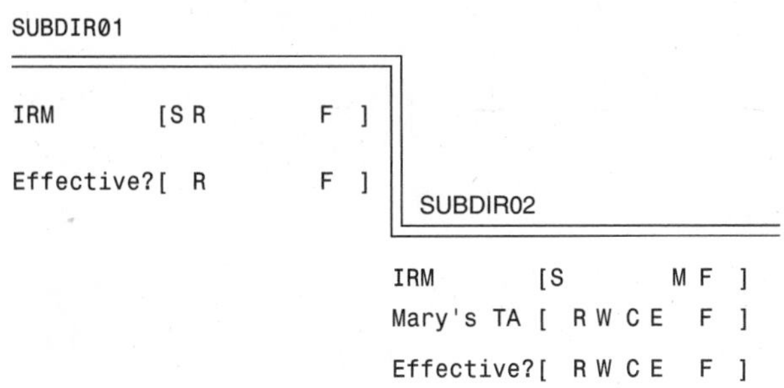

Figure 24.37
Trustee rights in subdirectory. (Courtesy of Learning Group International)

Example 3: If Supervisory Rights are granted to the parent directory, the user has all rights for the subdirectories and files regardless of a subdirectory's Trustee Assignment and Inherited Rights Mask (see fig. 24.38). (You must be careful when you assign Supervisory rights.)

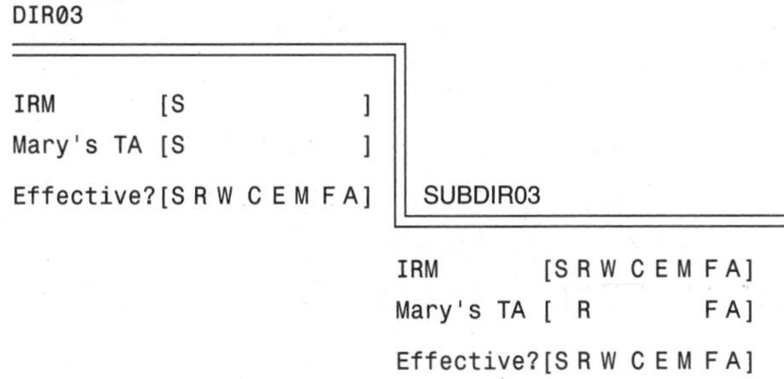

Figure 24.38
Supervisory rights in parent directory. (Graphic courtesy of Learning Group International)

You can examine the effective rights by using the NetWare utility FILER or the command-line utility RIGHTS.

To view the effective rights for the current directory for the user issuing the command, type:

RIGHTS

To view the effective rights of user ATHENA for directory SYS:USERS, type:

RIGHTS SYS:USERS/ATHENA

The rules of combination are designed so that effective rights flow down subdirectories. If no explicit TA is made, the effective rights are modified by the IRM. When an explicit TA is made, a new set of effective rights flows down subdirectories. This is different from pre-NetWare 2.2 versions in which Trustee Assignments rather than Effective Rights flow down subdirectories. When this happens, unexpected rights can be inherited by users when they create new subdirectories. The Inherited Rights Mask and the rules of combination were introduced in NetWare 2.2 and NetWare 3.*x* to overcome these problems. If you are familiar with NetWare 2.1*x*, the Inherited Rights Mask replaces the Maximum Rights Mask used in the earlier NetWare versions.

Attribute Security

Individual files or directories can be assigned attributes that override a user's effective rights (see fig. 24.39). USER1 has Read, Create, Erase, Write effective rights to SYS:PUBLIC/DATA. But the file is flagged with a Delete Inhibit attribute that prevents the file from being deleted even though the user has the Erase effective right for the directory.

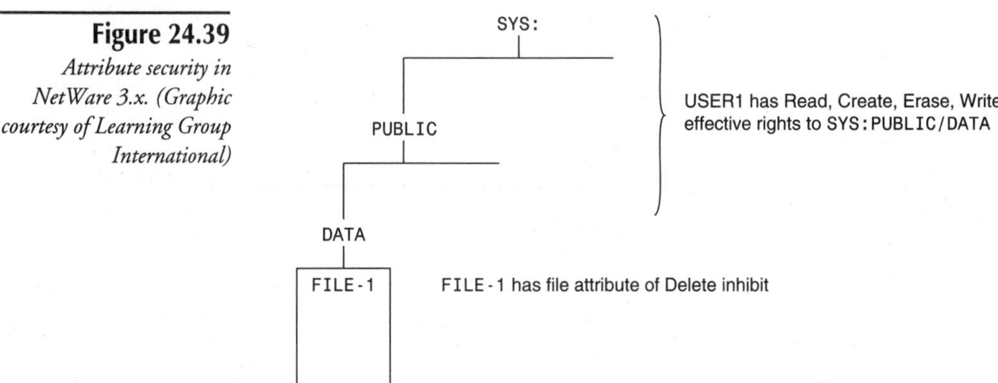

Figure 24.39 *Attribute security in NetWare 3.x. (Graphic courtesy of Learning Group International)*

24

Directory attributes and file attributes common to both NetWare 3.*x* and NetWare 4.*x* are illustrated in tables 24.11 and 24.12. In NetWare 3.*x*, directory attributes are set by the FLAGDIR command and file attributes are set by the FLAG command. In NetWare 4.*x*, the FLAG command can be used for setting attributes of files and directories.

Table 24.13 shows additional NetWare 4.*x* directory and file attributes.

Table 24.11
Directory Attributes for NetWare 3.*x*

Directory Attribute	Meaning
D	The *Delete Inhibit* attribute prevents directory from being erased.
H	The *Hidden* attribute hides a directory from a DOS DIR command.
P	The *Purge* attribute purges all files in directory when deleted.
R	The *Rename Inhibit* attribute prevents a directory from being renamed.
Sy	The *System* attribute similar to H; used for system directories.

Table 24.12
File Attributes for NetWare 3.*x*

File Attribute	Meaning
A	The *Archive Needed* attribute is automatically assigned to files modified after backups.
CI	The *Copy Inhibit* attribute restricts copy rights for Macintosh users.
DI	The *Delete Inhibit* attribute prevents file from being erased.
X	The *Execute Only* attribute prevents files from being copies; is permanent.
H	The *Hidden* attribute hides a file from a DOS DIR scan.
I	The *Indexed* attribute speeds access to large files; automatically assigned for files with over 64 FAT entries.
P	The *Purge* attribute purges a file when deleted.
Ra	The *Read audit* attribute audits reads to a file.
Ro	The *Read only* attribute cannot write to, erase, or rename files.
Rw	The *Read Write* attribute is the default setting for a file.
R	The *Rename Inhibit* attribute prevents a file from being renamed.
S	The *Sharable* attributes file can be used by more than one user.
Sy	The *System* attribute is similar to H; used for system files.
T	The *Transactional* attribute protects against incomplete operations on files.
Wa	The *Write audit* attribute audits writes to a file.

Table 24.13
Additional NetWare 4.*x* Attributes

Attribute	File/Directory	Abbreviation	Description
Migrate	File	M	Indicates that the file has migrated to near-line storage.

continues

Table 24.13, Continued
Additional NetWare 4.*x* Attributes

Attribute	File/Directory	Abbreviation	Description
Don't Migrate	File/Directory	Dm	Prevents a file or the files in a directory from migrating.
Compress	File	Co	Indicates if a file has been compressed.
Don't Compress	File/Directory	Dc	Prevents a file or the files in a directory from being compressed.
Immediate Compress	File/Directory	Ic	Specified file or files in a directory are marked for compression as soon as the OD can perform compression.
Can't compress	File	Cc	Indicates that a file cannot be compressed because of limited space-saving benefit.

The attributes Migrate (M), Compress (Co), Can't Compress (Cc) are status attributes and indicate the status of individual files only. The other attributes Don't Migrate (Dm), Don't Compress (Dc), and Immediate Compress (Ic) apply to both files an directories and specify actions that are to be performed or prevented from occurring.

The Data Migration feature is installed using INSTALL.NLM and requires a near-line-storage media that acts as a secondary to the primary hard disk storage area.

The compression feature is enabled or disabled on a volume-by-volume basis during installation. It can be further controlled by a variety of SET parameters.

SALVAGE and FILER

In NetWare 3.*x* there are two utilities to manage the file system—SALVAGE and FILER. In NetWare 4.*x* the salvage and file management functions are performed in a single integrated utility called FILER. There is no separate SALVAGE utility under NetWare 4.*x*.

SALVAGE restores files that have been deleted. In NetWare 2.*x*, SALVAGE has a command-line interface and can recover files that were deleted in the last delete command for the current log-in session. The NetWare 3.*x* SALVAGE is more flexible and enables the recovery of files that have been deleted but whose disk space has not been reallocated for other purposes.

The FILER utility can be used to change a user's rights to a file or a directory. FILER enables you to set a Trustee Assignment to a directory (or file) and to modify the IRM (or IRF in NetWare 4.*x*).

SALVAGE (NetWare 2.2 and NetWare 3.*x*)

NetWare 2.2's SALVAGE command enables you to select a volume and then recover files last deleted. NetWare 3.*x*'s SALVAGE utility is more powerful and a superset of the NetWare 2.2's SALVAGE utility. This section discusses the NetWare 3.*x* SALVAGE utility.

The SALVAGE utility can be used to:

- Recover or purge a file
- Restore files
- View/Recover deleted files

When SALVAGE is invoked from the command line, the Main Menu Options screen displays with the following options:

Salvage From Deleted Directories. This option recovers erased files from directories that do not exist.

Select Current Directory. This option enables you to change to another directory or volume/server to view the files that can be salvaged.

Set Salvage Options. This option enables you to change the way files are displayed on the screen. For example, you can display files sorted by deletion date, file size, file name, or owner name.

View/Recover Deleted Files. This option enables you to view files in the current directory. You can then recover or purge these files.

Recovered files are placed in the directory from which they were deleted. But if the directory has been deleted, the recovered files are placed in a hidden directory in the root called DELETED.SAV. NetWare currently does not track deleted directories, but it does track files by date and time. Because of this, you can have several versions of a file with the same name. If the file being recovered to a directory already exists, SALVAGE prompts you to rename the file being salvaged.

If you select View/Recover Deleted Files, the default pattern (*) shows all files. When you highlight a file for recovery and press Enter, information appears that tells you when the file was deleted, when it was last modified, who the owner of the file was, and who deleted it. To restore a file, choose Yes when the question Recover This File? appears.

To purge a file, highlight the file and press Del. Figure 24.40 shows the purge screen.

The files to be viewed can be sorted by a number of options shown in figure 24.41. Use Set Salvage Options in the SALVAGE main menu to determine these options.

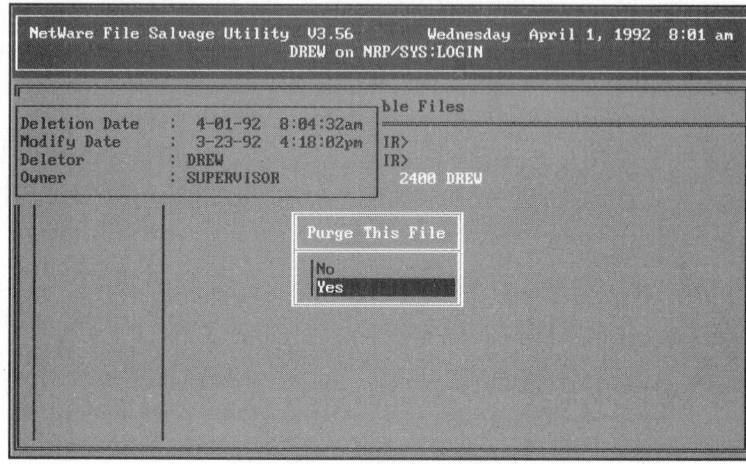

Figure 24.40 *The NetWare 3.x Salvage purge screen.*

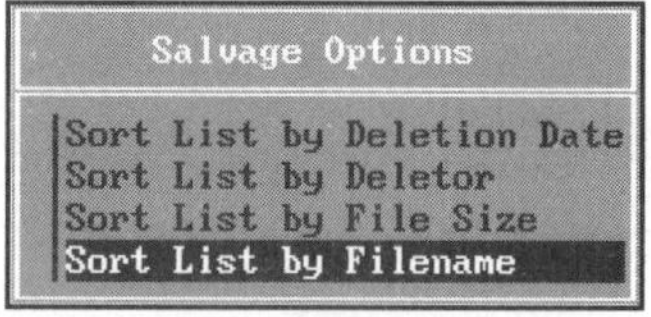

Figure 24.41 *The NetWare 3.x Salvage file list options.*

FILER (in NetWare 3.*x*)

The FILER utility is used to control volume, directory, and file information, to change directories, and to set file security.

To invoke the utility, type **FILER**. Figure 24.42 shows the NetWare 3.*x* FILER's main screen. The main options are briefly explained in the following list:

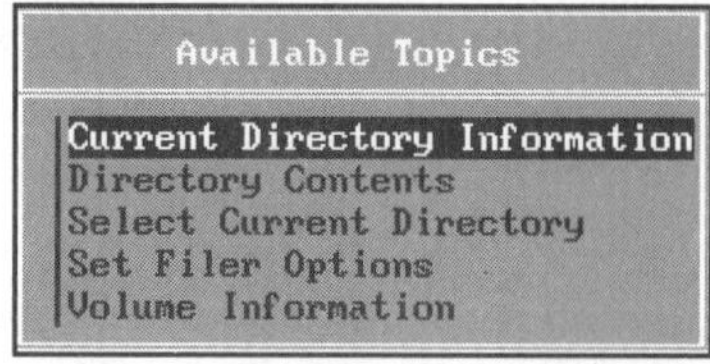

Figure 24.42 *NetWare 3.x FILER main menu.*

Current Directory Information. This option displays information about a directory such as:

Creation date

Directory owner

Inherited Rights Mask

Maximum Rights Mask (pre-NetWare 2.2)

Trustee Assignments

Effective Rights

Directory Contents. This option shows information on files and subdirectories for the current directory. Your effective rights determine which files and directories you can see.

Select Current Directory. This option enables you to change the current directory from FILER.

Set Filer Options. This option enables you to change the defaults for Directory Contents.

Volume Information. This option enables you to view the following information on the volume on which the current directory is located:

Total size of volume

Free space on volume

Maximum number of directories allowed

Unused directory entries

Figure 24.43 shows the screen that appears when you select Current Directory Information from the FILER main menu. If you can highlight a field, you can change the field.

```
Directory Information for

Owner: SUPERVISOR

Creation Date:  March 24, 1992
Creation Time:  2:38 pm
Directory Attributes: (see list)
Current Effective Rights: [SRWCEMFA]
Inherited Rights Mask: [        ]

Trustees:  (see list)
```

Figure 24.43
NetWare 3.x FILER directory information.

On the screen in figure 24.44, the following fields can be changed:

Owner

Creation Date

Creation Time

Directory Attributes

Inherited Rights Mask

Trustees

When FILER runs on pre-NetWare 2.2 versions, it displays the Maximum Rights Mask information instead of the Inherited Rights Mask.

To change directory rights for a current directory, select the Directory Attributes field, and press Enter. A list of Current Attributes displays. To add an attribute, press Ins; to delete an attribute, highlight it, and press Del. Figure 24.44 shows the list of directory attributes that can be added to SYS: directory. Table 24.11 describes these attributes.

The Inherited Rights Mask field can be changed in a manner similar to the Directory Attributes. Figure 24.45 shows the screen that appears after you highlight this field and press Enter and Ins. The rights displayed were discussed earlier in this chapter.

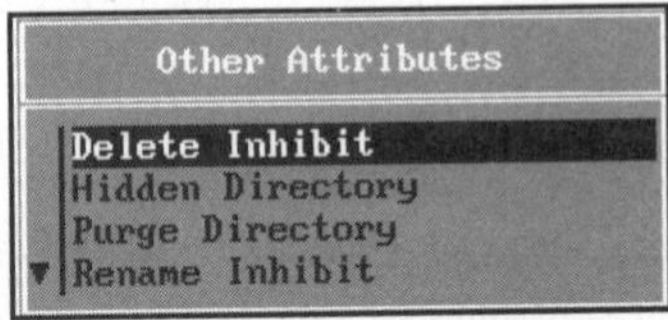

Figure 24.44
NetWare 3.x FILER Setting directory rights.

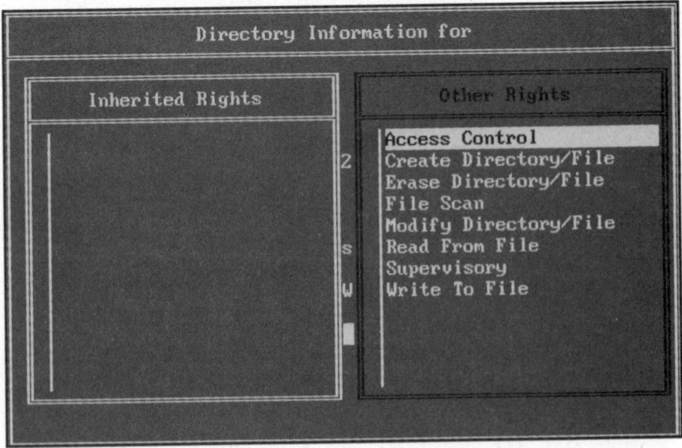

Figure 24.45
NetWare 3.x FILER Setting Inherited Rights Mask.

The Trustees field can be used to change the trustees (users or groups) assigned to the directory. Figure 24.46 shows the screen that displays after you highlight this field and press Enter and Ins. The list of users and groups that can become trustees to this directory appears.

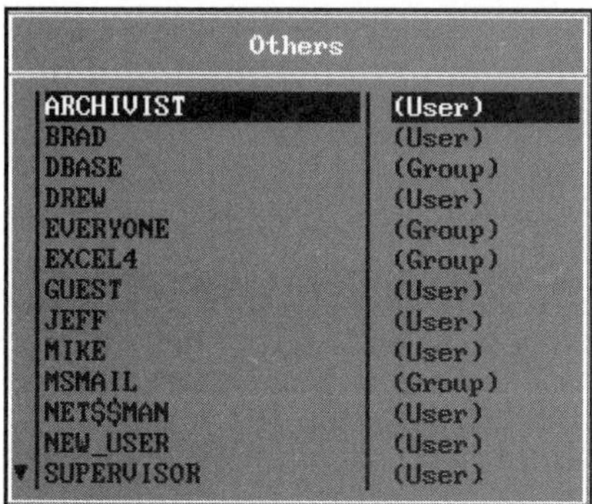

Figure 24.46
NetWare 3.x FILER Setting trustees.

The Directory Contents option on the FILER Available Topics menu can be used to display a list of the subdirectories and files contained by the current directory. Figure 24.47 shows the subdirectories and files that are displayed by selecting Directory Contents.

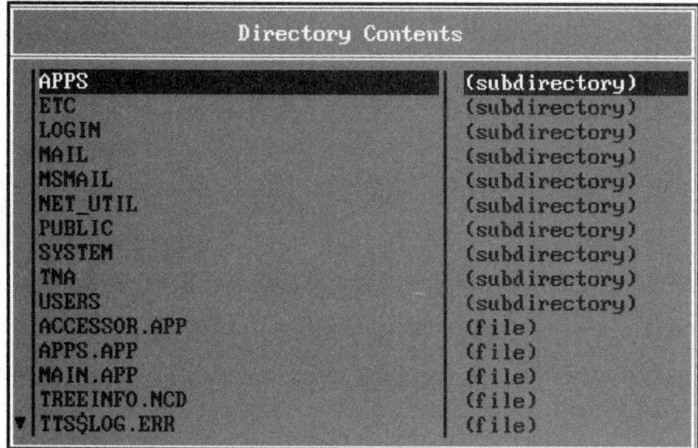

Figure 24.47
NetWare 3.x FILER Directory Contents.

To manage subdirectories, highlight the subdirectory name, and press Enter. This action displays the Subdirectory Options menu shown in figure 24.48. Selections in this box enable you to copy, move, and view subdirectories as well as enter subdirectory rights. This menu also has the Make This Your Current Directory option, which is an easy way to change FILER's current directory.

Figure 24.48
NetWare 3.x FILER Subdirectory Options.

If a file is highlighted in the Directory Contents box, FILER displays the menu shown in figure 24.49. This menu supports copying, moving, and viewing of files as well as setting file rights and file information.

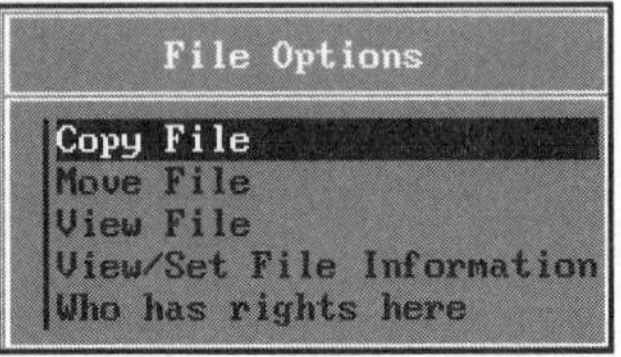

Figure 24.49
NetWare 3.x FILER File Options.

Figure 24.50 shows the screen when Set Filer Options is selected from the FILER main menu. If you can highlight a field, you can change the field.

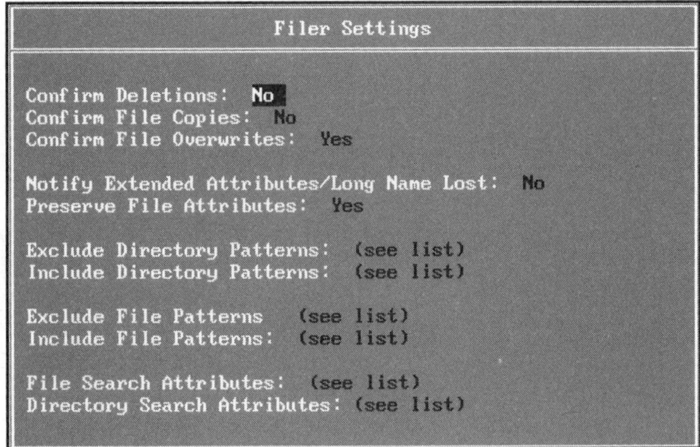

Figure 24.50
NetWare 3.x FILER File Settings.

On this screen, the following options can be changed:

Confirm Deletions

Confirm File Copies

Confirm File Overwrites

Notify Extended Attributes/Long Name Lost

Preserve File Attributes

Exclude/Include Directory Patterns

Exclude/Include File Patterns

File/Directory Search Attributes

Figure 24.51 shows the screen that appears when you select Volume Information from the FILER main menu.

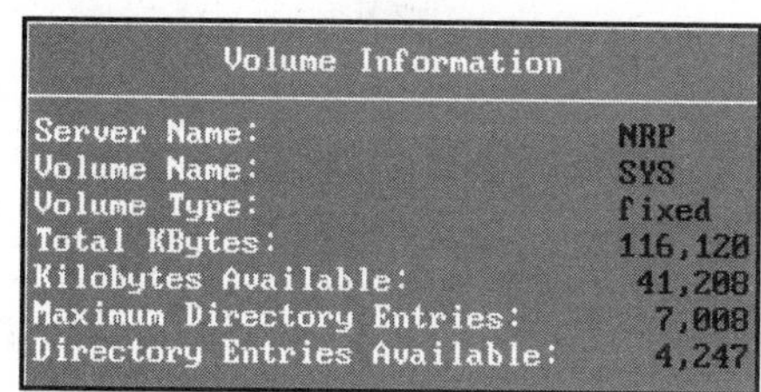

Figure 24.51
NetWare 3.x FILER Volume Information.

The FILER Utility in NetWare 4.*x*

The FILER utility, in NetWare 4.*x*, combines the functions of the NetWare 3.*x* FILER, SALVAGE, DSPACE, and VOLINFO.

FILER can be used to perform many of the file, directory and volume related tasks.

Some of the tasks that can be performed using FILER are the following:

- View file contents and directories
- View/set directory and file rights
- View/set directory and file attributes
- Copy, move, and delete files
- Delete entire subdirectory structure (including non-empty subdirectories)
- Limit disk space on a volume and directory
- Purge and savage files and directories

Figure 24.52 shows the main menu for FILER when the command FILER is run at a workstation.

The Manage files and directories option in the main menu shows you a list of directories and files in the current directory (see fig. 26.53).

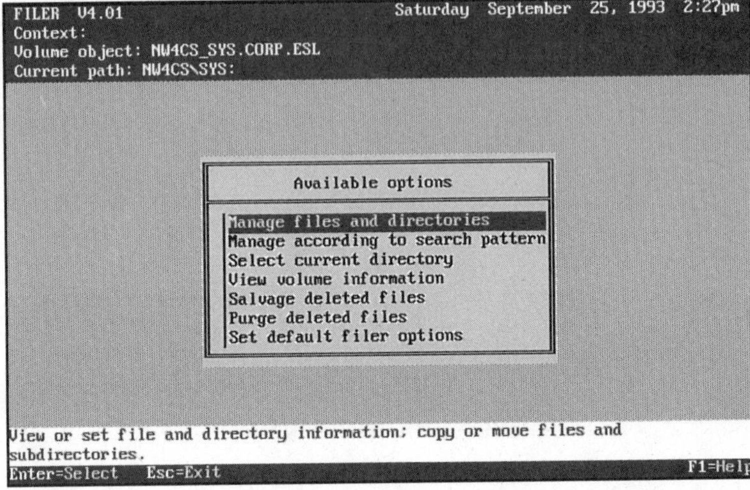

Figure 24.52
NetWare 4.x FILER Main Menu.

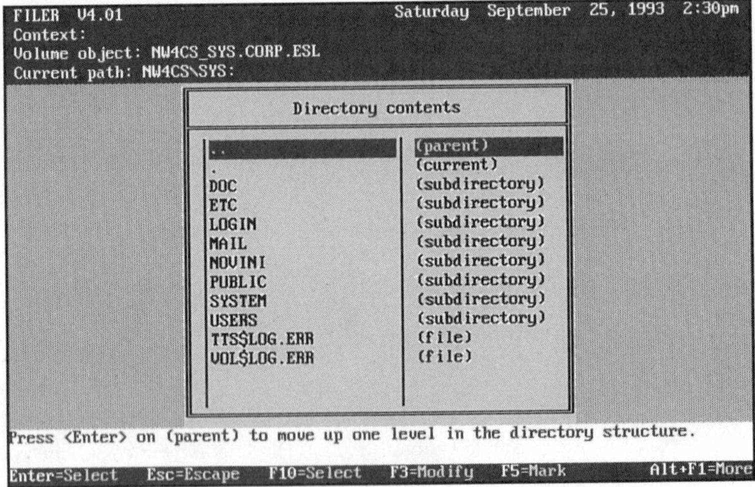

Figure 24.53
FILER Directory Content.

The Manage according to search pattern option in the main menu gives you the ability to set search patterns for the files and directories to view (see fig. 26.54).

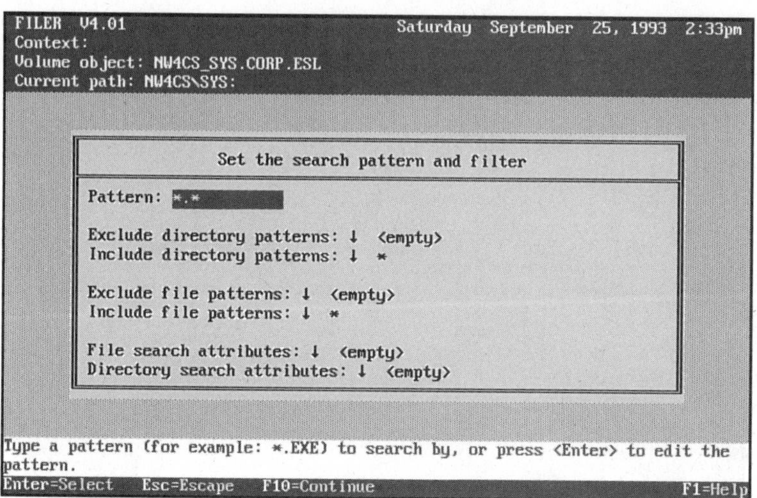

Figure 24.54
NetWare 4.x FILER Managing according to search patterns.

The Select current directory option in the main menu gives you the ability to set the current directory (see fig. 26.55). The current path is displayed on the top of the screen.

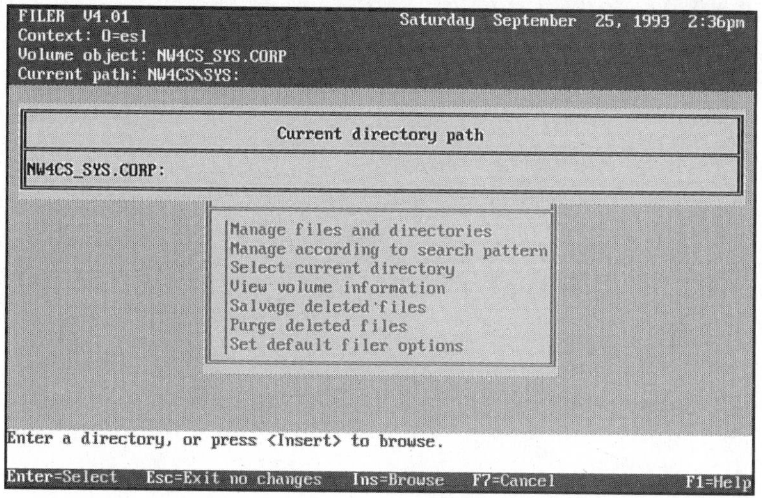

Figure 24.55
NetWare 4.x FILER Select Current Directory.

The View volume information option in the main menu gives you the ability to view statistics, features, date and time information for a volume (see fig. 26.56). The volume information is shown in figures 26.57, 26.58, and 26.59.

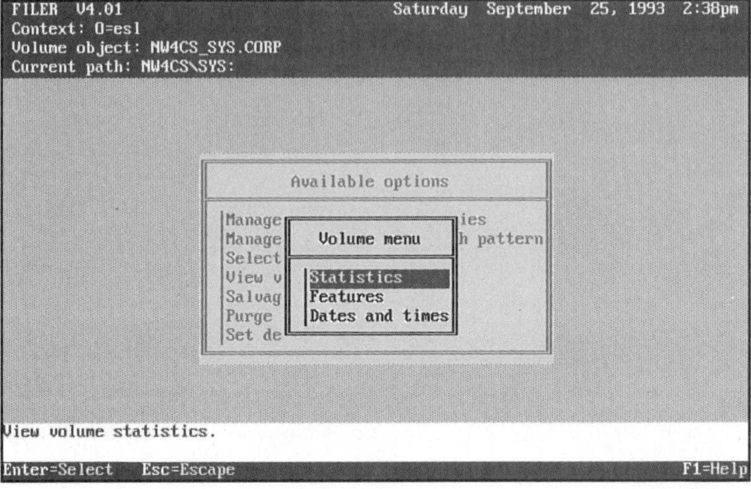

Figure 24.56
NetWare 4.x FILER View volume information.

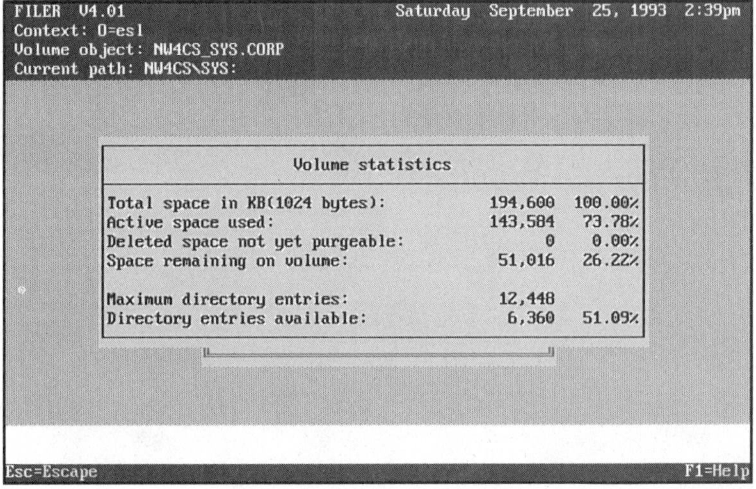

Figure 24.57
NetWare 4.x FILER Volume Statistics.

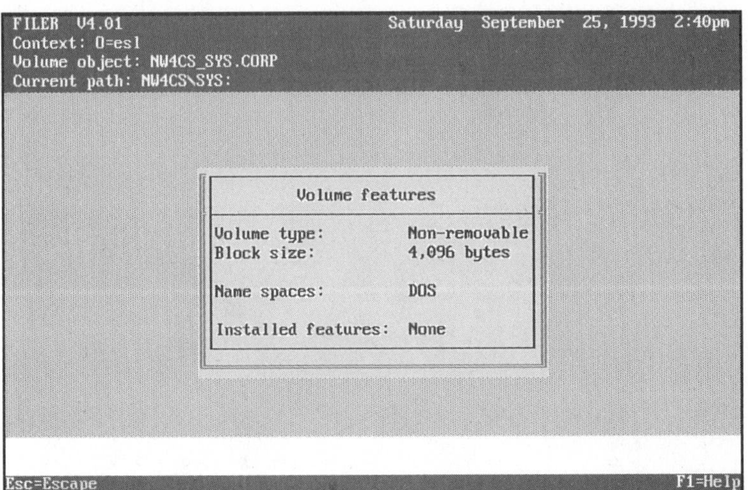

Figure 24.58
NetWare 4.x FILER Volume Features.

```
FILER  V4.01                              Saturday  September  25, 1993  2:40pm
Context: O=esl
Volume object: NW4CS_SYS.CORP
Current path: NW4CS\SYS:

                Volume dates and times

           Creation date: 8-21-1993
           Creation time: 7:31am
           Owner: [Supervisor]

           Last modified date: 9-25-1993
           Last modified time: 12:58pm

           Last archived date: (Not archived)
           Last archived time: (Not archived)
           Last archived by: Unknown

Esc=Escape                                                              F1=Help
```

Figure 24.59
NetWare 4.x FILER Volume Date and Times.

The Salvage deleted files option in the main menu gives you the ability to view/recover deleted files, salvage from deleted directories, and set salvage options (see fig. 26.60). The Purge deleted files option in the main menu gives you the ability to set a file pattern for all files to be purged (see fig. 26.61).

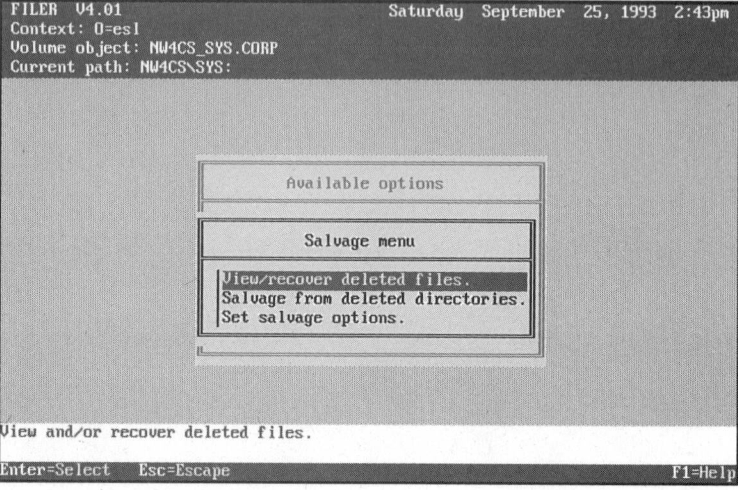

Figure 24.60
NetWare 4.x FILER Salvage deleted files options.

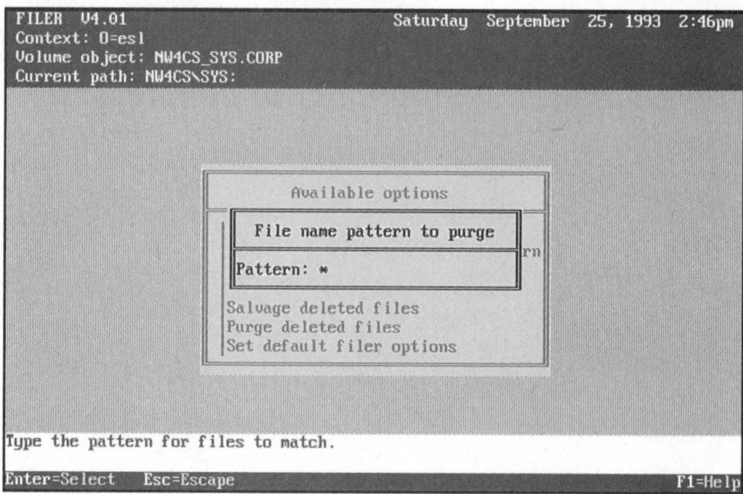

Figure 24.61
NetWare 4.x FILER Purge deleted files options.

The Set default filer options option in the main menu gives you the ability to confirm deletions, copy operations, overwrites (see fig. 26.62). It also allows you to specify of file attributes should be preserved, and if you should be notified if you are going to lose file attribute information when copying from one name space to another. NetWare 4.*x* allows the implementation of *sparse* files. Sparse files are common in database applications when a file may currently contain only a few of the total records that the file can contain. Because the valuable data is a small portion of the overall file size, a sparse representation of a file that occupies much less space can be designed. You can specify that if the files should be copied in their sparse format or not. You can also specify of the compressed files should be copied in the compressed state or not.

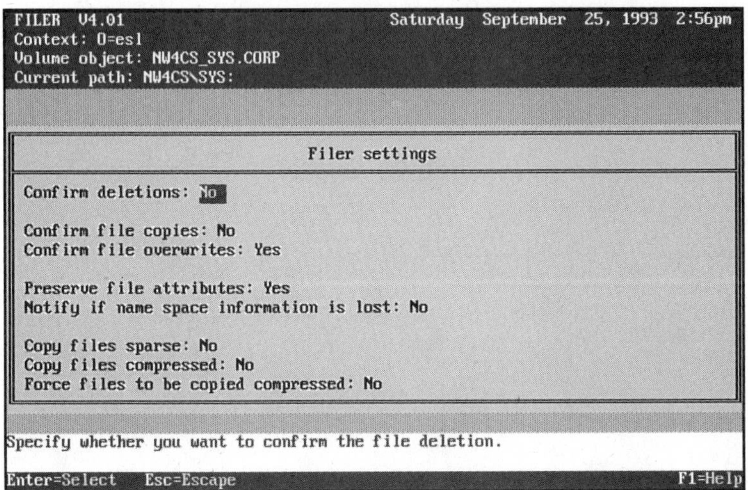

Figure 24.62
NetWare 4.x FILER Settings.

Summary

In this chapter, you have learned about the organization of the NetWare file system. The NetWare file system resides on physical hard disks at the server and is, therefore, effected by the performance of the server hard disk. You learned the characteristics of common server hard disks such as MFM, IDE, ESDI, and SCSI. This chapter also covered the use of the NetWare file system through network drives. Drive mappings and search drives were discussed, as well as the file security system.

NetWare Printing

In this chapter, you learn the fundamental concepts behind NetWare printing. You learn about the NetWare printing model, how to install print servers and remote printers, and how to configure core print services. You also are shown how to use NetWare printing utilities. As in previous chapters, some of the more important and intricate steps of network printing are covered in several examples.

The first part of this chapter covers general printing concepts that apply to all versions of NetWare. This is followed by coverage on NetWare 3.*x* printing services. Toward the end of the chapter, NetWare 4.*x* printing is discussed.

Understanding NetWare Printing

NetWare enables a printer to be shared by several users. An entire print job must be completed before another can start; otherwise, you get unreadable output consisting of characters from different print jobs. To be printed in a serial fashion, the jobs might have to wait in a queue.

NetWare enables users to share printers attached either to servers or workstations. Figure 25.1 shows a simple model for printing to a network printer attached to the file server. In the case of intelligent print devices, such as the HP LaserJet III Si, the printer can be attached directly to the network because it has the network interface and processing power to participate as a station on the network.

In earlier versions of NetWare, the only way a printer could be shared was to attach it to a server. Up to five printers could be attached in this manner. This type of configuration is called *core print services.* Core print services still are available in NetWare 2.2, but NetWare 2.2 uses a more flexible approach that enables most of the configuration to be done by console commands.

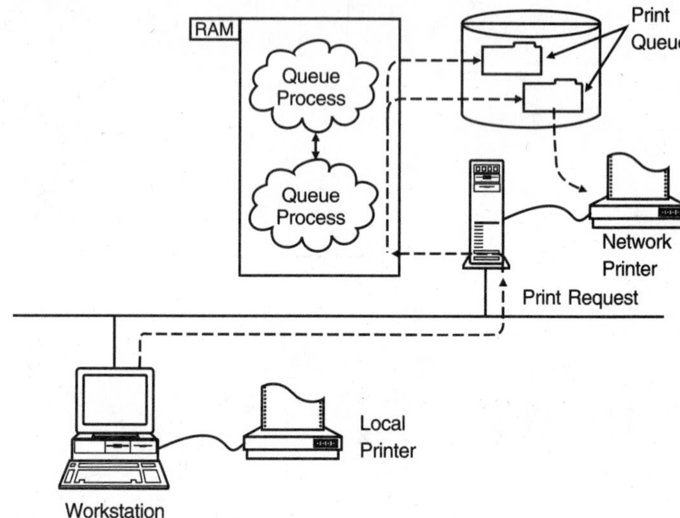

Figure 25.1
Network printer attached to the file server.

In earlier versions of NetWare (version 2.15 and below), the only way to configure the core print services was to bring down the server and run NETGEN in the custom mode, and then select Printer Options from the Miscellaneous Options box. It was difficult to manage NetWare Core Printing Services, so many outside vendors have produced utilities to fill this gap. These products work in conjunction with the NetWare printing mechanism and provide many useful features.

With the release of NetWare 3.*x*/4.*x*, a more flexible technique has been added that enables you to configure print servers at the server, a bridge, or a dedicated print server PC.

The print server configurations that currently are available in NetWare are as follows:

Print server VAP

Print server NLM

Dedicated print server at workstation

Nondedicated print server at workstation

Core print services

These print server configurations are examined in the sections that follow.

NetWare printing requests can be made from the workstation in several ways:

Using NPRINT

Using PRINTCON

Using CAPTURE and ENDCAP

NetWare-aware applications

NETUSER (in NetWare 4.*x*)

Figure 25.2 also shows some of these methods.

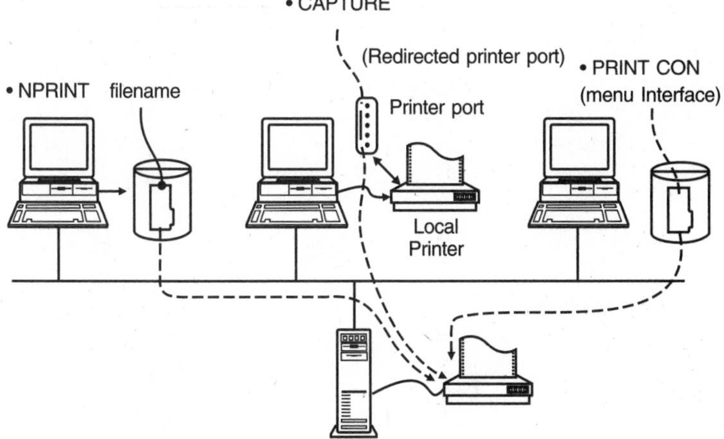

Figure 25.2
Common methods of printing from workstations.

25

In each of these methods, the data to be printed is directed from the workstation to a queue on the connected server. A print server process services the queue and directs the print job to a local printer or a remote printer (see fig. 25.3).

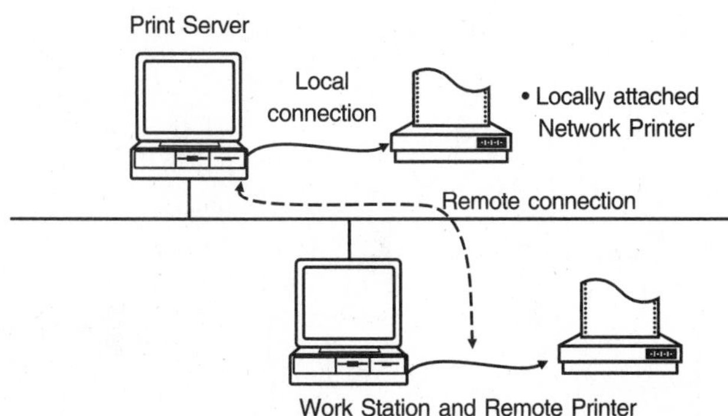

Figure 25.3
Network printers can be local or remote.

Using Local and Network Printers

Figure 25.4 shows a network that has a combination of local and network printers. Local printers can be used only by the workstations to which they are attached. Network printers can be shared by more than one user on the network.

After a print job leaves a workstation, it is stored temporarily in a print queue at the file server, and then is sent to the print server. If the print server is on a different machine than the file server, the print job is sent from the queue on the file server across the network to the printer. Figure 25.5 illustrates this concept.

Print Queues

Every print job sent to a network printer is sent to a print queue on the file server first. The queue stores the print job temporarily until the network printer is ready.

The print queues are created as subdirectories on the file server. In NetWare 3.*x* the print queues are created in the SYS:SYSTEM subdirectory. In NetWare 4.*x* print queues can be stored on any server writeable volume in the QUEUES directory. The print jobs are stored as files in the print queue subdirectory. After the print job is completed, the file containing the print job is removed.

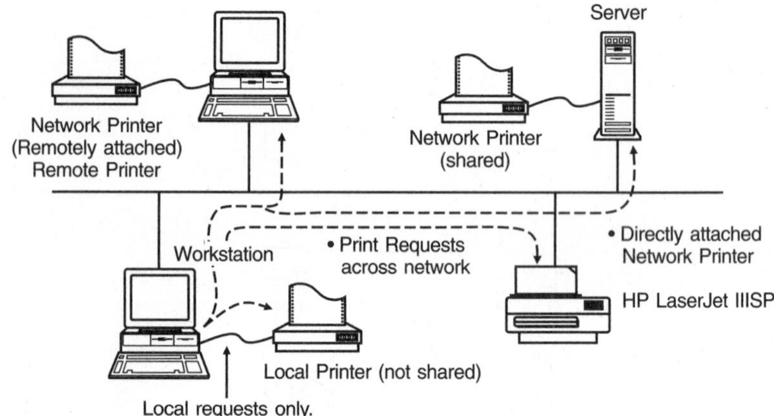

Figure 25.4
Local and network printers.

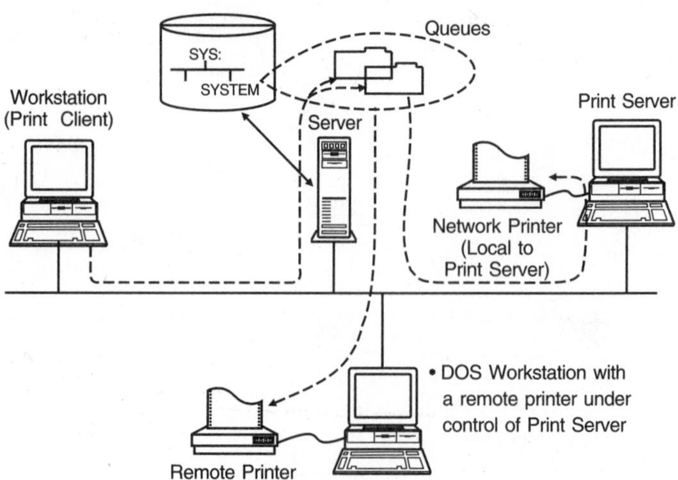

Figure 25.5
Routing print jobs from a print queue to a printer through a print server.

Print queues must be created by using the PCONSOLE utility or the NetWare 2.2 QUEUE command, and they must be created before defining a print server. Before queues can be created on a NetWare 2.2 server, core printing services must be installed by the INSTALL program.

The important concept to remember is that print queues are serviced by print servers; a *logical association* or *assignment* exists between a print queue and printers defined by the print server. The print server also can be considered a queue server because it prints jobs in the queue.

For the sake of simplicity and ease of management, it often is best to keep this logical association between a queue and a printer on a one-to-one basis, as shown in figure 25.6. Other types of logical associations, such as many-to-one, one-to-many, or many-to-many, also are possible. These are illustrated in figures 25.7 and 25.8.

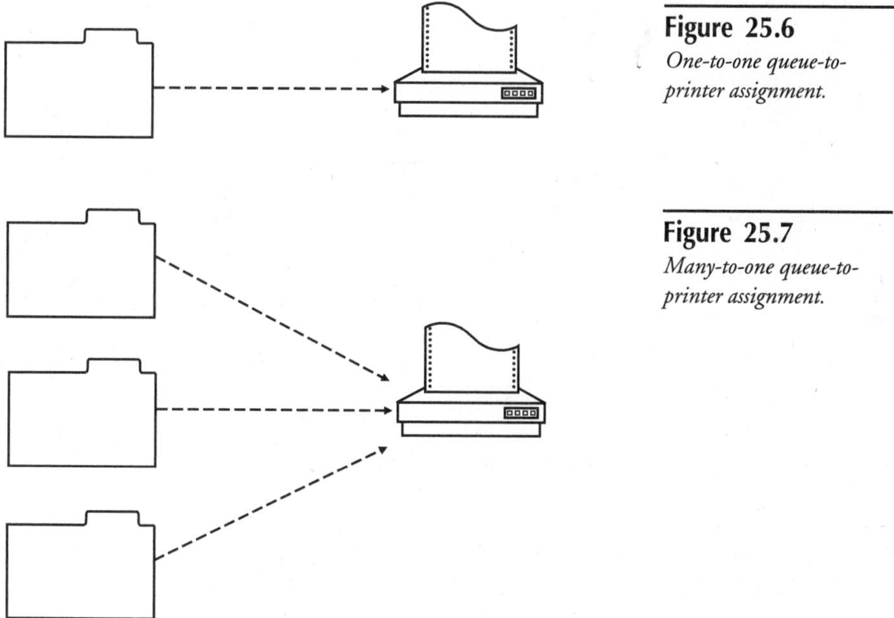

Figure 25.6
One-to-one queue-to-printer assignment.

Figure 25.7
Many-to-one queue-to-printer assignment.

In complex logical associations, you might need to use the *queue priority feature.* When a printer is assigned to a queue through PCONSOLE, you can select a priority number from 1 to 10 that determines the order in which the queue is serviced. Figure 25.9 shows a many-to-one printer setup in which queues are assigned at different priorities. The higher priority queue is serviced first, and the lower priority queues are serviced only when no print jobs are in the higher priority queues.

It is best to keep a one-to-one logical association between print queues and printers; that is, one print queue is serviced by one printer. Print queues and print servers should be given names that make it easy to identify this logical association. Also, the names selected must be indicative of the type of print jobs associated with print queues and print servers.

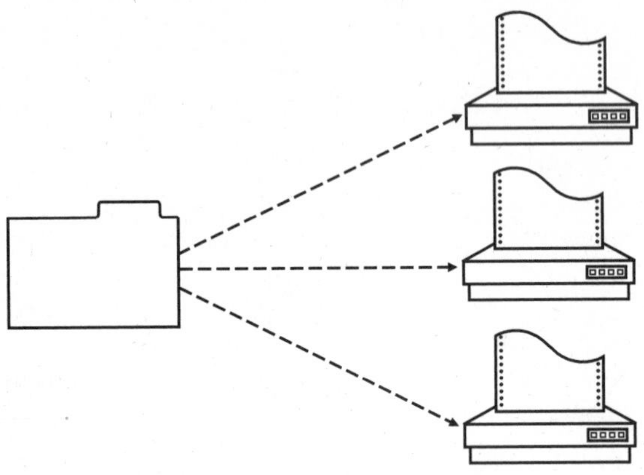

Figure 25.8
One-to-many queue-to-printer assignment.

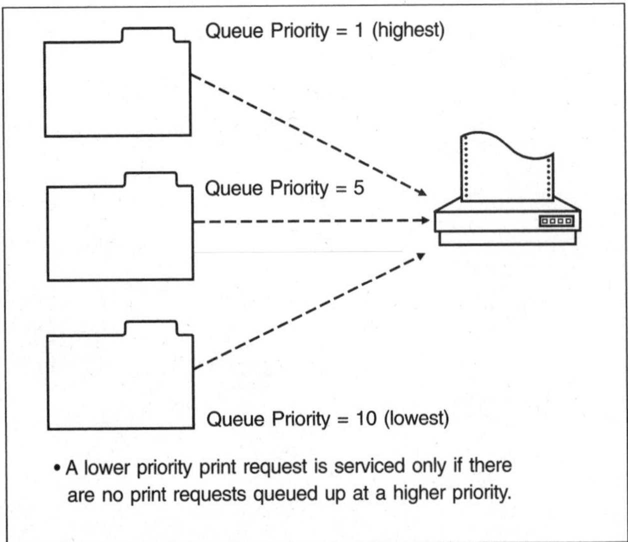

Figure 25.9
Queue priorities.

The discussion that follows covers printing in NetWare 2.*x* and 3.*x*. NetWare 4.*x* printing is covered in the latter part of his chapter.

Queue Operators and Queue Users in NetWare 3.*x*

Queues are managed by queue operators. Queue operators can perform the following tasks:

Assign other users to be queue operators

Edit a print job in the queue

Delete a print job, even while it is being printed

Modify queue status of the print job

Change the order in which print jobs are printed from the normal *First Come First Serviced* (FCFS) basis

After a print queue is created, the user SUPERVISOR is automatically assigned as a queue operator, and members of the group EVERYONE are assigned as print queue users. This is the default setup and works well for small networks.

In larger networks, it might become necessary to delegate responsibility for managing queues to other users. The supervisor can assign other users as queue operators through the PCONSOLE utility.

Figure 25.10 shows a print queue assigned for the group engineers located on the second floor of a building. The queue is defined on a file server located on the second floor, and the print server that services this queue also is on the second floor. The printing device might use special print paper, and because you do not want all users on the network to print to the engineering print server, the queue users will be members of group ENGINEERING and not group EVERYONE. These changes can be made by using the PCONSOLE utility.

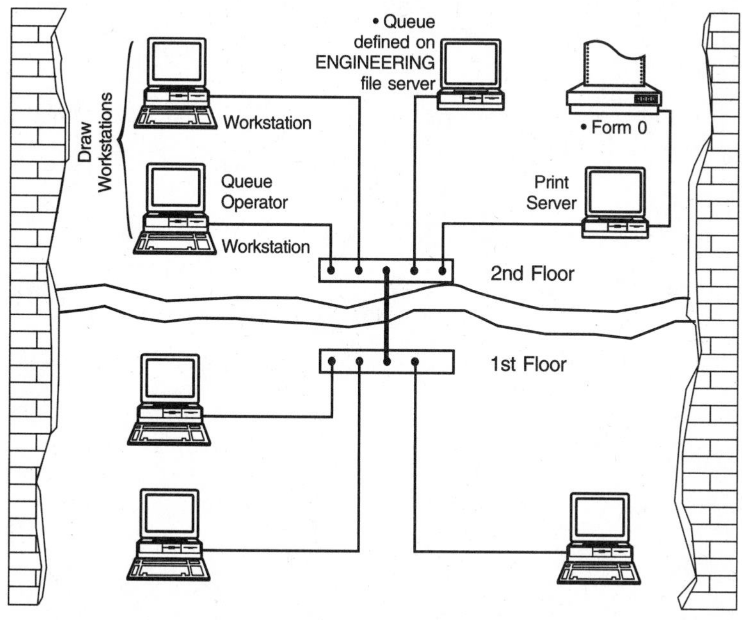

Figure 25.10
Organizing printers for groups and users.

Only users who are designated as queue users can submit jobs to the print queue.

In larger networks, delegate responsibility to queue operators for a department and make only the members of this department queue users. The queue operators then can manage the print jobs for their department. The queue can be defined on the departmental file server. If such a server does not exist, the queue might have to be defined on a central file server.

Print Servers in NetWare 3.*x*

A print server can be a workstation or a file server that has printers attached to its parallel or serial ports. A remote printer configuration also can be defined so that the print server sends the print job to a printer attached to another workstation. This workstation must be running the RPRINTER utility.

The print server takes the print jobs out of the queues assigned to it and sends them to the appropriate network printer. The print server must be created by using the PCONSOLE utility, *after* creating the print queues it will service. Before running the print server, you must use PCONSOLE to provide the following configuration information for the print server:

The queues that will be serviced by the printers

The file servers the print server must attach to service the queues

The print server operators

The printers that a print server will support

A print server can service queues from as many as eight file servers. If the print server must serve queues on other file servers, you must create a print-server user account on each file server so you can attach to them to access the queues on that file server.

Normally, any user can examine the status of a print server; you do not need special privileges to do this. If you want to print to a print server, however, you must be a *queue user* to insert your job in the queue serviced by the print server.

A *print server operator* is a special user who can perform the following tasks by using PCONSOLE:

Change queues serviced by the printer

Change queue priority

Attach print server to other file servers

Assign users to be notified if printer needs service

Change forms for the printer

Issue commands to the printer

Down the print server

A print server can specify and support up to 16 printers, including local and remote printers.

For local printers, you need to specify to which port the printer is connected. Up to five local printers can be defined. Most IBM PCs and compatibles can support up to three parallel printer ports (LPT1, LPT2, and LPT3) and two serial ports (COM1 and COM2). For serial printers, you must define the communication parameter settings in your printer configuration. These include the following:

Baud rate (bits per second)

Data bits (8 or 7 bits)

Stop bits (1 or 2)

Parity (Odd, Even, or None)

XON/XOFF (for flow control)

Remote printers are workstations that run a terminate-and-stay-resident (TSR) program called RPRINTER. A remote printer accepts the print jobs sent to it by the print server and directs them to the printer attached to the workstation.

NetWare Printing Utilities in NetWare 3.*x*

Table 25.1 shows a list of NetWare's printing utilities with a brief summary of their functions. These utilities are used depending on the situation at hand. These situations are discussed later in this chapter.

Table 25.1
NetWare Printing Utilities and Commands

Utility	Function
PCONSOLE	Print Console. Creates or modifies print queues and print server definitions, controls network printing, and views information about network printing.
PRINTDEF	Printer Definition. Creates a database to store print device definitions and print forms.
PRINTCON	Printer Console. Uses information stored in PRINTDEF to create customized print job configurations that control the way a job is printed. These print job configurations can be used with CAPTURE, NPRINT, and PCONSOLE.
CAPTURE	Captures local ports. Redirects output to local printer ports to printer queues on the file server. Used for applications and situations that do not have an understanding of printer queues.
ENDCAP	Ends capture of local printer ports. A printer attached to a local port can be used as a local printer.
SPOOL	Maps a network printer number to a printer queue to support older applications that print to a network printer number.

continues

Table 25.1, Continued
NetWare Printing Utilities and Commands

Utility	Function
NPRINT	Network Print. Modeled after the DOS PRINT command but works with network print queues. Used from the command line to submit a job to a file to be printed on a network printer.
PSC	Print Server Command. Controls print server from the command line as opposed to using PCONSOLE.

Print servers can be set up in one of four major ways. These methods correspond to the programs PSERVER.EXE, PSERVER.NLM, PSERVER.VAP, and RPRINTER.EXE. These print server configurations are described in table 25.2. RPRINTER.EXE can be used only if a print server has been set up in one of the other three ways. Technically, RPRINTER.EXE is not a print server program because it relies on either PSERVER.EXE, PSERVER.NLM, or PSERVER.VAP to act as a print server. RPRINTER.EXE supports a remote printer connection to a print server.

Table 25.2
NetWare Print Server Programs and Configurations

Print Server	Function
RSERVER.EXE	Runs at a DOS workstation in the nondedicated mode. Workstation can be used for running applications while printing takes place in the background. Must be used in conjunction with the PSERVER program running at a workstation or server.
PSERVER.EXE	Runs on a dedicated workstation and converts the workstation to a dedicated print server.
PSERVER.NLM	Print Server NetWare Loadbale Module. Runs on a NetWare 3.*x* server that can act as a print server.
PSERVER.VAP	Print Server Value Added Process. Runs on a NetWare 2.2 server that can act as a print server.

One easy way to remember which print server program corresponds to which machine platform is to examine the extension of these file names. The EXE print server programs run at the workstation. PSERVER.EXE runs at a dedicated station and converts it to a print server as the name of the program suggests. The R in RPRINTER.EXE stands for *remote.* This program is called RPRINTER, not RSERVER as it often is mistakenly referred to. This underscores the point made earlier, that RPRINTER is not really a print server program. It relies on the other PSERVER programs to direct a print job to it. The program with an NLM extension is a NetWare loadable module and can run only on a NetWare 3.*x* server. The program with a VAP extension is a value added process and can run only with a NetWare 2.*x* server.

Installing Print Servers in NetWare 3.*x*

Figure 25.11 shows an outline of the steps necessary to install a print server. In greater detail, these steps are as follows:

1. Create network print queues on the file server by using PCONSOLE.
2. Assign queue operators and queue users to the printer queue.
3. Create a print server definition.
4. Specify the file servers that have the queues that the print server will service.
5. Define printers used by the print server.
6. Assign queues to printers defined for the print server.
7. Optionally, set up printing for additional file servers.
8. Run one of the print server programs: PSERVER.EXE, PSERVER.VAP, or PSERVER.NLM on the appropriate hardware platform.
9. If a remote printer was assigned to the print server, run RPRINTER.EXE at the workstation (see fig. 25.11).

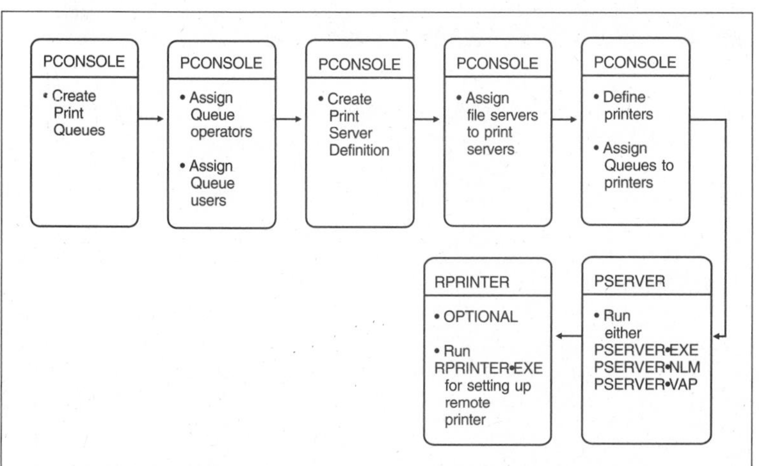

Figure 25.11
Print server installation chart.

Using PRINTDEF for Printer and Form Definitions in NetWare 3.*x*

PRINTDEF is used to define forms and printer definitions. The printer definitions include different modes of printer operation, such as letter quality, standard print mode, courier, and so on. The functions necessary to place the printer in a certain mode are defined in terms of escape code sequences that are sent to the printer.

NetWare comes with standard printer definitions for the major brands of printers. You can import and include them in the printer definition database, as follows:

1. Log in as a supervisor to a NetWare server. (This exercise shows the screens for a NetWare 3.11 server.) Type **PRINTDEF** to invoke the PRINTDEF utility. A screen similar to the one in figure 25.12 appears.

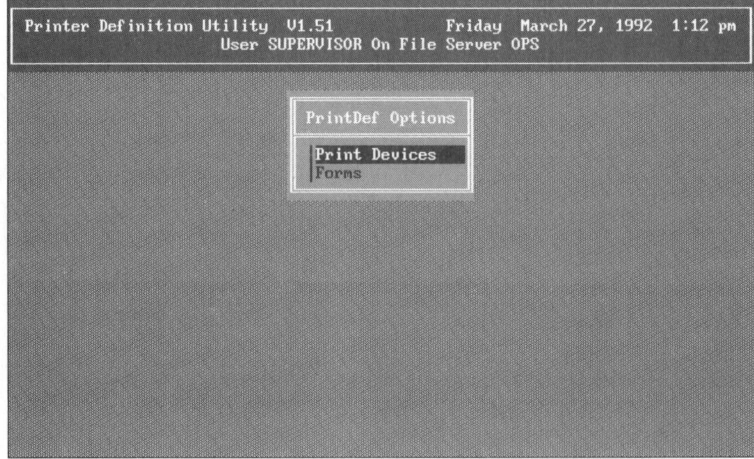

Figure 25.12
The PrintDef Options box.

2. Highlight the Forms option and press Enter. A screen showing a list of forms that have been defined appears (see fig. 25.13).

3. The screen shows a form that already has been defined. To add a new form, press Ins. A Form Definition box similar to the one shown in figure 25.14 displays.

4. Use the cursor keys to enter the following values:

   Name of form

   Form number

Length of form in number of lines per page

Width of form in number of characters per line

After entering the name of the form, press Esc and answer Yes to save the changes.

The new form that has been added appears (see fig. 25.15).

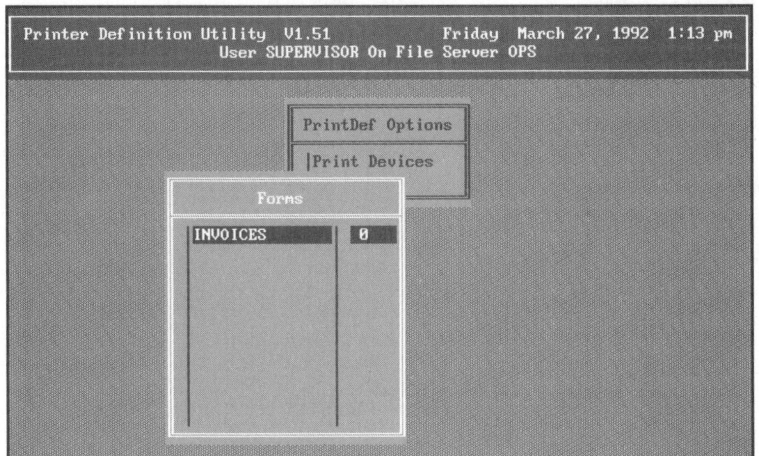

Figure 25.13
The Forms box.

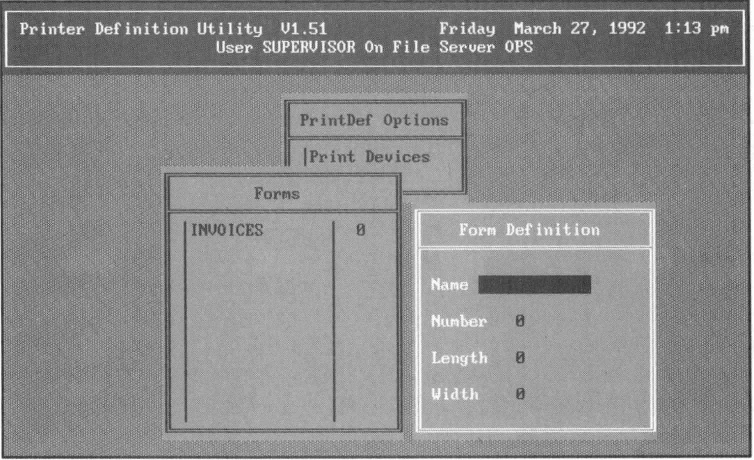

Figure 25.14
The Form Definition box.

25

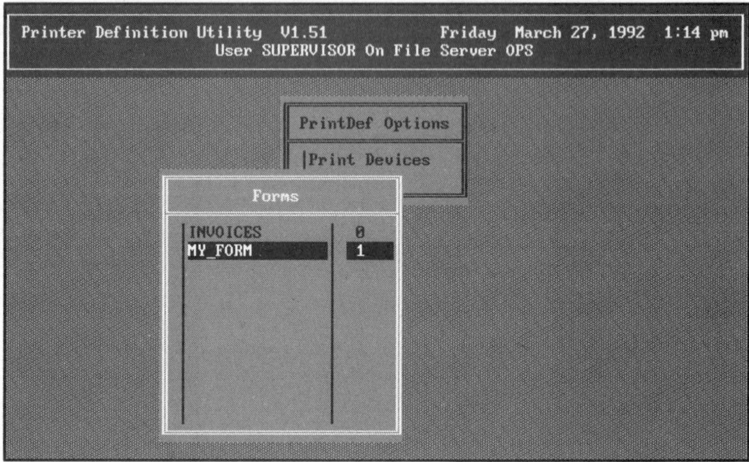

Figure 25.15
The Forms box.

5. Press Esc to go back to the PrintDef Options list. You now are finished creating a new form that can be used later on.

   NetWare comes with several printer device definitions for most standard printers. The printer definition you want probably has already been defined in the *Printer Definition Files* (PDF) that can be found in SYS:PUBLIC. The PDF files are easily recognizable because they have a PDF extension. Even if you want to create a new printer definition file, you can almost always start with an existing PDF file and customize it to suit your needs.

6. From the PrintDef Options box, select the Print Devices option. The Print Device Options box is displayed (see fig. 25.16).

   The Edit Print Devices option can be used for editing an existing definition. It also can be used for viewing an existing definition. The Import Print Device option can be used to insert a previously exported printer definition into the printer database. The Export Print Device option can be used to save a printer definition in the database to an external PDF file that can be used later on for importing to another printer definition database.

7. Select the Import Print Device option. When prompted for the Source Directory, enter **SYS:PUBLIC** or the name of the directory containing the PDF files, and press Enter. A list of available PDFs displays (see fig. 25.17).

8. Highlight the PDF file that you want to import and press Enter. For this exercise, import the APPLASER.PDF file.

9. You should be back to the Print Device Options list after the selected PDF file has been imported. Select the Edit Print Devices option to view the printer definitions. You should see a list of printer definitions in the database. In figure 25.18, for example, you also see an Epson Ex-800 printer definition that already was defined in this printer definition database.

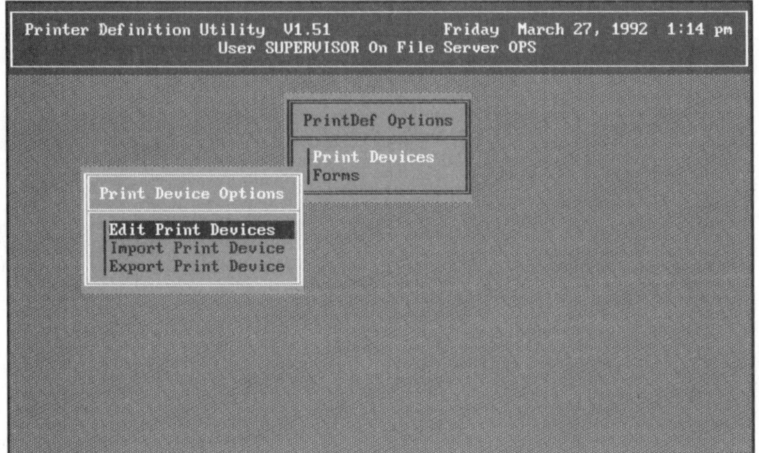

Figure 25.16
The Print Device Options box.

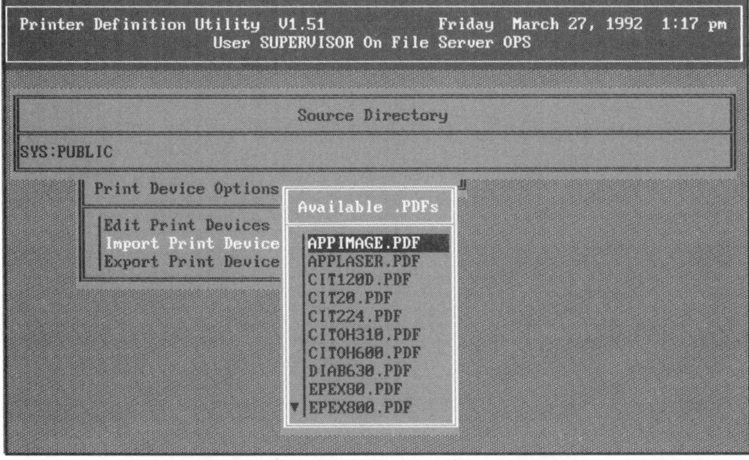

Figure 25.17
The Available .PDFs box.

10. Highlight the newly defined printer and press Enter to see its definition. The Edit Device Options box displays (see fig. 25.19).

11. Select the Device Modes option. A list of device modes for the selected printer definition displays (see fig. 25.20).

12. Select one of the device modes and press Enter. The functions defined in the selected device mode appear (see fig. 25.21).

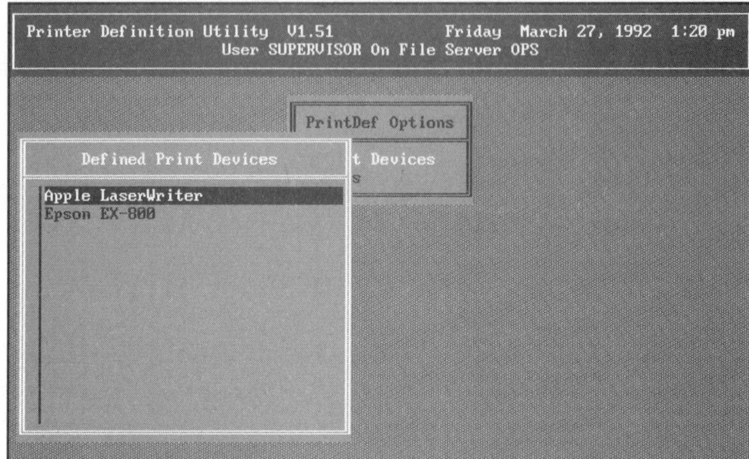

Figure 25.18
The Defined Print Devices box.

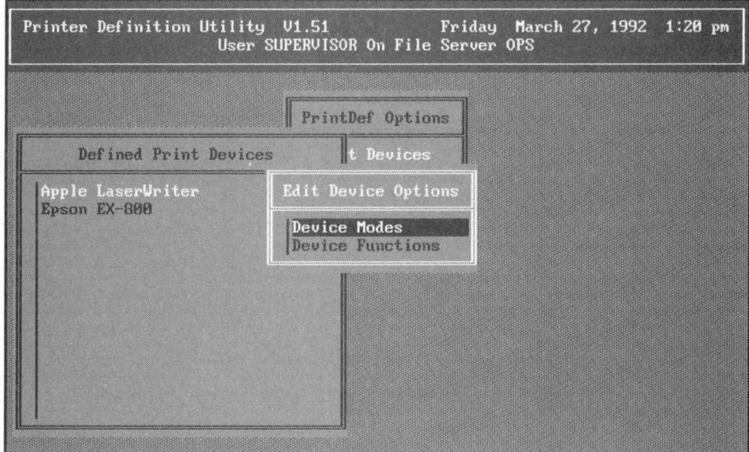

Figure 25.19
The Edit Device Options box.

13. Select one of the functions and press Enter. The escape codes defined for that function are listed, as shown in figure 25.22.

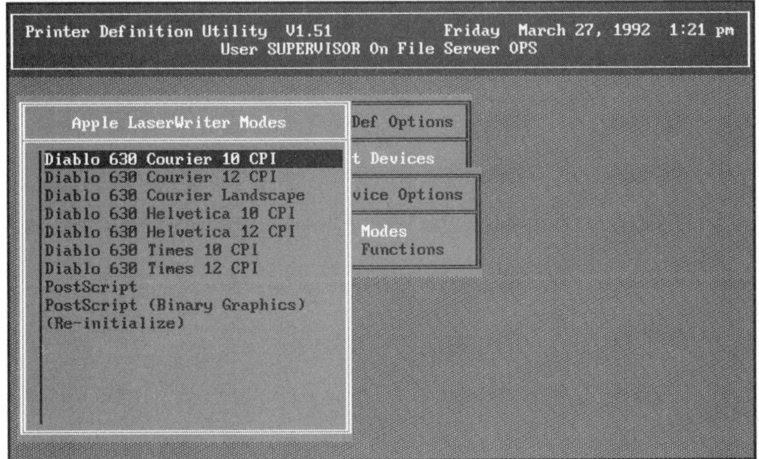

Figure 25.20
Device modes for the selected printer definition.

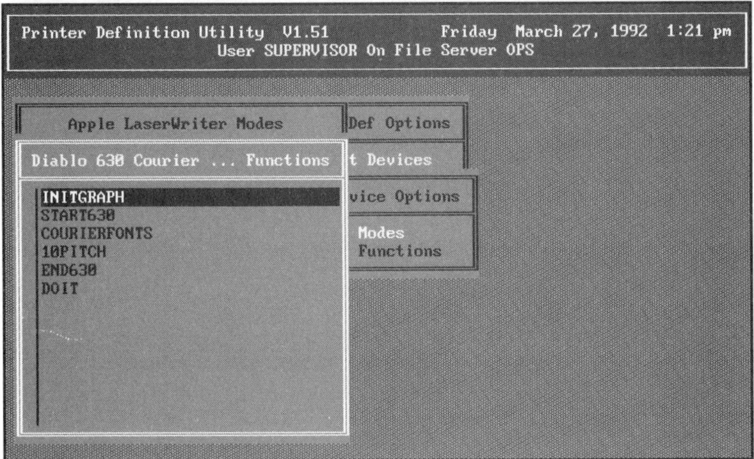

Figure 25.21
Device mode functions.

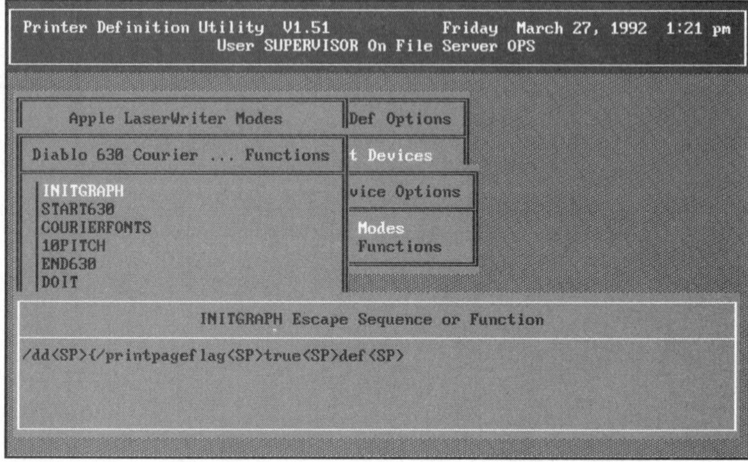

Figure 25.22
The Escape Sequence or Function box.

14. Press Esc enough times to get back to the Edit Device Options box and select Device Functions. The list of functions and their corresponding escape codes are listed, along with the function you viewed earlier (see fig. 25.23).

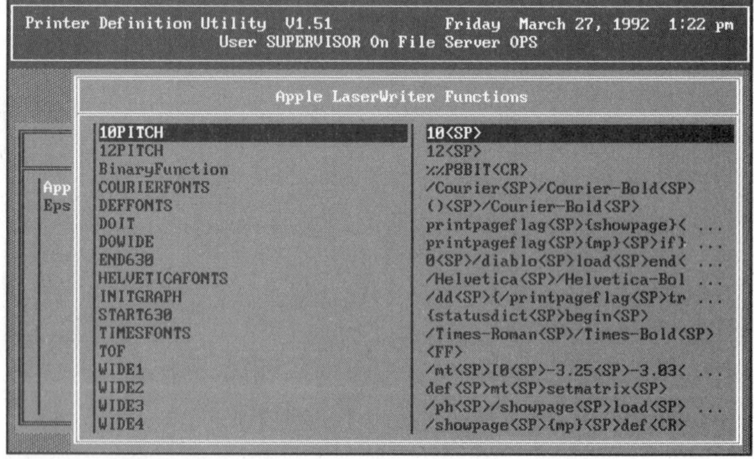

Figure 25.23
Functions and escape codes.

The ellipses (...) indicate more escape codes are available, which can be viewed by highlighting the function and pressing Enter.

15. Press Esc enough times until the Exit PRINTDEF query appears. Answer Yes, select Save Data Base, and then select Exit.

Using PRINTCON in NetWare 3.*x*

The PRINTCON utility can be used to define printer job configurations that can be used in utilities such as CAPTURE, NPRINT, and PCONSOLE. Use the following steps:

1. Log in as a supervisor to a NetWare server. (This exercise shows the screens for a NetWare 3.11 server.) Type **PRINTCON** to invoke the PRINTCON utility. The Available Options box displays (see fig. 25.24).

Figure 25.24
The Available Options box.

2. To create a print job configuration, select the Edit Print Job Configurations option. The Print Job Configurations box appears (see fig. 25.25).

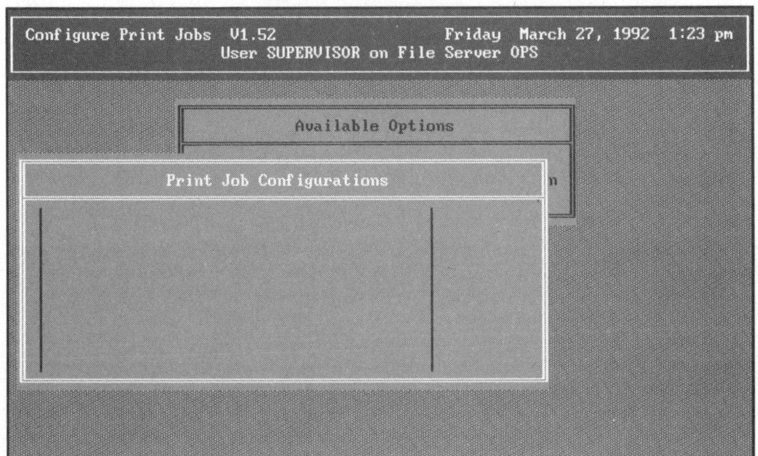

Figure 25.25
The Print Job Configurations box.

3. Press Ins to define a new printer configuration, and enter the name (up to 31 characters) of the print job configuration. A screen showing details of the print job configuration appears, as shown in figure 25.26.

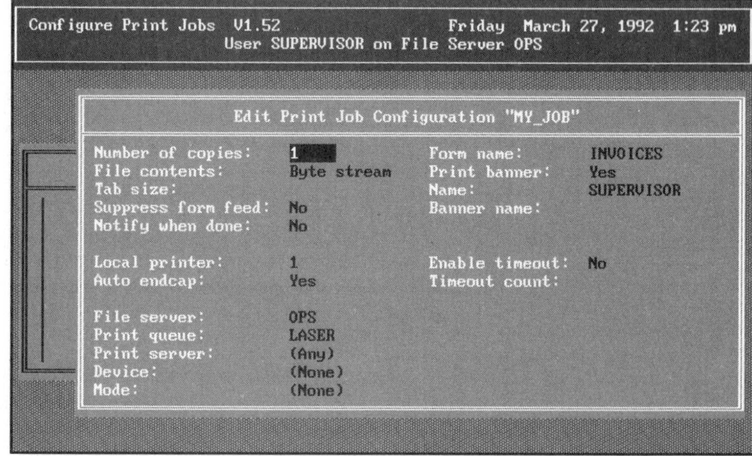

Figure 25.26
The Edit Print Job Configuration box.

The important fields and their meanings are described in table 25.3.

Table 25.3
Edit Print Job Configuration Box Fields

Field	Meaning
Number of copies	The number of copies to be printed for a print job.
File Contents	The type of print job. Values are Text and Byte stream. For jobs containing graphic data, Byte stream should be selected. For jobs consisting of text files, Text should selected. If Text is selected, you can define the Tab size field that has a default value of 8.
Suppress form feed	After the print job ends, should a form feed be suppressed (Yes) or issued (No)?
Notify when done	After the print job ends, should the workstation be notified (Yes) or not (No)?
Local printer	Which LPT printer (1, 2, or 3) should be used for the CAP-TURE command by default?
Auto endcap	Should the shell wait until ENDCAP is run before printing (No), or should it print whenever a program is exited (Yes)?

Field	Meaning
File server	The target file server where the print job should be sent.
Print queue	The queue on the specified target file server to which the print job should be sent. The print queue is defined by PCONSOLE.
Print server	Which print server associated with the print queue should service the print job? Default is (Any), but a specific print server can be specified.
Device	The print job must be customized for the specified printer.
Mode	After the Device field is selected, you can specify the print mode that was defined for the printer (using PRINTDEF).
Form name	The default form name (form 0) is shown here. An alternate form (defined by PRINTDEF) can be selected.
Print banner	Should a banner be printed before printing every job?
Name	If Print banner is set to Yes, the name on the banner can be specified here. When left empty, the name of the user printing the job is used; otherwise, whatever text is entered in this field is printed in the banner name.
Banner name	The banner includes the name of the file being printed. This field specifies the name of the file to be included in the banner. If the field is left blank, the name of the file being printed will be in the banner. If text is included here, that text will be printed in the banner, instead of the file name.
Enable timeout	When set to Yes, the shell automatically prints captured data after the time specified in the Timeout count field. When set to No, captured data is printed based on what the Auto endcap is set to. If the Auto endcap is set to Yes, printing occurs only after exiting the program. If Auto endcap is set to No, printing begins immediately.
Timeout count	Specifies the number of seconds the shell waits before printing saved data if nothing has been sent to the captured LPT. Timeout count is only applicable if Enable timeout field is set to Yes.

4. After making the desired changes to the print job, press Esc and answer Yes to save changes. A screen showing a list of print job configurations including the new one just defined appears, as shown in figure 25.27.

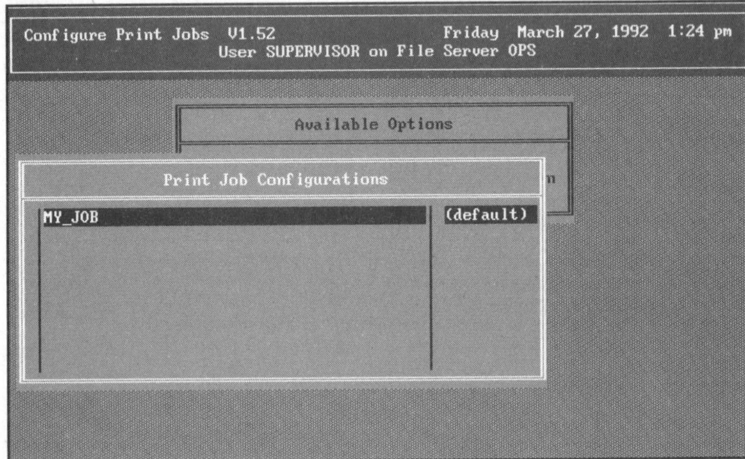

Figure 25.27
The Print Job Configurations box.

5. Press Esc to return to the Available Options box. To select the default print job configuration, select Select Default Print Job Configuration from the Available Options box.

6. To copy the print job configuration to another user, select Copy Print Job Configuration. A screen showing the source user to copy the print job from is displayed.

7. Enter a user for whom a print job configuration has already been defined and saved in the database. A screen displays the target user to copy the print job to.

8. Enter a user to which the print job configuration needs to be copied. This user must have been defined already. The Copy Print Job Configuration option is a quick way to replicate a print job configuration to other users.

9. Press Esc until the Exit Printcon query appears. Answer Yes to exit and Yes again to save changes in the database.

Using PCONSOLE To Define Queues and Print Server Definitions in NetWare 3.*x*

The PCONSOLE utility can be used to set up print queues and print servers, control network printing, and view information about network printing, as follows:

1. Log in as a supervisor to a NetWare server. (This exercise shows the screens for a NetWare 3.11 server.) Type **PCONSOLE** to invoke the PCONSOLE utility. The Available Options box appears (see fig. 25.28).

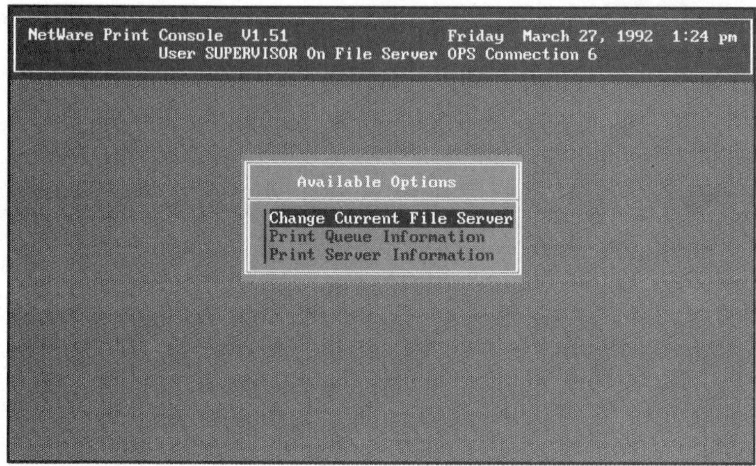

Figure 25.28
The Available Options box.

The options in the PCONSOLE box perform the following tasks:

Change Current File Server:

Selects the current file server

Attaches to file servers

Changes to a different user name on additional file servers

Logs out of additional file servers

Print Queue Information:

Creates/deletes/renames print queues

Assigns/removes queue operators

Assigns/removes queue users

Changes operator flags

Assigns print server to service a queue

Removes a print server from a queue

Views currently attached print servers

Lists the jobs in a queue

Prints a file

Sets/changes print job parameters

Deletes a print job

Changes order of print jobs

Places a hold on a print job

Views print queue status, queue object ID, print queue servers

Print Server Information:

Creates/deletes/renames print servers

Selects the password for the print server

Assigns the print server's full name

Attaches file servers to a print server

Views print server information, object ID

Downs a print server

Adds printers to the print server

Removes printers from the print server

Temporarily sets service mode of printer and mounted form number

Sets notify list of users for printers

Lists printers and queues serviced by printer

Assigns/removes print server operators

Assigns/removes print server users

Assigns queues to printers

Removes queues from printers

As you can see, PCONSOLE can perform a wide variety of tasks. In this exercise, only the tasks necessary to set up a new print server are performed.

2. To create a print queue, select Print Queue Information. A screen showing the print queues should be displayed. The Print Queues box appears (see fig. 25.29).

3. To create a queue, press Ins. When prompted for a print queue name, enter a queue name with a maximum of 47 characters, and press Enter. The name of the print queue should now appear in the Print Queues box, as shown in figure 25.30.

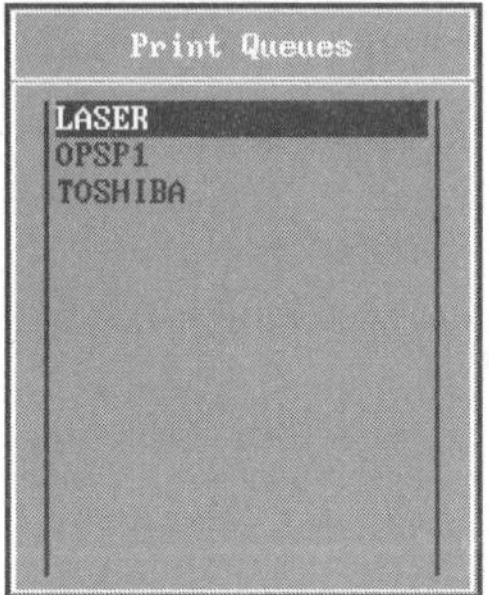

Figure 25.29
The Print Queues box.

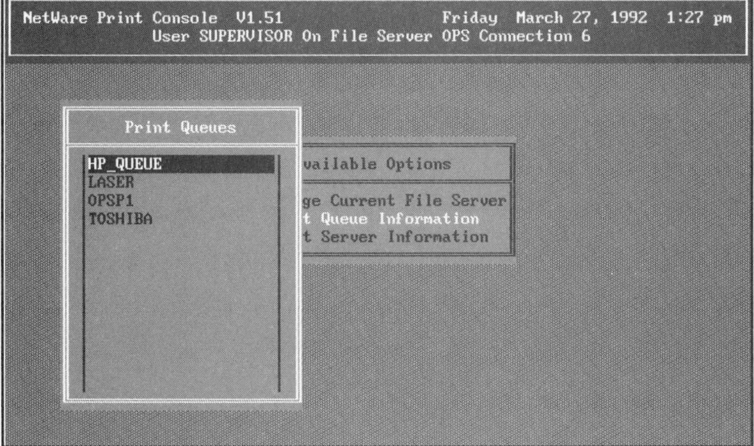

Figure 25.30
Displaying the name of the print queue.

4. Highlight the name of the print queue you just created and press Enter. The Print Queue Information box appears, as shown in figure 25.31.

5. Explore the options that follow. Most of these should indicate that no print jobs and entries in the queues exist. The Print Queue ID name can be recorded because it is the name of the subdirectory in SYS:SYSTEM that implements the print queue.

   Current Print Job Entries

   Current Queue Status

   Currently Attached Servers

   Print Queue ID

6. Select the Queue Users option. The Queue Users box displays (see fig. 25.32).

   By default, group EVERYONE (all users) can submit jobs to the print queue. This usually is adequate. If you want to restrict the queue users, highlight group EVERYONE and press Del. You can press Ins to add additional users.

25

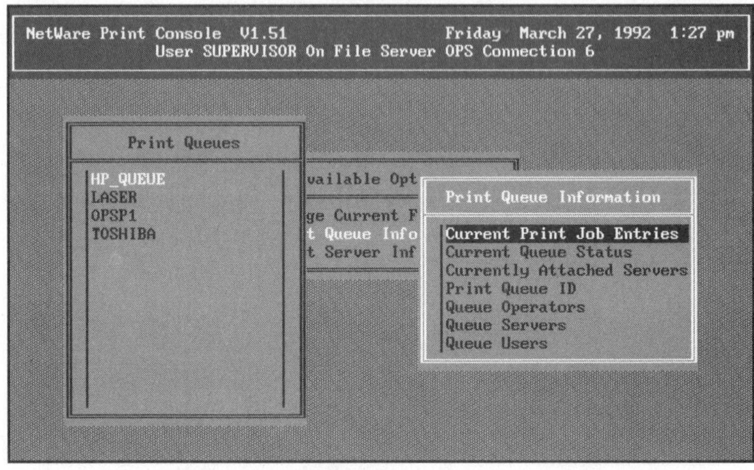

Figure 25.31
Print Queue Information box.

7. Press Esc to return to the Print Queue Information box.

8. Select the Queue Operators option. A screen showing the list of queue operators appears (see fig. 25.33).

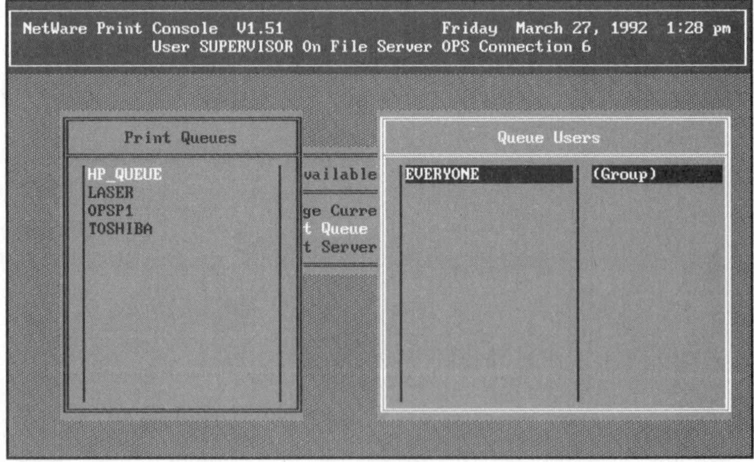

Figure 25.32
The Queue Users box.

By default, SUPERVISOR is always a queue operator. To assign other queue operators press Ins.

9. Press Ins at the Queue Operators list. A list of potential queue operators appears, as shown in figure 25.34.

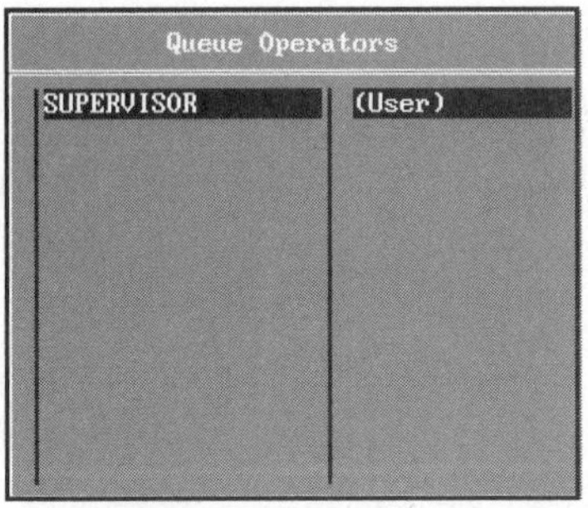

Figure 25.33
The Queue Operators box.

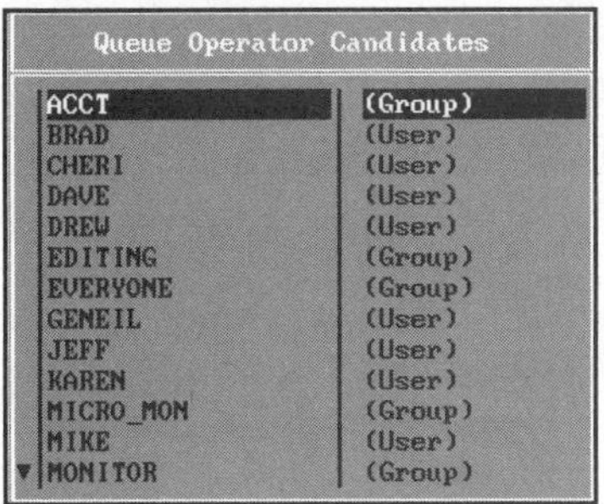

Figure 25.34
The Queue Operator Candidates box.

10. Mark the users to be made queue operators by pressing F5 and then pressing Ins. The selected users and groups that are the new queue operators appear in the Queue Operators box (see fig. 25.35).

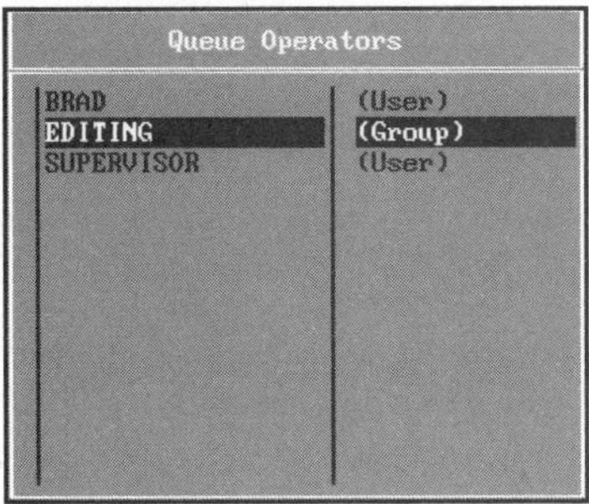

Figure 25.35
Displaying new queue operators in the Queue Operators box.

11. Press Esc to return to the Print Queue Information box.

12. Select the Queue Servers option. A screen showing the list of queue servers (print servers) appears, as shown in figure 25.36.

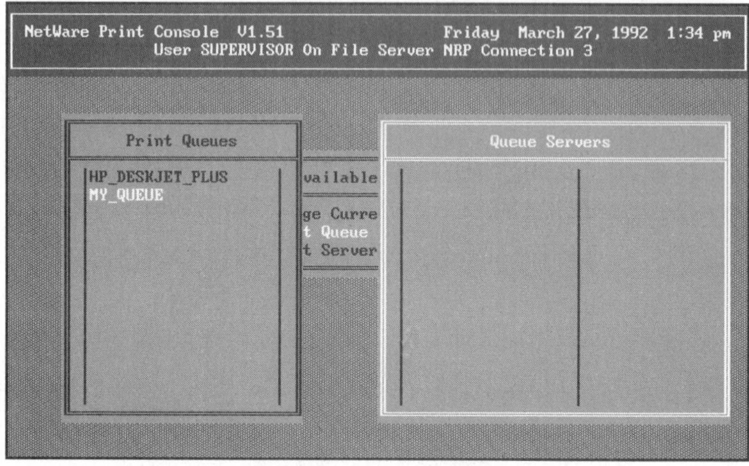

Figure 25.36
The Queue Servers box.

This list initially should be empty. If queue servers, which are the same as print servers, have been defined, they can be assigned to service the queue at this point by pressing Ins.

13. Press Esc until you return to the Available Options box. The print queue has been defined at this point. The next step is to define a print server.

14. Select the Print Server Information option. The Print Servers box displays, showing a list of the print servers that already are created (see fig. 25.37).

Figure 25.37
The Print Servers box.

15. To create a print server, press Ins. When prompted for a print server name, enter a name with a maximum of 47 characters, and then press Enter. The name of the print server you just created appears, as shown in figure 25.38.

16. Highlight the name of the print server you just created and press Enter. The Print Server Information box displays (see fig. 25.39).

17. Explore the Print Server ID option. The print server is the name of the subdirectory in SYS:SYSTEM that holds the print server information.

Figure 25.38
Displaying the new print server.

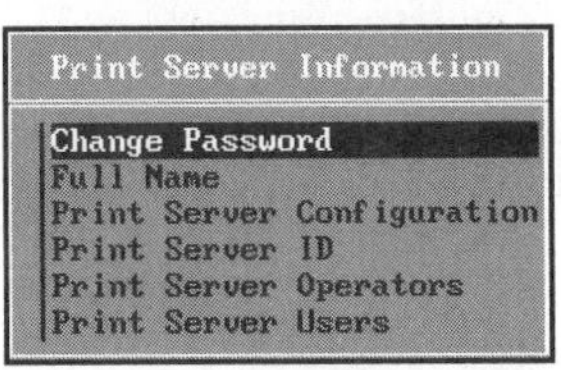

Figure 25.39
The Print Server Information box.

18. Select the Print Server Users option. The Server Users box, which shows the list of print server users, appears on-screen (see fig. 25.40).

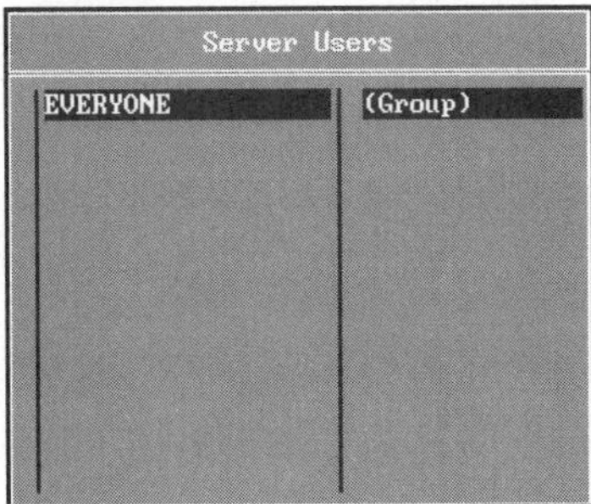

Figure 25.40
The Server Users box.

By default, all users (group EVERYONE) are users of print servers. This is adequate in most circumstances. If you want to restrict the print server users, highlight group EVERYONE and press Delete to delete group EVERYONE from the list of print server users. You can press Ins to add additional users.

19. Press Esc to return to the Print Server Information box.

20. Select the Print Server Operators option. A box showing the list of print server operators appears, as shown in figure 25.41.

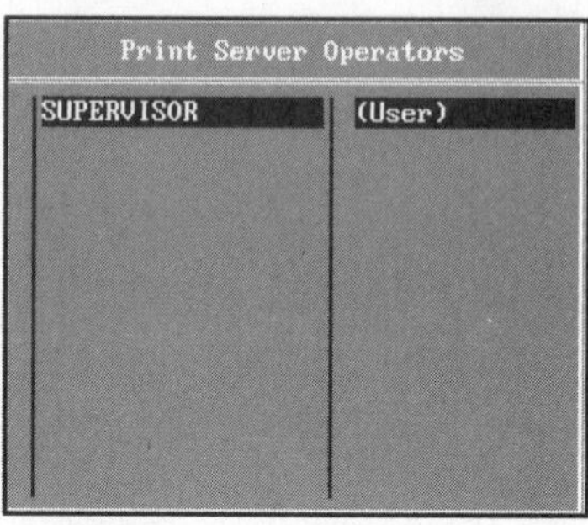

Figure 25.41
The Print Server Operators box.

By default, SUPERVISOR is always a print server operator. To assign other print server operators, press Ins.

21. Press Ins at the Print Server Operators list. A list of the potential print server operators displays (see fig. 25.42).

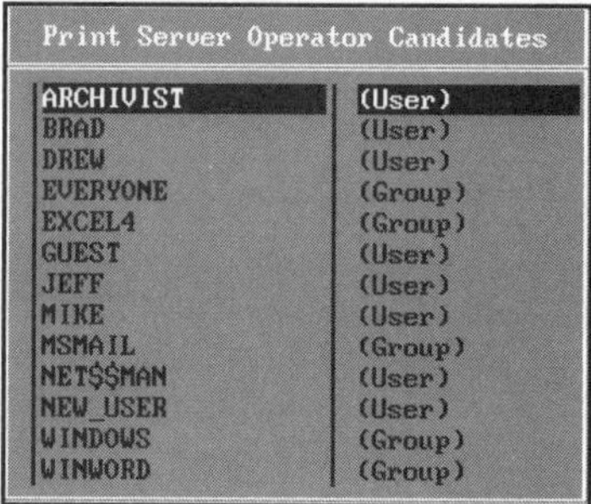

Figure 25.42
Print Server Operator Candidates box.

22. Press Esc enough times to get back to the Print Server Information box.

23. Select Change Password and enter a print server password for added security.

24. Select Full Name and enter a descriptive name for the print server.

25. Select Print Server Configuration and press Enter. The Print Server Configuration Menu box displays (see fig. 25.43).

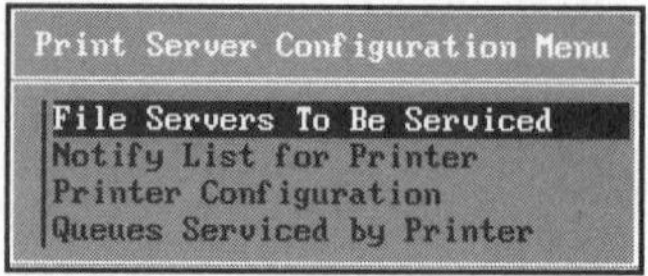

Figure 25.43
The Print Server Configuration Menu box.

26. Select the File Servers To Be Serviced option. A screen similar to the one shown in figure 25.44 appears.

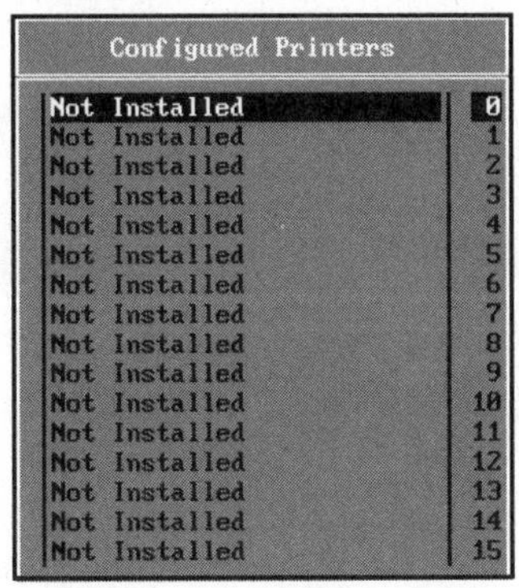

Figure 25.44
The Configured Printers box.

The default server is displayed. This is the server mapped to by the current default network drive. The available file servers can be obtained by pressing Ins.

27. Press Esc to return to the Print Server Configuration Menu. The print server has been created. The printer(s) for the print server must be defined at this point.

28. Select the Printer Configuration option. A list showing the configured printers appears. Initially, this list shows that no printers have been installed, as shown in figure 25.44.

You now must configure a printer, as follows:

Printer	0
Type	Parallel
Port	LPT1
IRG	7
Forms	0
Queue service mode	Change forms as needed

29. Highlight the first item on the list and press Enter. A screen showing the printer configuration appears (see fig. 25.45).

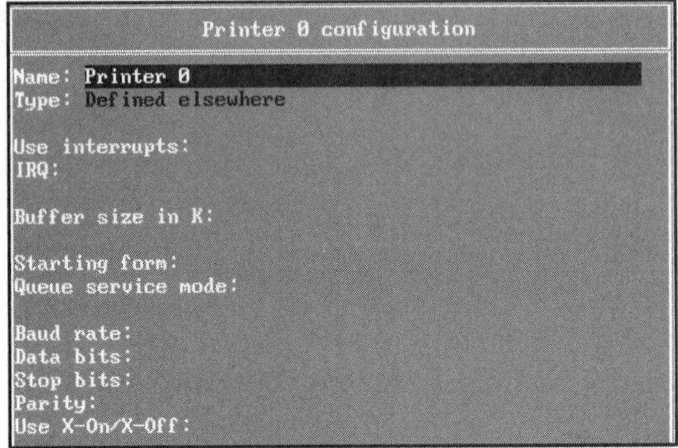

Figure 25.45
The Printer Configuration box.

The Printer Configuration box fields have the meanings as shown in table 25.4.

Table 25.4
Printer Configuration Box Fields

Fields	Meaning
Name	Enter a name for the printer, with a maximum of 47 characters.
Type	Defines a local or remote printer. In each category you have a choice of three parallel printer ports (LPT1, LPT2, LPT3) and four serial ports (COM1, COM2, COM3, COM4).
Use Interrupts	Enables the use of interrupts when you answer Yes. Interrupts are more efficient than polling techniques. The only reason to disable printer interrupts is to solve interrupt conflict problems.
IRQ	The Interrupt Request Line setting for the printer.
Buffer size in KB	The size of the print server's internal buffer. 3 KB is adequate for most purposes. If the printer does not run smoothly, increasing the print buffer size might help.
Starting form	Denotes the number of the form that must be mounted on the printer when the print server starts.
Queue Service Mode	Defines the queue service modes, as follows: Change forms as needed, Minimize form changes across queues, Minimize form changes within queues, and Service only currently mounted form.

The baud rate, data bits, stop bits, parity, and Use X-On/X-Off (flow control) are defined for serial printers and define the serial printer configuration.

30. Make the changes to the printer configuration. Press Esc once and answer Yes to the Save Changes query.

31. Return to the Print Server Configuration Menu by pressing Esc once.

    Now that a printer has been defined for the print server, you can designate a list of users that can be notified should the printer require service. For defining additional printers, you can repeat the previous steps for defining printers.

32. Select the Notify List for Printer option. When the defined printers list appears, highlight a printer and press Enter. A box similar to the one shown in figure 25.46 displays with a box that initially is empty.

33. Press Ins and the Notify Candidates box appears. Mark the users/group by pressing F5, and then press Enter. A screen indicating the notify intervals appears, as shown in figure 25.47.

Figure 25.46
File server notification list display.

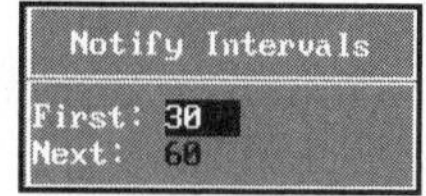

Figure 25.47
The Notify Intervals box.

The First field defines the time in seconds the first notification is sent. The Next field defines the intervals at which this message should be sent.

34. Press Esc to save changes. A box similar to the one shown in figure 25.48 displays.

35. Press Esc enough times to get back to the Print Server Configuration Menu. The next step is to assign a queue to the printer just defined.

36. Select the Queues Serviced by Printer option. After a list of defined printers appears, highlight a printer and press Enter. A screen similar to the one shown in figure 25.49 appears.

37. Press Ins. After the list of available queues appears, highlight the queue to be serviced by the printer and press Enter. Repeat this process for additional queues to be serviced by the printer attached to the print server.

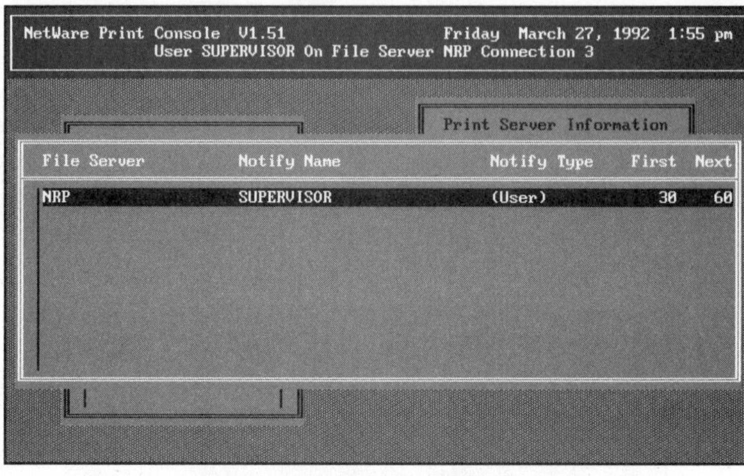

Figure 25.48
File server notification list display.

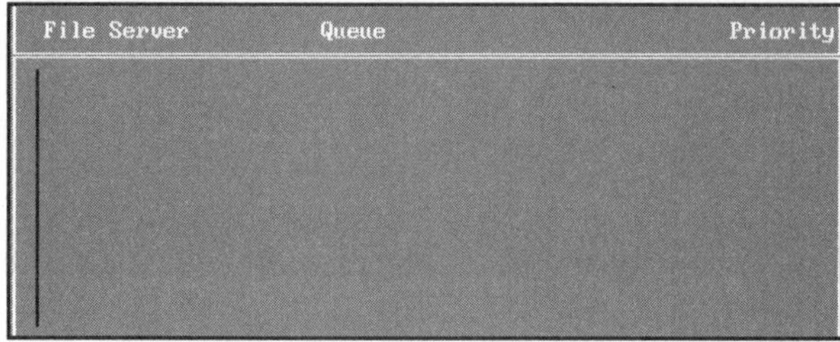

Figure 25.49
File server queues display.

After making the queue assignment for a printer, you are prompted for a priority. The priority value is from 1 to 10, with 1 being the highest priority.

After completing the queue assignment for a printer, a screen similar to the one shown in figure 25.50 appears.

38. Press Esc until the Exit Pconsole box appears. Select Yes to exit PCONSOLE.

The printer definition is complete. The next step is to install a print server. The print server program can be installed using any of the three PSERVER programs.

Running the PSERVER Program in NetWare 3.*x*

The PSERVER program can be installed at the NetWare 3.*x* server, NetWare 2.*x* server, or a dedicated workstation. To install the program, follow these steps:

1. At the NetWare 3.*x* server console, enter the following command:

```
LOAD PSERVER fileserver/printserver
```

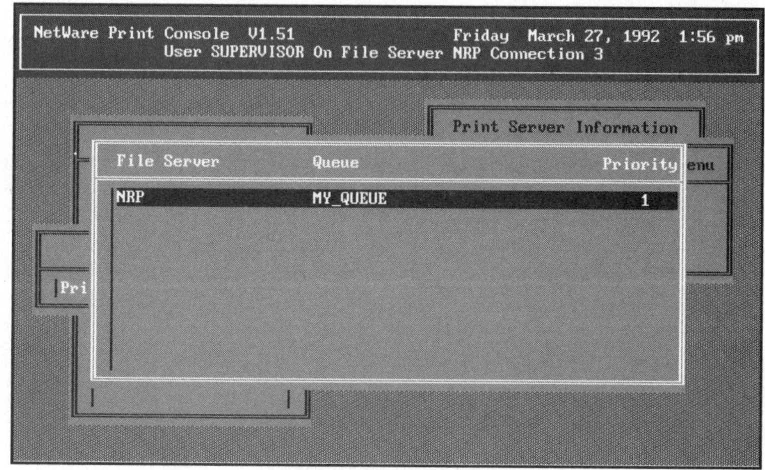

Figure 25.50
File server queues display.

The LOAD PSERVER command loads the PSERVER.NLM at the NetWare 3.*x* server. The arguments specify the name of the print server. The file server name can be left out.

2. For a dedicated workstation, create a user with the same name as the print server. Set the SPX connections to 60 or more. You can do this by entering the following line in the NET.CFG file:

   ```
   SPX Connections=60
   ```

   Load IPX and the shell with the new value for SPX connections. Log in to the file server on which the print server was defined and enter the following command:

   PSERVER ***fileserver/printserver***

3. For a NetWare 2.2 server, make sure that the PSERVER.VAP is in the SYS:SYSTEM directory. Then bring down the server and bring it up again. During the boot process, it asks if you want to load the VAPs. Answer Yes and enter the server name when prompted to do so.

4. If prompted for the password, enter the password set for the print server through PCONSOLE. A screen displays.

To see the next group of printers (8–15), press the spacebar.

Installing Remote Printers in NetWare 3.*x*

To install a remote printer, you must have defined a remote printer as one of the printers in the print server definition by using PCONSOLE. A maximum of 25 printers, including local and remote printers, can be defined for each print server.

The print server that is defining the remote printer must be running.

Perform the following steps to set up a remote printer at the workstation:

1. Attach a printer to be configured as a remote printer at the workstation. The printer settings must match those selected when defining the remote printer through PCONSOLE.

2. Log in as a user at the remote printer workstation and invoke the remote printer command by typing **RPRINTER**.

3. Select the print server that defines the remote printer. A list of remote printers assigned to the selected print server displays.

4. Select the remote printer. You should see a message informing you that the remote printer is installed.

The RPRINTER program takes up approximately 9 KB at the workstation.

Using Core Print Services in NetWare 2.*x*

Core print services are available only in the NetWare 2.*x* version. In NetWare 2.2, core print services can be configured at the server console without bringing the server down. In earlier versions of NetWare (2.15 and below), the server had to be brought down and the NETGEN utility used to configure print services.

Core Print Services Console Commands in NetWare 2.2

The NetWare 2.2 console commands for managing core print services are as follows:

QUEUE *queuename* CREATE

PRINTER *n* CREATE *port*

PRINTER *n* ADD *queuename* [[AT] [PRIORITY] *nn*]

SPOOL n queuename

The first keyword in these commands can be abbreviated using the first letter of the keyword—P for PRINTER, Q for QUEUE, and S for SPOOL.

These commands can be placed in the AUTOEXEC.SYS file in the SYS:SYSTEM directory so that they can be executed each time the server is booted. If a command is issued to create a queue or print definition that already exists, a harmless error message is generated on the server console.

Creating Print Queues in NetWare 2.2

The create queues command (QUEUE *queuename* CREATE) creates a queue with the name you provide on the NetWare server. Issuing this command creates a subdirectory with a name that is the queue ID (hexadecimal number) in SYS:SYSTEM. This subdirectory holds the print jobs submitted for printing. Some examples follow:

```
Q ENG_QUEUE CREATE
Q ACCT_QUEUE CREATE
Q URGENT_QUEUE CREATE
```

These commands create print queues named ENG_QUEUE, ACCT_QUEUE, and URGENT_QUEUE.

Creating a Printer Definition in NetWare 2.2

The printer definition command (PRINTER *n* CREATE *port*) creates a printer definition for the specified print number at the server's printer ports. The value of *n* specifies one of five printers and must be between 0 and 4. The ports could be serial (COM*x*) or parallel ports (LPT*x*). Issuing this command creates a subdirectory whose name is the print server ID (hexadecimal number) in SYS:SYSTEM. This subdirectory holds the printer definition. When a serial port (COM*x*) is specified, a default configuration is installed with the following values:

```
Poll     15
XONXOFF     No
Baud     9600
Stopbits     1
Wordsize     8
Parity     None
```

To change any of the default settings, specify any of the preceding parameters following the PRINTER *n* CREATE *port* command. The following is an example:

```
P 0 CREATE COM1 XONXOFF=YES WORDSIZE=7 PARITY=EVEN
```

Notice that the PRINTER command is abbreviated by the letter P. The XON/XOFF parameters are set to Yes, meaning XON/XOFF flow control is used. The word size is set to 7 bits, with even parity.

Other examples are as follows:

```
P 0 CREATE LPT1
P 1 CREATE COM2
```

These create printer numbers 0 and 1, which are defined on ports LPT1 and COM2

Assigning Printers to Queues in NetWare 2.2

The assign printers to queues command (PRINTER *n* ADD *queuename* [[AT] [PRIORITY] *nn*]) assigns a printer to a queue. When this assignment is made, the priority level at which the queue will be serviced can be specified. This priority (*nn*) can have a value between 1 and 10, with 1 the highest priority.

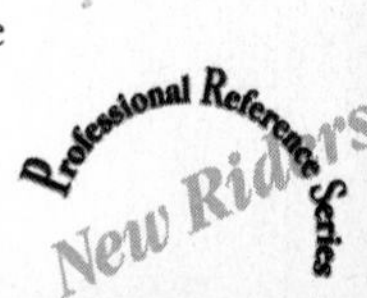

Queues at the highest priority are serviced before those at lower priorities. Normally a queue is assigned to one printer to keep this logical association simple. As explained earlier in this chapter, more complex mappings such as one-to-many, many-to-one, and many-to-many are possible.

Examples of the assign printers to queues command follow:

```
P 0 ADD ACCT_QUEUE
P 1 ADD ENG_QUEUE AT PRIORITY 4
```

The first command assigns printer number 0 to the queue ACCT_QUEUE. The second command assigns printer 1 to the queue ENG_QUEUE at a priority level of 4.

Using the SPOOL Command in NetWare 2.2

The SPOOL command (SPOOL *n queueName*) supports older applications that send their print jobs to print numbers rather than queues. If the printer number *n* is specified, the spooler with the name *queueName* is used. Printer number 0 is the default printer, so at least one SPOOL command must be given with printer number 0. The NPRINT and CAPTURE commands also have a default printer number when not explicitly specified.

Examples of the SPOOL command follow:

```
S 0 ENG_QUEUE
S 1 MY_QUEUE
```

The printer number 0 (default network printer) is assigned to the ENG_QUEUE, and printer 1 is assigned to MY_QUEUE. This assignment means that older applications that use printer numbers to direct the printer output will have their jobs directed to these queues and will be printed by the printers assigned to service this queue.

Using One Printer with Multiple Queues in NetWare 2.2

Figure 25.51 shows an example of one printer that services four queues. The queues are set to priority levels ranging from 1 to 4. Applications generate print jobs that can go in either one of these queues. When a high-priority job enters QUEUE_1, which is to be serviced at the highest priority level of 1, the current print job in progress is completed, and the new high-priority job is sent to the printer.

To implement this queue structure, the following commands should be issued at the server console:

```
Q QUEUE_1 CREATE
Q QUEUE_2 CREATE
Q QUEUE_3 CREATE
Q QUEUE_4 CREATE
P 0 CREATE LPT1
P 0 ADD QUEUE_1 AT PRIORITY 1
```

```
P 0 ADD QUEUE_2 AT PRIORITY 2
P 0 ADD QUEUE_3 AT PRIORITY 3
P 0 ADD QUEUE_4 AT PRIORITY 1
```

This is an example of one-to-many mapping

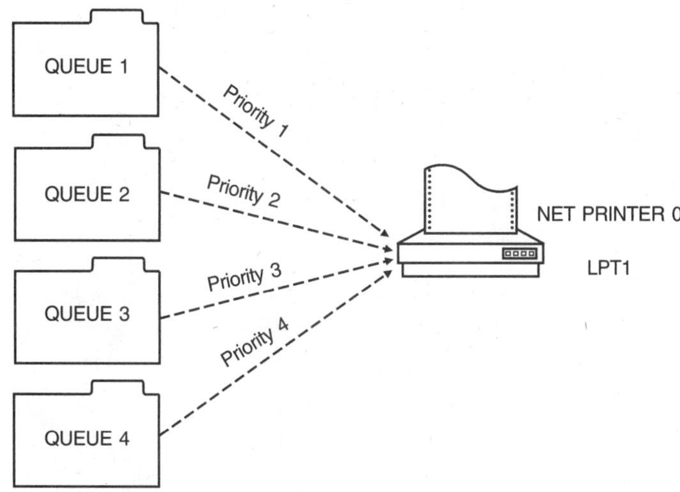

Figure 25.51
One printer with multiple queues.

Using One Queue with Multiple Printers in NetWare 2.2

Figure 25.52 shows an example of one queue being serviced by three printers. The printers are identical and assigned to ports LPT1, LPT2, and LPT3. Applications generate print jobs that can go in the single queue. The print job is serviced by the next printer that becomes free.

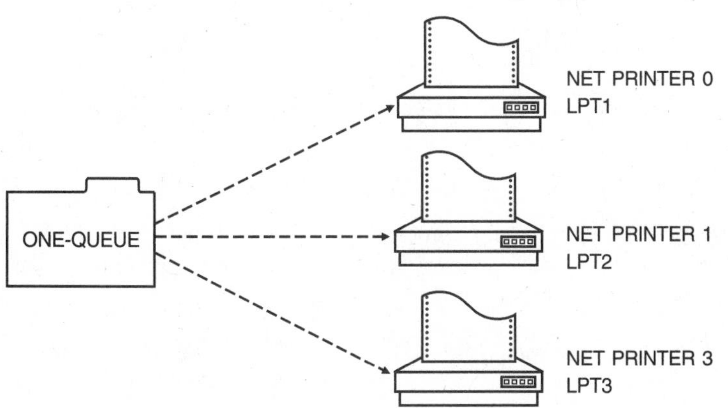

Figure 25.52
One queue with multiple printers.

To implement this queue structure, the following commands should be issued at the server console:

```
Q ONE_QUEUE CREATE
P 0 CREATE LPT1
P 1 CREATE LPT2
P 2 CREATE LPT3
P 0 ADD ONE_QUEUE
P 1 ADD ONE_QUEUE
P 2 ADD ONE_QUEUE
```

This is an example of many-to-one mapping

Using Multiple Queues with Multiple Printers in NetWare 2.2

Suppose that three queues are serviced by two printers. The printers are identical and assigned to ports LPT1 and LPT2. Applications generate print jobs that can go in the queues. The print jobs are serviced by the next printer that becomes free. QUEUE_2 is serviced by both PRINTER_1 and PRINTER_2 and is serviced at a higher priority than the other queues.

To implement this queue structure, the following commands should be issued at the server console:

```
Q QUEUE_1 CREATE
Q QUEUE_2 CREATE
Q QUEUE_3 CREATE
P 0 CREATE LPT1
P 1 CREATE LPT2
P 0 ADD QUEUE_1 AT PRIORITY 2
P 0 ADD QUEUE_2 AT PRIORITY 1
P 1 ADD QUEUE_2 AT PRIORITY 1
P 1 ADD QUEUE_3 AT PRIORITY 2
```

This is an example of many-to-many mapping

Generating Print Jobs in NetWare 2.*x* and 3.*x*

Print jobs are generated by applications running at the workstation or using print utilities to print files. These print jobs are sent to queues defined on a file server. From the queues, they are processed by the print servers assigned to the queue and sent to local or remote printers.

The utilities to generate print jobs are as follows:

CAPTURE and ENDCAP

NPRINT

PCONSOLE

Using CAPTURE and ENDCAP in NetWare 3.*x*

Applications designed to work with NetWare are compatible with the NetWare print queue and print support mechanisms. During the installation of these applications, you can define the interface to network printers. This should be all the printer configuration necessary.

Many applications, however, do not have a direct interface to NetWare printers; they require additional support and configuration. The command-line utilities CAPTURE and ENDCAP provide this support.

After you issue the CAPTURE command, it captures printer output directed at a parallel local port and sends it across the network to a print queue.

In earlier versions of NetWare, the print job from CAPTURE had to be redirected to a network printer. With NetWare 2.2 and NetWare 3.*x*, Novell has made the print queue the focal point for submitting jobs. The print job in the queue is printed on a network printer depending on how print queues have been assigned to print servers. This is a more flexible approach. The SPOOL command bridges the gap for applications that do not have awareness of print queues.

The SPOOL command must be used to associate a print number with a print queue if CAPTURE on pre-NetWare 2.2 or older applications is being used.

To associate the default printer (network printer 0) with the queue DEFAULT_QUEUE, for example, issue the following command at the server console:

```
S 0 DEFAULT_QUEUE
```

After the CAPTURE command is issued, it controls the print jobs sent to the local parallel port until another CAPTURE or ENDCAP command is issued or the user logs out. It is common to place the CAPTURE command in the login script file so that it holds for the duration of the session. If placed in the login script, CAPTURE (and external commands, in general) must be preceded by the numeral character (#) to indicate to the login processing that this is an external program or utility.

The following command directs printer output sent to the local port to the print queue HIGH_SPEED by using the job configuration MY_JOB.

```
CAPTURE L=1 Q=HIGH_SPEED J=MY_JOB
```

The following command is the same as the earlier CAPTURE command but is executed from the login script.

```
#CAPTURE L=1 Q=HIGH_SPEED J=MY_JOB
```

Job configurations contain many of the parameters that can be specified in the CAPTURE command. If the job configuration is set up appropriately, the other parameters are not necessary. If the parameters are specified explicitly on the command line, they override any settings in the job configuration.

Table 25.5 shows a list of parameters (options) that can be set up for both the CAPTURE and NPRINT commands (discussed later). Only the abbreviated forms of these parameters are shown because they tend to get used more often. The full form of these parameters can be determined from the description column. Unless explicitly stated or implied in the description, many of the parameters are common to both CAPTURE and NPRINT.

Table 25.5
CAPTURE and NPRINT Options and Parameters

Option	Description
SH	Shows the current CAPTURE settings.
?	Shows the list of options for CAPTURE.
NOTI	NOTIfies when the print job is done.
NNOTI	NoNOTIfy. Does not notify when print job is done (default setting).
TI=*n*	TImeout. Specifies timeout period *n* in seconds before job is printed. Default is TI=0 (disabled). Only for CAPTURE.
AU	AUtoEndcap. ENDCAP is automatically issued when application exits. Default setting. Only for CAPTURE.
NA	No AutoEndcap. ENDCAP is not automatically issued when application exits. Only for CAPTURE.
L=*n*	Specifies the Local parallel printer *n* to be used for capturing. Only for CAPTURE.
S=*fs*	Server. Specifies the file server *fs* where the print job should be sent. Default is the default file server.
PS=*ps*	PrintServer. Specifies the print server *ps* where the print job should be sent. Only for NPRINT.
Q=*qn*	Queue. Specifies the queue name *qn* where the print job is sent. If queue name is not specified, the print job is sent to the queue that spooler 0 has been assigned to.
CR=*path*	CReate. Specifies the path for the file that will store the print job, instead of being sent to the print queue. Only for CAPTURE.
J=*jc*	Job. Specifies the job configuration *jc* to be used for printing.
F=*n*	Form. Specifies the form number or name to be used for printing.
C=*n*	Copies. Specifies the number of copies (1 to 999) for printing. Default is 1.
T=*n*	Tabs. Specifies the tab size in the text mode of printing. Default is 8.
NT	No Tabs. Specifies no tabs should be used for the byte stream mode of printing.

Option	Description
NB	No Banner. No banner separator pages are generated.
NAM=*n*	NAMe. Indicates the text *n* that appears on the banner page instead of the default user name.
B=*n*	Banner. Specifies the banner name to be printed in the lower part of the banner instead of the default value of the file name being printed or LST: (for CAPTURE).
FF	FormFeed. Generates a form feed at the end of a print job. Default is form feed enabled. Only for CAPTURE.
NFF	NoFormFeed. Disables form feed at end of print job. Only for CAPTURE.
K	Keep. Keeps the received portion of the print job on the file server until it is printed, even if the workstation crashes. Only for CAPTURE.
D	Delete. Automatically erases the file after printing. Only for NPRINT.

The following are some other uses of the CAPTURE command:

In the following command, the local parallel port LPT1 is redirected to the print queue assigned by the Spooler 0 command (S 0 *queueName*):

```
CAPTURE NOTI
```

In the following command, the local parallel port LPT1 is redirected to the queue HP_QUEUE on file server KSS:

```
CAPTURE S=KSS Q=HP_QUEUE
```

In the following command, the local parallel port LPT2 is redirected to the queue and file server specified by the job configuration MY_JOB (set by using PRINTCON) and two copies of the print job are to be printed:

```
CAPTURE J=MY_JOB L=2 C=2
```

In the following command, the local parallel port LPT3 is redirected to the queue EPSON_QUEUE on the default file server and no form feed is to be issued at the end of the print job. Also, the job should be printed on form number 2. If this form is not mounted, a notification message is sent to mount the correct form.

```
CAPTURE L=3 Q=EPSON_QUEUE F=2 NFF
```

In the following command, the local parallel port LPT1 is redirected to the queue HP_QUEUE on the default file server, and the tab size to be used for text printing is 8. You should use tabs for text jobs to speed up printing.

```
CAPTURE L=1 Q=HP_QUEUE T=8
```

In the following command, the local parallel port LPT1 is redirected to the queue HP_QUEUE on the default file server, and the tabs and other control characters have special meanings for the application. This is the byte stream mode and is slightly slower than the text mode.

```
CAPTURE L=1 Q=HP_QUEUE
```

In the following command, the local parallel port LPT1 is redirected to the queue HP_QUEUE on the default file server, and the banner page separating print jobs is suppressed.

```
CAPTURE Q=HP_QUEUE NB
```

In the following command, the local parallel port LPT2 is redirected by using the job configuration SPL_JOB, and the banner page separating print jobs has the text SPECIAL_JOBS printed on top. Instead of the default LST: that appears below the banner name, the string SPELL appears.


```
CAPTURE J=SPL_JOB L=2 NAM=SPECIAL_JOBS B=SPELL
```

In the following command, the local parallel port LPT1 is redirected to the file REPORT.1 in the directory SYS:APPS/DATA:

```
CAPTURE CR=SYS:APPS/DATA/REPORT.1
```

In the following command, the local parallel port LPT1 is redirected to the queue MY_QUEUE and the job is sent to the queue after a timeout period of 12 seconds, if no further output is received. Also, the print job is kept in queue for printing, in case the workstation crashes.

```
CAPTURE Q=MY_QUEUE TI=12 K
```

To end the capture of the local parallel port, use the ENDCAP command. A number of options can be specified by using the ENDCAP command. These are listed in table 25.6.

Table 25.6

ENDCAP Options and Parameters

Option	Description
L=*n*	Local. Ends the capture for parallel port *n*. When not specified, local port LPT1 is assumed.
A	All. Ends capture for all local parallel ports.
C	Cancel. Ends capture of LPT1 and discards any data without printing.
CL	CancelLocal. Ends capture for LPT port *n* and discards any data without printing.
CA	CancelAll. Ends capture for all LPT ports and discards any data without printing.

Some examples of how to use the ENDCAP command are listed next:

The following command ends the capture of LPT1 port:

```
ENDCAP
```

The following command ends the capture of LPT3 port:

```
ENDCAP L=3
```

The following command ends the capture of LPT1 port and discards any spooled data without printing:

```
ENDCAP C
```

The following command ends the capture of LPT2 port and discards any spooled data without printing:


```
ENDCAP CL=2
```

The following command ends the capture of all parallel ports:

```
ENDCAP A
```

The following command ends the capture of all parallel ports and discards any spooled data for printing:

```
ENDCAP CA
```

NPRINT in NetWare 3.*x*

The NPRINT command is similar to the DOS PRINT command, in that it can be invoked from the command line to print a file. The parameters for NPRINT were discussed in table 10.3, together with the parameters for CAPTURE. As was explained in that section, many of these parameters are the same as that for CAPTURE, and many of the examples of CAPTURE command in the preceding section also can be used with NPRINT.

The following examples make use of parameters that are unique to NPRINT or that behave differently from CAPTURE.

The following command prints the FILE.TXT file to the queue HP_QUEUE on file server KSS to be processed by HP_PSERVER. The banner name is SCS and the tab size is set to 4 for text printing. The lower part of the banner shows the file name FILE.TXT being printed.

```
NPRINT FILE.TXT Q=HP_QUEUE PS=HP_PSERVER S=KSS NAM=SCS T=4
```

The following command prints the FILE.TXT file to the queue set by the Spooler 0 command and suppresses the banner page:

```
NPRINT FILE.TXT NB
```

PCONSOLE for Printing in NetWare 3.*x*

The versatile PCONSOLE utility also can be used for printing jobs, as shown in the following steps:

1. Type **PCONSOLE**.
2. Make the following selections:

   Print queue information

   Select a queue for printing

   Current print job entries
3. A list of print jobs in progress displays.
4. To print a job, press Ins. Enter the directory to be used for printing, and a list of files in that directory displays. Highlight a file to be printed and select it. To print several files, mark them by using F5 and press Enter to select them.
5. Select the print job configuration to be used for printing. The job configuration screen appears. You can edit any of the job configuration parameters. When done, press Esc to select the current settings and to submit the files for printing.
6. You can highlight any job in the print queue to obtain more detailed information on that job. The meanings of the individual fields are described in table 25.7.

Table 25.7
Print Queue Entry Information

Field	Description
Print job	Denotes job number of print job in queue
File size	Denotes size in bytes of print job
Client	Denotes user who sent the print job
Description	Denotes name of job
Status	Denotes condition of job
User hold	Indicates if job is held in queue by user or queue operator
Operator hold	Indicates if job is held by queue operator
Service Sequence	Specifies the order in which the job is printed
Number of Copies	Specifies number of copies to be printed

Field	Description
File contents	Specifies text or byte stream mode, text mode converts tabs to spaces, byte stream enables application to determine printer codes
Tab size	Specifies number of spaces per tab
Suppress form feed	Controls form feed generation at end of print job
Notify when done	Determines if user is notified at end of print job
Target server	Denotes print server that can process print job
Form	Denotes form type used for print job
Print Banner	Controls banner generation
Name	Specifies name to be printed in upper part of banner
Banner name	Specifies name to be printed in lower part of banner
Defer printing	Enables you to defer printing
Target date and time	If printing is to be deferred, it sets the date and time for printing (default is 2:00 a.m. on the following day)
Job entry date and time	Information on when the job was submitted

Monitoring and Controlling Print Jobs in NetWare 3.*x*

The following are commands that you can use to monitor and control print jobs:

PSTAT

PSC

PCONSOLE

Printer Status PSTAT in NetWare 3.*x*

The printer status command PSTAT can be used only for core print services. PSTAT reveals information on printers attached directly to the NetWare 2.*x* server, such as the following:

Ready status: on-line and off-line

Active status: active and stopped

Forms: Form number and name currently mounted

Print Server Command PSC in NetWare 3.*x*

The PSC command is a quick way of controlling print servers and network printers. It can be used for monitoring and controlling printers. Many of the functions in PSC also can be done by PCONSOLE. The difference is that PSC is used at the command line, whereas PCONSOLE is interactive.

Table 25.8 shows the list of flags that can be used with the PSC command. The general form of the PSC command is as follows:

```
PSC [PS=printserver] [P=printnumber] flaglist
```


Table 25.8
PSC Flags and Options

Flags	Description
STAT	STATus. Shows status of connected printers.
PAU	PAUse. Stops the printer temporarily.
STAR	STARt. Restarts a printer that was paused or stopped.
AB	ABort. Aborts the print job.
STO [K]	STOp [Keep]. Stops the printer. To resubmit the job, specify Keep.
MA [*char*]	MArk. Marks an asterisk (*) at print head. To use another character, specify the *char* value. Used for form alignment.
FF	FormFeed. Sends a form feed to the printer. The printer must be paused or stopped to do a form feed.
MO F=*n*	MOunt Form=*n*. Specifies a different mount form.
PRI	PRIvate. Specifies that the printer is private. It removes the remote printer from the list of network printers used by a print server and changes the remote printer to a local printer.
SH	SHared. Undoes the PRIvate option. Makes the remote printer available to others.
CD	CancelDown. Cancels the command to down the server if Going down after current jobs was selected in PCONSOLE.

You can use the DOS SET command to define the environment variable PSC to set the default values of the PS (print server) and P (printer). This simplifies the use of the PSC command by reducing the number of keystrokes that you have to enter.

At the DOS prompt, you can use the following command to set PSC:

```
SET PSC=PSPrintserver PPrinternumber
```

To specify PSC in a login script, use the following command:

```
SET PSC="PSprintserver PPrinternumber"
```

Replace *printserver* and *Printernumber* with the name of the print server and printer number. Then, you can issue the following command without having to specify the PS and the P parameters:

```
PSC flagList
```

The following are examples of using the preceding commands. The following command sets the print server to HP_PSERVER and the printer number to 0:


```
SET PSC=PSHP_PSERVER P0
```

To pause the printer, use the following command:

```
PSC PAU
```

To restart the printer, use the following command:

```
PSC STAR
```

In the preceding commands, the print server is HP_PSERVER and the printer number is 0 because these parameters were set in the DOS environment variable.

To display statistics on print server EP_PSERVER and printer 1, use the following command:

```
PSC PS=EP_SERVER P=1 STAT
```

The explicit use of PS and P parameters at the command line override any default settings.

Form Control and Management in NetWare 3.*x*

The PRINTDEF utility can be used to create and manage a database of forms. You were shown how to use PRINTDEF earlier in the chapter. Forms are useful when there is a need to share a printer with different types of forms, such as sales invoices, checks, and word processing documents. The print server keeps track of the current form that is in use at the printer. When a print job specifies a different type of form, it waits until the right form is mounted. Once the correct form is mounted on the printer, any of the following commands can be issued to indicate to the print server that a new form has been mounted:

```
PRINTER n MOUNT formnumber
```

or

```
PSC PS=printsever P=printernumber MO=formnumber
```

The *formnumber* parameter in the preceding commands can be replaced by a numeric value for the form number or by the form name.

PCONSOLE in NetWare 3.*x*

You also can use the PCONSOLE to view the status of print queues, as shown in the following steps:

1. Enter **PCONSOLE**.
2. Make the following selections:

   Print queue information

   Select a queue for printing

   Current queue status

3. The current queue status of the selected queue appears on-screen.

Printing in NetWare 4.*x*

In earlier versions of NetWare, the only way a printer could be shared was to attach it to a server. Up to 5 printers could be attached in this fashion. This type of configuration was called *core print services*. Core print services are still available in NetWare 2.2, but were removed from NetWare 3.*x*. In NetWare 4.*x*, there are no core (built-in) print services.

You have to explicitly add print services to NetWare 4.*x* before you can enable network printing. The primary tools to add print services are:

- NetWare Administrator Tool
- PCONSOLE

Other support utilities such as PRINTDEF, PRINTCON, and PSC still exist in NetWare 4.*x*. Since the scope of this book is to describe only the differences between NetWare 3.*x* and NetWare 4.*x*, these tools will not be described.

To enable printing in NetWare 4.*x* you need:

- Printers
- Print queues
- Print servers

Administrators of NetWare 3.*x* networks will recognize that these are the same concepts that were used with NetWare 3.*x*. The *big* difference here is that these components are objects in the NDS tree. The objects model physical and logical concepts. Thus the printer object corresponds to the printer device attached to the network (directly or via a server or workstation). In NetWare 4.*x* you can submit a job to the printer object. This is done by specifying the NDS name of the printer object when printing a job.

The printer object contains a logical association with the print queue and print server object so that the job ends up being processed by the appropriate print server and ends up in the correct network queue.

Figure 25.53 shows the physical components of network printing and figure 25.54 shows the logical components as part of the NDS tree. Figure 25.53 shows that print jobs submitted by the workstation are processed by the print server and are stored in a queue on some storage volume, and then printed to a network printer. These physical print components are represented as objects in the NDS tree in figure 25.54. The print jobs are submitted by the user objects User A and User B, to the printer object HP_PRINTER. Printer jobs can also be submitted to the print queue object HP_QUEUE, which is the traditional way printing is done in NetWare 3.*x*.

If an application does not understand the network printer objects or print queue objects, the CAPTURE command can be used to redirect (map) a local printer to a printer object or print queue object. The CAPTURE command for NetWare 4.*x* contains appropriate options to support this mode of operation.

25

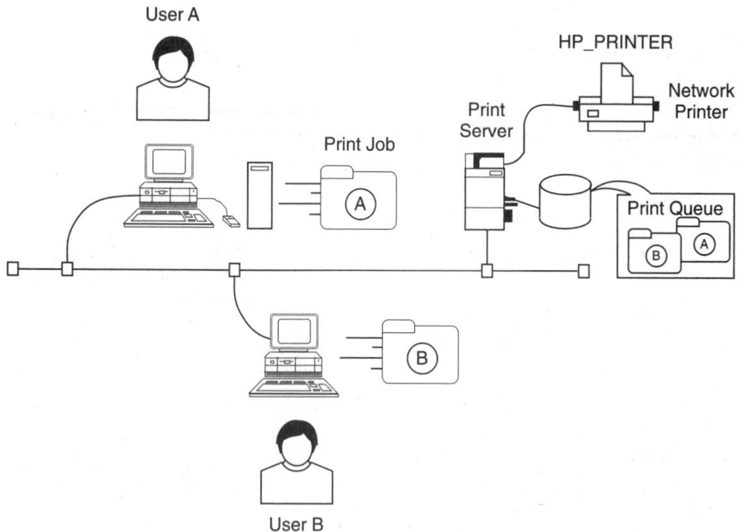

Figure 25.53
Physical components of network printing.

Print Queue Object

The Print Queue object is a logical representation of the physical print queue. The physical print queue is a directory on a storage volume where the print jobs are kept while they are waiting to be printed. The Print Queue object can be created using the NetWare Administrator or the PCONSOLE utility. The print queue object should be placed in the context it is most likely to be used. One of the properties of a print queue object is the physical location of the queue. This queue is always located on a storage volume that must be specified at the time of creating the print queue object. The print queue is placed in a subdirectory of the QUEUES directory. If the QUEUES directory does not exist at the time of creating the queue, it is automatically created.

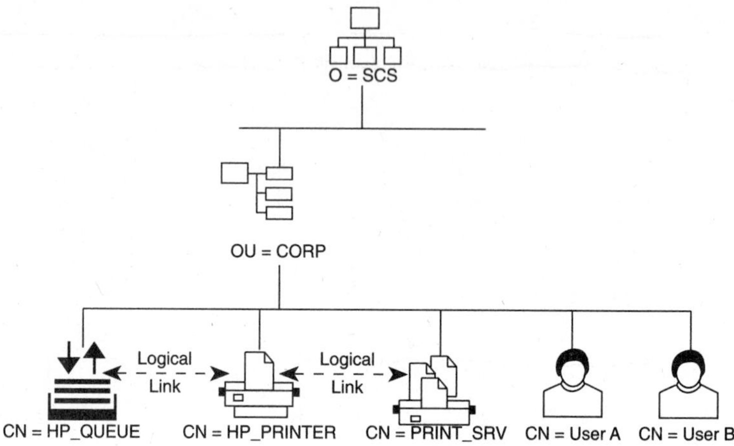

Figure 25.54
Logical (NDS) components of network printing.

25

Printer Object

The Printer object is a logical representation of the physical printer. The physical printer can be directly connected to the network (if it has a network interface), or to a workstation or a file server. The Printer object can be created using the NetWare Administrator or the PCONSOLE utility. The printer object should be placed in the context it is most likely to be used.

Figure 25.55 shows some of the configuration properties for the printer object. This shows the printer type (LPT1, Serial, AppleTalk, UNIX, AIO, XNP). The option types besides LPT1 and Serial are for direct network connection. The Banner Type can be Text or Postscript. The Service Interval shows how often the print server checks the print queue for print jobs assigned to this printer. This can be a value from 1 second to 15 seconds (default). The Buffer Size represents how large each a segment of print data sent to the printer can be. The buffer size can range from 1 KB to 20 KB and has a default value of 3 KB. The Network Address Restrictions show the network address the printer can use. The Service Mode for Forms property is the policy for changing forms.

The Print Server and PSERVER.NLM

The Print Server object describes the print server. The print server object is activated by the PSERVER.NLM, and can therefore run on NetWare servers only. This program takes the print server object name as a parameter when it is loaded.

```
LOAD PSERVER  PrintServerObjectName
```

The above command can be run on any NetWare server that is in the NDS tree. The *PrintServerObjectName* is replaced by the complete name of the print server object. Thus to activate the print server object CN=PS-CORP.OU=CORP.O=SCS, you would have to run the following on the NetWare servers the PSERVER.NLM as shown:

```
LOAD PSERVER .CN=PS-CORP.OU=CORP.O=SCS
```

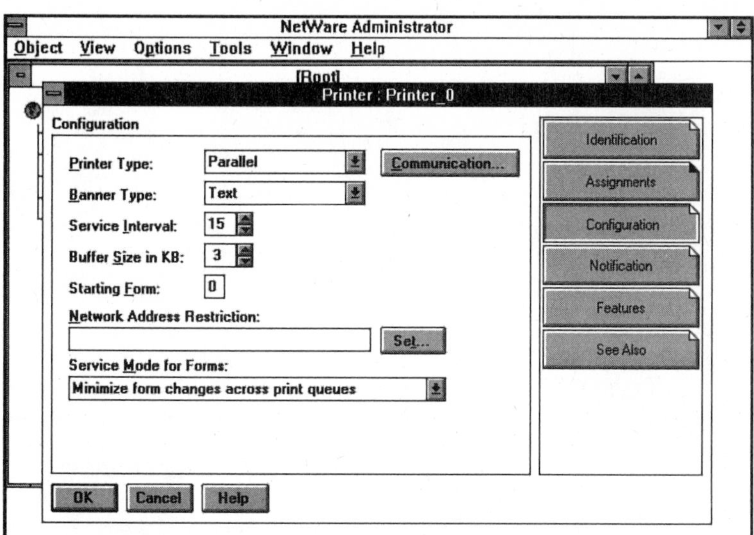

Figure 25.55
Configuration properties for printer object.

The PSERVER.NLM is the only type of print server that exists. The PSERVER.EXE of NetWare 3.*x* is no longer supported in NetWare 4.*x*.

The PSERVER.NLM can support up to 256 printers. Up to 5 of the 256 printers can be attached to the server where PSERVER.NLM is run (local printers). The remaining 251 printers can be attached anywhere else on the network (remote printer). These remote printers can be on other NetWare servers, workstations or directly attached to the network.

Figure 25.56 shows the types of printers used with a print server and figure 25.57 shows the operation of the PSERVER.NLM. The PSERVER.NLM monitors the queue and the printer, and directs print jobs in the network print queue to the appropriate network printer.

Print Server Object

The Print Server object is a logical representation of the print server program (PSERVER.NLM) running at a server. The Print Server object can be created using the NetWare Administrator or the PCONSOLE utility. The printer object should be placed in the context it is most likely to be used.

Figure 25.58 shows the properties of the printer object. Besides the Name property (Common Name), the only property that is set on this screen is the Advertising Name. Server programs in the NetWare environment, such as the PSERVER.NLM that activates a print server from the description in the print server object, advertise their existence using the Service Advertising Protocol (SAP). The other properties such as Other Names, Description, Location, Department and Organization are not set when the queue is initially created via PCONSOLE. It is a good practice to set these values to a meaningful description of the queue object. The Network Address property is only set when the print server is running. The print server in figure 25.58 is running. This is shown by the status fields and the Version property that reports the version number of the PSERVER.NLM that is running. The Network Address property shows that the print server is at F0000055:000000000001. The F0000055 is the internal network number of the NetWare server on which the PSERVER is running and 000000000001 is its node address.

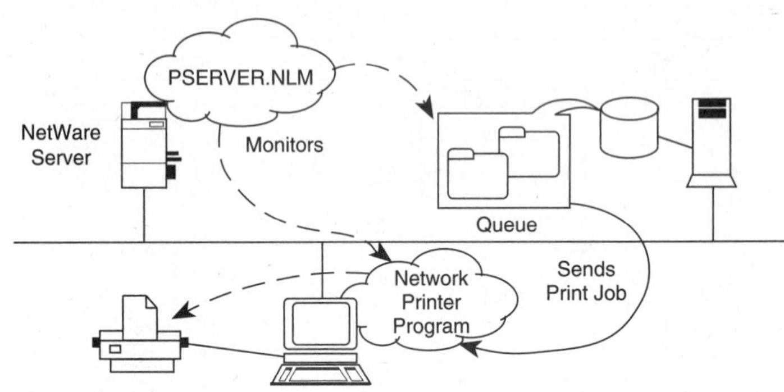

Figure 25.56
Types of printers used with Print Server.

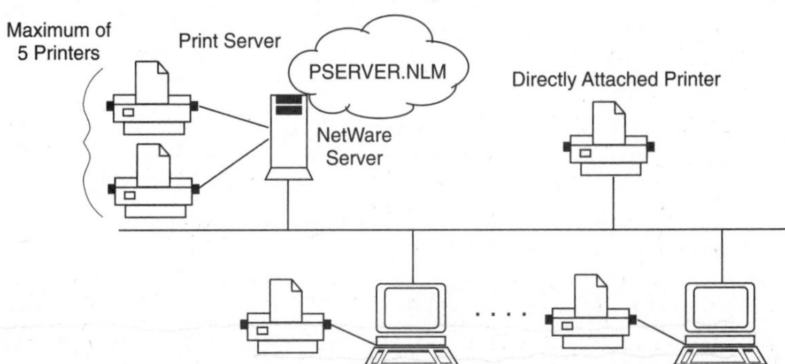

Figure 25.57
Print Server operation.

Figure 25.58
Print Server object properties.

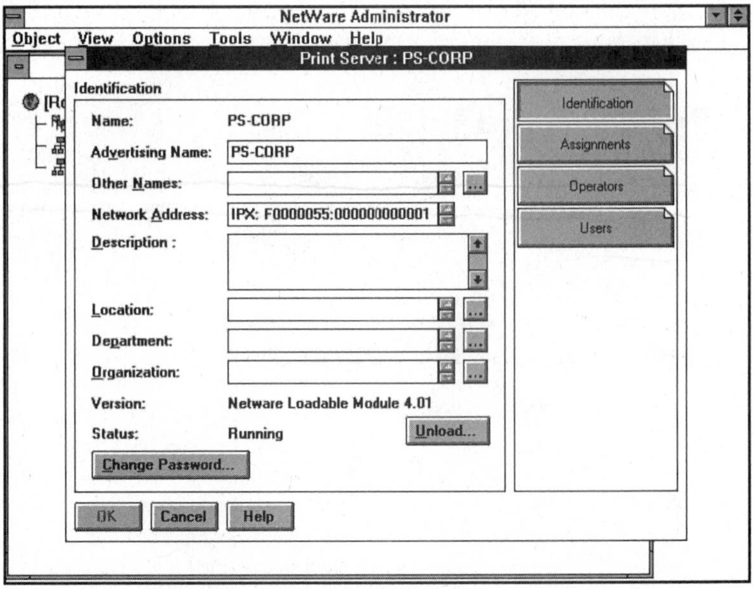

NetWare Administrator
Object View Options Tools Window Help
Print Server : PS-CORP

Identification

Name: PS-CORP
Advertising Name: PS-CORP
Other Names:
Network Address: IPX: F0000055:000000000001
Description :
Location:
Department:
Organization:
Version: Netware Loadable Module 4.01
Status: Running Unload...
Change Password...

Identification
Assignments
Operators
Users

OK Cancel Help

You can unload the print server by selecting the Unload button (see fig. 25.58). The print server can also be unloaded directly from the NetWare console on which it was loaded or through the PCONSOLE program. The print server password is used to secure access to the print server object and can be changed via the Change Password button.

Loading of Printer Definition

When the PSERVER.NLM loads, it activates the printer objects defined in the specified print server object's *printers* property list. If the printer is defined local to the PSERVER.NLM, a program called NPRINTER.NLM is autoloaded to activate any attached local printers (see fig. 25.59). For this reason, printers attached locally to the NetWare Server on which PSERVER.NLM is run are called *Autoload* printers. In figure 25.59, you can see that the Printer_0 was loaded successfully, but the second printer failed to load because, it too was trying to use interrupt line 7 that was already in use by the first printer. If the second printer was defined on a different port from LPT1, this problem would not exist.

Printers that are attached to other NetWare servers or workstations are called remote printers. These must have the NPRINTER program manually loaded on them. For NetWare servers the NPRINTER program is NPRINTER.NLM and for workstations it is NPRINTER.EXE. Because the NPRINTER program has to be manually loaded, for remote printers they are referred to as *Manual load* printers.

```
Loading module PSERVER.NLM
  NetWare 386 Print Server
  Version 4.01    June 14, 1993
  Copyright (c) 1992-1993 Novell, Inc. All rights reserved.
      Loading module NPRINTER.NLM
  NetWare Network Printer Driver v4.01
  Version 4.01    June 30, 1993
  Copyright (c) 1992-1993 Novell, Inc. All rights reserved.
  90 program messages in ENGLISH (language #4) were loaded.
Loading module NPRINTER.NLM
  NetWare Network Printer Driver v4.01
  Version 4.01    June 30, 1993
  Copyright (c) 1992-1993 Novell, Inc. All rights reserved.
  90 program messages in ENGLISH (language #4) were loaded.

Network printer Printer_0 (number 0) loaded
and attached to print server PS-CORP.

NPRINTER-NLM-4.1-10: Interrupt number 7 or the printer port requested
by printer 1 on print server PS-CORP is not available.
(Error code 3)

Network printer not loaded.
NW4KS:
```

Figure 25.59
Load PSERVER.NLM console messages.

The NPRINTER Program

The syntax for loading the NPRINTER program is

```
NPRINTER [PrintServerObjectName]   [PrinterObjectName]
```

or

```
LOAD NPRINTER PrintServerObjectName  PrinterObjectName
```

The first form is used for DOS and OS/2 workstations and the second form is used for loading the printer definition on a NetWare server. Multiple printers can be serviced at the NetWare server by running the LOAD NPRINTER command several times and specifying a different printer number each time.

The *PrintServerObjectName* refers to the print server object to which the printer is assigned. Since a print server object could have more than one printer object assigned to it, the second parameter, *PrinterObjectName,* further qualifies the statement by specifying the actual printer object name. You can also load the printer definition directly by leaving out the print server object name. Thus, to load printer object CN=HP_PRINTER.O=SCS at a workstation as a remote printer, you can use:

```
NPRINTER   .CN=HP_PRINTER.O=SCS
```


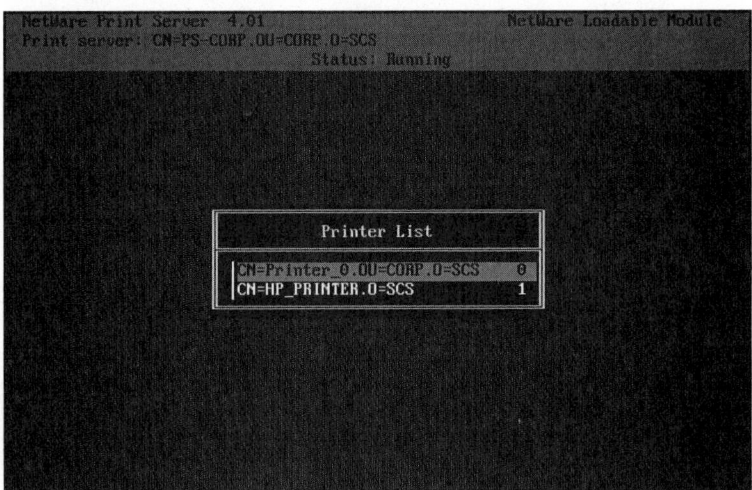

Figure 25.60
Printer List on the print server.

If NPRINTER is used without any options, it runs as a menu utility.

To unload the NPRINTER.EXE, use the command:

```
NPRINTER /U
```

To see the status of a printer, use the command

```
NPRINTER /S
```

The following shows the output produced by running NPRINTER /S on a workstation that had NPRINTER loaded in a prior step:

```
NetWare Network Printer Driver v4.01.
 Copyright 1988 - 1993, Novell, Inc.  All Rights Reserved.

Print server:             PS-CORP
Printer name:            HP_PRINTER
```

```
Printer number:          1
Printer port:            Unknown
Using IRQ:               None (Polled Mode)
TSR status:              Shared Mode
NPRINTER status:         Waiting for Print Job
Printer status:          Out of Paper
```

Figure 25.61 shows a summary of the different types of NPRINTER programs that are possible.

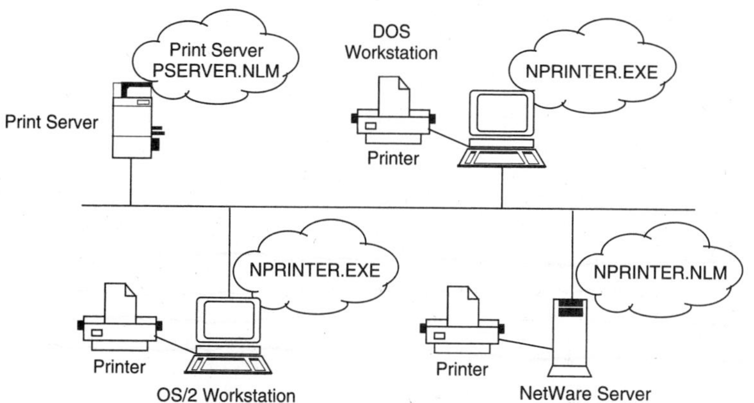

Figure 25.61
Different NPRINTER types.

Interactions between Print Queue, Print Server, and Printer Objects

When configuring network printing objects, certain critical properties for each of these objects need to be set up. You saw the use of some of these critical properties in the earlier discussion on print queue, printer and print server objects.

Figure 25.62 shows the important or *critical* properties for the print queue, printer and print server objects. The print queue is assigned to the Print Queues property of the printer object, and the printer object is assigned to the Printers property of the print server object. This assignment allows a link to be made between the different printing objects, regardless of their context. That is, the network print configuration objects (printer queue, print and print server objects) can be placed in the same context or different context. You should, however, try to create them in contexts that they are most likely to be used.

The diagram in figure 25.61 shows a one-to-one correspondence between the print queue, printer and print server object. This is the simplest and most often used setup. More complex, many-to-one assignments can be made. Figure 25.63 shows that multiple queues can be assigned to a single printer object, and multiple printer objects can be assigned to a single print server object.

To create the print configuration objects, you should have the Create object right to the container where these objects will be placed. The quickest way to create these objects is to use the Quick Setup option under PCONSOLE. If you do not have the Create object right, this option will not be shown on the PCONSOLE menu.

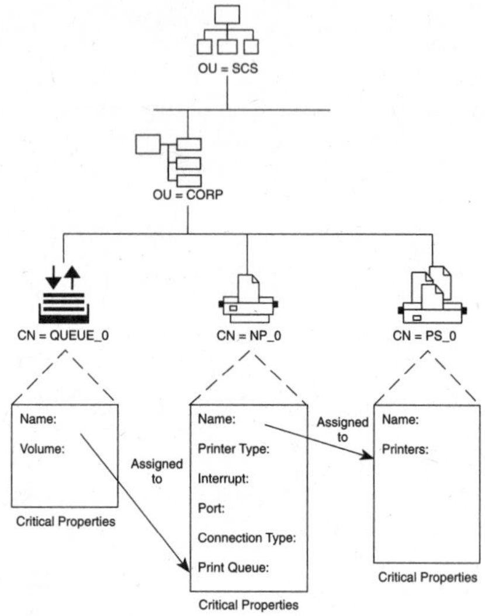

Figure 25.62 *Setting of Critical Properties for print objects.*

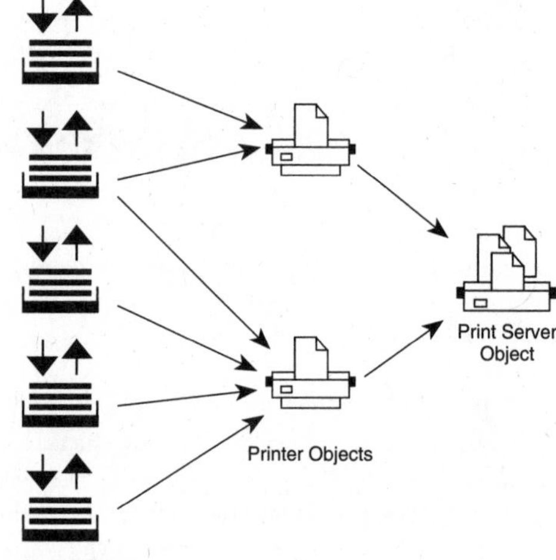

Figure 25.63 *Many-to-1 relationship between print objects.*

By default, the creator of the print objects is made a trustee and given all object rights and property rights to that object. Figure 25.64 shows the trustee rights to object PS-CORP. The creator of the object is Admin.ESL. This user has all rights to Object Rights (Supervisor, Browse, Delete, Rename) and the All Properties rights (Supervisor, Compare, Read, Write, Add Self).

Configuring Network Print Services

As mentioned earlier, the primary tools for configuring network services are PCONSOLE and Network Administrator. But only PCONSOLE has the Quick Setup option. The other options in PCONSOLE are the same as in the PCONSOLE for NetWare 3.*x*, with the exception that they have been modified to work with NDS objects.

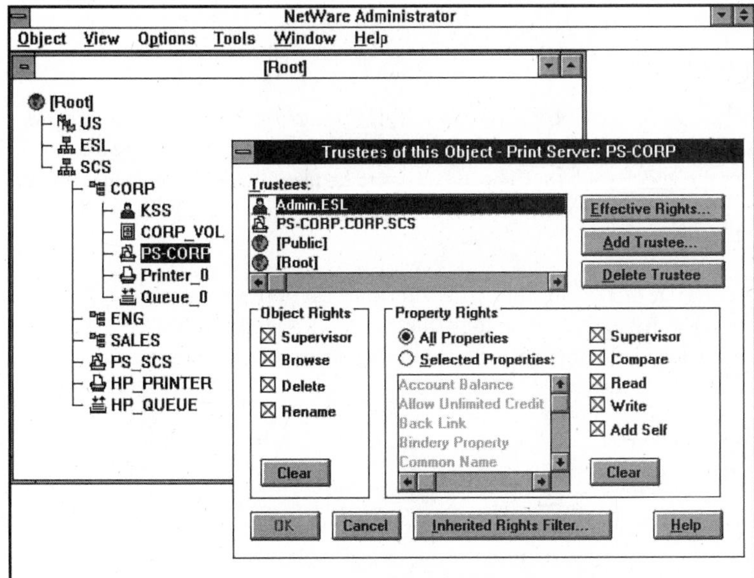

Figure 25.64
Trustee right of owner to print server object.

If you use the NetWare Administrator tool to create print objects, you have to make sure that their critical properties are defined, and the logical links between them are properly defined.

The NETADMIN.EXE program cannot be used to create print objects. You cannot use this tool to view or edit properties of print objects.

The PCONSOLE Utility

You will now be given a guided tour on implement network printing by using the PCONSOLE utility by creating print queues, printer and print server objects, and configuring them.

1. Login as an Admin user and run PCONSOLE. You can login as another user as long as you have create, delete and browse privileges to the container where you are creating the print objects. Should you wish to rename any print objects you create, you may also wish to have Rename object rights to leaf objects in the container.

2. Select Change Context from PCONSOLE and change your context to the container where you wish to place the print objects. In this guided tour the container name is OU=CORP.O=ESL_*XXX*. If you are practicing using PCONSOLE, you may wish to create an organization with a similar name. Substitute any characters for *XXX*, so you can experiment with different organization trees. You can always delete these trees at a later point.

   You can see your context reported on the top half of the PCONSOLE screen.

3. Select Print Queues from Available Options. You should see a list of print queue objects defined in the OU=CORP.O=ESL_*XXX* context. The list should initially be empty unless you have already created print queue objects in this container.

4. Press Ins to create a queue object. You should see a screen asking you to enter the new queue name:

5. Enter the name of the print queue object as QUEUE_1. (You can chose any other name, but for the purpose of this exercise, it will be referred to as QUEUE_1.) You should see a screen asking you to enter the queue's volume. The queue has to be placed on a volume objects. It is created as a subdirectory (with the name of the *Print Queue ID*) under the QUEUES directory.

6. ACTION: Enter the name of a volume object. For the purpose of this exercise the volume name is referred to as CORP_VOL. You can use the volume object name on your NetWare 4.*x* server, or create an alias in your current context to the server volume, name it CORP_VOL and use this name.

   You can also press Ins and browse through the NDS directory tree, searching for the volume to place the queue on.

   After you enter the volume name to used with the print queue object, you should see the newly created print queue object in the Print Queues list.

7. Your next step is to create a printer object. Return to the main PCONSOLE menu by pressing Esc.

   Select the Printers option from Available Options.

   You should see a list of printer objects defined in the OU=CORP.O=ESL_*XXX* context. The list should initially be empty.

8. Press Ins to create a printer object. You should see a screen asking you to enter the new printer name.

9. Enter the name of the print queue object as PRINTER_1. (You can choose any other name, but for the purpose of this exercise, it will be referred to as PRINTER_1.)

   You should see the newly created printer object in the Printers list.

10. Select the printer object you have created from the Printers list. You should see a screen on the printer configuration.

11. Assuming that you have a parallel printer, configure the printer as follows. If you have a serial printer use one of the COM*x* ports.

Printer Type:	Parallel
Configuration:	Port: LPT1
Location:	Manual Load or Autoload
Interrupt:	7
Address restriction:	No
Print Queues Assigned:	Assign QUEUE_1 to this printer

When you assign the queue object that you created earlier, you will select the Print queues assigned: (list) field from the Printer Configuration screen. You will see a Print Queue list. Press Ins and select the name of the queue object. You can also browse the directory tree, looking for queue objects, by selecting on the ".." (parent) entry.

The priority column displays the priority for jobs in queue. You can select the queue name entry to change its priority from 1 (highest) to 10 (lowest).

The state column displays codes that have the following meaning:

A = Printer is actively servicing the queue.

C = Printer is configured to service this queue.

D = This is the default print queue.

In the print configuration screen, you can also select the Notification field to select the users/groups that should be notified when a a print job has been completed. The default Notification list contains the Print job owner value.

12. Press Esc a few times, and save printer configuration changes when asked to do so.

    Return to the main Available Options menu.

13. The last step is to create a print server object.

    Select the Print Servers option from Available Options.

    You should see a list of print server objects defined in the OU=CORP.O=ESL_*XXX* context. The list should initially be empty.

14. Press Ins to create a printer object. You should see a screen asking you to enter the new print server name:

15. Enter the name of the print server as PSRV_1 (or any other print server name). You will see a message that you should wait while the print server object is being created. You should see the newly created printer object in the Print Servers list.

16. Your next step is to configure the print server object. Select the Print Server object you have created from the Print Servers list. You should see a list of Print Server Information options.

17. Select the Printers option from the Print Server Information list. You should see a list of Serviced Printers. Initially the list should be empty.

    Press Ins. You should see a list of printer objects that can be assigned to the print server.

18. Select the printer object you created earlier (PRINTER_1) and assign it to the print server. You should see a list of serviced printer objects that are assigned to the print server.

    You can assign up to 256 printer objects to a print server object. If you need to assign more than 256 printers, define another print server object.

19. Return to the main Available Options menu by pressing Esc a few times. You have created a print queue, printer and print server object and configured them properly.

The next step is to load the print server (PSERVER.NLM) on a server.

The LOAD PSERVER Command

The PSERVER command syntax is as follows:

```
LOAD PSERVER PrintServerObject
```

To load the PSERVER.NLM for the print server object CN=PSRV_1.OU=CORP.O=ESL_*XXX* that you created in the pervious section, use the command:

```
LOAD PSERVER     .CN=PSRV_1.OU=CORP.O=ESL_XXX
```

When the PSERVER.NLM loads, you should see a list of Available Options for the PSERVER.NLM (see fig. 25.65). Selecting Printer Status should show the list of printers that are defined for the print server object (see fig. 25.66). Selecting any of the printers listed shows the printer status (see fig. 25.67). Selecting Print Server Information from Available Options shows the print server information and status (see fig. 25.68).

You can change the Current Status field in the Print Server Information (see fig. 25.68) from Running to Unload to unload the print server immediately. If you wish to wait till all print jobs are finished before unloading the print server, you can set Current status filed to Unload after active print jobs.

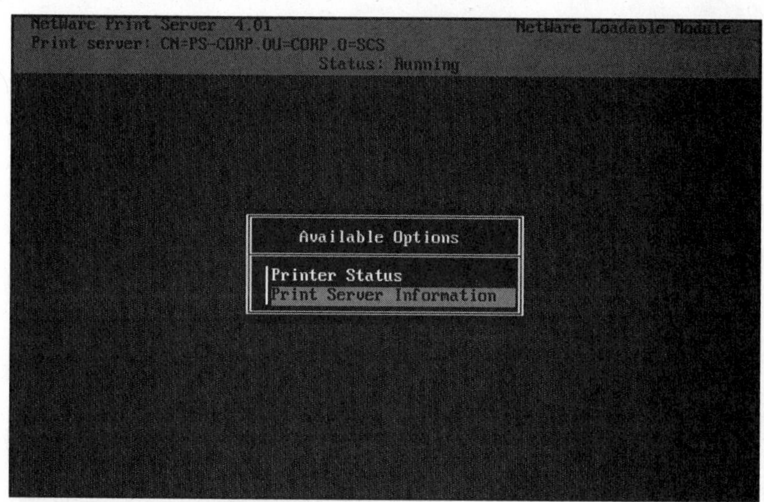

Figure 25.65
PSERVER Main Screen.

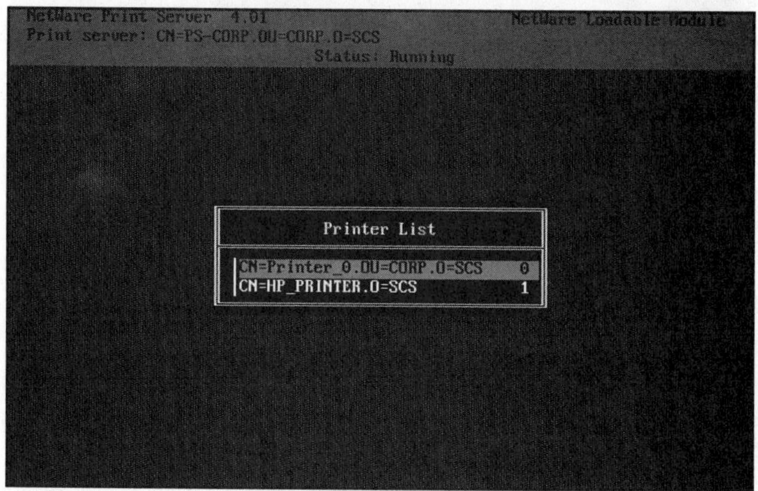

Figure 25.66
PSERVER Printer List.

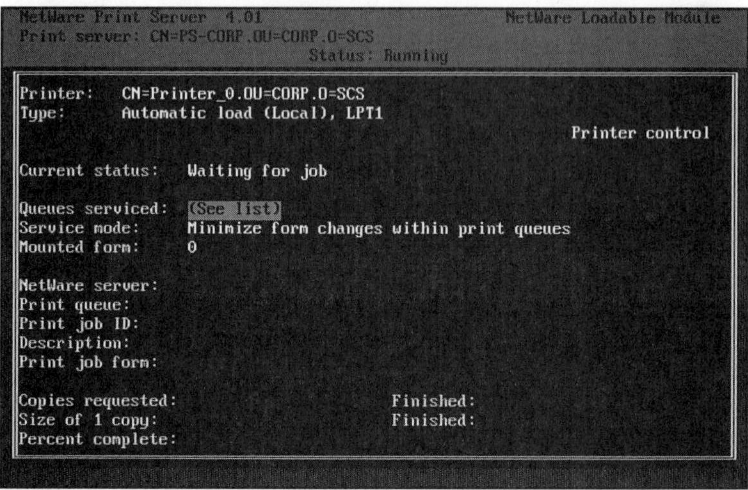

Figure 25.67
PSERVER Printer Status.

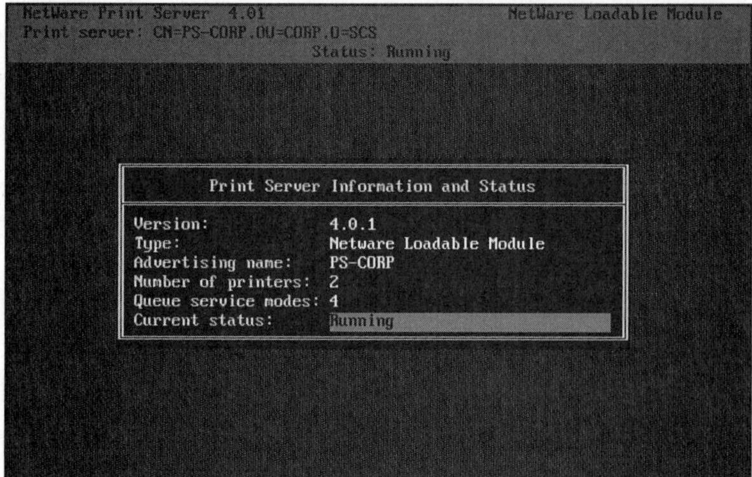

Figure 25.68
PSERVER Print Server Information and Status.

Quick Setup Configuration

The Quick Setup information option in PCONSOLE can be used to create in a single step a print queue, printer and print server object that have all of their critical properties defined. The print objects are created to have the proper logical links between themselves. This means that the print queue object is assigned to the printer object's Print Queues list property, and the printer object is assigned to the print server object's Printers list property.

The print objects that are created have default names of Q1 for print queue object, P1 for printer object and PS-*container* for the print server object. The *container* in the print server name PS-*container* is the name of the container in which the print server is defined. At the time of creation of these objects, you can change the default names to any other names (as long as they do not conflict with leaf names of other objects in the container).

Quick Setup will also make assumptions about the printer properties. For the printer object it defines the following property values.

Printer type:	Parallel
Location:	Auto Load (Local)
Interrupt:	None (polled mode)
Port:	LPT1

These values can be modified during Quick Setup, but they should match your physical printer configuration.

You will now be presented with a guide tour on using the Quick Setup Option of PCONSOLE.

1. Login as an Admin user and run PCONSOLE.
2. If your context is not OU=CORP.O=ESL_*XXX* where *XXX* is replaced by your group identity, select Change Context and change your context to where you wish to create the print objects.
3. Select Quick Setup from Available Options.

   If your context is a container, such as [Root], where print objects cannot be created, you will not see the quick Setup option in the Available Options menu.

   After selecting the Quick Setup option, you should see the Print Services Quick Setup screen (see fig. 25.69).

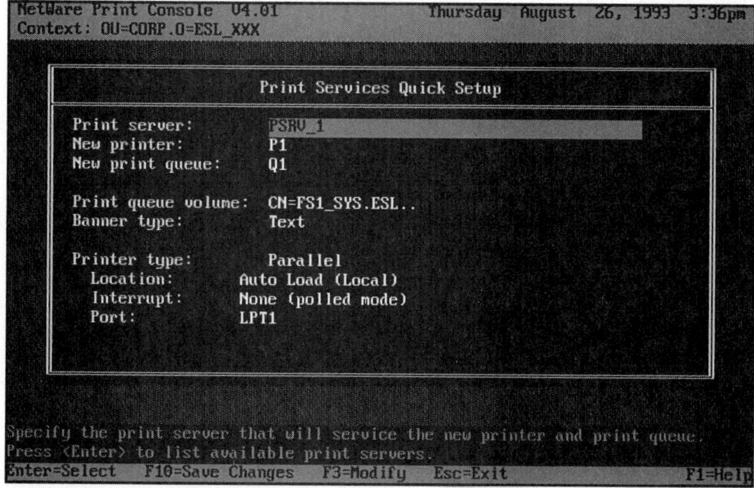

Figure 25.69
Print Services Quick Setup screen.

4. Change the names of these objects to whatever names you wish to use.

5. Change printer configuration to match your needs.

   The printer location to Auto Load (Local) means local printer, and a value of Manual Load means remote printer.

6. Press F10 to save changes. The printer objects will be created after a short wait.

Sending a Print Job

Once the network printing is setup, print jobs can be submitted using:

- NETUSER
- CAPTURE
- NPRINT
- PCONSOLE

The NETUSER is a menu-driven tool that can be used to perform common network related tasks such as network printing, messaging, drive mappings, attaching to other servers. This is a new tool that was first introduced with NetWare 4.0.

The NPRINT and CAPTURE are commands that take a number of options and can be used for sending a print job to network printer.

These printing tools will be briefly examined next.

Printing Using NETUSER

Figure 25.70 shows that one of the options available to NETUSER is Printing. Selecting the Printing option shows you a list of available printer ports local to your workstation. You can select any of these ports for network redirection. After selecting a port, you are given a choice of examining Print Jobs or redirecting the selected port by using Change Printers (see fig. 25.71). You cannot examine print jobs on a printer port that has not been *captured* (redirected to a network printer).

After selecting Change Printers, you are given a list of printers and queues in the current context. If no printers or queues are shown, you can use Ins to browse the NDS tree. Figure 25.72 shows that a queue Queue_0 and a printer Printer_0 NDS objects were found in the context OU=CORP.O=SCS. You can select either the Printer_0 or the Queue_0 object to direct the network print jobs. After redirecting a local printer, the Available Ports menu in NETUSER will show the queue name to which the port is redirected. You can now select the Print Jobs option to send a print job to the network queue. from this point on the procedure for sending print jobs is similar to that for PCONSOLE. That is, you can press Ins and browse directories for files to print.

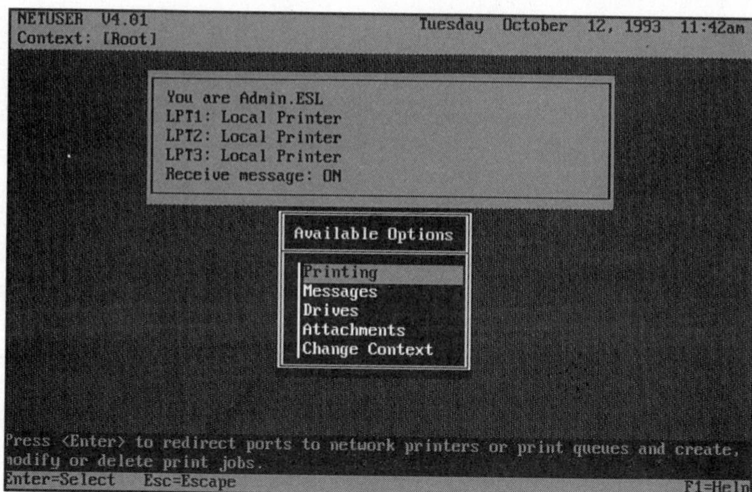

Figure 25.70
NETUSER options.

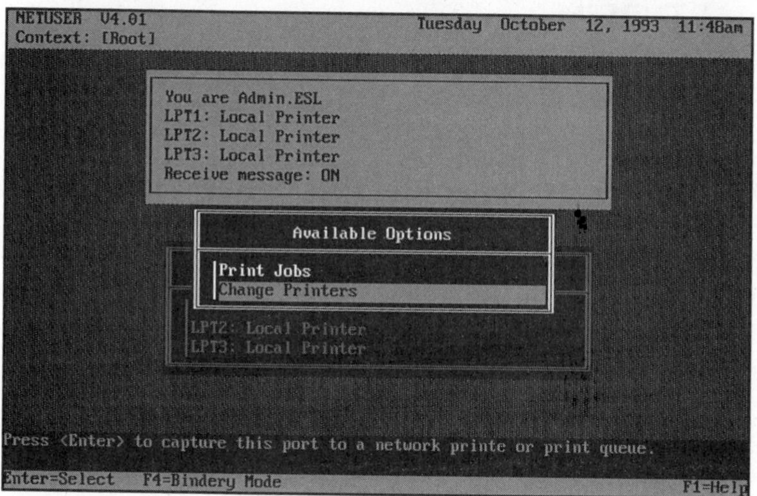

Figure 25.71
Available Printer Ports.

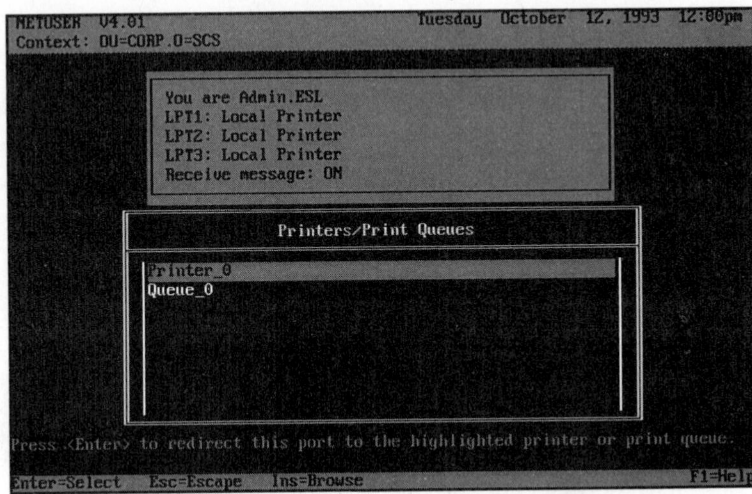

Figure 25.72
Printers/ Print Queues.

Printing Using CAPTURE

The CAPTURE command is used to redirect a local printer port to a network queue or network printer. Table 25.9 shows the CAPTURE options. The options that are new to CAPTURE in NetWare 4.*x* (compared with NetWare 3.*x*) have been highlighted. Option abbreviations are shown in bold. Therefore, the option EndCap can be abbreviated as EC.

The **P**rinter=*name* option can be used to specify the network printer object name to send print jobs to.

The ENDCAP command is no longer used with NetWare 4.*x*. Instead CAPTURE has a new EndCap option to stop printer redirection. To stop the capture of local printer port LPT1:, you can use:

```
CAPTURE EndCap
```

or

```
CAPTURE  EC
```

To stop printer redirection for all local printers, you can use the EndCap ALL option in one of two ways:

```
CAPTURE EndCap ALL
```

or

```
CAPTURE EC ALL
```

Table 25.9
CAPTURE Options

Option	Description
SHow	Shows current status of local printer ports. Used as an option by itself.
Printer=*name*	Specifies network printer to which redirected print jobs should be sent. If *name* is a complete NDS name with embedded blanks, quotes can be used.
Local=*n*	Redirects local LPT port *n*.
Queue=*name*	Indicates queue object to which print job should be sent.
EndCap	Ends redirection to local ports.
EndCap ALL	Ends redirection of all local printer ports.
CReate=*path*	Sends print job to file *path*.
Keep	Retains print job in queue, if workstation fails.
Job=*jc*	Specifies print job configuration to use. No need to specify other options.
NoBanner	Suppresses printing of banner page.
Banner=*name*	Prints banner page. Limit is 12 character for banner *name*. Appears in lower half of page.
NAMe=*name*	Default is name of file being printed. Indicates text in upper part of banner page. Limit is a 12 character name.
Form=*n*	Specifies form number or name that is to be used for print job.
Copies=*n*	Specifies number of copies for print job (1 - 255).
Tabs=*n*	Number of spaces to use for a tab character.
No **T**abs	Suppresses tab expansion to space characters.
TImeout=*n*	Number of seconds to wait before closing job.
Form **F**eed	Generates a form feed character at end of print job.
No **F**orm **F**eed	Suppresses form feed character at end of job.

continues

Table 25.9, Continued
CAPTURE Options

Option	Description
AUtoendcap	Captured data should be closed and sent to printer on exiting application.
NoAutoendcap	Captured data should *not* be closed and sent to printer on exiting application.
NOTIfy	Specifies that user receive notification of print job completion.
NoNOTIfy	Specifies that user not receive notification of print job completion.
/?	Help.
/? ALL	Displays all help screens.
Verbose	Provides detailed information on command as it is executed.

Printing Using NPRINT

To print a job using NPRINT, use the following syntax:

```
NPRINT    filename    [option]
```

The *option* can be replaced by any of the options in table 25.10. The options that are new to NPRINT in NetWare 4.*x* (compared with NetWare 3.*x*) have been highlighted.

Table 25.10
NPRINT Options

Option	Description
Server=*name*	Specifies a non-NDS server (bindery server) whose bindery contains the print queue definition.
Printer=*name*	Specifies network printer to which redirected print jobs should be sent. If *name* is a complete NDS name with embedded blanks, quotes can be used.
Local=*n*	Redirects local LPT port *n*.
Queue=*name*	Indicates queue object to which print job should be sent.

Option	Description
Job=*jc*	Specifies print job configuration to use. No need to specify other options.
NoBanner	Suppresses printing of banner page.
Banner=*name*	Prints banner page. Limit is 12 character for banner *name.* Appears in lower half of page.
NAMe=*name*	Default is name of file being printed. Indicates text in upper part of banner page. Limit is a 12 character name.
Form=*n*	Specifies form number or name that is to be used for print job.
Copies=*n*	Specifies number of copies for print job (1 - 255).
Tabs=*n*	Number of spaces to use for a tab character.
No Tabs	Suppresses tab expansion to space characters.
Form Feed	Generates a form feed character at end of print job.
No Form Feed	Suppresses form feed character at end of job.
NOTIfy	Specifies that user receive notification of print job completion.
NoNOTIfy	Specifies that user not receive notification of print job completion.
/?	Help.
/? ALL	Displays all help screens.
Verbose	Provides detailed information on command as it is executed.

Printing Using PCONSOLE

To print using PCONSOLE, select the Print Queues option from Available Options in PCONSOLE. If the print queue you want to print to is not displayed, use Change Context to change context to the container that has the queue object.

After selecting the Queue name from the Print Queues list you will see a menu on Print Queue Information. Select Print Jobs option. You should see the jobs in the current queue. Press Ins, enter a directory name to print from and press Enter. Select the files that you wish to print. You will be given a choice of Print Job Configurations to use for printing. If no print job configurations have been defined for the current container, you can select the (Defaults) print job configuration.

Network Printing Tools

Table 25.11 shows the list of network printing tools that are available for NetWare 4.*x*. The PCONSOLE, PSERVER, NPRINTER, and NWADMIN (Network Administrator) have been discussed so far. The PRINTCON and PRINTDEF tools will be discussed briefly.

Table 25.11
Network Printing Tools

Program	Extension	Executed On	Used For
PCONSOLE	EXE	Workstation	Creating and configuring print servers, print queues, and printer objects.
PRINTCON	EXE	Workstation	Creating and configuring print job configurations.
PRINTDEF	EXE	Workstation	Defining print forms, importing/ exporting print device definitions.
PSERVER	NLM	Server	Activating the print server object.
NPRINTER	EXE	Workstation	Allowing network printer attached to a station to be shared.
NPRINTER	NLM	Server	Allowing network printer attached to a server not running PSERVER.NLM to be shared.
NWADMIN	EXE	Workstation	GUI utility to perform printer management functions.
PSC	EXE	Workstation	Command-line utility to control and see status of printers and print servers.

NetWare 4.*x* offers PRINTCON and for PRINTDEF print job configuration. The print job configurations can be used as the Job Configuration parameter in CAPTURE and NPRINT to simplify the options by aggregating them under a print job configuration template. It is also used when submitting jobs to a queue using the Print Job option in NETUSER and PCONSOLE.

The PRINTCON Utility

Figure 25.73 shows the main menu for PRINTCON. The Edit Print Job Configuration is used to create new print job configurations. The Select Default Print Job Configuration allows you to select the print job configuration that will be used as a default. The Change Current Object allows you to change the container object or user object for which the print job configuration will be defined.

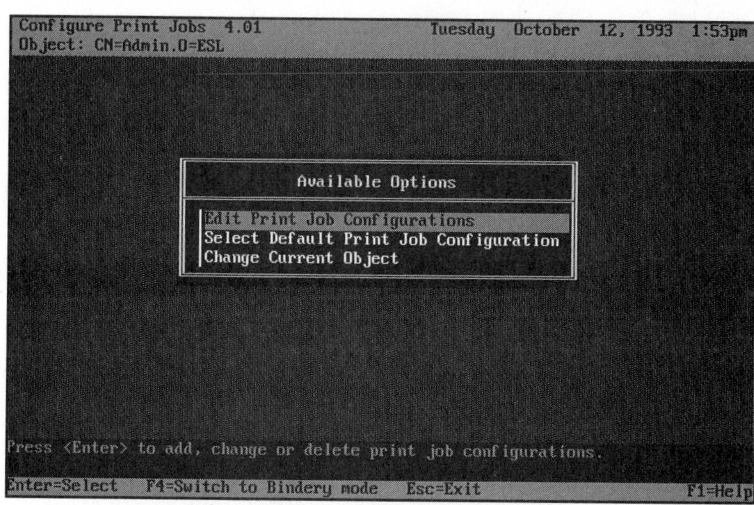

Print job configurations are stored as the Print Job Configuration property of an organization, organization unit or user object. If stored in a container, all users within the container can use the print job configuration. If the print job configuration is stored as a property of a user object, only that user can make use of the print job configuration.

The PRINTCON can operate in the directory mode (default) or the bindery mode. F4 can be used to toggle between these two modes. This allows the NetWare 4.*x* PRINTCON to be used with NetWare 3.*x* bindery. In NetWare 3.*x* print job configurations are stored in the bindery.

The PRINTDEF Utility

Figure 25.74 shows the main menu for PRINTDEF. The Print Devices option is used to modify printer definitions for print devices. The Print Forms option allows you to create and modify printer form definitions. The Change Current Context allows you to change the container object for which the form definition will be defined.

Print device definitions and forms are stored in the Print Devices and Print Forms property of the container object. If stored in a container, all users and print job configurations within the container can use the print device definition.

The PRINTDEF can operate in the directory mode (default) or the bindery mode. F4 can be used to toggle between these two modes. This allows the NetWare 4.*x* PRINTDEF to be used with NetWare 3.*x* bindery. In NetWare 3.*x* print device definitions are stored in the bindery.

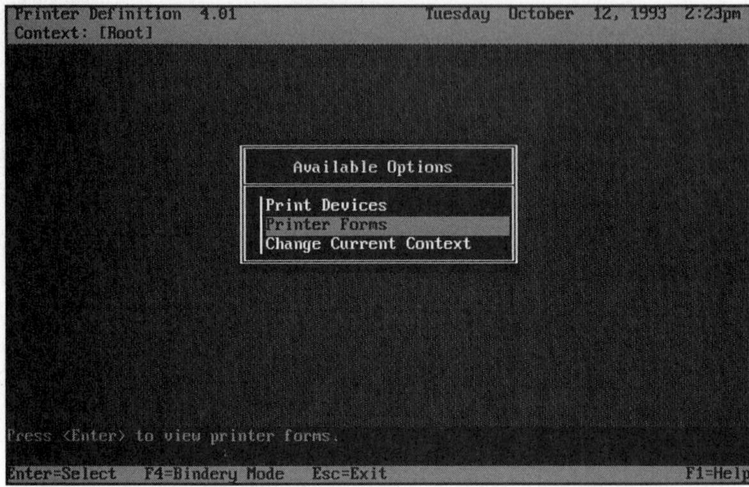

Figure 25.74
PRINTDEF Main Menu.

Summary

In this chapter, you have learned how to use and set up NetWare's printing mechanisms. NetWare supports a variety of printing methods to suit the needs of different printing applications. NetWare-aware applications designed to make use of the NetWare printer function *Application Programming Interfaces* (APIs) require very little configuration support. Applications that do not work as intimately with the NetWare printing mechanisms, however, require additional support.

Most of the printing chores can be done by using the PCONSOLE utility. A detailed guided tour of how to use PCONSOLE in NetWare 3.*x* and NetWare 4.*x* is presented in this chapter, along with examples on using many of NetWare's command-line utilities for printer support.

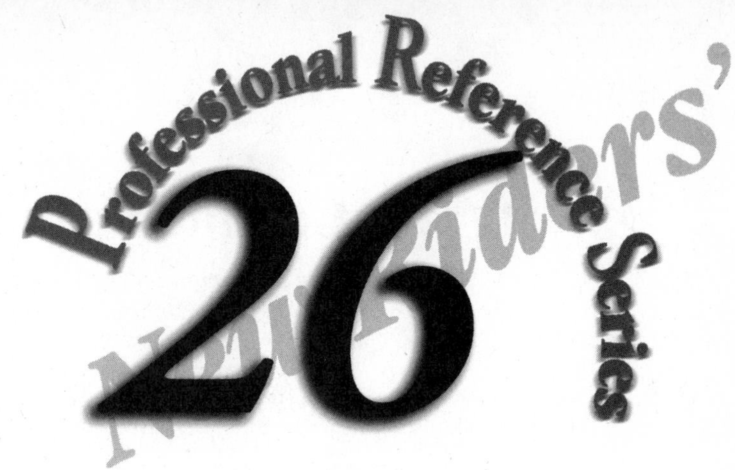

Internetworking

This chapter examines considerations for connecting NetWare in an internet environment that consists of non-NetWare networks and devices. The topics discussed include communications connectivity of NetWare LANs to the following networks:

- TCP/IP networks
- X.25 networks
- T1 networks
- Asynchronous links
- Synchronous links
- IBM SNA networks
- OSI networks
- UNIX networks

This chapter also discusses the installation of Novell's LAN WorkPlace for DOS, NetWare for NFS, and NetWare for FTAM.

NetWare Communications Connectivity

Novell has made a strong commitment to support current major networking architectures. Some of these network architectures (such as IBM SNA) are proprietary, others (such as TCP/IP networks) are industry standards, and some (such as OSI networks) are international standards.

These different networks are likely to coexist in the near future, so the capability to integrate multivendor networks is a key requirement for many network environments.

TCP/IP Connectivity

TCP/IP has become a de facto protocol standard for connecting different computing platforms, and it currently has the largest support among communication vendors. It is predicted that TCP/IP protocols eventually will be replaced by OSI protocols, but in the meantime, TCP/IP-based products, and the vendor and user support for them, show no signs of declining.

TCP/IP is not one protocol; it consists of two protocols: TCP and IP. *Transmission Control Protocol* (TCP) is a transport protocol that fits into layer 4 of the OSI model. *Internet Protocol* (IP) is a network protocol that fits into layer 3 of the OSI model. Often, *TCP/IP* is used as a term to describe the transport and network protocols and also the application protocols that make use of it. The basic TCP/IP protocols are shown in figure 26.1. The OSI model comparison is meant for categorizing the functions of the protocols and does not indicate OSI compliance.

In the figure, TCP represents a transport protocol that provides reliable communications through *virtual circuits.* This means that any errors occurring in the underlying network are corrected by TCP. TCP provides automatic acknowledgments and retransmissions of data (in case of errors), so that the users of the TCP layer do not have to worry about unreliable transmissions. In many ways, TCP is similar to Novell's SPX protocol, but it also is designed to work effectively over *wide area networks* (WANs). Besides data-transmission integrity, TCP also provides software addressing (port numbers) for applications that make use of it.

The *User Datagram Protocol* (UDP) in figure 26.1 provides a "best-efforts" datagram delivery service. It is used for network environments that are essentially quite reliable, such as LANs. If greater reliability is desired, the network application layer is responsible for implementing it. UDP is used by the *Simple Network Management Protocol* (SNMP), *Network File System* (NFS), and *Trivial File Transfer Protocol* (TFTP). It also is used to encapsulate NetWare IPX packets for IP tunneling.

The IP protocol can run on a wide variety of networking technologies, such as LANs, X.25, Frame Relay, Packet Radio, and Point-To-Point links. It provides a uniform interface to these networking technologies, as well as a uniform network address, routing of the transport protocols, fragmentation, and reassembly for long messages.

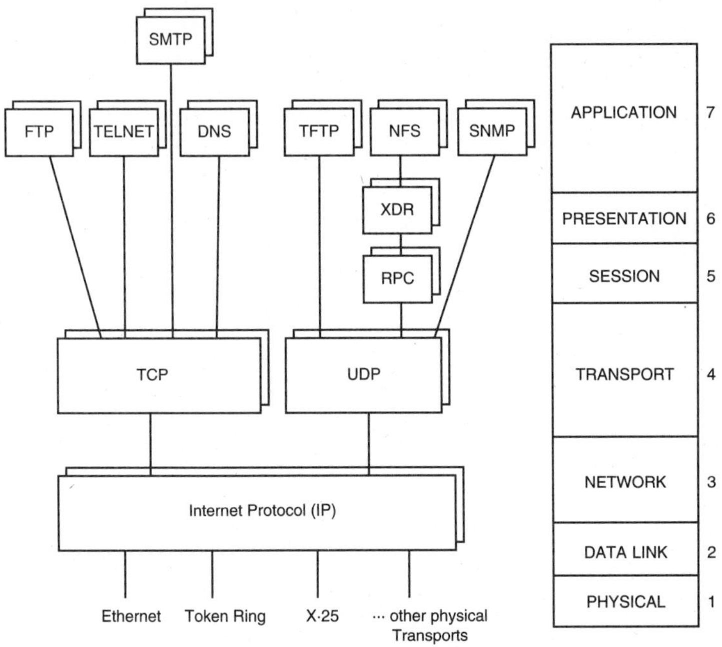

Figure 26.1
TCP/IP protocols and the OSI model.

Novell provides a variety of products for TCP/IP networks, which makes it easy to integrate NetWare-based networks with TCP/IP-based networks. Novell obtained much of its TCP/IP experience through its merger with Excelan. Novell's TCP/IP products enable different operating system platforms (DOS, OS/2, Macintosh, and UNIX) to be integrated. On the workstation side, these products are known collectively as the *LAN WorkPlace* products.

The goal of these TCP/IP-based products is to provide high-speed communications between dissimilar computers, which is the first step for running distributed applications across multiple dissimilar computers. Many vendors have begun providing this capability because they realize that they cannot lock a customer into one application architecture. Novell calls this concept *Network Integrated Computing Architecture* (NICA), which also means that applications written to TCP/IP can be distributed over the network.

Novell also provides MultiNet, a hardware-independent implementation of TCP/IP networking, for remote connectivity to VAX/VMS environments. NetWare 3.11 and above includes the TCP/IP Transport, a collection of NLMs that provides NetWare with TCP/IP transport protocols, *application programming interfaces* (APIs)—such as BSD Sockets, STREAMS, and AT&T's *Transport Layer Interface* (TLI)—and tools for managing those protocols. The IP routing that the TCP/IP Transport provides enables TCP/IP packets to be routed from one NetWare 3.*x* network to another. Tunneling IPX packets through IP subnets enables NetWare 3.11 (and above) servers to be connected through a TCP/IP internet.

TCP/IP support is provided through the *Open Datalink Interface* (ODI) drivers. These drivers can support multiple protocols, such as IPX and TCP/IP, through a single network adapter. This is valuable for the workstation that needs to run several client applications to communicate with servers using different protocols through a single network adapter. Without ODI (or a similar scheme), you would need multiple adapters in the workstation to provide multiple protocol stack functionality, resulting in higher cost and fewer free adapter slots at the workstation.

LAN WorkPlace for DOS

LAN WorkPlace for DOS provides access to TCP/IP hosts for DOS workstations and for Windows 3.*x* users who have DOS workstations. As mentioned in the previous section, TCP/IP has become a vendor-independent protocol, so the communications subnet and hardware can be implemented with products from a variety of sources.

The TCP/IP host machines can be UNIX systems, Digital VAXs running VMS or Ultrix, IBM mainframes running MVS or VM, or NetWare running NetWare for NFS. For DOS users, access is provided by a command-line interface; for Windows users, access is provided by the Windows graphical user interface (GUI).

Besides the basic TCP/IP application services, LAN WorkPlace can be used to run other TCP/IP-based applications, such as Quarterdeck's DESQview/X, VisionWare's X-Vision (a Windows-based X-Server), ORACLE's SQL*Net TCP/IP for MS-DOS, and the SYBASE PC Net-Library for DOS. Memory (RAM) space available for running these applications on the workstation is critical. Currently, the combined TCP/IP and ODI network drivers consume about 45 KB of conventional RAM. IPX and the NetWare shell require an additional 16 KB on machines that support extended or expanded memory. By using ODI, protocol stacks can be dynamically loaded or unloaded from memory without having to reboot.

The capabilities provided by LAN WorkPlace (for DOS and OS/2) are listed in table 26.1.

Table 26.1
LAN WorkPlace Features

Features	Description
FTP	*File Transfer Protocol* enables clients to transfer files between TCP/IP hosts supporting an FTP server. The FTP server can be a UNIX host or NetWare running the FTPSRV NLM.
TFTP	*Trivial File Transfer Protocol* utilities provide a simplified version of the FTP protocol using UDP/IP services.
rcp	A UNIX-like command-line utility, *remote copy* (rcp) provides an alternate method of file transfer.

Features	Description
Telnet VT220	Terminal emulation through *Telnet.* DEC VT100 and terminal emulators are included for both Windows and DOS. These emulators support up to 10 concurrent sessions to multiple hosts. *Telnet Application Programming Interface* (TelAPI) can be used to employ other vendors' communications programs and terminal emulators for communicating with TCP/IP-equipped hosts through Telnet.
Remote execution	UNIX-style commands including *remote shell* (rsh) and *remote execute* (rexec) enable users to invoke programs on remote systems from the DOS prompt and see the results on their own screen.
Remote printing	*Remote Printing* (rpr) provides printing of files to UNIX and VMS hosts.
NetBIOS on TCP/IP	The recommendations of standard documents RFC-1001/RFC-1002 NetBIOS API (B-node implementation) that provide a standard NetBIOS session layer interface over TCP/IP.

For users running Windows 3.*x* for DOS, LAN WorkPlace provides the following features:

- Up to 10 Telnet sessions can be provided through one workstation. The Host Presenter provides up to 10 simultaneous Telnet session windows (emulating a VT220, VT52, or VT100 terminal) to multiple TCP/IP-equipped hosts. It supports data transfer to and from the Telnet session through the Windows Clipboard. The Host Presenter also includes a scripting language called *Script Director.* Script Director makes conventional host-based applications easier to use.

- FTP server (FTPd—daemon) that runs in the background under Windows and accepts file requests from multiple FTP clients.

- File Express provides a graphical front end, instead of the traditional command-line user interface.

LAN WorkPlace uses ODI driver interfaces to run TCP/IP and NetWare IPX/SPX protocols concurrently on Ethernet, Token Ring, and ARCnet LANs. Because NetWare 3.11 (and above) can act as an IP router, LAN WorkPlace can connect NetWare clients on ARCnet and Token Ring LANs to TCP/IP hosts on Ethernet segments (see fig. 26.2). NetWare 2.*x* IPX routers do not support IP routing and must be on the same network segment as the target TCP/IP host.

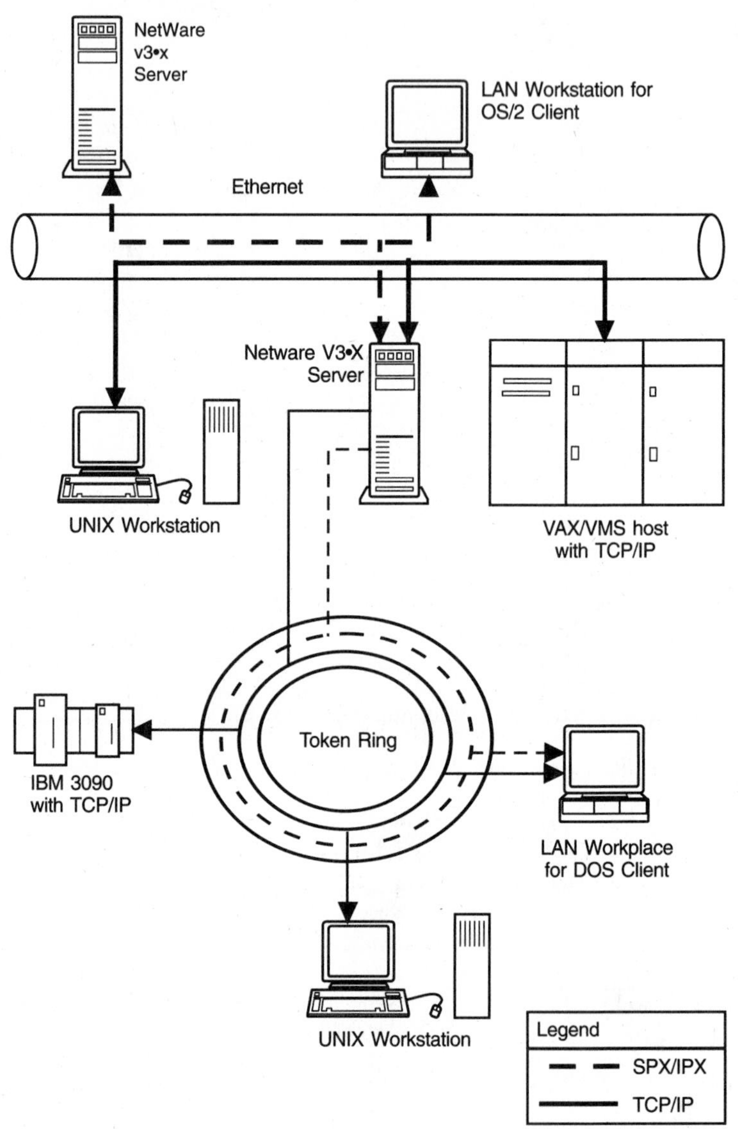

Figure 26.2
LAN WorkPlace for DOS.

LAN WorkPlace supports the Internet standards listed in table 26.2. This list applies to the LAN WorkPlace products for DOS, OS/2, and Macintosh.

Table 26.2
Standards Supported by LAN WorkPlace

Standard Name	Standard Number
IP (Internet Protocol)	RFC 791
IP Subnet Extension	RFC 950
IP Broadcast Datagrams	RFC 919IP
Broadcast Datagrams with Subnets	RFC 922
TCP (Transmission Control Protocol)	RFC 793
UDP (User Datagram Protocol)	RFC 768
IP-IEEE (Internet Protocol on IEEE 802)	RFC 1042
NetBIOS (NetBIOS Service Protocol on TCP/IP)	RFC 1001, 1002
ARP (Address Resolution Protocol)	RFC 826
RARP (Reverse Address Resolution Protocol)	RFC 903
ICMP (Internet Control Message Protocol)	RFC 792
DNS (Domain Name System) Resolver	RFC 1034, 1035
TELNET (Telnet Protocol)	RFC 854
FTP (File Transfer Protocol)	RFC 959
TFTP (Trivial File Transfer Protocol)	RFC 783

LAN WorkPlace for OS/2

LAN WorkPlace for OS/2 (see fig. 26.3) provides the capabilities of LAN WorkPlace for DOS on an OS/2 workstation. Because OS/2 is a multitasking operating system, multiple concurrent TCP/IP connections are easy to provide at an OS/2 workstation.

LAN WorkPlace for OS/2 supports the features listed in table 26.1 and the standards documents listed in table 26.2.

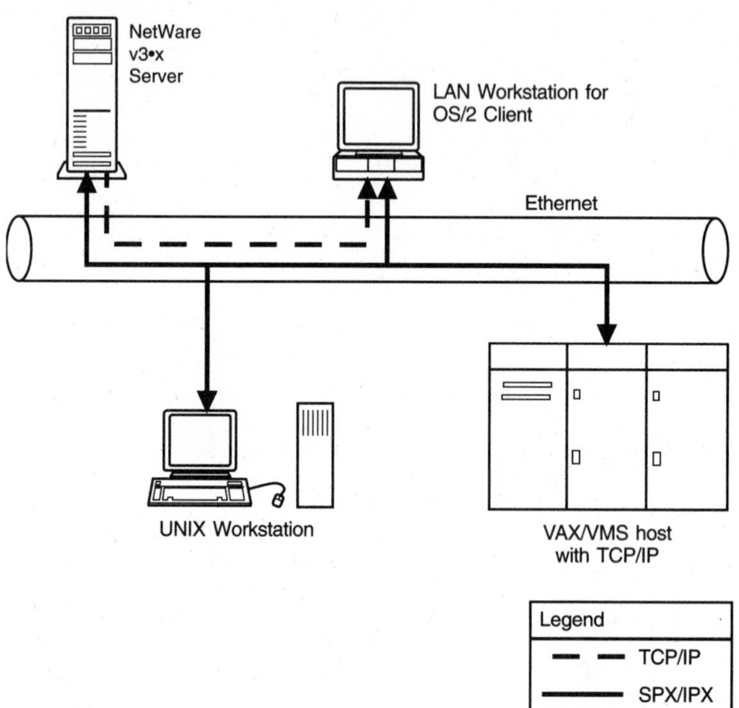

Figure 26.3
LAN WorkPlace for OS/2.

For third-party developers, an OS/2 developer's kit provides an application programming interface to the TCP/IP interface. The API can access the network drivers and the TCP/IP protocols through the BSD socket interface.

LAN WorkPlace for Macintosh

LAN WorkPlace for Macintosh provides Macintosh users with access to TCP/IP hosts such as IBM mainframes, VAX minicomputers, and PCs (see fig. 26.4). The users use the familiar Macintosh interface to access the remote hosts. The product consists of the TCPport transport system software, HostAccess, and NetStat desk accessory. HostAccess provides Telnet and FTP capability.

The physical transport mechanism for LAN WorkPlace for Macintosh can be EtherTalk (Ethernet) or LocalTalk. The Macintosh Plus can use the built-in LocalTalk connection, whereas the Macintosh SE, SE30, II, IIcx, and so on can use either LocalTalk or EtherTalk.

The features and standards supported by LAN WorkPlace for Macintosh are listed in tables 26.1 and 26.2.

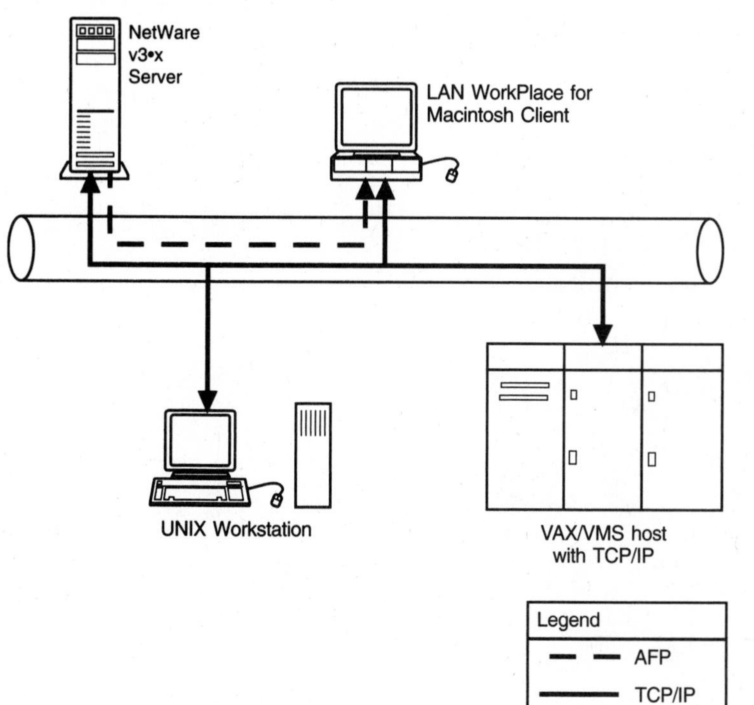

Figure 26.4
LAN WorkPlace for Macintosh.

Installing and Configuring LAN WorkPlace for DOS

This section presents you with a specific method for installing LAN WorkPlace for DOS. Follow these steps:

1. Install the ODI driver programs for your LAN NIC in the root directory or a directory that is on the DOS search path. Start the installation by running the program INSTALL from the LAN WorkPlace for DOS disk, in drive A, as follows:

   A:INSTALL

2. When the installation screen appears, do the following:

   Select drive for installing LAN WorkPlace (drive C or D). Install LAN WorkPlace Windows applications.

   To install Windows applications, you must have Windows 3.*x* installed because several Windows INI files need to be modified.

3. If the Windows directory is not on the DOS search path, you are prompted for the directory path that contains Windows.

If you do not have sufficient disk space to do a full installation, you are asked whether or not you want to stop the installation. If you are reinstalling LAN WorkPlace for DOS, and you know that the installation overwrites existing files, select No.

4. The list of information you need to know to complete the installation is shown in figure 26.5.

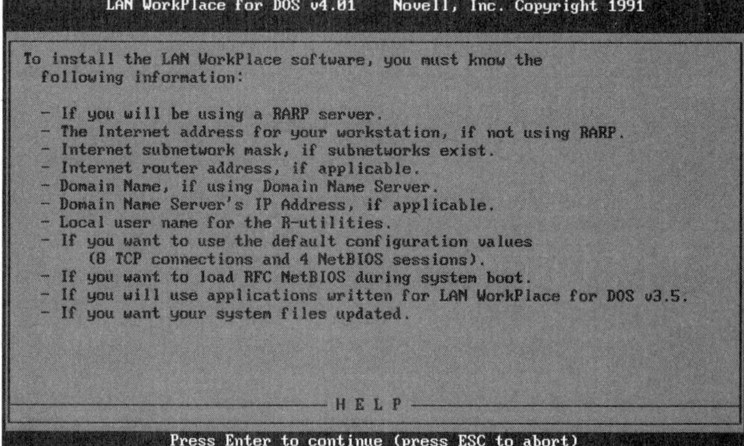

Figure 26.5
Information needed for LAN WorkPlace software installation.

26

5. After you know the answers to the configuration information, press Enter to continue.

6. If you are using a Reverse Address Resolution Protocol (RARP) to specify your IP address, you do not need to specify your IP address. Otherwise, you are asked to specify your IP address.

7. If you selected No for RARP server, you must specify your IP address, which must be unique. (Consult your network administrator for a unique IP address.)

   IP addresses are entered in the dotted decimal notation as four decimal digits, separated by a period (.).

8. If you are using subnets to logically partition your network, you must specify a subnet mask. The IP address is a two-part address, consisting of a network ID and a host ID, as shown in figure 26.6. There are different IP address formats (Class A, B, C, D, and E) that determine how many bits of the 32-bit IP address are used for the network ID and the host ID. For instance, a class B address in figure 26.6 has 16 bits for the host ID, enabling it to have 64,000 hosts (computers) on one network. Because this number is so large for most single networks, it is much easier to logically partition a single IP network into subnetworks. This can be done by superimposing your own meaning on the host ID. For example, in figure 26.7 the host ID can be further divided into a subnet field and a host ID field. The subnet field is the logical address you assign to a network smaller than the original single network, consisting of 64,000 hosts.

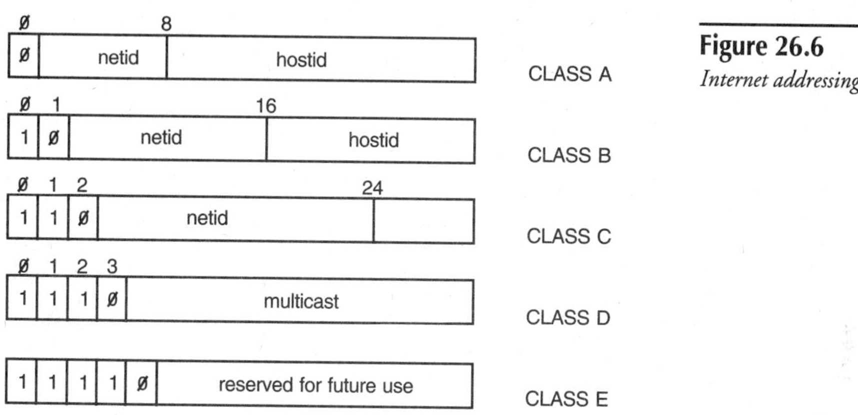

Figure 26.6
Internet addressing.

The subnet mask is also specified in the dotted decimal form, in which a binary 1 in the mask corresponds to the network and a binary 0 corresponds to the host. For instance, a subnet mask of 255.255.255.0 means that the last 8 bits are assigned to the host ID (computer), and the remaining 24 bits are split between the net ID and the subnet ID. If you are using a class B address, the first 16 bits are used for the net ID, leaving 8 bits for the subnet ID.

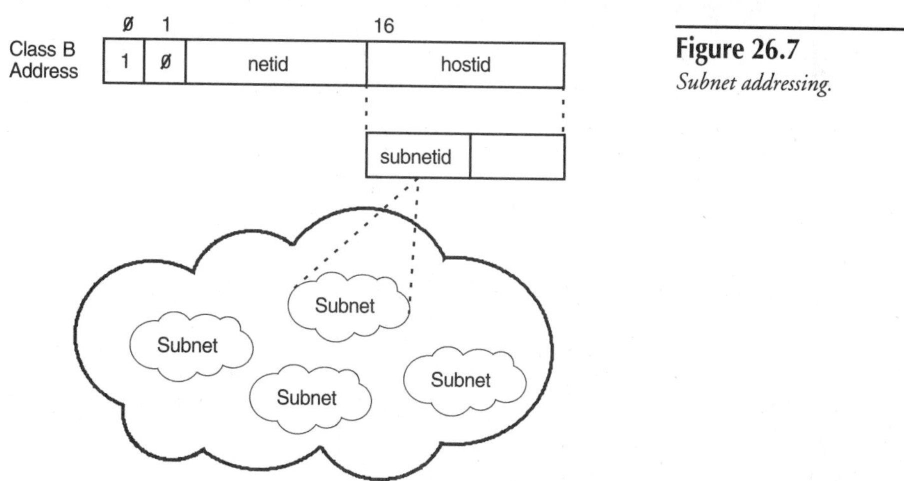

Figure 26.7
Subnet addressing.

9. If you answered Yes for subnet masks, you must specify the subnet mask and press Enter. You are then asked if you have an IP router.

10. If you are connecting to another TCP/IP internetwork, you probably have at least one IP router. You must specify the IP address of the default router. All packets with IP addresses not known to the current network are then sent to this default IP router.

11. If you answered Yes for an IP router, enter the IP router internet address.

12. You are asked if you want to accept the default TCP/IP configuration parameters. If you are not sure about these parameters, accept the defaults. Otherwise, specify TCP/IP parameters. If you need to have more than eight TCP connections or four NetBIOS sessions, you have to override the default parameters. The configuration parameters that can be changed are the following:

    TCP connections

    UDP sockets

    IP raw connections

    NetBIOS sessions

    NetBIOS commands

13. You are asked if your network has a *Domain Name Server* (DNS), which automatically translates symbolic names to their equivalent IP addresses. For many UNIX-based hosts, this is popularly implemented by the *Berkeley Internet Name Domain Server* (BIND) program. If you have such a server, you must specify its IP address.

14. If you selected Yes to the DNS server, you must enter its IP address.

15. If you want to load NetBIOS to run applications developed by third-party vendors, you can answer Yes to the question on loading NetBIOS during system boot.

16. If you answer Yes to the question on using applications from an earlier release of LAN WorkPlace, a converter program is loaded through AUTOEXEC.BAT to support the older applications.

17. Enter the user name you use to run the R-utilities (rcp, rsh, rexec, rpr, rpd, rps) to access a remote host. The user name you enter is stored in the DOS environment variable NAME, using the set NAME= command in your AUTOEXEC.BAT file.

18. To save your configuration information, answer Yes to update system files. System files are AUTOEXEC.BAT, CONFIG.SYS, NET.CFG, PROGRAM.INI, SYSTEM.INI, and WIN.INI.

19. Follow the instructions for inserting the LAN WorkPlace disks until the installation is complete.

Public Data Network Connectivity

When LANs are separated by large distances, connecting them requires a physical transport medium. Because it is not always possible to install cables to span large distances separating LANs, it is easier and cheaper to use existing facilities to connect the LANs.

A common facility that most LANs have access to is the telephone circuit. Telephone lines are normally used for voice (analog) signals. *Modems* can be used to convert the digital data in packets to an analog signal for transmission across telephone lines. When *Integrated Services Digital Network* (ISDN) becomes widely available, the modem device will no longer be necessary, because data is sent in digital form across the physical transport. Telephone circuits can be used on a dial-up basis or the telephone circuit can be dedicated for data connections. The dedicated telephone circuits are called *leased lines* and can be cheaper if they are in use constantly. A disadvantage of the telephone circuit is its limited data bandwidth. For higher data-transfer rate, synchronous circuits such as T1 can be used to connect LANs.

Another type of technology that is popular for transporting data across long distances is the *X.25 network*, which is traditionally used for terminal access to remote hosts (minicomputers and mainframes) and file transfers. X.25 speeds are not adequate for network-intensive LANs (the typical maximum is 64 Kbps), but they can be used for file transfer between LANs. X.25 is an international standard and is implemented by many public data networks. Many countries have public X.25 data networks, called *Public Data Networks* (PDNs).

This section explores Novell-based solutions for connecting LANs across large distances. The products that implement these solutions are the following:

- NetWare Link/X.25
- NetWare X.25 Gateway
- NetWare Asynchronous Remote Router
- NetWare Link/64
- NetWare Link/T1
- NetWare Connect

NetWare Link/X.25

In figure 26.8, NetWare Link/X.25 simultaneously connects a NetWare network with up to 11 remote networks. The X.25 connection provides NetWare with access to a packet-switching PDN. Any host or computer system connected to the X.25 network, as well as any public or private databases, can be accessed by NetWare users.

An example of a public database is CompuServe, which has information on stock market prices, airline schedules, computer forums, and so on. Novell's NetWire forum also is on CompuServe. The CompuServe forum can be reached by ordinary dial-up lines using local telephone access numbers. Asynchronous modems can be used for dialing from your PC, but your data eventually goes into a *Packet Assembler/Disassembler* (PAD) or a synchronous modem for transmission across the X.25 network.

The NetWare Link/X.25 connection acts as a router and enables NetWare users to be connected to other NetWare LANs and users. Figure 26.8 illustrates three NetWare LANs connected by X.25 networks using NetWare Link/X.25. A maximum of 11 remote networks can be connected in this

manner. The PDN multiplexes up to 11 connections (virtual circuits) over a single line, and it performs routing functions to send the traffic for each virtual circuit to its proper destination. NetWare X.25 works with private networks and public networks, such as SprintNet and Tymnet. Some of the PDN networks supported are listed in table 26.3.

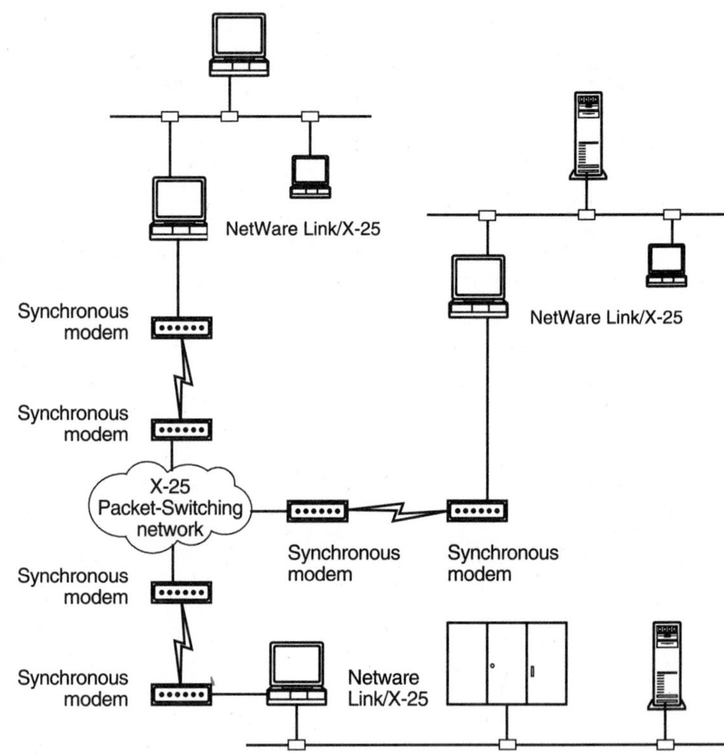

Figure 26.8
NetWare Link/X.25.

Table 26.3
Certified Public Data Networks for NetWare/X.25 Products

Country	Network Name
Australia	Austpac
Austria	Radaus Data
Belgium	DCS
Canada	Datapac, Infoswitch CNCP

Country	Network Name
Chile	Entel
Denmark	Datapak
Finland	Datapak, Digipak
France	Transpac
Germany	Datex-P
Hong Kong	Datapak, Intelpac
Netherlands	Datanet-1
New Zealand	Pacnet
Norway	Datapak
Portugal	Telepac
Singapore	Telepac
Spain	Iberpac
Sweden	Datapak
Switzerland	Telepac
U.K.	Packet Switch Stream
U.S.	Accunet, CompuServe, Infonet, SprintNet (formerly Telenet), Tymnet

The X.25 protocol recommendations are published every four years. NetWare X.25 supports the 1980 and 1984 CCITT recommendations for X.25 and X.75 (for connecting X.25 networks). Because most PDNs support these recommendations, NetWare Link/X.25 can be used with most of the international PDNs.

NetWare Link/X.25 operates as an external router that runs in either dedicated or nondedicated mode. The actual router interface and mechanisms are transparent to the user, enabling local network users to access remote resources as if they were local. Router connections are established or terminated using the X.25 CALL, ANSWER, and HANGUP commands.

Though any IBM PC, XT, AT, PS/2, or compatible can be used for NetWare Link/X.25, an 80286- or 80386-based machine is recommended. The minimum RAM requirements are 320 KB. For installation, one floppy disk drive is needed. Network connections include a network adapter for the local network and an X.25 board for the WAN link. The X.25 board is called the Novell *X.25 Extended Adapter.* The X.25 adapter is connected to a synchronous modem by means of a modem cable.

The external connections that are supported through the synchronous modem include leased lines and dial-up connections with speeds of 56 or 64 Kbps. For LAN-to-LAN connections the transport protocol is SPX/IPX. This is not surprising because this is the native protocol used to connect NetWare workstations to servers. Because of limited speeds, this type of network connection limits the applications to file transfers and terminal access. For situations in which remote-server-based applications are run at the workstation, the X.25 speeds are inadequate.

NetWare X.25 Gateway

NetWare X.25 Gateway software, running on a PC workstation with a Novell X.25 adapter, can turn the workstation to an X.25 Gateway for NetWare users. Gateway software enables multiple NetWare users to share a single link to a public or private X.25 Packet Data Network (PDN) and can be used by most major public data networks. Table 26.3 contains a list of X.25 networks that are also supported by the NetWare X.25 Gateway.

The NetWare X.25 Gateway can communicate with any host device that supports X.25 communications for asynchronous sessions. NetWare users must run terminal-emulation software in order to enable PCs to emulate asynchronous terminals, which are used to access other X.25 hosts. Many vendors, including Hewlett-Packard, IBM, Digital Equipment Corporation, Data General, Prime, Stratus, and Tandem, support X.25 communications on some or all of their computers. The X.25 Gateway supports a variety of terminal emulation packages. Depending on the emulation software used, a workstation can have up to eight simultaneous sessions. The terminal emulation software uses SPX/IPX or NetBIOS protocol to access the Gateway. The terminal emulation software selected must support the interrupt 14h (BIOS level) interface. Table 26.4 lists terminal-emulation packages that support the interrupt 14h interface and have been tested with the NetWare X.25 Gateway.

Table 26.4
Terminal-Emulation Software Tested with NetWare X.25 Gateway

Product	Vendor
AdvanceLink	Hewlett-Packard
CROSSTALK Mk.4	DCA/Crosstalk Communications
PROCOMM PLUS	Datastorm Technologies, Inc.
Reflection /+	Walker Richer & Quinn, Inc.
SimPC Master	Simware, Inc.

Product	Vendor
Softerm PC	Softronics
ZSTEM 240	KEA Systems, Ltd.

Figure 26.9 shows an X.25 Gateway connection to a NetWare LAN. The Gateway is typically connected to the packet-switching network through a high-speed synchronous modem. The X.25 Gateway PC provides the connection to the X.25 network, which is then shared by multiple LAN users.

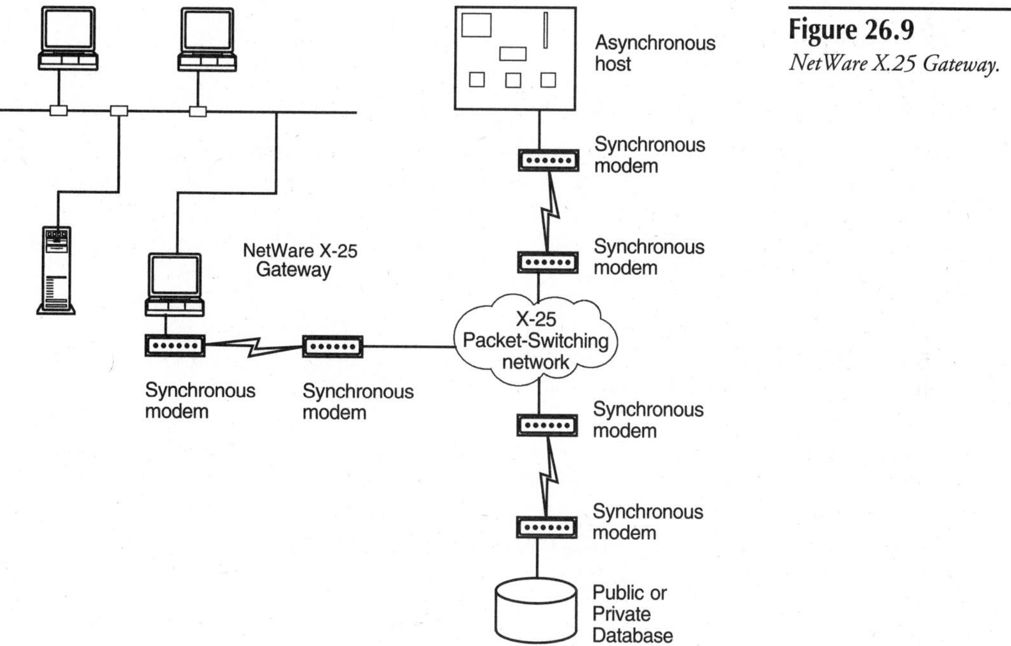

Figure 26.9
NetWare X.25 Gateway.

The NetWare X.25 Gateway supports speeds from 1.2 Kbps to 64 Kbps. At speeds of 56 Kbps and above, the X.25 Gateway is usually connected to the packet-switching network through a *Channel Service Unit/Data Service Unit* (CSU/DSU). If the CSU/DSU is equipped with a V.35 interface, a V.35-to-RS-232-C converter is used. The data transfer rate across the X.25 Gateway is considerably faster than the 19.2 Kbps maximum speed of asynchronous gateways.

There are a number of considerations for selecting software for communicating with an X.25 Gateway.

- **Choice of supported terminal-emulation software.** To work with the NetWare X.25 Gateway, the software must support the interrupt 14h (BIOS level) interface.
- **Multiple gateway support.** In large installations, multiple gateways may be necessary for performance, reliability, and higher availability.

- **Number of host-terminal sessions.** Some terminal-emulation software enables a single user to access multiple hosts.

- **Script language.** Automating the login connection to a host is a very useful feature. A script language within an asynchronous terminal-emulation package can be used to implement this and many common chores, such as interacting with menus on the host.

- **Keyboard mapping.** Differences usually exist between the keyboard of a PC and an asynchronous terminal that the host expects to communicate with. Most terminal-emulation products provide a mapping of terminal function keys to keys on the PC keyboard. Macro-mapping features also can enable users to represent a sequence of keystrokes with a single keystroke.

- **International language support.** If NetWare workstations are to be used in an international network, the terminal emulation product should have translation tables for international language support.

- **Management.** Remote management of the connection is an important issue in host connectivity. Both the host system manager and the PC network supervisor need information about gateway activity, which can be used to solve gateway-related problems.

- **File transfer.** Users who need a host connection often need to transfer files between their workstation and the host. At least XMODEM and Kermit transfer protocol should be supported.

- **Memory constraints.** Memory requirements can become critical in a network environment. Terminal-emulation software can take up to 100 KB of PC memory, in addition to memory used by DOS and network software. The NetWare shell requires about 50 KB of memory. Because of the 640 KB restriction of DOS, users can quickly run out of memory necessary for running applications. OS/2 workstations do not suffer from the 640 KB restriction, but the OS/2 operating system and applications require more memory themselves, further increasing the need for memory. In any environment, memory-efficient terminal-emulation software is needed to optimize available memory.

Other features of NetWare X.25 Gateway include utilities for frame and packet-level statistics with trace capabilities; support for up to eight simultaneous sessions per workstation; assignment of *Switched Virtual Circuits* (SVCs); and support for dial-up X.25 connections, which offer occasional users a less expensive alternative to leased lines. The transport protocols used to access the NetWare X.25 Gateway are SPX/IPX or NetBIOS. The maximum number of workstations and X.25 sessions supported by using Novell SPX/IPX are 97 users and 97 virtual circuits (sessions). If NetBIOS is used, the limits are 97 users and 254 virtual circuits. The X.25 line speeds are 1.2 Kbps to 64 Kbps, and the CCITT specifications supported are 1984 LAPB CCITT Recommendations X.25, X.3, X.28, X.29, and X.121. All 22 X.3 parameters are supported, both for mandatory and optional values. Parameters 1, 6, and 11 support the mandatory values only.

NetWare X.25 Gateway software requires an IBM PC, PS/2, or compatible with a network adapter, a connection to the network, at least one disk drive, and 512 KB of RAM. The NetWare X.25 Gateway also requires a synchronous modem and the Novell X.25 Extended Adapter.

NetWare Asynchronous Remote NetWare Communications Connectivity Router

The NetWare Asynchronous Remote Router software enables LANs to be connected over asynchronous dial-up lines to form a wide area network (see fig. 26.10). This product enables multiple asynchronous communications lines to be installed on a network, providing connections with other remote networks at speeds of up to 9.6 Kbps.

The link is transparent to users on either network from a procedural point of view, but because of its low speeds, users are usually aware of the longer time it takes to transfer data. Also, because of the lower speeds, applications requiring direct file access, such as databases, should not be run across asynchronous communications lines.

With NetWare Asynchronous Remote Router, the physical connections are made over voice-grade dial-up telephone lines. Because such connections are widely available, the network connections can be installed and reconfigured quickly; that is, networks can be connected to the WAN without waiting for installation of leased lines. With dial-up circuits, connections are made on demand, and if the usage is low, this can be an economical solution. For constant usage, leased lines (dedicated circuits) may turn out to be more economical.

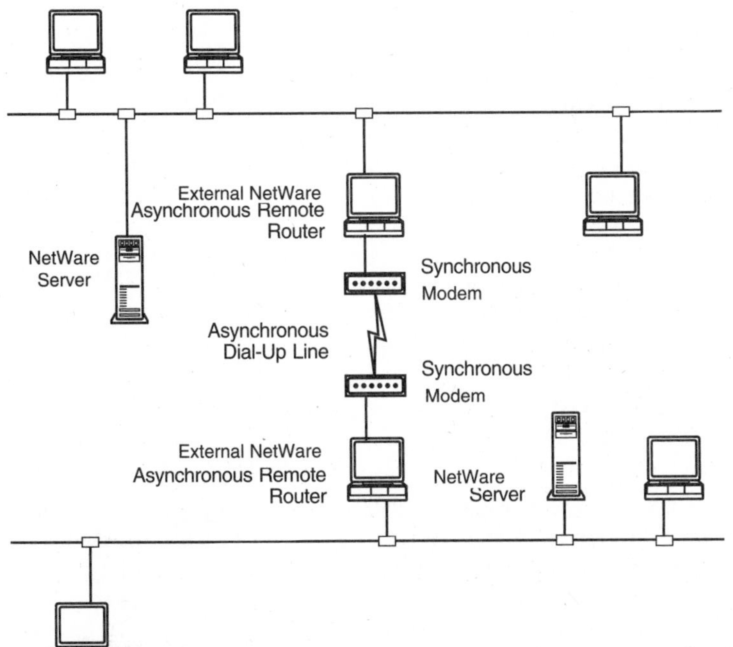

Figure 26.10
NetWare Asynchronous Remote Router.

The NetWare Asynchronous Remote Router can be configured in any one of the following ways:

- A COM1 or COM2 port of a NetWare External Router can be used as a single-line asynchronous router.
- A communications adapter, called the *Wide Area Network Interface Module*+ (WNIM+) can be installed in a NetWare file server. Each WNIM+ has an onboard processor, memory, and four asynchronous ports. A maximum of one WNIM+ can be installed in a NetWare file server.
- The WNIM+ can be installed in a network workstation, turning the workstation into an external router. A maximum of two WNIM+ adapters can be installed in a single external router, bringing the total number of lines supported to eight.

Support for both the server and external asynchronous router using COM1, COM2, or the WNIM+ is bundled with NetWare 2.*x* and NetWare 3.*x*. Additional copies of the NetWare Asynchronous Remote Router are required for additional external routers and must be purchased separately.

Novell does not recommend that the NetWare file server be used as a remote router, except in very small networks that use low-line speeds. The NetWare operating system has to process every character or group of characters it receives. For a high volume of asynchronous traffic, the server performance for other operations is seriously degraded.

When installing the NetWare Asynchronous Remote Router software in an external router, an IBM PC, XT, AT, or compatible can be used to run the router software. Novell recommends using an 80286- or 80386-based machine. The asynchronous router needs a network adapter for the local network and an asynchronous port. The asynchronous port can be COM1 or COM2 serial ports or the ports on WNIM+ adapters. The WNIM+ is connected to asynchronous modems through RS-232 cables. If COM1 or COM2 ports are used, the maximum speeds are 2400 bps. With WNIM+ boards, speeds up to 9600 bps are possible.

A dedicated router operating in real mode requires a minimum of 512 KB of RAM, and a nondedicated bridge operating in real mode requires a minimum of 640 KB. Dedicated 80286 and 80386 bridges running in protected mode require a minimum of 1 MB of RAM.

NetWare Link/64

NetWare Link/64 enables remote NetWare LANs to be connected through synchronous communications lines (see fig. 26.11). This product supports speeds from 9600 bps to 64 Kbps. NetWare Link/64 routes SPX/IPX and NetBIOS protocols over wide area networks. NetWare routing protocol (RIP) dynamically determines the shortest path for each packet, based on the current network topology. Inactive links are automatically bypassed.

NetWare Link/64 software can run in the file server with NetWare or in an external router. The external router can run in either a dedicated or non-dedicated mode. The Link/64 software communicates with a synchronous adapter that can support the V.35, RS-422, and RS-232 interfaces. Any one of the following synchronous adapters can be used:

- Novell Synchronous/V.35+ (up to 2.048 Mbps)
- Novell Synchronous/RS-422+ (up to 2.048 Mbps)
- Novell Synchronous/RS-232+ (19.2 Kbps)

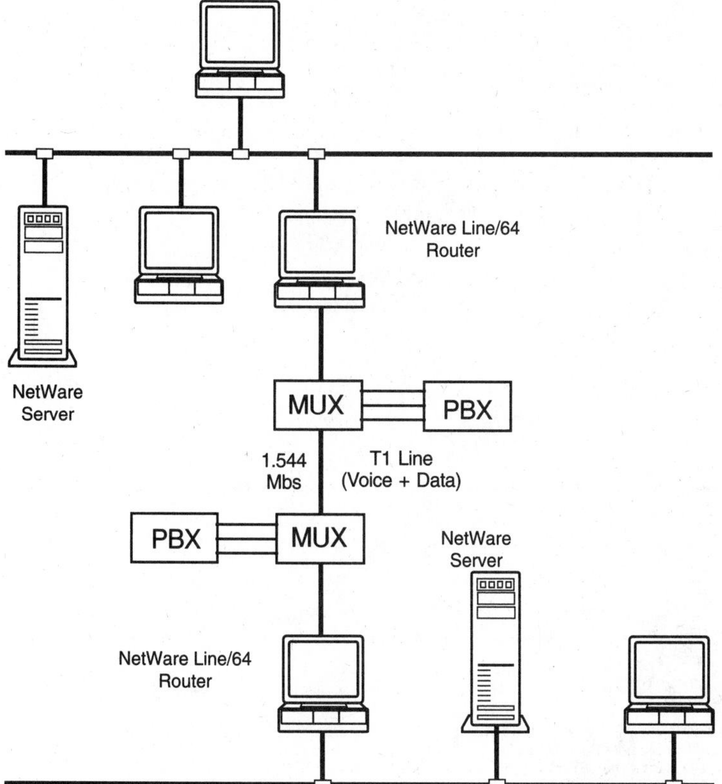

Figure 26.11
NetWare Link/64.

These Novell products can work with existing customer equipment, including *Data Service Units/ Channel Service Units* (DSUs/CSUs), synchronous modems, multiplexers, and data switches. A summary of the functions and features of NetWare Link/64 follows:

- Diagnostic programs for installation verification and online troubleshooting.
- Utilities for generating network loads and checking error rates under normal loads or stress testing.
- Support for V.35, RS-422, and RS-232 interfaces.
- NetWare Link/64 can work with any NetWare-supported network, including Ethernet, Token Ring, and ARCnet.

NetWare Link/64 is designed to run at a maximum speed of 64 Kbps. If applications requiring high throughput are used on the network, the higher performance provided by NetWare Link/T1 may be needed.

NetWare Link/T1

NetWare Link/T1 enables remote NetWare LANs to be connected by a T1 network. If a T1 network is not available, a point-to-point T1-circuit can be used. The connection is by synchronous communications lines over speeds ranging from 9,600 bps to 1.544 or 2.048 Mbps. In North America, T1 speeds are 1.544 Mbps, whereas in Europe they are set to 2.048 Mbps.

Figure 26.12 shows NetWare LANs connected by using NetWare Link/T1. This product enables connectivity at LAN speeds (greater than 1 Mbps), which means that applications can run across remote LANs connected by NetWare Link/T1. NetWare Link/T1 is designed for users who need high-speed LAN-to-LAN communications. Examples of these communications are applications requiring high throughput, such as databases, direct-file access, and rapid file transfers.

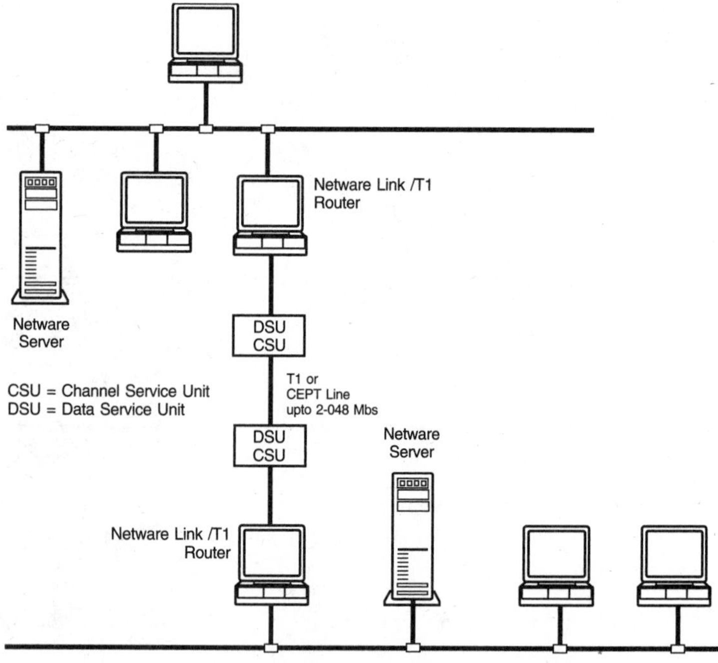

Figure 26.12
NetWare Link/T1.

The T1 circuit acts as the physical transport medium on which IPX/SPX and NetBIOS packet traffic can run. NetWare routing protocols (RIP—Routing Information Protocol) are used to dynamically determine the shortest path and fastest route for each packet, based on the current network topology. Failed links are automatically bypassed by the routing protocol.

NetWare Link/T1 software can run in the file server with NetWare (internal router) or in an external router. If performance is a consideration, the external router configuration gives better performance. The external router can run in either a dedicated or nondedicated mode. When running in an external router, the NetWare Link/T1 software requires DOS 3.*x* or higher. It also can run on the NetWare 3.*x* as an NLM or on NetWare 2.*x* server as a VAP.

NetWare Link/T1 software can be used with T1 network adapters, such as Novell's Synchronous/+ Adapters, which support the V.35, RS-422, and RS-232 interfaces. These adapters are the following:

- Novell Synchronous/V.35+ (up to 2.048 Mbps)
- Novell Synchronous/RS-422+ (up to 2.048 Mbps)
- Novell Synchronous/RS-232+ (19.2 Kbps)

These network adapters can work with existing customer equipment such as DSU/CSUs, synchronous modems, multiplexers, and data switches.

NetWare Link/T1 comes with diagnostic programs that can be used for installation verification and on-line troubleshooting. Utilities are provided for generating network loads and checking error rates under normal loads or stress loads. NetWare Link/T1 can be used to connect any NetWare-supported network such as Ethernet, Token Ring, and ARCnet.

NetWare Connect

NetWare Connect uses a NetWare server to provide remote computing needs. The product installs on the server as a series of NLMs, and is installed using the System Options of the INSTALL NLM. NetWare Connect allows multiple remote users to access network resources by dialing in to the server, and also allows workstations to dial out (see fig. 26.13).

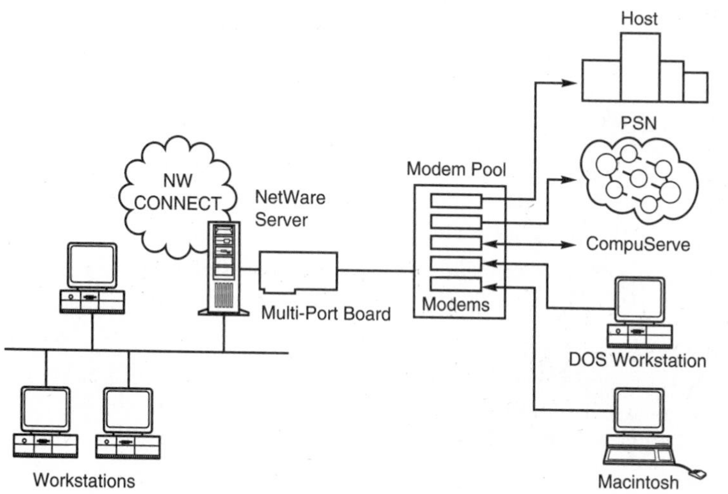

Figure 26.13
NetWare Connect inbound and outbound connections.

Features of NetWare Connect include the following:

- Dynamic port allocation
- Resource pooling
- Support for *AppleTalk Remote Access Services* (ARAS), *NASI Connection Service* (NCS), *Remote Node Service* (RNS)
- Port sharing
- Port security
- Audit trail maintenance
- X.25 support
- Support for NACS configuration and services

In a number of communication products, ports are dedicated for inbound and outbound operations. NetWare Connect's dynamic port allocation enables communication ports to be assigned on demand for inbound or outbound communication links. You also have the option of dedicating certain ports as inbound or outbound ports. Hardware resources, such as modems, telephone lines, modems, communication ports, can be treated as a pool of resources ("resource pooling") that are allocated on demand. You also can define several levels of port access and security that restrict access to services, ports, users, and AppleTalk zones, time users remain inline and enforcing dialback.

NetWare Connect supports three types of services: *AppleTalk Remote Access Services* (ARAS), *NASI Connection Service* (NCS) and *Remote Node Service* (RNS). ARAS and RNS support Macintosh and DOS workstations, respectively to login to a NetWare network from a remote location. These workstations act as remote nodes. Dialback can be used go enhance network security. In dialback, after the incoming call is authenticated by *NetWare Connect Services* (NCS), the NCS disconnects the user and dials back the user. Another advantage of dialback is to reverse the user charges to a central billing account.

NetWare Connect supports AppleTalk, IPX and TCP/IP protocols. Workstations on the network can use NetWare Connect running at the server to dial out via the communication ports at the server. Protocols such as X.25 can be used to connect to Packet Switched Networks.

NetWare Connect maintains an audit trail that records information about a connection, such as user name, time of connection, port name, telephone number dialed (outgoing call), dialback number, service used, session name, and alerts generated by NCS. The audit trail can be used to ensure proper usage of NetWare Connect services.

You can use NetWare Connect with *NetWare Asynchronous Communications Services* (NACS). NetWare Connect converts NACS configurations to configurations for NetWare Connect. You can also use NetWare Connect with NetWare Access Services that allows a PC on the LAN, called the application server, to run as multiple PCs.

IBM Host Connectivity

Novell provides a variety of products to connect with IBM's *Systems Network Architecture* (SNA) network environment. These products have made NetWare LANs acceptable in the IBM network environment. Novell gained much of its earlier expertise in SNA products through the acquisition of CXI, which was known for its SNA connectivity products.

This section discusses solutions for connecting NetWare LANs to IBM minicomputers and mainframes. Before discussing these solutions, a few words concerning IBM's SNA architecture and the vocabulary and terminology used to describe their communication products makes the discussion that follows more understandable.

The network architecture used by IBM for connecting its mainframe computers, IBM hosts, to terminals is called *SNA*. Figure 26.14 shows an example of an IBM SNA network that has a single domain. A *domain* consists of an IBM host and the communications network that provides access to it. Users interact to IBM hosts through terminals such as the IBM 3278 and IBM 3279. The terminals are managed by a specialized device called the *cluster controller*. The cluster controller (*terminal controller* in other network architectures) is needed because, by themselves, the terminals are "dumb"; the cluster controller handles the networking and connectivity chores on behalf of the terminals. The cluster controllers are managed by a *Front End Processor* (FEP) called the *communications controller*. The communications controller talks to the IBM host and offloads many of the communications functions that would otherwise have to be performed by the IBM host. The communication in this type of architecture is managed by the *Virtual Telecommunication Access Method* (VTAM) program, which runs on the host, and the *Network Control Program* (NCP), which runs on the communications controller.

26

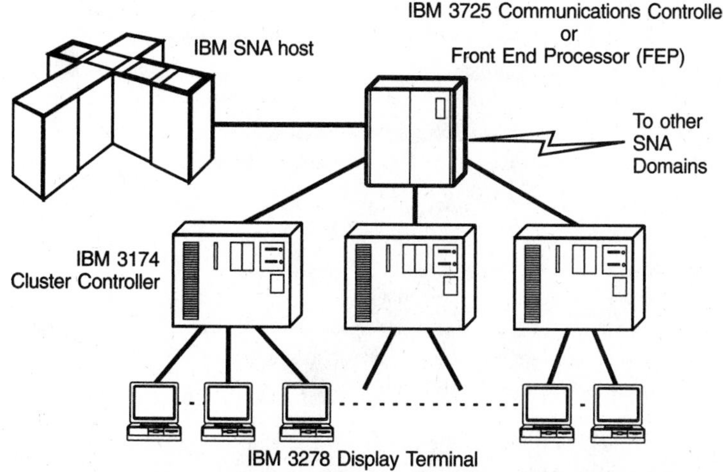

Figure 26.14
IBM SNA network.

Many of the techniques used to provide connections to the IBM SNA network involve some form of device emulation. The devices that are popularly emulated are the IBM 3278 and 3279 terminals, and the IBM cluster controller. Emulating the IBM terminals is called *3270 emulation*. When you hear a

product name, such as the NetWare 3270 CUT Workstation, you can tell from the use of the 3270 that this product involves terminal emulation.

The device that emulates an IBM cluster controller is called an *SNA gateway* because it can be connected to the IBM communications controller, and it can provide access to an SNA network from a non-SNA network.

NetWare for SAA

NetWare for SAA provides LAN-to-host connectivity for SNA networks. These connectivity options are integrated with the NetWare 3.*x* operating system. The host communications are managed by NLMs running on the NetWare server. At the heart of this product is the *Communications Executive* (see fig. 26.15), which provides communications-specific extensions to the NetWare operating system. Other services, such as X.25, wide area network routing, and remote LAN access, run on top of the Communications Executive.

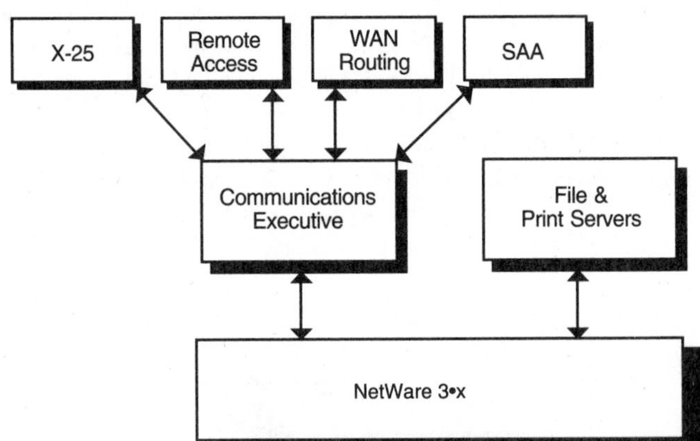

Figure 26.15
NetWare for SAA Communications Executive.

The Communications Executive provides a core set of functions available to applications services located on the server and to client applications running on workstations. The Communication Executive and NetWare for SAA are implemented as *NetWare Loadable Modules* (NLMs). These NLMs can be configured to run in conjunction with file and print services on a single server, or they can be installed on a NetWare 3.11 server dedicated to communications services (see fig. 26.16). NetWare for SAA comes with a kernel version of NetWare 3.*x* that does not provide any file services. The NetWare kernel can be used to configure dedicated communications services, as shown in figure 26.16.

The network connections supported by NetWare for SAA are either Token Ring or SDLC connections to the host. Token Ring connections can be made through 3174 cluster controllers, 37xx front-end processors, or integrated Token Ring controllers on the 9370 and AS/400 systems. SDLC connections can use synchronous modems to a 37xx front-end processor at speeds of up to 64 Kbps.

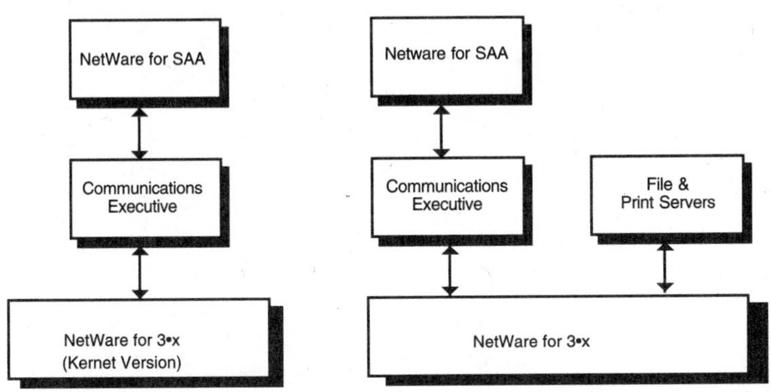

Figure 26.16
Dedicated versus integrated configuration for NetWare for SAA.

Access to the NetWare for SAA services can be made by using the NetWare 3270 LAN Workstation for DOS. The total number of host connections supported by NetWare for SAA can be up to 64. These sessions can be any combination of display, printer, or *Advanced Program-to-Program Communications* (APPC) sessions.

Additionally, NetWare for SAA can emulate a PU 2.0 (cluster controller) device when accessing host applications. It also can emulate PU2.1 (smart cluster controller) peer-to-peer connections between LAN workstations hosts and workstations on the Token Ring LAN.

Because NetWare for SAA runs on a NetWare server, any workstation that can access the server can make use of its services. This access can be provided by any of the LANs supported by NetWare such as ARCnet, Ethernet, and Token Ring. The native NetWare protocols such as SPX/IPX are used to provide a connection to NetWare for SAA. Figures 26.17 and 26.18 show NetWare for SAA configured for a Token Ring and an SDLC connection.

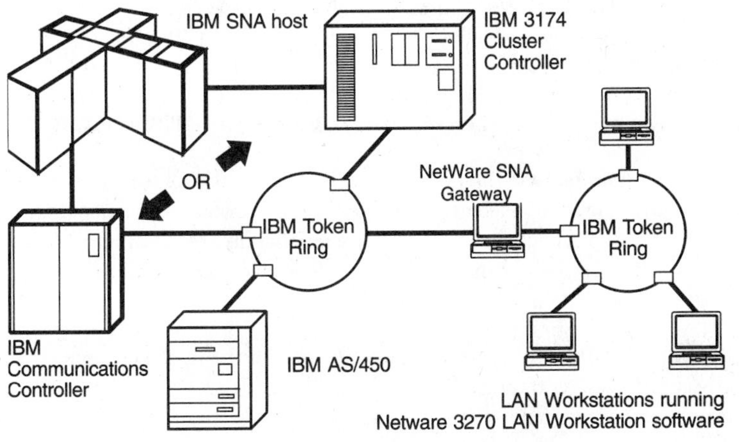

Figure 26.17
NetWare for SAA configured for Token Ring.

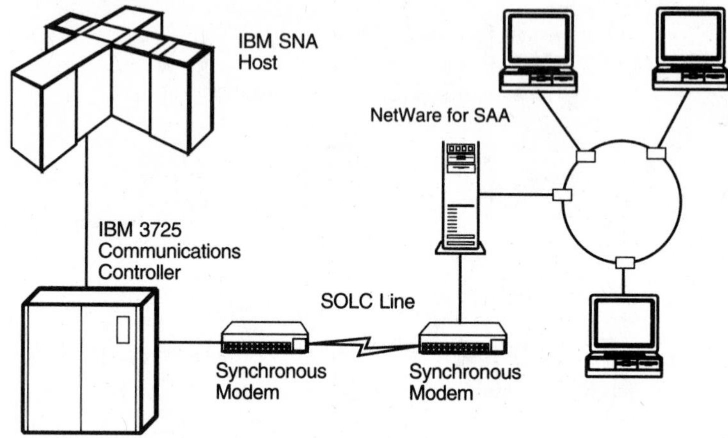

Figure 26.18
NetWare for SAA configured for SDLC.

In function, the NetWare for SAA acts as a gateway, but it is more versatile than the NetWare Gateway products. The features and functions of NetWare for SAA are enumerated in the following list:

- **Integrated with NetWare 3.x.** Because NetWare 3.*x* is a multi-tasking operating system, the limitations of running on a DOS platform are eliminated. NetWare for SAA is implemented as a collection of NLMs.

- **There is a choice of dedicated or nondedicated configurations for NetWare for SAA.** The dedicated configuration uses a NetWare kernel version that does not have the overhead of file services; it provides better performance than the nondedicated configuration.

- **The NetWare for SAA NLM configuration can be done dynamically.** That is, the NLMS can be loaded and unloaded even while the server is running.

- **SAA runs on a NetWare 3.x platform.** NetWare can, therefore, for SAA can make use of the fault-tolerance capabilities of NetWare 3.*x*, including SFT Levels I, II, III, and TTS, and the security and management services of NetWare.

- **The 64 host sessions can be any combination of display, printer, and APPC sessions.**

- **Support for both pooled and dedicated LUs.** *LU Groups* are pools of LUs for which a user or group of users has access rights. A user can reference these LU Groups by name when requesting host sessions. Based on the user's access rights, the LUs are dynamically allocated from the named group on a first-come, first-served basis. With dedicated LUs, LUs are allocated to specific users, and they can simultaneously access LU Groups and dedicated LUs.

- **Communication-specific security.** Besides NetWare security, administrators also can implement communication-security measures through the use of *Access Control Lists* (ACLs). ACLs are lists of NetWare users or groups authorized to use communications resources, such as specific host connections, LU Groups, and dedicated LUs. The communication-security mechanism is integrated with the NetWare bindery for ease of management.

- **NetView interface.** NetWare for SAA includes an interface to IBM's NetView, so that management can be integrated with the host-based network-management system. The interface to NetView is based on IBM's Entry Point model and makes the server running the NetWare Communication Services software appear to the host as an IBM device.

- **Name service.** NetWare for SAA extends NetWare Name Service to address communications resources such as hosts and links by name. This enables access to a communications resource without knowing which route to take. It also supports single network logins.

- **Diagnostic trace utility.** The trace utility enables a network manager to request a trace for all LUs or for a specific LU.

- **Menu-driven CSCON configuration utility.**

Configuring NetWare for SAA involves configuring the connected mainframes to recognize NetWare for SAA. The *Virtual Telecommunications Access Method* (VTAM) software on the host—which controls the host network, and/or the *Network Control Program* (NCP) software, running on a front-end processor—must be configured to recognize the server running NetWare for SAA and the sessions it supports. Configuration information about the host and the host link must be entered through the CSCON configuration utility.

NetWare for SAA requires an IBM PC 386 (or higher) or a PS/2 (cr compatible), installed with the NetWare 3.*x* operating system. The server must have a minimum of 6 MB of RAM. In addition, the server must have a LAN adapter for communicating with the workstations on the network and a communications adapter for the host connection.

Novell has tested a variety of hardware configurations for the NetWare for SAA product. Before installing the product, you might wish to obtain the most recent list of tested hardware from Novell. For host connections, Novell recommends the following:

- Novell Synchronous Adapter for the PC or the IBM Multiprotocol Adapter/A for Micro Channel for speeds up to 19.2 Kbps.

- Novell Synchronous/V.35 Adapter for the PC for speeds up to 64 Kbps.

For Token Ring connections, Novell recommends the following:

- Cabling type: Type A (shielded twisted-pair) cabling in the IBM Cabling System or an equivalent.

- Two Token Ring adapters to split loads on a heavily used NetWare for SAA computer. One adapter can be used for host communications, and the second can be used for LAN communications.

- Host connections to Token Ring: A 3174 cluster controller with the Token Ring Network Gateway Feature (IBM Feature #3025); a 3720/25/45 front-end processor with a Token Ring Interface Coupler or Token Ring Adapter; an IBM AS/400 with the IBM Token Ring Network Adapter (#6160) or the IBM Token Ring Network Subsystem (#6240); or a 937x with the IBM Token Ring Subsystem Controller Option.

Users who need to access the host device through NetWare for SAA need the NetWare 3270 LAN Workstation for DOS software, which enables their workstations to emulate 3270 terminals and 3287 printers, transfer files to and from the host, and run LU6.2 transaction programs. The limits for NetWare for SAA are currently 64 remote connections to the host and 64 connections through Token Ring. Up to 250 users can be defined as users of the communications services but no more than 64 can simultaneously access NetWare for SAA. Maximum line speeds supported are 64 Kbps for remote SDLC and 16 Mbps for Token Ring.

NetWare for SAA provides access to IBM AS/400 minicomputers through the Token Ring Connection. The AS/400 must be connected with an IBM or compatible Token Ring Adapter. Although most AS/400 applications are supported by NetWare for SAA, the following applications have been certified by Novell:

- IBM OfficeVision/400
- IBM AS/400 Query
- IBM AS/400 Online Education
- IBM AS/400 Utilities

NetWare SNA Gateway

The NetWare SNA Gateway software can run on any IBM PC or PS/2 and convert it into an SNA Gateway server. The NetWare SNA Gateway emulates an IBM cluster controller, and enables DOS machines on a LAN, such as Token Ring, to connect to the NetWare SNA Gateway and, through it, to the SNA host. Essentially, the NetWare SNA Gateway emulation is that of a Node Type 2.0 (PU) or 2.1 device, such as a cluster controller.

Depending on the type of host connection used, the NetWare SNA Gateway enables as many as 97 PCs or PS/2s on a LAN to communicate with an IBM or compatible SNA mainframe or midrange computer. The DOS machines communicate with the NetWare SNA Gateway software by using SPX or NetBIOS protocols. The NetWare SNA Gateway itself supports four different host connection options: Coaxial, CoaxMux, Remote, or Token Ring. Selecting the right option is an issue of cost and budget. These four options are discussed in the following sections:

- **Coaxial.** This option supports up to five host display and 3287 printer sessions through a coaxial connection between an emulator adapter in the Gateway server and an SNA DFT port on a 3x74 cluster controller. This connection is illustrated in figure 26.19.

- **CoaxMux.** This option supports up to 40 display and printer sessions. The required PC-emulation adapter is connected through coaxial to a 3299 multiplexer port on a 3x74 cluster controller. This type of connection enables the gateway to multiplex eight five-session DFT lines over a single coaxial connection. This connection is illustrated in figure 26.20.

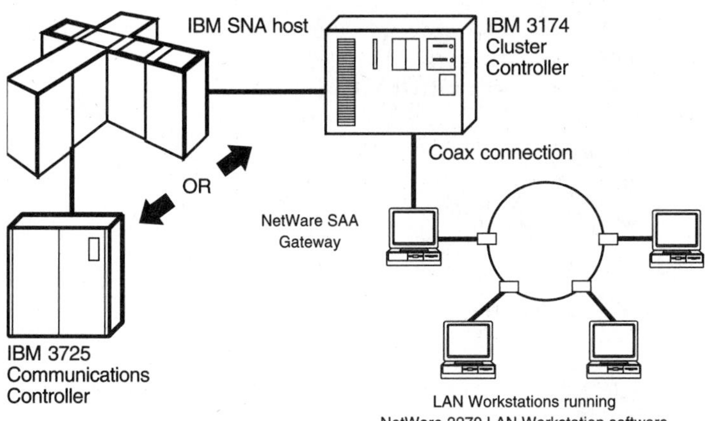

Figure 26.19
NetWare SNA Gateway: Coaxial connection.

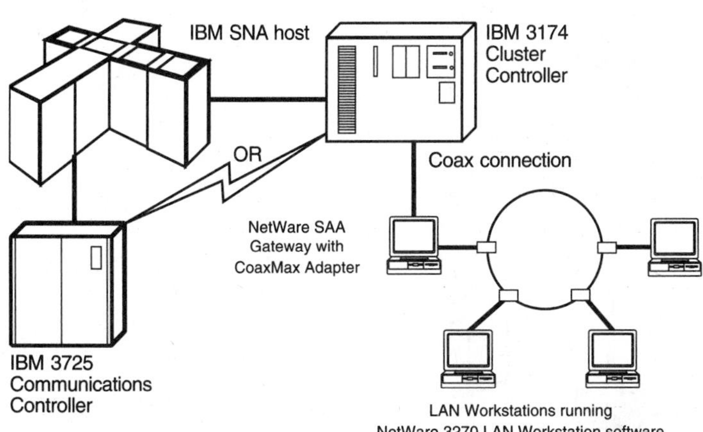

Figure 26.20
NetWare SNA Gateway: CoaxMux connection.

- **Remote.** This option supports up to 128 SNA host display and printer sessions on up to 97 workstations by means of an asynchronous modem connection to a 37xx front-end processor at speeds of up to 64 Kbps. This connection is illustrated in figure 26.21.
- **Token Ring.** Up to 128 host terminal and printer sessions are available to 97 workstations on a Token Ring network. The host connection can be made through the IBM 3174, 3720, 3725, 3745, 9370, or AS/400 if they are capable of Token Ring access. This connection is illustrated in figure 26.22.

For Coaxial connections, the Novell Coax Adapter for the PC or PS/2 can be used. This adapter is connected to an IBM 3x74 or compatible cluster controller with coaxial cable such as RG-62 A/U.

Alternatively, the IBM 3278/79 Adapter, the IBM 3270 Connection Adapter, the IRMA Convertible, or an IRMA I prom-based adapter with Novell-supplied IRMA PROMS can be used. The cluster controller must be configured for *Dual Function Terminal* (DFT) mode.

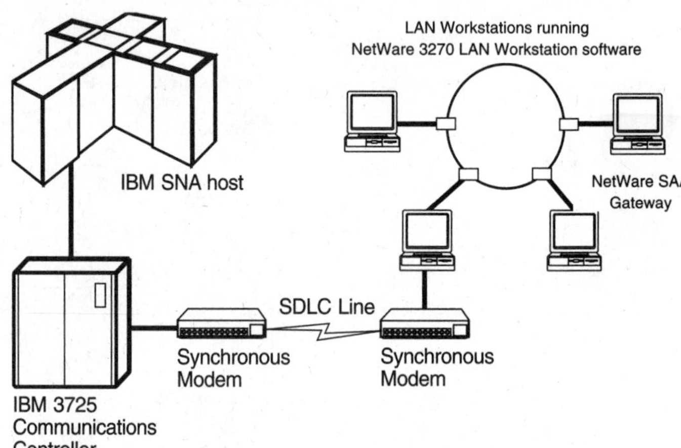

Figure 26.21
NetWare SNA Gateway: Remote connection.

For CoaxMux connections, the Novell CoaxMux Adapter for the PC can be used. This adapter is connected to a 3299 port on an IBM SNA 3174 or 3274 controller by means of a RG-62 A/U coaxial cable.

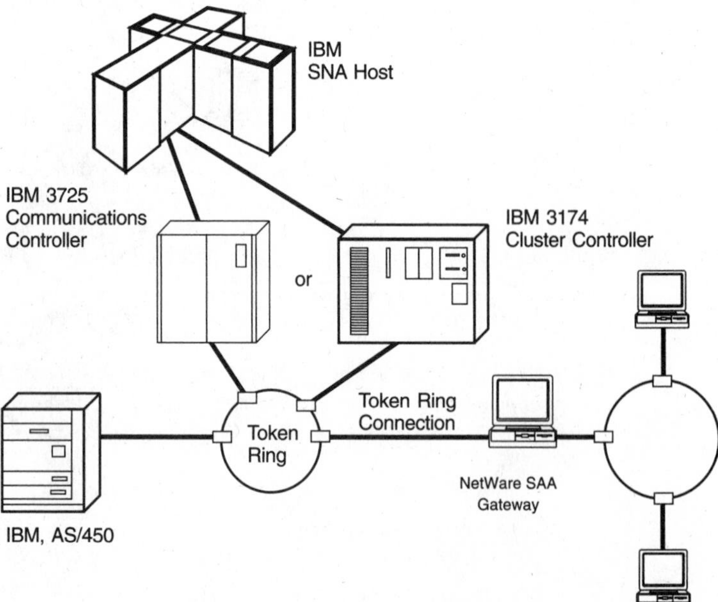

Figure 26.22
NetWare SNA Gateway: Token Ring connection.

For Remote connections, you can use a remote communications adapter that connects by means of synchronous, externally clocked modems over SNA/SDLC lines to an IBM 37xx front-end processor or equivalent. Depending on the adapter, it is either connected to the modem by means of an RS-232 modem cable or a V.35 cable.

The Novell Synchronous Adapter for the PC or the IBM Multiprotocol Adapter/A for the Micro Channel can be used for speeds of up to 19.2 Kbps. For speeds of up to 64 Kbps, the Novell Synchronous/V.35 Adapter for the PC can be used. Tests have shown that both the Novell Synchronous Adapter and the Novell Synchronous/V.35 Adapter perform best when used in a 386-based or better machine. Although this configuration can support up to 97 workstations and 128 sessions, decreasing the number of host sessions frees more memory and processing power for gateway operations.

For Token Ring connections, an IBM or compatible Token Ring adapter can be used. The Token Ring Network requires Type A (shielded twisted-pair) cabling in the IBM Cabling System or an equivalent. One of the following host devices must be connected to the Token Ring network: a 3174 cluster controller with the Token Ring Network Gateway Feature (IBM Feature #3025); a 3720/25/45 front-end processor with a Token Ring Interface Coupler or Token Ring Adapter; an IBM AS/400 with the IBM Token Ring Network Adapter (IBM Feature #6160) or the IBM Token Ring Network Subsystem (IBM Feature #6240); or a 937x with the IBM Token Ring Subsystem Controller Option.

For a Token Ring connection to the SNA network, the IEEE 802.2 protocol is used to communicate with the host. This means that the NetWare SNA Gateway must be on the same ring as the host device or connected to the host ring through an IBM Token Ring Bridge using source routing.

For workstation-to-NetWare gateway communications, SPX/IPX or NetBIOS protocols are used.

Any one of these adapters must be placed in the PC to act as the NetWare SNA Gateway. A second LAN adapter must also be placed in the gateway for LAN communications. For reasonable performance, a realistic number of host sessions must be used. Configuring with a maximum of 97 workstations and 128 sessions usually results in sluggish performance.

NetWare SNA Gateway includes NetWare LU6.2 for supporting distributed applications that operate in a peer-to-peer fashion using the *Advanced Peer to Peer Communications* (APPC). LU 6.2 is an implementation of IBM's APPC architecture, which supports peer-to-peer connections to PU2.1 devices. The NetWare SNA Gateway product includes keyboard files, templates, and documentation to facilitate connection to an IBM AS/400 through a Token Ring attachment. A Gateway Status utility provides status information on available host sessions, host-link status, session (LU) identification, and workstation status. There are management tools that include an internal trace facility for quick diagnosis and a self-test that isolates LAN problems between the gateway and the workstation.

NetWare SNA Gateway uses the *Service Advertising Protocol* (SAP) to broadcast its existence, meaning that all interconnected NetWare LANs are aware of the existence of the NetWare SNA Gateways and can make use of their services.

Multiple NetWare SNA Gateways can coexist on a single LAN, which enables access to multiple hosts and the capability to distribute the session load across several gateways. The NetWare SNA Gateway also enables implementation of backup gateways for redundancy and load-sharing among several gateways connected to a heavily used host.

Access to the SNA Gateway for PC users is provided by Token Ring LANs, which provide high-speed IBM host access and gateway capabilities to other LAN topologies. The NetWare SNA Gateway can bridge Novell-supported environments, such as Ethernet, by using both a Token Ring and an Ethernet adapter in the gateway machine.

NetWare SNA Gateway supports both pooled and dedicated LUs. Pooled LUs can be accessed by users on a first-come, first-served basis. Dedicated LUs enable network supervisors to assign LUs to specific users. The SNA gateway can be run as either a dedicated or nondedicated server. Because of the processing power needed to perform the gateway functions, it is recommended that the dedicated server configuration be used.

Before the gateway can be connected to the SNA host, the *Virtual Telecommunications Access Method* (VTAM) software on the host, which controls the host network and the *Network Control Program* (NCP) software, which runs on a communications controller (IBM 37XX), must be configured to recognize the SNA Gateway and the sessions it supports. This may require the help of the SNA host personnel. The product does come with worksheets that help the NetWare SNA Gateway installer to obtain information on the SNA host.

One key decision to make before installing NetWare SNA Gateway is the type of connection that makes the most sense for your environment—remote, coaxial, or Token Ring. This decision dictates the type of communications hardware to use with the gateway software. The same software package works with all three connections.

In general, a remote connection is required whenever the SNA host is at a distance from the users and cannot be easily connected by other means.

Coaxial connections provide a middle ground for connecting to local hosts, and they provide higher performance than remote connections (and usually cost less than Token Ring connections).

Token Ring connections provide the highest performance currently available, but they also have the highest cost. They give greater flexibility because the Token Ring also can be used for general LAN connectivity.

Regardless of the type of connection used, all configurations of the NetWare SNA Gateway require an IBM PC, PS/2, or recommended compatible with a network adapter and a connection to the SNA network. Because the performance of the gateway machine affects both gateway throughput and performance, this should be a high-performance machine, such as an 80486-based PC. The gateway configuration can operate in nondedicated mode in any workstation. Although the nondedicated gateway makes the solution more economical, the gateway is at the mercy of the workstation users and is susceptible to rebooting when it is used in nondedicated mode. The software requires 202 KB to 502 KB of RAM, depending on the connectivity option chosen and the number of sessions for which the software is configured.

Novell publishes a list of PCs and network hardware for which the SNA Gateway has been tested. Before buying the hardware, it is a good idea to obtain the most current list to avoid hardware/software compatibility problems.

In addition to the NetWare SNA Gateway software that provides connection to the SNA environment, users need to run the NetWare 3270 LAN Workstation software, which enables workstations to emulate 3270 terminals, and 3287 printers, and to transfer files to and from the host. The applications tested and certified by Novell that can be run at the workstations are the following: IBM OfficeVision/400, IBM AS/400 Query, IBM AS/400 Online Education, and IBM AS/400 Utilities.

Optional software for AS/400 communications also can be used, which includes the AS/400 Token Ring Gateway connection with additional keyboard files to create 5,250 keyboard layouts on the NetWare 3270 LAN Workstations. The keys supported are 3270 keys, with the exception of special function keys provided by the IBM 3270 Remote Attachment Feature. Novell also recommends the use of Spectrum Concepts' XCOM6.2 File Transfer software for file transfer between the 3270 LAN Workstations and the AS/400 through a separate NetWare SNA Gateway configured for LU6.2. The XCOM6.2 software is required on the PC and on the AS/400.

NetWare 3270 LAN Workstation for DOS

In the discussion on NetWare SNA Gateway, it was mentioned that the user needs terminal-emulation software to access the SNA host. The NetWare 3270 LAN Workstation for DOS provides this terminal-emulation capability, along with printer emulation. This product can be used with NetWare SNA Gateway or NetWare for SAA.

The emulation software supports up to five host sessions per workstation, which can be any combination of display, printer, *Advanced Program-to-Program Communications* (APPC) sessions, DOS session, file transfer, and keyboard-remapping utility. The data traffic from the workstation is sent across the LAN by using SPX/IPX or NetBIOS. The product is currently sold on a server license, which allows one copy of the software per file server, regardless of the number of workstations that use it.

File transfers between workstation and host are accomplished by using the SEND/RECEIVE or TRANSFER utilities, which are included with the software. The SEND/RECEIVE utilities upload and download files to and from the host by working with IBM's IND$FILE host file-transfer software in the TSO, CMS, and CICS environments. The TRANSFER utility can be used for the transfer of RFT and FFT data between the PC and the host when running SAA office applications, such as OfficeVision and DISOSS.

The features and functions of NetWare 3270 LAN workstation for DOS include the following:

- NetWare LU6.2 for support of LU6.2 applications.
- Automatic reattach that can reestablish the connection between the workstation and gateway if the gateway fails and is brought back up.
- Printer-session customization, which enables users to assign a printer to either a network or local printer, specify the number of lines-per-page, and configure software to automatically invoke a host printer session whenever it is loaded.
- Emulation of IBM 3270 terminals and 3287 printers.

- Support for up to five display and printer sessions per LAN workstation. These five sessions can be established with multiple hosts simultaneously when using NetWare for SAA.
- SEND/RECEIVE or TRANSFER software enables files to be transferred between the PC and the host.
- Support for commonly used APIs such as IBM's EEHLLAPI and Low-Level API, as well as for Novell's NetWare 3270 API.
- Keyboard-mapping capability and international language keyboard support.
- Redirection of host screen prints and 3287 printing-to-network printers.
- Support for extended data stream, including reverse video, underlining, highlighting, and seven colors.

- Internal trace and diagnostic facility.
- Support for pointing devices, such as light pens and Microsoft mouse-compatible devices.

NetWare 3270 LAN Workstation for DOS software emulates up to five display (LU2), printer (LU1 or LU3), and APPC (LU6.2) sessions per workstation. These LUs must be defined in the VTAM software, which runs on the host and controls the host network; and/or the Network Control Program, which runs on a front-end processor.

The NetWare 3270 LAN Workstation software is designed to work with NetWare operating systems 2.*x* and above by using SPX or any IBM NetBIOS network. At the workstation, DOS 3.1 or above and the appropriate NetWare adapter driver are required. For PS/2 workstations, DOS 3.3 or above must be used.

When loaded at the workstation, the software takes up a minimum of 121 KB of RAM for a single session to a NetWare SNA Gateway or NetWare for SAA. More memory is required to support additional sessions and functionality.

An option in the NetWare 3270 LAN Workstation for DOS is the NetWare 3270 Vector Graphics Option, which adds graphics capability to one host display session. The Vector Graphics Option supports the features and functions of an IBM 3179G color graphics terminal and of the IBM 3270 PC G. This option enables the use of host graphics applications such as GDDM, SAS/GRAPH, DISSPLA, and TELLAGRAF.

Remote user connection can be provided by using the *NetWare Access Server* (NAS), which enables up to six remote users to dial in to a NetWare network and run NetWare 3270 LAN Workstation for DOS software.

Application developers can make use of the development tools and APIs provided by the NetWare 3270 Tools. The API support includes DOS-supported APIs, such as NetWare 3270 API, IBM EEHLLAPI, and IBM Low-Level API.

NetWare 3270 CUT Workstation

The NetWare 3270 LAN products require workstations to be connected by a LAN. If a single stand-alone PC workstation needs to be connected to an SNA host, the LAN solution can become cost-prohibitive. A product called the *NetWare 3270 Control Unit Terminal* (CUT) *Workstation* can be used instead (see fig. 26.23). It is a software package that provides 3270 terminal-emulation and enables IBM PC, PS/2, and compatible workstations to emulate an IBM display terminal for communications with IBM mainframes.

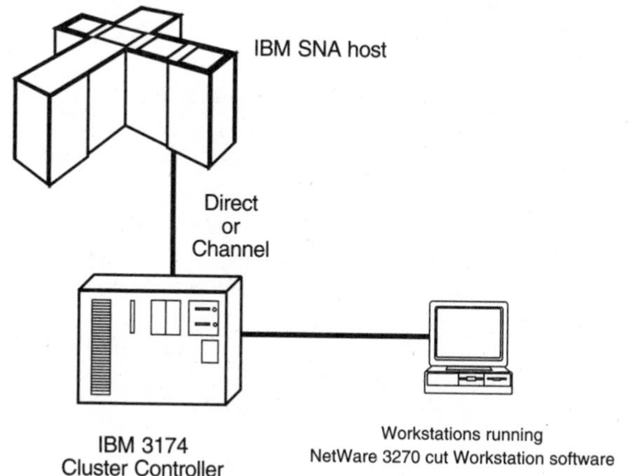

Figure 26.23
NetWare 3270 CUT Workstation.

The workstation communicates with the host by means of a direct coaxial connection to a 3x74 or compatible cluster controller. Users can transfer files to and from the host by using the SEND/RECEIVE utilities. The SEND/RECEIVE utilities upload and download files to and from the host, by working with IBM's IND$FILE host file transfer software in the TSO, CMS, and CICS environments. Other features and functions of the product include the following:

- Stand-alone PC users can access and run 3270 applications.
- Support for an extended data stream, including reverse video, underlining, highlighting, and seven colors.
- Support for common application-programming interfaces, including NetWare 3270 API, IBM EEHLLAPI and LLAPI, and DCA IRMA Subroutines.
- Support for one host and one DOS session.
- Support for file transfer through NetWare 3270 SEND/RECEIVE commands.
- Keyboard-mapping utility and international language keyboard support.
- Support for pointing devices, such as light pens and Microsoft-compatible mice.

A coaxial interface adapter is required for each workstation that needs access to the host. This adapter is connected to an IBM 3x74 or compatible cluster controller with coaxial cable, such as the RG-62 A/U. The coaxial interface adapter can be the Novell Coax Adapter (for the PC or PS/2),the IBM 3278/79 Adapter, the IBM 3270 Connection Adapter, or the IRMA Convertible.

The NetWare 3270 CUT Workstation software is designed to run in a stand-alone workstation running DOS 3.1 or above; it takes up a minimum 58 KB of RAM.

NetWare 3270 Multiworkstation

The NetWare 3270 CUT Workstation software enables only a single session to the SNA host. The *NetWare 3270 Multiworkstation* is designed to overcome the single-session limitation. It is a single station terminal-emulation software, but it enables IBM PC, PS/2, and compatible workstations to emulate up to five IBM display terminals and printers for communications with IBM mainframes.

These workstations are directly connected to the host by means of one of three connectivity options: coaxial, Token Ring, or SDLC (see fig. 26.24). The product includes file-transfer support, support for multiple application-programming interfaces, and workstation-customization tools.

The coaxial option requires a coaxial adapter for each PC that needs a host connection. This adapter is connected to an IBM 3x74 or compatible cluster controller with coaxial cable, such as the RG-62 A/U. The coaxial adapter can be the Novell Coax Adapter for the PC or PS/2, the IBM 3278/79 Adapter, the IBM 3270 Connection Adapter, or the DCA Convertible Adapter. An IRMA I PROM-based adapter with Novell-supplied PROMS also can be used. The cluster controller must be configured for DFT mode.

A remote connection to the host also is possible, requiring a remote communications adapter that connects through synchronous, externally clocked modems over SNA/SDLC lines to an IBM 37xx communications controller. This adapter is connected to the modem through an RS-232 modem cable. For PC and AT bus machines, the Novell Synchronous Adapter for the PC is required. The IBM Multiprotocol Adapter/A for the Micro Channel Architecture bus can be used in PS/2 or compatible machines.

An IBM Token Ring stand-alone connection requires an IBM or compatible Token Ring adapter. The Token Ring Network requires Type A (shielded twisted-pair) cabling in the IBM Cabling System or an equivalent. One of the following host devices must be connected to the Token Ring network: a 3174 cluster controller with the Token Ring Network Gateway Feature (IBM Feature # 3025); a 3720/25/45 front-end processor with a *Token Ring Interface Coupler* (TIC) or *Token Ring Adapter* (TRA); or a 937x with the IBM Token Ring Subsystem Controller Option. The IEEE 802.2 protocol is used to communicate with the host. Because of this, users of the Token Ring connection option must be on the same ring with the host device or be connected to the host ring through the 802.3 bridge using source routing.

With the NetWare 3270 Multiworkstation option, users can transfer files to and from the host by using the SEND/RECEIVE or TRANSFER utilities. The SEND/RECEIVE utilities upload and download files to and from the host by working with IBM's IND$FILE host file-transfer software in the TSO, CMS, and CICS environments. The TRANSFER program enables the transfer of RFT and FFT data between the PC and the host when running *Systems Application Architecture* (SAA) office applications such as OfficeVision and DISOSS. Features and functions of the multiworkstation product include the following:

- Emulation of IBM 3278/9 terminals and 3287 printers and support of up to five concurrent host terminal and printer sessions and a DOS session on a single workstation.
- File Transfer Utilities. SEND/RECEIVE or TRANSFER software.
- Support for many common application programming interfaces, including NetWare 3270 API, IBM EEHLLAPI and LLAPI, and DCA IRMA Subroutines.
- Keyboard-mapping utility and international language support.
- Redirection of host screen prints and 3287 printing-to-network printers.
- Extended data stream, including reverse video, underlining, highlighting, and seven colors.
- Internal trace facility for problem diagnosis.
- Support for pointing devices, such as the light pen and Microsoft mouse-compatible devices.

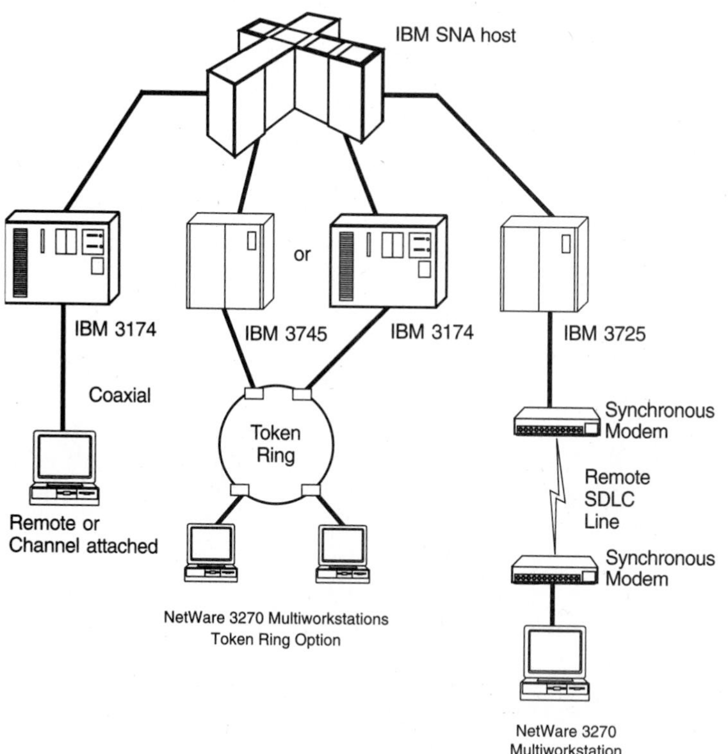

Figure 26.24
NetWare 3270 Multiworkstation.

For a large number of users, installing a LAN and a gateway may be more cost-effective than the Multiworkstation option.

The NetWare 3270 Multiworkstation requires an IBM PC, PS/2, or recommended compatible, with at least one disk drive and 256 KB of RAM. The type of communications hardware needed for the software depends on the type of connection: coaxial, SDLC, or Token Ring.

An option of the NetWare 3270 Multiworkstation and the Token Ring Server Option supports the use of the NetWare 3270 Vector Graphics Option, which adds graphics capability to one host display session. The Vector Graphics Option supports the features and functions of an IBM 3179G color graphics terminal, as well as those of the IBM 3270 PC G. This allows network users to run host graphics applications such as GDDM, SAS/GRAPH, DISSPLA, and TELLAGRAF.

NetWare 5250 Gateway

The NetWare 5250 Twinax Gateway turns a PC or PS/2 on a NetWare LAN into a gateway server that can be used to access an IBM AS/400 or System/3X minicomputer (see fig. 26.25). The gateway communicates with the AS/400 or System/3X through a local twinaxial or remote SDLC connection. IBM PCs on a NetWare LAN can then use this gateway to access information and applications on the minicomputer. In essence, the NetWare 5250 Gateway enables AS/400 or System/3X users to combine the functions of their personal computer with those of a midrange terminal.

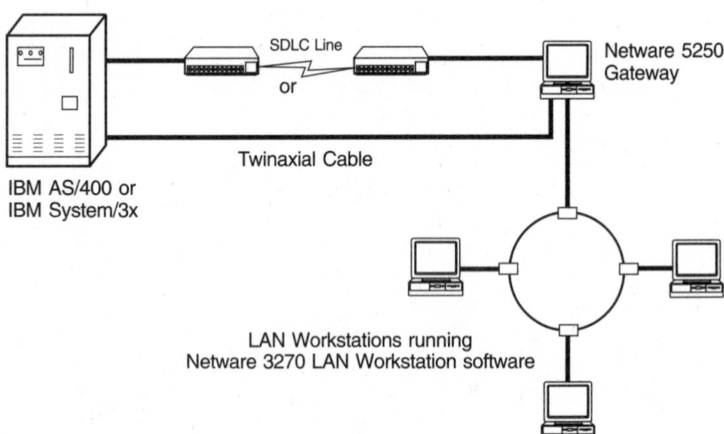

Figure 26.25
NetWare 5250 Gateway.

The NetWare 5250 Gateway supports up to seven local or nine remote concurrent display or host-addressable printer sessions to PCs attached to the network, with up to five of those available concurrently to any single workstation.

The features offered by the NetWare 5250 Gateway include the following:

- **Connects NetWare LANs to IBM minicomputers through local twinaxial or remote SDLC connections.** The NetWare 5250 Gateway distributes up to seven local or nine remote concurrent 5250 display and host-addressable printer sessions to PC and PS/2 workstations on a NetWare network.

- **Allows multiple gateways to run on a single LAN.** Additional gateways can be used for redundancy, load sharing, and support for multiple minicomputers.
- **NetWare SPX transport protocol is used by workstations to communicate with the NetWare 5250 Gateway.** Use of the SPX protocol eliminates the need for the NetBIOS protocol, which avoids the overhead of NetBIOS. Also, SPX is a higher-performance protocol.
- **The NetWare 5250 Gateway can be configured in the dedicated or nondedicated mode of operation.** You can choose to run the gateway server as a dedicated server or as a combination gateway server and NetWare 5250 LAN Workstation. Dedicated mode delivers optimal performance and reliability; nondedicated mode reduces the amount of equipment required.

To use the NetWare 5250 Gateway, users must run the NetWare 5250 LAN Workstation software on their workstations (described in the next section). Also, the AS/400 or System/3X minicomputers need to be configured to understand the NetWare 5250 Gateway.

The NetWare 5250 Gateway requires an IBM PC, PS/2, or compatible computer with a network adapter, a communications adapter, and a connection to the network. The communications link to the host is provided by a twinax adapter or an SDLC adapter. These adapters must be installed in the gateway server PC.

The twinax adapters supported are the Novell Twinax Adapter (for PCs) and the Micro-Integration STwinax MCA Adapter (for PS/2s).

The SDLC adapters supported are the Novell Synchronous Adapter for PCs, the Novell Synchronous/V.35 Adapter for PCs, and the IBM Multiprotocol Adapter/A. In addition to the adapter for host communications, a network adapter is necessary to connect the gateway PC to the NetWare LAN and the workstations.

Novell has published a list of hardware components that have been tested by Novell and recommended for use with its NetWare 5250 Gateway. Before proceeding with the installation you may wish to consult the most recent version of this list.

To summarize the sessions capability of the NetWare 5250 Gateway, the maximum number of host sessions-per-connection is seven for local twinax connections and nine for remote SDLC connections. The maximum number of NetWare 5250 Gateways that can be specified on a NetWare 5250 LAN Workstation is four. The maximum line speed supported for local twinax connection is one Mbps, 56 Kbps for remote SDLC connection. The RAM requirement on the gateway PC is 355-370 KB for running the Gateway software.

NetWare 5250 LAN Workstation

To use the NetWare 5250 Gateway on a NetWare LAN, terminal-emulation software must be used on the NetWare workstations. The NetWare 5250 LAN Workstation provides this terminal-emulation

capability, as shown in figure 26.25. The product provides PCs and PS/2s on a NetWare LAN with access to IBM AS/400 or System/3X minicomputers.

The NetWare 5250 LAN Workstation provides multisession capability. It supports five host display and printer sessions per workstation, hot-key transfer of control to and from DOS, and normal operations from the DOS session. The NetWare 5250 LAN Workstation features include the following:

- Multiple device-emulation types for the IBM AS/400 and System/3X environments. Current support includes IBM 3180, 3196, 5251, 5291, and 5292 displays; and IBM 3812, 5219, 5224, 5225, and 5256 printers.
- Capability to run multiple AS/400 and System/3X applications and utilities.
- Support for up to seven local or nine remote host sessions and one DOS session per workstation when used with NetWare 5250 Gateway.
- Keyboard-remapping capability enables an entire keyboard to be easily mapped to a 5250 or PC layout.
- Keyboard macro support enables users to record and play back frequently used keystroke sequences.
- Support for file transfer to AS/400 or System/3X hosts.

The NetWare 5250 LAN Workstation is sold on a per-server basis; it may be loaded on a file server or on individual 5250 LAN Workstations. Each host session must be configured on the minicomputer before it can be activated. The terminal emulation requires the use of the NetWare SPX transport protocol.

Asynchronous Servers

Asynchronous servers enable dial-in or dial-out access to a LAN. A problem that has to be solved for dial-in access is that the communications links have low speeds (compared to LAN speeds) and are inadequate for direct data file or program access. Invoking a 500 KB program from a remote PC connected to the network over a 19.2 Kbps link can take over three minutes. These delays are unacceptable to most users.

One solution is to use workstations on the LAN as proxy for the remote user. When the remote user, connected by a low-speed link, makes a direct network request for a data or program file, the request is executed on the proxy workstation. Only the screen changes are transferred to the remote workstation. Keystrokes generated at the remote workstation appear as if they are generated by the proxy workstation.

NetWare Asynchronous Communications Server (NACS)

The *NetWare Asynchronous Communications Server* (NACS) turns any IBM PC, AT, or compatible into an asynchronous communications server that enables up to 16 network workstations to simultaneously dial in or out of a NetWare LAN. The NACS software enables a pool of asynchronous modems, attached to the NACS, to be shared for a variety of communications tasks (see fig. 26.26).

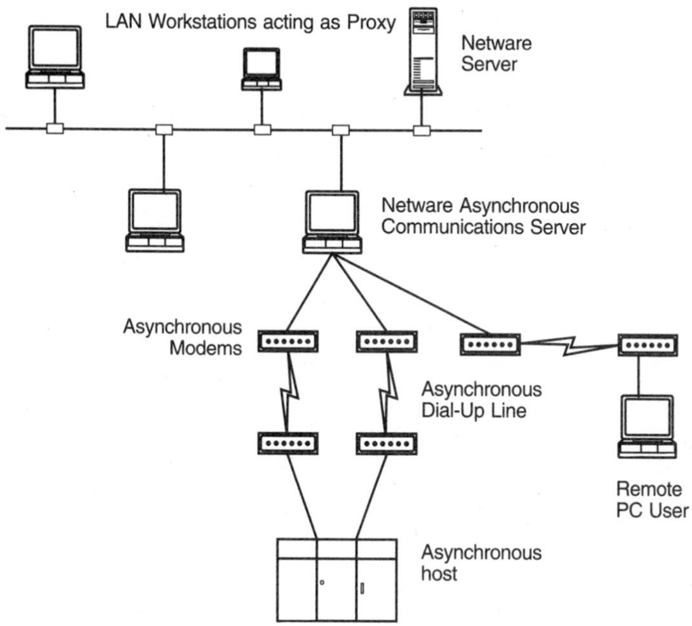

Figure 26.26
NetWare Asynchronous Communications Server (NACS).

Users run terminal-emulation software and access asynchronous hosts by means of the NACS: the NACS Control Program, which runs in a communications server PC, and the *NetWare Asynchronous Interface* (NASI) software, which runs in a user's workstation. The *NACS Control Program* manages the serial ports and all connection activities; the NASI software provides the application interface that enables workstation software, such as asynchronous terminal-emulation packages, to access the ports managed by the Control Program. The NASI software enables the NACS to work with a variety of asynchronous communications software packages.

Access to the communications server is simplified by the use of the *Distributed Asynchronous Name Service* implemented by the NACS program. Users can access a connection simply by requesting it by name. When users request a connection by name, the NACS software connects them with that resource, wherever it is located on the network, making the support of multiple NACSs simple and transparent. Other features and functions include the following:

- 16 asynchronous connections per NACS.
- Line speeds up to 19.2 Kbps-per-port.
- Multiple NACSs on a single network.
- Dial-out capability, so that users can share access to host computers and public computer services.
- Resource names defined through the Distributed Asynchronous Name Service.

- Communications ports are rotored across groups of ports and NACSs. Connection requests are pooled among groups of ports and NACS servers.
- A workstation can access multiple NACSs simultaneously.
- Support for a variety of asynchronous communications packages.
- User has full modem control, including hardware-flow control.
- Inactive session timeout feature frees up ports for other users.

The NACS server software requires a dedicated IBM PC or compatible with 256 KB of RAM, a network adapter, and a connection to the network. Asynchronous communications are implemented by the *NetWare Wide Area Network Interface Module+* (WNIM+), a communications adapter that supports up to four asynchronous ports. As many as four WNIM+ adapters can be installed in a single NACS, bringing the total number of supported ports to 16. Asynchronous modems are connected to the WNIM+ through RS-232 modem cables.

Users who want to access the NACS as an asynchronous gateway to dial-out need an asynchronous terminal-emulation software package. Novell recommends any one of the following terminal-emulation packages:

- Columbia University—MS Kermit
- Crosstalk/DCA—Crosstalk Mark IV
- Crystal Point Software—PCTerm
- Datastorm—ProComm
- Diversified Computer Systems—EM 220, EM 4010, or EM 4105
- Dynamic Microprocessor Associates—ASCOM IV
- The M/H Group—VSComm
- Persoft—SmarTerm
- Polygon Software—PolyTerm
- Relay Communications—Relay Gold
- Softklone—Mirror
- Softronics—Softerm PC
- Telemark—PC TEK
- Walker, Richer and Quinn—Reflection Series

Remote PC users who need to dial in to the LAN through the NACS can use either of the two following supported packages:

- Dynamic Microprocessor Associates—pcANYWHERE
- Triton Technologies—Cosession

NetWare Access Server

The NetWare Access Server software runs on an Intel 80386 or higher machine and enables up to 15 remote users to dial in to a NetWare network and access all the services and files available on the network—including applications, electronic mail, and access to mainframes and minicomputers. In addition to the 15 remote user sessions, a single session is reserved for network supervisors, enabling them to manage the network and remote connections. A security feature in the NetWare Access Server prevents unauthorized remote access. Figure 26.27 illustrates a network configuration using the NetWare Access Server.

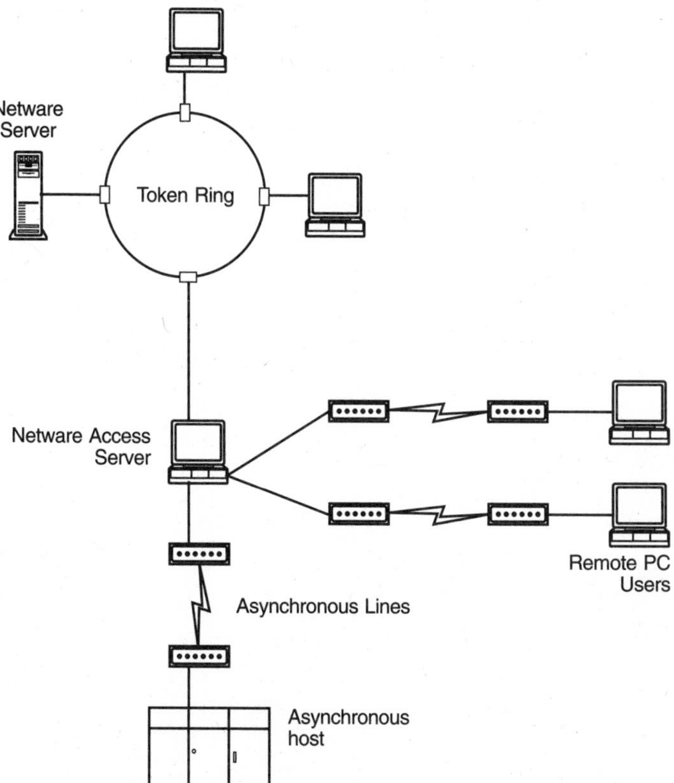

Figure 26.27
NetWare Access Server.

The NetWare Access Server software runs in the protected mode of the Intel 80386 microprocessor. It divides the CPU and RAM into virtual Intel 80386 machines, with each machine using 640 KB of RAM. The total number of such machines is 15. When a remote user dials in, one or more of the virtual machines is used for executing user requests.

Remote users can dial in to the NetWare Access Server through asynchronous modems. Software for remote PC connections is included with the NetWare Access Server.

Network requests sent by remote users are executed by one of the virtual 8086 machines on the NetWare Access Server. Only screen updates and keystrokes travel over the asynchronous lines; data file and program access occur at LAN speeds.

NetWare security access is controlled by the security features of the NetWare file server. An optional dial-back feature is included, which enables the Access Server to grant a network session to a remote user only after the server has called the user back (after initial contact) at a number specified by the network supervisor. This makes it difficult for unauthorized users to gain access to the network from a remote dial-up link. Other features and functions of NAS include the following:

- Support for 15 remote users and one supervisor session.
- Designed for heavy dial-in use without tying up local network workstations for executing remote requests.
- Dial-back capability for additional security. This feature can be implemented on a user-by-user basis.
- Audit trails are maintained on the NetWare Access Server, enabling the administrator to review remote access.
- Monitoring utilities. Session and status control utilities enable supervisors to monitor, the NAS server, session, and modem status; to view the work being done by a user; and to disconnect a user when necessary.
- Remote users can disconnect from the NAS server after starting long-running tasks and call back later to take follow-up action.
- Print jobs can be directed to network or remote printers.
- File-transfer capability.

The NetWare Access Server requires a network adapter and an asynchronous communications adapter for remote dial-up links. The amount of RAM needed can be estimated by the following rule of thumb: 3 MB of RAM is required for every 4 active sessions. For a total of 15 sessions, 12 MB of RAM is necessary.

The asynchronous connections can be provided by Novell's WNIM+ adapter, which is a high-performance asynchronous communications adapter that supports up to 4 asynchronous connections. As many as 4 WNIM+ adapters can be installed in a single NetWare Access Server for a total of 16 connections (15 remote users and one supervisor). The WNIM+ adapters are connected to asynchronous modems by means of RS-232 cables.

Distributed File System and NetWare Integration

Novell offers two products that offer solutions to the problem of interoperability between multivendor platforms: *NetWare for NFS* and *NetWare for FTAM.*

One of the most important resources that needs to be shared in a multivendor network is a universal file system. Such a file system can be distributed across a variety of platforms and provide transparent access to files anywhere on the network. Also, if this access is transparent to the user, the user does not have to be concerned about the location of the files. The two products, NetWare for NFS and NetWare for FTAM, implement a distributed file system that is transparent to the users, but they do this using fundamentally different approaches.

NFS was originally developed by Sun Microsystems. It was designed to enable file systems on UNIX hosts to be distributed and shared in a LAN environment. Sun Microsystems made the specifications to NFS and some key source code available to other vendors. There are over 150 vendors, including Novell, that have licensed the NFS technology. Novell's implementation of NFS is called NetWare for NFS. NFS is not an international standard the way FTAM is, but it has become a popular de facto standard.

FTAM (File Transfer Access Management) is an application layer (layer 7) international standard from the International Organization of Standards (ISO) committee. It is part of *Government Open Systems Interconnect Profile* (GOSIP).

GOSIP is a procurement standard for all federal agencies; different countries have their own GOSIP standard. For example, there is a US GOSIP, a UK GOSIP, a JAPAN GOSIP, and so on. GOSIP makes sure that network equipment purchased by different federal agencies can interoperate.

FTAM, which is part of GOSIP, implements a common virtual store capability that can be accessed by other computers. This *virtual store capability* can be used as a distributed file system, just as NFS can. The protocols used by FTAM are OSI protocols; NFS is based on TCP/IP protocols. Another difference is that NFS uses a typically connectionless mechanism; FTAM requires connections to be established between any two computers involved in an FTAM exchange.

NetWare NFS

NetWare NFS runs on NetWare 3.*x* servers and provides a distributed file system that can be used by any computer that has a client implementation of NFS. Specifically, it allows UNIX workstations transparent access to the NetWare 3.*x* file system and other services. NetWare NFS implements the protocols listed in table 26.5. Therefore, any NFS client that implements these protocols can access the files exported by the NetWare server running NetWare for NFS.

Table 26.5
Protocols Supported by NetWare for NFS

Protocol Abbreviation	Protocol's Full Name
XDR	Sun Microsystems External Data Representation Protocol
RPC	Sun Microsystems Remote Procedure Call (RPC)
NFS v.2	Sun Microsystems, Inc. Network File System version 2
MOUNT	Sun Microsystems, Inc. Mount Protocol
PORTMAPPER	Sun Microsystems, Inc. Portmapper Protocol
LPD	Berkeley UNIX Line Printer Daemon Protocol
FTP	DARPA (RFC 959) File Transfer Protocol

NetWare NFS consists of several NLMs that add NFS server capability to the NetWare server. Once NetWare NFS is installed, workstations with NFS client services can share files with other NetWare clients. These clients include DOS, Macintosh, OS/2, and UNIX workstations. The clients issue a MOUNT command to share the files exported by NetWare NFS. Besides file services, NetWare print services are also available, which enables a NetWare 3.*x* server to function as the single, centralized repository for all client files and to simplify file management in a complex network environment.

NetWare NFS runs on any server machine that can run the NetWare 3.*x* operating system; that is, a PC using an Intel 80386 or higher microprocessor. The minimum server RAM is 5 MB, and 3 MB of disk space are required on the volume that supports NFS name space. Because NFS makes use of the TCP/IP protocols, the TCP NLM must be loaded and running prior to activating NetWare for NFS.

NetWare NFS provides the following services over the TCP/IP transport:

- NFS for file sharing
- Line Printer Daemon (LPD) for print services
- File Transfer Protocol Daemon (FTPD)
- LOCKD, a standard UNIX file-and record-locking service

NetWare NFS features are described in the following list:

- The NFS Server NLM provides the mechanism that enables UNIX clients to view the NetWare 3.*x* file system as an extension of their native NFS environment. UNIX clients use the standard UNIX/NFS mount command to access NetWare volumes. Key NFS Server elements include transparent support of authentication, file-attribute mapping, file-name mapping, file locking, permissions mapping, and remote server-based system administration.

- The UNIX Namespace NLM provides the NetWare 3.*x* file system with native UNIX file attributes and naming conventions, enabling transparent file access from UNIX environments and file sharing across all NetWare 3.*x*-supported name spaces, including DOS, Macintosh, and OS/2.
- The LPD NLM enables UNIX-TCP/IP clients to submit print jobs to NetWare 3.*x* print queues.
- The FTPD NLM enables any FTP client with valid NetWare access to connect to a NetWare 3.*x* server and to initiate file transfers to and from any NetWare volume or directory.
- The Lock Manager NLM supports file and record locking in the NFS environment. Applications that perform UNIX advisory file and record locking are fully supported through the Lock Manager program within NetWare NFS.
- NFSCON NLM management and configuration utility enables monitoring of the NFS server. The tasks performed by management utilities include the following:

  System configuration and parameter initialization

  Statistics on NFS server utilization

  Fine-tuning of software parameters to enhance server performance

  Logging of error conditions

  Manipulation of the NFS file and directory permissions

DOS clients can access NetWare NFS services by using the following NFS client implementations for DOS:

- Sun Microsystem's PC-NFS
- Beam & Whiteside's DOS NFS
- FTP Software's Interdrive that comes with the PC/TCP Plus package

Installing NetWare NFS

The following steps are a guided tour for installing NetWare NFS:

1. From the server console, load the INSTALL NLM.
2. Select Product Options and press Ins.
3. When prompted for the drive/path name of the product source media, enter it. This is normally the floppy disk containing NetWare for NFS, unless you have copied it to NetWare volume. In that case, enter the source path name on the volume (example: **SYS:NFS**, if NetWare for NFS has been copied to this path).

4. When prompted to do so, enter the path name of the directory containing the SERVER.EXE program. This enables the installation process to copy the NFS name space to the DOS partition used to boot NetWare.

5. Select the INSTALL option from NFS Installation Options, which copies the NFS files to the proper directories (**SYS:SYSTEM**, for example) until the screen in figure 26.28 appears.

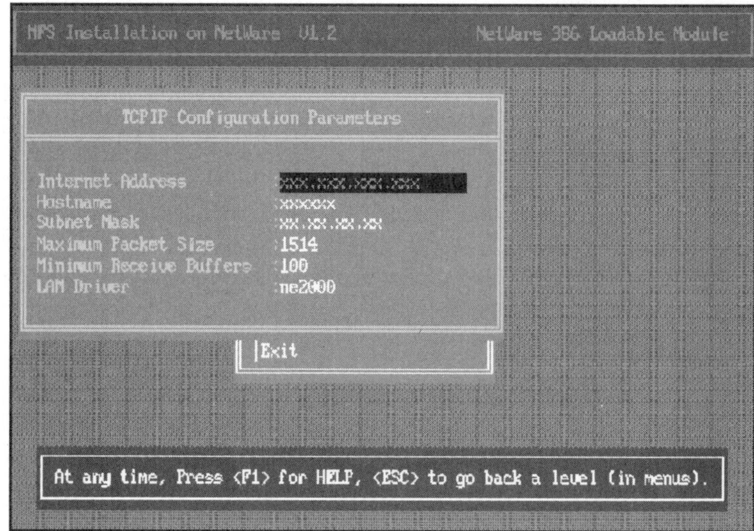

Figure 26.28
NFS TCP/IP Configuration Parameters.

6. Fill out the TCP/IP parameters based on your network setting, press Esc, and answer Yes to update configuration files.

7. When asked if you want to activate the following services, answer Yes (unless you do not want the services because of lack of RAM at server). You are prompted for the following services:

   UNIX to NetWare Print Service

   NetWare to UNIX Print Service

   Remote Console for UNIX (XCONSOLE)

   FTP Server

   Lock Manager

8. If you are reminded to restart the server to install the NFS name space, take note and press Esc.

9. Exit NFS INSTALL, and the list of NFS products that have been installed should appear.

10. Use Alt+Esc to switch to the system console. If you are doing the install from a remote console, use the asterisk (*) key on the numeric keypad.

11. Add the NFS name space from the system console. Execute the following commands to perform this step:

```
LOAD NFS
MOUNT volumeName
ADD NAME SPACE NFS TO SYS
```

12. Return to the INSTALL screen, by pressing Alt+Esc (or the * key on the numeric keypad).

13. Select the NetWare for NFS product name to invoke the NFSADMIN to be used for configuring the NetWare server.

    At this point, you must configure the user and group tables, NFS exports, host tables, file attributes for exported NetWare directories, and NetWare-to-UNIX LPR Gateway. The configuration information is kept in SYS:ETC and follows the UNIX/NFS style and convention as closely as possible.

14. Answer Yes to modify the following files in SYS:ETC.

    NFSUSERS

    NFSGROUP

    HOSTS

    EXPORTS

    LPR$PSRV.NAM (LPR Print Gateway, NetWare-to-UNIX print service)

15. Add user names of NetWare users to the list of NFS users by pressing Ins. This list is used by NetWare to map the NFS uid (user ID) to the NetWare user name to determine the user's trustee rights. When finished adding users, press Esc and confirm changes.

    Add group names of NetWare groups to the list of NFS groups by using the Ins key. This NFSGROUP file is used by NetWare to map the NFS gid (group ID) to the NetWare group name. When finished adding groups, press Esc and confirm changes.

    Add the host names (file HOSTS) and the internet address of each computer that is explicitly authorized to mount the NetWare file system by the EXPORTS file. When finished adding groups, press Esc and confirm changes.

16. Add the directories that can be exported from the NetWare file system to other computers. This list is written out to the file EXPORTS. This file is read automatically by the mounted NLM. Exported names must follow the UNIX naming convention and be entered in lowercase. All exported names in a volume must begin with */volname.* To export the SYS: root directory, use **/sys/**.

17. Configure the LPR Gateway. For this part you must know the Printer Description, UNIX Host Name, UNIX Printer Name, and NetWare Print Queue Name.

18. When finished configuring printers, exit NFSAdmin and INSTALL.

19. If you missed a step, you can use LOAD NFSADMIN from the console to configure any of the configuration files in SYS:ETC.

NetWare FTAM

File Transfer Access and Management (FTAM) provides a network-wide common view of a *virtual file store system* (see fig. 26.29). The virtual file store system provides a common view of the file system to all FTAM clients, who are called *initiators*. The virtual store file system is mapped to the real file system by FTAM. In general, the FTAM system enables copying of files to another system, reading and writing of individual records in the file, and changing attributes of a virtual store file.

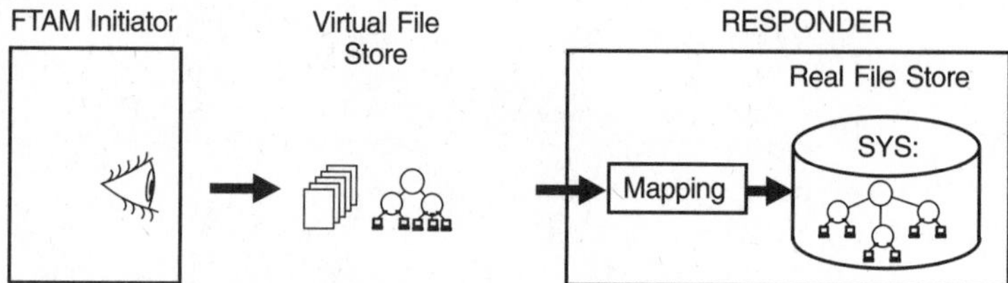

Figure 26.29
File transfer, access, and management (FTAM).

NetWare FTAM is an OSI FTAM server that runs on top of NetWare 3.*x* and enables a variety of FTAM clients to access the NetWare 3.*x* file system. In OSI terminology, the FTAM server is called the *responder* and the FTAM client is called the *initiator*. NetWare FTAM implements all seven layers of the OSI protocol suite and enables file transfer between NetWare and any other complementary OSI FTAM initiator, regardless of the hardware or software platform being used. FTAM initiators also can send files to NetWare print queues.

Figure 26.30 shows the NetWare FTAM components. The FTAM.EXE program runs on a NetWare workstation and communicates with the FTAM initiator, implemented by the FTAMCLI.NLM. The FTAM responder is implemented by the FTAMSVR.NLM. The FTAM initiator and responder can run on a single NetWare 3.*x* server or on different servers.

NetWare FTAM is implemented as a set of NLMs that runs on the NetWare 3.*x* operating system (see fig. 26.31).

The data flow between a FTAM user and FTAM initiator is shown in figure 26.32.

NetWare FTAM complies with U.S. GOSIP; it can be used with third-party X.400 mail gateways to satisfy the basic profile and service requirements of GOSIP 1.0. It implements the standard OSI protocol specifications for FTAM, ACSE, ASN.1, OSI Session, TP Class 4, and CLNP, and it conforms to the following *National Institute of Standards and Technology* (NIST) specifications:

FTAM T1 and M1
Directory Access: NBS-9 document type

U.S. GOSIP
Conforms to limited FTAM specification
Interoperates with full FTAM implementation

TOP 3.0
Conforms to limited FTAM specification
Interoperates with full FTAM implementation

U.K. GOSIP
Interoperates with U.K. GOSIP-conformant implementations

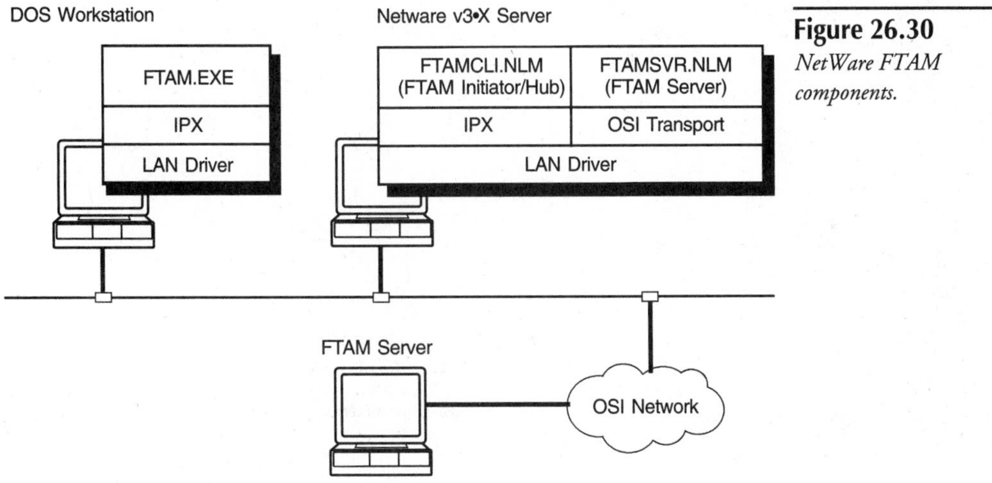

Figure 26.30
NetWare FTAM components.

Standards Conformance:

Directories:	**NBS-9 Document Type**
FTAM:	ISO 8671 (file types 1 and 3, limited and enhanced management)
ACSE:	ISO 8650
Presentation:	ISO 882x3
ASN.1:	ISO 8825
Session:	ISO 8327

continues

Directories:	NBS-9 Document Type
Transport:	ISO 8072 (COTP), ISO 8602 (CLTP)
Network:	ISO 8473 (CLNP), ISO 9542 (ES/IS)
Link:	ISO 802.2
Physical:	ISO 802.3 (CSMA/CD), ISO 802.5 (TR)

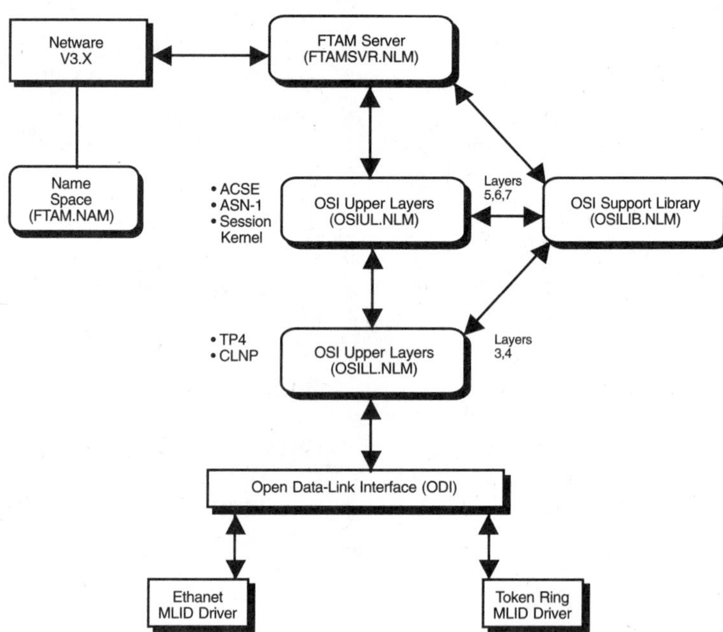

Figure 26.31
Data flow between NetWare 3.x and FTAM server.

NetWare FTAM features include the following:

- Provides file storage, retrieval, and management services to FTAM clients, depending on the capabilities of their FTAM client software:

  Users can transfer and retrieve whole files to the servers disk for storage.

  Users can delete files from the server's disk.

  Users can read a file's attributes.

  Users can rename files.

- Clients using NBS-9 can create and delete directories and list directory contents.
- NetWare FTAM enables FTAM clients to send files to NetWare print queues.
- NetWare FTAM runs on NetWare 3.*x* and requires at least 6 MB of memory and 1 MB of free disk space. The NetWare server must be connected to an Ethernet or Token Ring network and configured for IEEE 802.2 framing.

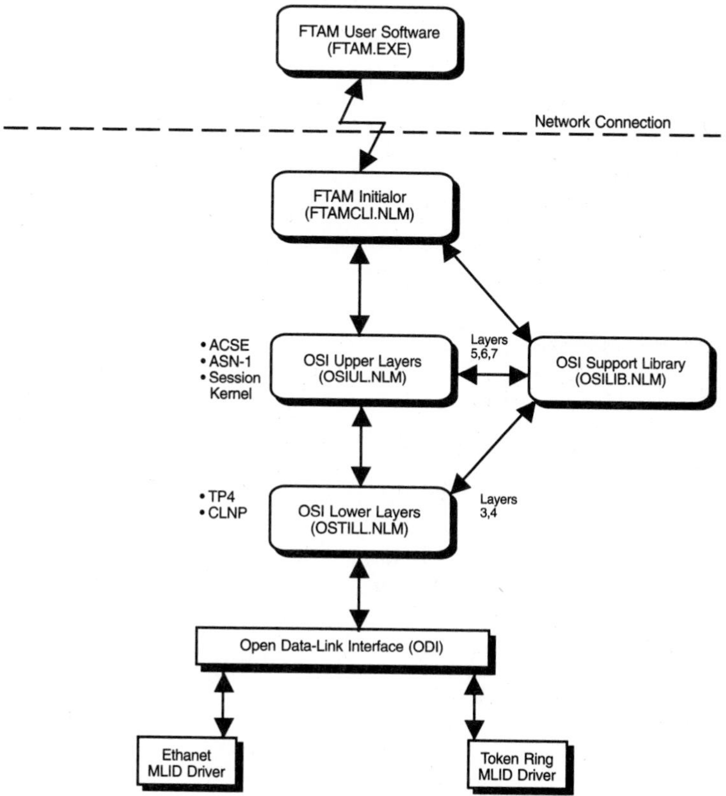

Figure 26.32
Data flow between FTAM user and FTAM initiator.

Installing NetWare FTAM

The following steps give you a guided tour for installing NetWare FTAM:

1. From the server console, load the INSTALL NLM.
2. Select Product Options, and then press Ins.
3. When prompted for the drive/path name of the product source media, enter it. This is normally the floppy disk containing NetWare for FTAM, unless you have copied it to NetWare volume. In that case, enter the source path name on the volume.

You have a choice of installing the FTAM server, FTAM client, or both. These instructions assume that you want to install both.

4. When prompted to do so, enter the path name of the directory containing the SERVER.EXE program. This enables the installation process to copy the FTAM name space to the DOS partition used to boot NetWare.

   You see a screen for NetWare FTAM configuration.

5. Select Volumes for FTAM Name Space.

6. Press Ins and add the volumes that you want to use for FTAM.

7. Select Set Configuration File Parameters from NetWare FTAM Configuration.

8. Select Set Default Directory from Configuration File Options. Accept the default SYS:LOGIN directory if you want user files to be stored there. Otherwise, select another directory.

9. Select Set Default NSAP from NetWare FTAM Configuration. The default NSAP address, as shown in figure 26.33, displays. Press Esc to select it.

Figure 26.33
FTAM default NSAP address.

10. Back out of the menus by selecting the Return option and save configuration changes. Press Esc until asked if you want to exit NetWare for FTAM installation. Answer Yes.

    The screen shown in figure 26.34, showing the installed products, displays.

11. Exit INSTALL.

12. Run the script ADDFTMNS.NCF to load the FTAM name space and add it to the volumes selected.

```
ADDFTMNS
```

13. Load the LAN driver with IEEE 802.2 encapsulation. For example, you can load the NE2000 driver on port 340 (hex), interrupt 4 by using the following:

```
LOAD NE2000 PORT=340 INT=4 FRAME=ETHERNET_802.2 NAME=OSI
```

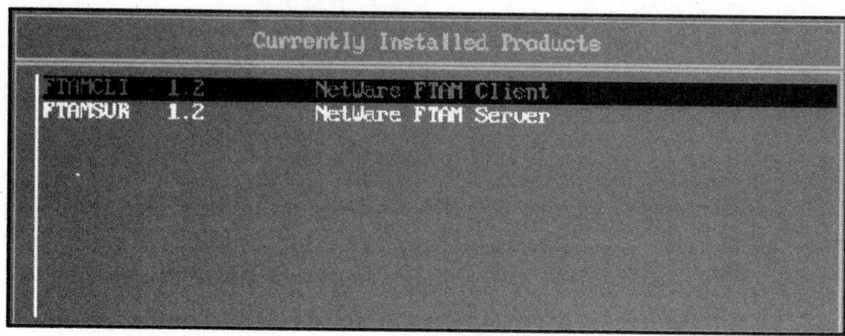

Figure 26.34
FTAM installed products.

14. Load the NetWare FTAM NLMs in the following order:

    LOAD OSIINIT

    LOAD OSILIB

    LOAD OSILL

    BIND CLNP TO *NAME*

    LOAD OSIUL

    LOAD FTAMSVR

    LOAD FTAMCLI

    Replace *NAME* with the value used in the BIND command.

15. Add the following command to load the FTAM name space to STARTUP.NCF:

    ```
    LOAD FTAM
    ```

16. To load FTAM automatically, add the commands in step 13 to 14 in the AUTOEXEC.NCF file.

17. Use the OSICON utility to perform configuration or maintenance tasks for FTAM clients and FTAM server. OSICON also can be used to configure ISO Lower Layers, Local NSAP, and Local OSI environment. For example, the screen in figure 26.35 is obtained by using OSICON -> FTAM Client. The P-Selector, S-Selector, and T-Selector are used to support multiple protocol entities at a given OSI layer. In NetWare FTAM, the T-Selector values can be changed to support multiple applications by using the OSI transport layer.

Figure 26.35
FTAM client options.

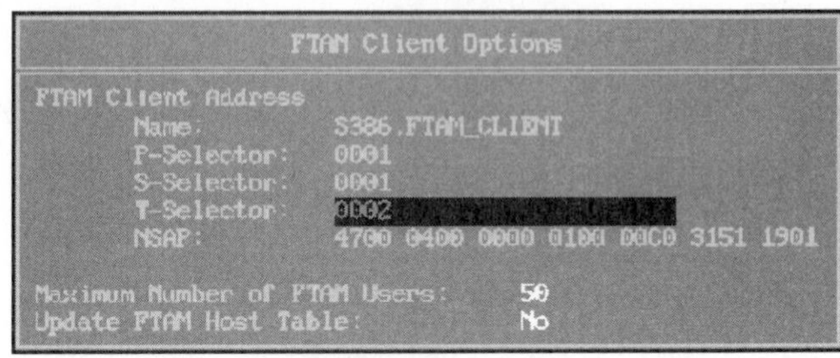

18. To Update the FTAM Host table, use the following selections:

    OSICON -> FTAM Client -> Update FTAM Host Table = Yes

    -> Select FTAM Host.

The screen shown in figure 26.36 shows the FTAM Host Information that can be changed. The addressing format is OSINET. Other formats are possible and can be selected by setting the field Change NSAP Format to Yes. These address formats are shown in figure 26.37. One of these address formats, the U.S.GOSIP format, is shown in figure 26.38.

Figure 26.36
FTAM host information.

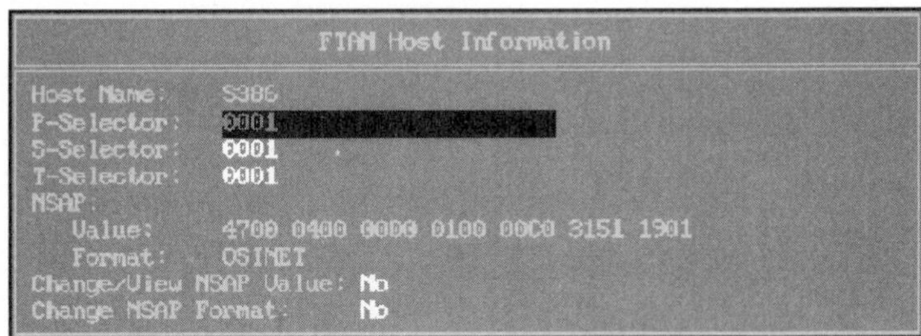

Figure 26.37
FTAM NSAP format options.

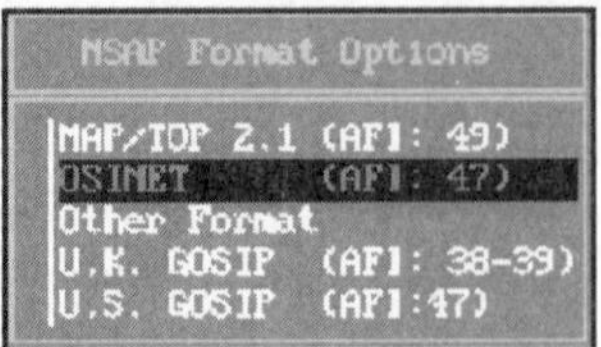

Figure 26.38
FTAM U.S. GOSIP format.

NetWare Ports to Other Platforms

It is Novell's intention to port NetWare on every major computing platform. The agreement with Hewlett-Packard to do a native port of NetWare 3.*x* to the HP High Precision Architecture is an example of Novell's strategy. As other RISC platforms become more dominant, you can expect to see more NetWare ports to these platforms.

This section examines ports of NetWare to the VMS and UNIX environments.

Port of NetWare to VAX/VMS

A company called Interconnections has ported NetWare to the VMS platform. NetWare runs as a process on top of the VMS operating system on a VAX. File services, server management, and NetWare security are mapped to equivalent functions on the VMS operating system.

NetWare for VMS enables a DEC VAX/VMS system to function as a NetWare server, which enables the integration of PC-based LANs and VAX/VMS-based minicomputer networks. DOS and OS/2 users can share data, applications, and printer services with VAX terminal users. DOS users also can make use of *Terminal Emulation Service* (TES) to access VMS applications. The VAX can be used as a large and secure disk storage with reliable and regular file backups. NetWare files are stored as standard RMS files, with automatic and dynamic translation of differences in file attributes and naming conventions among DOS, OS/2, and VMS.

NetWare for VMS enables as many as 254 DOS and OS/2 users to access the server concurrently. SPX/IPX packets can be transported across DECnet by using tunneling. This gives NetWare PC users on DECnet transparent access to remote VAXs or NetWare file servers by using the wide area networking features of DECnet. The SPX/IPX packets are encapsulated in DECnet packets that are then carried to any NetWare for VMS file server on the DECnet network. Once received, the DECnet envelope is removed and the SPX/IPX packets are forwarded to the desired NetWare server. This effectively creates a virtual IPX network over DECnet.

NetWare for VMS is installed on the VAX by using the standard VMSINSTAL utility, and it requires a minimum of 2 MB of memory (4 MB is recommended). It requires 10,000 blocks of disk space to operate, but 20,000 blocks are needed temporarily during installation.

A DEC Ethernet controller and the DEC-supplied Ethernet controller driver must be installed in the VAX, providing an Ethernet connection to the network. The NetWare workstations must be configured to use Ethernet II frame encapsulation, rather than the default IEEE 802.3 encapsulation. For ODI drivers, the frame encapsulation can be specified in the NET.CFG file. For non-ODI drivers, the ECONFIG utility can be used to configure the IPX.COM file for Ethernet II encapsulation. The TES feature on workstations requires 33 KB of RAM, but it can be unloaded when not in use. TES supports third-party emulation software written to use interrupt 14, including the following products:

EM 220 by Diversified Computer Systems, Inc.

poly-STAR by Polygon Software, Inc.

PCTerm by Crystal Point Software, Inc.

Reflection Series by Walker, Richer and Quinn

SmarTerm by Persoft, Inc.

SofTermPC by Softronics, Inc.

TNET-05 by Grafpoint

ZSTerm by KEA Systems Ltd.

NetWare for VMS supports DEC's standard DEC Ethernet controllers, including the DEUNA, DELUA, DESQA, DELQA, DEQNA, DESVA, DEBNT, DEBNI, and DEBNA controllers.

Digital Equipment Corporation also has a product called PATHWORKS for NetWare. This product implements NetWare on VMS and Ultrix operating systems and enables NetWare users to make use of high-performance server hardware.

NetWare for UNIX

With the development of NetWare 3.*x*, the NetWare operating system was written in the portable C language and compiled using a 32-bit C compiler (Watcom C compiler). Figure 26.39 illustrates that NetWare services can be considered to be independent of the multitasking features of the NetWare operating system. Because the NetWare services were rewritten in the portable C language, the multitasking NetWare operating system can be replaced by some other general-purpose operating system such as UNIX, VMS, or OS/2. Several of Novell's strategic partners have done that, but have focused their attention on porting NetWare services to the UNIX operating system. This version of NetWare was called Portable NetWare; its new name is NetWare for UNIX.

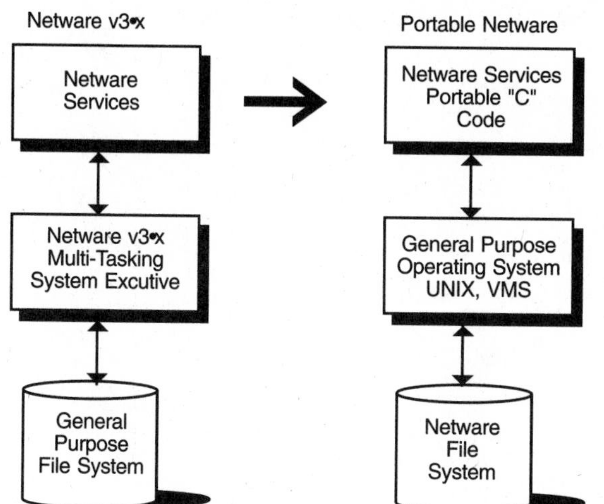

Figure 26.39
Portable NetWare.

Novell's strategic partners in the effort to run NetWare on UNIX platforms include NCR, Prime, Data General, Unisys, Hewlett-Packard, Innovus, Wang Labs, Mips, Altos Computers, Pyramid, ICL, Interactive, Integraph, and Rational Data.

Summary

This chapter has examined solutions for connecting NetWare to non-NetWare networks and devices. The topics discussed include the communications connectivity of NetWare LANs to TCP/IP networks, X.25 networks, T1 networks, Asynchronous Links, Synchronous Links, IBM SNA networks, OSI networks, and UNIX networks.

This chapter also discussed distributed file system solutions such as NetWare NFS, NetWare FTAM, and NetWare support on other platforms such as VMS and UNIX.

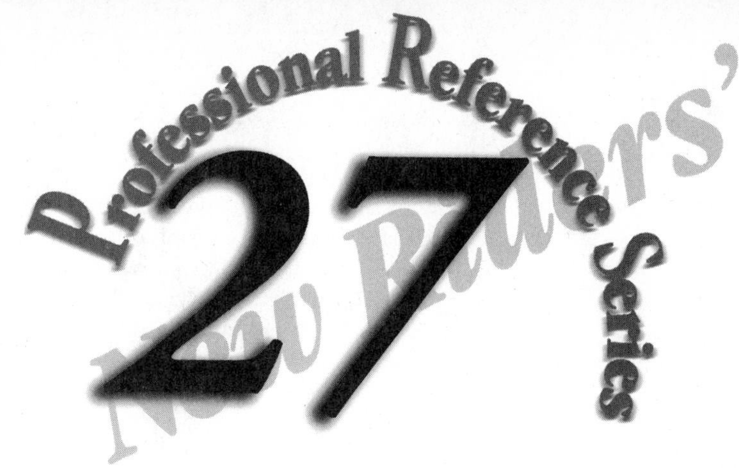

NetWare/IP

The communication between a NetWare workstation and NetWare server takes place using the IPX network layer (OSI layer 3) protocol. When NetWare was originally designed, Novell developed IPX based on the *Internet Datagram Protocol* (IDP) found in the *Xerox Network System* (XNS) network protocols used in Xerox networks. In the mid-1980s TCP/IP, which originated as a protocol used on the old ARPANET, became a de facto standard not only in universities and research organizations, but also in the commercial sector. Although TCP/IP has traditionally been used in UNIX networks, it is not limited to running on UNIX networks. Today, TCP/IP is available on all major computer/operating-system platforms ranging from microcomputers to mainframes. This chapter examines how a product called NetWare/IP can be used to provide access to NCP services using TCP/IP.

Understanding the Need for NetWare/IP

Novell began supporting TCP/IP at the NetWare server in 1988 using technology it obtained through the purchase of Excelan of San Jose. Today every NetWare 3.1*x* and 4.*x* server ships with a TCPIP.NLM that implements the TCP/IP protocol at the server. The TCPIP.NLM can be used to convert a NetWare server to an IP router and provide transport services for TCP/IP applications that can run at the server. An example of TCP/IP applications that run at the NetWare server is the NetWare NFS (Network File System) product. The NetWare NFS product must be purchased separately and implements NFS server, FTP (File Transfer Protocol) server, UNIX-to-NetWare, and NetWare-to-UNIX print gateways.

Until the development of NetWare/IP there was no way to send NCP requests to a NetWare server using TCP/IP. The LAN Workplace products or third-party products from FTP Software, Chameleon, Beam & Whiteside, and so on can be used to talk to TCP/IP applications such as FTP, NFS, and print gateways at the server, but they cannot be used to obtain NCP services from a NetWare server.

NetWare/IP allows the native IPX protocol service to be replaced by the TCP/IP transport services (see fig. 27.1). Many organizations have a mix of TCP/IP and IPX protocols running on their networks. Typically, TCP/IP is used by engineering workstations and large machines, and IPX is used by NetWare workstations and servers. Network managers have to support and understand both types of protocols. With NetWare/IP, IPX can be replaced by TCP/IP and this allows an organization to support only one protocol: the de facto TCP/IP.

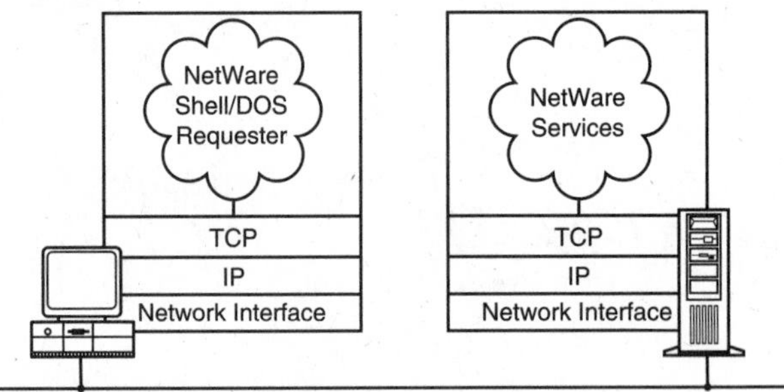

Figure 27.1
Use of TCP/IP in NetWare/IP.

NetWare/IP consists of a set of NLMs and client software that allows NetWare 3.1*x* and 4.*x* servers to use TCP/IP as their transport protocol for communicating with NetWare workstations. The NetWare workstations can be configured to use TCP/IP exclusively, or they can use TCP/IP in addition to the native IPX protocol.

NetWare/IP is currently available as a separate product not bundled with NetWare server software—it must be purchased separately. The NetWare/IP product comes with the DOS TCP/IP transport stack (TCPIP.EXE) from the LAN Workplace for DOS product.

Some of the benefits of NetWare/IP include the following:

- Network managers have the option of running IP-only networks. This is valuable for those organizations that standardized on TCP/IP as their protocol of choice. Routers on such networks can be configured to handle the IP packet only.

- Existing NetWare 3.1*x* and 4.*x* applications can continue to run and use TCP/IP as their transport protocol. These applications that use the standard NetWare APIs can run unmodified on a NetWare/IP node.

- Cost in managing network protocols is reduced because the network engineers who troubleshoot and configure network nodes have to understand and configure only one protocol—TCP/IP.

- NetWare/IPX and NetWare/IP networks can coexist. NetWare/IP has a feature called the NetWare/IP gateway that can be used to transparently connect native NetWare IPX networks with NetWare/IP networks. This gateway allows NetWare IPX clients to access NetWare/IP servers, and also allows NetWare/IP clients to access NetWare servers on the IPX network.

- The NetWare/IP gateway enables you to gradually convert NetWare clients to use NetWare/IP while allowing the network to function.

- NetWare/IP includes an application called XCONSOLE. This runs as an NLM at the server, and allows an X-Windows terminal to act as a console from which NetWare/IP can be managed. UNIX workstations or terminals that have X-Windows can manage a NetWare/IP server. These UNIX users have a choice of Windows manager such as MOTIF, OpenLook, or TWM.

Configurations Using NetWare/IP

Examples of network configurations that use NetWare/IP can clarify how NetWare/IP can be used. The following sections give some examples.

IP Backbone with IPX Islands

Consider an organization that standardized on using TCP/IP on their backbone network. A good reason for doing this, besides the fact that TCP/IP is now a de facto standard, is that the organization also has connectivity to the Internet, which is predominantly based on TCP/IP. It is also possible for such an organization to have a policy in which IPX can be used on local networks as long as the backbone only uses TCP/IP. Reasons for using TCP/IP exclusively on the backbone include the reduced costs of configuring backbone devices and of training personnel to administer the backbone. Another reason to use TCP/IP on the backbone is that TCP/IP has been proven to work efficiently on a WAN that has long delays in transmission and a variability in the delay. Local departments within the organization may, however, prefer the ease of configuration of IPX networks that do not require an explicit IPX network address assignment per workstation. Also managers of NetWare LANs are traditionally unfamiliar with the configuration requirements of TCP/IP networks. Because of this, it may be preferable for departmental networks to continue using IPX for accessing NetWare servers.

Figure 27.2 shows a campus network that has an IP backbone used to connect departmental networks. The departmental LANs run IPX to access NetWare servers. These departmental LANs can be joined to the IP backbone using the NetWare/IP gateway. This network configuration allows local departments to continue using IPX while IP is used on the backbone. The users in a department can continue using IPX locally and access servers in other departments using the IP backbone and the NetWare/IP servers configured as IPX-to-IP gateways.

This configuration also gives the organization the option of gradually converting the local NetWare IPX environment to one based on using IP entirely. After all the servers in a department are converted to NetWare/IP servers, the workstations can be configured to use TCP/IP as their transport protocol. The NetWare/IP server configured as an IPX-to-IP gateway can then be configured as an IP router instead. Alternatively, you can replace the IPX-to-IP gateway function with a dedicated IP router.

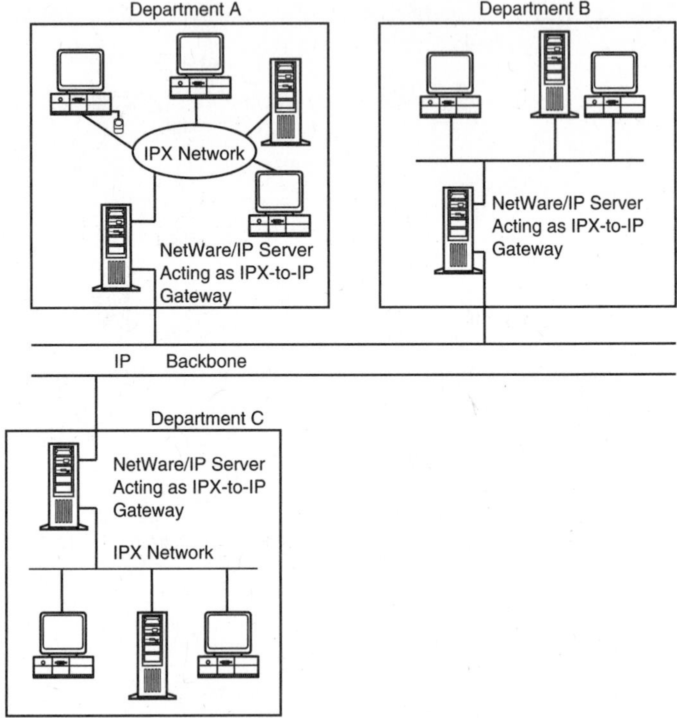

Figure 27.2
IP Backbone with IPX islands.

An IP-Only Network

Figure 27.3 shows a network that uses IP only. This configuration can be used by a department that has many locations scattered over long distances. NetWare/IP allows each NetWare server and workstation to use the TCP/IP protocols, which work equally well on LAN and WAN links. The NetWare workstations at each location have access to all NetWare servers on the local network and other locations.

The networks in figure 27.3 also can support non-NetWare workstations and servers that also use TCP/IP protocols. This allows the entire enterprise to be based on a single TCP/IP protocol.

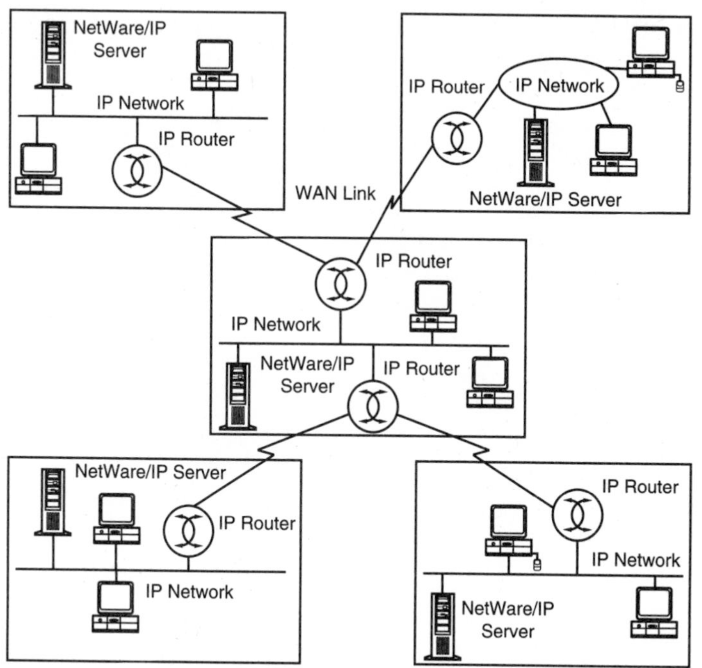

Figure 27.3
An IP-only NetWare network.

Examining NetWare/IP

NetWare/IP has the following components:

- **NetWare/IP server.** This is a series of NLMs that run on a NetWare 3.1*x* or 4.*x* server. These NLMs enable NetWare applications that previously used IPX to use TCP/IP as their transport protocol.

- **NetWare/IP client.** This allows a network workstation configured with an NIC to use TCP/IP protocols instead of (or in addition to) the IPX protocol. The NetWare client must be configured to use ODI drivers. The NetWare client support includes a TCP/IP stack implemented by TCPIP.EXE. Additional modules needed are NWIP.EXE, used for emulating the IPX Far Call interface, and a shell (NETX.EXE) or DOS Requester. If the VLMs are used, the NETX.VLM can be used to access bindery based servers. To access NetWare 4.*x* servers, the DOS Requester VLMs are needed.

- **Domain Name System (DNS) server.** A NetWare server can be set up as a DNS server. The DNS server provides a distributed name look-up service that resolves symbolic names of hosts to their IP addresses. NetWare/IP clients use the DNS to look up the name of their nearest *Domain SAP Servers* (DSS).

- **Domain SAP/RIP Servers (DSS).** These are used as repositories of SAP/RIP information on the network. *Service Advertising Protocol* (SAP) is used in NetWare networks by NetWare services to advertise themselves to the rest of the network. *Routing Information Protocol* (RIP) is used to exchange IPX routing information. Using DSS, it is possible to partition networks into domains called NetWare/IP domains so that NetWare/IP clients and servers know of services in their NetWare/IP domain only.

Novell estimates, based on an internal study, that NetWare/IP provides comparable performance to NetWare IPX-based networks. On the average, the throughput of NetWare/IP is eight percent less than using IPX for the network transport. Most applications will not notice a performance loss.

Understanding NetWare/IP Domains

NetWare/IP domains should not be confused with DNS domains used in IP networks as a general purpose name look-up service for host names. Whereas DNS can be used by a mix of NetWare workstations, NetWare servers, and UNIX-based machines, DSS is used only in NetWare networks. DSS and DNS servers can coexist on a network without any conflict.

Figure 27.4 shows an IP network for three separate departments of the hypothetical organization SCS. These department networks can be in different locations and are connected using IP routers. Department A has server NWS1 and workstation WS1; Department B has server NWS2 and workstation WS2; and department C has server NWS3 and client WS3.

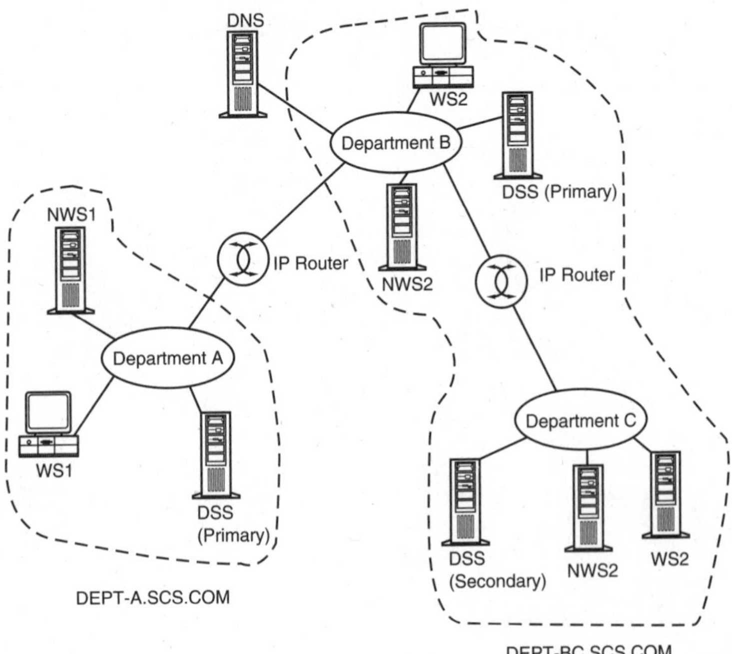

Figure 27.4
NetWare/IP domains.

You can have one logical NetWare/IP domain encompassing the entire network or break the network into several logical domains.

The NetWare/IP domain must have at least one Domain SAP/RIP Server, called the *primary* DSS server. The DSS server acts as a repository for all SAP/RIP information. It broadcasts SAP/RIP information at periodic intervals to workstations and servers within the NetWare/IP domain. By performing this action, it emulates the requirements for SAP/RIP broadcasts for an IPX network. NetWare/IP nodes learn of services on a NetWare network from the DSS. NetWare/IP servers communicate with the DSS periodically to obtain and update SAP/RIP updates. When a NetWare/IP client uses commands such as SLIST (NetWare 3.*x*), NLIST SERVER (NetWare 4.*x*), or DISPLAY SERVERS (console command) that require SAP information, the NetWare/IP server responds with information obtained from a DSS server.

It is not necessary for a DSS server to also be a NetWare/IP server. In other words, the DSS server does not have to be running NWIP.NLM, the component that implements the NetWare/IP server. The NLM needed for implementing DSS is DSS.NLM.

The primary DSS server supports all NetWare/IP nodes (clients and servers) in its NetWare/IP domain. The NetWare/IP nodes use DNS to find the name of the nearest DSS for obtaining SAP/RIP information.

You may decide to divide the IP network into several logical NetWare/IP domains. Reasons for doing this include the following:

- To limit the amount of SAP/RIP information that must be maintained by DSS servers for a domain
- To reduce the processing overhead on a DSS server

You also can increase efficiency by spreading the processing load across multiple DSS servers deployed throughout the network.

Figure 27.4 shows a network divided into two NetWare/IP domains. One NetWare/IP domain encompasses the department A network, and the other NetWare/IP domain encompasses the department B and department C networks. The NetWare/IP domains are shown with the following names:

- DEPT-A.SCS.COM (Department A network)
- DEPT-BC.SCS.COM (Department B and Department C networks)

The choice of names for the NetWare/IP domain such as DEPT-A or DEPT-BC is arbitrary. Use a convention that meets the needs of your organization. Novell documentation suggests Department B and Department C networks NWIP.SCS.COM and NWIP2.SCS.COM as names for the NetWare/IP domain.

The NetWare/IP domain DEPT-A.SCS.COM has a single primary DSS. The NetWare/IP domain DEPT-BC.SCS.COM has a primary DSS and a secondary DSS. The secondary DSS is located in the department C network. This makes it possible for the department C network to obtain SAP/RIP

information by contacting a local DSS server rather than going across a router (and potentially slow and expensive WAN links) to obtain SAP/RIP information from the primary DSS server for domain DEPT-BC.SCS.COM.

If a NetWare/IP client in a NetWare/IP domain needs access to a server in another domain, you can use the NWIPMAP.EXE utility that comes with NetWare/IP to create a drive mapping to the server. In the example in figure 27.4, if WS1 needs to access the PUBLIC directory on server NWS2 in domain DEPT-BC.SCS.COM, it can do so by creating a drive mapping H: to the PUBLIC directory of S2 as follows:

```
NWIPMAP H: = S2/SYS:PUBLIC@DEPT-BC.NOVELL.COM
```

Figure 27.4 shows a DNS server outside the NetWare/IP domains. This emphasizes the point that NetWare/IP domains are used for NetWare-based networks, and DNS servers can be used by NetWare and non-NetWare nodes (UNIX, VMS, MVS, and so on).

NetWare/IP Workstation Components

Figure 27.5 shows the NetWare workstation architecture that uses IPX only, and figure 27.6 shows the workstation architecture that uses TCP/IP to access NetWare services.

In figure 27.5, the bottom layer consists of the NIC hardware that represents layers 2 and 1 of the OSI model. The ODI interface is implemented by the Link Support Layer (LSL.COM), which communicates with the *Multiple Link Interface Driver* (MLID) for the NIC. The MLID communicates with the NIC hardware and with the Link Support Layer. The Link Support Layer provides a universal interface to the network adapter that allows a single protocol stack to establish communications with multiple NICs or multiple protocol stacks to communicate with a single NIC. For more details on the ODI interface see Chapter 1, "NetWare Protocols."

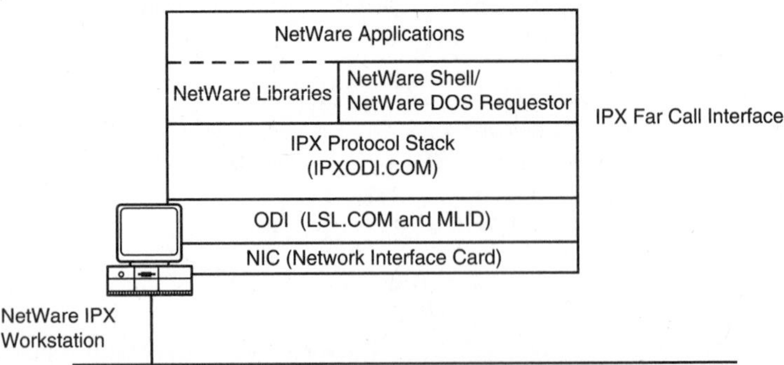

Figure 27.5
NetWare IPX client.

The IPXODI.COM implements the SPX/IPX protocols and provides the end-to-end transport protocols used by NetWare workstations. The IPXODI.COM exports an *Application Binary Interface* (ABI) called the *IPX Far Call Interface* that is backwards compatible with earlier versions of IPX.

The NetWare libraries can be used by applications to access the transport protocols directly. The NetWare shell and the DOS Requester are special purpose applications that provide file and print redirection.

The IPX Far Call Interface mechanism is needed for future and existing applications to run over TCP/IP. It also ensures backwards compatibility with earlier versions of IPX.

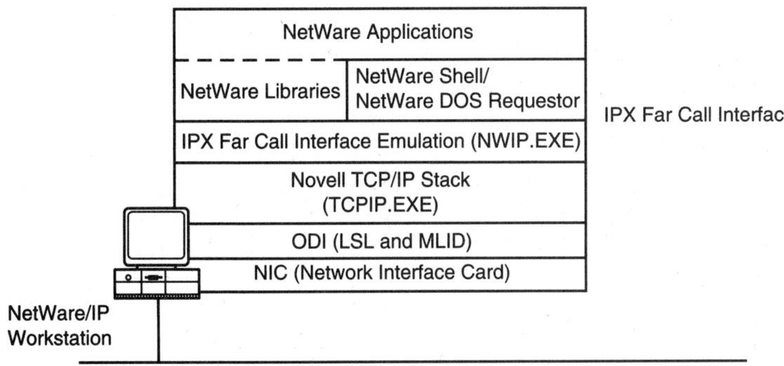

Figure 27.6
NetWare/IP client.

Comparing figure 27.6 with figure 27.5 shows that the IPXODI.COM is replaced with TCPIP.EXE. The TCPIP.EXE TSR implements the TCP/IP protocol stack. The TCP/IP protocol stack contains a transport layer (OSI layer 4) protocol called *User Datagram Protocol* (UDP). UDP is a simpler transport protocol than TCP and is more efficient for broadcasts and the request/reply nature of IP traffic.

Simple replacement of IPXODI.COM with TCPIP.EXE, however, is not sufficient to connect to a NetWare server because the ABI used by TCPIP.EXE is different from that used by the shell/DOS Requester and other NetWare applications for using IPXODI.COM. The goal is to leave the existing applications unmodified and yet be able to use TCPIP.EXE, which uses a different ABI. Remember that IPXODI.COM exports the IPX Far Call Interface used by existing NetWare applications. A new module called NWIP.EXE interfaces with TCPIP.EXE and is used to export the IPX Far Call Interface. This allows existing NetWare applications to use the IPX Far Call Interface. NWIP.EXE translates this into the ABI used by TCPIP.EXE. This architecture allows future NetWare applications to work transparently with TCP/IP as long as they use the IPX Far Call Interface ABI. You can use the NETX.EXE or the NetWare DOS Requester with TCPIP.EXE.

The only limitation to the NetWare/IP architecture is applications that use IPX-based NetBIOS. NetBIOS applications use the IPX broadcast mechanism. If TCP/IP is used as the transport protocol, these broadcasts are confined to the local IP subnet because IP routers do not forward non-directed UDP/IP broadcasts to other IP networks.

The memory used by TCPIP.EXE and NWIP.EXE is 17.2 KB and 15.1 KB, respectively.

The TCPIP.EXE used in NetWare/IP is the same protocol stack used in the LAN WorkPlace for DOS product. Novell claims the following advantages/features in using this TCP/IP implementation:

- Support for 64 TCP and 32 UDP sockets

- IP support for up to four ODI interfaces
- Support for up to three default routers on each interface
- Duplicate IP Address prevention because of the *Address Resolution Protocol* (ARP) mechanism detecting this problem
- Support for network interfaces that use ODI Drivers for Ethernet, Token-Ring, FDDI, ARCnet, SLIP, PPP, and IBM Broadband
- IP configuration options through a choice of BOOTP, RARP, or ASCII text file
- Troubleshooting utilities and support for SNMP
- Support for NetBIOS over TCP/IP using the enhanced "B-node" implementation of RFCs 1001 and 1002
- Support for the BSD Socket interface and WinSock interface

The Domain Name System

NetWare/IP contains the file NAMED.NLM that implements the *Domain Name System* (DNS). DNS is a distributed name-to-IP address database used on many TCP/IP-based networks including the Internet. When a workstation issues a TCP/IP command such as the following:

```
ftp ftp.novell.com
```

the name of the host ftp.novell.com needs to be resolved to the IP address of the host. The IP address is then used by the TCP/IP protocols to interact with the host. Users in general find the symbolic host name easier to remember than the IP address (32-bit number) of the host. The function of DNS is to translate the symbolic host name to an IP address number that can be used by the protocol software. The term *host* refers to any machine that implements a TCP/IP stack. The resolution of the host name to its equivalent IP address is performed by DNS protocols. These protocols and mechanisms are described in RFCs 1034, 1035, 1101, and 1183.

The IP address is a four-byte (32-bit) number assigned to every interface used by the IP protocol. If a NetWare server has two network interfaces to which IP is bound, a different IP address must be assigned to each of the boards. Most workstations have a single NIC, and if IP is used over this interface, a unique IP address must be assigned for the network interface.

The 32-bit IP address is usually written in a special format called the *dotted decimal notation.* In this notation, each of the four bytes that make up the IP address is expressed as a decimal number. The largest number contained in a byte is 255, and the smallest 0. Therefore, each of the bytes in the dotted decimal notation is a number between 0 and 255, inclusive.

The following is an example of an IP address in a dotted decimal notation:

144.19.74.201

The decimal number 144 corresponds to the most significant byte (left-most byte) of the 32-bit IP address, and the number 201 corresponds to the least significant byte (right-most byte) of the IP address. The dotted decimal number notation is much simpler to read than the 32-bit number translated as one decimal number. For example, the IP address also can be represented as the single decimal number: 2417183433.

DNS is implemented as a distributed database for looking up name-to-IP address correspondence. Another way of performing the name look up is to keep the name-to-IP address information in a static file. On UNIX systems, this static file is the /etc/hosts file. On NetWare servers, this static file is kept in the SYS:ETC/HOSTS file.

A sample host file format is shown next:

```
# Local network host addresses
#ident "@(#)hosts 1.1 - 88/05/17"
#
127.0.0.1       local localhost
144.19.74.1     sparc1 sp1
144.19.74.2     sparc2 sp2
144.19.74.3     sparc3 sp3
144.19.74.4     sparc4 sp4
144.19.74.5     sparc5 sp5
144.19.74.6     sparc6 sp6
144.19.74.7     sparc7 sp7
144.19.75.1     sparc8 sp8
144.19.75.2     sparc9 sp9
144.19.75.3     sparc10 sp10
144.19.75.4     sparc11 sp11
144.19.75.5     sparc12 sp12
144.19.75.6     sparc13 sp13
144.19.75.7     sparc14 sp14
144.19.74.101   cdos
144.19.74.102   server1 s386 nw
144.19.74.103   spws sparcsrv sps ss
144.19.74.201   sparcc1 spc1
144.19.74.202   sparcc2 spc2
```

The IP address 127.0.0.1 is a special address called the *loopback address.* Packets sent to this address never reach the network cable. The loopback address can be used for diagnostic purposes to verify that the internal code path through the TCP/IP protocols is working. It also can be used by client applications to communicate with software programs running on the same machine.

Each <IP Address, Host name> pair is expressed on a single line using the style shown in the host file. The multiple host names for the host are alias names. The protocol software, if configured to perform name resolution using this static host file, looks up the information for resolving a name. Consider the following command:

```
telnet sp14
```

The protocol software uses the following entry in the host file to resolve the name sp14:

```
144.19.75.7      sparc14 sp14
```

The name sp14 is an alias for the host name sparc14. The corresponding IP address is 144.19.75.7. The protocol software resolves the name sp14 to 144.19.75.7. The preceding command then becomes the following:

```
telnet 144.19.75.7
```

A number of problems exist with the static host file approach. As the number of hosts on a network becomes large. It becomes increasingly difficult to keep this file up to date. Also, many organizations have more than one network Administrator. It is difficult for these Administrators to coordinate with each other every time host files need to be changed. Even keeping this information in a large central static file becomes quickly unmanageable as the number of entries in this file becomes large.

The DNS system was developed to overcome the problems of name resolution on a large IP network. It provides a distributed database of names and IP addresses. The names could be host names or names of mail exchanger hosts. It also has provisions for keeping text descriptions of host names and for providing name resolution for other protocol families besides TCP/IP (such as Chaos net, XNS, and so on). It is, however, used predominantly for resolving host names for the TCP/IP protocols.

Part of the scheme used in DNS refers to the use of hierarchical names, in which names are organized into a hierarchical tree. At the top of the tree is the root domain named by the period symbol (.). Because all names have this common root, the period is omitted when specifying the hierarchical name in most TCP/IP applications. Below the root domain are top-level domains (see fig. 27.7). These reflect how names are organized. Table 27.1 shows examples of top level domains.

The two-letter designations are assigned to the country as per the CCITT standards. These are the same country designation used for specifying country objects in NetWare Directory Services. Below the top level domains are middle level domains. A number of middle level names can exist. Each name is separated from each other by use of the period (which can never occur as part of the name of a domain). The length of a complete domain name such as the following:

```
world.std.com
```

cannot exceed 255 characters. In the name world.std.com, the name of the host is as follows:

```
world
```

The following name is in the domain:

```
std.com
```

If another host is in the same domain whose name is "sparky," its *fully qualified name* (FQN) is as follows:

```
sparky.std.com
```

Many of the middle-level names refer to names of organizations. An organization is free to define subdomains within the organization. If it does this, it should provide appropriate name services to resolve names in these subdomains. For example, consider the organization SCS that has the following domain name:

```
scs.com
```

If this organization has separate networks for its Corporate, Marketing, and Research arms, it can define three separate subdomains named CORP, MKTG, RESCH, and provide a DNS server or a number of DNS servers to resolve names on its networks. The domains in this case are as follows:

```
corp.scs.com
mktg.scs.com
resch.scs.com
```

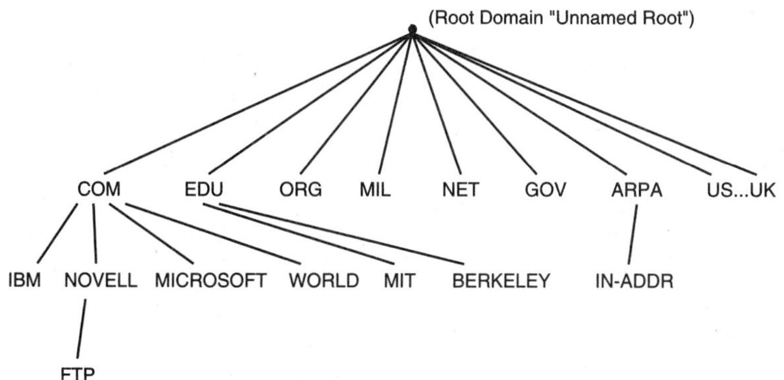

Figure 27.7
Hierarchical names in DNS.

27

Table 27.1
Top-Level Domains

Top Level Domain	Description
COM	Commercial organization
EDU	Education institution. Universities, schools, and so on
MIL	Military
GOV	Government (United States)
NET	Network provider
ORG	Organization

continues

Table 27.1, Continued
Top-Level Domains

Top Level Domain	Description
ARPA	ARPANET; now historical; still used for inverse address mapping
US	Country U.S.A
CA	Country Canada
UK	Country United Kingdom
DE	Country Germany
SE	Country Sweden
FR	Country France
IN	Country India
CN	Country China
JA	Country Japan

Although a DNS server is not required for each domain, it is common to have one or more for each domain being served. Figure 27.7 shows several DNS servers for the root domain. These servers would know about names of the top-level domains such as COM, EDU, MIL, ORG, NET, and so on. Several DNS servers can be used for a domain to perform load balancing, avoid unnecessary network traffic, and for reliability in case the primary DNS server was not available. The COM domain would have one or more DNS servers that knows the names of all commercial organizations in the COM domain. Within the COM domain, a subdomain such as IBM.COM has its own DNS servers for that domain. Hosts within a domain query the local DNS server for the domain to resolve names. For example, the host WORLD.STD.COM queries the DNS server for the domain STD.COM to find out the IP address of the host FTP.NOVELL.COM or the IP address of ATHENA.SCS.ORG. When this query is resolved, the results are usually cached locally for a configurable period of time.

The DNS servers for a domain need to resolve names of hosts in their domains. They do not need to know about hosts in subdomains if DNS servers are defined for subdomains. Secondary DNS servers in a domain must know the IP address of the primary server in the domain it can contact for resolving a name query. A DNS server must also know the IP address of the parent DNS server.

Relationship between DNS Domains and NetWare/IP Domains

A NetWare/IP domain is defined as a collection of NetWare/IP servers and clients that receive SAP/RIP information provided by one or more DSS servers in that domain. A NetWare network can be partitioned into multiple NetWare/IP domains. A NetWare/IP domain must exist in the context of a DNS domain. A NetWare/IP domain is created by creating a DNS subdomain with the following properties:

- The DNS subdomain must be a subdomain of an existing DNS domain.
- The DNS subdomain cannot have subdomains.

After creating the NetWare/IP domain, you must configure NetWare/IP nodes that belong to this domain with the NetWare/IP domain name.

The organization SCS has a registered domain SCS.ORG. This organization has two existing DNS subdomains for two separate networks for the Engineering and Marketing department as follows:

```
ENG.SCS.ORG
MKTG.SCS.ORG
```

SCS decides to have a NetWare/IP domain cover the entire Engineering network and two NetWare/IP domains for the Marketing network. To create these NetWare/IP domains, you must first create DNS subdomains. For the DNS domain ENG.SCS.ORG, you can create a NetWare/IP domain called the following:


```
NWIP.ENG.SCS.ORG
```

For the Marketing network, you must create two NetWare/IP domains. Therefore, you must first create two DNS subdomains of MKTG.SCS.ORG. You can do this by creating the following domains:

```
NWIP1.MKTG.SCS.ORG
NWIP2.MKTG.SCS.ORG
```

After creating these DNS subdomains, you must configure the NetWare/IP nodes and DSS servers that are in the NetWare/IP domain with the names of these subdomains.

Examining the DSS Server

To provide SAP/RIP information to a NetWare/IP network, you must have at least one DSS server in a NetWare/IP domain. The DSS server holds a database of SAP/RIP information for a NetWare/IP domain. The information in the DSS server can be replicated on multiple DSS servers to improve performance across WAN links and to increase reliability. This section helps you understand how the DSS server updates its information and how this information is disseminated to other NetWare/IP nodes. It also covers the issue of DSS database replication for improved reliability.

Updating DSS Servers

In a IPX-based NetWare server, NetWare services such as File, Print, and Database services advertise their existence using the SAP protocol. These services send SAP broadcast packets every 60 seconds. (The actual value is configurable, but 60 seconds is the default.) The broadcast packets are sent out over every network interface to which IPX is bound.

In NetWare/IP networks, NetWare services also advertise themselves using SAP. These SAP packets are sent directly to the DSS servers using UDP/IP packets.

When a NetWare server boots, it sends a SAP broadcast advertising its existence. If the server is configured as a NetWare/IP server, it also sends a SAP packet directly to the nearest DSS server using the UDP/IP protocol. The NetWare/IP server sends this information to the DSS server every five minutes (the value is configurable). If the DSS server does not receive the SAP refresh information, it times out the information.

Disseminating DSS Information

In an IPX-based network, NetWare servers listen for SAP packets and cache this information. They then create temporary bindery entries that list the services seen by the server. NetWare IPX clients and applications locate these services by looking up the bindery information stored on the server.

NetWare/IP servers also keep a list of available services in the NetWare bindery. They do this by periodically requesting a download of this information from the DSS server. The download occurs at a configurable time interval whose default value is five minutes.

Replicating the DSS Database

To increase the reliability and availability of the DSS information, you can have several secondary DSS servers in a NetWare/IP domain. If the primary DSS server is unavailable or too busy to respond to requests by NetWare/IP servers, the secondary server can be used to provide the desired information.

To provide consistency of the DSS information, the DSS database is replicated to all the DSS servers in the NetWare/IP domain. In a large network consisting of slow WAN links, performance can be improved by avoiding sending requests for DSS information across the WAN links. This can be achieved by installing a local DSS server on each network so that NetWare/IP nodes can query the local DSS server instead of querying a remote DSS server separated by the slow WAN link. The primary DSS server holds the master copy of the DSS server, and the secondary DSS servers hold a Read/Write replica.

SAP/RIP information can be received by DSS servers at different times. This can result in the DSS servers not having the same information. To keep the DSS servers synchronized, the secondary DSS servers contact the primary DSS server at periodic intervals to synchronize their information. If the DSS databases are out of synchronization, the synchronization process commences. If at any time, connectivity between primary and secondary DSS servers is lost, the secondary DSS server periodically attempts to establish a connection and initiate synchronization. If the secondary DSS server is activated after being down, it attempts to synchronize with the primary DSS when it comes up.

To ensure that synchronization is done correctly, each DSS server maintains a database version number for the information stored on it at any time. The database version number is changed whenever the database is changed by new information. The database version numbers help the DSS servers determine if the database is out of synchronization. During synchronization, the secondary DSS server uploads to the primary DSS any new records received since the last synchronization. It also downloads any records not in its database. Only changed, deleted, or new records are exchanged and not the entire database.

Understanding NetWare/IP Installation

The amount of memory needed to run a NetWare/IP server depends on the components loaded at the NetWare server, and the number of NetWare/IP servers configured in its NetWare/IP domain. If *N* is the number of NetWare/IP servers, the server memory requirements can be calculated using the formulas in table 27.2. The amount of disk space needed on the NetWare server is about 2 MB on the SYS: volume.

Table 27.2
Memory Requirements on a NetWare/IP Server
N = Number of NetWare/IP Servers in a NetWare/IP Domain

Type of NetWare Service	Memory Requirements (Bytes)
NetWare/IP	*N**380 + 75000
DSS on NetWare 3.1*x*	*N**440 + 450000
DSS on NetWare 4.*x*	*N**440 + 710000

NetWare/IP at the workstation requires approximately 2 MB of free disk space for DOS and 3.2 MB of free disk space for Windows. The TCPIP.EXE requires 17.2 KB of RAM, and the NWIP.EXE requires 15.1 KB of RAM. Using memory managers, these components can be loaded in upper memory.

Installing NetWare/IP

You must log in as SUPERVISOR (NetWare 3.1*x*) or Admin (NetWare 4.*x*). If installing on a NetWare 4.*x* server, you must have the bindery context set using the following server console command:

```
SET BINDERY CONTEXT = context
```

The bindery context is normally set in the AUTOEXEC.NCF file. To view the current server bindery context, use the following command:

```
SET BINDERY CONTEXT
```

You can install the NetWare/IP from a DOS workstation or the NetWare server.

Installing NetWare/IP from a DOS Workstation

To install from a DOS workstation, you must have REMOTE and RSPX running at the server. This can be done using the following commands:

```
LOAD REMOTE password
LOAD RSPX
```

The steps for installing are as follows:

1. Log in with Supervisor access to the server.

2. Create a directory called NWIP1 on one of the NetWare volumes.

3. Use NCOPY to copy the diskette labeled NWIP1 to the NWIP1 directory as follows:

   ```
   NCOPY A: SYS:NWIP1 /S /E
   ```

4. Run RCONSOLE.

5. Select the server to install NetWare/IP.

6. Enter **REMOTE** ***password*** to connect to the server console.

7. Proceed with instructions in the following section "Installing NetWare/IP from a Server."

Installing NetWare/IP from a Server

The steps for installing are as follows:

1. At the server console, run the INSTALL program by issuing the following command:

   ```
   LOAD INSTALL
   ```

2. On a NetWare 3.*1x* server, make the following selections:

   - Select Product Options.
   - Press Ins.

   On a NetWare 4.*x* server, make the following selections:

   - Select Maintenance/Selective Install.
   - Select Product Options.
   - Press Ins.

3. When prompted to insert the disk, enter the disk or alternate location for the source files.

On a NetWare 3.1*x* server, you can simply override the default source location (A:) by typing in the new path.

On a NetWare 4.*x* server, you can press F3 to specify a different source (such as SYS:NWIP1).

4. You are informed about a README file. Press Esc to continue.
5. Select No when asked if you want to exit installation. Select Yes if you want to read the README file and start the installation again.
6. If TCP/IP has not been configured, you are asked to switch to the console screen and configure it. You should also make changes to the AUTOEXEC.NCF file to configure TCP/IP. Press Esc to continue.

   If you are performing installation locally at the server, press ALT+ESC to switch to the console.

   If you are performing installations remotely, use the numeric key pad <+> or <-> key on NetWare 3.1*x* servers, and ALT+F3 or ALT+F4 on NetWare 4.*x* servers.

   To configure TCP/IP perform the following commands:

```
LOAD LANDriver NAME=IPNET FRAME=ETHERNET_II (for Ethernet)
LOAD LANDriver NAME=IPNET FRAME=TOKEN-RING_SNAP (for Token Ring)
BIND IP TO IPNET ADDR=IPAddress
```

   If you need to configure for subnetting, read Chapter 3, "Bridging and Routing," to see how to perform subnetting. Also, Chapter 26, "Internetworking," contains insights on performing subnetting.

7. Enter the local host name. The default is the name of the server. Accept the default.

   The INSTALL program begins copying the NetWare/IP files to hard disk and displays the file name being copied.

8. Enter the drive path for booting the server. This should be the C: drive on the NetWare server. Accept this value and press Enter.
9. Press Esc a few times to exit the INSTALL program. Confirm that you want to exit installation.
10. Make sure that your AUTOEXEC.NCF file contains the TCP/IP configuration.
11. Down the server.
12. Restart the server.

Proceed to the next section on configuring NetWare/IP software.

Configuring NetWare/IP

After you install NetWare/IP, it must be configured before it can be used. Configuring NetWare/IP involves a number of steps. One of the first steps is using the UNICON utility to perform the following:

- Configure NetWare/IP servers
- Configure DNS servers
- Configure DSS servers
- Monitor and fine-tune performance

Using UNICON

You can start UNICON by typing the following command at the server console:


```
LOAD UNICON
```

If asked to log in, specify the server name on which you want to perform NetWare/IP configuration. You must also specify the Supervisor account name and password.

Figure 27.8 shows the main UNICON screen. You can use the option on this screen to perform most NetWare/IP configuration tasks.

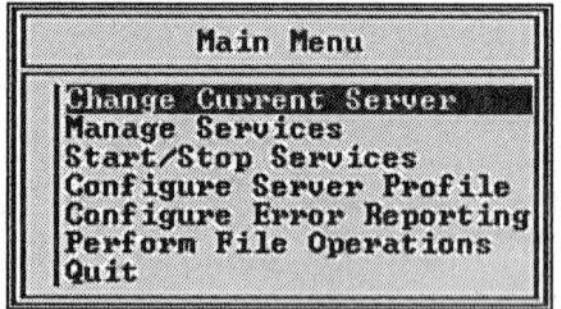

Figure 27.8
Main UNICON screen.

The *Change Current Server* option is used to log in to other NetWare servers for performing NetWare/IP configuration.

The *Manage Services* option is used to configure DNS server and Host information and NetWare/IP domains.

The *Start/Stop Services* option starts services not running, and stops services that are running.

The *Configure Server Profile* option is used to configure server parameters.

The *Configure Error Reporting* option is used to set the error reporting level for messages reported to the Product Kernel screen or the AUDIT.LOG file. It also can be used to specify the maximum size of the AUDIT.LOG file. Setting the error levels can be useful for troubleshooting NetWare/IP configuration.

The *Performing File Operations* option is used to copy files through FTP, edit files, set up the DNS nameserver database, and create text files from the database.

Configuring DNS Server

The DNS server must be configured before a NetWare/IP server or DSS server can be activated. You can configure DNS servers in the following two ways:

- Configure DNS server to run on a NetWare server.
- Configure DNS server to run on another operating system. An example choice is to use *Berkeley Internet Domain Service* (BIND) available on UNIX or DOS (from FTP Software, Inc).

Configuring DNS on a NetWare Server and Creating NetWare/IP Domains

The DNS server must contain IP Address and Host name mappings. You can enter these names directly into the DNS database. Each entry in the DNS database is called a *resource record.*

You must first create the DNS Master Database. You can do this by performing the following steps:

1. LOAD UNICON.
2. Select Perform File Operations (see fig. 27.9).
3. Select Initialize Local Nameservers (see fig. 27.10).

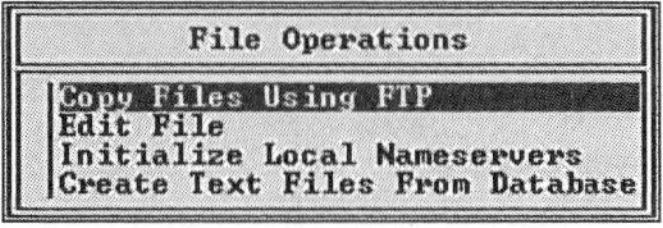

Figure 27.9
File Operations screen.

Figure 27.10
DNS Server Initialization Data screen.

4. Enter the *Fully Qualified Name* (FQN) for the DNS domain. The following is an example:

   SCS.COM

5. Wait a few seconds for the `Please Wait` message to disappear, and press Esc.
6. You are asked if you want to initialize the DNS database. Select Yes.
7. You see a status message similar to figure 27.11. Press Esc to continue.

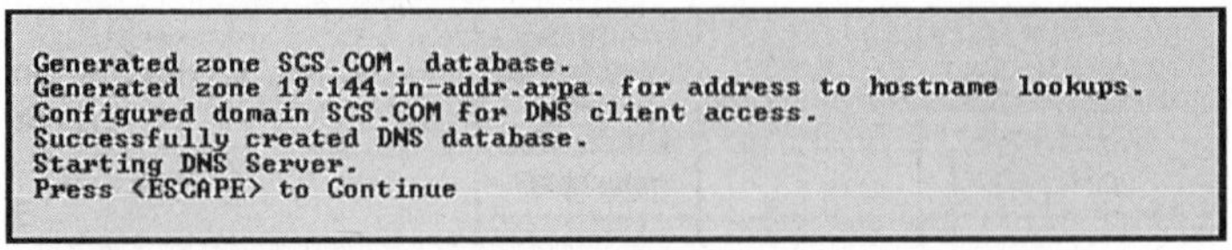

Figure 27.11
DNS database creation status messages.

```
Generated zone SCS.COM. database.
Generated zone 19.144.in-addr.arpa. for address to hostname lookups.
Configured domain SCS.COM for DNS client access.
Successfully created DNS database.
Starting DNS Server.
Press <ESCAPE> to Continue
```

At this point, you created the database for the domain name and started the DNS server. The database initially contains just the hostname record for the NetWare/IP server.

8. Press Esc a few times to get back to the main UNICON menu.

You can now enter hosts information for DSS severs in the domain that you just created by performing the following steps:

1. Select Manage Services.
2. Select Hosts. You should see a list of DSS server hosts in the DNS database (see fig. 27.12).

27

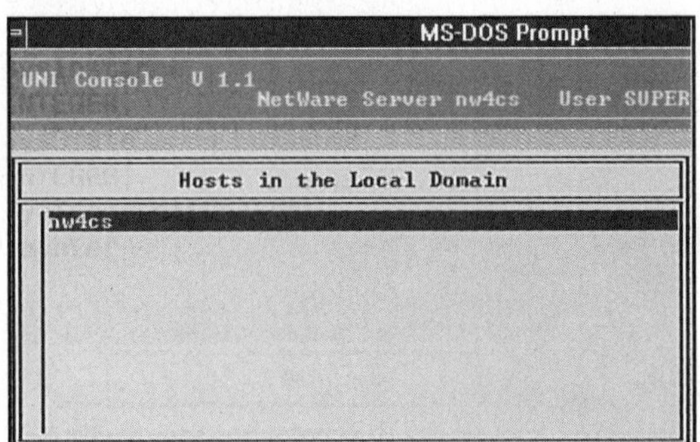

Figure 27.12
Hosts in local domain.

You can display information about a specific DSS host by highlighting a host and pressing Enter (see fig. 27.13).

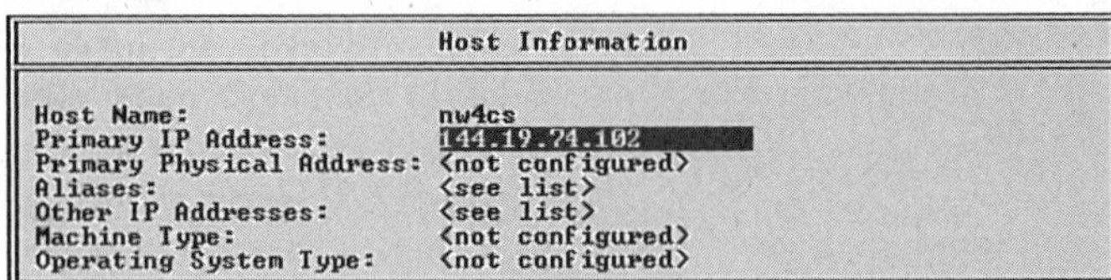

Figure 27.13
Host Information screen.

3. To add additional secondary DSS servers' host names, press Ins on the screen in figure 27.12. To modify entries for a host, use the screen shown in figure 27.13.
4. Go to the Manger Services menu option. (Press Esc if you have just performed step 12.)
5. Select DNS Server (see fig. 27.14).

Figure 27.14
DNS Server Administration screen.

6. Select Configure Master Database (see fig. 27.15).

7. The list shows the master domain you have just created. You need to add to it a DNS subdomain for the NetWare/IP domain. To do this press Ins and enter the name of the NetWare/IP domain. If the master domain zone name was SCS.COM., you can enter the NetWare/IP domain as follows:

   ```
   NWIP.SCS.COM.
   ```

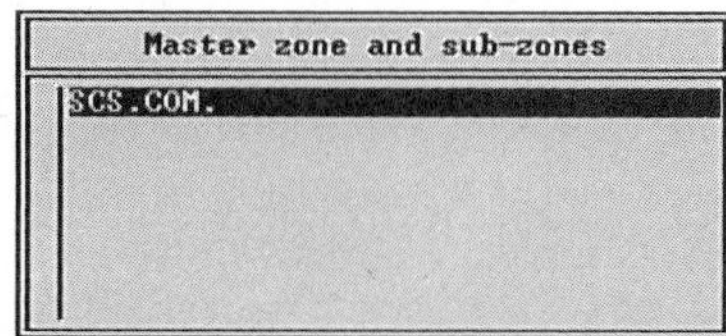

Figure 27.15
Master zone and sub-zone list.

8. Highlight the newly created NetWare/IP domain from the list of master zones and sub-zones and press Enter.

   You should see an empty list of nameservers for this subdomain (see fig. 27.16).

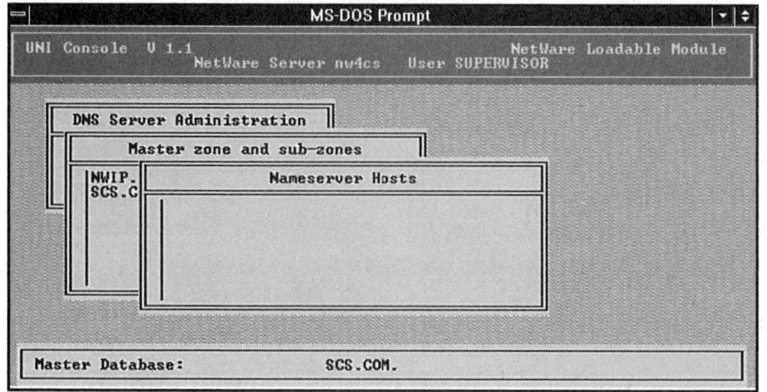

Figure 27.16
Nameservers in subdomain.

9. Press Ins.

   You are asked to enter the fully qualified name of the nameserver host (see fig. 27.17). Enter the name of the primary DSS server for the NetWare/IP domain. On a small network, this

DSS server can be the same as the DNS server. For example, if the name of the DSS server is NW4CS, its fully qualified name is as follows:

```
NW4CS.SCS.COM
```

UNICON automatically appends a period for the root domain.

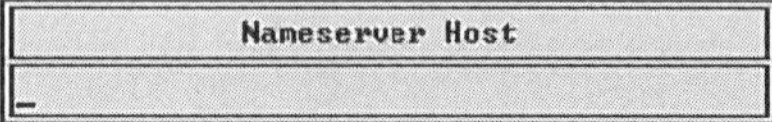

Figure 27.17
Adding DSS server to the NetWare/IP domain.

10. Press Enter after adding the name. You should see the name server added to the list of nameservers for the NetWare/IP domain (see fig. 27.18).

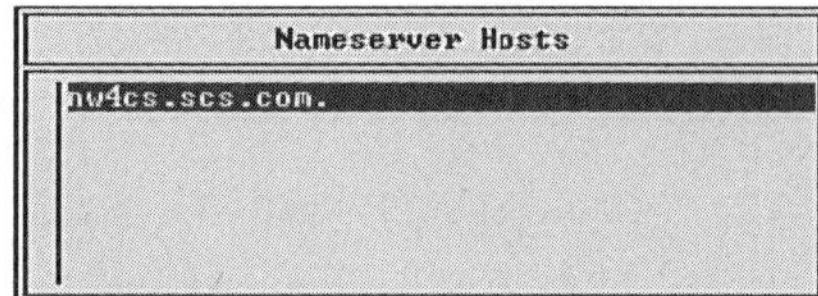

Figure 27.18
DSS server added to the NetWare/IP domain.

11. Repeat the steps 9 and 10 to add optional secondary DSS servers to the NetWare/IP domain.

12. Repeat steps 6 to 8 to create other NetWare/IP domains.

13. After creating a NetWare/IP subdomain (also DNS subdomain), you must inform the DNS server for the parent domain about the new DNS subdomain you just created. The parent DNS server can be on another node administered by someone else. You have to request the DNS administrator for the parent domain to add your subdomain to the parent's database. In the example in this guided tour, the parent DNS server is on the same server as the DSS server, and figure 27.19 shows that the master domain SCS.COM. knows about the subdomain (subzone) NWIP.SCS.COM.

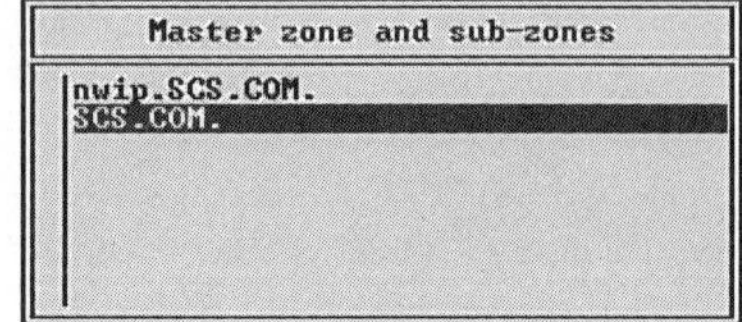

Figure 27.19
Master domain knows about new NetWare/IP domain.

When a new domain record is added to the parent DNS server, the NetWare DNS server automatically links into the DNS hierarchy by using the information stored in SYS:ETC\DNS\ROOT.DB.

14. Any time you add records in the DNS database, you must restart the DNS service, so that it can initialize its cache with the new information.

To restart the DNS service, you must first stop it and then start it again. The following steps outline how you can accomplish this:

1. Go to the main menu of UNICON.

2. Select Start/Stop Services.

3. If the DNS service appears in the list of Running Services (see fig. 27.20), highlight it and press Del. Answer Yes to the query verifying if you want to stop the service.

Figure 27.20
List of running services.

4. To start the DNS service again, press Ins on the list of running services. You should see a list of available services that you can run (see fig. 27.21). Highlight DNS Server and press Enter. This activates the DNS Service, and it appears in the list of Running Services.

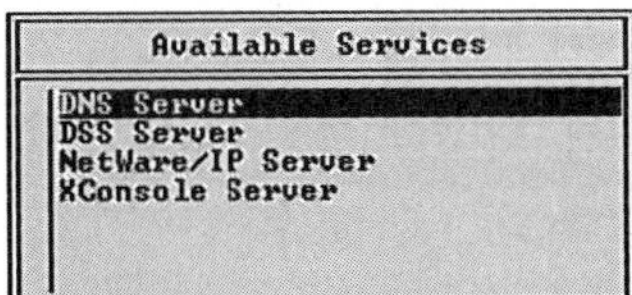

Figure 27.21
List of Available Services to run.

Creating a Replica of the DNS Database

For reliability, you may want to create one or more replicas of the DNS database on other servers. The following steps outline how you can do this:

1. LOAD UNICON.

2. Select Manage Services.

3. Select DNS Server.

4. Select Configure Replica Databases. You should see list of replica databases that initially is empty.

5. Press Ins to create a replica of the DNS database on the server. A form for importing database information appears (see fig. 27.12).

Figure 27.22
Replica Database Information form.

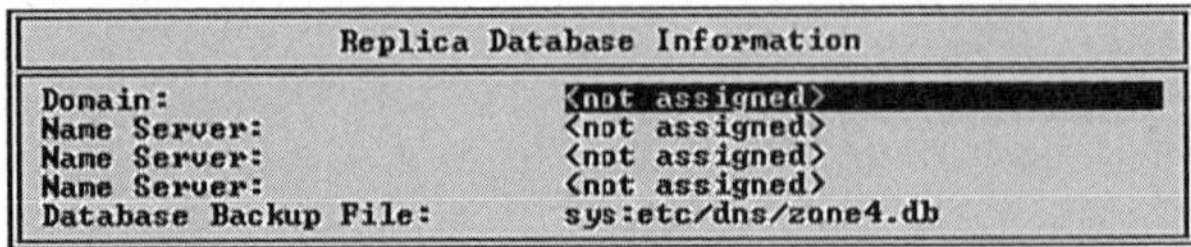

```
Replica Database Information

Domain:                      <not assigned>
Name Server:                 <not assigned>
Name Server:                 <not assigned>
Name Server:                 <not assigned>
Database Backup File:        sys:etc/dns/zone4.db
```

The *Domain* field specifies the name of the domain for which this replica has a copy.

The *Nameserver* field contains the IP address of the DNS master nameserver. Three Nameserver fields are provided to enter IP addresses of additional DNS nameservers.

The *Database Backup File* field contains the name of the file that contains the backup copy of the database. The default file name is sys:etc/doc/zones.dbf. You can change this to specify a different file name.

6. After filling in the form, press Esc. If asked to save your changes, answer Yes.

Configuring DNS Servers on Non-NetWare Platforms

If you are using a non-NetWare platform as a DNS server for a domain, you need to consult the documentation for DNS services for that operating system.

On UNIX systems, DNS is implemented by BIND. On BSD-derived UNIX, this is implemented by running the following program:

```
named
```

On SVR4 UNIX, the following is implemented by the program:

```
in.named
```

DOS-based implementation of BIND is available from FTP Software, Inc. It runs as a TSR called NAMED.

BIND uses a file called /etc/named.boot that contains a list of other files for holding the zone records for the DNS database. FTP Software's BIND uses the file name NAMED.BOO.

The DNS zone files are text files and have a special format. You can refer to the DNS RFCs referenced earlier for information on the syntax of these text records, or consult your operating system's implementation.

If you are using non-NetWare DNS servers for the master domain, you must add a record in its database for the new subdomains that you created for NetWare/IP. This usually involves using a text editor and adding a record to the zone data file for the DNS server. If you created a primary DSS named nw4cs.scs.com (IP address 144.19.73.102) and a secondary DSS named ucs.scs.com (IP address 144.19.74.103) for the NetWare/IP domain nwip.scs.com, add the following records to the zone data file for non-NetWare DNS:

```
# Domain/Host    Class    RR Type    Data
nwip.scs.com.    IN        NS         nw4cs.scs.com.# Primary DSS
```

```
nwip.scs.com.     IN      NS      ucs.scs.com.     # Secondary DSS
nw4cs.scs.com.    IN      A       144.19.74.102    # Host record
ucs.scs.com.      IN      A       144.19.74.103    # Host record
```

On most DNS implementations, you must restart the DNS service before the changes are registered.

Configuring DSS Server

After the DNS server is configured, you can configure the DSS server. This involves configuring the primary and secondary DSS servers and starting the DSS service.

Configuring Primary and Secondary DSS Servers

The following steps outline the DSS configuration procedure:

1. LOAD UNICON.

2. Select Manage Services.

3. Select NetWare/IP.

   If your DNS server is set up on a different server from the DSS server, you see a form that enables you to make the DSS server a client of the DNS server (on another machine). This form has a DNS Domain field and three Nameserver fields.

   The DNS Domain field is used to specify the name of your DNS domain. The first Nameserver field specifies the IP address of the server to contact to resolve name queries. The other Nameserver fields represent the order in which other DNS servers are contacted to resolve names, if the answer is not found in the first name server.

4. Select Configure Primary DSS. The Primary DSS Configuration form appears (see fig. 27.23).

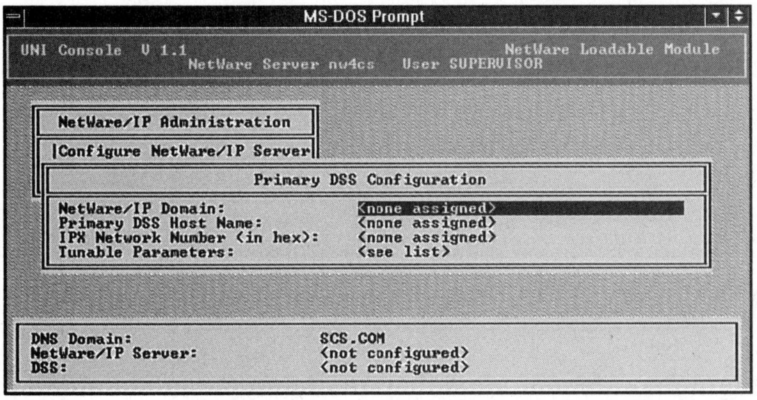

Figure 27.23
Primary DSS Configuration form.

The NetWare/IP Domain field contains the name of the NetWare/IP domain. All NetWare/ IP nodes (clients and servers) are members of this NetWare/IP domain. The NetWare/IP Domain, for example, can be the following:

```
nwip.scs.com.
```

The Primary DSS Hostname field contains the fully qualified name of the primary DSS host. For example, it can have a name such as the following:

```
nw4cs.SCS.COM.
```

The IPX Network Number (in hex) field contains the IPX network number assigned to the DSS service. This number must be different from the IPX internal network numbers assigned to NetWare 3.*x* and 4.*x* servers and from network numbers assigned to any IPX interface.

Selecting the Tunable Parameter field brings up a form for tuning DSS parameters (see fig. 27.24).


```
Tunable Parameters

UDP Port Number for NetWare/IP Service:          43981
SAP/RIP Database Synchronization Interval:       5        minutes
Maximum UDP Retransmissions:                     3
UDP Checksum?                                    No
```

Figure 27.24
Tunable DSS Parameters form.

The UDP Port Number for NetWare/IP Service field can be used to specify the UDP port number used by the NetWare/IP service. The default value is 43981. Two successive port numbers are assigned. The first port number 43981 (default) is used for packet transmission. The second port number 43982 (default) is used for SAP/RIP queries.

The SAP/RIP Database Synchronization Interval field can be used to specify how often a NetWare/IP server queries DSS for updated information. The value can range from 1 to 60 minutes with a default of five minutes.

The Maximum UDP Retransmissions field can be used to specify how many times a packet should be resent if no acknowledgment is received for the packet. The value can range from 1 to 48 minutes with a default of three minutes.

The UDP Checksum? field determines whether the UDP packet uses the checksum field (set to Yes or No). The default value is No. LANs have a reliable transmission rate, and a value of No gives maximum performance. If you suspect that the physical network transport is unreliable, you may want to set the value to Yes. If set to Yes, UDP checksums are performed over the data packet. Checksum errors cause a packet to be rejected and retransmitted.

If any of the DSS tunable parameters are changed, you must stop and restart all DSS servers for the domain. You should also unload NWIP.EXE and reload it at each workstation.

5. After configuring the primary DSS, press Esc. If asked to verify that you want to set up this host as a primary DSS server, answer Yes.

6. The next step is to configure any optional secondary DSS servers.

To configure Secondary DSS servers make the following selections:

1. Select Managing Services.
2. Select NetWare/IP.
3. Select Configure Secondary DSS. A secondary DSS server form with the following fields appears:

   Field NetWare/IP Domain contains the name of the NetWare/IP domain to which the secondary DSS belongs.

   Field DSS Primary Host specifies the name or IP address of the primary DSS server.

After the DSS servers are configured, you must start them by performing the following steps:

1. Go to the main menu of UNICON.
2. Select Start/Stop Services.
3. If the DSS server appears in the list of Running Services, highlight it and press Del. Answer Yes to the query confirming that you want to stop the service.
4. To start the DSS service again, press Ins on the list of Running Services. A list of available services that you can run appears. Highlight DSS Server and press Enter. This activates the DSS Service, and it appears in the list of Running Services. Starting the DSS server also starts the DNS server (if the DNS server is not running).

Changing DNS Servers Associated with DSS Servers

UNICON provides a Server Profile Form that can be used to change DNS server names accessed by DSS servers.

To access the Server Profile Form, perform the following steps:

1. LOAD UNICON.
2. Select Configure Server Profile from the main menu (see fig. 27.25).

```
                       Server Profile
Host IP Name                 :  nw4cs
Primary IP Address           :  144.19.74.102
Primary Subnet Mask          :  255.255.0.0
Operating System Version     :  NetWare 4.1
Time Zone                    :  US Pacific Standard Time
Synchronization Interval     :  60         seconds
DNS Access                   :  <enabled>
   Domain                    :  SCS.COM
   Primary Server            :  144.19.74.102
   Secondary Server          :  <not assigned>
   Tertiary Server           :  <not assigned>
```

Figure 27.25
Server Profile form.

The Host IP Name field contains the IP hostname of the NetWare/IP server created during NetWare/IP installation. This field cannot be selected. It is for informational purposes only.

The Primary IP Address field contains the IP address of the NetWare/IP server created during NetWare/IP installation. This field cannot be selected. It is for informational purposes only.

The Primary Subnet Mask field contains the subnet mask for the IP interface for the NetWare/IP server created during installation. This field cannot be selected. It is for informational purposes only.

The Operating System Version field contains the name of the operating system on the specified host. This field cannot be selected. It is for informational purposes only.

The Time Zone field is used to select one of the listed time zones. Selecting this field displays a list of available time zones (see fig. 27.26).

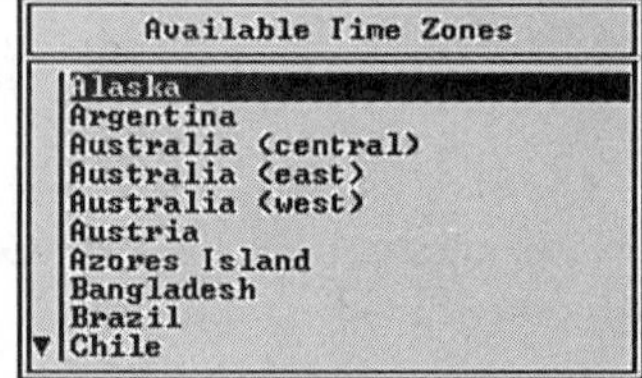

Figure 27.26
Time Zones for the NetWare/IP server.

You can add additional time zones by editing the text file SYS:ETC/TIMEZN. This editing can be performed by selecting the following options in UNICON:

1. Select Perform File Operations.
2. Select Edit File.

The contents of this file are as follows. The first column displays the hour offset and the second column the minute offset from GMT. Negative offsets are used for the Eastern hemisphere, and positive offsets are used for the Western hemisphere.

```
0  00     England
0  00     Portugal
-1 00     Austria
-1 00     France
-1 00     Germany
-1 00     Italy
-1 00     Spain
-2 00     Egypt
-2 00     Finland
-2 00     Greece
-2 00     Turkey
-2 00     Israel
-3 00     Kenya
-3 00     Saudi
-4 00     UAE
```

```
-5    00    Maldives
-4    30    Pakistan
-6    00    Bangladesh
-5    30    India
-6    00    Myanmar
-7    00    Thailand
-7    00    Indonesia
-8    00    Australia (west)
-9    30    Australia (central)
-8    00    China
-8    00    HongKong
-8    00    Singapore
-9    00    Japan
-9    00    Korea
-10   00    Australia (east)
-10   00    Guam
-11   00    New Caledonia
-12   00    Fiji
-12   00    New Zealand
11    00    Western Samoa
10    00    Hawaii
9 00        Alaska
8 00        US Pacific Standard Time
7 00        US Mountain Standard Time
6 00        US Central Standard Time
5 00        US Eastern Standard Time
9 00        US PST + daylight savings
8 00        US MST + daylight savings
7 00        US CST + daylight savings
6 00        US EST + daylight savings
4 00        Chile
4 00        Venezuela
3 00        Argentina
3 00        Brazil
2 00        Fernando de Noronha
1 00        Azores Island
-12   00    GMT -12
-11   00    GMT -11
-10   00    GMT -10
-9 00       GMT -9
-8 00       GMT -8
-7 00       GMT -7
-6 00       GMT -6
-5 00       GMT -5
-4 00       GMT -4
-3 00       GMT -3
-2 00       GMT -2
-1 00       GMT -1
0 00        GMT
1 00        GMT +1
2 00        GMT +2
3 00        GMT +3
```

```
4  00      | GMT +4  |
5  00      | GMT +5  |
6  00      | GMT +6  |
7  00      | GMT +7  |
8  00      | GMT +8  |
9  00      | GMT +9  |
10 00      | GMT +10 |
11 00      | GMT +11 |
12 00      | GMT +12 |
```

The Synchronization Interval field is the number of seconds at which the NetWare/IP server checks the SYS:ETC\NFSUSERS, SYS:NFSGROUP, and SYS:NWPARAM for changes. The first two files are used by the NetWare NFS product. The parameter ranges from 1 to 1,000 seconds and has a default value of 60 seconds.

The DNS Access field informs you if DNS is enabled or disabled.

The Domain field in the DNS Access group displays the DNS name configured during installation. You can enter a different value to change the domain name.

The Primary Server field in the DNS Access group can be set to the IP address of the first DNS server to contact for name resolution.

The Secondary Server field in the DNS Access group can be set to the IP address of the second DNS server to contact for name resolution if the other DNS servers fail to respond with the desired answer.

The Tertiary Server field in the DNS Access group can be set to the IP address of the third DNS server to contact for name resolution if the other DNS servers fail to respond with the desired answer.

Configuring the NetWare/IP Servers

After the DNS and DSS servers are configured, the next step is to configure the NetWare/IP servers.

The following is an outline of the steps needed to configure NetWare/IP:

1. LOAD UNICON.

2. Select Manage Services.

3. Select NetWare/IP.

   If your DNS server is set up on a different server from the DSS server, you see a form that enables you to make the DSS server a client of the DNS server (on another machine). This form has a DNS Domain field and three Nameserver fields.

   The DNS Domain field is used to specify the name of your DNS domain. The first Nameserver field specifies the IP address of the server to contact to resolve name queries. The other Nameserver fields represent the order in which other DNS servers are contacted to resolve names if the answer is not found in the first name server.

4. Select Configure NetWare/IP Server.

   The NetWare/IP configuration form appears (see fig. 27.27). In the NetWare/IP domain field, you should enter the fully qualified NetWare/IP domain to which this NetWare/IP server belongs. In the example for this guided tour, this value is as follows:

   `NWIP.SCS.COM.`

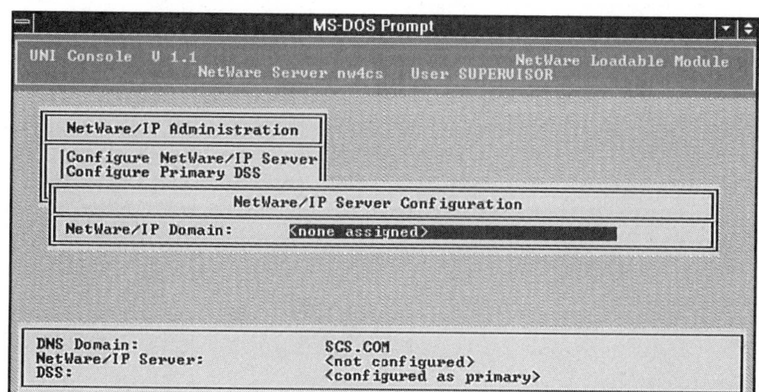

Figure 27.27
NetWare/IP Server Configuration form.

   If the NetWare server has two network boards to which the IP protocol is bound, you also see a Preferred IP Address field. You have the choice of associating any one of the IP addresses for the network interface with the NetWare/IP server. The decision to select the IP address must be based on the network interface through which you want NetWare/IP to communicate with the rest of the network.

5. Press Esc when done making changes and answer Yes to use this server as a NetWare/IP server. The status box at the bottom of the screen changes to indicate that the NetWare/IP server is configured.

You must start the NetWare/IP service. Before starting the NetWare/IP server, you must make sure that DNS and DSS are setup. To do so, follow these steps:

1. Go to the main menu of UNICON.

2. Select Start/Stop Services.

3. If the NetWare/IP server appears in the list of Running Services, highlight it and press Del. Answer Yes to the query verifying that you want to stop the service.

4. To start the NetWare/IP server again, press Ins on the list of Running Services. A list of available services that you can run appears. Highlight NetWare/IP Server and press Enter. This activates the NetWare/IP Server, and it appears in the list of Running Services.

Disabling the NetWare/IP Gateway

If the IPX protocol is bound to a network interface, the NetWare/IP server acts as an IPX-to-IP gateway. If you are on a purely IP-based network, you do not need the NetWare/IP gateway. You can disable this by unbinding IPX from the network interface. You can do this from the server console by typing the following command:

UNBIND IPX FROM *network_board*

Alternatively, you can comment out the BIND command in the AUTOEXEC.NCF files. You also can "comment out" the LOAD statement for the network drivers that use frame types used for IPX only.

Changes to AUTOEXEC.NCF

The NetWare/IP installation at the server adds a command called UNISTART.NCF at the end of the AUTOEXEC.NCF file. The UNISTART.NCF file contains the commands to start DNS, DSS, and NetWare/IP services. The following is an example of the contents of the UNISTART.NCF file:


```
load dispatch
load NAMED
load NISBIND
load NISSERV
load DSS
load NWIP.NLM
```

Installing and Configuring NetWare/IP Clients

The last phase in NetWare/IP installation is installing and configuring the NetWare/IP client. Before running the NetWare/IP client, you must do the following:

1. Set the CONFIG.SYS files to the following:

   `FILES=40` (or higher)

   `BUFFERS=20` (or higher)

2. Do not use the DOS APPEND command. To cancel any APPEND commands, you can use the following:

   `APPEND ;`

3. Disable the SHARE command, if it is in effect.

4. If you plan to run LAN WorkPlace or LAN WorkGroup, install these products before installing the NetWare/IP client. NetWare/IP is compatible with these products, but has files that include additional functionality.

Installing NetWare/IP Client

To install the NetWare/IP client software, perform the following steps:

1. Insert the disk labeled WSDOS_1 in drive A: and type the following command:

   INSTALL

   The INSTALL screen appears (see fig. 27.28).

```
STEP 1. Type target directory name for NetWare Client Files.
        C:\NWCLIENT

STEP 2. Client installation requires "LASTDRIVE=Z" in the
        CONFIG.SYS file and "CALL STARTNET.BAT" added to
        AUTOEXEC.BAT.  Install will make backup copies.
        Allow changes?  (Y/N):  No

STEP 3. Do you wish to install support for Windows? (Y/N):  No
        Windows Subdirectory:

STEP 4. Press <Enter> to install the driver for your network
        board.  You may then use arrow keys to find the
        board name.
        Press <Enter> to see list.

STEP 5. Press <Enter> to continue.

Esc-exit  Enter-select  ↑↓-move  Alt F10-exit
```

Figure 27.28
NetWare/IP INSTALL screen.

2. For STEP 1, type in the directory that contains NetWare/IP files. The default directory is C:\NWCLIENT.

3. For STEP 2, enter **Y** to have the INSTALL program modify the CONFIG.SYS and AUTOEXEC.BAT files. Enter **N** if you want to change these files manually.

4. For STEP 3, enter **Y** to install MS-Windows support; otherwise, enter **N.** If you entered **Y,** enter the pathname where MS Windows is installed.

5. In STEP 4, select the driver for your interface board.

   If you already have a driver loaded, INSTALL recognizes it. You can install the latest version of this driver or continue with the next step.

6. In STEP 5, continue with the installation by pressing Enter. The second form showing the remainder of the steps appears (see fig. 27.29).

7. In STEP 6, enter the NetWare/IP client information in each field.

8. In STEP 7, enter the name of the NetWare/IP domain to which this NetWare/IP client belongs. Figure 27.30 shows some sample values.

9. In STEP 8, press Enter to continue with installation. Follow instructions to enter appropriate diskettes.

Figure 27.29
Rest of NetWare/IP INSTALL screen.

```
STEP 6. Provide the following information for configuring TCP/IP.

    TCP/IP Directory:           C:\NET
    Using Boot Protocol?        No
    Client IP Address:          <none assigned>
    Subnetwork Mask:            <none assigned>
    Default Router Address:     <none assigned>
    DNS Domain:                 <none assigned>
    Name Server Address:        <none assigned>
    Name Server Address:        <none assigned>
    Name Server Address:        <none assigned>

STEP 7. Configure this host to access NetWare/IP service.

    NetWare/IP Domain:          <none assigned>

STEP 8. Press <Enter> to install.
```

Figure 27.30
NetWare/IP Client Configuration values.

```
STEP 6. Provide the following information for configuring TCP/IP.

    TCP/IP Directory:           C:\NET
    Using Boot Protocol?        No
    Client IP Address:          144.19.74.44
    Subnetwork Mask:            255.255.0.0
    Default Router Address:     144.19.74.91
    DNS Domain:                 SCS.COM.
    Name Server Address:        144.19.74.102
    Name Server Address:        144.19.74.201
    Name Server Address:        <none assigned>

STEP 7. Configure this host to access NetWare/IP service.

    NetWare/IP Domain:          NWIP.SCS.COM.

STEP 8. Press <Enter> to install.
```


Checking Frame Types

The NetWare/IP client uses any of the following frame types for TCP/IP:

- Ethernet: ETHERNET_II or ETHERNET_SNAP
- Token Ring: TOKEN-RING_SNAP
- FDDI: FDDI_SNAP
- ARCnet: NOVELL_RX-NET
- PCN or PCN II: IBM_PCN2_SNAP

Checking NET.CFG File

The NetWare/IP client installation modifies the NET.CFG file. The following is an example of the modified NET.CFG file:

```
#Link Driver CEODI
Link Driver CEODI
    FRAME Ethernet_802.2
    FRAME Ethernet_802.3
    FRAME Ethernet_II
```

```
    INT          5
    PORT        300
    MEM        d0000
    SOCKET        1
    IOWORDSIZE     16
    SOCKETSERVICES    Y
    CARDSERVICES    Y
Protocol IPX
    bind 1
;    bind 2
NetWare DOS Requester
    PB BUFFERS=4            ; Default is 3. 4 provides best throughput
    FIRST NETWORK DRIVE = F
    PREFERRED SERVER = NW4CS
    NAME CONTEXT = "OU=CORP.O=ESL"
Link Support
    Buffers    8 1500
    MemPool    4096
Protocol TCPIP
    PATH TCP_CFG        C:\NET\TCP
    ip_address    144.19.74.44
    ip_netmask    255.255.0.0
    ip_router    144.19.74.91
NWIP
    NWIP_DOMAIN_NAME    NWIP.SCS.COM.
    NSQ_BROADCAST    ON
```

The new sections added are the Protocol TCPIP and the NWIP. These contain the IP address interface and the NetWare/IP domain information.

Checking STARTNET.BAT File

The STARTNET.BAT file contains a line to load NWIP.EXE, the IPX Far Call Interface module.

The following is a sample STARTNET.BAT:

```
C:\NET\bin\yesno "Load Networking Software? [y/n]"
@ECHO OFF
if errorlevel 1 goto nonet
C:
CD \NWCLIENT
SET NWLANGUAGE=ENGLISH
LSL
CEODI
C:\NET\BIN\TCPIP
NWIP
if errorlevel -1 goto err_loading_nwip
VLM
CD \
:err_loading_nwip
:nonet
```

27

Summary

This chapter covers the essential concepts needed to design, install, and configure NetWare/IP-based networks.

NetWare/IP solves a very important problem. It allows network designers to use the TCP/IP protocol for transport services on a NetWare network. This allows large networks currently based on TCP/IP to use this protocol for all their network services.

NetWare/IP also can be used as a gateway to link IPX networks with a backbone network based on TCP/IP only.

Network Management

As LANs grow in scope, you can encounter significant problems in managing the user environments and operating the network. This chapter examines the tools you can use to manage larger networks.

Many third-party tools use proprietary schemes to manage a NetWare LAN. Some interesting developments have occurred in network management based on standard protocols. Products that comply with these standards can be mixed on a NetWare LAN and should be compatible. This section discusses these network management protocols.

Simple Network Management Protocol (SNMP)

The *Simple Network Management Protocol* (SNMP) is perhaps the most widely implemented vendor-independent network management protocol. SNMP originated in Internet, which is used to connect universities, government, and commercial organizations. Internet primarily uses the TCP/IP-based suite of protocols and is the largest computer network in the world.

SNMP has seen rapid deployment since it was first published. It is based on an earlier protocol called *Simple Gateway Monitoring Protocol* (SGMP). One reason for SNMP's popularity is that it is easier to implement than other competing protocols, such as OSI's CMIS/CMIP. Perhaps another subtle reason for its popularity is that the SNMP document (RFC 1098) is easier to read and understand than the OSI management protocol documents.

Many network vendors, including Novell, offer SNMP-based network management products. Today, most LAN hub vendors proudly announce that their hubs are SNMP-compliant. In fact, SNMP compliance has become a determining factor in many a network manager's decision to buy a specific product. Vendors such as DEC (which has its own proprietary network management protocols) or AT&T (which was interested only in OSI network management protocols) have announced or reengineered their products to implement SNMP.

With SNMP's popularity, it seems to have unstoppable momentum. It will be interesting to see if SNMP can be replaced by the more comprehensive and complex OSI management protocols.

Introduction to SNMP

The SNMP protocol is a layer 7 protocol. SNMP reports network management information over the network itself, but in case the network is down, it is possible to report management information over serial links such as RS-232 by using the *Serial Line Interface Protocol* (SLIP).

SNMP's attraction is its simplicity. Only four operations are defined that operate on SNMP objects. These operations are shown in table 28.1.

Table 28.1
SNMP Operations

Operation	Meaning
GET	Retrieves specific management information
GET-NEXT	Retrieves by traversal the next item of management information
SET	Manipulates the management information
TRAP	Reports events

Device parameters that describe management information are called *managed objects.* The collection of managed objects describe a *virtual store.* You can view this virtual store as a database. This database is called the *Management Information Base* (MIB). The MIB objects are described in a formal language called *Abstract Syntax Notation, Rev 1* (ASN.1). ASN.1 also is used to represent application layer data in the OSI model and is part of the presentation layer (layer 6).

Vendors can add device-specific MIBs through private enterprise extensions. MIB compilers are available to compile these definitions for inclusion in the SNMP managers. The MIB definitions (both I and II) are oriented toward management of TCP/IP-based networks; therefore, many vendors add private enterprise extensions to manage the features of their products. Ethernet and Token Ring parameters are managed by SNMP extensions. Vendors such as Synoptic Communications and Racal Interlan have published their extensions so that third-party SNMP managers can include these extensions.

Though SNMP originated on the TCP/IP-based Internet, RFC standards exist for use on OSI and SPX/IPX (Novell)-based networks. For example, RFC-1298 describes how SNMP can run over SPX/IPX protocols.

SNMP Agents and Managers

The nodes in a network that are to be managed run an implementation of the SNMP protocol that enables an external entity to manage the device. An *SNMP agent* enables these nodes to be managed by an external entity called an *SNMP manager.* The Novell LANtern product, discussed later in this chapter, is an example of an SNMP manager.

All managed devices do not need to directly support SNMP protocols. Repeaters and amplifiers on the network, for example, may not have sufficient processing capability to run SNMP protocols. Other devices on the network may implement other management protocols. These devices are called *foreign devices.* Foreign devices and devices that do not support SNMP can be managed by proxy SNMP agents.

SNMP agents and managers communicate through specially formatted messages called *Protocol Data Units* (SNMP PDUs). SNMP PDU requests are sent by managers to agents, and the agents respond with the requested values. Communication is driven by the managers, but agents are expected to respond. Because network events occur asynchronously, agents use the SNMP trap operation to report these events to the manager. The SNMP protocol is symmetrical; that is, SNMP GetRequest messages can be initiated by any SNMP device.

SNMP defines the notion of a community. A *community* is a relationship between an SNMP agent and one or more of its SNMP managers. All SNMP messages contain this community name. The community name is used to authenticate if the message is sent by an SNMP entity that belongs to the community.

SNMP agents are popularly implemented on, but not limited to, network hubs, concentrators, bridges, routers, and gateways. SNMP commands can be issued to disable malfunctioning concentrator ports, filter packets based on source or destination address, and report on packet statistics.

The SNMP protocol is concerned with the transfer of SNMP messages. The way that the MIB information is presented to the user and stored for analysis is an implementation issue left for the SNMP manager. This is where product differentiation between the SNMP managers take place. PC-based SNMP managers tend to use the Microsoft Windows graphical user interface (GUI), and UNIX-based SNMP managers use X-Windows.

SNMP Tools and Utilities

SNMP building blocks in the form of tools, compilers, and utilities are available from a number of vendors, such as Epilogue Technology Corp., Performance Systems International, and SNMP Research, Castle Rock Computing, Chameleon, Hewlett Packard, Sun Microsystems, and so on.

SNMP Research offers NETMON, which can run on a PC-based or UNIX workstation platform and displays a real-time geographical or logical map of the network. NETMON displays the status of links that are up or down (green for up and red for down), and then logs events to a disk. The SNMP manager requires support for UDP/IP. In most cases, this support is an appropriate TCP/IP driver that can work with the network interface. TCP/IP drivers include support for UDP.

SNMP can be used with non-TCP/IP-based networks. Only the SNMP managers and agents use UDP/IP, but other devices on the network can use their own protocols that coexist with UDP/IP. SNMP managers and agents, for example, can be used in a NetWare LAN. The NetWare nodes can use SPX/IPX and the SNMP devices can use UDP/IP. Both sets of protocols can co-exist on the same Ethernet or Token Ring LAN.

To demonstrate that SNMP is not restricted to computers running TCP/IP, some vendors have gone to extreme lengths. At an Interop show, Epilogue Technology demonstrated an SNMP agent controlling a toaster. SNMP Research demonstrated a SNMP-controlled electronic dog complete with a canine MIB! Users clicking on an X-Windows icon could cause this dog to bark.

Novell's LANtern

Novell's LANtern system contains the LANtern Network Monitor and the LANtern Services Manager. The LANtern Network Monitor is an SNMP agent from Novell that is designed to work with one or more SNMP managers to manage Ethernet networks. Novell's SNMP manager is called LANtern Services Manager.

The LANtern Network Monitor

The LANtern Network Monitor acts as a dedicated listener that gathers comprehensive statistical information about network performance utilization. Alarms implemented as SNMP trap messages also report the status of a network or warn you when parameter values exceed a predefined threshold. Communication with the LANtern monitor takes place over the network. In case of network failure, this communication also can be performed through an RS-232 serial interface. The LANtern monitor's hardware specifications are described in table 28.2.

Table 28.2
LANtern Network Monitor Hardware Specifications

Parameter	Description
CPU	Motorola 68020, 16 MHz with zero wait states
RAM	Up to 2 MB dual ported RAM; 8 KB of battery-backed static RAM
EPROM	256 KB of flash EPROM (expandable to 512 KB) for program storage
NIC	Intel 82586 LAN coprocessor (Ethernet)

Parameter	Description
Serial Port	CCITT V.24/V.28. DB-9 IBM AT compatible RS-232
Power	30 Watts. 95 to 264 VAC

The primary communication with a LANtern network monitor takes place over the network. You also can use a secondary communication channel over the serial interface port.

The LANtern monitor requires three pieces of information to communicate over the monitored network: its own IP address (adminNetworkIPAddr), the subnet mask (adminNetworkSubnetMask), and the address of one (any) directly connected gateway (adminNetworkGateway). When power is first applied to the LANtern monitor, it does not have this information. It obtains it by employing either the *Bootstrap Protocol* (BOOTP) or *Reverse Address Resolution Protocol* (RARP).

For LANtern monitors on an isolated remote LAN segment, the serial link running a data link protocol is specified in MIB object adminSerialDataLink. The default encapsulation is SLIP.

LANtern monitors all network traffic and gathers statistics on general network events and station-to-station traffic. A *network event* is any activity on the network that can cause the carrier sense (Ethernet) to be active for more than 0.5 microseconds. Table 28.3 lists the network events.

Table 28.3
LANtern Monitors General Network Events

MIB variable	Meaning
eGoodPackets	Total number of good packets
eBroadcastPackets	Broadcasts
eMulticastPackets	Multicasts
eUnicastPackets	Unicasts
eCRCAlignmentErrors	Faulty CRC
eOversize	Frame > 1518 bytes with good CRC
eUndersize	Frame < 64 bytes with good CRC
eJabbers	Frame > 1518 bytes with bad CRC
eLocalCollisions	Local collision or Signal Quality Error
eCollisionFragments	Frame < 64 bytes with bad CRC

The LANtern monitor keeps statistics for transmitting and receiving stations that include total packets transmitted, total bytes transmitted, total errors transmitted, protocols used, the date and time of first transmission, and the date and time of most recent transmission. The MIB defines two tables, eStnToStnTableSD and eStnToStnTableDS, through which this information can be accessed. These tables are identical, except that eStnToStnTableSD is organized with the source address as the major key and the destination address as the minor key, and that eStnToStnTableSD is organized with the destination address as the major key and the same address as the minor key. You can use these tables to get statistics on packets received by a station or transmitted from a station.

The LANtern Services Manager

LANtern Services Manager (LSM) is an SNMP manager that runs on a standard 80386, 80386SX, or 80486 IBM-compatible PC under the MS-Windows environment. Designed to work with the LANtern Monitor, the LSM can communicate with the LANtern Monitors through the monitored network or an RS-232 interface.

LSM detects and polls LANtern monitors, looks for stations, and can gather long-term trend data at user-definable intervals. LSM polls LANtern for real-time statistic data only if requested to do so, so that the impact of SNMP traffic on normal network activity is minimized. LSM stores information about alarms, events, station configuration, and long-term trends in Novell's popular Btrieve database.

Figure 28.1 shows the data flow between LANtern monitors and an LSM. This figure shows that LSM connections can be made through the monitored LAN, modem, or direct RS-232 link. The modem uses the RS-232 interface on the LANtern monitor and LSM. Real-time data can be displayed by means of messages, graphs, or tables. LANtern configuration data is stored in a configuration database that can be edited through LSM. Alarms and trend data are stored in the Btrieve database and can be displayed as trend table, trend graph, and alarm log.

You enable real-time data gathering by selecting the network segment and requesting the data that you want to display. LSM displays the data in the form of a graph or a table. As long as the data window is active, LSM continues to gather and update the display. Even if you minimize the real-time data window (turn it into an icon), the LSM continues to gather and store information in the background. LSM gathers and displays data in the form of counters, gauges, conversations, and station information.

Nineteen counters are available that can keep track of numbers of certain events. You can display the counters individually, in combination, or by profiles. *Profiles* contain several counters of the same type, such as packet counts broken by packet size. Gauges measure percentages of utilization, broadcast packets, collisions, and errors, and can be defined with an alarm threshold. If activity exceeds the threshold, an alarm notice can be generated. Conversations to and from a station can be monitored in the form of packets sent to and received from a station. These packets are displayed in the form of a table that can be updated at the rate you want or sorted by any column as a key.

Long-term trend data can be gathered and stored by the LSM in user- definable intervals. LSM displays this data as trend graphs or trend tables. A *trend graph* is a line graph that displays trend data in percentages for a selected network segment. The same counters and profiles are available as are available for real-time data. The trend data can be stored for 25 hours (100 15-minute intervals) before it is overwritten. The trend table lists the information gathered in the form of a table. It can be sorted automatically using any column as the sort key.

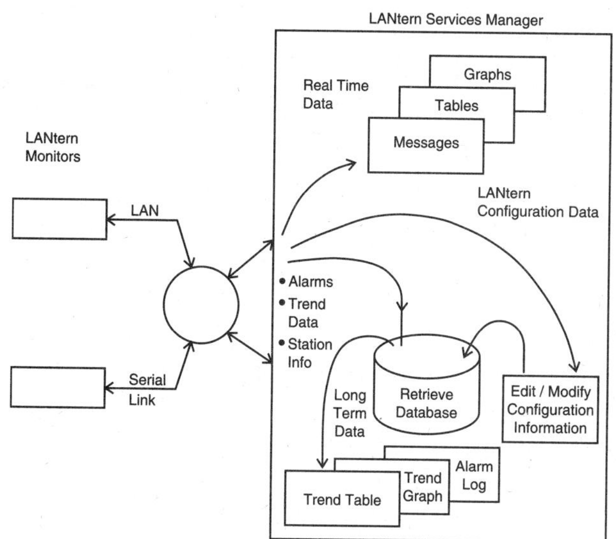

Figure 28.1
LANtern service manager data flow.

28

LSM provides two forms of alarm notices: gauge threshold alarms and activity event alarms. *Gauge threshold alarms* occur whenever the percentage value (gauge) exceeds the predefined threshold for utilization, broadcasts, collisions, and errors. *Activity event alarms* are related to specific lists of events or conditions that the LANtern monitor can detect. These events are listed in table 28.4.

Table 28.4
General Events Reported by LANtern Monitors

Event	Meaning
New station	Indicates when a station first starts transmitting
Duplicate IP address	Indicates two stations with same IP address
Station active	Indicates when a critical active station begins transmitting again
Authentication failure	Indicates an invalid community name in SNMP message
Cable failure	Indicates a cable fault on Ethernet or transceiver drop

continues

Table 28.4, Continued
General Events Reported by LANtern Monitors

Event	Meaning
Ping notification	Indicates when a LANtern monitor receives response to an echo-test message sent to a station
Warm start	Indicates that the LANtern was warm started
Utilization	Indicates that utilization exceeds threshold
Broadcasts	Indicates that broadcast packets exceed threshold
Collisions	Indicates that collisions exceed threshold
Errors	Indicates that packet errors exceed threshold

Figures 28.2 to 28.4 depict a scenario in which the LSM can be used to manage a network. The MIS manager sees a bright red alarm on the LSM console. A glance at the LSM gauges (fig. 28.2) reveals that the alarm was caused by a high number of CRC/Alignment errors. The MIS manager selects Station Monitor from the pull-down menu and sorts the table by using the Errors out column (fig. 28.3). The first six lines on this table show an unusually high number of errors. The MIS manager double-clicks on the icons that represent these stations. The location field indicates that the six stations are in the same building. Closer examination of the 10BASE-T network in the building (using a 10BASE-T tester) network reveals that faulty twisted-pair wiring is causing the errors (fig. 28.4).

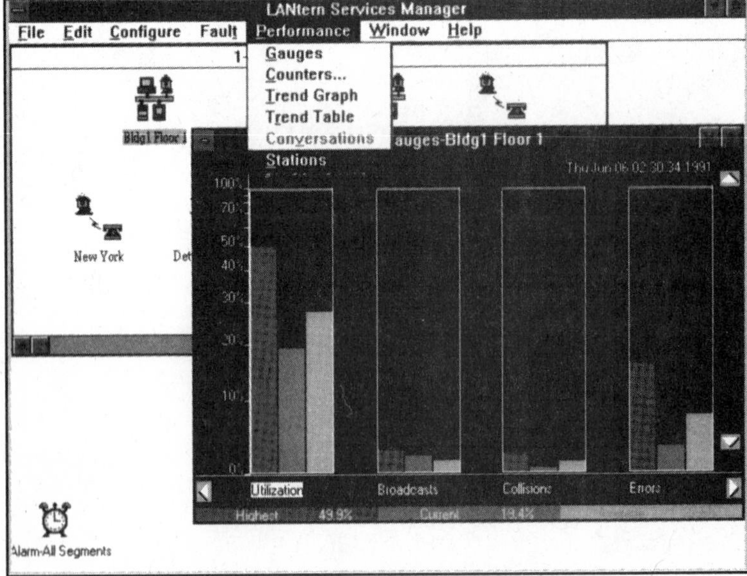

Figure 28.2
LANtern Services Manager reveals a high number of CRC/Alignment errors.

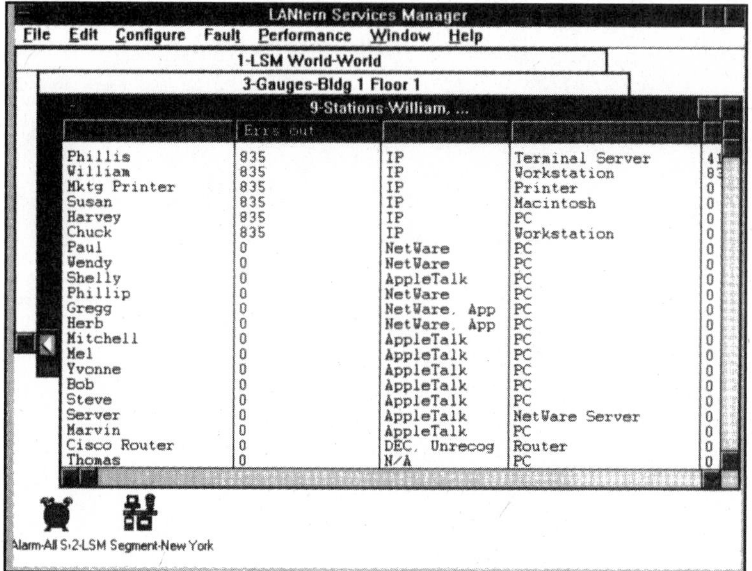

Figure 28.3
Sorting of station table by Errors out reveals six stations with a high amount of errors.

Remote Monitoring (RMON)

A number of organizations, including Novell, support an extension to SNMP MIBs that can be used for remote monitoring. This extension is called the RMON MIB. RMON specifies the way in which data can be monitored remotely from a central site. Although this process sounds similar to what SNMP does, SNMP MIBs typically focus on device configuration.

The RMON MIB defines more comprehensive monitoring and analysis than SNMP MIBs. A network vendor can implement RMON MIBs in devices such as hubs, bridges, and routers. The RMON MIB will provide the kind of information that Novell's LANtern product currently provides, which may lessen the need for dedicated probes such as LANtern Network Monitor. Gathering information for RMON MIBs is a process-intensive task, however, and the market for dedicated probes will still exist.

RMON defines nine categories of MIB objects. A vendor needs to implement only one category to comply with the RMON specification. Newer versions of Novell's LANtern monitor implement these categories.

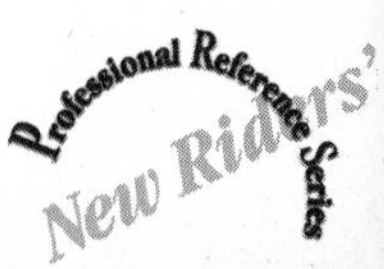

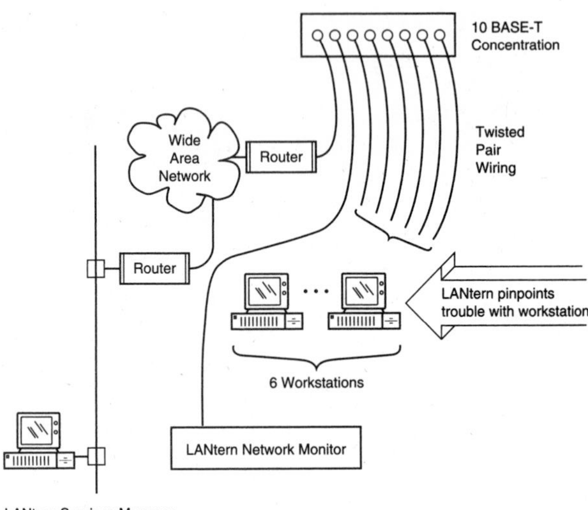

Figure 28.4
LANtern Services Manager pinpoints trouble with twisted-pair wiring.

NetWare Management System

NetWare Management System (NMS) is a distributed management system from Novell that can be used to monitor performance of NetWare servers, Ethernet and Token Ring network segments, routers and hubs that comply with the *Hub Management Interface* (HMI). It can also be used to explore and discover devices on the network and create a map of the devices attached to your network.

The NMS family of products consist of NMS agents that report on information on devices on the network, a NMS management console, a NMS Explorer server that can discover devices on a network. Figure 28.5 shows the type of network environment on which NMS can be used. This network consists of a number of NMS agents that report information on server alarms, alerts, network traffic, network hubs, and so on.

Understanding NMS Agents

The NMS agents perform the following main tasks:

1. Gather information on devices on the network. In order to do this, the NMS agents have intimate knowledge of the device and the critical parameters in the device being monitored.

2. Report alerts and problem conditions to the NMS console.

3. Execute commands for controlling the devices from the NMS console.

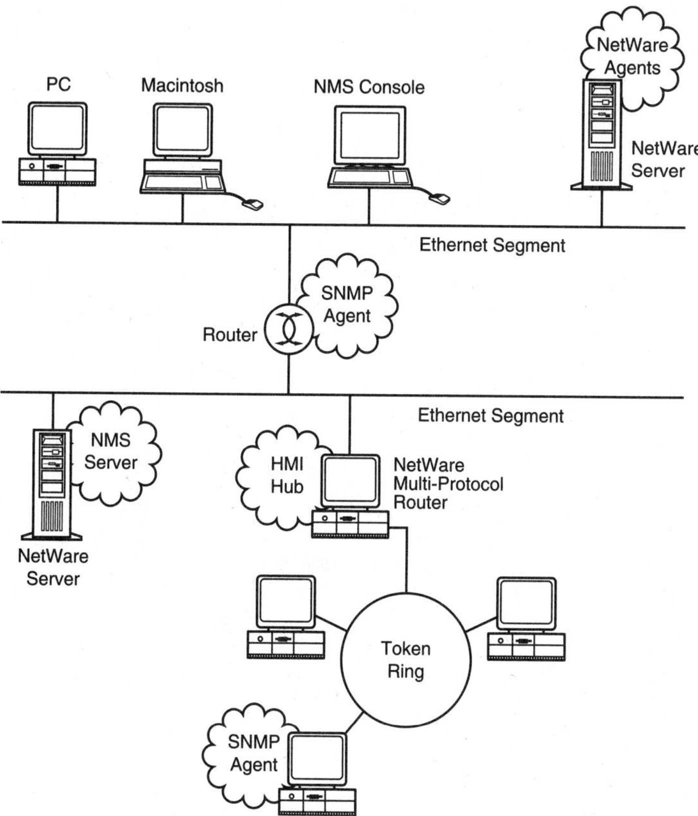

Figure 28.5
Example of an NMS-managed network.

The NMS agents that come with NMS are as follows:

- NetWare Management Agent software
- NetWare LANalyzer Agent
- LANtern network monitor
- NetWare Hub Services Manager

Understanding what these agents do will give you an insight into the types of activities that NMS can monitor.

The NetWare Management Agent provides information in server alarms and performance data on NetWare servers. These agents are typically deployed on each NetWare server that is to be managed.

The NetWare LANalyzer agent enables NMS to monitor network traffic on network segments. It is an implementation of the RMON MIB specification. These agents can monitor network traffic on any Ethernet and Token Ring segment. This agent runs on a NetWare server and can monitor traffic on all network segments connected to the server. The LANalyzer agent can be used for:

1. Obtain network traffic statistics related to performance and usage on network segments.
2. Statistics on each station on the network segment, such as the stations generating the most traffic, or conversation patterns between workstations.
3. Capture and decoded packets. You can capture packets on a network segment and decode them at the NMS console.
4. Find problems such as network traffic overload, stations with duplicate IP address, excessive errors on network segments. These errors are reported to the NMS console.

The LANtern monitor is a hardware device (discussed earlier in this chapter). It can be used to report information to the NMS console. In many ways, this device provides similar functionality to the LANalyzer agent with the difference that the LANtern device uses TCP/IP packets and requires IP routers to send this information, whereas the LANalyzer can communicate via IPX or TCP/IP. The LANtern device is dedicated for the segment to which it is attached and has a capture data buffer of 100 KB. NetWare LANalyzer agents are limited by the free memory available at the server.

The NetWare Hub Services software communicates with hub devices that support the HMI specification. This specification can be used to monitor hub performance and statistics. The NetWare Hub services agent can also be used with the NetWare MultiProtocol Router.

Network Management Functions of NMS

NMS functions are performed from the NMS Console. The NMS Console is an MS Windows-based application that provides a graphical front end to the NMS features and functions. The NMS Console includes a component called the NetExplorer Manager and a database (see fig. 28.6). The NetExplorer Manager communicates with a NMS server running on a NetWare server. The database in the NMS Console is used to store information obtained through the NetExplorer Manager. This NMS database contains a logical map of the network, configuration information on all "discovered" stations on the network, alarm log and NMS configuration information.

The NMS server implements a discovery system called the NetExplorer. The NetExplorer gathers information by communicating with NetWare servers, and NMS agents. The NetExplorer discovers the topology of the network, workstations on segments, routers, hubs and organizes this information in its local database (NETXPLOR.DAT). It then sends information from its database to the NMS Console. The NetExplorer needs a separate database to store its information and is separate from the NMS

Console database, because the NMS database is maintained by NMS Console, an MS Windows application, that may not be running all the time. When the NMS Console comes on-line, it polls the NetExplorer for information stored in the NetExplorer's database.

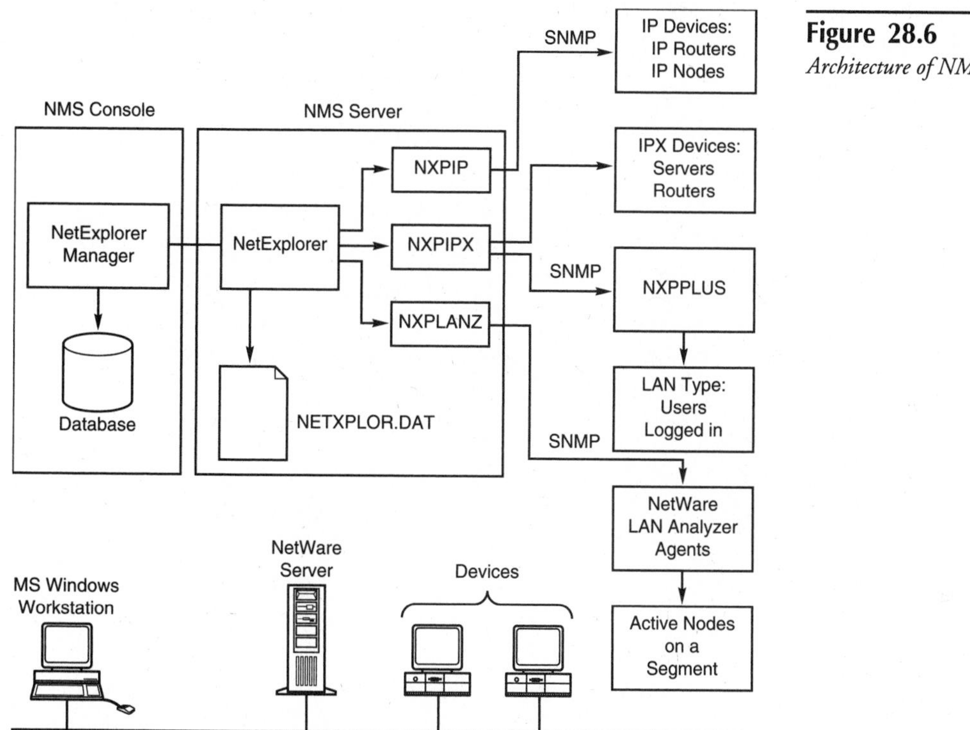

Figure 28.6
Architecture of NMS.

28

The NetExplorer component in the NMS Server is made up of a series of NLMs called *discovery* or *explorer NLMs*. These NLMs are the NXPIPX.NLM, NXPIP.NLM, NXPLANZ,NLM, NXPPLUS.NLM. The descriptions of each of these NLMs are shown in table 28.5.

Table 28.5
Explorer NLMs

Explorer NLM	Description
NXPIPX.NLM	This discovers information on IPX devices (servers, routers, and so forth) on the network. It reports when a new IPX device comes on-line and when it is no longer available.

continues

Table 28.5, Continued
Explorer NLMs

Explorer NLM	Description
NXPIP.NLM	This discovers information on IP devices (servers, routers, hubs, and so on) on the network. It reports when a new IP device comes on-line and when it is no longer available. It performs this discovery process using SNMP.
NXPLANZ.NLM	This communicates with NetWare LANanlayzer agents, and LANtern network monitors to discover information on devices on the segment. It reports on new, changed, or deleted devices on the network.
NXPPLUS.NLM	This can runs on all NetWare servers and reports on network interfaces at the server and users logged in or attached to the server.

Once the network management data is collected from the NMS Server, it is written in the NMS database. NMS uses this information to build a map of the network. NMS provides the following types of maps of your network:

- Logical Maps
- Locational Maps

NMS provides two types of logical maps: internet map and segment maps. An internet map shows the segments and routers and the logical interconnections between segments. The segment map shows the servers, workstations and other devices attached to the segment.

When alarms occur on the network, an alarm icon will appear next to the device on the logical map of the network. You can select the icon for the device to see an alarm report, or see details about the device's configuration.

Locational maps are physical maps of the network. NMS comes with an editor that you can use to create a customized physical map with floor plans, buildings, and so on.

The types of alarms that are reported and can be recorded are determined by the *Management Information Bases* (MIBs) that NMS has compiled. The NMS Tools menu provides a utility to compile MIBs.

NMS allows third-party developers to add new classes of objects to the object classes NMS knows about. This allows the functionality of NMS to be extended.

SNMP Support

NMS can be used to manage any device that has an SNMP agent on the network. You can use NMS to receive SNMP traps and use the SNMP MIB Browser tool to display and set values.

NMS comes with compiled MIBs that define traps and MIB variables. If you need to support a new type of device that uses custom MIBs, you must obtain a copy of the MIB definition from the manufacturer device. This MIB definition is an ASCII text file written using the ASN.1 (Abstract Syntax Notation, 1) syntax. It is similar in many ways to the schema definition for databases. You must then compile this MIB definition.

NMS provides many standard and vendor-proprietary MIB definitions. These are located in the NMS\SNMPMIBS\ALLMIBS directory. The following is an example of the ripsap.mib definition written using ASN.1:

```
RIPSAP DEFINITIONS ::= BEGIN
— This MIB defines the management information for the RIP and SAP
— protocols running in an IPX enviroment.  It provides information in
— addition to that contained in the IPX MIB itself.  All tables in this
— MIB are linked to an instance of IPX via the system instance
— identifier as defined in the IPX MIB.

IMPORTS
   enterprises, Counter
            FROM RFC1155-SMI
   OBJECT-TYPE
            FROM RFC-1212
   PhysAddress
            FROM RFC1213-MIB;

novell  OBJECT IDENTIFIER ::= {enterprises 23}
mibDoc  OBJECT IDENTIFIER ::= { novell 2 }
ripsap  OBJECT IDENTIFIER ::= {mibDoc 20}

— Groups

ripsapSystem  OBJECT IDENTIFIER ::= {ripsap 1}
ripsapCircuit OBJECT IDENTIFIER ::= {ripsap 2}

— Types

NetNumber ::= OCTET STRING (SIZE(4))

— System Group
—   This group contains global information about each instance of
—   RIP/SAP running on one system.
```

```
— RIP System Table
—   This table contains an entry for each instance of RIP
—   running on the system.

ripSysTable OBJECT-TYPE
   SYNTAX      SEQUENCE OF RIPSysEntry
   ACCESS      not-accessible
   STATUS      mandatory
   DESCRIPTION "The RIP system table."
   ::= {ripsapSystem 1}

ripSysEntry OBJECT-TYPE
   SYNTAX      RIPSysEntry
   ACCESS      not-accessible
   STATUS      mandatory
   DESCRIPTION "Each entry corresponds to one instance of RIP
                running on the system."
   INDEX       {ripSysInstance}
   ::= {ripSysTable 1}

RIPSysEntry ::= SEQUENCE {
                        ripSysInstance
                           INTEGER,
                        ripSysState
                           INTEGER,
                        ripSysIncorrectPackets
                           Counter
                       }


ripSysInstance OBJECT-TYPE
   SYNTAX      INTEGER
   ACCESS      read-write
   STATUS      mandatory
   DESCRIPTION "The unique identifier of the instance of RIP to
                which this row corresponds.  This value links the
                instance of RIP to an instance of IPX running on the
                system  (i.e. the value of ripSysInstance should be the
                same as a value of ipxSysInstance).  This value may be
                written only when creating a new entry in the table."
   ::= {ripSysEntry 1}

ripSysState OBJECT-TYPE
   SYNTAX      INTEGER {
                        off(1),
                        on(2)
                       }
```

28

```
    ACCESS      read-write
    STATUS      mandatory
    DESCRIPTION "Indicates the operational state of this instance of RIP."
    ::= {ripSysEntry 2}

ripSysIncorrectPackets OBJECT-TYPE
    SYNTAX      Counter
    ACCESS      read-only
    STATUS      mandatory
    DESCRIPTION "The number of times that an incorrectly formatted RIP
                 packet was received."
    ::= {ripSysEntry 3}

— SAP System Table
—   This table contains an entry for each instance of SAP
—   running on the system.

sapSysTable OBJECT-TYPE
    SYNTAX      SEQUENCE OF SAPSysEntry
    ACCESS      not-accessible
    STATUS      mandatory
    DESCRIPTION "The SAP system table."
    ::= {ripsapSystem 2}

sapSysEntry OBJECT-TYPE
    SYNTAX      SAPSysEntry
    ACCESS      not-accessible
    STATUS      mandatory
    DESCRIPTION "Each entry corresponds to one instance of SAP
                 running on the system."
    INDEX       {sapSysInstance}
    ::= {sapSysTable 1}

SAPSysEntry ::= SEQUENCE {
                        sapSysInstance
                           INTEGER,
                        sapSysState
                           INTEGER,
                        sapSysIncorrectPackets
                           Counter
                       }

sapSysInstance OBJECT-TYPE
    SYNTAX      INTEGER
    ACCESS      read-write
    STATUS      mandatory
    DESCRIPTION "The unique identifier of the instance of SAP to
                 which this row corresponds.  This value links the
                 instance of SAP to an instance of IPX running on the
```

28

```
                system  (i.e. the value of SApSysInstance should be the
                same as a value of ipxSysInstance).  This value may be
                written only when creating a new entry in the table."
   ::= {sapSysEntry 1}

sapSysState OBJECT-TYPE
   SYNTAX      INTEGER {
                        off(1),
                        on(2)
                       }
   ACCESS      read-write
   STATUS      mandatory
   DESCRIPTION "Indicates the operational state of this instance of SAP."
   ::= {sapSysEntry 2}

sapSysIncorrectPackets OBJECT-TYPE
   SYNTAX      Counter
   ACCESS      read-only
   STATUS      mandatory
   DESCRIPTION "The number of times that an incorrectly formatted SAP
                packet was received."
   ::= {sapSysEntry 3}
```



```
— Circuit Group
—   This group contains RIP and SAP management information for each
—   circuit known to this system.

— RIP Circuit Table
—   The RIP Circuit table contains an entry for the RIP information for
—   each circuit known to the system.

ripCircTable OBJECT-TYPE
   SYNTAX      SEQUENCE OF RIPCircEntry
   ACCESS      not-accessible
   STATUS      mandatory
   DESCRIPTION "The RIP Circuit table."
   ::= {ripsapCircuit 1}

ripCircEntry OBJECT-TYPE
   SYNTAX      RIPCircEntry
   ACCESS      not-accessible
   STATUS      mandatory
   DESCRIPTION "Each entry corresponds to one circuit known to the
                system."
   INDEX       {
                ripCircSysInstance,
                ripCircIndex
               }
   ::= {ripCircTable 1}
```

```
RIPCircEntry ::= SEQUENCE {
                            ripCircSysInstance
                               INTEGER,
                            ripCircIndex
                               INTEGER,
                            ripCircState
                               INTEGER,
                            ripCircPace
                               INTEGER,
                            ripCircUpdate
                               INTEGER,
                            ripCircAgeMultiplier
                               INTEGER,
                            ripCircPacketSize
                               INTEGER,
                            ripCircOutPackets
                               Counter,
                            ripCircInPackets
                               Counter
                           }

ripCircSysInstance OBJECT-TYPE
   SYNTAX      INTEGER
   ACCESS      read-write
   STATUS      mandatory
   DESCRIPTION "The unique identifier of the instance of RIP and IPX
                (via ipxSysInstance) to which this entry corresponds.
               This value may be written only when creating a new entry in
               the table."
   ::= {ripCircEntry 1}

ripCircIndex OBJECT-TYPE
   SYNTAX      INTEGER
   ACCESS      read-write
   STATUS      mandatory
   DESCRIPTION "The identifier of this circuit, unique within the
               instance of RIP.  This value corresponds to the circuit
               identifier found in ipxCircIndex.   This value may be
               written only when creating a new entry in the table."
   ::= {ripCircEntry 2}

ripCircState OBJECT-TYPE
   SYNTAX      INTEGER {
                        off(1),
                        on(2),
                        auto-on(3),
                        auto-off(4)
                       }
   ACCESS      read-write
   STATUS      mandatory
```

```
    DESCRIPTION "Indicates whether RIP information may be sent/received
                 over this circuit."
    DEFVAL      { auto-off }
    ::= {ripCircEntry 3}

ripCircPace OBJECT-TYPE
    SYNTAX      INTEGER
    ACCESS      read-write
    STATUS      mandatory
    DESCRIPTION "The maximum pace, in packets per second, at which RIP
                 packets may be sent on this circuit."
    ::= {ripCircEntry 4}

ripCircUpdate OBJECT-TYPE
    SYNTAX      INTEGER
    ACCESS      read-write
    STATUS      mandatory
    DESCRIPTION "The RIP periodic update interval, in seconds."
    DEFVAL      { 60 }
    ::= {ripCircEntry 5}

ripCircAgeMultiplier OBJECT-TYPE
    SYNTAX      INTEGER
    ACCESS      read-write
    STATUS      mandatory
    DESCRIPTION "The holding multiplier for information received in RIP
                 periodic updates."
    DEFVAL      { 4 }
    ::= {ripCircEntry 6}

ripCircPacketSize OBJECT-TYPE
    SYNTAX      INTEGER
    ACCESS      read-write
    STATUS      mandatory
    DESCRIPTION "The RIP packet size used on this circuit."
    ::= {ripCircEntry 7}

ripCircOutPackets OBJECT-TYPE
    SYNTAX      Counter
    ACCESS      read-only
    STATUS      mandatory
    DESCRIPTION "The number of RIP packets sent on this circuit."
    ::= {ripCircEntry 8}

ripCircInPackets OBJECT-TYPE
    SYNTAX      Counter
    ACCESS      read-only
    STATUS      mandatory
    DESCRIPTION "The number of RIP packets received on this circuit."
    ::= {ripCircEntry 9}
```

```
— SAP Circuit Table
—   The SAP Circuit table contains an entry for the SAP information for
—   each circuit known to the system.

sapCircTable OBJECT-TYPE
   SYNTAX      SEQUENCE OF SAPCircEntry
   ACCESS      not-accessible
   STATUS      mandatory
   DESCRIPTION "The SAP Circuit table."
   ::= {ripsapCircuit 2}

sapCircEntry OBJECT-TYPE
   SYNTAX      SAPCircEntry
   ACCESS      not-accessible
   STATUS      mandatory
   DESCRIPTION "Each entry corresponds to one circuit known to the
                system."
   INDEX       {
                sapCircSysInstance,
                sapCircIndex
               }
   ::= {sapCircTable 1}

SAPCircEntry ::= SEQUENCE {
                        sapCircSysInstance
                           INTEGER,
                        sapCircIndex
                           INTEGER,
                        sapCircState
                           INTEGER,
                        sapCircPace
                           INTEGER,
                        sapCircUpdate
                           INTEGER,
                        sapCircAgeMultiplier
                           INTEGER,
                        sapCircPacketSize
                           INTEGER,
                        sapCircGetNearestServerReply
                           INTEGER,
                        sapCircOutPackets
                           Counter,
                        sapCircInPackets
                           Counter
                       }

sapCircSysInstance OBJECT-TYPE
   SYNTAX      INTEGER
   ACCESS      read-write
```

```
   STATUS      mandatory
   DESCRIPTION "The unique identifier of the instance of SAP and IPX
                (via ipxSysInstance) to which this entry corresponds.
                This value may be written only when creating a new entry in
                the table."
   ::= {sapCircEntry 1}

sapCircIndex OBJECT-TYPE
   SYNTAX      INTEGER
   ACCESS      read-write
   STATUS      mandatory
   DESCRIPTION "The identifier of this circuit, unique within the
                instance of SAP.  This value corresponds to the circuit
                identifier found in ipxCircIndex.   This value may be
                written only when creating a new entry in the table."
   ::= {sapCircEntry 2}

sapCircState OBJECT-TYPE
   SYNTAX      INTEGER {
                       off(1),
                       on(2),
                       auto-on(3),
                       auto-off(4)
                      }
   ACCESS      read-write
   STATUS      mandatory
   DESCRIPTION "Indicates whether SAP information may be sent/received
                over this circuit."
   DEFVAL      { auto-off }
   ::= {sapCircEntry 3}

sapCircPace OBJECT-TYPE
   SYNTAX      INTEGER
   ACCESS      read-write
   STATUS      mandatory
   DESCRIPTION "The maximum pace, in packets per second, at which SAP
                packets may be sent on this circuit."
   ::= {sapCircEntry 4}

sapCircUpdate OBJECT-TYPE
   SYNTAX      INTEGER
   ACCESS      read-write
   STATUS      mandatory
   DESCRIPTION "The SAP periodic update interval, in seconds."
   DEFVAL      { 60 }
   ::= {sapCircEntry 5}

sapCircAgeMultiplier OBJECT-TYPE
   SYNTAX      INTEGER
   ACCESS      read-write
   STATUS      mandatory
```

```
    DESCRIPTION "The holding multiplier for information received in SAP
                 periodic updates."
    DEFVAL      { 4 }
    ::= {sapCircEntry 6}

sapCircPacketSize OBJECT-TYPE
    SYNTAX      INTEGER
    ACCESS      read-write
    STATUS      mandatory
    DESCRIPTION "The SAP packet size used on this circuit."
    ::= {sapCircEntry 7}

sapCircGetNearestServerReply OBJECT-TYPE
    SYNTAX      INTEGER {
                         no(1),
                         yes(2)
                        }
    ACCESS      read-write
    STATUS      mandatory
    DESCRIPTION "Indicates whether to respond to SAP get nearest server
                 requests received on this circuit."
    DEFVAL      { yes }
    ::= {sapCircEntry 8}

sapCircOutPackets OBJECT-TYPE
    SYNTAX      Counter
    ACCESS      read-only
    STATUS      mandatory
    DESCRIPTION "The number of SAP packets sent on this circuit."
    ::= {sapCircEntry 9}

sapCircInPackets OBJECT-TYPE
    SYNTAX      Counter
    ACCESS      read-only
    STATUS      mandatory
    DESCRIPTION "The number of SAP packets received on this circuit."
    ::= {sapCircEntry 10}
```

When an MIB is compiled that contains trap definitions, this information is added to the NMS database. When NMS receives this new type of trap, it looks up the NMS database to resolve the type of error trap.

When you compile MIB definitions, all MIB files in the CURRENT directory are compiled into a binary file called NMS\BIN\SNMPMIBS.BIN. This file is used by the MIB Browser and the SNMP protocol decoder. NMS allows you to talk to any SNMP-device using either TCP/IP or IPX.

The MIB Browser allows you to create profiles for devices. A profile is a set of MIB variable definitions that are of interest to you. It can be selected from the compiled MIBs and saved as named profile. You can select this profile from a list of profiles and instruct the MIB Browser to send SNMP queries to obtain the values of MIB variables in the profile. If a MIB variable in the profile is writeable, you can set a value for it. The MIB Browser uses the SNMP SET command to write this variable to the device.

Using NMS

After NMS has been installed, a program group for NMS is created that lists the tools for NMS (see fig. 28.7).

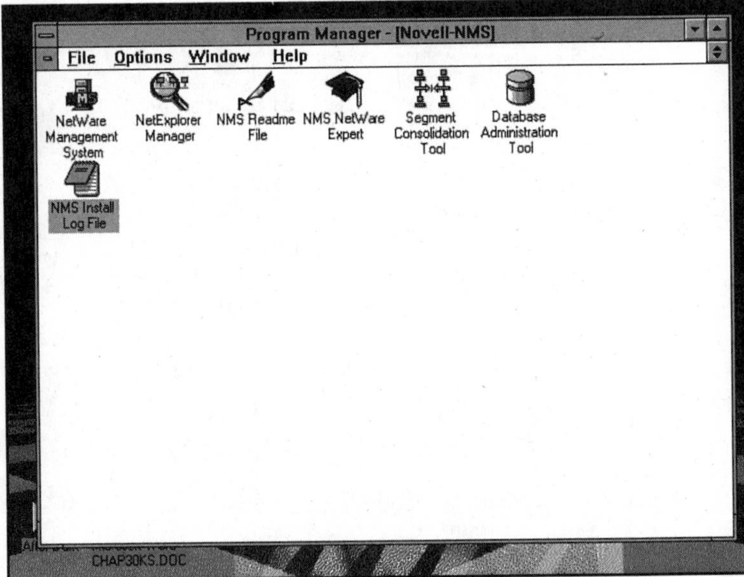

Figure 28.7
NMS Program Tools.

The discovery of nodes on the network is performed by NetExplorer. You can run NetExplorer manually or schedule for it to be run at specific times. To run NetExplorer manually, you should select the NetExplorer icon.

To schedule NetExplorer to run at a specific time, perform the following:

1. Start NMS by double-clicking on its icon in the NMS program group.
2. Select Configure from the NMS menus.
3. Select Global Preferences (see fig. 28.8).
4. Scroll through the list of icons in the Global Preference dialog book, and click on the NetExplorer icon. You should see the NetExplorer configuration screen (see fig. 28.9).
5. Click the option button labeled Run NetExplorer Manager Intermittently.
6. Enter the time to start the NetExplorer Manager.
7. Click on Save and double click the control-menu box to close the dialog book.

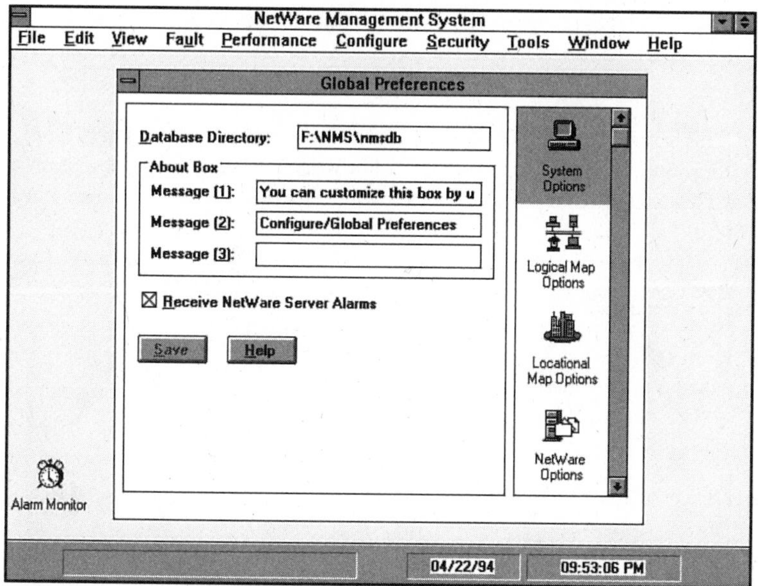

Figure 28.8
NMS Global Preferences.

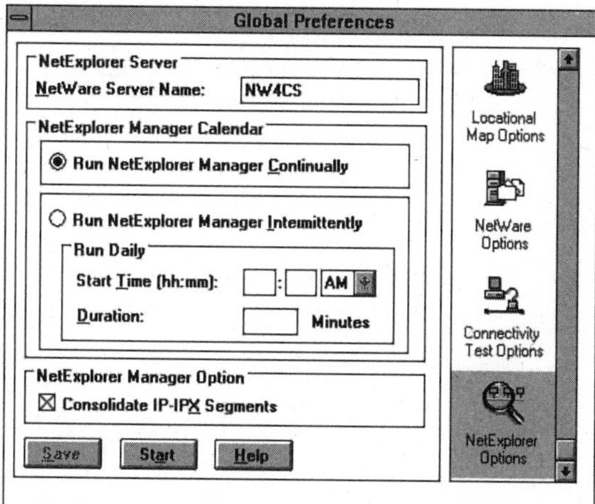

Figure 28.9
NMS NetExplorer Configuration.

NMS Discovery Process

After NetExplorer starts, discovery of the nodes on the networks takes place by three independent methods.

Method 1: IP Discovery. This is started by the NXPIP module and starts with the routing information on the NMS server. From the routing table, it looks up the IP address of each router contacts them using

SNMP. After reading the routing tables of the routers it contacts, it discovers IP addresses of other routers. It repeats the previous steps after discovering a new router. This allows it to discover all routers that are in a routing table.

Method 2: IPX Discovery. This is started by the NXPIPX module and starts with the IPX address, LAN type of each network interface on the NMS server. It uses SAP information stored in the server to learn about other IPX services. It then contacts the IPX devices and repeats this process each time it discovers a new IPX device (see fig. 28.10).

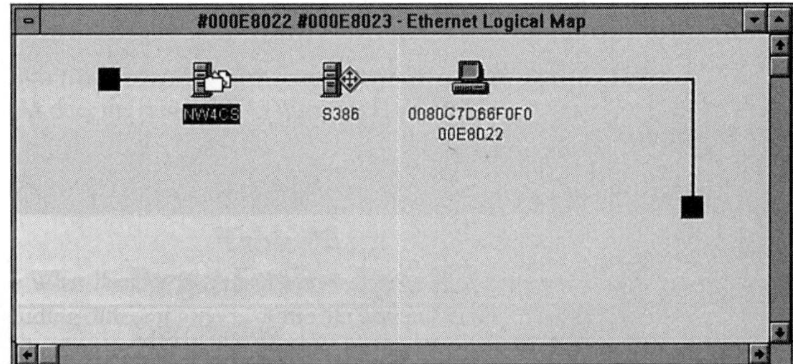

Figure 28.10
IPX Ethernet Logical Map.

Method 3: Protocol-independent Discovery. This is started by identifying all remote LANalyzer Agents and LANtern monitors. These agents and devices monitor MAC addresses of packets on the segments. The NXPLANZ.NLM on the NMS server uses SNMP to access data stored by the LANanalyzer Agents and the LANtern monitors.

Using NMS MIB Browser

You can use the MIB browser and predefined MIB profiles to query SNMP-manageable devices. To accomplish this you must perform the following steps:

1. Start the NMS Console
2. Select Tools from the menu bar
3. Select SNMP MIB Browser

You should see the MIB Browser screen (see fig. 28.11)

This screen shows that the IPX address option is used to poll a target device. If you are contacting an IP device, you should use the IPX address option, by selecting the IP button (see fig. 28.11).

Figure 28.12 shows that the selected device at address 144.10.74.55 was not reachable using the ARP interface profile.

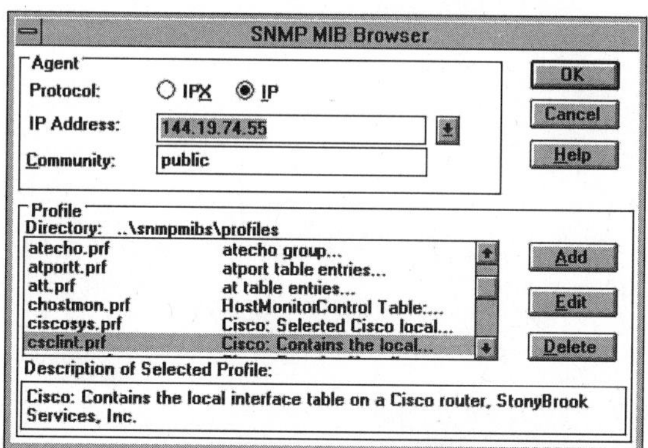

Figure 28.11
NMS MIB Browser using IPX address.

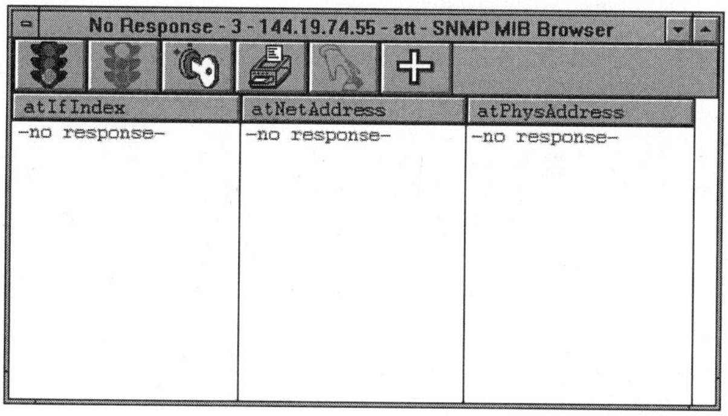

Figure 28.12
Unreachable interface.

Finding nodes

A useful feature of NMS is finding nodes based on:

- Name
- IPX address
- IP address
- MAC address
- Net Address
- Host Address

To use this feature:

1. Start the NMS Console

2. Select View from the menu bar
3. Select Find

   You should see the Find screen (see fig. 28.13).

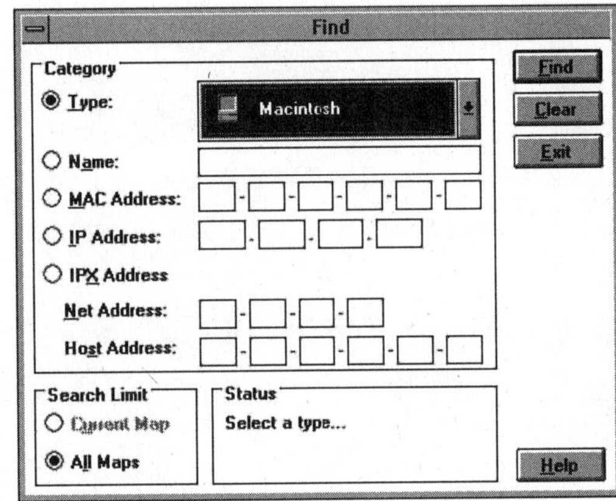

Figure 28.13
NMS Find screen.

28

4. Enter the criteria by which you wish to find the device, and select the Find button.

OSI-Based Management

OSI network management is ambitious and complex. It makes use of a protocol called *Common Management Information Protocol* (CMIP). In concept, it is similar to the SNMP-based approach except that it has a wider scope. Comparisons between these two sets of protocols have resulted in heated debates. Proponents of both systems realize that each protocol has a role to play in managing future networks. Both protocol families use a management-information base and vendor-specific extensions to the MIB.

Scope of OSI Management

Figure 28.14 shows the OSI network management model. The *Network Management Application Process* (NMAP) implements the network management services consisting of five elements:

- Fault management
- Performance management
- Security management

- Configuration management
- Accounting management

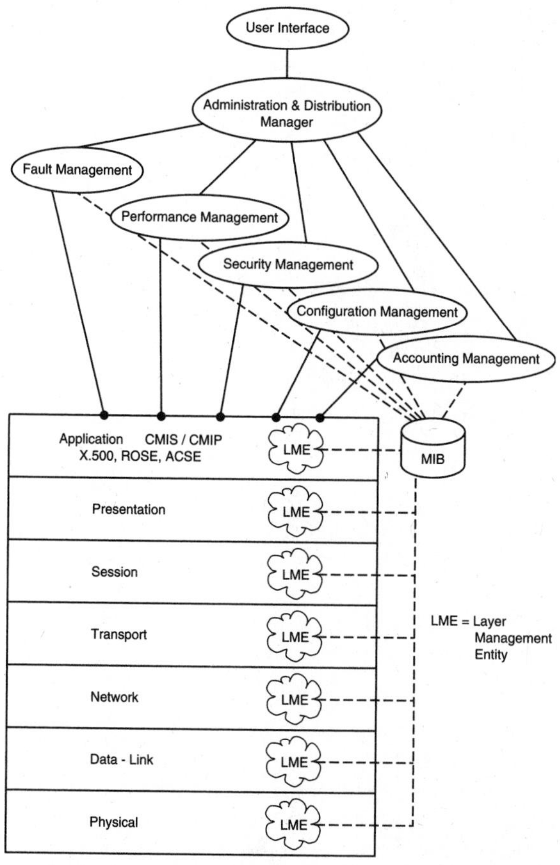

Figure 28.14
OSI network management model.

Each layer of the OSI model has a *Layer Management Entity* (LME) that sends management information on these five aspects to the NMAP. This management information is stored in the MIB, which is a virtual store that describes the different parameters to be managed.

The management operations that you can perform on MIBs are similar in concept to SNMP, but more complex. SNMP has four operations, but CMIP includes operations such as M-INITIALIZE, M-GET, M-SET, M-ACTION, M-ABORT, M-CREATE, M-DELETE, M-EVENT-REPORT, and M-TERMINATE.

OSI Management Protocols

Common Management Information Services (CMIS) and *Common Management Information Protocol* (CMIP) are the protocols used at the application layer. CMIS describes the management services provided to NMAP. The implementation of CMIS is done by the CMIP, which is a peer-to-peer protocol used to exchange management information (fig. 28.14).

The CMIP protocols make use of other OSI protocols. *Application Common Services Element* (ACSE) is used to provide communications binding, and *Remote Operation Services Element* (ROSE) implements a *Remote Procedure Call* (RPC) mechanism. At the other layers, full OSI-based services are used.

An Interim Approach CMOT

Because full OSI-based services are implemented on few networks, an attempt has been made to run OSI network management protocols on TCP/IP-based networks. TCP/IP was chosen for this experiment because it is a de facto industry standard, and it is the hope of OSI advocates that TCP/IP will be replaced by OSI protocols. Implementing CMIP on TCP/IP-based networks will make the transition to full OSI management protocols easier. The management protocol for this interim approach is called *Common Management Over TCP/IP* (CMOT).

The networking model for a CMOT management system is shown in figure 28.15. Only a minimal set of presentation-layer services needed for connection establishment, release, and data exchange are implemented. These minimal presentation services are referred to as *Lightweight Presentation Protocol* (LPP). The LPP services run on the TCP/UDP at the transport layer, which in turn run on *Internet Protocol* (IP) at the network layer. The CMIP protocol is implemented by *Common Management Information Services Element* (CMISE). A peer-to-peer session exists between CMISE on management systems over which CMIP messages are exchanged.

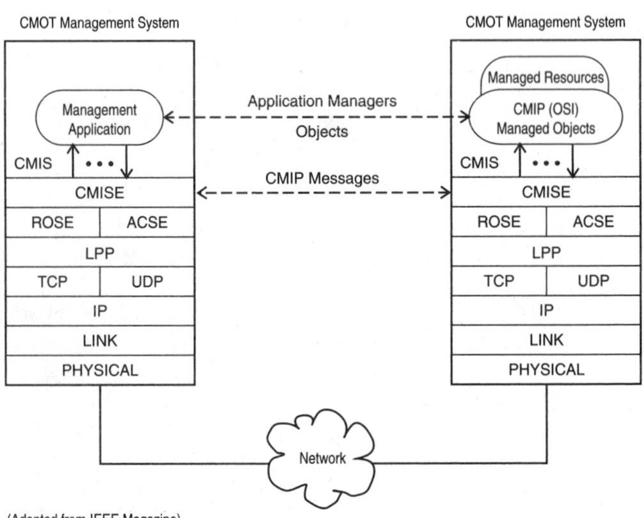

Figure 28.15
CMOT Management System.

Although there is a large commercial interest in SNMP, there is little in CMOT. CMOT may have missed its window of opportunity because SNMP delivered a working network management protocol with a powerful functionality that is much faster.

SNMP versus CMIP

Both SNMP and CMIP have strong proponents. Although CMIP offers features missing in SNMP, SNMP is widely deployed, and CMIP implementations are few at this time.

CMIP is association-oriented and requires that two CMIP application entities be connected before they can exchange management information. Although management information is sent reliably, there is greater overhead in CMIP. SNMP, on the other hand, does not need an established connection to send information. It has less protocol overhead and is faster than CMIP. You cannot be assured, however, that SNMP messages will reach their destination. You may have to build an acknowledgment strategy for certain applications.

CMIP enables multiple-object selection with conditional commands. For example, in CMIP you can request port information for all bridges that have a badPacketCount >= 50. SNMP does not support this capability directly. In SNMP, every bridge must be queried separately for badPacketCount, and the SNMP manager must check to see if the badPacketCount >= 50. CMIP returns more information from a single command than is needed in some situations, and filtering would have to be done anyway. SNMP tends to deliver just the information requested and nothing else.

Both CMIP and SNMP can specify multiple operations of the same type within a single request. In SNMP, the requests are carried out, in an atomic fashion-either they are all done, or none are carried out and an error code is returned. In CMIP, a best-efforts approach is used to carry out operations on multiple instances of the same object.

You can use CMIP to send a single request to get large amounts of data. If the data cannot be accommodated in a single reply, the data is sent in a series of linked replies. SNMP does not support linked replies and can be in-efficient for retrieving large amounts of data, such as addressing tables. SNMP proponents argue that the need for transfer of tables of information is less frequent than reading or writing to a simple MIB object.

You can use CMIP and SNMP to sequence or browse through an MIB. In CMIP, you can use wild cards to get multiple-object selection capabilities. With SNMP, the GET-NEXT command can traverse the MIB in a column-row order. To support the complex CMIP operations, MIB object organization gets more difficult and complex. SNMP GET-NEXT operation and MIB object organization is simpler.

CMIP uses object-specific commands such as "reboot system." SNMP makes use of the SET operation to set a Boolean flag to reboot the system.

CMIP event reports can be confirmed or unconfirmed. SNMP events are always unconfirmed. CMIP objects are more complex and comprehensive than SNMP objects. On the other hand, CMIP objects are more difficult to implement.

SNMP uses a polling method to access critical MIB parameters. CMIP uses an event-based reporting mechanism, which expects the managed device to report events. Polling introduces traffic overhead when the number of managed devices become large. Polling, however, keeps the SNMP-managed devices simple. CMIP is more efficient for managing large numbers of network devices, but these devices tend to be more complex because they have to take care of reporting events.

In general, CMIP more efficiently communicates large amounts of management information of the type that occurs between two CMIP managers. SNMP is better suited for manager-to-managed-device communications.

Summary

This chapter discussed a number of network management schemes, including SNMP, CMOT, and CMIS/CMIP. SNMP is the most widely supported technology. Novell has two products, the LANtern Services Manager and the LANtern Monitor, that implement SNMP.

Network Applications

Before LANs became popular, most applications for DOS were written under the assumption that only one user would be operating the machine at a time. Because there was no way to share resources under DOS on a single machine, this seemed like a reasonable assumption. After LANs became commonplace, many users tried to run these single-user applications on a network. They discovered that sometimes the applications ran without any problems, but they sometimes crashed or lost data. This chapter explores why these problems occur with single-user software and how multiuser software overcomes these problems. The different types of multiuser software also are examined.

Running Single-User Software on a Network

Normally, single-user applications are designed to run on machines without any network connections. Is it then possible for the single-user application to run on a network? Consider a single-user application that is stored at the workstation. When the name of the startup program for the application is typed at the DOS prompt, the DOS loader loads the application from the local media on which it is stored, and control is then transferred to the application that runs on the workstation.

If the single-user application is stored on a directory on the server, the user must first log in to a server on the network to run the application. The user must have a minimum of Read and File scan privileges in the directory in which the single-user application is stored. That directory can be set in the user's search path. The search path can be set making use of the MAP command at the command line, or the MAP commands can be placed in the login script files, as discussed in Chapter 23, "Managing User Sessions." Alternatively, the user can change the current directory to the directory in which the application is stored by using the MAP command or the DOS CD command.

When the name of the startup file for the application is typed, DOS does not know that the application is stored on a network directory; DOS issues a request to load the application program in the workstation's memory. The NetWare shell monitors all DOS system calls by placing itself between the request for DOS services—by means of the INT 21 (hex) interrupt—and the DOS services. If the NetWare shell determines that the request is for a file on the server, it issues a *NetWare Core Protocol* (NCP) packet to implement this request. The server (on which the file resides) processes the NCP request and returns an NCP reply indicating the status of the processed request.

When DOS issues a request to load the application program into memory, that request is translated by the NetWare shell into an NCP request to fetch a copy of the application program from the server (see fig. 29.1). A number of *packet transmissions* are performed to get the entire application program from the server directory to the workstation. The application program is then loaded in the workstation memory, and execution takes place without DOS being aware that the program was downloaded from the server.

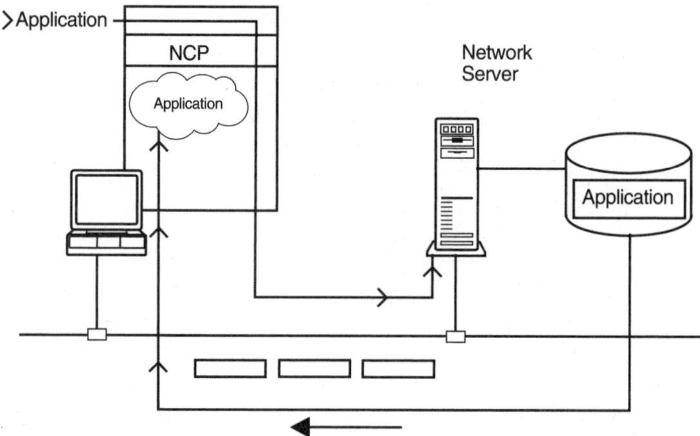

Figure 29.1
Loading an application from a NetWare server.

When the single-user application loads from the NetWare server, a typical operation is to access a data file. The data file may be on the network, and the single-user application is not aware that it is opening a network file. (It issues a DOS request to open a file.) The NetWare shell intercepts this request. After determining that the open file request is for a data file on the network, the NetWare shell directs the request to the server. The file is opened on the server, and the application is ready to perform file operations on it.

If the application needs to read a portion of a data file, it can open the file, read the data, and close the file again. The application also can open the file, and then keep it opened until the application ends normally.

If the application has been written to perform the first option, another station on the network running the same single-user application can open the file after it has been closed (see fig. 29.2) and modify the data in the file. When the first station reopens the file, the file will have been changed by the second station, but the first station will not be aware of this change. The two applications can easily step over each other and destroy each other's changes.

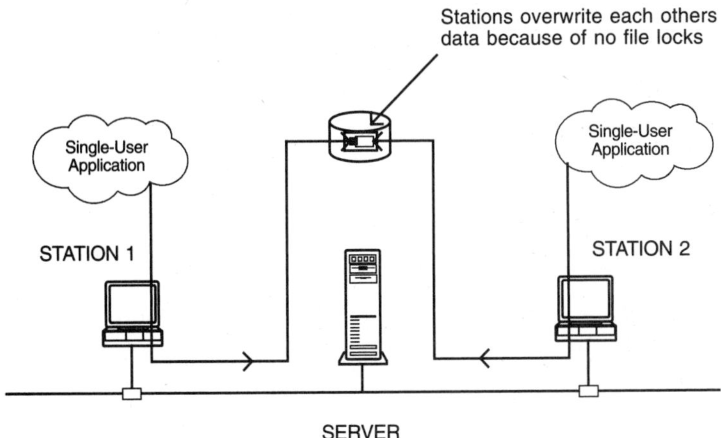

Figure 29.2
Data file conflicts when multiple users use a single-user application on a network.

The real problem is that there is no mechanism to enable the applications to communicate with each other when sharing data. Each application runs independently of other applications and is not aware of changes made to shared data.

To solve the single-user data access problem, there must be a concurrency-control mechanism that enables an application to place a lock on a data file so that other applications cannot modify the data file. A *lock* is a mechanism that is placed on a shared resource. It grants control over the resource to the application issuing the lock.

If the second option is being used by the application software, the single-user application can lock the data file by making use of NetWare features. When a data file is copied or created on a NetWare server, it has the default Non-sharable Read Write attributes. (This means that the file can be opened for read/write operations but, as long as the file is open, NetWare locks the file for you.) Therefore, if the file has Non-shareable Read Write attributes, the first station that opens the file locks the file (other stations are denied access to this file). This is one way to ensure that single-user applications can operate on a NetWare LAN.

To enable single-user applications to have the same file opened by a number of applications, the data file must have the Shared attribute. File attributes for NetWare files can be changed by using the FLAG command or the FILER utility.

Running Multiuser Applications

Multiuser applications are designed with *concurrency control* mechanisms. This means that applications are able to share data without writing over each other's data. Examples of applications that require this type of concurrency control are database applications, spreadsheets, electronic mail, and group productivity tools.

Concurrency-Control Mechanisms

Three concurrency-control mechanisms can be used for data file sharing:

- File locking
- Record locking
- Field locking

Figure 29.3 presents a conceptual view of these mechanisms. *File locking* makes the entire file unavailable to other users. If a word processor locks a file, for example, the file is unavailable for update operations. It may still be available for viewing (read operation), but other users cannot update the file in use. This is how networking versions of word processor applications, such as WordPerfect, implement file locks.

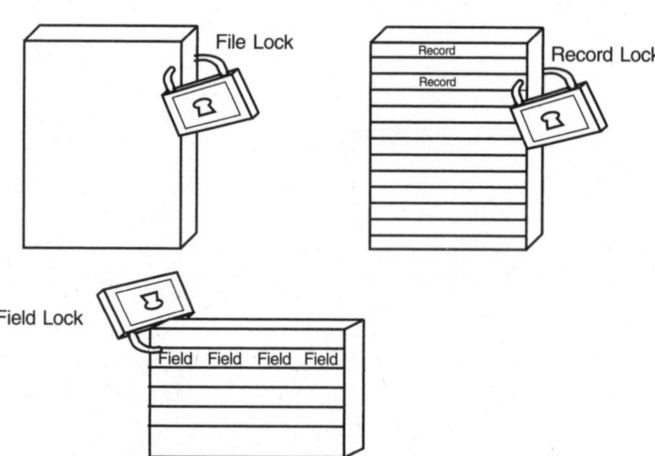

Figure 29.3
Concurrency-controlled mechanisms.

Record locking locks a range of bytes, rather than the entire file. This is a very useful feature in database applications in which different workstations may be working on different parts of the same data file. DOS 3.3 and later versions contain system services to support record locking. If the DOS record-locking services are used, the NetWare shell translates them into NCP requests that implement the locking through NetWare APIs. NetWare provides record-locking APIs that can be used directly by multiuser applications.

Field locking is a further refinement of the record-locking concept. Several users may be working on the same record but on different fields of that record. In an employee database, for example, one data-entry clerk can be updating the address and phone numbers of an employee while someone else is updating salary information for that employee. You also can have a higher-level lock so that certain fields can be viewed and updated by certain users only. A good example of this is the employee database, in which the salary information can be hidden from most users.

Logical Records versus Physical Locks

NetWare provides two types of locking mechanisms that are important for applications: logical and physical locks.

You can implement a *logical lock* by assigning a logical name to a resource and locking that name. Other applications check for a lock on the name before accessing the resource. A logical record is enforced by applications. It is not enforced by the NetWare operating system.

Physical locks are different from logical locks because they are enforced by the network operating system. Physical locks can be used to lock a range of bytes in a file. (This is the way to implement record and field locking.) If another user attempts to access a range of bytes that is physically locked, the user receives an `Access denied` message.

Logical and physical locks on a NetWare 3.*x* server can be displayed by using the MONITOR NLM. NetWare defines the following types of physical locks:

- **Locked Exclusive.** Locked so that no one else can read or write to the specified range of bytes.
- **Locked Shareable.** Locked so that reads are OK but only one station can write.
- **Locked.** Logged for future locking.
- **TTS Holding Lock.** Unlocked by application, but still locked by TTS because transactions are not complete.

SET Parameters That Control Application Locks

NetWare 3.*x* has a number of record-locking parameters that are important for applications that make use of file and record locking. You can use the SET command to set these parameters on the server console. These parameters are as follows:

- MAXIMUM RECORD LOCKS
- MAXIMUM FILE LOCKS
- MAXIMUM RECORD LOCKS PER CONNECTION
- MAXIMUM FILE LOCKS PER CONNECTION

Limits are placed on the total number of system-wide and per-connection file and record locks because implementing locks takes up server resources that can be used for other functions. In most situations, the default limits are adequate for applications that make use of record and file locking. If applications fail because of messages about insufficient file and record locks, consider increasing these limits.

- **MAXIMUM RECORD LOCKS.** This parameter sets a limit on the total number of record locks that are possible on a NetWare server at the same time.

- **MAXIMUM FILE LOCKS.** This parameter sets the limit on the total number of opened and locked files NetWare can simultaneously handle at the server.
- **MAXIMUM RECORD LOCKS PER CONNECTION.** This parameter controls the maximum number of record locks a station can use per connection.
- **MAXIMUM FILE LOCKS PER CONNECTION.** This parameter controls the maximum number of opened and locked files a station can use per connection.

Database Applications in a LAN Environment

Databases that run on LANs must be able to support multiple-user access to the database. This means that all of the network and database protocols needed for remote access of the database must be supported. For NetWare LANs, the preferred protocols are the SPX/IPX for transport. Because the database software makes use of NetWare files to implement its database, the NetWare Core Protocols also are used. Database servers, such as SQL Server from Microsoft, require the Named Pipes protocol. (This must be supported at the workstation that accesses the SQL Server.)

The database also must be able to implement file and record locking and, optionally, field-level locking. Security mechanisms should be in place that enable access to files, records, and fields on a per-user or per-user group basis.

Another important requirement is the automated recovery and backup facility. If data files get corrupted, there should be a way of making the data files consistent. A transaction tracking capability, as implemented in the NetWare SQL product, also is desirable. Such *transaction tracking services* (TTSs) are available in NetWare. When used in the context of databases, TTS means that a log is made of the transaction before the transaction is actually executed. This transaction log is called the *transaction backout file.* If the transaction fails because of a server, workstation, or network crash, the transaction can be rolled back to the point before the transaction, so that the integrity of the database is preserved.

There are two types of technologies used to implement databases on a LAN: file server-based technology and database server-based technology.

File Server-Based Technology

Figure 29.4 shows a LAN in which file server-based technology is used. In this technology, the file server provides remote file services used for storing the database files. Most of the database processing is done at the workstation. The file server provides only reading/writing of data blocks and support for record and file locks. The algorithms for record manipulation are executed at the workstation.

With file server-based databases, records have to be transported from the file server to the workstation for processing. Tasks that require processing many records at a time can generate a large amount of traffic. The network bandwidth and the delays involved in record transfer can easily become a bottleneck. For every record update, the record must first be transferred to the workstation. The record copy is changed at the workstation and then sent back to the server to be written into the database, which results in at least two record transfers per update operation. If the record is larger than the maximum packet size configured for the LAN, additional packet transfers may occur as the record is broken into smaller pieces and sent across the network.

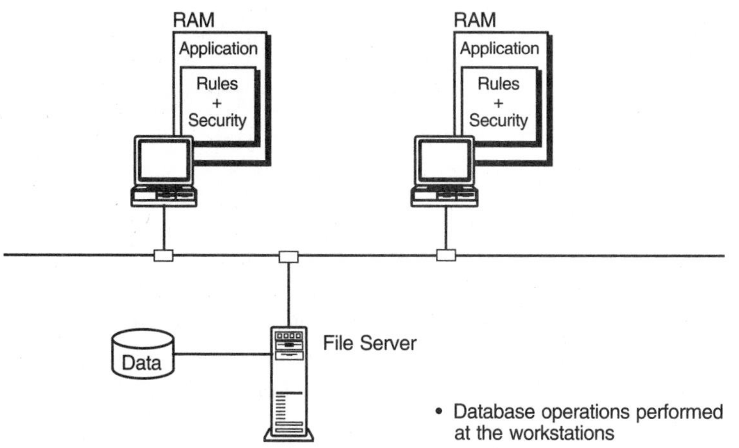

Figure 29.4
File server-based technology.

Consider a situation in which the database consists of 500,000 employee records. A query is sent to the file server-based database asking for a list of all employees who earn more than $200,000 per year. Although only a few individuals satisfy this criterion, this query still means that each of the 500,000 records is transported to the workstation, where the salary field is compared to the $200,000 criterion. This is not a very efficient way to process this information.

Database files on the server are implemented as B+ or B* trees, which are database technologies in which the indices used to access the records are kept in pages of a fixed size and organized in the form of a tree. As part of the database operation, it may be necessary to perform operations, such as splitting and recombining, on these index blocks. In file server-based databases, the index block operations have to be performed at the workstation. This creates its own traffic, and when splitting and recombining lead to other blocks being split or recombined, the network traffic increases.

File server-based technology, though not very efficient, is adequate for small databases. For larger databases, a different type of technology is needed: database server-based technology.

Examples of file server-based products are Paradox, dBASE from Borland, Rbase from MIcrorim, ZIM from Zanthe, Foxbase from Fox Software, Clipper from Nantucket, Focus from Information Builders, Dataflex from Data Access, and DataEase from DataEase International.

Database Servers

In database servers (see fig. 29.5), database operations are split into front-end and back-end operations. The back end is run on a server and performs all database operations. The front end is used to provide a graphical interface to the user and to perform minor processing. Actually, this is very similar to the way traditional database processing takes place on mainframe databases, in which all processing is done on the mainframe.

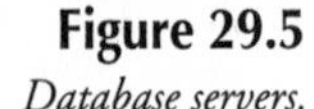

Figure 29.5
Database servers.

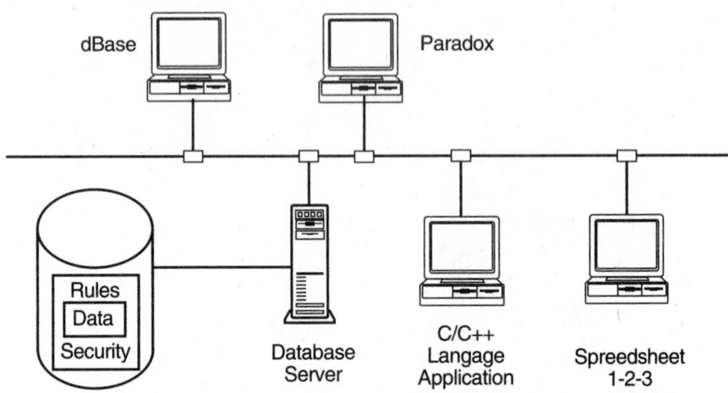

In many ways, database servers are a happy marriage of mainframe database technology and PC technology. The PC used as a workstation performs all graphical user interface processing, and database operations are performed on a centralized machine. The rules and integrity checks for database processing are kept on a central computer, which provides the best kind of security.

Consider the example in which the database consists of 500,000 employee records and a query is sent to the file server-based database for a list of all employees that have a salary greater than $200,000 per year. In the database server example, because all database processing takes place at the database server, there is no requirement to transfer each one of the 500,000 records to the workstation. The database server can sequence through each record and compare the salary field against the $200,000 criteria. Only the handful of records that satisfy the criterion is sent to the workstation. This is a much more efficient way of processing this information.

Another advantage of using a database server is not having to transfer B+/B* tree index pages to the workstation for splitting and recombining.

Examples of database server products are NetWare SQL from Novell, LAN Server from Oracle, SQL Server from Microsoft, INGRES from Ingres Corporation, SQL Base from Gupta Technologies, and XDB Server from Novell.

LAN-Based Word Processing

The advantages of using network versions of word processors is that PC users can easily share files across the network. A network operating system such as NetWare can be used for implementing security and file sharing, so that personal information is kept safe from others. Figure 29.6 shows a LAN-based word processing application.

The NetWare server can be used for sharing common document templates and group documents, and for document consolidation. Popular LAN-based word processing applications are WordPerfect, Microsoft Word, and many others.

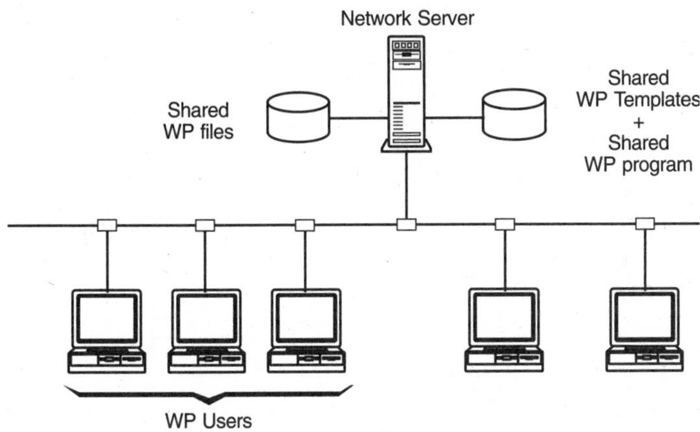

Figure 29.6
LAN-based word processing.

LAN-Based Spreadsheets

The NetWare server can be used to share spreadsheets among several users (see fig. 29.7). At the basic level, at least file locking should be implemented, which prevents users from updating the spreadsheet at the same time. If users are working on different areas of a large spreadsheet, it may be desirable to have cell-level locking, so that individual users can work on the same spreadsheet without overwriting each other's work.

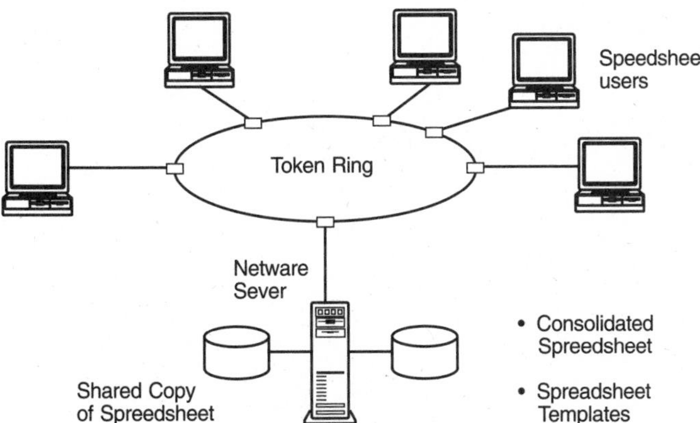

Figure 29.7
LAN-based spreadsheets.

Some LAN spreadsheets support intelligent consolidation, in which groups of spreadsheets can be rolled up and consolidated across the network. The NetWare server also enables the sharing of common templates and financial models that have all the formulas predefined—all that is required is data entry.

Electronic Mail

Figure 29.8 shows the model for electronic mail running on a LAN. The NetWare server acts as a post office where the mail boxes for the users are kept. Electronic mail is sent by posting a mail message to the server. Users can log in to the server at any time and run the electronic mail application, which enables them to read the messages waiting for them.

Figure 29.8 shows that mail-gateways are necessary to access other electronic mail systems. It also is possible for users to dial in to the LAN to read their electronic mail.

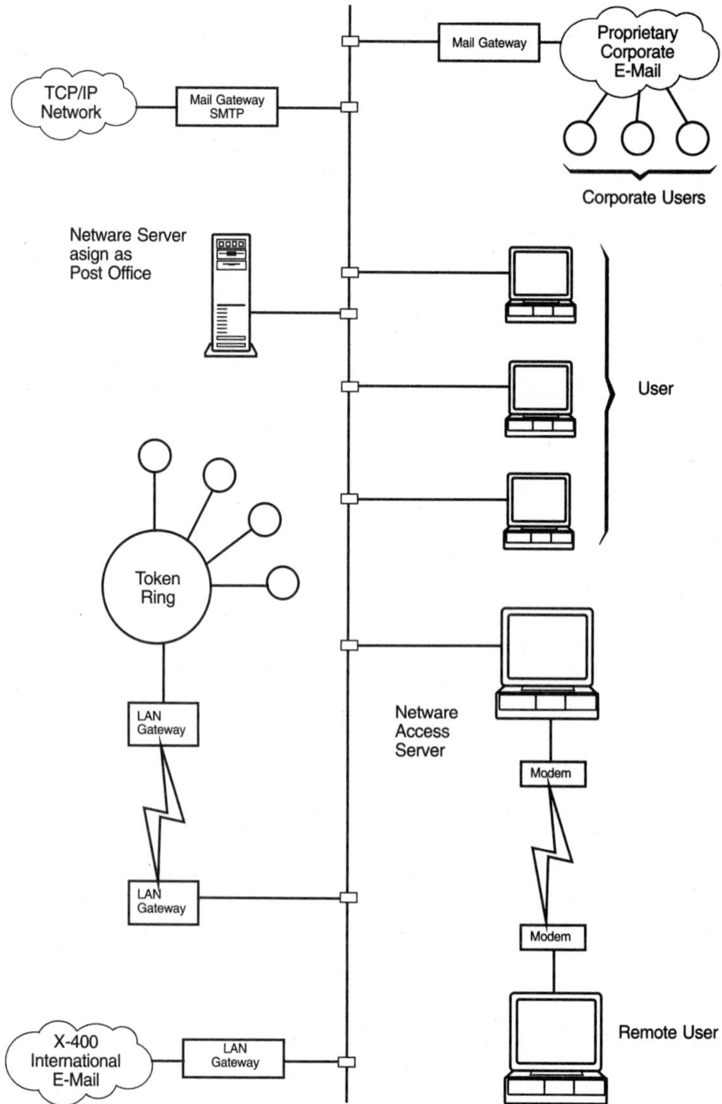

Figure 29.8
A large LAN-based electronic mail configuration.

The most popular electronic mail protocol for LANs is *Message Handling System* (MHS). MHS was originally developed by Action Technologies of Emeryville, California, but its specification and future evolution is now under the control of Novell.

Some of the popular electronic mail products include Da Vinci Mail from Da Vinci Systems, Banyan Mail from Banyan Systems, Higgins Mail from Enable/Higgins Group, Herald Mail from Emissary Systems, Quick Mail from CE Software, and ALL-IN-1 mail from DEC.

Many of the electronic mail systems provide electronic mail gateways to other systems such as IBM PROFS, IBM DISOSS, DEC ALL-IN-1, X.400, and SMTP. For international mail networks, the standard is X.400. When evaluating electronic mail systems, support for X.400 gateways should be on the top of your list because this is the way most electronic mail systems are evolving.

Many electronic mail packages are feature-rich. Some of the features that are supported are the following:

- Carbon copy and blind copy. *Carbon copy* is sent to the designated user. A *blind copy* of the message is sent to other recipients that do not show up in the electronic mail.
- Distribution list. These can be personal or system wide.
- Attachments. Files, graphic data, and screen captures can be attached and sent.
- File folders. For organizing personal mail.
- Delivery receipt and read receipt on a per-electronic-mail basis.
- Auto forwarding and express delivery.
- Message encryption and compression.
- Pop-up notification of new mail.
- Electronic mail gateways to other electronic mail systems.
- Remote user access.

Workgroup Software

Workgroup software enables a group of users to coordinate their efforts as a team. It has a combination of features such as electronic mail, word processing, to-do-list, project tracking/management/scheduling, financial planning, and electronic accessories (calculators, notepads, clocks, alarms).

Examples of such applications include Notes from Lotus, Office Vision from IBM, WordPerfect Office from WordPerfect Corporation (now Novell GroupWare from Novell), Rhapsody from AT&T, and Total Office Manager from Network Technology.

MHS

Do not confuse Message Handling System—originally created by Action Technologies—with MHS specified in the X.400 MHS standard, even though they have the same name.

MHS does not provide a user interface; it is a messaging standard that specifies the mechanism as to how messages are to be represented and exchanged. It can be used by application developers to develop distributed applications. MHS handles the collection, routing, and delivery of any message or file across dissimilar environments. Applications that use MHS do not have to worry about the mechanics of data transfer such as transport protocols, error checking, sequencing, and so on. MHS handles these low-level details by properly interfacing with appropriate transport protocols. MHS provides transparent store-and-forward capabilities. It is designed to run on Novell networks, though stand-alone versions of MHS for DOS also are available. When MHS is run on a server, it takes approximately 300K of RAM.

Because the communication method is store-and-forward, a message can be held at an electronic post-office box before it is transmitted. Therefore, MHS is not suited for realtime interprocess communication. When implemented on a server, MHS provides a back-end store-and-forward message server.

MHS is similar in concept to X.400, but is much simpler. It does not require the extensive computing resources required by X.400, and it has a much simpler API. It is typically used to transmit electronic messages, but also can be used for transmitting text and binary files. To send mail from an MHS system to a non-MHS system such as ALL-IN-1, Easylink, X.400, or SMTP, you need a mail gateway to convert the different mail formats.

Details of the MHS structure are documented in the NetWare MHS Developer's Kit which contains a description of the *Message Control Block* (MCB), and *Standard Message Format* (SMF) interface.

An example of an MHS-based network is shown in figure 29.9. The MHS post offices also are called MHS hubs because they act as a central site for exchanging electronic mail.

This network shows that a mobile user can dial into the network with a laptop and a modem and receive or send mail on the MHS network. The laptop user needs the personal edition of MHS up and running on his system; this enables the user to log in to the network at any one of the hubs and collect or send mail. The mail is stored at an MHS hub from which it is sent to the destination directly or through intervening MHS hubs.

Electronic mail can be composed and sent by the laptop user while the user is logged in to the network. However, this approach can be costly in terms of long-distance telephone charges. A better way is to configure the MHS on the laptop so that long-distance connection time is reduced to electronic-mail transfer only. This can be done by setting up default routing information in configuration files on the laptop.

The following sample batch file can be used to start the MHS connectivity manager on your laptop:

```
@echo off
rem Go to the MHS directory installed on your laptop
cd  \ mhs\exe
rem Invoke MHS
```

```
mhs -l
rem Invoke the E-mail user agent
call uagent.bat
rem Save log files and then delete them
copy \sdrege.*    \log\*.*   >  nul
del  \sdrege.*   >  nul
```

The use of the -l option causes the MHS program to run and terminate if there is no more mail to deliver. The connectivity manager (user agent) is run after the electronic-mail transfer. The log files are then backed up and deleted for the next session.

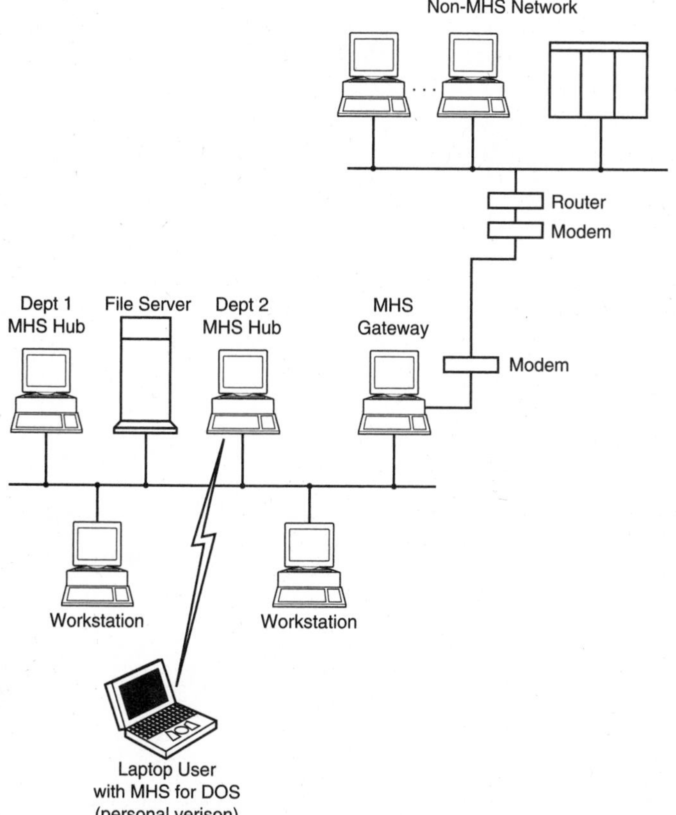

Figure 29.9
An example of an MHS network.

To set up a menu driven system using Novell menus, one can set up a menu script similar to the following:

```
%MHS Dialup,29,60
SCS Corporate Office
....@echo off
....set MHSPHONE=1,406-333-4471
....call MHSCON.BAT....CORPMHS   2
```

```
....set MHSPHONE=
Your MHS Choice
....@echo off
....set MHSPHONE=@1"Please enter the MHS dial number"
....call MHSCON.BAT   CORPMHS   2
....set MHSPHONE=
```

The MHSCON.BAT file can use the MHSUSER command and accept arguments to make the connection. The phone number is passed as an environment string variable to the MHSCON.BAT batch file to make it possible to pass comma (,) values for delays. The use of commas is useful when dialing out using the number 9 or causing delays for credit card numbers.

NetWare 3.12 comes with a single server version of the Basic MHS package and an e-mail client utility called FIRSTMAIL. The Basic MHS can be installed from the CD-ROM distribution or the BASICMHS-1 and BASICMHS-2 floppy disks. The installation procedure uses the System Options of the INSTALL NLM that allows NLM applications to be installed directly on the server. Once installed, Basic MHS services are started by loading the BASICMHS.NLM at the server. The following is a guideline in starting the Basic MHS server:

1. Ensure that CLIB.NLM, BTRIEVE.NLM, and BSPXCOM.NLM are loaded at the server.

2. Load BASICMHS.NLM by entering the following command:


```
LOAD SYS:MHS\EXE\BASICMHS
          [-Nserver/vol:path\MHS\MAIL] [-Snnn]
          [-Vxy]
```

The[-N*server*/ *vol*:*path*\MHS\MAIL] path identifies the path to the MHS's MAIL directory if you decided to locate it at different location than the root of the SYS: volume.

The -S*nnn* parameter is used to specify the minimum disk space (in KB, default is 200 KB) required for message delivery. If the amount of space available is less than the specified parameter value, mail delivery is suspended, until more disk space becomes available.

The -V*xy* is used to display the verbosity of system level messages. The *x* and *y* values can range from 0 to 9. Default is 5 for *x* and 3 for *y*. The *x* represents verbosity level for the file server console messages and *y* represents the verbosity system log. A larger numeric value means that more messages will be displayed. To disable messages set verbosity level to 0.

Btrieve

The Btrieve record manager was originally developed by Softcraft which was later purchased by Novell in the mid-1980s. Btrieve is bundled with every version of NetWare. It is a complete record manager system that enables you to build in an indexed data file. You can build a master index and several supplementary indexes for each data file. The indexed files are maintained in the same file as the data file. Btrieve has been used as the basis for building applications by many third-party vendors (including many accounting packages) primarily because it is fast. Some of Btrieve's features are the following:

- Up to 24 indexes per file
- 14 different data types (Integer, String, Zstring, Float, BCD, Money, Date, and so on)
- Ascending/Descending keys with user-defined collating sequences
- 4G data-file size
- Volume spanning
- Data-file encryption and file ownership
- Single and multiple record-level locks
- File-level locks
- Defining atomicity of operations using Transaction Tracking
- Logging and Rollforward processes to recover from corrupt files
- Dead-lock detection in a server-based environment

Integrated into Btrieve is its own cache manager that can be used for optimizing I/O performance. When Btrieve is loaded at the workstation, you can specify the size of this cache. The cache can dramatically improve I/O performance. If cache space is over-committed, a least-recently-used (LRU) algorithm is used.

Btrieve can run either as a server-based program or a workstation-based program. The workstation-based program has to be purchased separately, whereas the server-based is bundled with NetWare. At the workstation, Btrieve can run on DOS/MS Windows and OS/2 platforms. Future support for other dominant workstation operating system platforms is expected.

In the workstation-based version, Btrieve is loaded as a TSR for DOS and as a device driver for OS/2. The application program calls the Btrieve interface through a system call. These system calls are trapped by Btrieve. This approach allows an application written in any language that can issue a system call to access the Btrieve record manager. Btrieve comes with software wrappers (libraries or DLLs) for languages such as C, Pascal, COBOL, and BASIC.

In the server-based version, Btrieve runs on the NetWare server and is accessed by workstations that must run the Btrieve requester component. The Btrieve requester is responsible for sending data requests to the Btrieve server component and receiving results from the Btrieve server and communicating it to the application. Figure 29.10 shows the possibilities of the different workstation clients communicating with the NetWare Btrieve server component.

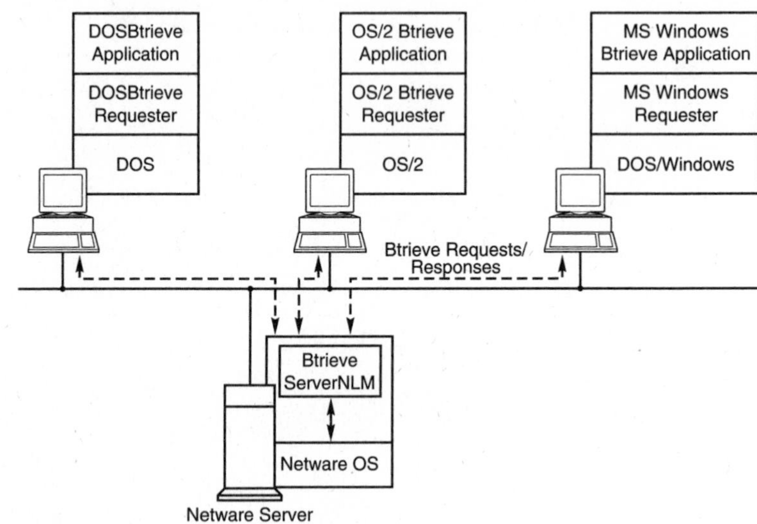

Figure 29.10
Btrieve requester/server architecture.

Btrieve Programs

The NetWare Btrieve package consists of the following programs:

29

BSERVER

BROUTER

Btrieve Requester

BSERVER is the Btrieve record manager, which runs at the server. It can be set up to run using the console LOAD command in the AUTOEXEC.NCF file. The BROUTER also loads at the server and allows other server-based applications loaded at the server to communicate with the BSERVER. Essentially, it provides server-to-server Btrieve operation. The Btrieve requester must be loaded at each workstation, and its name is specific to the work-station operating system on which it runs. The BSERVER and BROUTER programs are available as NLMs for NetWare 3.*x* and VAPs for NetWare 2.*x*.

In addition to the preceding components, a utility called BSETUP.EXE is available that runs at a workstation and can be used for configuring the BSERVER and BROUTER programs. Some of the parameters BSETUP can configure are the following:

- Number of open files, handles, locks, transactions, files per transaction, sessions
- Largest record size, page size, compressed record size
- Create file as transactional
- Logging of selected files

least two record transfers per update operation. If the record is larger than the maximum packet size configured for the LAN, additional packet transfers may occur as the record is broken into smaller pieces and sent across the network.

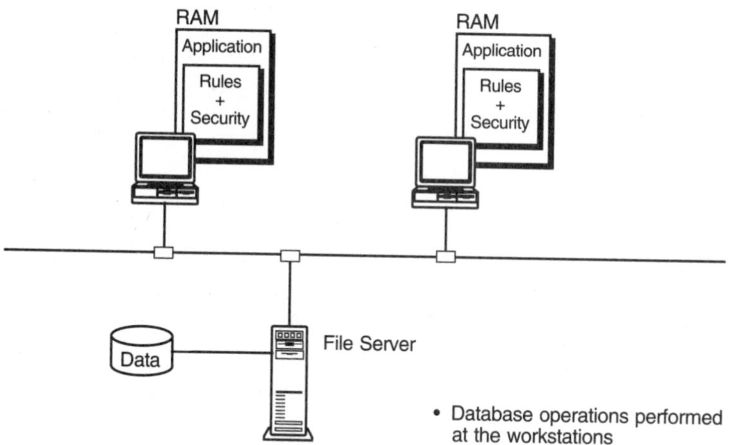

Figure 29.4
File server-based technology.

Consider a situation in which the database consists of 500,000 employee records. A query is sent to the file server-based database asking for a list of all employees who earn more than $200,000 per year. Although only a few individuals satisfy this criterion, this query still means that each of the 500,000 records is transported to the workstation, where the salary field is compared to the $200,000 criterion. This is not a very efficient way to process this information.

Database files on the server are implemented as B+ or B* trees, which are database technologies in which the indices used to access the records are kept in pages of a fixed size and organized in the form of a tree. As part of the database operation, it may be necessary to perform operations, such as splitting and recombining, on these index blocks. In file server-based databases, the index block operations have to be performed at the workstation. This creates its own traffic, and when splitting and recombining lead to other blocks being split or recombined, the network traffic increases.

File server-based technology, though not very efficient, is adequate for small databases. For larger databases, a different type of technology is needed: database server-based technology.

Examples of file server-based products are Paradox, dBASE from Borland, Rbase from MIcrorim, ZIM from Zanthe, Foxbase from Fox Software, Clipper from Nantucket, Focus from Information Builders, Dataflex from Data Access, and DataEase from DataEase International.

Database Servers

In database servers (see fig. 29.5), database operations are split into front-end and back-end operations. The back end is run on a server and performs all database operations. The front end is used to provide a graphical interface to the user and to perform minor processing. Actually, this is very similar to the way traditional database processing takes place on mainframe databases, in which all processing is done on the mainframe.

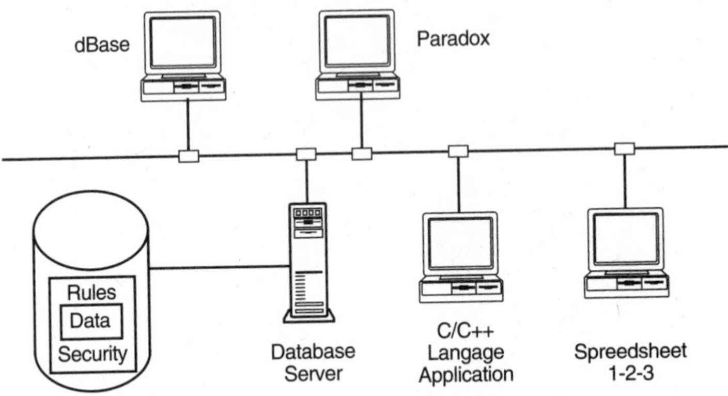

Figure 29.5
Database servers.

In many ways, database servers are a happy marriage of mainframe database technology and PC technology. The PC used as a workstation performs all graphical user interface processing, and database operations are performed on a centralized machine. The rules and integrity checks for database processing are kept on a central computer, which provides the best kind of security.

Consider the example in which the database consists of 500,000 employee records and a query is sent to the file server-based database for a list of all employees that have a salary greater than $200,000 per year. In the database server example, because all database processing takes place at the database server, there is no requirement to transfer each one of the 500,000 records to the workstation. The database server can sequence through each record and compare the salary field against the $200,000 criteria. Only the handful of records that satisfy the criterion is sent to the workstation. This is a much more efficient way of processing this information.

Another advantage of using a database server is not having to transfer B+/B* tree index pages to the workstation for splitting and recombining.

Examples of database server products are NetWare SQL from Novell, LAN Server from Oracle, SQL Server from Microsoft, INGRES from Ingres Corporation, SQL Base from Gupta Technologies, and XDB Server from Novell.

LAN-Based Word Processing

The advantages of using network versions of word processors is that PC users can easily share files across the network. A network operating system such as NetWare can be used for implementing security and file sharing, so that personal information is kept safe from others. Figure 29.6 shows a LAN-based word processing application.

The NetWare server can be used for sharing common document templates and group documents, and for document consolidation. Popular LAN-based word processing applications are WordPerfect, Microsoft Word, and many others.

NetWare SQL

NetWare SQL comprises a number of components that can be used to convert a NetWare server to an SQL server. Figure 2.11 shows the architecture of the NetWare SQL server.

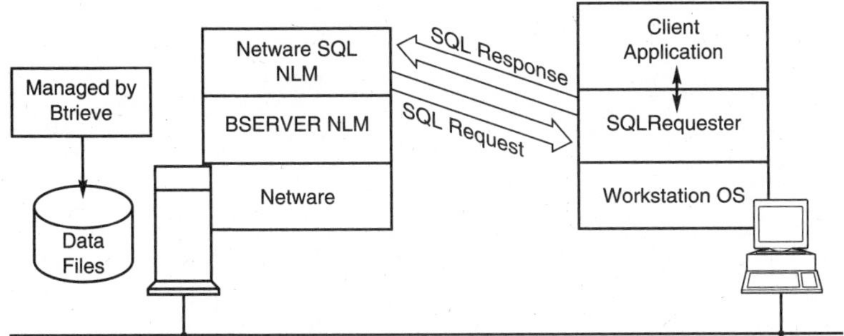

Figure 29.11
NetWare SQL architecture.

NetWare SQL relies on the Btrieve NLM component (BSERVER NLM) to perform the record manager operations. NetWare SQL runs on top of this and provides an SQL database server functionality. This SQL server can accept SQL requests from other workstations that must be running the SQL requester. An XQLI program is available that can run at the workstation and be used to compose and issue SQL queries against NetWare SQL.

29

Client applications can be written to make use of embedded SQL queries to the NetWare SQL server.

Although NetWare SQL is available from Novell, its performance is lower than that of other SQL servers from database vendors such as Oracle and Gupta Technologies.

Building Networking Applications

An interesting trend in networking applications is for the developer and the user to develop customized applications rapidly. Among the tools leading this trend are Visual Basic, Power Builder and Visual AppBuilder.

Both Visual Basic and Power Builder use a high-level script language to describe the actions to be performed. Visual Basic uses a Basic language look-alike and Power Builder uses Power Script. While it is easy to build small applications quickly using these tools they suffer from the following disadvantage for large applications. It is easy to hide large segments of code in places which become difficult to trace or follow especially when maintaining someone else's code.

Visual AppBuilder

Visual AppBuilder is a product now available from Novell, and it uses high level objects and functions to link them into a visual program (see fig. 29.12) that can be compiled to generate an executable file. In this figure, the bottom part of the screen show a palette of objects that you can use and the functions associated with them. These objects are dropped into a worksheet called the *subject.* When certain events occur such as clicking of a mouse button or pressing of a key, you can specify a sequence of operations that need to be performed. An operation is implemented by a function that you also select from the function palette at the bottom of the screen. A sequence of operations can be represented by linking a series of functions together. This is called a *function-chain.* The functions take arguments. These arguments are the objects on which operations are to be performed.

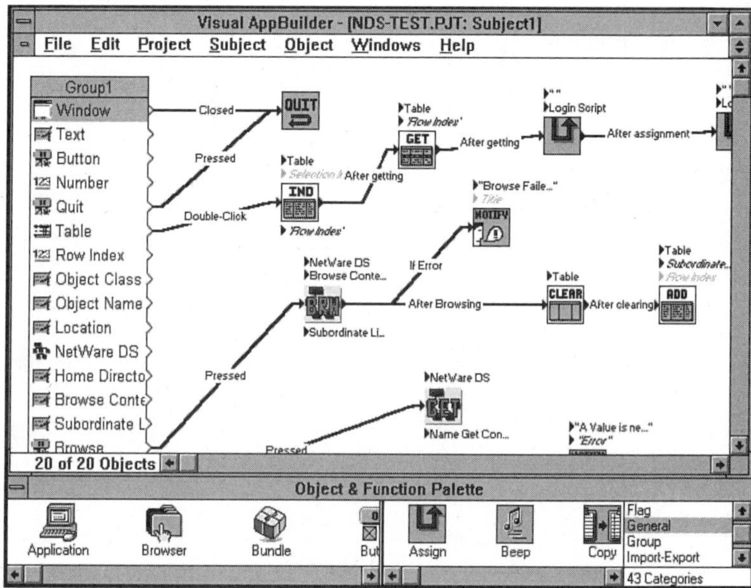

Figure 29.12
Visual AppBuilder Program.

Visual AppBuilder is written for the Macintosh and MS Windows environment. Programs written in either of these environments can run on the other environment where Visual AppBuilder is supported provided the objects used in the program are supported in both environments.

The initial implementation of Visual AppBuilder was written for the Macintosh and MS Windows environment. It is to become available for other operating system environments such as OS/2, Windows NT and UNIX (all major versions) using the AppWare Foundation.

The components used for building applications using Visual AppBuilder are called *AppWare Loadable Modules* (ALMs). A common misconception is that these components are used for building NLMs. While it will be possible eventually to use AppWare for building NLMs, ALMs are meant for developing networked applications that run at workstations such as DOS/Windows, Macintosh, OS/2, UNIX and Windows NT. The ALMs are software objects that encompass program code with associated data storage and functions to achieve a desired task. For example, there are ALM objects for Oracle database, SQL Base (Gupta) database, NetWare Directory Services, Serial Communications, Inter-Application Communications, DDE, Multimedia, Telephony, HyperCard XCMDS, and so forth. You can also take an existing DLL (Dynamic Link Library) for MS/Windows and wrap it around a special DLL that makes the composite object behave as an ALM. This enables you to leverage existing DLLs in your application.

Using ALMs which are pre-written pieces of code you can build powerful network applications without writing a single line of code. These ALMs are available through Novell and third-party developers.

The ALMs are rewritten using a toolkit that consist of C/C++ compilers and tools for their fabrication. If an ALM for performing a task is not available, it can be written using a traditional 3-GL language such as C/C++.

AppWare Foundation

The AppWare Foundation is a set of programming library APIs from Novell, that insulates programmers from the complexity of GUI and network programming on multiple platforms. The AppWare Foundation APIs are designed to run on multiple platforms such as DOS/Windows, Macintosh, UNIX, OS/2, and Windows NT. By writing to this common API set, developers can access existing GUIs, operating system and network resources.

The advantage of using AppWare Foundation is to make your applications portable across the many platforms on which AppWare Foundation runs. The WordPerfect division of Novell is using AppWare Foundation to speed up the development times for developing cross-platform applications. PowerSoft which makes PowerBuilder, a competitor to Visual AppBuilder, is also porting PowerBuilder to use AppWare Foundation. The Object Windows C++ Library from Borland also uses AppWare Foundation.

AppWare Bus

Figure 29.13 shows the relationship between Visual AppBuilder and AppWare Foundation.

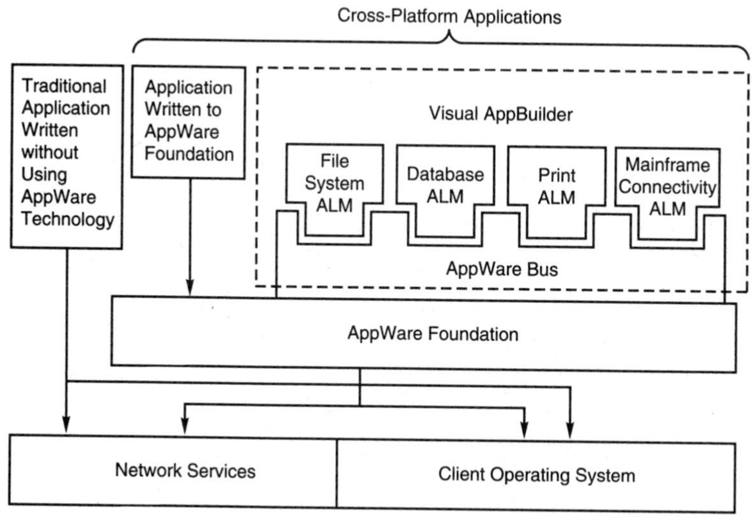

Figure 29.13
AppWare Architecture.

The AppWare Bus is used by the ALMs that comprise a Visual AppBuilder program to communicate between themselves. It allows ALMs to plug into this AppWare Bus much in the same manner and ease of plug-in boards on the system bus of a PC.

Another interesting concept is the Distributed AppWare Bus. This is an application bus that extends beyond the confines of a single workstation to other machines on the network (see fig. 29.14). It makes it possible to have ALMs running on different machines on the network and working in a cooperative fashion to achieve the desired goals of the application. This makes it possible for an application written for a single machine, to be split so that parts of the application (ALMs) run on other machines. It can be used for building client/server applications.

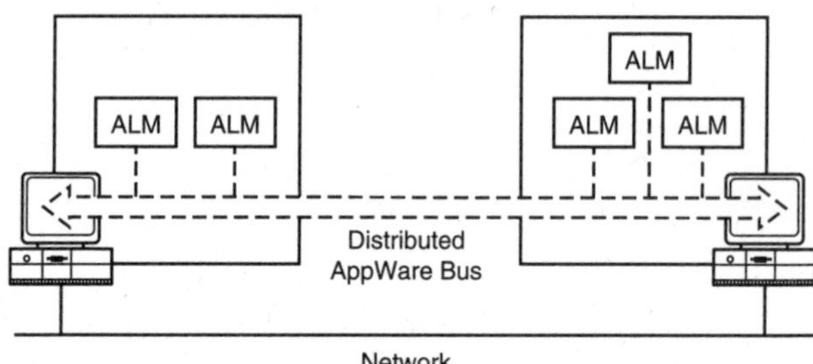

Figure 29.14
Distributed AppWare Bus.

The AppWare bus defines a standard application protocol for interaction between ALMs. This standard protocol guarantees that all ALMs written to conform to it can work together. It eliminates the need to program low-level interactions between ALMs.

SBACKUP

A very important consideration in managing applications and their associated data files is preserving files in case of catastrophic events such as a disk crash, fire, or earthquake. Backup is a very traditional means for assuring that one can recover from these unfortunate events.

Novell's SBACKUP utility runs as an NLM on the NetWare 3.*x* and 4.*x* servers and is used to provide a server-based backup. This means that the tape-drive hardware can be attached directly to the NetWare server instead of to a workstation, and the server's file system can be backed up locally. Prior to the availability of SBACKUP, the only backup option available from Novell was to use a workstation as a backup. There were and still are a variety of third-party backup methods that provide server-based backup, such as ArcServe from Cheyenne Software.

The distinction between server-based and workstation-based backup methods is seen in figure 29.15. In workstation-based backups, the file system has to be backed up across the network. This generates a large amount of network traffic that can seriously impact the normal work of other users on the network. For this reason, workstation-based backup methods are confined to the early hours of the morning when there are likely to be few users on the network. If the workstation and server are separated by router and bridge devices, performing workstation-based backups can stress these components and further reduce the throughput of the network. In a server-based backup, the file system is backed up using the bus used to connect the backup device to the server. The server bus is generally faster than most common networks in use today, and, therefore, backups can be performed at speeds generally not possible using workstation-based methods. For SBACKUP, transfer rates have been reported that are four times faster than backing up a remote server. If the server disk and backup device are attached to the same internal bus, and the backup is done at the same time as heavy access to the server's disk subsystem by other users, there will be a small performance degradation because of bus contention.

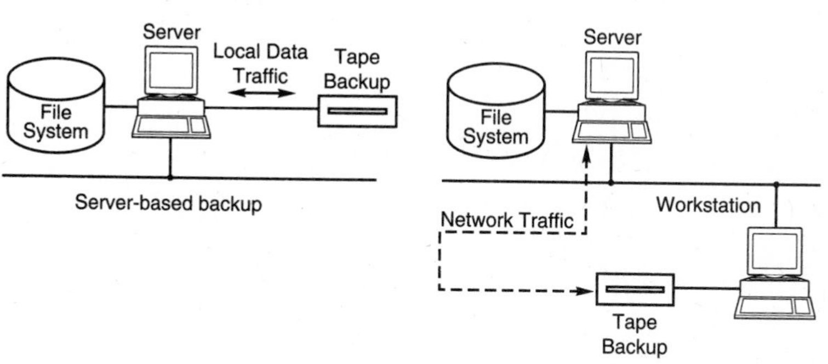

Figure 29.15
Server-based versus workstation-based backup.

In addition to performing server-based backup, SBACKUP can file systems of other NetWare servers across the network. The comments made earlier about backups across the networks apply to backing up other servers; however, this feature is a great convenience to the network administrator because it makes remote backups of other servers possible.

The SBACKUP architecture consists of a number of components necessary to perform local and remote backups. Figure 29.16 illustrates the SBACKUP architecture. The server that is connected to the backup device is called a *host*. Other servers that can be backed up across the network are called *targets*. A backup device needs to be connected only to the host and not to the targets. However, for the host to back up its own file system, it must have the host and target components loaded.

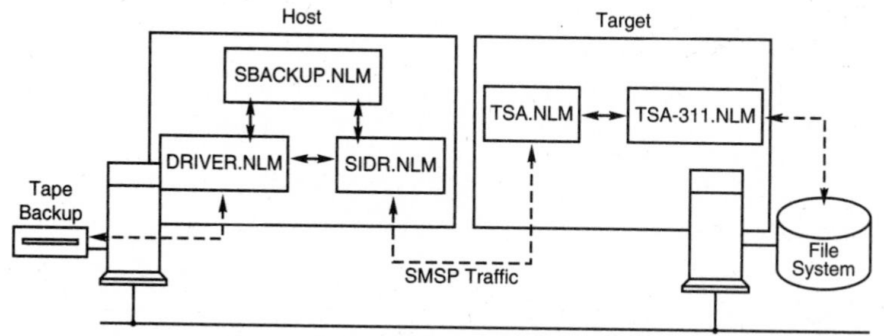

Figure 29.16
SBACKUP architecture.

The host server backup system consists of the following NLM components:

SBACKUP.NLM

SIDR.NLM

DRIVER.NLM

The SBACKUP.NLM provides the user interface to SBACKUP and also serves as the backup engine. It interfaces with the disk driver NLM. The DRIVER.NLM is a generic name; the actual driver NLM name is specific to the tape drive being used. Examples of tape driver NLMs are WANGTEK.NLM, ASPIDIBI.NLM, and TAPEDC00.NLM.

For the host server to back up the target server, it needs to establish a network connection to the target server. A special NLM called SIDR.NLM provides this capability. SIDR.NLM is a backup requestor very much like the requestor and redirector components used in NetWare DOS or OS/2 workstations. It makes the connection to the target server and uses Novell's *Storage Management Services Protocol* (SMSP) to backup the target server's file system. The SMSP protocol has the capability of specifying parent data sets, child data sets, trustee information, bindery information, disk space restriction, and directory and file attributes. The *parent data set* is a term used to describe a directory, subdirectory, or a bindery. A parent data set has subordinate data sets such as child data sets. *Child data sets* do not have any subordinates. An example of a child data set would be a file.

The TSA.NLM is the target server agent and provides the end point to the connection request from the SIDR.NLM. It provides the link between the SIDR data requester and the target-specific module running on the target called TSA-311.NLM. The TSA-311.NLM has the awareness of the target's file system data structure and passes this information on to the TSA.NLM. Other TSAs are available to back up DOS, OS/2 workstations and the NDS for NetWare 4.*x*. For NetWare 4.*x* TSA_NDS.NLM is used for backing up the NetWare Directory Services and TSA400.NLM is used for backing up the NetWare 4.*x* file system. NetWare 3.12 and NetWare 4.*x* provide a TSA_SMS.COM that runs on DOS workstations using VLMs that can be used to back up the workstation.

A number of auxiliary NLMs are needed to support the operation of SBACKUP. These NLMs are installed when the file server is installed, and include the following:

STREAMS.NLM

SPXS.NLM

TLI.NLM

CLIB.NLM

NUT.NLM

The STREAMS, SPSX, and TLI NLMs provide the communications components needed to connect the host SIDR and target TSA NLMs. The CLIB is the base C-Language library and OS interface. The NUT NLM provides an interface for other NLMs in the form of a template so that NLMs can call up a menu interface.

If the host server needs to back up its own file system, it must have the host and target components loaded.

All of the SBACKUP components together consume a fairly substantial chunk of server memory. You need at least 3 MB of memory above and beyond the server's requirements to run the SBACKUP system on the host.

NetWare comes with drivers for most of the major backup devices. The current trend is to use backup devices that connect using SCSI controllers. SCSI devices give higher transfer data rates and provide the ability to daisy-chain several SCSI devices. SBACKUP supports the following tape devices:

- Devices that use a DIBI-2 certified driver
- Wangtek tape drive with Quik O2 controller
- Wangtek tape drive with PC36 (60, 125, or 150/125) controller

Although the operation of SBACKUP is similar to NBACKUP (only available in NetWare 3.11 and below), the two use different data-storage formats and, therefore, are incompatible with each other. For this reason, you should never mix the two storage formats. Data backed up using SBACKUP must be restored with SBACKUP only, and data backed up with NBACKUP must be restored with NBACKUP. NBACKUP supports DOS and Macintosh file-name spaces only, whereas SBACKUP supports these and additional name spaces such as NFS and OS/2. NBACKUP is not available in NetWare 3.12 and NetWare 4.*x*.

The SBACKUP can be run in parallel with other console commands you can issue from the server. You must, therefore, never accidentally mount or dismount a volume while SBACKUP is in progress. Doing so can permanently damage the volume, corrupt the data, or crash the server.

SBACKUP Operation in NetWare 3.*x*

SBACKUP is automatically installed during NetWare installation. It is contained on the disks labeled BACKUP. Device driver and parameter information are stored in the directory SYS:SYSTEM\DIBI under the file name DIBI2$DV.DAT. This file also contains information about all the supported device drivers and can be edited using a text editor run from a workstation. Alternatively, you can use the EDIT NLM from the server console to edit this file. The following is an example of the command that enables you to edit from the server console:

```
LOAD EDIT SYS:SYSTEM\DIBI\DIBI2$DV.DAT
```

New device driver information can be added by adding a line for the driver. You can use existing driver information as an example for adding new drivers.

To load SBACKUP, you must perform the following load sequences from the server console:

1. **LOAD TSA** (This loads all applicable modules and configuration files.)
2. LOAD SBACKUP.

3. Enter the user name (SUPERVISOR/Admin or backup operator) and password.
4. If more than one backup device driver is loaded, you will be prompted to select one of the device drivers.

To back up a server you must have SBACKUP NLM loaded and running. Then you need to perform the following tasks:

1. From the Main menu use the Select Target to Backup/Restore option.

   `Select the target server` appears. Only those servers that have the target component NLMs loaded appear on the list. If you select a target server that is different from the host server, you must provide a user name and password to log in to the server.

2. Select the Backup Menu option from the Main Menu.
3. From the Backup Menu, choose the Select Working Directory option.

   Enter the path name of the working directory. This is the working directory that must be in the host file server.

4. From the Backup Menu, select Backup Selected Directory.

   When the Backup Options window appears, enter the following information for backing up a file system:

What to backup:	(Directory name)
Session Description:	(For documentation purposes)
Exclude Options:	(See list)
Include/Exclude Options:	(See list)
Clear modify bit:	No
Append This Session:	Yes

5. Back out of this screen by pressing Esc. Save the settings and answer Yes to proceed with the backup.
6. From the Start Backup Menu prompt, select the option to back up now or later.

Note that if files are in use by users, they will not be backed up and will be reported in the SBACKUP error log. You can use the View Error Log option from the SBACKUP Main Menu to view the error log.

To restore a server, you must have SBACKUP NLM loaded and running and perform the following tasks:

1. Select the Restore Menu option from the Main Menu.

2. From the Restore menu, choose the Select Working Directory option.

   Enter the path name of the working directory. This is the working directory which must be in the host file server.

3. From the Restore Menu, select either the Restore Session or Restore Without Session Files option.

   The Restore Without Session Files option checks through a backup of entries on tape to find a session to restore.

4. When the Restore Options window appears, select the desired option for restoring the file system:

Overwrite Existing Parent:	Yes
Overwrite Existing Child:	Yes
Include Exclude Options:	(See List)
Destination Paths:	None

   The default is to restore all trustee, attributes, and data as they were during backup.

5. Back out of the preceding screen by pressing Esc, and save the settings. Answer Yes to proceed with the restore.

6. At the Start Restore prompt, select Yes.

SBACKUP in NetWare 4.*x*

NetWare 4.*x* implements back up services using Storage Management Service. SMS allows data to be backed up and restored independent of the backup hardware and file system. The Storage Management supports a variety of backup hardware devices and it can serve as back up file systems for DOS, OS/2, Macintosh and UNIX. This capability to backup different file systems is particularly important because NetWare based networks support a heterogeneous workstation operating system environment. SMS provides support for the following workstations and data representation:

- DOS workstations
- OS/2 workstations
- Macintosh workstations (Macintosh name space)
- UNIX workstations (NFS name space)
- NetWare Directory Service

- NetWare File Systems (2.2 to 4.*x*)
- Btrieve (SQL) database

The primary tool that uses SMS is SBACKUP. SBACKUP runs as an NLM and relies on target serviced agents to communicate a data representation to it. The SBACKUP.NLM runs on the server that has the backup device. The SBACKUP NLM is responsible for backup and restore operations. The NBACKUP functionality of earlier NetWare releases is now consolidated in SBACKUP.

The target service agents can run on NetWare servers and communicate with the workstations on the network. The target service agents have knowledge of different data representations. For example a target service agent called TSA400.NLM is used to backup/restore NetWare 4.*x* file system, and the target service agent TSA311.NLM does the same for NetWare 3.*x*. Table 29.1 contains a list of TSA's that are installed with NetWare 4.*x*. These TSA's can be found in the SYS:SYSTEM directory.

Table 29.1
Target Service Agents

TSA Name	Description
TSA311.NLM	NetWare 3.*x* file system TSA
TSA400.NLM	NetWare 4.*x* file system TSA
TSA_DOS.NLM	TSA for backing up DOS files
TSA_NDS.NLM	TSA for backing up NDS
TSA_OS2.NLM	TSA for backing up OS/2 file system

29

SMS Architecture

Besides SBACKUP.NLM and TSA's, SMS consists of a number of other support NLMs that work together to provide backup and restore operations. Figure 29.17 shows how this can be done.

SMS consists of a number of other modules such as the *Storage Management Data Requester* (SMDR) that is used to pass commands between the SBACKUP and the TSAs, device drivers that use the *Storage Device Interface* (SDI) to communicate between the SBACKUP program and the storage devices (see fig. 29.17).

The SBACKUP uses the SMDR to access the TSA. If the TSA is on the same server as the SBACKUP NLM, then the data source is on the same server. An example of this would be using the TSA400.NLM on the host server to back up the host file system. Another example would be to use the TSA_NDS.NLM on the host to backup the NDS data base on the host server.

The term *host* refers to the server that has the backup device. The term *target* refers to the network device (workstation or server) that has the data to be backed up or restored.

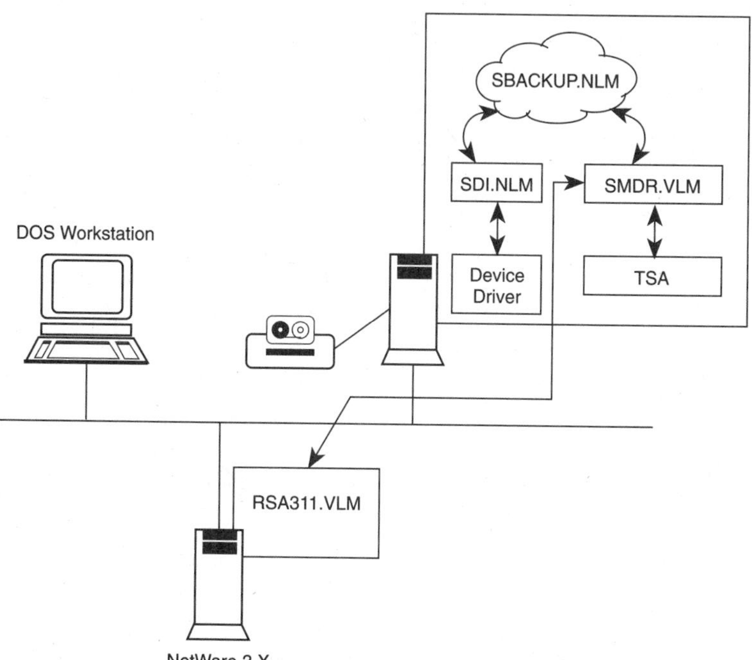

Figure 29.17
SMS components.

If the TSA is on a remote machine, such as a NetWare 3.*x* server running TSA311.NLM, then the file system on the remote machine can be backed up. It is the responsibility of the TSA to obtain the requested data and pass it on to SBACKUP via the SMDR. The TSA is the agent that is *closest* to the source data that is being backed up and restored. It has knowledge of the file system or data representation of the source data.

SBACKUP is able to backup or restore the data by communicating with the backup device via the Storage Device Interface NLM (SDI.NLM) and the backup device drivers. The Storage Device Interface is used to detect the presence of the device and media and presents a list of devices that are available to the SBACKUP program. The backup operator can then select the appropriate backup device via the SBACKUP interface. The SMDR NLM provides a high level interface to the backup device drivers. The backup device drivers have knowledge of the backup device hardware, and use commands for reading, writing, rewinding, and ejecting the storage media. The SDI.NLM, SMDR.NLM, STREAMS.NLM, CLIB.NLM, SPXS.NLM, and NWSNUT.NLM are autoloaded when SBACKUP loads.

To backup and restore workstations, another component called the Workstation Manager (WS_MAN.NLM) must be loaded on the host server. WS_MAN NLM is autoloaded when TSA_DOS or TSA_OS2 load. The Workstation Manager keeps an internal list of DOS TSRs (or OS/2 and UNIX daemons) that have contacted it and are available for backup/restore operation.

The NetWare 4.*x* SBACKUP Tool

The SBACKUP.NLM is loaded at the server. It is similar to the SBACKUP.NLM for NetWare 3.*x* servers but has been customized for the NetWare 4.*x* operating system.

In order to use SBACKUP, you must first load all the necessary drivers and TSAs for the target being backed up. NetWare 4.*x* ships with the tape drivers listed in table 29.2. The TAPEDAI.DSK can work with any tape device on a SCSI controller.

If the TAPEDAI.DSK driver is not installed in the SYS:SYSTEM directory on the server, you can find a copy of it in the \NETWARE.40________\DISKDRV directory on the NetWare 4.*x* CD-ROM distribution.

Specialized tape device drivers are optimized for speed and can be expected to work more efficiently than generic device drivers. Contact the tape vendor to find if they have specialized tape device drivers that work with NetWare 4.*x* SBACKUP. The list of drivers that are bundled with NetWare 4.*x* can be expected to change with time. Contact your Novell reseller or Novell at (800) NETWARE or (801) 429-7000 for a list of the latest drivers that are supported.

Table 29.2
Backup Device Drivers

Device Driver	Description
TAPEDAI.DSK	This is a generic ASPI-compatible tape driver for SCSI controllers. It is designed to use the Advanced SCSI Programming Interface (ASPI).
MNS16S.NLM and MNSDAT.DSK	These are device drivers for Mountain Network Solutions, Inc., SCSI controllers and tape devices.
PS2SCSI.DSK	These work with PS/2 SCSI controllers and IBM 2.2 GB 8mm tape devices.
AHA1540.DSK, AHA1640.DSK, AHA1740.DSK, ASPITRAN.DSK	These work with devices that usethe Adaptec 1540, 1640 and 1740 controllers.

Steps for Using SBACKUP in NetWare 4.*x*

The steps outlined below guide you through the basics of performing an SBACKUP.

The actual screens that are presented using SBACKUP often depend on the selections you make from the SBACKUP menu for your network environment. For instance, you can select the Backup option, without logging in to the Target Service first. In this case, you will be presented with a screen to log in to the target service first before performing the backup operation. Another example is the writing of labels on tapes. If you are using a new tape or completely rewriting the tape, and you have not written a new label on the tape, you will be presented with a screen to label the tape.

1. First load the appropriate backup device drivers on the server console. If you are using a SCSI controller, you may be able to use the generic TAPEDAI.DSK device driver.

   ```
   LOAD TAPEDAI.
   ```

   Figure 29.18 shows the server console screen when this device drive loads. The version number of the TAPEDAI.DSK and its date of creation are displayed. In this particular version of the TAPEDAI driver there were three outdated API calls, so a warning message was generated.

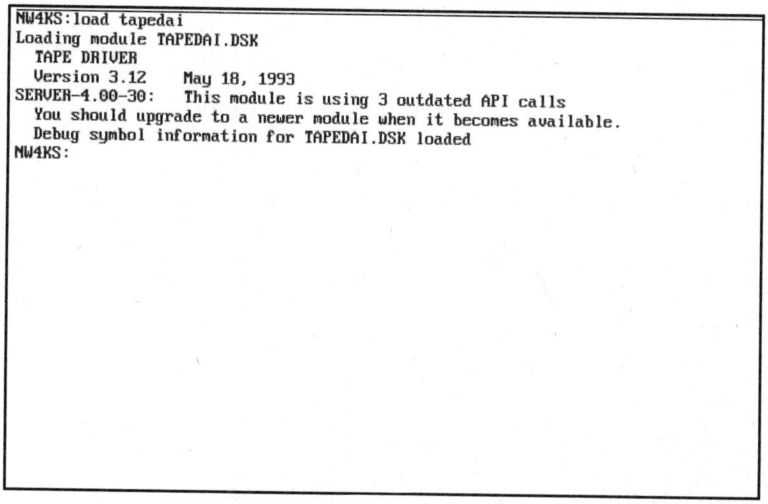

```
NW4KS:load tapedai
Loading module TAPEDAI.DSK
  TAPE DRIVER
  Version 3.12    May 18, 1993
SERVER-4.00-30:   This module is using 3 outdated API calls
  You should upgrade to a newer module when it becomes available.
  Debug symbol information for TAPEDAI.DSK loaded
NW4KS:
```

Figure 29.18
LOAD TAPEDAI Messages.

   TAPEDAI uses the ASPI interface. ASPI does not provide sharing of a tape device between competing applications. You should not load any other device that uses ASPI, when you are using the TAPEDAI driver.

2. Optional: Load any other device drivers required by the manufacturer's hardware.

3. Load the TSA agents on the target. In the example on these steps, we wish to backup the NetWare 4.*x* file system and the NDS database. Therefore, you must load the TSA400.NLM and the TSA_NDS.NLM.

   ```
   LOAD TSA400
   ```

   Figure 29.19 shows the server console screen when the TSA for the NetWare 4.*x* file system loads. The version number of the TSA agent and its date of creation are displayed.

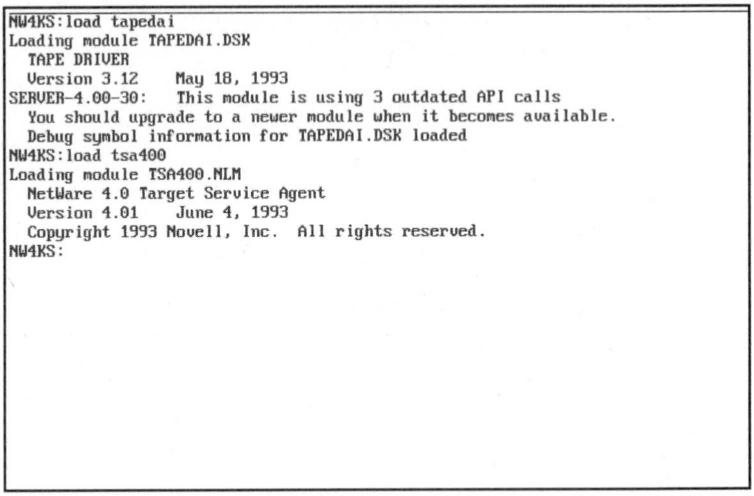

Figure 29.19
LOAD TSA400 Messages.

```
NW4KS:load tapedai
Loading module TAPEDAI.DSK
  TAPE DRIVER
  Version 3.12    May 18, 1993
SERVER-4.00-30:   This module is using 3 outdated API calls
  You should upgrade to a newer module when it becomes available.
  Debug symbol information for TAPEDAI.DSK loaded
NW4KS:load tsa400
Loading module TSA400.NLM
  NetWare 4.0 Target Service Agent
  Version 4.01    June 4, 1993
  Copyright 1993 Novell, Inc.  All rights reserved.
NW4KS:
```

Figure 29.20 shows the server console screen when the TSA for the NDS database loads. The version number of the TSA agent and it's date of creation are displayed.

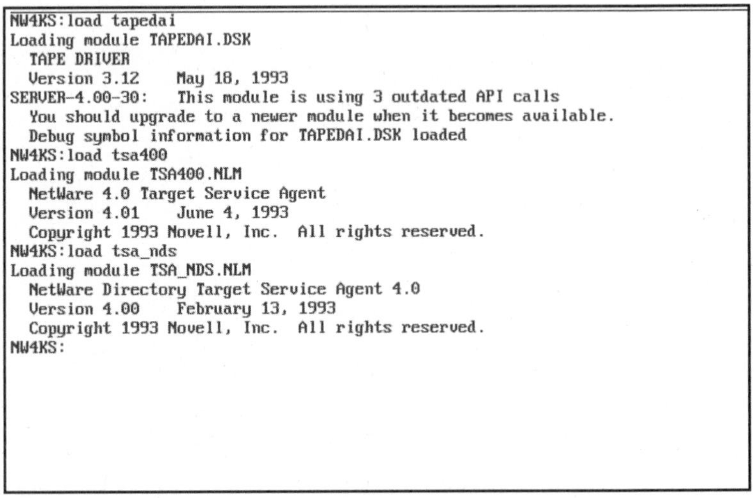

29

Figure 29.20
LOAD TSA_NDS Messages.

```
NW4KS:load tapedai
Loading module TAPEDAI.DSK
  TAPE DRIVER
  Version 3.12    May 18, 1993
SERVER-4.00-30:   This module is using 3 outdated API calls
  You should upgrade to a newer module when it becomes available.
  Debug symbol information for TAPEDAI.DSK loaded
NW4KS:load tsa400
Loading module TSA400.NLM
  NetWare 4.0 Target Service Agent
  Version 4.01    June 4, 1993
  Copyright 1993 Novell, Inc.  All rights reserved.
NW4KS:load tsa_nds
Loading module TSA_NDS.NLM
  NetWare Directory Target Service Agent 4.0
  Version 4.00    February 13, 1993
  Copyright 1993 Novell, Inc.  All rights reserved.
NW4KS:
```

4. Before loading the SBACKUP NLM, you must issue the command SCAN FOR NEW DEVICES. This assures that the tape device recognized by TAPEDAI is registered by NetWare 4.*x*. The command LIST DEVICES can be used to see current devices. The commands below show the list of devices before and after executing the SCAN FOR NEW DEVICES command.

```
LIST DEVICES
```

Figure 29.21 shows the output of the LIST DEVICES command. Only one device, device # 0, is listed. This is the Micropolis 1528 hard disk with 1.2 GB capacity.

```
SCAN FOR NEW DEVICES
```

Figure 29.22 shows the SCAN FOR NEW DEVICES command. No output is generated, but the command takes a few seconds.

When the SCAN FOR NEW DEVICES command is executed, you should see the light indicators on the backup device light up when the device is accessed. If this does not happen, you should check for a lose cable or incorrect hardware configuration for the tape device.

```
LIST DEVICES
```

Figure 29.23 shows the output of the LIST DEVICES command, after the SCAN FOR NEW DEVICES recognizes the backup device. An additional device, device # 1, is listed. This is the HP 35470A tape drive unit for DAT tapes.

```
NW4KS:load tapedai
Loading module TAPEDAI.DSK
  TAPE DRIVER
  Version 3.12     May 18, 1993
SERVER-4.00-30:   This module is using 3 outdated API calls
  You should upgrade to a newer module when it becomes available.
  Debug symbol information for TAPEDAI.DSK loaded
NW4KS:load tsa400
Loading module TSA400.NLM
  NetWare 4.0 Target Service Agent
  Version 4.01     June 4, 1993
  Copyright 1993 Novell, Inc.  All rights reserved.
NW4KS:load tsa_nds
Loading module TSA_NDS.NLM
  NetWare Directory Target Service Agent 4.0
  Version 4.00     February 13, 1993
  Copyright 1993 Novell, Inc.  All rights reserved.
NW4KS:list devices
 1. Device #  0 MICROP   1528-15MD1076301 DD24 (5D000000).
NW4KS:
```

Figure 29.21
LIST DEVICES command before scanning for new devices.

29

5. The next step is to load the SBACKUP NLM.

   LOAD SBACKUP

   SBACKUP has a SIZE and BUFFERS option, as shown below:

   LOAD SBACKUP SIZE=*sizeInKB* BUFFERS=*numberOfBuffers*

   The SIZE parameter is the buffer size used by SBACKUP in kilobytes. The value can range from 16, 32, 64, 128, 256 KB. The default value is 64 KB.

Figure 29.22
SCAN FOR NEW DEVICES.

```
NW4KS:scan for new devices
NW4KS:
```

Figure 29.23
LIST DEVICES command after scanning for new devices.

```
NW4KS:scan for new devices
NW4KS:list devices
 8. Device #  1 HP - HP35470A (020000FF).
 1. Device #  0 MICROP   1528-15MD1076301 DD24 (5D000000).
NW4KS:
```


The BUFFERS parameter is the number of buffers reserved by SBACKUP. The value can range from 2 to 29. The default value is 4.

You may wish to experiment with higher values to improve backup performance. If you do, take into account the additional memory required by SBACKUP. This could adversely affect server performance. For example, selecting a buffer size of 256 KB and 29 buffers will require an additional 2.56 MB of server RAM. Since NetWare 4.*x* does not use virtual memory, this is real RAM requirement.

Once SBACKUP is loaded, you can use it to perform backup and restores.

To unload SBACKUP and the support NLMs, they should be unloaded in the reverse order of their load sequence; that is, you must unload SBACKUP first, then the TSA NLMs and finally the backup device drivers. The following is an example of this unload sequence:

```
UNLOAD SBACKUP
UNLOAD TSA400
UNLOAD  TSA_NDS
UNLOAD TAPEDAI
```

Using NetWare 4.*x* SBACKUP To Perform a Backup

The following steps show the sequence of steps needed for performing a backup operation. The steps assume that all the necessary drivers have already been loaded.

1. The SBACKUP NLM must be loaded on the host server.

   ```
   LOAD SBACKUP
   ```

   After SBACKUP loads, you should see the SBACKUP main menu as shown in figure 29.24.

   The *Backup* option is used to specify a target to backup. It will also ask you to specify the location of the session log, the device and media to use and the type of backup to perform.

   The *Restore* option is used to specify the target to restore to. It will ask you to specify what data you wish to restore and the location to restore to. If a session log has been maintained, you can restore based on the session name. Alternatively, you can select the data directly from the tape. One reason for restoring directly from tape is the session log file has been deleted or is corrupt. Restoring from a session log is convenient and quicker to do.

   The *Log/Error File Administration* option allows you to browse through the error log file that is created when a backup or restore session is done. This is a quick way to determine if any errors have occurred during backup or restore operations.

   The *Storage Device Administration* option allows you to choose the device and media to be used for the backup or restore operation. This option is useful if you have more than one backup device. This option can also be used for checking the status of the media in the backup device.

   The *Change Target to Back Up From or Restore To* is used to display the names of the targets to which you are attached. You can select a target for performing an operation. When you do this, you will be asked to specify a username/password for logging on to the target.

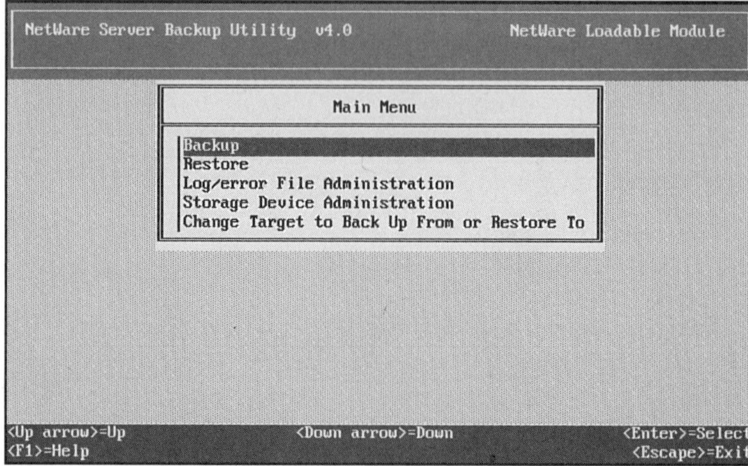

Figure 29.24
SBACKUP Main Menu.

2. Select the *Storage Device Administration* to see the list of devices to back up to. You should see a list of devices (see fig. 29.25) that you can use. In figure 29.25, only one backup device is shown, since there is only one backup unit attached to the host server. From figure 29.25, you can see that the HP - 35470A device is available for use. Using Tab displays the status of the device.

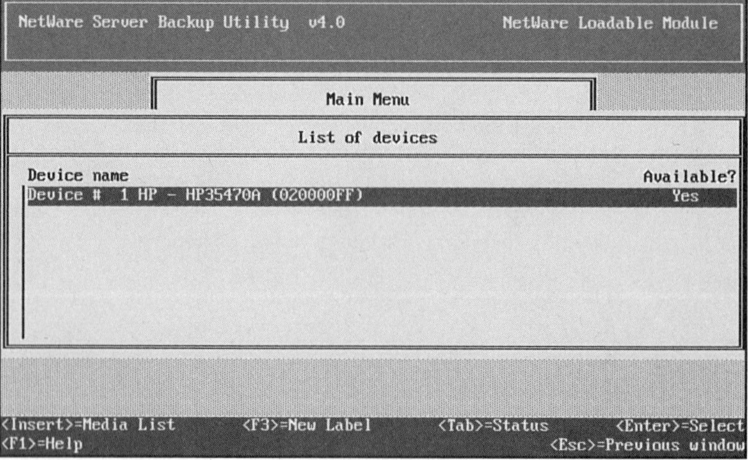

Figure 29.25
List of devices.

Figure 29.26 shows the status of the device. The *current operation* indicates if the device is currently reading, writing or formatting the media. Its value is shown as None, if no operation is being performed by the device. The *Device mode* indicates if the device is selected for reading, writing or both. The *Maximum capacity* indicates the storage capacity of the media in the backup device. In figure 29.26, both the Device mode and the Maximum capacity have a value of "unknown", as the tape device driver does not report the media status.

```
NetWare Server Backup Utility  v4.0            NetWare Loadable Module

                         Main Menu
                      List of devices
 Status of: Device #  1 HP - HP35470A (020000FF)
  Current operation:      None
  Device mode:            unknown
  Maximum capacity:       unknown

<F1>=Help                                        <Esc>=Previous window
```

Figure 29.26
Device Status.

The media in the device needs to be labeled. If the media has never been labeled, you can do this task here or postpone it to a later point in the *Backup* option, when you will be prompted to label the media. To label the media, highlight the backup device from the *List of devices* menu, and press Ins. You should see the media for the device as shown in figure 29.27. In figure 29.27, the media has the label NDS_LABEL which means that it was labeled in an SBACKUP operation earlier.

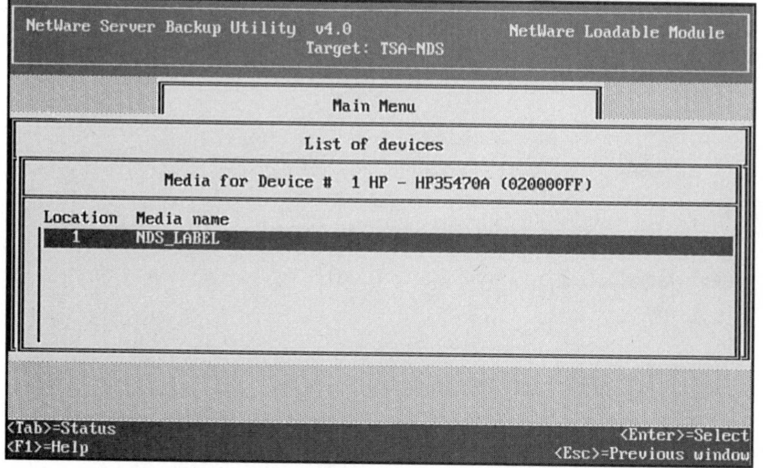

Figure 29.27
Media List.

Pressing Tab on the media that is listed shows the status of the media. This is shown in figure 29.28. If the media was written by an SMS application (such as SBACKUP), the media owner is not displayed. If the media was written by a non-SMS application, or if it was initially "blank," then the *Media owner* is listed as "Unidentified".

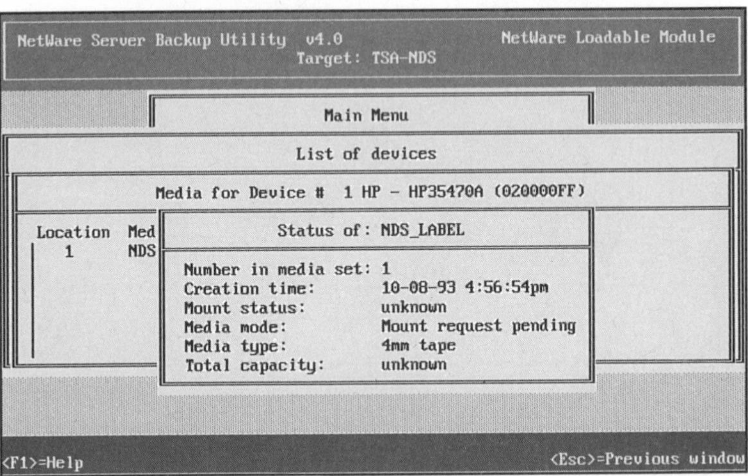

Figure 29.28
Status of media in backup device.

The *Number in media set* shows the media (tape) number within a particular media set. If the backup session takes more than one tape, the tapes are numbered consecutively in the order in which they are used. In figure 29.28, the first of these tapes has been identified and has a number of 1.

The *Current date* shows the time when the media label was created and used.

The *Media status* indicates a value of "Mounted," "Mount Pending," "Not Mounted," or "unknown". A *Mounted* value indicates that the media is ready for reading or writing. A *Mount Pending* value indicates that the request to mount is waiting in a queue to be processed. A *Not Mounted* indicates that the media is not mounted in the device.

The *Media mode* indicates if the media is selected for reading, writing, reading and writing, or if the mount requests pending.

The *Media type* indicates the type of media in the device, such as a 4mm or 8mm tape.

The *Total capacity* indicates the capacity of the media. If the driver does not report this value, a value of "unknown" is shown.

You should select the media you want to use by highlighting it and pressing Enter. You will be informed that you have selected the media (see fig. 29.29).

3. Select the *Change Target to Back Up From or Restore To* option from the SBACKUP Main Menu. Figure 29.30 shows the choices of target service that are running. Since the TSA400.NLM and TSA_NDS.NLM were loaded, you see that the target services are NetWare 4.0 Directory (NDS) and the NetWare 4.0 File System.

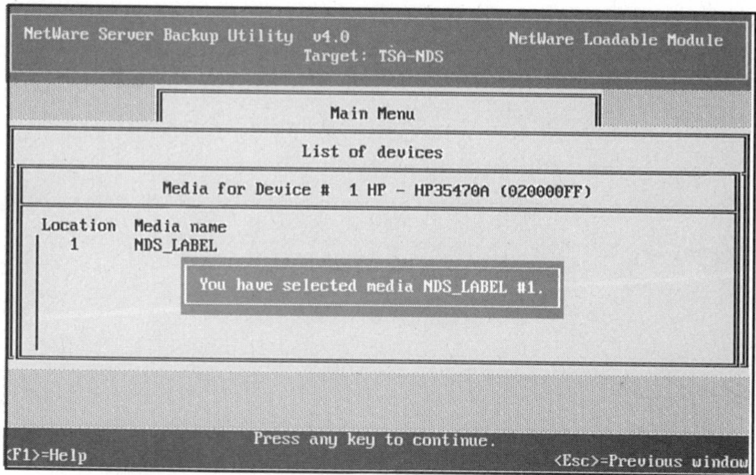

Figure 29.29
Selected media.

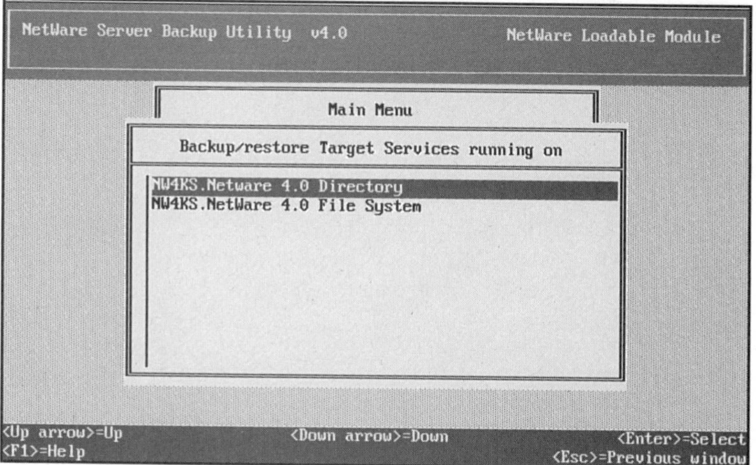

Figure 29.30
Target Services.

4. In this backup example, we will select the NDS database for backing up. Selecting the NetWare 4.0 Directory option will result in you being prompted for the user name for the target NDSTS (NDS target service) and the password as shown in figures 29.31 and 29.32.

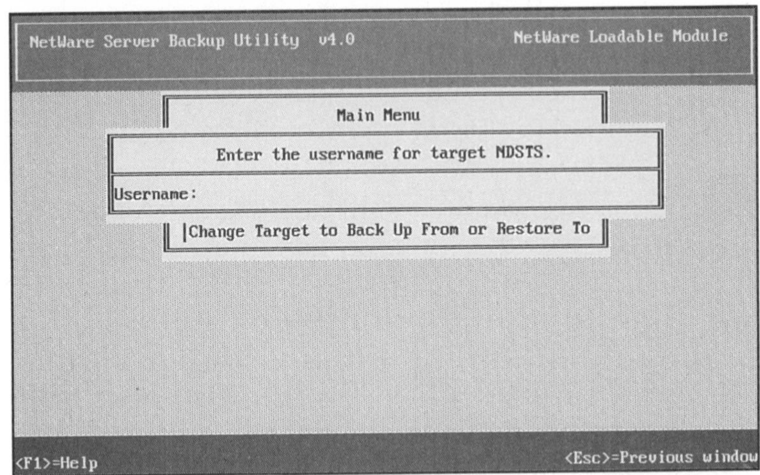

Figure 29.31 *User Name for Target Service.*

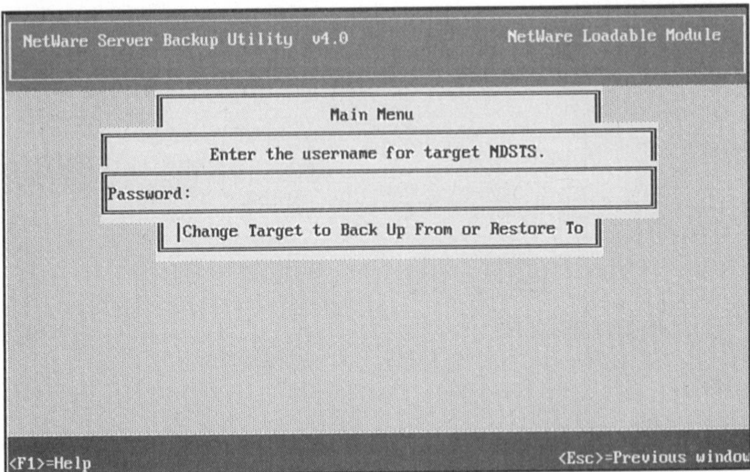

Figure 29.32 *Password for User Name/ Target Service.*

29

If you are having a problem logging in as a user name, use the complete name. For example, if you are logging in as user Admin in container O=ESL, use the name:

```
.CN=Admin.O=ESL
```

If you are logged in correctly, you will see a status message, informing you that you are connected to the target service. If you do not see this message, check to see if the complete user name you have typed in exists, or if you have entered the password correctly.

The target you are connected to is always reported on the top part of the SBACKUP screen.

5. From the SBACKUP Main Menu, select *Backup*. You will be asked to select the device and media to back up to, if you have not done this already. Figure 29.33 shows the media and backup device to be used. This screen will only appear if you have not selected the media type in step 2.

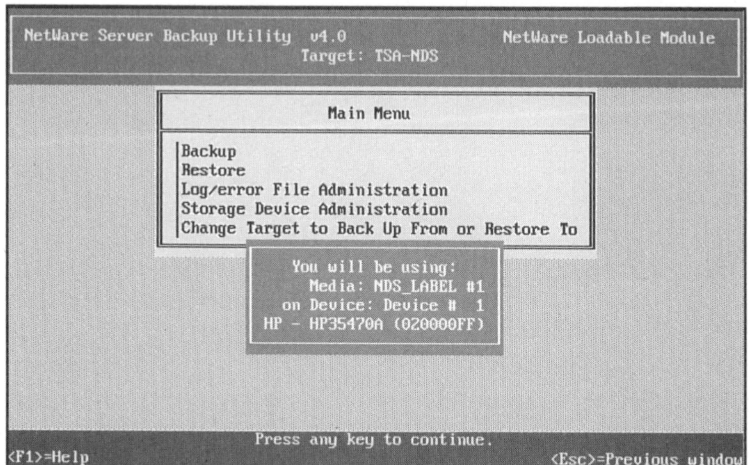

Figure 29.33
Device media to be used for backup.

You will be asked to select a location for the log and error file (see fig. 29.34). If you have been using SBACKUP for some time and have already selected this option, this screen will be bypassed. The default location is SYS:SYSTEM/TSA/LOG. You can however, select any other location.

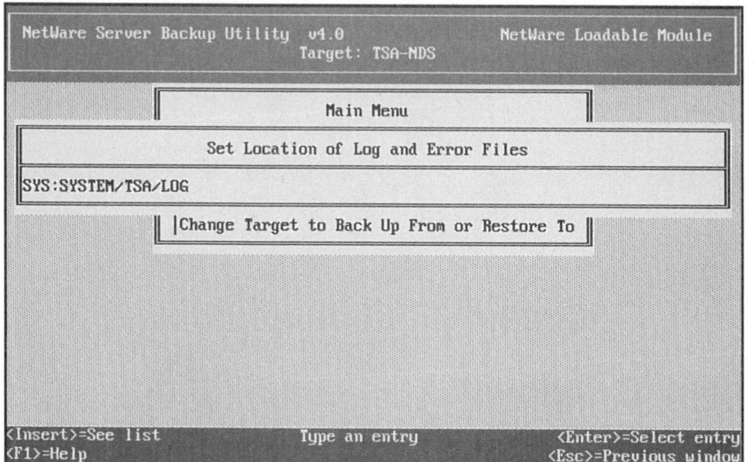

Figure 29.34
Location of log/error files.

6. Next, you will be asked if you want to perform a full backup or a custom backup (see fig. 29.35). In general the choices are Full, Differential, Incremental and Custom. For backing up NDS database, you have a choice of Full and Custom only. The different backup types were explained earlier in the chapter.

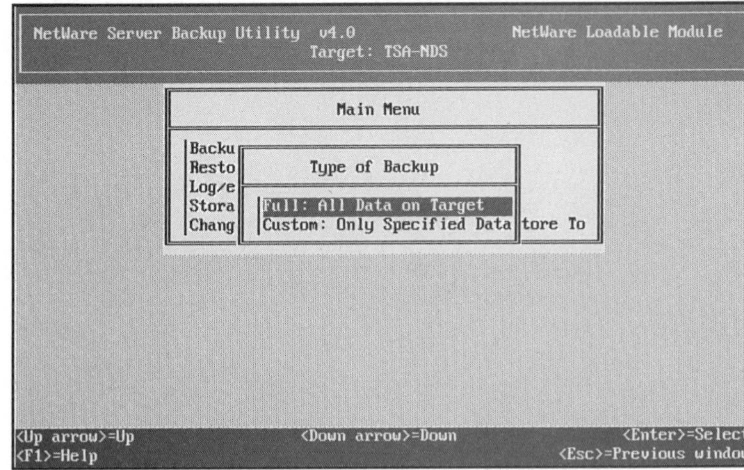

Figure 29.35
Type of Backup.

29

7. In our example, we will select the Full backup method. You will be presented with backup options (see fig 29.36).

Figure 29.36
Backup Options.

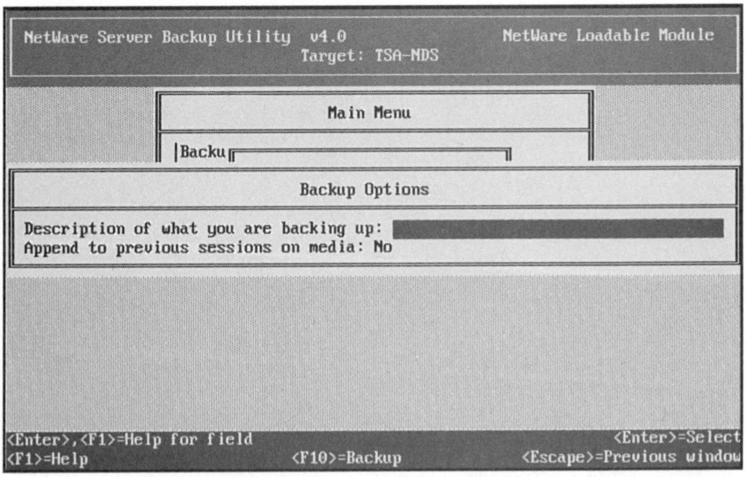

```
NetWare Server Backup Utility  v4.0                NetWare Loadable Module
                         Target: TSA-NDS
                Main Menu
      Backu
                        Backup Options
 Description of what you are backing up:
 Append to previous sessions on media: No
<Enter>,<F1>=Help for field                                  <Enter>=Select
<F1>=Help                    <F10>=Backup        <Escape>=Previous window
```

Enter a description of what you want to backup and whether you wish to append to data on the tape (Yes) or start writing from the beginning of the tape (No). It is important to keep the description informative, because when you select data to be restored, you will be presented with a choice of the backup descriptions that you enter at this step.

8. To start the backup, press F29. You will be presented with a choice of when to start the backup (see fig. 29.37).

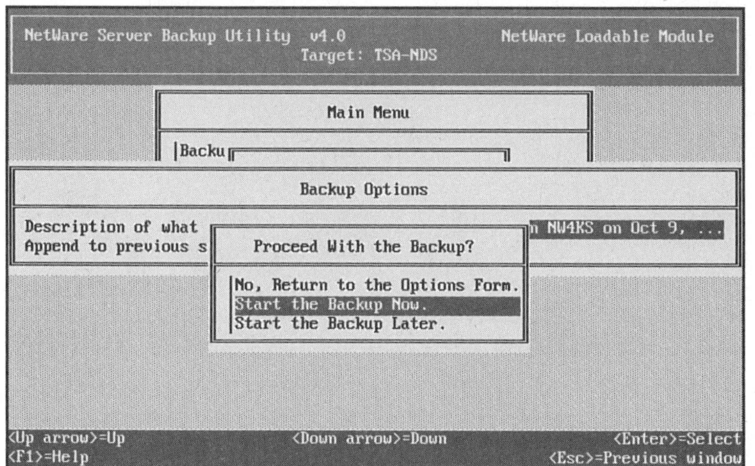

Figure 29.37
Proceed with Backup options.

If you wish to start the backup later, you can select "Start the Backup Later" and you will be presented with a form to schedule a backup at a future date and time (see fig. 29.38).

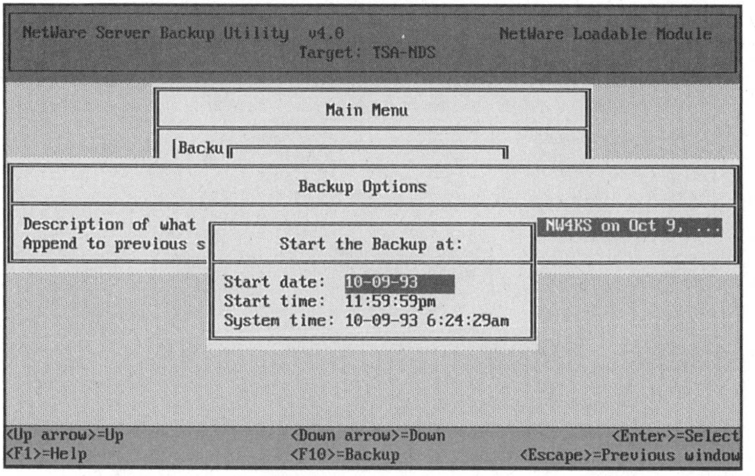

Figure 29.38
Schedule a Backup.

If you select the backup now option, you will be presented with a status screen (see fig. 29.39). Press Enter to proceed to the next step. Enter the name of the label for the media set, if you are prompted for it. If the media is being completely overwritten, you will be prompted for it.

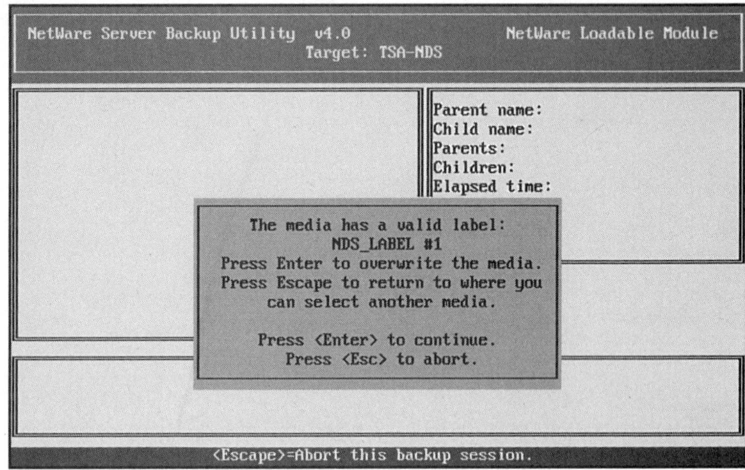

Figure 29.39
Status screen on media label.

As the backup proceeds, you will see a status window on the top right hand corner of the screen that will inform you of the status of the backup. Among other things you are shown the elapsed time and the amount of data backed up. The data that is backed up will be shown on the top left hand corner of the screen.

At the end of the backup, you will see a message informing you that the backup is complete (see fig. 29.40). Press Enter to continue and exit SBACKUP.

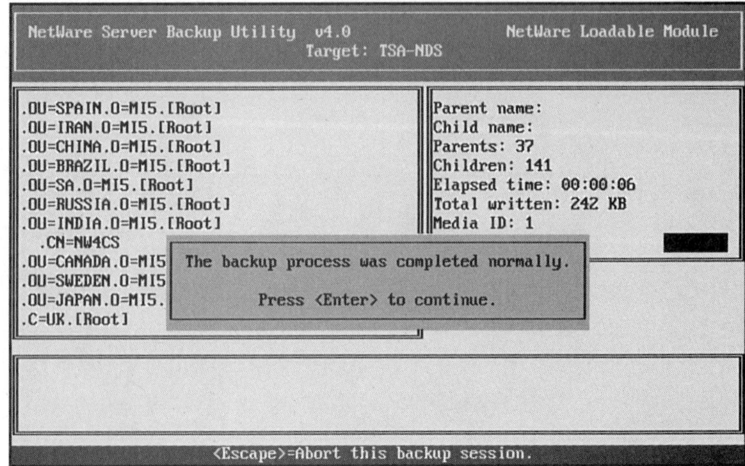

Figure 29.40
Backup completion.

Using NetWare 4.x SBACKUP To Perform a Restore

The following steps show the sequence of steps needed for performing a restore operation. The steps assume that all the necessary drivers have already been loaded.

1. The SBACKUP NLM must be loaded on the host server.

   ```
   LOAD SBACKUP
   ```

   After SBACKUP loads, you should see the SBACKUP main menu. The different SBACKUP options are described in the previous section.

2. Select the *Storage Device Administration* to see the list of devices to back up to. You should see a list of devices that you can use.

   Press Ins to see the media in the device (see fig. 29.41). Highlight the media and press Enter to select the media to restore from (see fig. 29.42).

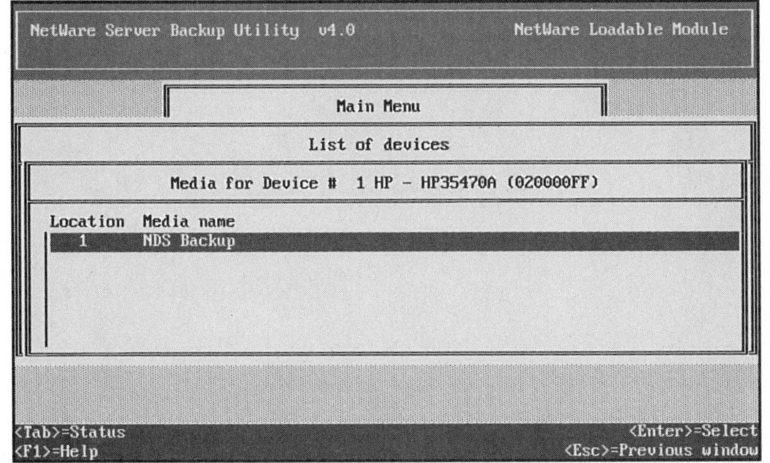

Figure 29.41
Media List for restore.

   Pressing Tab on the media that is listed shows the status of the media. Please refer to the previous section on performing backup using SBACKUP to see a description of the media status.

3. Select the *Change Target to Back Up From or Restore To* option from the SBACKUP Main Menu. Figure 29.43 shows the choices of target service that are running. Since the TSA400.NLM and TSA_NDS.NLM were loaded, you see that the target services are NetWare 4.0 Directory (NDS) and the NetWare 4.0 File System.

Figure 29.42
Selected media.

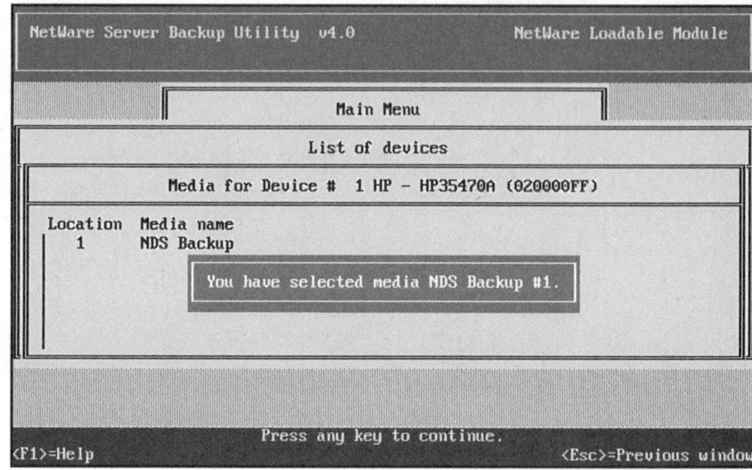

Figure 29.43
Backup/Restore Target Services.

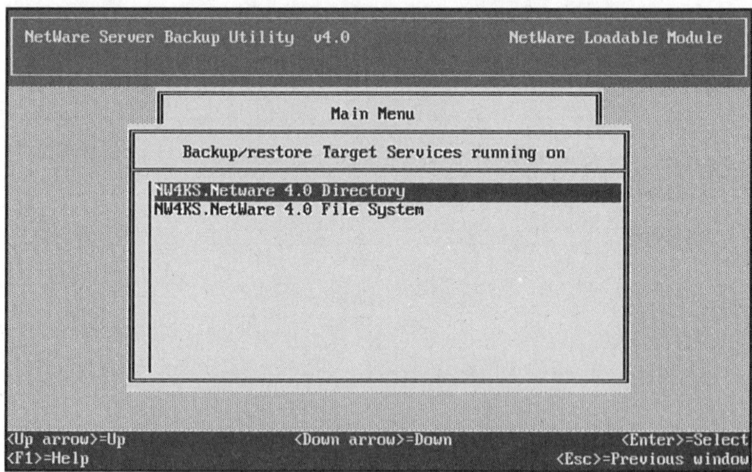

4. In this restore example, we will select the NDS database for restoring. Selecting the NetWare 4.0 Directory option will result in you being prompted for the user name for the target NDSTS (NDS target service) and the password as shown in figures 29.44 and 29.45.

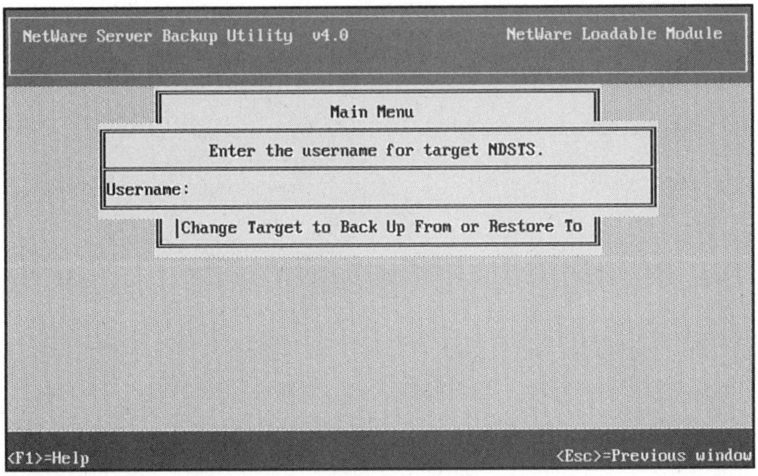

Figure 29.44
Username for Target Service for Restoring.

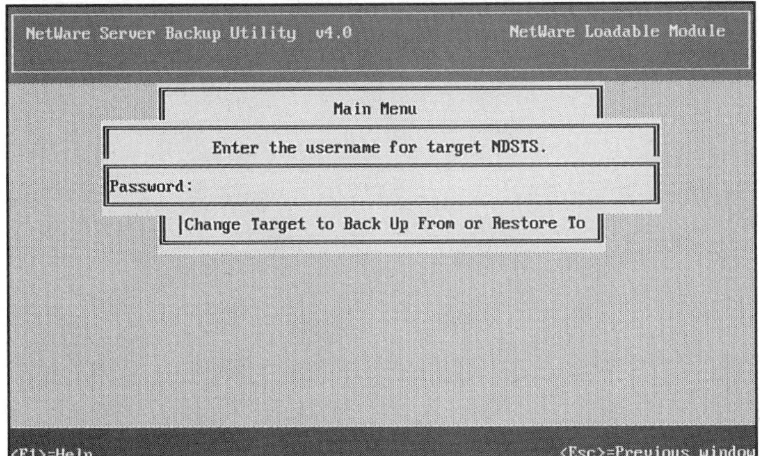

Figure 29.45
Password for Username/ Target Service.

If you are logged in correctly, you will see a status message informing you that you are connected to the target service. If you do not see this message, check to see if the complete user name you have typed in exists, or you have entered the password correctly.

5. From the SBACKUP Main Menu, select *Restore*. You will be presented with a choice of restoring with session files or without session files (see fig. 29.46). Restoring with session files is simpler, but you may have to select restoring without session files if the log file has been deleted or has been corrupted.

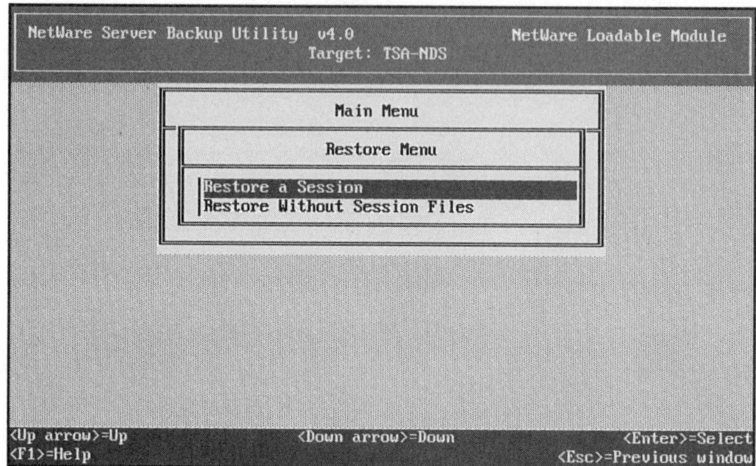

Figure 29.46
Session restore options.

If you select "Restore a session", you will be asked to select a location for the log and error file (see fig. 29.47). If you have been using SBACKUP for some time and have already selected this option, this screen will be bypassed. The default location is SYS:SYSTEM/TSA/LOG. If you had selected a different location at the time of performing a backup, you must specify this location.

29

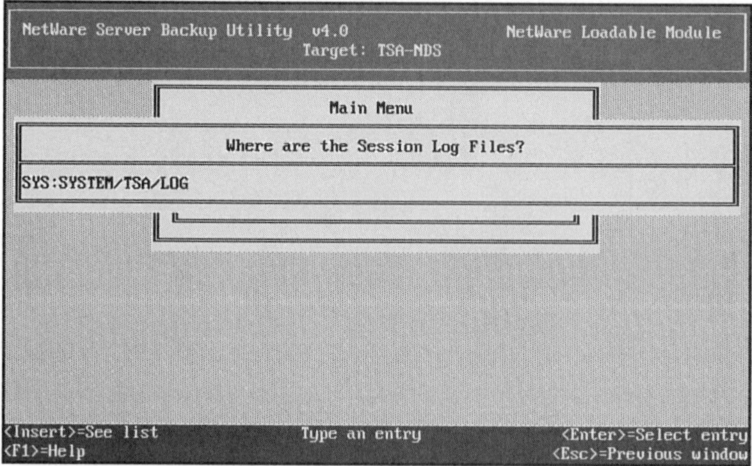

Figure 29.47
Location of log/error files for restoring.

Figure 29.48 shows the different backup sessions that have been performed. The most recent session is listed first. Highlight the session that you wish to restore and press Enter.

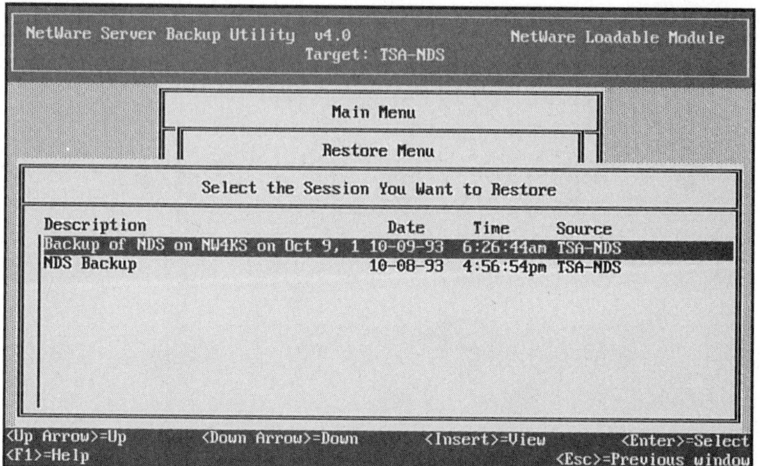

Figure 29.48
List of sessions to restore from.

6. Next, you will be asked to select a device and media to restore from (see fig. 29.49). This gives you an opportunity to insert the media in the device, if you have not done so already. Press Enter to continue. You will see a "Please wait" message as the media is read. You will be shown the backup device and the media that you will be using (see fig. 29.50).

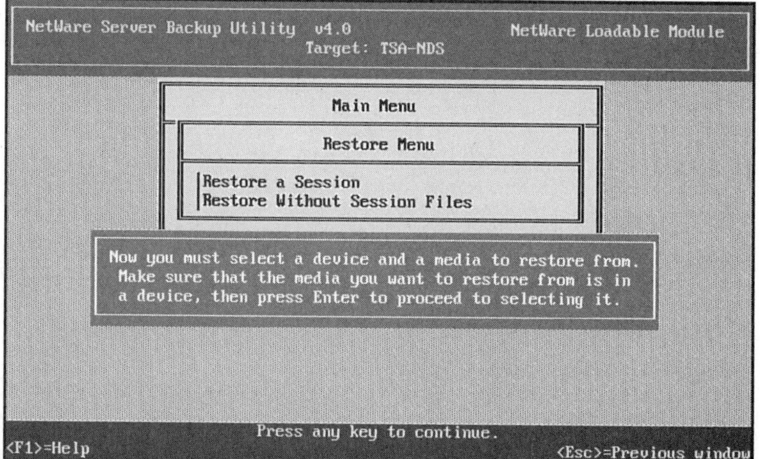

Figure 29.49
Status message for selecting device and media.

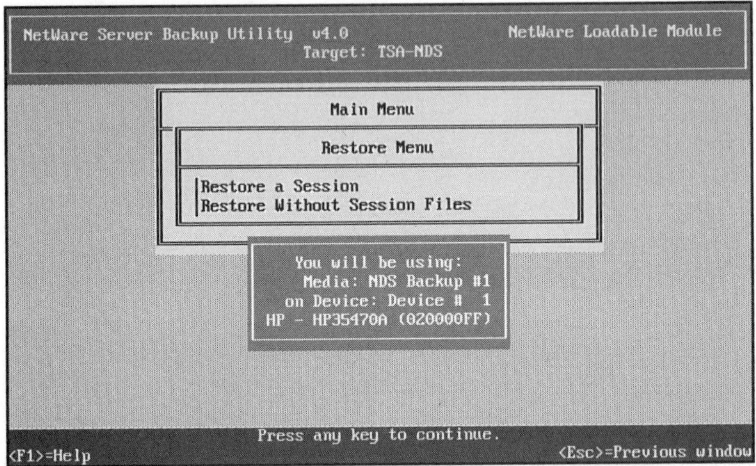

Figure 29.50
Media and device to be used for restoring.

You will be presented with Restore options that will ask you if you wish to override the parent and child during restore (see fig. 29.51). Figure 29.51 shows only the options that apply to restoring the NDS database. Within SBACKUP, a parent can be a server, a volume, a file directory, or an NDS container directory. The child is the lowest level of the tree structure such as a file or a leaf object.

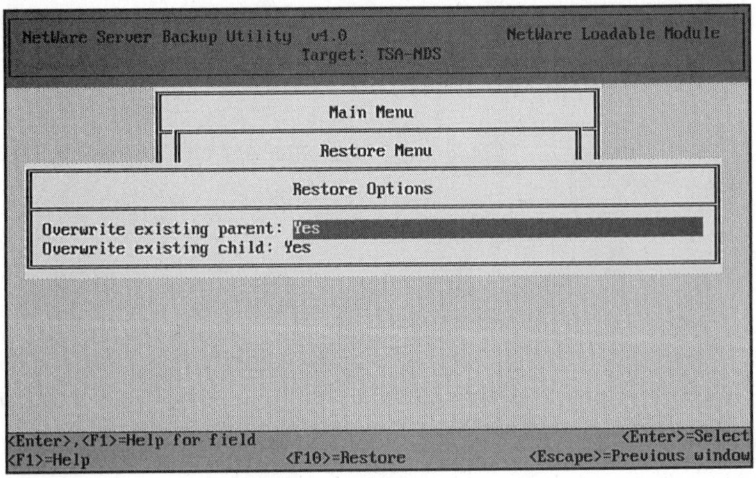

Figure 29.51
Restore options for NDS.

For restoring a file system, you should see a different set of restore options, dealing with how to scan for what you are restoring and the different subsets that you are restoring (see fig. 29.52).

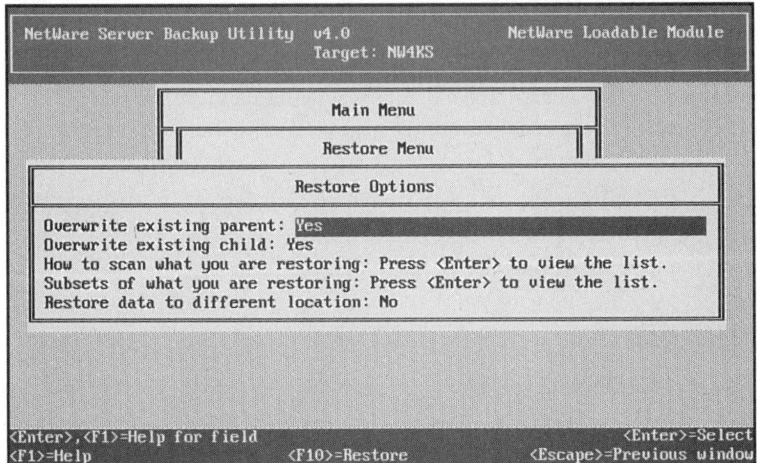

Figure 29.52
Restore Options for file system.

Press F29 to commence the restore. You will be asked to verify your choice. Select Yes.

As the restore proceeds, you will see a status window on the top right hand corner of the screen that will inform you of the status of the restore. Among other things you are shown the elapsed time and the amount of data restored. The data that is restored will be shown on the top left hand corner of the screen.

At the end of the restore, you will see a message informing you that the restore is complete (see fig. 29.53). Press Enter to continue and exit SBACKUP.

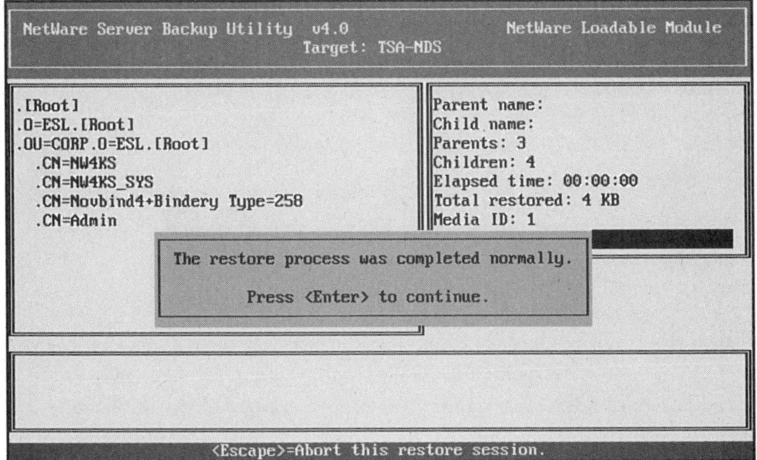

Figure 29.53
Restore Completion.

Restoring without Session Files

Occasionally you may have a corrupt session log or the session log may have been accidentally deleted. In this case you must perform the restore without a session log. The steps outlined below show you the sequence of steps to be performed. These steps complement the steps outlined in the previous section.

1. Perform steps 1 to 4 from the previous section.

2. From the SBACKUP Main Menu, select *Restore.* You will be presented with a choice of restoring with session files or without session files. Select "Restore Without Session Files" if the session files are corrupt or have been deleted. You will be shown a message (see fig. 29.54) that you will have to select the device and media to restore from.

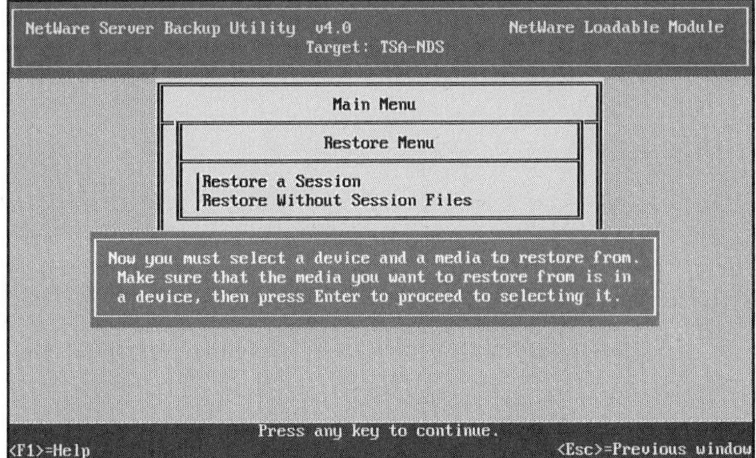

Figure 29.54
Message on selecting device and media to restore from.

   Press Enter to continue to the next step.

   The SBACKUP program will identify the media you have inserted (see fig. 29.55). Press Enter to continue.

   You will be given a selection of restore options. Make appropriate choices, and press F29. Verify that you wish to continue.

3. The SBACKUP program will read the sessions from the media. Figure 29.56 shows the first session that it found. If this is not the session that you wish to restore, you will have to select No, Go on to the Next Session on the media. If there are many sessions on the media, this could take some time. If you found the session that you wish to restore, select Yes, Restore This Session.

4. Proceed with the restore operations outlined in the previous section.

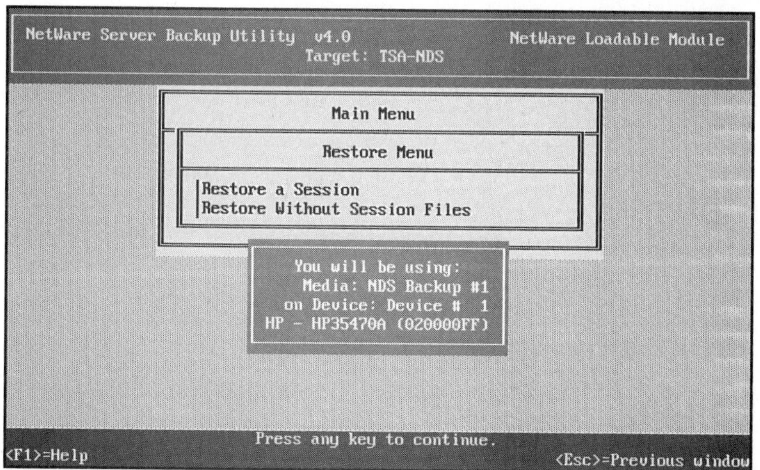

Figure 29.55
Media identified by Restore.

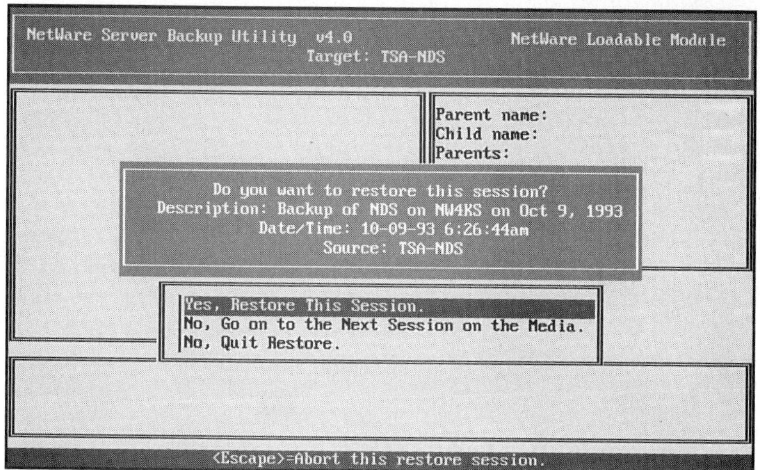

Figure 29.56
Session description read from media and restore choices.

Restore Options for Restoring a File System

The example of the restore operation was given in the context of restoring an NDS database. The restore options that are presented are quite different for restoring a file system. This section will discuss the restore options that are peculiar to restoring a file system.

When you select the "Restore a Session " option from the Restore Menu for a restoring a file system, you will be asked to select the device/media and the name of the session to restore from. You will then see the restore options of figure 29.57.

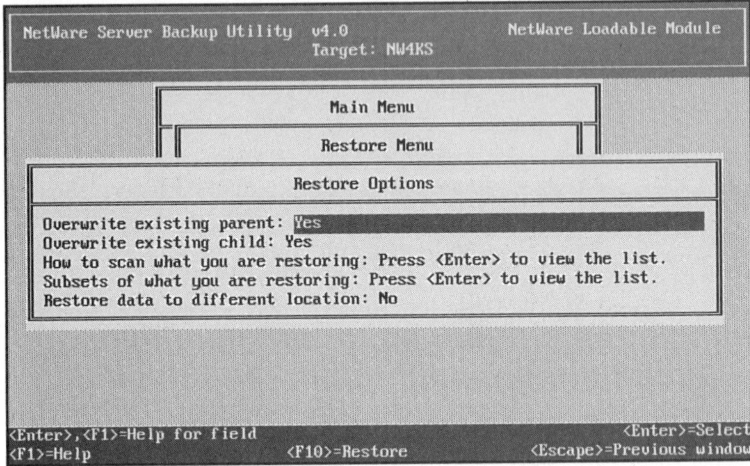

Figure 29.57
Restore Options for a File System.

Selecting the *Subsets of what you are restoring* option from the Restore Options form will show you the data items (also called data structure) that are available for restoring (see fig. 29.58). This option classifies data items as Major TSA or Minor TSA resources. A Major TSA resource contains data that can be backed as a whole when selected. Examples of Major TSAs are the File Server and the Volume. When you select a Major TSA resource such as a Volume, all directories and files within it are considered for restore operation. A Minor TSA resource is contained within a directory structure of a Major TSA resource. An example of this would be the directories and files within a volume.

In figure 29.58, if you wish to include an entire volume for a restore operation, you would select *Include major TSA resource* (see fig. 29.59) and press Ins to see a list of major TSA resources that are available for selection (see fig. 29.60).

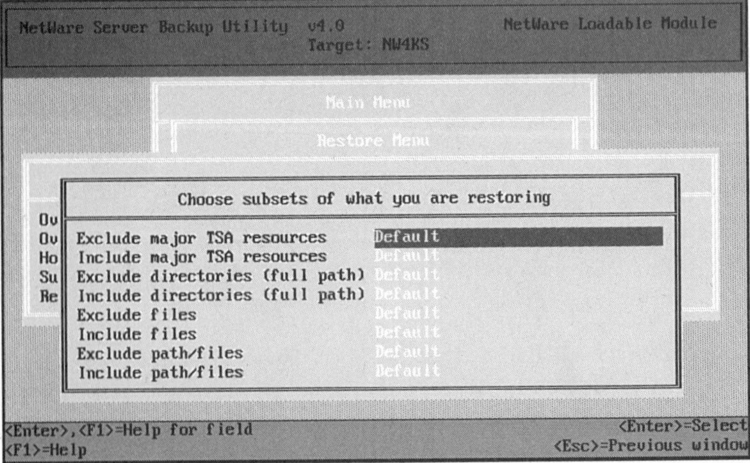

Figure 29.58
Subsets of what you are restoring option.

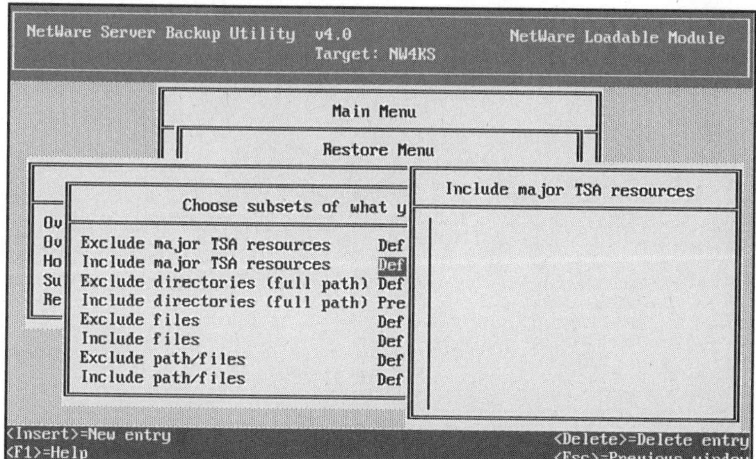

Figure 29.59
Include major TSA resources.

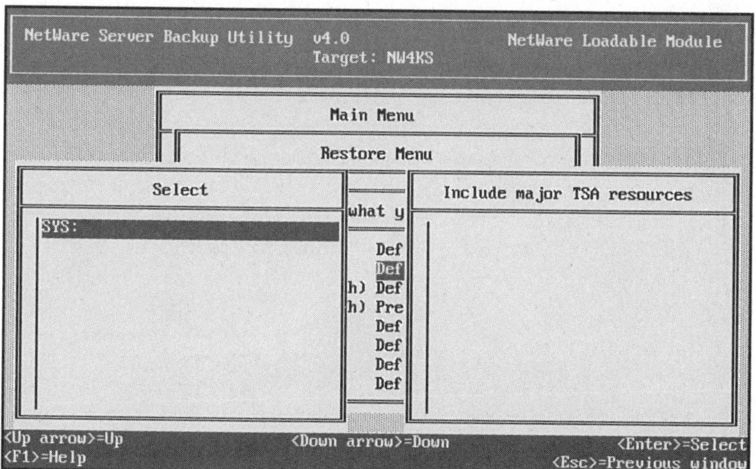

Figure 29.60
Selections for major TSA resources.

You can use the other options for excluding or including directories or files. If you wish to include a specific directory for backup, you can select *Include directories (full path)* and press Ins to add a directory name. Figure 29.61 shows the directory SYS:SYSTEM is selected for restore operation.

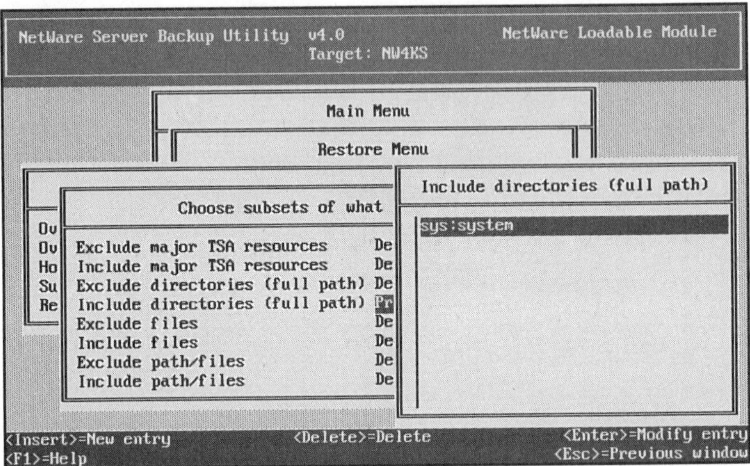

Figure 29.61
Using Include directories option.

Selecting the *How to scan for what you are restoring* option from the Restore Options form, will show you options for excluding different aspects of the file system (see fig. 29.62). This option shows the type of data contained in the data sets for the type of target (NetWare 4.*x* file system, in this case) that is being restored. The group of data files and directories that you are restoring is called a data set. You can select the data sets that you wish to exclude from the restore operation. If you wish to restore a type of data from this list, select a value of No, otherwise select a value of Yes. By default all of the Exclude options have a value of No. This means that all aspects of the data set should be scanned for the restore operation. The data stream refers to the data that is being restored. This option works with the other options "Subsets of what you are restoring" and the "Overwrite" option. It narrows the types of data sets that should be scanned for in the restore operation. For example, you can use this to exclude or include any of the following:

- Extended attributes
- Directory trustees
- File trustees
- Volume restrictions
- Directory space restrictions

If you wish to restore data to a different location from where it was backed up, you should set the field *Restore data to different location* to Yes. The default value for this field is No, which means that data will be restored on top of existing data.

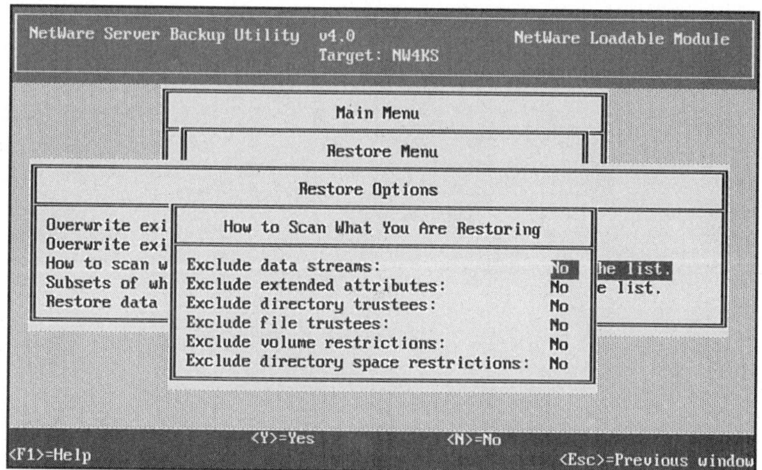

Figure 29.62
The How to Scan What You Are Restoring options.

Custom Backup Options

The example of the backup operation was given in the context of backing an NDS database. The backup options that are presented are quite different when the Custom Backup Method is selected for file systems.

When you select the "Custom: Only Specified Data " option from the Type of Backup Menu, you will then see the custom backup options of figure 29.63.

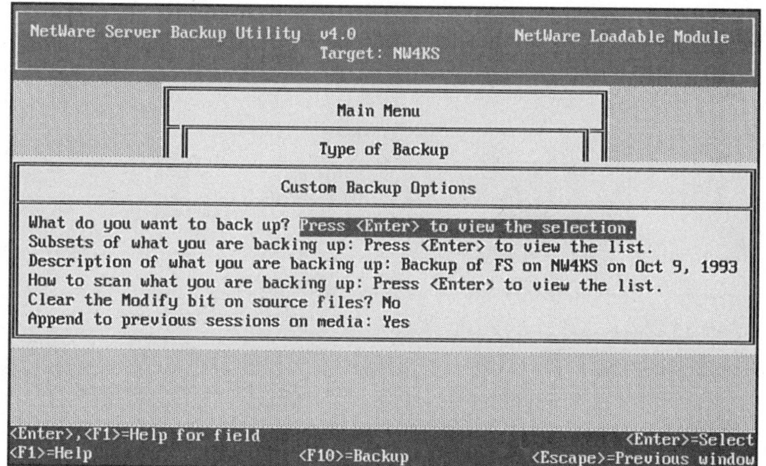

Figure 29.63
Custom Backup Options for a File System.

Selecting *What do you want to backup?* shows the Major TSA resource that is to be backed up (see fig. 29.64). Pressing Ins gives you a choice of other Major TSAs that can be backed up.

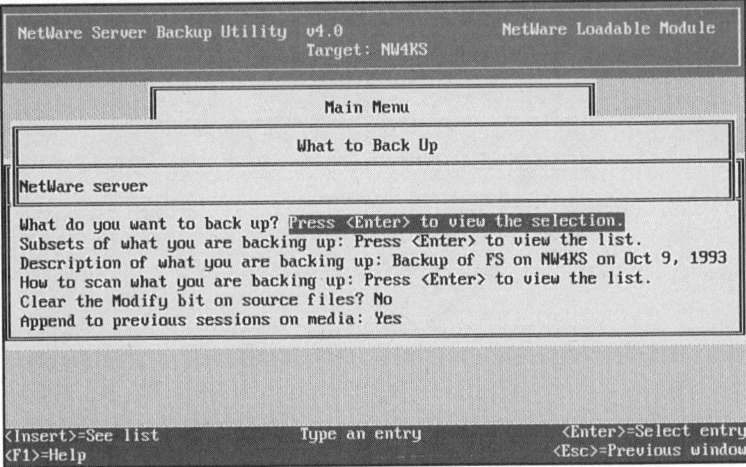

Figure 29.64
What do you want to back up? option.

A Major TSA resource contains data that can be backed as a whole when selected. Examples of Major TSAs are the File Server and the Volume. When you select a Major TSA resource such as a Volume, all directories and files within it are considered for restore operation. A Minor TSA resource is contained within a directory structure of a Major TSA resource. An example of this would be the directories and files within a volume.

Selecting *Subsets of what you are backing up* option from the Custom Backup Options form, will show you the data items (also called data structure) that are available for backing up (see fig. 29.65). This option classifies data items as Major TSA or Minor TSA resources.

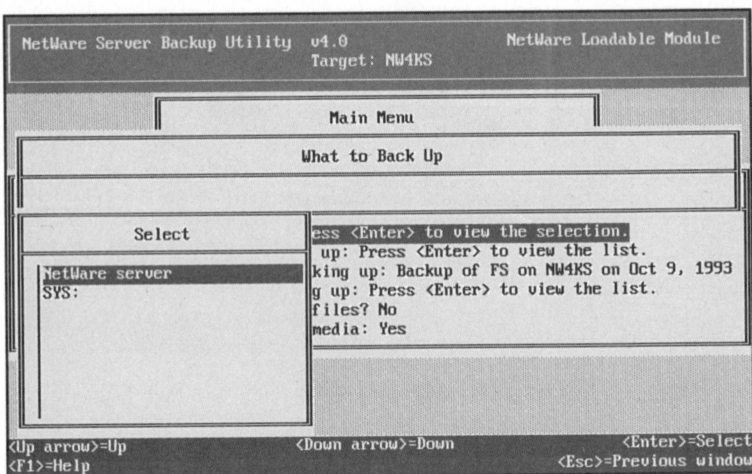

Figure 29.65
Selections for What do you want to back up? option.

In figure 29.66, if you wish to include an entire volume for a restore operation, you would select *Include major TSA resource* (see fig. 29.67) and press Ins to see a list of major TSA resources that are available for selection (see fig. 29.68).

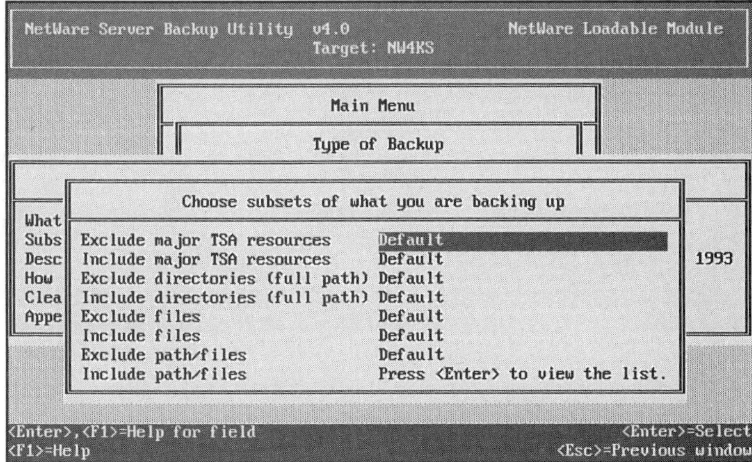

Figure 29.66
Subsets of what you are backing up option.

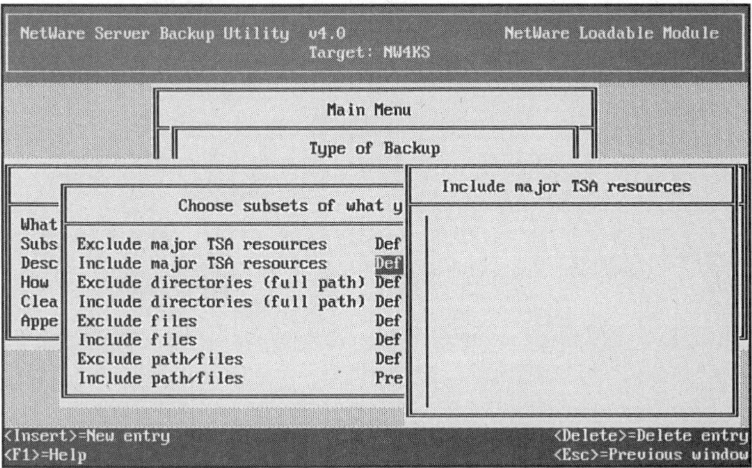

Figure 29.67
Include Major TSA resource for Backup.

29

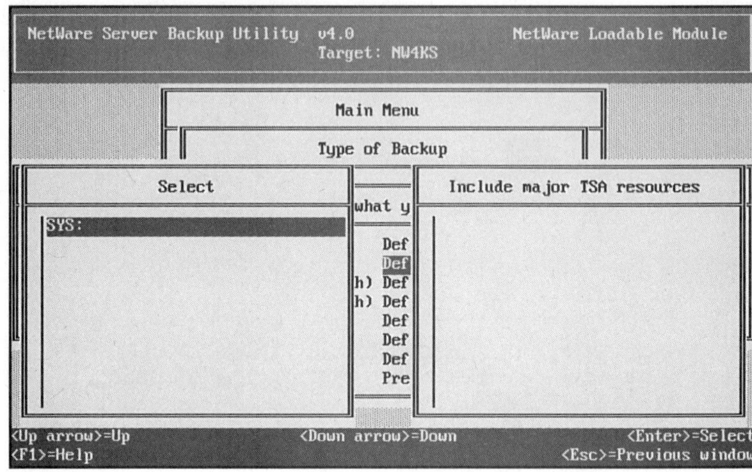

Figure 29.68
Selections for major TSA resource for Backup.

Selecting the *How to Scan What You Are Backing Up* option from the Custom Backup Options form will show you options for excluding different aspects of the file system (see fig. 29.69). This option shows the type of data contained in the data sets for the type of target (NetWare 4.*x* file system, in this case) that is being backed up. A group of data files and directories that you are restoring is called a data set.

29

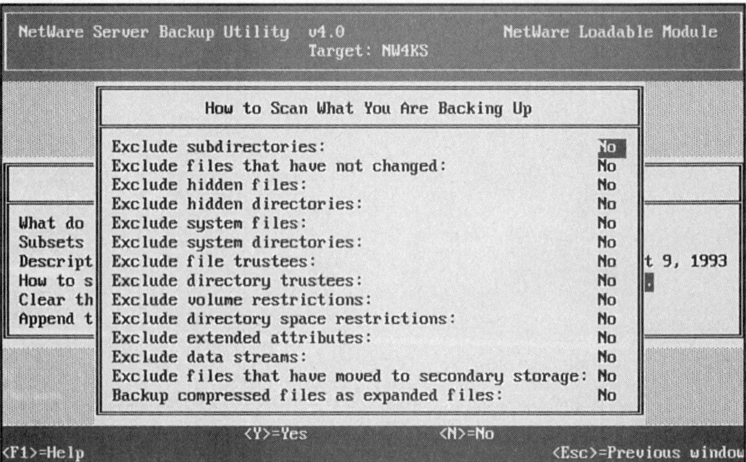

Figure 29.69
How to Scan What You Are Backing Up options.

You can select the data sets that you wish to exclude from the backup operation. If you wish to backup a type of data from this list, select a value of No, otherwise select a value of Yes. By default all of the Exclude options have a value of No. This means that all aspects of the data set should be scanned for the backup operation. This option works with the option "Subsets of what you are backing up" option. It narrows the types of data sets that should be scanned for in the backup operation. For example, you can use this to exclude (Yes) or include (No) any of the following:

- Subdirectories
- Files that have not changed
- Hidden files and directories
- File and directory trustees
- System files and directories
- Directory and volume space restrictions
- Extended attributes
- Files that have been moved to secondary storage
- Backup compressed files as expanded files

NetWare 4.*x* SBACKUP and Compressed Files

Using SBACKUP, you can specify if the files that you wish to backup should be backed up in a compressed state or not. The default on NetWare 4.*x* volumes is that compression is enabled. This default is set at the time a volume is first created as part of the server installation.

In general, you should back up compressed files in their compressed state, as the backup is faster. If you backup compressed files in the compressed state, you cannot restore it to a NetWare 3.*x* server that does not support the NetWare 4.*x* compression.

It is not a good idea to run SBACKUP when file compression is occurring on the volume. This would degrade the performance of SBACKUP. Since both the default time for compressing newly created/modified files and scheduling a delayed backup is 12:00 AM., you should schedule an SBACKUP several hours after volume compression begins.

NetWare 4.*x* SBACKUP Log and Error Files

The SBACKUP session files can be administered by selecting the *Log/error File Administration* option from the SBACKUP main menu. Figure 29.70 shows the options that are available when this option is selected. You can select a log file to view by selecting the *View a log file* option (see fig. 29.71). Similarly, the error file can be viewed by selecting the *View an Error File option.* You can specify the location of log and error files by selecting the *Set Location of Log and Error Files* option (see fig. 29.72).

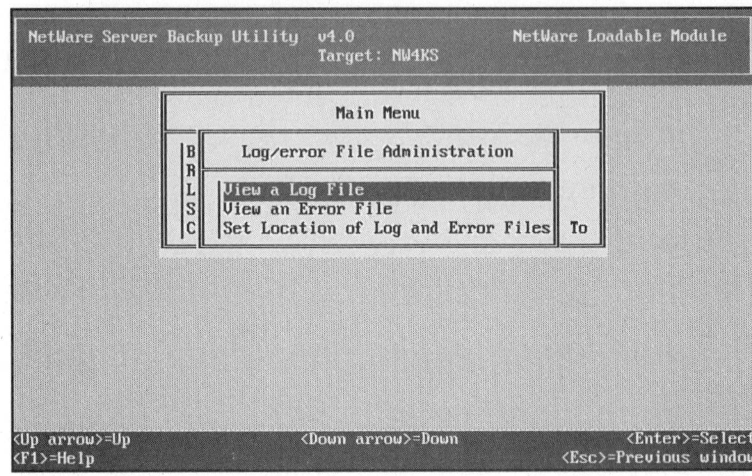

Figure 29.70 *Log/Error File Administration Menu.*

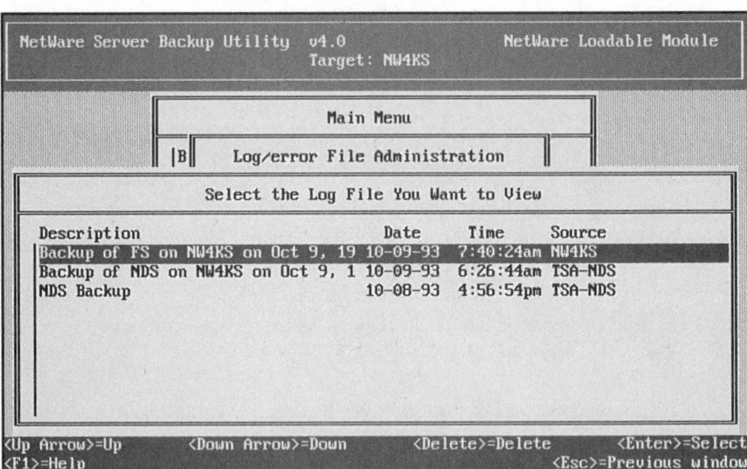

Figure 29.71 *View a Log file.*

29

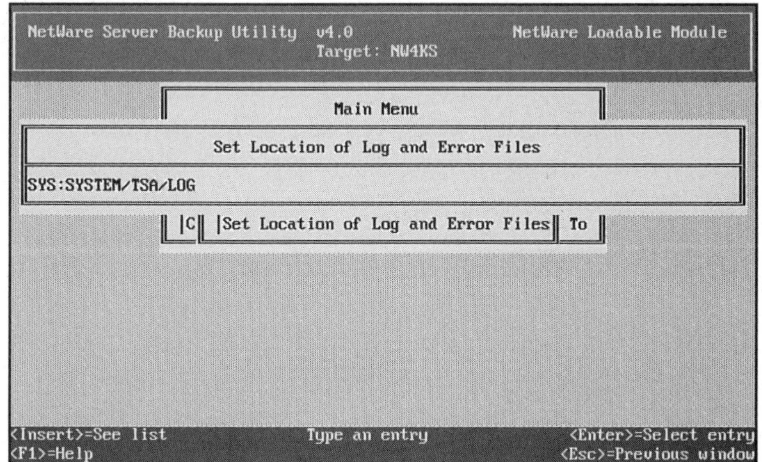

Figure 29.72
Setting location of log and error files.

NetWare 4.*x* SBACKUP Rights and Security Issues

Before SMS can be used, the backup operator must be able to log into NDS. In addition to this, to perform SBACKUP, you need Read and File Scan rights to the file system being backed up. These rights allow the operator to read the files and scan for names of files in directories being backed.

If you are performing an Incremental or Full Backup, the archive bit is cleared at the end of the back up pass. To perform this, the backup operator must have Modify right.

To back up the NDS database, you must be able to view the NDS tree structure and read the property values of the NDS object. To perform these operations, the backup operator must have Browse object trustee right to the NDS tree, and the Read property right to All Properties. Since the Browse right is assigned to the implicit group [public], no special considerations need to be made, unless this right is blocked by the IRF. The Read All Properties right must be assigned to the root of the NDS sub-tree that the backup operator has the authority for.

If the TSA at the workstation has a password set, the backup operator must have knowledge of this password.

Guideline for Using NetWare 4.*x* SBACKUP

There are a number of useful caveats to keep in mind when performing SBACKUP. These are listed below for your reference.

1. SBACKUP uses temporary files that can be as large as 7 MB. Make sure that you have enough free disk space on the server for these temporary files.

2. Switching to the system console when running SBACKUP and manually unloading the drivers is potentially dangerous. It could crash the server.

3. Do not mount or dismount volumes during an SBACKUP session. This could corrupt data and crash the server.

4. When backing up a system that has global compression enabled, wait for a period of time until the compression has been completed, before backing up the file system. This will allow a maximum number of files to be backed up in the compressed state.

5. In general, be aware of the name space formats supported by the file system being backed up. SBACKUP currently supports name spaces for:

   - DOS
   - OS/2
   - FS
   - Macintosh
   - FTAM

6. The NetWare server where SBACKUP is run requires a minimum of 3 MB of RAM in addition to other server RAM requirements.

7. If backing up other workstations (DOS, OS/2, etc.), you must know the workstation password, if it has been set.

8. SBACKUP logs out when the SBACKUP session finishes. If the SBACKUP session requires more than one media (tape), it will wait for one to be inserted before continuing. If no one is on hand to feed another tape drive to the backup device, SBACKUP will be logged into the target. This could pose a security weakness.

Summary

In this chapter, you learned about the basic differences between single-user and multiuser software and the different concurrency-control mechanisms that are needed to support multiuser applications.

The different types of application technologies, such as file server-based databases and database servers, also were discussed. The kinds of services offered by LAN-based versions of spreadsheets and word processing software were examined.

Network Troubleshooting

Network Cable Troubleshooting

A surprisingly large number of the problems associated with networks turn out to be cable-related. NetWare-based networks are typically built using twisted-pair, coaxial, or fiber-optic technology. It is easier to troubleshoot problems related to physical cabling if you understand the characteristics of the cable and adhere to the installation requirements of the cable. This chapter provides information that helps you to troubleshoot cable related problems.

Examining Twisted-Pair Cables

Twisted-pair cables are fast becoming a popular media choice for LANs because of low cost, relative ease of installation, and provision for bandwidths of up to 100 Mbps. Twisted-pair is also used to provide the physical cable for POTS (Plain Old Telephone Service). In its simplest form, a twisted-pair cable consists of two copper wires that together form a pair. A device using such a twisted-pair cable uses one of the wires in the pair for sending an electrical signal, whereas the other wire provides an electrical return signal needed to complete the circuit (see fig. 30.1). The wires are twisted to reduce the amount of electrical interference between the wires and their external surroundings.

To provide bi-directional communications between devices, one pair is used for sending data, and the other pair is used for receiving data (see fig. 30.2). A twisted-pair cable can consist of a number of such pairs. Plain old telephone service uses two pairs. LAN cables typically have four pairs, although all the pairs may not be used.

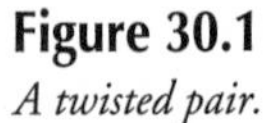

Figure 30.1
A twisted pair.

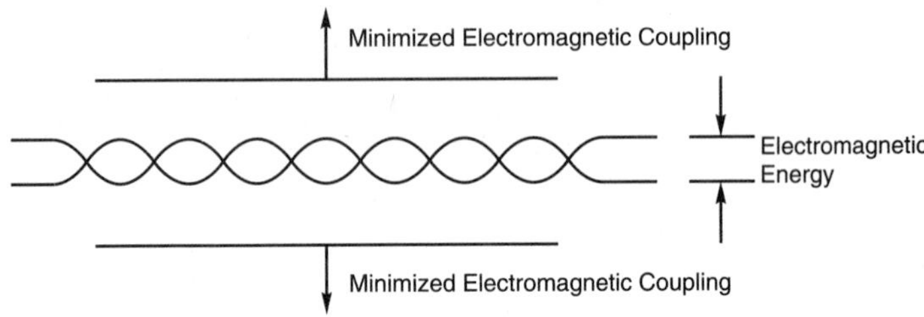

Figure 30.2
Twisted pairs for sending and receiving.

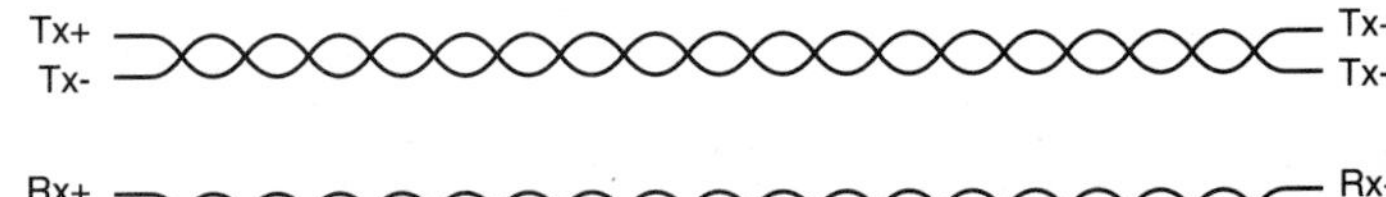

- Tx+ Transmit Signal
- Tx- Transmit Signal Return
- Rx+ Receive Signal
- Rx- Receive Signal Return

Twisted pairs can be shielded or unshielded. These are called *Shielded Twisted Pair* (STP) and *Unshielded Twisted Pair* (UTP), respectively.

Classifying Twisted-Pair Wiring

The *Telecommunications Industry Association* (TIA) and *Electronics Industry Association* (EIA) classify the twisted-pair wiring used in data networks based on its electrical characteristics. These specifications are described in the EIA/TIA 568, TSB-36, and TSB-40 documents and their successor document, the SP2840. Table 30.1 summarizes these classifications.

Table 30.1
Categories of UTP

Classification	Description
Category 1	This is intended for basic communications and is not rated for any application. There is no performance criteria for this category. These cables are unsuited for LAN data transmission.
Category 2	This is a low performance UTP cable not suited for LAN data transmission. It can be used for voice/PBX, alarm wiring, and low speed data transmission. The IBM cable type 3 is rated as Category 2.

Classification	Description
Category 3	This is suitable for data transmission speeds up to 16 MHz. This classification applies to the UTP cable and the connecting hardware. Typical applications are IEEE 802.3 10BASE-T, ARCnet, IEEE 802.5 16 Mbps UTP annex, and 100BASE-VG (IEEE 802.12).
Category 4	This is suitable for data transmission speeds up to 20 MHz. This classification applies to the UTP cable and the connecting hardware. Category 4 connecting hardware is suitable for Category 3 UTP. Typical applications are IEEE 802.3 10BASE-T, and IEEE 802.5 16 Mbps UTP annex.
Category 5	This is suitable for data transmission speeds up to 100 MHz. This classification applies to the UTP cable and the connecting hardware. Category 5 connecting hardware is suitable for Category 3 and Category 4 UTP. Typical applications are IEEE 802.14 100BASE-X, LATM (LAN ATM), TP-PMD (Twisted Pair-Physical Media Dependent) for CDDI (Copper Distributed Data Interface).

Categories 1, 2, and 3 are non-datagrade cables, even though Category 3 can be used in LAN applications. Categories 4 and 5 are rated as datagrade cables. Because Category 5 can be used for existing Category 3 applications, it is recommended that new wiring installations use Category 5 cables and connectors. This allows your networks to be upgraded to faster LANs (LATM, 100BASE-TX, CDDI) that can run on Category 5.

A common misconception about the UTP classifications is that a category of cable specifies a minimum *twists per inch* (TPI). That is, Category 3 requires 3 TPI, and Category 5 requires 5 TPI. This is not so. The criteria used to determine a category classification is based on the electrical and transmission characteristics of the cable. These electrical and transmission characteristics include the following:

- Mutual capacitance
- Characteristic impedance
- Structural return loss
- Attenuation
- Near end crosstalk

These transmission characteristics are discussed in the sections that follow for Categories 3, 4, and 5. The UTP cables for these categories are four unshielded twisted-pair wires of 24 AWG (American Wire Gauge) thermoplastic insulated conductors. These four conductor pairs can be solid or stranded and are enclosed in a thermoplastic jacket. The standards document also allows the use of four-pair 22 AWG cables that meet or exceed the electrical and transmission requirements.

Mutual Capacitance

Between any two conductors separated by an insulator (called *dielectric*) exists an electrical coupling that allows the transfer of energy (see fig. 30.3) from one conductor to another. The measure of how much electrical charge can be transferred from one conductor to another when a certain amount of voltage is applied is called *capacitance.* Capacitance is defined as the ratio of the electrical charge on the conductors and the voltage difference between the conductors. The capacitance for any twisted pair should be below a certain minimum value to achieve good transmission. The capacitance for any pair measured at or corrected for temperature at 20 degrees Celsius should not exceed the values indicated in table 30.2. The unit of measurement of capacitance is the *farad.* This is a very large unit, and it is usual to see capacitance measured in micro-farads (0.0000001 farad) or nano-farads (0.0000000001 farad).

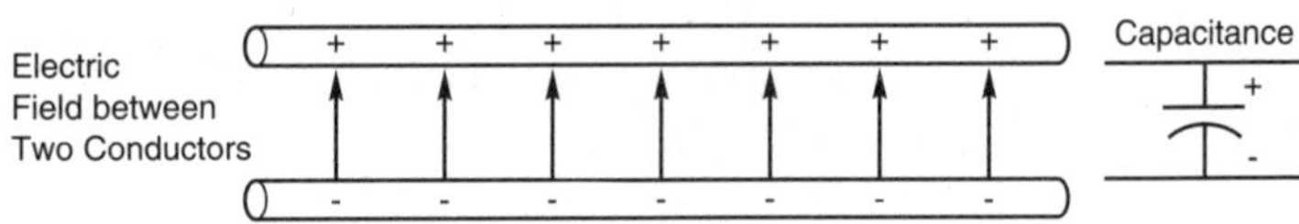

Figure 30.3
Electrical coupling between wires.

Table 30.2
Mutual Capacitance Measured at 1 KHz and 20 Degrees Celsius

Cable Type	Mutual Capacitance (Nano-Farads per 1,000 ft. or 305 Meters of cable)
Category 1, Category 2	No requirements
Category 3	20
Category 4	17
Category 5	17

30

Characteristic Impedance

Cables are rated by their characteristic impedance. *Impedance* of cable is defined as the opposition to the flow of an electrical signal at a particular frequency. For cables used in data communications, the impedance is measured in *ohms.* Each cable type has an impedance value considered to be characteristic of the cable, and hence the term *characteristic impedance* is used to describe this value. When a cable is terminated by its characteristic impedance, there are no signal reflections from the termination. Without a proper termination (equal to the characteristic impedance), when a signal reaches the extremity, it is reflected back. The reflected signal can cause interference with the data signal and should be avoided. Terminating the cable with its characteristic impedance makes the cable appear as if it is infinitely long (in electrical terms), and this prevents any reflected energy.

For Category 3, 4, and 5 cables the characteristic impedance should be 100 ohms plus or minus 15 percent variation, in the frequency range from 1 MHz to the highest frequency used for that cable type.

Characteristic impedance is a function of the geometry of the cable and the composition of its materials. Because structural variations exist in the geometry and material composition, the characteristic impedance actually varies with frequency. Also the cable for which the characteristic impedance is measured should be greater than one-eighth the wavelength. For frequencies of 100 MHz, one-eighth of the wavelength of the signal is approximately three meters.

Structural Return Loss

The fluctuation of input impedance of a cable is related to the *Structural Return Loss* (SRL) for a cable terminated in its own characteristic impedance. The degree of mismatch between the characteristic impedance of the cable and the connector is called the Structural Return Loss. SRL is measured by applying a balanced input signal (the inverted signal is placed on the other wire of the pair) to the connector pair, measuring the reflected signal, and taking the ratio of the input signal and the reflected signal. A higher SRL value is therefore better.

Table 30.3 shows the requirements for the different cables. Typically, SRL values for UTP cables are greater than 14 dB (decibels). Decibels are calculated as the logarithmic ratio (to the base ten) of the power signals multiplied by ten. From the calculations shown next, you can see that the value of 14 dB implies a ratio of 25 between input and reflected signal power, and a value of 23 dB implies a ratio of 200 between input and reflected signal power.

Assume that the following is true:

Pi = Input signal power

Pr = Reflected signal power

Vi = Input signal voltage

Vr = Reflected signal voltage

Therefore a decibel value of 14 implies the following:

10 log (Pi/Pr) = 14

log (Pi/Pr) = 1.4

Pi/Pr = 10**1.4 = 25.11

Vi/Vr = $\sqrt{Pi/Pr}$ = 5.01

Vr = 0.2 Vi

Reflected signal voltage (Vr) should be less than 20 percent of input signal voltage (Vi).

A decibel value of 23 implies the following:

10 log (Pi/Pr) = 23

log (Pi/Pr) = 2.3

Pi/Pr = 10**2.3 = 199.53

Vi/Vr = $\sqrt{Pi/Pr}$ = 14.13

Vr = 0.07 Vi

Reflected signal voltage (Vr) should be less than 27 percent of input signal voltage (Vi).

Table 30.3
Mutual Capacitance Measured at 1 KHz and 20 Degrees Celsius

Cable Type	Frequency	SRL (Decibels — dB)
Category 1, 2, 3	Not Applicable	No requirements
Category 4, 5	1 to 20 MHz	23 (or greater)
Category 5	20 to 100 MHz	14 (or greater)

Attenuation

30

As data signals propagate through the cable, some of their energy is dissipated. Table 30.4 shows the maximum attenuation for any pair of cables. This attenuation is measured for 1,000 feet (305 meters) of UTP cable at a temperature of 20 degrees Celsius. Attenuation values of 0.512 MHz and below in table 30.4 are for engineering design and are not used in conformance tests.

Table 30.4
Maximum Attenuation of 1,000 Feet UTP @ 20 Degrees Celsius

Frequency (MHz)	Category 3 (dB)	Category 4 (dB)	Category 5 (dB)
0.064	2.8	2.3	2.2
0.256	4.0	3.4	3.2
0.512	5.6	4.6	4.5
0.772	6.8	5.7	5.5
1.0	7.8	6.5	6.3
4.0	17	13	13

Frequency (MHz)	Category 3 (dB)	Category 4 (dB)	Category 5 (dB)
8.0	26	19	18
10.0	30	22	20
16.0	40	27	25
20.0	—	31	28
25.0	—	—	32
31.25	—	—	36
62.5	—	—	52
100.0	—	—	67

The introduction of connectors needed at end points of the cable further increases this loss (because of signal reflections). The worst case attenuation for Category 3, 4, and 5 UTP connectors that have a characteristic impedance of 100 ohms is shown in table 30.5.

Table 30.5
Attenuation of Connecting Hardware for 100 ohm UTP

Frequency (MHz)	Category 3 (dB)	Category 4 (dB)	Category 5 (dB)
1	0.4	0.1	0.1
4	0.4	0.1	0.1
8	0.4	0.1	0.1
10	0.4	0.1	0.1
16	0.4	0.2	0.2
20	—	0.2	0.2
25	—	—	0.2
31.25	—	—	0.2
62.5	—	—	0.3
100	—	—	0.4

Near End Crosstalk

Because the twisted-pair wires are close together in the UTP cable, a certain amount of electrical coupling is between them. Because of this electrical coupling, a signal applied to one of the pairs induces a smaller signal on the other pair (see fig. 30.4). This is called *crosstalk,* and it is quite common with poor-quality analog voice lines in which you can hear another telephone conversation. For UTP cables used for data transmission, the crosstalk must be below a certain level. A high degree of crosstalk can distort the data signal and make it unintelligible.

In UTP cables, a parameter called *Near End Crosstalk* (NEXT) is important. This parameter is measured by applying a balanced input signal on a wire pair and measuring the output on the other pairs. The pair to which the signal is applied is called the *disturbing pair,* and the pair on which crosstalk is being measured is called the *disturbed pair.* In the measurement of NEXT, both the disturbed and disturbing pairs are terminated by 100 ohms, the nominal characteristic impedance of UTP cable.

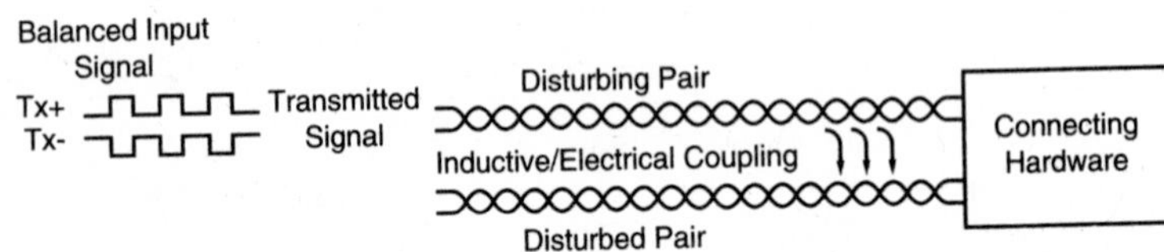

Figure 30.4
Near End Crosstalk.

30

NEXT is defined in terms of decibels and is the logarithmic ratio (to the base ten) of the power levels of the disturbing signal and the crosstalk signal, scaled by a factor of ten. As a formula, this can be expressed as follows:

NEXT = 10 log (Pi/Pc)

in which

Pi = Power of the balanced disturbing signal

Pc = Power of the disturbed crosstalk signal

As the crosstalk signal decreases, the NEXT value should increase. Therefore, a larger NEXT value is better for data transmission because large NEXT values imply small crosstalk signals. As the frequency of the transmitted signal increases, the value of NEXT decreases—that is, the crosstalk signal increases.

The minimum NEXT value at 0.772 MHz should be 43 dB for Category 3 cable; 58 dB for Category 4; and 64 dB for Category 5.

Table 30.6 shows the minimum NEXT values for Category 3, 4, and 5 cables over a range of frequencies.

At any operating frequency, the minimum NEXT at room temperature (defined as 20 degrees Celsius) should be greater than the value determined by the following formula for all operating frequencies for a length of UTP 305 meters (1,000 feet) long:

NEXT(0.772) – 15 log (F/0.772)

The notation NEXT(0.772) means the value of NEXT at 0.772 MHz and the F in the equation refers to the frequency. If NEXT(F) is the value of NEXT at frequency F, the preceding condition can be stated as follows:

NEXT(F) >= NEXT(0.772) – 15 log (F/0.772)

The values in table 30.6 must satisfy the condition just stated. These values are actually derived from the preceding formula truncated to the nearest decibel. Consider the NEXT for Category 5 at frequency 100 MHz.

NEXT(100) >= NEXT(0.772) – 15 log (100/0.772)

NEXT (100) >= 64 – 15 log (100/0.772)

NEXT (100) >= 64 – 15*2.11

NEXT (100) >= 32

This shows that NEXT(100) for Category 5 should be 32 dB, and this agrees with the value in table 30.6.

Table 30.6
NEXT for Horizontal UTP Cable

Frequency (MHz)	Category 3 (dB)	Category 4 (dB)	Category 5 (dB)
0.150	54	68	74
0.772	43	58	64
1.0	41	56	62
4.0	32	47	53
8.0	28	42	48
10.0	26	41	47
16.0	23	38	44
20.0	—	36	42

continues

Table 30.6, Continued
NEXT for Horizontal UTP Cable

Frequency (MHz)	Category 32 (dB)	Category 4 (dB)	Category 5 (dB)
25.0	—	—	41
31.25	—	—	40
62.5	—	—	35
100	—	—	32

Table 30.6 shows the requirements for UTP cable. The NEXT requirements for connecting hardware used with UTP cables are different, and these are shown in table 30.7. The NEXT for connecting hardware should exceed or equal the following value:

$$\text{NEXT}(16) - 20 \log (F/16)$$

where NEXT(16) is the minimum loss at 16 MHz. If the loss at frequency F is NEXT(F), the following is true:

$$\text{NEXT}(F) >= \text{NEXT}(16) - 20 \log (F/16)$$

The minimum NEXT value for the connecting hardware at 16 MHz is 34 dB for Category 3 connector; 46 dB for Category 4 connector; and 56 dB for Category 5 connector. The values for connector loss in table 30.7 are in agreement with the preceding formula.

Table 30.7
NEXT for UTP Connecting Hardware

Frequency (MHz)	Category 3 (dB)	Category 4 (dB)	Category 5 (dB)
1.0	58	65	65
4.0	46	58	65
8.0	40	52	62
10.0	38	50	60
16.0	34	46	56
20.0	—	44	54
25.0	—	—	52

Frequency (MHz)	Category 3 (dB)	Category 4 (dB)	Category 5 (dB)
31.25	—	—	50
62.5	—	—	40

Direct Current Resistance

The *Direct Current* (DC) resistance between the input and output connectors of the connecting hardware, not including the cable, should not exceed 0.3 ohm for Category 3, 4, and 5 UTP cables. DC resistance should not be confused with characteristic impedance. Characteristic impedance is a measurement of opposition to the flow of alternating current at a particular frequency. DC resistance is the measurement of flow of a direct current (or current of zero frequency) and is an indication of the connectors' capability to transmit DC current and low frequency currents.

Connector Termination and Cable Installation Practices

To minimize loss at the connectors in which twisted-pair wires are terminated, the stripped leads should not exceed 0.55 inch (14 mm) (see fig. 30.5). The length of the jacket portion should not exceed 0.5 inch (13 mm), with the flat portion of the jacket less than or equal to 0.3 inch (8 mm). The general strategy for terminating UTP with connectors should be to reduce the amount of untwisted wire and the separation between the conductor pairs at the connectors. The amount of untwisting when terminating to connecting hardware should not exceed 0.5 inch (13 mm) for Category 5 cables, and 1.0 inch (25 mm) for Category 4 cables. While untwisting the cable, strip back as small an amount as possible of the cable needed for termination.

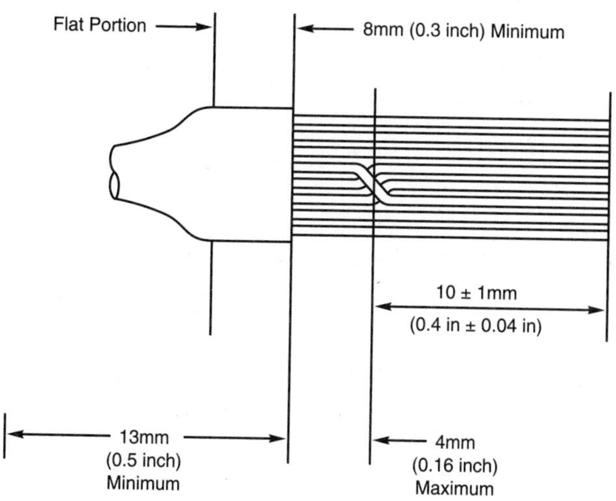

Figure 30.5
Dimensions of UTP leads at connector end.

For cross-connect cables used to connect hubs, use factory terminated UTP cables because this reduces performance variations in UTP connections. During installation and after the UTP cable is installed, take care to avoid subjecting the UTP cables to physical stress. The maximum pulling stress or force that a four-pair UTP horizontal 24 AWG (0.5 mm) cable can be subjected to is 110 Newtons (25 lb_f). The bend radius of UTP cable should not be less than four times the cable diameter for horizontal UTP.

Also be aware that when installing cables on a conducting surface, such as a ground plane or metal conduit, the mutual capacitance, characteristic impedance, return loss, and attenuation can worsen by two to three percent. This normally is not a problem, but you should be aware of this fact.

Color Code Requirements

The color codes of standard UTP (also called *straight-through*) cables should conform to either Color Code Option 1 or Color Code Option 2, shown in table 30.8.

Table 30.8
Color Codes for 100 Ohm, Standard UTP Cable

Pair	Color Code Option 1	Color Code Option 2
1	White with Blue stripe (W-B)	Green (G)
1	Blue (BL) or Blue with White (BL-W) stripe	Red (R)
2	White with Orange (W-O) stripe	Black (BK)
2	Orange (O) or Orange with White (O-W) stripe	Yellow (Y)
3	White with Green (W-G) stripe	Blue (BL)
3	Green (G) or Green with White (G-W) stripe	Orange (O)
4	White with Brown (W-BR) stripe	Brown (BR)
4	Brown (BR) or Brown with White (BR-W) stripe	Slate (S)

Two types of jacks may be used—T568A and T568B. In UTP jacks with the T568A designation, pair 1 is assigned to pins 4 and 5 of the jack, pair 2 is assigned to pins 3 and 6, pair 3 is assigned to pins 1 and 2, and pair 4 is assigned to pins 7 and 8. In UTP jacks with the T568B designation, pair 1 is assigned to pins 4 and 5, pair 2 is assigned to pins 1 and 2, pair 3 is assigned to pins 3 and 6, and pair 4 is assigned to pins 7 and 8. Both ends of the UTP cable must use the same type of jack.

Troubleshooting Tips for UTP

Problems associated with UTP generally fall into the following groups:

- Attenuation
- Crossed pairs
- Split pairs
- Connector problems
- Termination practices
- Crosstalk

Attenuation Problems

Attenuation is measured in decibels and represents loss in power of the transmitted signal. If you are using the correct UTP cable category and are within the distance limits of the network type, you should not normally have a problem because of attenuation. If your cable suffers from excessive attenuation (measured by wire testing tools discussed later), you should check for any of the following:

- **Excessive length of UTP cable.** The maximum length depends on the network type being used and is usually 100 meters for most networks.
- **Installation of an inferior category cable.** Install only cables rated for the network type and the data transfer rate used. For example, do not install a Category 3 cable when a Category 5 cable is required.
- **Poorly installed connectors.** Poorly installed connectors can produce excessive attenuation. Keep the lengths of untwisted twisted-pair wire at the connectors as small as possible. Excessive lengths of untwisted wires can result in significant signal loss.
- **Rising temperature.** Cables are usually rated for a maximum of 40 degrees Celsius. Avoid installing cables near heat sources or areas that have high temperatures.

Crossed Pair Problems

Crossed pairs are formed when each pair of wire has conductors crossed at the connectors. Normally, a conductor connecting pin 1 at one connector should be terminated on pin 1 of the other connector. In a crossed pair, pin 1 is connected to pin 2 of the remote connector, and pin 2 is connected to pin 1 of the remote connector; pin 3 is connected to pin 6 of the remote connector, and pin 6 is connected to pin 3 of the remote connector (see fig. 30.6). For normal connections between a workstation and network hub, a straight-through cable is used (see fig. 30.7). The pair connecting pins 1 and 2 is used for

transmission, and the wire pair connecting pins 3 and 6 is used for receiving (see table 30.9). Hub-ports have an X marking on them indicating that the connectors at the hub are wired to perform cross-over functions. Cross over is actually needed in the signal path between the workstation NIC and the hub electronics so that a signal transmitted on, say pin 1, appears on the receive line at the hub. Similarly, a signal transmitted on pin 1 at the hub should appear on the receive line (pin 2) at the workstation. If a cross-over cable is used between the workstation and the hub, the X function at the hub also performs a cross-over function, and the workstation and hub ends up transmitting and receiving on the same line. This prevents the hub and workstation from communicating. Usually one of the ports on a hub can be programmed as a straight port or an X port. This can then be used to link the hubs using a straight-through cable.

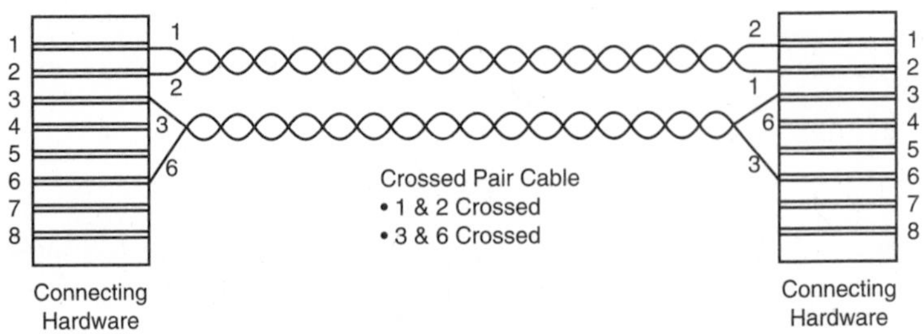

Figure 30.6
Crossed-pair cable.

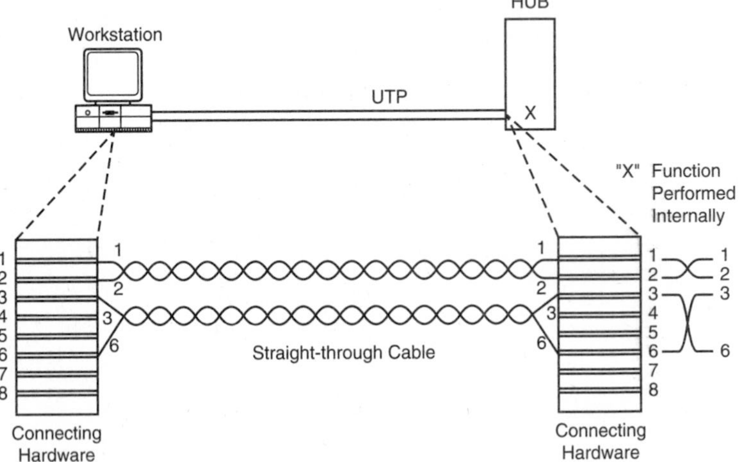

Figure 30.7
Straight-through cable.

Cross-over cables can be used to connect hubs. When used in this manner, each end of the cross-over cable should be connected either to an X-port or a straight-through port on the hub.

Another little-known use of cross-over cable is to form a low cost UTP LAN consisting of two stations, by connecting the cross-over cable between the NICs of the two stations (server and workstation). This allows a LAN to be formed using UTP wiring and no hub! Such a network can be used for test purposes (such as the one used by the author while traveling on the road) and does not require the availability of a hub. For such a network to work reliably you should not use long cable lengths of the cross-over cable.

Table 30.9
Pairs Used in 10BASE-T and 100BASE-TX

Contact	MDI signal
1	TD+
2	TD_
3	RD+
4	Not used by 10BASE-T/100BASE-TX
5	Not used by 10BASE-T/100BASE-TX
6	RD
7	Not used by 10BASE-T/100BASE-TX
8	Not used by 10BASE-T/100BASE-TX

Crossed-pair cable problems can be detected with a simple continuity check using an ohm meter (or multimeter with a DC continuity check).

Split Pair Problems

In split pairs, physical continuity is maintained, but the conductors from different pairs are combined. This leads to pairs that do not have the required twists to minimize signal loss and electrical coupling. These types of problems are difficult to detect with simple continuity checks that show the necessary pin-to-pin correspondence. Split pairs in Category 5 cable reduce its performance to that of a Category 2 cable. Split pair cables also can support 10BASE-T for short distances. If cable testers used on a cable reveal unusually low values for NEXT (22 dB or lower), you may suspect a split pair problem. Remember that a lower NEXT implies larger amounts of crosstalk.

Figure 30.8 shows a split pair cable in which the pin 2 conductor is twisted with the pin 6 conductor, and the pin 3 conductor is twisted with the pin 1 conductor. For 10BASE-T and 100BASE-TX UTP cables, the pin 1 conductor should be twisted with the pin 2 conductor, and the pin 3 conductor should be twisted with the pin 6 conductor.

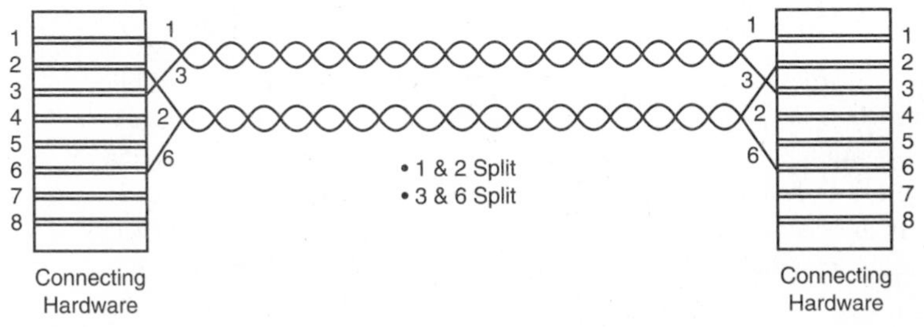

Figure 30.8
Split pair cable.

30

Connector Problems

You must use the right type of connector with the UTP cable. UTP cables can use solid wire conductors or stranded wire connectors. Each of these UTP types requires its own type of connector. For solid wire connectors, two blades in the pin connector make a firm grip on the conductor. For stranded wire UTP cables, use connectors in which the blade is designed to pierce the strand.

If an incorrect type of connector is used, it can create intermittent contact with the conductor.

Termination Problems

Use proper tools for the category type you are connecting. Use the dimensions specified in the section, "Connector Termination and Cable Installation Practices," earlier in this chapter. Some of the items to watch out for include the following:

- Use tight wire twist in the connector.
- Minimize the length of cable untwisted at the connectors.
- Do not use old 66 type blocks that have high attenuation and crosstalk.
- Terminate voice and data cables on different punch blocks.

Crosstalk Problems

Measurement of NEXT can reveal if the cable can be used at a particular frequency. A high NEXT implies a good cable (small crosstalk), and a low NEXT implies any of the following problems due to large amounts of crosstalk:

- **Split pairs.** This problem is caused if conductors in different pair twists are grouped together.
- **Use of silkline cables.** Silkline cables are untwisted cables that have a low NEXT value (large amounts of crosstalk).
- **Mixing voice and data.** You may be running voice and data applications running in the same UTP cable. This can lead to low NEXT values.
- **Improper terminations.** Large lengths of untwisted cable at end connectors.

Troubleshooting Tools

One of the simplest tools is the *continuity tester*. Most multimeters have a continuity tester option. Continuity testers are made by Fluke, Paladin, Seimon, Progressive Electronics, Micronta, and many others. These types of tools measure the DC characteristics of the cable, but not the transmission characteristics such as NEXT. To measure NEXT, you can use tools from Fluke, Wavetek, and Microtest. Another class of tools is *certification tools*. These tools are available from Hewlett Packard, Fluke, and Microtest. Certification tools perform a battery of tests on a cable and certify the cable as being Category 5, 4, or 3 compliant. Certification tools also include tests for Ethernet, Token Ring, ARCnet, Fast Ethernet, CDDI, and other types of LANs. An example of a cable certification tool is the PentaScanner from Microtest (call 800-526-9675 or 602-952-6401). In addition to finding cable faults, the PentaScanner analyzes LAN traffic.

Understanding Coaxial Cables

Coaxial cables are the earliest form of cables used for LANs. They have largely been superseded by the more popular UTP cables discussed in this chapter. Coaxial cables consist of a central conductor with a shield around it. Different types of cables are available for different types of LANs. For example, Thin Wire Ethernet, Thick Wire Ethernet, and ARCnet all use different types of cables. One way to tell the cables apart is their physical diameter and characteristic impedance.

Both Thick Wire and Thin Wire Ethernet use cables with characteristic impedance of 50 ohms. However, Thin Wire cables have greater loss and are rated for shorter distances of 185 meters. Thick Wire cables, on the other hand, are rated at distances up to 500 meters. Broadband Ethernet (10BROAD36) uses cables with characteristic impedance of 75 ohms, and ARCnet cables have a characteristic impedance of 93 ohms.

Problems associated with coaxial cables are typically the following:

- Exceeding distance specifications
- Opens and shorts in a cable
- Mismatch in characteristic impedance

Exceeding Distance Specifications

Coaxial cables are rated for different lengths of operations. If the distance rating of the coaxial cable is exceeded, the transmitted signal attenuates below the level needed for successful reception. The maximum length of a cable type depends on the type of LAN. Chapter 2, "LAN Standards for Physical and Data Link Layers," described the details of configurations for many types of LANs. Table 30.10 summarizes the distance limitations for different types of LANs.

Make sure that the maximum length of cable segments is not exceeded. Several cable scanners are available on the market that enable you to measure cable lengths, such as the MicroTest cable scanner. When measuring cable lengths, make sure that no LAN traffic is on the cable. One end of the cable is kept open or short-circuited through a specially wired terminator that has zero resistance. (The resistor component is replaced by a small length of conducting wire.) The cable scanner is attached to the other end of the cable (see fig. 30.9). The cable scanner is programmed with information on the cable type, such as RG-58 for 100BASE-2, and RG-62 for ARCnet. The cable scanner uses the cable type to look up the speed of the transmission signal on the cable. It then sends a pulse signal, starts a timer, and waits for the reflection to come back. Knowing the time it takes a signal to come back and the speed of transmitted signal, the cable scanner can estimate the cable length. This type of technique is called *Time Domain Reflection,* and the instruments that perform them are called *Time Domain Reflectometers* (TDRs).

Figure 30.9

Estimating cable length.

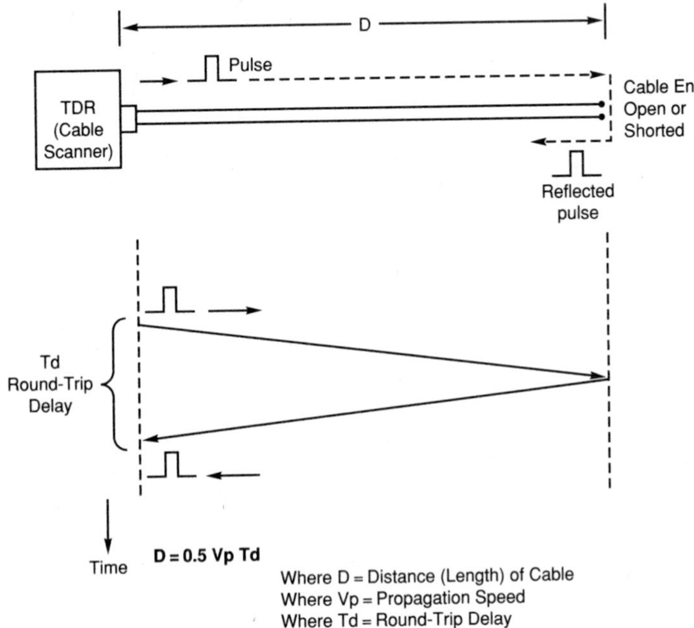

30

Assume that the cable length is *D*; the time for signal to come back is *Td*; and propagation speed in cable is *Vp*. The formula can be used for computing length of cable (D).

$$2D = VpTd$$

and

$$D = 0.5\,VpTd$$

Cable scanners contain the logic to compute the preceding formula and display the results.

For a 10BASE2 cable minimum *Vp* is 0.65c (c= velocity of light in vacuum = 300,000,000 meters/sec). Consult table 2.5 in Chapter 2, "LAN Standards for Physical and Data Link Layers," for cable velocities.

Assume that the pulse comes back within two microseconds and use the preceding formula for estimating distance, as follows:

$$D = 0.5\ VpTd$$

$$= 0.5 * 0.65 * 300{,}000{,}000 * 0.000002$$

$$= 195 \text{ meters}$$

Comparing this length with that in table 30.10, you can see that this cable exceeds the maximum segment length for 10BASE2 (185 meters). The figures in table 30.10 are based on cable types with certain attenuation characteristics. Many manufacturers supply superior cables, and it is possible for 10BASE2 LANs with 195-meter cable segments to work, but there is no guarantee that it will always work as new types of devices are added. Many networks enable the use of repeaters to overcome distance limitations.

Table 30.10
Coaxial Cable Lengths for Different LANs

LAN Type	Type of Measurement	Length
10BASE2 (Thin Wire Ethernet)	Coax segment	185 meters (maximum)
10BASE2 (Thin Wire Ethernet)	Distance between workstations	0.5 meters (minimum)
10BASE5 (Thick Wire Ethernet)	Coax segment	500 meters (maximum)
10BASE5 (Thick Wire Ethernet)	Distance between workstations	Multiples of 2.5 meters
10BASE5 (Thick Wire Ethernet)	Transceiver cable	50 meters (maximum)
ARCnet	Distance between workstation and hub	100 feet (maximum)
ARCnet	Distance between hubs	2,000 feet (maximum)
10BASE-T	Unshielded Twisted Pair	100 meters between work-station and concentrator

Opens and Shorts in Cables

It is possible for cables to become damaged and produce an open circuit or short circuit within the cable. Figure 30.10 shows cables with an open circuit and a short circuit. These types of cable faults are often found at the cable extremities and are caused by poorly installed connectors. An open circuit can be caused by the connector not making proper contact with the cable conductor or the outer shield. A short circuit can be caused by a strand of wire from the shield making contact with the central conductor when the connector is crimped at the cable end. Proper cable crimping tools that apply even pressure (such as those made by AMP) and attention to detail while crimping the connectors can prevent many of these problems.

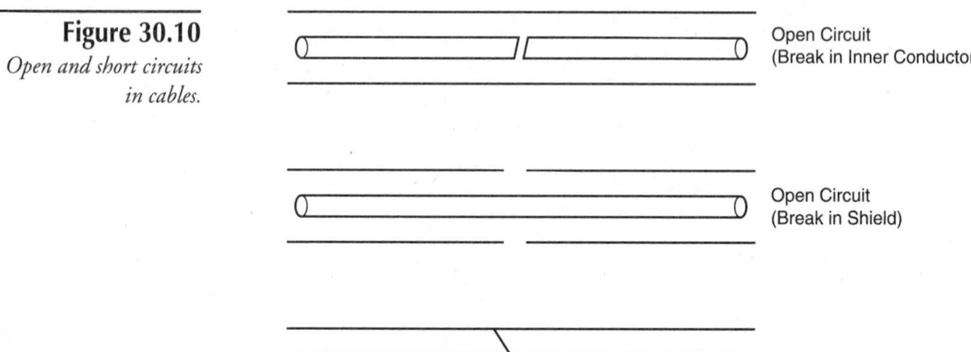

Figure 30.10
Open and short circuits in cables.

An open or short circuit also can occur in the middle of a cable run. This can be caused by manufacturing defects or damage to the cable. Cables can be damaged when a piece of heavy equipment falls on the cable. This can cause a break in the shield or central conductor, which results in an open circuit. The shearing action that damages the cable also can cause the insulation material between the shield and the conductor to extrude from the cable, causing the shield and conductor to make contact producing a short circuit. Damage to the cable can sometimes be discovered by inspection, but a cable run may be in an area difficult to inspect (false ceilings, under carpet, within walls, and so on). You can use a cable scanner, described in the preceding section, to estimate the distance to an open or short circuit.

If the polarity of the reflected signal is the same as the polarity of the transmitted signal, the cable has an *open-circuit fault* (see fig. 30.11). If the polarity of the reflected signal is the opposite polarity of the transmitted signal, the cable has a *short-circuit fault* (see fig. 30.12). The type of fault can be detected by using the time domain reflection technique in which one end of the cable is terminated by the characteristic impedance of the cable, and a TDR is used to send a pulse from the other end. The TDR uses the polarity of the return signal to classify the fault as an open circuit or short circuit. It uses the time it takes the reflected signal to come back to estimate distance to the fault (see fig. 30.13). It is possible to have a damaged cable that has neither an open nor a short circuit, but still has a reflected signal (see fig. 30.14). Most TDRs classify this as either an open circuit or short circuit depending on whether the positive or negative polarity signal is stronger.

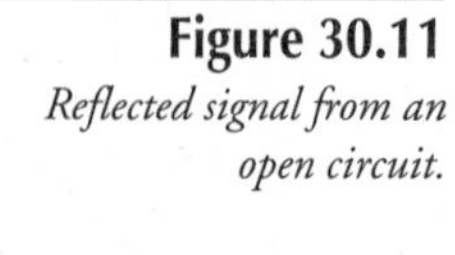

Figure 30.11
Reflected signal from an open circuit.

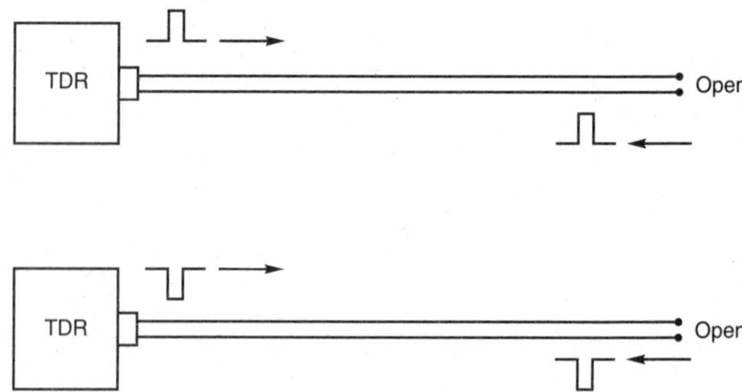

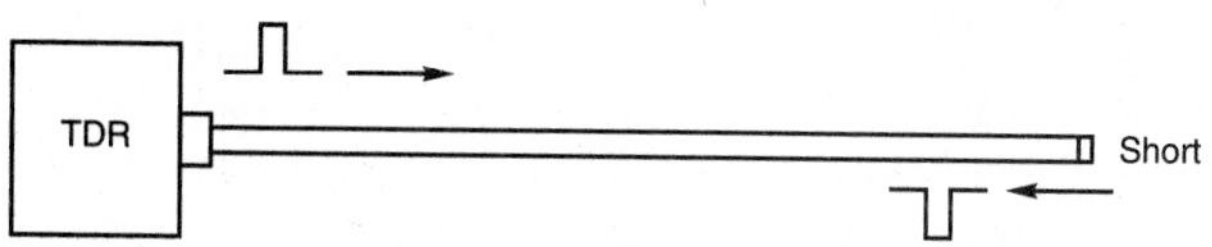

Figure 30.12
Reflected signal from a short circuit.

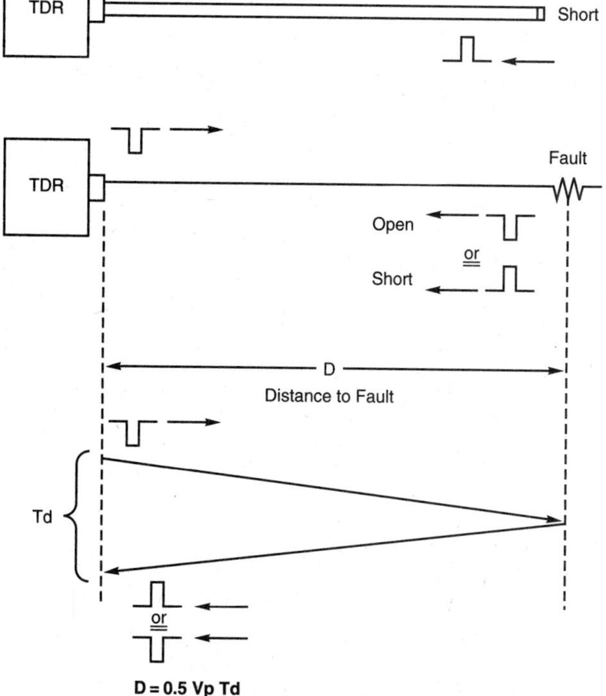

Figure 30.13
Determining an open circuit/short circuit fault.

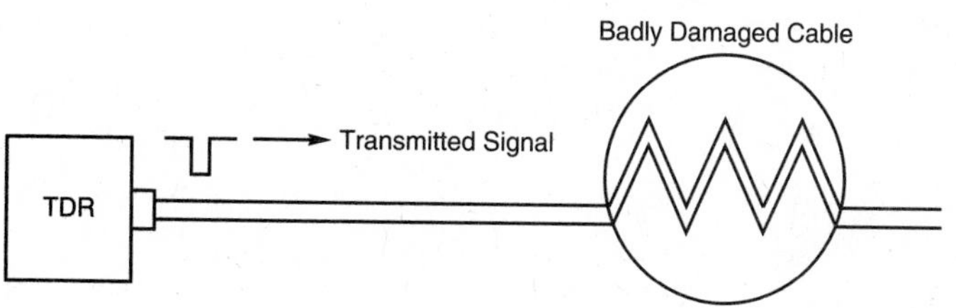

Figure 30.14
Reflected signal from a damaged cable that has neither an open nor short circuit.

Consider the following example of detecting a fault. A negative signal is sent from a TDR, and the reflected signal comes back after three microseconds on a 10BASE5 cable. The reflected signal has a positive polarity. From this, you can determine that a short is in the cable. Minimum propagation velocity of a 10BASE5 cable is 0.77c (c= velocity of light in vacuum = 300,000,000 meters/sec). To estimate distance of fault from the TDR, use the following formula:

$$D = 0.5\ VpTd$$

$$= 0.5 * 0.77 * 300{,}000{,}000 * 0.000003$$

$$= 346.5 \text{ meters}$$

Therefore, the short circuit is 347 meters away from the TDR.

It must be emphasized that TDRs have an error value of plus or minus a few meters. Consult the manufacturers' technical specifications for this error value.

Mismatch in Characteristic Impedance

You must use cables with the correct characteristic impedance for a LAN type. Some of these cables such as RG-62 and RG-58 use similar BNC connectors. It is possible to connect these, but doing so creates an impedance mismatch because RG-62, used in ARCnet, has a characteristic impedance of 93 ohms; and RG-58, used in 10BASE2, has a characteristic impedance of 50 ohms.

When a mismatch in characteristic impedance occurs, unexpected reflections in the cable can interfere with the transmitted signal (see fig. 30.15).

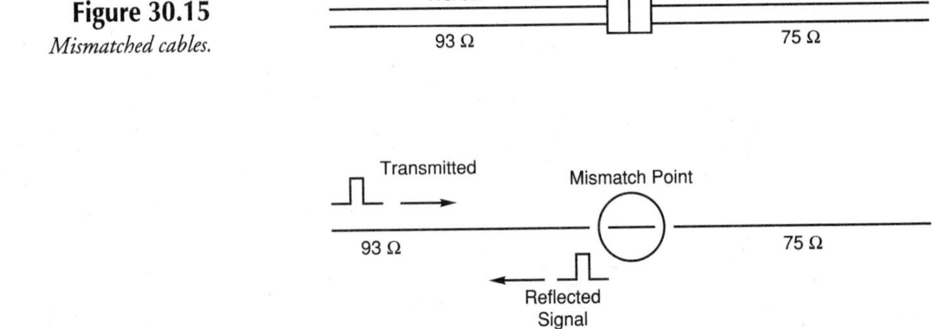

Figure 30.15
Mismatched cables.

Most LAN cables have an RG (Recommended Gauge) rating shown in table 30.11. Use this to determine if you are using the correct cable type.

Table 30.11
Recommended Gauge Rating

Cable Type	Application	Characteristic Impedance
RG-58U	10BASE2	50 ohm
RG-59U	CATV	75 ohm
RG-62U	ARCnet	93 ohm

Fiber-Optic Cables

Fiber-optic cables can be used in Ethernet, Token Ring, and ARCnet LANs to extend the range because these cables have very low attenuation. Another advantage is that these cables are difficult to tap and consequently are more secure. Also, they do not suffer from electromagnetic interference.

Two types of equipment are used in troubleshooting fiber-optic cables: Power Meter and Optical TDR. The Power Meter is used to measure loss in power of light signal. This is caused by signal absorption, diffraction, and other problems owing to imperfection in cable geometry and fiber-optic material. The Optical TDR is used to measure distance and location of faults.

Most problems with fiber are caused at end connections and locations at which two fiber-optic cables are spliced together. To avoid these problems, use the best quality fiber-optic splicing tools. The manufacturer of your fiber-optic cable can advise you on the type of equipment to use.

Summary

A surprisingly large number of problems associated with networks are cable-related. Most LANs use twisted-pair, coaxial, or fiber-optic technology. To help you troubleshoot problems related to physical cabling, this chapter discussed the characteristics of these cable types. You also were provided with information and tips to troubleshoot cable problems. Much of the emphasis in this chapter was on twisted-pair wiring, although coaxial cables and fiber optics also were discussed.

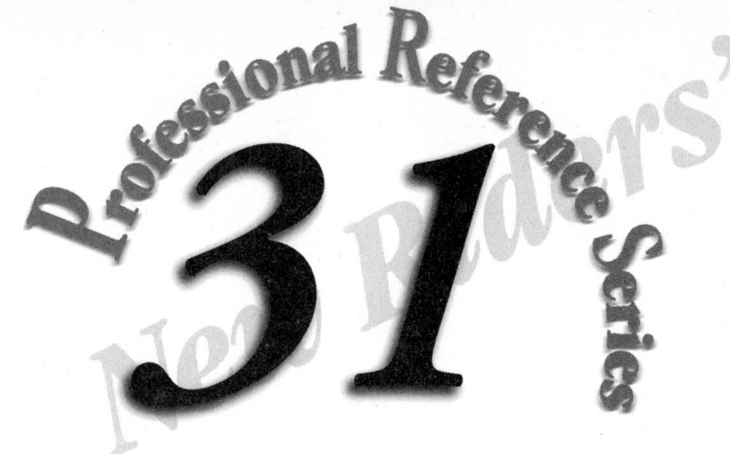

Network Troubleshooting

Connectivity problems are among the most common problems encountered on networks. These connectivity problems can be physical problems with cables or problems related to network software configuration. This chapter provides some insights on how you can troubleshoot networks.

Understanding Troubleshooting

When people talk about troubleshooting they often expect to see a magic formula or a set of procedures so precise that when followed exactly, they yield the solution to the problem. In well-defined relatively simple systems, it is possible to come up with a set of procedures that can always solve the problem. On a system as complex and varied as a network, it is not easy to come up with exact procedures.

Troubleshooting is based on understanding the principles and details of networking and applying these principles to troubleshoot problems. The earlier chapters covered many of the principles and operations of networks. One of the first tasks that you need to perform is to isolate or categorize the problem. The problem could be any of the following:

- Network hardware or computer related
- Application software related
- Network Operating System environment related
- Combination of all the above.

The last category is the most challenging type of problem because of possible complex interactions between the network hardware, application software, and the Network Operating System.

As you proceed through applying your knowledge to solving a problem, you should, like any good scientist, document your work. This helps you to avoid making assumptions about the problem scenario that are not justified. Making such assumptions can lead to "blind-alleys" or lead you astray in understanding the cause of the problem. Making incorrect assumptions about a problem is perhaps the single most important factor that contributes to lengthy troubleshooting experiences. Documenting your work also helps you develop insights into how to troubleshoot problems, and helps you discuss your troubleshooting attempts with others—such as a product's technical support personnel.

Understanding Product-Specific Troubleshooting

As new versions of software and hardware products are released, they may not always work together in the desired way. Troubleshooting these problems involves knowing which versions of software/hardware combination do not work with each other. It is not very useful to list the versions of software and hardware combinations that have conflicts in a book of this nature because such lists become outdated quickly. You can obtain this information from the vendor or participate in user groups that discuss these problems.

Using CompuServe

For Novell products, the most popular method of obtaining troubleshooting support is *NETWIRE*—a forum available through CompuServe. *CompuServe* is an information utility that you can access using a modem and communications software. In general, CompuServe is a popular method with vendors for providing technical support. If you do not have access to CompuServe, you can receive a free CompuServe Introductory Kit by calling the following number:

(800) 848-8199 (ask for representative number 597)

The general number for CompuServe from North America is the following:

(800) 848-8990

To call CompuServe headquarters in the United States from outside North America, use the following number:

(614) 457-8650

Table 31.1 gives a partial list of CompuServe numbers outside North America.

Table 31.1
CompuServe Service Numbers Outside North America

Country	Direct	Toll-Free
Argentina	(+54) 1-372-7817	
Australia	(+61) 2-410-4260	008-023-158
Chile	(+56) 2-696-8807	
Germany	(+49) 89-66-55-0-222	0130-3732
Hungary	(+36) 1-156-5366	
Hong Kong	(+852) 867-0118	
Israel	(+972) 3-29-0466	
Japan	(+81) 3-5471-5906	0120-22-1200
New Zealand	(+61) 2-410-4260	0800-441-082
South Korea	(+82) 2-569-5400	080-022-7400
Switzerland	(+49)89-66-55-0-222	155-31-79
Taiwan	(+886) 2- 651-6899	
United Kingdom	(+44) 272-760-680	0800-289-378
Venezuela	(+58) 2-793-2384	

The pricing structure is subject to change and is not mentioned in this book. Contact CompuServe for the most recent price plans.

The NETWIRE forums are organized into groups and can be accessed by typing the following command on the CompuServe forum:

```
GO NETWIRE
```

The NETWIRE forum continues to evolve and expand and has been reorganized several times over the years. As a result, most books that attempt to explain the menus are out of date quickly. The menu interface is fairly intuitive. If you prefer, you can use a MS-Windows front-end to the CompuServe menus, obtainable from CompuServe.

To obtain a list of local access phone numbers in your area, issue the following command from the CompuServe prompt:

```
GO PHONES
```

If you have an Internet access connection, and access to the TELNET program, you can access CompuServe by typing the following command:

```
TELNET COMPUSERVE.COM
```

The Network Support Encyclopedia

Another source of Novell-specific product information is the *Network Support Encyclopedia* (NSE), which contains much of the information available through NETWIRE libraries on CD-ROMs. New versions of these NSE CD-ROMs are released several times a year. You can contact Novell for more information on subscribing to the NSE.

The Internet

If you have access to the Internet, you can use anonymous FTP to connect to the Novell FTP site at the following address:

```
FTP.NOVELL.COM
```

Other "mirror" sites that provide the same information through FTP access are as follows:

- SJF-LWP.NOVELL.COM (San Jose, California, U.S.A)
- NETLAB2.USU.EDU (Logan, Utah, U.S.A)
- RISC.UA.EDU (Tuscaloosa, Alabama, U.S.A)
- BNUG.PROTEON.COM (Boston, Mass., U.S.A)
- NOVELL.NRC.CA (Ottawa, Canada)
- FTP.SALFORD.AC.UK (U.K.)
- FTP.RUG.NL (Netherlands)
- TUI.LINCAN.AC.NZ (New Zealand)
- FTP.NOVELL.DE (Germany)

The FTP sites contain almost all NETWIRE file areas; the NETWIRE SysOp mediated forums are missing.

Novell also has a World Wide Web server at the following address:

```
http://www.novell.com/
```

If you have Gopher client software (from Chameleon or another source), you can access the Gopher server at this address:

```
gopher.novell.com
```

Troubleshooting with LANalyzer for Windows

A protocol analyzer can not only offer many insights into the workings of a LAN, but also can be used as a powerful network troubleshooting tool. Many choices for protocol analyzers are available, including the following more common ones:

- Network General's Sniffer
- LANalyzer (Hardware-based product)
- LANWatch
- LAN Decoder
- LANalyzer for Windows

The first two choices are hardware based, and therefore more capable and also more expensive. The last three choices are software based and can work on any DOS workstation that has a network adapter. The LANalyzer for Windows is a Novell product and requires that MS Windows be installed.

The troubleshooting tips in this chapter are based on LANalyzer for Windows. The LANalyzer for Windows product is described next.

LANalyzer for Windows is installed in its own program group and contains the program items shown in figure 31.1.

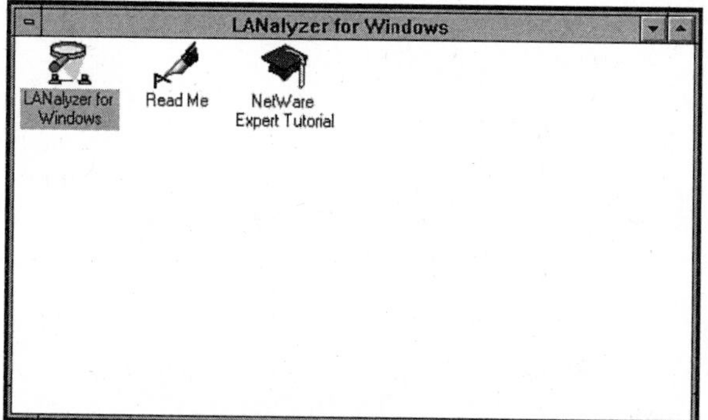

Figure 31.1
LANalyzer for Windows program items.

When you activate the LANalyzer program, you see a dashboard (see fig. 31.2) that displays packets/second, utilization, errors/second. *Packets/second* is an instantaneous measurement of throughput rate. *Utilization* is network utilization and is the ratio of the current data rate to the maximum data rate on the network. *Errors/second* measures the frequency of errors on the network. Errors/second is a useful parameter to observe in troubleshooting your network. If this rate is high, it indicates a network that could have severe problems.

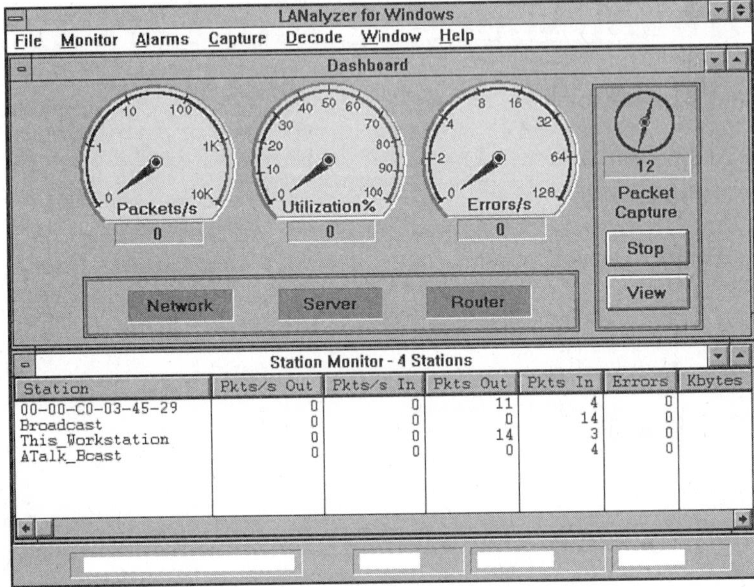

Figure 31.2
LANalyzer for Windows main screen.

The LANalyzer product is designed to work with Ethernet and Token Ring networks. Besides measuring the data rate, utilization, and error rate, LANalyzer can be used to capture packets. Figure 31.3 shows that the LANalyzer is capturing packets. The bottom half of the screen also shows the Station Monitor window. This window lists the different stations/nodes on the network that have been seen on the network. The MAC addresses of the stations are shown in the Stations column. You can associate names to MAC addresses, in which case the names that you assign are displayed instead of the MAC addresses. LANalyzer classifies packets seen as general broadcasts or AppleTalk protocol broadcasts. The other columns indicate statistics on the number of input and output packets, and kilobytes of data.

31

As you scroll through the window to see other columns, you see columns such as Address that display the MAC addresses of the stations (see fig. 31.3). Using this, you can discover the MAC addresses of all stations seen on the network. An Alarm ticker tape and icon at the bottom of the screen alert you to abnormal conditions on the network, such as over-size or under-size packets. These conditions can be caused by malfunctions of network cards or the network driver.

Double-clicking on any station in the Station Monitor window shows detailed statistics on the station.

Troubleshooting Networks Using Baseline Performance

As part of troubleshooting networks, you should create a baseline for your network. A *baseline* is a measurement of your network performance under normal operating conditions on the network. N*ormal operating conditions on the network* are conditions under which you typically operate the network for long periods of times. These conditions include the users running applications and performing network tasks that they normally perform on any day.

LANalyzer for Windows - [Station Monitor - 10 Stations]

File Monitor Alarms Capture Decode Window Help

In	Errors	Kbytes Out	Kbytes In	Bytes/s Out	Bytes/s In	Address
23	0	5	2	0	0	00-80-C7-D6-6F-0F
38	0	19	2	0	0	00-00-C0-03-45-29
100	0	0	18	0	0	FF-FF-FF-FF-FF-FF
4	0	0	0	0	0	09-00-07-FF-FF-FF
0	0	0	0	0	0	00-01-02-6B-43-4E
2	0	0	0	0	0	F0-00-00-00-00-01
0	0	0	0	0	0	00-00-00-00-01-40
2	0	0	0	0	0	00-F0-00-00-01-00
0	0	0	0	0	0	48-00-00-01-01-07
2	0	0	0	0	0	00-00-00-00-00-01

Figure 31.3
Observing other columns in the Station Monitor window.

LANalyzer for Windows enables you to measure baseline performance by displaying and printing graphs for the following network parameters:

- Utilization percentage
- Packets per second
- Errors per second
- Kilobytes per second
- Most active stations

Trend Analysis of Utilization Percentage

Compare the current values of these network performance parameters against the baseline for determining which conditions are unusual in the network you are troubleshooting. A useful feature within LANalyzer is trend analysis. *Trend analysis* can be done on any of the previously stated network parameters. Figure 31.4 shows the Trend - Utilization% screen. The percentage utilization is defined as the KB/sec transferred to the maximum KB/sec transfer possible on the network. When examining peak percentage utilization, look for peaks and lows. Peaks indicate activities of high network utilization, and you should set an alarm threshold to a value greater than the baseline peak value. For example, you can set the alarm threshold for a parameter to be five percent greater than the baseline peak value.

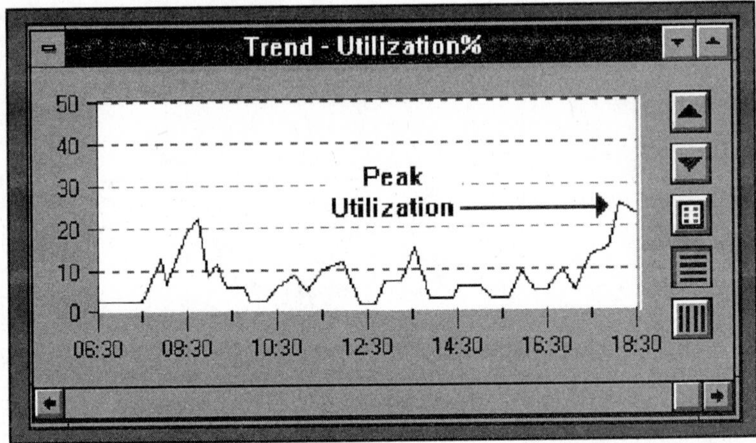

Figure 31.4
Trend - Utilization% screen.

Trend Analysis of Packets Per Second

Packets per second also is an indication of network activity. Like percentage utilization, it also is a measure of network activity. When the peak packets per second increases, you can usually expect percentage utilization to also increase. If the percentage utilization does not increase with an increase in packets per second, it indicates an increase in the number of small packets on the network. When examining peak packets per second (see fig. 31.5), you should look for peaks and lows. Peaks indicate activities of high network utilization, and you should set an alarm threshold to a value greater than the baseline peak value. For example, you can set the alarm threshold for a parameter to be five percent greater than the baseline peak value.

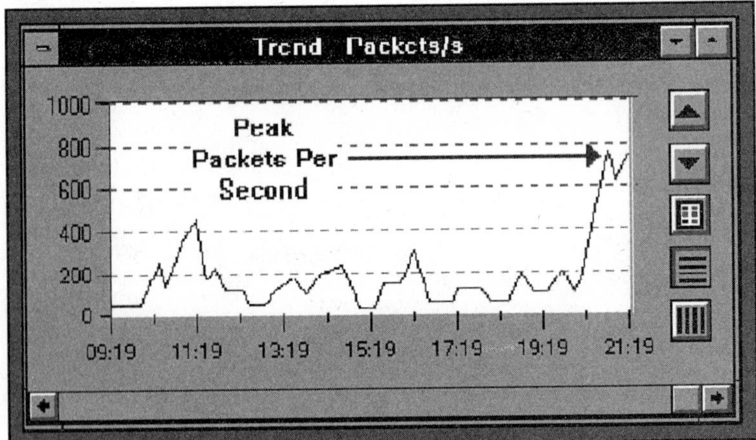

Figure 31.5
Trend - Packets per second.

A high packet per second rate can indicate a broadcast storm, which is caused by incorrectly configured bridges on the network, or problems with routing broadcast messages sent due to rapidly changing status of network links.

Trend Analysis of Errors Per Second

Errors per second is the number of errors over the last 15 minutes. This value should normally be low. When the errors per second increase, it indicates a problem on the network. Check for the type of errors encountered, such as under-size or over-size packets, routers unreachable, and so on. When examining peak errors per second (see fig. 31.6), look for peaks and lows. Peaks indicate high error rate, and you should set an alarm threshold to a value greater than the baseline peak value. For example, set the alarm threshold for a parameter to be five percent greater than the baseline peak value.

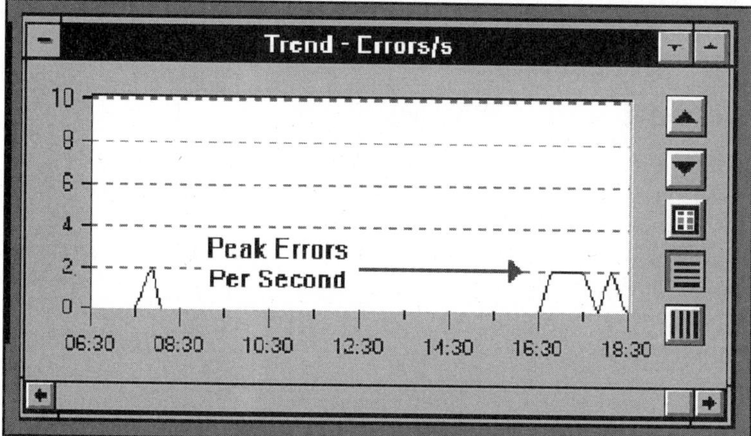

Figure 31.6
Trend - Errors per second.

Trend Analysis of Kilobytes Per Second

Kilobytes per second is the data throughput on the network. This value follows the percentage utilization graph. High KB/sec indicates periods of high network activity. Monitor this parameter to alert yourself of excessive network traffic. When examining kilobytes per second (see fig. 31.7), look for peaks and lows. Peaks indicate high network activity, and you should set an alarm threshold to a value greater than the baseline peak value. For example, set the alarm threshold for a parameter to be five percent greater than the baseline peak value.

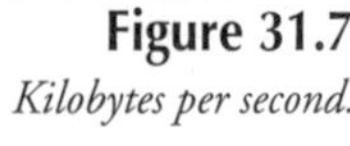

Figure 31.7
Kilobytes per second.

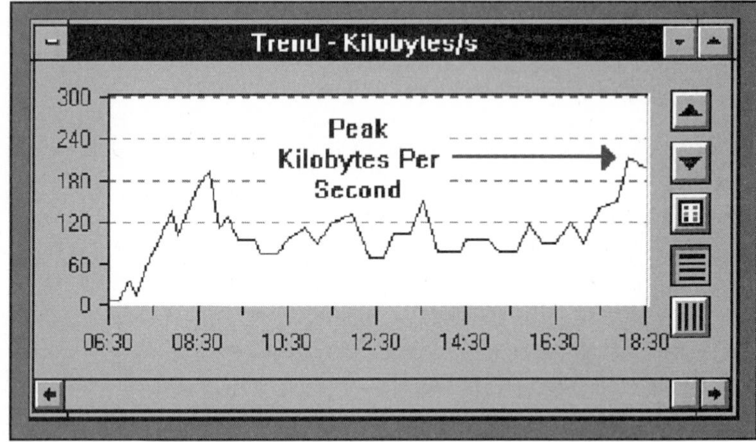

Trend Analysis for Most Active Stations

Double-clicking on a column heading in the Station Monitor window sorts the table based on the column value. You can, therefore, double-click on the Kbytes Out column to find the stations transmitting the largest amount of data, or double-click on Packets Out to find the stations transmitting the largest number of packets. This information can help you detect the most active stations on the network, and help you isolate the source of excessive network traffic.

Exporting Trend Graphs

Use the Export Trend menu item in the File menu to export the trend values of a graph to a *Comma Separated Value* (CSV) form, which can be read into a database or spreadsheet for further analysis. For example, you can do an analysis to see how adding additional users, workstations, or servers impacts percentage utilization or errors per second parameters.

Using Alarms in LANalyzer To Troubleshoot Network Problems

Two types of alarms can be set: *General Network* alarms and *Network Specific* alarms that can be Ethernet or Token Ring specific. Examples of General Network alarms are as follows:

- Packets per second
- Percentage utilization
- Broadcasts per second
- CRC errors per second
- Server overload

- Server down
- Router down

You can set alarms to indicate exceptional conditions on the network. An alarm condition occurs if the parameter value exceeds a threshold value.

When an alarm occurs, the alarm icon is activated with an audible sound. You can see the ticker-tape message at the bottom of the screen indicating the type of alarm. If several alarms trigger at once, it usually indicates a serious condition on the network. Because NetWare servers can act as IPX routers, a NetWare server becoming unreachable generates multiple alarms, such as a NetWare server down and an IPX router down alarm.

Troubleshooting Packets Per Second Utilization Alarms

When the *packets per second utilization alarm* is triggered it does not necessarily indicate a serious condition on the network. This alarm can be triggered by a change in network traffic type or network application on the network. For example, running TCP/IP applications such as TELNET can generate a packet for every character typed by a user. This can create a large number of small-sized packets. A more useful indicator of excessive network traffic is the percentage utilization of the network.

Troubleshooting Percentage Utilization Alarms

The *percentage utilization alarm* indicates a situation in which the network is being saturated with data traffic. To reduce network traffic on the network, consider segmenting the network at the data link or network layer of the OSI model. Segmenting the network at the data link layer implies partitioning the network using bridges. Segmenting the network at the network layer can be done using routers. You may want to review Chapter 3, "Bridging and Routing," for the relative merits of partitioning networks using bridges and routers.

Troubleshooting Broadcasts Per Second Alarms

The *broadcasts per second alarm* can be triggered by an excessive number of broadcasts on the network. Certain network services, such as SAP, RIP and NetBIOS, ARP (Address Resolution Protocol—part of TCP/IP), AARP (AppleTalk Address Resolution Protocol), and BOOTP (Boot Protocol—part of TCP/IP) generate broadcast traffic. A router or bridge problem can result in a *broadcast storm* in which the majority of the packets on the network are broadcast storms that leave little room on the network for normal data packets. If certain types of broadcast traffic are not needed on network segments, you can filter out these packets at a bridge or router; for example, you can prevent a SAP or an IPX RIP broadcast to an AppleTalk or TCP/IP network segment. You may also use SAP filtering at the NetWare server or increase the interval at which RIP broadcasts can take place. On networks consisting of WAN links, you may want to use NetWare/IP that replaces the NetWare IPX protocol with IP protocol in TCP/IP. NetWare/IP uses DSS servers that can be used to control SAP/RIP broadcasts for a network segment. You also can eliminate SAP/RIP by exclusively using the *NetWare Link State Protocol* (NLSP) on your network (see Chapter 3, "Bridging and Routing").

Troubleshooting Server/Router Down Alarm Messages

If a server or router no longer responds to packets on the network, LANalyzer detects this condition and reports this problem as a server down or router alarm message. A *server* on an IPX network is any node that broadcasts SAP packets for the services running on it. Common examples of servers are file servers, print servers, and database servers. A *router* is a node that originates RIP packets. All NetWare servers have IPX routing software.

The most common cause of a "server down" alarm message is a break in the network connection to the server. Occasionally, you may see this message if the server is too busy to respond to a message from the LANalyzer workstation. Upon receiving a "server no longer responds message," go to the Server Monitor window in LANalyzer and double-click on the server that triggered the alarm to see its transmission statistics. If no packets are outgoing from the server, check the connection to the server and verify if the server is still up. A misconfiguration at the server, such as the IPX protocol being "unbound" or "bound" to an incorrect frame type, also can cause the server down alarm message.

If the server transmission statistics show that the server is transmitting packets, it indicates that the server is slow to respond, or there may be network bandwidth bottlenecks. To verify if you are experiencing network bandwidth bottlenecks, you may want to examine the Detail utilization graph for percentage utilization to observe if the network is experiencing high network utilization percentages.

You also may see a server alarm with a ticker-tape message `Overload on server` *`XXXX`*. This is caused by congestion control packets received from the server. When the number of requests received at the server are very high, it can respond with a special NCP `Request being processed` congestion reply packet. This informs the client that the server is busy, and the client should not time-out too early and break the network connection. Congestion at a NetWare server can be caused by insufficient memory for file caching, server disk I/O channel bottleneck, or high CPU utilization. You can avoid congestion control packets from the server by adding more server memory, using faster disks with greater data bandwidth, or using a faster CPU.

If you see a `Router` *`xxx`* `no longer responds` alarm message, it indicates that there might be a break in the network connection to the router or that the router has gone down. The router here indicates an IPX router or an AppleTalk Phase I or Phase II router. Occasionally, you may see this message if the router is too busy to respond to a message from the LANalyzer workstation. Upon receiving a `router no longer responds message`, go to the Router Monitor window in LANalyzer; double-click on the router that triggered the alarm; and observe its transmission statistics. If no packets are outgoing from the router, check the connection to the router and verify that the router is still operational. A misconfiguration at the router, such as the IPX protocol or the AppleTalk protocols being "unbound" or "bound" to an incorrect frame type, also can cause the `router no longer responds` alarm message. Remember that if the NetWare server is acting as an AppleTalk router on an Ethernet network, it uses the ETHERNET_SNAP frame type.

Troubleshooting Ethernet-Specific Alarms

Network Specific alarms can be Ethernet-specific or Token Ring-specific. The Ethernet-specific alarms are as follows:

- CRC errors
- Short packet error
- Long packet error
- Fragment error
- Jabber error

CRC Errors

In Ethernet networks, no special station monitors errors in transmission on the network. The receiving node must detect an error by calculating the CRC of the packet and comparing it with the CRC value computed by the sender. If the sender's CRC and the receiver's CRC values for a packet are different, it indicates a transmission error. This error is reported to upper-layer protocols that may request another packet, or time-out and wait for the packet to be retransmitted.

Not all CRC errors are caused by noise on the transmission medium. CRC errors also can be caused by faulty network adapters/transceivers, corrupt network drivers, and badly configured cabling systems.

Short Packet Errors on Ethernet Networks

A *short packet error* is caused by a faulty LAN driver or card transmitting an Ethernet packet less than 64 bytes, the minimum size of Ethernet packets on the network. This type of error is sometimes referred to as an *undersized packet error.*

You can solve this problem by updating to later drivers that can fix this error or by replacing the network card. You can use LANalyzer to detect the workstation that generated a short packet.

Long Packet Errors on Ethernet Networks

A *long packet error* is caused by a faulty LAN driver or card transmitting an Ethernet packet more than 1,518 bytes, the maximum size of Ethernet packets on the network. This type of error is sometimes referred to as an *oversized packet error.*

You can solve this problem by updating to later drivers that can fix the error or by replacing the network card. You can use LANalyzer to detect the workstation that generated a long packet.

Fragment Errors

Fragments are caused by collisions on the network. When packets collide, the resulting signal transmission constitutes one or more badly formed packets detected by LANalyzer as fragments. A high number of fragments on the network indicates excessive collisions possibly caused by overloading of the system. Observe the percentage utilization statistic to see if high fragment rates are accompanied by a rise in percentage utilization. If no change in network traffic occurs and a large number of fragments exist, you should suspect faulty NICs or a cabling system not properly installed.

Jabber Errors on Ethernet Networks

A *jabber error* occurs when a network card continually transmits on the network and prevents other stations from gaining access to the network. Ethernet operation is CSMA/CD based. As part of this access mechanism, other stations must wait until no activity is on the network before transmitting. If a station transmits continually, it prevents other stations from transmitting.

This error usually indicates a malfunctioning transceiver. You can replace the external transceiver for 10BASE5 networks or replace the cards that use internal transceiver (10BASE2, 10BASE-T, 100BASE-TX, and so on).

Troubleshooting Token Ring-Specific Alarms

Token ring errors detected by nodes on the ring are sent to the Ring Error Monitor station at the *functional address* C0 00 00 00 00 08. The Ring Error Monitor station is a special node that receives errors reported on the ring. Besides the Ring Error Monitor, other special token ring nodes provide specific functions. These are listed in table 31.2. Typical token ring networks have Active Monitor and Standby Monitor stations only. To create other types of Monitor stations you must load special software (obtainable through IBM or vendor of hardware) on a workstation.

With the exception of the Standby Monitor, each station in table 31.2 uses a functional address. LANalyzer records all errors reported to the Ring Error Monitor (functional address C0 00 00 00 00 08). These errors contain information on the station that reported the error, the station suspected as the cause of the error, and the fault domain. The *fault domain* is the area in which the fault is located and includes the network boards, cables, and MAU (Multistation Access Unit) ports. This area is between the station that reported the error and the NAUN (Nearest Active Upstream Neighbor). For additional details on token ring fault domains, see Chapter 2, “LAN Standards for Physical and Data Link Layers.” By tracking the errors reported to the Ring Error Monitor, LANalyzer can generate reports and alarms provided by the token ring management protocols.

Table 31.2
Special Token Ring Stations

Station	Functional Address	Description
Active Monitor	C0 00 00 00 00 01	Maintains master clock for ring. Monitors ring for good tokens and frames. Performs ring purges and places new token on ring when necessary. Initiates Ring Poll process every 7 seconds to receive responses from other Standby Monitors and establishes the Ring Order.
Standby Monitor	No Functional address	All stations that are not Active Monitors are Standby Monitors. Standby Monitors monitor the Active Monitor. If Active Monitor fails to send the Active Monitor Present (AMP) frame, Standby Monitors use the Monitor Contention process to determine the new Active Monitor.
Ring Error	C0 00 00 00 00 08	Maintains error Monitor statistics on the ring. Every station reports errors encountered in the last 2 seconds (default) to the Ring Error Monitor. After reporting the errors, the station resets its error counter. Stations report errors to the functional address C0-00-00-00-00-08 even if the Ring Error Monitor station does not exist.

continues

Table 31.2, Continued
Special Token Ring Stations

Station	Functional Address	Description
Ring Parameter	C0 00 00 00 00 02	Maintains and monitors Server station parameters during the ring insertion process. When a station inserts into the ring, it sends a request frame to the Ring Parameter Server requesting adapter settings, ring number, and error report timer. If a Ring Parameter Server is configured for the token ring, it responds to the station's request with the station settings. If there is no Ring Parameter server reply, the station uses its default settings.
Network Manager	C0 00 00 00 00 10	Collects configuration information and measures network performance. It can modify other networks' adapter configurations or force an adapter to remove itself from the ring, if necessary.

Using LANalyzer, you can monitor token ring station details by double-clicking on a station in the Station Monitor window and selecting the Ring Information button. The station information includes the following:

- **Station address/name.** MAC address or text string assigned to the station name.
- **Status.** This indicates whether the station is currently in the ring or off the ring. You can use it to dynamically watch station insertion and removal.
- **Last Entry/Exit.** The date and time the station entered the ring or exited the ring. This helps you to correlate the time a problem occurred with the time a station entered or exited the ring.
- **Insertions.** The number of times a station entered or exited the ring. A large number of insertions indicates a problem with the card or the MAU port and/or cable to workstation.
- **Internal errors.** These are errors detected by the token ring adapter's hardware or firmware. Internal errors cause the token ring adapter to remove itself from the ring and attempt reinsertion into the ring.

- **Congestion.** This indicates that a station cannot copy a frame because of lack of buffer space. This could be caused by a misconfigured adapter or driver or a problem with the application not freeing up unused buffer space.

- **Abort Delimiter.** This indicates the number of times a station aborted a transmission by issuing an Abort Delimiter. Abort Delimiters are issued by a station when it can recover from an error automatically. If the station cannot recover from the error automatically, it removes itself from the ring permanently.

- **A/C Errors.** These errors indicate that a station cannot set the *Address Recognized Indicator* (ARI) and the *Frame Copied Indicator* (FCI) bits in a frame that it has copied. These errors are typically caused by faulty token ring adapters.

- **Lost Frames.** This error indicates that a transmitting station did not receive the frame it sent. Token ring networks perform a hardware acknowledgment in which the transmitting station receives the frame it sent and uses the flags modified by the stations on the token ring to assess if the packet was received correctly. A large number of these errors indicates a cabling problem. Lost frames also can be caused by stations inserting and removing themselves from the ring at the time the frame was crossing that station.

- **Frequency Errors.** These errors indicate that the ring clock and the adapter clock are not properly synchronized and differ by an excessive amount. When a station detects a frequency error, it automatically enters a Monitor Contention phase to reestablish ring integrity.

- **Frames Copied.** This indicates that a station received an address sent to it, but the ARI bit was already set. This might be because of a duplicate node address on the ring, or a transmission error that caused the ARI bit to be set. The ARI bit is not covered by the CRC flag. It is duplicated in the frame to detect if there was an error in the ARI bit.

- **Token Errors.** These errors are detected and reported if this station is an Active Monitor. These errors can be caused by encoding violations. Token ring uses Differential Manchester Encoding, and certain non-data symbols can occur only in designated parts of the token ring frame. Other reasons for token errors are that no token or frame is received within 10 milliseconds or Monitor Count bit is set to 1 when a 0 value is expected. When the Active Monitor detects a token ring error, it issues a Ring Purge frame and releases a new token.

- **Beacons.** Beacon frames are generated by a station when it detects a serious error in the ring, such as broken cable link. Manual intervention may be required to restore ring integrity.

- **Line error.** This is equivalent to the CRC error in Ethernet. It is generated when the receiver detects code violations in the frame/token or when the received frame contains an invalid *Frame Check Sequence* (FCS). The term FCS is used in a token ring frame to indicate a CRC value.

- **Burst Error.** This error occurs when a token ring adapter detects an absence of transitions in the signal. Transitions are used for encoding clocking information and encoding data (using Differential Manchester Encoding). A large number of burst errors can occur when an adapter is inserting or removing itself from the ring because of component failure.

- **Physical.** This number indicates the number of the currently viewed station in relationship to the physical ring.
- **Active.** This is set to ON if the station is currently active. If a station is not currently on the ring, it is set to OFF. This also indicates the number of the active station.
- **Upstream/Downstream Buttons.** You can use the Upstream and Downstream buttons to traverse the ring and view information on the nodes on the ring. If you suspect the error to be directly upstream from the current station being viewed, you can use the Upstream button to "walk" upstream and view the neighbor's node information.

Both the Upstream and Downstream buttons are very powerful methods of determining fault domains. Figures 31.8 to 31.11 indicate how "walking" the tree upstream or downstream can be used to isolate faults. In figure 31.8, the Beacons, Line errors, and Burst errors are shown at station A. These indicate that the fault is downstream from A, in the direction of station B. If you walk the tree downstream from A, you arrive at station B. If you walk upstream from A, you arrive at station D. You skip station E because it is inactive. Statistics at B (see fig. 31.9) reveal that the fault is upstream from B, in the direction of A. From this, you can conclude that the fault is between stations A and B. The remaining figures 31.10 and 31.11 show statistics at stations C and D. These reveal that the link between these stations and their neighbors do not have any errors.

Figure 31.8
Error statistics at station A.

Station A	Upstream	Downstream
Beacons	0	0
Line Errors	4	30
Burst Errors	3	4361

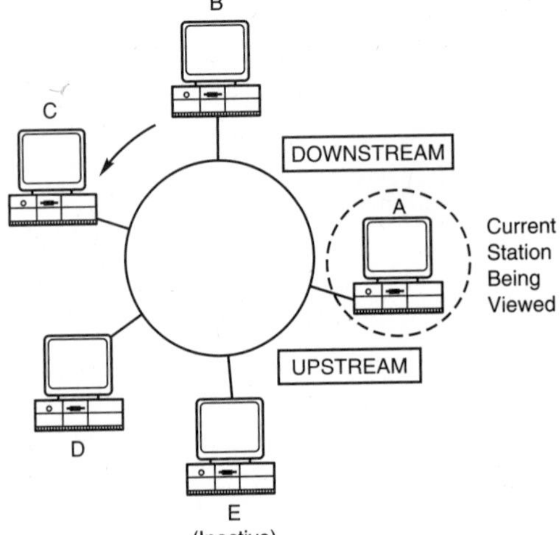

Station B

	Upstream	Downstream
Beacons	0	0
Line Errors	30	0
Burst Errors	4361	0

Current Station Being Viewed
B
DOWNSTREAM
UPSTREAM
C
A
D
E (Inactive)

Figure 31.9
Error statistics at station B.

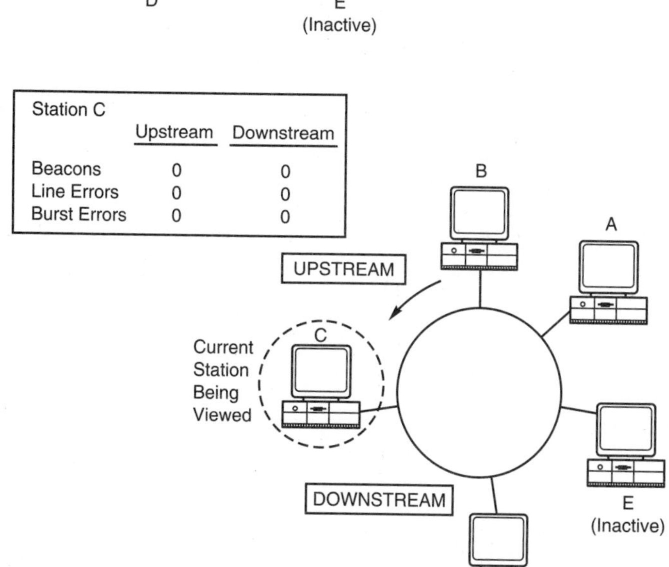

Station C

	Upstream	Downstream
Beacons	0	0
Line Errors	0	0
Burst Errors	0	0

Figure 31.10
Error statistics at station C.

31

Figure 31.11
Error statistics at station D.

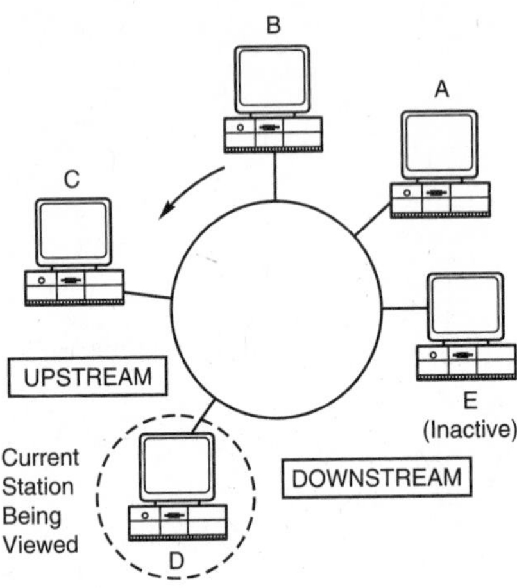

Station D	Upstream	Downstream
Beacons	0	0
Line Errors	0	0
Burst Errors	0	0

Other Troubleshooting Methods

A surprisingly large number of problems are related to network connectivity. Most NetWare Administrators have encountered the following common problem:

```
A File Server Could not be found
```

The preceding chapter discussed cabling issues that must be resolved to ensure physical connectivity. You can use the methods discussed in that chapter to ensure physical integrity of the network. There might, however, be nothing wrong with the physical layer of the network, and you still might not be able to connect to the network. The problem might be with any of the upper-layers (data link, network, transport, session, presentation, or application layers).

The following is a useful checklist that can help you isolate and solve some of your connectivity problems:

1. Make sure that your network adapter is working correctly.
2. Make sure that you are using the correct version of the network adapter driver.
3. Make sure that you are using the correct version of the transport protocol and client network software.
4. Check your network driver configuration parameters.

5. Make sure that you are using correct frame types at workstations and server.

6. Use the TRACK ON command at the server console to see if SAP requests such as Get Nearest Server and Give Nearest Server are being received.

The following tools can help you solve the preceding problems:

- A multimeter with a continuity check and ohmmeter option
- Diagnostic software for the network cards
- Software troubleshooting tools: CheckIt, Manifest, Norton Utilities, and so on
- Protocol Analyzers

Summary

Connectivity problems are among the most common network problems. This chapter discussed how a tool such as LANalyzer for Windows can be used to troubleshoot a large variety of Ethernet and Token Ring related problems. This chapter emphasized physical connectivity problems. Information about troubleshooting specific types of problems, such as Time Synchronization on a NetWare 4.*x* network and using MONITOR to prevent problems from occurring are found in other parts of this book.

Appendix

Installing and Using the On-Line Command References

Your *NetWare: The Professional Reference, Third Edition* companion disk includes two NetWare command references in the form of Windows Help files. Two different files are provided: one for NetWare versions 2.2 and 3.1*x* and another for NetWare 4.01. This appendix covers installation of the help files and some special features of the command reference help files.

Installing the Command Reference Help Files

1. Insert your companion disk in a floppy disk drive.
2. In Windows, select **F**ile, **R**un.
3. When Run prompts for a command line, enter **`A:INSTALL`**. Specify the disk drive letter in which your companion disk resides.
4. The screen shown in figure A.1 enables you to specify the directory in which the help files will be installed. Edit this path if desired.

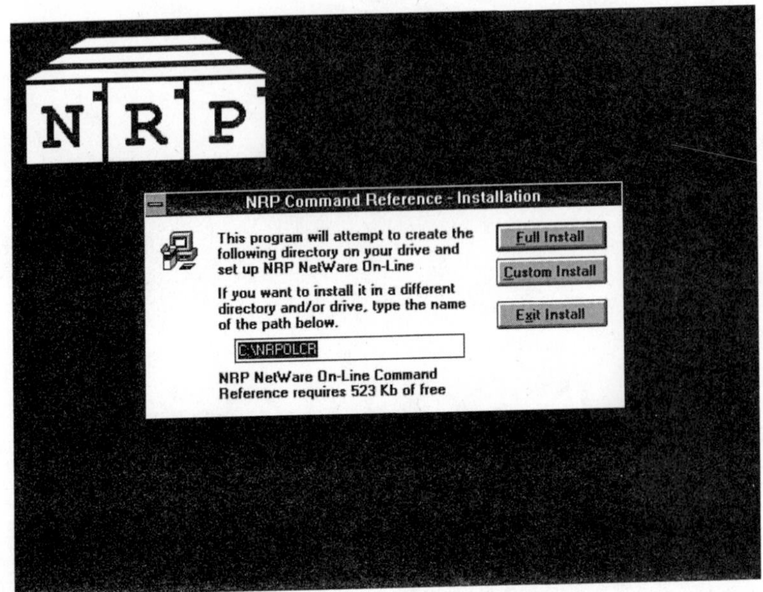

Figure A.1 *Specifying the installation directory.*

You can also specify a **F**ull Install, which installs both help files, or a **C**ustom Install which enables you to select one or both files.

5. If you select **C**ustom Install, the screen in Figure A.2 enables you to specify which files will be installed. Click on program descriptions to highlight the ones you wish to install. Then click on Continue.

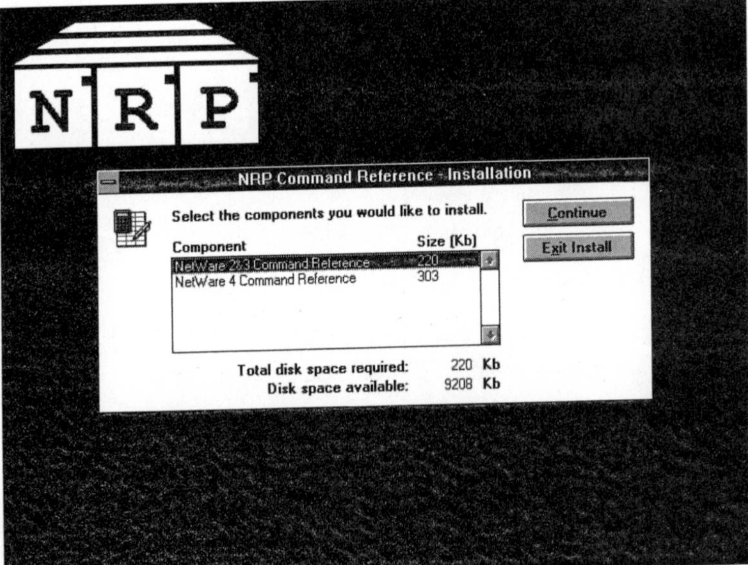

Figure A.2 *Selecting files to be installed.*

6. After files are copied, the next screen (see Fig. A.3) prompts you to specify the Program Manager group in which the help icons will be installed. Edit the group name that appears in the text field if desired. Then click on **Create** to complete the installation.

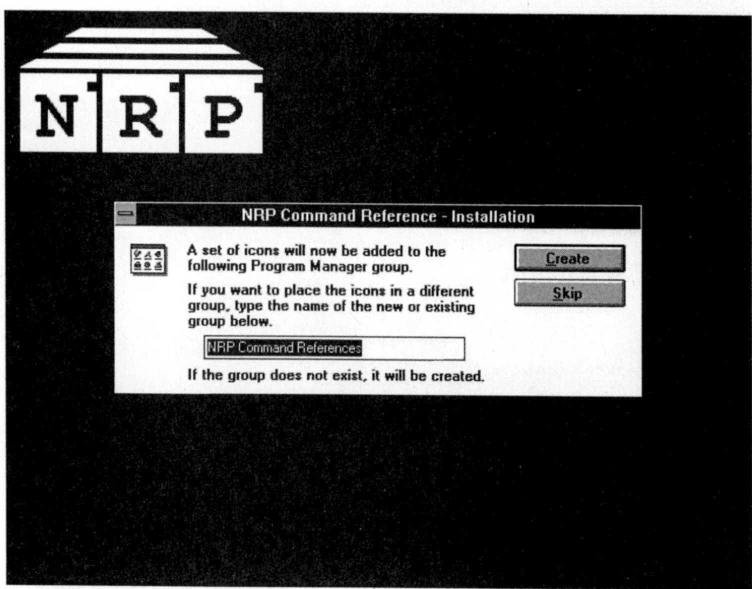

Figure A.3
Specifying the Program Manager group.

After you complete installation, a new program group is created with two help icons, similar to the group shown in Figure A.4.

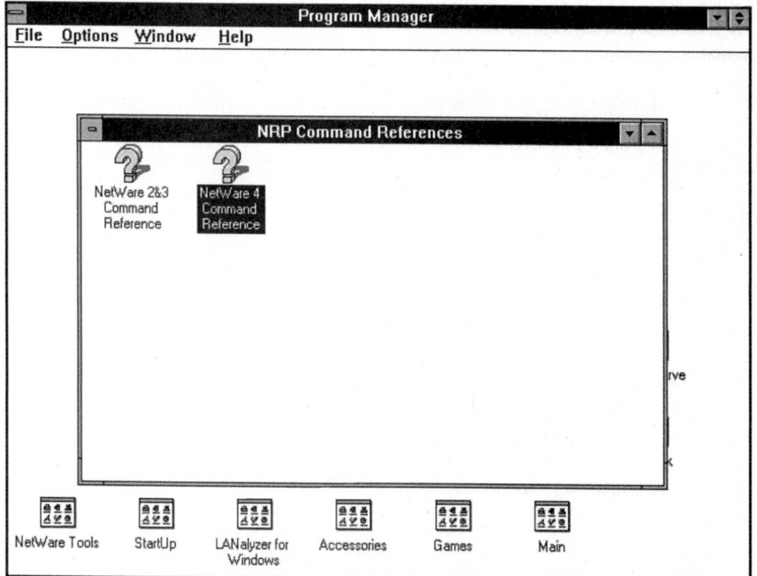

Figure A.4
The Program Manager group that is created.

Using the On-Line Command References

The command references are standard Windows help files with some special features. This appendix will concentrate on those special features.

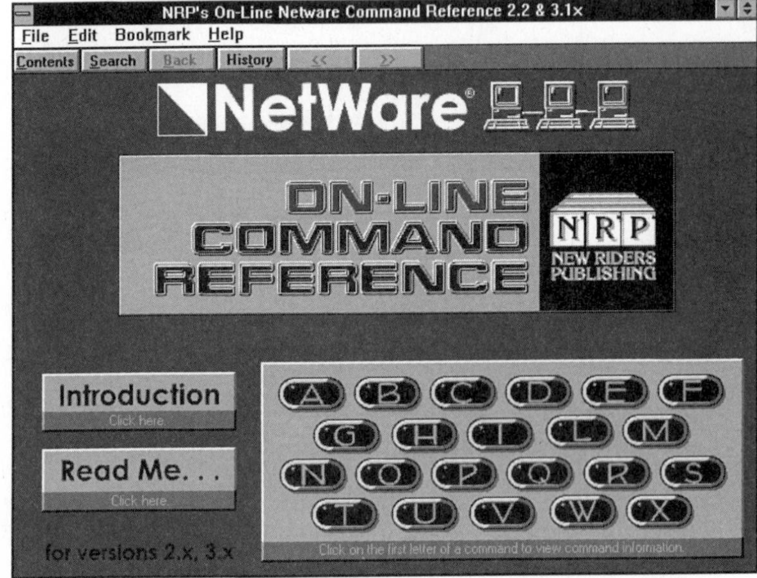

Figure A.5
A command reference main screen.

Figure A.5 shows the main screen that is displayed when you start a command reference. This screen has three special options:

1. Clicking on Introduction displays a description of the help program.
2. Clicking on Read Me displays a menu of informational topics such as copyright notices.
3. Click on a key letter to display a menu of commands starting with that letter.

Figure A.6 shows the display for a typical command. All commands contain the following sections:

- Purpose
- Syntax
- Options

- Rules and Considerations
- Examples
- Important Messages
- Notes
- See Also

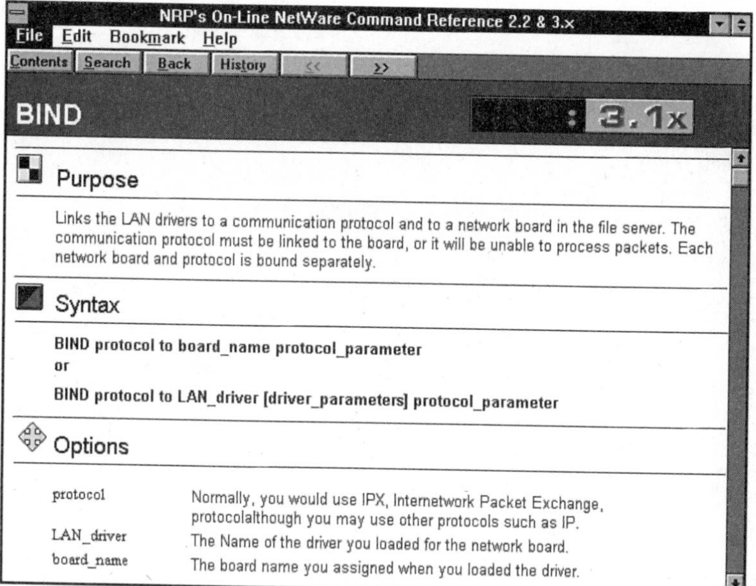

Figure A.6
Example of a command entry.

Entries in See Also are all cross-referenced to the appropriate command entries. Any time you see green text, click on the text to cross-link to the related entry.

Icons appear at the top right of the screen that describe when and where a particular command is valid. Click on these icons for more information. Figure A.7 shows an example in which the 3.1x icon has been clicked.

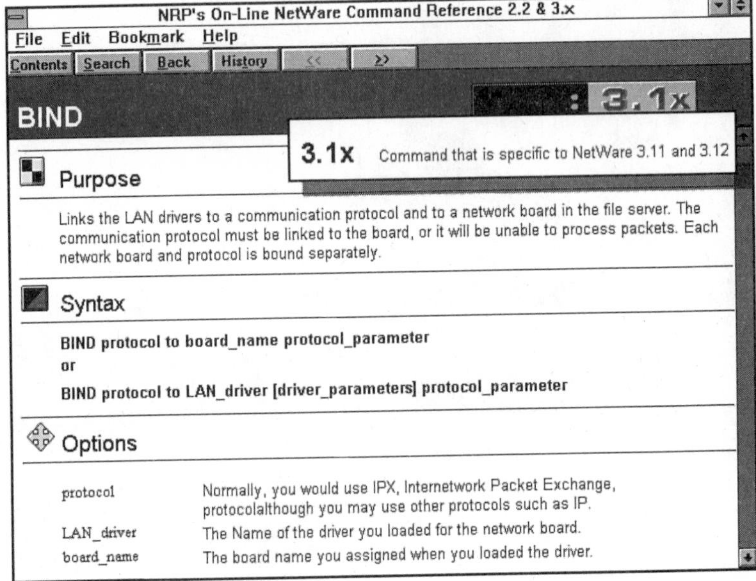

Figure A.7 *Example of an icon description.*

INDEX

Symbols

A

D

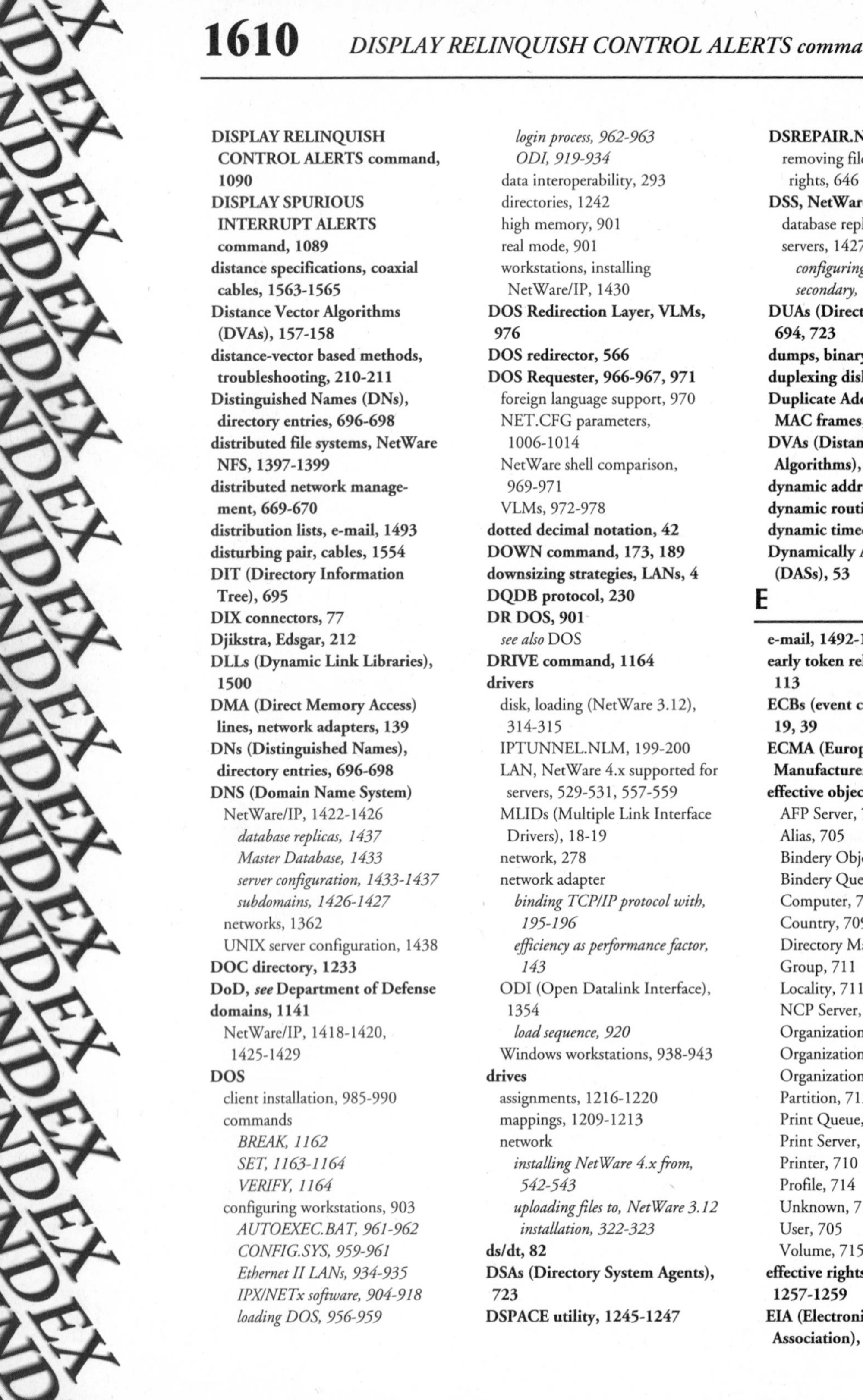

E

F

G

H

J–K

L

O

S

U

V

NetWare: The Professional Reference

REGISTRATION CARD

Fill out this card to receive information about future NetWare books and other New Riders titles!

Name ______________________ **Title** ______________

Company ______________________

Address ______________________

City/State/ZIP ______________________

I bought this book because: ______________________

____

I purchased this book from:

☐ A bookstore (Name ______________________)

☐ A software or electronics store (Name ______________)

☐ A mail order (Name of Catalog ______________)

I purchase this many computer books each year:

☐ 1–5 ☐ 6 or more

I currently use these applications: ______________________

____

____

____

I found these chapters to be the most informative: ______________

____

I found these chapters to be the least informative: ______________

____

Additional comments: ______________________

____

☐ I would like to see my name in print! You may use my name and quote me in future New Riders products and promotions. My daytime phone number is: ______________

New Riders Publishing 201 West 103rd Street • Indianapolis, Indiana 46290 USA

Fold Here

PLACE
STAMP
HERE

New Riders Publishing
201 West 103rd Street
Indianapolis, Indiana 46290
USA